THE
TV ENCYCLOPEDIA

David Inman

A Perigee Book

Perigee Books
are published by
The Putnam Publishing Group
200 Madison Avenue
New York, NY 10016

Library of Congress Cataloging-in-Publication Data

Inman, David, 1957 - .
    The TV Encyclopedia / David Inman
        p.   cm.
        1. Television broadcasting—United States—Biography—Dictionaries
I. Title
Dictionaries. I. Title.
PN1992.4.A2I66 1991 90-24917 CIP
791.45'092273—dc20
[B]
ISBN 0-399-51718-9
ISBN 0-399-51704-9 (PBK)

Cover design by Jack Ribik

Printed in the United States of America

1 2 3 4 5 6 7 8 9 10

INTRODUCTION

Being a guy, I like to switch channels as I watch TV. Incessantly. It's a guy thing, I know, and I'm okay with that. I own it. But when you switch channels, or even when you watch a TV program all the way through, you often catch certain guest stars who look familiar.

This book is designed to provide answers to questions like, "Hey, isn't that Richard Dreyfuss on that 'Bewitched' episode?" (Yes.) Or, "Say, that looks like Robert Redford on that 'Twilight Zone.' Is it?" (Sure is.) Or, "Boy, I wonder if that's Clark Gable on that episode of 'The Muppet Show'?" (No, it isn't, and if you think it is you need the kind of help that this book can't provide.)

In other words, *The TV Encyclopedia* tells you more than the easy stuff—that Dick Van Dyke starred in "The Dick Van Dyke Show," for instance. Any TV book worth its salt could tell you that. But how many will tell you that he did two guest shots on "The Phil Silvers Show" in the fifties, or that Van Dyke and Mary Tyler Moore revived the characters of Rob and Laura Petrie on Moore's 1979 variety series? Just one, we hope. Because TV is much more than who starred in what series, although that information is certainly important. TV is also guest appearances on sitcoms and variety shows and specials. It's director John Frankenheimer chasing some kids off a "Playhouse 90" set in 1959 and getting bawled out on the air by Art Linkletter, whose "House Party" show the kids were appearing on. It's Bob Barker deciding to quit coloring his hair. It's Marlo Thomas appearing on "Bonanza" as a Chinese mail-order bride destined for Hoss Cartwright (Dan Blocker). It's the writers who put the words in the actors' mouths, and the directors who kept them from running into the camera.

Yes, the good, the bad and the weird. That's TV. And that's what this book proposes to examine. Inside you'll find extensive information concerning thousands of performers, directors and writers and their work. There are also several trivia quizzes designed to test your own TV knowledge, and a few highly opinionated essays about selected TV shows that have either been highly influential or extremely popular or both. And now, if you'll excuse me, there's a good episode of "The Dick Van Dyke Show" coming on....

ABOUT THE SYMBOLS

The symbols CBS, ABC, FOX, etc. after most entries are self-explanatory. However, a few symbols may be less familiar. A syndicated (non-network) program is indicated by the symbol SYN, and the symbol DUM stands for the DuMont television network, which was in existence from 1946-55. Also, PBS was known as NET during the 1960's.

ACKNOWLEDGMENTS

The story of this book—and of my life—begins with family. My parents, David and Marilyn Inman, offered endless encouragement, support and love to me as I pursued my goal of being a writer. My brother and sister, Steve and Amy Inman, were always there as well. Without them, this book would not exist. Neither would I.

Jena Monahan hired me almost ten years ago to write the television trivia column that would lead to this book. Greg Johnson offered help and encouragement in his position as features editor of *The Courier-Journal* in Louisville, Kentucky, where I work as a reporter and critic. My sister-in-law, Mindy Inman, helped me with soap opera information.

My agent, Kris Dahl of ICM, was a tireless represenative on my behalf, as was her assistant Gordon Kato. Technical help came willingly from computer experts and friends Jim Reed and Kevin Barnes. Kevin spent many a night babysitting my computer system when I was convinced the machine would work for anyone except me. He often brought his delightful son Jody, who thought the best thing about my writing a TV book was the collection of pictures from "ALF" that I amassed. Boz Johnson and Kelly O'Loane did the typesetting and page layouts with professionalism and style. Judy Linden has been a helpful and supportive editor, and the assistance of her assistant, Sharon Stahl, has also been appreciated.

I was fortunate to have conscientious and thorough researchers working for me: Sherri Arnett, Jeff Ashley, Holly Hinson and Kory Wilcoxson.

Program information was provided by the following: George Faber and Betsy Vorce of Viacom, Andy Samet and James Wood of Worldvision Enterprises, Mandy Murphy of Paramount, Renee Clinkunbroomer of MCA Television, Sharon Jacobson of The Nostalgia Channel, Anna Umbach of King World, Celeste Hicks of the USA Network, Julianne Causey of The Family Channel and Jeff Straw of WLKY–TV in Louisville. Additional information was provided by helpful folks at TNT and Louisville TV stations WHAS, WAVE and WDRB.

Finally, my thanks go to Vince Staten, formerly the TV critic with *The Louisville Times*. Vince and I conceived this idea about five years ago. By the time the project became a reality, Vince was working on several books of his own and couldn't share authorship with me. But his help, advice, support and friendship are—and always have been—very special to me.

To Becky

Who's shown me there's life beyond television

A

AAKER, LEE
b. Los Angeles, CA, September 24, 1943. Fifties child actor who played Rusty on "The Adventures of Rin Tin Tin."
AS A REGULAR: "The Adventures of Rin Tin Tin," ABC, 1954-59.
AND: "Jewelers Showcase: Teacher of the Year," CBS, 1952; "A Letter to Loretta: Kid Stuff," NBC, 1953; "Fireside Theatre: The Boy Down the Road," NBC, 1953; "Ford Theatre: And Suddenly You Knew," NBC, 1953; "Schlitz Playhouse of Stars: Pearl-Handled Guns," CBS, 1954; "Screen Directors Playhouse: The Brush Roper," NBC, 1954; "The Loretta Young Show: The Refinement of Ab," NBC, 1956; "The Ford Show," NBC, 1956; "The Ford Show," NBC, 1957; "The Red Skelton Show," CBS, 1959; "The Millionaire: Millionaire Henry Banning," CBS, 1959; "The Danny Thomas Show: Rusty Meets Little Lord Fauntleroy," CBS, 1960; "The Donna Reed Show: The Electrical Storm," ABC, 1961; "The Lucy Show: Lucy and the Military Academy," CBS, 1963.

TRIVIA QUIZ #1: WHAT'S IN A NAME?
Each of these shows had a one-word title that is a proper name.

1. A 1972 CBS sitcom with Beatrice Arthur as an outspoken housewife.
2. A 1987 ABC sitcom with Alan Arkin as the head of a hospital purchasing department.
3. A 1961 NBC sitcom with Shirley Booth as an unflappable maid.
4. A 1978 CBS cop show with Mark Harmon playing second fiddle to a labrador retriever.
5. A 1975 NBC sitcom with Lee Grant as a divorcee.
6. A 1979 ABC sitcom with Donna Pescow as the new wife of Robert Hays.
7. A 1968 NBC sitcom with Diahann Carroll as a widowed nurse.
8. A 1979 CBS sitcom with Steve Guttenberg as a daydreamer.
9. A 1954 CBS sitcom with June Havoc as an attorney.
10. A 1964 ABC sitcom with Mickey Rooney as a hotel owner.

(Answers at end of book.)

AAMES, WILLIE
b. Los Angeles, CA, 1962. Actor who began as a child and still plays childlike dimwits, notably Buddy Lembeck on "Charles in Charge"; he played Tommy Bradford on "Eight Is Enough."
AS A REGULAR: "We'll Get By," CBS, 1975; "Swiss Family Robinson," ABC, 1975-76; "Eight Is Enough," ABC, 1977-81; "The Edge of Night," ABC, 1983; "Charles in Charge," CBS, 1984-85; SYN, 1987- .
AND: "Medical Center: The Nowhere Child," CBS, 1971; "The Odd Couple: Win One for Felix," ABC, 1971; "The Courtship of Eddie's Father: The Karate Story," ABC, 1972; "The Courtship of Eddie's Father: In the Eye of the Beholder," ABC, 1972; "Gunsmoke: Quiet Day in Dodge," CBS, 1973; "Medical Center: The Enemies," CBS, 1974; "Medical Center: Torment," CBS, 1975; "Little House on the Prairie: Injun Kid," NBC, 1977; "Blacke's Magic: Revenge of the Esperanza," NBC, 1986.
TV MOVIES AND MINISERIES: "Frankenstein," ABC, 1973; "Unwed Father," ABC, 1974; "The Family Nobody Wanted," ABC, 1975; "Eight Is Enough: A Family Reunion," NBC, 1987; "An Eight Is Enough Wedding," NBC, 1989.

ABBOTT, BUD
b. William Abbott, Asbury Park, NJ, October 2, 1895; d. 1974. Straight man to Lou Costello through dozens of successful pictures in the 1940s; their last appearance together was when Costello was honored on "This Is Your Life."
AS A REGULAR: "The Colgate Comedy Hour," NBC, 1951-54; "The Abbott and Costello Show," CBS, 1952-54; SYN, 1966.
AND: "The Steve Allen Show," NBC, 1956; "This Is Your Life," NBC, 1957; "G.E. Theatre: The Joke's on Me," CBS, 1961.
* Abbott lent his voice to Abbott and Costello animated cartoons in 1966.
* See also Lou Costello.

ABBOTT, GEORGE
b. Forestville, NY, June 25, 1887. Playwright and director who did little television.
AS A REGULAR: "The U.S. Royal Showcase," NBC, 1952.
AND: "Tattinger's: Rest in Peas," NBC, 1988.

ABBOTT, PHILIP
b. Lincoln, NB, March 21, 1923. Actor-director who played agent Arthur Ward on "The FBI"; he got his start in New York-based fifties television.
AS A REGULAR: "The House on High Street," NBC, 1959-60; "Search for Tomorrow," CBS, 1961-

63; "The FBI," ABC, 1965-74; "Rich Man, Poor Man—Book II," ABC, 1976-77.
AND: "Kaiser Aluminum Hour: The Army Game," NBC, 1956; "Kraft Television Theatre: Shadow of Suspicion," NBC, 1956; "True Story: The Alibi," NBC, 1957; "U.S. Steel Hour: A Matter of Pride," CBS, 1957; "Modern Romances: The Long Night," NBC, 1957; "Goodyear TV Playhouse: The Legacy," NBC, 1957; "Modern Romances: The Accursed," NBC, 1957; "Studio One: The Undiscovered," CBS, 1958; "Armstrong Circle Theatre: ... And Bring Home a Baby," CBS, 1959; "Playhouse 90: In Lonely Expectation," CBS, 1959; "Dillinger: A Year to Kill," CBS, 1960; "Perry Mason: The Case of the Envious Editor," CBS, 1961; "Naked City: The Well-Dressed Termites," ABC, 1961; "The Twilight Zone: Long-Distance Call," CBS, 1961; "Naked City: A Memory of Crying," ABC, 1961; "The Detectives Starring Robert Taylor: The Airtight Case," ABC, 1961; "Armstrong Circle Theatre: Parole Granted," CBS, 1961; "The Defenders: Quality of Mercy," CBS, 1961; "Bus Stop: A Lion Walks Among Us," ABC, 1961; "Saints and Sinners: A Night of Horns and Bells," NBC, 1962; "G.E. True: O.S.I.," CBS, 1963; "Route 66: Suppose I Said I Was the Queen of Spain," CBS, 1963; "The Twilight Zone: The Parallel," CBS, 1963; "The Outer Limits: The Borderland," ABC, 1963; "The Outer Limits: ZZZZZZ," ABC, 1964; "Walt Disney's Wonderful World of Color: Kilroy," NBC, 1965; "Medical Center: Torment," CBS, 1975; "Salvage I: Mermadon," ABC, 1979; "Quincy: Last Rights," NBC, 1980; "Lou Grant: Business," CBS, 1981; "Quincy: Women of Valor," NBC, 1983; "St. Elsewhere: Handoff," NBC, 1987; "thirtysomething: Payment Due," ABC, 1989.
TV MOVIES AND MINISERIES: "Escape From Bogen County," CBS, 1977.
AS A DIRECTOR: "The FBI," ABC, 1970-73.

ABERLIN, BETTY

Singer who's a familiar face to millions of kids across America as Lady Aberlin on "Mister Rogers' Neighborhood."
AS A REGULAR: "Mister Rogers' Neighborhood," PBS, 1970- ; "The Smothers Brothers Comedy Hour," NBC, 1975.

ACE, GOODMAN

b. Kansas City, MO, January 15, 1899; d. 1982. Ace comedy writer who created "Easy Aces" and was a longtime writer for Perry Como.
AS WRITER: "Easy Aces," DUM, 1949-50; "Texaco Star Theatre," NBC, 1952-53; "The Buick Berle Show," NBC, 1953-55; "The Perry Como Show," NBC, 1955-59; "The Big Party," CBS, 1959; "Perry Como's Kraft Music Hall,"

NBC, 1960-63; "The Jimmy Durante Show," NBC, 1961.

ACE, JANE

b. 1900; d. 1974. Comedienne and wife of Goodman Ace.
AS A REGULAR: "Easy Aces," DUM, 1949-50.

ACKER, SHARON

b. Canada, April 2, 1935. Blonde actress who was a "new" Della Street to the "new" Perry Mason (Monte Markham) in a short-lived series; she also played Erin, wife of heroic liberal Senator Hays Stowe (Hal Holbrook) on "The Bold Ones."
AS A REGULAR: "The Bold Ones," NBC, 1970-71; "The New Adventures of Perry Mason," CBS, 1973-74; "Executive Suite," CBS, 1976-77; "Texas," NBC, 1982.
AND: "It Takes a Thief: The Thingamabob Heist," ABC, 1968; "The Wild Wild West: Night of the Sedgewick Curse," CBS, 1968; "Star Trek: The Mark of Gideon," NBC, 1969; "Lancer: The Gifts," CBS, 1969; "Mission: Impossible: Decoy," CBS, 1970; "Cannon: Salinas Jackpot," CBS, 1971; "Gunsmoke: Trafton," CBS, 1971; "The FBI: The Watchdog," ABC, 1971; "Alias Smith and Jones: The Fifth Victim," ABC, 1972; "Mission: Impossible: Trapped," CBS, 1972; "The Mod Squad: Big George," ABC, 1972; "McMillan and Wife: Night of the Wizard," NBC, 1972; "Marcus Welby, M.D.: Ask Me Again Tomorrow," ABC, 1972; "Marcus Welby, M.D.: The Other Martin Loring," ABC, 1972; "Barnaby Jones: Perchance to Kill," CBS, 1973; "Cannon: Death of a Hunter," CBS, 1974; "The Streets of San Francisco: The Programming of Charlie Blake," ABC, 1975; "Barnaby Jones: Jeopardy for Two," CBS, 1975; "Barnaby Jones: The Deadly Conspiracy," CBS, 1975; "The Streets of San Francisco: Breakup," ABC, 1976; "The Rockford Files: Rosendahl and Gilda Stern Are Dead," NBC, 1978; "The Love Boat: The Kissing Bandit," ABC, 1978; "The Rockford Files: The Man Who Saw the Alligators," NBC, 1979; "Murder, She Wrote: Keep the Home Fries Burning," CBS, 1986.
TV MOVIES AND MINISERIES: "A Clear and Present Danger," NBC, 1970; "Hec Ramsey," NBC, 1972; "The Strangler," NBC, 1973; "The Hanged Man," ABC, 1974; "Dead on Target," ABC, 1976; "The Murder That Wouldn't Die," NBC, 1980.

ACKERMAN, BETTYE

b. Cottageville, SC, February 28, 1928. Actress who played Dr. Maggie Graham on "Ben Casey" and was married to Sam Jaffe, who played Dr. Zorba on the show and was 37 years her senior.

AS A REGULAR: "Ben Casey," ABC, 1961-66; "Return to Peyton Place," NBC, 1972-74.
AND: "Alcoa Premiere: The Jail," ABC, 1962; "Alcoa Premiere: Chain Reaction," ABC, 1963; "The Breaking Point: Better Than a Dead Lion," ABC, 1964; "Perry Mason: The Case of the Thermal Thief," CBS, 1965; "The FBI: The Homecoming," ABC, 1968; "Mannix: Only Giants Can Play," CBS, 1969; "The FBI: The Prey," ABC, 1969; "Medical Center: Twenty-Four Hours," CBS, 1969; "Medical Center: Deadly Encounter," CBS, 1970; "The FBI: Antennae of Death," ABC, 1970; "Columbo: Blueprint For Murder," NBC, 1972; "Medical Center: Question of Guilt," CBS, 1973; "The Rookies: Sound of Silence," ABC, 1973; "Gunsmoke: The Golden Land," CBS, 1973; "Police Story: Glamour Boy," NBC, 1974; "Ironside: Setup: Danger," NBC, 1974; "Lucas Tanner: Bonus Baby," NBC, 1974; "The Streets of San Francisco: Asylum," ABC, 1975; "Police Story: Three Days to Thirty," NBC, 1976; "Police Woman: Good Old Uncle Ben," NBC, 1978; "The Love Boat: The Professor Has Class," ABC, 1983.
TV MOVIES AND MINISERIES: "Companions in Nightmare," NBC, 1968; "Heat of Anger," CBS, 1972; "Murder or Mercy," ABC, 1974.

ACKERMAN, LESLIE

Actress who played the daughter of steelworker Pete "Skag" Skagsa (Karl Malden).
AS A REGULAR: "Skag," NBC, 1980.
AND: "Welcome Back, Kotter: Pilot," ABC, 1975; "Barnaby Jones: Fatal Witness," CBS, 1975; "All in the Family: Archie the Baby-Sitter," CBS, 1976; "The Streets of San Francisco: Child of Anger," ABC, 1977; "Cagney & Lacey: Con Games," CBS, 1985; "Heartbeat: Paradise Lost," ABC, 1989.
TV MOVIES AND MINISERIES: "Studs Lonigan," NBC, 1979; "Women at West Point," CBS, 1979; "Young Love, First Love," CBS, 1979; "Malice in Wonderland," CBS, 1985; "Perry Mason: The Case of the Lethal Lesson," NBC, 1989.

ACKROYD, DAVID

b. Orange, NJ, May 30, 1940. Actor usually in intense roles; he played Dr. Dave Gilchrest on "Another World" and the sullen Dr. Boyer on "AfterMASH."
AS A REGULAR: "The Secret Storm," CBS, 1971-74; "Another World," NBC, 1974-77; "Dallas," CBS, 1978-79; "Little Women," NBC, 1979; "AfterMASH," CBS, 1984.
AND: "Kojak: Close Cover Before Killing," CBS, 1975; "Lou Grant: Sports," CBS, 1978; "Riptide: Catch a Fallen Star," NBC, 1984; "Hardcastle and McCormick: Undercover McCormick," ABC, 1985; "St. Elsewhere: Lost and Found in Space,"

NBC, 1985; "St. Elsewhere: Close Encounter," NBC, 1985; "St. Elsewhere: Watch the Skies," NBC, 1985; "Cagney & Lacey: Extradition," CBS, 1986; "The A-Team: Dishpan Man," NBC, 1986; "Cagney & Lacey: Turn, Turn, Turn," CBS, 1987; "Highway to Heaven: Hello and Farewell," NBC, 1988; "Highway to Heaven: Hello and Farewell," NBC, 1988; "Studio 5B: Surro-Gate," ABC, 1989; "Studio 5B: The Perfect View," ABC, 1989.
TV MOVIES AND MINISERIES: "The Dark Secret of Harvest Home," NBC, 1978; "The Word," CBS, 1978; "And I Alone Survived," NBC, 1978; "Mind Over Murder," CBS, 1979; "A Gun in the House," CBS, 1981; "Cocaine: One Man's Seduction," NBC, 1983; "Deadly Lessons," ABC, 1983; "When Your Lover Leaves," NBC, 1983; "The Sky's No Limit," CBS, 1984; "Picking Up the Pieces," CBS, 1985; "Stark: Mirror Image," CBS, 1986; "The Children of Times Square," ABC, 1986; "A Smoky Mountain Christmas," ABC, 1986; "Poor Little Rich Girl: The Barbara Hutton Story," NBC, 1987; "Windmills of the Gods," CBS, 1988.

ACOVONE, JAY

b. Mahopac, NY, August 20, 1955. Hunky actor who played deputy D.A. Joe Maxwell on "Beauty and the Beast."
AS A REGULAR: "Search for Tomorrow," NBC, 1983-84; "Hollywood Beat," ABC, 1985; "Beauty and the Beast," CBS, 1987-89.
AND: "Matlock: The Doctors," NBC, 1987.

ACTMAN, JANE

b. New York City, NY, April 6, 1949. Seventies actress who played Paul Lynde's daughter on his sitcom.
AS A REGULAR: "The Paul Lynde Show," ABC, 1972-73.
AND: "The Virginian: A Women of Stone," NBC, 1969; "Love, American Style: Love and the Young Unmarrieds," ABC, 1969; "Room 222: The Laughing Majority," ABC, 1970; "The Partridge Family: My Son the Feminist," ABC, 1970; "Hawaii Five-O: R & R & R," CBS, 1972; "Room 222: Bleep," ABC, 1972; "Medical Center: Tainted Lady," CBS, 1974; "Marcus Welby, M.D.: No Gods in Sight," ABC, 1974; "The Rookies: A Deadly Image," ABC, 1975; "Three for the Road: Odyssey in Jeans," CBS, 1975; "Joe Forrester: Weekend," NBC, 1975; "Barnaby Jones: Price of Terror," CBS, 1975.
TV MOVIES AND MINISERIES: "The Chadwick Family," ABC, 1974; "Black Beauty," NBC, 1978.

ACUFF, ROY

b. Roy Claxton Acuff, Maynardsville, TN, September 15, 1903. Country-western singer.

AS A REGULAR: "Grand Ole Opry," ABC, 1955-56; "Hee Haw," SYN, 1980-85.
AND: "George Burns in Nashville?," NBC, 1980.
TV MOVIES AND MINISERIES: "The Concrete Cowboys," CBS, 1979.

ADAIR, DEBORAH

b. Lynchburg, VA. Actress who played Jill Foster Abbott on "The Young and the Restless" and Tracy Kendall on "Dynasty."
AS A REGULAR: "The Young and the Restless," CBS, 1980-83; "Dynasty," ABC, 1983-84; "Finder of Lost Loves," ABC, 1984-85.
AND: "The Love Boat: Starting Over," ABC, 1984; "Hotel: Fantasies," ABC, 1984; "The Love Boat: Egyptian Cruise," ABC, 1986.
TV MOVIES AND MINISERIES: "Gore Vidal's Lincoln," NBC, 1988.

ADAIR, JEAN

Actress usually in spinster roles.
AS A GUEST: "Summer Theatre: At Mrs. Beam's," CBS, 1951; "Kraft Television Theatre: Never Be the Same," NBC, 1951; "Broadway Theatre: Outward Bound," SYN, 1952.

ADAM, NOELLE

b. France, 1935. Singer-dancer.
AS A REGULAR: "The Keefe Brasselle Show," CBS, 1963.
AND: "The Ed Sullivan Show," CBS, 1960; "Jonathan Winters Special," NBC, 1964; "Trials of O'Brien: A Gaggle of Girls," CBS, 1965.

ADAMS, BEVERLY—See Beverly Sassoon.

ADAMS, BROOKE

b. New York City, NY, February 8, 1949. Gamin-like actress of films ("Days of Heaven") and TV; she played one of the sorority-sisters-with-a-past ("Which one of you bitches is my mother?") in "Lace."
AS A REGULAR: "O.K. Crackerby," ABC, 1965-66.
AND: "Police Woman: For the Love of Angela," NBC, 1975; "Kojak: Dead Again," CBS, 1977; "Family: A Love Story for Willie," ABC, 1977; "Family: Acts of Love," ABC, 1977; "Moonlighting: Fetal Attraction," ABC, 1988.
TV MOVIES AND MINISERIES: "The Daughters of Joshua Cabe Return," ABC, 1975; "James Dean," NBC, 1976; "Lace," ABC, 1984; "Special People: Based on a True Story," CBS, 1984; "Lace II," ABC, 1985; "Bridesmaids," CBS, 1989.

ADAMS, CASEY — See Max Showalter.

ADAMS, DON

b. New York City, NY, April 19, 1926. Comic who parlayed his arch, William Powell-style of delivery into one of TVs most remembered comic creations: Maxwell Smart. And he hasn't done much worth remembering since.
AS A REGULAR: "Perry Como's Kraft Music Hall," NBC, 1961-63; "The Bill Dana Show," NBC, 1963-65; "Get Smart," NBC, 1965-69, CBS, 1969-70; "The Partners," NBC, 1971-72; "Don Adams Screen Test," SYN, 1974-75; "Check It Out," USA & SYN, 1985-89.
AND: "Saturday Spectacular: Esther Williams Aqua Spectacale," NBC, 1956; "The Steve Allen Show," NBC, 1957; "The Steve Allen Show," NBC, 1958; "The Lux Show with Rosemary Clooney," NBC, 1958; "Steve Allen Presents The Steve Lawrence and Eydie Gorme Show," NBC, 1958; "The Chevy Show," NBC, 1959; "Perry Como's Kraft Music Hall," NBC, 1960; "Startime: Soldiers in Greasepaint," NBC, 1960; "The Ed Sullivan Show," CBS, 1960; "The Ed Sullivan Show," CBS, 1961; "The Garry Moore Show," CBS, 1961; "Playboy's Penthouse," SYN, 1961; "The Jimmy Dean Show," ABC, 1964; "The Tonight Show Starring Johnny Carson," NBC, 1965; "Hullabaloo," NBC, 1965; "Combat!: The Long Wait," ABC, 1965; "The Tonight Show Starring Johnny Carson," NBC, 1965; "Bob Hope Chrysler Theatre: Murder at NBC," NBC, 1967; "The Danny Thomas Hour: Instant Money," NBC, 1967; "Hollywood Squares," NBC, 1968; "Bob Newhart Special: A Last Laugh at the 60's," ABC, 1970; "Don Adams Special: Hooray for Hollywood," CBS, 1970; "The Comedians," SYN, 1971; "The Saga of Sonora," NBC, 1973; "The Sonny and Cher Comedy Hour," CBS, 1973; "A Couple of Dons," NBC, 1973; "Celebrity Sweepstakes," NBC, 1974; "Wait Till Your Father Gets Home: Don for the Defense," SYN, 1974; "The Mike Douglas Show," SYN, 1975; "Sammy and Company," SYN, 1975; "Joys," NBC, 1976; "Three Times Daily," CBS, 1976; "The Mike Douglas Show," SYN, 1977; "The Love Boat: Safety Last," ABC, 1982; "The Love Boat: The Very Temporary Secretary," ABC, 1983; "The Love Boat: Novelties," ABC, 1984; "The Fall Guy: Losers Weepers," ABC, 1984.
TV MOVIES AND MINISERIES: "The Exterminators," CBS, 1973; "The Love Boat," ABC, 1976; "Get Smart, Again!," ABC, 1989.
* Emmies: 1967, 1968, 1969.

ADAMS, EDIE

b. Elizabeth Edith Enke, Kingston, PA, April 16, 1927. Sexy blonde actress-singer of the fifties and sixties, famous for her "Why don't you pick one up and—smoke it sometime" Muriel cigar commercials of the sixties; widow of Ernie Kovacs.

AS A REGULAR: "Kovacs on the Corner," NBC, 1951-52; "It's Time for Ernie," NBC, 1951; "Ernie in Kovacsland," NBC, 1951; "The Jack Paar Show," CBS, 1953-56; "The Ernie Kovacs Show," NBC, 1955-56; "The Chevy Show," NBC, 1958; "Take a Good Look," ABC, 1959-61; "Here's Edie," ABC, 1962-63; "The Edie Adams Show," ABC, 1963-64.

AND: "Appointment with Adventure: The Royal Treatment," CBS, 1955; "The Walter Winchell Show," NBC, 1956; "The Jonathan Winters Show," NBC, 1956; "The Ed Sullivan Show," CBS, 1957; "Cinderella," CBS, 1957; "The Frank Sinatra Show," ABC, 1958; "The Gisele MacKenzie Show," NBC, 1958; "The Ed Sullivan Show," CBS, 1958; "Kovacs on Music," NBC, 1959; "G.E. Theatre: The Falling Angel," CBS, 1959; "Art Carney Special: Small World, Isn't It?," NBC, 1959; "Bell Telephone Hour: The Golden West," NBC, 1959; "Dick Clark's World of Talent," ABC, 1959; "Arthur Murray Party," NBC, 1959; "U.S. Steel Hour: The American Cowboy," CBS, 1960; "Revlon Revue," CBS, 1960; "Westinghouse Lucille Ball-Desi Arnaz Show: Lucy Meets the Mustache," CBS, 1960; "Perry Como's Kraft Music Hall," NBC, 1960; "The Jack Paar Show," NBC, 1961; "Here's Hollywood," NBC, 1961; "U.S. Steel Hour: Private Eye, Private Eye," CBS, 1961; "The Dick Powell Show: Thunder in a Forgotten Town," NBC, 1963; "Sid Caesar and Edie Adams Together," ABC, 1963; "The Jack Paar Program," NBC, 1965; "Hollywood Palace," ABC, 1965; "ABC Nightlife," ABC, 1965; "The Danny Kaye Show," CBS, 1966; "The Lucy Show: Mooney's Other Wife," CBS, 1968; "The Carol Burnett Show," CBS, 1968; "Don Adams Special: Hooray for Hollywood," CBS, 1970; "The Don Knotts Show," NBC, 1971; "Love, American Style: Love and the Hotel Caper," ABC, 1971; "McMillan and Wife: Blues for Sally M," NBC, 1972; "Harry O: Past Imperfect," ABC, 1976; "Rosetti and Ryan: Is There a Lawyer in the House?," NBC, 1977; "Police Woman: Blind Terror," NBC, 1978; "The Love Boat: Marooned," ABC, 1978; "A Man Called Sloane: Lady Bug," NBC, 1979; "Bosom Buddies: Pilot," ABC, 1980; "The Mike Douglas Show," SYN, 1981; "Fantasy Island: The World's Most Desirable Woman," ABC, 1981; "Murder, She Wrote: Capitol Offense," CBS, 1985.

TV MOVIES AND MINISERIES: "Evil Roy Slade," NBC, 1972; "Fast Friends," NBC, 1979; "Make Me an Offer," ABC, 1980; "Portrait of an Escort," CBS, 1980.

ADAMS, FRANKLIN P.

b. Chicago, IL, 1881; d. 1960. Newspaper columnist and panelist on the radio and TV versions of "Information Please."

AS A REGULAR: "Information Please," CBS, 1952.

ADAMS, JEB

b. Hollywood, CA, April 10, 1961. Blond actor who played Lt. Jeb Pruitt on "Baa Baa Black Sheep"; son of Nick Adams.

AS A REGULAR: "Baa Baa Black Sheep," NBC, 1978.

AND: "Highway to Heaven: Normal People," NBC, 1986.

ADAMS, JOEY

b. New York City, NY, January 6, 1911.

AS A REGULAR: "Back That Fact," ABC, 1953.

AND: "Strike It Rich," CBS, 1957; "The Jackie Gleason Show," CBS, 1957; "The Julius LaRosa Show," NBC, 1957; "Make Me Laugh," ABC, 1958; "Your First Impression," NBC, 1963; "The Steve Allen Show," SYN, 1968.

ADAMS, JULIE

b. Betty May Adams, Waterloo, IA, October 17, 1926. Fifties movie starlet ("The Creature From the Black Lagoon") who played Jimmy Stewart's wife on his sitcom and Paula Denning on "Capitol."

AS A REGULAR: "Yancy Derringer," CBS, 1958-59; "General Hospital," ABC, 1969-70; "The Jimmy Stewart Show," NBC, 1971-72; "Code Red," ABC, 1981-82; "Capitol," CBS, 1983-87.

AND: "Lux Video Theatre: Appointment with Love," NBC, 1955; "Studio One: Circle of Guilt," CBS, 1956; "The Loretta Young Show: The Hidden One," NBC, 1956; "Climax!: Two Tests for Tuesday," CBS, 1957; "Goodyear Theatre: Points Beyond," NBC, 1958; "Maverick: The Brasada Spur," ABC, 1959; "Ellery Queen: The Curse of Aden," NBC, 1959; "Maverick: The White Widow," ABC, 1960; "Alcoa Theatre: Minister Accused," NBC, 1960; "77 Sunset Strip: Safari," ABC, 1960; "Hawaiian Eye: Murder, Anyone?," ABC, 1960; "The Rifleman: Nora," ABC, 1960; "The Wrangler: The Affair with Browning's Woman," NBC, 1960; "SurfSide 6: Laugh for the Lady," ABC, 1961; "The Andy Griffith Show: The County Nurse," CBS, 1962; "King of Diamonds: A Girl's Best Friend," SYN, 1962; "The Dick Powell Show: 330 Independence Square," NBC, 1962; "Dr. Kildare: Horn of Plenty," NBC, 1962; "Checkmate: The Someday Man," CBS, 1962; "Kraft Suspense Theatre: The Robrioz Ring," NBC, 1964; "You Don't Say," NBC, 1964; "Perry Mason: The Case of the Missing Bottle," CBS, 1964; "You Don't Say," NBC, 1965; "Kraft Suspense Theatre: Kill No More," NBC, 1965; "Perry Mason: The Case of the Fatal Fortune," CBS, 1965; "Twelve O'Clock High: Big Brother," ABC, 1965; "Amos Burke, Secret Agent: Deadlier Than the Male," ABC, 1965; "The Long Hot Summer: Bitter Harvest," ABC, 1965; "The Virginian: No Drums, No

Trumpets," NBC, 1966; "The Big Valley: Target," ABC, 1966; "The Big Valley: Emperor of Rice," ABC, 1968; "The Mod Squad: You Can't Tell the Players Without a Programmer," ABC, 1968; "Ironside: I, the People," NBC, 1968; "The Outsider: One Long-Stemmed American Beauty," NBC, 1968; "My Friend Tony: Voices," NBC, 1969; "The Doris Day Show: Married for a Day," CBS, 1969; "Marcus Welby, M.D.: Don't Ignore the Miracles," ABC, 1970; "The Young Lawyers: And the Walls Came Tumbling Down," ABC, 1971; "Night Gallery: The Miracle at Camefeo," NBC, 1972; "The Doris Day Show: The Press Secretary," CBS, 1972; "Cannon: Child of Fear," CBS, 1972; "The Mod Squad: Scion of Death," ABC, 1973; "The Streets of San Francisco: Labyrinth," ABC, 1975; "Marcus Welby, M.D.: An End and a Beginning," ABC, 1975; "Ellery Queen: Veronica's Veils," NBC, 1975; "Medical Center: The Stranger," CBS, 1976; "Police Woman: Murder with Pretty People," NBC, 1978; "Cross Wits," SYN, 1978; "Quincy: Honor Thy Elders," NBC, 1980; "Quincy: Sleeping Dogs," NBC, 1982; "Murder, She Wrote: If It's Thursday, It Must Be Beverly," CBS, 1987; "Murder, She Wrote: Benedict Arnold Slipped Here," CBS, 1988; "Murder, She Wrote: Sins of Castle Cove," CBS, 1989.

TV MOVIES AND MINISERIES: "The Trackers," ABC, 1971; "Go Ask Alice," ABC, 1973.

ADAMS, MARLA
Soap actress who plays Helen on "Generations"; she formerly played Dina Abbott Mergeron on "The Young and the Restless."

AS A REGULAR: "The Secret Storm," CBS, 1968-74; "Capitol," CBS, 1983; "The Young and the Restless," CBS, 1983-89; "Generations," NBC, 1989- .

AND: "Barnaby Jones: Conspiracy of Terror," CBS, 1974; "Adam 12: Dana Hall," NBC, 1975; "The Streets of San Francisco: Breakup," ABC, 1976; "Marcus Welby, M.D.: Prisoner of the Island Cell," ABC, 1976; "Barnaby Jones: Deadly Charade," CBS, 1977; "Barnaby Jones: Academy of Evil," CBS, 1978; "The Love Boat: Rocky," ABC, 1978; "Carter Country: Teddy's Folly," ABC, 1979.

TV MOVIES AND MINISERIES: "The Secret Night Caller," NBC, 1975.

ADAMS, MASON
b. New York City, NY, February 26, 1919. Former radio actor usually in fatherly or distinguished roles; he played Los Angeles Tribune managing editor Charlie Hume on "Lou Grant" and has provided the folksy voice for hundreds of commercials.

AS A REGULAR: "Lou Grant," CBS, 1977-82; "Morningstar/Eveningstar," CBS, 1986; "Knight and Daye," NBC, 1989.

AND: "The Phil Silvers Show: Bilko the Genius," CBS, 1958; "The Love Boat: Daddy's Little Girl," ABC, 1981; "Family Ties: Paper Lion," NBC, 1986; "Murder, She Wrote: The Search for Peter Kerry," CBS, 1989.

TV MOVIES AND MINISERIES: "The Deadliest Season," CBS, 1977; "And Baby Makes Six," NBC, 1979; "The Revenge of the Stepford Wives," NBC, 1980; "Flamingo Road," NBC, 1980; "Adam," NBC, 1983; "Passions," CBS, 1984; "The Night They Saved Christmas," ABC, 1984; "Who Is Julia?" CBS, 1986; "Under Siege," NBC, 1986; "Rage of Angels: The Story Continues," NBC, 1986.

* On the radio, Adams was Pepper Young on the serial "Pepper Young's Family."

ADAMS, MAUD
b. Maud Wikstrom, Sweden, February 12, 1945. Sexy actress who got her first big break selling Lip Quencher lip gloss in the seventies, back when women wore that kind of stuff.

AS A REGULAR: "Chicago Story," NBC, 1982; "Emerald Point NAS," CBS, 1983-84.

AND: "Love, American Style: Love and the Monsters," ABC, 1971; "Kojak: Kojak's Days," CBS, 1977; "The John Davidson Show," SYN, 1980; "The Mike Douglas Show," SYN, 1981; "Hotel: Recriminations," ABC, 1986; "Mission: Impossible: The Plague," ABC, 1989.

TV MOVIES AND MINISERIES: "The Hostage Tower," CBS, 1980; "Playing for Time," CBS, 1980; "Nairobi Affair," CBS, 1984.

ADAMS, NEILE
b. Ruby Neilan Salvador Adams, Manila, 1935. Actress and dancer; former wife of Steve McQueen, with whom she appeared in the "Alfred Hitchcock Presents" episode "The Man From the South."

AS A GUEST: "Pat Boone Chevy Showroom," ABC, 1958; "The Patrice Munsel Show," ABC, 1958; "The Eddie Fisher Show," NBC, 1958; "Alfred Hitchcock Presents: The Man From the South," CBS, 1960; "Perry Como's Kraft Music Hall," NBC, 1960; "Alfred Hitchcock Presents: One Grave Too Many," CBS, 1960; "The Bob Hope Buick Show," NBC, 1960; "The Man From UNCLE: The Yellow Scarf Affair," NBC, 1965.

TV MOVIES AND MINISERIES: "Women in Chains," ABC, 1972.

ADAMS, NICK
b. Nicholas Aloysius Adamshock, Nanticoke, PA, July 10, 1931; d. 1968. Handsome actor who played Johnny Yuma, "The Rebel"; he died of an overdose of drugs he was taking for a nervous disorder.

AS A REGULAR: "The Rebel," ABC, 1959-61; "Saints and Sinners," NBC, 1962-63.

AND: "The People's Choice: Sock vs. Stone Kenyon," NBC, 1956; "Playhouse 90: The Troublemakers," CBS, 1957; "Dick Powell's Zane Grey Theatre: Showdown at Bitter Creek," CBS, 1958; "The Dick Clark Saturday Night Beechnut Show," ABC, 1960; "Steve Allen Plymouth Show," NBC, 1960; "What's My Line?," CBS, 1960; "Here's Hollywood," NBC, 1961; "The Dick Powell Show: Who Killed Julie Greer?," NBC, 1961; "The Dick Powell Show: Savage Sunday," NBC, 1962; "Combat!: Bridgehead," ABC, 1963; "77 Sunset Strip: By His Own Verdict," ABC, 1963; "Burke's Law: Who Killed Billy Jo?," ABC, 1963; "Burke's Law: Who Killed Eleanora Davis?," ABC, 1963; "Object Is," ABC, 1964; "Stump the Stars," CBS, 1964; "Arrest and Trial: A Roll of the Dice," ABC, 1964; "The Outer Limits: Fun and Games," ABC, 1964; "The Tonight Show Starring Johnny Carson," NBC, 1964; "The Reporter: How Much for a Prince?," CBS, 1964; "Burke's Law: Who Killed Mr. Cartwheel?," ABC, 1964; "Voyage to the Bottom of the Sea: Turn Back the Clock," ABC, 1964; "Burke's Law: Who Killed Merlin the Great?," ABC, 1964; "Rawhide: Corporal Dasovik," CBS, 1964; "The Mike Douglas Show," SYN, 1965; "Burke's Law: Who Killed Wimbeldon Hastings?," ABC, 1965; "Ben Casey: Three Li'l Lambs," ABC, 1965; "The Wild, Wild West: The Night of the Two-Legged Buffalo," CBS, 1966; "Walt Disney's Wonderful World of Color: Willie and the Yank," NBC, 1967; "Combat!: The Masquers," ABC, 1967; "Hondo: Hondo and the Apache Trail," ABC, 1967; "The Wild Wild West: The Night of the Vipers," CBS, 1968.

ADAMS, STANLEY
b. 1920. Rotund character actor usually in comic conman roles, but occasionally as a convincing low-life type.
AS A REGULAR: "How To," CBS, 1951; "The Adventures of Hiram Holliday," NBC, 1956-57.
AND: "My Friend Flicka: Golden Promise," CBS, 1956; "Pied Piper of Hamelin," NBC, 1957; "Court of Last Resort: The Frank Clark Case," NBC, 1958; "The Thin Man: The Pre-Incan Caper," CBS, 1958; "The Jane Wyman Show: Swindler's Inn," NBC, 1958; "The Thin Man: The Bronze Bonze," NBC, 1959; "Science Series: The Alphabet Conspiracy," NBC, 1959; "December Bride: The Texan, Rory Calhoun," CBS, 1959; "Mr. Lucky: That Stands for Pool," CBS, 1959; "Riverboat: That Taylor Affair," NBC, 1960; "Dan Raven: The Empty Frame," NBC, 1960; "Pete and Gladys: Gladys Rents the House," CBS, 1961; "The Law and Mr. Jones: The Big Gambling Raid," ABC, 1961; "The Twilight Zone: Once Upon a Time," CBS, 1961; "Robert Taylor's Detectives: Night Boat," NBC, 1962;

"The New Breed: The Torch," ABC, 1962; "The Andy Griffith Show: Deputy Otis," CBS, 1962; "Have Gun, Will Travel: Cream of the Jest," CBS, 1962; "Mr. Smith Goes to Washington: The Country Sculptor," ABC, 1962; "McKeever and the Colonel: Straight and Narrow," NBC, 1962; "Alcoa Premiere: Impact of an Execution," ABC, 1963; "The Gallant Men: Next of Kin," ABC, 1963; "Wagon Train: The Trace McCloud Story," ABC, 1964; "Bob Hope Chrysler Theatre: The Square Peg," NBC, 1964; "Bonanza: The Pure Truth," NBC, 1964; "The Twilight Zone: Mr. Garrity and the Graves," CBS, 1964; "The Dick Van Dyke Show: Your Home Sweet Home Is My Home," CBS, 1965; "The Bing Crosby Show: Moonlighting Becomes You," ABC, 1965; "McHale's Navy: Will the Real Admiral Please Stand Up?," ABC, 1965; "My Mother the Car: Lights, Camera, Mother," NBC, 1965; "The Donna Reed Show: All This and Voltaire, Too?," ABC, 1966; "McHale's Navy: Wally for Congress," ABC, 1966; "Pistols 'n' Petticoats: No Sale," CBS, 1966; "The Lucy Show: Lucy the Fight Manager," CBS, 1967; "T.H.E. Cat: Matter Over Mind," NBC, 1967; "Gilligan's Island: Gilligan, the Goddess," CBS, 1967; "The Lucy Show: Lucy and the Pool Hustler," CBS, 1968; "The Lucy Show: Lucy and Ken Berry," CBS, 1968; "Barefoot in the Park: You'll Never Walk Alone," ABC, 1970; "Love, American Style: Love and the Man Next Door," ABC, 1970; "Love, American Style: Love and the New Act," ABC, 1972; "The Odd Couple: The Hustler," ABC, 1973; "Mannix: Out of the Night," CBS, 1973; "The Odd Couple: The Big Broadcast," ABC, 1974; "Medical Center: Life, Death, and Mrs. Armbruster," CBS, 1976; "One Day at a Time: Julie's Job," CBS, 1976.
TV MOVIES AND MINISERIES: "Love, Hate, Love," ABC, 1971; "Banyon," NBC, 1971; "The Night Stalker," ABC, 1972; "Every Man Needs One," ABC, 1972.
AS WRITER: "T.H.E. Cat: Marked for Death," NBC, 1966.

ADDAMS, DAWN
b. Felixstowe, England, September 21, 1930. Fifties starlet.
AS A REGULAR: "The Alan Young Show," CBS, 1953.
AND: "Ford Theatre: Sweet Talk Me, Jackson," NBC, 1953; "The Saint: The Fellow Traveler," SYN, 1964.
* Addams appeared in Charlie Chaplin's 1957 film "A King in New York," but her other movie credits were negligible, including "Where the Bullets Fly" and "The Vault of Horror."

ADDY, WESLEY
b. Omaha, NB, August 4, 1913. Actor usually

in distinguished roles; he plays Cabot Alden on "Loving."

AS A REGULAR: "The Edge of Night," CBS, 1958-59; "Ryan's Hope," ABC, 1977-78; "Loving," ABC, 1983- .

AND: "CBS Television Workshop: The Brick and the Rose," CBS, 1960; "John Brown's Raid," NBC, 1960; "The Eternal Light: Pages From the Talmud," NBC, 1960; "Armstrong Circle Theatre: The Spy Next Door," CBS, 1961; "The Eternal Light: The Search," NBC, 1961; "Perry Mason: The Case of the Weary Watchdog," CBS, 1962; "Look Up and Live: The History of Asceticism," CBS, 1964; "The Outer Limits: The Brain of Colonel Barham," ABC, 1965; "The Fugitive: Conspiracy of Silence," ABC, 1965; "The FBI: All the Streets Are Silent," ABC, 1965; "The FBI: The Plunderers," ABC, 1966; "Love on a Rooftop: Murder in Apartment D," ABC, 1967; "The FBI: The Fraud," ABC, 1969; "The FBI: Silent Partners," ABC, 1969; "Medical Center: No Margin for Error," CBS, 1973; "The Rockford Files: Dirty Money, Black Light," NBC, 1977.

ADLER, LUTHER

b. New York City, NY, May 4, 1903. Stage actor whose career thrived when most TV was being produced in New York.

AS A REGULAR: "The Psychiatrist," NBC, 1971.
AND: "U.S. Steel Hour: Hedda Gabler," ABC, 1954; "Studio One: A Criminal Design," CBS, 1954; "Robert Montgomery Presents: The Killers," NBC, 1955; "Star Stage: The Sainted General," NBC, 1956; "U.S. Steel Hour: The Partners," CBS, 1956; "Studio One: The Cauliflower Heart," CBS, 1956; "Playhouse 90: The Last Clear Chance," CBS, 1958; "Playhouse 90: The Plot to Kill Stalin," CBS, 1958; "The Twilight Zone: The Man in the Bottle," CBS, 1960; "The Untouchables: Nicky," ABC, 1960; "Naked City: The Man Who Bit the Diamond in Half," ABC, 1960; "The Islanders: Escape From Kaledau," ABC, 1961; "Play of the Week: A Month in the Country," SYN, 1961; "DuPont Show of the Month: The Lincoln Murder Case," CBS, 1961; "The Untouchables: Murder Under Glass," ABC, 1961; "Naked City: A Memory of Crying," ABC, 1961; "Ben Casey: The Insolent Heart," ABC, 1961; "Naked City: The Fingers of Henri Tourelle," ABC, 1961; "Target: The Corruptors: The Silent Partner," ABC, 1961; "The Untouchables: Takeover," ABC, 1962; "Target: The Corruptors: The Wrecker," ABC, 1962; "Route 66: Man Out of Time," CBS, 1962; "Naked City: Make It Fifty Dollars, and Add Love to Nona," ABC, 1962; "Ben Casey: The White Ones Are Dolphins," ABC, 1963; "Kraft Suspense Theatre: Doesn't Anyone Know Who I Am?," NBC, 1964; "Mission: Impossible: Phantoms," CBS, 1970; "The Name of the Game: Tarot," NBC, 1970; "Hawaii Five-O: V Is for Vashion," CBS, 1972; "D.H.O.," ABC, 1973; "Hec Ramsey: The Detroit Connection," NBC, 1973; "Hawaii Five-0: How to Steal a Masterpiece," CBS, 1974; "The Streets of San Francisco: Mister Nobody," ABC, 1974.

TV MOVIES AND MINISERIES: "The Sunshine Patriot," NBC, 1968; "The Psychiatrist: God Bless the Children," NBC, 1970.
* Adler's sister is acting teacher Stella Adler.

ADRIAN, IRIS

b. Los Angeles, CA, May 29, 1912. Wisecracking character actress usually in tough comic roles.

AS A REGULAR: "The Abbott and Costello Show," CBS, 1952-54; "The Ted Knight Show," CBS, 1978.

AND: "Racket Squad: Three Ring Circus," CBS, 1953; "The Jack Benny Program," CBS, 1961; "The Munsters: Grandpa Leaves Home," CBS, 1964; "The Bing Crosby Show: The Test," ABC, 1965; "The Beverly Hillbillies: Jed's Temptation," CBS, 1965; "Green Acres: Lisa's First Day on the Farm," CBS, 1965; "Get Smart: The Day Smart Turned Chicken," NBC, 1965; "The Beverly Hillbillies: Clampett Cha Cha Cha," CBS, 1966; "The Lucy Show: Lucy Meets the Law," CBS, 1967; "The Doris Day Show: Buck Visits the Big City," CBS, 1970; "The Doris Day Show: Doris vs. Pollution," CBS, 1970; "The Doris Day Show: A Weighty Problem," CBS, 1971; "The Love Boat: The Tour Guide," ABC, 1986.

THE ADVENTURES OF OZZIE AND HARRIET, ABC, 1952-66.

"Uh-uh, Dave, uh-uh Rick, uh-uh Harriet...."

So went the call of Ozzie every week on "The Adventures of Ozzie and Harriet," as America watched little Ricky Nelson grow into a rock and roll idol, little Dave grow into Rick's slightly boring older brother and Ozzie stay pretty much the same benign, bumbling pop he'd been the week, or year, or even decade before.

In reality, of course, Ozzie Nelson was one sharp businessman and the producer-director and occasional writer for "The Adventures of Ozzie and Harriet," which had begun on radio in 1944. In 1949, Ozzie brought on his own young sons to play his sons, and on television it was always a family affair, even as Rick and Dave grew older and married—their real-life wives played their wives on the show.

The plots on "Ozzie and Harriet" were 1950's sitcom stuff all the way, but the show had its own kind of special wit. And the scrapes everyone got into at least had some sort of basis in reality. At its worst, the show was just kind of, well, relaxing and familiar.

When Ricky wasn't banging on his guitar or drums, that is. In late 1956, Ricky performed "I'm Walkin'" on the "Ricky, the Drummer" episode and a rock and roll legend was born. For virtually all the rest of the show's run, Ricky sang a song a week, usually in a short sequence tacked on to the end of the show.

"The Adventures of Ozzie and Harriet" was never a hit; it was never even in the top 25 shows. But it was a dependable performer at a time when ABC was hungry for hits. By the time it went off the air in 1966, Dave and Rick were married and practicing lawyers. In later years, both men would divorce and Rick would die in a 1985 plane crash in which drugs may have been involved.

AGAR, JOHN

b. *Chicago, IL, January 31, 1921.* Hunky actor of the 1950s.

AS A GUEST: "Fireside Theatre: The Next to Crash," NBC, 1952; "The Unexpected: Desert Honeymoon," NBC, 1952; "Ford Theatre: The Old Man's Bride," NBC, 1953; "Fireside Theatre: The Farnsworth Case," NBC, 1954; "Schlitz Playhouse of Stars: Little War in San Dede," CBS, 1954; "Climax!: The First and the Last," CBS, 1955; "The Loretta Young Show: Earthquake," NBC, 1956; "G.E. Theatre: The Thousand-Dollar Gun," CBS, 1957; "The Gale Storm Show: Diamonds Are a Girl's Best," CBS, 1958; "Perry Mason: The Case of the Caretaker's Cat," CBS, 1959; "Rawhide: Incident at the Buffalo Smoke House," CBS, 1959; "Rawhide: Incident of the Slavemaster," CBS, 1960; "Best of the Post: Band of Brothers," SYN, 1960; "Bat Masterson: Farmer with a Badge," NBC, 1961; "Death Valley Days: Pioneer Doctor," SYN, 1963; "The Virginian: Walk in Another's Footsteps," NBC, 1964; "Branded: $10,000 for Durango," NBC, 1965; "Combat!: The Mockingbird," ABC, 1966; "Hondo: Hondo and the Judas," ABC, 1967; "Family Affair: What Did You Do in the West, Uncle?," CBS, 1967; "The Name of the Game: Nightmare," NBC, 1968; "The Virginian: The Mustangers," NBC, 1968; "Highway to Heaven: The Return of the Masked Rider," NBC, 1984.

AGUTTER, JENNY

b. *England, December 20, 1952.* Actress who won an Emmy for her sensitive portrayal in "The Snow Goose."

AS A GUEST: "Hallmark Hall of Fame: The Snow Goose," NBC, 1971; "Magnum P.I.: Little Games," CBS, 1985; "Murder, She Wrote: One White Rose for Death," CBS, 1986; "The Twilight Zone: The Last Defender of Camelot," CBS, 1986; "The Equalizer: The Visitation," CBS, 1989; "Dear John: The British Are Coming," NBC, 1989.

TV MOVIES AND MINISERIES: "A War of Children," CBS, 1972; "The Man in the Iron Mask," NBC, 1977; "Mayflower: The Pilgrims' Adventure," CBS, 1979; "Beulah Land," NBC, 1980.

* Emmies: 1972.

AHERNE, BRIAN

b. *Kings Norton, England, May 2, 1902; d. 1986.* Actor often in dapper, in-control roles.

AS A GUEST: "Theatre Hour: Dear Brutus," CBS, 1950; "Armstrong Circle Theatre: The Magnificent Gesture," NBC, 1950; "Lux Video Theatre: A Well-Remembered Voice," CBS, 1951; "Pulitzer Prize Playhouse: The Buccaneer," ABC, 1951; "Lux Video Theatre: Two for Tea," CBS, 1953; "Robert Montgomery Presents: Element of Risk," NBC, 1953; "Robert Montgomery Presents: Breakdown," NBC, 1953; "The Old Flame," CBS, 1955; "G.E. Theatre: The Martyr," CBS, 1955; "Rheingold Theatre: The Round Dozen," NBC, 1955; "Producers Showcase: Reunion in Vienna," NBC, 1955; "Crossroads: Chinese Checkers," ABC, 1955; "Rheingold Theatre: Appearance and Reality," NBC, 1956; "Crossroads: The Sacred Trust," ABC, 1956; "Climax!: Night Shriek," CBS, 1956; "Du Pont Theatre: Pursuit of a Princess," ABC, 1956; "Crossroads: The Lamp of Father Cataldo," ABC, 1956; "Studio 57: Safe Enough," SYN, 1957; "Errol Flynn Theatre: The Transfer," SYN, 1957; "Goodyear Theatre: Story Without a Moral," NBC, 1959; "The Twilight Zone: The Trouble with Templeton," CBS, 1960; "Wagon Train: The Bruce Saybrook Story," NBC, 1961; "Rawhide: The Gentleman's Gentleman," CBS, 1961; "Walt Disney's Wonderful World of Color: The Waltz King," NBC, 1963.

AHN, PHILIP

b. *Los Angeles, CA, March 29, 1911; d. 1978.* Actor of Korean descent usually cast as an inscrutable type; he played Master Kan on "Kung Fu."

AS A REGULAR: "The Garlund Touch (Mr. Garlund)," CBS, 1960; "Kung Fu," ABC, 1972-75.

AND: "Four Star Playhouse: Stuffed Shirt," CBS, 1955; "TV Reader's Digest: Mr. Pak Takes

Over," ABC, 1955; "Hey, Jeannie!: Jeannie the Proprietor," CBS, 1956; "Navy Log: Commander and the Kid," ABC, 1957; "The Californians: Death by Proxy," NBC, 1958; "Lawman: The Intruders," ABC, 1958; "Have Gun, Will Travel: Hey Boy's Revenge," CBS, 1958; "The Adventures of Rin Tin Tin: The Ming Vase," ABC, 1959; "Bonanza: Day of the Dragon," NBC, 1961; "Follow the Sun: Ghost Story," ABC, 1962; "Adventures in Paradise: Build My Gallows Low," ABC, 1962; "The Brothers Brannagan: Key of Jade," SYN, 1962; "Hawaiian Eye: The Broken Thread," ABC, 1962; "Mr. Smith Goes to Washington: The Fork in the Road," ABC, 1962; "Ensign O'Toole: Operation: Intrigue," NBC, 1963; "Bonanza: A Pink Cloud Comes From Old Cathay," NBC, 1964; "The Rogues: Our Men in Marawat," NBC, 1965; "I Spy: Carry Me Back to Old Tsing-Tao," NBC, 1965; "The Wild Wild West: The Night the Dragon Screamed," CBS, 1966; "The Man From UNCLE: The Abominable Snowman Affair," NBC, 1966; "The Man From UNCLE: The Five Daughters Affair," NBC, 1967; "I Spy: An American Empress," NBC, 1967; "My Three Sons: Honorable Guest," CBS, 1968; "Hawaii Five-O: Full Fathom Five," CBS, 1968; "Mission: Impossible: Doomsday," CBS, 1969; "Ironside: Love My Enemy," NBC, 1969; "The Streets of San Francisco: The Year of the Locusts," ABC, 1973; "Love, American Style: Love and the Golden Worm," ABC, 1974; "The Magician: The Illusion of the Lost Dragon," NBC, 1974; "ABC Theatre: Judgment: The Courtmartial of the Tiger of Malaya-General Yamashita," ABC, 1974; "M*A*S*H: Hawkeye," CBS, 1976; "M*A*S*H: Exorcism," CBS, 1976; "Sanford & Son: Chinese Torture," NBC, 1977; "M*A*S*H: Change Day," CBS, 1977; "Switch: The Tong," CBS, 1978; "Police Woman: The Human Rights of Tiki Kim," NBC, 1978.
TV MOVIES AND MINISERIES: "Hawaii Five-O," CBS, 1968; "Kung Fu," ABC, 1972.

AIDMAN, CHARLES
  b. Frankfort, IN, January 31, 1925. Actor with a cool, calming voice, usually in intelligent roles; he was the narrator on the revival of "The Twilight Zone" and played a hypnotist who unwittingly put Rob Petrie under a spell on a memorable episode of "The Dick Van Dyke Show."
AS A REGULAR: "The Twilight Zone," CBS, 1985-87.
AND: "Kraft Television Theatre: Give Me the Courage," NBC, 1957; "Big Story: Young Lovers," NBC, 1957; "Kraft Television Theatre: Circle of Fear," NBC, 1957; "Studio One: The Left-Hand Welcome," CBS, 1958; "The Twilight Zone: And When the Sky Was Opened," CBS, 1959; "U.S. Marshal: The Miracle," SYN, 1959; "Wichita Town: Ruby Dawes," NBC, 1960;

"Riverboat: Fight at New Canal," NBC, 1960; "Gunsmoke: Unwanted Deputy," CBS, 1960; "Playhouse 90: Tomorrow," CBS, 1960; "Gunsmoke: About Chester," CBS, 1961; "The Law and Mr. Jones: Mea Culpa," ABC, 1961; "Bonanza: The Rival," NBC, 1961; "Thriller: Terror in Teakwood," NBC, 1961; "The Dick Van Dyke Show: My Husband Is Not a Drunk," CBS, 1962; "The Virginian: The Devil's Children," NBC, 1962; "The Dick Van Dyke Show: Laura's Little Lie," CBS, 1963; "The Virginian: The Girl From Yesterday," NBC, 1964; "Slattery's People: Question-Do the Ignorant Sleep in Pure White Beds?," CBS, 1964; "The Andy Griffith Show: Andy's Rival," CBS, 1965; "The Fugitive: Trial by Fire," ABC, 1965; "Gomer Pyle, USMC: A Visit From Cousin Goober," CBS, 1965; "The Hero: The Day They Shot Sam Garrett," NBC, 1966; "Gunsmoke: The Money Store," CBS, 1968; "The FBI: The Tunnel," ABC, 1968; "Gunsmoke: The Intruder," CBS, 1969; "The Bold Ones: The Rockford Riddle," NBC, 1969; "The Virginian: No War for the Warrior," NBC, 1970; "Medical Center: The Clash," CBS, 1970; "The Rookies: Rabbits on the Runway," ABC, 1972; "The Streets of San Francisco: The Unicorn," ABC, 1973; "Kolchak the Night Stalker: The Zombie," ABC, 1974; "The Streets of San Francisco: Most Likely to Succeed," ABC, 1975; "The Rockford Files: The Mayor's Committee from Deer Lick Falls," NBC, 1977; "M*A*S*H: The Grim Reaper," CBS, 1977; "Little House on the Prairie: The Election," NBC, 1977; "Kojak: Justice for All," CBS, 1978; "Police Woman: A Shadow on the Sea," NBC, 1978; "Lou Grant: Andrew," CBS, 1979; "Quincy: Walk Softly Through the Night," NBC, 1979; "Quincy: Mode of Death," NBC, 1979; "Bosom Buddies: Waterballoongate," ABC, 1981; "Today's FBI: Blue Collar," ABC, 1982.
TV MOVIES AND MINISERIES: "The Sound of Anger," NBC, 1968; "The Picture of Dorian Gray," ABC, 1973; "Deliver Us From Evil," ABC, 1973; "The Red Badge of Courage," NBC, 1974; "The Barbary Coast," ABC, 1975; "Amelia Earhart," NBC, 1976; "The New Adventures of Heidi," NBC, 1978.

AIELLO, DANNY
  b. New York City, NY, June 20, 1933. Heavyset actor usually in ethnic roles; in the movies he played Sal, the pizzaria owner in "Do the Right Thing."
AS A REGULAR: "Lady Blue," ABC, 1985-86.
AND: "Kojak: Black Thorn," CBS, 1977; "Tales From the Darkside: The Odds," SYN, 1984.
TV MOVIES AND MINISERIES: "Lovey: A Circle of Children, Part II," CBS, 1978; "Lady Blue," ABC, 1985; "Daddy," ABC, 1987; "Alone in the Neon Jungle," CBS, 1988; "The Preppie Murder," ABC, 1989.

AJAYE, FRANKLYN

b. *Brooklyn, NY, May 13, 1949*. Comedian and comic writer.
AS A REGULAR: "Keep on Truckin'," ABC, 1975.
AND: "Barney Miller: You Dirty Rat," ABC, 1975; "The Merv Griffin Show," SYN, 1977; "Don Kirshner's Rock Concert," SYN, 1979; "The Tonight Show Starring Johnny Carson," NBC, 1988; "227: Tenants, Anyone?," NBC, 1989; "Jonathan Winters and Friends," SHO, 1989.
AS WRITER: "In Living Color," FOX, 1990- .

AKINS, CLAUDE

b. *Nelson, GA, May 25, 1918*. Burly actor who went from playing heavies to soft-hearted good guys; best known as Sonny Pruitt on "Movin' On" and as Sheriff Lobo.
AS A REGULAR: "Movin' On," NBC, 1974-76; "Nashville 99," CBS, 1977; "B.J. and the Bear," NBC, 1979; "Lobo (The Misadventures of Sheriff Lobo)," NBC, 1979-81; "Legmen," NBC, 1984.
AND: "I Love Lucy: Desert Island," CBS, 1956; "Gunsmoke: Greater Love," CBS, 1956; "Have Gun, Will Travel: The Great Mojave Chase," CBS, 1957; "Gunsmoke: The Cabin," CBS, 1958; "The Adventures of McGraw: Mojave," NBC, 1958; "Dick Powell's Zane Grey Theatre: Man Unforgiving," CBS, 1958; "Schlitz Playhouse of Stars: Way of the West," CBS, 1958; "Restless Gun: Thicker Than Water," NBC, 1958; "The Twilight Zone: The Monsters Are Due on Maple Street," CBS, 1960; "Bonanza: Desert Justice," NBC, 1960; "The Overland Trail: Fire in the Hole," NBC, 1960; "Wanted Dead or Alive: Prison Trail," CBS, 1960; "SurfSide 6: A Matter of Seconds," ABC, 1961; "The Roaring Twenties: So's Your Old Man," ABC, 1961; "Bus Stop: The Stubborn Stumbos," ABC, 1962; "Gunsmoke: He Learned About Women," CBS, 1962; "The Outlaws: Charge!," NBC, 1962; "The Twilight Zone: The Little People," CBS, 1962; "Empire: Ride to a Fall," NBC, 1962; "Mr. Novak: One Monday Afternoon," NBC, 1964; "Kraft Suspense Theatre: Operation Grief," NBC, 1964; "Branded: The Vindicator," NBC, 1965; "Daniel Boone: The Place of 1,000 Spirits," NBC, 1965; "Slattery's People: When Do We Hang the Good Samaritan?," CBS, 1965; "Rawhide: Walk Into Terror," CBS, 1965; "Gunsmoke: The Ladies From St. Louis," CBS, 1967; "The Lucy Show: Lucy Meets the Law," CBS, 1967; "Combat!: Nightmare on the Red Ball Run," ABC, 1967; "Hondo: Hondo and the Gladiators," ABC, 1967; "The Outsider: Along Came a Spider," NBC, 1968; "McMillan and Wife: Till Death Do Us Part," NBC, 1972; "Gunsmoke: The Predators," CBS, 1972; "The FBI: Dark Journey," ABC, 1972; "Mission: Impossible: Speed," CBS, 1973; "Love, American Style: Love and the First Kiss," ABC, 1973; "Police Story: The Ten-Year Honeymoon," NBC,

1973; "McCloud: The Colorado Cattle Caper," NBC, 1974; "The Mike Douglas Show," SYN, 1974; "Police Story: The Long Ball," NBC, 1976; "The Love Boat: Looking for Mr. Wilson," ABC, 1983; "The Master: Juggernaut," NBC, 1984; "Murder, She Wrote: Deadly Lady," CBS, 1984; "Murder, She Wrote: Hit, Run and Homicide," CBS, 1984; "The Love Boat: Country Blues," ABC, 1985; "The New Mike Hammer: Green Blizzard," CBS, 1987; "Hunter: The Legion," NBC, 1989.
TV MOVIES AND MINISERIES: "Lock, Stock and Barrel," ABC, 1971; "River of Mystery," NBC, 1971; "The Night Stalker," ABC, 1972; "The Norliss Tapes," NBC, 1973; "The Death Squad," ABC, 1973; "In Tandem," NBC, 1974; "Medical Story," NBC, 1975; "Hallmark Hall of Fame: Eric," NBC, 1975; "Kiss Me, Kill Me," ABC, 1976; "Yesterday's Child," NBC, 1977; "Best Sellers: The Rhinemann Exchange," NBC, 1977; "B.J. and the Bear," NBC, 1978; "Little Mo," NBC, 1978; "Murder in Music City," NBC, 1979; "The Concrete Cowboys," CBS, 1979; "Manhunt for Claude Dallas," CBS, 1986; "If It's Tuesday, It Still Must Be Belgium," NBC, 1987; "Mothers, Daughters and Lovers," NBC, 1989.

ALADDIN

b. *Aladdin Abdullah Achmed Anthony Pallante, New York City, NY, 1917*. Violinist with the Lawrence Welk orchestra.
AS A REGULAR: "The Lawrence Welk Show," ABC, 1955-67.
AND: "The Rebel: The Threat," ABC, 1961.

ALBERGHETTI, ANNA MARIA

b. *Pesaro, Italy, May 15, 1936*. Actress-singer who played the gamin on TV.
AS A GUEST: "Make Room for Daddy: Danny Helps Anna Maria," ABC, 1954; "Texaco Star Theatre," NBC, 1955; "Ford Theatre: Never Lend Money to a Woman," NBC, 1956; "G.E. Theatre: The Song Caruso Sang," CBS, 1956; "Ford Star Jubilee: A Bell for Adano," CBS, 1956; "The Loretta Young Show: Song of Rome," NBC, 1956; "Climax!: The Secret Thread," CBS, 1956; "Schlitz Playhouse of Stars: The Enchanted," CBS, 1957; "The Perry Como Show," NBC, 1957; "The Loretta Young Show: Emergency," NBC, 1957; "Climax!: Bait for the Tiger," CBS, 1957; "The Steve Allen Show," NBC, 1957; "Climax!: The Secret of the Red Room," CBS, 1957; "Pat Boone Chevy Showroom," ABC, 1957; "The Ed Sullivan Show," CBS, 1957; "The Gisele MacKenzie Show," NBC, 1957; "The Chevy Show," NBC, 1958; "The du Pont Show of the Month: Aladdin," CBS, 1958; "The George Burns Show," NBC, 1959; "The Music Shop," NBC, 1959; "Wagon Train: The Conchita

Vasquez Story," NBC, 1959; "The Voice of Firestone: The Music of Cole Porter," ABC, 1959; "The Garry Moore Show," CBS, 1959; "Startime: The Jazz Singer," NBC, 1959; "The Ed Sullivan Show," CBS, 1960; "Here's Hollywood," NBC, 1960; "The Garry Moore Show," CBS, 1960; "Checkmate: Runaway," CBS, 1960; "The Ed Sullivan Show," CBS, 1961; "The Garry Moore Show," CBS, 1961; "Perry Como's Kraft Music Hall," NBC, 1962; "The Jack Paar Program," NBC, 1964; "The Mike Douglas Show," SYN, 1964; "Bob Hope Christmas Special," NBC, 1965; "Kismet," ABC, 1967; "The Mike Douglas Show," SYN, 1967; "The Ed Sullivan Show," CBS, 1968; "To Rome with Love: Anything Can Happen in Rome," CBS, 1970.

* Alberghetti made her debut in Carnegie Hall at age 14.

ALBERONI, SHERRY
b. 1946. Child actress of the fifties and sixties.
AS A REGULAR: "The Ed Wynn Show," NBC, 1958-59; "The Tom Ewell Show," CBS, 1960-61.
AND: "The Real McCoys: First Date," ABC, 1960; "The Andy Williams Show," NBC, 1962; "The Farmer's Daughter: Miss Cheese," ABC, 1963; "Mr. Novak: Hello, Miss Phipps," NBC, 1963; "The Man From UNCLE: The Pop Art Affair," NBC, 1966; "Family Affair: Beware the Other Woman," CBS, 1966; "The Monkees: The Chaperone," NBC, 1966; "My Three Sons: A Real Nice Time," CBS, 1966; "Family Affair: The Candy Striper," CBS, 1967; "Make Room for Granddaddy: The Teen Idol," ABC, 1970; "My Three Sons: After the Honeymoon," CBS, 1971.

ALBERT, EDDIE
b. Edward Albert Heimberger, Rock Island, IL, April 22, 1908. Actor with extensive TV credits, best known as lawyer-turned-farmer Oliver Wendell Douglas, the best-dressed man in Hooterville, on "Green Acres;" more recently he played the father of Elliot Weston (Timothy Busfield) on "thirtysomething."
AS A REGULAR: "Leave It to Larry," CBS, 1952; "Nothing But the Best," NBC, 1953; "On Your Account," NBC, 1953-54; "Saturday Night Revue," NBC, 1954; "Petticoat Junction," CBS, 1965; "Green Acres," CBS, 1965-71; "Switch," CBS, 1975-78; "Falcon Crest," CBS, 1987.
AND: "Somerset Maugham TV Theatre: Smith Serves," NBC, 1951; "Schlitz Playhouse of Stars: Enchanted Evening," CBS, 1952; "The Early Bird," CBS, 1952; "Studio One: The Trial of John Peter Zenger," CBS, 1953; "G.E. Theatre: I'm a Fool," CBS, 1954; "A Connecticut Yankee," NBC, 1955; "G.E. Theatre: Into the Night," CBS, 1955; "Schlitz Playhouse of Stars: Too Many

Nelsons," CBS, 1955; "The Chocolate Soldier," NBC, 1955; "Front Row Center: Johnny Belinda," CBS, 1955; "Our Mr. Sun," CBS, 1956; "The Ed Sullivan Show," CBS, 1956; "Climax!: Let It Be Me," CBS, 1957; "Dick Powell's Zane Grey Theatre: Fugitive," CBS, 1957; "Schlitz Playhouse of Stars: Pattern for Death," CBS, 1957; "Studio 57: An End to Fear," SYN, 1958; "The Patrice Munsel Show," ABC, 1958; "Alcoa Theatre: Lazarus Walks Again," NBC, 1958; "Schlitz Playhouse of Stars: Last Edition," CBS, 1958; "Dick Powell's Zane Grey Theatre: The Vaunted," CBS, 1958; "The Loretta Young Show: The Last Witness," NBC, 1958; "This Is Your Life," NBC, 1958; "The Jack Paar Show," NBC, 1959; "U.S. Steel Hour: The Apple of His Eye," CBS, 1959; "Laramie: Glory Road," NBC, 1959; "Riverboat: The Unwilling," NBC, 1959; "Phil Silvers Special: The Ballad of Louie the Louse," CBS, 1959; "Dick Clark's World of Talent," ABC, 1959; "Pat Boone Chevy Showroom," ABC, 1959; "Playhouse 90: The Silver Whistle," CBS, 1959; "Mother's March," SYN, 1960; "Sunday Showcase: Hollywood Sings," NBC, 1960; "Ben Casey: An Uncommonly Innocent Killing," ABC, 1962; "The New Breed: A Motive Named Waler," ABC, 1962; "The Virginian: Impasse," NBC, 1962; "Wagon Train: The Kurt Davos Story," ABC, 1962; "Naked City: Robin Hood and Clarence Darrow, They Went Out with Bow and Arrow," ABC, 1963; "The du Pont Show: Windfall," NBC, 1963; "Voyage to the Bottom of the Sea: Eleven Days to Zero," ABC, 1964; "The Outer Limits: Cry of Silence," ABC, 1964; "The Reporter: A Time to Be Silent," CBS, 1964; "Rawhide: The Photographer," CBS, 1964; "Kraft Suspense Theatre: The Gun," NBC, 1964; "Mr. Novak: Visons of Sugar Plums," NBC, 1964; "Art Linkletter's House Party," CBS, 1965; "The Rogues: The Golden Ocean," NBC, 1965; "Burke's Law: Who Killed Rosie Sunset?," ABC, 1965; "The Man From UNCLE: The Love Affair," NBC, 1965; "Petticoat Junction: Kate Bradley, Peacemaker," CBS, 1966; "The Smothers Brothers Comedy Hour," CBS, 1967; "Petticoat Junction: The Valley Has a Baby," CBS, 1968; "The Ed Sullivan Show," CBS, 1968; "The Beverly Hillbilles: The Thanksgiving Story," CBS, 1968; "Mouse on the Mayflower," NBC, 1968; "What's It All About, World?," ABC, 1969; "Columbo: Dead Weight," NBC, 1971; "The David Frost Show," SYN, 1971; "McCloud: The Park Avenue Hustlers," NBC, 1972; "Daddy's Girls," CBS, 1973; "Here's Lucy: Lucy Gives Eddie Albert the Old Song and Dance," CBS, 1973; "Kung Fu: Blood of the Dragon," ABC, 1974; "Benjamin Franklin: The Ambassador," CBS, 1974; "Simon & Simon: Pirate's Key," CBS, 1983; "The Love Boat: The Dean and the Flunkee," ABC, 1983; "Murder, She Wrote: Hit, Run and Homicide," CBS, 1984; "Highway to Heaven: Jonathan Smith Goes to

Washington," NBC, 1985; "The Twilight Zone: Dream Me a Life," CBS, 1986; "Murder, She Wrote: The Body Politic," CBS, 1988; "thirtysomething: Elliot's Dad," ABC, 1989.

TV MOVIES AND MINISERIES: "See the Man Run," ABC, 1971; "Fireball Forward," ABC, 1972; "The Borrowers," NBC, 1973; "Killer Bees," ABC, 1974; "Promise Him Anything," ABC, 1975; "Switch," CBS, 1975; "Evening in Byzantium," SYN, 1978; "The Word," CBS, 1978; "Trouble in High Timber Country," ABC, 1980; "Beulah Land," NBC, 1980; "The Demon Murder Case," NBC, 1983; "Burning Rage," CBS, 1984; "In Like Flynn," ABC, 1985; "Dress Gray," NBC, 1986; "Mercy or Murder?" NBC, 1987.

* Albert was announced as a co-host for "Candid Camera" before it premiered in 1960, but he was dropped in favor of Arthur Godfrey.
* See also "Green Acres."

ALBERT, EDWARD
b. Los Angeles, February 20, 1951. Actor and son of Eddie Albert.

AS A REGULAR: "The Yellow Rose," NBC, 1983-84; "Falcon Crest," CBS, 1986.

AND: "This Is Your Life (Eddie Albert)," NBC, 1958; "Orson Welles' Great Mysteries: A Terribly Strange Bell," SYN, 1973; "Kung Fu: Blood of the Dragon," ABC, 1974; "Hollywood Squares," NBC, 1974; "The Rookies: Nightmare," ABC, 1975; "Meidcal Story: A Life in Balance," NBC, 1975; "Police Story: Test of Brotherhood," NBC, 1975; "Police Story: Bought and Paid For," NBC, 1976; "Ellery Queen: Caesar's Last Siege," NBC, 1976; "The Love Boat: Little People," ABC, 1979; "The New Mike Hammer: Deadly Collection," CBS, 1987; "ABC Afterschool Special: Daddy Can't Read," ABC, 1989.

TV MOVIES AND MINISERIES: "Death Cruise," ABC, 1974; "Killer Bees," ABC, 1974; "Black Beauty," NBC, 1978; "The Millionaire," CBS, 1978; "Silent Victory: The Kitty O'Neil Story," CBS, 1979; "The Last Convertible," NBC, 1981.

ALBERTSON, FRANK
b. Fergus Falls, MN, February 2, 1909; d. 1964. Comic-oriented character actor.

AS A REGULAR: "My Friend Flicka," CBS, 1956; "Bringing Up Buddy," CBS, 1960-61.

AND: "Armstrong Circle Theatre: Three Cents Worth of Fear," NBC, 1957; "Sugarfoot: Misfire," ABC, 1957; "Alfred Hitchcock Presents: Disappearing Trick," CBS, 1958; "Restless Gun: The Englishman," NBC, 1958; "The Californians: Bella Union," NBC, 1958; "Sugarfoot: The Canary Kid," ABC, 1958; "The Phil Silvers Show: Bilko's Giveaway," CBS, 1958; "For Better or Worse: The Case of the Childish Bride," CBS, 1959; "Dick Powell's Zane Grey Theatre:

Welcome Home a Stranger," CBS, 1959; "Bronco: The Masquerade," ABC, 1960; "Hawaiian Eye: Cut of Ice," ABC, 1960; "Cheyenne: The Long Rope," ABC, 1960; "Wanted Dead or Alive: To the Victor," CBS, 1960; "The Aquanauts: The Frameup Adventure," CBS, 1960; "Thriller: Man in the Middle," NBC, 1960; "Michael Shayne: The Heiress," NBC, 1961; "The Tom Ewell Show: The Prying Eye," CBS, 1961; "Alfred Hitchcock Presents: You Can't Trust a Man," NBC, 1961; "Lassie: Double Trouble," CBS, 1962; "The Real McCoys: Actress in the House," CBS, 1962; "Sam Benedict: Green Room, Gray Morning," NBC, 1963; "The Andy Griffith Show: Gomer Pyle, USMC," CBS, 1964; "Mr. Novak: The Death of a Teacher," NBC, 1964.

ALBERTSON, GRACE
Actress and wife of Frank.

AS A REGULAR: "Our Private World," CBS, 1965.

AND: "Peter Gunn: The Vicious Dog," NBC, 1958; "For Better or Worse: The Case of the Childish Bride," CBS, 1959; "The Tom Ewell Show: The Prying Eye," CBS, 1961; "Bringing Up Buddy: Buddy and the Teenager," CBS, 1961; "My Three Sons: The Crush," ABC, 1961; "Cheyenne: The Equalizer," ABC, 1961; "Dr. Kildare: The Bed I've Made," NBC, 1962; "Dragnet: The Big Blank," NBC, 1967; "Mannix: To Cage a Seagull," CBS, 1970; "Mannix: A Step in Time," CBS, 1971; "Mission: Impossible: Shape-Up," CBS, 1971; "Marcus Welby, M.D.: Of Magic Shadow Shapes," ABC, 1972; "Empty Nest: What's a Father to Do?," NBC, 1988.

TV'S TOP TEN, 1974-75
1. All in the Family (CBS)
2. Sanford & Son (NBC)
.3. Chico and the Man (NBC)
4. The Jeffersons (CBS)
5. M*A*S*H (CBS)
6. Rhoda (CBS)
7. Good Times (CBS)
8. The Waltons (CBS)
9. Maude (CBS)
10. Hawaii Five-O (CBS)

ALBERTSON, JACK
b. Malden, MA, June 16, 1907; d. 1981. Vaudeville hoofer who was a familiar face on sitcoms; he played garage owner Ed Brown on "Chico and the Man."

AS A REGULAR: "The Thin Man," NBC, 1958-59; "The Donna Reed Show," ABC, 1960; "The Tab Hunter Show," NBC, 1961; "Room for One More," ABC, 1962; "Ensign O'Toole," NBC, 1962-63; "Dr. Simon Locke," SYN, 1971-72; "Chico and the Man," NBC, 1974-78; "Grandpa Goes to Washington," NBC, 1978-79.

AND: "Our Miss Brooks: Travel Crazy," CBS, 1956; "I Love Lucy: Bon Voyage," CBS, 1956; "The 20th Century-Fox Hour: City in Flames," CBS, 1957; "Have Gun, Will Travel: High Wire," CBS, 1957; "Shirley Temple's Storybook: The Land of Green Ginger," NBC, 1958; "December Bride: Fred MacMurray Show," CBS, 1958; "The Jack Benny Program," CBS, 1960; "The Many Loves of Dobie Gillis: Maynard G. Krebs, Boy Millionaire," CBS, 1960; "Riverboat: Listen to the Nightingale," NBC, 1961; "The Red Skelton Show: San Fernando's Diet Formula," CBS, 1961; "The Twilight Zone: The Shelter," CBS, 1961; "Margie: Pity the Poor Working Girl," ABC, 1961; "87th Precinct: Killer's Payoff," NBC, 1961; "Mr. Ed: Ed the Songwriter," CBS, 1961; "The Danny Thomas Show: Danny Weaves a Web," CBS, 1961; "The Joey Bishop Show: The Ham in the Family," NBC, 1961; "Wagon Train: The Martin Onyx Story," NBC, 1962; "Father of the Bride: The Souvenir," CBS, 1962; "The Dick Van Dyke Show: The Twizzle," CBS, 1962; "The Twilight Zone: I Dream of Genie," CBS, 1963; "Mr. Ed: Ed the Musician," CBS, 1964; "The Doctors and the Nurses: The Outpost," CBS, 1964; "The Defenders: The Objector," CBS, 1965; "Run, Buddy, Run: The Death of Buddy Overstreet," CBS, 1966; "Hey, Landlord!: The Long, Hot Bus," NBC, 1966; "Gunsmoke: Danny," CBS, 1969; "The Virginian: The Girl in the Shadows," NBC, 1969; "Marcus Welby, M.D.: Go Get 'Em, Tiger," ABC, 1970; "Nanny and the Professor: The Haunted House," ABC, 1970; "Ironside: Blackout," NBC, 1970; "Love, American Style: Love and the Second Time," ABC, 1971; "Gunsmoke: One for the Road," CBS, 1972; "Alias Smith and Jones: Jailbreak at Junction City," ABC, 1972; "Gunsmoke: Cowtown Hustler," CBS, 1974; "The Streets of San Francsisco: The Set-Up," ABC, 1973; "The Tonight Show Starring Johnny Carson," NBC, 1974; "Hollywood Squares," NBC, 1974; "Tattletales," CBS, 1975; "Mitzi and a Hundred Guys," CBS, 1975; "Cher," CBS, 1975; "Paul Lynde Special," ABC, 1975; "Tattletales," CBS, 1976; "Inaugural Eve Special," CBS, 1977; "Charlie's Angels: From Street Models to Hawaiian Angels," ABC, 1980; "Over Easy," PBS, 1981.

TV MOVIES AND MINISERIES: "The Monk," ABC, 1969; "A Clear and Present Danger," NBC, 1970; "Once Upon a Dead Man," NBC, 1971; "Congratulations, It's a Boy!," ABC, 1971; "Lock, Stock and Barrel," NBC, 1971; "Valentine," ABC, 1979.

* Albertson's career got a big boost when he appeared in a Los Angeles production of "Waiting for Godot" in 1957.
* Alberton won a Tony and an Oscar for his role in "The Subject Was Roses"; his 1975 Emmy Award was for a "Cher" guest appearance.
* Emmies: 1975, 1976.

ALBERTSON, MABEL

b. 1901; d. 1982. Character actress who's played the mother of Darrin Stephens, Howard Sprague, Donald Hollinger and other TV milquetoasts.

AS A REGULAR: "That's My Boy," CBS, 1954-55; "Those Whiting Girls," CBS, 1955; "The Tom Ewell Show," CBS, 1960-61.

AND: "The Loretta Young Show: Double Trouble," NBC, 1954; "December Bride: Ruth's Haircut," CBS, 1956; "The Loretta Young Show: Little League," NBC, 1956; "The Millionaire: The Story of Virginia Lennart," CBS, 1956; "The 20th Century-Fox Hour: Threat to a Happy Ending," CBS, 1957; "Have Gun, Will Travel: Les Girls," CBS, 1959; "Rawhide: Incident of the Dancing Death," CBS, 1960; "The Jack Benny Program: Musicale," CBS, 1961; "The Tab Hunter Show: Those Happy College Days," NBC, 1961; "The Roaring Twenties: So's Your Old Man," ABC, 1961; "The Dick Powell Show: The Fifth Caller," NBC, 1961; "The Danny Thomas Show: Teacher for a Day," CBS, 1961; "Cheyenne: Rendezvous with a Miracle," ABC, 1962; "Perry Mason: The Case of the Hateful Hero," CBS, 1962; "Fair Exchange: Innocents Abroad," CBS, 1962; "Hazel: The Reluctant Witness," NBC, 1964; "My Three Sons: The Substitute Teacher," ABC, 1964; "Mr. Novak: Moonlighting," NBC, 1964; "The Munsters: Munster Masquerade," CBS, 1964; "Bewitched: Samantha Meets the Folks," ABC, 1964; "The Lucy Show: Lucy and the Missing Stamp," CBS, 1964; "Bewitched: A Nice Little Dinner Party," ABC, 1965; "No Time for Sergeants: Andy Meets His Match," ABC, 1965; "The Smothers Brothers Show: Is Your Wig Wam?," CBS, 1965; "Hazel: Hazel Sits It Out," CBS, 1965; "Bewitched: The Dancing Bear," ABC, 1966; "The Adventures of Ozzie and Harriet: Ozzie a Go-Go," ABC, 1966; "The Andy Griffith Show: The County Clerk," CBS, 1966; "That Girl: Soap Gets in Your Eyes," ABC, 1966; "The Wild Wild West: The Night of the Bottomless Pit," CBS, 1966; "The Andy Griffith Show: The Lodge," CBS, 1966; "The Andy Griffith Show: Dinner at Eight," CBS, 1967; "Dragnet: The Big Bullet," NBC, 1967; "That Girl: Thanksgiving Comes But Once a Year, Hopefully," ABC, 1967; "The Ghost and Mrs. Muir: Here Today, Gone Tomorrow," NBC, 1968; "That Girl: Odpdypahimcaifss," ABC, 1968; "The Virginian: Big Tiny," NBC, 1968; "Bewitched: Tabitha's Weekend," ABC, 1969; "Gomer Pyle, USMC: Gomer Maneuvers," CBS, 1969; "Bewitched: Sam's Double Mother Trouble," ABC, 1969; "Bewitched: Samantha's Secret Is Discovered," ABC, 1970; "That Girl: There Are a Bunch of Cards in St. Louis," ABC, 1971; "The Paul Lynde Show: Is This Trip Necessary?," ABC, 1973; "The Paul Lynde Show: Everything You Wanted to Know About Your Mother-in-Law But Were Afraid to Ask," ABC, 1973; "Bob

& Carol & Ted & Alice: Premiere," ABC, 1973; "The Mary Tyler Moore Show: Anyone Who Hates Kids and Dogs," CBS, 1975.
TV MOVIES AND MINISERIES: "The House That Would Not Die," ABC, 1970.

ALBRIGHT, LOLA

b. Akron, OH, July 20, 1924. Sexy actress of the fifties who played Edie Hart, girlfriend of "Peter Gunn."
AS A REGULAR: "Peter Gunn," NBC, 1958-60; ABC, 1960-61; "Peyton Place," ABC, 1965.
AND: "Lux Video Theatre: Inside Story," CBS, 1951; "Lux Video Theatre: Stolen Years," CBS, 1951; "Tales of Tommorow: The Miraculous Serum," ABC, 1952; "Fireside Theatre: Invitation to Marriage," NBC, 1954; "Pepsi Cola Playhouse: Borrow My Car," ABC, 1954; "The Bob Cummings Show: Too Many Cooks," CBS, 1955; "Screen Directors Playhouse: Arroyo," NBC, 1955; "The Bob Cummings Show: Bob Falls in Love," CBS, 1956; "The Bob Cummings Show: Hawaii Calls," CBS, 1956; "The Red Skelton Show," CBS, 1957; "Panic!: Fingerprints," NBC, 1957; "The Thin Man: The Tennis Champ," NBC, 1958; "Target: The Jewel Thief," SYN, 1958; "Art Linkletter's House Party," CBS, 1958; "Steve Allen Plymouth Show," NBC, 1959; "The George Gobel Show," CBS, 1960; "Michael Shayne: Framed in Blood," NBC, 1960; "Robert Taylor's Detectives: The Queen of Craven Point," NBC, 1961; "Alfred Hitchcock Presents: The Woman Who Wanted to Live," NBC, 1962; "Comedy Spot: The Mighty O," CBS, 1962; "Saints and Sinners: Dear George, the Siamese Cat Is Missing," NBC, 1962; "The Alfred Hitchcock Hour: The Black Curtain," CBS, 1962; "My Three Sons: Going Steady," ABC, 1962; "The Beverly Hillbillies: Granny's Spring Tonic," CBS, 1963; "Kraft Mystery Theatre: Go Look at Roses," NBC, 1963; "The Eleventh Hour: Cold Hands, Warm Heart," NBC, 1963; "Burke's Law: Who Killed Harris Crown?," ABC, 1963; "The Dick Van Dyke Show: How to Spank a Star," CBS, 1964; "Burke's Law: Who Killed Cassandra Cass?," ABC, 1964; "The Alfred Hitchcock Hour: Misadventure," NBC, 1964; "Wagon Train: Those Who Stay Behind," ABC, 1964; "Mr. Broadway: Sticks and Stones May Break My Bones," CBS, 1964; "Burke's Law: Who Killed Nobody Somehow?," ABC, 1965; "Bonanza: The Search," NBC, 1965; "Burke's Law: Who Killed Mother Goose?," ABC, 1965; "Rawhide: The Gray Rock Hotel," CBS, 1965; "Branded: Mightier Than the Sword," NBC, 1965; "Branded: Cowards Die Many Times," NBC, 1966; "Bob Hope Chrysler Theatre: Runaway Bay," NBC, 1966; "Bonanza: A Bride for Buford," NBC, 1967; "Bob Hope Chrysler Theatre: To Sleep, Perchance to Scream," NBC, 1967; "The Man From UNCLE: The Prince of Darkness Affair," NBC, 1967;

"Medical Center: Condemned," CBS, 1972; "Kojak: The Corrupter," CBS, 1973; "ABC Matinee Today: My Secret Mother," ABC, 1973; "Ready and Willing," NBC, 1974; "Medical Center: No Escape," CBS, 1974; "Wide World of Mystery: The Nurse Killer," ABC, 1975; "Police Story: The Cutting Edge," NBC, 1975; "Medical Center: Condemned," CBS, 1975; "McMillan and Wife: The Deadly Cure," NBC, 1976; "Columbo: Fade in to Murder," NBC, 1976; "Switch: Who Killed Lila Craig?," CBS, 1977; "The Eddie Capra Mysteries: Where There's Smoke," NBC, 1978; "Quincy: Murder on Ice," NBC, 1983.
TV MOVIES AND MINISERIES: "How I Spent My Summer Vacation," NBC, 1967.

ALDA, ALAN,

b. New York City, NY, January 28, 1936. Tall, lanky actor-writer who played Dr. Benjamin Franklin "Hawkeye" Pierce on "M*A*S*H" and helped usher in the age of the "sensitive" guy; now he writes and directs movies, each of which seems more forgettable than the last.
AS A REGULAR: "That Was the Week That Was," NBC, 1964; "M*A*S*H," CBS, 1972-83.
AND: "The Phil Silvers Show: Bilko, the Art Lover," CBS, 1958; "The Nurses: Many a Sullivan," CBS, 1963; "The Nurses: Night Sounds, CBS, 1963; "Route 66: Soda Pop and Paper Flags," CBS, 1963; "The Trials of O'Brien: Picture Me a Murder," CBS, 1965; "Where's Everett?," CBS, 1966; "Coronet Blue: Six Months to Mars," CBS, 1967; "Higher and Higher," CBS, 1968; "The Match Game," NBC, 1968; "What's My Line?," SYN, 1970; "Hotel Ninety," CBS, 1973; "6 Rms Riv Vu," CBS, 1974; "Free to Be You and Me," ABC, 1974; "The Mike Douglas Show," SYN, 1974; "The Merv Griffin Show," SYN, 1974; "Annie and the Hoods," ABC, 1974; "The Carol Burnett Show," CBS, 1974.
TV MOVIES AND MINISERIES: "Truman Capote's The Glass House," CBS, 1972; "Playmates," ABC, 1972; "Isn't It Shocking?," ABC, 1973; "Kill Me if You Can," NBC, 1977.
AS EXECUTIVE PRODUCER: "The Four Seasons," CBS, 1984.
AS WRITER: "M*A*S*H," CBS, 1973-83.
AS DIRECTOR: "M*A*S*H," CBS, 1974-83.
* Emmies: 1974, 1977, 1979, 1982.

ALDA, ANTONEY

b. New York City, NY. Actor who plays Johnny Corelli on "Days of Our Lives"; brother of Alan Alda.
AS A REGULAR: "Days of Our Lives," NBC, 1990- .
AND: "Columbo: Murder Under Glass," NBC, 1978; "M*A*S*H: Lend a Hand," CBS, 1980.

ALDA, BEATRICE

b. New York City, NY, August 10, 1961. Young

actress whose dad, Alan, created her only credit.

AS A REGULAR: "The Four Seasons," CBS, 1984.

TV'S TOP TEN, 1982-83

1. 60 Minutes (CBS)
2. Dallas (CBS)
3. M*A*S*H (CBS)
4. Magnum P.I. (CBS)
5. Dynasty (ABC)
6. Three's Company (ABC)
7. Simon & Simon (CBS)
8. Falcon Crest (CBS)
9. The Love Boat (ABC)
10. The A-Team (NBC)
10. Monday Night Football (ABC)

ALDA, ELIZABETH

b. New York City, August 20, 1960. See Beatrice Alda.

AS A REGULAR: "The Four Seasons," CBS, 1984.

ALDA, ROBERT

b. Alphonso Giuseppe Giovanni Roberto d'Abruzzo, New York City, February 26, 1914; d. 1986. Leading man of films ("Rhapsody in Blue") and stage ("Guys and Dolls") in sporadic TV; father of Alan and Antoney Alda.

AS A REGULAR: "By Popular Demand," CBS, 1950; "Personality Puzzle," ABC, 1953; "What's Your Bid," DUM, 1953; "Secret File, USA," SYN, 1954; "Can Do," NBC, 1956; "Love of Life," CBS, 1966-67; "Supertrain," NBC, 1979; "Days of Our Lives," NBC, 1981.

AND: "The Substitute," SYN, 1950; "Faith Baldwin Playhouse: Inspiration," ABC, 1951; "Lux Video Theatre: I Can't Remember," CBS, 1952; "Tales of Tomorrow: Youth on Tap," ABC, 1952; "Gulf Playhouse: One Afternoon on Caribou," NBC, 1952; "Robert Montgomery Presents: Tomorrow Will Sing," NBC, 1953; "Salute to Baseball," NBC, 1957; "Club 60," NBC, 1957; "Pantomime Quiz," CBS, 1957; "Playhouse 90: The Gentleman From Seventh Avenue," CBS, 1958; "Schlitz Playhouse of Stars: Curfew at Midnight," CBS, 1958; "Pursuit: Eagle in the Cage," CBS, 1958; "The Millionaire: Millionaire Julia Conrad," CBS, 1959; "Naked City: Fallen Star," ABC, 1959; "The Vikings: Shipwreck," SYN, 1960; "The Lucy Show: Lucy Goes to Art Class," CBS, 1964; "Ironside: The Taker," NBC, 1967; "That Girl: Just Spell the Name Right," ABC, 1968; "Ironside: The Sacrifice," NBC, 1968; "NYPD: The Case of the Shady Lady," ABC, 1968; "Ironside: A Bullet for Mark," NBC, 1969; "Here's Lucy: Secretary Beautiful," CBS, 1970; "The Name of the Game: Man of the People," NBC, 1970; "Mission: Impossible: Flip Side," CBS, 1970; "Here's Lucy: Lucy the Coed," CBS, 1970; "Here's Lucy: Lucy

Goes Hawaiian," CBS, 1971; "The Merv Griffin Show," SYN, 1974; "Rhoda: Parents' Day," CBS, 1974; "Rhoda: Anything Wrong?," CBS, 1974; "Police Story: War Games," NBC, 1975; "Kojak: No Immunity for Murder," CBS, 1975; "M*A*S*H: The Consultant," CBS, 1975; "Rhyme and Reason," ABC, 1975; "The Rockford Files: A Three Day Affair with a Thirty Day Escrow," NBC, 1978; "Cross Wits," SYN, 1978; "Laverne & Shirley: Shirley and the Old Man," ABC, 1979; "The White Shadow: Links," CBS, 1980; "M*A*S*H: Lend a Hand," CBS, 1980; "Quincy: Jury Duty," NBC, 1981; "Quincy: Murder on Ice," NBC, 1983.

TV MOVIES AND MINISERIES: "Last Hours Before Morning," NBC, 1975.

ALDEN, NORMAN

b. Fort Worth, TX, September 13, 1924. Character actor usually in gruff roles; he played the exasperated boss of hopeless Texas Ranger Rango (Tim Conway) and the father of Polly (Ronne Troup), wife of Chip Douglas (Stanley Livingston) on "My Three Sons."

AS A REGULAR: "Hennesey," CBS, 1960-62; "The Life and Legend of Wyatt Earp," ABC, 1961; "Rango," ABC, 1967; "My Three Sons," CBS, 1970-71; "Fay," NBC, 1975-76.

AND: "The 20th Century-Fox Hour: Threat to a Happy Ending," CBS, 1957; "Circus Boy: The Marvelous Manellis," ABC, 1957; "Goodyear Theatre: The Giant Step," NBC, 1958; "The George Burns and Gracie Allen Show: Grammar School Dance," CBS, 1958; "Alcoa Theatre: Decoy Duck," NBC, 1958; "The Adventures of Rin Tin Tin: The Foot Soldier," ABC, 1959; "Guestward Ho!: The Beatniks," ABC, 1961; "Lawman: The Four," ABC, 1961; "Cain's Hundred: Comeback," NBC, 1961; "Bonanza: The Friendship," NBC, 1961; "Ripcord: The Helicopter Race," SYN, 1962; "Combat!: Masquerade," ABC, 1963; "Temple Houston: The Law and Big Annie," NBC, 1964; "Combat!: The Silver Service," ABC, 1964; "Mr. Broadway: Between the Rats and the Finks," CBS, 1964; "My Favorite Martian: Hate Me a Little," CBS, 1965; "Hogan's Heroes: Happines Is a Warm Sergeant," CBS, 1965; "Honey West: How Brillig, O Beamish Boy?," ABC, 1966; "Honey West: Like Visions and Omens-and All That Jazz," ABC, 1966; "The Smothers Brothers Show: Harried, Italian Style," CBS, 1966; "The Andy Griffith Show: The Battle of Mayberry," CBS, 1966; "Batman: The Joker Trumps an Ace/ Batman Sets the Pace," ABC, 1966; "The Mod Squad: Bad Man on Campus," ABC, 1968; "Gunsmoke: The Night Riders," CBS, 1969; "To Rome with Love: The Secret Day," CBS, 1969; "Mannix: To Cage a Seagull," CBS, 1970; "Hawaii Five-O: Rest in Peace, Somebody," CBS, 1971; "Mission: Impossible: Double Dead," CBS,

1972; "The FBI: The Wizard," ABC, 1972; "Mannix: See No Evil," CBS, 1973; "The Rookies: Tarnished Idol," ABC, 1973; "Gunsmoke: Lynch Town," CBS, 1973; "The Streets of San Francisco: The Bullet," ABC, 1973; "Kung Fu: The Praying Mantis Kills," ABC, 1973; "Planet of the Apes: The Trap," CBS, 1974; "Kojak: The Nicest Guys on the Block," CBS, 1975; "Adam 12: Something Worth Dying For," NBC, 1975; "The Rookies: Cliffy," ABC, 1975; "Alice: Big Daddy Dawson's Coming," CBS, 1976; "McMillan: All Bets Are Off," NBC, 1976; "Alice: Alice by Moonlight," CBS, 1977; "Switch: Dangerous Curves," CBS, 1977; "The Rockford Files: Heartaches of a Fool," NBC, 1978; "One Day at a Time: Fear of Success," CBS, 1979; "Barnaby Jones: The Medium," CBS, 1979; "The Love Boat: Honeymoon Pressure," ABC, 1980; "Nero Wolfe: Murder in Question," NBC, 1981; "Webster: Consulting Adults," ABC, 1983; "Hardcastle and McCormick: Pennies From a Dead Man's Eyes," ABC, 1984; "Silver Spoons: Uncle Harry," NBC, 1985; "Sledge Hammer!: To Sledge, with Love," ABC, 1986; "Murder, She Wrote: Mr. Penroy's Vacation," CBS, 1988; "Cagney & Lacey: Land of the Free," CBS, 1988; "Cagney & Lacey: A Class Act," CBS, 1988.
TV MOVIES AND MINISERIES: "The Pigeon," ABC, 1969; "The Psychiatrist: God Bless the Children," NBC, 1970; "The Trackers," ABC, 1971; "Murdock's Gang," ABC, 1973; "Cry Panic!," ABC, 1974; "No Other Love," CBS, 1979; "Samurai," ABC, 1979; "Destination: America," ABC; 1987; "Lady Mobster," ABC, 1988; "Man Against the Mob," NBC, 1988.

ALEONG, AKI
Asian actor usually in threatening roles; best known as Mr. Chaing on "V."
AS A REGULAR: "V," NBC, 1984-85.
AND: "Producers Showcase: The Letter," NBC, 1956; "Robert Montgomery Presents: The Enemy," NBC, 1957; "Love That Jill: Find Your Perfect Mate," ABC, 1958; "The Islanders: Our Girl in Saigon," ABC, 1960; "Adventures in Paradise: Incident in Suva," ABC, 1960; "The Islanders: The Strange Courtship of Danny Koo," ABC, 1961; "Hong Kong: Love, Honor and Perish," ABC, 1961; "Hawaiian Eye: Maid in America," ABC, 1961; "The Brothers Brannagan: Key of Jade," SYN, 1962; "The Outer Limits: The Hundred Days of the Dragon," ABC, 1963; "The Outer Limits: Expanding Human," ABC, 1964; "Hazel: Hazel's Inquisitive Mind," NBC, 1965; "The Virginian: Ah Sing Vs. Wyoming," NBC, 1967; "Cagney & Lacey: Capitalism," CBS, 1986; "Scarecrow and Mrs. King: The Man Who Died Twice," CBS, 1986; "Hunter: An Honorable Profession," NBC, 1988; "Mancuso FBI: Little Saigon," NBC, 1989.

ALETTER, FRANK
b. College Point, NY, January 14, 1926. Clean-cut leading man of several sixties sitcoms; he played Cara Williams' husband and time-traveling astronaut Mac on "It's About Time."
AS A REGULAR: "Bringing Up Buddy," CBS, 1960-61; "The Cara Williams Show," CBS, 1964-65; "It's About Time," CBS, 1966-67; "Nancy," NBC, 1970-71.
AND: "U.S. Steel Hour: Trouble-in-Law," CBS, 1959; "Armstrong Circle Theatre: Dishonor System, CBS, 1960; "G.E. Theatre: Tippy-Top," CBS, 1961; "The Gertrude Berg Show: The Bird," CBS, 1962; "The Lloyd Bridges Show: The Testing Ground," CBS, 1962; "Alcoa Premiere: Mr. Lucifer," ABC, 1962; "The Lucy Show: Lucy the Music Lover," CBS, 1962; "Hazel: Ain't Walter Nice?," NBC, 1963; "The Wide Country: The Girl From Nob Hill," NBC, 1963; "Ben Casey: With the Rich and Mighty, Always a Little Patience," ABC, 1963; "My Favorite Martian: Russians R in Season," CBS, 1963; "The Twilight Zone: The Parallel," CBS, 1963; "Twelve O'Clock High: Grant Me No Favor," ABC, 1965; "Twelve O'Clock High: Angel Babe," ABC, 1966; "Petticoat Junction: The Invisible Mr. Dobble," CBS, 1966; "The FBI: Act of Violence," ABC, 1968; "The Doris Day Show: The Flyboy," CBS, 1969; "Petticoat Junction: The Tenant," CBS, 1969; "Medical Center: Danger Point," CBS, 1971; "Nanny and the Professor: Nanny and Her Witch's Brew," ABC, 1971; "The FBI: A Second Life," ABC, 1972; "The Bold Ones: By Reason of Insanity," NBC, 1972; "Love, American Style: Love and the Naked Stranger," ABC, 1972; "Maude: Love and Marriage," CBS, 1972; "M*A*S*H: For the Good of the Outfit," CBS, 1973; "Ironside: Class of '40," NBC, 1973; "Marcus Welby, M.D.: A Question of Fault," ABC, 1973; "Marcus Welby, M.D.: The Last Rip-Off," ABC, 1974; "Adam 12: Suspect #1," NBC, 1974; "Kolchak, the Night Stalker: Chopper," ABC, 1975; "Marcus Welby, M.D.: Dark Fury," ABC, 1975; "Kojak: My Brother, My Enemy," CBS, 1975; "Police Woman: Broken Angels," NBC, 1976; "Switch: Come Die With Me," CBS, 1976; "Emergency!: Rules of Order," NBC, 1976; "What's Happening!: The Maid Did It," ABC, 1977; "Switch: 30,000 Witnesses," CBS, 1978; "All in the Family: The Commercial," CBS, 1978; "Columbo: How to Dial a Murder," NBC, 1978; "Police Woman: Good Old Uncle Ben," NBC, 1978; "The Love Boat: They Tried to Tell Us We're Too Young," ABC, 1979; "Lou Grant: Venice," CBS, 1981; "Three's Company: Professor Jack," ABC, 1981; "Simon & Simon: Almost Completely Out to Sea," CBS, 1984; "Murder, She Wrote: Capitol Offense," CBS, 1985; "The Golden Girls: Premiere," NBC, 1985.
TV MOVIES AND MINISERIES: "Rich Man, Poor Man," ABC, 1976; "The Star Maker," NBC, 1981.

ALETTER, KYLE

b. Los Angeles, CA. Daughter of Frank Aletter and Lee Meriwether.

AS A GUEST: "The Love Boat: Clothes Make the Girl," ABC, 1981.

TV MOVIES AND MINISERIES: "The Day After," ABC, 1983.

ALEXANDER, BEN

b. Nicholas Benton Alexander, Goldfield, NV, May 26, 1911; d. 1969. Radio announcer who became a familiar TV face as Jack Webb's partner Frank Smith on the first "Dragnet."

AS A REGULAR: "Party Time at Club Roma," NBC, 1950-51; "Dragnet," NBC, 1953-59; "Take a Good Look," ABC, 1960; "About Faces," ABC, 1960-61; "Felony Squad," ABC, 1966-69.

AND: "Noah's Ark: Once Upon a Midnight," NBC, 1956; "The Ford Show," NBC, 1957; "The Joseph Cotten Show: The Lie Detector Case," NBC, 1957; "Queen for a Day," NBC, 1957; "The Perry Como Show," NBC, 1957; "Queen for a Day," NBC, 1958; "The Tennessee Ernie Ford Show," ABC, 1962; "Batman: An Egg Grows in Gotham/The Yegg Foes in Gotham," ABC, 1966.
* Alexander was a child actor in silent films.

ALEXANDER, DENISE

b. New York City, NY, November 11, 1939. Soap actress who played Susan Martin on "Days of Our Lives," Dr. Lesley Williams Weber on "General Hospital" and Mary McKinnon on "Another World."

AS A REGULAR: "The Clear Horizon," CBS, 1960-61, 1962; "Days of Our Lives," NBC, 1966-73; "General Hospital," ABC, 1973-84; "Another World," NBC, 1986-89.

AND: "Father Knows Best: No Apron Strings," NBC, 1957; "The Danny Thomas Show: Terry's Girlfriend," CBS, 1958; "The Twilight Zone: Third From the Sun," CBS, 1960; "The Many Loves of Dobie Gillis: Almost a Father," CBS, 1960; "The Loretta Young Show: Plain, Unmarked Envelope," NBC, 1960; "The Detectives Starring Robert Taylor: The Frightened Ones," ABC, 1961; "The Way: The Crowd," SYN, 1961; "The Barbara Stanwyck Show: Call Me Annie," NBC, 1961; "Angel: Goodbye, Young Lovers," CBS, 1961; "Ben Casey: A Memory of Candy Stripes," ABC, 1962; "The Blue Angels: Blind Flight," SYN, 1962; "The Virginian: Impasse," NBC, 1962; "Combat!: No Time for Pity," ABC, 1963; "Combat!: The General and the Sergeant," ABC, 1964; "Hollywood Squares," NBC, 1976.

ALEXANDER, JANE

b. Jane Quigley, Boston, MA, October 28, 1939. Leading lady whose performances always indicate intelligence as well as talent; an Emmy winner for "Playing for Time."

AS A GUEST: "Repertory Theatre: St. Patrick's Day," NET, 1965; "NYPD: The Night Watch," ABC, 1969.

TV MOVIES AND MINISERIES: "Welcome Home, Johnny Bristol," CBS, 1972; "Miracle on 34th Street," CBS, 1973; "This Is the West That Was," NBC, 1974; "Death Be Not Proud," ABC, 1975; "Eleanor and Franklin," ABC, 1976; "Eleanor and Franklin: The White House Years," ABC, 1977; "A Circle of Children," CBS, 1977; "Lovey: A Circle of Children, Part II," CBS, 1978; "A Question of Love," ABC, 1978; "Playing for Time," CBS, 1980; "When She Says No," ABC, 1984; "Calamity Jane," CBS, 1984; "Malice in Wonderland," CBS, 1985; "Blood and Orchids," CBS, 1986; "In Love and War," NBC, 1987; "A Friendship in Vienna," DIS, 1988; "Open Admissions," CBS, 1988.
* Emmies: 1981.

ALEXANDER, ROD

b. Los Angeles, CA. Dancer-choreographer, often with Bambi Linn.

AS A REGULAR: "Your Show of Shows," NBC, 1952-54.

AND: "The Steve Allen Show," NBC, 1956; "Strike It Rich," CBS, 1957; "The Steve Allen Show," NBC, 1957; "Arthur Murray Party," NBC, 1957; "The Vic Damone Show," CBS, 1957; "Texaco Star Theatre: Command Appearance," NBC, 1957; "The Ed Sullivan Show," CBS, 1958; "Victor Borge Special," CBS, 1958; "Swing Into Spring," NBC, 1958; "Arthur Godfrey's Talent Scouts," CBS, 1958; "At the Movies," NBC, 1959; "U.S. Steel Hour: Step on the Gas," CBS, 1960; "The Ed Sullivan Show," CBS, 1960.

AS CHOREOGRAPHER: "No Place Like Home," NBC, 1960; "Connie Francis Special: Kicking Sound Around," ABC, 1961.
* See also Bambi Linn.

ALFONSO, KRISTIAN

Soap goddess/vixen who played Hope Brady on "Days of Our Lives" who left the show in 1987 to sail around the world with husband Bo (Peter Reckell) and came back when the money was good enough; in the meantime she played Pilar Cumson on "Falcon Crest."

AS A REGULAR: "Days of Our Lives," NBC, 1983-87, 1990; "Falcon Crest," CBS, 1987-90.

AND: "Murder, She Wrote: A Very Good Year for Murder," CBS, 1988; "MacGyver: Unfinished Business," ABC, 1989; "Candid Camera on Wheels," CBS, 1989; "The Pat Sajak Show," CBS, 1989.

TV MOVIES AND MINISERIES: "The Star Maker," NBC, 1981.

ALI, MUHAMMAD
b. Cassius Clay, Louisville, Ky. Boxing great.
AS A GUEST: "The Jerry Lewis Show," ABC, 1963; "ABC Nightlife," ABC, 1964; "Lola Falana Special," ABC, 1975; "The Jacksons," CBS, 1977; "Diff'rent Strokes: Arnold's Hero," NBC, 1979.
TV MOVIES AND MINISERIES: "Freedom Road," NBC, 1979;

ALICE, MARY
Black actress who plays Lettie Bostic on "A Different World."
AS A REGULAR: "A Different World," NBC, 1988-.
AND: "Sanford & Son: My Brother-in-Law's Keeper," NBC, 1975; "Police Woman: Target Black," NBC, 1975; "Doctors' Hospital: Knives of Chance," NBC, 1975; "Sanford & Son: Brother, Can You Spare an Act?," NBC, 1975; "Serpico: The Traitor in Our Midst," NBC, 1976.
TV MOVIES AND MINISERIES: "Just an Old Sweet Song," CBS, 1976; "This Man Stands Alone," NBC, 1979; "The Women of Brewster Place," ABC, 1989.

ALICIA, ANA
b. Ana Alicia Ortiz, Mexico City, Mexico, December 12, 1956. Pouty sexpot of the soaps; she played Melissa on "Falcon Crest."
AS A REGULAR: "Ryan's Hope," ABC, 1977-78; "Falcon Crest," CBS, 1982-90.
AND: "Buck Rogers in the 25th Century: Vegas in Space," NBC, 1979; "B.J. and the Bear: Seven Lady Captives," NBC, 1981; "The Love Boat: My Mother, the Chaperone," ABC, 1984; "The Byron Allen Show," SYN, 1989.
TV MOVIES AND MINISERIES: "Coward of the County," CBS, 1981; "The Ordeal of Bill Carney," CBS, 1981; "Happy Endings," CBS, 1983.

ALL IN THE FAMILY, CBS, 1971-79.

Archie Bunker made television history. He called a spade a spade, so to speak, and had a racial epithet for every minority. Producers Norman Lear and Bud Yorkin intended for Archie to be a character we laughed at, but many of the viewers who made the Bunker's America's favorite family for almost all the 1970s were laughing with Archie, not at him. Carroll O'Connor played Archie to a turn; his supporting cast—Jean Stapleton as wife Edith, Rob Reiner as son-in-law Mike "Meathead" Stivic, Sally Struthers as daughter Gloria—were his equals. By 1979, Stapleton, Reiner and Struthers had left the show, but O'Connor didn't know when to quit. "Archie Bunker's Place" ran into the mid-1980s, and became just another TV show—not a very good one at that. Strangely enough, however, the issues "All in the Family" addressed are just as prevalent today; ironically, the show now seems shrill and dated.

ALLAN, JED
b. Bronx, NY. Soap actor; he played Don Craig on "Days of Our Lives" and now plays C.C. Capwell on "Santa Barbara."
AS A REGULAR: "Love of Life," CBS, 1964; "The Secret Storm," CBS, 1964-65; "Lassie," CBS, 1968-70; "Love, American Style," ABC, 1973-74; "Days of Our Lives," NBC, 1975-85; "Santa Barbara," NBC, 1987- .
AND: "Mannix: To the Swiftest Death," CBS, 1968; "The Mary Tyler Moore Show: And Now, Sitting in for Ted Baxter," CBS, 1971; "Love, American Style: Love and the Bathtub," ABC, 1972; "Marcus Welby, M.D.: A Question of Fault," ABC, 1973; "Chase: The Scene Stealers," NBC, 1973; "Marcus Welby, M.D.: The 266 Days," ABC, 1974; "Kojak: Dead on His Feet," CBS, 1974; "The Streets of San Francisco: Interlude," ABC, 1976; "McMillan: Affair of the Heart," NBC, 1977; "Goodnight Beantown: The Out-of-Towner," CBS, 1983; "Simon & Simon: Almost Completely Out to Sea," CBS, 1984; "Hardcastle and McCormick: There Goes the Neighborhood," ABC, 1985.
TV MOVIES AND MINISERIES: "Ransom for a Dead Man," NBC, 1971; "The Specialists," NBC, 1975; "Brenda Starr," ABC, 1976; "Fast Friends," NBC, 1979.

ALLBRITTON, LOUISE
b. Oklahoma City, OK, July 3, 1920; d. 1979. Actress who played teen roles in several forties B-features.
AS A REGULAR: "The Stage Door," CBS, 1950; "I've Got a Secret," CBS, 1952; "Concerning Miss Marlowe," NBC, 1954-55.
AND: "Tele-Theatre: Hart to Hart," NBC, 1950; "Studio One: The Rockingham Tea Set," CBS, 1950; "Robert Montgomery Presents: The Champion," NBC, 1950; "Armstrong Circle Theatre: The Other Woman," NBC, 1950; "Armstrong Circle Theatre: The Darkroom," NBC, 1952; "Armstrong Circle Theatre: City Editor," NBC, 1952; "Appointment with Adventure: Stage Fright," CBS, 1955; "Alfred Hitchcock Presents: Never Again," CBS, 1956; "The Invisible Man: The Gunrunners," CBS, 1960; "U.S. Steel Hour: Famous," CBS, 1961; "Naked City: Show Me the Way to Go Home," ABC, 1961; "Girl Talk," SYN, 1963.

ALLEGRETTI, COSMO
Puppeteer.

AS A REGULAR: "Captain Kangaroo," CBS, 1955-85; "Mister Mayor," CBS, 1964-65.

ALLEN, BYRON
b. Detroit, MI, April 22, 1961. Young comedian.
AS A REGULAR: "Real People," NBC, 1979-84; "The Byron Allen Show," SYN, 1989- .
AND: "Hollywood Squares," NBC, 1980; "Animal Crack-Ups," ABC, 1989.
TV MOVIES AND MINISERIES: "Case Closed," CBS, 1988.
AS CO-WRITER: "Case Closed," CBS, 1988.

ALLEN, CHAD
b. Cerritos, CA, June 5, 1974. Young blond actor who played David Witherspoon on "Our House"; memorable as Tommy, the autistic son of Dr. Donald Westphall (Ed Flanders) on "St. Elsewhere."
AS A REGULAR: "St. Elsewhere," NBC, 1983-88; "Webster," ABC, 1985-86; "Our House," NBC, 1986-88.
AND: "Hunter: Heir of Neglect," NBC, 1988; "Highway to Heaven: The Whole Nine Yards," NBC, 1988; "My Two Dads: Blast from the Past," NBC, 1989; "My Two Dads: Who's on First?," NBC, 1989.

ALLEN, CHET
b. Chickasaw, OK, August 17, 1932; d. 1984. Young actor of the fifties.
AS A REGULAR: "Bonino," NBC, 1953; "Trouble-shooters," NBC, 1959-60.

ALLEN, DAYTON
b. New York City, NY, September 24, 1919. Comic whose trademark was a snide, sing-song delivery of his lines; best known for his tenure with Steve Allen.
AS A REGULAR: "Adventures of Oky Doky," DUM, 1948-49; "The Steve Allen Show," NBC, 1956-59; "The Steve Allen Plymouth Show," NBC, 1959-60; "Deputy Dawg," SYN, 1960-61; "The Dayton Allen Show," SYN, 1960-61.
AND: "Art Linkletter's House Party," CBS, 1961; "The Munsters: Operation Herman," CBS, 1965; "The Great American Dream Machine," NET, 1971.

ALLEN, DEBBIE
b. Houston, TX, January 16, 1950. Dancer-choreographer who now works behind the camera.
AS A REGULAR: "3 Girls 3," NBC, 1977; "Fame," NBC, 1982-83, SYN, 1983-87.
AND: "Good Times: J.J.'s Fiancee," CBS, 1976; "The Love Boat: Isaac's Aegean Affair," ABC, 1983; "The Cosby Show: If the Dress Fits, Wear It," NBC, 1988; "The Debbie Allen Special," ABC, 1989.

TV MOVIES AND MINISERIES: "The Greatest Thing That Almost Happened," CBS, 1977; "Roots: The Next Generations," ABC, 1979.
AS DIRECTOR: "The Bronx Zoo: Lost and Found," NBC, 1987; "The Magical World of Disney: Polly," NBC, 1989.
AS PRODUCER-DIRECTOR: "A Different World," NBC, 1988- .

ALLEN, DENNIS
b. Kansas City, MO. Long-faced comic of the late sixties, best known for his tenure with Rowan and Martin.
AS A REGULAR: "What's It All About, World?," ABC, 1969; "The Leslie Uggams Show," CBS, 1969; "Rowan & Martin's Laugh-In," NBC, 1970-73.

ALLEN, ELIZABETH
b. Elizabeth Gillease, Jersey City, NJ, January 25, 1934. Former model, and the young woman who said "And Away We Go!" on Jackie Gleason's show; she played Victoria Bellman on "Texas."
AS A REGULAR: "The Jackie Gleason Show," CBS, 1954-55, 1956-57; "Bracken's World," NBC, 1969-70; "The Paul Lynde Show," ABC, 1972-73; "CPO Sharkey," NBC, 1976-77; "Texas," NBC, 1980-82.
AND: "The Jack Paar Show," NBC, 1959; "Tales of Wells Fargo: Threat of Death," NBC, 1960; "The Twilight Zone: The After Hours," CBS, 1960; "Naked City: The Man Who Bit the Diamond in Half," ABC, 1960; "Checkmate: Murder Game," CBS, 1960; "Thriller: The Hungry Glass," NBC, 1961; "Route 66: Most Vanquished, Most Victorious," CBS, 1961; "Bachelor Father: The House at Smuggler's Cove," NBC, 1961; "Thriller: The Grim Reaper," NBC, 1961; "77 Sunset Strip: The Desert Spa Caper," ABC, 1961; "Alcoa Premiere: The Fugitive Eye," ABC, 1961; "Bachelor Father: The Law and Kelly Gregg," ABC, 1961; "The Alfred Hitchcock Hour: The Thirty-First of February," CBS, 1963; "Ben Casey: Suffer the Little Children," ABC, 1963; "Combat!: No Hallelujah for Glory," ABC, 1963; "Slattery's People: Question-What Is Truth?," CBS, 1964; "Burke's Law: Who Killed Victor Barrows?," ABC, 1964; "The FBI: The Death Wind," ABC, 1966; "The Man From UNCLE: The Waverly Ring Affair," NBC, 1966; "Mannix: Days Beyond Recall," CBS, 1971; "Password," ABC, 1972; "Kojak: Therapy in Dynamite," CBS, 1974.
TV MOVIES AND MINISERIES: "No Other Love," CBS, 1979.

ALLEN, FRED
b. John Florence Sullivan, Cambridge, MA, May 31, 1894, d. 1956. Legendary comic and

wit whose sour appearance and reliance on words meant he was better suited for the radio; he reluctantly entered TV in the early fifties.
AS A REGULAR: "The Colgate Comedy Hour," NBC, 1950; "Chesterfield Sound Off Time," NBC, 1951-52; "Judge for Yourself," NBC, 1953-54; "What's My Line?," CBS, 1954-56.
AND: "Armstrong Circle Theatre: Fred Allen's Sketchbook," NBC, 1954; "Project 20: The Jazz Age," NBC, 1956.

ALLEN, GRACIE

b. *Grace Ethel Cecile Rosalie Allen, San Francisco, CA, July 26, 1902; d. 1964.* Beloved comedienne who was dumb in front of an audience and smart as a whip in private; partner of George Burns for 36 years and his wife for 38.
AS A REGULAR: "The George Burns and Gracie Allen Show," CBS, 1950-58.
AND: "The Jackie Gleason Show," CBS, 1957; "The Bob Cummings Show: Bob Meets the Mortons," CBS, 1957; "The Ed Sullivan Show," CBS, 1957.

ALLEN, IRWIN

b. *New York City, NY, June 12, 1916.* Producer of TV and movie projects that rely on jazzy special effects and gadgetry.
AS PRODUCER: "Voyage to the Bottom of the Sea," ABC, 1964-68; "Lost in Space," CBS, 1965-68; "Land of the Giants," ABC, 1968-70; "Swiss Family Robinson," ABC, 1975-76; "Code Red," ABC, 1981-82.
AS DIRECTOR - TV MOVIES AND MINISERIES: "City Beneath the Sea," NBC, 1971.
* Allen also produced or directed the films "The Poseidon Adventure," "The Towering Inferno" and "The Swarm."

ALLEN, JONELLE

b. *New York City, NY, July 18, 1944.* Actress who plays mean Doreen on "Generations."
AS A REGULAR: "Palmerstown, USA," CBS, 1980-81; "Berrenger's," NBC, 1985; "Generations," NBC, 1988- .
AND: "Hallmark Hall of Fame: Green Pastures," NBC, 1956; "Police Story: The Execution," NBC, 1975; "Police Story: Company Man," NBC, 1975; "Barney Miller: Hot Dogs," ABC, 1975; "Police Woman: Above and Beyond," NBC, 1975; "Joe Forrester: The Boy Next Door," NBC, 1976; "What's Happening!: Rerun Sees the Light," ABC, 1978; "All in the Family: Archie's Other Wife," CBS, 1978; "The White Shadow: Air Ball," CBS, 1979; "Cagney & Lacey: A Killer's Dream," CBS, 1984; "Hill Street Blues: The Count of Monte Tasco," NBC, 1984.
TV MOVIES AND MINISERIES: "Cage Without a Key," CBS, 1975; "Foster and Laurie," CBS,

1975; "Vampire," ABC, 1979; "Victims," ABC, 1982; "The Midnight Hour," ABC, 1985; "Penalty Phase," CBS, 1986.

ALLEN, KAREN

b. *October 5, 1951.* Actress of films ("Raiders of the Lost Ark") and the odd miniseries.
TV MOVIES AND MINISERIES: "Lovey: A Circle of Children, Part II," CBS, 1978; "East of Eden," ABC, 1981.

ALLEN, MARTY

b. *Pittsburgh, PA, March 23, 1922.* Pudgy, bug-eyed comic with Brillo-pad hair whose trademark was the phrase "Hello Dere!"; teamed with singer Steve Rossi until 1968.
AS A REGULAR: "The $1.98 Beauty Show," SYN, 1978-80.
AS A GUEST WITH STEVE ROSSI: "Perry Como's Kraft Music Hall," NBC, 1959; "Perry Como's Kraft Music Hall," NBC, 1960; "The Garry Moore Show," CBS, 1962; "The Garry Moore Show," CBS, 1963; "Vacation Playhouse: Hello Dere!," CBS, 1963; "Password," CBS, 1963; "The Garry Moore Show," CBS, 1964; "The Ed Sullivan Show," CBS, 1964; "To Tell the Truth," CBS, 1964; "Get the Message," ABC, 1964; "The Ed Sullivan Show," CBS, 1965; "To Tell the Truth," CBS, 1965; "Hollywood Palace," ABC, 1965; "The Merv Griffin Show," SYN, 1966; "The Dean Martin Show," NBC, 1967; "Operation: Entertainment," ABC, 1968; "Hollywood Squares," NBC, 1968; "The Ed Sullivan Show," CBS, 1968.
SOLO: "Funny You Should Ask," ABC, 1968; "The Merv Griffin Show," SYN, 1968; "Personality," NBC, 1969; "You're Putting Me On," NBC, 1969; "You Don't Say," NBC, 1969; "Love, American Style: Love and the Athlete," ABC, 1969; "The Tonight Show Starring Johnny Carson," NBC, 1969; "The Merv Griffin Show," CBS, 1969; "The Merv Griffin Show," CBS, 1970; "Changing Scene II," ABC, 1970; "Night Gallery: Quoth the Raven," NBC, 1971; "The Merv Griffin Show," SYN, 1973; "Hollywood Squares," NBC, 1974; "Hollywood Squares," NBC, 1975; "Mitzi and a Hundred Guys," CBS, 1975; "The Magnificent Marble Machine," NBC, 1975; "Beat the Clock," SYN, 1975; "The $20,000 Pyramid," ABC, 1976; "Junior Almost Anything Goes," ABC, 1977; "Sha Na Na," SYN, 1981; "It's Garry Shandling's Show: Force Boxman," FOX, 1988.
TV MOVIES AND MINISERIES: "Mister Jerico," ABC, 1970; "Benny and Barney: Las Vegas Undercover," NBC, 1977; "Murder Can Hurt You!," ABC, 1980.

ALLEN, RAYMOND G.

Actor who played Uncle Woody, cowering

husband of Aunt Esther (Lawanda Page) on "Sanford & Son" and its spinoff.
AS A REGULAR: "Sanford & Son," NBC, 1976-77; "The Sanford Arms," NBC, 1977.
AND: "Good Times: Springtime in the Ghetto," CBS, 1974; "Sanford & Son: Aunt Esther and Uncle Woodrow-Phffft," NBC, 1974; "Good Times: The House Guest," CBS, 1975; "Doctors Hospital: Knives of Chance," NBC, 1975; "Sanford & Son: Divorce, Sanford Style," NBC, 1975; "The Jeffersons: George Finds a Father," CBS, 1978.

ALLEN, REX
b. Wilcox, AZ, December 31, 1922. Actor with a folksy voice and manner; probably best known for the Walt Disney nature films he narrated and for the Purina Dog Chow commercials ("All you add is love") he did in the sixties.
AS A REGULAR: "Frontier Doctor," SYN, 1958; "Five Star Jubilee," NBC, 1961.
AND: "The Rosemary Clooney Show," SYN, 1957; "Ozark Jubilee," ABC, 1957; "The Red Skelton Show," CBS, 1957; "The Lux Show with Rosemary Clooney," NBC, 1958; "Country Music Jubilee," ABC, 1958; "Disneyland: The Horse of the West," ABC, 1958; "Hoedown," NBC, 1959; "Jubilee USA," ABC, 1959; "Mother's March," SYN, 1960; "About Faces," ABC, 1960; "Jubilee USA," ABC, 1960; "Kraft Music Hall Goes West," NBC, 1962; "The Jimmy Dean Show," ABC, 1965.

ALLEN, REX JR.
b. Chicago, IL, August 23, 1947. Son of Rex, now a country-western singer.
AS A REGULAR: "The CBS Newcomers," CBS, 1971; "Nashville on the Road," SYN, 1981-83.
AND: "The Smothers Brothers Show: Heaven Help the Dropout," CBS, 1966.

ALLEN, RICKY
Sixties child actor who played Chip's pal Sudsy Pfieffer on "My Three Sons," and not much else.
AS A REGULAR: "My Three Sons," ABC, 1960-62.
And: "Many Happy Returns: Mother Burnley's Chickens," CBS, 1964; "My Three Sons: Back to Earth," CBS, 1968; "My Three Sons: Rough on Dodie," CBS, 1969.

ALLEN, STEVE
b. New York City, NY, December 16, 1921. Gifted comic writer and performer who pretty much originated the contemporary talk-show format. Best known as the host of a witty, well-written prime-time variety show of the fifties, he also played Lech Oseransky, father of Victor Ehrlich (Ed Begley, Jr.) on "St. Elsewhere."

AS A REGULAR: "Songs for Sale," CBS, 1951-52; "Talent Patrol," ABC, 1953; "What's My Line?," CBS, 1953-54; "The Tonight Show (Tonight)," NBC, 1954-57; "The Steve Allen Show," NBC, 1956-59; SYN, 1963-72; "The Steve Allen Plymouth Show," NBC, 1959-60; "The New Steve Allen Show," ABC, 1961; "I've Got a Secret," CBS, 1964-67; SYN, 1972-73; "The Steve Allen Comedy Hour," CBS, 1967; NBC, 1980-81; "The Sounds of Summer," NET, 1969; "I've Got a Secret," SYN, 1972-73; "Steve Allen's Laugh Back," SYN, 1976; "Meeting of Minds," PBS, 1977-78; "Life's Most Embarrassing Moments," ABC, 1985; "The Start of Something Big," SYN, 1985-86.
AND: "Danger: Five Minutes to Die," CBS, 1953; "Danger: Flamingo," CBS, 1953; "The Follies of Susy," NBC, 1954; "Kraft Television Theatre: Man on Roller Skates," NBC, 1956; "The Ford Show," NBC, 1957; "Mike Wallace Interviews," ABC, 1957; "Texaco Star Theatre: Command Appearance," NBC, 1957; "The Perry Como Show," NBC, 1957; "All-Star Jazz," NBC, 1957; "Wide Wide World: The Sound of Laughter," NBC, 1958; "This Is Your Life," NBC, 1958; "Pat Boone Chevy Showroom," ABC, 1958; "The Bob Cummings Show: Bob Clashes with Steve Allen," NBC, 1959; "The Music Shop," NBC, 1959; "What's My Line?," CBS, 1959; "I've Got a Secret," CBS, 1960; "What's My Line?," CBS, 1960; "The Spike Jones Show," CBS, 1960; "G.E. Theatre: The Man Who Thought for Himself," CBS, 1960; "The du Pont Show with June Allyson: Play-Acting," CBS, 1960; "Here's Hollywood," NBC, 1960; "Person to Person," CBS, 1960; "The Nation's Future: Should There Be Any Taboos for Comedians?," NBC, 1960; "What's My Line?," CBS, 1961; "Nothing to Sneeze At," ABC, 1962; "Dinah Shore Special," NBC, 1962; "The Bob Hope Show," NBC, 1962; "The Ed Sullivan Show," CBS, 1962; "What's My Line?," CBS, 1962; "I've Got a Secret," CBS, 1962; "The Judy Garland Show," CBS, 1964; "What's My Line?," CBS, 1964; "Summer Playhouse: The Apartment House," CBS, 1964; "The Ed Sullivan Show," CBS, 1965; "The Dean Martin Show," NBC, 1965; "Batman: The Cat's Meow/The Bat's Kow Tow," ABC, 1966; "The Match Game," NBC, 1967; "Get Smart: The Mild Ones," NBC, 1967; "You Don't Say," NBC, 1968; "Hollywood Squares," NBC, 1968; "Paulsen for President," CBS, 1968; "Kraft Music Hall: Roast for Johnny Carson," NBC, 1968; "Love, American Style: Love and the Many-Married Couple," ABC, 1970; "Evening at Pops," NET, 1972; "The Merv Griffin Show," SYN, 1973; "Hi-Ho, Steverino: A 25th Anniversary Salute to Steve Allen," ABC, 1974; "The Tonight Show Starring Johnny Carson," NBC, 1974; "Tattletales," CBS, 1974; "The Merv Griffin Show," SYN, 1974; "The Snoop Sisters: Fear Is a

Free Throw," NBC, 1974; "What's My Line?," SYN, 1975; "Mitzi and a Hundred Guys," CBS, 1975; "Medical Center: The Velvet Knife," CBS, 1975; "The Mike Douglas Show," SYN, 1975; "Joys," NBC, 1976; "Something Spectacular with Steve Allen," PBS, 1981; "Dummies," HBO, 1981; "St. Elsewhere: Russian Roulette," NBC, 1987; "St. Elsewhere: Visiting Daze," NBC, 1987; "St. Elsewhere: The Abby Singer Show," NBC, 1988; "It's Garry Shandling's Show: Save Mr. Peck's," FOX, 1989; "Later with Bob Costas," NBC, 1989; "The People Next Door: I Do, I Do," CBS, 1989.

TV MOVIES AND MINISERIES: "Now You See It, Now You Don't," NBC, 1968; "Rich Man, Poor Man," ABC, 1976.

* An example of Allen's quick-wittedness: Once, doing a commercial for Plexiglas, Allen hit a sheet of it with a hammer—and the sheet shattered. Allen paused for a moment and then said, "Yes, that's right, ladies and gentlemen, this hammer is made out of Plexiglas!"

* The producers of "St. Elsewhere" saluted Allen and his variety show regulars by casting many of them as the parents of "St. Elsewhere" doctors: Allen and real-life wife Jayne Meadows played Ehrlich's parents, Louis Nye played the father of Elliott Axelrod (Stephen Furst), Tom Poston the father of Jack Morrison (David Morse) and Bill Dana the father of Wayne Fiscus (Howie Mandel).

ALLEN, WOODY
b. Allen Stewart Konigsberg, Brooklyn, NY, December 1, 1935. Bespectacled comedian with a neurotic persona; he gained fame through TV and club appearances. Now he sticks to feature films ("Annie Hall," "Crimes and Misdemeanors") and shuns the tube.

AS A REGULAR: "Hot Dog," NBC, 1970-71.

AND: "The Jack Paar Program," NBC, 1962; "The Merv Griffin Show," NBC, 1962; "The Merv Griffin Show," NBC, 1963; "The Tonight Show Starring Johnny Carson," NBC, 1963; "The Jack Paar Program," NBC, 1964; "The Tonight Show Starring Johnny Carson," NBC, 1964; "Hullabaloo," NBC, 1965; "The Andy Williams Show," NBC, 1965; "The Ed Sullivan Show," CBS, 1965; "Hippodrome," CBS, 1966; "Personality," NBC, 1967; "The Tonight Show Starring Johnny Carson," NBC, 1968; "Woody Allen Special," CBS, 1969; "The Ed Sullivan Show," CBS, 1969; "The Dick Cavett Show," ABC, 1969; "The Merv Griffin Show," CBS, 1970; "The Dick Cavett Show," ABC, 1971.

ALLENBY, PEGGY
Actress who played Matttie on "The Edge of Night."

AS A REGULAR: "First Love," NBC, 1954-55; "The Edge of Night," CBS, 1957-66.

AND: "U.S. Steel Hour: Trouble-in-Law," CBS, 1959.

ALLEY, KIRSTIE
b. Wichita, KS, January 12, 1955. Lushly sexy actress who plays Rebecca Howe on "Cheers."

AS A REGULAR: "Masquerade," ABC, 1983-84; "Cheers," NBC, 1987- .

TV MOVIES AND MINISERIES: "Sins of the Past," ABC, 1984; "A Bunny's Tale," ABC, 1985; "North and South," ABC, 1985; "North and South, Book II," ABC, 1986; "Stark: Mirror Image," CBS, 1986; "Prince of Bel Air," ABC, 1986; "Infidelity," ABC, 1987.

ALLISON, FRAN
b. LaPorte City, IA, 1908; d. 1989. Pert actress who played straightwoman to puppets Kukla and Oliver J. Dragon; on radio and early TV with Don McNeill she played the gossipy Aunt Fanny.

AS A REGULAR: "Kukla, Fran & Ollie," NBC, 1948-52; ABC, 1954-57; SYN, 1961-62; "Don McNeill TV Club," ABC, 1950-51; "Down You Go," DUM, 1954; "It's About Time," ABC, 1954; "Let's Dance," ABC, 1954.

AND: "Many Moons," ABC, 1954; "The George Gobel Show," NBC, 1957; "Pinocchio," NBC, 1957; "The Tonight Show," NBC, 1957; "The Jack Paar Show," NBC, 1958; "Jubilee USA," ABC, 1958; "The Jack Paar Show," NBC, 1959; "The Jack Paar Show," NBC, 1961; "Perry Como's Kraft Music Hall," NBC, 1962; "The Roy Rogers and Dale Evans Show," ABC, 1962; "Damn Yankees," NBC, 1967; "Miss Pickerell," NBC, 1972.

ALLMAN, ELVIA
b. Spencer, NC, 1905. Tall, skinny actress who played the schemeing Selma Plout on "The Beverly Hillbillies."

AS A REGULAR: "The Abbott and Costello Show," CBS, 1952-54; "Blondie," NBC, 1957; "Petticoat Junction," CBS, 1965-70; "The Beverly Hillbillies," CBS, 1969-71.

AND: "I Love Lucy: Job Switching," CBS, 1952; "I Love Lucy: Fan Magazine Interview," CBS, 1954; "I Love Lucy: Homecoming," CBS, 1955; "The Bob Cummings Show: Mrs. Montague's Niece," NBC, 1955; "The Bob Cummings Show: Too Many Cooks," CBS, 1956; "The Adventures of Ozzie and Harriet: A Doctor in the House," ABC, 1956; "December Bride: The Homecoming," CBS, 1957; "The Bob Cummings Show: Bob for Mayor," NBC, 1957; "The Lucille Ball-Desi Arnaz Show: The Celebrity Next Door," CBS, 1957; "December Bride: Wedding Float," CBS, 1958; "The Ann Sothern Show: Two Too Many," CBS, 1958; "December Bride: Beatnik

Show," CBS, 1959; "The Lucille Ball-Desi Arnaz Show: Milton Berle Hides Out at the Ricardos," CBS, 1959; "The Jack Benny Program," CBS, 1960; "Pete and Gladys: For Pete's Sake," CBS, 1960; "Bachelor Father: It Happened in November," NBC, 1960; "Dennis the Menace: Dennis' Birthday," CBS, 1961; "The Real McCoys: Pepino's Wedding," ABC, 1961; "Pete and Gladys: Pete's Hobby," CBS, 1962; "Calvin and the Colonel: The Colonel's Old Flame," ABC, 1962; "The Red Skelton Show: Calling Dr. Kadiddlehopper," CBS, 1962; "Dennis the Menace: John Wilson's Cushion," CBS, 1962; "Wagon Train: The Donna Fuller Story," ABC, 1962; "The Beverly Hillbillies: Jed Rescues Pearl," CBS, 1963; "The Dick Van Dyke Show: Uncle George," CBS, 1963; "Many Happy Returns: Pop Goes the Easel," CBS, 1965; "The Addams Family: Morticia Meets Royalty," ABC, 1965; "The Dick Van Dyke Show: The Great Petrie Fortune," CBS, 1965; "The Munsters: The Most Beautiful Ghoul in the World," CBS, 1966; "The Patty Duke Show: Patty the Psychic," ABC, 1966; "McHale's Navy: La Dolce 73," ABC, 1966; "The Adventures of Ozzie and Harriet: Dave's Other Office," ABC, 1966; "Bewitched: Maid to Order," ABC, 1966; "My Three Sons: Both Your Houses," CBS, 1967; "The Doris Day Show: The Feminist," CBS, 1970; "The Doris Day Show: Jimmy the Gent," CBS, 1973; "The Odd Couple: The Oddyssey Couple," ABC, 1973; "Gimme a Break: Grandma Fools Around," NBC, 1982.

ALLYSON, JUNE
b. Ella Geisman, Bronx, NY, October 7, 1923. Forties and fifties film actress, usually in fresh-faced roles ("Good News," "The Stratton Story"); now best known as the commercial spokeswoman for an adult diaper.
AS A REGULAR: "The du Pont Show with June Allyson," CBS, 1959-61.
AND: "General Motors 50th Anniversary Show," NBC, 1957; "Dick Powell's Zane Grey Theatre: Cry Hope! Cry Hate!," CBS, 1960; "I've Got a Secret," CBS, 1961; "The Dick Powell Show: A Time to Die," NBC, 1962; "The Dick Powell Show: Special Assignment," NBC, 1962; "The Dick Powell Show: Project X," NBC, 1963; "The Dick Powell Show: The Third Side of the Coin," NBC, 1963; "Burke's Law: Who Killed Beau Sparrow?," ABC, 1963; "The Match Game," NBC, 1964; "The Mike Douglas Show," SYN, 1964; "The Name of the Game: High on a Rainbow," NBC, 1968; "The Mike Douglas Show," SYN, 1971; "Hollywood Squares," NBC, 1973; "The Love Boat: Her Own Two Feet," ABC, 1978; "House Calls: I'll Be Suing You," CBS, 1980; "Simon & Simon: The Last Time I Saw Michael," CBS, 1982; "The Love Boat: Discount Romance," ABC, 1983; "Murder, She

Wrote: Hit, Run and Homicide," CBS, 1984.
TV MOVIES AND MINISERIES: "See the Man Run," ABC, 1971; "Letters From Three Lovers," ABC, 1973.
* "The du Pont Show" was not a happy experience for Allyson. She told interviewers that her husband, producer Dick Powell, had talked her into the project, and the scripts and production values were never up to her standards. She walked off the set several times and made only rare appearances on episodes of the show.

ALTMAN, JEFF
Comic of various variety shows who shared the stage with Japanese pop vocalists Pink Lady on a memorably bad series; NBC executives signed the sexy singers to a contract without realizing they didn't speak English.
AS A REGULAR: "Cos," ABC, 1976; "The Starland Vocal Band Show," CBS, 1977; "Pink Lady," NBC, 1980; "Solid Gold," SYN, 1982-83.
AND: "WKRP in Cincinnati: Johnny Comes Back," CBS, 1979; "The John Davidson Show," SYN, 1981; "thirtysomething: Trust Me," ABC, 1989; "Animal Crack-Ups," ABC, 1989; "Late Night with David Letterman," NBC, 1989.
TV MOVIES AND MINISERIES: "In Love with an Older Woman," CBS, 1982; "Little White Lies," NBC, 1989.

ALYN, KIRK
b. Oxford, NJ, October 8, 1910. Actor who played Superman in 1940s movie serials.
AS A GUEST: "Grindl: Grindl Goes West," NBC, 1964; "The Donna Reed Show: No More Parties-Almost," ABC, 1966.

AMECHE, DON
b. Dominic Felix Amici, Kenosha, WI, May 31, 1908. Actor and radio announcer who was a familiar face on TV in the fifties and sixties, falling out of sight until making an Oscar-winning comeback with "Cocoon" in the eighties.
AS A REGULAR: "Take a Chance," NBC, 1950; "Holiday Hotel," ABC, 1950-51; "Coke Time with Eddie Fisher," NBC, 1953-57; "International Showtime," NBC, 1961-65.
AND: "Saturday Spectacular: High Button Shoes," NBC, 1956; "The Ed Sullivan Show," CBS, 1957; "Arthur Murray Party," NBC, 1957; "Goodyear TV Playhouse: Your Every Wish," NBC, 1957; "Strike It Rich," CBS, 1957; "The Polly Bergen Show," NBC, 1957; "General Motors 75th Anniversary Show," NBC, 1957; "Art Linkletter's House Party," CBS, 1957; "Du Pont Show of the Month: Junior Miss," CBS, 1957; "To Tell the Truth," CBS, 1957; "Climax!: Albert Anastasia: His Life and Death," CBS, 1958; "To Tell the

Truth," CBS, 1958; "To Tell the Truth," CBS, 1959; "Pat Boone Chevy Showroom," ABC, 1960; "Christophers: Making Government Your Business," SYN, 1960; "Frances Langford Special," NBC, 1960; "To Tell the Truth," CBS, 1961; "Perry Como's Kraft Music Hall," NBC, 1961; "Our American Heritage: Woodrow Wilson and the Unknown Soldier," NBC, 1961; "Password," CBS, 1961; "The Match Game," NBC, 1964; "To Tell the Truth," CBS, 1964; "The Greatest Show on Earth: The Glorious Days of Used to Be," ABC, 1964; "Burke's Law: Who Killed Annie Doran?," ABC, 1964; "Petticoat Junction: Steve's Uncle George," CBS, 1970; "Alias Smith and Jones: Dreadful Sorry, Clementine," ABC, 1971; "Columbo: Suitable for Framing," NBC, 1971; "McCloud: The Man in the Golden Hat," NBC, 1975; "Quincy: The Eye of the Needle," NBC, 1978; "The Love Boat: One Rose a Day," ABC, 1979; "The Love Boat: Aunt Hilly," ABC, 1981; "Mr. Smith: Mr. Smith Goes Public," NBC, 1983; "The Love Boat: The Lady and the Maid," ABC, 1984.

TV MOVIES AND MINISERIES: "Shadow Over Elveron," NBC, 1968; "Gidget Gets Married," ABC, 1972; "A Masterpiece of Murder," NBC, 1986; "Pals," CBS, 1987.

AMECHE, JIM
b. 1914; d. 1983. Former radio actor and brother of Don.
AS A REGULAR: "Festival of Stars," NBC, 1957.
AND: "The Hathaways: Waltzing with Walter," ABC, 1962.

AMES, ED
b. Malden, MA, July 9, 1927. Pop singer of the forties and fifties with the Ames brothers; still, best known to audiences for his dramatic roles, including that of Mingo on "Daniel Boone."
AS A REGULAR: "Daniel Boone," NBC, 1964-68.
AND: "The Ed Sullivan Show," CBS, 1957; "The Steve Allen Show," NBC, 1957; "Pat Boone Chevy Showroom," ABC, 1957; "American Bandstand," ABC, 1958; "The Ed Sullivan Show," CBS, 1959; "New Year's Eve Party," CBS, 1959; "The Ed Sullivan Show," CBS, 1960; "The Ed Sullivan Show," CBS, 1961; "The Rifleman: Quiet Night, Deadly Night," ABC, 1962; "The Travels of Jaimie McPheeters: The Day of the Pawnees," ABC, 1963; "The Tonight Show Starring Johnny Carson," NBC, 1966; "You Don't Say," NBC, 1966; "The Ed Sullivan Show," CBS, 1967; "Personality," NBC, 1967; "Kraft Music Hall," NBC, 1968; "Hollywood Squares," NBC, 1969; "Stand Up and Cheer," SYN, 1971; "McCloud: The Colorado Cattle Caper," NBC, 1974; "Murder, She Wrote: Murder at the Oasis," CBS, 1985; "It's Garry Shandling's Show: Sarah," FOX, 1988; "In the Heat of the Night: Prisoners," NBC, 1988.

AMES, FLORENZ
Fatherly actor of fifties TV; he played Ellery Queen's father and Mr. Dithers on "Blondie."
AS A REGULAR: "Ellery Queen," DUM, 1950-51; ABC, 1951-52; SYN, 1954-56; "Blondie," NBC, 1957.
AND: "The People's Choice: Sock Gives Gus Away," NBC, 1956; "Broken Arrow: The Conspirators," ABC, 1956; "Father Knows Best: Margaret Hires a Gardener," NBC, 1956; "Telephone Time: Revenge," ABC, 1957.

AMES, LEON
b. Leon Waycoff, Portland, IN, January 20, 1903. Mustachioed actor who played lots of dads, as well as wisecracking neighbor Gordon Kirkwood on "Mr. Ed."
AS A REGULAR: "Life with Father," CBS, 1953-55; "Father of the Bride," CBS, 1961-62; "Mr. Ed," CBS, 1963-65.
AND: "Twilight Theatre: Ace of Spades," ABC, 1953; "Front Row Center: Ah, Wilderness!," CBS, 1955; "Screen Directors Playhouse: Want-Ad Wedding," NBC, 1955; "Matinee Theatre: Daughter of the Seventh," NBC, 1957; "Lux Video Theatre: Adam Had Four Sons," NBC, 1957; "Studio One: Tongues of Angels," CBS, 1958; "No Warning!: Amnesiac," NBC, 1958; "G.E. Theatre: The Odd Ball," CBS, 1958; "Playhouse 90: The Raider," CBS, 1959; "G.E. Theatre: Adams' Apples," CBS, 1960; "New Comedy Showcase: Maggie," CBS, 1960; "The Barbara Stanwyck Show: The Assassin," NBC, 1961; "The Lucy Show: Lucy and the Military Academy," CBS, 1963; "Please Don't Eat the Daisies: The Monster in the Basement," NBC, 1966; "The Beverly Hillbillies: The Badger Game," CBS, 1966; "The Beverly Hillbillies: Jethro Takes Love Lessons," CBS, 1966; "The Andy Griffith Show: The Senior Play," CBS, 1966; "ABC Stage '67: The Wide Open Door," ABC, 1967; "My Three Sons: Dr. Osborne, M.D.," CBS, 1968; "My Three Sons: Big Ol' Katie," CBS, 1968; "My Three Sons: Expendable Katie," CBS, 1968; "Bewitched: What Makes Darren Run?," ABC, 1970; "The Ghost and Mrs. Muir: Wedding Day????," ABC, 1970; "The Storefront Lawyers: The Electric Kid," CBS, 1970; "The Name of the Game: Capitol Affair," NBC, 1971; "The Jeffersons: Jenny's Grandparents," CBS, 1975.
TV MOVIES AND MINISERIES: "Sherlock Holmes in

New York," NBC, 1976.

* Ames played Margaret O'Brien's father in the 1944 classic "Meet Me in St. Louis"; he also played her father in "Tongues of Angels" on "Studio One" and in the sitcom pilot "Maggie."

AMES, NANCY

b. *Washington, D.C., 1937*. Sixties singer who opened each episode of the satirical revue "That Was the Week That Was."

AS A REGULAR: "That Was the Week That Was," NBC, 1964-65.

AND: "Hootenanny," ABC, 1963; "Hullabaloo," NBC, 1965; "The Mike Douglas Show," SYN, 1965; "Perry Como Special," NBC, 1965; "Kraft Music Hall," NBC, 1967; "The Red Skelton Hour," CBS, 1967; "Operation: Entertainment," ABC, 1968; "It's Happening," ABC, 1968; "Bob Hope Special," NBC, 1968; "The Name of the Game: Pineapple Rose," NBC, 1968; "The Jerry Lewis Show," NBC, 1969; "The Andy Williams Show," SYN, 1977.

AMES, RACHEL

Actress who plays Audrey March Hardy Hobart on "General Hospital."

AS A REGULAR: "The Lineup," CBS, 1959-60; "General Hospital," ABC, 1964- .

AND: "The Millionaire: Millionaire Jessica Marsh," CBS, 1960; "Laramie: Cemetery Road," NBC, 1960; "Stagecoach West: The Root of Evil," ABC, 1961; "Wagon Train: The Saul Bevins Story," NBC, 1961; "G.E. True: Circle of Death," CBS, 1962; "Wagon Train: The Trace McCloud Story," ABC, 1964; "Arrest and Trial: Funny Man with a Monkey," ABC, 1964; "The Virginian: Death Wait," NBC, 1969.

AMORY, CLEVELAND

b. *Nahant, MA, September 2, 1917*. Best-selling author ("The Cat Who Came for Christmas") and former critic for TV Guide, with some television experience of his own.

AS A REGULAR: "One Minute Please," D, 54-55.

AND: "The Last Word," CBS, 1957; "The Jack Paar Show," NBC, 1959; "Person to Person," CBS, 1959; "The Last Word," CBS, 1959.

AS CREATOR: "O.K. Crackerby," ABC, 1965-66.

AMOS, JOHN

b. *Newark, NJ, December 27, 1941*. Husky actor who played Gordy the weatherman on "The Mary Tyler Moore Show" and James Evans, husband of Florida (Esther Rolle) and father of big-mouthed J.J. (Jimmie Walker) on "Good Times."

AS A REGULAR: "The Mary Tyler Moore Show," CBS, 1970-73; "The Funny Side," NBC, 1971; "Maude," CBS, 1973-74; "Good Times," CBS, 1974-76; "Hunter," NBC, 1984-85.

AND: "The Bill Cosby Show: Swan's Way," NBC, 1970; "Love, American Style: Love and the Split-Up," ABC, 1971; "Love, American Style: Love and the Hiccups," ABC, 1971; "Keeping Up with the Joneses," NBC, 1972; "Sanford and Son: The Big Party," NBC, 1973; "Maude: Florida's Problem," CBS, 1973; "Two's Company," CBS, 1973; "Maude: Florida's Affair," CBS, 1973; "Maude: Florida's Goodbye," CBS, 1974; "Police Story: Oxford Gray," NBC, 1976; "The Mary Tyler Moore Show: Hail the Conquering Gordy," CBS, 1977; "The Love Boat: Final Score," ABC, 1983; "The A-Team: Pur-Dee Poison," NBC, 1984; "Hardcastle and McCormick: The Homecoming," ABC, 1984; "The Cosby Show: The Physical," NBC, 1988; "Gideon Oliver: Tongs," ABC, 1989.

TV MOVIES AND MINISERIES: "Future Cop," ABC, 1976; "Roots," ABC, 1977; "Willa," CBS, 1979; "Bonanza: The Next Generation," SYN, 1988.

AMSTERDAM, MOREY

b. *Chicago, IL, December 14, 1914*. Wise-cracking vaudeville-trained comic who was just perfect as Buddy Sorrell, wisecracking vaudeville-trained comic writer, on "The Dick Van Dyke Show."

AS A REGULAR: "Stop Me If You've Heard This One," NBC, 1948; "The Morey Amsterdam Show," CBS, 1948-49; DUM, 1949-50; "Texaco Star Theatre," NBC, 1948; "Broadway Open House," NBC, 1950; "Can You Top This?," ABC, 1950-51; "Battle of the Ages," CBS, 1952; "Who Said That?," NBC, 1954; "Make Me Laugh," ABC, 1958; "Keep Talking," CBS, 1958-59; ABC, 1959-60; "The Dick Van Dyke Show," CBS, 1961-66; "Can You Top This?," SYN, 1970; "Honeymoon Suite," ABC, 1973; "The Young and the Restless," CBS, 1990.

AND: "The Tonight Show," NBC, 1956; "The Gale Storm Show: Checkmate," CBS, 1957; "December Bride: Mountain Climbing," CBS, 1957; "The Jackie Gleason Show," CBS, 1957; "The Danny Thomas Show: The Honeymoon Flashback," CBS, 1957; "How to Marry a Millionaire: The Three Pretenders," SYN, 1957; "The Adventures of Jim Bowie: Choctaw Honor," ABC, 1958; "Gunsmoke: Joe Phy," CBS, 1958; "Schlitz Playhouse of Stars: I Shot a Prowler," CBS, 1958; "The Ed Sullivan Show: Man of the Hour," CBS, 1958; "The Phil Silvers Show: Bilko's Give-away," CBS, 1958; "Have Gun, Will Travel: The Moor's Revenge," CBS, 1959; "Pete and Gladys: Gladys Rents the House," CBS, 1961; "Art Linkletter's House Party," CBS, 1961; "The Garry Moore Show," CBS, 1961; "Art Linkletter's House Party," CBS, 1962; "Your First Impression," NBC, 1962; "Stump the Stars," CBS, 1962; "Mr. Magoo's Christmas Carol,"

NBC, 1962; "The Danny Thomas Show: The Woman Behind the Jokes," CBS, 1963; "The Match Game," NBC, 1964; "What's This Song?," NBC, 1965; "PDQ," NBC, 1965; "PDQ," NBC, 1966; "Daktari: The Chimp Who Cried Wolf," CBS, 1966; "Kraft Music Hall," NBC, 1967; "Hollywood Squares," NBC, 1968; "The Match Game," NBC, 1968; "That's Life: Life in Suburbia," ABC, 1968; "The Merv Griffin Show," SYN, 1968; "Love, American Style: Love and Mother," ABC, 1969; "The Partridge Family: Did You Hear the One About Danny Partridge?," ABC, 1970; "Love, American Style: Love and the See-Thru Mind," ABC, 1973; "Match Game '74," CBS, 1974; "Rudolph's Shiny New Year," ABC, 1976; "Alice: Alice by Moonlight," CBS, 1977.

TV MOVIES AND MINISERIES: "Sooner or Later," NBC, 1979; "Side by Side," CBS, 1988.

* Amsterdam also played Buddy on "The Woman Behind the Jokes" episode of "The Danny Thomas Show."

ANDERMAN, MAUREEN
Actress who plays Molly Dodd's pal, Nina Shapiro; she also played restaurant owner Pete O'Phelan on "The Equalizer."

AS A REGULAR: "Search for Tomorrow," CBS, 1981; "The Equalizer," CBS, 1987-89; "The Days and Nights of Molly Dodd," NBC, 1987-88; LIF, 1988- .

AND: "Kojak: Where Do You Go When You Have No Place to Go?," CBS, 1977; "St. Elsewhere: Down's Syndrome," NBC, 1982.

TV MOVIES AND MINISERIES: "Cocaine and Blue Eyes," NBC, 1983.

ANDERS, MERRY
b. Chicago, IL, 1932. Starlet who did lots of TV and low-grade movies in the fifties and sixties.

AS A REGULAR: "The Stu Erwin Show," ABC, 1954-55; "It's Always Jan," CBS, 1955-56; "How to Marry a Millionaire," SYN, 1958-59; "Never Too Young," ABC, 1965-66.

AND: "The Millionaire: The Jay Powers Story," CBS, 1956; "Cheyenne: Big Ghost Basin," ABC, 1957; "77 Sunset Strip: All Our Yesterdays," ABC, 1958; "Sugarfoot: Outlaw Island," ABC, 1959; "Maverick: The People's Friend," ABC, 1960; "Maverick: Destination Devil's Flat," ABC, 1960; "Cheyenne: Ordeal at Dead Tree," ABC, 1961; "The Loretta Young Show: Enter at Your Own Risk," NBC, 1961; "SurfSide 6: Yesterday's Hero," ABC, 1961; "77 Sunset Strip: Face in the Window," ABC, 1961; "77 Sunset Strip: Tiger by the Tail," ABC, 1961; "Hawaiian Eye: Don't Kiss Me Goodbye," ABC, 1961; "Bringing Up Buddy: Buddy and the Amazon," CBS, 1961; "Michael Shayne: Dead Air," NBC, 1961; "77 Sunset Strip: The Lady Has the Answers," ABC, 1961; "The Bob Cummings Show: The Oxtail Incident," CBS, 1961; "Hawaiian Eye: Pill in the Box,"

ABC, 1961; "Maverick: Three Queens Full," ABC, 1961; "Ichabod and Me: The Visit," CBS, 1961; "Perry Mason: The Case of the Glamorous Ghost," CBS, 1962; "Straightaway: Tiger by the Tail," ABC, 1962; "Death Valley Days: Way Station," SYN, 1962; "Death Valley Days: The Vintage Years," SYN, 1962; "77 Sunset Strip: The Odds on Odette," ABC, 1962; "The Joey Bishop Show: Freddie Goes Highbrow," NBC, 1963; "The Joey Bishop Show: Jack Carter Helps Joey Propose," NBC, 1964; "Arrest and Trial: The Best There Is," ABC, 1964; "The Virginian: A Man Called Kane," NBC, 1964; "The Addams Family: Fester's Punctured Romance," ABC, 1964; "Gunsmoke: Waste," CBS, 1971.

ANDERSON, BARBARA
b. Brooklyn, NY, November 27, 1945. Popular actress of the late sixties; she won an Emmy as officer Eve Whitfield on "Ironside" and later played Mimi Davis on "Mission: Impossible."

AS A REGULAR: "Ironside," NBC, 1967-71; "Mission: Impossible," CBS, 1972-73.

AND: "The Virginian: The Challenge," NBC, 1966; "Star Trek: Conscience of the King," NBC, 1966; "Mannix: The Name is Mannix," CBS, 1967; "Paris 7000: Call Me Lee," ABC, 1970; "Paris 7000: Call Me Ellen," ABC, 1970; "Marcus Welby, M.D.: To Get Through the Night," ABC, 1970; "Night Gallery: Fright Night," NBC, 1972; "Medical Center: The Casualty," CBS, 1973; "Marcus Welby, M.D.: Out of Control," ABC, 1974; "Owen Marshall, Conselor at Law: To Keep and Bear Arms," ABC, 1974; "Amy Prentiss: Profile in Evil," NBC, 1975; "Police Story: To Steal a Million," NBC, 1975; "The Invisible Man: Eyes Only," NBC, 1975; "Switch: Net Loss," CBS, 1977; "The Love Boat: Ship of Ghouls," ABC, 1978; "Simon & Simon: Design for Murder," CBS, 1983.

TV MOVIES AND MINISERIES: "Ironside," NBC, 1967; "Split Second to an Epitaph," NBC, 1968; "Visions...," CBS, 1972; "The Six Million Dollar Man," ABC, 1973; "Don't Be Afraid of the Dark," ABC, 1973; "Murder in the Comptuer," ABC, 1973; "Strange Homecoming," NBC, 1974; "You Lie So Deep, My Love," ABC, 1975; "SST-Death Flight," ABC, 1977.

* Emmies: 1968.

ANDERSON, BILL
Country-western singer turned game show host.

AS A REGULAR: "The Better Sex," ABC, 1977-78; "Backstage at the Grand Ole Opry," SYN, 1980-81; "Fandango," TNN, 1983- .

AND: "The Jimmy Dean Show," ABC, 1965; "The Mike Douglas Show," SYN, 1970; "The Merv Griffin Show," SYN, 1975; "The Grand Ole Opry at 50," ABC, 1975; "Music Hall America," SYN, 1977.

ANDERSON, G.M. "BRONCHO BILLY"

b. Max Aronson, Little Rock, March 21, 1882; d. 1971. Cowboy actor-director who began his career in the 1903 film "The Great Train Robbery."

AS A GUEST: "Wide, Wide World: The Western," NBC, 1958; "Alias Smith and Jones: The Men That Corrupted Hadleyburg," ABC, 1972.

ANDERSON, DARYL

b. Seattle, WA, July 1, 1951. Lanky actor who played the slovenly-but-sensitive photographer Dennis "Animal" Price on "Lou Grant."

AS A REGULAR: "Lou Grant," CBS, 1977-82.

AND: "Match Game '79," CBS, 1979; "Dance Fever," SYN, 1980; "The Love Boat: Teach Me Tonight," ABC, 1981; "The A-Team: The A-Team Is Coming, the A-Team Is Coming," NBC, 1986; "Blacke's Magic: Death Goes to the Movies," NBC, 1986.

TV MOVIES AND MINISERIES: "The Phoenix," ABC, 1981.

ANDERSON, EDDIE "ROCHESTER"

b. Oakland, CA, September 18, 1905; d. 1977. Black comic actor best known as Jack Benny's wisecracking valet.

AS A REGULAR: "The Jack Benny Program," CBS, 1950-64; NBC, 1964-65.

AND: "The Red Skelton Show," CBS, 1957; "The George Gobel Show," NBC, 1957; "Hallmark Hall of Fame: Green Pastures," NBC, 1957; "Shower of Stars: Jack Benny's 40th Birthday Celebration," CBS, 1958; "Hallmark Hall of Fame: Green Pastures," NBC, 1959; "Bachelor Father: Pinch That Penny," ABC, 1962; "The Dick Powell Show: The Last of the Private Eyes," NBC, 1963; "Love, American Style: Love and the Hustler," ABC, 1969.

* Anderson began working with Jack Benny in 1937.

ANDERSON, HARRY

b. Newport, RI, October 14, 1952. Talented comic magician who traded his witty act for the security of the lead in a popular, totally mediocre sitcom.

AS A REGULAR: "Night Court," NBC, 1984- ; "Our Time," NBC, 1985.

AND: "The John Davidson Show," SYN, 1981; "Cheers: Sam at Eleven," NBC, 1982; "Cheers: The Boys in the Bar," NBC, 1983; "Cheers: Pick a Con ... Any Con," NBC, 1983; "Cheers: How Do I Love Thee, Let Me Call You Back," NBC, 1983; "Saturday Night Live," NBC, 1985; "Harry Anderson's 'Hello, Sucker!,'" SHO, 1985; "The Smothers Brothers Comedy Hour," CBS, 1988; "The Magical World of Disney: The Absent-Minded Professor," NBC, 1988; "The Tonight Show Starring Johnny Carson," NBC, 1989.

ANDERSON, HERBERT

b. Oakland, CA, March 30, 1917. Lanky actor who played Henry Mitchell, father of "Dennis the Menace" (Jay North).

AS A REGULAR: "Dennis the Menace," CBS, 1959-63.

AND: "Navy Log: Ping Happy Spit Kit," ABC, 1957; "Suspicion: The Other Side of the Curtain," NBC, 1957; "G.E. Theatre: The Coward of Fort Bennett," CBS, 1958; "Goodyear Theatre: The Obenauf Story," NBC, 1959; "Rawhide: Incident of the Rusty Shotgun," CBS, 1964; "The Man From UNCLE: The Shark Affair," NBC, 1964; "Many Happy Returns: Walter Meets the Machine," CBS, 1964; "The Bing Crosby Show: Genius at Work," ABC, 1964; "The Smothers Brothers Show: Here Comes the Bridegroom," CBS, 1965; "Petticoat Junction: Better Never Than Late," CBS, 1966; "I Dream of Jeannie: Watch the Birdie," NBC, 1966; "Batman: The Clock King's Crazy Crimes/The King Gets Crowned," ABC, 1966; "My Three Sons: My Dad the Athlete," CBS, 1967; "Batman: The Sport of Penguins/A Horse of Another Color," ABC, 1967; "The Man From UNCLE: The Suburbia Affair," NBC, 1967; "Dragnet: The Big Bank," NBC, 1967; "My Three Sons: The Grandfathers," CBS, 1968; "Family Affair: No Uncle Is an Island," CBS, 1969; "The Brady Bunch: Is There a Doctor in the House?," ABC, 1969; "Nanny and the Professor: A Diller, a Dollar," ABC, 1970; "The Paul Lynde Show: Back Talk," ABC, 1973; "The Magician: The Illusion of the Evil Spikes," NBC, 1974.

TV MOVIES AND MINISERIES: "Virginia Hill," NBC, 1974.

ANDERSON, JOHN

b. Clayton, IL, October 20, 1922. Lean, craggy character actor who played Virgil Earp on "Wyatt Earp" and guested on dozens of other westerns.

AS A REGULAR: "The Life and Legend of Wyatt Earp," ABC, 1959-61; "The Rifleman," ABC, 1959-61; "Rich Man, Poor Man - Book II," ABC, 1976-77.

AND: "The Phil Silvers Show: Reunion," CBS, 1955; "Dick Powell's Zane Grey Theatre: Episode in Darkness," CBS, 1957; "Trackdown: End of an Outlaw," CBS, 1957; "Law of the Plainsman: Appointment in Santa Fe," NBC, 1959; "Tales of Wells Fargo: The Quiet Village," NBC, 1960; "The Detectives Starring Robert Taylor: Karate," ABC, 1960; "Lawman: Left Hand of the Law," ABC, 1960; "Law of the Plainsman: Jeb's Daughter," NBC, 1960; "Harrigan and Son: Non Compos Mentis," ABC, 1960; "Maverick: Benefit of a Doubt," ABC, 1961; "Assassination Plot at Teheran," ABC, 1961; "87th Precinct: The Modus Man," NBC, 1961; "Cheyenne: Retaliation," ABC, 1961; "Alfred Hitchcock Presents: The Old

Pro," NBC, 1961; "King of Diamonds: The Uncivil Servant," SYN, 1962; "Laramie: The Perfect Gift," NBC, 1962; "Tales of Wells Fargo: Reward for Gaine," NBC, 1962; "Death Valley Days: A Girl Named Virginia," SYN, 1962; "The Tall Man: Night of the Hawk," NBC, 1962; "Alcoa Premiere: Second Chance," ABC, 1962; "Dr. Kildare: The Visitors," NBC, 1962; "The Eleventh Hour: I Don't Belong in a White-Painted House," NBC, 1962; "The Twilight Zone: Of Late I Think of Cliffordville," CBS, 1963; "The Outer Limits: Nightmare," ABC, 1963; "The Twilight Zone: The Old Man in the Cave," CBS, 1963; "The Lieutenant: Gone the Sun," NBC, 1964; "The Fugitive: Come Watch Me Die," ABC, 1964; "Walt Disney's Wonderful World of Color: A Taste of Melon," NBC, 1964; "Ben Casey: But Who Shall Beat the Drums?," ABC, 1964; "The Fugitive: Scapegoat," ABC, 1965; "The FBI: The Forests of the Night," ABC, 1966; "Gunsmoke: Mail Drop," CBS, 1967; "The Road West: Road to Glory," NBC, 1967; "The Iron Horse: Five Days to Washtiba," ABC, 1967; "The Virginian: Bitter Autumn," NBC, 1967; "Lancer: Blood Rock," CBS, 1968; "Hollywood Television Theatre: The Andersonville Trial," NET, 1970; "McMillan and Wife: Death Is a Seven-Point Favorite," NBC, 1971; "The FBI: The Wizard," ABC, 1972; "Kung Fu: Blood Brothers," ABC, 1973; "Gunsmoke: Kimbrough," CBS, 1973; "The Bob Newhart Show: The Gray Flannel Shrink," CBS, 1974; "Little House on the Prairie: Haunted House," NBC, 1975; "Emergency!: The Smoke Eater," NBC, 1975; "The Rockford Files: Coulter City Wildcat," NBC, 1976; "The Quest: Shanklin," NBC, 1976; "Lou Grant: Take-Over," CBS, 1977; "Silver Spoons: The Great Computer Caper," NBC, 1982; "M*A*S*H: Say No More," CBS, 1983; "Riptide: Diamonds Are for Never," NBC, 1984; "Scarecrow and Mrs. King: The Mole," CBS, 1984; "Aaron's Way: The Harvest," NBC, 1988; "Knightwatch: Lost Weekend," ABC, 1988; "Baby Boom: The Club," NBC, 1988; "Hunter: No Good Deed Ever Goes Unpunished," NBC, 1988; "Knightwatch: Cops," ABC, 1989.
TV MOVIES AND MINISERIES: "Scalplock," NBC, 1966; "Set This Town on Fire," NBC, 1973; "Call to Danger," CBS, 1973; "Brock's Last Case," NBC, 1973; "Partners in Crime," NBC, 1973; "Heat Wave," ABC, 1974; "Smile, Jenny, You're Dead," ABC, 1974; "Manhunter," CBS, 1974; "Dead Man on the Run," ABC, 1975; "Death Among Friends," NBC, 1975; "The Dark Side of Innocence," NBC, 1976; "Bridger," ABC, 1976; "Best Sellers: Once an Eagle," NBC, 1977; "Donner Pass: The Road to Survival," NBC, 1978; "The Deerslayer," NBC, 1978; "Backstairs at the White House," NBC, 1979; "In Search of Historic Jesus," NBC, 1981; "Full Exposure: The Sex Tapes Scandal," NBC, 1989.

* Anderson played Franklin D. Roosevelt in "Backstairs at the White House" and Abraham Lincoln in the feature film "The Lincoln Conspiracy."

ANDERSON, DAME JUDITH

b. Frances Margaret Anderson, Adelaide, Australia, February 10, 1898. Film and stage actress who played the evil Mrs. Danvers in "Rebecca" and the evil Minx Capwell on "Santa Barbara"; an Emmy winner for "Macbeth."

AS A REGULAR: "Santa Barbara," NBC, 1984-87.
AND: "Pulitzer Prize Playhouse: The Silver Cord," ABC, 1951; "Motorola TV Hour: Black Chiffon," ABC, 1954; "Light's Diamond Jubilee," ABC, CBS, NBC, 1954; "Hallmark Hall of Fame: Macbeth," NBC, 1954; "Elgin TV Hour: Yesterday's Magic," ABC, 1954; "The Christmas Story," CBS, 1954; "Rheingold Theatre: Louise," NBC, 1955; "Rheingold Theatre: Virtue," NBC, 1955; "Neighbor Theatre: The Senora," NBC, 1955; "Rheingold Theatre: The Creative Impulse," NBC, 1955; "Producers Showcase: Caesar and Cleopatra," NBC, 1956; "Hallmark Hall of Fame: Cradle Song," NBC, 1956; "Climax!: The Circular Staircase," CBS, 1956; "Playhouse 90: The Clouded Image," CBS, 1957; "Telephone Time: Abby, Julia and the Seven Pet Cows," ABC, 1958; "Du Pont Show of the Month: The Bridge of San Luis Rey," CBS, 1958; "Playhouse 90: The Second Happiest Day," CBS, 1959; "The Moon and Sixpence," NBC, 1959; "Wagon Train: The Felezia Kingdom Story," NBC, 1959; "Hallmark Hall of Fame: The Hallmark Christmas Festival," NBC, 1959; "Playhouse 90: To the Sound of Trumpets," CBS, 1960; "Arthur Murray Party," NBC, 1960; "Hallmark Hall of Fame: Cradle Song," NBC, 1960; "Our American Heritage: Millionaire's Mite," NBC, 1960; "Play of the Week: Medea," SYN, 1960; "Hallmark Hall of Fame: Macbeth," NBC, 1960; "Hallmark Hall of Fame: Elizabeth the Queen," NBC, 1968; "Hallmark Hall of Fame: The File on Devlin," NBC, 1969; "Hallmark Hall of Fame: Hamlet," NBC, 1970; "A Salute to Television's 25th Anniversary," ABC, 1972; "Hollywood Television Theatre: The Chinese Prime Minister," PBS, 1974.
TV MOVIES AND MINISERIES: "The Borrowers," NBC, 1973; "The Underground Man," NBC, 1974.
* Emmies: 1955.

ANDERSON, LONI

b. St. Paul, MN, August 5, 1945. Blonde bombshell who has a way with a funny line; best known as receptionist Jennifer Marlowe on "WKRP in Cincinnati."

AS A REGULAR: "WKRP in Cincinnati," CBS, 1978-82; "Partners in Crime" NBC, 1984; "Easy Street," NBC, 1986-87.

AND: "Barnaby Jones: Deadly Reunion," CBS, 1976; "The Bob Newhart Show: Carlin's New Suit," CBS, 1977; "Three's Company: Coffee, Tea or Jack?," ABC, 1978; "Hollywood Squares," NBC, 1978; "The Love Boat: Kin Folk," ABC, 1979; "Amazing Stories: Guilt Trip," NBC, 1985; "The Jim Henson Hour: The Heartless Giant," NBC, 1989; "Blondie & Dagwood Second Wedding Workout," CBS, 1989.

TV MOVIES AND MINISERIES: "Sizzle," ABC, 1981; "Country Gold," CBS, 1982; "My Mother's Secret Life," ABC, 1984; "A Letter to Three Wives," NBC, 1985; "Stranded," NBC, 1986; "Necessity," CBS, 1988; "A Whisper Kills," ABC, 1988; "Sorry, Wrong Number," USA, 1989.

ANDERSON, LYNN

b. Grand Forks, ND, September 26, 1947.
Singer of middle-of-the-road country tunes.

AS A REGULAR: "The Lawrence Welk Show," ABC, 1967-68; "Dean Martin Presents," NBC, 1973.

AND: "Hee Haw," SYN, 1971; "The Dean Martin Show," NBC, 1972; "Country Music Hit Parade," NBC, 1973; "Music Country USA," NBC, 1974; "The Wacky World of Jonathan Winters," SYN, 1974; "Midnight Special," NBC, 1974; "The Peter Marshall Variety Show," SYN, 1976; "Hollywood Squares," NBC, 1976; "Pop! Goes the Country," SYN, 1982.

ANDERSON, MARIAN

b. Philadelphia, PA, February 17, 1902.
Gifted operatic singer.

AS A GUEST: "See It Now: The Lady From Philadelphia: Through Asia with Marian Anderson," CBS, 1957; "America Pauses for the Merry Month of May," CBS, 1959; "A Tribute to Eleanor Roosevelt on Her Diamond Jubilee," NBC, 1959; "Startime: Christmas Startime," NBC, 1959; "Startime: Well, What About You?," NBC, 1960.

ANDERSON, MELISSA SUE

b. Berkeley, CA, September 26, 1962. Actress who played Mary Ingalls on "Little House on the Prairie"; she won an Emmy for an "ABC Afterschool Special."

AS A REGULAR: "Little House on the Prairie," NBC, 1974-81.

AND: "The Love Boat: Chubs," ABC, 1978; "The Love Boat: Cindy," ABC, 1979; "ABC Afterschool Special: Which Mother Is Mine?," ABC, 1980; "Finder of Lost Loves: Premiere," ABC, 1984; "Murder, She Wrote: Hooray for Homicide," CBS, 1984; "Hotel: Imperfect Union," ABC, 1985; "The Equalizer: Memories of Manon," CBS, 1987; "The Equalizer: The

Mystery of Manon," CBS, 1988.

TV MOVIES AND MINISERIES: "Survival of Dana," CBS, 1979.

* Emmies: 1980.

ANDERSON, MELODY

b. Canada, December 3, 1955. Attractive blonde actress who's appeared in several TV movies with titles that sound like they came out of "True Romance" magazine.

AS A REGULAR: "Manimal," NBC, 1983.

AND: "B.J. and the Bear: Wheels of Fortune," NBC, 1979; "St. Elsewhere: Brothers," NBC, 1983; "St. Elsewhere: Remission," NBC, 1983; "St. Elsewhere: Working," NBC, 1983; "St. Elsewhere: Addiction," NBC, 1983; "Philip Marlowe, Private Eye: Blackmailers Don't Shoot," HBO, 1987; "Murder, She Wrote: Prediction: Murder," CBS, 1988.

TV MOVIES AND MINISERIES: "Pleasure Cove," NBC, 1979; "Policewoman Centerfold," NBC, 1983; "Beverly Hills Madam," NBC, 1986; "Deep Dark Secrets," NBC, 1987.

ANDERSON, MICHAEL JR.

b. England, December 3, 1945. Actor who played Clayt Monroe, head of a brood of parentless children in the wild west on "The Monroes."

AS A REGULAR: "The Monroes," ABC, 1966-67.

AND: "Fair Exchange: A Young Man's Fancy," CBS, 1962; "Stoney Burke: Gold-Plated Maverick," ABC, 1963; "The John Forsythe Show: Miss Culver, Won't You Please Come Home?," NBC, 1965; "Medical Center: Junkie," CBS, 1970; "Love, American Style: Love and the Fuzz," ABC, 1971; "Love, American Style: Love and the Eyewitness," ABC, 1971; "Hawaii Five-O: The Sunday Torch," CBS, 1973; "Hawaii Five-O: How to Steal a Masterpiece," CBS, 1974; "Ironside: Raise the Devil," NBC, 1974; "The Streets of San Francisco: Asylum," ABC, 1975; "Police Story: Headhunter," NBC, 1975; "Quincy: An Ounce of Prevention," NBC, 1979; "Jesse Hawkes: Premiere," CBS, 1989.

TV MOVIES AND MINISERIES: "The House That Would Not Die," ABC, 1970; "In Search of America," ABC, 1971; "The Family Rico," CBS, 1972; "The Daughters of Joshua Cabe," ABC, 1972; "Coffee, Tea or Me?," CBS, 1973; "Shootout in a One-Dog Town," ABC, 1974; "Kiss Me, Kill Me," ABC, 1976; "Washington: Behind Closed Doors," ABC, 1977.

ANDERSON, RICHARD

b. August 8, 1926. Actor who often plays official types, best known as Oscar on "The Six Million Dollar Man" and "The Bionic Woman."

AS A REGULAR: "Mama Rosa," ABC, 1950; "The Rifleman," ABC, 1960-61; "Bus Stop," ABC, 1961-62; "The Lieutenant," NBC, 1963-64; "Perry Mason," CBS, 1965-66; "Dan August," ABC, 1970-71; "The Six Million Dollar Man," ABC, 1974-78; "The Bionic Woman," ABC, 1976-77; NBC, 1977-78; "Cover Up," CBS, 1984-85; "Dynasty," ABC, 1986-87.

AND: "The Millionaire: Millionaire Rod Matthews," CBS, 1956; "Schlitz Playhouse of Stars: The Lonely Wizard," CBS, 1957; "Matinee Theatre: Love Out of Town," NBC, 1958; "Command Performance: The Lone Hand," SYN, 1958; "Zorro: Amnesty for Zorro," ABC, 1959; "Law of the Plainsman: Cavern of the Wind," NBC, 1960; "Stagecoach West: The Land Beyond," ABC, 1960; "Mr. Garlund: The Towers," CBS, 1960; "Thriller: The Purple Room," NBC, 1960; "Checkmate: Murder Game," CBS, 1960; "Wanted Dead or Alive: Epitaph," CBS, 1961; "Hong Kong: Murder by Proxy," ABC, 1961; "The Rifleman: The Bullet," ABC, 1963; "Dr. Kildare: Whoever Heard of a Two-Headed Doll?," NBC, 1963; "The Virginian: Strangers at Sundown," NBC, 1963; "Perry Mason: The Case of the Accosted Accountant," CBS, 1964; "The Eleventh Hour: Who Chopped Down the Cherry Tree?," NBC, 1964; "Perry Mason: The Case of the Paper Bullets," CBS, 1964; "The Man From UNCLE: The Quadripartite Affair," NBC, 1964; "Slattery's People: Does Nero Still at Ringside Sit?," CBS, 1965; "The Man From UNCLE: The Candidate's Wife Affair," NBC, 1966; "The FBI: The Enemies," ABC, 1968; "Mannix: Fear I to Fall," CBS, 1968; "The Big Valley: Bounty on a Barkley," ABC, 1968; "The Mod Squad: A Town Called Sincere," ABC, 1969; "The FBI: The Challenge," ABC, 1969; "Gunsmoke: The War Priest," CBS, 1970; "Alias Smith and Jones: Never Trust an Honest Man," ABC, 1971; "Ironside: License to Kill," NBC, 1971; "The FBI: The Franklin Papers," ABC, 1972; "The FBI: The Big Job," ABC, 1973; "The Streets of San Francisco: A Room with a View," ABC, 1973; "The New Adventures of Perry Mason: The Case of the Telltale Trunk," CBS, 1973; "Barnaby Jones: Fatal Flight," CBS, 1973; "Owen Marshall, Counselor at Law: A Killer with a Badge," ABC, 1974; "Gunsmoke: The Guns of Cibola Blanca," CBS, 1974; "The Love Boat: Aftermath," ABC, 1979; "Lobo: The Dirtiest Girls in Town," NBC, 1980; "Charlie's Angels: Wakiki Angels," ABC, 1981; "Nero Wolfe: What Happened to April?," NBC, 1981; "Fantasy Island: Wuthering Heights," ABC, 1982; "The Fall Guy: Inside, Outside," ABC, 1983; "Simon & Simon: The List," CBS, 1983; "Simon & Simon: Full Moon Blues," CBS, 1986; "Simon & Simon: Ancient Echoes," CBS, 1987; "Murder, She Wrote: Mirror, Mirror, on the Wall," CBS, 1989.

TV MOVIES AND MINISERIES: "Along Came a Spider," ABC, 1970; "Dead Men Tell No Tales," CBS, 1971; "The Astronaut," NBC, 1972; "The Longest Night," ABC, 1972; "Say Goodbye, Maggie Cole," ABC, 1972; "The Night Strangler," ABC, 1973; "Jarrett," ABC, 1973; "The Immigrants," SYN, 1978; "Pearl," ABC, 1978; "Murder by Natural Causes," CBS, 1979; "Perry Mason Returns," NBC, 1985; "The Return of the Six-Million Dollar Man and the Bionic Woman," NBC, 1987; "Stranger on My Land," ABC, 1988; "Bionic Showdown: The Six Million Dollar Man and the Bionic Woman," NBC, 1989.

ANDERSON, RICHARD DEAN

b. Minneapolis, MN, January 23, 1950. Hunky TV actor who played Dr. Jeff Webber on "General Hospital" and now plays scientist-adventurer Stace MacGyver.

AS A REGULAR: "General Hospital," ABC, 1976-81; "Seven Brides for Seven Brothers," CBS, 1982-83; "Emerald Point NAS," CBS, 1983-84; "MacGyver," ABC, 1985- .

TV MOVIES AND MINISERIES: "Ordinary Heroes," ABC, 1986.

ANDERSON, SAM

Actor who plays Gorpley on "Perfect Strangers."

AS A REGULAR: "Mama Malone," CBS, 1984; "Perfect Strangers," ABC, 1988- .

AND: "WKRP in Cincinnati: The Americanization of Ivan," CBS, 1980; "WKRP in Cincinnati: The Secrets of Dayton Heights," CBS, 1981; "St. Elsewhere: Dog Day Hospital," NBC, 1983; "E/R: All's Well That Ends," CBS, 1984; "Hill Street Blues: Last Chance Salon," NBC, 1984; "Magnum P.I.: Ms. Jones," CBS, 1985; "Simon & Simon: Down-Home Country Blues," CBS, 1985; "Hardcastle and McCormick: McCormick's Bar and Grill," ABC, 1986; "Growing Pains: How the West Was Won," ABC, 1988; "Growing Pains: Homecoming Queen," ABC, 1988; "Growing Pains: Carol's Papers," ABC, 1989; "Growing Pains: Ben and Mike's Excellent Adventure," ABC, 1989; "Alien Nation: The Game," FOX, 1989.

ANDERSON, WARNER

b. Brooklyn, NY, March 10, 1911; d. 1976. Actor who played Det. Lt. Ben Guthrie on "The Lineup," CBS's answer to "Dragnet."

AS A REGULAR: "The Doctor," NBC, 1952-53; "The Lineup," CBS, 1954-60; "Peyton Place," ABC, 1964-65.

AND: "Ford Theatre: Alias Nora Hale," NBC, 1953; "Climax!: Nightmare by Day," CBS, 1956; "Climax!: The Garsten Case," CBS, 1956; "Pursuit: Calculated Risk," CBS, 1958; "Death Valley Days: The Strangers," SYN, 1960; "Play

41

of the Week: Night of the Auk," SYN, 1961; "The Red Skelton Show: The Nine Lives of Freddie," CBS, 1962; "Mannix: A Game of Shadows," CBS, 1972; "The Rockford Files: Charlie Harris at Large," NBC, 1975.
TV MOVIES AND MINISERIES: "Gidget Grows Up," ABC, 1969.

ANDES, KEITH
b. John Charles Andes, Ocean City, NJ, July 12, 1920. Lean actor with an athletic build and rock-hard jaw.
AS A REGULAR: "This Man Dawson," SYN, 1959-60; "Glynis," CBS, 1963; "Paradise Bay," NBC, 1965-66; "Search," NBC, 1973.
AND: "Ford Theatre: Pretend You're You," NBC, 1955; "Ford Theatre: Johnny, Where Are You?," NBC, 1955; "The Great Waltz," NBC, 1955; "The Loretta Young Show: The Challenge," NBC, 1956; "Producers Showcase: Bloomer Girl," NBC, 1956; "Holiday," NBC, 1956; "Conflict: Blind Drop: Warsaw," ABC, 1957; "Playhouse 90: Homeward Borne," CBS, 1957; "The Eve Arden Show: The Budget," CBS, 1957; "The Jane Wyman Show: The Doctor Was a Lady," NBC, 1958; "Goodyear Theatre: The Lady Takes the Stand," NBC, 1958; "Alcoa Theatre: Ten Miles to Doomsday," NBC, 1959; "Bell Telephone Hour: And There Shall Be Music," NBC, 1961; "Have Gun, Will Travel: The Piano," CBS, 1961; "Follow the Sun: Marine of the Month," ABC, 1962; "The Rifleman: The Debit," ABC, 1962; "G.E. True: Firebug," CBS, 1963; "Perry Mason: The Case of the Skeleton's Closet," CBS, 1962; "Vacation Playhouse: Hide and Seek," CBS, 1963; "The Lucy Show: Lucy Goes Duck Hunting," CBS, 1963; "77 Sunset Strip: The Target," ABC, 1964; "Perry Mason: The Case of the Illicit Illusion," CBS, 1964; "The Lucy Show: Lucy and the Winter Sports," CBS, 1964; "The Outer Limits: Expanding Human," ABC, 1964; "Day in Court," ABC, 1964; "Mickey: Norma's Old Flame," ABC, 1964; "The Littlest Hobo: High Society," SYN, 1964; "Death Valley Days: Paid in Full," SYN, 1965; "Day in Court," ABC, 1965; "The Lucy Show: Lucy and the Golden Greek," CBS, 1965; "Run for Your Life: Where Mystery Begins," NBC, 1965; "The Andy Griffith Show: Helen the Authoress," CBS, 1967; "I Spy: A Room with a Rack," NBC, 1967; "I Spy: Laya," NBC, 1967; "Star Trek: The Apple," NBC, 1967; "I Spy: Now You See Her, Now You Don't," NBC, 1967; "Petticoat Junction: No, No, You Can't Take Her Away," CBS, 1970; "The Bold Ones: Killer on the Loose," NBC, 1970; "Dan August: The Manufactured Man," ABC, 1971; "Cannon: A Deadly Quiet Town," CBS, 1972; "Cannon: Moving Targets," CBS, 1973; "Gunsmoke: Matt's Love Story," CBS, 1973; "The Streets of San Francisco: Act of Duty," ABC, 1973; "The Wonderful World of Disney:

Twister, Bull From the Sky," NBC, 1976.
TV MOVIES AND MINISERIES: "The Ultimate Imposter," CBS, 1979; "Blinded by the Light," CBS, 1980.
* Andes' name was changed by producer David Selznick, who had Andes under contract.

ANDRESS, URSULA
b. Switzerland, March 19, 1938. Statusque actress whose big break came in the 1962 James Bond film "Dr. No."
AS A GUEST: "Thriller: La Strega," NBC, 1962; "The Steve Lawrence Show," CBS, 1965; "The Love Boat: China Cruise," ABC, 1983.
TV MOVIES AND MINISERIES: "Peter the Great," NBC, 1986; "Man Against the Mob: The Chinatown Murders," NBC, 1989.

ANDREWS SISTERS
b. Minneapolis, MN. La Verne, b. July 6, 1915; d. 1967. Maxene, b. January 3, 1918. Patricia, b. February 16, 1920. Popular vocal trio of the forties.
AS GUESTS: "The Perry Como Show," NBC, 1957; "The Steve Allen Show," NBC, 1957; "Washington Square," NBC, 1957; "The Julius LaRosa Show," NBC, 1957; "The Jimmy Dean Show," CBS, 1957; "The Ed Sullivan Show," CBS, 1957; "The Bob Crosby Show," NBC, 1958; "The Jimmie Rodgers Show," NBC, 1959; "The Golden Circle," ABC, 1959; "The Joey Bishop Show: Joey and the Andrews Sisters," NBC, 1963; "The Dean Martin Show," NBC, 1965; "The Jimmy Dean Show," ABC, 1966; "Here's Lucy: Lucy and the Andrews Sisters," CBS, 1969.

ANDREWS, ANTHONY
Blond actor usually in debonair roles; he first attracted attention as the doomed Sebastian in "Brideshead Revisited."
AS A REGULAR: "Columbo: Columbo Goes to the Guillotine," ABC, 1989; "Nightmare Classics: The Strange Case of Dr. Jekyll and Mr. Hyde," SHO, 1989.
TV MOVIES AND MINISERIES: "A War of Children," CBS, 1972; "QB VII," ABC, 1974; "Mistress of Paradise," ABC, 1981; "Ivanhoe," CBS, 1982; "Agatha Christie's Sparkling Cyanide," CBS, 1983; "Great Performances: Brideshead Revisited," PBS, 1984; "A.D.," NBC, 1985; "Bluegrass," CBS, 1988; "The Woman He Loved," CBS, 1988.

ANDREWS, DANA
b. Carver Dana Andrews, Collins, MS, January 1, 1909. Hollywood veteran who turned to TV as his film career faded; he played Tom Boswell on the soap "Bright Promise."
AS A REGULAR: "Bright Promise," NBC, 1969-72.

AND: "The Perry Como Show," NBC, 1957; "Playhouse 90: The Right Hand Man," CBS, 1958; "What's My Line?," CBS, 1958; "What's My Line?," CBS, 1960; "Playhouse 90: Alas, Babylon," CBS, 1960; "Person to Person," CBS, 1960; "G.E. Theatre: The Playoff," CBS, 1960; "Bob Hope Buick Show," NBC, 1961; "Here's Hollywood," NBC, 1961; "The Barbara Stanwyck Show: Yanqui Go Home," NBC, 1961; "Checkmate: Trial by Midnight," CBS, 1962; "The du Pont Show: Emergency Ward," NBC, 1962; "The du Pont Show: Mutiny," NBC, 1962; "The Dick Powell Show: Crazy Sunday," NBC, 1962; "The Twilight Zone: No Time Like the Past," CBS, 1963; "The Dick Powell Show: Last of the Big Spenders," NBC, 1963; "Alcoa Premiere: The Town that Died," ABC, 1963; "To Tell the Truth," CBS, 1963; "Ben Casey: The Light That Loses, the Light That Wins," ABC, 1964; "Exploring," NBC, 1964; "Bob Hope Chrysler Theatre: A Wind of Hurricane Force," NBC, 1964; "The Presidency: A Splendid Misery," CBS, 1964; "Family Affair: The Wings of an Angel," CBS, 1969; "The Name of the Game: The Time Is Now," NBC, 1970; "Night Gallery: The Different Ones," NBC, 1971; "Ironside: The Last Cotillion," NBC, 1974; "The American Girls: Pilot," CBS, 1978.

TV MOVIES AND MINISERIES: "The Failing of Raymond," ABC, 1971; "Shadow in the Street," NBC, 1975; "The First 36 Hours of Dr. Durant," ABC, 1975; "The Last Hurrah," NBC, 1977; "Ike," ABC, 1979.

ANDREWS, EDWARD

b. Edward Bryan Andrews Jr., Griffin, GA, October 9, 1914; d. 1985. Roly-poly actor who excelled as blustery, officious types or as the small-town hypocrite.

AS A REGULAR: "Broadside," ABC, 1964-65; "The Doris Day Show," CBS, 1970-72; "Supertrain," NBC, 1979.

AND: "Studio One: Miss Turner's Decision," CBS, 1955; "Kaiser Aluminum Hour: The Army Game," NBC, 1956; "Climax!: Night of the Heat Wave," CBS, 1956; "Alcoa Hour: Ride the Wild Mare," NBC, 1957; "Omnibus: The Trial of Captain Kidd," ABC, 1957; "Goodyear TV Playhouse: The Gene Austin Story," NBC, 1957; "Robert Montgomery Presents: The Weather Lover," NBC, 1957; "Suspicion: Someone Is After Me," NBC, 1958; "Playhouse 90: Point of No Return," CBS, 1958; "Adventures in Paradise: The Raft," ABC, 1959; "The Twilight Zone: Third From the Sun," CBS, 1960; "The Untouchables: Portrait of a Thief," ABC, 1960; "Hong Kong: Catch a Star," ABC, 1960; "O'Conner's Ocean," NBC, 1960; "The Outlaws: The Waiting Game," NBC, 1961; "Robert Herridge Theatre: The Lottery," SYN, 1961; "Route 66: Eleven, the Hard Way," CBS, 1961; "Thriller: A Good Imagination," NBC, 1961; "Rawhide: Incident in Rio Salado," CBS, 1961; "Dr. Kildare: Shining Image," NBC, 1961; "Thriller: A Third for Pinochle," ABC, 1961; "The Dick Powell Show: The Court-Martial of Captain Wycliff," NBC, 1962; "Ben Casey: Pack Up All My Care and Woe," ABC, 1962; "Bonanza: Song in the Dark," NBC, 1963; "The Twilight Zone: You Drive," CBS, 1964; "Mr. Novak: The Song of Songs," NBC, 1964; "The FBI: Courage of a Conviction," ABC, 1965; "The Beverly Hillbillies: Foggy Mountain Soap," CBS, 1966; "Hey, Landlord!: Roommate, Stay Away From My Door," NBC, 1967; "The Wild Wild West: The Night of the Brain," CBS, 1967; "The Guns of Will Sonnett: What's in a Name?," ABC, 1968; "I Dream of Jeannie: Genie, Genie, Who's Got the Genie?," NBC, 1968; "The FBI: Breakthrough," ABC, 1968; "Insight: Don't Let Me Catch You Praying," SYN, 1968; "Bewitched: The Battle of Burning Oak," ABC, 1969; "Bewitched: Samantha's Pet Warlock," ABC, 1970; "Hawaii Five-O: Time and Memories," CBS, 1970; "The FBI: Three Way Split," ABC, 1971; "Bonanza: Rock-a-Bye Hoss," NBC, 1971; "McMillan and Wife: Till Death Do Us Part," NBC, 1972; "Love, American Style: Love and the Lost Dog," ABC, 1972; "Love, American Style: Love and Formula 26B," ABC, 1972; "The Paul Lynde Show: Pollution Solution," ABC, 1972; "The Bold Ones: Moment of Crisis," NBC, 1972; "Love, American Style: Love and the Memento," ABC, 1973; "McMillan and Wife: Free Fall to Terror," NBC, 1973; "Barbary Coast: Guns for a Queen," ABC, 1975; "Ellery Queen: The Mad Tea Party," NBC, 1975; "Sanford & Son: Committee Man," NBC, 1976; "The McLean Stevenson Show: Grandma's Secret," NBC, 1977; "Chico and the Man: Ed Talks to God," NBC, 1977; "Charlie's Angels: Angels on Ice," ABC, 1977; "One Day at a Time: Ann's Out-of-Town Client," CBS, 1977; "The Bob Newhart Show: Crisis in Education," CBS, 1978; "Three's Company: Doctor in the House," ABC, 1982.

TV MOVIES AND MINISERIES: "The Over-the-Hill Gang," ABC, 1969; "The Intruders," NBC, 1970; "Travis Logan, D.A.," CBS, 1971; "The Streets of San Francisco," ABC, 1972; "How to Break Up a Happy Divorce," NBC, 1976; "Undercover with the KKK," NBC, 1979.

ANDREWS, JULIE

b. Julia Elizabeth Wells, Walton-on-Thames, England, October 1, 1935. Award-winning musical-comedy performer who does television just often enough to remind people how tastefully talented she is.

AS A REGULAR: "The Julie Andrews Hour," ABC, 1972-73.

AND: "Ford Star Jubilee: High Tor," CBS, 1956; "The Ed Sullivan Show," CBS, 1956;

"Cinderella," CBS, 1957; "Dinah Shore Chevy Show," NBC, 1958; "The Big Record," CBS, 1958; "Jack Benny Special," CBS, 1959; "The Fabulous Fifties," CBS, 1960; "Bell Telephone Hour: Portraits in Music," NBC, 1960; "The Ed Sullivan Show," CBS, 1961; "The Garry Moore Show," CBS, 1961; "The Broadway of Lerner and Loewe," NBC, 1962; "Julie and Carol at Carnegie Hall," CBS, 1962; "The David Frost Show," SYN, 1971; "Julie and Carol at Lincoln Center," CBS, 1971; "Julie Andrews on Sesame Street," ABC, 1973; "Julie Andrews: The Sound of Christmas," ABC, 1987; "Great Performances: An Evening with Alan Jay Lerner," PBS, 1989; "AT&T Presents: Julie & Carol: Together Again," ABC, 1989.
* Emmies: 1973.

ANDREWS, STANLEY

b. 1891; d. 1969. Grizzled actor who played the oooooold ranger, longtime host of "Death Valley Days" until he was booted out in favor of Ronald Reagan, who lent more conviction to the Boraxo commercials.

AS A REGULAR: "Death Valley Days," SYN, 1952-65.
AND: "The Abbott and Costello Show: Jail," CBS, 1952; "Circus Boy: Elmer, the Rainmaker," ABC, 1958.

ANDREWS, TIGE

b. Brooklyn, NY, March 19, 1923. Actor usually in tough-guy roles; he played Capt. Adam Greer, who oversaw "The Mod Squad."

AS A REGULAR: "The Detectives Starring Robert Taylor," ABC, 1959-61; "Robert Taylor's Detectives," NBC, 1961-62; "The Mod Squad," ABC, 1968-73.
AND: "Playhouse 90: Seven Against the Wall," CBS, 1958; "Adventures in Paradise: Wild Mangoes," ABC, 1961; "The Dick Powell Show: Somebody's Waiting," NBC, 1961; "Alcoa Premiere: Flashing Spikes," ABC, 1962; "Ensign O'Toole: Operation: Holdout," NBC, 1962; "Sam Benedict: Green Room, Gray Morning," NBC, 1963; "Mr. Novak: A Single Isolated Incident," NBC, 1963; "Twelve O'Clock High: Rx for a Sick Bird," ABC, 1965; "Gomer Pyle, USMC: Cat Overboard," CBS, 1965; "Gomer Pyle, USMC: Gomer Captures a Submarine," CBS, 1965; "Gomer Pyle, USMC: The Grudge Fight," CBS, 1965; "The FBI: Force of Nature," ABC, 1967; "Gunsmoke: The Jackals," CBS, 1968; "Hollywood Squares," NBC, 1970; "Marcus Welby, M.D.: For Services Rendered," ABC, 1973; "Police Story: Countdown," NBC, 1974; "Kojak: The Chinatown Murders," CBS, 1974; "Amy Prentiss: Profile in Evil," NBC, 1975; "Police Story: Face for a Shadow," NBC, 1975; "Kojak: Deadly Innocence," CBS, 1976; "Kojak: Photo Must Credit Joe Paxton," CBS, 1978; "Quincy: Expert in Murder," NBC, 1982.

TV MOVIES AND MINISERIES: "The Return of Mod Squad," ABC, 1979.

ANDREWS, TOD

b. Buffalo, NY, 1920; d. 1972. Beefy actor who played Confederate Major John Singleton Mosby, "The Gray Ghost."

AS A REGULAR: "First Love," NBC, 1954-55; "The Gray Ghost," SYN, 1957-58; "Bright Promise," NBC, 1969-72.
AND: "The Gale Storm Show: The Witch Doctor," CBS, 1956; "Boots and Saddles: Pound of Flesh," SYN, 1957; "The Millionaire: Millionaire Dr. Joseph Frye," CBS, 1959; "Checkmate: The Mask of Vengeance," CBS, 1960; "77 Sunset Strip: The Space Caper," ABC, 1961; "The Ann Sothern Show: The Beginning," CBS, 1961; "The Andy Griffith Show: The Inspector," CBS, 1961; "Gunsmoke: The Love of Money," CBS, 1961; "Frontier Circus: Karina," CBS, 1961; "Grindl: Dial G for Grindl," NBC, 1964; "The Twilight Zone: The Bewitchin' Pool," CBS, 1964; "The FBI: Target of Interest," ABC, 1969.
TV MOVIES AND MINISERIES: "Weekend of Terror," ABC, 1970; "The President's Plane Is Missing," ABC, 1973.

THE ANDY GRIFFITH SHOW
CBS, 1960-68.
How does a sitcom end an eight-season run as the nation's top show? Easy. Just make the humor gentle, the characters true-to-life and offer a rural haven from a fractured America, vintage 1968.

The quality of "The Andy Griffith Show" is as undisputed now as it was virtually unrecognized throughout much of the 1960s, and it was, overall, the doing of one man—Andy Griffith. By the late 1950s Griffith was a hit with his comedy albums and on Broadway, so could pick the best for his television vehicle—producer Sheldon Leonard (working with Danny Thomas) and writers such as Aaron Ruben, Arthur Stander and Bob Ross. Griffith didn't want a show that made fun of country people, and he didn't get one. He wanted a TV equivalent to the gentle radio comedy "Lum and Abner," and that's what he got. Griffith played Andy Taylor, a widower and sheriff of Mayberry, North Carolina; Ronny Howard was son Opie, Francis Bavier Andy's Aunt Bee, and Don Knotts was Andy's faithful deputy, one-bullet (kept in his pocket) Barney Fife. Barney left town, Andy romanced the local schoolteacher (Aneta Corseaut) and after a while we even got to see how Mayberry looked in color. The nation was changing, as well, but Mayberry remained an island of sanity and decency. And it still is.

ANGEL, HEATHER

b. February 9, 1909; d. 1986. British actress who played Miss Faversham on "Family Affair."
AS A REGULAR: "Peyton Place," ABC, 1965-66; "Family Affair," CBS, 1966-71.
AND: "Disneyland: Alice in Wonderland," ABC, 1954; "Studio 57: Stopover in Bombay," SYN, 1958; "Suspicion: The Woman Turned to Salt," NBC, 1958; "Perry Mason: The Case of the Lucky Loser," CBS, 1958; "Lawman: The Grubstake," ABC, 1961; "Here's Hollywood," NBC, 1962; "Mr. Novak: The Tower," NBC, 1964; "The Guns of Will Sonnett: A Fool and His Money," ABC, 1968.
TV MOVIES AND MINISERIES: "Backstairs at the White House," NBC, 1979.

ANGELI, PIER

b. Anna Maria Pierangeli, Italy, June 19, 1932; d. 1971. Leading lady of the fifties, in the fragile Audrey Hepburn mold; she died of a barbituate overdose.
AS A GUEST: "Westinghouse Desilu Playhouse: Bernadette," CBS, 1958; "The Perry Como Show," NBC, 1958; "Pat Boone Chevy Showroom," ABC, 1960.

ANGLIM, PHILIP

b. San Francisco, CA, February 11, 1953. Actor who played "The Elephant Man" on stage and TV.
TV MOVIES AND MINISERIES: "ABC Theatre of the Month: The Elephant Man," ABC, 1982; "The Thorn Birds," ABC, 1983.

ANGUSTAIN, IRA

Actor who played Ricky Gomez on "The White Shadow" and doomed comic Freddie Prinze in a TV movie.
AS A REGULAR: "The White Shadow," CBS, 1978-80.
TV MOVIES AND MINISERIES: "Can You Hear the Laughter? The Story of Freddie Prinze," CBS, 1979.

ANKA, PAUL

b. Ottawa, Canada, July 30, 1941. Pop singer-songwriter whose most famous work might well be the theme from "The Tonight Show"—or maybe "Havin' My Baby."
AS A GUEST: "The Ed Sullivan Show," CBS, 1957; "The Big Record," CBS, 1957; "The Dick Clark Saturday Night Beechnut Show," ABC, 1958; "The Perry Como Show," NBC, 1958; "The Perry Como Show," NBC, 1959; "The Dick Clark Saturday Night Beechnut Show," ABC, 1959; "The Ed Sullivan Show," CBS, 1959; "Arthur Murray Party," NBC, 1959; "Perry Como's Kraft Music Hall," NBC, 1960; "The Dick Clark Saturday Night Beechnut Show," ABC, 1960; "Coke Time," ABC, 1960; "Dan Raven: L.A. 46," NBC, 1960; "American Bandstand," ABC, 1960; "Dan Raven: The Satchel Man," NBC, 1960; "Perry Como's Kraft Music Hall," NBC, 1961; "The Ed Sullivan Show," CBS, 1961; "The Dinah Shore Chevy Show," NBC, 1961; "American Bandstand," ABC, 1961; "The Danny Thomas Show: Old Man Danny," CBS, 1961; "Seasons of Youth," ABC, 1961; "We, the People - 1961," NBC, 1961; "The Ed Sullivan Show," CBS, 1962; "American Bandstand," ABC, 1962; "I've Got a Secret," CBS, 1962; "Jackie Gleason and His American Scene Magazine," CBS, 1962; "Password," CBS, 1964; "Hullabaloo," NBC, 1965; "On Broadway Tonight," CBS, 1965; "The Young Set," ABC, 1965; "Hullabaloo," NBC, 1965; "Hollywood Palace," ABC, 1966; "The Merv Griffin Show," SYN, 1968; "The Tonight Show Starring Johnny Carson," NBC, 1969; "The David Frost Show," SYN, 1971; "Hollywood Squares," NBC, 1974; "Kojak: The Betrayal," CBS, 1974; "Donny and Marie," ABC, 1977; "Sha Na Na," SYN, 1981; "The Fall Guy: Dirty Laundry," ABC, 1983.

ANNA-LISA

b. Ana-Lisa Ruud, Oslo, Norway, 1934. Fifties starlet.
AS A REGULAR: "Black Saddle," NBC, 1959-60.
AND: "Sugarfoot: Mail Order Bride," ABC, 1958; "Lux Playhouse: Small Wonder," CBS, 1958; "Maverick: The Judas Mask," ABC, 1958; "Cheyenne: Brand of Courage," ABC, 1958;

"Secret Agent 7: Prussian Jewel Case," SYN, 1959; "77 Sunset Strip: Spark of Freedom," ABC, 1960; "The Millionaire: Millionaire Mark Fleming," CBS, 1960; "Day in Court," ABC, 1960; "Gunsmoke: The Blacksmith," CBS, 1960; "Laramie: .45 Calibre," NBC, 1960; "The Islanders: Our Girl in Saigon," ABC, 1960; "SurfSide 6: The International Net," ABC, 1960; "Bonanza: The Savage," NBC, 1960; "Assignment: Underwater: The Disappearance," SYN, 1961; "G.E. True: Code Name: Christopher," CBS, 1962; "Voyage to the Bottom of the Sea: Village of Guilt," ABC, 1964; "The Man From UNCLE: The Candidate's Wife Affair," NBC, 1966.

ANNIS, FRANCESCA

b. *London, England, 1944.* Actress who played Lillie Langtry on "Masterpiece Theatre."

AS A GUEST: "Magnum P.I.: Mad Dogs & Englishmen," CBS, 1985.

TV MOVIES AND MINISERIES: "Masterpiece Theatre: Lillie," PBS, 1981; "I'll Take Manhattan," CBS, 1987; "Onassis: The Richest Man in the World," ABC, 1988.

ANN-MARGRET

b. *Ann-Margret Olsson, Valsjobyn, Sweden, April 28, 1941.* Sixties sex symbol who has matured into an actress of power and style.

AS A GUEST: "Ted Mack Amateur Hour," CBS, 1957; "The Jack Benny Program: Variety Show," CBS, 1961; "The Flintstones: Ann-Margrock Presents," ABC, 1963; "The Tonight Show Starring Johnny Carson," NBC, 1968; "The Joey Bishop Show," ABC, 1968; "Bob Hope Christmas Special," NBC, 1969; "Ann-Margret Special," NBC, 1969; "The Dean Martin Show," NBC, 1970; "Here's Lucy: Lucy and Ann-Margret," CBS, 1970; "This Is Your Life," SYN, 1971; "Bell System Family Theatre: Dames at Sea," NBC, 1971; "Ann-Margret Special," NBC, 1973; "The Mike Douglas Show," SYN, 1975; "Bob Hope Special," NBC, 1977; "Ann-Margret Special," NBC, 1977; "The Merv Griffin Show," SYN, 1980; "America's Tribute to Bob Hope," NBC, 1988.

TV MOVIES AND MINISERIES: "Who Will Love My Children?," ABC, 1983; "A Streetcar Named Desire," ABC, 1984; "The Two Mrs. Grenvilles," NBC, 1987.

* On the 1962 Oscar telecast, Ann-Margret sang and danced to one of the nominated songs, "Bachelor in Paradise." Almost immediately, she was offered a role in the movie version of "Bye Bye Birdie."

* On September 10, 1972, just before she made her entrance at a Lake Tahoe club, Ann-Margret fell head first from a 22-foot platform, crushing the left side of her face and driving pieces of her shattered cheekbone into her sinuses. Eleven weeks later she was performing again.

* Ann-Margret deserved an Emmy for her role as a dying mother in "Who Will Love My Children?," and the actress who won the Emmy in that category—Barbara Stanwyck for "The Thorn Birds"—admitted as much when she accepted the award.

ANSARA, MICHAEL

b. *Lowell, MA, April 15, 1922.* Actor of Lebanese ancestry who played Cochise on "Broken Arrow."

AS A REGULAR: "Broken Arrow," ABC, 1956-58; "Law of the Plainsman," NBC, 1959-60; "Buck Rogers in the 25th Century," NBC, 1979-80.

AND: "Medic: The Laughter and the Weeping," NBC, 1956; "Alfred Hitchcock Presents: Shopping for Death," CBS, 1956; "Alfred Hitchcock Presents: The Orderly World of Mr. Appleby," CBS, 1956; "Alfred Hitchcock Presents: The Baby Sitter," CBS, 1956; "The Adventures of Rin Tin Tin: Yo-o Rinty!," ABC, 1956; "Playhouse 90: The Killers of Mussolini," CBS, 1959; "The Rebel: The Champ," ABC, 1960; "The Untouchables: Nicky," ABC, 1960; "The Barbara Stanwyck Show: Night Visitors," NBC, 1961; "The Wide Country: Devil in the Chute," NBC, 1962; "Wagon Train: The Adam MacKenzie Story," ABC, 1963; "Rawhide: Incident at Rio Doloroso," CBS, 1963; "Rawhide: Incident of Iron Bull," CBS, 1963; "The Farmer's Daughter: Comes the Revolution," ABC, 1963; "Kraft Suspense Theatre: A Truce to Terror," NBC, 1964; "Burke's Law: Who Killed Carrie Cornell?," ABC, 1964; "Perry Mason: The Case of the Antic Angel," CBS, 1964; "The Outer Limits: Soldier," ABC, 1964; "Rawhide: Canliss," CBS, 1964; "I Dream of Jeannie: Happy Anniversary," NBC, 1966; "The Girl From UNCLE: The Prisoner of Zalamar Affair," NBC, 1966; "Bewitched: A Most Unusual Wood Nymph," ABC, 1966; "Star Trek: Day of the Dove," NBC, 1968; "It Takes a Thief: Guess Who's Coming to Rio?," ABC, 1969; "The High Chapparal: For the Love of Carlos," NBC, 1969; "I Dream of Jeannie: My Sister, the Homemaker," NBC, 1969; "The Name of the Game: The Takeover," NBC, 1970; "The Bill Cosby Show: The Artist," NBC, 1970; "The Name of the Game: The Garden," NBC, 1970; "Mission: Impossible: The Western," CBS, 1973; "Shaft: The Killing," CBS, 1973; "Police Story: Requiem for an Informer," NBC, 1973; "Police Story: Chief," NBC, 1974; "McMillan and Wife: Reunion in Terror," NBC, 1974; "The Rockford Files: Joey Blue Eyes," NBC, 1976; "Kojak: Justice Deferred," CBS, 1976; "Gavilan: Designated Hero," NBC, 1982; "Hardcastle and McCormick: Mirage a Trois," ABC, 1985; "Hunter: Rape and

Revenge," NBC, 1985; "The New Mike Hammer: A Blinding Fear," CBS, 1987; "Murder, She Wrote: The Last Flight of the Dizzy Damsel," CBS, 1988.

TV MOVIES AND MINISERIES: "How I Spent My Summer Vacation," NBC, 1967; "Powderkeg," CBS, 1971; "Call to Danger," CBS, 1973; "Ordeal," ABC, 1973; "Shootout in a One-Dog Town," ABC, 1974; "The Barbary Coast," ABC, 1975; "Centennial," NBC, 1978-79.

* Ansara, a hairy fellow, had to shave his chest while filming "Broken Arrow" episodes.

ANSPACH, SUSAN
b. *New York City, NY, 1939.* Blonde actress of sixties and seventies films ("Five Easy Pieces," "Blume in Love"); she played Jenny, ex-wife of sportswriter Slap Maxwell (Dabney Coleman).

AS A REGULAR: "The Yellow Rose," NBC, 1983; "The Slap Maxwell Story," ABC, 1987-88.

AND: "The Patty Duke Show: Cathy the Rebel," ABC, 1965; "Love Story: All My Tomorrows," NBC, 1973; "McMillan and Wife: Point for Law," NBC, 1976; "Empty Nest: Here's a Howdy-Do," NBC, 1989.

TV MOVIES AND MINISERIES: "I Want to Keep My Baby," CBS, 1976; "Portrait of an Escort," CBS, 1980; "Deadly Encounter," CBS, 1982; "Space," CBS, 1985.

ANTHONY, RAY
b. *January 20, 1922.* Bandleader.

AS A REGULAR: "TV's Top Tunes," CBS, 1953-54; "The Ray Anthony Show," ABC, 1956-57.

AND: "The Spike Jones Show," CBS, 1957; "The Vic Damone Show," CBS, 1957; "The Big Record," CBS, 1958; "The Steve Allen Show," NBC, 1958; "Studio 57: Take Five," SYN, 1958; "The Steve Allen Show," NBC, 1958; "The Music Shop," NBC, 1959; "Five Fingers: Operation Ramrod," NBC, 1959; "Here's Hollywood," NBC, 1961; "The Chevy Show," NBC, 1961.

ANTON, SUSAN
b. *Oak Glen, CA, October 12, 1950.* Tall, attractive singer-actress who was given the star treatment by NBC in the late seventies; virtually nothing came of it, except maybe a few dates with Dudley Moore.

AS A REGULAR: "Stop Susan Williams," NBC, 1979; "Presenting Susan Anton," NBC, 1979.

AND: "The Merv Griffin Show," SYN, 1977; "Switch: Go for Broke," CBS, 1977; "The Merv Griffin Show," SYN, 1978; "Midnight Special," NBC, 1980; "The Love Boat: China Cruise," ABC, 1983; "Murder, She Wrote: Corned Beef and Carnage," CBS, 1986; "It's Garry Shandling's Show: No Baby, No Show," FOX, 1988.

ANTONIO, LOU
b. *Oklahoma City, OK, January 23, 1934.* Actor-director who played Barney, chauffeur and guardian to "The Snoop Sisters" (Helen Hayes and Mildred Natwick).

AS A REGULAR: "The Snoop Sisters," NBC, 1973-74; "Dog and Cat," ABC, 1977; "Makin' It," ABC, 1979.

AND: "True Story: The Runaway," NBC, 1959; "Have Gun, Will Travel: The Calf," CBS, 1960; "Naked City: A Hole in the City," ABC, 1961; "The Defenders: The Riot," CBS, 1961; "The Power and the Glory," CBS, 1961; "Naked City: Portrait of a Painter," ABC, 1962; "The Defenders: Death Takes the Stand," CBS, 1962; "Route 66: And Make Thunder His Tribute," CBS, 1963; "Twelve O'Clock High: The Men and the Boys," ABC, 1964; "The Virginian: The Inchworm's Got No Wings at All," NBC, 1966; "Gunsmoke: Prairie Wolfer," CBS, 1967; "The Monkees: Hillbilly Honeymoon," NBC, 1967; "Gunsmoke: O'Quillian," CBS, 1968; "I Dream of Jeannie: Genie, Genie, Who's Got the Genie?," NBC, 1968; "Bewitched: Going Ape," ABC, 1969; "Gunsmoke: Goldtown," CBS, 1969; "Gunsmoke: The Long Night," CBS, 1969; "Mission: Impossible: The Hostage," CBS, 1971; "The FBI: Superstition Rock," ABC, 1971; "The FBI: Fool's Gold," ABC, 1973; "The Rookies: Tarnished Idol," ABC, 1973.

TV MOVIES AND MINISERIES: "Sole Survivor," CBS, 1970; "Partners in Crime," NBC, 1973; "Where the Ladies Go," ABC, 1980.

AS DIRECTOR: "The Outside Woman," CBS, 1989.

APPLEGATE, CHRISTINA
b. *Hollywood, CA, November 25, 1972.* Blonde actress who plays Kelly Bundy on "Married with Children."

AS A REGULAR: "Charles in Charge," CBS, 1983; "Heart of the City," ABC, 1986-87; "Married with Children," FOX, 1987- .

AND: "Father Murphy: A Horse From Heaven," NBC, 1982; "Amazing Stories: Welcome to My Nightmare," NBC, 1986; "Family Ties: Band on the Run," NBC, 1987; "21 Jump Street: I'm Okay, You Need Work," FOX, 1988; "The Pat Sajak Show," CBS, 1989.

TV MOVIES AND MINISERIES: "Dance 'Til Dawn," NBC, 1988.

* Applegate made her TV debut at the age of three months, in the arms of mother, actress Nancy Priddy, on a segment of "Days of Our Lives."

APPLEGATE, EDDIE
b. *Edward Robert Applegate, Wyncote, PA, 1935.* Clean-cut actor who played Richard, gawky teenage boyfriend of Patty Lane on "The Patty Duke Show," even though he was pushing thirty at the time.

AS A REGULAR: "The Patty Duke Show," ABC, 1963-66; "Nancy," NBC, 1970-71.
AND: "Mr. Novak: My Name Is Not Legion," NBC, 1963; "Daktari: Adam and Jenny," CBS, 1968.

APPLEGATE, FRED

Pudgy actor who played TV director J.J. Wall on "Newhart."
AS A REGULAR: "Newhart," CBS, 1985-87; "9 to 5," SYN, 1987-88; "FM," NBC, 1989, 1990.
AND: "Hooperman: Who Do You Truss?," ABC, 1988; "Anything But Love: This Is Not a Date," ABC, 1989.

APREA, JOHN

Actor usually in Italian or Hispanic roles; he played Sheriff Jack North on "Falcon Crest" and Manny Vasquez on "Knots Landing."
AS A REGULAR: "The Montefuscos," NBC, 1975; "Matt Houston," ABC, 1982-83; "Falcon Crest," CBS, 1987; "Knots Landing," CBS, 1988; "Full House," ABC, 1988- .
AND: "Mannix: Murder Revisited," CBS, 1970; "The FBI: Night of the Long Knives," ABC, 1973; "The Rookies: Shadow of a Man," ABC, 1975; "The Powers of Matthew Star: Accused," NBC, 1982; "The A-Team: There Goes the Neighborhood," NBC, 1985; "Private Eye: Blue Movies," NBC, 1987.
TV MOVIES AND MINISERIES: "Crazy Times," ABC, 1981; "Getting Physical," CBS, 1984; "Blood Vows: The Story of a Mafia Wife," NBC, 1987.

ARBUS, ALLAN

b. *New York City, NY, February 15, 1918.*
Slight, curly-haired character actor best known as visiting shrink Dr. Sidney Freedman on "M*A*S*H."
AS A REGULAR: "Working Stiffs," CBS, 1979; "The Gangster Chronicles," NBC, 1981; "The Four Seasons," CBS, 1984.
AND: "M*A*S*H: Radar's Report," CBS, 1973; "M*A*S*H: Deal Me Out," CBS, 1973; "The Odd Couple: Cleanliness Is Next to Impossible," ABC, 1974; "The Odd Couple: The Hollywood Story," ABC, 1974; "M*A*S*H: O.R.," CBS, 1974; "M*A*S*H: Quo Vadis, Captain Chandler?," CBS, 1975; "M*A*S*H: Dear Sigmund," CBS, 1976; "M*A*S*H: Hawk's Nightmare," CBS, 1976; "M*A*S*H: War Of Nerves," CBS, 1977; "M*A*S*H: The Billfold Syndrome," CBS, 1978; "Taxi: One-Punch Banta," ABC, 1978; "The Rockford Files: Black Mirror," ABC, 1978; "M*A*S*H: Good-bye, Cruel World," CBS, 1980; "M*A*S*H: Bless You, Hawkeye," CBS, 1981; "M*A*S*H: Pressure Points," CBS, 1982; "M*A*S*H: Good-bye, Farewell and Amen," CBS, 1983; "Cagney &

Lacey: Violation," CBS, 1985; "L.A. Law: I'm in the Nude for Love," NBC, 1989; "Matlock: The Star," NBC, 1989; "Chicken Soup: Operation Jackie," ABC, 1989.
TV MOVIES AND MINISERIES: "Scream, Pretty Peggy," ABC, 1973; "The Law," NBC, 1974; "Stalk the Wild Child," NBC, 1976; "The Preppie Murder," ABC, 1989; "When He's Not a Stranger," CBS, 1989.

ARCHER, ANNE

b. *Los Angeles, CA, August 25, 1947.*
Attractive actress of films ("Fatal Attraction," "The Narrow Margin") and some TV; daughter of Marjorie Lord and John Archer.
AS A REGULAR: "Bob & Carol & Ted & Alice," ABC, 1973; "The Family Tree," NBC, 1983; "Falcon Crest," CBS, 1985.
AND: "The FBI: Downfall," ABC, 1971; "Ironside: Murder Impromptu," NBC, 1971; "The Mod Squad: Color of Laughter, Color of Tears," ABC, 1971; "Alias Smith and Jones: Shootout at Diablo Station," ABC, 1972; "Love, American Style: Love and the Fountain of Youth," ABC, 1972; "Mannix: A Problem of Innocence," CBS, 1973; "Harry O: Guardian at the Gates," ABC, 1974; "Switch: The Old Diamond Game," CBS, 1975; "Petrocelli: Shadow of Fear," NBC, 1975; "Switch: The Cold War Con," CBS, 1975; "Little House on the Prairie: Doctor's Lady," NBC, 1975; "Harry O: The Mysterious Case of Lester and Dr. Fong," ABC, 1976; "Switch: Big Deal in Paradise," CBS, 1976.
TV MOVIES AND MINISERIES: "The Blue Knight," CBS, 1973; "The Mark of Zorro," ABC, 1974; "The Log of the Black Pearl," NBC, 1975; "A Matter of Wife and Death," NBC, 1975; "The Dark Side of Innocence," NBC, 1976; "Best Sellers: Seventh Avenue," NBC, 1977; "The Pirate," CBS, 1978; "The Sky's No Limit," CBS, 1984; "A Different Affair," CBS, 1987.

ARCHER, BEVERLY

b. *Oak Park, IL, July 19, 1948.* Lanky comedienne, usually as sharp-but-gawky types; best known as Iola on "Mama's Family."
AS A REGULAR: "The Nancy Walker Show," ABC, 1976; "We've Got Each Other," CBS, 1977-78; "Spencer," NBC, 1984-85; "Mama's Family," SYN, 1986-89; "Major Dad," CBS, 1990- .
AND: "My Sister Sam: Camp Burn-Out," CBS, 1987; "ALF: Someone to Watch Over Me," NBC, 1988; "ALF: Breaking Up Is Hard to Do," NBC, 1988.

ARCHER, JOHN

b. *Ralph Bowman, Osceola, NB, May 8, 1915.*
Actor who's also the father of Anne Archer.
AS A GUEST: "The Loretta Young Show: The Case of Mrs. Bannister," NBC, 1955; "Science Fiction

Theatre: 100 Years Long," SYN, 1955; "The Bob Cummings Show: Bob Goes to the Moon," NBC, 1958; "The Californians: J. Jimmerson Jones, Inc.," NBC, 1958; "Laramie: The Run to Tumavaca," NBC, 1959; "The Man and the Challenge: Killer River," NBC, 1960; "Colt .45: Phantom Trail," ABC, 1960; "The Twilight Zone: Will the Real Martian Please Stand Up," CBS, 1961; "Lassie: Timmy vs. Martians," CBS, 1961; "Perry Mason: The Case of the Sardonic Sergeant," CBS, 1961; "87th Precinct: Killer's Payoff," NBC, 1961; "77 Sunset Strip: The Cold Cash Caper," ABC, 1961; "Hawaiian Eye: Big Fever," ABC, 1962; "Bonanza: The Jackknife," NBC, 1962; "Hawaiian Eye: Boar Hunt," ABC, 1963; "Hazel: Hazel Scores a Touchdown," NBC, 1963; "Hazel: The Reluctant Witness," NBC, 1964; "McHale's Navy: Fuji's Big Romance," ABC, 1964; "Perry Mason: The Case of the Candy Queen," CBS, 1965; "The Virginian: Beloved Outlaw," NBC, 1966; "Batman: A Riddle a Day Keeps the Riddler Away/When the Rat's Away, the Mice Will Play," ABC, 1966; "The Virginian: The Girl on the Glass Mountain," NBC, 1966; "Batman: Ice Spy/The Duo Defy," ABC, 1967; "Mannix: The Solid Gold Web," CBS, 1969; "Columbo: Requiem for a Falling Star," NBC, 1973.

ARCHERD, ARMY
Show-biz columnist who usually plays himself on TV.
AS A REGULAR: "The Movie Game," SYN, 1969-72.
AND: "77 Sunset Strip: Six Superior Skirts," ABC, 1959; "Batman: The Minstrel's Shakedown/Barbecued Batman," ABC, 1966; "That Girl: Opening Night," ABC, 1970; "Columbo: Forgotten Lady," NBC, 1975; "James at 15: Fast and Loose," NBC, 1977.
TV MOVIES AND MINISERIES: "More Than Friends," ABC, 1978.

ARDEN, EVE
b. Eunice Queedens, Mill Valley, CA, April 30, 1912; d. 1990. Actress at her best in wisecracking roles, which she played as schoolteacher Connie Brooks "Our Miss Brooks" and as one of "The Mothers-in-Law."
AS A REGULAR: "Our Miss Brooks," CBS, 1952-56; "The Eve Arden Show," CBS, 1957-58; "The Mothers-in-Law," NBC, 1967-69; "Falcon Crest," CBS, 1987.
AND: "Starlight Theatre: Julie," CBS, 1951; "I Love Lucy: L.A. at Last!," CBS, 1955; "Dinah Shore Chevy Show," NBC, 1958; "The Perry Como Show," NBC, 1958; "Dinah Shore Chevy Show," NBC, 1959; "Perry Como's Kraft Music Hall," NBC, 1959; "The Red Skelton Show: Appleby's Bird Woman," CBS, 1959; "The George Gobel Show," CBS, 1959; "Startime: Meet

Cyd Charisse," NBC, 1959; "The Ford Show," NBC, 1960; "Checkmate: Death by Design," CBS, 1961; "The Red Skelton Show," CBS, 1961; "Here's Hollywood," NBC, 1961; "My Three Sons: Steve Meets Marissa," ABC, 1962; "The Red Skelton Hour," CBS, 1963; "Careful, It's My Art," NBC, 1963; "Vacation Playhouse: He's All Yours," CBS, 1964; "The Red Skelton Hour," CBS, 1965; "Laredo: Which Way Did They Go?," NBC, 1965; "You Don't Say," NBC, 1966; "Bewitched: And Then There Were Three," ABC, 1966; "Run for Your Life: Who's Watching the Fleshpot?," NBC, 1966; "The Man From UNCLE: The Minus X Affair," NBC, 1966; "Personality," NBC, 1968; "What's It All About, World?," ABC, 1969; "Love, American Style: Love and the New Roommate," ABC, 1971; "The Movie Game," SYN, 1971; "Love, American Style: Love and the Contact Lens," ABC, 1971; "The Girl with Something Extra: The Greening of Aunt Fran," NBC, 1974; "ABC Afternoon Playbreak: Mother of the Bride," ABC, 1974; "Harry and Maggie," CBS, 1975; "Ellery Queen: Miss Aggie's Farewell Performance," NBC, 1975; "Maude: Maude's Aunt," CBS, 1977; "Alice: Alice in TV Land," CBS, 1979; "The Love Boat: Kin Folk," ABC, 1979; "B.J. and the Bear: The Girls of Hollywood High," NBC, 1980; "Amazing Stories: Secret Cinema," NBC, 1986.
TV MOVIES AND MINISERIES: "In Name Only," ABC, 1969; "A Very Missing Person," NBC, 1972; "All My Darling Daughters," ABC, 1972; "A Guide for the Married Woman," ABC, 1978.
* Emmies: 1954.

ARGENZIANO, CARMEN
Heavyset actor who plays softies and tough types.
AS A REGULAR: "Booker," FOX, 1989-90.
AND: "Mannix: Murder Revisited," CBS, 1970; "The FBI: Night of the Long Knives," ABC, 1973; "Columbo: Identity Crisis," NBC, 1975; "The Rockford Files: A Different Drummer," ABC, 1978; "Lou Grant: Mob," CBS, 1978; "Lou Grant: Charlatan," CBS, 1979; "Lou Grant: Friends," CBS, 1981; "The Powers of Matthew Star: Accused," NBC, 1982; "T.J. Hooker: Vengeance Is Mine," ABC, 1983; "The A-Team: In Plane Sight," NBC, 1984; "Cheers: Sam Turns the Other Cheek," NBC, 1984; "Hill Street Blues: Last Chance Salon," NBC, 1984; "Hunter: A Child Is Born," NBC, 1988; "L.A. Law: Chariots of Meyer," NBC, 1988.
TV MOVIES AND MINISERIES: "Waco & Rhinehart," ABC; 1987; "Liberace," ABC, 1988; "Police Story: The Watch Commander," ABC, 1988.

ARKIN, ADAM
b. Brooklyn, NY, August 19, 1956. Son of Alan. Actor usually in likable roles; he played the

49

neurotic Jim Eisenberg, husband of Lindley Gardner (Jayne Atkinson) on "A Year in the Life."

AS A REGULAR: "Busting Loose," CBS, 1977; "Teachers Only," NBC, 1982; "Tough Cookies," CBS, 1986; "Harry," ABC, 1987; "A Year in the Life," NBC, 1987-88.

AND: "Happy Days: Fonzie Joins the Band," ABC, 1975; "Harry O: Portrait of a Murder," ABC, 1975; "Barney Miller: Hotel," ABC, 1975; "Hawaii Five-O: A Touch of Guilt," CBS, 1975; "The Love Boat: Heads or Tails," ABC, 1979; "St. Elsewhere: Newheart," NBC, 1983; "St. Elsewhere: Fathers and Sons," NBC, 1985; "The Twilight Zone: A Matter of Minutes," CBS, 1986; "All Is Forgiven: Past Perfect," NBC, 1986; "MacGyver: The Invisible Killer," ABC, 1989.

TV MOVIES AND MINISERIES: "It Couldn't Happen to a Nicer Guy," ABC, 1974; "All Together Now," ABC, 1975; "Pearl," ABC, 1978; "A Year in the Life," NBC, 1986.

ARKIN, ALAN

b. New York City, NY, March 26, 1934. Former folksinger and member of the Second City comedy troupe; his movie performances ("The In-Laws") sparkle with offbeat humor, but his television work has been on the dramatic side—including "Harry," a misbegotten sitcom.

AS A REGULAR: "Harry," ABC, 1987.

AND: "Camera Three," CBS, 1959; "The Eternal Light: How They Knocked the Devil Out of Ezra," NBC, 1963; "East Side/West Side: The Beatnik and the Politician," CBS, 1964; "ABC Nightlife," ABC, 1964; "ABC Stage '67: The Love Song of Barney Kempinski," ABC, 1966; "The Trouble with People," NBC, 1972; "Captain Kangaroo," CBS, 1975; "Love, Life, Liberty and Lunch," ABC, 1976; "To America," CBS, 1976; "St. Elsewhere: Ties That Bind," NBC, 1983; "St. Elsewhere: Lust Et Veritas," NBC, 1983; "The Fourth Wise Man," ABC, 1985.

TV MOVIES AND MINISERIES: "The Defection of Simas Kudirka," CBS, 1978; "A Deadly Business," CBS, 1986; "Escape From Sobibor," CBS, 1987.

AS DIRECTOR: "Trying Times: The Visit," PBS, 1988; "Trying Times: The Boss," PBS, 1989.

ARLEN, RICHARD

b. Richard Cornelius van Mattimore, Charlottesville, VA, September 1, 1899; d. 1976. Actor whose career began in silent films.

AS A GUEST: "The Loretta Young Show: He Always Comes Home," NBC, 1955; "Science Fiction Theatre: Out of Nowhere," SYN, 1955; "The Whistler: Cancelled Flight," SYN, 1955; "Crossroads: St. George and the Dragon," ABC, 1956; "Climax!: Flight to Tommorow," CBS, 1956; "Crossroads: Weekend Minister," ABC, 1957; "The 20th Century-Fox Hour: Deep Water," CBS, 1957; "Playhouse 90: Child of Trouble," CBS, 1957; "Crossroads: 9:30 Action," ABC, 1957; "O. Henry Playhouse: Georgia's Ruling," SYN, 1957; "Christophers: Harness That Power," SYN, 1958; "Wanted Dead or Alive: Rope Law," CBS, 1959; "Lawman: The Gunman," ABC, 1959; "Yancy Derringer: A State of Crisis," CBS, 1959; "Bat Masterson: Death and Taxes," NBC, 1959; "Art Linkletter's House Party," CBS, 1959; "Lawman: Last Stop," ABC, 1960; "Bat Masterson: The Price of Paradise," NBC, 1961; "This Is Your Life," NBC, 1961; "Lawman: The Man From New York," ABC, 1961; "Here's Hollywood," NBC, 1961; "Perry Mason: The Case of the Misguided Missle," CBS, 1961; "The New Breed: To Sell a Human Being," ABC, 1962; "Branded: Coward, Step Aside," NBC, 1965; "The Lucy Show: Lucy and Carol Burnett," CBS, 1967; "Petticoat Junction: Wings," CBS, 1968; "The Wonderful World of Disney: Sky's the Limit," NBC, 1975.

* Arlen and Charles "Buddy" Rogers played themselves on "Petticoat Junction": the occasion was the Hooterville premiere of the 1927 film "Wings," in which Arlen co-starred.

ARLEN, ROXANNE

b. Dolores Rosedale, Detroit, MI, 1935. Fifties starlet—and as simply Roxanne, she was the assistant on "Beat the Clock."

AS A REGULAR: "Beat the Clock," CBS, 1950-58; ABC, 1958-61.

AND: "Broadway Television Theatre: The Patsy," SYN, 1954; "Ford Theatre: Model Wife," ABC, 1956; "Ford Theatre: The Marriage Plan," ABC, 1956; "Playhouse 90: Topaze," CBS, 1957; "U.S. Steel Hour: The Square Egghead," CBS, 1959; "The Detectives Starring Robert Taylor: The New Man," ABC, 1960; "The Roaring Twenties: The Prairie Flower," ABC, 1960; "Witness: Arnold Rothstein," CBS, 1960; "The Roaring Twenties: Bold Edition," ABC, 1960; "SurfSide 6: A Slight Case of Chivalry," ABC, 1961; "87th Precinct: The Missing Person," NBC, 1962; "The Roaring Twenties: The People People Marry," ABC, 1962; "Hennesey: Calling Dr. Good-Deed," CBS, 1962; "SurfSide 6: Portrait of Nicole," ABC, 1962; "Naked City: Make It Fifty Dollars, and Add Love to Nona," ABC, 1962.

ARLISS, DIMITRA

b. October 23, 1932. Actress usually in dour roles; she played Maria Falconetti on the series spinoff of "Rich Man, Poor Man."

AS A REGULAR: "Rich Man, Poor Man–Book II," ABC, 1976-77.

AND: "Kojak: A Killing in the Second House," CBS, 1974; "Marcus Welby, M.D.: The One Face in the World," ABC, 1975; "Quincy: Go Fight

City Hall To the Death," NBC, 1976.
TV MOVIES AND MINISERIES: "The Art of Crime,"
NBC, 1975; "Onassis: The Richest Man in the
World," ABC, 1988.

ARMEN, KAY
Fifties singer.
AS A REGULAR: "Washington Square," NBC,
1956-57; "The Ray Bolger Show," NBC, 1957;
"Love and Marriage," NBC, 1959-60.
AND: "The Vic Damone Show," CBS, 1957;
"Music for a Spring Night: Concert in the Park,"
ABC, 1960; "The Jack Paar Show," NBC, 1960;
"The Jack Paar Show," NBC, 1961; "The Jack
Paar Show," NBC, 1962; "Play Your Hunch,"
NBC, 1963; "Girl Talk," SYN, 1963.
TV MOVIES AND MINISERIES: "Jimmy B. and
Andre," CBS, 1980.

ARMS, RUSSELL
b. Berkeley, CA, February 3, 1929. Actor-
singer who was a regular on "Your Hit
Parade."
AS A REGULAR: "School House," DUM, 1949;
"The Fifty-Fourth Street Revue," CBS, 1949-
50; "Chance of a Lifetime," ABC, 1950-51;
"Your Hit Parade," NBC, 1952-57.
AND: "The Ed Sullivan Show," CBS, 1957; "The
Jonathan Winters Show," NBC, 1957; "Art
Linkletter's House Party," CBS, 1957; "Hidden
Treasure," SYN, 1957; "The Arlene Francis
Show," NBC, 1957; "The Gisele MacKenzie
Show," NBC, 1958; "The Gale Storm Show:
Lovey-dovey," CBS, 1958; "Matinee Theatre:
The Long, Long Laugh," NBC, 1958; "Matinee
Theatre: The Broom and the Groom," NBC, 1958;
"Your Hit Parade," CBS, 1958; "Have Gun, Will
Travel: Death of a Gunfighter," CBS, 1959;
"Buckskin: I'll Sing at Your Wedding," NBC,
1959; "America Pauses for the Merry Month of
May," CBS, 1959; "Perry Mason: The Case of the
Credulous Quarry," CBS, 1960; "Rawhide: Arana
Sacar," CBS, 1960; "Gunsmoke: Bad Sheriff,"
CBS, 1961; "The Barbara Stanwyck Show:
Dragon by the Tail," NBC, 1961; "Bell Telephone
Hour: Almanac for February," NBC, 1961; "Have
Gun, Will Travel: The Revenger," CBS, 1961;
"Rawhide: Incident of the Surrender," CBS, 1962;
"Marcus Welby, M.D.: The Legacy," ABC, 1970;
"A Salute to Television's 25th Anniversary,"
ABC, 1972.

ARMSTRONG, BESS
b. Baltimore, MD, December 11, 1953. Pert
actress in pert roles; currently she plays
Elizabeth Meyers on "Married People."
AS A REGULAR: "On Our Own," CBS, 1977-78;
"All Is Forgiven," NBC, 1986; "Married
People," ABC, 1990- .
AND: "The Love Boat: A Different Girl," ABC,

1978; "Barefoot in the Park," SHO, 1982.
TV MOVIES AND MINISERIES: "How to Pick Up
Girls," ABC, 1978; "Walking Through the
Fire," CBS, 1979; "The 11th Victim," CBS,
1979; "This Girl for Hire," CBS, 1983; "Lace,"
ABC, 1984.

ARMSTRONG, CURTIS
Stocky actor who played Bert Viola, detective
whose heart belonged to Agnes di Pesto
(Allyce Beasley) on "Moonlighting."
AS A REGULAR: "Moonlighting," ABC, 1986-89.

ARMSTRONG, LOUIS
b. New Orleans, LA, July 4, 1900; d. 1971.
Legendary jazz trumpeter and vocalist with a
style all his own.
AS A GUEST: "Producers Showcase: The Lord
Don't Play Favorites," NBC, 1956; "Ford Star
Jubilee: You're the Top," CBS, 1956; "The Ed
Sullivan Show," CBS, 1956; "The Perry Como
Show," NBC, 1956; "The Twentieth Century:
Satchmo the Great," CBS, 1957; "The Ed
Sullivan Show," CBS, 1957; "Du Pont Show of
the Month: Crescendo," CBS, 1957; "The
Edsel Show," CBS, 1957; "All-Star Jazz,"
NBC, 1957; "All-Star Jazz," CBS, 1958; "The
Steve Allen Show," NBC, 1958; "You Asked
for It," ABC, 1958; "All-Star Jazz: The Golden
Age of Jazz," CBS, 1959; "Ed Sullivan
Presents the Spoleto Festival," CBS, 1959;
"The Ed Sullivan Show," CBS, 1959; "Bing
Crosby Special," ABC, 1959; "Bell Telephone
Hour: Our Musical Ambassadors," NBC, 1960;
"An Hour with Danny Kaye," CBS, 1960;
"The Chevy Show: Swinging at the Summit,"
NBC, 1961; "Here's Hollywood," NBC, 1961;
"The Ed Sullivan Show," CBS, 1961;
"Westinghouse Presents: Carnival at Sun
Valley," ABC, 1962; "The Ed Sullivan Show,"
CBS, 1964; "Walt Disney's Wonderful World
of Color: Disneyland's 10th Anniversary,"
NBC, 1965; "Bell Telephone Hour," NBC,
1965; "Hollywood Palace," ABC, 1965; "The
Dean Martin Show," NBC, 1965; "The Ed
Sullivan Show," CBS, 1966; "The Dean Martin
Show," NBC, 1967; "Operation: Entertain-
ment," ABC, 1968; "Johnny Carson Special:
The Sun City Scandals," NBC, 1970.

ARMSTRONG, R.G.
*b. Robert Golden Armstrong, Birmingham, AL,
April 7, 1917.* Deep-voiced, heavyset actor
who often plays heavies, or good guys who act
a lot like heavies.
AS A REGULAR: "T.H.E. Cat," NBC, 1966-67.
AND: "Kraft Television Theatre: Fire and Ice,"
NBC, 1957; "Have Gun, Will Travel: Killer's
Widow," CBS, 1958; "Have Gun, Will Travel:
Deliver the Body," CBS, 1958; "Alfred Hitchcock

Presents: The Tall Man Who Found the Money," NBC, 1960; "The Garlund Touch: Rachel," CBS, 1961; "Walt Disney Presents: Texas John Slaughter–A Holster Full of Law," ABC, 1961; "The Andy Griffith Show: Ellie Saves a Female," CBS, 1961; "Bonanza: The Horse Breaker," NBC, 1961; "Gunsmoke: Chester's Indian," CBS, 1961; "Laramie: The Jailbreakers," NBC, 1961; "Frontier Circus: Coals of Fire," CBS, 1962; "The Twilight Zone: Nothing in the Dark," CBS, 1962; "G.E. Theatre: The Little Hours," CBS, 1962; "Tales of Wells Fargo: Winter Storm," NBC, 1962; "The Wide Country: Don't Cry for Johnny Devlin, NBC, 1963; "The Virginian: The Small Parade," NBC, 1963; "Kraft Suspense Theatre: My Enemy, This Town," NBC, 1964; "Slattery's People: Question-How Do You Fall in Love with a Town?," CBS, 1965; "The Fugitive: Corner of Hell," ABC, 1965; "Rawhide: Six Weeks to Bent Fork," CBS, 1965; "The FBI: A Mouthful of Dust," ABC, 1965; "The Guns of Will Sonnett: The Turkey Shoot," ABC, 1967; "The Virginian: The Girl on the Pinto," NBC, 1967; "Alias Smith and Jones: The Bounty Hunter," ABC, 1971; "Cannon: A Lonely Place to Die," CBS, 1971; "Marcus Welby, M.D.: No Charity for the MacAllisters," ABC, 1974; "Gunsmoke: The Disciple," CBS, 1974; "McMillan and Wife: Downshift to Danger," NBC, 1974; "Police Story: Love, Mabel," NBC, 1974; "Friday the 13th: The Series: Hellowe'en," SYN, 1988; "Matlock: The Hunting Party," NBC, 1989.

TV MOVIES AND MINISERIES: "Hec Ramsey," NBC, 1972; "Reflections on Murder," ABC, 1974; "Kingston: The Power Play," NBC, 1976; "Devil Dog: The Hound of Hell," CBS, 1978; "The Time Machine," NBC, 1978; "The Legend of the Golden Gun," NBC, 1979; "The Last Ride of the Dalton Gang," NBC, 1979; "Oceans of Fire," CBS, 1986; "Independence," NBC, 1987; "LBJ: The Early Years," NBC, 1987; "War and Remembrance," ABC, 1988, 1989.

ARMSTRONG, ROBERT

b. *Saginaw, MI, November 20, 1880; d. 1973.* Fast-talking actor who played the man who brought "King Kong" to New York in the 1933 classic.

AS A REGULAR: "The First Hundred Years," CBS, 1950-52; "State Trooper," SYN, 1957-59.

AND: "The Red Skelton Show," CBS, 1957; "The Adventures of Ozzie and Harriet: Volunteer Fireman," ABC, 1958; "Climax!: Shooting for the Moon," CBS, 1958; "The Adventures of McGraw: Mojave," NBC, 1958; "Tales of Wells Fargo: The Prisoner," NBC, 1958; "Have Gun, Will Travel: The Hanging of Roy Carter," CBS, 1958; "Cimarron City: The Town Is a Prisoner," NBC, 1959; "Lawman: The Hardcase," ABC, 1959; "Wagon Train: The Estaban Zamora Story,"

NBC, 1959; "Riverboat: The Wichita Arrows," NBC, 1960; "Cheyenne: The Mustangers," ABC, 1960; "Lawman: The Catcher," ABC, 1960; "The Barbara Stanwyck Show: Along the Barbary Coast," NBC, 1961; "Tales of Wells Fargo: Lady Trouble," NBC, 1961; "Rawhide: Incident Before Black Pass," CBS, 1961; "Lassie: Lassie and the Grand Canyon," CBS, 1961; "Perry Mason: The Case of the Sardonic Sergeant," CBS, 1961; "Alfred Hitchcock Presents: The Faith of Aaron Menefee," NBC, 1962; "Perry Mason: The Case of the Accosted Accountant," CBS, 1964.

ARNAZ, DESI

b. *Desiderio Arnaz III, Santiago, Cuba, March 2, 1917; d. 1986.* Bandleader-singer and husband of Lucille Ball; he played her husband, Ricky Ricardo, on "I Love Lucy" and was largely responsible for accumulating their fortune in television production.

AS A REGULAR: "I Love Lucy," CBS, 1951-57; "The Lucille Ball-Desi Arnaz Show," CBS, 1957-59; "Westinghouse Desilu Playhouse," CBS, 1958-60.

AND: "Our Miss Brooks: Miss Brooks and the King," CBS, 1955; "The Ed Sullivan Show," CBS, 1956; "The Bob Hope Show," NBC, 1956; "December Bride: Sunken Den," CBS, 1956; "The Danny Thomas Show: Lucille Ball Upsets the Williams Household," CBS, 1959; "Westinghouse Desilu Playhouse: So Tender, So Profane," CBS, 1959; "Milton Berle Special," NBC, 1959; "Westinghouse Desilu Playhouse: Thunder in the Night," CBS, 1960; "The Red Skelton Show," CBS, 1961; "The Mothers-in-Law: A Night to Forget," NBC, 1967; "The Mothers-in-Law: The Hombre Who Came to Dinner," NBC, 1968; "The Mothers-in-Law: The Matador Makes a Movie," NBC, 1968; "The Men From Shiloh: The Best Man," NBC, 1970; "Hollywood Squares," NBC, 1972; "Ironside: Riddle at 24,000," NBC, 1974; "Medical Center: The Rip-Off," CBS, 1975; "The Mike Douglas Show," SYN, 1976; "Saturday Night Live," NBC, 1976; "Joys," NBC, 1976; "Alice: The Cuban Connection," CBS, 1978.

AS DIRECTOR: "Milton Berle Special," NBC, 1959.

AS PRODUCER-DIRECTOR: "The Mothers-in-Law," NBC, 1967-69.

ARNAZ, DESI JR.

b. *Desiderio Arnaz IV, Los Angeles, CA, January 19, 1953.* Son of Desi Sr. and Lucille Ball, he was born the same day Little Ricky arrived on "I Love Lucy" and starred opposite his mother sixteen years later.

AS A REGULAR: "Here's Lucy," CBS, 1968-71; "Automan," ABC, 1983-84.

AND: "I Love Lucy: The Ricardos Dedicate a Statue," CBS, 1957; "Dinah Shore Chevy Show," NBC, 1960; "The Lucy Show: Lucy and the Scout

Trip," CBS, 1964; "The Mothers-in-Law: The Hombre Who Came to Dinner," NBC, 1968; "The Mothers-in-Law: The Matador Makes a Movie," NBC, 1968; "The Brady Bunch: The Possible Dream," ABC, 1970; "The Mod Squad: Feet of Clay," ABC, 1971; "Love, American Style: Love and the Motel Mixup," ABC, 1971; "Here's Lucy: Lucy and Joe Namath," CBS, 1972; "Medical Story: A Life in Balance," NBC, 1975; "Police Story: Spanish Class," NBC, 1976; "The Mike Douglas Show," SYN, 1976; "Police Story: The Other Side of the Badge," NBC, 1976; "The Streets of San Francisco: In Case of Madness," ABC, 1976; "Saturday Night Live," NBC, 1976; "The Love Boat: Eyes of Love," ABC, 1978.

TV MOVIES AND MINISERIES: "Mr. and Mrs. Bo Jo Jones," ABC, 1971; "The Voyage of the Yes," CBS, 1973; "She Lives," ABC, 1973; "Having Babies," ABC, 1976; "Flight to Holocaust," NBC, 1977; "Black Market Baby," ABC, 1977; "How to Pick Up Girls," ABC, 1978; "Crisis in Mid-Air," CBS, 1979; "The Great American Traffic Jam," NBC, 1980; "The Night the Bridge Fell Down," NBC, 1983.

ARNAZ, LUCIE

b. *Los Angeles, CA, July 17, 1951*. Daughter of Lucille Ball and Desi Arnaz, with mixed TV success on her own; memorable in the title role of the TV movie "Who Is the Black Dahlia?," about an unsolved murder case in forties Hollywood.

AS A REGULAR: "Here's Lucy," CBS, 1968-74; "The Lucie Arnaz Show," CBS, 1985; "Sons and Daughters," CBS, 1990- .

AND: "I Love Lucy: The Ricardos Dedicate a Statue," CBS, 1957; "The Lucy Show: Lucy Is a Soda Jerk," CBS, 1963; "The Lucy Show: Lucy Is a Chaperone," CBS, 1963; "The Lucy Show: Lucy and the Ring-a-Ding Ring," CBS, 1966; "The Lucy Show: Lucy Gets Her Diploma," CBS, 1967; "The Lucy Show: Lucy and Robert Goulet," CBS, 1967; "The Dating Game," ABC, 1968; "What's My Line?," SYN, 1974; "The Mike Douglas Show," SYN, 1974; "The $10,000 Pyramid," CBS, 1974; "Marcus Welby, M.D.: The Time Bomb," ABC, 1975; "Don Adams Screen Test," SYN, 1975; "Dinah!," SYN, 1975; "The John Davidson Show," SYN, 1981; "Murder, She Wrote: The Wearing of the Green," CBS, 1988.

TV MOVIES AND MINISERIES: "Who Is the Black Dahlia?," NBC, 1975; "Death Scream," ABC, 1975; "The Mating Season," CBS, 1980; "Washington Mistress," CBS, 1982; "Who Gets the Friends?," CBS, 1988.

ARNDT, DENIS

b. *Canada*. Solid actor who played Mary Tyler Moore's husband on her most recent TV series attempt.

AS A REGULAR: "Annie McGuire," CBS, 1988-89.

AND: "Wiseguy: Dirty Little Wars," CBS, 1988; "TV 101: Premiere," CBS, 1988; "The Wonder Years: The Walkout," ABC, 1989; "Mancuso FBI: Suspicious Minds," NBC, 1989; "Life Goes On: Corky Witnesses a Crime," ABC, 1989.

ARNESS, JAMES

b. *James Aurness, Minneapolis, MN, May 26, 1923*. Physically commanding hero who played rock-solid Marshal Matt Dillon on "Gunsmoke," the most popular TV western ever.

AS A REGULAR: "Gunsmoke," CBS, 1955-75; "How the West Was Won," ABC, 1978-79; "McClain's Law," NBC, 1981-82.

AND: "Lux Video Theatre: The Chase," NBC, 1954; "The Ed Sullivan Show," CBS, 1958; "Wide, Wide World: The Western," NBC, 1958; "Art Linkletter's House Party," CBS, 1958; "Red Skelton Chevy Special," CBS, 1959; "Christmas at the Circus," CBS, 1959; "The Chevrolet Golden Anniversary Show," CBS, 1961; "A Salute to Television's 25th Anniversary," ABC, 1972.

TV MOVIES AND MINISERIES: "The Macahans," ABC, 1976; "Gunsmoke: Return to Dodge," CBS, 1987; "Red River," CBS, 1988.

* Arness was cast as Matt Dillon on the recommendation of John Wayne, who turned down the role.
* Arness stands six feet, six inches tall.
* Brother of Peter Graves.

TV'S TOP TEN, 1958-59
1. Gunsmoke (CBS)
2. Wagon Train (NBC)
3. Have Gun, Will Travel (CBS)
4. The Rifleman (ABC)
5. The Danny Thomas Show (CBS)
6. Maverick (ABC)
7. Tales of Wells Fargo (NBC)
8. The Real McCoys (ABC)
9. I've Got a Secret (CBS)
10. The Life and Legend of Wyatt Earp (ABC)

ARNETTE, JEANETTA

Blonde actress who plays assistant principal Bernadette Meara on "Head of the Class."

AS A REGULAR: "Head of the Class," ABC, 1986- .

AND: "Hill Street Blues: Jungle Madness," NBC, 1981; "St. Elsewhere: Qui Transtulit Sustinct," NBC, 1983; "The Bay City Blues: Beautiful Peoples," NBC, 1983; "Riptide: Girls' Night Out," NBC, 1985.

TV MOVIES AND MINISERIES: "Flight #90: Disaster on the Potomac," NBC, 1984; "Sister Margaret and the Saturday Night Ladies," CBS, 1987; "Single Women, Married Men," CBS, 1989.

ARNGRIM, ALISON

b. New York City, 1962. Young actress who played bratty Nellie Oleson on "Little House on the Prairie."

AS A REGULAR: "Little House on the Prairie," NBC, 1974-81.

AND: "Room 222: Triple Date," ABC, 1969; "Dance Fever," SYN, 1981.

ARNGRIM, STEFAN

b. 1955. Young actor of the sixties.

AS A REGULAR: "Land of the Giants," ABC, 1968-70.

AND: "T.H.E. Cat: King of Limpets," NBC, 1966; "Combat!: Gulliver," ABC, 1966; "The Virginian: The Gauntlet," NBC, 1967; "Dragnet: Juvenile," NBC, 1968.

TV MOVIES AND MINISERIES: "Silent Night, Lonely Night," NBC, 1969.

ARNO, SIG

b. Siegfried Aron, Germany, 1895; d. 1975. Comic actor.

AS A REGULAR: "My Friend Irma," CBS, 1952-53.

AND: "December Bride: Lily, the Artist," CBS, 1955; "Counterpoint: The Wedding," SYN, 1955; "Hallmark Hall of Fame: Time Remembered," NBC, 1961.

ARNOLD, DANNY

Emmy-award winning writer and producer.

AS PRODUCER-DIRECTOR: "My World and Welcome to It," NBC, 1969-70; "Barney Miller," ABC, 1975-82.

AS CREATOR: "Barney Miller," ABC, 1974-82; "Joe Bash," ABC, 1986.

* Emmies: 1970, 1982.

ARNOLD, EDDY

b. Henderson, TN, May 15, 1918. Popular country-western singer on dozens of variety shows.

AS A REGULAR: "The Eddy Arnold Show," CBS, 1952; NBC, 1953; "Eddy Arnold Time," ABC, 1956; "Today on the Farm," NBC, 1960-61; "Kraft Music Hall," NBC, 1968-72.

AND: "Du Pont Show of the Month: Crescendo," CBS, 1957; "Jubilee USA," ABC, 1958; "Hoedown," NBC, 1959; "Jubilee USA," ABC, 1959; "The Chevy Show," NBC, 1959; "Jubilee USA," ABC, 1960; "The Chevy Show," NBC, 1961; "Highways of Melody," NBC, 1961; "The Ed Sullivan Show," CBS, 1964; "The Jimmy Dean Show," ABC, 1964; "Hootenanny," ABC, 1964; "The Jimmy Dean Show," ABC, 1965; "The Steve Lawrence Show," CBS, 1965; "The Danny Kaye Show," CBS, 1967; "The Mike Douglas Show," SYN, 1967; "The Mike Douglas Show," SYN, 1968; "Carol Channing Special," CBS, 1968; "The Merv Griffin Show," CBS,

1970; "Country Music Hit Parade," NBC, 1973; "Sammy and Company," SYN, 1976; "A Conversation with Dinah," TNN, 1989.

ARNOLD, EDWARD

b. New York City, 1890; d. 1956. Rotund character actor, in movies from 1915.

AS A REGULAR: "Edward Arnold Theatre," SYN, 1954-55.

AND: "Pulitzer Prize Playhouse: Our Town," ABC, 1950; "Ford Theatre: Junior," NBC, 1952; "Hollywood Opening Night: Thirty Days," NBC, 1952; "Schlitz Playhouse of Stars: Lost and Found," CBS, 1953; "Ford Theatre: Ever Since the Day," NBC, 1953; "G.E. Theatre: Walking John Stopped Here," CBS, 1954; "Ford Theatre: The Tryst," NBC, 1954; "Studio One: Twelve Angry Men," CBS, 1954; "Climax!: South of the Sun," CBS, 1955; "Eddie Cantor Theatre: Starbound," ABC, 1955; "Climax!: Deal a Blow," CBS, 1955; "Ford Theatre: Twelve to Eternity," NBC, 1955; "Ethel Barrymore Theatre: The Victim," SYN, 1956.

ARQUETTE, CLIFF

b. Toledo, OH, 1905; d. 1974. Actor who created the character of homespun humorist Charley Weaver of Mount Idy, Ohio, famous for his letters from Mama, on local Los Angeles television and portrayed him throughout the fifties and sixties.

AS A REGULAR: "The RCA Victor Show," NBC, 1952-54; "Do it Yourself," NBC, 1955; "The Jack Paar Show," NBC, 1958-62; "Hobby Lobby (The Charley Weaver Show)," ABC, 1959-60; "The Roy Rogers and Dale Evans Show," ABC, 1962; "Hollywood Squares," NBC, 1968-73; "The Jonathan Winters Show," CBS, 1968-69.

AND: "Dragnet: The Big Trio," NBC, 1952; "Drama at Eight: Uncle Charley," SYN, 1953; "The Loretta Young Show: Time and Yuletide," NBC, 1955; "I've Got a Secret," CBS, 1958; "The Ford Show," NBC, 1958; "The Ford Show," NBC, 1959; "Dinah Shore Chevy Show," NBC, 1959; "The Garry Moore Show," CBS, 1959; "Arthur Murray Party," NBC, 1959; "The Ford Show," NBC, 1960; "Mother's March," SYN, 1960; "The Arthur Murray Party for Bob Hope," NBC, 1960; "Person to Person," CBS, 1960; "Jack Paar Presents," NBC, 1960; "Startime: Fun Fair," NBC, 1960; "The Garry Moore Show," CBS, 1960; "Person to Person," CBS, 1960; "This Is Your Life," NBC, 1960; "The Ford Show," NBC, 1961; "The Square World of Jack Paar," NBC, 1961; "The Chevy Show," NBC, 1961; "I've Got a Secret," CBS, 1961; "Perry Como's Kraft Music Hall," NBC, 1961; "Truth or Consequences," NBC, 1964; "The Tennessee Ernie Ford Show," ABC, 1965; "The Joey Bishop Show: The Weed City Story," CBS, 1965; "The

Mike Douglas Show," SYN, 1965; "The Farmer's Daughter: Babe in the Woods," ABC, 1965; "The Andy Williams Show," NBC, 1965; "The Jimmy Dean Show," ABC, 1965; "F Troop: Our Brave in F Troop," ABC, 1967; "The Steve Allen Show," SYN, 1968; "The Glen Campbell Goodtime Hour," CBS, 1969.

ARQUETTE, LEWIS

Actor who's the son of Cliff Arquette and father of Rosanna; he played J.D. Pickett on "The Waltons."

AS A REGULAR: "The Marilyn McCoo and Billy Davis, Jr. Show," CBS, 1977; "The Waltons," CBS, 1978-81.

AND: "Alice: The Second Time 'Round," CBS, 1977; "Barney Miller: Wojo's Girl," ABC, 1979; "Tenspeed and Brown Shoe: The Sixteen Byte Data Chip and the Brown-Eyed Fox," ABC, 1980; "Foul Play: Postage Due," ABC, 1981; "House Calls: Son of Emergency," CBS, 1981; "Harper Valley PTA: The $500 Misunderstanding," NBC, 1981; "Remington Steele: Red Holt Steele," NBC, 1983; "Codename: Foxfire: Tell Me That You Love Me," NBC, 1985; "E/R: A Cold Night in Chicago," CBS, 1985; "Sledge Hammer!: Witless," ABC, 1986; "Paradise: Ghost Dance," CBS, 1988.

TV MOVIES AND MINISERIES: "My First Love," ABC, 1988; "A Very Brady Christmas," CBS, 1988.

ARQUETTE, ROSANNA

b. New York City, August 10, 1959. Elfin actress in films ("Baby, It's You," "Desperately Seeking Susan") and TV, especially memorable as the girlfriend of Gary Gilmore (Tommy Lee Jones) in "The Executioner's Song"; granddaughter of Cliff Arquette.

AS A REGULAR: "Shirley," NBC, 1979-80.

AND: "James at 16: An Hour Before Midnight," NBC, 1978; "Saturday Night Live," NBC, 1986; "Trying Times: A Family Tree," PBS, 1988.

TV MOVIES AND MINISERIES: "The Dark Secret of Harvest Home," NBC, 1978; "G.E. Theatre: A Long Way Home," ABC, 1981; "The Wall," CBS, 1982; "The Executioner's Song," NBC, 1982; "One Cooks, the Other Doesn't," CBS, 1983; "The Parade," CBS, 1984; "Promised a Miracle," CBS, 1988.

ARRANTS, ROD

Soap hunk who plays Richard Cates on "Days of Our Lives."

AS A REGULAR: "The Young and the Restless," CBS, 1974; "Lovers and Friends (For Richer, for Poorer)," NBC, 1977-78; "Search for Tomorrow," CBS, 1978-82; NBC, 1982-84; "Days of Our Lives," NBC, 1985- .

AND: "Remington Steele: Steele of Approval," NBC, 1985.

ARTHUR, BEATRICE

b. New York City, NY, May 13, 1926. T actress, usually in cutting comic roles; s played Maude Findlay and now plays D Zbornak on "The Golden Girls."

AS A REGULAR: "Perry Como's Kraft Music F NBC, 1961; "Maude," CBS, 1972-78; "Amanda's," ABC, 1983; "The Golden Girl NBC, 1985- .

AND: "The Seven Lively Arts: Gold Rush," CBS 1958; "Omnibus: Mrs. McThing," NBC, 1958; "The Gift of the Magi," CBS, 1958; "Connie Francis Special: Kicking Sound Around," ABC, 1961; "All in the Family: Cousin Maude's Visit," CBS, 1971; "All in the Family: Maude," CBS, 1972; "The Merv Griffin Show," SYN, 1975; "Cos," ABC, 1976; "Saturday Night Live," NBC, 1979; "The Mary Tyler Moore Hour," CBS, 1979; "Irving Berlin's 100th Birthday Celebration," CBS, 1988; "Empty Nest: Dumped," NBC, 1989; "Ooh-La-La-It's Bob Hope's Fun Birthday Spectacular From Paris' Bicentennial," NBC, 1989; "Later with Bob Costas," NBC, 1989.

TV MOVIES AND MINISERIES: "My First Love," ABC, 1988.

* Emmies: 1977.

TV'S TOP TEN, 1988-89

1. The Cosby Show (NBC)
2. A Different World (NBC)
3. Cheers (NBC)
4. Roseanne (ABC)
4. The Golden Girls (NBC)
6. 60 Minutes (CBS)
7. Who's the Boss? (ABC)
8. Growing Pains (ABC)
9. Empty Nest (NBC)
10. Murder, She Wrote (CBS)

ARTHUR, JEAN

b. Gladys Greene, New York City, NY, October 17, 1905. Screen actress ("Mr. Deeds Goes to Town," "Shane") who tried TV in the mid-sixties.

AS A REGULAR: "The Jean Arthur Show," CBS, 1966.

AND: "Gunsmoke: Thursday's Child," CBS, 1965.

ARTHUR, MAUREEN

b. San Jose, CA, 1934. Blonde actress, usually in sexy comic roles.

AS A REGULAR: "The Tonight Show," NBC, 1956-57; "The Jan Murray Show (Charge Account)," NBC, 1960-61; "Holiday Lodge," CBS, 1961; "What's It All About, World?," ABC, 1969; "Empire," CBS, 1984.

AND: "Bourbon Street Beat: If a Body," ABC, 1960; "Celebrity Talent Scouts," CBS, 1960; "Bachelor Father: Bentley and the Homebody," ABC, 1962; "Branded: Mightier Than the word," NBC, 1965; "Get Smart: Hoo Done It," NBC, 1966; "The Hero: Who Needs a Friend in Need?," NBC, 1966; "Please Don't Eat the Daisies: Remember Lake Serene," NBC, 1967; "The Flying Nun: Ah Love, Could You and I Conspire," ABC, 1967; "That's Life: Pilot," ABC, 1968; "Gomer Pyle, USMC: Freddy's Friendly Computer," CBS, 1969; "Bob Hope Special," NBC, 1969; "Hollywood Squares," NBC, 1969; "Love, American Style: Love and Who?," ABC, 1969; "Love, American Style: Love and the Longest Night," ABC, 1971; "Sanford & Son: Lamont as Othello," NBC, 1973; "Laverne & Shirley: Tough in the Middle," ABC, 1977; "Alice: Mel's in Love," CBS, 1977; "CPO Sharkey: Sharkey Meets Pruitt's Sister," NBC, 1978; "Mork & Mindy: P.S. 2001," ABC, 1981; "Mork & Mindy: Pajama Game II," ABC, 1982; "Murder, She Wrote: J.B. ... As in Jailbird," CBS, 1988; "Highway to Heaven: The Reunion," NBC, 1989.

TV MOVIES AND MINISERIES: "Like Normal People," ABC, 1979.

ARVAN, JAN
b. 1912; d. 1979. Character actor and frequent supporting performer opposite Red Skelton.
AS A REGULAR: "Zorro," ABC, 1957-59; "Red," NBC, 1970-71.
AND: "Telephone Time: Passport to Life," CBS, 1957; "The Adventures of Rin Tin Tin: Bitter Medicine," ABC, 1957; "Telephone Time: A Picture of the Magi," ABC, 1957; "The Adventures of Rin Tin Tin: Running Horse," ABC, 1958; "Restless Gun: Ride with the Devil," NBC, 1959; "The Detectives Starring Robert Taylor: My Name Is Tommy," ABC, 1959; "The Adventures of Ozzie and Harriet: Happy Anniversary," ABC, 1960; "Startime: Crime, Inc.," NBC, 1960; "The Red Skelton Show: Clem's Fountain of Youth," CBS, 1960; "The Power of the Resurrection," NBC, 1960; "The Loretta Young Show: The Eternal Now," NBC, 1960; "The Tom Ewell Show: Tom Cuts Off the Credit," CBS, 1960; "Holiday Lodge: The Kid," CBS, 1961; "The Virginian: Man From the Sea," NBC, 1962; "I'm Dickens, He's Fenster: How Not to Succeed in Business," ABC, 1963; "The Adventures of Ozzie and Harriet: Dave Takes a Client to Dinner," ABC, 1963; "Hazel: All Mixed Up," NBC, 1964; "My Favorite Martian: Three to Make Ready," CBS, 1964; "Green Acres: One of Our Assemblymen Is Missing," CBS, 1966; "Captain Nice: How Shiek Can You Get?," NBC, 1967; "Petticoat Junction: Don't Call Us," CBS, 1967; "Love on a Rooftop: Low Calorie Love," ABC, 1967; "Batman: Pop Goes the Joker/Flop Goes the Joker," ABC, 1967; "Family Affair: A Waltz From Vienna," CBS, 1968; "Mannix: To Catch a Rabbit," CBS, 1969; "Room 222: Funny Boy," ABC, 1969; "Love, American Style: Love

and the Nuisance," ABC, 1970; "Family: Gifts," ABC, 1978.
TV MOVIES AND MINISERIES: "Winchester '73," NBC, 1967; "The Screaming Woman," ABC, 1972.

ASHBROOK, DANA
Young actor who plays Bobby Briggs on "Twin Peaks."
AS A REGULAR: "Twin Peaks," ABC, 1990- .
AND: "21 Jump Street: Whose Choice Is It Anyway?," FOX, 1988; "21 Jump Street: Play Now, Pay Later," FOX, 1988.
TV MOVIES AND MINISERIES: "Longarm," ABC, 1988.

ASHER, WILLIAM
b. 1919. Emmy-winning producer-director.
AS PRODUCER: "Dinah Shore Chevy Show," NBC, 1956-58.
AS PRODUCER--DIRECTOR: "Bewitched," ABC, 1964-72.
AS DIRECTOR: "I Love Lucy," CBS, 1952-57; "Alice," CBS, 1977-79; "Foul Play: Sins of the Fathers," ABC, 1981; "Foul Play: Play It Again, Tuck," ABC, 1981.
* Asher directed "Beach Party," "Muscle Beach Party," "Bikini Beach," "Beach Blanket Bingo" and "How to Stuff a Wild Bikini."
* Emmies: 1966.

ASHLEY, ELIZABETH
b. Ocala, FL, August 30, 1939. Deep-voiced actress in film ("Ship of Fools," "92 in the Shade") and TV; she plays crazy Aunt Frieda on "Evening Shade."
AS A REGULAR: "Another World," NBC, 1990; "Evening Shade," CBS, 1990- .
AND: "Du Pont Show of the Month: Heaven Can Wait," CBS, 1960; "U.S. Steel Hour: The Big Splash," CBS, 1961; "The Defenders: The Prowler," CBS, 1961; "The Nurses: The Barb Bowers Story," CBS, 1962; "Ben Casey: And Even Death Shall Die," ABC, 1962; "U.S. Steel Hour: The Young Avengers," CBS, 1963; "Girl Talk," SYN, 1963; "Sam Benedict: Season of Vengeance," NBC, 1963; "Stoney Burke: Tigress by the Tail," NBC, 1963; "Missing Links," NBC, 1964; "Password," CBS, 1964; "Password," CBS, 1966; "Run for Your Life: The Grotenberg Mask," NBC, 1966; "Hallmark Hall of Fame: The File on Devlin," NBC, 1969; "Love, American Style: Love and the Banned Book," ABC, 1970; "Love, American Style: Love and the Other Love," ABC, 1970; "The Men From Shiloh: The West vs. Colonel MacKenzie," NBC, 1970; "Medical Center: Brink of Doom," CBS, 1970; "Mission: Impossible: Encounter," CBS, 1971; "Ghost Story: At the Cradle Foot," NBC, 1972; "Mission: Impossible: The Question," CBS, 1973;

"Police Story: Dangerous Games," NBC, 1973; "Mannix: The Dark Hours," CBS, 1974; "Ironside: Close to the Heart," NBC, 1974; "The FBI: Diamond Run," ABC, 1974; "Sandburg's Lincoln: Sad Figure Laughing," NBC, 1975; "Saturday Night Live," NBC, 1982; "Cagney & Lacey: The Psychic," CBS, 1985; "The Love Boat: The Perfect Divorce," ABC, 1985; "Miami Vice: Knock, Knock, Who's There?," NBC, 1987; "Murder, She Wrote: Truck Stop," CBS, 1989.
TV MOVIES AND MINISERIES: "Harpy," CBS, 1971; "The Face of Fear," CBS, 1971; "When Michael Calls," ABC, 1972; "Second Chance," ABC, 1972; "The Heist," ABC, 1972; "Your Money or Your Wife," CBS, 1972; "The Magician," NBC, 1973; "One of My Wives is Missing," ABC, 1976; "A Fire in the Sky," NBC, 1978; "Svengali," CBS, 1983; "He's Fired, She's Hired," CBS, 1984; "Stagecoach," CBS, 1986; "The Two Mrs. Grenvilles," NBC, 1987; "Warm Hearts, Cold Feet," CBS, 1987.

ASHTON, JOHN
Mustachioed actor best known as the exasperated partner of Eddie Murphy in the "Beverly Hills Cop" movies.
AS A REGULAR: "Dallas," CBS, 1978-79; "Breaking Away," ABC, 1980-81; "Hardball," NBC, 1989-90.
AND: "Columbo: Negative Reaction," NBC, 1974; "Police Story: The Other Side of the Badge," NBC, 1976; "M*A*S*H: Last Laugh," CBS, 1977; "Police Woman: Once a Snitch," NBC, 1977.
TV MOVIES AND MINISERIES: "A Death in California," ABC, 1985; "The Deliberate Stranger," NBC, 1986; "I Know My First Name Is Steven," NBC, 1989.

ASKIN, LEON
b. Vienna, 1907. Corpulent character actor who played Gen. Burkhalter on "Hogan's Heroes."
AS A REGULAR: "Hogan's Heroes," CBS, 1965-71.
AND: "The 20th Century-Fox Hour: Operation Cicero," CBS, 1956; "Telephone Time: Passport to Life," CBS, 1957; "Restless Gun: The Shooting of Jett King," NBC, 1957; "Matinee Theatre: The Heart's Desire," NBC, 1958; "Walt Disney Presents: The Peter Tchaikovsky Story," ABC, 1959; "Saints and Sinners: The Year Joan Crawford Won the Oscar," NBC, 1963; "The Outer Limits: The Inheritors," ABC, 1964; "My Favorite Martian: Martin of the Movies," CBS, 1965; "Honey West: The Abominable Snowman," ABC, 1965; "The Man From UNCLE: The Project Deephole Affair," NBC, 1966; "My Favorite Martian: Pay the Man the $24," CBS, 1966; "The Man From UNCLE: The Off-Broadway Affair," NBC, 1966; "It's About Time: The Stone Age Diplomats," CBS, 1967; "The Monkees: The Card-Carrying Red Shoes," NBC,

1967; "Happy Days: Fearless Malph," ABC, 1978; "Three's Company: The Bake-Off," ABC, 1979.
TV MOVIES AND MINISERIES: "Genesis II," ABC, 1973.

ASNER, EDWARD
b. Kansas City, MO, November 15, 1929. Bald, burly actor who began in tough character roles and became an Emmy-winning star as newsroom boss Lou Grant of "The Mary Tyler Moore Show" and his own series; also an Emmy winner for "Rich Man, Poor Man" and "Roots."
AS A REGULAR: "Slattery's People," CBS, 1964-65; "The Mary Tyler Moore Show," CBS, 1970-77; "Lou Grant," CBS, 1977-82; "Off the Rack," ABC, 1985; "The Bronx Zoo," NBC, 1987-88; "Captain Planet and the Planeteers," TBS, 1990- .
AND: "Studio One: The Night America Trembled," CBS, 1957; "Omnibus: Capital Punishment," NBC, 1958; "Naked City: A Hole in the City," ABC, 1961; "Naked City: New York to L.A.," ABC, 1961; "Route 66: The Opponent," CBS, 1961; "Route 66: The Mud Nest," CBS, 1961; "Target: The Corruptors: The Golden Carpet," ABC, 1961; "Cain's Hundred: Blues for a Junkman," NBC, 1962; "Route 66: Shoulder the Sky, My Lad," CBS, 1962; "Route 66: Welcome to the Wedding," CBS, 1962; "Dr. Kildare: The Legacy," NBC, 1962; "The Untouchables: Search for a Dead Man," ABC, 1963; "The Alfred Hitchcock Hour: To Catch a Butterfly," CBS, 1963; "Stoney Burke: Tigress by the Tail," ABC, 1963; "The Breaking Point: Last Summer We Didn't Go Away," ABC, 1963; "Mr. Novak: First Year, First Day," NBC, 1963; "The Outer Limits: It Crawled Out of the Woodwork," ABC, 1963; "The Virginian: Echo From Another Day," NBC, 1963; "The Farmer's Daughter: Like Father, Like Son," ABC, 1964; "The Defenders: Hero of the People," CBS, 1964; "Gunsmoke: Hung High," CBS, 1964; "Mr. Novak: An Elephant Is Like a Tree," NBC, 1965; "Please Don't Eat the Daisies: My Good Friend What's-His-Name," NBC, 1966; "Gunsmoke: Whispering Tree," CBS, 1966; "The FBI: The Tormentors," ABC, 1966; "The Iron Horse: The Prisoners," ABC, 1967; "The FBI: The Dynasty," ABC, 1968; "The Wild Wild West: The Night of the Amnesiac," CBS, 1968; "Mission: Impossible: The Mind of Stefan Miklos," CBS, 1969; "The FBI: The Attorney," ABC, 1969; "Medical Center: The Last Ten Yards," CBS, 1969; "The Mod Squad: Color of Laughter, Color of Tears," ABC, 1971; "The Mod Squad: The Connection," ABC, 1972; "Police Story: A Dangerous Age," NBC, 1974; "Password," ABC, 1974; "Match Game '75," CBS, 1975; "Match Game '76," CBS, 1976; "Police Story: Three Days to Thirty," NBC, 1976;

"Dinah!," SYN, 1976; "Saturday Night Live," NBC, 1984; "Later With Bob Costas," NBC, 1989.

TV MOVIES AND MINISERIES: "The Doomsday Flight," NBC, 1966; "Daughter of the Mind," ABC, 1969; "The House on Greenapple Road," ABC, 1970; "The Old Man Who Cried Wolf," ABC, 1970; "The Last Child," ABC, 1971; "They Call It Murder," NBC, 1971; "Haunts of the Very Rich," ABC, 1972; "The Police Story," NBC, 1973; "The Girl Most Likely To...," ABC, 1973; "The Imposter," NBC, 1975; "Hey, I'm Alive!," ABC, 1975; "Rich Man, Poor Man," ABC, 1976; "Roots," ABC, 1977; "The Life and Assassination of the Kingfish," NBC, 1977; "Vital Signs," CBS, 1986; "Kate's Secret," NBC, 1986; "Cracked Up," ABC, 1987; "A Friendship in Vienna," DIS, 1988.

* Emmies: 1971, 1972, 1975, 1976, 1977, 1978, 1980.

ASSANTE, ARMAND

Actor who usually plays continental miniseries smoothies; he played Dr. Mike Powers on "The Doctors."

AS A REGULAR: "How to Survive a Marriage," NBC, 1974-75; "The Doctors," NBC, 1975-77.

AND: "Kojak: Caper on a Quiet Street," CBS, 1977; "Kate Loves a Mystery: A Chilling Surprise," NBC, 1979.

TV MOVIES AND MINISERIES: "Lady of the House," NBC, 1978; "The Pirate," CBS, 1978; "Human Feelings," NBC, 1978; "Rage of Angels," NBC, 1983; "Why Me?," ABC, 1984; "Evergreen," NBC, 1985; "A Deadly Business," CBS, 1986; "Stranger in My Bed," NBC, 1987; "Hands of a Stranger," NBC, 1987; "Passion and Paradise," ABC, 1989.

ASTAIRE, FRED

b. Frederick Austerlitz, Omaha, NB, May 10, 1899; d. 1987. Dancer with an infinite grace and wit. His first TV special, in 1958, won nine Emmy awards; he won a dramatic Emmy for "A Family Upside Down."

AS A REGULAR: "Alcoa Premiere," ABC, 1961-63; "It Takes a Thief," ABC, 1968-70.

AND: "Art Linkletter's House Party," CBS, 1957; "The Ed Sullivan Show," CBS, 1957; "Person to Person," CBS, 1957; "G.E. Theatre: Imp on a Cobweb Leash," CBS, 1957; "An Evening with Fred Astaire," NBC, 1958; "G.E. Theatre: Man on a Bicycle," CBS, 1959; "Another Evening with Fred Astaire," NBC, 1959; "Steve Allen Plymouth Show," NBC, 1959; "Astaire Time," NBC, 1960; "Here's Hollywood," NBC, 1961; "Bob Hope Chrysler Theatre: Think Pretty," NBC, 1964; "Hollywood Palace," ABC, 1965; "Dr. Kildare: Fathers and Daughters/A Gift of Love/The Tent-Dwellers/Going Home," NBC, 1965; "Hollywood Palace," ABC, 1966; "Fred Astaire Special," NBC, 1968; "The Dick Cavett Show," ABC, 1970; "The Dick Cavett Show," ABC, 1971; "Santa Claus Is Coming to Town," ABC, 1971; "Make Mine Red, White and Blue," NBC, 1972; "The Merv Griffin Show," SYN, 1975; "The Mike Douglas Show," SYN, 1976; "A Family Upside Down," NBC, 1978.

TV MOVIES AND MINISERIES: "The Over-the-Hill Gang Rides Again," ABC, 1970; "The Man in the Santa Claus Suit," NBC, 1979.

* Astaire made his Broadway debut in 1917, and his film debut in 1933.
* Emmies: 1959, 1961, 1978.

ASTIN, JOHN

b. Baltimore, MD, March 30, 1930. Comedic actor who played Gomez Addams on "The Addams Family" and "Evil Roy Slade" in the TV movie; currently he plays Buddy, the father of Harry Stone (Harry Anderson) on "Night Court."

AS A REGULAR: "I'm Dickens, He's Fenster," ABC, 1962-63; "The Addams Family," ABC, 1964-66; "The Pruitts of Southhampton," ABC, 1967; "McMillan and Wife," NBC, 1972-73; "Operation Petticoat," ABC, 1977-78; "Mary," CBS, 1985-86; "Attack of the Killer Tomatoes," FOX, 1990- .

AND: "Maverick: The Town That Wasn't There," ABC, 1960; "Peter Loves Mary: Wilma's Phantom Lover," CBS, 1960; "The Twilight Zone: A Hundred Yards Over the Rim," CBS, 1961; "The Donna Reed Show: Mouse at Play," ABC, 1961; "Hennesey: Remember Pearl Harbor?," CBS, 1961; "Route 66: Journey to Nineveh," CBS, 1962; "The Farmer's Daughter: Bless Our Happy Home," ABC, 1964; "Destry: The Infernal Triangle," ABC, 1964; "I'll Bet," NBC, 1965; "The Danny Kaye Show," CBS, 1965; "Occasional Wife: The Wedding," NBC, 1966; "The Wild Wild West: Night of the Tartar," CBS, 1967; "Batman: Batman's Anniversary/A Riddling Controversy," ABC, 1967; "Hey, Landlord!: Czech Your Wife, Sir?," NBC, 1967; "The Pat Boone Show," NBC, 1967; "Sheriff Who?," NBC, 1967; "The Flying Nun: Flight of the Dodo Bird," ABC, 1967; "Gunsmoke: Hard-Luck Henry," CBS, 1967; "He & She: The Coming Out Party," CBS, 1967; "CBS Playhouse: The Experiment," CBS, 1969; "Bonanza: Abner Willoughby's Return," NBC, 1969; "Love, American Style: Love and the Intruder," ABC, 1970; "Night Gallery: Pamela's Voice," NBC, 1970; "The Odd Couple: Oscar's New Life," ABC, 1971; "The Doris Day Show: The Father-Son Weekend," CBS, 1971; "The Men From Shiloh: Jump-Up," NBC, 1971; "Love, American Style: Love and the Happy Medium," ABC, 1972; "Night Gallery: The Girl with the Hungry Eyes," NBC, 1972; "The Partridge Family: Diary of a

Mad Millionaire," ABC, 1973; "ABC Afternoon Playbreak: Miss Kline, We Love You," ABC, 1974; "Police Woman: Nothing Left to Lose," NBC, 1975; "Marcus Welby, M.D.: Unindicted Wife," ABC, 1975; "The Bob Crane Show: A Case of Misdiagnosis," NBC, 1975; "Police Story: Firebird," NBC, 1976; "Welcome Back, Kotter: The Museum," ABC, 1976; "The Love Boat: Marooned," ABC, 1978; "Password Plus," NBC, 1980; "Simon & Simon: Revolution #9 1/2," CBS, 1984; "Diff'rent Strokes: A Haunting We Will Go," NBC, 1984; "The Facts of Life: Summer of '84," NBC, 1984; "Riptide: Baxter and Boz," NBC, 1985; "Murder, She Wrote: Joshua Peabody Died Here-Possibly," CBS, 1985; "Murder, She Wrote: A Lady in the Lake," CBS, 1986; "The Love Boat: Egyptian Cruise," ABC, 1986; "Murder, She Wrote: Sticks and Stones," CBS, 1986; "St. Elsewhere: Visiting Daze," NBC, 1987; "Webster: Rich Man, Poor Man," SYN, 1988; "Webster: Simple Gifts," SYN, 1988; "Night Court: The Night Court Before Christmas," NBC, 1988; "Night Court: From Snoop to Nuts," NBC, 1989; "Night Court: Life with Buddy," NBC, 1989; "Night Court: For Love or Money," NBC, 1989.

TV MOVIES AND MINISERIES: "Two on a Bench," ABC, 1971; "Evil Roy Slade," NBC, 1972; "Skyway to Death," ABC, 1974; "Hard Day at Blue Nose," ABC, 1974; "Only with Married Men," ABC, 1974; "The Dream Makers," NBC, 1975.

ASTIN, MACKENZIE

b. *Hollywood, CA, 1973.* Young actor, son of John Astin and Patty Duke; he played Andy on "The Facts of Life."

AS A REGULAR: "The Facts of Life," NBC, 1985-89.

TV MOVIES AND MINISERIES: "I Dream of Jeannie: 15 Years Later," NBC, 1985; "The Facts of Life Down Under," NBC, 1987.

ASTOR, MARY

b. *Lucille Langhanke, Quincy, IL, 1906; d. 1987.* Screen star who made her career in "women's films" of the 1930s and 40s and as the scheming Brigid in "The Maltese Falcon." On television she tended to appear in plays and on dramatic series.

AS A GUEST: "Kraft Television Theatre: The Missing Years," NBC, 1954; "Studio One: Jack Sparling, 46," CBS, 1954; "Danger: Circle of Doom," CBS, 1954; "Best of Broadway: The Philadelphia Story," CBS, 1954; "Philco TV Playhouse: Miss America of 1955," NBC, 1954; "U.S. Steel Hour: The Thief," ABC, 1955; "Kraft Television Theatre: The Hickory Limb," ABC, 1955; "Producers Showcase: The Women," NBC, 1955; "Elgin TV Hour: The $1,000 Window," CBS, 1955; "Front Row

Center: Dinner at Eight," CBS, 1955; "Climax!: Wild Stallion," CBS, 1955; "Studio 57: A Farewell Appearance," SYN, 1956; "Climax!: Nightmare by Day," CBS, 1956; "Star Stage: I Am Her Nurse," NBC, 1956; "Playwrights '56: You and Me and the Gatepost," NBC, 1956; "Matinee Theatre: The Catamaran," NBC, 1956; "Climax!: Phone Call for Matthew Quade," CBS, 1956; "Matinee Theatre: The Lovers," NBC, 1956; "Robert Montgomery Presents: Sunset Boulevard," NBC, 1956; "Playhouse 90: Mr. and Mrs. McAdam," CBS, 1957; "Lux Video Theatre: The Man Who Played God," NBC, 1957; "Climax!: The High Jungle," CBS, 1957; "Playhouse 90: The Troublemakers," CBS, 1957; "Studio One: The Lonely Stage," CBS, 1958; "Dick Powell's Zane Grey Theatre: Black Is for Grief," CBS, 1958; "Playhouse 90: The Return of Ansel Gibbs," CBS, 1958; "Alfred Hitchcock Presents: Mrs. Herman and Mrs. Fennimore," CBS, 1958; "Alfred Hitchcock Presents: The Impossible Dream," CBS, 1959; "Playhouse 90: Diary of a Nurse," CBS, 1959; "G.E. Theatre: The Last Dance," CBS, 1959; "Special Tonight: The Phildelphia Story," NBC, 1959; "U.S. Steel Hour: The Women of Hadley," CBS, 1960; "U.S. Marshal: My Sons," SYN, 1960; "U.S. Steel Hour: Revolt in Hadley," CBS, 1960; "Buick Electra Playhouse: The Snows of Kilimanjaro," CBS, 1960; "Playhouse 90: Journey to the Day," CBS, 1960; "Thriller: Rose's Last Summer," NBC, 1960; "Person to Person," CBS, 1960; "Rawhide: Incident of the Promised Land," CBS, 1961; "Checkmate: A Brooding Fixation," CBS, 1962; "Dr. Kildare: Operation Lazarus," NBC, 1962; "The Defenders: Poltergeist," CBS, 1963; "Dr. Kildare: Face of Fear," CBS, 1963; "Burke's Law: Who Killed Cable Roberts?," ABC, 1963; "Ben Casey: Dispel the Black Cycle," ABC, 1963.

ATES, ROSCOE

b. *Grange, MS, January 20, 1892; d. 1962.* Actor who usually played the dim sidekicks of movie and TV cowboys.

AS A REGULAR: "The Marshal of Gunsight Pass," ABC, 1950.

AND: "G.E. Theatre: Moment of Fear," CBS, 1956; "Buckskin: A Well of Gold," NBC, 1958; "Restless Gun: The Painted Beauty," NBC, 1958; "Alfred Hitchcock Presents: Post Mortem," CBS, 1958; "Wagon Train: The Sacramento Story," NBC, 1958; "Alfred Hitchcock Presents: The Jokester," CBS, 1958; "Alfred Hitchcock Presents: The Desert Shall Blossom," CBS, 1958; "Tales of Wells Fargo: Long Odds," NBC, 1959; "Wagon Train: The Clara Duncan Story," NBC, 1959; "Hotel De Paree: Sundance and the Bare-

Knuckled Fighters," CBS, 1959; "Alfred Hitchcock Presents: Road Hog," CBS, 1959.

ATHERTON, WILLIAM
b. *Orange, CT, July 30, 1947.* Movie actor in intense roles ("To Live and Die in L.A.," "Cousins") who's done some TV.
AS A GUEST: "Murder, She Wrote: Death in the Afternoon," CBS, 1985; "The Twilight Zone: Night of the Meek," CBS, 1985; "The Equalizer: Blood and Wine," CBS, 1987; "Murder, She Wrote: Murder, She Spoke," CBS, 1987; "The Equalizer: Zebra 17," CBS, 1989.
TV MOVIES AND MINISERIES: "Centennial," NBC, 1978-79; "Malibu," ABC, 1983.

ATKINS, CHET
b. *Luttrell, TN, June 20, 1924.* Talented guitarist.
AS A REGULAR: "Grand Ole Opry," ABC, 1955-56.
AND: "Country Music Jubilee," ABC, 1958; "Jubilee USA," ABC, 1958; "Jubilee USA," ABC, 1959; "Today on the Farm," NBC, 1961; "The Jimmy Dean Show," ABC, 1964; "The Mike Douglas Show," SYN, 1968; "Hee Haw," CBS, 1970; "Hee Haw," SYN, 1974; "Como Country-Perry and His Nashville Friends," CBS, 1975; "The Grand Ole Opry at 50," ABC, 1975.

ATKINS, CHRISTOPHER
b. *Rye, NY, February 21, 1961.* Pretty-boy actor who got his big break opposite Brooke Shields in "The Blue Lagoon"; he played Peter Richards, young lover of Sue Ellen (Linda Gray) on "Dallas."
AS A REGULAR: "Dallas," CBS, 1983-84; "Rock 'n' Roll Summer Action," ABC, 1985.
TV MOVIES AND MINISERIES: "Child Bride of Short Creek," NBC, 1981; "Secret Weapons," NBC, 1985.

ATKINS, TOM
b. *Pittsburgh, PA.* Actor usually in stern roles, often as cops; he was the no-nonsense boss of Det. Dennis Becker (Joe Santos) on "The Rockford Files."
AS A REGULAR: "The Rockford Files," NBC, 1974-76; "Serpico," NBC, 1976-77.
AND: "Rhoda: Pop Goes the Question," CBS, 1974; "Hawaii Five-O: Sing a Song of Suspense," CBS, 1975; "The Rookies: Lamb to the Slaughter," ABC, 1976; "The Rockford Files: Battle of Canoga Park," NBC, 1977; "Lou Grant: Fire," CBS, 1979; "Skag: Pilot," NBC, 1980; "Lou Grant: Strike," CBS, 1981; "Lou Grant: Drifters," CBS, 1981; "M*A*S*H: The Tooth Shall Set You Free," CBS, 1982; "Quincy: Guns Don't Die," NBC, 1982; "St. Elsewhere: Dog Day Hospital," NBC, 1983; "The Equalizer: Blood and

Wine," CBS, 1987.
TV MOVIES AND MINISERIES: "G.E. Theatre: Miles to Go Before I Sleep," CBS, 1975; "Shell Game," CBS, 1975; "The Deadly Game," NBC, 1976; "Skeezer," NBC, 1982; "Mickey Spillane's Murder Me, Murder You," CBS, 1983; "Blind Justice," CBS, 1986; "A Stranger Waits," CBS, 1987; "American Playhouse: Lemon Sky," PBS, 1988; "Gang of Four," ABC, 1989; "The Heist," SHO, 1989.

ATKINSON, JAYNE
Actress who played Lindley on "A Year in the Life" and now plays Karen Buckman on "Parenthood."
AS A REGULAR: "A Year in the Life," NBC, 1987-88; "Parenthood," NBC, 1990- .
AND: "Moonlighting: Shirts and Skins," ABC, 1989.
TV MOVIES AND MINISERIES: "A Year in the Life," NBC, 1986; "The Revenge of Al Capone," NBC, 1989.

ATTERBURY, MALCOLM
b. *Philadelphia, PA, February 20, 1907.* Character actor who usually played old timers.
AS A REGULAR: "Thicker Than Water," ABC, 1973; "Apple's Way," CBS, 1974-75.
AND: "Wire Service: Night of August 7," ABC, 1956; "Noah's Ark: Talking Ostrich," NBC, 1957; "Wire Service: Ninety and Nine," ABC, 1957; "The Thin Man: The Paris Pendant," NBC, 1957; "Schlitz Playhouse of Stars: One Way Out," CBS, 1957; "Alcoa Theatre: The Face of Truth," NBC, 1957; "Wagon Train: The Riley Gratton Story," NBC, 1957; "The Twilight Zone: Mr. Denton on Doomsday," CBS, 1959; "Have Gun, Will Travel: Something to Live for," CBS, 1959; "Have Gun, Will Travel: Shot by Request," CBS, 1959; "M Squad: The Velvet Stakeout," NBC, 1960; "Stagecoach West: The Guardian Angels," ABC, 1961; "Straightaway: Heat Wave," ABC, 1961; "The Dick Powell Show: Somebody's Waiting," NBC, 1961; "Window on Main Street: The Charity Drive," CBS, 1961; "Perry Mason: The Case of the Tarnished Trademark," CBS, 1962; "The Andy Griffith Show: The Cow Thief," CBS, 1962; "The Twilight Zone: No Time Like the Past," CBS, 1963; "The Virginian: Strangers at Sundown," NBC, 1963; "The Fugitive: Man on a String," ABC, 1964; "Rawhide: Incident at Boot Hill," CBS, 1965; "The FBI: Pound of Flesh," ABC, 1965; "Hazel: Hazel Sits It Out," CBS, 1965; "The FBI: Collision Course," ABC, 1966; "Run, Buddy, Run: Did You Ever Have One of Those Days?," CBS, 1966; "Judd for the Defense: The Worst of Both Worlds," ABC, 1968; "Gunsmoke: The Good Indian," CBS, 1971; "The Odd Couple: A Barnacle Adventure," ABC, 1973; "The Rookies: Trial by Doubt," ABC, 1974; "The Bob Newhart Show: No Sale," CBS, 1976.

ATWATER, EDITH

b. Chicago, April 22, 1911. Actress who played Judy Carne's mother on "Love on a Rooftop" and the aunt of Parker Stevenson and Shaun Cassidy on "The Hardy Boys Mysteries."

AS A REGULAR: "Love on a Rooftop," ABC, 1966-67; "The Hardy Boys Mysteries," ABC, 1977-78; "Kaz," CBS, 1978-79.

AND: "The Eternal Light: Between Two Eternities," NBC, 1960; "Stoney Burke: A Matter of Pride," ABC, 1962; "The Eleventh Hour: Cry a Little for Mary, Too," NBC, 1962; "The Eleventh Hour: Along About Late in the Afternoon," NBC, 1962; "Hazel: Do Not Disturb the Occupants," CBS, 1965; "Nanny and the Professor: Nanny Will Do," ABC, 1970; "Room 222: Can Nun Be One Too Many?," ABC, 1973; "The Rockford Files: The Four Pound Brick," NBC, 1975; "Family Ties: Auntie Up," NBC, 1985.

AUBERJONOIS, RENE

b. New York City, NY, June 1, 1940. Stage actor who found TV fame as fussbudget Clayton Endicott on "Benson."

AS A REGULAR: "Benson," ABC, 1980-86.

AND: "Night Gallery: Camera Obscura," NBC, 1971; "Love, American Style: Love and the Spaced-Out Chick," ABC, 1973; "The Bob Newhart Show: Shrinks Across the Sea," CBS, 1975; "The Rookies: The Voice of Thunder," ABC, 1975; "The Jeffersons: Harry and Daphne," CBS, 1975; "Rhoda: Two Little Words: Marriage Counselor," CBS, 1976; "Baa Baa Black Sheep: One Little War," NBC, 1976; "Rhoda: The Ultimatum," CBS, 1977; "Rosetti and Ryan: Is There a Lawyer in the House?," NBC, 1977; "The Rockford Files: With the French Heel Back, Can the Nehru Jacket Be Far Behind?," NBC, 1979; "Charlie's Angels: Angels on Skates," ABC, 1979; "Blacke's Magic: Wax Poetic," NBC, 1986; "Murder, She Wrote: Murder in the Minor Key," CBS, 1987; "Murder, She Wrote: Mourning Among the Wisterias," CBS, 1988; "Cadets," ABC, 1988; "L.A. Law: The Son Also Rises," NBC, 1988.

TV MOVIES AND MINISERIES: "Once Upon a Dead Man," NBC, 1971; "The Birdmen," CBS, 1971; "Shirts/Skins," ABC, 1973; "Panache," ABC, 1976; "Best Sellers: The Rhinemann Exchange," NBC, 1977; "The Dark Secret of Harvest Home," NBC, 1978; "The Wild Wild West Revisited," CBS, 1979; "More Wild Wild West," CBS, 1980; "Longarm," ABC, 1988; "A Connecticut Yankee in King Arthur's Court," NBC, 1989.

AUBREY, SKYE

Attractive actress of the seventies; daughter of former CBS president James Aubrey.

AS A GUEST: "Love, American Style: Love and the Good Deal," ABC, 1969; "Marcus Welby, M.D.: The Merely Syndrome," ABC, 1970; "Green Acres: Eb Elopes," CBS, 1970; "The Interns: Some Things Don't Change," CBS, 1970; "The Most Deadly Game: The Classic Burial Position," ABC, 1971; "Marcus Welby, M.D.: A Yellow Bird," ABC, 1972; "Emergency!: Virus," NBC, 1972; "Assignment: Vienna: Hot Potato," ABC, 1972; "Jigsaw: The Bradley Affair," ABC, 1972; "Owen Marshall, Counselor at Law: Who Saw Him Die?," ABC, 1972; "Banyon: The Murder Game," NBC, 1972; "Toma: Stakeout," ABC, 1973; "Love, American Style: Love and the Flying Finletters," ABC, 1974; "Switch: Lady of the Deep," CBS, 1978.

TV MOVIES AND MINISERIES: "Vanished," NBC, 1971; "The City," ABC, 1971; "Ellery Queen: Don't Look Behind You," NBC, 1971; "A Very Missing Person," NBC, 1972; "The Longest Night," ABC, 1972; "The Phantom of Hollywood," CBS, 1974; "In the Steps of a Dead Man," ABC, 1974.

AUBUCHON, JACQUES

Actor who usually plays continental types.

AS A REGULAR: "McHale's Navy," ABC, 1962-64; "Paris 7000," ABC, 1970.

AND: "You Are There: Mr. Christian Sizes the Bounty," CBS, 1956; "The Adventures of Hiram Holliday: Wrong Rembrandt," NBC, 1956; "Lux Video Theatre: Paris Calling," NBC, 1957; "Westinghouse Desilu Playhouse: Bernadette," CBS, 1958; "Bat Masterson: River Boat," NBC, 1959; "Rawhide: Incident at Spanish Rock," CBS, 1959; "Have Gun, Will Travel: Incident at Borrasca End," CBS, 1959; "77 Sunset Strip: Who Killed Cock Robin?," ABC, 1960; "Shirley Temple's Storybook: The Black Arrow," NBC, 1960; "Maverick: Dutchman's Gold," ABC, 1961; "Cheyenne: Duel at Judas Basin," ABC, 1961; "The Outlaws: The Bill Doolin Story," NBC, 1961; "Cheyenne: Stranger in Town," ABC, 1961; "Checkmate: The Crimson Pool," CBS, 1961; "Have Gun, Will Travel: The Kid," CBS, 1961; "Target: The Corruptors: A Man Is Waiting to be Murdered," ABC, 1962; "The Twilight Zone: Valley of the Shadow," CBS, 1963; "The Virginian: The Final Hour," NBC, 1963; "Perry Mason: The Case of the Betrayed Bride," CBS, 1964; "The Man From UNCLE: The Terbur Affair," NBC, 1964; "Daniel Boone: The Sound of Fear," NBC, 1965; "Combat!: Evasion," ABC, 1965; "F Troop: Yellow Bird," ABC, 1966; "Hogan's Heroes: The Battle of Stalag 13," CBS, 1966; "The Man From UNCLE.: The Come with Me to the Casbah Affair," NBC, 1966; "The Monkees: The Spy Who Came in From the Cool," NBC, 1966; "Bewitched: Samantha's Thanksgiving to Remember," ABC, 1967; "Columbo: Publish or Perish," NBC, 1974; "Marcus Welby, M.D.: The

Faith of Childish Things," ABC, 1974; "Hawaii
Five-0: Steal Now, Pay Later," CBS, 1974; "Kung
Fu: Barbary House," ABC, 1975; "Switch: The
Walking Bomb," CBS, 1975; "Remington Steele:
Small Town Steele," NBC, 1984.
TV MOVIES AND MINISERIES: "Black Water Gold,"
ABC, 1970; "September Gun," CBS, 1983.

AUDLEY, ELEANOR
Character actress who specialized in playing
snooty rich ladies, including the mother of Lisa
Douglas (Eva Gabor) on "Green Acres."
AS A REGULAR: "Green Acres," CBS, 1965-71.
AND: "G.E. Theatre: That's the Man," CBS, 1956;
"Father Knows Best: Betty's Birthday," NBC,
1956; "I Love Lucy: Lucy Wants to Move to the
Country," CBS, 1957; "I Love Lucy: Lucy Raises
Tulips," CBS, 1957; "How to Marry a Million-
aire: Society Mother," SYN, 1958; "Have Gun,
Will Travel: Day of the Badman," CBS, 1960;
"Peter Gunn: Witness in the Window," NBC,
1960; "The Joey Bishop Show: Charity Begins at
Home," NBC, 1961; "The Dick Van Dyke Show:
Forty-Four Tickets," CBS, 1961; "The Joey
Bishop Show: Follow That Mink," NBC, 1961;
"The Many Loves of Dobie Gillis: An American
Strategy," CBS, 1962; "The Joey Bishop Show:
The Fashion Show," NBC, 1962; "The Beverly
Hillbillies: Jethro Goes to School," CBS, 1962;
"The Joey Bishop Show: A Woman's Place,"
NBC, 1962; "The Dick Van Dyke Show:
Somebody Has to Play Cleopatra," CBS, 1962;
"Have Gun, Will Travel: The Debutante," CBS,
1963; "The Dick Van Dyke Show: Too Many
Stars," CBS, 1963; "The Beverly Hillbillies: Elly
Needs a Maw," CBS, 1963; "McHale's Navy:
Marryin' Chuck," ABC, 1964; "The Beverly
Hillbillies: Jethro's Graduation," CBS, 1964;
"The Farmer's Daughter: Scandal in Washing-
ton," ABC, 1964; "Mr. Ed: Animal Jury," CBS,
1965; "The Farmer's Daughter: Katy's Cam-
paign," ABC, 1965; "The Man From UNCLE:
The Love Affair," NBC, 1965; "The Smothers
Brothers Show: The Rise and Fall of the Wedding
Cake," CBS, 1965; "Honey West: Little Green
Robin Hood," ABC, 1966; "Pistols 'n' Petticoats:
No Sale," CBS, 1966; "Love on a Rooftop: The
Fifty Dollar Misunderstanding," ABC, 1966; "My
Three Sons: Instant Co-Worker," CBS, 1969.

AUER, MISCHA
*b. Mischa Ounskowski, St. Petersburg, Russia,
November 17, 1905; d. 1967.* Pop-eyed, dark-
featured actor usually in comic roles.
AS A GUEST: "Westinghouse Desilu Playhouse:
Ballad for a Bad Man," CBS, 1959; "The
Dennis O'Keefe Show: Maid to Order,"
CBS, 1960; "Special Tonight: Ninotchka,"
ABC, 1960; "The Mike Douglas Show,"
SYN, 1964.

AUMONT, JEAN-PIERRE
*b. Jean-Pierre Salomons, Paris, France,
January 5, 1913.* Actor usually in sensitive,
romantic roles.
AS A GUEST: "Celanese Theatre: No Time for
Comedy," ABC, 1951; "Robert Montgomery
Presents: A Christmas Gift," NBC, 1951;
"Goodyear Theatre: A Softness in the Wind,"
NBC, 1952; "Studio One: Letter to an
Unknown Woman," CBS, 1952; "Omnibus:
Arms and the Man," CBS, 1953; "Philco TV
Playhouse: The Way of the Eagle," NBC,
1953; "Orient Express: European Edition,"
SYN, 1954; "Climax!: The Sound of Silence,"
CBS, 1956; "Studio 57: Integrity," SYN, 1956;
"Errol Flynn Theatre: First Come, First
Loved," SYN, 1957; "Arthur Murray Party,"
NBC, 1957; "Kraft Television Theatre: Sing a
Song," NBC, 1957; "Playhouse 90: Word From
a Sealed-Off Box," CBS, 1958; "U.S. Steel
Hour: Family Happiness," CBS, 1959; "Arthur
Murray Party," NBC, 1959; "Person to
Person," CBS, 1959; "Arthur Murray Party,"
NBC, 1960; "What's My Line?," CBS, 1960;
"The Jack Paar Show," NBC, 1960; "The
Loretta Young Show: The Eternal Now," NBC,
1960; "Startime: The Nanette Fabray Show-So
Help Me, Aphrodite," NBC, 1960; "U.S. Steel
Hour: The Impostor," CBS, 1960; "Here's
Hollywood," NBC, 1961; "Theatre '62: The
Spiral Staircase," NBC, 1961; "Theatre '62:
Intermezzo," NBC, 1961; "Password," CBS,
1961; "Walt Disney's Wonderful World of
Color: The Horse Without a Head," NBC,
1963; "The Patty Duke Show: The French
Teacher," ABC, 1963; "The Mike Douglas
Show," SYN, 1964; "The Name of the Game:
The White Birch," NBC, 1968; "Starsky and
Hutch: Murder at Sea," ABC, 1976; "The Love
Boat: The Reunion," ABC, 1979; "Simon &
Simon: C'est Simon," CBS, 1984.
TV MOVIES AND MINISERIES: "Beggarman, Thief,"
NBC, 1979; "The Memory of Eva Ryker,"
CBS, 1980; "A Time for Miracles," ABC,
1980; "Melba," PBS, 1989; "Masterpiece
Theatre: A Tale of Two Cities," PBS, 1989.

AUSTIN, GENE
Country-western singer of the thirties who
enjoyed a brief career revival after his life story
was dramatized in the fifties.
AS A GUEST: "Goodyear TV Playhouse: The Gene
Austin Story," NBC, 1957; "The Ed Sullivan
Show," CBS, 1957; "The Big Record," CBS,
1957.
* George Grizzard played Austin in "The Gene
Austin Story."

AUSTIN, KAREN
Actress who played Lana, the first clerk on
"Night Court."

AS A REGULAR: "The Quest," ABC, 1982; "Night Court," NBC, 1984.

AS A GUEST: "Happy Days: Kid Stuff," ABC, 1978; "The Rockford Files: White on White and Nearly Perfect," NBC, 1978; "Three's Company: Chrissy's Cousin," ABC, 1980; "Hill Street Blues: Blood Money," NBC, 1981; "Quincy: The Shadow of Death," NBC, 1982; "Three's Company: Jack's 10," ABC, 1982; "St. Elsewhere: Give the Boy a Hand," NBC, 1985; "The Twilight Zone: A Matter of Minutes," CBS, 1986; "L.A. Law: Simian Enchanted Evening," NBC, 1986; "L.A. Law: Raiders of the Lost Bark," NBC, 1986; "Jake and the Fatman: Pilot," CBS, 1987; "Columbo: Columbo Goes to the Guillotine," ABC, 1989.

TV MOVIES AND MINISERIES: "Assassin," CBS, 1986; "Penalty Phase," CBS, 1986; "When the Time Comes," ABC, 1987; "Laura Lansing Slept Here," NBC, 1988; "Two of a Kind: The Case of the Hillside Stranglers," NBC, 1989.

AUSTIN, PAMELA

Young actress of the sixties, best known as the "Dodge Rebellion" girl ("The Dodge Rebellion wants you!") in TV commercials.

AS A GUEST: "The Adventures of Ozzie and Harriet: Rick Sends a Picture," ABC, 1962; "The Adventures of Ozzie and Harriet: Any Date in a Storm," ABC, 1963; "The Virginian: It Takes a Big Man," NBC, 1963; "The Twilight Zone: Number Twelve Looks Just Like You," CBS, 1964; "The Bing Crosby Show: Bugged by the Love Bugs," ABC, 1965; "The Bing Crosby Show: Are Parents People?," ABC, 1965; "The Bing Crosby Show: The Image," ABC, 1965; "My Three Sons: Robbie and the Chorus Girl," CBS, 1965; "The Wild Wild West: The Night of the Whirring Death," CBS, 1966; "The Virginian: The Girl on the Glass Mountain," NBC, 1966; "Love, American Style: Love and the Phone Booth," ABC, 1969; "Columbo: Blueprint for Murder," NBC, 1972.

TV MOVIES AND MINISERIES: "Evil Roy Slade," NBC, 1972.

AUSTIN, TERI

b. Canada, April 17, 1959. Actress who played Jill Bennett on "Knots Landing."

AS A REGULAR: "Knots Landing," CBS, 1985-89.

AND: "Free Spirit: Guess Who's Staying for Dinner," ABC, 1989.

TV MOVIES AND MINISERIES: "False Witness," NBC, 1989.

AUTRY, ALAN

Beefy actor who plays good old boy Bubba on "In the Heat of the Night"; no relation to Gene Autry.

AS A REGULAR: "In the Heat of the Night," NBC, 1988- .

AND: "Cheers: The Boys in the Bar," NBC, 1983; "The A-Team: Labor Pains," NBC, 1983; "Webster: How the West Was Won," ABC, 1985; "St. Elsewhere: Out on a Limb," NBC, 1986; "Newhart: Will the Real Dick Loudon Please Shut Up," CBS, 1986; "The A-Team: Quarterback Sneak," NBC, 1986; "The Facts of Life: Peeksill Law," NBC, 1988.

TV MOVIES AND MINISERIES: "Blue de Ville," NBC, 1986; "Destination: America," ABC, 1987; "Proud Men," ABC, 1987; "Street of Dreams," CBS, 1988.

AUTRY, GENE

b. Tioga, TX, September 29, 1907. Cowboy actor and tycoon.

AS A REGULAR: "The Gene Autry Show," CBS, 1950-56.

AND: "The Steve Allen Show," NBC, 1956; "The Big Record," CBS, 1957; "Wide, Wide World: The Western," NBC, 1958; "Arthur Murray Party," NBC, 1959; "Steve Allen Plymouth Show," NBC, 1959; "Person to Person," CBS, 1960; "Summer Sports Spectacular: Birth of a Ball Club," CBS, 1961; "The Mike Douglas Show," SYN, 1967.

AVALON, FRANKIE

b. Francis Thomas Avallone, Philadelphia, PA, September 18, 1940. Teen idol of the fifties and star of sixties beach movies who still shows up occasionally on the tube.

AS A REGULAR: "Easy Does It ... Starring Frankie Avalon," CBS, 1976.

AND: "American Bandstand," ABC, 1957; "The Big Record," CBS, 1958; "The Perry Como Show," NBC, 1958; "The Dick Clark Saturday Night Beechnut Show," ABC, 1958; "The Dick Clark Saturday Night Beechnut Show," ABC, 1959; "The Dick Clark Saturday Night Beechnut Show," ABC, 1960; "Coke Time," ABC, 1960; "Perry Como's Kraft Music Hall," NBC, 1960; "Shirley Temple's Storybook: Emmy Lou," NBC, 1960; "The Spirit of the Alamo," ABC, 1960; "The Chevy Show: Four in One," NBC, 1961; "My Sister Eileen: Ruth Becomes a Success," CBS, 1961; "Dinah Shore Special," NBC, 1961; "The New Steve Allen Show," ABC, 1961; "Here's Hollywood," NBC, 1962; "The Eleventh Hour: A Tumble From a High White Horse," NBC, 1963; "The Patty Duke Show: How to Be Popular," ABC, 1963; "Rawhide: Incident at Farragut Pass," CBS, 1963; "Burke's Law: Who Killed Cynthia Royal?," ABC, 1963; "Mr. Novak: A Thousand Voices," NBC, 1963; "Mr. Novak: A Thousand Voices," NBC, 1963; "Burke's Law: Who Killed the Strangler?," ABC, 1965; "American Bandstand," ABC, 1965; "Hullaba-loo," NBC, 1965; "The Bing Crosby Show: The

Keefers Come Calling," ABC, 1965; "Combat!: Brother, Brother," ABC, 1965; "The Patty Duke Show: A Foggy Day in Brooklyn Heights," ABC, 1965; "The Steve Lawrence Show," CBS, 1965; "The Lucy Show: Lucy the Star Maker," CBS, 1967; "Off to See the Wizard: Who's Afraid of Mother Goose?," ABC, 1967; "Hollywood Squares," NBC, 1968; "The Jackie Gleason Show," CBS, 1968; "It Takes a Thief: A Friend in the Deep," ABC, 1969; "Love, American Style: Love and the Tuba," ABC, 1971; "The Tonight Show Starring Johnny Carson," NBC, 1972; "The Saga of Sonora," NBC, 1973; "Here's Lucy: The Carters Meet Frankie Avalon," CBS, 1973; "Police Story: Requiem for C.Z. Smith," NBC, 1974; "The Sonny Comedy Revue," ABC, 1974; "The Merv Griffin Show," SYN, 1975; "Dinah!," SYN, 1976; "$weepstake$: Dewey and Harold and Sarah and Maggie," NBC, 1979; "American Bandstand's 33 1/3 Anniversary," ABC, 1985; "On Stage at Wolf Trap: The Golden Boys of Bandstand," PBS, 1986.

AVALOS, LUIS
b. *Havana, Cuba*. Slight, bald actor usually in comic roles.
AS A REGULAR: "The Electric Company," PBS, 1970-80; "Highcliffe Manor," NBC, 1979; "Condo," ABC, 1983; "E/R," CBS, 1984-85; "I Had Three Wives," CBS, 1985; "You Again?," NBC, 1986-87.
AND: "Barney Miller: Chase," ABC, 1977; "The Jeffersons: Joltin' George," CBS, 1979; "Barney Miller: Bones," ABC, 1982; "Benson: It Ain't Sheik," ABC, 1983; "CBS Summer Playhouse: Some Kinda Woman," CBS, 1988; "Full House: Luck Be a Lady," ABC, 1989.
TV MOVIES AND MINISERIES: "Long Journey Back," ABC, 1978; "Ghost Fever," CBS, 1985; "Fresno," CBS, 1986.

AVERBACK, HY
b. *Minneapolis, MN, 1920*. Former radio announcer and comic actor who turned to directing.
AS A REGULAR: "The Tonight Show (Tonight)," NBC, 1955; "Our Miss Brooks," CBS, 1955-56; "NBC Comedy Hour," NBC, 1956.
AND: "I Love Lucy: The Hedda Hopper Story," CBS, 1955; "Love That Jill: Find Your Perfect Mate," ABC, 1958; "The Jack Paar Show," NBC, 1958; "Columbo: Suitable for Framing," NBC, 1971.
AS DIRECTOR-PRODUCER: "The Real McCoys," ABC, 1957-60; "The Tom Ewell Show," CBS, 1960-61; "Mrs. G. Goes to College (The Gertrude Berg Show)," CBS, 1961-62; "Columbo: Suitable for Framing," NBC, 1971; "M*A*S*H," CBS, 1972-82; "Columbo: A Stitch in Crime," NBC, 1973.

AVERY, PHYLLIS
b. *New York City, NY, November 14, 1924*. All-purpose actress of fifties TV; she played George Gobel's wife Alice for a time on his variety show.
AS A REGULAR: "The Ray Milland Show (Meet Mr. McNutley)," CBS, 1953-55; "The George Gobel/Eddie Fisher Show," NBC, 1957-59; "Clear Horizon," CBS, 1960-61, 1962; "Mr. Novak," NBC, 1964-65.
AND: "The Unexpected: House of Shadows," NBC, 1952; "The Millionaire: The Story of Vickie Lawson," CBS, 1955; "Schlitz Playhouse of Stars: The Girl Who Scared Men Off," CBS, 1955; "Schlitz Playhouse of Stars: Midnight Kill," CBS, 1955; "Schlitz Playhouse of Stars: Christmas Guest," CBS, 1955; "Playhouse 90: The Jet-Propelled Couch," CBS, 1957; "Perry Mason: The Case of the Half-Wakened Wife," CBS, 1957; "Broken Arrow: The Teacher," ABC, 1957; "Trackdown: Look for the Woman," CBS, 1957; "Studio 57: A Little Care," SYN, 1957; "Studio One: The Other Place," CBS, 1958; "G.E. Theatre: Silent Ambush," CBS, 1958; "Schlitz Playhouse of Stars: Bluebeard's Seventh Wife," CBS, 1958; "The Millionaire: Millionaire Jim Hayes," CBS, 1959; "The Deputy: Queen Bea," NBC, 1960; "Peter Gunn: Send a Thief," NBC, 1960; "Rawhide: Incident in No Man's Land," CBS, 1960; "Laramie: Ride Into Darkness," NBC, 1960; "Assignment: Underwater: The Sea Cave," SYN, 1961; "Comedy Spot: I Love My Doctor," CBS, 1962; "Alcoa Premiere: Guest in the House," ABC, 1962; "Sam Benedict: The View From an Ivory Tower," NBC, 1962; "Laramie: The Fugitives," NBC, 1963; "The Virginian: If You Have Tears," NBC, 1963; "Dr. Kildare: Four Feet in the Morning," NBC, 1963; "The Eleventh Hour: Four Feet in the Morning," NBC, 1963; "The Greatest Show on Earth: Man in a Hole," ABC, 1964; "Vacation Playhouse: The Human Comedy," CBS, 1964; "Bob Hope Chrysler Theatre: Massacre at Ft. Phil Kearney," NBC, 1966; "All in the Family: Edith's Conversion," CBS, 1973; "Maude: Walter's Crisis," CBS, 1976.
TV MOVIES AND MINISERIES: "The Last Child," ABC, 1971.

AVERY, TOL
d. *1973*. Heavyset character actor who often played cops or other stern roles; on an episode of "Gomer Pyle, USMC" he played the macho father of Lou Ann Poovie (Elizabeth MacRae), who thought Gomer was a sissy boy.
AS A REGULAR: "The Thin Man," NBC, 1957-58; "Slattery's People," CBS, 1964-65.
AND: "Science Fiction Theatre: The World Below," SYN, 1955; "M Squad: The System," NBC, 1958; "Maverick: Maverick Springs," ABC, 1959; "Bourbon Street Beat: Key to the

City," ABC, 1960; "Bourbon Street Beat: False Identity," ABC, 1960; "Johnny Midnight: Golf Clubbed," SYN, 1960; "Maverick: Last Wire From Stop Gap," ABC, 1960; "Hawaiian Eye: Talk and You're Dead," ABC, 1961; "Maverick: Maverick at Law," ABC, 1961; "The Virginian: If You Have Tears," NBC, 1963; "The Eleventh Hour: Who Chopped Down the Cherry Tree?," NBC, 1964; "The Andy Griffith Show: The Shoplifters," CBS, 1964; "Profiles in Courage: The Oscar W. Underwood Story," NBC, 1964; "The Rogues: Bless You, G. Carter Huntington," NBC, 1965; "Gomer Pyle, USMC: Gomer Minds His Sergeants' Car," CBS, 1965; "Batman: The Joker Trumps an Ace/Batman Sets the Pace," ABC, 1966; "My Three Sons: Our Boy in Washington," CBS, 1966; "The Smothers Brothers Show: His Honor the Crook," CBS, 1966; "F Troop: The Ballot of Corporal Agarn," ABC, 1966; "Batman: King Tut's Coup/Batman's Waterloo," ABC, 1967; "Gomer Pyle, USMC: The Better Man," CBS, 1967; "Dragnet: The Big Badge," NBC, 1967; "Mannix: Fear I to Fall," CBS, 1968; "The FBI: The Flaw," ABC, 1968; "The FBI: Journey Into Night," ABC, 1969; "Here's Lucy: Lucy Cuts Vincent's Price," CBS, 1970; "Love, American Style: Love and the Hypnotist," ABC, 1970; "Mannix: Round Trip to Nowhere," CBS, 1970; "Room 222: I Gave My Love," ABC, 1972.
TV MOVIES AND MINISERIES: "Set This Town on Fire," NBC, 1973.

AXTON, HOYT
b. Duncan, OK, March 25, 1938. Deep-voiced singer and songwriter who often plays lovable, bearish types.
AS A REGULAR: "The Rousters," NBC, 1983-84; "Domestic Life," CBS, 1984.
AND: "Hootenanny," ABC, 1964; "I Dream of Jeannie: Fastest Gun in the East," NBC, 1966; "The Iron Horse: Right of Way Through Paradise," ABC, 1966; "McCloud: The Moscow Connection," NBC, 1977; "WKRP in Cincinnati: I Do, I Do-For Now," CBS, 1979; "The Tonight Show Starring Johnny Carson," NBC, 1980; "Star Search," SYN, 1985; "Diff'rent Strokes: A Camping We Will Go," NBC, 1985; "Murder, She Wrote: Coal Miner's Slaughter," CBS, 1988; "Doodle's," ABC, 1988.
TV MOVIES AND MINISERIES: "Dallas: The Early Years," CBS, 1986; "Guilty of Innocence: The Lenell Geter Story," CBS, 1987; "Christmas Comes to Willow Creek," CBS, 1987; "Desperado: Avalanche at Devil's Ridge," NBC, 1988.

AYKROYD, DAN
b. Ottawa, Canada, July 1, 1952. Gifted comic performer of seventies TV.

AS A REGULAR AND WRITER: "Saturday Night Live," NBC, 1975-79.
AND: "Saturday Night Live's 15th Anniversary," NBC, 1989.
* Emmies: 1977.

AYRES, LEAH
Attractive young actress often in temptress roles; she played Valerie Bryson on "The Edge of Night."
AS A REGULAR: "The Edge of Night," ABC, 1981-83; "9 to 5," ABC, 1983.
AND: "The Love Boat: For Better or Worse," ABC, 1984; "The A-Team: Double Heat," NBC, 1984; "The Love Boat: Country Blues," ABC, 1985; "St. Elsewhere: Sanctuary," NBC, 1985; "St. Elsewhere: Loss of Power," NBC, 1985; "St. Elsewhere: To Tell the Truth," NBC, 1986; "St. Elsewhere: Family Ties," NBC, 1986; "St. Elsewhere: Family Feud," NBC, 1986; "21 Jump Street: Don't Pet the Teacher," FOX, 1987; "Who's the Boss?: Heather Can Wait," ABC, 1989.
TV MOVIES AND MINISERIES: "Police Story: The Watch Commander," ABC, 1988.

AYRES, LEW
b. Minneapolis, MN, December 28, 1908.
AS A REGULAR: "Frontier Justice," CBS, 1958; "Lime Street," ABC, 1985.
AND: "Omnibus: Nothing So Monstrous," CBS, 1954; "Screen Directors Playhouse: One Against Many," NBC, 1956; "Ford Theatre: Measure of Faith," ABC, 1956; "Dick Powell's Zane Grey Theatre: Unrelenting Sky," CBS, 1956; "Playhouse 90: The Family Nobody Wanted," CBS, 1956; "Westinghouse Desilu Playhouse: The Case for Dr. Mudd," CBS, 1958; "Pursuit: The Silent Night," CBS, 1958; "Alcoa Theatre: Cpl. Hardy," NBC, 1959; "Dick Powell's Zane Grey Theatre: A Man to Look Up To," CBS, 1960; "Route 66: The Man on the Monkey Board," CBS, 1960; "Saints and Sinners: Judgment in Jazz Alley," NBC, 1962; "Laramie: Time of the Traitor," NBC, 1962; "Channing: A Rich, Famous, Glamorous Folk Singer Like Me," ABC, 1964; "Ben Casey: For a Just Man Falleth Seven Times," ABC, 1964; "Kraft Suspense Theatre: Kill No More," NBC, 1965; "I Spy: Tiger," NBC, 1966; "The FBI: The Tormentors," ABC, 1966; "The Big Valley: Presumed Dead," ABC, 1968; "The Doris Day Show: Doris Hires a Millioniare," CBS, 1970; "My Three Sons: Mister X," CBS, 1970; "The Doris Day Show: Doris Leaves Today's World," CBS, 1970; "The Men From Shiloh: The Price of the Hanging," NBC, 1970; "San Francisco International Airport: Supersonic Transport," NBC, 1970; "The Interns: The Guardian," CBS, 1971; "The Streets of San Francisco: The House on Hyde Street," ABC, 1973; "Hawaii Five-O: Anyone Can Build a

Bomb," CBS, 1973; "Hawkins: Blood Feud," CBS, 1973; "Columbo: Mind Over Mayhem," NBC, 1974; "The Magician: The Illusion of the Evil Spikes," NBC, 1974; "Kung Fu: The Vanishing Image," ABC, 1974; "McMillan and Wife: Requiem for a Bride," NBC, 1975; "The Mary Tyler Moore Show: Mary and the Sexagenarian," CBS, 1977; "The Love Boat: A Frugal Pair," ABC, 1981; "Magnum, P.I.: The Curse of the King Kamahameha Club," CBS, 1981; "Little House: A New Beginning: Welcome to Olsenville," NBC, 1982; "Quincy: The Law Is a Fool," NBC, 1983; "Cagney & Lacey: Old Flames," CBS, 1988; "Highway to Heaven: Goodbye, Mr. Zelinka," NBC, 1989; "L.A. Law: Leave It to Geezer," NBC, 1989.

TV MOVIES AND MINISERIES: "Hawaii Five-O," CBS, 1968; "Marcus Welby, M.D.," ABC, 1969; "Earth II," ABC, 1971; "She Waits," CBS, 1972; "The Strangler," NBC, 1973; "The Questor Tapes," NBC, 1974; "Heat Wave," ABC, 1974; "Francis Gary Powers: The True Story of the U-2 Spy Incident," NBC, 1976; "Suddenly, Love," NBC, 1978; "Reunion," CBS, 1980; "Under Siege," NBC, 1986; "Cast the First Stone," NBC, 1989.

AZZARA, CANDY

b. Brooklyn, NY, May 18, 1947. Blonde actress usually in Bronx-accented, good-hearted dame roles.

AS A REGULAR: "Calucci's Department," CBS, 1973; "Rhoda," CBS, 1974-75; "Soap," ABC, 1979.

AND: "Kojak: Close Cover Before Killing," CBS, 1975; "Barney Miller: The Layoff," ABC, 1975; "The Montefuscos: Nunzie's Girl," NBC, 1975; "Barney Miller: Bus Stop," ABC, 1976; "Kojak: Caper on a Quiet Street," CBS, 1977; "Rhoda: The Jack Story," CBS, 1978; "Turnabout: Crass Reunion," NBC, 1979; "House Calls: Paging Dr. Michaels," CBS, 1979; "The Merv Griffin Show," SYN, 1980; "Barney Miller: Dietrich's Arrest," ABC, 1980; "Tenspeed and Brown Shoe: Loose Larry's List of Losers," ABC, 1980; "CHiPS: Satan's Angels," NBC, 1980; "The Love Boat: Venetian Love Song," ABC, 1982; "E/R: Both Sides Now," CBS, 1985; "Murder, She Wrote: Mr. Penroy's Vacation," CBS, 1988.

TV MOVIES AND MINISERIES: "Love Boat II," ABC, 1977; "Divorce Wars: A Love Story," ABC, 1982.

B

BABCOCK, BARBARA

b. February 27, 1937. Actress best known for her Emmy-winning role as Grace Gardner, lover of Phil Esterhaus (Michael Conrad) on "Hill Street Blues"; she also played Liz Craig on "Dallas."

AS A REGULAR: "Search for Tomorrow," CBS, 1976; "Dallas," CBS, 1978-82; "Hill Street Blues," NBC, 1981-85; "The Four Seasons," CBS, 1984; "Mr. Sunshine," ABC, 1986; "The Law and Harry McGraw," CBS, 1987-88.

AND: "Our American Heritage: Gentleman's Decision," NBC, 1961; "The Many Loves of Dobie Gillis: The Devil and Dobie Gillis," CBS, 1963; "The Munsters: Bats of a Feather," CBS, 1965; "Mission: Impossible: The Cardinal," CBS, 1968; "Mannix: In Need of a Friend," CBS, 1968; "Hogan's Heroes: Happy Birthday, Dear Hogan," CBS, 1969; "Family Affair: Oh, to Be in England," CBS, 1969; "The Streets of San Francisco: The Cat's Paw," ABC, 1975; "The Rockford Files: Irving the Explainer," NBC, 1977; "McMillan: Affair of the Heart," NBC, 1977; "The White Shadow: Mainstream," CBS, 1979; "Paris: Pilot," CBS, 1979; "Benson: Katie's Romance," ABC, 1981; "McClain's Law: A Time of Peril," NBC, 1981; "Taxi: Like Father, Like Son," ABC, 1981; "Best of the West: Frog Gets Lucky," ABC, 1982; "Cheers: Now Pitching: Sam Malone," NBC, 1983; "Hotel: Promises," ABC, 1985; "Empty Nest: The First Time Again," NBC, 1989.

TV MOVIES AND MINISERIES: "The Last Child," ABC, 1971; "Survival of Dana," CBS, 1979; "Memories Never Die," CBS, 1982; "Quarterback Princess," CBS, 1983; "Attack on Fear," CBS, 1984; "News at Eleven," CBS, 1986.

* Emmies: 1981.

BACALL, LAUREN

b. Betty Joan Perske, New York City, NY, September 16, 1924. Film actress and widow of Humphery Bogart who shows up on TV now and then.

AS A GUEST: "Light's Diamond Jubilee: The Girls in Their Summer Dresses," ABC, CBS, NBC, 1954; "Producers Showcase: The Petrified Forest," NBC, 1955; "Ford Star Jubilee: Blithe Spirit," CBS, 1956; "I've Got a Secret," CBS, 1960; "Perry Como's Kraft Music Hall," NBC, 1963; "Dr. Kildare: The Oracle," NBC, 1963; "Get the Message," ABC, 1964; "Mr. Broadway: Something to Sing About," CBS, 1964; "Bob Hope Chrysler Theatre: Double Jeopardy," NBC, 1965; "Password," CBS, 1965; "The Match Game," NBC, 1965; "ABC Stage '67: How to Tell Your Past, Present and Maybe Even Your Future Through Social Dancing," ABC, 1967; "Applause!," CBS, 1973; "Happy Endings: A Commercial Break," ABC, 1975; "The Rockford Files: Lions, Tigers, Monkeys and Dogs," NBC, 1979; "Great Performances: Bacall on Bogart," PBS, 1988; "Late Night with David Letterman," NBC, 1989.

TV MOVIES AND MINISERIES: "Dinner at Eight," TNT, 1989.

BACH, CATHERINE

b. Warren, OH, March 1, 1954. Young actress who played the skimpily dressed Daisy Duke on "The Dukes of Hazzard"; on "Trying Times" she played a bubbleheaded TV sexpot.

AS A REGULAR: "The Dukes of Hazzard," CBS, 1979-85.

AND: "The Merv Griffin Show," SYN, 1980; "The Love Boat: Witness for the Prosecution," ABC, 1980; "Dance Fever," SYN, 1981; "The Love Boat: Whose Dog Is It, Anyway?" ABC, 1983; "Trying Times: Drive, She Said," PBS, 1988.

TV MOVIES AND MINISERIES: "Strange New World," ABC, 1975.

BACKUS, JIM

b. James Gilmore Backus, Cleveland, OH, February 25, 1913; d. 1989. Character actor was the voice of Mr. Magoo, the husband of Joan Davis on "I Married Joan" and millionaire Thurston Howell III on "Gilligan's Island."

AS A REGULAR: "Hollywood House," ABC, 1949-50; "I Married Joan," NBC, 1952-55; "The Jim Backus Show (Hot Off the Wire)," SYN, 1960-61; "Talent Scouts," CBS, 1962; "The Famous Adventures of Mr. Magoo," NBC, 1964-65; "Gilligan's Island," CBS, 1964-67; "Continental Showcase," CBS, 1966; "Blondie," CBS, 1968-69; "The Good Guys," CBS, 1969; "The New Adventures of Gilligan," ABC, 1974-76.

AND: "TV Reader's Digest: If I Were Rich," ABC, 1955; "Front Row Center: Uncle Barney," CBS, 1956; "Warner Bros. Presents Conflict: Survival," ABC, 1956; "The Pied Piper of Hamelin," NBC, 1957; "To Tell the Truth," CBS, 1958; "Studio One: The McTaggart Succession," CBS, 1958; "The Gale Storm Show: Susannah Plays Cupid," CBS, 1958; "Playhouse 90: Free Weekend," CBS, 1958; "The Today Show," NBC, 1958; "The George Gobel Show," NBC, 1958; "The Music Shop," NBC, 1959; "The Danny Thomas Show:

The Deerfield Story," CBS, 1960; "Mr. Magoo's Christmas Carol," NBC, 1962; "McKeever and the Colonel: The Millionaire," NBC, 1963; "The Beverly Hillbillies: The Clampetts Entertain," CBS, 1963; "Burke's Law: Who Killed Carrie Cornell?," ABC, 1964; "The du Pont Show: Jeremy Rabbit, the Secret Avenger," NBC, 1964; "Arrest and Trial: Birds of a Feather," ABC, 1964; "Espionage: A Tiny Drop of Poison," NBC, 1964; "Burke's Law: Who Killed Vaudeville?," ABC, 1964; "PDQ," NBC, 1965; "ABC Nightlife," ABC, 1965; "Damn Yankees," NBC, 1967; "Password," CBS, 1967; "Funny You Should Ask," ABC, 1969; "The Wild, Wild West: The Night of the Sabatini Death," CBS, 1969; "Love, American Style: Love and the Understanding," ABC, 1970; "I Dream of Jeannie: Help, Help, a Shark," NBC, 1970; "Uncle Sam Magoo," NBC, 1970; "Love, American Style: Love and the Marriage Counselor," ABC, 1970; "Nanny and the Professor: The Tyrannosaurus Tibia," ABC, 1970; "The Brady Bunch: Grand Canyon or Bust," ABC, 1970; "Love, American Style: Love and the Understanding," ABC, 1970; "Alias Smith and Jones: The Biggest Game in the West," ABC, 1972; "Of Thee I Sing," CBS, 1972; "The Mod Squad: And Once for My Baby," ABC, 1973; "Match Game '73," CBS, 1973; "Medical Center: The Vortex," CBS, 1973; "The Brady Bunch: The Hustler," ABC, 1974; "The Merv Griffin Show," SYN, 1974; "Marcus Welby, M.D.: Last Flight to Babylon," ABC, 1974; "Yes, Virginia, There Is a Santa Claus," ABC, 1974; "Chico and the Man: The Beard," NBC, 1975; "Kolchak, the Night Stalker: Chopper," ABC, 1975; "Gunsmoke: Brides and Grooms," CBS, 1975; "Police Story: The Return of Joe Forrester," NBC, 1975; "Joe Forrester: Pilot," NBC, 1975; "Ellery Queen: The Mad Tea Party," NBC, 1975; "ABC Afterschool Special: The Amazing Cosmic Adventures of Duffy Moon," ABC, 1976; "Charlie's Angels: Angels on Ice," ABC, 1977; "$weepstake$: Billy, Wally and Ludmilla, and Theodore," NBC, 1979; "Eischied: Angels of Terror," NBC, 1979; "Fantasy Island: Eagleman," ABC, 1980; "St. Elsewhere: Cheek to Cheek," NBC, 1986.

TV MOVIES AND MINISERIES: "Wake Me When the War Is Over," ABC, 1969; "Getting Away From It All," ABC, 1972; "Magic Carpet," NBC, 1972; "The Girl Most Likely To...," ABC, 1973; "Miracle on 34th Street," CBS, 1973; "The Return of Joe Forrester," NBC, 1975; "Rescue From Gilligan's Island," NBC, 1978; "The Castaways on Gilligan's Island," NBC, 1979; "The Rebels," SYN, 1979; "The Harlem Globetrotters on Gilligan's Island," NBC, 1981.

BADDELEY, HERMOINE
b. England, November 13, 1906; d. 1986. Tiny British actress who played the randy Mrs. Naugatuck on "Maude."

AS A REGULAR: "Camp Runamuck," NBC, 1965-66; "The Good Life," NBC, 1971-72; "Maude," CBS, 1974-77.

AND: "Playhouse 90: Dark as the Night," CBS, 1959; "Startime: Dear Arthur," NBC, 1960; "Mr. Novak: Chin Up, Mr. Novak," NBC, 1964; "Bewitched: I Get Your Nannie, You Get My Goat," ABC, 1967; "Batman: The Great Escape/ The Great Train Robbery," ABC, 1968; "Journey to the Unknown: Eve," ABC, 1968; "Night Gallery: A Feast of Blood," NBC, 1972; "Dean Martin's Red Hot Scandals of 1926," NBC, 1976; "Little House on the Prairie: Castoffs," NBC, 1977; "Charlie's Angels: Mother Angel," ABC, 1978; "Little House on the Prairie: The Lake Kezia Monster," NBC, 1979; "$weepstake$: Victor, Billy and Bobby, 'Sometimes,' " NBC, 1979; "Magnum P.I.: The Case of the Red-Faced Thespian," CBS, 1984; "Shadow Chasers: Pilot," ABC, 1985.

TV MOVIES AND MINISERIES: "I Take These Men," CBS, 1983; "This Girl for Hire," CBS, 1983.

BADLER, JANE
b. Long Island, NY. Former soap vixen— Melinda on "One Life to Live" and Natalie on "The Doctors"—best known as hamster-snacking Diana, the sexy alien on "V."

AS A REGULAR: "One Life to Live," ABC, 1977-81, 1983; "The Doctors," NBC, 1981-82; "V," NBC, 1984-85; "Falcon Crest," CBS, 1986-87; "The Highwayman," NBC, 1988; "Mission: Impossible," ABC, 1989-90.

AND: "Blacke's Magic: Ten Tons of Trouble," NBC, 1986; "Murder, She Wrote: Curse of the Daanav," CBS, 1987.

TV MOVIES AND MINISERIES: "V," NBC, 1983; "V: The Final Battle," NBC, 1984; "Penalty Phase," CBS, 1986.

BAER, MAX JR.
b. Oakland, CA, December 4, 1937. Beefy actor who played Jethro on "The Beverly Hillbillies."

AS A REGULAR: "The Beverly Hillbillies," CBS, 1962-71.

AND: "Maverick: The Bundle From Britain," ABC, 1960; "Maverick: A Bullet for the Teacher," ABC, 1960; "77 Sunset Strip: The Corsican Caper," ABC, 1961; "77 Sunset Strip: The Chrome Coffin," ABC, 1961; "Follow the Sun: A Choice of Weapons," ABC, 1962; "It's a Man's World: Drive Over to Exeter," NBC, 1962; "Love, American Style: Love and the Fullback," ABC, 1972; "Love, American Style: Love and the Games People Play," ABC, 1974; "Matt Houston: Return to 'Nam," ABC, 1984.

TV MOVIES AND MINISERIES: "The Birdmen," CBS, 1971.

BAER, PARLEY

b. Florida. Bald, portly character actor who often played exasperated types, including Mayor Stoner of Mayberry on "The Andy Griffith Show"; he's also worked as a circus ringmaster.

AS A REGULAR: "The Adventures of Ozzie and Harriet," ABC, 1955-61; "The Andy Griffith Show," CBS, 1962-63; "The Addams Family," ABC, 1965-66; "The Double Life of Henry Phyfe," ABC, 1966.

AND: "Father Knows Best: A Friend of Old George's," CBS, 1955; "I Love Lucy: Ricky Needs an Agent," CBS, 1955; "The Charlie Farrell Show: Hamburger Heaven," CBS, 1956; "Make Room for Daddy: Problem Father," ABC, 1956; "The Jane Wyman Show: The Hidden People," NBC, 1957; "Matinee Theatre: The Little Minister," NBC, 1957; "Have Gun, Will Travel: Tiger," CBS, 1959; "Phil Silvers Special: The Slowest Gun in the West," CBS, 1960; "Hawaiian Eye: The Classic Cab," ABC, 1961; "Bus Stop: The Runaways," ABC, 1961; "The Rifleman: A Friend in Need," ABC, 1961; "Perry Mason: The Case of the Captain's Coins," CBS, 1962; "Dennis the Menace: Calling All Bird Lovers," CBS, 1962; "Rawhide: Incident at Crooked Hat," CBS, 1963; "Walt Disney's Wonderful World of Color: Bristle Face," NBC, 1964; "77 Sunset Strip: Queen of the Cats," ABC, 1964; "The Outer Limits: Behold, Eck!," ABC, 1964; "The Lucy Show: Lucy the Meter Maid," CBS, 1964; "The Farmer's Daughter: Katy's Castle," ABC, 1965; "F Troop: The 86 Proof Spring," ABC, 1965; "Green Acres: Lisa the Helpmate," CBS, 1965; "The Lucy Show: Lucy the Undercover Agent," CBS, 1965; "Hogan's Heroes: The Scientist," CBS, 1965; "Amos Burke, Secret Agent: A Very Important Russian Is Missing," ABC, 1966; "The Farmer's Daughter: Moe Hill and the Mountains," ABC, 1966; "Petticoat Junction: Jury at the Shady Rest," CBS, 1966; "The Lucy Show: Lucy the Superwoman," CBS, 1966; "Hogan's Heroes: Everyone Has a Brother-in-Law," CBS, 1967; "Bewitched: Cheap, Cheap!," ABC, 1967; "Petticoat Junction: Kate's Day in Court," CBS, 1967; "The FBI: False Witness," ABC, 1967; "The Virginian: A Bad Place to Die," NBC, 1967; "The Virginian: Halfway Back From Hell," NBC, 1969; "Bewitched: Tabitha's Very Own Samantha," ABC, 1970; "Petticoat Junction: Last Train to Pixley," CBS, 1970; "The FBI: The Quest," ABC, 1970; "Mannix: Walk with a Dead Man," CBS, 1970; "The Bill Cosby Show: The Deluge," NBC, 1970; "Here's Lucy: Lucy's Bonus Bounces," CBS, 1971; "The Mod Squad: Color of Laughter, Color of Tears," ABC, 1971; "Bewitched: The Truth, Nothing But the Truth, So Help Me Sam," ABC, 1972; "Apple's Way: The Circus," CBS, 1974; "Three for the Road: Trail of Bigfoot," CBS, 1975; "Lou Grant: Kidnap," CBS, 1979; "Charlie's Angels: Angels at the Altar," ABC, 1979; "Little House on the Prairie: Sweet Sixteen," NBC, 1980; "Lou Grant: Goop," CBS, 1980; "Newhart: But Seriously Beavers," CBS, 1984; "Simon & Simon: The Case of Don Diablo," CBS, 1986; "The Twilight Zone: The Storyteller," CBS, 1986; "Newhart: Much to Do Without Muffin," CBS, 1987; "Life Goes On: The Babysitter," ABC, 1989.

TV MOVIES AND MINISERIES: "Wake Me When the War Is Over," ABC, 1969; "The Over-the-Hill Gang Rides Again," ABC, 1970; "The Sheriff," ABC, 1971; "Punch and Jody," CBS, 1974; "The Time Machine," NBC, 1978; "Norman Rockwell's Breaking Home Ties," ABC, 1987.

BAGGETTA, VINCENT

b. Paterson, NJ, December 7, 1947. Actor who played crime-solving Eddie Capra and was assistant D.A. John Moretti on "The Colbys."

AS A REGULAR: "The Eddie Capra Mysteries," NBC, 1978-79; "Chicago Story," NBC, 1982; "The Colbys," ABC, 1986; "Jack and Mike," ABC, 1986-87.

AND: "The Twilight Zone: The Thirty-Fathom Grave," CBS, 1963; "Actors Company: The Winter's Tale," NET, 1967; "The Rookies: Take Over," ABC, 1974; "Kojak: The Chinatown Murders," CBS, 1974; "Kojak: A Long Way From Times Square," CBS, 1975; "The Rockford Files: Drought at Indianhead River," NBC, 1976; "The Rockford Files: Hotel of Fear," NBC, 1977; "Foul Play: Play It Again, Tuck," ABC, 1981; "Lou Grant: Fireworks," CBS, 1981; "Remington Steele: Steele Away with Me," NBC, 1983; "Hill Street Blues: Nichols From Heaven," NBC, 1984; "Simon & Simon: Reunion at Alcatraz," CBS, 1985; "Murder, She Wrote: Footnote to Murder," CBS, 1985; "Murder, She Wrote: Steal Me a Story," CBS, 1987; "Heartbeat: Where's Solomon When You Need Him?," ABC, 1988.

TV MOVIES AND MINISERIES: "I Want to Keep My Baby," CBS, 1976; "The Chicago Story," NBC, 1981; "The Ordeal of Bill Carney," CBS, 1981; "Doubletake," CBS, 1985; "Perry Mason: The Case of the Murdered Madam," NBC, 1987; "Police Story: The Freeway Killings," NBC, 1987; "Shakedown on the Sunset Strip," CBS, 1988.

BAILEY, F. LEE

b. Waltham, MA, June 10, 1933. Famed attorney who hosted a talk show and two crime-related programs.

AS A REGULAR: "Good Company," ABC, 1967; "Whodunnit?," NBC, 1979; "Lie Detector," SYN, 1983.

BAILEY, G.W.

b. Port Arthur, TX. Curly-haired, bespectacled actor who played Luther Rizzo on "M*A*S*H" and Dr. Hugh Beale on "St. Elsewhere"; in the movies he plays the nemesis of the "Police Academy" misfits.

AS A REGULAR: "M*A*S*H," CBS, 1979-83; "St. Elsewhere," NBC, 1982-83; "Goodnight Beantown," CBS, 1983-84.

AND: "Lou Grant: Fire," CBS, 1979; "Happy Days: Joanie Busts Out," ABC, 1979; "Simon & Simon: Under the Knife," CBS, 1984; "Riptide: Prisoner of War," NBC, 1985; "Simon & Simon: Out-of-Town Brown," CBS, 1985.

TV MOVIES AND MINISERIES: "Murder in Texas," NBC, 1981; "A Winner Never Quits," ABC, 1986; "Downpayment on Murder," NBC, 1987; "War and Remembrance," ABC, 1988, 1989.

BAILEY, JACK

b. Hampton, IA, September 15, 1907. Patronizing game-show host of the fifties and the sixties.

AS A REGULAR: "Place the Face," CBS, 1953-54; "Truth or Consequences," NBC, 1954-56; "Queen for a Day," NBC, 1955-60; ABC, 1960-64.

AND: "The Ford Show," NBC, 1956; "The Ford Show," NBC, 1957; "County Fair," NBC, 1958; "The Ford Show," NBC, 1959; "The Ford Show," NBC, 1960; "Christophers: Social Work," SYN, 1960; "Christophers: Robert E. Lee," SYN, 1960; "The Tonight Show Starring Johnny Carson," NBC, 1962; "Mr. Ed: Stowaway Horse," CBS, 1965; "Batman: Hizzoner the Penguin/Dizzoner the Penguin," ABC, 1966; "Green Acres: His Honor," CBS, 1966; "Gunsmoke: Noose of Gold," CBS, 1967; "Lancer: Little Darling of the Sierras," CBS, 1969; "Marcus Welby, M.D.: A More Exciting Case," ABC, 1972.

BAILEY, PEARL

b. Newport News, VA, March 29, 1918; d. 1990. Singer and comic actress with an ingratiating, no-nonsense manner, "Pearlie Mae" to her fans.

AS A REGULAR: "The Pearl Bailey Show," ABC, 1971.

AND: "The Perry Como Show," NBC, 1956; "The Steve Allen Show," NBC, 1957; "Arthur Murray Party," NBC, 1957; "The Nat King Cole Show," NBC, 1957; "The Perry Como Show," NBC, 1957; "The Perry Como Show," NBC, 1958; "The Big Record," CBS, 1958; "Pat Boone Chevy Showroom," ABC, 1958; "The Big Party," CBS, 1959; "Dinah Shore Chevy Showroom," NBC, 1960; "The Ed Sullivan Show," CBS, 1961; "The Ed Sullivan Show," CBS, 1962; "The Jack Paar Program," NBC, 1963; "The Andy Williams Show," NBC, 1963; "The Ed Sullivan Show," CBS, 1967; "The Mike Douglas Show," SYN, 1968; "The Flip Wilson Show," NBC, 1972; "Hollywood Squares," NBC, 1973; "Hollywood Squares," NBC, 1974; "Bing Crosby and His Friends," CBS, 1974; "Feeling Good," PBS, 1974; "The Merv Griffin Show," SYN, 1975; "Donny and Marie," ABC, 1976; "Hollywood Squares," NBC, 1977; "The John Davidson Show," SYN, 1981; "Silver Spoons: Lulu's Back in Town," NBC, 1984; "Silver Spoons: What's Cookin'?," NBC, 1985.

TV MOVIES AND MINISERIES: "Peter Gunn," ABC, 1989.

BAILEY, RAYMOND

b. San Francisco, CA, 1904; d. 1980. Mustachioed actor who played Mr. Drysdale on "The Beverly Hillbillies."

AS A REGULAR: "My Sister Eileen," CBS, 1960-61; "The Many Loves of Dobie Gillis," CBS, 1961-63; "Margie," ABC, 1961-62; "The Beverly Hillbillies," CBS, 1962-71.

AND: "Gunsmoke: General Parsley Smith," CBS, 1955; "Matinee Theatre: Starmaster," NBC, 1956; "Warner Bros. Presents Conflict: People Against McQuade," ABC, 1956; "Alfred Hitchcock Presents: Disappearing Trick," CBS, 1958; "Goodyear Theatre: Decision by Terror," NBC, 1958; "The Jack Benny Program: Jack Goes to a Nightclub," CBS, 1959; "Yancy Derringer: Mayhem in the Market," CBS, 1959; "The Millionaire: Millionaire Julia Conrad," CBS, 1959; "The Donna Reed Show: A Penny Saved," ABC, 1959; "Bronco: The Burning Springs," ABC, 1959; "The Tom Ewell Show: Tom Cuts Off the Credit," CBS, 1960; "SurfSide 6: Par-a-kee," ABC, 1960; "77 Sunset Strip: The Dresden Doll," ABC, 1960; "The Twilight Zone: Back There," CBS, 1961; "Lassie: The Pigeon," CBS, 1961; "Bachelor Father: Bentley and the Great Debate," NBC, 1961; "Have Gun, Will Travel: Cream of the Jest," CBS, 1962; "Laramie: The Runt," NBC, 1962; "Going My Way: The Parish Car," ABC, 1962; "Bonanza: The Colonel," NBC, 1963; "The Twilight Zone: From Agnes-With Love," CBS, 1964.

BAIN, BARBARA

b. Chicago, IL, September 13, 1931. Emmy-winning actress who played Cinammon Carter on "Mission: Impossible"; she and her husband Martin Landau left the show in a salary dispute.

AS A REGULAR: "Richard Diamond, Private Detective," CBS, 1959; "Mission: Impossible," CBS, 1966-69; "Space: 1999," SYN, 1975-77.

AND: "Alcoa Theatre: Small Bouquet," NBC, 1959; "Perry Mason: The Case of the Wary Wildcatter," CBS, 1960; "The Law and Mr. Jones: Christmas Is a Legal Holiday," ABC, 1960;

"Adventures in Paradise: Nightmare in the Sun," ABC, 1961; "Straightaway: The Craziest Game in Town," ABC, 1962; "Hawaiian Eye: Two Million Too Much," ABC, 1963; "The Many Loves of Dobie Gillis: I Was a Spy for the F.O.B.," CBS, 1963; "The Dick Van Dyke Show: Will You Two Be My Wife?," CBS, 1963; "The Lieutenant: A Touch of Hands," NBC, 1963; "Valentine's Day: The Old School Tie," ABC, 1964; "Summer Playhouse: Young in Heart," CBS, 1964; "My Mother the Car: I'm Through Being a Nice Guy," NBC, 1965; "Get Smart: KAOS in Control," NBC, 1965; "My Mother the Car: Desperate Minutes," NBC, 1966; "Password," CBS, 1966; "Hollywood Squares," NBC, 1968; "The Carol Burnett Show," CBS, 1968; "The Red Skelton Hour," CBS, 1969; "Moonlighting: My Fair David," ABC, 1985; "Scarecrow and Mrs. King: The Kruschev List," CBS, 1987; "Murder, She Wrote: Coal Miner's Slaughter," CBS, 1988.

TV MOVIES AND MINISERIES: "Murder Once Removed," NBC, 1971; "Goodnight My Love," ABC, 1972; "Savage," NBC, 1973; "A Summer Without Boys," ABC, 1973; "The Harlem Globetrotters on Gilligan's Island," NBC, 1981.

* Emmies: 1967, 1968, 1969.

BAIN, CONRAD
b. Canada, February 4, 1923. Bland-looking actor in bland roles, including Dr. Arthur Harmon, neighbor of "Maude" (Beatrice Arthur) and Philip Drummond, adoptive dad of Arnold (Gary Coleman) on "Diff'rent Strokes."

AS A REGULAR: "The Edge of Night," CBS, 1970; "Maude," CBS, 1972-78; "Diff'rent Strokes," NBC, 1978-85; ABC, 1985-86; "Mr. President," FOX, 1987-88.

AND: "Tattletales," CBS, 1974; "Grandpa Goes to Washington: Kelley at the Bat," NBC, 1978; "The Love Boat: Locked Away," ABC, 1978; "The Love Boat: Unmade for Each Other," ABC, 1985.

TV MOVIES AND MINISERIES: "Child Bride of Short Creek," NBC, 1981.

BAINTER, FAY
b. Los Angeles, CA, December 7, 1892; d. 1968. Character actress, usually in matronly roles.

AS A GUEST: "Lux Video Theatre: A Child Is Born," CBS, 1950; "Schlitz Playhouse of Stars: Two Living and One Dead," CBS, 1951; "Robert Montgomery Presents: O Evening Star," NBC, 1952; "Lux Video Theatre: Ile," CBS, 1952; "Schlitz Playhouse of Stars: Jenny," CBS, 1953; "Studio One: Black Rain," CBS, 1953; "Suspense: Career," CBS, 1953; "Robert Montgomery Presents: All Things Glad and Beautiful," NBC, 1953; "Ford Theatre: The Happiest Day," NBC, 1954; "Lux Video Theatre: Shall Not Perish," CBS, 1954; "Hallmark Hall of Fame: The Story of Ruth,"

NBC, 1954; "Ford Theatre: The Unlocked Door," NBC, 1954; "The Web: The Face on the Shadow," CBS, 1954; "Kraft Television Theatre: The Sears Girl," NBC, 1956; "Matinee Theatre: The Book of Ruth," NBC, 1956; "Studio One: The Dark Corner," CBS, 1957; "Adventures in Paradise: Prisoner in Paradise," ABC, 1960; "Art Linkletter's House Party," CBS, 1960; "Thriller: Girl with a Secret," NBC, 1960; "The Donna Reed Show: The Baby Buggy," ABC, 1962; "Dr. Kildare: Sister Mike," NBC, 1963; "Bob Hope Chrysler Theatre: Out on the Outskirts of Town," NBC, 1964; "The Alfred Hitchcock Hour: Power of Attorney," NBC, 1965.

BAIO, JIMMY
b. Brooklyn, NY, March 15, 1963. Former child actor who played Billy Tate on "Soap"; cousin of Scott Baio and brother of Joey.

AS A REGULAR: "Joe and Sons," CBS, 1975-76; "Soap," ABC, 1977-81.

AND: "The Love Boat: Rocky," ABC, 1978; "Dance Fever," SYN, 1980.

BAIO, JOEY
b. Brooklyn, NY, 1957. Former child actor.

AS A REGULAR: "The Hero," NBC, 1966-67.

AND: "The Monkees: Captain Crocodile," NBC, 1967.

BAIO, SCOTT
b. Brooklyn, NY, September 22, 1961. Cousin of Jimmy and Joey; if all goes according to plan, he'll play teen babysitter-butler Charles on "Charles in Charge" until he's about 60. Formerly Chachi, love of Joanie Cunningham (Erin Moran) on "Happy Days."

AS A REGULAR: "Blansky's Beauties," ABC, 1977; "Happy Days," ABC, 1977-84; "Who's Watching the Kids?," NBC, 1978; "Joanie Loves Chachi," ABC, 1982-83; "Charles in Charge," CBS, 1984-85, SYN, 1987- .

AND: "ABC Afterschool Special: Stoned," ABC, 1980; "Hotel: Faith, Hope and Charity," ABC, 1983; "The Fall Guy: Femme Fatale," ABC, 1985; "Full House: Dr. Dare Rides Again," ABC, 1989.

TV MOVIES AND MINISERIES: "The Boy Who Drank Too Much," CBS, 1980; "Senior Trip!," NBC, 1981.

BAKER, ART
b. Arthur Shank, New York City, NY, January 7, 1898; d. 1966. Actor turned fifties emcee; he was Dinah Shore's commercial announcer.

AS A REGULAR: "You Asked for It," DUM, 1950-51, ABC, 1951-58; "Dinah Shore Chevy Show," NBC, 1951-57; "End of the Rainbow," NBC, 1958.

AND: "Adventures in Paradise: The Baby Sitters," ABC, 1962.

BAKER, BLANCHE
  b. New York City, NY, December 20, 1956. Daughter of Carroll Baker; an Emmy winner for "Holocaust."
  AS A GUEST: "The Equalizer: Desperately," CBS, 1986.
  TV MOVIES AND MINISERIES: "Holocaust," NBC, 1978; "Mary and Joseph: A Story of Faith," NBC, 1979; "Embassy," ABC, 1985; "Nobody's Child," CBS, 1986.
  * Emmies: 1978.

BAKER, CARROLL
  b. Johnstown, PA, May 28, 1931. Film starlet of the fifties and sixties ("Baby Doll," "Harlow"); in some TV.
  AS A GUEST: "Danger: Season for Murder," CBS, 1955; "Person to Person," CBS, 1958; "Here's Hollywood," NBC, 1961; "Bob Hope Special," NBC, 1965; "Wide World of Mystery: The Next Victim," ABC, 1975.
  TV MOVIES AND MINISERIES: "Hitler's SS: Portrait in Evil," NBC, 1985; "On Fire," ABC, 1987.

BAKER, CATHY
  b. 1947. Blonde actress who says "That's all!" at the end of every stellar episode of "Hee Haw."
  AS A REGULAR: "Hee Haw," CBS, 1969-71, SYN, 1971- .

BAKER, DIANE
  b. Hollywood, CA, February 25, 1938. Actress in fifties and sixties television who's now turned to directing and writing.
  AS A REGULAR: "Here We Go Again," ABC, 1973.
  AND: "Della," SYN, 1959; "Playhouse 90: In Lonely Expectation," CBS, 1959; "Buick Electra Playhouse: The Killers," CBS, 1959; "Du Pont Show of the Month: Arrowsmith," CBS, 1960; "Adventures in Paradise: Passage to Tua," ABC, 1960; "Follow the Sun: Journey Into Darkness," ABC, 1961; "Bus Stop: The Resurrection of Annie Ahern," ABC, 1961; "Dr. Kildare: The Heart, An Imperfect Machine," NBC, 1963; "Mr. Novak: A Feeling for Friday," NBC, 1963; "Wagon Train: The Alice Whitetree Story," ABC, 1964; "Bob Hope Chrysler Theatre: Perilous Times," NBC, 1965; "Bob Hope Chrysler Theatre: Free of Charge," NBC, 1967; "The FBI: The Harvest," ABC, 1968; "The FBI: Target of Interest," ABC, 1969; "The Virginian: A Love to Remember," NBC, 1969; "The Name of the Game: Pay Till It Hurts," NBC, 1969; "Mission: Impossible: The Falcon," CBS, 1970; "Paris 7000: Journey to Nowhere," ABC, 1970; "Night Gallery: They're Tearing Down Tim Riley's Bar,"

NBC, 1971; "Love, American Style: Love and the Small Wedding," ABC, 1972; "Wheeler and Murdock," ABC, 1972; "Bonanza: Cassie," NBC, 1972; "Medical Story: Test Case," NBC, 1975; "The Streets of San Francisco: The Cat's Paw," ABC, 1975; "Wide World of Mystery: Halfway to Danger," ABC, 1975; "Marcus Welby, M.D.: The Medea Factor," ABC, 1975; "Police Woman: The Pawnshop," NBC, 1976; "Columbo: Last Salute to the Commodore," NBC, 1976; "Kojak: The Summer of '69," CBS, 1977; "Barnaby Jones: The Wife Beater," CBS, 1977; "ABC Afterschool Special: One of a Kind," ABC, 1978; "Fantasy Island: Saturday's Child," ABC, 1983; "Murder, She Wrote: Simon Says, Color Me Dead," CBS, 1987.
  TV MOVIES AND MINISERIES: "The Dangerous Days of Kiowa Jones," ABC, 1966; "Trial Run," NBC, 1969; "The D.A.: Murder One," NBC, 1969; "The Old Man Who Cried Wolf," ABC, 1970; "Do You Take This Stranger?," NBC, 1971; "Sarge: The Badge or the Cross," NBC, 1971; "Congratulations, It's a Boy!," ABC, 1971; "A Little Game," ABC, 1971; "Killer by Night," CBS, 1972; "The Police Story," NBC, 1973; "A Tree Grows in Brooklyn," NBC, 1974; "The Dream Makers," NBC, 1975; "The Last Survivors," NBC, 1975; "Masterpiece Theatre: How Green Was My Valley," PBS, 1976.
  AS WRITER: "ABC Afterschool Special: One of a Kind," ABC, 1978.

BAKER, JOE DON
  b. Groesbeck, TX, February 12, 1943. Bulky actor usually in macho roles; he played tough cop Earl Eischied and substituted for Carroll O'Connor for a time on "In the Heat of the Night."
  AS A REGULAR: "Eischied," NBC, 1979-80; "In the Heat of the Night," NBC, 1989.
  AND: "Judd for the Defense: Shadow of a Killer," ABC, 1967; "Lancer: The Homecoming," CBS, 1968; "The Outsider: A Wild Place in the Road," NBC, 1968; "Gunsmoke: Reprisal," CBS, 1969; "Bonanza: The Real People of Muddy Creek," NBC, 1969; "The Mod Squad: Willie Poor Boy," ABC, 1969; "Bracken's World: Focus on a Gun," NBC, 1970; "Lancer: A Person Unknown," CBS, 1970; "The FBI: Summer of Terror," ABC, 1970; "Mission: Impossible: The Miracle," CBS, 1971; "The High Chapparal: The Hostage," NBC, 1971; "The Streets of San Francisco: Beyond Vengeance," ABC, 1973.
  TV MOVIES AND MINISERIES: "Mongo's Back in Town," CBS, 1971; "That Certain Summer," ABC, 1972; "The Abduction of Kari Swenson," NBC, 1987.

BAKULA, SCOTT
  b. St. Louis, MO, 1955. Talented actor who

plays time-traveling Sam Beckett on "Quantum Leap."

AS A REGULAR: "Gung Ho," ABC, 1986-87; "Eisenhower & Lutz," CBS, 1988; "Quantum Leap," NBC, 1989- .

AND: "Designing Women: Pilot," CBS, 1986; "The Pat Sajak Show," CBS, 1989.

TV MOVIES AND MINISERIES: "The Last Fling," ABC, 1987.

* Bakula's name rhymes with "Dracula."

BAL, JEANNE

b. Santa Monica, CA, May 3, 1928. Sixties actress, usually in supporting roles as teachers or secretaries.

AS A REGULAR: "The Sid Caesar Show," ABC, 1958; "Love and Marriage," NBC, 1959-60; "NBC Playhouse," NBC, 1960; "Bachelor Father," NBC, 1961; ABC, 1961-62; "Mr. Novak," NBC, 1963-64.

AND: "Diagnosis: Unknown: The Parasite," CBS, 1960; "Riverboat: Listen to the Nightingale," NBC, 1961; "Thriller: Papa Benjamin," NBC, 1961; "Route 66: Effigy in Snow," CBS, 1961; "Checkmate: State of Shock," CBS, 1961; "Bachelor Father: Star Light, Star Not So Bright," ABC, 1961; "The Fugitive: Tiger Left, Tiger Right," ABC, 1964; "Perry Mason: The Case of the Telltale Tap," CBS, 1965; "McHale's Navy: The Great Necklace Caper," ABC, 1965; "Perry Mason: The Case of the Wrathful Wraith," CBS, 1965; "Hey, Landlord!: Instant Family," NBC, 1966; "Star Trek: The Man Trap," NBC, 1966.

BALDWIN, ALEC

b. Amityville, NY, April 3, 1958. Screen hunk ("The Hunt for Red October") who played Billy on "The Doctors" and Joshua on "Knots Landing."

AS A REGULAR: "The Doctors," NBC, 1980-82; "Cutter to Houston," CBS, 1983; "Knots Landing," CBS, 1984-85.

AND: "Hotel: Distortions," ABC, 1985.

TV MOVIES AND MINISERIES: "Sweet Revenge," CBS, 1984; "Love on the Run," NBC, 1985; "Dress Gray," NBC, 1986; "The Alamo: 13 Days to Glory," NBC, 1987.

BALDWIN, BILL

b. 1913; d. 1982. Actor who often appeared as a radio or TV announcer.

AS A REGULAR: "Mayor of Hollywood," NBC, 1952.

AND: "Leave It to Beaver: A Horse Named Nick," ABC, 1959; "Leave It to Beaver: Forgotten Party," ABC, 1959; "Bronco: The Masquerade," ABC, 1960; "Mr. Lucky: The Tax Man," CBS, 1960; "The Red Skelton Show: San Fernando's Diet Formula," CBS, 1961; "The Jack Benny Program: Don's Anniversary," CBS, 1961; "The

Danny Thomas Show: Linda's Crush," CBS, 1963; "The Beverly Hillbillies: The Bank Raising," CBS, 1964; "The Beverly Hillbillies: Hedda Hopper's Hollywood," CBS, 1964; "The Beverly Hillbillies: The Sheik," CBS, 1965; "Mannix: A Question of Midnight," CBS, 1969; "Mannix: Who Is Sylvia?," CBS, 1970; "Here's Lucy: Lucy the Skydiver," CBS, 1970; "Marcus Welby, M.D.: They Grow Up," ABC, 1972; "Barnaby Jones: Mystery Cycle," CBS, 1974; "Lou Grant: Inheritance," CBS, 1980; "Lou Grant: Execution," CBS, 1981.

TV MOVIES AND MINISERIES: "McCloud: Who Killed Miss USA?," NBC, 1970.

BALIN, INA

b. Ina Rosenberg, Brooklyn, NY, November 12, 1937; d. 1990. Actress in ingenue roles during the late fifties; her real-life involvment with Vietnemese orphans was dramatized in "The Children of An Lac."

AS A GUEST: "New York Confidential: Massacre," SYN, 1958; "Kraft Television Theatre: Angry Harvest," NBC, 1958; "Du Pont Show of the Month: The Count of Monte Cristo," CBS, 1958; "U.S. Steel Hour: Bride of the Fox," CBS, 1960; "Our American Heritage: The Invincible Teddy," NBC, 1961; "Westinghouse Presents: Come Again to Carthage," CBS, 1961; "Adventures in Paradise: Once There Was a Princess," ABC, 1962; "The du Pont Show: The Interrogator," NBC, 1962; "Stoney Burke: Child of Luxury," ABC, 1962; "The Lieutenant: A Touching of Hands," NBC, 1963; "The Defenders: The Uncivil War," CBS, 1964; "Voyage to the Bottom of the Sea: Time Bomb," ABC, 1965; "Bonanza: Devil on Her Shoulder," NBC, 1965; "The Dick Van Dyke Show: Draw Me a Pear," CBS, 1965; "It Takes a Thief: The Randomiz Miniature," ABC, 1968; "The FBI: The Maze," ABC, 1969; "The Name of the Game: The Tradition," NBC, 1970; "Mannix: Woman in the Shadows," CBS, 1971; "Alias Smith and Jones: Miracle at Santa Marta," ABC, 1971; "Cool Million: Million Dollar Misunderstanding," NBC, 1972; "The Streets of San Francisco: A Wrongful Death," ABC, 1973; "Mannix: A Matter of the Heart," CBS, 1974; "Police Story: Countdown," NBC, 1974; "The Streets of San Francisco: Dead Air," ABC, 1975; "Barnaby Jones: Beware the Dog," CBS, 1975; "Barnaby Jones: The Picture Pirates," CBS, 1978; "Quincy: Dying for a Drink," NBC, 1982; "Magnum, P.I.: L.A.," CBS, 1986; "Murder, She Wrote: A Very Good Year for Murder," CBS, 1988.

TV MOVIES AND MINISERIES: "The Lonely Profession," NBC, 1969; "Desperate Mission," NBC, 1971; "Call to Danger," CBS, 1973; "The Police Story," NBC, 1973; "Panic on the

5:22," ABC, 1974; "The Immigrants," SYN, 1978; "The Children of An Lac," CBS, 1980.

BALL, LUCILLE
b. Lucille Desiree Ball, Jamestown, NY, August 6, 1911; d. 1989. Comic princess of fifties television, a woman who combined beauty with an amazing aptitude for physical schtick.
AS A REGULAR: "I Love Lucy," CBS, 1951-57; "The Lucille Ball-Desi Arnaz Show," CBS, 1957-59; "The Lucy Show," CBS, 1962-68; "Here's Lucy," CBS, 1968-74; "Life with Lucy," ABC, 1986.
AND: "The Ed Sullivan Show," CBS, 1956; "The Bob Hope Show," NBC, 1956; "Westinghouse Desilu Playhouse: K.O. Kitty," CBS, 1958; "The Danny Thomas Show: Lucille Ball Upsets the Williams Household," CBS, 1959; "The Arthur Godfrey Show," CBS, 1959; "The Phil Silvers Show: Bilko's Ape Man," CBS, 1959; "The Ann Sothern Show: The Lucy Story," CBS, 1959; "Milton Berle Special," NBC, 1959; "Hedda Hopper's Hollywood," NBC, 1960; "Celebrity Talent Scouts," CBS, 1960; "The Garry Moore Show," CBS, 1960; "Eleanor Roosevelt's Jubilee," NBC, 1960; "The Jack Paar Show," NBC, 1961; "Bob Hope Buick Show," NBC, 1961; "The Ed Sullivan Show," CBS, 1961; "The Good Years," CBS, 1962; "Opening Night," CBS, 1962; "The Bob Hope Show," NBC, 1962; "The Danny Kaye Show," NBC, 1962; "Opening Night," CBS, 1963; "Password," CBS, 1963; "The Greatest Show on Earth: Lady in Limbo," ABC, 1963; "Password," CBS, 1964; "The Jack Benny Program," NBC, 1964; "Bob Hope Chrysler Theatre: Have Girls, Will Travel," NBC, 1964; "The Danny Kaye Show," CBS, 1964; "The Steve Lawrence Show," CBS, 1965; "A Salute to Stan Laurel," CBS, 1965; "Jack Benny Special," NBC, 1968; "Dinah Shore Special," NBC, 1969; "The Tonight Show Starring Johnny Carson," NBC, 1970; "The Carol Burnett Show," CBS, 1970; "Dinah's Place," NBC, 1970; "The Glen Campbell Goodtime Hour," CBS, 1971; "A Salute to Television's 25th Anniversary," ABC, 1972; "Dinah's Place," NBC, 1972; "Happy Anniversary and Goodbye," CBS, 1974; "Lucille Ball," CBS, 1975; "Two for Three," CBS, 1975; "Dinah!," SYN, 1975; "What Now, Catherine Curtis?," CBS, 1976; "The Practice: The Dream," NBC, 1976; "General Electric's All-Star Anniversary," ABC, 1978; "The Mary Tyler Moore Hour," CBS, 1979; "Cher ... and Other Fantasies," NBC, 1979; "Lucy Comes to NBC," NBC, 1980; "Magic of the Stars," HBO, 1981; "The Best of Three's Company," ABC, 1982; "America's Tribute to Bob Hope," NBC, 1988.
TV MOVIES AND MINISERIES: "Stone Pillow," CBS, 1985.
* In 1974, when "Here's Lucy" went off the air, *TV Guide* estimated that Ball had appeared in 495 episodes of her three sitcoms and that more than 3,000 actors and actresses had appeared on her shows.
* See also "I Love Lucy."
* Emmies: 1953, 1956, 1967, 1968.

TV'S TOP TEN, 1951-52
1. Arthur Godfrey's Talent Scouts (CBS)
2. Texaco Star Theatre (NBC)
3. I Love Lucy (CBS)
4. The Red Skelton Show (NBC)
5. The Colgate Comedy Hour (NBC)
6. Arthur Godfrey and His Friends (CBS)
7. Fireside Theatre (NBC)
8. Your Show of Shows (NBC)
9. The Jack Benny Program (CBS)
10. You Bet Your Life (NBC)

BALLANTINE, CARL
b. Brooklyn, NY. Bald, dumpy comic actor and magician; he played Lester Gruber on "McHale's Navy."
AS A REGULAR: "McHale's Navy," ABC, 1962-66; "The Queen and I," CBS, 1969; "One in a Million," ABC, 1980.
AND: "The Garry Moore Show," CBS, 1957; "Circus Time," ABC, 1957; "The Jackie Gleason Show," CBS, 1957; "The Garry Moore Show," CBS, 1958; "The Steve Allen Show," NBC, 1959; "The Garry Moore Show," CBS, 1959; "The Andy Williams Show," CBS, 1959; "Dick Clark's New Year's Eve Party," ABC, 1959; "The Chevy Show," NBC, 1960; "Startime: Fun Fair," NBC, 1960; "Car 54, Where Are You?: The Taming of Lucille," NBC, 1961; "Car 54, Where Are You?: Christmas at the 53rd," NBC, 1961; "Kraft Music Hall Goes West," NBC, 1962; "Hollywood Palace," ABC, 1964; "Object Is," ABC, 1964; "Hollywood Palace," ABC, 1965; "That Girl: I'll Be Suing You," ABC, 1966; "The Monkees: Find the Monkees," NBC, 1967; "I Dream of Jeannie: The Used Car Salesman," NBC, 1968; "Mayberry RFD: The Copy Machine," CBS, 1968; "Love, American Style: Love and the Shower," ABC, 1969; "The Partridge Family: Partridge Up a Pear Tree," ABC, 1971; "CHiPS: Rustling," NBC, 1978; "Alice: Spell Mel's," CBS, 1982; "The Cosby Show: The Show Must Go On," NBC, 1987.
TV MOVIES AND MINISERIES: "The Girl Most Likely To...," ABC, 1973.

BALLARD, KAYE
b. Catherine Gloria Balotta, Cleveland, OH, November 20, 1926. Short comic actress who specializes in loudmouth ethnic types.
AS A REGULAR: "Henry Morgan's Great Talent Hunt," NBC, 1951; "Perry Como's Kraft Music Hall," NBC, 1961-63; "The Mothers-in-Law," NBC, 1967-69; "The Doris Day Show,"

CBS, 1970-71; "The Steve Allen Comedy Hour," NBC, 1980-81; "What a Dummy," SYN, 1990- .

AND: "The Ed Sullivan Show," CBS, 1956; "Cinderella," CBS, 1957; "Club 60," NBC, 1957; "The Garry Moore Show," CBS, 1957; "The Ed Sullivan Show," CBS, 1957; "American Bandstand," ABC, 1957; "The Garry Moore Show," CBS, 1958; "The Jack Paar Show," NBC, 1958; "The Patrice Munsel Show," ABC, 1958; "Make Me Laugh," ABC, 1958; "The Garry Moore Show," CBS, 1959; "The Jack Paar Show," NBC, 1960; "The Merv Griffin Show," NBC, 1963; "Girl Talk," SYN, 1963; "Candid Camera," CBS, 1963; "Play Your Hunch," NBC, 1963; "The Patty Duke Show: The Perfect Teenager," ABC, 1964; "The Price Is Right," ABC, 1964; "Get the Message," ABC, 1964; "The Tonight Show Starring Johnny Carson," NBC, 1965; "The Mike Douglas Show," SYN, 1965; "Hollywood Squares," NBC, 1968; "The Jerry Lewis Show," NBC, 1968; "Hollywood Squares," NBC, 1969; "What's It All About, World?," ABC, 1969; "Jimmy Durante Presents the Lennon Sisters Hour," ABC, 1970; "Love, American Style: Love and the VIP Restaurant," ABC, 1971; "Here's Lucy: Lucy and Harry's Italian Bombshell," CBS, 1971; "Love, American Style: Love and the Dream Burglar," ABC, 1973; "Love, American Style: Love and the Soap Opera," ABC, 1973; "Dinah!," SYN, 1975; "Hollywood Squares," NBC, 1975; "Police Story: Officer Dooly," NBC, 1976; "The Love Boat: Happy Ending," ABC, 1979; "All Star Secrets," NBC, 1979; "Monsters!: Rerun," SYN, 1989.

BALSAM, MARTIN

b. New York City, NY, November 4, 1919. Short, stocky actor with extensive TV and film experience; he played Murray Klein, partner in "Archie Bunker's Place."

AS A REGULAR: "Valiant Lady," CBS, 1953-57; "The Greatest Gift," NBC, 1954-55; "Archie Bunker's Place," CBS, 1979-81.

AND: "Philco TV Playhouse: Statute of Limitations," NBC, 1954; "Philco TV Playhouse: The Joker," NBC, 1954; "Goodyear TV Playhouse: Last Boat to Messina," NBC, 1954; "U.S. Steel Hour: Freighter," CBS, 1955; "Goodyear TV Playhouse: The Taker," NBC, 1955; "Philco TV Playhouse: A Man Is Ten Feet Tall," NBC, 1955; "The Ed Sullivan Show," CBS, 1956; "Studio One: The Defender," CBS, 1957; "Alfred Hitchcock Presents: The Equalizer," CBS, 1958; "Kraft Theatre: Dog in a Bush Tunnel," NBC, 1958; "Studio One: The Desperate Age," CBS, 1958; "Playhouse 90: Bomber's Moon," CBS, 1958; "Westinghouse Desilu Playhouse: The Time Element," CBS, 1958; "The Twilight Zone: The 16 Millimeter Shrine," CBS, 1959; "Have Gun, Will Travel: Saturday Night," CBS, 1960;

"Naked City: New York to L.A.," ABC, 1961; "Way Out: The Overnight Case," CBS, 1961; "Alfred Hitchcock Presents: Final Arrangements," NBC, 1961; "Route 66: First Class Mouliak," CBS, 1961; "The Untouchables: Tunnel of Horrors," ABC, 1961; "Naked City: Which Is Joseph Creeley?," ABC, 1961; "The New Breed: Lady Killer," ABC, 1961; "The Defenders: The Best Defense," CBS, 1961; "The Eleventh Hour: Something Crazy's Going On in the Back Room," NBC, 1963; "The Twilight Zone: The New Exhibit," CBS, 1963; "The Breaking Point: A Pelican in the Wilderness," ABC, 1963; "Arrest and Trial: Signal of an Ancient Flame," ABC, 1964; "The Defenders: The Seven-Hundred-Year-Old Gang," CBS, 1964; "Wagon Train: The Whipping," ABC, 1964; "Mr. Broadway: Something to Sing About," CBS, 1964; "The Man From UNCLE: The Odd Man Affair," NBC, 1965; "Dr. Kildare: The Encroachment/A Patient Lost/What Happened to All the Sunshine and Roses?/The Taste of Crow/Out of a Concrete Tower," NBC, 1966; "The Fugitive: There Goes the Ball Game," ABC, 1967; "Among the Paths to Eden," ABC, 1967; "The Name of the Game: Nightmare," NBC, 1968; "The Name of the Game: The Enemy Before Us," NBC, 1970; "Police Story: Man on a Rack," NBC, 1973; "Kojak: A Killing in the Second House," CBS, 1974; "Maude: Maude and Chester," CBS, 1976; "The Twilight Zone: Personal Demons," CBS, 1986.

TV MOVIES AND MINISERIES: "Hunters Are for Killing," CBS, 1970; "The Old Man Who Cried Wolf," ABC, 1970; "Night of Terror," ABC, 1972; "A Brand New Life," ABC, 1973; "The Six Million Dollar Man," ABC, 1973; "Trapped Beneath the Sea," ABC, 1974; "G.E. Theatre: Miles to Go Before I Sleep," CBS, 1975; "Death Among Friends," NBC, 1975; "The Lindbergh Kidnapping Case," NBC, 1976; "Raid on Entebbe," NBC, 1977; "The Millionaire," CBS, 1978; "Rainbow," NBC, 1978; "The Seeding of Sarah Burns," CBS, 1979; "The House on Garibaldi Street," SYN, 1979; "Hallmark Hall of Fame: Aunt Mary," CBS, 1979; "The People vs. Jean Harris," NBC, 1981; "I Want to Live!," ABC, 1983; "Little Gloria ... Happy at Last," NBC, 1982; "Space," CBS, 1985; "Second Serve," CBS, 1986; "Queenie," ABC, 1987; "Kids Like These," CBS, 1987; "The Child Saver," NBC, 1988.

BANANA MAN—See A. Robbins.

BANCROFT, ANNE

b. Anna Maria Louise Italiano, New York City, NY, September 17, 1931. Oscar-winning actress ("The Miracle Worker," "The Graduate") whose two musical-comedy TV specials in the seventies were well received; wife of Mel Brooks.

AS A GUEST: "Studio One: Torrents of Spring," CBS, 1950; "Kraft Television Theatre: To Live in Peace," NBC, 1953; "Lux Video Theatre: A Medal for Benny," CBS, 1954; "Lux Video Theatre: Hired Wife," NBC, 1956; "Alcoa Hour: Hostages to Fortune," NBC, 1957; "Dick Powell's Zane Grey Theatre: Episode in Darkness," CBS, 1957; "The Frank Sinatra Show: A Time to Cry," ABC, 1958; "The Arlene Francis Show," NBC, 1958; "The Jack Paar Show," NBC, 1959; "The Jack Paar Show," NBC, 1960; "Perry Como's Kraft Music Hall," NBC, 1960; "Person to Person," CBS, 1960; "Perry Como's Kraft Music Hall," NBC, 1961; "Perry Como's Kraft Music Hall," NBC, 1962; "Bob Hope Special," NBC, 1964; "Perry Como Special," NBC, 1964; "Kraft Music Hall," NBC, 1969; "Annie: The Women in the Life of a Man," CBS, 1970; "Annie and the Hoods," ABC, 1974; "The Merv Griffin Show," SYN, 1980.

TV MOVIES AND MINISERIES: "Jesus of Nazareth," NBC, 1977.

BANK, FRANK

b. Hollywood, CA, April 12, 1942. Former child actor who played Lumpy Rutherford on "Leave It to Beaver."

AS A REGULAR: "Leave It to Beaver," ABC, 1958-63; "The New Leave It to Beaver," DIS, 1985-86, WTBS, 1986-89.

AND: "Yes, Yes Nanette: Country Club," NBC, 1961.

BANKHEAD, TALLULAH

b. Huntsville, AL, January 31, 1903; d. 1968. Deep-voiced stage and film actress who did some TV.

AS A REGULAR: "All Star Revue," NBC, 1952-53.

AND: "U.S. Steel Hour: Hedda Gabler," ABC, 1954; "Shower of Stars," CBS, 1957; "The Steve Allen Show," NBC, 1957; "Arthur Murray Party," NBC, 1957; "The George Gobel Show," NBC, 1957; "Schlitz Playhouse of Stars: The Hole Card," CBS, 1957; "Command Appearance," NBC, 1957; "The Polly Bergen Show," NBC, 1957; "The Lucille Ball-Desi Arnaz Show: The Celebrity Next Door," CBS, 1957; "Destiny: Eyes of a Stranger," CBS, 1958; "Milton Berle Starring in the Kraft Music Hall," NBC, 1959; "The Ed Sullivan Show," CBS, 1959; "The Big Party," CBS, 1959; "I've Got a Secret," CBS, 1960; "The Tonight Show Starring Johnny Carson," NBC, 1962; "The Merv Griffin Show," SYN, 1966; "Batman: Black Widow Strikes Again/Caught in the Spider's Den," ABC, 1967.

BANNER, JOHN

b. Vienna, Austria, January 28, 1910; d. 1973. Clownish comic actor best known as the lovable, gullible Sgt. Schultz on "Hogan's Heroes."

AS A REGULAR: "Hogan's Heroes," CBS, 1965-71; "The Chicago Teddy Bears," CBS, 1971.

AND: "Member of the Jury," SYN, 1956; "Father Knows Best: Brief Holiday," NBC, 1957; "Cimarron City: I, the Jury," NBC, 1958; "The Roaring Twenties: The Velvet Frame," ABC, 1960; "My Sister Eileen: Ruth Becomes a Waitress," CBS, 1960; "Michael Shayne: The Poison Pen Club," NBC, 1960; "Dante: The Bavarian Barbarians," NBC, 1960; "77 Sunset Strip: The Antwerp Caper," ABC, 1960; "The du Pont Show with June Allyson: Silent Panic," CBS, 1960; "The Untouchables: Takeover," ABC, 1962; "The Many Loves of Dobie Gillis: I Was a Spy for the F.O.B.," CBS, 1963; "The Virginian: The Small Parade," NBC, 1963; "My Three Sons: What's the Princess Really Like?," ABC, 1964; "The Man From UNCLE: The Neptune Affair," NBC, 1964; "The Donna Reed Show: Moon Shot," ABC, 1963; "Hazel: The Investor," NBC, 1965; "The Lucy Show: Lucy and Bob Crane," CBS, 1966; "The Doris Day Show: The Crapshooter Who Would Be King," CBS, 1971; "The Partridge Family: Who Is Max Ledbetter and Why Is He Saying All Those Terrible Things?," ABC, 1972.

BANNON, JACK

b. Hollywood, CA, June 14, 1940. Versatile actor who's played TV characters from wisecracking editor Art Donovan on "Lou Grant" to the inmate who raped Jack Morrison (David Morse) on "St. Elsewhere."

AS A REGULAR: "Lou Grant," CBS, 1977-82; "Trauma Center," ABC, 1983.

AND: "The Beverly Hillbillies: Cabin in Beverly Hills," CBS, 1964; "The Beverly Hillbillies: Dash Riprock, You Cad," CBS, 1965; "Green Acres: The Price of Apples," CBS, 1966; "Petticoat Junction: Girls! Girls! Girls!," CBS, 1967; "Petticoat Junction: Kate's Day in Court," CBS, 1967; "The Beverly Hillbillies: Something for the Queen," CBS, 1968; "Mannix: To Catch a Rabbit," CBS, 1969; "Petticoat Junction: One of Our Chickens Is Missing," CBS, 1969; "Mannix: Who Killed Me?," CBS, 1969; "Barney Miller: The Sighting," ABC, 1978; "The Love Boat: He's My Brother," ABC, 1981; "St. Elsewhere: Down's Syndrome," NBC, 1982; "St. Elsewhere: Cora and Arnie," NBC, 1982; "Simon & Simon: Our Fair City," CBS, 1984; "Remington Steele: Steele in the Family," NBC, 1984; "Newhart: Lady in Waiting," CBS, 1985; "Moonlighting: The Dream Sequence Always Rings Twice," ABC, 1985; "Hunter: The Castro Connection," NBC, 1986; "St. Elsewhere: Cheek to Cheek," NBC, 1986; "Matlock: Diary of a Perfect Murder," NBC, 1986; "Cagney & Lacey: Friendly Smoke," CBS, 1988; "Cagney & Lacey: Don't I Know You?,"

CBS, 1988; "Dynasty: Broken Krystle," ABC, 1988; "Dynasty: She's Back," ABC, 1988; "Murphy's Law: Never Play Leapfrog with a Unicorn," ABC, 1989; "Murder, She Wrote: From Russia-with Blood," CBS, 1989; "Midnight Caller: End of the Innocence," NBC, 1989; "Living Dolls: C Is for Model," ABC, 1989.

TV MOVIES AND MINISERIES: "Take Your Best Shot," CBS, 1982; "Diary of a Perfect Murder," NBC, 1986; "Perry Mason: The Case of the Sinister Spirit," NBC, 1987.

AS DIALOGUE COACH: "Green Acres," CBS, 1965-66.

* Bannon is the son of Bea Benedaret, who played Kate Bradley on "Petticoat Junction."

BARA, NINA
b. *Argentina, 1925; d. 1990.* Actress who played Tonga on "Space Patrol" and then promptly got out of show biz to become a librarian.
AS A REGULAR: "Space Patrol," ABC, 1951-52.

BARBEAU, ADRIENNE
b. *Sacramento, CA, June 11, 1947.* Pneumatic actress who played Carol, daughter of Maude Findlay (Beatrice Arthur).
AS A REGULAR: "Maude," CBS, 1972-78.
AND: "The Tonight Show Starring Johnny Carson," NBC, 1974; "Match Game '74," CBS, 1974; "Celebrity Sweepstakes," NBC, 1975; "The Mike Douglas Show," SYN, 1975; "The Bobby Vinton Show," SYN, 1975; "The $20,000 Pyramid," ABC, 1978; "The Love Boat: Masquerade," ABC, 1978; "Hotel: Cinderella," ABC, 1984; "The Twilight Zone: Teacher's Aide," CBS, 1985; "Murder, She Wrote: Jessica Behind Bars," CBS, 1986; "Head of the Class: The Little Sister," ABC, 1989.
TV MOVIES AND MINISERIES: "The Great Houdinis," ABC, 1976; "Having Babies," ABC, 1976; "Crash," ABC, 1978; "Someone Is Watching Me!," NBC, 1978; "The Darker Side of Terror," CBS, 1979; "Valentine Magic on Love Island," NBC, 1980; "Bridge Across Time," NBC, 1985; "Seduced," CBS, 1985.

BARBOUR, JOHN
b. *Canada, April 24, 1934.* Comic and TV personality.
AS A REGULAR: "Real People," NBC, 1979-82; "On Stage America," SYN, 1984.
AND: "The Dean Martin Show," NBC, 1967; "The Merv Griffin Show," SYN, 1968; "Get Smart: The Apes of Rath," CBS, 1969; "The Odd Couple: Two on the Aisle," ABC, 1974; "Sanford & Son: The Masquerade Party," NBC, 1975.
TV MOVIES AND MINISERIES: "Pray for the Wildcats," ABC, 1974; "Body of Evidence," CBS, 1988.

BARBUTTI, PETE
b. *Scranton, PA, May 4, 1934.* Comedian.
AS A REGULAR: "The Garry Moore Show," CBS, 1966-67; "The John Davidson Show," NBC, 1976.
AND: "On Broadway Tonight," CBS, 1965; "The Joey Bishop Show," ABC, 1968; "Get Smart: Closely Watched Planes," NBC, 1968; "The Della Reese Show," SYN, 1969; "The Merv Griffin Show," SYN, 1973.

BARCROFT, ROY
b. *Howard N. Ravenscroft, Crab Orchard, NB, September 7, 1902; d. 1969.* Actor usually in cowboy roles.
AS A REGULAR: "Laramie," NBC, 1959-63.
AND: "Cowboy G-Men: Sidewinder," SYN, 1952; "Death Valley Days: Birth of a Boom," SYN, 1956; "Maverick: The Jeweled Gun," ABC, 1957; "Have Gun, Will Travel: The Haunted Trees," CBS, 1959; "Dick Powell's Zane Grey Theatre: Man Alone," CBS, 1959; "M Squad: The Human Bond," NBC, 1959; "Riverboat: The Wichita Arrows," NBC, 1960; "Empire: The Fire Dancer," NBC, 1962; "Gunsmoke: Clarey Cotter," CBS, 1963; "Rawhide: Incident of the Mountain Man," CBS, 1963; "The Virginian: The Small Parade," NBC, 1963; "The Andy Griffith Show: Dogs, Dogs, Dogs," CBS, 1963; "Bonanza: The Lonely Runner," NBC, 1965; "Gunsmoke: The Returning," CBS, 1967; "The Iron Horse: Leopards Try, But Leopards Can't," ABC, 1967; "Gunsmoke: O'Quillian," CBS, 1968; "Gunsmoke: Mannon," CBS, 1969; "Gunsmoke: The Mark of Cain," CBS, 1969.

BARDETTE, TREVOR
b. *Nashville, AR, November 19, 1902; d. 1977.* Weatherbeaten actor who played Old Man Clanton, enemy of Wyatt Earp (Hugh O'Brian).
AS A REGULAR: "The Life and Legend of Wyatt Earp," ABC, 1959-61.
AND: "Ford Theatre: Sudden Silence," ABC, 1956; "Broken Arrow: The Captive," ABC, 1956; "Cheyenne: Lone Gun," ABC, 1956; "The Life and Legend of Wyatt Earp: The Sharpshooter," ABC, 1957; "The 20th Century-Fox Hour: Man of the Law," CBS, 1957; "Panic!: Courage," NBC, 1957; "Panic!: The Prisoner," NBC, 1957; "Restless Gun: The Child," NBC, 1957; "Restless Gun: Hiram Grover's Strike," NBC, 1958; "O. Henry Playhouse: The Emancipation of Billy," SYN, 1958; "Rough Riders: The Maccabites," ABC, 1958; "Restless Gun: Peligroso," NBC, 1958; "The Rebel: The Unwanted," ABC, 1959; "Gunsmoke: Small Water," CBS, 1960; "Have Gun, Will Travel: Jenny," CBS, 1960; "Have Gun, Will Travel: A Head of Hair," CBS, 1960; "The Rebel: The Threat," ABC, 1961; "Maverick: Benefit of Doubt," ABC, 1961; "The Joey Bishop

Show: The Big Date," NBC, 1962; "Wagon Train: The Lily Legend Story," ABC, 1963; "Perry Mason: The Case of the Two-Faced Turnabout," CBS, 1963; "The Andy Griffith Show: Gomer the House Guest," CBS, 1963; "The FBI: To Free My Enemy," ABC, 1965; "Slattery's People: The Unborn," CBS, 1965; "My Favorite Martian: Horse and Buggy Martin," CBS, 1966; "Daktari: Shoot to Kill," CBS, 1966; "Gunsmoke: The Wreckers," CBS, 1967; "Gomer Pyle, USMC: Goodbye, Dolly," CBS, 1968.

BARI, LYNN

b. *Marjorie Schuyler Fisher, Roanoke, VA, December 18, 1913.* Forties film actress often in sultry or sinister roles; she stayed busy on TV during the fifties.
AS A REGULAR: "Detective's Wife," CBS, 1950; "Boss Lady," NBC, 1952.
AND: "Bigelow Theatre: Agent From Scotland Yard," CBS, 1951; "Lux Video Theatre: Weather for Today," CBS, 1951; "Schaefer Century Theatre: The Other Woman," NBC, 1952; "Ford Theatre: All's Fair in Love," NBC, 1953; "Four Star Playhouse: Stake My Life," CBS, 1954; "Science Fiction Theatre: Hour of Nightmare," SYN, 1955; "Screen Directors Playhouse: Arroyo," NBC, 1955; "The Red Skelton Show," CBS, 1958; "Walt Disney Presents: The Nine Lives of Elfego Baca—Attorney at Law," ABC, 1959; "Law of the Plainsman: The Matriarch," NBC, 1959; "The Overland Trail: Perilous Passage," NBC, 1960; "The Aquanauts: The Atlantis Adventure," CBS, 1960; "Michael Shayne: The Heiress," NBC, 1961; "Checkmate: Goodbye, Griff," CBS, 1961; "The New Breed: The Butcher," ABC, 1961; "Ben Casey: A Certain Time, a Certain Darkness," ABC, 1961; "Perry Mason: The Case of the Accosted Accountant," CBS, 1964; "Perry Mason: The Case of the Fatal Fetish," CBS, 1965; "The FBI: Line of Fire," ABC, 1967; "The FBI: The Mechanized Accomplice," ABC, 1968.

BARKER, BOB

b. *Darrington, WA, December 12, 1923.* Smiling emcee and animal-rights activist who, in a controversial move, stopped dying his hair a few years ago.
AS A REGULAR: "Truth or Consequences," NBC, 1956-64; SYN, 1966-74; "End of the Rainbow," NBC, 1958; "Family Game," ABC, 1967-68; "The Price Is Right," CBS, 1972 - , SYN, 1972-79, 1985-86; "That's My Line," CBS, 1980-81.
AND: "The Mike Douglas Show," SYN, 1967; "Tattletales," CBS, 1975; "Dinah!," SYN, 1978; "Match Game P.M.," SYN, 1980.

BARKIN, ELLEN

b. *1957.* Actress more active these days in

movies ("Diner," "Sea of Love") than TV.
TV MOVIES AND MINISERIES: "We're Fighting Back," CBS, 1981; "Parole," CBS, 1982; "Terrible Joe Moran," CBS, 1984.

BARNES, C.B.

b. *Portland, ME, November 7, 1972.* Young actor in fresh-faced roles; he played Ross Harper on "Day by Day."
AS A REGULAR: "Starman," ABC, 1986-87; "Day by Day," NBC, 1988-89.
AND: "ABC Afterschool Special: Private Affairs," ABC, 1989.

BARNES, JOANNA

b. *Boston, MA, November 15, 1934.* Sexy actress of the sixties.
AS A REGULAR: "21 Beacon Street," NBC, 1959; "The Trials of O'Brien," CBS, 1965-66; "Dateline: Hollywood," ABC, 1967.
AND: "Ford Theatre: The Man Who Beat Lupo," ABC, 1957; "Warner Bros. Presents Conflict: The Velvet Cage," ABC, 1957; "Warner Bros. Presents Conflict: Anything for Money, ABC, 1957; "Maverick: Ghost Rider," ABC, 1957; "Hawaiian Eye: A Dime a Dozen," ABC, 1959; "The Man From Blackhawk: Remember Me Not," ABC, 1960; "Maverick: The Resurrection of Joe November," ABC, 1960; "M Squad: The Twisted Way," NBC, 1960; "The Bob Cummings Show: Executive Sweet," CBS, 1961; "The Investigators: In a Mirror, Darkly," CBS, 1961; "Target: The Corruptors: The Golden Carpet," ABC, 1961; "Follow the Sun: The Primitive Clay," ABC, 1961; "Have Gun, Will Travel: Penelope," CBS, 1962; "Sam Benedict: Tears for a Nobody Doll," NBC, 1962; "The Eleventh Hour: My Name Is Judith, I'm Lost, You See," NBC, 1963; "The Beverly Hillbillies: Elly Starts to School," CBS, 1963; "The Beverly Hillbillies: The Clampett Look," CBS, 1963; "Arrest and Trial: A Circle of Strangers," ABC, 1964; "The Farmer's Daughter: The Next Mrs. Morley," ABC, 1964; "Snap Judgment," NBC, 1967; "Mannix: Fear I to Fall," CBS, 1968; "Nanny and the Professor: The Scientific Approach," ABC, 1970; "Alias Smith and Jones: Miracle at Santa Marta," ABC, 1971; "Alias Smith and Jones: How to Rob a Bank in One Hard Lesson," ABC, 1972; "Quincy: Who's Who in Neverland," NBC, 1976; "Charlie's Angels: Angels on Skates," ABC, 1979; "When the Whistle Blows: Macho Man," ABC, 1980; "Barney Miller: Chinatown," ABC, 1982; "Remington Steele: My Fair Steele," NBC, 1983; "Murder, She Wrote: The Way to Dusty Death," CBS, 1987; "Cheers: The Visiting Lecher," NBC, 1989.
TV MOVIES AND MINISERIES: "Secrets of a Mother and Daughter," CBS, 1983.

BARNES, PRISCILLA

b. *Fort Dix, NJ, December 7, 1955*. Blonde actress who replaced the irreplacable Suzanne Somers (yeah, right) on "Three's Company."

AS A REGULAR: "The American Girls," CBS, 1978; "Three's Company," ABC, 1981-84.

AND: "The Rockford Files: The Mayor's Committee from Deer Lick Falls," NBC, 1977; "Kojak: Sixty Miles to Hell," CBS, 1978; "Hollywood Squares," SYN, 1979; "The Love Boat: Pride of the Pacific," ABC, 1982; "The Love Boat: Mr. Smith Goes to Stockhom," ABC, 1985; "Murder, She Wrote: Dead Heat," CBS, 1986; "Blacke's Magic: Revenge of the Esperanza," NBC, 1986; "Highway to Heaven: Summer Camp," NBC, 1988.

TV MOVIES AND MINISERIES: "The Time Machine," NBC, 1978; "A Vacation in Hell," ABC, 1979; "The Wild Women of Chastity Gulch," ABC, 1982; "Perfect People," ABC, 1988.

BARON, SANDY

b. *1938*. Fast-talking comic who showed up on game and talk shows.

AS A REGULAR: "That Was the Week That Was," NBC, 1964; "Hey Landlord," NBC, 1966-67; "The Della Reese Show," SYN, 1969-70.

AND: "Naked City: Torment Him Much and Hold Him Long," ABC, 1962; "The Mike Douglas Show," SYN, 1965; "Hollywood Squares," NBC, 1967; "How's Your Mother-in-Law?," ABC, 1968; "Love, American Style: Love and the Good Samaritan," ABC, 1969; "Hollywood Squares," NBC, 1970; "Name Droppers," NBC, 1970; "The Game Game," SYN, 1970; "Love, American Style: Love and the Guilty Conscience," ABC, 1972; "What's My Line?," SYN, 1972; "Ironside: Countdown," NBC, 1973.

TV MOVIES AND MINISERIES: "The Police Story," NBC, 1973; "Anatomy of a Seduction," CBS, 1979.

BARR, DOUGLAS

b. *Cedar Rapids, IA, May 1, 1949*. Beefy, generic TV actor who plays Bill Stillfield, husband of Charlene (Jean Smart) on "Designing Women."

AS A REGULAR: "When the Whistle Blows," ABC, 1980; "The Fall Guy," ABC, 1981-86; "The Wizard," CBS, 1986-87; "Designing Women," CBS, 1987- .

AND: "Fantasy Island: Snow Bird," ABC, 1980; "The Love Boat: Pride of the Pacific," ABC, 1982; "Hotel: Resolutions," ABC, 1984; "The Love Boat: The Last Heist," ABC, 1984; "Murder, She Wrote: Curse of the Daanav," CBS, 1987.

BARR, LEONARD

b. *1903; d. 1980*. Skinny, deadpan comic whose roots were in vaudeville; Dean Martin's uncle.

AS A REGULAR: "Szysznyk," CBS, 1977-78.

AND: "Hollywood Palace," ABC, 1964; "The Dean Martin Show," NBC, 1969; "Love, American Style: Love and the Longest Night," ABC, 1971; "The Odd Couple: The Hollywood Story," ABC, 1974; "The Odd Couple: Old Flames Never Die," ABC, 1975; "The Tony Randall Show: Case: His Honor vs. Her Honor," ABC, 1976.

TV MOVIES AND MINISERIES: "Evil Roy Slade," NBC, 1972.

BARR, ROSEANNE

b. *Salt Lake City, UT, November 3, 1952*. Comedienne whose personal trials have almost obscured the fact that she still puts out a decent sitcom each week.

AS A REGULAR: "Roseanne," ABC, 1988- .

AND: "Hollywood Squares," SYN, 1987; "Hollywood Squares," SYN, 1988; "Late Night with David Letterman," NBC, 1989.

TV'S TOP TEN, 1989-90

1. Roseanne (ABC)
2. The Cosby Show (NBC)
3. Cheers (NBC)
4. A Different World (NBC)
5. America's Funniest Home Videos (ABC)
6. The Golden Girls (NBC)
7. 60 Minutes (CBS)
8. The Wonder Years (ABC)
9. Empty Nest (NBC)
10. Chicken Soup (ABC)

BARRETT, MAJEL

b. *Cleveland, OH*. Actress who played nurse Christine Chapel on "Star Trek."

AS A REGULAR: "Star Trek," NBC, 1966-69.

AND: "Westinghouse Desilu Playhouse: Christmas Surprise Package," CBS, 1959; "Pete and Gladys: Eyewitness," CBS, 1961; "Window on Main Street: The Charity Drive," CBS, 1961; "Bonanza: Gift of Water," NBC, 1962; "The Lucy Show: Lucy Is a Kangaroo for a Day," CBS, 1962; "The Lieutenant: In the Highest Tradition," NBC, 1964; "Many Happy Returns: Bye Bye Cupid," CBS, 1964; "Love on a Rooftop: 117 Ways to Cook Hamburger," ABC, 1966; "The FBI: The Animal," ABC, 1974; "Star Trek: The Next Generation: Manhunt," SYN, 1989.

TV MOVIES AND MINISERIES: "Genesis II," ABC, 1973; "Planet Earth," ABC, 1974.

BARRETT, RONA

b. *New York City, NY, October 8, 1936*. Professional gossipmonger who seems to have fallen from favor.

AS A REGULAR: "Tomorrow," NBC, 1980-81; "Television: Inside and Out," NBC, 1981-82.

BARRIE, BARBARA

b. Chicago, IL, May 23, 1931. Slight, talented actress best known as the wife of Barney Miller (Hal Linden) for a time and as Evelyn, the sensitive mother of Dave Stohler in the film and TV versions of "Breaking Away."

AS A REGULAR: "Love of Life," CBS, 1960; "Diana," NBC, 1973-74; "Barney Miller," ABC, 1975-76; "Breaking Away," ABC, 1980-81; "Tucker's Witch," CBS, 1982-83; "Reggie," ABC, 1983; "Double Trouble," NBC, 1984-85.

AND: "The Phil Silvers Show: WAC," CBS, 1955; "Kraft Television Theatre: The Grapefruit to Lisbon," NBC, 1956; "Robert Montgomery Presents: Wait for Me," NBC, 1957; "Kaiser Aluminum Hour: Whereabouts Unknown," NBC, 1957; "The Phil Silvers Show: The Big Man Hunt," CBS, 1957; "Suspicion: Hand in Glove," NBC, 1957; "Suspicion: Heartbeat," NBC, 1957; "Kraft Theatre: The Sound of Trouble," NBC, 1957; "The Phil Silvers Show: Bilko's Valentine," CBS, 1958; "Art Carney Special: Full Moon Over Brooklyn," NBC, 1960; "Play of the Week: A Palm Tree in a Rose Garden," SYN, 1960; "Armstrong Circle Theatre: Black-Market Babies," CBS, 1961; "U.S. Steel Hour: Delayed Honeymoon," CBS, 1961; "The Defenders: The Attack," CBS, 1961; "Route 66: Even Stones Have Eyes," CBS, 1962; "Naked City: Dust Devil on a Quiet Street," ABC, 1962; "Dr. Kildare: The Mosaic," NBC, 1963; "The Twilight Zone: Miniature," CBS, 1963; "The Virginian: The Small Parade," NBC, 1963; "Mr. Novak: How Does Your Garden Grow," NBC, 1964; "The Defenders: The Seven-Hundred-Year-Old Gang," CBS, 1964; "Ben Casey: A Rambling Discourse on Egyptian Water Clocks," ABC, 1965; "The Trials of O'Brien: A Horse Called Destiny," CBS, 1966; "NET Playhouse: To Be Young, Gifted and Black," NET, 1972; "ABC's Matinee Today: A Mask of Love," ABC, 1973; "Koska ... and His Family," NBC, 1973; "The Mary Tyler Moore Show: I Love a Piano," CBS, 1974; "Hollywood Television Theatre: For the Use of the Hall," PBS, 1975; "McMillan and Wife: Aftershock," NBC, 1975; "Barney Miller: 'Quo Vadis?'," ABC, 1978; "Barney Miller: Toys," ABC, 1978; "Lou Grant: Andrew," CBS, 1979; "Kate & Allie: Late Bloomer," CBS, 1986; "Family Ties: The Way We Were," NBC, 1987; "A Fine Romance: A Horse Is a Horse-of Course, of Course," ABC, 1989; "Island Son: Role Models," CBS, 1989.

TV MOVIES AND MINISERIES: "Harold Robbins' 79 Park Avenue," NBC, 1977; "Backstairs at the White House," NBC, 1979; "Roots: The Next Generations," ABC, 1979; "To Race the Wind," CBS, 1980; "The Children Nobody Wanted," CBS, 1981; "Not Just Another Affair," CBS, 1982; "G.E. Theater: Two of a Kind," CBS, 1982; "The Execution," NBC, 1985; "Vital Signs," CBS, 1986; "My First Love," ABC, 1988.

BARRIE, WENDY

b. Wendy Jenkins, Hong Kong, April 18, 1912; d. 1978. Actress in British films who became a personality on early TV.

AS A REGULAR: "Adventures of Oky Doky," DUM, 1948-49; "Picture This," NBC, 1948-49; "The Wendy Barrie Show," DUM, 1949; ABC, 1949-50; NBC, 1950.

AND: "The Garry Moore Show," CBS, 1958; "Beachcomber: Mr. Winters," SYN, 1962.

BARRIS, CHUCK

b. Philadelphia, PA, June 3, 1928. Producer of game shows that relied on innuendo, put-down humor and crudity all during the sixties and seventies; of course, he made a mint on them.

AS A REGULAR: "The Gong Show," SYN, 1977-80; "The Chuck Barris Rah Rah Show," NBC, 1978.

AND: "Sanford & Son: Sanford and Gong," NBC, 1976; "What's Happening!: Going, Going, Gong," ABC, 1978.

AS PRODUCER: "The Dating Game," ABC, 1966-70; "Dream Girl of '67," ABC, 1966-67; "The Newlywed Game," ABC, 1967-71; "Operation: Entertainment," ABC, 1968-69; "The Parent Game," SYN, 1972-74; "The Gong Show," NBC, 1976-79; SYN, 1977-80; "The Chuck Barris Rah Rah Show," NBC, 1978; "The $1.98 Beauty Show," SYN, 1978-80.

BARRIS, MARTI

b. Maureen Barris, Hollywood, CA, 1938. Singer.

AS A REGULAR: "Howdy Doody," NBC, 1959-60.

AND: "The Bob Crosby Show," NBC, 1958; "American Bandstand," ABC, 1959; "The Lawrence Welk Show," ABC, 1959; "Music on Ice," NBC, 1960.

BARRY, GENE

b. Eugene Klass, New York City, June 14, 1921. Actor who played suave western lawman Bat Masterson, suave cop/spy Amos Burke and suave crimebusting reporter Glenn Howard on "The Name of the Game."

AS A REGULAR: "Our Miss Brooks," CBS, 1955-56; "Bat Masterson," NBC, 1958-61; "Burke's Law," ABC, 1963-65; "Amos Burke, Secret Agent," ABC, 1965-66; "The Name of the Game," NBC, 1968-71.

AND: "The Loretta Young Show: Something About Love," NBC, 1954; "Ford Theatre: Touch of Spring," NBC, 1955; "Stage 7: Debt to a Stranger," CBS, 1955; "Science Fiction Theatre:

Spider, Incorporated," NBC, 1955; "Alfred Hitchcock Presents: Salvage," CBS, 1955; "Ford Theatre: The Blue Ribbon," NBC, 1955; "The Millionaire: The Story of Steve Carey," CBS, 1955; "Damon Runyon Theatre: The Good Luck Kid," CBS, 1956; "G.E Theatre: Return to Guam," CBS, 1956; "Ford Theatre: The Women Who Dared," ABC, 1956; "The Jane Wyman Show: A Place on the Bay," NBC, 1956; "The Jane Wyman Show: The Pendulum," NBC, 1957; "The Perry Como Show," NBC, 1959; "Dinah Shore Chevy Show," NBC, 1959; "Pete and Gladys: Crossed Wires," CBS, 1961; "Westinghouse Presents: An Old-Fashioned Thanksgiving," ABC, 1961; "The Dick Powell Show: Seeds of April," NBC, 1962; "G.E. Theatre: The Roman Kind," CBS, 1962; "The Alfred Hitchcock Hour: Dear Uncle George," CBS, 1963; "Hollywood Palace," ABC, 1964; "Hollywood Palace," ABC, 1965; "The Andy Williams Show," NBC, 1965; "ABC Nightlife," ABC, 1965; "The Tonight Show Starring Johnny Carson," NBC, 1974; "The Love Boat: Going by the Book," ABC, 1978; "Charlie's Angels: Hula Angels," ABC, 1981; "The Pat Sajak Show," CBS, 1989; "Paradise: A Gathering of Guns," CBS, 1989.

TV MOVIES AND MINISERIES: "Prescription: Murder," NBC, 1968; "Istanbul Express," NBC, 1968; "Do You Take This Stranger?," NBC, 1971; "The Devil and Miss Sarah," ABC, 1971; "Perry Mason: The Case of the Lost Love," NBC, 1988; "Turn Back the Clock," NBC, 1989.

BARRY, JACK

b. Lindenhurst, NY, March 20, 1918; d. 1984. Game-show emcee whose career was hampered a bit by the quiz-show scandals of the fifties; in the seventies he made a comeback with "The Joker's Wild."

AS A REGULAR: "Juvenile Jury," NBC, 1947-48, 1951-53; CBS, 1953-54; NBC, 1955; SYN, 1971-72; "Life Begins at Eighty," NBC, 1950; ABC, 1950-52; DUM, 1952-55; ABC, 1955-56; "Wisdom of the Ages," DUM, 1952-53; "Winky Dink and You," CBS, 1953-57; "The Big Surprise," NBC, 1955-56; "Twenty-One," NBC, 1956-58; "High-Low," NBC, 1956; "Concentration," NBC, 1958-59; "Tic Tac Dough," NBC, 1958-59; "The Generation Gap," ABC, 1969; "The Reel Game," ABC, 1971; "Break the Bank," ABC, 1976; "The Joker's Wild," CBS, 1972-75; SYN, 1976-84; "Joker! Joker! Joker!," SYN, 1979-80.

AND: "Batman: Hi Diddle Riddle/Smack in the Middle," ABC, 1966.

* After accusations surfaced, it was found that some contestants on "Twenty-One" were given answers before the show; Barry, however, was never implicated.

BARRY, PATRICIA

b. Patricia White, Davenport, IA. Actress who played Jack Kulgman's understanding wife on "Harris Against the World"; more recently she played Sally Gleason on "The Guiding Light."

AS A REGULAR: "First Love," NBC, 1954-55; "Harris Against the World," NBC, 1964-65; "Days of Our Lives," NBC, 1971-74; "Lovers and Friends (For Richer, for Poorer)," NBC, 1977-78; "All My Children," ABC, 1980-81; "The Guiding Light," CBS, 1984-86.

AND: "Alcoa Hour: Flight Into Danger," NBC, 1956; "Goodyear TV Playhouse: Weekend in Vermont," NBC, 1957; "Playhouse 90: Reunion," CBS, 1957; "Studio One: The Shadow of a Genius," CBS, 1958; "Gunsmoke: The Cabin," CBS, 1958; "G.E. Theatre: Bill Bailey, Won't You Please Come Home," CBS, 1959; "Westinghouse Desilu Playhouse: The Hard Road," CBS, 1959; "Laramie: The Star Trail," NBC, 1959; "Goodyear Theatre: The Golden Shanty," NBC, 1959; "Startime: The Wicked Scheme of Jebal Deeks," NBC, 1959; "G.E. Theatre: They Liked Me Fine," CBS, 1960; "Bachelor Father: Bentley Meets the Perfect Woman," NBC, 1960; "Tales of Wells Fargo: Dealer's Choice," NBC, 1960; "Ben Casey: The Sweet Kiss of Madness," ABC, 1961; "My Three Sons: Second Time Around," ABC, 1962; "Thriller: A Wig for Miss DeVore," NBC, 1962; "Walt Disney's Wonderful World of Color: Sammy the Way-Out Seal," NBC, 1962; "Rawhide: Incident of the Married Widow," CBS, 1963; "The Twilight Zone: I Dream of Genie," CBS, 1963; "The Virginian: The Judgement," NBC, 1963; "The Farmer's Daughter: Rendez-vous for Two," ABC, 1964; "The Guns of Will Sonnett: The Hero," ABC, 1967; "Mannix: Only Giants Can Play," CBS, 1969; "Columbo: Playback," NBC, 1975; "Police Woman: Nothing Left to Lose," NBC, 1975; "Three's Company: The Reverend Steps Out," ABC, 1979; "Quincy: Vigil of Fear," NBC, 1981; "Hardcastle and McCormick: Whatever Happened to Guts?," ABC, 1984; "Simon & Simon: Still Phil After All These Years," CBS, 1986; "Murder, She Wrote: Something Borrowed, Someone Blue," CBS, 1989.

TV MOVIES AND MINISERIES: "Crowhaven Farm," ABC, 1970; "Dead Men Tell No Tales," CBS, 1971; "The Great American Beauty Contest," ABC, 1973; "First You Cry," CBS, 1978; "Bogie," CBS, 1980; "The Jerk, Too," NBC, 1984.

BARRYMORE, ETHEL

b. Ethel Mae Blyth, Philadelphia, PA, August 15, 1879; d. 1959. Stage and screen legend.

AS A REGULAR: "Ethel Barrymore Theatre," SYN, 1956-57.

AND: "Hollywood Opening Night: Mysterious Ways," NBC, 1952; "Climax!: The Thirteenth Chair," CBS, 1954; "Remember: White Oaks," NBC, 1955; "Svengali and the Blonde," NBC, 1955; "G.E. Theatre: Prosper's Old Mother," CBS, 1955; "Playhouse 90: Eloise," CBS, 1956; "Texaco Star Theatre: Command Appearance," NBC, 1957; "World's Greatest Mother," SYN, 1958.

BARRYMORE, JOHN JR.
b. *John Blythe Barrymore, Jr., Beverly Hills, CA, June 4, 1932.* Son of the movies' "Great Profile," a performer who inherited his father's love of drink and penchant for getting in trouble. He went into seclusion in the late sixties and then did some more TV work. Also known as John Drew Barrymore; father of Drew.
AS A REGULAR: "Pantomime Quiz," CBS, 1953; DUM, 1953-54; CBS, 1954.
AND: "Schlitz Playhouse of Stars: Boomerang," CBS, 1953; "Matinee Theatre: The Runaways," NBC, 1956; "Climax!: The Secret Thread," CBS, 1956; "The 20th Century-Fox Hour: End of a Gun," CBS, 1957; "Playhouse 90: The Miracle Worker," CBS, 1957; "Matinee Theatre: End of the Rope," NBC, 1957; "Playhouse 90: Ain't no Time for Glory," CBS, 1957; "Rawhide: Incident of the Haunted Hills," CBS, 1959; "The Dick Powell Show: Colossus," NBC, 1962; "Rawhide: Corporal Dasovik," CBS, 1964; "The Wild Wild West: The Night of the Double-Edged Knife," CBS, 1965; "Run for Your Life: Hoodlums on Wheels," NBC, 1966; "The Road West: This Savage Land," NBC, 1966; "Dundee and the Culhane: The Turn the Other Cheek Brief," CBS, 1967; "The Wild Wild West: Night of the Double Knife," CBS, 1969; "Kung Fu: Barbary House," ABC, 1975; "Lou Grant: Dogs," CBS, 1980.
TV MOVIES AND MINISERIES: "Winchester '73," NBC, 1967.

BARTH, EDDIE
b. *Philadelphia, PA, September 29, 1931.* Portly, gravel-voiced character actor, usually playing cops or blue-collar types. He's also provided voices for hundreds of commercial voice-overs.
AS A REGULAR: "Shaft," CBS, 1973-74; "Husbands, Wives & Lovers," CBS, 1978; "Number 96," NBC, 1980-81; "Simon & Simon," CBS, 1981-83; "Mickey Spillane's Mike Hammer," CBS, 1984-85.
AND: "The Twilight Zone: The New Exhibit," CBS, 1963; "The FBI: Overload," ABC, 1967; "Mannix: The Sound of Darkness," CBS, 1969; "The Streets of San Francisco: Cry Help," ABC, 1974; "Barney Miller: Stakeout," ABC, 1975; "Kojak: A House of Prayer, A Den of Thieves," CBS, 1975; "Alice: Auld Acquaintances Should be Forgot," CBS, 1979; "Scarecrow and Mrs.

King: Car Wars," CBS, 1985; "Perfect Strangers: Baby, You Can Drive My Car," ABC, 1986; "The New Mike Hammer: Kill John Doe," CBS, 1987.
TV MOVIES AND MINISERIES: "Amelia Earhart," NBC, 1976; "Rich Man, Poor Man," ABC, 1976; "Jimmy B. and Andre," CBS, 1980.

BARTLETT, BONNIE
b. *1935.* Emmy-winning actress who played Ellen, long-suffering wife of Dr. Mark Craig (William Daniels) on "St. Elsewhere"; also the real-life wife of Daniels. In the fifties she played Vanessa on "Love of Life."
AS A REGULAR: "Love of Life," CBS, 1955-59; "Little House on the Prairie," NBC, 1976-77; "St. Elsewhere," NBC, 1982-88.
AND: "The Patty Duke Show: My Cousin the Hero," ABC, 1965; "Gunsmoke: In Performance of Duty," CBS, 1974; "Little House on the Prairie: Ma's Holiday," NBC, 1974; "Kojak: The Good Luck Bomber," CBS, 1975; "Barney Miller: The Delegate," ABC, 1980; "Lou Grant: Unthinkable," CBS, 1981; "Barney Miller: Inquiry," ABC, 1982; "Midnight Caller: Promise to a Dead Man," NBC, 1989; "Murder, She Wrote: Seal of the Confessional," CBS, 1990; "Wiseguy: Sanctuary," CBS, 1990; "Wiseguy: Brrrump-Bump," CBS, 1990.
TV MOVIES AND MINISERIES: "The Legend of Lizzie Borden," ABC, 1975; "Ike," ABC, 1979; "G.E. Theatre: A Long Way Home," ABC, 1981; "Malice in Wonderland," CBS, 1985; "The Deliberate Stranger," NBC, 1986; "Deadly Deception," CBS, 1987; "Right to Die," NBC, 1987; "Police Story: The Watch Commander," ABC, 1988.
* Emmies: 1986, 1987.

BARTON, JAMES
b. *Gloucester City, NJ, November 1, 1890; d. 1962.* Dancer-comic who grew up in vaudeville; he did bits as elderly men in TV dramas.
AS A GUEST: "Kaiser Aluminum Hour: Man on a White Horse," NBC, 1956; "Kraft Television Theatre: The Big Break," NBC, 1957; "Playhouse 90: The Time of Your Life," CBS, 1958; "New York Confidential: The Captain Kenesaw Story," SYN, 1958; "Naked City: Goodbye, My Lady Love," ABC, 1959; "Naked City: A Little of the Action," ABC, 1959; "Hotel De Paree: A Fool and His Gold," CBS, 1959; "The Loretta Young Show: Switchblade," NBC, 1960; "The Americans: Half Moon Road," NBC, 1961; "Adventures in Paradise: Hill of Ghosts," ABC, 1961; "Naked City: Bridge Party," ABC, 1961; "Alcoa Premiere: The Jail," ABC, 1962.

BARTY, BILLY
b. *Millsboro, PA, October 25, 1924.* Dwarf

actor who was a regular performer with the oh-so-refined Spike Jones.

AS A REGULAR: "Ford Festival," NBC, 1951-52; "Circus Boy," NBC, 1956-57; ABC, 1957-58; "The Spike Jones Show," NBC, 1954; CBS, 1957; "Club Oasis," NBC, 1958; "Sigmund and the Sea Monsters," NBC, 1974-76; "Ace Crawford, Private Eye," CBS, 1983.

AND: "Mr. Lucky: Taking a Chance," CBS, 1960; "This Is Your Life," NBC, 1960; "Peter Gunn: Baby Shoes," NBC, 1960; "Art Linkletter's House Party," CBS, 1960; "Rawhide: Prairie Elephant," CBS, 1961; "My Three Sons: Coincidence," ABC, 1962; "Get Smart: Ironhand," CBS, 1969; "Get Smart: Is This Trip Necessary?," CBS, 1969; "Get Smart: Hello Columbus, Goodbye America," CBS, 1970; "Love, American Style: Love and the Wee He," ABC, 1972; "Barney Miller: Sex Surrogate," ABC, 1977; "The Love Boat: Murder on the High Seas," ABC, 1979; "Little House on the Prairie: Annabelle," NBC, 1979; "CHiPS: Counterfeit," NBC, 1979; "Little House: A New Beginning: Little Lou," NBC, 1982.

TV MOVIES AND MINISERIES: "Punch and Jody," CBS, 1974.

BARUCH, ANDRE

b. Paris, France, 1906. Velvet-voiced announcer of radio and early TV; later a New York deejay with wife Bea Wain.

AS A REGULAR: "Masters of Magic," CBS, 1949; "Your Hit Parade," NBC, 1950-57.

BASEHART, RICHARD

b. Zanesville, OH, August 31, 1914; d. 1984. Actor best known as Admiral Harriman Nelson on "Voyage to the Bottom of the Sea."

AS A REGULAR: "Voyage to the Bottom of the Sea," ABC, 1964-68; "WEB," NBC, 1978.

AND: "Playhouse 90: So Soon to Die," CBS, 1957; "Studio One: Mutiny on the Shark," CBS, 1957; "Dick Powell's Zane Grey Theatre: Medal for Valor," CBS, 1958; "Playhouse 90: A Dream of Treason," CBS, 1960; "Playhouse 90: The Hiding Place," CBS, 1960; "Du Pont Show of the Month: Men in White," CBS, 1960; "Hallmark Hall of Fame: Shangri-La," NBC, 1960; "Play of the Week: He Who Gets Slapped," SYN, 1961; "Family Classics: The Light That Failed," CBS, 1961; "Here's Hollywood," NBC, 1961; "Rawhide: Black Sheep," CBS, 1961; "Theatre '62: The Paradine Case," NBC, 1962; "Naked City: Dust Devil on a Quiet Street," ABC, 1962; "Ben Casey: Light Up the Dark Corners," ABC, 1963; "Arrest and Trial: In Question to a Bleeding Heart," ABC, 1963; "The Alfred Hitchcock Hour: Starring the Defense," CBS, 1963; "The Twilight Zone: Probe Seven," CBS, 1963; "Combat!: The Long Way Home," ABC, 1963; "The American Woman in the 20th Century," CBS, 1964; "Hans

Brinker," NBC, 1969; "Hollywood Television Theatre: The Andersonville Trial," NET, 1970; "Ironside: Noel's Gonna Fly," NBC, 1970; "Gunsmoke: Captain Sligo," CBS, 1971; "The Bold Ones: Is This Operation Necessary?," NBC, 1972; "Columbo: Dagger of the Mind," NBC, 1972; "Hawaii Five-O: The Odd Lot Caper," CBS, 1973; "Marcus Welby, M.D.: A Full Life," ABC, 1974; "Marcus Welby, M.D.: The Last Rip-Off," ABC, 1974; "The First Woman President," ABC, 1974; "ABC Theatre: The Court-Martial of Lt. Calley," ABC, 1975; "American Parade: The Case Against Milligan," CBS, 1975; "Medical Story: The God Syndrome," NBC, 1975; "Hallmark Hall of Fame: Valley Forge," NBC, 1975; "The Streets of San Francisco: Requiem for Murder," ABC, 1976; "Little House on the Prairie: Troublemaker," NBC, 1976; "Knight Rider: Pilot," NBC, 1982.

TV MOVIES AND MINISERIES: "Sole Survivor," CBS, 1970; "City Beneath the Sea," NBC, 1971; "The Birdmen," ABC, 1971; "The Death of Me Yet," ABC, 1971; "Assignment: Munich," ABC, 1972; "The Bounty Man," ABC, 1972; "Maneater," CBS, 1973; "Time Travelers," ABC, 1976; "21 Hours at Munich," ABC, 1976; "Flood," NBC, 1976; "Stonestreet: Who Killed the Centerfold Model?," NBC, 1977; "The Critical List," NBC, 1978; "The Rebels," SYN, 1979.

BASINGER, KIM

b. Athens, GA, December 8, 1953. Movie sex symbol ("Batman," "9 1/2 Weeks").

AS A REGULAR: "Dog and Cat," ABC, 1977; "From Here to Eternity," NBC, 1980.

TV MOVIES AND MINISERIES: "Katie: Portrait of a Centerfold," NBC, 1978; "From Here to Eternity," NBC, 1979; "Killjoy," CBS, 1981.

BATEMAN, JASON

b. New York City, NY, January 14, 1969. Young actor who plays David Hogan on "The Hogan Family."

AS A REGULAR: "Little House on the Prairie," NBC, 1981-82; "Silver Spoons," NBC, 1982-84; "It's Your Move," NBC, 1984-85; "Valerie," NBC, 1986-87; "Valerie's Family," NBC, 1987; "The Hogan Family," NBC, 1988-90; CBS, 1990- .

AND: "Knight Rider: Lost Knight," NBC, 1984; "St. Elsewhere: You Beta Your Life," NBC, 1986; "Matlock: The Producer," NBC, 1987; "Candid Camera: Eat! Eat! Eat!," CBS, 1989; "The Pat Sajak Show," CBS, 1989; "The Ice Capades with Jason Bateman and Alyssa Milano," ABC, 1989.

TV MOVIES AND MINISERIES: "The Fantastic World of D.C. Collins," NBC, 1984; "Can You Feel Me Dancing?," NBC, 1986; "Philly Boy," NBC, 1988; "Moving Target," NBC, 1988.

BATEMAN, JUSTINE

b. Rye, NY, February 19, 1966. Sister of Jason; she played Mallory Keaton on "Family Ties."
AS A REGULAR: "Family Ties," NBC, 1982-89.
AND: "Glitter: On Your Toes," ABC, 1984; "Saturday Night Live," NBC, 1988; "Candid Camera: Eat! Eat! Eat!," CBS, 1989; "The Jim Henson Hour: Miss Piggy's Hollywood," NBC, 1989.
TV MOVIES AND MINISERIES: "Right to Kill?," ABC, 1985; "Family Ties Vacation," NBC, 1985; "Can You Feel Me Dancing?," NBC, 1986.

BATES, RHONDA

Tall, big-mouthed actress of late seventies TV.
AS A REGULAR: "Keep on Truckin'," ABC, 1975; "Blansky's Beauties," ABC, 1977; "The Roller Girls," NBC, 1978; "Speak Up, America," NBC, 1980.
AND: "CPO Sharkey: Sharkey Boogies on Down," NBC, 1977; "CPO Sharkey: Sharkey the Marriage Counselor," NBC, 1977; "The Love Boat: What's a Brother For?," ABC, 1979; "The John Davidson Show," SYN, 1980.

BATMAN, ABC, 1966-68.

ABC brought the concept of "camp" to television with this 1966 comedy series that wasn't a comedy at all to the millions of kids who watched it and made it the hottest thing since white "Hullabaloo" boots. But to adults, "Batman" was a stiffly acted, deadpan spoof of movie serials that still stands up as so-bad-it's-good TV. Example: In the show's first episode, villainess Jill St. John dies by falling into an atomic pit in the Batcave. Batman, who tried to save her: "What a way to go-go."

An immediate hit, "Batman" spawned bat-paraphenalia, a theatrical bat-movie and even a new Arthur Murray dance, the "Batusi." Adam West, who played Batman, alias Bruce Wayne, and Burt Ward, who played Robin, alias Dick Grayson, became superstars for about a year. Big names lined up to play villians: Vincent Price as Egghead, George Sanders, Otto Preminger and Eli Wallach as Mr. Freeze, Burgess Meredith as the Penguin, Julie Newmar and Eartha Kitt as Catwoman (played in the movie by Lee Meriwether), David Wayne as the Mad Hatter, Roddy MacDowall as the Bookworm, Joan Collins as the Siren, Van Johnson as the Minstrel, Cesar Romero as the Joker and most notably, Frank Gorshin as the Riddler. Other stars appeared in cameos, usually popping out of windows in walls the Dynamic Duo were scaling. "Batman" aired twice a week at first, each

Wednesday episode ending with a cliffhanger that was resolved on Thursday nights. By the fall of 1967, however, Batmania was cooling and the show went to once-a-week, adding Batgirl (Yvonne Craig) to keep those young male fans who were starting to get interested in the opposite sex. "Batman" didn't fade from public consciousness, however; when Tim Burton made a darker version of the story in 1989, it became the year's highest-grossing film. And a lot of people wanted it to be as witty and silly as the TV show was.

TRIVIA QUIZ #3: "BATMAN"
1. What was all over the Riddler's outfit?
2. What was the name of Bruce Wayne's aunt?
3. What was Batgirl's secret identity?
4. True or false: On the TV show, Bruce Wayne's butler, Alfred, knew the secret identity of his boss.
5. Who created Batman?
6. Neil Hamilton played police commissioner ___.
7. Stafford Repp played police chief ___.
8. The "Batman" theme song had a one-word lyric. What was it?
9. Fill in the blank: "Tune in tomorrow night: Same ___, same _____."
10. True or false: Sean Connery once popped out of a window on the show.

(Answers at end of book.)

BAUER, CHARITA

b. Newark, NJ, December 20, 1923; d. 1985. Plump, motherly actress who played Bert Bauer on "The Guiding Light" for 32 years.
AS A REGULAR: "The Aldrich Family," NBC, 1949-50; "The Guiding Light," CBS, 1952-84.
AND: "Look Up and Live: An Enemy of the People," CBS, 1962.
TV MOVIES AND MINISERIES: "The Cradle Will Fall," CBS, 1983.

BAUER, JAIME LYN

b. Phoenix, AZ, March 9, 1949. Actress who played Lauralee Brooks Prentiss on "The Young and the Restless."
AS A REGULAR: "The Young and the Restless," CBS, 1973-82, 1984; "Bare Essence," NBC, 1983.
AND: "The Love Boat: Too Rich and Too Thin," ABC, 1984; "The Love Boat: Baby Sister," ABC, 1985.
TV MOVIES AND MINISERIES: "The Mysterious Island of Beautiful Women," CBS, 1979; "Where the Hell's That Gold?," CBS, 1988.

BAUMAN, JON "BOWSER"

b. *Queens, NY, September 14, 1947*. Former member of Sha Na Na turned game-show host.

AS A REGULAR: "Sha Na Na," SYN, 1977-81; "The Match Game/Hollywood Squares Hour," NBC, 1983-84; "Pop 'n' Rocker Game," SYN, 1983-84.

BAUR, ELIZABETH

b. *Los Angeles, CA, December 11, 1948*. Actress who played policewoman Fran Belding on "Ironside."

AS A REGULAR: "Lancer," CBS, 1968-71; "Ironside," NBC, 1971-75.

AND: "Room 222: Cheating," ABC, 1970; "Nanny and the Professor: The Communication Gap," ABC, 1971; "Emergency!: School Days," NBC, 1972; "Police Woman: Flip of a Coin," NBC, 1978; "Fantasy Island: The World's Most Desirable Woman," ABC, 1981.

BAVIER, FRANCES

b. *New York City, NY, January 14, 1902; d. 1990*. Actress best known as Aunt Bee on "The Andy Griffith Show."

AS A REGULAR: "It's a Great Life," NBC, 1954-56; "The Eve Arden Show," CBS, 1957-58; "The Andy Griffith Show," CBS, 1960-68; "Mayberry RFD," CBS, 1968-70.

AND: "Damon Runyon Theatre: It Comes Up Money," CBS, 1955; "Alfred Hitchcock Presents: Revenge," CBS, 1955; "The Loretta Young Show: The First Man to Ask Her," NBC, 1956; "The Jane Wyman Show: Small Talk," NBC, 1957; "Schlitz Playhouse of Stars: One Left Over," CBS, 1957; "Perry Mason: The Crimson Kiss," CBS, 1957; "G.E. Theatre: With Malice Toward One," CBS, 1957; "The Gale Storm Show: A Trip for Auntie," CBS, 1958; "Sugarfoot: The Trial of the Canary Kid," ABC, 1959; "The Danny Thomas Show: Danny Meets Andy Griffith," CBS, 1960; "Gomer Pyle, USMC: A Visit From Aunt Bee," CBS, 1967.

* Bavier appeared in the pilot for "The Andy Griffith Show" that appeared on "The Danny Thomas Show," but not as Aunt Bee; she was a Mayberry resident whose husband had just been buried—in a rented suit.
* After Bavier retired from show business, she settled in North Carolina, in a small town not unlike Mayberry.
* Emmies: 1967.

BAXLEY, BARBARA

b. *1924; d. 1990*. Actress who played many a raspy-voiced, hard-bitten woman.

AS A REGULAR: "Search for Tomorrow," CBS, 1962, 1969; "Where the Heart Is," CBS, 1969-73.

AND: "Broadway Television Theatre: It Pays to Advertise," SYN, 1952; "Robert Montgomery Presents: Keane vs. Keane," NBC, 1952; "Armstrong Circle Theatre: A Volcano is Dancing Here," CBS, 1952; "Kraft Television Theatre: The Twilight Road," NBC, 1953; "Mirror Theatre: One Summer's Rain," NBC, 1953; "Goodyear TV Playhouse: Moment of Panic," NBC, 1954; "Philco TV Playhouse: Write Me Out Forever," NBC, 1954; "Alfred Hitchcock Presents: Nightmare in 4-D," CBS, 1957; "Kaiser Aluminum Hour: The Story of a Crime," NBC, 1957; "Alfred Hitchcock Presents: The Three Dreams of Mr. Findlater," CBS, 1957; "True Story: Marriage of Convenience," NBC, 1957; "New York Confidential: Sudden Money," SYN, 1958; "Shirley Temple's Storybook: Beauty and the Beast," NBC, 1958; "Alfred Hitchcock Presents: Design for Loving," CBS, 1958; "Alcoa Presents: Message From Clara," ABC, 1959; "Alfred Hitchcock Presents: Anniversary Gift," CBS, 1959; "Alfred Hitchcock Presents: Across the Threshold," CBS, 1960; "Have Gun, Will Travel: Full Circle," CBS, 1960; "Diagnosis: Unknown: A Sudden Stillness," CBS, 1960; "Play of the Week: A Palm Tree in a Rose Garden," SYN, 1960; "Special for Women: The Single Woman," NBC, 1961; "Way Out: The Overnight Case," CBS, 1961; "The Defenders: The Seven Ghosts of Simon Gray," CBS, 1962; "The Twilight Zone: Mute," CBS, 1963; "The Defenders: Claire Cheval Died in Boston," CBS, 1964; "The Fugitive: Nobody Loses All the Time," ABC, 1966; "The Streets of San Francisco: The Takers," ABC, 1972; "Marcus Welby, M.D.: The Circles of Shame," ABC, 1973; "Hawaii Five-O: One Big Happy Family," CBS, 1973; "Owen Marshall, Counselor at Law: House of Friends," ABC, 1974; "The Rookies: Take Over," ABC, 1974; "The Snoop Sisters: The Devil Made Me Do It," NBC, 1974; "Hotel: Vantage Point," ABC, 1984; "The Twilight Zone: Button, Button," CBS, 1986; "Murder, She Wrote: Jessica Behind Bars," CBS, 1986.

TV MOVIES AND MINISERIES: "The Law," NBC, 1974; "The Imposter," NBC, 1975.

BAXTER, ANNE

b. *Michigan City, IN, May 7, 1923; d. 1985*. Screen actress ("All About Eve") who usually played refined types, including Victoria Cabot on "Hotel."

AS A REGULAR: "Marcus Welby, M.D.," ABC, 1969-70; "Hotel," ABC, 1983-86.

AND: "G.E. Theatre: Bitter Choice," CBS, 1957; "Playhouse 90: The Right Hand Man," CBS, 1958; "G.E. Theatre: Stopover," CBS, 1958; "Art Linkletter's House Party," CBS, 1958; "Lux Playhouse: The Four," CBS, 1958; "Arthur Murray Party," NBC, 1958; "Wagon Train: The Kitty Angel Story," NBC, 1959; "Riverboat: Race to Cincinnati," NBC, 1959; "Dick Powell's Zane

Grey Theatre: Hand on the Latch," CBS, 1959; "Checkmate: Death Runs Wild," CBS, 1960; "The Du Pont Show with June Allyson: The Dance Man," CBS, 1960; "G.E. Theatre: Goodbye, My Love," CBS, 1960; "Dr. Kildare: A Day to Remember," NBC, 1964; "Batman: Zelda the Great/A Death Worse Than Fate," ABC, 1966; "My Three Sons: Designing Woman," CBS, 1967; "Batman: The Ogg and I/How to Hatch a Dinosaur," ABC, 1967; "Batman: The Ogg Couple," ABC, 1967; "The Danny Thomas Hour: Measure of a Man," NBC, 1968; "The FBI: Region of Peril," ABC, 1968; "Run for Your Life: Life Among the Maneaters," NBC, 1968; "Ironside: An Obvious Case of Guilt," NBC, 1968; "The FBI: Region of Peril," ABC, 1968; "The Name of the Game: The Protector," NBC, 1968; "The Virginian: Nora," NBC, 1968; "The Big Valley: The 25 Graves of Midas," ABC, 1969; "The Name of the Game: The Bobby Currier Story," NBC, 1969; "Hollywood Squares," NBC, 1969; "Ironside: Programmed for Death," NBC, 1969; "The Name of the Game: The Takeover," NBC, 1970; "The Name of the Game: All the Old Familiar Faces," NBC, 1970; "Columbo: Requiem for a Falling Star," NBC, 1973; "Cannon: He Who Digs a Grave," CBS, 1973; "Love Story: All My Tomorrows," NBC, 1973; "Banacek: If Max Is So Smart, Why Doesn't He Tell Us Where He Is?," NBC, 1973; "Tomorrow," NBC, 1976; "The Love Boat: Letting Go," ABC, 1985.

TV MOVIES AND MINISERIES: "Stranger on the Run," NBC, 1967; "Companions in Nightmare," NBC, 1968; "Marcus Welby, M.D.," ABC, 1969; "The Challengers," CBS, 1970; "Ritual of Evil," NBC, 1970; "If Tomorrow Comes," ABC, 1971; "The Catcher," ABC, 1972; "Lisa, Bright and Dark," NBC, 1973; "The Moneychangers," NBC, 1976; "Little Mo," NBC, 1978; "East of Eden," ABC, 1981.

BAXTER, DR. FRANK

Shakespeare lecturer and professor who was a TV personality for a time; best known for "Our Mr. Sun."

AS A REGULAR: "Telephone Time," ABC, 1957-58.

AND: "The George Burns and Gracie Allen Show: The Shakespeare Paper," CBS, 1956; "Our Mr. Sun," CBS, 1956; "Hemo the Magnificent," CBS, 1957; "The Ford Show," NBC, 1957; "The Strange Case of the Cosmic Rays," NBC, 1957; "The Unchained Goddess," NBC, 1958; "Gateways to the Mind," NBC, 1958; "The Alphabet Conspiracy," NBC, 1959; "Art Linkletter's House Party," CBS, 1959; "The Thread of Life," NBC, 1960; "Bell Telephone Hour: Much Ado About Music," NBC, 1961; "About Time," NBC, 1962; "My Three Sons: Robbie Valentino," ABC, 1962; "Mr. Novak: X Is

the Unknown Factor," NBC, 1963; "You Don't Say," NBC, 1967.

BAXTER BIRNEY, MEREDITH

b. Los Angeles, CA, June 21, 1947. Blonde actress who played Nancy Lawrence Maitland on "Family" and Elyse Keaton on "Family Ties"; daughter of Whitney Blake.

AS A REGULAR: "Bridget Loves Bernie," CBS, 1972-73; "Family," ABC, 1976-80; "Family Ties," NBC, 1982-89.

AND: "The Interns: The Secret," CBS, 1971; "The Young Lawyers: The Victim," ABC, 1971; "The Doris Day Show: Young Love," CBS, 1971; "The Partridge Family: Where Do Mermaids Go?," ABC, 1971; "Owen Marshall, Counselor at Law: Words of Summer," ABC, 1972; "Barnaby Jones: The Deadly Jinx," CBS, 1974; "Young Love," CBS, 1974; "Medical Center: The Demi-God," CBS, 1974; "Wide World of Mystery: The Invasion of Carol Enders," ABC, 1975; "Medical Center: The Velvet Knife," CBS, 1975; "The Streets of San Francisco: Deadly Silence," ABC, 1975; "Medical Story: A Life in the Balance," NBC, 1975; "McMillan and Wife: Secrets for Sale," NBC, 1975; "City of Angels: The November Plan," NBC, 1976; "ABC Mystery of the Week: Terror in the Night," ABC, 1976; "Police Woman: Sara Who?," NBC, 1976; "The Love Boat: The Captain and the Lady," ABC, 1977; "What Really Happened to the Class of '65?: The Class Jock," NBC, 1978; "The Love Boat: The Gigolo," ABC, 1982; "The Pat Sajak Show," CBS, 1989.

TV MOVIES AND MINISERIES: "The Cat Creature," ABC, 1973; "The Stranger Who Looks Like Me," ABC, 1974; "Target Risk," NBC, 1975; "The Imposter," NBC, 1975; "The Night That Panicked America," ABC, 1975; "Little Women," NBC, 1978; "Beulah Land," NBC, 1980; "Take Your Best Shot," CBS, 1982; "ABC Theater: The Rape of Richard Beck," ABC, 1985; "Family Ties Vacation," NBC, 1985; "Kate's Secret," NBC, 1986; "The Long Journey Home," NBC, 1987; "She Knows Too Much," NBC, 1989.

BEACHAM, STEPHANIE

b. Casablanca, Morocco, August 23, 1949. British actress who wallowed in witchery as the nasty Sable Colby on "The Colbys" and "Dynasty."

AS A REGULAR: "The Colbys," ABC, 1985-87; "Dynasty," ABC, 1988-89; "Sister Kate," NBC, 1989-90.

AND: "ALF Takes Over the Network," NBC, 1989.

BEAIRD, BARBARA

b. Waco, TX, 1948. Former child actress.

AS A REGULAR: "Fibber McGee and Molly," NBC, 1959-60.
AND: "Steve Canyon: Iron Curtain," NBC, 1959; "Startime: Incident at a Corner," NBC, 1960; "The Danny Thomas Show: Rusty and the Tomboy," CBS, 1960; "The Chevy Show: Ghosts, Goblins and Kids," NBC, 1960; "Wagon Train: The Will Santee Story," NBC, 1961; "Rawhide: The Boss's Daughters," CBS, 1962.

BEAIRD, BETTY
b. El Paso, TX, 1939. Actress who played Marie Waggedorn, mother of Earl J. Waggedorn (Michael Link) and friend of Julia Baker (Diahann Carroll).
AS A REGULAR: "Julia," NBC, 1968-71.

BEAIRD, PAMELA
b. 1942. Cousin of Barbara, another young actress; she played Mary Ellen Rogers, occasional girlfriend of Wally Cleaver (Tony Dow) on "Leave It to Beaver."
AS A REGULAR: "The Mickey Mouse Club," ABC, 1956; "My Friend Flicka," CBS, 1956-57.
AND: "Fury: Trial by Jury," NBC, 1956; "The Adventures of Jim Bowie: Thieves' Market," ABC, 1957; "Telephone Time: Stranded," ABC, 1957; "Circus Boy: Royal Roustabout," NBC, 1958; "Leave It to Beaver: Eddie's Girl," ABC, 1959; "Leave It to Beaver: Wally's Orchid," ABC, 1960; "Leave It to Beaver: Wally's Weekend Job," ABC, 1961; "The Danny Thomas Show: Casanova Junior," CBS, 1962; "Mr. Novak: I Don't Even Live Here," NBC, 1963; "Mr. Novak: How Does Your Garden Grow," NBC, 1964.

BEAN, ORSON
b. Dallas Frederick Burrows, Burlington, VT, July 22, 1928. Comic with a dry style; best known as a quiz-show panelist.
AS A REGULAR: "I've Got a Secret," CBS, 1952; "The Blue Angel," CBS, 1954; "Keep Talking," ABC, 1959-60; "To Tell the Truth," CBS, 1964-67; "Mary Hartman, Mary Hartman," SYN, 1977-78; "One Life to Live," ABC, 1984.
AND: "Broadway Television Theatre: Three Men on a Horse," SYN, 1952; "Broadway Television Theatre: Nothing But the Truth," SYN, 1952; "Studio One: The Square Peg," CBS, 1952; "U.S. Steel Hour: Good for You," ABC, 1954; "Robert Montgomery Presents: It Happened in Paris," NBC, 1954; "Studio One: Joye," CBS, 1954; "U.S. Steel Hour: The Fifth Wheel," ABC, 1954; "Best of Broadway: Arsenic and Old Lace," CBS, 1955; "Elgin TV Hour: San Francisco Fracas," ABC, 1955; "Studio One: A Christmas Surprise," CBS, 1956; "The Phil Silvers Show: Bilko's Insurance Company," CBS, 1958; "Pantomime

Quiz," ABC, 1958; "The Millionaire: The Newman Johnson Story," CBS, 1958; "Laugh Line," NBC, 1959; "Miracle on 34th Street," NBC, 1959; "Art Carney Special: The Man in the Dog Suit," NBC, 1960; "The Twilight Zone: Mr. Bevis," CBS, 1960; "Play of the Week: Once Around the Block," SYN, 1960; "The du Pont Show with June Allyson: The Secret Life of James Thurber," CBS, 1961; "The Jack Paar Show," NBC, 1961; "Password," CBS, 1962; "Naked City: To Walk Like a Lion," ABC, 1962; "To Tell the Truth," CBS, 1963; "Hootenanny," ABC, 1964; "To Tell the Truth," CBS, 1964; "The Match Game," NBC, 1964; "Get the Message," ABC, 1964; "To Tell the Truth," CBS, 1965; "The Young Set," ABC, 1965; "The Merv Griffin Show," SYN, 1966; "NET Playhouse: The Star Wagon," NET, 1967; "Ghostbreaker," NBC, 1967; "The Dean Martin Show," NBC, 1969; "Love, American Style: Love and the Teacher," ABC, 1970; "The Tonight Show Starring Johnny Carson," NBC, 1971; "Tattletales," CBS, 1975; "Match Game '75," CBS, 1975; "Ellery Queen: The Chinese Dog," NBC, 1975; "The Tonight Show Starring Johnny Carson," NBC, 1976; "Stumpers," NBC, 1976; "The Love Boat: Mona of the Movies," ABC, 1979.

BEASLEY, ALLYCE
b. Brooklyn, NY, July 6, 1954. Actress who played Agnes di Pesto, rhyming receptionist for the Blue Moon Detective Agency on "Moonlighting"; she also played the daughter of Coach (Nicholas Colasanto) on an early episode of "Cheers."
AS A REGULAR: "Moonlighting," ABC, 1985-89.
AND: "Taxi: Scenskees From a Marriage," NBC, 1982; "Cheers: The Coach's Daughter," NBC, 1982; "Remington Steele: Steele Crazy After All These Years," NBC, 1983; "Shaping Up: Pilot," ABC, 1984.

THE BEATLES
Revolutionary rock group of the sixties; they made their live U.S. TV debut with Ed Sullivan, but Jack Paar ran film of them performing in England shortly before they appeared with Sullivan.
AS GUESTS: "The Jack Paar Program," NBC, 1964; "The Ed Sullivan Show," CBS, 1964; "Shindig," ABC, 1964; "Around The Beatles," ABC, 1964; "The Ed Sullivan Show," CBS, 1965; "The Smothers Brothers Comedy Hour," CBS, 1968; "The Music Scene," ABC, 1969.
* See also George Harrison, John Lennon, Paul McCartney and Ringo Starr.

BEATTY, NED
b. Louisville, KY, July 6, 1937. Stocky character actor of films ("Deliverance,"

"Network") and TV; lately he's played the father of Dan Connor (John Goodman) on "Roseanne."

AS A REGULAR: "Szysznyk," CBS, 1977-78.
AND: "The Rockford Files: Profit and Loss," NBC, 1974; "M*A*S*H: Dear Peggy," CBS, 1975; "Petrocelli: Death Ride," NBC, 1975; "The Rookies: Shadow of a Man," ABC, 1975; "The Rockford Files: Return to the 38th Parallel," NBC, 1976; "The Streets of San Francisco: Hang Tough," ABC, 1977; "Gunsmoke: The Hiders," CBS, 1975; "Hawaii Five-O: Oldest Profession-Latest Price," CBS, 1976; "The Mike Douglas Show," SYN, 1981; "Murder, She Wrote: The Murder of Sherlock Holmes," CBS, 1984; "Alfred Hitchcock Presents: Incident in a Small Jail," NBC, 1985; "Highway to Heaven: That's Our Dad," NBC, 1985; "Roseanne: Father's Day," ABC, 1989; "B.L. Stryker: The King of Jazz," ABC, 1989; "Roseanne: We Gather Together," ABC, 1989.

TV MOVIES AND MINISERIES: "Footsteps," CBS, 1972; "The Marcus-Nelson Murders," CBS, 1973; "Dying Room Only," ABC, 1973; "The Execution of Private Slovik," NBC, 1974; "Attack on Terror: The FBI Versus the Ku Klux Klan," CBS, 1975; "The Deadly Tower," NBC, 1975; "A Question of Love," ABC, 1978; "ABC Theatre: Friendly Fire," ABC, 1979; "All God's Children," ABC, 1980; "A Woman Called Golda," SYN, 1982; "Kentucky Woman," CBS, 1983; "Hostage Flight," NBC, 1985.

BEATTY, WARREN

b. Warren Beaty, Richmond, VA, March 30, 1937. Screen hunk for thirty years; for a brief time he played rich kid Milton Armitage on "The Many Loves of Dobie Gillis."

AS A REGULAR: "The Many Loves of Dobie Gillis," CBS, 1959-60.
AND: "Kraft Television Theatre: The Curly-Headed Kid," NBC, 1957; "Studio One: The Night America Trembled," CBS, 1957; "Suspicion: Heartbeat," NBC, 1957; "Alcoa Presents One Step Beyond: The Visitor," ABC, 1960.

BEAUMONT, HUGH

b. Lawrence, KS, February 16, 1909; d. 1982. Arguably TV's most famous dad; as Ward Cleaver on "Leave It to Beaver" he dispensed wisdom and advice and even kept a sense of humor about himself. And he wore a tie to read the newspaper.

AS A REGULAR: "Leave It to Beaver," CBS, 1957-58; ABC, 1958-63.
AND: "Teledrama: Danger Zone," CBS, 1953; "Fireside Theatre: The Traitor," NBC, 1953; "Topper: Hypnotist," CBS, 1953; "Studio 57: Trap Mates," SYN, 1954; "Four Star Playhouse: The Adolescent," CBS, 1954; "The Lineup: Cop

Shooting Story," CBS, 1954; "Four Star Playhouse: Stake My Life," CBS, 1954; "Four Star Playhouse: The Frightened Woman," CBS, 1955; "The Adventures of Superman: The Big Squeeze," SYN, 1955; "Science Fiction Theatre: Conversation with an Ape," SYN, 1955; "Cavalcade Theatre: A Time for Courage," ABC, 1955; "Four Star Playhouse: The Firing Squad," CBS, 1955; "Crossroads: With All My Love," ABC, 1955; "Medic: The World So High," NBC, 1955; "Cavalcade Theatre: The Boy Who Walked to America," ABC, 1956; "Ford Theatre: The Silent Stranger," NBC, 1956; "Four Star Playhouse: Command," CBS, 1956; "Schlitz Playhouse of Stars: Web of Circumstance," CBS, 1956; "The Loretta Young Show: But for God's Grace," NBC, 1956; "The Loretta Young Show: The Refinement of Ab," NBC, 1956; "The Loretta Young Show: The Bronte Story," NBC, 1956; "The Loretta Young Show: Take Care of My Child," NBC, 1956; "The Loretta Young Show: The Girl Who Knew," NBC, 1957; "Meet McGraw: Border City," NBC, 1957; "Art Linkletter's House Party," CBS, 1958; "The George Gobel Show," NBC, 1958; "Wagon Train: The Pearlie Garnet Story," ABC, 1964; "The Virginian: The Showdown," NBC, 1965; "The Virginian: The Girl on the Glass Mountain," NBC, 1966; "Petticoat Junction: Every Bachelor Should Have a Family," CBS, 1966; "Petticoat Junction: Meet the In-Laws," CBS, 1967; "Petticoat Junction: With This Gown I Thee Wed," CBS, 1967; "The Virginian: With Help From Ulysses," NBC, 1968; "Mannix: To the Swiftest Death," CBS, 1968; "The Virginian: Nora," NBC, 1968; "Marcus Welby, M.D.: The Merely Syndrome," ABC, 1970; "Mannix: War of Nerves," CBS, 1970; "Mannix: The Mouse That Died," CBS, 1970; "The Most Deadly Game: The Classic Burial Position," ABC, 1971.
* Beaumont also played the father of Steve Bradley (Mike Minor) on several episodes of "Petticoat Junction."

BEAVERS, LOUISE

b. Cincinnati, OH, March 8, 1902; d. 1962. Actress who became one of television's first black stars.

AS A REGULAR: "Beulah," ABC, 1952-53.
AND: "Star Stage: Cleopatra Collins," NBC, 1956; "Playhouse 90: The Hostess with the Mostess," CBS, 1957; "Walt Disney Presents: The Birth of the Swamp Fox," ABC, 1959; "You Bet Your Life," NBC, 1960; "Room for One More: Happiness Is Just a State of Mind," ABC, 1962.

BECK, JOHN

b. Chicago, IL, 1944. Mustachioed actor usually in macho soap roles; he played Sam Curtis on "Flamingo Road" and Mark Graison on "Dallas."

AS A REGULAR: "James Garner as Nichols," NBC, 1971-72; "Flamingo Road," NBC, 1981-82; "Dallas," CBS, 1983-84; 1985-86.
AND: "The Mod Squad: A Seat by the Window," ABC, 1969; "The FBI: Boomerang," ABC, 1969; "Mannix: Color Her Missing," CBS, 1969; "Gunsmoke: Kiowa," CBS, 1970; "Gunsmoke: Tycoon," CBS, 1971; "Mission: Impossible: The Missile," CBS, 1971; "Hawaii Five-O: Nightmare in Blue," CBS, 1974; "Gunsmoke: The Busters," CBS, 1975; "Matt Houston: Killing Isn't Everything," ABC, 1982; "The Love Boat: No Dad of Mine," ABC, 1985; "Hunter: The Castro Connection," NBC, 1986; "Matlock: The Quarterback," NBC, 1986; "Magnum, P.I.: Limbo," CBS, 1987.
TV MOVIES AND MINISERIES: "The Silent Gun," ABC, 1969; "Lock, Stock and Barrel," NBC, 1971; "The Law," NBC, 1974; "Attack on Terror: The FBI Versus the Ku Klux Klan," CBS, 1975; "The Call of the Wild," NBC, 1976; "Arthur Hailey's Wheels," NBC, 1978; "The Time Machine," NBC, 1978; "Flamingo Road," NBC, 1980; "The Great American Traffic Jam," NBC, 1980; "Peyton Place: The Next Generation," NBC, 1985; "Perry Mason: The Case of the Lady in the Lake," NBC, 1988.

BECK, MICHAEL

b. *Memphis, TN, February 4, 1949*. Hunky actor who played police Sgt. Levon Lundy on "Houston Knights."
AS A REGULAR: "Houston Knights," CBS, 1987-88.
AND: "Murder, She Wrote: The Search for Peter Kerry," CBS, 1989.
TV MOVIES AND MINISERIES: "Holocaust," NBC, 1978; "Mayflower: The Pilgrims' Adventure," CBS, 1979; "Fly Away Home," ABC, 1981; "Chiller," CBS, 1985; "Houston: The Legend of Texas," CBS, 1986.

BECKETT, SCOTTY

b. *Oakland, CA, October 4, 1929; d. 1968*. Former member of "Our Gang" who turned to television as his career waned.
AS A REGULAR: "Rocky Jones, Space Ranger," NBC, 1954.
AND: "Armstrong Circle Theatre: Before Breakfast," NBC, 1953; "Backbone of America," NBC, 1953; "Telephone Time: Away Boarders," CBS, 1956; "Navy Log: Survive," ABC, 1957; "George Sanders Mystery Theatre: The Night I Died," NBC, 1957.

BECKHAM, BRICE

b. *Long Beach, CA, February 11, 1976*. Young actor known as Wesley on "Mr. Belvedere."
AS A REGULAR: "Mr. Belvedere," ABC, 1985-90.

BEDELIA, BONNIE

b. *New York City, NY, March 25, 1946*. Gifted actress in film ("Heart Like a Wheel," "Presumed Innocent") and TV; she played Sandy Porter on "Love of Life" and the love interest of Little Joe (Michael Landon) on "Bonanza."
AS A REGULAR: "Love of Life," CBS, 1961-67; "The New Land," ABC, 1974.
AND: "CBS Playhouse: My Father and My Mother," CBS, 1968; "Judd for the Defense: The Death Farm," ABC, 1968; "The High Chaparral: The Deliverers," NBC, 1968; "Bonanza: Forever," NBC, 1972; "Love Story: Love Came Laughing," NBC, 1973.
TV MOVIES AND MINISERIES: "Then Came Bronson," NBC, 1969; "Sandcastles," CBS, 1972; "A Time for Love," NBC, 1973; "Hawkins on Murder," CBS, 1973; "Message to My Daughter," ABC, 1973; "Heat Wave," ABC, 1974; "A Question of Love," ABC, 1978; "Walking Through the Fire," CBS, 1979; "Salem's Lot," CBS, 1979; "Memorial Day," CBS, 1983; "Lady From Yesterday," CBS, 1985; "Alex: The Life of a Child," ABC, 1986; "When the Time Comes," ABC, 1987.

BEDFORD, BRIAN

b. *England, February 16, 1935*.
AS A REGULAR: "Coronet Blue," CBS, 1967.
AND: "Nanny and the Professor: Cholmondeley Featherstonehaugh," ABC, 1971; "Alfred Hitchcock Presents: Murder Me Twice," NBC, 1985; "The Equalizer: Bump and Run," CBS, 1986; "The Equalizer: Beyond Control," CBS, 1987; "Cheers: How to Recede in Business," NBC, 1988; "Murder, She Wrote: Benedict Arnold Slipped Here," CBS, 1988; "The Equalizer: Time Present, Time Past," CBS, 1989.

BEE, MOLLY,

b. *Mollie Beachboard, Washington, D.C., August 18, 1939*. Fifties and sixties country-western singer.
AS A REGULAR: "The Tennessee Ernie Ford Show," NBC, 1955-57; "Swingin' Country," NBC, 1966.
AND: "The Ray Anthony Show," ABC, 1957; "The Ford Show," NBC, 1957; "The Spike Jones Show," CBS, 1957; "The Gisele MacKenzie Show," NBC, 1958; "The Ford Show," NBC, 1958; "Bob Hope Special," NBC, 1959; "The Liberace Show," ABC, 1959; "The Ford Show," NBC, 1959; "America Pauses for the Merry Month of May," CBS, 1959; "The Jimmie Rodgers Show," NBC, 1959; "The Lawrence Welk Show," ABC, 1959; "The Jack Benny Program," CBS, 1960; "The Chevy Show: County Fair USA," NBC, 1960; "Here's Hollywood," NBC, 1960; "The Ford Show," NBC, 1960; "The Jimmy Dean Show," ABC, 1964; "What's This

Song?," NBC, 1965; "The Mike Douglas Show," SYN, 1967; "Hee Haw," SYN, 1975.

BEER, JACQUELINE
b. France, 1932. Actress who played secretary Suzanne Fabray, who worked for the guys of "77 Sunset Strip"; a Miss Universe finalist, she was Miss France 1954.
AS A REGULAR: "77 Sunset Strip," ABC, 1958-63.
AND: "Do You Trust Your Wife?," CBS, 1956; "The Adventures of Hiram Holliday: The Adventure of the Unkissed Bride," NBC, 1957; "The Alaskans: The Seal Skin Game," ABC, 1960; "Cheyenne: Manitoba Manhunt," ABC, 1961; "Cheyenne: Until Kingdom Come," ABC, 1962; "The Twilight Zone: Come Wander with Me," CBS, 1964; "The Rogues: Gambit by the Golden Gate," NBC, 1965; "The Man From UNCLE: The Recollectors Affair," NBC, 1965; "Run for Your Life: The Cold, Cold War of Paul Bryan," NBC, 1965.
* Beer appeared on "Do You Trust Your Wife?" with husband Jean Garcia-Roady, who was arrested after the show for embezzling $8,200 from the Bank of America and served a year in prison.

BEERY, NOAH JR.
b. New York City, NY, August 10, 1913. Ruddy actor who played Joseph "Rocky" Rockford, father of private eye Jim Rockford (James Garner).
AS A REGULAR: "Circus Boy," NBC, 1956-57; ABC, 1957-58; "Riverboat," NBC, 1960-61; "Hondo," ABC, 1967; "Doc Elliot," ABC, 1974; "The Rockford Files," NBC, 1974-80; "The Quest," ABC, 1982; "The Yellow Rose," NBC, 1983-84.
AND: "Schlitz Playhouse of Stars: The Quitter," CBS, 1954; "Studio One: The Enemy Within," CBS, 1958; "Wagon Train: The Jonas Murdock Story," NBC, 1960; "Wagon Train: Path of the Serpent," NBC, 1961; "Wanted Dead or Alive: El Gato," CBS, 1961; "The Real McCoys: The Investors," ABC, 1961; "Wanted Dead or Alive: Barney's Bounty," CBS, 1961; "Adventures in Paradise: Nightmare in the Sun," ABC, 1961; "Route 66: 1800 Days to Justice," CBS, 1962; "The Wide Country: A Guy for Clementine," NBC, 1962; "Gunsmoke: Prairie Wolfer," CBS, 1964; "Wagon Train: The Kate Crawley Story," ABC, 1964; "Perry Mason: The Case of the Golden Venom," CBS, 1965; "Branded: Now Join the Human Race," NBC, 1965; "The Littlest Hobo: My Client-A Dog," SYN, 1966; "The Virginian: The Long Way Home," NBC, 1966; "The Monroes: Lost in the Wilderness," ABC, 1966; "Combat!: A Little Jazz," ABC, 1967; "The Virginian: You Can Lead a Horse to Water," NBC, 1970; "The Streets of San Francisco: The Hard Breed," ABC, 1973; "Police Story: The Big

Walk," NBC, 1973; "The Waltons: The Heritage," CBS, 1974; "The Love Boat: Celebration," ABC, 1980; "Magnum, P.I.: J. Digger Doyle," CBS, 1981; "Hot Pursuit: Gillian," NBC, 1984; "Murder, She Wrote: Funeral at Fifty-Mile," CBS, 1985; "The Love Boat: The Winning Number," ABC, 1986.
TV MOVIES AND MINISERIES: "The Alpha Caper," ABC, 1973; "Sidekicks," CBS, 1974; "Savages," ABC, 1974; "Francis Gary Powers: The True Story of the U-2 Spy Incident," NBC, 1976; "The Bastard," SYN, 1978; "The Capture of Grizzly Adams," NBC, 1982.
* Beery is the nephew of Wallace Beery. His nickname, "Pidge," was given to him by Josie Cohan shortly after he was born.

BEGLEY, ED
b. Hartford, CT, March 25, 1901; d. 1970. Oscar-winning actor ("Sweet Bird of Youth"), a stocky, heavyset type who played small-town hypocrites and villianous tycoons on everything from "Lights Out" to "The Lucy Show"; he even served a stint as a sportscaster on "Roller Derby."
AS A REGULAR: "Roller Derby," ABC, 1951; "Leave It to Larry," CBS, 1952.
AND: "Lights Out: The Posthumous Dead," NBC, 1950; "Armstrong Circle Theatre: Super Highway," NBC, 1951; "The Early Bird," CBS, 1952; "Armstrong Circle Theatre: Before Breakfast," NBC, 1953; "Robert Montgomery Presents: Harvest," NBC, 1953; "Goodyear TV Playhouse: Ernie Barger is Fifty," NBC, 1953; "Armstrong Circle Theatre: Tour of Duty," NBC, 1953; "Philip Morris Playhouse: The Wager," SYN, 1954; "Motorola TV Hour: The Muldoon Matter," ABC, 1954; "Philco TV Playhouse: This Land Is Mine," NBC, 1956; "Alcoa Hour: Man on Fire," NBC, 1956; "Alcoa Hour: The Big Vote," NBC, 1956; "U.S. Steel Hour: Windfall," CBS, 1957; "Kraft Television Theatre: Smart Boy," NBC, 1957; "U.S. Steel Hour: Walk with a Stranger," CBS, 1958; "Kraft Theatre: Look What's Going On!," NBC, 1958; "The Garry Moore Show," CBS, 1958; "Climax!: The Big Success," CBS, 1958; "U.S. Steel Hour: The Enemies," CBS, 1958; "Westinghouse Desilu Playhouse: City in Bondage," CBS, 1960; "U.S. Steel Hour: The Great Gold Mountain," CBS, 1960; "Cain's Hundred: Blue Water, White Beach," NBC, 1961; "Target: The Corruptors: Bite of a Tiger," ABC, 1961; "My Three Sons: Romance of the Silver Pines," ABC, 1962; "The New Breed: Policemen Die Alone," ABC, 1962; "Ben Casey: Victory Wears a Cruel Smile," ABC, 1962; "Cain's Hundred: Blood Money," NBC, 1962; "The Dick Powell Show: The Hook," NBC, 1962; "Going My Way: My Son, the Social Worker," ABC, 1963; "Route 66: In the Closing of a Trunk," CBS, 1963; "Ben Casey: Hang No

Hats On Dreams," ABC, 1963; "The du Pont Show: The Last Hangman," NBC, 1963; "Burke's Law: Who Killed Julian Buck?," ABC, 1963; "Wagon Train: The Sam Spicer Story," ABC, 1963; "The Virginian: The Invaders," NBC, 1964; "Wagon Train: The Reno Sutton Story," ABC, 1964; "The Fugitive: Man in a Chariot," ABC, 1964; "The Presidency: A Splendid Misery," CBS, 1964; "Burke's Law: Who Killed Mr. Cartwheel?," ABC, 1964; "The Alfred Hitchcock Hour: Triumph," NBC, 1964; "Burke's Law: Who Killed Supersleuth?," ABC, 1964; "The Dick Van Dyke Show: The Case of the Pillow," CBS, 1965; "The Virginian: Chaff in the Wind," NBC, 1966; "Slattery's People: Is Democracy Too Expensive?," CBS, 1966; "Bob Hope Chrysler Theatre: In Pursuit of Excellence," NBC, 1966; "Bonanza: A Time to Step Down," NBC, 1966; "The Lucy Show: Lucy the Bean Queen," CBS, 1966; "The Wild Wild West: The Night of the Infernal Machine," CBS, 1966; "The Invaders: The Betrayed," ABC, 1967; "The Invaders: Labrynth," ABC, 1967; "Gunsmoke: The Water Witch," CBS, 1968; "Gunsmoke: Mr. Sam'l," CBS, 1968; "The High Chapparal: Follow Your Heart," NBC, 1968; "The Name of the Game: Lola in Lipstick," NBC, 1968; "My Three Sons: The New Room," CBS, 1968; "The Mod Squad: Child of Sorrow, Child of Light," ABC, 1969; "The Ghost and Mrs. Muir: Madam Candidate," NBC, 1969; "Walt Disney's Wonderful World of Color: Secrets of the Pirate's Inn," NBC, 1969; "Hallmark Hall of Fame: Neither Are We Enemies," NBC, 1970; "The FBI: The Deadly Gift," ABC, 1971.
TV MOVIES AND MINISERIES: "The Silent Gun," ABC, 1969.

BEGLEY, ED JR.
b. Los Angeles, CA, September 16, 1949. Tall, blonde, bespectacled actor who looks nothing at all like his father (see above); he played Dr. Victor Ehrlich on "St. Elsewhere."
AS A REGULAR: "Roll Out," CBS, 1973-74; "St. Elsewhere," NBC, 1982-88; "Parenthood," NBC, 1990.
AND: "My Three Sons: The Computer Picnic," CBS, 1967; "Room 222: Alice in Blunderland," ABC, 1969; "Nanny and the Professor: The Great Debate," ABC, 1971; "Room 222: The Nichols Girl," ABC, 1972; "Love, American Style: Love and the Happy Family," ABC, 1973; "Happy Days: The Deadly Dares," ABC, 1974; "Medical Center: Survivors," CBS, 1975; "Columbo: How to Dial a Murder," NBC, 1978; "M*A*S*H: Too Many Cooks," CBS, 1979; "Laverne & Shirley: A Drunken Sailor," ABC, 1979; "Charlie's Angels: Angels on Skates," ABC, 1979; "Barnaby Jones: Death Is the Punchline," CBS, 1980; "Quincy: Dear Mummy," NBC, 1981; "Riker: Pilot," CBS, 1981; "Voyagers!: Pilot," NBC, 1982; "Saturday Night Live," NBC, 1984; "The Love Boat: A Fish

Out of Water," ABC, 1984; "Late Night with David Letterman," NBC, 1989.
TV MOVIES AND MINISERIES: "Hot Rod," NBC, 1979; "Rascals and Robbers," CBS, 1982; "An Uncommon Love," CBS, 1983; "Celebration Family," ABC, 1987.

BEL GEDDES, BARBARA
b. Barbara Geddes, New York City, NY, October 31, 1922. Stage and film actress best known as Miss Ellie Southworth Ewing, matriarch of the "Dallas" clan.
AS A REGULAR: "Dallas," CBS, 1978-84, 1985- .
AND: "Robert Montgomery Presents: Rebecca," NBC, 1950; "Robert Montgomery Presents: The Philadelphia Story," NBC, 1950; "Nash Airflyte Theatre: Molly Morgan," CBS, 1950; "Campbell TV Soundstage: Isn't Everything?," NBC, 1954; "The Ed Sullivan Show," CBS, 1956; "The Joseph Cotten Show: The Gentle Voice of Murder," NBC, 1957; "Schlitz Playhouse of Stars: Fifty Beautiful Girls," CBS, 1957; "Studio One: The Morning Face," CBS, 1957; "Schlitz Playhouse of Stars: French Provincial," CBS, 1957; "Alfred Hitchcock Presents: Foghorn," CBS, 1958; "Alfred Hitchcock Presents: Lamb to the Slaughter," CBS, 1958; "Playhouse 90: Rumors of Evening," CBS, 1958; "Studio One: The Desperate Age," CBS, 1958; "U.S. Steel Hour: Mid-Summer," CBS, 1958; "Du Pont Show of the Month: The Hasty Heart," CBS, 1958; "Alfred Hitchcock Presents: The Morning of the Bride," CBS, 1959; "Riverboat: Payment in Full," NBC, 1959; "Dow Hour of Great Mysteries: The Burning Court," NBC, 1960; "Alfred Hitchcock Presents: Sybilla," NBC, 1960; "Dr. Kildare: Miracle for Margaret," NBC, 1966; "CBS Playhouse: Secrets," CBS, 1968; "Journey to the Unknown: The Madison Equation," ABC, 1969.
* Bel Geddes starred in one of the best-known episodes of "Alfred Hitchcock Presents." In "Lamb to the Slaughter"—made the same year she appeared in Hitchcock's film "Vertigo"—she played a wronged wife who killed her unfaithful husband by beating him with a leg of lamb. When the police arrived to investigate, she cooked the evidence and served it to them.
* In 1984, Bel Geddes underwent heart surgery and left "Dallas," to be replaced by Donna Reed. But she was back in a year.
* Emmies: 1980.
* See also Donna Reed.

BELAFONTE, HARRY
b. New York City, NY, March 1, 1927. Singer and performer whose Jamaican-flavored songs were hot as hi-fi in the fifties; an Emmy winner for "Tonight with Belafonte."
AS A REGULAR: "Sugar Hill Times," CBS, 1949.
AND: "Three for Tonight," CBS, 1955; "G.E. Theatre: Winner by Decision," CBS, 1955; "The

Nat King Cole Show," NBC, 1957; "The Steve Allen Show," NBC, 1958; "Bell Telephone Hour: Adventures in Music," NBC, 1959; "Person to Person," CBS, 1959; "Tonight with Belafonte," CBS, 1959; "Belafonte ... New York 19, New York," CBS, 1960; "Perry Como's Kraft Music Hall," NBC, 1961; "What's My Line?," CBS, 1961; "Dinah Shore Special," ABC, 1965; "The Danny Kaye Show," CBS, 1965; "The Tonight Show Starring Johnny Carson," NBC, 1968; "The Smothers Brothers Comedy Hour," CBS, 1968; "The Great American Dream Machine," NET, 1970; "The New Bill Cosby Show," CBS, 1972; "The Mike Douglas Show," SYN, 1973; "Today Is Ours," CBS, 1974; "Free to Be You and Me," ABC, 1974; "The Muppet Show," SYN, 1979.
TV MOVIES AND MINISERIES: "Grambling's White Tiger," NBC, 1981.
* Emmies: 1960.

BELAFONTE, SHARI
b. New York City, NY, September 22, 1954. Pert actress who played Julie Gillette on "Hotel"; daughter of Harry Belanfonte.
AS A REGULAR: "Hotel," ABC, 1983-88.
AND: "Lobo: What Are Girls Like You Doing in a Bank Like This?," NBC, 1981; "The Love Boat: Love Is Blind," ABC, 1984; "Candid Camera: Eat! Eat! Eat!," CBS, 1989.
TV MOVIES AND MINISERIES: "Kate's Secret," NBC, 1986; "Perry Mason: The Case of the All-Star Assassin," NBC, 1989.

BELFORD, CHRISTINE
b. Amityville, NY, January 14, 1949. Attractive actress most active in seventies TV.
AS A REGULAR: "Banacek," NBC, 1972-74; "Married: The First Year," CBS, 1979; "Empire," CBS, 1984; "Outlaws," CBS, 1986-87.
AND: "Marcus Welby, M.D.: The Basic Moment," ABC, 1971; "Alias Smith and Jones: Bush-whack!," ABC, 1972; "Mannix: Light and Shadow," CBS, 1973; "Marcus Welby, M.D.: Last Flight to Babylon," ABC, 1974; "The White Shadow: Here's Mud in Your Eye," CBS, 1978; "CHiPS: Wheels of Justice," NBC, 1980; "Magnum, P.I.: Adelaide," CBS, 1981; "Nero Wolfe: Death and the Dolls," NBC, 1981; "Silver Spoons: Evelyn Returns," NBC, 1982; "Hart to Hart: Bahama-Bound Harts," ABC, 1983; "It's Not Easy: Pilot," ABC, 1983; "Goodnight Beantown: An Old Flame Flickers," CBS, 1984; "Murder, She Wrote: We're Off to Kill the Wizard," CBS, 1984; "Family Ties: Art Lover," NBC, 1986; "ABC Afterschool Specials: The Day My Kid Went Punk," ABC, 1987; "Murphy's Law: Do Someone a Favor and It Becomes Your Job," ABC, 1988; "Murder, She Wrote: Double Exposure," CBS, 1989; "Living Dolls: And I Thought Modeling Was Hard," ABC, 1989.

TV MOVIES AND MINISERIES: "Vanished," NBC, 1971; "Banacek: Detour to Nowhere," NBC, 1972; "Kate McShane," CBS, 1975; "The Million Dollar Rip-Off," NBC, 1976; "High Midnight," CBS, 1979; "Agatha Christie's Sparkling Cyanide," CBS, 1983.

BELLAMY, RALPH
b. Chicago, IL, June 17, 1904. Actor whose career spans six decades; on television he's best known as Mike Barnett of "Man Against Crime," as psychiatrist Richard Starke on "The Eleventh Hour" and as Franklin Roosevelt in "The Winds of War" and "War and Remembrance."
AS A REGULAR: "Man Against Crime," CBS, 1949-53; DUM, 1953-54; NBC 1953-54; "To Tell the Truth," CBS, 1957-59; "Frontier Justice," CBS, 1961; "The Eleventh Hour," NBC, 1963-64; "Harold Robbins' The Survivors," ABC, 1969-70; "The Most Deadly Game," ABC, 1970-71; "Hunter," CBS, 1977; "Christine Cromwell," ABC, 1989-90.
AND: "U.S. Steel Hour: Fearful Decision," ABC, 1954; "Elgin TV Hour: High Man," ABC, 1954; "Studio One: Like Father, Like Son," CBS, 1955; "G.E. Theatre: Outpost of Home," CBS, 1955; "Playwrights '56: Honor," NBC, 1956; "Goodyear TV Playhouse: The Film Maker," NBC, 1956; "Climax!: The Fog," CBS, 1956; "Playhouse 90: Heritage of Anger," CBS, 1956; "Ford Theatre: Model Wife," ABC, 1956; "Dick Powell's Zane Grey Theatre: Stars Over Texas," CBS, 1956; "Schlitz Playhouse of Stars: The Big Payoff," CBS, 1956; "Studio One: The Defender," CBS, 1957; "The Perry Como Show," NBC, 1958; "Hallmark Hall of Fame: Hallmark Christmas Tree —Light One Candle," NBC, 1958; "The Eternal Light: The Land of the Book," NBC, 1959; "Our American Heritage: Divided We Stand," NBC, 1959; "A Tribute to Eleanor Roosevelt On Her Diamond Jubilee," NBC, 1959; "Bell Telephone Hour: Concert Hall," NBC, 1960; "Our American Heritage: Not Without Honor," NBC, 1960; "Checkmate: Portrait of a Man Running," CBS, 1961; "Rawhide: Judgment at Hondo Seco," CBS, 1961; "Westinghouse Presents: The Dispossessed," CBS, 1961; "Here's Hollywood," NBC, 1961; "Breck Golden Showcase: Saturday's Children," CBS, 1962; "Westinghouse Presents: The First Day," CBS, 1962; "Death Valley Days: The Vintage Years," SYN, 1962; "Alcoa Premiere: Impact of an Execution," ABC, 1963; "Alcoa Premiere: Chain Reaction," ABC, 1963; "Dr. Kildare: Four Feet in the Morning," NBC, 1963; "Rawhide: The Pursuit," CBS, 1965; "The FBI: The Death Wind," ABC, 1966; "Bob Hope Chrysler Theatre: A Time to Love," NBC, 1967; "Run for Your Life: Trip to the Far Side," NBC, 1967; "Owen Marshall, Counselor at Law: Once a Lion," ABC,

1973; "Medical Story: Wasteland," NBC, 1975; "Medical Center: The Eighth Deadly Sin," CBS, 1975; "The Bob Newhart Show: You're Fired, Mr. Chips," CBS, 1977; "The Love Boat: The Lone Ranger," ABC, 1981; "Little House: A New Beginning: Marvin's Garden," NBC, 1983; "The Love Boat: Story of the Century," ABC, 1984; "The Twilight Zone: Monsters," CBS, 1986; "Matlock: The Power Brokers," NBC, 1987.

TV MOVIES AND MINISERIES: "Wings of Fire," NBC, 1967; "The Immortal," ABC, 1969; "Something Evil," CBS, 1972; "The Missiles of October," ABC, 1974; "The Log of the Black Pearl," NBC, 1975; "Adventures of a Queen," CBS, 1975; "Search for the Gods," NBC, 1975; "Murder on Flight 502," ABC, 1975; "McNaughton's Daughter," NBC, 1976; "Nightmare in Badham County," ABC, 1976; "The Boy in the Plastic Bubble," ABC, 1976; "The Moneychangers," NBC, 1976; "Return to Earth," ABC, 1976; "Best Sellers: Once an Eagle," NBC, 1977; "Testimony of Two Men," SYN, 1977; "Arthur Hailey's Wheels," NBC, 1978; "The Clone Master," NBC, 1978; "The Billion Dollar Threat," ABC, 1979; "The Memory of Eva Ryker," CBS, 1980; "The Winds of War," ABC, 1983; "War and Remembrance," ABC, 1988, 1989.

BELLAVER, HARRY
b. February 12, 1905. Actor who played tough cop Frank Arcaro on "Naked City."

AS A REGULAR: "Naked City," ABC, 1958-59; 1960-63.

AND: "Studio One: The Open Door," CBS, 1956; "Climax!: Murder Has a Deadline," CBS, 1957; "Wanted Dead or Alive: Bad Gun," CBS, 1959; "The Man From Blackhawk: Death at Noon," ABC, 1960; "Tightrope!: Achilles and His Heels," CBS, 1960; "The Nurses: Is There Room for Edward?," CBS, 1964; "The Eternal Light: Inscription for a Blank Page," NBC, 1964; "The FBI: The Hijackers," ABC, 1965; "Honey West: A Million Bucks in Anybody's Language," ABC, 1965; "The FBI: Overload," ABC, 1967; "Kojak: An Unfair Trade," CBS, 1976.

TV MOVIES AND MINISERIES: "Murder in Music City," NBC, 1979.

BELLER, KATHLEEN
b. Queens, NY, February 10, 1955. Dark-featured, wide-eyed actress who often plays fragile types; she played Kirby on "Dynasty" and teacher Mary Callahan on "The Bronx Zoo."

AS A REGULAR: "Search for Tomorrow," CBS, 1971-74; "Dynasty," ABC, 1982-84; "The Bronx Zoo," NBC, 1987-88.

AND: "Hawaii Five-O: The Waterfront Stealing," CBS, 1975; "Medical Center: You Can't Annul My Baby," CBS, 1976; "What Really Happened

to the Class of '65?: The Class Misfit," NBC, 1978; "American Short Story: Rappaccini's Daughter," PBS, 1980; "Murder, She Wrote: Funeral at Fifty-Mile," CBS, 1985; "Blacke's Magic: Breathing Room," NBC, 1986.

TV MOVIES AND MINISERIES: "Something for Joey," CBS, 1977; "Are You in the House Alone?," CBS, 1978; "No Place to Hide," CBS, 1981; "Manions of America," ABC, 1981; "The Blue and the Gray," CBS, 1982; "Deadly Messages," ABC, 1985.

BELLSON, LOUIS
b. Rock Falls, IL, July 26, 1924. Jazz drummer and bandleader; widower of Pearl Bailey.

AS A REGULAR: "The Pearl Bailey Show," ABC, 1971.

AND: "The Ed Sullivan Show," CBS, 1962; "The Lively Ones," NBC, 1962; "The Tonight Show Starring Johnny Carson," NBC, 1964; "Lou Grant: Jazz," CBS, 1981.

BELLWOOD, PAMELA
b. New York City, NY, June 26, 1951. Actress who played Claudia Blaisdel on "Dynasty."

AS A REGULAR: "WEB," NBC, 1978; "Dynasty," ABC, 1981-86.

AND: "Ironside: Once More for Joey," NBC, 1974; "Rhoda: 9-E Is Available," CBS, 1974; "Serpico: The Party of Your Choice," NBC, 1977; "Switch: The Siege at the Bouziki Bar," CBS, 1978; "Finder of Lost Loves: Losing Touch," ABC, 1984; "Murder, She Wrote: Weave a Tangled Web," CBS, 1989.

TV MOVIES AND MINISERIES: "The Wild Women of Chastity Gulch," ABC, 1982; "Cocaine: One Man's Seduction," NBC, 1983; "Baby Sister," ABC, 1983; "Agatha Christie's Sparkling Cyanide," CBS, 1983; "Deep Dark Secrets," NBC, 1987.

BELUSHI, JIM
b. Chicago, IL, June 15, 1954. Comic actor who has the same build and persona—but not quite the same level of talent—as his late brother, John.

AS A REGULAR: "Who's Watching the Kids?," NBC, 1978; "Working Stiffs," CBS, 1979; "Saturday Night Live," NBC, 1983-85.

BELUSHI, JOHN
b. Chicago, IL, January 24, 1949; d. 1982. Comic dynamo whose manic performances onstage as one of the Blues Brothers, Samauri delicatessen owner and the leader of the Killer Bees, among others, were paired with a fast-lane private life that blew up on him in his early thirties.

AS A REGULAR AND WRITER: "Saturday Night Live," NBC, 1975-79.

* Emmies: 1977.

BENADERET, BEA

b. New York City, NY, April 4, 1906; d. 1968.
Blonde character actress who played Blanche
Morton, Gracie Allen's next-door neighbor and
best pal; after a stint as the voice of Betty
Rubble on "The Flintstones" she came into her
own as Kate Bradley, owner of the Shady Rest
Hotel on "Petticoat Junction."

AS A REGULAR: "The George Burns and Gracie
Allen Show," CBS, 1950-58; "The George
Burns Show," NBC, 1958-59; "The
Flintstones," ABC, 1960-64; "Peter Loves
Mary," NBC, 1960-61; "The Beverly
Hillbillies," CBS, 1962-63; "Petticoat
Junction," CBS, 1963-68; "Green Acres," CBS,
1965-66.

AND: "I Love Lucy: Lucy Plays Cupid," CBS,
1952; "The Lineup: The Falling Out of Thieves,"
CBS, 1955; "Screen Directors Playhouse: A
Midsummer Daydream," NBC, 1955; "The Bob
Cummings Show: Bob Meets the Mortons," CBS,
1957; "The Bob Cummings Show: Scramble for
Grandpa," CBS, 1957; "Restless Gun: Madame
Brimstone," NBC, 1959; "77 Sunset Strip: Two
Cents a Death," ABC, 1960; "The Chevy Show:
The Happiest Day," NBC, 1961; "The Many
Loves of Dobie Gillis: Spaceville," CBS, 1961;
"Top Cat: A Visit From Mother," ABC, 1961;
"The New Breed: A Motive Named Walter," ABC,
1962; "Talent Scouts," CBS, 1963; "Art
Linkletter's House Party," CBS, 1963; "The
Danny Kaye Show," CBS, 1964; "The Beverly
Hillbillies: Greetings From the President," CBS,
1967.

* Benaderet was Lucille Ball's original choice to
play Ethel Mertz on "I Love Lucy."

BENDIX, WILLIAM

*b. New York City, NY, January 4, 1906; d.
1964.* Character actor who excelled at dim-
witted, heart-of-gold types and who played one
of the most famous of them, Chester A. Riley.

AS A REGULAR: "The Life of Riley," NBC, 1953-
58; "The Overland Trail," NBC, 1960.

AND: "Lights Out: The Hollow Man," NBC, 1952;
"Hollywood Opening Night: Terrible Tempered
Tolliver," NBC, 1952; "Lux Video Theatre: The
Mechanical Cook," CBS, 1954; "Ford Theatre: A
Past Remembered," NBC, 1954; "Fireside Theatre:
Sgt. Sullivan Speaking," NBC, 1955; "Fireside
Theatre: Mr. Onion," NBC, 1955; "Philco TV
Playhouse: Kyrai Katina," NBC, 1956; "Goodyear
TV Playhouse: Footlight Frenzy," NBC, 1956;
"Screen Directors Playhouse: High Air," ABC,
1956; "What's My Line?," CBS, 1956; "Robert
Montgomery Presents: The Misfortunes of Mr.
Minihan," NBC, 1956; "The 20th Century-Fox
Hour: Threat to a Happy Ending," CBS, 1957;
"Youth Wants to Know," NBC, 1957; "The Lux
Show with Rosemary Clooney," NBC, 1957; "The
Steve Allen Show," NBC, 1957; "The Jane

Wyman Show: Prime Suspect," NBC, 1958;
"Wagon Train: Around the Horn," NBC, 1958;
"The Garry Moore Show," CBS, 1958; "The
Unknown: Desperation," SYN, 1958; "The Ford
Show," NBC, 1958; "Westinghouse Desilu
Playhouse: The Time Element," CBS, 1958;
"Playhouse 90: A Quiet Game of Cards," CBS,
1959; "Milton Berle Starring in the Kraft Music
Hall," NBC, 1959; "Schlitz Playhouse of Stars: Ivy
League," CBS, 1959; "The Ransom of Red Chief,"
NBC, 1959; "Riverboat: The Barrier," NBC, 1959;
"The Ford Show," NBC, 1959; "Steve Allen
Plymouth Show," NBC, 1959; "The Untouchables:
The Tri-State Gang," ABC, 1959; "What's My
Line?," CBS, 1960; "I've Got a Secret," CBS,
1960; "Candid Camera," CBS, 1960; "G.E.
Theatre: We're Holding Your Son," CBS, 1961;
"Follow the Sun: Sergeant Kolchak Fades Away,"
ABC, 1962; "The Dick Powell Show: 330
Independence Square," NBC, 1962; "The Dick
Powell Show: Last of the Private Eyes," NBC,
1963; "Burke's Law: Who Killed Holly Howard?,"
ABC, 1963; "Burke's Law: Who Killed Cassandra
Cass?," ABC, 1964.

* Bendix's father was a conductor and violinist
with the Metropolitan Opera orchestra.

BENEDICT, DIRK

b. Helena, MT, March 1, 1944. Hunky actor
who played Templeton "Faceman" Peck on
"The A-Team."

AS A REGULAR: "Chopper One," ABC, 1974;
"Battlestar Galactica," ABC, 1978-79; "The
A-Team," NBC, 1983-87.

AND: "Hawaii Five-O: Little Girl Blue," CBS,
1973; "The Mike Douglas Show," SYN, 1978;
"Donny and Marie," ABC, 1978; "The Love Boat:
Captive Audience," ABC, 1980; "The Love Boat:
Whose Dog Is It, Anyway," ABC, 1983; "Murder,
She Wrote: Smooth Operator," CBS, 1989; "The
Pat Sajak Show," CBS, 1989.

TV MOVIES AND MINISERIES: "Journey From
Darkness," NBC, 1975; "Georgia Peaches,"
CBS, 1980; "Trenchcoat in Paradise," CBS,
1989.

BENEDICT, PAUL

b. Silver City, NM, September 17, 1938. Long-
faced, jut-jawed actor who played Harry
Bentley, silly next-door neighbor of "The
Jeffersons."

AS A REGULAR: "Sesame Street," NET, 1969-74;
"The Jeffersons," CBS, 1975-81, 1983-85.

AND: "Kojak: Slay Ride," CBS, 1974; "Maude: All
Psyched Out," CBS, 1975; "All in the Family: The
Jeffersons Move Up," CBS, 1975.

TV MOVIES AND MINISERIES: "The Blue and the
Gray," CBS, 1982; "Babycakes," CBS, 1989.

* On "Sesame Street," Benedict was the guy in
the derby hat and trenchcoat who'd walk
around painting numbers on things.

BENET, BRENDA
b. Brenda Nelson, Los Angeles, 1945; d. 1982.
Attractive actress who began as a starlet, later best known as Lee Carmichael on "Days of Our Lives." Depressed over failed marriages to actors Paul Petersen and Bill Bixby, and over the death of her young son, she committed suicide.
AS A REGULAR: "The Young Marrieds," ABC, 1964-66; "Days of Our Lives," NBC, 1979-82.
AND: "Hollywood Deb Stars Ball," ABC, 1963; "Wendy & Me: East Is East and West Is Wendy," ABC, 1964; "Wendy & Me: How Not to Succeed in Stealing," ABC, 1965; "McHale's Navy: Will the Real Admiral Please Stand Up?," ABC, 1965; "My Three Sons: Happy Birthday, World," CBS, 1966; "I Dream of Jeannie: Jeannie Goes to Honolulu," NBC, 1967; "The FBI: Flight," ABC, 1969; "My Three Sons: Come the Day," CBS, 1969; "It Takes a Thief: The Scorpio Drop," ABC, 1969; "My Three Sons: Double Jealousy," CBS, 1970; "Love, American Style: Love and the Young Executive," ABC, 1970; "Mannix: The Judas Touch," CBS, 1970; "The Courtship of Eddie's Father: The Lonely Weekend," ABC, 1971; "Love, American Style: Love and the Test of Manhood," ABC, 1972; "The Magician: Illusion in Terror," NBC, 1973; "The Love Boat: Message for Maureen," ABC, 1977.
TV MOVIES AND MINISERIES: "Horror at 37,000 Feet," CBS, 1973.
* Petersen blamed Hollywood for Benet's death. He told *TV Guide*, "In Hollywood, people make a great pretense at understanding the human condition. Particularly people on the soap operas. And they themselves are so poisoned by false values that they cannot, even with a co-worker, see the pain and lonliness and suffering."

BENET, VICKI
b. France. Cabaret singer who did some variety shows; actress Brenda Nelson liked Benet's surname and adopted it as her own.
AS A GUEST: "Pontiac Star Parade: The Future Lies Ahead," NBC, 1960; "Art Linkletter's House Party," CBS, 1960; "Art Linkletter's House Party," CBS, 1961; "Have Gun, Will Travel: The Invasion," CBS, 1962.

BENJAMIN, RICHARD
b. New York City, NY, May 22, 1938. Slight, likable actor who stopped to do a good sitcom, "He & She" on his way to movie stardom in the seventies and directing in the eighties.
AS A REGULAR: "He & She," CBS, 1967-68; "Quark," NBC, 1978.
AND: "Dr. Kildare: A Hand Held Out in Darkness," NBC, 1964; "Vacation Playhouse: My Lucky Penny," CBS, 1966; "The Merv Griffin Show," SYN, 1969; "Bob Newhart Special: A Last Laugh

at the 60's," ABC, 1970; "Saturday Night Live," NBC, 1979; "Saturday Night Live," NBC, 1980.
TV MOVIES AND MINISERIES: "Packin' It In," CBS, 1983.

BENNETT, BRUCE
b. Herman Brix, Tacoma, WA, May 19, 1909. Burly baritone-voiced actor, former shot-putter.
AS A GUEST: "Ford Theatre: So Many Things Happen," NBC, 1952; "A Letter to Loretta: Prisoner at One O'Clock," NBC, 1953; "Cavalcade of Stars: Moonlight Witness," ABC, 1954; "Schlitz Playhouse of Stars: Mystery of Murder," CBS, 1954; "Science Fiction Theatre: Beyond," SYN, 1955; "Damon Runyon Theatre: Pick the Winner," CBS, 1955; "Science Fiction Theatre: Signals From the Moon," SYN, 1956; "Science Fiction Theatre: Bolt of Lightning," SYN, 1957; "Playhouse 90: Ain't No Time for Glory," CBS, 1957; "West Point: White Fury," ABC, 1958; "No Warning: Survivors," NBC, 1958; "Perry Mason: The Case of the Lucky Loser," CBS, 1958; "Laramie: Hour After Dawn," NBC, 1960; "Perry Mason: The Case of the Misguided Missile," CBS, 1960; "The Case of the Dangerous Robin: Invitation to Murder," SYN, 1960; "Perry Mason: The Case of the Roving River," CBS, 1961; "Perry Mason: The Case of the Reckless Rock Hound," CBS, 1964; "Kraft Suspense Theatre: The Last Clear Chance," NBC, 1965; "Branded: I Killed Jason McCord," NBC, 1965; "Perry Mason: The Case of the Carefree Coronary," CBS, 1965; "The Virginian: Yesterday's Timepiece," NBC, 1967; "The Virginian: The Gauntlet," NBC, 1967; "Daktari: The Killer Cub," CBS, 1968; "Daktari: The Divining Rods," CBS, 1968.

BENNETT, CONSTANCE
b. New York City, NY, October 22, 1904; d. 1965. Movie actress of the thirties ("Topper") who did a little television.
AS A GUEST: "Faith Baldwin Theatre: Love Letters," ABC, 1951; "Robert Montgomery Presents: Senora Isobel," NBC, 1952; "Broadway Television Theatre: Twentieth Century," SYN, 1953; "Robert Montgomery Presents: Oysters in the Stew," NBC, 1956; "Arthur Murray Party," NBC, 1959; "The Ann Sothern Show: Always April," CBS, 1961; "The Reporter: The Man Behind the Man," CBS, 1964; "The Price Is Right," ABC, 1965.

BENNETT, JOAN
b. Palisades, NJ, February 27, 1910; d. 1990. Blonde actress of thirties and forties films who found a new generation of fans as Elizabeth/Flora Collins on "Dark Shadows."
AS A REGULAR: "Too Young to Go Steady," NBC, 1959; "Dark Shadows," ABC, 1966-71.
AND: "Nash Airflyte Theatre: Peggy," CBS, 1951;

"Somerset Maugham Theatre: The Dream," CBS, 1951; "Danger: A Clear Case of Suicide," CBS, 1951; "G.E. Theatre: You're Only Young Once," CBS, 1954; "Best of Broadway: The Man Who Came to Dinner," CBS, 1954; "Ford Theatre: Letters Marked Personal," NBC, 1955; "Shower of Stars: The Dark Fleece," CBS, 1955; "I've Got a Secret," CBS, 1957; "Playhouse 90: The Thundering Wave," CBS, 1957; "Du Pont Show of the Month: Junior Miss," CBS, 1957; "Pursuit: Epitaph for a Golden Girl," CBS, 1959; "Arthur Murray Party," NBC, 1959; "Password," CBS, 1961; "The Match Game," NBC, 1964; "Mr. Broadway: Don't Mention My Name in Sheboygan," CBS, 1964; "Burke's Law: Who Killed Mr. Colby in Ladies' Lingerie?," ABC, 1965; "The Mike Douglas Show," SYN, 1970; "Love, American Style: Love and the Second Time," ABC, 1971.

TV MOVIES AND MINISERIES: "Gidget Gets Married," ABC, 1972; "The Eyes of Charles Sand," ABC, 1972; "Suddenly, Love," NBC, 1978; "This House Possessed," ABC, 1981; "Divorce Wars: A Love Story," ABC, 1982.

BENNETT, TONY

b. Anthony Benedetto, Astoria, Queens, NY, August 3, 1926. Classically elegant song stylist.

AS A REGULAR: "Songs for Sale," CBS, 1950; "The Tony Bennett Show," NBC, 1956; "Perry Presents," NBC, 1959.

AND: "Arthur Godfrey's Talent Scouts," CBS, 1950; "The Steve Allen Show," NBC, 1956; "The Perry Como Show," NBC, 1957; "Salute to Baseball," NBC, 1957; "The Jackie Gleason Show," CBS, 1957; "The Steve Allen Show," NBC, 1957; "The Big Record," CBS, 1957; "The Nat King Cole Show," NBC, 1957; "The Ed Sullivan Show," CBS, 1957; "The Perry Como Show," NBC, 1958; "The Patrice Munsel Show," ABC, 1958; "The Big Record," CBS, 1958; "Pat Boone Chevy Showroom," ABC, 1958; "The Dick Clark Saturday Night Beechnut Show," ABC, 1958; "The Steve Allen Show," NBC, 1958; "Steve Allen Presents the Steve Lawrence-Eydie Gorme Show," NBC, 1958; "The Danny Thomas Show: Tony Bennett Gets Danny's Help," CBS, 1959; "The Perry Como Show," NBC, 1959; "The Garry Moore Show," CBS, 1959; "Dinah Shore Chevy Show," NBC, 1959; "Steve Allen Plymouth Show," NBC, 1959; "Steve Allen Plymouth Show," NBC, 1960; "Playboy's Penthouse," SYN, 1961; "American Bandstand," ABC, 1961; "The Tonight Show Starring Johnny Carson," NBC, 1962; "Jackie Gleason and His American Scene Magazine," CBS, 1962; "The Ed Sullivan Show," CBS, 1962; "Hollywood Palace," ABC, 1964; "The Twentieth Century: The Songs of Harold Arlen," CBS, 1964; "The Music Scene," ABC, 1969; "The Mike Douglas Show," SYN, 1970; "The Doris Day

Show: Tony Bennett Is Eating Here," CBS, 1971; "The Merv Griffin Show," SYN, 1974; "The Merv Griffin Show," SYN, 1975; "The Mike Douglas Show," SYN, 1976; "Skag: The Working Girl," NBC, 1980; "Bennett & Basie Together," PBS, 1982; "Irving Berlin's 100th Birthday Celebration," CBS, 1988; "Later with Bob Costas," NBC, 1989.

TV MOVIES AND MINISERIES: "King," NBC, 1978.
* Bennett was a guest on Johnny Carson's first "Tonight" show.

BENNY, JACK

b. Benjamin Kubelsky, Waukegan, IL, February 14, 1894; d. 1974. Violin player less-than-extraordinare, fussbudget, pinchpenny boss to Rochester, Dennis Day and Don Wilson, a Sunday night tradition for decades and one of America's most timeless comic figures.

AS A REGULAR: "The Jack Benny Program," CBS, 1950-64; NBC, 1964-65; "Shower of Stars," CBS, 1956-58; "Jack Benny Special," CBS, 1959-62; NBC, 1965-73.

AND: "G.E. Theatre: The Face Is Familiar," CBS, 1954; "Four Star Playhouse: The House Always Wins," CBS, 1955; "The George Burns and Gracie Allen Show: Gracie Thinks She's Not Married to George," CBS, 1955; "G.E. Theatre: The Honest Man," CBS, 1956; "The George Gobel Show," NBC, 1957; "G.E. Theatre: The Fenton Touch," CBS, 1957; "The George Burns and Gracie Allen Show: Ronnie Gets an Agent," CBS, 1957; "The Marge and Gower Champion Show," CBS, 1957; "The Danny Thomas Show: Lose Me in Las Vegas," CBS, 1957; "The Gisele MacKenzie Show," NBC, 1957; "The Perry Como Show," NBC, 1957; "Bachelor Father: Bentley the Homemaker," CBS, 1958; "The Danny Thomas Show: Jack Benny Takes Danny's Job," CBS, 1958; "The George Burns Show," NBC, 1958; "Bob Hope Special," NBC, 1959; "Startime: George Burns in the Big Time," NBC, 1959; "The George Gobel Show," CBS, 1959; "The Danny Thomas Show: That Old Devil, Jack Benny," CBS, 1960; "The Garry Moore Show," CBS, 1960; "Phil Silvers Special: The Slowest Gun in the West," CBS, 1960; "George Burns Special," NBC, 1960; "Eleanor Roosevelt's Jubilee," NBC, 1960; "Remember How Great," NBC, 1961; "Checkmate: A Funny Thing Happened to Me on the Way to the Game," CBS, 1962; "The Milton Berle Show," NBC, 1962; "Opening Night," CBS, 1962; "The Bob Hope Show," NBC, 1962; "I've Got a Secret," CBS, 1963; "Opening Night," CBS, 1963; "The Tonight Show Starring Johnny Carson," NBC, 1964; "Bob Hope Special," NBC, 1964; "The Lucy Show: Lucy and the Plumber," CBS, 1964; "The Andy Williams Show," NBC, 1964; "Bob Hope Chrysler Theatre: Have Girls, Will Travel," NBC,

1964; "The Smothers Brothers Comedy Hour," CBS, 1967; "The Lucy Show: Lucy Gets Jack Benny's Account," CBS, 1967; "Kraft Music Hall," NBC, 1967; "The Beautiful Phyllis Diller Show," NBC, 1968; "Here's Lucy: Lucy Visits Jack Benny," CBS, 1968; "Jimmy Durante Presents the Lennon Sisters Hour," ABC, 1969; "Here's Lucy: Lucy and Jack Benny's Biography," CBS, 1970; "Bob Hope Special," NBC, 1970; "Here's Lucy: Lucy the Crusader," CBS, 1971; "Here's Lucy: Lucy and the Celebrities," CBS, 1971; "The Funny Side," NBC, 1971; "The Flip Wilson Show," NBC, 1972; "The Dean Martin Show," NBC, 1972; "Playhouse New York: The 1940s-The Great Radio Comedians," NET, 1973; "The Dean Martin Show," NBC, 1973; "Music Country USA," NBC, 1974; "Annie and the Hoods," NBC, 1974.

* Who drove Benny off the air? Jim Nabors—or, more specifically, Gomer Pyle. Benny's program aired opposite "Gomer Pyle USMC" when the show was number three in the country. And after fifteen years on TV and another ten or so on radio, Benny decided to end his weekly show.
* In 1958, Benny won an Emmy in this category: "Best continuing performance (male) in a series by a comedian, singer, host, dancer, MC, announcer, narrator, panelist or any person who essentially plays himself."
* Emmies: 1958, 1959.

BENSON, LUCILLE
b. Scottsboro, AL, July 17, 1922; d. 1984. Actress who broke into TV in her late forties; usually she played good-hearted, wise older women.

AS A REGULAR: "Nashville 99," CBS, 1977; "Bosom Buddies," ABC, 1980-81.

AND: "Paper Moon: Birthday," ABC, 1974; "Kolchak, the Night Stalker: The Knightly Murders," ABC, 1975; "Petrocelli: Face of Evil," NBC, 1975; "Switch: Ain't Nobody Here Named Barney," CBS, 1976; "The Ropers: Family Planning," ABC, 1979; "Little House on the Prairie: Sweet Sixteen," NBC, 1980; "Nero Wolfe: Wolfe at the Door," NBC, 1981; "The Love Boat: Teach Me Tonight," ABC, 1981.

TV MOVIES AND MINISERIES: "Escape," ABC, 1971; "Duel," ABC, 1971; "Women in Chains," ABC, 1972; "The Delphi Bureau," ABC, 1972; "The Devil's Daughter," ABC, 1973; "Message to My Daughter," ABC, 1973; "The Day the Earth Moved," ABC, 1974; "Reflections on Murder," ABC, 1974; "Betrayal," ABC, 1974; "The Runaway Barge," NBC, 1975; "The Killer Who Wouldn't Die," ABC, 1976; "The Strange Possession of Mrs. Oliver," NBC, 1977; "Black Market Baby," ABC, 1977; "Charleston," NBC, 1979; "Murder in Music City," NBC, 1979; "The Concrete Cowboys," CBS, 1979.

BENSON, ROBBY
b. Dallas, TX, January 21, 1956. Elfin-faced actor of films ("One on One") and TV, usually in wholesome roles.

AS A REGULAR: "Search for Tomorrow," CBS, 1971-73; "Tough Cookies," CBS, 1986.

AND: "One Day at a Time: The College Man," CBS, 1976; "Dinah!," SYN, 1977; "Alfred Hitchcock Presents: The Method Actor," NBC, 1985; "No Earthly Reason: For Jenny with Love," CBN, 1989.

TV MOVIES AND MINISERIES: "Remember When," NBC, 1974; "All the Kind Strangers," ABC, 1974; "Virginia Hill," NBC, 1974; "Death Be Not Proud," ABC, 1975; "The Death of Richie," NBC, 1977; "G.E. Theater: Two of a Kind," CBS, 1982; "California Girls," ABC, 1985.

BENTON, BARBI
b. Sacramento, CA, January 28, 1950. Playboy bunny, former paramour of Hugh Hefner and an "actress" who's made a stab at a "singing" career.

AS A REGULAR: "Hee Haw," SYN, 1971-76; "Sugar Time," ABC, 1977-78.

AND: "The Mike Douglas Show," SYN, 1974; "Celebrity Sweepstakes," NBC, 1974; "The Mike Douglas Show," SYN, 1975; "McCloud: The Park Avenue Pirates," NBC, 1975; "Nashville on the Road," SYN, 1975; "Dinah!," SYN, 1976; "The Love Boat: Marooned," ABC, 1978; "The Love Boat: Not Now, I'm Dying," ABC, 1979; "Charlie's Angels: Island Angels," ABC, 1980; "Sha Na Na," SYN, 1980; "Fantasy Island: Pleasure Palace," ABC, 1980; "Fantasy Island: The World's Most Desirable Woman," ABC, 1981; "CHiPS: Ponch's Angels," NBC, 1981; "Fantasy Island: House of Dolls," ABC, 1982; "Murder, She Wrote: Murder in the Electric Cathedral," CBS, 1986.

TV MOVIES AND MINISERIES: "The Great American Beauty Contest," ABC, 1973; "The Third Girl From the Left," ABC, 1973.

BERADINO, JOHN
b. Los Angeles, LA, May 1, 1917. Actor who's played Dr. Steve Hardy on "General Hospital" for lo these many years.

AS A REGULAR: "I Led Three Lives," SYN, 1953-56; "The New Breed," ABC, 1961-62; "General Hospital," ABC, 1963- ; "One Life to Live," ABC, 1969.

AND: "Cavalcade Theatre: Monument to a Young Man," ABC, 1956; "Ford Theatre: Paris Edition," ABC, 1956; "West Point: His Brother's Keeper," CBS, 1956; "Wire Service: High Adventure," ABC, 1956; "Broken Arrow: Rebellion," ABC, 1957; "Ford Theatre: Cross Hairs," ABC, 1957; "Richard Diamond, Private Detective: The Torch

Carriers," CBS, 1957; "Colt .45: One Good Turn," ABC, 1957; "The Jane Wyman Show: Death Rides the 12:15," NBC, 1957; "The Thin Man: The Dead Duck," NBC, 1957; "The Adventures of McGraw: The Cheat," NBC, 1958; "Cimarron City: A Respectable Girl," NBC, 1958; "Have Gun, Will Travel: Juliet," CBS, 1959; "The Texan: Blue Norther," CBS, 1959; "77 Sunset Strip: The Widow and the Web," ABC, 1959; "The Untouchables: One-Armed Bandit," ABC, 1960; "Tightrope!: Bullets and Ballet," CBS, 1960; "Lawman: Dilemma," ABC, 1960; "Checkmate: The Dark Divide," CBS, 1960; "Tales of Wells Fargo: The Border Renegade," NBC, 1961; "Route 66: Sleep on Four Pillows," CBS, 1961; "Dante: Not as a Canary," NBC, 1961; "Miami Undercover: Tricked," SYN, 1961; "SurfSide 6: Circumstantial Evidence," ABC, 1961; "Manhunt: The Disappearance," SYN, 1961; "Cheyenne: The Cousin From Atlanta," ABC, 1961; "Batman: Penguin's Clean Sweep," ABC, 1968; "The Love Boat: Hometown Doc," ABC, 1981.

TV MOVIES AND MINISERIES: "Do Not Fold, Spindle or Mutilate," ABC, 1971; "Moon of the Wolf," ABC, 1972; "A Guide for the Married Woman," ABC, 1978.

* Beradino played pro baseball for the St. Louis Browns from 1939-48 and for the Cleveland Indians from 1948-52.

BERG, GERTRUDE

b. New York City, NY, October 3, 1899; d. 1966. Comic actress and writer who played the good-hearted Molly Goldberg on the radio and TV for decades.

AS A REGULAR: "The Goldbergs," CBS, 1949-51; NBC, 1952-53; DUM, 1954; "Mrs. G. Goes to College (The Gertrude Berg Show)," CBS, 1961-62.

AND: "U.S. Steel Hour: Morning Star," ABC, 1954; "Elgin TV Hour: Hearts and Hollywood," ABC, 1954; "U.S. Steel Hour: Six O'Clock Call," ABC, 1955; "Elgin TV Hour: Mind Over Mama," ABC, 1955; "Alcoa Hour: Paris and Mrs. Perlman," NBC, 1956; "The Perry Como Show," NBC, 1957; "Washington Square," NBC, 1957; "Matinee Theatre: The Golden Door," NBC, 1957; "Kate Smith Hour," ABC, 1957; "The George Gobel Show," NBC, 1958; "The Ford Show," NBC, 1958; "Pat Boone Chevy Showroom," ABC, 1958; "The Perry Como Show," NBC, 1958; "The Garry Moore Show," CBS, 1958; "Eye on New York," CBS, 1959; "Pontiac Star Parade: An Evening with Perry Como," NBC, 1959; "U.S. Steel Hour: Trouble-in-Law," CBS, 1959; "The Ed Sullivan Show," CBS, 1959; "The Garry Moore Show," CBS, 1959; "A Tribute to Eleanor Roosevelt on Her Diamond Jubilee," NBC, 1959; "The Garry Moore Show," CBS, 1960; "Arthur Murray

Party," NBC, 1960; "Play of the Week: The World of Sholom Aleichem," SYN, 1960; "The Jack Paar Show," NBC, 1961; "Hennesey: Aunt Sarah," CBS, 1961; "Here's Hollywood," NBC, 1961; "The Ed Sullivan Show," CBS, 1965.

* Emmies: 1951.

BERGEN, CANDICE

b. Beverly Hills, CA, May 9, 1946. Striking actress who turned to a sitcom when her movie prospects began to dry up; by all accounts, TV is delighted to have her.

AS A REGULAR: "Murphy Brown," CBS, 1988- .

AND: "Coronet Blue: The Rebel," CBS, 1967; "Woody Allen Special," CBS, 1969; "The Dick Cavett Show," ABC, 1969; "Saturday Night Live," NBC, 1975; "Saturday Night Live," NBC, 1976; "Best of Brazilian Television," PBS, 1980; "Saturday Night Live," NBC, 1987; "Trying Times: Moving Day," PBS, 1988; "Late Night with David Letterman," NBC, 1988; "The Pat Sajak Show," CBS, 1989.

TV MOVIES AND MINISERIES: "Arthur the King," CBS, 1985; "Hollywood Wives," ABC, 1985; "Murder: By Reason of Insanity," CBS, 1985; "Mayflower Madam," CBS, 1987.

* Emmies: 1989, 1990.

BERGEN, EDGAR

b. Chicago, IL, February 16, 1903; d. 1978. A performer whose comic ability was such that he succeeded as a ventriloquist—on the radio. The father of Charlie McCarthy, Mortimer Snerd and Candice, Bergen's success continued in television and he began to get work as a character actor.

AS A REGULAR: "Do You Trust Your Wife?," CBS, 1956-57.

AND: "Kraft Television Theatre: A Connecticut Yankee in King Arthur's Court," ABC, 1954; "Shower of Stars: Lend an Ear," CBS, 1954; "The Jack Benny Program," CBS, 1956; "The Kate Smith Hour," ABC, 1957; "Club Oasis," NBC, 1957; "The Steve Allen Show," NBC, 1958; "The Bob Crosby Show," NBC, 1958; "December Bride: Edgar Bergen Show," CBS, 1958; "The Perry Como Show," NBC, 1958; "Frances Langford Special," NBC, 1959; "Milton Berle Starring in the Kraft Music Hall," NBC, 1959; "The Ford Show," NBC, 1959; "Five Fingers: Dossier," NBC, 1959; "The Strawberry Blonde," NBC, 1959; "The du Pont Show with June Allyson: Moment of Fear," CBS, 1960; "The Devil and Daniel Webster," NBC, 1960; "The Ed Sullivan Show," CBS, 1960; "The Ed Sullivan Show," CBS, 1961; "Here's Hollywood," NBC, 1961; "I've Got A Secret," CBS, 1961; "The Dick Powell Show: Who Killed Julie Greer?," NBC, 1961; "The Dick Powell Show: A Time to Die," NBC, 1962; "Bachelor Father: A Visit to the Bergens," ABC, 1962; "The Dick Powell Show:

Special Assignment," NBC, 1962; "The Roy Rogers and Dale Evans Show," ABC, 1962; "The Joey Bishop Show: Joey's Mustache," NBC, 1963; "Burke's Law: Who Killed Victor Barrows?," ABC, 1964; "The Greatest Show on Earth: There Are No Problems, Only Opportunities," ABC, 1964; "Voyage to the Bottom of the Sea: The Fear-Makers," ABC, 1964; "The Tonight Show Starring Johnny Carson," NBC, 1964; "Burke's Law: Who Killed Cornelius Gilbert?," ABC, 1964; "Burke's Law: Who Killed Wimbledon Hastings?," ABC, 1965; "The Littlest Hobo: A Doll Talks," SYN, 1965; "My Sister Hank," ABC, 1972; "Playhouse New York: The 1940s-The Great Radio Comedians," NET, 1973; "The Boston Pops in Hollywood," PBS, 1976; "The Muppet Show," SYN, 1976.

TV MOVIES AND MINISERIES: "The Hanged Man," NBC, 1964; "The Homecoming," CBS, 1971.

BERGEN, POLLY
b. Nellie Pauline Burgin, Knoxville, TN, July 14, 1930. Fifties glamour girl who turned serious actress with an Emmy-winning performance as Helen Morgan in 1957; best known to today's audiences as Rhoda, long-suffering wife of Pug Henry (Robert Mitchum) in "The Winds of War" and "War and Remembrance."

AS A REGULAR: "Pepsi Cola Playhouse," ABC, 1954-55; "To Tell the Truth," CBS, 1956-61; "The Polly Bergen Show," NBC, 1957-58.

AND: "Schlitz Playhouse of Stars: The Haunted Heart," CBS, 1952; "Schlitz Playhouse of Stars: Autumn in New York," CBS, 1952; "Studio One: Fatal in My Fashion," CBS, 1954; "Elgin TV Hour: Falling Star," ABC, 1954; "Appointment with Adventure: Rendezvous in Paris," CBS, 1955; "Elgin TV Hour: San Francisco Fracas," ABC, 1955; "Playhouse 90: Helen Morgan," CBS, 1957; "The Ed Sullivan Show," CBS, 1957; "The Big Record," CBS, 1957; "The Chevy Show," NBC, 1958; "Lux Playhouse: The Best House in the Valley," CBS, 1958; "The Ed Sullivan Show," CBS, 1959; "Dinah Shore Chevy Show," NBC, 1960; "Bell Telephone Hour: The Music Makers," NBC, 1960; "Jack Benny Special," CBS, 1960; "Startime: Well, What About You?," NBC, 1960; "George Burns Special," NBC, 1960; "U.S. Steel Hour: The Great Gold Mountain," CBS, 1960; "I've Got a Secret," CBS, 1960; "Phil Silvers Special: Just Polly and Me," CBS, 1960; "The Garry Moore Show," CBS, 1960; "Person to Person," CBS, 1960; "Bob Hope Buick Show," NBC, 1960; "Bell Telephone Hour: Almanac for February," NBC, 1961; "Dinah Shore Chevy Show," NBC, 1961; "Alfred Hitchcock Presents: You Can't Trust a Man," NBC, 1961; "Here's Hollywood," NBC, 1961; "Wagon Train: The Kitty Albright Story," NBC, 1961; "Yves Montand Special,"

ABC, 1961; "Perry Como's Kraft Music Hall," NBC, 1962; "Bell Telephone Hour: Weavers of Song," NBC, 1962; "The Dick Powell Show: Tissue of Hate," NBC, 1963; "Dr. Kildare: The Dark Side of the Mirror," NBC, 1963; "Bob Hope Chrysler Theatre: The Loving Cup," NBC, 1965; "The Ed Sullivan Show," CBS, 1965; "The Dean Martin Show," NBC, 1967; "The Ed Sullivan Show," CBS, 1967; "Hollywood Palace," ABC, 1968; "Murder, She Wrote: School for Scandal," CBS, 1985.

TV MOVIES AND MINISERIES: "Death Cruise," ABC, 1974; "Murder on Flight 502," ABC, 1975; "Harold Robbins' 79 Park Avenue," NBC, 1977; "The Million-Dollar Face," NBC, 1981; "Born Beautiful," NBC, 1982; "The Winds of War," ABC, 1983; "Addicted to His Love," ABC, 1988; "War and Remembrance," ABC, 1988, 1989; "Marked for Murder," NBC, 1988; "My Brother's Wife," ABC, 1989.

* Emmies: 1958.

BERGERAC, JACQUES
b. France, May 26, 1927. Actor usually in dashing continental roles.

AS A GUEST: "Alfred Hitchcock Presents: Safe Conduct," CBS, 1956; "Alfred Hitchcock Presents: The Legacy," CBS, 1956; "The Millionaire: The Story of Virginia Lennart," CBS, 1956; "Playhouse 90: Made in Heaven," CBS, 1956; "Climax!: The Long Count," CBS, 1957; "G.E. Theatre: I Will Not Die," CBS, 1957; "Matinee Theatre: The Vagabond," NBC, 1958; "Studio One: Mrs. 'arris Goes to Paris," CBS, 1958; "The Gale Storm Show: Heaven Scent," CBS, 1958; "The David Niven Show: The Lady From Winnetka," NBC, 1959; "Peck's Bad Girl: The Visitor," CBS, 1959; "Pantomime Quiz," ABC, 1959; "The Dick Van Dyke Show: The Square Triangle," CBS, 1963; "77 Sunset Strip: 5," ABC, 1963; "Perry Mason: The Case of the Fifty Millionth Frenchman," CBS, 1964; "Run for Your Life: The Cold, Cold War of Paul Bryan," NBC, 1965; "Bob Hope Chrysler Theatre: Mr. Governess," NBC, 1965; "Art Linkletter's House Party," CBS, 1966; "The Beverly Hillbillies: His Royal Highness," CBS, 1967; "Batman: Catwoman Goes to College/Batman Displays His Knowledge," ABC, 1967; "The Lucy Show: Lucy and the French Movie Star," CBS, 1967; "Get Smart: 99 Loses Control," NBC, 1968; "Run for Your Life: Life Among the Maneaters," NBC, 1968; "Batman: Minerva, Mayhem, and Millionaires," ABC, 1968; "The Doris Day Show: Doris Strikes Out," CBS, 1969.

BERGMAN, INGRID
b. Stockholm, Sweden, August 29, 1915; d. 1982. Legendary film beauty who made only a

few memorable TV appearances; an Emmy winner as Golda Meir and for "The Turn of the Screw."

AS A GUEST: "The Steve Allen Show," NBC, 1957; "The Steve Allen Show," NBC, 1958; "Small World," CBS, 1959; "Startime: The Turn of the Screw," NBC, 1959; "Twenty-Four Hours in a Woman's Life," CBS, 1961; "Hedda Gabler," CBS, 1963; "ABC Stage '67: The Human Voice," ABC, 1967.

TV MOVIES AND MINISERIES: "A Woman Called Golda," SYN, 1982.

* Emmies: 1960, 1982.

BERGMAN, PETER

b. Guantanamo Bay, Cuba, June 11, 1943. Formely Dr. Cliff Warner on "All My Children," now Jack Abbott on "The Young and the Restless."

AS A REGULAR: "The Starland Vocal Band Show," CBS, 1977; "All My Children," ABC, 1979-89; "The Young and the Restless," CBS, 1989- .

TV MOVIES AND MINISERIES: "Almost Partners," PBS, 1989.

* Bergman did those "I'm-not-a-doctor-but-I-play-one-on-TV" cough-syrup commercials.

BERLE, MILTON

b. Milton Berlinger, New York City, NY, July 12, 1908. Anything-for-a-laugh "Uncle Miltie" who was television's first star; since his variety shows in the fifties, he's done practically nothing but guest shots, including a couple of episodes of "Batman" as Louie the Lilac.

AS A REGULAR: "Texaco Star Theatre," NBC, 1948-53; "The Buick Berle Show," 1953-54; "The Milton Berle Show," NBC, 1954-56; ABC, 1966-67; "Milton Berle Starring in the Kraft Music Hall," NBC, 1958-59; "Milton Berle Special," NBC, 1959-60; "Jackpot Bowling Starring Milton Berle," NBC, 1960-61; "General Hospital," ABC, 1981-82.

AND: "Washington Square," NBC, 1957; "Wide, Wide World: The Fabulous Infant," NBC, 1957; "Kraft Television Theatre: Material Witness," NBC, 1958; "Person to Person," CBS, 1959; "Arthur Murray Party," NBC, 1959; "The Westinghouse Lucille Ball-Desi Arnaz Show: Milton Berle Hides Out at the Ricardos," CBS, 1959; "A Tribute to Eleanor Roosevelt on her Diamond Jubilee," NBC, 1959; "The Danny Thomas Show: Danny and Milton Berle Quit Show Biz," CBS, 1959; "The Dick Powell Show: Doyle Against the House," NBC, 1961; "The Andy Williams Show," NBC, 1962; "The Dick Powell Show: Thunder in a Forgotten Town," NBC, 1963; "The Joey Bishop Show: Joey and Milton and Baby Makes Three," NBC, 1963; "Bob Hope Chrysler Theatre: The Candidate,"

NBC, 1963; "Sing Along with Mitch," NBC, 1964; "Kraft Suspense Theatre: That He Should Weep for Me," NBC, 1964; "Bob Hope Special," NBC, 1964; "The Jack Benny Program," NBC, 1965; "The Lucy Show: Lucy Saves Milton Berle," CBS, 1965; "The Ed Sullivan Show," CBS, 1965; "Trials of O'Brien: Dead End on Flugel Street," CBS, 1965; "Batman: The Greatest Mother of Them All/Ma Parker," ABC, 1966; "F Troop: The Great Troop Robbery," ABC, 1966; "The Lucy Show: Lucy and John Wayne," CBS, 1966; "Bob Hope Chrysler Theatre: Murder at NBC," NBC, 1967; "The Lucy Show: Lucy Meets the Berles," CBS, 1967; "Hollywood Palace," ABC, 1967; "The Big Valley: A Flock of Trouble," ABC, 1967; "The Jackie Gleason Show," CBS, 1967; "I Dream of Jeannie: The Second Greatest Con Artist in the World," NBC, 1967; "Batman: Louie the Lilac," ABC, 1967; "Hollywood Squares," NBC, 1968; "Batman: Louie's Lethal Lilac Time," ABC, 1968; "Get Smart: Don't Look Back," NBC, 1968; "Ironside: I, the People," NBC, 1968; "Here's Lucy: Lucy and the Used Car Dealer," CBS, 1969; "The Merv Griffin Show," CBS, 1970; "The Engelbert Humperdinck Show," ABC, 1970; "That Girl: Those Friars," ABC, 1971; "Love, American Style: Love and the Vacation," ABC, 1971; "The Mod Squad: Wild Weekend," ABC, 1971; "Love, American Style: Love and the Old Boyfriend," ABC, 1971; "The Mod Squad: Exit the Closer," ABC, 1971; "The Glen Campbell Goodtime Hour," CBS, 1972; "Mannix: Nightshade," CBS, 1972; "A Salute to Television's 25th Anniversary," ABC, 1972; "McCloud: Give My Regards to Broadway," NBC, 1972; "The Bold Ones: A Purge of Madness," NBC, 1972; "Hi-Ho, Steverino: A 25th Anniversary Salute to Steve Allen," ABC, 1974; "Here's Lucy: Milton Berle Is the Life of the Party," CBS, 1974; "The David Susskind Show: Portrait of a Funny Man-Milton Berle," SYN, 1974; "Hollywood Squares," NBC, 1976; "Joys," NBC, 1976; "The Love Boat: Gotcha!," ABC, 1977; "The Love Boat: The Harder They Fall," ABC, 1979; "Saturday Night Live," NBC, 1979; "CHiPS: The Great 5K Star Race and Boulder Wrap Party," NBC, 1980; "Sha Na Na," SYN, 1981; "Something Spectacular with Steve Allen," PBS, 1981; "The Love Boat: Zeke and Zelda," ABC, 1981; "The Love Boat: CPR, IOU," ABC, 1983; "Fantasy Island: Curtain Call," ABC, 1983; "Gimme a Break: Grandpa's Secret Life," NBC, 1984; "Amazing Stories: Fine Tuning," NBC, 1985; "The Love Boat: Hidden Treasure," ABC, 1985.

TV MOVIES AND MINISERIES: "Seven in Darkness," ABC, 1969; "Two on a Bench," ABC, 1971; "Evil Roy Slade," NBC, 1972; "The Legend of Valentino," ABC, 1975; "Side by Side," CBS, 1988.

* Emmies: 1950.

100

BERLINGER, WARREN

b. *Brooklyn, NY, August 31, 1937*. Chubby, impish actor, usually in comic roles; he began as a teenager in live TV.

AS A REGULAR: "The Secret Storm," CBS, 1954-57; "The Joey Bishop Show," NBC, 1961-62; "The Funny Side," NBC, 1971; "A Touch of Grace," ABC, 1973; "Operation Petticoat," ABC, 1978-79; "Small & Frye," CBS, 1983.

AND: "Goodyear TV Playhouse: Your Every Wish," NBC, 1957; "Kraft Mystery Theatre: Death Wears Many Faces," NBC, 1958; "Look Up and Live: Diary of a Teenager," CBS, 1958; "Westginhouse Desilu Playhouse: The Hanging Judge," CBS, 1959; "Johnny Staccato: Angry Young Man," NBC, 1960; "Startime: Incident at a Corner," NBC, 1960; "The FBI: The Defector," ABC, 1966; "The Smothers Brothers Show: How to Succeed in Business and Be Really Trying," CBS, 1966; "That Girl: The Honeymoon Apartment," ABC, 1967; "Gunsmoke: Wonder," CBS, 1967; "Family Affair: The Flip Side," CBS, 1969; "Gomer Pyle, USMC: Proxy Pappas," CBS, 1969; "Walt Disney's Wonderful World of Color: Kilroy," NBC, 1969; "Bracken's World: Focus on a Gun," NBC, 1970; "Love, American Style: Love and the Proposal," ABC, 1970; "That Girl: Easy Faller," ABC, 1970; "Love, American Style: Love and the Triple Threat," ABC, 1971; "Keeping Up with the Joneses," NBC, 1972; "Love, American Style: Love and the Singing Suitor," ABC, 1972; "Love, American Style: Love and the Weighty Problem," ABC, 1973; "Emergency!: Inheritance Tax," NBC, 1973; "Happy Days: Richie's Flip Side," ABC, 1975; "Shaughnessy," NBC, 1976; "Gemini Man: Run, Sam, Run," NBC, 1976; "What's Happening!: The Incomplete Shakespeare," ABC, 1977; "Happy Days: The Physical," ABC, 1977; "Alice: The Pain of No Return," CBS, 1977; "The Love Boat: A Home Is Not a Home," ABC, 1979; "Happy Days: The Hucksters," ABC, 1980; "Alice: Dog Day Evening," CBS, 1980; "CHiPS: Suicide Stunt," NBC, 1981; "Making a Living: The Boys of Summer," ABC, 1981; "E/R: Say It Ain't So," CBS, 1984; "The A-Team: The Road to Hope," NBC, 1985; "Simon & Simon: Deep Water Death," CBS, 1986.

TV MOVIES AND MINISERIES: "The Girl Most Likely To...," ABC, 1973; "The Red Badge of Courage," NBC, 1974; "Wanted: The Sundance Woman," ABC, 1976; "Sex and the Single Parent," CBS, 1979; "The Other Woman," CBS, 1983; "What Price Victory," ABC, 1988.

BERMAN, SHELLEY

b. *Sheldon Berman, Chicago, IL, February 3, 1926*. Cerebral stand-up comic of the fifties and sixties.

AS A REGULAR: "Mary Hartman, Mary Hartman," SYN, 1977-78.

AND: "The Steve Allen Show," NBC, 1957; "The Steve Allen Show," NBC, 1958; "The Lux Show with Rosemary Clooney," NBC, 1958; "The Jack Paar Show," NBC, 1958; "The Chevy Show," NBC, 1958; "The Ed Sullivan Show," CBS, 1959; "Celebrity Talent Scouts," CBS, 1960; "Mike Wallace Interviews," CBS, 1960; "Perry Como's Kraft Music Hall," NBC, 1960; "Person to Person," CBS, 1960; "The Jack Paar Show," NBC, 1961; "Perry Como's Kraft Music Hall," NBC, 1961; "What's My Line?," CBS, 1961; "The Twilight Zone: The Mind and the Matter," CBS, 1961; "G.E. Theatre: The $200 Parlay," CBS, 1961; "Here's Hollywood," NBC, 1961; "Rawhide: The Peddler," CBS, 1962; "The Ed Sullivan Show," CBS, 1962; "The Jack Paar Program," NBC, 1963; "Password," CBS, 1963; "The du Pont Show: Comedian Backstage," NBC, 1963; "The Judy Garland Show," CBS, 1964; "Burke's Law: Who Killed Cassandra Cass?," ABC, 1964; "The Mike Douglas Show," SYN, 1964; "Bewitched: The Witches Are Out," ABC, 1964; "The Ed Sullivan Show," CBS, 1965; "Mr. Roberts: The Replacement," NBC, 1966; "The Hero: The Truth Never Hurts-Much," NBC, 1966; "The Man From UNCLE: The Super-Colossal Affair," NBC, 1966; "Kraft Music Hall," NBC, 1968; "The Steve Allen Show," SYN, 1968; "The Tonight Show Starring Johnny Carson," NBC, 1969; "What's It All About, World?," ABC, 1969; "It Takes Two," NBC, 1969; "The Mary Tyler Moore Show: Divorce Isn't Everything," CBS, 1970; "Love, American Style: Love and the V.I.P. Restaurant," ABC, 1971; "Love, American Style: Love and the College Professor," ABC, 1971; "Love, American Style: Love and the Ledge," ABC, 1972; "Emergency!: The Screenwriter," NBC, 1974; "Police Woman: The Company," NBC, 1975; "The Comedy Shop," SYN, 1978; "Eischied: Angels of Terror," NBC, 1979; "CHiPS: Fast Money," NBC, 1981; "St. Elsewhere: Getting Ahead," NBC, 1987; "The New Mike Hammer: The Last Laugh," CBS, 1987; "What's Alan Watching?," CBS, 1989.

BERNARD, BUTCH—See Tommy Nolan.

BERNARD, ED

b. Philadelphia, PA, July 4, 1939. Heavyset actor best known as Det. Joe Styles on "Police Woman."

AS A REGULAR: "Cool Million," NBC, 1972-73; "Police Woman," NBC, 1974-78; "The White Shadow," CBS, 1978-80; "Hardcastle and McCormick," ABC, 1985-87.

AND: "Police Story: Dangerous Games," NBC, 1973; "Love Story: A Glow of Dying Embers," NBC, 1973; "Police Story: The Gamble," NBC, 1974; "That's My Mama: Pilot," ABC, 1974; "Kojak: Dead on His Feet," CBS, 1974; "Mork & Mindy: Gullible Mork," ABC, 1978; "Hardcastle and McCormick: Whistler's Pride," ABC, 1984.

TV MOVIES AND MINISERIES: "Murdock's Gang," ABC, 1973; "Unwed Father," ABC, 1974; "Reflections on Murder," ABC, 1974.

BERNARDI, HERSCHEL

b. New York City, NY, October 30, 1923; d. 1986. Bald, mustachioed actor of the stage and live TV; best known as Lt. Jacoby on "Peter Gunn," the "Miami Vice" of its day, and as blue-collar worker turned executive Arnie Nuvo on "Arnie."

AS A REGULAR: "Matinee Theatre," NBC, 1955-56; "Peter Gunn," NBC, 1958-60; ABC, 1960-61; "The Jetsons," ABC, 1962-63; "Arnie," CBS, 1970-72; "Hail to the Chief," ABC, 1985.

AND: "Studio 57: A Little Care," SYN, 1957; "The Walter Winchell File: Terror," ABC, 1958; "Suspicion: Comfort for the Grave," NBC, 1958; "Bonanza: The Smiler," NBC, 1961; "Dr. Kildare: Winter Harvest," NBC, 1961; "Cain's Hundred: Penitent," NBC, 1961; "Dr. Kildare: My Brother, the Doctor," NBC, 1962; "Sam Benedict: Twenty Aching Years," NBC, 1962; "Naked City: Five Cranks for Winter, Ten Cranks for Spring," ABC, 1962; "The Untouchables: Bird in the Hand," ABC, 1962; "The Eleventh Hour: Like a Diamond in the Sky," NBC, 1963; "The Dick Powell Show: The Last of the Big Spenders," NBC, 1963; "Mr. Novak: I Don't Even Live Here," NBC, 1963; "The Eleventh Hour: There Should Be an Outfit Called Families Anonymous," NBC, 1963; "Route 66: Child of a Night," CBS, 1964; "The Defenders: Claire Cheval Died in Boston," CBS, 1964; "Grindl: The Lucky Piece," NBC, 1964; "Object Is," ABC, 1964; "Burke's Law: Who Killed Marty Kelso?," ABC, 1964; "Kraft Suspense Theatre: Their Own Executioner," NBC, 1964; "The Defenders: The Sixth Alarm," CBS, 1964; "Bob Hope Chrysler Theatre: The Sojourner," NBC, 1964; "Profiles in Courage: Edmund G. Ross," NBC, 1965; "The Doctors and the Nurses: The Witness," CBS, 1965; "Honey West: The Owl and the Eye," ABC, 1965; "The Fugitive: Landscape with Running Figures," ABC, 1965; "Insight: The Ragpicker," SYN, 1966; "The Red Skelton Hour," CBS, 1968; "The Mike Douglas Show," SYN,

1968; "A Hatful of Rain," ABC, 1968; "The Merv Griffin Show," SYN, 1969; "The Mike Douglas Show," SYN, 1971; "ABC Theatre: Judgment: The Trial of Julius and Ethel Rosenberg," ABC, 1974; "The Story of Jacob and Joseph," ABC, 1974; "Lucas Tanner: Those Who Cannot, Teach," NBC, 1975; "Newman's Drugstore," NBC, 1976; "Murder, She Wrote: Capitol Offense," CBS, 1985.

TV MOVIES AND MINISERIES: "But I Don't Want to Get Married!," ABC, 1970; "No Place to Run," ABC, 1972; "Sandcastles," CBS, 1972; "The Story of Jacob and Joseph," ABC, 1974; "Best Sellers: Seventh Avenue," NBC, 1977; "The Million-Dollar Face," NBC, 1981.

BERNAU, CHRISTOPHER

b. 1940; d. 1989. Actor who played Alan Spaulding on "The Guiding Light."

AS A REGULAR: "The Guiding Light," CBS, 1977-84, 1986-88.

BERNSEN, CORBIN

b. Los Angeles, CA. Blond actor who plays attorney Arnie Becker on "L.A. Law"; the son of soap stalwart Jeanne Cooper of "The Young and the Restless."

AS A REGULAR: "Ryan's Hope," ABC, 1984-85; "L.A. Law," NBC, 1986- .

AND: "Matlock: The Producer," NBC, 1987; "Anything But Love: Bang, You're Dead," ABC, 1989; "The Arsenio Hall Show," SYN, 1989.

BERRY, CHUCK

b. Charles Edward Berry, San Jose, CA, January 15, 1926. Rock 'n' roll legend.

AS A GUEST: "The Big Beat," ABC, 1957; "American Bandstand," ABC, 1957; "The Guy Mitchell Show," ABC, 1957; "The Dick Clark Saturday Night Beechnut Show," ABC, 1958; "American Bandstand," ABC, 1959; "Midnight Special," NBC, 1973; "Saturday Night Live," NBC, 1976; "The John Davidson Show," SYN, 1981.

BERRY, KEN

b. Moline, IL, 1930. Light comic leading man who played Capt. Parmenter on "F Troop," Sam Jones on "Mayberry RFD" and now plays Vint on "Mama's Family."

AS A REGULAR: "The Ann Sothern Show," CBS, 1960-61; "The Bob Newhart Show," NBC, 1962; "F Troop," ABC, 1965-67; "Mayberry RFD," CBS, 1968-71; "The Ken Berry 'WOW' Show," ABC, 1972; "Mama's Family," NBC, 1983-85; SYN, 1986- .

AND: "The Andy Williams Show," CBS, 1959; "Harrigan and Son: Young Man's World," ABC, 1960; "Michael Shayne: The Trouble with Ernie," NBC, 1961; "The Garry Moore Show," CBS,

1961; "Father of the Bride: The Engagement Party," CBS, 1961; "Father of the Bride: The New Watch," CBS, 1962; "The Dick Van Dyke Show: The Brave and the Backache," CBS, 1964; "The Dick Van Dyke Show: My Mother Can Beat Up My Father," CBS, 1964; "Hazel: The Marriage Trap," NBC, 1964; "Combat!: The Hostages," ABC, 1964; "Wendy & Me: Wendy's Secret Wedding," ABC, 1964; "No Time for Sergeants: Stockdale's Island," ABC, 1964; "No Time for Sergeants: Stockdale's Millions," ABC, 1964; "No Time for Sergeants: Two for the Show," ABC, 1965; "The Danny Thomas Hour: The Royal Follies of 1933," NBC, 1967; "You Don't Say," NBC, 1967; "The Mike Douglas Show," SYN, 1968; "The Lucy Show: Lucy and Ken Berry," CBS, 1968; "The Andy Griffith Show: Mayberry RFD," CBS, 1968; "The Andy Griffith Show: Sam for Town Council," CBS, 1968; "The Carol Burnett Show," CBS, 1969; "Rowan & Martin's Laugh-In," NBC, 1970; "The Carol Burnett Show," CBS, 1970; "Love, American Style: Love and the Penal Code," ABC, 1971; "The Carol Burnett Show," CBS, 1971; "Love, American Style: Love and the Jinx," ABC, 1972; "Once Upon a Mattress," CBS, 1972; "Love, American Style: Love and the Teller's Tale," ABC, 1973; "Mitzi Gaynor: The First Time," CBS, 1973; "The Carol Burnett Show," CBS, 1973; "NBC Follies," NBC, 1973; "The Brady Bunch: Kelly's Kids," ABC, 1974; "Tattletales," CBS, 1974; "Medical Center: Half a Life," CBS, 1975; "The Sonny and Cher Comedy Hour," CBS, 1977; "The Life and Times of Grizzly Adams: The Fugitive," NBC, 1977; "Little House on the Prairie: Annabelle," NBC, 1979; "All Star Secrets," NBC, 1979; "Gimme a Break: The Man From Zoron," NBC, 1985.

TV MOVIES AND MINISERIES: "Wake Me When The War Is Over," ABC, 1969; "The Reluctant Heroes," ABC, 1971; "Every Man Needs One," ABC, 1972; "Letters From Three Lovers," ABC, 1973; "Love Boat II," ABC, 1977.

TV'S TOP TEN, 1969-70

1. Rowan & Martin's Laugh-In (NBC)
2. Gunsmoke (CBS)
3. Bonanza (NBC)
4. Mayberry RFD (CBS)
5. Family Affair (CBS)
6. Here's Lucy (CBS)
7. The Red Skelton Hour (CBS)
8. Marcus Welby, M.D. (ABC)
9. Walt Disney's Wonderful World of Color (NBC)
10. The Doris Day Show (CBS)

BERTINELLI, VALERIE

b. Wilmington, DE, April 23, 1960. Actress who grew up (and in other directions) on TV as Barbara Cooper on "One Day at a Time."

AS A REGULAR: "One Day at a Time," CBS, 1975-84; "Sydney," CBS, 1990.

AND: "The Peter Marshall Variety Show," SYN, 1977; "Hollywood Squares," SYN, 1979; "Saturday Night Live," NBC, 1987; "The Pat Sajak Show," CBS, 1989.

TV MOVIES AND MINISERIES: "Young Love, First Love," CBS, 1979; "The Promise of Love," CBS, 1980; "The Princess and the Cabbie," CBS, 1981; "I Was a Mail Order Bride," CBS, 1982; "The Seduction of Gina," CBS, 1984; "Shattered Vows," NBC, 1984; "Silent Witness," NBC, 1985; "Rockabye," CBS, 1986; "Ordinary Heroes," ABC, 1986; "I'll Take Manhattan," CBS, 1987; "Taken Away," CBS, 1989.

* Bertinelli met husband Eddie Van Halen at a rock concert in Shreveport, Louisiana, in August 1980.

BESSELL, TED

b. Flushing, NY, March 20, 1935. Light comic leading man who was Donald Hollinger, boyfriend of Ann Marie on "That Girl" (Marlo Thomas) and later Mary Tyler Moore's TV paramour; now he's a respected comedy director.

AS A REGULAR: "It's a Man's World," NBC, 1962-63; "Gomer Pyle, USMC," CBS, 1966; "That Girl," ABC, 1966-71; "Me and the Chimp," CBS, 1972; "Good Time Harry," NBC, 1980; "Hail to the Chief," ABC, 1985.

AND: "The Lieutenant: Alert," NBC, 1963; "The Greatest Show on Earth: You're All Right, Ivy," ABC, 1963; "The Great Adventure: Rodger Young," CBS, 1964; "Ben Casey: August Is the Month Before Christmas," ABC, 1964; "The Bill Dana Show: The Movie Star," NBC, 1965; "The Littlest Hobo: A.W.O.L. Louie," SYN, 1965; "The Alfred Hitchcock Hour: Thou Still Unravished Bride," NBC, 1965; "Love, American Style: Love and the Roommate," ABC, 1969; "Marcus Welby, M.D.: Echo From Another World," ABC, 1972; "The Ted Bessell Show," CBS, 1973; "Bobby Parker and Company," NBC, 1974; "The Mary Tyler Moore Show: Mary Richards Falls in Love," CBS, 1975; "The Mary Tyler Moore Show: One Boyfriend Too Many," CBS, 1975.

TV MOVIES AND MINISERIES: "Two on a Bench," ABC, 1971; "Your Money or Your Wife," CBS, 1972; "Scream, Pretty Peggy," ABC, 1973; "What Are Best Friends For?," ABC, 1973.

AS DIRECTOR: "The Tracey Ullman Show," FOX, 1986-90.

BESSER, JOE

b. St. Louis, MO, August 12, 1907; d. 1988. Pudgy comic actor and former member of the

Three Stooges, whose trademark line was "Y'craaaazy." He played Stinky on "The Abbott and Costello Show" and Mr. Jillson on "The Joey Bishop Show."

AS A REGULAR: "The Ken Murray Show," CBS, 1950-51; "The Abbott and Costello Show," CBS, 1952-54; "The Joey Bishop Show," NBC, 1962-64; CBS, 1964-65.

AND: "Favorite Story: No Tears," SYN, 1952; "December Bride: Skid Row," CBS, 1955; "My Sister Eileen: The Lease-Breakers," CBS, 1960; "Shirley Temple's Storybook: Babes in Toyland," NBC, 1960; "The Jack Benny Program: Tennessee Ernie Ford Visits," CBS, 1961; "Batman: Hizzoner the Penguin/Dizzoner the Penguin," ABC, 1966; "Hollywood Palace," ABC, 1967; "The Mothers-in-Law: How Not to Manage a Rock Group," NBC, 1968; "The Mothers-in-Law: The First Anniversary Is the Hardest," NBC, 1968; "That's Life: Bachelor Days," ABC, 1968; "The Mothers-in-Law: Two on the Aisle," NBC, 1969; "Love, American Style: Love and the Proposal," ABC, 1970; "Love, American Style: Love and the Lady Barber," ABC, 1972; "Love, American Style: Love and the Legend," ABC, 1973.

TV MOVIES AND MINISERIES: "The Monk," ABC, 1969.

BEST, JAMES

b. Corydon, IN, July 26, 1926. Actor and stuntman who played rugged, anonymous roles for years before becoming a household name—in some households, at least—as Sheriff Roscoe P. Coltrane on the goofy "The Dukes of Hazzard."

AS A REGULAR: "The Dukes of Hazzard," CBS, 1979-85.

AND: "Du Pont Theatre: Woman's Work," ABC, 1956; "West Point: Lost Cadet," CBS, 1957; "Du Pont Theatre: One Day at a Time," ABC, 1957; "Alfred Hitchcock Presents: Death Sentence," CBS, 1958; "Wanted Dead or Alive: Sheriff of Red Rock," CBS, 1958; "Restless Gun: Jebediah Bonner," NBC, 1958; "Target: Assassin," SYN, 1958; "Wanted Dead or Alive: Six-up to Bannach," CBS, 1959; "Alfred Hitchcock Presents: Cell 227," CBS, 1960; "Stagecoach West: High Lonesome," ABC, 1960; "The Andy Griffith Show: Guitar Player," CBS, 1960; "The Rebel: Deathwatch," ABC, 1960; "Pony Express: Boredom," SYN, 1960; "The du Pont Show with June Allyson: Love on Credit," CBS, 1960; "Have Gun, Will Travel: A Quiet Night in Town," CBS, 1961; "Bonanza: The Fugitive," NBC, 1961; "Stagecoach West: The Arsonist," ABC, 1961; "The Andy Griffith Show: The Guitar Player Returns," CBS, 1961; "Whispering Smith: The Hemp Reeger Case," NBC, 1961; "SurfSide 6: One for the Road," ABC, 1961; "The Twilight Zone: The Grave," CBS, 1961; "The Bob

Cummings Show: Twangy Won't Fly," CBS, 1961; "Laramie: The Runaway," NBC, 1962; "The Twilight Zone: The Last Rites of Jeff Myrtlebank," CBS, 1962; "77 Sunset Strip: The Long Shoe Caper," ABC, 1962; "The Twilight Zone: Jess-Belle," CBS, 1963; "The Gallant Men: The Warrior," ABC, 1963; "Death Valley Days: Sixty-Seven Miles of Gold," SYN, 1964; "Honey West: A Matter of Wife and Death," ABC, 1965; "The Virginian: Letter of the Law," NBC, 1965; "The Iron Horse: High Devil," ABC, 1966; "The Guns of Will Sonnett: Meeting at Devil's Fork," ABC, 1967; "The Mod Squad: The Price of Terror," ABC, 1968; "The Felony Squad: The Distant Shore," ABC, 1968; "The Guns of Will Sonnett: Robber's Roost," ABC, 1969; "Gunsmoke: Charlie Noon," CBS, 1969; "Hawkins: Blood Feud," CBS, 1973.

TV MOVIES AND MINISERIES: "Run, Simon, Run," ABC, 1970; "Savages," ABC, 1974; "The Runaway Barge," NBC, 1975; "The Savage Bees," NBC, 1976; "Centennial," NBC, 1978-79.

BEST, WILLIE

b. Mississippi, 1916; d. 1962. Black actor whose film and TV work was mostly limited to racist dimwit roles, except perhaps on "My Little Margie," where everyone acted brain-damaged.

AS A REGULAR: "The Stu Erwin Show," ABC, 1950-55; "My Little Margie," CBS, 1952; NBC, 1952; CBS, 1953; NBC, 1953-55; "Waterfront," SYN, 1954-55.

BETHUNE, ZINA

b. New York City, NY, February 17, 1946. Actress who began her career as a teenager on New York-based soaps; she played young nurse Gail Lucas on "The Nurses" and Barbara Sterling Latimer on "Love of Life."

AS A REGULAR: "The Guiding Light," CBS, 1956-58; "Young Doctor Malone," NBC, 1959-60; "The Nurses," CBS, 1962-65; "Love of Life," CBS, 1965-71.

AND: "Odyssey: Satan in Salem," CBS, 1957; "The Seven Lively Arts: The Nutcracker," CBS, 1957; "Kraft Theatre: Three Plays by Tennessee Williams—This Property Is Condemned," NBC, 1958; "Little Women," CBS, 1958; "Sunday Showcase: People Kill People Sometimes," NBC, 1959; "Special for Women: The Cold Woman," NBC, 1960; "Route 66: The Swan Bed," CBS, 1960; "Naked City: The Human Trap," ABC, 1960; "U.S. Steel Hour: Famous," CBS, 1961; "True Story: The Chance," NBC, 1961; "Cain's Hundred: The Swinger," NBC, 1962; "Route 66: Kiss the Maiden All Forlorn," CBS, 1962; "Confidential for Women: Eve," ABC, 1966; "The Invaders: The Prophet," ABC, 1967; "Gunsmoke: Family of Killers," CBS, 1973;

"Emergency!: Alley Cat," NBC, 1973; "Planet of the Apes: The Legacy," CBS, 1974.

BETTGER, LYLE

b. Philadelphia, PA, February 13, 1915. Stiff, charisma-less actor of movies and TV.

AS A REGULAR: "Court of Last Resort," NBC, 1957-58; "Grand Jury," SYN, 1959-60.

AND: "TV Reader's Digest: Return from Oblivion," ABC, 1956; "Schlitz Playhouse of Stars: Showdown at Painted Rock," CBS, 1956; "Ford Theatre: Appointment with Destiny," NBC, 1956; "Warner Bros. Presents Conflict: Explosion," ABC, 1956; "Schlitz Playhouse of Stars: Step Right Up and Die," CBS, 1956; "The 20th Century-Fox Hour: End of a Gun," CBS, 1957; "Pursuit: Last Night of August," CBS, 1958; "Law of the Plainsman: Full Circle," NBC, 1959; "Walt Disney Presents: Texas John Slaughter - Killers from Kansas," ABC, 1959; "Dick Powell's Zane Grey Theatre: The Law and the Gun," CBS, 1959; "Laramie: Night of the Quiet Men," NBC, 1959; "Laramie: Rimrock," NBC, 1961; "The Tall Man: Hard Justice," NBC, 1961; "Tales of Wells Fargo: Mr. Mute," NBC, 1961; "Rawhide: The Blue Spy," CBS, 1961; "Laramie: The Lawless Seven," NBC, 1961; "The Rifleman: Skull," ABC, 1962; "Bonanza: The Guilty," NBC, 1962; "Laramie: Beyond Justice," NBC, 1962; "Grindl: Grindl, Femme Fatale," NBC, 1963; "Kraft Suspense Theatre: A Truce to Terror," NBC, 1964; "Death Valley Days: Graydon's Charge," SYN, 1964; "Rawhide: Incident of the Dowry Dundee," CBS, 1964; "Combat: A Rare Vintage," ABC, 1964; "Mr. Novak: Beat the Plowshare: Edge the Sword," NBC, 1965; "Blue Light: A Traitor's Blood," ABC, 1966; "Bonanza: Something Hurt, Something Wild," NBC, 1966; "The Time Tunnel: Invasion," ABC, 1966; "Insight: Man in the Middle," SYN, 1968; "Hawaii Five-O: All the King's Horses," CBS, 1969; "The Men From Shiloh: Nightmare at New Life," NBC, 1970; "NET Playhouse: Biography-Portrait of the Hero as a Young Man," NET, 1972; "Mannix: Portrait of a Hero," CBS, 1972; "Ironside: Class of '40," NBC, 1973; "Police Story: Violent Homecoming," NBC, 1973; "Hawaii Five-O: The Sunday Torch," CBS, 1973; "Police Story: Incident in the Kill Zone," NBC, 1975; "Hawaii Five-O: Let Death Do Us Part," CBS, 1976.

TV MOVIES AND MINISERIES: "The Return of the Gunfighter," ABC, 1967.

BETZ, CARL

b. Pittsburgh, PA, March 9, 1920; d. 1978. Handsome, solid actor who hit TV paydirt as Dr. Alex Stone, husband of Donna Stone (Donna Reed); he won an Emmy as criminal attorney Clinton Judd.

AS A REGULAR: "Love of Life," CBS, 1950; "The Donna Reed Show," ABC, 1958-66; "Judd for the Defense," ABC, 1967-69.

AND: "Kraft Television Theatre: Party for Jonathan," NBC, 1954; "Robert Montgomery Presents: Two Wise Women," NBC, 1954; "Appointment with Adventure: Suburban Terror," CBS, 1956; "Crusader: The Boy on the Brink," CBS, 1956; "The Millionaire: The Story of Rose Russell," CBS, 1957; "Perry Mason: The Case of the Sunbather's Diary," CBS, 1958; "Alfred Hitchcock Presents: The Motive," CBS, 1958; "Alfred Hitchcock Presents: On the Nose," CBS, 1958; "The Millionaire: The Jack Garrison Story," CBS, 1958; "You Don't Say," NBC, 1968; "The FBI: Boomerang," ABC, 1969; "Love, American Style: Love and the Former Marriage," ABC, 1969; "It Takes Two," NBC, 1969; "Mission: Impossible: The Crane," CBS, 1970; "Medical Center: The VD Story," CBS, 1970; "Crisis," CBS, 1970; "Ironside: The Lonely Way to Go," NBC, 1970; "Night Gallery: The Dead Man," NBC, 1970; "The Mod Squad: A Bummer for R.J.," ABC, 1971; "The FBI: Downfall," ABC, 1971; "Mission: Impossible: Break!," CBS, 1972; "Cannon: The Endangered Species," CBS, 1972; "Love, American Style: Love and the Modern Wife," ABC, 1972; "The Streets of San Francisco: The Bullet," ABC, 1973; "Barnaby Jones: Stand In for Death," CBS, 1973; "The Magician: Man on Fire," NBC, 1973; "The New Adventures of Perry Mason: The Case of the Spurious Spouse," CBS, 1973; "Marcus Welby, M.D.: No Gods in Sight," ABC, 1974; "SWAT: Criss-Cross," ABC, 1975; "Quincy: Visitors in Paradise," NBC, 1977.

TV MOVIES AND MINISERIES: "The Monk," ABC, 1969; "In Search of America," ABC, 1971; "The Deadly Dream," ABC, 1971; "Set This Town on Fire," NBC, 1973; "Killdozer," ABC, 1974; "The Daughters of Joshua Cabe Return," ABC, 1975; "Brinks: The Great Robbery," NBC, 1976.

* Emmies: 1969.

TRIVIA QUIZ #4:
"THE BEVERLY HILLBILLIES"
1. What was Jethro's twin sister's name?
2. What bank did Mr. Drysdale head?
3. What was Mr. Drysdale's son's name?
4. Who played him?
5. What was Dash Riprock's real name?
6. What did the Clampetts call their swimming pool?
7. What movie company did Jed Clampett own?
8. Which cereal company sponsored the show?
9. Which cigarette sponsored the show?
10. Nancy Kulp played Mr. Drysdale's secretary, Jane _____.

(Answers at end of book.)

THE BEVERLY HILLBILLIES
CBS, 1962-71.

This hugely successful sitcom set audience records that stood for years. It was about an Ozark family who struck oil and moved to the hills of Beverly: Buddy Ebsen was Jed Clampett, Donna Douglas his daughter Elly May, Max Baer Jr. his nephew Jethro and Irene Ryan the grandma of the batch. Paul Henning, the show's creator, was a Missouri native and had fiddled with cornpone humor while writing for Bob Cummings and for George Burns and Gracie Allen. In its Wednesday night time spot, the show was the first to give Perry Como fits (he was competing on NBC) and its success probably helped keep "The Dick Van Dyke Show," which followed it, on the air. In 1970 the show fell out of TV's top 25 shows for the first time and when CBS cleaned house of its rural-oriented shows in 1971, "The Beverly Hillbillies"—which had begun poking fun at women's liberation— bit the dust.

TV'S TOP TEN, 1962-63

1. The Beverly Hillbillies (CBS)
2. Candid Camera (CBS)
2. The Red Skelton Hour (CBS)
4. Bonanza (NBC)
4. The Lucy Show (CBS)
6. The Andy Griffith Show (CBS)
7. Ben Casey (ABC)
7. The Danny Thomas Show (CBS)
9. The Dick Van Dyke Show (CBS)
10. Gunsmoke (CBS)

TRIVIA QUIZ #5: "BEWITCHED"

1. What was the name of the advertising agency Darrin Stephens worked for?
2. What automobile company sponsored the show?
3. What was Mr. Kravitz' first name?
4. What was Mrs. Kravitz' first name?
5. What was the name of Samantha's crafty cousin?
6. Who played her?
7. Who was Samantha's physician?
8. Tabitha was the Stephens' daughter. What was their son's name?
9. All grown up, Tabitha had her own ABC series in 1977. Who played her?
10. Which body part did Samantha twitch to implement her powers?

(Answers at end of book.)

BEYMER, RICHARD
b. George Richard Beymer, Avoca, IA, February 21, 1939. Actor who began in soulful juvenile roles and who now plays depraved hotel and brothel owner Benjamin Horne on "Twin Peaks."

AS A REGULAR: "Paper Dolls," ABC, 1984; "Twin Peaks," ABC, 1990- .
AND: "Sky King: Man Hunt," ABC, 1955; "Make Room for Daddy: Terry Has a Date," ABC, 1956; "Navy Log: The Soapbox Kid," ABC, 1958; "The Jane Wyman Show: On the Brink," NBC, 1958; "Walt Disney Presents: Boston Tea Party," ABC, 1958; "Playhouse 90: Dark December," CBS, 1959; "Here's Hollywood," NBC, 1961; "The Virginian: You Take the High Road," NBC, 1965; "Kraft Suspense Theatre: The Easter Breach," NBC, 1965; "Walt Disney's Wonderful World of Color: Johnny Tremain," NBC, 1965; "Dr. Kildare: Mercy of Murder/A Strange Sort of Accident/New Doctor in Town/Reckoning," NBC, 1966; "The Man From UNCLE: The Survival School Affair," NBC, 1967; "Moonlighting: All Creatures Great and Not-So-Great," ABC, 1986; "Murder, She Wrote: The Way to Dusty Death," CBS, 1987; "Murder, She Wrote: The Days Dwindle Down," CBS, 1987; "The Bronx Zoo: The Gospel Truth," NBC, 1988.
TV MOVIES AND MINISERIES: "Generation," ABC, 1985.

BICKFORD, CHARLES
b. Cambridge, MA, January 1, 1889; d. 1967. Rugged actor in movies ("The Farmer's Daughter," "The Days of Wine and Roses") and TV, usually in taciturn roles; he played Shiloh Ranch owner John Grainger on "The Virginian."

AS A REGULAR: "Man Behind the Badge," SYN, 1955-56; "The Virginian," NBC, 1966-67.
AND: "Ford Theatre: Sunk," NBC, 1952; "Schlitz Playhouse of Stars: The Copper Ring," CBS, 1953; "Schlitz Playhouse of Stars: The Viking," CBS, 1954; "Playhouse 90: Forbidden Area," CBS, 1956; "Ford Theatre: Front Page Father," ABC, 1956; "Playhouse 90: Sincerely, Willis Wayde," CBS, 1956; "The 20th Century-Fox Hour: The Man Who Couldn't Wait," CBS, 1957; "Playhouse 90: Free Weekend," CBS, 1958; "Playhouse 90: The Days of Wine and Roses," CBS, 1958; "Hallmark Hall of Fame: Cradle Song," NBC, 1960; "Buick Electra Playhouse: The Gambler, the Nun and the Radio," CBS, 1960; "Checkmate: Target ... Tycoon," CBS, 1960; "The Barbara Stanwyck Show: Ironback's Bride," NBC, 1960; "The Islanders: The Cold War of Adam Smith," ABC, 1960; "The Americans: Long Way Back," NBC, 1961; "G.E. Theatre: The Golden Years," CBS, 1961; "Dr. Kildare: Winter Harvest," NBC, 1961; "The Dick Powell Show: The Geetas Box," NBC, 1961;

"Theatre '62: The Farmer's Daughter," NBC, 1962; "The Virginian: The Devil's Children," NBC, 1962; "Alcoa Premiere: Million Dollar Hospital," ABC, 1963; "The Dick Powell Show: The Old Man and the City," NBC, 1963; "The Eleventh Hour: The Silence of Good Men," NBC, 1963; "Suspense Theatre: I, Christopher Bell," CBS, 1964.

BIEHN, MICHAEL
b. Arizona, 1957. Actor in films ("The Terminator") and some TV.
AS A REGULAR: "The Runaways," NBC, 1978-79.
AND: "Hill Street Blues: Fowl Play," NBC, 1984.
TV MOVIES AND MINISERIES: "Zuma Beach," NBC, 1978; "A Fire in the Sky," NBC, 1978; "The Paradise Connection," CBS, 1979; "China Rose," CBS, 1983; "Deadly Intentions," ABC, 1985.

BILL, TONY
b. San Diego, CA, August 23, 1940. Actor who began as a juvenile and now produces movies ("My Bodyguard").
AS A REGULAR: "What Really Happened to the Class of '65?," NBC, 1977-78.
AND: "Ben Casey: A Boy Is Standing Outside the Door," ABC, 1965; "Mr. Novak: An Elephant Is Like a Tree," NBC, 1965; "For the People: Dangerous to the Public Peace and Safety," CBS, 1965; "The Loner: An Echo of Bugles," CBS, 1965; "Dr. Kildare: The Bell in the Schoolhouse Tolls for Thee, Kildare/Life in the Dance Hall: F-U-N/Some Doors Are Slamming/Enough la Boheme for Everybody/A Pyrotechnic Display," NBC, 1965; "Run for Your life: The Time of the Sharks," NBC, 1965; "The Virginian: Chaff in the Wind," NBC, 1966; "Bonanza: The Oath," NBC, 1966; "I Spy: Father Abraham," NBC, 1966; "The Road West: The Predators," NBC, 1967; "Bob Hope Chrysler Theatre: Dead Wrong," NBC, 1967; "The Man from UNCLE: The Seven Wonders of the World Affair," NBC, 1968; "Bracken's World: Love It or Leave It, Change It or Lose," NBC, 1970; "Cade's County: Slay Ride," CBS, 1972; "St. Elsewhere: Down's Syndrome," NBC, 1982; "Hotel: Intimate Stranger," ABC, 1984; "Alfred Hitchcock Presents: The Night Caller," NBC, 1985; "Murder, She Wrote: Trial by Error," CBS, 1986; "Moonlighting: Cool Hand Dave," ABC, 1987.
TV MOVIES AND MINISERIES: "Haunts of the Very Rich," ABC, 1972; "Having Babies II," ABC, 1977; "Washington: Behind Closed Doors," ABC, 1977; "Are You in the House Alone?," CBS, 1978; "Portrait of an Escort," CBS, 1980; "Washington Mistress," CBS, 1982; "Running Out," CBS, 1983.

BILLINGSLEY, BARBARA
b. Barbara Lillian Combes, Los Angeles, CA,

December 22, 1922. Pert actress who was perfect mom June Cleaver on "Leave It to Beaver."
AS A REGULAR: "Profesional Father," CBS, 1955; "Leave It to Beaver," CBS, 1957-58; ABC, 1958-63; "The New Leave It to Beaver," DIS, 1985-86; TBS, 1986-89.
AS A GUEST: "Schlitz Playhouse of Stars: The Doctor Goes Home," CBS, 1953; "Four Star Playhouse: Sound Off, My Love," CBS, 1953; "Cavalcade of America: The Stolen General," ABC, 1953; "Pride of the Family: Albie's Old Flame," ABC, 1953; "Schlitz Playhouse of Stars: The Jungle Trap," CBS, 1954; "Fireside Theatre: The Whole Truth," NBC, 1954; "Schlitz Playhouse of Stars: Small Delay at Fort Bess," CBS, 1954; "Star Theatre: Golden Opportunity," CBS, 1954; "Four Star Playhouse: Breakfast in Bed," CBS, 1955; "Schlitz Playhouse of Stars: Gift of Life," CBS, 1955; "The Loretta Young Show: Tightwad Millionaire," NBC, 1956; "The Brothers: The Brave One," CBS, 1957; "Make Room for Daddy: Danny's Date," ABC, 1957; "Du Pont Theatre: Frightened Witness," ABC, 1957; "Mr. Adams and Eve: That Magazine," CBS, 1957; "Studio 57: It's a Small World," SYN, 1957; "The George Gobel Show," NBC, 1958; "Mother's March," SYN, 1960; "The FBI: The Fatal Connection," ABC, 1971; "The FBI: Recurring Nightmare," ABC, 1971; "Mork & Mindy: Cheerleaders in Chains," ABC, 1982; "Silver Spoons: I Won't Dance," NBC, 1984; "The New Mike Hammer: Who Killed Sister Lorna?," CBS, 1987; "Baby Boom: Guilt," NBC, 1988.
TV MOVIES AND MINISERIES: "Still the Beaver," CBS, 1983; "Bay Coven," NBC, 1987.

BILLINGSLEY, PETER
b. New York City, NY, 1972. Young actor, blonde and bespectacled, memorable as the lead in the film "A Christmas Story"; he's the brother of young actress Melissa Michaelsen.
AS A REGULAR: "Real People," NBC, 1982-84.
AND: "Little House on the Prairie: No Beast So Fierce," NBC, 1982.
TV MOVIES AND MINISERIES: "Memories Never Die," CBS, 1982.

BIRD, BILLIE
b. Pocatello, ID. Elderly actress who's played old ladies who say outrageous things on three sitcoms.
AS A REGULAR: "It Takes Two," ABC, 1982-83; "Benson," ABC, 1985-86; "Dear John," NBC, 1988- .
AND: "Gunsmoke: The Hanging of Newly O'Brien," CBS, 1973; "House Calls: Deafenwolf," CBS, 1982; "Goodnight Beantown: Popsicle," CBS, 1983; "Three's a Crowd: Aunt

Mae Visits," ABC, 1984; "Max Headroom: Blipverts," ABC, 1987; "Newhart: Telethon Man," CBS, 1987; "The Charmings: Cindy's Back in Town," ABC, 1987; "First Impressions: Poor Clara," CBS, 1988.

BIRNEY, DAVID

b. Washington, D.C., April 23, 1939. Actor who played Bernie Steinberg, wife of Bridget (Meredith Baxter Birney); then he played supercop Serpico and Dr. Ben Samuels on "St. Elsewhere."

AS A REGULAR: "A World Apart," ABC, 1970-71; "Bridget Loves Bernie," CBS, 1972-73; "Serpico," NBC, 1976-77; "St. Elsewhere," NBC, 1982-83; "Glitter," ABC, 1984-85.

AND: "Hallmark Hall of Fame: Saint Joan," NBC, 1967; "The FBI: The Minerva Tapes," ABC, 1971; "Hawaii Five-O: Follow the White Brick Road," CBS, 1972; "Orson Welles' Great Mysteries: The Ingenious Reporter," SYN, 1973; "Wide World of Mystery: The Haunting of Penthouse D," ABC, 1974; "Police Story: Captain Hook," NBC, 1974; "McMillan and Wife: Love, Honor and Swindle," NBC, 1975; "Medical Center: If Mine Eye Offends Me," CBS, 1975; "Police Woman: Bloody Nose," NBC, 1975; "Medical Center: The Touch of Sight," CBS, 1976; "Bronk: Cancelled," CBS, 1976; "The Streets of San Francisco: Clown of Death," ABC, 1976; "Police Story: Officer Dooly," NBC, 1976; "The Love Boat: Marooned," ABC, 1978; "Family: Malicious Mischief," ABC, 1979; "The Twilight Zone: Tooth or Consequences," CBS, 1986; "Murder, She Wrote: Prediction: Murder," CBS, 1988; "CBS Schoolbreak Special: 15 and Getting Straight," CBS, 1989; "Matlock: The Con Man," NBC, 1989.

TV MOVIES AND MINISERIES: "Murder or Mercy?," ABC, 1974; "Only with Married Men," ABC, 1974; "Bronk," CBS, 1975; "The Deadly Game," NBC, 1976; "Testimony of Two Men," SYN, 1977; "Someone Is Watching Me!," NBC, 1978; "High Midnight," CBS, 1979; "The Five of Me," CBS, 1981; "Master of the Game," CBS, 1984; "The Long Journey Home," NBC, 1987; "Love and Betrayal," CBS, 1989.

BISHOP, JOEY

b. Joseph Abraham Gottlieb, Bronx, NY, February 3, 1918. Nebbishy comic, mascot of Sinatra's "rat pack," who was hot in the late fifties and early sixties.

AS A REGULAR: "Keep Talking," CBS, 1958-59; ABC, 1959-60; "The Jack Paar Show," NBC, 1958-62; "The Joey Bishop Show," NBC, 1961-64; CBS, 1964-65; ABC, 1967-69; "Celebrity Sweepstakes," NBC, 1974-76; "Liar's Club," SYN, 1976-78.

AS A GUEST: "Dinah Shore Chevy Show," NBC, 1957; "The Perry Como Show," NBC, 1957; "The Perry Como Show," NBC, 1958; "The Frank Sinatra Show," ABC, 1958; "The Bob Crosby Show," NBC, 1958; "The Garry Moore Show," CBS, 1959; "Arthur Murray Party," NBC, 1959; "Richard Diamond, Private Detective: No Laughing Matter," NBC, 1959; "Dinah Shore Chevy Show," NBC, 1960; "Arthur Murray Party," NBC, 1960; "The Frank Sinatra Timex Show," ABC, 1960; "What's My Line?," CBS, 1960; "Esther Williams at Cypress Gardens, NBC, 1960; "Candid Camera," CBS, 1960; "Du Pont Show of the Month: Heaven Can Wait," CBS, 1960; "The Jack Benny Program," CBS, 1960; "Person to Person," CBS, 1960; "Open End," NBC, 1960; "The Danny Thomas Show: Everything Happens to Me," CBS, 1961; "Dinah Shore Chevy Show: Like Young," NBC, 1961; "Here's Hollywood," NBC, 1961; "Password," CBS, 1962; "The Dick Powell Show: Thunder in a Forgotten Town," NBC, 1963; "The Tonight Show Starring Johnny Carson," NBC, 1965; "Get Smart: Viva Smart," NBC, 1967; "The Name of the Game: I Love You, Billy Baker," NBC, 1970; "The Barbara McNair Show," SYN, 1970; "The Mike Douglas Show," SYN, 1971; "The Dean Martin Show," NBC, 1971; "The Tonight Show Starring Johnny Carson," NBC, 1973; "The Tonight Show Starring Johnny Carson," NBC, 1974; "Chico and the Man: Too Many Crooks," NBC, 1976; "Break the Bank," SYN, 1976; "Dinah!," SYN, 1978; "Dinah!," SYN, 1979; "Hardcastle and McCormick: What's So Funny?," ABC, 1985; "Murder, She Wrote: Murder at the Oasis," CBS, 1985.

BISHOP, JULIE

b. Jacqueline Brown, Denver, CO, August 30, 1914. Former child actress who played Bob Cummings' girlfriend on his first sitcom.

AS A REGULAR: "My Hero," NBC, 1952-53.

AS A GUEST: "Fireside Theatre: Juror on Trial," NBC, 1954; "The Bob Cummings Show: The Sergeant Wore Skirts," CBS, 1956; "Warner Bros. Presents Conflict: Survival," ABC, 1956.

BISHOP, WILLIAM

b. Oak Park, IL, July 16, 1917; d. 1959. Pleasant, forgettable leading man of the fifties.

AS A REGULAR: "It's a Great Life," NBC, 1954-55.

AND: "Schlitz Playhouse of Stars: Drawing Room ABC," CBS, 1952; "Easy Chair Theatre: Brown of Calaveras," SYN, 1953; "Firside Theatre: Unexpected Wife," NBC, 1953; "Fireside Theatre: Mission to Algeria," NBC, 1953; "Cavalcade of America: Pirate's Choice," ABC, 1953; "Fireside Theatre: Bless the Man," NBC, 1953; "Ford Theatre: Mantrap," NBC, 1954;

"Schlitz Playhouse of Stars: Night Ride to Butte," CBS, 1954; "Pepsi Cola Playhouse: And the Beasts Were There," ABC, 1954; "Cavalcade Theatre: Spindletop," ABC, 1954; "Pepsi Cola Playhouse: Grenadine," ABC, 1954; "I Married Joan: Double Wedding," NBC, 1954; "Hallmark Hall of Fame: Ethan Allen," NBC, 1955; "Science Fiction Theatre: Hour of Nightmare," SYN, 1955; "Playhouse 90: The Star Wagon," CBS, 1957; "The 20th Century-Fox Hour: The Marriage Broker," CBS, 1957; "Ford Theatre: Desperation," ABC, 1957; "Schlitz Playhouse of Stars: The Dead Are Silent," CBS, 1957; "The Millionaire: Millionaire Pete Hopper," CBS, 1958; "The Gale Storm Show: A Lass in Alaska," CBS, 1958.

BISOGLIO, VAL
b. New York City, NY, May 7, 1926. Burly actor who usually plays good-hearted types; he was bar owner Danny Tovo on "Quincy."
AS A REGULAR: "Roll Out," CBS, 1973-74; "Police Woman," NBC, 1974-76; "Quincy," NBC, 1976-83; "Working Stiffs," CBS, 1979.
AS A GUEST: "The Mary Tyler Moore Show: Room 223," CBS, 1971; "All in the Family: Archie Sees a Mugging," CBS, 1972; "All in the Family: Archie and the Editorial," CBS, 1972; "Ironside: Downhill All the Way," NBC, 1973; "Kojak: The Chinatown Murders," CBS, 1974; "Barney Miller: The Life and Times of Barney Miller," ABC, 1974; "Ironside: The Rolling Y," NBC, 1974; "Barney Miller: You Dirty Rat," ABC, 1975; "Get Christie Love!: Uncle Harry," ABC, 1975; "McMillan and Wife: Aftershock," NBC, 1975; "Police Woman: Ice," NBC, 1975; "McCloud: The Night New York Turned Blue," NBC, 1976; "The Rockford Files: Sticks and Stones May Break Your Bones, But Waterbury Will Bury You," NBC, 1977; "B.J. and the Bear: Wheels of Fortune," NBC, 1979; "B.J. and the Bear: The Friendly Double Cross," NBC, 1980; "M*A*S*H: The Life You Save," CBS, 1981; "M*A*S*H: 'Twas the Day After Christmas," CBS, 1981; "M*A*S*H: A Holy Mess," CBS, 1982; "Miami Vice: Forgive Us Our Debts," NBC, 1986.
TV MOVIES AND MINISERIES: "The Marcus-Nelson Murders," CBS, 1973; "Matt Helm," ABC, 1975; "Flying High," CBS, 1978.

BISSELL, WHIT
b. Whitner Bissell, New York City, NY, October 25, 1909; d. 1981. Familiar character actor who usually plays doctors or other figures of authority.
AS A REGULAR: "The Time Tunnel," ABC, 1966-67.
AND: "Science Fiction Theatre: The Green Bomb," SYN, 1956; "The Jane Wyman Show: Two Sides to Everything," NBC, 1956; "Schlitz Playhouse of Stars: The Night They Won the Oscar," CBS, 1956; "Science Fiction Theatre: Dr. Robot," SYN, 1956; "Playhouse 90: The Comedian," CBS, 1957; "Have Gun, Will Travel: No Visitors," CBS, 1957; "Have Gun, Will Travel: The Silver Queen," CBS, 1958; "Suspicion: Fraction of a Second," NBC, 1958; "Goodyear Theatre: The White Flag," NBC, 1958; "No Warning!: Parole," NBC, 1958; "Peter Gunn: The Frog," NBC, 1958; "The Californians: Pipeline," NBC, 1959; "The Lineup: The Strange Return of Army Armitage," CBS, 1959; "Men Into Space: Christmas on the Moon," CBS, 1959; "Tightrope!: Night of the Gun," CBS, 1960; "Hawaiian Eye: Hong Kong Passage," ABC, 1960; "Wagon Train: The Jane Hawkins Story," NBC, 1960; "Maverick: Kiz," ABC, 1960; "The Tom Ewell Show: Advice to the Lovelorn," CBS, 1961; "Happy: All in a Day's Work," NBC, 1961; "Stagecoach West: Not in Our Stars," ABC, 1961; "Guestward Ho!: Bill the Candidate," ABC, 1961; "The Law and Mr. Jones: A Fool for a Client," ABC, 1961; "Lawman: The Threat," ABC, 1961; "The Deputy: Enemy of the Town," NBC, 1961; "Stagecoach West: Blind Man's Buff," ABC, 1961; "The Bob Cummings Show: Very Warm for Mayan," CBS, 1961; "Hawaiian Eye: Total Eclipse," ABC, 1962; "Alfred Hitchcock Presents: Burglar Proof," NBC, 1962; "Have Gun, Will Travel: The Burning Tree," CBS, 1963; "The Virginian: The Final Hour," NBC, 1963; "The Donna Reed Show: Whatever You Wish," ABC, 1963; "The Outer Limits: Nightmare," ABC, 1963; "The Great Adventure: The Colonel From Connecticut," CBS, 1964; "The Virginian: The Long Quest," NBC, 1964; "Wagon Train: The John Gillman Story," ABC, 1964; "Slattery's People: Question-What Did You Do All Day, Mr. Slattery?," CBS, 1965; "The Man From UNCLE: The Bat Cave Affair," NBC, 1966; "Camp Runamuck: Senior Citizens," NBC, 1966; "The FBI: The Spy-Master," ABC, 1966; "Hogan's Heroes: The Rise and Fall of Sergeant Schultz," CBS, 1966; "I Dream of Jeannie: Fastest Gun in the East," NBC, 1966; "Please Don't Eat the Daisies: The Silent Butler Spoke," NBC, 1967; "Gomer Pyle, USMC: To Watch a Thief," CBS, 1967; "The Man From UNCLE: The 'J' for Judas Affair," NBC, 1967; "Here's Lucy: Lucy Goes on Strike," CBS, 1969; "Mannix: The Solid Gold Web," CBS, 1969; "Marcus Welby, M.D.: The Other Side of the Chart," ABC, 1970; "Hollywood Television Theatre: The Andersonville Trial," NET, 1970; "Marcus Welby, M.D.: The Working Heart," ABC, 1973; "Barnaby Jones: Murder in the Doll's House, " CBS, 1973; "Ironside: The Taste of Ashes," NBC, 1974; "McCloud: The Barefoot Girls," NBC, 1974; "Kojak: Deadly Innocence," CBS, 1976.
TV MOVIES AND MINISERIES: "In Broad Daylight,"

ABC, 1971; "Cry Rape!," CBS, 1973; "Flood," NBC, 1976; "The Time Machine," NBC, 1978; "Ike," ABC, 1979; "Strangers: The Story of a Mother and Daughter," CBS, 1979.

BIXBY, BILL
b. Wilfred Bailey Bixby, San Francisco, CA, January 22, 1934. Popular TV leading man whose material has been highly variable, from the thoughtful "Courtship of Eddie's Father" to the frantic "My Favorite Martian" to the weak "Goodnight Beantown." Recognizable to today's generation as the guy who gets mad just before a green Lou Ferrigno shows up and starts ramming into walls.

AS A REGULAR: "The Joey Bishop Show," NBC, 1962; "My Favorite Martian," CBS, 1963-66; "The Courtship of Eddie's Father," ABC, 1969-72; "The Magician," NBC, 1973-74; "The New Masquerade Party," SYN, 1974-75; "The Incredible Hulk," CBS, 1978-82; "The Book of Lists," CBS, 1982; "Goodnight Beantown," CBS, 1983-84.

AS A GUEST: "Hennesey: Welcome Home, Dr. Blair," CBS, 1961; "Straightaway: The Tin Caesar," ABC, 1961; "The Many Loves of Dobie Gillis: The Gigolo," CBS, 1961; "The Danny Thomas Show: Danny Weaves a Web," CBS, 1961; "The Danny Thomas Show: Danny and Durante," CBS, 1961; "Ben Casey: A Few Brief Lines for Dave," ABC, 1961; "Bachelor Father: The Law and Kelly Gregg," ABC, 1961; "Checkmate: To the Best of My Knowledge," CBS, 1961; "The Joey Bishop Show: Home Sweet Home," NBC, 1962; "The Andy Griffith Show: Bailey's Bad Boy," CBS, 1962; "The Joey Bishop Show: A Man's Best Friend," NBC, 1962; "Alcoa Premiere: The Voice of Charlie Pont," ABC, 1962; "Dr. Kildare: The Soul Killer," NBC, 1962; "The Eleventh Hour: Try to Keep Alive Until Next Tuesday," NBC, 1963; "The Danny Thomas Show: Jose's Rival," CBS, 1963; "The Lieutenant: A Million Miles From Clary," NBC, 1963; "The Twilight Zone: The Thirty-Fathom Grave," CBS, 1963; "Password," CBS, 1965; "You Don't Say," NBC, 1965; "Combat!: The Losers," ABC, 1966; "The Iron Horse: Appointment with an Epitaph," ABC, 1967; "That Girl: The Honeymoon Apartment," ABC, 1967; "The Danny Thomas Hour: Two for Penny," NBC, 1968; "Ironside: Tom Dayton Is Loose Among Us," NBC, 1970; "Love, American Style: Love and the Eskimo," ABC, 1970; "Hollywood Television Theatre: Big Fish, Little Fish," NET, 1971; "Love, American Style: Love and the Rug," ABC, 1971; "Night Gallery: Last Rites for a Dead Druid," NBC, 1972; "Hollywood Squares," NBC, 1972; "Night Gallery: The Return of the Sorcerer," NBC, 1972; "Love, American Style:

Love and the Overnight Guests," ABC, 1972; "Of Men and Women: Why He Was Late to Work," ABC, 1972; "Medical Center: Pressure Point," CBS, 1972; "Barnaby Jones: To Denise, with Love & Murder," CBS, 1974; "Hollywood Television Theatre: Steambath," PBS, 1974; "Short Stories of Love: Epicac," NBC, 1974; "Ironside: Raise the Devil," NBC, 1974; "The Streets of San Francisco: Target: Red," ABC, 1974; "Magic Man," NBC, 1974; "Password," ABC, 1974; "Password All-Stars," ABC, 1975; "Mitzi and a Hundred Guys," CBS, 1975; "The Streets of San Francisco: Police Buff," ABC, 1976; "The Love Boat: Message for Maureen," ABC, 1977; "J.J. Starbuck: Pilot," NBC, 1987.

TV MOVIES AND MINISERIES: "Congratulations, It's a Boy!," ABC, 1971; "The Couple Takes a Wife," ABC, 1972; "The Magician," NBC, 1973; "Shirts/Skins," ABC, 1973; "Rich Man, Poor Man," ABC, 1976; "Spencer's Pilots," CBS, 1976; "The Great Houdinis," ABC, 1976; "Fantasy Island," ABC, 1977; "Black Market Baby," ABC, 1977; "Murder Is Easy," CBS, 1982; "Sins of Innocence," CBS, 1986; "The Incredible Hulk Returns," NBC, 1988; "The Trial of the Incredible Hulk," NBC, 1989.

AS DIRECTOR: "The Incredible Hulk Returns," NBC, 1988.

* See also Brenda Benet.

BLACK, KAREN
b. Karen Ziegler, Park Ridge, IL, July 1, 1942. Actress whose TV work is divided into two periods: Before and After "Five Easy Pieces" and movie stardom.

AS A REGULAR: "The Second Hundred Years," ABC, 1967-68.

AND: "Run for Your Life: Tell It to the Dead," NBC, 1967; "The Iron Horse: The Prisoners," ABC, 1967; "The Big Valley: Day of Grace," ABC, 1967; "The FBI: The Satellite," ABC, 1967; "The Invaders: The Ransom," ABC, 1968; "Judd for the Defense: The Devil's Surrogate," ABC, 1968; "The Name of the Game: Give Till It Hurts," NBC, 1969; "The Shameful Secrets of Hastings Corners," NBC, 1970; "Rollin' on the River," SYN, 1971; "Ghost Story: Bad Connection," NBC, 1972; "Saturday Night Live," NBC, 1976; "Saturday Night Live," NBC, 1981; "E/R: Enter Romance," CBS, 1985; "E/R: The Many Wives of Sheinfeld," CBS, 1985; "Murder, She Wrote: One Good Bid Deserves a Murder," CBS, 1986; "Miami Vice: Victims of Circumstance," NBC, 1989; "The Pat Sajak Show," CBS, 1989.

TV MOVIES AND MINISERIES: "Trilogy of Terror," NBC, 1975; "The Strange Possession of Mrs. Oliver," NBC, 1977; "Where the Ladies Go," ABC, 1980.

* In "Trilogy of Terror," Black played a woman pursued and attacked by a spear-wielding doll.

Sounds silly, but it's one of the few TV movies vividly recalled by practically everyone who saw it. (The other is "Evil Roy Slade.")

BLACK, SHIRLEY TEMPLE—See Shirley Temple.

BLACKMAN, JOAN
b. 1938. Actress who played Marian Fowler on "Peyton Place."
AS A REGULAR: "Peyton Place," ABC, 1965-66.
AND: "Goodyear Theatre: Disappearance," NBC, 1958; "Slattery's People: Question-Remember the Dark Sins of Youth?," CBS, 1964; "Doc Elliot: Things That Might Have Been," ABC, 1974.

BLACKMER, SIDNEY
b. Salisbury, NC, July 13, 1895; d. 1973. Smooth, experienced actor who tended to play sinister types.
AS A REGULAR: "Ben Casey," ABC, 1966.
AND: "Pulitzer Prize Playhouse: The Pen," ABC, 1951; "Armstrong Circle Theatre: Last Chance," NBC, 1951; "Philco TV Playhouse: Television Story," NBC, 1951; "Suspense: This Is Your Confession," CBS, 1951; "Tales of Tomorrow: The Dark Angel," ABC, 1951; "The Web: Kill with Kindness," CBS, 1952; "U.S. Steel Hour: The Notebook Warrior," ABC, 1954; "Ford Theatre: Shadow of Truth," NBC, 1954; "Damon Runyon Theatre: The Big Fix," CBS, 1955; "Alfred Hitchcock Presents: Don't Come Back Alive," CBS, 1955; "Robert Montgomery Presents: One Bright Day," NBC, 1956; "Hallmark Hall of Fame: The Little Foxes," NBC, 1956; "Climax!: Scream in Silence," CBS, 1958; "The Texan: Edge of the Cliff," CBS, 1958; "Dick Powell's Zane Grey Theatre: The Sharpshooter," CBS, 1958; "The Adventures of Jim Bowie: Horse Thief," ABC, 1958; "Matinee Theatre: The Cause," NBC, 1958; "Westinghouse Desilu Playhouse: The Night the Phone Rang," CBS, 1958; "Walt Disney Presents: Texas John Slaughter—The Slaughter Trail," ABC, 1959; "Sunday Showcase: What Makes Sammy Run?," NBC, 1959; "Best of the Post: Early Americana," SYN, 1960; "Bonanza: The Dream Riders," NBC, 1961; "Thriller: The Premature Burial," NBC, 1961; "Alfred Hitchcock Presents: The Faith of Aaron Menefee," NBC, 1962; "Cain's Hundred: The Manipulator," NBC, 1962; "Target: The Corruptors: The Malignant Hearts," ABC, 1962; "Dr. Kildare: Operation Lazarus," NBC, 1962; "The du Pont Show: Diamond Fever," NBC, 1963; "The Outer Limits: The Hundred Days of the Dragon," ABC, 1963; "The Defenders: The Empty Heart," CBS, 1963; "The Ed Sullivan Show," CBS, 1964; "Look Up and Live: The Promised World," CBS, 1964; "Profiles in Courage: The Oscar W. Underwood Story," NBC, 1964; "The Reporter: A Time to Be

Silent," CBS, 1964; "Bonanza: The Late Ben Cartwright," NBC, 1968; "The Name of the Game: Pineapple Rose," NBC, 1968; "Walt Disney's Wonderful World of Color: The Man From Bitter Creek," NBC, 1969; "The Name of the Game: Chains of Command," NBC, 1969.
TV MOVIES AND MINISERIES: "Do You Take This Stranger?," NBC, 1971.

BLACQUE, TAUREAN
b. Herbert Middleton, Jr., Newark, NJ. Actor who was detective Neal Washington on "Hill Street Blues" and Henry Marshall on "Generations."
AS A REGULAR: "Hill Street Blues," NBC, 1981-87; "Generations," NBC, 1989.
AND: "Sanford & Son: Fred the Activist," NBC, 1977; "The Bob Newhart Show: Ex-Con Job," CBS, 1977; "The Bob Newhart Show: Son of Ex-Con Job," CBS, 1978; "Taxi: Bobby's Acting Career," ABC, 1978; "The White Shadow: Delores, of Course," CBS, 1979; "Paris: Dear John," CBS, 1979; "CBS Summer Playhouse: Off Duty," CBS, 1988.
* Blacque has ten adopted children.

BLAINE, JIMMY
b. 1924; d. 1967. Young actor-singer-kid-show-host of the fifties.
AS A REGULAR: "Stop the Music," ABC, 1949-52; "The Paul Winchell/Jerry Mahoney Show," NBC, 1950; "Hold That Camera," DUM, 1950; "Jimmy Blaine's Junior Edition," ABC, 1951; "Those Two," NBC, 1951-52; "The Billy Daniels Show," ABC, 1952; "Music at the Meadowbrook," ABC, 1953; 1956; "Ruff and Reddy," NBC, 1957-59.
AND: "The Big Payoff," CBS, 1957.

BLAINE, VIVIAN
b. Vivienne Stapleton, Newark, NJ, November 21, 1924. Actress-singer of the fifties.
AS A REGULAR: "Mary Hartman, Mary Hartman," SYN, 1976.
AND: "Philco TV Playhouse: Double Jeopardy," NBC, 1953; "Center Stage: The Heart of a Clown," ABC, 1954; "Damon Runyon Theatre: Pick the Winner," CBS, 1955; "Hallmark Hall of Fame: Dream Girl," NBC, 1955; "The Ed Sullivan Show," CBS, 1956; "Lux Video Theatre: The Undesirable," NBC, 1957; "The Ray Bolger Show," NBC, 1957; "The Ed Sullivan Show," CBS, 1958; "Person to Person," CBS, 1958; "Steve Allen Presents the Steve Lawrence-Eydie Gorme Show," NBC, 1958; "The Perry Como Show," NBC, 1958; "Patti Page Olds Show," ABC, 1958; "Your Hit Parade," CBS, 1959; "The Garry Moore Show," CBS, 1959; "Arthur Murray Party," NBC, 1959; "Route 66: A Bunch of Lonely Pagliaccis," CBS, 1963; "The Love Boat: Man of

the Cloth," ABC, 1978; "Murder, She Wrote: Broadway Malady," CBS, 1985.

TV MOVIES AND MINISERIES: "Katie: Portrait of a Centerfold," NBC, 1978; "The Cracker Factory," ABC, 1979; "Fast Friends," NBC, 1979; "Sooner or Later," NBC, 1979.

BLAIR, BETSY

b. Betsy Boger, New York City, NY, December 11, 1923. Former film and stage actress who now plays the mother of Ellyn (Polly Draper) on "thirtysomething."

AS A GUEST: "Philco TV Playhouse: The Charmed Circle," NBC, 1950; "Goodyear TV Playhouse: A Will to Live," NBC, 1957; "thirtysomething: No Promises," ABC, 1989.

TV MOVIES AND MINISERIES: "Marcus Welby, M.D.: A Family Affair," NBC, 1988.

BLAIR, JANET

b. Martha Jane Lafferty, Altoona, PA, April 23, 1921.

AS A REGULAR: "Leave It to the Girls," NBC, 1949-51; ABC, 1953-54; "Caesar's Hour," NBC, 1956-57; "The Chevy Show," NBC, 1958; 1959; "The Smith Family," ABC, 1971-72.

AND: "Armstrong Circle Theatre: The Beautiful Wife," NBC, 1954; "Elgin TV Hour: Flood," ABC, 1954; "U.S. Steel Hour: King's Pawn," ABC, 1954; "Goodyear TV Playhouse: Doing Her Bit," NBC, 1955; "A Connecticut Yankee," NBC, 1955; "Climax!: The Dance," CBS, 1955; "Front Row Center: Kitty Foyle," CBS, 1955; "One Touch of Venus," NBC, 1955; "The Ed Sullivan Show," CBS, 1958; "Alcoa Theatre: The First Star," NBC, 1958; "This Is Your Life," NBC, 1959; "Chevy Show Special," NBC, 1959; "Dinah Shore Chevy Show," NBC, 1959; "The Strawberry Blonde," NBC, 1959; "Pat Boone Chevy Showroom," ABC, 1959; "The Chevy Show: Around the World with Nellie Bly," NBC, 1960; "The Chevy Show," NBC, 1960; "Pat Boone Chevy Showroom," ABC, 1960; "The Chevy Show: Mexican Fiesta," NBC, 1960; "Chevy Mystery Show: Femme Fatale," NBC, 1960; "Chevy Mystery Show: A Perfect Alibi," NBC, 1960; "The Ed Sullivan Show," CBS, 1961; "Bell Telephone Hour: Weavers of Song," NBC, 1962; "Bell Telephone Hour: The Songs of Irving Berlin," NBC, 1962; "Stump the Stars," CBS, 1962; "The Ed Sullivan Show," CBS, 1963; "Girl Talk," SYN, 1963; "The Outer Limits: Tourist Attraction," ABC, 1963; "Burke's Law: Who Killed Purity Mather?," ABC, 1963; "Bob Hope Chrysler Theatre: Wake Up, Darling," NBC, 1964; "Burke's Law: Who Killed Merlin the Great?," ABC, 1964; "Ben Casey: Then, Suddenly, Panic," ABC, 1966; "Marcus Welby, M.D.: The Legacy," ABC, 1970; "Marcus Welby, M.D.: The Tortoise Dance," ABC, 1973.

BLAIR, JUNE

b. Margaret June Blair, San Francisco, CA, October 30. 1936. Actress who married Dave Nelson in real life, thereby becoming a part of the Nelson TV family.

AS A REGULAR: "Two Faces West," SYN, 1960; "The Adventures of Ozzie and Harriet," ABC, 1960-66.

AS A GUEST: "M Squad: The Bad Apple," NBC, 1959; "Hawaiian Eye: Three Tickets to Lani," ABC, 1959; "The Texan: Town Divided," CBS, 1960; "Bat Masterson: Death by Decree," NBC, 1960; "The Aquanauts: The Defective Tank Adventure," CBS, 1961; "Here's Hollywood," NBC, 1961.

* It's somewhat ironic that Blair became a part of one of television's best-known families—she was abandoned by her father at eight months of age and by her mother at three years of age. She lived with eight foster families as she grew up.

* See also "The Adventures of Ozzie and Harriet."

BLAIR, LINDA

b. Westport, CT, 1959. Actress who grossed out American moviegoers in "The Exorcist" and then grossed out TV viewers by getting raped with a plunger handle in the girls-in-prison TV movie "Born Innocent."

AS A REGULAR: "Hidden Faces," NBC, 1968-69.

AND: "Fantasy Island: Shadow Games," ABC, 1982; "Murder, She Wrote: Murder Takes the Bus," CBS, 1985.

TV MOVIES AND MINISERIES: "Born Innocent," NBC, 1974; "Sarah T.: Portrait of a Teenage Alcholic," NBC, 1975; "Sweet Hostage," ABC, 1975; "Victory at Entebbe," ABC, 1976; "Stranger in Our House," NBC, 1978.

BLAIR, PATRICIA

b. Fort Worth, TX, 1938. Actress who played Rebecca, wife of Daniel Boone (Fess Parker).

AS A REGULAR: "The Rifleman," ABC, 1962-63; "Daniel Boone," NBC, 1964-70.

AND: "The Dennis O'Keefe Show: What's in a Name?," CBS, 1960; "The Loretta Young Show: Unconditional Surrender," NBC, 1960; "The Law and Mr. Jones: The Storyville Gang," ABC, 1960; "The Case of the Dangerous Robin: Serum," SYN, 1961; "Comedy Spot: You're Only Young Once," CBS, 1962; "The Joey Bishop Show: The Image," NBC, 1962; "The Virginian: The Evil That Men Do," NBC, 1963; "Bonanza: The Lila Conrad Story," NBC, 1964; "Temple Houston: Thy Name Is Woman," NBC, 1964.

BLAKE, AMANDA

b. Beverly Louise Neill, Buffalo, NY, February 20, 1929; d. 1989. Redheaded actress who was

Miss Kitty Russell of the Long Branch Saloon, Dodge City, Kansas.

AS A REGULAR: "Gunsmoke," CBS, 1955-74; "The Edge of Night," ABC, 1984.

AND: "Schlitz Playhouse of Stars: Double Exposure," CBS, 1952; "Fireside Theatre: Nine Quarts of Water," NBC, 1954; "Four Star Playhouse: Vote of Confidence," CBS, 1954; "Matinee Theatre: Sound of Fear," NBC, 1956; "The Red Skelton Show," CBS, 1957; "The Red Skelton Show," CBS, 1958; "Art Linkletter's House Party," CBS, 1958; "G.E. Theatre: Night Club," CBS, 1959; "The Red Skelton Show: San Fernando's Treasure Hunt," CBS, 1959; "The Red Skelton Show: San Fernando for Governor," CBS, 1960; "Here's Hollywood," NBC, 1960; "The Red Skelton Show: San Fernando and Herbie," CBS, 1961; "The Red Skelton Show: San Fernando and the Kaaka Maami Island," CBS, 1961; "Stump the Stars," CBS, 1963; "Art Linkletter's House Party," CBS, 1964; "Password," CBS, 1965; "Password," CBS, 1967; "Hee Haw," CBS, 1970; "Hee Haw," SYN, 1972; "Tattletales," CBS, 1974; "The Quest: Day of Outrage," NBC, 1976; "The Love Boat: Oldies But Goodies," ABC, 1979.

TV MOVIES AND MINISERIES: "Betrayal," ABC, 1974; "Gunsmoke: Return to Dodge," CBS, 1987.

BLAKE, MADGE

b. 1900; d. 1969. Actress usually in dotty roles who didn't begin her career until age 46; she played Flora MacMichael on "The Real McCoys," Aunt Harriet on "Batman" and the mother of apple-eating Larry Mondello (Rusty Stevens) on "Leave It to Beaver."

AS A REGULAR: "The Real McCoys," ABC, 1957-62; CBS, 1962-63; "The Joey Bishop Show," NBC, 1961-62; "Batman," ABC, 1966-68.

AND: "I Love Lucy: Ricky Loses His Temper," CBS, 1954; "Schlitz Playhouse of Stars: False Alarm," CBS, 1956; "Du Pont Theatre: Date with a Stranger," ABC, 1956; "I Love Lucy: Lucy and Superman," CBS, 1957; "December Bride: The Homecoming," CBS, 1957; "Lassie: The Artist," CBS, 1957; "The Adventures of Ozzie and Harriet: The Trophy," ABC, 1958; "Leave It to Beaver: Beaver's Guest," ABC, 1958; "Leave It to Beaver: June's Birthday," ABC, 1960; "Guestward Ho: No Vacancy," ABC, 1961; "Angel: Call Me Mother," CBS, 1961; "The Danny Thomas Show: Everything Happens to Me," CBS, 1961; "Holiday Lodge: The Kissing Bug," CBS, 1961; "Room for One More: Girl From Sweden," ABC, 1962; "The Jack Benny Program," CBS, 1962; "The Dick Van Dyke Show: Very Old Shoes, Very Old Rice," CBS, 1963; "My Favorite Martian: Raffles No. 2," CBS, 1963; "Channing: Where Are the Snows ...?," ABC, 1964; "Harris Against the World:

Pilot," NBC, 1964; "Bewitched: The Witches Are Out," ABC, 1964; "The Lucy Show: Lucy the Camp Cook," CBS, 1964; "The Addams Family: The Addams Family Goes to School," ABC, 1964; "The Dick Van Dyke Show: Brother, Can You Spare $2,500?," CBS, 1965; "My Favorite Martian: Once Upon a Martian Mother's Day," CBS, 1965; "The Dick Van Dyke Show: Uhny Uftz," CBS, 1965; "The Smothers Brothers Show: A Boarding House Is Not a Home," CBS, 1965; "Gomer Pyle, USMC: Gomer, the Good Samaritan," CBS, 1967.

BLAKE, ROBERT

b. Michael J. Vijencio Gubitosi, Nutley, NJ, Sept, 18, 1933. Diminutive, macho actor who was, undoubtedly, the baddest man ever on "Hollywood Squares"; an Emmy-winner as tough cop Tony Baretta.

AS A REGULAR: "The Richard Boone Show," NBC, 1963-64; "Baretta," ABC, 1975-78; "Hell Town," NBC, 1985.

AND: "Favorite Story: Born Unto Trouble," SYN, 1953; "Fireside Theatre: Night in the Warehouse," NBC, 1953; "Court of Last Resort: The Case of Tomas Mendoza," NBC, 1957; "The Rebel: He's Only a Boy," ABC, 1960; "Alcoa Presents One Step Beyond: Gypsy," ABC, 1960; "Have Gun, Will Travel: The Fatalist," CBS, 1960; "Have Gun, Will Travel: The Shooting of Jessie May," CBS, 1960; "Bat Masterson: No Amnesty for Death," NBC, 1961; "Wagon Train: The Joe Muharich Story," NBC, 1961; "Naked City: New York to L.A.," ABC, 1961; "Laramie: Wolf Cub," NBC, 1961; "Ben Casey: Imagine a Long, Bright Corridor," ABC, 1962; "Straightaway: A Moment in the Sun," ABC, 1962; "The New Breed: My Brother's Keeper," ABC, 1962; "Have Gun, Will Travel: A Place for Abel Hix," CBS, 1962; "Slattery's People: Does Nero Still at Ringside Sit?," CBS, 1965; "Rawhide: The Winter Soldier," CBS, 1965; "The FBI: A Mouthful of Dust," ABC, 1965; "Trials of O'Brien: Bargain Day on the Street of Regret," CBS, 1965; "The FBI: The Price of Death," ABC, 1966; "Twelve O'Clock High: A Distant Cry," ABC, 1966; "Death Valley Days: The Kid from Hell's Kitchen," SYN, 1972; "Tattletales," CBS, 1974; "Hollywood Squares," NBC, 1975; "Saturday Night Live," NBC, 1982.

TV MOVIES AND MINISERIES: "The Monkey Mission," NBC, 1981; "Of Mice and Men," NBC, 1985; "Hell Town," NBC, 1985; "Heart of a Champion: The Ray Mancini Story," CBS, 1985.

* Emmies: 1975.

BLAKE, WHITNEY

b. McMinnville, OR. Attractive blonde actress who played Dorothy Baxter, mistress over the not-easily-dominated maid for all seasons Hazel Burke (Shirley Booth).

AS A REGULAR: "Hazel," NBC, 1961-65; "The David Frost Revue," SYN, 1971-73.

AND: "Du Pont Theatre: The Man Who Asked No Favors," ABC, 1957; "Cheyenne: Hired Gun," ABC, 1957; "Wire Service: The Indictment," ABC, 1957; "O. Henry Playhouse: A Trick of Nature," SYN, 1957; "Perry Mason: The Case of the Careless Redhead," CBS, 1957; "Dick Powell's Zane Grey Theatre: The Promise," CBS, 1957; "The Millionaire: The Pete Marlow Story," CBS, 1957; "M Squad: The Frightened Wife," NBC, 1958; "Maverick: The Burning Sky," ABC, 1958; "Alcoa Theatre: Coast to Coast," NBC, 1958; "Pursuit: Last Night of August," CBS, 1958; "Ellery Queen: The Hollow Man," NBC, 1958; "The Lineup: The Charles Cleveland Case," CBS, 1959; "Bachelor Father: Bentley and the Bartered Bride," NBC, 1959; "Westinghouse Desilu Playhouse: Two Counts of Murder," CBS, 1959; "77 Sunset Strip: The One That Got Away," ABC, 1960; "Cheyenne: Riot at Arroyo Soco," ABC, 1960; "Riverboat: The Blowup," NBC, 1960; "Perry Mason: The Case of the Black-Eyed Blonde," CBS, 1960; "M Squad: The Velvet Stakeout," NBC, 1960; "The Millionaire: Millionaire Nancy Cortez," CBS, 1960; "Rawhide: Incident of the Murder Steer," CBS, 1960; "The Overland Trail: High Bridge," NBC, 1960; "Michael Shayne: Dolls Are Deadly," NBC, 1960; "Pony Express: Landgrab," SYN, 1960; "Cheyenne: The Mustangers," ABC, 1960; "Adventures in Paradise: The Krishmen," ABC, 1960; "Pete and Gladys: Pete's Personality Change," CBS, 1960; "Thriller: The Fatal Impulse," NBC, 1960; "Route 66: Sheba," CBS, 1961; "The Aquanauts: Niagara Drive," CBS, 1961; "Cheyenne: Yankee Tornado," ABC, 1961; "The Man From UNCLE: The Take Me To Your Leader Affair," NBC, 1966; "Batman: Catwoman Goes to College/Batman Displays His Knowledge," ABC, 1967; "The Virginian: Bitter Harvest," NBC, 1967.

TV MOVIES AND MINISERIES: "The Stranger Who Looks Like Me," ABC, 1974; "Strange Homecoming," NBC, 1974; "Returning Home," ABC, 1975.

* Blake played the first defendant on "Perry Mason."
* Blake and her husband, producer-writer Alan Manings, created "One Day at a Time."

BLAKELY, SUSAN

b. Frankfurt, Germany, September 7, 1948. Model-turned-actress who scored as Julie Prescott Abbott Jordache in "Rich Man, Poor Man"; since then she's proven herself an actress of substance.

AS A REGULAR: "Falcon Crest," CBS, 1990.

AND: "Rich Man, Poor Man, Book 2: Pilot," ABC,

1976; "The Love Boat: The Accident," ABC, 1985; "The Twilight Zone: The Card," CBS, 1986; "Private Eye: Nicky the Rose," NBC, 1987; "Wonderworks: Hiroshima Maiden," PBS, 1988; "In the Heat of the Night: Family Secrets," NBC, 1988; "ABC Afterschool Special: Torn Between Two Fathers," ABC, 1989.

TV MOVIES AND MINISERIES: "Rich Man, Poor Man," ABC, 1976; "Secrets," ABC, 1977; "Make Me an Offer," ABC, 1980; "The Bunker," CBS, 1981; "Will There Really Be a Morning?," CBS, 1983; "Blood and Orchids," CBS, 1986; "The Ted Kennedy Jr. Story," NBC, 1986; "The Annihilator," NBC, 1986; "Broken Angel," ABC, 1988; "Hallmark Hall of Fame: April Morning," CBS, 1988; "Ladykillers," ABC, 1988; "Fatal Confession: A Father Dowling Mystery," NBC, 1988; "AT&T Presents: The Incident," CBS, 1990.

BLANC, MEL

b. Melvin Jerome Blanc, San Francisco, May 30, 1908; d. 1989. Versatile comic actor and man of a thousand voices; he was Mr. Fingue on the radio and TV versions of "The Jack Benny Program" and he provided the coughing noises that Benny's Maxwell would make; best known, of course, as Barney Rubble and Bugs Bunny.

AS A REGULAR: "The Jack Benny Program," CBS, 1950-64; NBC, 1964-65; "The Bugs Bunny Show," ABC, 1960-62; "The Flintstones," ABC, 1960-66; "The Jetsons," ABC, 1962-63; "Where's Huddles?," CBS, 1970; "The Bugs Bunny/Roadrunner Show," CBS, 1976; "Buck Rogers in the 25th Century," NBC, 1979-81.

AND: "The Unchained Goddess," NBC, 1958; "Shower of Stars: Jack Benny's 40th Birthday Celebration," CBS, 1958; "The Garry Moore Show," CBS, 1958; "Angel: The Argument," CBS, 1960; "Here's Hollywood," NBC, 1961; "The Beverly Hillbillies: Granny Learns to Drive," CBS, 1964; "The Mothers-in-Law: The Birth of Everything But the Blues," NBC, 1968; "Too Close for Comfort: A Thanksgiving Tale," ABC, 1982.

BLANCHARD, MARI

b. Mary Blanchard, Long Beach, CA, April 13, 1927; d. 1970. Fifties bombshell.

AS A REGULAR: "Terry and the Pirates," NBC, 1957; "Klondike," NBC, 1960-61.

AND: "Warner Bros. Presents Conflict: Siren Song," ABC, 1956; "The Millionaire: The Laura Hunter Story," CBS, 1958; "Rawhide: Incident of the Stalking Death," CBS, 1959; "Sugarfoot: Apollo with a Gun," ABC, 1959; "Not for Hire: The Binge," SYN, 1959; "Laramie: Rope of Steel," NBC, 1960; "Mr. Lucky: I Bet Your Life," CBS, 1960; "Bronco: Montana Passage," ABC,

1960; "77 Sunset Strip: The Positive Negative," ABC, 1961; "Rawhide: Incident of the Big Blowout," CBS, 1961; "The Roaring Twenties: The Vamp," ABC, 1961; "Gunslinger: Road of the Dead," CBS, 1961; "77 Sunset Strip: The Cold Cash Caper," ABC, 1961; "Robert Taylor's Detectives: Night on the Town," NBC, 1962; "Perry Mason: The Case of the Melancholy Marksman," CBS, 1962; "The Breaking Point: So Many Pretty Girls, So Little Time," ABC, 1964; "The Virginian: Doctor Pat," NBC, 1967.

BLANE, SALLY

b. *Elizabeth Jane Young, Salida, CO, July 11, 1910.* Sister of Loretta Young; she made a few movies in the thirties and did a little TV in the fifties.

AS A GUEST: "Pepsi Cola Playhouse: Grenadine," ABC, 1954; "Star Stage: On Trial," NBC, 1955; "Schlitz Playhouse of Stars: On a Dark Night," CBS, 1955; "The Loretta Young Show: Oh, My Aching Heart," NBC, 1956.

BLEDSOE, TEMPESTT

b. *Chicago, IL, August 1, 1973.* Actress who plays Vanessa on "The Cosby Show."

AS A REGULAR: "The Cosby Show," NBC, 1984- .
AND: "A Different World: Risky Business," NBC, 1989; "Friday Night Videos," NBC, 1989.
TV MOVIES AND MINISERIES: "Dance 'Til Dawn," NBC, 1988; "Dream Date," NBC, 1989.

BLESSING, JACK

b. *Baltimore, MD.* Slight blond actor who played detective MacGillicuddy on "Moonlighting."

AS A REGULAR: "Small & Frye," CBS, 1983; "Moonlighting," ABC, 1987-89.
AND: "Quincy: Slow Boat to Madness," NBC, 1981; "Remington Steele: Steele Away with Me," NBC, 1983; "Mr. President: Uncle Sam," FOX, 1987; "Day by Day: Out for a Stretch," NBC, 1988; "Amen: Get 'Em Up, Scout," NBC, 1988; "Living Dolls: The Not-So-Sweet Smell of Success," ABC, 1989.
TV MOVIES AND MINISERIES: "Women at West Point," CBS, 1979; "Miracle on Ice," ABC. 1981; "Tonight's the Night," ABC, 1987; "LBJ: The Early Years," NBC, 1987; "Strange Voices," NBC, 1987; "Mothers, Daughters and Lovers," NBC, 1989.

BLEYER, ARCHIE

b. *Corona, NY, June 12, 1909.* Bandleader with Arthur Godfrey who ran his own record label; Godfrey dumped him when he threatened to get too successful.

AS A REGULAR: "Arthur Godfrey's Talent Scouts," CBS, 1948-54; "Arthur Godfrey and His Friends," CBS, 1949-54.

BLOCKER, DAN

b. *Texas, December 10, 1932; d. 1972.* Actor who began his career as a heavy before becoming best known and loved as gentle giant Hoss Cartwright on "Bonanza."

AS A REGULAR: "Cimarron City," NBC, 1958-59; "Bonanza," NBC, 1959-72.
AND: "Cheyenne: Land Beyond the Law," ABC, 1957; "Restless Gun: Jody," NBC, 1957; "Restless Gun: The Child," NBC, 1957; "The Thin Man: The Departed Doctor," NBC, 1958; "Sgt. Preston of the Yukon: Underground Ambush," CBS, 1958; "Restless Gun: The Way Back," NBC, 1958; "Restless Gun: Mercyday," NBC, 1958; "Maverick: The Jail at Junction Flats," ABC, 1958; "The Rifleman: The Sister," ABC, 1958; "Wagon Train: The Duta Grey Story," NBC, 1958; "Have Gun, Will Travel: Gun Shy," CBS, 1958; "Westinghouse Desilu Playhouse: Chez Rouge," CBS, 1959; "Here's Hollywood," NBC, 1960; "Perry Como's Kraft Music Hall," NBC, 1962; "Henry Fonda and the Family," CBS, 1962; "The Andy Williams Show," NBC, 1963; "Exploring," NBC, 1963.
TV MOVIES AND MINISERIES: "Something for a Lonely Man," NBC, 1968.

BLOCKER, DIRK

b. *Los Angeles, CA, July 31, 1957.* Husky actor; son of Dan Blocker.

AS A REGULAR: "Baa Baa Black Sheep (Black Sheep Squadron)," NBC, 1976-78; "Ryan's Four," ABC, 1983.
AND: "Little House on the Prairie: School Mom," NBC, 1974; "Marcus Welby, M.D.: Out of Control," ABC, 1974; "Lucas Tanner: Winners and Losers," NBC, 1974; "M*A*S*H: Identity Crisis," CBS, 1981; "Simon & Simon: Opposite Attack," CBS, 1987; "Hunter: The Jade Woman," NBC, 1987; "MacGyver: Blood Brothers," ABC, 1988; "Hunter: Dead on Target," NBC, 1988.
TV MOVIES AND MINISERIES: "Bridger," ABC, 1976; "Desperado," NBC, 1987; "My Father, My Son," CBS, 1988.

BLONDELL, JOAN

b. *New York City, NY, August 30, 1909; d. 1979.* Movie veteran who worked just as hard in television.

AS A REGULAR: "The Real McCoys," CBS, 1963; "Here Come the Brides," ABC, 1968-70; "Banyon," NBC, 1972-73.
AND: "Nash Airflyte Theatre: Pot of Gold," CBS, 1951; "Tales of Tomrrow: Little Black Bag," ABC, 1952; "Schlitz Playhouse of Stars: The Pussyfootin' Rocks," CBS, 1952; "Shower of Stars: Burlesque," CBS, 1955; "G.E. Theatre: Star in the House," CBS, 1955; "U.S. Steel Hour: White Gloves," CBS, 1955; "Playhouse 90: Child of Trouble," CBS, 1957; "The Ed Sullivan

Show," CBS, 1958; "Studio One: The Funny-Looking Kid," CBS, 1958; "Person to Person," CBS, 1959; "Playhouse 90: A Marriage of Strangers," CBS, 1959; "About Faces," ABC, 1960; "Adventures in Paradise: Forbidden Sea," ABC, 1960; "Witness: Ma Barker," CBS, 1961; "Burke's Law: Who Killed Harris Crown?," ABC, 1963; "Wagon Train: The Bleecker Story," ABC, 1963; "The Twilight Zone: What's in the Box?," CBS, 1964; "The Greatest Show on Earth: You're All Right, Ivy," ABC, 1964; "Burke's Law: Who Killed Half of Glory Lee?," ABC, 1964; "Bonanza: The Pressure Game," NBC, 1964; "Dr. Kildare: Dolly's Dilemma," NBC, 1964; "Walt Disney's Wonderful World of Color: Kilroy," NBC, 1965; "The Lucy Show: Lucy the Stunt Man," CBS, 1965; "The Girl from UNCLE: The UFO Affair," NBC, 1967; "Family Affair: Somebody Upstairs," CBS, 1967; "The Guns of Will Sonnett: A Sunday in Paradise," ABC, 1967; "Petticoat Junction: Girl of Our Dreams," CBS, 1968; "The Outsider: There Was a Little Girl," NBC, 1968; "The Dating Game," ABC, 1968; "The Name of the Game: Battle at Gannon's Bridge," NBC, 1970; "McCloud: The New Mexican Connection," NBC, 1971; "Love, American Style: Love and the Lovesick Sailor," ABC, 1971; "The Rookies: Cry Wolf," ABC, 1973; "Three for the Girls: Sonny Boy," CBS, 1973; "Medical Center: Stranger in Two Worlds," CBS, 1973; "The New Dick Van Dyke Show: Fun Funeral," CBS, 1973; "The Snoop Sisters: The Devil Made Me Do It," NBC, 1974; "Police Story: Little Boy Lost," NBC, 1975; "Switch: One of Our Zeppelins Is Missing," CBS, 1976; "Starsky and Hutch: The Las Vegas Strangler," ABC, 1976; "The Love Boat: Ship of Ghouls," ABC, 1978; "$weepstake$: Dewey and Harold and Sarah and Maggie," NBC, 1979.
TV MOVIES AND MINISERIES: "Winchester '73," NBC, 1967; "The Dead Don't Die," NBC, 1975; "Winner Take All," NBC, 1975; "Death at Love House," ABC, 1976; "Battered," NBC, 1978; "The Rebels," SYN, 1979.

BLOOM, CLAIRE
b. London, England, February 15, 1931. Delicately beautiful actress of film and TV.
AS A GUEST: "Producers Showcase: Cyrano de Bergerac," NBC, 1955; "Producers Showcase: Caesar and Cleopatra," NBC, 1956; "Producers Showcase: Romeo and Juliet," NBC, 1957; "Goodyear TV Playhouse: First Love," NBC, 1957; "Robert Montgomery Presents: Victoria Regina," NBC, 1957; "Shirley Temple's Storybook: Beauty and the Beast," NBC, 1958; "Person to Person," CBS, 1959; "Playhouse 90: Misalliance," CBS, 1959; "Checkmate: Through a Dark Glass," CBS, 1961; "Jo Stafford Special," SYN, 1964; "BBC Drama: Anna Karenina," NET, 1964; "Festival of the Arts: Wuthering Heights," NET, 1965; "Bob Hope Chrysler Theatre: A Time to Love," NBC, 1967; "Hallmark Hall of Fame: Soldier in Love," NBC, 1967; "Ivanov," CBS, 1967; "The Dick Cavett Show," ABC, 1968; "The Growing Up of David Lev," NBC, 1973; "Orson Welles' Great Mysteries: Ice Storm," SYN, 1974.
TV MOVIES AND MINISERIES: "Backstairs at the White House," NBC, 1979; "Florence Nightingale," NBC, 1985; "Promises to Keep," CBS, 1985; "Shadowlands," PBS, 1986; "Queenie," ABC, 1987; "Beryl Markham: A Shadow on the Sun," CBS, 1988.

BLOOM, LINDSAY
b. Omaha, NB, 1952. Former Ding-a-Ling Sister on "The Dean Martin Show" who played Velda, the stacked secretary of the macho Mr. Mike Hammer (Stacy Keach), private eye.
AS A REGULAR: "The Dean Martin Show," NBC, 1973-74; "Dallas," CBS, 1982; "Mickey Spillane's Mike Hammer (The New Mike Hammer)," CBS, 1984-87.
AND: "Rhoda: I Won't Dance," CBS, 1976; "Police Story: Ice Time," NBC, 1977; "Switch: 30,000 Witnesses," CBS, 1978;
TV MOVIES AND MINISERIES: "Bridge Across Time," NBC, 1985; "The Return of Mickey Spillane's Mike Hammer," CBS, 1986.

BLUE, BEN
b. Benjamin Bernstein, Montreal, Canada, September 12, 1901; d. 1975. Mime who excelled at physical comedy.
AS A REGULAR: "The Frank Sinatra Show," CBS, 1950-51; "Saturday Night Revue," NBC, 1954; "Accidental Family," NBC, 1967-68.
AS A GUEST: "Squeegee," SYN, 1956; "The Ed Sullivan Show," CBS, 1956; "The Ed Sullivan Show," CBS, 1957; "Five Star Comedy Party," ABC, 1957; "The Julius LaRosa Show," NBC, 1957; "Arthur Murray Party," NBC, 1957; "I've Got a Secret," CBS, 1957; "Art Linkletter's House Party," CBS, 1958; "People Are Funny," NBC, 1958; "The Jack Benny Program," CBS, 1960; "Comedy Spot: Ben Blue's Brothers," CBS, 1960; "Shirley Temple's Storybook: The Land of Oz," NBC, 1960; "Harrigan and Son: The Comics," ABC, 1961; "Keyhole: Hollywood Racketeers," SYN, 1962; "The Ed Sullivan Show," CBS, 1963; "Hollywood Palace," ABC, 1964; "Hollywood Palace," ABC, 1965; "Hollywood Palace," ABC, 1966.

BLYDEN, LARRY
b. Houston, TX, 1925; d. 1975. Light leading man who played hustler Sammy Glick in a TV production of "What Makes Sammy Run"; best

known as the emcee of several game shows of the sixties and seventies.

AS A REGULAR: "Joe and Mabel," CBS, 1956; "Harry's Girls," NBC, 1963-64; "Personality," NBC, 1967-69; "You're Putting Me On," NBC, 1969; "The Movie Game," SYN, 1969-72; "What's My Line?," SYN, 1972-75.

AS A GUEST: "Armstrong Circle Theatre: Herman," NBC, 1953; "Goodyear TV Playhouse: Suitable for Framing," NBC, 1954; "Elgin TV Hour: The $1,000 Window," CBS, 1955; "Playwrights '56: You Sometimes Get Rich," NBC, 1956; "Playhouse 90: One Coat of White," CBS, 1957; "Playhouse 90: Three Men on a Horse," CBS, 1957; "Alcoa Hour: He's for Me," NBC, 1957; "Studio One: My Mother and How She Undid Me," CBS, 1957; "U.S. Steel Hour: Never Know the End," CBS, 1958; "U.S. Steel Hour: Be My Guest," CBS, 1958; "Du Pont Show of the Month: Harvey," CBS, 1958; "Your Hit Parade," CBS, 1959; "Arthur Murray Party," NBC, 1959; "America Pauses for the Merry Month of May," CBS, 1959; "Sunday Showcase: What Makes Sammy Run," NBC, 1959; "The Garry Moore Show," CBS, 1959; "The Ed Sullivan Show," CBS, 1960; "Sunday Showcase: One Loud, Clear Voice," NBC, 1960; "The Garry Moore Show," CBS, 1960; "The Twilight Zone: A Nice Place to Visit," CBS, 1960; "Arthur Murray Party," NBC, 1960; "Chevy Mystery Show: The Machine Calls It Murder," NBC, 1960; "Moment of Fear: Conjure Wife," NBC, 1960; "Omnibus: He Shall Have Power," NBC, 1960; "Play of the Week: A Very Special Baby," SYN, 1960; "Play of the Week: Thieves' Carnival," SYN, 1960; "Play of the Week: The Girls in 509," SYN, 1961; "Thriller: Choose a Victim," NBC, 1961; "The Loretta Young Show: Double Edge," NBC, 1961; "The Loretta Young Show: 13 Donner Street," NBC, 1961; "U.S. Steel Hour: Watching Out for Dulie," CBS, 1961; "U.S. Steel Hour: Delayed Honeymoon," CBS, 1961; "Target: The Corruptors: The Golden Carpet," ABC, 1961; "G.E. Theatre: Call to Danger," CBS, 1961; "U.S. Steel Hour: My Wife's Best Friend," CBS, 1961; "The Twilight Zone: Showdown with Rance McGrew," CBS, 1962; "Cain's Hundred: Blood Money," NBC, 1962; "Adventures in Paradise: The Dream Merchant," ABC, 1962; "U.S. Steel Hour: Male Call," CBS, 1962; "The Dick Powell Show: Tomorrow, the Man," NBC, 1962; "Sam Benedict: Hear the Mellow Wedding Bells," NBC, 1962; "The du Pont Show: Two Faces of Treason," NBC, 1963; "The Reporter: Murder by Scandal," CBS, 1964; "Dr. Kildare: Take Care of My Little Girl," NBC, 1965; "The Alfred Hitchcock Hour: Wally the Beard," NBC, 1965; "12 O'Clock High: Mutiny at 10,000 Feet," ABC, 1965; "Kraft Suspense Theatre: Twixt the Cup and the Lip," NBC, 1965; "The Fugitive: Crack in a Crystal Ball," ABC, 1965; "Slattery's People: The Hero," CBS, 1965; "The Man from UNCLE: The Waverly Ring Affair," NBC, 1966; "ABC Stage '67: Olympus 7000," ABC, 1966; "The Tonight Show Starring Johnny Carson," NBC, 1967; "Ghostbreaker," NBC, 1967; "The FBI: The Innocents," ABC, 1970; "Medical Center: Terror," CBS, 1972; "Cannon: The Torch," CBS, 1972; "Drink, Drank, Drunk," PBS, 1974.

TV MOVIES AND MINISERIES: "The Satin Murders," ABC, 1974.

* Blyden died of injuries he recieved in an auto accident.

BLYTH, ANN
b. Mt. Kisco, NY, August 16, 1928. Actress with a pleasant singing voice who hawked Hostess snack cakes on commercials in the mid-seventies.

AS A GUEST: "RCA Victor Show," NBC, 1953; "Lux Video Theatre: A Place in the Sun," CBS, 1954; "Dinah Shore Chevy Show," NBC, 1958; "The Eddie Fisher Show," NBC, 1958; "The Ed Sullivan Show," CBS, 1958; "Art Linkletter's House Party," CBS, 1958; "This Is Your Life," NBC, 1958; "The Perry Como Show," NBC, 1958; "Bell Telephone Hour," NBC, 1959; "Wagon Train: The Jenny Tannen Story," NBC, 1959; "Startime: Art Linkletter's Secret World of Kids," NBC, 1959; "Wagon Train: The Martha Barham Story," NBC, 1959; "Christophers: The Importance of Guiding the Reading of Young People," SYN, 1959; "The du Pont Show with June Allyson: Suspected," CBS, 1959; "The Citadel," ABC, 1960; "Steve Allen Plymouth Show," NBC, 1960; "The Triumphant Hour," SYN, 1960; "Wagon Train: The Clementine Jones Story," NBC, 1961; "The Dick Powell Show: Savage Sunday," NBC, 1962; "Wagon Train: The Eva Newhope Story," ABC, 1962; "Saints and Sinners: The Year Joan Crawford Won the Oscar," NBC, 1963; "Wagon Train: The Fort Pierce Story," ABC, 1963; "The Twilight Zone: Queen of the Nile," CBS, 1964; "Burke's Law: Who Killed Andy Zygmunt?," ABC, 1964; "Burke's Law: Who Killed Mother Goose?," ABC, 1965; "Kraft Suspense Theatre: Jungle of Fear," NBC, 1965; "The Name of the Game: Swingers Only," NBC, 1969; "The Mike Douglas Show," SYN, 1970; "Switch: Mistresses, Murder and Millions," CBS, 1975; "Quincy: The Eye of the Needle," NBC, 1978; "Quincy: Murder on Ice," NBC, 1983; "Murder, She Wrote: Reflections of the Mind," CBS, 1985.

BOB & RAY

Bob Elliott, b. Boston, MA, March 26, 1923; and Ray Goulding, b. Lowell, MA, March 20, 1922; d. 1990. Sublimely witty comedy team whose literate humor played as well, or better, on the radio than on TV; best known on the tube for their Piels beer commercials of the fifties and sixties.

AS REGULARS: "Bob and Ray," NBC, 1951-53; "Club Embassy," NBC, 1952-53; "The Name's the Same," ABC, 1955; "Happy Days," CBS, 1970.

AND: "The Ed Sullivan Show," CBS, 1957; "The Perry Como Show," NBC, 1958; "The Jack Paar Show," NBC, 1958; "Night Clubs, New York," CBS, 1960; "The Jack Paar Show," NBC, 1961; "Westinghouse Presents: An Old-Fashioned Thanksgiving," ABC, 1961; "The Tonight Show Starring Johnny Carson," NBC, 1975; "The Tonight Show Starring Johnny Carson," NBC, 1976.

* See also Bob Elliott.

BOCHCO, STEVEN

Emmy-winning producer-writer responsible for some of the better television of the eighties.

AS WRITER: "Columbo: Murder by the Book," NBC, 1971; "Columbo: Blueprint for Murder," NBC, 1972; "Columbo: Etude in Black," NBC, 1972; "Columbo: Double Shock," NBC, 1973; "Columbo: Mind Over Mayhem," NBC, 1974.

TV MOVIES AND MINISERIES: "Lieutenant Schuster's Wife," ABC, 1972; "Double Indemnity," ABC, 1973.

AS PRODUCER-CREATOR OR CO-CREATOR: "Paris," CBS, 1979-80; "Hill Street Blues," NBC, 1981-87; "L.A. Law," NBC, 1986- ; "Hooperman," ABC, 1987-89; "Cop Rock," ABC, 1990- .

AS A GUEST: "L.A. Law: Pilot," NBC, 1986; "Later with Bob Costas," NBC, 1989; "Fifty Years of Television: A Golden Celebration," CBS, 1989.

* Bochco was a guest at a cocktail party in the "L.A. Law" pilot.

* Emmies: 1981, 1982, 1983, 1984, 1987.

BOCHNER, HART

b. Canada, 1956. Handsome actor who played Byron Henry in "War and Remembrance."

TV MOVIES AND MINISERIES: "East of Eden," ABC, 1981; "Having It All," ABC, 1982; "The Sun Also Rises," NBC, 1984; "War and Remembrance," ABC, 1988, 1989.

BOCHNER, LLOYD

b. Canada, July 29, 1924. Lantern-jawed actor, usually in suave roles; he played Cecil Colby on "Dynasty" and C.C. Capwell on "Santa Barbara."

AS A REGULAR: "One Man's Family," NBC, 1952;

"Hong Kong," ABC, 1960-61; "The Richard Boone Show," NBC, 1963-64; "Dynasty," ABC, 1981-82; "Santa Barbara," NBC, 1984-85; "Avonlea," DIS, 1990- .

AND: "Hallmark Hall of Fame: Twelfth Night," NBC, 1957; "Encounter: Breakthrough," ABC, 1958; "The Citadel," ABC, 1960; "Thriller: The Prisoner in the Mirror," NBC, 1961; "U.S. Steel Hour: Watching Out for Dulie," CBS, 1961; "U.S. Steel Hour: The Bitter Sex," CBS, 1961; "Sam Benedict: Hannigan," NBC, 1962; "G.E. True: Code Name: Christopher," CBS, 1962; "The Dick Powell Show: Days of Glory," NBC, 1962; "Voyage to the Bottom of the Sea: The Fear-Makers," ABC, 1964; "Bob Hope Chrysler Theatre: Murder in the First," NBC, 1964; "The Man From UNCLE: The See-Paris-and-Die Affair," NBC, 1965; "The Legend of Jesse James: The Dead Man's Hand," ABC, 1965; "Honey West: The Owl and the Eye," ABC, 1965; "The Wild Wild West: The Night of the Puppeteer," CBS, 1966; "T.H.E. Cat: Curtains for Miss Winslow," NBC, 1966; "The Man From UNCLE: The Summit-5 Affair," NBC, 1967; "Hogan's Heroes: Some of Their Planes Are Missing," CBS, 1967; "The Virginian: Ah Sing Vs. Wyoming," NBC, 1967; "Bewitched: Marriage, Witch's Style," ABC, 1969; "The FBI: The Inside Man," ABC, 1969; "Mannix: To Kill a Butcherbird," CBS, 1969; "Medical Center: Jeopardy," CBS, 1969; "Mission: Impossible: Takeover," CBS, 1971; "The Bold Ones: Moment of Crisis," NBC, 1972; "B.J. and the Bear: The Girls of Hollywood High," NBC, 1980; "Columbo: Lady in Waiting," NBC, 1971; "Columbo: The Most Dangerous Match," NBC, 1973; "Mannix: To Quote a Dead Man," CBS, 1973; "The Magician: Man on Fire," NBC, 1973; "The New Adventures of Perry Mason: The Case of the Frenzied Feminist," CBS, 1973; "Gunsmoke: The Iron Blood of Courage," CBS, 1974; "Medical Center: Tainted Lady," CBS, 1974; "Police Story: Chief," NBC, 1974; "Switch: The Cruise Ship Murders," CBS, 1975; "Barnaby Jones: Double Vengeance," CBS, 1975; "Wide World of Mystery: The Nurse Killer," ABC, 1975; "McCloud: Night of the Shark," NBC, 1976; "McMillan: Philip's Game," NBC, 1977; "Matt Houston: Heritage," ABC, 1983; "The A-Team: The Big Squeeze," NBC, 1985; "Murder, She Wrote: Unfinished Business," CBS, 1986; "Murder, She Wrote: Deadpan," CBS, 1988; "Highway to Heaven: The Reunion," NBC, 1989; "The Golden Girls: Rites of Spring," NBC, 1989.

TV MOVIES AND MINISERIES: "Scalplock," NBC, 1966; "Stranger on the Run," NBC, 1967; "Crowhaven Farm," ABC, 1970; "They Call It Murder," NBC, 1971; "Satan's School for Girls," ABC, 1973; "Richie Brockelman, Private Eye," NBC, 1976; "The Immigrants," SYN, 1978; "A Fire in the Sky," NBC, 1978; "Mary and Joseph: A Story of Faith," NBC, 1979;

"Haywire," CBS, 1980; "Rona Jaffe's Mazes and Monsters," CBS, 1982.

BOGART, HUMPHREY
b. Humphrey De Forest Bogart, New York City, NY, January 23, 1899; d. 1957. Movie idol whose only TV dramatic appearance was a reprise of the Broadway and film role that had helped make him famous: Gangster Duke Mantee.
AS A GUEST: "Producers Showcase: The Petrified Forest," NBC, 1955.

BOGART, PAUL
b. New York City, NY, November 21, 1919. Emmy-winning director who helmed live dramas and "All in the Family."
AS DIRECTOR: "Shirley Temple's Storybook: The Legend of Sleepy Hollow," NBC, 1958; "U.S. Steel Hour: Flint and Fire," CBS, 1958; "Ten Little Indians," NBC, 1959; "U.S. Steel Hour: The Impostor," CBS, 1960; "Music for a Summer Night: Tribute to a Poet," ABC, 1960; "Armstrong Circle Theatre: Engineer of Death: The Eichmann Story," CBS, 1960; "U.S. Steel Hour: Famous," CBS, 1961; "U.S. Steel Hour: Watching Out for Dulie," CBS, 1961; "U.S. Steel Hour: Delayed Honeymoon," CBS, 1961; "The Breck Golden Showcase: The Picture of Dorian Gray," CBS, 1961; "Armstrong Circle Theatre: Spin a Crooked Record," CBS, 1961; "Theatre '62: Spellbound," NBC, 1962; "The Defenders: The 700-Year-Old Gang," CBS, 1964; "CBS Playhouse: Dear Friends," CBS, 1968; "CBS Playhouse: Shadow Game," CBS, 1969; "All in the Family," CBS, 1975-79; "Alice: Pilot," CBS, 1976.
* Emmies: 1965, 1968, 1969, 1978.

BOHAY, HEIDI
b. Somerset County, NJ, December 15, 1959. Forgettable cutie-pie actress who played Megan on "Hotel."
AS A REGULAR: "Hotel," ABC, 1983-87.
AND: "Teachers Only: A Case of Entrapment," NBC, 1982; "The Love Boat: Revenge with the Proper Stranger," ABC, 1984; "Finder of Lost Loves: Wayward Dreams," ABC, 1985; "The Love Boat: Three Faces of Love," ABC, 1985; "Murder, She Wrote: Indian Giver," CBS, 1987.

BOHRER, CORINNE
b. North Carolina. Dimpled actress who played nurse Cory Smith on "E/R" and good witch Winnie on "Free Spirit."
AS A REGULAR: "E/R," CBS, 1984-85; "Free Spirit," ABC, 1989-90.
AND: "The Powers of Matthew Star: Daredevil," NBC, 1982; "Hardcastle and McCormick: Third Down and Twenty Years to Life," ABC, 1984; "St. Elsewhere: Brand New Bag," NBC, 1986.

TV MOVIES AND MINISERIES: "Her Secret Life," ABC, 1987; "Destination: America," ABC, 1987.

BOLAND, MARY
b. Philadelphia, PA, January 28, 1880; d. 1965. Actress who specialized in playing domineering wives and society dowagers.
AS A GUEST: "Masterpiece Playhouse: The Rivals," NBC, 1950; "Musical Comedy Time: Mme. Modiste," NBC, 1951; "Armstrong Circle Theatre: The First Born," NBC, 1954; "Producers Showcase: The Women," NBC, 1955; "Best of Broadway: The Guardsman," CBS, 1955; "The Jack Paar Show," NBC, 1958.

BOLGER, RAY
b. Dorchester, MA, January 10, 1904; d. 1987. Dancer-comic who brightened many a movie or stage musical, but who had only iffy success with series television; he played the father of Shirley Partridge (Shirley Jones) on "The Partridge Family."
AS A REGULAR: "The Ray Bolger Show (Where's Raymond?)," ABC, 1953-55; "Washington Square," NBC, 1956-57; "The Ray Bolger Show," NBC, 1957.
AND: "The Perry Como Show," NBC, 1956; "The George Gobel Show," NBC, 1957; "Art Linkletter's House Party," CBS, 1957; "Christophers: The Meaning of Excellence," SYN, 1958; "The Perry Como Show," NBC, 1958; "Dinah Shore Chevy Show," NBC, 1958; "Christophers: Washington's Inner Life During the Revolution," SYN, 1958; "I've Got a Secret," CBS, 1958; "The Big Record," CBS, 1958; "Pontiac Star Parade: The Ginger Rogers Show," CBS, 1958; "G.E. Theatre: The Girl with Flaxen Hair," CBS, 1958; "Dinah Shore Chevy Show," NBC, 1959; "Jimmy Durante Special: Give My Regards to Broadway," NBC, 1959; "G.E. Theatre: Silhouette," CBS, 1959; "Bell Telephone Hour: The Four of Us," NBC, 1960; "Bell Telephone Hour: The Music of Richard Rodgers," NBC, 1961; "What's My Line?," CBS, 1961; "I've Got a Secret," CBS, 1961; "Walt Disney's Wonderful World of Color: Backstage Party," NBC, 1961; "The Red Skelton Hour," CBS, 1962; "I've Got a Secret," CBS, 1962; "Perry Como's Kraft Music Hall," NBC, 1963; "The Judy Garland Show," CBS, 1964; "Password," CBS, 1964; "Password," CBS, 1965; "Bell Telephone Hour," NBC, 1965; "Password," CBS, 1967; "The Partridge Family: Whatever Happened to the Old Songs?," ABC, 1970; "The Movie Game," SYN, 1970; "The Partridge Family: The Forty-Year Itch," ABC, 1971; "Nanny and the Professor: South Sea Island Sweetheart," ABC, 1971; "The Partridge Family: The Mod Father," ABC, 1972; "The Mike Douglas Show," SYN, 1976; "Little House on the Prairie: There's No Place Like Home," NBC, 1978; "The Love Boat:

Second Time Around," ABC, 1979; "Little House on the Prairie: Dance with Me," NBC, 1979; "Diff'rent Strokes: A Haunting We Will Go," NBC, 1984.

TV MOVIES AND MINISERIES: "The Entertainer," NBC, 1976; "Best Sellers: Captains and the Kings," NBC, 1976.

BONADUCE, DANNY

b. August 13, 1959. Carrot-topped child actor of the late sixties; he played wisecracking Danny Partridge on "The Partridge Family" and now works as an FM deejay.

AS A REGULAR: "The Partridge Family," ABC, 1970-74.

AND: "Mayberry RFD: The Camper," CBS, 1969; "Mayberry RFD: Mike's Birthday Party," CBS, 1969; "Hollywood Television Theatre: Invitation to a March," NET, 1972.

TV MOVIES AND MINISERIES: "Murder on Flight 502," ABC, 1975.

BONANOVA, FORTUNIO

b. Spain, January 13, 1893; d. 1969. Opera singer who turned to comedy in films and on television, specializing in blustery ethnic types.

AS A REGULAR: "Count of Monte Cristo," SYN, 1955.

AND: "The Abbott and Costello Show: Uncle Bozzo's Visit," CBS, 1953; "The Abbott and Costello Show: Fencing Master," CBS, 1953; "I Love Lucy: Lucy's Mother-in-Law," CBS, 1954; "December Bride: The Gigolo," CBS, 1954.

BONANZA, NBC, 1959-73.

The Ponderosa, a zillion-acre ranch (it was supposed to be a thousand square miles) in Nevada, was a man's world. Here was where rancher Ben Cartwright lived with his sons—serious Adam (Pernell Roberts), gentle Hoss (Dan Blocker) and romantic Little Joe (Michael Landon).

There weren't many woman around, and with good reason. They all kept dying. Each of Ben's sons had a different mother: Adam's was Elizabeth, played by Geraldine Brooks in the 1961 episode "Elizabeth, My Love"; Hoss' was Inger, played by Inga Swenson in the 1962 episode "Inger, My Love"; Joe's was Marie, played by Felicia Farr in the 1963 episode "Marie, My Love." And no sooner did each of them give birth than they were plowed down by a runaway stagecoach or something.

Not that it mattered to viewers: From 1961 to 1967, "Bonanza" was among the nation's top five shows. The relationships between the Cartwrights were what made "Bonanza" special—that and every fall, you could see

---

what the new Chevrolets looked like.

In 1972, "Bonanza" was moved from its Sunday night timeslot to Tuesdays, opposite the new sitcom "Maude" on CBS. The new competition, and the loss of Dan Blocker in 1972, drove "Bonanza" off the air the next year.

In 1988, the TV-movie "Bonanza: The Next Generation" premiered, with none of the original cast. The characters included Ben Cartwright's brother (John Ireland), Little Joe's son (Michael Landon, Jr.), Joe's wife (Marianne Rogers, apparently avoiding stagecoaches) and Hoss' son (Brian A. Smith).

BOND, RALEIGH

b. 1935; d. 1989. Actor who played diner regular Raleigh on "Alice" and informant T.P. Aquinas on "Scarecrow and Mrs. King."

AS A REGULAR: "Alice," CBS, 1979-81; "Scarecrow and Mrs. King," CBS, 1986-87.

AND: "Lou Grant: Dying," CBS, 1978; "Lou Grant: Witness," CBS, 1979; "Barney Miller: Middle Age," ABC, 1979; "Lou Grant: Kidnap," CBS, 1979; "Lou Grant: Immigrants," CBS, 1981; "Bosom Buddies: Who's on Thirst," ABC, 1982; "The Powers of Matthew Star: Thirty-Six Hours," NBC, 1983; "Family Ties: Baby Boy Doe," NBC, 1984; "Family Ties: Basic Training," NBC, 1989; "Mr. Belvedere: Stakeout," ABC, 1989.

TV MOVIES AND MINISERIES: "Salvage I," ABC, 1979.

BOND, SUDIE

b. Louisville, KY, July 13, 1925; d. 1984.

AS A REGULAR: "Temperatures Rising," ABC, 1973-74; "The Guiding Light," CBS, 1975; "Flo," CBS, 1980-81.

AND: "Omnibus: Fierce, Funny and Far Out," NBC, 1961; "Look Up and Live: The Sandbox," CBS, 1961; "Look Up and Live: Brand," CBS, 1961; "Camera Three: Through Monocle: The Politcal Spectacle," CBS, 1964; "The Doctors and the Nurses: The Patient Nurse," CBS, 1965; "All in the Family: Birth of the Baby," CBS, 1975; "Maude: Poor Albert," CBS, 1975; "All in the Family: Mike the Pacifist," CBS, 1977.

TV MOVIES AND MINISERIES: "The Borgia Stick," NBC, 1967.

BOND, WARD

b. Denver, CO, April 9, 1903; d. 1960. Veteran cowboy actor whose role as Major Adams on "Wagon Train" was the culmination of thirty years of filmmaking, often with good buddy John Wayne.

AS A REGULAR: "Wagon Train," NBC, 1957-61.

AND: "Silver Theatre: My Brother's Keeper," CBS, 1950; "Schlitz Playhouse of Stars: Apple of His Eye," CBS, 1952; "Gulf Playhouse: You Can't Look It Up," NBC, 1952; "Ford Theatre: Gun Job," NBC, 1953; "G.E. Theatre: Winners Never Lose," CBS, 1953; "Ford Theatre: Segment," NBC, 1954; "Cavalcade of America: The Marine Who Was 200 Years Old," ABC, 1955; "Climax!: The Mojave Kid," CBS, 1955; "Screen Directors Playhouse: Rookie of the Year," NBC, 1955; "Star Stage: The Marshal and the Mob," NBC, 1956; "Schlitz Playhouse of Stars: Plague Ship," CBS, 1956; "Schlitz Playhouse of Stars: Moment of Vengeance," CBS, 1956; "Du Pont Theatre: Once a Hero," ABC, 1956; "The Steve Allen Show," NBC, 1957; "The Steve Allen Show," NBC, 1958; "Wide Wide World: The Western," NBC, 1958; "G.E. Theatre: A Turkey for the President," CBS, 1958; "Christophers: Writing Opportunities in Every Field," SYN, 1958.

> ## TV'S TOP TEN, 1959-60
> 1. Gunsmoke (CBS)
> 2. Wagon Train (NBC)
> 3. Have Gun, Will Travel (CBS)
> 4. The Danny Thomas Show (CBS)
> 5. The Red Skelton Show (CBS)
> 6. Father Knows Best (CBS)
> 6. 77 Sunset Strip (ABC)
> 8. The Price Is Right (NBC)
> 9. Wanted Dead or Alive (CBS)
> 10. Perry Mason (CBS)

BONDI, BEULAH
b. Chicago, IL, May 3, 1883; d. 1981. Actress who played Jimmy Stewart's mother in "It's a Wonderful Life" and won an Emmy for a guest shot on "The Waltons."
AS A GUEST: "Medallion Theatre: Gran'ma Rebel," CBS, 1953; "Alfred Hitchcock Theatre: Our Cook's a Treasure," CBS, 1955; "Front Row Center: Finley's Fan Club," CBS, 1956; "Climax!: The Secret of River Lane," CBS, 1956; "Goodyear TV Playhouse: Ark of Safety," NBC, 1956; "Climax!: Circle of Destruction," CBS, 1957; "G.E. Theatre: The Town with a Past," CBS, 1957; "Hallmark Hall of Fame: On Borrowed Time," NBC, 1957; "Climax!: Hurricane Dianne," CBS, 1957; "This Is Your Life" (Lowell Thomas), NBC, 1959; "Playhouse 90: Tomorrow," CBS, 1960; "Best of the Post: Antidote for Hatred," SYN, 1960; "Harrigan and Son: Non Compos Mentis," ABC, 1960; "Wagon Train: The Prairie Story," NBC, 1961; "Alcoa Premiere: The Hands of Danofrio," ABC, 1962; "Perry Mason: The Case of the Nebulous Nephew," CBS, 1963; "The Waltons: The Conflict," CBS, 1974; "Sandburg's Lincoln: Crossing

Fox River," NBC, 1976; "The Waltons: The Pony Cart," CBS, 1976.
TV MOVIES AND MINISERIES: "She Waits," CBS, 1972.
* See also Lowell Thomas.
* Emmies: 1977.

BONERZ, PETER
b. Portsmouth, NH, August 6, 1938. Comic actor and director; he played dentist Jerry Robinson on "The Bob Newhart Show."
AS A REGULAR: "Story Theatre," SYN, 1971-72; "The Bob Newhart Show," CBS, 1972-78; "9 to 5," ABC, 1982-83.
AND: "The Addams Family: Morticia the Writer," ABC, 1965; "Hey, Landlord!: The Big Fumble," NBC, 1966; "McMillan and Wife: Death Is a Seven-Point Favorite," NBC, 1971; "Sanford & Son: TV or Not TV," NBC, 1972; "Password All-Stars," ABC, 1974; "The $20,000 Pyramid," ABC, 1977; "Shoot for the Stars," NBC, 1977; "Murder, She Wrote: The Perfect Foil," CBS, 1986.
TV MOVIES AND MINISERIES: "How to Break Up a Happy Divorce," NBC, 1976; "The Bastard," SYN, 1978; "Mirror, Mirror," NBC, 1979; "Your Place or Mine," CBS, 1983; "Circle of Violence: A Family Drama," CBS, 1986.
AS DIRECTOR: "The Bob Newhart Show," CBS, 1974-78; "The Mary Tyler Moore Show: The Outsider," CBS, 1974; "Sharing Richard," CBS, 1988; "1st & Ten," HBO, 1989- .

BONET, LISA
b. San Francisco, CA, November 16, 1967. Young actress who plays Denise, one of Bill Cosby's TV daughters; she was given a series of her own in 1987, but it was decided her character worked better as a second banana, so Denise came home from college, and college (in the form of "A Different World") continues without her.
AS A REGULAR: "The Cosby Show," NBC, 1984-87, 1988- ; "A Different World," NBC, 1987-88.

BONNE, SHIRLEY
b. Shirley Mae Tanner, Inglewood, CA, 1934. Actress who played the ditsy Eileen Sherwood on a short-lived sixties sitcom.
AS A REGULAR: "My Sister Eileen," CBS, 1960-61.
AND: "Mr. Novak: Sparrow on the Wire," NBC, 1964; "The Joey Bishop Show: The Perfect Girl," CBS, 1964; "Many Happy Returns: A Date for Walter," CBS, 1965; "Medical Center: The Adversaries," CBS, 1969.

BONNER, FRANK
b. Little Rock, AR, February 28, 1942. Actor who played supersalesman Herb Tarlek, who wore sportcoats that looked like they were made

out of carpet remnants, on "WKRP in Cincinnati."

AS A REGULAR: "WKRP in Cincinnati," CBS, 1978-82; "Sidekicks," ABC, 1986-87; "Just the Ten of Us," ABC, 1988-90.

AND: "The FBI: The Confession," ABC, 1973; "Emergency!: Fools," NBC, 1973; "Love, American Style: Love and the Extra Job," ABC, 1974; "The Love Boat: Daddy's Little Girl," ABC, 1981; "The Love Boat: Sly as a Fox," ABC, 1983; "Legmen: I Shall Be Re-Released," NBC, 1984; "Newhart: Kirk Pops the Question," CBS, 1984; "Scarecrow and Mrs. King: Tale of the Dancing Weasel," CBS, 1985; "Night Court: Mac and Quon Le-No Reservations," NBC, 1985; "Scarecrow and Mrs. King: Utopia Now," CBS, 1985; "Blacke's Magic: Death Goes to the Movies," NBC, 1986.

TV MOVIES AND MINISERIES: "The Facts of Life Goes to Paris," NBC, 1982.

BONO, SONNY

b. Salvatore Bono, Detroit, MI, February 16, 1935. Mayor of Palm Springs, CA, former singing partner of Cher and host of his own short-lived solo variety show of the seventies, not necessarily in that order.

AS A REGULAR: "Shindig," ABC, 1964-66; "The Sonny and Cher Comedy Hour," CBS, 1971-74; 1976-77; "The Sonny Comedy Revue," ABC, 1974.

AND: "Hullabaloo," NBC, 1965; "Hollywood Palace," ABC, 1966; "The Man From UNCLE: The Hot Number Affair," NBC, 1967; "Rowan & Martin's Laugh-In," NBC, 1968; "Kraft Music Hall," NBC, 1968; "The Tonight Show Starring Johnny Carson," NBC, 1968; "The Joey Bishop Show," ABC, 1968; "Love, American Style: Love and the Sack," ABC, 1971; "The Secret of Shark Island," CBS, 1973; "Marcus Welby, M.D.: Blood Kin," ABC, 1973; "The Mike Douglas Show," SYN, 1975; "The Love Boat: Oh, My Aching Brother," ABC, 1978; "The Love Boat: Sounds of Silence," ABC, 1979; "The Mike Douglas Show," SYN, 1979; "The Love Boat: Happy Ending," ABC, 1979; "The Love Boat: Pride of the Pacific," ABC, 1982; "Murder, She Wrote: Just Another Fish Story," CBS, 1988; "Late Night with David Letterman," NBC, 1989.

TV MOVIES AND MINISERIES: "Murder on Flight 502," ABC, 1975; "Murder in Music City," NBC, 1979.

BOOKE, SORRELL

b. Buffalo, NY, January 4, 1930. A lifetime of impressive credits, and all anyone remembers him as is Boss Hogg of "Dukes of Hazzard" fame.

AS A REGULAR: "Rich Man, Poor Man—Book II," ABC, 1976-77; "The Dukes of Hazzard," CBS, 1979-85.

AND: "Naked City: The Day It Rained Mink," ABC, 1961; "Cry Vengeance!," NBC, 1961; "Jackie Gleason Special: The Million Dollar Incident," CBS, 1961; "Naked City: A Corpse Ran Down Mulberry Street," ABC, 1961; "Naked City: Beyond This Place There Be Dragons," ABC, 1963; "Look Up and Live: The Horse and His Rider," CBS, 1963; "The Eternal Light: The Kaddish of Levi Yitzhok," NBC, 1963; "NBC Children's Theatre: Robin Hood," NBC, 1964; "The Patty Duke Show: Block That Statue," ABC, 1964; "Bob Hope Chrysler Theatre: Exit From a Plane in Flight," NBC, 1965; "Twelve O'Clock High: Faith, Hope and Sergeant Aronson," ABC, 1965; "Dr. Kildare: With Hellfire and Thunder/Daily Flights to Olympus," NBC, 1965; "The Wild Wild West: The Night of the Egyptian Queen," CBS, 1968; "Room 222: Mr. Bomberg," ABC, 1971; "Hawaii Five-O: To Kill or Be Killed," CBS, 1971; "The FBI: The Fatal Connection," ABC, 1971; "All in the Family: Archie and the Editorial," CBS, 1972; "M*A*S*H: Requiem For A Lightweight," CBS, 1972; "M*A*S*H: Chief Surgeon Who?," CBS, 1972; "Alias Smith and Jones: The Strange Fate of Conrad Meyer Zulick," ABC, 1973; "The New Adventures of Perry Mason: The Case of the Horoscope Homicide," CBS, 1973; "Columbo: Swan Song," NBC, 1974; "The Streets of San Francisco: Murder by Proxy," ABC, 1975; "Kolchak, the Night Stalker: Legacy of Terror," ABC, 1975; "All in the Family: Archie the Donor," CBS, 1975; "All in the Family: Grandpa Blues," CBS, 1975; "Harry O: The Mysterious Case of Lester and Dr. Fong," ABC, 1976; "The Bob Newhart Show: Send This Boy to Camp," CBS, 1976; "Columbo: The Bye-Bye Sky High I.Q. Murder Case," NBC, 1977; "Baa Baa Black Sheep: Poor Little Lambs," NBC, 1977; "All in the Family: Archie's Grand Opening," CBS, 1977; "Little House on the Prairie: I Remember, I Remember," NBC, 1978; "The Rockford Files: The Jersey Bounce," NBC, 1978; "What's Happening!: Basketball Brain," ABC, 1978; "Cross Wits," SYN, 1980; "Blacke's Magic: Last Flight From Moscow," NBC, 1986; "Full House: Our Very First Christmas Show," ABC, 1988.

TV MOVIES AND MINISERIES: "The Borgia Stick," NBC, 1967; "Owen Marshall, Counselor at Law," ABC, 1971; "The Adventures of Nick Carter," ABC, 1972; "Dr. Max," CBS, 1974; "The Last Angry Man," ABC, 1974; "Adventures of the Queen," CBS, 1975; "Brenda Starr," ABC, 1976.

BOOMER, LINWOOD

b. Canada, 1955. Actor who played Adam Kendall on "Little House."

AS A REGULAR: "Little House on the Prairie," NBC, 1978-81.

TV MOVIES AND MINISERIES: "Suddenly, Love,"
NBC, 1978.

BOONE, PAT
b. *Charles Eugene Boone, Jacksonville, FL,
June 1, 1934.* Arthur Godfrey protégé and
born-again Christian; the clean-cut singing idol
of the fifties your parents liked while you
preferred Elvis.
AS A REGULAR: "Arthur Godfrey and His Friends,"
CBS, 1955-57; "Pat Boone Chevy Showroom,"
ABC, 1957-60; "The Pat Boone Show," NBC,
1966-67; SYN, 1967-68.
AND: "Dinah Shore Chevy Show," NBC, 1957;
"The Perry Como Show," NBC, 1957; "The
Chevy Show," NBC, 1957; "The Steve Allen
Show," NBC, 1957; "The Gale Storm Show: Pat
on the Back," CBS, 1957; "General Motors 50th
Anniversary Show," NBC, 1957; "The Steve
Allen Show," NBC, 1958; "Hoedown," NBC,
1959; "Dinah Shore Chevy Show," NBC, 1959;
"I've Got a Secret," CBS, 1959; "Bulova Watch
Time with Pat Boone," ABC, 1961; "The Jack
Paar Show," NBC, 1961; "The Pat Boone Show,"
NBC, 1962; "Bell Telephone Hour," NBC, 1963;
"The Ed Sullivan Show," CBS, 1964; "The Ed
Sullivan Show," CBS, 1965; "The Ed Sullivan
Show," CBS, 1967; "The Joey Bishop Show,"
ABC, 1968; "The Beverly Hillbillies: Collard
Greens an' Fatback," CBS, 1969; "That Girl: I
Don't Have the Vegas Notion," ABC, 1969;
"Night Gallery: The Academy," NBC, 1969;
"Dinah's Place," NBC, 1970; "Festival at Ford's,"
NBC, 1971; "The Tonight Show Starring Johnny
Carson," NBC, 1973; "Owen Marshall, Counselor
at Law: Child of Wednesday," ABC, 1973; "Good
News, America," SYN, 1975; "Dinah!," SYN,
1976.
TV MOVIES AND MINISERIES: "The Pigeon," ABC,
1969.
* Boone wore white buck shoes on television for
a simple reason: They were the only good
shoes he had at the time. And they became his
trademark.
* Boone and his wife Shirley visited Rock
Hudson to pray over him just before he died of
AIDS in 1987. Later Shirley told reporters
she'd spoken in tongues at Hudson's deathbed.

BOONE, RANDY
b. *Fayetteville, NC, January 17, 1942.* Young
actor who played Randy on "The Virginian."
AS A REGULAR: "It's a Man's World," NBC, 1962-
63; "The Virginian," NBC, 1963-66;
"Cimarron Strip," CBS, 1967-68.
AND: "The Twilight Zone: The Seventh Is Made
Up of Phantoms," CBS, 1963; "The Fugitive:
Come Watch Me Die," ABC, 1964; "Combat!:
The Letter," ABC, 1966; "Hondo: Hondo and the
Eagle Claw," ABC, 1967; "Hondo: Hondo and the
War Cry," ABC, 1967; "Emergency!: Fools,"

NBC, 1973; "Kolchak, the Night Stalker: The
Spanish Moss Murders," ABC, 1974.
TV MOVIES AND MINISERIES: "The Hanged Man,"
NBC, 1964.

BOONE, RICHARD
b. *Los Angeles, CA, June 18, 1916; d. 1981.*
Mustachioed, slightly homely actor who was a
memorable TV hero as no-first-name Paladin,
"a knight without armor in a savage land," on
"Have Gun, Will Travel."
AS A REGULAR: "Medic," NBC, 1954-56; "Have
Gun, Will Travel," CBS, 1957-63; "The
Richard Boone Show," NBC, 1963-64; "Hec
Ramsey," NBC, 1972-74.
AND: "G.E. Theatre: Love Is Eternal," CBS, 1955;
"Frontier: Salt War," NBC, 1955; "Matinee
Theatre: Wuthering Heights," NBC, 1955;
"Climax!: Bail Out at 43,000," CBS, 1955; "Lux
Video Theatre: The Shadow of Evil," CBS, 1956; "Lux
Video Theatre: A House of His Own," NBC,
1956; "Studio One: Dead of Noon," CBS, 1957;
"Climax!: Don't Ever Come Back," CBS, 1957;
"Lux Video Theatre: A House of His Own,"
NBC, 1957; "Climax!: To Walk the Night," CBS,
1957; "I've Got a Secret," CBS, 1958; "The Ed
Sullivan Show," CBS, 1959; "U.S. Steel Hour:
Little Tin God," CBS, 1959; "Playhouse 90: The
Tunnel," CBS, 1959; "Playhouse 90: Tomorrow,"
CBS, 1960; "What's My Line?," CBS, 1960;
"U.S. Steel Hour: The Charlie and the Kid," CBS,
1960; "The Right Man," CBS, 1960; "The Spirit
of the Alamo," ABC, 1960; "The Wizard of Oz,"
CBS, 1960; "High Hopes," SYN, 1961; "The Ed
Sullivan Show," CBS, 1961; "Art Linkletter's
House Party," CBS, 1961; "Let Freedom Ring,"
CBS, 1961; "What's My Line?," CBS, 1962;
"John Brown's Body," CBS, 1962; "Art
Linkletter's House Party," CBS, 1962; "Cimarron
Strip: The Roarer," CBS, 1967; "From Sea to
Shining Sea: The Unwanted," SYN, 1975.
TV MOVIES AND MINISERIES: "In Broad Daylight,"
ABC, 1971; "Deadly Harvest," CBS, 1972;
"Hec Ramsey," NBC, 1972; "Goodnight My
Love," ABC, 1972; "The Great Niagara,"
ABC, 1974.
* Boone was a seventh-generation nephew of
Daniel Boone.

123

* In 1960, CBS paid Boone $1.1 million to stay with "Have Gun, Will Travel" for another season.

BOOTH, SHIRLEY
b. Thelma Booth Ford, Hartford, CT, August 30, 1907. Stage actress who came to television when she was good and ready, and left when she was likewise; an Emmy winner as unflappable maid Hazel Burke.
AS A REGULAR: "Hazel," NBC, 1961-65; CBS, 1965-66; "A Touch of Grace," ABC, 1973.
AND: "Playhouse 90: The Hostess with the Mostess," CBS, 1957; "The Perry Como Show," NBC, 1958; "The Dinah Shore Chevy Show," NBC, 1958; "The Garry Moore Show," CBS, 1960; "U.S. Steel Hour: Welcome Home," CBS, 1961; "U.S. Steel Hour: The Haven," CBS, 1961; "Art Linkletter's House Party," CBS, 1961; "Here's Hollywood," NBC, 1961; "Perry Como's Kraft Music Hall," NBC, 1961; "Here's Hollywood," NBC, 1962; "The Jack Paar Program," NBC, 1964; "The Andy Williams Show," NBC, 1964; "The Glass Menagerie," CBS, 1966; "CBS Playhouse: Do Not Go Gentle Into That Good Night," CBS, 1967; "The Ghost and Mrs. Muir: Medium Well Done," ABC, 1970; "The Year Without a Santa Claus," ABC, 1974.
TV MOVIES AND MINISERIES: "The Smugglers," NBC, 1968.
* Emmies: 1962, 1963.

TV'S TOP TEN, 1961-62
1. Wagon Train (NBC)
2. Bonanza (NBC)
3. Gunsmoke (CBS)
4. Hazel (NBC)
5. Perry Mason (CBS)
6. The Red Skelton Show (CBS)
7. The Andy Griffith Show (CBS)
8. The Danny Thomas Show (CBS)
9. Dr. Kildare (NBC)
10. Candid Camera (CBS)

BOOTHE, POWERS
b. Synder, TX, 1949. Actor who won an Emmy as cult leader Jim Jones; he hasn't been heard from much lately.
AS A REGULAR: "Skag," NBC, 1980; "Philip Marlowe, Private Eye," HBO, 1986-87.
TV MOVIES AND MINISERIES: "The Plutonium Incident," CBS, 1980; "The Guyana Tragedy," CBS, 1980.
* Emmies: 1980.

BORDEN, LYNN
b. Lynn Freyse, Detroit, MI, 1935. Miss Arizona 1957; she played Hazel's mistress, Barbara Baxter, when the show moved to CBS.

AS A REGULAR: "Hazel," CBS, 1965-66.
AND: "The Dick Van Dyke Show: Stretch Petrie Versus Kid Schenk," CBS, 1964; "Family Affair: The Way It Was," CBS, 1967; "The FBI: The Phone Call," ABC, 1968; "Ironside: A World of Jackals," NBC, 1969; "Get Smart: Greer Window," NBC, 1969; "The Mod Squad: A Town Called Sincere," ABC, 1969; "McMillan and Wife: Requiem for a Bride," NBC, 1975.
TV MOVIES AND MINISERIES: "The Big Rip-Off," NBC, 1975; "Centennial," NBC, 1978-79.

BORG, VEDA ANN
b. Boston, MA, January 11, 1915; d. 1973. Character actress with a forgettable manner and memorable name.
AS A REGULAR: "The Abbott and Costello Show," CBS, 1952-54.
AND: "The Red Skelton Show," CBS, 1957; "Navy Log: The Decoy," ABC, 1957; "The 20th Century-Fox Hour: The Marriage Broker," CBS, 1957; "The Thin Man: That's the Spirit," NBC, 1957; "Sugarfoot: The Dead Hills," ABC, 1958; "Restless Gun: More Than Kin," NBC, 1958; "Restless Gun: Mercyday," NBC, 1958; "Restless Gun: Jenny," NBC, 1959; "This Is the Life: The Will to Live," SYN, 1959; "This Is the Life: Party Line," SYN, 1962.

BORGE, VICTOR
b. Copenhagen, Denmark, January 3, 1909. Sublimely witty pianist and entertainer.
AS A REGULAR: "The Victor Borge Show," NBC, 1951.
AND: "Victor Borge Special," CBS, 1956; "The Ed Sullivan Show," CBS, 1957; "Victor Borge Special," CBS, 1958; "What's My Line?," CBS, 1958; "Pontiac Star Parade: The Victor Borge Show," CBS, 1958; "Small World," CBS, 1959; "Pontiac Star Parade: Victor Borge Show," NBC, 1959; "Pontiac Star Parade: Victor Borge's Accent on Music," NBC, 1960; "The Ed Sullivan Show," CBS, 1960; "Victor Borge Special," ABC, 1960; "I've Got a Secret," CBS, 1961; "The Jack Paar Program," NBC, 1962; "What's My Line?," CBS, 1962; "The Merv Griffin Show," NBC, 1962; "The Merv Griffin Show," NBC, 1963; "Victor Borge Special," ABC, 1964; "The Jack Paar Program," NBC, 1964; "Perry Como Special," NBC, 1964; "What's My Line?," CBS, 1964; "The Tonight Show Starring Johnny Carson," NBC, 1964; "Hollywood Palace," ABC, 1964; "What's My Line?," CBS, 1965; "The Ed Sullivan Show," CBS, 1965; "The Man From UNCLE: The Suburbia Affair," NBC, 1967; "Hollywood Palace," ABC, 1967; "Kraft Music Hall," NBC, 1968; "The Andy Williams Show," NBC, 1969; "This Is Tom Jones," ABC, 1970; "The David Frost Show," SYN, 1970; "The Tonight Show Starring Johnny Carson," NBC, 1976; "The Pat Sajak Show," CBS, 1989.

BORGNINE, ERNEST

b. Ermes Effron Borgnine, Hamden, CT, January 24, 1917. Bulldog-faced actor who won an Oscar for "Marty" and played fun-loving Lt. Cdr. Quinton McHale on "McHale's Navy"; later he played Dominic Santini on "Airwolf."

AS A REGULAR: "McHale's Navy," ABC, 1962-66; "Airwolf," CBS, 1984-86.

AND: "Ford Theatre: Night Visitor," NBC, 1954; "Fireside Theatre: The Poachers," NBC, 1955; "Make Room for Daddy: Rusty Runs Away," ABC, 1955; "The Ed Sullivan Show," CBS, 1956; "Dick Powell's Zane Grey Theatre: Black Creek Encounter," CBS, 1957; "Wagon Train: The Willy Moran Story," NBC, 1957; "Navy Log: Human Bomb," ABC, 1957; "The General Motors 50th Anniversary Show," NBC, 1957; "The Ed Sullivan Show," CBS, 1957; "Schlitz Playhouse of Stars: Two Lives Have I," CBS, 1958; "O. Henry Playhouse: Reformation of Calliope," SYN, 1958; "Wagon Train: Around the Horn," NBC, 1958; "Laramie: Circle of Fire," NBC, 1959; "Wagon Train: The Estaban Zamora Story," NBC, 1959; "Here's Hollywood," NBC, 1960; "Dick Powell's Zane Grey Theatre: A Gun for Willie," CBS, 1960; "Laramie: Ride the Wild Wind," NBC, 1960; "Wagon Train: The Earl Packer Story," NBC, 1961; "G.E. Theatre: The Legend That Walks Like a Man," CBS, 1961; "The Blue Angels: Blue Leaders," SYN, 1961; "Alcoa Premiere: Seven Against the Sea," ABC, 1962; "G.E. Theatre: The Bar Mitzvah of Major Orlovsky," CBS, 1962; "Hollywood Palace," ABC, 1964; "Wagon Train: The Chief Crazy Bear Story," ABC, 1965; "Bob Hope Chrysler Theatre: The Blue-Eyed Horse," NBC, 1966; "The Jerry Lewis Show," NBC, 1968; "Get Smart: The Little Black Book," NBC, 1968; "Portrait: Legend in Granite," ABC, 1973; "NBC Follies," NBC, 1973; "Sandy in Disneyland," CBS, 1974; "Little House on the Prairie: The Lord Is My Shepherd," NBC, 1974; "Hollywood Squares," SYN, 1975; "Don Adams Screen Test," SYN, 1975; "The Mike Douglas Show," SYN, 1981; "The Love Boat: Venetian Love Song," ABC, 1982; "Highway to Heaven: Another Kind of War, Another Kind of Peace," NBC, 1985; "Jake and the Fatman: Key Witness," CBS, 1989.

TV MOVIES AND MINISERIES: "Sam Hill: Who Killed The Mysterious Mr. Foster?," NBC, 1971; "The Trackers," ABC, 1971; "Twice in a Lifetime," NBC, 1974; "Little House on the Prairie," NBC, 1974; "Future Cop," ABC, 1976; "Jesus of Nazareth," NBC, 1977; "Carpool," CBS, 1983; "The Dirty Dozen: Next Mission," NBC, 1985; "The Dirty Dozen: The Deadly Mission," NBC, 1987; "The Dirty Dozen: The Fatal Mission," NBC, 1988.

BOSLEY, TOM

b. Chicago, IL, October 1, 1927. Roly-poly actor who's played Richie Cunninghan's dad Howard on "Happy Days," Sheriff Amos Tupper on "Murder, She Wrote" and crime-solving Father Dowling.

AS A REGULAR: "That Was the Week That Was," NBC, 1964; "The Debbie Reynolds Show," NBC, 1969-70; "The Dean Martin Show," NBC, 1971-72; "The Sandy Duncan Show," CBS, 1972; "Wait Till Your Father Gets Home," SYN, 1972-74; "Happy Days," ABC, 1974-84; "That's Hollywood," SYN, 1976-82; "Murder, She Wrote," CBS, 1984-88; "The Father Dowling Mysteries," NBC, 1988; ABC, 1989- .

AND: "Diagnosis: Unknown: A Case of Radiant Wine," CBS, 1960; "The Right Man," CBS, 1960; "Perry Como's Kraft Music Hall," NBC, 1961; "The Eternal Light: A Cup of Light," NBC, 1961; "Hallmark Hall of Fame: Arsenic and Old Lace," NBC, 1962; "The Shari Lewis Show," NBC, 1962; "Car 54, Where Are You?: The Star Boarder," NBC, 1963; "The du Pont Show: The Gambling Heart," NBC, 1964; "Jericho: Dutch and Go," CBS, 1966; "The FBI: Ring of Steel," ABC, 1968; "Get Smart: The Frakas Fracas," NBC, 1968; "Bonanza: The Last Vote," NBC, 1968; "The Donald O'Connor Show," SYN, 1968; "The Virginian: Crime Wave in Buffalo Springs," NBC, 1969; "The Bill Cosby Show: The Gumball Incident," NBC, 1970; "Bewitched: Samantha's Magic Mirror," ABC, 1970; "Love, American Style: Love and the Artful Codger," ABC, 1971; "The Paul Lynde Show: The Congressman's Son," ABC, 1973; "Maude: The Medical Profession," CBS, 1973; "Tenafly: Joyride to Nowhere," NBC, 1973; "Chase: Gang War," NBC, 1973; "McMillan and Wife: Free Fall to Terror," NBC, 1973; "The Streets of San Francisco: Going Home," ABC, 1973; "Love, American Style: Love and the Comedienne," ABC, 1973; "Kolchak, the Night Stalker: The Sentry," ABC, 1975; "Tattletales," CBS, 1975; "The Rich Little Show," NBC, 1976; "The Streets of San Francisco: Dead or Alive," ABC, 1976; "Joanie Loves Chachi: Who Gives a Hootenanny?," ABC, 1982; "The Love Boat: Pride of the Pacific," ABC, 1982; "The Love Boat: Intensive Care," ABC, 1983; "Murder, She Wrote: Hit, Run and Homicide," CBS, 1984; "Murder, She Wrote: Death Takes a Curtain Call," CBS, 1985; "The Love Boat: Picture From the Past," ABC, 1985.

TV MOVIES AND MINISERIES: "Marcus Welby, M.D.," ABC, 1969; "Night Gallery," NBC, 1969; "A Step Out of Line," CBS, 1971; "Vanished," NBC, 1971; "Congratulations, It's a Boy!," ABC, 1971; "Mr. and Mrs. Bo Jo Jones," ABC, 1971; "The Streets of San Francisco," ABC, 1972; "No Place to Run,"

ABC, 1972; "Miracle on 34th Street," CBS, 1973; "The Girl Who Came Gift-Wrapped," ABC, 1974; "Death Cruise," ABC, 1974; "The Last Survivors," NBC, 1975; "The Night That Panicked America," ABC, 1975; "The Love Boat," ABC, 1976; "Black Market Baby," ABC, 1977; "Testimony of Two Men," SYN, 1977; "The Bastard," SYN, 1978; "The Triangle Factory Fire Scandal," NBC, 1979; "The Rebels," SYN, 1979; "The Return of Mod Squad," ABC, 1979; "Private Sessions," NBC, 1985; "Perry Mason: The Case of the Notorious Nun," NBC, 1986; "Fatal Confession: A Father Dowling Mystery," NBC, 1988.

BOSSON, BARBARA

b. Bellvernon, PA, November 1, 1939. Actress often in shrill roles; she played Fay Furillo on "Hill Street Blues" and continues to pop up in shows produced by her husband, Steven Bochco.
AS A REGULAR: "Richie Brockelman, Private Eye," NBC, 1978; "Hill Street Blues," NBC, 1981-86; "Hooperman," ABC, 1987-89; "Cop Rock," ABC, 1990.
AND: "Mannix: A Question of Midnight," CBS, 1969; "Emergency!: School Days," NBC, 1972; "Alias Smith and Jones: The Ten Days That Shook Kid Curry," ABC, 1973; "Griff: Countdown to Terror," ABC, 1973; "McMillan and Wife: Downshift to Danger," NBC, 1974; "McMillan and Wife: The Deadly Cure," NBC, 1976; "The New Mike Hammer: Requiem for Billy," CBS, 1986; "L.A. Law: Raiders of the Lost Bark," NBC, 1986; "Murder, She Wrote: The Wearing of the Green," CBS, 1988; "CBS Schoolbreak Special: Words to Live By," CBS, 1989.
TV MOVIES AND MINISERIES: "Richie Brockelman, Private Eye," NBC, 1976; "Calender Girl Murders," ABC, 1984; "Hostage Flight," NBC, 1985.

BOSTWICK, BARRY

b. San Mateo, CA, February 24, 1935. Actor who began his career as a song-and-dance man; nowadays he plays decidedly more macho characters, including George Washington and grizzled sub commander "Lady" Aster in "War and Remembrance."
AS A REGULAR: "Foul Play," ABC, 1981; "Dads," ABC, 1986-87.
AND: "Saturday Night Live," NBC, 1984; "Irving Berlin's 100th Birthday Celebration," CBS, 1988; "The Magical World of Disney: Parent Trap III," NBC, 1989; "The Magical World of Disney: Parent Trap Hawaiian Honeymoon," NBC, 1989.
TV MOVIES AND MINISERIES: "The Chadwick Family," ABC, 1974; "Murder By Natural Causes," CBS, 1979; "Scruples," CBS, 1980; "Red Flag: The Ultimate Game," CBS, 1981;

"Summer Girl," CBS, 1983; "An Uncommon Love," CBS, 1983; "George Washington," CBS, 1984; "Deceptions," NBC, 1985; "Betrayed by Innocence," CBS, 1986; "Pleasures," ABC, 1986; "George Washington II: The Forging of a Nation," CBS, 1986; "I'll Take Manhattan," CBS, 1987; "Addicted to His Love," ABC, 1988; "Body of Evidence," CBS, 1988; "War and Remembrance," ABC, 1988, 1989; "Till We Meet Again," CBS, 1989.

BOSWELL, CONNEE

b. New Orleans, LA, December 3, 1907; d. 1976. Jazz vocalist who appeared on a few variety programs.
AS A REGULAR: "Pete Kelly's Blues," NBC, 1959.
AND: "The Tony Bennett Show," NBC, 1956; "Club 60," NBC, 1957; "Art Linkletter's House Party," CBS, 1957; "The Ed Sullivan Show," CBS, 1957; "The Julius LaRosa Show," NBC, 1957; "Art Linklétter's House Party," CBS, 1958; "Stars of Jazz," ABC, 1958; "Music for a Summer Night: Tin Pan Alley," ABC, 1959; "Bell Telephone Hour: A Night of Music," NBC, 1959; "Play Your Hunch," NBC, 1963.

BOTTOMS, JOSEPH

b. Santa Barbara, CA, April 22, 1954. One of the hunky Bottoms brothers.
AS A GUEST: "Owen Marshall, Counselor at Law: A Piece of God," ABC, 1972; "Murder, She Wrote: Murder at the Oasis," CBS, 1985.
TV MOVIES AND MINISERIES: "Trouble Comes to Town," ABC, 1973; "Unwed Father," ABC, 1974; "Stalk the Wild Child," NBC, 1976; "Holocaust," NBC, 1978; "The Intruder Within," ABC, 1981; "The Sins of Dorian Gray," ABC, 1983; "Time Bomb," NBC, 1984; "Island Sons," ABC, 1987; "Police Story: Cop Killers," ABC, 1988.

BOTTOMS, SAM

b. Santa Barbara, CA, October 17, 1955. Another one.
AS A REGULAR: "Santa Barbara," NBC, 1985.
AND: "Marcus Welby, M.D.: Aspects of Love," ABC, 1976; "Murder, She Wrote: The Search for Peter Kerry," CBS, 1989.
TV MOVIES AND MINISERIES: "Savages," ABC, 1974; "Cage Without a Key," CBS, 1975; "East of Eden," ABC, 1981; "Desperate Lives," CBS, 1982; "Island Sons," ABC, 1987.

BOTTOMS, TIMOTHY

b. Santa Barbara, CA, August 30, 1950. Another one.
AS A GUEST: "Freddy's Nightmares: Missing Persons," SYN, 1989.
TV MOVIES AND MINISERIES: "The

Moneychangers," NBC, 1976; "The Gift of Love," ABC, 1978; "East of Eden," ABC, 1981; "Perry Mason: The Case of the Notorious Nun," NBC, 1986; "Island Sons," ABC, 1987.

BOUTON, JIM
b. Newark, NJ, March 8, 1939. Baseball player who turned to sportscasting, then to writing, and finally to appearing in an incredibly short-lived sitcom based on his book.
AS A REGULAR: "Ball Four," CBS, 1976.

BOWEN, ROGER
b. Attleboro, MA. Bespectacled actor usually in comic roles; he played Hamilton Majors, Herschel Bernardi's pompous boss on "Arnie" and was Henry Blake in the movie version of "M*A*S*H."
AS A REGULAR: "Arnie," CBS, 1970-72; "The Brian Keith Show," NBC, 1973-74; "At Ease," ABC, 1983; "Suzanne Pleshette Is Maggie Briggs," CBS, 1984.
AND: "Nanny and the Professor: Nanny and the Smoke-Filled Room," ABC, 1970; "Love, American Style: Love and Dear Old Mom and Dad," ABC, 1972; "Barney Miller: The Arsonist," ABC, 1975; "Maude: Maude's Reunion," CBS, 1977; "All in the Family: Archie and the Ku Klux Klan," CBS, 1977; "Alice: The Fourth Time Around," CBS, 1979; "House Calls: Side to Side," CBS, 1979; "House Calls: The Hostage Situation," CBS, 1981; "House Calls: Lust Weekend," CBS, 1981.
TV MOVIES AND MINISERIES: "Deadlock," NBC, 1969; "Playmates," ABC, 1972; "Hunter," CBS, 1973; "It Couldn't Happen to a Nicer Guy," ABC, 1974; "The Rangers," NBC, 1974; "The Moneychangers," NBC, 1976; "The Bastard," SYN, 1978; "The Murder That Wouldn't Die," NBC, 1980.

BOWMAN, LEE
b. Cincinnati, OH, December 28, 1914; d. 1979. Actor who played detective Ellery Queen and was a member of the panel on "Masquerade Party."
AS A REGULAR: "Ellery Queen," ABC, 1951-52; "What's Going On?," ABC, 1954; "Masquerade Party," CBS, 1958; NBC, 1958-59; CBS, 1959-60; NBC, 1960; "Miami Undercover," SYN, 1960-61.
AND: "Silver Theatre: Bad Guy," CBS, 1950; "Robert Montgomery Presents: The Awful Truth," NBC, 1950; "Studio One: The Blonde Comes First," CBS, 1950; "Nash Airflyte Theatre: Suppressed Desires," CBS, 1950; "Lux Video Theatre: Weather for Today," CBS, 1951; "Curtain Call: Summer Evening," SYN, 1952; "Robert Montgomery Presents: The Glass Cage,"

NBC, 1953; "Lux Video Theatre: Borrowed Wife," NBC, 1954; "Love Story: The Arms of the Law," SYN, 1954; "Robert Montgomery Presents: Halfway House," NBC, 1955; "Stage 7: Emergency," CBS, 1955; "Robert Montgomery Presents: The Great Gatsby," NBC, 1955; "Robert Montgomery Presents: All Expenses Paid," NBC, 1956; "Lux Video Theatre: Top Rung," NBC, 1956; "Schlitz Playhouse of Stars: Top Secret," CBS, 1956; "The Loretta Young Show: New Slant," NBC, 1956; "The Loretta Young Show: The Bad Apple," NBC, 1957; "Kraft Television Theatre: The Category Is Murder," NBC, 1957; "Suspicion: Someone Is After Me," NBC, 1958; "Studio One: The Laughing Willow," CBS, 1958; "77 Sunset Strip: The Raiders," ABC, 1962; "The Fugitive: Detour on a Road Going Nowhere," ABC, 1964.
TV MOVIES AND MINISERIES: "Fame Is the Name of the Game," NBC, 1966.

BOXLEITNER, BRUCE
b. Elgin, IL, May 12, 1950. Rather styleless TV hunk who played agent Lee Stetson on "Scarecrow and Mrs. King."
AS A REGULAR: "How The West Was Won," ABC, 1978-79; "Bring 'Em Back Alive," CBS, 1982-83; "Scarecrow and Mrs. King," CBS, 1983-87.
AND: "The Mary Tyler Moore Show: I Gave at the Office," CBS, 1973; "Hawaii Five-0: Right Grave, Wrong Body," CBS, 1974; "Hawaii Five-0: And the Horse Jumped Over the Moon," CBS, 1975; Police Woman: Paradise Mall," NBC, 1975; "Hawaii Five-0: Capsule Kidnapping," CBS, 1976.
TV MOVIES AND MINISERIES: "A Cry for Help," ABC, 1975; "The Macahans," ABC, 1976; "Kiss Me, Kill Me," ABC, 1976; "Murder at the World Series," ABC, 1977; "Happily Ever After," CBS, 1978; "The Last Convertible," NBC, 1981; "Fly Away Home," ABC, 1981; "East of Eden," ABC, 1981; "Bare Essence," CBS, 1982; "The Gambler II: The Adventure Continues," CBS, 1983; "Passion Flower," CBS, 1986; "Angel in Green," CBS, 1987; "The Gambler III: The Legend Continues," CBS, 1987; "Red River," CBS, 1988; "The Town Bully," ABC, 1988; "From the Dead of the Night," NBC, 1989; "The Road Raiders," CBS, 1989; "Till We Meet Again," CBS, 1989.

BOYD, JIMMY
b. McComb, MO, January 9, 1940. Former child performer whose 1952 recording of "I Saw Mommy Kissing Santa Claus" was a huge hit.
AS A REGULAR: "Date with the Angels," ABC, 1957-58; "The Betty White Show," ABC, 1958; "Bachelor Father," CBS, 1958-59; NBC, 1959-61; "Broadside," ABC, 1964-65.

AND: "U.S. Steel Hour: Huck Finn," CBS, 1957; "Shirley Temple's Storybook: Emmy Lou," NBC, 1960; "My Three Sons: The Substitute Teacher," ABC, 1964; "The Bing Crosby Show: Hoop Shots," ABC, 1964; "The John Forsythe Show: Tis Better to Have Loved and Lost," NBC, 1965; "Batman: Louie the Lilac," ABC, 1967; "The Donald O'Connor Show," SYN, 1968.

BOYD, STEPHEN

b. William Millar, Belfast, N. Ireland, July 4, 1928; d. 1977. Hunky actor in films ("Ben Hur") and TV.

AS A GUEST: "Lilli Palmer Theatre: The Stolen Pearl," SYN, 1955; "This Is Your Life," NBC, 1959; "Hedda Hopper's Hollywood," NBC, 1960; "Playhouse 90: To the Sound of Trumpets," CBS, 1960; "Dinah Shore Chevy Show," NBC, 1960; "Here's Hollywood," NBC, 1961; "G.E. Theatre: The Wall Between," CBS, 1962; "Bob Hope Chrysler Theatre: War of Nerves," NBC, 1964; "The Poppy Is Also a Flower," ABC, 1966; "I've Got a Secret," CBS, 1966; "The Steve Allen Show," SYN, 1968; "The Movie Game," SYN, 1970; "Hallmark Hall of Fame: The Hands of Cormac Joyce," NBC, 1972; "Of Men and Women: The Interview," ABC, 1973.

TV MOVIES AND MINISERIES: "Carter's Army," ABC, 1970; "Key West," NBC, 1973; "The Lives of Jenny Dolan," NBC, 1975.

BOYD, WILLIAM

b. Cambridge, OH, June 5, 1895; d. 1972.
AS A REGULAR: "Hopalong Cassidy," NBC, 1949-51.

BOYER, CHARLES

b. Figeac, France, August 28, 1897; d. 1978. Matinee idol who turned to TV in the fifties.

AS A REGULAR: "Four Star Playhouse," CBS, 1952-55; "Alcoa-Goodyear Theatre (A Turn of Fate)," NBC, 1957-58; "The Rogues," NBC, 1964-65.

AND: "Stage 7: Madeira! Madeira!," CBS, 1955; "I Love Lucy: Lucy Meets Charles Boyer," CBS, 1956; "Hallmark Hall of Fame: There Shall Be No Night," NBC, 1957; "Dinah Shore Chevy Show," NBC, 1960; "The Dick Powell Show: The Prison," NBC, 1962; "The Dick Powell Show: Days of Glory," NBC, 1962; "The Name of the Game: The Emissary," NBC, 1969.

BOYLE, LARA FLYNN

b. Chicago, IL, March 24, 1970. Actress who plays Donna Hayward on "Twin Peaks."

AS A REGULAR: "Twin Peaks," ABC, 1990- .

TV MOVIES AND MINISERIES: "Amerika," ABC, 1987; "Terror on Highway 91," CBS, 1989; "Gang of Four," ABC, 1989; "The Preppie Murder," ABC, 1989.

BOYLE, PETER

b. Philadelphia, PA, October 18, 1933. Beefy, bald actor of film ("Young Frankenstein," "The Dream Team") and TV; usually in comic roles.

AS A REGULAR: "Comedy Tonight," CBS, 1970; "Joe Bash," ABC, 1986.

AND: "Saturday Night Live," NBC, 1976; "Cagney & Lacey: A Class Act," CBS, 1988; "Midnight Caller: Fathers and Sons," NBC, 1989.

TV MOVIES AND MINISERIES: "The Man Who Could Talk to Kids," CBS, 1973; "Tailgunner Joe," NBC, 1977; "From Here to Eternity," NBC, 1979; "Echoes in the Darkness," CBS, 1987; "Disaster at Silo 7," ABC, 1988; "The Rise and Fall of Oliver North," CBS, 1989.

BRACKEN, EDDIE

b. Astoria, Queens, NY, February 7, 1920. Comic actor in the movies ("Hail the Conquering Hero," "The Miracle of Morgan's Creek") and TV, usually playing frantic characters.

AS A REGULAR: "I've Got a Secret," CBS, 1952; "Make the Connection," NBC, 1955; "Masquerade Party," ABC, 1954-56, NBC, 1957.

AND: "Gulf Playhouse: A Question of Rank," NBC, 1952; "Gulf Playhouse: Mr. Breger," NBC, 1952; "Schlitz Playhouse of Stars: Simplon Express," CBS, 1953; "Goodyear TV Playhouse: Suit Yourself," NBC, 1955; "Studio One: A Likely Story," CBS, 1955; "Schlitz Playhouse of Stars: The Rising Wind," CBS, 1955; "The 20th Century-Fox Hour: The Genius," CBS, 1956; "Schlitz Playhouse of Stars: Formosa Affair," CBS, 1956; "Climax!: False Witness," CBS, 1957; "Studio One: My Mother and How She Undid Me," CBS, 1957; "General Motors 50th Anniversary Show," NBC, 1957; "The Patrice Munsel Show," ABC, 1958; "Studio One: The Award Winner," CBS, 1958; "Dinah Shore Chevy Show," NBC, 1958; "Steve Allen Presents The Steve Lawrence and Eydie Gorme Show," NBC, 1958; "Dinah Shore Chevy Show," NBC, 1959; "Pat Boone Chevy Showroom," ABC, 1959; "The David Niven Show: A Day of Small Miracles," NBC, 1959; "The Strawberry Blonde," NBC, 1959; "Play of the Week: Archy and Mehitabel," SYN, 1960; "The Roaring Twenties: Another Time, Another War," ABC, 1961; "Going My Way: Like My Own Brother," ABC, 1962; "Lamp Unto My Feet: Mr. Jones and Monday," CBS, 1963; "Rawhide: Incident of the Clown," CBS, 1963; "Burke's Law: Who Killed April?," ABC, 1964; "Rawhide: Incident of the Pied Piper," CBS, 1964; "Burke's Law: Who Killed the Card?," ABC, 1965; "Ellery Queen: The Hard-Headed Huckster," NBC, 1976; "Murder, She Wrote: Armed Response," CBS, 1985; "Amazing Stories: Boo!," NBC, 1986; "Blacke's Magic: A Friendly Game of Showdown," NBC, 1986;

"Great Performances: Show Boat," PBS, 1989; "Wiseguy: Sanctuary," CBS, 1990; "Wiseguy: Brrrump-Bump," CBS, 1990.

BRADDOCK, MICKEY—See Mickey Dolenz.

BRADLEY, ED
b. *Philadelphia, PA, June 22, 1941.* CBS correspondent.
AS A REGULAR: "60 Minutes," CBS, 1981- .
* Emmies: 1980, 1981, 1982.

BRADLEY, TRUMAN
b. *1905; d. 1974.* Former radio announcer who hosted "Science Fiction Theatre."
AS A REGULAR: "Science Fiction Theater," SYN, 1955-57.

THE BRADY BUNCH
ABC, 1969-74, 1977; NBC, 1981; CBS, 1990.
This suburban family that won't go away was created by Sherwood Schwartz, a former writer for Red Skelton who also was responsible for "Gilligan's Island" (Did this guy have his finger on America's pulse or what?). Mike Brady (Robert Reed) married Carol something-or-other. He had three boys, all brunettes like dad; she had three girls, all blondes like mom. They lived together in a big house with the maid, Alice (Ann B. Davis). ABC brought them back for a variety show in 1977, and then NBC brought them back and had two of the daughters get married. Then CBS brought them back for a smash reunion movie and gave them another series chance. For about two weeks.

BRADY, PAT
b. *Robert Patrick Brady, Toledo, OH, December 31, 1914; d. 1972.* Longtime sidekick to Roy Rogers and Dale Evans.
AS A REGULAR: "The Roy Rogers Show," NBC, 1951-57; "The Roy Rogers and Dale Evans Show," ABC, 1962.

BRADY, SCOTT
b. *Gerald Tierney, Brooklyn, NY, September 13, 1924; d. 1985.* Reliable movie and TV actor, usually in action roles; he also played the father of Shirley Feeney (Cindy Williams) in an episode of "Laverne & Shirley."
AS A REGULAR: "Shotgun Slade," SYN, 1959-61.
AND: "Ford Theatre: Just What the Doctor Ordered," NBC, 1953; "Lux Video Theatre: Return to Alsace," CBS, 1953; "Schlitz Playhouse of Stars: Night in the Big Swamp," CBS, 1955; "Studio 57: Night Tune," SYN, 1955; "The Loretta

Young Show: Man in the Ring," NBC, 1955; "Lux Video Theatre: Tabloid," NBC, 1956; "Crossroads: Barbed-Wire Preacher," ABC, 1957; "Dick Powell's Zane Grey Theatre: Man on the Run," CBS, 1957; "Playhouse 90: Lone Woman," CBS, 1957; "Schlitz Playhouse of Stars: Papa Said No," CBS, 1958; "Climax!: The Big Success," CBS, 1958; "Schlitz Playhouse of Stars: The Salted Mine," CBS, 1959; "The Ed Sullivan Show," CBS, 1959; "Checkmate: Voyage Into Fear," CBS, 1961; "G.E. Theatre: We're Holding Your Son," CBS, 1961; "The Untouchables: The Floyd Gibbons Story," ABC, 1962; "The Alfred Hitchcock Hour: Run for Doom," CBS, 1963; "The Virginian: The Storm Gate," NBC, 1968; "The Name of the Game: High on a Rainbow," NBC, 1968; "Gunsmoke: Danny," CBS, 1969; "Mannix: A Chance at the Roses," CBS, 1970; "The High Chaparral: Wind," NBC, 1970; "The Name of the Game: The War Merchants," NBC, 1970; "San Francisco International Airport: Hostage," NBC, 1970; "The Immortal: Paradise Bay," ABC, 1970; "The Men From Shiloh: The Animal," NBC, 1971; "Gunsmoke: Jubilee," CBS, 1972; "McMillan and Wife: No Hearts, No Flowers," NBC, 1973; "Dirty Sally: Right of Way," CBS, 1974; "Police Story: Countdown," NBC, 1974; "Police Story: The Wyatt Earp Syndrome," NBC, 1974; "Police Story: A Dangerous Age," NBC, 1974; "Police Story: Cop in the Middle," NBC, 1974; "Police Story: Across the Line," NBC, 1974; "Police Story: Incident in the Kill Zone," NBC, 1975; "Police Story: Headhunter," NBC, 1975; "Hawaii Five-O: The Hostage," CBS, 1975; "The Rockford Files: Gearjammers," NBC, 1975; "All in the Family: Edith's Night Out," CBS, 1976; "All in the Family: Archie's Brief Encounter," CBS, 1976; "Welcome Back, Kotter: Caruso's Way," ABC, 1977; "The Rockford Files: The Trees, the Bees and T.T. Flowers," NBC, 1977; "Laverne & Shirley: Buddy, Can You Spare a Father," ABC, 1977; "The Rockford Files: Local Man Eaten by Newspaper," NBC, 1978; "Eischied: Do They Really Need to Die?," NBC, 1979; "Taxi: The Great Race," ABC, 1979; "Charlie's Angels: Taxi Angels," ABC, 1981; "McClain's Law: Pilot," NBC, 1981; "McClain's Law: Green Light," NBC, 1982; "Matt Houston: Killing Isn't Everything," ABC, 1982; "Cagney & Lacey: The Informant," CBS, 1983; "Simon & Simon: The Shadow of Sam Penny," CBS, 1983.
TV MOVIES AND MINISERIES: "The D.A.: Murder One," NBC, 1969; "The Night Strangler," ABC, 1973; "Roll, Freddy, Roll," ABC, 1974; "The Kansas City Massacre," ABC, 1975; "Law and Order," ABC, 1976; "Arthur Hailey's Wheels," NBC, 1978; "This Girl for Hire," CBS, 1983.

BRAEDEN, ERIC
b. *Hans Gudengast, Germany.* Charismatic, craggy-faced actor who got his start playing

Nazis; now he's the enigmatic Victor Newman on "The Young and the Restless."

AS A REGULAR: "Combat!," ABC, 1963-64; "The Rat Patrol," ABC, 1966-68; "The Young and the Restless," CBS, 1980- .

AND: "The Man From UNCLE: The Discotheque Affair," NBC, 1965; "Run for Your Life: The Cold, Cold War of Paul Bryan," NBC, 1965; "Twelve O'Clock High: Rx for a Sick Bird," ABC, 1965; "Run for Your Life: How to Sell Your Soul for Fun and Profit," NBC, 1965; "The Virginian: No Drums, No Trumpets," NBC, 1966; "Mission: Impossible: The Short Tail Spy," CBS, 1966; "Mission: Impossible: Echo of Yesterday," CBS, 1967; "Hawaii Five-O: The Second Shot," CBS, 1970; "The FBI: The Target," ABC, 1970; "Gunsmoke: Jaekel," CBS, 1971; "Gunsmoke: The Bullet," CBS, 1971; "Mannix: Woman in the Shadows," CBS, 1971; "Marcus Welby, M.D.: In Sickness and in Health," ABC, 1972; "McCloud: The Million Dollar Round Up," NBC, 1973; "Barnaby Jones: Perchance to Kill," CBS, 1973; "Owen Marshall, Counselor at Law: N Is for Nightmare," ABC, 1973; "Banacek: The Vanishing Chalice," NBC, 1974; "Gunsmoke: The Iron Blood of Courage," CBS, 1974; "Kolchak, the Night Stalker: The Werewolf," ABC, 1974; "The FBI: Diamond Run," ABC, 1974; "Marcus Welby, M.D.: A Fevered Angel," ABC, 1974; "The Rookies: The Assassin," ABC, 1974; "The Mary Tyler Moore Show: The Critic," CBS, 1977; "Kojak: When You Hear the Beep, Drop Dead," CBS, 1977; "Switch: Net Loss," CBS, 1977; "The Eddie Capra Mysteries: Murder, Murder," NBC, 1978; "Switch: 30,000 Witnesses," CBS, 1978; "Hagen: Pilot," CBS, 1980.

TV MOVIES AND MINISERIES: "Honeymoon with a Stranger," ABC, 1969; "The Mask of Sheba," NBC, 1970; "The Judge and Jake Wyler," NBC, 1972; "Death Race," ABC, 1973; "The New, Original Wonder Woman," ABC, 1975; "Happily Ever After," CBS, 1978; "The Power Within," ABC, 1979; "The Aliens Are Coming," NBC, 1980.

BRAND, JOLENE

b. Los Angeles, CA, 1935. Starlet who played Zorro's girlfriend Anna Maira Verdugo and was a female foil for Ernie Kovacs.

AS A REGULAR: "Zorro," ABC, 1958-59; "Take a Good Look," ABC, 1959-61; "Guestward Ho!," ABC, 1960-61; "The New Ernie Kovacs Show," ABC, 1961-62.

AND: "The Detectives Starring Robert Taylor: Anatomy of Fear," ABC, 1960; "Hennesey: Senior Nurse," CBS, 1960; "Maverick: A Technical Error," ABC, 1961.

BRAND, NEVILLE

b. Kewanee, IL, August 13, 1921. Weatherbeaten actor with a gravelly voice; he played Al Capone on "The Untouchables" and was Texas Ranger Reese Bennet on "Laredo."

AS A REGULAR: "Laredo," NBC, 1965-67.

AND: "Favorite Story: The Gold Bug," SYN, 1952; "Footlights Theatre: The Man Who Had Nothing to Lose," CBS, 1952; "Schlitz Playhouse of Stars: The Edge of Battle," CBS, 1954; "Schlitz Playhouse of Stars: The Dumbest Man in the Army," CBS, 1954; "Appointment with Adventure: The Quiet Gun," CBS, 1955; "Stage 7: Armed," CBS, 1955; "The Jane Wyman Show: Between Jobs," NBC, 1956; "Climax!: Ten Minutes to Curfew," CBS, 1956; "The Jane Wyman Show: Harbor Patrol," NBC, 1957; "Climax!: Walk a Tightrope," CBS, 1957; "Playhouse 90: Galvanized Yankee," CBS, 1957; "Schlitz Playhouse of Stars: Guys Like O'Malley," CBS, 1958; "G.E. Theatre: The Coward of Fort Bennett," CBS, 1958; "Kraft Theatre: Run, Joe, Run," NBC, 1958; "Kraft Theatre: All the King's Men," NBC, 1958; "U.S. Steel Hour: Goodbye ... But It Doesn't Go Away," CBS, 1958; "Dick Powell's Zane Grey Theatre: Trouble at Tres Cruces," CBS, 1959; "Westinghouse Desilu Playhouse: The Untouchables," CBS, 1959; "Bonanza: The Last Viking," NBC, 1960; "The Untouchables: The Organization," ABC, 1961; "The Untouchables: The Big Train," ABC, 1961; "Straightaway: The Tin Caesar," ABC, 1961; "Cain's Hundred: The Debasers," NBC, 1962; "Death Valley Days: Preacher with a Past," SYN, 1962; "The du Pont Show: The Outpost," NBC, 1962; "The Joey Bishop Show: Double Exposure," NBC, 1962; "Naked City: Lament for a Dead Indian," ABC, 1962; "Weekend," SYN, 1963; "Ben Casey: Will Everyone Who Believes in Terry Dunne Please Applaud?," ABC, 1963; "Rawhide: Incident of the Red Wind," CBS, 1963; "The Lieutenant: The Two-Star Giant," NBC, 1963; "Bob Hope Chrysler Theatre: Seven Miles of Bad Road," NBC, 1963; "Wagon Train: The William Carr Story," ABC, 1964; "Arrest and Trial: An Echo of Conscience," ABC, 1964; "Destry: The Solid Gold Girl," ABC, 1964; "Wagon Train: The Zebedee Titus Story," ABC, 1964; "Suspense Theatre: The Savage," CBS, 1964; "Combat: Fly Away Home," ABC, 1964; "The Twilight Zone: The Encounter," CBS, 1964; "The Virginian: We've Lost a Train," NBC, 1965; "Tarzan: Alex the Great," NBC, 1968; "The Men From Shiloh: Gun Quest," NBC, 1970; "Bonanza: The Luck of Pepper Shannon," NBC, 1970; "Alias Smith and Jones: Shootout at Diablo Station," ABC, 1971; "Bonanza: The Rattlesnake Brigade," NBC, 1971; "McCloud: Fifth Man in a String Quartet," NBC, 1972; "Alias Smith and Jones: Which Way to the OK Corral?," ABC, 1972; "Marcus Welby. M.D.: Don't Talk About Darkness," ABC, 1972; "The Magician: Lightning on a Dry Day," NBC, 1973; "McCloud: The Solid Gold Swingers," NBC,

1973; "Police Story: War Games," NBC, 1975; "Police Woman: The Loner," NBC, 1975; "Kojak: Sweeter Than Life," CBS, 1975; "McCloud: Three Guns for New York," NBC, 1975; "Swiss Family Robinson: Jean Lafitte," ABC, 1976; "Quincy: Dark Angel," NBC, 1979.
TV MOVIES AND MINISERIES: "Lock, Stock and Barrel," NBC, 1971; "Marriage: Year One," NBC, 1971; "The Adventures of Nick Carter," ABC, 1972; "Two for the Money," ABC, 1972; "No Place to Run," ABC, 1972; "Hitched," NBC, 1973; "Killdozer," ABC, 1974; "Death Stalk," NBC, 1974; "Barbary Coast," ABC, 1975; "Best Sellers: Captains and the Kings," NBC, 1976; "The Quest," NBC, 1976.

BRANDO, MARLON
b. Omaha, NB, April 3, 1924. Screen and stage legend; he won an Emmy as Nazi George Lincoln Rockwell on the "Roots" sequel.
AS A GUEST: "The Ed Sullivan Show," CBS, 1956.
TV MOVIES AND MINISERIES: "Roots: The Next Generations," ABC, 1979.
* Emmies: 1979.

BRANDON, CLARK
b. New York City, NY, December 30, 1958. Fresh-faced actor, usually in light roles.
AS A REGULAR: "The Fitzpatricks," CBS, 1977-78; "Out of the Blue," ABC, 1979; "Mr. Merlin," CBS, 1981-82.
AND: "The Love Boat: Dee Dee's Dilemma," ABC, 1983.
TV MOVIES AND MINISERIES: "Like Mom, Like Me," CBS, 1978; "In Love with an Older Woman," CBS, 1982.

BRANDON, HENRY
b. Henry Kleinbach, Germany, 1912; d. 1990. Actor with extensive film and TV credits, usually as a sinister type.
AS A GUEST: "Broken Arrow: Passage Deferred," ABC, 1956; "Robert Montgomery Presents: Victoria Regina," NBC, 1957; "Suspicion: The Flight," NBC, 1957; "Wagon Train: The Charles Avery Story," NBC, 1957; "Have Gun, Will Travel: The Yuma Treasure," CBS, 1957; "Westinghouse Desilu Playhouse: The Case for Dr. Mudd," CBS, 1958; "Lawman: To Capture the West," ABC, 1959; "Wagon Train: The Martha Barham Story," NBC, 1959; "Maverick: A Bullet for the Teacher," ABC, 1960; "77 Sunset Strip: Trouble in the Middle East," ABC, 1960; "Adventures in Paradise: Angel of Death," ABC, 1961; "Gunsmoke: Stolen Horses," CBS, 1961; "Gunslinger: The Death of Yellow Singer," CBS, 1961; "Whispering Smith: The Mortal Coil," NBC, 1961; "Adventures in Paradise: The Assassins," ABC, 1961; "77 Sunset Strip: The Diplomatic

Caper," ABC, 1962; "Combat!: Mountain Man," ABC, 1964; "Grindl: Grindl, Girl Wac," NBC, 1964; "Temple Houston: The Gun That Swept the West," NBC, 1964; "Mickey: The Big Jump," ABC, 1964; "The Outer Limits: The Chameleon," ABC, 1964; "Get Smart: School Days," NBC, 1965; "Mr. Ed: Ed Breaks the Hip Code," CBS, 1965; "Branded: Fill No Glass for Me," NBC, 1965; "Combat!: A Child's Game," ABC, 1966; "Mr. Terrific: Harley and the Killer," CBS, 1967; "Get Smart: Pheasant Under Glass," CBS, 1969; "E/R: Say It Ain't So," CBS, 1984.

BRANDON, MICHAEL
b. Brooklyn, NY. Handsome actor who played Yank-cop-in-London James Dempsey on "Dempsey & Makepeace."
AS A REGULAR: "Emerald Point NAS," CBS, 1983-84; "Dempsey & Makepeace," SYN, 1985.
AND: "Man in the Middle," CBS, 1972; "Love, American Style: Love and the Secret Habit," ABC, 1972; "Love Story: Love Came Laughing," NBC, 1973; "Medical Center: Web of Intrigue," CBS, 1974; "Police Story: A Community of Victims," NBC, 1975; "St. Elsewhere: Aids and Comfort," NBC, 1983.
TV MOVIES AND MINISERIES: "The Impatient Heart," NBC, 1971; "The Strangers in 7A," CBS, 1972; "The Third Girl From the Left," ABC, 1973; "Hitchhike," ABC, 1974; "The Red Badge of Courage," NBC, 1974; "Queen of the Stardust Ballroom," CBS, 1975; "Cage Without a Key," ABC, 1975; "James Dean," NBC, 1976; "Scott Free," NBC, 1976; "A Vacation in Hell," ABC, 1979; "A Perfect Match," CBS, 1980; "Between Two Brothers," CBS, 1982; "Deadly Messages," ABC, 1985; "ABC Family Classic: Rock 'N' Roll Mom," ABC, 1989.

BRANDS, X
b. Jay X Brands, Kansas City, MO, July 24, 1927. Caucasian actor who almost always played Indians, including Pahoo-Ka-Ta-Wah, sidekick of Yancy Derringer (Jock Mahoney).
AS A REGULAR: "Yancy Derringer," CBS, 1958-59.
AND: "The Adventures of Rin Tin Tin: Return of Rin Tin Tin," ABC, 1956; "Sgt. Preston of the Yukon: Lost River Roundup," CBS, 1957; "The Adventures of Rin Tin Tin: The Invaders," ABC, 1957; "The Adventures of Rin Tin Tin: Brave Bow," ABC, 1958; "Tales of Wells Fargo: The Trading Post," NBC, 1960; "Bat Masterson: Masterson's Arcadia Club," NBC, 1960; "The Tall Man: Rovin' Gambler," NBC, 1961; "The Life and Legend of Wyatt Earp: Wyatt Takes the Primrose Path," ABC, 1961; "Rawhide: Incident in the Middle of Nowhere," CBS, 1961;

"Cheyenne: Massacre at Gunsight Pass," ABC, 1961; "Laramie: The Day of the Savage," NBC, 1962; "Bonanza: The Far, Far Better Thing," NBC, 1965; "Laredo: Yahoo," NBC, 1965; "Gunsmoke: Buffalo Man," CBS, 1968; "Gunsmoke: Hawk," CBS, 1969; "The FBI: The Doll Courier," ABC, 1969; "Gunsmoke: Snow Train," CBS, 1970; "The FBI: The Replacement," ABC, 1971.

BRANNUM, HUGH "LUMPY"
b. Sandwich, IL, 1910; d. 1987. Mr. Green Jeans.
AS A REGULAR: "Captain Kangaroo," CBS, 1955-84.

BRASSELLE, KEEFE
b. John Brasselli, Elyria, OH, February 7, 1923; d. 1981. Charmless singer and comic who somehow sold CBS brass on his talent in the mid-1960s.
AS A REGULAR: "Keep It in the Family," ABC, 1957; "Be Our Guest," CBS, 1960; "The Keefe Brasselle Show," CBS, 1963.
AND: "Ford Theatre: Shadow of Truth," NBC, 1954; "Rheingold Theatre: A Matter of Courage," NBC, 1955; "Lux Video Theatre: The Eyes of Father Tomasino," NBC, 1955; "Science Fiction Theatre: Postcard From Barcelona," SYN, 1955; "Ford Theatre: Never Lend Money to a Woman," NBC, 1956; "Club 60," NBC, 1957; "Celebrity Playhouse: I Never Belived in Miracles," SYN, 1957; "The Loretta Young Show: Conflict," NBC, 1958; "The Phil Silvers Show: Bilko vs. Covington," CBS, 1958; "The Red Skelton Show: Clem in Miami Beach," CBS, 1959; "The David Niven Show: Good Deed," NBC, 1959; "Concentration," NBC, 1959; "The Ed Sullivan Show," CBS, 1959; "Pantomime Quiz," ABC, 1959; "The Red Skelton Show," CBS, 1960; "U.S. Steel Hour: The Go-Between," CBS, 1962; "Variety Gardens," CBS, 1962; "The Young Set," ABC, 1965; "Adam 12: Night Watch," NBC, 1973.
AS PRODUCER: "The Baileys of Balboa," CBS, 1964-65; "The Cara Williams Show," CBS, 1964-65; "The Reporter," CBS, 1964.
* When Brasselle sold three shows to CBS in 1964 without the benefit of pilot episodes, tongues wagged. Brasselle had close personal ties to controversial CBS president James Aubrey, who was dumped in 1965, partly as a result of the uproar. And the shows were awful—even worse, they were unsuccessful.

BRAUN, BOB
b. Ludlow, KY, April 20, 1929. Cincinnati TV personality who had his own talk show for decades; his schtick in the fifties was lip-synching to records and his schtick in the eighties is doing commercials to sell adjustable beds and the like.
AS A REGULAR: "The Dotty Mack Show," DUM, 1953; ABC, 1953-56; "ValueTelevision," SYN, 1987.

BRAVERMAN, BART
b. Los Angeles, CA, February 1, 1946. Actor who played Bobby "Binzer" Borso on "Vega$."
AS A REGULAR: "Vega$," ABC, 1978-81; "The New Odd Couple," ABC, 1982-83.
AND: "Columbo: A Case of Immunity," NBC, 1975; "M*A*S*H: Dear Sigmund," CBS, 1976; "Murder, She Wrote: Birds of a Feather," CBS, 1984; "Riptide: Be True to Your School," NBC, 1984; "Baywatch: Heat Wave," NBC, 1989; "Freddy's Nightmares: Silence Is Golden," SYN, 1989.
TV MOVIES AND MINISERIES: "Prince of Bel Air," ABC, 1986; "A Very Brady Christmas," CBS, 1988.

BRAY, ROBERT
b. Kalispell, MT, October 23, 1917; d. 1983. Generic actor who played ranger Corey Stuart, master of "Lassie."
AS A REGULAR: "Stagecoach West," ABC, 1960-61; "Lassie," CBS, 1964-69.
AND: "Frontier: The Hanging at Thunder Butte Creek," NBC, 1956; "Cheyenne: Noose at Noon," ABC, 1958; "Kraft Mystery Theatre: 87th Precinct," NBC, 1958; "Maverick: The Spanish Dancer," ABC, 1959; "The Man From Blackhawk: The Trouble with Tolliver," ABC, 1959; "Riverboat: Three Graves," NBC, 1960; "Alfred Hitchcock Presents: Not the Running Type," CBS, 1960; "The Overland Trail: Fire in the Hole," NBC, 1960; "Laramie: The Protectors," NBC, 1960; "The Loretta Young Show: The Unwanted," NBC, 1960; "Alfred Hitchcock Presents: Letter of Credit," CBS, 1960; "Here's Hollywood," NBC, 1961; "Alfred Hitchcock Presents: A Jury of Her Peers," NBC, 1961; "Laramie: The Dynamiters," NBC, 1962; "Gunsmoke: Quint's Indian," CBS, 1963; "Laramie: The Dispossessed," NBC, 1963; "The Twilight Zone: The Seventh Is Made Up of Phantoms," CBS, 1963.

BRAY, THOM
b. Camden, NJ. Tall, thin actor who played the nerdy Murray "Boz" Bozinsky on "Riptide."
AS A REGULAR: "Breaking Away," ABC, 1980-81; "Riptide," NBC, 1984-86; "Harry," ABC, 1987.
AND: "Lou Grant: Hometown," CBS, 1981; "Remington Steele: Sign, Steeled and Delivered," NBC, 1982; "Quincy: Cry for Help," NBC, 1983; "Murder, She Wrote: Night of the Headless Horseman," CBS, 1986; "The Love Boat: The Prodigy," ABC, 1986.

TV MOVIES AND MINISERIES: "Last of the Great Survivors," CBS, 1984; "Lady Mobster," ABC, 1988.

BRAZZI, ROSSANO
b. Bologna, Italy, September 18, 1916. Actor-singer specializing in continental types.
AS A REGULAR: "Harold Robbins' The Survivors," ABC, 1969-70.
AND: "Rheingold Theatre: Big Nick," NBC, 1955; "Dinah Shore Chevy Show," NBC, 1957; "People Are Funny," NBC, 1958; "Dinah Shore Chevy Show," NBC, 1960; "The du Pont Show with June Allyson: Slip of the Tongue," CBS, 1960; "Here's Hollywood," NBC, 1960; "The Du Pont Show with June Allyson: Our Man in Rome," CBS, 1961; "Run for Your Life: Keep My Share of the World," NBC, 1966; "The Mike Douglas Show," SYN, 1967; "The Name of the Game: The Skin Game," NBC, 1970; "Madigan: The Naples Beat," NBC, 1973; "Police Woman: The Young and the Fair," NBC, 1978; "The Love Boat: The Gigolo," ABC, 1982.
TV MOVIES AND MINISERIES: "Honeymoon with a Stranger," ABC, 1969; "A Time for Miracles," ABC, 1980; "Christopher Columbus," CBS, 1985.

BRECK, PETER
b. Rochester, NY, 1929. Brawny actor who played Nick Barkley on "The Big Valley."
AS A REGULAR: "Black Saddle," NBC, 1959; ABC, 1959-60; "The Big Valley," ABC, 1965-69; "The Secret Empire," NBC, 1979.
AND: "Restless Gun: Take Me Home," NBC, 1958; "Dick Powell's Zane Grey Theatre: Showdown at Bitter Creek," CBS, 1958; "77 Sunset Strip: Lovely Lady, Pity Me," ABC, 1958; "Have Gun, Will Travel: The Teacher," CBS, 1958; "Have Gun, Will Travel: The Protege," CBS, 1958; "Cheyenne: Man From Medora," ABC, 1960; "Maverick: Destination Devil's Flat," ABC, 1960; "Hawaiian Eye: Baker's Half Dozen," ABC, 1960; "The Roaring Twenties: Big-Town Blues," ABC, 1961; "SurfSide 6: Thieves Among Honor," ABC, 1961; "77 Sunset Strip: Face in the Window," ABC, 1961; "Maverick: The Maverick Report," ABC, 1962; "Maverick: Marshal Maverick," ABC, 1962; "SurfSide 6: Portrait of Nicole," ABC, 1962; "Cheyenne: Indian Gold," ABC, 1962; "Cheyenne: Dark Decision," ABC, 1962; "77 Sunset Strip: Wolf! Cried the Blonde," ABC, 1962; "Perry Mason: The Case of the Bluffing Blast," CBS, 1963; "Mr. Novak: A Feeling for Friday," NBC, 1963; "The Outer Limits: O.B.I.T.," ABC, 1963; "Bonanza: The Cheating Game," NBC, 1964; "The Virginian: Rope of Lies," NBC, 1964; "Alias Smith and Jones: The Great Shell Game," ABC, 1972; "Mission: Impossible: Crack-Up," CBS, 1972; "The Fall Guy: King of the Cowboys," ABC, 1984.

TV MOVIES AND MINISERIES: "Black Beauty," NBC, 1978.

BREEDING, LARRY
b. Winchester, IL, September 28, 1946; d. 1982. Slight actor, usually in comic roles.
AS A REGULAR: "Who's Watching the Kids?," NBC, 1978; "The Last Resort," CBS, 1979-80.
AND: "Alice: My Fair Vera," CBS, 1979; "The Love Boat: The Caller," ABC, 1980; "The Love Boat: Clothes Make the Girl," ABC, 1981; "Lou Grant: Friends," CBS, 1981.
TV MOVIES AND MINISERIES: "The Love Tapes," ABC, 1980.

BRENDEL, EL
b. Elmer G. Brendel, Philadelphia, PA, March 25, 1890; d. 1964. Comedian who used a Swedish dialect. Constantly.
AS A GUEST: "Cowboy G-Men: Sidewinder," SYN, 1952; "The People's Choice: Mandy's Male Animal," NBC, 1956; "The Bob Cummings Show: Bob Clahses with His Landlady," NBC, 1957; "The Adventures of Rin Tin Tin: Swedish Cook," ABC, 1957; "McKeever and the Colonel: The Cookie Crumbles," NBC, 1962.

BRENNAN, EILEEN
b. Los Angeles, CA, September 3, 1937. Actress usually in comic roles; she won an Emmy and an Oscar as mean Captain Doreen Lewis in the movie and TV versions of "Private Benjamin."
AS A REGULAR: "Rowan & Martin's Laugh-In," NBC, 1968; "13 Queens Boulevard," ABC, 1979; "A New Kind of Family," ABC, 1979-80; "Private Benjamin," CBS, 1981-83; "Off the Rack," ABC, 1985.
AND: "The Ed Sullivan Show," CBS, 1960; "Music for a Summer Night: Theatre Under the Stars," ABC, 1960; "All in the Family: The Elevator Story," CBS, 1972; "Love, American Style: Love and the Lucky Couple," ABC, 1972; "Dinah!," SYN, 1977; "Taxi: Thy Boss's Wife," ABC, 1981; "The Love Boat: Dutch Treat," ABC, 1984; "Newhart: Draw Partner," CBS, 1988; "Murder, She Wrote: Old Habits Die Hard," CBS, 1987; "CBS Summer Playhouse: Off Duty," CBS, 1988.
TV MOVIES AND MINISERIES: "Playmates," ABC, 1972; "The Blue Knight," CBS, 1973; "My Father's House," NBC, 1975; "The Night That Panicked America," ABC, 1975; "The Death of Richie," NBC, 1977; "Black Beauty," NBC, 1978; "When She Was Bad," ABC, 1979; "My Old Man," CBS, 1979; "Blood Vows: The Story of a Mafia Wife," NBC, 1987.
* Emmies: 1981.

BRENNAN, WALTER
b. Swampscott, MA, July 25, 1894; d. 1974. Oscar-winning actor who starred in dozens of

films ("Meet John Doe," "Rio Bravo") before making a mint on TV as Grandpappy Amos McCoy on one of the ABC network's first major hits.
AS A REGULAR: "The Real McCoys," ABC, 1957-62; CBS, 1962-63; "The Tycoon," ABC, 1964-65; "The Guns of Will Sonnett," ABC, 1967-69; "To Rome with Love," CBS, 1970-71.
AND: "Schlitz Playhouse of Stars: Lucky Thirteen," CBS, 1953; "Light's Diamond Jubilee: The Leader of the People," ABC, CBS, NBC, 1954; "Schlitz Playhouse of Stars: Mr. Ears," CBS, 1955; "Screen Directors Playhouse: The Brush Roper," NBC, 1955; "Schlitz Playhouse of Stars: The Happy Sun," CBS, 1956; "Ethel Barrymore Theatre: The Gentle Years," SYN, 1956; "Du Pont Theatre: Woman's Work," ABC, 1956; "Dick Powell's Zane Grey Theatre: Vengeance Canyon," CBS, 1956; "Ford Theatre: Duffy's Man," ABC, 1956; "The Ford Show," NBC, 1957; "Dick Powell's Zane Grey Theatre: Ride a Lonely Trail," CBS, 1957; "Have Gun, Will Travel: Show of Force," CBS, 1957; "The Ford Show," NBC, 1958; "Christophers: George Washington's Difficulties," SYN, 1958; "I've Got a Secret," CBS, 1959; "Perry Como's Kraft Music Hall," NBC, 1959; "The Chevy Show: County Fair USA," NBC, 1960; "A Date with Debbie," ABC, 1960; "The Chevy Show," NBC, 1961; "What's This Song?," NBC, 1965; "The Glen Campbell Goodtime Hour," CBS, 1970; "Jimmy Durante Presents the Lennon Sisters Hour," ABC, 1970; "Red," NBC, 1970; "Alias Smith and Jones: The Day They Hanged Kid Curry," ABC, 1971; "Alias Smith and Jones: Twenty-One Days to Tenstrike," ABC, 1972; "Alias Smith and Jones: Don't Get Mad, Get Even," ABC, 1972.
TV MOVIES AND MINISERIES: "The Over-the-Hill Gang," ABC, 1969; "The Young Country," ABC, 1970; "The Over-the-Hill Gang Rides Again," ABC, 1970; "Two for the Money," ABC, 1972; "Home for the Holidays," ABC, 1972.

BRENNER, DAVID
b. Philadelphia, PA. Lean stand-up comic.
AS A REGULAR: "Nightlife," SYN, 1986-87.
AND: "The Golddiggers," SYN, 1971; "The Tonight Show Starring Johnny Carson," NBC, 1973; "The Merv Griffin Show," SYN, 1974; "The Mike Douglas Show," SYN, 1974; "The Mike Douglas Show," SYN, 1975; "Hollywood Squares," NBC, 1976; "The Pat Sajak Show," CBS, 1989; "The Tonight Show Starring Johnny Carson," NBC, 1989.

BRENT, GEORGE
b. Dublin, Ireland, March 15, 1904; d. 1979. Mustachioed matinee idol of thirties and forties films ("Dark Victory," "The Great Lie") who

did a little TV; he played a globe-trotting reporter on his only series.
AS A REGULAR: "Wire Service," ABC, 1956-57.
AND: "Ford Theatre: Double Exposure," NBC, 1953; "Schlitz Playhouse of Stars: Medicine Woman," CBS, 1953; "Mirror Theatre: Key in the Lock," CBS, 1953; "Ford Theatre: Unbroken Promise," NBC, 1954; "Fireside Theatre: The Indiscreet Mrs. Jarvis," NBC, 1955; "Gloria Swanson Theatre: A Fond Farewell," SYN, 1955; "Fireside Theatre: Return in Triumph," NBC, 1955; "Fireside Theatre: It's Easy to Get Ahead," NBC, 1955; "Stage 7: The Magic Hat," CBS, 1955; "Studio 57: Diagnosis of a Selfish Lady," SYN, 1955; "Studio 57: Death Dream," SYN, 1955; "Science Fiction Theatre: The Long Day," SYN, 1955; "Crossroads: The Inner Light," ABC, 1956; "Crossroads: The Kid Had a Gun," ABC, 1956; "Rawhide: Incident of the Chubasco," CBS, 1959; "Chevy Mystery Show: I Know What I'd Have Done," NBC, 1960.

BREWER, TERESA
b. Toledo, OH, May 7, 1931. Tiny fifties singer who belted her songs.
AS A REGULAR: "Summertime USA," CBS, 1953; "Perry Presents," NBC, 1959.
AND: "The Arthur Murray Show," CBS, 1956; "The Ed Sullivan Show," CBS, 1956; "The Perry Como Show," NBC, 1956; "Arthur Godfrey and His Friends," CBS, 1957; "The Perry Como Show," NBC, 1957; "The Jackie Gleason Show," CBS, 1957; "The Ed Sullivan Show," CBS, 1957; "The Big Record," CBS, 1957; "The Perry Como Show," NBC, 1958; "The Dick Clark Saturday Night Beechnut Show," ABC, 1958; "Pat Boone Chevy Showroom," NBC, 1958; "The Ford Show," NBC, 1958; "The Ed Sullivan Show," CBS, 1958; "Patti Page Olds Show," ABC, 1958; "The Ed Sullivan Show," CBS, 1959; "Patti Page Olds Show," ABC, 1959; "Pat Boone Chevy Showroom," ABC, 1959; "The Perry Como Show," NBC, 1959; "The Ed Sullivan Show," CBS, 1959; "Steve Allen Plymouth Show," NBC, 1959; "The Ed Sullivan Show," CBS, 1960; "Celebrity Talent Scouts," CBS, 1960; "The Ed Sullivan Show," CBS, 1961; "The Tonight Show Starring Johnny Carson," NBC, 1962; "Jackie Gleason and His American Scene Magazine," CBS, 1962; "To Tell the Truth," CBS, 1963; "The Merv Griffin Show," SYN, 1973; "Dinah!," SYN, 1975.

BREWSTER, DIANE
b. Kansas City, KS, 1931. Sexy starlet of the fifties and sixties; she played con artist Samantha Crawford, who fleeced the Maverick brothers (James Garner and Jack Kelly) more than once—she also played Beaver Cleaver's first teacher, Miss Canfield.

AS A REGULAR: "The Ina Ray Hutton Show," NBC, 1956; "Maverick," ABC, 1957-59; "Leave It to Beaver," CBS, 1957-58; "The Islanders," ABC, 1960-61.

AND: "Warner Bros. Presents Cheyenne: Dark Rider," ABC, 1956; "Dick Powell's Zane Grey Theatre: Time of Decision," CBS, 1957; "Studio 57: It's a Small World," SYN, 1957; "Wire Service: Death at Twin Pines," ABC, 1957; "Wagon Train: The Honorable Don Charlie Story," NBC, 1958; "Schlitz Playhouse of Stars: The Lonely Wizard," CBS, 1958; "Restless Gun: The Whip," NBC, 1958; "Schlitz Playhouse of Stars: The Town That Slept with the Lights On," CBS, 1958; "Studio 57: Who's Been Sitting in My Chair?," SYN, 1958; "Death Valley Days: Faro Bill's Layout," SYN, 1959; "Cimarron City: Runaway Train," NBC, 1959; "Wanted Dead or Alive: Double Fee," CBS, 1959; "Wagon Train: The Lita Foldaire Story," NBC, 1960; "Dick Powell's Zane Grey Theatre: A Man to Look Up To," CBS, 1960; "Best of the Post: I'm No Hero," SYN, 1960; "The Rifleman: Jealous Man," ABC, 1962; "Cheyenne: Dark Decision," ABC, 1962; "77 Sunset Strip: The Dark Wood," ABC, 1962; "The Dakotas: Fargo," ABC, 1963; "Arrest and Trial: Signals of an Ancient Flame," ABC, 1964; "77 Sunset Strip: Dead as in Dude," ABC, 1964; "Kentucky Jones: Pilot," NBC, 1964; "Ironside: Force of Arms," NBC, 1968.

* In addition to appearing on "Leave It to Beaver," Brewster had a role in the show's pilot film, "It's a Small World"—but not as Miss Canfield.

BRIAN, DAVID

b. New York City, NY, August 5, 1914. Actor in stern roles, including the incorruptable Mr. District Attorney.

AS A REGULAR: "Mr. District Attorney," SYN, 1954; "The Immortal," ABC, 1970-71.

AND: "Schlitz Playhouse of Stars: 19 Rue Marie," CBS, 1953; "Mirror Theatre: Flight From Home," CBS, 1953; "G.E. Theatre: That Other Sunlight," CBS, 1954; "Ford Theatre: Taming of the Shrewd," NBC, 1954; "Crossroads: Timber-land Preacher," ABC, 1956; "Celebrity Play-house: The Twelve-Year Secret," SYN, 1957; "Crossroads: The Wreath," ABC, 1957; "G.E. Theatre: Bold Loser," CBS, 1958; "Johnson's Wax Theatre: Strange Defense," CBS, 1958; "Bat Masterson: The Conspiracy," NBC, 1959; "Alcoa Theatre: Shadow of Evil," NBC, 1959; "Rawhide: Incident at Jacob's Well," CBS, 1960; "The Untouchables: The St. Louis Story," ABC, 1960; "Westinghouse Desilu Playhouse: Murder Is a Private Affair," CBS, 1960; "G.E. Theatre: Labor of Love," CBS, 1961; "The Untouchables: Testi-mony of Evil," ABC, 1961; "Rawhide: Incident of the Painted Lady," CBS, 1961; "Cain's Hundred: Degrees of Guilt," NBC, 1961;

"Target: The Corruptors: One for the Road," ABC, 1962; "Laramie: Protective Custody," NBC, 1963; "The Dakotas: Fargo," ABC, 1963; "Death Valley Days: The Peacemaker," SYN, 1963; "Kraft Suspense Theatre: Who Is Jennifer?," NBC, 1964; "Daniel Boone: The Choosing," NBC, 1964; "Profiles in Courage: Judge Benjamin Barr Lindsey," NBC, 1965; "Laredo: Three's Company," NBC, 1965; "I Dream of Jeannie: The Yacht Murder Case," NBC, 1965; "Honey West: The Perfect Un-Crime," ABC, 1966; "Branded: Call to Glory," NBC, 1966; "Please Don't Eat the Daisies: A-Hunting We Will Go," NBC, 1966; "The Iron Horse: The Silver Bullet," ABC, 1967; "Love on a Rooftop: Going Home to Daughter," ABC, 1967; "Hondo: Hondo and the Ghost of Ed Dow," ABC, 1967; "Star Trek: Patterns of Force," NBC, 1968; "Cimarron Strip: The Greeners," CBS, 1968; "Mannix: Blackout," CBS, 1968; "Gunsmoke: Lobo," CBS, 1968; "The Name of the Game: Keep the Doctor Away," NBC, 1969; "The Name of the Game: The Time is Now," NBC, 1970; "Gunsmoke: McCabe," CBS, 1970; "O'Hara, U.S. Treasury: Operation: Spread," CBS, 1971; "Mission: Impossible: Movie," CBS, 1972; "Police Story: Death on Credit," NBC, 1973; "Hec Ramsey: The Mystery of the Yellow Rose," NBC, 1973; "Gunsmoke: Thirty a Month and Found," CBS, 1974; "Archer: Shades of Blue," NBC, 1975.

BRICKELL, BETH

b. Camden, AR, 1941. Actress who played Ellen Wedloe, wife of Tom (Dennis Weaver) and mother of Mark (Clint Howard), who was the master of the 650-pound black bear "Gentle Ben."

AS A REGULAR: "Gentle Ben," CBS, 1967-69.

AND: "The Man From UNCLE: The Suburbia Affair," NBC, 1967; "Love, American Style: Love and the Safely Married Man," ABC, 1970; "Marcus Welby, M.D.: The Worth of a Man," ABC, 1970; "Alias Smith and Jones: The Wrong Train to Brimstone," ABC, 1971; "Hawaii Five-O: Good Night Baby, Time to Die," CBS, 1972; "Gunsmoke: The Widow and the Rogue," CBS, 1973; "Ironside: The Over-the-Hill Blues," NBC, 1974; "Three for the Road: Adventure in Los Angeles," CBS, 1975; "Matt Helm: The Deadly Breed," ABC, 1975.

TV MOVIES AND MINISERIES: "San Francisco International," NBC, 1970; "The Great Man's Whiskers," NBC, 1973; "Brock's Last Case," NBC, 1973.

BRIDGES, BEAU

b. Lloyd Vernet Bridges III, Los Angeles, CA, December 9, 1941. Son of Lloyd and brother of Jeff; he paid his dues in TV and came back to appear in several above-average TV movies and miniseries.

AS A REGULAR: "My Three Sons," ABC, 1960-61; "Ensign O'Toole," NBC, 1962-63; "United States," NBC, 1980.

AND: "Dick Powell's Zane Grey Theatre: Image of a Drawn Sword," CBS, 1961; "The Real McCoys: The Rich Boy," ABC, 1962; "The Lloyd Bridges Show: A Pair of Boots," CBS, 1962; "The Lloyd Bridges Show: Gentleman in Blue," CBS, 1962; "The Lloyd Bridges Show: The Skippy Mannox Story," CBS, 1963; "Ben Casey: The Echo of a Silent Cheer," ABC, 1963; "Rawhide: Incident at Paradise," CBS, 1963; "Mr. Novak: Pay the Two Dollars," NBC, 1963; "Mr. Novak: Sparrow on the Wire," NBC, 1964; "My Three Sons: Marriage by Proxy," ABC, 1964; "The Eleventh Hour: Cannibal Plants, They Eat You Alive," NBC, 1964; "Dr. Kildare: The Child Between," NBC, 1964; "Combat: The Short Day of Private Putnam," ABC, 1964; "My Three Sons: Mike Wears the Pants," ABC, 1964; "Mr. Novak: Honor-and All That," NBC, 1965; "The FBI: An Elephant Is Like a Rope," ABC, 1965; "Twelve O'Clock High: Then Came the Mighty Hunter," ABC, 1965; "The FBI: An Elephant Is Like a Rope," ABC, 1965; "The Fugitive: Stroke of Genius," ABC, 1966; "The Loner: The Mourners for Johnny Sharp," CBS, 1966; "Branded: Nice Day for a Hanging," NBC, 1966; "Gunsmoke: Jason," CBS, 1966; "Vacation Playhouse: Frank Merriwell," CBS, 1966; "Bonanza: Justice," NBC, 1967; "The Fugitive: The Other Side of the Coin," ABC, 1967; "Walt Disney's Wonderful World of Color: 'Atta Girl, Kelly," NBC, 1967; "Cimarron Strip: The Legend of Jud Starr," CBS, 1967; "Insight: The Last of My Brothers," SYN, 1969; "Robert Young and the Family," CBS, 1973; "ABC Afterschool Special: My Dad Lives in a Downtown Hotel," ABC, 1973; "Benjamin Franklin: The Whirlwind," CBS, 1974; "Dinah!," SYN, 1980; "Saturday Night Live," NBC, 1983; "Amazing Stories: Vanessa in the Garden," NBC, 1985; "Late Night with David Letterman," NBC, 1989.

TV MOVIES AND MINISERIES: "The Man Without a Country," ABC, 1973; "The Stranger Who Looks Like Me," ABC, 1974; "Medical Story," NBC, 1975; "The Child-Stealer," ABC, 1979; "The Kid From Nowhere," NBC, 1982; "Hallmark Hall of Fame: Witness for the Prosecution," CBS, 1982; "The Red-Light Sting," CBS, 1984; "Space," CBS, 1985; "Outrage!," CBS, 1986; "Everybody's Baby: The Rescue of Jessica McClure," ABC, 1989; "Three of a Kind," ABC, 1989.

BRIDGES, JEFF

b. Los Angeles, CA, December 4, 1949. Son of Lloyd, and an accomplished film actor ("The Last Picture Show," "The Fabulous Baker Boys") in his own right.

AS A GUEST: "The Lloyd Bridges Show: Gentleman in Blue," CBS, 1962; "The Lloyd Bridges Show: To Walk with the Stars," CBS, 1963; "The FBI: Boomerang," ABC, 1969; "The Most Deadly Game: Nightbirds," ABC, 1970; "Saturday Night Live," NBC, 1983; "Faerie Tale Theatre: Rapunzel," SHO, 1983.

TV MOVIES AND MINISERIES: "Silent Night, Lonely Night," NBC, 1969; "In Search of America," ABC, 1971.

BRIDGES, LLOYD

b. Petaluma, CA, January 15, 1913. Solid actor who made his TV mark as skindiving Mike Nelson on "Sea Hunt."

AS A REGULAR: "Sea Hunt," SYN, 1958-61; "The Lloyd Bridges Show," CBS, 1962-63; "The Loner," CBS, 1965-66; "San Francisco Internationl Airport," NBC, 1970-71; "Joe Forrester," NBC, 1975-76; "Paper Dolls," ABC, 1984; "Capital News," ABC, 1990.

AND: "Bigelow-Sanford Theatre: A Man's First Debt," SYN, 1951; "Robert Montgomery Presents: Rise Up and Walk," NBC, 1952; "Studio One: International Incident," CBS, 1952; "Stage 7: Prairie Dog Court," CBS, 1955; "Shower of Stars: The Dark Fleece," CBS, 1955; "Climax!: Edge of Terror," CBS, 1955; "Front Row Center: The Ainsley Case," CBS, 1956; "Dick Powell's Zane Grey Theatre: Wire," CBS, 1956; "Alcoa Hour: Tragedy in a Temporary Town," NBC, 1956; "Climax!: The Sound of Silence," CBS, 1956; "Studio 57: The Regula-tors," SYN, 1956; "Climax!: Figures in Clay," CBS, 1956; "Studio One: American Primitive," CBS, 1956; "Playhouse 90: Heritage of Anger," CBS, 1956; "Dick Powell's Zane Grey Theatre: Time of Decision," CBS, 1957; "Alcoa Hour: Ride the Wild Mare," NBC, 1957; "Studio 57: Man on the Outside," SYN, 1957; "U.S. Steel Hour: They Never Forget," CBS, 1957; "Climax!: Disappearance of Amanda Hale," CBS, 1957; "Playhouse 90: Clash by Night," CBS, 1957; "Studio One: First Prize for Murder," CBS, 1957; "The Frank Sinatra Show: A Time to Cry," ABC, 1958; "The Steve Allen Show," NBC, 1958; "The Ford Show," NBC, 1959; "Westinghouse Desilu Playhouse: Lepke," CBS, 1959; "I've Got a Secret," CBS, 1960; "Special Tonight: The Valley of Decision," CBS, 1960; "About Faces," ABC, 1960; "Art Linkletter's House Party," CBS, 1960; "Dick Powell's Zane Grey Theatre: Ransom," CBS, 1960; "Here's Hollywood," NBC, 1961; "Marineland Circus," NBC, 1961; "The du Pont Show with June Allyson: Death of the Temple Bay," CBS, 1961; "Dick Powell's Zane Grey Theatre: Image of a Drawn Sword," CBS, 1961; "Dinah Shore Chevy Show," NBC, 1961; "The Dick Powell Show: Who Killed Julie Greer?," NBC, 1961; "Alcoa Premiere: The Fortress," ABC, 1961; "G.E. Theatre: Star Witness," CBS,

1961; "The Ed Sullivan Show," CBS, 1962; "Kraft Suspense Theatre: A Hero for Our Times," NBC, 1963; "The Great Adventure: Wild Bill Hickok-The Legend and the Man," CBS, 1964; "The Eleventh Hour: Cannibal Plants, They Eat You Alive," NBC, 1964; "Bob Hope Chrysler Theatre: Exit From a Plane in Flight," NBC, 1965; "Password," CBS, 1966; "Mission: Impossible: Fakeout," CBS, 1966; "A Case of Libel," ABC, 1968; "CBS Playhouse: The People Next Door," CBS, 1968; "Here's Lucy: Lucy's Big Break," CBS, 1972; "Police Story: Wolf," NBC, 1974; "Police Story: The Return of Joe Forrester," NBC, 1974; "Benjamin Franklin: The Whirlwind," CBS, 1974; "Hollywood Squares," SYN, 1975; "The Love Boat: Farnsworth's Fling," ABC, 1982; "Matt Houston: Heritage," ABC, 1983.

TV MOVIES AND MINISERIES: "Lost Flight," ABC, 1969; "Silent Night, Lonely Night," NBC, 1969; "The Silent Gun," ABC, 1969; "The Love War," ABC, 1970; "Do You Take This Stranger?," NBC, 1971; "A Tattered Weh," CBS, 1971; "The Deadly Dream," ABC, 1971; "Haunts of the Very Rich," ABC, 1972; "Trouble Comes to Town," ABC, 1973; "Crime Club," CBS, 1973; "Death Race," ABC, 1973; "Stowaway to the Moon," CBS, 1975; "Roots," ABC, 1977; "The Return of Joe Forrester," NBC, 1975; "The Critical List," NBC, 1978; "Disaster on the Coastliner," ABC, 1979; "East of Eden," ABC, 1981; "Life of the Party: The Story of Beatrice," CBS, 1982; "Grace Kelly," ABC, 1983; "George Washington," CBS, 1984; "North and South, Book II," ABC, 1986; "Dress Gray," NBC, 1986; "Marked for Murder," NBC, 1988; "Cross of Fire," NBC, 1989.

* In 1956, during the live performance of the anti-lynching drama "Tragedy in a Temporary Town," Bridges got a little carried away. During a fierce speech, he called a crowd of extras "goddamn stinking pigs."

BRIDGES, TODD
b. San Francisco, CA, May 27, 1966. Former child actor who played Willis, brother of Arnold (Gary Coleman) on "Diff'rent Strokes".
AS A REGULAR: "Fish," ABC, 1977-78; "Diff'rent Strokes," NBC, 1978-85; ABC, 1985-86.
AND: "Barney Miller: The Hero," ABC, 1975; "Little House on the Prairie: To Wisdom of Solomon," NBC, 1977; "The Love Boat: Mike and Ike," ABC, 1978; "The Return of Mod Squad," ABC, 1979; "Here's Boomer: The Stableboy," NBC, 1980;
TV MOVIES AND MINISERIES: "Roots," ABC, 1977; "High School USA," NBC, 1983.

BRIMLEY, WILFORD
b. Salt Lake City, UT, September 27, 1934.

Walrus-mustached actor and TV oatmeal pitchman who specializes in playing lovable old codgers, including Gus Witherspoon of "Our House"; funny thing is, he isn't that old.
AS A REGULAR: "Our House," NBC, 1986-88.
AND: "The Waltons: The Ghost Story," CBS, 1974.
TV MOVIES AND MINISERIES: "The Wild Wild West Revisited," CBS, 1979; "Amber Waves," ABC, 1980; "Thompson's Last Run," CBS, 1986.

BRINKLEY, DAVID
b. Wilmington, NC, July 10, 1920. Erudite, witty news anchor and writer.
AS A REGULAR: "The Huntley-Brinkley Report," NBC, 1956-71; "David Brinkley's Journal," NBC, 1961-63; "NBC Evening News," 1976-79; "NBC Magazine with David Brinkley," NBC, 1980-81; "This Week with David Brinkley," ABC, 1981- .

BRISEBOIS, DANIELLE
b. Brooklyn, NY, June 28, 1969. Former child actress who played Stephanie on "All in the Family" and "Archie Bunker's Place"; she played Mary Frances Sumner for a time on "Knots Landing."
AS A REGULAR: "All in the Family," CBS, 1978-79; "Archie Bunker's Place," CBS, 1979-83; "Knots Landing," CBS, 1983-84.
AND: "The Love Boat: The Reluctant Father," ABC, 1983; "Murder, She Wrote: No Fashionable Way to Die," CBS, 1987.

BRISSETTE, TIFFANY
b. December 26, 1974. Child actress who played Vicki, the disgustingly cute robot on "Small Wonder."
AS A REGULAR: "Small Wonder," SYN, 1985-88.
AND: "Webster: The Uh-Oh Feeling," ABC, 1984; "Webster: Too Much Class," ABC, 1984; "Webster: Strike Up the Band," ABC, 1985.

BRITTANY, MORGAN
b. Suzanne Cupito, Hollywood, CA, December 5, 1951. Former child actress-dancer usually in glossy prime-time soaps; she played Katherine Wentworth on "Dallas."
AS A REGULAR: "Dallas," CBS, 1981-84; "Glitter," ABC, 1984-85.
AS A GUEST: "The Twilight Zone: Nightmare as a Child," CBS, 1960; "The Chevy Show: Ghosts, Goblins and Kids," NBC, 1960; "My Three Sons: Daughter for a Day," ABC, 1962; "The Lloyd Bridges Show: My Child Is Yet a Stranger," CBS, 1962; "The Lloyd Bridges Show: The Wonder of Wanda," CBS, 1963; "The Twilight Zone: Valley of the Shadow,"

CBS, 1963; "The Twilight Zone: Caesar and Me," CBS, 1964; "The Outer Limits: The Inheritors," ABC, 1964; "Special for Women: Child in Danger," ABC, 1964; "My Three Sons: Mary Lou," CBS, 1965; "The Andy Griffith Show: Look, Paw, I'm Dancing," CBS, 1966; "My Three Sons: Melinda," CBS, 1967; "Buck Rogers in the 25th Century: Happy Birthday, Buck," NBC, 1980; "The Fall Guy: Inside, Outside," ABC, 1983; "The Love Boat: Misunderstanding," ABC, 1983; "Hotel: Prisms," ABC, 1984; "The Love Boat: I'll Never Forget What's-Her-Name," ABC, 1984; "The Love Boat: Charmed, I'm Sure," ABC, 1985; "Star Search," SYN, 1985; "Half Nelson: Pilot," ABC, 1985; "Murder, She Wrote: Footnote to Murder," CBS, 1985; "The Love Boat: Gothic Romance," ABC, 1986; "Married with Children: Life's a Beach," FOX, 1988.
TV MOVIES AND MINISERIES: "Samurai," ABC, 1979; "Stunt Seven," CBS, 1979; "In Search of Historic Jesus," NBC, 1981; "Perry Mason: The Case of the Scandalous Scoundrel," NBC, 1987; "LBJ: The Early Years," NBC, 1987.

BRITTON, BARBARA

b. *Long Beach, CA, September 26, 1919; d. 1980.* Actress who playing the crime-solving Pamela North, wife of Jerry North (Richard Denning) on "Mr. and Mrs. North"; she was also the first actress to play Laura Petrie in "Head of the Family," which would be transformed into "The Dick Van Dyke Show."
AS A REGULAR: "Mr. and Mrs. North," CBS, 1952-53; NBC, 1954; "One Life to Live," ABC, 1979.
AND: "Robert Montgomery Presents: Mrs. Mike," NBC, 1950; "Armstrong Circle Theatre: Christopher Beach," NBC, 1950; "Pulitzer Prize Playhouse: Haunted House," ABC, 1951; "Lux Video Theatre: Treasure Trove," CBS, 1951; "Schlitz Playhouse of Stars: Say Hello to Pamela," CBS, 1952; "Robert Montgomery Presents: Til Next We Meet," NBC, 1952; "Climax!: Flight 951," CBS, 1955; "Robert Montgomery Presents: Now or Never," NBC, 1955; "Appointment with Adventure: Five Star Crisis," CBS, 1955; "Robert Montgomery Presents: The Stranger," NBC, 1955; "Ford Theatre: Twelve to Eternity," NBC, 1955; "Ford Theatre: The Fabulous Sycamores," NBC, 1955; "Frontiers of Faith: The Whalebone Locket," NBC, 1959; "The Big Party," CBS, 1959; "New Year's Eve Party," CBS, 1959; "Comedy Spot: Head of the Family," CBS, 1960.

BRITTON, PAMELA

b. *Armilda Jane Britton, Milwaukee, 1923; d. 1974.* Blonde actress who played spacy

landlady Lorelei Brown on "My Favorte Martian."
AS A REGULAR: "Blondie," NBC, 1957; "My Favorite Martian," CBS, 1963-66.
AND: "77 Sunset Strip: Publicity Brat," ABC, 1960; "Peter Gunn: ... Than a Serpent's Tooth," ABC, 1961; "Gunslinger: Golden Circle," CBS, 1961; "Password," CBS, 1965; "The Magician: The Man Who Lost Himself," NBC, 1973.

BRODERICK, JAMES

b. *Charleston, SC, March 7, 1930; d. 1982.* Actor with extensive stage and TV experience who didn't become a star until he played pop Doug Lawrence on "Family"; father of Matthew Broderick.
AS A REGULAR: "Brenner," CBS, 1959, 1964; "As the World Turns," CBS, 1962; "Family," ABC, 1976-80.
AND: "Kraft Television Theatre: The 9th Hour," NBC, 1956; "Kraft Television Theatre: No Warning," NBC, 1957; "Studio One: A Member of the Family," CBS, 1957; "Armstrong Circle Theatre: The Complex Mummy Complex," CBS, 1958; "Look Up and Live," Diary of a Teenager," CBS, 1958; "John Brown's Raid," NBC, 1960; "U.S. Steel Hour: Delayed Honeymoon," CBS, 1961; "The Defenders: Storm at Birch Glen," CBS, 1962; "The Defenders: Blood Country," CBS, 1962; "Armstrong Circle Theatre: Escape to Nowhere," CBS, 1962; "The Twilight Zone: On Thursday We Leave for Home," CBS, 1963; "Hallmark Hall of Fame: Abe Lincoln in Illinois," NBC, 1964; "For the People: ... the killing of one human being ...," CBS, 1965; "The FBI: Anatomy of a Prison Break," ABC, 1966; "The Love Boat: The Remake," ABC, 1980.
TV MOVIES AND MINISERIES: "Roots: The Next Generations," ABC, 1979; "The Shadow Box," ABC, 1980.

BRODIE, STEVE

b. *John Stevens, Eldorado, KS, November 25, 1919.* Actor in rugged roles.
AS A REGULAR: "The Life and Legend of Wyatt Earp," ABC, 1959-61; "Everglades," SYN, 1961-62.
AND: "The Adventures of Wild Bill Hickok: A Close Shave for Wild Bill," SYN, 1955; "Science Fiction Theatre: Dead Reckoning," SYN, 1955; "Science Fiction Theatre: The Long Day," SYN, 1955; "Alfred Hitchcock Presents: The Creeper," CBS, 1956; "Schlitz Playhouse of Stars: One Left Over," CBS, 1957; "Crossroads: 9:30 Action," ABC, 1957; "Panic!: Twenty-Six Hours to Sunrise," NBC, 1957; "Undercurrent: Live Bait," CBS, 1957; "Navy Log: American U-Boat III," ABC, 1958; "Alfred Hitchcock Presents: Death Sentence," CBS, 1958; "The Alaskans: Peril at Caribou Crossing," ABC,

1960; "Tightrope!: A Matter of Money," CBS, 1960; "Pony Express: The Branson Brothers," SYN, 1960; "Thriller: The Fatal Impulse," NBC, 1960; "Stagecoach West: The Saga of Jeremy Boone," ABC, 1960; "Tales of Wells Fargo: Fraud," NBC, 1961; "Maverick: Devil's Necklace," ABC, 1961; "The Brothers Brannagan: Love Me, Love My Dog," SYN, 1961; "SurfSide 6: A Matter of Seconds," ABC, 1961; "Cheyenne: The Equalizer," ABC, 1961; "Laramie: The Confederate Express," NBC, 1962; "Rawhide: Incident of the Dogfaces," CBS, 1962; "Wagon Train: The Orly French Story," ABC, 1962; "The Virginian: Run Away Home," NBC, 1963; "Burke's Law: Who Killed Nobody Somehow?," ABC, 1965; "The Beverly Hillbillies: Drysdale's Dog Days," CBS, 1965; "Daktari: Return of the Killer," CBS, 1966; "Gunsmoke: No Tomorrow," CBS, 1971; "Police Woman: Sons," NBC, 1978.

BROGAN, JIMMY
b. Boston, MA. Young comic whom ABC officials pegged as the next Robin Williams; they introduced him on "Happy Days" and then put him in a sitcom as an angel and even brought Williams in to guest star in the first episode, but no dice.
AS A REGULAR: "Out of the Blue," ABC, 1979.
AND: "Happy Days: Chachi Sells His Soul," ABC, 1979.

BROKAW, TOM
b. Yankton, SD, February 6, 1940.
AS A REGULAR: "NBC Weekend News," NBC, 1975-76; "Today," NBC, 1976-82; "NBC Nightly News with Tom Brokaw," NBC, 1982- .

BROLIN, JAMES
b. Los Angeles, CA, July 18, 1940. Handsome actor who played Dr. Steven Kiley on "Marcus Welby, M.D." and Peter McDermott on "Hotel."
AS A REGULAR: "Marcus Welby, M.D.," ABC, 1969-76; "Hotel," ABC, 1983-88; "Reunion," SYN, 1990- .
AND: "Follow the Sun: The Highest Wall," ABC, 1961; "Bus Stop: The Resurrection of Annie Ahern," ABC, 1961; "Follow the Sun: The Longest Crap Game in History," ABC, 1961; "Margie: Madame President," ABC, 1962; "The Patty Duke Show: Patty Meets the Great Outdoors," ABC, 1965; "The Long Hot Summer: Man with Two Faces," ABC, 1966; "Batman: Hot Off the Griddle/The Cat and the Fiddle," ABC, 1966; "The Monroes: Incident of the Hanging Tree," ABC, 1966; "Batman: The Sandman Cometh/The Catwoman Goeth (A Stitch in Time)," ABC, 1966; "The Monroes: Range War,"

ABC, 1966; "Batman: Ring Around the Riddler," ABC, 1967; "The Virginian: Crime Wave in Buffalo Springs," NBC, 1969; "Love, American Style: Love and the Note," ABC, 1971; "Owen Marshall, Counselor at Law: Men Who Care," ABC, 1972; "Hollywood Squares," NBC, 1973; "The Merv Griffin Show," SYN, 1974; "The Sonny Comedy Revue," ABC, 1974; "Owen Marshall, Counselor at Law: I've Promised You a Father," ABC, 1974; "The Mike Douglas Show," SYN, 1977.
TV MOVIES AND MINISERIES: "Marcus Welby, M.D.," ABC, 1969; "Short Walk to Daylight," ABC, 1972; "Class of '63," ABC, 1973; "Trapped," ABC, 1973; "Steel Cowboy," NBC, 1978; "The Ambush Murders," CBS, 1982; "Mae West," ABC, 1982; "Cowboy," CBS, 1983; "Beverly Hills Cowgirl Blues," CBS, 1985; "Deep Dark Secrets," NBC, 1987.
* Emmies: 1970.

BROLIN, JOSH
b. Los Angeles, CA. Son of James, usually in roles which allow him to glower; he plays Wild Bill Hickok on "The Young Riders."
AS A REGULAR: "Private Eye," NBC, 1987-88; "The Young Riders," ABC, 1989- .
AND: "Highway to Heaven: A Match Made in Heaven," NBC, 1985; "21 Jump Street: My Future's So Bright, I Gotta Wear Shades," FOX, 1987.

BROMFIELD, JOHN
b. Farron Bromfield, South Bend, IN, June 11, 1922. Nondescript action hero who played lawman Frank Morgan in a nondescript action series; apparently he liked to dance, which is why he wound up on Arthur Murray's show.
AS A REGULAR: "Sheriff of Cochise (U.S. Marshal)," SYN, 1956-60.
AND: "Arthur Murray Party," NBC, 1959; "This Is Your Life," NBC, 1960; "Arthur Murray Party," NBC, 1960.
* Bromfield was on "This Is Your Life" to salute Toni Lee Scott, a singer who lost her leg in a motocycle accident.

BROMFIELD, VALRI
b. Canada. Comic actress and writer.
AS A REGULAR: "The Bobbie Gentry Show," CBS, 1974; "Angie," ABC, 1979-80; "Best of the West," ABC, 1981-82; "The New Show," NBC, 1984.
AND: "Lily," ABC, 1975; "Head of the Class: The Hot Seat," ABC, 1989; "Head of the Class: Labor Daze," ABC, 1989.
AS PRODUCER-WRITER: "Head of the Class," ABC, 1986- .

BRONSON, CHARLES

b. Charles Buchinsky, Ehrenfield, PA, November 3, 1921. Film and TV actor whose pockmarked face and beady eyes are his fortune.

AS A REGULAR: "Man with a Camera," ABC, 1958-60; "Empire," NBC, 1963; "The Travels of Jaimie McPheeters," ABC, 1963-64.

AND: "The Doctor: Take the Odds," NBC, 1953; "Four Star Playhouse: The Witness," CBS, 1954; "Waterfront: Trestle Point," SYN, 1954; "Public Defender: Cornered," CBS, 1955; "Treasury Men in Action: The Case of the Deadly Dilemma," ABC, 1955; "Stage 7: The Time of Day," CBS, 1955; "Treasury Men in Action: The Case of the Shot in the Dark," ABC, 1955; "Pepsi Cola Playhouse: The Woman in the Mine," ABC, 1955; "Crusader: A Boxing Match," CBS, 1955; "Cavalcade Theatre: Chain of Hearts," ABC, 1955; "Hey, Jeannie!: Jeannie the Policewoman," CBS, 1956; "Telephone Time: She Sette Her Little Foote," CBS, 1956; "The Millionaire: The Story of Jerry Bell," CBS, 1957; "Wire Service: The Avengers," ABC, 1957; "Have Gun, Will Travel: The Outlaw," CBS, 1957; "M Squad: Fight," NBC, 1958; "Sugarfoot: The Bullet and the Cross," ABC, 1958; "Have Gun, Will Travel: The Man Who Wouldn't Talk," CBS, 1958; "Yancy Derringer: Hell and High Water," CBS, 1959; "U.S. Marshal: Pursuit," SYN, 1959; "Playhouse 90: Rank and File," CBS, 1959; "Playhouse 90: The Cruel Day," CBS, 1960; "Laramie: Street of Hate," NBC, 1960; "Hennesey: Hennesey a la Gunn," CBS, 1960; "The Aquanauts: The Cave Divers," CBS, 1960; "Riverboat: Zigzag," NBC, 1960; "G.E. Theatre: Memory in White," CBS, 1961; "Alcoa Presents One Step Beyond: The Last Round," ABC, 1961; "The Islanders: The Generous Politician," ABC, 1961; "G.E. Theatre: Memory in White," CBS, 1961; "The Loretta Young Show: Woodlot," NBC, 1961; "The New Breed: The Valley of the 3 Charlies," ABC, 1961; "Adventures in Paradise: Survival," ABC, 1961; "Alfred Hitchcock Presents: The Woman Who Wanted to Live," NBC, 1962; "The Untouchables: The Death Tree," ABC, 1962; "Have Gun, Will Travel: Brotherhood," CBS, 1962; "Dr. Kildare: Whoever Heard of a Two-Headed Doll?," NBC, 1963; "Bonanza: The Underdog," NBC, 1964; "Combat!: Heritage," ABC, 1965; "Vacation Playhouse: Luke and the Tenderfoot," CBS, 1965; "The Big Valley: Earthquake," ABC, 1965; "The Virginian: The Nobility of Kings," NBC, 1965; "Rawhide: Duel at Daybreak," CBS, 1965; "The FBI: The Animal," ABC, 1966; "The Fugitive: The Judgement," ABC, 1967; "The Virginian: Reckoning," NBC, 1967; "The Mike Douglas Show," SYN, 1976.

TV MOVIES AND MINISERIES: "Raid on Entebbe," NBC, 1977.

BROOKE, HILLARY

b. Beatrice Peterson, Astoria, Queens, NY, September 8, 1914. Actress usually in comic roles; she was a foil to Abbott and Costello and the lady friend of Vern Albright (Charles Farrell), father of "My Little Margie" (Gale Storm).

AS A REGULAR: "My Little Margie," CBS, 1952; NBC, 1952; CBS, 1953; NBC, 1953-55; "The Abbott and Costello Show," CBS, 1952-54.

AND: "Racket Squad: Fair Exchange," CBS, 1952; "Dark Adventure: The Second Mrs. Sands," ABC, 1953; "Four Star Playhouse: The Ladies on His Mind," CBS, 1953; "Twilight Time: That Time in Boston," ABC, 1953; "Four Star Playhouse: Backstage," CBS, 1954; "Pepsi Cola Playhouse: Before the Police Arrive," ABC, 1954; "Cavalcade Theatre: A Man's Home," ABC, 1954; "Public Defender: Jackpot," CBS, 1955; "Fireside Theatre: Luxurious Ladies," NBC, 1955; "Ford Theatre: Cardboard Casanova," NBC, 1955; "The Millionaire: The Story of Vickie Lawson," CBS, 1955; "Crossroads: Vivi Shining Bright," ABC, 1955; "I Love Lucy: The Fox Hunt," CBS, 1956; "Screen Directors Playhouse: The Sword of Villon," NBC, 1956; "West Point: The Right to Choose," CBS, 1956; "Private Secretary: That's No Lady—That's an Agent, CBS, 1957; "Perry Mason: The Case of the Sleepwalker's Niece," CBS, 1957; "Meet McGraw: Kiss of Death," NBC, 1957; "December Bride: The Other Woman," CBS, 1957; "Bob Hope Special," NBC, 1958; "Christophers: You Can Strengthen Education," SYN, 1959; "Yancy Derringer: The Louisiana Dude," CBS, 1959; "Michael Shayne: This Is It, Michael Shayne," NBC, 1960.

BROOKS, ALBERT

b. Albert Einstein, Los Angeles, CA, July 22, 1947. Comic actor-writer-director ("Lost in America") with his own unique style; he hasn't had much of a chance to strut his stuff on TV, but he used to make commercial parodies and short films for "Saturday Night Live." The son of comic "Parkyakarkus" Einstein and brother of Bob Einstein, aka "Super Dave" Osborne.

AS A REGULAR: "Dean Martin Presents," NBC, 1969; "Saturday Night Live," NBC, 1975-76.

AND: "Love, American Style: Love and Operation Model," ABC, 1969; "The Odd Couple: Oscar the Model," ABC, 1970; "The Odd Couple: Felix Is Missing," ABC, 1970; "The Tonight Show Starring Johnny Carson," NBC, 1971; "The Comedians," SYN, 1971; "The Tonight Show Starring Johnny Carson," NBC, 1973; "General Electric All-Star Anniversary," ABC, 1978.

BROOKS, AVERY

b. Evansville, IN. Black actor with a menacing style; he played Hawk, sidekick of private eye

Spenser (Robert Urich) and then got his own series.

AS A REGULAR: "Spenser: For Hire," ABC, 1985-89; "A Man Called Hawk," ABC, 1989.

TV MOVIES AND MINISERIES: "Roots: The Gift," ABC, 1988.

BROOKS, FOSTER

b. Louisville, KY, May 11, 1912. Former deejay whose comic drunk act led to his being dubbed "The Lovable Lush" and made a regular on Bill Cosby's variety show and Dean Martin's celebrity roasts; in these days of M.A.D.D., the act doesn't seem all that funny anymore.

AS A REGULAR: "The New Bill Cosby Show," CBS, 1972-73; "The Dean Martin Show," NBC, 1973-75; "Mork & Mindy," ABC, 1981.

AND: "The Munsters: Happy 100th Anniversary," CBS, 1965; "Bewitched: Disappearing Samantha," ABC, 1966; "The Flying Nun: A Young Man with a Coronet," ABC, 1967; "The Beverly Hillbillies: The Clampetts Fiddle Around," CBS, 1968; "It Takes a Thief: A Case of Red Turnips," ABC, 1968; "The Beverly Hillbillies: The Grun Incident," CBS, 1971; "The Mod Squad: Death of a Nobody," ABC, 1971; "Here's Lucy: Tipsy Through the Tulips," CBS, 1973; "The Mike Douglas Show," SYN, 1974; "The Merv Griffin Show," SYN, 1977; "Police Woman: Ambition," NBC, 1977; "Switch: Legends of the Macunas," CBS, 1977; "The Mike Douglas Show," SYN, 1978; "Quincy: Murder on Ice," NBC, 1983; "Murder, She Wrote: Simon Says, Color Me Dead," CBS, 1987; "The New Mike Hammer: Elegy for a Tramp," CBS, 1987.

* The producers of "Rhoda" asked Brooks to play Carlton, the drunken doorman, but he turned down the role.

BROOKS, GERALDINE

b. Geraldine Stroock, New York City, NY, October 29, 1925; d. 1977. Heavyset actress with a long stage and TV career; in her last series she played Angela Dumpling, loving wife of Joe (James Coco).

AS A REGULAR: "Woman with a Past," CBS, 1954; "Faraday and Company," NBC, 1973-74; "The Dumplings," NBC, 1976.

AND: "Starlight Theatre: Magic Wire," SYN, 1951; "Lights Out: The Chamber of Gloom," NBC, 1951; "Lux Video Theatre: Kelly," NBC, 1952; "Broadway Television Theatre: Seventh Heaven," SYN, 1953; "Armstrong Circle Theatre: The Honor of Littorno," NBC, 1953; "Studio One: A Criminal Design," CBS, 1954; "Appointment with Adventure: When in Rome," CBS, 1955; "Studio One: Manhattan Duet," CBS, 1956; "U.S. Steel Hour: This Day in Fear," CBS, 1959; "Johnny Staccato: The Only Witness," NBC, 1959; "Richard Diamond, Private

Detective: Dead to the World," NBC, 1960; "U.S. Steel Hour: The Charlie and the Kid," CBS, 1960; "Have Gun, Will Travel: Love and a Bad Woman," CBS, 1960; "Naked City: Down the Long Night," ABC, 1960; "U.S. Steel Hour: The Mating Machine," CBS, 1961; "Adventures in Paradise: Who Is Sylvia?," ABC, 1961; "Bonanza: Elizabeth, My Love," NBC, 1961; "Stoney Burke: Death Rides a Pale Horse," ABC, 1963; "Alcoa Premire: Five, Six, Pick Up Sticks," ABC, 1963; "The Dick Powell Show: Colossus," NBC, 1963; "Laramie: The Stranger," NBC, 1963; "Combat!: The Walking Wounded," ABC, 1963; "The Defenders: Everybody Else Is Dead," CBS, 1963; "Kraft Suspense Theatre: The Image Merchants," NBC, 1963; "Kraft Suspense Theatre: A Hero for Our Times," NBC, 1963; "The Fugitive: A Ticket to Alaska," ABC, 1963; "The Greatest Show on Earth: A Black Dress for Gina," ABC, 1963; "The Outer Limits: The Architects of Fear," ABC, 1963; "The Nurses: The Rainbow Ride," CBS, 1964; "Ben Casey: Keep Out of Reach of Adults," ABC, 1964; "The Outer Limits: Cold Hands, Warm Heart," ABC, 1964; "Dr. Kildare: The Elusive Dik-Dik," NBC, 1964; "A Man Called Shenandoah: A Long Way Home," ABC, 1966; "Hawk: Thanks for the Honeymoon," ABC, 1966; "Bonanza: To Bloom for Thee," NBC, 1966; "Get Smart: Kiss of Death," NBC, 1966; "Run for Your Life: The List of Alice McKenna," NBC, 1967; "The Fugitive: Goodbye, My Love," ABC, 1967; "The Danny Thomas Hour: Fame is a Four-Letter Word," NBC, 1967; "My Friend Tony: Encounter," NBC, 1969; "To Rome with Love: The Secret Day," CBS, 1969; "Insight: The Oleander Years," SYN, 1970; "Dan August: Circle of Lies," ABC, 1971; "Marcus Welby, M.D.: Contract," ABC, 1971; "You Are There: The Mystery of Amelia Earhart," CBS, 1971; "Ironside: Hey, Buddy, Can You Spare a Life?," NBC, 1972; "The Streets of San Francisco: The Bullet," ABC, 1973; "Cannon: Prisoners," CBS, 1973; "Barnaby Jones: The Murdering Class," CBS, 1973; "Barnaby Jones: Sunday: Doomsday," CBS, 1973; "Ellery Queen: The Chinese Dog," NBC, 1975; "McMillan and Wife: Requiem for a Bride," NBC, 1975; "Celebrity Sweepstakes," NBC, 1976.

TV MOVIES AND MINISERIES: "Ironside," NBC, 1967; "A Mask of Love," ABC, 1973.

BROOKS, JAMES L.

b. New York City, NY. Emmy winning writer and producer; co-creator of "The Mary Tyler Moore Show," arguably the most influential situation comedy of the last twenty-five years.

AS WRITER: "My Mother the Car: It Might As Well Be Spring As Not," NBC, 1966; "My Three Sons: The Perfect Separation," CBS, 1967; "The Andy Griffith Show: Emmett's

141

Brother-in-Law," CBS, 1968; "The Andy Griffith Show: The Mayberry Chef," CBS, 1968; "Room 222: Richie's Story (Pilot)," ABC, 1969; "Room 222: Arizona State Loves You," ABC, 1969.

AS CO-WRITER: "My Mother the Car: The Blabbermouth," NBC, 1966; "The Mary Tyler Moore Show: Love Is All Around," CBS, 1970; "The MTM Show: Support Your Local Mother," CBS, 1970; "The MTM Show: Christmas and the Hard-Luck Kid," CBS, 1970; "The MTM Show: The Good Time News," CBS, 1971; "Paul Sand in Friends and Lovers: Pilot," CBS, 1974; "The New Lorenzo Music Show," ABC, 1976; "The MTM Show: The Last Show," CBS, 1977; "Taxi: Like Father, Like Daughter (Pilot)," ABC, 1978.

AS CREATOR: "Room 222," ABC, 1969-74.

AS CO-CREATOR: "The Mary Tyler Moore Show," CBS, 1970-77; "Rhoda," CBS, 1974-78; "Lou Grant," CBS, 1977-82; "Taxi," ABC, 1978-82; NBC, 1982-83; "The Associates," ABC, 1979-80; "The Tracey Ullman Show," FOX, 1987-90.

AS CO-PRODUCER: "The Mary Tyler Moore Show," CBS, 1970-77.

AS CO-EXECUTIVE PRODUCER: "Paul Sand in Friends and Lovers," CBS, 1974-75; "Rhoda," CBS, 1974-78; "Lou Grant," CBS, 1977-78; "Taxi," ABC, 1978-82; NBC, 1982-83; "The Tracey Ullman Show," FOX, 1987-90; "The Simpsons," FOX, 1990- .

AS A RABBI: "The Mary Tyler Moore Show: Enter Rhoda's Parents," CBS, 1972.

* Brooks worked briefly as a writer for CBS News in New York before going west in the mid-1960's.
* Brooks' distinctive, high-pitched laugh can be heard off-camera in the audience of dozens of episodes of "The Mary Tyler Moore Show" and "Taxi."
* Emmies: 1971, 1975, 1976, 1977, 1979, 1980, 1981.

BROOKS, JOEL
b. New York City, NY. Stocky, mustachioed actor who played wishy-washy photography agent J.D. Lucas on "My Sister Sam."

AS A REGULAR: "Private Benjamin," CBS, 1982; "Teachers Only," NBC, 1983; "Hail to the Chief," ABC, 1985; "My Sister Sam," CBS, 1986-88; "Good Grief," FOX, 1990- .

AND: "Three's Company: Jack the Ripper," ABC, 1979; "Three's Company: The Root of All Evil," ABC, 1980; "M*A*S*H: Cementing Relationships," CBS, 1980; "Taxi: Tony's Lady," ABC, 1982; "Goodnight Beantown: Hooking for Mr. Goodbar," CBS, 1983; "Night Court: Billie and the Cat," NBC, 1984; "Duet: Too Many Cooks," FOX, 1989; "Hunter: Investment in Death," NBC, 1989; "Homeroom: Who Is Captain Fitness? (And

Why Is He Saying All Those Terrible Things About Me?)," ABC, 1989.

TV MOVIES AND MINISERIES: "The Mating Season," CBS, 1980; "Stranded," NBC, 1986; "Dinner at Eight," TNT, 1989.

BROOKS, MEL
b. Melvin Kamisky, Brooklyn, NY, 1926. Comic writer and director in film ("Blazing Saddles," "Young Frankenstein") and TV; his guest shots were often as a team with Carl Reiner.

AS A GUEST: "The Ed Sullivan Show," CBS, 1961; "The New Steve Allen Show," ABC, 1961; "The Tonight Show Starring Johnny Carson," NBC, 1962; "The Tonight Show Starring Johnny Carson," NBC, 1963; "Hollywood Palace," ABC, 1964; "The Tonight Show Starring Johnny Carson," NBC, 1964; "Hollywood Palace," ABC, 1965; "Hollywood Squares," NBC, 1967; "The Comedians," SYN, 1971; "Free to Be You and Me," ABC, 1974; "Annie and the Hoods," ABC, 1974; "The 2000 Year Old Man," CBS, 1975; "The Tonight Show Starring Johnny Carson," NBC, 1975.

AS CO-WRITER: "Your Show of Shows," NBC, 1950-54; "Caesar's Hour," NBC, 1954-57.

AS CO-CREATOR/CO-WRITER: "Get Smart," NBC, 1965-69; CBS, 1969-70; "The Sid Caesar, Imogene Coca, Carl Reiner, Howard Morris Special," CBS, 1967; "When Things Were Rotten," ABC, 1975; "The Nutt House," NBC, 1989.

* Brooks was a guest on Johnny Carson's first "Tonight" show.
* Emmies: 1967.

BROOKS, RAND
b. St. Louis, MO, September 21, 1918. Actor who played Corporal Boone on "The Adventures of Rin Tin Tin."

AS A REGULAR: "The Adventures of Rin Tin Tin," ABC, 1954-58.

AND: "The Roy Rogers Show: Jailbreak," NBC, 1955; "Sky King: Money Has Wings," ABC, 1955; "Sgt. Preston of the Yukon: Ghost Mine," CBS, 1958; "Maverick: Stampede," ABC, 1958; "The Real McCoys: Batter Up," ABC, 1959; "Bat Masterson: Pigeon and Hawk," NBC, 1960; "Manhunt: The Model," SYN, 1960; "Checkmate: A Slight Touch of Venom," CBS, 1961; "Shannon: Saints and Sinners," SYN, 1962; "Combat!: Crossfire," ABC, 1965; "My Three Sons: Mary Lou," CBS, 1965; "Petticoat Junction: What's a Trajectory?," CBS, 1965.

TV MOVIES AND MINISERIES: "Double Indemnity," ABC, 1973.

BROOKS, STEPHEN
b. Columbus, OH, 1942. Clean-cut actor usually in straight-arrow roles; he played

special agent Jim Rhodes on "The FBI" and Joshua Fallon on "Days of Our Lives."
AS A REGULAR: "The Nurses," CBS, 1963-64; "The FBI," ABC, 1965-67; "The Interns," CBS, 1970-71; "Days of Our Lives," NBC, 1980-82.
AND: "Look Up and Live: The Journal of Vera Grey," CBS, 1963; "Owen Marshall, Counselor at Law: The Triangle," ABC, 1972; "Barnaby Jones: Stand-In for Death," CBS, 1973; "Vega$: Dan Tanna Is Dead," ABC, 1979; "Barnaby Jones: Deadline for Murder," CBS, 1980; "House Calls: It Ain't Necessary to Sew," CBS, 1982.
TV MOVIES AND MINISERIES: "Two for the Money," ABC, 1972.

BROSNAN, PIERCE
b. Ireland, May 16, 1952. Slim, attractive actor who played detective Remington Steele and now has turned his energies toward miniseries.
AS A REGULAR: "Remington Steele," NBC, 1982-87.
TV MOVIES AND MINISERIES: "Manions of America," ABC, 1981; "Remington Steele: The Steele That Wouldn't Die," NBC, 1987; "James Clavell's Noble House," NBC, 1988; "Around the World in 80 Days," NBC, 1989; "The Heist," SHO, 1989.
* Brosnan came within a hair's breadth of being the next James Bond, but the "Remington Steele" producers, who still had him under contract, wouldn't turn Brosnan loose. And Timothy Dalton became the new 007.

BROTHERS, DR. JOYCE
b. Joyce Bauer, New York City, NY, 1927. Psychologist who has a few obessions of her own, namely appearing on any crappy TV show that pays cash.
AS A REGULAR: "One Life to Live," ABC, 1972; "The Gong Show," SYN, 1976-80.
AND: "The $64,000 Question," CBS, 1955; "The $64,000 Challenge," CBS, 1956; "The Merv Griffin Show," NBC, 1962; "The Merv Griffin Show," NBC, 1963; "The Tonight Show Starring Johnny Carson," NBC, 1963; "Art Linkletter's House Party," CBS, 1964; "You Don't Say," NBC, 1967; "The Mike Douglas Show," SYN, 1967; "The Smothers Brothers Comedy Hour," CBS, 1968; "The Merv Griffin Show," CBS, 1969; "Love, American Style: Love and the Clinical Problem," ABC, 1974; "Police Woman: Fish," NBC, 1974; "Celebrity Sweepstakes," NBC, 1975; "Match Game '75," CBS, 1975; "Cross Wits," SYN, 1975; "Police Woman: Task Force: Cop Killer," NBC, 1976; "The Sonny and Cher Comedy Hour," CBS, 1977; "Police Woman: Do You Still Beat Your Wife?," NBC, 1977; "Happy Days: Spunkless Spunky," ABC, 1978; "The Love Boat: Aftermath," ABC, 1979; "WKRP in Cincinnati: Hotel Oceanview," CBS,

1980; "Taxi: The Wedding of Latka and Simka," ABC, 1982; "Simon & Simon: Room 3502," CBS, 1983; "Hardcastle and McCormick: Hate the Picture, Love the Frame," ABC, 1984; "Moonlighting: A Trip to the Moon," ABC, 1987; "The New Mike Hammer: Lady Killer," CBS, 1987; "ALF: Tonight, Tonight," NBC, 1988; "The Munsters Today: One Flew Over the Munster's Nest," SYN, 1989; "TV 101: First Love," CBS, 1989; "The People Next Door: House and Home," CBS, 1989.
* Brothers won $134,000 answering questions about boxing on "The $64,000 Question" and "The $64,000 Challenge."

BROWN, BLAIR
b. Washington, D.C., 1952. Attractive redheaded actress who plays Molly Dodd, single woman loose in the Big Apple.
AS A REGULAR: "The Days and Nights of Molly Dodd," NBC, 1987-88; LIF, 1988- .
AND: "Marcus Welby, M.D.: The One Face in the World," ABC, 1975; "The Rockford Files: The Girl in the Bay City Boys Club," NBC, 1975; "Kojak: Where Do You Go When You Have No Place to Go?" CBS, 1977; "The Tonight Show Starring Johnny Carson," NBC, 1989.
TV MOVIES AND MINISERIES: "The Oregon Trail," NBC, 1976; "Best Sellers: Captains and the Kings," NBC, 1976; "Eleanor and Franklin: The White House Years," ABC, 1977; "Arthur Hailey's Wheels," NBC, 1978; "And I Alone Survived," NBC, 1978; "The Child-Stealer," ABC, 1979; "Kennedy," NBC, 1983; "The Bad Seed," ABC, 1985; "Space," CBS, 1986; "Hands of a Stranger," NBC, 1987.

BROWN, CHELSEA
b. Chicago, IL. Actress who began her career as a bikinied dancer on "Rowan & Martin's Laugh-In."
AS A REGULAR: "Rowan & Martin's Laugh-In," NBC, 1968-69; "Matt Lincoln," ABC, 1970-71.
AND: "The Game Game," SYN, 1969; "The Flying Nun: The Paolo Story," ABC, 1969; "Marcus Welby, M.D.: Once There Was a Bantu Prince," ABC, 1972; "Police Story: Dangerous Games," NBC, 1973; "Mission: Impossible: Reprisal," ABC, 1989.
TV MOVIES AND MINISERIES: "Dial Hot Line," ABC, 1970.

BROWN, GEORG STANFORD
b. Cuba, June 24, 1943. Actor who played officer Terry Webster on "The Rookies"; nowadays he directs more than he acts.
AS A REGULAR: "The Rookies," ABC, 1972-76.
AND: "The FBI: The Intermediary," ABC, 1968; "Dragnet: The Big Problem," NBC, 1968;

"Mannix: Eagles Sometimes Can't Fly," CBS, 1969; "Medical Center: Rebel in White," CBS, 1970; "The Bold Ones: Killer on the Loose," NBC, 1970; "Medical Center: Man in Hiding," CBS, 1971; "Mannix: A Choice of Evils," CBS, 1971; "Mission: Impossible: Bag Woman," CBS, 1971; "Room 222: And in This Corner," ABC, 1972; "Paris: Dead Men Don't Kill," CBS, 1979; "Hill Street Blues: Chipped Beef," NBC, 1981; "Cagney & Lacey: Choices," CBS, 1984; "Matlock: The Mayor," NBC, 1989.

TV MOVIES AND MINISERIES: "The Young Lawyers," CBS, 1969; "Ritual of Evil," NBC, 1970; "The Rookies," ABC, 1972; "Dawn: Portrait of a Teenage Runaway," NBC, 1976; "Roots," ABC, 1977; "Roots: The Next Generations," ABC, 1979; "The Night the City Screamed," ABC, 1980; "In Defense of Kids," CBS, 1983; "North and South," ABC, 1985; "Alone in the Neon Jungle," CBS, 1988.

AS DIRECTOR: "Hill Street Blues," NBC, 1982-84; "Cagney & Lacey," CBS, 1984-87.
* Emmies: 1986.

BROWN, JAMES

b. Augusta, GA, May 3, 1934. Soul brother number one, Mr. Please Please Please, the hardest-working man in show business.

AS A GUEST: "American Bandstand," ABC, 1961; "Where the Action Is," ABC, 1965; "The Ed Sullivan Show," CBS, 1966; "American Bandstand," ABC, 1968; "Hollywood Palace," ABC, 1968; "The Match Game," NBC, 1968; "The Joey Bishop Show," ABC, 1968; "The Mike Douglas Show," SYN, 1969; "The Jerry Lewis Show," NBC, 1969; "The Music Scene," ABC, 1969; "Tattletales," CBS, 1975; "Midnight Special," NBC, 1976; "Saturday Night Live," NBC, 1980; "Sha Na Na," SYN, 1980.
* Yipes Dept.: James Brown on "The Match Game," with co-celebrity guest Meredith MacRae. Enough said.

BROWN, JAMES L.

b. Desdemona, TX, March 22, 1920. Rugged actor who played Lt. Rip Masters on "The Adventures of Rin Tin Tin" and crooked detective Harry McSween on "Dallas."

AS A REGULAR: "The Adventures of Rin Tin Tin," ABC, 1954-59; "Dallas," CBS, 1984-88.

AND: "Ozark Jubilee," ABC, 1957; "Route 66: A Fury Slinging Flame," CBS, 1960; "Laramie: Strange Company," NBC, 1961; "Route 66: Aren't You Surprised to See Me?," CBS, 1962; "Have Gun, Will Travel: Penelope," CBS, 1962; "The Virginian: West," NBC, 1962; "The Virginian: The Money Cage," NBC, 1963; "Honey West: Come to Me, My Litigation Baby," ABC, 1966; "Murder, She Wrote: Mourning Among the Wisterias," CBS, 1988.

TV MOVIES AND MINISERIES: "Powderkeg," CBS, 1971.

BROWN, JIM

b. St. Simon Island, GA, February 17, 1935. Former football player with the Cleveland Browns.

AS A GUEST: "The Fugitive: Passage to Helena," ABC, 1964; "Valentine's Day: For Me and My Sal," ABC, 1965; "I Spy: Cops and Robbers," NBC, 1967; "Hollywood Squares," NBC, 1967; "Operation: Entertainment," ABC, 1968; "The FBI: The Maze," ABC, 1969; "The Sonny and Cher Comedy Hour," CBS, 1972; "Police Story: End of the Line," NBC, 1977; "CHiPS: Roller Disco," NBC, 1979; "Knight Rider: Knight of the Drones," NBC, 1984; "The A-Team: Quarterback Sneak," NBC, 1986.

TV MOVIES AND MINISERIES: "Lady Blue," ABC, 1985.

BROWN, JIM ED

b. Sparkman, AR, March 1, 1934.

AS A REGULAR: "Nashville on the Road," SYN, 1975-81.

BROWN, JOE E.

b. Holgate, OH, July 28, 1892; d. 1973. Broad, satchel-mouthed comic of films ("Alibi Ike," "Some Like It Hot") and TV.

AS A REGULAR: "The Buick Circus Hour," NBC, 1952-53.

AND: "Schlitz Playhouse of Stars: Meet Mr. Justice," CBS, 1955; "Screen Directors Playhouse: The Silent Partner," NBC, 1955; "G.E. Theatre: The Golden Key," CBS, 1956; "Do You Trust Your Wife?," CBS, 1956; "The Steve Allen Show," NBC, 1957; "Masquerade Party," NBC, 1957; "Strike It Rich," CBS, 1957; "Art Linkletter's House Party," CBS, 1958; "Christophers: Benjamin Franklin," SYN, 1958; "The Ann Sothern Show: Olive's Dream Man," CBS, 1960; "Arthur Murray Party," NBC, 1960; "All-Star Circus," ABC, 1960; "All-Star Circus," NBC, 1961; "Art Linkletter's House Party," CBS, 1961; "Here's Hollywood," NBC, 1961; "Preview Theatre: Five's a Family," NBC, 1961; "Route 66: Journey to Nineveh," CBS, 1962; "The Greatest Show on Earth: You're All Right, Ivy," ABC, 1964.

BROWN, JOHN MASON

b. Louisville, KY, July 3, 1900. Commentator and panelist on early TV shows.

AS A REGULAR: "Americana," NBC, 1947-48; "Critic at Large," ABC, 1948-49; "Tonight on Broadway," CBS, 1948-49; "Who Said That?," ABC, 1955.

BROWN, JOHNNY

b. *St. Petersburg, FL, June 11, 1937*. Rotund comic who played bulding superintendent Nathan Bookman on "Good Times."

AS A REGULAR: "The Leslie Uggams Show," CBS, 1969; "Rowan & Martin's Laugh-In," NBC, 1970-72; "Good Times," CBS, 1976-79.

AND: "The Mike Douglas Show," SYN, 1965; "The Sammy Davis Jr. Show," NBC, 1966; "The Rookies: Prayers Unanswered, Prayers Unheard," ABC, 1973; "Maude: Walter's Holiday," CBS, 1973; "Baffle," NBC, 1973; "Good Times: The Family Business," CBS, 1975; "Where's the Fire?," ABC, 1975; "Rhyme and Reason," ABC, 1976; "Chico and the Man: Della Moves In/Second Coming of Della," NBC, 1976; "Sammy and Company," SYN, 1976; "Cross Wits," SYN, 1979; "227: Play It Again, Stan," NBC, 1989.

BROWN, OLIVIA

b. *West Germany*. Actress who's played Lt. Trudy Joplin on "Miami Vice" and Vanessa, the outrageous girlfriend of Anthony (Meshach Taylor) on a couple of "Designing Women" episodes.

AS A REGULAR: "Miami Vice," NBC, 1984-89.

AND: "Paradise: Orphan Train," CBS, 1989; "Family Matters: Stakeout," ABC, 1989; "Designing Women: The First Day of the Last Decade of the Entire Twentieth Century," CBS, 1990; "Designing Women: Anthony and Vanessa," CBS, 1990.

BROWN, PAMELA

b. *London, July 8, 1917; d. 1975*. Actress who won an Emmy for "Victoria Regina."

AS A GUEST: "Celanese Theatre: Susan and God," ABC, 1951; "Playhouse 90: The Violent Heart," CBS, 1958; "Suspicion: The Woman Turned to Salt," NBC, 1958; "Alcoa Presents One Step Beyond: The Tiger," ABC, 1961; "Hallmark Hall of Fame: Victoria Regina," NBC, 1961; "Espionage: Never Turn Your Back on a Friend," NBC, 1964; "Hallmark Hall of Fame: The Admirable Crichton," NBC, 1968.

TV MOVIES AND MINISERIES: "Dracula," CBS, 1974; "In This House of Brede," CBS, 1975.

* Emmies: 1962.

BROWN, PETER

b. *Pierre de Lappe, Brooklyn, NY, 1935*. Actor who began as a child radio performer; more recently he played Greg Peters on "Days of Our Lives" and Roger Forbes on "General Hospital."

AS A REGULAR: "Lawman," ABC, 1958-62; "Laredo," NBC, 1965-67; "Days of Our Lives," NBC, 1972-79; "The Young and the Restless," CBS, 1981-82; "Loving," ABC,

1983-84; "General Hospital," ABC, 1984-86.

AND: "Cheyenne: Top Hand," ABC, 1957; "Maverick: Stage West," ABC, 1957; "Cheyenne: Renegades," ABC, 1958; "Sugarfoot: Hideout," ABC, 1958; "Sugarfoot: The Trial of the Canary Kid," ABC, 1959; "The Pat Boone Chevy Showroom," ABC, 1959; "Cheyenne: Ghost of Cimarron," ABC, 1960; "Maverick: Hadley's Hunters," ABC, 1960; "Here's Hollywood," NBC, 1961; "Cheyenne: Pocketful of Stars," ABC, 1962; "77 Sunset Strip: Wolf! Cried the Blonde," ABC, 1962; "The Gallant Men: The Bridge," ABC, 1963; "Kraft Suspense Theatre: The Action of the Tiger," NBC, 1964; "The Virginian: Return a Stranger," NBC, 1964; "Wagon Train: Those Who Stay Behind," ABC, 1964; "The Virginian: We've Lost a Train," NBC, 1965; "The Virginian: A Small Taste of Justice," NBC, 1967; "The Mod Squad: The Debt," ABC, 1969; "The Bob Newhart Show: Tennis, Emily?," CBS, 1972; "Medical Center: Deadlock," CBS, 1972; "The Magician: The Vanishing Lady," NBC, 1973; "Police Story: The Gamble," NBC, 1974; "Police Story: Love, Mabel," NBC, 1974; "Police Woman: Above and Beyond," NBC, 1975; "The Streets of San Francisco: One Last Trick," ABC, 1977; "Lobo: Airsick 1981," NBC, 1981; "Magnum, P.I.: Heal Thyself," CBS, 1982; "Simon & Simon: The Dillinger Print," CBS, 1984; "Riptide: Peter Pan Is Alive and Well," NBC, 1984; "Knight Rider: Knight Behind Bars," NBC, 1985; "Aaron's Way: New Patterns," NBC, 1988; "Hunter: Partners," NBC, 1989.

TV MOVIES AND MINISERIES: "Hunters Are for Killing," CBS, 1970; "Salvage I," ABC, 1979.

BROWN, ROBERT

b. *Scotland, 1927*. Curly headed, jut-jawed actor; he played Jason Bolt, who brought women to love-starved 1880s Seattle on "Here Come the Brides."

AS A REGULAR: "Here Come the Brides," ABC, 1968-70; "Primus," SYN, 1971.

AND: "Perry Mason: The Case of the Sleepy Slayer," CBS, 1964; "Bewitched: Darrin on a Pedestal," ABC, 1970; "Mannix: The Girl in the Polka Dot Dress," CBS, 1973; "Columbo: Playback," NBC, 1975; "Police Story: To Steal a Million," NBC, 1975; "Police Story: Little Boy Lost," NBC, 1975.

TV MOVIES AND MINISERIES: "Games Mother Never Taught You," CBS, 1982.

BROWN, TIMOTHY

b. *Chicago, IL, 1937*. Handsome black actor in occasional films ("Nashville") and TV; he played Spearchucker Jones in the TV version of "M*A*S*H" before the character was dropped.

AS A REGULAR: "M*A*S*H," CBS, 1972.

AND: "The Wild Wild West: The Night of the

Bubbling Death," CBS, 1967; "The Mary Tyler Moore Show: Keep Your Guard Up," CBS, 1970; "Gimme a Break: The Answering Machine," NBC, 1985.

TV MOVIES AND MINISERIES: "Glory Days," CBS, 1988.

BROWN, TOM

b. January 6, 1913; d. 1990. Actor who played rancher Ed O'Connor on "Gunsmoke" and Al Weeks on "General Hospital."

AS A REGULAR: "Gunsmoke," CBS, 1955-75; "Mr. Lucky," CBS, 1959-60; "General Hospital," ABC, 1975-79.

AND: "Playhouse 90: Heritage of Anger," CBS, 1956; "Hey, Jeannie!: Jeannie the Big Sister," CBS, 1957; "Matinee Theatre: Daughter of the Seventh," NBC, 1957; "West Point: Only Witness," CBS, 1957; "O. Henry Playhouse: Fourth in Salvador," SYN, 1957; "Circus Boy: The Tumbling Clown," ABC, 1958; "American Legend: The Tenderfoot," SYN, 1958; "Peter Gunn: The Dirty Word," NBC, 1959; "Have Gun, Will Travel: Something to Live for," CBS, 1959; "Guestward Ho!: The Hooton Statue," ABC, 1961; "Pete and Gladys: Gladys Cooks Pete's Goose," CBS, 1961; "77 Sunset Strip: The Lady Has the Answers," ABC, 1961; "The Rifleman: Skull," ABC, 1962; "Ripcord: The Helicopter Race," SYN, 1962; "Mr. Roberts: Undercover Cook," NBC, 1966.

TV MOVIES AND MINISERIES: "Cutter's Trail," CBS, 1970.

BROWN, VANESSA

b. Smylla Brind, Vienna, Austria, March 24, 1928. Actress who was one of those gabby gal panelists on "Leave It to the Girls"; she played nutty housewife Liz Cooper for a time on "My Favorite Husband"—a role Lucille Ball had played on the radio.

AS A REGULAR: "Leave It to the Girls," NBC, 1949-51; ABC, 1953-54; "My Favorite Husband," CBS, 1955; "All That Glitters," SYN, 1977.

AND: "Pulitzer Prize Playhouse: Blockade," ABC, 1951; "Robert Montgomery Presents: The Kimballs," NBC, 1951; "Philco TV Playhouse: The Monument," NBC, 1952; "Stage 7: The Legacy," CBS, 1955; "Climax!: The Box of Chocolates," CBS, 1955; "Climax!: The Dance," CBS, 1955; "The Millionaire: The Louise Williams Story," CBS, 1956; "The Loretta Young Show: Incident in Kawi," NBC, 1956; "Schlitz Playhouse of Stars: One Way Out," CBS, 1957; "Climax!: Hurricane Diane," CBS, 1957; "Dick Powell's Zane Grey Theatre: Three Days to Death," CBS, 1958; "Wagon Train: The Sally Potter Story," NBC, 1958; "Matinee Theatre: The Man with Pointed Toes," NBC, 1958; "The Red Skelton Show: Deadeye the Indian Scout," CBS,

1958; "Goodyear Theatre: Any Friend of Julie's," NBC, 1959; "G.E. Theatre: Silhouette," CBS, 1959; "Alcoa Presents One Step Beyond: The Lovers," ABC, 1960; "Chevy Mystery Show: Murder by the Book," NBC, 1960; "Murder, She Wrote: The Search for Peter Kerry," CBS, 1989.

* On one episode of "Climax!," Brown's character was stabbed in the, um, climax. She then got up, sat at a dressing table and began combing her hair—which is where the camera caught her at the end of the show, when she was still supposed to be "dead."

BROWNE, ROSCOE LEE

b. Woodbury, NJ, May 2, 1925. Bald black actor, usually in distinguished roles or as butlers; he played Rosemont on "Falcon Crest" and replaced Robert Guillaume as the Tate family butler on "Soap." He won an Emmy for reciting Shakespeare on a very awkward episode of "The Cosby Show."

AS A REGULAR: "McCoy," NBC, 1975-76; "Miss Winslow and Son," CBS, 1979; "Soap," ABC, 1980-81; "Falcon Crest," CBS, 1988-90.

AND: "Espionage: The Whistling Shrimp," NBC, 1963; "Look Up and Live: The History of Asceticism," CBS, 1964; "Festival of the Arts: Benito Cereno," NET, 1965; "Mannix: Deadfall," CBS, 1968; "The Invaders: The Vise," ABC, 1968; "The Name of the Game: The Third Choice," NBC, 1969; "The Name of the Game: The Time is Now," NBC, 1970; "All in the Family: The Elevator Story," CBS, 1972; "Sanford & Son: Jealousy," NBC, 1972; "The Streets of San Francisco: A Trout in the Milk," ABC, 1973; "All in the Family: Archie in the Hospital," CBS, 1973; "Good Times: God's Business is Good Business," CBS, 1974; "Short Stories of Love: Epicac," NBC, 1974; "Barney Miller: Escape Artist," ABC, 1975; "Maude: Victoria's Boyfriend," CBS, 1977; "Starsky and Hutch: Starsky and Hutch on Playboy Island," ABC, 1977; "Maude: Mr. Butterfield's Return," CBS, 1978; "Magnum, P.I.: Legacy From a Friend," CBS, 1983; "Blacke's Magic: Death Goes to the Movies," NBC, 1986; "Highway to Heaven: Country Doctor," NBC, 1986; "The Cosby Show: Shakespeare," NBC, 1986; "A Different World: All's Fair," NBC, 1988.

TV MOVIES AND MINISERIES: "The Big Ripoff," NBC, 1975; "King," NBC, 1978; "Stuck with Each Other," NBC, 1989; "Lady in a Corner," NBC, 1989.

* Emmies: 1986.

BRUCE, CAROL

b. Great Neck, NY, November 15, 1919. Stage and TV performer who played Mamma Carlson on "WKRP in Cincinnati."

AS A REGULAR: "WKRP in Cincinnati," CBS, 1979-82.

AND: "Silver Theatre: Happy Marriage," CBS, 1950; "Musical Comedy Time: Miss Liberty," NBC, 1951; "Curtain Call: The Promise," NBC, 1952; "Armstrong Circle Theatre: Thief of Diamonds," CBS, 1957; "Music for a Summer Night: Tribute to a Poet," ABC, 1960; "Girl Talk," SYN, 1963; "The Twilight Zone: Dead Woman's Shoes," CBS, 1985; "Perfect Strangers: Tux for Two," ABC, 1987; "Perfect Strangers: High Society," ABC, 1988; "Hooperman: In the Still of My Pants," ABC, 1989.

BRUCE, DAVID

b. Andrew McBroom, Kankakee, IL, January 6, 1914; d. 1976. Actor who played Harry Henderson, bumbling master of the household where maid Beulah (Louise Beavers) ruled.
AS A REGULAR: "Beulah," ABC, 1952-53.

BRUCE, VIRGINIA

b. Helen Virginia Briggs, Minneapolis, MN, September 29, 1910. Film actress who did little TV.
AS A GUEST: "Silver Theatre: Wedding Anniversary," CBS, 1950; "Lux Video Theatre: Something to Live For," CBS, 1953; "G.E. Theatre: Woman's World," CBS, 1953; "Science Fiction Theatre: Dead Storage," SYN, 1955; "Science Fiction Theatre: Friend of a Raven," SYN, 1955; "The Loretta Young Show: Weekend in Winnetka," NBC, 1956; "Studio 57: Who's Calling?," SYN, 1956; "Matinee Theatre: People in Glass Houses," NBC, 1956; "Lux Video Theatre: Mildred Pierce," NBC, 1956; "Ford Theatre: The Connoisseur," ABC, 1957.

BRYAN, ARTHUR Q.

b. 1900; d. 1959. Character actor and, most importantly, the voice of Elmer J. Fudd.
AS A REGULAR: "Movieland Quiz," ABC, 1948; "The Hank McCune Show," NBC, 1950.
AND: "I Love Lucy: Ricky Loses His Voice," CBS, 1952; "Producers Showcase: The Lord Don't Play Favorites," NBC, 1956.

BRYANT, ANITA

b. Barnsdall, OK, March 25, 1940. Singer of sugary ballads and orange juice pitchwoman.
AS A REGULAR: "The George Gobel Show," CBS, 1959-60.
AND: "The Peter Lind Hayes Show," ABC, 1958; "The Garry Moore Show," CBS, 1958; "The Jimmy Dean Show," CBS, 1958; "American Bandstand," ABC, 1959; "The Dick Clark Saturday Night Beechnut Show," ABC, 1959; "The Jimmie Rodgers Show," NBC, 1959; "The Dick Clark Saturday Night Beechnut Show," ABC, 1960; "Coke Time," ABC, 1960; "Saturday Prom," NBC, 1960; "American Bandstand," ABC, 1960; "Bob Hope Buick Show," NBC, 1961; "The Ed Sullivan Show," CBS, 1961; "The Ford Show," NBC, 1961; "Bell Telephone Hour: Salute to Autumn," NBC, 1961; "The Bob Hope Christmas Show," NBC, 1962; "American Bandstand," ABC, 1962; "The Bob Hope Christmas Show," NBC, 1963; "Perry Como's Kraft Music Hall," NBC, 1963; "Bob Hope Christmas Special," NBC, 1964; "The Ed Sullivan Show," CBS, 1964; "Bob Hope Christmas Special," NBC, 1965; "The Red Skelton Hour," CBS, 1965; "Art Linkletter's House Party," CBS, 1969; "Kraft Music Hall," NBC, 1970; "The Mike Douglas Show," SYN, 1976.

BRYANT, NANA

b. Cincinnati, OH, 1888; d. 1955.
AS A REGULAR: "The First Hundred Years," CBS, 1950-52; "Our Miss Brooks," CBS, 1955.
AND: "Make Room for Daddy: Julia's Birthday," ABC, 1955.

BRYGGMAN, LARRY

b. Concord, CA, December 21, 1938. Actor who plays grouchy Dr. John Dixon on "As the World Turns."
AS A REGULAR: "As the World Turns," CBS, 1969- .

BRYNNER, YUL

b. Taidje Khan, Sakhalin Island, Russia, July 12, 1915; d. 1985. The once and future King of Siam.
AS A REGULAR: "Anna and the King," CBS, 1972.
AND: "Omnibus: Lodging for the Night," CBS, 1953; "CBS Reports: Rescue-with Yul Brynner," CBS, 1960; "Keyhole: Hollywood Abroad," SYN, 1962; "The Poppy Is Also a Flower," ABC, 1966.
AS PRODUCER-DIRECTOR: "Life with Snarky Parker," CBS, 1950.

BUCHANAN, EDGAR

b. Humansville, MO, March 21, 1903; d. 1979. Character actor who played the laid-back Uncle Joe Carson on "Petticoat Junction."
AS A REGULAR: "Hopalong Cassidy," NBC, 1949-51; "Judge Roy Bean," SYN, 1956; "Petticoat Junction," CBS, 1963-70; "Green Acres," CBS, 1965-66; "Cade's County," CBS, 1971-72.
AND: "Schlitz Playhouse of Stars: The Brush Roper," CBS, 1954; "The Millionaire: Millionaire William Vaughn," CBS, 1955; "G.E. Theatre: The Road That Led Afar," CBS, 1956; "Climax!: Avalanche at Devil's Pass," CBS, 1957; "Climax!: Deadly Climate," CBS, 1957; "Restless Gun: Aunt Emma," NBC, 1958; "Maverick: Duel at Sundown," ABC, 1959; "The Californians: One Ton of Peppercorns," NBC, 1959; "Wanted Dead

or Alive: Railroaded," CBS, 1959; "Wanted Dead or Alive: Amos Carter," CBS, 1959; "Leave it to Beaver: Uncle Billy," ABC, 1960; "Maverick: The Cactus Switch," ABC, 1961; "Klondike: The Golden Burro," NBC, 1961; "Laramie: Stolen Tribute," NBC, 1961; "National Velvet: Grandpa," NBC, 1961; "National Velvet: Grandpa Returns," NBC, 1961; "Tales of Wells Fargo: The Repentant Outlaw," NBC, 1961; "Bringing Up Buddy: Big-Game Hunter," CBS, 1961; "Bonanza: Sam Hill," NBC, 1961; "The Barbara Stanwyck Show: A Man's Game," NBC, 1961; "The Tall Man: The Judas Palm," NBC, 1961; "The Bob Cummings Show: The Oxtail Incident," CBS, 1961; "Ichabod and Me: The Printer," CBS, 1961; "Bus Stop: The Man From Bootstrap," ABC, 1961; "The Rifleman: The Long Goodbye," ABC, 1961; "The Andy Griffith Show: Aunt Bee's Brief Encounter," CBS, 1961; "Dr. Kildare: The Administrator," NBC, 1962; "Gunsmoke: Old Dan," CBS, 1962; "The Twilight Zone: The Last Rites of Jeff Myrtlebank," CBS, 1962; "Thriller: Til Death Do Us Part," NBC, 1962; "Dennis the Menace: Dennis and the Hermit," CBS, 1962; "Alcoa Premiere: Flashing Spikes," ABC, 1962; "Leave It to Beaver: Uncle Billy's Visit," ABC, 1963; "The Beverly Hillbillies: Granny Goes to Hooterville," CBS, 1968; "The Beverly Hillbillies: The Thanksgiving Story," CBS, 1968; "Green Acres: Hail to the Fire Chief," CBS, 1968; "The Beverly Hillbillies: Christmas in Hooterville," CBS, 1968; "Green Acres: How Hooterville Was Floundered," CBS, 1968; "Green Acres: Everybody Tries to Love a Countess," CBS, 1969; "Love, American Style: Love and the Family Hour," ABC, 1973.
TV MOVIES AND MINISERIES: "Something for a Lonely Man," NBC, 1968; "The Over-the-Hill Gang," ABC, 1969; "The Over-the-Hill Gang Rides Again," ABC, 1970; "Yuma," ABC, 1971.

BUCKLEY, BETTY
b. Big Springs, TX, July 3, 1947. Stage actress ("Cats") who played Abby Bradford, second wife of Tom (Dick Van Patten) on "Eight Is Enough."
AS A REGULAR: "Eight Is Enough," ABC, 1977-81.
AND: "The Mike Douglas Show," SYN, 1980; "Cagney & Lacey: You've Come a Long Way, Baby," CBS, 1987; "ABC Afterschool Specials: Taking a Stand," ABC, 1989.
TV MOVIES AND MINISERIES: "The Ordeal of Bill Carney," CBS, 1981; "The Three Wishes of Billy Grier," ABC, 1984; "Roses Are for the Rich," CBS, 1987; "Babycakes," CBS, 1989.

BUCKLEY, HAL
b. 1936; d. 1986. Slim actor, usually in comic roles; he played St. John Quincy, who tutored

the children of millionaire O.K. Crackerby (Burl Ives).
AS A REGULAR: "O.K. Crackerby," ABC, 1965-66.
AND: "That Girl: The Detective Story," ABC, 1968; "Nanny and the Professor: The Games Families Play," ABC, 1970; "The Partridge Family: The Princess and the Partridge," ABC, 1972; "Banacek: The Three Million Dollar Piracy," NBC, 1973.

BUJOLD, GENEVIEVE
b. Montreal, Canada, July 1, 1942. Attractive, dark-featured actress of films and TV.
AS A GUEST: "Saint Joan," NET, 1967; "New York Playhouse: Antigone," NET, 1972; "Caesar and Cleopatra," NBC, 1976.
TV MOVIES AND MINISERIES: "Mistress of Paradise," ABC, 1981; "Red Earth, White Earth," CBS, 1989.

BUKTENICA, RAY
b. New York City, NY, August 6, 1943. Slim, bespectacled actor who played Dr. Norman Solomon on "House Calls" and Benny, boyfriend of Brenda Morgenstern on "Rhoda."
AS A REGULAR: "Rhoda," CBS, 1977-78; "House Calls," CBS, 1979-82; "Open House," FOX, 1989-90.
AND: "Hawaii Five-O: Little Girl Blue," CBS, 1973; "The Partridge Family: The Diplomat," ABC, 1973; "Hawaii Five-O: Jury of One," CBS, 1973; "The Love Boat: The Scoop," ABC, 1979; "The Love Boat: Putting on the Dog," ABC, 1983; "The Love Boat: Don't Get Mad, Get Even," ABC, 1984; "Hardcastle and McCormick: You and the Horse You Rode in On," ABC, 1984; "Simon & Simon: Simon Without Diplomat," CBS, 1985; "The Twilight Zone: Take My Life-Please!," CBS, 1986; "Mutts," ABC, 1988; "Murder, She Wrote: Something Borrowed, Someone Blue," CBS, 1989; "Head of the Class: King of Remedial," ABC, 1989; "Life Goes On: Paige's Date," ABC, 1989.
TV MOVIES AND MINISERIES: "Mary Jane Harper Cried Last Night," CBS, 1977; "Wait Til Your Mother Gets Home," NBC, 1983; "Heart of a Champion: The Ray Mancini Story," CBS, 1985; "The George McKenna Story," CBS, 1986.

BULIFANT, JOYCE
b. Joyce Boulifant, Newport News, VA, December 16, 1937. Blonde actress who played the wife of Murray Slaughter (Gavin MacLeod) on "The Mary Tyler Moore Show."
AS A REGULAR: "Tom, Dick and Mary," NBC, 1964-65; "The Bill Cosby Show," NBC, 1969-71; "Love Thy Neighbor," ABC, 1973; "Flo," CBS, 1980-81.

AND: "Thriller: An Attractive Family," NBC, 1962; "The Tall Man: The Four Queens," NBC, 1962; "The Wide Country: A Guy for Clementine," NBC, 1962; "Alcoa Premiere: Mr. Lucifer," ABC, 1962; "Gunsmoke: Uncle Sunday," CBS, 1962; "Empire: The Tiger Inside," NBC, 1963; "My Three Sons: Flashback," ABC, 1963; "Perry Mason: The Case of the Surplus Suitor," CBS, 1963; "McHale's Navy: Today I Am a Man!," ABC, 1963; "The Real McCoys: The Peacemakers," CBS, 1963; "Wagon Train: The Michael Malone Story," ABC, 1964; "Perry Mason: The Case of the Ice-Cold Hands," CBS, 1964; "Arrest and Trial: A Roll of the Dice," ABC, 1964; "The Virginian: Roar From the Mountain," NBC, 1964; "Dr. Kildare: The Atheist and the True Believer/A Quick Look at Glory/A Sort of Falling in Love/The Last to Believe in Miracles/The Next Thing to Murder/Never So Happy," NBC, 1966; "The Mary Tyler Moore Show: Just a Lunch," CBS, 1971; "The Mary Tyler Moore Show: The Slaughter Affair," CBS, 1972; "Love, American Style: Love and the Awkward Age," ABC, 1973; "Match Game '74," CBS, 1974; "Tattletales," CBS, 1974; "Password," ABC, 1974; "The Mary Tyler Moore Show: What Do You Want To Do When You Produce?," CBS, 1975; "The Mary Tyler Moore Show: Murray Takes a Stand," CBS, 1976; "The Mary Tyler Moore Show: Murray Can't Lose," CBS, 1976; "Police Story: Monster Manor," NBC, 1976; "Three's Company: Chrissy's Date," ABC, 1977; "Alice: Who Ordered the Hot Turkey?," CBS, 1978; "Turnabout: We're a Little Late, Folks," NBC, 1979.
TV MOVIES AND MINISERIES: "Hanging by a Thread," NBC, 1979.

BULLOCK, JIM J.
b. Casper, WY. Comic who became the substitute Paul Lynde on "Hollywood Squares."
AS A REGULAR: "Hollywood Squares," SYN, 1978-80; "Too Close for Comfort," ABC, 1980-83; SYN, 1984-86; "ALF," NBC, 1989-90.

BUNCE, ALAN
b. Westfield, NJ, June 28, 1903; d. 1965. Actor who played Ethel's husband, Albert.
AS A REGULAR: "Ethel and Albert," NBC, 1953-54; CBS, 1955; ABC, 1955-56.
AND: "Hallmark Hall of Fame: The Real Glory," NBC, 1952; "Kraft Television Theatre: The New Tenant," NBC, 1952; "Armstrong Circle Theatre: The 38th President," NBC, 1953; "The Web: Dark Meeting," NBC, 1953; "Kraft Television Theatre: Autumn Story," NBC, 1953; "Mirror Theatre: The Party," NBC, 1953; "The Web: The Bait," CBS, 1954; "Elgin TV Hour: Family Meeting," ABC, 1955; "Studio One: Operation Home," CBS,

1955; "Frontiers of Faith: Channels," NBC, 1959; "The Right Man," CBS, 1960; "Naked City: To Walk in Silence," ABC, 1960; "Perry Mason: The Case of the Guilty Clients," CBS, 1961; "U.S. Steel Hour: The Woman Across the Hall," CBS, 1961; "The Good Years," CBS, 1962; "U.S. Steel Hour: The Perfect Accident," CBS, 1962; "The Defenders: The Crusader," CBS, 1962; "Stoney Burke: Fight Night," ABC, 1962; "The Nurses: You Could Die Laughing," CBS, 1963; "The Patty Duke Show: Patty the People's Voice," ABC, 1964; "The Defenders: Whitewash," CBS, 1964; "For the People: ... to prosecute all crimes ...," CBS, 1965.

BUNDY, BROOKE
b. 1947. Actress who played teen roles on sixties TV; later she played Diana Maynard Taylor on "General Hospital."
AS A REGULAR: "General Hospital," ABC, 1973-76; "Days of Our Lives," NBC, 1976-77.
AND: "The Donna Reed Show: To Be a Boy," ABC, 1962; "The Donna Reed Show: Big Sixteen," ABC, 1963; "The Adventures of Ozzie and Harriet: The Torn Dress," ABC, 1963; "My Three Sons: High on the Hog," ABC, 1963; "Mr. Novak: X Is the Unknown Factor," NBC, 1963; "Mr. Novak: The Song of Songs," NBC, 1964; "Gidget: Gidget's Foreign Policy," ABC, 1965; "The Virginian: The Mark of a Man," NBC, 1966; "Dragnet: The Big Little Victim," NBC, 1968; "The FBI: Ring of Steel," ABC, 1968; "The FBI: Death of a Fixer," ABC, 1968; "Medical Center: Thousands and Thousands of Miles," CBS, 1969; "Mission: Impossible: The Controllers," CBS, 1969; "The FBI: Boomerang," ABC, 1969; "The Mod Squad: Fever," ABC, 1970; "Mannix: To Save a Dead Man," CBS, 1971; "Medical Center: Countdown," CBS, 1971; "The Mod Squad: Home Is the Street," ABC, 1971; "The Rookies: A Bloody Shade of Blue," ABC, 1972; "The Mod Squad: The Night Holds Terror," ABC, 1973; "The FBI: The Rap Taker," ABC, 1973; "Owen Marshall, Counselor at Law: The Camerons Are a Special Clan," ABC, 1973; "Police Story: Line of Fire," NBC, 1973; "The Magician: The Illusion of the Queen's Gambit," NBC, 1974; "The Brady Bunch: Kelly's Kids," ABC, 1974; "Medical Center: Midwife," CBS, 1974; "Emergency!: Nagging Suspicion," NBC, 1974; "Police Story: War Games," NBC, 1975; "Police Woman: Mother Love," NBC, 1976; "Barnaby Jones: Anatomy of Fear," CBS, 1977; "Simon & Simon: Have a Little Wine with Your Murder?," CBS, 1984; "Moonlighting: Yours Very Deadly," ABC, 1986; "Webster: Hello Nicky," SYN, 1987.
TV MOVIES AND MINISERIES: "Along Came a Spider," ABC, 1970; "Travis Logan, D.A.," CBS, 1971; "The Adventures of Nick Carter," ABC, 1972; "Short Walk to Daylight," ABC, 1972; "A Beautiful Killing," ABC, 1974; "Man

on the Outside," ABC, 1975; "Francis Gary Powers: The True Story of the U-2 Spy Incident," NBC, 1976; "Crash," ABC, 1978; "Two Fathers' Justice," NBC, 1985; "News at Eleven," CBS, 1986.

BUNTROCK, BOBBY

b. Denver, CO, August 4, 1952. Blonde child actor who played Harold Baxter on "Hazel."

AS A REGULAR: "Hazel," NBC, 1961-65; CBS, 1965-66.

AND: "The Virginian: The Masquerade," NBC, 1967.

BUONO, VICTOR

b. San Diego, CA, 1938; d. 1982. Three-hundred pound actor who played King Tut on "Batman" and other roles as—heh, heh—heavies; he was also the father of Reverend Jim (Christopher Lloyd) on "Taxi."

AS A REGULAR: "Man From Atlantis," NBC, 1977-78.

AND: "On the Go," CBS, 1959; "SurfSide 6: Deadly Male," ABC, 1960; "The Rebel: Blind Marriage," ABC, 1960; "Checkmate: Moment of Truth," CBS, 1960; "77 Sunset Strip: The Legend of Leckonby," ABC, 1961; "The Untouchables: Mister Moon," ABC, 1961; "Michael Shayne: The Trouble with Ernie," NBC, 1961; "The Untouchables: The Gang War," ABC, 1962; "Perry Mason: The Case of the Absent Artist," CBS, 1962; "G.E. True: Firebug," CBS, 1963; "The New Loretta Young Show: Hey, Rube," CBS, 1963; "77 Sunset Strip: 5," ABC, 1963; "Perry Mason: The Case of the Simple Simon," CBS, 1964; "Bob Hope Chrysler Theatre: Memorandum for a Spy," NBC, 1965; "Perry Mason: The Case of the Grinning Gorilla," CBS, 1965; "The Wild Wild West: The Night of the Inferno," CBS, 1965; "Voyage to the Bottom of the Sea: Cyborg," ABC, 1965; "The Man From UNCLE: The Deadly Goddess Affair," NBC, 1966; "I Spy: Turkish Delight," NBC, 1966; "Perry Mason: The Case of the Twice-Told Twist," CBS, 1966; "Batman: The Curse of Tut/The Pharoah's in a Rut," ABC, 1966; "The Wild Wild West: The Night of the Eccentrics," CBS, 1966; "Batman: The Spell of Tut/The Case is Shut," ABC, 1966; "The Wild Wild West: Night of the Feathered Fury," CBS, 1967; "Batman: King Tut's Coup/Batman's Waterloo," ABC, 1967; "T.H.E. Cat: Lisa," NBC, 1967; "The Danny Thomas Hour: The Scene," NBC, 1967; "Batman: The Unkindest Tut of All," ABC, 1967; "The Legend of Robin Hood," NBC, 1968; "Batman: I'll Be a Mummy's Uncle," ABC, 1968; "Dinah Shore Special," NBC, 1969; "The Tonight Show Starring Johnny Carson," NBC, 1969; "Here's Lucy: Lucy Gets Her Man," CBS, 1969; "The Flying Nun: Sisters Socko in San Tanco," ABC, 1969; "It Takes a Thief: The Three Virgins

of Rome," ABC, 1969; "Get Smart: Moonlighting Becomes You," CBS, 1970; "O'Hara, U.S. Treasury: Operation Bribery," CBS, 1971; "Night Gallery: A Midnight Visit to the Neighborhood Blood Bank," NBC, 1971; "Assigment: Vienna: Annalisa," ABC, 1972; "The Mod Squad: Kristie," ABC, 1972; "CBS Playhouse 90: The Lie," CBS, 1973; "The Odd Couple: The Exorcists," ABC, 1973; "Hawaii Five-O: The $100,000 Nickel," CBS, 1973; "Orson Welles' Great Mysteries: Money to Burn," SYN, 1974; "Benjamin Franklin: The Ambassador," CBS, 1974; "The Odd Couple: The Rent Strike," ABC, 1975; "Khan!: Cloud of Guilt," CBS, 1975; "Ellery Queen: Two-Faced Woman," NBC, 1976; "The Practice: Jules and the Bum," NBC, 1976; "Alice: The Last Review," CBS, 1976; "Sirota's Court: Pilot," NBC, 1976; "Taxi: Going Home," ABC, 1980; "Fantasy Island: With Affection, Jack the Ripper," ABC, 1980; "Vega$: Black Cat Killer," ABC, 1980.

TV MOVIES AND MINISERIES: "Goodnight My Love," ABC, 1972; "Crime Club," CBS, 1973; "High Risk," ABC, 1976; "Brenda Starr," ABC, 1976; "Backstairs at the White House," NBC, 1979; "The Return of Mod Squad," ABC, 1979; "Better Late Than Never," NBC, 1979; "Murder Can Hurt You!," ABC, 1980; "More Wild Wild West," CBS, 1980.

BURGHOFF, GARY

b. Bristol, CT, May 24, 1940. Actor who won an Emmy as Radar O'Reilly on "M*A*S*H"; he returned as the character to try and put some life into the stillborn sitcom "AfterMASH."

AS A REGULAR: "The Don Knotts Show," NBC, 1970-71; "M*A*S*H," CBS, 1972-79; "AfterMASH," CBS, 1984.

AND: "Love, American Style: Love and the Crisis Line," ABC, 1973; "Match Game '74," CBS, 1974; "Twigs," CBS, 1975; "Match Game '75," CBS, 1975; "Match Game '76," CBS, 1976; "Fantasy Island: Pleasure Palace," ABC, 1980; "Tales of the Unexpected: The Best Policy," SYN, 1981; "The Love Boat: Lost and Found," ABC, 1981.

TV MOVIES AND MINISERIES: "The Man in the Santa Claus Suit," NBC, 1979; "Casino," ABC, 1980.

* Emmies: 1977.

BURKE, BILLIE

b. Mary William Ethelbert Appleton Burke, Washington, D.C., August 7, 1885; d. 1970. Film actress (Glinda the Good Witch in "The Wizard of Oz") who did a bit of TV.

AS A REGULAR: "Doc Corkle," NBC, 1952.

AND: "Lights Out: Dr. Heidigger's Experiment," NBC, 1950; "Bigelow Theatre: Dear Amanda," CBS, 1951; "Best of Broadway: Arsenic and Old Lace," CBS, 1955; "Matinee Theatre: Mother

Was a Bachelor," NBC, 1956; "Playhouse 90: The Star Wagon," CBS, 1957; "Texaco Star Theatre: Command Appearance," NBC, 1957; "Playhouse 90: Rumors of Evening," CBS, 1958; "Art Linkletter's House Party," CBS, 1958; "77 Sunset Strip: Publicity Brat," ABC, 1960.

BURKE, DELTA
b. Orlando, FL, July 30, 1956. Actress who plays the outrageous, much-married former beauty queen Suzanne Sugarbaker on "Designing Women"; one gets the feeling she's just as outrageous in real life.
AS A REGULAR: "The Chisholms," CBS, 1980; "Filthy Rich," CBS, 1982-83; "1st & Ten," HBO, 1983-86; "Designing Women," CBS, 1986- .
AND: "Nero Wolfe: Murder by the Book," NBC, 1981; "Remington Steele: Altered Steele," NBC, 1983; "The Love Boat: The End Is Near," ABC, 1983; "The Love Boat: Out of My Hair," ABC, 1983; "Simon & Simon: Sudden Storm," CBS, 1987.
TV MOVIES AND MINISERIES: "Charleston," NBC, 1979; "Mickey Spillane's Murder Me, Murder You," CBS, 1983; "A Bunny's Tale," ABC, 1985; "Where the Hell's That Gold?," CBS, 1988.
* Miss Florida 1974.

BURKE, PAUL
b. New Orleans, LA, July 21, 1926. Actor who played detective Adam Flint on "Naked City," officer Joe Gallagher on "Twelve O'Clock High" and congressman Neal McVane on "Dynasty."
AS A REGULAR: "Noah's Ark," NBC, 1956-57; "Harbourmaster (Adventures at Scott Island)," CBS, 1957; ABC, 1958; "Five Fingers," NBC, 1959-60; "Naked City," ABC, 1960-63; "Twelve O'Clock High," ABC, 1964-67; "Dynasty," ABC, 1982-84, 1987; "Santa Barbara," NBC, 1984; "Hot Shots," CBS, 1986-87.
AND: "Favorite Story: Man on a Bike," SYN, 1951; "Big Town: The Blood Profiteer," NBC, 1955; "The Adventures of Superman: Superman Week," SYN, 1955; "Frontier: Georgia Gold," NBC, 1955; "Stage 7: The Fox Hunt," CBS, 1955; "Navy Log: Sky Pilot," CBS, 1955; "Matinee Theatre: Hold My Hand and Run," NBC, 1956; "Panic!: Courage," NBC, 1957; "The Lineup: The Winner Takes Nothing Case," CBS, 1958; "Tightrope!: The Money Fight," CBS, 1959; "Hotel De Paree: Sundance and the Long Trek," CBS, 1960; "Hawaiian Eye: Second Fiddle," ABC, 1960; "Black Saddle: End of the Line," ABC, 1960; "Wanted Dead or Alive: The Trial," CBS, 1960; "Wagon Train: Path of the Sergeant," NBC, 1961; "The Lieutenant: Captain Thomson," NBC, 1963; "The Eleventh Hour: What Did She

Mean by 'Good Luck'?," NBC, 1963; "The Great Adventure: The Special Courage of Captain Pratt," CBS, 1964; "Dr. Kildare: A Hundred Million Tomorrows," NBC, 1964; "The Eleventh Hour: A Pattern of Sundays," NBC, 1964; "Combat!: Point of View," ABC, 1964; "Slattery's People: Question-What's a Genius Worth This Week?," CBS, 1964; "Medical Center: Undercurrent," CBS, 1970; "Hawaii Five-O: The Gunrunner," CBS, 1971; "Medical Center: The Doctor and Mr. Harper," CBS, 1972; "Marcus Welby, M.D.: The Panic Path," ABC, 1973; "Police Story: The Ten-Year Honeymoon," NBC, 1973; "The New Adventures of Perry Mason: The Case of the Murdered Murderer," CBS, 1973; "Shaft: The Kidnapping," CBS, 1973; "Medical Center: A Choice of Evils," CBS, 1974; "Ironside: Two Hundred Large," NBC, 1974; "Owen Marshall, Counselor at Law: To Keep and Bear Arms," ABC, 1974; "Hawkins: Candidate for Murder," CBS, 1974; "Police Story: World Full of Hurt," NBC, 1974; "Ironside: Act of Vengeance," NBC, 1974; "McMillan and Wife: Night Train to L.A.," NBC, 1975; "Police Story: Vice: 24 Hours," NBC, 1975; "Petrocelli: Any Number Can Die," NBC, 1976; "Police Story: Officer Dooly," NBC, 1976; "Starsky and Hutch: The Las Vegas Strangler," ABC, 1976; "The Love Boat: Ages of Man," ABC, 1979; "Magnum, P.I.: Mr. White Death," CBS, 1982; "Fantasy Island: Fantasy Island Girl," ABC, 1983; "T.J. Hooker: Blue Murder," ABC, 1983.
TV MOVIES AND MINISERIES: "Crowhaven Farm," ABC, 1970; "The Rookies," ABC, 1972; "Lieutenant Schuster's Wife," ABC, 1972; "Crime Club," CBS, 1973; "An Echo of Theresa," ABC, 1973; "Little Ladies of the Night," ABC, 1977; "Beach Patrol," ABC, 1979; "The Red-Light Sting," CBS, 1984.

BURKLEY, DENNIS
b. Van Nuys, CA. Rotund actor best known as Mac Slattery on "Mary Hartman, Mary Hartman" and as Cal, an overweight junkyard worker who was the butt of Redd Foxx's putdowns on "Sanford."
AS A REGULAR: "The Texas Wheelers," ABC, 1974-75; "Mary Hartman, Mary Hartman," SYN, 1977-78; "Hanging In," CBS, 1979; "Sanford," NBC, 1980-81; "Flipside," NBC, 1988.
AND: "The Rockford Files: Coulter City Wildcat," NBC, 1976; "Family: A Point of Departure," ABC, 1976; "McCloud: Bonnie and McCloud," NBC, 1976; "The Rockford Files: The Return of the Black Shadow," NBC, 1979; "Tenspeed and Brown Shoe: The Sixteen Byte Data Chip and the Brown-Eyed Fox," ABC, 1980; "Hill Street Blues: The Belles of St. Mary's," NBC, 1983; "Hill Street Blues: Eugene's Comedy Empire Strikes Back," NBC, 1983; "Hill Street Blues:

151

Spotlight on Rico," NBC, 1983; "Scarecrow and Mrs. King: Always Look a Gift Horse in the Mouth," CBS, 1983; "E/R: Growing Pains," CBS, 1984; "Who's the Boss?: Tony and the Professor," ABC, 1989.

TV MOVIES AND MINISERIES: "The Call of the Wild," NBC, 1976; "Best Sellers: Once an Eagle," NBC, 1977; "Charleston," NBC, 1979; "Mrs. R's Daughter," NBC, 1979.

BURMESTER, LEO
b. Louisville, KY.
AS A REGULAR: "Flo," CBS, 1980-81; "True Blue," NBC, 1989-90.
AND: "Nurse: A Place to Die," CBS, 1982; "The Equalizer: No Place Like Home," CBS, 1988.
TV MOVIES AND MINISERIES: "Chiefs," CBS, 1983; "George Washinton II: The Forging of a Nation," CBS, 1986.

BURNETT, CAROL
b. San Antonio, TX, April 26, 1933. Gifted comedienne who helmed one of the most successful variety shows ever at a time when the genre was breathing its last and then performed in some memorable TV drama ("Friendly Fire," "The Tenth Month"); she was an Emmy winner for two specials, "Julie and Carol at Carnegie Hall" and "Carol & Company."
AS A REGULAR: "Stanley," NBC, 1956-57; "Pantomime Quiz," ABC, 1958; 1959; "The Garry Moore Show," CBS, 1958; 1959-62; "The Entertainers," CBS, 1964-65; "The Carol Burnett Show," CBS, 1967-78; ABC, 1979; "Mama's Family," NBC, 1983-85; "Carol & Company," NBC, 1990- .
AND: "The Garry Moore Show," CBS, 1956; "The Ed Sullivan Show," CBS, 1957; "The Jonathan Winters Show," NBC, 1957; "The Garry Moore Show," CBS, 1957; "The Arlene Francis Show," NBC, 1957; "The General Motors 50th Anniversary Show," NBC, 1957; "The Arlene Francis Show," NBC, 1958; "Dinah Shore Chevy Show," NBC, 1958; "The Jack Paar Show," NBC, 1958; "The Ed Sullivan Show," CBS, 1958; "The Chevy Show," NBC, 1958; "I've Got a Secret," CBS, 1960; "U.S. Steel Hour: The American Cowboy," CBS, 1960; "Play Your Hunch," NBC, 1960; "I've Got a Secret," CBS, 1960; "No Place Like Home," NBC, 1960; "I've Got a Secret," CBS, 1961; "The du Pont Show: The Wonderful World of Toys," NBC, 1961; "Password," CBS, 1961; "Password," CBS, 1962; "The Twilight Zone: Cavender Is Coming," CBS, 1962; "I've Got a Secret," CBS, 1962; "The Jack Benny Program: Jack Plays Tarzan," CBS, 1962; "Julie and Carol at Carnegie Hall," CBS, 1962; "The Garry Moore Show," CBS, 1963; "Carol & Company," CBS, 1963; "Talent Scouts," CBS, 1963; "Calamity Jane," CBS, 1963; "The Garry Moore Show,"

CBS, 1964; "Password," CBS, 1964; "Once Upon a Mattress," CBS, 1964; "Password," CBS, 1965; "The Lucy Show: Lucy Gets a Roommate/Lucy and Carol in Palm Springs," CBS, 1966; "Password," CBS, 1966; "Gomer Pyle, USMC: Corporal Carol," CBS, 1967; "Get Smart: One of Our Olives Is Missing," NBC, 1967; "The Lucy Show: Lucy and Carol Burnett," CBS, 1967; "Girlfriends and Nabors," CBS, 1968; "Art Linkletter's House Party," CBS, 1968; "Here's Lucy: Lucy and Carol Burnett," CBS, 1969; "Gomer Pyle, USMC: Showtime with Sgt. Carol," CBS, 1969; "Carol Channing Special," ABC, 1969; "Here's Lucy: Lucy and Carol Burnett," CBS, 1970; "The Movie Game," SYN, 1970; "Here's Lucy: Lucy the Crusader," CBS, 1971; "Julie and Carol at Lincoln Center," CBS, 1971; "Once Upon a Mattress," CBS, 1972; "6 Rms Riv Vu," CBS, 1974; "Drink, Drank, Drunk," PBS, 1974; "Shirley MacLaine Special," CBS, 1974; "The Merv Griffin Show," SYN, 1974; "Twigs," CBS, 1975; "The Mike Douglas Show," SYN, 1975; "All My Children," ABC, 1976; "Van Dyke and Company," NBC, 1976; "Dinah!," SYN, 1978; "The Muppet Show," SYN, 1981; "All My Children," ABC, 1983; "Magnum P.I.: Rembrandt's Girl," CBS, 1984; "The Laundromat," HBO, 1985; "Carol, Carl, Whoopi and Robin," ABC, 1986; "A Conversation with Dinah," TNN, 1989; "AT&T Presents: Julie & Carol: Together Again," ABC, 1989.
TV MOVIES AND MINISERIES: "The Grass Is Always Greener Over the Septic Tank," CBS, 1978; "ABC Theatre: Friendly Fire," ABC, 1979; "The Tenth Month," CBS, 1979; "Life of the Party: The Story of Beatrice," CBS, 1982; "Between Friends," HBO, 1983; "Fresno," CBS, 1986; "Hostage," CBS, 1988.
* Burnett made a splash in 1955 when she recorded the comedy song "I Made a Fool of Myself Over John Foster Dulles." Dulles was President Eisenhower's dour secretary of state.
* Emmies: 1962, 1963.

BURNETTE, SMILEY
b. Lester Alvin Burnette, Summum, IL, March 18, 1911; d. 1967. Former sidekick of Gene Autry who played Charlie Pratt, one of the engineers of the Cannonball, on "Petticoat Junction."
AS A REGULAR: "Ozark Jubilee," ABC, 1959; "Petticoat Junction," CBS, 1963-67.
AND: "Country Music Jubilee," ABC, 1957; "Jubilee USA," ABC, 1958; "Jubilee USA," ABC, 1960; "Green Acres: The Day of Decision," CBS, 1966.

BURNS, ALLAN
Comic writer and producer, formerly in partnership with James L. Brooks.
AS WRITER: "He & She," CBS, 1967-68.

AS CO-CREATOR: "The Mary Tyler Moore Show,"
CBS, 1970-77.
AS CREATOR: "The Duck Factory," NBC, 1984;
"Eisenhower and Lutz," CBS, 1988; "FM,"
NBC, 1988, 1989.
* Emmies: 1968, 1971, 1975, 1976, 1977.
* See also James L. Brooks.

BURNS, CATHERINE

b. New York City, NY, September 25, 1945.
Attractive young actress in late sixties TV and
movies ("Red Sky at Morning").
AS A REGULAR: "One Life to Live," ABC, 1969-70.
AND: "The Mod Squad: Belinda-The End of Little
Miss Bubble Gum," ABC, 1972; "Love, American
Style: Love and Lady Luck," ABC, 1972; "The
Waltons: The Substitute," CBS, 1973; "Emer-
gency!: Rumors," NBC, 1974; "Sandburg's
Lincoln: Prairie Lawyer," NBC, 1975; "Medical
Story: Million Dollar Baby," NBC, 1975;
"Medical Center: The Stranger," CBS, 1976;
"Police Woman: Double Image," NBC, 1976.
TV MOVIES AND MINISERIES: "Two for the Money,"
ABC, 1972; "The Catcher," NBC, 1972; "Night
of Terror," ABC, 1972; "Amelia Earhart,"
NBC, 1976; "The Word," CBS, 1978.

BURNS, DAVID

b. New York City, June 22, 1902; d. 1971. Stage
and TV actor, often in blustery roles; he won an
Emmy for "The Price."
AS A REGULAR: "The Imogene Coca Show," NBC,
1955; "My Favorite Husband," CBS, 1955;
"The Trials of O'Brien," CBS, 1965-66.
AND: "The Ed Sullivan Show," CBS, 1957; "The
Jack Paar Show," NBC, 1958; "The Charley
Weaver Show," ABC, 1960; "The Merv Griffin
Show," SYN, 1966; "Then Came Bronson: The
Ninety-Nine Mile Creek," NBC, 1970; "Hallmark
Hall of Fame: The Price," NBC, 1971.
* Burns formed a comedy team with Kay
Medford briefly in 1958.
* Emmies: 1971.

BURNS, GEORGE

*b. Nathan Birnbaum, New York City, NY, January
20, 1896.* Longtime straight man to Gracie
Allen, Oscar-winning actor ("The Sunshine
Boys") and a show business figure vener-
able enough to be cast as God in three movies.
AS A REGULAR: "The George Burns and Gracie
Allen Show," CBS, 1950-58; "The George
Burns Show," NBC, 1958-59; "Wendy & Me,"
ABC, 1964-65; "George Burns Comedy Week,"
CBS, 1985.
AND: "The Bob Cummings Show: Hawaii Calls,"
CBS, 1955; "The Jack Benny Program," CBS,
1956; "The Jackie Gleason Show," CBS, 1957;
"The Bob Cummings Show: Bob Meets the
Mortons," CBS, 1957; "The Ed Sullivan Show,"

CBS, 1957; "The Jack Paar Show," NBC, 1958;
"The Jack Benny Program," CBS, 1958; "The
Bob Cummings Show: Bob Butters Beck - Beck
Butters Better," NBC, 1958; "The George Gobel
Show," NBC, 1958; "The Bob Cummings Show:
Bob Helps Martha," NBC, 1959; "The Bob
Cummings Show: Bob Helps Von Zell," NBC,
1959; "Startime: George Burns in the Big Time,"
NBC, 1959; "G.E. Theatre: Platinum on the
Rocks," CBS, 1959; "The Jack Benny Program,"
CBS, 1959; "Dinah Shore Chevy Show," NBC,
1960; "George Burns Special," NBC, 1960;
"Eleanor Roosevelt's Jubilee," NBC, 1960; "Open
End," NBC, 1960; "The Garry Moore Show,"
CBS, 1961; "The Jack Benny Program: Variety
Show," CBS, 1961; "The Jack Paar Show," NBC,
1961; "Dinah Shore Special," NBC, 1961; "Perry
Como's Kraft Music Hall," NBC, 1962; "Mr. Ed:
George Burns Meets Mr. Ed," CBS, 1962; "The
Jack Paar Program," NBC, 1962; "The Jack Paar
Program," NBC, 1963; "The Jack Benny
Program," CBS, 1964; "Sing Along with Mitch,"
NBC, 1964; "Hollywood Palace," ABC, 1965;
"The Tonight Show Starring Johnny Carson,"
NBC, 1965; "The Lucy Show: Lucy and George
Burns," CBS, 1966; "The Smothers Brothers
Comedy Hour," CBS, 1967; "Kraft Music Hall,"
NBC, 1967; "Carol Channing Special," CBS,
1968; "That's Life: Pilot," ABC, 1968; "The
Jackie Gleason Show," CBS, 1969; "This Is Tom
Jones," ABC, 1969; "The Dean Martin Show,"
NBC, 1969; "Here's Lucy: Lucy and Jack
Benny's Biography," CBS, 1970; "Playhouse
New York: The 1940s-The Great Radio
Comedians," NET, 1973; "Midnight Special,"
NBC, 1973; "Hi-Ho, Steverino: A 25th Anniver-
sary Salute to Steve Allen," ABC, 1974; "The
Smothers Brothers Comedy Hour," NBC, 1975;
"Ellery Queen: Veronica's Veils," NBC, 1975;
"The Mike Douglas Show," SYN, 1976; "Joys,"
NBC, 1976; "Alice: Oh, George Burns," CBS,
1978; "George Burns in Nashville?," NBC, 1980;
"Bob Hope Lampoons Television 1985," NBC,
1985; "America's Tribute to Bob Hope," NBC,
1988; "Bob Hope's Super Bowl Party," NBC,
1989; "Fifty Years of Television: A Golden
Celebration," CBS, 1989.
TV MOVIES AND MINISERIES: "G.E. Theater: Two of
a Kind," CBS, 1982.
* Burns appeared on "The Jack Benny Program"
in 1961 to introduce his newest discovery:
Ann-Margret.
* Yipes Dept.: This was the actual plot for "Oh,
George Burns": Waitress Vera (Beth Howland)
has seen the movie "Oh, God" several times,
and so she naturally thinks that when George
Burns walks into Mel's Diner, God is paying a
visit.

BURNS, JACK

b. Boston, MA, November 15, 1933. Long-faced

comedian who played deputy Warren Ferguson on "The Andy Griffith Show"; he also teamed for a time with Avery Schreiber, and nowadays he works more as a writer than a performer.
AS A REGULAR: "The Andy Griffith Show," CBS, 1965-66; "Our Place," CBS, 1967; "Getting Together," ABC, 1971-72; "Wait Till Your Father Gets Home," SYN, 1972-74; "The Burns and Schreiber Comedy Hour," ABC, 1973.
AND: "The Jack Paar Program," NBC, 1965; "Hollywood Palace," ABC, 1965; "Perry Como Special," NBC, 1967; "That's Life: Bachelor Days," ABC, 1968; "The Glen Campbell Goodtime Hour," CBS, 1969; "Love, American Style: Love and the Eyewitness," ABC, 1971; "Nanny and the Professor: Goodbye Arabella Hello," ABC, 1971; "Love, American Style: Love and the Lady Killers," ABC, 1972; "Love, American Style: Love and the Perfect Wife," ABC, 1972; "The Dean Martin Show," NBC, 1973; "The Mike Douglas Show," SYN, 1974; "Love, American Style: Love and the Opera Singer," ABC, 1974; "Saturday Night Live," NBC, 1976.
AS WRITER: "The Muppet Show," SYN, 1976-81; "Fridays," ABC, 1980-82.

BURNS, MICHAEL
b. New York City, NY, December 30, 1947. Former child actor who grew up on TV and thereafter found it harder to get work; he played orphan Barnaby West on "Wagon Train."
AS A REGULAR: "It's a Man's World," NBC, 1962-63; "Wagon Train," ABC, 1963-65.
AND: "Alfred Hitchcock Presents: Special Delivery," CBS, 1959; "The Many Loves of Dobie Gillis: The Right Triangle," CBS, 1960; "The Wrangler: The Affair with Browning's Woman," NBC, 1960; "Alfred Hitchcock Presents: The Doubtful Doctor," NBC, 1960; "Wagon Train: The Allison Justis Story," NBC, 1960; "G.E. Theatre: Learn to Say Goodbye," CBS, 1960; "Tales of Wells Fargo: Frightened Witness," NBC, 1960; "Wagon Train: The Jeremy Dow Story," NBC, 1960; "The Loretta Young Show: Quiet Desperation," NBC, 1961; "G.E. Theatre: Louie and the Horseless Buggy," CBS, 1961; "The Tall Man: Ransom of a Town," NBC, 1961; "Wagon Train: The Odyssey of Flint McCullough," NBC, 1961; "Alfred Hitchcock Presents: A Pearl Necklace," NBC, 1961; "Preview Theatre: Harry's Business," NBC, 1961; "The Twilight Zone: The Shelter," CBS, 1961; "Alcoa Premiere: Family Outing," ABC, 1961; "Wagon Train: The Mark Minor Story," NBC, 1961; "Lassie: Joey," CBS, 1961; "Wagon Train: The Dr. Denker Story," NBC, 1962; "Kraft Suspense Theatre: Charlie, He Couldn't Kill a Fly," NBC, 1964; "The Farmer's Daughter: The Fall and Rise of Steven Morley," ABC, 1966;

"The Virginian: The Challenge," NBC, 1966; "Dragnet: The Big LSD," NBC, 1967; "Bonanza: Napoleon's Children," NBC, 1967; "Tarzan: The Last of the Supermen," NBC, 1967; "Gunsmoke: Nowhere to Run," CBS, 1968; "The Big Valley: Run of the Savage," ABC, 1968; "Gunsmoke: The Head Cutters," CBS, 1968; "The Virginian: Seth," NBC, 1968; "The Virginian: The Bugler," NBC, 1969; "The FBI: Scapegoat," ABC, 1969; "Medical Center: Jeopardy," CBS, 1969; "Hollywood Television Theatre: The Andersonville Trial," NET, 1970; "Here's Lucy: Lucy and Aladdin's Lamp," CBS, 1971; "The FBI: Downfall," ABC, 1971; "The Partridge Family: The Undergraduate," ABC, 1971; "Hawaii Five-O: And I Want Some Candy, and a Gun That Shoots," CBS, 1971; "Medical Center: Circle of Power," CBS, 1971; "Love, American Style: Love and the Scroungers," ABC, 1972; "The Streets of San Francisco: Act of Duty," ABC, 1973; "The Mod Squad: Put Out the Welcome Mat for Death," ABC, 1973; "Love, American Style: Love and the Mail Room," ABC, 1973; "Barnaby Jones: Programmed for Killing," CBS, 1974; "Young Love," CBS, 1974; "The Manhunter: The Baby-Faced Killers," CBS, 1974; "The Streets of San Francisco: I Ain't Marching Anymore," ABC, 1974; "The Streets of San Francisco: Judgement Day," ABC, 1976; "Police Woman: Ambition," NBC, 1977.
TV MOVIES AND MINISERIES: "Stranger on the Run," NBC, 1967; "Gidget Gets Married," ABC, 1972; "Brock's Last Case," NBC, 1973.

BURNS, RONNIE
b. Evanston, IL, July 9, 1935. Adopted son of George Burns and Gracie Allen who had a mildly successful TV career in the late fifties.
AS A REGULAR: "The George Burns and Gracie Allen Show," CBS, 1955-58; "The George Burns Show," NBC, 1958-59; "Happy," NBC, 1960; 1961.
AND: "Playhouse 90: Helen Morgan," CBS, 1957; "American Bandstand," ABC, 1958; "G.E. Theatre: The World's Greatest Quarterback," CBS, 1958; "The Jack Benny Program," CBS, 1958; "Bachelor Father: Woman of the House," CBS, 1958; "No Warning!: Double Identity," NBC, 1958; "The Perry Como Show," NBC, 1959; "The Millionaire: Millionaire Ann Griffin," CBS, 1959; "The Red Skelton Show: Mr. K. Goes to College," CBS, 1961.

BURR, RAYMOND
b. William Stacey Burr, New Westminster, British Columbia, May 21, 1917. Rotund actor of distinguished bearing and a former movie heavy, he's now once again playing Perry Mason a couple times a year.
AS A REGULAR: "Perry Mason," CBS, 1957-66; "Ironside," NBC, 1967-75; "Kingston:

Confidential," NBC, 1977.
AND: "Dragnet: The Human Bomb," NBC, 1951; "Gruen Guild Playhouse: The Tiger," SYN, 1952; "Favorite Story: How Much Land Does a Man Need?," SYN, 1952; "Gruen Guild Playhouse: Face Value," SYN, 1952; "Gruen Guild Playhouse: The Leather Coat," SYN, 1952; "Mr. Lucky at Seven: Pearls From Paris," ABC, 1952; "Twilight Theatre: The Mask of Medusa," ABC, 1953; "Ford Theatre: The Fugitives," NBC, 1954; "Four Star Playhouse: The Room," CBS, 1954; "Schlitz Playhouse of Stars: The Ordeal of Dr. Sutton," CBS, 1955; "Counterpoint: The Wreck," SYN, 1955; "The 20th Century-Fox Hour: The Ox Bow Incident," CBS, 1955; "Lux Video Theatre: The Web," NBC, 1955; "Ford Theatre: Man Without a Fear," NBC, 1956; "Climax!: The Sound of Silence," CBS, 1956; "Climax!: The Shadow of Evil," CBS, 1956; "Lux Video Theatre: Flamingo Road," NBC, 1956; "Climax!: Savage Portrait," CBS, 1956; "Playhouse 90: The Greer Case," CBS, 1957; "Undercurrent: No Escape," CBS, 1957; "Playhouse 90: Lone Woman," CBS, 1957; "A Star Shall Rise," SYN, 1959; "The Triumphant Hour," SYN, 1960; "Person to Person," CBS, 1960; "The Jack Benny Program: Jack on Trial for Murder," CBS, 1961; "The Jack Benny Program," CBS, 1962; "Art Linkletter's House Party," CBS, 1964; "Hollywood Squares," NBC, 1968; "It Takes a Thief: A Thief Is a Thief Is a Thief," ABC, 1968; "The Flip Wilson Show," NBC, 1970; "The Flip Wilson Show," NBC, 1971; "Festival at Ford's," NBC, 1971; "The Bold Ones: Five Days in the Death of Sgt. Brown," NBC, 1972; "Portrait: A Man Named John," ABC, 1973; "The Sonny and Cher Comedy Hour," CBS, 1976; "The Inventing of America," NBC, 1976; "The Love Boat: Reunion Cruise," ABC, 1979.
TV MOVIES AND MINISERIES: "Ironside," NBC, 1967; "Split Second to an Epitaph," NBC, 1968; "The Priest Killer," NBC, 1971; "Mallory: Circumstantial Evidence," NBC, 1976; "Kingston: The Power Play," NBC, 1976; "Harold Robbins' 79 Park Avenue," NBC, 1977; "The Jordan Chance," CBS, 1978; "Centennial," NBC, 1978-79; "Love's Savage Fury," ABC, 1979; "Disaster on the Coastliner," ABC, 1979; "The Curse of King Tut's Tomb," NBC, 1980; "The Night the City Screamed," ABC, 1980; "Peter and Paul," CBS, 1981; "Perry Mason Returns," NBC, 1985; "Perry Mason: The Case of the Notorious Nun," NBC, 1986; "Perry Mason: The Case of the Shooting Star," NBC, 1986; "Perry Mason: The Case of the Sinister Spirit," NBC, 1987; "Perry Mason: The Case of the Scandalous Scoundrel," NBC, 1987; "Perry Mason: The Case of the Murdered Madam," NBC, 1987; "Perry Mason: The Case of the Avenging Ace," NBC, 1988; "Perry Mason:

The Case of the Lost Love," NBC, 1988; "Perry Mason: The Case of the Lethal Lesson," NBC, 1989; "Perry Mason: The Case of the Musical Murder," NBC, 1989; "Perry Mason: The Case of the All-Star Assassin," NBC, 1989.
* When the pilot for "Perry Mason" was shot, Burr wasn't in the role. One story says he played prosecutor Hamilton Berger, another says he was playing private eye Paul Drake. Whoever he was playing, he was recast as Mason.
* Emmies: 1959, 1961.

BURROWS, ABE
b. New York, NY, December 18, 1910; d. 1985. Playwright and TV personality of the fifties; father of TV producer-director James Burrows.
AS A REGULAR: "This Is Show Business," CBS, 1949-51, NBC, 1956; "Abe Burrows' Almanac," CBS, 1950; "We Take Your Word," CBS, 1950-51; "The Name's The Same," ABC, 1951-52; "What's It For," NBC, 1957-58.
AND: "The Steve Allen Show," NBC, 1958; "New Year's Eve Party," CBS, 1959; "What's My Line?," CBS, 1961; "Password," CBS, 1961; "Password," CBS, 1962; "To Tell the Truth," CBS, 1962; "The Match Game," NBC, 1963; "The Match Game," NBC, 1964; "Missing Links," NBC, 1964; "To Tell the Truth," CBS, 1964; "To Tell the Truth," CBS, 1965; "The Match Game," NBC, 1965; "Call My Bluff," NBC, 1965; "The Match Game," NBC, 1966.
AS PRODUCER-DIRECTOR: "The Big Party," CBS, 1959; "New Year's Eve Party," CBS, 1959; "Revlon Revue," CBS, 1960.
AS CREATOR: "O.K. Crackerby," ABC, 1965-66.

BURROWS, JAMES
b. New York City, NY. Emmy-winning director and producer who's been involved with some of the better sitcoms of the last twenty years; an Emmy winner for "Taxi" and "Cheers."
AS DIRECTOR: "The Mary Tyler Moore Show: Neighbors," CBS, 1974; "The Mary Tyler Moore Show: The Happy Homemaker Takes Lou Home," CBS, 1975; "The Bob Newhart Show," CBS, 1975-77; "The Mary Tyler Moore Show: Mary the Writer," CBS, 1976; "The Mary Tyler Moore Show: Mary's Insomnia," CBS, 1976; "Taxi," ABC, 1978-80; "Cheers," NBC, 1982- .
AND: "Rhoda: The Lady in Red," CBS, 1974.
* Emmies: 1980, 1981, 1983, 1984.

BURRUD, BILL
b. Hollywood, CA, January 12, 1925. Animal-show host.
AS A REGULAR: "Treasure," SYN, 1959-60;

"Animal World," NBC, 1968, CBS, 1969; 1971; ABC, 1970; "Safari to Adventure," SYN, 1969-75.

BURSTYN, ELLEN

b. *Edna Rae Gillooly, Detroit, MI, December 7, 1932*. Oscar-winning film actress ("Alice Doesn't Live Here Anymore") who began in TV.

AS A REGULAR: "The Doctors," NBC, 1965; "The Iron Horse," ABC, 1967-68; "The Ellen Burstyn Show," ABC, 1986-87.

AND: "Hallmark Hall of Fame: Hallmark Christmas Tree —Before the Stores Close," NBC, 1958; "Du Pont Show of the Month: Arrowsmith," CBS, 1960; "Michael Shayne: Strike Out," NBC, 1961; "The Loretta Young Show: Woodlot," NBC, 1961; "SurfSide 6: Double Image," ABC, 1961; "The Dick Powell Show: Ricochet," NBC, 1961; "Cheyenne: Day's Pay," ABC, 1961; "Dr. Kildare: Second Chance," NBC, 1961; "77 Sunset Strip: The Navy Caper," ABC, 1961; "Bus Stop: Cry to Heaven," ABC, 1962; "Window on Main Street: The Psychic," CBS, 1962; "I'm Dickens, He's Fenster: Harry, the Father Image," ABC, 1962; "Perry Mason: The Case of the Dodging Domino," CBS, 1962; "The Real McCoys: The Girl Veterinarian," CBS, 1962; "77 Sunset Strip: Dial S for Spencer," ABC, 1963; "Kraft Suspense Theatre: The Deep End," NBC, 1964; "The Greatest Show on Earth: Big Man From Nairobi," ABC, 1964; "The Virginian: Last Grave at Socorro Creek," NBC, 1969; "Gunsmoke: Waste," CBS, 1971; "The Bold Ones: Lisa, I Hardly Knew You," NBC, 1972; "Saturday Night Live," NBC, 1980.

TV MOVIES AND MINISERIES: "Thursday's Game," ABC, 1974; "The People Vs. Jean Harris," NBC, 1981; "Surviving," ABC, 1985; "Into Thin Air," CBS, 1985; "Something in Common," CBS, 1986.

* Burstyn also acted under the names Ellen McCrea and Ellen McRae.

BURTON, LEVAR

b. *Germany, February 16, 1957*. Actor who became an international celebrity after playing Kunta Kinte on "Roots"; steady employment, however, was another matter. Now he plays Lt. Geordi La Forge on "Star Trek: The Next Generation."

AS A REGULAR: "Star Trek: The Next Generation," SYN, 1987- .

AND: "The $20,000 Pyramid," ABC, 1978; "The Osmond Family," ABC, 1979; "The Love Boat: Love Is Blind," ABC, 1984.

TV MOVIES AND MINISERIES: "Roots," ABC, 1977; "Battered," NBC, 1978; "One in a Million: The Ron LeFlore Story," CBS, 1978; "Dummy," CBS, 1979; "The Acorn People," NBC, 1981; "Grambling's White Tiger," NBC, 1981; "The

Midnight Hour," ABC, 1985; "A Special Friendship," CBS; 1987; "Roots: The Gift," ABC, 1988.

BURTON, RICHARD

b. *Richard Jenkins, Pontrhydfen, Wales, November 10, 1925; d. 1984*. Powerful actor best known for his screen roles ("Who's Afraid of Virginia Woolf?," "Equus"); he did TV either as a favor to friends (Sammy Davis Jr., Lucille Ball) or for the dough ("Ellis Island").

AS A REGULAR: "Winston Churchill-The Valiant Years," ABC, 1960-63.

AND: "Du Pont Show of the Month: Wuthering Heights," CBS, 1958; "Buick Electra Playhouse: The Fifth Column," CBS, 1960; "Hallmark Hall of Fame: The Tempest," NBC, 1960; "The Ed Sullivan Show," CBS, 1961; "Camera Three: A Child's Christmas in Wales," CBS, 1961; "The Broadway of Lerner and Loewe," NBC, 1962; "The Sammy Davis Jr. Show," NBC, 1966; "Here's Lucy: Lucy Meets the Burtons," CBS, 1970; "Hallmark Hall of Fame: The Gathering Storm," NBC, 1974.

TV MOVIES AND MINISERIES: "Divorce His/Divorce Hers," ABC, 1973; "Brief Encounter," NBC, 1974; "Ellis Island," CBS, 1984.

* See also Elizabeth Taylor.

BURTON, WENDELL

b. *San Antonio, TX, July 21, 1947*. Young actor usually in fresh-faced roles; he played Charlie Brown in the Broadway musical "You're a Good Man, Charlie Brown."

AS A REGULAR: "The New Dick Van Dyke Show," CBS, 1973.

AND: "Medical Center: The VD Story," CBS, 1970; "Medical Center: Fatal Decision," CBS, 1972; "Longstreet: Leave the Wreck for Others to Enjoy," ABC, 1972; "Room 222: The Rights of Others," ABC, 1973; "Love, American Style: Love and the Face Bow," ABC, 1973; "Kung Fu: The Praying Mantis Kills," ABC, 1973; "The Rookies: Eyewitness," ABC, 1974.

TV MOVIES AND MINISERIES: "Murder Once Removed," NBC, 1971; "Go Ask Alice," ABC, 1973; "The Red Badge of Courage," NBC, 1974; "Journey From Darkness," NBC, 1975; "Medical Story," NBC, 1975.

BUSEY, GARY

b. *Goose Creek, TX, June 29, 1944*. Husky, rawboned actor of film ("The Buddy Holly Story") and some TV.

AS A REGULAR: "The Texas Wheelers," ABC, 1974-75.

AND: "Gunsmoke: The Busters," CBS, 1975; "Saturday Night Live," NBC, 1979.

TV MOVIES AND MINISERIES: "Bloodsport," ABC, 1973; "The Execution of Private Slovik," NBC,

1974; "The Law," NBC, 1974; "The Neon Empire," SHO, 1989.

BUSFIELD, TIMOTHY
b. East Lansing, MI. Bearded actor who's a ball of wound-up creative energy as Elliot Weston on "thirtysomething."
AS A REGULAR: "Reggie," ABC, 1983; "Trapper John, M.D.," CBS, 1984-86; "thirtysomething," ABC, 1987- .
AND: "Family Ties: Best Man," NBC, 1984; "Hotel: Imperfect Union," ABC, 1985.

BUSHMAN, FRANCIS X.
b. Norfolk, VA, January 10, 1883; d. 1966. Silent screen legend who was rediscovered by television in the fifties.
AS A GUEST: "Pepsi Cola Playhouse: Hollywood, Home Sweet Home," ABC, 1954; "Schlitz Playhouse of Stars: The Secret," CBS, 1954; "The Big Surprise," NBC, 1955; "The George Burns and Gracie Allen Show: The Interview," CBS, 1956; "Bob Hope Special," NBC, 1957; "Mr. Adams and Eve: The Business Manager," CBS, 1957; "You Bet Your Life," NBC, 1958; "77 Sunset Strip: All Our Yesterdays," ABC, 1958; "The Danny Thomas Show: Rusty's Day in Court," CBS, 1959; "Perry Mason: The Case of the Nine Dolls," CBS, 1960; "Hedda Hopper's Hollywood," NBC, 1960; "Perry Mason: The Case of the Flighty Father," CBS, 1960; "Here's Hollywood," NBC, 1960; "G.E. Theatre: The Other Wise Man," CBS, 1960; "Happy: The Weekend Nothing Happened," NBC, 1961; "Peter Gunn: Last Resort," ABC, 1961; "Dr. Kildare: The Bell in the School-house Tolls for Thee, Kildare/Life in the Dance Hall: F-U-N/Some Doors Are Slamming/Enough la Boheme for Everybody," NBC, 1965; "Batman: Death in Slow Motion/The Riddler's False Notion," ABC, 1966; "Voyage to the Bottom of the Sea: The Terrible Toys," ABC, 1966.

BUTKUS, DICK
b. Chicago, NY, December 9, 1942. Beefy actor, former football star.
AS A REGULAR: "Blue Thunder," ABC, 1984; "Half Nelson," NBC, 1985; "The Star Games," SYN, 1985; "My Two Dads," NBC, 1987-90.
AND: "Emergency!: Body Language," NBC, 1974; "McMillan and Wife: Guilt by Association," NBC, 1974; "Joe Forrester: Weekend," NBC, 1975; "The Rockford Files: The No-Cut Contract," NBC, 1976; "Taxi: The Apartment," ABC, 1979; "Simon & Simon: It's Only a Game," CBS, 1982; "Matt Houston: Killing Isn't Everything," ABC, 1982; "The Love Boat: Ace Meets the Champ," ABC, 1984; "Blacke's Magic: Vanishing Act," NBC, 1986; "Matlock: The

Annihilator," NBC, 1987; "Growing Pains: The Marrying Kind," ABC, 1988; "Kate & Allie: Wedding Belle Blues," CBS, 1988; "The Tonight Show Starring Johnny Carson," NBC, 1989.
TV MOVIES AND MINISERIES: "Brian's Song," ABC, 1971; "Rich Man, Poor Man," ABC, 1976; "The Stepford Children," NBC, 1987.

BUTLER, DAWS
b. Toledo, OH, November 16, 1916; d. 1989. Actor with a long career in animated cartoons, speaking for everyone from Yogi Bear to Elroy Jetson.
AS A REGULAR: "Yogi Bear," SYN, 1958-59; "The Jetsons," ABC, 1962-63, many others.

BUTLER, DEAN
b. Canada, May 20, 1956. Handsome actor who played Almanzo Wilder, husband of Laura (Melissa Gilbert) on "Little House on the Prairie."
AS A REGULAR: "Little House on the Prairie," NBC, 1979-83; "The New Gidget," SYN, 1986-88.
AND: "The Love Boat: Familar Faces," ABC, 1982; "The Love Boat: Long Time, No See," ABC, 1983; "Who's the Boss?: Mona Gets Pinned," ABC, 1984; "The Love Boat: Made for Each Other," ABC, 1986; "ABC Afterschool Special: Private Affairs," ABC, 1989.
TV MOVIES AND MINISERIES: "Forever," NBC, 1978; "The Kid with the 200 I.Q.," NBC, 1983; "Little House: Look Back to Yesterday," NBC, 1983; "Little House: The Last Farewell," NBC, 1984; "Little House: Bless All the Dear Children," NBC, 1984.

BUTTERWORTH, SHANE
b. Riverside, CA, October 3, 1969.
AS A REGULAR: "The Bad News Bears," CBS, 1979-80.
TV MOVIES AND MINISERIES: "The Dark Side of Innocence," NBC, 1976; "The Cracker Factory," ABC, 1979.

BUTTONS, RED
b. Aaron Chwatt, New York City, NY, February 5, 1919. Catskills comic whose rapid-fire style made him a TV hit for about three weeks; then he re-emerged as a character actor, winning an Oscar in 1957 for "Sayanora."
AS A REGULAR: "The Red Buttons Show," CBS, 1952-53; "The Double Life of Henry Phyfe," ABC, 1966; "Knots Landing," CBS, 1987.
AND: "Studio One: The Tale of St. Emergency," CBS, 1956; "The Perry Como Show," NBC, 1956; "The Perry Como Show," NBC, 1957; "Arthur Murray Party," NBC, 1957; "Tony Martin Special," NBC, 1957; "The Ed Sullivan Show," CBS, 1957; "The Eddie Fisher Show,"

NBC, 1958; "Hansel and Gretel," NBC, 1958; "Dinah Shore Chevy Show," NBC, 1958; "Patti Page Olds Show," ABC, 1958; "Playhouse 90: A Marriage of Strangers," CBS, 1959; "Arthur Murray Party," NBC, 1959; "I've Got a Secret," CBS, 1959; "The Jack Paar Show," NBC, 1959; "G.E. Theatre: The Tallest Marine," CBS, 1959; "The Ed Sullivan Show," CBS, 1960; "U.S. Steel Hour: The Case of the Missing Wife," CBS, 1960; "G.E. Theatre: Tippy-Top," CBS, 1961; "Saints and Sinners: All the Hard Young Men," NBC, 1962; "The Tonight Show Starring Johnny Carson," NBC, 1962; "Password," CBS, 1962; "The Eleventh Hour: Sunday Father," NBC, 1964; "Hollywood Palace," ABC, 1964; "The Greatest Show on Earth: The Last of the Strongmen," ABC, 1964; "Ben Casey: Journey's End in Lovers' Meeting," ABC, 1965; "Bob Hope Chrysler Theatre: Murder at NBC," NBC, 1967; "The Danny Thomas Hour: The Zero Man," NBC, 1967; "The Dean Martin Show," NBC, 1968; "The Jackie Gleason Show," CBS, 1968; "Love, American Style: Love and the Geisha," ABC, 1969; "The Mike Douglas Show," SYN, 1970; "George M!," NBC, 1970; "ABC Afterschool Special: Alexander," ABC, 1973; "Little House on the Prairie: The Circus Man," NBC, 1975; "Joys," NBC, 1976; "Don Adams Screen Test," SYN, 1976; "The Love Boat: A Friendly Little Game," ABC, 1978; "The Love Boat: Happy Ending," ABC, 1979; "The Love Boat: Discount Romance," ABC, 1983; "It's Garry Shandling's Show: Force Boxman," FOX, 1988; "It's Garry Shandling's Show: Save Mr. Peck's," FOX, 1989.
TV MOVIES AND MINISERIES: "Breakout," NBC, 1970; "The New, Original Wonder Woman," ABC, 1975; "Louis Armstrong-Chicago Style," ABC, 1976; "The Users," ABC, 1978; "Leave 'Em Laughing," CBS, 1981.

BUTTRAM, PAT
b. *Addison, AL, 1917.* Squeaky-voiced comic who played Gene Autry's TV sidekick and the sidewinding Mr. Haney on "Green Acres."
AS A REGULAR: "The Gene Autry Show," CBS, 1950-56; "Green Acres," CBS, 1965-71.
AND: "The George Gobel Show," NBC, 1957; "The George Gobel Show," NBC, 1958; "The Jim Backus Show: Once Upon a Moose," SYN, 1961; "The Jack Paar Show," NBC, 1961; "The Real McCoys: Luke the Reporter," CBS, 1962; "Arthur Godfrey in Hollywood," CBS, 1962; "Art Linkletter's House Party," CBS, 1963; "The Ed Sullivan Show," CBS, 1963; "The Real McCoys: The Partners," CBS, 1963; "The Danny Thomas Show: Here's the $50 Back," CBS, 1963; "The Ed Sullivan Show," CBS, 1964; "Art Linkletter's House Party," CBS, 1964; "The Munsters: All-Star Munster," CBS, 1965; "Petticoat Junction: The County Fair," CBS, 1966; "The Dean Martin Show," NBC, 1968; "Petticoat Junction: The

Other Woman," CBS, 1969; "Petticoat Junction: A Most Momentous Occasion," CBS, 1969; "Love, American Style: Love and the Longest Night," ABC, 1971; "Love, American Style: Love and the Country Girl," ABC, 1971; "Love, American Style: Love and the Competitors," ABC, 1973; "Chico and the Man: Gregory Peck Is a Rooster," NBC, 1977; "Darkroom: Catnip," ABC, 1981; "Simon & Simon: The Rough Rider Rides Again," CBS, 1982.
TV MOVIES AND MINISERIES: "The Hanged Man," NBC, 1964.
* On "The Danny Thomas Show," Buttram played a no-good vaudevillian named Harvey Bullock—an inside joke because Bullock was a long-time writer for Thomas and "The Andy Griffith Show," among many others.

BUX, KUDA
b. *Khudah Bukhsh, 1905; d. 1981.* Mystic who was an early TV curiosity.
AS A REGULAR: "I'd Like to See," NBC, 1948-49; "Kuda Bux, Hindu Mystic," CBS, 1950.
AND: "Captain Kangaroo," CBS, 1957; "Captain Kangaroo," CBS, 1958.

BUZZI, RUTH
b. *Wequetequock, CT, July 24, 1936.* Rubber-faced comic actress with a broad style; best known as little old lady Gladys Hornsby on "Rowan & Martin's Laugh-In."
AS A REGULAR: "The Entertainers," CBS, 1964-65; "The Steve Allen Comedy Hour," CBS, 1967; "That Girl," ABC, 1967-68; "Rowan & Martin's Laugh-In," NBC, 1968-73; "The Lost Saucer," ABC, 1975-77; "Days of Our Lives," NBC, 1983.
AND: "The Monkees: A Coffin Too Frequent," NBC, 1967; "The Mike Douglas Show," SYN, 1967; "Love, American Style: Love and the Haunted House," ABC, 1970; "The Glen Campbell Goodtime Hour," CBS, 1970; "Bob Hope Special," NBC, 1970; "The Dean Martin Show," NBC, 1971; "Night Gallery: Witches' Feast," NBC, 1971; "The Golddiggers," SYN, 1972; "The Flip Wilson Show," NBC, 1972; "Singles," CBS, 1972; "Here's Lucy: My Fair Buzzi," CBS, 1972; "Medical Center: The Judgement," CBS, 1973; "Love, American Style: Love and the Missing Mister," ABC, 1973; "Lotsa Luck: The Rich Widow," NBC, 1974; "Sandy in Disneyland," CBS, 1974; "Paradise," CBS, 1974; "ABC Afterschool Special: The Crazy Comedy Concert," ABC, 1974; "Funshine Saturday Sneakpeek," ABC, 1975; "The Bobby Vinton Show," SYN, 1975; "The Flip Wilson Comedy Special," CBS, 1975; "Cher," CBS, 1975; "Emergency!: Grateful," NBC, 1976; "Donny and Marie," ABC, 1976; "Medical Center: The Happy State of Depression," CBS, 1976; "The Love Boat: The Dummies," ABC, 1978; "Alice:

Henry's Bitter Half," CBS, 1981; "Dance Fever," SYN, 1982; "Life with Lucy: Lucy Makes a Hit with John Ritter," ABC, 1986.

TV MOVIES AND MINISERIES: "In Name Only," ABC, 1969.

BYINGTON, SPRING
b. Colorado Springs, CO, October 17, 1893; d. 1971. Actress remembered as Lily Ruskin on "December Bride," a popular sitcom of the fifties that is virtually unseen today.

AS A REGULAR: "December Bride," CBS, 1954-59; "Laramie," NBC, 1961-63.

AND: "Bigelow Theatre: Charming Billy," CBS, 1951; "Make Room for Daddy: Wonderland," ABC, 1954; "Ford Theatre: Wonderful Day for a Wedding," NBC, 1954; "The 20th Century-Fox Hour: A Trip to Paris," CBS, 1955; "The 20th Century-Fox Hour: Safety in Numbers," CBS, 1956; "Studio 57: The Great Wide World," SYN, 1956; "The Vic Damone Show," CBS, 1956; "The 20th Century-Fox Hour: The Moneymaker," CBS, 1956; "The Ford Show," NBC, 1956; "The Lux Show with Rosemary Clooney," NBC, 1958; "Christophers: Some Christopher Ideas," SYN, 1959; "Christophers: The Unique Position of the Teenager," SYN, 1960; "The Detectives Starring Robert Taylor: Face Down, Floating," ABC, 1960; "Goodyear Theatre: The Sitter's Baby," NBC, 1960; "The Tab Hunter Show: The Matchmaker," NBC, 1960; "Alfred Hitchcock Presents: The Man with Two Faces," NBC, 1960; "Dennis the Menace: Dennis' Birthday," CBS, 1961; "Mr. Ed: Oh, Those Hats!," CBS, 1964; "The Greatest Show on Earth: This Train Doesn't Stop Until It Gets There," ABC, 1964; "Bob Hope Chrysler Theatre: The Timothy Heist," NBC, 1964; "Dr. Kildare: Fathers and Daughters/A Gift of Love/The Tent-Dwellers/Going Home," NBC, 1965; "Batman: The Sandman Cometh/The Catwoman Goeth (A Stitch in Time)," ABC, 1966; "I Dream of Jeannie: Meet My Master's Mother," NBC, 1967; "The Flying Nun: To Fly or Not to Fly," ABC, 1968.

BYNER, JOHN
Comic and impersonator.

AS A REGULAR: "The Garry Moore Show," CBS, 1966-67; "The Steve Allen Comedy Hour," CBS, 1967; "Accidental Family," NBC, 1968; "The John Byner Comedy Hour," CBS, 1972; "The Practice," NBC, 1976-77; "Soap," ABC, 1978-80; "Bizarre," SHO, 1982-87.

AND: "The Ed Sullivan Show," CBS, 1964; "The Ed Sullivan Show," CBS, 1967; "Get Smart: The Hot Line," NBC, 1968; "The Mothers-in-Law: It's a Dog's Life," NBC, 1968; "The Don Rickles Show," ABC, 1968; "Operation: Entertainment," ABC, 1968; "The Steve Allen Show," SYN, 1968; "That's Life: Chalk Can Be Sexy," ABC, 1969; "The Ed Sullivan Show," CBS, 1969; "This Is Tom Jones," ABC, 1969; "The Glen Campbell Goodtime Hour," CBS, 1970; "The Glen Campbell Goodtime Hour," CBS, 1972; "Singles," CBS, 1972; "The Odd Couple: The New Car," ABC, 1973; "Love, American Style: Love and the Lifter," ABC, 1973; "The Carol Burnett Show," CBS, 1973; "Hawaii Five-O: Killer at Sea," CBS, 1974; "The Odd Couple: The Bigger They Are," ABC, 1975; "Dinah!," SYN, 1975; "When Things Were Rotten: The Ultimate Weapon," ABC, 1975; "The Bobby Vinton Show," SYN, 1976; "Joys," NBC, 1976; "The Bobby Vinton Show," SYN, 1977; "The Donna Fargo Show," SYN, 1978.

TV MOVIES AND MINISERIES: "A Guide for the Married Woman," ABC, 1978; "The Man in the Santa Claus Suit," NBC, 1979; "Murder Can Hurt You!," ABC, 1980.

BYRD, RALPH
b. Dayton, OH, April 22, 1909; d. 1952. Actor who played Dick Tracy in the movies and TV, not to be confused with Warren Beatty.

AS A REGULAR: "Dick Tracy," ABC, 1950-51.

AND: "Fireside Theatre: Operation Mona Lisa," NBC, 1950; "Fireside Theatre: The Man Without a Country," NBC, 1950; "Cinema Theatre: The Bunker," SYN, 1952.

BYRNES, EDD
b. Ed Breitenberger, New York City, NY, July 30, 1933. Actor who was a late fifties sensation as parking-attendant-turned-private-eye Kookie on "77 Sunset Strip."

AS A REGULAR: "77 Sunset Strip," ABC, 1958-63; "$weepstake$," NBC, 1979.

AND: "The Gale Storm Show: Not So Innocents Abroad," CBS, 1956; "Cheyenne: The Brand," ABC, 1957; "Maverick: Stage West," ABC, 1957; "Cheyenne: The Last Comanchero," ABC, 1958; "Sugarfoot: Ring of Sand," ABC, 1958; "The Steve Allen Show," NBC, 1959; "Pat Boone Chevy Showroom," ABC, 1959; "American Bandstand," ABC, 1959; "Coke Time," ABC, 1960; "Maverick: Hadley's Hunters," ABC, 1960; "Lawman: The Mad Bunch," ABC, 1960; "The Alfred Hitchcock Hour: Final Escape," CBS, 1964; "Burke's Law: Who Killed Mr. Colby in Ladies' Lingerie?," ABC, 1965; "Mr. Roberts: The Reluctant Draggin'," NBC, 1966; "Honey West: Little Green Robin Hood," ABC, 1966; "Mannix: Penny for a Peep-Show," CBS, 1969; "Love, American Style: Love and the Pickup," ABC, 1971; "Alias Smith and Jones: The Ten Days That Shook Kid Curry," ABC, 1973; "Faraday and Company: A Wheelbarrow Full of Trouble," NBC, 1973; "Police Woman: Wednesday's Child," NBC, 1976; "Sword of Justice: The Skywaymen," NBC, 1978; "B.J. and the Bear: Crackers," NBC, 1979; "B.J. and the Bear: The Friendly Double Cross," NBC, 1980;

"CHiPS: Off-Road," NBC, 1980; "House Calls: Muggers and Other Strangers," CBS, 1980; "Charlie's Angels: Wakiki Angels," ABC, 1981; "The Love Boat: Palimony O' Mine," ABC, 1982; "Quincy: On Dying High," NBC, 1983; "Simon & Simon: Corpus Delecti," CBS, 1984; "Simon & Simon: The Last Big Break," CBS, 1986.

TV MOVIES AND MINISERIES: "The Silent Gun," ABC, 1969; "Mobile Two," ABC, 1975.

* Byrnes was cast in "77 Sunset Strip" pilot as a killer. But when the producers saw the response to the actor, they cast him as Kookie (Real name: Gerald Lloyd Kookson III).

* On October 16, 1959, Byrnes introduced the song "Kookie, Kookie, Lend Me Your Comb" on "77 Sunset Strip." The tune hit number four on the pop charts.

BYRON, JEAN

b. Louisville, KY. Actress best known as Natalie Lane, Patty Duke's TV mom (and aunt—she played cousins, identical cousins).

AS A REGULAR: "Mayor of the Town," SYN, 1954; "The Many Loves of Dobie Gillis," CBS, 1959-60; 1961-63; "Full Circle," CBS, 1960-61; "The Patty Duke Show," ABC, 1963-66; "Pat Paulsen's Half a Comedy Hour," ABC, 1970.

AND: "Science Fiction Theatre: The Human Equation," SYN, 1955; "Science Fiction Theatre: The Long Day," SYN, 1955; "Science Fiction Theatre: One Thousand Eyes," SYN, 1956; "Science Fiction Theatre: The Miracle Hour," SYN, 1956; "My Friend Flicka: Big Red," CBS, 1957; "The 20th Century-Fox Hour: Threat to a Happy Ending," CBS, 1957; "Cheyenne: Blind Spot," ABC, 1959; "77 Sunset Strip: Created He Them," ABC, 1960; "Bus Stop: The Man From Bootstrap," ABC, 1961; "Robert Taylor's Detectives: Crossed Wires," NBC, 1962; "Cheyenne: The Idol," ABC, 1962; "Laramie: Bad Blood," NBC, 1962; "Batman: Nora Clavicle and the Ladies' Crime Club," ABC, 1968; "Marcus Welby, M.D.: I Can Hardly Tell You Apart," ABC, 1972; "The Rookies: Reading, Writing and Angel Dust," ABC, 1975; "Police Woman: The Lifeline Agency," NBC, 1976.

TV MOVIES AND MINISERIES: "Ransom for a Dead Man," NBC, 1971.

C

CAAN, JAMES

b. Bronx, NY, March 26, 1939. Actor who broke into movies through TV; he played doomed football player Brian Piccolo in the TV-movie "Brian's Song."

AS A GUEST: "Naked City: Bullets Cost Too Much," ABC, 1961; "Route 66: And the Cat Jumped Over the Moon," CBS, 1961; "Alcoa Premiere: The Masked Marine," ABC, 1962; "The Untouchables: A Fist of Five," ABC, 1962; "Dr. Kildare: The Mosaic," NBC, 1963; "Ben Casey: Justice to a Microbe," ABC, 1963; "Death Valley Days: Deadly Decision," SYN, 1963; "Combat!: Anatomy of a Patrol," ABC, 1963; "Kraft Suspense Theatre: The Hunt," NBC, 1963; "The Breaking Point: Glass Flowers Never Drop Petals," ABC, 1964; "Channing: My Son, the All-American," ABC, 1964; "The Alfred Hitchcock Hour: Memo From Purgatory," NBC, 1964; "Wagon Train: The Lee Barton Story," ABC, 1965; "The FBI: A Life in the Balance," ABC, 1969; "The David Frost Show," SYN, 1971; "The Virginia Graham Show," SYN, 1972; "Rowan & Martin's Laugh-In," NBC, 1972.

TV MOVIES AND MINISERIES: "Brian's Song," ABC, 1971.

CABOT, BRUCE

b. Jacques Etienne de Bujac, Carlsbad, NM, April 20, 1904; d. 1972. B-movie actor who played Ellery Queen for a time.

AS A REGULAR: "Ellery Queen," DUM, 1955.
AND: "Stars Over Hollywood: Not a Bad Guy," NBC, 1950; "Stars Over Hollywood: Merry Christmas From Sweeney," NBC, 1950; "Lux Video Theatre: Treasure Trove," CBS, 1951; "Gruen Guild Playhouse: Driven Snow," ABC, 1951; "Tales of Tomorrow: Dune Roller," ABC, 1952; "Tales of Tomorrow: The Seeing-Eye Surgeon," ABC, 1952; "Half Hour Theatre: Tails for Jeb Mulcahy," ABC, 1953; "Phil Silvers Special: The Slowest Gun in the West," CBS, 1960; "77 Sunset Strip: Double Trouble," ABC, 1960; "Here's Hollywood," NBC, 1961; "Burke's Law: Who Killed Hollywood?," ABC, 1963; "Bob Hope Chrysler Theatre: Have Girls, Will Travel," NBC, 1964; "Bonanza: A Dime's Worth of Glory," NBC, 1964; "Daniel Boone: The Devil's Four," NBC, 1965.

CABOT, SEBASTIAN

b. Charles Sebastian Thomas Cabot, London, England, July 6, 1918; d. 1977. Bearded, corpulent actor who was Mr. French on the less-than-scintillating sitcom "Family Affair."

AS A REGULAR: "Checkmate," CBS, 1960-62; "Stump the Stars," CBS, 1964; "Suspense," CBS, 1964; "Family Affair," CBS, 1966-71; "Ghost Story," NBC, 1972-73.

AND: "Gunsmoke: The Queue," CBS, 1955; "Alfred Hitchcock Presents: A Bullet for Baldwin," CBS, 1956; "Fireside Theatre: The Liberator," NBC, 1956; "Disneyland: Dog Grayson—Along the Oregon Trail," ABC, 1956; "The Adventures of Hiram Holliday: The Sea Cucumber," NBC, 1956; "Studio 57: A Hero Returns," SYN, 1956; "The Adventures of Hiram Holliday: Adventure of the Moroccan Hawk Moth," NBC, 1957; "Playhouse 90: So Soon to Die," CBS, 1957; "The Adventures of Hiram Holliday: Ersatz Joe," NBC, 1957; "Schlitz Playhouse of Stars: Rich Man, Poor Man," CBS, 1957; "The Jane Wyman Show: Contact," NBC, 1957; "Hotel De Paree: A Fool and His Gold," CBS, 1959; "Bonanza: The Spanish Grant," NBC, 1960; "The Twilight Zone: A Nice Place to Visit," CBS, 1960; "Cheyenne: Border Affair," ABC, 1960; "The Islanders: Five O'Clock Friday," ABC, 1960; "Here's Hollywood," NBC, 1961; "The Dick Powell Show: The Last of the Private Eyes," NBC, 1963; "My Three Sons: The In-Law Whammy," ABC, 1964; "Mr. Ed: Whiskers and Tails," CBS, 1965; "Vacation Playhouse: Duke," CBS, 1965; "The Beverly Hillbillies: The Poor Farmer," CBS, 1965; "Walt Disney's Wonderful World of Color: One Day on Beetle Rock," NBC, 1967; "Art Linkletter's House Party," CBS, 1968; "The Mike Douglas Show," SYN, 1968; "The Mike Douglas Show," SYN, 1969; "It Takes Two," NBC, 1969; "To Rome with Love: Roman Affair," CBS, 1970; "McCloud: Encounter with Aries," CBS, 1971; "Hollywood Squares," NBC, 1972.

TV MOVIES AND MINISERIES: "The Spy Killer," ABC, 1969; "Foreign Exchange," ABC, 1970; "Miracle on 34th Street," CBS, 1973.

* Hard to imagine, but Cabot's beard was considered a real novelty in the clean-shaven early sixties; *TV Guide* even ran a picture article on how Cabot cared for his whiskers.

CADORETTE, MARY

b. East Hartford, CT, March 31, 1957. Pert actress who played Vicky Bradford, fiancee of Jack Tripper (John Ritter) in a short-lived "Three's Company" spinoff.

AS A REGULAR: "Three's a Crowd," ABC, 1984-85.

And: "The Love Boat: Made for Each Other," ABC, 1986; "Simon & Simon: For the People," CBS, 1986; "My Two Dads: Whose Night Is It, Anyway?," NBC, 1987.

TV MOVIES AND MINISERIES: "Perry Mason: The Case of the Musical Murder," NBC, 1989.

CADY, FRANK

b. Susanville, CA, 1915. Lean, bald actor who played storekeeper Sam Drucker on "Petticoat Junction" and "Green Acres"; he was also Doc Williams on "The Adventures of Ozzie and Harriet" and the original Mayberry town drunk on the pilot for "The Andy Griffith Show."

AS A REGULAR: "The Adventures of Ozzie and Harriet," ABC, 1954-65; "Petticoat Junction," CBS, 1963-70; "Green Acres," CBS, 1965-71; "The Beverly Hillbillies," CBS, 1968-69.

AND: "December Bride: Lily in a Gas Station," CBS, 1956; "You Are There: The Great Diamond Fraud," CBS, 1956; "The Jane Wyman Show: A Dangerous Thing," NBC, 1957; "December Bride: Ruth the Brain," CBS, 1959; "Markham: Crash in the Desert," CBS, 1960; "The Danny Thomas Show: Danny Meets Andy Griffith," CBS, 1960; "The Alaskans: The Last Bullet," ABC, 1960; "Guestward Ho!: The Hooton Statue," ABC, 1961; "Guestward Ho!: Bill the Fireman," ABC, 1961; "Guestward Ho!: The Wrestler," ABC, 1961; "Perry Mason: The Case of the Pathetic Patient," CBS, 1961; "Pete and Gladys: The Live-In Couple," CBS, 1961; "Dennis the Menace: The Club Initiation," CBS, 1962; "G.E. Theatre: My Dark Days," CBS, 1962; "The Virginian: The Exiles," NBC, 1963; "Grindl: The Great Bank Robbery," NBC, 1963; "Hazel: The Flagpole," NBC, 1964; "The Andy Griffith Show: The Legend of Barney Fife," CBS, 1966; "Hawaii Five-O: Mother's Deadly Helper," CBS, 1974.

CAESAR, SID

b. Yonkers, NY, September 8, 1922. Perhaps the most gifted comic on early TV, expert at physical comedy and verbal wit; sketches from "Your Show of Shows" still stand up today.

AS A REGULAR: "The Admiral Broadway Revue," NBC, 1949; "The Saturday Night Revue," NBC, 1950; "Your Show of Shows," NBC, 1950-54; "Caesar's Hour," NBC, 1954-57; "The Sid Caesar Show," ABC, 1958, 1963-64; "As Caesar Sees It," ABC, 1962-63.

AND: "The Ed Sullivan Show," CBS, 1956; "Dinah Shore Chevy Show," NBC, 1958; "Some of Manie's Friends," NBC, 1959; "At the Movies," NBC, 1959; "U.S. Steel Hour: Holiday on Wheels," CBS, 1959; "U.S. Steel Hour: Marriage ... Handle with Care," CBS, 1959; "Sid Caesar Special: Tiptoe Through TV," CBS, 1960; "Sid Caesar Special: Variety—World of Show Biz," CBS, 1960; "Perry Como's Kraft Music Hall," NBC, 1960; "G.E. Theatre: The Devil You Say," CBS, 1961; "25 Years of Life Magazine," NBC, 1961; "The Ed Sullivan Show," CBS, 1961; "Checkmate: Kill the Sound," CBS, 1961; "The Ed Sullivan Show," CBS, 1962; "Sid Caesar and Edie Adams Together," ABC, 1963; "The Ed Sullivan Show," CBS, 1964; "The Ed Sullivan Show," CBS, 1965; "The Andy Williams Show," NBC, 1965; "The Sid Caesar, Imogene Coca, Carl Reiner, Howard Morris Special," CBS, 1967; "The Danny Thomas Hour: Instant Money," NBC, 1967; "The Carol Burnett Show," CBS, 1967; "The Lucy Show: Lucy and Sid Caesar," CBS, 1968; "The Carol Burnett Show," CBS, 1968; "Hollywood Palace," ABC, 1968; "That Girl: The Drunkard," ABC, 1968; "That's Life: Buying a House," ABC, 1968; "The Jackie Gleason Show," CBS, 1968; "That's Life: Bringing Baby Home," ABC, 1968; "The Steve Allen Show," SYN, 1968; "That's Life: You Never Take Me Anyplace," ABC, 1969; "Love, American Style: Love and Who?," ABC, 1969; "Love, American Style: Love and the Bowling Ball," ABC, 1970; "A Salute to Television's 25th Anniversary," ABC, 1972; "The Julie Andrews Hour," ABC, 1973; "When Things Were Rotten: The French Disconnection," ABC, 1975; "Joys," NBC, 1976; "The Love Boat: The Dummies," ABC, 1978; "Saturday Night Live," NBC, 1983; "Amazing Stories: Mr. Magic," NBC, 1985; "Ooh-La-La-It's Bob Hope's Fun Birthday Spectacular From Paris' Bicentennial," NBC, 1989.

TV MOVIES AND MINISERIES: "Flight to Holocaust," NBC, 1977; "Found Money," NBC, 1983; "Hallmark Hall of Fame: Love Is Never Silent," NBC, 1985; "Freedom Fighter," NBC, 1988; "Side by Side," CBS, 1988.

* Emmies: 1952, 1957.

CAGNEY, JAMES

b. New York City, NY, July 17, 1899; d. 1986. Screen legend who did little TV, but was talked out of retirement for a sentimental TV movie just before his death.

AS A GUEST: "Robert Montgomery Presents: Soldier from the Wars Returning," NBC, 1956; "The Bob Hope Show," NBC, 1956; "Christophers: A Link in the Chain," SYN, 1957; "Navy Log: The Lonely Watch," ABC, 1958; "The Ed Sullivan Show," CBS, 1960; "The Jack Paar Show," NBC, 1960; "Biography of the Fight," ABC, 1960; "The Ballad of Smokey the Bear," NBC, 1966; "The American Film Institute Salute to James Cagney," CBS, 1974.

TV MOVIES AND MINISERIES: "Terrible Joe Moran," CBS, 1984.

* For "Biography of the Fight," Cagney narrated films about the lives of Floyd Patterson and Ingemar Johansson.

CAGNEY, JEANNE

b. New York City, NY, March 25, 1919. Sister of James; she was a co-host on "Queen for a Day."

AS A REGULAR: "Queen for a Day," ABC, 1956-60.

AND: "Lux Video Theatre: Satan's Waitin'," NBC, 1949; "Drama: A Capture," SYN, 1950; "Bigelow Theatre: The Big Hello," CBS, 1951; "The Unexpected: Legal Tender," NBC, 1952; "TV Reader's Digest: I'll Pick More Daisies," ABC, 1955; "Trial at Tara," SYN, 1962.

CAINE, HOWARD

b. Nashville, TN, January 2, 1928. Slight, dark-featured character actor who played Major Hochstedder on "Hogan's Heroes."

AS A REGULAR: "The Californians," NBC, 1957-58; "Hogan's Heroes," CBS, 1966-71.

AND: "Goodyear Theatre: The Ticket," NBC, 1960; "Hallmark Hall of Fame: Captain Brassbound's Conversion," NBC, 1960; "Michael Shayne: Dolls Are Deadly," NBC, 1960; "Bringing Up Buddy: The Girls in Court," CBS, 1960; "Pete and Gladys: Pete Takes Up Golf," CBS, 1960; "Alcoa Premiere: Pattern of Guilt," ABC, 1962; "Straightaway: Full Circle," ABC, 1962; "Leave It to Beaver: Eddie the Businessman," ABC, 1962; "Fair Exchange: No More Transatlantic Calls!," CBS, 1962; "McKeever and the Colonel: The Bugle Sounds," NBC, 1962; "The Lucy Show: Lucy Goes to Art Class," CBS, 1964; "The Lucy Show: Lucy Goes Into Politics," CBS, 1964; "The Outer Limits: The Chameleon," ABC, 1964; "Slattery's People: A Sitting Duck Named Slattery," CBS, 1965; "My Favorite Martian: Bottled Martin," CBS, 1965; "Get Smart: The Day Smart Turned Chicken," NBC, 1965; "The FBI: The Hijackers," ABC, 1965; "Rango: Gunfight at the K.O. Saloon," ABC, 1967; "Get Smart: A Man Called Smart," NBC, 1967; "Adam's Rib: Illegal Aid," ABC, 1973; "Bret Maverick: The Ballad of Bret Maverick," NBC, 1982.

TV MOVIES AND MINISERIES: "The Doomsday Flight," NBC, 1966; "War and Remembrance," ABC, 1988, 1989.

CALHOUN, RORY

b. Francis Timothy Durgin, Los Angeles, CA, August 8, 1922. Rough-and-tumble actor who played gunfighter Bill Longley on "The Texan."

AS A REGULAR: "The Texan," CBS, 1958-60; "Capitol," CBS, 1982-87.

AND: "Ford Theatre: The Road Ahead," NBC, 1954; "Ford Theatre: Garrity's Sons," NBC, 1955; "Climax!: Champion," CBS, 1955; "Screen Directors Playhouse: Day Is Done," NBC, 1955; "Ford Theatre: Bet the Queen," NBC, 1955; "Screen Directors Playhouse: Hot Cargo," NBC, 1956; "This Is Your Life" (Gilbert Roland), NBC, 1956; "December Bride: Rory Calhoun Show," CBS, 1956; "Can Do," NBC, 1956; "Dick Powell's Zane Grey Theatre: Muletown Gold Strike," CBS, 1956; "December Bride: The Texan, Rory Calhoun," CBS, 1959; "Westinghouse Desilu Playhouse: The Killer Instinct," CBS, 1959; "Wagon Train: The Artie Matthewson Story," NBC, 1961; "The Dick Powell Show: Measure of a Man," NBC, 1963; "Death Valley Days: Measure of a Man," SYN, 1963; "The Greatest Show on Earth: This Train Doesn't Stop Till It Gets There," ABC, 1964; "Bonanza: Thanks for Everything, Friend," NBC, 1964; "The Virginian: A Father for Toby," NBC, 1964; "Burke's Law: Who Killed Nobody Somehow?," ABC, 1965; "Wagon Train: The Jarbo Pierce Story," ABC, 1965; "Rawhide: The Testing Post," CBS, 1965; "I Spy: A Day Called Four Jaguar," NBC, 1966; "Death Valley Days: The Water Bringer," SYN, 1966; "Gilligan's Island: The Hunter," CBS, 1967; "Land's End," NBC, 1968; "Alias Smith and Jones: Night of the Red Dog," ABC, 1972; "The Doris Day Show: Cover Girl," CBS, 1972; "Owen Marshall, Counselor at Law: Charlie Gave Me Your Number," ABC, 1972; "Hec Ramsey: The Green Feather," NBC, 1972; "Circle of Fear: Death's Head," NBC, 1973; "Police Story: Death on Credit," NBC, 1973; "Police Story: The Shoefly Days," NBC, 1974; "Jigsaw John: Follow the Yellow Brick Road," NBC, 1976.

TV MOVIES AND MINISERIES: "Flight to Holocaust," NBC, 1977; "Flatbed Annie and Sweetiepie: Lady Truckers," CBS, 1979; "The Rebels," SYN, 1979.

AS WRITER: "The Texan: The Nomad," CBS, 1960.

CALLAN, MICHAEL

b. Martin Calinieff, Philadelphia, PA, November 22, 1935. Light leading man of the sixties who moved into bad-guy roles on seventies cop shows.

AS A REGULAR: "Occasional Wife," NBC, 1966-67; "Superboy," SYN, 1989- .

AND: "Here's Hollywood," NBC, 1961; "Arrest and Trial: Tears From a Silver Dipper," ABC, 1963; "Dr. Kildare: Quid Pro Quo," NBC, 1964; "Hazel: Welcome Back, Kevin," NBC, 1964; "Twelve O'Clock High: The Suspected," ABC, 1964; "American Bandstand," ABC, 1965; "The FBI: Quantico," ABC, 1966; "Twelve O'Clock High: Decoy," ABC, 1966; "The Mike Douglas Show," SYN, 1966; "The FBI: Ring of Steel," ABC, 1968; "The Felony Squad: The Love Victim," ABC, 1968; "Kiss Me, Kate!," ABC, 1968; "Love, American Style: Love and the Man Next Door," ABC, 1970; "The Mary Tyler Moore Show: Smokey the Bear Wants You," CBS, 1971;

"Love, American Style: Love and Women's Lib,"
ABC, 1971; "Love, American Style: Love and the
Loudmouth," ABC, 1971; "Ironside: Good
Samaritan," NBC, 1971; "The FBI: The Outcast,"
ABC, 1972; "ABC Afternoon Playbreak: The Gift
of Terror," ABC, 1973; "Police Surgeon: The
Judas Goat of Ebony Street," SYN, 1973; "Love,
American Style: Love and the Single Husband,"
ABC, 1973; "Honeymoon Suite," ABC, 1973;
"Police Story: Countdown," NBC, 1974; "Police
Story: Glamour Boy," NBC, 1974; "McMillan
and Wife: Night Train to L.A.,", NBC, 1975;
"Police Story: The Man in the Shadows," NBC,
1975; "Barnaby Jones: Poisoned Pigeon," CBS,
1975; "Medical Story: An Air Full of Death,"
NBC, 1975; "Switch: The Girl on the Golden
Strip," CBS, 1976; "Quincy: Sullied Be Thy
Name," NBC, 1977; "Simon & Simon: Caught
Between the Devil and the Deep Blue Sea," CBS,
1983; "Hardcastle and McCormick: Once Again
with Vigorish," ABC, 1983; "E/R: Growing
Pains," CBS, 1984; "Hardcastle and McCormick:
McCormick's Bar and Grill," ABC, 1986;
"Murder, She Wrote: J.B.... As in Jailbird," CBS,
1988.
TV MOVIES AND MINISERIES: "In Name Only,"
ABC, 1969; "Donner Pass: The Road to
Survival," NBC, 1978; "Blind Ambition,"
CBS, 1979; "Scruples," CBS, 1980; "Last of
the Great Survivors," CBS, 1984.

CALLAS, CHARLIE
b. Brooklyn, NY. Rubber-faced comic, a
protégé of Jerry Lewis; his mechanical shtick
was a hot item in the seventies.
AS A REGULAR: "The Andy Williams Show,"
NBC, 1970-71; "ABC Comedy Hour," ABC,
1972; "Switch," CBS, 1975-78; "The Dom
DeLuise Show," SYN, 1987-88.
AND: "The Jimmy Dean Show," ABC, 1964; "The
Munsters: Herman Picks a Winner," CBS, 1966;
"The Flip Wilson Show," NBC, 1970; "Rowan &
Martin's Laugh-In," NBC, 1972; "Love,
American Style: Love and the Bathtub," ABC,
1972; "Rowan & Martin's Laugh-In," NBC,
1973; "The Bobby Vinton Show," SYN, 1975;
"Hollywood Squares," NBC, 1977; "The Merv
Griffin Show," SYN, 1979; "The Love Boat:
Cyrano De Bricker," ABC, 1979; "Hart to Hart:
Murder Is a Drag," ABC, 1981; "It Takes Two:
Inside Lisa Quinn," ABC, 1983; "Cagney &
Lacey: Lady Luck," CBS, 1984; "It's Garry
Shandling's Show: Save Mr. Peck's," FOX, 1989.
TV MOVIES AND MINISERIES: "The Snoop Sisters,"
NBC, 1972; "Switch," CBS, 1975.

CALVET, CORINNE
b. Corinne Dibos, Paris, France, April 30,
1936. Sexy film and TV actress of the fifties,
usually in temptress roles.
AS A GUEST: "Lux Video Theatre: Legacy of
Love," CBS, 1952; "Lux Video Theatre:
Babette," CBS, 1953; "Ford Theatre: Indirect
Approach," NBC, 1954; "The Red Skelton
Show," CBS, 1956; "The Ford Show," NBC,
1956; "Do You Trust Your Wife?," CBS,
1956; "Climax!: Bait for the Tiger," CBS,
1957; "The Steve Allen Show," NBC, 1957;
"Studio One: Balance of Terror," CBS, 1958;
"Pantomime Quiz," ABC, 1959; "Keep
Talking," ABC, 1960; "Burke's Law: Who
Killed Julian Buck?," ABC, 1963; "Burke's
Law: Who Killed Everybody?," ABC, 1964;
"Burke's Law: Who Killed the 13th Clown?,"
ABC, 1965; "Batman: The Joker's Flying
Saucer," ABC, 1968; "Police Story: The
Gamble," NBC, 1974.
TV MOVIES AND MINISERIES: "The Phantom of
Hollywood," CBS, 1974.

CAMBRIDGE, GODFREY
b. New York City, NY, February 26, 1933; d.
1976. Comedian-actor who died of a heart
attack on the set of the TV-movie "Victory at
Entebbe," in which he was going to play
Ugandan president Idi Amin.
AS A GUEST: "U.S. Steel Hour: Male Call," CBS,
1962; "The Jack Paar Program," NBC, 1964;
"Get the Message," ABC, 1964; "The
Tennessee Ernie Ford Show," ABC, 1965;
"Hollywood Palace," ABC, 1965; "The Man
From UNCLE: The My Friend the Gorilla
Affair," NBC, 1966; "The Dick Van Dyke
Show: The Man From My Uncle," CBS, 1966;
"Daktari: Cry for Help," CBS, 1966; "I Spy:
Court of the Lion," NBC, 1967; "The Jonathan
Winters Show," CBS, 1968; "Kraft Music
Hall," NBC, 1969; "Hollywood Palace," ABC,
1969; "The Red Skelton Hour," CBS, 1969;
"Bob Newhart Special: A Last Laugh at the
60's," ABC, 1970; "Love, American Style:
Love and the Champ," ABC, 1970; "The
Golddiggers," SYN, 1971; "Night Gallery:
Make Me Laugh," NBC, 1971; "The David
Frost Show," SYN, 1971; "Jack Paar Tonight,"
ABC, 1973; "Furst Family of Washington,"
ABC, 1973; "ABC Theatre: Ceremonies in
Dark Old Men," ABC, 1975; "Police Story:
Year of the Dragon," NBC, 1975.

CAMERON, CANDACE
Young actress, sister of Kirk; she plays Donna
Jo "D.J." Tanner on "Full House."
AS A REGULAR: "Full House," ABC, 1987- .
AND: "St. Elsewhere: My Aim Is True," NBC,
1984; "Punky Brewster: Milk Does a Body
Good," NBC, 1985; "Growing Pains: Fool for
Love," ABC, 1988.
TV MOVIES AND MINISERIES: "Disney Sunday
Movie: The Little Spies," ABC, 1986; "I Saw
What You Did," CBS, 1988.

CAMERON, KIRK

b. Panorama City, CA, October 12, 1970. Teen heartthrob who plays Mike Seaver on "Growing Pains."

AS A REGULAR: "Two Marriages," ABC, 1983-84; "Growing Pains," ABC, 1985- .

AND: "ABC Afterschool Special: The Woman Who Willed a Miracle," ABC, 1982; "ABC Afterschool Special: Andrea's Story: A Hitchhiking Tragedy," ABC, 1983; "Full House: Just One of the Guys," ABC, 1988; "Animal Crack-Ups," ABC, 1989; "Dick Clark's New Year's Rockin' Eve '90," ABC, 1989.

TV MOVIES AND MINISERIES: "Goliath Awaits," SYN, 1981.

CAMERON, ROD

b. Roderick Cox, Calgary, Alberta, Canada, December 7, 1910; d. 1983. Husky actor who played basically the same role—that of an upright cop—on three syndicated series in the fifties.

AS A REGULAR: "City Detective," SYN, 1953; "State Trooper," SYN, 1957-59; "Coronado 9," SYN, 1959-60; "Star Route, USA," SYN, 1964-65.

AND: "Pepsi Cola Playhouse: The Silence," ABC, 1954; "Fireside Theatre: Gusher City," NBC, 1955; "Studio 57: Win a Cigar," SYN, 1955; "The Loretta Young Show: Tropical Secretary," NBC, 1955; "Star Stage: Killer on Horseback," NBC, 1956; "Studio 57: Tombstone for Taro," SYN, 1956; "Crossroads: Deadly Fear," ABC, 1956; "The Loretta Young Show: New Slant," NBC, 1956; "Laramie: Drifter's Gold," NBC, 1960; "Alfred Hitchcock Presents: The Tall Man Who Found the Money," NBC, 1960; "Laramie: Men in Shadows," NBC, 1961; "Laramie: The Last Journey," NBC, 1961; "Tales of Wells Fargo: Assignment in Gloribee," NBC, 1962; "Laramie: Lost Allegiance," NBC, 1962; "Laramie: Broken Honor," NBC, 1963; "Burke's Law: Who Killed Holly Howard?," ABC, 1963; "Perry Mason: The Case of the Bouncing Boomerang," CBS, 1963; "Bob Hope Chrysler Theatre: Have Girls, Will Travel," NBC, 1964; "Bonanza: Ride the Wind," NBC, 1966; "Hondo: Hondo and the Sudden Town," ABC, 1967; "The Name of the Game: The Civilized Man," NBC, 1969; "Alias Smith and Jones: The Biggest Game in the West," ABC, 1972; "Alias Smith and Jones: High Lonesome Country," ABC, 1972; "Police Story: Glamour Boy," NBC, 1974; "The Rockford Files: A Bad Deal in the Valley," NBC, 1976.

CAMP, HAMILTON

b. London, England, October 30, 1934. Slight actor who's been memorable as wisecracking handyman Andrew Hummel on "He & She" and as a too-short date for Mary Richards on an episode of "The Mary Tyler Moore Show."

AS A REGULAR: "He & She," CBS, 1967-68; "Turn-On," ABC, 1969; "Story Theatre," SYN, 1971-72; "Co-ed Fever," CBS, 1979; "Too Close for Comfort," ABC, 1981; "The Nashville Palace," NBC, 1981-82; "Just Our Luck," ABC, 1983.

AND: "The Andy Griffith Show: The Barbershop Quartet," CBS, 1966; "Hey, Landlord!: When You Need a Hidden Room You Can Never Find One," NBC, 1966; "Bewitched: Samantha's Secret Saucer," ABC, 1968; "Gomer Pyle, USMC: A Star Is Not Born," CBS, 1968; "Make Room for Granddaddy: This Granddaddy Rated X," ABC, 1970; "The Mary Tyler Moore Show: Toulouse-Lautrec is One of My Favorite Artists," CBS, 1970; "Love, American Style: Love and the Super Lover," ABC, 1972; "Love, American Style: Love and the Positive Man," ABC, 1973; "Alice: The Accident," CBS, 1977; "M*A*S*H: Major Topper," CBS, 1978; "WKRP in Cincinnati: Hold-Up," CBS, 1978; "Laverne & Shirley: O Come All Ye Bums," ABC, 1978; "Alice: Flo Finds Her Father," CBS, 1979; "Alice: Bet-a-Million Mel," CBS, 1981; "Three's Company: Furley vs. Furley," ABC, 1981; "Mork & Mindy: Present Tense," ABC, 1982; "M*A*S*H: The Moon Is Not Blue," CBS, 1982; "Jennifer Slept Here: Risky Weekend," NBC, 1984; "The Twilight Zone: The Little People," CBS, 1986; "Cheers: Suspicion," NBC, 1986; "Murphy Brown: The Strike," CBS, 1989.

TV MOVIES AND MINISERIES: "Portrait of a Showgirl," CBS, 1982.

CAMPANELLA, JOSEPH

b. New York City, NY, November 21, 1927. Jut-jawed, graying actor usually in good-guy roles; he was lawyer Brian Darrell on "The Bold Ones," the ex-husband of Ann Romano (Bonnie Franklin) on "One Day at a Time" and, most recently, Harper Deveraux on "Days of Our Lives."

AS A REGULAR: "The Guiding Light," CBS, 1959-60; "The Doctors," NBC, 1963-64; "The Doctors and the Nurses," CBS, 1964-65; "Mannix," CBS, 1967-68; "The Bold Ones," NBC, 1969-72; "The Undersea World of Jacques Cousteau," ABC, 1976; "The Colbys," ABC, 1985-86; "Days of Our Lives," NBC, 1987, 1990.

AND: "Robert Montgomery Presents: In a Foreign City," NBC, 1955; "Kraft Television Theatre: Anna Santonello," NBC, 1956; "Robert Montgomery Presents: The Weather Lover," NBC, 1957; "Studio One: Rudy," CBS, 1957; "U.S. Steel Hour: Haunted Harbor," CBS, 1957; "Naked City: Take Off Your Hat When a Funeral Passes," ABC, 1961; "Route 66: To Walk with the Serpent," CBS, 1962; "The Virginian: Siege," NBC, 1963; "The Nurses: The Walls Came

Tumbling Down," CBS, 1963; "Bob Hope Chrysler Theatre: Corridor 400," NBC, 1963; "The Nurses: Credo," CBS, 1964; "The Nurses: The Rainbow Ride," CBS, 1964; "Espionage: We, the Hunted," NBC, 1964; "The Eleventh Hour: 87 Different Kinds of Love," NBC, 1964; "The Fugitive: Set Fire to a Straw Man," ABC, 1965; "Confidential for Women: The Divorcee," ABC, 1966; "The FBI: Anatomy of a Prison Break," ABC, 1966; "The Fugitive: The Other Side of the Coin," ABC, 1967; "Mission: Impossible: The Reluctant Dragon," CBS, 1967; "Captain Nice: Beware of Hidden Prophets," NBC, 1967; "The Wild Wild West: The Night of the Wolf," CBS, 1967; "The Invaders: The Storm," ABC, 1967; "The Virginian: Ride the Misadventure," NBC, 1968; "Mission: Impossible: The Spy," CBS, 1968; "The Name of the Game: Witness," NBC, 1968; "Gunsmoke: The Hide-Cutters," CBS, 1968; "The FBI: Death of a Fixer," ABC, 1968; "Ironside: Alias Mr. Baithwaite," NBC, 1969; "Paris 7000: No Place to Hide," ABC, 1970; "Marcus Welby, M.D.: Dance to No Music," ABC, 1970; "The Name of the Game: The Other Kind of a Spy," NBC, 1970; "Ironside: The Happy Dreams of Hollow Men," NBC, 1970; "Night Gallery: The Nature of the Enemy," NBC, 1970; "Marcus Welby, M.D.: A Spanish Saying I Made Up," ABC, 1970; "Owen Marshall, Counselor at Law: Smiles From Yesterday," ABC, 1972; "Alias Smith and Jones: The Fifth Victim," ABC, 1972; "Night Gallery: Miss Lovecraft Sent Me," NBC, 1972; "ABC Afternoon Playbreak: Things I Never Said," ABC, 1973; "Police Story: The Gamble," NBC, 1973; "Assignment: Vienna: Soldier of Fortune," ABC, 1973; "Tenafly: Man Running," NBC, 1974; "One Day at a Time: Dad Comes Back," CBS, 1976; "One Day at a Time: The New Car," CBS, 1977; "One Day at a Time: The Older Man," CBS, 1977; "One Day at a Time: Father, Dear Father," CBS, 1978; "What Really Happened to the Class of '65?: The Class Misfit," NBC, 1978; "Quincy: No Way to Treat a Patient," NBC, 1980; "One Day at a Time: The Wedding," CBS, 1982; "Hotel: Illusions," ABC, 1984; "The Love Boat: Egyptian Cruise," ABC, 1986; "Murder, She Wrote: The Cemetery Vote," CBS, 1987; "21 Jump Street: The Dreaded Return of Russell Buckins," FOX, 1989; "Paradise: The Devil's Escort," CBS, 1989.

TV MOVIES AND MINISERIES: "Any Second Now," NBC, 1969; "The Whole World is Watching," NBC, 1969; "A Clear and Present Danger," NBC, 1970; "Owen Marshall, Counselor at Law," ABC, 1971; "Murder Once Removed," NBC, 1971; "You'll Never See Me Again," ABC, 1973; "Drive Hard, Drive Fast," NBC, 1973; "The President's Plane is Missing," ABC, 1973; "Skyway to Death," ABC, 1974; "Unwed Father," ABC, 1974; "Terror on the 40th Floor," NBC, 1974; "Hit Lady," ABC, 1974; "Journey From Darkness," NBC, 1975; "Sky Hei$t," NBC, 1975; "The Plutonium Incident," CBS, 1980.

CAMPBELL, ARCHIE

b. Bullsgap, TN, November 17, 1914; d. 1987. Cornpone comic whose big routine was the story of "Rindercella"; he was a "Hee Haw" staple until his death.

AS A REGULAR: "Hee Haw," CBS, 1969-71; SYN, 1971-87.

AND: "Jubilee USA," ABC, 1959; "The Ed Sullivan Show," CBS, 1970.

CAMPBELL, FLORA

b. 1911; d. 1978.

AS A REGULAR: "Faraway Hill," DUM, 1946; "A Date with Judy," ABC, 1952-53; "Valiant Lady," CBS, 1953-57; "The Seeking Heart," CBS, 1954.

CAMPBELL, GLEN

b. Delight, AR, April 22, 1935. Mainstream pop singer whose country-flavored hits made him a hot recording and TV property in the late sixties; CBS thought his down-home style was just the thing to replace the controversial Smothers Brothers, who'd helped Campbell get his start.

AS A REGULAR: "Shindig," ABC, 1964-66; "Summer Smothers Brothers Show," CBS, 1968; "The Glen Campbell Goodtime Hour," CBS, 1969-72; "The Glen Campbell Music Show," SYN, 1982-83.

AND: "American Bandstand," ABC, 1961; "American Bandstand," ABC, 1965; "The Smothers Brothers Comedy Hour," CBS, 1968; "The Beautiful Phyllis Diller Show," NBC, 1968; "The Steve Allen Show," SYN, 1968; "Bob Hope Special," NBC, 1968; "Operation: Entertainment," ABC, 1968; "Feliciano-Very Special," NBC, 1969; "The Merv Griffin Show," CBS, 1970; "The Jim Nabors Hour," CBS, 1970; "The Tonight Show Starring Johnny Carson," NBC, 1971; "Jack Paar Tonight," ABC, 1973; "The Mike Douglas Show," SYN, 1975; "Cher," CBS, 1975; "Dinah!," SYN, 1976; "The Carol Burnett Show," CBS, 1977; "The Mike Douglas Show," SYN, 1977; "The Merv Griffin Show," SYN, 1980; "The Tom and Dick Smothers Brothers Special," NBC, 1980; "Glen Campbell and Tanya Tucker," HBO, 1981; "American Bandstand's 33 1/3 Anniversary," ABC, 1985.

TV MOVIES AND MINISERIES: "Strange Homecoming," NBC, 1974.

CAMPBELL, NICHOLAS

b. Canada, March 24, 1952. Would-be TV

hunk who played detective Mike Devitt on "Diamonds."
AS A REGULAR: "The Insiders," ABC, 1985-86; "Diamonds," CBS, 1987-88; USA, 1988-90.
AND: "T.J. Hooker: Death Strip," ABC, 1983; "Night Heat: Obie's Law," CBS, 1985.
TV MOVIES AND MINISERIES: "Children of the Night," CBS, 1985.

CAMPBELL, WILLIAM

b. Newark, NJ, October 30, 1926. Actor whose long career has ranged from playing truck driver Jerry Austin on "Cannonball" to Det. Joey Indelli on "Crime Story."
AS A REGULAR: "Cannonball," SYN, 1958-59; "Dynasty," ABC, 1984-85; "Crime Story," NBC, 1986-88.
AND: "Schlitz Playhouse of Stars: Fresh Start," CBS, 1953; "A Letter to Loretta: Thanksgiving in Beaver Run," NBC, 1953; "Four Star Playhouse: The Wallet," CBS, 1954; "The Loretta Young Show: The Flood," NBC, 1955; "The Loretta Young Show: Prison at One O'Clock," NBC, 1956; "Cavalcade Theatre: The Man on the Beat," ABC, 1956; "The Millionaire: The Nick Cannon Story," CBS, 1956; "West Point: Thicker Than Water," CBS, 1956; "Telephone Time: Passport to Life," CBS, 1957; "The Millionaire: Millionaire Tom Hampton," CBS, 1959; "Goodyear Theatre: Squeeze Play," NBC, 1960; "Tales of Wells Fargo: Threat of Death," NBC, 1960; "Perry Mason: The Case of the Ill-Fated Faker," CBS, 1960; "Philip Marlowe: Murder in the Stars," ABC, 1960; "The Garlund Touch: Double, Double," CBS, 1960; "Stagecoach West: Never Walk Alone," ABC, 1961; "Gunsmoke: Old Dan," CBS, 1962; "Combat: Soldier of Fortune," ABC, 1965; "The Wild, Wild West: The Night of the Freebooters," CBS, 1966; "Star Trek: The Squire of Gothos," NBC, 1967; "Combat: Nightmare on the Red Ball Run," ABC, 1967; "Garrison's Gorillas: The Magnificent Forger," ABC, 1967; "Star Trek: The Trouble with Tribbles," NBC, 1967; "Bonanza: The Late Ben Cartwright," NBC, 1968; "It Takes a Thief: A Spot of Trouble," ABC, 1968; "O'Hara, U.S. Treasury: Operation: Big Stakes," CBS, 1971; "The Rookies: The Wheel of Death," ABC, 1973; "The Streets of San Francisco: Chapel of the Damned," ABC, 1973; "The Streets of San Francisco: Flags of Terror," ABC, 1974; "Emergency!: Messin' Around," NBC, 1974; "Medical Center: A Choice of Evils," CBS, 1974; "Hec Ramsey: Scar Tissue," NBC, 1974; "Chase: The People Parlay," NBC, 1974; "Mr. and Mrs. Cop," CBS, 1974; "Police Woman: Ice," NBC, 1975; "Medical Center: Aftershock," CBS, 1975; "Marcus Welby, M.D.: Dark Fury," ABC, 1975; "Quincy: Quincy's Wedding," NBC, 1983; "Hotel: Promises," ABC, 1985.

CANARY, DAVID

b. Elwood, IN, August 25, 1938. Actor who played ranch hand Candy on "Bonanza"; now he's Adam Chandler on "All My Children."
AS A REGULAR: "Peyton Place," ABC, 1965-66; "Bonanza," NBC, 1967-70; 1972-73; "Another World," NBC, 1981-83; "All My Children," ABC, 1983- .
AND: "Gunsmoke: Nitro," CBS, 1967; "Gunsmoke: Tiger by the Tail," CBS, 1967; "The FBI: The Last Job," ABC, 1971; "Hawaii Five-O: 3,000 Crooked Miles to Town," CBS, 1971; "Bearcats!: Hostages," CBS, 1971; "Alias Smith and Jones: Everything Else You Can Steal," ABC, 1971; "Alias Smith and Jones: The Strange Fate of Conrad Meyer Zulick," ABC, 1972; "The Rookies: Down Home Boy," ABC, 1973; "Police Story: Death on Credit," NBC, 1973; "Kung Fu: Theodora," ABC, 1973; "The Rookies: A Test of Courage," ABC, 1974.
TV MOVIES AND MINISERIES: "Incident on a Dark Street," CBS, 1973; "Melvin Purvis-G-Man," ABC, 1974; "The Dain Curse," CBS, 1978.
* Emmies: 1986.

CANDY, JOHN

b. Canada, October 31, 1950. Emmy-winning rotund comic actor whose "SCTV" characters include Johnny LaRue, talk-show sidekick William B. and porn king Harry, the Guy with the Snake on His Face; nowadays he's mostly in movies ("Uncle Buck").
AS A REGULAR: "Second City TV," SYN, 1977-79; "SCTV Network 90," NBC, 1981-83; "Camp Candy," NBC, 1988-89.
AND: "Saturday Night Live," NBC, 1983; "Really Weird Tales," HBO, 1986; "The Dave Thomas Comedy Show," CBS, 1990.
* Emmies: 1982, 1983.

CANFIELD, MARY GRACE

b. Rochester, NY. Actress usually in plain-Jane roles; she played handywoman Ralph Monroe on "Green Acres."
AS A REGULAR: "The Hathaways," ABC, 1961-62; "Green Acres," CBS, 1966-71; "Family," ABC, 1976-78.
AND: "Robert Montgomery Presents: One Smart Apple," NBC, 1957; "Dan Raven: Penny," NBC, 1960; "My Sister Eileen: Monkey Shines," CBS, 1960; "My Sister Eileen: Ebenezer Scrooge Appopolous," CBS, 1960; "Thriller: A Good Imagination," NBC, 1961; "Alfred Hitchcock Presents: Bang, You're Dead," NBC, 1961; "Hazel: Rock-a-Bye Baby," NBC, 1962; "The Joey Bishop Show: The Baby Formula," NBC, 1963; "The Andy Griffith Show: A Date for Gomer," CBS, 1963; "The Farmer's Daughter: Jewel Beyond Compare," ABC, 1965; "The Farmer's Daughter: Twelve Angry Women,"

ABC, 1966; "Bewitched: Follow That Witch," ABC, 1966; "Run, Buddy, Run: Buddy the Life Saver," CBS, 1966.

TV MOVIES AND MINISERIES: "Night of Terror," ABC, 1972.

CANNELL, STEPHEN J.

Influential producer of light, fast-moving crime shows.

AS PRODUCER: "The Rockford Files," NBC, 1974-80; "Tenspeed and Brown Shoe," ABC, 1980; "The A-Team," NBC, 1983-87; "Hardcastle and McCormick," ABC, 1983-86; "Riptide," NBC, 1984-86; "Hunter," NBC, 1984- ; "21 Jump Street," FOX, 1987-90; SYN, 1990- ; "Booker," FOX, 1989-90;

* Emmies: 1978.

CANNON, DYAN

b. Camille Diane Friesen, Tacoma, WA, January 4, 1937. Film actress ("Bob & Carol & Ted & Alice," "Heaven Can Wait") with some TV experience; former wife of Cary Grant.

AS A REGULAR: "Full Circle," CBS, 1960-61.

AND: "Have Gun, Will Travel: The Man Who Wouldn't Talk," CBS, 1958; "For Better or Worse: The Case of the Childish Bride," CBS, 1959; "Bat Masterson: Lady Luck," NBC, 1959; "Wanted Dead or Alive: Vanishing Act," CBS, 1959; "Acapulco: The Gentleman From Brazil," NBC, 1961; "Malibu Run: The Radioactive-Object Adventure," CBS, 1961; "Hawaiian Eye: The Big Dealer," ABC, 1961; "Guestward Ho!: The Wrestler," ABC, 1961; "Malibu Run: The Diana Adventure," CBS, 1961; "Follow the Sun: The Woman Who Never Was," ABC, 1961; "The Untouchables: The Silent Partner," ABC, 1962; "77 Sunset Strip: The Bridal Trail Caper," ABC, 1962; "Stoney Burke: Death Rides a Pale Horse," ABC, 1963; "Mr. Broadway: Between the Rats and the Finks," CBS, 1964; "The Reporter: The Man Behind the Man," CBS, 1964; "Profiles in Courage: Sam Houston," NBC, 1964; "The Danny Kaye Show," CBS, 1965; "Amos Burke, Secret Agent: The Weapon," ABC, 1965; "The Movie Game," SYN, 1969; "Medical Center: Victim," CBS, 1969; "The Mike Douglas Show," SYN, 1973; "Saturday Night Live," NBC, 1976; "The Muppet Show," SYN, 1980.

TV MOVIES AND MINISERIES: "Virginia Hill," NBC, 1974; "Lady of the House," NBC, 1978; "Having It All," ABC, 1982; "Master of the Game," CBS, 1984; "Arthur the King," CBS, 1985; "ABC Family Classic: Rock 'N' Roll Mom," ABC, 1989.

* Cary Grant first saw Cannon in 1961 on "Malibu Run."

CANNON, J.D.

b. Salmon, ID, April 24, 1932. Actor who played the gruff chief Peter B. Clifford on "McCloud."

AS A REGULAR: "McCloud," NBC, 1970-77; "Alias Smith and Jones," ABC, 1971-72; "Call to Glory," ABC, 1984-85.

AND: "Frontiers of Faith: Beautiful Johnny," NBC, 1960; "Omnibus: He Shall Have Power," NBC, 1960; "U.S. Steel Hour: Operation Northstar," CBS, 1960; "Naked City: C3H5(NO3)3," ABC, 1961; "The Defenders: The Attack," CBS, 1961; "The Defenders: The Voices of Death," CBS, 1962; "The Untouchables: Cooker in the Sky," ABC, 1962; "Armstrong Circle Theatre: The Friendly Thieves," CBS, 1962; "Wagon Train: The Abel Weatherly Story," ABC, 1963; "The Nurses: No Score," CBS, 1963; "Combat!: The Quiet Warrior," ABC, 1963; "East Side/West Side: One Drink at a Time," CBS, 1964; "The Defenders: Drink Like a Lady," CBS, 1964; "Kraft Suspense Theatre: Operation Grief," NBC, 1964; "Rawhide: Piney," CBS, 1964; "Rawhide: The Book," CBS, 1965; "The Doctors and the Nurses: A Question of Murder," CBS, 1965; "The Defenders: The Unwritten Law," CBS, 1965; "Twelve O'Clock High: Rx for a Sick Bird," ABC, 1965; "The Fugitive: Middle of a Heat Wave," ABC, 1965; "The Wild Wild West: The Night of the Deadly Bed," CBS, 1965; "The FBI: The Man Who Went Mad by Mistake," ABC, 1966; "The FBI: Flight Plan," ABC, 1967; "The FBI: The Runaways," ABC, 1968; "Lancer: Blood Rock," CBS, 1968; "Gunsmoke: Jake MacGraw," CBS, 1969; "The FBI: Conspiracy of Corruption," ABC, 1970; "The Fall Guy: Soldiers of Misfortune," ABC, 1982; "Remington Steele: Steele in the News," NBC, 1983; "Remington Steele: Hounded Steele," NBC, 1984; "Murder, She Wrote: Funeral at Fifty-Mile," CBS, 1985; "Blacke's Magic: Address Unknown," NBC, 1986.

TV MOVIES AND MINISERIES: "U.M.C.," CBS, 1969; "The D.A.: Murder One," NBC, 1969; "Sam Hill: Who Killed the Mysterious Mr. Foster?," NBC, 1971; "Cannon," CBS, 1971; "Testimony of Two Men," SYN, 1977; "Ike," ABC, 1979; "Walking Through the Fire," CBS, 1979.

CANNON, KATHERINE

b. Hartford, CT, September 6, 1953. Actress usually in wholesome roles; she played schoolteacher Mae Woodward on "Father Muprhy."

AS A REGULAR: "Harold Robbins' The Survivors," ABC, 1969-70; "Baa Baa Black Sheep," NBC, 1977-78; "The Contender," CBS, 1980; "Father Murphy," NBC, 1981-84; "Heartbeat," ABC, 1988-89.

AND: "Hawaii Five-O: Time and Memories," CBS, 1970; "Medical Center: The VD Story," CBS, 1970; "Gunsmoke: Susan Was Evil," CBS, 1974; "The Streets of San Francisco: Flags of

Terror," ABC, 1974; "Barnaby Jones: Dangerous Summer," CBS, 1975; "Barnaby Jones: Killer on Campus," CBS, 1977; "Barnaby Jones: The Mercenaries," CBS, 1977; "Sword of Justice: Judgement Day," NBC, 1978; "B.J. and the Bear: The Murphy Contingent," NBC, 1979; "Magnum, P.I.: Thank Heavens for Little Girls-and Big Ones, Too," CBS, 1980; "Magnum, P.I.: I Do?," CBS, 1983; "Murder, She Wrote: Deadline for Murder," CBS, 1986; "Empty Nest: Blame It on the Moon," NBC, 1989; "Hardball: A Killer Date," NBC, 1989.

TV MOVIES AND MINISERIES: "Women in Chains," ABC, 1972; "Can Ellen Be Saved?," ABC, 1974; "Will: G. Gordon Liddy," NBC, 1982.

CANOVA, DIANA
b. West Palm Beach, FL, June 1, 1953. Actress who's the daughter of Judy Canova, usually in comic roles; she played Corrine Tate on "Soap."

AS A REGULAR: "Dinah and Her New Best Friends," CBS, 1976; "Soap," ABC, 1977-80; "I'm a Big Girl Now," ABC, 1980-81; "Foot in the Door," CBS, 1983; "Throb," SYN, 1986-88.

AND: "Happy Days: Because She's There," ABC, 1974; "Chico and the Man: Life Style," NBC, 1974; "Chico and the Man: The Giveaway," NBC, 1975; "Barney Miller: Strip Joint," ABC, 1979; "The Mike Douglas Show," SYN, 1980; "The Love Boat: Heartbreaker," ABC, 1985; "Murder, She Wrote: Death Casts a Spell," CBS, 1985; "St. Elsewhere: Family Ties," NBC, 1986; "Murder, She Wrote: Murder-According to Maggie," CBS, 1990.

TV MOVIES AND MINISERIES: "The Death of Ocean View Park," ABC, 1979; "Night Partners," CBS, 1983.

CANOVA, JUDY
b. Jacksonville, FL, November 20, 1916; d. 1983. Comic actress who did hillbilly humor long before anyone had thought of Jed Clampett.

AND: "The Tony Bennett Show," NBC, 1956; "The Rosemary Clooney Show," SYN, 1957; "The Steve Allen Show," NBC, 1957; "The Danny Thomas Show: The Country Girl," CBS, 1958; "The Big Record," CBS, 1958; "Milton Berle Starring in the Kraft Music Hall," NBC, 1958; "Alfred Hitchcock Presents: Party Line," CBS, 1960; "Vacation Playhouse: Tallie," CBS, 1965; "Li'l Abner," NBC, 1967; "The Murdocks and McClays," ABC, 1970.

CANTOR, EDDIE
b. Edward Iskowitz, New York City, NY, January 31, 1892; d. 1964. Legendary comic and singer of movies, radio, stage and TV; he was one of the most popular performers of the thirties.

AS A REGULAR: "The Colgate Comedy Hour," NBC, 1950-54; "Eddie Cantor Comedy Theatre," SYN, 1954-55.

AND: "Playhouse 90: Sizeman and Son," CBS, 1956; "Matinee Theatre: George Has a Birthday," NBC, 1956; "The Jackie Gleason Show," CBS, 1957; "Art Linkletter's House Party," CBS, 1957; "I've Got a Secret," CBS, 1957; "The Arlene Francis Show," NBC, 1957; "The Big Record," CBS, 1957; "The Eddie Fisher Show," NBC, 1958; "Christophers: The Career of James Otis," SYN, 1959; "A Tribute to Eleanor Roosevelt on Her Diamond Jubilee," NBC, 1959; "Art Linkletter's House Party," CBS, 1959; "Startime: George Burns in the Big Time," NBC, 1959; "Pontiac Star Parade: The Future Lies Ahead," NBC, 1960; "Christophers: The Importance of Participation," SYN, 1960; "Christophers: Biblical Readings," SYN, 1960.

CAPOTE, TRUMAN
b. New Orleans, LA, September 30, 1924; d. 1984. Author ("Breakfast at Tiffany's," "In Cold Blood") who did occasional TV; he won an Emmy for "A Christmas Memory."

AS A GUEST: "The Last Word," CBS, 1957; "The Sonny and Cher Comedy Hour," CBS, 1973; "The Merv Griffin Show," SYN, 1975.

AS CO-WRITER: "ABC Stage '67: A Christmas Memory," ABC, 1966.

* Emmies: 1967.

CAPP, AL
b. Alfred Gerald Caplin, New Haven, CT, September 28, 1909; d. 1979. Artist responsible for the "Li'l Abner" comic strip.

AS A REGULAR: "What's the Story?," DUM, 1953; "Anyone Can Win," CBS, 1953.

AND: "Small World," CBS, 1959; "The Red Skelton Show: Clem in Dogpatch," CBS, 1960.

CAPRA, FRANK
b. Palermo, Sicily, May 18, 1897. Movie director ("Mr. Smith Goes to Washington," "It's a Wonderful Life") who turned to TV in the fifties.

AS PRODUCER-DIRECTOR: "Our Mr. Sun," CBS, 1956; "Hemo the Magnificent," CBS, 1957; "The Strange Case of the Cosmic Rays," NBC, 1957; "The Unchained Goddess," NBC, 1958.

AS HIMSELF: "This Is Your Life," NBC, 1959.

CARA, IRENE
b. Bronx, NY, March 18, 1959. Grammy-winning actress ("Fame").

AS A REGULAR: "Love of Life," CBS, 1970-71; "The Electric Company," PBS, 1972.

AS A GUEST: "Kojak: A Hair-Trigger Away," CBS, 1976; "What's Happening!: Rerun Gets Married," ABC, 1977.

TV MOVIES AND MINISERIES: "Roots: The Next
Generations," ABC, 1979.

CARERE, CHRISTINE
b. France, July 27, 1930.
AS A REGULAR: "Blue Light," ABC, 1966.

CAREY, HARRY JR.
b. Saugus, CA, May 16, 1921. Veteran cowboy
actor who's the son of another veteran cowboy
actor.
AS A REGULAR: "Walt Disney Presents: Texas
John Slaughter," ABC, 1958-59.
AND: "Wire Service: The Oilman," ABC, 1957;
"The Lineup: The Fleet Queen Case," CBS, 1957;
"Playhouse 90: Lone Woman," CBS, 1957; "Have
Gun, Will Travel: The Man Who Wouldn't Talk,"
CBS, 1958; "Bonanza: The Mission," NBC, 1960;
"The Tall Man: One of One Thousand," NBC,
1960; "Have Gun, Will Travel: Misguided
Father," CBS, 1960; "Have Gun, Will Travel: The
Marshal's Boy," CBS, 1960; "Have Gun, Will
Travel: The Legacy," CBS, 1960; "Gunsmoke:
Bad Sheriff," CBS, 1961; "Have Gun, Will
Travel: The Taxgatherer," CBS, 1961; "Wagon
Train: The George B. Hanrahan Story," NBC,
1962; "Have Gun, Will Travel: Taylor's Woman,"
CBS, 1962; "Gunsmoke: Abe Blocker," CBS,
1962; "Laramie: Time of the Traitor," NBC,
1962; "Ripcord: A Free-Falling Star," SYN, 1963;
"Have Gun, Will Travel: Sweet Lady in the
Moon," CBS, 1963; "Have Gun, Will Travel:
Face of a Shadow," CBS, 1963; "Branded: The
Vindicator," NBC, 1965; "Bonanza: The Flannel-
Mouth Gun," NBC, 1965; "Gunsmoke: Waco,"
CBS, 1968; "Mannix: Missing: Sun and Sky,"
CBS, 1969; "Gunsmoke: The Lost," CBS, 1971;
"Gunsmoke: The Bullet," CBS, 1971; "The
Streets of San Francisco: The Hard Breed," ABC,
1973; "Gunsmoke: A Trail of Bloodshed," CBS,
1974; "Police Woman: Sons," NBC, 1978; "Little
House on the Prairie: A New Beginning," NBC,
1980; "B.L. Stryker: Auntie Sue," NBC, 1989.
TV MOVIES AND MINISERIES: "Black Beauty," NBC,
1978.

CAREY, MACDONALD
b. Sioux City, IA, Mar. 15, 1913. Dependable
actor who plays patriarch Tom Horton on
"Days of Our Lives."
AS A REGULAR: "Doctor Christian," SYN, 1956-
57; "Lock Up," SYN, 1959-61; "Days of Our
Lives," NBC, 1965- .
AND: "Celanese Theatre: Yellow Jack," ABC,
1952; "Lux Video Theatre: You Be the Bad Guy,"
CBS, 1952; "Ford Theatre: Edge of the Law,"
NBC, 1952; "Hollywood Opening Night: Apples
on the Lilac Tree," NBC, 1952; "Ford Theatre:
The Sermon of the Gun," NBC, 1953; "Climax!:
Unimportant Man," CBS, 1955; "Climax!: Deal a

Blow," CBS, 1955; "Stage 7: Where You Love
Me," CBS, 1955; "Stage 7: The Hayfield," CBS,
1955; "Science Fiction Theatre: The Human
Equation," SYN, 1955; "Climax!: Gamble on a
Thief," CBS, 1955; "The 20th Century-Fox Hour:
Meet Mr. Kringle," CBS, 1955; "G.E. Theatre:
Easter Gift," CBS, 1956; "Ford Theatre: The
Kill," NBC, 1956; "Undercurrent: The Plugged
Nickel," CBS, 1956; "Alcoa Hour: Flight Into
Danger," NBC, 1956; "Climax!: The Chinese
Game," CBS, 1956; "Kaiser Aluminum Hour:
Whereabouts Unknown," NBC, 1957; "Ford
Theatre: Broken Barrier," ABC, 1957; "The
Joseph Cotten Show: Alibi for Murder," NBC,
1957; "Dr. Hudson's Secret Journal: Caroline
Story," SYN, 1957; "Undercurrent: Live Bait,"
CBS, 1957; "The Jane Wyman Show: Man on the
35th Floor," NBC, 1957; "Suspicion: Diary for
Death," NBC, 1957; "The Ford Show," NBC,
1957; "Dick Powell's Zane Grey Theatre: License
to Kill," CBS, 1958; "Wagon Train: The Bill
Tawnee Story," NBC, 1958; "Studio One: The
Lonely Stage," CBS, 1958; "Playhouse 90:
Natchez," CBS, 1958; "Schlitz Playhouse of
Stars: False Impression," CBS, 1958; "Rawhide:
Incident of the Golden Calf," CBS, 1959; "Alfred
Hitchcock Presents: Coyote Moon," CBS, 1959;
"Checkmate: Rendezvous in Washington," CBS,
1962; "The Alfred Hitchcock Hour: House
Guest," CBS, 1962; "The Dick Powell Show: The
Last of the Private Eyes," NBC, 1963; "Kraft
Mystery Theatre: The Image Merchants," NBC,
1963; "Daniel Boone: The Place of 1,000 Spirits,"
NBC, 1965; "Burke's Law: Who Killed the Fat
Cat?," ABC, 1965; "Branded: The Mission,"
NBC, 1965; "Kraft Suspense Theatre: The Green
Felt Jungle," NBC, 1965; "Run for Your Life:
The Girl Next Door is a Spy," NBC, 1965; "Run
for Your Life: Our Man in Limbo," NBC, 1965;
"Ben Casey: The Importance of Being 65937,"
ABC, 1965; "Bewitched: Birdies, Bogeys and
Baxter," ABC, 1967; "The Magician: Illusion in
Terror," NBC, 1973; "Police Story: Fingerprint,"
NBC, 1974; "Owen Marshall, Counselor at Law:
The Desertion of Keith Ryder," ABC, 1974;
"McMillan and Wife: The Deadly Cure," NBC,
1976; "Police Story: Firebird," NBC, 1976;
"Switch: Formula for Murder," CBS, 1977;
"Murder, She Wrote: Trouble in Eden," CBS,
1987.
TV MOVIES AND MINISERIES: "Gidget Gets
Married," ABC, 1972; "Ordeal," ABC, 1973;
"Who Is the Black Dahlia?," NBC, 1975;
"Roots," ABC, 1977; "Stranger in Our House,"
NBC, 1978; "The Rebels," SYN, 1979.

CAREY, OLIVE
b. Olive Fuller Golden, 1896; d. 1989. Actress
and wife of Harey Carey.
AS A REGULAR: "Mr. Adams and Eve," CBS,
1957-58; "Lock Up," SYN, 1960-61.

170

AND: "Schlitz Playhouse: The Brush Roper," CBS, 1954; "The Lineup: The Strange Return of Army Armitage," CBS, 1959; "Dennis the Menace: Man of the House," CBS, 1960; "Laramie: Deadly is the Night," NBC, 1961; "Have Gun, Will Travel: Mark of Cain," CBS, 1962; "Alcoa Premiere: Pattern of Guilt," ABC, 1962; "Lawman: The Youngest," ABC, 1962.

TV MOVIES AND MINISERIES: "The Norliss Tapes," NBC, 1973.

CAREY, PHILIP

b. Hackensack, NJ, July 15, 1925. Actor who plays Asa Buchanan on "One Life to Live."

AS A REGULAR: "Tales of the 77th Bengal Lancers," NBC, 1956-57; "Philip Marlowe," ABC, 1959-60; "Laredo," NBC, 1965-67; "Untamed World," SYN, 1968-75; "Bright Promise," NBC, 1969-72; "One Life to Live," ABC, 1979- .

AND: "Ford Theatre: Madame .44," NBC, 1953; "Ford Theatre: Gun Job," NBC, 1953; "Ford Theatre: The Unlocked Door, NBC, 1954; "Ford Theatre: Stars Don't Shine," NBC, 1955; "Pond's Theatre: Billy Budd," ABC, 1955; "Ford Theatre: Twelve to Eternity," NBC, 1955; "Ford Theatre: Panic," NBC, 1956; "Ford Theatre: Duffy's Man," ABC, 1956; "Ford Theatre: Torn," ABC, 1957; "Undercurrent: Known But to God," CBS, 1957; "Undercurrent: I'll Make the Arrest," CBS, 1957; "Lux Playhouse: A Deadly Guest," CBS, 1959; "Michael Shayne: Shoot the Works," NBC, 1960; "Dick Powell's Zane Grey Theatre: One Must Die," CBS, 1961; "Thriller: Man in the Cage," NBC, 1961; "Stagecoach West: The Root of Evil," ABC, 1961; "The Rifleman: Death Trap," ABC, 1961; "The Asphalt Jungle: The Professor," ABC, 1961; "Tales of Wells Fargo: The Dodger," NBC, 1961; "The Roaring Twenties: Kitty Goes West," ABC, 1961; "Here's Hollywood," NBC, 1961; "Lawman: Change of Venue," ABC, 1962; "Cheyenne: One Way Ticket," ABC, 1962; "Cheyenne: Until Kingdom Come," ABC, 1962; "77 Sunset Strip: Violence for Your Furs," ABC, 1962; "Cheyenne: Johnny Brassbuttons," ABC, 1962; "The Gallant Men: The Leathernecks," ABC, 1963; "The Lucy Show: Lucy and the Runaway Butterfly," CBS, 1963; "77 Sunset Strip: Flight 307," ABC, 1963; "G.E. True: Nitro," CBS, 1963; "Insight: Face of Tyranny," SYN, 1963; "The Virginian: Siege," NBC, 1963; "Kraft Suspense Theatre: My Enemy, This Town," NBC, 1964; "The Virginian: We've Lost a Train," NBC, 1965; "The Felony Squad: No Sad Songs for Charlie," ABC, 1967; "Ironside: Barbara Who?," NBC, 1968; "Ironside: Goodbye to Yesterday," NBC, 1969; "All in the Family: Judging Books by Covers," CBS, 1971; "Gunsmoke: Trapton," CBS, 1971; "Gunsmoke: Trafton," CBS, 1971; "Room 222: I've Got the Hammer, If You've Got the Thumb," ABC, 1973;

"Banacek: Rocket to Oblivion," NBC, 1974; "Police Woman: Anatomy of Two Rapes," NBC, 1974; "Kolchak, the Night Stalker: Firefall," ABC, 1974; "McCloud: The Man with the Golden Hat," NBC, 1975; "Little House on the Prairie: The Halloween Dream," NBC, 1979.

TV MOVIES AND MINISERIES: "Scream of the Wolf," ABC, 1974.

CAREY, RON

b. Newark, NJ, December 11, 1935. Round-faced actor, usually in comic roles; he played officer Carl Levitt on "Barney Miller."

AS A REGULAR: "The Melba Moore-Clifton Davis Show," CBS, 1972; "The Corner Bar," ABC, 1973; "The Montefuscos," NBC, 1975; "Barney Miller," ABC, 1976-82; "Have Faith," ABC, 1989.

AND: "The Merv Griffin Show," SYN, 1968; "Operation: Entertainment," ABC, 1968; "The Merv Griffin Show," SYN, 1969; "The Comedians," SYN, 1971; "ABC Comedy Hour," ABC, 1972; "The Merv Griffin Show," SYN, 1980.

CARLIN, GEORGE

b. Bronx, NY, May 12, 1937. Comedian.

AS A REGULAR: "The Kraft Summer Music Hall," NBC, 1966; "That Girl," ABC, 1966-67; "Away We Go," CBS, 1967; "Tony Orlando and Dawn," CBS, 1976.

AND: "On Broadway Tonight," CBS, 1965; "The Mike Douglas Show," SYN, 1966; "The Merv Griffin Show," SYN, 1966; "The Smothers Brothers Comedy Hour," CBS, 1968; "The Steve Allen Show," SYN, 1969; "The David Frost Show," SYN, 1970; "The Movie Game," SYN, 1970; "Saturday Night Live," NBC, 1975; "The Flip Wilson Comedy Special," CBS, 1975; "Welcome Back, Kotter: Radio Free Freddie," ABC, 1977; "The Tonight Show Starring Johnny Carson," NBC, 1979; "Saturday Night Live," NBC, 1984; "What's Alan Watching?," CBS, 1989.

TV MOVIES AND MINISERIES: "Disney Sunday Movie: Justin Case," ABC, 1988.

CARLISLE, KITTY

b. New Orleans, LA, September 3, 1915. Leading lady of gracious bearing and a longtime quiz show regular.

AS A REGULAR: "I've Got a Secret," CBS, 1952-53; "What's Going On?," ABC, 1954; "To Tell the Truth," CBS, 1956-67; SYN, 1969-77.

AND: "Nash Airflyte Theatre: Waltz Dream," CBS, 1951; "Holiday," NBC, 1956; "The Last Word," CBS, 1957; "The Last Word," CBS, 1958; "Music for a Summer Night: Theatre Under the Stars," ABC, 1960; "Music for New Year's Night: Class of '61," ABC, 1961; "Password," CBS, 1961; "Play Your Hunch," NBC, 1963; "Missing

Links," NBC, 1963; "The Match Game," NBC, 1964; "Missing Links," NBC, 1964.
* Carlisle was the first female guest on "Password"; the first male guest was Tom Poston.

CARLSON, LINDA
b. *Knoxville, TN, May 12, 1945.*
AS A REGULAR: "Westside," ABC, 1977; "Kaz," CBS, 1978-79; "Newhart," CBS, 1984-89.
AND: "Kojak: Cry for the Kids," CBS, 1977; "WKRP in Cincinnati: Hotel Oceanview," CBS, 1980; "Lou Grant: Rape," CBS, 1981; "Remington Steele: Hearts of Steele," NBC, 1983; "St. Elsewhere: A Pig Too Far," NBC, 1984; "Cagney & Lacey: Entrapment," CBS, 1985; "My Two Dads: SoHo's by You?," NBC, 1987.
TV MOVIES AND MINISERIES: "Victims for Victims: The Theresa Saldana Story," NBC, 1984.

CARLSON, RICHARD
b. *Albert Lea, MN, April 29, 1912; d. 1977.* Actor best remembered as agent Herbert Philbrick, the man who exposed America's Communist "menace" on the historical—and hysterical—series "I Led Three Lives."
AS A REGULAR: "I Led Three Lives," SYN, 1953-56; "MacKenzie's Raiders," SYN, 1958-59.
AND: "Pulitzer Prize Playhouse: The Canton Story," ABC, 1950; "Studio One: The Road to Jericho," CBS, 1950; "Theatre Hour: Heart of Darkness," CBS, 1950; "Prudential Playhouse: One Sunday Afternoon," CBS, 1951; "Lights Out: The Devil in Glencairn," NBC, 1951; "Robert Montgomery Presents: Eva? Caroline?," NBC, 1952; "Studio One: Captain-General of the Armies," CBS, 1952; "Celanese Theatre: When Ladies Meet," ABC, 1952; "Schlitz Playhouse of Stars: The Playwright," CBS, 1952; "Ford Theatre: Adventure in Connecticut," NBC, 1953; "Hollywood Opening Night: My Boss and I," NBC, 1953; "Eye Witness: Statement of the Accused," NBC, 1953; "Schlitz Playhouse of Stars: Pursuit," CBS, 1953; "Lux Video Theatre: All Dressed in White," CBS, 1954; "G.E. Theatre: Pardon My Aunt," CBS, 1954; "Schlitz Playhouse of Stars: Hemmed In," CBS, 1954; "Best of Broadway: The Philadelphia Story," CBS, 1954; "Kraft Television Theatre: Haunted," NBC, 1955; "Omnibus: The Billy Mitchell Court-Martial," CBS, 1956; "Climax!: Flame-Out on T-6," CBS, 1956; "Schlitz Playhouse of Stars: The Night They Won the Oscar," CBS, 1956; "Hemo the Magnificent," CBS, 1957; "The Strange Case of the Cosmic Rays," NBC, 1957; "The Unchained Goddess," NBC, 1958; "Riverboat: The Faithless," NBC, 1959; "The Loretta Young Show: The Best Season," NBC, 1960; "Chevy Mystery Show: Enough Rope," NBC, 1960; "The Aquanauts: Submarine Adventure," CBS, 1960;

"Burke's Law: Who Killed Sweet Betsy?," ABC, 1963; "Arrest and Trial: Onward and Upward," ABC, 1964; "The Virginian: Smile of a Dragon," NBC, 1964; "The Fugitive: The Homecoming," ABC, 1964; "Burke's Law: Who Killed My Girl?," ABC, 1964; "Voyage to the Bottom of the Sea: The Village of Guilt," ABC, 1964; "Perry Mason: The Case of the Tragic Trophy," CBS, 1964; "Perry Mason: The Case of the Avenging Angel," CBS, 1966; "Bonanza: The Thirteenth Man," NBC, 1968; "It Takes a Thief: The Naked Billionaire," ABC, 1969; "The FBI: Moment of Truth," NBC, 1969; "Owen Marshall, Counselor at Law: Eighteen Years Next April," ABC, 1971; "Cannon: The Torch," CBS, 1972.
TV MOVIES AND MINISERIES: "The Doomsday Flight," NBC, 1966.
AS DIRECTOR: "The Loretta Young Show: The Best Season," NBC, 1960; "The Loretta Young Show: Linda," NBC, 1960.

CARMEL, ROGER C.
b. *Brooklyn, NY, 1932; d. 1986.* Corpulent, mustachioed character actor who played con man Harry Mudd on "Star Trek."
AS A REGULAR: "The Mothers-in-Law," NBC, 1967-68; "Fitz and Bones," NBC, 1981.
AND: "Naked City: The Pedigree Sheet," ABC, 1960; "Armstrong Circle Theatre: The Antique Swindle," CBS, 1960; "True Story: Murder to Measure," NBC, 1960; "Armstrong Circle Theatre: The Crime Without a Country," CBS, 1961; "Naked City: The Day the Island Almost Sank," ABC, 1961; "Look Up and Live: Comedies of Terror—A Likely Story," CBS, 1961; "Naked City: Today the Man Who Kills the Ants is Coming!," ABC, 1962; "Route 66: Where There's a Will, There's a Way," CBS, 1964; "The Patty Duke Show: Author, Author," ABC, 1964; "The Dick Van Dyke Show: It Wouldn't Hurt Them to Give Us a Raise," CBS, 1964; "The Man From UNCLE: The Quadripartite Affair," NBC, 1964; "The Alfred Hitchcock Hour: The Crimson Witness," NBC, 1965; "The Munsters: Lily Munster, Girl Model," CBS, 1965; "The Man From UNCLE: The Ultimate Computer Affair," NBC, 1965; "Hogan's Heroes: The Prisoner's Prisoner," CBS, 1965; "The Smothers Brothers Show: A Wolf in Sheik's Clothing," CBS, 1966; "Star Trek: Mudd's Women," NBC, 1966; "Batman: A Piece of the Action/Batman's Satisfaction," ABC, 1967; "Star Trek: The Trouble with Tribbles," NBC, 1967; "Star Trek: I, Mudd," NBC, 1968; "Hawaii Five-O: FOB Honolulu," CBS, 1971; "The Doris Day Show: Detective Story," CBS, 1972; "Owen Marshall, Counselor at Law: Sigh No More, Lady," ABC, 1972; "The Paul Lynde Show: Springtime for Paul," ABC, 1973; "McMillan and Wife: Death of a Monster," NBC, 1973; "McCloud: The Man with the Golden Hat," NBC, 1975; "Chico and the

Man: The Giveaway," NBC, 1975; "Chico and the Man: Long Live the Man," NBC, 1975; "Switch: The Late Show Murders," CBS, 1975; "All in the Family: Fire," CBS, 1977; "Three's Company: Ralph's Rival," ABC, 1979; "B.J. and the Bear: Run for the Money," NBC, 1979; "Laverne & Shirley: Murder on the Moose Jaw Express," ABC, 1980; "Hart to Hart: Tis the Season to Be Murdered," ABC, 1980.

TV MOVIES AND MINISERIES: "Anatomy of a Seduction," CBS, 1979.

CARMEN, JULIE

b. Millburn, NJ, April 4, 1954. Actress who played Sofia Stavros on "Falcon Crest."

AS A REGULAR: "Condo," ABC, 1983; "Falcon Crest," CBS, 1986-90.

AND: "Lou Grant: Indians," CBS, 1980; "Nero Wolfe: What Happened to April?," NBC, 1981; "Remington Steele: Steele Knuckles and Glass Jaws," NBC, 1983; "The Twilight Zone: Wish Bank," CBS, 1985.

TV MOVIES AND MINISERIES: "Can You Hear the Laughter? The Story of Freddie Prinze," CBS, 1979; "300 Miles for Stephanie," NBC, 1981; "The Neon Empire," SHO, 1989; "Manhunt: Search for the Night Stalker," NBC, 1989.

CARMICHAEL, HOAGY

b. Hoagland Howard Carmichael, Bloomington, IN, November 22, 1899; d. 1981. Gifted songwriter and screen actor who did a bit of TV, including a stint as ranch hand Jonesy on "Laramie."

AS A REGULAR: "Saturday Night Revue," NBC, 1953; "Laramie," NBC, 1959-60.

AND: "Gulf Playhouse: The Whale on the Beach," NBC, 1952; "The Joseph Cotten Show: Death in the Snow," NBC, 1956; "Playhouse 90: Helen Morgan," CBS, 1957; "The Rosemary Clooney Show," SYN, 1957; "The Big Record," CBS, 1957; "Telephone Time: I Get Along Without You Very Well," ABC, 1957; "Command Appearance," NBC, 1957; "Climax!: The Sound of the Moon," CBS, 1958; "All-Star Jazz," CBS, 1958; "Celebrity Talent Scouts," CBS, 1960; "Project 20: Those Ragtime Years," NBC, 1960; "The Ford Show," NBC, 1961; "The Flintstones: The Hit Songwriters," ABC, 1961; "Burke's Law: Who Killed Snooky Martinelli?," ABC, 1964; "Burke's Law: Who Killed Molly?," ABC, 1964; "The Man Who Bought Paradise," CBS, 1965; "The Farmer's Daughter: Oh Boy, Is the Honeymoon Over," ABC, 1966; "The Name of the Game: Echo of a Nightmare," NBC, 1970; "Owen Marshall, Counselor at Law: Smiles From Yesterday," ABC, 1972.

* Carmichael appeared, memorably, in the movies "Topper," "To Have and Have Not," "The Best Years of Our Lives" and "Young Man with a Horn." His songs include

"Stardust," "Old Rockin' Chair," "Lazybones," "Two Sleepy People," "Heart and Soul," "I Get Along Without You Very Well," "How Little We Know," "Ole Buttermilk Sky" and "In the Cool, Cool, Cool of the Evening."

CARNE, JUDY

b. Joyce Botterill, Northampton, England, 1939. Slight English actress who was the "Sock it to me" girl on "Rowan & Martin's Laugh-In."

AS A REGULAR: "Fair Exchange," CBS, 1962-63; "The Baileys of Balboa," CBS, 1964-65; "Love on a Rooftop," ABC, 1966-67; "Rowan & Martin's Laugh-In," NBC, 1968-70; "Kraft Music Hall Presents Sandler & Young," NBC, 1969.

AND: "Bonanza: A Question of Strength," NBC, 1963; "The Man From UNCLE: The Ultimate Computer Affair," NBC, 1965; "The Farmer's Daughter: A Sonny Honeymoon," ABC, 1965; "Gunsmoke: Sweet Billy," CBS, 1966; "I Dream of Jeannie: Is There an Extra Jeannie in the House?," NBC, 1966; "The Patty Duke Show: Fiancee for a Day," ABC, 1966; "Hollywood Squares," NBC, 1967; "The Big Valley: Explosion," ABC, 1967; "The Man From UNCLE: The Gurnius Affair," NBC, 1967; "PDQ," NBC, 1967; "Run for Your Life: A Dangerous Proposal," NBC, 1968; "I Dream of Jeannie: The Biggest Star in Hollywood," NBC, 1969; "This Is Tom Jones," ABC, 1969; "Love, American Style: Love and the Burglar," ABC, 1969; "The Andy Williams Show," NBC, 1970; "The Andy Williams Show," NBC, 1971; "Love, American Style: Love and the Vampire," ABC, 1971; "Alias Smith and Jones: The Root of It All," ABC, 1971; "Love, American Style: Love and the Advice Column," ABC, 1972; "Love, American Style: Love and the Single Sister," ABC, 1972; "Someone at the Top of the Stairs," ABC, 1973; "Love, American Style: Love and the Last Joke," ABC, 1974; "Ironside: Once More for Joey," NBC, 1974; "ABC Afternoon Playbreak: Oh! Baby, Baby, Baby ...," ABC, 1974; "Cross Wits," SYN, 1976.

TV MOVIES AND MINISERIES: "Dead Men Tell No Tales," CBS, 1971; "Only with Married Men," ABC, 1974.

CARNEY, ALAN

b. Brooklyn, NY, 1911; d. 1973.

AS A REGULAR: "Take It From Me," ABC, 1953-54.

AND: "Have Gun, Will Travel: The Five Books of Owen Deaver," CBS, 1958; "Goodyear Theatre: Coogan's Reward," NBC, 1959; "Frontier Circus: The Shaggy Kings," CBS, 1961; "Have Gun, Will Travel: Justice in Hell," CBS, 1962; "The Hathaways: The Paint Job," ABC, 1962; "The Donna Reed Show: The Golden Trap," ABC,

1962; "The Hathaways: Pop Goes the Budget," ABC, 1962; "The Donna Reed Show: Mister Nice Guy," ABC, 1962.

CARNEY, ART

b. Mt. Vernon, NY, November 4, 1918. Oscar and Emmy-winning performer as effective in drama as in comedy; even if he hadn't done anything else, however, he'll still be remembered as Ralph Kramden's loyal friend, neighbor and fellow Beaver, Ed Norton.

AS A REGULAR: "The Morey Amsterdam Show," CBS, 1948-49; DUM, 1949-50; "Cavalcade of Stars," DUM, 1950-52; "Henry Morgan's Great Talent Hunt," NBC, 1951; "The Jackie Gleason Show," CBS, 1952-55; 1956-57; 1961; 1966-70; "The Honeymooners," CBS, 1955-56; 1971; Art Carney Specials, NBC, 1959-61; "Lanigan's Rabbi," NBC, 1977.

AND: "Lux Video Theatre: Thanks for a Lovely Evening," CBS, 1953; "Studio One: The Laugh Maker," CBS, 1953; "Danger: I'll Be Waiting," CBS, 1953; "Campbell TV Soundstage: The Square Hole," NBC, 1953; "Studio One: Confessions of a Nervous Man," CBS, 1953; "Suspense: Mr. Nobody," NBC, 1953; "Kraft Television Theatre: Burlesque," NBC, 1954; "Suspense: The Return Journey," CBS, 1954; "Kraft Television Theatre: Alice in Wonderland," NBC, 1954; "Studio One: A Letter to Mr. Gubbins," CBS, 1954; "Kraft Television Theatre: Uncle Harry," NBC, 1954; "Best of Broadway: Panama Hattie," CBS, 1954; "Climax!: The Bigger They Come," CBS, 1955; "Studio One: The Incredible World of Horace Ford," CBS, 1955; "Star Stage: The Man Who Was Irrestible to Women," NBC, 1956; "Air Power: Fools, Daredevils and Genuises," CBS, 1956; "Dinah Shore Chevy Show," NBC, 1957; "Playhouse 90: Charley's Aunt," CBS, 1957; "Playhouse 90: The Fabulous Irishman," CBS, 1957; "The Tonight Show," NBC, 1957; "The Arlene Francis Show," NBC, 1958; "Dinah Shore Chevy Show," NBC, 1958; "The Perry Como Show," NBC, 1958; "The Jack Paar Show," NBC, 1958; "Du Pont Show of the Month: Harvey," CBS, 1958; "Christophers: Some Facts About Benedict Arnold," SYN, 1958; "The Sid Caesar Show," NBC, 1958; "Alfred Hitchcock Presents: Safety for the Witness," CBS, 1958; "Art Carney Meets Peter and the Wolf," ABC, 1958; "Playhouse 90: The Velvet Alley," CBS, 1959; "Chevy Show Special," NBC, 1959; "Art Carney Meets the Sorcerer's Apprentice," ABC, 1959; "At the Movies," NBC, 1959; "America Pauses for the Merry Month of May," CBS, 1959; "A Tribute to Eleanor Roosevelt on Her Diamond Jubilee," NBC, 1959; "Dinah Shore Chevy Show," NBC, 1960; "Hooray for Love," CBS, 1960; "The Right Man," CBS, 1960; "The Twilight Zone: Night of the Meek," CBS, 1960; "The Jackie Gleason Show," CBS, 1961; "Chevy Show: O'Halloran's Luck," NBC, 1961; "Jane Powell Special: Young at Heart," NBC, 1961; "Connie Francis Special: Kicking Sound Around," ABC, 1961; "Westinghouse Presents: The Sound of the Sixties," NBC, 1961; "The Chevrolet Golden Anniversary Show," CBS, 1961; "The Ed Sullivan Show," CBS, 1961; "Jackie Gleason and His American Scene Magazine," CBS, 1962; "Andy Williams Special," NBC, 1963; "The Danny Kaye Show," CBS, 1963; "Jackie Gleason and His American Scene Magazine," CBS, 1964; "The Danny Kaye Show," CBS, 1964; "A Wild Winters Night," NBC, 1964; "The du Pont Show: A Day Like Today," NBC, 1964; "Bob Hope Chrysler Theatre: The Timothy Heist," NBC, 1964; "Mr. Broadway: Smelling Like a Rose," CBS, 1964; "Batman: Shoot a Crooked Arrow/Walk the Straight and Narrow," ABC, 1966; "The Dick Cavett Show," ABC, 1968; "The David Frost Show," SYN, 1970; "The Men From Shiloh: With Love, Bullets and Valentines," NBC, 1970; "The David Frost Revue," SYN, 1971; "The Dean Martin Show," NBC, 1971; "Perry Como's Winter Show," NBC, 1971; "ABC Comedy Hour," ABC, 1972; "Jackie Gleason Special," CBS, 1973; "Happy Anniversary and Goodbye," CBS, 1974; "Happy Endings: Kidnapped," ABC, 1975; "The Honeymooners-The Second Honeymoon," ABC, 1976; "What Now, Catherine Curtis?," CBS, 1976; "Christmas in Disneyland," ABC, 1976; "Alice: My Cousin, Art Carney," CBS, 1979.

TV MOVIES AND MINISERIES: "The Snoop Sisters," NBC, 1972; "Death Scream," ABC, 1975; "Katherine," ABC, 1975; "Lanigan's Rabbi," NBC, 1976; "Letters From Frank," CBS, 1979; "Terrible Joe Moran," CBS, 1984; "The Night They Saved Christmas," ABC, 1984; "Izzy and Moe," CBS, 1985.

* Emmies: 1954, 1955, 1956, 1967, 1968, 1984.

CARPENTER, KAREN

b. New Haven, CT, March 2, 1950; d. 1983;
& RICHARD

b. New Haven, CT, October 15, 1946. Brother and sister who scored as a soft-pop duo in the seventies, even getting their own summer variety show; rigid professional and emotional expectations drove Karen Carpenter to anorexia and an early death.

AS A REGULAR: "Make Your Own Kind of Music," NBC, 1971.

AND: "The Johnny Cash Show," ABC, 1971; "The Perry Como Christmas Show," CBS, 1974.

CARR, DARLENE

b. Chicago, IL, 1950. Actress who began in teen roles, usually as a lovestruck kid with a crush on the series star.

AS A REGULAR: "The John Forsythe Show," NBC, 1965-66; "Dean Martin Presents," NBC, 1969; "The Smith Family," ABC, 1971-72; "The Streets of San Francisco," ABC, 1973-77; "The Oregon Trail," NBC, 1977; "Miss Winslow and Son," CBS, 1979; "Bret Maverick," NBC, 1981-82.

AND: "Mayberry RFD: Sam and the Teenager," CBS, 1968; "The Virginian: Family Man," NBC, 1969; "Family Affair: Uncle Prince Charming," CBS, 1969; "Marcus Welby, M.D.: Madonna with Knapsack and Flute," ABC, 1969; "The FBI: The Savage Wilderness," ABC, 1970; "The FBI: End of a Nightmare," ABC, 1972; "The Rookies: The Commitment," ABC, 1972; "Barnaby Jones: To Catch a Dead Man, " CBS, 1973; "Alias Smith and Jones: McGuffin," ABC, 1973; "Marcus Welby, M.D.: The Tortoise Dance," ABC, 1973; "Barnaby Jones: The Last Contract," CBS, 1974; "The Rookies: The Late Mr. Brent," ABC, 1974; "The Rookies: The Assassin," ABC, 1974; "Medical Center: The Eighth Deadly Sin," CBS, 1975; "SWAT: Pressure Cooker," ABC, 1975; "Medical Center: Survivors," CBS, 1975; "Jigsaw John: Follow the Yellow Brick Road," NBC, 1976; "Hollywood Squares," NBC, 1977; "The Merv Griffin Show," SYN, 1977; "The White Shadow: Salami's Affair," CBS, 1980; "Vega$: The Man Who Was Twice," ABC, 1980; "Simon & Simon: Who Killed the Sixties?," CBS, 1984; "Murder, She Wrote: School for Scandal," CBS, 1985; "Blacke's Magic: A Friendly Game of Showdown," NBC, 1986; "Simon & Simon: The Case of Don Diablo," CBS, 1986.

TV MOVIES AND MINISERIES: "All My Darling Daughters," ABC, 1972; "Horror at 37,000 Feet," CBS, 1973; "Runaway!," ABC, 1973; "My Darling Daughters' Anniversary," ABC, 1973; "The Chadwick Family," ABC, 1974; "Law of the Land," NBC, 1976; "Best Sellers: Once an Eagle," NBC, 1977; "Young Joe, the Forgotten Kennedy," ABC, 1977.

CARRADINE, DAVID

b. Hollywood, December 8, 1936. Actor who played the peaceful Caine, a student of life and nonviolence who spent three years trudging through wild west on the Eastern western "Kung Fu."

AS A REGULAR: "Shane," ABC, 1966; "Kung Fu," ABC, 1972-75.

AND: "Arrest and Trial: The Black Flower," ABC, 1964; "The Virginian: The Intruders," NBC, 1964; "Bob Hope Chrysler Theatre: The War and Eric Kurtz," NBC, 1965; "The Alfred Hitchcock Hour: Thou Still Unravished Bride," NBC, 1965; "Trials of O'Brien: The Greatest Game," CBS, 1966; "Saga of Western Man: Cortez and the Legend," NET, 1967; "Coronet Blue: The Rebel," CBS, 1967; "Johnny Belinda," ABC, 1967; "Ironside: Due Process of Law," NBC, 1968;

"The Name of the Game: Tarot," NBC, 1970; "Ironside: The Quincunx," NBC, 1971; "Gunsmoke: The Lavery," CBS, 1971; "Night Gallery: The Phantom Farmhouse," NBC, 1971; "Ironside: License to Kill," NBC, 1971; "John Denver Special," ABC, 1974; "The Family Holvak: The Long Way Home," NBC, 1975; "Saturday Night Live," NBC, 1980; "Darkroom: Catnip," ABC, 1981; "Today's FBI: Hostage," ABC, 1981; "Amazing Stories: Thanksgiving," NBC, 1986; "Matlock: The Country Boy," NBC, 1987; "Matlock: The Prisoner," NBC, 1989.

TV MOVIES AND MINISERIES: "Maybe I'll Come Home in the Spring," ABC, 1971; "Kung Fu," ABC, 1972; "Gauguin the Savage," CBS, 1980; "Jealousy," ABC, 1984; "The Bad Seed," ABC, 1985; "North and South," ABC, 1985; "North and South, Book II," ABC, 1986; "Kung Fu," CBS, 1986; "Oceans of Fire," CBS, 1986; "Six Against the Rock," NBC, 1987; "I Saw What You Did," CBS, 1988; "The Cover Girl and the Cop," NBC, 1989.

CARRADINE, JOHN

b. Richmond Reed Carradine, New York City, NY, February 5, 1906; d. 1988. Long-faced character actor, often in creepy roles; even when he wasn't, he was still capable of a haunting performance.

AS A REGULAR: "Trapped," SYN, 1951; "My Friend Irma," CBS, 1953-54.

AND: "Lights Out: The Half-Pint Flask," NBC, 1950; "The Web: Stone Cold Dead," CBS, 1950; "Lights Out: Meddlers," CBS, 1951; "Suspense: Come Into My Parlor," CBS, 1953; "Climax!: The First and the Last," CBS, 1955; "Climax!: The Adventures of Huckleberry Finn," CBS, 1955; "Gunsmoke: Reed Survives," CBS, 1955; "Climax!: The Hanging Judge," CBS, 1956; "Front Row Center: Deadlock," CBS, 1956; "Studio 57: The Rarest Stamp," SYN, 1956; "Alfred Hitchcock Presents: The Appointment of Eleanor," CBS, 1956; "Du Pont Show of the Month: The Prince and the Pauper," CBS, 1957; "Studio One: Please Report Any Odd Characters," CBS, 1957; "Telephone Time: Novel Appeal," ABC, 1957; "The Red Skelton Show," CBS, 1958; "Wagon Train: The Dora Gray Story," NBC, 1958; "77 Sunset Strip: All Our Yester-days," ABC, 1958; "The Rifleman: The Mind Reader," ABC, 1959; "Rough Riders: The End of Nowhere," ABC, 1959; "Bat Masterson: Tumbleweed Wagon," NBC, 1959; "The Millionaire: Millionaire Karl Miller," CBS, 1959; "The Red Skelton Show," CBS, 1959; "The Twilight Zone: The Howling Man," CBS, 1960; "Harrigan and Son: A Matter of Dignity," ABC, 1960; "Wagon Train: The Colter Craven Story," NBC, 1960; "Maverick: Red Dog," ABC, 1961; "Here's Hollywood," NBC, 1961; "Bonanza: Springtime," NBC, 1961; "Thriller: Masquerade,"

NBC, 1961; "The Red Skelton Show: The Great Brain Robbery," CBS, 1961; "Thriller: The Remarkable Mrs. Hawk," NBC, 1961; "Death Valley Days: Miracle at Boot Hill," SYN, 1962; "The Red Skelton Show: Appleby's Bearded Boarder," CBS, 1962; "The Lucy Show: Lucy Goes to Art Class," CBS, 1964; "The Legend of Jesse James: As Far as the Sea," ABC, 1966; "Laredo: Sound of Terror," NBC, 1966; "The Girl From UNCLE: The Montori Device Affair," NBC, 1966; "The Man From UNCLE: The Prince of Darkness Affair," NBC, 1967; "Hondo: Hondo and the Judas," ABC, 1967; "The Big Valley: Town of No Exit," ABC, 1969; "Decisions, Decisions!," NBC, 1969; "Night Gallery: The Big Surprise," NBC, 1971; "Ironside: Gentle Oaks," NBC, 1971; "Love, American Style: Love and the Anniversary," ABC, 1973; "Emergency!: I'll Fix It," NBC, 1974; "Hollywood Television Theatre: The Lady's Not for Burning," PBS, 1974; "McCloud: McCloud Meets Dracula," NBC, 1977.

TV MOVIES AND MINISERIES: "Daughter of the Mind," ABC, 1969; "Crowhaven Farm," ABC, 1970; "The Night Strangler," ABC, 1973; "The Cat Creature," ABC, 1973; "Stowaway to the Moon," CBS, 1975; "Death at Love House," ABC, 1976; "Best Sellers: Captains and the Kings," NBC, 1976.

CARRADINE, KEITH
b. San Mateo, CA, August 8, 1949. Carradine brother who's made his TV mark in several memorable movies and miniseries.

AS A GUEST: "Love, American Style: Love and the Anniversary," ABC, 1973.

TV MOVIES AND MINISERIES: "Man on a String," ABC, 1972; "Kung Fu," ABC, 1972; "The Godchild," ABC, 1974; "Scorned and Swindled," CBS, 1984; "Blackout," HBO, 1985; "A Winner Never Quits," ABC, 1986; "Eye on the Sparrow," NBC, 1987; "My Father, My Son," CBS, 1988; "The Revenge of Al Capone," NBC, 1989; "The Forgotten," USA, 1989.

CARRADINE, ROBERT
b. Los Angeles, CA, March 24, 1954. The youngest Carradine brother, best known for his roles in the "Revenge of the Nerds" movies.

AS A REGULAR: "The Cowboys," ABC, 1974.

AND: "Alfred Hitchcock Presents: Night Fever," NBC, 1985; "The Twilight Zone: Still Life," CBS, 1986.

TV MOVIES AND MINISERIES: "Footsteps," CBS, 1972; "Go Ask Alice," ABC, 1973; "Survival of Dana," CBS, 1979; "The Sun Also Rises," NBC, 1984; "Monte Carlo," CBS, 1986; "I Saw What You Did," CBS, 1988.

CARREY, JIM
b. Canada, January 17, 1962. Comic and impressionist.

AS A REGULAR: "The Duck Factory," NBC, 1984; "In Living Color," FOX, 1990- .

CARRILLO, LEO
b. Los Angeles, CA, August 6, 1880; d. 1961. Character actor who played Pancho, the Cisco kid's sidekick.

AS A REGULAR: "The Cisco Kid," SYN, 1950-56.

CARROLL, DIAHANN
b. Carol Diahann Johnson, Bronx, NY, July 17, 1935. Actress who made TV history as the first black to play a leading role as a non-domestic in a situation comedy.

AS A REGULAR: "Julia," NBC, 1968-71; "The Diahann Carroll Show," CBS, 1976; "Dynasty," ABC, 1984-87.

AND: "The Red Skelton Show," CBS, 1954; "Circus Time," ABC, 1956; "The Steve Allen Show," NBC, 1957; "The Ed Sullivan Show," CBS, 1957; "Du Pont Show of the Month: Crescendo," CBS, 1957; "The Tonight Show," NBC, 1957; "The Jack Paar Show," NBC, 1958; "Music USA," CBS, 1958; "The Jack Paar Show," NBC, 1959; "The Garry Moore Show," CBS, 1959; "The Steve Allen Show," NBC, 1959; "The Andy Williams Show," CBS, 1959; "The Garry Moore Show," CBS, 1960; "Peter Gunn: Sing a Song of Murder," NBC, 1960; "Pontiac Star Parade: The Man in the Moon," NBC, 1960; "The Garry Moore Show," CBS, 1961; "Naked City: A Horse Has a Big Head-Let Him Worry," ABC, 1962; "The Ed Sullivan Show," CBS, 1962; "Exploring," NBC, 1963; "The Merv Griffin Show," NBC, 1963; "The Eleventh Hour: And Man Created Vanity," NBC, 1963; "The Danny Kaye Show," CBS, 1964; "The Judy Garland Show," CBS, 1964; "Hollywood Palace," ABC, 1964; "The Dean Martin Show," NBC, 1965; "The Steve Lawrence Show," CBS, 1965; "ABC Stage '67: C'est la Vie," ABC, 1967; "The Tonight Show Starring Johnny Carson," NBC, 1968; "Hollywood Palace," ABC, 1968; "Francis Albert Sinatra Does His Thing," CBS, 1968; "Movin'," NBC, 1970; "Jack Lemmon-Get Happy," NBC, 1973; "Hotel Ninety," CBS, 1973; "The Love Boat: Isaac the Groupie," ABC, 1977; "Hollywood Squares," SYN, 1980; "Webster: Strike Up the Band," ABC, 1985; "America's Tribute to Bob Hope," NBC, 1988; "A Different World: For She's Only a Bird in a Gilded Cage," NBC, 1989; "Christmas in Washington," NBC, 1989; "A Different World: For Whom the Jingle Bell Tolls," NBC, 1989.

TV MOVIES AND MINISERIES: "Death Scream," ABC, 1975; "Roots: The Next Generations," ABC, 1979; "I Know Why the Caged Bird

Sings," CBS, 1979; "From the Dead of the Night," NBC, 1989.

* "Julia," the first weekly series to be "built around the character of a contemporary negro," as NBC called it, began after the show's creator, Hal Kantor, heard NAACP director Roy Wilkins preach nonviolence at the Beverly Hilton Hotel on May 22, 1967.

CARROLL, LEO G.
b. Weedon, England, 1892; d. 1972. British actor who played fuddy British types; best known as Mr. Waverly, the head of UNCLE (United Network Command for Law and Enforcement) and as banker Cosmo Topper, whose life was complicated by two ghosts that were always hanging around.

AS A REGULAR: "Topper," CBS, 1953-55; "Going My Way," ABC, 1962-63; "The Man From UNCLE," NBC, 1964-68; "The Girl From UNCLE," NBC, 1966-67.

AND: "Billy Rose's Playbill: The Benefit of the Doubt," SYN, 1950; "Danger: Head Print," CBS, 1951; "Cavalcade of America: The Splendid Dream," ABC, 1954; "Star Tonight: Can You Coffee Pot on Ice Skates?," ABC, 1956; "Cheyenne: Dark Rider," ABC, 1956; "Matinee Theatre: Angel Street," NBC, 1958; "Shirley Temple's Storybook: The Magic Fishbone," NBC, 1958; "Studio One: Bellingham," CBS, 1958; "Command Performance: Mr. November," SYN, 1960; "U.S. Steel Hour: Double-Edged Sword," CBS, 1961; "Alcoa Premiere: The Fugitive Eye," ABC, 1961; "U.S. Steel Hour: Bury Me Twice," CBS, 1961; "Thriller: An Attractive Family," NBC, 1962; "Mystery Theatre: Dead on Nine," NBC, 1962; "Hazel: Hazel's Midas Touch," NBC, 1964; "Channing: Where Are the Snows ...?," ABC, 1964; "Bob Hope Chrysler Theatre: Wind Fever," NBC, 1966; "Walt Disney's Wonderful World of Color: A Boy Called Nuthin'," NBC, 1967; "Ironside: Little Dog, Gone," NBC, 1970.

CARROLL, PAT
b. Shreveport, LA, May 5, 1927. Heavyset blonde actress who played Bunny, wife of Charlie Halper (Sid Melton) on "The Danny Thomas Show," as well as lending solid support to a number of other sitcoms and game shows.

AS A REGULAR: "The Red Buttons Show," CBS, 1952-53; "Saturday Night Revue," NBC, 1954; "Caesar's Hour," NBC, 1956-57; "Masquerade Party," CBS, 1958; "Keep Talking," CBS, 1958-59; ABC, 1959-60; "You're in the Picture," CBS, 1961; "The Danny Thomas Show," CBS, 1961-64; "Getting Together," ABC, 1971-72; "Busting Loose," CBS, 1977; "Too Close for Comfort," SYN, 1986; "She's the Sheriff," SYN, 1987-89.

AND: "Pepsi Cola Playhouse: The Black Purse,"

ABC, 1954; "Best Foot Forward," NBC, 1954; "Studio 57: Fish Widow," SYN, 1954; "Producers Showcase: The Women," NBC, 1955; "Kraft Television Theatre: The Gramercy Ghost," NBC, 1955; "Damon Runyon Theatre: Broadway Dateline," CBS, 1955; "Masquerade Party," NBC, 1957; "Two for the Money," CBS, 1957; "The Ford Show," NBC, 1958; "The Patrice Munsel Show," ABC, 1958; "Steve Allen Presents the Steve Lawrence-Eydie Gorme Show," NBC, 1958; "U.S. Steel Hour: Private Eye, Private Eye," CBS, 1961; "The Ann Sothern Show: Pandora," CBS, 1961; "To Tell the Truth," CBS, 1961; "Here's Hollywood," NBC, 1961; "Password," CBS, 1961; "The Investigators: The Dead End Men," CBS, 1961; "Password," CBS, 1962; "Art Linkletter's House Party," CBS, 1962; "The Ed Sullivan Show," CBS, 1963; "Your First Impression," NBC, 1963; "You Don't Say," NBC, 1963; "Object Is," ABC, 1964; "The Red Skelton Hour," CBS, 1964; "You Don't Say," NBC, 1964; "You Don't Say," NBC, 1965; "The Danny Kaye Show," CBS, 1965; "Please Don't Eat the Daisies: Wring Out the Welcome Mat," NBC, 1966; "You Don't Say," NBC, 1967; "Snap Judgment," NBC, 1968; "Personality," NBC, 1968; "The Red Skelton Hour," CBS, 1968; "Letters to Laugh-In," NBC, 1969; "The Carol Burnett Show," CBS, 1970; "Love, American Style: Love and the Great Catch," ABC, 1970; "The Mary Tyler Moore Show: Hi!," CBS, 1971; "My Three Sons: After the Honeymoon," CBS, 1971; "Love, American Style: Love and the Free Weekend," ABC, 1971; "Oh, Nurse!," CBS, 1972; "Honeymoon Suite," ABC, 1973; "Honeymoon Suite," ABC, 1974; "Police Story: The Ripper," NBC, 1974; "Police Woman: Do You Still Beat Your Wife?," NBC, 1977.

TV MOVIES AND MINISERIES: "Second Chance," ABC, 1972.

* Emmies: 1957.

CARSON, JACK
b. John Elmer Carson, Canada, October 27, 1910; d. 1963. Film and TV actor in bigmouth roles.

AS A REGULAR: "All Star Revue," NBC, 1950-52; "The U.S. Royal Showcase," NBC, 1952.

AND: "Theatre Hour: Room Service," CBS, 1950; "Lux Video Theatre: No Shoes," CBS, 1951; "Lux Video Theatre: For Heaven's Sake," CBS, 1952; "G.E. Theatre: The Marriage Fix," CBS, 1953; "G.E. Theatre: Here Comes Calvin," CBS, 1954; "U.S. Steel Hour: Goodbye ... But It Doesn't Go Away," ABC, 1954; "U.S. Steel Hour: Man in the Corner," ABC, 1955; "Screen Directors Playhouse: Arroyo," NBC, 1955; "U.S. Steel Hour: The Gambler," CBS, 1955; "Fireside Theatre: The Director," NBC, 1955; "Climax!: Portrait in Celluloid," CBS, 1955; "Damon Runyon Theatre: Broadway Dateline," CBS,

1956; "Alfred Hitchcock Presents: The Children of Aldo Nuevon," CBS, 1956; "The Bob Cummings Show: Hawaii Calls," CBS, 1956; "Schlitz Playhouse of Stars: False Alarm," CBS, 1956; "Schlitz Playhouse of Stars: The Press Agent," CBS, 1956; "Schlitz Playhouse of Stars: The Trophy," CBS, 1956; "Ford Theatre: Paris Edition," ABC, 1956; "The George Gobel Show," NBC, 1957; "Playhouse 90: Three Men on a Horse," CBS, 1957; "The Steve Allen Show," NBC, 1957; "The Guy Mitchell Show," ABC, 1957; "Climax!: Tunnel of Fear," CBS, 1957; "U.S. Steel Hour: Huck Finn," CBS, 1957; "Date with the Angels: Cousin Herbie," ABC, 1957; "The Betty White Show," ABC, 1958; "Studio One: The Funny-Looking Kid," CBS, 1958; "Studio 57: Who's Been Sitting in My Chair," SYN, 1958; "Playhouse 90: The Long March," CBS, 1958; "The Garry Moore Show," CBS, 1958; "Alcoa Theatre: High Class Type of Mongrel," NBC, 1959; "Alcoa Theatre: Another Day, Another Dollar," NBC, 1959; "Bonanza: Mr. Henry Comstock," NBC, 1959; "Startime: Something Special," NBC, 1959; "Alcoa Theatre: How's Business?," NBC, 1959; "Dick Powell's Zane Grey Theatre: Sundown Smith," CBS, 1960; "Take a Good Look," ABC, 1960; "Thriller: The Big Blackout," NBC, 1960; "The Twilight Zone: The Whole Truth," CBS, 1961; "U.S. Steel Hour: The Big Splash," CBS, 1961; "The Chevy Show: The Happiest Day," NBC, 1961; "The Dick Powell Show: Who Killed Julie Greer?," NBC, 1961; "Bus Stop: The Man From Bootstrap," ABC, 1961; "U.S. Steel Hour: Far From the Shade Tree," CBS, 1962; "Walt Disney's Wonderful World of Color: Sammy, the Way-Out Seal," NBC, 1962.

CARSON, JEAN
b. Charleston, WV, 1925. Deep-voiced actress usually in comic roles; she played Daphne, one of the "Fun Girls" who plagued Andy and Barney on "The Andy Griffith Show."
AS A REGULAR: "The Red Buttons Show," CBS, 1952-53; "The Betty Hutton Show," CBS, 1959-60.
AND: "Court of Last Resort: The Darlene Fitzgerald Case," NBC, 1957; "Wagon Train: The Riley Gratton Story," NBC, 1957; "Sugarfoot: Small War at Custer Junction," ABC, 1958; "Matinee Theatre: Love Out of Town," NBC, 1958; "Chevy Mystery Show: Thunder of Silence," NBC, 1960; "The Twilight Zone: A Most Unusual Camera," CBS, 1960; "The Tom Ewell Show: A Fellow Needs a Friend," CBS, 1961; "Dante: Light Lady, Dark Room," NBC, 1961; "The Tom Ewell Show: The Prying Eye," CBS, 1961; "The Tom Ewell Show: Put It On, Take It Off," CBS, 1961; "The Untouchables: The Nero Rankin Story," ABC, 1961; "The Joey Bishop Show: Home Sweet Home," NBC, 1962;

"The Andy Griffith Show: Convicts at Large," CBS, 1962; "Perry Mason: The Case of the Bountiful Beauty," CBS, 1964; "The Andy Griffith Show: Fun Girls," CBS, 1964; "Gomer Pyle, USMC: Love Letters to the Sarge," CBS, 1965; "The Andy Griffith Show: The Arrest of the Fun Girls," CBS, 1965; "Wendy & Me: Wendy's $5,000 Chair," ABC, 1965.

CARSON, JEANNIE
b. England, May 23, 1928. Pert redheaded actress of fifties TV, often as an innocent Englishwoman abroad.
AS A REGULAR: "Hey, Jeannie!," CBS, 1956-57.
AND: "The Ed Sullivan Show," CBS, 1957; "What's My Line?," CBS, 1957; "The Jane Wyman Show: A Dangerous Thing," NBC, 1957; "The Ford Show," NBC, 1957; "The Ray Bolger Show," NBC, 1957; "The George Gobel Show," NBC, 1957; "Club Oasis," NBC, 1957; "G.E. Theatre: Time to Go Now," CBS, 1958; "Wagon Train: The Annie MacGregor Story," NBC, 1958; "The Frank Sinatra Show," ABC, 1958; "Little Women," CBS, 1958; "Pat Boone Chevy Showroom," ABC, 1958; "Hallmark Hall of Fame: Berkeley Square," NBC, 1959; "Startime: Something Special," NBC, 1959; "Arthur Murray Party," NBC, 1960;

CARSON, JOHNNY
b. Corning, IA, October 23, 1925. Teflon-coated comic who defies age and audience dropoff.
AS A REGULAR: "Earn Your Vacation," CBS, 1954; "The Johnny Carson Show," CBS, 1955-56; "Who Do You Trust?," ABC, 1958-62; "To Tell the Truth," CBS, 1961-62; "The Tonight Show Starring Johnny Carson," NBC, 1962- .
AND: "The Ed Sullivan Show," CBS, 1956; "The Ed Sullivan Show," CBS, 1957; "Playhouse 90: Three Men on a Horse," CBS, 1957; "The Polly Bergen Show," NBC, 1958; "The Jack Paar Show," NBC, 1958; "Pantomime Quiz," ABC, 1958; "The Steve Allen Show," NBC, 1958; "The Steve Allen Show," NBC, 1959; "Arthur Murray Party," NBC, 1959; "The Garry Moore Show," CBS, 1959; "The Andy Williams Show," CBS, 1959; "I've Got a Secret," CBS, 1959; "Steve Allen Plymouth Show," NBC, 1959; "Dick Clark's World of Talent," ABC, 1959; "U.S. Steel Hour: Queen of the Orange Bowl," CBS, 1960; "Dinah Shore Chevy Show," NBC, 1960; "I've Got a Secret," CBS, 1960; "The Arthur Murray Party for Bob Hope," NBC, 1960; "Steve Allen Plymouth Show," NBC, 1960; "U.S. Steel Hour: Girl in the Gold Bathtub," CBS, 1960; "Perry Como's Kraft Music Hall," NBC, 1960; "The Garry Moore Show," CBS, 1960; "Celebrity Talent Scouts," CBS, 1960; "New Comedy Showcase: Johnny Come Lately," CBS, 1960; "To Tell the Truth," CBS, 1960; "The Garry

Moore Show," CBS, 1961; "The Ed Sullivan Show," CBS, 1961; "I've Got a Secret," CBS, 1961; "Here's Hollywood," NBC, 1961; "The Garry Moore Show," CBS, 1962; "Password," CBS, 1962; "Perry Como's Kraft Music Hall," NBC, 1962; "Bob Hope Special," NBC, 1965; "Get Smart: Aboard the Orient Express," NBC, 1965; "Bob Hope Chrysler Theatre: Murder at NBC," NBC, 1967; "Jack Benny Special," NBC, 1968; "The Don Rickles Show," ABC, 1968; "Kraft Music Hall: Roast for Johnny Carson," NBC, 1968; "Get Smart: The King Lives?," NBC, 1968; "Here's Lucy: Lucy and Johnny Carson," CBS, 1969; "Red," NBC, 1970; "Johnny Carson Special: The Sun City Scandals," NBC, 1970; "Rowan & Martin's Laugh-In," NBC, 1973; "The Smothers Brothers Comedy Hour," NBC, 1975; "Joys," NBC, 1976; "The Mary Tyler Moore Show: Mary's Big Party," CBS, 1977; "Night Court: Russkie Business," NBC, 1988.
AS WRITER: "The Red Skelton Show," CBS, 1953-54.

* Carson's first appearance as a host in a late night slot came four years before he took over "The Tonight Show"; in 1958, he was a guest and host for Jack Paar.
* Carson tried his hand at sitcoms before going to talk shows—the 1960 pilot "Johnny Come Lately" cast him as Johnny Martin, go-getting TV reporter, but no network bought it. Carson was also considered for another sitcom role— that of Rob Petrie on what would become "The Dick Van Dyke Show."
* Carson's "roast" in 1968 spurred dozens of imitations; Dean Martin liked the idea so much that he began weekly roasts in the mid-seventies, providing employment for dozens of has-been comics.
* Emmies: 1976, 1977, 1978, 1979.

CARSON, KEN
b. Coalgate, OK, November 14, 1914. Singer.
AS A REGULAR: "The Garry Moore Show," CBS, 1950-64; "The Garry Moore Evening Show," CBS, 1951.
AND: "The Tonight Show Starring Johnny Carson," NBC, 1964.

CARSON, MINDY
b. New York City, NY, July 16, 1927. Fifties vocalist.
AS A REGULAR: "Ford Star Revue," NBC, 1951; "Club Embassy," NBC, 1952-53; "Perry Como's Kraft Music Hall," NBC, 1961-63.
AND: "The Guy Mitchell Show," ABC, 1957; "The Big Record," CBS, 1958; "The Voice of Firestone: An Evening with Paul Whiteman," ABC, 1959; "Bell Telephone Hour: And Freedom Sings," NBC, 1960; "Music for a Winter Night: The Sounds of Christmas," ABC, 1960; "Armstrong Circle Theatre: Spin a Crooked Record," CBS, 1961; "Bell Telephone Hour: The Songs of Irving Berlin," NBC, 1962; "Bell Telephone Hour," NBC, 1963.

CARTER, DIXIE
b. McLemoresville, TX, May 25, 1939. Actress who plays Julia Sugarbaker on "Designing Women."
AS A REGULAR: "The Edge of Night," CBS, 1974-75; ABC, 1975-76; "On Our Own," CBS, 1977-78; "Out of the Blue," ABC, 1979; "Filthy Rich," CBS, 1982-83; "Diff'rent Strokes," NBC, 1984-85; "Designing Women," CBS, 1986- .
AND: "Lou Grant: Suspect," CBS, 1981; "Bret Maverick: Hallie," NBC, 1982; "Best of the West: The Pretty Prisoner," ABC, 1982.
TV MOVIES AND MINISERIES: "The Killing of Randy Webster," CBS, 1981.

CARTER, JACK
b. New York City, NY, June 24, 1923. Scrawny comedian.
AS A REGULAR: "Texaco Star Theatre," NBC, 1948; "American Minstrels of 1949," ABC, 1949; "Cavalcade of Stars," DUM, 1949-50; "The Jack Carter Show," NBC, 1950-51.
AND: "The Perry Como Show," NBC, 1957; "Arthur Murray Party," NBC, 1957; "The Big Record," CBS, 1957; "The Perry Como Show," NBC, 1958; "The Ed Sullivan Show," CBS, 1958; "Pat Boone Chevy Showroom," ABC, 1958; "The Big Party," CBS, 1959; "Dick Clark's World of Talent," ABC, 1959; "The Ed Sullivan Show," CBS, 1960; "Revlon Revue," CBS, 1960; "Diagnosis: Unknown: Main Course—Murder," CBS, 1960; "Westinghouse Presents: Carnival at Sun Valley," ABC, 1962; "Password," CBS, 1962; "Hennesey: Buttons and Bones," CBS, 1962; "The Ed Sullivan Show," CBS, 1962; "Dr. Kildare: Guest Appearance," NBC, 1962; "Mr. Smith Goes to Washington: That's Show Business," ABC, 1963; "Ensign O'Toole: Operation: Geisha," NBC, 1963; "Dr. Kildare: The Great Guy," NBC, 1963; "The Danny Thomas Show: Danny's Replacement," CBS, 1963; "Burke's Law: Who Killed April?," ABC, 1964; "The Ed Sullivan Show," CBS, 1964; "Password," CBS, 1964; "The Joey Bishop Show: Jack Carter Helps Joey Propose," NBC, 1964; "Hollywood Palace," ABC, 1964; "The Dick Van Dyke Show: Stretch Petrie Versus Kid Schenk," CBS, 1964; "Hollywood Palace," ABC, 1965; "Password," CBS, 1965; "Combat!: Main Event," ABC, 1965; "The Ed Sullivan Show," CBS, 1965; "The Merv Griffin Show," SYN, 1966; "Batman: Come Back, Shame/It's the Way You Play the Game," ABC, 1966; "Hollywood Squares," NBC, 1967; "Dream Girl of '67," ABC, 1967; "The Lucy Show: Lucy Sues Mooney," CBS, 1967; "The Ed Sullivan Show," CBS, 1968; "Holly-

wood Squares," NBC, 1968; "I Dream of Jeannie: My Master the Ghost Breaker," NBC, 1968; "Funny You Should Ask," ABC, 1968; "The Merv Griffin Show," SYN, 1969; "The Wild Wild West: The Night of the Janus," CBS, 1969; "Alan King Special," NBC, 1969; "The Jackie Gleason Show," CBS, 1969; "Hollywood Palace," ABC, 1969; "Personality," NBC, 1969; "Love, American Style: Love and the Comedy Team," ABC, 1969; "The David Frost Show," SYN, 1969; "The Merv Griffin Show," CBS, 1970; "Mannix: One for the Lady," CBS, 1970; "Medical Center: Edge of Violence," CBS, 1971; "Rowan & Martin's Laugh-In," NBC, 1972; "Love, American Style: Love and the Bachelor Party," ABC, 1972; "Cade's County: Ragged Edge," CBS, 1972; "Love, American Style: Love and the Cryptic Gift," ABC, 1973; "Police Story: Man on a Rack," NBC, 1973; "Hawaii Five-O: Try to Die on Time," CBS, 1973; "The $10,000 Pyramid," CBS, 1974; "The Odd Couple: Your Mother Wears Army Boots," ABC, 1975; "Ellery Queen: Veronica's Veils," NBC, 1975; "Sammy and Company," SYN, 1976; "The Rockford Files: The Becker Connection," NBC, 1976; "Tattletales," CBS, 1977; "Break the Bank," SYN, 1977; "Sanford & Son: Fred Meets Redd," NBC, 1977; "Switch: Who Killed Lila Craig?," CBS, 1977; "Police Woman: Blind Terror," NBC, 1978; "Carter Country: Baker's First Day," ABC, 1979; "Big Shamus, Little Shamus: Pilot," CBS, 1979; "Gimme a Break: Nell Goes to Jail," NBC, 1982; "The New Mike Hammer: Murder in the Cards," CBS, 1986; "Murder, She Wrote: Dead Heat," CBS, 1986; "Murder, She Wrote: Just Another Fish Story," CBS, 1988.
TV MOVIES AND MINISERIES: "The Lonely Profession," NBC, 1969; "The Family Rico," CBS, 1972; "The Sex Symbol," ABC, 1974; "The Last Hurrah," NBC, 1977; "Human Feelings," NBC, 1978; "Rainbow," NBC, 1978; "The Hustler of Muscle Beach," ABC, 1980.

CARTER, JUNE
b. Maces Spring, VA, June 23, 1929.
AS A REGULAR: "Grand Ole Opry," ABC, 1955-56; "The Johnny Cash Show," ABC, 1969-71; CBS, 1976.
AND: "The Garry Moore Show," CBS, 1957; "Jubilee USA," ABC, 1959; "The Ford Show," NBC, 1959; "Jubilee USA," ABC, 1960; "Five Star Jubilee," NBC, 1961; "Hootenanny," ABC, 1964; "The Glen Campbell Goodtime Hour," CBS, 1969; "Little House on the Prairie: The Collection," NBC, 1976; "Inaugural Eve Special," CBS, 1977.
TV MOVIES AND MINISERIES: "Murder in Coweta County," CBS, 1983; "The Last Days of Frank and Jesse James," NBC, 1986; "Stagecoach," CBS, 1986.

CARTER, LYNDA
b. Phoenix, AZ, July 24, 1951. Statuesque actress who's supposed to be a star, but nobody can figure out just what she ever did to become one.
AS A REGULAR: "Wonder Woman," ABC, 1976-77; CBS, 1977-79; "Partners in Crime," NBC, 1984.
AND: "Starsky and Hutch: The Las Vegas Strangler," ABC, 1976; "Dinah!," SYN, 1976; "The Mike Douglas Show," SYN, 1977.
TV MOVIES AND MINISERIES: "The New, Original Wonder Woman," ABC, 1975; "Born to Be Sold," NBC, 1981; "Rita Hayworth: The Love Goddess," CBS, 1983; "Stillwatch," CBS, 1987.

CARTER, NELL
b. Birmingham, AL, September 13, 1948. Heavy actress who became a TV success by uttering juvenile putdowns on the neanderthal sitcom "Gimme a Break"; an Emmy winner for "Ain't Misbehavin'."
AS A REGULAR: "Ryan's Hope," ABC, 1979; "Lobo," NBC, 1980-81; "Gimme a Break," NBC, 1981-87.
AND: "Ain't Misbehavin'," NBC, 1981; "Irving Berlin's 100th Birthday Celebration," CBS, 1988; "The Presidential Inaugural Gala," CBS, 1989; "Morton's by the Bay," NBC, 1989; "227: Take My Diva-Please," NBC, 1989.
* Emmies: 1982.

CARTER, RALPH
b. New York City, May 30, 1961. Actor who played Michael Evans on "Good Times."
AS A REGULAR: "Good Times," CBS, 1974-79.

CARTER, T.K.
b. Los Angeles, CA, December 14, 1956. Black comic actor.
AS A REGULAR: "Just Our Luck," ABC, 1983; "Punky Brewster," NBC, 1985-86.
AND: "The Jeffersons: Homecoming," CBS, 1978; "The Magical World of Disney: Polly," NBC, 1989.
TV MOVIES AND MINISERIES: "Carpool," CBS, 1983.

CARTER, TERRY
b. Brooklyn, NY. Actor who played Sgt. Joe Broadhurst, sidekick of Sam McCloud (Dennis Weaver).
AS A REGULAR: "McCloud," NBC, 1970-77; "Battlestar Galactica," ABC, 1978-79.
AND: "The Phil Silvers Show: Bilko's Engagement," CBS, 1956; "Hallmark Hall of Fame: Green Pastures," CBS, 1957; "Playhouse 90: The Time of Your Life," CBS, 1958; "Hallmark Hall of Fame: Green Pastures," NBC, 1959; "Naked City: C3H5(NO3)3," ABC, 1961; "That Girl: The

Defiant One," ABC, 1969; "Mannix: Medal for a Hero," CBS, 1969; "Mr. Belvedere: Marsha's Job," ABC, 1987; "227: The Roommate," NBC, 1988.

TV MOVIES AND MINISERIES: "McCloud: Who Killed Miss USA?," NBC, 1970; "Two on a Bench," ABC, 1971.

CARTER, THOMAS
b. Naples, Italy. Actor-director; he played Hayward on "The White Shadow."

AS A REGULAR: "Szysznyk," CBS, 1977-78; "The White Shadow," CBS, 1978-80.

AND: "M*A*S*H: The Winchester Tapes," CBS, 1977; "What's Happening!: One Strike and You're Out," ABC, 1977; "Hill Street Blues: Invasion of the Third World Mutant Body Snatchers," NBC, 1982.

AS DIRECTOR-PRODUCER: "Equal Justice," ABC, 1990- .

CARTWRIGHT, ANGELA
b. England, September 9, 1952. Former child actress who played Linda Williams on "The Danny Thomas Show" and then played Penny Robinson on "Lost in Space."

AS A REGULAR: "The Danny Thomas Show," CBS, 1957-64; "Lost in Space," CBS, 1965-68; "Make Room for Grandaddy," ABC, 1970-71.

AND: "The Lucille Ball-Desi Arnaz Show: Lucy Makes Room for Danny," CBS, 1958; "The Chevy Show: Children Are People?," NBC, 1960; "The Chevy Show: Ghosts, Goblins and Kids," NBC, 1960; "Shirley Temple's Storybook: Babes in Toyland," NBC, 1960; "The Red Skelton Show," CBS, 1961; "Your First Impression," NBC, 1964; "Danny Thomas Special," NBC, 1965; "My Three Sons: The Glass Sneaker," ABC, 1965; "The John Forsythe Show: Little Miss Egghead," NBC, 1965; "My Three Sons: Chip and Debbie," CBS, 1969; "Room 222: The Nichols Girl," ABC, 1972; "The Love Boat: Baby Talk," ABC, 1982.

TV MOVIES AND MINISERIES: "U.M.C.," CBS, 1969; "High School USA," NBC, 1983.

CARTWRIGHT, VERONICA
b. England, 1949. Sister of Angela; she played Jemima Boone on "Daniel Boone" and violent Violet Rutherford on a couple of "Leave It to Beaver" episodes.

AS A REGULAR: "Daniel Boone," NBC, 1964-66.

AND: "Dick Powell's Zane Grey Theatre: Lone Woman," CBS, 1959; "Leave It to Beaver: The Tooth," ABC, 1959; "Leave It to Beaver: Beaver and Violet," ABC, 1960; "Leave It to Beaver: Beaver's Rat," ABC, 1961; "The Twilight Zone: I Sing the Body Electric," CBS, 1962; "The Eleventh Hour: My Name Is Judith, I'm Lost, You See," NBC, 1963; "Leave It to Beaver: Don

Juan Beaver," ABC, 1963; "Dr. Kildare: Take Case of My Little Girl," NBC, 1965; "Who Has Seen the Wind?," ABC, 1965; "The Dating Game," ABC, 1968; "Mannix: Edge of the Knife," CBS, 1968; "Dragnet: Personnel-The Shooting," NBC, 1969; "Family Affair: Flower Power," CBS, 1969; "Then Came Bronson: Still Waters," NBC, 1969; "My Three Sons: The Honeymoon," CBS, 1970; "Serpico: Dawn of the Furies," NBC, 1976.

TV MOVIES AND MINISERIES: "Desperate for Love," CBS, 1989.

CARVER, MARY
b. Los Angeles, CA, May 3, 1924. Actress who played the mother of the private-eye Simon boys.

AS A REGULAR: "Simon & Simon," CBS, 1981-89.

AND: "Gunsmoke: Chester's Mail Order Bride," CBS, 1956; "The Law and Mr. Jones: Semper Fidelis," ABC, 1960; "The Twilight Zone: The Incredible World of Horace Ford," CBS, 1963; "The Man From UNCLE: The Moonglow Affair," NBC, 1966; "The Virginian: To Bear Witness," NBC, 1967; "McCloud: This Must Be the Alamo," NBC, 1974; "Lou Grant: Schools," CBS, 1978; "Quincy: The Law Is a Fool," NBC, 1983; "Head of the Class: We Love You, Mrs. Russell," ABC, 1988.

CARVEY, DANA
b. Missoula, MT, June 6, 1955. Gifted mimic and comedian; he savages George Bush on "Saturday Night Live."

AS A REGULAR: "One of the Boys," NBC, 1982; "Blue Thunder," ABC, 1984; "Saturday Night Live," NBC, 1986- .

AND: "Late Night with David Letterman," NBC, 1989.

CASE, ALLEN
b. Dallas, TX, 1935; d. 1986. Actor in western roles, also known as song-and-dance man.

AS A REGULAR: "The Deputy," NBC, 1959-61; "The Legend of Jesse James," ABC, 1965-66.

AND: "The Tonight Show," NBC, 1958; "Have Gun, Will Travel: Juliet," CBS, 1959; "Have Gun, Will Travel: Alaska," CBS, 1959; "The Ford Show," NBC, 1959; "The Garry Moore Show," CBS, 1960; "The Garry Moore Show," CBS, 1961; "Here's Hollywood," NBC, 1961; "The Chevrolet Golden Anniversary Show," CBS, 1961; "The Virginian: West," NBC, 1962; "Bell Telephone Hour: Salute to Veterans Day," NBC, 1965; "Gunsmoke: The Good People," CBS, 1966; "The Bob Newhart Show: Ex-Con Job," CBS, 1977; "The Bob Newhart Show: Son of Ex-Con Job," CBS, 1978.

TV MOVIES AND MINISERIES: "The Magician," NBC, 1973; "Man From Atlantis," NBC, 1977.

CASE, NELSON

b. Long Beach, CA, February 3, 1910; d. 1976.
AS A REGULAR: "Armstrong Circle Theatre," NBC, 1950-51; "What's It Worth," DUM, 1952-53; "Summer Playhouse," NBC, 1954; "Sneak Preview," NBC, 1956.

CASEY, BERNIE

b. Wyco, WV, June 8, 1939. Former pro football star with the San Francisco 49ers and the L.A. Rams.
AS A REGULAR: "Harris and Company," NBC, 1979; "The Bay City Blues," NBC, 1983.
AND: "The Streets of San Francisco: Timelock," ABC, 1973; "The Snoop Sisters: Fear Is a Free Throw," NBC, 1974; "Police Story: Company Man," NBC, 1975; "Police Story: Six Foot Stretch," NBC, 1977; "Police Woman: Once a Snitch," NBC, 1977; "Alfred Hitchcock Presents: The Method Actor," NBC, 1985; "Hunter: Investment in Death," NBC, 1989.
TV MOVIES AND MINISERIES: "Brian's Song," ABC, 1971; "Gargoyles," CBS, 1972; "Panic on the 5:22," ABC, 1974; "Mary Jane Harper Cried Last Night," CBS, 1977; "Roots: The Next Generations," ABC, 1979; "The Sophisticated Gents," NBC, 1981; "Hear No Evil," CBS, 1982; "The Fantastic World of D.C. Collins," NBC, 1984; "Mother's Day," FAM, 1989.

CASH, JOHNNY

b. Kingsland, AR, February 26, 1932.
AS A REGULAR: "The Johnny Cash Show," ABC, 1969-71; CBS, 1976.
AND: "The Jackie Gleason Show," CBS, 1957; "The Jimmy Dean Show," CBS, 1957; "Country Music Jubilee," ABC, 1957; "American Bandstand," ABC, 1958; "The Dick Clark Saturday Night Beechnut Show," ABC, 1958; "Country Music Jubilee," ABC, 1958; "The Peter Lind Hayes Show," ABC, 1958; "Jubilee USA," ABC, 1959; "The George Gobel Show," NBC, 1959; "The Chevy Show," NBC, 1959; "The Jimmie Rodgers Show," NBC, 1959; "Bell Telephone Hour: The Golden West," NBC, 1959; "Jubilee USA," ABC, 1960; "The Ford Show," NBC, 1960; "The Deputy: The Deathly Quiet," NBC, 1961; "Hootenanny," ABC, 1964; "The Jimmy Dean Show," ABC, 1964; "Shindig," ABC, 1965; "The Steve Lawrence Show," CBS, 1965; "Kraft Music Hall," NBC, 1969; "The Glen Campbell Goodtime Hour," CBS, 1969; "NET Playhouse: The Trail of Tears," NET, 1970; "The Partridge Family: What? And Get Out of Show Business?," ABC, 1970; "Rowan & Martin's Laugh-In," NBC, 1972; "Columbo: Swan Song," NBC, 1974; "The Grand Ole Opry at 50," ABC, 1975; "Little House on the Prairie: The Collection," NBC, 1976; "Inaugural Eve Special," CBS, 1977; "Saturday Night Live," NBC, 1982;

"Johnny Cash: An Inside Look," TNN, 1989.
TV MOVIES AND MINISERIES: "The Pride of Jesse Hallam," CBS, 1981; "Murder in Coweta County," CBS, 1983; "North and South," ABC, 1985; "The Last Days of Frank and Jesse James," NBC, 1986; "Stagecoach," CBS, 1986.

CASH, ROSALIND

b. Atlantic City, NJ, December 31, 1938.
AS A REGULAR: "Knightwatch," ABC, 1988; "A Different World," NBC, 1989- .
AND: "The Mary Tyler Moore Show: A Girl Like Mary," CBS, 1974; "Harry O: Shadows at Noon," ABC, 1974; "Good Times: J.J. and the Older Woman," CBS, 1976; "Kojak: The Godson," CBS, 1977; "Police Woman: Shadow of Doubt," NBC, 1977; "Barney Miller: Dog Days," ABC, 1978; "Hardcastle and McCormick: The Homecoming," ABC, 1984; "Highway to Heaven: A Song of Songs," NBC, 1986; "The Golden Girls: Mixed Blessing," NBC, 1988; "thirtysomething: We'll Meet Again," ABC, 1988; "Family Ties: All in the Neighborhood," NBC, 1989; "thirtysomething: New Job," ABC, 1989; "227: Gone Fishing," NBC, 1989.
TV MOVIES AND MINISERIES: "A Killing Affair," CBS, 1977; "The Sophisticated Gents," NBC, 1981; "Special Bulletin," NBC, 1983.

CASON, BARBARA

b. Memphis, TN, November 15, 1933; d. 1990. Actress who played Ruth Shandling, Garry's mom on "It's Garry Shandling's Show."
AS A REGULAR: "Comedy Tonight," CBS, 1970; "Temperatures Rising," ABC, 1973-74; "Carter Country," ABC, 1977-79; "It's Garry Shandling's Show," FOX, 1988-90.
AND: "All in the Family: The Election Story," CBS, 1971; "The Courtship of Eddie's Father: Time for a Change," ABC, 1972; "All in the Family: Birth of the Baby," CBS, 1975; "Family: Thursday's Child Has Far to Go," ABC, 1976; "The Jeffersons: A Case of Black and White," CBS, 1977; "Lou Grant: Double-Cross," CBS, 1981; "Quincy: Next Stop Nowhere," NBC, 1982; "Remington Steele: Red Holt Steele," NBC, 1983; "Scarecrow and Mrs. King: Life of the Party," CBS, 1985; "Hollywood Beat: Pilot," ABC, 1985; "Murder, She Wrote: Benedict Arnold Slipped Here," CBS, 1988.
TV MOVIES AND MINISERIES: "It Couldn't Happen to a Nicer Guy," ABC, 1974; "She's Dressed to Kill," NBC, 1979; "A Matter of Life and Death," CBS, 1981; "Memories Never Die," CBS, 1982.

CASS, PEGGY

b. Boston, MA, May 21, 1924. Comedienne and game-show regular.
AS A REGULAR: "The Jack Paar Show," NBC,

1958-62; "Keep Talking," CBS, 1958-59; ABC, 1959-60; "The Hathaways," ABC, 1961-62; "To Tell the Truth," CBS, 1964-67; SYN, 1969-77; "Jack Paar Tonight," ABC, 1973; "The Doctors," NBC, 1978-79; "Women in Prison," FOX, 1987-88.

AND: "The Phil Silvers Show: Operation Love," CBS, 1958; "Alfred Hitchcock Presents: Six People, No Music," CBS, 1958; "The Phil Silvers Show: Bilko's Sharpshooter," CBS, 1959; "Arthur Murray Party," NBC, 1960; "25 Years of Life Magazine," NBC, 1961; "To Tell the Truth," CBS, 1961; "The Barbara Stanwyck Show: Call Me Annie," NBC, 1961; "To Tell the Truth," CBS, 1962; "Password," CBS, 1962; "The Jack Paar Program," NBC, 1962; "The Garry Moore Show," CBS, 1962; "The Match Game," NBC, 1963; "To Tell the Truth," CBS, 1963; "Password," CBS, 1964; "The Match Game," NBC, 1964; "Password," CBS, 1965; "The Merv Griffin Show," SYN, 1967; "The Tonight Show Starring Johnny Carson," NBC, 1968; "That's Life: Life in Suburbia," ABC, 1968; "The Merv Griffin Show," SYN, 1969; "You're Putting Me On," NBC, 1969; "The Comedians," SYN, 1971; "Love, American Style: Love and the Unbearable Fiancee," ABC, 1972; "The Love Boat: The Invisible Maniac," ABC, 1980; "Hotel: Charades," ABC, 1983; "Tales From the Darkside: Painkiller," SYN, 1984.

CASSAVETES, JOHN

b. *New York City, NY, December 9, 1929; d. 1989.* Intense actor-director whose only TV series was a "Peter Gunn" ripoff and whose best work was on the big screen.

AS A REGULAR: "Johnny Staccato," NBC, 1959-60.

AND: "Robert Montgomery Presents: Diary," NBC, 1954; "Armstrong Circle Theatre: Ladder of Lies," NBC, 1955; "Elgin TV Hour: Crime in the Street," ABC, 1955; "You Are There: The Death of Socrates," CBS, 1955; "Kraft Television Theatre: Judge Costain's Hotel," NBC, 1955; "Climax!: Savage Portrait," CBS, 1956; "Playhouse 90: Winter Dreams," CBS, 1957; "Person to Person," CBS, 1958; "Studio One: Kurishiki Incident," CBS, 1958; "Alcoa Theatre: The First Star," NBC, 1958; "Pursuit: Calculated Risk," CBS, 1958; "G.E. Theatre: Ticket for Tecumseh," CBS, 1959; "Lux Playhouse: The Dreamer," CBS, 1959; "Hedda Hopper's Hollywood," NBC, 1960; "Rawhide: Incident Near Gloomy River," CBS, 1961; "Dr. Kildare: The Visitors," NBC, 1962; "The Lloyd Bridges Show: El Medico," CBS, 1962; "Channing: Message From the Tin Room," ABC, 1963; "The Breaking Point: There Are the Hip and There Are the Square," ABC, 1963; "The Alfred Hitchcock Hour: Murder Case," CBS, 1964; "Burke's Law: Who Killed Annie Foran?," ABC, 1964; "Burke's

Law: Who Killed Don Pablo?," ABC, 1964; "Combat: S.I.W.," ABC, 1965; "The Legend of Jesse James: The Quest," ABC, 1965; "Voyage to the Bottom of the Sea: The Peacemaker," ABC, 1965; "The Virginian: Long Ride to Wind River," NBC, 1966; "The Long, Hot Summer: The Intruders," ABC, 1966; "Bob Hope Chrysler Theatre: Time of Change," NBC, 1966; "Bob Hope Chrysler Theatre: Free of Charge," NBC, 1967; "Alexander the Great," ABC, 1968; "The Merv Griffin Show," SYN, 1969; "New York Playhouse: Hollywood: You Must Remember This," PBS, 1972; "Columbo: Etude in Black," NBC, 1972; "Nightside," ABC, 1973.

TV MOVIES AND MINISERIES: "Flesh and Blood," CBS, 1979.

CASSIDY, DAVID

b. *New York City, NY, April 12, 1950.* Hey, girls! It's Keith "I Think I Love You" Partridge!

AS A REGULAR: "Harold Robbins' The Survivors," ABC, 1969; "The Partridge Family," ABC, 1970-74; "David Cassidy—Man Undercover," NBC, 1978-79.

AND: "Ironside: Stolen on Demand," NBC, 1969; "Marcus Welby, M.D.: Fun and Games," ABC, 1970; "The FBI: Fatal Impostor," ABC, 1970; "Bonanza: The Law and Billy Burgess," NBC, 1970; "Medical Center: His Brother's Keeper," CBS, 1970; "This Is Your Life (Shirley Jones)," SYN, 1971; "The Love Boat: Target Gopher," ABC, 1980.

TV MOVIES AND MINISERIES: "The Night the City Screamed," ABC, 1980.

CASSIDY, JACK

b. *Richmond Hill, Queens, NY, March 5, 1927; d. 1976.* Performer who excelled at playing dashing, conceited types; he shone as Oscar North, star of the "Jetman" TV show, on "He & She" and as murderers who matched wits with Lt. Columbo.

AS A REGULAR: "He & She," CBS, 1967-68.

AND: "Lux Video Theatre: Movie Songs," NBC, 1956; "Lux Video Theatre: Dark Victory," NBC, 1957; "U.S. Steel Hour: Shadow of Evil," CBS, 1957; "Lux Video Theatre: The Last Act," NBC, 1957; "The Garry Moore Show," CBS, 1959; "Bell Telephone Hour: Our Musical Ambassadors," NBC, 1960; "Wagon Train: The Nancy Palmer Story," NBC, 1961; "G.E. Theatre: Sis Bowls 'Em Over," CBS, 1961; "Alfred Hitchcock Presents: A Pearl Necklace," NBC, 1961; "Maverick: The Art Lovers," ABC, 1961; "Cheyenne: The Harrigan," ABC, 1961; "Hawaiian Eye: Concert in Hawaii," ABC, 1961; "77 Sunset Strip: The Bridal Trail Caper," ABC, 1962; "SurfSide 6: Who is Sylvia?," ABC, 1962; "Everglades: Black Honeymoon," SYN, 1962; "Cheyenne: One Evening in Abilene," ABC, 1962; "Hennesey: I Thee Wed," CBS, 1962; "Mr.

Magoo's Christmas Carol," NBC, 1962; "The Dick Powell Show: The Big Day," NBC, 1962; "Bell Telephone Hour," NBC, 1964; "Mr. Broadway: The He-She Chemistry," CBS, 1964; "Bell Telephone Hour," NBC, 1965; "The Alfred Hitchcock Hour: The Photographer and the Undertaker," NBC, 1965; "The Lucy Show: Lucy the Undercover Agent," CBS, 1965; "The Garry Moore Show: High Button Shoes," CBS, 1966; "Coronet Blue: A Charade for Murder," CBS, 1967; "Bewitched: Samantha Goes South for a Spell," ABC, 1968; "Get Smart: The Return of the Ancient Mariner," NBC, 1968; "That Girl: I Don't Have the Vegas Notion," ABC, 1969; "Personality," NBC, 1969; "Hollywood Squares," NBC, 1969; "Love, American Style: Love and the Many-Married Couple," ABC, 1970; "Bewitched: A Chance on Love," ABC, 1970; "Hollywood Television Theatre: The Andersonville Trial," NET, 1970; "George M!," NBC, 1970; "Night Gallery: The Last Laurel," NBC, 1971; "This Is Your Life (Shirley Jones)," SYN, 1971; "Love, American Style: Love and the Big Game," ABC, 1971; "Men at Law: Marathon," CBS, 1971; "The Mourner," NBC, 1971; "Columbo: Murder by the Book," NBC, 1971; "Sarge: John Michael O'Flaherty Presents the Eleven O'Clock War," NBC, 1971; "The Mary Tyler Moore Show: Cover Boy," CBS, 1971; "Orson Welles' Great Mysteries: For Sale-Silence," SYN, 1973; "Celebrity Sweepstakes," NBC, 1974; "Columbo: Publish or Perish," NBC, 1974; "The Merv Griffin Show," SYN, 1974; "Theatre in America: June Moon," PBS, 1974; "I've Gotta Be Me," NBC, 1974; "Hollywood Television Theatre: Knuckle," PBS, 1975; "Dean's Place," NBC, 1975; "Hawaii Five-O: How to Steal a Submarine," CBS, 1975; "Dean's Place," NBC, 1976; "Columbo: Now You See Him," NBC, 1976; "Rhyme and Reason," ABC, 1976; "McCloud: London Bridges," NBC, 1977.
TV MOVIES AND MINISERIES: "Your Money or Your Wife," CBS, 1972; "A Time for Love," NBC, 1973; "The Phantom of Hollywood," CBS, 1974; "Death Among Friends," NBC, 1975; "Benny and Barney: Las Vegas Undercover," NBC, 1977.
* Cassidy died when fire destroyed his apartment.

CASSIDY, JOANNA
b. Camden, NJ, August 2, 1944. Attractive actress who played Jo Jo, long-suffering lady friend of "Buffalo" Bill Bittinger (Dabney Coleman).
AS A REGULAR: "Shields and Yarnell," CBS, 1977; "The Roller Girls," NBC, 1978; "240-Robert," ABC, 1979-80; "The Family Tree," NBC, 1983; "Buffalo Bill," NBC, 1983-84; "Code Name: Foxfire," NBC, 1985.
AND: "Taxi: High School Reunion," ABC, 1978;

"The Love Boat: The Vacation," ABC, 1979; "Hart to Hart: Slow Boat to Murder," ABC, 1981; "Charlie's Angels: Hula Angels," ABC, 1981; "Lou Grant: Twenty-Two," CBS, 1982; "Second Stage," ABC, 1988.
TV MOVIES AND MINISERIES: "She's Dressed to Kill," NBC, 1979; "Reunion," CBS, 1980; "Invitation to Hell," ABC, 1984; "Hollywood Wives," ABC, 1985; "Code Name: Foxfire," NBC, 1986; "Pleasures," ABC, 1986; "The Children of Times Square," ABC, 1986; "Nightmare at Bitter Creek," CBS, 1988; "A Father's Revenge," ABC, 1988.

CASSIDY, PATRICK
b. Los Angeles, CA. Brother of David and Shaun.
AS A BROTHER: "The Bay City Blues," NBC, 1983; "Dirty Dancing," CBS, 1988.
AND: "The Love Boat: Vicki and the Fugitive," ABC, 1984.
TV MOVIES AND MINISERIES: "Angel Dusted," NBC, 1981; "Dress Gray," NBC, 1986; "Something in Common," CBS, 1986; "Christmas Eve," NBC, 1986; "Three on a Match," NBC, 1987.

CASSIDY, SHAUN
b. Los Angeles, CA, September 27, 1958. Hey, girls! It's Joe "Da Doo Ron Ron" Hardy!
AS A REGULAR: "The Hardy Boys Mysteries," ABC, 1977-79; "Breaking Away," ABC, 1980-81.
AND: "This Is Your Life (Shirley Jones)," SYN, 1971; "Murder, She Wrote: Murder in the Minor Key," CBS, 1987; "Matlock: The Investigation," NBC, 1988.
TV MOVIES AND MINISERIES: "Like Normal People," ABC, 1979; "Roots: The Gift," ABC, 1988.

CASSIDY, TED
b. Pittsburgh, PA, 1932; d. 1979. Tall, gaunt actor who played the Addams family butler, Lurch.
AS A REGULAR: "The Addams Family," BC, 1964-66; "The New Adventures of Huck Finn," NBC, 1968-69.
AND: "Batman: The Penguin's Nest/The Bird's Last Jest," ABC, 1966; "Star Trek: What Are Little Girls Made Of?," NBC, 1966; "The Man From UNCLE: The Napoleon's Tomb Affair," NBC, 1967; "The Beverly Hillbillies: The Dahlia Feud," CBS, 1967; "I Dream of Jeannie: Please Don't Feed the Astronauts," NBC, 1968; "The Bionic Woman: The Return of Bigfoot," ABC, 1976.
TV MOVIES AND MINISERIES: "Genesis II," ABC, 1973; "Planet Earth," ABC, 1974; "Benny and Barney: Las Vegas Undercover," NBC, 1977.

184

CASTELLANO, RICHARD S.

b. New York City, NY, September 4, 1934; d. 1988. Stocky bald actor who came to fame via the "Godfather" movies.

AS A REGULAR: "The Super," ABC, 1972; "Joe and Sons," CBS, 1975-76; "The Gangster Chronicles," NBC, 1981.

AND: "NYPD: Nothing Is Real But the Dead," ABC, 1968; "On Stage: The Choice," NBC, 1969; "Hollywood Squares," NBC, 1971.

TV MOVIES AND MINISERIES: "Incident on a Dark Street," CBS, 1973; "Honor Thy Father," CBS, 1973.

CASTLE, PEGGIE

b. Peggie Thomas Blair, Appalachia, VA, December 22, 1927; d. 1973.

AS A REGULAR: "Lawman," ABC, 1959-62.

AND: "Warner Bros. Presents Conflict: The Money," ABC, 1957; "Cheyenne: The Spanish Grant," ABC, 1957; "Perry Mason: The Case of the Negligent Nymph," CBS, 1957; "Dick Powell's Zane Grey Theatre: Quiet Sunday in San Ardo," CBS, 1957; "Restless Gun: Hornitas Town," NBC, 1958; "The Texan: The First Notch," CBS, 1958; "77 Sunset Strip: The Well-Selected Frame," ABC, 1958; "Restless Gun: Lady by Law," NBC, 1958; "The Virginian: Morgan Starr," NBC, 1966.

CAULFIELD, JOAN

b. Beatrice Joan Caulfield, Orange, NJ, June 1, 1922. Comic actress.

AS A REGULAR: "My Favorite Husband," CBS, 1953-55; "Sally," NBC, 1957-58.

AND: "Saturday's Children," CBS, 1950; "Schlitz Playhouse of Stars: Girl in a Million," CBS, 1951; "Robert Montgomery Presents: The Longest Night," NBC, 1952; "Hollywood Opening Night: Apples on the Lilac Tree," NBC, 1952; "Ford Theatre: Girl in the Park," NBC, 1952; "Schlitz Playhouse of Stars: A String of Beads," CBS, 1952; "Schlitz Playhouse of Stars: The Bankmouse," CBS, 1956; "Lux Video Theatre: Only Yesterday," NBC, 1957; "Ford Theatre: House of Glass," ABC, 1957; "Art Linkletter's House Party," CBS, 1958; "Pursuit: Eagle in the Cage," CBS, 1958; "G.E. Theatre: The Lady's Choice," CBS, 1959; "Bob Hope Special," NBC, 1960; "Hong Kong: Love, Honor and Perish," ABC, 1961; "Cheyenne: Showdown at Oxbend," ABC, 1962; "Burke's Law: Who Killed the Kind Doctor?," ABC, 1963; "Burke's Law: Who Killed the Toy Soldier?," ABC, 1965; "Burke's Law: Who Killed the 13th Clown?," ABC, 1965; "My Three Sons: Forget Me Not," CBS, 1966; "Murder, She Wrote: Trouble in Eden," CBS, 1987.

TV MOVIES AND MINISERIES: "The Magician," NBC, 1973.

CAVETT, DICK

b. Gibbon, NB, November 19, 1936.

AS A REGULAR: "This Morning," ABC, 1968; "The Dick Cavett Show," ABC, 1968-72; CBS, 1975; PBS, 1977-82; USA, 1985-86; ABC, 1986; "The Edge of Night," ABC, 1983.

AND: "The Phil Silvers Show: Boxer," CBS, 1956; "The Tonight Show Starring Johnny Carson," NBC, 1966; "The Mike Douglas Show," SYN, 1967; "Kraft Music Hall," NBC, 1967; "Operation: Entertainment," ABC, 1968; "Kraft Music Hall: Roast for Johnny Carson," NBC, 1968; "The Tonight Show Starring Johnny Carson," NBC, 1969; "This Is Tom Jones," ABC, 1969; "Alias Smith and Jones: Twenty-One Days to Tenstrike," ABC, 1972; "Rowan & Martin's Laugh-In," NBC, 1972; "The Odd Couple: Two Men on a Hoarse," ABC, 1975; "Saturday Night Live," NBC, 1976; "Cheers: They Called Me Mayday," NBC, 1983; "Hotel: Outsiders," ABC, 1984; "Amazing Stories: Mirror, Mirror," NBC, 1986; "Kate & Allie: High Anxiety," CBS, 1986.

CAZENOVE, CHRISTOPHER

b. England, December 17, 1945.

AS A REGULAR: "Dynasty," ABC, 1986-87; "A Fine Romance," ABC, 1989.

AND: "Lou Grant: Execution," CBS, 1981.

TV MOVIES AND MINISERIES: "From a Far Country: Pope John Paul II," NBC, 1981; "The Letter," ABC, 1982; "Lace II," ABC, 1985; "Windmills of the Gods," CBS, 1988.

TRIVIA QUIZ #6: NAME THAT CAR

Match the TV detective with the make of car he or she drove:

1. Continental	a. Jim Rockford
2. Oldsmobile	b. Thomas Magnum
3. Firebird	c. Jonathan Hart
4. Camaro	d. Joe Mannix
5. VW Rabbit	e. Frank Cannon
6. Mercury	f. Dave Starsky
7. Ferrari	g. Steve McGarrett
8. Torino	h. Frank Furillo
9. Mercedes	i. Kelly Garrett
10. Mustang	j. Laura Holt

(Answers at end of book.)

CERF, BENNETT

b. New York City, NY, 1898; d. 1971. Panelist and publishing executive.

AS A REGULAR: "Whats My Line?," CBS, 1951-67.

AND: "Tex and Jinx," NBC, 1957; "Mike Wallace Interviews," ABC, 1957; "The Arlene Francis Show," NBC, 1957; "Person to Person," CBS, 1958; "The Last Word," CBS, 1958; "I've Got a Secret," CBS, 1961; "Password," CBS, 1961;

"The Match Game," NBC, 1964; "Get the Message," ABC, 1964; "The Match Game," NBC, 1966.

CERUSICO, ENZO
b. Rome, 1943.
AS A REGULAR: "My Friend Tony," NBC, 1969.
TV MOVIES AND MINISERIES: "Magic Carpet," NBC, 1972.

CESANA, RENZO
b. Rome, 1907; d. 1970. Actor who cooed sweet nothings to the TV screen as the Continental.
AS A REGULAR: "The Continental," CBS, 1952; ABC, 1952-53.
AND: "Peter Loves Mary: Mr. Satini Writes a Letter," NBC, 1961; "The Gallant Men: Robertino," ABC, 1962; "Voyage to the Bottom of the Sea: Escape From Venice," ABC, 1965; "Bewitched: Business, Italian Style," ABC, 1967.

CHAKIRIS, GEORGE
b. Norwood, OH, September 16, 1933.
AS A REGULAR: "Dallas," CBS, 1985-86.
AND: "Ford Star Jubilee: You're the Top," CBS, 1956; "The Garry Moore Show," CBS, 1961; "Highways of Melody," NBC, 1961; "Dinah Shore Special," NBC, 1962; "Shindig," ABC, 1965; "Shindig," ABC, 1966; "Kismet," ABC, 1967; "Medical Center: Trial by Terror," CBS, 1970; "Hawaii Five-O: Death is a Company Policy," CBS, 1972; "A Salute to Television's 25th Anniversary," ABC, 1972; "Medical Center: Tio Taco, M.D.," CBS, 1972; "Police Surgeon: Dangerous Windfall," SYN, 1973; "The Partridge Family: S.O.S.," ABC, 1973; "Medical Center: The Last Performance," CBS, 1975; "Masterpiece Theatre: Notorious Woman," PBS, 1975; "Scarecrow and Mrs. King: Lost and Found," CBS, 1984; "Murder, She Wrote: Weave a Tangled Web," CBS, 1989.
TV MOVIES AND MINISERIES: "Kiss Me and Die," ABC, 1974.

CHAMBERLAIN, RICHARD
b. George Richard Chamberlain, Los Angeles, CA, March 31, 1935. Good-looking, seemingly ageless actor who was Dr. James Kildare in the sixties and TV's miniseries king in the eighties.
AS A REGULAR: "Dr. Kildare," NBC, 1961-66; "Island Son," CBS, 1989-90.
AND: "Alfred Hitchcock Presents: Road Hog," CBS, 1959; "Bourbon Street Beat: Target of Hate," ABC, 1960; "Mr. Lucky: Anniversary Party," CBS, 1960; "Thriller: The Watcher," NBC, 1960; "The Deputy: The Edge of Doubt," NBC, 1961; "Whispering Smith: Stain of Justice," NBC, 1961; "Here's Hollywood," NBC,

1961; "Play Your Hunch," NBC, 1962; "The Eleventh Hour: Four Feet in the Morning," NBC, 1963; "You Don't Say," NBC, 1964; "The Tonight Show Starring Johnny Carson," NBC, 1964; "Hallmark Hall of Fame: Hamlet," NBC, 1970; "The Little Mermaid," CBS, 1974; "Hollywood Television Theatre: The Lady's Not for Burning," PBS, 1974; "The Merv Griffin Show," SYN, 1974.
TV MOVIES AND MINISERIES: "F. Scott Fitzgerald and The Last of the Belles," ABC, 1973; "The Woman I Love," ABC, 1974; "The Count of Monte Cristo," NBC, 1975; "The Man in the Iron Mask," NBC, 1977; "Centennial," NBC, 1978-79; "Shogun," NBC, 1980; "The Thorn Birds," ABC, 1983; "Cook & Peary: The Race to the Pole," CBS, 1983; "Wallenberg: A Hero's Story," NBC, 1985; "Casanova," ABC, 1987; "The Bourne Identity," ABC, 1988.
* Chamberlain's recording of the theme song from "Dr. Kildare" was a hit in July 1962.

CHAMPION, GOWER
b. Geneva, IL, June 21, 1921; d. 1980;
& MARGE
b. Marjorie Celeste Belcher, Los Angeles, CA, September 2, 1921. Dancers-choreographers.
AS REGULARS: "The Admiral Broadway Revue," NBC, 1949; "The Marge and Gower Champion Show," CBS, 1957.
AND: "Lux Video Theatre: Bouquet for Millie," CBS, 1953; "Three for Tonight," CBS, 1955; "G.E. Theatre: The Rider on the Pale Horse," CBS, 1956; "The Standard Oil 75th Anniversary Show," NBC, 1957; "G.E. Theatre: Mischief at Bandy Leg," CBS, 1957; "Dinah Shore Chevy Show," NBC, 1957; "Dinah Shore Chevy Show," NBC, 1958; "The Perry Como Show," NBC, 1958; "The Eddie Fisher Show," NBC, 1958; "The Garry Moore Show," CBS, 1958; "Art Linkletter's House Party," CBS, 1958; "Dinah Shore Chevy Show," NBC, 1959.
GOWER SOLO:
AS CHOREOGRAPHER: "Pontiac Star Parade: Accent on Love," NBC, 1959.
MARGE SOLO:
AS A GUEST: "Candid Camera," CBS, 1963; "NET Playhouse: New Theatre for Now," NET, 1969.
AS CHOREOGRAPHER: "Queen of the Stardust Ballroom," CBS, 1975.
* The Champions married in 1947 and divorced in 1973.
* Gower choreographed the Broadway shows "Bye, Bye Birdie," "Hello, Dolly!," "I Do! I Do!," "Sugar," and "Mack and Mabel." He died on the day his last production, "42nd Street," opened; his death wasn't announced until the final curtain.
* Emmies: 1975, to Marge for choreographing "Queen of the Stardust Ballroom."

186

CHANCELLOR, JOHN

b. Chicago, IL, July 14, 1927.

AS A REGULAR: "NBC Evening News," NBC, 1970-82; "NBC Nightly News with Tom Brokaw," NBC, 1982- .

CHANDLER, CHICK

b. Kingston, NY, January 18, 1905; d. 1988. Character actor who usually played homespun types.

AS A REGULAR: "Soliders of Fortune," SYN, 1955-56; "One Happy Family," NBC, 1961.

AND: "I Love Lucy: Ethel's Home Town," CBS, 1955; "Screen Directors Playhouse: It's Always Sunday," CBS, 1956; "Crossroads: The Patton Prayer," ABC, 1957; "The Brothers: Gilly and the Movie Star," CBS, 1957; "December Bride: Piano Show," CBS, 1957; "Schlitz Playhouse of Stars: The Blue Hotel," CBS, 1957; "The Danny Thomas Show: The Country Girl," CBS, 1958; "Richard Diamond, Private Detective: The Purple Penguin," CBS, 1958; "The Thin Man: Bat McKidderick, Esq.," NBC, 1959; "Johnny Staccato: The Naked Truth," NBC, 1959; "The Ann Sothern Show: Go-Go Gordon," CBS, 1960; "The Real McCoys: Father and Son Day," ABC, 1960; "Lassie: Long Chase," CBS, 1961; "Frontier Circus: The Balloon Girl," CBS, 1962; "The Joey Bishop Show: Route 78," NBC, 1962; "This Is the Life: Skid Row Rescue," SYN, 1962; "Mr. Ed: Horse Talk," CBS, 1963; "Mr. Ed: Ed the Desert Rat," CBS, 1964; "The Littlest Hobo: Sniff Me a Murder," SYN, 1964; "Walt Disney's Wonderful World of Color: Kilroy," NBC, 1965; "Gomer Pyle, USMC: Gomer and the Phone Company," CBS, 1966; "Love on a Rooftop: One Too Many Cooks," ABC, 1967; "Bonanza: My Friend, My Enemy," NBC, 1969; "Mannix: To Cage a Seagull," CBS, 1970.

CHANDLER, GEORGE

b. Waukegan, IL, June 30, 1899. Actor who played Uncle Petrie Martin on "Lassie."

AS A REGULAR: "The Abbott and Costello Show," CBS, 1952-54; "Lassie," CBS, 1958-59; "Ichabod and Me," CBS, 1961-62.

AND: "Robert Montgomery Presents: Ichabod," NBC, 1956; "Wire Service: Until I Die," ABC, 1956; "Fury: Joey and the Stranger," NBC, 1956; "Robert Montgomery Presents: One Smart Apple," NBC, 1957; "Schlitz Playhouse of Stars: The Three Dollar Bill," CBS, 1957; "Wagon Train: The Cassie Tanner Story," NBC, 1958; "G.E. Theatre: Adams' Apples," CBS, 1960; "Phil Silvers Special: The Slowest Gun in the West," CBS, 1960; "Buick Electra Playhouse: The Gambler, the Nun and the Radio," CBS, 1960; "The Twilight Zone: The Whole Truth," CBS, 1961; "Bringing Up Buddy: Cynthia's Boy Friend," CBS, 1961; "The Donna Reed Show:

Post Time, 1963; "Petticoat Junction: Birdman of Shady Rest," CBS, 1966; "Run, Buddy, Run: Down on the Farm," CBS, 1966; "Batman: Black Widow Strikes Again/Caught in the Spider's Den," ABC, 1967; "Mannix: Killjoy," CBS, 1969; "Love, American Style: Love and the Monsters," ABC, 1971; "Gunsmoke: Waste," CBS, 1971; "Here's Lucy: Meanwhile, Back at the Office," CBS, 1974; "Switch: Coronado Circle," CBS, 1977; "Lou Grant: Hollywood," CBS, 1979.

TV MOVIES AND MINISERIES: "Griffin and Phoenix," ABC, 1976.

CHANDLER, JEFF

b. Ira Grossel, Brooklyn, NY, December 15, 1918; d. 1961. Fifties screen actor.

AS A GUEST: "The Steve Allen Show," NBC, 1957; "The Perry Como Show," NBC, 1957; "The American Jew: A Tribute to Freedom," CBS, 1958; "Here's Hollywood," NBC, 1960; "Art Linkletter's House Party," CBS, 1960; "National Velvet: Epidemic," NBC, 1961.

CHANDLER, ROBIN

b. 1921.

AS A REGULAR: "Who's Whose," CBS, 1951; "Quick on the Draw," DUM, 1952; "Revlon Mirror Theatre," NBC, CBS, 1953; "Take a Guess," CBS, 1953.

CHANEY, LON JR.

b. Creighton Chaney, Oklahoma City, OK, February 10, 1906; d. 1973. Hulking character actor.

AS A REGULAR: "Hawkeye and the Last of the Mohicans," SYN, 1957; "Pistols 'n' Petticoats," CBS, 1966-67.

AND: "Tales of Tomorrow: Frankenstein," ABC, 1952; "Schlitz Playhouse of Stars: The Trial," CBS, 1952; "Cavalcade Theatre: Moonlight School," ABC, 1954; "Cavalcade Theatre: Stay On, Stranger," ABC, 1955; "Telephone Time: The Golden Junkman," CBS, 1956; "Studio 57: The Ballad of Jubal Puckett," SYN, 1956; "Climax!: The Necessary Evil," CBS, 1957; "Tombstone Territory: The Black Marshal From Deadwood," ABC, 1957; "The Red Skelton Show," CBS, 1958; "Rough Riders: An Eye for an Eye," ABC, 1959; "The Red Skelton Show: Appleby and the Ice Man," CBS, 1959; "Have Gun, Will Travel: The Scorched Feather," CBS, 1959; "G.E. Theatre: The Family Man," CBS, 1959; "Adventures in Paradise: The Black Pearl," ABC, 1959; "Johnny Ringo: The Raffertys," CBS, 1960; "Bat Masterson: Bat Trap," NBC, 1960; "Wagon Train: The Jose Morales Story," NBC, 1960; "Stagecoach West: Not in Our Stars," ABC, 1961; "Klondike: The Hostages," NBC, 1961; "Dick Powell's Zane Grey Theatre: A Warm Day in Heaven," CBS, 1961; "The Deputy: Brother in

Arms," NBC, 1961; "Wagon Train: The Chalice," NBC, 1961; "SurfSide 6: Witness for the Defense," ABC, 1961; "Route 66: The Mud Nest," CBS, 1961; "The Rifleman: Gunfire," ABC, 1962; "Lawman: The Tarnished Badge," ABC, 1962; "Route 66: Lizard's Leg and Owlet's Wing," CBS, 1962; "Rawhide: Incident at Spider Rock," CBS, 1963; "Have Gun, Will Travel: Cage at McNaab," CBS, 1963; "Empire: Hidden Asset," NBC, 1963; "Route 66: Come Out, Come Out," CBS, 1963; "The Monkees: Monkees in a Ghost Town," NBC, 1966; "What's New: The Children's West," NET, 1971.

CHANNING, CAROL

b. Seattle, WA, January 31, 1921. Pop-eyed musical-comedy legend.

AS A GUEST: "Omnibus: This Little Kitty Stayed Cool," CBS, 1953; "Svengali and the Blonde," NBC, 1955; "The Ford Show," NBC, 1956; "The Perry Como Show," NBC, 1956; "The Red Skelton Show," CBS, 1957; "Playhouse 90: Three Men on a Horse," CBS, 1957; "The Spike Jones Show," CBS, 1957; "The Rosemary Clooney Show," SYN, 1957; "The Ed Sullivan Show," CBS, 1957; "Du Pont Show of the Month: Crescendo," CBS, 1957; "Shower of Stars," CBS, 1957; "The Lux Show with Rosemary Clooney," NBC, 1957; "Arthur Murray Party," NBC, 1958; "The George Burns Show," NBC, 1959; "Arthur Murray Party," NBC, 1959; "The Jack Paar Show," NBC, 1959; "The Sam Levenson Show," CBS, 1959; "The Ed Sullivan Show," CBS, 1959; "A Toast to Jerome Kern," NBC, 1959; "The Ed Sullivan Show," CBS, 1961; "Dinah Shore Chevy Show," NBC, 1961; "The Garry Moore Show," CBS, 1962; "The Merv Griffin Show," NBC, 1962; "I've Got a Secret," CBS, 1963; "The Andy Williams Show," NBC, 1963; "Password," CBS, 1963; "Password," CBS, 1964; "The Price Is Right," ABC, 1964; "What's My Line?," CBS, 1964; "Carol Channing Special," CBS, 1968; "The Carol Burnett Show," CBS, 1968; "Carol Channing Special," ABC, 1969; "Festival at Ford's," NBC, 1971; "The Carol Burnett Show," CBS, 1971; "The Love Boat: The Love Boat Musical," ABC, 1982; "The Love Boat: My Friend, The Executrix," ABC, 1982; "The Love Boat: Authoress, Authoress," ABC, 1984; "Animal Crack-Ups," ABC, 1989.

CHANNING, STOCKARD

b. Susan Stockard, New York City, 1944. Actress who network executives were hot on in the late seventies; now she appears in above-average TV movies and miniseries.

AS A REGULAR: "Stockard Channing in Just Friends," CBS, 1979; "The Stockard Channing Show," CBS, 1980.

AND: "Medical Center: The Spectre," CBS, 1974; "Trying Times: The Sad Professor," PBS, 1989.

TV MOVIES AND MINISERIES: "The Girl Most Likely To...," ABC, 1973; "Silent Victory: The Kitty O'Neil Story," CBS, 1979; "Not My Kid," CBS, 1985; "The Room Upstairs," CBS, 1987; "Echoes in the Darkness," CBS, 1987; "Perfect Witness," HBO, 1989.

CHAO, ROSALIND

b. Los Angeles, CA. Actress who played Soon-Lee Klinger on "M*A*S*H."

AS A REGULAR: "Diff'rent Strokes," NBC, 1982-83; "M*A*S*H," CBS, 1983; "AfterMASH," CBS, 1983-84; "Against the Law," FOX, 1990- .

AND: "ABC Afterschool Special: P.J. and the President's Son," ABC, 1976; "Lobo: The Roller Disco Karate Kaper," NBC, 1981; "St. Elsewhere: Not My Type," NBC, 1986; "Private Eye: Chinatown," NBC, 1987; "Miami Vice: Heart of Night," NBC, 1988; "Jake and the Fatman: The Way You Look Tonight," CBS, 1989; "Island Son: Icarus Falling," CBS, 1989.

TV MOVIES AND MINISERIES: "The Ultimate Imposter," CBS, 1979.

CHAPIN, LAUREN

b. Los Angeles, CA, May 23, 1945. Actress who played Kathy Anderson, aka Kitten, on "Father Knows Best"; she recovered from an adolescence of drug addiction and is now involved in religious causes.

AS A REGULAR: "Father Knows Best," CBS, 1954-55; NBC, 1955-58; CBS, 1958-60.

AND: "Fireside Theatre: The 99th Day," NBC, 1955; "The Steve Allen Show," NBC, 1956; "G.E. Theatre: The Man Who Thought for Himself," CBS, 1960; "The Mike Douglas Show," SYN, 1981.

CHAPLIN, SYDNEY

b. Los Angeles, CA, March 31, 1926. The son of Charlie Chaplin and Lita Grey; a stage actor who's done a little TV.

AS A GUEST: "The 20th Century-Fox Hour: Carnival," CBS, 1956; "Wonderful Town," CBS, 1958; "Pontiac Star Parade Presents Phil Silvers," CBS, 1959; "The Match Game," NBC, 1964; "Password," CBS, 1964; "The Match Game," NBC, 1965; "Police Woman: Pawns of Power," NBC, 1975; "Switch: Before the Holocaust," CBS, 1976.

TV MOVIES AND MINISERIES: "The Woman Hunter," CBS, 1972; "Medical Story," NBC, 1975.

CHAPMAN, GRAHAM

b. England, 1940; d. 1989. Member of the Monty Python troupe.

AS A REGULAR: "The Big Show," NBC, 1980.

TV MOVIES AND MINISERIES: "Still Crazy Like a Fox," CBS, 1987.

CHAPMAN, LONNY

b. Tulsa, OK, October 1, 1920.
AS A REGULAR: "The Investigator," NBC, 1958; "For the People," CBS, 1965.
AND: "Studio One: The Open Door," CBS, 1956; "Kraft Television Theatre: The Sound of Trouble," NBC, 1957; "Suspicion: End in Violence," NBC, 1958; "Decoy: Cry Revenge," SYN, 1958; "Salute to the American Theatre," CBS, 1959; "The Secret of Freedom," NBC, 1960; "The Americans: The Gun," NBC, 1961; "The Defenders: The Accident," CBS, 1961; "The Outlaws: The Brathwaite Brothers," NBC, 1961; "The Nurses: Dr. Lillian," CBS, 1962; "The Rifleman: And the Devil Makes Five," ABC, 1963; "The Wide Country: To Cindy with Love," NBC, 1963; "The Defenders: Eyewitness," CBS, 1965; "The Virginian: Chaff in the Wind," NBC, 1966; "The Virginian: Without Mercy," NBC, 1967; "The Guns of Will Sonnett: Message at Noon," ABC, 1967; "Mission: Impossible: Shape-Up," CBS, 1971; "Mannix: A Walk in the Shadows," CBS, 1972; "Marcus Welby, M.D.: Cross-Match," ABC, 1972; "The Rookies: Easy Money," ABC, 1973; "Medical Center: Time of Darkness," CBS, 1973; "Doc Elliot: The Carrier," ABC, 1974; "Owen Marshall, Counselor at Law: To Keep and Bear Arms," ABC, 1974; "Kodiak: Death Chase," ABC, 1974; "Lucas Tanner: Winners and Losers," NBC, 1974; "McCloud: The Concrete Jungle Caper," NBC, 1974; "The Streets of San Francisco: Merchants of Death," ABC, 1975; "Medical Center: Two Against Death," CBS, 1975; "The Rookies: Cliffy," ABC, 1975; "McCloud: Fire!," NBC, 1975; "The Blue Knight: Copycats," CBS, 1976; "Simon & Simon: Thin Air," CBS, 1982; "Quincy: Across the Line," NBC, 1982; "Murder, She Wrote: Dead Heat," CBS, 1986; "Murder, She Wrote: Indian Giver," CBS, 1987; "Jake and the Fatman: Key Witness," CBS, 1989.
TV MOVIES AND MINISERIES: "The Dangerous Days of Kiowa Jones," ABC, 1966; "Marriage: Year One," NBC, 1971; "The Screaming Woman," ABC, 1972; "Visions...," CBS, 1972; "Hunter," CBS, 1973; "Big Rose," CBS, 1974; "Terror Out of the Sky," CBS, 1978; "Black Beauty," NBC, 1978; "King," NBC, 1978; "Blind Ambition," CBS, 1979; "Hanging By a Thread," NBC, 1979; "This Man Stands Alone," NBC, 1979; "Who Will Love My Children?," ABC, 1983.

CHARISSE, CYD

b. Tula Ellice Finklea, Amarillo, TX, March 8, 1921. Dancer in fifties movie musicals whose TV work has been of the "Oh, look how well she's aged" variety.

AS A GUEST: "Wide, Wide World," NBC, 1957; "Startime: Meet Cyd Charisse," NBC, 1959; "Checkmate: Dance of Death," CBS, 1961; "Dinah Shore Special," NBC, 1962; "Hollywood Palace," ABC, 1965; "Hollywood Squares," NBC, 1967; "Medical Center: No Way Home," CBS, 1975; "The Love Boat: I'll See You Again," ABC, 1979; "Fantasy Island: The Big Show," ABC, 1983; "Glitter: In Tennis Love Means Nothing," ABC, 1984; "Murder, She Wrote: Widow, Weep for Me," CBS, 1985.
TV MOVIES AND MINISERIES: "Call Her Mom," ABC, 1972; "Portrait of an Escort," CBS, 1980; "Swimsuit," NBC, 1989.

CHARLES, RAY

b. Ray Charles Robinson, Albany, GA, September 23, 1930. Gifted bluesman-pianist.
AS A GUEST: "Perry Como's Kraft Music Hall," NBC, 1961; "Dinah Shore Special," NBC, 1963; "Kraft Music Hall," NBC, 1967; "The Jerry Lewis Show," NBC, 1968; "This Is Tom Jones," ABC, 1970; "The Englebert Humperdinck Show," ABC, 1970; "The Carol Burnett Show," CBS, 1972; "Cotton Club '75," NBC, 1974; "The Mac Davis Show," NBC, 1975; "Saturday Night Live," NBC, 1977; "St. Elsewhere: Jose, Can You See?," NBC, 1987; "Moonlighting: A Trip to the Moon," ABC, 1987; "Who's the Boss?: Hit the Road, Chad," ABC, 1987; "Willie Nelson: Texas Style," CBS, 1988; "Irving Berlin's 100th Birthday Celebration," CBS, 1988; "Sesame Street 20... And Still Counting," NBC, 1989.

CHARLES, RAY

b. Chicago, September 13, 1918. Chorus and orchestra director.
AS A REGULAR: "The Perry Como Show," NBC, 1955-60; "Perry Como's Kraft Music Hall," NBC, 1960-61; "Pontiac Star Parade: An Evening with Perry Como," NBC, 1959; "The Funny Side," NBC, 1971; "The John Byner Comedy Hour," CBS, 1972.
* Emmies: 1971, 1972.

CHARLESON, IAN

d. 1990.
TV MOVIES AND MINISERIES: "The Sun Also Rises," NBC, 1984; "Master of the Game," CBS, 1984.

CHARLIE'S ANGELS, ABC, 1976-81.
"Charlie's Angels"—three sexy woman detectives—always seemed to get cases where they'd have to pose as prostitutes, or cheerleaders, or ice skaters, or aerobics instructors, or hula girls, or stewardesses, or bikini models. They were sent on these cases by the unseen Charlie Townsend

---

(John Forsythe), who would call them every week (how personal).

Created by Aaron Spelling, a TV magnate who has quit feeling ashamed of himself a long time ago, "Charlie's Angels" was agressively mindless TV fodder. Every so often there'd be a spicy scene, like the time the Angels went undercover in a women's prison and had to have their bodies fumigated while the fumigator, a gay warden, drooled over their forms.

Sabrina Duncan (Kate Jackson) was the "smart" one, which meant she could read without moving her lips. Jill (Farrah Fawcett) was the athletic, spunky one; when she left after one season after becoming a low-grade sex goddess, her just-as-athletic, equally-spunky sister Kris (Cheryl Ladd) took over. Kelly Garrett (Jaclyn Smith) was the one who'd "been around," whatever that meant. Jackson left the show in 1979 and was replaced by Tiffany Welles (Shelley Hack). Hack has the distinction of being the only Angel to be dumped by the producers, rather than vice-versa; she was replaced by Tanya Roberts, as Julie Rogers. But by then it was 1980, and people had been watching this junk for four years; by 1981 it was gone.

TRIVIA QUIZ #7:
"CHARLIE'S ANGELS"

1. David Doyle played Charlie's assistant, Bosley. What was Bosley's first name?
2. What movie did Farrah Fawcett make when she left the show?
3. Who's Farrah Fawcett's ex-husband?
4. True or false: All the Angels slept with Bosley.
5. The show's creator, Aaron Spelling, decided to try an all-male version of "Charlie's Angels," which ran as an episode called "Toni's Boys." Which well-known screen actress played Toni?
6. Kate Jackson had played nurse Kate Danko in a series before "Charlie's Angels." Name it.
7. Jaclyn Smith appeared in another ABC detective show in the 1989-90 season. Name it.
8. Farrah Fawcett's reputation as a serious actress grew when she appeared in this 1984 TV-movie about a battered wife. Name it.
9. Each episode of "Charlie's Angels" began with which phrase?
10. What perfume did Shelley Hack sell on TV before joining the show?

(Answers at end of book.)

CHARO
b. Spain, January 15, 1951. Blonde sort-of-singer, kind-of-actress. She and Florence Henderson appeared most often as "Love Boat" guests.
AS A REGULAR: "Chico and the Man," NBC, 1977-78.
AND: "The Danny Kaye Show," CBS, 1965; "The Mike Douglas Show," SYN, 1971; "The Wacky World of Jonathan Winters," SYN, 1973; "Hollywood Squares," NBC, 1973; "Hollywood Squares," NBC, 1974; "The Merv Griffin Show," SYN, 1974; "Hollywood Squares," NBC, 1975; "Joys," NBC, 1976; "Charo," ABC, 1976; "Bob Hope Special," NBC, 1977; "The Peter Marshall Variety Show," SYN, 1977; "The Love Boat: The Acapulco Connection," ABC, 1977; "The Love Boat: April's Return," ABC, 1979; "The Love Boat: April's Love," ABC, 1979; "The John Davidson Show," SYN, 1981; "The Love Boat: April the Nanny," ABC, 1981; "Sha Na Na," SYN, 1982; "The John Davidson Show," SYN, 1982; "The Love Boat: April in Boston," ABC, 1982; "The Love Boat: I Like to Be in America," ABC, 1983; "The Jeffersons: You'll Never Get Rich," CBS, 1983; "The Love Boat: Aerobic April," ABC, 1984; "The Love Boat: Forties Fantasy," ABC, 1985.

CHARTOFF, MELANIE
b. New Haven, CT. Actress usually in comic roles; she plays Parker Lewis' principal, Ms. Musso.
AS A REGULAR: "Fridays," ABC, 1980-82; "Take Five," CBS, 1987; "Parker Lewis Can't Lose," FOX, 1990- .
AND: "St. Elsewhere: Fathers and Sons," NBC, 1985; "The Love Boat: Hippies and Yuppies," ABC, 1986; "Newhart: Til Depth Do Us Part," CBS, 1987; "Wiseguy: Phantom Pain," CBS, 1988.
TV MOVIES AND MINISERIES: "Having It All," ABC, 1982; "The Gambler III: The Legend Continues," CBS, 1987.

CHASE, BARRIE
b. Kings Point, NY, 1935. Dancer who was Fred Astaire's TV partner.
AS A GUEST: "The Lucille Ball-Desi Arnaz Show: Lucy Takes a Cruise to Havana," CBS, 1957; "An Evening with Fred Astaire," NBC, 1958; "Have Gun, Will Travel: A Sense of Justice," CBS, 1959; "Another Evening with Fred Astaire," NBC, 1958; "Person to Person," CBS, 1960; "Astaire Time," NBC, 1960; "Seasons of Youth," ABC, 1961; "Perry Como's Kraft Music Hall," NBC, 1962; "Burke's Law: Who Killed Mr. X?," ABC, 1963; "Hollywood Palace," ABC, 1964; "Bob Hope Chrysler Theatre: Think Pretty," NBC,

1964; "Bonanza: The Ballerina," NBC, 1965; "Mr. Roberts: Unwelcome Aboard," NBC, 1966; "Mr. Terrific: Fly, Ballerina, Fly," CBS, 1967; "The Mike Douglas Show," SYN, 1967; "Fred Astaire Special," NBC, 1968; "Operation: Entertainment," ABC, 1968; "The Steve Allen Show," SYN, 1968.

CHASE, CHEVY
b. Cornelius Crane Chase, New York City, NY, October 8, 1943.
AS A REGULAR: "Saturday Night Live," NBC, 1975-76.
AND: "Inaugural Eve Special," CBS, 1977; "Saturday Night Live," NBC, 1978; "Saturday Night Live," NBC, 1980; "Saturday Night Live," NBC, 1982; "Saturday Night Live," NBC, 1985; "Saturday Night Live," NBC, 1986; "It's Garry Shandling's Show: Save Mr. Peck's," FOX, 1989; "Saturday Night Live's 15th Anniversary," NBC, 1989.
* Emmies: 1976.

CHASE, ILKA
b. New York City, NY, April 8, 1903; d. 1978. Actress, author and, on talk and panel shows, a symbol of New York chic.
AS A REGULAR: "Celebrity Time," CBS, 1949-50; "Glamour-Go-Round," CBS, 1950; "Masquerade Party," NBC, 1952; CBS, 1953-54; ABC, 1954-56; NBC, 1957; "Keep Talking," CBS, 1958-59; "Trials of O'Brien," CBS, 1965-66.
AND: "Silver Theatre: Concerning the Soul of Felicity," CBS, 1950; "Pulitzer Prize Playhouse: Robert E. Lee," ABC, 1952; "Cinderella," CBS, 1957; "Kraft Theatre: The Spell of the Tigress," NBC, 1958; "The Last Word," CBS, 1958; "The Jack Paar Show," NBC, 1959; "Person to Person," CBS, 1959; "The Defenders: The Boy Between," CBS, 1961; "The New Breed: I Remember Murder," ABC, 1961; "Girl Talk," SYN, 1963; "The Patty Duke Show: The House Guest," ABC, 1963; "The Mike Douglas Show," SYN, 1965; "Cool Million: Assault on Gavaloni," NBC, 1972.

CHECKER, CHUBBY
b. Ernest Evans, Philadelphia, PA, October 3, 1941. Twister.
AS A GUEST: "American Bandstand," ABC, 1959; "The Dick Clark Saturday Night Beechnut Show," ABC, 1959; "The Dick Clark Saturday Night Beechnut Show," ABC, 1960; "American Bandstand," ABC, 1960; "American Bandstand," ABC, 1962; "Later with Bob Costas," NBC, 1989; "Quantum Leap: Good Morning, Peoria," NBC, 1989.
* Checker played at Bob Costas' wedding reception.

CHEEK, MOLLY
b. Bronxville, NY.
AS A REGULAR: "Chicago Story," NBC, 1982; "It's Garry Shandling's Show," FOX, 1988-90.
AND: "St. Elsewhere: Tweety and Ralph," NBC, 1982; "Hardcastle and McCormick: Never My Love," ABC, 1984.
TV MOVIES AND MINISERIES: "Torn Between Two Lovers," CBS, 1979; "To Find My Son," CBS, 1980; "A Summer to Remember," CBS, 1985.

TRIVIA QUIZ #8: "CHEERS"
1. What was Sam Malone's baseball nickname?
2. One of the actors in the running to play Sam Malone ended up over at "Knots Landing" playing Gregory Sumner. Name him.
3. What was Norm's original occupation?
4. Sam had a lucky symbol that he gave to another ballplayer in one episode. What was it?
5. When Nicholas Colasanto died in 1985, he was replaced by Woody Harrelson as another bartender, Woody Boyd. What state is Woody from?
6. What town?
7. In what state does Cliff always take his vacation?
8. What was the name of Rebecca Howe's boss, on whom she had a crush?
9. What did Carla's husband, Eddie LeBec, do for a living?
10. How was he killed?

(Answers at end of book.)

CHER
b. Cherilyn LaPiere, El Centro, CA, May 20, 1946. Singer, Oscar-winning actress ("Moonstruck") and the livelihood of several Beverly Hills plastic surgeons.
AS A REGULAR: "Shindig," ABC, 1964-66; "The Sonny and Cher Comedy Hour," CBS, 1971-74, 1976-77; "Cher," CBS, 1975-76.
AND: "Hullabaloo," NBC, 1965; "Hollywood Palace," ABC, 1966; "The Man From UNCLE: The Hot Number Affair," NBC, 1967; "Rowan & Martin's Laugh-In," NBC, 1968; "Kraft Music Hall," NBC, 1968; "The Tonight Show Starring Johnny Carson," NBC, 1968; "The Joey Bishop Show," ABC, 1968; "The Glen Campbell Goodtime Hour," CBS, 1969; "Love, American Style: Love and the Sack," ABC, 1971; "Cher ... and Other Fantasies," NBC, 1979.
* "Cher ... and Other Fantasies." What a nice, self-effacing title.

CHERRY, DON
b. Wichita, TX, January 11, 1924. Singer.

191

AS A REGULAR: "Penthouse Party," ABC, 1950-51; "The Peter Lind Hayes Show," ABC, 1958-59; "The Dean Martin Summer Show," NBC, 1967.
AND: "The Walter Winchell Show," NBC, 1956; "The Ed Sullivan Show," CBS, 1957; "The Jack Paar Show," NBC, 1958; "Arthur Murray Party," NBC, 1958; "The Tennessee Ernie Ford Show," ABC, 1964; "The Tennessee Ernie Ford Show," ABC, 1965; "The Dean Martin Show," NBC, 1967.

CHESHIRE, ELIZABETH
b. Burbank, CA, March 3, 1967.
AS A REGULAR: "Sunshine," NBC, 1975; "The Family Holvak," NBC, 1975.
TV MOVIES AND MINISERIES: "And I Alone Survived," NBC, 1978; "The Seduction of Miss Leona," CBS, 1980.

CHEVALIER, MAURICE
b. Paris, France, September 12, 1888; d. 1972.
AS A GUEST: "Maurice Chevalier's Paris," NBC, 1957; "The Jack Benny Program: Jack in Paris," CBS, 1957; "The Ed Sullivan Show," CBS, 1958; "Person to Person," CBS, 1958; "The Ed Sullivan Show," CBS, 1958; "The Lucille Ball-Desi Arnaz Show: Lucy Goes to Mexico," CBS, 1958; "Dinah Shore Chevy Show," NBC, 1958; "The Ed Sullivan Show," CBS, 1959; "Startime: The Wonderful World of Entertainment," NBC, 1959; "A Tribute to Eleanor Roosevelt on Her Diamond Jubilee," NBC, 1959; "Person to Person," CBS, 1960; "Mother's March," SYN, 1960; "A Musical Bouquet From Maurice Chevalier," CBS, 1960; "An Invitation to Paris," ABC, 1960; "The Gershwin Years," CBS, 1961; "Bing Crosby Special," ABC, 1961; "The Broadway of Lerner and Loewe," NBC, 1962; "The World of Maurice Chevalier," NBC, 1963; "Hollywood Palace," ABC, 1964; "The Red Skelton Hour," CBS, 1965; "ABC Stage '67: C'est la Vie," ABC, 1967; "The Dick Cavett Show," ABC, 1970; "The David Frost Show," SYN, 1970.

CHILDRESS, ALVIN
b. Meridian, MS, 1907; d. 1986. Actor who played Amos Jones on "Amos 'n Andy."
AS A REGULAR: "Amos 'n Andy," CBS, 1951-53.
AND: "Sanford & Son: Crossed Swords," NBC, 1972; "Good Times: The Windfall," CBS, 1974; "The Jeffersons: Mother Jefferson's Boyfriend," CBS, 1975; "Fish: Fish Behind Bars," ABC, 1977.
TV MOVIES AND MINISERIES: "Banyon," NBC, 1971.

CHING, WILLIAM
b. 1912.
AS A REGULAR: "Our Miss Brooks," CBS, 1955-56.
AND: "The Loretta Young Show: A Shadow Between," NBC, 1955; "Science Fiction Theatre: Friend of a Raven," SYN, 1955; "Science Fiction Theatre: The Last Barrier," SYN, 1956; "The Jane Wyman Show: Technical Charge of Homicide," NBC, 1956; "Science Fiction Theatre: The Human Circuit," SYN, 1956; "Love That Jill: Kiss Me, Sergeant," ABC, 1958; "The Californians: Murietta," NBC, 1958.

CHRISTIE, AUDREY
b. June 27, 1912; d. 1989.
AS A REGULAR: "Joey Faye's Frolics," CBS, 1950; "Guess What," DUM, 1952; "The Seeking Heart," CBS, 1954; "Today Is Ours," NBC, 1958; "Fair Exchange," CBS, 1962-63; "The Cara Williams Show," CBS, 1964-65.
AS A GUEST: "Goodyear TV Playhouse: Your Every Wish," NBC, 1957; "Studio One: In Love with a Stranger," CBS, 1957; "Alcoa Hour: The Trouble with Women," NBC, 1957; "Profiles in Courage: The Mary S. McDowell Story," NBC, 1964; "Dr. Kildare: Marriage of Convenience," NBC, 1965; "The Adventures of Ozzie and Harriet: The Tangled Web," ABC, 1965; "Honey West: Whatever Lola Wants," ABC, 1965; "Barney Miller: The Courtesans," ABC, 1975; "Medical Center: The Last Performance," CBS, 1975; "Barney Miller: Old Love," ABC, 1982.
TV MOVIES AND MINISERIES: "Shirts/Skins," ABC, 1973; "F. Scott Fitzgerald in Hollywood," ABC, 1976.

CHRISTOPHER, GERARD
b. Jerry Dinome.
AS A REGULAR: "Superboy," SYN, 1989- .
AND: "Murphy's Law: Where Are My Socks and Other Mysteries of Love," ABC, 1988.

CHRISTOPHER, JORDAN
b. Youngstown, OH, October 23, 1940.
AS A REGULAR: "Secrets of Midland Heights," CBS, 1980-81.
AND: "Scarecrow and Mrs. King: The Triumvirate," CBS, 1986; "Scarecrow and Mrs. King: Mission of Gold," CBS, 1987.
TV MOVIES AND MINISERIES: "Seduced," CBS, 1985.

CHRISTOPHER, WILLIAM
b. Evanston, IL, October 20, 1932. Actor usually in mild-mannered roles, including that of Father Francis Mulcahy on "M*A*S*H" and its spinoff.
AS A REGULAR: "Gomer Pyle, USMC," CBS,

1964-70; "M*A*S*H," CBS, 1972-83; "AfterMASH," CBS, 1983-84.
AND: "Hogan's Heroes: Movies Are Your Best Escape," CBS, 1965; "The Patty Duke Show: The Three Little Kittens," ABC, 1966; "The Andy Griffith Show: A New Doctor in Town," CBS, 1966; "That Girl: I Am Curious Lemon," ABC, 1969; "Columbo: Mind Over Mayhem," NBC, 1974; "Good Times: The Enlistment," CBS, 1975; "The Love Boat: The Reluctant Father," ABC, 1983; "The Love Boat: Watching the Master," ABC, 1984; "Murder, She Wrote: A Lady in the Lake," CBS, 1986.

CHUNG, CONNIE
b. Washington, D.C., August 20, 1946.
AS A REGULAR: "NBC Weekend News," NBC, 1983-88; "NBC News at Sunrise," NBC, 1983-86; "1986," NBC, 1986; "Saturday Night with Connie Chung," CBS, 1989-90; "Face to Face with Connie Chung," CBS, 1990.
AND: "David Letterman's Old-Fashioned Christmas," NBC, 1987; "Murphy Brown: TV or Not TV," CBS, 1989.

CHURCHILL, SARAH
b. Sarah Millicent Hermione Churchill, London, England, October 7, 1914; d. 1982. Stage actress and daughter of Winston Churchill who turned to television drama.
AS A REGULAR: "Hallmark Hall of Fame," NBC, 1952-55.
AND: "Lux Video Theatre: Sweet Sorrow," CBS, 1951; "Faith Baldwin Theatre: We Have These Hours," ABC, 1951; "Matinee Theatre: The Old Maid," NBC, 1956; "Matinee Theatre: Susan and God," NBC, 1956; "Matinee Theatre: Skylark," NBC, 1956; "Lux Video Theatre: Temptation," NBC, 1956; "Matinee Theatre: Savrola," NBC, 1956; "Playhouse 90: Sincerely, Willis Wayde," CBS, 1956; "Matinee Theatre: The Others," NBC, 1957; "Matinee Theatre: The Tone of Time," NBC, 1957; "Matinee Theatre: Aesop and Rhodope," NBC, 1957; "Matinee Theatre: No Time for Comedy," NBC, 1957; "Matinee Theatre: The Makropoulous Secret," NBC, 1958; "Matinee Theatre: Love Out of Town," NBC, 1958.

CIOFFI, CHARLES
b. 1935.
AS A REGULAR: "Where the Heart Is," CBS, 1969-73; "Assignment Vienna," ABC, 1972-73; "Get Christie Love!," ABC, 1974; "Another World," NBC, 1979; "Days of Our Lives," NBC, 1990- .
AND: "Medical Center: The Pawn," CBS, 1971; "The FBI: The Break-up," ABC, 1972; "The FBI: A Piece of the Action," ABC, 1974; "Hawaii Five-O: We Hang Our Own," CBS, 1974;

"Hawaii Five-O: McGarrett Is Missing," CBS, 1975; "The Streets of San Francisco: Spooks for Sale," ABC, 1975; "Medical Center: The Silent Witness," CBS, 1976; "Kojak: The Queen of Hearts is Wild," CBS, 1977; "Little House on the Prairie: Someone Please Love Me," NBC, 1979; "Nero Wolfe: To Catch a Dead Man," NBC, 1981; "Lou Grant: Law," CBS, 1981; "Taxi: The Road Not Taken," ABC, 1982; "The A-Team: The Rabbit Who Ate Las Vegas," NBC, 1983; "St. Elsewhere: Family Feud," NBC, 1986; "Simon & Simon: Family Forecast," CBS, 1986; "The Equalizer: Counterfire," CBS, 1986; "The Equalizer: Suspicion of Innocence," CBS, 1987; "Midnight Caller: Bank Job," NBC, 1989; "thirtysomething: No Promises," ABC, 1989; "Kojak: Fatal Flaw," ABC, 1989.
TV MOVIES AND MINISERIES: "Mongo's Back in Town," CBS, 1971; "See the Man Run," ABC, 1971; "Nicky's World," CBS, 1974; "Kate McShane," CBS, 1975; "Return to Earth," ABC, 1976; "Just a Little Inconvenience," NBC, 1977; "Samurai," ABC, 1979; "Dream Breakers," CBS, 1989; "Peter Gunn," ABC, 1989.

CLAIR, DICK
b. San Francisco, CA. Comic actor and writer, often with Jenna McMahon.
AS A REGULAR: "The Many Loves of Dobie Gillis," CBS, 1961; "What's It All About, World?," ABC, 1969; "The Funny Side," NBC, 1971.
AND: "My Three Sons: Too Much in Common," ABC, 1962; "The Mary Tyler Moore Show: Party Is Such Sweet Sorrow," CBS, 1971; "Love, American Style: Love and the Little Black Book," ABC, 1972; "The Bob Newhart Show: A Home Is Not Necessarily a House," CBS, 1973; "Dinah!," SYN, 1978.
AS CO-WRITER: "The Mary Tyler Moore Show: Feeb," CBS, 1972; "The Bob Newhart Show: Mom, I L-L-Love You," CBS, 1972; "The Mary Tyler Moore Show: My Brother's Keeper," CBS, 1973; "The Mary Tyler Moore Show: Remembrance of Things Past," CBS, 1973; "The Carol Burnett Show," CBS, 1973-78.
* Emmies: 1974, 1975, 1978.

CLAIRE, DOROTHY
b. LaPorte, IN, June 5, 1925.
AS A REGULAR: "Henry Morgan's Great Talent Hunt," NBC, 1951; "The Paul Winchell-Jerry Mahoney Show," NBC, 1951-52.

CLARK, CANDY
b. Norman, OK, 1950.
AS A GUEST: "Room 222: The Witch of Whitman High," ABC, 1972; "Banacek: No Stone

Unturned," NBC, 1973; "Simon & Simon: Full Moon Blues," CBS, 1986; "Starman: Different Drummer," ABC, 1986; "Matlock: The Country Boy," NBC, 1987; "St. Elsewhere: Their Town," NBC, 1988.

TV MOVIES AND MINISERIES: "James Dean," NBC, 1976; "Amateur Night at the Dixie Bar and Grill," NBC, 1979; "Where the Ladies Go," ABC, 1980; "Cocaine and Blue Eyes," NBC, 1983.

CLARK, DANE

b. Bernard Zanville, Brooklyn, NY, February 18, 1913.

AS A REGULAR: "Justice," SYN, 1952-53; "Wire Service," ABC, 1956-57; "Bold Venture," SYN, 1959; "The New Adventures of Perry Mason," CBS, 1973-74.

AND: "Mystery Theatre: The Dark Door," ABC, 1950; "Nash Airflyte Theatre: I Won't Take a Minute," CBS, 1950; "Nash Airflyte Theatre: Pearls Are a Nuisance," CBS, 1951; "Lux Video Theatre: Not Guilty—of Much," CBS, 1951; "Gruen Guild Theatre: Unfinished Business," ABC, 1951; "Philco TV Playhouse: The Recluse," NBC, 1953; "Medallion Theatre: Columbo Discovers Italy," CBS, 1953; "Fireside Theatre: The Little Guy," NBC, 1955; "Damon Runyon Theatre: A Job for the Macrone," CBS, 1955; "Science Fiction Theatre: Before the Beginning," SYN, 1955; "Climax!: The Mad Bomber," CBS, 1957; "Impact: Remember to Live," SYN, 1957; "Playhouse 90: Reunion," CBS, 1958; "Schlitz Playhouse of Stars: Heroes Never Grow Up," CBS, 1958; "Suspicion: The Hollow Man," NBC, 1958; "Studio One: The Enemy Within," CBS, 1958; "Wagon Train: The John Wilbot Story," NBC, 1958; "Special for Women: The Indiscriminate Woman," NBC, 1962; "The Untouchables: Bird in the Hand," ABC, 1962; "Burke's Law: Who Killed Cornelius Gilbert?," ABC, 1964; "The Defenders: The Silent Killer," CBS, 1965; "Kraft Suspense Theatre: The Safe House," NBC, 1965; "Ben Casey: For San Diego, You Need a Different Bus," ABC, 1966; "I Spy: One Thousand Fine," NBC, 1966; "The Danny Thomas Hour: The Last Hunters," NBC, 1968; "Ironside: I, the People," NBC, 1968; "The Name of the Game: Goodbye, Harry," NBC, 1969; "Bracken's World: Stop Date," NBC, 1969; "Mannix: Walk with a Dead Man," CBS, 1970; "Ironside: A Killing Will Occur," NBC, 1970; "Mannix: A Ticket to the Eclipse," CBS, 1970; "The Men From Shiloh: The Mysterious Mr. Tate," NBC, 1970; "Mannix: With Intent to Kill," CBS, 1971; "Dan August: The Meal Ticket," ABC, 1971; "Owen Marshall, Counselor at Law: Legacy of Fear," ABC, 1971; "Night Gallery: Spectre in Tap Shoes," NBC, 1972; "The Mod Squad: Belinda-End of Little Miss Bubblegum," ABC, 1972; "Police Story: Explosion!," NBC,

1974; "Medical Story: Test Case," NBC, 1975; "Police Woman: Task Force: Cop Killer," NBC, 1976; "McMillan: All Bets Are Off," NBC, 1976; "Hawaii Five-O: Blood Money Is Hard to Wash," CBS, 1977; "Switch: 30,000 Witnesses," CBS, 1978; "The Hardy Boys Mysteries: Search for Atlantis," ABC, 1978; "Simon & Simon: The Shadow of Sam Penny," CBS, 1983.

TV MOVIES AND MINISERIES: "The Face of Fear," CBS, 1971; "The Family Rico," CBS, 1972; "Say Goodbye, Maggie Cole," ABC, 1972; "Murder on Flight 502," ABC, 1975; "James Dean," NBC, 1976; "Best Sellers: Once an Eagle," NBC, 1977.

CLARK, DICK

b. Mount Vernon, NY, November 30, 1929.

AS A REGULAR: "American Bandstand," ABC, 1957-87; "The Dick Clark Saturday Night Beechnut Show," ABC, 1958-60; "Dick Clark's World of Talent," ABC, 1959; "The Object Is," ABC, 1963-64; "Missing Links," ABC, 1964; "Dick Clark Presents The Rock and Roll Years," ABC, 1973-74; "Dick Clark's Live Wednesday," NBC, 1978; "The $25,000 Pyramid (The $10,000 Pyramid)," CBS, 1973-74; ABC, 1974-80; SYN, 1974-79, 1981; CBS, 1982- ; SYN, 1985- ; "The Krypton Factor," ABC, 1981; "Inside America," ABC, 1982; "TV's Bloopers & Practical Jokes," NBC, 1984- ; "Dick Clark's Nighttime," SYN, 1985-86; "The Challengers," SYN, 1990- .

AND: "Person to Person," CBS, 1958; "The Steve Allen Show," NBC, 1958; "What's My Line?," CBS, 1958; "Pantomime Quiz," ABC, 1958; "Patti Page Olds Show," ABC, 1958; "This Is Your Life," NBC, 1959; "The Record Years," ABC, 1959; "Dick Clark's New Year's Eve Party," ABC, 1959; "This Is Your Life (Connie Francis)," NBC, 1961; "The Gift of Talent," ABC, 1962; "Talent Scouts," CBS, 1963; "Burke's Law: Who Killed Victor Barrows?," ABC, 1964; "Burke's Law: Who Killed the Swinger on a Hook?," ABC, 1964; "Honey West: There's a Long, Long Fuse a-Burning," ABC, 1966; "Batman: Shoot a Crooked Arrow/Walk the Straight and Narrow," ABC, 1966; "The Partridge Family: Star Quality," ABC, 1970; "The Odd Couple: The New Car," ABC, 1973; "The Merv Griffin Show," SYN, 1974; "Dinah!," SYN, 1975; "Sha Na Na," SYN, 1979; "The Pat Sajak Show," CBS, 1989; "The People Next Door: Dream Date," CBS, 1989; "Fifty Years of Television: A Golden Celebration," CBS, 1989; "Dick Clark's New Year's Rockin' Eve '90," ABC, 1989.

AS EXECUTIVE PRODUCER: "Rock 'n' Roll Summer Action," ABC, 1985; "Puttin' on the Hits," SYN, 1985-89; "Dick Clark's Nighttime," SYN, 1985-86; "In Person From the Palace," CBS, 1987; "Keep On Cruisin'," CBS, 1987.

CLARK, FRED

*b. Frederic Leonard Clark, Lincoln, CA,
March 9, 1914; d. 1968.* Bald character actor,
usually in comic roles.

AS A REGULAR: "The George Burns and Gracie
Allen Show," CBS, 1951-53; "The Beverly
Hillbillies," CBS, 1963; "The Double Life of
Henry Phyfe," ABC, 1966.

AND: "Broadway Television Theatre: Twentieth
Century," SYN, 1953; "Lux Video Theatre:
Forever Female," NBC, 1955; "Screen Directors
Playhouse: Want-Ad Wedding," NBC, 1955;
"Studio One: Circle of Guilt," CBS, 1956; "Alcoa
Hour: President," NBC, 1956; "Du Pont Theatre:
Pursuit of a Princess," ABC, 1956; "Kraft
Television Theatre: The Singin' Idol," NBC,
1957; "The Arlene Francis Show," NBC, 1957;
"Do You Trust Your Wife?," ABC, 1957; "Lux
Playhouse: The Case of the Two Sisters," CBS,
1959; "The Untouchables: Little Egypt," ABC,
1960; "Startime: Well, What About You?," NBC,
1960; "Shirley Temple's Storybook: Emmy Lou,"
NBC, 1960; "The Twilight Zone: A Most Unusual
Camera," CBS, 1960; "G.E. Theatre: My Darling
Judge," CBS, 1961; "Bus Stop: The Runaways,"
ABC, 1961; "Naked City: Bridge Party," ABC,
1961; "G.E. Theatre: The Holdout," CBS, 1962;
"Armstrong Circle Theatre: Securities for
Suckers," CBS, 1962; "U.S. Steel Hour: Male
Call," CBS, 1962; "Wagon Train: The Martin
Gatsby Story," ABC, 1962; "Going My Way: A
Matter of Principle," ABC, 1962; "Burke's Law:
Who Killed Holly Howard?," ABC, 1963;
"Burke's Law: Who Killed Mr. Cartwheel?,"
ABC, 1964; "Slattery's People: Question: Bill
Bailey, Why Did You Come Home?," CBS, 1965;
"The Dick Van Dyke Show: 100 Terrible Hours,"
CBS, 1965; "Bob Hope Chrysler Theatre: Mr.
Governess," NBC, 1965; "The Addams Family:
Feud in the Addams Family," ABC, 1965;
"Laredo: The Land Grabbers," NBC, 1965; "ABC
Stage '67: Olympus 7-0000," ABC, 1966; "The
Beverly Hillbillies: Granny Retires," CBS, 1967;
"F Troop: The Day They Shot Agarn," ABC,
1967; "The Beverly Hillbillies: The Doctors,"
CBS, 1967; "Off to See the Wizard: Who's Afraid
of Mother Goose?," ABC, 1967; "Bonanza: A
Girl Named George," NBC, 1968; "Eddie
Skinner," CBS, 1971.

CLARK, OLIVER

b. Buffalo, NY. Actor who played amnesia
victim John Doe No. 6 on "St. Elsewhere."

AS A REGULAR: "Karen," ABC, 1975; "The Bob
Newhart Show," CBS, 1976-77; "3 Girls 3,"
NBC, 1977; "We've Got Each Other," CBS,
1977-78; "The Two of Us," CBS, 1981-82; "St.
Elsewhere," NBC, 1985-86.

AND: "NYPD: Naked in the Streets," ABC, 1968;
"Love, American Style: Love and the Generation
Gap," ABC, 1973; "Tenafly: Joy Ride to

Nowhere," NBC, 1973; "The Bob Newhart Show:
The New Look," CBS, 1975; "Barney Miller: The
Layoff," ABC, 1975; "Doctors' Hospital: But
Who Will Bless Thy Daughter Norah?," NBC,
1975; "Barney Miller: Noninvolvement," ABC,
1976; "M*A*S*H: Thirty-Eight Across," CBS,
1977; "M*A*S*H: Mail Call Three," CBS, 1978;
"Barney Miller: Hostage," ABC, 1978; "Barney
Miller: The Dentist," ABC, 1979; "Barney Miller:
The Doll," ABC, 1981; "Barney Miller:
Landmark," ABC, 1982; "St. Elsewhere: Getting
Ahead," NBC, 1987; "Mr. Belvedere: Moonlight-
ing," ABC, 1987; "Rags to Riches: That's
Cheating," NBC, 1987; "Mr. Belvedere: Hooky,"
ABC, 1988; "Life Goes On: Corky for President,"
ABC, 1989; "The Golden Girls: Comedy of
Errors," NBC, 1989; "Dear John: The Secret of
Success," NBC, 1989.

TV MOVIES AND MINISERIES: "Hanging by a
Thread," NBC, 1979; "Happy Endings," NBC,
1983.

* As John Doe No. 6, Clark spent all of one "St.
Elsewhere" episode imagining he was Mary
Richards, the character Mary Tyler Moore
played on her seventies sitcom. The episode
climaxed when John met guest star Betty
White in a hallway. "Sue Ann!" he ex-
claimed—and ended the episode by tossing his
hat in the air a la the opening credits of "The
Mary Tyler Moore Show."

CLARK, PETULA

b. Epsom, England, November 15, 1932.

AS A GUEST: "Shindig," ABC, 1965; "The Ed
Sullivan Show," CBS, 1965; "Where the
Action Is," ABC, 1966; "The Tonight Show
Starring Johnny Carson," NBC, 1968; "Petula
Clark Special," NBC, 1968; "The Andy
Williams Show," NBC, 1969; "The Dean
Martin Show," NBC, 1970; "Petula," ABC,
1970; "The Glen Campbell Goodtime Hour,"
CBS, 1971; "Dinah!," SYN, 1974; "The
Tonight Show Starring Johnny Carson," NBC,
1975; "The Mike Douglas Show," SYN, 1975;
"Midnight Special," NBC, 1975; "Sammy and
Company," SYN, 1976.

* On her 1968 special, Petula Clark was singing
a number with Harry Belafonte, she put her
hand on Belafonte's arm and the sponsor
objected.

CLARK, ROY

b. Meherrin, WV, April 15, 1933.

AS A REGULAR: "The George Hamilton IV Show,"
ABC, 1959; "Swingin' Country," NBC, 1966;
"Hee Haw," CBS, 1969-71; SYN, 1971- .

AND: "Arthur Godfrey's Talent Scouts," CBS,
1956; "The Jimmy Dean Show," ABC, 1964;
"The Jimmy Dean Show," ABC, 1965; "The Mike
Douglas Show," SYN, 1967; "The Beverly

Hillbillies: Cousin Roy," CBS, 1968; "The Jonathan Winters Show," CBS, 1968; "The Beverly Hillbillies: Jethro the Flesh Peddler," CBS, 1969; "The Beverly Hillbillies: Cousin Roy in Movieland," CBS, 1969; "The Glen Campbell Goodtime Hour," CBS, 1969; "Movin'," NBC, 1970; "The Glen Campbell Goodtime Hour," CBS, 1970; "Love, American Style: Love and the Twanger Tutor," ABC, 1973; "The Merv Griffin Show," SYN, 1973; "Midnight Special," NBC, 1974; "Dinah!," SYN, 1975; "The Mac Davis Show," NBC, 1975; "Saturday Night Live with Howard Cosell," ABC, 1975; "The Grand Ole Opry at 50," ABC, 1975; "Mac Davis Special," NBC, 1975; "Hee Haw Honeys," SYN, 1978; "Hollywood Squares," SYN, 1980; "Roy Clark's Friendship Tour: USSR," TNN, 1989.

CLARK, SUSAN

b. Canada, March 8, 1940. Actress who won an Emmy as Babe Zaharias and played Katherine on "Webster."

AS A REGULAR: "McNaughton's Daughter," NBC, 1976; "Webster," ABC, 1983-87; SYN, 1987-89.

AND: "Bob Hope Chrysler Theatre: Blind Man's Bluff," NBC, 1967; "The Virginian: Melanie," NBC, 1967; "Run for Your Life: Cry Hard, Cry Fast," NBC, 1967; "Marcus Welby, M.D.: Hello, Goodbye, Hello," ABC, 1969; "The Bold Ones: In the Defense of Ellen McKay," NBC, 1971; "Columbo: Lady in Waiting," NBC, 1971; "Marcus Welby, M.D.: Please Don't Send Flowers," ABC, 1972; "The Bold Ones: The Inalienable Right to Die," NBC, 1972; "Conflicts: Double Solitaire," PBS, 1974; "Barnaby Jones: Woman in the Shadows," CBS, 1974; "Hollywood Squares," NBC, 1975; "Hollywood Squares," NBC, 1976.

TV MOVIES AND MINISERIES: "Something for a Lonely Man," NBC, 1968; "The Challengers," CBS, 1970; "The Astronaut," NBC, 1972; "Trapped," ABC, 1973; "Babe," CBS, 1975; "McNaughton's Daughter," NBC, 1976; "Amelia Earhart," NBC, 1976; "Jimmy B. and Andre," CBS, 1980; "The Choice," CBS, 1981; "Maid in America," CBS, 1982.

* Emmies: 1976.

CLARKE, BRIAN PATRICK

b. Belmont, NC, August 1, 1952. Blonde hunk who plays a guy named Storm on "The Bold and the Beautiful."

AS A REGULAR: "Delta House," ABC, 1979; "Eight Is Enough," ABC, 1979-81; "General Hospital," ABC, 1983-87; "The Bold and the Beautiful," CBS, 1990- .

TV MOVIES AND MINISERIES: "Eight Is Enough: A Family Reunion," NBC, 1987.

CLARKE, GARY

b. Los Angeles, CA, August 16, 1936.

AS A REGULAR: "Michael Shayne," NBC, 1960-61; "The Virginian," NBC, 1962-64; "Hondo," ABC, 1967.

AND: "Sky King: Rodeo Decathalon," CBS, 1958; "Tales of Wells Fargo: Death Raffle," NBC, 1961; "Laramie: The Fatal Step," NBC, 1961; "G.E. Theatre: The Little Hours," CBS, 1962; "Wagon Train: The Lonnie Fallon Story," NBC, 1962; "Bachelor Father: Summer Romance," ABC, 1962; "The Tall Man: Quarantine," NBC, 1962; "My Three Sons: The New Room," CBS, 1968; "Then Came Bronson: The Forest Primeval," NBC, 1970; "The Streets of San Francisco: The Takers," ABC, 1973; "Chase: The Dealer-Wheelers," NBC, 1973; "The FBI: Survival," ABC, 1974.

TV MOVIES AND MINISERIES: "Revenge," ABC, 1971; "The Eyes of Charles Sand," ABC, 1972.

CLARKE, MAE

b. Mary Klotz, Philadelphia, PA, August 16, 1907. Supporting actress in the movies and on the tube; the woman into whose kisser James Cagney pushed a grapefruit half in "The Public Enemy."

AS A GUEST: "The Loretta Young Show: The Judgment," NBC, 1954; "Four Star Playhouse: Man in the Cellar," CBS, 1954; "Public Defender: Gunpoint," CBS, 1955; "Medic: When I Was Young," NBC, 1955; "Matinee Theatre: George Has a Birthday," NBC, 1956; "Ford Theatre: Front Page Father," ABC, 1956; "The Jane Wyman Show: Killer's Pride," NBC, 1957; "The Loretta Young Show: A Greater Strength," NBC, 1958; "George Sanders Mystery Theatre: And the Birds Still Sing," NBC, 1959; "Batman: An Egg Grows in Gotham/The Yegg Foes in Gotham," ABC, 1966.

CLARY, ROBERT

b. Paris, France, March 1, 1926. Slight actor who played LeBeau on "Hogan's Heroes" and is now a soap actor.

AS A REGULAR: "Pantomime Quiz," CBS, 1954; ABC, 1955; CBS, 1955; 1956; 1957; "Stump the Stars," CBS, 1962-63; "Hogan's Heroes," CBS, 1965-71; "Days of Our Lives," NBC, 1972-73, 1975-83; "The Young and the Restless," CBS, 1973-74; "The Bold and the Beautiful," CBS, 1990- .

AND: "The Rosemary Clooney Show," SYN, 1956; "The Spike Jones Show," CBS, 1957; "Art Linkletter's House Party," CBS, 1957; "The Gisele MacKenzie Show," NBC, 1958; "The Jimmy Dean Show," CBS, 1958; "The Garry Moore Show," CBS, 1958; "Pat Boone Chevy Showroom," ABC, 1958; "Your Hit Parade,"

CBS, 1959; "The Peter Lind Hayes Show," ABC, 1959; "Pantomime Quiz," ABC, 1959; "Playboy's Penthouse," SYN, 1961; "The Merv Griffin Show," NBC, 1962; "The Joey Bishop Show," ABC, 1967; "Love, American Style: Love and the Letter," ABC, 1969; "Cross Wits," SYN, 1976.
TV MOVIES AND MINISERIES: "Remembrance of Love," NBC, 1982.

CLAYBURGH, JILL

b. New York City, NY, April 30, 1944. Attractive actress who began in TV, left it for the movies, and now seems to be making her way back to the tube.
AS A REGULAR: "Search for Tomorrow," CBS, 1969-70.
AND: "NYPD: Deadly Circle of Violence," ABC, 1968; "On Stage: The Choice," NET, 1969; "Going Places," NBC, 1973; "Medical Center: A Choice of Evils," CBS, 1974; "The Rockford Files: The Big Ripoff," NBC, 1974; "Saturday Night Live," NBC, 1976; "Saturday Night Live," NBC, 1978.
TV MOVIES AND MINISERIES: "The Snoop Sisters," NBC, 1972; "Shock-a-Bye, Baby," ABC, 1973; "Hustling," ABC, 1975; "The Art of Crime," NBC, 1975; "Griffin and Phoenix," ABC, 1976; "Miles to Go," CBS, 1986; "Who Gets the Friends?," CBS, 1988.

CLAYTON, JAN

b. Tularosa, NM, August 26, 1917; d. 1983.
AS A REGULAR: "Pantomime Quiz," CBS, 1953; DUM, 1953-54; CBS, 1954; "Lassie," CBS, 1954-57; "Stump the Stars," CBS, 1962-63.
AND: "Story Theatre: The Manchester Marriage," SYN, 1951; "Jewelers Showcase: Three and One-Half Musketeers," CBS, 1953; "Make Room for Daddy: School Festival," ABC, 1954; "Matinee Theatre: Wednesday's Child," NBC, 1958; "Dinah Shore Chevy Show," NBC, 1958; "The Millionaire: Millionaire Irene Marshall," CBS, 1959; "The Ed Sullivan Show," CBS, 1959; "The Deputy: Lady with a Mission," NBC, 1960; "Tales of Wells Fargo: The Bride and the Bandit," NBC, 1960; "The Danny Thomas Show: The Singing Sisters," CBS, 1960; "Wagon Train: The Prairie Story," NBC, 1961; "Here's Hollywood," NBC, 1961; "My Three Sons: Romance of the Silver Pines," ABC, 1962; "The Tall Man: St. Louis Woman," NBC, 1962; "Wagon Train: The William Carr Story," ABC, 1964; "Daktari: Return of the Killer," CBS, 1966; "My Three Sons: Charley O'the Seven Seas," CBS, 1967; "Daktari: Miracle in the Jungle," CBS, 1968; "Archer: The Turkish Connection," NBC, 1975; "The Streets of San Francisco: The Thrill Killers," ABC, 1976; "The Love Boat: Teach Me Tonight," ABC, 1981.

CLEVELAND, GEORGE

b. Canada, 1886; d. 1957. Actor who played Gramps Miller on "Lassie."
AS A REGULAR: "Lassie," CBS, 1954-57.

CLINE, PATSY

d. 1963. Country-western singer.
AS A GUEST: "Arthur Godfrey's Talent Scouts," CBS, 1957; "The Big Beat," ABC, 1957; "Country Music Jubilee," ABC, 1957; "Country Music Jubilee," ABC, 1958; "Jubilee USA," ABC, 1959; "Ranch Party," SYN, 1960; "Jubilee USA," ABC, 1960; "American Bandstand," ABC, 1962; "The Tennessee Ernie Ford Show," ABC, 1962.

CLOONEY, BETTY

b. Maysville, KY, 1930. Singer; sister of Rosemary.
AS A REGULAR: "The Jack Paar Show," CBS, 1953-56.
AND: "The Lux Show with Rosemary Clooney," NBC, 1957; "The Lawrence Welk Show," ABC, 1960.

CLOONEY, ROSEMARY

b. Maysville, KY, May 23, 1928. Talented singer with a rich, warm voice who appeared in TV and movies. At the beginning of her career she was saddled with silly novelty songs but now performs tasteful, swinging versions of standards.
AS A REGULAR: "Songs for Sale," CBS, 1950-51; "The Rosemary Clooney Show," SYN, 1956-57; "The Lux Show with Rosemary Clooney," NBC, 1957-58.
AND: "Arthur Godfrey's Talent Scouts," CBS, 1950; "The Ed Sullivan Show," CBS, 1956; "The Perry Como Show," NBC, 1956; "The Ford Show," NBC, 1957; "The Bob Hope Show," NBC, 1957; "The Steve Allen Show," NBC, 1957; "The Edsel Show," CBS, 1957; "The George Gobel Show," NBC, 1958; "The Steve Allen Show," NBC, 1958; "The Perry Como Show," NBC, 1959; "The George Burns Show," NBC, 1959; "The Voice of Firestone: Mardi Gras Night," ABC, 1959; "Some of Manie's Friends," NBC, 1959; "The Garry Moore Show," CBS, 1959; "Bell Telephone Hour," NBC, 1959; "Bob Hope Special," NBC, 1959; "Summer on Ice," NBC, 1959; "The Ford Show," NBC, 1959; "The Ed Sullivan Show," CBS, 1959; "Perry Como's Kraft Music Hall," NBC, 1959; "Bell Telephone Hour: The Gift of Music," NBC, 1959; "The Ed Sullivan Show," CBS, 1960; "The Bing Crosby Show," ABC, 1960; "Perry Como's Kraft Music Hall," NBC, 1960; "No Place Like Home," NBC, 1960; "Bell Telephone Hour: Music Hath Charms," NBC, 1961; "Marineland Circus," NBC, 1961; "The Ed Sullivan Show," CBS, 1961;

"The Ed Sullivan Show," CBS, 1962; "The Red Skelton Hour," CBS, 1962; "Password," CBS, 1963; "The Dick Powell Show: The Losers," NBC, 1963; "The Jimmy Dean Show," ABC, 1963; "Hollywood Palace," ABC, 1964; "I've Got a Secret," CBS, 1964; "The Tonight Show Starring Johnny Carson," NBC, 1964; "The Bing Crosby Show," CBS, 1964; "The Entertainers," CBS, 1965; "The Tonight Show Starring Johnny Carson," NBC, 1965; "The Merv Griffin Show," SYN, 1974; "Dinah!," SYN, 1975; "The Merv Griffin Show," SYN, 1975; "The Merv Griffin Show," SYN, 1980; "Hardcastle and McCormick: If You Could See What I See," ABC, 1986; "Irving Berlin's 100th Birthday Celebration," CBS, 1988; "A Conversation with Dinah," TNN, 1989.

TV MOVIES AND MINISERIES: "Sister Margaret and the Saturday Night Ladies," CBS, 1987.

* Clooney's life story—which involved a nervous breakdown in the late 1960s and a tempestuous marriage to Jose Ferrer—was dramatized in the 1982 TV-movie "Rosie," in which Clooney was played by Sondra Locke.

CLOSE, GLENN
b. Greenwich, CT, March 19, 1947.
AS A GUEST: "Saturday Night Live," NBC, 1989.
TV MOVIES AND MINISERIES: "Too Far to Go," NBC, 1979; "Something About Amelia," ABC, 1984.

CLOWER, JERRY
b. Missisippi, September 28, 1926. Country-flavored comic.
AS A REGULAR: "Nashville on the Road," SYN, 1975-81.

CLUTE, SIDNEY
b. Brooklyn, NY, April 21, 1916; d. 1985.
AS A REGULAR: "Lou Grant," CBS, 1977-79; "Cagney & Lacey," CBS, 1982-85.
AND: "Perry Mason: The Case of the Cautious Coquette," CBS, 1958; "The Millionaire: The Laura Hunter Story," CBS, 1958; "Steve Canyon: Operation Towline," NBC, 1958; "The Millionaire: Millionaire Gilbert Burton," CBS, 1959; "Harrigan and Son: Senior Goes to Hollywood," ABC, 1961; "Holiday Lodge: The Champ," CBS, 1961; "Hennesey: The Sightseers," CBS, 1961; "The Dick Powell Show: Open Season," NBC, 1961; "Father of the Bride: The Souvenir," CBS, 1962; "Slattery's People: How Do You Catch a Cool Bird of Paradise?," CBS, 1965; "Wendy & Me: Wendy Lends a Helping Voice," ABC, 1965; "Petticoat Junction: The Baffling Raffle," CBS, 1965; "Bewitched: The Horse's Mouth," ABC, 1966; "Hogan's Heroes: Hogan Springs," CBS, 1966; "Bewitched: Endora Moves in for a Spell," ABC, 1966; "Love on a Rooftop: King of the

Castle," ABC, 1967; "Get Smart: The Girls From KAOS," NBC, 1967; "The FBI: Passage Into Fear," ABC, 1967; "Dragnet: The Big Search," NBC, 1968; "Room 222: Naked Came We Into the World," ABC, 1969; "Medical Center: The Adversaries," CBS, 1969; "Dragnet: Frauds-DR-28," NBC, 1969; "Dragnet: Robbery-The Harrassing Wife," NBC, 1970; "Dragnet: D.H.Q.-Night School," NBC, 1970; "Room 222: Adams' Lib," ABC, 1970; "Marcus Welby, M.D.: All the Pretty People," ABC, 1972; "Here's Lucy: Lucy and Chuck Connors Have a Surprise Slumber Party," CBS, 1973; "Chase: Vacation for a President," NBC, 1974; "The Streets of San Francisco: Jacob's Boy," ABC, 1974; "McCloud: The Concrete Jungle Caper," NBC, 1974; "McCloud: The Park Avenue Pirates," NBC, 1975; "All in the Family: Prisoner in the House," CBS, 1975; "That's My Mama: The Witness," ABC, 1975; "McCloud: Three Guns for New York," NBC, 1975; "McCloud: The Great Taxicab Stampede," NBC, 1977.

CLYDE, ANDY
b. Scotland, March 25, 1892; d. 1967. Wiry, mustachioed character actor who played Amos McCoy's friend/enemy George McMichael on "The Real McCoys" and the kindly Cully Wilson on "Lassie."
AS A REGULAR: "Circus Boy," NBC, 1956-57; "The Real McCoys," ABC, 1957-62; CBS, 1962-63; "Lassie," CBS, 1958-64; "No Time for Sergeants," ABC, 1964-65.
AND: "The Adventures of Rin Tin Tin: Homer the Great," ABC, 1957; "Wagon Train: The Jennifer Churchill Story," NBC, 1958; "The Texan: Troubled Town," CBS, 1958; "Restless Gun: A Very Special Investigator," NBC, 1959; "Shotgun Slade: The Hermit," SYN, 1959; "The Millionaire: Millionaire Andrew C. Cooley," CBS, 1959; "The Tall Man: McBean Rides Again," NBC, 1960; "The Life and Legend of Wyatt Earp: Billy Buckett, Incorporated," ABC, 1961; "The Tall Man: The Reluctant Bridegroom," NBC, 1961; "The Tall Man: Millionaire McBean," NBC, 1961; "The Andy Griffith Show: Mayberry Goes Bankrupt," CBS, 1961; "The Tall Man: Substitute Sheriff," NBC, 1962.

COBB, BUFF
b. Italy, October 19, 1928.
AS A REGULAR: "All Around The Town," CBS, 1951-52; "Masquerade Party," CBS, 1953-54; ABC, 1954-55.

COBB, JULIE
b. Los Angeles, CA. Actress and daughter of Lee J. Cobb.
AS A REGULAR: "The D.A.," NBC, 1971-72; "A

Year at the Top," CBS, 1977; "Charles in Charge," CBS, 1984-85.

AND: "The Waltons: The Air Mail Man," CBS, 1973; "Gunsmoke: The Colonel," CBS, 1974; "Little House on the Prairie: Money Crop," NBC, 1975; "Marcus Welby, M.D.: The Fruitfulness of Mrs. Steffie Rhodes," ABC, 1975; "Rosetti and Ryan: If You Can't Trust Your Lawyers ...," NBC, 1977; "Lou Grant: Expose," CBS, 1979; "Magnum P.I.: Going Home," CBS, 1985; "MacGruder and Loud: A Very Scary Man," ABC, 1985; "MacGyver: Eagles," ABC, 1986; "St. Elsewhere: You Beta Your Life," NBC, 1986; "Family Ties: O, Brother," NBC, 1987; "Newhart: Inn This Corner," CBS, 1987; "Growing Pains: Mom of the Year," ABC, 1989; "Duet: Role Call," FOX, 1989; "Heartbeat: Gestalt and Battery," ABC, 1989; "Doogie Howser, M.D.: Blood and Remembrance," ABC, 1989.

TV MOVIES AND MINISERIES: "The Death Squad," ABC, 1973; "Steel Cowboy," NBC, 1978; "Salem's Lot," CBS, 1979; "Brave New World," NBC, 1980; "To Find My Son," CBS, 1980; "Baby Girl Scott," CBS, 1987.

COBB, LEE J.
b. Leo Jacob Cobb, New York City, NY, December 8, 1911; d. 1976. Actor who excelled at hard-shell, soft-hearted types; best known as Judge Henry Garth on "The Virginian" and as Willy Loman in a 1966 TV production of "Death of a Salessmman."

AS A REGULAR: "The Virginian," NBC, 1962-66; "The Young Lawyers," ABC, 1970-71.

AND: "Somerset Maugham Theatre: The Moon and Sixpence," NBC, 1951; "Tales of Tomorrow: Test Flight," ABC, 1951; "Lights Out: The Veil," NBC, 1951; "Ford Theatre: Night Visitor," NBC, 1954; "Producers Showcase: Darkness at Noon," NBC, 1955; "Medic: Break Through the Bars," NBC, 1955; "Goodyear TV Playhouse: A Patch on Faith," NBC, 1956; "Dick Powell's Zane Grey Theatre: Death Watch," CBS, 1956; "Playhouse 90: Panic Button," CBS, 1957; "Studio One: No Deadly Medicine," CBS, 1957; "Dick Powell's Zane Grey Theatre: Legacy of a Legend," CBS, 1958; "Westinghouse Desilu Playhouse: Trial at Devil's Canyon," CBS, 1959; "Playhouse 90: Project Immortality," CBS, 1959; "Du Pont Show of the Month: I, Don Quixote," CBS, 1959; "G.E. Theatre: Lear vs. the Committeemen," CBS, 1960; "Du Pont Show of the Month: Men in White," CBS, 1960; "The du Pont Show with June Allyson: School of the Soldier," CBS, 1961; "Naked City: Take Off Your Hat When a Funeral Passes," ABC, 1961; "Self-Portrait: Vincent Van Gogh," NBC, 1961; "Westinghouse Presents: Footnote to Fame," CBS, 1962; "G.E. Theatre: The Unstoppable Gray Fox," CBS, 1962; "Bob Hope Chrysler Theatre: It's Mental Work," NBC,

1963; "Death of a Salesman," CBS, 1966; "On Stage: To Confuse the Angel," SYN, 1970; "McCloud: The Park Avenue Rustlers," NBC, 1973; "Gunsmoke: The Colonel," CBS, 1974; "Suddenly an Eagle," ABC, 1976.

TV MOVIES AND MINISERIES: "Heat of Anger," CBS, 1972; "Double Indemnity," ABC, 1973; "Dr. Max," CBS, 1974; "Trapped Beneath the Sea," ABC, 1974; "The Great Ice Ripoff," ABC, 1974.

AS DIRECTOR: "Startime: Tennesse Ernie Meets King Arthur," NBC, 1960.

COBURN, CHARLES
b. Charles Douville Coburn, Savannah, GA, 1877; d. 1961. Portly character actor who came to TV after a prolific movie career.

AS A GUEST: "Pulitzer Prize Playhouse: You Can't Take It With You," ABC, 1950; "Ford Theatre: The World's My Oyster," NBC, 1953; "Center Stage: The Worthy Opponent," ABC, 1954; "Best of Broadway: The Royal Family," CBS, 1954; "U.S. Steel Hour: One for the Road," ABC, 1954; "Studio One: The Cuckoo in Spring," CBS, 1954; "Ford Theatre: Pretend You're You," NBC, 1955; "Studio 57: Sam," SYN, 1955; "Rheingold Theatre: The Lady's Game," NBC, 1955; "Eddie Cantor Theatre: Family Affair," ABC, 1955; "December Bride: Lily and the Wolf," CBS, 1955; "Rheingold Theatre: A Difficult Age," NBC, 1956; "The Jane Wyman Show: Kristi," NBC, 1956; "Ford Theatre: Mr. Kagle and the Baby Sitter," NBC, 1956; "Ethel Barrymore Theatre: Winter and Spring," SYN, 1956; "The Rosemary Clooney Show," SYN, 1956; "The Betty White Show," ABC, 1958; "The Jack Paar Show," NBC, 1958; "Art Linkletter's House Party," CBS, 1959; "The Danny Thomas Show: Grandpa's Diet," CBS, 1959; "The Today Show," NBC, 1959; "Startime: The Wicked Scheme of Jebal Deeks," NBC, 1959; "Best of the Post: Six Months to Live," SYN, 1960; "Here's Hollywood," NBC, 1961.

COBURN, JAMES
b. Laurel, NB, August 31, 1928. Tall, leather-faced actor who ordered Schlitz Light beer on TV commercials.

AS A REGULAR: "Klondike," NBC, 1960-61; "Acapulco," NBC, 1961; "Darkroom," ABC, 1981-82.

AND: "Studio One: The Night America Trembled," CBS, 1957; "Wagon Train: The Millie Davis Story," NBC, 1958; "Alfred Hitchcock Presents: The Jokester," CBS, 1958; "Wanted Dead or Alive: Reunion for Revenge," CBS, 1959; "Dick Powell's Zane Grey Theatre: A Thread of Respect," CBS, 1959; "M Squad: The Firemakers," NBC, 1959; "The Californians: One Ton of Peppercorns," NBC, 1959; "Wanted Dead

or Alive: The Kovack Affair," CBS, 1959; "Tate: Home Town," NBC, 1960; "Wanted Dead or Alive: The Trial," CBS, 1960; "Dick Powell's Zane Grey Theatre: Desert Flight," CBS, 1960; "Lawman: The Catcher," ABC, 1960; "The Aquanauts: River Gold," CBS, 1961; "The Detectives Starring Robert Taylor: The Frightened Ones," ABC, 1961; "Perry Mason: The Case of the Envious Editor," CBS, 1961; "Ripcord: Double Drop," SYN, 1962; "Cain's Hundred: Blues for a Junkman," NBC, 1962; "King of Diamonds: Backlash," SYN, 1962; "Rawhide: The Hostage Child," CBS, 1962; "Checkmate: A Chant of Silence," CBS, 1962; "Perry Mason: The Case of the Angry Astronaut," CBS, 1962; "Bonanza: The Long Night," NBC, 1962; "The Twilight Zone: The Old Man in the Cave," CBS, 1963; "Route 66: Kiss the Monster, Make Him Sleep," CBS, 1964; "Combat!: Masquerade," ABC, 1964; "The Defenders: The Man Who Saved His Country," CBS, 1964; "The Dick Cavett Show," ABC, 1969; "The David Frost Show," SYN, 1971; "The John Davidson Show," SYN, 1980; "Saturday Night Live," NBC, 1982; "Faerie Tale Theatre: Pinocchio," SHO, 1984.
TV MOVIES AND MINISERIES: "The Dain Curse," CBS, 1978; "Malibu," ABC, 1983; "Sins of the Father," NBC, 1985; "Death of a Soldier," CBS, 1986.

COCA, IMOGENE
b. Philadelphia, PA, November 18, 1908. Gifted comic actress and peerless foil of Sid Caesar.
AS A REGULAR: "Buzzy Wuzzy," ABC, 1948; "The Admiral Broadway Revue," NBC, 1949; "Your Show of Shows," NBC, 1950-54; "The Imogene Coca Show," NBC, 1954-55; "The Sid Caesar Show," ABC, 1958; "Grindl," NBC, 1963-64; "It's About Time," CBS, 1966-67.
AND: "U.S. Steel Hour: The Funny Heart," CBS, 1956; "The Jane Wyman Show: Helpmate," NBC, 1956; "Playhouse 90: Made in Heaven," CBS, 1956; "The Ed Sullivan Show," CBS, 1957; "Ruggles of Red Gap," NBC, 1957; "G.E. Theatre: Cab Driver," CBS, 1957; "Arthur Murray Party," NBC, 1958; "The Ed Sullivan Show," CBS, 1959; "Arthur Murray Party," NBC, 1959; "I've Got a Secret," CBS, 1959; "The George Gobel Show," CBS, 1959; "Perry Como's Kraft Music Hall," NBC, 1959; "The George Gobel Show," CBS, 1960; "Art Linkletter's House Party," CBS, 1960; "About Faces," ABC, 1960; "Shirley Temple's Storybook: Madeline," NBC, 1960; "The Danny Kaye Show," CBS, 1964; "The Danny Kaye Show," CBS, 1965; "The Sid Caesar, Imogene Coca, Carl Reiner, Howard Morris Special," CBS, 1967; "The Carol Burnett Show," CBS, 1967; "The Jackie Gleason Show," CBS, 1968; "Hollywood Palace," ABC, 1968; "Love, American Style: Love and the Out-of-

Town Client," ABC, 1970; "Bewitched: Mary, the Good Fairy/The Good Fairy Strikes Again," ABC, 1971; "Night Gallery: The Merciful," NBC, 1971; "The Brady Bunch: Jan's Aunt Jenny," ABC, 1972; "The Emporer's New Clothes," ABC, 1972; "Love, American Style: Love and the Fighting Couple," ABC, 1972; "Wide World of Mystery: Too Easy to Kill," ABC, 1975; "Freddy the Freeloader's Christmas Dinner," HBO, 1981; "Fantasy Island: Curtain Call," ABC, 1983; "Moonlighting: Los Dos Dipestos," ABC, 1987.
TV MOVIES AND MINISERIES: "The Return of the Beverly Hillbillies," CBS, 1981.
* Emmies: 1952.

COCHRAN, RON
b. Canada, 1912. TV Personality and ABC newsman; the man on duty at the network when President John F. Kennedy was shot.
AS A REGULAR: "Man of the Week," CBS, 1954; "Armstrong Circle Theatre," CBS, 1961-62; "ABC Evening News," ABC, 1963-65.

COCHRAN, STEVE
b. Robert Alexander Cochran, Eureka, CA, May 25, 1917; d. 1965. Beefy leading man who often played not-so-pleasant types.
AS A GUEST: "Studio One: Letter of Love," CBS, 1953; "Medallion Theatre: The 39th Bomb," CBS, 1954; "Studio One: The Role of Lover," CBS, 1954; "Ford Theatre: Trip Around the Block," NBC, 1954; "Climax!: The After House," CBS, 1954; "Studio One: A Most Contagious Game," CBS, 1955; "Climax!: Fear is the Hunter," CBS, 1956; "Art Linkletter's House Party," CBS, 1958; "The Twilight Zone: What You Need," CBS, 1959; "Naked City: Debt of Honor," ABC, 1960; "The Untouchables: The Purple Gang," ABC, 1960; "Shirley Temple's Storybook: The Indian Captive," NBC, 1960; "The Renegade," NBC, 1960; "The Untouchables: 90-Proof Dame," ABC, 1961; "Here's Hollywood," NBC, 1961; "Bus Stop: Afternoon of a Cowboy," ABC, 1961; "The Dick Powell Show: Obituary for Mr. X," NBC, 1962; "The Virginian: West," NBC, 1962; "The Virginian: West," NBC, 1962; "Stoney Burke: Death Rides a Pale Horse," ABC, 1963; "Route 66: ... Shall Forfeit His Dog and Ten Shillings to the King," CBS, 1963; "Death Valley Days: West Side of Heaven," SYN, 1964; "Mr. Broadway: Keep an Eye on Emily," CBS, 1964; "Burke's Law: Who Killed the Tall One in the Middle?," ABC, 1964; "Burke's Law: Who Killed the Rest?," ABC, 1965; "Bonanza: The Rap," NBC, 1965.

COCO, JAMES
b. New York City, NY, March 21, 1929; d. 1987. Bald, roly-poly comic actor with stage

roots who won an Emmy as a mentally handicapped, homeless man on "St. Elsewhere" just before his death.
AS A REGULAR: "Calucci's Department," CBS, 1973; "The Dumplings," NBC, 1976.
AND: "Playboy's Penthouse," SYN, 1961; "Directions '66: The Bigger They Are," ABC, 1966; "Directions '67: From Here on It's Downhill All the Way," ABC, 1967; "NET Playwrights: La Mama Playwrights," NET, 1967; "New York Television Theatre: Apple Pie," NET, 1968; "NYPD: Who's Got the Bundle?," ABC, 1969; "Hallmark Hall of Fame: The Littlest Angel," NBC, 1969; "The Dick Cavett Show," ABC, 1970; "Kraft Music Hall," NBC, 1970; "The Trouble with People," NBC, 1972; "V.D. Blues," NET, 1973; "Marcus Welby, M.D.: Gemini Descending," ABC, 1973; "The Merv Griffin Show," SYN, 1974; "The Mike Douglas Show," SYN, 1975; "Medical Center: The Rip-Off," CBS, 1975; "Maude: Maude's New Friends," CBS, 1976; "The Love Boat: Who's Who," ABC, 1978; "$weepstake$: Vince, Pete and Jessie, Jessica and Rodney," NBC, 1979; "St. Elsewhere: Cora and Arnie," NBC, 1982; "Murder, She Wrote: We're Off to Kill the Wizard," CBS, 1984; "The Love Boat: Partners to the End," ABC, 1985; "The Twilight Zone: Play Time," CBS, 1985; "Who's the Boss?: Junior Executive," ABC, 1985.
TV MOVIES AND MINISERIES: "There Must Be a Pony," ABC, 1986; "The Stepford Children," NBC, 1987.

CODY, IRON EYES
b. Oklahoma, 1916. Cherokee Indian of many TV roles, but best remembered as the noble chief who shed a tear at seeing the polluted world in a TV spot.
AS A GUEST: "The Life and Legend of Wyatt Earp: Wyatt and the Captain," ABC, 1957; "Disneyland: Along the Oregon Trail," ABC, 1957; "Disneyland: The Saga of Andy Burnett," ABC, 1957; "Restless Gun: Pressing Engagement," NBC, 1958; "The Adventures of Rin Tin Tin: Miracle of the Mission," ABC, 1958; "The Lucille Ball-Desi Arnaz Show: Lucy Goes to Alaska," CBS, 1959; "Guestward Ho!: Bill the Candidate," ABC, 1961; "The Rebel: The Burying of Sammy Hart," ABC, 1961; "The Virginian: The Intruders," NBC, 1964; "The FBI: A Mouthful of Dust," ABC, 1965.
TV MOVIES AND MINISERIES: "Something for a Lonely Man," NBC, 1968; "The Quest," NBC, 1976.

COFFIELD, PETER
b. 1946; d. 1983.
AS A REGULAR: "WEB," NBC, 1978.
AND: "Medical Center: Trial by Knife," CBS,

1974; "The Rookies: Solomon's Dilemma," ABC, 1975; "Barnaby Jones: A Simple Case of Terror," CBS, 1977; "The Love Boat: Chubs," ABC, 1978; "Nurse: The Gift," CBS, 1981; "Love, Sidney: Father's Day," NBC, 1982.
TV MOVIES AND MINISERIES: "Cry Rape!," CBS, 1973; "Washington: Behind Closed Doors," ABC, 1977.

COHN, MINDY
b. Los Angeles, CA, May 20, 1966. Actress who played Natalie Green, first to lose her virginity of the "Facts of Life" girls, in case you were wondering.
AS A REGULAR: "The Facts of Life," NBC, 1979-88.
AND: "Diff'rent Strokes: Slumber Party," NBC, 1979; "Diff'rent Strokes: The Older Man," NBC, 1981; "21 Jump Street: Chapel of Love," FOX, 1988;
TV MOVIES AND MINISERIES: "The Facts of Life Goes to Paris," NBC, 1982; "The Facts of Life Down Under," NBC, 1987.

COHOON, PATTI
b. Whittier, CA, January 27, 1959.
AS A REGULAR: "Here Come the Brides," ABC, 1969-70; "Apple's Way," CBS, 1974-75; "The Runaways," NBC, 1979.
AND: "The FBI: The Innocents," ABC, 1970; "Mannix: Bang, Bang, You're Dead," CBS, 1971; "The Courtship of Eddie's Father: My Son, the Artist," ABC, 1971; "Gunsmoke: Trafton," CBS, 1971; "Gunsmoke: P.S. Murry Christmas," CBS, 1971; "Gunsmoke: The River," CBS, 1972; "The Girl with Something Extra: Sugar and Spice and a Quarterback Sneak," NBC, 1973; "Gunsmoke: The Iron Blood of Courage," CBS, 1974; "ABC Afterschool Special: P.J. and the President's Son," ABC, 1976.
TV MOVIES AND MINISERIES: "Acceptable Risks," ABC, 1986.

COLASANTO, NICHOLAS
b. Nicholas Colossanto, Providence, RI, January 19, 1924; d. 1985. Coach Ernie Pantusso of "Cheers."
AS A REGULAR: "Cheers," NBC, 1982-85.
AND: "Playhouse 90: For Whom the Bell Tolls," CBS, 1959; "Car 54, Where Are You?: Je T'Adore Muldoon," NBC, 1963; "The Alfred Hitchcock Hour: Final Escape," CBS, 1964; "My Favorite Martian: Martin's Revoltin' Development," CBS, 1966; "The Man From UNCLE: The Indian Indians Affair," NBC, 1966; "The FBI: The Camel's Nose," ABC, 1966; "Run for Your Life: The Day Time Stopped," NBC, 1966; "Ironside: The Challenge," NBC, 1968; "Mannix: To the Swiftest Death," CBS, 1968; "The FBI: Bitter Harbor," ABC, 1971; "The Streets of San

Francisco: Deathwatch," ABC, 1973; "Kojak: Conspiracy of Fear," CBS, 1974; "Lou Grant: Mob," CBS, 1978.
TV MOVIES AND MINISERIES: "Fame is the Name of the Game," NBC, 1966; "Toma," ABC, 1973; "The Return of the World's Greatest Detective," NBC, 1976.
AS DIRECTOR: "Columbo: Etude in Black," NBC, 1972; "Columbo: Swan Song," NBC, 1974.

COLBERT, CLAUDETTE
b. Lily Chauchoin, Paris, France, September 13, 1903. Oscar-winning screen beauty who came out of retirement in 1987 to play one of "The Two Mrs. Grenvilles."
AS A REGULAR: "Woman!," CBS, 1959.
AND: "Best of Broadway: The Royal Family," CBS, 1954; "Climax!: The White Carnation," CBS, 1954; "Ford Theatre: Magic Formula," NBC, 1955; "Best of Broadway: The Guardsman," CBS, 1955; "Climax!: Private Worlds," CBS, 1955; "Ford Theatre: While We're Young," NBC, 1955; "Climax!: The Deliverance of Sister Cecilia," CBS, 1955; "The Loretta Young Show: A Pattern of Deceit," NBC, 1955; "Ford Star Jubilee: Blithe Spirit," CBS, 1956; "Robert Montgomery Presents: After All These Years," NBC, 1956; "The Steve Allen Show," NBC, 1956; "Playhouse 90: One Coat of White," CBS, 1957; "Dick Powell's Zane Grey Theatre: Blood in the Dust," CBS, 1957; "The General Motors 50th Anniversary Show," NBC, 1957; "Telephone Time: Novel Appeal," ABC, 1957; "G.E. Theatre: The Last Town Car," CBS, 1958; "The Steve Allen Show," NBC, 1958; "Colgate Theatre: Welcome to Washington," NBC, 1958; "Pontiac Star Parade: An Evening with Perry Como," NBC, 1959; "The Bells of St. Mary's," CBS, 1959; "Dick Powell's Zane Grey Theatre: So Young the Savage Land," CBS, 1960.
TV MOVIES AND MINISERIES: "The Two Mrs. Grenvilles," NBC, 1987.

COLBERT, ROBERT
b. Long Beach, CA. Actor who played Stuart Brooks on "The Young and the Restless."
AS A REGULAR: "Maverick," ABC, 1961; "The Time Tunnel," ABC, 1966-67; "The Young and the Restless," CBS, 1973-83.
AND: "Secret Agent 7: Prussian Jewel Case," SYN, 1959; "Hawaiian Eye: The Kamehameha Cloak," ABC, 1960; "Sugarfoot: Blackwater Swamp," ABC, 1960; "Bourbon Street Beat: Twice Betrayed," ABC, 1960; "Colt .45: Attack," ABC, 1960; "The Alaskans: White Vengeance," ABC, 1960; "Bronco: End of a Rope," ABC, 1960; "Colt .45: Showdown at Goldtown," ABC, 1960; "77 Sunset Strip: The Attic," ABC, 1960; "SurfSide 6: The Impractical Joker," ABC, 1961; "77 Sunset Strip: Old Cardsharps Never Die," ABC, 1961; "Hawaiian Eye: A Taste for Money,"

ABC, 1961; "77 Sunset Strip: The Man in the Crowd," ABC, 1961; "Hawaiian Eye: Kill a Grey Fox," ABC, 1961; "Lawman: The Locket," ABC, 1962; "Hawaiian Eye: Little Miss Rich Witch," ABC, 1962; "The Roaring Twenties: Footlights," ABC, 1962; "Checkmate: Ride a Wild Horse," CBS, 1962; "Bus Stop: Door Without a Key," ABC, 1962; "The Virginian: Impasse," NBC, 1962; "Thriller: The Bride Who Died Twice," NBC, 1962; "Alcoa Premiere: Impact of an Execution," ABC, 1963; "My Favorite Martian: That Little Old Matchmaker, Martin," CBS, 1963; "77 Sunset Strip: Dead as in Dude," ABC, 1964; "The Virginian: Return a Stranger," NBC, 1964; "Twelve O'Clock High: The Loneliest Place in the World," ABC, 1965; "Twelve O'Clock High: Big Brother," ABC, 1965; "The FBI: The Forests of the Night," ABC, 1966; "Dream Girl of '67," ABC, 1967; "That Girl: Fly Me to the Moon," ABC, 1969; "Mannix: Who Is Sylvia?," CBS, 1970; "Mannix: Duet for Three," CBS, 1970; "Mission: Impossible: Bag Woman," CBS, 1971; "Mannix: A Choice of Evils," CBS, 1971; "Mannix: A Walk in the Shadows," CBS, 1972; "Alias Smith and Jones: Twenty-One Days to Tenstrike," ABC, 1972; "Archer: Shades of Blue," NBC, 1975; "Knight Rider: Mouth of the Snake," NBC, 1983; "Simon & Simon: Simon Without Simon," CBS, 1985.
TV MOVIES AND MINISERIES: "City Beneath the Sea," NBC, 1971.

COLBY, BARBARA
d. 1975. Actress who was murdered right after being cast as Julie Erskine, boss of Phyllis Lindstrom (Cloris Leachman).
AS A REGULAR: "Phyllis," CBS, 1975.
AND: "Columbo: Murder by the Book," NBC, 1971; "The FBI: The Exchange," ABC, 1973; "McMillan and Wife: The Devil You Say," NBC, 1973; "Gunsmoke: The Iron Men," CBS, 1974; "The Mary Tyler Moore Show: Will Mary Richards Go to Jail?," CBS, 1974; "Medical Center: Trial by Knife," CBS, 1974; "The Mary Tyler Moore Show: You Try to Be a Nice Guy," CBS, 1975.
TV MOVIES AND MINISERIES: "A Brand New Life," ABC, 1973.

COLBY, MARION
b. 1922; d. 1987. Singer.
AS A REGULAR: "Broadway Open House," NBC, 1951; "Doodles Weaver," NBC, 1951; "The Henny and Rocky Show," ABC, 1955.
AND: "American Bandstand," ABC, 1958; "Milton Berle Special," NBC, 1959.

COLE, CAROL
b. West Medford, MA, October 17, 1944.
AS A REGULAR: "Grady," NBC, 1975-76.

AND: "T.H.E. Cat: The Ninety Percent Blues,"
NBC, 1967; "Sanford & Son: The Family Man,"
NBC, 1975.

COLE, DENNIS
b. *Detroit, MI, 1940.* Generic TV hunk.
AS A REGULAR: "Paradise Bay," NBC, 1965-66;
"The Felony Squad," ABC, 1966-69;
"Bracken's World," NBC, 1969-70;
"Bearcats!," CBS, 1971; "The Young and the
Restless," CBS, 1981-82.
AND: "Medical Center: Pitfall," CBS, 1971;
"Love, American Style: Love and the Three-
Timer," ABC, 1974; "The Streets of San
Francisco: Bird of Prey," ABC, 1974; "Police
Story: Monster Manor," NBC, 1976; "The Quest:
The Captive," NBC, 1976; "The Love Boat: A
Tasteful Affair," ABC, 1977; "Police Woman:
Murder with Pretty People," NBC, 1978; "The
Eddie Capra Mysteries: Murder, Murder," NBC,
1978; "Charlie's Angels: Angels on Skis," ABC,
1979; "Vega$; All Kinds of Love," ABC, 1980;
"Fantasy Island: Jungle Man," ABC, 1980; "The
Love Boat: From Here to Maternity," ABC, 1980;
"The Fall Guy: The Winner," ABC, 1984; "The
A-Team: Where's the Monster When You Need
Him?," NBC, 1985; "Simon & Simon: The Last
Big Break," CBS, 1986; "The New Mike
Hammer: Lady Killer," CBS, 1987.
TV MOVIES AND MINISERIES:: "Powderkeg," CBS,
1971; "Connection," ABC, 1973; "The Barbary
Coast," ABC, 1975.

COLE, GARY
Actor who plays cop-turned-talk-radio-host
Jack Killian, the midnight caller.
AS A REGULAR: "Midnight Caller," NBC, 1988- .
AND: "Miami Vice: Trust Fund," NBC, 1986.
TV MOVIES AND MINISERIES: "Heart of Steel," ABC,
1983; "Fatal Vision," NBC, 1984; "Vital
Signs," CBS, 1986; "Echoes in the Darkness,"
CBS, 1987; "Those She Left Behind," NBC,
1989.

COLE, MICHAEL
b. *Madison, WI, 1945.* Actor who played Pete
Cochran on "The Mod Squad."
AS A REGULAR: "The Mod Squad," ABC, 1968-73.
AND: "Gunsmoke: Snap Decision," CBS, 1966;
"The Dating Game," ABC, 1969; "Police Story:
The Ripper," NBC, 1974; "Police Story: The
Witness," NBC, 1975; "The Love Boat: Reunion
Cruise," ABC, 1979; "Vega$: No Way to Treat a
Victim," ABC, 1981; "Murder, She Wrote:
Murder, She Spoke," CBS, 1987.
TV MOVIES AND MINISERIES: "The Last Child,"
ABC, 1971; "Beg, Borrow ... or Steal," CBS,
1973; "Evening in Byzantium," SYN, 1978;
"The Return of Mod Squad," ABC, 1979.

COLE, NAT "KING"
b. *Nathaniel Adams Coles, Montgomery, AL,
1919; d. 1965.* Jazz singer and pianist with
timeless talent whose TV show was dropped
for lack of sponsorship. He made numerous
guest appearances after that and died of lung
cancer.
AS A REGULAR: "The Nat King Cole Show," NBC,
1956.
AND: "President's Birthday Party," CBS, 1956;
"The Perry Como Show," NBC, 1956; "The
Walter Winchell Show," NBC, 1956; "Five Stars
in Springtime," NBC, 1957; "Person to Person,"
CBS, 1957; "Tony Martin Special," NBC, 1957;
"The Ed Sullivan Show," CBS, 1958; "The Perry
Como Show," NBC, 1959; "The George Gobel
Show," NBC, 1959; "Some of Manie's Friends,"
NBC, 1959; "Pat Boone Chevy Showroom,"
ABC, 1959; "Perry Como's Kraft Music Hall,"
NBC, 1959; "The Golden Circle," ABC, 1959;
"This Is Your Life," NBC, 1960; "Steve Allen
Plymouth Show," NBC, 1960; "Startime:
Academy Award Songs," NBC, 1960; "Eleanor
Roosevelt's Jubilee," NBC, 1960; "Dinah Shore
Chevy Show," NBC, 1960; "Something Special,"
NBC, 1960; "The Ed Sullivan Show," CBS, 1961;
"The Garry Moore Show," CBS, 1961; "The Jack
Paar Show," NBC, 1961; "Here's Hollywood,"
NBC, 1961; "Dinah Shore Special," NBC, 1961;
"The Jack Paar Program," NBC, 1962; "The
Garry Moore Show," CBS, 1962; "The Jack
Benny Program," CBS, 1964; "The Garry Moore
Show," CBS, 1964; "The Jack Paar Program,"
NBC, 1964.

COLE, TINA
b. *Hollywood, CA, 1943.* Actress who played
Katie Douglas, wife of Robbie (Don Grady) on
"My Three Sons."
AS A REGULAR: "Hawaiian Eye," ABC, 1963; "My
Three Sons," CBS, 1967-72.
AND: "My Three Sons: House for Sale," ABC,
1964; "My Three Sons: Robbie Works the Coffee
House Set," ABC, 1964; "My Three Sons: Robbie
and the Little Stranger," CBS, 1966; "To Rome
with Love: Rome Is Where You Find It," CBS,
1970; "The Rookies: Point of Impact," ABC,
1973.

COLEMAN, DABNEY
b. *Austin, TX, January 2, 1932.* Actor who's
played TV heels Buffalo Bill Bittinger and
Slap Maxwell.
AS A REGULAR: "That Girl," ABC, 1966-67;
"Bright Promise," NBC, 1969-72; "Mary
Hartman, Mary Hartman," SYN, 1976-78;
"Apple Pie," ABC, 1978; "Buffalo Bill," NBC,
1983-84; "The Slap Maxwell Story," ABC,
1987-88.
AND: "The Outer Limits: Specimen Unknown,"

ABC, 1964; "The Fugitive: World's End," ABC, 1964; "The Outer Limits: The Mice," ABC, 1964; "The Outer Limits: Wolf 359," ABC, 1964; "The Fugitive: Nicest Fella You'd Ever Want to Meet," ABC, 1965; "The FBI: Slow March Up a Steep Hill," ABC, 1965; "I Dream of Jeannie: Anybody Here Seen Jeannie?," NBC, 1965; "The Donna Reed Show: Rally Round the Girls, Boys," ABC, 1965; "The FBI: The Hijackers," ABC, 1965; "Hazel: A-Hunting We Will Go," CBS, 1965; "The FBI: The Conspirators," ABC, 1967; "The FBI: Flight," ABC, 1969; "Room 222: Choose One: And They Lived Happily/Unhappily Ever After," ABC, 1970; "Nanny and the Professor: The Humanization of Herbert T. Peabody," ABC, 1970; "The FBI: Incident in the Desert," ABC, 1970; "Dan August: The King Is Dead," ABC, 1970; "The FBI: The Game of Terror," ABC, 1971; "Mannix: Portrait of a Hero," CBS, 1972; "Owen Marshall, Counselor at Law: Who Saw Him Die?," ABC, 1972; "Room 222: The Rights of Others," ABC, 1973; "Griff: All the Lonely People," ABC, 1973; "Columbo: Double Shock," NBC, 1973; "The FBI: Survival," ABC, 1974; "The Streets of San Francisco: Jacob's Boy," ABC, 1974; "Kojak: Therapy in Dynamite," CBS, 1974; "McMillan and Wife: Aftershock," NBC, 1975; "The Mary Tyler Moore Show: The Seminar," CBS, 1976; "Bert D'Angelo/Superstar: The Brown Horse Connection," ABC, 1976; "The Streets of San Francisco: The Drop," ABC, 1976; "Police Story: Three Days to Thirty," NBC, 1976; "Switch: One of Our Zeppelins Is Missing," CBS, 1976; "Barnaby Jones: Final Judgement," CBS, 1978; "Diff'rent Strokes: Arnold's Girlfriend," NBC, 1979; "The Love Boat: Poor Little Rich Girl," ABC, 1979; "Barnaby Jones: Indoctrination in Evil," CBS, 1979; "Saturday Night Live," NBC, 1987; "Dolly," ABC, 1988; "It's Garry Shandling's Show: Save Mr. Peck's," FOX, 1989.
TV MOVIES AND MINISERIES: "The Brotherhood of the Bell," CBS, 1970; "Savage," NBC, 1973; "Dying Room Only," ABC, 1973; "The President's Plane Is Missing," ABC, 1973; "Medical Center: Aftershock," CBS, 1975; "Attack on Terror: The FBI Versus the Ku Klux Klan," CBS, 1975; "Returning Home," ABC, 1975; "Kiss Me, Kill Me," ABC, 1976; "More Than Friends," ABC, 1978; "When She Was Bad," ABC, 1979; "Callie & Son," CBS, 1981; "Murrow," HBO, 1986; "Fresno," CBS, 1986; "Guilty of Innocence: The Lenell Geter Story," CBS, 1987; "Sworn to Silence," ABC, 1987; "Baby M," ABC, 1988; "Maybe Baby," NBC, 1988.
* Emmies: 1987.

COLEMAN, GARY
b. Zion, IL, February 8, 1968. Short, stocky child actor who's virtually disappeared from the show-biz scene.

AS A REGULAR: "Diff'rent Strokes," NBC, 1978-85; ABC, 1985-86.
AND: "Fernwood 2-Night," SYN, 1977; "The Tonight Show Starring Johnny Carson," NBC, 1978; "Buck Rogers in the 25th Century: Cosmic Whiz Kid," NBC, 1979; "Lucy Comes to NBC," NBC, 1980; "Silver Spoons: The Great Computer Caper," NBC, 1982; "Simon & Simon: Like Father, Like Son," CBS, 1986.
TV MOVIES AND MINISERIES: "The Kid From Left Field," NBC, 1979; "The Fantastic World of D.C. Collins," NBC, 1984; "Playing with Fire," NBC, 1985.
* Coleman broke into show biz at age 5, when he did some modeling for a fashion show. Then he appeared in several TV commercials and was spotted by producer Norman Lear, who was planning a modern-day remake of "The Little Rascals." Lear ended up casting him as Arnold on "Diff'rent Strokes."

COLEMAN, JACK
b. Easton, PA, February 21, 1958. Steven Carrington on "Dynasty."
AS A REGULAR: "Days of Our Lives," NBC, 1981-82; "Dynasty," ABC, 1982-89.
AND: "Glitter: In Tennis Love Means Nothing," ABC, 1984; "Finder of Lost Loves: Wayward Dreams," ABC, 1985; "The Love Boat: The Racer's Edge," ABC, 1985.
TV MOVIES AND MINISERIES: "Bridesmaids," CBS, 1989.

COLICOS, JOHN
b. Canada, December 10, 1928. Actor who played Mikkos Cassadine on "General Hospital."
AS A REGULAR: "The Adventures of Hiram Holliday," NBC, 1956; "Battlestar Galactica," ABC, 1978-79; "General Hospital," ABC, 1981.
AND: "You Are There: Mr. Christian Seizes the Bounty," CBS, 1956; "Studio One: The Rice Sprout Song," CBS, 1957; "Du Pont Show of the Month: The Count of Monte Cristo," CBS, 1958; "Hallmark Hall of Fame: Berkeley Square," NBC, 1959; "Du Pont Show of the Month: Oliver Twist," CBS, 1959; "U.S. Steel Hour: The Impostor," CBS, 1960; "U.S. Steel Hour: The Case of the Missing Wife, CBS, 1960; "Our American Heritage: Not Without Honor," NBC, 1960; "Omnibus: He Shall Have Power," NBC, 1960; "Family Classics: The Three Musketeers," CBS, 1960; "Our American Heritage: Born a Giant," NBC, 1960; "Directions '62: The Saintmaker's Christmas Eve," ABC, 1961; "Look Up and Live: Many Voices," CBS, 1961; "Hallmark Hall of Fame: Cyrano de Bergerac," NBC, 1962; "U.S. Steel Hour: The Troubled Heart," CBS, 1963; "The Defenders: The Silent Killers," CBS, 1965; "T.H.E. Cat: A Slight

Family Trait," NBC, 1967; "Mannix: In Need of a Friend," CBS, 1968; "Then Came Bronson: Still Waters," NBC, 1969; "Mission: Impossible: Flight," CBS, 1970; "Mannix: A Day Filled with Shadows," CBS, 1970; "The FBI: The Test," ABC, 1972; "Mannix: Cry Pigeon," CBS, 1972; "Mannix: The Inside Man," CBS, 1972; "The Magician: Ripoff," NBC, 1974; "Medical Center: Heel of the Tyrant," CBS, 1974; "Gunsmoke: Hard Labor," CBS, 1975; "Hawaii Five-O: Death's Name is Sam," CBS, 1975; "Petrocelli: Terror on Wheels," NBC, 1975; "Medical Center: You Can't Annul My Baby," CBS, 1976; "Switch: Coronado Circle," CBS, 1977; "Charlie's Angels: Angels in a Box," ABC, 1978; "Vega$: Dan Tanna Is Dead," ABC, 1979; "The Yellow Rose: Sport of Kings," NBC, 1984; "Scarecrow and Mrs. King: Playing Possum," CBS, 1984; "Night Heat: The Victim," CBS, 1987; "Night Heat: Blowing Bubbles," CBS, 1988.
TV MOVIES AND MINISERIES: "Goodbye Raggedy Ann," CBS, 1971; "A Matter of Wife and Death," NBC, 1975; "The Bastard," SYN, 1978; "The Paradise Connection," CBS, 1979.

COLLIER, DON
b. Inglewood, CA, 1928. Rough-hewn actor who shows up in a lot of westerns, most recently as Tompkins on "The Young Riders."
AS A REGULAR: "The Outlaws," NBC, 1960-62; "The High Chaparral," NBC, 1967-71; "The Young Riders," ABC, 1989- .
AND: "Here's Hollywood," NBC, 1961; "The Wide Country: Our Ernie Kills People," NBC, 1962; "Bonanza: The Good Samaritan," NBC, 1962; "Death Valley Days: Loss of Faith," SYN, 1963; "Temple Houston: The Dark Madonna," NBC, 1963; "Perry Mason: The Case of the Fifty Millionth Frenchman," CBS, 1964; "The Virginian: The Girl From Yesterday," NBC, 1964; "Bonanza: The Flannel-Mouth Gun," NBC, 1965; "Little House on the Prairie: The Runaway Caboose," NBC, 1976; "Highway to Heaven: A Dream of Wild Horses," NBC, 1987.
TV MOVIES AND MINISERIES: "Key West," NBC, 1973; "The Last Ride of the Dalton Gang," NBC, 1979; "War and Remembrance," ABC, 1988, 1989.

COLLIER, LOIS
b. Madelyn Jones, Salley, SC, March 21, 1919.
AS A REGULAR: "Boston Blackie," SYN, 1951-53.

COLLINGE, PATRICIA
b. Dublin, Ireland, September 20, 1894; d. 1974. Stage actress who played the mother of Teresa Wright in Alfred Hitchcock's "Shadow of a Doubt" and whose association with Hitchcock extended to her TV work.

AS A GUEST: "The Web: Midnight Guest," CBS, 1953; "Studio One: The River Garden," CBS, 1953; "Goodyear TV Playhouse: The Rumor," NBC, 1953; "Studio One: Crime at Blossom's," CBS, 1953; "Love Story: The Wedding Dress," SYN, 1954; "Appointment with Adventure: A Sword Has Two Edges," CBS, 1955; "Alfred Hitchcock Presents: The Cheney Vase," CBS, 1955; "Armstrong Circle Theatre: Ward Three: 4 P.M. to Midnight," NBC, 1956; "Front Row Center: Hawk's Head," CBS, 1956; "Alfred Hitchcock Presents: The Rose Garden," CBS, 1956; "Climax!: The Trouble at Number 5," CBS, 1957; "Alfred Hitchcock Presents: Across the Threshhold," CBS, 1960; "Alfred Hitchcock Presents: The Landlady," NBC, 1961; "U.S. Steel Hour: Scene of the Crime," CBS, 1962; "The Alfred Hitchcock Hour: Bonfire," CBS, 1962; "East Side/West Side: Creeps Live Here," CBS, 1963; "The Alfred Hitchcock Hour: The Ordeal of Mrs. Snow," NBC, 1964.

COLLINGWOOD, CHARLES
b. Three Rivers, MI, June 4, 1917; d. 1985.
AS A REGULAR: "The Big Question," CBS, 1951; "Adventure," CBS, 1953; "Odyssey," CBS, 1957; "Conquest," CBS, 1959-60; "Person to Person," CBS, 1959-61; "Portrait," CBS, 1963; "Chronicle," CBS, 1963-64.

COLLINS, DOROTHY
b. Marjorie Chandler, Windsor, Ontario, Canada, November 18, 1926. Musical-comedy performer who's best remembered as the brunette on "Candid Camera" who was always pulling jokes on hapless victims.
AS A REGULAR: "Your Hit Parade," NBC, 1950-57; CBS, 1958-59; "Candid Camera," CBS, 1960-61.
AND: "The Jonathan Winters Show," NBC, 1956; "The Jonathan Winters Show," NBC, 1957; "The Steve Allen Show," NBC, 1957; "U.S. Steel Hour: Who's Earnest?," CBS, 1957; "The Perry Como Show," NBC, 1957; "The Jimmy Dean Show," CBS, 1957; "Get Set, Go!," SYN, 1957; "The Big Record," CBS, 1958; "Pat Boone Chevy Showroom," ABC, 1958; "The Steve Allen Show," NBC, 1958; "Pat Boone Chevy Showroom," ABC, 1959; "The Ed Sullivan Show," CBS, 1959; "Bell Telephone Hour: We Two," NBC, 1960; "Perry Como's Kraft Music Hall," NBC, 1960; "Pat Boone Chevy Show-room," ABC, 1960; "The Arthur Murray Party for Bob Hope," NBC, 1960; "American Bandstand," ABC, 1960; "The Garry Moore Show," CBS, 1960; "Bell Telephone Hour: Designs in Music," NBC, 1961; "Password," CBS, 1961; "Password," CBS, 1962; "Perry Como's Kraft Music Hall," NBC, 1962; "To Tell the Truth," CBS, 1962; "The Garry Moore Show," CBS, 1962; "The

Garry Moore Show," CBS, 1963; "The Match Game," NBC, 1963; "The Danny Kaye Show," CBS, 1964; "Hollywood Palace," ABC, 1964; "The Jimmy Dean Show," ABC, 1964; "The Danny Kaye Show," CBS, 1965.

COLLINS, GARY
b. Venice, CA, April 30, 1938. Antiseptic actor and talk-show host.

AS A REGULAR: "The Wackiest Ship in the Army," NBC, 1965-66; "The Iron Horse," ABC, 1966-68; "The Sixth Sense," ABC, 1972; "Born Free," NBC, 1974; "Hour Magazine," SYN, 1985-88; "Home," ABC, 1990- .

AND: "Love, American Style: Love and the Other Guy," ABC, 1969; "Love, American Style: Love and the Tattoo," ABC, 1969; "The Virginian: Incident at Diablo Crossing," NBC, 1969; "The FBI: Center of Peril," ABC, 1971; "McCloud: Fifth Man in a String Quartet," NBC, 1972; "Marcus Welby, M.D.: I'm Really Trying," ABC, 1972; "Love, American Style: Love and the Sex Survey," ABC, 1972; "Tattletales," CBS, 1974; "Love, American Style: Love and the Seven-Year Wait," ABC, 1974; "Police Story: Country Boy," NBC, 1974; "Police Story: Bought and Paid For," NBC, 1976; "Alice: The Principal of the Thing," CBS, 1978; "Police Woman: Flip of a Coin," NBC, 1978; "Charlie's Angels: Mother Angel," ABC, 1978; "The Love Boat: Ship of Ghouls," ABC, 1978; "Gimme a Break: Second Chance," NBC, 1986.

TV MOVIES AND MINISERIES: "Quarantined," ABC, 1970; "Getting Away From It All," ABC, 1972; "Houston, We've Got a Problem," ABC, 1974; "The Night They Took Miss Beautiful," NBC, 1977; "Roots," ABC, 1977; "The Kid From Left Field," NBC, 1979.

COLLINS, JOAN
b. London, England, May 23, 1933. Sexpot actress of the fifties who was in deserved obscurity when her career was resurrected with the role of the evil Alexis on "Dynasty." After milking that for all it was worth, Collins seems headed for no-name city once again.

AS A REGULAR: "Dynasty," ABC, 1981-88.

AND: "The Steve Allen Show," NBC, 1957; "The Ed Sullivan Show," CBS, 1957; "Bob Hope Special," NBC, 1959; "Person to Person," CBS, 1961; "The Bob Hope Show," NBC, 1962; "Here's Hollywood," NBC, 1962; "Run for Your Life: The Borders of Barbarism," NBC, 1966; "The Man From UNCLE: The Galatea Affair," NBC, 1966; "Star Trek: The City on the Edge of Forever," NBC, 1967; "Batman: Ring Around the Riddler," ABC, 1967; "Batman: The Wail of the Siren," ABC, 1967; "The Virginian: The Lady From Wichita," NBC, 1967; "The Danny Thomas Hour: The Demon Under the Bed," NBC, 1967; "Mission: Impossible: Nicole," CBS, 1969; "The

Persuaders: Five Miles to Midnight," ABC, 1972; "Hallmark Hall of Fame: The Man Who Came to Dinner," NBC, 1972; "Orson Welles' Great Mysteries: The Dinner Party," SYN, 1973; "Showoffs," ABC, 1975; "Switch: Stung From Beyond," CBS, 1975; "Police Woman: The Pawnshop," NBC, 1976; "Police Woman: The Trick Book," NBC, 1976; "Starsky and Hutch: Starsky and Hutch on Playboy Island," ABC, 1977; "The John Davidson Show," SYN, 1981; "The Love Boat: The Captain's Crush," ABC, 1983; "The Tonight Show Starring Johnny Carson," NBC, 1986; "Hour Magazine," SYN, 1986.

TV MOVIES AND MINISERIES: "Drive Hard, Drive Fast," NBC, 1973; "The Moneychangers," NBC, 1976; "The Wild Women of Chastity Gulch," ABC, 1982; "The Making of a Male Model," ABC, 1983; "Her Life as a Man," NBC, 1984; "The Cartier Affair," NBC, 1984; "Sins," CBS, 1986; "Monte Carlo," CBS, 1986.

TV'S TOP TEN, 1984-85

1. Dynasty (ABC)
2. Dallas (CBS)
3. The Cosby Show (NBC)
4. 60 Minutes (CBS)
5. Family Ties (NBC)
6. The A-Team (NBC)
7. Simon & Simon (CBS)
8. Murder, She Wrote (CBS)
9. Knots Landing (CBS)
10. Falcon Crest (CBS)
10. Crazy Like a Fox (CBS)

COLLINS, RAY
b. Sacramento, CA, 1888; d. 1965. Prolific movie actor who played Lt. Arthur Tragg on "Perry Mason."

AS A REGULAR: "The Halls of Ivy," CBS, 1954; "Perry Mason," CBS, 1957-64.

AND: "Cavalcade of America: The Last Will of Daniel Webster," ABC, 1953; "Climax!: Champion," CBS, 1955; "You Are There: P.T. Barnum Presents Jenny Lind," CBS, 1955; "Science Fiction Theatre: The Frozen Sound," SYN, 1955; "The 20th Century-Fox Hour: Miracle on 34th Street," CBS, 1955; "Science Fiction Theatre: Target: Hurricane," SYN, 1956; "The 20th Century-Fox Hour: Gun in His Hand," CBS, 1956; "Ford Star Jubilee: Twentieth Century," CBS, 1956; "Science Fiction Theatre: The Sound That Kills," SYN, 1956; "Studio One: The Star Spangled Soldier," CBS, 1956; "Studio One: A Special Announcement," CBS, 1956; "Alfred Hitchcock Presents: Conversation with a Corpse," CBS, 1956; "On Trial: The Trial of Mary Suratt," NBC, 1956; "Playhouse 90:

Invitation to a Gunfighter," CBS, 1957; "Father Knows Best: Betty Goes to College," CBS, 1960.

COLLINS, RUSSELL

b. *Indianapolis, IN, October 8, 1897; d. 1965.*
AS A REGULAR: "Ichabod and Me," CBS, 1961-62; "Many Happy Returns," CBS, 1964-65.
AND: "Science Fiction Theatre: The Sound of Murder," SYN, 1955; "Kraft Television Theatre: Shadow of Suspicion," NBC, 1956; "Alfred Hitchcock Presents: John Brown's Body," CBS, 1956; "U.S. Steel Hour: Shadow of Evil," CBS, 1957; "Kraft Theatre: The Velvet Trap," NBC, 1958; "Shirley Temple's Storybook: The Nightingale," NBC, 1958; "Du Pont Show of the Month: The Human Comedy," CBS, 1959; "The Ransom of Red Chief," NBC, 1959; "Have Gun, Will Travel: Crowbait," CBS, 1960; "The Tall Man: Big Sam's Boy," NBC, 1961; "The Islanders: A Rope for Charlie Munday," ABC, 1961; "Acapulco: Carbon Copy-Cat," NBC, 1961; "Wagon Train: The Tiburcio Mendez Story," NBC, 1961; "Alfred Hitchcock Presents: Deathmate," NBC, 1961; "The Twilight Zone: Kick the Can," CBS, 1962; "The Many Loves of Dobie Gillis: Names My Mother Called Me," CBS, 1962; "Hazel: Potluck a la Mode," NBC, 1963; "The Dick Van Dyke Show: Very Old Shoes, Very Old Rice," CBS, 1963; "The Fugitive: Come Watch Me Die," ABC, 1964; "The Outer Limits: Don't Open Till Doomsday," ABC, 1964; "Channing: Where Are the Snows ...?," ABC, 1964; "Ben Casey: A Falcon's Eye, a Lion's Heart, a Girl's Hand," ABC, 1964; "Hazel: The Countess," NBC, 1964; "The Breaking Point: Shadow of a Starless Night," ABC, 1964; "The Beverly Hillbillies: The Critter Doctor," CBS, 1964; "Ben Casey: But Who Shall Beat the Drums?," ABC, 1964; "The Fugitive: Man on a String," ABC, 1964; "The Farmer's Daughter: Forever Is a Cast-Iron Mess," ABC, 1965.

COLLINS, STEPHEN

b. *Des Moines, IA, October 1, 1949.* Handsome TV action hero.
AS A REGULAR: "Tales of the Gold Monkey," ABC, 1982-83; "Tattinger's," NBC, 1988; "Nick & Hillary," NBC, 1989; "Working It Out," NBC, 1990- .
AND: "Jigsaw John: The Mourning Line," NBC, 1976.
TV MOVIES AND MINISERIES: "Best Sellers: The Rhinemann Exchange," NBC, 1977; "The Henderson Monster," CBS, 1980; "Threesome," CBS, 1984; "Dark Mirror," ABC, 1984; "The Two Mrs. Grenvilles," NBC, 1987; "Weekend War," ABC, 1988.

COLLYER, BUD

b. *New York City, NY, June 18, 1908; d. 1969.*

Game show emcee who was Superman on the radio.
AS A REGULAR: "Missus Goes a-Shopping," CBS, 1944-49; "Break the Bank," ABC, 1948-49; NBC, 1949-52; CBS, 1952-53; "Winner Take All," CBS, 1948-50; "Talent Jackpot," DUM, 1949; "Beat the Clock," CBS, 1950-58; ABC, 1958-61; "Say It with Acting," NBC, 1949-50, ABC, 1951-52; "Masquerade Party," NBC, 1952; "Quick As a Flash," ABC, 1953-54; "On Your Way," DUM, 1953-54; "Talent Patrol," ABC, 1953; "Feather Your Nest," NBC, 1954-56; "To Tell the Truth," CBS, 1956-67; "Number Please," ABC, 1961.
AND: "I've Got a Secret," CBS, 1956; "Five Stars in Springtime," NBC, 1957.

COLLYER, JUNE

b. *Dorothea Heermance, New York City, NY, August 19, 1907; d. 1968.* Actress who was married to Stu Erwin in real life and on his TV series; the sister of Bud Collyer.
AS A REGULAR: "The Stu Erwin Show," ABC, 1950-55.

COLMAN, RONALD

b. *Richmond, England, February 9, 1891; d. 1958.* Silken-voiced matinee idol who brought his succesful radio series to television for one season; Colman played Ivy College president William Todhunter Hall.
AS A REGULAR: "The Halls of Ivy," CBS, 1954-55.
AND: "Four Star Playhouse: The Lost Silk Hat," CBS, 1952; "Four Star Playhouse: The Man Who Walked Out on Himself," CBS, 1953; "Four Star Playhouse: The Ladies on His Mind," CBS, 1953; "Four Star Playhouse: A String of Pearls," CBS, 1954; "The Jack Benny Program," CBS, 1956; "G.E. Theatre: The Chess Game," CBS, 1956; "Studio 57: Perfect Likeness," SYN, 1957.

COLOMBY, SCOTT

b. *Brooklyn, NY, September 19, 1952.*
AS A REGULAR: "Sons and Daughters," CBS, 1974; "Szysznyk," CBS, 1977-78.
AND: "Ironside: Act of Vengeance," NBC, 1974; "One Day at a Time: Barbara Plus Two," CBS, 1977; "One Day at a Time: Bob's New Girl," CBS, 1978; "Quincy: Unhappy Hour," NBC, 1980; "St. Elsewhere: Give the Boy a Hand," NBC, 1985; "The A-Team: Members Only," NBC, 1986.
TV MOVIES AND MINISERIES: "Can Ellen Be Saved?," ABC, 1974; "Senior Year," CBS, 1974; "Are You in the House Alone?," CBS, 1978; "Angel on My Shoulder," ABC, 1980.

COLONNA, JERRY

b. *Gerald Colonna, Boston, MA, 1904; d. 1986.* Bug-eyed, fast-talking comic ("Amazing, isn't

it?") who was Bob Hope's longtime sidekick.
AS A REGULAR: "The Jerry Colonna Show," ABC,
1951; "Bob Hope Special," NBC, 1951-66.
AND: "The Rosemary Clooney Show," SYN, 1957;
"Five Star Comedy Party," ABC, 1957; "Climax!:
The Giant Killer," CBS, 1957; "I've Got a Secret,"
CBS, 1957; "Pinocchio," NBC, 1957; "The Gale
Storm Show: Come Home, Little Beatnik," CBS,
1958; "Christophers: Everyone Has a Job to Do,"
SYN, 1958; "Frances Langford Special," NBC,
1959; "Christophers: Some Insights on George
Washington," SYN, 1959; "Shirley Temple's
Storybook: Babes in Toyland," NBC, 1960;
"Here's Hollywood," NBC, 1962; "McHale's
Navy: Hello, McHale? Colonna!," ABC, 1965;
"The Monkees: Gift Horse," NBC, 1966.

COLT, MARSHALL
b. New Orleans, LA, 1948.
AS A REGULAR: "McClain's Law," NBC, 1981-82;
"Lottery," ABC, 1983-84.
AND: "Barnaby Jones: The Protectors," CBS, 1979;
"Barnaby Jones: Indoctrination in Evil," CBS,
1979.
TV MOVIES AND MINISERIES: "Beverly Hills
Madam," NBC, 1986; "Mercy or Murder?"
NBC, 1987; "Guilty of Innocence: The Lenell
Geter Story," CBS, 1987.

COMO, PERRY
*b. Pierno Como, Canonsburg, PA, May 18,
1912.* Beloved singer with a relaxed style and
amiable manner; a TV staple for more than
twenty years.
AS A REGULAR: "The Chesterfield Supper Club,"
NBC, 1948-50; "The Perry Como Show," CBS,
1950-55; NBC, 1955-59; "Perry Como's Kraft
Music Hall," NBC, 1959-63; "Perry Como
Special," NBC, 1963-73; CBS, 1974-76; ABC,
1976- .
AND: "The Walter Winchell Show," NBC, 1956;
"The Bob Hope Show," NBC, 1956; "The Ed
Sullivan Show," CBS, 1956; "The Dinah Shore
Chevy Show," NBC, 1957; "Tenth Annual Emmy
Awards," NBC, 1958; "Some of Manie's Friends,"
NBC, 1959; "Pontiac Star Parade: An Evening
with Perry Como," NBC, 1959; "Bing Crosby
Special," ABC, 1960; "Here's Hollywood," NBC,
1960; "Celebrity Golf," NBC, 1960; "Bob Hope
Special: Potomac Madness," NBC, 1960; "Danny
Thomas Special," NBC, 1965; "The Flip Wilson
Show," NBC, 1970; "The Pearl Bailey Show,"
ABC, 1971; "A Salute to Television's 25th
Anniversary," ABC, 1972; "Julie Andrews on
Sesame Street," ABC, 1973; "Ann-Margret
Special," NBC, 1977.
* Emmies: 1955, 1956, 1957, 1959.

COMPTON, FORREST
b. Reading, PA, September 15, 1925. Actor who

played Mike Karr on "The Edge of Night."
AS A REGULAR: "The Brighter Day," CBS, 1961-
62; "Gomer Pyle, USMC," CBS, 1964-70;
"Bright Promise," NBC, 1969-71; "The Edge
of Night," CBS, 1972-75; ABC, 1975-84.
AND: "Hennesey: Big Brother," CBS, 1960;
"Hennesey: Bonjour, Mr. Hennesey," CBS, 1960;
"Route 66: An Absence of Tears," CBS, 1961;
"Checkmate: A Slight Touch of Venom," CBS,
1961; "G.E. Theatre: Call to Danger," CBS, 1961;
"Hawaiian Eye: My Love, But Lightly," ABC,
1962; "77 Sunset Strip: The Bridal Trail Caper,"
ABC, 1962; "The Twilight Zone: The Thirty-
Fathom Grave," CBS, 1963; "The FBI: Pound of
Flesh," ABC, 1965; "Hogan's Heroes: Will the
Real Adolf Please Stand Up?," CBS, 1966; "The
FBI: Passage Into Fear," ABC, 1967; "The FBI:
False Witness," ABC, 1967; "The FBI: Wind It
Up and It Betrays You," ABC, 1968; "The FBI:
The Challenge," ABC, 1969; "Mannix: One for
the Lady," CBS, 1970; "The FBI: The Traitor,"
ABC, 1970; "That Girl: That Senorita," ABC,
1970; "The FBI: The Hitchhiker," ABC, 1971;
"The FBI: Desperate Journey," ABC, 1973.

COMPTON, JOHN
b. Tennessee, June 21, 1923. Clean-cut actor
who was pegged for stardom as the star of a
Jack Webb series, but the show didn't last out a
season.
AS A REGULAR: "The D.A.'s Man, NBC, 1959.
AND: "Navy Log: Man Alone," ABC, 1956;
"Fury: The Pulling Contest," NBC, 1958; "Sgt.
Preston of the Yukon: Battle at Bradley's," CBS,
1958; "Steve Canyon: Operation B-52," NBC,
1959; "The Real McCoys: Aunt Win Steps In,"
CBS, 1963.

CONAWAY, JEFF
b. New York City, NY, October 5, 1950. Actor
who played actor Bobby Wheeler on "Taxi."
AS A REGULAR: "Taxi," ABC, 1978-81; "Wizards
and Warriors," CBS, 1983; "Berrenger's,"
NBC, 1985; "The Bold and the Beautiful,"
CBS, 1989- .
AND: "Happy Days: Richie Fights Back," ABC,
1975; "The Mary Tyler Moore Show: Menage a
Lou," CBS, 1976; "Barnaby Jones: Wipeout,"
CBS, 1976; "Kojak: May the Horse Be With
You," CBS, 1978; "Barnaby Jones: Killer on
Campus," CBS, 1977; "Murder, She Wrote: Birds
of a Feather," CBS, 1984; "The Love Boat:
Heartbreaker," ABC, 1985; "Murder, She Wrote:
Corned Beef and Carnage," CBS, 1986;
"Matlock: The Affair," NBC, 1986; "The New
Mike Hammer: Little Miss Murder," CBS, 1987;
"Freddy's Nightmares: Identity Crisis," SYN,
1989.
TV MOVIES AND MINISERIES: "The Making of a
Male Model," ABC, 1983; "Bay Coven," NBC,
1987.

CONDON, EDDIE
b. *Goodland, IN, 1904; d. 1973.*
AS A REGULAR: "Eddie Condon's Floor Show,"
NBC, 1949; CBS, 1950.
AND: "The Garry Moore Show," CBS, 1958.

CONKLIN, CHESTER
b. *Oskaloosa, IA, January 11, 1888; d. 1971.*
Former Keystone Cop in a bit of TV.
AS A REGULAR: "Doc Corkle," NBC, 1952.
AND: "Make Room for Daddy: The First
Hollywood Show," ABC, 1954.

CONN, DIDI
b. *Brooklyn, NY, July 13, 1951.* Impish young
actress, star of the movie "You Light Up My
Life," who played Denise Stevens Downey on
"Benson."
AS A REGULAR: "Keep on Truckin'," ABC, 1975;
"The Practice," NBC, 1976-77; "Benson,"
ABC, 1981-85.
AND: "Happy Days: Kiss Me Sickly," ABC, 1975;
"$weepstake$: Cowboy, Linda and Angie, Mark,"
NBC, 1979; "The $20,000 Pyramid," ABC, 1980;
"The Love Boat: Love on Strike," ABC, 1983;
"Highway to Heaven: All That Glitters," NBC,
1985; "Highway to Heaven: Ghost Rider," NBC,
1986; "Cagney & Lacey: Waste Deep," CBS,
1987.

CONNELL, JANE
b. *Oakland, CA, October 27, 1925.*
AS A REGULAR: "Stanley," NBC, 1956-57; "As
Caesar Sees It," ABC, 1962-63; "Mister
Mayor," CBS, 1964-65; "The Dumplings,"
NBC, 1976.
AND: "The Garry Moore Show," CBS, 1957; "The
Jack Paar Show," NBC, 1959; "Bewitched: Aunt
Clara's Victoria Victory," ABC, 1967; "Be-
witched: Sam's Double Mother Trouble," ABC,
1969; "Bewitched: To Go or Not to Go, That Is
the Question," ABC, 1970; "Bewitched: Salem,
Here We Come," ABC, 1970; "That Girl: Chef's
Night Out," ABC, 1970; "The Mary Tyler Moore
Show: Divorce Isn't Everything," CBS, 1970;
"Bewitched: George Washington Zapped Here,"
ABC, 1972; "Love, American Style: Love and the
Suspicious Husband," ABC, 1974; "Maude: The
Game Show," CBS, 1976; "All in the Family:
Edith's Fiftieth Birthday," CBS, 1977;
"M*A*S*H: Old Soldiers," CBS, 1980.

CONNELLY, CHRISTOPHER
b. *1941; d. 1988.* Actor who played Norman
Harrington, brother of Ryan O'Neal on
"Peyton Place"; then Connelly played the Ryan
O'Neal role in the TV version of "Paper
Moon."
AS A REGULAR: "Peyton Place," ABC, 1964-69;
"Paper Moon," ABC, 1974-75.

AND: "Mr. Novak: The Tower," NBC, 1964;
"Love, American Style: Love and Mother," ABC,
1969; "Love, American Style: Love and the New
Roommate," ABC, 1971; "Love, American Style:
Love and the Triple Threat," ABC, 1971;
"Mannix: One Step to Midnight," CBS, 1972;
"Barnaby Jones: The Deadly Jinx," CBS, 1974;
"The Brian Keith Show: Here Comes the What?,"
NBC, 1974; "Marcus Welby, M.D.: Fear of
Silence," ABC, 1974; "Police Story: Wolf," NBC,
1974; "Ironside: Speak No Evil," NBC, 1974;
"Medical Story: Wasteland," NBC, 1975; "Police
Story: Company Man," NBC, 1975; "Petrocelli:
Survival," NBC, 1976; "Police Story: The Jar,"
NBC, 1976; "The Quest: The Captive," NBC,
1976; "Hawaii Five-O: To Die in Paradise," CBS,
1977; "Fantasy Island: Magnolia Blossoms,"
ABC, 1979; "The Love Boat: Brotherhood of the
Sea," ABC, 1979; "B.J. and the Bear: Crackers,"
NBC, 1979; "The Fall Guy: Inside, Outside,"
ABC, 1983.
TV MOVIES AND MINISERIES: "In Name Only,"
ABC, 1969; "Incident in San Francisco," ABC,
1971; "The Last Day," NBC, 1975; "Murder in
Peyton Place," NBC, 1977; "Crash," ABC,
1978; "Stunt Seven," CBS, 1979; "Peyton
Place: The Next Generation," NBC, 1985;
"The Ted Kennedy Jr. Story," NBC, 1986.

CONNELLY, MARC
b. *Marcus Cook, McKeesport, PA, December
13, 1890; d. 1980.* Playwright, actor and
storyteller who made the game-show rounds
and played a judge on "The Defenders."
AS A REGULAR: "Droodles," NBC, 1954; "One
Minute Please," DUM, 1954-55.
AND: "Broadway Television Theatre: The Village
Green," SYN, 1953; "The Jack Paar Show," NBC,
1959; "The Bells of St. Mary's," CBS, 1959; "The
Jack Paar Show," NBC, 1960; "Play of the Week:
Black Monday," SYN, 1961; "Du Pont Show of
the Month: The Night of the Storm," CBS, 1961;
"The Defenders: Man Against Himself," CBS,
1963; "The Defenders: A Taste of Vengeance,"
CBS, 1963; "The Defenders: Conflict of
Interests," CBS, 1964; "The Dick Cavett Show,"
PBS, 1978.
TV MOVIES AND MINISERIES: "The Borgia Stick,"
NBC, 1967.

CONNORS, CHUCK
b. *Kevin Joseph Connors, Brooklyn, NY, April
10, 1921.* Actor who had a way with a glower
and no sense of humor, a combination that
served him well as tough-but-fair Lucas
McCain on "The Rifleman."
AS A REGULAR: "Dear Phoebe," NBC, 1954; "The
Rifleman," ABC, 1958-63; "Arrest and Trial,"
ABC, 1963-64; "Branded," NBC, 1965-66;
"Cowboy in Africa," ABC, 1967-68; "Thrill
Seekers," SYN, 1973-74; "The Yellow Rose,"

NBC, 1983-84; "Werewolf," FOX, 1987-88.
AND: "G.E. Theatre: The Road to Edinburgh,"
CBS, 1954; "Four Star Playhouse: Vote of
Confidence," CBS, 1954; "The Loretta Young
Show: The Girl Who Knew," NBC, 1955; "Four
Star Playhouse: The Good Sisters," CBS, 1955;
"The Adventures of Superman: Flight to the
North," SYN, 1955; "TV Reader's Digest: The
Manufactured Clue," ABC, 1955; "Schlitz
Playhouse of Stars: O'Connor and the Blue-Eyed
Felon," CBS, 1955; "Screen Directors Playhouse:
The Brush Roper," NBC, 1955; "Cavalcade
Theatre: Barbed Wire Christmas," ABC, 1955;
"Fireside Theatre: The Thread," NBC, 1956;
"Gunsmoke: The Preacher," CBS, 1956; "West
Point: The Operator," CBS, 1956; "The Gale
Storm Show: The Witch Doctor," CBS, 1956;
"Tales of Wells Fargo: The Thin Rope," NBC,
1957; "O. Henry Playhouse: Only the Horse
Would Know," SYN, 1957; "Restless Gun: Silver
Threads," NBC, 1957; "The Millionaire: The Hub
Grimes Story," CBS, 1957; "West Point: Army-
Navy Game," CBS, 1957; "Wagon Train: The
Charles Avery Story," NBC, 1957; "Date with the
Angels: Double Trouble," ABC, 1958; "Love
That Jill: They Went Thataway," ABC, 1958;
"The Adventures of Jim Bowie: Horse Thief,"
ABC, 1958; "Tales of Wells Fargo: Sam Bass,"
NBC, 1958; "G.E. Theatre: The Thousand-Dollar
Gun," CBS, 1958; "Bob Hope Special," NBC,
1959; "What's My Line?," CBS, 1959; "The
Steve Allen Plymouth Show," NBC, 1959; "The
Big Party," CBS, 1959; "The du Pont Show with
June Allyson: Trial by Fear," CBS, 1960; "The
Dinah Shore Chevy Show," NBC, 1960; "What's
My Line?," CBS, 1960; "The Chevy Show: Love
is Funny," NBC, 1960; "Person to Person," CBS,
1961; "Password," CBS, 1961; "Here's
Hollywood," NBC, 1961; "Play Your Hunch,"
NBC, 1962; "The Hero: A Night to Remember to
Forget," NBC, 1966; "The Joey Bishop Show,"
ABC, 1968; "The Men From Shiloh: The
Animal," NBC, 1970; "The Name of the Game:
The Broken Puzzle," NBC, 1971; "Night Gallery:
The Ring with the Red Velvet Ropes," NBC,
1973; "The Sonny and Cher Comedy Hour," CBS,
1973; "Here's Lucy: Lucy and Chuck Connors
Have a Surprise Slumber Party," CBS, 1973;
"Police Story: Across the Line," NBC, 1974;
"Police Story: The Cutting Edge," CBS, 1975;
"The Six Million Dollar Man: The Price of
Liberty," ABC, 1975; "Police Story: Trash Detail,
Front and Center," NBC, 1976; "Stone:
Homicide," ABC, 1980; "Best of the West: Frog
Gets Lucky," ABC, 1982; "The Love Boat: The
Hustlers," ABC, 1983; "Murder, She Wrote: Coal
Miner's Slaughter," CBS, 1988; "The Pat Sajak
Show," CBS, 1989; "Paradise: A Gathering of
Guns," CBS, 1989.
TV MOVIES AND MINISERIES: "The Birdmen," CBS,
1971; "Night of Terror," ABC, 1972; "Set This

Town on Fire," NBC, 1973; "Horror at 37,000
Feet," CBS, 1973; "The Police Story," NBC,
1973; "Banjo Hackett," NBC, 1976; "Nightmare in Badham County," ABC, 1976; "The
Night They Took Miss Beautiful," NBC, 1977;
"Roots," ABC, 1977; "Standing Tall," NBC,
1978; "The Capture of Grizzly Adams," NBC,
1982; "High Desert Kill," USA, 1989.

CONNORS, MIKE
*b. Krekor Ohanian, Fresno, CA, August 15,
1925.* He-man action hero, most notably as
private dick Joe Mannix.
AS A REGULAR: "Tightrope!," CBS, 1959-60;
"Mannix," CBS, 1967-75; "Today's FBI,"
ABC, 1981-82.
AND: "Ford Theatre: Yours for a Dream," NBC,
1954; "Schlitz Playhouse of Stars: The Last Out,"
CBS, 1955; "Schlitz Playhouse of Stars: No Trial
by Jury," CBS, 1955; "The Life and Legend of
Wyatt Earp: Big Baby Contest," ABC, 1955; "The
Millionaire: The Story of Victor Volante," CBS,
1956; "The Loretta Young Show: Now a Brief
Word," NBC, 1956; "Frontier: Tomas and the
Widow," NBC, 1956; "The People's Choice:
Sock and the Law," NBC, 1956; "Lux Video
Theatre: The Latch Key," NBC, 1957; "The
Walter Winchell File: The Steep Hill," ABC,
1957; "Maverick: Point Blank," ABC, 1957; "M
Squad: Peter Loves Mary," NBC, 1957; "Have
Gun, Will Travel: The Bride," CBS, 1957; "The
Gale Storm Show: Mardi Gras," CBS, 1957;
"Maverick: The Naked Gallows," ABC, 1957;
"Wagon Train: The Dora Gray Story," NBC,
1958; "The Texan: Edge of the Cliff," CBS, 1958;
"Cheyenne: Dead to Rights," ABC, 1958; "Studio
57: Getaway Car," SYN, 1958; "Cimarron City:
Hired Hand," NBC, 1958; "Jefferson Drum:
Simon Pitt," NBC, 1958; "Lawman: Lady in
Question," ABC, 1958; "Alcoa Presents One Step
Beyond: The Aerialist," ABC, 1959; "About
Faces," ABC, 1960; "The Expendables," ABC,
1962; "The Untouchables: The Eddie O'Gara
Story," ABC, 1962; "The Whirlybirds: Rita Ames
Is Missing," SYN, 1963; "Perry Mason: The Case
of the Bullied Bowler," CBS, 1964; "Hollywood
Squares," NBC, 1967; "You Don't Say," NBC,
1968; "The Red Skelton Hour," CBS, 1968; "The
Jonathan Winters Show," CBS, 1968; "Red,"
NBC, 1970; "The Merv Griffin Show," CBS,
1970; "Dinah's Place," NBC, 1970; "The Movie
Game," SYN, 1970; "Here's Lucy: Lucy and
Mannix Are Held Hostage," CBS, 1971; "Mitzi
Gaynor: The First Time," CBS, 1973; "Holly-
wood Squares," SYN, 1975; "Joys," NBC, 1976;
"The Mike Douglas Show," SYN, 1976; "The
John Davidson Show," SYN, 1981; "Glitter:
Premiere," ABC, 1984; "Murder, She Wrote:
Truck Stop," CBS, 1989.
TV MOVIES AND MINISERIES: "Beg, Borrow ... or

Steal," CBS, 1973; "The Killer Who Wouldn't Die," ABC, 1976; "Revenge for a Rape," ABC, 1976; "Long Journey Back," ABC, 1978; "The Death of Ocean View Park," ABC, 1979; "High Midnight," CBS, 1979; "Casino," ABC, 1980; "Nightkill," NBC, 1980; "War and Remembrance," ABC, 1988, 1989.

CONRAD, MICHAEL

b. New York City, NY, October 16, 1925; d. 1983. Actor who long labored in the television vineyard; best known as Sgt. Phillip Freemason Esterhaus on "Hill Street Blues."

AS A REGULAR: "Delvecchio," CBS, 1976-77; "Hill Street Blues," NBC, 1981-84.

AND: "Naked City: Fire Island," ABC, 1959; "Armstrong Circle Theatre: Merchants of Evil," CBS, 1962; "Wagon Train: The Sandra Cummings Story," ABC, 1963; "The Twilight Zone: Black Leather Jackets," CBS, 1964; "The Dick Van Dyke Show: The Ugliest Dog in the World," CBS, 1965; "The Dick Van Dyke Show: Body and Sol," CBS, 1965; "I Spy: Carry Me Back to Old Tsing-Tao," NBC, 1965; "My Favorite Martian: Martin's Revoltin' Development," CBS, 1966; "The FBI: The Man Who Went Mad by Mistake," ABC, 1966; "Gomer Pyle, USMC: Gomer and the Beast," CBS, 1966; "Laredo: No Bugles, One Drum," NBC, 1966; "Bonanza: The Fighters," NBC, 1966; "I Spy: So Coldly Sweet," NBC, 1966; "Bob Hope Chrysler Theatre: Time of Flight," NBC, 1966; "Gunsmoke: Gunfighter, R.I.P.," CBS, 1966; "That Girl: Little Auction Annie," ABC, 1966; "The Fugitive: The Sharp Edge of Chivalry," ABC, 1966; "The Felony Squad: Arrangement with Death," ABC, 1967; "The Desperate Hours," ABC, 1967; "Lost in Space: Fugitives in Space," CBS, 1968; "The Outcasts: The Man From Bennington," ABC, 1968; "The Virginian: The Stranger," NBC, 1969; "Mannix: Once Upon a Saturday," CBS, 1969; "The Immortal: By Gift of Chase," ABC, 1970; "The Virginian: Nightmare," NBC, 1970; "The Bold Ones: The Letter of the Law," NBC, 1970; "Mission: Impossible: TOD-5," CBS, 1972; "Alias Smith and Jones: Bushwack!," ABC, 1972; "Hawaii Five-O: Fools Die Twice," CBS, 1972; "All in the Family: Flashback: Mike and Gloria's Wedding," CBS, 1972; "The FBI: Ransom," ABC, 1973; "Hawaii Five-O: Fools Die Twice," CBS, 1972; "The Bob Newhart Show: Backlash," CBS, 1973; "Emergency!: Alley Cat," NBC, 1973; "The Bob Newhart Show: A Matter of Principal," CBS, 1974; "Emergency!: Quicker Than the Eye," NBC, 1974; "Marcus Welby, M.D.: Save the Last Dance for Me," ABC, 1975; "Emergency!: 905-Wild," NBC, 1975; "The Family Holvak: The Long Way Home," NBC, 1975; "Barney Miller: Wojo's Girl," ABC, 1979; "Paris: Once More for Free," CBS, 1979.

TV MOVIES AND MINISERIES: "The Third Girl From the Left," ABC, 1973; "The Rangers," NBC, 1974; "Delancey Street," NBC, 1975; "Starsky and Hutch," ABC, 1975; "The First 36 Hours of Dr. Durant," ABC, 1975; "Satan's Triangle," ABC, 1975.

* Emmies: 1981, 1982.

CONRAD, ROBERT

b. Conrad Robert Falk, Chicago, IL, March 1, 1935. Actor whose ultra-macho posturings on TV as well as in real life are strictly a matter of taste. Best known as secret agent Jim West, "Baa Baa Black Sheep" hero "Pappy" Boyington and as the guy who put batteries on his shoulder and dared you to knock them off in TV commercials.

AS A REGULAR: "Hawaiian Eye," ABC, 1959-63; "The Wild Wild West," CBS, 1965-70; "The D.A.," NBC, 1971-72; "Assignment Vienna," ABC, 1972-73; "Baa Baa Black Sheep," NBC, 1976-78; "The Duke," NBC, 1979; "A Man Called Sloane," NBC, 1979-80; "High Mountain Rangers," CBS, 1988; "Jesse Hawkes," CBS, 1989.

AND: "Maverick: Yellow River," ABC, 1959; "Colt .45: Amnesty," ABC, 1959; "The Man and the Challenge: White Out," NBC, 1959; "77 Sunset Strip: Only Zeroes Count," ABC, 1959; "77 Sunset Strip: Who Killed Cock Robin?," ABC, 1960; "The Gallant Men: And Cain Cried Out," ABC, 1962; "American Bandstand," ABC, 1962; "Temple Houston: The Town That Trespassed," NBC, 1964; "American Bandstand," ABC, 1965; "Kraft Suspense Theatre: Four Into Zero," NBC, 1965; "Mannix: Playground," CBS, 1969; "Mission: Impossible: The Killer," CBS, 1970; "Mission: Impossible: Break!," CBS, 1972; "Columbo: An Exercise in Fatality," NBC, 1974; "The Mike Douglas Show," SYN, 1976; "Saturday Night Live," NBC, 1982; "J.J. Starbuck: A Killing in the Market," NBC, 1987.

TV MOVIES AND MINISERIES: "The D.A.: Murder One," NBC, 1969; "Weekend of Terror," ABC, 1970; "The D.A.: Conspiracy to Kill," NBC, 1971; "Five Desperate Women," ABC, 1971; "The Adventures of Nick Carter," ABC, 1972; "The Last Day," NBC, 1975; "Smash-Up on Interstate 5," ABC, 1976; "Centennial," NBC, 1978-79; "The Wild Wild West Revisited," CBS, 1979; "More Wild Wild West," CBS, 1980; "Coach of the Year," NBC, 1980; "Hard Knox," NBC, 1984; "Two Fathers' Justice," NBC, 1985; "Charley Hannah," ABC, 1986; "One Police Plaza," CBS, 1986; "The Fifth Missile," NBC, 1986; "Assassin," CBS, 1986; "One Police Plaza," CBS, 1986; "High Mountain Rangers," CBS, 1987; "Police Story: Gladiator School," ABC, 1988; "Glory Days," CBS, 1988.

* When "High Mountain Rangers" showed signs

of strength against NBC's "The Facts of Life" on Saturday nights, Conrad wasted no time gloating about it. "Don't push it—I'm the only hit you've got," he told embarrassed CBS officials at one affiliate meeting. The show was yanked soon afterwards.

CONRAD, WILLIAM

b. *Louisville, KY, September 27, 1920.* Rotund actor with a resonant voice who played Matt Dillon in the radio version of "Gunsmoke" and then unexpectedly became a TV star as cops Frank Cannon and then as Jason "Fatman" McCabe.

AS A REGULAR: "The Bullwinkle Show," NBC, 1961-62; "The Fugitive," ABC, 1963-67; "Cannon," CBS, 1971-76; "The Wild, Wild World of Animals," SYN, 1973-78; "Tales of the Unexpected," NBC, 1977; "Nero Wolfe," NBC, 1981; "Jake and the Fatman," CBS, 1987- .

AND: "Bat Masterson: Stampede at Tent City," NBC, 1958; "The Man and the Challenge: Invisible Force," NBC, 1959; "The Aquanauts: The Trophy Adventure," CBS, 1961; "Bat Masterson: Terror on the Trinity," NBC, 1961; "Have Gun, Will Travel: The Man Who Struck Moonshine," CBS, 1962; "Have Gun, Will Travel: Genesis," CBS, 1962; "G.E. True: Circle of Death," CBS, 1962; "The Alfred Hitchcock Hour: The Thirty-First of February," CBS, 1963; "The Name of the Game: The Power," NBC, 1969; "The Name of the Game: The Skin Game," NBC, 1970; "The Storefront Lawyers: Survivors Will Be Prosecuted," CBS, 1970; "Barnaby Jones: Requiem for a Son," CBS, 1973; "Barnaby Jones: Blood Relations," CBS, 1975; "Break the Bank," SYN, 1976; "The Big Event: Christmas Around the World," NBC, 1976; "Murder, She Wrote: Death Takes a Curtain Call," CBS, 1985; "Matlock: The Don," NBC, 1986.

TV MOVIES AND MINISERIES: "The Brotherhood of the Bell," CBS, 1970; "The D.A.: Conspiracy to Kill," NBC, 1971; "Cannon," CBS, 1971; "O'Hara, United States Treasury: Operation Cobra," CBS, 1971; "The Murder That Wouldn't Die," NBC, 1980; "Turnover Smith," ABC, 1980; "In Like Flynn," ABC, 1985; "Vengeance: The Story of Tony Cimo," CBS, 1986.

AS DIRECTOR: "77 Sunset Strip," ABC, 1963-64.
AS PRODUCER: "Klondike," NBC, 1960-61.

CONRIED, HANS

b. *Frank Foster, Baltimore, MD, April 15, 1917; d. 1982.* Character actor with impeccable diction and a way with dialects who was Uncle Tonoose on "The Danny Thomas Show," the voice of Snidely Whiplash on "Dudley Do Right" and Wrong-Way Feldman on "Gilligan's Island," among others.

AS A REGULAR: "Pantomime Quiz," CBS, 1950, 1951; NBC, 1952; ABC, 1955; CBS, 1956, 1957; "Take a Guess," CBS, 1953; "The Danny Thomas Show (Make Room for Daddy)," ABC, 1957; CBS, 1957-64; "What's It For?," NBC, 1957-58; "The Jack Paar Show," NBC, 1958-62; "Take a Good Look," ABC, 1959-61; "The Bullwinkle Show," NBC, 1961-62; "Stump the Stars," CBS, 1962-63; "Made in America," CBS, 1964; "Make Room for Granddaddy," ABC, 1970-71; "The Tony Randall Show," CBS, 1977-78; "American Dream," ABC, 1981.

AND: "I Love Lucy: Redecorating," CBS, 1952; "I Love Lucy: Lucy Hires an English Tutor," CBS, 1952; "Make Room for Daddy: Cousin Carl," ABC, 1954; "Make Room for Daddy: The Actor," ABC, 1955; "The Bob Cummings Show: Bob Escapes Schultzy's Trap," CBS, 1956; "Saturday Spectacular: Manhattan Tower," NBC, 1956; "Playhouse 90: Eloise," CBS, 1956; "The Red Skelton Show," CBS, 1957; "The General Motors 50th Anniversary Show," NBC, 1957; "The Unchained Goddess," NBC, 1958; "Maverick: Black Fire," ABC, 1958; "To Tell the Truth," CBS, 1958; "The Donna Reed Show: It's the Principle of the Thing," ABC, 1959; "Perry Presents," NBC, 1959; "The Real McCoys: The Actor," ABC, 1959; "The Ransom of Red Chief," NBC, 1959; "U.S. Steel Hour: A Taste of Champagne," CBS, 1959; "Art Carney Special: Small World, Isn't It," NBC, 1959; "Love and Marriage: Childe of Capricorn," NBC, 1959; "U.S. Steel Hour: Step on the Gas," CBS, 1960; "Art Linkletter's House Party," CBS, 1960; "The Islanders: Escape From Kaledau," ABC, 1961; "The Square World of Jack Paar," NBC, 1961; "U.S. Steel Hour: Private Eye, Private Eye," CBS, 1961; "Have Gun, Will Travel: The Knight," CBS, 1961; "The Jack Paar Program," NBC, 1962; "Mr. Ed: Ed and Paul Revere," CBS, 1962; "The Lucy Show: Lucy's Barbershop Quartet," CBS, 1963; "The Jack Paar Program," NBC, 1963; "The du Pont Show: Holdup!," NBC, 1963; "The Lucy Show: Lucy Plays Cleopatra," CBS, 1963; "Object Is," ABC, 1963; "Truth or Consequences," NBC, 1964; "Burke's Law: Who Killed April?," ABC, 1964; "Dr. Kildare: The Last Leaves on the Tree," NBC, 1964; "Gilligan's Island: Wrong Way Feldman," CBS, 1964; "Burke's Law: Who Killed 711?," ABC, 1964; "Burke's Law: Who Killed Rosie Sunset?," ABC, 1965; "Danny Thomas Special," NBC, 1965; "Gilligan's Island: The Return of Wrong Way Feldman," CBS, 1965; "Please Don't Eat the Daisies: At Home with the Faculty," NBC, 1966; "The Monkees: The Monkees' Paw," NBC, 1968; "The Beverly Hillbillies: The Clampetts Fiddle Around," CBS, 1968; "Love, American Style: Love and the Good Deal," ABC, 1969; "The Mike Douglas Show," SYN, 1970; "Love, American Style: Love and the Tuba," ABC, 1971; "Love,

American Style: Love and the Split-Up," ABC, 1971; "Here's Lucy: Lucy and Danny Thomas," CBS, 1973; "Love, American Style: Love and the Footlight Fiance," ABC, 1973; "Kolchak, the Night Stalker: The Knightly Murders," ABC, 1975; "The Mike Douglas Show," SYN, 1977; "Quark: May the Source Be With You," NBC, 1978; "Laverne & Shirley: Laverne and Shirley Go to Night School," ABC, 1978; "The Love Boat: Dream Boat," ABC, 1979; "Alice: The Last Stow It," CBS, 1979; "Fantasy Island: A Very Strange Affair," ABC, 1982; "Barefoot in the Park," SHO, 1982.

TV MOVIES AND MINISERIES: "Wake Me When the War Is Over," ABC, 1969.

CONSIDINE, TIM
b. *Louisville, KY, December 10, 1941*. Actor who got his first break as Marty of "Spin and Marty" action serial fame on "The Mickey Mouse Club," and then played the oldest Douglas son, Mike, on "My Three Sons."
AS A REGULAR: "The Mickey Mouse Club," ABC, 1956-59; "Walt Disney Presents: The Swamp Fox," ABC, 1959-60; "My Three Sons," ABC, 1960-65; CBS, 1965.
AND: "Disneyland: Fourth Anniversary Show," ABC, 1957; "Medical Center: The Crooked Circle," CBS, 1969; "Gunsmoke: Snow Train," CBS, 1970; "Ironside: Noel's Gonna Fly," NBC, 1970; "Simon & Simon: Design for Murder," CBS, 1983.
AS CO-WRITER: "My Three Sons: Goodbye Again," ABC, 1964.
AS DIRECTOR: "My Three Sons: The Leopard's Spots," ABC, 1965.

CONSTANTINE, MICHAEL
b. *Reading, PA, May 22, 1927*. Actor who won an Emmy as wise, downtrodden principal Seymour Kaufman on "Room 222."
AS A REGULAR: "Hey Landlord," NBC, 1966-67; "Room 222," ABC, 1969-74; "Sirota's Court," NBC, 1976-77.
AND: "Armstrong Circle Theatre: The New Class - The Book Heard Round the World," CBS, 1958; "The Untouchables: The King of Champagne," ABC, 1961; "The Asphalt Jungle: The Fighter," ABC, 1961; "Target: The Corruptors: To Wear a Badge," ABC, 1961; "The Defenders: The Attack," CBS, 1961; "Naked City: Let Me Die Before I Wake," ABC, 1962; "Ben Casey: The Night That Nothing Happened," ABC, 1962; "Sam Benedict: Tears for a Nobody Doll," NBC, 1962; "The Twilight Zone: I Am the Night-Color Me Black," CBS, 1964; "The Outer Limits: Counterweight," ABC, 1964; "Slattery's People: Question-Remember the Dark Sins of Youth?," CBS, 1964; "The Dick Van Dyke Show: You Ought to Be in Pictures," CBS, 1966; "T.H.E. Cat: Marked for Death," NBC, 1966; "Combat!:

Entombed," ABC, 1967; "The Flying Nun: Sister Lucky," ABC, 1968; "The Virginian: A Touch of Hands," NBC, 1969; "The Odd Couple: Engrave Trouble," ABC, 1971; "The Mary Tyler Moore Show: I Am Curious Cooper," CBS, 1971; "McMillan and Wife: The Deadly Cure," NBC, 1976; "Quincy: Walk Softly Through the Night," NBC, 1979; "Lou Grant: Boomerang," CBS, 1981; "Lou Grant: Beachhead," CBS, 1981; "Quincy: Gentle Into That Good Night," NBC, 1981; "Darkroom: Guillotine," ABC, 1982; "The Powers of Matthew Star: The Italian Caper," NBC, 1982; "Quincy: Give Me Your Weak," NBC, 1982; "Hotel: Faith, Hope and Charity," ABC, 1983; "The Love Boat: China Cruise," ABC, 1983; "Simon & Simon: The Disappearance of Harry," CBS, 1984; "Remington Steele: Cast in Steele," NBC, 1984; "Murder She Wrote: Murder Takes the Bus," CBS, 1985; "Magnum, P.I.: Mentor," CBS, 1986; "Simon & Simon: Walking Point," CBS, 1987; "MacGyver: Out in the Cold," ABC, 1987; "Hunter: Payback," NBC, 1988; "Murder, She Wrote: The Wearing of the Green," CBS, 1988; "Simon & Simon: Second Swell," CBS, 1988; "Mancuso FBI: I Cover the Waterfront," NBC, 1989.
TV MOVIES AND MINISERIES: "Suddenly Single," ABC, 1971; "Deadly Harvest," CBS, 1972; "Say Goodbye, Maggie Cole," ABC, 1972; "The Bait," ABC, 1973; "Big Rose," CBS, 1974; "Death Cruise," ABC, 1974; "The Secret Night Caller," NBC, 1975; "The Night That Panicked America," ABC, 1975; "Conspiracy of Terror," CBS, 1976; "Twin Detectives," ABC, 1976; "Wanted: The Sundance Woman," ABC, 1976; "Harold Robbins' 79 Park Avenue," NBC, 1977; "The Pirate," CBS, 1978; "Crisis in Mid-Air," CBS, 1979; "Roots: The Next Generations," ABC, 1979; "The Love Tapes," ABC, 1980.
* Emmies: 1970.

CONTE, JOHN
b. *Palmer, MA, September 15, 1915*.
AS A REGULAR: "Van Camp's Little Show," NBC, 1950-51; "Matinee Theatre," NBC, 1955-58; "Mantovani," SYN, 1959.
AND: "Musical Comedy Time: Anything Goes," CBS, 1950; "Naughty Marietta," NBC, 1955; "A Connecticut Yankee," NBC, 1955; "The Merry Widow," NBC, 1955; "The Desert Song," NBC, 1955; "Goodyear TV Playhouse: Tangled Web," NBC, 1955; "Climax!: Fear Strikes Out," CBS, 1955; "Target: Lost Identity," SYN, 1958; "Perry Mason: The Case of the Madcap Modiste," CBS, 1960; "77 Sunset Strip: The Positive Negative," ABC, 1961; "Perry Mason: The Case of the Blind Man's Bluff," CBS, 1961; "Perry Mason: The Case of the Injured Innocent," CBS, 1961; "Here's Hollywood," NBC, 1962; "Perry Mason: The Case of the Lover's Leap," CBS, 1963; "Bonanza: The Return," NBC, 1965.

CONTE, RICHARD

b. Nicolas Peter Conte, New York City, NY, March 24, 1914; d. 1975.

AS A REGULAR: "Four Just Men," SYN, 1959; "The Jean Arthur Show," CBS, 1966.

AND: "G.E. Theatre: The Eye of the Beholder," CBS, 1953; "Ford Theatre: Turn Back the Clock," NBC, 1954; "Ford Theatre: The Silent Stranger," NBC, 1956; "U.S. Steel Hour: Overnight Haul," CBS, 1956; "The 20th Century-Fox Hour: End of a Gun," CBS, 1957; "The Twilight Zone: Perchance to Dream," CBS, 1959; "Buick Electra Playhouse: The Gambler, the Nun and the Radio," CBS, 1960; "Checkmate: Moment of Truth," CBS, 1960; "The Untouchables: The Organization," ABC, 1961; "Alfred Hitchcock Presents: The Old Pro," NBC, 1961; "Bus Stop: Cry to Heaven," ABC, 1962; "Naked City: One of the Most Important Men in the Whole World," ABC, 1962; "Checkmate: An Assassin Arrives, Andante," CBS, 1962; "The Untouchables: The Chess Game," ABC, 1962; "Alcoa Premiere: Ordeal in Darkness," ABC, 1962; "Frontier Circus: Naomi Champagne," CBS, 1962; "The du Pont Show: The Outpost," NBC, 1962; "Going My Way: A Saint for Mama," ABC, 1962; "77 Sunset Strip: 5," ABC, 1963; "Arrest and Trial: Tigers are for Jungles," ABC, 1964; "The Reporter: Hideout," CBS, 1964; "The Donna Reed Show: Who's Who on 202?," ABC, 1964; "Kraft Suspense Theatre: The Green Felt Jungle," NBC, 1965; "The Danny Thomas Hour: Fame is a Four-Letter Word," NBC, 1967; "The Bold Ones: Trial of a Mafiosa," NBC, 1970.

TV MOVIES AND MINISERIES: "The Challengers," CBS, 1970.

CONTI, TOM

b. Paisley, Scotland, November 22, 1941.

TV MOVIES AND MINISERIES: "The Wall," CBS, 1982; "Nazi Hunter: The Beate Klarsfeld Story," ABC, 1986.

CONVERSE, FRANK

b. St. Louis, May 22, 1938.

AS A REGULAR: "Coronet Blue," CBS, 1967; "NYPD," ABC, 1967-69; "Movin' On," NBC, 1974-76; "The Family Tree," NBC, 1983; "One Life to Live," ABC, 1984-85; "Dolphin Cove," CBS, 1989.

AND: "Hawk: H Is a Dirty Letter," ABC, 1966; "The Young Lawyers: Is There a Good Samaritan in the House?," ABC, 1970; "The Most Deadly Game: Model for Murder," ABC, 1970; "Medical Center: Trial by Terror," CBS, 1970; "The FBI: Death on Sunday," ABC, 1971; "The Sixth Sense: Whisper of Evil," ABC, 1972; "CBS Children's Hour: Summer Is Forever," CBS, 1972; "Columbo: Requiem for a Falling Star," NBC, 1973; "D.H.O.," ABC, 1973; "Theatre in

America: The Widowing of Mrs. Halroyd," PBS, 1974; "Stat!," CBS, 1975; "Starsky and Hutch: The Las Vegas Strangler," ABC, 1976; "Police Story: Thanksgiving," NBC, 1976; "Rhoda: The Second Time Around," CBS, 1977; "Kingston: Confidential: The Boston Shamrock," NBC, 1977; "Police Woman: The Killer Cowboys," NBC, 1977; "Magnum P.I.: A Little Bit of Luck, a Little Bit of Grief," CBS, 1985; "The Equalizer: Back Home," CBS, 1986; "Wonderworks: Home at Last," PBS, 1988.

TV MOVIES AND MINISERIES: "Dr. Cook's Garden," ABC, 1971; "A Tattered Web," CBS, 1971; "The Haunting of Rosalind," ABC, 1973; "In Tandem," NBC, 1974; "Sergeant Matlovich vs. the U.S. Air Force," NBC, 1978; "The Miracle of Kathy Miller," CBS, 1981; "Alone in the Neon Jungle," CBS, 1988.

CONVY, BERT

b. St. Louis, MO, July 23, 1933; d. 1991. Light actor and game show host.

AS A REGULAR: "Father of the Bride," CBS, 1961-62; "Love of Life," CBS, 1963; "The Snoop Sisters," NBC, 1973-74; "Tattletales," CBS, 1974-78, 1983-84; "The Late Summer Early Fall Bert Convy Show," CBS, 1976; "Password," NBC, 1979-82, 1984- ; "It's Not Easy," ABC, 1983; "People Do the Craziest Things," ABC, 1984-85; "Win, Lose or Draw," NBC & SYN, 1987-89; "3rd Degree," SYN, 1989-90.

AND: "77 Sunset Strip: Vicious Circle," ABC, 1958; "Alcoa Presents One Step Beyond: The Explorer," ABC, 1960; "Perry Mason: The Case of the Nimble Nephew," CBS, 1960; "Hawaiian Eye: The Humuhumunukunukuapuaa Kid," ABC, 1961; "The Defenders: Survival," CBS, 1964; "The Cliff Dwellers," ABC, 1966; "Hawk: Game with a Dead End," ABC, 1966; "Snap Judgment," NBC, 1967; "Bewitched: Paul Revere Rides Again," ABC, 1970; "The Partridge Family: Whatever Happened to Moby Dick?," ABC, 1971; "Night Gallery: They're Tearing Down Tim Riley's Bar," NBC, 1971; "You Are There: Paul Revere's Ride," CBS, 1972; "The Mary Tyler Moore Show: Have I Found a Guy for You," CBS, 1972; "Love, American Style: Love and the Cryptic Gift," ABC, 1973; "McMillan and Wife: Downshift to Danger," NBC, 1974; "ABC Afternoon Playbreak: Oh! Baby Baby Baby ...," ABC, 1974; "Match Game '75," CBS, 1975; "Dinah!," SYN, 1975; "Medical Story: Woman in White," NBC, 1975; "Charlie's Angels: Love Boat Angels," ABC, 1979; "The Love Boat: What a Drag," ABC, 1984; "Hotel: Fantasies," ABC, 1984; "Murder, She Wrote: Christopher Bundy-Died on Sunday," CBS, 1986; "It's Garry Shandling's Show: Go Go Goldblum," FOX, 1988.

TV MOVIES AND MINISERIES: "Death Takes a Holiday," ABC, 1971; "Love Boat II," ABC,

1977; "SST-Death Flight," ABC, 1977; "Thou Shalt Not Commit Adultery," NBC, 1978; "Dallas Cowboy Cheerleaders," ABC, 1979; "Hanging by a Thread," NBC, 1979; "The Man in the Santa Claus Suit," NBC, 1979; "Help Wanted: Male," CBS, 1982; "Love Thy Neighbor," ABC, 1984.
* Emmies: 1977.

CONWAY, GARY
b. Boston, MA, February 4, 1936. Hunky actor who played Capt. Steve Burton on "Land of the Giants."
AS A REGULAR: "Burke's Law," ABC, 1963-65; "Land of the Giants," ABC, 1968-70.
AND: "Colt .45: Absent Without Leave," ABC, 1958; "Hawaiian Eye: Baker's Half Dozen," ABC, 1960; "77 Sunset Strip: The Rice Estate," ABC, 1960; "It's a Man's World: The Bravest Man in Cordella," NBC, 1962; "Columbo: Any Old Port in a Storm," NBC, 1973; "Police Story: Chief," NBC, 1974; "The Love Boat: Sally's Paradise," ABC, 1981.
TV MOVIES AND MINISERIES: "The Judge and Jake Wyler," NBC, 1972.

CONWAY, SHIRL
b. Franklinville, NY, 1916.
AS A REGULAR: "Joe and Mabel," CBS, 1956; "Caesar's Hour," NBC, 1956-57; "The Nurses," CBS, 1962-65.
AND: "Bride and Groom," NBC, 1957; "Frontiers of Faith: Grab and Grace," NBC, 1960; "Route 66: Some of the People, Some of the Time," CBS, 1961; "The Defenders: Gideon's Follies," CBS, 1961; "The Match Game," NBC, 1964; "The Mike Douglas Show," SYN, 1964; "I've Got a Secret," CBS, 1965; "NET Showcase: The Beggar's Opera," NET, 1967.

CONWAY, TIM
b. Chagrin Falls, OH, December 15, 1933. Skilled second banana to such comics as Steve Allen and Carol Burnett, and much less successful when it came to headlining his own shows.
AS A REGULAR: "The New Steve Allen Show," ABC, 1961; "McHale's Navy," ABC, 1962-66; "Rango," ABC, 1967; "The Tim Conway Show," CBS, 1970; CBS, 1980-81; "The Tim Conway Comedy Hour," CBS, 1970; "The Carol Burnett Show," CBS, 1975-78; ABC, 1979; "Ace Crawford, Private Eye," CBS, 1983; "Tim Conway's Funny America," ABC, 1990.
AND: "Broadside: Pilot," ABC, 1964; "Hollywood Palace," ABC, 1964; "Hollywood Palace," ABC, 1965; "The Danny Kaye Show," CBS, 1967; "Hollywood Squares," NBC, 1967; "The Red Skelton Hour," CBS, 1967; "Rowan & Martin's

Laugh-In," NBC, 1968; "Operation: Entertainment," ABC, 1968; "The Carol Burnett Show," CBS, 1968; "That's Life: Bachelor Days," ABC, 1968; "That's Life: Our First Baby," ABC, 1968; "Operation: Entertainment," ABC, 1969; "Turn On," ABC, 1969; "The Glen Campbell Goodtime Hour," CBS, 1969; "The Carol Burnett Show," CBS, 1969; "Rowan & Martin's Laugh-In," NBC, 1970; "The Carol Burnett Show," CBS, 1972; "The New Bill Cosby Show," CBS, 1972; "The Carol Burnett Show," CBS, 1973; "The New Bill Cosby Show," CBS, 1973; "The Flip Wilson Show," NBC, 1973; "Hotel Ninety," CBS, 1973; "The Carol Burnett Show," CBS, 1974; "Hi-Ho, Steverino: A 25th Anniversary Salute to Steve Allen," ABC, 1974; "The Boys," CBS, 1974; "ABC Afternoon Special: The Crazy Comedy Concert," ABC, 1974; "The Carol Burnett Show," CBS, 1974; "Doris Day Today," CBS, 1975.
TV MOVIES AND MINISERIES: "Roll, Freddy, Roll," ABC, 1974.
* Conway was the first and only guest host of "Turn On," an ABC "Laugh-In" ripoff that was so tasteless it was cancelled after one episode.
* Emmies: 1973, 1977, 1978.

CONWAY, TOM
b. Thomas Charles Sanders, Russia, September 15, 1904; d. 1967. Actor who played crimefighter Mark Saber.
AS A REGULAR: "The Vise/Mark Saber," ABC, 1951-54; "The Betty Hutton Show," CBS, 1959-60.
AND: "The 20th Century-Fox Hour: Stranger in the Night," CBS, 1956; "The Jane Wyman Show: Not for Publication," NBC, 1957; "O. Henry Playhouse: A Madison Square Arabian Knight," SYN, 1957; "Alfred Hitchcock Presents: The Glass Eye," CBS, 1957; "Rawhide: Incident of the Tumbleweed Wagon," CBS, 1959; "Cheyenne: The Conspirators," ABC, 1960; "Alfred Hitchcock Presents: Relative View," CBS, 1959; "Alfred Hitchcock Presents: The Schartz-Metterklume Method," CBS, 1960; "The Dick Powell Show: The Fifth Caller," NBC, 1961; "Perry Mason: The Case of the Simple Simon," CBS, 1964.

COOGAN, JACKIE
b. Jack Leslie Coogan, Los Angeles, October 24, 1914; d. 1984. Former child star who appeared opposite Charlie Chaplin in "The Kid" at age seven; later he turned to character roles, most notably that of bald, dumpy Uncle Fester, who lit up light bulbs by putting them in his mouth on "The Addams Family."
AS A REGULAR: "Pantomime Quiz," CBS, 1950; CBS, 1951; NBC, 1952; CBS, 1953; DUM, 1953-54; ABC, 1955; CBS, 1955; "Cowboy G-Men," SYN, 1952; "McKeever and the Colonel," NBC, 1962-63; "The Addams

Family," ABC, 1964-66; NBC, 1973-74.
AND: "Racket Squad: Christmas Caper," CBS, 1952; "So This Is Hollywood: Reunion in Hollywood," NBC, 1955; "Damon Runyon Theatre: Honorary Degree," CBS, 1955; "Matinee Theatre: The Old Payola," NBC, 1956; "Playhouse 90: Forbidden Area," CBS, 1956; "Playhouse 90: The Star Wagon," CBS, 1957; "Playhouse 90: Charley's Aunt," CBS, 1957; "Studio One: Trial by Slander," CBS, 1958; "The Red Skelton Show," CBS, 1958; "Peter Gunn: Keep Smiling," NBC, 1959; "The Red Skelton Show," CBS, 1959; "The Ann Sothern Show: Surprise, Surprise," CBS, 1960; "The Ann Sothern Show: Wedding March," CBS, 1960; "Mr. Lucky: Dangerous Lady," CBS, 1960; "Shirley Temple's Storybook: Rebel Gun," NBC, 1961; "Perry Mason: The Case of the Crying Comedian," CBS, 1961; "The Andy Griffith Show: Barney on the Rebound," CBS, 1961; "The Joey Bishop Show: A Show of His Own," NBC, 1962; "The Red Skelton Hour," CBS, 1962; "The Dick Powell Show: Thunder in a Forgotten Town," NBC, 1963; "The Jack Paar Program," NBC, 1964; "Burke's Law: Who Killed Annie Foran?," ABC, 1964; "Family Affair: Fat, Fat, the Water Rat," CBS, 1967; "I Dream of Jeannie: Guess Who's Going to Be a Bride," NBC, 1969; "The Name of the Game: Man of the People," NBC, 1970; "The Partridge Family: Did You Hear the One About Danny Partridge?," ABC, 1970; "The Name of the Game: The Glory Shouter," NBC, 1970; "Barefoot in the Park: Disorder in the Court," ABC, 1970; "Alias Smith and Jones: Which Way to the OK Corral?," ABC, 1972; "Love, American Style: Love and the Happy Day," ABC, 1972; "The Brady Bunch: The Fender Benders," ABC, 1972; "Cool Million: Assault on Gavaloni," NBC, 1972; "Emergency!: Trainee," NBC, 1972; "Love, American Style: Love and the Newscasters," ABC, 1972; "Marcus Welby, M.D.: The Problem with Charlie," ABC, 1973; "McMillan and Wife: Two Dollars' Trouble," NBC, 1973; "Alias Smith and Jones: McGuffin," ABC, 1973; "Hawaii Five-O: Here Today, Gone Tonight," CBS, 1973; "Ironside: Friend or Foe," NBC, 1974; "McMillan and Wife: Cross and Double," NBC, 1974; "Dirty Sally: The Hanging of Cyrus Pike," CBS, 1974; "Gunsmoke: The Guns of Cibola Blanca," CBS, 1974; "Lucille Ball Special," CBS, 1975; "McCoy: Doubletake," NBC, 1975; "$weepstake$: Victor, Billy and Bobby, 'Sometimes,'" NBC, 1979.
TV MOVIES AND MINISERIES: "Cool Million," NBC, 1972; "The Phantom of Hollywood," CBS, 1974; "Sherlock Holmes in New York," NBC, 1976.

COOGAN, KEITH
b. Palm Springs, CA, January 13, 1970. Former child actor who played Jeffrey Burton on "The Waltons"; he's the grandson of Jackie Coogan.

AS A REGULAR: "The MacKenzies of Paradise Cove," ABC, 1979; "The Waltons," CBS, 1979-80; "Gun Shy," CBS, 1983.
AND: "The Love Boat: Tug of War," ABC, 1979; "Strike Force: Magic Man," ABC, 1981; "ABC Afterschool Special: A Town's Revenge," ABC, 1989.
TV MOVIES AND MINISERIES: "A Question of Love," ABC, 1978; "Memorial Day," CBS, 1983.

COOGAN, RICHARD
b. Short Hills, NY.
AS A REGULAR: "Captain Video and his Video Rangers," DUM, 1949-50; "Love of Life," CBS, 1951-56; "The Californians," NBC, 1957-59; "The Clear Horizon," CBS, 1960-61, 1962.
AND: "Bronco: Shadow of Jesse James," ABC, 1960; "Cheyenne: Alibi for a Scalped Man," ABC, 1960; "Sugarfoot: Wolf Pack," ABC, 1960; "Maverick: Thunder From the North," ABC, 1960; "Laramie: No Second Chance," NBC, 1960; "The Loretta Young Show: This Subtle Danger," NBC, 1961; "Bonanza: The Rescue," NBC, 1961; "Laramie: Riders of the Night," NBC, 1961; "Laramie: Widow in White," NBC, 1961; "Laramie: The Barefoot Kid," NBC, 1962; "Laramie: The Replacement," NBC, 1962.

COOK, DONALD
b. Portland, OR, September 26, 1900; d. 1961. Stage and film actor who did some New York-based TV.
AS A REGULAR: "Plymouth Playhouse," ABC, 1953; "Too Young to Go Steady," NBC, 1959.
AND: "Prudential Family Playhouse: Skylark," CBS, 1951; "Lux Video Theatre: The Magnolia Touch," CBS, 1952; "Lux Video Theatre: One of Those Things," CBS, 1953; "The Doctor: The Way of Hope," ABC, 1953; "P.M. Playhouse: Make Me Happy, Make Me Sad," CBS, 1954; "Goodyear TV Playhouse: The Tresaure Hunters," NBC, 1957; "Schlitz Playhouse of Stars: No Answer," CBS, 1958.

COOK, ELISHA, JR.
b. San Francisco, CA, December 26, 1906. Legendary movie heavy or henchman, appearing memorably as Wilmer in "The Maltese Falcon"; best known on TV as Frances "Ice Pick" Hofstetler on "Magnum, P.I."
AS A REGULAR: "Magnum P.I.," CBS, 1983-88.
AND: "Motorola TV Hour: Brandenburg Gate," ABC, 1953; "Treasury Men in Action: The Case of the Elder Brother," ABC, 1955; "Alfred Hitchcock Presents: Salvage," CBS, 1955; "TV Reader's Digest: The Trigger Finger Clue," ABC, 1956; "Climax!: The Secret Thread," CBS,

1956; "The Millionaire: The Story of Judge William Westholme," CBS, 1957; "The Life and Legend of Wyatt Earp: The Equalizer," ABC, 1957; "G.E. Theatre: Silent Ambush," CBS, 1958; "Trackdown: The Trail," CBS, 1958; "Johnny Staccato: Evil," NBC, 1959; "Tightrope!: The Long Odds," CBS, 1960; "Johnny Staccato: Solomon," NBC, 1960; "Wagon Train: The Tracy Sadler Story," NBC, 1960; "Peter Gunn: The Long, Long Ride," NBC, 1960; "Startime: The Young Juggler," NBC, 1960; "The Rebel: The Bequest," ABC, 1960; "Thriller: The Fatal Impulse," NBC, 1960; "SurfSide 6: Witness for the Defense," ABC, 1961; "The Outlaws: The Dark Sunrise of Griff Kincaid," NBC, 1962; "The Dick Powell Show: Borderline," NBC, 1962; "The Fugitive: The Witch," ABC, 1963; "Destry: Law and Order Day," ABC, 1964; "Rawhide: Piney," CBS, 1964; "Perry Mason: The Case of the Reckless Rockhound," CBS, 1964; "Summer Fun: McNab's Lab," ABC, 1966; "The Road West: The Wild Man," NBC, 1966; "Star Trek: Courtmartial," NBC, 1967; "Batman: Ice Spy/The Duo Defy," ABC, 1967; "Dinah Shore Special," NBC, 1969; "The Ghost and Mrs. Muir: Not So Desperate Hours," ABC, 1969; "Bonanza: The Weary Willies," NBC, 1970; "McCloud: Encounter with Aries," NBC, 1971; "Movin' On: Pilot," NBC, 1974; "The Odd Couple: Our Fathers," ABC, 1974; "Ironside: A Matter of Life or Death," NBC, 1974; "SWAT: Coven of Killers," ABC, 1975; "McCoy: In Again, Out Again," NBC, 1976; "Simon & Simon: The Shadow of Sam Penny," CBS, 1983; "The A-Team: The Road to Hope," NBC, 1985; "The Twilight Zone: Quarantine," CBS, 1986.
TV MOVIES AND MINISERIES: "The Movie Murderer," NBC, 1970; "Night Chase," CBS, 1970; "The Night Stalker," ABC, 1972; "The Phantom of Hollywood," CBS, 1974; "Salem's Lot," CBS, 1979; "Leave 'Em Laughing," CBS, 1981; "This Girl for Hire," CBS, 1983.

COOK, FIELDER
b. Atlanta, GA, March 9, 1923. Producer and director of notable live drama shows.
AS PRODUCER-DIRECTOR: "Kraft Television Theatre (Kraft Theatre)," NBC, 1947-58; ABC, 1953-55; "Kaiser Aluminum Hour," NBC, 1956-57; "Playhouse 90: The Dingaling Girl," CBS, 1959; "The Phildelphia Story," NBC, 1959; "Playhouse 90: In the Presence of Mine Enemies," CBS, 1960; "Focus," NBC, 1962; "Hallmark Hall of Fame: The Price," NBC, 1971; "The Pool Hall," A&E, 1989.
TV MOVIES AND MINISERIES: "Sam Hill: Who Killed The Mysterious Mr. Foster?," NBC, 1971; "Goodbye Raggedy Ann," CBS, 1971; "The Homecoming," CBS, 1971; "Miracle on 34th Street," CBS, 1973.
* Emmies: 1971.

COOK, NATHAN
b. Philadelphia, PA, April 9, 1950. Actor who played Billy Griffin on "Hotel."
AS A REGULAR: "The White Shadow," CBS, 1978-80; "Hotel," ABC, 1983-88.
AND: "Hill Street Blues: Blood Money," NBC, 1981; "Hill Street Blues: Hearts and Minds," NBC, 1981; "Hill Street Blues: The Last White Man on East Ferry Avenue," NBC, 1981; "The Love Boat: Forties Fantasy," ABC, 1985.

COOK, PETER
b. England, November 17, 1937. Urbane-looking English comic who was teamed with Dudley Moore for a time; best known to TV audiences as proper butler Robert Brentwood on "The Two of Us."
AS A REGULAR: "The Two of Us," CBS, 1981-82.
AND: "The Jack Paar Program," NBC, 1962; "What's My Line?," CBS, 1963; "The Merv Griffin Show," NBC, 1963; "Chronicle: A Trip to the Moon," CBS, 1964; "The Mike Douglas Show," SYN, 1968; "Kraft Music Hall," NBC, 1969; "Saturday Night Live," NBC, 1976.

COOKE, ALSTAIR
b. Alfred Alistair Cooke, Manchester, England, November 20, 1908. Urbane host and TV personality.
AS A REGULAR: "Omnibus," CBS, 1952-56; ABC, 1956-57; NBC, 1957-61; "The Dow Hour of Great Mysteries," NBC, 1960-61; "Masterpiece Theatre," PBS, 1970- ; "America," NBC, 1972-73.
AND: "The Last Word," CBS, 1957; "The Perry Como Show," NBC, 1957; "The Last Word," CBS, 1958; "Space—Man's Last Frontier," NBC, 1959.
* Emmies: 1973, 1975.

COOKSEY, DANNY
b. Moore, OK, November 2, 1975.
AS A REGULAR: "Diff'rent Strokes," NBC, 1984-85; ABC, 1985-86; "The Cavanaughs," CBS, 1986-88.
AND: "MacGyver: Eagles," ABC, 1986; "Werewolf: The Boy Who Cried Werewolf," FOX, 1987.
TV MOVIES AND MINISERIES: "A Smokey Mountain Christmas," ABC, 1986.

COOPER, GARY
b. Frank James Cooper, Helena, MT, May 7, 1901; d. 1961. Movie legend.
AS A GUEST: "Wide, Wide World: The Western," NBC, 1958; "The Jack Benny Program," CBS, 1958; "The Perry Como Show," NBC, 1959; "Hedda Hopper's Hollywood," NBC, 1960; "Project 20: The Real West," NBC, 1961.

COOPER, DAME GLADYS

b. England, December 18, 1888; d. 1971.
AS A REGULAR: "The Rogues," NBC, 1964-65.
AND: "Alcoa Hour: Sister," NBC, 1956; "The
Joseph Cotten Show: The Tichborne Claimant,"
NBC, 1957; "Alfred Hitchcock Presents: The End
of Indian Summer," CBS, 1957; "Playhouse 90:
Circle of the Day," CBS, 1957; "Playhouse 90: The
Mystery of 13," CBS, 1957; "Suspicion: Lord
Arthur Saville's Crime," NBC, 1958; "Playhouse
90: Verdict of Three," CBS, 1958; "Theatre '59:
The Stray Cat," NBC, 1959; "Adventures in
Paradise: Paradise Lost," ABC, 1959; "The
Twilight Zone: Nothing in the Dark," CBS, 1962;
"Naked City: Memory of a Red Trolley Car,"
ABC, 1962; "The Dick Powell Show: In Search of
a Son," NBC, 1962; "Fair Exchange: Dorothy's
Trip to Europe," CBS, 1962; "The Alfred
Hitchcock Hour: What Really Happened?," CBS,
1963; "Hallmark Hall of Fame: Pygmalion," NBC,
1963; "Going My Way: The Custody of the Child,"
ABC, 1963; "The Twilight Zone: Passage on the
Lady Anne," CBS, 1963; "Burke's Law: Who
Killed Sweet Betsy?," ABC, 1963; "The Twilight
Zone: Night Call," CBS, 1963; "The Twilight
Zone: Passage on the Lady Anne," CBS, 1963;
"The Outer Limits: Borderland," ABC, 1963; "The
Alfred Hitchcock Hour: Consider Her Ways,"
NBC, 1964; "The Twilight Zone: Night Call,"
CBS, 1964; "Ben Casey: Because of the Needle,
the Haystack Was Lost," ABC, 1965; "Run,
Buddy, Run: Killer Cassidy," CBS, 1966.

COOPER, JACKIE

*b. John Cooper, Jr., Los Angeles, CA, September
15, 1922.* Former child star who made the jump
to adult stardom. On TV he was councilman
Socrates Miller on "The People's Choice" and
Navy doctor Chick Hennessey. Now he directs.
AS A REGULAR: "The People's Choice," NBC,
1955-58; "Hennesey," CBS, 1959-62; "The
Dean Martin Comedy World," NBC, 1974;
"Mobile One," ABC, 1975.
AND: "Lux Video Theatre: Life, Liberty and Orrin
Dooley," NBC, 1952; "Tales of Tomorrow: The
Cocoon," ABC, 1952; "Lux Video Theatre: A
Message for Janice," CBS, 1952; "Robert
Montgomery Presents: The Fall Guy," NBC, 1952;
"Armstrong Circle Theatre: The Middle Son,"
NBC, 1953; "Danger: Towerman," CBS, 1953;
"Medallion Theatre: Twenty-Four Men to a Plane,"
CBS, 1953; "Robert Montgomery Presents: A
Dreamer of a Summer," NBC, 1954; "Producers
Showcase: Yellow Jack," NBC, 1955; "G.E.
Theatre: Yankee Peddler," CBS, 1955; "Armstrong
Circle Theatre: I Found 60 Million Dollars," NBC,
1955; "Robert Montgomery Presents: It Depends
on You," NBC, 1955; "U.S. Steel Hour: The Old
Lady Shows Her Medals," CBS, 1956; "The Steve
Allen Show," NBC, 1957; "Studio One: The Fair-
Haired Boy," CBS, 1958; "The George Gobel

Show," NBC, 1958; "To Tell the Truth," CBS,
1958; "Steve Allen Presents the Steve Lawrence
and Eydie Gorme Show," NBC, 1958; "The Arthur
Godfrey Show," CBS, 1958; "Oldsmobile Music
Theatre: A Nice Place to Hide," NBC, 1959; "Pat
Boone Chevy Showroom," ABC, 1959; "Dick
Clark's World of Talent," ABC, 1959; "Arthur
Murray Party," NBC, 1959; "Dinah Shore Chevy
Show," NBC, 1959; "Revlon Revue," CBS, 1960;
"U.S. Steel Hour: Step on the Gas," CBS, 1960;
"Best of the Post: Martha," SYN, 1961; "Mrs. G.
Goes to College: Mrs. G. Meets Dr. Hennesey,"
CBS, 1961; "The Danny Kaye Show," CBS, 1963;
"The Great Adventure: The Hunley," CBS, 1963;
"The Twilight Zone: Caesar and Me," CBS, 1964;
"McCloud: Encounter with Aries," NBC, 1972;
"Ironside: The Countdown," NBC, 1972; "Ghost
Story: Cry of the Cat," NBC, 1972; "Keep an Eye
on Denise," CBS, 1973; "Columbo: Candidate for
Crime," NBC, 1973; "Kojak: Last Rites for a Dead
Priest," CBS, 1974; "Police Story: Robbery: 48
Hours," NBC, 1974; "The Rockford Files: Claire,"
NBC, 1975; "The Merv Griffin Show," SYN,
1975; "Police Story: Eamon Kinsella Royce,"
NBC, 1976; "Police Story: The Blue Fog," NBC,
1977; "The Rockford Files: The House on Willis
Avenue," NBC, 1978; "St. Elsewhere: Time
Heals," NBC, 1986; "Murder, She Wrote: Death
Stalks the Big Top," CBS, 1986.
TV MOVIES AND MINISERIES: "The Astronaut," NBC,
1972; "The Day the Earth Moved," ABC, 1974;
"The Invisible Man," NBC, 1975; "Mobile
Two," ABC, 1975.
AS DIRECTOR: "The People's Choice," NBC, 1956-
58; "M*A*S*H," CBS, 1973-74; "The Mary
Tyler Moore Show: You Sometimes Hurt the
One You Hate," CBS, 1974; "The White
Shadow," CBS, 1978-80.
TV MOVIES AND MINISERIES: "Shadow on the Land,"
NBC, 1968; "Maybe I'll Come Home in the
Spring," ABC, 1971; "The Invisible Man,"
NBC, 1975.
* Emmies: 1974, 1979.

COOPER, JEANNE

b. Taft, CA. Experienced character actress who
plays Kay Chancellor on "The Young and the
Restless"; mother of Corbin Bernsen.
AS A REGULAR: "Bracken's World," NBC, 1970;
"The Young and the Restless," CBS, 1973- .
AND: "Ford Theatre: Sometimes It Happens," ABC,
1956; "Playhouse 90: The Country Husband,"
CBS, 1956; "The Web: Last Chance," NBC, 1957;
"Cheyenne: Top Hand," ABC, 1957; "Death
Valley Days: I Am Joaquin," SYN, 1958; "The
Jane Wyman Show: A Widow's Kiss," NBC,
1958; "M Squad: The Cover-Up," NBC, 1958;
"Dick Powell's Zane Grey Theatre: Showdown at
Bitter Creek," CBS, 1958; "77 Sunset Strip:
Lovely Lady, Pity Me," ABC, 1958; "Tales of
Wells Fargo: Belle Starr," NBC, 1958; "Schlitz

Playhouse of Stars: The Man Who Had No Friends," CBS, 1959; "Death Valley Days: Sixth Sense," SYN, 1959; "The Twilight Zone: Mr. Denton on Doomsday," CBS, 1959; "Wanted Dead or Alive: Man on Horseback," CBS, 1959; "The Man From Blackhawk: Death at Noon," ABC, 1960; "Bronco: Shadow of Jesse James," ABC, 1960; "M Squad: Grenade for a Summer Evening," NBC, 1960; "Thriller: The Big Blackout," NBC, 1960; "The Tall Man: The Reversed Blade," NBC, 1961; "Maverick: Flood's Folly," ABC, 1961; "Rawhide: Incident on the Road Back," CBS, 1961; "Ben Casey: But Linda Only Smiled," ABC, 1961; "87th Precinct: Killer's Payoff," NBC, 1961; "The New Breed: The Butcher," ABC, 1961; "The Roaring Twenties: Asparagus Tips," ABC, 1961; "Wagon Train: The Traitor," NBC, 1961; "SurfSide 6: Anniversary Special," ABC, 1962; "Hawaiian Eye: My Love, But Lightly," ABC, 1962; "Perry Mason: The Case of the Glamorous Ghost," CBS, 1962; "Have Gun, Will Travel: Protects Ex-Con's Wife," CBS, 1962; "Cheyenne: The Quick and the Deadly," ABC, 1962; "Wagon Train: The Donna Fuller Story," ABC, 1962; "Bonanza: The Good Samaritan," NBC, 1962; "The Eleventh Hour: My Name Is Judith, I'm Lost, You See," NBC, 1963; "The Dakotas: Mutiny at Fort Mercy," ABC, 1963; "Rawhide: Incident at Crooked Hat," CBS, 1963; "Stoney Burke: Web of Fear," ABC, 1963; "Hawaiian Eye: The Long Way Home," ABC, 1963; "Bonanza: She Walks in Beauty," NBC, 1963; "Mr. Novak: The Boy Without a Country," NBC, 1963; "The Virginian: The Fortunes of J. Jimerson Jones," NBC, 1964; "77 Sunset Strip: The Target," ABC, 1964; "Perry Mason: The Case of the Nervous Neighbor," CBS, 1964; "Dr. Kildare: The Child Between," NBC, 1964; "A Man Called Shenandoah: Survival," ABC, 1965; "The Loner: The Lonely Calico Queen," CBS, 1965; "The Big Valley: Heritage," ABC, 1965; "The Man From UNCLE: The Children's Day Affair," NBC, 1965; "The Monroes: Ride with Terror," ABC, 1966; "Ironside: Officer Bobby," NBC, 1968; "Nanny and the Professor: The Balloon Ladies," ABC, 1971; "Mannix: A Walk in the Shadows," CBS, 1972; "Hawkins: A Life for a Life," CBS, 1973; "Doc Elliot: The Carrier," ABC, 1974; "Kolchak, the Night Stalker: The Devil's Platform," ABC, 1974; "The Mike Douglas Show," SYN, 1981; "L.A. Law: Fry Me to the Moon," NBC, 1986.
TV MOVIES AND MINISERIES: "Sweet Hostage," ABC, 1975.
* When Cooper had a facelift in the early eighties, the producers of "The Young and the Restless" wrote it into the script, and the cameras filmed the procedure.

COOPER, MELVILLE
b. England, October 15, 1896; d. 1973.

AS A REGULAR: "I've Got a Secret," CBS, 1952.
AND: "Musical Comedy Time: The Merry Widow," NBC, 1950; "Musical Comedy Time: Mme. Modiste," NBC, 1951; "Robert Montgomery Presents: Cashel Byron's Profession," NBC, 1952; "Kraft Television Theatre: The Peaceful Warrior," NBC, 1952; "Kraft Television Theatre: A Christmas Carol," NBC, 1952; "Armstrong Circle Theatre: The Marmalade Scandal," NBC, 1953; "Summer Studio One: The Gathering Night," CBS, 1953; "Telephone Time: Keely's Wonderful Machine," CBS, 1956; "Alfred Hitchcock Presents: I Killed the Count," CBS, 1956; "Playhouse 90: Charley's Aunt," CBS, 1957; "West Point: Jet Flight," ABC, 1957; "Shirley Temple's Storybook: The Wild Swans," NBC, 1958; "U.S. Steel Hour: Night of Betrayal," CBS, 1959; "Dow Hour of Great Mysteries: The Datchet Diamonds," NBC, 1960; "Best of the Post: Six Months to Live," SYN, 1960.

COOTE, ROBERT
b. London, England, February 4, 1909.
AS A REGULAR: "Who's There?," CBS, 1952; "The Rogues," NBC, 1964-65; "Nero Wolfe," NBC, 1981.
AND: "Westinghouse Desilu Playhouse: Murder in Gratitude," CBS, 1959; "Playhouse 90: To the Sound of Trumpets," CBS, 1960; "Rawhide: Incident in the Garden of Eden," CBS, 1960; "$weepstake$: Billy, Wally and Ludmilla, and Theodore," NBC, 1979.
TV MOVIES AND MINISERIES: "Target Risk," NBC, 1975.

COPAGE, MARC
b. Los Angeles, CA, June 21, 1962. Child actor who played Corey Baker, daughter of "Julia" (Diahann Carroll).
AS A REGULAR: "Julia," NBC, 1968-71.
AND: "Hollywood Palace," ABC, 1968; "Sanford & Son: Ebenezer Sanford," NBC, 1975.

COPELAND, MAURICE
b. Rector, AR, 1911; d. 1985.
AS A REGULAR: "Hawkins Falls," NBC, 1951-55; "Those Endearing Young Charms," NBC, 1952.

COPLEY, TERI
b. 1961. Blonde starlet.
AS A REGULAR: "We Got It Made," NBC, 1983-84; SYN, 1987-88; "I Had Three Wives," CBS, 1985.
AND: "The Love Boat: Dutch Treat," ABC, 1984; "The Love Boat: The Tour Guide," ABC, 1986; "Quantum Leap: October 24, 1974," NBC, 1989.
TV MOVIES AND MINISERIES: "The Star Maker," NBC, 1981; "I Married a Centerfold," NBC, 1984; "In the Line of Duty: The FBI Murders," NBC, 1988.

CORBETT, GLENN

b. El Monte, CA, 1929. Generically handsome leading man who replaced George Maharis on "Route 66" as Linc Case, and who plays Paul Morgan on "Dallas."

AS A REGULAR: "It's a Man's World," NBC, 1962-63; "Route 66," CBS, 1963-64; "The Road West," NBC, 1966-67; "The Doctors," NBC, 1976-81; "Dallas," CBS, 1983-84, 1988- .

AND: "Silver Theatre: My Brother's Keeper," CBS, 1950; "Gunsmoke: Chicken," CBS, 1964; "Twelve O'Clock High: The Men and the Boys," ABC, 1964; "Twelve O'Clock High: Those Who Are About to Die," ABC, 1965; "The Man From UNCLE: The Hong Kong Shilling Affair," NBC, 1965; "Kraft Suspense Theatre: The Last Clear Chance," NBC, 1965; "The Virginian: The Awakening," NBC, 1965; "Bonanza: Mighty Is the Word," NBC, 1965; "Bob Hope Chrysler Theatre: In Pursuit of Excellence," NBC, 1966; "Garrison's Gorillas: Now I Lay Me Down to Die," ABC, 1967; "Star Trek: Metamorphosis," NBC, 1967; "Marcus Welby, M.D.: Another Buckle for Wesley Hill," ABC, 1971; "The FBI: Death Watch," ABC, 1971; "Bonanza: Winter Kill," NBC, 1971; "Owen Marshall, Counselor at Law: Legacy of Fear," ABC, 1971; "Barnaby Jones: Divorce-Murderer's Style," CBS, 1973; "Cannon: Murder by the Numbers," CBS, 1973; "The Streets of San Francisco: Inferno," ABC, 1973; "Gunsmoke: Family of Killers," CBS, 1974; "Police Story: Cop in the Middle," NBC, 1974; "Police Story: Robbery: 48 Hours," NBC, 1974; "Born Free: The Masai Rebels," NBC, 1974; "Police Woman: Sidewinder," NBC, 1975; "Petrocelli: Five Yards of Trouble," NBC, 1975; "Police Story: Sniper," NBC, 1975; "Police Story: The Empty Weapon," NBC, 1975; "Police Story: The Other Side of the Fence," NBC, 1976; "Barnaby Jones: Master of Deception," CBS, 1979; "The Rockford Files: The Battle-Ax and the Exploding Cigar," NBC, 1979.

TV MOVIES AND MINISERIES: "The Stranger," NBC, 1973; "Log of the Black Pearl," NBC, 1975; "The Law of the Land," NBC, 1976.

CORBETT, GRETCHEN

b. Camp Sherman, OR, August 13, 1947. Actress who played attorney Beth Davenport on "The Rockford Files."

AS A REGULAR: "The Rockford Files," NBC, 1974-78; "Otherworld," CBS, 1985.

AND: "Marcus Welby, M.D.: Fear of Silence," ABC, 1974; "Banacek: Now You See Me, Now You Don't," NBC, 1974; "Ironside: The Taste of Ashes," NBC, 1974; "Columbo: An Exercise in Fatality," NBC, 1974; "Kojak: Conspiracy of Fear," CBS, 1974; "Gunsmoke: A Town in Chains," CBS, 1974; "Marcus Welby, M.D.: The Outrage," ABC, 1974; "McMillan and Wife: Love, Honor and Swindle," NBC, 1975; "Hawaii Five-O: Study in Rage," CBS, 1975; "Marcus Welby, M.D.: Aspects of Love," ABC, 1976; "Emergency!: The Nuisance," NBC, 1976; "Marcus Welby, M.D.: Vanity Case," ABC, 1976; "Switch: Come Die With Me," CBS, 1976; "Hollywood Television Theatre: The Fatal Weakness," PBS, 1976; "Family: Acts of Love," ABC, 1977; "Barnaby Jones: Blind Jeopardy," CBS, 1978; "One Day at a Time: Plain Favorite," CBS, 1981; "Magnum, P.I.: The Curse of the King Kamahameha Club," CBS, 1981; "Cheers: Diane's Perfect Date," NBC, 1983; "Magnum P.I.: Limited Engagement," CBS, 1983; "Murder, She Wrote: Deadline for Murder," CBS, 1986; "21 Jump Street: Higher Education," FOX, 1987.

TV MOVIES AND MINISERIES: "The Savage Bees," NBC, 1976; "Secrets of Three Hungry Wives," NBC, 1978; "Mandrake," NBC, 1979; "She's Dressed to Kill," NBC, 1979; "North Beach and Rawhide," CBS, 1985.

CORBY, ELLEN

b. Ellen Hansen, Racine, WI, June 3, 1913. Actress who, after years of playing spinsters, found recognition as Grandma Walton.

AS A REGULAR: "Trackdown," CBS, 1958-59; "Please Don't Eat the Daisies," NBC, 1965-67; "The Waltons," CBS, 1972-79.

AND: "The Millionaire: Millionaire Bedelia Buckley," CBS, 1956; "Telephone Time: Mr. and Mrs. Browning," CBS, 1956; "Matinee Theatre: The Hollow Woman," NBC, 1956; "I Love Lucy: Lucy Meets Orson Welles," CBS, 1956; "The Life and Legend of Wyatt Earp: Shootin' Woman," ABC, 1957; "Mr. Adams and Eve: Howard Goes to Jail," CBS, 1957; "Restless Gun: Crisis at Easter Creek," NBC, 1958; "Peter Gunn: Love Me to Death," NBC, 1958; "Wagon Train: The Greenhorn Story," NBC, 1959; "The Betty Hutton Show: Gullible Goldie," CBS, 1960; "Hennesey: We're Glad It's You," CBS, 1960; "Wagon Train: Wagons Ho!," NBC, 1960; "Follow the Sun: Mele Kalikmaka to You," ABC, 1961; "The Bob Cummings Show: Kay Largo," CBS, 1962; "Cheyenne: The Durango Brothers," ABC, 1962; "Fair Exchange: Innocents Abroad," CBS, 1962; "Bonanza: The Hayburner," NBC, 1963; "The Andy Griffith Show: Barney's First Car," CBS, 1963; "Hazel: You Ain't Fully Dressed Without a Smile," NBC, 1963; "McKeever and the Colonel: Make Room for Mother," NBC, 1963; "The Lucy Show: Lucy Gets Locked in the Vault," CBS, 1963; "Hazel: Hot Potato a la Hazel," NBC, 1964; "The Beverly Hillbillies: The Widow Poke Arrives," CBS, 1964; "Gomer Pyle, USMC: The Case of the Marine Bandit," CBS, 1964; "The Virginian: All Nice and Legal," NBC, 1964; "Ben Casey: A Woods Full of Question Marks," ABC, 1964; "The Littlest Hobo: Two Against Two," SYN, 1965; "The Addams Family: Mother Lurch Visits the Addams Family," ABC, 1965; "The

Donna Reed Show: The Gift Shop," ABC, 1965; "The Farmer's Daughter: The Woman Behind the Man," ABC, 1965; "Hazel: The Hold Out," CBS, 1965; "The FBI: The Forests of the Night," ABC, 1966; "Honey West: Come to Me, My Litigation Baby," ABC, 1966; "Get Smart: Dear Diary," NBC, 1966; "The FBI: Collision Course," ABC, 1966; "The FBI: The Satellite," ABC, 1967; "The FBI: The Nightmare," ABC, 1968; "The FBI: The Butcher," ABC, 1968; "Batman: The Joker's Flying Saucer," ABC, 1968; "Gomer Pyle, USMC: The Short Voyage Home," CBS, 1969; "Nanny and the Professor: I Think That I Shall Never See a Tree," ABC, 1970; "The FBI: The Savage Wilderness," ABC, 1970; "Tenafly: Joyride to Nowhere," NBC, 1973.

TV MOVIES AND MINISERIES: "A Tattered Web," CBS, 1971; "The Homecoming," CBS, 1971; "The Story of Pretty Boy Floyd," ABC, 1974; "A Day for Thanks on Walton's Mountain," NBC, 1982.

* A stroke kept Corby off "The Waltons" for a time in 1977; she returned in 1978 but her frail condition forced her off the show for good in 1979.
* Emmies: 1973, 1975, 1976.

CORCORAN, BRIAN
b. California, 1951.
AS A REGULAR: "Walt Disney Presents: Texas John Slaughter," ABC, 1958-61; "O.K. Crackerby," ABC, 1965-66.
AND: "Suspicion: Four O'Clock," NBC, 1957; "Wagon Train: The Estaban Zamora Story," NBC, 1959; "Walt Disney Presents: The Nine Lives of Elfego Baca—Gus Tomlin Is Dead," ABC, 1960; "Here's Hollywood," NBC, 1961; "Bachelor Father: Blossom Comes to Visit," ABC, 1962; "The Munsters: Hot Rod Herman," CBS, 1965.

CORCORAN, DONNA
b. 1941.
AS A GUEST: "Tales of Wells Fargo: All That Glitters," NBC, 1960; "Here's Hollywood," NBC, 1961; "My Three Sons: First Things First," ABC, 1963.

CORCORAN, KELLY
b. California, 1958. Young actor.
AS A REGULAR: "The Road West," NBC, 1966-67.
AND: "The Adventures of Ozzie and Harriet: The Chess Set," ABC, 1964.

CORCORAN, KEVIN
b. Santa Monica, CA, June 10, 1949. Child actor who played Moochie in serials on the "Mickey Mouse Club" and appeared in other Walt Disney projects.
AS A GUEST: "Mickey Mouse Club," ABC, 1957;

"Disneyland: Fourth Anniversary Show," ABC, 1957; "Walt Disney Presents: A Diamond Is a Boy's Best Friend," ABC, 1959; "The Ed Sullivan Show," CBS, 1960; "Walt Disney Presents: Moochie of Pop Warner Football," ABC, 1960; "Walt Disney Presents: Daniel Boone—... And Chase the Buffalo," ABC, 1960; "Here's Hollywood," NBC, 1961; "Walt Disney Presents: Daniel Boone—The Wilderness Road," ABC, 1961; "Walt Disney's Wonderful World of Color: Backstage Party," NBC, 1961; "Walt Disney's Wonderful World of Color: The Mooncussers," NBC, 1962; "Walt Disney's Wonderful World of Color: Johnny Shiloh," NBC, 1963; "My Three Sons: Both Your Houses," CBS, 1967.

CORCORAN, NOREEN
b. Los Angeles, CA, 1943. Young actress who played Kelly Gregg, the girl who made her uncle, swinging bachelor Bentley Gregg (John Forsythe) a "Bachelor Father"; one of a whole family of young actors and actresses of the fifties and sixties.
AS A REGULAR: "Bachelor Father," CBS, 1957-59; NBC, 1959-61; ABC, 1961-62.
AND: "G.E. Theatre: A New Girl in His Life," CBS, 1957; "Here's Hollywood," NBC, 1961; "Going My Way: Don't Forget to Say Goodbye," ABC, 1963; "Channing: Exercise in a Shark Tank," ABC, 1963; "The Eleventh Hour: You're So Smart, Why Can't You Be Good?," NBC, 1964; "Mr. Novak: Fare Thee Well," NBC, 1964.

CORD, ALEX
b. Alexander Viespi, Floral Park, NY, August 3, 1931. Former rodeo performer who specializes in action-oriented roles.
AS A REGULAR: "WEB," NBC, 1978; "Cassie and Company," NBC, 1982; "Airwolf," CBS, 1984-86; USA, 1986-87.
AND: "Branded: Survival," NBC, 1965; "ABC Nightlife," ABC, 1965; "Bob Hope Chrysler Theatre: The Lady Is My Wife," NBC, 1967; "Room 222: Clothes Make the Boy," ABC, 1969; "Night Gallery: Keep in Touch, We'll Think of Something," NBC, 1971; "Mission: Impossible: Crack-Up," CBS, 1972; "Gunsmoke: The Sodbusters," CBS, 1972; "Mission: Impossible: Crack-Up," CBS, 1972; "The FBI: Night of the Long Knives," ABC, 1973; "Police Story: Line of Fire," NBC, 1973; "Born Free: The Trespassers," NBC, 1974; "Police Story: To Steal a Million," NBC, 1975; "Police Story: The Losing Game," NBC, 1975; "Police Story: Officer Dooly," NBC, 1976; "Police Woman: Tennis Bum," NBC, 1976; "Hollywood Squares," NBC, 1978; "The Love Boat: Doc's Dismissal," ABC, 1981; "Jake and the Fatman: Key Witness," CBS, 1989; "Mission: Impossible: For Art's Sake," ABC, 1989.

TV MOVIES AND MINISERIES: "The Scorpio Letters,"

ABC, 1967; "Your Money or Your Wife," CBS, 1972; "Genesis II," ABC, 1973; "Beggarman, Thief," NBC, 1979; "The Dirty Dozen: The Fatal Mission," NBC, 1988.

COREY, PROF. IRWIN
b. Brooklyn, NY, January 29, 1912. Comedian.
AS A REGULAR: "The Andy Williams Show," NBC, 1969-70; "Doc," CBS, 1975-76.
AND: "The Steve Allen Show," NBC, 1956; "The Steve Allen Show," NBC, 1957; "Omnibus: Mrs. McThing," NBC, 1958; "The Phil Silvers Show: Bilko's Grand Hotel," CBS, 1959; "The Tonight Show Starring Johnny Carson," NBC, 1962; "The Mike Douglas Show," SYN, 1968; "The Merv Griffin Show," SYN, 1973; "The Mike Douglas Show," SYN, 1975.

COREY, JEFF
b. New York City, NY, August 10, 1914. Actor and acting teacher who specializes in kindly elderly types.
AS A REGULAR: "Hell Town," NBC, 1985; "Morningstar/Eveningstar," CBS, 1986.
AND: "Beachcomber: The Shark Affair," SYN, 1962; "The Outer Limits: O.B.I.T.," ABC, 1963; "The Doctors and the Nurses: No Shadow Where There Is No Sun," CBS, 1964; "Rawhide: Incident at Boot Hill," CBS, 1965; "Gomer Pyle, USMC: Supply Sergeants Never Die," CBS, 1965; "The Wild Wild West: The Night of a Thousand Eyes," CBS, 1965; "The Wild Wild West: The Night of the Underground Terror, 1968; "Hawaii Five-O: King of the Hill," CBS, 1968; "Gunsmoke: The Night Riders," CBS, 1969; "Mannix: Overkill," CBS, 1971; "Hawaii Five-O: Highest Castle, Deepest Grave," CBS, 1971; "Alias Smith and Jones: The Day the Amnesty Came Through," ABC, 1973; "The Bob Newhart Show: Old Man Rivers," CBS, 1973; "The Streets of San Francisco: Shattered Image," ABC, 1973; "Paper Moon: The Imposter," ABC, 1974; "Starsky and Hutch: Death Ride," ABC, 1975; "Barney Miller: The Prisoner," ABC, 1978; "What's Happening!: Diplomatic Immunity," ABC, 1978; "Little House on the Prairie: Barn Burner," NBC, 1979; "Barney Miller: The Desk," ABC, 1979; "Lou Grant: Brushfire," CBS, 1980; "Lou Grant: Compesinos," CBS, 1981; "Lou Grant: Blacklist," CBS, 1981; "Newhart: Tickets, Please," CBS, 1984; "Night Court: Santa Goes Downtown," NBC, 1984; "Perfect Strangers: Taking Stock," ABC, 1987; "Wolf: Curtains of Silence," CBS, 1989.
TV MOVIES AND MINISERIES: "The Movie Murderer," NBC, 1970; "A Clear and Present Danger," NBC, 1970; "Something Evil," CBS, 1972; "Set This Town on Fire," NBC, 1973; "Banjo Hackett," NBC, 1976; "The Pirate," CBS, 1978; "Testimony of Two Men," SYN, 1977; "Final Jeopardy," NBC, 1985; "Hell Town," NBC, 1985; "Second Serve," CBS, 1986; "A Deadly Silence," ABC, 1989.

COREY, JOSEPH
b. Joseph Martorano; d. 1972.
AS A REGULAR: "Private Secretary," CBS, 1953-54, 1955-57; "Dear Phoebe," NBC, 1954-55.
AND: "Hennesey: The Christmas Show," CBS, 1959; "M Squad: Anything for Joe," NBC, 1960; "Fair Exchange: Lieutenant's Paradise," CBS, 1962; "Gomer Pyle, USMC: Guest in the Barracks," CBS, 1964; "M*A*S*H: Cowboy," CBS, 1972.
TV MOVIES AND MINISERIES: "Now You See It, Now You Don't," NBC, 1968.

COREY, JILL
b. Avonmore, PA, September 30, 1935. Popular singer of the fifties.
AS A REGULAR: "The Dave Garroway Show," NBC, 1953-54; "The Johnny Carson Daytime Show," CBS, 1955; "The Johnny Carson Show," CBS, 1955-56; "The Jill Corey Show," SYN, 1957; "Your Hit Parade," NBC, 1957-58.
AND: "The Walter Winchell Show," NBC, 1956; "The Jonathan Winters Show," NBC, 1957; "Climax!: Let It Be Me," CBS, 1957; "The Steve Allen Show," NBC, 1957; "Arthur Murray Party," NBC, 1957; "The Vic Damone Show," CBS, 1957; "The Ed Sullivan Show," CBS, 1957; "Texaco Star Theatre: Command Appearnace," NBC, 1957; "Person to Person," CBS, 1957; "Kraft Television Theatre: The Sound of Trouble," NBC, 1957; "The Big Record," CBS, 1957; "The Steve Allen Show," NBC, 1958; "The Dick Clark Saturday Night Beechnut Show," ABC, 1958; "The Ed Sullivan Show," CBS, 1958; "The Jack Paar Show," NBC, 1959; "The George Burns Show," NBC, 1959; "The Jimmie Rodgers Show," NBC, 1959; "The Dick Clark Saturday Night Beechnut Show," ABC, 1960; "The Ed Sullivan Show," CBS, 1960; "Be Our Guest," CBS, 1960; "Music on Ice," NBC, 1960; "Sing Along with Mitch," NBC, 1961; "Seasons of Youth," ABC, 1961.

COREY, WENDELL
b. Dracut, MA, March 20, 1914; d. 1968. Actor who played solid or sardonic types; on TV he was straight man to Patty McCormack ("Peck's Bad Girl") and Nanette Fabray.
AS A REGULAR: "Harbor Command," SYN, 1957-58; "Peck's Bad Girl," CBS, 1959; "Westinghouse Playhouse Starring Nanette Fabray and Wendell Corey (Yes, Yes Nanette)," NBC, 1961; "The Eleventh Hour," NBC, 1962-63.
AND: "Celanese Theatre: Susan and God," ABC, 1951; "C.O.D.," NBC, 1952; "Celanese Theatre: The Animal Kingdom," NBC, 1952; "Curtain

Call: Swell Girl," NBC, 1952; "Gulf Playhouse: The Duel," NBC, 1952; "Hollywood Opening Night: The Lucky Coin," NBC, 1952; "Lux Video Theatre: With Glory and Honor," CBS, 1953; "Plymouth Playhouse: A Tale of Two Cities," ABC, 1953; "Robert Montgomery Presents: Half a Kingdom," NBC, 1953; "Backbone of America: Stagecoach to Paradise," NBC, 1953; "Robert Montgomery Presents: The 17th of June," NBC, 1954; "Studio One: Donovan's Brain," CBS, 1955; "U.S. Steel Hour: The Rack," ABC, 1955; "Climax!: To Wake at Midnight," CBS, 1955; "Alcoa Hour: The Black Wings," NBC, 1955; "Studio One: My Son Johnny," CBS, 1956; "Studio One: The Arena," CBS, 1956; "Climax!: The Lou Gehrig Story," CBS, 1956; "The Tonight Show," NBC, 1956; "The 20th Century-Fox Hour: Man of the Law," CBS, 1957; "Dick Powell's Zane Grey Theatre: Quiet Sunday in San Ardo," CBS, 1957; "Studio One: The Desperate Age," CBS, 1958; "Art Linkletter's House Party," CBS, 1958; "Alfred Hitchcock Presents: Poison," CBS, 1958; "Bob Hope Special," NBC, 1959; "Sunday Showcase: One Loud, Clear Voice," NBC, 1960; "Dick Powell's Zane Grey Theatre: Killer Instinct," CBS, 1960; "Dick Powell's Zane Grey Theatre: The Man From Yesterday," CBS, 1960; "Target: The Corruptors: Mr. Megaloma- nia," ABC, 1961; "The Untouchables: Power Play," ABC, 1961; "The New Breed: Till Death Do Us Part," ABC, 1961; "Walt Disney's Wonderful World of Color: The Light in the Forest," NBC, 1961; "Here's Hollywood," NBC, 1961; "Bus Stop: Turn Again Home," ABC, 1962; "Tell It to Groucho," CBS, 1962; "Channing: A Window on the War," ABC, 1963; "Burke's Law: Who Killed Annie Foran?," ABC, 1964; "Branded: The Mission," NBC, 1965; "Perry Mason: The Case of the Unwelcome Well," CBS, 1966; "Run for Your Life: The Committee for the 25th," NBC, 1966; "The Road West: Piece of Tin," NBC, 1966; "The Guns of Will Sonnett: The Natural Way," ABC, 1967; "The Wild Wild West: Night of the Death-Maker," CBS, 1968.

CORLEY, PAT
b. *Texas*. Actor who plays Phil the bartender on "Murphy Brown"; memorable as coroner Wally Niedorf on "Hill Street Blues."
AS A REGULAR: "The Bay City Blues," NBC, 1983; "He's the Mayor," ABC, 1986; "Murphy Brown," CBS, 1988- .
AND: "Barnaby Jones: The Price of Anger," CBS, 1979; "Lou Grant: Andrew," CBS, 1979; "Lou Grant: Dogs," CBS, 1980; "House Calls: The Ducks of Hazard," CBS, 1982; "Hill Street Blues: A Hair of the Dog," NBC, 1982; "Hill Street Blues: The Phantom of the Hill," NBC, 1982; "Hill Street Blues: No Body's Perfect," NBC, 1982; "The Powers of Matthew Star: Matthew Star: D.O.A.," NBC, 1983; "Hill Street Blues:

The Belles of St. Mary's," NBC, 1983; "St. Elsewhere: Release," NBC, 1983; "Hill Street Blues: Life in the Minors," NBC, 1983; "Simon & Simon: Our Fair City," CBS, 1984; "Hardcastle and McCormick: She Ain't Deep But She Sure Runs Fast," ABC, 1985; "Simon & Simon: Still Phil After All These Years," CBS, 1986; "Murder, She Wrote: Power Keg," CBS, 1986; "Simon & Simon: Sudden Storm," CBS, 1987; "L.A. Law: Pigmalion," NBC, 1987; "J.J. Starbuck: Cactus Jack's Last Call," NBC, 1988; "Cagney & Lacey: A Fair Shake," CBS, 1988.
TV MOVIES AND MINISERIES: "And I Alone Survived," NBC, 1978; "The Executioner's Song," NBC, 1982; "Scorned and Swindled," CBS, 1984; "Stormin' Home," CBS, 1985; "Silent Witness," NBC, 1985; "Stark: Mirror Image," CBS, 1986; "Fresno," CBS, 1986; "The Christmas Gift," CBS, 1986; "The Stepford Children," NBC, 1987; "Poker Alice," CBS, 1987.

CORNELIUS, HELEN
b. *Missouri, December 6, 1941*.
AS A REGULAR: "Nashville on the Road," SYN, 1977-81.

CORNELL, KATHARINE
b. *Berlin, 1893; d. 1974*.
AS A GUEST: "Producers Showcase: The Barretts of Wimpole Street," NBC, 1956; "Hallmark Hall of Fame: There Shall Be No Night," NBC, 1957.

CORNELL, LYDIA
b. *El Paso, TX*.
AS A REGULAR: "Too Close for Comfort," ABC, 1980-83, SYN, 1984-85.
AND: "The Love Boat: Lotions of Love," ABC, 1983; "The A-Team: Wheel of Fortune," NBC, 1985; "Hunter: Straight to the Heart," NBC, 1987; "Full House: El Problema Grande de D.J.," ABC, 1989; "Monsters!: A Bond of Silk," SYN, 1989; "Hagar the Horrible," CBS, 1989.

CORNTHWAITE, ROBERT
b. *St. Helens, OR, April 28, 1917*.
AS A GUEST: "You Are There: The First Moscow Purge Trial," CBS, 1956; "Dick Powell's Zane Grey Theatre: Dangerous Orders," CBS, 1957; "Suspicion: Doomsday," NBC, 1957; "The Thin Man: The Robot Client," NBC, 1958; "The Adventures of Jim Bowie: Adventure with Audubon," ABC, 1958; "Perry Mason: The Case of the Wandering Widow," CBS, 1960; "The Law and Mr. Jones: The Storyville Gang," ABC, 1960; "Maverick: Family Pride," ABC, 1961; "Hong Kong: The Hunted," ABC, 1961; "Lawman: The Grubstake," ABC, 1961; "Adventures in Paradise: The Secret Place,"

ABC, 1962; "Laramie: Naked Steel," NBC, 1963; "The Andy Griffith Show: Dogs, Dogs, Dogs," CBS, 1963; "The Twilight Zone: No Time Like the Past," CBS, 1963; "The Virginian: It Takes a Big Man," NBC, 1963; "Wagon Train: The Fenton Canaby Story," ABC, 1963; "The Alfred Hitchcock Hour: Three Wives Too Many," CBS, 1964; "Rawhide: Incident at Zebulon," CBS, 1964; "Amos Burke, Secret Agent: The Prisoners of Mr. Sin," ABC, 1965; "The Munsters: Happy 100th Anniversary," CBS, 1965; "The Farmer's Daughter: Lo, the Smart Indian," ABC, 1966; "Batman: Shoot a Crooked Arrow/ Walk the Straight and Narrow," ABC, 1966; "The FBI: The Defector," ABC, 1966; "The Virginian: Ride to Delphi," NBC, 1966; "Gidget: Don't Defrost the Alligator," ABC, 1966; "The High Chaparral: No Irish Need Apply," NBC, 1969; "The FBI: Center of Peril," ABC, 1971; "The FBI: Break-in," ABC, 1973; "Laverne & Shirley: Guinea Pig," ABC, 1977; "Buck Rogers in the 25th Century: Unchained Woman," NBC, 1979; "Kate & Allie: Picture of an Affair," CBS, 1985; "Cagney & Lacey: Favors," CBS, 1987; "Perfect Strangers: High Society," ABC, 1988.
TV MOVIES AND MINISERIES: "Two on a Bench," ABC, 1971; "Killer by Night," CBS, 1972; "The Longest Night," ABC, 1972; "The Devil's Daughter," ABC, 1973; "The Six Million Dollar Man," ABC, 1973; "Love's Savage Fury," ABC, 1979.

CORRELL, CHARLES
b. Peoria, IL, February 3, 1890; d. 1972. Performer who played Andy Brown on the radio version of "Amos 'n Andy"; he and partner Freeman Gosden tried to recreate the characters in a sixties animated cartoon.
AS A REGULAR: "Calvin and the Colonel," ABC, 1961-62.
AND: "Art Linkletter's House Party," CBS, 1958.

CORRELL, RICHARD
b. Los Angeles, CA. Son of Charles Correll; he played Richard on "Leave It to Beaver."
AS A REGULAR: "Leave It to Beaver," ABC, 1960-63.
AND: "The Danny Thomas Show: The Report Card," CBS, 1960; "The Adventures of Ozzie and Harriet: Our Man in Alaska," ABC, 1961; "The Adventures of Ozzie and Harriet: Selling Rick's Drums," ABC, 1961; "Lassie: Lassie and the Greyhound," CBS, 1961; "Lassie: Timmy vs. Martians," CBS, 1961; "National Velvet: The Bully," NBC, 1961; "National Velvet: The Club," NBC, 1961; "National Velvet: The Test," NBC, 1962;
TV MOVIES AND MINISERIES: "Still the Beaver," CBS, 1983.

CORRIGAN, LLOYD
b. San Francisco, CA, October 16, 1900; d. 1969. Actor and screenwriter who did character roles and whose steady TV employment came on sitcoms with one-word titles.
AS A REGULAR: "Willy," CBS, 1954-55; "Happy," NBC, 1960; 1961; "Hank," NBC, 1965-66.
AND: "The 20th Century-Fox Hour: Young Man From Kentucky," CBS, 1957; "The Life and Legend of Wyatt Earp: Command Performance," ABC, 1957; "The Adventures of Ozzie and Harriet: The Sculpturing Class," ABC, 1957; "The Adventures of Ozzie and Harriet: The Fishing Lure," ABC, 1957; "The 20th Century-Fox Hour: The Marriage Broker," CBS, 1957; "Crossroads: A Green Hill Far Away," ABC, 1957; "Father Knows Best: An Evening to Remember," NBC, 1957; "The Eve Arden Show: The New Liza Hammond," CBS, 1957; "The Life and Legend of Wyatt Earp: Mr. Buntline's Vacation," ABC, 1957; "Restless Gun: The Battle of Tower Rock," NBC, 1958; "Shirley Temple's Storybook: Mother Goose," NBC, 1958; "How to Marry a Millionaire: For the Love of Mink," SYN, 1959; "Restless Gun: The Lady and the Gun," NBC, 1959; "Tombstone Territory: Marked for Murder," ABC, 1959; "Johnny Staccato: Evil," NBC, 1959; "Riverboat: Race to Cincinnati," NBC, 1959; "Milton Berle Special," NBC, 1959; "The Life and Legend of Wyatt Earp: The Noble Outlaws," ABC, 1959; "The Adventures of Ozzie and Harriet: The T-Shirts," ABC, 1960; "Peter Gunn: The Candidate," ABC, 1960; "Lock Up: Theft on Skid Row," SYN, 1960; "Life and Legend of Wyatt Earp: Woman of Tucson," ABC, 1960; "Gunslinger: The Diehards," CBS, 1961; "Rawhide: Incident of the Running Man," CBS, 1961; "Lassie: A Christmas Story," CBS, 1961; "The Real McCoys: Honesty is the Best Policy," ABC, 1962; "Have Gun, Will Travel: One, Two, Three," CBS, 1962; "Maverick: The Maverick Report," ABC, 1962; "Death Valley Days: A Sponge Full of Vinegar," SYN, 1962; "Dennis the Menace: Junior Pathfinders Ride Again," CBS, 1962; "Death Valley Days: Money to Burn," SYN, 1962; "My Three Sons: Kibitzers," ABC, 1962; "The Lucy Show: Lucy Puts Up a TV Antenna," CBS, 1962; "The Jack Benny Program," CBS, 1963; "77 Sunset Strip: Alimony League," ABC, 1964; "Bonanza: The Pure Truth," NBC, 1964; "The Lucy Show: Lucy and the Great Bank Robbery," CBS, 1964; "The Donna Reed Show: Do Me a Favor-Don't Do Me Any Favors," ABC, 1965; "The Lucy Show: Lucy the Choirmaster," CBS, 1965; "Petticoat Junction: Hooterville, You're All Heart," CBS, 1966.

CORRIGAN, RAY "CRASH"
b. Raymond Bernard, Milwaukee, February 14, 1907; d. 1976. Movie cowboy who took a stab at kiddie TV.

AS A REGULAR: "Crash Corrigan's Ranch," ABC, 1950.

CORSEAUT, ANETA

b. Hutchinson, KS, November 3, 1933. Actress who played schoolteacher Helen Crump on "The Andy Griffith Show."

AS A REGULAR: "The Gertrude Berg Show (Mrs. G. Goes to College)," CBS, 1961-62; "The Andy Griffith Show," CBS, 1964-68; "House Calls," CBS, 1979-82.

AND: "Black Saddle: Client: Peter Warren," ABC, 1959; "Johnny Ringo: Black Harvest," CBS, 1960; "Dick Powell's Zane Grey Theatre: Ransom," CBS, 1960; "Harrigan and Son: The Man Who Wouldn't Stay Dead," ABC, 1961; "The Real McCoys: The McCoy Hex," CBS, 1963; "The Eleventh Hour: The Secret in the Stone," NBC, 1964; "Death Valley Days: Paid in Full," SYN, 1965; "The Farmer's Daughter: Katy by Moonlight," ABC, 1965; "Gunsmoke: The Ladies From St. Louis," CBS, 1967; "Mayberry RFD: Andy and Helen Get Married," CBS, 1968; "Mayberry RFD: Andy's Baby," CBS, 1969; "Nanny and the Professor: My Son the Sitter," ABC, 1970; "Columbo: A Stitch in Crime," NBC, 1973; "Marcus Welby, M.D.: Gemini Descending," ABC, 1973; "Adam 12: Something Worth Dying For," NBC, 1975.

TV MOVIES AND MINISERIES: "Return to Mayberry," NBC, 1986.

COSBY, BILL

b. Philadelphia, PA, July 12, 1937. Comic actor who broke the color barrier, becoming the first black to star in a dramatic series with "I Spy." Then in 1984, he almost singlehandedly made NBC the number one network with his well-written family sitcom.

AS A REGULAR: "I Spy," NBC, 1965-68; "The Bill Cosby Show," NBC, 1969-71; "The New Bill Cosby Show," CBS, 1972-73; "Fat Albert and the Cosby Kids," CBS, 1972-77; "Cos," ABC, 1976; "The Cosby Show," NBC, 1984- .

AND: "The Jack Paar Program," NBC, 1963; "The Garry Moore Show," CBS, 1964; "The Jack Paar Program," NBC, 1964; "The Tonight Show Starring Johnny Carson," NBC, 1964; "The Tonight Show Starring Johnny Carson," NBC, 1965; "The Jack Paar Program," NBC, 1965; "The Match Game," NBC, 1965; "The Mike Douglas Show," SYN, 1965; "The Jimmy Dean Show," ABC, 1965; "You Don't Say," NBC, 1966; "Perry Como Special," NBC, 1966; "The Roger Miller Show," NBC, 1966; "Bob Hope Chrysler Theatre: Murder at NBC," NBC, 1967; "The Tonight Show Starring Johnny Carson," NBC, 1968; "The Mike Douglas Show," SYN, 1968; "Sesame Street," NET, 1970; "Dick Van Dyke Meets Bill Cosby," NBC, 1970; "Aesop's Fables," CBS, 1971; "The Electric Company,"

NET, 1972; "Dinah's Place," NBC, 1972; "The Wacky World of Jonathan Winters," SYN, 1973; "Feeling Good," PBS, 1974; "The Merv Griffin Show," SYN, 1975; "Bill Cosby Special," ABC, 1975; "Sammy and Company," SYN, 1976; "The Tonight Show Starring Johnny Carson," NBC, 1976; "Friends," NBC, 1976; "The John Davidson Show," SYN, 1980; "The Mike Douglas Show," SYN, 1981; "Sesame Street 20... And Still Counting," NBC, 1989.

TV MOVIES AND MINISERIES: "To All My Friends on Shore," CBS, 1972.

* Emmies: 1966, 1967, 1968, 1981.

TV'S TOP TEN, 1985-86

1. The Cosby Show (NBC)
2. Family Ties (NBC)
3. Murder, She Wrote (CBS)
4. 60 Minutes (CBS)
5. Cheers (NBC)
6. Dallas (CBS)
7. Dynasty (ABC)
7. The Golden Girls (NBC)
9. Miami Vice (NBC)
10. Who's the Boss? (ABC)

COSELL, HOWARD

b. Howard Cohen, Winston-Salem, NC, Mar. 25, 1920. Controversial sportscaster and commentator.

AS A REGULAR: "Sports Focus," ABC, 1957-58; "Monday Night Football," ABC, 1970-83; "Saturday Night Live with Howard Cosell," ABC, 1975-76; "Monday Night Baseball," ABC, 1977-85; "Speaking of Everything," SYN, 1988- .

AND: "Strike It Rich," CBS, 1957; "World Series Special," ABC, 1961; "Nanny and the Professor: Sunday's Hero," ABC, 1971; "The Partridge Family: Whatever Happened to Moby Dick?," ABC, 1971; "The Odd Couple: Big Mouth," ABC, 1972; "The Sonny and Cher Comedy Hour," CBS, 1973; "The Odd Couple: Your Mother Wears Army Boots," ABC, 1975; "Saturday Night Live," NBC, 1985; "The Tonight Show Starring Johnny Carson," NBC, 1988.

TV MOVIES AND MINISERIES: "The 500-Pound Jerk," CBS, 1973; "Connection," ABC, 1973.

* Emmies: 1983, 1986.

COSSART, VALERIE

b. England, June 27, 1907.

AS A REGULAR: "The Hartmans," NBC, 1949; "The First Hundred Years," CBS, 1950-52; "Love of Life," CBS, 1979-80.

AND: "Kraft Television Theatre: The Wonderful Gift," NBC, 1956; "Alfred Hitchcock Presents: Impromptu Murder," CBS, 1958; "Naked City: To Walk in Silence," ABC, 1960; "The Defenders: The Accident," CBS, 1961.

COSTELLO, LOU

b. Louis Francis Cristillo, Paterson, NJ, 1908; d. 1959. Longtime partner with Bud Abbott as one of Hollywood's most successful comedy teams; he had split with his partner and was playing dramatic TV roles when he died of a heart attack.

AS A REGULAR: "The Colgate Comedy Hour," NBC, 1951-54; "The Abbott and Costello Show," CBS, 1952-54.

AND: "The Steve Allen Show," NBC, 1956; "The Steve Allen Show," NBC, 1957; "This Is Your Life," NBC, 1957; "The Steve Allen Show," NBC, 1958; "The Lux Show with Rosemary Clooney," NBC, 1958; "G.E. Theatre: Blaze of Glory," CBS, 1958; "Wagon Train: The Tobias Jones Story," NBC, 1958; "The Ed Sullivan Show," CBS, 1958.

* Beginning with his appearance on "The Steve Allen Show" in 1957, Costello was a solo act.

COSTER, NICOLAS

b. England, December 30, 1934. Actor who usually plays rich smoothies on soaps.

AS A REGULAR: "Young Doctor Malone," NBC, 1958-63; "The Secret Storm," CBS, 1964, 1968-69; "Our Private World," CBS, 1965; "As the World Turns," CBS, 1966; "Somerset," NBC, 1970-76; "Another World," NBC, 1972-76, 1980; "Lobo," NBC, 1980-81; "Ryan's Four," ABC, 1983; "One Life to Live," ABC, 1983-84; "Santa Barbara," NBC, 1984-88, 1990- .

AND: "U.S. Steel Hour: No Leave for the Captain," CBS, 1959; "The Defenders: The Accident," CBS, 1961; "Directions '63: Thou Art Woman," ABC, 1962; "No Time for Sergeants: The Living End," ABC, 1965; "One Day at a Time: The Dating Game," CBS, 1978; "Little House on the Prairie: I Remember, I Remember," NBC, 1978; "The Rockford Files: A Good Clean Bust with Sequel Rights," NBC, 1978; "Kate Loves a Mystery: A Chilling Surprise," NBC, 1979; "Paris: The Ghost Maker," CBS, 1979; "Tenspeed and Brown Shoe: Loose Larry's List of Losers," ABC, 1980; "Today's FBI: Blue Collar," ABC, 1982; "Magnum, P.I.: I Do?," CBS, 1983; "Hardcastle and McCormick: Crystal Duck," ABC, 1983; "L.A. Law: Brackman Vasektimzed," NBC, 1987; "Murder, She Wrote: Smooth Operator," CBS, 1989; "Hooperman: Rashomanny," ABC, 1989; "thirtysomething: First Day/Last Day," ABC, 1989; "Who's the Boss?: Tony Does Golf," ABC, 1989; "Life Goes On: Call of the Wild," ABC, 1989.

TV MOVIES AND MINISERIES: "The Word," CBS, 1978; "A Fire in the Sky," NBC, 1978; "Long Journey Back," ABC, 1978; "The Solitary Man," CBS, 1979; "Incident at Dark River," TNT, 1989.

COSTIGAN, JAMES

b. Los Angeles, CA, 1929. Emmy-winning writer with "Hallmark Hall of Fame."

AS WRITER: "Hallmark Hall of Fame," NBC, 1957-60.

TV MOVIES AND MINISERIES: "A War of Children," CBS, 1972; "F. Scott Fitzgerald and the Last of the Belles," ABC, 1973; "Love Among the Ruins," ABC, 1974; "Eleanor and Franklin," ABC, 1976.

AS ACTOR: "Armstrong Circle Theatre: The Trusted Thief," CBS, 1958; "Paper Moon: Birthday," ABC, 1974.

* Emmies: 1959, 1975, 1976.

COTLER, KAMI

b. Long Beach, CA, June 17, 1965.

AS A REGULAR: "Me and the Chimp," CBS, 1972; "The Waltons," CBS, 1972-81.

TV MOVIES AND MINISERIES: "The Homecoming," CBS, 1971; "The Heist," ABC, 1972; "A Wedding on Walton's Mountain," NBC, 1982; "A Day for Thanks on Walton's Mountain," NBC, 1982.

COTTEN, JOSEPH

b. Petersburg, VA, May 15, 1905. All-purpose leading man, as effective in good roles as in villainous ones. Perhaps his most memorable TV appearance was in the "Alfred Hitchcock Presents" episode "Breakdown." He played a cold-hearted man who had been paralyzed in a car crash, mistaken for dead and about to be buried—until the immobile man began to cry.

AS A REGULAR: "The 20th Century-Fox Hour," CBS, 1955-56; "The Joseph Cotten Show (On Trial)," NBC, 1956-57; "The Joseph Cotten Show," CBS, 1959; "Hollywood and the Stars," NBC, 1963-64.

AND: "G.E. Theatre: The High Green Wall," CBS, 54; "Producers Showcase: State of the Union," NBC, 1954; "Best of Broadway: Broadway," CBS, 1955; "Star Stage: On Trial," NBC, 1955; "The Loretta Young Show: Reunion," NBC, 1955; "Alfred Hitchcock Presents: Breakdown," CBS, 1955; "Ford Theatre: Man Without Fear," NBC, 1956; "G.E. Theatre: HMS Marlborough," CBS, 1956; "Star Stage: The Man in the Black Robe," NBC, 1956; "Star Stage: U.S. vs. Alexander Holmes," NBC, 1956; "G.E. Theatre: The Enemies," CBS, 1956; "The Ford Show," NBC, 1957; "The Jane Wyman Show: Contact," NBC, 1957; "Telephone Time: The Man the Navy Couldn't Sink," ABC, 1957; "Alfred Hitchcock Presents: Together," CBS, 1958; "Suspicion: The Eye of Truth," NBC, 1958; "Arthur Murray Party," NBC, 1958; "Westinghouse Desilu Playhouse: The Day the Town Stood Up," CBS, 1959; "Alfred Hitchcock Presents: Dead Weight," CBS, 1959; "The du Pont Show with June Allyson: The Blue Goose," CBS, 1960; "The du

Pont Show with June Allyson: Dark Fear," CBS, 1960; "Checkmate: Face in the Window," CBS, 1960; "The Barbara Stanwyck Show: The Hitchhiker," NBC, 1961; "Wagon Train: The Captain Dan Brady Story," NBC, 1961; "Bus Stop: Cherie," ABC, 1961; "Theatre '62: Notorious," NBC, 1961; "Dr. Kildare: The Administrator," NBC, 1962; "Saints and Sinners: The Man on the Rim," NBC, 1962; "Wagon Train: The John Augustus Story," NBC, 1962; "To Tell the Truth," CBS, 1963; "The Great Adventure: The Death of Sitting Bull," CBS, 1963; "77 Sunset Strip: By His Own Verdict," ABC, 1963; "Cimarron Strip: The Search," CBS, 1967; "Some May Live," ABC, 1967; "Alexander the Great," ABC, 1968; "It Takes a Thief: Hands Across the Border," ABC, 1968; "It Takes a Thief: To Lure a Man," ABC, 1969; "The Virginian: A Time of Terror," NBC, 1970; "The Name of the Game: The King of Denmark," NBC, 1970; "It Takes a Thief: Beyond a Treasonable Doubt," ABC, 1970; "NET Playhouse: The Trail of Tears," NET, 1970; "The Men From Shiloh: Gun Quest," NBC, 1970; "The Streets of San Francisco: A Collection of Eagles," ABC, 1973; "The Rockford Files: This Case Is Closed," NBC, 1974; "Freedom Is," SYN, 1976; "The Love Boat: Aunt Hilly," ABC, 1981.

TV MOVIES AND MINISERIES: "Split Second to an Epitaph," NBC, 1968; "The Lonely Profession," NBC, 1969; "Cutter's Trail," CBS, 1970; "Assault on the Wayne," ABC, 1971; "Do You Take This Stranger?," NBC, 1971; "City Beneath the Sea," CBS, 1971; "The Screaming Woman," ABC, 1972; "The Devil's Daughter," ABC, 1973; "The Lindbergh Kidnapping Case," NBC, 1976.

COUGHLIN, KEVIN

b. 1945; d. 1976. Former child actor who played T.R. Ryan on "Mama."

AS A REGULAR: "Mama," CBS, 1952-56.

AND: "Armstrong Circle Theatre: For Ever and Ever," NBC, 1954; "Goodyear TV Playhouse: Old Tosselfoot," NBC, 1954; "Robert Montgomery Presents: Don't You Ever Go Home?," NBC, 1954; "Philco TV Playhouse: Man in the Middle of the Ocean," NBC, 1954; "Center Stage: The Heart of a Clown," ABC, 1954; "Studio One: A Christmas Surprise," CBS, 1956; "Harbourmaster: Sanctuary," CBS, 1957; "Harbourmaster: Enemy Unknown," CBS, 1957; "U.S. Steel Hour: Old Marshals Never Die," CBS, 1958; "Robert Herridge Theatre: A Trip to Czardis," SYN, 1960; "Play of the Week: The Closing Door," SYN, 1960; "Play of the Week: The Climate of Eden," SYN, 1960; "Robert Herridge Theatre: The Ballad of Huck Finn," SYN, 1960; "Armstrong Circle Theatre: Runaway Road: Story of Missing Persons," CBS, 1962; "The Patty Duke Show: The Green-Eyed Monster," ABC, 1964;

"Combat!: The First Day," ABC, 1965; "The Virginian: The Crooked Path," NBC, 1968; "Dragnet: The Big Departure," NBC, 1968; "Dragnet: Homicide-The Student," NBC, 1969; "The Virginian: Last Grave at Sorocco Creek," NBC, 1969; "Gunsmoke: The Commandment," CBS, 1969; "Gunsmoke: The Mark of Cain," CBS, 1969; "Gunsmoke: Coreyville," CBS, 1969; "Gunsmoke: The Gun," CBS, 1970; "O'Hara, U.S. Tresaury: Operation Time Fuse," CBS, 1971; "Gunsmoke: This Golden Land," CBS, 1973; "The FBI: Break-In," ABC, 1973.

COURT, HAZEL

b. England, February 10, 1926. Attractive redheaded actress who went from English TV productions to American ones.

AS A REGULAR: "Dick and the Duchess," CBS, 1957-58.

AND: "The Buccaneers: Gentleman Jack and the Lady," CBS, 1956; "Playhouse 90: Bomber's Moon," CBS, 1958; "Alfred Hitchcock Presents: Arthur," CBS, 1959; "Alcoa Theatre: The Tweed Hat," NBC, 1960; "Bonanza: The Last Trophy," NBC, 1960; "G.E. Theatre: Hot Footage," CBS, 1960; "Stagecoach West: Finn McCool," ABC, 1961; "Danger Man: The Lonely Chair," CBS, 1961; "Alfred Hitchcock Presents: A Pearl Necklace," NBC, 1961; "Thriller: Terror in Teakwood," NBC, 1961; "Kraft Mystery Theatre: Breakout," NBC, 1961; "The Dick Powell Show: A Swiss Affair," NBC, 1961; "The Dick Powell Show: Borderline," NBC, 1962; "Sam Benedict: So Various, So Beautiful," NBC, 1962; "Rawhide: Incident of the Dowry Dundee," CBS, 1964; "The Farmer's Daughter: Speak for Yourself, John Katy," ABC, 1964; "The Twilight Zone: The Fear," CBS, 1964; "Twelve O'Clock High: The Men and the Boys," ABC, 1964; "Burke's Law: Who Killed the Eleventh Best-Dressed Woman in the World?," ABC, 1964; "Dr. Kildare: The Life Machine/ Toast the Golden Couple/Wives and Losers/ Welcome Home, Dear Anna/Hour of Decision/ Aftermath," NBC, 1965; "Gidget: In and Out with the In-Laws," ABC, 1966; "The Wild Wild West: The Night of the Returning Dead," CBS, 1966; "Mission: Impossible: Charity," CBS, 1967; "Mannix: A View of Nowhere," CBS, 1968; "McMillan and Wife: Till Death Do Us Part," NBC, 1972.

COURTNEY, JACQUELINE

b. East Orange, NJ, September 24, 1946. Actress who played Alice Matthews on "Another World" and Pat Ashley on "One Life to Live."

AS A REGULAR: "The Edge of Night," CBS, 1961; "Our Five Daughters," NBC, 1962; "Another World," NBC, 1964-75, 1984-85; "One Life to Live," ABC, 1975-83.

COVER, FRANKLIN

b. Cleveland, OH, November 20, 1928. Actor who played Tom Wills on "The Jeffersons."
AS A REGULAR: "The Jeffersons," CBS, 1975-85.
AND: "All in the Family: The Jeffersons Move Up," CBS, 1975; "The Love Boat: Your Money or Your Wife," ABC, 1985; "227: The Butler Did It," NBC, 1988.
TV MOVIES AND MINISERIES: "Short Walk to Daylight," ABC, 1972; "A Woman Called Golda," SYN, 1982.

COWAN, JEROME

b. New York City, NY, October 6, 1897; d. 1972.
AS A REGULAR: "Not for Publication," DUM, 1951-52; "Valiant Lady," CBS, 1953-57; "The Tab Hunter Show," NBC, 1960-61; "The Tycoon," ABC, 1964-65.
AND: "Stage 7: Conflict," CBS, 1955; "Goodyear TV Playhouse: The Gene Austin Story," NBC, 1957; "Armstrong Circle Theatre: Counterfeit, Inc.," NBC, 1957; "Studio One: Love Me to Pieces," CBS, 1957; "Telephone Time: The Frying Pan," ABC, 1957; "Look Up and Live: Diary of a Teenager," CBS, 1958; "New York Confidential: Medallion," SYN, 1958; "Bat Masterson: The Conspiracy," NBC, 1959; "Tightrope!: Three to Make Ready," CBS, 1960; "Adventures in Paradise: The Violent Journey," ABC, 1960; "The Millionaire: Millionaire Katherine Boland," CBS, 1960; "The Dennis O'Keefe Show: What's in a Name?," CBS, 1960; "G.E. Theatre: Hot Footage," CBS, 1960; "Chevy Mystery Show: The Last Six Blocks," NBC, 1960; "Chevy Mystery Show: Blind Man's Bluff," NBC, 1960; "The Outlaws: Ballad for a Badman," NBC, 1960; "The Real McCoys: Executive Wife," ABC, 1960; "Target: The Corruptors: My Native Land," ABC, 1962; "Mr. Smith Goes to Washington: But What Are You Doing for Your Country?," ABC, 1962; "The Wide Country: What Are Friends For?," NBC, 1962; "The Real McCoys: Luke in the Ivy League," CBS, 1963; "Grindl: Grindl, She-Wolf of Wall Street," NBC, 1963; "My Favorite Martian: The Atom Misers," CBS, 1963; "Destry: Law and Order Day," ABC, 1964; "The Lucy Show: Lucy and Art Linkletter," CBS, 1966; "Gomer Pyle, USMC: A Star Is Born," CBS, 1966; "The Munsters: Herman's Lawsuit," CBS, 1966; "The Mothers-in-Law: Herb's Little Helpers," NBC, 1968; "The Debbie Reynolds Show: How to Succeed in the Stock Market Without Really Trying," NBC, 1970; "Here's Lucy: Lucy's Vacuum," CBS, 1970.

COWARD, SIR NOEL

b. Teddington, England, December 16, 1899; d. 1973.
AS A GUEST: "Ford Star Jubilee: Blithe Spirit," CBS, 1956; "Ford Star Jubilee: This Happy Breed," CBS, 1956; "The Ed Sullivan Show," CBS, 1957; "Small World," CBS, 1959; "Androcles and the Lion," NBC, 1967.

COX, RONNY

b. Cloudcroft, NM, July 23, 1938.
AS A REGULAR: "Apple's Way," CBS, 1974-75; "Spencer," NBC, 1984-85; "St. Elsewhere," NBC, 1987-88; "Cop Rock," ABC, 1990.
AND: "Madigan: The Manhattan Beat," NBC, 1972; "Hernandes: Houston P.D.," NBC, 1973; "Rx for the Defense," ABC, 1973; "The Tonight Show Starring Johnny Carson," NBC, 1975; "Hollywood Television Theatre: The Chicago Conspiracy Trial," PBS, 1975; "The Life and Times of Grizzly Adams: Unwelcome Neighbor," NBC, 1977; "Darkroom: The Siege of 31 August," ABC, 1981; "Family Ties: Where's Poppa?," NBC, 1986; "Murder, She Wrote: Death Stalks the Big Top," CBS, 1986; "Alfred Hitchcock Presents: Road Hog," NBC, 1986; "ABC Afterschool Specials: Just Another Kid: An AIDS Story," ABC, 1987; "CBS Summer Playhouse: Roughhouse," CBS, 1988.
TV MOVIES AND MINISERIES: "Connection," ABC, 1973; "A Case of Rape," CBS, 1974; "Who Is the Black Dahlia?," NBC, 1975; "Having Babies," ABC, 1976; "Lovey: A Circle of Children, Part II," CBS, 1978; "Transplant," CBS, 1979; "GE Theater: Two of a Kind," CBS, 1982; "The Abduction of Kari Swenson," NBC, 1987; "Baby Girl Scott," CBS, 1987; "Scandal in a Small Town," NBC, 1988; "In the Line of Duty: The FBI Murders," NBC, 1988; "The Comeback," CBS, 1989.

COX, WALLY

b. Wallace M. Cox, Detroit, MI, December 6, 1924; d. 1973. Bespectacled comic actor with a small frame and high-pitched voice, fondly remembered as mild-mannered teacher Mr. Peepers and as the man who said, "There's no need to fear—Underdog is here!"
AS A REGULAR: "School House," DUM, 1949; "Mr. Peepers," NBC, 1952-55; "The Adventures of Hiram Holliday," NBC, 1956-57; "Underdog," NBC, 1968-70; "Hollywood Squares," NBC, 1967-73.
AND: "Danger: Ask Me Another," CBS, 1951; "Starlight Theatre: I Guess There Are Other Girls," CBS, 1951; "Goodyear TV Playhouse: The Copper," NBC, 1951; "Goodyear TV Playhouse: Tigers Don't Sing," NBC, 1952; "Babes in Toyland," NBC, 1954; "Producers Showcase: Yellow Jack," NBC, 1955; "Heidi," NBC, 1955; "Babes in Toyland," NBC, 1955; "The Bob Hope Show," NBC, 1957; "Matinee Theatre: The 19th Hole," NBC, 1957; "Kraft Television Theatre: The Roaring 20th," NBC,

1957; "The Steve Allen Show," NBC, 1957; "The Arlene Francis Show," NBC, 1957; "The Frank Sinatra Show: The Green Grass of St. Theresa," ABC, 1958; "The Garry Moore Show," CBS, 1958; "Wagon Train: The Vincent Eaglewood Story," NBC, 1959; "The Chevy Show," NBC, 1959; "The Jack Paar Show," NBC, 1959; "U.S. Steel Hour: The American Cowboy," CBS, 1960; "The Adventures of Ozzie and Harriet: The Fraternity Rents Out a Room," ABC, 1961; "Follow the Sun: The Inhuman Equation," ABC, 1962; "Car 54, Where Are You?: No More Pickpockets," NBC, 1962; "Candid Camera," CBS, 1962; "The Merv Griffin Show," NBC, 1963; "The Tonight Show Starring Johnny Carson," NBC, 1963; "77 Sunset Strip: 5," ABC, 1963; "Burke's Law: Who Killed Purity Mather?," ABC, 1963; "The Twilight Zone: From Agnes-With Love," CBS, 1964; "Burke's Law: Who Killed the Card?," ABC, 1965; "The Match Game," NBC, 1965; "The Mike Douglas Show," SYN, 1965; "The Dick Van Dyke Show: The Making of a Councilman," CBS, 1966; "The Beverly Hillbillies: The Bird Watchers," CBS, 1966; "The Beverly Hillbillies: Granny Tonics a Birdwatcher," CBS, 1966; "Mission: Impossible: Pilot," CBS, 1966; "Lost in Space: Forbidden World," CBS, 1966; "The Girl From UNCLE: The Little John Doe Affair," NBC, 1966; "Bob Hope Chrysler Theatre: Murder at NBC," NBC, 1967; "The Mike Douglas Show," SYN, 1967; "I Spy: Casanova From Canarsie," NBC, 1967; "Get Smart: Dr. Yes," NBC, 1968; "The Dick Cavett Show," ABC, 1968; "The Merv Griffin Show," SYN, 1968; "Bonanza: The Last Vote," NBC, 1968; "Snap Judgment," NBC, 1968; "Here's Lucy: Lucy and the Ex-Con," CBS, 1969; "Love, American Style: Love and Mr. Nice Guy," ABC, 1970; "The Bill Cosby Show: Goodbye, Cruel World," NBC, 1970; "Here's Lucy: Lucy and Wally Cox," CBS, 1970; "It Takes a Thief: Project X," ABC, 1970; "Walt Disney's Wonderful World of Color: The Wacky Zoo of Morgan City," NBC, 1970; "Here's Lucy: Lucy and the Diamond Cutter," CBS, 1970; "Night Gallery: Junior," NBC, 1971; "McMillan and Wife: The Easy Sunday Murder Case," NBC, 1971; "Alias Smith and Jones: The Men Who Corrupted Hadleyburg," ABC, 1972; "Here's Lucy: Lucy Sublets the Office," CBS, 1972; "The Odd Couple: The Pen is Mightier Than the Pencil," ABC, 1972; "Once Upon a Mattress," CBS, 1972; "The Mouse Factory," SYN, 1972.
TV MOVIES AND MINISERIES: "Ironside," NBC, 1967; "Quarantined," ABC, 1970; "The Young Country," ABC, 1970; "Magic Carpet," NBC, 1972; "The Night Strangler," ABC, 1973.

CRABBE, BUSTER

b. Clarence Lindon Crabbe, Oakland, CA, February 17, 1907; d. 1983. Former Olympic swimmer who played, rather woodenly, Tarzan and Buck Rogers in the thirties.
AS A REGULAR: "Foreign Legionnaire," NBC, 1955-57.
AND: "Philco TV Playhouse: A Cowboy for Chris," NBC, 1952; "Pond's Theatre: The Cornered Man," ABC, 1955; "The Steve Allen Show," NBC, 1956; "Ellery Queen: This Murder Comes to You Live," NBC, 1959; "The Red Skelton Show," CBS, 1959; "Marineland Circus," NBC, 1961; "Buck Rogers in the 25th Century: Planet of the Slave Girls," NBC, 1979.

CRABBE, CULLEN

b. Santa Monica, CA, September 4, 1944. Son of actor Buster Crabbe, who played his young ward, Cuffy, on "Foreign Legionnaire."
AS A REGULAR: "Foreign Legionnaire," NBC, 1955-57.

CRAIG, YVONNE

b. Dallas, TX, 1938. Starlet who played Barbara Gordon, aka Batgirl.
AS A REGULAR: "Batman," ABC, 1967-68.
AND: "Schlitz Playhouse of Stars: The Honor System," CBS, 1958; "Schlitz Playhouse of Stars: Papa Said No," CBS, 1958; "Mr. Lucky: Little Miss Wow," CBS, 1959; "The Many Loves of Dobie Gillis: Dobie's Navy Blues," CBS, 1960; "Hennesey: Scarlet Woman in White," CBS, 1960; "77 Sunset Strip: Family Skeleton," ABC, 1960; "Checkmate: The Cyanide Touch," CBS, 1960; "The Barbara Stanwyck Show: House in Order," NBC, 1960; "The Detectives Starring Robert Taylor: Quiet Night," ABC, 1961; "Peter Loves Mary: That Certain Age," NBC, 1961; "Tales of Wells Fargo: The Remittance Man," NBC, 1961; "Malibu Run: The Rainbow Adventure," CBS, 1961; "The Many Loves of Dobie Gillis: Like Mother, Like Daughter, Like Wow," CBS, 1961; "Follow the Sun: A Ghost in Her Gazebo," ABC, 1962; "The Many Loves of Dobie Gillis: The Sweet Success of Smell," CBS, 1962; "Laramie: The Long Road Back," NBC, 1962; "Sam Benedict: Sugar and Spice and Everything," NBC, 1963; "Object Is," ABC, 1963; "77 Sunset Strip: Lovers' Lane," ABC, 1964; "My Favorite Martian: Martin of the Movies," CBS, 1965; "Ben Casey: If You Play Your Cards Right, You Too Can Be a Loser," ABC, 1965; "The Big Valley: Night of the Wolf," ABC, 1965; "The Man From UNCLE: The Brain Killer Affair," NBC, 1965; "The Wild Wild West: The Night of the Grand Emir," CBS, 1966; "Mr. Roberts: #*@% the Torpedos," NBC, 1966; "My Three Sons: If at First ...," CBS, 1966; "The Ghost and Mrs. Muir: Haunted Honeymoon," NBC, 1968; "The Mod Squad: Find Tara Chapman," ABC, 1968; "Star Trek: Whom Gods Destroy," NBC, 1969; "Love, American Style: Love and a Couple of Couples," ABC,

1969; "Mannix: Who Killed Me?," CBS, 1969; "The Courtship of Eddie's Father: They're Either Too Young or Too Old," ABC, 1970; "Land of the Giants: Wild Journey," ABC, 1970; "Three Coins in a Fountain," NBC, 1970; "Love, American Style: Love and the Big Game," ABC, 1971; "Love, American Style: Love and the Loudmouth," ABC, 1971; "Love, American Style: Love and the Confession," ABC, 1972; "Mannix: Search for a Whisper," CBS, 1973; "Emergency!: Alley Cat," NBC, 1973; "The Magician: The Man Who Lost Himself," NBC, 1973; "Kojak: Dark Sunday," CBS, 1973.

TV MOVIES AND MINISERIES: "Jarrett," ABC, 1973.

CRANE, BOB

b. Waterbury, CT, July 13, 1928; d. 1978. Former radio disk jockey with a glib style that served him well as Col. Robert Hogan, leader of a group of POW commandos.

AS A REGULAR: "The Donna Reed Show," ABC, 1963-65; "Hogan's Heroes," CBS, 1965-71; "The Bob Crane Show," NBC, 1975.

AND: "The Twilight Zone: Static," CBS, 1961; "G.E. Theatre: The $200 Parlay," CBS, 1961; "The Dick Van Dyke Show: Somebody Has to Play Cleopatra," CBS, 1962; "The Alfred Hitchcock Hour: The Thirty-First of February," CBS, 1963; "Channing: Hall Full of Strangers," ABC, 1963; "Your First Impression," NBC, 1964; "Password," CBS, 1965; "The Lucy Show: Lucy and Bob Crane," CBS, 1966; "PDQ," NBC, 1967; "The John Gary Show," SYN, 1968; "Funny You Should Ask," ABC, 1968; "Arsenic and Old Lace," ABC, 1969; "Love, American Style: Love and the Modern Wife," ABC, 1969; "The Barbara McNair Show," SYN, 1970; "Love, American Style: Love and the Logical Explanation," ABC, 1971; "The Doris Day Show: And Here's ... Doris," CBS, 1971; "Night Gallery: House with Ghost," NBC, 1971; "Rollin' on the River," SYN, 1971; "Love, American Style: Love and the Waitress," ABC, 1971; "Make Mine Red, White and Blue," NBC, 1972; "Rowan & Martin's Laugh-In," NBC, 1972; "Baffle," NBC, 1973; "Tenafly: Man Running," NBC, 1974; "Police Woman: Requiem for Bored Wives," NBC, 1974; "Mitzi and a Hundred Guys," CBS, 1975; "Ellery Queen: The Hard-Headed Huckster," NBC, 1976; "Gibbsville: Trapped," NBC, 1976; "Break the Bank," SYN, 1976.

TV MOVIES AND MINISERIES: "The Delphi Bureau," ABC, 1972.

* Crane was found bludgeoned to death in his Scottsdale, Arizona hotel room, and the murder has never been solved.

CRAWFORD, BRODERICK

b. William Broderick Crawford, Philadelphia, December 9, 1911; d. 1986. Pudgy actor

usually in grouchy, in-command roles; he played Dan Matthews on "Highway Patrol."

AS A REGULAR: "Highway Patrol," SYN, 1955-59; "King of Diamonds," SYN, 1961-62; "The Interns," CBS, 1970-71.

AND: "Lux Video Theatre: Hunt the Man Down," CBS, 1952; "G.E. Theatre: Ride the River," CBS, 1953; "Ford Theatre: Margin for Fear," NBC, 1953; "Schlitz Playhouse of Stars: The Widow Makes Three," CBS, 1953; "Schlitz Playhouse of Stars: Desert Tragedy," CBS, 1953; "Schlitz Playhouse of Stars: Man From the Outside," CBS, 1954; "Producers Showcase: Yellow Jack," NBC, 1955; "Damon Runyon Theatre: Dancing Dan's Christmas," CBS, 1955; "The Marge and Gower Champion Show," CBS, 1957; "Rough Riders: Quantrill," ABC, 1959; "Bat Masterson: Two Graves for Swan Valley," NBC, 1959; "The Virginian: A Killer in Town," NBC, 1963; "Arrest and Trial: Flame in the Dark," ABC, 1963; "Burke's Law: Who Killed Snooky Martinelli?," ABC, 1964; "Destry: The Solid Gold Girl," ABC, 1964; "Burke's Law: Who Killed Avery Lord?," ABC, 1964; "Bob Hope Chrysler Theatre: The Meal Ticket," NBC, 1964; "Rawhide: Incident at Deadhorse," CBS, 1964; "Burke's Law: Who Killed 711?," ABC, 1964; "Burke's Law: Who Killed Davidian Jones?," ABC, 1964; "The Rogues: Gambit by the Golden Gate," NBC, 1965; "Kraft Suspense Theatre: The Long Ravine," NBC, 1965; "Bob Hope Chrysler Theatre: March From Camp Tyler," NBC, 1965; "Bob Hope Chrysler Theatre: Brilliant Benjamin Boggs," NBC, 1966; "The Man From UNCLE: The J Is for Judas Affair," NBC, 1967; "Cimarron Strip: The Blue Moon Train," CBS, 1967; "The Name of the Game: Blind Man's Bluff," NBC, 1969; "Get Smart: The Treasure of C. Errol Madre," CBS, 1969; "Love, American Style: Love and the Dating Computer," ABC, 1969; "The Name of the Game: The Power," NBC, 1969; "Bracken's World: A Perfect Piece of Casting," NBC, 1970; "It Takes a Thief: Fortune City," ABC, 1970; "The Man and the City: Disaster on Turner Street," ABC, 1971; "Alias Smith and Jones: The Man Who Broke the Bank at Red Gap," ABC, 1972; "Night Gallery: You Can't Get Help Like That Anymore," NBC, 1972; "Banacek: No Sign of the Cross," NBC, 1972; "Paradise," CBS, 1974; "Medical Story: A Right to Die," NBC, 1975; "Saturday Night Live," NBC, 1976; "City of Angels: The Losers," NBC, 1976; "Simon & Simon: The Rough Rider Rides Again," CBS, 1982.

TV MOVIES AND MINISERIES: "The Challenge," ABC, 1970; "A Tattered Web," CBS, 1971; "The Adventures of Nick Carter," ABC, 1972; "The Phantom of Hollywood," CBS, 1974; "Look What's Happened to Rosemary's Baby," ABC, 1976; "Mayday at 40,000 Feet," CBS, 1976.

CRAWFORD, JOAN

b. Lucille LeSueur, San Antonio, TX, March 23, 1904; d. 1977. Oscar-winning actress whose rather overwrought performances date badly; her sporadic TV appearances weren't particulary memorable.

AS A REGULAR: "The Secret Storm," CBS, 1968.
AND: "Mirror Theatre: Beacause I Love Him," CBS, 1953; "G.E. Theatre: The Road to Edinburgh," CBS, 1954; "G.E. Theatre: Strange Witness," CBS, 1958; "Bob Hope Special," NBC, 1958; "G.E. Theatre: And One Was Loyal," CBS, 1959; "Della," SYN, 1959; "Dick Powell's Zane Grey Theatre: Rebel Range," CBS, 1959; "Startime: Talent Scouts," NBC, 1960; "Bob Hope Buick Show," NBC, 1960; "Dick Powell's Zane Grey Theatre: One Must Die," CBS, 1961; "I've Got A Secret," CBS, 1961; "The du Pont Show: The Ziegfeld Touch," NBC, 1961; "The Tonight Show Starring Johnny Carson," NBC, 1962; "Password," CBS, 1962; "The Tonight Show Starring Johnny Carson," NBC, 1963; "Route 66: Same Picture, Different Frame," CBS, 1963; "Hollywood Palace," ABC, 1965; "The Man From UNCLE: The Five Daughters Affair," NBC, 1967; "The Merv Griffin Show," SYN, 1968; "The Lucy Show: Lucy and the Lost Star," CBS, 1968; "The Merv Griffin Show," CBS, 1969; "The Virginian: Nightmare," NBC, 1970; "The Tim Conway Show," CBS, 1970; "The Sixth Sense: Dear John: We're Going to Scare You to Death," ABC, 1972.

* Crawford was a guest on Johnny Carson's first "Tonight" show.
* On "Hollywood Palace," Crawford read "A Prayer for Little Children." It is not known whether the phrase "wire hangers" appeared in it.
* Crawford's appearance on "The Secret Storm" for four episodes in 1968 was to fill in for daughter Christina, who was hospitalized. Reportedly, Crawford did all her scenes drunk.

CRAWFORD, JOHNNY

b. John Ernest Crawford, 1947. Child actor who played Mark McCain, son of the rifleman, Lucas McCain (Chuck Connors).

AS A REGULAR: "Mickey Mouse Club," ABC, 1956-58; "The Rifleman," ABC, 1958-63.
AND: "Stage 7: A Man Named March," CBS, 1955; "Cavalcade Theatre: The Boy Nobody Wanted," ABC, 1956; "The Adventures of Rin Tin Tin: Second Chance," ABC, 1956; "Lux Video Theatre: Little Boy Lost," NBC, 1956; "Telephone Time: Hatfield the Rainmaker," CBS, 1956; "The Loretta Young Show: The End of the Week," NBC, 1956; "Ford Theatre: The Marriage Plan," ABC, 1956; "American Bandstand," ABC, 1957; "Matinee Theatre: The Serpent's Tooth," NBC, 1957; "Telephone Time: Bullet Lou Kirn," ABC, 1957; "The Millionaire: The Story of Frank Keegan," CBS, 1957; "The Loretta Young Show:

The Little Witness," NBC, 1957; "Matinee Theatre: The Iceman," NBC, 1958; "Dick Powell's Zane Grey Theatre: Man Unforgiving," CBS, 1958; "Restless Gun: Gratitude," NBC, 1958; "Dick Powell's Zane Grey Theatre: The Sharpshooter," CBS, 1958; "Wagon Train: The Sally Potter Story," NBC, 1958; "Trackdown: The Deal," CBS, 1958; "The Untouchables: Ring of Terror," ABC, 1962; "The Donna Reed Show: A Very Bright Boy," ABC, 1961; "American Bandstand," ABC, 1962; "The Dick Powell Show: Apples Don't Fall Far," NBC, 1963; "American Bandstand," ABC, 1964; "Mr. Novak: Let's Dig a Little Grammar," NBC, 1964; "Mr. Novak: The Tender Twigs," NBC, 1965; "Branded: A Coward Steps Aside," NBC, 1965; "Rawhide: Crossing at White Feather," CBS, 1965; "The Time Tunnel: The Revenge of Robin Hood," ABC, 1966; "Star Trek: The Galileo 7," NBC, 1967; "Bonanza: The Trouble with Amy," NBC, 1970; "The Pat Sajak Show," CBS, 1989; "Paradise: A Gathering of Guns," CBS, 1989.
TV MOVIES AND MINISERIES: "The Gambler II: The Adventure Continues," CBS, 1983.

CRENNA, RICHARD

b. Los Angeles, CA, November 30, 1927. Actor-director who played squeaky-voiced Walter Denton on "Our Miss Brooks" and Luke McCoy. Recently, he's gravitated toward miniseries and feature films; an Emmy winner for "The Rape of Richard Beck."

AS A REGULAR: "Our Miss Brooks," CBS, 1952-55; "The Real McCoys," ABC, 1957-62; CBS, 1962-63; "Slattery's People," CBS, 1964-65; "All's Fair," CBS, 1976-77; "It Takes Two," ABC, 1982-83.
AND: "I Love Lucy: The Young Fans," CBS, 1952; "Frontier: The Ten Days of John Leslie," NBC, 1955; "Medic: Don't Count the Stars," NBC, 1956; "Father Knows Best: The Promising Young Man," NBC, 1956; "The Millionaire: The Ralph McKnight Story," CBS, 1956; "Matinee Theatre: Barricade on the Big Black," NBC, 1957; "Cheyenne: Hard Bargain," ABC, 1957; "Sally: Sally vs. Feudalism," NBC, 1958; "Matinee Theatre: The Cause," NBC, 1958; "The Deputy: A Time to Sow," NBC, 1960; "Here's Holly-wood," NBC, 1961; "Kraft Suspense Theatre: The Long Lost Life of Edward Smalley," NBC, 1963; "Art Linkletter's House Party," CBS, 1964; "ABC Nightlife," ABC, 1965; "The Danny Kaye Show," CBS, 1965; "The Tonight Show Starring Johnny Carson," NBC, 1968; "The Dick Cavett Show," ABC, 1968; "Conflicts: Double Solitaire," PBS, 1974; "Hollywood Squares," NBC, 1974; "Dinah!," SYN, 1980.
TV MOVIES AND MINISERIES: "Thief," ABC, 1971; "Footsteps," CBS, 1972; "Double Indemnity," ABC, 1973; "Nightmare," CBS, 1973; "Shootout in a One-Dog Town," ABC, 1974;

"Honky Tonk," NBC, 1974; "A Girl Named Sooner," NBC, 1975; "Devil Dog: The Hound of Hell," CBS, 1978; "First You Cry," CBS, 1978; "A Fire in the Sky," NBC, 1978; "Centennial," NBC, 1978-79; "Mayflower: The Pilgrims' Adventure," CBS, 1979; "The Ordeal of Bill Carney," CBS, 1981; "Passions," CBS, 1984; "ABC Theater: The Rape of Richard Beck," ABC, 1985; "Doubletake," CBS; 1985; "On Wings of Eagles," NBC, 1986; "A Case of Deadly Force," CBS, 1986; "The High Price of Passion," NBC, 1986; "Police Story: The Freeway Killings," NBC, 1987; "Kids Like These," CBS, 1987; "Two of a Kind: The Case of the Hillside Stranglers," NBC, 1989; "Stuck with Each Other," NBC, 1989.

AS DIRECTOR: "The Andy Griffith Show," CBS, 1963-64.

* Emmies: 1985.

CRISTAL, LINDA
b. Victoria Moya, Argentina, February 23, 1935. Actress who played Victoria Cannon, wife of Big John Cannon (Leif Erickson) on "The High Chaparral."

AS A REGULAR: "County Fair," NBC, 1958; "The High Chaparral," NBC, 1967-71.

AND: "Rawhide: Incident on a Burst of Evil," CBS, 1959; "The Spirit of the Alamo," ABC, 1960; "The Tab Hunter Show: Holiday in Spain," NBC, 1961; "Voyage to the Bottom of the Sea: The City Beneath the Sea," ABC, 1964; "T.H.E. Cat: Moment of Truth," NBC, 1966; "Call Holme," NBC, 1972; "Search: Flight to Nowhere," NBC, 1972; "Police Story: Across the Line," NBC, 1974; "Barnaby Jones: Homecoming for a Dead Man," CBS, 1979; "The Love Boat: The Duel," ABC, 1981.

TV MOVIES AND MINISERIES: "The Dead Don't Die," NBC, 1975; "Best Sellers: Seventh Avenue," NBC, 1977.

CROFT, MARY JANE
b. Muncie, IN. Blonde actress with a edge to her voice; she spoke for Cleo the bassett hound on "The People's Choice" and later was Lucille Ball's pal on "The Lucy Show."

AS A REGULAR: "I Married Joan," NBC, 1952-55; "Our Miss Brooks," CBS, 1952-54; "The Life of Riley," NBC, 1953-58; "The Adventures of Ozzie and Harriet," ABC, 1954-66; "The People's Choice," NBC, 1955-58; "I Love Lucy," CBS, 1957; "The Lucy Show," CBS, 1965-68; "Here's Lucy," CBS, 1968-74.

AND: "I Love Lucy: Lucy Is Envious," CBS, 1954; "I Love Lucy: Return Home From Europe," CBS, 1956; "The Brothers: The Crush," CBS, 1957; "The Perry Como Show," NBC, 1957; "December Bride: Hot Meal," CBS, 1957; "The Lucy Show: Lucy Drives a Dump Truck," CBS, 1963; "The Lucy Show: Lucy and the Little League," CBS,

1963; "The Mothers-in-Law: The Not-So-Grand Opera," NBC, 1969.

* Actually, Croft didn't appear in person on "The Perry Como Show"; her voice did, as Cleo.

CROMWELL, JAMES
Tall, skinny actor who played Stretch Cunningham on "All in the Family."

AS A REGULAR: "All in the Family," CBS, 1974; "Hot L Baltimore," ABC, 1975; "The Nancy Walker Show," ABC, 1976; "The Last Precinct," NBC, 1986; "Easy Street," NBC, 1986-87; "Mama's Boy," NBC, 1988-89.

AND: "Maude: Last Tango in Tuckahoe," CBS, 1974; "The Rockford Files: The Countess," NBC, 1974; "M*A*S*H: Last Laugh," CBS, 1977; "Police Story: Ice Time," NBC, 1977; "Three's Company: Chrissy's Night Out," ABC, 1977; "Alice: Who Ordered the Hot Turkey?," CBS, 1978; "The White Shadow: Mainstream," CBS, 1979; "Diff'rent Strokes: Arnold's Hero," NBC, 1979; "Barney Miller: Strip Joint," ABC, 1979; "The White Shadow: The Death of Me Yet," CBS, 1980; "Barney Miller: Liquidation," ABC, 1981; "Barney Miller: Stress Analyzer," ABC, 1981; "Foul Play: Hit and Run," ABC, 1981; "Riptide: Girls' Night Out," NBC, 1985; "Night Court: Nuts About Harry," NBC, 1985; "Hardcastle and McCormick: Undercover McCormick," ABC, 1985; "Hunter: Sniper," NBC, 1985; "Scarecrow and Mrs. King: Tale of the Dancing Weasel," CBS, 1985; "Amazing Stories: One for the Road," NBC, 1986; "Mr. Belvedere: Fat Cats," ABC, 1989; "Christine Cromwell: Things That Go Bump in the Night," ABC, 1989; "Star Trek: The Next Generation: The Hunted," SYN, 1990.

TV MOVIES AND MINISERIES: "The Girl in the Empty Grave," NBC, 1977; "Best Sellers: Once an Eagle," NBC, 1977.

CRONKITE, WALTER
Newsman.

AS A REGULAR: "Pick the Winner," CBS, 1952; CBS/DUM, 1956; "Man of the Week," CBS, 1952-53; "You Are There," CBS, 1953-57; "It's News to Me," CBS, 1954; "Air Power," CBS, 1956-58; "The 20th Century (The 21st Century)," CBS, 1957-70; "Eyewitness to History," CBS, 1959-60; "The CBS Evening News with Walter Cronkite," CBS, 1962-80; "Universe," CBS, 1980-82.

AND: "Mike Todd Party," CBS, 1957; "The Ed Sullivan Show: Man of the Hour," CBS, 1958; "Steve Allen Plymouth Show," NBC, 1959; "The Mary Tyler Moore Show: Ted Baxter Meets Walter Cronkite," CBS, 1974; "Later with Bob Costas," NBC, 1989; "From Vienna: The New Year's Celebration 1989," PBS, 1989; "Fifty Years of Television: A Golden Celebration," CBS, 1989; "Murphy Brown: The Roasting,"

CBS, 1989.
* Emmies: 1973.

CRONYN, HUME

b. Canada, July 18, 1911.

AS A REGULAR: "The Marriage," NBC, 1954. AND: "Philco TV Playhouse: The Reluctant Landlord," NBC, 1950; "Suspense: Strike Me Dead," CBS, 1950; "Studio One: Public Servant," CBS, 1951; "Omnibus: Glory in the Flower," CBS, 1953; "Motorola TV Hour: The Family Man," ABC, 1954; "Omnibus: John Quincy Adams," CBS, 1955; "Producers Showcase: The Fourposter," NBC, 1955; "Philco TV Playhouse: Christmas 'til Closing," NBC, 1955; "U.S. Steel Hour: The Great Adventure," CBS, 1956; "Climax!: The Fifth Wheel," CBS, 1956; "Omnibus: The Better Half," CBS, 1956; "Alcoa Hour: The Confidence Man," NBC, 1956; "Alcoa Theatre: The Big Wave," NBC, 1956; "G.E. Theatre: Pot of Gold," CBS, 1956; "Alfred Hitchcock Presents: Kill with Kindness," CBS, 1956; "Studio One: The Five Dollar Bill," CBS, 1957; "Alcoa Hour: No License to Kill," NBC, 1957; "Studio One: A Member of the Family," CBS, 1957; "Schlitz Playhouse of Stars: Clothes Make the Man," CBS, 1957; "Studio 57: Little Miss Bedford," SYN, 1957; "Person to Person," CBS, 1958; "Du Pont Show of the Month: The Bridge of San Luis Rey," CBS, 1958; "Telephone Time: War Against War," ABC, 1958; "The Loretta Young Show: Windfall," NBC, 1958; "The Loretta Young Show: Thanks to You," NBC, 1958; "G.E. Theatre: Ah There, Beau Brimmel," CBS, 1958; "Alfred Hitchcock Presents: Impromptu Murder," CBS, 1958; "The Ed Sullivan Show," CBS, 1959; "The Moon and Sixpence," NBC, 1959; "Hallmark Hall of Fame: A Doll's House," NBC, 1959; "The Barbara Stanwyck Show: Good Citizen," NBC, 1960; "Here's Hollywood," NBC, 1960; "Play of the Week: Juno and the Paycock," SYN, 1960; "Naked City: C3H5(NO3)3," ABC, 1961; "Get the Message," ABC, 1964; "Password," CBS, 1964; "The Oath: 33 Hours in the Life of God," ABC, 1976.

TV MOVIES AND MINISERIES: "Hallmark Hall of Fame: Foxfire," CBS, 1987; "AT&T Presents: Day One," CBS, 1989.

CROSBY, BING

b. Harry Lillis Crosby, Tacoma, WA, May 2, 1904; d. 1977. Famed crooner whose relaxed onstage manner betrayed a complex, sometimes stern personality.

AS A REGULAR: "The Bing Crosby Show" (specials), ABC, 1958-61; "The Bing Crosby Show," ABC, 1964-65; "Hollywood Palace," ABC, 1964-70. AND: "Ford Star Jubilee: High Tor," CBS, 1956; "Ford Star Jubilee: You're the Top," CBS, 1956; "The Ed Sullivan Show," CBS, 1956; "The Phil Silvers Show: Sgt. Bilko Presents Bing Crosby," CBS, 1957; "The Edsel Show," CBS, 1957; "The Frank Sinatra Show," ABC, 1957; "The Perry Como Show," NBC, 1957; "Bing Crosby and His Friends," CBS, 1958; "Bob Hope Special," NBC, 1958; "Dean Martin Special," NBC, 1958; "Dean Martin Special," NBC, 1959; "Frank Sinatra Timex Show," ABC, 1959; "Perry Como's Kraft Music Hall," NBC, 1960; "The du Pont Show: Happy With the Blues," NBC, 1961; "The Bob Hope Show," NBC, 1962; "Dinah Shore Special," NBC, 1963; "The Bing Crosby Show," CBS, 1964; "Bell Telephone Hour," NBC, 1964; "The Jackie Gleason Show," CBS, 1967; "The Danny Thomas Hour: The Demon Under the Bed," NBC, 1967; "The Dean Martin Show," NBC, 1967; "Playhouse New York: The 1940s-The Great Radio Comedians," NET, 1973; "Bing Crosby and His Friends," CBS, 1974; "Bell System Family Theatre: Christmas with the Bing Crosbys," NBC, 1974.

TV MOVIES AND MINISERIES: "Dr. Cook's Garden," ABC, 1971.
* Crosby was the first choice to play Lt. Columbo, but he turned down the role.
* Crosby's production company produced "Hogan's Heroes," "Ben Casey" and the film "Final Chapter—Walking Tall."
* Crosby died of a heart attack while golfing in Spain.

CROSBY, BOB

b. George Robert Crosby, Spokane, WA, August 23, 1913. Bandleader and brother of Bing.

AS A REGULAR: "The Bob Crosby Show," CBS, 1953-54; CBS, 1956; NBC, 1958. AND: "Climax!: One Night Stand," CBS, 1955; "Arthur Godfrey's Talent Scouts," CBS, 1956; "Shower of Stars," CBS, 1956; "The Jack Benny Program," CBS, 1957; "Shower of Stars: Jack Benny's 40th Birthday Celebration," CBS, 1958; "Art Linkletter's House Party," CBS, 1958; "Whats My Line?," CBS, 1958; "The Jack Benny Program: Autolight," CBS, 1959; "Startime: The Swingin' Years," NBC, 1960; "Big Band Cavalcade," PBS, 1975.

CROSBY, CATHY LEE

AS A REGULAR: "That's Incredible," ABC, 1980-84. AND: "Marcus Welby, M.D.: In Sickness and in Health," ABC, 1972; "Emergency!: Virus," NBC, 1972; "Barnaby Jones: Murder in the Doll's House," CBS, 1973; "Shaft: The Capricorn Murders," CBS, 1974; "Kolchak: The Night Stalker: The Youth Killer," ABC, 1975; "The Love Boat: Like Father, Like Son," ABC, 1979; "The John Davidson Show," SYN, 1981; "Hardcastle and McCormick: The Homecoming,"

ABC, 1984; "The Love Boat: The Captain Wears Pantyhose," ABC, 1985.

TV MOVIES AND MINISERIES: "Wonder Woman," ABC, 1974; "World War III," NBC, 1982; "Intimate Strangers," CBS, 1986.

CROSBY, DENISE

Shapely actress and granddaughter of Bing.

AS A REGULAR: "Star Trek: The Next Generation," SYN, 1987-88.

AND: "Mancuso FBI: I Cover the Waterfront," NBC, 1989.

CROSBY, DENNIS

b. Hollywood, CA, 1935; d. 1989

& PHILIP

b. Hollywood, CA, 1935. Twin sons of Bing Crosby.

AS REGULARS: "The Bing Crosby Show (Specials)," ABC, 1959-60.

AND: "The Phil Silvers Show: The Bilkos and the Crosbys," CBS, 1958; "Pat Boone Chevy Showroom," ABC, 1959; "Perry Como's Kraft Music Hall," NBC, 1960; "The Dick Clark Saturday Night Beechnut Show," ABC, 1960; "The Ed Sullivan Show," CBS, 1960; "Person to Person," CBS, 1961; "I've Got a Secret," CBS, 1961; "The Ed Sullivan Show," CBS, 1961; "The Ed Sullivan Show," CBS, 1962.

CROSBY, GARY

b. Hollywood, CA, 1934. Son of Bing who began performing with his father and then became estranged from him.

AS A REGULAR: "The Bill Dana Show," NBC, 1963-65; "Adam 12," NBC, 1968-75; "Chase," NBC, 1973-74.

AND: "The Bob Hope Show," NBC, 1957; "Pat Boone Chevy Showroom," ABC, 1958; "The Bob Crosby Show," NBC, 1958; "Milton Berle Starring in the Kraft Music Hall," NBC, 1958; "The Eddie Fisher Show," NBC, 1958; "The Phil Silvers Show: The Bilkos and the Crosbys," CBS, 1958; "The Ford Show," NBC, 1960; "Here's Hollywood," NBC, 1961; "American Bandstand," ABC, 1962; "Ben Casey: A Cardinal Act of Mercy," ABC, 1963; "Ensign O'Toole: Operation: Boxer," NBC, 1963; "Ensign O'Toole: Operation: Physical," NBC, 1963; "Hollywood Palace," ABC, 1964; "The Twilight Zone: Come Wander with Me," CBS, 1964; "The Bing Crosby Show: Exactly Like Who?," ABC, 1964; "The Bing Crosby Show: The Dominant Male," ABC, 1964; "Perry Mason: The Case of the Frustrated Folk Singer," CBS, 1965; "Hullabaloo," NBC, 1965; "The Farmer's Daughter: Have You Ever Thought of Building?," ABC, 1966; "Hondo: Hondo and the Hanging Town," ABC, 1967; "The Flying Nun: Speak the Speech, I Pray You," ABC, 1969; "Dragnet: Forgery-DR-33," NBC,

1969; "Love, American Style: Love and the Tuba," ABC, 1971; "The FBI: The Fatal Connection," ABC, 1971; "Ironside: Class of '57," NBC, 1971; "Here's Lucy: Lucy Plays Cops and Robbers," CBS, 1973; "The Wacky World of Jonathan Winters," SYN, 1974; "Tattletales," CBS, 1974; "Ironside: Trial of Terror," NBC, 1974; "Marcus Welby, M.D.: The Medea Factor," ABC, 1975; "Emergency!: Daisy's Pick," NBC, 1975; "The Bionic Woman: Bionic Beauty," ABC, 1976; "The Rockford Files: Never Send a Boy King to Do a Man's Job," NBC, 1979; "Simon & Simon: It's Only a Game," CBS, 1982; "Matlock: The Court-Martial," NBC, 1987.

TV MOVIES AND MINISERIES: "Wings of Fire," NBC, 1967; "O'Hara, United States Treasury: Operation Cobra," CBS, 1971; "Sandcastles," CBS, 1972; "Partners in Crime," NBC, 1973.

* Crosby wrote "Going My Own Way" after his father died, describing him as a cold, uncaring father and cruel taskmaster.

CROSBY, KATHRYN

b. Olive Kathryn Grandstaff, Houston, TX, November 25, 1933. Actress who married Bing Crosby in 1957 and pretty much retired from show biz.

AND: "The Eddie Fisher Show," NBC, 1957; "Ford Theatre: The Connoisseur," ABC, 1957; "Bing Crosby and His Friends," CBS, 1958; "Studio 30: A Kiss for Santa," SYN, 1958; "Mother's March," SYN, 1960; "The Tonight Show Starring Johnny Carson," NBC, 1964; "The Bing Crosby Show," CBS, 1964; "The Bing Crosby Show: The Image," ABC, 1965; "Dream Girl of '67," ABC, 1967; "Bell System Family Theatre: Christmas with the Bing Crosbys," NBC, 1974.

CROSBY, MARY

b. Los Angeles, CA, 1959. Daughter of Bing and, as the sexy and evil Kristin Shepard on "Dallas," the woman who shot J.R. Ewing and reaped record ratings for the show; she made her TV debut with her dad on "The Danny Thomas Hour."

AS A REGULAR: "Brothers and Sisters," NBC, 1979; "Dallas," CBS, 1979-81; "Knots Landing," CBS, 1980.

AND: "The Danny Thomas Hour: The Demon Under the Bed," NBC, 1967; "Bell System Family Theatre: Christmas with the Bing Crosbys," NBC, 1974; "Three's Company: ... And Justice for Jack," ABC, 1980; "The John Davidson Show," SYN, 1981; "The Love Boat: Pride of the Pacific," ABC, 1982; "The Love Boat: A Fish Out of Water," ABC, 1984; "Hotel: The Wedding," ABC, 1984; "Glitter: On Your Toes," ABC, 1984; "Hotel: Distortions," ABC,

1985; "Hotel: Saving Grace," ABC, 1985; "Freddy's Nightmares: Lucky Stiff," SYN, 1989.

TV MOVIES AND MINISERIES: "Pearl," ABC, 1978; "A Guide for the Married Woman," ABC, 1978; "Midnight Lace," NBC, 1981; "Hollywood Wives," ABC, 1985; "Final Jeopardy," NBC, 1985; "Stagecoach," CBS, 1986; "In the Heat of the Night," NBC, 1989.

CROTHERS, SCATMAN

b. Benjamin Crothers, Terre Haute, 1911; d. 1986. Black actor who played Louie the garbageman on "Chico and the Man."

AS A REGULAR: "The Beany and Cecil Show," SYN, 1961; ABC, 1964-66; "Chico and the Man," NBC, 1974-78; "Hong Kong Phooey," ABC, 1974-75; "One of the Boys," NBC, 1982; "Casablanca," NBC, 1983; "Morningstar/Eveningstar," CBS, 1986.

AND: "Bonanza: The Smiler," NBC, 1961; "Barefoot in the Park: Somethin' Fishy," ABC, 1970; "Bewitched: Three Men and a Witch on a Horse," ABC, 1971; "Love, American Style: Love and the Dummies," ABC, 1971; "Love, American Style: Love and the Perfect Wedding," ABC, 1972; "Kojak: The Corrupter," CBS, 1973; "The New Temperatures Rising Show: The Mothers," ABC, 1973; "Hollywood Television Theatre: The Sty of the Blind Pig," PBS, 1974; "Kolchak, the Night Stalker: The Zombie," ABC, 1974; "The Odd Couple: The Subway Story," ABC, 1974; "Sanford & Son: The Stand-In," NBC, 1975; "The Merv Griffin Show," SYN, 1975; "Joys," NBC, 1976; "Laverne & Shirley: Murder on the Moose Jaw Express," ABC, 1980; "NBC Special Treat: Sunshine's on the Way," NBC, 1980; "Dance Fever," SYN, 1981; "It Takes Two: Death Penalty," ABC, 1982; "Taxi: A Grand Gesture," NBC, 1983; "Hill Street Blues: The End of Logan's Run," NBC, 1984; "The Love Boat: Santa, Santa, Santa," ABC, 1985.

TV MOVIES AND MINISERIES: "Roots," ABC, 1977; "The Harlem Globetrotters on Gilligan's Island," NBC, 1981; "Missing Children: A Mother's Story," CBS, 1982.

*   Crothers got his nickname in 1932, while auditioning as a scat singer for a radio job in Dayton, Ohio.

CROWLEY, PATRICIA

b. Olyphant, PA, September 17, 1933. Actress who played Joan Nash on "Please Don't Eat the Daisies."

AS A REGULAR: "A Date with Judy," ABC, 1951; "Please Don't Eat the Daisies," NBC, 1965-67; "Joe Forrester," NBC, 1975-76; "Dynasty," ABC, 1986; "Generations," NBC, 1989.

AND: "Kraft Television Theatre: Sixteen," NBC, 1950; "Goodyear TV Playhouse: Tresaure Chest," NBC, 1952; "Suspense: Night of Evil," CBS,

1952; "Armstrong Circle Theatre: The Laughing Shoes," NBC, 1952; "Armstrong Circle Theatre: Fairy Tale," NBC, 1952; "Armstrong Circle Theatre: Caprice," NBC, 1952; "Lux Video Theatre: The Pretext," CBS, 1954; "U.S. Steel Hour: Two," ABC, 1954; "Goodyear TV Playhouse: Guilty Is the Stranger," NBC, 1954; "G.E. Theatre: Bachelor's Bride," CBS, 1955; "Lux Video Theatre: Here Comes the Groom," NBC, 1956; "Climax!: The 78th Floor," CBS, 1956; "West Point: Heat of Anger," CBS, 1956; "Schlitz Playhouse of Stars: Girl With a Glow," CBS, 1957; "Crossroads: The Deadline," ABC, 1957; "The Frank Sinatra Show: A Gun at His Back," ABC, 1957; "77 Sunset Strip: Conspiracy of Silence," ABC, 1959; "Maverick: Betrayal," ABC, 1959; "Westinghouse Desilu Playhouse: The Untouchables," CBS, 1959; "Goodyear Theatre: I Remember Caviar," NBC, 1959; "Bronco: Game at the Beacon Club," ABC, 1959; "Riverboat: Tampico Raid," NBC, 1960; "Goodyear Theatre: All in the Family," NBC, 1960; "Maverick: A Tale of Three Cities," ABC, 1960; "Robert Taylor's Detectives: Escort," NBC, 1961; "Dr. Kildare: A Very Present Help," NBC, 1962; "Cain's Hundred: The Quick Brown Fox," NBC, 1962; "Rawhide: Incident of the Mountain Man," CBS, 1963; "Bonanza: The Actress," NBC, 1963; "The Twilight Zone: Printer's Devil," CBS, 1963; "The Eleventh Hour: Five Moments of Time," NBC, 1963; "The Fugitive: The Witch," ABC, 1963; "Mr. Novak: Love in the Wrong Season," NBC, 1963; "77 Sunset Strip: The Toy Jungle," ABC, 1963; "The Lieutenant: Between Music and Laughter," NBC, 1964; "Arrest and Trial: The Black Flower," ABC, 1964; "Chain Letter," NBC, 1966; "The Virginian: The Hell Wind," NBC, 1968; "You Don't Say," NBC, 1968; "Walt Disney's Wonderful World of Color: Boomerang," NBC, 1969; "Love, American Style: Love and the Modern Wife," ABC, 1969; "Walt Disney's Wonderful World of Color: Menace on the Mountain," NBC, 1970; "Marcus Welby, M.D.: A Portrait of Debbie," ABC, 1971; "Columbo: Death Lends a Hand," NBC, 1971; "The Bold Ones: One Lonely Step," NBC, 1971; "Alias Smith and Jones: Miracle at Santa Marta," ABC, 1971; "The Bold Ones: One Lonely Step," NBC, 1971; "Owen Marshall, Counselor at Law: Warlock at Mach 3," ABC, 1972; "Griff: All the Lonely People," ABC, 1973; "Police Story: Fingerprint," NBC, 1974; "Police Story: The Man in the Shadows," NBC, 1975; "Matt Helm: The Game of the Century," ABC, 1975; "Police Story: The Long Ball," NBC, 1976; "Police Woman: Trial by Prejudice," NBC, 1976; "The Streets of San Francisco: Castle of Fear," ABC, 1976; "Family: Return Engagement," ABC, 1977; "The Rockford Files: Guilt," NBC, 1978; "Happy Days: A Potsie Is Born," ABC, 1980; "Charlie's Angels: Hula Angels," ABC, 1981; "Today's FBI: Skyjack," ABC, 1981; "Fantasy Island:

Saturday's Child," ABC, 1983; "Blacke's Magic: Knave of Diamonds, Ace of Hearts," NBC, 1986.
TV MOVIES AND MINISERIES: "The Return of Joe Forrester," NBC, 1975; "The Millionaire," CBS, 1978.

CRUZ, BRANDON
b. *Bakersfield, CA, May 28, 1962.* Child actor who played Eddie.
AS A REGULAR: "The Courtship of Eddie's Father," ABC, 1969-72.
AND: "Medical Center: Night Cry," CBS, 1973; "The Growing Up of David Lev," NBC, 1973; "Gunsmoke: The Dreamer," CBS, 1973; "Love, American Style: Love and the Unsteady Steady," ABC, 1973; "Police Story: Cop in the Middle," NBC, 1974; "Doc Elliott: A Time to Grow," ABC, 1974; "ABC Afterschool Special: Mighty Moose and the Quarterback," ABC, 1974.
TV MOVIES AND MINISERIES: "But I Don't Want to Get Married!," ABC, 1970.

CRYSTAL, BILLY
Comedian; an Emmy winner for "Midnight Train to Moscow."
AS A REGULAR: "Soap," ABC, 1977-81; "The Billy Crystal Comedy Hour," NBC, 1982; "Saturday Night Live," NBC, 1984-85.
AND: "The Merv Griffin Show," SYN, 1977; "Midnight Special," NBC, 1977; "Hollywood Squares," SYN, 1978; "The Love Boat: The Kissing Bandit," ABC, 1978; "Sha Na Na," SYN, 1978; "Midnight Special," NBC, 1980; "The John Davidson Show," SYN, 1981; "Saturday Night Live," NBC, 1984; "All Star Tribute to Kareem Abdul-Jabbar," NBC, 1989; "Late Night with David Letterman," NBC, 1989; "Billy Crystal: Midnight Train to Moscow," HBO, 1989.
TV MOVIES AND MINISERIES: "Human Feelings," NBC, 1978; "SST-Death Flight," ABC, 1977.
* Emmies: 1990.

CULLEN, BILL
b. *William Lawrence Cullen, Pittsburgh, February 18, 1920; d. 1990.* Longtime game show host with a decency and understated humor that set him apart from many of his flashier contemporaries.
AS A REGULAR: "Act It Out," NBC, 1949; "Winner Take All," CBS, 1951; "Who's There?," CBS, 1952; "Give and Take," CBS, 1952; "I've Got a Secret," CBS, 1952-67; 1976; "Where Was I?," DUM, 1953; "Why?," ABC, 1953; "Bank on the Stars," CBS, 1953, NBC, 1954; "Place the Face," NBC, 1954-55; "Name That Tune," CBS, 1954-55; "Down You Go," NBC, 1956; "The Price Is Right," NBC, 1956-63; ABC, 1963-64; "Eye Guess," NBC, 1966-69; "To Tell the Truth," SYN, 1969-77; 1980; "Three

on a Match," NBC, 1971-74; "The $25,000 Pyramid," SYN, 1974-79; "Winning Streak," NBC, 1974-75; "Blankety Blanks," ABC, 1975; "Pass the Buck," CBS, 1978; "The Love Experts," SYN, 1978-79; "Chain Reaction," NBC, 1980; "Blockbusters," NBC, 1980-82; "Child's Play," CBS, 1982-83; "Hot Potato," NBC, 1984; "The Joker's Wild," SYN, 1984-86.
AND: "Password," CBS, 1962; "Personality," NBC, 1967; "Personality," NBC, 1968; "You're Putting Me On," NBC, 1969; "What's My Line?," SYN, 1974; "Break the Bank," SYN, 1976; "Cross Wits," SYN, 1977; "The $20,000 Pyramid," ABC, 1979; "Password Plus," NBC, 1980.

CULP, ROBERT
b. *Berkeley, CA, August 16, 1930.* Talented light leading man who played Texas Ranger Hoby Gilman in "Trackdown," swinging spy Kelly Robinson in "I Spy" and put-upon FBI agent Bill Maxwell in "The Greatest American Hero."
AS A REGULAR: "Trackdown," CBS, 1957-59; "I Spy," NBC, 1965-68; "The Greatest American Hero," ABC, 1981-83.
AND: "Star Tonight: The Chevigny Man," ABC, 1956; "U.S. Steel Hour: The Funny Heart," CBS, 1956; "Playwrights '56: Nick and Letty," NBC, 1956; "Tate: The Bounty Hunter," NBC, 1960; "Chevy Mystery Show: Dead Man's Walk," NBC, 1960; "The Outlaws: Thirty a Month," NBC, 1960; "Shirley Temple's Storybook: The House of the Seven Gables," NBC, 1960; "Dick Powell's Zane Grey Theatre: Morning Incident," CBS, 1960; "Hennesey: The Specialist," CBS, 1961; "Walt Disney's Wonderful World of Color: Sammy, the Way-Out Seal," NBC, 1962; "Empire: Where the Hawk Is Wheeling," NBC, 1963; "Naked City: The Highest of Prizes," ABC, 1963; "You Don't Say," NBC, 1966; "Get Smart: Die, Spy," NBC, 1968; "The Name of the Game: Little Bear Died Running," NBC, 1970; "Columbo: Death Lends a Hand," NBC, 1971; "Columbo: The Most Crucial Game," NBC, 1972; "CBS Playhouse 90: The Lie," CBS, 1973; "Columbo: Double Exposure," NBC, 1973; "Shaft: The Executioners," CBS, 1973; "From Sea to Shining Sea," SYN, 1974; "Password All-Stars," ABC, 1974; "Police Story: Year of the Dragon," NBC, 1975; "Give Me Liberty," SYN, 1975; "A Man Called Sloane: The Seduction Squad," NBC, 1979; "The Love Boat: The Major's Wife," ABC, 1980; "Saturday Night Live," NBC, 1982; "Hardcastle and McCormick: School for Scandal," ABC, 1984; "Murder, She Wrote: Murder by Appointment Only," CBS, 1986; "Highway to Heaven: Parent's Day," NBC, 1986; "The Cosby Show: The Bald and the

Beautiful," NBC, 1987; "Matlock: The Power Brokers," NBC, 1987; "Who's the Boss?: Gambling Jag," ABC, 1989.

TV MOVIES AND MINISERIES: "The Hanged Man," NBC, 1964; "See the Man Run," ABC, 1971; "A Cold Night's Death," ABC, 1973; "Outrage!," ABC, 1973; "Houston, We've Got a Problem," ABC, 1974; "Strange Homecoming," NBC, 1974; "A Cry for Help," ABC, 1975; "Flood," NBC, 1976; "Roots: The Next Generations," ABC, 1979; "Hot Rod," NBC, 1979; "The Night the City Screamed," ABC, 1980; "Killjoy," CBS, 1981; "Her Life as a Man," NBC, 1984; "Calender Girl Murders," ABC, 1984; "Brothers-in-Law," ABC, 1985; "The Gladiator," ABC, 1986; "The Blue Lightning," CBS, 1986; "Combat High," NBC, 1986; "What Price Victory," ABC, 1988.

AS WRITER: "The Rifleman: Waste," ABC, 1962; "I Spy: So Long, Patrick Henry," NBC, 1965.

CUMMINGS, BOB

b. *Clarence Robert Orville Cummings, Joplin, MO, June 9, 1908; d. 1990.* Light romantic leading man who began his television career with good work in dramas and then turned to a limp sitcom as ladies' man Bob Collins; an Emmy winner for "Twelve Angry Men."

AS A REGULAR: "My Hero," NBC, 1952-53; "The Bob Cummings Show," NBC, 1955; CBS, 1955-57; NBC, 1957-59; CBS, 1961-62; "My Living Doll," CBS, 1964-65.

AND: "Sure as Fate: Run From the Sun," ABC, 1950; "Lux Video Theatre: The Shiny People," CBS, 1951; "Robert Montgomery Presents: Lila, My Love," NBC, 1952; "Lux Video Theatre: Pattern for Glory," CBS, 1952; "Campbell TV Soundstage: The Test Case," NBC, 1954; "Studio One: Twelve Angry Men," CBS, 1954; "Elgin TV Hour: Flood," ABC, 1954; "Best Foot Forward," NBC, 1954; "Studio One: A Special Announcement," CBS, 1956; "Schlitz Playhouse of Stars: One Left Over," CBS, 1957; "G.E. Theatre: Too Good with a Gun," CBS, 1957; "The Steve Allen Show," NBC, 1957; "Dinah Shore Chevy Show," NBC, 1957; "Schlitz Playhouse of Stars: Dual Control," CBS, 1957; "Person to Person," CBS, 1957; "Dinah Shore Chevy Show," NBC, 1958; "Playhouse 90: Bomber's Moon," CBS, 1958; "The Twilight Zone: King Nine Will Not Return," CBS, 1960; "Dick Powell's Zane Grey Theatre: The Last Bugle," CBS, 1960; "What About Linda?," SYN, 1961; "Art Linkletter's House Party," CBS, 1961; "Here's Hollywood," NBC, 1961; "The du Pont Show: The Action in New Orleans," NBC, 1962; "Perry Como's Kraft Music Hall," NBC, 1962; "The Dick Powell Show: The Last of the Private Eyes," NBC, 1963;

"Hollywood Palace," ABC, 1964; "The Beverly Hillbillies: The Race for Queen," CBS, 1964; "The Great Adventure: Plague," CBS, 1964; "Bob Hope Chrysler Theatre: The Square Peg," NBC, 1964; "The Flying Nun: Speak the Speech, I Pray You," ABC, 1969; "Green Acres: Rest and Relaxation," CBS, 1970; "Bewitched: Samantha and the Troll," ABC, 1971; "Love, American Style: Love and the Second Time," ABC, 1971; "Here's Lucy: Lucy and Her Genuine Twimby," CBS, 1973; "Love, American Style: Love and the Secret Spouse," ABC, 1973.

TV Movies and Miniseries: "Gidget Grows Up," ABC, 1969; "The Great American Beauty Contest," ABC, 1973; "Partners in Crime," NBC, 1973.

CURTIN, JANE

b. *Cambridge, MA, September 6, 1947.* Emmy winning actress with a scene-saving style on sitcoms that she never had much of a chance to show on "Saturday Night Live."

AS A REGULAR: "Saturday Night Live," NBC, 1975-80; "Kate & Allie," CBS, 1984-89; "Working It Out," NBC, 1990- .

AND: "What Really Happened to the Class of '65?: The Class Hustler," NBC, 1977; "Tattinger's: Broken Windows," NBC, 1988; "Saturday Night Live's 15th Anniversary," NBC, 1989.

TV Movies and Miniseries: "Divorce Wars: A Love Story," ABC, 1982; "Maybe Baby," NBC, 1988.

* Emmies: 1984, 1985.

CURTIS, KEN

b. *Curtis Gates, Lamar, CO, July 12, 1916; d. 1991.* Scrawny cowboy actor who played deputy Festus Haggen on "Gunsmoke."

AS A REGULAR: "Ripcord," SYN, 1961-63; "Gunsmoke," CBS, 1964-75; "The Yellow Rose," NBC, 1983-84.

AND: "Have Gun, Will Travel: The Posse," CBS, 1959; "Have Gun, Will Travel: Naked Gun," CBS, 1959; "Gunsmoke: The Ex-Urbanites," CBS, 1960; "Gunsmoke: Speak Me Fair," CBS, 1960; "Wagon Train: The Horace Best Story," NBC, 1960; "Perry Mason: The Case of the Clumsy Clown," CBS, 1960; "The Spirit of the Alamo," ABC, 1960; "Have Gun, Will Travel: Love's Young Dream," CBS, 1960; "The Case of the Dangerous Robin: Disaster at Sea," SYN, 1961; "Have Gun, Will Travel: Soledad Crossing," CBS, 1961; "Have Gun, Will Travel: Pandora's Box," CBS, 1962; "Gunsmoke: Us Haggens," CBS, 1962; "Death Valley Days: Greydon's Charge," SYN, 1964.

TV MOVIES AND MINISERIES: "Black Beauty," NBC, 1978.

D

DAGMAR

b. *Jennie Lewis, Huntington, WV, November 29, 1926.* Blonde comic actress who was extremely popular in the early fifties.

AS A REGULAR: "Broadway Open House," NBC, 1950-51; "Dagmar's Canteen," NBC, 1952; "Masquerade Party," ABC, 1955-56; NBC, 1959.

AND: "Bob Hope Special," NBC, 1950; "The Phil Silvers Show: Bilko's Television Idea," CBS, 1957; "Mike Wallace Interviews," ABC, 1957; "Arthur Murray Party," NBC, 1958; "Person to Person," CBS, 1959.

DAHL, ARLENE

b. *Minneapolis, MN, August 11, 1924.* Leading lady of the fifties whose talent lay more in self-promotion as a beauty expert than acting.

AS A REGULAR: "Pepsi Cola Playhouse," ABC, 1953-54; "Opening Night," NBC, 1958; "One Life to Live," ABC, 1981-84.

AND: "Ford Theatre: Wedding March," NBC, 1954; "Lux Video Theatre: September Affair," NBC, 1954; "Ford Theatre: All That Glitters," NBC, 1955; "Ford Theatre: Sometimes It Happens," ABC, 1956; "The Steve Allen Show," NBC, 1957; "The Perry Como Show," NBC, 1957; "Person to Person," CBS, 1957; "Dick Clark's World of Talent," ABC, 1959; "Celebrity Talent Scouts," CBS, 1960; "Riverboat: That Taylor Affair," NBC, 1960; "Here's Hollywood," NBC, 1960; "Burke's Law: Who Killed Alex Debbs?," ABC, 1963; "Burke's Law: Who Killed Snooky Martinelli?," ABC, 1964; "You Don't Say," NBC, 1964; "Object Is," ABC, 1964; "Burke's Law: Who Killed Everybody?," ABC, 1964; "Burke's Law: Who Killed Mr. Colby in Ladies' Lingerie?," ABC, 1965; "Bob Hope Chrysler Theatre: Perilous Times," NBC, 1965; "The Merv Griffin Show," SYN, 1966; "Love, American Style: Love and the Teddy Bear," ABC, 1971; "Tattletales," CBS, 1974; "Beat the Clock," SYN, 1975; "The Love Boat: Bo 'n Sam," ABC, 1979; "The Love Boat: Love Below Decks," ABC, 1983.

DAILEY, DAN

b. *New York City, NY, December 14, 1914; d. 1978.* Song and dance man of movies and TV.

AS A REGULAR: "Four Just Men," SYN, 1959; "The Governor & J.J.," CBS, 1969-70; "Faraday and Company," NBC, 1973-74.

AND: "Shower of Stars: Burlesque," CBS, 1955; "Paris in the Springtime," NBC, 1956; "The Ed Sullivan Show," CBS, 1956; "Dinah Shore Chevy Show," NBC, 1957; "The Ed Sullivan Show," CBS, 1957; "The General Motors 50th Anniversary Show," NBC, 1957; "G.E. Theatre: Bill Bailey, Won't You Please Come Home?," CBS, 1959; "The Untouchables: Come and Kill Me," ABC, 1962; "The Alfred Hitchcock Hour: The Tender Poisoner," CBS, 1962; "Stump the Stars," CBS, 1962; "Vacation Playhouse: Papa GI," CBS, 1964; "Summer Playhouse: Low Man on a Totem Pole," CBS, 1964; "Hollywood Palace," ABC, 1964; "The Mike Douglas Show," SYN, 1965; "Here's Lucy: Won't You Calm Down, Dan Dailey?," ABC, 1971; "The Wonderful World of Disney: Michael O'Hara, the Fourth," NBC, 1972; "Mitzi Gaynor: The First Time," CBS, 1973.

TV MOVIES AND MINISERIES: "Mr. and Mrs. Bo Jo Jones," ABC, 1971; "The Daughters of Joshua Cabe Return," ABC, 1975; "Testimony of Two Men," SYN, 1977.

DAILY, BILL

b. *Des Moines, IA, August 30, 1928.* Light comic actor who played Howard Borden on "The Bob Newhart Show" and Roger Healey on "I Dream of Jeannie."

AS A REGULAR: "I Dream of Jeannie," NBC, 1965-70; "The Bob Newhart Show," CBS, 1972-78; "Aloha Paradise," ABC, 1981; "Small & Frye," CBS, 1983; "Starting From Scratch," SYN, 1987-89.

AND: "The Mike Douglas Show," SYN, 1964; "Bewitched: A Vision of Sugar Plums," ABC, 1964; "The Mike Douglas Show," SYN, 1965; "The Farmer's Daughter: Katy by Moonlight," ABC, 1965; "My Mother the Car: The Defenders," NBC, 1965; "The Farmer's Daughter: Forever Is a Cast-Iron Mess," ABC, 1965; "Love, American Style: Love and the Country Girl," ABC, 1971; "Love, American Style: Love and the Single Sister," ABC, 1972; "The Mary Tyler Moore Show: His Two Right Arms," CBS, 1972; "Dinah!," SYN, 1975; "Match Game '75," CBS, 1975; "Cross Wits," SYN, 1975; "Flying High: Pilot," CBS, 1978; "CHiPs: Roller Disco," NBC, 1979; "The Love Boat: Rent-a-Family," ABC, 1979; "The Powers of Matthew Star: Daredevil," NBC, 1982; "ALF: We Are Family," NBC, 1988; "ALF: Mind Games," NBC, 1989.

TV MOVIES AND MINISERIES: "In Name Only," ABC, 1969; "Valentine Magic on Love Island," NBC, 1980; "I Dream of Jeannie: 15 Years Later," NBC, 1985.

DALIO, MARCEL

b. *Paris, July 17, 1900; d. 1983*. French film actor ("Rules of the Game") who came to America during World War II.
AS A REGULAR: "Warner Bros. Presents Casablanca," ABC, 1955-56.
AND: "TV Reader's Digest: The Baron and His Uranium Killing," ABC, 1955; "77 Sunset Strip: Spark of Freedom," ABC, 1960; "G.E. Theatre: At Your Service," CBS, 1960; "Bringing Up Buddy: Cynthia's Concert Tour," CBS, 1961.
* Dalio was the only cast member of the movie "Casablanca" to appear in the television series. In the movie, he played the croupier at Rick's; on the series he played police Captain Louis Renault, played in the movie by Claude Rains.

DALTON, ABBY

b. *Marlene Wasden, Glendale, CA, August 15, 1932*. Attractive actress who played Joey Bishop's TV wife and Julia Cumson on "Falcon Crest."
AS A REGULAR: "Hennesey," CBS, 1959-62; "The Joey Bishop Show," NBC, 1962-64; CBS, 1964-65; "The Jonathan Winters Show," CBS, 1967-69; "Falcon Crest," CBS, 1981-86.
AND: "Schlitz Playhouse of Stars: Way of the West," CBS, 1958; "Maverick: Duel at Sundown," ABC, 1959; "Sugarfoot: The Desperadoes," ABC, 1959; "Have Gun, Will Travel: Young Gun," CBS, 1959; "Chevy Mystery Show: Dead Man's Walk," NBC, 1960; "Here's Hollywood," NBC, 1961; "Hawaiian Eye: Nightmare in Paradise," ABC, 1962; "Password," CBS, 1962; "You Don't Say," NBC, 1964; "PDQ," NBC, 1965; "You Don't Say," NBC, 1965; "You Don't Say," NBC, 1966; "Hollywood Squares," NBC, 1967; "Hollywood Squares," NBC, 1968; "My Three Sons: Gossip, Inc.," CBS, 1968; "Hollywood Squares," NBC, 1969; "It Takes Two," NBC, 1970; "Love, American Style: Love and the Intruder," ABC, 1970; "Nanny and the Professor: The Masculine-Feminine Mystique," ABC, 1970; "Love, American Style: Love and the Waitress," ABC, 1971; "Password," ABC, 1972; "Love, American Style: Love and the Flying Finletters," ABC, 1974; "The Life and Times of Barney Miller," ABC, 1974; "Police Story: Cop in the Middle," NBC, 1974; "Showoffs," ABC, 1975; "The Love Boat: The Prize Winner," ABC, 1983; "Hardcastle and McCormick: Round Up the Old Gang," ABC, 1986; "Murder, She Wrote: Obituary for a Dead Anchor," CBS, 1986.
TV MOVIES AND MINISERIES: "Magic Carpet," NBC, 1972.

DALTON, TIMOTHY

b. *Wales, March 21, 1944*. Actor who now plays Bond—James Bond.

AS A REGULAR: "Charlie's Angels: Fallen Angels," ABC, 1979.
TV MOVIES AND MINISERIES: "Centennial," NBC, 1978-79; "The Flame Is Love," NBC, 1979; "The Master of Ballantrae," CBS, 1984; "Florence Nightingale," NBC, 1985; "Sins," CBS, 1986.

DALY, JAMES

b. *Wisconsin Rapids, WI, October 23, 1918; d. 1978*. Actor who played Dr. Paul Lochner on "Medical Center."
AS A REGULAR: "The Front Page," CBS, 1949-50; "Foreign Intrigue," NBC, 1953; "Medical Center," CBS, 1969-76.
AND: "Pulitzer Prize Playhouse: The Return of Mr. Moto," NBC, 1952; "The Web: The Vanished Horse," CBS, 1952; "Robert Montgomery Presents: Til Next We Meet," NBC, 1952; "Studio One: The Great Lady," CBS, 1952; "Studio One: To a Moment of Triumph," CBS, 1953; "Goodyear TV Playhouse: Doing Her Bit," NBC, 1955; "Omnibus: The Art of Murder," ABC, 1956; "Studio One: Goodbye, Picadilly," CBS, 1956; "Du Pont Theatre: One Day at a Time," ABC, 1957; "Goodyear TV Playhouse: First Love," NBC, 1957; "The Loretta Young Show: This Is the Moment," NBC, 1959; "Our American Heritage: Destiny West," NBC, 1960; "The Ann Sothern Show: Katy Meets Danger," CBS, 1960; "The Twilight Zone: A Stop at Willoughby," CBS, 1960; "The Breaking Point: And If Thy Hand Offend Thee," ABC, 1964; "The Nurses: The Human Transition," CBS, 1964; "The du Pont Show: Don't Go Upstairs," NBC, 1964; "Hallmark Hall of Fame: The Magnificent Yankee," NBC, 1965; "Dr. Kildare: With Hellfire and Thunder/Daily Flights to Olympus," NBC, 1965; "Hallmark Hall of Fame: Eagle in a Cage," NBC, 1965; "Dr. Kildare: Toast the Governess," NBC, 1965; "The Autumn Garden," NET, 1966; "The FBI: The Chameleon," ABC, 1966; "The Road West: The Gunfighter," NBC, 1966; "The Fugitive: The Evil Men Do," ABC, 1966; "Bob Hope Chrsyler Theatre: Storm Crossing," NBC, 1966; "NET Playhouse: An Enemy of the People," NET, 1966; "The Invaders: Beachhead," ABC, 1967; "The Felony Squad: The Night of the Shark," ABC, 1967; "The FBI: The Gold Card," ABC, 1967; "The Virginian: Nightmare at Fort Killman," NBC, 1967; "Gunsmoke: The Favor," CBS, 1967; "Mission: Impossible: Shock," CBS, 1967; "Mission: Impossible: The Bank," CBS, 1967; "Judd for the Defense: Conspiracy," ABC, 1967; "Hallmark Hall of Fame: Saint Joan," NBC, 1967; "CBS Playhouse: Dear Friends," CBS, 1967; "Combat!: Encounter," ABC, 1967; "The Invaders: The Peacemaker," ABC, 1968; "Walt Disney's Wonderful World of Color: The Treasure of San Bosco," NBC, 1968; "Judd for the Defense: Punishments, Cruel and Unusual,"

ABC, 1968; "The Virginian: Silver Image," NBC, 1968; "Star Trek: Requiem for Methuselah," NBC, 1969; "The FBI: Conspiracy of Silence," ABC, 1969; "Ironside: The People Against Judge McIntire," NBC, 1970.
TV MOVIES AND MINISERIES: "U.M.C.," CBS, 1969; "The Resurrection of Zachary Wheeler," ABC, 1971; "Roots: The Next Generations," ABC, 1979.
* Emmies: 1966.

DALY, JOHN
b. Johannesburg, South Africa, February 20, 1914. Newsman and TV personality.
AS A REGULAR: "Celebrity Time," CBS, 1949-50; "The Front Page," CBS, 1949-50; "We Take Your Word," CBS, 1950-51; "What's My Line?," CBS, 1950-67; "It's News to Me," CBS, 1951-53; "America's Town Meeting," ABC, 1952; "Open Hearing," ABC, 1954; "Who Said That?," ABC, 1955; "The Voice of Firestone," ABC, 1958-59.
AND: "Bing Crosby and His Friends," CBS, 1958; "Navy Log: And Then There Were None," ABC, 1958; "Prolog 1959," ABC, 1958; "Investigators and the Law," ABC, 1959; "The Splendid American," ABC, 1959; "The Jack Benny Program: Don's Anniversary," CBS, 1961; "Miss Universe Pageant," CBS, 1961; "Westinghouse Presents: The Sound of the Sixties," NBC, 1961; "The Merv Griffin Show," NBC, 1963; "Green Acres: Oliver Buys a Farm," CBS, 1965.
* Emmies: 1955.

DALY, TYNE
b. Madison, WI, February 21, 1947. Emmy winning actress who usually plays intense characters, including cop Mary Beth Lacey on the overrated "Cagney & Lacey."
AS A REGULAR: "Cagney & Lacey," CBS, 1982-88.
AND: "The Virginian: The Orchard," NBC, 1968; "Medical Center: Moment of Decision," CBS, 1970; "Ironside: The People Against Judge McIntire," NBC, 1970; "McMillan and Wife: Husbands, Wives and Thieves," NBC, 1971; "Mission: Impossible: Nerves," CBS, 1971; "Longstreet: One in the Reality Column," ABC, 1971; "Hollywood Television Theatre: Young Marrieds at Play," NET, 1971; "Doc Elliot: The Touch of God," ABC, 1974; "The Rookies: Time Lock," ABC, 1974; "The Streets of San Francisco: Commitment," ABC, 1974; "Barnaby Jones: A Gathering of Thieves," CBS, 1974; "Medical Center: Gift From a Killer," CBS, 1975; "The Law: Prior Consent," NBC, 1975; "The Rookies: Cliffy," ABC, 1975; "The Rookies: From Out of Darkness," ABC, 1976; "Lou Grant: Violence," CBS, 1981; "Quincy: Vigil of Fear," NBC, 1981; "Quincy: Gentle Into That Good Night," NBC, 1981; "Magnum, P.I.: The Jororo Kill," CBS, 1982.

TV MOVIES AND MINISERIES: "A Howling in the Woods," NBC, 1971; "Heat of Anger," CBS, 1972; "The Man Who Could Talk to Kids," CBS, 1973; "Larry," CBS, 1974; "The Entertainer," NBC, 1976; "Better Late Than Never," NBC, 1979; "A Matter of Life and Death," CBS, 1981; "Cagney & Lacey," CBS, 1981; "Your Place or Mine," CBS, 1983; "Kids Like These," CBS, 1987; "Stuck with Each Other," NBC, 1989.
* Emmies: 1983, 1984, 1985.

DAMON, CATHRYN
b. Seattle, WA, September 11, 1930; d. 1987. Emmy winning actress who played Mary Campbell on "Soap."
AS A REGULAR: "Soap," ABC, 1977-81; "Webster," ABC, 1984-86.
AND: "The Love Boat: The Man Who Loved Women," ABC, 1978; "The Love Boat: Friend of the Family," ABC, 1983; "Simon & Simon: Dear Lovesick," CBS, 1984; "Murder, She Wrote: It's a Dog's Life," CBS, 1984; "Matlock: The Chef," NBC, 1987; "The New Mike Hammer: Who Killed Sister Lorna?," CBS, 1987.
TV MOVIES AND MINISERIES: "Friendships, Secrets and Lies," NBC, 1979; "Not in Front of the Children," CBS, 1982; "Who Will Love My Children?," ABC, 1983.
* Emmies: 1980.

DAMON, STUART
b. Brooklyn, NY, February 5, 1937. Prince Charming in "Cinderella" and Dr. Alan Quartermaine on "General Hospital."
AS A REGULAR: "The Champions," NBC, 1968; "General Hospital," ABC, 1977- .
AND: "Cinderella," CBS, 1965; "The Toni Tennille Show," SYN, 1980; "The Mike Douglas Show," SYN, 1981; "Fantasy Island: Three's a Crowd," ABC, 1983; "The New Mike Hammer: Green Lipstick," CBS, 1987.
TV MOVIES AND MINISERIES: "Fantasies," ABC, 1982.

DAMONE, VIC
b. Vito Farinola, Brooklyn, NY, June 12, 1928. Singer.
AS A REGULAR: "The Vic Damone Show," CBS, 1956, 1957; "The Lively Ones," NBC, 1962-63; "The Dean Martin Summer Show," NBC, 1967.
AND: "Alcoa Hour: The Stingiest Man in Town," NBC, 1956; "The Ed Sullivan Show," CBS, 1957; "The Perry Como Show," NBC, 1957; "Arthur Godfrey and His Friends," CBS, 1957; "The Jackie Gleason Show," CBS, 1957; "The du Pont Show with June Allyson: Piano Man," CBS, 1960; "The du Pont Show: Happy With the Blues," NBC, 1961; "Westinghouse Presents: The Sound of the Sixties," NBC, 1961; "Playboy's

Penthouse," SYN, 1961; "The Ed Sullivan Show," CBS, 1961; "The Jack Paar Show," NBC, 1961; "The Jack Paar Show," NBC, 1962; "The Dick Van Dyke Show: Like a Sister," CBS, 1962; "The Garry Moore Show," CBS, 1962; "The Joey Bishop Show: Joey Gets Brainwashed," NBC, 1964; "The Judy Garland Show," CBS, 1964; "Hollywood Palace," ABC, 1964; "The Red Skelton Hour," CBS, 1964; "The Andy Williams Show," NBC, 1965; "Hollywood Palace," ABC, 1965; "The Mike Douglas Show," SYN, 1965; "The Dean Martin Show," NBC, 1965; "The Dangerous Christmas of Little Red Riding Hood," ABC, 1965; "Jericho: Two for the Road," CBS, 1966; "The Danny Thomas Hour: It's Greek to Me," NBC, 1967; "Danny Thomas Special," NBC, 1967; "The Tonight Show Starring Johnny Carson," NBC, 1968; "Hollywood Squares," NBC, 1974; "The Mike Douglas Show," SYN, 1975; "The Mike Douglas Show," SYN, 1976; "America's Tribute to Bob Hope," NBC, 1988; "Christmas in Washington," NBC, 1989.

DANA, BILL
b. William Szathmary, Quincy, MA, October 5, 1934. Comedian and comic writer who created Jose Jimenez; later he played the father of Wayne Fiscus (Howie Mandel) on "St. Elsewhere."
AS A REGULAR: "The Steve Allen Show," NBC, 1956-59; "Steve Allen Plymouth Show," NBC, 1959-60; "The Spike Jones Show," CBS, 1960; "The Danny Thomas Show," CBS, 1960-61; "The New Steve Allen Show," ABC, 1961; "The Bill Dana Show," NBC, 1963-65; "Steve Allen's Laugh Back," SYN, 1976; "No Soap, Radio," ABC, 1982; "Zorro and Son," CBS, 1983.
AND: "The Garry Moore Show," CBS, 1960; "The Garry Moore Show," CBS, 1961; "The Ed Sullivan Show," CBS, 1962; "The Ed Sullivan Show," CBS, 1963; "The Tonight Show Starring Johnny Carson," NBC, 1963; "Andy Williams Special," NBC, 1964; "Hollywood Palace," ABC, 1964; "The Mike Douglas Show," SYN, 1964; "The Jack Paar Program," NBC, 1965; "Batman: An Egg Grows in Gotham/The Yegg Foes in Gotham," ABC, 1966; "Get Smart: Supersonic Boom," NBC, 1967; "The Man From UNCLE: The Matterhorn Affair," NBC, 1967; "That's Life: The Ninth Month," ABC, 1968; "Hollywood Palace," ABC, 1968; "Get Smart: Ice Station Siegfried," CBS, 1970; "Love, American Style: Love and Las Vegas," ABC, 1970; "The Mouse Factory," SYN, 1973; "Police Woman: Side-winder," NBC, 1975; "McMillan and Wife: Aftershock," NBC, 1975; "Rosetti and Ryan: Is There a Lawyer in the House?," NBC, 1977; "Something Spectacular with Steve Allen," PBS, 1981; "Too Close for Comfort: Rafkin's Bum," ABC, 1982; "St. Elsewhere: Once Upon a Mattress," NBC, 1986; "St. Elsewhere: No Chemo, Sabe?," NBC, 1987; "The Golden Girls: My Brother, My Father," NBC, 1988; "St. Elsewhere: The Abby Singer Show," NBC, 1988; "The Smothers Brothers Comedy Hour," CBS, 1989.
TV MOVIES AND MINISERIES: "The Snoop Sisters," NBC, 1972; "A Guide for the Married Woman," ABC, 1978.
AS WRITER: "The Steve Allen Show," NBC, 1956-59; "The Steve Allen Plymouth Show," NBC, 1959-60; "The New Steve Allen Show," ABC, 1961; "All in the Family: Sammy's Visit," CBS, 1972.
AS WRITER-PRODUCER: "The Spike Jones Show," CBS, 1960; "The Tim Conway Comedy Hour," CBS, 1970.
* Dana used a variation of his mother's first name—Dena—for his stage name.
* See also Steve Allen.

D'ANDREA, TOM
b. Chicago, IL, May 15, 1909. Actor who played neighbor Jim Gillis on "The Life of Riley."
AS A REGULAR: "The Life of Riley," NBC, 1953-55; 1956-58; "The Soldiers," NBC, 1955; "Dante," NBC, 1960-61.
AND: "Appointment with Love: Never Laugh at a Lady," ABC, 1953; "The George Gobel Show," NBC, 1958; "My Living Doll: Rhoda Cures a Gambler," CBS, 1964; "The Addams Family: Portrait of Gomez," ABC, 1965; "The Farmer's Daughter: Jewel Beyond Compare," ABC, 1965; "The Dick Van Dyke Show: Bad Reception In Albany," CBS, 1966; "The Smothers Brothers Show: The Big Newsboy War," CBS, 1966; "The Andy Griffith Show: A Singer in Town," CBS, 1966; "The Beverly Hillbillies: The Folk Singers," CBS, 1966; "Green Acres: A Pig in a Poke," CBS, 1966; "Green Acres: Not Guilty," CBS, 1968; "That Girl: Chef's Night Out," ABC, 1970; "That Girl: That Shoplifter," ABC, 1971.

DANDRIDGE, RUBY
b. Memphis, TN, March 3, 1902; d. 1987.
AS A REGULAR: "Beulah," ABC, 1952-53; "Father of the Bride," CBS, 1961-62.

DANGERFIELD, RODNEY
b. Babylon, NY, November 22, 1921. Comedian.
AS A REGULAR: "The Dean Martin Show," NBC, 1972-73.
AND: "On Broadway Tonight," CBS, 1965; "The Ed Sullivan Show," CBS, 1967; "The Merv Griffin Show," SYN, 1968; "Operation: Entertainment," ABC, 1968; "The Ed Sullivan Show," CBS, 1968; "The Merv Griffin Show," CBS, 1969; "The Ed Sullivan Show," CBS, 1970; "The Tonight Show Starring Johnny Carson,"

NBC, 1972; "The Tonight Show Starring Johnny Carson," NBC, 1974; "The Gong Show," SYN, 1976; "Saturday Night Live," NBC, 1980.
TV MOVIES AND MINISERIES: "Benny and Barney: Las Vegas Undercover," NBC, 1977.

DANIELS, WILLIAM

b. Brooklyn, NY, March 31, 1927. Character actor who played John Adams on stage, in films and on TV; best known, however, for his rich, Emmy-winning portrayal of the arrogant Dr. Mark Craig on "St. Elsewhere."
AS A REGULAR: "Captain Nice," NBC, 1967; "The Adams Chronicles," PBS, 1976; "The Nancy Walker Show," ABC, 1976; "Freebie and the Bean," CBS, 1980-81; "Knight Rider," NBC, 1982-86; "St. Elsewhere," NBC, 1982-88.
AND: "Studio One: Portrait of a Citizen," CBS, 1956; "Brenner: Man in the Middle," CBS, 1959; "Armstrong Circle Theatre: The Spy Next Door," CBS, 1961; "Directions '62: The Saintmaker's Christmas Eve," ABC, 1961; "The Munsters: Family Portrait," CBS, 1964; "The Doctors and the Nurses: A Couple of Dozen Tiny Pills," CBS, 1965; "Profiles in Courage: Woodrow Wilson," NBC, 1965; "T.H.E. Cat: The Ring of Anasis," NBC, 1966; "The Ghost and Mrs. Muir: Mister Perfect," NBC, 1968; "Judd for the Defense: Epitaph on a Computer Card," ABC, 1969; "My Friend Tony: Let George Do It," NBC, 1969; "Love, American Style: Love and the Old Lover," ABC, 1973; "Ironside: The Savage Sentry," NBC, 1973; "CBS Playhouse 90: The Lie," CBS, 1973; "The Fabulous Dr. Fable," ABC, 1973; "McCloud: Butch Cassidy Rides Again," NBC, 1973; "Kolchak, the Night Stalker: The Vampire," ABC, 1974; "Medical Story: Wasteland," NBC, 1975; "The Bob Newhart Show: Fathers and Sons and Mothers," CBS, 1975; "Barbary Coast: Guns for a Queen," ABC, 1975; "McCloud: The Night New York Turned Blue," NBC, 1976; "McMillan and Wife: Point for Law," NBC, 1976; "The Rockford Files: So Help Me God," NBC, 1976; "The Rockford Files: The Italian Bird Fiasco," NBC, 1976; "Quincy: A Star Is Dead," NBC, 1976; "Quincy: Last Rights," NBC, 1980.
TV MOVIES AND MINISERIES: "Murdock's Gang," ABC, 1973; "A Case of Rape," NBC, 1974; "Sarah T.: Portrait of a Teenage Alcoholic," NBC, 1975; "One of Our Own," ABC, 1975; "Francis Gary Powers: The True Story of the U-2 Spy Incident," NBC, 1976; "Sergeant Matlovich vs. the U.S. Air Force," NBC, 1978; "The Bastard," SYN, 1978; "The Rebels," SYN, 1979; "Blind Ambition," CBS, 1979; "City in Fear," ABC, 1980; "The Million-Dollar Face," NBC, 1981; "Dropout Father," CBS, 1982; "The Little Match Girl," NBC, 1987; "Howard Beach: Making the Case for Murder," NBC, 1989.
* Emmies: 1985, 1986.

DANNER, BLYTHE

b. Philadelphia, PA, February 3, 1943. Distinctive actress who plays comedy and drama equally well; her most recent TV work was the goofy "Tattinger's," resurrected as "Nick and Hillary."
AS A REGULAR: "Adam's Rib," ABC, 1973; "Tattinger's," NBC, 1988; "Nick and Hillary," NBC, 1989.
AND: "NYPD: Day Tripper," ABC, 1968; "On Stage: To Confuse the Angel," NBC, 1970; "George M!," NBC, 1970; "Hollywood Television Theatre: The Scarecrow," NET, 1972; "Columbo: Etude in Black," NBC, 1972; "NET Playhouse: To Be Young, Gifted and Black," NET, 1972; "Theatre in America: The Seagull," PBS, 1975; "M*A*S*H: The More I See You," CBS, 1976; "Saturday Night Live," NBC, 1982; "St. Elsewhere: The Women," NBC, 1984.
TV MOVIES AND MINISERIES: "Dr. Cook's Garden," ABC, 1971; "F. Scott Fitzgerald and the Last of the Belles," ABC, 1974; "Sidekicks," CBS, 1974; "Are You in the House Alone?," CBS, 1978; "Too Far to Go," NBC, 1979; "In Defense of Kids," CBS, 1983; "Guilty Conscience," CBS, 1985; "Helen Keller: The Miracle Continues," SYN, 1985.

DANO, LINDA

b. 1943. Actress who plays clothes horse Felicia Gallant on "Another World" and is the all-too-involved co-hostess of the talk show "Attitudes."
AS A REGULAR: "The Montefuscos," NBC, 1975; "One Life to Live," ABC, 1978-80; "As the World Turns," CBS, 1981-82; "Another World," NBC, 1983- ; "Attitudes," LIF, 1987- .
AND: "Wide World of Mystery: The Nurse Killer," ABC, 1975; "The Rockford Files: Sticks and Stones May Break Your Bones, But Waterbury Will Bury You," NBC, 1977; "Barney Miller: Rape," ABC, 1978.
TV MOVIES AND MINISERIES: "Rage of Angels: The Story Continues," NBC, 1986.

DANOVA, CESARE

b. Italy, March 1, 1926.
AS A REGULAR: "Garrison's Gorillas," ABC, 1967-68.
AND: "Five Fingers: The Final Dream," NBC, 1959; "Tales of Wells Fargo: Vasquez," NBC, 1960; "The Rifleman: Baranca," ABC, 1960; "Adventures in Paradise: Treasure Hunt," ABC, 1961; "The Roaring Twenties: Lucky Charm," ABC, 1961; "The Outlaws: The Sooner," NBC, 1961; "Dick Powell's Zane Grey Theatre: The Release," CBS, 1961; "The Breaking Point: A Child of the Center Ring," ABC, 1964; "The Lucy Show: Lucy Meets a Millionaire," CBS, 1964; "Bonanza: Woman of Fire," NBC, 1965; "The

Mod Squad: The Girl in Chair Nine," ABC, 1969; "The Doris Day Show: Doris Meets a Prince," CBS, 1970; "The Doris Day Show: When in Rome, Don't," CBS, 1971; "McMillan and Wife: Husbands, Wives and Thieves," NBC, 1971; "The Doris Day Show: Cover Girl," CBS, 1972; "Mannix: Light and Shadow," CBS, 1973; "McMillan and Wife: The Fine Art of Staying Alive," NBC, 1973; "Police Story: The Gamble," NBC, 1974; "McCloud: Shivaree on Delancey Street," NBC, 1974; "Medical Center: Half a Life," CBS, 1975; "Police Story: The Losing Game," NBC, 1975; "Sanford & Son: Can You Chop This?," NBC, 1976; "Chico and the Man: The Return of Aunt Connie," NBC, 1976; "Charlie's Angels: Angels on Skis," ABC, 1979; "Barnaby Jones: A Desperate Pursuit," CBS, 1979; "The Love Boat: The Lady From Laramie," ABC, 1981; "Nero Wolfe: To Catch a Dead Man," NBC, 1981; "Blacke's Magic: Breathing Room," NBC, 1986; "Magnum, P.I.: Who Is Don Luis and Why Is He Trying to Kill Me?," CBS, 1986; "Murder, She Wrote: The Perfect Foil," CBS, 1986; "Hunter: Requiem for Sergeant McCall," NBC, 1987; "Mission: Impossible: The Greek," ABC, 1989.
TV MOVIES AND MINISERIES: "Honeymoon with a Stranger," ABC, 1969.

DANSON, TED
Talented, Emmy winning actor who plays Sam Malone on "Cheers."
AS A REGULAR: "Cheers," NBC, 1982- .
AND: "Laverne & Shirley: Why Did the Fireman Wear Red Suspenders?," ABC, 1980; "Magnum, P.I.: Beauty Knows No Pain," CBS, 1981; "Taxi: The Unkindest Cut," ABC, 1982; "Late Night with David Letterman," NBC, 1989; "Saturday Night Live," NBC, 1989; "The Jim Henson Hour: Lighthouse Hour," NBC, 1989.
TV MOVIES AND MINISERIES: "Cowboy," CBS, 1983; "Something About Amelia," ABC, 1984; "When the Bough Breaks," NBC, 1986.
* Emmies: 1990.

TV'S TOP TEN, 1987-88
1. The Cosby Show (NBC)
2. A Different World (NBC)
3. Cheers (NBC)
4. The Golden Girls (NBC)
5. Growing Pains (ABC)
6. Who's the Boss? (ABC)
7. Night Court (NBC)
8. 60 Minutes (CBS)
9. Murder, She Wrote (CBS)
10. ALF (NBC)
10. The Wonder Years (ABC)

DANTE, MICHAEL
b. Ralph Vitti, Stamford, CT, 1935.
AS A REGULAR: "Custer," ABC, 1967.

AND: "Colt .45: One Good Turn," ABC, 1957; "Sugarfoot: The Dead Hills," ABC, 1958; "Westinghouse Desilu Playhouse: The Killer Instinct," CBS, 1959; "The Texan: Stampede," CBS, 1959; "The Texan: Trouble on the Trail," CBS, 1959; "The Texan: The Reluctant Bridegroom," CBS, 1959; "Perry Mason: The Case of the Dangerous Dowager," CBS, 1959; "G.E. Theatre: The Story of Judith," CBS, 1960; "The Detectives Starring Robert Taylor: The Champ," ABC, 1961; "Cain's Hundred: Final Judgement," NBC, 1961; "Hawaiian Eye: Go Steady with Danger," ABC, 1963; "Perry Mason: The Case of the Feather Cloak," CBS, 1965; "Branded: Mightier Than the Sword," NBC, 1965; "Get Smart: Kisses for KAOS," NBC, 1966; "Cagney & Lacey: Right to Remain Silent," CBS, 1987.

DANTINE, HELMUT
b. Vienna, October 7, 1917; d. 1982.
AS A REGULAR: "Shadow of the Cloak," DUM, 1951-52.
AND: "Ford Theatre: The Bet," NBC, 1953; "Studio 57: The Alibi," SYN, 1957; "Climax!: The Long Count," CBS, 1957; "G.E. Theatre: Flight From Tormendero," CBS, 1957; "Playhouse 90: Clipper Ship," CBS, 1957; "The Millionaire: The Josef Marton Story," CBS, 1957; "Studio 57: The Alibi," SYN, 1957; "The Joseph Cotten Show: The Gentle Voice of Murder," NBC, 1957; "Schlitz Playhouse of Stars: I Shot a Prowler," CBS, 1958; "Studio 57: A Source of Irritation," SYN, 1958; "The Thin Man: Design for Murder," NBC, 1958; "Playhouse 90: The Hiding Place," CBS, 1960; "The Rogues: Run for the Money," NBC, 1965; "Hallmark Hall of Fame: The File on Devlin," NBC, 1969; "Night Gallery: The Devil Is Not Mocked," NBC, 1971; "Call Holme," NBC, 1972.

DANZA, TONY
b. Brooklyn, NY, April 21, 1951. Light comic actor who's a TV staple; he plays Tony Micelli on "Who's the Boss?"
AS A REGULAR: "Taxi," ABC, 1978-82; NBC, 1982-83; "Who's the Boss?," ABC, 1984- .
AND: "The Love Boat: When Worlds Collide," ABC, 1983; "The Tonight Show Starring Johnny Carson," NBC, 1986; "Saturday Night Live," NBC, 1986; "Saturday Night Live," NBC, 1989; "Living Dolls: It's My Party," ABC, 1989; "A Conversation with Dinah," TNN, 1989.
TV MOVIES AND MINISERIES: "Murder Can Hurt You!," ABC, 1980; "Single Bars, Single Women," ABC, 1984; "Doing Life," NBC, 1986; "Freedom Fighter," NBC, 1988.

DARDEN, SEVERN
b. November 9, 1929.
AS A REGULAR: "Mary Hartman, Mary Hartman," SYN, 1977-78; "Beyond Westworld," CBS,

1980; "Take Five," CBS, 1987.

AND: "Alfred Hitchcock Presents: Beta Delta Gamma," NBC, 1961; "Car 54, Where Are You?: Toody and the Art World," NBC, 1962; "Honey West: Little Green Robin Hood," ABC, 1966; "The Monkees: Monkee vs. Machine," NBC, 1966; "I Dream of Jeannie: Jeannie and the Great Bank Robbery," NBC, 1967; "Barefoot in the Park: Nothin' But the Truth," ABC, 1970; "Alias Smith and Jones: Never Trust an Honest Man," ABC, 1971; "The Man and the City: I Should Have Let Him Die," ABC, 1971; "Bonanza: The Rattlesnake Brigade," NBC, 1971; "Kolchak, the Night Stalker: The Spanish Moss Murders," ABC, 1974; "The Practice: The Vote," NBC, 1976; "City of Angels: The House on Orange Grove Avenue," NBC, 1976; "Jigsaw John: Follow the Yellow Brick Road," NBC, 1976; "Barney Miller: The Mole," ABC, 1976; "The Quest: Day of Outrage," NBC, 1976; "Laverne & Shirley: Look Before You Leap," ABC, 1977; "Cheers: Homicidal Ham," NBC, 1983.

TV MOVIES AND MINISERIES: "The Movie Murderer," NBC, 1970; "Playmates," ABC, 1972; "The Man Who Died Twice," CBS, 1973; "Skyway to Death," ABC, 1974; "The New, Original Wonder Woman," ABC, 1975; "The Disappearance of Aimee," NBC, 1976; "Best Sellers: Captains and the Kings," NBC, 1976; "Outside Chance," CBS, 1978.

DARIN, BOBBY

b. Robert Walden Cassotto, New York City, NY, May 14, 1936; d. 1973. Fifties finger-popping singer ("Mack the Knife") and actor who swung, man.

AS A REGULAR: "Dean Martin Presents," NBC, 1972; "The Bobby Darin Show," NBC, 1973.

AND: "Stage Show," CBS, 1956; "The Big Beat," ABC, 1957; "American Bandstand," ABC, 1957; "The Dick Clark Saturday Night Beechnut Show," ABC, 1958; "The Bob Crosby Show," NBC, 1958; "The Dick Clark Saturday Night Beechnut Show," ABC, 1959; "The Perry Como Show," NBC, 1959; "The Ed Sullivan Show," CBS, 1959; "An Evening with Durante," NBC, 1959; "Hennesey: Hennesey Meets Honeyboy," CBS, 1959; "Louis Jourdan Presents the Timex Show," NBC, 1959; "Startime: George Burns in the Big Time," NBC, 1959; "This Is Your Life," NBC, 1959; "The Big Party," CBS, 1959; "The Ed Sullivan Show," CBS, 1960; "Arthur Murray Party," NBC, 1960; "George Burns Special," NBC, 1960; "Coke Time," ABC, 1960; "Dan Raven: The High Cost of Fame," NBC, 1960; "Bob Hope Buick Show," NBC, 1960; "Bobby Darin and Friends," NBC, 1961; "This Is Your Life (Connie Francis)," NBC, 1961; "The Jackie Gleason Show," CBS, 1961; "Here's Hollywood," NBC, 1962; "Play Your Hunch," NBC, 1962; "The Merv Griffin Show," NBC, 1962; "The Bob

Hope Show," NBC, 1962; "Password," CBS, 1963; "The Judy Garland Show," CBS, 1963; "The Jack Benny Program," CBS, 1964; "The Edie Adams Show," ABC, 1964; "I've Got a Secret," CBS, 1964; "Wagon Train: The John Gillman Story," ABC, 1964; "Bob Hope Chrysler Theatre: Murder in the First," NBC, 1964; "American Bandstand," ABC, 1964; "The Andy Williams Show," NBC, 1965; "The Match Game," NBC, 1965; "The Red Skelton Hour," CBS, 1965; "The Steve Lawrence Show," CBS, 1965; "Run for Your Life: Who's Watching the Fleshpot?," NBC, 1966; "The Danny Thomas Hour: The Cage," NBC, 1968; "Ironside: The Gambling Game," NBC, 1971; "The Tonight Show Starring Johnny Carson," NBC, 1972; "Night Gallery: Dead Weight," NBC, 1972.

* In 1959, Darin—at age 22—became the youngest performer ever to headline in Las Vegas.
* Darin died following a heart operation.

DARLING, JOAN

b. Boston, MA, April 15, 1935. Actress who played secretary Frieda Krause on "Owen Marshall, Counselor at Law."

AS A REGULAR: "Owen Marshall, Counselor At Law," ABC, 1971-74.

AND: "Seasons of Youth," ABC, 1961; "Marcus Welby, M.D.: Dance to No Music," ABC, 1970; "Marcus Welby, M.D.: Men Who Care, Part II," ABC, 1971; "Paris: Pawn," CBS, 1979; "Quincy: Jury Duty," NBC, 1981.

TV MOVIES AND MINISERIES: "Owen Marshall, Counselor at Law," ABC, 1971; "The Two Worlds of Jennie Logan," CBS, 1979.

AS CO-WRITER: "The Dick Van Dyke Show: Your Home Sweet Home Is My Home," CBS, 1965.

AS DIRECTOR: "The Mary Tyler Moore Show: Chuckle's Bites The Dust," CBS, 1975; "M*A*S*H: The Nurses," CBS, 1976; "Taxi: Nina Loves Alex," ABC, 1982.

DARNELL, LINDA

b. Monetta Eloyse Darnell, Dallas, TX, October 16, 1921; d. 1965. Sulty actress of the forties who, like many other stars, turned to TV later in her career.

AS A GUEST: "G.E. Theatre: White Corridors," CBS, 1955; "The 20th Century-Fox Hour: Deception," CBS, 1956; "Ford Theatre: All for a Man," NBC, 1956; "Schlitz Playhouse of Stars: Terror in the Streets," CBS, 1957; "Ford Theatre: Fate Travels East," ABC, 1957; "Playhouse 90: Homeward Borne," CBS, 1957; "Climax!: Trial by Fire," CBS, 1957; "Art Linkletter's House Party," CBS, 1957; "The Jane Wyman Show: The Elevator," NBC, 1958; "Studio 57: My Little Girl," SYN, 1958; "Wagon Train: The Dora Gray Story," NBC, 1958; "Wagon Train: The Sacramento Story," NBC, 1958; "Pursuit: Free Ride," CBS, 1958; "Cimarron City: Kid on a Calico Horse," NBC, 1958; "77 Sunset Strip: Sing Something Simple," ABC, 1959; "Here's Hollywood," NBC, 1961; "Play Your Hunch," NBC, 1962; "Burke's Law: Who Killed His Royal Highness?," ABC, 1964.

* Darnell died in a Chicago house fire.

DARREN, JAMES
b. James Ercolani, Philadelphia, PA, June 8, 1936. Teen idol who turned to serious acting, more or less, as Officer Jim Corrigan on "T.J. Hooker."

AS A REGULAR: "The Time Tunnel," ABC, 1966-67; "T.J. Hooker," ABC, 1983-85; CBS, 1985-86.

AND: "The Web: Kill and Run," NBC, 1957; "The Steve Allen Show," NBC, 1959; "The Donna Reed Show: April Fool," ABC, 1959; "The Dick Clark Saturday Night Beechnut Show," ABC, 1959; "Bob Hope Special," NBC, 1959; "Bob Hope Buick Show," NBC, 1961; "The Donna Reed Show: One Starry Night," ABC, 1961; "Here's Hollywood," NBC, 1961; "American Bandstand," ABC, 1963; "American Bandstand," ABC, 1965; "The Flintstones: Surfin' Fred," ABC, 1965; "Voyage to the Bottom of the Sea: The Mechanical Man," ABC, 1966; "Love, American Style: Love and the Monsters," ABC, 1971; "Celebrity Sweepstakes," NBC, 1976; "Police Woman: Task Force: Cop Killer," NBC, 1976; "The Mike Douglas Show," SYN, 1976; "Baa Baa Black Sheep: Show Biz Warrior," NBC, 1977; "Hollywood Squares," NBC, 1980; "The Mike Douglas Show," SYN, 1980; "The Love Boat: For the Record," ABC, 1981; "T.J. Hooker: King of the Hill," ABC, 1982; "One Day at a Time: The Cruise," CBS, 1983.

TV MOVIES AND MINISERIES: "City Beneath the Sea," NBC, 1971; "The Lives of Jenny Dolan," NBC, 1975; "Turnover Smith," ABC, 1980.

DARROW, HENRY
b. New York City, NY, September 15, 1933. Actor who played Manolito Montoya on "The High Chaparral" and now tends to play deposed South American dictators in guest shots.

AS A REGULAR: "The High Chaparral," NBC, 1967-71; "The New Dick Van Dyke Show," CBS, 1973-74; "Harry O," ABC, 1974-75; "Zorro and Son," CBS, 1983; "Me and Mom," ABC, 1985; "Santa Barbara," NBC, 1989- .

AND: "T.H.E. Cat: To Bell T.H.E. Cat," NBC, 1966; "The Iron Horse: Cougar Man," ABC, 1966; "T.H.E. Cat: Design for Death," NBC, 1967; "Gunsmoke: The Hanging," CBS, 1967; "The Wild Wild West: The Night of the Tottering Tontine," CBS, 1967; "Mission: Impossible: Blast," CBS, 1971; "The FBI: Canyon of No Return," ABC, 1972; "The Mod Squad: No More Oak Leaves for Ernie Holland," ABC, 1972; "Kung Fu: The Brujo," ABC, 1973; "Chase:

Vacation for a President," NBC, 1974; "Kojak: Before the Devil Knows," CBS, 1974; "Hawaii Five-O: Legacy of Terror," CBS, 1975; "McMillan and Wife: Requiem for a Bride," NBC, 1975; "The Streets of San Francisco: Alien Country," ABC, 1976; "Quincy: Go Fight City Hall-To the Death," NBC, 1976; "Hawaii Five-O: The Cop on the Cover," CBS, 1977; "Police Woman: The Inside Connection," NBC, 1977; "B.J. and the Bear: Seven Lady Captives," NBC, 1981; "Quincy: Scream to the Skies," NBC, 1981; "Scarecrow and Mrs. King: If Thoughts Could Kill," CBS, 1983; "Scarecrow and Mrs. King: Remembrance of Things Past," CBS, 1983; "Scarecrow and Mrs. King: Lost and Found," CBS, 1984; "Easy Street: Friends for Life," NBC, 1986; "Magnum P.I.: Way of the Stalking Horse," CBS, 1985; "Simon & Simon: Nuevo Salvador," CBS, 1988; "The Golden Girls: Yes, We Have No Havanas," NBC, 1988.

TV MOVIES AND MINISERIES: "Brock's Last Case," NBC, 1973; "Hitchhike!," ABC, 1974; "Night Games," NBC, 1974; "Aloha Means Goodbye," CBS, 1974; "The Invisible Man," NBC, 1975; "Centennial," NBC, 1978-79; "ABC Theatre: Attica," ABC, 1980.

DARWELL, JANE
b. Patti Woodward, Palmyra, MO, October 15, 1879; d. 1967. Heavy-set movie character actress who played mothers and nurses and who was just as prolific on TV.

AS A GUEST: "Hollywood Opening Night: Josie," NBC, 1952; "Ford Theatre: Good of His Soul," NBC, 1954; "Fireside Theatre: Nine Quarts of Water," NBC, 1954; "Ford Theatre: Slide, Darling, Slide," NBC, 1954; "Climax!: The Bigger They Come," CBS, 1955; "Studio 57: Center Ring," SYN, 1955; "Ford Theatre: Second Sight," NBC, 1955; "Ford Theatre: The Mumbys," NBC, 1955; "Climax!: House of Shadows," CBS, 1955; "Screen Directors Playhouse: The Prima Donna," NBC, 1956; "The Adventures of Rin Tin Tin: Rin Tin Tin Meets O'Hara's Mother," ABC, 1956; "Du Pont Theatre: Woman's Work," ABC, 1956; "Playhouse 90: Sincerely, Willis Wayde," CBS, 1956; "Playhouse 90: The Greer Case," CBS, 1957; "Playhouse 90: Three Men on a Horse," CBS, 1957; "Maverick: Black Fire," ABC, 1958; "Studio One: A Dead Ringer," CBS, 1958; "Buckskin: Mr. Rush's Secretary," NBC, 1959; "Wagon Train: The Vivian Carter Story," NBC, 1959; "Wagon Train: The Andrew Hale Story," NBC, 1959; "New Comedy Showcase: You're Only Young Twice," CBS, 1960; "Shirley Temple's Storybook: The Fawn," NBC, 1961; "The Real McCoys: Back to West Virginny," ABC, 1961; "The Real McCoys: Fly Away Home," ABC, 1961; "Wagon Train: The Artie Matthewson

Story," NBC, 1961; "Lassie: Lassie's Wild Baby," CBS, 1961; "Follow the Sun: The Far Edge of Nowhere," ABC, 1961; "Burke's Law: Who Killed Eleanor Davis?," ABC, 1963; "The Alfred Hitchcock Hour: The Jar," NBC, 1964; "Lassie: Lassie the Voyager," CBS, 1966.
* Darwell's film credits included "Design for Living," "The Adventures of Jesse James," "The Ox-Bow Incident," "The Last Hurrah," "The Grapes of Wrath" and "Mary Poppins."

DA SILVA, HOWARD
b. *Cleveland, OH, May 4, 1909; d. 1986.* Blacklisted actor who began to get TV work in the sixties; an Emmy winner for "Verna, USO Girl."
AS A REGULAR: "For the People," CBS, 1965.
AND: "Silver Theatre: My Heart's in the Highlands," CBS, 1950; "The Defenders: The Bagman," CBS, 1963; "East Side/West Side: I Before E," CBS, 1963; "Hamlet," CBS, 1964; "The Defenders: The Man Who," CBS, 1964; "The Outer Limits: I, Robot," ABC, 1964; "Ben Casey: The Day They Stole County General," ABC, 1965; "Ben Casey: A Nightingale Named Nathan," ABC, 1965; "The Man From UNCLE: The Foreign Legion Affair," NBC, 1966; "The Loner: To Hang a Dead Man," CBS, 1966; "The Fugitive: Death is the Door Prize," ABC, 1966; "NET Showcase: The Trial Begins," NET, 1967; "NET Showcase: The Beggar's Opera," NET, 1967; "NYPD: Old Gangsters Never Die," ABC, 1967; "Gentle Ben: Battle of Wedloe Woods," CBS, 1967; "Keep the Faith," CBS, 1972; "Love, American Style: Love and the End of the Line," ABC, 1973; "Kung Fu: The Hoots," ABC, 1973; "ABC Theatre: The Missiles of October," ABC, 1974; "The American Parade: Stop, Thief!," CBS, 1976; "Great Performances: Verna: USO Girl," PBS, 1978.
* Emmies: 1978.

DAUPHIN, CLAUDE
b. *Corbeil, France, August 19, 1903; d. 1978.*
AS A REGULAR: "Paris Precinct," ABC, 1955-56.
AND: "Suspense: Betrayal in Vienna," CBS, 1952; "Summer Studio One: Shadow of a Man," CBS, 1953; "Lux Video Theatre: The Moment of the Rose," CBS, 1953; "U.S. Steel Hour: The Vanishing Point," ABC, 1953; "Philco TV Playhouse: The Broken Fist," NBC, 1954; "Omnibus: The Apollo of Bellac," CBS, 1954; "Schlitz Playhouse of Stars: Something Wonderful," CBS, 1954; "Schlitz Playhouse of Stars: On Leave," CBS, 1954; "Studio One: Cardinal Mindszenty," CBS, 1954; "Schlitz Playhouse of Stars: How the Brigadier Won His Medals," CBS, 1954; "Studio One: Sail with the Tide," CBS, 1955; "Appointment with Adventure: Minus Three Thousand," CBS, 1955; "Front Row Center: Meeting at Mayerling," CBS, 1955;

"Alcoa Hour: Paris and Mrs. Perlman," NBC, 1956; "G.E. Summer Originals: The Green Parrot," CBS, 1956; "Arthur Murray Party," NBC, 1960; "Frontiers of Faith: Self-Portrait," NBC, 1960; "U.S. Steel Hour: How to Make a Killing," CBS, 1960; "Play of the Week: Crime of Passion," SYN, 1961; "Mystery Theatre: The Problem in Cell Thirteen," NBC, 1962; "Naked City: The Virtues of Madame Douvay," ABC, 1962; "Harry's Girls: Collector's Item," NBC, 1963; "World Theatre: France: The Faces of Love," SYN, 1964.
TV MOVIES AND MINISERIES: "Berlin Affair," ABC, 1970; "Les Miserables," CBS, 1978.

DAVALOS, DICK
b. *Bronx, NY, November 5, 1935.*
AS A REGULAR: "The Americans," NBC, 1961.
AND: "West Point: One Command," CBS, 1957; "U.S. Steel Hour: A Loud Laugh," CBS, 1957; "Armstrong Circle Theatre: Thirty Days to Reconsider," CBS, 1958; "Alcoa Presents One Step Beyond: The Return," ABC, 1960; "Bonanza: The Trail Gang," NBC, 1960; "Hawaiian Eye: A Touch of Velvet," ABC, 1961; "Laramie: The Last Journey," NBC, 1961; "Perry Mason: The Case of the Hateful Hero," CBS, 1962; "Hawaiian Eye: Lament for a Saturday Warrior," ABC, 1962; "Dr. Kildare: An Ancient Office," NBC, 1962; "Perry Mason: The Case of the Ice-Cold Hands," CBS, 1964; "The Littlest Hobo: Blue Water Sailor," SYN, 1964; "Mannix: Missing: Sun and Sky," CBS, 1969; "The FBI: The Replacement," ABC, 1971; "SWAT: Ordeal," ABC, 1975; "The Rockford Files: Foul on the First Play," NBC, 1976; "Hawaii Five-O: A Capitol Crime," CBS, 1977; "B.J. and the Bear: Pogo Lil," NBC, 1979; "Hart to Hart: Heart-Shaped Murder," ABC, 1981.
TV MOVIES AND MINISERIES: "Snatched," ABC, 1973.

DAVIDSON, BEN
b. *Los Angeles, CA, June 14, 1940.* Former Oakland Raiders defensive end.
AS A REGULAR: "Ball Four," CBS, 1976; "Code R," CBS, 1977.
AND: "Banacek: Let's Hear It for a Living Legend," NBC, 1972; "B.J. and the Bear: A Bear in the Hand," NBC, 1981.
TV MOVIES AND MINISERIES: "The Rebels," SYN, 1979.

DAVIDSON, JOHN
b. *Pittsburgh, PA, December 13, 1941.* Clean-cut singer and entertainer.
AS A REGULAR: "The Entertainers," CBS, 1964-65; "The Kraft Summer Music Hall," NBC, 1966; "The John Davidson Show," ABC, 1969, NBC, 1976; SYN, 1980-82; "The Girl with Something Extra," NBC, 1973-74; "That's Incredible," ABC, 1980-84; "The Time Machine," NBC,

1985; "Hollywood Squares," SYN, 1986-89; "Incredible Sunday," ABC, 1988-89; "Holiday Gourmet," TNN, 1989- .

AND: "Hallmark Hall of Fame: The Fantasticks," NBC, 1964; "The Young Set," ABC, 1965; "The Jimmy Dean Show," ABC, 1965; "Bell Telephone Hour: The Music of Jerome Kern," NBC, 1965; "This Is Tom Jones," ABC, 1969; "Roberta," NBC, 1969; "Love, American Style: Love and the Young Executive," ABC, 1970; "The FBI: Judas Goat," ABC, 1972; "Love, American Style: Love and the Scroungers," ABC, 1972; "The Julie Andrews Hour," ABC, 1973; "NBC Follies," NBC, 1973; "Here's Lucy: Lucy and the Professor," CBS, 1973; "The Sonny and Cher Comedy Hour," CBS, 1973; "Love, American Style: Love and the Baby Derby," ABC, 1973; "The Tonight Show Starring Johnny Carson," NBC, 1974; "Sandy in Disneyland," CBS, 1974; "The Streets of San Francisco: Mask of Death," ABC, 1974; "The Mike Douglas Show," SYN, 1975; "Feeling Good," PBS, 1975; "The Tonight Show Starring Johnny Carson," NBC, 1976; "The Mike Douglas Show," SYN, 1978; "Hotel: Deceptions," ABC, 1983; "Hotel: Vantage Point," ABC, 1984; "The Love Boat: Girl of the Midnight Sun," ABC, 1985; "Search for Haunted Hollywood," SYN, 1989.

TV MOVIES AND MINISERIES: "A Time for Love," NBC, 1973; "Coffee, Tea, or Me?," CBS, 1973; "Shell Game," CBS, 1975.

DAVIS, ANN B.

b. Schenectady, NY, May 5, 1926. Comedienne whose career spans almost 40 years, without any noticable improvement in her material.

AS A REGULAR: "The Bob Cummings Show," NBC, 1955; CBS, 1955-57; NBC, 1957-59; "The Keefe Brasselle Show," CBS, 1963; "The John Forsythe Show," NBC, 1965-66; "The Brady Bunch," ABC, 1969-74; "The Brady Bunch Hour," ABC, 1977; "The Brady Brides," NBC, 1981; "The Bradys," CBS, 1990.

AND: "Art Linkletter's House Party," CBS, 1957; "The Perry Como Show," NBC, 1958; "Arthur Murray Party," NBC, 1959; "Wagon Train: The Countess Baranof Story," NBC, 1960; "McKeever and the Colonel: Too Many Sergeants," NBC, 1963; "Bob Hope Chrysler Theatre: Wake Up, Darling," NBC, 1964; "The Dating Game," ABC, 1969; "Love, American Style: Love and the Trip," ABC, 1971; "The Love Boat: The Invisible Maniac," ABC, 1980; "Day by Day: A Very Brady Episode," NBC, 1989; "The People Next Door: Make Room for Abby," CBS, 1989.

TV MOVIES AND MINISERIES: "The Brady Girls Get Married," NBC, 1981; "A Very Brady Christmas," CBS, 1988.

* Emmies: 1958, 1959.

DAVIS, BETTE

b. Ruth Elizabeth Davis, Lowell, MA, April 5,

1908; d. 1989. Movie icon who had a simple attitude regarding television—it was work that paid well. An Emmy winner for "Strangers: The Story of a Mother and Daughter."

AS A GUEST: "The 20th Century-Fox Hour: Crack-Up," CBS, 1956; "Person to Person," CBS, 1956; "G.E. Theatre: With Malice Toward One," CBS, 1957; "Schlitz Playhouse of Stars: For Better, for Worse," CBS, 1957; "Telephone Time: Stranded," ABC, 1957; "Dinah Shore Chevy Show," NBC, 1958; "Studio 57: The Starmaker," SYN, 1958; "G.E. Theatre: The Cold Touch," CBS, 1958; "Suspicion: Fraction of a Second," NBC, 1958; "Alfred Hitchcock Presents: Out There - Darkness," CBS, 1959; "Wagon Train: The Ella Lindstrom Story," NBC, 1959; "The du Pont Show with June Allyson: Dark Morning," CBS, 1959; "The Jack Paar Show," NBC, 1959; "Wagon Train: The Elizabeth McQueeney Story," NBC, 1960; "The Jack Paar Show," NBC, 1960; "Wagon Train: The Bettina May Story," NBC, 1961; "Here's Hollywood," NBC, 1962; "The Jack Paar Program," NBC, 1962; "The Virginian: The Accomplice," NBC, 1962; "The Andy Williams Show," NBC, 1962; "Perry Mason: The Case of Constant Doyle," CBS, 1963; "Hollywood Palace," ABC, 1964; "Hollywood Palace," ABC, 1965; "Gunsmoke: The Jailer," CBS, 1966; "It Takes a Thief: Touch of Magic," ABC, 1970; "Hello Mother, Goodbye," NBC, 1974; "Inaugural Eve Special," CBS, 1977; "Hotel: Premiere," ABC, 1983; "The Tonight Show Starring Johnny Carson," NBC, 1986; "The Tonight Show Starring Johnny Carson," NBC, 1988; "Late Night with David Letterman," NBC, 1989.

TV MOVIES AND MINISERIES: "Madame Sin," ABC, 1972; "The Judge and Jake Wyler," NBC, 1972; "Scream, Pretty Peggy," ABC, 1973; "The Disappearance of Aimee," NBC, 1976; "The Dark Secret of Harvest Home," NBC, 1978; "Strangers: The Story of a Mother and Daughter," CBS, 1979; "White Mama," CBS, 1980; "Little Gloria ...Happy at Last," NBC, 1982; "Agatha Christie's Murder with Mirrors," CBS, 1985.

* Emmies: 1979.

DAVIS, BILLY JR.

b. St. Louis, MO, June 26, 1940. Pop singer, former member of the Fifth Dimension.

AS A REGULAR: "The Marilyn McCoo and Billy Davis, Jr. Show," CBS, 1977.

AND: "The Love Boat: Mike and Ike," ABC, 1978; "Dance Fever," SYN, 1979.

DAVIS, BRAD

b. Tallahassee, FL, November 6, 1949. Intense actor often in psychotic roles.

AS A REGULAR: "How to Survive a Marriage,"

NBC, 1974-75.
AND: "The Rookies: Rolling Thunder," ABC, 1974; "Alfred Hitchcock Presents: Arthur," NBC, 1985; "The Twilight Zone: Button, Button," CBS, 1986.
TV MOVIES AND MINISERIES: "Sybil," NBC, 1976; "Roots," ABC, 1977; "Chiefs," CBS, 1983; "Vengeance: The Story of Tony Cimo," CBS, 1986; "When the Time Comes," ABC, 1987; "The Caine Mutiny Court-Martial," CBS, 1988.

DAVIS, CLIFTON
b. Chicago, IL, October 4, 1945.
AS A REGULAR: "A World Apart," ABC, 1970-71; "Love, American Style," ABC, 1971; "The Melba Moore-Clifton Davis Show," CBS, 1972; "That's My Mama," ABC, 1974-75; "Amen," NBC, 1986- .
AND: "Police Story: The Ho Chi Minh Trail," NBC, 1973; "Love Story: A Glow of Dying Embers," NBC, 1973; "Cotton Club '75," NBC, 1974; "Mitzi and a Hundred Guys," CBS, 1975; "The $10,000 Pyramid," ABC, 1975; "The Mike Douglas Show," SYN, 1977; "Police Story: The Malflores," NBC, 1977; "The Love Boat: Peek-a-Boo," ABC, 1980; "Super Password," NBC, 1989; "Animal Crack-Ups," ABC, 1989.
TV MOVIES AND MINISERIES: "Little Ladies of the Night," ABC, 1977; "The Night the City Screamed," ABC, 1980; "Dream Date," NBC, 1989.

DAVIS, GAIL
b. Betty Jeanne Grayson, Little Rock, AR, October 5, 1925.
AS A REGULAR: "Annie Oakley," ABC, 1955-58.
AND: "Wide, Wide World: The Western," NBC, 1958; "Bob Hope Special," NBC, 1959; "Perry Como's Kraft Music Hall," NBC, 1959; "Mother's March," SYN, 1960; "The Andy Griffith Show: The Perfect Female," CBS, 1961.

DAVIS, GEENA
b. Wareham, MA, January 21, 1957. Oscar-winning actress ("The Accidental Tourist") who's a TV sitcom veteran.
AS A REGULAR: "Buffalo Bill," NBC, 1983-84; "Sara," NBC, 1985.
AND: "Family Ties: Help Wanted," NBC, 1984; "Family Ties: Karen II, Alex 0," NBC, 1984; "Riptide: Raiders of the Lost Sub," NBC, 1984; "Remington Steele: Steele in the Chips," NBC, 1984; "Saturday Night Live," NBC, 1989; "Trying Times: The Hit List," PBS, 1989.
TV MOVIES AND MINISERIES: "Secret Weapons," NBC, 1985.
AS WRITER: "Buffalo Bill: The Search High and Low for Miss WBFL," NBC, 1984.

DAVIS, JANETTE
b. Pine Bluff, TN, 1924. One of the few singers

associated with Arthur Godfrey who didn't get dumped by the old redhead.
AS A REGULAR: "Arthur Godfrey and His Friends," CBS, 1949-57.

DAVIS, JIM
b. Dearborn, MI, August 26, 1915; d. 1981. Rough-hewn actor with a no-nonsense manner, best known as patriarch Jock Ewing on "Dallas."
AS A REGULAR: "Stories of the Century," SYN, 1956; "Rescue 8," SYN, 1958-60; "The Cowboys," ABC, 1974; "Dallas," CBS, 1978-81.
AND: "The Millionaire: The Story of Jim Driskill," CBS, 1957; "Royal Playhouse: White Violet," SYN, 1957; "O. Henry Playhouse: After 20 Years," SYN, 1957; "Yancy Derringer: Two Tickets to Promontory," CBS, 1959; "Laramie: Trail Drive," NBC, 1960; "Markham: The Snowman," CBS, 1960; "The Tall Man: The Lonely Star," NBC, 1960; "G.E. Theatre: Journey to a Wedding," CBS, 1960; "Wagon Train: The Candy O'Hara Story," NBC, 1960; "Bonanza: The Gift," NBC, 1961; "Tales of Wells Fargo: The Lobo," NBC, 1961; "The Outlaws: The Brothers," NBC, 1961; "Gunsmoke: The Imposter," CBS, 1961; "Gunslinger: The New Savannah Story," CBS, 1961; "Malibu Run: The Diana Adventure," CBS, 1961; "Here's Hollywood," NBC, 1961; "Rawhide: The Greedy Town," CBS, 1962; "The Donna Reed Show: Pioneer Woman," ABC, 1963; "Wagon Train: The Melanie Craig Story," ABC, 1964; "Death Valley Days: Three Minutes to Eternity," SYN, 1964; "The Lucy Show: Lucy and Viv in Las Vegas," CBS, 1965; "F Troop: The Loco Brothers," ABC, 1966; "Gunsmoke: The Mission," CBS, 1966; "The Virginian: The Heritage," NBC, 1968; "Gunsmoke: Buffalo Man," CBS, 1968; "Kung Fu: The Soul Is the Warrior," ABC, 1973; "The Streets of San Francisco: Shattered Image," ABC, 1973; "Kung Fu: The Well," ABC, 1973; "Banacek: If Max Is So Smart, Why Doesn't He Tell Us Where He Is?," NBC, 1973; "The Streets of San Francisco: The Hard Breed," ABC, 1973; "Gunsmoke: Jesse," CBS, 1973.
TV MOVIES AND MINISERIES: "Vanished," NBC, 1971; "The Trackers," ABC, 1971; "Deliver Us From Evil," ABC, 1973; "Satan's Triangle," ABC, 1975; "The Runaway Barge," NBC, 1975; "Law of the Land," NBC, 1976; "Just a Little Inconvenience," NBC, 1977.

DAVIS, JOAN
b. Madonna Josephine Davis, St. Paul, MN, June 29, 1912; d. 1961. Comic actress who was the poor man's Lucille Ball, in the movies and on TV.
AS A REGULAR: "I Married Joan," NBC, 1952-55.
AND: "Campbell TV Soundstage: The Psychopathic

Nurse," NBC, 1954; "The Bob Hope Show," NBC, 1956; "Tony Martin Special," NBC, 1957; "The George Gobel Show," NBC, 1958; "The Steve Allen Show," NBC, 1958; "Dinah Shore Chevy Show," NBC, 1958; "Milton Berle Starring in the Kraft Music Hall," NBC, 1959; "The Garry Moore Show," CBS, 1959.

* Davis was performing in vaudeville at age 3; she had her own radio show before television, and both her series were written by her ex-husband and ex-vaudeville partner, Serenus "Si" Wills.

DAVIS, MAC
b. Lubbock, TX, January 21, 1942. Pop singer and actor who was popular in the seventies.
AS A REGULAR: "The Mac Davis Show," NBC, 1974-76.
AND: "The Johnny Cash Show," ABC, 1970; "Stand Up and Cheer," SYN, 1974; "Bell System Family Theatre: Christmas with the Bing Crosbys," NBC, 1974; "Mac Davis Special," NBC, 1975; "Bob Hope Special," NBC, 1977; "Webster: Almost Home," ABC, 1985.
TV MOVIES AND MINISERIES: "Brothers-in-Law," ABC, 1985; "What Price Victory," ABC, 1988.

DAVIS, OSSIE
b. Cogdell, GA, December 18, 1917. Distinguished actor-writer who's played a sidekick to Burt Reynolds on two TV series.
AS A REGULAR: "With Ossie & Ruby," PBS, 1981-82; "B.L. Stryker," ABC, 1989-90; "Evening Shade," CBS, 1990- .
AND: "Showtime U.S.A.: Green Pastures," SYN, 1951; "Kraft Television Theatre: The Emporer Jones," NBC, 1955; "Salute to the American Theatre," CBS, 1959; "CBS Television Workshop: Brown Girl, Brownstones," CBS, 1960; "John Brown's Raid," NBC, 1960; "Camera Three," CBS, 1960; "Play of the Week: Seven Times Monday," SYN, 1961; "The Defenders: The Riot," CBS, 1961; "Car 54, Where Are You?: Here Comes Charlie," NBC, 1963; "The Defenders: Metamorphosis," CBS, 1963; "The Great Adventure: Go Down, Moses," CBS, 1963; "The Defenders: Star-Spangled Ghetto," CBS, 1963; "The Defenders: Mind Over Murder," CBS, 1964; "The Defenders: Turning Point," CBS, 1964; "The Doctors and the Nurses: A Family Resemblance," CBS, 1964; "The Defenders: Fires of the Mind," CBS, 1965; "The Defenders: Nobody Asks What Side You're On," CBS, 1965; "The Defenders: The Sworn Twelve," CBS, 1965; "Slattery's People: What Can You Do with a Wounded Tiger?," CBS, 1965; "Look Up and Live: The Continuity of Despair," CBS, 1966; "The Fugitive: Death Is the Door Prize," ABC, 1966; "Run for Your Life: A Game of Violence," NBC, 1966; "NYPD: Nothing Is Real but the Dead," ABC, 1968; "Hallmark Hall of Fame: Teacher, Teacher,"

NBC, 1969; "The Name of the Game: The Third Choice," NBC, 1969; "Bonanza: The Wish," NBC, 1969; "Today Is Ours," CBS, 1974; "The Tenth Level," CBS, 1976.
TV MOVIES AND MINISERIES: "The Outsider," NBC, 1967; "Night Gallery," NBC, 1969; "The Sheriff," ABC, 1971; "King," NBC, 1978; "Roots: The Next Generations," ABC, 1979; "Freedom Road," NBC, 1979; "All God's Children," ABC, 1980.

DAVIS, PATTI
b. Los Angeles, CA. Daughter of Nancy and Ronald Reagan; as an actress, she's appeared in less-than-stellar TV.
AS A REGULAR: "Rituals," SYN, 1984.
AND: "Here's Boomer: Boomer and Miss 21st Century," NBC, 1980; "Nero Wolfe: Gambit," NBC, 1981; "The Love Boat: The Prodigy," ABC, 1986; "The Pat Sajak Show," CBS, 1989.

DAVIS, PHYLLIS
b. Port Arthur, TX, July 17, 1940. Actress who played Beatrice on "Vega$."
AS A REGULAR: "Love, American Style," ABC, 1970-74; "Vegas," ABC, 1978-81.
AND: "The Beverly Hillbillies: Brewster's Baby," CBS, 1966; "The Beverly Hillbillies: Jethro's Pad," CBS, 1966; "Hey, Landlord!: The Big Fumble," NBC, 1966; "The Streets of San Francisco: The Hard Breed," ABC, 1973; "The Odd Couple: Moonlighter," ABC, 1974; "The Love Boat: The Now Marriage," ABC, 1979; "The Love Boat: Making the Grade," ABC, 1980; "Fantasy Island: Diamond Lil," ABC, 1981; "Knight Rider: Pilot," NBC, 1982; "Matt Houston: Killing Isn't Everything," ABC, 1982; "The Love Boat: All the Congressman's Women," ABC, 1985; "Magnum P.I.: A Little Bit of Luck, a Little Bit of Grief," CBS, 1985.
TV MOVIES AND MINISERIES: "The Wild Women of Chastity Gulch," ABC, 1982.

DAVIS, ROGER
Generic TV hunk.
AS A REGULAR: "The Gallant Men," ABC, 1962-63; "Redigo," NBC, 1963; "Dark Shadows," ABC, 1966-71; "Alias Smith and Jones," ABC, 1971-73.
AND: "The Twilight Zone: Spur of the Moment," CBS, 1964; "Medical Center: Web of Darkness," CBS, 1971; "Medical Center: The Idol-Maker," CBS, 1971; "The Bold Ones: The Long Morning After," NBC, 1971; "You Are There: The Siege of the Alamo," CBS, 1971; "The Bold Ones: Moment of Crisis," NBC, 1972; "McCloud: Butch Cassidy Rides Again," NBC, 1973; "The New Adventures of Perry Mason: The Case of the Murdered Murderer," CBS, 1973; "Ironside: Once More for Joey," NBC, 1974; "Firehouse:

Randall's Pride," ABC, 1974; "The Rockford Files: The Kirkoff Case," NBC, 1974; "Quincy: The Two Sides of Truth," NBC, 1977.

TV MOVIES AND MINISERIES: "The Young Country," ABC, 1970; "River of Gold," ABC, 1971; "Killer Bees," ABC, 1974.

DAVIS, RUFE

b. Dinson, OK, 1908; d. 1974. Character actor who played Fred Smoot, one of the engineers of the Cannonball, on "Petticoat Junction."

AS A REGULAR: "Petticoat Junction," CBS, 1963-68; "Green Acres," CBS, 1965-66.

DAVIS, SAMMY JR.

b. New York City, NY, December 8, 1925; d. 1990. Dancer, actor and singer who exemplified almost everything good and bad about twentieth century show business.

AS A REGULAR: "The Sammy Davis Jr. Show," NBC, 1966; "NBC Follies," NBC, 1973; "Sammy and Company," SYN, 1975-77; "One Life to Live," ABC, 1980-81; "General Hospital," ABC, 1982.

AND: "The Steve Allen Show," NBC, 1956; "The Walter Winchell Show," NBC, 1956; "Washington Square," NBC, 1956; "The Perry Como Show," NBC, 1956; "Jerry Lewis Special," NBC, 1957; "The Frank Sinatra Show," ABC, 1958; "The Big Record," CBS, 1958; "G.E. Theatre: Auf Wiedersehen," CBS, 1958; "Milton Berle Starring in the Kraft Music Hall," NBC, 1958; "The Steve Allen Show," NBC, 1959; "G.E. Theatre: The Patsy," CBS, 1960; "The Frank Sinatra Timex Show," ABC, 1960; "G.E. Theatre: Memory in White," CBS, 1961; "Lawman: Blue Boss and Willie Shay," ABC, 1961; "Stump the Stars," CBS, 1962; "The Rifleman: The Most Amazing Man," ABC, 1962; "The Ed Sullivan Show," CBS, 1963; "The Andy Williams Show," NBC, 1963; "The Danny Thomas Show: Rusty's Birthday," CBS, 1963; "Ben Casey: Allie," ABC, 1963; "Burke's Law: Who Killed Alex Debbs?," ABC, 1963; "What's My Line?," CBS, 1964; "The Ed Sullivan Show," CBS, 1964; "Password," CBS, 1965; "The Patty Duke Show: Will the Real Sammy Davis Please Hang Up?," ABC, 1965; "Hullabaloo," NBC, 1965; "Alice in Wonderland," ABC, 1966; "The Wild Wild West: The Night of the Returning Dead," CBS, 1966; "Batman: The Clock King's Crazy Crimes/The King Gets Crowned," ABC, 1966; "Hollywood Palace," ABC, 1967; "I Dream of Jeannie: The Greatest Entertainer in the World," NBC, 1967; "The Danny Thomas Hour: The Enemy," NBC, 1967; "Danny Thomas Special," NBC, 1967; "Personality," NBC, 1968; "The Joey Bishop Show," ABC, 1968; "Hollywood Palace," ABC, 1969; "The Mod Squad: Keep the Faith, Baby," ABC, 1969; "The Mike Douglas Show," SYN, 1969; "This Is Tom Jones," ABC, 1969;

"Hollywood Palace," ABC, 1969; "The Beverly Hillbillies: The Clampetts in New York," CBS, 1969; "The Mod Squad: Survival House," ABC, 1970; "Here's Lucy: Lucy and Sammy Davis Jr.," CBS, 1970; "The Mod Squad: The Song of Willie," ABC, 1970; "The Name of the Game: I Love You, Billy Baker," NBC, 1970; "The Tonight Show Starring Johnny Carson," NBC, 1970; "The David Frost Show," SYN, 1971; "All in the Family: Sammy's Visit," CBS, 1972; "The Courtship of Eddie's Father: A Little Help From My Friend," ABC, 1972; "Old Faithful," ABC, 1973; "Chico and the Man: Sammy Stops In," NBC, 1975; "The Carol Burnett Show," CBS, 1976; "Bob Hope Special," NBC, 1977; "Dinah!," SYN, 1977; "The Mike Douglas Show," SYN, 1978; "Dance Fever," SYN, 1982; "Star Search," SYN, 1985; "Gimme a Break: The Lookalike," NBC, 1985; "Bob Hope's Super Bowl Party," NBC, 1989; "The Cosby Show: No Way Baby," NBC, 1989; "Hunter: Ring of Honor," NBC, 1989; "Frank, Liza, & Sammy: The Ultimate Event," SHO, 1989; "HBO Comedy Hour: Sammy Davis Jr. and Jerry Lewis," HBO, 1989.

TV MOVIES AND MINISERIES: "The Pigeon," ABC, 1969; "The Trackers," ABC, 1971; "Poor Devil," NBC, 1973.

DAVISON, BRUCE

b. Philadelphia, PA, 1948.

AS A REGULAR: "Hunter," NBC, 1985-86.

AND: "Medical Center: A Duel with Doom," CBS, 1970; "Marcus Welby, M.D.: Love Is When They Say They Need You," ABC, 1972; "Love, American Style: Love and the Secret Spouse," ABC, 1973; "Love Story: Time for Love," NBC, 1974; "Police Story: Requiem for C.Z. Smith," NBC, 1974; "Lou Grant: Andrew," CBS, 1979; "Police Woman: Bait," NBC, 1976; "Tales From the Darkside: The Word Processor of the Gods," SYN, 1984; "V: The Betrayal," NBC, 1985; "Amazing Stories: Boo!," NBC, 1986; "Murder, She Wrote: The Cemetery Vote," CBS, 1987; "Dakota's Way," ABC, 1988.

TV MOVIES AND MINISERIES: "Owen Marshall, Counselor at Law," ABC, 1971; "The Affair," ABC, 1973; "The Last Survivors," NBC, 1975; "Mind Over Murder," CBS, 1979; "The Gathering, Part II," NBC, 1979; "The Lathe of Heaven," PBS, 1980; "Theater for Young Americans: The Wave," ABC, 1981; "Poor Little Rich Girl: The Barbara Hutton Story," NBC, 1987; "Lady in a Corner," NBC, 1989.

DAWBER, PAM

b. Farmington Hills, MI, October 18, 1951. Attractive actress who was Mindy to Robin Williams' Mork.

AS A REGULAR: "Mork & Mindy," ABC, 1978-82; "My Sister Sam," CBS, 1986-88.

AND: "The Twilight Zone: But Can She Type?,"

CBS, 1985.

TV MOVIES AND MINISERIES: "Remembrance of Love," NBC, 1982; "Through Naked Eyes," ABC, 1983; "Last of the Great Survivors," CBS, 1984; "This Wife for Hire," CBS, 1985; "Wild Horses," CBS, 1985; "Quiet Victory: the Charlie Wedemeyer Story," CBS, 1988; "Do You Know the Muffin Man?," CBS, 1989.

DAWSON, RICHARD

b. England, November 20, 1932.

AS A REGULAR: "Hogan's Heroes," CBS, 1965-71; "Rowan & Martin's Laugh-In," NBC, 1971-73; "The New Dick Van Dyke Show," CBS, 1973-74; "Match Game," CBS, 1973-78; "The New Masquerade Party," SYN, 1974-75; "Match Game P.M.," SYN, 1975-78; "I've Got a Secret," CBS, 1976; "Family Feud," ABC, 1976-85; SYN, 1977-85.

AND: "The Dick Van Dyke Show: Racy Tracy Rattigan," CBS, 1963; "The Outer Limits: The Invisibles," ABC, 1964; "How's Your Mother-in-Law?," ABC, 1968; "McCloud: The Stage Is All the World," NBC, 1970; "Love, American Style: Love and the Groupie," ABC, 1971; "Love, American Style: Love and the Hiccups," ABC, 1971; "Password," ABC, 1974; "Password All-Stars," ABC, 1975; "The Odd Couple: Laugh, Clown, Laugh," ABC, 1975; "McMillan and Wife: Aftershock," NBC, 1975; "The Merv Griffin Show," SYN, 1975; "The Love Boat: The Song Is Ended," ABC, 1978; "Mama's Family: Family Feud," NBC, 1983.

TV MOVIES AND MINISERIES: "How to Pick Up Girls," ABC, 1978.

DAY, DENNIS

b. New York City, NY, May 21, 1917; d. 1988.

AS A REGULAR: "The Jack Benny Program," CBS, 1950-64; NBC, 1964-65; "The RCA Victor Show," NBC, 1952-54.

AND: "Babes in Toyland," NBC, 1954; "Babes in Toyland," NBC, 1955; "The Spike Jones Show," CBS, 1957; "Date with the Angels: Star Struck," ABC, 1957; "The Steve Allen Show," NBC, 1957; "Pat Boone Chevy Showroom," ABC, 1958; "Shower of Stars: Jack Benny's 40th Birthday Celebration," CBS, 1958; "Navy Log: The Soapbox Kid," ABC, 1958; "The Big Record," CBS, 1958; "Studio One: The McTaggart Succession," CBS, 1958; "Way Back in 1960," ABC, 1960; "The George Gobel Show," CBS, 1960; "The Ed Sullivan Show," CBS, 1960; "Death Valley Days: Way Station," SYN, 1962; "Burke's Law: Who Killed Davidian Jones?," ABC, 1964; "Burke's Law: Who Killed Rosie Sunset?," ABC, 1965; "The Bing Crosby Show: Operation Man Save," ABC, 1965; "The Lucy Show: Little Old Lady," CBS, 1967; "Danny Thomas Special," NBC, 1967; "Love, American

Style: Love and the Big Leap," ABC, 1969; "Frosty's Wonderland," ABC, 1976.

DAY, DORIS

b. Doris von Kappelhoff, Cincinnati, OH, April 3, 1924. Popular actress and singer who hasn't really needed television to be successful.

AS A REGULAR: "The Doris Day Show," CBS, 1968-73; "Doris Day's Best Friends," CBN, 1985-86.

AND: "The Ed Sullivan Show," CBS, 1956; "I've Got a Secret," CBS, 1959; "Doris Day Today," CBS, 1975.

* Day's husband and manager, Martin Melcher, had committed her to her CBS series without her knowledge. When he died in 1968, however, she discovered she was broke and did the show.

DAY, LARAINE

b. La Raine Johnson, Roosevelt, UT, October 13, 1917.

AS A REGULAR: "Day Dreaming with Laraine Day," ABC, 1951; "I've Got a Secret," CBS, 1952; "Masquerade Party," NBC, 1958-59.

AND: "Nash Airflyte Theatre: The Crisis," CBS, 1951; "Lux Video Theatre: Column Item," CBS, 1951; "Lux Video Theatre: It's a Promise," CBS, 1951; "Lux Video Theatre: Double Indemnity," NBC, 1954; "Ford Theatre: Too Old for Dolls," NBC, 1955; "The Loretta Young Show: Slander," NBC, 1955; "Screen Directors Playhouse: The Final Tribute," NBC, 1955; "Undercurrent: Kelly," CBS, 1957; "Schlitz Playhouse of Stars: Bitter Parting," CBS, 1957; "Person to Person," CBS, 1957; "The Ford Show," NBC, 1957; "The Loretta Young Show: Man in a Hurry," NBC, 1957; "I've Got a Secret," CBS, 1958; "Swiss Family Robinson," NBC, 1958; "Pursuit: Tiger on a Bicycle," CBS, 1958; "Playhouse 90: Dark as the Night," CBS, 1959; "Have Gun, Will Travel: Out at the Old Ballpark," CBS, 1960; "Celebrity Talent Scouts," CBS, 1960; "To Tell the Truth," CBS, 1961; "Chckmate: To the Best of My Knowledge," CBS, 1961; "Let Freedom Ring," CBS, 1961; "Follow the Sun: Not Aunt Charlotte!," ABC, 1962; "The New Breed: A Motive Named Walter," ABC, 1962; "The Alfred Hitchcock Hour: Death and the Joyful Woman," NBC, 1963; "Burke's Law: Who Killed Billy Jo?," ABC, 1963; "You Don't Say," NBC, 1964; "You Don't Say," NBC, 1965; "The Name of the Game: The Taker," NBC, 1968; "The FBI: Gamble with Death," ABC, 1969; "The Sixth Sense: The Heart that Wouldn't Stay Buried," ABC, 1972; "Medical Center: Broken Image," CBS, 1973; "The Love Boat: Marooned," ABC, 1978; "Lou Grant: Hollywood," CBS, 1979.

TV MOVIES AND MINISERIES: "Murder on Flight 502," ABC, 1975.

DAY, LYNDA—See Lynda Day George.

DEACON, RICHARD
b. Binghamton, NY, 1922; d. 1984. Bald, portly, bespectacled character actor who was born to play officious clerks and pompous know-it-alls; best known as Mel Cooley on "The Dick Van Dyke Show" and Fred, father of Clarence "Lumpy" Rutherford (Frank Bank) on "Leave It to Beaver."
AS A REGULAR: "The Charlie Farrell Show," CBS, 1956; "Date with the Angels," ABC, 1957-58; "Leave It to Beaver," CBS, 1957-58; ABC, 1958-63; "The Dick Van Dyke Show," CBS, 1961-66; "The Pruitts of Southhampton," ABC, 1967; "The Mothers-in-Law," NBC, 1968-69; "The Beverly Hillbillies," CBS, 1970-71; "B.J. and the Bear," NBC, 1979.
AND: "December Bride: Sunken Den," CBS, 1956; "December Bride: Lily the Matchmaker," CBS, 1956; "Studio 57: It's a Small World," SYN, 1957; "The 20th Century-Fox Hour: The Great American Hoax," CBS, 1957; "The Lucille Ball-Desi Arnaz Show: The Celebrity Next Door," CBS, 1957; "Navy Log: The Big White Albatross," ABC, 1957; "Tales of Wells Fargo: The Gambler," NBC, 1958; "The Real McCoys: The Tax Man Cometh," ABC, 1959; "How to Marry a Millionaire: Loco Goes to Night School," SYN, 1959; "Guestward Ho!: Too Many Cooks," ABC, 1961; "National Velvet: The Riding Mistress," NBC, 1961; "The Real McCoys: Money in the Bank," ABC, 1961; "The Donna Reed Show: The Electrical Storm," ABC, 1961; "The Jack Benny Program: Jack Gets a Passport," CBS, 1962; "About Time," NBC, 1962; "Pete and Gladys: The Prize," CBS, 1962; "McKeever and the Colonel: The Bugle Sounds," NBC, 1962; "My Favorite Martian: Russians R in Season," CBS, 1963; "The Twilight Zone: The Brain Center at Whipple's," CBS, 1964; "My Favorite Martian: My Nephew, the Artist," CBS, 1964; "Bob Hope Chrysler Theatre: Have Girls, Will Travel," NBC, 1964; "The Munsters: Pike's Pique," CBS, 1964; "The Addams Family: Cousin Itt and the Vocational Counselor," ABC, 1965; "The Farmer's Daughter: Have You Ever Thought of Building?," ABC, 1966; "I Dream of Jeannie: Who Are You Calling a Jeannie?," NBC, 1967; "How's Your Mother-in-Law?," ABC, 1968; "Love, American Style: Love and the Phonies," ABC, 1970; "Here's Lucy: Lucy the Crusader," CBS, 1971; "Green Acres: The Ex-Secretary," CBS, 1971; "Love, American Style: Love and the Oldy Weds," ABC, 1971; "McMillan and Wife: Till Death Do Us Part," NBC, 1972; "Here's Lucy: Lucy Sublets the Office," CBS, 1972; "Love, American Style: Love and the Fountain of Youth," ABC, 1972; "McMillan and Wife: Love, Honor and Swindle," NBC, 1975; "Maude: Tuckahoe Bicentennial," CBS, 1976; "What's

Happening!: Dee the Cheerleader," ABC, 1979.
TV MOVIES AND MINISERIES: "Still the Beaver," CBS, 1983.

DEAN, JAMES
b. Marion, IN, February 8, 1931; d. 1955. Fifties screen icon who was trained in live television drama.
AS A GUEST: "Father Peyton's TV Theatre: Hill Number One," SYN, 1951; "The Web: Sleeping Dogs," CBS, 1952; "U.S. Steel Hour: Prologue to Glory," ABC, 1952; "Studio One: Abraham Lincoln," CBS, 1952; "The Kate Smith Hour: Hound of Heaven," NBC, 1953; "Treasury Men in Action: The Case of the Watchful Dog," NBC, 1953; "You Are There: The Capture of Jesse James," CBS, 1953; "Danger: No Room," CBS, 1953; "Treasury Men in Action: The Case of the Sawed Off Shotgun," NBC, 1953; "Campbell TV Soundstage: Something for an Empty Briefcase," NBC, 1953; "Summer Studio One: Sentence of Death," CBS, 1953; "Danger: The Little Woman," CBS, 1953; "Danger: Death Is My Neighbor," CBS, 1953; "Kraft Television Theatre: Keep Our Honor Bright," NBC, 1953; "Campbell TV Soundstage: Life Sentence," NBC, 1953; "Kraft Television Theatre: A Long Time Till Dawn," NBC, 1953; "Armstrong Circle Theatre: The Bells of Cockaigne," NBC, 1953; "Robert Montgomery Presents: Harvest," NBC, 1953; "Philco TV Playhouse: Run Like a Thief," NBC, 1954; "Danger: Padlocks," CBS, 1954; "G.E. Theatre: I'm a Fool," CBS, 1954; "G.E. Theatre: The Dark, Dark Hours," CBS, 1954; "U.S. Steel Hour: The Thief," ABC, 1955; "Schlitz Playhouse of Stars: The Unlighted Road," CBS, 1955.
* Dean also worked behind the scenes in TV—in the early fifties he tested stunts for "Beat the Clock."

DEAN, JIMMY
b. Seth Ward, Plainview, TX, August 10, 1928. Country-western singer, variety show host, sausage maker.
AS A REGULAR: "The Jimmy Dean Show," CBS, 1957-58; 1958-59; ABC, 1963-66; "Daniel Boone," NBC, 1968-70; "J.J. Starbuck," NBC, 1987-88.
AND: "The Vic Damone Show," CBS, 1957; "The Steve Allen Show," NBC, 1957; "The Steve Allen Show," NBC, 1958; "Pat Boone Chevy Showroom," ABC, 1958; "The Perry Como Show," NBC, 1958; "The Chevy Show," NBC, 1959; "Arthur Murray Party," NBC, 1960; "Five Star Jubilee," NBC, 1961; "The Ed Sullivan Show," CBS, 1961; "Candid Camera," CBS, 1962; "The Tonight Show Starring Johnny Carson," NBC, 1962; "The Jack Paar Program," NBC, 1963; "The Patty Duke Show: The Song

Writers," ABC, 1963; "The Ed Sullivan Show," CBS, 1967; "Operation: Entertainment," ABC, 1968; "The Mike Douglas Show," SYN, 1969; "Jimmy Durante Presents the Lennon Sisters Hour," ABC, 1969; "The Merv Griffin Show," CBS, 1970; "Dinah!," SYN, 1976.

TV MOVIES AND MINISERIES: "The Ballad of Andy Crocker," ABC, 1969; "Rolling Man," ABC, 1972; "The City," NBC, 1977.

DEAN, LARRY

b. 1936. Singer.

AS A REGULAR: "The Lawrence Welk Show," ABC, 1956-60.

AND: "American Bandstand," ABC, 1958; "The Lucy Show: Lucy and the Ceramic Cat," CBS, 1965; "The Lucy Show: Lucy and Bob Crane," CBS, 1966; "The Lucy Show: Lucy and the Robot," CBS, 1966.

DECAMP, ROSEMARY

b. Prescott, AZ, November 14, 1914. Pleasant, wholesome actress who went from playing Jackie Gleason's wife to Bob Cummings' sister to Marlo Thomas' and Shirley Jones' mother to Noah Beery's girlfriend on "The Rockford Files."

AS A REGULAR: "The Life of Riley," NBC, 1949-50; "The Bob Cummings Show," NBC, 1955; CBS, 1955-57; NBC, 1957-59; "The Baileys of Balboa," CBS, 1964; "That Girl," ABC, 1966-70; "Petticoat Junction," CBS, 1968.

AND: "Ford Theatre: Madame .44," NBC, 1953; "Ford Theatre: Alias Nora Hale," NBC, 1953; "Ford Theatre: Good of His Soul," NBC, 1954; "Ford Theatre: Segment," NBC, 1954; "Caval-cade Theatre: Nobody's Fool," ABC, 1955; "TV Reader's Digest: The Sad Death of a Hero," ABC, 1955; "TV Reader's Digest: The Old, Old Story," ABC, 1956; "Climax!: The 78th Floor," CBS, 1956; "Studio One: Trial by Slander," CBS, 1958; "Studio One: No Place to Run," CBS, 1958; "G.E. Theatre: Night Club," CBS, 1959; "The Red Skelton Show: Clem's Other Clem," CBS, 1961; "87th Precinct: Killer's Payoff," NBC, 1962; "Follow the Sun: Chalk One Up for Johnny," ABC, 1962; "Rawhide: The House of the Hunter," CBS, 1962; "Hazel: Hazel's Cousin," NBC, 1962; "Ensign O'Toole: Operation: Swindle," NBC, 1962; "The Beverly Hillbillies: The Family Tree," CBS, 1963; "The Beverly Hillbillies: Jed Cuts the Family Tree," CBS, 1963; "The Breaking Point: A Little Anger Is a Good Thing," ABC, 1964; "The Littlest Hobo: You Can't Buy a Friend," SYN, 1965; "Dr. Kildare: Music Hath Charms," NBC, 1965; "Amos Burke, Secret Agent: Operation Long Shadow," ABC, 1965; "Death Valley Days: Mrs. Romney and the Outlaws," SYN, 1966; "Death Valley Days: Canary Harris vs. the Almighty," SYN, 1967; "Love, American Style: Love and the Other Love," ABC, 1969;

"The Partridge Family: Whatever Happened to the Old Songs?," ABC, 1970; "Mannix: The Crime that Wasn't," CBS, 1971; "Night Gallery: The Painted Mirror," NBC, 1971; "The Partridge Family: The Forty-Year Itch," ABC, 1971; "Longstreet: Long Way Home," ABC, 1971; "Call Holme," NBC, 1972; "The Partridge Family: The Mod Father," ABC, 1972; "Mannix: Little Girl Lost," CBS, 1973; "Love, American Style: Love and the Anniversary," ABC, 1973; "The Partridge Family: Made in San Pueblo," ABC, 1973; "Marcus Welby, M.D.: Dark Corridors," ABC, 1975; "The Rockford Files: Gearjammers," NBC, 1975; "B.J. and the Bear: For Adults Only," NBC, 1981; "Quincy: Whatever Happened to Morris Perlmutter?" NBC, 1983; "St. Elsewhere: A Room with a View," NBC, 1986.

TV MOVIES AND MINISERIES: "The Time Machine," NBC, 1978; "Blind Ambition," CBS, 1979.

DE CARLO, YVONNE

b. Peggy Yvonne Middleton, Vancouver, September 1, 1922. Actress who made her mark in Arabian-nights movies in the forties and as Lily Munster in the sixties.

AS A REGULAR: "Backbone of America," NBC, 1953; "The Munsters," CBS, 1964-66.

AND: "Lights Out: Another Country," NBC, 1952; "Ford Theatre: Madame 44," NBC, 1953; "Screen Directors Playhouse: Hot Cargo," NBC, 1956; "Star Stage: The Sainted General," NBC, 1956; "The Perry Como Show," NBC, 1956; "Shower of Stars," CBS, 1957; "The Steve Allen Show," NBC, 1957; "Schlitz Playhouse of Stars: Storm Over Rapallo," CBS, 1957; "Playhouse 90: Verdict of Three," CBS, 1958; "Milton Berle Starring in the Kraft Music Hall," NBC, 1959; "Bonanza: A Rose for Lotta," NBC, 1959; "Adventures in Paradise: Isle of Eden," ABC, 1960; "Death Valley Days: The Lady Was an M.D.," SYN, 1961; "Follow the Sun: The Longest Crap Game in History," ABC, 1961; "Follow the Sun: Annie Beeler's Place," ABC, 1962; "Stump the Stars," CBS, 1962; "The Virginian: A Time Remembered," NBC, 1963; "Burke's Law: Who Killed Beau Sparrow?," ABC, 1963; "The Greatest Show on Earth: The Night the Monkey Died," ABC, 1964; "The Girl From UNCLE: The Moulin Ruse Affair," NBC, 1967; "Custer: The Raiders," ABC, 1967; "The Virginian: Crime Wave at Buffalo Springs," NBC, 1969; "The Name of the Game: Island of Gold and Precious Stones," NBC, 1970; "Murder, She Wrote: Jessica Behind Bars," CBS, 1986.

TV MOVIES AND MINISERIES: "The Mark of Zorro," ABC, 1974; "The Girl on the Late-Late Show," NBC, 1974.

* De Carlo's films include "Kismet," "Salome-Where She Danced," "Song of Scheherazade," "Slave Girl," "Casbah" and "Flame of the Islands."

253

DE CORDOVA, FRED

b. New York City, NY, October 27, 1910.
Longtime producer-director.

AS PRODUCER-DIRECTOR: "The George Burns and Gracie Allen Show," CBS, 1951-58; "December Bride," CBS, 1958-59; "My Three Sons," ABC, 1960-65.

AS PRODUCER: "The Tonight Show Starring Johnny Carson," NBC, 1971- .

AS PERFORMER: "December Bride: Child of Nature," CBS, 1958; "ALF: Tonight, Tonight," NBC, 1988.

DEE, RUBY

b. Ruby Ann Wallace, Cleveland, October 27, 1924. Gifted actress and longtime wife of Ossie Davis.

AS A REGULAR: "The Guiding Light," CBS, 1967; "Peyton Place," ABC, 1968-69; "With Ossie & Ruby," PBS, 1981-82.

AND: "Salute to the American Theatre," CBS, 1959; "Camera Three," CBS, 1960; "Play of the Week: Seven Times Monday," SYN, 1961; "Play of the Week: Black Monday," SYN, 1961; "Alcoa Premiere: Impact of an Execution," ABC, 1962; "The Nurses: Express Stop From Lenox Avenue," CBS, 1963; "The Fugitive: Decision in the Ring," ABC, 1963; "The Great Adventure: Go Down, Moses," CBS, 1963; "East Side/West Side: No Hiding Place," CBS, 1963; "The Defenders: The Sworn Twelve," CBS, 1965; "Look Up and Live: Continuity of Despair," CBS, 1966; "NET Playhouse: To Be Young, Gifted and Black," NET, 1972; "D.H.O.," ABC, 1973; "Tenafly: The Window That Wasn't," NBC, 1973; "Today Is Ours," CBS, 1974; "Wedding Band," ABC, 1974; "Police Woman: Target Black," NBC, 1975.

TV MOVIES AND MINISERIES: "Deadlock," NBC, 1969; "The Sheriff," ABC, 1971; "It's Good to Be Alive," CBS, 1974; "Roots: The Next Generations," ABC, 1979; "I Know Why the Caged Bird Sings," CBS, 1979; "All God's Children," ABC, 1980; "The Atlanta Child Murders," CBS, 1985; "Windmills of the Gods," CBS, 1988; "Gore Vidal's Lincoln," NBC, 1988. •

DEE, SANDRA

b. Alexandra Zuck, Bayonne, NJ, April 23, 1942. Teen actress who popped up on TV into the seventies.

AS A GUEST: "The Steve Allen Show," NBC, 1959; "Perry Como's Kraft Music Hall," NBC, 1962; "Night Gallery: Tell David ...," NBC, 1971; "The Sixth Sense: Through a Flame Darkly," ABC, 1972; "Love, American Style: Love and the Sensuous Twin," ABC, 1972; "Police Woman: Blind Terror," NBC, 1978.

TV MOVIES AND MINISERIES: "The Man Hunter," ABC, 1969; "The Daughters of Joshua Cabe," ABC, 1972; "Houston, We've Got a Problem," ABC, 1974; "The Manhunter," NBC, 1976; "Fantasy Island," ABC, 1977.

DEES, RICK

b. Memphis, TN, 1950. Deejay who had a novelty hit in the seventies called "Disco Duck."

AS A REGULAR: "Solid Gold," SYN, 1984-85; "Into the Night with Rick Dees," ABC, 1990- .

AND: "Cheers: Sam at Eleven," NBC, 1982.

TV MOVIES AND MINISERIES: "The Gladiator," ABC, 1986.

DEFORE, DON

b. Cedar Rapids, IA, August 25, 1917. Actor with the clean-cut manner you'd expect from a Cedar Rapids fellow. Best known as Ozzie Nelson's neighbor, Thorny Thornberry, and as George "Mr. B" Baxter, the exasperated master of Hazel the maid.

AS A REGULAR: "The Adventures of Ozzie and Harriet," ABC, 1952-58; "Hazel," NBC, 1961-65.

AND: "Silver Theatre: Double Feature," CBS, 1950; "Silver Theatre: Walt and Lavinia," CBS, 1950; "Hollywood Premiere Theatre: Mr. and Mrs. Detective," ABC, 1950; "Bigelow Theatre: A Woman's Privilege," CBS, 1951; "Science Fiction Theatre: Time Is Just a Place," SYN, 1955; "Schlitz Playhouse of Stars: A Gift of Life," CBS, 1955; "Crossroads: The Comeback," ABC, 1956; "Ford Theatre: The Idea Man," ABC, 1957; "Studio One: The Enemy Within," CBS, 1958; "Queen for a Day," NBC, 1958; "G.E. Theatre: The Lady's Choice," CBS, 1959; "The Philadelphia Story," NBC, 1959; "The Loretta Young Show: Plain, Unmarked Envelope," NBC, 1960; "Michael Shayne: Dolls Are Deadly," NBC, 1960; "Best of the Post: Suicide Flight," SYN, 1960; "Alfred Hitchcock Presents: Coming, Mama," NBC, 1961; "The Merv Griffin Show," SYN, 1968; "Hallmark Hall of Fame: A Punt, a Pass and a Prayer," NBC, 1968; "My Three Sons: The Matchmakers," CBS, 1969; "The Mod Squad: A Place to Run," ABC, 1969; "Mannix: Murder Revisited," CBS, 1970; "The Men From Shiloh: The West vs. Colonel Mackenzie," NBC, 1970; "Marcus Welby, M.D.: Go Ahead and Cry," ABC, 1975; "Murder, She Wrote: Unfinished Business," CBS, 1986; "St. Elsewhere: Visiting Daze," NBC, 1987.

TV MOVIES AND MINISERIES: "Black Beauty," NBC, 1978.

DEFOREST, CALVERT

b. Brooklyn, NY. Stocky, bald performer known to his legion of fans as Larry "Bud" Melman, a man who is as essential to the success of "Late Night with David Letterman" as mayonnaise is to deviled eggs.

AS A REGULAR: "Late Night with David Letterman," NBC, 1982- .

DEHAVEN, GLORIA

b. Los Angeles, CA, July 23, 1924. Starlet of the fifties; she played Bess Shelby on "Ryan's Hope."

AS A REGULAR: "Make the Connection," NBC, 1955; "As the World Turns," CBS, 1966-67; "Nakia," ABC, 1974; "Ryan's Hope," ABC, 1983-89.

AND: "Musical Comedy Time: Miss Liberty," NBC, 1951; "Apoointment with Adventure: The Snow People," CBS, 1955; "Robert Montgomery Presents: The Briefcase," NBC, 1956; "The George Gobel Show," NBC, 1956; "Arthur Murray Party," NBC, 1957; "Mr. Broadway," NBC, 1957; "The Guy Mitchell Show," ABC, 1957; "The Jimmy Dean Show," CBS, 1958; "Pantomime Quiz," ABC, 1958; "Ellery Queen: Body of the Crime," NBC, 1959; "Revlon Revue: The Many Sides of Mickey Rooney," CBS, 1960; "Wagon Train: The Allison Justis Story," NBC, 1960; "Adventures in Paradise: The Jonah Stone," ABC, 1961; "Perry Como's Kraft Music Hall," NBC, 1961; "The Defenders: Gideon's Follies," CBS, 1961; "Burke's Law: Who Killed the Swinger on a Hook?," ABC, 1964; "What's This Song?," NBC, 1964; "You Don't Say," NBC, 1965; "The Mike Douglas Show," SYN, 1968; "The Jimmy Stewart Show: Old School Ties," NBC, 1972; "Wednesday Night Out," NBC, 1972; "Honeymoon Suite," ABC, 1972; "Marcus Welby, M.D.: Catch a Ring That Isn't There," ABC, 1973; "Gunsmoke: Like Old Times," CBS, 1974; "Cross Wits," SYN, 1976; "Harris and Company: A Very Special Person," NBC, 1979; "B.J. and the Bear: Eighteen Wheel Ripoff," NBC, 1980; "Fantasy Island: My Man Friday," ABC, 1982; "The Love Boat: Don't Leave Home Without It," ABC, 1983; "Mama's Family: Positive Thinking," NBC, 1983; "Highway to Heaven: A Mother and a Daughter," NBC, 1986; "The Love Boat: Second Banana," ABC, 1986; "Murder, She Wrote: If It's Thursday, It Must Be Beverly," CBS, 1987; "Murder, She Wrote: Sins of Castle Cove," CBS, 1989.

TV MOVIES AND MINISERIES: "Call Her Mom," ABC, 1972; "Evening in Byzantium," SYN, 1978.

DE HAVILLAND, OLIVIA

b. Tokyo, Japan, July 1, 1916. Durable actress whose TV work has tended toward the quality side—not counting "The Love Boat," that is.

AS A GUEST: "The Jack Paar Show," NBC, 1958; "The Last Word," CBS, 1958; "I've Got a Secret," CBS, 1958; "Youth Wants to Know," NBC, 1958; "Person to Person," CBS, 1960; "I've Got a Secret," CBS, 1960; "Hollywood Palace," ABC, 1964; "ABC Stage '67: Noon Wine," ABC, 1966; "The Danny Thomas Hour: The Last Hunters," NBC, 1968; "The Love Boat: Aunt Hilly," ABC, 1981.

TV MOVIES AND MINISERIES: "The Screaming Woman," ABC, 1972; "Roots: The Next Generations," ABC, 1979; "Murder Is Easy," CBS, 1982; "The Royal Romance of Charles and Diana," CBS, 1982; "Anastasia: The Mystery of Anna," NBC, 1986; "The Woman He Loved," CBS, 1988.

DEHNER, JOHN

b. New York City, NY, November 23, 1915. Actor with piercing eyes and a resonant voice; he often plays pompous bosses or other figures of authority.

AS A REGULAR: "The Westerner," NBC, 1960; "The Roaring Twenties," ABC, 1960-62; "The Baileys of Balboa," CBS, 1964-65; "Morning Star," NBC, 1965-66; "The Don Knotts Show," NBC, 1970-71; "The Doris Day Show," CBS, 1971-73; "Temperatures Rising," ABC, 1973-74; "Big Hawaii," NBC, 1977; "Young Maverick," CBS, 1979-80; "Enos," CBS, 1980-81; "Bare Essence," NBC, 1983.

AND: "The Loretta Young Show: Top Man," NBC, 1955; "Frontier: Georgia Gold," NBC, 1955; "Gunsmoke: Tap Day for Kitty," CBS, 1956; "The Jane Wyman Show: Farmer's Wife," NBC, 1957; "Dick Powell's Zane Grey Theatre: Decision at Wilson's Creek," CBS, 1957; "Restless Gun: Hill of Death," NBC, 1957; "Wagon Train: The Emily Rossiter Story," NBC, 1957; "Dick Powell's Zane Grey Theatre: Legacy of a Legend," CBS, 1958; "Wagon Train: The Annie Griffith Story," NBC, 1959; "Cheyenne: Payroll of the Dead," ABC, 1959; "Wichita Town: Death Watch," NBC, 1959; "Playhouse 90: The Killers of Mussolini," CBS, 1959; "The Twilight Zone: The Lonely," CBS, 1959; "Bat Masterson: The Prescott Campaign," NBC, 1961; "Stagecoach West: The Root of Evil," ABC, 1961; "Rawhide: Incident of the New Start," CBS, 1961; "The Rifleman: The Prisoner," ABC, 1961; "Stagecoach West: El Carnicero," ABC, 1961; "Maverick: Devil's Necklace," ABC, 1961; "77 Sunset Strip: Caper in E Flat," ABC, 1961; "The Untouchables: The Nero Rankin Story," ABC, 1961; "77 Sunset Strip: Leap, My Lovely," ABC, 1962; "Rawhide: Incident of the Four Horsemen," CBS, 1962; "The Gallant Men: One Moderately Peaceful Sunday," ABC, 1962; "Empire: Echo of a Man," NBC, 1962; "Stoney Burke: King of the Hill," ABC, 1963; "Rawhide: Incident of Judgment Day," CBS, 1963; "The Andy Griffith Show: Aunt Bee's Medicine Man," CBS, 1963; "The Virginian: Echo From Another Day," NBC, 1963; "The Virginian: To Make This Place Remember," NBC, 1963; "The Greatest Show on Earth: Where the Wire Ends," ABC, 1964; "Combat!: The General and the Sergeant," ABC,

1964; "The Twilight Zone: Mr. Garrity and the Graves," CBS, 1964; "Hogan's Heroes: The Late Inspector General," CBS, 1965; "F Troop: Honest Injun," ABC, 1965; "The Wild Wild West: The Night of the Casual Killer," CBS, 1965; "The Big Valley: Night of the Wolf," ABC, 1965; "T.H.E. Cat: King of Limpets," NBC, 1966; "The Virginian: Harvest of Strangers," NBC, 1966; "The Virginian: One Spring Like Long Ago," NBC, 1966; "Captain Nice: Beware of Hidden Prophets," NBC, 1967; "The Beverly Hillbillies: The Soap Opera," CBS, 1968; "Then Came Bronson: The Gleam of the Eagle Mind," NBC, 1970; "Love, American Style: Love and the Secret Spouse," ABC, 1973; "Columbo: Swan Song," NBC, 1974; "Kolchak, the Night Stalker: The Knightly Murders," ABC, 1975; "Switch: Stung From Beyond," CBS, 1975; "Columbo: Last Salute to the Commodore," NBC, 1976; "The Rockford Files: There's One in Every Port," NBC, 1976; "Quincy: Physician, Heal Thyself," NBC, 1979; "Hardcastle and McCormick: Surprise on Seagull Beach," ABC, 1985.

TV MOVIES AND MINISERIES: "Winchester '73," NBC, 1967; "Something for a Lonely Man," NBC, 1968; "Quarantined," ABC, 1970; "Honky Tonk," NBC, 1974; "The Big Rip-Off," NBC, 1975; "The New Daughters of Joshua Cabe," ABC, 1976; "Bare Essence," CBS, 1982; "War and Remembrance," ABC, 1988, 1989.

DE KOVA, FRANK
b. 1910; d. 1981. Swarthy character actor who played endless straight Indian roles on TV westerns until he got a chance to spoof the image as Chief Wild Eagle of the Hekawi Indians on "F Troop."
AS A REGULAR: "F Troop," ABC, 1965-67.
AND: "Tales of the 77th Bengal Lancers: Hostage," NBC, 1956; "Gunsmoke: Greater Love," CBS, 1956; "Buckskin: Coup Stick," NBC, 1958; "Cheyenne: The Rebellion," ABC, 1959; "The Detectives Starring Robert Taylor: Karate," ABC, 1959; "The Alaskans: Contest at Gold Bottom," ABC, 1959; "Johnny Staccato: Night of Jeopardy," NBC, 1959; "The Deputy: Back to Glory," NBC, 1959; "The Untouchables: Unhired Assassin," ABC, 1960; "The Rifleman: Meeting at Midnight," ABC, 1960; "SurfSide 6: Country Gentleman," ABC, 1960; "The Untouchables: The Waxey Gordon Story," ABC, 1960; "Hawaiian Eye: The Contenders," ABC, 1960; "The Roaring Twenties: The White Carnation," ABC, 1960; "Lawman: Cornered," ABC, 1960; "The Islanders: The Widow From Richmond," ABC, 1960; "Hong Kong: Double Jeopardy," ABC, 1961; "The Untouchables: The Underground Court," ABC, 1961; "Hawaiian Eye: The Stanhope Brand," ABC, 1961; "Rawhide: Incident of the Boomerang," CBS, 1961; "Route 66: Most Vanquished,

Most Victorious," CBS, 1961; "The Tall Man: The Cloudbuster," NBC, 1961; "Gunslinger: The New Savannah Story," CBS, 1961; "The Roaring Twenties: Million-Dollar Suit," ABC, 1961; "Frontier Circus: The Shaggy Kings," CBS, 1961; "Cheyenne: Cross Purpose," ABC, 1961; "Maverick: A Technical Error," ABC, 1961; "Wagon Train: Clyde," NBC, 1961; "The Bob Cummings Show: La Dolce Roma," CBS, 1961; "Thriller: La Strega," NBC, 1962; "The Outlaws: Charge!," NBC, 1962; "Wagon Train: The George B. Hanrahan Story," NBC, 1962; "The Gallant Men: The Ninety-Eight Cent Man," ABC, 1962; "Cheyenne: Pocketful of Stars," ABC, 1962; "The Untouchables: A Fist of Five," ABC, 1962; "The Greatest Show on Earth: Corsicans Don't Cry," ABC, 1964; "Daniel Boone: The Sound of Wings," NBC, 1964; "Hawaii Five-O: Golden Boy in Black Trunks," CBS, 1969; "Love, American Style: Love and the Eskimo's Wife," ABC, 1972; "The FBI: Night of the Long Knives," ABC, 1973; "The FBI: The Bought Jury," ABC, 1973; "Police Story: Across the Line," NBC, 1974; "Police Woman: The Company," NBC, 1975; "The Rockford Files: Hotel of Fear," NBC, 1977; "Little House on the Prairie: The Craftsman," NBC, 1979; "Little House on the Prairie: The Halloween Dream," NBC, 1979.

TV MOVIES AND MINISERIES: "Crossfire," NBC, 1975.

DELANY, DANA
Emmy winning actress who plays nurse Colleen McMurphy on "China Beach."
AS A REGULAR: "Love of Life," CBS, 1979-80; "As the World Turns," CBS, 1981; "Sweet Surrender," NBC, 1987; "China Beach," ABC, 1988- .
AND: "Moonlighting: Gillian," ABC, 1985; "Magnum, P.I.: L.A.," CBS, 1986; "Magnum, P.I.: One Picture Is Worth...," CBS, 1987.
TV MOVIES AND MINISERIES: "Threesome," CBS, 1984.
* Emmies: 1989.

DELL, GABRIEL
b. British West Indies, October 7, 1919.
AS A REGULAR: "The Corner Bar," ABC, 1972; "A Year at the Top," CBS, 1977.
AND: "Naked City: Man Without a Skin," ABC, 1963; "Ben Casey: Francini? Who Is Francini?," ABC, 1965; "The Fugitive: There Goes the Ball Game," ABC, 1967; "Then Came Bronson: Old Tigers Never Die: They Just Run Away," NBC, 1969; "I Dream of Jeannie: My Master, the Chili King," NBC, 1970; "The Name of the Game: Appointment in Paradise," NBC, 1971; "McCloud: Somebody's Out to Get Jennie," NBC, 1971; "Sanford & Son: The Suitcase Case," NBC, 1972; "Sanford & Son: The Big Party," NBC, 1972;

"Barney Miller: Vigilante," ABC, 1975; "Risko," CBS, 1976; "Serpico: Sanctuary," NBC, 1976.
TV MOVIES AND MINISERIES: "Cutter," NBC, 1972.

DELMAR, KENNY
b. Boston, MA, 1910; d. 1984. Actor who often played pompous Southerners; on the radio he was Senator, I say Senator Claghorn on "Alley's Alley."
AS A REGULAR: "School House," DUM, 1949; "The Ernie Kovacs Show," NBC, 1955-56.
AND: "U.S. Steel Hour: Good for You?," ABC, 1954; "Elgin TV Hour: The $1,000 Window," CBS, 1955; "U.S. Steel Hour: The Meanest Man in the World," CBS, 1955; "Goodyear TV Playhouse: Suit Yourself," NBC, 1955; "Studio One: A Most Contagious Game," CBS, 1955; "U.S. Steel Hour: Shoot It Again," CBS, 1955; "Armstrong Circle Theatre: Actual," NBC, 1955; "Kraft Television Theatre: Paper Foxhole," NBC, 1956; "Kraft Television Theatre: The Gentle Grafter," NBC, 1956; "Studio One: The Star Spangled Soldier," CBS, 1956; "Playhouse 90: Snow Shoes," CBS, 1957; "Kraft Television Theatre: Sextuplets!," NBC, 1957; "Car 54, Where Are You?: A Star is Born—In the Bronx," NBC, 1962.

DEL RIO, DOLORES
b. Lolita Dolores Martinez Ansunsolo Lopez Negrette, Durango, Mexico, August 3, 1905; d. 1983. Screen siren who made her debut in silent-movie days and did a little TV.
AS A GUEST: "Schlitz Playhouse of Stars: Old Spanish Custom," CBS, 1957; "U.S. Steel Hour: The Public Prosecutor," CBS, 1958; "The Chevy Show: Mexican Fiesta," NBC, 1960; "The Man Who Bought Paradise," CBS, 1965; "I Spy: Return to Glory," NBC, 1966; "Branded: The Ghost of Murietta," NBC, 1966; "Marcus Welby, M.D.: The Legacy," ABC, 1970.

DELUISE, DOM
b. Brooklyn, NY, August 1, 1933. Roly-poly comic whose "The Great Dominick" magic routine got him attention in the early 1960s.
AS A REGULAR: "The Entertainers," CBS, 1964-65; "The Dean Martin Show," NBC, 1965-74; "The Dean Martin Summer Show," NBC, 1966; "The Dom DeLuise Show," CBS, 1968; SYN, 1987-88; "The Glen Campbell Goodtime Hour," CBS, 1971-72; "Lotsa Luck," NBC, 1973-74; "The Dom DeLuise Show," SYN, 1988-89.
AND: "The Shari Lewis Show," NBC, 1962; "The Munsters: Just Another Pretty Face," CBS, 1966; "The Merv Griffin Show," SYN, 1966; "Please Don't Eat the Daisies: The Purple Avenger," NBC, 1966; "The Girl From UNCLE: The Danish Blue Affair," NBC, 1966; "Hollywood Palace," ABC, 1967; "The Dean Martin Show," NBC, 1967; "The

Mike Douglas Show," SYN, 1967; "The Dean Martin Show," NBC, 1968; "The Merv Griffin Show," SYN, 1968; "Experiment in Television: This is Sholom Aleichem," NBC, 1969; "The Ghost and Mrs. Muir: Today I Am a Ghost," ABC, 1969; "The Glen Campbell Goodtime Hour," CBS, 1972; "Arthur Godfrey," NBC, 1972; "The Flip Wilson Show," NBC, 1973; "Medical Center: The World's a Balloon," CBS, 1974; "The Mac Davis Show," NBC, 1975; "Tony Orlando and Dawn," CBS, 1975; "Dean Martin's Red Hot Scandals of 1926," NBC, 1976; "The Jacksons," CBS, 1977; "The Mike Douglas Show," SYN, 1980; "Amazing Stories: Guilt Trip," NBC, 1985; "Easy Street: Too Many Cooks," NBC, 1987; "21 Jump Street: Woolly Bullies," FOX, 1989; "B.L. Stryker: Die Laughing," ABC, 1989.
TV MOVIES AND MINISERIES: "Evil Roy Slade," NBC, 1972; "Only with Married Men," ABC, 1974.

DEMAREST, WILLIAM
b. St. Paul, MN, Feb, 27, 1892; d. 1983. Gruff character actor remembered as Uncle Charley on "My Three Sons."
AS A REGULAR: "The Danny Thomas Show," CBS, 1957-58; "Love and Marriage," NBC, 1959-60; "Tales of Wells Fargo," NBC, 1961-62; "My Three Sons," ABC, 1965; CBS, 1965-72.
AND: "The Red Skelton Show," CBS, 1960; "Red Skelton Special," CBS, 1960; "The Rebel: A Wife for Johnny Yuma," ABC, 1960; "Here's Hollywood," NBC, 1961; "The Danny Thomas Show: Tonoose vs. Daly," CBS, 1961; "Going My Way: The Slasher," ABC, 1963; "Bonanza: The Hayburner," NBC, 1963; "Dr. Kildare: Why Won't Anyone Listen?," NBC, 1964; "The Farmer's Daughter: The One-Eyed Sloth," ABC, 1964; "The Twilight Zone: What's in the Box?," CBS, 1964; "Burke's Law: Who Killed Vaudeville?," ABC, 1964; "To Rome with Love: Rome Is Where You Find It," CBS, 1970; "McMillan and Wife: Two Dollars' Trouble," NBC, 1973; "The Merv Griffin Show," SYN, 1974; "The Tonight Show Starring Johnny Carson," NBC, 1975; "McMillan and Wife: Greed," NBC, 1975; "Ellery Queen: Veronica's Veils," NBC, 1975; "The Tonight Show Starring Johnny Carson," NBC, 1981.
TV MOVIES AND MINISERIES: "Don't Be Afraid of the Dark," ABC, 1973.

DENISON, ANTHONY JOHN
b. Bronx, NY.
AS A REGULAR: "Crime Story," NBC, 1986-88; "Wiseguy," CBS, 1987; 1990- .
TV MOVIES AND MINISERIES: "Full Exposure: The Sex Tapes Scandal," NBC, 1989; "I Love You Perfect," ABC, 1989.

DENNEHY, BRIAN

b. Bridgeport, CT, July 9, 1940. Burly actor who plays good and bad guys with aplomb; memorable as the sympathetic bartender in the film "10."

AS A REGULAR: "Big Shamus, Little Shamus," CBS, 1979; "Star of the Family," ABC, 1982.

AND: "M*A*S*H: Souvenirs," CBS, 1977; "Lou Grant: Nazi," CBS, 1977; "Cagney & Lacey: Bounty Hunter," CBS, 1984; "Hunter: Pilot," NBC, 1984.

TV MOVIES AND MINISERIES: "Pearl," ABC, 1978; "A Real American Hero," CBS, 1978; "Silent Victory: The Kitty O'Neil Story," CBS, 1979; "The Jericho Mile," ABC, 1979; "Dummy," CBS, 1979; "The Seduction of Miss Leona," CBS, 1980; "Fly Away Home," ABC, 1981; "Skokie," CBS, 1981; "I Take These Men," CBS, 1983; "Acceptable Risks," ABC, 1986; "AT&T Presents: Day One," CBS, 1989; "Perfect Witness," HBO, 1989.

DENNING, RICHARD

b. Louis Denninger, Poughkeepsie, NY, 1914. Lantern-jawed actor who played the governor on "Hawaii Five-O."

AS A REGULAR: "Mr. and Mrs. North," CBS, 1952-53; NBC, 1954; "Flying Doctor," SYN, 1958; "Michael Shayne," NBC, 1960-61; "Karen," NBC, 1964-65; "Hawaii Five-O," CBS, 1968-80.

AND: "Cavalcade of America: The Man Who Took a Chance," NBC, 1952; "Ford Theatre: The Doctor's Downfall," NBC, 1953; "Schlitz Playhouse of Stars: Tapu," CBS, 1954; "Pitfall: The Hot Welcome," SYN, 1954; "Ford Theatre: The Legal Beagles," NBC, 1954; "Ford Theatre: All That Glitters," NBC, 1955; "Crossroads: Chinese Checkers," ABC, 1955; "Ford Theatre: Bachelor Husband," NBC, 1955; "Ford Theatre: Double Trouble," NBC, 1956; "Ford Theatre: On the Beach," ABC, 1956; "Cheyenne: The Spanish Grant," ABC, 1956; "Lux Video Theatre: The Undesirable," NBC, 1957; "Ford Theatre: The Idea Man," ABC, 1957; "G.E. Theatre: Eyes of a Stranger," CBS, 1957; "G.E. Theatre: Letters From Cairo," CBS, 1958; "Studio One: The Laughing Willow," CBS, 1958; "Destiny: Eyes of a Stranger," CBS, 1958; "Here's Hollywood," NBC, 1960; "Going My Way: Don't Forget to Say Goodbye," ABC, 1963; "Alice Through the Looking Glass," NBC, 1966; "McCloud: Cowboy in Paradise," NBC, 1974.

DENNIS, MATT

b. Seattle, WA, February 11, 1914. Pianist-composer.

AS A REGULAR: "The Matt Dennis Show," NBC, 1955; "The Ernie Kovacs Show," NBC, 1955-56.

AND: "The Ray Anthony Show," ABC, 1957; "The Rosemary Clooney Show," SYN, 1957; "The Big Record," CBS, 1958; "Patti Page Olds Show," ABC, 1959; "The Chevy Show," NBC, 1959; "The Big Party," CBS, 1959; "Johnny Ringo: Border Town," CBS, 1960.

DENNIS, SANDY

b. Hastings, NB, April 27, 1937.

AS A REGULAR: "The Guiding Light," CBS, 1956.

AND: "Music for New Year's Night: Class of '61," ABC, 1961; "Naked City: Idylls of a Running Back," ABC, 1962; "Naked City: Carrier," ABC, 1963; "The Fugitive: The Other Side of the Mountain," ABC, 1963; "Arrest and Trial: Somewhat Lower than Angels," ABC, 1964; "Mr. Broadway: Don't Mention My Name in Sheboygan," CBS, 1964; "A Hatful of Rain," ABC, 1968; "Alfred Hitchcock Presents: Arthur," NBC, 1985; "The Love Boat: Out of the Blue," ABC, 1985; "The Equalizer: Out of the Past," CBS, 1986.

TV MOVIES AND MINISERIES: "The Man Who Wanted to Live Forever," ABC, 1970; "Something Evil," CBS, 1972; "The Execution," NBC, 1985.

DENNISON, RACHEL

b. Knoxville, TN, August 31, 1959. Sister of Dolly Parton; she played the role Parton played in the film "9 to 5" on the TV series.

AS A REGULAR: "9 to 5," ABC, 1982-83; SYN, 1986-88.

DENVER, BOB

b. New Rochelle, NY, January 9, 1935. Gilligan, of island fame.

AS A REGULAR: "The Many Loves of Dobie Gillis," CBS, 1959-63; "Gilligan's Island," CBS, 1964-67; "The Good Guys," CBS, 1968-70; "Dusty's Trail," SYN, 1973; "The New Adventures of Gilligan," ABC, 1974-76; "Far Out Space Nuts," CBS, 1975-76.

AND: "Perry Como's Kraft Music Hall," NBC, 1960; "Coke Time," ABC, 1960; "Dr. Kildare: If You Can't Believe the Truth," NBC, 1963; "The Farmer's Daughter: An Enterprising Young Man," ABC, 1963; "The Andy Griffith Show: Divorce, Mountain Style," CBS, 1964; "Art Linkletter's House Party," CBS, 1964; "Password," CBS, 1965; "Password," CBS, 1966; "I Dream of Jeannie: My Son, the Genie," NBC, 1967; "PDQ," NBC, 1967; "Love, American Style: Love and the Cake," ABC, 1970; "Love, American Style: Love and the Hitchhiker," ABC, 1971; "Whatever Happened to Dobie Gillis?," CBS, 1977; "The Love Boat: Reunion Cruise," ABC, 1979; "Fantasy Island: Eagleman," ABC, 1980; "The Love Boat: A Dress to Remember," ABC, 1981; "Fantasy Island: House of Dolls,"

ABC, 1982; "Win, Lose or Draw," SYN, 1988; "Hollywood Squares," SYN, 1988; "The Pat Sajak Show," CBS, 1989.

TV MOVIES AND MINISERIES: "Rescue From Gilligan's Island," NBC, 1978; "The Castaways on Gilligan's Island," NBC, 1979; "The Harlem Globetrotters on Gilligan's Island," NBC, 1981; "The Invisible Woman," NBC, 1983; "High School USA," NBC, 1983; "Bring Me the Head of Dobie Gillis," CBS, 1988.

DENVER, JOHN

b. Henry John Deutschendorf, Jr., Roswell, NM, December 31, 1943. Singer of wholesome pop ballads who was big in the seventies.

AS A GUEST: "Owen Marshall, Counselor at Law: The Camerons Are a Special Clan," ABC, 1973; "John Denver Special," ABC, 1974; "McCloud: The Colorado Cattle Caper," NBC, 1974; "An Evening with John Denver," ABC, 1975; "Doris Day Today," CBS, 1975; "Van Dyke and Company," NBC, 1976; "John Denver and the Ladies," ABC, 1979; "Donahue," SYN, 1980; "The John Davidson Show," SYN, 1980; "Julie Andrews: The Sound of Christmas," ABC, 1987.

TV MOVIES AND MINISERIES: "The Christmas Gift," CBS, 1986; "Hallmark Hall of Fame: Foxfire," CBS, 1987.

DEPP, JOHNNY

Glowering teen actor; he played police officer Tom Hanson on "21 Jump Street."

AS A REGULAR: "21 Jump Street," FOX, 1987-90.

AND: "Lady Blue: The Hunter," ABC, 1985.

DER, RICKY

b. 1953. Child actor.

AS A REGULAR: "Kentucky Jones," NBC, 1964-65.

DEREK, JOHN

b. Derek Harris, Hollywood, August 12, 1926. Former juvenile actor who's turned his energies toward marrying beautiful women.

AS A REGULAR: "Frontier Circus," CBS, 1961-62.

AND: "Ford Theatre: Tomorrow's Men," NBC, 1953; "Ford Theatre: Black Jim Hawk," ABC, 1956; "Playhouse 90: Massacre at Sand Creek," CBS, 1956; "Dick Powell's Zane Grey Theatre: There Were Four," CBS, 1957; "Dick Powell's Zane Grey Theatre: Storm Over Eden," CBS, 1961.

DERN, BRUCE

b. Chicago, IL, June 4, 1936. Actor typecast for years as psychotics, but who can also handle comedy and straight drama.

AS A REGULAR: "Stoney Burke," ABC, 1962-63.

AND: "Naked City: Bullets Cost Too Much," ABC, 1961; "SurfSide 6: Daphne, Girl Detective," ABC, 1961; "Ben Casey: A Dark Night for Billy Harris," ABC, 1961; "Robert Taylor's Detectives: Act of God," NBC, 1961; "The Law and Mr. Jones: Poor Eddie's Dead," ABC, 1962; "The Fugitive: The Other Side of the Mountain," ABC, 1963; "The Dick Powell Show: The Old Man and the City," NBC, 1963; "The Virginian: First to Thine Own Self," NBC, 1964; "The Virginian: The Payment," NBC, 1964; "The Virginian: The Payment," NBC, 1964; "Twelve O'Clock High: The Lorelei," ABC, 1965; "The Fugitive: Corner of Hell," ABC, 1965; "The FBI: Pound of Flesh," ABC, 1965; "Twelve O'Clock High: The Mission," ABC, 1965; "Wagon Train: The Chief Crazy Bear Story," ABC, 1965; "Rawhide: Walk Into Terror," CBS, 1965; "The Virginian: A Little Learning," NBC, 1965; "Laredo: Rendezvous at Arillo," NBC, 1965; "Shenandoah: The Verdict," ABC, 1965; "Twelve O'Clock High: The Jones Boy," ABC, 1965; "The Fugitive: The Good Guys and the Bad Guys," ABC, 1965; "The Big Valley: Under a Dark Star," ABC, 1966; "The Loner; To Hang a Dead Man," CBS, 1966; "The Big Valley: By Force of Violence," ABC, 1966; "The Big Valley: The Lost Treasure," ABC, 1966; "The Big Valley: Fallen Hawk," ABC, 1966; "Gunsmoke: The Jailer," CBS, 1966; "Walt Disney's Wonderful World of Color: Gallagher Goes West," NBC, 1966; "Run for Your Life: The Treasure Seekers," NBC, 1966; "The Fugitive: The Devil's Disciples," ABC, 1966; "The Big Valley: Four Days to Furnace Hill," ABC, 1967; "The Big Valley: The Prize," ABC, 1968; "The FBI: The Nightmare," ABC, 1968; "Gunsmoke: The Long Night," CBS, 1969; "Then Came Bronson: Amid Splinters of the Thunderbolt," NBC, 1969; "Land of the Giants: Wild Journey," ABC, 1970; "Bonanza: The Gold Mine," NBC, 1970; "The High Chapparal: Only the Bad Come to Sonora," NBC, 1970; "Saturday Night Live," NBC, 1982; "Saturday Night Live," NBC, 1983.

TV MOVIES AND MINISERIES: "Sam Hill: Who Killed the Mysterious Mr. Foster?," NBC, 1971; "ABC Theatre: Tough Love," ABC, 1985; "Space," CBS, 1985; "Roses Are for the Rich," CBS, 1987; "Trenchcoat in Paradise," CBS, 1989.

DESIDERIO, ROBERT

b. Bronx, NY, 1951.

AS A REGULAR: "Search for Tomorrow," CBS, 1979-80; "One Life to Live," ABC, 1981-82; "Ryan's Hope," ABC, 1982; "Heart of the City," ABC, 1986-87.

AND: "Hardcastle and McCormick: Goin' Nowhere Fast," ABC, 1983; "Scarecrow and Mrs. King: The Mole," CBS, 1984; "Hotel: Illusions," ABC, 1984; "The A-Team: The Bells of St.

Mary's," NBC, 1984; "Remington Steele: Springtime for Steele," NBC, 1985; "The Fall Guy: A Fistful of Lire," ABC, 1985; "MacGruder and Loud: Stepover Man," ABC, 1985; "Hardcastle and McCormick: Angie's Choice," ABC, 1985; "Family Ties: Just One Look," NBC, 1985; "Murder, She Wrote: Doom with a View," CBS, 1987; "Cheers: Bar Wars," NBC, 1988; "Island Son: Painkillers," CBS, 1989.

TV MOVIES AND MINISERIES: "The Princess and the Cabbie," CBS, 1981; "Moonlight," CBS, 1982; "Baby Girl Scott," CBS, 1987; "Original Sin," NBC, 1989.

DESMOND, JOHN

b. Detroit, MI, 1920; d. 1985. Singer.

AS A REGULAR: "Face the Music," CBS, 1948; "Tin Pan Alley TV," ABC, 1950; "Don McNeill TV Club," ABC, 1950-51; "The Jack Paar Show," CBS, 1953-56; CBS, 1954; "Sally," NBC, 1958; "Your Hit Parade," CBS, 1958-59; "Music on Ice," NBC, 1960; "Glenn Miller Time," CBS, 1961; "Blansky's Beauties," ABC, 1977.

AND: "Danger: Sing for Your Life," CBS, 1953; "Philco TV Playhouse: Hearts and Flowers," NBC, 1955; "Robert Montgomery Presents: Don't Do Me Any Favors," NBC, 1955; "Philco TV Playhouse: The Miss America Story," NBC, 1955; "Alcoa Hour: The Stingiest Man in Town," NBC, 1956; "Climax!: Let It Be Me," CBS, 1957; "The Ray Anthony Show," ABC, 1957; "Art Linkletter's House Party," CBS, 1957; "The Nat King Cole Show," NBC, 1957; "Climax!: Keep Me in Mind," CBS, 1957; "The Jack Paar Show," NBC, 1958; "The Bob Crosby Show," NBC, 1958; "The Jimmy Dean Show," CBS, 1958; "The Garry Moore Show," CBS, 1959; "Westinghouse Desilu Playhouse: A Diamond for Carla," CBS, 1959; "Bell Telephone Hour: On Stage with Music," NBC, 1959; "Steve Allen Plymouth Show," NBC, 1960; "The Dick Clark Saturday Night Beechnut Show," ABC, 1960; "Bell Telephone Hour: The Music of Romance," NBC, 1960; "Bell Telephone Hour: The Songs of Irving Berlin," NBC, 1962; "U.S. Steel Hour: Dry Rain," CBS, 1962; "The Mike Douglas Show," SYN, 1964; "The Young Set," ABC, 1965; "Over Easy," PBS, 1980.

AS DIRECTOR: "U.S. Steel Hour: Wish on the Moon," CBS, 1959; "Accent: Ethan Allen and the Green Mountain Boys," CBS, 1962.

DEUEL, PETER

b. Rochester, NY, 1940; d. 1971. Actor in sixties TV; he played Hannibal Heyes on "Alias Smith and Jones."

AS A REGULAR: "Gidget," ABC, 1965-66; "Love on a Rooftop," ABC, 1966-67; "Alias Smith and Jones," ABC, 1971-72.

AND: "Combat!: Vendetta," ABC, 1964; "Twelve O'Clock High: The Hours Before Dawn," NBC, 1964; "The Mickey Rooney Show: Crazy Hips McNish," ABC, 1964; "The Fugitive: Fun and Games and Party Favors," ABC, 1965; "The FBI: Slow March Up a Steep Hill," ABC, 1965; "The FBI: False Witness," ABC, 1967; "The Virginian: The Good-Hearted Badman," NBC, 1968; "The Name of the Game: The White Birch," NBC, 1968; "The Virginian: The Price of Love," NBC, 1969; "The Interns: The Price of Life," CBS, 1970; "The Young Lawyers: The Glass Prison," ABC, 1970; "The Bold Ones: Trial of a PFC," NBC, 1970; "Marcus Welby, M.D.: A Passing of Torches," ABC, 1970; "The Name of the Game: The Savage Eye," NBC, 1971; "Hollywood Television Theatre: The Scarecrow," NET, 1972.

TV MOVIES AND MINISERIES: "Marcus Welby, M.D.," ABC, 1969; "Only One Day Left Before Tomorrow," NBC, 1969; "The Young Country," ABC, 1970; "The Psychiatrist: God Bless the Children," NBC, 1970; "Alias Smith and Jones," ABC, 1971; "How to Steal an Airplane," NBC, 1971.

* Deuel died of a gunshot wound in his Hollywood apartment on December 30, 1971. Police said the gun Deuel used had also been used to shoot a framed telegram telling Deuel that he hadn't been elected to the board of directors of the Screen Actors Guild.

DEUTSCH, PATTI

b. Pittsburgh, PA. Comic actress.

AS A REGULAR: "The John Byner Comedy Hour," CBS, 1972; "Rowan & Martin's Laugh-In," NBC, 1972-73.

AND: "The Merv Griffin Show," SYN, 1968; "The Girl with Something Extra: It's So Peaceful in the Country," NBC, 1973; "Match Game '73," CBS, 1973; "Celebrity Sweepstakes," NBC, 1974; "Tattletales," CBS, 1974; "Match Game '75," CBS, 1975; "Cross Wits," SYN, 1976.

DEVANE, WILLIAM

b. Albany, NY, September 5, 1939. Actor whose big TV break came as John F. Kennedy in "The Missiles of October"; he now plays one of television's better bad guys, Greg Sumner on "Knots Landing."

AS A REGULAR: "Where the Heart Is," CBS, 1969-73; "From Here to Eternity," NBC, 1979-80; "Knots Landing," CBS, 1983- .

AND: "On Stage: This Town Will Never Be the Same Again," NBC, 1969; "Medical Center: Ghetto Clinic," CBS, 1970; "You Are There: Galileo," CBS, 1972; "Medical Center: The Gladiator," CBS, 1972; "Ironside: Riddle Me Death," NBC, 1972; "Gunsmoke: Kimbrough," CBS, 1973; "Ironside: Downhill All the Way," NBC, 1973; "Medical Center: Nightmare," CBS, 1973; "Mannix: The Dark Hours," CBS, 1974; "Hawaii Five-O: Killer at Sea," CBS, 1974; "The

Snoop Sisters: A Black Day for Bluebeard," NBC, 1974; "ABC Theatre: Judgment: The Court Martial of the Tiger of Malaya–General Yamashita," ABC, 1974; "ABC Theatre: The Missles of October," ABC, 1974.

TV MOVIES AND MINISERIES: "Crime Club," CBS, 1973; "The Bait," ABC, 1973; "Shirts/Skins," ABC, 1973; "Fear on Trial," CBS, 1975; "Black Beauty," NBC, 1978; "From Here to Eternity," NBC, 1979; "Red Flag: The Ultimate Game," CBS, 1981; "The Other Victim," CBS, 1981; "Jane Doe," CBS, 1983; "With Intent to Kill," CBS, 1984; "The Preppie Murder," ABC, 1989.

DEVINE, ANDY

b. Jeremiah Schwartz, Flagstaff, AZ, October 7, 1905; d. 1977. Western actor and kid-show host whose trademark was a raspy voice, the result of having a stick rammed down his throat in a fall as a child.

AS A REGULAR: "The Adventures of Wild Bill Hickok," SYN, 1951-58; "Andy's Gang," NBC, 1955-60; "Flipper," NBC, 1964-65.

AND: "The Ford Show," NBC, 1957; "Shower of Stars: Jack Benny's 40th Birthday Celebration," CBS, 1958; "The Lux Show with Rosemary Clooney," NBC, 1958; "The Ford Show," NBC, 1958; "The Garry Moore Show," CBS, 1958; "The Ford Show," NBC, 1959; "Wagon Train: The Jess MacAbbee Story," NBC, 1959; "The Ford Show," NBC, 1960; "The Ford Show," NBC, 1961; "The Barbara Stanwyck Show: Big Jake," NBC, 1961; "G.E. Theatre: Ten Days in the Sun," CBS, 1962; "The Twilight Zone: Hocus Pocus and Frisby," CBS, 1962; "Burke's Law: Who Killed Victor Barrows?," ABC, 1964; "What's This Song?," NBC, 1964; "My Three Sons: The Sure Thing," ABC, 1965; "The Virginian: Yesterday's Timepiece," NBC, 1967; "Bonanza: A Girl Named George," NBC, 1968; "Walt Disney's Wonderful World of Color: Ride a Northbound Horse," NBC, 1969; "Gunsmoke: Stryker," CBS, 1969; "Love, American Style: Love and the Mountain Cabin," ABC, 1969; "Life with Linkletter," NBC, 1970; "Walt Disney's Wonderful World of Color: Smoke," NBC, 1970; "The Men From Shiloh: The Animal," NBC, 1971; "Alias Smith and Jones: The Men That Corrupted Hadleyburg," ABC, 1972.

TV MOVIES AND MINISERIES: "The Over-the-Hill Gang," ABC, 1969; "The Over-the-Hill Gang Rides Again," ABC, 1970.

DEVITO, DANNY

b. Daniel Michael DeVito, Neptune, NJ, November 17, 1944. Pint-sized actor-director who played Louie on "Taxi" and now helms big-screen flicks ("The War of the Roses").

AS A REGULAR: "Taxi," ABC, 1978-82, NBC, 1982-83.

AND: "Police Woman: Death Game," NBC, 1977; "Saturday Night Live," NBC, 1982; "Saturday Night Live," NBC, 1983; "Amazing Stories: The Wedding Ring," NBC, 1986; "Saturday Night Live," NBC, 1987; "The Tonight Show Starring Johnny Carson," NBC, 1987; "Wonderworks: Two Daddies?," PBS, 1989; "Friday Night Videos," NBC, 1989.

TV MOVIES AND MINISERIES: "Valentine," ABC, 1979.

AS DIRECTOR: "Taxi: Elaine and the Monk," NBC, 1982; "Taxi: Sugar Ray Nardo," NBC, 1983; "Taxi: Jim's Mario's," NBC, 1983; "Mary," CBS, 1985.

* Emmies: 1981.

DE VOL, FRANK

b. Moundsville, WV, September 20, 1911. Composer and comic actor; he played Happy Kyne, leader of the Mirthmakers, on "Fernwood 2-Night" and wrote the "My Three Sons" theme song.

AS A REGULAR: "I'm Dickens, He's Fenster," ABC, 1962-63; "Fernwood 2-Night," SYN, 1977-78.

AND: "The Betty White Show," ABC, 1958; "The Jack Paar Show," NBC, 1959; "Grindl: Grindl's Day Off," NBC, 1964; "My Favorite Martian: The Disastro-Nauts," CBS, 1964; "Get Smart: The Diplomat's Daughter," NBC, 1965; "Get Smart: I'm Only Human," NBC, 1966; "Gidget: A Hard Night's Night," ABC, 1966; "I Dream of Jeannie: My Master the Great Caruso," NBC, 1966; "Please Don't Eat the Daisies: Trouble Right Here in Ridgemont City," NBC, 1966; "Petticoat Junction: That Was the Night That Was," CBS, 1967; "That Girl: 7 1/4," ABC, 1968; "Petticoat Junction: The Christening," CBS, 1969; "I Dream of Jeannie: Guess Who's Going to Be a Bride," NBC, 1969; "One Day at a Time: Wicked Ann," CBS, 1981.

AS ORCHESTRA LEADER: "Kollege of Musical Knowledge," NBC, 1954; "Dinah Shore Special," NBC, 1961.

DEWHURST, COLEEN

b. Montreal, Canada, June 3, 1926. Gifted actress who often plays strong women; currently she shows up on "Murphy Brown" now and then as Murphy's mother, Avery. She won an Emmy for that role and for "Between Two Women."

AS A REGULAR: "Avonlea," DIS, 1990- .

AND: "Du Pont Show of the Month: The Count of Monte Cristo," CBS, 1958; "U.S. Steel Hour: The Hours Before Dawn," CBS, 1959; "How Long the Night," SYN, 1959; "Du Pont Show of the Month: I, Don Quixote," CBS, 1959; "Startime: Talent Scouts," NBC, 1960; "Play of the Week: Burning Bright," SYN, 1960; "Ben Casey: I Remember a Lemon Tree," ABC, 1961; "The Virginian: The Executioners," NBC, 1962;

261

"Focus," NBC, 1962; "The Nurses: The Fly Shadow," CBS, 1962; "The Eleventh Hour: I Don't Belong in a White-Painted House," NBC, 1962; "U.S. Steel Hour: Night Run to the West," CBS, 1963; "The du Pont Show: Something to Hide," NBC, 1963; "East Side/West Side: Nothing But the Half-Truth," CBS, 1963; "Dr. Kildare: All Brides Should Be Beautiful," NBC, 1965; "The Virginian: The Executioners," NBC, 1965; "The Alfred Hitchcock Hour: Night Fever," NBC, 1965; "The FBI: The Babysitter," ABC, 1966; "Play of the Week: Burning Bright," NET, 1966; "The FBI: The Baby Sitter," ABC, 1966; "The Big Valley: A Day of Terror," ABC, 1966; "The Big Valley: Day of Terror," ABC, 1966; "The Crucible," CBS, 1967; "NET Playhouse: My Mother's House," NET, 1967; "Hallmark Hall of Fame: The Price," NBC, 1971; "You Are There: The Trial of Susan B. Anthony," CBS, 1972; "Hallmark Hall of Fame: The Hands of Cormac," NBC, 1972; "Portait: Legend in Granite," ABC, 1973; "Three Women Alone," PBS, 1974; "ABC Theatre: A Moon for the Misbegotten," ABC, 1975; "The Love Boat: The Death and Life of Sir Albert Demarest," ABC, 1984; "Moonlighting: Take My Wife, for Instance," ABC, 1989; "Murphy Brown: Mama Said," CBS, 1989; "Murphy Brown: Brown Like Me," CBS, 1989.

TV MOVIES AND MINISERIES: "A Prowler in the Heat," ABC, 1973; "The Story of Jacob and Joseph," ABC, 1974; "Studs Lonigan," NBC, 1979; "Silent Victory: The Kitty O'Neil Story," CBS, 1979; "Mary and Joseph: A Story of Faith," NBC, 1979; "And Baby Makes Six," NBC, 1979; "A Perfect Match," CBS, 1980; "Baby Comes Home," CBS, 1980; "A.D.," NBC, 1985; "Between Two Women," ABC, 1986; "Johnny Bull," ABC, 1986; "Those She Left Behind," NBC, 1989.

* Emmies: 1986, 1989.

DE WILDE, BRANDON

b. Brooklyn, NY, April 9, 1942; d. 1972.
AS A REGULAR: "Jamie," ABC, 1953-54.
AND: "Philco TV Playhouse: No Medals on Pop," NBC, 1951; "Philco TV Playhouse: A Cowboy for Chris," NBC, 1952; "Plymouth Playhouse: Jamie," ABC, 1953; "Light's Diamond Jubilee: The Leader of the People," ABC, CBS, NBC, 1954; "Climax!: The Day They Gave Babies Away," CBS, 1955; "Climax!: An Episode of Sparrows," CBS, 1956; "Star Stage: Bend to the Wind," NBC, 1956; "Screen Directors Playhouse: Partners," ABC, 1956; "The Standard Oil 75th Anniversary Show," NBC, 1957; "U.S. Steel Hour: The Locked Door," CBS, 1957; "Alcoa Theatre: Man of His House," NBC, 1959; "Arthur Murray Party," NBC, 1959; "Wagon Train: The Danny Benedict Story," NBC, 1959; "Alfred Hitchcock Presents: The Sorcerer's Apprentice," CBS, 1960; "CBS Television Workshop: My

Theory About Girls," CBS, 1960; "Thriller: Pigeons From Hell," NBC, 1961; "Wagon Train: The Mark Minor Story," NBC, 1961; "The Virginian: 50 Days to Moose Jaw," NBC, 1962; "The Nurses: Ordeal," CBS, 1963; "The Greatest Show on Earth: Love the Giver," ABC, 1964; "Walt Disney's Wonderful World of Color: The Tenderfoot," NBC, 1964; "Twelve O'Clock High: Here's to Courageous Cowards," ABC, 1964; "The Defenders: The Objector," CBS, 1965; "The Young Set," ABC, 1965; "Combat!: A Sudden Terror," ABC, 1966; "ABC Stage '67: The Confession," ABC, 1966; "The Virginian: The Orchard," NBC, 1968; "Journey to the Unknown: One on a Desert Island," ABC, 1968; "The Name of the Game: The Bobby Currier Story," NBC, 1969; "Hawaii Five-O: The King Kamehameha Blues," CBS, 1969; "Love, American Style: Love and the Bachelor," ABC, 1969; "The Young Rebels: To Hang a Hero," ABC, 1970; "Night Gallery: The Class of '99," NBC, 1971; "Ironside: In the Line of Duty," NBC, 1971.

* De Wilde died in a traffic accident.

DE WITT, GEORGE

b. Atlantic City, NJ, 1923; d. 1979.
AS A REGULAR: "Seven at Eleven," NBC, 1951; "All in One," CBS, 1952-53; "Name That Tune," CBS, 1955-59; "Be Our Guest," CBS, 1960.
AND: "The Perry Como Show," NBC, 1956; "The Ed Sullivan Show," CBS, 1957; "The Julius LaRosa Show," NBC, 1957; "Masquerade Party," NBC, 1957; "The Vic Damone Show," CBS, 1957; "The Gisele MacKenzie Show," NBC, 1957; "The Gisele MacKenzie Show," NBC, 1958; "The Bob Crosby Show," NBC, 1958; "Arthur Murray Party," NBC, 1959; "Arthur Murray Party," NBC, 1960; "Hawaiian Eye: The Sign-Off," ABC, 1962.

DE WITT, JOYCE

b. Wheeling, WV, April 23, 1949. Actress who played Janet Wood, the nice (as opposed to the sexy) roommate of Jack Tripper (John Ritter) on "Three's Company." She seemed worried about heading into obscurity after "Three's Company" went off the air, and seems to have hit the nail on the head.
AS A REGULAR: "Three's Company," ABC, 1977-84.
AND: "Hollywood Squares," SYN, 1978; "The Love Boat: The Scoop," ABC, 1979; "The Osmond Family," ABC, 1979.

DE WOLFE, BILLY

b. William Andrew Jones, Wollaston, MA, February 18, 1907; d. 1974. Comic character actor with a fussy manner and clipped voice.
AS A REGULAR: "The Imogene Coca Show," NBC,

1954-55; "That Girl," ABC, 1966; "The Pruitts of Southhampton," ABC, 1967; "Good Morning, World," CBS, 1967-68; "The Queen and I," CBS, 1969; "The Doris Day Show," CBS, 1970-72.
AND: "The Ed Sullivan Show," CBS, 1957; "Arthur Murray Party," NBC, 1957; "The Betty White Show," ABC, 1958; "The Jack Paar Show," NBC, 1958; "This Is Your Life (Hermione Gingold)," NBC, 1960; "Here's Hollywood," NBC, 1961; "Burke's Law: Who Killed the Fat Cat?," ABC, 1965; "Bob Hope Chrysler Theatre: Cops and Robbers," NBC, 1965; "The Dick Van Dyke Show: The Ugliest Dog in the World," CBS, 1965; "Rango: Requiem for a Ranger," ABC, 1967; "Arsenic and Old Lace," ABC, 1969; "The Tonight Show Starring Johnny Carson," NBC, 1970; "The Mike Douglas Show," SYN, 1971; "Frosty the Snowman," CBS, 1971; "Love, American Style: Love and the Fractured Fibula," ABC, 1974; "Free to Be You and Me," ABC, 1974.

DEY, SUSAN
b. *Pekin, IL, December 10, 1952.* Actress who made many an adolescent boy's heart pump as Laurie Partridge; now she has much the same effect on those some boys as Grace Van Owen on "L.A. Law."
AS A REGULAR: "The Partridge Family," ABC, 1970-74; "Loves Me, Loves Me Not," CBS, 1977; "Emerald Point NAS," CBS, 1983-84; "L.A. Law," NBC, 1986- .
AND: "This Is Your Life (Shirley Jones)," SYN, 1971; "Circle of Fear: Doorway to Death," NBC, 1973; "Celebrity Sweepstakes," NBC, 1974; "Born Free: A Matter of Survival," NBC, 1974; "The Rookies: Angel," ABC, 1975; "SWAT: Deadly Tide," ABC, 1975; "The Quest: The Captive," NBC, 1976; "The Streets of San Francisco: The Thrill Killers," ABC, 1976; "Barnaby Jones: Testament of Power," CBS, 1977; "Late Night with David Letterman," NBC, 1988; "A Place at the Table," NBC, 1988.
TV MOVIES AND MINISERIES: "Terror on the Beach," CBS, 1973; "Cage Without a Key," ABC, 1975; "Mary Jane Harper Cried Last Night," CBS, 1977; "Little Women," NBC, 1978; "Malibu," ABC, 1983; "Sunset Limousine," CBS, 1983; "Angel in Green," CBS, 1987; "I Love You Perfect," ABC, 1989.

DE YOUNG, CLIFF
b. *Inglewood, CA, February 12, 1945.*
AS A REGULAR: "Sunshine," NBC, 1975.
AND: "Sticks and Bones," CBS, 1973; "Marcus Welby, M.D.: Last Flight to Babylon," ABC, 1974; "The Twilight Zone: The Road Less Traveled," CBS, 1986; "Murder, She Wrote: Murder Through the Looking Glass," CBS, 1988; "Murder, She Wrote: Coal Miner's Slaughter," CBS, 1988.
TV MOVIES AND MINISERIES: "Sunshine," NBC,

1973; "The Night That America Panicked," ABC, 1975; "The Lindbergh Kidnapping Case," NBC, 1976; "Best Sellers: Captains and the Kings," NBC, 1976;, "King," NBC, 1978; "Centennial," NBC, 1978-79; "The Seeding of Sarah Burns," CBS, 1979; "Fun and Games," ABC, 1980; "This Girl for Hire," CBS, 1983; "Master of the Game," CBS, 1984; "Deadly Intentions," ABC, 1985; "Her Secret Life," ABC, 1987; "Dance 'Til Dawn," NBC, 1988.

DHEIGH, KHIGH
b. *New Jersey, 1910.* Asian actor who played Wo Fat, arch-enemy of Steve McGarrett (Jack Lord) on "Hawaii Five-O."
AS A REGULAR: "Hawaii Five-O," CBS, 1968-80; "Khan!," CBS, 1975.
AND: "The Wild Wild West: The Night of the Samauri," CBS, 1967; "The Wild Wild West: The Night of the Pelican," CBS, 1968; "Ironside: Love My Enemy," NBC, 1969; "Mission: Impossible: Butterfly," CBS, 1970; "Kung Fu: Spirit Helper," ABC, 1973; "The FBI: The Two Million Dollar Hit," ABC, 1974; "Kung Fu: Ordeal by Love," ABC, 1974.
TV MOVIES AND MINISERIES: "Hawaii Five-O," CBS, 1968; "Judge Dee in the Monastery Murders," ABC, 1974; "James Clavell's Noble House," NBC, 1988.

DIAMOND, BOBBY
b. *Los Angeles, CA, August 23, 1943.* Former child actor who played Joey, young master of "Fury."
AS A REGULAR: "Fury," NBC, 1955-60; "Westinghouse Playhouse Starring Nanette Fabray and Wendell Corey (Yes, Yes Nanette)," NBC, 1961; "The Many Loves of Dobie Gillis," CBS, 1962-63.
AND: "Wagon Train: The Dick Jarvis Story," NBC, 1960; "Pete and Gladys: Continental Dinner," CBS, 1961; "The Twilight Zone: In Praise of Pip," CBS, 1963; "Mr. Novak: The Private Life of Douglas Morgan, Jr.," NBC, 1964; "Mr. Novak: Visons of Sugar Plums," NBC, 1964; "The Patty Duke Show: The Greatest Speaker in the Whole Wide World," ABC, 1966; "The Patty Duke Show: Too Young and Foolish to Go Steady," ABC, 1966; "The Bill Cosby Show: Really Cool," NBC, 1970.

DIAMOND, DON
b. *Brooklyn, NY.* Actor usually in westerns; he played Hekawi Indian Crazy Cat on "F Troop."
AS A REGULAR: "The Adventures of Kit Carson," SYN, 1951-55; "Zorro," ABC, 1957-59; "F Troop," ABC, 1965-67.
AND: "The Life and Legend of Wyatt Earp: Wyatt Earp Meets Doc Holliday," ABC, 1957; "Redigo: The Hunters," NBC, 1963; "The Dick Van Dyke

Show: Remember the Alimony," CBS, 1966; "That Girl: I'll Be Suing You," ABC, 1966; "The Big Valley: Tunnel of Gold," ABC, 1966; "The Flying Nun: Flight of the Dodo Bird," ABC, 1967; "The Guns of Will Sonnett: A Grave for Jim Sonnett," ABC, 1967; "The Flying Nun: The Crooked Convent," ABC, 1968; "Gomer Pyle, USMC: Marriage, Sgt. Carter-Style," CBS, 1969; "Get Smart: The Treasure of C. Errol Madre," CBS, 1969; "Love, American Style: Love and the Optimist," ABC, 1970; "Here's Lucy: Lucy and Viv Visit Tijuana," CBS, 1970; "Columbo: Candidate for Crime," NBC, 1973; "The Odd Couple: Felix the Horse Player," ABC, 1975; "Chico and the Man: Charo and the Matador," NBC, 1979; "Lou Grant: Expose'," CBS, 1979; "The White Shadow: A Christmas Present," CBS, 1979; "WKRP in Cincinnati: Jennifer's Home for Christmas," CBS, 1979; "WKRP in Cincinnati: Bah, Humbug," CBS, 1980; "Hill Street Blues: Here's Adventure, Here's Romance," NBC, 1983.

DIAMOND, SELMA

b. Canada, August 5, 1920; d. 1985. Gravel-voiced comic writer and actress, the real-life role model for Sally Rogers (Rose Marie) on "The Dick Van Dyke Show"; best known as Selma on "Night Court."

AS A REGULAR: "Night Court," NBC, 1984-85.
AND: "The Jack Paar Show," NBC, 1961; "Jackie Gleason and His American Scene Magazine," CBS, 1963; "Get the Message," ABC, 1964; "The Match Game," NBC, 1966; "Personality," NBC, 1969; "The Merv Griffin Show," CBS, 1969; "The Steve Allen Show," SYN, 1970; "Too Close for Comfort: Break Out the Pampers," ABC, 1982.
TV MOVIES AND MINISERIES: "Magic Carpet," NBC, 1972; "The Other Woman," CBS, 1983.
AS WRITER: "The Perry Como Show," NBC, 1955-59; "The Big Party," CBS, 1959; "Perry Como's Kraft Music Hall," NBC, 1960-63; "Aqua Varieties," ABC, 1965.

THE DICK VAN DYKE SHOW,

CBS, 1961-66.

This landmark sitcom was one of the first to examine a character's home and work life. It's just as notable for what it didn't have: No nagging wife, no imbecilic husband, no mother-in-law, no overly cute kids (if anything, Richie Petrie got a little uglier as he got older).

The people on "The Dick Van Dyke Show" acted like real people—witty, but real. Rob and Laura Petrie embodied the spirit of the early sixties in that they were young, attractive and successful. And they did what all young, attractive successful people did in those days: They moved to suburbia.

"The Dick Van Dyke Show" did have slapstick, make no mistake. But unlike almost any other sitcom, it combined pratfalls with sharp funny dialogue. And the gifted Dick Van Dyke delivered them both with ease. As his wife, Mary Tyler Moore learned comic skills that put her above just about any other actress working in a sixties sitcom—or a seventies sitcom, for that matter.

"The Dick Van Dyke Show" went out on top—Van Dyke and Moore wanted to try movies, but supporting players Rose Marie (Sally Rogers) and Morey Amsterdam (Buddy Sorrell) would've been happy if the show had run another five years. In the long run, the show's short run was best. It makes the memory of it all the more vivid: The first sitcom to deal with the subconscious in episodes about dreams and nightmares, the first to use flashbacks to explore Rob Petrie's Army stint and his days as a rookie comedy writer, the first to have as its hero and heroine a couple who looked and acted as though they'd actually made love before. If we're lucky, there won't be a reunion show.

TRIVIA QUIZ #9: "THE DICK VAN DYKE SHOW"

1. Where was Rob Petrie stationed in the Army?
2. In what city did the Petries live? Bonus: On what street?
3. What did the Petries' next-door neighbor, Jerry Helper do for a living?
4. What kind of sports car did Rob Petrie own?
5. How did Rob and Laura meet?
6. Richard Deacon played producer Mel _____.
7. What was Richie Petrie's middle name?
8. What was Buddy Sorrell's wife's name?
9. In the "It May Look Like a Walnut" episode, Rob thought that aliens were trying to take over the world. Who did their leader look like?
10. What was Laura Petrie's maiden name?

(Answers at end of book.)

DICKINSON, ANGIE

b. Angeline Brown, Kulm, ND, September 30, 1932. Fifties starlet who's still thought of as a sex symbol in some quarters; she played Pepper Anderson, policewoman.

AS A REGULAR: "Police Woman," NBC, 1974-78; "Cassie and Company," NBC, 1982.

AND: "Matinee Theatre: Technique," NBC, 1955; "G.E. Theatre: Try to Remember," CBS, 1956; "It's a Great Life: The Voice," NBC, 1956; "The Life and Legend of Wyatt Earp: One of Jesse's Gang," ABC, 1956; "Cheyenne: War Party," ABC, 1957; "Wire Service: Confirm or Deny," ABC, 1957; "Meet McGraw: Tycoon," NBC, 1957; "Alcoa Theatre: Circumstantial," NBC, 1957; "Meet McGraw: McGraw in Reno," NBC, 1957; "M Squad: Diamond Hard," NBC, 1957; "Have Gun, Will Travel: A Matter of Ethics," CBS, 1957; "Mickey Spillane's Mike Hammer: A Letter Edged in Blackmail," SYN, 1958; "Perry Mason: The Case of the One-Eyed Witness," CBS, 1958; "Restless Gun: Imposter for a Day," NBC, 1958; "The Bob Cummings Show: Bob and Automation," NBC, 1958; "Men Into Space: Moon Probe," CBS, 1959; "Checkmate: Remembrance of Crimes Past," CBS, 1962; "The Dick Powell Show: No Strings Attached," NBC, 1962; "The Alfred Hitchcock Hour: Captive Audience," CBS, 1962; "Stump the Stars," CBS, 1962; "Stump the Stars," CBS, 1963; "Bob Hope Chrysler Theatre: A Killing at Sundial," NBC, 1963; "This Is the Life: Bright Shadows," SYN, 1964; "Password," CBS, 1964; "You Don't Say," NBC, 1965; "The Fugitive: Brass Ring," ABC, 1965; "The Man Who Bought Paradise," CBS, 1965; "Password," CBS, 1965; "The Alfred Hitchcock Hour: The Thanatos Palace Hotel," NBC, 1965; "Dr. Kildare: Do You Trust Your Doctor?," NBC, 1965; "Dr. Kildare: She Loves Me, She Loves Me Not," NBC, 1965; "Password," CBS, 1966; "The Poppy Is Also a Flower," ABC, 1966; "The Virginian: Ride to Delphi," NBC, 1966; "Bob Hope Chrysler Theatre: And Baby Makes Five," NBC, 1966; "The Merv Griffin Show," SYN, 1968; "A Case of Libel," ABC, 1968; "The Man and the City: Running Scared," ABC, 1971; "Ghost Story: Creature of the Canyon," NBC, 1972; "Hec Ramsey: The Detroit Connection," NBC, 1973; "Police Story: The Gamble," NBC, 1974; "Dean's Place," NBC, 1975; "Bob Hope's Christmas Party," NBC, 1975; "Joys," NBC, 1976; "Saturday Night Live," NBC, 1987; "Kojak: Fatal Flaw," ABC, 1989.

TV MOVIES AND MINISERIES: "The Love War," ABC, 1970; "Thief," ABC, 1971; "The Resurrection of Zachary Wheeler," ABC, 1971; "See the Man Run," ABC, 1971; "The Norliss Tapes," NBC, 1973; "Pray for the Wildcats," ABC, 1974; "Overboard," NBC, 1978; "Pearl," ABC, 1978; "The Suicide's Wife," CBS, 1979; "Dial M for Murder," NBC, 1981; "One Shoe Makes It Murder," CBS, 1982; "Jealousy," ABC, 1984; "A Touch of

Scandal," CBS, 1984; "Hollywood Wives," ABC, 1985; "Stillwatch," CBS, 1987; "Police Story: The Freeway Killings," NBC; 1987; "Prime Target," NBC, 1989.

DIERKOP, CHARLES

b. LaCrosse, WI, September 11, 1936.

AS A REGULAR: "Police Woman," NBC, 1974-78.

AND: "Mr. Broadway: Try to Find a Spy," CBS, 1964; "The Man From UNCLE: The Off-Broadway Affair," NBC, 1966; "Gunsmoke: The Newcomers," CBS, 1966; "The Andy Griffith Show: Otis the Deputy," CBS, 1966; "Mr. Terrific: Stanley the Fighter," CBS, 1967; "Batman: Penguin's Clean Sweep," ABC, 1968; "Mannix: Penny for a Peep-Show," CBS, 1969; "The FBI: Escape to Terror," ABC, 1970; "Love, American Style: Love and the Eyewitness," ABC, 1971; "Bearcats!: Bitter Flats," CBS, 1971; "Mission: Impossible: The Bride," CBS, 1972; "Alias Smith and Jones: The Day the Amnesty Came Through," ABC, 1973; "Mannix: Desert Run," CBS, 1973; "Kung Fu: The Chalice," ABC, 1973; "Kojak: Dead on His Feet," CBS, 1974; "Police Story: The Gamble," NBC, 1974; "CHiPS: Satan's Angels," NBC, 1980; "Simon & Simon: The Rookie," CBS, 1986; "Simon & Simon: Little Boy Dead," CBS, 1988.

TV MOVIES AND MINISERIES: "Alias Smith and Jones," ABC, 1971; "City Beneath the Sea," NBC, 1971; "Lock, Stock and Barrel," NBC, 1971; "The Face of Fear," CBS, 1971; "Female Artillery," ABC, 1973; "Murdock's Gang," ABC, 1973; "The Deerslayer," NBC, 1978.

DIETRICH, DENA

b. Pittsburgh, PA. Actress who played Mother Nature in soft margarine commercials of the sixties.

AS A REGULAR: "Adam's Rib," ABC, 1973; "Paul Sand in Friends and Lovers," CBS, 1974; "Karen," ABC, 1975; "The Practice," NBC, 1976-77; "The Ropers," ABC, 1979-80.

AND: "The Trouble with People," NBC, 1972; "Emergency!: Surprise," NBC, 1974; "It's Garry Shandling's Show: Home Sweet Home," FOX, 1989; "Life Goes On: Break a Leg, Mom," ABC, 1989.

TV MOVIES AND MINISERIES: "The Strange and Deadly Occurrence," NBC, 1974; "Battle of the Generations," NBC, 1979; "Baby Comes Home," CBS, 1980.

DILLER, PHYLLIS

b. Phyllis Driver, Lima, OH, July 17, 1917. Cackling, fright-wigged comedienne of the sixties, a Jack Paar discovery.

AS A REGULAR: "The Jack Paar Show," NBC, 1959-62; "The Pruitts of Southhampton," ABC, 1966-67; "The Beautiful Phyllis Diller

265

Show," NBC, 1968; "The Gong Show," SYN, 1976-80.

AND: "I Take Thee," NBC, 1959; "Playboy's Penthouse," SYN, 1961; "The Ed Sullivan Show," CBS, 1962; "Art Linkletter's House Party," CBS, 1962; "The Jack Paar Program," NBC, 1962; "The Merv Griffin Show," NBC, 1963; "Play Your Hunch," NBC, 1963; "I've Got a Secret," CBS, 1964; "The Jack Paar Program," NBC, 1964; "Password," CBS, 1964; "The Price Is Right," ABC, 1964; "Your First Impression," NBC, 1964; "Bob Hope Special," NBC, 1964; "Art Linkletter's House Party," CBS, 1964; "The Mike Douglas Show," SYN, 1964; "To Tell the Truth," CBS, 1964; "The Jack Paar Program," NBC, 1965; "The Match Game," NBC, 1965; "The Dean Martin Show," NBC, 1965; "The Mike Douglas Show," SYN, 1965; "The Andy Williams Show," NBC, 1966; "Bob Hope Special," NBC, 1966; "Batman: The Minstrel's Shakedown/ Barbecued Batman," ABC, 1966; "The Andy Williams Show," NBC, 1967; "Hollywood Palace," ABC, 1968; "Paulsen for President," CBS, 1968; "The Tonight Show Starring Johnny Carson," NBC, 1968; "Funny You Should Ask," ABC, 1968; "Rowan & Martin's Laugh-In," NBC, 1968; "The Movie Game," SYN, 1969; "Love, American Style: Love and the Heist," ABC, 1969; "The Merv Griffin Show," CBS, 1969; "Love, American Style: Love and the Phonies," ABC, 1970; "Night Gallery: Pamela's Voice," NBC, 1971; "Love, American Style: Love and the Vacation," ABC, 1971; "Rowan & Martin's Laugh-In," NBC, 1973; "A Good Medium Is Rare," CBS, 1973; "Love, American Style: Love and the Comedienne," ABC, 1973; "The Shape of Things," CBS, 1973; "Wait Till Your Father Gets Home: The Lady Detective," SYN, 1974; "Hollywood Squares," NBC, 1975; "Joys," NBC, 1976; "The Mike Douglas Show," SYN, 1977; "Junior Almost Anything Goes," ABC, 1977; "The Love Boat: The Audit Couple," ABC, 1979; "Battlestars," NBC, 1982; "The Muppet Show," SYN, 1982; "The Jeffersons: You'll Never Get Rich," CBS, 1983; "America's Tribute to Bob Hope," NBC, 1988; "Animal Crack-ups," ABC, 1989.

DILLMAN, BRADFORD

b. San Francisco, CA, April 14, 1930.
Handsome actor in dozens of TV guest shots and movies, few of them memorable.

AS A REGULAR: "Court-Martial," ABC, 1966; "King's Crossing," ABC, 1982; "Falcon Crest," CBS, 1982-83.

AND: "Kraft Television Theatre: Strangers in Hiding," NBC, 1954; "Pond's Theatre: The Kingdom of Andrew Jones," ABC, 1955; "Hallmark Hall of Fame: There Shall Be No Night," NBC, 1957; "Omnibus: Stover at Yale," NBC, 1957; "Climax!: A Matter of Life and Death," CBS, 1957; "Here's Hollywood," NBC, 1961; "Alcoa Premiere: The Voice of Charlie Pont," ABC, 1962; "The Eleventh Hour: Eat Little Fishie, Eat," NBC, 1962; "Naked City: Her Life in Moving Pictures," ABC, 1963; "Ben Casey: The Bark of a Three-Headed Hound," ABC, 1964; "The Breaking Point: Shadows of a Starless Night," ABC, 1964; "The Alfred Hitchcock Hour: Isabel," NBC, 1964; "Profiles in Courage: Edmund G. Ross," NBC, 1965; "Dr. Kildare: The Atheist and the True Believer/A Quick Look at Glory/A Sort of Falling in Love/The Last to Believe in Miracles/The Next Thing to Murder/ Never So Happy," NBC, 1966; "The Man From UNCLE: The Prince of Darkness Affair," NBC, 1967; "The FBI: The Mastermind," ABC, 1971; "Bonanza: Face of Fear," NBC, 1971; "Night Gallery: Pickman's Model," NBC, 1971; "Mission: Impossible: Stone Pillow," CBS, 1972; "Alias Smith and Jones: The McCreedy Bust: Going, Going, Gone," ABC, 1972; "Cannon: Cain's Mark," CBS, 1972; "The Sixth Sense: Face of Ice," ABC, 1972; "The Mod Squad: The Combination," ABC, 1972; "The Mary Tyler Moore Show: You Certainly Are a Big Boy," CBS, 1972; "Columbo: The Greenhouse Jungle," NBC, 1972; "The Mod Squad: The Connection," ABC, 1972; "McCloud: The Park Avenue Rustlers," NBC, 1973; "Barnaby Jones: Requiem for a Son," CBS, 1973; "Medical Center: A Life at Stake," CBS, 1973; "Barnaby Jones: Image in a Cracked Mirror," CBS, 1974; "ABC Afternoon Playbreak: The Last Bride of Salem," ABC, 1974; "Barnaby Jones: The Deadlier Species," CBS, 1975; "Wide World of Mystery: Please Call it Murder," ABC, 1975; "Wide World of Mystery: Death in Deep Water," ABC, 1975; "Medical Story: The God Syndrome," NBC, 1975; "Three for the Road: The Fugitives," CBS, 1975; "The Streets of San Francisco: Murder by Proxy," ABC, 1975; "Wide World of Mystery: Demon! Demon!," ABC, 1975; "Barnaby Jones: Final Judgment," CBS, 1977; "The Love Boat: Set-Up for Romance," ABC, 1983; "Hotel: Prisms," ABC, 1984; "Hot Pursuit: Pilot," NBC, 1984; "Murder, She Wrote: Murder to a Jazz Beat," CBS, 1985; "Murder, She Wrote: Steal Me a Story," CBS, 1987; "Christine Cromwell: Easy Come, Easy Go," ABC, 1989.

TV MOVIES AND MINISERIES: "Fear No Evil," NBC, 1969; "Black Water Gold," ABC, 1970; "Longstreet," ABC, 1971; "Five Desperate Women," ABC, 1971; "Revenge," ABC, 1971; "The Eyes of Charles Sand," ABC, 1972; "The Delphi Bureau," ABC, 1972; "Moon of the Wolf," ABC, 1972; "Deliver Us From Evil," ABC, 1973; "Murder or Mercy," ABC, 1974; "The Disappearance of Flight 412," NBC, 1974; "Adventures of the Queen," CBS, 1975; "Force Five," CBS, 1975; "Widow," NBC,

1976; "Street Killing," ABC, 1976; "Kingston: Power Play," NBC, 1976; "Jennifer: A Woman's Story," NBC, 1979; "Before and After," ABC, 1979; "The Memory of Eva Ryker," CBS, 1980.

DINOME, JERRY—See Gerard Christopher.

DINSDALE, SHIRLEY
b. San Francisco, CA, October 31, 1926. Ventriloquist on early TV.
AS A REGULAR: "Judy Splinters," NBC, 1949.
* Emmies: 1948.

DISHY, BOB
b. Brooklyn, NY. Comic actor.
AS A REGULAR: "That Was the Week That Was," NBC, 1964-65.
AND: "Damn Yankees," NBC, 1967; "That Girl: The Russians Are Staying," ABC, 1971; "Hollywood Television Theatre: The Police," NET, 1971; "The Mary Tyler Moore Show: Second-Story Story," CBS, 1971; "Columbo: The Greenhouse Jungle," NBC, 1972; "All in the Family: Maude," CBS, 1972; "Love, American Style: Love and the Love Nest," ABC, 1973; "Barney Miller: The Layoff," ABC, 1975; "McCoy: Bless the Big Fish," NBC, 1975; "Columbo: Now You See Him," NBC, 1976; "Alice: The Pharmacist," CBS, 1977; "Barney Miller: The Delegate," ABC, 1980; "The Twilight Zone: Play Time," CBS, 1985; "The Golden Girls: Mr. Terrific," NBC, 1988.
TV MOVIES AND MINISERIES: "It Couldn't Happen to a Nicer Guy," ABC, 1974.

DISNEY, WALT
b. Walter Elias Disney, Chicago, December 5, 1901; d. 1966. Animator-producer who's arguably had more impact on contemporary pop culture than anyone.
AS A REGULAR: "Disneyland," ABC, 1954-58; "Walt Disney Presents," ABC, 1958-61; "Walt Disney's Wonderful World of Color," NBC, 1961-66.
AND: "The Ed Sullivan Show," CBS, 1956; "Hedda Hopper's Hollywood," NBC, 1960; "Art Linkletter's House Party," CBS, 1960.
* Emmies: 1956.

DIXON, DONNA
b. Alexandria, VA, July 20, 1957. Blonde actress; wife of Dan Aykroyd.
AS A REGULAR: "Bosom Buddies," ABC, 1980-82; "Berrenger's," NBC, 1985.
TV MOVIES AND MINISERIES: "Beverly Hills Madam," NBC, 1986.

DIXON, IVAN
b. New York City, NY, April 6, 1931. Actor who played Kinchloe on "Hogan's Heroes."
AS A REGULAR: "Hogan's Heroes," CBS, 1965-70.
AND: "Studio One: Career," CBS, 1956; "Studio One: Walk Down the Hill," CBS, 1957; "Du Pont Show of the Month: Arrowsmith," CBS, 1960; "The Twilight Zone: The Big, Tall Wish," CBS, 1960; "Have Gun, Will Travel: Long Way Home," CBS, 1961; "Follow the Sun: The Hunters," ABC, 1961; "The New Breed: Policemen Die Alone," ABC, 1962; "Cain's Hundred: Blues for a Junkman," NBC, 1962; "Target: The Corruptors: Journey Into Mourning," ABC, 1962; "Dr. Kildare: Something of Importance," NBC, 1962; "Laramie: Among the Missing," NBC, 1962; "The Defenders: Man Against Himself," CBS, 1963; "Stoney Burke: The Test," ABC, 1963; "Perry Mason: The Case of the Nebulous Nephew," CBS, 1963; "The Outer Limits: The Human Factor," ABC, 1963; "The Great Adventure: The Special Courage of Captain Pratt," CBS, 1964; "The Twilight Zone: I Am the Night-Color Me Black," CBS, 1964; "The Man From UNCLE: The Vulcan Affair," NBC, 1964; "Bob Hope Chrysler Theatre: Murder in the First," NBC, 1964; "The Fugitive: Escape Into Black," ABC, 1964; "The Outer Limits: The Inheritors," ABC, 1964; "The Defenders: The Non-Violent," CBS, 1965; "I Spy: So Long, Patrick Henry," NBC, 1965; "NET Playhouse: The Final War of Ollie Winter," NET, 1967; "The Fugitive: Dossier on a Diplomat," ABC, 1967; "The Felony Squad: The Deadly Junkman," ABC, 1967; "Ironside: Backfire," NBC, 1967; "It Takes a Thief: Get Me to the Resurrection on Time," ABC, 1968; "The Name of the Game: The Black Answer," NBC, 1968; "The Name of the Game: The Incomparable Connie Walker," NBC, 1969; "The Mod Squad: Return to Darkness, Return to Light," ABC, 1970; "The FBI: The Deadly Pact," ABC, 1970; "Love, American Style: Love and the Baby," ABC, 1971.
TV MOVIES AND MINISERIES: "Fer-De-Lance," CBS, 1974; "Amerika," ABC, 1987.

DIZON, JESSE
b. Oceanside, CA, June 16, 1950.
AS A REGULAR: "Operation Petticoat," ABC, 1977-78.
AND: "Room 222: Just Call Me Mr. Shigematsu," ABC, 1972; "Kojak: The Chinatown Murders," CBS, 1974; "Baa Baa Black Sheep: Poor Little Lambs," NBC, 1977; "The White Shadow: That Old Gang of Mine," CBS, 1979; "The Rockford Files: Only Rock'n'Roll Will Never Die," NBC, 1979; "Misfits of Science: The Missing Link," NBC, 1985; "Cagney & Lacey: Capitalism," CBS, 1986; "Island Son: Fathers and Sons," CBS, 1989.
TV MOVIES AND MINISERIES: "Lady of the House," NBC, 1978; "Thou Shalt Not Commit Adultery," NBC, 1978.

DOBSON, KEVIN

b. *Jackson Heights, NY, March 18, 1943.*
Formerly Kojak's sidekick Crocker, now plays
M. "Mack" Patrick MacKenzie on "Knots
Landing."
AS A REGULAR: "Kojak," CBS, 1973-78; "Shan-
non," CBS, 1981-82; "Knots Landing," CBS,
1982- .
AND: "Miami Vice: The Lost Madonna," NBC,
1989.
TV MOVIES AND MINISERIES: "The Immigrants,"
SYN, 1978; "Transplant," CBS, 1979; "Hardhat
and Legs," CBS, 1980; "Reunion," CBS, 1980;
"Sweet Revenge," CBS, 1984.

DOBYNS, LLOYD

b. *Newport News, VA, March 12, 1936.*
AS A REGULAR: "Weekend," NBC, 1974-79; "NBC
News Overnight," NBC, 1982; "Monitor,"
NBC, 1983-84.

DODSON, JACK

b. *Pittsburgh, PA, 1931.* Actor who played
country clerk Howard Sprague on "The Andy
Griffith Show" and its sequel.
AS A REGULAR: "The Andy Griffith Show," CBS,
1966-68; "Mayberry RFD," CBS, 1968-71;
"All's Fair," CBS, 1976-77; "In the Beginning,"
CBS, 1978; "Phyl & Mikhy," CBS, 1980.
AND: "The Lucy Show: Lucy the Undercover
Agent," CBS, 1965; "The Virginian: The
Inchworm's Got No Wings at All," NBC, 1966;
"The Andy Griffith Show: Lost and Found," CBS,
1966; "Room 222: Who Is Benedict Arnold?,"
ABC, 1971; "The Doris Day Show: Doris' House
Guest," CBS, 1972; "Hawaii Five-O: Murder is a
Taxing Affair," CBS, 1973; "Barney Miller: Horse
Thief," ABC, 1975; "Happy Days: A Sight for
Sore Eyes," ABC, 1976; "The Nancy Walker
Show: Pilot," ABC, 1976; "Happy Days: The Last
of the Bigtime Malphs," ABC, 1977; "Maude:
Phillip and Sam," CBS, 1977; "Happy Days:
Ralph's Problem," ABC, 1979; "Lou Grant:
Guns," CBS, 1980; "Barney Miller: Guns," ABC,
1980; "Mork & Mindy: Raided Mind-Skis," ABC,
1980; "One Day at a Time: Social Security," CBS,
1983; "Cagney & Lacey: Lottery," CBS, 1985; "St.
Elsewhere: The Naked and the Dead," NBC, 1985;
"St. Elsewhere: The Idiot and the Odyssey," NBC,
1987; "St. Elsewhere: Curtains," NBC, 1988;
"Duet: Partners," FOX, 1988; "Mr. Belvedere:
Stakeout," ABC, 1989; "Mr. Belvedere: A Happy
Guys Christmas," ABC, 1989.
TV MOVIES AND MINISERIES: "Return to Mayberry,"
NBC, 1986.
* Excruciatingly trivial trivia: Dodson's first
  appearance on "The Andy Griffith Show"
  wasn't as county clerk Howard Sprague, but as a
  guy named Ed Jenkins.

DOHERTY, SHANNEN

b. *Memphis, TN, April 12, 1971.* Actress who
played Jenny Wilder on "Little House" and
Kris Witherspoon on "Our House."
AS A REGULAR: "Little House on the Prairie,"
NBC, 1982-83; "Our House," NBC, 1986-88;
"Beverly Hills 90210," FOX, 1990- .
AND: "Father Murphy: By the Bear That Bit Me,"
NBC, 1981; "Magnum P.I.: A Sense of Doubt,"
CBS, 1983.
TV MOVIES AND MINISERIES: "The Other Lover,"
CBS, 1985.

DOLENZ, GEORGE

Actor who was Mickey Dolenz's father.
AS A REGULAR: "The Count of Monte Cristo,"
SYN, 1955.
AND: "Favorite Story: God Sees the Truth," SYN,
1952; "Restless Gun: The Outlander," NBC,
1958; "Cimarron City: The Town is a Prisoner,"
NBC, 1959; "The Islanders: Talent for Danger,"
ABC, 1960; "The Rebel: The Uncourageous,"
ABC, 1961; "The Deputy: Brand of Honesty,"
NBC, 1961; "Tales of Wells Fargo: Moneyrun,"
NBC, 1962; "Bonanza: Marie, My Love," NBC,
1963.

DOLENZ, MICKEY

b. *George Michael Dolenz, Los Angeles, CA,
March 8, 1945.* Former child actor (as Mickey
Braddock), later that crazy drummer with The
Monkees.
AS A REGULAR: "Circus Boy," NBC, 1956-57;
ABC, 1957-58; "The Monkees," NBC, 1966-
68.
AND: "Mr. Novak: One Monday Afternoon,"
NBC, 1964; "Mr. Novak: Born of Kings and
Angels," NBC, 1964; "The Monkees Special,"
NBC, 1969; "My Three Sons: Polly the Pigeon,"
CBS, 1972; "Owen Marshall, Counselor at Law:
The Camerons Are a Special Clan," ABC, 1973;
"The New Mike Hammer: Deadly Collection,"
CBS, 1987.

DOLLAR, LYNN

b. *North Dakota, 1930.* The Vanna White of
her day, lovely assistant on "The $64,000
Question."
AS A REGULAR: "The $64,000 Question," CBS,
1955-58.
AND: "The Phil Silvers Show: It's for the Birds,"
CBS, 1956.

DONAHUE, ELINOR

b. *Tacoma, WA, April 19, 1937.* Former child
actress who was singing on the radio at age
two; she played Betty "Princess" Anderson on
"Father Knows Best," girlfriends to Andy
Griffith and Tony Randall and the mom of

Chris Elliott on "Get a Life."

AS A REGULAR: "Father Knows Best," CBS, 1954-55; NBC, 1955-58; CBS, 1958-60; "The Andy Griffith Show," CBS, 1960-61; "Many Happy Returns," CBS, 1964-65; "The Odd Couple," ABC, 1972-74; "Mulligan's Stew," NBC, 1977; "Please Stand By," SYN, 1978-79; "Days of Our Lives," NBC, 1984-85; "The New Adventures of Beans Baxter," FOX, 1987-88; "Get a Life," FOX, 1990- .

AND: "Schlitz Playhouse of Stars: I Want to Be a Star," CBS, 1952; "The Loretta Young Show: He Always Comes Home," NBC, 1955; "The Loretta Young Show: Weekend in Winnetka," NBC, 1955; "The George Burns and Gracie Allen Show: The Mistaken Marriage of Emily Vanderlip and Roger," CBS, 1956; "Ford Theatre: Sheila," NBC, 1956; "The Steve Allen Show," NBC, 1956; "Goodyear Theatre: Marked Down for Connie," NBC, 1960; "Dennis the Menace: Dennis and the Wedding," CBS, 1960; "U.S. Steel Hour: Delayed Honeymoon," CBS, 1961; "G.E. Theatre: A Voice on the Phone," CBS, 1961; "The Brothers Brannagan: Duet," SYN, 1962; "77 Sunset Strip: Scream Softly, Dear," ABC, 1963; "Have Gun, Will Travel: The Burning Tree," CBS, 1963; "U.S. Steel Hour: The Secrets of Stella Crozier," CBS, 1963; "Dr. Kildare: Ship's Doctor," NBC, 1963; "Redigo: Hostage Hero Hiding," NBC, 1963; "The Virginian: Siege," NBC, 1963; "The Eleventh Hour: The Secret in the Stone," NBC, 1964; "A Man Called Shenandoah: Town on Fire," ABC, 1965; "Star Trek: Metamorphosis," NBC, 1967; "The Flying Nun: My Sister the Sister," ABC, 1968; "The Flying Nun: How to Be a Spanish Grandmother," ABC, 1968; "The Flying Nun: My Sister the Doctor," ABC, 1970; "If I Love You, Am I Trapped Forever?," CBS, 1974; "The Rookies: Blue Christmas," ABC, 1974; "Police Story: Ice Time," NBC, 1977; "$weepstake$: Victor, Billy and Bobby, Sometimes,'" NBC, 1979; "The Love Boat: A Home Is Not a Home," ABC, 1979; "Diff'rent Strokes: The Woman," NBC, 1979; "Barnaby Jones: The Silent Accuser," CBS, 1980; "The Love Boat: Zeke and Zelda," ABC, 1981; "Hotel: Deceptions," ABC, 1983; "Newhart: The Lady or the Tiger," CBS, 1988; "The Golden Girls: Stan Takes a Wife," NBC, 1989; "CBS Schoolbreak Special: Never Say Goodbye," CBS, 1989.

TV MOVIES AND MINISERIES: "In Name Only," ABC, 1969; "Gidget Gets Married," ABC, 1972.

DONAHUE, PHIL

b. Cleveland, OH, December 21, 1935. Talk-show host.

AS A REGULAR: "Donahue," SYN, 1972- ; "The Last Word," ABC, 1982-83.

AND: "The Arsenio Hall Show," SYN, 1989.

DONAHUE, TROY

b. Merle Johnson, Jr., Bayport, NY, January 27, 1936. Hunky blonde actor of long, long ago.

AS A REGULAR: "SurfSide 6," ABC, 1960-62; "Hawaiian Eye," ABC, 1962-63; "The Secret Storm," CBS, 1970.

AND: "Wagon Train: The Hunter Malloy Story," NBC, 1959; "Tales of Wells Fargo: The Rawhide Kid," NBC, 1959; "Maverick: Pappy," ABC, 1959; "Sugarfoot: The Wild Bunch," ABC, 1959; "Hawaiian Eye: Beach Boy," ABC, 1959; "Bronco: The Devil's Spawn," ABC, 1959; "Bob Hope Special," NBC, 1960; "77 Sunset Strip: Condor's Lair," ABC, 1960; "Hawaiian Eye: A Birthday Boy," ABC, 1960; "The Alaskans: Heart of Gold," ABC, 1960; "Lawman: The Payment," ABC, 1960; "Colt .45: The Hothead," ABC, 1960; "77 Sunset Strip: The Hot Tamale Caper," ABC, 1961; "Here's Hollywood," NBC, 1961; "American Bandstand," ABC, 1961; "The Ed Sullivan Show," CBS, 1962; "Hawaiian Eye: The After Hours Heart," ABC, 1962; "The Patty Duke Show: Operation: Tonsils," ABC, 1965; "The Name of the Game: Nightmare," NBC, 1968; "The Tonight Show Starring Johnny Carson," NBC, 1969; "The Virginian: Fox, Hound and the Widow McCloud," NBC, 1969.

TV MOVIES AND MINISERIES: "Ironside: Split Second to an Epitaph," NBC, 1968; "The Lonely Profession," NBC, 1969.

DONALD, PETER

b. England, 1918; d. 1979. Comedian and quiz-show regular; he was one of five possible hosts tried out on "Texaco Star Theatre"—Milton Berle won. (The others included Henny Youngman, Morey Amsterdam and Jack Carter.)

AS A REGULAR: "Texaco Star Theatre," NBC, 1948; "Prize Performance," CBS, 1950; "Can You Top This?," ABC, 1950-51; "Ad Libbers," CBS, 1951; "Masquerade Party," NBC, 1952; CBS, 1953; DUM, 1953-54; ABC, 1955; CBS, 1955; CBS, 1957; "Where Was I?," DUM, 1952-53.

DONALDSON, SAM

b. El Paso, TX, March 11, 1934.

AS A REGULAR: "ABC Weekend News," ABC, 1979- ; "PrimeTime Live," ABC, 1989- .

AND: "Late Night with David Letterman," NBC, 1989.

DONLEVY, BRIAN

b. Ireland, February 9, 1899; d. 1972.

AS A REGULAR: "Dangerous Assignment," SYN, 1951-52.

AND: "Pulitzer Prize Playhouse: The Pharmacist's Mate," ABC, 1950; "Lux Video Theatre: Tunnel

Job," CBS, 1953; "Robert Montgomery Presents: First Vice-President," NBC, 1953; "Medallion Theatre: Safari," CBS, 1954; "Lux Video Theatre: The Great McGinty," NBC, 1955; "Ford Theatre: Policy of Joe Aladdin," NBC, 1955; "Climax!: Pink Cloud," CBS, 1955; "Crossroads: Mr. Liberty Bell," ABC, 1955; "Damon Runyon Theatre: Barbecue," CBS, 1955; "Kraft Television Theatre: Home is the Hero," NBC, 1956; "Studio One: The Laughter of Giants," CBS, 1956; "Ford Theatre: Double Trouble," NBC, 1956; "Lux Video Theatre: Impact," NBC, 1956; "Crossroads: The Judge," ABC, 1956; "Crossroads: God of Kandikur," ABC, 1957; "Du Pont Show of the Month: Beyond This Place," CBS, 1957; "I've Got a Secret," CBS, 1957; "The Texan: The Man Behind the Star," CBS, 1959; "Rawhide: Incident of the Power and the Plow," CBS, 1959; "Wagon Train: The Joseph Cato Story," NBC, 1959; "Hotel De Paree: Sundance and the Hard Sell," CBS, 1959; "The Texan: Trail Dust," CBS, 1959; "Du Pont Show with June Allyson: Escape," CBS, 1960; "Dick Powell's Zane Grey Theatre: The Sunday Man," CBS, 1960; "Here's Hollywood," NBC, 1961; "Target: The Corruptors: A Man Waiting to Be Murdered," ABC, 1962; "Saints and Sinners: Dear George, the Siamese Cat Is Missing," NBC, 1962; "The du Pont Show: Jeremy Rabbitt, the Secret Avenger," NBC, 1964; "Perry Mason: The Case of the Positive Negative," CBS, 1966; "Family Affair: Hard Hat Jody," CBS, 1967.

DONNELL, JEFF

b. Jean Marie Donnell, South Windham, ME, July 10, 1921; d. 1988. Actress who played George Gobel's wife, Alice, on his variety series and was Stella Fields on "General Hospital."

AS A REGULAR: "The George Gobel Show," NBC, 1954-58; "Matt Helm," ABC, 1975-76; "General Hospital," ABC, 1980-89.

AND: "Bigelow Theatre: Make Your Bed," CBS, 1951; "Schlitz Playhouse of Stars: Girl of My Dreams," CBS, 1953; "Ford Theatre: Taming of the Shrewd," NBC, 1954; "U.S. Steel Hour: One for the Road," ABC, 1954; "Counterpoint: It Wouldn't Be Fair," SYN, 1955; "Cavalcade of America: The New Salem Story," ABC, 1955; "Gloria Swanson Theatre: The Antique Shop," SYN, 1955; "Climax!: No Stone Unturned," CBS, 1955; "Matinee Theatre: The Old Payola," NBC, 1956; "Ethel Barrymore Theatre: The Peabodys," SYN, 1956; "Studio 57: Swing Your Partner, Hector," SYN, 1956; "Playhouse 90: Sincerely, Willis Wayde," CBS, 1956; "The Chevy Show," NBC, 1957; "U.S. Steel Hour: Goodbye ... But It Doesn't Go Away," CBS, 1958; "U.S. Steel Hour: Little Tin God," CBS, 1959; "Pantomime Quiz," ABC, 1959; "Ellery Queen: The Chemistry Set," NBC, 1959; "U.S. Steel Hour: Game of Hearts,"

CBS, 1960; "The Overland Trail: The Most Dangerous Gentleman," NBC, 1960; "The Ann Sothern Show: The Girls," CBS, 1960; "The du Pont Show with June Allyson: A Thief or Two," CBS, 1960; "Play of the Week: Uncle Harry," SYN, 1960; "Here's Hollywood," NBC, 1961; "U.S. Steel Hour: Tangle of Truth," CBS, 1961; "Mr. Ed: A Man for Velma," CBS, 1962; "Perry Mason: The Case of the Melancholy Marksman," CBS, 1962; "U.S. Steel Hour: Farewell to Innocence," CBS, 1962; "Walt Disney's Wonderful World of Color: Bristle Face," NBC, 1964; "Your First Impression," NBC, 1964; "Perry Mason: The Case of the Bullied Bowler," CBS, 1964; "Special for Women: The Atheist and the True Believer," NBC, 1966; "The Addams Family: Morticia the Decorator," ABC, 1966; "Gidget: Take a Lesson," ABC, 1966; "Julia: The Grass Is Sometimes Greener," NBC, 1968; "The Mothers-in-Law: Herb's Little Helpers," NBC, 1968; "The FBI: Blood Tie," ABC, 1969; "Bracken's World: Together Again-For the Last Time," NBC, 1970; "Medical Center: Witch Hunt," CBS, 1970; "Sanford & Son: The Piano Movers," NBC, 1972; "Cannon: The Seventh Grave," CBS, 1972; "Emergency!: Crash," NBC, 1972; "The FBI: Holiday with Terror," ABC, 1972; "Barnaby Jones: The Murdering Class," CBS, 1973; "ABC Afternoon Playbreak: The Gift of Terror," ABC, 1973; "The Girl with Something Extra: Mind-Ing Mama," NBC, 1973; "Marcus Welby, M.D.: Last Flight to Babylon," ABC, 1974; "Chico and the Man: Matchmaker, Matchmaker," NBC, 1977; "The Bob Newhart Show: Freudian Ship," CBS, 1978.

TV MOVIES AND MINISERIES: "Love, Hate, Love," ABC, 1971; "Congratulations, It's a Boy!," ABC, 1971; "Murder by Natural Causes," CBS, 1979.

DONOVAN, KING

b. 1919. Actor who played Bob Cummings' TV pal, Harvey Helm.

AS A REGULAR: "The Bob Cummings Show," NBC, 1955; CBS, 1956-57; NBC, 1957-58; "Please Don't Eat the Daisies," NBC, 1966-67.

AND: "Frontier: Paper Gunman," NBC, 1955; "December Bride: Jaywalker," CBS, 1956; "The George Burns and Gracie Allen Show: The Costume Party," CBS, 1956; "Navy Log: After You, Ludwig," ABC, 1957; "Tales of Wells Fargo: The Feud," NBC, 1957; "The People's Choice: The Wrong Indians," NBC, 1958; "Alcoa Theatre: Most Likely to Succeed," NBC, 1958; "Richard Diamond, Private Detective: The Counselor," NBC, 1959; "Wanted Dead or Alive: Bad Gun," CBS, 1959; "Mr. Lucky: My Little Gray Home," CBS, 1959; "Maverick: Maverick Springs," ABC, 1959; "Shotgun Slade: The Embezzler," SYN, 1959; "77 Sunset Strip: The

270

Kookie Caper," ABC, 1959; "Riverboat: The Boy From Pittsburgh," NBC, 1959; "Art Linkletter's House Party," CBS, 1960; "Laramie: Cemetery Road," NBC, 1960; "Hotel De Paree: Bounty for Sundance," CBS, 1960; "Rawhide: Incident of the Buryin' Man," CBS, 1963; "The Beverly Hillbillies: The Clampetts Are Overdrawn," CBS, 1963; "The Beverly Hillbillies: The Clampetts Go Hollywood," CBS, 1963; "The Smothers Brothers Show: The Boss Who Came to Breakfast, Lunch and Dinner," CBS, 1966; "Daktari: Wall of Flames," CBS, 1966; "The Big Valley: Into the Widow's Web," ABC, 1966; "The Beverly Hillbillies: The Army Game," CBS, 1967.

DOOHAN, JAMES
b. Canada, March 3, 1920. Burly actor who played Scotty on "Star Trek."
AS A REGULAR: "Star Trek," NBC, 1966-69, 1973-75; "Jason of Star Command," CBS, 1978-79.
AND: "Hazel: Hazel's Highland Fling," NBC, 1963; "G.E. True: Escape," CBS, 1963; "The Gallant Men: The Warrior," ABC, 1963; "The Twilight Zone: Valley of the Shadow," CBS, 1963; "The Virginian: The Man Who Couldn't Die," NBC, 1963; "The Outer Limits: Expanding Human," ABC, 1964; "The Man From UNCLE: The Shark Affair," NBC, 1964; "Bewitched: A Strange Little Visitor," ABC, 1965; "The Man From UNCLE: The Bride of Lions Affair," NBC, 1966; "Then Came Bronson: Amid Splinters of the Thunderbolt," NBC, 1969; "Marcus Welby, M.D.: Let Ernest Come Over," ABC, 1970; "Marcus Welby, M.D.: Don't Talk About Darkness," ABC, 1972; "Magnum, P.I.: The Big Blow," CBS, 1983; "Hotel: Resolutions," ABC, 1984.
TV MOVIES AND MINISERIES: "Scalplock," NBC, 1966.

DOOLEY, PAUL
b. Parkersburg, WV, February 22, 1938. Stocky character actor who played reluctant retiree Dick Hale on the underrated sitcom "Coming of Age."
AS A REGULAR: "The Dom DeLuise Show," CBS, 1968; "Coming of Age," CBS, 1988.
AND: "Weekend," SYN, 1963; "Kraft Suspense Theatre: A Lion Amongst Men," NBC, 1964; "Bewitched: Oedipus Hex," ABC, 1966; "Get Smart: The Greatest Spy on Earth," NBC, 1966; "ALF: Break Up to Make Up," NBC, 1989.
TV MOVIES AND MINISERIES: "The Rise and Fall of Oliver North," CBS, 1989; "When He's Not a Stranger," CBS, 1989.

DOONICAN, VAL
b. Ireland, 1932.
AS A REGULAR: "The Val Doonican Show," ABC, 1971.

DOQUI, ROBERT
Black actor who, in order to get steady TV work in Hollywood, had to play a few noble savages on "Daktari."
AS A REGULAR: "Felony Squad," ABC, 1968-69.
AND: "The Outer Limits: The Invisible Enemy," ABC, 1964; "Daktari: The Trial," CBS, 1966; "Daktari: Trail of the Cheetah," CBS, 1966; "Daktari: Crime Wave at Wameru," CBS, 1967; "The Man From UNCLE: The Yo Ho Ho and a Bottle of Rum Affair," NBC, 1967; "Daktari: The Monster of Wameru," CBS, 1968; "Get Smart: The Hot Line," NBC, 1968; "The Guns of Will Sonnett: The Trap," ABC, 1968; "Gunsmoke: The Mark of Cain," CBS, 1969; "Gunsmoke: The Good Samaritans," CBS, 1969; "Happy Days: Best Man," ABC, 1974; "Sanford & Son: The Headache," NBC, 1975; "The Jeffersons: Florence in Love," CBS, 1976; "The Streets of San Francisco: Dead or Alive," ABC, 1976; "Maude: Maude's Desperate Hours," CBS, 1977; "The White Shadow: A Silent Cheer," CBS, 1979; "The Fall Guy: The Winner," ABC, 1984; "Webster: God Bless the Child," ABC, 1984; "Punky Brewster: Punky Finds a Home," NBC, 1984; "Cagney & Lacey: Sorry, Right Number," CBS, 1986; "Frank's Place: Eligible Bachelor," CBS, 1987.
TV MOVIES AND MINISERIES: "Visions...," CBS, 1972; "Lieutenant Schuster's Wife," ABC, 1972; "A Dream for Christmas," CBS, 1973; "Centennial," NBC, 1978-79; "The Child-Stealer," ABC, 1979; "Dark Mirror," ABC, 1984.

DORAN, ANN
b. Amarillo, TX, July 28, 1913. Actress who played the mother of Jesse James, James Dean in "Rebel Without a Cause" and Eddie Haskell on "Leave It to Beaver."
AS A REGULAR: "National Velvet," NBC, 1960-62; "The Legend of Jesse James," ABC, 1965-66; "Longstreet," ABC, 1971-72; "Shirley," NBC, 1979-80.
AND: "The Loretta Young Show: Understanding Heart," NBC, 1956; "Matinee Theatre: The Outing," NBC, 1956; "The 20th Century-Fox Hour: Men in Her Life," CBS, 1957; "Leave It to Beaver: Voodoo Magic," CBS, 1958; "This Is the Life: The Wrong Way Out," SYN, 1958; "The Loretta Young Show: The Accused," NBC, 1959; "G.E. Theatre: Adams' Apples," CBS, 1960; "Perry Mason: The Case of the Prodigal Parent," CBS, 1960; "The Jack Benny Program: Dennis's Surprise Party," ABC, 1962; "The Virginian: Run Away Home," NBC, 1963; "The Virginian: Portrait of a Widow," NBC, 1964; "The Virginian: The Fortunes of J. Jimerson Jones," NBC, 1964; "McHale's Navy: Pumpkin Takes Over," ABC, 1965; "Hey, Landlord!: Instant Family," NBC, 1966; "Hey, Landlord!: Woody,

Can You Spare a Sister?," NBC, 1967; "Petticoat Junction: Meet the In-Laws," CBS, 1967; "The Virginian: The Lady from Wichita," NBC, 1967; "The Guns of Will Sonnett: He Shall Lead the Children," ABC, 1968; "Ironside: Dora," NBC, 1970; "The Virginian: A King's Ransom," NBC, 1970; "Ironside: This Could Blow Your Mind," NBC, 1970; "The Bold Ones: The Day the Lion Died," NBC, 1970; "The Odd Couple: Where's Grandpa?," ABC, 1972; "Alias Smith and Jones: Witness to a Lynching," ABC, 1972; "Marcus Welby, M.D.: We'll Walk Out of Here Together," ABC, 1972; "Ironside: Setup: Danger," NBC, 1974; "M*A*S*H: The Kids," CBS, 1975; "Little House on the Praire: Founder's Day," NBC, 1975; "The A-Team: Duke of Whispering Pines," NBC, 1986; "Heartbeat: Critical Overload," ABC, 1989.
TV MOVIES AND MINISERIES: "Weekend of Terror," ABC, 1970; "The Priest Killer," CBS, 1971; "The Last Angry Man," ABC, 1974; "Flood," NBC, 1976; "Little Mo," NBC, 1978; "Backstairs at the White House," NBC, 1979.

DOREMUS, DAVID
Child actor; he played Hal on "Nanny and the Professor."
AS A REGULAR: "Nanny and the Professor," ABC, 1970-71.

DORSEY, JIMMY
b. Shenandoah, PA, February 29, 1904; d. 1957. Bandleader.
AS A REGULAR: "Stage Show," CBS, 1954-56.

DORSEY, TOMMY
d. Mahonoy Plains, PA, November 19, 1905; d. 1956. Bandleader.
AS A REGULAR: "Stage Show," CBS, 1954-56.

DOTRICE, ROY
b. England, May 26, 1923. Actor who played Father on "Beauty and the Beast."
AS A REGULAR: "Beauty and the Beast," CBS, 1987-90.
AND: "Hart to Hart: Max's Waltz," ABC, 1984; "Remington Steele: Steele Eligible," NBC, 1984; "The A-Team: The Spy Who Mugged Me," NBC, 1986; "The Equalizer: Trial by Ordeal," CBS, 1989; "Nightmare Classics: Carmilla," SHO, 1989.
TV MOVIES AND MINISERIES: "The Lady Forgets," CBS, 1989.

DOUGLAS, DIANA
b. Bermuda, Jan 22, 1923.
AS A REGULAR: "Photocrime," ABC, 1949; "Three Steps to Heaven," NBC, 1953-54; "The Cowboys," ABC, 1974.
AND: "Science Fiction Theatre: End of Tomorrow," SYN, 1956; "Robert Montgomery Presents:

Wait for Me," NBC, 1957; "Robert Montgomery Presents: One Smart Apple," NBC, 1957; "Salute to the American Theatre: The Male Animal," CBS, 1959; "The Defenders: Drink Like a Lady," CBS, 1964; "Ben Casey: War of Nerves," ABC, 1965; "The Streets of San Francisco: Chapel of the Damned," ABC, 1973; "Owen Marshall, Counselor at Law: A Lesson in Loving," ABC, 1973; "Hawkins: Die, Darling, Die," CBS, 1973; "Kung Fu: The Tong," ABC, 1973; "Lou Grant: Hoax," CBS, 1977; "Lou Grant: Review," CBS, 1981; "Nero Wolfe: In the Best Families," NBC, 1981; "Remington Steele: Tempered Steele," NBC, 1982; "Scarecrow and Mrs. King: I Am Not Now, Nor Have I Even Been, a Spy," CBS, 1984.
TV MOVIES AND MINISERIES: "Dead Man on the Run," ABC, 1975; "A Fire in the Sky," NBC, 1978; "Roots: The Next Generations," ABC, 1979.

DOUGLAS, DONNA
b. Dorothy Smith, Baton Rouge, LA, 1933. Sixties starlet who was just like all the other starlets until she was cast as Elly May Clampett.
AS A REGULAR: "The Beverly Hillbillies," CBS, 1962-71.
AND: "The Detectives Starring Robert Taylor: Alibis," ABC, 1960; "The Twilight Zone: The Eye of the Beholder," CBS, 1960; "The Aquanauts: The Big Swim," CBS, 1960; "Thriller: The Hungry Glass," NBC, 1961; "Michael Shayne: Murder Is a Fine Art," NBC, 1961; "Checkmate: The Paper Killer," CBS, 1961; "Checkmate: The Deadly Silence," CBS, 1961; "77 Sunset Strip: The Celluloid Cowboy," ABC, 1961; "Pete and Gladys: The Manikin Merry-go-Round," CBS, 1961; "Hennesey: His Honor, Dr. Blair," CBS, 1961; "Malibu Run: The Stakeout Adventure," CBS, 1961; "SurfSide 6: Jonathan Wembley is Missing," ABC, 1961; "Mr. Ed: Clint Eastwood Meets Mr. Ed," CBS, 1962; "The Twilight Zone: Cavender Is Coming," CBS, 1962; "Love, American Style: Love and the Other Guy," ABC, 1969; "Love, American Style: Love and the Love Kit," ABC, 1973; "McMillan and Wife: Man Without a Face," NBC, 1974.
TV MOVIES AND MINISERIES: "The Return of the Beverly Hillbillies," CBS, 1981.
* "Eye of the Beholder" was a memorable "Twilight Zone"; Douglas played a woman covered in bandages who's undergone plastic surgery to repair her hideous looks. She spends the episode agonizing over whether the operation was a success and when the wraps are removed, she's beautiful—but not to the pig-faced doctors who operated on her.

DOUGLAS, JAMES
b. Los Angeles, CA, 1933. Actor who played Steven Cord on "Peyton Place" and Grant

Coleman on "As the World Turns."

AS A REGULAR: "Peyton Place," ABC, 1964-69; "Another World," NBC, 1972-74; "As the World Turns," CBS, 1974-81.

AND: "West Point: Operation Survival," ABC, 1957; "Death Valley Days: Sam Kee and Uncle Sam," SYN, 1959; "Death Valley Days: The Legend of Tule Joe," SYN, 1960; "Philip Marlowe: Last Call for Murder," ABC, 1960; "T.H.E. Cat: Crossing at Destino Bay," NBC, 1966.

TV MOVIES AND MINISERIES: "A Clear and Present Danger," NBC, 1970; "Peyton Place: The Next Generation," NBC, 1985.

DOUGLAS, KIRK

b. Issur Danielovitch, Amsterdam, NY, December 9, 1916.

AS A GUEST: "The Perry Como Show," NBC, 1956; "The Ed Sullivan Show," CBS, 1956; "Person to Person," CBS, 1957; "Mike Wallace Interviews," ABC, 1957; "The General Motors 50th Anniversary Show," NBC, 1957; "The Ed Sullivan Show," CBS, 1957; "The Steve Allen Show," NBC, 1958; "Person to Person," CBS, 1960; "Here's Hollywood," NBC, 1960; "The Lucy Show: Lucy Goes to a Hollywood Premiere," CBS, 1966; "Saga of Western Man: Cortez and the Legend," NET, 1967; "The Don Rickles Show," ABC, 1968; "The Legend of Silent Night," ABC, 1968; "Dr. Jekyll and Mr. Hyde," NBC, 1973; "The Dean Martin Show," NBC, 1973; "The Mike Douglas Show," SYN, 1975; "Saturday Night Live," NBC, 1980.

TV MOVIES AND MINISERIES: "Mousey," ABC, 1974; "The Moneychangers," NBC, 1976; "Victory at Entebbe," ABC, 1976; "Remembrance of Love," NBC, 1982; "Amos," CBS, 1985; "Queenie," ABC, 1987; "AT&T Presents: Inherit the Wind," NBC, 1988.

DOUGLAS, MELVYN

b. Melvyn Hesselberg, Macon, GA, April 5, 1901; d. 1981.

AS A REGULAR: "Hollywood Off Beat," ABC, 1952; "Steve Randall," DUM, 1952-53; "Blind Date," DUM, 1953; "Frontier Justice," CBS, 1959.

AND: "Ford Theatre Hour: Cause for Suspicion," ABC, 1950; "Starlight Theatre: Relatively Speaking," CBS, 1951; "Lights Out: Private, Keep Out," NBC, 1952; "Ford Theatre: Letters Marked Personal," NBC, 1955; "Kraft Theatre: The Chess Game," NBC, 1955; "Alcoa Hour: Thunder in Washington," NBC, 1955; "Alcoa Hour: Man on a Tiger," NBC, 1956; "Playhouse 90: The Greer Case," CBS, 1957; "U.S. Steel Hour: The Hill Wife," CBS, 1957; "The Garry Moore Show," CBS, 1957; "Arthur Murray Party," NBC, 1957; "Goodyear TV Playhouse: The Legacy," NBC, 1957; "G.E. Theatre: Love

Came Late," CBS, 1957; "Wide, Wide World: American Theatre '58," NBC, 1958; "Playhouse 90: The Plot to Kill Stalin," CBS, 1958; "U.S. Steel Hour: Second Chance," CBS, 1958; "Playhouse 90: The Return of Ansel Gibbs," CBS, 1958; "Playhouse 90: Judgement at Nuremberg," CBS, 1959; "The Ed Sullivan Show," CBS, 1959; "Our American Heritage: Shadow of a Soldier," NBC, 1960; "Person to Person," CBS, 1960; "Land of Promise," SYN, 1960; "Ben Casey: Rage Against the Dying Light," ABC, 1963; "Kraft Suspense Theatre: The Image Merchants," NBC, 1963; "Bob Hope Chrysler Theatre: A Killing at Sundial," NBC, 1963; "Hallmark Hall of Fame: Inherit the Wind," NBC, 1965; "The Fugitive: The 2130," ABC, 1966; "Hallmark Hall of Fame: Lamp at Midnight," NBC, 1966; "The Crucible," CBS, 1967; "CBS Playhouse: Do Not Go Gentle Into That Good Night," CBS, 1967; "This Morning," ABC, 1968; "On Stage: The Choice," NBC, 1969; "Ghost Story: House of Evil," NBC, 1972; "The Growing Up of David Lev," NBC, 1973; "Benjamin Franklin: The Statesman," CBS, 1975.

TV MOVIES AND MINISERIES: "Companions in Nightmare," NBC, 1968; "Hunters Are for Killing," CBS, 1970; "Death Takes a Holiday," ABC, 1971; "The Death Squad," ABC, 1973; "Murder or Mercy," ABC, 1974.

* Douglas' wife, congresswoman Helen Gahagan Douglas, died 14 months before her husband.
* Douglas' films include "Ninotchka," "Theodora Goes Wild," "Mr. Blandings Builds His Dream House," "Hud," "The Americanization of Emily," "The Candidate" and "Being There."
* Emmies: 1968.

DOUGLAS, MICHAEL

b. New Brunswick, NJ, September 25, 1944. Oscar winning ("Wall Street") son of Kirk Douglas; he played Inspector Steve Keller on "The Streets of San Francisco."

AS A REGULAR: "The Streets of San Francisco," ABC, 1972-76.

AND: "Person to Person," CBS, 1960; "CBS Playhouse: The Experiment," CBS, 1969; "The FBI: The Hitchhiker," ABC, 1971; "Medical Center: The Albatross," CBS, 1971; "The Mike Douglas Show," SYN, 1975; "The Mike Douglas Show," SYN, 1977; "Saturday Night Live," NBC, 1984; "Friday Night Videos," NBC, 1989.

TV MOVIES AND MINISERIES: "When Michael Calls," ABC, 1972; "The Streets of San Francisco," ABC, 1972.

DOUGLAS, MIKE

b. Michael D. Dowd, Jr., Chicago, August 11, 1925. Singer and talk-show host.

AS A REGULAR: "Kay Kyser's Kollege of Musical Knowledge," NBC, 1949-50, 1954; "The

Music Show," DUM, 1953-54; "The Mike Douglas Show," SYN, 1963-82.
AND: "Club 60," NBC, 1957; "The Man From UNCLE: The Nowhere Affair," NBC, 1966; "The Carol Burnett Show," CBS, 1968; "The Jackie Gleason Show," CBS, 1968; "The Mary Tyler Moore Hour," CBS, 1979; "The Love Boat: Rhino of the Year," ABC, 1983.

DOUGLAS, PAUL
b. Philadelphia, PA, April 11, 1907; d. 1959. Actor often in gruff roles in film ("A Letter to Three Wives," "The Solid Gold Cadillac") and TV.
AS A REGULAR: "Adventure Theatre," NBC, 1956-57.
AND: "Hollywood Opening Night: The Living Image," NBC, 1953; "Omnibus: The Oyster and the Pearl," CBS, 1953; "Plymouth Playhouse: Justice," ABC, 1953; "Medallion Theatre: The Magic Touch," CBS, 1954; "Lux Video Theatre: Casablanca," NBC, 1955; "Elgin TV Hour: Black Eagle Pass," ABC, 1955; "Request Performance: The Trouble with Youth," NBC, 1955; "Climax!: Flight 951," CBS, 1955; "Damon Runyon Theatre: Numbers and Figures," CBS, 1955; "Playwrights '56: The Answer," NBC, 1955; "Suspicion: Comfort for the Grave," NBC, 1958; "Studio One: The Edge of Truth," CBS, 1958; "Shower of Stars: Jack Benny's 40th Birthday Celebration," CBS, 1958; "Schlitz Playhouse of Stars: The Honor System," CBS, 1958; "Climax!: On the Take," CBS, 1958; "Playhouse 90: The Dungeon," CBS, 1958; "Studio One: The Lady Died at Midnight," CBS, 1958; "Goodyear Theatre: The Chain and the River," NBC, 1958; "Dick Powell's Zane Grey Theatre: Day of the Killing," CBS, 1959; "Playhouse 90: The Raider," CBS, 1959; "The Lucille Ball-Desi Arnaz Show: Lucy Wants a Career," CBS, 1959; "Playhouse 90: Judgment at Nuremberg," CBS, 1959; "Alfred Hitchcock Presents: Touche," CBS, 1959; "Goodyear Theatre: The Incorrigibles," NBC, 1959.
* Just before his death, Douglas was signed to do "The Mighty Casey" episode of "The Twilight Zone." But by then he was so weakened by a heart condition that his scenes had to be reshot with Lee Marvin in the role.

DOUGLASS, ROBYN
b. Japan, June 21. 1953.
AS A REGULAR: "Battlestar Galactica," ABC, 1980; "Houston Knights," CBS, 1987-88.
AND: "Tenspeed and Brown Shoe: Pilot," ABC, 1980; "The New Mike Hammer: Mike's Baby," CBS, 1986.
TV MOVIES AND MINISERIES: "The Clone Master," NBC, 1978; "The Girls in the Office," ABC, 1979; "Her Life as a Man," NBC, 1984.

DOW, TONY
b. Hollywood, CA, April 13, 1945. Former child star who played Wally Cleaver on "Leave It to Beaver" in the fifties, sixties and eighties. Recently he's turned to TV directing.
AS A REGULAR: "Leave It to Beaver," CBS, 1957-58; ABC, 1958-63; "Never Too Young," ABC, 1965-66; "The New Leave It to Beaver," DIS, 1985-86; TBS, 1986-89.
AND: "The George Gobel Show," NBC, 1958; "Here's Hollywood," NBC, 1961; "Dr. Kildare: Four Feet in the Morning," NBC, 1963; "The Eleventh Hour: Four Feet in the Morning," NBC, 1963; "Mr. Novak: To Lodge and Dislodge," NBC, 1963; "The Greatest Show on Earth: The Show Must Go On-to Orange City," ABC, 1964; "Mr. Novak: The Death of a Teacher," NBC, 1964; "Mr. Novak: Fear Is a Handful of Dust," NBC, 1964; "My Three Sons: A Guest in the House," ABC, 1964; "Mr. Novak: Johnny Ride the Pony," NBC, 1964; "Mr. Novak: The Tender Twigs," NBC, 1965; "Love, American Style: Love and the Only Child," ABC, 1971; "The Love Boat: Looking for Mr. Wilson," ABC, 1983; "Quincy: Suffer the Little Children," NBC, 1983; "Murder, She Wrote: The Bottom Line Is Murder," CBS, 1987; "The New Mike Hammer: Kill John Doe," CBS, 1987.
TV MOVIES AND MINISERIES: "A Great American Tragedy," ABC, 1972; "Still the Beaver," CBS, 1983.

DOWN, LESLEY-ANNE
b. London, England, March 17, 1954. English actress whose career seems to parallel that of soap vixens Stephanie Beacham and Joan Collins.
AS A REGULAR: "Masterpiece Theatre: Upstairs, Downstairs," PBS, 1974-77; "Dallas," CBS, 1989-.
AND: "Dinah!," SYN, 1979.
TV MOVIES AND MINISERIES: "Murder Is Easy," CBS, 1982; "North and South," ABC, 1985; "Arch of Triumph," CBS, 1985; "North and South, Book II," ABC, 1986; "Indiscreet," CBS, 1988; "Ladykillers," ABC, 1988; "Night Walk," CBS, 1989.

DOWNEY, MORTON
b. Wallingford, CT, November 14, 1901; d. 1985.
AS A REGULAR: "Mohawk Showroom," NBC, 1949; "Star of the Family," CBS, 1950-51.
AND: "The Jack Paar Show," NBC, 1959.

DOWNEY, MORTON JR
Big-mouthed talk show host of the eighties.
AS A REGULAR: "The Morton Downey Jr. Show," SYN, 1987-89.
AND: "The Dick Clark Saturday Night Beechnut Show," ABC, 1959.

DOWNEY, ROBERT JR.
b. New York City, NY, April 4, 1965.
AS A REGULAR: "Saturday Night Live," NBC, 1985-86.

DOWNS, HUGH
b. Lima, OH, February 14, 1921.
AS A REGULAR: "Home," NBC, 1954-57; "The Tonight Show (The Jack Paar Show)," NBC, 1957-62; "Concentration," NBC, 1958-69; "The Tonight Show," NBC, 1962; "20/20," ABC, 1978- .
AND: "The Chevy Show," NBC, 1958; "A Toast to Jerome Kern," NBC, 1959; "World Wide 60: The Shape of Things," NBC, 1960; "Riverboat: The Night of the Faceless Men," NBC, 1960; "Esther Williams at Cypress Gardens," NBC, 1960; "Perry Como's Kraft Music Hall," NBC, 1960; "Here's Hollywood," NBC, 1961; "Car 54, Where Are You?: Catch Me on the Paar Show," NBC, 1961; "The Jack Benny Program: Rock Hudson Visits," CBS, 1962; "Play Your Hunch," NBC, 1962; "The Merv Griffin Show," NBC, 1963; "Perry Como's Kraft Music Hall," NBC, 1963; "The Jack Paar Program," NBC, 1964; "The Jack Paar Program," NBC, 1965; "The Dick Cavett Show," ABC, 1968; "The Pat Sajak Show," CBS, 1989.
TV MOVIES AND MINISERIES: "Woman of the Year," CBS, 1976.

DOWNS, JOHNNY
b. Brooklyn, NY, October 10, 1913. Musical-comedy performer of TV's early days.
AS A REGULAR: "Captain Billy's Mississippi Music Hall," CBS, 1948; "Girl About Town," NBC, 1948; "Manhattan Showcase," CBS, 1949.
AND: "Racket Squad: Fair Exchange," CBS, 1952.

DOYLE, DAVID
b. Omaha, NB, December 1, 1925. Roly-poly actor who played Bosley, supervisor of "Charlie's Angels."
AS A REGULAR: "The New Dick Van Dyke Show," CBS, 1972-73; "Bridget Loves Bernie," CBS, 1972-73; "Charlie's Angels," ABC, 1976-81; "Sweet Surrender," NBC, 1987.
AND: "Art Carney Special: Very Important People," NBC, 1959; "The Right Man," CBS, 1960; "Art Carney Special: Everybody's Doin' It," NBC, 1961; "Car 54, Where Are You?: A Star Is Born-In the Bronx," NBC, 1962; "Car 54, Where Are You?: The Loves of Sylvia Schnauser," NBC, 1963; "The Defenders: The Seven-Hundred-Year-Old Gang," CBS, 1964; "The Patty Duke Show: Going Steady," ABC, 1964; "The Patty Duke Show: The Dropout," ABC, 1964; "The Patty Duke Show: Patty the Folk Singer," ABC, 1965; "Trials of O'Brien: A Gaggle of Girls," CBS, 1965; "That Girl: That King," ABC, 1971; "Love, American Style: Love and the Golden Memory," ABC, 1973; "M*A*S*H: The Army-Navy Game," CBS, 1973; "Adam's Rib: French Pastry," ABC, 1973; "Love Story: Mirabelle's Summer," NBC, 1973; "All in the Family: Et Tu Archie," CBS, 1974; "Kolchak, the Night Stalker: Firefall," ABC, 1974; "Kojak: Best War in Town," CBS, 1974; "Barney Miller: Ambush," ABC, 1975; "Police Story: Vice: 24 Hours," NBC, 1975; "McCoy: Bless the Big Fish," NBC, 1975; "Match Game '78," CBS, 1978; "The Love Boat: The Man Who Loved Women," ABC, 1978; "Cross Wits," SYN, 1979; "Hollywood Squares," SYN, 1980; "The Love Boat: Winning Isn't Everything," ABC, 1982; "The Love Boat: Don't Take My Wife, Please," ABC, 1983; "The Love Boat: Partners to the End," ABC, 1985; "Starman: The Grifters," ABC, 1987; "Let Me Hear You Whisper," A&E, 1989.
TV MOVIES AND MINISERIES: "Incident on a Dark Street," CBS, 1973; "The Police Story," NBC, 1973; "Money to Burn," ABC, 1973; "Bloodsport," ABC, 1973; "Miracle on 34th Street," CBS, 1973; "The Stranger Within," ABC, 1974; "The Secret Night Caller," NBC, 1975; "The First 36 Hours of Dr. Durant," ABC, 1975; "Charlie's Angels," ABC, 1976; "Black Market Baby," ABC, 1977; "Wait Til Your Mother Gets Home," NBC, 1983; "The Invisible Woman," NBC, 1983; "Maybe Baby," NBC, 1988.

DRAKE, TOM
b. Alfred Alderdice, Brooklyn, NY, August 5, 1918. Former MGM contract player (Judy Garland's love in "Meet Me in St. Louis") who did lots of television to pay the bills.
AS A GUEST: "Suspense: 1,000 to One for Your Money," CBS, 1950; "Suspense: Murder at the Mardi Gras," CBS, 1950; "Suspense: Red Wine," CBS, 1950; "Lights Out: The Power of the Brute," NBC, 1951; "Tales of Tomorrow: Fountain of Youth," ABC, 1952; "The Unexpected: Bright Boy," NBC, 1952; "Schlitz Playhouse of Stars: A String of Beads," CBS, 1952; "Mirror Theatre: Lullaby," CBS, 1953; "Schlitz Playhouse of Stars: The Secret," CBS, 1954; "Climax!: The Long Goodbye," CBS, 1954; "Playhouse 90: Rendezvous in Black," CBS, 1956; "77 Sunset Strip: The Treehouse Caper," ABC, 1959; "The Whirlybirds: Challenge," SYN, 1959; "Laramie: Duel at Alta Mesa," NBC, 1959; "Wagon Train: The Lita Foldaire Story," NBC, 1960; "Riverboat: Face of Courage," NBC, 1960; "The Alaskans: Black Sand," ABC, 1960; "Philip Marlowe: Murder Is Dead Wrong," ABC, 1960; "Hawaiian Eye: The Pretty People," ABC, 1961; "Follow the Sun: The Far Edge of Nowhere," ABC, 1961; "Hawaiian Eye: Big Fever," ABC, 1962; "King of Diamonds:

Diamonds Don't Burn," SYN, 1962; "Ben Casey: Eulogy in Four Flats," ABC, 1965; "Branded: Very Few Heroes," NBC, 1965; "Mr. Novak: Once a Clown," NBC, 1965; "The Alfred Hitchcock Hour: Off Season," NBC, 1965; "Branded: Judge Not," NBC, 1965; "Combat!: The Old Men," ABC, 1965; "The Wild Wild West: Night of the Bottomless Pit," CBS, 1966; "Gunsmoke: Ring of Darkness," CBS, 1969; "Land of the Giants: Doomsday," ABC, 1970; "The Name of the Game: Echo of a Nightmare," NBC, 1970; "Walt Disney's Wonderful World of Color: The Boy Who Stole the Elephants," NBC, 1970; "The Bold Ones: Killer on the Loose," NBC, 1970; "The Young Lawyers: Down at the House of Truth, Visiting," ABC, 1971; "Mannix: The Man Outside," CBS, 1971; "Marcus Welby, M.D.: A Necessary End," ABC, 1972; "Police Story: A Dangerous Age," NBC, 1974; "Medical Story: An Air Full of Death," NBC, 1975; "Matt Helm: The Deadly Breed," ABC, 1975; "Marcus Welby, M.D.: The Highest Mountain, Part I," ABC, 1976; "The Streets of San Francisco: Child of Anger," ABC, 1977.

TV MOVIES AND MINISERIES: "City Beneath the Sea," NBC, 1971; "Tight as a Drum," ABC, 1974; "A Matter of Wife and Death," NBC, 1975; "Mayday at 40,000 Feet!," CBS, 1976.

DREYFUSS, RICHARD

b. Brooklyn, NY, October 29, 1947. Cuddly leading man of the movies who had to start somewhere, after all.

AS A REGULAR: "Karen," NBC, 1964-65.

AND: "Gidget: Ego a Go-Go," ABC, 1966; "Bewitched: Man's Best Friend," ABC, 1966; "Please Don't Eat the Daisies: My Son the Actor," NBC, 1966; "The Big Valley: Boy Into Man," ABC, 1967; "Hey, Landlord!: Big Brother Is Watching You," NBC, 1967; "Hey, Landlord!: Testing, One, Two," NBC, 1967; "Judd for the Defense: Weep the Hunter Home," ABC, 1969; "The Ghost and Mrs. Muir: Buried on Page One," NBC, 1969; "The New People: Marriage in Basic Black," ABC, 1969; "The Mod Squad: Mother of Sorrow," ABC, 1970; "The Bold Ones: No Harm to the Patient," NBC, 1970; "Room 222: The Valedictorian," ABC, 1970; "The Young Lawyers: Down at the House of Truth, Visiting," ABC, 1971; "You Are There: The Mystery of Amelia Earhart," CBS, 1971; "Hollywood Television Theatre: Shadow of a Gunman," NET, 1972; "Gunsmoke: This Golden Land," CBS, 1973; "Catch-22," ABC, 1973; "The Mod Squad: The Night Holds Terror," ABC, 1973; "Hollywood Television Theatre: Me," NET, 1973; "Lily," ABC, 1975; "Saturday Night Live," NBC, 1978.

TV MOVIES AND MINISERIES: "Two for the Money," ABC, 1972; "Victory at Entebbe," ABC, 1976.

DRIER, MOOSIE

b. Chicago, IL, August 6, 1964.

AS A REGULAR: "Rowan & Martin's Laugh-In," NBC, 1971-73; "Executive Suite," CBS, 1976-77.

AND: "The Bob Newhart Show: Father Knows Worst," CBS, 1972; "The Bob Newhart Show: Blues for Mr. Borden," CBS, 1973; "The FBI: The Betrayal," ABC, 1974; "ABC Afterschool Special: The Runaways," ABC, 1974; "The Bob Newhart Show: Sorry, Wrong Mother," CBS, 1974; "Police Story: Little Boy Lost," NBC, 1975; "The Bob Newhart Show: The Boy Next Door," CBS, 1976; "The Bob Newhart Show: My Son the Comedian," CBS, 1977; "Family Ties: The Fifth Wheel," NBC, 1983; "The A-Team: Beneath the Surface," NBC, 1986; "Cagney & Lacey: A Safe Place," CBS, 1986.

TV MOVIES AND MINISERIES: "Roll, Freddy, Roll," ABC, 1974; "Royce," CBS, 1976; "Rainbow," NBC, 1978.

DRISCOLL, BOBBY

b. Cedar Rapids, IA, May 3, 1937; d. 1968. Former child actor ("Song of the South") who turned to TV as his voice changed. But parts weren't plentiful enough, Driscoll turned to drugs, was arrested several times and finally died of a heart attack.

AS A GUEST: "Schlitz Playhouse of Stars: Space Conquerors," CBS, 1952; "The Loretta Young Show: Big Jim," NBC, 1954; "Fireside Theatre: His Father's Keeper," NBC, 1954; "Fireside Theatre: The Double Life of Barney Peters," NBC, 1955; "Gloria Swanson Theatre: The Best Years," SYN, 1955; "TV Reader's Digest: A Matter of Life and Death," ABC, 1955; "Front Row Center: Ah, Wilderness!," CBS, 1955; "Medic: Laughter Is a Boy," NBC, 1955; "Schlitz Playhouse of Stars: Too Late to Run," CBS, 1955; "Screen Directors Playhouse: Day Is Done," NBC, 1955; "Navy Log: Navy Corpsman," CBS, 1955; "Crusader: Fear," CBS, 1956; "Ford Theatre: Try Me for Size," NBC, 1956; "TV Reader's Digest: No Horse, No Wife, No Mustache," ABC, 1956; "Studio One: I Do," CBS, 1956; "TV Reader's Digest: The Smuggler," ABC, 1956; "Dick Powell's Zane Grey Theatre: Death Watch," CBS, 1956; "Navy Log: Navy Corpsman," ABC, 1956; "M Squad: Pete Loves Mary," NBC, 1957; "Men of Annapolis: The Irwin Brown Story," SYN, 1958; "Chevy Mystery Show: Summer Hero," NBC, 1960; "Best of the Post: Cop Without a Badge," SYN, 1961.

DRU, JOANNE

b. Joanne Letitia Lacock, Logan, WV, January 31, 1923.

AS A REGULAR: "Guestward Ho!," ABC, 1960-61.

AND: "Pulitzer Prize Playhouse: The Silver Cord," ABC, 1951; "Robert Montgomery Presents: Betrayed," NBC, 1953; "Ford Theatre: Just What the Doctor Ordered," NBC, 1953; "Schlitz Playhouse of Stars: Richard and the Lion," CBS, 1953; "Lux Video Theatre: Call Off the Wedding," CBS, 1954; "Ford Theatre: Yours for a Dream," NBC, 1954; "Matinee Theatre: Celebrity," NBC, 1956; "Lux Video Theatre: Flamingo Road," NBC, 1956; "Climax!: Night Shriek," CBS, 1956; "Playhouse 90: The Blackwell Story," CBS, 1957; "Lux Video Theatre: Paris Calling," NBC, 1957; "Studio 57: Palm Springs Incident," SYN, 1957; "The Steve Allen Show," NBC, 1957; "Studio One: The Brotherhood of the Bell," CBS, 1958; "G.E. Theatre: All I Survey," CBS, 1958; "Wagon Train: The Nels Stack Story," NBC, 1958; "The Red Skelton Show," CBS, 1958; "Arthur Murray Party," NBC, 1959; "The David Niven Show: The Lady From Winnetka," NBC, 1959; "Goodyear Theatre: Capital Gains," NBC, 1960; "Comedy Spot: Adventures of a Model," CBS, 1960; "Walt Disney's Wonderful World of Color: The Light in the Forest," NBC, 1961; "Burke's Law: Who Killed the Eleventh Best-Dressed Woman in the World?," ABC, 1964; "The Long, Hot Summer: Nor Hell a Fury," ABC, 1965; "The Green Hornet: Corpse of the Year," ABC, 1967; "Bob Hope Chrysler Theatre: To Sleep, Perchance to Scream," NBC, 1967; "It Takes Two," NBC, 1969; "Marcus Welby, M.D.: Dark Corridors," ABC, 1975.

DRURY, JAMES
b. New York City, NY, April 18, 1934. Actor who played the Virginian.
AS A REGULAR: "The Virginian," NBC, 1962-70; "The Men From Shiloh," NBC, 1970-71; "Firehouse," ABC, 1974.
AND: "The 20th Century-Fox Hour: Times Like These," CBS, 1956; "Decision: The Virginian," NBC, 1958; "Broken Arrow: Power," ABC, 1958; "Cheyenne: Freeze-Out," ABC, 1958; "The Texan: Troubled Town," CBS, 1958; "The Ed Wynn Show: A Date with Mrs. Creavy," NBC, 1958; "Have Gun, Will Travel: Hunt the Man Down," CBS, 1959; "Gunsmoke: Johnny Red," CBS, 1959; "Men Into Space: Tankers in Space," CBS, 1960; "The Rebel: Fair Game," ABC, 1960; "Bourbon Street Beat: Wall of Silence," ABC, 1960; "The Loretta Young Show: Linda," NBC, 1960; "Wagon Train: The Bleymier Story," NBC, 1960; "The Rebel: Vindication," ABC, 1960; "Gunsmoke: Old Faces," CBS, 1961; "The Loretta Young Show: The Preliminaries," NBC, 1961; "Rawhide: Incident of the Boomerang," CBS, 1961; "Michael Shayne: No Shroud for Shayne," NBC, 1961; "The Rifleman: Death Trap," ABC, 1961; "Stagecoach West: Blind Man's Buff," ABC, 1961; "Rawhide: Incident of the Night on the Town,"

CBS, 1961; "Perry Mason: The Case of the Missing Melody," CBS, 1961; "Robert Taylor's Detectives: Walk a Crooked Line," NBC, 1962; "Wagon Train: The Cole Crawford Story," NBC, 1962; "It Takes a Thief: A Thief Is a Thief Is a Thief," ABC, 1968; "It Takes Two," NBC, 1969; "Name Droppers," NBC, 1969; "Hollywood Squares," NBC, 1970; "Ironside: The Professionals," NBC, 1971; "Alias Smith and Jones: The Long Chase," ABC, 1972.
TV MOVIES AND MINISERIES: "Breakout," NBC, 1970; "Alias Smith and Jones," ABC, 1971; "The Devil and Miss Sarah," ABC, 1971.

DRYER, FRED
b. Hawthorne, CA, July 6, 1946. Husky actor who plays detective Sgt. Rick Hunter.
AS A REGULAR: "Hunter," NBC, 1984- .
AND: "Lou Grant: Violence," CBS, 1981; "CHiPs: Force Seven," NBC, 1982; "Cheers: Sam at Eleven," NBC, 1982; "Cheers: Old Flames," NBC, 1983.
TV MOVIES AND MINISERIES: "The Star Maker," NBC, 1981; "Something So Right," CBS, 1982; "The Fantastic World of D.C. Collins," NBC, 1984.
* Dryer played pro football for 14 seasons with the New York Giants and Los Angeles Rams.
* Dryer was one of several actors considered for the role of Sam Malone on "Cheers."

DRYSDALE, DON
b. Van Nuys, CA, July 23, 1936. Pitcher with the Brooklyn and Los Angeles Dodgers, retired in 1969.
AS A REGULAR: "Monday Night Baseball," ABC, 1978-85.
AND: "Lawman: The Hardcase," ABC, 1960; "The Millionaire: Millionaire Larry Maxwell," CBS, 1960; "Leave It to Beaver: The Long Distance Call," ABC, 1962; "Alcoa Premiere: Flashing Spikes," ABC, 1962; "The Donna Reed Show: The Man Behind the Mask," ABC, 1962; "Art Linkletter's House Party," CBS, 1963; "The Donna Reed Show: All Those Dreams," ABC, 1963; "The Donna Reed Show: My Son, the Catcher," ABC, 1964; "The Joey Bishop Show: Joey and the Los Angeles Dodgers," NBC, 1964; "The Donna Reed Show: Play Ball," ABC, 1964; "The Flying Nun: The Big Game," ABC, 1969; "Then Came Bronson: The Spitball Kid," NBC, 1969; "The Brady Bunch: The Dropout," ABC, 1970; "Lucas Tanner: Instant Replay," NBC, 1974.

DUBOIS, JA'NET
b. Philadelphia, PA, August 5, 1938.
AS A REGULAR: "Love of Life," CBS, 1970-72; "Good Times," CBS, 1974-79; "Laughs!," SHO, 1990- .

AND: "CBS Children's Hour: J.T.," CBS, 1970; "Sanford & Son: Sanford and Son and Sister Makes Three,"NBC, 1972; "Shaft: The Killing," CBS, 1973; "The Resolution of Mossie Way," PBS, 1974; "Kojak: Loser Takes All," CBS, 1974; "Sammy and Company," SYN, 1976; "The Love Boat: The Matchmaker," ABC, 1980; "Magnum, P.I.: Little Girl Who," CBS, 1986.

TV MOVIES AND MINISERIES: "The Blue Knight," NBC, 1973; "A Beautful Killing," ABC, 1974; "Roots: The Next Generations," ABC, 1979; "Hellinger's Law," CBS, 1981; "The Sophisticated Gents," NBC, 1981.

DUEL, PETER—See Peter Deuel.

DUFF, HOWARD

b. Bremerton, WA, November 24, 1917; d. 1990. Sardonic actor who played nightclub owner Willie Dante, Det. Sam Stone on "The Felony Squad," Sheriff Titus Semple on "Flamingo Road," Paul Galveston on "Knots Landing" and Sen. Henry O'Dell on "Dallas."

AS A REGULAR: "Mr. Adams and Eve," CBS, 1957-58; "Dante," NBC, 1960-61; "The Felony Squad," ABC, 1966-69; "Flamingo Road," NBC, 1981-82; "Knots Landing," CBS, 1984-85; "Dallas," CBS, 1988-89.

AND: "Ford Theatre: The Ming Lama," NBC, 1953; "Ford Theatre: A Season to Love," NBC, 1954; "Schlitz Playhouse of Stars: Woman Expert," CBS, 1954; "Climax!: Escape From Fear," CBS, 1955; "Rheingold Theatre: First Offense," NBC, 1955; "Science Fiction Theatre: The Sound of Murder," SYN, 1955; "Climax!: Fury at Dawn," CBS, 1956; "I've Got a Secret," CBS, 1957; "The Ed Sullivan Show," CBS, 1957; "Art Linkletter's House Party," CBS, 1958; "Dinah Shore Chevy Show," NBC, 1958; "The Twilight Zone: A World of Difference," CBS, 1960; "Here's Hollywood," NBC, 1960; "Bus Stop: Door Without a Key," ABC, 1962; "Combat: Missing in Action," ABC, 1962; "The Alfred Hitchcock Hour: The Tender Poisoner," CBS, 1962; "Combat!: Missing in Action," ABC, 1962; "Sam Benedict: Not Even the Gulls Shall Weep," NBC, 1963; "The Virginian: Distant Fury," NBC, 1963; "Arrest and Trial: Isn't It a Lovely View?," ABC, 1963; "Burke's Law: Who Killed Billy Jo?," ABC, 1963; "You Don't Say," NBC, 1964; "The Eleventh Hour: Prodigy," NBC, 1964; "Burke's Law: Who Killed The Paper Dragon?," ABC, 1964; "Bob Hope Chrysler Theatre: The Sojourner," NBC, 1964; "The Rogues: Bless You, G. Carter Huntington," NBC, 1964; "I Spy: Crusade to Limbo," NBC, 1966; "Batman: The Impractical Joker/the Joker's Provokers," ABC, 1966; "Batman: The Entrancing Dr. Cassandra," ABC, 1968; "The Bold Ones: Man Without a Heart," NBC, 1969; "The Immortal: Paradise Bay," ABC, 1970; "The Name

of the Game: The Glory Shouter," NBC, 1970; "The Mod Squad: Put Out the Welcome Mat for Death," ABC, 1973; "Medical Story: An Air Full of Death," NBC, 1975; "Marcus Welby, M.D.: The One Face in the World," ABC, 1975; "Police Story: Headhunter," NBC, 1975; "The Rockford Files: There's One in Every Port," NBC, 1976; "Switch: Who Killed Lila Craig?," CBS, 1977; "Lou Grant: Hollywood," CBS, 1979; "The Love Boat: The Tomorrow Lady," ABC, 1982; "St. Elsewhere: Addiction," NBC, 1983; "Murder, She Wrote: Deadly Lady," CBS, 1984; "Scarecrow and Mrs. King: Tale of the Dancing Weasel," CBS, 1985; "Scarecrow and Mrs. King: The Kruschev List," CBS, 1987.

TV MOVIES AND MINISERIES: "The D.A.: Murder One," NBC, 1969; "In Search of America," ABC, 1971; "A Little Game," ABC, 1971; "The Heist," ABC, 1972; "Snatched," ABC, 1973; "In the Glitter Palace," NBC, 1977; "Battered," NBC, 1978; "Valentine Magic on Love Island," NBC, 1980; "Flamingo Road," NBC, 1980; "East of Eden," ABC, 1981; "The Wild Women of Chastity Gulch," ABC, 1982; "This Girl for Hire," CBS, 1983; "Love on the Run," NBC, 1985; "Roses Are for the Rich," CBS, 1987; "War and Remembrance," ABC, 1988, 1989; "Settle the Score," NBC, 1989.

AS DIRECTOR: "Camp Runamuck," NBC, 1965-66.

DUFFY, JULIA

b. Minneapolis, MN, June 27, 1950. Petite blonde actress who deserved an Emmy as spoiled maid Stephanie Vanderkellen on "Newhart."

AS A REGULAR: "The Doctors," NBC, 1973-77; "Wizards and Warriors," CBS, 1983; "Newhart," CBS, 1983-90; "Baby Talk," ABC, 1990- .

AND: "The Love Boat: The Wedding," ABC, 1979; "Lou Grant: Rape," CBS, 1981; "Cheers: Any Friend of Diane's," NBC, 1982; "Simon & Simon: Room 3502," CBS, 1983; "The Love Boat: The Last Heist," ABC, 1984.

TV MOVIES AND MINISERIES: "Maybe Baby," NBC, 1988; "The Cover Girl and the Cop," NBC, 1989.

DUFFY, PATRICK

b. Townsend, MT, March 17, 1949. Bobby Ewing, dead and alive.

AS A REGULAR: "Man From Atlantis," NBC, 1977-78; "Dallas," CBS, 1978-85, 1986- .

AND: "Charlie's Angels: Angel in Love," ABC, 1980; "Hotel: Missing Pieces," ABC, 1985; "A Conversation with Dinah," TNN, 1989.

TV MOVIES AND MINISERIES: "Man From Atlantis," NBC, 1977; "Cry for the Strangers," CBS, 1982.

278

DUGAN, DENNIS

b. Wheaton, IL, 1948. Fresh-faced actor who played young private eye Richie Brockelman and Walter, the nice guy Maddie Hayes (Cybill Shepherd) married and divorced on "Moonlighting."

AS A REGULAR: "Richie Brockelman, Private Eye," NBC, 1978; "Empire," CBS, 1984; "Shadow Chasers," ABC, 1985-86; "Moonlighting," ABC, 1987-88.

AND: "Love, American Style: Love and the Lie," ABC, 1973; "M*A*S*H: Love and Marriage," CBS, 1975; "Columbo: Last Salute to the Commodore," NBC, 1976; "Alice: Pilot," CBS, 1976; "Hollywood Television Theatre: The Fatal Weakness," PBS, 1976; "The Rockford Files: The House on Willis Avenue," NBC, 1978; "The Rockford Files: Never Send a Boy King to Do a Man's Job," NBC, 1979; "Hill Street Blues: The World According to Freedom," NBC, 1981; "Hill Street Blues: The Spy Who Came From Delgado," NBC, 1982; "Hill Street Blues: Pestolozzi's Revenge," NBC, 1982; "Hill Street Blues: Freedom's Last Stand," NBC, 1982; "M*A*S*H: Strange Bedfellows," CBS, 1983; "St. Elsewhere: Tears of a Clown," NBC, 1985.

TV MOVIES AND MINISERIES: "Richie Brockelman, Private Eye," NBC, 1976; "Rich Man, Poor Man," ABC, 1976; "Country Gold," CBS, 1982; "The Toughest Man in the World," CBS, 1984.

DUGGAN, ANDREW

b. Franklin, IN, December 28, 1923; d. 1987. Lantern-jawed actor who played rancher Murdoch Lancer.

AS A REGULAR: "Bourbon Street Beat," ABC, 1959-60; "Room for One More," ABC, 1962; "Twelve O'Clock High," ABC, 1965-67; "Lancer," CBS, 1968-71.

AND: "Stage 7: The Double Cross," CBS, 1955; "Cheyenne: The Bounty Killers," ABC, 1956; "Gunsmoke: How to Cure a Friend," CBS, 1956; "Cheyenne: Land Beyond the Law," ABC, 1957; "Matinee Theatre: The Iceman," NBC, 1958; "Suspicion: Eye for an Eye," NBC, 1958; "Have Gun, Will Travel: The Teacher," CBS, 1958; "Dow Hour of Great Mysteries: The Cat and the Canary," NBC, 1960; "The Roaring Twenties: Brother's Keeper," ABC, 1960; "77 Sunset Strip: The Hamlet Caper," ABC, 1961; "Lawman: Marked Man," ABC, 1961; "Maverick: The Ice Man," ABC, 1961; "Cheyenne: The Frightened Town," ABC, 1961; "77 Sunset Strip: The Celluloid Cowboy," ABC, 1961; "77 Sunset Strip: Baker Street Caper," ABC, 1962; "Cheyenne: Satonka," ABC, 1962; "Hawaiian Eye: The Broken Thread," ABC, 1962; "Cheyenne: Showdown at Oxbend," ABC, 1962; "The Dakotas: Red Sky Over Bismarck," ABC, 1963; "Hawaiian Eye: Maybe Menehunes," ABC, 1963;

"Dr. Kildare: Four Feet in the Morning," NBC, 1963; "The Eleventh Hour: Four Feet in the Morning," NBC, 1963; "Slattery's People: Question-Do the Ignorant Sleep in Pure White Beds?," CBS, 1964; "The Fugitive: The End Is But the Beginning," ABC, 1965; "The Big Valley: Brawlers," ABC, 1965; "F Troop: The New I.G.," ABC, 1966; "The FBI: A Question of Guilt," ABC, 1967; "Medical Center: Undercurrent," CBS, 1970; "Medical Center: Man at Bay," CBS, 1970; "McMillan and Wife: Death Is a Seven-Point Favorite," NBC, 1971; "Mannix: The Man Outside," CBS, 1971; "Hollywood Television Theatre: Neighbors," NET, 1971; "Banacek: The Two Million Clams of Cap'n Jack," NBC, 1973; "Medical Center: Stranger in Two Worlds," CBS, 1973; "Hawaii Five-O: Death with Father," CBS, 1974; "Barnaby Jones: Foul Play," CBS, 1974; "The Streets of San Francisco: Target: Red," ABC, 1974; "McMillan and Wife: Game of Survival," NBC, 1974; "McMillan and Wife: Point for Law," NBC, 1976; "Switch: Fade Out," CBS, 1977; "Lou Grant: Skids," CBS, 1979; "Vega$: Redhanded," ABC, 1979; "CHiPS: Counterfeit," NBC, 1979; "M*A*S*H: Father's Day," CBS, 1980; "Hart to Hart: Bahama-Bound Harts," ABC, 1983; "Hardcastle and McCormick: The Georgia Street Motors," ABC, 1984.

TV MOVIES AND MINISERIES: "Hawaii Five-O," CBS, 1968; "The Forgotten Man," ABC, 1971; "Two on a Bench," ABC, 1971; "The Homecoming," CBS, 1971; "Jigsaw," ABC, 1972; "The Streets of San Francisco," ABC, 1972; "Firehouse," ABC, 1973; "Panic on the 5:22," ABC, 1974; "The Last Angry Man," ABC, 1974; "Attack on Terror: The FBI Versus the Ku Klux Klan," CBS, 1975; "Rich Man, Poor Man," ABC, 1976; "The Deadliest Season," CBS, 1977; "Best Sellers: Once an Eagle," NBC, 1977; "Overboard," NBC, 1978; "The Time Machine," NBC, 1978; "A Fire in the Sky," NBC, 1978; "Backstairs at the White House," NBC, 1979; "The Long Days of Summer," ABC, 1980; "M Station: Hawaii," CBS, 1980.

DUKE, PATTY

b. Anna Marie Duke, Elmhurst, NY, December 14, 1946. Actress whose TV and movie roles have ranged from Helen Keller to teenager Patty Lane to Martha Washington.

AS A REGULAR: "Kitty Foyle," NBC, 1958; "The Brighter Day," CBS, 1958-59; "The Patty Duke Show," ABC, 1963-66; "It Takes Two," ABC, 1982-83; "Hail to the Chief," ABC, 1985; "Karen's Song," FOX, 1987.

AND: "Kraft Television Theatre: The Big Heist," NBC, 1957; "Armstrong Circle Theatre: Have Jacket: Will Travel," CBS, 1957; "U.S. Steel Hour: The Reward," CBS, 1958; "Du Pont Show of the Month: Wuthering Heights," CBS, 1958;

"An American Girl," NBC, 1958; "The $64,000 Challenge," CBS, 1958; "Du Pont Show of the Month: The Prince and the Pauper," CBS, 1958; "Kraft Mystery Theatre: Death Wears Many Faces," NBC, 1958; "Swiss Family Robinson," NBC, 1958; "U.S. Steel Hour: One Red Rose for Christmas," CBS, 1958; "U.S. Steel Hour: Family Happiness," CBS, 1959; "Meet Me in St. Louis," CBS, 1959; "Armstrong Circle Theatre: Zone of Silence," CBS, 1959; "U.S. Steel Hour: Seed of Guilt," CBS, 1959; "Once Upon a Christmas Fable," NBC, 1959; "U.S. Steel Hour: One Red Rose for Christmas," CBS, 1959; "The Power and the Glory," CBS, 1961; "Ben Casey: Mrs. McBroom and the Cloud Watcher," ABC, 1962; "U.S. Steel Hour: The Duchess and the Smugs," CBS, 1962; "The Wide Country: To Cindy, with Love," NBC, 1963; "Hollywood Television Theatre: Birdbath," NET, 1971; "The Sixth Sense: With Affection, Jack the Ripper," ABC, 1972; "Police Story: Sniper," NBC, 1975; "Police Woman: Nothing Left to Lose," NBC, 1975; "Marcus Welby, M.D.: Unindicted Wife," ABC, 1975; "The Love Boat: What a Drag," ABC, 1984; "J.J. Starbuck: Pilot," NBC, 1987.

TV MOVIES AND MINISERIES: "My Sweet Charlie," NBC, 1970; "Two On a Bench," ABC, 1971; "If Tomorrow Comes," ABC, 1971; "She Waits," CBS, 1972; "Deadly Harvest," CBS, 1972; "Nightmare," CBS, 1973; "Hard Day at Blue Nose," ABC, 1974; "Look What's Happened to Rosemary's Baby," ABC, 1976; "Best Sellers: Captains and the Kings," NBC, 1976; "Hanging by a Thread," NBC, 1979; "Before and After," ABC, 1979; "The Miracle Worker," NBC, 1979; "Something So Right," CBS, 1982; "September Gun," CBS, 1983; "George Washington," CBS, 1984; "Best Kept Secrets," ABC, 1984; "A Time to Triumph," CBS, 1986; "George Washington II: The Forging of a Nation," CBS, 1986; "Fight for Life," ABC, 1987; "Perry Mason: The Case of the Avenging Ace," NBC, 1988; "Everybody's Baby: The Rescue of Jessica McClure," ABC, 1989; "Amityville: The Evil Escapes," NBC, 1989.
* Duke and co-contestant Eddie Hodges each won $8,000 answering show-biz questions on "The $64,000 Challenge."
* Duke won an Oscar for playing Helen Keller in the film version of "The Miracle Worker"; in 1979 she played Keller's teacher, Annie Sullivan, in a TV-movie remake and won an Emmy.
* Emmies: 1970, 1977, 1980.

DUKE, ROBIN
b. Canada, March 13, 1954.
AS A REGULAR: "Second City TV," SYN, 1980-81; "Saturday Night Live," NBC, 1981-84.

DULLEA, KEIR
b. Cleveland, OH, May 30, 1936.
AS A REGULAR: "The Starlost," SYN, 1973-74.
AND: "Special Tonight: Mrs. Miniver," CBS, 1960; "Frontiers of Faith: From the Dark Source," NBC, 1960; "Route 66: Black November," CBS, 1960; "Naked City: Murder Is a Face I Know," ABC, 1961; "U.S. Steel Hour: The Big Splash," CBS, 1961; "Hallmark Hall of Fame: Give Us Barabbas!," NBC, 1961; "Play of the Week: All Summer Long," SYN, 1961; "U.S. Steel Hour: The Golden Thirty," CBS, 1961; "The New Breed: Prime Target," ABC, 1961; "Alcoa Premiere: People Need People," ABC, 1961; "Checkmate: A Very Rough Sketch," CBS, 1961; "U.S. Steel Hour: Far From the Shade Tree," CBS, 1962; "Alcoa Premiere: Tiger," ABC, 1962; "Mystery Theatre: Cry Ruin," NBC, 1962; "Alcoa Premiere: Ordeal in Darkness," ABC, 1962; "The du Pont Show: The Outpost," NBC, 1962; "The Eleventh Hour: Cry a Little for Mary, Too," NBC, 1962; "Empire: Stopover on the Way to the Moon," NBC, 1963; "U.S. Steel Hour: The Young Avengers," CBS, 1963; "Bonanza: Elegy for a Hangman," NBC, 1963; "Naked City: The Apple Falls Not Far From the Tree," ABC, 1963; "Going My Way: One Small, Unhappy Family," ABC, 1963; "Alcoa Premiere: The Broken Year," ABC, 1963; "Channing: The Trouble with Girls," ABC, 1964; "Twelve O'Clock High: To Heinie with Love," ABC, 1965; "Hollywood Television Theatre: Montserrat," NET, 1971; "McMillan and Wife: Blues for Sally M," NBC, 1972; "Switch: James Caan Con," CBS, 1975.

TV MOVIES AND MINISERIES: "Black Water Gold," ABC, 1970; "Law and Order," NBC, 1976; "The Legend of the Golden Gun," NBC, 1979; "The Hostage Tower," CBS, 1980; "Brave New World," NBC, 1980; "No Place to Hide," CBS, 1981.

DUMBRILLE, DOUGLASS
b. Canada, October 13, 1890; d. 1974.
Character actor who specialized in playing grouchy bosses and slick, evil types.
AS A REGULAR: "China Smith," SYN, 1952-55; "The Life of Riley," NBC, 1953-58; "Grand Jury," SYN, 1959-60; "The New Phil Silvers Show," CBS, 1963-64.
AND: "Fireside Theatre: The Devil's Due," NBC, 1950; "Racket Squad: The Case of the Fabulous Mr. Jones," CBS, 1951; "Ford Theatre: The Fugitives," NBC, 1954; "Public Defender: The Do-Gooder," CBS, 1954; "Gloria Swanson Theatre: My Last Duchess," SYN, 1955; "Treasury Men in Action: The Case of the Slippery Eel," ABC, 1955; "Disneyland: Davy Crockett and the River Pirates," ABC, 1955; "TV Reader's Digest: The Sad Death of a Hero," ABC, 1955; "Fireside Theatre: Big Joe's Comin' Home," NBC, 1955; "Crossroads: Through the

Window," ABC, 1956; "Cavalcade Theatre: Young Andy Jackson," ABC, 1956; "The Charlie Farrell Show: Private War," CBS, 1956; "Hey, Jeannie!: Jeannie the WAC," CBS, 1956; "Tales of the Bengal Lancers: The Traitor," NBC, 1956; "Crossroads: The Thanksgiving Prayer," ABC, 1956; "The George Burns and Gracie Allen Show: Blanche Gets a Jury Notice," CBS, 1958; "Laramie: Duel at Alta Mesa," NBC, 1959; "The George Burns Show: The Landlord Visits," NBC, 1959; "The Untouchables: Syndicate Sanctuary," ABC, 1959; "The Many Loves of Dobie Gillis: I Was a High School Scrooge," CBS, 1961; "The Many Loves of Dobie Gillis: Move Over, Perry Mason," CBS, 1961; "The Many Loves of Dobie Gillis: Like Low Noon," CBS, 1962; "The Twilight Zone: The Self-Improvement of Salvadore Ross," CBS, 1964; "Perry Mason: The Case of the Latent Lover," CBS, 1964; "Perry Mason: The Case of the Duplicate Case," CBS, 1965; "The Beverly Hillbillies: The Richest Woman," CBS, 1966; "Batman: Zelda the Great/ A Death Worse Than Fate," ABC, 1966.

DUMONT, MARGARET

b. Margaret Baker, October 20, 1889; d. 1965. Actress who was a legendary straightwoman for the Marx Brothers in several movies, and for good reason—she didn't get their jokes.
AS A REGULAR: "My Friend Irma," CBS, 1952-53.
AND: "The Donna Reed Show: Miss Lovelace Comes to Tea," ABC, 1959; "The Chevy Show: Around the World with Nellie Bly," NBC, 1960.

DUNAWAY, FAYE

b. Bascom, FL, January 14, 1941. Blonde, somewhat mannered actress who was the toast of Hollywood moviemakers in the seventies and has since drifted to television.
AS A GUEST: "Trials of O'Brien: The 10-Foot, Six-Inch Pole," CBS, 1966; "Hogan's Goat," NET, 1971; "After the Fall," NBC, 1974.
TV MOVIES AND MINISERIES: "Portrait: The Woman I Love," ABC, 1974; "The Disappearance of Aimee," NBC, 1976; "Christopher Columbus," CBS, 1985; "Agatha Christie's Thirteen at Dinner," CBS, 1985; "Casanova," ABC, 1987; "Cold Sassy Tree," TNT, 1989.

DUNCAN, SANDY

b. Henderson, TX, February 20, 1946. Perky actress who plays Sandy Hogan on "The Hogan Family."
AS A REGULAR: "Funny Face," CBS, 1971; "The Sandy Duncan Show," CBS, 1972; "Valerie's Family," NBC, 1987; "The Hogan Family," NBC, 1987-90; CBS, 1990- .
AND: "Bonanza: An Earthquake Called Callahan," NBC, 1971; "The Sonny and Cher Comedy Hour," CBS, 1972; "Sandy's Jekyll and Hyde,"

CBS, 1973; "Rowan & Martin's Laugh-In," NBC, 1973; "The Flip Wilson Show," NBC, 1973; "Password," ABC, 1973; "The Tonight Show Starring Johnny Carson," NBC, 1974; "Sandy in Disneyland," CBS, 1974; "Bing Crosby and His Friends," CBS, 1974; "Dinah!," SYN, 1975; "Sammy and Company," SYN, 1975; "Pinocchio," CBS, 1976; "The Six Million Dollar Man: Return of Big Foot," ABC, 1976; "The Bionic Woman: Return of Big Foot," ABC, 1976; "Christmas in Disneyland," ABC, 1976; "Bonkers!," SYN, 1978; "ALF: We Are Family," NBC, 1988; "The Pat Sajak Show," CBS, 1989.
TV MOVIES AND MINISERIES: "Roots," ABC, 1977; "My Boyfriend's Back," NBC, 1989.

DUNN, JAMES

b. Santa Monica, CA, November 2, 1905; d. 1967. Actor who played young go-getters in thirties movies and then moved to character roles.
AS A REGULAR: "It's a Great Life," NBC, 1954-56.
AND: "Curtain Call: The Summer People," NBC, 1952; "Schlitz Playhouse of Stars: I Want to be a Star," CBS, 1952; "Hollywood Opening Night: Quite a Viking," NBC, 1952; "Hollywood Opening Night: Josie," NBC, 1952; "Goodyear TV Playhouse: Medal in the Family," NBC, 1953; "Studio One: The Show Piece," CBS, 1953; "Studio One: Shadow of the Devil," CBS, 1953; "Studio One: The Magic Lantern," CBS, 1953; "Goodyear TV Playhouse: Her Prince Charming," NBC, 1953; "First Person: One Night Stand," NBC, 1953; "Robert Montgomery Presents: Paradise Cafe," NBC, 1954; "Robert Montgomery Presents: My Little Girl," NBC, 1954; "Schlitz Playhouse of Stars: The Treasure of Santa Domingo," CBS, 1954; "G.E. Theatre: Desert Crossing," CBS, 1954; "Armstrong Circle Theatre: Jody and Me," NBC, 1954; "Robert Montgomery Presents: Joe's Boy," NBC, 1955; "The Red Skelton Show," CBS, 1957; "Mr. Broadway," NBC, 1957; "Climax!: Keep Me in Mind," CBS, 1957; "Walt Disney Presents: The Nine Lives of Elfego Baca-Law and Order, Inc.," ABC, 1958; "Wanted Dead or Alive: Call Your Shot," CBS, 1959; "Naked City: Sweet Prince of Delancey Street," ABC, 1961; "Route 66: Bridge Across Five Days," CBS, 1961; "The Investigators: The Mind's Own Fire," CBS, 1961; "Going My Way: Keep an Eye on Santa Claus," ABC, 1962; "Ben Casey: Saturday, Surgery and Stanley Schultz," ABC, 1962; "Slattery's People: Question-How Do You Fall in Love with a Town?," CBS, 1965; "Branded: The First Kill," NBC, 1965; "T.H.E. Cat: The Canary Who Lost His Voice," NBC, 1966.
TV MOVIES AND MINISERIES: "The Movie Maker," NBC, 1967; "Shadow Over Elveron," NBC, 1968.

DUNN, LIAM
b. 1916; d. 1976. Slight, wiry character actor often in exasperated roles; he played the father of Ted Baxter (Ted Knight) on a memorable episode of "The Mary Tyler Moore Show."
AS A REGULAR: "Captain Nice," NBC, 1967; "The Queen and I," CBS, 1969; "Diana," NBC, 1973-74.
AND: "Room 222: Funny Boy," ABC, 1969; "Room 222: Once Upon a Time, There Was Air You Couldn't See," ABC, 1970; "Mannix: Days Beyond Recall," CBS, 1971; "Gunsmoke: No Tomorrow," CBS, 1972; "Sanford & Son: A Guest in the Yard," NBC, 1972; "Banacek: The Two Million Clams of Cap'n Jack," NBC, 1972; "The Paul Lynde Show: Out of Bounds," ABC, 1973; "Faraday and Company: Premiere," NBC, 1973; "The Girl with Something Extra: A Gift for the Gifted," NBC, 1973; "The Mary Tyler Moore Show: Father's Day," CBS, 1973; "The Snoop Sisters: Corpse and Robbers," NBC, 1973; "Koska ... and His Family," NBC, 1973; "The Partridge Family: Art for Mom's Sake," ABC, 1974; "If I Love You, Am I Trapped Forever?," CBS, 1974; "McMillan and Wife: Love, Honor and Swindle," NBC, 1975; "Twigs," CBS, 1975; "Barney Miller: Horse Thief," ABC, 1975; "Kojak: The Trade-Off," CBS, 1975; "McCoy: In Again, Out Again," NBC, 1976; "Rhoda: Don't Give Up the Office," CBS, 1976; "McMillan and Wife: The Deadly Cure," NBC, 1976; "Three Times Daley," CBS, 1976.
TV MOVIES AND MINISERIES: "The Crooked Hearts," ABC, 1972; "Genesis II," ABC, 1973; "Isn't It Shocking?," ABC, 1973; "Miracle on 34th Street," CBS, 1973; "A Cry in the Wilderness," ABC, 1974; "A Tree Grows in Brooklyn," NBC, 1974; "Panache," ABC, 1976.

DUNN, MICHAEL
b. Gary Neil Miller, Shattuck, OK, October 20, 1934; d. 1973. Dwarf actor who played the evil Dr. Lovelace on "The Wild Wild West."
AS A REGULAR: "The Wild Wild West," CBS, 1965-68.
AND: "The Jack Paar Program," NBC, 1964; "Arrest and Trial: Revenge of the Worm," ABC, 1964; "East Side/West Side: Here Today," CBS, 1964; "Get Smart: Mr. Big," NBC, 1965; "Amos Burke, Secret Agent: The Prisoners of Mr. Sin," ABC, 1965; "Run for Your Life: The Dark Beyond the Door," NBC, 1966; "Tarzan: Alex the Great," NBC, 1968; "Star Trek: Plato's Stepchildren," NBC, 1968; "Bonanza: It's a Small World," NBC, 1970; "Night Gallery: The Sins of the Fathers," NBC, 1972; "A Homely Place," CBS, 1973.
TV MOVIES AND MINISERIES: "Goodnight My Love," ABC, 1972.

DUNN, NORA
b. Chicago, IL, April 29, 1952. Actress who led a one-woman protest against comedian Andrew "Dice" Clay; she refused to appear on "Saturday Night Live" the night he hosted the show and her contract wasn't renewed.
AS A REGULAR: "Saturday Night Live," NBC, 1985-90.

DUNN, RALPH
b. Titusville, PA, 1902; d. 1968.
AS A REGULAR: "Norby," NBC, 1955; "Kitty Foyle," NBC, 1958.
AND: "The Phil Silvers Show: Investigation," CBS, 1956; "Kraft Theatre: Fifty Grand," NBC, 1958; "Hallmark Hall of Fame: Arsenic and Old Lace," NBC, 1962; "The Doctors and the Nurses: The Outpost," CBS, 1964; "NYPD: Money Man," ABC, 1967.

DUNNE, IRENE
b. Louisville, KY, December 20, 1904; d. 1990. Genteel actress who could do comedy with the best of them, but her TV work was more along the lines of refined drama.
AS A REGULAR: "Schlitz Playhouse of Stars," CBS, 1952.
AND: "Ford Theatre: Sister Veronica," NBC, 1954; "Ford Theatre: Touch of Spring," NBC, 1955; "Ford Theatre: On the Beach," NBC, 1956; "Ford Theatre: Sheila," NBC, 1956; "The Perry Como Show," NBC, 1956; "President's Birthday Party," CBS, 1956; "The Jack Benny Program," CBS, 1958; "Christophers: The Story of Two Men," SYN, 1958; "The du Pont Show with June Allyson: The Opening Door," CBS, 1959; "The Big Party," CBS, 1959; "Christophers: The Importance of Libraries," SYN, 1959; "Christophers: The Importance of Just Laws," SYN, 1960; "Eleanor Roosevelt's Jubilee," NBC, 1960; "Frontier Circus: Dr. Sam," CBS, 1961; "G.E. Theatre: Go Fight City Hall," CBS, 1962; "Saints and Sinners: Source of Information," NBC, 1962.

DUNNE, STEVE
b. Northampton, MA, Jan 13, 1916. Smiling actor who was also an emcee.
AS A REGULAR: "Profesional Father," CBS, 1955; "You're On Your Own," CBS, 1956-57; "Truth or Consequences," NBC, 1957-58; "The Liberace Show," ABC, 1958-59; "The Brothers Brannagan," SYN, 1960-61; "Double Exposure," CBS, 1961.
AND: "Lux Video Theatre: The Hard Way," NBC, 1957; "Lux Video Theatre: Who is Picasso?," NBC, 1957; "Matinee Theatre: The Forbidden Search," NBC, 1957; "Kraft Theatre: Come to Me," NBC, 1957; "The Millionaire: Millionaire Dan Howell," CBS, 1958; "Goodyear Theatre: A

Light in the Fruit Closet," NBC, 1959; "Alfred Hitchcock Presents: Bang, You're Dead," NBC, 1961; "Alfred Hitchcock Presents: Services Rendered," NBC, 1961; "Your First Impression," NBC, 1962; "The Beverly Hillbillies: The Soup Contest," CBS, 1966; "Petticoat Junction: Second Honeymoon," CBS, 1966; "Batman: An Egg Grows in Gotham/The Yegg Foes in Gotham," ABC, 1966; "Nanny and the Professor: A Fowl Episode," ABC, 1970.

TV MOVIES AND MINISERIES: "Suddenly Single," ABC, 1971; "The Death of Me Yet," ABC, 1971.

DUNNINGER, JOSEPH
b. New York City, NY, April 28, 1892; d. 1975. Mentalist.
AS A REGULAR: "The Bigelow Show," NBC, 1948-49; CBS, 1949; "The Dunninger Show," NBC, 1955; "The Amazing Dunninger," ABC, 1956.

DUNNOCK, MILDRED
b. Baltimore, MD, January 25, 1906.
AS A GUEST: "Kraft Television Theatre: The Last Step," NBC, 1950; "The Web: The Handcuff," CBS, 1952; "Celanese Theatre: On Borrowed Time," ABC, 1952; "Goodyear TV Playhouse: A Game of Hide and Seek," NBC, 1954; "Inner Sanctum: The Sinners," SYN, 1954; "Armstrong Circle Theatre: Treasure Trove," NBC, 1954; "Campbell TV Soundstage: The Almighty Dollar," NBC, 1954; "Kraft Television Theatre: The Worried Songbirds," ABC, 1954; "Alfred Hitchcock Presents: None Are So Blind," CBS, 1956; "Kraft Television Theatre: The Wonderful Gift," NBC, 1956; "Playhouse 90: The Playroom," CBS, 1957; "Alfred Hitchcock Presents: Heart of Gold," CBS, 1957; "Kraft Theatre: The Sound of Trouble," NBC, 1957; "Playhouse 90: Diary of a Nurse," CBS, 1959; "Robert Herridge Theatre: A Trip to Czardis," SYN, 1960; "The Eternal Light: About Sophie Meier," NBC, 1960; "The Tom Ewell Show: The Friendly Man," CBS, 1960; "The Investigators: The Mind's Own Fire," CBS, 1961; "Westinghouse Presents: The First Day," CBS, 1962; "The Alfred Hitchcock Hour: Beyond the Sea of Death," CBS, 1964; "The Defenders: The Man Who Saved His Country," CBS, 1964; "The Reporter: A Time to Be Silent," CBS, 1964; "Death of a Salesman," CBS, 1966; "Experiment in Television: The Hamster of Happiness," NBC, 1968; "The FBI: The Prey," ABC, 1969.

TV MOVIES AND MINISERIES: "A Brand New Life," ABC, 1973; "A Summer Without Boys," ABC, 1973; "Murder or Mercy," ABC, 1974; "And Baby Makes Six," NBC, 1979; "Baby Comes Home," CBS, 1980; "The Patricia Neal Story," CBS, 1981; "Isabel's Choice," CBS, 1981.

DURANTE, JIMMY
b. James Francis Durante, New York City, NY, February 10, 1893; d. 1980. The "Schnozzola," beloved comedian with a protruding proboscis, remembered more for his guest appearances than any regular series. His trademark: "Goodnight, Mrs. Calabash, wherever you are."
AS A REGULAR: "All Star Revue," NBC, 1950-53; "Buick Circus Hour," NBC, 1952-53; "The Colgate Comedy Hour," NBC, 1953-54; "Texaco Star Theatre," NBC, 1954-55; "The Jimmy Durante Show," NBC, 1954-57; "Jimmy Durante Presents the Lennon Sisters Hour," ABC, 1969-70.
AND: "The Walter Winchell Show," NBC, 1956; "The Standard Oil 75th Anniversary Show," NBC, 1957; "Dinah Shore Chevy Show," NBC, 1957; "The Eddie Fisher Show," NBC, 1958; "Club Oasis," NBC, 1958; "Dinah Shore Chevy Show," NBC, 1958; "Milton Berle Starring in the Kraft Music Hall," NBC, 1958; "An Evening with Durante," NBC, 1959; "A Tribute to Eleanor Roosevelt on Her Diamond Jubilee," NBC, 1959; "Jimmy Durante Special: Give My Regards to Broadway," NBC, 1959; "Steve Allen Plymouth Show," NBC, 1960; "The Garry Moore Show," CBS, 1960; "Eleanor Roosevelt's Jubilee," NBC, 1960; "Open End," NBC, 1960; "Bob Hope Buick Show," NBC, 1960; "Perry Como's Kraft Music Hall," NBC, 1961; "The Jimmy Durante Show," NBC, 1961; "The Danny Thomas Show: Danny and Durante," CBS, 1961; "Scene Stealers," SYN, 1962; "The Ed Sullivan Show," CBS, 1962; "The Ed Sullivan Show," CBS, 1963; "Perry Como Special," NBC, 1964; "The Ed Sullivan Show," CBS, 1964; "The Ed Sullivan Show," CBS, 1965; "Jimmy Durante Meets the Lively Arts," ABC, 1965; "The Lucy Show: Lucy Goes to a Hollywood Premiere," CBS, 1966; "Alice Through the Looking Glass," NBC, 1966; "Bob Hope Chrysler Theatre: Murder at NBC," NBC, 1967; "Danny Thomas Special," NBC, 1967; "Personality," NBC, 1968; "Hollywood Palace," ABC, 1968; "Hollywood Palace," ABC, 1969; "The Mothers-in-Law: Every In-Law Wants to Get Into the Act," NBC, 1969; "Bob Hope Special," NBC, 1969; "The Andy Williams Show," NBC, 1970; "Frosty the Snowman," CBS, 1971; "A Salute to Television's 25th Anniversary," ABC, 1972.

* In 1961, Durante and his wife, Margie, wanted to adopt a baby, but adoption officials said Durante, then 68, was too old. A judge overruled them, saying, "I have heard this man sing "Young at Heart.""
* Durante suffered a stroke in 1972 and spent his last years in a wheelchair.
* Emmies: 1953.

DURNING, CHARLES

b. Highland Falls, NY, February 28, 1933.
Heavyweight character actor with a sense of physical grace who excelled as the dancing partner of Maureen Stapleton in the TV-movie "Queen of the Stardust Ballroom."

AS A REGULAR: "Another World," NBC, 1972; "The Cop and the Kid," NBC, 1975-76; "Eye to Eye," ABC, 1985; "Evening Shade," CBS, 1990- .

AND: "Madigan: The Midtown Beat," NBC, 1972; "All in the Family: Gloria, The Victim," CBS, 1973; "Cannon: The Deadly Conspiracy," CBS, 1975; "Barnaby Jones: The Deadly Conspiracy," CBS, 1975; "Hawaii Five-O: Retire in Sunny Hawaii Forever," CBS, 1975; "Amazing Stories: Guilt Trip," NBC, 1985; "Amazing Stories: You Gotta Believe Me," NBC, 1986.

TV MOVIES AND MINISERIES: "Connection," ABC, 1973; "The Trial of Chaplain Jensen," ABC, 1975; "Queen of the Stardust Ballroom," CBS, 1975; "Switch," CBS, 1975; "Best Sellers: Captains and the Kings," NBC, 1976; "Studs Lonigan," NBC, 1979; "ABC Theatre: Attica," ABC, 1980; "A Perfect Match," CBS, 1980; "Crisis at Central High," CBS, 1981; "The Best Little Girl in the World," ABC, 1981; "Death of a Salesman," CBS, 1985; "The Man Who Broke 1,000 Chains," HBO, 1987; "The Gambler III: The Legend Continues," CBS, 1987; "Case Closed," CBS, 1988; "Prime Target," NBC, 1989; "Dinner at Eight," TNT, 1989.

DUROCHER, LEO

b. West Springfield, MA, July 27, 1906.
Baseball player and manager.

AS A REGULAR: "Jackpot Bowling Starring Milton Berle," NBC, 1959.

AND: "Command Appearance," NBC, 1957; "Person to Person," CBS, 1957; "The George Gobel Show," NBC, 1958; "The Beverly Hillbillies: The Clampetts and the Dodgers," CBS, 1963; "Mr. Ed: Leo Durocher Meets Mr. Ed," CBS, 1963; "The Joey Bishop Show: Double Play From Foster to Durocher to Joey," NBC, 1964; "The Donna Reed Show: My Son, the Catcher," ABC, 1964; "The Donna Reed Show: Play Ball," ABC, 1964; "Mr. Novak: Boy Under Glass," NBC, 1964; "The Munsters: Herman the Rookie," CBS, 1965.

DURRELL, MICHAEL

b. Brooklyn, NY, October 6, 1943.

AS A REGULAR: "Nobody's Perfect," ABC, 1980; "I'm a Big Girl Now," ABC, 1980-81; "Shannon," CBS, 1981-82; "Alice," CBS, 1984-85; "Matlock," NBC, 1986-89.

AND: "Kojak: Laid Off," CBS, 1977; "Barney Miller: Appendicitis," ABC, 1978; "Barney Miller: The Baby Broker," ABC, 1978; "Barnaby Jones: Girl, on the Road," CBS, 1979; "Quincy: Cover-Up," NBC, 1980; "House Calls: Campaign in the Neck," CBS, 1982; "Cagney & Lacey: Internal Affairs," CBS, 1982; "Hill Street Blues: Midway to What?," NBC, 1983; "Hill Street Blues: Honk if You're a Goose," NBC, 1983; "Goodnight Beantown: Looking Forward to the Past," CBS, 1983; "Remington Steele: Steele Sweet on You," NBC, 1984; "Scarecrow and Mrs. King: Unfinished Business," CBS, 1986; "Cagney & Lacey: Shadow of Doubt," CBS, 1988; "Who's the Boss?: Mother and Child Disunion," ABC, 1989.

TV MOVIES AND MINISERIES: "The Immigrants," SYN, 1978; "V," NBC, 1983; "Diary of a Perfect Murder," NBC, 1986; "Family Sins," CBS, 1987.

DURYEA, DAN

b. White Plains, NY, January 23, 1907; d. 1968.

AS A REGULAR: "China Smith," SYN, 1952; "Peyton Place," ABC, 1967-68.

AND: "Schlitz Playhouse of Stars: P.G.," CBS, 1952; "Schlitz Playhouse of Stars: Singapore Souvenir," CBS, 1952; "Ford Theatre: Double Exposure," NBC, 1953; "Schlitz Playhouse of Stars: O'Brien," CBS, 1955; "Rheingold Theatre: The Lie," NBC, 1955; "Fireside Theatre: Nailed Down," NBC, 1955; "December Bride: High Sierras," CBS, 1955; "Star Stage: The Marshal and the Mob," NBC, 1956; "Schlitz Playhouse of Stars: Repercussion," CBS, 1956; "The 20th Century-Fox Hour: Smoke Jumpers," CBS, 1956; "G.E. Theatre: The Road That Led Afar," CBS, 1956; "Climax!: Four Hours in White," CBS, 1958; "Laramie: Stage Stop," NBC, 1959; "The Twilight Zone: Mr. Denton on Doomsday," CBS, 1959; "Adventures in Paradise: Judith," ABC, 1960; "Riverboat: The Wichita Arrows," NBC, 1960; "Riverboat: Fort Epitaph," NBC, 1960; "Wagon Train: The Joshua Gilliam Story," NBC, 1960; "Dick Powell's Zane Grey Theatre: Knight of the Sun," CBS, 1961; "The Barbara Stanwyck Show: Sign of the Zodiac," NBC, 1961; "Route 66: Don't Count Stars," CBS, 1961; "Checkmate: Tight as a Drum," CBS, 1961; "Rawhide: Incident of the Wolvers," CBS, 1962; "The Wide Country: Tears on a Painted Face," NBC, 1962; "The Eleventh Hour: Why Am I Grown So Cold?," NBC, 1963; "Alcoa Premiere: Blow High, Blow Clear," ABC, 1963; "U.S. Steel Hour: The Many Ways of Heaven," CBS, 1963; "Rawhide: Incident of the Prophecy," CBS, 1963; "The Alfred Hitchcock Hour: Three Wives Too Many," CBS, 1964; "Burke's Law: Who Killed 711?," ABC, 1964; "Daniel Boone: The Sound of Fear," NBC, 1965; "Combat: Dateline," ABC, 1965; "The Long, Hot Summer: The Return of the Quicks," ABC, 1965; "The Virginian: The

Challenge," NBC, 1966; "The Loner: A Little Stroll to the End of the Line," CBS, 1966; "The Monroes: Gold Fever," ABC, 1966; "Combat!: A Little Jazz," ABC, 1967; "Combat!: Jonah," ABC, 1967; "Dragnet: The Big Trial," NBC, 1967.
TV MOVIES AND MINISERIES: "Winchester '73," NBC, 1967; "Stranger on the Run," NBC, 1967.

DUSAY, MARJ
b. Russell, KS, February 20, 1936.
AS A REGULAR: "Stop Susan Williams," NBC, 1979; "Bret Maverick," NBC, 1981-82; "Capitol," CBS, 1983-87.
AND: "The Wild Wild West: The Night of the Turncoat," CBS, 1967; "Hogan's Heroes: Guess Who Came to Dinner," CBS, 1968; "The Wild Wild West: The Night of the Kraken," CBS, 1968; "The Mod Squad: The Debt," ABC, 1969; "Medical Center: A Duel With Doom," CBS, 1970; "The FBI: The Impersonator," ABC, 1970; "Family Affair: The Unsinkable Mr. French," CBS, 1970; "The Mod Squad: The Judas Trap," ABC, 1970; "Alias Smith and Jones: Never Trust an Honest Man," ABC, 1971; "The Odd Couple: What Does a Naked Lady Say to You?," ABC, 1971; "Mannix: Mask for a Charade," CBS, 1973; "The Manhunter: The Doomsday Gang," CBS, 1974; "Barnaby Jones: The Deadlier Species," CBS, 1975; "The Streets of San Francisco: Murder by Proxy," ABC, 1975; "The Bionic Woman: In This Corner, Jamie Sommers," ABC, 1976; "Barnaby Jones: Final Judgment," CBS, 1978; A Friend Indeed," NBC, 1981; "The Facts of Life: Graduation," NBC, 1983; "E/R: All's Well That Ends," CBS, 1984; "Mancuso FBI: Elections," NBC, 1989.
TV MOVIES AND MINISERIES: "Climb an Angry Mountain," NBC, 1972; "Most Wanted," ABC, 1976; "Murder in Peyton Place," NBC, 1977; "Arthur Hailey's Wheels," NBC, 1978; "The Child-Stealer," ABC, 1979; "The Paradise Connection," CBS, 1979; "The Murder That Wouldn't Die," NBC, 1980.

DUSSAULT, NANCY
b. Pensacola, FL, June 30, 1936. Actress who was David Hartman's original co-host on "Good Morning, America" and played Muriel Rush on "Too Close for Comfort."
AS A REGULAR: "The New Dick Van Dyke Show," CBS, 1971-73; "Good Morning, America," ABC, 1976-78; "Too Close for Comfort," ABC, 1980-83; SYN, 1984-86.
AND: "The Ed Sullivan Show," CBS, 1961; "The Ed Sullivan Show," CBS, 1962; "To Tell the Truth," CBS, 1964; "Bell Telephone Hour: The Music of Jerome Kern," NBC, 1965; "Love, American Style: Love and the See-Through Man," ABC, 1971; "Love, American Style: Love and the Fractured Fibula," ABC, 1974; "The Mike Douglas Show," SYN, 1974; "Barney Miller: The Courtesans," ABC, 1975; "The Love Boat: The Lady From

Laramie," ABC, 1981; "The Love Boat: What Goes Around," ABC, 1986; "Murder, She Wrote: The Way to Dusty Death," CBS, 1987; "Matlock: The Power Brokers," NBC, 1987; "Full House: Aftershocks," ABC, 1989.

DUVALL, ROBERT
b. San Diego, CA, January 5, 1931. Oscar winning actor ("Tender Mercies") who began in TV; he came back to play Dwight D. Eisenhower in a miniseries.
AS A GUEST: "Armstrong Circle Theatre: Jailbreak," CBS, 1959; "Destiny's Tot," NBC, 1960; "Armstrong Circle Theatre: Positive Identification," CBS, 1960; "John Brown's Raid," NBC, 1960; "Naked City: A Hole in the City," ABC, 1961; "Robert Herridge Theatre: The Bartender," SYN, 1961; "Great Ghost Tales: William Wilson," NBC, 1961; "Route 66: Birdcage on My Foot," CBS, 1961; "Cain's Hundred: King of the Mountain," NBC, 1961; "The Defenders: Perjury," CBS, 1961; "Alfred Hitchcock Presents: Bad Actor," NBC, 1962; "Shannon: The Big Fish," SYN, 1962; "Naked City: The One Marked Hot Gives Cold," ABC, 1962; "The Twilight Zone: Miniature," CBS, 1963; "The Outer Limits: The Chameleon," ABC, 1964; "The Outer Limits: The Inheritors," ABC, 1964; "The FBI: The Giant Killer," ABC, 1965; "Combat: The Enemy," ABC, 1965; "Shane: Poor Tom's A-Cold," ABC, 1966; "Combat!: Cry for Help," ABC, 1966; "T.H.E. Cat: The Long Chase," NBC, 1967; "Combat!: The Partisan," ABC, 1967; "Cimarron Strip: The Roarer," CBS, 1967; "The Wild Wild West: Night of the Falcon," CBS, 1967; "The FBI: The Executioners," ABC, 1967; "Run for Your Life: The Killing Scene," NBC, 1968; "Judd for the Defense: Murder in a Square Hole," ABC, 1968; "The FBI: The Harvest," ABC, 1968; "The Mod Squad: Keep the Faith, Baby," ABC, 1969; "The FBI: Nightmare Road," ABC, 1969.
TV MOVIES AND MINISERIES: "Fame is the Name of the Game," NBC, 1966; "Ike," ABC, 1979; "The Terry Fox Story," HBO, 1982; "Lonesome Dove," CBS, 1989.

DUVALL, SHELLEY
b. Houston, TX, 1950. Actress and producer.
AS A REGULAR: "Faerie Tale Theatre," SHO, 1982-86.
AND: "Love, American Style: Love and the Mr. and Mrs.," ABC, 1973; "Saturday Night Live," NBC, 1976; "The Twilight Zone: Saucer of Lonliness," CBS, 1986; "Wonderworks: Frog," PBS, 1988.
AS PRODUCER: "Faerie Tale Theatre," SHO, 1982-86.
TV MOVIES AND MINISERIES: "Dinner at Eight," TNT, 1989.

DYSART, RICHARD

b. *Brighton, MA*. Actor usually in distinguished roles; he plays Leland MacKenzie on "L.A. Law."

AS A REGULAR: "L.A. Law," NBC, 1986- .

AND: "Art Carney Special: Our Town," NBC, 1959; "Camera Three: In Tilbury Town," CBS, 1960; "Du Pont Show of the Month: The Lincoln Murder Case," CBS, 1961; "Look Up and Live: The Horse and His Rider," CBS, 1963; "East Side/West Side: The Sinner," CBS, 1963; "The Doctors and the Nurses: The Outpost," CBS, 1964; "The Defenders: Eyewitness," CBS, 1965; "NET Playhouse: Harriet," NET, 1972; "All in the Family: Edith Gets a Mink," CBS, 1972; "McCoy: Bless the Big Fish," NBC, 1975; "Columbo: Murder Under Glass," NBC, 1978; "Lou Grant: Censored," CBS, 1980.

TV MOVIES AND MINISERIES: "Gemini Man," NBC, 1976; "First You Cry," CBS, 1978; "Bogie," CBS, 1980; "The Ordeal of Dr. Mudd," CBS, 1980; "The People vs. Jean Harris," NBC, 1981; "Missing Children: A Mother's Story," CBS, 1982; "The Last Days of Patton," CBS, 1986; "Blood and Orchids," CBS, 1986; "Six Against the Rock," NBC, 1987; "Moving Target," NBC, 1988; "AT&T Presents: Day One," CBS, 1989.

E

EASTWOOD, CLINT

b. San Francisco, CA, May 31, 1930.
International film star usuaully in tightly-
wound roles; he made his TV mark as Rowdy
Yates on "Rawhide."
AS A REGULAR: "Rawhide," CBS, 1959-66.
AND: "West Point: White Fury," CBS, 1957;
"Navy Log: The Lonely Watch," ABC, 1958;
"Maverick: Duel at Sundown," ABC, 1959;
"Here's Hollywood," NBC, 1960; "Mr. Ed: Clint
Eastwood Meets Mr. Ed," CBS, 1962; "Here's
Hollywood," NBC, 1962; "Stump the Stars,"
CBS, 1962; "The Danny Kaye Show," CBS,
1965; "The Merv Griffin Show," CBS, 1969;
"The Merv Griffin Show," CBS, 1971; "The
Presidential Inaugural Gala," CBS, 1989.
AS DIRECTOR: "Amazing Stories: Vanessa in the
Garden," NBC, 1985.

EBSEN, BONNIE

b. 1952. Daughter of Buddy.
AS A REGULAR: "The Kallikaks," NBC, 1977.
AND: "Barnaby Jones: Venus As in Fly Trap,"
CBS, 1974; "Barnaby Jones: The Last Contract,"
CBS, 1974; "Marcus Welby, M.D.: No Charity
for the MacAllisters," ABC, 1974; "Barnaby
Jones: Taste for Murder," CBS, 1975; "Barnaby
Jones: The Coronado Triangle," CBS, 1978;
"Barnaby Jones: Target for a Wedding," CBS,
1979; "Barnaby Jones: Murder in the Key of C,"
CBS, 1980.
TV MOVIES AND MINISERIES: "Smash-Up on
Interstate 5," ABC, 1976; "The Paradise
Connection," CBS, 1979.

EBSEN, BUDDY

b. Christian L. Ebsen, Jr., Belleville, IL, April
2, 1908. Vaudeville hoofer who had mild
success in movies, and achieved a kind of pop
immortality as Jed Clampett, resident of
Beverly ... Hills, that is.
AS A REGULAR: "Disneyland: The Adventures of
Davy Crockett," ABC, 1954-55; "Northwest
Passage," NBC, 1958-59; "The Beverly
Hillbillies," CBS, 1962-71; "Barnaby Jones,"
CBS, 1973-80; "Matt Houston," ABC, 1984-
85.
AND: "Gruen Guild Playhouse: Al Haddon's
Lamp," SYN, 1952; "Broadway Television
Theatre: Burlesque," SYN, 1952; "Broadway
Television Theatre: The Nervous Wreck," SYN,
1952; "Broadway Television Theatre: Seven Keys
to Baldpate," SYN, 1952; "Schlitz Playhouse of
Stars: The Pussyfooting Rocks," CBS, 1952;

"Climax!: Tunnel of Fear," CBS, 1957;
"Playhouse 90: Free Weekend," CBS, 1958;
"Playhouse 90: A Trip to Paradise," CBS, 1959;
"Black Saddle: The Apprentice," ABC, 1960;
"Rawhide: Incident of the Stargazer," CBS, 1960;
"Johnny Ringo: The Killing Bug," CBS, 1960;
"Maverick: Cats of Paradise," ABC, 1960; "G.E.
Theatre: Graduation Dress," CBS, 1960;
"Riverboat: The Water at Gorgeous Springs,"
NBC, 1960; "Cheyenne: Apache Treasure," ABC,
1960; "Maverick: The Maverick Line," ABC,
1960; "Gunsmoke: Old Fool," CBS, 1960; "77
Sunset Strip: Open and Close in One," ABC,
1961; "The Twilight Zone: The Prime Mover,"
CBS, 1961; "The Andy Griffith Show: Opie's
Hobo Friend," CBS, 1961; "Have Gun, Will
Travel: The Brothers," CBS, 1961; "Have Gun,
Will Travel: A Knight to Remember," CBS, 1961;
"Bus Stop: The Man From Bootstrap," ABC,
1961; "Adventures in Paradise: One-Way Ticket,"
ABC, 1961; "Highways of Melody," NBC, 1961;
"The Danny Kaye Show," CBS, 1964; "Holly-
wood Palace," ABC, 1964; "The Entertainers,"
CBS, 1965; "Hollywood Palace," ABC, 1965;
"The Danny Kaye Show," CBS, 1965; "Art
Linkletter's House Party," CBS, 1968; "Cowsills
Special," NBC, 1968; "Jimmy Durante Presents
the Lennon Sisters Hour," ABC, 1969; "Holly-
wood Television Theatre: The Andersonville
Trial," NET, 1970; "Hawaii Five-O: 3,000
Crooked Miles to Honolulu," CBS, 1971;
"Gunsmoke: Drago," CBS, 1971; "Bonanza:
Saddle Stiff," NBC, 1972; "Night Gallery: The
Waiting Room," NBC, 1972; "Alias Smith and
Jones: What's in it for Mia?," ABC, 1972; "Alias
Smith and Jones: High Lonesome Country,"
ABC, 1972; "The Mac Davis Show," NBC, 1975;
"Tiny Tree," NBC, 1976; "Tattletales," CBS,
1977; "Hardcastle and McCormick: Killer B's,"
ABC, 1983; "The Yellow Rose: Deadline," NBC,
1984.
TV MOVIES AND MINISERIES: "The Daughters of
Joshua Cabe," ABC, 1972; "Horror at 37,000
Feet," CBS, 1973; "Tom Sawyer," CBS, 1973;
"The President's Plane is Missing," ABC,
1973; "Smash-Up on Interstate 5," ABC, 1976;
"The Bastard," SYN, 1978; "The Critical List,"
NBC, 1978; "The Paradise Connection," CBS,
1979; "The Return of the Beverly Hillbillies,"
CBS, 1981; "Stone Fox," NBC, 1987.
* See also "The Beverly Hillbillies," Nancy
Kulp.

EDELMAN, HERB

b. Brooklyn, NY, November 5, 1930. Bald,

portly character actor usually in likable roles; he plays Stan, ex-husband of Dorothy (Beatrice Arthur) on "The Golden Girls."

AS A REGULAR: "The Good Guys," CBS, 1968-70; "Ladies' Man," CBS, 1980-81; "Strike Force," ABC, 1981-82; "9 to 5," ABC, 1982-83; "St. Elsewhere," NBC, 1984-85; "The Golden Girls," NBC, 1985- ; "Knots Landing," CBS, 1990.

AND: "The Reporter: How Much for a Prince?," CBS, 1964; "Hey, Landlord!: The Long, Hot Bus," NBC, 1966; "That Girl: Time for Arrest," ABC, 1966; "It's About Time: The Stone Age Diplomats," CBS, 1967; "The Flying Nun: Ah Love, Could You and I Conspire," ABC, 1967; "The Mothers-in-Law: The Not-Cold-Enough War," NBC, 1967; "Love, American Style: Love and the King," ABC, 1969; "Love, American Style: Love and the Dating Computer," ABC, 1969; "Bewitched: This Little Piggy," ABC, 1971; "The Bill Cosby Show: Tobacco Road," NBC, 1971; "Mission: Impossible: Run for the Money," CBS, 1971; "Ironside: Murder by One," NBC, 1973; "Love, American Style: Love and Other Mistakes," ABC, 1973; "The Partridge Family: The Strikeout King," ABC, 1973; "Diana: Queen for a Night," NBC, 1973; "Police Story: The Ho Chi Minh Trail," NBC, 1973; "Maude: Maude the Boss," CBS, 1974; "The Streets of San Francsisco: Mask of Death," ABC, 1974; "Happy Days: The Cunningham Caper," ABC, 1975; "Medical Center: Gift From a Killer," CBS, 1975; "Barney Miller: The Guest," ABC, 1975; "Kojak: The Pride and the Princess," CBS, 1976; "Police Story: The Long Ball," NBC, 1976; "Welcome Back, Kotter: What a Move!," ABC, 1977; "The San Pedro Beach Bums: The Angels and the Bums," ABC, 1977; "Kojak: Chains of Custody," CBS, 1978; "The Love Boat: Zeke and Zelda," ABC, 1981; "Matt Houston: The Crying Clown," ABC, 1983; "Cagney & Lacey: Thank God It's Monday," CBS, 1984; "Cagney & Lacey: Hooked," CBS, 1984; "Cagney & Lacey: Power," CBS, 1985; "The Love Boat: Picture Me a Spy," ABC, 1986; "St. Elsewhere: Down and Out in Beacon Hill," NBC, 1988; "St. Elsewhere: Requiem for a Heavyweight," NBC, 1988; "thirtysomething: Be a Good Girl," ABC, 1989.

TV MOVIES AND MINISERIES: "In Name Only," ABC, 1969; "The Feminist and the Fuzz," ABC, 1971; "The Neon Ceiling," NBC, 1971; "Banyon," NBC, 1971; "Once Upon a Dead Man," NBC, 1971; "The Strange and Deadly Occurrence," NBC, 1974; "Crossfire," NBC, 1975; "Picking Up the Pieces," CBS, 1985; "Marathon," CBS, 1980.

EDEN, BARBARA

b. Barbara Jean Moorhead, San Francisco, CA, August 23, 1934. Blonde actress who played Jeannie and still tends toward sexpot roles.

AS A REGULAR: "How to Marry a Millionaire," SYN, 1958-59; "I Dream of Jeannie," NBC, 1965-70; "Harper Valley PTA," NBC, 1981-82; "The Magical World of Disney: Brand New Life," NBC, 1989-90; "Dallas," CBS, 1990- .

AND: "West Point: Decision," CBS, 1956; "I Love Lucy: Country Club Dance," CBS, 1957; "The Millionaire: The Ted McAllister Story," CBS, 1957; "Perry Mason: The Case of the Angry Mourner," CBS, 1957; "December Bride: The Other Woman," CBS, 1957; "Father Knows Best: The Rivals," NBC, 1958; "Here's Hollywood," NBC, 1961; "Adventures in Paradise: The Inheritance," ABC, 1961; "The Andy Griffith Show: The Manicurist," CBS, 1962; "Target: The Corruptors: Babes in Wall Street," ABC, 1962; "Cain's Hundred: Savage in Darkness," NBC, 1962; "Saints and Sinners: Daddy's Girl," NBC, 1962; "Dr. Kildare: If You Can't Believe the Truth," NBC, 1963; "Burke's Law: Who Killed Harris Crown?," ABC, 1963; "Rawhide: Incident at Confidence Rock," CBS, 1963; "Object Is," ABC, 1964; "Route 66: Where There's a Will, There's a Way," CBS, 1964; "Burke's Law: Who Killed the Paper Dragon?," ABC, 1964; "The Virginian: The Brazos Kid," NBC, 1964; "Burke's Law: Who Killed Cornelius Gilbert?," ABC, 1964; "Rawhide: Damon's Road," CBS, 1964; "Burke's Law: Who Killed the Man on the White Horse?," ABC, 1965; "Slattery's People: When Do We Hang the Good Samaritan?," CBS, 1965; "The Rogues: Wherefore Art Thou, Harold?," NBC, 1965; "The Pat Boone Show," NBC, 1967; "Kismet," ABC, 1967; "Password," CBS, 1968; "The Tonight Show Starring Johnny Carson," NBC, 1970; "Changing Scene II," ABC, 1970; "Bob Hope Special," NBC, 1971; "The Glen Campbell Goodtime Hour," CBS, 1972; "The Barbara Eden Show," ABC, 1973; "Out to Lunch," ABC, 1974; "The Sonny Comedy Revue," ABC, 1974; "Celebrity Sweepstakes," NBC, 1975; "The Sonny and Cher Comedy Hour," CBS, 1976; "Break the Bank," SYN, 1978; "The Mike Douglas Show," SYN, 1978; "Hollywood Squares," SYN, 1979; "The Pat Sajak Show," CBS, 1989.

TV MOVIES AND MINISERIES: "The Feminist and the Fuzz," ABC, 1971; "A Howling in the Woods," NBC, 1971; "The Woman Hunter," CBS, 1972; "Guess Who's Sleeping in My Bed?," ABC, 1973; "The Stranger Within," ABC, 1974; "Let's Switch," ABC, 1975; "How to Break Up a Happy Divorce," NBC, 1976; "Stonestreet: Who Killed the Centerfold Model?," NBC, 1977; "The Girls in the Office," ABC, 1979; "I Dream of Jeannie: 15 Years Later," NBC, 1985; "The Stepford Children," NBC, 1987; "Your Mother Wears Combat Boots," NBC, 1989.

THE ED SULLIVAN SHOW,

CBS, 1948-71.

A Sunday-night tradition for an amazing 23 years, "The Ed Sullivan Show" was hosted by a man with no real talent or camera presence who seemed to want to make up for that by introducing some of the most talented people in show business every week. Ed would have something for everyone: Jewish storyteller Myron Cohen for grandma, Robert Goulet for mom, Abbe Lane for dad, the singing Herman's Hermits for sis, the guy who spun plates to the "Saber Dance" for the older kids and the puppet mouse Topo Gigio ("Kees me goodnight, Eddie") for the little kids.

Sullivan also presented his share of cultural programming; in the mid-1950s, the show regularly featured scenes from Broadway shows, and the Bolshoi Ballet also appeared, as did performing bears from Russia. And Ed has his own favorite guests, people who almost never appeared on any other shows—dancer Peg Leg Bates, comics Johnny Wayne and Frank Shuster, ventriloquist Ricky Layne and his dummy Velvel. And the guy who spun the plates.

A few notable shows:

* The Beatles appeared on February 9, 1964, along with 30 policemen to control the screaming crowds. In New York, the show drew 59 percent of the viewing audience.

* Elvis Presley was on the show September 9, 1956; he was photographed from the waist up so his pelvic thrusts and leg wobbles wouldn't incite a sexual frenzy among American teenagers. Incidentally, Sullivan didn't emcee that show because he didn't like the idea of booking Presley; Charles Laughton did, announcing simply: "Ladies and gentlemen, Elvis Presley."

* Irving Berlin made a rare TV appearance with Sullivan to celebrate his 80th birthday in 1968. The show was expanded to 90 minutes and ended with an American flag in fireworks as everyone—except Ed, perhaps—sang "God Bless America."

* On January 5, 1964, Sullivan presented Sister Sourire, a Belgian nun whose recording of the song "Dominique" was a big hit. Sullivan traveled to Sourire's convent to hear her sing, and the incident was later dramatized—with Sullivan as himself—in the Debbie Reynolds film "The Singing Nun." On that same show, in the classic Sullivan tradition of offering something for everyone, our host also brought us the Nazareth Boys Choir from Israel, and Stevie Wonder.

EDWARDS, BLAKE

b. Tulsa, OK, July 26, 1922. Writer-director of films ("The Pink Panther," "10") and TV; he created the jazz-oriented detective show "Peter Gunn."

AS CREATOR-WRITER-DIRECTOR: "Peter Gunn," NBC, 1958-60; ABC, 1960-61; "Mr. Lucky," CBS, 1959-60.

AS WRITER-TV MOVIES AND MINISERIES: "The Monk," ABC, 1969; "Peter Gunn," ABC, 1989.

AS WRITER-DIRECTOR-TV MOVIES AND MINISERIES: "Disney Sunday Movie: Justin Case," ABC, 1988.

EDWARDS, CLIFF

b. Hannibal, MO, June 14, 1895; d. 1971. Actor and singer (known as "Ukelele Ike") who did some TV variety.

AS A REGULAR: "The Fifty-Fourth Street Revue," CBS, 1949; "The Cliff Edwards Show," CBS, 1949.

AND: "Playhouse 90: No Time at All," CBS, 1958.
* Edwards supplied the voice of Jiminy Cricket.

EDWARDS, DOUGLAS

b. Ada, OK, July 14, 1917.

AS A REGULAR: "Douglas Edwards and the News," CBS, 1948-62; "Celebrity Time," CBS, 1950-52; "Masquerade Party," CBS, 1953-54; "Armstrong Circle Theatre," CBS, 1957-61; "F.Y.I.," CBS, 1960.

EDWARDS, GEOFF

b. Westfield, NJ. Actor and game show emcee.

AS A REGULAR: "Petticoat Junction," CBS, 1968; "The Bobby Darin Show," NBC, 1973; "Hollywood's Talking," CBS, 1973; "Jackpot," NBC, 1974-75; "Treasure Hunt," SYN, 1974-77; "Shoot for the Stars," NBC, 1977; "Play the Percentages," SYN, 1980; "Starcade," SYN, 1983-85.

AND: "The Love Experts," SYN, 1978.

EDWARDS, RALPH

b. Merino, CO, June 13, 1913. Game show host and producer; he surprised guests of honor on "This Is Your Life" for years.

AS A REGULAR: "Truth or Consequences," CBS, 1950-51; "This is Your Life," NBC, 1952-61; SYN, 1971; NBC, 1987-88.

AND: "Person to Person," CBS, 1956; "The Steve Allen Show," NBC, 1957; "The Eddie Fisher Show," NBC, 1958.

AS PRODUCER: "Truth or Consequences," CBS, 1950-51; NBC, 1954-65; SYN, 1966-74; 1977-78; "This is Your Life," NBC, 1952-61; SYN, 1971; NBC, 1987-88; "End of the Rainbow," NBC, 1958; "Cross Wits," SYN, 1974-80, 1986-87; "The People's Court," SYN, 1981- .

EDWARDS, VINCE
b. *Vincent Edward Zoino, Brooklyn, NY, July 9, 1928.* Actor with a brooding quality that led to his character, Ben Casey, being nicknamed "The Surly Surgeon." Still, the show was a huge hit, and for most of the sixties Vince-baby was on top of the world.
AS A REGULAR: "Ben Casey," ABC, 1961-66; "Matt Lincoln," ABC, 1970-71.
AND: "Ford Theatre: Garrity's Sons," NBC, 1955; "Fireside Theatre: The Smuggler," NBC, 1955; "The 20th Century-Fox Hour: The Last Patriarch," CBS, 1956; "G.E. Theatre: Bitter Choice," CBS, 1957; "The Deputy: The Choice," NBC, 1959; "The Untouchables: Mexican Standoff," ABC, 1959; "Laramie: The Protectors," NBC, 1960; "Queen for a Day," ABC, 1961; "Dinah Shore Special," NBC, 1962; "The Lucy Show: Lucy Goes to a Hollywood Premiere," CBS, 1966; "The Dean Martin Show," NBC, 1970; "The Merv Griffin Show," CBS, 1970; "Saga of Sonora," NBC, 1973; "Medical Story: Test Case," NBC, 1975; "Police Story: On the Street," NBC, 1976; "Police Story: Payment Deferred," NBC, 1976; "Knight Rider: Pilot," NBC, 1982.
TV MOVIES AND MINISERIES: "Sole Survivor," CBS, 1970; "Dial Hot Line," ABC, 1970; "Do Not Fold, Spindle or Mutilate," ABC, 1971; "Firehouse," ABC, 1973; "Maneater," CBS, 1973; "Deathstalk," NBC, 1974; "Best Sellers: The Rhinemann Exchange," NBC, 1977; "Evening in Byzantium," SYN, 1978; "The Return of Mickey Spillane's Mike Hammer," CBS, 1986; "The Dirty Dozen: The Deadly Mission," NBC, 1987.

EGAN, RICHARD
b. *San Francisco, CA, July 29, 1921; d. 1987.*
AS A REGULAR: "Empire," NBC, 1962-63; "Redigo," NBC, 1963; "Capitol," CBS, 1982-87.
AND: "Ford Theatre: Double Bet," NBC, 1953; "Schlitz Playhouse of Stars: Go Away a Winner," CBS, 1954; "Impact: Malaya Incident," SYN, 1958; "Play Your Hunch," NBC, 1962; "The Tonight Show Starring Johnny Carson," NBC, 1963; "Bob Hope Chrysler Theatre: Massacre at Ft. Phil Kearney," NBC, 1966; "The Streets of San Francisco: The Unicorn," ABC, 1973; "Police Story: Captain Hook," NBC, 1974; "Matt Helm: Pilot," ABC, 1975; "Police Story: Bought and Paid For," NBC, 1976; "The Quest: The Captive," NBC, 1976.

TV MOVIES AND MINISERIES: "Valley of Mystery," ABC, 1967; "The House that Would Not Die," ABC, 1970; "Shootout in a One-Dog Town," ABC, 1974.

EGGAR, SAMANTHA
b. *London, England, May 3, 1939.*
AS A REGULAR: "Anna and the King," CBS, 1972.
AND: "The Saint: Marcia," NBC, 1965; "Love Story: The Cardboard House," NBC, 1973; "Lucas Tanner: Shattered," NBC, 1975; "Smithsonian Institution Special: The Legendary Curse of the Hope Diamond," CBS, 1975; "Hollywood Television Theatre: The Man of Destiny," PBS, 1975; "Hollywood Television Theatre: The Hemingway Play," PBS, 1976; "Starsky and Hutch: Starsky and Hutch on Playboy Island," ABC, 1977; "The Love Boat: Funny Valentine," ABC, 1979; "Hagen: Pilot," CBS, 1980; "The Love Boat: First Voyage, Last Voyage," ABC, 1981; "Hart to Hart: Long Lost Love," ABC, 1983; "Murder, She Wrote: Hooray for Homicide," CBS, 1984; "Finder of Lost Loves: Wayward Dreams," ABC, 1985; "Heartbeat: Confidentially Yours," ABC, 1989.
TV MOVIES AND MINISERIES: "Double Indemnity," ABC, 1973; "All the Kind Strangers," ABC, 1974; "The Killer Who Wouldn't Die," ABC, 1976; "Love Among Thieves," ABC, 1987.

EIKENBERRY, JILL
b. *New Haven, CT, January 21, 1947.* Actress who plays Ann Kelsey on "L.A. Law."
AS A REGULAR: "L.A. Law," NBC, 1986- .
AND: "Nurse: Impressions," CBS, 1982; "ABC Family Theater: A Family Again," ABC, 1988.
TV MOVIES AND MINISERIES: "The Deadliest Season," CBS, 1977; "Swan Song," ABC, 1980; "Sessions," NBC, 1983; "Family Sins," CBS, 1987; "Assault and Matrimony," NBC, 1989; "My Boyfriend's Back," NBC, 1989; "Cast the First Stone," NBC, 1989.

EINSTEIN, BOB
b. *Los Angeles, CA, November 20, 1940.* Comedy writer and actor; he plays "Super Dave" Osborne on a cable comedy show and on Nike commercials. Brother of Albert Brooks.
AS A REGULAR: "The Smothers Brothers Comedy Hour," CBS, 1967-69, NBC, 1975; "Pat Paulsen's Half a Comedy Hour," ABC, 1970; "The Sonny and Cher Comedy Hour," CBS, 1973-74; "Joey & Dad," CBS, 1975; "Van Dyke and Company," NBC, 1976; "Super Dave," SHO, 1987- .
AND: "Late Night with David Letterman," NBC, 1989.
AS WRITER: "The Smothers Brothers Comedy Hour," CBS, 1967-69; "Van Dyke and Company," NBC, 1976-77; "Super Dave," SHO, 1987- .
* Emmies: 1969, 1977.

EINSTEIN, HARRY "PARKYAKARKUS"

b. Boston, MA, 1904; d. 1958. Radio comedian; the father of Bob Einstein and Albert Brooks.
AS A GUEST: "Playhouse 90: No Time at All," CBS, 1958.

EISENMANN, IKE

b. Houston, TX, July 21, 1962.
AS A REGULAR: "Fantastic Journey," NBC, 1977.
AND: "Mannix: The Upside Down Penny," CBS, 1972; "Gunsmoke: Eleven Dollars," CBS, 1972; "Gunsmoke: Patricia," CBS, 1973; "Doc Elliot: A Time to Grow," ABC, 1974; "Doctors' Hospital: Vital Signs," NBC, 1975; "Little House on the Prairie: Centennial," NBC, 1976; "Police Woman: Deadline: Death," NBC, 1977; "Little House on the Prairie: Harriet's Happings," NBC, 1978; "Strike Force: Magic Man," ABC, 1981; "Blondie & Dagwood Second Wedding Workout," CBS, 1989.
TV MOVIES AND MINISERIES: "Banjo Hackett," NBC, 1976; "Black Beauty," NBC, 1978; "The Bastard," SYN, 1978; "Devil Dog: The Hound of Hell," CBS, 1978.

EISLEY, ANTHONY

b. Fred Eisley, Philadelphia, 1925. Mustachioed actor who played private eye Tracy Steele.
AS A REGULAR: "Bonino," NBC, 1953; "Pete Kelly's Blues," NBC, 1959; "Hawaiian Eye," ABC, 1959-62; "Bright Promise," NBC, 1969-72.
AND: "Tales of the Texas Rangers: Kickback," CBS, 1956; "The Loretta Young Show: Second Rate Citizen," NBC, 1958; "77 Sunset Strip: Perfect Setup," ABC, 1960; "The Real McCoys: Aunt Win Steps In," CBS, 1963; "The Dick Van Dyke Show: The Lady and the Tiger and the Lawyer," CBS, 1964; "Combat!: A Gift of Hope," ABC, 1964; "The Farmer's Daughter: Katy's 76th Birthday," ABC, 1964; "Perry Mason: The Case of the Missing Button," CBS, 1964; "The Outer Limits: The Brain of Colonel Barham," ABC, 1965; "Honey West: A Nice Little Till to Tap," ABC, 1965; "The FBI: The Man Who Went Mad by Mistake," ABC, 1966; "The Wild Wild West: The Night of the Eccentrics," CBS, 1966; "Gomer Pyle, USMC: Marry Me, Marry Me," CBS, 1966; "The Doris Day Show: The Woman Hater," CBS, 1969; "Dragnet: Ad. Vice-DR-29," NBC, 1969; "Dragnet: Frauds-DR-36," NBC, 1969; "Dragnet: S.I.U.-The Ring," NBC, 1969; "The Wild Wild West: The Night of the Janus," CBS, 1969; "Dragnet: Missing Persons-The Body," NBC, 1970; "Ironside: The Riddle in Room Six," NBC, 1971; "The FBI: The Replacement," ABC, 1971; "Marcus Welby, M.D.: Dinner of Herbs," ABC, 1972; "The Rookies: Cry Wolf," ABC, 1973; "The Magician: Lady in a Trap," NBC, 1973;

"The Mary Tyler Moore Show: WJM Tries Harder," CBS, 1974; "The Streets of San Francisco: I Ain't Marching Anymore," ABC, 1974; "Ironside: Act of Vengeance," NBC, 1974; "The Rookies: A Deadly Image," ABC, 1975; "The Rookies: The Code Five Affair," ABC, 1975; "Barnaby Jones: False Witness," CBS, 1979; "A Man Called Sloane: The Seduction Squad," NBC, 1979.
AS WRITER: "Hawaiian Eye: Satan City," ABC, 1961.

ELAM, JACK

b. Phoenix, AZ, November 13, 1916. Burly character actor with a wandering left eye who began his career playing heavies, and now tends toward comic roles, such as Bully on "Easy Street."
AS A REGULAR: "The Dakotas," ABC, 1963; "Temple Houston," NBC, 1963-64; "The Texas Wheelers," ABC, 1974-75; "Struck by Lightning," CBS, 1979; "Detective in the House," CBS, 1985; "Easy Street," NBC, 1986-87.
AND: "Gangbusters: Billy Dirk," SYN, 1954; "Dick Powell's Zane Grey Theatre: Dangerous Orders," CBS, 1957; "Restless Gun: Hornitas Town," NBC, 1958; "Cheyenne: The Besieged," ABC, 1959; "Have Gun, Will Travel: The Man Who Lost," CBS, 1959; "Mr. Lucky: The Big Squeeze," CBS, 1960; "Gunsmoke: Where'd They Go?," CBS, 1960; "Lawman: Thirty Minutes," ABC, 1960; "The Rifleman: Shotgun Man," ABC, 1960; "Dick Powell's Zane Grey Theatre: Deception," CBS, 1960; "Phil Silvers Special: The Slowest Gun in the West," CBS, 1960; "Stagecoach West: The Fork in the Road," ABC, 1960; "Klondike: Queen of the Klondike," NBC, 1961; "Dick Powell's Zane Grey Theatre: Ambush," CBS, 1961; "The Twilight Zone: Will the Real Martian Please Stand Up," CBS, 1961; "Lawman: The Four," ABC, 1961; "The Rifleman: Knight Errant," ABC, 1961; "National Velvet: The Desperado," NBC, 1961; "The Rifleman: The Shattered Idol," ABC, 1961; "The Outlaws: The Outlaw Marshals," NBC, 1961; "Have Gun, Will Travel: One, Two, Three," CBS, 1962; "Rawhide: The Pitchwagon," CBS, 1962; "Daniel Boone: The Sound of Fear," NBC, 1965; "The Legend of Jesse James: Three Men From Now," ABC, 1965; "F Troop: Dirge for the Scourge," ABC, 1965; "Hondo: Hondo and the Rebel Hat," ABC, 1967; "The Wild Wild West: The Night of the Montezuma's Hordes," CBS, 1967; "Gunsmoke: First People," CBS, 1968; "Gunsmoke: The Sisters," CBS, 1969; "The Virginian: Rich Man, Poor Man," NBC, 1970; "Plimpton! Shootout at Rio Lobo," ABC, 1970; "Gunsmoke: Murdoch," CBS, 1971; "Gunsmoke: P.S. Murry Christmas," CBS, 1971; "$weepstake$: Billy, Wally and Ludmilla, and

Theodore," NBC, 1979; "Father Murphy: By the Bear That Bit Me," NBC, 1981; "Here's Boomer: Boomer and the Muskrat Cove Treasure," NBC, 1981; "Webster: How the West Was Won," ABC, 1985; "Simon & Simon: Love and/or Marriage," CBS, 1986.

TV MOVIES AND MINISERIES: "The Over-the-Hill Gang," ABC, 1969; "The Daughters of Joshua Cabe," ABC, 1972; "The Red Pony," ABC, 1973; "Shootout in a One-Dog Town," ABC, 1974; "Sidekicks," CBS, 1974; "Huckleberry Finn," ABC, 1975; "The New Daughters of Joshua Cabe," ABC, 1976; "Black Beauty," NBC, 1978; "Where the Hell's That Gold?," CBS, 1988.

ELCAR, DANA
b. Ferndale, MI. Actor who plays Peter Thornton on "MacGyver."

AS A REGULAR: "A Time to Live," NBC, 1954; "Baretta," ABC, 1975; "Baa Baa Black Sheep," NBC, 1976-78; "MacGyver," ABC, 1985- .

AND: "Art Carney Special: Our Town," NBC, 1959; "Sunday Showcase: The Margaret Bourke-White Story," NBC, 1960; "The Sacco-Vanzetti Story," NBC, 1960; "Omnibus: He Shall Have Power," NBC, 1960; "Our American Heritage: Woodrow Wilson and the Unknown Soldier," NBC, 1961; "U.S. Steel Hour: The Troubled Heart," CBS, 1963; "Car 54, Where Are You?: The Star Boarder," NBC, 1963; "Catholic Hour: In Word and in Song," NBC, 1963; "Mannix: Fear I to Fall," CBS, 1968; "The FBI: The Young Warriors," ABC, 1969; "Get Smart: And Baby Makes Four," CBS, 1969; "Medical Center: The Last Ten Yards," CBS, 1969; "The Virginian: The Power Seekers," NBC, 1969; "Mission: Impossible: Flip Side," CBS, 1970; "Mannix: The Search for Darrell Andrews," CBS, 1970; "Room 222: The Lincoln Story," ABC, 1970; "Storefront Lawyers: The Electric Kid," CBS, 1970; "Medical Center: Man at Bay," CBS, 1970; "Alias Smith and Jones: Only Three to a Bed," ABC, 1972; "The FBI: Fatal Reunion," ABC, 1973; "Chase: Hot Beef," NBC, 1974; "The Manhunter: The Doomsday Gang," CBS, 1974; "The Rockford Files: The Great Blue Lake Land and Development Company," NBC, 1975; "One Day at a Time: A Little Larceny," CBS, 1979; "Foul Play: Double Play," ABC, 1981; "Newhart: The Visitors," CBS, 1983; "The A-Team: Double Heat," NBC, 1984; "Hardcastle and McCormick: The Georgia Street Motors," ABC, 1984; "Scarecrow and Mrs. King: Spiderweb," CBS, 1985.

TV MOVIES AND MINISERIES: "The Borgia Stick," NBC, 1967; "The D.A.: Murder One," NBC, 1969; "The Sound of Anger," NBC, 1968; "Deadlock," NBC, 1969; "The Whole World Is Watching," NBC, 1969; "San Francisco

International," NBC, 1970; "Sarge: The Badge or the Cross," NBC, 1971; "The Death of Me Yet," ABC, 1971; "The Bravos," ABC, 1972; "Fireball Forward," ABC, 1972; "Hawkins on Murder," CBS, 1973; "Dying Room Only," ABC, 1973; "Heat Wave," ABC, 1974; "Senior Year," CBS, 1974; "Panic on the 5:22," ABC, 1974; "Law of the Land," NBC, 1976; "Gemini Man," NBC, 1976; "Centennial," NBC, 1978-79; "Samurai," ABC, 1979; "Quarterback Princess," CBS, 1983; "ABC Theatre: Tough Love," ABC, 1985; "Agatha Christie's Murder in Three Acts," CBS, 1986.

ELDER, ANN
b. Cleveland, OH, September 21, 1942. Comic actress and writer.

AS A REGULAR: "The Smothers Brothers Show," CBS, 1965-66; "Rowan & Martin's Laugh-In," NBC, 1970-72.

AND: "McHale's Navy: The Vampire of Taratupa," ABC, 1965; "The Farmer's Daughter: Nej, Nej, a Thousand Times Nej," ABC, 1965; "Ben Casey: For San Diego, You Need a Different Bus," ABC, 1966; "The Man From UNCLE: The Bridge of Lions Affair," NBC, 1966; "Run, Buddy, Run: Death with Father," CBS, 1966; "The Wild Wild West: The Night of the Druid's Blood," CBS, 1966; "Hey, Landlord!: Sharin' Sharon," NBC, 1967; "Get Smart: The Impossible Mission," NBC, 1968; "The Don Knotts Show," NBC, 1970; "The Odd Couple: The Flight of the Felix," ABC, 1970; "Match Game '74," CBS, 1974; "You Don't Say," ABC, 1975.

AS CO-WRITER: "Lily," CBS, 1973; "Lily Tomlin," ABC, 1976.

* Emmies: 1974, 1976.

ELIZONDO, HECTOR
b. New York City, NY, December 22, 1936. Actor who usually plays bosses, irate or wise; best known as the hotel manager in the film "Pretty Woman."

AS A REGULAR: "Adventures of Oky Doky," DUM, 1948-49; "Popi," CBS, 1976; "Freebie and the Bean," CBS, 1980-81; "Casablanca," NBC, 1983; "A.K.A. Pablo," ABC, 1984; "Foley Square," CBS, 1985-86; "Down and Out in Beverly Hills," FOX, 1987.

AND: "All in the Family: The Elevator Story," CBS, 1972; "Kojak: Web of Death," CBS, 1973; "Maude: Speed Trap," CBS, 1974; "The Rockford Files: Say Goodbye to Jennifer," NBC, 1975; "Baretta: Jurisdiction," ABC, 1975; "Columbo: A Case of Immunity," NBC, 1975; "Kojak: A Need to Know," CBS, 1976; "The Rockford Files: A Good Clean Bust with Sequel Rights," NBC, 1978; "Bret Maverick: The Hidalgo Thing," NBC, 1982; "Amazing Stories: Life on Death Row," NBC, 1986; "Matlock: The Cop," NBC, 1986;

"The Equalizer: Past Imperfect," CBS, 1989; "Kojak: Ariana," ABC, 1989.
TV MOVIES AND MINISERIES: "The Impatient Heart," NBC, 1971; "Wanted: The Sundance Woman," ABC, 1976; "The Dain Curse," CBS, 1978; "Out of the Darkness," CBS, 1985; "Murder: By Reason of Insanity," CBS, 1985; "Addicted to His Love," ABC, 1988; "Your Mother Wears Combat Boots," NBC, 1989.

ELLERBEE, LINDA
b. Bryan, TX, August 15, 1944.
AS A REGULAR: "Weekend," NBC, 1978-79; "NBC News Overnight," NBC, 1982-83; "Summer Sunday USA," NBC, 1984; "Our World," ABC, 1986-87.

ELLIOT, "MAMA" CASS
b. Ellen Naomi Cohen, Baltimore, MD, September 19, 1943; d. 1974. Former singer with the Mamas and Papas who struck out on her own; she died of a heart attack, not by choking on food, as was widely reported at the time.
AS A REGULAR: "Andy Williams Presents Ray Stevens," NBC, 1970.
AND: "The Smothers Brothers Comedy Hour," CBS, 1968; "The Johnny Cash Show," ABC, 1969; "The Carol Burnett Show," CBS, 1970; "The Carol Burnett Show," CBS, 1971; "Love, American Style: Love and the New You," ABC, 1972; "Hollywood Squares," NBC, 1972; "Young Dr. Kildare: Charlotte Wade Makes Lots of Shade," SYN, 1972; "Saga of Sonora," NBC, 1973; "Don't Call Me Mama Anymore," CBS, 1973; "Jack Lemmon-Get Happy," NBC, 1973; "The Carol Burnett Show," CBS, 1973.
TV MOVIES AND MINISERIES: "The Haunted Candy Factory," CBS, 1973.

ELLIOTT, BOB
Comedian.
AS A REGULAR: "Get a Life," FOX, 1990- .
* See also Bob & Ray.

ELLIOTT, CHRIS
b. New York City, NY. Emmy winning comedy writer and actor, son of Bob Elliott; he plays thirty-year-old paperboy Chris Peterson on "Get a Life."
AS A REGULAR: "Late Night with David Letterman," NBC, 1982-89; "Nick & Hillary," NBC, 1989; "Get a Life," FOX, 1990- .
AS WRITER: "Late Night with David Letterman," NBC, 1983-89.
* Emmies: 1984, 1985, 1986, 1987.

ELLIOTT, DAVID
b. New York City, NY, 1959.
AS A REGULAR: "Joe & Valerie," NBC, 1978-79.
AND: "St. Elsewhere: Remission," NBC, 1983;

"St. Elsewhere: Monday, Tuesday, Sven's Day," NBC, 1983; "Simon & Simon: Grand Illusion," CBS, 1983; "Knightwatch: The Knights Before Christmas," ABC, 1988.
TV MOVIES AND MINISERIES: "Pearl," ABC, 1978.

ELLIOTT, SAM
b. Sacramento, CA, August 9, 1944.
AS A REGULAR: "Mission: Impossible," CBS, 1970-71; "The Yellow Rose," NBC, 1983-84.
AND: "Lancer: Yesterday's Vengeance," CBS, 1969; "The FBI: The Prey," ABC, 1969; "Mission: Impossible: The Innocent," CBS, 1970; "Gunsmoke: The Wedding," CBS, 1972; "Hawkins: Die, Darling, Die," CBS, 1973; "The Streets of San Francisco: The Hard Breed," ABC, 1973; "Mannix: Little Girl Lost," CBS, 1973; "Doc Elliot: A Time to Live," ABC, 1974; "Hawaii Five-0: The Two-Faced Corpse," CBS, 1974; "The Manhunter: The Ma Gentry Gang," CBS, 1974; "Police Woman: Farewell, Mary Jane," NBC, 1975.
TV MOVIES AND MINISERIES: "The Challenge," ABC, 1970; "Assault on the Wayne," ABC, 1971; "The Blue Knight," NBC, 1973; "I Will Fight No More Forever," ABC, 1975; "Best Sellers: Once an Eagle," NBC, 1977; "Murder in Texas," NBC, 1981; "The Shadow Riders," CBS, 1982; "Travis McGee," ABC, 1983; "A Death in California," ABC, 1985; "The Blue Lightning," CBS, 1986; "Houston: The Legend of Texas," CBS, 1986.

ELLIOTT, STEPHEN
b. New York City, NY.
AS A REGULAR: "Young Doctor Malone," NBC, 1958-63; "A World Apart," ABC, 1970-71; "Beacon Hill," CBS, 1975; "Executive Suite," CBS, 1976-77; "Falcon Crest," CBS, 1981-82; "Dallas," CBS, 1985-86; "Trial and Error," CBS, 1988.
AND: "Armstrong Circle Theatre: Raid in Beatnik Village," CBS, 1960; "Columbo: A Deadly State of Mind," NBC, 1975; "Kojak: Elegy in an Asplat Graveyard," CBS, 1975; "City of Angels: The November Plan," NBC, 1976; "The Rockford Files: The Competitive Edge," NBC, 1977; "Lou Grant: Slaughter," CBS, 1978; "Quincy: Sweet Land of Liberty," NBC, 1979; "Hagen: Pilot," CBS, 1980; "Taxi: Thy Boss's Wife," ABC, 1981; "Magnum, P.I.: Almost Home," CBS, 1982; "Nero Wolfe: Might as Well Be Dead," NBC, 1981; "Quincy: To Clear the Air," NBC, 1982; "Little House: A New Beginning: The Empire Builders," NBC, 1982; "Remington Steele: My Fair Steele," NBC, 1983; "Hardcastle and McCormick: The Homecoming," ABC, 1984; "St. Elsewhere: Playing God," NBC, 1984; "St. Elsewhere: Two Balls and a Strike," NBC, 1984; "St. Elsewhere: Strike Out," NBC, 1984; "St. Elsewhere: Breathless," NBC, 1984; "St.

Elsewhere: My Aim Is True," NBC, 1984; "St. Elsewhere: Up on the Roof," NBC, 1984; "Scarecrow and Mrs. King: Weekend," CBS, 1984; "Murder, She Wrote: Armed Response," CBS, 1985; "Scarecrow and Mrs. King: The Triumvirate," CBS, 1986; "Columbo: Grand Deceptions," ABC, 1989; "Dear John: Fathers Know Best," NBC, 1989.

TV MOVIES AND MINISERIES: "The Gun," ABC, 1974; "Young Joe, the Forgotten Kennedy," ABC, 1977; "Overboard," NBC, 1978; "Betrayal," NBC, 1978; "Sergeant Matlovich vs. the U.S. Air Force," NBC, 1978; "Some Kind of Miracle," CBS, 1979; "The Ordeal of Patty Hearst," ABC, 1979; "Son Rise: A Miracle of Love," NBC, 1979; "Can You Hear the Laughter? The Story of Freddie Prinze," CBS, 1979; "Mrs. R's Daughter," NBC, 1979; "Jacqueline Bouvier Kennedy," ABC, 1981; "Not in Front of the Children," CBS, 1982; "When He's Not a Stranger," CBS, 1989.

ELLIOTT, WILLIAM
b. 1934; d. 1983. Black actor who played Otis Foster on "Bridget Loves Bernie."
AS A REGULAR: "Bridget Loves Bernie," CBS, 1972-73; "Adam 12," NBC, 1974-75.
AND: "The Rookies: Concrete Valley, Neon Sky," ABC, 1972; "Ironside: The Rolling Y," NBC, 1974.
TV MOVIES AND MINISERIES: "The Old Man Who Cried Wolf," ABC, 1970.

ELSON, ANDREA
b. New York City, NY, March 6, 1969. Actress who played Lynn Tanner of "ALF."
AS A REGULAR: "Whiz Kids," CBS, 1983-84; "ALF," NBC, 1986-90.
TV MOVIES AND MINISERIES: "Class Cruise," NBC, 1989.

ELY, RON
b. Ronald Pierce, Hereford, TX, June 21, 1938. Silo-sized leading man who was Tarzan on TV; also, the guy the Miss America people turned to when they dumped Bert Parks in 1980.
AS A REGULAR: "The Aquanauts (Malibu Run)," CBS, 1961; "Tarzan," NBC, 1966-68; "Face the Music," SYN, 1980-81; "Sea Hunt," SYN, 1987-88.
AND: "Father Knows Best: Crisis Over a Kiss," CBS, 1959; "How to Marry a Millionaire: The Method," SYN, 1959; "The Millionaire: Millionaire Sgt. Matthew Brogan," CBS, 1959; "The Life and Legend of Wyatt Earp: The Posse," ABC, 1960; "Thriller: Waxworks," NBC, 1962; "The Courtship of Eddie's Father: Pain," ABC, 1969; "Ironside: A Killing at the Track," NBC, 1971; "Marcus Welby, M.D.: To Father a Child," ABC, 1974; "The Love Boat: Does Father Know

Best?," ABC, 1982; "Hotel: Charades," ABC, 1983; "The Love Boat: Off Course Romance," ABC, 1983.

EMERSON, FAYE
b. Elizabeth, LA, July 8, 1917; d. 1983. Actress and socialite who was one of early television's most popular personalities, partly because of her beauty and smarts and partly because of the plunging necklines on the gowns she wore on TV.
AS A REGULAR: "Paris Cavalcade of Fashions," NBC, 1948; "The Faye Emerson Show," CBS, 1950; "Fifteen with Faye," NBC, 1950; "Faye Emerson's Wonderful Town," CBS, 1951-52; "Author Meets the Critics," DUM, 1952; "I've Got a Secret," CBS, 1952-58; "Quick as a Flash," ABC, 1953-54; "What's in a Word," CBS, 1954; "Masquerade Party," CBS, 1958; NBC, 1958-59; CBS, 1959-60; NBC, 1960.
AND: "Billy Rose's Playbill: George III Once Drooled in This Plate," SYN, 1950; "Chesterfield Presents: Count Victor Lustig," NBC, 1952; "Goodyear TV Playhouse: Catch a Falling Stry," NBC, 1953; "U.S. Steel Hour: Hope for a Harvest," ABC, 1953; "Studio One: Melissa," CBS, 1954; "U.S. Steel Hour: The Fifth Wheel," ABC, 1954; "U.S. Steel Hour: Secret in the Family," CBS, 1958; "U.S. Steel Hour: Call It a Day," CBS, 1959; "The Jack Paar Show," NBC, 1960; "U.S. Steel Hour: The Oddball," CBS, 1961; "Girl Talk," SYN, 1963; "The du Pont Show: The Bachelor Game," NBC, 1963.
* Emerson was married to Elliott Roosevelt, son of Franklin, from 1944-50.

EMERSON, HOPE
b. Hawarden, IA, October 27, 1897; d. 1960. Beefy character actress who played jazz club owner Mother on "Peter Gunn" and kindly housekeeper Sarge on "The Dennis O'Keefe Show."
AS A REGULAR: "Kobb's Korner," CBS, 1948-49; "Doc Corkle," NBC, 1952; "Peter Gunn," NBC, 1958-59; "The Dennis O'Keefe Show," CBS, 1959-60.
AND: "The Bob Cummings Show: How to Handle Women," CBS, 1956; "Kaiser Aluminum Hour: So Short a Season," NBC, 1957; "Goodyear TV Playhouse: The House," NBC, 1957; "The Bob Cummings Show: Bob Clashes with His Land-lady," NBC, 1957; "Jerry Lewis Special," NBC, 1957; "Studio One: The McTaggart Succession," CBS, 1958; "Playhouse 90: The Innocent Sleep," CBS, 1958; "Death Valley Days: Big Liz," SYN, 1958; "G.E. Theatre: Night Club," CBS, 1959; "Shannon: The Florentine Prince," SYN, 1960.

ENBERG, DICK
b. Mt. Clemens, MI, January 9, 1935. NBC

sports commentator since 1975.
AS A REGULAR: "The Perfect Match," SYN, 1967-68; "Where's Huddles?," CBS, 1970; "Baffle," NBC, 1973-74; "Three for the Money," NBC, 1975.
* Emmies: 1978, 1981, 1983.

ENGEL, GEORGIA
b. Washington, D.C., July 28, 1948. Tall blonde actress who played Georgette, loving wife of Ted Baxter on "The Mary Tyler Moore Show."
AS A REGULAR: "The Mary Tyler Moore Show," CBS, 1973-77; "The Betty White Show," CBS, 1977-78; "Goodtime Girls," ABC, 1980; "Jennifer Slept Here," NBC, 1983-84.
AND: "Rhoda: Rhoda's Wedding," CBS, 1974; "Dean's Place," NBC, 1975; "Dean Martin Special," NBC, 1975; "Dean Martin's Red Hot Scandals of 1926," NBC, 1976; "Mork & Mindy: The Exidor Affair," ABC, 1979; "The Love Boat: Seal of Approval," ABC, 1981; "The Love Boat: Meet the Author," ABC, 1982.
* See also Lorna Patterson.

ENGLUND, ROBERT
b. Glendale, CA. Actor who plays Freddie Krueger, the killer who looks like his face was pushed into a cauldron of hot grease, in the "Nightmare on Elm Street" movies.
AS A REGULAR: "V," NBC, 1984-85; "Downtown," CBS, 1986-87; "Freddie's Nightmares," SYN, 1988- ; "Shadow Theatre," USA, 1990- .
AND: "Police Woman: Sons," NBC, 1978; "Hart to Hart: Rhinestone Harts," ABC, 1981; "Hollywood Beat: Pilot," ABC, 1985; "The Pat Sajak Show," CBS, 1989.
TV MOVIES AND MINISERIES: "Young Joe, the Forgotten Kennedy," ABC, 1977; "The Fighter," CBS, 1983; "Hobson's Choice," CBS, 1983; "V: The Final Battle," NBC, 1984; "Infidelity," ABC, 1987.

ENRIQUEZ, RENE
b. San Francisco, CA, November 25, 1933; d. 1990. Actor who played Lt. Ray Calletano on "Hill Street Blues."
AS A REGULAR: "Hill Street Blues," NBC, 1981-87.
AND: "NYPD: The Witch of 116th Street," ABC, 1968; "Chico and the Man: E. Pluribus Used Car," NBC, 1974; "Police Story: Hard Rock Brown," NBC, 1977; "WKRP in Cincinnati: Tornado," CBS, 1979; "Benson: Trust Me," ABC, 1979; "Lou Grant: Sweep," CBS, 1979; "Barnaby Jones: Killer Without a Name," CBS, 1980.
TV MOVIES AND MINISERIES: "Nicky's World," CBS, 1974; "Foster and Laurie," CBS, 1975; "High Risk," ABC, 1976; "Centennial," NBC, 1978-79; "Hostage Flight," NBC, 1985; "Perry

Mason: The Case of the Scandalous Scoundrel," NBC, 1987; "Full Exposure: The Sex Tapes Scandal," NBC, 1989.

ERDMAN, RICHARD
b. Waynoka, OK, June 1, 1925. Actor-director who often plays cynical types.
AS A REGULAR: "The Ray Bolger Show," ABC, 1953-55; "The Tab Hunter Show," NBC, 1960-61; "Saints and Sinners," NBC, 1962-63; "From Here to Eternity," NBC, 1980; "Dallas," CBS, 1988-89.
AND: "Medic: Glass of Fear," NBC, 1955; "West Point: Jet Flight," CBS, 1957; "The Jane Wyman Show: Hide and Seek," NBC, 1958; "Navy Log: Helldivers Over Greece," ABC, 1958; "Perry Mason: The Case of the Gilded Lily," CBS, 1958; "Accused: The Pookey Nagler Case," ABC, 1959; "The David Niven Show: Lifeline," NBC, 1959; "Not For Hire: Ticket to a Gas Chamber," SYN, 1959; "Perry Mason: The Case of the Lost Act," CBS, 1960; "Perry Mason: The Case of the Absent Artist," CBS, 1962; "Mr. Ed: Unemployment Show," CBS, 1963; "The Twilight Zone: A Kind of a Stopwatch," CBS, 1963; "The Dick Van Dyke Show: Baby Fat," CBS, 1965; "Green Acres: A Home Isn't Built in a Day," CBS, 1966; "Gomer Pyle, USMC: Go Blow Your Horn," CBS, 1967; "The Man From UNCLE: The Suburbia Affair," NBC, 1967; "The Beverly Hillbillies: The Clampetts in Washington," CBS, 1970; "Here's Lucy: Lucy and Art Linkletter," CBS, 1970; "Lou Grant: Sect," CBS, 1978; "Alice: The Reporter," CBS, 1979; "Lou Grant: Nightside," CBS, 1980; "Lou Grant: Business," CBS, 1981; "Lou Grant: Jazz," CBS, 1981.
TV MOVIES AND MINISERIES: "Visions...," CBS, 1972; "The Great Man's Whiskers," NBC, 1973.
AS DIRECTOR: "The Dick Van Dyke Show: Dear Sally Rogers," CBS, 1966; "The Dick Van Dyke Show: Buddy Sorrell—Man and Boy," CBS, 1966.

ERICKSON, LEIF
b. Alameda, CA, October 27, 1911; d. 1986. Big actor who played Big John Cannon on "The High Chaparral."
AS A REGULAR: "The High Chaparral," NBC, 1967-71.
AND: "Story Theatre: The Marquis," SYN, 1951; "Schlitz Playhouse of Stars: Say Hello to Pamela," CBS, 1952; "Schlitz Playhouse of Stars: Homecoming," CBS, 1952; "The Unexpected: Blackmail," NBC, 1952; "The Millionaire: Millionaire Norman Conover," CBS, 1955; "The Millionaire: The Brian Hendricks Story," CBS, 1956; "Climax!: The Gold Dress," CBS, 1957; "Hill Number One," SYN, 1957; "Playhouse 90: One Coat of White," CBS, 1957; "Climax!: Walk a Tightrope," CBS, 1957; "Playhouse 90: The

Shape of the River," CBS, 1960; "Bonanza: The Rescue," NBC, 1961; "Rawhide: Incident Near Gloomy River," CBS, 1961; "The Rebel: Helping Hand," ABC, 1961; "The New Breed: Care Is No Cure," ABC, 1962; "Target: The Corruptors: Goodbye, Children," ABC, 1962; "Hazel: Hazel and the Vanishing Hero," NBC, 1963; "The Great Adventure: The Outlaw and the Nun," CBS, 1963; "The Travels of Jaimie McPheeters: The Day of the Toll Takers," ABC, 1964; "The Virginian: The Drifter," NBC, 1964; "The Great Adventure: The President Vanishes," CBS, 1964; "Grindl: The Moon Killer," NBC, 1964; "The Alfred Hitchcock Hour: The Monkey's Paw: A Retelling," NBC, 1965; "Paris 7000: To Cage a Lion," ABC, 1970; "The Name of the Game: Seek and Destroy," NBC, 1971; "Night Gallery: The Academy," NBC, 1971; "The Sixth Sense: The Heart That Wouldn't Stay Buried," ABC, 1972; "Insight: The Governor's Mansion," SYN, 1972; "The New Healers," ABC, 1972; "The Mod Squad: Yesterday's Ashes," ABC, 1972; "Owen Marshall, Counselor at Law: Love Child," ABC, 1972; "Marcus Welby, M.D.: With a Shout Not a Whimper," ABC, 1972; "Night Gallery: Something in the Woodwork," NBC, 1973; "The Streets of San Francisco: For the Love of God," ABC, 1973; "Medical Story: The Moonlight Healer," NBC, 1975; "Cannon: Daddy's Little Girl," CBS, 1976; "The Rockford Files: Trouble in Paradise Cove," NBC, 1979.

TV MOVIES AND MINISERIES: "Terror in the Sky," ABC, 1971; "The Deadly Dream," ABC, 1971; "The Family Rico," CBS, 1972; "The Daughters of Joshua Cabe," ABC, 1972; "Force Five," CBS, 1975.

ERICSON, JOHN
b. Joseph Meibes, Antwerp, Belgium, September 25, 1926. Handsome actor who played Sam Bolt, sidekick of female private eye Honey West (Anne Francis).

AS A REGULAR: "Honey West," ABC, 1965-66.
AND: "Saturday's Children," CBS, 1950; "Goodyear TV Playhouse: A Matter of Life and Death," NBC, 1951; "Kraft Television Theatre: Delicate Story," NBC, 1951; "G.E. Theatre: Shadow on the Heart," CBS, 1955; "Star Stage: The Girl Who Wasn't Wanted," NBC, 1955; "Stage 7: Cold Harbor," CBS, 1955; "The Loretta Young Show: A Ticket for May," NBC, 1956; "Dick Powell's Zane Grey Theatre: License to Kill," CBS, 1958; "Shirley Temple's Storybook: The Legend of Sleepy Hollow," NBC, 1958; "Playhouse 90: The Innocent Sleep," CBS, 1958; "Shirley Temple's Storybook: Hiawatha," NBC, 1958; "Dick Powell's Zane Grey Theatre: The Tall Shadow," CBS, 1958; "Restless Gun: Four Lives," NBC, 1958; "The Loretta Young Show: The Grenade," NBC, 1960; "Chevy Mystery Show: Blind Man's Bluff," NBC, 1960;

"Bonanza: Breed of Violence," NBC, 1960; "U.S. Steel Hour: The Mating Machine," CBS, 1961; "Rawhide: Incident Near Gloomy River," CBS, 1961; "Burke's Law: Who Killed Marty Kelso?," ABC, 1964; "The Fugitive: Brass Ring," ABC, 1965; "Profiles in Courage: Prudence Crandall," NBC, 1965; "Burke's Law: Who Killed the Jackpot?," ABC, 1965; "Bob Hope Chrysler Theatre: Guilty or Not Guilty," NBC, 1966; "Bonanza: Journey to Terror," NBC, 1967; "The Invaders: Moonshot," ABC, 1967; "Ironside: Beware the Wiles of the Stranger," NBC, 1970; "The Men From Shiloh: The Politician," NBC, 1971; "Medical Center: The Albatross," CBS, 1971; "Longstreet: The Old Team Spirit," ABC, 1971; "The FBI: The Wedding Gift," ABC, 1973; "Hawkins: Candidate for Murder," CBS, 1974; "Police Story: Cop in the Middle," NBC, 1974; "Police Story: The Execution," NBC, 1975; "Police Woman: Means to an End," NBC, 1977; "The A-Team: Till Death Do Us Part," NBC, 1983.

TV MOVIES AND MINISERIES: "The Bounty Man," ABC, 1972; "Tenafly," NBC, 1973.

ERWIN, STUART
b. Squaw Valley, CA, February 14, 1902; d. 1967. Character actor who often played Joe Average types and was the star of his own family sitcom for five seasons.

AS A REGULAR: "The Stu Erwin Show," ABC, 1950-55; "The Greatest Show on Earth," ABC, 1963-64.
AND: "Armstrong Circle Theatre: Jackpot," NBC, 1950; "Armstrong Circle Theatre: The Lucky Suit," NBC, 1952; "Playhouse 90: Snow Shoes," CBS, 1957; "Crossroads: Patchwork Family," ABC, 1957; "Art Linkletter's House Party," CBS, 1957; "Playhouse 90: The Right Hand Man," CBS, 1958; "Pursuit: The Vengeance," CBS, 1958; "Walt Disney Presents: A Diamond Is a Boy's Best Friend," ABC, 1959; "Father Knows Best: Family Contest," CBS, 1960; "Walt Disney Presents: Wrong Way Moochie," ABC, 1960; "Thriller: The Watcher," NBC, 1960; "The Andy Griffith Show: Opie's Charity," CBS, 1960; "King of Diamonds: The Swindler," SYN, 1962; "Perry Mason: The Case of the Double-Entry Mind," CBS, 1962; "The Untouchables: The Floyd Gibbons Story," ABC, 1962; "Our Man Higgins: The Milkman Cometh," ABC, 1963; "The Defenders: The Poisoned Fruit Doctrine," CBS, 1963; "The Donna Reed Show: The Playmate," ABC, 1963; "Perry Mason: The Case of the Scandalous Sculptor," CBS, 1964; "The Farmer's Daughter: A Locket for Agatha," ABC, 1964; "Dr. Kildare: Take Care of My Little Girl," NBC, 1965; "Perry Mason: The Case of the Impetuous Imp," CBS, 1965; "Gentle Ben: Wayward Bear," CBS, 1967.

TV MOVIES AND MINISERIES: "Shadow Over Elveron," NBC, 1968.

ESTRADA, ERIK

b. New York City, NY, March 16, 1949. Dark-featured actor who played Ponch on "CHiPS"; he was TV hunk flavor of the month for a while and then viewers moved on to someone else.
AS A REGULAR: "CHiPS," NBC, 1977-83.
AND: "Hawaii Five-O: Engaged to Be Buried," CBS, 1973; "Owen Marshall, Counselor at Law: Once a Lion," ABC, 1973; "Kolchak, the Night Stalker: Legacy of Terror," ABC, 1975; "Medical Center: The High Cost of Winning," CBS, 1975; "Police Woman: Don't Feed the Pigeons," NBC, 1975; "The Love Boat: Going by the Book," ABC, 1978; "The Mike Douglas Show," SYN, 1980; "Women Who Rate a 10," NBC, 1981.
TV MOVIES AND MINISERIES: "Honeyboy," NBC, 1982; "The Dirty Dozen: The Fatal Mission," NBC, 1988; "She Knows Too Much," NBC, 1989.

EUBANKS, BOB

b. Flint, MI. Longtime emcee of the sleazy "Newlywed Game."
AS A REGULAR: "The Newlywed Game," ABC, 1966-74, SYN, 1977-80, 1985-88; "The Diamond Head Game," SYN, 1975; "Rhyme and Reason," ABC, 1975-76; "All-Star Secrets," NBC, 1979; "Dream House," NBC, 1983-84; "Trivial Trap," ABC, 1984-85; "Card Sharks," CBS & SYN, 1986- .
AND: "The Adventures of Ozzie and Harriet: The Housemother," ABC, 1964; "The Adventures of Ozzie and Harriet: The Chess Set," ABC, 1964; "Riptide: Games People Play," NBC, 1985.

EVANS, DR. BERGEN

b. Ohio, 1904; d. 1978. Game show host.
AS A REGULAR: "Down You Go," DUM, 1951-55, CBS, 1955, ABC, 1955-56; "Ghost," NBC, 1952; "Super Ghost," NBC, 1952-53; "Of Many Things," ABC, 1953-54; "It's About Time," ABC, 1954; "The $64,000 Question," CBS, 1955-58; "The Last Word," CBS, 1956-59; "Top Dollar," CBS, 1958.

EVANS, DALE

b. Frances Butts, Uvalde, TX, October 31, 1912. Actress who's been the longtime saddlemate of cowboy star Roy Rogers on and off screen.
AS A REGULAR: "The Roy Rogers Show," NBC, 1951-57; "The Chevy Show," NBC, 1958-62; "The Roy Rogers and Dale Evans Show," ABC, 1962.
AND: "Matinee Theatre: Anxious Night," NBC, 1958; "Saga of Sonora," NBC, 1973.
* Evans wrote Roy Rogers' theme, "Happy Trails."
* Her horse on "The Roy Rogers Show" was named Buttermilk.

* Evans married Rogers in 1947.
* See also Roy Rogers.

EVANS, DAMON

b. Baltimore, MD, November 24, 1950.
AS A REGULAR: "The Jeffersons," CBS, 1975-78;
TV MOVIES AND MINISERIES: "Roots: The Next Generations," ABC, 1979.

EVANS, DAME EDITH

b. London, England, February 8, 1888; d. 1976. Distinguished British actress.
AS A GUEST: "Hallmark Hall of Fame: Time Remembered," NBC, 1961; "Pursue and Destroy," ABC, 1966.
TV MOVIES AND MINISERIES: "David Copperfield," ABC, 1970; "Masterpiece Theatre: The Gambler," NET, 1971; "QB VII," ABC, 1974.

EVANS, GENE

b. Holbrook, AZ, July 11, 1922.
AS A REGULAR: "My Friend Flicka," CBS, 1956-57; "Spencer's Pilots," CBS, 1976.
AND: "Newsstand Theatre: Tantrum-Size 12," ABC, 1952; "Science Fiction Theatre: Stranger in the Desert," SYN, 1955; "Schlitz Playhouse of Stars: Ambitious Cop," CBS, 1956; "Bonanza: The Fear Merchants," NBC, 1959; "Rawhide: Incident at the Buffalo Smoke House," CBS, 1959; "Walt Disney Presents: Texas John Slaughter-Apache Friendship," CBS, 1960; "Route 66: Blue Murder," CBS, 1961; "Follow the Sun: Ghost Story," ABC, 1962; "The Alfred Hitchcock Hour: A Piece of the Action," CBS, 1962; "The Virginian: The Accomplice," NBC, 1962; "G.E. True: The Moonshiners," CBS, 1963; "Gunsmoke: First People," CBS, 1968; "Gunsmoke: Snow Train," CBS, 1970; "Mannix: Murder Times Three," CBS, 1971; "Alias Smith and Jones: The Men That Corrupted Hadleyburg," ABC, 1972; "Gunsmoke: Tatum," CBS, 1972; "Gunsmoke: The Iron Blood of Courage," CBS, 1974; "Gunsmoke: Thirty a Month and Found," CBS, 1974; "Fantasy Island Magnolia Blossoms," ABC, 1979; "Here's Boomer: The Stableboy," NBC, 1980; "M*A*S*H: Blood and Guts," CBS, 1982; "Simon & Simon: For the People," CBS, 1986; "Simon & Simon: Treasure," CBS, 1987; "Scarecrow and Mrs. King: Mission of Gold," CBS, 1987.
TV MOVIES AND MINISERIES: "Dragnet," NBC, 1969; "The Intruders," NBC, 1970; "The Bounty Man," ABC, 1972; "Shootout in a One-Dog Town," ABC, 1974; "Sidekicks," CBS, 1974; "The Last Day," NBC, 1975; "Matt Helm," ABC, 1975; "Best Sellers: The Rhinemann Exchange," NBC, 1977; "The Concrete Cowboys," CBS, 1979; "Casino," ABC, 1980; "The Shadow Riders," CBS, 1982; "Travis McGee," ABC, 1983; "The Alamo: 13 Days to Glory," NBC, 1987.

EVANS, LINDA

b. *Linda Evanstad, Hartford, CT, November 18, 1942*. Blonde actress who played Audra Barkley on "The Big Valley" and Krystle Carrington on "Dynasty."

AS A REGULAR: "The Adventures of Ozzie and Harriet," ABC, 1960-61; "The Big Valley," ABC, 1965-69; "Hunter," CBS, 1977; "Dynasty," ABC, 1981-89.

AND: "Bachelor Father: A Crush on Bentley," NBC, 1960; "The Eleventh Hour: Where Ignorant Armies Clash by Night, NBC, 1963; "The Lieutenant: Two Star Giant," NBC, 1963; "Wagon Train: The Jamison Hershey Story," ABC, 1965; "My Favorite Martian: Martin's Favorite Martian," CBS, 1965; "McCloud: Butch Cassidy Rides Again," NBC, 1973; "Banacek: Rocket to Oblivion," NBC, 1974; "Harry O: Guardian at the Gates," ABC, 1974; "McMillan and Wife: Night Train to L.A.," NBC, 1975; "The Rockford Files: Claire," NBC, 1975; "The Rockford Files: The Farnsworth Stratagem," NBC, 1975; "The Love Boat: Three in a Bed," ABC, 1982; "The Love Boat: China Cruise," ABC, 1983; "Ooh-La-La-It's Bob Hope's Fun Birthday Spectacular From Paris' Bicentennial," NBC, 1989.

TV MOVIES AND MINISERIES: "Female Artillery," ABC, 1973; "Nakia," ABC, 1974; "Standing Tall," NBC, 1978; "Bare Essence," CBS, 1982; "The Gambler II: The Adventure Continues," CBS, 1983; "The Last Frontier," CBS, 1986.

* On "Bachelor Father," Evans was a teenager who had a crush on John Forsythe, whom she'd later be "married" to on "Dynasty." Awwww.

EVANS, MAURICE

b. *Dorchester, England, June 3, 1901; d. 1989*. Shakespearean actor who found TV success as the father of Samantha (Elizabeth Montgomery) on "Bewitched."

AS A REGULAR: "Bewitched," ABC, 1964-72.

AND: "Hallmark Hall of Fame: Hamlet," NBC, 1953; "Hallmark Hall of Fame: King Richard II," NBC, 1954; "Hallmark Hall of Fame: The Devil's Disciple," NBC, 1955; "Hallmark Hall of Fame: The Taming of the Shrew," NBC, 1956; "The Ed Sullivan Show," CBS, 1956; "Hallmark Hall of Fame: Man and Superman," NBC, 1956; "Hallmark Hall of Fame: Twelfth Night," NBC, 1957; "U.S. Steel Hour: No Leave for the Captain," CBS, 1959; "Perry Como's Kraft Music Hall," NBC, 1959; "Hallmark Hall of Fame: The Tempest," NBC, 1960; "Steve Allen Plymouth Show," NBC, 1960; "Hallmark Hall of Fame: Macbeth," NBC, 1960; "Candid Camera," CBS, 1961; "Westinghouse Presents: Come Again to Carthage," CBS, 1961; "U.S. Steel Hour: The Loves of Claire Amber," CBS, 1962; "The Red Skelton Hour," CBS, 1964; "Bob Hope Chrysler

Theatre: The Game," NBC, 1965; "The Man From UNCLE: The Bridge of Lions Affair," NBC, 1966; "The War of the Roses," NET, 1966; "Heartbreak House," NET, 1966; "Batman: The Puzzles Are Coming/The Duo Is Slumming," ABC, 1966; "Tarzan: Basil of the Jungle," NBC, 1967; "The Big Valley: Danger Road," ABC, 1969; "The Mod Squad: Never Give the Fuzz an Even Break," ABC, 1969; "Search: The Murrow Disappearance," NBC, 1972; "The Snoop Sisters: Fear Is a Free Throw," NBC, 1974; "Columbo: Forgotten Lady," NBC, 1975; "The Streets of San Francisco: School of Fear," ABC, 1975; "The Love Boat: Marriage of Convenience," ABC, 1980.

TV MOVIES AND MINISERIES: "U.M.C.," CBS, 1969; "The Brotherhood of the Bell," CBS, 1970; "Bell System Family Theatre: The Canterville Ghost," NBC, 1975.

* Evans' soliloquy as Hamlet in a live production was interrupted by a stagehand who wandered into the shot accidentally. He then tiptoed off camera.

EVANS, MIKE

b. *Salisbury, NC, November 3, 1949*. Actor who played Lionel Jefferson, one-time neighbor of Archie Bunker (Carroll O'Connor).

AS A REGULAR: "All in the Family," CBS, 1971-75; "The Jeffersons," CBS, 1975; 1979-81; "The Practice," NBC, 1976-77.

AND: "Love, American Style: Love and the Perfect Wedding," ABC, 1972; "The New Adventures of Perry Mason: The Case of the Tortured Titan," CBS, 1973; "The Streets of San Francisco: For Good or Evil," ABC, 1974; "Dinah!," SYN, 1975.

TV MOVIES AND MINISERIES: "Call Her Mom," ABC, 1972; "The Voyage of the Yes," CBS, 1973; "Rich Man, Poor Man," ABC, 1976.

EVERETT, CHAD

b. *Raymond Lee Cramton, South Bend, IN, June 11, 1936*. Hunky actor who began his TV career at the Warner Bros. film factory and then became one of MGM's last contract players; best known as Dr. Joe Gannon on "Medical Center."

AS A REGULAR: "The Dakotas," ABC, 1963; "Medical Center," CBS, 1969-76; "Hagen," CBS, 1980; "The Rousters," NBC, 1983-84.

AND: "Cheyenne: Apache Treasure," ABC, 1960; "Hawaiian Eye: The Kahuna Curtain," ABC, 1960; "77 Sunset Strip: The College Caper," ABC, 1961; "77 Sunset Strip: The Rival Eye Caper," ABC, 1961; "Lawman: The Son," ABC, 1961; "SurfSide 6: The Artful Deceit," ABC, 1962; "77 Sunset Strip: The Diplomatic Caper," ABC, 1962; "Hawaiian Eye: The Four-Cornered Triangle," ABC, 1962; "Cheyenne: A Man Called Ragan," ABC, 1962; "Hawaiian Eye: Cricket," ABC, 1962; "SurfSide 6: The Neutral Corner,"

ABC, 1962; "Redigo: Papa-San," NBC, 1963; "Route 66: Come Home, Greta Inger Gruenschaffen," CBS, 1963; "The Lieutenant: Man with an Edge," NBC, 1964; "Branded: The First Kill," NBC, 1965; "The Man From UNCLE: The J Is for Judas Affair," NBC, 1967; "Dream Girl of '67," ABC, 1967; "The FBI: The Hero," ABC, 1968; "Journey to the Unknown: Poor Butterfly," ABC, 1969; "Ironside: And Be My Love," NBC, 1969; "The Merv Griffin Show," CBS, 1970; "Rowan & Martin's Laugh-In," NBC, 1972; "It Takes a Lot of Love," CBS, 1973; "Dinah!," SYN, 1976; "Glory Road West," ABC, 1976; "Donny and Marie," ABC, 1976; "Murder, She Wrote: Obituary for a Dead Anchor," CBS, 1986; "The Love Boat: Egyptian Cruise," ABC, 1986.

TV MOVIES AND MINISERIES: "The Return of the Gunfighter," ABC, 1967; "In the Glitter Palace," NBC, 1977; "Centennial," NBC, 1978-79; "The Intruder Within," ABC, 1981; "Mistress of Paradise," ABC, 1981; "Thunder Boat Row," ABC, 1989.

EVIGAN, GREG

b. South Amboy, NJ, October 14, 1953.

AS A REGULAR: "A Year at the Top," CBS, 1977; "B.J. and the Bear," NBC, 1979-81; "Masquerade," ABC, 1983-84; "My Two Dads," NBC, 1987-90.

AND: "One Day at a Time: Jealousy," CBS, 1978; "Barnaby Jones: Target for a Wedding," CBS, 1979; "The Misadventures of Sheriff Lobo: Pilot," NBC, 1979; "Murder, She Wrote: Death Stalks the Big Top," CBS, 1986; "The New Mike Hammer: Mike Gets Married," CBS, 1987; "Matlock: The Billionaire," NBC, 1987.

TV MOVIES AND MINISERIES: "B.J. and the Bear," NBC, 1978; "Private Sessions," NBC, 1985; "The Lady Forgets," CBS, 1989.

EWELL, TOM

b. Yewell Tompkins, Owensboro, KY, April 29, 1909. Craggy-faced comic actor who played the family man tempted by Marilyn Monroe in "The Seven Year Itch"; on TV, best known as Billy on "Baretta."

AS A REGULAR: "The Tom Ewell Show," CBS, 1960-61; "Baretta," ABC, 1975-78; "Best of the West," ABC, 1981-82;

AND: "Billy Rose's Playbill: The Whirligig of Life," SYN, 1951; "Studio One: Mighty Like a Rogue," CBS, 1951; "Lights Out: The Deal," NBC, 1951; "Robert Montgomery Presents: See No Evil," NBC, 1952; "Playwrights '56: Daisy, Daisy," NBC, 1955; "Alfred Hitchcock Presents: The Case of Mr. Pelham," CBS, 1956; "The Patrice Munsel Show," ABC, 1957; "The Chevy Show," NBC, 1958; "U.S. Steel Hour: The Square Egghead," CBS, 1959; "G.E. Theatre: The Day of the Hanging," CBS, 1959; "Breck Golden Showcase: The Fourposter," CBS, 1962; "Art Linkletter's House Party," CBS, 1962; "To Tell the Truth," CBS, 1962; "The Dick Powell Show: The Honorable Albert Higgins," NBC, 1963; "Get the Message," ABC, 1964; "Wagon Train: The Story of Hector Heatherington," ABC, 1964; "Burke's Law: Who Killed Nobody Somehow?," ABC, 1965; "Summer Fun: The Kwimpers of New Jersey," ABC, 1966; "The Men From Shiloh: With Love, Bullets and Valentines," NBC, 1970; "The Name of the Game: A Sister From Napoli," NBC, 1971; "Alias Smith and Jones: The Root of It All," ABC, 1971; "Taxi: Nardo Loses Her Marbles," ABC, 1979.

TV MOVIES AND MINISERIES: "The Spy Who Returned From the Dead," ABC, 1974; "Promise Him Anything," ABC, 1975; "The Return of Mod Squad," ABC, 1979.

F

FABARES, SHELLEY

b. Santa Monica, CA, January 19, 1942.
Actress who grew up on TV, beginning as
Mary Stone, Donna Reed's TV daughter; now
she plays Christine Armstrong on "Coach."

AS A REGULAR: "The Donna Reed Show," ABC,
1958-63; "The Brian Keith Show (The Little
People)," NBC, 1972-74; "The Practice,"
NBC, 1976-77; "Mary Hartman, Mary
Hartman," SYN, 1977-78; "Highcliffe Manor,"
NBC, 1979; "One Day at a Time," CBS, 1981-
84; "Coach," ABC, 1989- .

AND: "Matinee Theatre: Wuthering Heights,"
NBC, 1955; "Captain Midnight: Flight Into the
Unknown," CBS, 1955; "The Loretta Young
Show: Day of Rest," NBC, 1958; "The Mickey
Mouse Club: The Adventures of Annette," ABC,
1958; "Colgate Theatre: Welcome to Washing-
ton," NBC, 1958; "Mr. Novak: I Don't Even Live
Here," NBC, 1963; "The Donna Reed Show:
Mary Comes Home," ABC, 1963; "Mr. Novak:
My Name Is Not Legion," NBC, 1963; "The
Eleventh Hour: How Do I Say 'I Love You,'?"
NBC, 1964; "Arrest and Trial: An Echo of
Conscience," ABC, 1964; "The Twilight Zone:
Black Leather Jackets," CBS, 1964; "American
Bandstand," ABC, 1964; "The Donna Reed
Show: The Daughter Complex," ABC, 1964;
"The Donna Reed Show: Old Faithful," ABC,
1964; "The Donna Reed Show: Indoor Outing,"
ABC, 1965; "Summer Fun: Meet Me in St.
Louis," ABC, 1966; "The Ghost and Mrs. Muir:
Vanessa," ABC, 1968; "Bracken's World: A
Package Deal," NBC, 1969; "Love, American
Style: Love and Mother," ABC, 1969; "The
Interns: The Guardian," CBS, 1971; "Love,
American Style: Love and the Fuzz," ABC, 1971;
"Ironside: A Matter of Life or Death," NBC,
1974; "The Rockford Files: Caledonia, It's Worth
a Fortune!," NBC, 1974; "The Rookies:
Solomon's Dilemma," ABC, 1975; "Barnaby
Jones: Flight to Danger," CBS, 1975; "Marcus
Welby, M.D.: Strike II," ABC, 1975; "Hollywood
Squares," NBC, 1976; "Hello, Larry: The Seattle
Story—Marion Returns," NBC, 1979; "The Love
Boat: September Song," ABC, 1980; "The Love
Boat: Sly as a Fox," ABC, 1983; "The Love Boat:
Her Honor the Mayor," ABC, 1985; "Newhart:
The First of the Belles," CBS, 1987; "Murder, She
Wrote: Mirror, Mirror, On the Wall," CBS, 1989.

TV MOVIES AND MINISERIES: "U.M.C.," CBS, 1969;
"Brian's Song," ABC, 1971; "Two for the
Money," ABC, 1972; "Sky Hei$t," NBC, 1975;
"Pleasure Cove," NBC, 1979; "Friendships,
Secrets and Lies," NBC, 1979; "The Great

American Traffic Jam," NBC, 1980; "Memorial Day," CBS, 1983; "Class Cruise," NBC,
1989.

* In 1962, Fabares sang "Johnny Angel" on "The
Donna Reed Show" and it became a hit single.
* Fabares is the niece of Nanette Fabray.

FABIAN

*b. Fabian Anthony Forte, Philadelphia, PA,
February 6, 1943.* Teen singer of the fifties and
sixties whose bookings these days are limited
to nostalgia shows.

AS A GUEST: "American Bandstand," ABC, 1958;
"The Dick Clark Saturday Night Beechnut
Show," ABC, 1958; "The Dick Clark Saturday
Night Beechnut Show," ABC, 1959; "Ameri-
can Bandstand," ABC, 1959; "The Perry Como
Show," NBC, 1959; "The Ed Sullivan Show,"
CBS, 1959; "The Record Years," ABC, 1959;
"Pat Boone Chevy Showroom," ABC, 1959;
"The Red Skelton Show: Freddie and Fabian,"
CBS, 1959; "Dick Clark's New Year's Eve
Party," ABC, 1959; "Startime: The Dean
Martin Show," NBC, 1960; "The Red Skelton
Show," CBS, 1960; "The Dick Clark Saturday
Night Beechnut Show," ABC, 1960; "Person to
Person," CBS, 1960; "Perry Como's Kraft
Music Hall," NBC, 1960; "American
Bandstand," ABC, 1960; "Dinah Shore Chevy
Show," NBC, 1961; "Bulova Watch Time with
Pat Boone," ABC, 1961; "Candid Camera,"
CBS, 1961; "Bus Stop: A Lion Walks Among
Us," ABC, 1961; "The Gertrude Berg Show:
Peace Corps," CBS, 1962; "The Bob Hope
Show," NBC, 1962; "The Dick Powell Show:
Run Till It's Dark," NBC, 1962; "American
Bandstand," ABC, 1962; "The Virginian: Say
Goodbye to All That," NBC, 1963; "Wagon
Train: The Molly Kincaid Story," ABC, 1963;
"The Eleventh Hour: You're So Smart, Why
Can't You Be Good?," NBC, 1964; "The
Virginian: Two Men Named Laredo," NBC,
1965; "The Virginian: Outcast," NBC, 1966;
"The FBI: Unknown Victim," ABC, 1971;
"Love, American Style: Love and the Crisis
Line," ABC, 1973; "Laverne & Shirley:
Laverne and Shirley Meet Fabian," ABC,
1977; "The Love Boat: Palimony O'Mine,"
ABC, 1982; "American Bandstand's 33 1/3
Anniversary," ABC, 1985; "On Stage at Wolf
Trap: The Golden Boys of Bandstand," PBS,
1986; "The Facts of Life: '62 Pick-Up," NBC,
1986; "Hollywood Squares," SYN, 1988.

TV MOVIES AND MINISERIES: "Katie: Portrait of a
Centerfold," NBC, 1978.

* Fabian's dramatic debut on "Bus Stop" was a real cause celebre at the time. Directed by Robert Altman, "A Lion Walks Among Us" featured our boy as a remorseless psychotic killer. The show was one of those that spurred FCC chairman Newton Minow to call network TV "a vast wasteland." Then on "The Dick Powell Show," he got the chance to play a good guy, prompting critic Harriet Van Horne to write, "Fabian has a neat, but tiny, talent."

FABRAY, NANETTE
b. *Ruby Bernadette Nanette Therese Fabares, San Diego, October 17, 1920.* Musical-comedy performer with extensive TV experiences; she played Katherine Romano, mother of Ann (Bonnie Franklin) on "One Day at a Time" and won Emmies for her work with Sid Caesar.

AS A REGULAR: "Caesar's Hour," NBC, 1954-56; "Westinghouse Playhouse Starring Nanette Fabray and Wendell Corey (Yes, Yes Nanette)," NBC, 1961; "One Day at a Time," CBS, 1979-84.

AND: "Omnibus: Arms and the Man," CBS, 1953; "Shower of Stars," CBS, 1956; "Saturday Spectacular: High Button Shoes," NBC, 1956; "Playhouse 90: The Family Nobody Wanted," CBS, 1956; "Alcoa Hour: The Original Miss Chase," NBC, 1957; "Kaiser Aluminum Hour: A Man's Game," NBC, 1957; "Dinah Shore Chevy Show," NBC, 1957; "I've Got a Secret," CBS, 1957; "The Patrice Munsel Show," ABC, 1957; "The Chevy Show," NBC, 1957; "Dinah Shore Chevy Show," NBC, 1958; "Shower of Stars," CBS, 1958; "The Perry Como Show," NBC, 1959; "Laramie: Glory Road," NBC, 1959; "Startime: The Dean Martin Show," NBC, 1960; "Bell Telephone Hour: Portraits in Music," NBC, 1960; "Startime: The Nanette Fabray Show–So Help Me, Aphrodite," NBC, 1960; "The Jack Benny Program," CBS, 1960; "Here's Holly-wood," NBC, 1961; "Password," CBS, 1963; "Burke's Law: Who Killed Molly?," ABC, 1964; "Burke's Law: Who Killed Cornelius Gilbert?," ABC, 1964; "The Andy Williams Show," NBC, 1965; "Bob Hope Chrysler Theatre: In Any Language," NBC, 1965; "Alice Through the Looking Glass," ABC, 1966; "Hollywood Squares," NBC, 1967; "The Jerry Lewis Show," NBC, 1968; "The Smothers Brothers Comedy Hour," CBS, 1969; "Funny You Should Ask," ABC, 1969; "The Carol Burnett Show," CBS, 1969; "The Movie Game," SYN, 1969; "Name Droppers," NBC, 1969; "Love, American Style: Love and the Heist," ABC, 1969; "Hollywood Squares," NBC, 1970; "Love, American Style: Love and the Liberated Lady Boss," ABC, 1970; "George M!," NBC, 1970; "The Carol Burnett Show," CBS, 1970; "The Carol Burnett Show," CBS, 1971; "The Mary Tyler Moore Show: Just Around the Corner," CBS, 1972; "Rowan & Martin's Laugh-In," NBC, 1972; "The Mary Tyler Moore Show: You've Got a Friend," CBS, 1972; "Love, American Style: Love and the Parent's Sake," ABC, 1974; "Happy Anniversary and Goodbye," CBS, 1974; "The Mac Davis Show," NBC, 1975; "Hollywood Squares," NBC, 1975; "Dinah!," SYN, 1976; "Maude: Maude's Reunion," CBS, 1977; "The Love Boat: Teach Me Tonight," ABC, 1981; "Hotel: Charades," ABC, 1983.

TV MOVIES AND MINISERIES: "Fame Is the Name of the Game," NBC, 1966; "But I Don't Want to Get Married!," ABC, 1970; "Magic Carpet," NBC, 1972; "The Couple Takes a Wife," ABC, 1972; "The Man in the Santa Claus Suit," NBC, 1979.

* Emmies: 1956, 1957.

FADIMAN, CLIFTON
b. *Brooklyn, NY, May 15, 1904.* Quiz show panelist and commentator.

AS A REGULAR: "This Is Show Business," CBS, 1949-54, NBC, 1956; "Information Please," CBS, 1952; "What's in a Word," CBS, 1954; "The Name's the Same," ABC, 1955; "Quiz Kids," CBS, 1956.

AND: "Whats My Line?," CBS, 1958; "The Jerry Lewis Show," ABC, 1963.

FAIRBANKS, DOUGLAS JR.
b. *New York City, NY, December 9, 1909.* Screen star usually in suave roles.

AS A REGULAR: "Douglas Fairbanks Jr. Presents," SYN, 1952-57.

AND: "The Bob Hope Show," NBC, 1950; "Rheingold Theatre: Counterfeit," NBC, 1955; "What's My Line?," CBS, 1956; "The Steve Allen Show," NBC, 1956; "I've Got a Secret," CBS, 1956; "I've Got a Secret," CBS, 1957; "The Ed Sullivan Show," CBS, 1957; "The Ed Sullivan Show," CBS, 1958; "Person to Person," CBS, 1958; "Dinah Shore Chevy Show," NBC, 1959; "The Big Party," CBS, 1959; "I've Got a Secret," CBS, 1959; "The Chevy Show: Home for Christmas," NBC, 1960; "We, the People–1961," NBC, 1961; "U.S. Steel Hour: Nightmare at Bleak Hill," CBS, 1962; "Route 66: Kiss the Maiden All Forlorn," CBS, 1962; "The du Pont Show: The Shadowed Affair," NBC, 1962; "Password," CBS, 1963; "To Tell the Truth," CBS, 1963; "The Red Skelton Hour," CBS, 1964; "Password," CBS, 1964; "Dr. Kildare: An Ungodly Act," NBC, 1964; "The Price Is Right," ABC, 1965; "Password," CBS, 1965; "Bob Hope Special," NBC, 1965; "Shindig," ABC, 1965; "ABC Stage '67: The Canterville Ghost," ABC, 1966; "The Legend of Robin Hood," NBC, 1968; "The Donald O'Connor Show," SYN, 1968; "Rowan & Martin's Laugh-In," NBC, 1968; "The Love Boat: Critical Success," ABC, 1979; "B.L. Stryker: Auntie Sue," NBC, 1989.

TV MOVIES AND MINISERIES: "The Crooked Hearts,"
ABC, 1972; "The Hostage Tower," CBS, 1980.

FAIRCHILD, MORGAN

b. *Dallas, TX, February 3, 1950*. Blonde soap
vixen whose career was built on appareances in
the kind of glossy TV junk that's fallen out of
fashion; she played Constance Carlyle on
"Flamingo Road."

AS A REGULAR: "Search for Tomorrow," CBS,
1973-77; "Flamingo Road," NBC, 1981-82;
"Paper Dolls," ABC, 1984; "Falcon Crest,"
CBS, 1985-86.

AND: "Kojak: A Hair-Trigger Away," CBS, 1976;
"The Bob Newhart Show: Grand Delusion," CBS,
1977; "Happy Days: My Fair Fonzie," ABC,
1977; "Switch: Downshift," CBS, 1977; "Mork &
Mindy: Mork's Seduction," ABC, 1978; "Police
Woman: Murder with Pretty People," NBC, 1978;
"Barnaby Jones: A Dangerous Affair," CBS,
1978; "The Mike Douglas Show," SYN, 1981;
"Hotel: Premiere," ABC, 1983; "Bob Hope
Lampoons Television 1985," NBC, 1985; "CBS
Summer Playhouse: Some Kinda Woman," CBS,
1988; "My Two Dads: Macho Stupid Guy Time,"
NBC, 1989; "Murphy Brown: TV or Not TV,"
CBS, 1989.

TV MOVIES AND MINISERIES: "Honeyboy," NBC,
1978; "Murder in Music City," NBC, 1979;
"The Concrete Cowboys," CBS, 1979; "The
Memory of Eva Ryker," CBS, 1980;
"Flamingo Road," NBC, 1980; "Time Bomb,"
NBC, 1984; "North and South," ABC, 1985;
"Street of Dreams," CBS, 1988.

FALANA, LOLA

b. *Camden, NJ, September 11, 1943*. High
energy singer-dancer.

AS A REGULAR: "The New Bill Cosby Show,"
CBS, 1972-73; "Ben Vereen... Comin' at Ya,"
NBC, 1975.

AND: "The FBI: The Sanctuary," ABC, 1969;
"Hollywood Palace," ABC, 1969; "The Flip
Wilson Show," NBC, 1970; "The Pearl Bailey
Show," ABC, 1971; "The Streets of San
Francisco: A String of Puppets," ABC, 1973;
"Lola Falana Special," ABC, 1975; "Sammy and
Company," SYN, 1976; "The Tonight Show
Starring Johnny Carson," NBC, 1976; "Lola!,"
ABC, 1976; "The Love Boat: Marooned," ABC,
1978; "Vega$: Redhanded," ABC, 1979.

FALK, PETER

b. *New York City, NY, September 16, 1927*.
Multiple-Emmy winning actor who plays
shuffling-on-the-outside, sharp-on-the-inside
Lt. Columbo. And judging by the way he
seems in real life, Falk isn't acting all that
much.

AS A REGULAR: "Trials of O'Brien," CBS, 1965-

66; "Columbo," NBC, 1971-78; ABC, 1989-
90.

AND: "Robert Montgomery Presents: Return
Visit," NBC, 1957; "Studio One: The Mother
Bit," CBS, 1957; "Studio One: Rudy," CBS,
1957; "Kraft Mystery Theatre: Night Cry,"
NBC, 1958; "Play of the Week: The Power and
the Glory," SYN, 1959; "Play of the Week: The
Emporer's New Clothes," SYN, 1960; "The
Untouchables: Underworld Bank," ABC, 1960;
"The Islanders: Hostage Island," ABC, 1960;
"The Sacco-Vanzetti Story," NBC, 1960;
"Witness: Abe 'Kid Twist' Reles," CBS, 1960;
"Have Gun, Will Travel: The Poker Fiend,"
CBS, 1960; "Cry Vengeance!," NBC, 1961;
"Malibu Run: The Jeremiah Adventure," CBS,
1961; "The Law and Mr. Jones: Cold Turkey,"
ABC, 1961; "Malibu Run: The Double
Adventure," CBS, 1961; "Here's Hollywood,"
NBC, 1961; "Jackie Gleason Special: The
Million Dollar Incident," CBS, 1961; "Alfred
Hitchcock Presents: Gratitude," NBC, 1961;
"Naked City: A Very Cautious Boy," ABC,
1961; "The Barbara Stanwyck Show: The
Assassin," NBC, 1961; "Target: The Corrupters:
The Million-Dollar Dump," ABC, 1961; "The
Untouchables: The Troubleshooter," ABC,
1961; "The Twilight Zone: The Mirror," CBS,
1961; "The New Breed: Cross the Little Line,"
ABC, 1962; "The Dick Powell Show: The Price
of Tomatoes," NBC, 1962; "87th Precinct: The
Pigeon," NBC, 1962; "Naked City: Lament for a
Dead Indian," ABC, 1962; "The Dick Powell
Show: The Doomsday Boys," NBC, 1962; "The
Alfred Hitchcock Hour: Bonfire," CBS, 1962;
"Dr. Kildare: The Balance and the Crucible,"
NBC, 1963; "Wagon Train: The Gus Morgan
Story," ABC, 1963; "Bob Hope Chrysler
Theatre: Four Kings," NBC, 1963; "The Danny
Kaye Show," CBS, 1964; "The du Pont Show:
Ambassador at Large," NBC, 1964; "Ben Casey:
For Jimmy, the Best of Everything," ABC, 1964;
"The Danny Kaye Show," CBS, 1965; "Bob
Hope Chrysler Theatre: Perilous Times," NBC,
1965; "Brigadoon," ABC, 1966; "Bob Hope
Chrysler Theatre: Dear Deductable," NBC,
1966; "Hollywood Squares," NBC, 1967;
"Dream Girl of '67," ABC, 1967; "Personality,"
NBC, 1967; "A Hatful of Rain," ABC, 1968;
"The Name of the Game: A Sister From Napoli,"
NBC, 1971; "The Merv Griffin Show," SYN,
1973; "The Mike Douglas Show," SYN, 1974;
"Scared Straight!," SYN, 1979; "The Tonight
Show Starring Johnny Carson," NBC, 1989.

TV MOVIES AND MINISERIES: "Prescription:
Murder," NBC, 1968; "A Step Out of Line,"
CBS, 1971; "Ransom for a Dead Man," NBC,
1971; "Griffin and Phoenix," ABC, 1976.

AS DIRECTOR: "Columbo: Blueprint for Murder,"
NBC, 1972.

* Emmies: 1962, 1972, 1975, 1976, 1990.

FALKENBERG, JINX
b. *Spain, January 21, 1919.* Early TV personality.
AS A REGULAR: "Tex and Jinx," NBC, 1947; CBS, 1949; "Masquerade Party," CBS, 1958.
AND: "To Tell the Truth," CBS, 1961; "Theatre '62: Intermezzo," NBC, 1961; "Girl Talk," SYN, 1963.

FARENTINO, JAMES
b. *Brooklyn, NY, February 24, 1938.* Generically handsome actor who played lawyer Neil Darrell on "The Bold Ones" and adventurer Jefferson Keyes, who'd solve cases for a cool million; he showed a flair for comedy as newspaper editor Frank DeMarco on Mary Tyler Moore's mid-eighties sitcom.
AS A REGULAR: "The Bold Ones," NBC, 1969-72; "Cool Million," NBC, 1972-73; "Dynasty," ABC, 1981-82; "Blue Thunder," ABC, 1984; "Mary," CBS, 1985-86.
AND: "The Alfred Hitchcock Hour: The Black Curtain," CBS, 1962; "The Defenders: The Last Illusion," CBS, 1963; "77 Sunset Strip: Bonus Baby," ABC, 1963; "Route 66: Cries of Persons Close to One," CBS, 1964; "The Reporter: Super-Star," CBS, 1964; "The FBI: All the Streets Are Silent," ABC, 1965; "The Alfred Hitchcock Hour: Death Scene," NBC, 1965; "Twelve O'Clock High: P.O.W.," ABC, 1965; "Ben Casey: O, the Big Wheel Turns by Faith, by Faith," ABC, 1965; "Laredo: I See By Your Outfit," NBC, 1965; "The FBI: All the Streets Are Silent," ABC, 1965; "The Virginian: The Wolves Up Front, the Jackals Behind," NBC, 1966; "The Fugitive: Passage to Helena," ABC, 1967; "Run for Your Life: Cry Hard, Cry Fast," NBC, 1967; "Ironside: Something for Nothing," NBC, 1968; "Love, American Style: Love and the Neighbor," ABC, 1969; "The Men From Shiloh: The Best Man," NBC, 1970; "Night Gallery: Since Aunt Ada Came to Stay," NBC, 1971; "Hollywood Television Theatre: Birdbath," NET, 1971; "Night Gallery: The Girl with the Hungry Eyes," NBC, 1972; "Police Story: Dangerous Games," NBC, 1973; "Love Story: The Soft, Kind Brush," NBC, 1973; "Police Story: Requiem for C.Z. Smith," NBC, 1974; "Police Story: Incident in the Kill Zone," NBC, 1975; "My Wife Next Door," NBC, 1975.
TV MOVIES AND MINISERIES: "Wings of Fire," NBC, 1967; "The Sound of Anger," NBC, 1968; "The Whole World Is Watching," NBC, 1969; "Vanished," NBC, 1971; "The Longest Night," ABC, 1972; "The Family Rico," CBS, 1972; "Cool Million," NBC, 1972; "The Elevator," ABC, 1974; "Crossfire," NBC, 1975; "Jesus of Nazareth," NBC, 1977; "Silent Victory: The Kitty O'Neil Story," CBS, 1979; "Son Rise: A Miracle of Love," NBC, 1979; "Something So Right," CBS, 1982; "The Cradle Will Fall," CBS, 1983; "A Summer to Remember," CBS, 1985; "Picking Up the Pieces," CBS, 1985;

"Sins," CBS, 1986; "That Secret Sunday," CBS, 1986; "Family Sons," CBS, 1987; "The Red Spider," CBS, 1988; "Who Gets the Friends?," CBS, 1988; "Naked Lie," CBS, 1989.

FARGAS, ANTONIO
b. *Bronx, NY, August 14, 1946.* Actor who played the streetwise Huggy Bear on "Starsky and Hutch."
AS A REGULAR: "Starsky and Hutch," ABC, 1975-79; "All My Children," ABC, 1982-83.
AND: "The Bill Cosby Show: The Barber Shop," NBC, 1971; "Ironside: Downhill All the Way," NBC, 1973; "Sanford & Son: Fred Sanford, Legal Eagle," NBC, 1974; "Police Story: The Ho Chi Minh Trail," NBC, 1974; "Kolchak, the Night Stalker: The Zombie," ABC, 1974; "Kojak: Loser Takes All," CBS, 1974; "$weepstake$: Cowboy, Linda and Angie, Mark," NBC, 1979; "Nurse: Long Day's Journey Into Morning," CBS, 1981; "Hardcastle and McCormick: Once Again with Vigorish," ABC, 1983; "Miami Vice: Mirror Image," NBC, 1989.
TV MOVIES AND MINISERIES: "Huckleberry Finn," ABC, 1975; "Starsky and Hutch," ABC, 1975; "The Ambush Murders," CBS, 1982; "A Good Sport," CBS, 1984.

FARGE, ANNIE
b. *France, 1935.* French starlet who was pegged by some to be a sitcom star as the naive Angel.
AS A REGULAR: "Angel," CBS, 1960-61.
AND: "Here's Hollywood," NBC, 1960; "Art Linkletter's House Party," CBS, 1960; "The Garry Moore Show," CBS, 1960; "The Rifleman: The Princess," ABC, 1962; "Adventures in Paradise: Policeman's Holiday," ABC, 1962; "The Third Man: Hamburg Shakedown," SYN, 1962; "Perry Mason: The Case of the Betrayed Bride," CBS, 1964.

FARINA, DENNIS
b. *Chicago, IL, 1944.* Craggy-faced actor who played tough cop Mike Torello on "Crime Story."
AS A REGULAR: "Crime Story," NBC, 1986-88.
AND: "Miami Vice: One-Eyed Jack," NBC, 1984; "Hunter: The Snow Queen," NBC, 1985; "Miami Vice: Lombard," NBC, 1985; "Later with Bob Costas," NBC, 1989.
TV MOVIES AND MINISERIES: "Six Against the Rock," NBC, 1987; "Open Admissions," CBS, 1988; "Two of a Kind: The Case of the Hillside Stranglers," NBC, 1989.

FARMER, FRANCES
b. *Seattle, WA, September 19, 1913; d. 1970.* Actress whose alcoholism and rebellion against

the Hollywood studio system led to her "retirement" from movies and time in a mental institution. In the late fifties she attempted a comeback, and did some TV work—and was surprised by "This Is Your Life" host Ralph Edwards, who told a sanitized version of her story to America.

AS A GUEST: "The Ed Sullivan Show," CBS, 1957; "Playhouse 90: Reunion," CBS, 1958; "This Is Your Life," NBC, 1958; "Studio One: Tongues of Angels," CBS, 1958.

FARR, JAMIE

b. Toledo, OH, July 1, 1934. Dark-featured character actor who was headed toward sitcom obscurity when he was cast as cross-dressing Cpl. Max Klinger on "M*A*S*H."

AS A REGULAR: "The Dick Van Dyke Show," CBS, 1961; "The Chicago Teddy Bears," CBS, 1971; "M*A*S*H," CBS, 1973-83; "The Gong Show," SYN, 1976-80; "AfterMASH," CBS, 1983-84.

AND: "The Rebel: Two Weeks," ABC, 1961; "Holiday Lodge: The Actor," CBS, 1961; "Hazel: Let's Get Away From It All," NBC, 1964; "Gomer Pyle, USMC: Gomer Pyle, POW," CBS, 1965; "My Favorite Martian: The Avenue C Mob," CBS, 1965; "Amos Burke, Secret Agent: A Very Important Russian Is Missing," ABC, 1966; "I Dream of Jeannie: Get Me to Mecca on Time," NBC, 1966; "My Favorite Martian: Virus M for Martin," CBS, 1966; "Get Smart: The Impossible Mission," NBC, 1968; "Gomer Pyle, USMC: A Star Is Not Born," CBS, 1968; "Family Affair: Flower Power," CBS, 1969; "The Flying Nun: Cast Your Bread Upon the Waters," ABC, 1969; "Room 222: The New Boy," ABC, 1970; "Love, American Style: Love and Lover's Lane," ABC, 1972; "The Streets of San Francisco: A Collection of Eagles," ABC, 1973; "M*A*S*H: Chief Surgeon Who?," CBS, 1972; "Kolchak, the Night Stalker: Primal Scream," ABC, 1975; "Amy Prentiss: Profile in Evil," NBC, 1975; "Barnaby Jones: Doomed Alibi," CBS, 1975; "Tattletales," CBS, 1975; "Rhyme and Reason," ABC, 1975; "The Magnificent Marble Machine," NBC, 1976; "Joys," NBC, 1976; "The Mike Douglas Show," SYN, 1981; "The Love Boat: Youth Takes a Holiday," ABC, 1983; "Murder, She Wrote: A Little Night Work," CBS, 1988.

TV MOVIES AND MINISERIES: "The Blue Knight," NBC, 1973; "Amateur Night at the Dixie Bar and Grill," NBC, 1979; "Murder Can Hurt You!," ABC, 1980.

AS DIRECTOR: "M*A*S*H: Friends and Enemies," CBS, 1983.

FARRELL, CHARLES

b. Onset Bay, MA, August 9, 1901; d. 1990. Light leading man of thirties movies who played Vern, the exasperated father of Gale Storm on the monumentallly stupid sitcom "My Little Margie."

AS A REGULAR: "My Little Margie," CBS, 1952; NBC, 1952; CBS, 1953; NBC, 1953-55; "The Charlie Farrell Show," CBS, 1956.

AND: "The Saint: The Unkind Philanthropist," NBC, 1965.

FARRELL, GLENDA

b. Enid, OK, June 30, 1904; d. 1971. Screen and TV actress who played wisecracking types; she won an Emmy for a "Ben Casey" guest shot.

AS A GUEST: "Silver Theatre: Gaudy Lady," CBS, 1950; "Prudential Family Playhouse: Ruggles of Red Gap," CBS, 1951; "Armstrong Circle Theatre: The Straightforward Narrow," NBC, 1952; "Tales of Tomorrow: The Build-Box," ABC, 1953; "Elgin TV Hour: Crime in the Streets," ABC, 1955; "Studio One: Miss Turner's Decision," CBS, 1955; "Studio One: The Other Place," CBS, 1958; "Studio One: The Edge of Truth," CBS, 1958; "Cimarron City: A Respectable Girl," NBC, 1958; "Ellery Queen: Confession of Murder," NBC, 1959; "G.E. Theatre: Night Club," CBS, 1959; "The Bells of St. Mary's," CBS, 1959; "Buick Electra Playhouse: The Killers," CBS, 1959; "Wagon Train: The Jess MacAbbee Story," NBC, 1959; "U.S. Steel Hour: Queen of the Orange Bowl," CBS, 1960; "Play of the Week: A Palm Tree in a Rose Garden," SYN, 1960; "The Islanders: The Widow From Richmond," ABC, 1960; "Our American Heritage: The Invincible Teddy," NBC, 1961; "A Story of Love: A String of Beads," NBC, 1961; "Yes, Yes Nanette: A Tale of Two Mothers," NBC, 1961; "U.S. Steel Hour: Summer Rhapsody," CBS, 1961; "U.S. Steel Hour: The Woman Across the Hall," CBS, 1961; "Frontier Circus: Mighty Like Rogues," CBS, 1962; "The Defenders: The Naked Heiress," CBS, 1962; "U.S. Steel Hour: The Inner Panic," CBS, 1962; "Route 66: Man Out of Time," CBS, 1962; "Empire: Stopover on the Way to the Moon," NBC, 1963; "Ben Casey: A Cardinal Act of Mercy," ABC, 1963; "U.S. Steel Hour: Moment of Rage," CBS, 1963; "Rawhide: Incident at Farragut Pass," CBS, 1963; "Dr. Kildare: The Exploiters," NBC, 1963; "The Fugitive: Fatso," ABC, 1963; "Bonanza: The Pure Truth," NBC, 1964; "The Bing Crosby Show: The Liberated Woman," ABC, 1964; "Directions '66: The Bigger They Are," ABC, 1966.

* Emmies: 1963.

FARRELL, MIKE

b. St. Paul, MN, February 6, 1939. Tall, long-faced actor who played Scott Banning on "Days of Our Lives" before joining "M*A*S*H" as B.J. Hunnicutt.

AS A REGULAR: "Days of Our Lives," NBC, 1968-70; "The Interns," CBS, 1970-71; "The Man and the City," ABC, 1971-72; "M*A*S*H," CBS, 1975-83.

AND: "McHale's Navy: Washing Machine Charlie," ABC, 1963; "Combat!: The Bankroll," ABC, 1966; "Mannix: Blind Mirror," CBS, 1969; "Sarge: A Terminal Case of Vengeance," NBC, 1971; "The Bold Ones: In Sudden Darkness," NBC, 1972; "Bonanza: The Hidden Enemy," NBC, 1972; "Ghost Story: Eulogy for a Vampire," NBC, 1972; "Love, American Style: Love and the Hot Spell," ABC, 1973; "The Rookies: The Wheel of Death," ABC, 1973; "Owen Marshall, Counselor at Law: The Camerons Are a Special Clan," ABC, 1973; "The New Land Pilot," ABC, 1974; "Ironside: The Faded Image," NBC, 1974; "Marcus Welby, M.D.: Hell Is Upstairs," ABC, 1974; "Hollywood Television Theatre: Ladies of the Corridor," PBS, 1975; "The $20,000 Pyramid," ABC, 1976; "Shoot for the Stars," NBC, 1977; "Dinah!," SYN, 1978.

TV MOVIES AND MINISERIES: "The Longest Night," ABC, 1972; "She Cried Murder," CBS, 1973; "The Questor Tapes," NBC, 1974; "Live Again, Die Again," ABC, 1974; "McNaughton's Daughter," NBC, 1976; "Battered," NBC, 1978; "Sex and the Single Parent," CBS, 1979; "Letters From Frank," CBS, 1979; "Memorial Day," CBS, 1983; "Private Sessions," NBC, 1985; "Vanishing Act," CBS, 1986; "A Deadly Silence," ABC, 1989; "Incident at Dark River," TNT, 1989.

AS DIRECTOR: "M*A*S*H: Ain't Love Grand," CBS, 1979; "M*A*S*H: Heal Thyself," CBS, 1980; "M*A*S*H: War Co-Respondent," CBS, 1980; "M*A*S*H: Death Takes a Holiday," CBS, 1980.

AS WRITER: "M*A*S*H: The Yalu Brick Road," CBS, 1979; "M*A*S*H: War Co-Respondent," CBS, 1980; "M*A*S*H: Death Takes a Holiday," CBS, 1980; "M*A*S*H: Run for the Money," CBS, 1982; "M*A*S*H: Strange Bedfellows," CBS, 1983.

FARROW, MIA

b. Los Angeles, CA, February 9, 1946. Elfin actress who was hot gossip-page fodder in the mid-sixties because of her free-spirited ways on the set of "Peyton Place," on which she played Allison MacKenzie, and her 1966 marriage to Frank Sinatra, who was thirty years her senior.

AS A REGULAR: "Peyton Place," ABC, 1964-66.

AND: "The Mike Douglas Show," SYN, 1965; "Johnny Belinda," ABC, 1967; "The Tonight Show Starring Johnny Carson," NBC, 1968; "Peter Pan," NBC, 1976.

TV MOVIES AND MINISERIES: "Goodbye Raggedy Ann," CBS, 1971.

FAULK, JOHN HENRY

b. 1918; d. 1990. Broadcaster/commentator who successfully fought blacklisting in the fifties.

AS A REGULAR: "It's News to Me," CBS, 1951-54; "Leave It to the Girls," ABC, 1954; "The Morning Show," CBS, 1955; "Hee Haw," SYN, 1975-82.

AND: "Get the Message," ABC, 1964.

TV MOVIES AND MINISERIES: "Adam," NBC, 1983.

* Faulk was named as a Communist by AWARE in the early fifties. He was fired from his job with CBS radio and denied other employment. Faulk sued AWARE, and in 1962, he won. Officials of AWARE were ordered to pay Faulk $3.5 million. The story was dramatized in the 1975 TV movie "Fear on Trial" with William Devane as Faulk and George C. Scott as attorney Louis Nizer.

FAWCETT, FARRAH

b. Corpus Christi, TX, February 2, 1946. Blonde sex symbol with windblown tresses who, in the mid-seventies, was as hot as platform shoes. She played private eye Jill Munroe, the "athletic" one of "Charlie's Angels" and has since proven herself as a serious actress.

AS A REGULAR: "Charlie's Angels," ABC, 1976-77.

AND: "I Dream of Jeannie: See You in C-U-B-A," NBC, 1969; "The Flying Nun: Marcello's Idol," ABC, 1969; "I Dream of Jeannie: My Sister, the Homemaker," NBC, 1969; "The Flying Nun: Armando and the Pool Table," ABC, 1970; "Inside O.U.T.," NBC, 1971; "The Girl with Something Extra: How Green Was Las Vegas," NBC, 1973; "McCloud: The Colorado Cattle Caper," NBC, 1974; "Marcus Welby, M.D.: I've Promised You a Father,.....," ABC, 1974; "Harry O: Forbidden City," ABC, 1976; "Charlie's Angels: Fallen Angels," ABC, 1979; "Charlie's Angels: The Prince and the Angel," ABC, 1980; "Charlie's Angels: An Angel's Trail," ABC, 1980; "The Arsenio Hall Show," SYN, 1989.

TV MOVIES AND MINISERIES: "The Feminist and the Fuzz," ABC, 1971; "The Great American Beauty Contest," ABC, 1973; "The Girl Who Came Gift-Wrapped," ABC, 1974; "Murder on Flight 502," ABC, 1975; "Charlie's Angels," ABC, 1976; "Murder in Texas," NBC, 1981; "The Burning Bed," NBC, 1984; "The Red-Light Sting," CBS, 1984; "Between Two Women," ABC, 1986; "Nazi Hunter: The Beate Klarsfeld Story," ABC, 1986; "Poor Little Rich Girl: The Barbara Hutton Story," NBC, 1987; "Margaret Bourke-White," TNT, 1989; "Small Sacrifices," ABC, 1989.

* See also "Charlie's Angels."

FAYE, ALICE
b. *Ann Leppert, New York City, NY, May 5, 1915.* Musical-comedy star who did a few TV guest shots, often with husband Phil Harris.
AS A GUEST: "Phil Harris Special," NBC, 1959; "Perry Como's Kraft Music Hall," NBC, 1962; "The Red Skelton Hour," CBS, 1963; "Hollywood Palace," ABC, 1964; "Hollywood Palace," ABC, 1967; "The Dean Martin Show," NBC, 1968; "The Mike Douglas Show," SYN, 1969; "The Love Boat: Celebration," ABC, 1980.

FAYE, HERBIE
b. *1899; d. 1980.* Comic actor; he played Pvt. Sam Fender on "The Phil Silvers Show."
AS A REGULAR: "Seven at Eleven," NBC, 1951; "You'll Never Get Rich (The Phil Silvers Show)," CBS, 1955-59; "The New Phil Silvers Show," CBS, 1963-64; "Love Thy Neighbor," ABC, 1973; "Doc," CBS, 1975-76.
AND: "Perry Como's Kraft Music Hall," NBC, 1959; "Phil Silvers Special: Summer in New York," CBS, 1960; "The Tom Ewell Show: Mr. Shrewd," CBS, 1961; "The Tom Ewell Show: Handy Man," CBS, 1961; "Mrs. G. Goes to College: Sam's Car," CBS, 1961; "The Danny Thomas Show: Danny Weaves a Web," CBS, 1961; "The Joey Bishop Show: The Ham in the Family," NBC, 1961; "The Dick Van Dyke Show: Where Did I Come From?," CBS, 1962; "The Joey Bishop Show: The Income Tax Caper," NBC, 1962; "The Dick Van Dyke Show: One Angry Man," CBS, 1962; "The Jack Benny Program," CBS, 1963; "The Dick Van Dyke Show: When a Bowling Pin Talks, Listen," CBS, 1963; "The Twilight Zone: A Kind of a Stopwatch," CBS, 1963; "My Favorite Martian: How You Gonna Keep Them Down on the Pharmacy?," CBS, 1964; "The Joey Bishop Show: The Do-It-Yourself Nursery," CBS, 1965; "The Dick Van Dyke Show: Brother, Can You Spare $2,500?," CBS, 1965; "The Dick Van Dyke Show: Stacey Petrie," CBS, 1965; "Burke's Law: Who Killed Cop Robin?," ABC, 1965; "Bewitched: A Bum Raps," ABC, 1966; "The Dick Van Dyke Show: The Last Chapter," CBS, 1966;

"Gomer Pyle, USMC: Gomer and the Little Men From Outer Space," CBS, 1966; "The Andy Griffith Show: Tape Recorder," CBS, 1967; "Petticoat Junction: It's Not Easy to Be a Mother," CBS, 1967; "The Lucy Show: Lucy and the Pool Hustler," CBS, 1968; "The Mothers-in-Law: Every In-Law Wants to Get Into the Act," NBC, 1969; "Petticoat Junction: Kathy Jo's First Birthday," CBS, 1969; "That Girl: That King," ABC, 1971; "All in the Family: Success Story," CBS, 1971; "Here's Lucy: Lucy and Harry's Italian Bombshell," CBS, 1971; "The Odd Couple: And Leave the Greyhound to Us," ABC, 1971; "Love, American Style: Love and the Lovely Evening," ABC, 1972; "Here's Lucy: Lucy the Other Woman," CBS, 1972; "The Mary Tyler Moore Show: Put on a Happy Face," CBS, 1973; "The Bob Newhart Show: Who's Been Sleeping on My Couch?," CBS, 1973; "The Odd Couple: The Exorcists," ABC, 1973; "Happy Days: Knock Around the Clock," ABC, 1974; "Barney Miller: The Social Worker," ABC, 1975.

FAYLEN, CAROL
b. *Los Angeles, CA, 1949.* Daughter of Frank Faylen.
AS A REGULAR: "The Bing Crosby Show," ABC, 1964-65.
AND: "Leave It to Beaver: Beaver the Hero," ABC, 1962; "Leave It to Beaver: The Book Report," ABC, 1963.

FAYLEN, FRANK
b. *St. Louis, MO, 1907.* Character actor who played Dobie Gillis' dad, Herbert, and the dad of Don Hollinger (Ted Bessell) on "That Girl."
AS A REGULAR: "The Many Loves of Dobie Gillis," CBS, 1959-63.
AND: "My Mother the Car: And Leave the Drive-in to Us," NBC, 1965; "The Beverly Hillbillies: Clampett Cha Cha Cha," CBS, 1966; "Petticoat Junction: Girl of Our Dreams," CBS, 1968; "That Girl: There Are a Bunch of Cards in St. Louis," ABC, 1971.

FAYLEN, KAY
b. *Los Angeles, CA.* Actress and daughter of Frank Faylen.
AS A REGULAR: "Dr. Christian," SYN, 1956.
AND: "Science Fiction Theatre: The Miracle of Dr. Dove," SYN, 1956.

FEINSTEIN, ALAN
b. *New York City, NY, September 8, 1941.*
AS A REGULAR: "Love of Life," CBS, 1965-68; "The Edge of Night," CBS, 1969-74; "Jigsaw John," NBC, 1976; "The Runaways," NBC, 1979; "The Family Tree," NBC, 1983; "Berrenger's," NBC, 1985.
AND: "Kojak: Wall Street Gunslinger," CBS,

1974; "Harry O: Portrait of a Murder," ABC, 1975; "Medical Story: Woman in White," NBC, 1975; "The Rookies: Death Lady," ABC, 1975; "The Streets of San Francisco: Interlude," ABC, 1976; "St. Elsewhere: Family History," NBC, 1983; "Hardcastle and McCormick: Flying Down to Rio," ABC, 1983; "Remington Steele: Diced Steele," NBC, 1985; "Heartbeat: Critical Overload," ABC, 1989.

TV MOVIES AND MINISERIES: "The Users," ABC, 1978; "The Two Worlds of Jennie Logan," CBS, 1979; "Masada," ABC, 1981; "Second Serve," CBS, 1986; "On Fire," ABC, 1987; "My Boyfriend's Back," NBC, 1989.

FELD, FRITZ

b. *Berlin, Germany, October 15, 1900*. Short, slight comic actor who usually played headwaiters, floorwalkers or other officious types, often capping his character by tapping his hand over his mouth to make a popping noise.

AS A GUEST: "December Bride: The Shoplifter," CBS, 1955; "I Love Lucy: Paris at Last," CBS, 1956; "The Red Skelton Show," CBS, 1958; "Accused: The Chandor Rona Case," CBS, 1959; "Bachelor Father: Paris in the Spring," NBC, 1961; "The Many Loves of Dobie Gillis: Will Success Spoil Dobie's Mother?," CBS, 1961; "Adventures in Paradise: Queens Back to Back," ABC, 1961; "The Farmer's Daughter: Rendezvous for Two," ABC, 1964; "The Donna Reed Show: Pandemonium in the Condominium," ABC, 1964; "The Farmer's Daughter: A Real Live Congressman," ABC, 1964; "The Farmer's Daughter: Helping Hand," ABC, 1964; "No Time for Sergeants: My Fair Andy," ABC, 1965; "The Man From UNCLE: The Sort of Do-It-Yourself Dreadful Affair," NBC, 1966; "The Man From UNCLE: The Napoleon's Tomb Affair," NBC, 1967; "Batman: Pop Goes the Joker/Flop Goes the Joker," ABC, 1967; "The Beverly Hillbillies: Jethro Proposes," CBS, 1968; "Batman: The Joker's Flying Saucer," ABC, 1968; "Bewitched: Samantha on the Keyboard," ABC, 1968; "Love, American Style: Love and the Boss," ABC, 1971; "The Odd Couple: Felix the Horse Player," ABC, 1975; "ABC Afterschool Special: P.J. and the President's Son," ABC, 1976; "Magnum, P.I.: Birdman of Budapest," CBS, 1983.

TV MOVIES AND MINISERIES: "Call Her Mom," ABC, 1972; "Last of the Great Survivors," CBS, 1984; "Get Smart, Again!," ABC, 1989.

FELDMAN, COREY

b. *Reseda, CA, July 16, 1971*.

AS A REGULAR: "The Bad News Bears," CBS, 1979-80; "Madame's Place," SYN, 1982.

AND: "Fernwood 2-Night," SYN, 1977; "The Love Boat: Super Mom," ABC, 1979; "Mork & Mindy:

Gunfight at the O.K. Corral," ABC, 1980; "Cheers: Manager Coach," NBC, 1983; "CBS Schoolbreak Special: 15 and Getting Straight," CBS, 1989; "Trying Times: The Boss," PBS, 1989.

TV MOVIES AND MINISERIES: "Still the Beaver," CBS, 1983.

FELDMAN, MARTY

b. *London, England, July 8, 1934; d. 1982*. Cockeyed comic actor.

AS A REGULAR: "Dean Martin Presents," NBC, 1970; "The Marty Feldman Comedy Machine," ABC, 1972.

AND: "The Dean Martin Show," NBC, 1970; "The Dean Martin Show," NBC, 1971; "Hallmark Hall of Fame: The Man Who Came to Dinner," NBC, 1972; "Hollywood Squares," NBC, 1973; "The Merv Griffin Show," SYN, 1974; "Celebrity Sweepstakes," NBC, 1974; "Cher," CBS, 1975; "Harlem Globetrotters Popcorn Machine: The Three Musketeers," CBS, 1976; "The Muppet Show," SYN, 1981.

AS DIRECTOR: "When Things Were Rotten: Wedding Belle Blue," ABC, 1975.

* Feldman also had a British television show, 1970's "Marty," and he was a writer for BBC shows featuring David Frost, John Cleese and Graham Chapman.

FELDON, BARBARA

b. *Pittsburgh, PA, March 12, 1941*. Brunette actress who played Agent 99 on "Get Smart."

AS A REGULAR: "Get Smart," NBC, 1965-69; CBS, 1969-70; "The Marty Feldman Comedy Machine," ABC, 1972; "Dean Martin's Comedy World," NBC, 1974.

AND: "The $64,000 Question," CBS, 1957; "Girl Talk," SYN, 1963; "The du Pont Show: The Bachelor Game," NBC, 1963; "Missing Links," NBC, 1964; "East Side/West Side: The Street," CBS, 1964; "Mr. Broadway: Try to Find a Spy," CBS, 1964; "The Doctors and the Nurses: Hildie," CBS, 1964; "Flipper: The Lady and the Dolphin," NBC, 1964; "Slattery's People: What's a Requiem for a Loser?," CBS, 1964; "Twelve O'Clock High: End of the Line," ABC, 1965; "The Man From UNCLE: The Never-Never Affair," NBC, 1965; "Profiles in Courage: Grover Cleveland," NBC, 1965; "The Mike Douglas Show," SYN, 1966; "The Mike Douglas Show," SYN, 1967; "Password," CBS, 1967; "The Jerry Lewis Show," NBC, 1967; "Rowan & Martin's Laugh-In," NBC, 1968; "The Smothers Brothers Comedy Hour," CBS, 1968; "What's It All About, World?," ABC, 1969; "The Name of the Game: Cynthia Is Alive and Living in Avalon," NBC, 1970; "The Dean Martin Show," NBC, 1970; "The Flip Wilson Show," NBC, 1972; "Father on Trial," NBC, 1972; "Search: In Search of Midas," NBC, 1972; "Medical Center:

Between Two Fires," CBS, 1973; "Of Men and Women: Never Trust a Lady," ABC, 1973; "Griff: Death by Prescription," ABC, 1973; "McMillan and Wife: Free Fall to Terror," NBC, 1973; "The Bear Who Slept Through Christmas," NBC, 1973; "Don Adams Screen Test," SYN, 1975; "Doctors Hospital: And Sorrow for Angels," NBC, 1975; "The Magnificent Marble Machine," NBC, 1975; "The $20,000 Pyramid," ABC, 1976; "The Gong Show," SYN, 1976.

TV MOVIES AND MINISERIES: "Getting Away From it All," ABC, 1972; "Playmates," ABC, 1972; "What Are Best Friends For?," ABC, 1973; "Lady Killer," ABC, 1973; "Let's Switch," ABC, 1975; "A Guide for the Married Woman," ABC, 1978; "Sooner or Later," NBC, 1979; "A Vacation in Hell," ABC, 1979; "Before and After," ABC, 1979; "Get Smart, Again!," ABC, 1989.

FELL, NORMAN
b. Philadelphia, PA, March 24, 1924. Character actor with a face like a bassett hound; he was Stanley Roper on "Three's Company" and a spinoff series.
AS A REGULAR: "87th Precinct," NBC, 1961-62; "Dan August," ABC, 1970-71; "Needles and Pins," NBC, 1973; "Three's Company," ABC, 1977-79; "The Ropers," ABC, 1979-80; "Teachers Only," NBC, 1982-83.
AND: "Sunday Showcase: What Makes Sammy Run?," NBC, 1959; "The Untouchables: The Rusty Heller Story," ABC, 1960; "The Tab Hunter Show: Me and My Shadow," NBC, 1961; "Sam Benedict: Where There's a Will," NBC, 1962; "The Lieutenant: Cool of the Evening," NBC, 1963; "Ben Casey: I'll Get on My Icefloe and Wave Goodbye," ABC, 1964; "Dr. Kildare: Fathers and Daughters/A Gift of Love/The Tent-Dwellers/Going Home," NBC, 1965; "Bewitched: I'd Rather Twitch Than Fight," ABC, 1966; "A Man Called Shenandoah: Muted Fifes, Muffled Drums," ABC, 1966; "The Man From UNCLE: The Moonglow Affair," NBC, 1966; "The Wild Wild West: The Night of the Whirring Death," CBS, 1966; "Judd for the Defense: The Sound of the Plastic Axe," ABC, 1968; "The FBI: The Catalyst," ABC, 1969; "Love, American Style: Love and the Good Deal," ABC, 1969; "Love, American Style: Love and the Clinic," ABC, 1973; "Marcus Welby, M.D.: Catch a Ring That Isn't There," ABC, 1973; "Medical Center: The World's a Balloon," CBS, 1974; "Police Story: Wolf," NBC, 1974; "McMillan and Wife: Love, Honor and Swindle," NBC, 1975; "Rhoda: Chest Pains," CBS, 1975; "Rhoda: Ida's Doctor," CBS, 1975; "Fay: Lillian's Separation," NBC, 1975; "The Bionic Woman: In This Corner, Jamie Sommers," ABC, 1976; "The Streets of San Francisco: The Thrill Killers," ABC, 1976; "The Life and Times of Grizzly Adams: The Redemp-

tion of Ben," NBC, 1977; "Police Story: One of Our Cops Is Crazy," NBC, 1977; "The Love Boat: Julie's Dilemma," ABC, 1978; "Simon & Simon: Facets," CBS, 1985; "Webster: Almost Home," ABC, 1985; "Murder, She Wrote: Dead Heat," CBS, 1986; "The Twilight Zone: The Convict's Piano," CBS, 1986; "Magnum, P.I.: Solo Flight," CBS, 1987; "Murder, She Wrote: Just Another Fish Story," CBS, 1988; "Murphy's Law: Never Play Leapfrog with a Unicorn," ABC, 1989.
TV MOVIES AND MINISERIES: "The Hanged Man," NBC, 1964; "Three's a Crowd," ABC, 1969; "The Heist," ABC, 1972; "Thursday's Game," ABC, 1974; "Death Stalk," NBC, 1974; "Richie Brockelman, Private Eye," NBC, 1976; "Rich Man, Poor Man," ABC, 1976; "Roots: The Next Generations," ABC, 1979; "Uncommon Valor," CBS, 1983.

FELTON, VERNA
b. Salina, CA, 1890; d. 1966. Older actress who took many a pratfall as Hilda Crocker, the crazy friend of Lily Ruskin (Spring Byington) on "December Bride"; also the voice of Fred Flintstone's mother-in-law.
AS A REGULAR: "The RCA Victor Show," NBC, 1952; "December Bride," CBS, 1954-59; "Pete and Gladys," CBS, 1960-61.
AND: "I Love Lucy: Sales Resistance," CBS, 1953; "The Vic Damone Show," CBS, 1956; "Climax!: Disappearance of Amanda Hale," CBS, 1957; "Art Linkletter's House Party," CBS, 1959; "The Ann Sothern Show: Devery's White Elephant," CBS, 1959; "Here's Hollywood," NBC, 1961; "The Jack Benny Program: Dennis's Surprise Party," ABC, 1962; "Henry Fonda and the Family," CBS, 1962; "The Flintstones: Trouble-in-Law," ABC, 1962; "My Three Sons: Coincidence," ABC, 1962; "Dennis the Menace: Aunt Emma Visits the Wilsons," CBS, 1963.

FEMIA, JOHN
b. Brooklyn, NY, 1967.
AS A REGULAR: "Hello, Larry," NBC, 1979-80; "Square Pegs," CBS, 1982-83.

FENNELLY, PARKER
b. Northeast Harbor, ME. Actor who played flinty New England types; he was Titus Moody on Fred Allen's radio show.
AS A REGULAR: "The Headmaster," CBS, 1970-71.
AND: "Lux Video Theatre: Bert's Wedding," NBC, 1950; "Nash Airflyte Theatre: Fiddling Fool," CBS, 1951; "Philco TV Playhouse: Ephraim Tutt's Clean Hands," NBC, 1951; "Philco TV Playhouse: Mr. Quimby's Christmas," NBC, 1952; "Kraft Television Theatre: The Southwest Corner," NBC, 1955; "U.S. Steel Hour: The Meanest Man in the World," CBS, 1955; "Lamp Unto My Feet: To Hold in Trust,"

CBS, 1955; "Robert Montgomery Presents: The Stranger," NBC, 1955; "American Inventory: Calculated Risk," NBC, 1955; "Robert Montgomery Presents: Mr. Tutt Baits a Hook," NBC, 1956; "Robert Montgomery Presents: Mr. Tutt Goes West," NBC, 1956; "The Jack Paar Show," NBC, 1958; "Have Gun, Will Travel: Three Sons," CBS, 1958; "New Comedy Showcase: The Trouble with Richard," CBS, 1960; "Play of the Week: The Girls in 509," SYN, 1960; "Have Gun, Will Travel: The Calf," CBS, 1960; "Harrigan and Son: Pay the Two Dollars," ABC, 1960; "Window on Main Street: The Curse," CBS, 1962.

FENNEMAN, GEORGE
b. San Francisco, CA, November 10, 1919. Longtime announcer with Groucho Marx; also the stern narrator who told you that the story you were about to see was true, but the names had been changed to protect the innocent, on "Dragnet."
AS A REGULAR: "You Bet Your Life (The Groucho Show)," NBC, 1951-61; "Dragnet," NBC, 1953-59; "Anybody Can Play," ABC, 1958; "Your Surprise Package," CBS, 1961-62; "Your Funny, Funny Films," ABC, 1963.
AND: "G.E Theatre: A Question of Romance," CBS, 1958; "Art Linkletter's House Party," CBS, 1959; "The Tom Ewell Show: The Prying Eye," CBS, 1960; "Batman: An Egg Grows in Gotham/ The Yegg Foes in Gotham," ABC, 1966; "Please Don't Eat the Daisies: And What Does Your Husband Do?," NBC, 1966; "Gomer Pyle, USMC: All You Need Is One Good Break," CBS, 1968.

FERRELL, CONCHATA
b. Charleston, WV, March 28, 1943. Heavyset character actress, usually in good-hearted roles. She played Nurse Thor on "E/R" and was memorable as a tough attorney ready to take the Chez Louisianne to court on an episode of "Frank's Place."
AS A REGULAR: "Hot L Baltimore," ABC, 1975; "B.J. and the Bear," NBC, 1979-80; "McClain's Law," NBC, 1981-82; "E/R," CBS, 1984-85.
AND: "Maude: Florida's Goodbye," CBS, 1974; "Good Times: Willona the Fuzz," CBS, 1977; "The Love Boat: Reunion Cruise," ABC, 1979; "Freebie and the Bean: Bolo's Lady," CBS, 1980; "Lou Grant: Drifters," CBS, 1981; "St. Elsewhere: Hearts," NBC, 1983; "Frank's Place: The Bridge," CBS, 1987; "CBS Summer Playhouse: Old Money," CBS, 1988; "ABC Afterschool Special: Runaway Ralph," ABC, 1988; "Murder, She Wrote: Something Borrowed, Someone Blue," CBS, 1989; "Hard Time on Planet Earth: Wrestlemania," CBS, 1989.
TV MOVIES AND MINISERIES: "Who'll Save Our Children?," CBS, 1978; "Before and After,"

ABC, 1979; "The Seduction of Miss Leona," CBS, 1980; "Reunion," CBS, 1980; "Life of the Party: The Story of Beatrice," CBS, 1982; "North Beach and Rawhide," CBS, 1985; "Samaritan: The Mitch Snyder Story," CBS, 1986; "Eye on the Sparrow," NBC, 1987.

FERRER, JOSE
b. Santurce, Puerto Rico, January 8, 1912. Balding, distinguished actor who won an Oscar as Cyrano de Bergerac and who played the fabulously rich father of Stephanie Vanderkellen (Julia Duffy) on "Newhart."
AS A REGULAR: "Another World," NBC, 1983; "Bridges to Cross," CBS, 1986.
AND: "Producers Showcase: Cyrano de Bergerac," NBC, 1955; "The George Burns and Gracie Allen Show: Cyrano de Bergerac," CBS, 1956; "Producers Showcase: The Letter," NBC, 1956; "Producers Showcase: Festival of Music," NBC, 1956; "The Rosemary Clooney Show," SYN, 1957; "The Lux Show with Rosemary Clooney," NBC, 1958; "The Ford Show," NBC, 1958; "Truth or Consequences," NBC, 1958; "The Ed Sullivan Show," CBS, 1958; "Bell Telephone Hour," NBC, 1959; "G.E. Theatre: Survival," CBS, 1959; "U.S. Steel Hour: Marriage ... Handle with Care," CBS, 1959; "Perry Como's Kraft Music Hall," NBC, 1960; "The Chevy Show: Pleasant Dreams," NBC, 1960; "No Place Like Home," NBC, 1960; "The Greatest Show on Earth: No Middle Ground for Harry Kyle," ABC, 1963; "The Garry Moore Show," CBS, 1964; "Password," CBS, 1964; "The Danny Kaye Show," CBS, 1964; "Kismet," ABC, 1967; "A Case of Libel," ABC, 1968; "The Name of the Game: Tarot," NBC, 1970; "The Name of the Game: Why I Blew Up Dakota," NBC, 1970; "Hallmark Hall of Fame: Gideon," NBC, 1971; "The Little Drummer Boy," NBC, 1971; "Orson Welles' Great Mysteries: In the Confessional," SYN, 1974; "Columbo: Mind Over Mayhem," NBC, 1974; "ABC Afterschool Special: Cyrano," ABC, 1974; "Medical Story: Pilot," NBC, 1975; "Hallmark Hall of Fame: Truman at Potsdam," NBC, 1976; "Starsky and Hutch: Murder at Sea," ABC, 1976; "Magnum, P.I.: Thicker Than Blood," CBS, 1981; "Quincy: Ghost of a Chance," NBC, 1982; "Fantasy Island Random Choices," ABC, 1983; "Murder, She Wrote: Death Casts a Spell," CBS, 1985; "Newhart: Look Homeward, Stephanie," CBS, 1985; "Newhart: Locks, Stocks and Noodlehead," CBS, 1985; "Newhart: Pre-Nups," CBS, 1986; "Matlock: The Don," NBC, 1986; "Newhart: Thanksgiving for the Memories," CBS, 1986; "Newhart: Til Depth Do Us Part," CBS, 1987; "Newhart: It's My Party and I'll Die If I Want to," CBS, 1987.
TV MOVIES AND MINISERIES: "The Aquarians," NBC, 1970; "Banyon," NBC, 1971; "The Cable Car Murder," CBS, 1971; "The Marcus-

Nelson Murders," CBS, 1973; "The Missing Are Deadly," ABC, 1975; "The Art of Crime," NBC, 1975; "Medical Story," NBC, 1975; "Best Sellers: The Rhinemann Exchange," NBC, 1977; "Gideon's Trumpet," CBS, 1980; "The Murder That Wouldn't Die," NBC, 1980; "Berlin Tunnel 21," CBS, 1981; "Peter and Paul," CBS, 1981; "This Girl for Hire," CBS, 1983; "Samson and Delilah," ABC, 1984; "George Washington," CBS, 1984; "Hitler's SS: Portrait in Evil," NBC, 1985; "Seduced," CBS, 1985.

FERRER, MEL
b. *Melchior Gaston Ferrer, Elberon, NJ, August 25, 1917.*
AS A REGULAR: "Behind the Screen," CBS, 1981-82; "Falcon Crest," CBS, 1981-84.
AND: "Lux Video Theatre: The Vigilantes," CBS, 1953; "Omnibus: Nature of the Beast," CBS, 1953; "Producers Showcase: Mayerling," NBC, 1957; "Dick Powell's Zane Grey Theatre: The Ghost," CBS, 1959; "Bob Hope Chrysler Theatre: The Fifth Passenger," NBC, 1963; "Columbo: Requiem for a Falling Star," NBC, 1973; "Hollywood Television Theatre: Carola," NET, 1973; "Police Story: The Wyatt Earp Syndrome," NBC, 1974; "Marcus Welby, M.D.: Designs," ABC, 1974; "Hawaii Five-O: To Kill a Mind," CBS, 1977; "Eischied: Spanish Eight," NBC, 1979; "Hotel: Resolutions," ABC, 1984; "Murder, She Wrote: Widow, Weep for Me," CBS, 1985; "The Love Boat: The Villa," ABC, 1985; "Murder, She Wrote: Weave a Tangled Web," CBS, 1989; "The Magical World of Disney: Wild Jack," NBC, 1989; "Christine Cromwell: Things That Go Bump in the Night," ABC, 1989.
TV MOVIES AND MINISERIES: "Tenafly," NBC, 1973; "Black Beauty," NBC, 1978; "The Memory of Eva Ryker," CBS, 1980; "One Shoe Makes It Murder," CBS, 1982; "Seduced," CBS, 1985; "Peter the Great," NBC, 1986; "Outrage!," CBS, 1986.

FERRIGNO, LOU
b. *Brooklyn, NY, November 9, 1952.* Incredibly hulky actor.
AS A REGULAR: "The Incredible Hulk," CBS, 1978-82; "Trauma Center," ABC, 1983.
AND: "The Fall Guy: License to Kill," ABC, 1981; "The Fall Guy: The Winner," ABC, 1984.
TV MOVIES AND MINISERIES: "The Incredible Hulk Returns," NBC, 1988; "The Trial of the Incredible Hulk," NBC, 1989.
* Ferrigno is 60 percent deaf, a result of severe ear infections.
* Ferrigno played football briefly in Canada, but dropped out after breaking a fellow player's legs during a scrimmage.

FIEDLER, ARTHUR
b. *Boston, MA, December 17, 1894; d. 1979.*

AS A REGULAR: "Evening at Pops," PBS, 1969-78.
AND: "Music for a Spring Night: To Boston with Love," ABC, 1960; "Music for the Young," ABC, 1962.

FIEDLER, JOHN
b. *Platville, WI, February 3, 1925.* Slight, bespectacled actor usually in milquetoast roles; he played Woody, stagehand and Audi dealer, on "Buffalo Bill."
AS A REGULAR: "The Bob Newhart Show," CBS, 1972-78; "Kolchak, the Night Stalker," ABC, 1974-75; "Buffalo Bill," NBC, 1983-84.
AND: "Studio One: Walk Down the Hill," CBS, 1957; "Studio One: Death and Taxes," CBS, 1957; "U.S. Steel Hour: You Can't Win," CBS, 1957; "Kraft Theatre: All the King's Men," NBC, 1958; "Sunday Showcase: After Hours," NBC, 1960; "The Twilight Zone: Night of the Meek," CBS, 1960; "Pete and Gladys: The Fur Coat Story," CBS, 1961; "Checkmate: A Slight Touch of Venom," CBS, 1961; "The Many Loves of Dobie Gills: The Ruptured Duck," CBS, 1961; "The Many Loves of Dobie Gillis: The Second Most Beautiful Girl in the World," CBS, 1961; "The Twilight Zone: Cavender Is Coming," CBS, 1962; "My Favorite Martian: Man or Amoeba?," CBS, 1963; "The Farmer's Daughter: The Swinger," ABC, 1964; "The Munsters: Pilot," CBS, 1964; "The Donna Reed Show: Painter, Go Home," ABC, 1965; "That Girl: Christmas and the Hard Luck Kid," ABC, 1966; "Bewitched: Nobody But a Frog Knows How to Live," ABC, 1967; "Captain Nice: Who's Afraid of Amanda Woolf?," NBC, 1967; "Please Don't Eat the Daisies: The Play's the Thing," NBC, 1967; "Get Smart: Classification: Dead," NBC, 1967; "Bewitched: Marriage, Witch's Style," ABC, 1969; "Bewitched: Daddy Comes to Visit," ABC, 1969; "Get Smart: Age Before Duty," CBS, 1969; "McMillan and Wife: The Devil You Say," NBC, 1973; "The Streets of San Francsisco: Mask of Death," ABC, 1974; "Police Story: The Ripper," NBC, 1974; "The Odd Couple: The Dog Story," ABC, 1974; "The Cop and the Kid: Weekend Guest," NBC, 1976; "Alice: Mel's Happy Burger," CBS, 1976; "Switch: Dancer," CBS, 1977; "Three's Company: Jack Looks for a Job," ABC, 1977; "B.J. and the Bear: Crackers," NBC, 1979; "The Misadventures of Sheriff Lobo: Perkins Bombs Out," NBC, 1980; "Love, Sidney: The Party," NBC, 1981; "The Golden Girls: Love Me Tender," NBC, 1989.
TV MOVIES AND MINISERIES: "Cannon," CBS, 1971; "A Tattered Web," CBS, 1971; "Hitched," NBC, 1973; "Double Indemnity," ABC, 1973; "Woman of the Year," CBS, 1976; "Human Feelings," NBC, 1978; "The Monkey Mission," NBC, 1981.

FIELD, BETTY
b. Boston, MA, February 8, 1918; d. 1973.
AS A GUEST: "Masterpiece Playhouse: Six
Characters in Search of an Author," NBC,
1950; "Lux Video Theatre: Local Storm,"
CBS, 1951; "Somerset Maugham Theatre:
Grace," NBC, 1951; "Robert Montgomery
Presents: See No Evil," NBC, 1952;"Motorola
TV Hour: The Sins of the Fathers," ABC,
1954; "Elgin TV Hour: Family Crisis," ABC,
1954; "Producers Showcase: Happy Birthday,"
NBC, 1956; "The Loretta Young Show: Take
Care of My Child," NBC, 1956; "Climax!:
Scream in Silence," CBS, 1958; "Hallmark
Hall of Fame: Ah, Wilderness!," NBC, 1959;
"The Untouchables: The White Slavers," ABC,
1960; "Alfred Hitchcock Presents: Very Moral
Theft," NBC, 1960; "Route 66: The Swan
Bed," CBS, 1960; "Play of the Week: Uncle
Harry," SYN, 1961; "Naked City: Bullets Cost
Too Much," ABC, 1961; "Route 66: Across
Walnuts and Wine," CBS, 1962; "Dr. Kildare:
A Time for Every Purpose," NBC, 1962; "Girl
Talk," SYN, 1963; "Sam Benedict: Some Fires
Die Slowly," NBC, 1963; "The Alfred
Hitchcock Hour: The Star Juror," CBS, 1963;
"Going My Way: Florence, Come Home,"
ABC, 1963; "The Defenders: A Taste of
Ashes," CBS, 1964; "The Outsider: One Long-
Stemmed American Beauty," NBC, 1968;
"Judd for the Defense: Thou Shalt Not Suffer a
Witch to Live," ABC, 1968.

FIELD, MARGARET—See Maggie Mahoney.

FIELD, SALLY
b. Pasadena, CA, November 6, 1946. Oscar-
winning actress who began her career on TV
sitcoms, most notably as Sister Bertrille, a
diminutive nun who flew when the breeze
lifted her wing-like habit; her path to movie
stardom began with an Emmy Award for
"Sybil."
AS A REGULAR: "Gidget," ABC, 1965-66; "The
Flying Nun," ABC, 1967-70; "The Girl with
Something Extra," NBC, 1973-74.
AND: "Hey, Landlord!: Woody, Can You Spare a
Sister?," NBC, 1967; "Hey, Landlord!: Sharin'
Sharon," NBC, 1967; "Hey, Landlord!: Big
Brother Is Watching You," NBC, 1967; "Hey,
Landlord!: A Little Off the Top," NBC, 1967;
"Hollywood Squares," NBC, 1967; "It's
Happening," ABC, 1968; "Bracken's World:
Jenny, Who Bombs Buildings," NBC, 1970;
"Night Gallery: Whisper," NBC, 1971; "Alias
Smith and Jones: Dreadful Sorry, Clementine,"
ABC, 1971; "Alias Smith and Jones: The
Clementine Ingredient," ABC, 1972; "Marcus
Welby, M.D.: I Can Hardly Tell You Apart,"
ABC, 1972; "Hollywood Squares," NBC, 1974;

"Hollywood Squares," SYN, 1975; "Donahue,"
SYN, 1979.
TV MOVIES AND MINISERIES: "Maybe I'll Come
Home in the Spring," ABC, 1971; "Marriage:
Year One," NBC, 1971; "Mongo's Back in
Town," CBS, 1971; "Home for the Holidays,"
ABC, 1972; "Hitched," NBC, 1973; "Bridger,"
ABC, 1976; "Sybil," NBC, 1976.
* Emmies: 1977.

FIELDS, DAME GRACIE
*b. Grace Stansfield, Rochdale, England,
January 9, 1898; d. 1979.* Popular British
entertainer who did some live TV drama.
AS A GUEST: "U.S. Steel Hour: The Old Lady
Shows Her Medals," CBS, 1956; "The Ed
Sullivan Show," CBS, 1956; "Goodyear TV
Playhouse: A Murder Is Announced," NBC,
1956; "Du Pont Show of the Month: A Tale of
Two Cities," CBS, 1958; "Studio One: Mrs.
'Arris Goes to Paris," CBS, 1958; "The Ed
Sullivan Show," CBS, 1959; "Arthur Murray
Party," NBC, 1959; "The Jack Paar Show,"
NBC, 1961; "Bell Telephone Hour: A Galaxy
of Music," NBC, 1961.

FIELDS, KIM
b. Los Angeles, CA, May 12, 1969. Actress
who played Tootie on "The Facts of Life."
AS A REGULAR: "Baby I'm Back," CBS, 1978;
"The Facts of Life," NBC, 1979-88.
AND: "Diff'rent Strokes: Slumber Party," NBC,
1979; "Diff'rent Strokes: Bank Job," NBC, 1980;
"227: The Roommate," NBC, 1988.
TV MOVIES AND MINISERIES: "The Facts of Life
Goes to Paris," NBC, 1982; "The Facts of Life
Down Under," NBC, 1987.

FIELDS, SID
b. 1898; d. 1975. Comedian.
AS A REGULAR: "The Frank Sinatra Show," CBS,
1950-51; "The Abbott and Costello Show,"
CBS, 1952-54; "Jackie Gleason and His
American Scene Magazine," CBS, 1962-66.

FIELDS, TOTIE
b. Hartford, CT, 1931; d. 1978. Rotund
comedienne who was a familiar face on talk
and game shows.
AS A GUEST: "The Ed Sullivan Show," CBS, 1964;
"The Mike Douglas Show," SYN, 1964; "The
Ed Sullivan Show," CBS, 1965; "The Merv
Griffin Show," SYN, 1966; "The Ed Sullivan
Show," CBS, 1967; "The Mike Douglas
Show," SYN, 1968; "Personality," NBC, 1968;
"The Joey Bishop Show," ABC, 1968; "The
Merv Griffin Show," SYN, 1969; "Hollywood
Squares," NBC, 1970; "Dinah's Place," NBC,
1971; "Here's Lucy: Lucy the Other Woman,"
CBS, 1972; "The Merv Griffin Show," SYN,

1972; "Hollywood Squares," NBC, 1974; "The Merv Griffin Show," SYN, 1975; "Tony Orlando and Dawn," CBS, 1975; "Medical Center: Life, Death and Mrs. Armbruster," CBS, 1976; "Tony Orlando and Dawn," CBS, 1976; "Dinah!," SYN, 1976.

FINLEY, PAT
b. *Asheville, NC, 1940*. Brunette actress who played Bob Newhart's sister on his seventies sitcom.
AS A REGULAR: "From a Bird's Eye View," NBC, 1971; "The Funny Side," NBC, 1971; "The Bob Newhart Show," CBS, 1974-76.
AND: "Music for New Year's Night: Class of '61," ABC, 1961; "The Mary Tyler Moore Show: Divorce Isn't Everything," CBS, 1970; "The Mary Tyler Moore Show: A Friend in Deed," CBS, 1971; "Love, American Style: Love and the Weighty Problem," ABC, 1973; "The Rockford Files: The Farnsworth Stratagem," NBC, 1975; "The Rockford Files: The Becker Connection," NBC, 1976; "The Rockford Files: To Protect and Serve," NBC, 1977; "The Rockford Files: The Paper Palace," NBC, 1977; "The Rockford Files: Kill the Messenger," NBC, 1978; "The Rockford Files: The No Fault Affair," NBC, 1979; "The Love Boat: Haven't I Seen You ...?," ABC, 1979; "Lou Grant: Censored," CBS, 1980; "Lou Grant: Stroke," CBS, 1981.
TV MOVIES AND MINISERIES: "An Innocent Love," CBS, 1982.

FINN, FRED E.
b. *San Francisco, CA, 1938*. Nightclub entertainer; husband of Mickie.
AS A REGULAR: "Mickie Finn's," NBC, 1966.

FINN, MICKIE
b. *Hugo, OK, June 16, 1938*. Nightclub entertainer; wife of Fred.
AS A REGULAR: "Mickie Finn's," NBC, 1966.

FIORE, BILL
b. *Williston Park, NY, 1940*. Comic actor.
AS A REGULAR: "The Corner Bar," ABC, 1972-73.
AND: "The Mary Tyler Moore: Anchorman Overboard," CBS, 1970; "Alice: 86 the Waitresses," CBS, 1977; "Three's Company: Jack Looks for a Job," ABC, 1977.
TV MOVIES AND MINISERIES: "Murder by Natural Causes," CBS, 1979.

FISHER, CARRIE
b. *Los Angeles, October 21, 1956*. Actress and author with a warped wit whose TV appearances have been in unique projects.
AS A GUEST: "This Is Your Life (Debbie Reynolds)," NBC, 1961; "Saturday Night Live," NBC, 1978; "Faerie Tale Theatre:

Thumbelina," SHO, 1984; "Amazing Stories: Gershwin's Trunk," NBC, 1987; "Late Night with David Letterman," NBC, 1988; "Wonderworks: Two Daddies?," PBS, 1989; "Trying Times: Hunger Chic," PBS, 1989.
* Fisher wrote "Postcards From the Edge" and "Surrender the Pink"; she's the daughter of Debbie Reynolds and Eddie Fisher.

FISHER, EDDIE
b. *Edwin Jack Fisher, Philadelphia, PA, August 10, 1928*. Popular singer of the fifties who's remembered most for divorcing that nice Debbie Reynolds in 1959 to marry that homewrecker Elizabeth Taylor.
AS A REGULAR: "Coke Time with Eddie Fisher," NBC, 1953-57; "The George Gobel/Eddie Fisher Show," NBC, 1957-59.
AND: "Light's Diamond Jubilee," ABC, CBS, NBC, 1954; "President's Birthday Party," NBC, 1956; "Can Do," NBC, 1956; "The Walter Winchell Show," NBC, 1956; "The George Gobel Show," NBC, 1956; "The Jackie Gleason Show," CBS, 1957; "The Bob Hope Show," NBC, 1957; "The Steve Allen Show," NBC, 1957; "The Gisele MacKenzie Show," NBC, 1957; "Club Oasis," NBC, 1957; "The Perry Como Show," NBC, 1958; "The Frank Sinatra Show," ABC, 1958; "The Gisele MacKenzie Show," NBC, 1958; "Club Oasis," NBC, 1958; "The George Burns Show," NBC, 1958; "The Music Shop," NBC, 1959; "Some of Manie's Friends," NBC, 1959; "American Bandstand," ABC, 1960; "The Jack Paar Show," NBC, 1960; "The Ed Sullivan Show," CBS, 1962; "The Merv Griffin Show," NBC, 1962; "Here's Edie," ABC, 1963; "The Dean Martin Show," NBC, 1965; "The Ed Sullivan Show," CBS, 1965; "The Andy Williams Show," NBC, 1965; "The Mike Douglas Show," SYN, 1975.

FISHER, GAIL
b. *Plainfield, NJ, August 18, 1935*. Emmy winning actress who played Joe Mannix's secretary, Peggy Fair.
AS A REGULAR: "Mannix," CBS, 1968-75.
AND: "Play of the Week: Simply Heavenly," SYN, 1960; "My Three Sons: Gossip, Inc.," CBS, 1968; "Love, American Style: Love and the Hustler," ABC, 1969; "Room 222: Welcome Back, Miss Brown," ABC, 1971; "Love, American Style: Love and the Baby," ABC, 1971; "Medical Center: Street Girl," CBS, 1975; "The White Shadow: The Russians Are Coming," CBS, 1980.
TV MOVIES AND MINISERIES: "Every Man Needs One," ABC, 1972.
* Emmies: 1970.

FITZGERALD, BARRY
b. *William Joseph Shields, Dublin, Ireland, March*

10, 1888; d. 1961. Character actor who gained fame playing Irish types, most notably Father Fitzgibbon in the film "Going My Way."
AS A GUEST: "Lux Video Theatre: The Man Who Struck It Rich," CBS, 1952; "The RCA Victor Show," NBC, 1953; "G.E. Theatre: The White Steed," CBS, 1954; "Alfred Hitchcock Presents: Santa Claus and the 10th Avenue Kid," CBS, 1955; "The Ed Sullivan Show," CBS, 1960.

FITZGERALD, GERALDINE
b. Dublin, Ireland, November 24, 1914. Fragile, beautiful actress who played the former lover of Dr. Auschlander (Norman Lloyd) on "St. Elsewhere" and has done several other finely etched guest roles.
AS A REGULAR: "Our Private World," CBS, 1965; "The Best of Everything," ABC, 1970.
AND: "Magnavox Theatre Hour: The Marble Faun," CBS, 1950; "Robert Montgomery Presents: To Walk the Night," NBC, 1951; "Schlitz Playhouse of Stars: The Daughter," CBS, 1952; "Studio One: Dark Possesion," CBS, 1954; "Robert Montgomery Presents: Love Story," NBC, 1954; "Goodyear TV Playhouse: The Lawn Party," NBC, 1954; "Robert Montgomery Presents: The Iron Cobweb," NBC, 1955; "Armstrong Circle Theatre: The Secret of Emily du Vane," NBC, 1955; "The Barretts of Wimpole Street," CBS, 1955; "Producers Showcase: Dodsworth," NBC, 1956; "Ellery Queen: This Murder Comes to You Live," NBC, 1959; "The Moon and Sixpence," NBC, 1959; "Music for a Summer Night: The Female of the Species," ABC, 1960; "Shirley Temple's Storybook: The Black Sheep," NBC, 1960; "Alfred Hitchcock Presents: A Woman's Help," NBC, 1960; "Naked City: Take Off Your Hat When a Funeral Passes," ABC, 1961; "Naked City: Today the Man Who Kills the Ants Is Coming!," ABC, 1962; "The Nurses: For the Mice and Rabbits," CBS, 1964; "The Defenders: A Voice Loud and Clear," CBS, 1964; "The Alfred Hitchcock Hour: Power of Attorney," NBC, 1965; "Conflict: Me," SYN, 1973; "The American Parade: We the Women," CBS, 1974; "Theatre in America: The Widowing of Mrs. Halroyd," NET, 1974; "Theatre in America: Forget-Me-Not Lane," PBS, 1975; "Lou Grant: Dying," CBS, 1978; "Captain Kangaroo," CBS, 1980; "St. Elsewhere: Attack," NBC, 1984; "Cagney & Lacey: Con Games," CBS, 1985; "St. Elsewhere: Jose, Can You See?," NBC, 1987; "The Golden Girls: Mother's Day," NBC, 1988; "The Golden Girls: Not Another Monday," NBC, 1989.
TV MOVIES AND MINISERIES: "Yesterday's Child," NBC, 1977; "Dixie: Changing Habits," CBS, 1983; "Kennedy," NBC, 1983; "Do You Remember Love," CBS, 1985; "Circle of Violence: A Family Drama," CBS, 1986;

"Night of Courage," ABC, 1987.
* Fitzgerald is the mother of film director Michael Lindsay-Hogg.

FITZSIMMONS, TOM
b. San Francisco, CA, October 28, 1947. Actor who played Bell on "The Paper Chase."
AS A REGULAR: "The Paper Chase," CBS, 1978-79; SHO, 1983-84.
AND: "All in the Family: Mike Goes Skiing," CBS, 1977; "Murder, She Wrote: Trouble in Eden," CBS, 1987.

FIX, PAUL
b. March 13, 1901; d. 1983. Character actor who played Marshal Micah Torrence on "The Rifleman."
AS A REGULAR: "The Rifleman," ABC, 1958-63.
AND: "The Abbott and Costello Show: Cheap-skates," CBS, 1953; "Gunsmoke: Cholera," CBS, 1956; "Playhouse 90: Clipper Ship," CBS, 1957; "Wire Service: Violence Preferred," ABC, 1957; "Perry Mason: The Case of the Angry Mourner," CBS, 1957; "Sugarfoot: Hideout," ABC, 1958; "The Texan: A Tree for Planting," CBS, 1958; "Law of the Plainsman: Toll Road," ABC, 1959; "Perry Mason: The Case of the Roving River," CBS, 1961; "Wagon Train: The Amos Billings Story," NBC, 1962; "The Travels of Jaimie McPheeters: The Day of the Picnic," ABC, 1964; "The Twilight Zone: I Am the Night-Color Me Black," CBS, 1964; "Slattery's People: Question-What Are You Doing Out There, Waldo?," CBS, 1964; "Star Trek: Where No Man Has Gone Before," NBC, 1966; "The Wild Wild West: The Night of the Green Terror," CBS, 1966; "Ironside: The Laying On of Hands," NBC, 1970; "Mannix: Scapegoat," CBS, 1972; "Alias Smith and Jones: Night of the Red Dog," ABC, 1972; "Alias Smith and Jones: Only Three to a Bed," ABC, 1972; "Emergency!: Rip-Off," NBC, 1973; "The Doris Day Show: Byline ... Alias Doris," CBS, 1973; "The FBI: The Big Job," ABC, 1973; "The New Adventures of Perry Mason: The Case of the Violent Valley," CBS, 1974; "The Streets of San Francisco: Winterkill," ABC, 1974; "The Streets of San Francisco: River of Fear," ABC, 1974; "Barnaby Jones: Dark Legacy," CBS, 1974; "Barnaby Jones: Death on Deposit," CBS, 1974; "Barnaby Jones: Double Vengeance," CBS, 1975; "The Rockford Files: The House on Willis Avenue," NBC, 1978.
TV MOVIES AND MINISERIES: "Winchester '73," NBC, 1967; "Set This Town on Fire," NBC, 1973; "The Rebels," SYN, 1979; "Hanging by a Thread," NBC, 1979.

FLAGG, FANNIE
b. Birmingham, AL. Comic actress usually in down-home roles.

AS A REGULAR: "The New Dick Van Dyke Show," CBS, 1971-73; "Match Game P.M.," SYN, 1975-82; "Liar's Club," SYN, 1976-78; "Harper Valley PTA," NBC, 1981-82.
AND: "Candid Camera," CBS, 1966; "The Match Game," NBC, 1968; "The Match Game," NBC, 1969; "The Merv Griffin Show," CBS, 1969; "Beat the Clock," SYN, 1969; "Bobbie Gentry Special," CBS, 1970; "Love, American Style: Love and the Bachelor Party," ABC, 1972; "Match Game '74," CBS, 1974; "Cross Wits," SYN, 1977; "Captain Kangaroo," CBS, 1981; "The Love Boat: The Very Temporary Secretary," ABC, 1983.
TV MOVIES AND MINISERIES: "The New, Original Wonder Woman," ABC, 1975.

FLAHERTY, JOE
b. Pittsburgh, PA, June 21, 1940.
AS A REGULAR: "Second City TV," SYN, 1977-81; "SCTV Network 90," NBC, 1981-83; "Maniac Mansion," FAM, 1990- .
AND: "Kojak: I Could Kill My Wife's Lawyer," CBS, 1977; "The White Shadow: Gonna Fly Now," CBS, 1980; "Married with Children: Tooth and Consequences," FOX, 1989.
* Emmies: 1983.

FLANAGAN, FIONNULA
b. Ireland, December 10, 1941. Redheaded actress usually in strong-woman roles; she won an Emmy as Clothilde in "Rich Man, Poor Man."
AS A REGULAR: "How the West Was Won," ABC, 1978-79; "Hard Copy," CBS, 1987; "H.E.L.P.," ABC, 1990.
AND: "Mannix: The Crimson Halo," CBS, 1972; "Marcus Welby, M.D.: A Joyful Song," ABC, 1973; "The New Adventures of Perry Mason: The Case of the Horoscope Homicide," CBS, 1973; "Shaft: The Murder Machine," CBS, 1974; "Hec Ramsey: Only Birds and Fools," NBC, 1974; "The Rookies: Trial by Doubt," ABC, 1974; "Police Story: Company Man," NBC, 1975; "The Streets of San Francisco: Requiem for Murder," ABC, 1976; "Medical Center: Child of Conflict," CBS, 1976; "Kojak: A Summer Madness," CBS, 1976; "Marcus Welby, M.D.: To Trump an Ace," ABC, 1976; "Serpico: Every Man Must Pay His Dues," NBC, 1976; "Riptide: Peter Pan Is Alive and Well," NBC, 1984; "Murder, She Wrote: Steal Me a Story," CBS, 1987; "Simon & Simon: A Firm Grasp on Reality," CBS, 1988; "Hunter: Shellelagh," NBC, 1989; "Columbo: Murder-A Self Portrait," ABC, 1989.
TV MOVIES AND MINISERIES: "The Picture of Dorian Gray," ABC, 1973; "The Godchild," ABC, 1974; "The Legend of Lizzie Borden," ABC, 1975; "Nightmare in Badham County," ABC, 1976; "Rich Man, Poor Man," ABC, 1976; "Young

Love, First Love," CBS, 1979; "Through Naked Eyes," ABC, 1983; "Scorned and Swindled," CBS, 1984; "A Winner Never Quits," ABC, 1986.
* Emmies: 1976.

FLANDERS, ED
b. Minneapolis, MN, December 29, 1934. Emmy winning actor; as Dr. Donald Westphall on "St. Elsewhere" he bristled when a for-profit corporation took over his hospital and took his leave after mooning the boss. He also won an Emmy as President Harry Truman and for "A Moon for the Misbegotten."
AS A REGULAR: "St. Elsewhere," NBC, 1982-88.
AND: "Cimarron Strip: The Roarer," CBS, 1967; "Hawaii Five-O: Uptight," CBS, 1969; "Hawaii Five-O: The Guarnerius Caper," CBS, 1970; "McMillan and Wife: Husbands, Wives and Thieves," NBC, 1971; "Bearcats!: Hostages," CBS, 1971; "M*A*S*H: Yankee Doodle Doctor," CBS, 1972; "Hawaii Five-O: While You're at It, Bring in the Moon," CBS, 1972; "Mannix: A Walk in the Shadows," CBS, 1972; "Marcus Welby, M.D.: The Comeback," ABC, 1973; "Barnaby Jones: Death on Deposit," CBS, 1974; "Hawaii Five-O: One Born Every Minute," CBS, 1974; "Hawaii Five-O: And the Horse Jumped Over the Moon," CBS, 1975; "The Mary Tyler Moore Show: Mary's Father," CBS, 1975; "ABC Theatre: A Moon for the Misbegotten," ABC, 1975; "Harry S Truman: Plain Speaking," PBS, 1976.
TV MOVIES AND MINISERIES: "Goodbye Raggedy Ann," CBS, 1971; "The Snoop Sisters," NBC, 1972; "Hunter," CBS, 1973; "Indict and Convict," ABC, 1973; "Things in Their Season," CBS, 1974; "The Legend of Lizzie Borden," ABC, 1975; "Attack on Terror: The FBI Versus the Ku Klux Klan," CBS, 1975; "Eleanor and Franklin," ABC, 1976; "The Amazing Howard Hughes," CBS, 1977; "Backstairs at the White House," NBC, 1979; "Blind Ambition," CBS, 1979; "Skokie," CBS, 1981; "Special Bulletin," NBC, 1983; "AT&T Presents: The Final Days," ABC, 1989.
* Emmies: 1976, 1977, 1983.

FLANNERY, SUSAN
b. New York City, NY, July 31, 1943. Actress who played Dr. Laura Spencer on "Days of Our Lives."
AS A REGULAR: "Days of Our Lives," NBC, 1966-75; "Dallas," CBS, 1981; "The Bold and the Beautiful," CBS, 1987- .
AND: "Voyage to the Bottom of the Sea: Time Bomb," ABC, 1965; "Mannix: Search for a Whisper," CBS, 1973.
TV MOVIES AND MINISERIES: "The Moneychangers," NBC, 1976; "Anatomy of a Seduction," CBS, 1979; "Money on the Side," ABC, 1982.

FLAVIN, JAMES

b. Portland, ME, May 14, 1906; d. 1976. Actor who often played Irish cops, in drama and comedy.

AS A REGULAR: "Man with a Camera," ABC, 1959-60; "The Roaring Twenties," ABC, 1960-62.

AND: "The Abbott and Costello Show: Beauty Contest Story," CBS, 1953; "I Love Lucy: Visitor From Italy," CBS, 1956; "Crossroads: The Patton Prayer," ABC, 1957; "Alcoa Theatre: Cupid Wore a Badge," NBC, 1957; "Schlitz Playhouse of Stars: Portrait of a Legend," CBS, 1958; "The Untouchables: Three Thousand Suspects," ABC, 1960; "Lassie: Gentle Tiger," CBS, 1960; "Harrigan and Son: 100 Proof," ABC, 1961; "The Real McCoys: The Bazaar," ABC, 1961; "The Twilight Zone: Once Upon a Time," CBS, 1961; "Pete and Gladys: The Chocolate Cake Caper," CBS, 1962; "SurfSide 6: Vendetta Arms," ABC, 1962; "McKeever and the Colonel: McKeever Meets Munroe," NBC, 1963; "Mr. Novak: Beyond a Reasonable Doubt," NBC, 1964; "Hazel: The Campaign Manager," NBC, 1964; "Burke's Law: Who Killed Cop Robin?," ABC, 1965; "Mr. Ed: Ed Breaks the Hip Code," CBS, 1965; "Walt Disney's Wonderful World of Color: The Further Adventures of Gallegher," NBC, 1965.

TV MOVIES AND MINISERIES: "Francis Gary Powers: The True Story of the U-2 Spy Incident," NBC, 1976.

FLEISCHER, CHARLES

b. Washington, D.C., August 27, 1950. Comic actor who also supplied the voice of Roger Rabbit in the movies.

AS A REGULAR: "Keep on Truckin'," ABC, 1975; "Welcome Back, Kotter," ABC, 1978-79; "Thicke of the Night," SYN, 1983-84.

AND: "Barney Miller: Hair," ABC, 1975; "Welcome Back, Kotter: Sweatside Story," ABC, 1976; "Welcome Back, Kotter: Horshack vs. Carvelli," ABC, 1975; "Hill Street Blues: Can World War III Be an Attitude?," NBC, 1981; "The Pat Sajak Show," CBS, 1989.

TV MOVIES AND MINISERIES: "The Death of Richie," NBC, 1977.

FLEMING, ARTHUR

b. New York City, NY. Down-to-earth, upright emcee of "Jeopardy!" for almost 15 years.

AS A REGULAR: "The Californians," NBC, 1958-59; "Jeopardy!," NBC, 1964-75, 1978-79; SYN, 1974-75; "NBC Adventure Theatre," NBC, 1971; "The G.E. College Bowl," SYN, 1978-79.

AND: "I'll Bet," NBC, 1965; "Hollywood Squares," NBC, 1972; "Kingston: Confidential: Seed of Corruption," NBC, 1977.

* Fleming was an usher at the wedding of David Eisenhower and Julie Nixon.
* "I was the first guy to say, 'Winston tastes good like a cigarette should,'" Fleming told *TV Guide.*

FLEMING, ERIC

b. Santa Paula, CA, 1925; d. 1966. Actor who played Gil Favor on "Rawhide"; he was killed while filming a stunt for a movie.

AS A REGULAR: "Major Dell Conway of the Flying Tigers," DUM, 1951; "The Golden Windows," NBC, 1954; "Rawhide," CBS, 1959-65.

AND: "The Phil Silvers Show: Investigation," CBS, 1956; "The Silent Service: Christmas Under Water," SYN, 1958; "Studio One: The Strong Man," CBS, 1958; "Stump the Stars," CBS, 1962; "Bonanza: Peace Officer," NBC, 1965; "Bonanza: Pursued," NBC, 1966.

FLEMING, RHONDA

b. Marilyn Louis, Los Angeles, CA, August 10, 1923. Redheaded bombshell of fifties movies and TV.

AS A GUEST: "Best of Broadway: Stage Door," CBS, 1955; "Ford Theatre: South of Selangor," NBC, 1955; "Person to Person," CBS, 1957; "The Big Record," CBS, 1957; "Bob Hope Special," NBC, 1957; "Wagon Train: The Jennifer Churchill Story," NBC, 1958; "Burke's Law: Who Killed Wade Walker?," ABC, 1963; "You Don't Say," NBC, 1964; "The Tonight Show Starring Johnny Carson," NBC, 1964; "Bob Hope Chrysler Theatre: Have Girls, Will Travel," NBC, 1964; "The Mike Douglas Show," SYN, 1964; "Burke's Law: Who Killed 711?," ABC, 1964; "The Virginian: We've Lost a Train," NBC, 1965; "Needles and Pins: The Silent Spring Line," NBC, 1973; "Search: The Clayton Lewis Document," NBC, 1973; "McMillan and Wife: Cross and Double," NBC, 1974; "Police Woman: Anatomy of Two Rapes," NBC, 1974; "Ellery Queen: The Mad Tea Party," NBC, 1975; "The Love Boat: Mona of the Movies," ABC, 1979.

TV MOVIES AND MINISERIES: "Last Hours Before Morning," NBC, 1975; "Love for Rent," ABC, 1979.

FLETCHER, JACK

b. Forest Hills, NY, 1922; d. 1990. Bespectacled character actor, usually in bumbling or overbearing boss roles.

AS A REGULAR: "Calucci's Department," CBS, 1973; "The Bob Crane Show," NBC, 1975; "Grady," NBC, 1975-76; "Presenting Susan Anton," NBC, 1979.

AND: "Wonderful Town," CBS, 1958; "The Alan King Show," CBS, 1961; "The Jack Paar

Program," NBC, 1963; "Once Upon a Mattress," CBS, 1964; "Bewitched: My Baby, the Tycoon," ABC, 1966; "Gidget: Don't Defrost the Alligator," ABC, 1966; "Welcome Back, Kotter: Goodbye, Mr. Kripps," ABC, 1978; "Gimme a Break: Nell Goes to Jail," NBC, 1982; "Gimme a Break: The Centerfold," NBC, 1983; "Gimme a Break: Glenlawn Street Blues," NBC, 1983; "Starman: Society's Pet," ABC, 1986.

FLETCHER, LOUISE

b. Birmingham, AL, 1934. Actress who began her career playing Southern belles on TV; after dropping out of show business, she made a triumphant return with an Oscar winning performance as Nurse Ratched in "One Flew Over the Cuckoo's Nest." When she accepted the award, she performed her acceptance speech in sign language to communicate with her deaf parents.

AS A GUEST: "Playhouse 90: The Last Man," CBS, 1958; "Yancy Derringer: Old Dixie," CBS, 1958; "Lawman: The Encounter," ABC, 1959; "Wagon Train: The Andrew Hale Story," NBC, 1959; "Maverick: The Saga of Waco Williams," ABC, 1959; "Perry Mason: The Case of the Mythical Monkeys," CBS, 1960; "Wagon Train: The Tom Tuckett Story," NBC, 1960; "Troubleshooters: The Landmark," NBC, 1960; "Sugarfoot: Funeral at Forty Mile," ABC, 1960; "Tate: The Bounty Hunter," NBC, 1960; "Perry Mason: The Case of the Larcenous Lady," CBS, 1960; "Best of the Post: Groper in the Dark," SYN, 1960; "The Life and Legend of Wyatt Earp: The Law Must Be Fair," ABC, 1961.

TV MOVIES AND MINISERIES: "Can Ellen Be Saved?," ABC, 1974; "Thou Shalt Not Commit Adultery," NBC, 1978; "A Summer to Remember," CBS, 1985.

FLIPPEN, JAY C.

b. Little Rock, AR, March 6, 1900; d. 1971. Dependable, weatherbeaten character actor, usually in charming con-artist roles.

AS A REGULAR: "Ensign O'Toole," NBC, 1962-63. **AND:** "Ford Theatre: Come On, Red," NBC, 1954; "Climax!: Pink Cloud," CBS, 1955; "Climax!: Faceless Enemy," CBS, 1956; "Climax!: The Stalker," CBS, 1957; "The 20th Century-Fox Hour: The Man Who Couldn't Wait," CBS, 1957; "Climax!: Mr. Runyon of Broadway," CBS, 1957; "Goodyear TV Playhouse: The House," NBC, 1957; "Playhouse 90: Before I Die," CBS, 1958; "Playhouse 90: No Time at All," CBS, 1958; "Wanted Dead or Alive: Miracle at Pot Hole," CBS, 1958; "Alcoa Theatre: The Best Way to Go," NBC, 1959; "The David Niven Show: Good Deed," NBC, 1959; "Rawhide: Incident of the Widowed Dove," CBS, 1959; "Follow the Sun: The Last of the Big Spenders," ABC, 1962; "Bus

Stop: Verdict of 12," ABC, 1962; "The Dick Van Dyke Show: The Return of Happy Spangler," CBS, 1962; "The Dick Powell Show: The Last of the Private Eyes," NBC, 1963; "Burke's Law: Who Killed Holly Howard?," ABC, 1963; "Burke's Law: Who Killed Wade Walker?," ABC, 1963; "Bonanza: The Prime of Life," NBC, 1963; "Rawhide: Incident at Hourglass," CBS, 1964; "Burke's Law: Who Killed Molly?," ABC, 1964; "The Road West: Charade of Justice," NBC, 1967; "The Virginian: The Barren Ground," NBC, 1967; "That Girl: Twas the Night Before Christmas, You're Under Arrest," ABC, 1967; "The Virginian: Stopover," NBC, 1969; "The Name of the Game: The Incomparable Connie Walker," NBC, 1969; "Judd for the Defense: Borderline Girl," ABC, 1969; "Bracken's World: King David," NBC, 1969; "The Name of the Game: Chains of Command," NBC, 1969.

TV MOVIES AND MINISERIES: "Fame Is the Name of the Game," NBC, 1966; "The Sound of Anger," NBC, 1968; "The Old Man Who Cried Wolf," ABC, 1970; "Sam Hill: Who Killed the Mysterious Mr. Foster?," NBC, 1971.

TRIVIA QUIZ #10: "THE FLINTSTONES"

1. Where were the Flinstones headed in the show's opening credits?
2. What cigarette sponsored the show for a time?
3. Who was the otherworldly little character who popped into Fred and Barney's life toward the end of the show's run?
4. To what fraternal lodge did Fred and Barney belong?
5. What was the name of the Flintstones' pet dinosaur?
6. What did Wilma use to vacuum her carpets?
7. What was the name of Fred's boss?
8. Who did Ann-Margret play in a guest shot?
9. What was Wilma's maiden name?
10. Toward the end of the show's run, the Rubbles got a pet. What was its name?

(Answers at end of book.)

FLOWERS, WAYLAND

d. 1989. Ventriloquist whose dummy was the outrageous Madame.

AS A REGULAR: "Keep on Truckin'," ABC, 1975; "Laugh-In," NBC, 1977-78; "Solid Gold," SYN, 1980-84; "Madame's Place," SYN, 1982.

AND: "Hollywood Squares," NBC, 1976.

FLYNN, ERROL

b. Hobart, Tasmania, June 20, 1909; d. 1959.

316

Swashbuckling screen star who lived hard and fast, and who did TV roles strictly for the cash.
AS A REGULAR: "Errol Flynn Theatre," SYN, 1957-58.
AND: "Screen Directors Playhouse: The Sword of Villon," NBC, 1956; "The Steve Allen Show," NBC, 1957; "Playhouse 90: Without Incident," CBS, 1957; "Arthur Murray Party," NBC, 1957; "The Red Skelton Show," CBS, 1959; "Goodyear Theatre: The Golden Shanty," NBC, 1959.

FLYNN, JOE

b. Youngstown, OH, November 8, 1924; d. 1974. Slight, bespecatcled comic actor with a tinny voice who excelled at the slow burn and the sarcastic comeback; best known as Captain Wallace Binghamton on "McHale's Navy."
AS A REGULAR: "The George Gobel/Eddie Fisher Show," NBC, 1958-59; "The George Gobel Show," CBS, 1959-60; "The Adventures of Ozzie and Harriet," ABC, 1959-62; "The Bob Newhart Show," NBC, 1961-62; "The Joey Bishop Show," NBC, 1961-62; "McHale's Navy," ABC, 1962-66; "The Tim Conway Show," CBS, 1970; "It Pays to Be Ignorant," SYN, 1972-73.
AND: "The Life of Riley: World's Greatest Grandson," NBC, 1956; "Ford Theatre: Fear Has Many Faces," ABC, 1957; "The Dennis O'Keefe Show: A Visit From the Major," CBS, 1959; "The Danny Thomas Show: Kathy Crashes TV," CBS, 1959; "Startime: Incident at a Corner," NBC, 1960; "M Squad: The Man with the Ice," NBC, 1960; "The Hathaways: Walter Takes a Partner," ABC, 1961; "McKeever and the Colonel: The Bugle Sounds," NBC, 1962; "The Jack Benny Program," CBS, 1963; "Object Is," ABC, 1964; "Hollywood Palace," ABC, 1964; "Broadside: Pilot," ABC, 1964; "Batman: The Cat's Meow/ The Bat's Kow Tow," ABC, 1966; "Captain Nice: Don't Take Any Wooden Indians," NBC, 1967; "I Dream of Jeannie: Dr. Bellows Goes Sane," NBC, 1968; "Family Affair: My Man, the Star," CBS, 1969; "Love, American Style: Love and the Shower," ABC, 1969; "The Ghost and Mrs. Muir: Not so Faust," ABC, 1970; "The Movie Game," SYN, 1970; "That Girl: An Uncle Herbert for All Seasons," ABC, 1970; "Love, American Style: Love and the Mixed Marriage," ABC, 1972; "Alias Smith and Jones: Night of the Red Dog," ABC, 1972; "Love, American Style: Love and the Eskimo's Wife," ABC, 1972; "Faraday and Company: A Wheelbarrow Full of Trouble," NBC, 1973; "The Magician: The Man Who Lost Himself," NBC, 1973; "The Merv Griffin Show," SYN, 1974.
TV MOVIES AND MINISERIES: "The Girl Most Likely To...," ABC, 1973.

FLYNN, MIRIAM

b. Cleveland, OH.

AS A REGULAR: "The Tim Conway Show," CBS, 1980-81; "Maggie," ABC, 1981-82; "Raising Miranda," CBS, 1988.
AND: "Gimme a Break: Glenlawn Street Blues," NBC, 1983; "Webster: The Uh-Oh Feeling," ABC, 1984; "Cheers: Love Thy Neighbor," NBC, 1985; "The Tracey Ullman Show: Changing Lanes," FOX, 1988; "CBS Summer Playhouse: Real Life," CBS, 1988; "Dear John: The Other Group," NBC, 1989; "Murder, She Wrote: Murder–According to Maggie," CBS, 1990.
TV MOVIES AND MINISERIES: "Her Life as a Man," NBC, 1984.

FOCH, NINA

b. Nina Consuelo Maud Fock, Leyden, Netherlands, April 20, 1924. Blonde actress usually in roles as chic women in control of their circumstances.
AS A REGULAR: "Two Girls Named Smith," ABC, 1951; "QED," ABC, 1951; "It's News to Me," CBS, 1954; "Shadow Chasers," ABC, 1985-86.
AND: "Suspense: One and One's a Lonesome," CBS, 1950; "Armstrong Circle Theatre: The Rose and the Shamrock," NBC, 1950; "Cameo Theatre: Betrayal," NBC, 1951; "Pulitzer Prize Playhouse: The Skin of Our Teeth," ABC, 1951; "Studio One: A Guest at the Embassy," CBS, 1954; "Suspense: Main Feature: Death," CBS, 1954; "Colgate Comedy Hour: Roberta," NBC, 1955; "The Loretta Young Show: Reunion," NBC, 1955; "Climax!: Night of Execution," CBS, 1955; "The 20th Century-Fox Hour: Our Life," CBS, 1955; "Warner Bros. Presents Conflict: One Life," ABC, 1956; "Studio One: At the Drop of a Hat," CBS, 1956; "Playhouse 90: Heritage of Anger," CBS, 1956; "Alcoa Hour: A Double Life," NBC, 1957; "Studio One: Image of Fear," CBS, 1958; "Pursuit: Ticket to Tangier," CBS, 1958; "Playhouse 90: Free Weekend," CBS, 1958; "Ten Little Indians," NBC, 1958; "U.S. Steel Hour: Whisper of Evil," CBS, 1959; "Rawhide: Incident of the Judas Trap," CBS, 1959; "Keep Talking," CBS, 1959; "U.S. Steel Hour: The Case of Julia Walton," CBS, 1959; "The Loretta Young Show: The Red Dress," NBC, 1959; "U.S. Steel Hour: A Time to Decide," CBS, 1960; "The Americans: The Rebellious Rose," NBC, 1961; "Theatre '62: Rebecca," NBC, 1962; "Naked City: The Sweetly Smiling Face of Truth," ABC, 1962; "Dr. Kildare: My Name Is Lisa and I Am Lost," NBC, 1965; "Combat!: The Casket," ABC, 1965; "A Man Called Shenandoah: Marlee," ABC, 1966; "The Long, Hot Summer: Carlotta, Come Home," ABC, 1966; "Bob Hope Chrsyler Theatre: And Baby Makes Five," NBC, 1966; "I Spy: Child Out of Time," NBC, 1967; "Bob Hope Chrysler Theatre: A Time to Love," NBC, 1967; "The Name of the Game: Collector's Edition," NBC, 1968; "The Mod Squad: Love," ABC, 1968;

"That Girl: That Script," ABC, 1971; "Men at Law: Marathon," CBS, 1971; "Hollywood Television Theatre: The Scarecrow," NET, 1972; "Police Surgeon: Confined Panic," SYN, 1972; "ABC Afternoon Playbreak: Oh! Baby, Baby, Baby ...," ABC, 1974; "Kolchak, the Night Stalker: The Trevi Collection," ABC, 1975; "Barnaby Jones: Stalking Horse," CBS, 1976; "McMillan: Philip's Game," NBC, 1977; "Lou Grant: Hollywood," CBS, 1979; "The New Mike Hammer: Golden Lady," CBS, 1986.
TV MOVIES AND MINISERIES: "Prescription: Murder," NBC, 1968; "Gidget Grows Up," ABC, 1969; "Female Artillery," ABC, 1973; "A Little Bit Like Murder," ABC, 1973; "Outback Bound," CBS, 1988; "War and Remembrance," ABC, 1988, 1989.

FOGEL, JERRY
b. Rochester, NY, January 17, 1936.
AS A REGULAR: "The Mothers-in-Law," NBC, 1967-69; "The White Shadow," CBS, 1978-79.
AND: "That Girl: Don't Just Do Something, Stand There," ABC, 1966; "That Girl: Chef's Night Out," ABC, 1970; "Love, American Style: Love and the Guru," ABC, 1972; "Marcus Welby, M.D.: It Is So Soon That I Am Done For," ABC, 1972; "The Paul Lynde Show: Pollution Solution," ABC, 1972; "Marcus Welby, M.D.: The Working Heart," ABC, 1973; "Marcus Welby, M.D.: Friends in High Places," ABC, 1973; "Here's Lucy: The Carters Meets Frankie Avalon," CBS, 1973; "The Bob Newhart Show: The Gray Flannel Shrink," CBS, 1974; "Marcus Welby, M.D.: The Last Rip-Off," ABC, 1974; "Marcus Welby, M.D.: Public Secrets," ABC, 1974; "Barnaby Jones: Image of Evil," CBS, 1975; "The Mary Tyler Moore Show: Ted's Change of Heart," CBS, 1976; "Lou Grant: Take-Over," CBS, 1977; "The Bob Newhart Show: Easy For You to Say," CBS, 1978.
TV MOVIES AND MINISERIES: "All My Darling Daughters," ABC, 1972; "My Darling Daughters' Anniversary," ABC, 1973; "Devil Dog: The Hound of Hell," CBS, 1978.

FOLEY, ELLEN
b. St. Louis, MO, 1951. Perky blonde actress who played public defender Billie Young on "Night Court."
AS A REGULAR: "3 Girls 3," NBC, 1977; "Night Court," NBC, 1984-85.

FOLEY, JOSEPH
b. 1910; d. 1955.
AS A REGULAR: "The Aldrich Family," NBC, 1950-53; "Mr. Peepers," NBC, 1952-53.

FOLEY, RED
b. Berea, KY, June 17, 1910; d. 1968. Country-

western singer, and Pat Boone's father-in-law.
AS A REGULAR: "Ozark Jubilee (Country Music Jubilee, Jubilee USA)," ABC, 1955-60; "Mr. Smith Goes to Washington," ABC, 1962-63.
AND: "Pat Boone Chevy Showroom," ABC, 1957; "Hoedown," NBC, 1959; "Pat Boone Chevy Showroom," ABC, 1959.

FONDA, HENRY
b. Grand Island, NB, May 16, 1905; d. 1982. Screen legend, usually in principled roles in film and on TV; he played cop and family man Chad Smith on "The Smith Family."
AS A REGULAR: "Rheingold Theatre," NBC, 1955; "The Deputy," NBC, 1959-61; "The Smith Family," ABC, 1971-72; "Decades of Decision," PBS, 1976.
AND: "Medallion Theatre: The Decision at Arrowsmith," CBS, 1953; "G.E. Theatre: Clown," CBS, 1955; "Producers Showcase: The Petrified Forest," NBC, 1955; "The Ed Sullivan Show," CBS, 1957; "The Steve Allen Show," NBC, 1958; "The George Gobel Show," CBS, 1959; "A Tribute to Eleanor Roosevelt on Her Diamond Jubilee," NBC, 1959; "The Fabulous Fifties," CBS, 1960; "Steve Allen Plymouth Show," NBC, 1960; "The Ed Sullivan Show," CBS, 1961; "I've Got a Secret," CBS, 1962; "The Good Years," CBS, 1962; "Henry Fonda and the Family," CBS, 1962; "Hollywood: The Fabulous Era," ABC, 1963; "The Dick Powell Show: Tissue of Hate," NBC, 1963; "Bell Telephone Hour: Lyrics by Oscar Hammerstein," NBC, 1964; "Paulsen for President," CBS, 1968; "Pat Paulsen's Half a Comedy Hour," ABC, 1970; "The Bill Cosby Show: The Elevator Doesn't Stop Here Anymore," NBC, 1970; "The Doris Day Show: Doris Goes to Hollywood," CBS, 1971; "The American West of John Ford," CBS, 1971; "America's Romance with the Land," ABC, 1973; "All in the Family: The Best of All in the Family," CBS, 1974; "Clarence Darrow," NBC, 1974; "The American Parade: FDR: The Man Who Changed America," CBS, 1975; "Maude: Maude's Moods," CBS, 1976; "Glory Road West," ABC, 1976; "General Electric's All-Star Anniversary," ABC, 1978; "Family: A Special Family Thanksgiving," ABC, 1979.
TV MOVIES AND MINISERIES: "Stranger on the Run," NBC, 1967; "The Red Pony," ABC, 1973; "The Alpha Caper," ABC, 1973; "ABC Theatre: Collision Course," ABC, 1976; "Best Sellers: Captains and the Kings," NBC, 1976; "Roots: The Next Generations," ABC, 1979; "Gideon's Trumpet," CBS, 1980.

FONDA, JANE
b. New York City, NY, December 21, 1937. Daughter of Henry, war protester, workout queen.
AS A GUEST: "Person to Person," CBS, 1960; "A

Story of Love: A String of Beads," NBC, **1961**; "Here's Hollywood," NBC, 1962; "Password," CBS, 1962; "The Merv Griffin Show," SYN, 1966; "9 to 5: Security Guard," ABC, **1982**; "The Tonight Show Starring Johnny Carson," NBC, 1989.

TV MOVIES AND MINISERIES: "A Doll's House," ABC, 1973; "The Dollmaker," ABC, 1984.

* Fonda had just moved into a new apartment when "Person to Person" came to visit, so the interview took place in her empty living room.
* Emmies: 1985.

FONDA, PETER

b. New York City, NY, February 23, 1939. Son of Henry, brother of Jane; he did more TV than his sister did before breaking into films ("Easy Rider").

AS A GUEST: "Naked City: The Night the Saints Lost their Halos," ABC, 1962; "The New Breed: Thousands and Thousands of Miles," ABC, 1962; "Wagon Train: The Orly French Story," ABC, 1962; "The Defenders: The Brother Killers," CBS, 1963; "Channing: An Obelisk for Benny," ABC, 1963; "Arrest and Trial: A Circle of Strangers," ABC, 1964; "The Alfred Hitchcock Hour: The Return of Verge Likens," NBC, 1964; "Twelve O'Clock High: The Sound of Distant Thunder," ABC, 1964; "Password," CBS, 1965; "Insight: Politics Can Become a Habit," SYN, 1967; "On Stage: Certain Honorable Men," NBC, 1968; "The Merv Griffin Show," SYN, 1968; "Celebrity Sweepstakes," NBC, 1974.

TV MOVIES AND MINISERIES: "The Hostage Tower," CBS, 1980; "A Reason to Live," NBC, 1985.

FONG, KAM

b. Hawaii. Actor who played Chin Ho on "Hawaii Five-O."

AS A REGULAR: "Hawaii Five-O," CBS, 1968-78.
AND: "Magnum, P.I.: Wave Goodbye," CBS, 1982.

TV MOVIES AND MINISERIES: "Hawaii Five-O," CBS, 1968.

FONTAINE, FRANK

b. Cambridge, MA, April 19, 1920; d. 1979. Singer whose most familiar role was that of jut-lipped, cockeyed Crazy Guggenheim on variety shows.

AS A REGULAR: "The Swift Show," NBC, 1949; "Scott Music Hall," NBC, 1952-53; "The Paul Winchell Show," ABC, 1957-60; "Jackie Gleason and His American Scene Magazine," CBS, 1962-66.
AND: "Salute to Baseball," NBC, 1957; "The Tonight Show," NBC, 1957; "Make Me Laugh," ABC, 1958; "The Jack Paar Show," NBC, 1958; "The Peter Lind Hayes Show," ABC, 1959; "The

Jack Benny Program," CBS, 1959; "Be Our Guest," CBS, 1960; "The Jack Benny Program," CBS, 1960; "The Jack Benny Program," CBS, 1961; "The Garry Moore Show," CBS, 1961; "The Ed Sullivan Show," CBS, 1962; "The Joey Bishop Show," ABC, **1968**.

FONTAINE, JOAN

b. Joan de Havilland, Tokyo, October 22, 1917. Actress who specializes in the same kind of refined roles as her sister, Olivia de Havilland, and who apparently used to love appearing on game shows.

AS A REGULAR: "Family Classics," CBS, 1960-61.
AND: "Four Star Playhouse: Girl on the Park Bench," CBS, 1953; "Four Star Playhouse: Trudy," CBS, 1955; "The Loretta Young Show: A Shadow Between," NBC, 1955; "G.E. Theatre: In Summer Promise," CBS, 1956; "Ford Theatre: Your Other Love," NBC, 1956; "Star Stage: The Shadowy Third," NBC, 1956; "The 20th Century-Fox Hour: Stranger in the Night," CBS, 1956; "On Trial: The de Santre Story," NBC, 1956; "G.E. Theatre: The Victorian Chaise Lounge," CBS, 1957; "The Joseph Cotten Show: Fatal Charm," NBC, 1957; "G.E. Theatre: At Miss Minner's," CBS, 1958; "Westinghouse Desilu Playhouse: Perilous," CBS, 1959; "Dick Clark's World of Talent," ABC, 1959; "Startime: Closed Set," NBC, 1960; "G.E. Theatre: The Story of Judith," CBS, 1960; "Alcoa Presents One Step Beyond: The Visitor," ABC, 1960; "G.E. Theatre: A Possibility of Oil," CBS, 1961; "Here's Hollywood," NBC, 1961; "Checkmate: Voyage Into Fear," CBS, 1961; "The Dick Powell Show: The Clocks," NBC, 1962; "To Tell the Truth," CBS, 1962; "To Tell the Truth," CBS, 1963; "Wagon Train: The Naomi Taylor Story," ABC, 1963; "The Alfred Hitchcock Hour: The Paragon," CBS, 1963; "Missing Links," NBC, 1963; "To Tell the Truth," CBS, 1964; "The Match Game," NBC, 1964; "To Tell the Truth," CBS, 1965; "The Match Game," NBC, 1965; "The Bing Crosby Show: Operation Man Save," ABC, 1965; "Personality," NBC, 1967; "Snap Judgment," NBC, 1968; "Personality," NBC, 1968.

TV MOVIES AND MINISERIES: "The Users," ABC, 1978; "Crossings," ABC, 1986.

THE FONTANE SISTERS

Marge, Bea and Geri, b. New Milford, NJ. Singing trio who usually worked with Perry Como.

AS REGULARS: "The Chesterfield Supper Club," NBC, 1948-50; "TV's Top Tunes," CBS, 1951; "The Perry Como Show," CBS, 1950-55; NBC, 1955-59.
AND: "Club 60," NBC, 1957; "The Jimmy Dean Show," CBS, 1957; "Pat Boone Chevy Show-room," ABC, 1957; "The Bob Crosby Show,"

NBC, 1958; "American Bandstand," ABC, 1958; "Dick Clark's New Year's Eve Party," ABC, 1959; "American Bandstand," ABC, 1960.

FONTANNE, LYNN

b. London, England, 1887; d. 1983. Stage actress who did a bit of TV; an Emmy winner for "The Magnificent Yankee."
AS A GUEST: "Producers Showcase: The Great Sebastians," NBC, 1957; "Peter Pan," NBC, 1960; "Hallmark Hall of Fame: The Magnificent Yankee," NBC, 1965; "Hallmark Hall of Fame: Anastasia," NBC, 1967.
* Emmies: 1965.

FORAN, DICK

b. John Nicholas Foran, Flemington, NJ, June 18, 1910; d. 1979.
AS A REGULAR: "Walt Disney Presents: The Swamp Fox," ABC, 1959-60; "O.K. Crackerby," ABC, 1965-66.
AND: "Studio One: The Loud Red Patrick," CBS, 1950; "Tele-Theatre: The Great Emptiness," NBC, 1950; "Kraft Television Theatre: Irish Eyes," NBC, 1951; "Kraft Television Theatre: The Peaceful Warrior," NBC, 1952; "Studio One: The Kill," CBS, 1952; "Best of Broadway: The Philadelphia Story," CBS, 1954; "Shower of Stars: Burlesque," CBS, 1955; "Stage 7: Billy and the Bride," CBS, 1955; "Public Defender: Condemned," CBS, 1955; "Public Defender: Operation CLEAT," CBS, 1955; "TV Reader's Digest: When the Wise Men Appeared," ABC, 1955; "Climax!: The Secret of River Lane," CBS, 1956; "Crossroads: Boomtown Padre," ABC, 1957; "Ford Theatre: Broken Barrier," ABC, 1957; "Crossroads: Coney Island Wedding," ABC, 1957; "Colt .45: Final Payment," ABC, 1957; "The Millionaire: Millionaire Hugh Waring," CBS, 1957; "Circus Boy: The Return of Buffalo Bill," ABC, 1957; "Matinee Theatre: The Gardenia Bush," NBC, 1958; "Have Gun, Will Travel: Young Gun," CBS, 1959; "Yancy Derringer: Two of a Kind," CBS, 1959; "The Red Skelton Show," CBS, 1959; "Lassie: The Partnership," CBS, 1962; "Perry Mason: The Case of the Garrulous Gambler," CBS, 1962; "Lawman: The Wanted Man," ABC, 1962; "Death Valley Days: Holy Terror," SYN, 1963; "The Virginian: A Man Called Kane," NBC, 1964; "Death Valley Days: Kate Melville and the Law," SYN, 1965; "Rawhide: The Testing Post," CBS, 1965; "Vacation Playhouse: Off We Go!," CBS, 1966; "The Virginian: Requiem for a Country Doctor," NBC, 1967; "The Virginian: Reckoning," NBC, 1967; "The Virginian: Big Tiny," NBC, 1968; "Mayberry, RFD: Palm Springs Cowboy," CBS, 1969.

FORBES, SCOTT

b. South Africa, 1921. Action-oriented hero who played Jim Bowie.
AS A REGULAR: "The Seeking Heart," CBS, 1954; "The Adventures of Jim Bowie," ABC, 1956-58.
AND: "Stage 7: To Kill a Man," CBS, 1955; "Schlitz Playhouse of Stars: Top Man," CBS, 1955; "Schlitz Playhouse of Stars: Fedar," CBS, 1955; "The Loretta Young Show: My Uncles O'Moore," NBC, 1955; "The Loretta Young Show: Gesundheit," NBC, 1956; "Telephone Time: Mr. and Mrs. Browning," CBS, 1956; "The Jane Wyman Show: In a Different Life," NBC, 1958; "Studio One: The Edge of Truth," CBS, 1958; "Dick Powell's Zane Grey Theatre: Man Alone," CBS, 1959; "Best of the Post: The Return," SYN, 1960; "U.S. Steel Hour: The Duchess and the Smugs," CBS, 1962.

FORD, ART

b. New York City, NY. Former deejay.
AS A REGULAR: "Art Ford on Broadway," ABC, 1950; "The Art Ford Show," NBC, 1951; "Who's Whose," CBS, 1951.

FORD, FAITH

Actress who plays Corky Sherwood Forest on "Murphy Brown."
AS A REGULAR: "Another World," NBC, 1983-84; "The Popcorn Kid," CBS, 1987; "Murphy Brown," CBS, 1988- .
AND: "Webster: Almost Home," ABC, 1985; "Cagney & Lacey: Rites of Passage," CBS, 1986; "The Pat Sajak Show," CBS, 1989; "Friday Night Videos," NBC, 1989; "Murder, She Wrote: Goodbye, Charlie," CBS, 1989.
TV MOVIES AND MINISERIES: "If It's Tuesday, It Still Must Be Belgium," NBC, 1987.

FORD, GLENN

b. Gwyllyn Ford, Quebec, Canada, May 1, 1916. Solid leading man of movies and TV.
AS A REGULAR: "Cade's County," CBS, 1971-72; "Friends of Man," SYN, 1973-74; "The Family Holvak," NBC, 1975.
AND: "Person to Person," CBS, 1957; "A Day Called X," CBS, 1957; "The Tonight Show Starring Johnny Carson," NBC, 1963; "The Dean Martin Show," NBC, 1970; "Hollywood Squares," NBC, 1972; "Hollywood Squares," NBC, 1973; "Hollywood Squares," NBC, 1974; "Celebrity Sweepstakes," NBC, 1974; "Hollywood Squares," SYN, 1975.
TV MOVIES AND MINISERIES: "The Brotherhood of the Bell," CBS, 1970; "Slayride," CBS, 1971; "Jarrett," ABC, 1973; "The Disappearance of Flight 412," NBC, 1974; "The Greatest Gift," NBC, 1974; "Punch and Jody," NBC, 1974; "Best Sellers: Once an Eagle," NBC, 1976; "Evening in Byzantium," SYN, 1978; "Beggarman, Thief," NBC, 1979.

FORD, HARRISON

b. *Chicago, IL, July 13, 1942.* Superstar known to movie audiences as Han Solo and Indiana Jones; he began in TV.

AS A GUEST: "The Virginian: The Moduc Kid," NBC, 1967; "Ironside: The Past Is Prologue, NBC, 1967; "The FBI: Caesar's Wife," ABC, 1969; "Love, American Style: Love and the Former Marriage," ABC, 1969; "The FBI: Scapegoat," ABC, 1969; "Gunsmoke: The Sodbusters," CBS, 1972; "Gunsmoke: Whelan's Men," CBS, 1973.

TV MOVIES AND MINISERIES: "The Intruders," NBC, 1970; "James A. Michener's Dynasty," NBC, 1976.

FORD, JOHN

b. *Sean Aloysius O'Feeney, Cape Elizabeth, ME, February 1, 1895; d. 1973.* Cantankerous, legendary film director with a true vision who turned his talents on occasion to TV.

AS A GUEST: "Wide Wide World: The Western," NBC, 1958; "The American West of John Ford," CBS, 1973.

AS DIRECTOR: "Screen Directors Playhouse: Rookie of the Year," NBC, 1955; "Wagon Train: The Colter Craven Story," NBC, 1960; "Alcoa Premiere: Flashing Spikes," ABC, 1962.

* Ford's films include "Stagecoach," "The Grapes of Wrath," "My Darling Clementine," "She Wore a Yellow Ribbon," "The Quiet Man," "The Last Hurrah" and many others.

FORD, PAUL

b. *Baltimore, MD, Paul Ford Weaver, November 2, 1901; d. 1976.* Former insurance salesman; a bald, blustery character actor who was at his best as the befuddled Colonel John Hall, commanding officer over Sgt. Ernie Bilko on "The Phil Silvers Show."

AS A REGULAR: "The Phil Silvers Show (You'll Never Get Rich)," CBS, 1955-59; "The Baileys of Balboa," CBS, 1964-65.

AND: "Norby: Overdrawn Account," NBC, 1955; "Studio One: The Tale of St. Emergency," CBS, 1956; "Producers Showcase: Bloomer Girl," NBC, 1956; "Kaiser Aluminum Hour: A Man's Game," NBC, 1957; "Art Linkletter's House Party," CBS, 1957; "Du Pont Show of the Month: Junior Miss," CBS, 1957; "Playhouse 90: Turn Left at Mt. Everest," CBS, 1958; "The Right Man," CBS, 1960; "Shirley Temple's Storybook: King Midas," NBC, 1961; "G.E. Theatre: Open House," CBS, 1961; "The Outlaws: Outrage at Pawnee Bend," NBC, 1961; "Alfred Hitchcock Presents: The Hat Box," NBC, 1961; "The Garry Moore Show," CBS, 1962; "Hallmark Hall of Fame: The Teahouse of the August Moon," NBC, 1962; "The Lloyd Bridges Show: Now You Take Your Average Rock," CBS, 1962; "The Merv Griffin Show," NBC, 1963; "The Tonight Show Starring Johnny Carson," NBC, 1963; "U.S. Steel Hour: Don't Shake the Family Tree," CBS, 1963; "The Red Skelton Hour," CBS, 1965; "Love, American Style: Love and Grandma," ABC, 1970; "Love, American Style: Love and the Old Flames," ABC, 1972.

TV MOVIES AND MINISERIES: "In Name Only," ABC, 1969.

FORD, TENNESSEE ERNIE

b. *Ernest Jennings Ford, Bristol, TN, February 13, 1919.* Singer-humorist whose country-style clowning on a couple of "I Love Lucy" episodes; made him a TV hit. His NBC variety show, however, featured everything from pop to country to abridged material from Gilbert and Sullivan operettas.

AS A REGULAR: "The Kollege of Musical Knowledge," NBC, 1954; "The Tennessee Ernie Ford Show," NBC, 1955-57; ABC, 1961-65; "The Ford Show," NBC, 1956-61.

AND: "I Love Lucy: Tennessee Ernie Visits," CBS, 1954; "I Love Lucy: Tennessee Ernie Hangs On," CBS, 1954; "I Love Lucy: Tennessee Bound," CBS, 1955; "This Is Your Life," NBC, 1956; "The George Gobel Show," NBC, 1957; "The Steve Allen Show," NBC, 1957; "The Rosemary Clooney Show," SYN, 1957; "The Lux Show with Rosemary Clooney," NBC, 1957; "The Perry Como Show," NBC, 1958; "The George Gobel Show," NBC, 1958; "The Danny Thomas Show: Tennessee Ernie Stays for Dinner," CBS, 1959; "The George Gobel Show," CBS, 1960; "Startime: Tennessee Ernie Meets King Arthur," NBC, 1960; "How Tall Is a Giant?," NBC, 1960; "Here's Hollywood," NBC, 1960; "Something Special," NBC, 1960; "The Jack Benny Program," CBS, 1961; "The Andy Williams Show," NBC, 1962; "The Andy Williams Show," NBC, 1964; "The Andy Williams Show," NBC, 1966; "Andy Griffith Special," CBS, 1967; "The Lucy Show: Lucy Meets Tennessee Ernie Ford," CBS, 1967; "The Red Skelton Hour," CBS, 1967; "Mouse on the Mayflower," NBC, 1968; "Here's Lucy: Lucy and Tennessee Ernie Ford," CBS, 1969; "The Jim Nabors Hour," CBS, 1970; "Country Music Hit Parade," NBC, 1973; "The Mike Douglas Show," SYN, 1973; "Password All-Stars," ABC, 1975; "Dinah!," SYN, 1975; "Dolly," SYN, 1976; "Hee Haw," SYN, 1977; "Hee Haw," SYN, 1978; "Hee Haw," SYN, 1979.

FORD, WALLACE

b. *Samuel Jones Grundy, England, February 12, 1898; d. 1966.* Actor who played older characters and sidekicks.

AS A REGULAR: "The Deputy," NBC, 1959-60.

AND: "Schlitz Playhouse of Stars: Come What May," CBS, 1952; "Goodyear TV Playhouse: The

Happy Rest," NBC, 1953; "The American Hour: Outlaw's Reckoning," ABC, 1953; "Armstrong Circle Theatre: The Marshal of Misery Gulch," NBC, 1953; "Studio One: Runaway," CBS, 1954; "Armstrong Circle Theatre: Treasure Trove," NBC, 1954; "Death Valley Days: Claim-Jumping Jenny," SYN, 1954; "Father Knows Best: The Christmas Story," CBS, 1954; "Fireside Theatre: Big Joe's Comin' Home," NBC, 1955; "Court of Last Resort: The Jim Thompson Case," NBC, 1957; "Playhouse 90: The Last Man," CBS, 1958; "Trackdown: A Stone for Benny French," CBS, 1959; "Tales of Wells Fargo: Dead Man's Street," NBC, 1960; "Klondike: 88 Keys to Trouble," NBC, 1960; "The Wide Country: Down a Dusty Road," NBC, 1962; "Alcoa Premiere: The Glass Palace," ABC, 1963; "Vacation Playhouse: Three Wishes," CBS, 1963; "The Great Adventure: The Colonel From Connecticut," CBS, 1964; "Walt Disney's Wonderful World of Color: Bristle Face," NBC, 1964; "The Travels of Jaimie McPheeters: The Day of the Tin Trumpet," ABC, 1964; "The Andy Griffith Show: Aunt Bee's Romance," CBS, 1964.

FORMAN, JOEY

b. 1929; d. 1982. Comic actor, frequently with Mickey Rooney; he played detective Harry Hoo on "Get Smart."

AS A REGULAR: "The Mickey Rooney Show," NBC, 1954-55; "The New Steve Allen Show," ABC, 1961; "The Sid Caesar Show," ABC, 1963-64; "The Joey Bishop Show," CBS, 1964-65; "The Steve Allen Comedy Hour," NBC, 1980-81.

AND: "The Steve Allen Show," NBC, 1956; "The Danny Thomas Show: Terry's Girlfriend," CBS, 1958; "The Ed Sullivan Show," CBS, 1958; "Revlon Revue: The Many Sides of Mickey Rooney," CBS, 1960; "Alcoa Theatre: You Should Meet My Sister," NBC, 1960; "Comedy Spot: The Sky's the Limit," CBS, 1960; "G.E. Theatre: Don't Let It Throw You," CBS, 1961; "The Ed Sullivan Show," CBS, 1961; "The Joey Bishop Show: On the Spot," NBC, 1961; "Bob Hope Chrysler Theatre: Kicks," NBC, 1965; "Get Smart: The Amazing Harry Hoo," NBC, 1966; "Get Smart: Hoo Done It," NBC, 1966; "Bewitched: Hoho the Clown," ABC, 1967; "The Monkees: Captain Crocodile," NBC, 1967; "The Monkees: Monkee Chow Mein," NBC, 1967; "Get Smart: The Little Black Book," NBC, 1968; "Nanny and the Professor: The Haunted House," ABC, 1970; "The Doris Day Show: Charity Begins at the Office," CBS, 1971; "Ironside: Murder Impromptu," NBC, 1971; "Love, American Style: Love and the Extra Job," ABC, 1974; "Celebrity Sweepstakes," NBC, 1974; "One Day at a Time: Julie's Job," CBS, 1976; "Three's Company: It's Only Money," ABC,

1977; "Nero Wolfe: Wolfe at the Door," NBC, 1981; "Fantasy Island: House of Dolls," ABC, 1982.

FORREST, STEVE

b. William Forrest Andrews, Huntsville, TX, September 29, 1924. Rough-and-ready actor who played SWAT commander Lt. Dan "Hondo" Harrelson and mystery man Wes Parmalee on "Dallas"; brother of Dana Andrews.

AS A REGULAR: "The Baron," ABC, 1966; "SWAT," ABC, 1975-76; "Dallas," CBS, 1986.

AND: "The Loretta Young Show: Saigon," NBC, 1956; "Climax!: Flight to Tomorrow," CBS, 1956; "Alfred Hitchcock Presents: The End of Indian Summer," CBS, 1957; "Climax!: Let It Be Me," CBS, 1957; "Playhouse 90: Clipper Ship," CBS, 1957; "Lux Video Theatre: The Armed Venus," NBC, 1957; "The Outlaws: Thirty a Month," NBC, 1960; "The Wide Country: The Royce Bennett Story," NBC, 1962; "The Dick Powell Show: Project X," NBC, 1963; "The Virginian: The Money Cage," NBC, 1963; "The Twilight Zone: The Parallel," CBS, 1963; "Rawhide: Blood Harvest," CBS, 1965; "The Fugitive: Last Second of a Big Dream," ABC, 1965; "Burke's Law: Who Killed the Jackpot?," ABC, 1965; "Cimarron Strip: Broken Wing," CBS, 1967; "Bonanza: Desperate Passage," NBC, 1967; "Cimarron Strip: Sound of a Drum," CBS, 1968; "Medical Center: Death Grip," CBS, 1970; "The Name of the Game: Little Bear Died Running," NBC, 1970; "The FBI: The Stalking Horse," ABC, 1971; "Men at Law: The View From the Top," CBS, 1971; "Mission: Impossible: The Visitors," CBS, 1971; "Alias Smith and Jones: Twenty-One Days to Tenstrike," ABC, 1972; "Night Gallery: The Waiting Room," NBC, 1972; The Sixth Sense: Echo of a Distant Scream," ABC, 1972; "Ghost Story: The Summer House," NBC, 1972; "Hec Ramsey: Hangman's Wages," NBC, 1972; "Love, American Style: Love and the Flying Finletters," ABC, 1974; "McMillan and Wife: Man Without a Face," NBC, 1974; "Hotel: The Wedding," ABC, 1984; "Finder of Lost Loves: Premiere," ABC, 1984; "Murder, She Wrote: Murder in the Electric Cathedral," CBS, 1986; "Murder, She Wrote: Trevor Hudson's Legacy," CBS, 1989.

TV MOVIES AND MINISERIES: "Chant of Silence," ABC, 1973; "The Hanged Man," ABC, 1974; "The Hatfields and the McCoys," ABC, 1975; "Wanted: The Sundance Woman," ABC, 1976; "Testimony of Two Men," SYN, 1977; "The Deerslayer," NBC, 1978; "Captain America," CBS, 1979; "Manions of America," ABC, 1981; "Malibu," ABC, 1983; "Hollywood Wives," ABC, 1985; "Gunsmoke: Return to Dodge," CBS, 1987.

FORSTER, ROBERT

b. Rochester, NY, July 13, 1941.

AS A REGULAR: "Banyon," NBC, 1972-73; "Nakia," ABC, 1974; "Once a Hero," ABC, 1987.

AND: "NYPD: Catch a Hero," ABC, 1967; "Higher and Higher, Attorneys at Law," CBS, 1968; "Judd for the Defense: In a Puff of Smoke," ABC, 1968; "Police Story: The Man in the Shadows," NBC, 1975; "Medical Story: The Moonlight Healer," NBC, 1975; "Police Story: Little Boy Lost," NBC, 1975; "Gibbsville: All the Young Girls," NBC, 1976; "Police Story: Ice Time," NBC, 1977; "Magnum P.I.: Deja Vu," CBS, 1985; "Murder, She Wrote: The Perfect Foil," CBS, 1986; "Jesse Hawkes: Premiere," CBS, 1989.

TV MOVIES AND MINISERIES: "Banyon," NBC, 1971; "The Death Squad," ABC, 1973; "Nakia," ABC, 1974; "Royce," CBS, 1976; "The City," NBC, 1977; "The Darker Side of Terror," CBS, 1979.

FORSYTHE, HENDERSON

Actor who played Dr. David Stewart on "As the World Turns" and was active in live TV drama.

AS A REGULAR: "As the World Turns," CBS, 1960-88; "Eisenhower & Lutz," CBS, 1988; "Nearly Departed," NBC, 1989.

AND: "Studio One: The Playwright and the Star," CBS, 1957; "Studio One: The Mother Bit," CBS, 1957; "Studio One: The Human Barrier," CBS, 1957; "Armstrong Circle Theatre: Kidnap Story: Hold for Release!," CBS, 1958; "U.S. Steel Hour: A Matter of Pride," CBS, 1958; "U.S. Steel Hour: Rachel's Summer," CBS, 1959; "U.S. Steel Hour: Bride of the Fox," CBS, 1960; "Du Pont Show of the Month: The Night of the Storm," CBS, 1961; "U.S. Steel Hour: Welcome Home," CBS, 1961; "The Defenders: The Riot," CBS, 1961; "U.S. Steel Hour: Who Is This Woman?," CBS, 1962; "U.S. Steel Hour: Night Run to the West," CBS, 1963; "Mr. Broadway: Between the Rats and the Finks," CBS, 1964.

TV MOVIES AND MINISERIES: "Word of Honor," CBS, 1981; "Crisis at Central High," CBS, 1981.

FORSYTHE, JOHN

b. John Freund, Carney's Point, NJ, January 29, 1918. Handsome actor who was bachelor father Bentley Gregg, the unseen Charlie who sent his angels out on cases, and Blake Carrington, who had a lot of trouble controlling his dynasty.

AS A REGULAR: "Bachelor Father," CBS, 1957-59; NBC, 1959-61; ABC, 1961-62; "The John Forsythe Show," NBC, 1965-66; "To Rome with Love," CBS, 1969-71; "Charlie's Angels," ABC, 1976-81; "Dynasty," ABC, 1981-89.

AND: "Studio One: None But My Foe," CBS, 1951; "Robert Montgomery Presents: Dark Victory," NBC, 1951; "Danger: A Clear Case of Suicide," CBS, 1951; "Lights Out: The Pattern," NBC, 1951; "Lights Out: The Upstairs Floor," NBC, 1952; "Studio One: Hold Back the Night," CBS, 1952; "Pulitzer Prize Playhouse: The American Leonardo," ABC, 1952; "Philco TV Playhouse: The Monument," NBC, 1952; "Suspense: The Beach at Falesa," CBS, 1952; "Elgin TV Hour: Driftwood," ABC, 1955; "Studio One: Operation Home," CBS, 1955; "Climax!: One Night Stand," CBS, 1955; "Alfred Hitchcock Presents: Premonition," CBS, 1955; "Playwrights '56: Return to Cassino," NBC, 1956; "Climax!: Pale Horse, Pale Rider," CBS, 1956; "G.E. Theatre: A New Girl in His Life," CBS, 1957; "The Jack Benny Program," CBS, 1957; "Climax!: Shooting for the Moon," CBS, 1958; "Schlitz Playhouse of Stars: Way of the West," CBS, 1958; "Christophers: The Story of Johnny Appleseed," SYN, 1958; "Lux Playhouse: The Miss and Missles," CBS, 1959; "Sunday Showcase: What Makes Sammy Run," NBC, 1959; "The Ford Show," NBC, 1960; "Here's Hollywood," NBC, 1961; "The Alfred Hitchcock Hour: I Saw the Whole Thing," CBS, 1962; "Hallmark Hall of Fame: Teahouse of the August Moon," NBC, 1962; "Alcoa Premiere: Five, Six, Pick Up Sticks," ABC, 1963; "ABC Stage '67: How to Tell Your Past, Present and Maybe Even Your Future Through Social Dancing," ABC, 1967; "Run for Your Life: A Choice of Evils," NBC, 1967; "Hallmark Hall of Fame: A Bell for Adano," NBC, 1967; "It Takes a Thief: When Good Friends Get Together," ABC, 1968; "Columbo: Murder by the Book," NBC, 1971; "Mannix: Dark So Early, Dark So Long," CBS, 1971; "Medical Story: Million Dollar Baby," NBC, 1975; "Dinah!," SYN, 1978; "The Love Boat: China Cruise," ABC, 1983; "America's Tribute to Bob Hope," NBC, 1988; "Ooh-La-La- It's Bob Hope's Fun Birthday Spectacular From Paris' Bicentennial," NBC, 1989.

TV MOVIES AND MINISERIES: "See How They Run," NBC, 1964; "Shadow on the Land," NBC, 1968; "Murder Once Removed," NBC, 1971; "The Letters," ABC, 1973; "Lisa, Bright and Dark," CBS, 1973; "Police Story: Chief," NBC, 1974; "Cry Panic!," ABC, 1974; "Terror on the 40th Floor," NBC, 1974; "The Healers," NBC, 1974; "The Deadly Tower," NBC, 1975; "Amelia Earhart," NBC, 1976; "The Users," ABC, 1978; "A Time for Miracles," ABC, 1980; "Sizzle," ABC, 1981; "On Fire," ABC, 1987.

FOSTER, BUDDY

b. July 12, 1957. Child actor who played Mike,

son of Sam Jones (Ken Berry) on "Mayberry RFD"; brother of Jodie.

AS A REGULAR: "Hondo," ABC, 1967; "Mayberry RFD," CBS, 1968-71.

AND: "Petticoat Junction: Temperance, Temperance," CBS, 1967; "The Andy Griffith Show: Mayberry RFD," CBS, 1968; "The Andy Griffith Show: Opie and Mike," CBS, 1968; "Dragnet: Juvenile Genius," NBC, 1969.

TV MOVIES AND MINISERIES: "Black Noon," CBS, 1971.

FOSTER, JODIE

b. Bronx, NY, November 19, 1962. Oscar-winning actress who's made the unlikely leap from TV child star to respected film performer.

AS A REGULAR: "Bob & Carol & Ted & Alice," ABC, 1973; "Paper Moon" ABC, 1974-75.

AND: "Mayberry RFD: The Pet Shop," CBS, 1969; "The Courtship of Eddie's Father: Bully for You," ABC, 1969; "Gunsmoke: Roots of Fear," CBS, 1969; "Julia: Romeo and Julia," NBC, 1969; "Nanny and the Professor: The Scientific Approach," ABC, 1970; "The Wonderful World of Disney: Menace on the Mountain," NBC, 1970; "The Courtship of Eddie's Father: A Loaf of Bread, a Bar of Soap and a Jar of Peanut Butter," ABC, 1970; "Mayberry RFD: Mike's Project," CBS, 1970; "My Three Sons: Everybody's Working for Peanuts," CBS, 1971; "My Three Sons: The Recital," CBS, 1971; "The Courtship of Eddie's Father: The Lonely Weekend," ABC, 1971; "Gunsmoke: P.S. Murry Christmas," CBS, 1971; "Gunsmoke: The Predators," CBS, 1972; "Ironside: Bubble, Bubble, Toil and Murder," NBC, 1972; "ABC Afterschool Special: Alexander," ABC, 1973; "The New Adventures of Perry Mason: The Case of the Deadly Deeds," CBS, 1973; "Love Story: The Youngest Lovers," NBC, 1973; "Medical Center: The Captives," CBS, 1975; "ABC Afterschool Special: The Life of T.K. Dearing," ABC, 1976; "The Wonderful World of Disney: One Little Indian," NBC, 1976; "Saturday Night Live," NBC, 1976; "Storybook Classics: The Fisherman's Wife," SHO, 1989.

TV MOVIES AND MINISERIES: "Smile, Jenny, You're Dead," ABC, 1974; "Svengali," CBS, 1983; "The Blood of Others," HBO, 1984.

FOSTER, MEG

b. Connecticut. Striking actress who played Chris Cagney on "Cagney & Lacey" until network executives complained that she seemed a little too butch in the role.

AS A REGULAR: "Sunshine," NBC, 1975; "Cagney & Lacey," CBS, 1982.

AND: "The Mod Squad: Death of a Nobody," ABC, 1971; "Medical Center: Conflict," CBS, 1972; "The FBI: A Second Life," ABC, 1972; "Mannix: A Game of Shadows," CBS, 1972;

"Barnaby Jones: A Little Glory, A Little Death," CBS, 1973; "Barnaby Jones: Gold Record for Murder," CBS, 1974; "Barnaby Jones: Blueprint for a Caper," CBS, 1974; "The FBI: The Animal," ABC, 1974; "Medical Center: Web of Intrigue," CBS, 1974; "The Streets of San Francisco: Trail of Terror," ABC, 1975; "Hawaii Five-O: Double Exposure," CBS, 1976; "Three for the Road: The Albatross," CBS, 1975; "The Twilight Zone: Dreams for Sale," CBS, 1985; "Murder, She Wrote: Joshua Peabody Died Here-Possibly," CBS, 1985; "Miami Vice: Blood & Roses," NBC, 1988.

TV MOVIES AND MINISERIES: "The Death of Me Yet," ABC, 1971; "Things in Their Season," CBS, 1974; "Promise Him Anything," ABC, 1975; "James Dean," NBC, 1976; "Washington: Behind Closed Doors," ABC, 1977; "Best Kept Secrets," ABC, 1984.

FOSTER, PHIL

b. Brooklyn, NY, March 29, 1913; d. 1985. Comedian who played Frank, father of Laverne De Fazio (Penny Marshall).

AS A REGULAR: "The Greatest Gift," NBC, 1954-55; "Laverne & Shirley," ABC, 1976-83.

AND: "Arthur Murray Party," NBC, 1957; "The Phil Silvers Show: Bilko the Genius," CBS, 1958; "The Garry Moore Show," CBS, 1958; "The Jimmy Dean Show," CBS, 1959; "The Ed Sullivan Show," CBS, 1960; "The Jack Paar Show," NBC, 1961; "The Merv Griffin Show," NBC, 1962; "Arthur Godfrey Special: The Sounds of New York," CBS, 1963; "Weekend," SYN, 1963; "The Joey Bishop Show: Double Play From Foster to Durocher to Joey," NBC, 1964; "The Tonight Show Starring Johnny Carson," NBC, 1965; "Trials of O'Brien: Never Bet on Anything That Talks," CBS, 1965; "This Morning," ABC, 1968; "The Odd Couple: Two Men on a Hoarse," ABC, 1975.

FOSTER, PRESTON

b. Ocean City, NJ, October 24, 1900; d. 1970. Actor in beefy roles.

AS A REGULAR: "Waterfront," SYN, 1954-55; "Gunslinger," CBS, 1961.

AND: "Schlitz Playhouse of Stars: Manhattan Robin Hood," CBS, 1953; "Ford Theatre: The Lady and the Champ," NBC, 1953; "G.E. Theatre: The Hunter," CBS, 1953; "The Loretta Young Show: Fear Me Not," NBC, 1955; "Star Stage: The Guardian," NBC, 1956; "Club 60," NBC, 1957; "The Ford Show," NBC, 1957; "O. Henry Playhouse: Between Rounds," SYN, 1957; "The Jane Wyman Show: Tunnel Eight," NBC, 1958; "Schlitz Playhouse of Stars: Portrait of a Legend," CBS, 1958; "Art Linkletter's House Party," CBS, 1961; "Target: The Corruptors: Prison Empire," ABC, 1961; "Going My Way: A Memorial for Finnegan," ABC, 1963; "The Eleventh Hour:

Cold Hands, Warm Heart," NBC, 1963; "77 Sunset Strip: Lovers' Lane," ABC, 1964.

FOWLEY, DOUGLAS
b. *Daniel Vincent Fowley, New York City, NY, May 30, 1911.* Actor who played western heavies and other cynical types, later becoming a specialist at grizzled old coots. Played Doc Holliday on "Wyatt Earp."
AS A REGULAR: "The Life and Legend of Wyatt Earp," ABC, 1955-56; 1957-61; "Pistols 'n' Petticoats," CBS, 1966-67; "Detective School," ABC, 1979.
AND: "The Abbott and Costello Show: Bank Holdup," CBS, 1953; "December Bride: High Sierras," CBS, 1955; "Damon Runyon Theatre: Bunny on the Beach," CBS, 1956; "The Red Skelton Show," CBS, 1957; "Richard Diamond, Private Detective: A Cup of Black Coffee," CBS, 1958; "The Adventures of Rin Tin Tin: Rusty's Opportunity," ABC, 1958; "The Gale Storm Show: The Case of the Chinese Puzzle," CBS, 1959; "Death Valley Days: Cap'n Pegleg," SYN, 1959; "The Andy Griffith Show: Opie and His Merry Men," CBS, 1963; "Temple Houston: Sam's Boy," NBC, 1964; "Gomer Pyle, USMC: Gomer and the Father Figure," CBS, 1966; "My Three Sons: The Standing Still Tour," CBS, 1968; "Mayberry RFD: The New Well," CBS, 1970; "The Streets of San Francisco: The Albatross," ABC, 1973; "Kung Fu: The Assassin," ABC, 1973; "Police Woman: The Cradle Robbers," NBC, 1974; "Kolchak, the Night Stalker: The Trevi Collection," ABC, 1975; "Marcus Welby, M.D.: Dark Corridors," ABC, 1975; "Father Murphy: Graduation," NBC, 1982.
TV MOVIES AND MINISERIES: "The Oregon Trail," NBC, 1976; "The Moneychangers," NBC, 1976.

FOX, BERNARD
Character actor who played Dr. Bombay on "Bewitched," Malcolm Meriwether on "The Andy Griffith Show" and Col. Crittendon on "Hogan's Heroes."
AS A REGULAR: "Bewitched," ABC, 1967-72.
AND: "The Danny Thomas Show: Shy Alfie," CBS, 1963; "The Andy Griffith Show: Andy's English Valet," CBS, 1963; "The Andy Griffith Show: Return of Malcolm Merriwether," CBS, 1964; "The Dick Van Dyke Show: Teacher's Petrie," CBS, 1964; "McHale's Navy: The British Also Have Ensigns," ABC, 1964; "Twelve O'Clock High: The Climate of Doubt," ABC, 1964; "The Farmer's Daughter: Crime of Passion," ABC, 1965; "The Dick Van Dyke Show: Girls Will Be Boys," CBS, 1965; "The Dick Van Dyke Show: Never Bathe on Saturday," CBS, 1965; "Perry Mason: The Case of the Laughing Lady," CBS, 1965; "F Troop: The Phantom Major," ABC, 1965; "The Andy Griffith

Show: Malcolm at the Crossroads," CBS, 1965; "I Spy: Carry Me Back to Old Tsing-Tao," NBC, 1965; "The Man From UNCLE: The Thor Affair," NBC, 1966; "Hogan's Heroes: The Crittenden Plan," CBS, 1967; "Hogan's Heroes: Hogan, Go Home," CBS, 1968; "The Monkees: The Monkees Mind Their Manor," NBC, 1968; "Hogan's Heroes: Hogan's Trucking Service—We Deliver the Factory to You," CBS, 1968; "The Wild Wild West: The Night of the Winged Terror," CBS, 1969; "Hogan's Heroes: Crittendon's Commandos," CBS, 1970; "Love, American Style: Love and the Liberated Lady Boss," ABC, 1970; "Hogan's Heroes: Lady Chitterly's Lover," CBS, 1970; "The Partridge Family: A Partridge by Any Other Name," ABC, 1971; "Columbo: Dagger of the Mind," NBC, 1972; "Love, American Style: Love and the Lady Athlete," ABC, 1972; "Love, American Style: Love and the Golden Memory," ABC, 1973; "Columbo: Troubled Waters," NBC, 1975; "Barbary Coast: Arson and Old Lace," ABC, 1975; "M*A*S*H: Tea and Empathy," CBS, 1978; "Lou Grant: Libel," CBS, 1980; "Simon & Simon: Revolution #9 1/2," CBS, 1984; "Murder, She Wrote: One White Rose for Death," CBS, 1986.
TV MOVIES AND MINISERIES: "The Hound of the Baskervilles," ABC, 1972; "Gauguin the Savage," CBS, 1980.

FOX, MICHAEL J.
b. *Edmonton, Canada, June 9, 1961.* Movie and TV performer who won two Emmies as Alex Keaton on "Family Ties."
AS A REGULAR: "Palmerstown, USA," CBS, 1980-81; "Family Ties," NBC, 1982-89.
AND: "Lou Grant: Kids," CBS, 1979; "The Love Boat: He Ain't Heavy," ABC, 1983; "Night Court: Santa Goes Downtown," NBC, 1984; "The Tonight Show Starring Johnny Carson," NBC, 1988; "Late Night with David Letterman," NBC, 1989.
TV MOVIES AND MINISERIES: "Letters From Frank," CBS, 1979; "High School USA," NBC, 1983; "Family Ties Vacation," NBC, 1985.
* Fox came to Hollywood after appearing in "Letters From Frank," which was filmed in Canada. He was encouraged to come to the U.S. by the stars of the movie—Art Carney and Maureen Stapleton.
* Emmies: 1986, 1987.

FOX, SONNY
b. *Brooklyn, NY.* Emcee.
AS A REGULAR: "The $64,000 Challenge," CBS, 1956; "On Your Mark," ABC, 1961; "The Movie Game," SYN, 1969-72; "Way Out Games," CBS, 1976-77.
AND: "The Price Is Right," NBC, 1958; "The Price Is Right," NBC, 1959; "Beat the Clock," ABC, 1959; "Beat the Clock," ABC, 1960.

FOXWORTH, ROBERT

b. Houston, TX, November 1, 1941. Actor who played Chase Gioberti on "Falcon Crest."

AS A REGULAR: "Storefront Lawyers," CBS, 1970-71; "Falcon Crest," CBS, 1981-87.

AND: "Hogan's Goat," NET, 1971; "The Mod Squad: Medicine Man," ABC, 1971; "Mannix: The Glass Trap," CBS, 1971; "The Bold Ones: An Inalienable Right to Die," NBC, 1971; "Medical Center: A Game for One Player," CBS, 1972; "Hawaii Five-O: Thanks for the Honeymoon," CBS, 1973; "Love Story: All My Tomorrows," NBC, 1973; "The FBI: The Double Play," ABC, 1973; "The Streets of San Francisco: Shield of Honor," ABC, 1974; "Kung Fu: The Lawman," ABC, 1974; "The Manhunter: The Carnival," CBS, 1974; "Sandburg's Lincoln: Prairie Lawyer," NBC, 1975; "Quincy: A Star Is Dead," NBC, 1976; "Cagney & Lacey: A Fair Shake," CBS, 1988; "Columbo: Grand Deceptions," ABC, 1989.

TV MOVIES AND MINISERIES: "The Devil's Daughter," ABC, 1973; "Frankenstein," ABC, 1973; "Mrs. Sundance," ABC, 1974; "The Questor Tapes," NBC, 1974; "The FBI Story: Alvin Karpis, Public Enemy Number One," CBS, 1974; "The Memory of Eva Ryker," CBS, 1980; "Peter and Paul," CBS, 1981; "The Return of Desperado," NBC, 1988.

FOXX, REDD

b. John Elroy Sanford, St. Louis, December 9, 1922. Nightclub comic who won TV fame as Fred Sanford; his efforts to resurrect the character, however, have met with little success.

AS A REGULAR: "Sanford & Son," NBC, 1972-77; "Redd Foxx," ABC, 1977-78; "Sanford," NBC, 1980-81; "The Redd Foxx Show," ABC, 1986.

AND: "The Lucy Show: Lucy and the Ceramic Cat," CBS, 1965; "The Lucy Show: My Fair Lucy," CBS, 1965; "The Name of the Game: I Love You, Billy Baker," NBC, 1970; "The Bobby Darin Show," NBC, 1973; "The Flip Wilson Show," NBC, 1973; "The Tonight Show Starring Johnny Carson," NBC, 1973; "Hollywood Squares," NBC, 1974; "Andy Williams Special," NBC, 1974; "Cotton Club '75," NBC, 1974; "The Smothers Brothers Comedy Hour," NBC, 1975; "Grady: Be It Ever So Humble," NBC, 1975; "The Mike Douglas Show," SYN, 1975; "Bob Hope's Christmas Party," NBC, 1975; "Lola!," ABC, 1976; "The John Davidson Show," SYN, 1981.

TV MOVIES AND MINISERIES: "Ghost of a Chance," CBS, 1987.

FRAKES, JONATHON

b. Bethlehem, PA. Actor who plays Cdr. William Riker on "Star Trek: The Next Generation."

AS A REGULAR: "The Doctors," NBC, 1977-78; "Bare Essence," NBC, 1983; "Paper Dolls,"

ABC, 1984; "Star Trek: The Next Generation," SYN, 1987- .

AND: "Paris: Pay the Two Bucks," CBS, 1980; "Here's Boomer: The Private Eye," NBC, 1980; "Hill Street Blues: Of Mouse and Man," NBC, 1982; "Voyagers!: An Arrow Pointing East," NBC, 1982; "Quincy: Ghost of a Chance," NBC, 1982; "Highway to Heaven: A Divine Madness," NBC, 1984.

TV MOVIES AND MINISERIES: "Beach Patrol," ABC, 1979; "Beulah Land," NBC, 1980; "The Cover Girl and the Cop," NBC, 1989.

TV'S TOP TEN, 1972-73

1. All in the Family (CBS)
2. Sanford & Son (NBC)
3. Hawaii Five-O (CBS)
4. Maude (CBS)
5. Bridget Loves Bernie (CBS)
5. NBC Sunday Mystery Movie (NBC)
7. The Mary Tyler Moore Show (CBS)
7. Gunsmoke (CBS)
9. The Wonderful World of Disney (NBC)
10. Ironside (NBC)

FRANCIOSA, ANTHONY

b. Anthony Papaleo, New York City, NY, October 28, 1928. Dashing actor who played crusading jet-setter Jeff Dillon on "The Name of the Game" and secret agent Matt Helm.

AS A REGULAR: "Valentine's Day," ABC, 1964-65; "The Name of the Game," NBC, 1968-71; "Search," NBC, 1972-73; "Matt Helm," ABC, 1975-76; "Finder of Lost Loves," ABC, 1984-85.

AND: "Goodyear TV Playhouse: The Arena," NBC, 1954; "Studio One: It Might Happen Tomorrow," CBS, 1955; "Hallmark Hall of Fame: The Cradle Song," NBC, 1956; "Goodyear TV Playhouse: County Fair Time," NBC, 1956; "The Steve Allen Show," NBC, 1957; "Du Pont Show of the Month: Heaven Can Wait," CBS, 1960; "The Dick Powell Show: Charlie's Duet," NBC, 1963; "The du Pont Show: The Shark," NBC, 1963; "Arrest and Trial: Call It a Lifetime," ABC, 1963; "The Breaking Point: Last Summer We Didn't Go Away," ABC, 1963; "The Greatest Show on Earth: An Echo of Faded Velvet," ABC, 1963; "Bob Hope Chrysler Theatre: A Case of Armed Robbery," NBC, 1964; "The Virginian: The Shiloh Years," NBC, 1970; "The Men From Shiloh: Follow the Leader," NBC, 1970; "This Is the West That Was," NBC, 1974; "The Twilight Zone: Crazy as a Soup Sandwich," SYN, 1988.

TV MOVIES AND MINISERIES: "Fame Is the Name of the Game," NBC, 1966; "The Deadly Hunt," CBS, 1971; "Earth II," ABC, 1971; "The Catcher," NBC, 1972; "This Is the West That Was," NBC, 1974; "Matt Helm," ABC, 1975; "Arthur Hailey's Wheels," NBC, 1978;

"Stagecoach," CBS, 1986; "Blood Vows: The Story of a Mafia Wife," NBC, 1987.

FRANCIS, ANNE
b. Ossining, NY, September 16, 1930. Attractive blonde actress with a distinctive beauty mark on her right cheek; she played private eye Honey West.
AS A REGULAR: "Versatile Varieties," NBC, 1949-50; "Honey West," ABC, 1965-66; "My Three Sons," CBS, 1971-72; "Dallas," CBS, 1981; "Riptide," NBC, 1984.
AND: "Lights Out: Faithful Heart," NBC, 1950; "Kraft Television Theatre: Black Sheep," NBC, 1950; "Ford Theatre: The Tryst," NBC, 1954; "Climax!: Scream in Silence," CBS, 1958; "U.S. Steel Hour: Queen of the Orange Bowl," CBS, 1960; "Alfred Hitchcock Presents: Hooked," CBS, 1960; "Startime: Jeff McLeod: The Last Reb," NBC, 1960; "Our American Heritage: Autocrat and Son," NBC, 1960; "The Untouchables: The Doreen Maney Story," ABC, 1960; "The Twilight Zone: The After Hours," CBS, 1960; "Route 66: A Month of Sundays," CBS, 1961; "Dr. Kildare: A Million-Dollar Property," NBC, 1961; "Burke's Law: Who Killed Wade Walker?," ABC, 1963; "Ben Casey: A Bird in the Solitude Singing," ABC, 1964; "The Reporter: Hideout," CBS, 1964; "The Man From UNCLE: The Quadripartite Affair," NBC, 1964; "Burke's Law: Who Killed the Jackpot?," ABC, 1965; "The Fugitive: The Judgement," ABC, 1967; "The Invaders: The Saucer," ABC, 1967; "The Name of the Game: Incident in Berlin," NBC, 1968; "Mission: Impossible: Double Circle," CBS, 1969; "The Name of the Game: The Garden," NBC, 1970; "Dan August: Murder by Proxy," ABC, 1970; "The Men From Shiloh: Gun Quest," NBC, 1970; "Love, American Style: Love and the Visitor," ABC, 1970; "Columbo: Short Fuse," NBC, 1972; "Banacek: Horse of a Slightly Different Color," NBC, 1974; "Ironside: Friend or Foe," NBC, 1974; "Kung Fu: Night of the Owls, Day of the Doves," ABC, 1974; "Movin' On: The Price of Loving," NBC, 1975; "Barnaby Jones: Theatre of Fear," CBS, 1975; "Flying High: Pilot," CBS, 1978; "Quincy: Physician, Heal Thyself," NBC, 1979; "CHiPS: In the Best of Families," NBC, 1982; "Simon & Simon: The Shadow of Sam Penny," CBS, 1983; "Murder, She Wrote: The Murder of Sherlock Holmes," CBS, 1984; "Hardcastle and McCormick: The Long-Ago Girl," ABC, 1985; "The Love Boat: Shea Farrell," ABC, 1985; "Jake and the Fatman: Pilot," CBS, 1987; "The Golden Girls: Till Death Do We Volley," NBC, 1989; "Matlock: The Starlet," NBC, 1989.
TV MOVIES AND MINISERIES: "Wild Women," ABC, 1970; "The Intruders," NBC, 1970; "The Forgotten Man," ABC, 1971; "Mongo's Back in Town," CBS, 1971; "Fireball Forward,"

ABC, 1972; "Haunts of the Very Rich," ABC, 1972; "Cry Panic," ABC, 1974; "The FBI Story: Alvin Karpis, Public Enemy Number One," CBS, 1974; "The Last Survivors," NBC, 1975; "A Girl Named Sooner," NBC, 1975; "Banjo Hackett," NBC, 1976; "Little Mo," NBC, 1978; "The Rebels," SYN, 1979; "Beggarman, Thief," NBC, 1979; "Rona Jaffe's Mazes and Monsters," CBS, 1982; "Poor Little Rich Girl: The Barbara Hutton Story," NBC, 1987; "My First Love," ABC, 1988.
* Francis' character of Honey West, a woman private eye, was introduced on the "Who Killed the Jackpot?" episode of "Burke's Law."

FRANCIS, ARLENE
b. Arlene Francis Kazanjian, Boston, MA, October 20, 1908. Actress best known to TV audiences for playing herself on quiz shows, specifically in a 17-year stint on "What's My Line?"
AS A REGULAR: "Blind Date," ABC, 1949-52; NBC, 1952, DUM, 1952-53; "By Popular Demand," CBS, 1950; "Prize Performance," CBS, 1950; "What's My Line?," CBS, 1950-67; "Who's There?," CBS, 1952; "Talent Patrol," ABC, 1953-55; "The Comeback Story," ABC, 1954; "Home," NBC, 1954-57; "The Arlene Francis Show," NBC, 1957-58.
AND: "Sure as Fate: The Dancing Doll," CBS, 1950; "Lux Video Theatre: Mr. Finchley vs. the Bomb," NBC, 1952; "With These Hands," NBC, 1952; "Suspense: Her Last Adventure," CBS, 1952; "Mike Wallace Interviews," ABC, 1957; "The Jack Paar Show," NBC, 1959; "Bell Telephone Hour: The Younger Generation," NBC, 1961; "The Jack Paar Show," NBC, 1961; "I've Got a Secret," CBS, 1961; "Password," CBS, 1961; "Here's Hollywood," NBC, 1961; "The Gertrude Berg Show: The Mother Affair," CBS, 1962; "Password," CBS, 1962; "The Merv Griffin Show," NBC, 1962; "The Match Game," NBC, 1962; "The Match Game," NBC, 1964; "Password," CBS, 1964; "Password," CBS, 1965; "Laura," ABC, 1968; "Hallmark Hall of Fame: Harvey," NBC, 1972; "Scarecrow and Mrs. King: Double Agent," CBS, 1984.

FRANCIS, CONNIE
b. Concetta Franconero, Belleville, NJ, December 12, 1938. Singer who won first prize on "Talent Scouts" and went on to become one of the most popular singers of the sixties.
AS A REGULAR: "The Jimmie Rodgers Show," NBC, 1959.
AND: "Arthur Godfrey's Talent Scouts," CBS, 1950; "The Big Beat," ABC, 1957; "American Bandstand," ABC, 1957; "American Bandstand," ABC, 1958; "The Big Record," CBS, 1958; "The Perry Como Show," NBC, 1958; "Your Hit Parade," CBS, 1959; "The Dick Clark Saturday

Night Beechnut Show," ABC, 1960; "Here's Hollywood," NBC, 1960; "Perry Como's Kraft Music Hall," NBC, 1960; "The New Steve Allen Show," ABC, 1961; "The Ed Sullivan Show," CBS, 1962; "Play Your Hunch," NBC, 1962; "The Jack Benny Program," CBS, 1963; "The Merv Griffin Show," NBC, 1963; "Jonathan Winters Special," NBC, 1964; "The Andy Williams Show," NBC, 1966; "Bob Hope Chrysler Theatre: The Sister and the Savage," NBC, 1966; "The Dean Martin Show," NBC, 1967; "The Mike Douglas Show," SYN, 1968; "The Ed Sullivan Show," CBS, 1969; "The Toni Tennille Show," SYN, 1981.

FRANCIS, GENIE

b. Englewood, NJ, May 26, 1962. Soap goddess, Laura on "General Hospital."

AS A REGULAR: "General Hospital," ABC, 1975-81, 1983-84; "Bare Essence," NBC, 1983; "Days of Our Lives," NBC, 1987-89; "All My Children," ABC, 1990- .

AND: "Murder, She Wrote: Birds of a Feather," CBS, 1984; "Hotel: Outsiders," ABC, 1984; "Murder, She Wrote: Corned Beef and Carnage," CBS, 1986; "The New Mike Hammer: Body Shot," CBS, 1987.

TV MOVIES AND MINISERIES: "Bare Essence," CBS, 1982; "North and South," ABC, 1985; "North and South, Book II," ABC, 1986.

FRANCIS, IVOR

b. Canada, 1918; d. 1986. White-haired, bespectacled actor who often played fussy types; the father of Genie Francis.

AS A REGULAR: "Bright Promise," NBC, 1969-72; "Room 222," ABC, 1969-72; "Dusty's Trail," SYN, 1973-74.

AND: "The Flying Nun: The Landlord Cometh," ABC, 1969; "Get Smart: Hurray for Hollywood," NBC, 1969; "Judd for the Defense: The View From the Ivy Tower," ABC, 1969; "The Flying Nun: When Generations Gap," ABC, 1970; "The Mary Tyler Moore Show: The Snow Must Go On," CBS, 1970; "The Bold Ones: Lisa, I Hardly Knew You," NBC, 1972; "Night Gallery: Little Girl Lost," NBC, 1972; "Maude: Maude and the Radical," CBS, 1972; "The Mod Squad: Eyes of the Beholder," ABC, 1972; "The Partridge Family: Heartbreak Keith," ABC, 1973; "Adam's Rib: Murder!," ABC, 1973; "Kojak: Deliver Us Some Evil," CBS, 1974; "Kung Fu: The Passion of Cher Yi," ABC, 1974; "Hawaii Five-O: I'll Kill 'Em Again," CBS, 1974; "Bronk: Cancelled," CBS, 1976; "Barney Miller: The Recluse," ABC, 1976; "Quincy: The Two Sides of Truth," NBC, 1977; "Fish: Fish Behind Bars," ABC, 1977; "Barnaby Jones: Duet for Dying," CBS, 1977; "Lou Grant: Pack," CBS, 1980; "Barney Miller: The Tontine," ABC, 1982; "Barney Miller: Bones," ABC, 1982.

TV MOVIES AND MINISERIES: "Hunters Are for Killing," CBS, 1970; "Killer by Night," CBS, 1972; "The Eyes of Charles Sand," ABC, 1972; "The Night Strangler," ABC, 1973; "Outrage!," ABC, 1973; "The Return of the World's Greatest Detective," NBC, 1976.

FRANCISCUS, JAMES

b. Clayton, MO, January 31, 1934; d. 1991 Clean-cut actor who, as young and idealistic John Novak, was to high school teaching what "Dr. Kildare" was to medicine.

AS A REGULAR: "Naked City," ABC, 1958-59; "The Investigators," CBS, 1961; "Mr. Novak," NBC, 1963-65; "Longstreet," ABC, 1971-72; "Doc Elliot," ABC, 1974; "Hunter," CBS, 1977.

AND: "Studio One: A Walk in the Forest," CBS, 1957; "Studio One: Kurishiki Incident," CBS, 1958; "Have Gun, Will Travel: Deliver the Body," CBS, 1958; "The Millionaire: Millionaire Margaret Stoneham," CBS, 1960; "Wagon Train: The Benjamin Burns Story," NBC, 1960; "Hennesey: Annapolis Man," CBS, 1960; "The Deputy: Mother and Son," NBC, 1960; "Alfred Hitchcock Presents: Summer Shade," NBC, 1961; "The du Pont Show with June Allyson: The Guilty Heart," CBS, 1961; "G.E. Theatre: Love Is a Lion's Roar," CBS, 1961; "The Americans: The Invaders," NBC, 1961; "Ben Casey: So Oft It Chances in Particular Men," ABC, 1962; "Dr. Kildare: Jail Ward," NBC, 1963; "The Eleventh Hour: Hang by One Hand," NBC, 1963; "The Tonight Show Starring Johnny Carson," NBC, 1963; "Twelve O'Clock High: Cross Hairs of Death," ABC, 1966; "Combat: The Gun," ABC, 1966; "Combat!: Decision," ABC, 1966; "The FBI: Force of Nature," ABC, 1967; "Judd for the Defense: The Devil's Surrogate," ABC, 1968; "The FBI: Out of Control," ABC, 1968; "Ghost Story: At the Cradle Foot," NBC, 1972; "Liars Club," SYN, 1978.

TV MOVIES AND MINISERIES: "Shadow Over Elveron," NBC, 1968; "Trial Run," NBC, 1969; "Night Slaves," ABC, 1970; "Longstreet," ABC, 1971; "The 500-Pound Jerk," CBS, 1973; "Aloha Means Goodbye," CBS, 1974; "The Dream Makers," NBC, 1975; "The Trial of Chaplain Jensen," ABC, 1975; "One of My Wives Is Missing," ABC, 1976; "The Pirate," CBS, 1978; "Secrets of Three Hungry Wives," NBC, 1978; "Nightkill," NBC, 1980; "Jacqueline Bouvier Kennedy," ABC, 1981; "Secret Weapons," NBC, 1985.

* Franciscus played a John F. Kennedy-style politican in the film "The Greek Tycoon" and Kennedy himself in "Jacqueline Bouvier Kennedy."

FRANK, GARY

b. Spokane, WA, October 9, 1950. Emmy

winning actor best known as that nice Willie Lawrence on "Family."

AS A REGULAR: "General Hospital," ABC, 1973; "Sons and Daughters," CBS, 1974; "Family," ABC, 1976-80.

AND: "Medical Center: The Fourth Sex," CBS, 1975; "The Streets of San Francisco: The Thrill Killers," ABC, 1976; "Hill Street Blues: Midway to What?," NBC, 1983; "Hill Street Blues: Honk if You're a Goose," NBC, 1983; "Remington Steele: Steele Framed," NBC, 1983; "Remington Steele: Stronger Than Steele," NBC, 1985; "Magnum, P.I.: Murder by Night," CBS, 1986; "The Last Precinct: Never Cross a Vampire," NBC, 1986; "Scarecrow and Mrs. King: It's in the Water," CBS, 1986; "Hunter: Dead on Target," NBC, 1988; "Matlock: The Clown," NBC, 1989.

TV MOVIES AND MINISERIES: "Senior Year," CBS, 1974; "The Night the City Screamed," ABC, 1980; "Midnight Lace," NBC, 1981.

* Emmies: 1977.

FRANKENHEIMER, JOHN

b. Malba, NY, February 19, 1930. Director of top-notch fifties TV drama who migrated to movies.

AS DIRECTOR: "Playhouse 90," CBS, 1956-59; "Studio One: The Last Summer," CBS, 1958; "Du Pont Show of the Month: The Browning Version," CBS, 1959; "Sunday Showcase: People Kill People Sometimes," NBC, 1959; "Startime: The Turn of the Screw," NBC, 1959; "Buick Electra Playhouse: The Fifth Column," CBS, 1960; "Buick Electra Playhouse: The Snows of Kilimanjaro," CBS, 1960; "Sunday Showcase: The American," NBC, 1960.

* Among Frankenheimer's "Playhouse 90" credits: "The Comedian," Rod Serling's drama with Mickey Rooney as an abrasive TV comic; "The Death of Manolete"; "Eloise"; "For Whom the Bell Tolls."

* In January 1959, Frankenheimer chased a kid away who'd wandered onto a "Playhouse 90" set at CBS Television City. The kid happened to be headed for a taping of "Art Linkletter's House Party," and that led to a feud with Linkletter, who, on the air, called Frankenheimer "a young genius who takes himself too seriously."

FRANKLIN, BONNIE

b. Santa Monica, CA, January 6, 1944. Pert actress who played divorcee Ann Romano on the amazingly successful "One Day at a Time"; no relation whatsoever to Aretha.

AS A REGULAR: "One Day at a Time," CBS, 1975-84.

AND: "Du Pont Theatre: The Man From St. Paul," ABC, 1957; "Mr. Novak: The People Doll: You Wind It Up and It Makes Mistakes," NBC, 1964;

"Gidget: Chivalry Isn't Dead, It's Just Hiding," ABC, 1965; "Please Don't Eat the Daisies: Very, Very Huckleberry," NBC, 1965; "Gidget: Too Many Cooks," ABC, 1965; "The Man From UNCLE: The Gazebo in the Maze Affair," NBC, 1965; "Please Don't Eat the Daisies: Big Man on Campus," NBC, 1966; "Please Don't Eat the Daisies: Night of Knights," NBC, 1966; "The Munsters: Herman's Sorority Caper," CBS, 1966; "The Man From UNCLE: The Her Master's Voice Affair," NBC, 1966; "Match Game '77," CBS, 1977; "The Love Boat: The Captain and the Lady," ABC, 1977; "The Mary Tyler Moore Hour," CBS, 1979; "Hollywood Squares," SYN, 1980.

TV MOVIES AND MINISERIES: "The Law," NBC, 1974; "A Guide for the Married Woman," ABC, 1978; "Portrait of a Rebel: Margaret Sanger," CBS, 1980; "Your Place or Mine," CBS, 1983; "Sister Margaret and the Saturday Night Ladies," CBS, 1987.

FRANKLIN, HUGH

b. 1916; d. 1986. Actor who played Dr. Charles Tyler on "All My Children."

AS A REGULAR: "Young Doctor Malone," NBC, 1958-63; "All My Children," ABC, 1970-83, 1985.

TV MOVIES AND MINISERIES: "The Borgia Stick," NBC, 1967.

FRANN, MARY

b. Mary Luecke, St. Louis, MO, February 27, 1943. Attractive actress who played Joanna Loudon, Bob Newhart's second TV wife.

AS A REGULAR: "Return to Peyton Place," NBC, 1972-74; "Days of Our Lives," NBC, 1974-79; "King's Crossing," ABC, 1982; "Newhart," CBS, 1982-90.

AND: "The Mary Tyler Moore Show: Some of My Best Friends Are Rhoda," CBS, 1972; "Hawaii Five-O: Little Girl Blue," CBS, 1973; "The FBI: Confessions of a Madman," ABC, 1974; "Apple's Way: The Circus," CBS, 1974; "The Rockford Files: Counter Gambit," NBC, 1975; "The Rockford Files: A Fast Count," NBC, 1978; "WKRP in Cincinnati: Dr. Fever and Mr. Tide," CBS, 1981; "Nero Wolfe: Wolfe at the Door," NBC, 1981; "Hotel: Missing Pieces," ABC, 1985; "The New Mike Hammer: A Face in the Night," CBS, 1987; "Animal Crack-Ups," ABC, 1989; "The Pat Sajak Show," CBS, 1989.

TV MOVIES AND MINISERIES: "Portrait of an Escort," CBS, 1980; "Eight Is Enough: A Family Reunion," NBC, 1987; "Dance 'Til Dawn," NBC, 1988; "Single Women, Married Men," CBS, 1989.

FRANZ, DENNIS

b. Chicago, IL, October 28, 1944. Actor who

excels at sleazy types, most notably as Det. Norman Buntz on "Hill Street Blues" and a short-lived spinoff.

AS A REGULAR: "Chicago Story," NBC, 1982; "The Bay City Blues," NBC, 1983; "Hill Street Blues," NBC, 1983-87; "Beverly Hills Buntz," NBC, 1987-88.

AND: "Hardcastle and McCormick: Did You See the One That Got Away?," ABC, 1984; "Riptide: Double Your Pleasure," NBC, 1984; "The A-Team: Chopping Spree," NBC, 1984; "E/R: The Sister," CBS, 1984; "Hunter: The Snow Queen," NBC, 1985; "MacGruder and Loud: The Odds Favor Death," ABC, 1985; "The A-Team: The Big Squeeze," NBC, 1985; "Hardcastle and McCormick: There Goes the Neighborhood," ABC, 1985; "Simon & Simon: Dark Side of the Street," CBS, 1985; "Matlock: The Mayor," NBC, 1989; "Christine Cromwell: Easy Come, Easy Go," ABC, 1989.

TV MOVIES AND MINISERIES: "The Chicago Story," NBC, 1981; "Deadly Messages," ABC, 1985; "Kiss Shot," CBS, 1989.

FRAWLEY, WILLIAM
b. Burlington, IA, February 26, 1887; d. 1966. Comic actor who rose from vaudeville through movies to television, settling in for long runs as the irascible Fred Mertz on "I Love Lucy" and the irascible Michael Francis "Bub" O'Casey on "My Three Sons."

AS A REGULAR: "The First Hundred Years," CBS, 1950-51; "I Love Lucy," CBS, 1951-57; "The Lucille Ball-Desi Arnaz Show," CBS, 1957-59; "My Three Sons," ABC, 1960-64.

AND: "Silver Theatre: The First Hundred Years," CBS, 1950; "Silver Theatre: Papa Romani," CBS, 1950; "Story Theatre: The Lady or the Tiger," SYN, 1951; "Demi-Tasse Tales: Wedding Morning," CBS, 1953; "Summer Night Theatre: Room for Improvement," SYN, 1954; "The Loretta Young Show: Dear Midge," NBC, 1954; "The Mickey Mouse Club: Spin and Marty," ABC, 1954; "Shower of Stars: High Pitch," CBS, 1955; "Damon Runyon Theatre: Bunny on the Beach," CBS, 1956; "The Bob Hope Show," NBC, 1956; "The Ford Show," NBC, 1957; "The Red Skelton Show," CBS, 1958; "Westinghouse Desilu Playhouse: Comeback," CBS, 1959; "The Gale Storm Show: The Card Sharp," ABC, 1959; "The Red Skelton Show: Freddie's Thanksgiving," CBS, 1960; "This Is Your Life," NBC, 1961; "Summer Playhouse: The Apartment House," CBS, 1964; "The Tonight Show Starring Johnny Carson," NBC, 1965; "The Lucy Show: Lucy and the Countess Have a Horse Guest," CBS, 1965.

FRAZEE, JANE
b. Duluth, MN, 1918; d. 1985.
AS A REGULAR: "Beulah," ABC, 1952-53.

AND: "The Abbott and Costello Show: The Paper Hangers," CBS, 1953; "Death Valley Days: The Rival Hash Houses," SYN, 1954; "Stage 7: Yesterday's Pawn Shop," CBS, 1955; "Matinee Theatre: Tin Wedding," NBC, 1956.

FREBERG, STAN
b. Los Angeles, CA, August 7, 1926. Satirist and comic; he now produces TV commercials.
AS A REGULAR: "The Chevy Show," NBC, 1958.

AND: "The Steve Allen Show," NBC, 1957; "The Frank Sinatra Show," ABC, 1958; "Club Oasis," NBC, 1958; "The Lux Show with Rosemary Clooney," NBC, 1958; "The Andy Williams Show," CBS, 1959; "The Jack Paar Show," NBC, 1961; "Stan Freberg Presents Chinese New Year's Eve," ABC, 1962; "The Jack Paar Program," NBC, 1964; "What's My Line?," CBS, 1964; "The Monkees: Monkee vs. Machine," NBC, 1966; "Everybody's Talking," ABC, 1967; "Amazing Stories: Family Dog," NBC, 1987.

FREED, ALAN
b. Johnstown, PA, December 15, 1922; d. 1965. Rock 'n' roll deejay.
AS A REGULAR: "Rock 'n' Roll," ABC, 1957; "The Big Beat," ABC, 1957.

AND: "Three O'Clock Hop," ABC, 1958.

FREEMAN, AL JR.
b. Albert Cornelius Freeman Jr., San Antonio, TX, March 21, 1934. Emmy winning actor who plays Capt. Ed Hall on "One Life to Live."
AS A REGULAR: "Hot L Baltimore," ABC, 1975; "One Life to Live," ABC, 1972- .

AND: "The Doctors and the Nurses: A Couple of Dozen Tiny Pills," CBS, 1965; "The Defenders: Nobody Asks You What Side You're On," CBS, 1965; "Mr. Novak: There's a Penguin in My Garden," NBC, 1965; "Slattery's People: What's a Swan Song for a Sparrow?," CBS, 1965; "The FBI: The Enemies," ABC, 1968; "The Merv Griffin Show," SYN, 1968; "Judd for the Defense: The View From the Ivy Tower," ABC, 1969; "On Being Black: Basis of Need," NET, 1969; "NET Playhouse: To Be Young, Gifted and Black," NET, 1972; "Maude: Speed Trap," CBS, 1974; "Hollywood Television Theatre: The Chicago Conspiracy Trial," PBS, 1975; "Kojak: A Need to Know," CBS, 1976; "The Cosby Show: Back to the Track, Jack," NBC, 1985.

TV MOVIES AND MINISERIES: "My Sweet Charlie," NBC, 1970; "King," NBC, 1978; "Roots: The Next Generations," ABC, 1979.
* Emmies: 1979.

FREEMAN, KATHLEEN
b. Chicago, IL, February 17, 1919. Character actress, usually in battle-axe roles.
AS A REGULAR: "Topper," CBS, 1953-54; "Mayor

330

of the Town," SYN, 1954; "It's About Time," CBS, 1966-67; "The Beverly Hillbillies," CBS, 1969-71; "Funny Face," CBS, 1971; "Lotsa Luck," NBC, 1973-74.

AND: "The Loretta Young Show: Inga," NBC, 1956; "The Donna Reed Show: Have Fun," ABC, 1959; "The Donna Reed Show: The Grateful Patient," ABC, 1959; "77 Sunset Strip: The Widow and the Web," ABC, 1959; "Hawaiian Eye: And Then There Were Three," ABC, 1960; "Bus Stop: The Man From Bootstrap," ABC, 1961; "Margie: Flaming Youth," ABC, 1962; "Robert Taylor's Detectives: Pandora's Box," NBC, 1962; "Margie: The Dangerous Age," ABC, 1962; "Laramie: Justice in a Hurry," NBC, 1962; "The Beverly Hillbillies: The Clampetts in Court," CBS, 1963; "The Lucy Show: Lucy Plays Florence Nightingale," CBS, 1964; "The Dick Van Dyke Show: Honeymoons Are for the Lucky," CBS, 1964; "The Lucy Show: Lucy Gets Her Maid," CBS, 1964; "The Bing Crosby Show: Real Estate Venture," ABC, 1965; "The Dick Van Dyke Show: Never Bathe on Saturday," CBS, 1965; "The Beverly Hillbillies: A Real Nice Neighbor," CBS, 1965; "Hogan's Heroes: Cupid Comes to Stalag 13," CBS, 1966; "Hey, Landlord!: The Big Fumble," NBC, 1966; "The Smothers Brothers Show: Her Number Is 36-22-35," CBS, 1966; "Gomer Pyle, USMC: Hit and Write," CBS, 1969; "Hogan's Heroes: Watch the Trains Go By," CBS, 1969; "Gomer Pyle, USMC: I'm Always Chasing Gomers," CBS, 1969; "The Bill Cosby Show: A Word From Our Sponsor," NBC, 1969; "Love, American Style: Love and the Doorknob," ABC, 1969; "Hogan's Heroes: Unfair Exchange," CBS, 1969; "The Beverly Hillbillies: The Clampetts in Washington," CBS, 1970; "The Beverly Hillbillies: Jed Buys the Capitol," CBS, 1970; "Kolchak, the Night Stalker: The Youth Killer," ABC, 1975; "Kojak: Case Without a File," CBS, 1977; "My Sister Sam: Patti's Party," CBS, 1986; "Growing Pains: Birth of a Seaver," ABC, 1988; "ALF: Alone Again, Naturally," NBC, 1988; "L.A. Law: Izzy Ackerman, Or Is He Not?," NBC, 1989; "TV 101: First Love," CBS, 1989; "Mr. Belvedere: Fear of Flying," ABC, 1989; "Head of the Class: Arvid Nose Best," ABC, 1989.

TV MOVIES AND MINISERIES: "But I Don't Want to Get Married!," ABC, 1970; "Call Her Mom," ABC, 1972; "Hitched," NBC, 1973.

FREEMAN, MORGAN

Actor ("Driving Miss Daisy") who began on stage and on TV; he played Easy Reader on "The Electric Company."

AS A REGULAR: "The Electric Company," PBS, 1972-76; "Another World," NBC, 1982-84.

AND: "New York Television Theatre: Hard Travelin'," NET, 1969.

TV MOVIES AND MINISERIES: "ABC Theatre:

Attica," ABC, 1980; "The Atlanta Child Murders," CBS, 1985; "Resting Place," CBS, 1986; "Fight for Life," ABC, 1987.

FREES, PAUL

b. Chicago, IL, June 22, 1920; d. 1986. Actor who provided the voice for two TV stalwarts, among others—the unseen John Beresford Tipton, who gave someone a million dollars each week, and Boris Badenov.

AS A REGULAR: "The Millionaire," CBS, 1955-60; "The Bullwinkle Show," NBC, 1961-62; "Calvin and the Colonel," ABC, 1961-62; "The Famous Adventures of Mr. Magoo," NBC, 1964-65.

AND: "The Adventures of Jim Bowie: German George," ABC, 1958; "Mr. Magoo's Christmas Carol," NBC, 1962.

FRENCH, VICTOR

b. Santa Barbara, CA, December 4, 1934; d. 1989. Actor long associated with Michael Landon, playing the same kind of gentle giants Dan Blocker might have played: Isiah Edwards on "Little House" and Mark Gordon on "Highway to Heaven."

AS A REGULAR: "Get Smart," NBC, 1965-69; CBS, 1969-70; "The Hero," NBC, 1966-67; "Little House on the Prairie," NBC, 1974-77, 1982-83; "Carter Country," ABC, 1977-79; "Highway to Heaven," NBC, 1984-89.

AND: "Hazel: A Matter of Principle," NBC, 1961; "The Virginian: The Accomplice," NBC, 1962; "The Virginian: The Secret of Brymar Hall," NBC, 1964; "No Time for Sergeants: The $100,000 Canteen," ABC, 1964; "My Favorite Martian: Loralie Brown vs. Everybody," CBS, 1965; "The Wild Wild West: The Night of a Thousand Eyes," CBS, 1965; "Batman: Zelda the Great/A Death Worse Than Fate," ABC, 1966; "Captain Nice: The Week They Stole Payday," NBC, 1967; "F Troop: The Day They Shot Agarn," ABC, 1967; "The Beverly Hillbillies: Robin Hood and the Sheriff," CBS, 1967; "The FBI: False Witness," ABC, 1967; "Gunsmoke: Vengeance," CBS, 1967; "Gunsmoke: Major Glory," CBS, 1967; "Gunsmoke: Hill Girl," CBS, 1968; "Gunsmoke: Uncle Finney," CBS, 1968; "Gunsmoke: O'Quillian," CBS, 1968; "Mission: Impossible: Trial by Fury," CBS, 1968; "The FBI: Moment of Truth," ABC, 1969; "Mannix: Figures in a Landscape," CBS, 1970; "Gunsmoke: Kiowa," CBS, 1970; "Gunsmoke: Trafton," CBS, 1971; "Mission: Impossible: The Tram," CBS, 1971; "The Streets of San Francisco: Death-watch," ABC, 1973; "The Rookies: Deadly Cage," ABC, 1973; "Gunsmoke: The Tarnished Badge," CBS, 1974; "Gunsmoke: The Sharecrop-pers," CBS, 1974; "Little House on the Prairie: The Christmas They Never Forgot," NBC, 1981.

TV MOVIES AND MINISERIES: "Cutter's Trail," CBS,

1970; "The Tribe," NBC, 1974; "Amateur Night at the Dixie Bar and Grill," NBC, 1979; "The Golden Moment: An Olympic Love Story," NBC, 1980; "Little House: Look Back to Yesterday," NBC, 1983; "Little House: Bless All the Dear Children," NBC, 1984.

FREWER, MATT
Actor who got his start as that next big thing that only lasted about ten minutes, computer-animated wiseguy Max Headroom.
AS A REGULAR: "Max Headroom," SHO, 1985-87; ABC, 1987; "Doctor, Doctor," CBS, 1989- .
AND: "Miami Vice: Redemption in Blood," NBC, 1988; "Miami Vice: Hostile Takeover," NBC, 1988.

FREY, LEONARD
b. Brooklyn, NY, September 4, 1938; d. 1988. Thin actor often in priggish comic roles; fondly remembered as town bad guy Parker Tillman on "Best of the West."
AS A REGULAR: "Best of the West," ABC, 1981-82; "Mr. Smith," NBC, 1983; "Mr. Sunshine," ABC, 1986.
AND: "Mission: Impossible: Mindbend," CBS, 1971; "Shaft: The Killing," CBS, 1973; "Medical Center: Girl From Bedlam," CBS, 1974; "The Mary Tyler Moore Show: Ted Baxter's Famous Broadcaster's School," CBS, 1975; "Barney Miller: Escape Artist," ABC, 1975; "Barney Miller: Vanished," ABC, 1980.
TV MOVIES AND MINISERIES: "Shirts/Skins," ABC, 1973; "Testimony of Two Men," SYN, 1977.

FRID, JONATHAN
Barnabas Collins, vampire.
AS A REGULAR: "Dark Shadows," ABC, 1966-71.
TV MOVIES AND MINISERIES: "The Devil's Daughter," ABC, 1973.

FRIDELL, SQUIRE
b. Oakland, CA, February 9, 1943. Actor who's best known to TV audiences as the fresh-faced guy on the Toyota commercials.
AS A REGULAR: "Rosetti and Ryan," NBC, 1977.
AND: "The Ropers: Days of Beer and Rosie," ABC, 1979; "M*A*S*H: Identity Crisis," CBS, 1981.
TV MOVIES AND MINISERIES: "The Strangers in 7A," CBS, 1972; "Human Feelings," NBC, 1978.

FRIEBUS, FLORIDA
Actress who played the mom of Dobie Gillis, and Mrs. Bakerman, the woman who knitted during group therapy on "The Bob Newhart Show."
AS A REGULAR: "The Many Loves of Dobie Gillis," CBS, 1959-63; "The Bob Newhart Show," CBS, 1972-78.

AND: "The Joseph Cotten Show: The Gentle Voice of Murder," NBC, 1957; "Father Knows Best: Big Sister," CBS, 1959; "Chevy Mystery Show: Summer Hero," NBC, 1960; "My Mother the Car: My Son the Judge," NBC, 1965; "The Mary Tyler Moore Show: Room 223," CBS, 1971; "Sanford & Son: The Suitcase Case," NBC, 1972; "The Mary Tyler Moore Show: Operation: Lou," CBS, 1972; "The Partridge Family: The Diplomat," ABC, 1973; "Barnaby Jones: Murder-Go-Round, " CBS, 1973; "Cannon: Catch Me If You Can," CBS, 1973; "The Rookies: Prayers Unanswered, Prayers Unheard," ABC, 1973; "Chico and the Man: Garage Sale," NBC, 1975; "Rhoda: Brenda Runs Away," CBS, 1978.
TV MOVIES AND MINISERIES: "G.E. Theatre: Miles to Go Before I Sleep," CBS, 1975.

FRISCHMAN, DAN
b. Whippany, NJ. Actor who plays Arvid Engen on "Head of the Class."
AS A REGULAR: "Head of the Class," ABC, 1986- .
AND: "The Facts of Life: Kids Can Be Cruel," NBC, 1982; "Webster: Who's to Blame," ABC, 1985; "Animal Crack-Ups," ABC, 1989.

FRIZZELL, LOU
b. 1920; d. 1979. Pudgy actor who usually played old-shoe characters.
AS A REGULAR: "Bonanza," NBC, 1970-72; "Chopper One," ABC, 1974; "The New Land," ABC, 1974.
AND: "Armstrong Circle Theatre: The Antique Swindle," CBS, 1960; "Armstrong Circle Theatre: Moment of Panic," CBS, 1961; "Profiles in Courage: The Robert Taft Story," NBC, 1965; "The FBI: Crisis Ground," ABC, 1968; "The FBI: The Quarry," ABC, 1968; "Owen Marshall, Counselor at Law: Eulogy for a Wide Receiver," ABC, 1971; "Owen Marshall, Counselor at Law: Until Proven Innocent," ABC, 1971; "The FBI: The Runner," ABC, 1972; "Marcus Welby, M.D.: A Question of Fault," ABC, 1973; "The FBI: Break-in," ABC, 1973; "Hawaii Five-O: Little Girl Blue," CBS, 1973; "Barnaby Jones: Murder-Go-Round," CBS, 1973; "Barnaby Jones: Programmed for Killing," CBS, 1974; "The Streets of San Francisco: The Victims," ABC, 1974; "The Streets of San Francisco: The Glass Dart Board," ABC, 1975; "Harry O: Portrait of a Murder," ABC, 1975; "The Streets of San Francisco: No Minor Vices," ABC, 1976; "Police Story: Odyssey of Death," NBC, 1976; "Barnaby Jones: Anatomy of Fear," CBS, 1977; "Alice: The Principal of the Thing," CBS, 1978; "Alice: The Fourth Time Around," CBS, 1979.
TV MOVIES AND MINISERIES: "Footsteps," CBS, 1972; "Runaway!," ABC, 1973; "Letters From Three Lovers," ABC, 1973; "Money to Burn," ABC, 1973; "Crossfire," NBC, 1975; "Returning Home," ABC, 1975; "Devil Dog:

The Hound of Hell," CBS, 1978; "Steel Cowboy," NBC, 1978; "Centennial," NBC, 1978-79.

FROMAN, JANE
b. *St. Louis, MO, November 10, 1907.* Singer who had her legs crushed in a World War II plane crash; she wrote a book, "With a Song in My Heart," about her recovery, and her career was revived when Susan Hayward played her in the movies.
AS A REGULAR: "Jane Froman's USA Canteen," CBS, 1952-55.
AND: "Texaco Star Theatre," NBC, 1955; "Bell Telephone Hour: Our Musical Ambassadors," NBC, 1960; "Arthur Murray Party," NBC, 1960; "The Ed Sullivan Show," CBS, 1960; "The Jack Paar Show," NBC, 1960.

FROST, DAVID
b. *Tenterden, England, Apr. 7, 1939.* Personality whose talk-show was a hot item in the late sixties; he brought "That Was the Week That Was" over from England.
AS A REGULAR: "That Was the Week That Was," NBC, 1964-65; "The David Frost Show," SYN, 1969-72; "The David Frost Revue," SYN, 1971-73; "Headliners with David Frost," NBC, 1978.
AND: "The Merv Griffin Show," SYN, 1968; "The Tonight Show Starring Johnny Carson," NBC, 1968; "Petula," ABC, 1970; "The Carol Burnett Show," CBS, 1971; "Here's Lucy: Lucy Helps David Frost Go Night-Night," CBS, 1971.
TV MOVIES AND MINISERIES: "Agatha Christie's Thirteen at Dinner," CBS, 1985.

FRYE, DAVID
b. *Brooklyn, NY, 1934.* Impressionist who did a mean Richard Nixon.
AS A GUEST: "Operation: Entertainment," ABC, 1968; "The Ed Sullivan Show," CBS, 1968; "The Tonight Show Starring Johnny Carson," NBC, 1968; "Kraft Music Hall," NBC, 1970; "ABC Comedy Hour," ABC, 1972; "The Tonight Show Starring Johnny Carson," NBC, 1973.

FRYE, SOLEIL MOON
b. *Glendora, CA, August 6, 1976.* Young actress.
AS A REGULAR: "Punky Brewster," NBC, 1984-86.
AND: "MacGruder and Loud: A Very Scary Man," ABC, 1985; "Cadets," ABC, 1988; "Animal Crack-Ups," ABC, 1989.
TV MOVIES AND MINISERIES: "Invitation to Hell," ABC, 1984.
* "Invitation to Hell" was not about visiting a taping of "Punky Brewster."

FUJIKAWA, HATSUO "JERRY"
b. *1911; d. 1983.*
AS A REGULAR: "Mr. T. and Tina," ABC, 1976;
AND: "Hong Kong: Murder by Proxy," ABC, 1961; "Bachelor Father: A Party for Peter," ABC, 1961; "The Twilight Zone: A Quality of Mercy," CBS, 1961; "The Untouchables: Kiss of Death," ABC, 1963; "The Man From UNCLE: The Cherry Blossom Affair," NBC, 1965; "I Spy: Always Say Goodbye," NBC, 1966; "Green Acres: Lisa's Mudder Comes for a Visit," CBS, 1969; "M*A*S*H: The Chosan People," CBS, 1974; "M*A*S*H: Officer of the Day," CBS, 1974; "M*A*S*H: Love and Marriage," CBS, 1975; "M*A*S*H: Back Pay," CBS, 1980; "Taxi: Louie's Mom Remarries," ABC, 1981; "M*A*S*H: The Birthday Girls," CBS, 1982.

FULLER, PENNY
b. *Durham, NC, 1940.* Actress usually in take-charge roles; an Emmy winner for "The Elephant Man."
AS A REGULAR: "The Edge of Night," CBS, 1964; "Bare Essence," NBC, 1983; "Fortune Dane," ABC, 1986.
AND: "Route 66: Welcome to the Wedding," CBS, 1962; "Love, American Style: Love and the Watchdog," ABC, 1969; "The FBI: The Doll Courier," ABC, 1969; "The FBI: The Deadly Species," ABC, 1972; "The Bob Newhart Show: Goodnight, Nancy," CBS, 1972; "The FBI: The Wedding Gift," ABC, 1973; "Love, American Style: Love and the Teller's Tale," ABC, 1973; "Marcus Welby, M.D.: The Comeback," ABC, 1973; "Barnaby Jones: The Platinum Connection," CBS, 1974; "Ann in Blue," ABC, 1974; "Medical Center: The Invisible Wife," CBS, 1975; "Barnaby Jones: Poisoned Pigeon," CBS, 1975; "McNaughton's Daughter: The Smashed Lady," NBC, 1976; "Newhart: The Senator's Wife Was Indiscreet," CBS, 1982; "Simon & Simon: Design for Murder," CBS, 1983; "The Love Boat: Julie and the Bachelor," ABC, 1983; "The Love Boat: Joint Custody," ABC, 1985; "Matlock: The Gigolo," NBC, 1988; "Murder, She Wrote: Mourning Among the Wisterias," CBS, 1988; "China Beach: The World," ABC, 1989.
TV MOVIES AND MINISERIES: "Women in Chains," ABC, 1972; "Amber Waves," ABC, 1980; "ABC Theatre of the Month: The Elephant Man," ABC, 1982; "Lois Gibbs and the Love Canal," CBS, 1982; "Your Place or Mine," CBS, 1983; "Intimate Agony," ABC, 1983; "George Washington II: The Forging of a Nation," CBS, 1986; "The Two Mrs. Grenvilles," NBC, 1987; "At Mother's Request," CBS, 1987.
* Emmies: 1982.

FULLER, ROBERT

b. *Troy, NY, July 29, 1933.* Rugged actor who played Jess Harper on "Laramie," Cooper Smith on "Wagon Train" and Dr. Kelly Brackett on "Emergency!"

AS A REGULAR: "Laramie," NBC, 1959-63; "Wagon Train," ABC, 1963-65; "Emergency!," NBC, 1972-77.

AND: "Buckskin: The Trial of Chrissy Miller," NBC, 1958; "The Californians: Pipeline," NBC, 1958; "No Warning!: Survivors," NBC, 1958; "Lux Playhouse: Coney Island Winter," CBS, 1958; "Restless Gun: Peligroso," NBC, 1958; "Mickey Spillane's Mike Hammer: I Ain't Talking," SYN, 1958; "Restless Gun: Shadow of a Gunfighter," NBC, 1958; "Wagon Train: The Ella Lindstrom Story," NBC, 1959; "Alcoa Presents One Step Beyond: Emergency Only," ABC, 1959; "Cimarron City: Blind Is the Killer," NBC, 1959; "Wagon Train: The Kate Parker Story," NBC, 1959; "The Lawless Years: The Cutie Jaffe Story," NBC, 1959; "Here's Hollywood," NBC, 1961; "High Hopes," SYN, 1961; "Alcoa Premiere: The Hour of the Bath," ABC, 1962; "Kraft Supsense Theatre: Jungle Fear," NBC, 1965; "Bob Hope Chrysler Theatre: Massacre at Ft. Phil Kearney," NBC, 1966; "The Virginian: A Welcoming Town," NBC, 1967; "The Big Valley: A Flock of Trouble," ABC, 1967; "Dan August: The Titan," ABC, 1971; "The Men From Shiloh: Flight From Memory," NBC, 1971; "Adam 12: Emergency!," NBC, 1972; "The Wonderful World of Disney: Carb, the Sierra Coyote," NBC, 1974; "Hollywood Squares," NBC, 1974; "Dinah!," SYN, 1975; "The Magnificent Marble Machine," NBC, 1976; "Hollywood Squares," SYN, 1980; "The Love Boat: A Business Affair," ABC, 1982; "The Love Boat: Her Honor the Mayor," ABC, 1985; "Finder of Lost Loves: Tricks," ABC, 1985; "Blacke's Magic: Vanishing Act," NBC, 1986; "Murder, She Wrote: The Body Politic," CBS, 1988.

TV MOVIES AND MINISERIES: "Emergency!," NBC, 1972; "Donner Pass: The Road to Survival," NBC, 1978; "Disaster on the Coastliner," ABC, 1979; "Bonanza: The Next Generation," SYN, 1988.

FULTON, EILEEN

b. *Margaret Elizabeth McLarty, Asheville, NC, September 13, 1933.* Actress who plays Lisa on "As the World Turns," who's been married so often we don't have space to list all her last names.

AS A REGULAR: "As the World Turns," CBS, 1960- ; "Our Private World," CBS, 1965.

AND: "Naked City: The Face of the Enemy," ABC, 1962.

* Fulton left "As the World Turns" for a time in 1983 because the writers were about to make her character a grandmother. Then she came back.

FUNICELLO, ANNETTE

b. *Utica, NY, October 22, 1942.* The bustiest Mouseketeer, a young actress idolized by America's girls and lusted after by America's boys in the fifties and sixties.

AS A REGULAR: "The Mickey Mouse Club," ABC, 1956-59; "The Danny Thomas Show," CBS, 1959; "Easy Does It ... Starring Frankie Avalon," CBS, 1976.

AND: "The Dick Clark Saturday Night Beechnut Show," ABC, 1959; "Walt Disney Presents: The Nine Lives of Elfego Baca-Attorney at Law," ABC, 1959; "Walt Disney Presents: The Nine Lives of Elfego Baca-The Griswold Murder," ABC, 1959; "Zorro: Missing Father," ABC, 1959; "The Music Shop," NBC, 1959; "Zorro: Please Believe Me," ABC, 1959; "Zorro: The Brooch," ABC, 1959; "American Bandstand," ABC, 1959; "The Dick Clark Saturday Night Beechnut Show," ABC, 1960; "Coke Time," ABC, 1960; "American Bandstand," ABC, 1960; "Walt Disney Presents: Zorro-The Postponed Wedding," ABC, 1961; "Walt Disney's Wonderful World of Color: The Horsemasters," NBC, 1961; "Walt Disney's Wonderful World of Color: Backstage Party," NBC, 1961; "Walt Disney's Wonderful World of Color: Golden Horseshoe Revue," NBC, 1962; "Concentration," NBC, 1962; "Walt Disney's Wonderful World of Color: Escapade in Florence," NBC, 1962; "Burke's Law: Who Killed the Kind Doctor?," ABC, 1963; "Burke's Law: Who Killed the Strangler?," ABC, 1965; "Hullabaloo," NBC, 1965; "Hondo: Hondo and the Apache Trail," ABC, 1967; "Love, American Style: Love and the Tuba," ABC, 1971; "Dinah!," SYN, 1975; "Fantasy Island: Mary Ann and Miss Sophisticate," ABC, 1980; "The Love Boat: Palimony O'Mine," ABC, 1982; "Growing Pains: The Seavers vs. the Cleavers," ABC, 1986.

TV MOVIES AND MINISERIES: "Lots of Luck," DIS, 1985.

FUNT, ALLEN

b. *Brooklyn, NY, September 16, 1914.* Performer whose long career is attributable more to his gimmick than any personal charm.

AS A REGULAR: "Candid Microphone," ABC, 1948; "Candid Camera," NBC, 1949; CBS, 1949-50; NBC, 1953; CBS, 1960-67; "The Garry Moore Show," CBS, 1959-60; "The New Candid Camera," SYN, 1974-78; "Candid Camera Special," CBS, 1987- .

AND: "The Jack Paar Show," NBC, 1958; "The Jerry Lewis Show," NBC, 1960; "The Garry Moore Show," CBS, 1962; "The Jack Paar Program," NBC, 1963; "The New Phil Silvers Show: Smile, Harry, You're on Candid Camera," CBS, 1964; "The Jack Paar Program," NBC, 1965; "Here's Lucy: Lucy and Candid Camera," CBS, 1971.

AS PRODUCER-CREATOR: "Tell It to the Camera," CBS, 1963-64.

FURLONG, KIRBY

b. Canoga Park, CA, 1963.
AS A REGULAR: "The Jimmy Stewart Show,"
NBC, 1971-72.
AND: "The FBI: Dark Christmas," ABC, 1972;
"Marcus Welby, M.D.: Please Don't Send
Flowers," ABC, 1972; "Medical Center: Crown
of Thorns," CBS, 1975.
TV MOVIES AND MINISERIES: "Off the Minnesota
Strip," ABC, 1980.

FURNESS, BETTY

b. Elizabeth Furness, New York City, NY,
January 3, 1916. Commercial spokeswoman
of the fifties, consumer advocate of the
seventies and eighties.
AS A REGULAR: "Studio One," CBS, 1949-58;
"Penthouse Party," ABC, 1950-51; "Byline,"
ABC, 1951; "Today," NBC, 1975- .
AND: "Studio One: Confessions of a Nervous Man,"
CBS, 1953; "Studio One: Affairs of State," CBS,
1955; "Climax!: Silent Decision," CBS, 1955;
"Studio One: Babe in the Woods," CBS, 1957;
"Art Linkletter's House Party," CBS, 1958;
"Climax!: The Thief with the Big Blue Eyes," CBS,
1958; "To Tell the Truth," CBS, 1962;
"Password," CBS, 1962; "To Tell the Truth,"
CBS, 1964; "Get the Message," ABC, 1964;
"ABC Stage '67: The People Trap," ABC,
1966.

FURST, STEPHEN

b. Norfolk, VA. Pudgy actor who played Dr.
Elliott Axelrod on "St. Elsewhere."
AS A REGULAR: "Delta House," ABC, 1979; "St.
Elsewhere," NBC, 1983-88.
AND: "MacGyver: Renegade," ABC, 1989.
TV MOVIES AND MINISERIES: "If It's Tuesday, It
Still Must Be Belgium," NBC, 1987.

FURTH, GEORGE

b. Chicago, IL, December 14, 1932. Actor

usually in snippy roles; he's turned almost
totally to playwriting.
AS A REGULAR: "Broadside," ABC, 1964-65;
"Tammy," ABC, 1965-66; "The Good Guys,"
CBS, 1968-69; "The Dumplings," NBC, 1976.
AND: "The Defenders: Claire Cheval Died in
Boston," CBS, 1964; "McHale's Navy: The Dart
Gun Wedding," ABC, 1964; "The Farmer's
Daughter: Katy and the Image Maker," ABC,
1964; "Profiles in Courage: The Robert Taft
Story," NBC, 1965; "Honey West: Pop Goes the
Easel," ABC, 1966; "Run for Your Life: In
Search of April," NBC, 1966; "The Road West:
This Dry and Thirsty Land," NBC, 1966;
"Batman: Hizzoner the Penguin/Dizzoner the
Penguin," ABC, 1966; "Run for Your Life: The
Grotenberg Mask," NBC, 1966; "F Troop:
Survival of the Fittest," ABC, 1966; "The
Monkees: One Man Shy," NBC, 1966; "Laredo:
Walk Softly," NBC, 1967; "The Monkees: A
Coffin Too Frequent," NBC, 1967; "Love,
American Style: Love and the Intruder," ABC,
1970; "The Odd Couple: I Do, I Don't," ABC,
1970; "Green Acres: The Ex-Secretary," CBS,
1971; "All in the Family: Archie's Aching Back,"
CBS, 1971; "That Girl: Stag Party," ABC, 1971;
"Bonanza: Rock-a-Bye Hoss," NBC, 1971;
"Love, American Style: Love and the Well-
Groomed Bride," ABC, 1972; "Happy Days:
Goin' to Chicago," ABC, 1975; "Hollywood
Television Theatre: For the Use of the Hall," PBS,
1975; "Ellery Queen: The Twelfth Floor
Express," NBC, 1975; "All in the Family: Mike
Faces Life," CBS, 1975; "Little House on the
Prairie: The Talking Machine," NBC, 1976;
"Murder, She Wrote: No Laughing Matter," CBS,
1987.
TV MOVIES AND MINISERIES: "Fame Is the Name of
the Game," NBC, 1966; "Sam Hill: Who
Killed the Mysterious Mr. Foster?," NBC,
1971; "The Third Girl From the Left," ABC,
1973; "What Are Best Friends For?," ABC,
1973; "Let's Switch," ABC, 1975.

G

GABOR, EVA

b. Budapest, Hungary, February 11, 1926.
Gabor sister who played Lisa Douglas, wife
of Oliver (Eddie Albert) on "Green Acres."

AS A REGULAR: "Green Acres," CBS, 1965-71;
"Petticoat Junction," CBS, 1965-66; "Bridges
to Cross," CBS, 1986.

AND: "Masterpiece Playhouse: Uncle Vanya,"
NBC, 1950; "Story Theatre: Lodging for the
Night," SYN, 1951; "Suspense: This Is Your
Confession," CBS, 1951; "Summer Theatre: At
Mrs. Beam's," CBS, 1951; "Suspense: The
Duel," CBS, 1953; "Studio One: Paul's
Apartment," CBS, 1954; "G.E. Theatre: Ah
There, Beau Brimmel," CBS, 1958; "Matinee
Theatre: Nine-Finger Jack," NBC, 1958; "The
Jack Paar Show," NBC, 1958; "You Asked for
It," ABC, 1958; "The Jack Paar Show," NBC,
1959; "Five Fingers: Station Break," NBC,
1959; "Arthur Murray Party," NBC, 1959;
"Adventures in Paradise: Peril at Pitcairn,"
ABC, 1959; "The Ann Sothern Show: Katy and
the New Girl," CBS, 1959; "The Big Party,"
CBS, 1959; "The Jack Paar Show," NBC, 1960;
"U.S. Steel Hour: How to Make a Killing," CBS,
1960; "Arthur Murray Party," NBC, 1960; "The
Detectives Starring Robert Taylor: The
Retirement of Maria Muir," ABC, 1960; "Here's
Hollywood," NBC, 1960; "Dow Hour of Great
Mysteries: The Great Impersonation," NBC,
1960; "Harrigan and Son: There's No Fool Like
an Old Fool," ABC, 1960; "Person to Person,"
CBS, 1960; "The Ann Sothern Show: The Royal
Visit," CBS, 1961; "Harrigan and Son: They
Were All in Step But Jim," ABC, 1961; "The
Jack Paar Show," NBC, 1961; "The Tonight
Show Starring Johnny Carson," NBC, 1963;
"Burke's Law: Who Killed Harris Crown?,"
ABC, 1963; "To Tell the Truth," CBS, 1964;
"Hollywood Squares," NBC, 1968; "The
Beverly Hillbillies: The Thanksgiving Story,"
CBS, 1968; "The Dean Martin Show," NBC,
1970; "Night Gallery: The Painted Mirror,"
NBC, 1971; "Here's Lucy: Lucy and Eva Gabor
Are Hospital Roommates," CBS, 1972;
"Hollywood Squares," NBC, 1973; "Hollywood
Squares," SYN, 1975; "Tattletales," CBS, 1975;
"Rosetti and Ryan: Ms. Bluebeard," NBC, 1977;
"Hart to Hart: With This Hart I Thee Wed,"
ABC, 1982; "The Love Boat: Mothers Don't Do
That," ABC, 1982; "Hotel: Prisms," ABC, 1984;
"The Love Boat: The Prediction," ABC, 1986.

TV MOVIES AND MINISERIES: "Wake Me When the
War Is Over," ABC, 1969.

* See also "Green Acres."

GABOR, ZSA ZSA

b. Budapest, Hungary, February 6, 1919.
Much-married actress who never learned the
meaning of the word "overexposure."

AS A GUEST: "Climax!: The Great Impersonation,"
CBS, 1955; "Climax!: Man of Taste," CBS,
1955; "G.E. Theatre: The Honest Man," CBS,
1956; "Matinee Theatre: The Tall Dark
Stranger," NBC, 1956; "Ford Theatre: Autumn
Fever," NBC, 1956; "Matinee Theatre: The
Babylonian Heart," NBC, 1956; "The Bob
Cummings Show: Grandpa Meets Zsa Zsa,"
CBS, 1956; "The Ford Show," NBC, 1956;
"The Herb Shriner Show," CBS, 1956;
"Playhouse 90: The Greer Case," CBS, 1957;
"The Life of Riley: Foriegn Intrigue," NBC,
1957; "Playhouse 90: Circle of the Day," CBS,
1957; "Matinee Theatre: The Last Voyage,"
NBC, 1957; "The Rosemary Clooney Show,"
SYN, 1957; "Art Linkletter's House Party,"
CBS, 1957; "Arthur Murray Party," NBC,
1957; "The George Gobel Show," NBC, 1957;
"Matinee Theatre: The Europeans," NBC,
1958; "Shower of Stars," CBS, 1958; "Matinee
Theatre: The Two Mrs. Carrolls," NBC, 1958;
"December Bride: Zsa Zsa Gabor Show," CBS,
1958; "Arthur Murray Party," NBC, 1959;
"The Steve Allen Show," NBC, 1959; "Take a
Good Look," ABC, 1959; "Bob Hope Special,"
NBC, 1959; "Pat Boone Chevy Showroom,"
ABC, 1960; "Special Tonight: Ninotchka,"
ABC, 1960; "Arthur Murray Party," NBC,
1960; "Burke's Law: Who Killed Cable
Roberts?," ABC, 1963; "The Joey Bishop
Show: Zsa Zsa Redecorates the Nursery,"
NBC, 1964; "Burke's Law: Who Killed
Supersleuth?," ABC, 1964; "Bob Hope
Chrysler Theatre: Double Jeopardy," NBC,
1965; "Gilligan's Island: Erika Tiffany
Smith to the Rescue," CBS, 1965; "The
Merv Griffin Show," SYN, 1966; "F Troop:
Play, Gypsy, Play," ABC, 1966; "Alice in
Wonderland," ABC, 1966; "Hollywood
Squares," NBC, 1967; "Bonanza: Maestro
Hoss," NBC, 1967; "My Three Sons: Ernie and
Zsa Zsa," CBS, 1968; "Batman: Minerva,
Mayhem and Millionaires," ABC, 1968; "The
Name of the Game: Fear of High Places,"
NBC, 1968; "The Mike Douglas Show,"
SYN, 1970; "Night Gallery: The Painted
Mirror," NBC, 1971; "The Wacky World
of Jonathan Winters," SYN, 1973; "The
Mike Douglas Show," SYN, 1974; "Dinah!,"
SYN, 1975; "Tattletales," CBS, 1976;
"Supertrain: A Very Formal Heist," NBC,

1979; "The Pat Sajak Show," CBS, 1989.

TV MOVIES AND MINISERIES: "California Girls," ABC, 1985.

* Gabor's 1989 trial on charges of slapping a Beverly Hills cop who'd pulled her over in her Rolls-Royce was covered worldwide, mostly by television. She was found guilty, performed some community service and spent a weekend in jail.
* In 1983, Gabor was appearing at a Philadelphia dinner theatre in "Forty Carats" when she walked off the stage, claiming that a group of handicapped patrons were making too much noise.

GAIL, MAX
b. *Grosse Pointe, MI, April 5, 1943.* Actor who played the dim Sgt. Wojohowicz on "Barney Miller."

AS A REGULAR: "Barney Miller," ABC, 1975-82; "Whiz Kids," CBS, 1983-84; "Normal Life," CBS, 1990.

AND: "Paul Sand in Friends and Lovers: The Big Fight," CBS, 1974; "The Streets of San Francisco: Dead or Alive," ABC, 1976; "The $20,000 Pyramid," ABC, 1976; "Matlock: The Investigation," NBC, 1988.

TV MOVIES AND MINISERIES: "The Priest Killer," CBS, 1971; "Like Mom, Like Me," CBS, 1978; "Desperate Women," NBC, 1978; "Pearl," ABC, 1978; "The 11th Victim," CBS, 1979; "The Aliens Are Coming," NBC, 1980; "Fun and Games," ABC, 1980; "Letting Go," ABC, 1985; "The Other Lover," CBS, 1985; "Killer in the Mirror," NBC, 1986; "Intimate Strangers," CBS, 1986; "Can You Feel Me Dancing?," NBC, 1986; "Tonight's the Night," ABC, 1987; "Man Against the Mob," NBC, 1988; "The Outside Woman," CBS, 1989.

AS DIRECTOR: "Barney Miller: Wojo's Problem," ABC, 1978; "Barney Miller: Accusation," ABC, 1978; "Barney Miller: The Counterfeiter," ABC, 1979; "Barney Miller: Computer Crime," ABC, 1979; "Barney Miller: Bones," ABC, 1982.

GALLAGHER, HELEN
b. *Brooklyn, NY, July 19, 1926.* Actress best known as Maeve Ryan on "Ryan's Hope."

AS A REGULAR: "Manhattan Showcase," CBS, 1949; "Ryan's Hope," ABC, 1975-89.

AND: "Kraft Television Theatre: Pardon My Prisoner," NBC, 1954; "Paris in the Springtime," NBC, 1956; "The Ed Sullivan Show," CBS, 1958; "Arthur Murray Party," NBC, 1958; "Arthur Murray Party," NBC, 1959; "Hallmark Hall of Fame: Shangri-La," NBC, 1960; "Bell Telephone Hour: The Music of Richard Rodgers," NBC, 1961; "Yves Montand Special," ABC, 1961.

GALLAGHER, MEGAN
b. *Pennsylvania, February 6, 1960.* Attractive redheaded actress who played cop Tina Russo on "Hill Street Blues" and Wayloo Marie on "China Beach."

AS A REGULAR: "Dallas," CBS, 1979-81; "Hill Street Blues," NBC, 1986-87; "The Slap Maxwell Story," ABC, 1987-88; "China Beach," ABC, 1988-89.

GALLOWAY, DON
b. *Brooksville, KY, July 27, 1937.* Actor who played Det. Sgt. Ed Brown on "Ironside"; as a performer he's almost as scintillating as that name.

AS A REGULAR: "The Secret Storm," CBS, 1962; "Arrest and Trial," ABC, 1963-64; "Tom, Dick and Mary," NBC, 1964-65; "Ironside," NBC, 1967-75; "The Guiness Game," SYN, 1979-80; "Hizzonner," NBC, 1979.

AND: "The Virginian: The Final Hour," NBC, 1963; "Convoy: The Man with the Saltwater Socks," NBC, 1965; "The John Forsythe Show: Is It a Bird? Is It a Plane? No, It's Miss Culver!," NBC, 1966; "Twelve O'Clock High: 25th Mission," ABC, 1966; "Run for Your Life: In Search of April," NBC, 1966; "The Virginian: The Challenge," NBC, 1966; "Marcus Welby, M.D.: The Girl From Rainbow Beach," ABC, 1970; "Love, American Style: Love and the Doctor's Honeymoon," ABC, 1971; "Love, American Style: Love and the Pretty Secretary," ABC, 1973; "Police Woman: Incident Near a Black and White," NBC, 1975; "Medical Story: A Right to Die," NBC, 1975; "The Life and Times of Grizzly Adams: Adams' Ark," NBC, 1977; "Police Woman: Tigress," NBC, 1978; "Fantasy Island: Mary Ann and Miss Sophisticate," ABC, 1980; "Knight Rider: The Long Way Home," NBC, 1983; "Hotel: Prisms," ABC, 1984; "E/R: Save the Last Dance for Me," CBS, 1984; "Scarecrow and Mrs. King: Odds on a Dead Pigeon," CBS, 1985; "MacGyver: Fraternity of Thieves," ABC, 1989; "Murder, She Wrote: Trevor Hudson's Legacy," CBS, 1989; "Matlock: The Bestseller," NBC, 1989.

TV MOVIES AND MINISERIES: "Ironside," NBC, 1967; "Split Second to an Epitaph," NBC, 1968; "The Priest Killer," CBS, 1971; "Lieutenant Schuster's Wife," ABC, 1972; "Portrait: A Man Named John," ABC, 1973; "This Child Is Mine," ABC, 1973; "You Lie So Deep, My Love," ABC, 1975; "Perry Mason: The Case of the Avenging Ace," NBC, 1988.

GANZEL, TERESA
b. *Toledo, OH, March 23, 1957.* Actress often in naive sexpot roles.

AS A REGULAR: "Teachers Only," NBC, 1983; "The Duck Factory," NBC, 1984; "Roxie,"

CBS, 1987; "The Dave Thomas Comedy Show," CBS, 1990.
AND: "Three's Company: Lies My Roommate Told Me," ABC, 1981; "The Love Boat: Ace Takes the Test," ABC, 1985; "Remington Steele: Steele Trying," NBC, 1985; "The Twilight Zone: Tooth or Consequences," CBS, 1986; "Hardcastle and McCormick: If You Could See What I See," ABC, 1986; "ALF: Tonight, Tonight," NBC, 1988; "The Tonight Show Starring Johnny Carson," NBC, 1988.
TV MOVIES AND MINISERIES: "Fresno," CBS, 1986.

GARAGIOLA, JOE
b. *Joseph Henry Garagiola, St. Louis, MO, February 12, 1926.* Baseball catcher turned TV personality.
AS A REGULAR: "Today," NBC, 1966-74; 1990- ; "He Said, She Said," SYN, 1969-71; "Sale of the Century," NBC, 1969-73; "Joe Garagiola's Memory Game," NBC, 1971; "Strike It Rich," SYN, 1986-87.
AND: "The Tonight Show," NBC, 1957; "The Jack Paar Show," NBC, 1958; "The Ed Sullivan Show," CBS, 1958; "The Jack Paar Show," NBC, 1960; "The Jack Paar Program," NBC, 1964; "The Match Game," NBC, 1964.
TV MOVIES AND MINISERIES: "Lucas Tanner," NBC, 1974.

GARDENIA, VINCENT
b. *Vincent Scognamiglio, Italy, January 7, 1922.* Stage actor who played Archie Bunker's neighbor Frank Lorenzo; later he was the station manager who fired everyone on the last episode of "The Mary Tyler Moore Show" and now occasionally appears as Murray, the father of Roxanne Melman (Susan Ruttan) on "L.A. Law."
AS A REGULAR: "All in the Family," CBS, 1973-74; "Breaking Away," ABC, 1980-81.
AND: "Studio One: The Night America Trembled," CBS, 1957; "Naked City: Baker's Dozen," ABC, 1959; "Armstrong Circle Theatre: Sound of Violence," CBS, 1959; "Witness: Huey P. Long," CBS, 1960; "The du Pont Show: The Forgery," NBC, 1962; "East Side/West Side: If Your Grandmother Had Wheels," CBS, 1964; "The Bing Crosby Show: The Green Couch," ABC, 1964; "The Defenders: Fires of the Mind," CBS, 1965; "Trials of O'Brien: Pilot," CBS, 1965; "The Big Valley: Palms of Glory," ABC, 1965; "Mission: Impossible: The Council," CBS, 1967; "NYPD: Money Man," ABC, 1967; "The Monkees: The Case of the Missing Monkee," NBC, 1967; "Gunsmoke: Noose of Gold," CBS, 1967; "All in the Family: Lionel Moves Into the Neighborhood," CBS, 1971; "All in the Family: The Bunkers and the Swingers," CBS, 1972; "The Rookies: Dirge for Sunday," ABC, 1972; "Love, American Style: Love and the Girlish Groom,"

ABC, 1973; "Kojak: A House of Prayer, A Den of Thieves," CBS, 1975; "The Mary Tyler Moore Show: The Last Show," CBS, 1977; "The Twilight Zone: Kentucky Rye," CBS, 1985.
TV MOVIES AND MINISERIES: "Marciano," ABC, 1979; "Muggable Mary: Street Cop," CBS, 1982; "Kennedy," NBC, 1983; "Dark Mirror," ABC, 1984.

GARDINER, REGINALD
b. *Wimbledon, Surrey, England, February 27, 1903; d. 1980.* Prim mustachioed actor, usually in comic roles.
AS A REGULAR: "The Pruitts of Southhampton," ABC, 1966-67.
AND: "Best of Broadway: The Man Who Came to Dinner," CBS, 1954; "Best of Broadway: The Guardsman," CBS, 1955; "Hallmark Hall of Fame: Alice in Wonderland," NBC, 1955; "The 20th Century-Fox Hour: Mr. Belvedere," CBS, 1956; "The Ford Show," NBC, 1956; "The Millionaire: The Story of Waldo Francis Turner," CBS, 1956; "The Tonight Show," NBC, 1957; "I've Got a Secret," CBS, 1957; "The Arlene Francis Show," NBC, 1957; "The Betty White Show," ABC, 1958; "Behind Closed Doors: Double Jeopardy," NBC, 1958; "Alfred Hitchcock Presents: Banquo's Chair," CBS, 1959; "U.S. Border Patrol: Appointment with Catastrophe," SYN, 1960; "Adventures in Paradise: Mr. Flotsam," ABC, 1961; "Mr. Smith Goes to Washington: Citizen Bellows," ABC, 1963; "Our Man Higgins: Will the Real Mr. Hargrave Please Stand Up?," ABC, 1963; "Laramie: The Marshals," NBC, 1963; "Burke's Law: Who Killed Victor Barrows?," ABC, 1964; "Hazel: The Fashion Show," NBC, 1964; "77 Sunset Strip: Dead as in Dude," ABC, 1964; "Summer Playhouse: The Apartment House," CBS, 1964; "Many Happy Returns: The House Divided," CBS, 1964; "Burke's Law: Who Killed Davidian Jones?," ABC, 1964; "Hazel: Stop Rockin' Our Reception," NBC, 1965; "The Man From UNCLE: The Round Table Affair," NBC, 1966; "Batman: Pop Goes the Joker/Flop Goes the Joker," ABC, 1967; "ABC Stage '67: The Wide Open Door," ABC, 1967; "Bewitched: I Get Your Nannie, You Get My Goat," ABC, 1967; "Petticoat Junction: Uncle Joe and the Master Plan," CBS, 1967; "The Monkees: The Monkees' Paw," NBC, 1968.

GARDNER, AVA
b. *Smithfield, NC, December 24, 1922; d. 1990.* Movie beauty who did a little TV toward the end of her career.
AS A REGULAR: "Knots Landing," CBS, 1985.
TV MOVIES AND MINISERIES: "The Kidnapping of the President," NBC, 1980; "A.D.," NBC, 1985; "The Long Hot Summer," NBC, 1985; "Harem," ABC, 1986.

338

GARGAN, WILLIAM

b. Brooklyn, NY, July 17, 1905; d. 1979. Actor who played private eye Martin Kane on two series.

AS A REGULAR: "Martin Kane, Private Eye," NBC, 1949-51; "The New Adventures of Martin Kane," SYN, 1957.

AND: "Pepsi Cola Playhouse: Death the Hard Way," ABC, 1954; "Pepsi Cola Playhouse: Lost Lullaby," ABC, 1954; "Ford Theatre: Favorite Son," NBC, 1955; "The 20th Century-Fox Hour: Man on the Ledge," CBS, 1956; "Studio One: The McTaggart Succession," CBS, 1958; "Christophers: Advice for Parents," SYN, 1959; "Christophers: Directing Public Opinion," SYN, 1960.

* Gargan had cancer of the larnyx, and it was removed in 1960. Speaking through an artificial voice box, he became an anti-smoking crusader.

GARLAND, BEVERLY

b. Beverly Fessenden, Santa Cruz, CA, October 17, 1926. Starlet of the fifties on the screen and on TV; in the sixties she played the wife of Bing Crosby on his sitcom, then married Fred MacMurray on "My Three Sons" and later played the mothers of Amanda King (Kate Jackson) of "Scarecrow and Mrs. King" and Laura Holt (Stephanie Zimbalist) of "Remington Steele."

AS A REGULAR: "Mama Rosa," ABC, 1950; "Decoy," SYN, 1957-58; "Walt Disney Presents: The Nine Lives of Elfego Baca," ABC, 1959; "The Bing Crosby Show," ABC, 1964-65; "My Three Sons," CBS, 1969-72; "Scarecrow and Mrs. King," CBS, 1983-87.

AND: "Hollywood Playhouse: Thirty Days," SYN, 1952; "Four Star Playhouse: Bourbon Street," CBS, 1954; "Medic: White Is the Color," NBC, 1955; "The Millionaire: Millionaire Carl Nelson," CBS, 1955; "Four Star Playhouse: Night of Lark Cottage," CBS, 1955; "Climax!: A Taste for Crime," CBS, 1957; "Telephone Time: The Other Van Gogh," ABC, 1957; "Playhouse 90: Edge of Innocence," CBS, 1957; "Yancy Derringer: The Fair Freebooter," CBS, 1958; "Yancy Derringer: The Wayward Warrior," CBS, 1959; "Laramie: Saddle and Spur," NBC, 1960; "Tales of Wells Fargo: Pearl Hart," NBC, 1960; "Wanted Dead or Alive: Prison Trail," CBS, 1960; "Rawhide: Incident of the Roman Candles," CBS, 1960; "Thriller: Knock Three-one-two," NBC, 1960; "Stagecoach West: The Storm," ABC, 1960; "The Nurses: The Walls Came Tumbling Down," CBS, 1963; "Rawhide: Incident of the Gallows Tree," CBS, 1963; "Sam Benedict: Image of a Toad," NBC, 1963; "The Dakotas: The Chooser of the Slain," ABC, 1963; "The Fugitive: Smoke Screen," ABC, 1963; "The Farmer's Daughter: The Stand-In," ABC, 1963; "The Eleventh Hour:

What Did She Mean by 'Good Luck'?," NBC, 1963; "Kraft Suspense Theatre: Charlie, He Couldn't Kill a Fly," NBC, 1964; "What's This Song?," NBC, 1964; "Hollywood Palace," ABC, 1965; "A Man Called Shenandoah: The Onslaught," ABC, 1965; "Laredo: Lazyfoot, Where Are You?," NBC, 1965; "PDQ," NBC, 1966; "The Loner: Incident in the Middle of Nowhere," CBS, 1966; "Gunsmoke: Time of the Jackals," CBS, 1969; "Then Came Bronson: The Mary R.," NBC, 1970; "The Game Game," SYN, 1970; "Gunsmoke: The Badge," CBS, 1970; "Marcus Welby, M.D.: A Fragile Possession," ABC, 1972; "The Rookies: Three Hours to Kill," ABC, 1973; "Cannon: Deadly Heritage," CBS, 1973; "Mannix: Little Girl Lost," CBS, 1973; "Love, American Style: Love and the Big Top," ABC, 1973; "Doc Elliot: A Small Hand of Friendship," ABC, 1974; "Medical Center: The World's a Balloon," CBS, 1974; "Ironside: The Over-the-Hill Blues," NBC, 1974; "Wide World of Mystery: The Deadly Volley," ABC, 1975; "Remington Steele: Thou Shall Not Steele," NBC, 1982; "Magnum, P.I.: Italian Ice," CBS, 1982; "Remington Steele: String of Steele," NBC, 1983; "Heartbeat: Prison," ABC, 1989.

TV MOVIES AND MINISERIES: "Cutter's Trail," CBS, 1970; "Say Goodbye, Maggie Cole," ABC, 1972; "The Weekend Nun," ABC, 1972; "The Voyage of the Yes," CBS, 1973; "Unwed Father," ABC, 1974; "The Day the Earth Moved," ABC, 1974; "This Girl for Hire," CBS, 1983.

GARLAND, JUDY

b. Frances Gumm, Grand Rapids, MN, June 10, 1922; d. 1969. Screen legend who tried a TV variety series, but it couldn't weather the harsh competition of "Bonanza."

AS A REGULAR: "The Judy Garland Show," CBS, 1963-64.

AND: "Here's Hollywood," NBC, 1961; "Judy Garland Special," CBS, 1962; "The Jack Paar Program," NBC, 1962; "The Jack Paar Program," NBC, 1963; "Talent Scouts," CBS, 1963; "On Broadway Tonight," CBS, 1965; "The Andy Williams Show," NBC, 1965; "The Ed Sullivan Show," CBS, 1965; "Perry Como Special," NBC, 1966; "Jack Paar Special," NBC, 1967; "The Merv Griffin Show," SYN, 1969.

GARNER, JAMES

b. James Baumgarner, Norman, OK, April 7, 1928. Charismatic leading man with a dry wit; star of arguably the best western series ever and undoubtedly the best detective series ever.

AS A REGULAR: "Maverick," ABC, 1957-60; "James Garner as Nichols," NBC, 1971-72; "The Rockford Files," NBC, 1974-80; "Bret Maverick," NBC, 1981-82.

AND: "Cheyenne: Mountain Fortess," ABC, 1955;

"Cheyenne: Decision," ABC, 1956; "Warner Bros. Presents Conflict: The Man From 1997," ABC, 1956; "Cheyenne: Last Train West," ABC, 1956; "Warner Bros. Presents Conflict: People Against McQuade," ABC, 1956; "Dick Powell's Zane Grey Theatre: Stars Over Texas," CBS, 1956; "Warner Bros. Presents Conflict: Girl on a Subway," ABC, 1957; "Cheyenne: War Party," ABC, 1957; "Wide, Wide World: The Western," NBC, 1958; "Pat Boone Chevy Showroom," ABC, 1959; "The Bing Crosby Show," ABC, 1959; "77 Sunset Strip: Downbeat," ABC, 1959; "Bob Hope Special," NBC, 1960; "Angel: The French Lesson," CBS, 1961; "Dinah Shore Chevy Show," NBC, 1961; "Bob Hope Buick Show," NBC, 1961; "The Bob Hope Show," NBC, 1961; "I've Got a Secret," CBS, 1962; "Dinah Shore Special," NBC, 1962; "Bob Hope Special," NBC, 1963; "The Merv Griffin Show," SYN, 1969; "The Andy Williams Show," NBC, 1970; "Rowan & Martin's Laugh-In," NBC, 1970; "The Tonight Show Starring Johnny Carson," NBC, 1974.
TV MOVIES AND MINISERIES: "The New Maverick," ABC, 1978; "Heartsounds," ABC, 1984; "Space," CBS, 1985; "Hallmark Hall of Fame: Promise," CBS, 1986; "Hallmark Hall of Fame: My Name Is Bill W.," ABC, 1989.
AS EXECUTIVE PRODUCER: "Hallmark Hall of Fame: Promise," CBS, 1986; "Hallmark Hall of Fame: My Name Is Bill W.," ABC, 1989.
* Emmies: 1977, 1987.

GARR, TERI
b. *Lakewood, OH, December 11, 1949*. Blonde actress who combines her regular film appearances with special TV projects and visits to her pal, David Letterman.
AS A REGULAR: "Shindig," ABC, 1965-66; "The Ken Berry "WOW" Show," ABC, 1972; "The Burns and Schreiber Comedy Hour," ABC, 1973; "The Girl with Something Extra," NBC, 1973-74; "The Sonny and Cher Comedy Hour," CBS, 1973-74; "The Sonny Comedy Revue," ABC, 1974.
AND: "Mr. Novak: How Does Your Garden Grow," NBC, 1964; "Batman: Instant Freeze/Rats Like Cheese," ABC, 1966; "Star Trek: Assignment Earth," NBC, 1968; "It Takes a Thief: Guess Who's Coming to Rio," ABC, 1969; "Room 222: Naked Came We Into the World," ABC, 1969; "McCloud: The Million Dollar Round Up," NBC, 1973; "The Odd Couple: Last Tango in Newark," ABC, 1973; "M*A*S*H: The Sniper," CBS, 1973; "The Bob Newhart Show: Emily in for Carol," CBS, 1973; "The Odd Couple: The Flying Felix," ABC, 1974; "The Bob Newhart Show: Confessions of an Orthodontist," CBS, 1974; "Barnaby Jones: Image in a Cracked Mirror," CBS, 1974; "McCloud: This Must Be the Alamo," NBC, 1974; "McCloud: The Concrete Jungle Caper," NBC, 1974; "Barnaby Jones: Image in a Cracked Mirror," CBS, 1974; "The Merv Griffin Show," SYN, 1975; "McCloud: Return to the Alamo," NBC, 1975; "Cher," CBS, 1975; "Maude: Viv's Dog," CBS, 1975; "Saturday Night Live," NBC, 1980; "Faerie Tale Theatre: Tale of the Frog Prince," SHO, 1982; "Saturday Night Live," NBC, 1983; "Late Night with David Letterman," NBC, 1983; "Saturday Night Live," NBC, 1985; "Late Night with David Letterman," NBC, 1986; "David Letterman's Old Fashioned Christmas," NBC, 1987; "Trying Times: Drive, She Said," PBS, 1988; "Late Night with David Letterman," NBC, 1989.
TV MOVIES AND MINISERIES: "Law and Order," NBC, 1976; "Hallmark Hall of Fame: The Winter of Our Discontent," CBS, 1983; "Intimate Strangers," CBS, 1986; "Fresno," CBS, 1986.
* Garr began her career as a dancer—she was a regular go-go girl on "Shindig"—and she danced in a couple of Elvis Presley movies. In the 1966 movie "The Swinger," Garr doubled for star Ann-Margret in a scene where Margret's character is doused in paint and rolls on a canvas.
* Garr also did dozens of commercials, playing, among other characters, Chiquita Banana.

GARRETT, BETTY
b. *St. Joseph, MO, May 23, 1919*. Musical-comedy performer who played Irene Lorenzo on "All in the Family" and landlady Edna Babish on "Laverne & Shirley."
AS A REGULAR: "All in the Family," CBS, 1973-75; "Laverne & Shirley," ABC, 1976-81.
AND: "Ford Theatre: A Smattering of Bliss," NBC, 1955; "Ford Theatre: The Penlands and the Poodle," ABC, 1957; "Arthur Murray Party," NBC, 1957; "Art Carney Special: Very Important People," NBC, 1959; "Art Carney Special: The Best of Anything," NBC, 1960; "The Chevy Show: Love Is Funny," NBC, 1960; "The Chevy Show: Autumn Crocus," NBC, 1961; "The Lloyd Bridges Show: Mr. Pennington's Machine," CBS, 1962; "The Fugitive: Escape Into Black," ABC, 1964; "Medical Center: The Prisoners," CBS, 1974; "Theatre in America: Who's Happy Now?," PBS, 1975; "The Tonight Show Starring Johnny Carson," NBC, 1975; "The Love Boat: Julie's Dilemma," ABC, 1978; "Murder, She Wrote: Trouble in Eden," CBS, 1987; "Blacke's Magic: Wax Poetic," NBC, 1986.

GARRETT, LEIF
b. *Hollywood, CA, November 8, 1961*.
AS A REGULAR: "Three for the Road," CBS, 1975.
AND: "Family Affair: Heroes Are Born," CBS, 1970; "Gunsmoke: The Sodbusters," CBS, 1972; "The FBI: The Deadly Species," ABC, 1972; "The Odd Couple: The Frog," ABC, 1974; "The Odd Couple: Felix Remarries," ABC, 1975;

"Family: All for Love," ABC, 1978; "CHiPS: Roller Disco," NBC, 1979; "Hunter: A Child Is Born," NBC, 1988.

TV MOVIES AND MINISERIES: "Strange Homecoming," NBC, 1974; "Flood," NBC, 1976.

GARROWAY, DAVE

b. *Schenectady, NY, July 13, 1913; d. 1982.* Personality of the "egghead" school with a pleasant, decent TV manner; he appeared on the tube only occasionally after he left as longtime host of "Today" in 1961.

AS A REGULAR: "Garroway at Large," NBC, 1949-51; "Today," NBC, 1952-61; "The Dave Garroway Show," NBC, 1953-54; "Wide, Wide World," NBC, 1955-59; "Garroway AM and PM," CBS, 1964-65; "Garroway," SYN, 1969; "The CBS Newcomers," CBS, 1971.

AND: "The Colgate Comedy Hour," NBC, 1951; "Babes in Toyland," NBC, 1954; "Babes in Toyland," NBC, 1955; "Christmas Eve with the Dave Garroways," NBC, 1957; "Swing Into Spring," NBC, 1958; "Bell Telephone Hour: Our Musical Ambassadors," NBC, 1960; "Startime: Talent Scouts," NBC, 1960; "Dave's Place," NBC, 1960; "Something Special," NBC, 1960; "The Merv Griffin Show," NBC, 1963; "The Young Set," ABC, 1965; "The Merv Griffin Show," SYN, 1968; "Alias Smith and Jones: The Man Who Corrupted Hadleyburg," ABC, 1972; "A Salute to Television's 25th Anniversary," ABC, 1972; "The Mike Douglas Show," SYN, 1975; "Today," NBC, 1982.

* Garroway died of a self-inflicted gunshot wound; reportedly he was despondent over his health after having open-heart surgery in 1981.

GARSON, GREER

b. *County Down, N. Ireland, September 29, 1912.* Excruciatingly prim leading lady who did some TV in the fifties and early sixties.

AS A REGULAR: "The Pallisers," PBS, 1974.

AND: "Producers Showcase: Reunion in Vienna," NBC, 1955; "Star Stage: Career," NBC, 1956; "G.E. Theatre: The Glorious Gift of Molly Malloy," CBS, 1956; "The Ford Show," NBC, 1956; "Hallmark Hall of Fame: The Little Foxes," NBC, 1956; "G.E. Theatre: The Earring," CBS, 1957; "The Steve Allen Show," NBC, 1957; "What's My Line?," CBS, 1957; "Telephone Time: Revenge," ABC, 1957; "Father Knows Best: Kathy's Big Chance," NBC, 1957; "This Is Your Life" (Mervyn LeRoy), NBC, 1959; "The Big Party," CBS, 1959; "G.E. Theatre: R.S.V.P.," CBS, 1960; "Hallmark Hall of Fame: Captain Brassbound's Conversion," NBC, 1960; "The du Pont Show: The Shadowed Affair," NBC, 1962; "Hallmark Hall of Fame: The Invincible Mr. Disraeli," NBC, 1963; "Hollywood Squares," NBC, 1967; "The Men From Shiloh: The Lady at the Bar," NBC, 1970; "The Little Drummer Boy,"

NBC, 1971; "Hallmark Hall of Fame: Crown Matrimonial," NBC, 1974; "The Little Drummer Boy, Book II," NBC, 1976; "The Love Boat: The Tomorrow Lady," ABC, 1982.

TV MOVIES AND MINISERIES: "Little Women," NBC, 1978.

GARVER, KATHY

b. *Long Beach, CA, 1948.* Actress who played Cissy, the teenager on "Family Affair."

AS A REGULAR: "Family Affair," ABC, 1966-71.

AND: "Telephone Time: Parents of a Stranger," CBS, 1957; "The Bing Crosby Show: The Keefers Come Calling," ABC, 1965; "Death Valley Days: The Magic Locket," SYN, 1965; "Dr. Kildare: Fathers and Daughters," NBC, 1965; "The Patty Duke Show: Patty the Diplomat," ABC, 1966; "The Big Valley: The Royal Road," ABC, 1969; "Matlock: The Bestseller," NBC, 1989.

GARY, JOHN

b. *Watertown, NY, November 29, 1932.* Folk singer.

AS A REGULAR: "The John Gary Show," CBS, 1966; SYN, 1968.

AND: "The Jack Paar Show," NBC, 1959; "The Lawrence Welk Show," ABC, 1959; "The Dick Clark Saturday Night Beechnut Show," ABC, 1960; "The Tonight Show Starring Johnny Carson," NBC, 1963; "The Tonight Show Starring Johnny Carson," NBC, 1964; "The Danny Kaye Show," CBS, 1964; "The Tennessee Ernie Ford Show," ABC, 1964; "The Danny Kaye Show," CBS, 1965; "Hollywood Squares," NBC, 1968; "The Joey Bishop Show," ABC, 1968.

GAUTIER, DICK

b. *Los Angeles, CA, October 30, 1931.* Actor who played Hymie the robot on "Get Smart"; he played Conrad Birdie in the stage production of "Bye Bye Birdie."

AS A REGULAR: "Get Smart," NBC, 1966-69; "Mr. Terrific," CBS, 1967; "It's Your Bet," SYN, 1969-73; "Here We Go Again," ABC, 1973; "When Things Were Rotten," ABC, 1975; "Liar's Club," SYN, 1976-78.

AND: "The Ed Sullivan Show," CBS, 1960; "The Patty Duke Show: Anywhere I Hang My Horn Is Home," ABC, 1966; "Bewitched: Samantha the Dressmaker," ABC, 1966; "Gidget: The Gidget Gadget," ABC, 1966; "Love on a Rooftop: Who Was That Husband I Saw You With?," ABC, 1967; "PDQ," NBC, 1967; "Vacation Playhouse: The Jones Boys," CBS, 1967; "The Flying Nun: The Great Casino Robbery," ABC, 1969; "It Takes Two," NBC, 1970; "The Doris Day Show: The Forward Pass," CBS, 1971; "Love, American Style: Love and Women's Lib," ABC, 1971; "Love, American Style: Love and the Security Building," ABC, 1971; "Love, American Style:

Love and the Traveling Salesman," ABC, 1971; "The Doris Day Show: The Sheik of Araby," CBS, 1971; "Love, American Style: Love and the Four-Sided Triangle," ABC, 1972; "Password," ABC, 1973; "Love, American Style: Love and the Sexpert," ABC, 1973; "Honeymoon Suite," ABC, 1973; "The Mary Tyler Moore Show: Hi There, Sports Fans," CBS, 1973; "Banacek: The Three Million Dollar Piracy," NBC, 1973; "Match Game '74," CBS, 1974; "Love, American Style: Love and the Fractured Fibula," ABC, 1974; "Hawkins: The Slave Trade," CBS, 1974; "Kolchak, the Night Stalker: The Werewolf," ABC, 1974; "Showoffs," ABC, 1975; "Celebrity Sweepstakes," NBC, 1976; "Marcus Welby, M.D.: All Passions Spent," ABC, 1976; "Good Heavens: I Want Nancy," ABC, 1976; "Stumpers," NBC, 1976; "The Love Boat: Musical Cabins," ABC, 1978; "$weepstake$: Victor, Billy and Bobby, 'Sometimes,'" NBC, 1979; "Eischied: Do They Really Need to Die?," NBC, 1979; "The Love Boat: We Three," ABC, 1979; "Happy Days: Nervous Romance," ABC, 1981; "Quincy: Cry for Help," NBC, 1983; "Goodnight Beantown: The Consumer's Best Friend," CBS, 1984; "Murder, She Wrote: Birds of a Feather," CBS, 1984; "Knight Rider: The Chameleon," NBC, 1984; "Matlock: The Gambler," NBC, 1987; "Murder, She Wrote: Just Another Fish Story," CBS, 1988.

TV MOVIES AND MINISERIES: "Benny and Barney: Las Vegas Undercover," NBC, 1977; "Marathon," CBS, 1980; "This Wife for Hire," CBS, 1985; "Get Smart, Again!," ABC, 1989.

GAVIN, JOHN
b. Jack Golenor, Los Angeles, CA, April 8, 1928. Hunky actor who dropped out of an unexceptional show biz career to become Ronald Reagan's ambassador to Mexico.

AS A REGULAR: "Destry," ABC, 1964; "Convoy," NBC, 1965; "Doctor's Private Lives," ABC, 1979.

AND: "Here's Hollywood," NBC, 1961; "Alcoa Premiere: The Jail," ABC, 1962; "The Alfred Hitchcock Hour: Run for Doom," CBS, 1963; "Kraft Suspense Theatre: A Truce to Terror," NBC, 1964; "The Virginian: Portrait of a Widow," NBC, 1964; "Kraft Suspense Theatre: Three Persons," NBC, 1964; "The Alfred Hitchcock Hour: Off Season," NBC, 1965; "The Mike Douglas Show," SYN, 1965; "The Mike Douglas Show," SYN, 1967; "The Doris Day Show: Skiing, Anyone?," CBS, 1971; "Mannix: The Danford File," CBS, 1973; "Medical Center: Major Annie, M.D.," CBS, 1976; "The Love Boat: Lonely at the Top," ABC, 1977.

TV MOVIES AND MINISERIES: "Cutter's Trail," CBS, 1970; "The New Adventures of Heidi," NBC, 1978.

GAYNES, GEORGE
b. Finland, May 16, 1917. Actor who played Henry Warnimot, guardian of Punky Brewster (Soleil Moon Frye).

AS A REGULAR: "Search for Tomorrow," CBS, 1971; "Rich Man, Poor Man—Book II," ABC, 1976-77; "General Hospital," ABC, 1980; "Punky Brewster," NBC, 1984-86; SYN, 1986-87.

AND: "Accent: Ethan Allen and the Green Mountain Boys," CBS, 1962; "Hawaiian Eye: The Broken Thread," ABC, 1962; "Cheyenne: Vengeance Is Mine," ABC, 1962; "The Patty Duke Show: The Perfect Hostess," ABC, 1965; "Mannix: Who Will Dig the Graves?," CBS, 1968; "Mission: Impossible: The Elixer," CBS, 1968; "Columbo: Etude in Black," NBC, 1972; "Columbo: Any Old Port in a Storm," NBC, 1973; "The Law: Complaint Amended," NBC, 1975; "McCloud: Fire!," NBC, 1975; "City of Angels: The Palm Springs Answer," NBC, 1976; "The Quest: Day of Outrage," NBC, 1976; "WKRP in Cincinnati: Jennifer's Home for Christmas," CBS, 1979; "Cheers: Where There's a Will," NBC, 1983; "Matlock: The Power Brokers," NBC, 1987.

TV MOVIES AND MINISERIES: "Trilogy of Terror," NBC, 1975; "Woman of the Year," CBS, 1976; "Best Sellers: Captains and the Kings," NBC, 1976; "Washington: Behind Closed Doors," ABC, 1977.

GAYNOR, JANET
b. Laura Gainor, Philadelphia, PA, October 6, 1906; d. 1984. Celebrated film actress of the thirties who did a little TV, including the inevitable "Love Boat" guest shot.

AS A GUEST: "Medallion Theatre: Dear Cynthia," CBS, 1953; "Lux Video Theatre: Two Dozen Roses," CBS, 1954; "G.E. Theatre: The Flying Wife," CBS, 1959; "Hedda Hopper's Hollywood," NBC, 1960; "Over Easy," PBS, 1980; "The Love Boat: A Frugal Pair," ABC, 1981.

GAYNOR, MITZI
b. Francesca Mitzi Marlene de Czanyi von Gerber, Chicago, IL, September 4, 1931. Musical-comedy actress whose Hollywood career peaked just as the movie musical was breathing its last; now she plays nightclubs and theatres and occasionally brings her act to television.

AS A GUEST: "The Ed Sullivan Show," CBS, 1958; "Jack Benny Special," CBS, 1959; "Frank Sinatra Timex Show," ABC, 1959; "The Dick Clark Beechnut Show," ABC, 1960; "The Donald O'Connor Show," NBC, 1960; "The Ed Sullivan Show," CBS, 1963; "The Ed Sullivan Show," CBS, 1964; "Mitzi Gaynor Special," NBC, 1968; "Mitzi's Second

Special," NBC, 1969; "Perry Como's Winter Show," NBC, 1971; "Mitzi Gaynor: The First Time," CBS, 1973; "Mitzi and a Hundred Guys," CBS, 1975.

GAZZARA, BEN
b. Biago Anthony Gazzara, New York City, NY, August 28, 1930. Brooding method actor who was a hit on TV as doomed lawyer Paul Bryan, packing all the adventure into his remaining days as he could in "Run for Your Life."
AS A REGULAR: "Arrest and Trial," ABC, 1963-64; "Run for Your Life," NBC, 1965-68.
AND: "Danger: Fresh as a Daisy," CBS, 1952; "Kraft Television Theatre: The Last Mile," NBC, 1952; "The Web: A Case of Escape," CBS, 1953; "Medallion Theatre: The Alibi Kid," CBS, 1954; "U.S. Steel Hour: The Notebook Warrior," ABC, 1954; "Playhouse 90: The Troublemakers," CBS, 1957; "Playhouse 90: The Violent Heart," CBS, 1958; "Kraft Theatre: Three Plays by Tennessee Williams-Moony's Kid Don't Cry," NBC, 1958; "What's My Line?," CBS, 1959; "I've Got a Secret," CBS, 1959; "Du Pont Show of the Month: Body and Soul," CBS, 1959; "Cry Vengeance!," NBC, 1961; "Here's Hollywood," NBC, 1962; "Password," CBS, 1962; "Carol for Another Christmas," ABC, 1964; "Kraft Suspense Theatre: Rapture at 240," NBC, 1965; "Bob Hope Chrysler Theatre: Free of Charge," NBC, 1967; "The Merv Griffin Show," SYN, 1968; "The American Dream: The General," CBS, 1974; "The Life of Leonardo Da Vinci," NET, 1974.
TV MOVIES AND MINISERIES: "When Michael Calls," ABC, 1972; "Fireball Forward," ABC, 1972; "The Family Rico," CBS, 1972; "Pursuit," ABC, 1972; "Maneater," CBS, 1973; "QB VII," ABC, 1974; "The Death of Richie," NBC, 1977; "The Trial of Lee Harvey Oswald," ABC, 1977; "An Early Frost," NBC, 1985; "A Letter to Three Wives," NBC, 1985; "Downpayment on Murder," NBC, 1987; "Police Story: The Freeway Killings," NBC, 1987.
AS DIRECTOR: "Columbo: A Friend in Deed," NBC, 1974.

GEAR, LUELLA
b. New York City, NY, September 5, 1897.
AS A REGULAR: "Joe and Mabel," CBS, 1955-56.
AND: "The Trap: The Chocolate Cobweb," CBS, 1950; "Sure as Fate: Tremolo," CBS, 1950; "Broadway Television Theatre: The Patsy," SYN, 1952; "The Web: The Poison Tree," CBS, 1952; "Elgin TV Hour: Falling Star," ABC, 1954; "Producers Showcase: Happy Birthday," NBC, 1956; "Play of the Week: Juno and the Paycock," SYN, 1960; "The Defenders: Conflict of Interests," CBS, 1964.

GEARY, ANTHONY
b. Coalville, UT, May 29, 1947. Actor who played Luke on "General Hospital."
AS A REGULAR: "Bright Promise," NBC, 1969-72; "The Young and the Restless," CBS, 1973; "General Hospital," ABC, 1978-84.
AND: "Room 222: Choose One: And They Lived Happily/Unhappily Ever After," ABC, 1970; "All in the Family: Judging Books by Covers," CBS, 1971; "The Partridge Family: Ain't Loveth Grand," ABC, 1972; "Mannix: A Way to Dusty Death," CBS, 1973; "Shaft: Hit-Run," CBS, 1973; "Doc Elliot: The Carrier," ABC, 1974; "The Streets of San Francisco: The Twenty-Five Caliber Plague," ABC, 1974; "The Streets of San Francisco: Poisoned Snow," ABC, 1975; "Marcus Welby, M.D.: Tidal Wave," ABC, 1975; "Barnaby Jones: Eyes of Terror," CBS, 1976; "Barnaby Jones: Voice in the Night," CBS, 1976; "Hizzonner: Mr. Perfect," NBC, 1979; "The Mike Douglas Show," SYN, 1981; "Murder, She Wrote: From Russia-with Blood," CBS, 1989.
TV MOVIES AND MINISERIES: "Intimate Agony," ABC, 1983; "Sins of the Past," ABC, 1984; "The Imposter," ABC, 1984; "Kicks," ABC, 1985; "Perry Mason: The Case of the Murdered Madam," NBC, 1987; "Do You Know the Muffin Man?," CBS, 1989; "High Desert Kill," USA, 1989.

GEER, WILL
b. Frankfort, IN, March 9, 1902; d. 1978. Emmy winning actor who played Grandpa Walton. His career was derailed for a time by blacklisting; but he made up for it with a vengeance.
AS A REGULAR: "The Waltons," CBS, 1972-78.
AND: "East Side/West Side: Here Today," CBS, 1964; "Trials of O'Brian: The 10-Foot, Six-Inch Pole," CBS, 1966; "Trials of O'Brian: The Only Game in Town," CBS, 1966; "The Crucible," CBS, 1967; "I Spy: Home to Judgment," NBC, 1968; "Of Mice and Men," ABC, 1968; "Mayberry, RFD: Aunt Bee's Cruise/Aunt Bee and the Captain," CBS, 1969; "Bonanza: The Running Man," NBC, 1969; "Hawaii Five-O: Forty Feet High, and It Kills," CBS, 1969; "Then Came Bronson: Old Tigers Never Die: They Just Run Away," NBC, 1969; "The Bold Ones: The Shattered Image," NBC, 1970; "Medical Center: Rebel in White," CBS, 1970; "The Name of the Game: One of the Girls in Research," NBC, 1970; "The Bold Ones: The Day the Lion Died," NBC, 1970; "The Bill Cosby Show: The Old Man of 4-C," NBC, 1970; "The Courtship of Eddie's Father: Who Wants to Sail Down the Amazon, Anyway?," ABC, 1970; "Bonanza: A Home for Jamie," NBC, 1971; "The Bold Ones: The Letter of the Law," NBC, 1971; "Alias Smith and Jones: Smiler with a Gun," ABC, 1972; "Hollywood Television Theatre: The Scarecrow," NET, 1972;

"Bewitched: George Washington Zapped Here," ABC, 1972; "Medical Center: No Way Out," CBS, 1972; "Columbo: A Stitch in Crime," NBC, 1973; "ABC Afternoon Playbreak: The Gift of Terror," ABC, 1973; "Kung Fu: The Ancient Warrior," ABC, 1973; "Medical Center: Hexed," CBS, 1974; "The Oath: The Sad and Lonely Sundays," ABC, 1976; "Starsky and Hutch: Murder at Sea," ABC, 1976; "Tony Orlando and Dawn," CBS, 1977.

TV MOVIES AND MINISERIES: "The Brotherhood of the Bell," CBS, 1970; "Brock's Last Case," NBC, 1973; "Harry O," ABC, 1973; "Savage," NBC, 1973; "Isn't It Shocking?," ABC, 1973; "The Hanged Man," ABC, 1974; "Honky Tonk," NBC, 1974; "Hurricane," ABC, 1974; "The Night That Panicked America," ABC, 1975; "Law and Order," NBC, 1976.

* Geer was a blacklist victim, called before the House Unamerican Activities Committee in 1951 because he had praised the Russian stage and cinema in a 1948 article in The Daily Worker, the Communist Party newspaper. Geer took the fifth amendment and didn't get another acting job until 1962, when director Otto Preminger hired him for the film "Advise and Consent."

* Emmies: 1975.

GENNARO, PETER
b. Metairie, LA, 1924. Dancer-choreographer of many TV shows.

AS A REGULAR: "The Polly Bergen Show," NBC, 1957-58; "Your Hit Parade," CBS, 1958-59.

AS A CHOREOGRAPHER: "Mr. Broadway," NBC, 1957; "The Polly Bergen Show," NBC, 1957-58; "The Bob Crosby Show," NBC, 1958; "The Andy Williams Show," CBS, 1959; "The Secret World of Eddie Hodges," CBS, 1960; "Perry Como's Kraft Music Hall," NBC, 1960-63; "The Judy Garland Show," CBS, 1963-64; "The Bing Crosby Show," CBS, 1964; "The Entertainers," CBS, 1965; "The Andy Griffith, Don Knotts, Jim Nabors Special," CBS, 1965; "Kraft Music Hall," NBC, 1967-71; "Off to See the Wizard: Who's Afraid of Mother Goose?," ABC, 1967.

GEORGE, ANTHONY
b. Endicott, NY, January 29, 1925. Actor who most recently played Will Vernon on "One Life to Live."

AS A REGULAR: "The Untouchables," ABC, 1960; "Checkmate," CBS, 1960-62; "Dark Shadows," ABC, 1966-70; "Search for Tomorrow," CBS, 1970-75; "One Life to Live," ABC, 1977-84.

AND: "Schlitz Playhouse of Stars: A Light in the Desert," CBS, 1956; "Tales of Wells Fargo: Bounty," NBC, 1957; "Cheyenne: The Spanish Grant," ABC, 1957; "Schlitz Playhouse of Stars:

Lottery for Revenge," CBS, 1958; "How to Marry a Millionaire: Prince Kaudim Story," SYN, 1958; "Sugarfoot: The Desperadoes," ABC, 1959; "Laramie: Fugitive Road," NBC, 1959; "Keyhole: Hollywood Hopefuls," SYN, 1962; "Wagon Train: The Johnny Masters Story," ABC, 1963; "Police Woman: Bondage," NBC, 1977.

GEORGE, CHRISTOPHER
b. Royal Oak, MN, February 25, 1929; d. 1983.

AS A REGULAR: "The Rat Patrol," ABC, 1966-68; "The Immortal," ABC, 1970-71.

AND: "Bewitched: George the Warlock," ABC, 1965; "Hollywood Squares," NBC, 1967; "The FBI: Return to Power," ABC, 1970; "Love, American Style: Love and Formula 26B," ABC, 1972; "Love, American Style: Love and the Burglar Joke," ABC, 1973; "Owen Marshall, Counselor at Law: The Break-in," ABC, 1974; "Police Story: Cop in the Middle," NBC, 1974; "McCloud: Sharks!," NBC, 1975; "SWAT: Deadly Tide," ABC, 1975; "Police Story: The Execution," NBC, 1975; "The Love Boat: Play by Play," ABC, 1979; "The Misadventures of Sheriff Lobo: Pilot," NBC, 1979; "The Love Boat: Reunion Cruise," ABC, 1979.

TV MOVIES AND MINISERIES: "The Immortal," ABC, 1969; "The House on Greenapple Road," ABC, 1970; "Escape," ABC, 1971; "Dead Men Tell No Tales," CBS, 1971; "Man on a String," ABC, 1972; "The Heist," ABC, 1972; "A Beautiful Killing," ABC, 1974; "The Last Survivors," NBC, 1975; "Mayday at 40,000 Feet!," CBS, 1976.

GEORGE, LYNDA DAY
b. San Marcos, TX, December 11, 1944. Actress who played Casey on "Mission: Impossible" and not much lately.

AS A REGULAR: "The Silent Force," ABC, 1970-71; "Mission: Impossible," CBS, 1971-73.

AND: "NBC Children's Theatre: Robin Hood," NBC, 1964; "T.H.E. Cat: The System," NBC, 1966; "The Fugitive: The Judgement," ABC, 1967; "The FBI: Sky on Fire," ABC, 1967; "The Virginian: A Welcoming Town," NBC, 1967; "The Invaders: The Trial," ABC, 1967; "The FBI: Line of Fire," ABC, 1967; "The Felony Squad: The Flip Side of Fear," ABC, 1968; "The FBI: The Widow," ABC, 1968; "It Takes a Thief: A Matter of Loyal Larceny," ABC, 1968; "The FBI: Return to Power," ABC, 1970; "The Immortal: Man on a Punched Card," ABC, 1970; "Hollywood Squares," NBC, 1972; "Marcus Welby, M.D.: I've Promised You a Father," ABC, 1974; "Owen Marshall, Counselor at Law: I've Promised You a Father," ABC, 1974; "Wide World of Mystery: Come Out, Come Out, Wherever You Are," ABC, 1974; "McCloud: Sharks!," NBC, 1975; "Barnaby Jones: Double Vengeance," CBS, 1975; "Cross Wits," SYN,

1975; "Wonder Woman: Fraulein Wonder Woman," ABC, 1976; "The Love Boat: Play by Play," ABC, 1979; "Fantasy Island: With Affection, Jack the Ripper," ABC, 1980; "Hardcastle and McCormick: Too Rich and Too Thin," ABC, 1985; "Blacke's Magic: Address Unknown," NBC, 1986; "Mission: Impossible: Reprisal," ABC, 1989.

TV MOVIES AND MINISERIES: "The Sound of Anger," NBC, 1968; "Fear No Evil," NBC, 1969; "The House on Greenapple Road," ABC, 1970; "Cannon," CBS, 1971; "The Sheriff," ABC, 1971; "She Cried Murder!," ABC, 1973; "Set This Town on Fire," NBC, 1973; "A Beautiful Killing," ABC, 1974; "Panic on the 5:22," ABC, 1974; "The Trial of Chaplain Jensen," ABC, 1975; "Death Among Friends," NBC, 1975; "The Barbary Coast," ABC, 1975; "Mayday at 40,000 Feet," CBS, 1976; "Rich Man, Poor Man," ABC, 1976; "Best Sellers: Once an Eagle," NBC, 1976; "Twin Detectives," ABC, 1976; "Murder at the World Series," ABC, 1977; "Roots," ABC, 1977; "Casino," ABC, 1980.

GEORGE, PHYLLIS

b. Denton, TX, June 25, 1949. Former Miss America (1971) who hasn't quite found her TV niche, though not due to a lack of trying. She was the co-host of the "CBS Morning News" in 1985.

AS A REGULAR: "Candid Camera," SYN, 1974-78; "People," CBS, 1978; "CBS Morning News," 1985.

AND: "The Pat Sajak Show," CBS, 1989.

* Two of the guests during George's infamous tenure on the "CBS Morning News" were Cathleen Crowell Webb, a woman who'd falsely accused a man of raping her and Gary Dotson, the man who'd served time in prison as the result of her accusation. George asked them to hug on the air.

GEORGIADE, NICK

b. New York City, NY, February 5, 1933. Rough-looking actor who played characters on both sides of the law.

AS A REGULAR: "The Untouchables," ABC, 1959-63; "Run, Buddy, Run," CBS, 1966-67.

AND: "Combat!: The Party," ABC, 1963; "The Travels of Jaimie McPheeters: The Day of the Toll Takers," ABC, 1964; "The Travels of Jaimie McPheeters: The Day of the Pretenders," ABC, 1964; "Batman: Ring Around the Riddler," ABC, 1967; "Get Smart: And Only Two Ninety-Nine," CBS, 1970; "Mission: Impossible: Squeeze Play," CBS, 1970; "Hawaii Five-O: The Second Shot," CBS, 1970; "Kojak: In Full Command," CBS, 1978.

GERARD, GIL

b. Little Rock, AR, January 23, 1943. Generic TV hunk.

AS A REGULAR: "The Doctors," NBC, 1974-76; "Buck Rogers in the 25th Century," NBC, 1979-81; "Sidekicks," ABC, 1986-87; "Nightingales," NBC, 1989; "EARTH Force," CBS, 1990.

AND: "Little House on the Prairie: The Handyman," NBC, 1977; "Hawaii Five-O: Deadly Doubles," CBS, 1977; "The Mike Douglas Show," SYN, 1981.

TV MOVIES AND MINISERIES: "Not Just Another Affair," CBS, 1982; "Hear No Evil," CBS, 1982; "Help Wanted: Male," CBS, 1982; "Stormin' Home," CBS, 1985.

GERRITSEN, LISA

b. Los Angeles, CA, December 21, 1957. Child actress of the sixties; she played Bess, daughter of Phyllis Lindstrom on "The Mary Tyler Moore Show" and "Phyllis."

AS A REGULAR: "My World and Welcome to It," NBC, 1969-70; "The Mary Tyler Moore Show," CBS, 1970-75; "Phyllis," CBS, 1975-77.

AND: "The Doris Day Show: The Black Eye," CBS, 1968; "Gunsmoke: The Miracle Man," CBS, 1968; "Family Affair: A Diller, A Dollar," CBS, 1969; "The Courtship of Eddie's Father: The Library Card," ABC, 1969; "Family Affair: Stamp of Approval," CBS, 1970; "Gunsmoke: Sam McTavish, M.D.," CBS, 1970; "Gunsmoke: Jenny," CBS, 1970; "The Men From Shiloh: Hannah," NBC, 1970; "The Odd Couple: Bunny Is Missing," ABC, 1971; "Bonanza: Cassie," NBC, 1971; "The Wonderful World of Disney: The Boy and the Bronc Buster," NBC, 1973; "Ironside: Come Eleven, Come Twelve," NBC, 1973; "Ironside: The Double Edged Corner," NBC, 1974; "Hollywood Squares," NBC, 1976.

TV MOVIES AND MINISERIES: "A Howling in the Woods," NBC, 1971; "Locusts," CBS, 1974.

GERTZ, JAMI

b. Chicago, IL, October 28, 1965.

AS A REGULAR: "Square Pegs," CBS, 1982-83; "Dreams," CBS, 1984.

AND: "Family Ties: Double Date," NBC, 1984.

GETTY, ESTELLE

b. New York City, NY, July 25, 1924. Actress who plays Sophia Petrillo on "The Golden Girls."

AS A REGULAR: "The Golden Girls," NBC, 1985- .

AND: "Hotel: Intimate Stranger," ABC, 1984; "Newhart: What Makes Dick Run?," CBS, 1985; "Empty Nest: Libby's Gift," NBC, 1988; "The Pat Sajak Show," CBS, 1989.

TV MOVIES AND MINISERIES: "Victims for Victims: The Theresa Saldana Story," NBC, 1984; "Copacabana," CBS, 1985.

GETZ, JOHN
  b. Davenport, IA.
AS A REGULAR: "Rafferty," CBS, 1977; "Suzanne
  Pleshette Is Maggie Briggs," CBS, 1984;
  "MacGruder and Loud," ABC, 1985;
  "Mariah," ABC, 1987.
AND: "Barney Miller: Atomic Bomb," ABC, 1977;
"The Associates: The First Day," ABC, 1979;
"Three's Company: Lee Ain't Heavy, He's My
Brother," ABC, 1980.
TV MOVIES AND MINISERIES: "Loose Change,"
  NBC, 1978; "Kent State," NBC, 1981;
  "Muggable Mary: Street Cop," CBS, 1982;
  "Not in Front of the Children," CBS, 1982.

GHOSTLEY, ALICE
  b. Eve, MO, August 14, 1926. Actress usually
  in comic roles as spacy types; currently she
  plays Berniece on "Designing Women."
AS A REGULAR: "Jackie Gleason and His American
  Scene Magazine," CBS, 1962-66; "Captain
  Nice," NBC, 1967; "The Jonathan Winters
  Show," CBS, 1968-69; "Bewitched," ABC,
  1969-72; "Mayberry, RFD," CBS, 1970-71;
  "James Garner as Nichols," NBC, 1971-72;
  "The Julie Andrews Hour," ABC, 1972-73;
  "Temperatures Rising," ABC, 1974; "Design-
  ing Women," CBS, 1988- .
AND: "Cinderella," CBS, 1957; "The Tonight
Show," NBC, 1957; "General Motors' 50th
Anniversary Show," NBC, 1957; "Hallmark Hall
of Fame: Twelfth Night," NBC, 1957; "The Jack
Paar Show," NBC, 1958; "The Chevy Show,"
NBC, 1959; "Dow Hour of Great Mysteries: The
Datchet Diamonds," NBC, 1960; "Hooray for
Love," CBS, 1960; "Hallmark Hall of Fame:
Shangri-La," NBC, 1960; "Art Carney Special:
Everybody's Doin' It," NBC, 1961; "The Tom
Ewell Show: I Don't See It," CBS, 1961; "The
Tom Ewell Show: The Chutney Caper," CBS,
1961; "Car 54, Where Are You?: Love Finds
Muldoon," NBC, 1961; "Car 54, Where Are
You?: Christmas at the 53rd," NBC, 1961;
"Please Don't Eat the Daisies: Move Over,
Mozart," NBC, 1966; "Bewitched: Maid to
Order," ABC, 1966; "Get Smart: Last One in Is a
Rotten Spy," NBC, 1966; "He & She: What's in
the Kitty?," CBS, 1968; "Get Smart: The Frakas
Fracas," NBC, 1968; "The John Gary Show,"
SYN, 1968; "The Mothers-in-Law: And Baby
Makes Four," NBC, 1969; "Love, American
Style: Love and the Unlikely Couple," ABC,
1969; "Hogan's Heroes: That's No Lady, That's
My Spy," CBS, 1970; "The Odd Couple: The
Breakup," ABC, 1970; "Love, American Style:
Love and the Boss," ABC, 1971; "Love,
American Style: Love and the Mixed Marriage,"
ABC, 1972; "Love, American Style: Love and the
High School Sweetheart," ABC, 1973; "Kolchak,
the Night Stalker: Bad Medicine," ABC, 1974;
"Cross Wits," SYN, 1976; "What's Happening!:

The Maid Did It," ABC, 1977; "Good Times: The
Evanses Get Involved," CBS, 1977; "One Day at
a Time: The Ghost Writer," CBS, 1977; "Gimme
a Break: Love Thy Neighbor," NBC, 1982; "The
Golden Girls: Mother's Day," NBC, 1988.
TV MOVIES AND MINISERIES: "Two on a Bench,"
  ABC, 1971.

GIAN, JOSEPH
  b. North Miami Beach, CA, July 13, 1961. Actor
  who played cop Rick Silardi on "Hooperman."
AS A REGULAR: "Hooperman," ABC, 1987-89;
  "Knots Landing," CBS, 1989- .
AND: "Star Search," SYN, 1986.
TV MOVIES AND MINISERIES: "Happy Endings,"
  NBC, 1983.

GIBB, ANDY
  b. England, March 5, 1958; d. 1988. Pop
  singer.
AS A REGULAR: "Solid Gold," SYN, 1981-82.
AND: "The John Davidson Show," SYN, 1981;
"The Merv Griffin Show," SYN, 1981; "Gimme a
Break: The Groupie," NBC, 1983; "Punky
Brewster: Play It Again, Punky," NBC, 1984;
"Punky Brewster: Miss Adorable," NBC, 1984;
"Punky Brewster: My Aged Valentine," NBC,
1985; "The Music of Your Life," SYN, 1985.

GIBB, CYNTHIA
  b. Bennington, VT, December 14, 1963.
AS A REGULAR: "Search for Tomorrow," CBS,
  1981-82; ABC, 1982-83; "Fame," NBC, 1982-
  83; SYN, 1983-86.

GIBBS, MARLA
  b. Chicago, IL, June 14, 1946. Actress who's
  appeared on two long-running sitcoms—as
  Florence on "The Jeffersons" and Mary on
  "227"—and luck, not talent, has had everything
  to do with it.
AS A REGULAR: "The Jeffersons," CBS, 1975-85;
  "Checking In," CBS, 1981; "227," NBC, 1985-
  90.
AND: "Barney Miller: Vigilante," ABC, 1975.

GIBSON, HENRY
  b. Germantown, PA, September 21, 1935.
  Poetry-spouting comedian who's also a capable
  dramatic actor.
AS A REGULAR: "The Joey Bishop Show," NBC,
  1963; "Rowan & Martin's Laugh-In," NBC,
  1968-71.
AND: "The Merv Griffin Show," NBC, 1962;
"Grindl: Grindl, Girl Wac," NBC, 1964; "My
Favorite Martian: Danger! High Voltage!," CBS,
1964; "The Beverly Hillbillies: A Man for Elly,"
CBS, 1964; "The Littlest Hobo: The Great
Manhunt," SYN, 1964; "Laredo: Pride of the
Rangers," NBC, 1965; "Mr. Roberts: Liberty,"

NBC, 1965; "Mr. Roberts: Physician, Heal Thyself," NBC, 1965; "F Troop: Wrongo Starr and the Lady in Black," ABC, 1966; "The Dick Van Dyke Show: Talk to the Snail," CBS, 1966; "F Troop: The Return of Wrongo Starr," ABC, 1966; "Hey, Landlord!: Aunt Harriet Wants You," NBC, 1967; "Bewitched: Samantha's French Pastry," ABC, 1968; "The John Gary Show," SYN, 1968; "Hollywood Squares," NBC, 1968; "Love, American Style: Love and the Shower," ABC, 1969; "Bewitched: If the Shoe Pinches," ABC, 1970; "The David Frost Show," SYN, 1970; "Love, American Style: Love and the Note," ABC, 1971; "ABC Afternoon Playbreak: Honeymoon Suite," ABC, 1972; "Love, American Style: Love and the Sweet Sixteen," ABC, 1972; "Love, American Style: Love and the Christmas Punch," ABC, 1972; "The Karen Valentine Show," ABC, 1973; "Love, American Style: Love and the Spendthrift," ABC, 1973; "Wide World of Mystery: Violence in Blue," ABC, 1975; "McCloud: The Man From Taos," NBC, 1975; "Dinah!," SYN, 1975; "Barbary Coast: Arson and Old Lace," ABC, 1975; "Police Woman: Don't Feed the Pigeons," NBC, 1975; "Little House on the Prairie: Annabelle," NBC, 1979; "$weepstake$: Victor, Billy and Bobby, 'Sometimes,'" NBC, 1979; "Simon & Simon: It's Only a Game," CBS, 1982; "Magnum, P.I.: Mixed Doubles," CBS, 1982; "The Love Boat: The Christmas Presence," ABC, 1982; "The Fall Guy: The Meek Shall Inherit Rhonda," ABC, 1983; "Quincy: Murder on Ice," NBC, 1983; "Half-Nelson: Diplomatic Immunity," NBC, 1985; "The Twilight Zone: Welcome to Winfield," CBS, 1986; "Murder, She Wrote: Who Threw the Barbitals in Mrs. Fletcher's Chowder?," CBS, 1987.

TV MOVIES AND MINISERIES: "Evil Roy Slade," NBC, 1972; "Every Man Needs One," ABC, 1972; "The New, Original Wonder Woman," ABC, 1975; "Escape From Bogen County," CBS, 1977; "The Night They Took Miss Beautiful," NBC, 1977; "Amateur Night at the Dixie Bar and Grill," NBC, 1979.

GIELGUD, SIR JOHN

b. London, England, Apr. 14, 1904. Distinguished actor of stage, screen and TV, as the saying goes.

AS A GUEST: "Du Pont Show of the Month: The Browning Version," CBS, 1959; "Ed Sullivan Presents the Spoleto Festival," CBS, 1959; "The Big Party," CBS, 1959; "Bell Telephone Hour: Much Ado About Music," NBC, 1961; "Ages of Man," CBS, 1966; "ABC Stage '67: The Love Song of Barney Kempinski," ABC, 1966; "From Chekov, with Love," CBS, 1968; "NET Playhouse: The May Fly and the King," NET, 1968; "Ivanov," CBS, 1967; "Hallmark Hall of Fame: Hamlet," NBC, 1970; "The David Frost Show," SYN, 1970; "Home,"

NET, 1971; "ABC Afterschool Special: William," ABC, 1973; "Shades of Greene: Special Duties," PBS, 1976; "Peter Pan," NBC, 1976.

TV MOVIES AND MINISERIES: "Probe," NBC, 1972; "Frankenstein: The True Story," NBC, 1973; "QB VII," ABC, 1974; "Les Miserables," CBS, 1978; "The Hunchback of Notre Dame," CBS, 1982; "The Master of Ballantrae," CBS, 1984; "Camille," CBS, 1984; "Romance on the Orient Express," NBC, 1985; "War and Remembrance," ABC, 1988, 1989.

GIFFORD, FRANCES

b. Mary Frances Gifford, Long Beach, CA, December 7, 1920. Actress who played "Jungle Girl" onscreen, and did a bit of TV.

AS A REGULAR: "A.E.S. Hudson Street," ABC, 1978.

AND: "Fireside Theatre: Grey Gardens," NBC, 1953; "G.E. Theatre: My Wife, Poor Wretch," CBS, 1953; "Drama at Eight: Adopted Son," SYN, 1953.

GIFFORD, FRANK

b. Santa Monica, CA, August 16, 1930. Former football star with the New York Giants.

AS A REGULAR: "Monday Night Football," ABC, 1971- .

AND: "Hazel: Hazel and the Halfback," NBC, 1963; "Password," CBS, 1964; "The Reporter: How Much for a Prince?," CBS, 1964; "Webster: You Can't Go Home Again," ABC, 1984; "Life Goes On: Corky Witnesses a Crime," ABC, 1989.

GIFFORD, KATHIE LEE

b. Kathie Lee Johnson, Paris, France. TV personality whose picture should be next to "perky" in the dictionary; adoring wife of Frank Gifford.

AS A REGULAR: "Hee Haw Honeys," SYN, 1978-79; "Good Morning, America," ABC, 1984-87; "Live with Regis & Kathie Lee," SYN, 1988- .

GILBERT, BILLY

b. Louisville, KY, September 12, 1894; d. 1971. Gifted corpulent comic actor, the perfect buffoon opposite such comics as Laurel and Hardy and Charlie Chaplin; he found steady TV employment on kiddie-oriented shows.

AS A REGULAR: "Smilin' Ed McConnell and His Gang," NBC, 1951-55; "Andy's Gang," NBC, 1955-60.

AND: "The Garry Moore Show," CBS, 1956; "Producers Showcase: Jack and the Beanstalk," NBC, 1956; "The Red Skelton Show," CBS, 1958; "Shirley Temple's Storybook: Mother Goose," NBC, 1958; "The Garry Moore Show," CBS, 1959; "The Jimmy Dean Show," CBS, 1959; "The Red Skelton Show: San Fernando for

Governor," CBS, 1960; "Shirley Temple's Storybook: Madeline," NBC, 1960; "The Roaring Twenties: Coney Red Hots," ABC, 1961; "The Danny Thomas Show: Everything Happens to Me," CBS, 1961; "The Red Skelton Show: Clem the Genius," CBS, 1961; "Johnny Carson Special: The Sun City Scandals," NBC, 1970.

GILBERT, MELISSA

b. *Los Angeles, CA, May 8, 1964*. Actress who played Laura Ingalls Wilder on "Little House"; when that series ended, she married into the mafia on a TV movie.

AS A REGULAR: "Little House on the Prairie," NBC, 1974-83.

AND: "The Love Boat: Rocky," ABC, 1978; " Dick Clark's Live Wednesday," NBC, 1978; "Faerie Tale Theatre: The Snow Queen," SHO, 1984.

TV MOVIES AND MINISERIES: "The Miracle Worker," NBC, 1979; "Little House: Look Back to Yesterday," NBC, 1983; "Little House: The Last Farewell," NBC, 1984; "Little House: Bless All the Dear Children," NBC, 1984; "Choices," ABC, 1986; "Penalty Phase," CBS, 1986; "Blood Vows: The Story of a Mafia Wife," NBC, 1987; "Killer Instinct," NBC, 1988.

GILFORD, JACK

b. *Jacob Gellman, New York City, NY, July 25, 1907; d. 1990*. Gifted comic actor, memorable as the rougish father of Alex Rieger (Judd Hirsch) on "Taxi," and on Cracker Jack commercials of the sixties.

AS A REGULAR: "The Arrow Show," NBC, 1948-49; "The David Frost Revue," SYN, 1971-73; "Paul Sand in Friends and Lovers," CBS, 1974-75; "Apple Pie," ABC, 1978; "The Duck Factory," NBC, 1984.

AND: "The Play's the Thing: Screwball," CBS, 1950; "The Arlene Francis Show," NBC, 1957; "Play of the Week: The World of Sholom Aleichem," SYN, 1960; "Car 54, Where Are You?: The Curse of the Snitkins," NBC, 1963; "The Cowboy and the Tiger," ABC, 1963; "The Defenders: Moment of Truth," CBS, 1964; "The Defenders: The Seven-Hundred-Year-Old Gang," CBS, 1964; "Mr. Broadway: Try to Find a Spy," NBC, 1964; "Allan Sherman's Funnyland," NBC, 1965; "The Defenders: No-Knock," CBS, 1965; "T.H.E. Cat: Little Arnie From Long Ago," NBC, 1966; "The Eternal Light: The Temptation of Reb Yisroel," NBC, 1967; "The Dean Martin Show," NBC, 1967; "The Ghost and Mrs. Muir: Uncle Arnold the Magnificent," NBC, 1968; "Here's Lucy: Lucy Helps Craig Get a Driver's License," CBS, 1969; "Arsenic and Old Lace," ABC, 1969; "The Dean Martin Show," NBC, 1969; "Get Smart: And Baby Makes Four," CBS, 1969; "NET Playhouse: They," NET, 1970; "Of Thee I

Sing," CBS, 1972; "Once Upon a Mattress," CBS, 1972; "Twigs," CBS, 1975; "Dinah!," SYN, 1975; "McMillan and Wife: Greed," NBC, 1975; "Captain Kangaroo," CBS, 1976; "Dinah!," SYN, 1976; "Rhoda: The Return of Billy Glass," CBS, 1976; "Police Woman: The Trick Book," NBC, 1976; "All in the Family: Archie Finds a Friend," CBS, 1976; "Lou Grant: Home," CBS, 1979; "The Associates: Tucker's Courtroom Coup," ABC, 1979; "Taxi: Honor Thy Father," ABC, 1979; "Taxi: Like Father, Like Son," ABC, 1981; "Alice: Mel's Christmas Carol," CBS, 1981; "The Love Boat: A Honeymoon for Horace," ABC, 1982; "Hotel: Premiere," ABC, 1983; "The Golden Girls: Sophia's Wedding," NBC, 1988; "thirtysomething: The Mike Van Dyke Show," ABC, 1988; "Head of the Class: Scuttlebutt," ABC, 1989; "B.L. Stryker: Auntie Sue," NBC, 1989.

TV MOVIES AND MINISERIES: "Best Sellers: Seventh Avenue," NBC, 1977; "Goldie and the Boxer Go to Hollywood," NBC, 1981; "Hostage Flight," NBC, 1985.

GILLETTE, ANITA

b. *Baltimore, MD, August 16, 1936*.

AS A REGULAR: "Me and the Chimp," CBS, 1972; "Bob & Carol & Ted & Alice," ABC, 1973; "The Baxters," SYN, 1979-80; "Another World," NBC, 1982; "Quincy," NBC, 1982-83; "Almost Grown," CBS, 1988.

AND: "The Garry Moore Show," CBS, 1962; "Bell Telephone Hour: Salute to Veterans Day," NBC, 1965; "The Merv Griffin Show," SYN, 1968; "Love, American Style: Love and the Water Bed," ABC, 1971; "Love, American Style: Love and the Boomerang," ABC, 1972; "Love, American Style: Love and the Know-It-All," ABC, 1972; "The $10,000 Pyramid," CBS, 1974; "St. Elsewhere: Time Heals," NBC, 1986.

TV MOVIES AND MINISERIES: "A Matter of Wife and Death," NBC, 1975; "Marathon," CBS, 1980.

GILLIGAN'S ISLAND, CBS, 1964-67.

"Gilligan's Island" deserves some sort of commendation—not for quality but because the show's creators were able to put seven people on a desert island for three seasons and totally ignore what seven people on a desert island for three years would really do. Suffice to say they wouldn't spend all their time trying to make radios out of coconuts.

Created by former Red Skelton writer Sherwood Schwartz, "G.I." featured Gilligan (Bob Denver), erstwhile first mate of the S.S. *Minnow*, which had run aground. Alan Hale was the skipper, Jonas Grumby; he and Gilligan did a lot of Laurel and Hardy-style pratfalls and they shared a hut. Hmmm ....

Jim Backus and Natalie Schafer were Mr. and Mrs. Thurston Howell III, Russell Johnson was the professor, Roy Hinckley by name, Tina Louise was movie star Ginger Grant and Dawn Wells was homespun Mary Ann Summers. When last heard from, in a 1981 TV-movie, the castaways had been rescued but were back on the island with the Harlem Globetrotters. Wonder if they were bunking with the Skipper and Gilligan ....

GILLILAND, RICHARD

b. Fort Worth, TX. Actor who plays J.D., boyfriend of Mary Jo (Annie Potts) on "Designing Women" and Jeffrey, bum boyfriend of Ellyn (Polly Draper) on "thirtysomething."

AS A REGULAR: "McMillan," NBC, 1976-77; "Operation Petticoat," ABC, 1977-78; "Little Women," NBC, 1979; "The Waltons," CBS, 1981; "Just Our Luck," ABC, 1983; "Designing Women," CBS, 1986- ; "Heartland," CBS, 1988.

AND: "The Streets of San Francisco: I Ain't Marching Anymore," ABC, 1974; "Medical Center: Heel of the Tyrant," CBS, 1974; "Marcus Welby, M.D.: An End and a Beginning," ABC, 1975; "The Blue Knight: Minnesota," CBS, 1976; "The Love Boat: Heads or Tails," ABC, 1979; "The Love Boat: Out of My Hair," ABC, 1983; "The Love Boat: The Counterfeit Couple," ABC, 1985; "Heartbeat: Stress," ABC, 1989; "thirtysomething: Legacy," ABC, 1989; "thirtysomething: The Burning Bush," ABC, 1989.

TV MOVIES AND MINISERIES: "The Family Kovack," CBS, 1974; "Little Women," NBC, 1978; "A Wedding on Walton's Mountain," NBC, 1982; "The Night the Bridge Fell Down," NBC, 1983; "Challenge of a Lifetime," ABC, 1985; "Embassy," ABC, 1985; "Acceptable Risks," ABC, 1986; "Police Story: Monster Manor," ABC, 1988.

GILLIAM, STU

b. Detroit, MI, July 27, 1943. Black comedian most popular in the late sixties; on "Dean Martin Presents" he'd make his entrance each week at the end of a chorus line of men in Ku Klux Klan robes and hoods.

AS A REGULAR: "Dean Martin Presents," NBC, 1968; "Harris and Company," NBC, 1979.

AND: "The Ed Sullivan Show," CBS, 1968; "Get Smart: Die, Spy," NBC, 1968; "Funny You Should Ask," ABC, 1968; "The Steve Allen Show," SYN, 1968; "Funny You Should Ask," ABC, 1969; "Hollywood Squares," NBC, 1970; "Can You Top This?," SYN, 1970; "Rowan & Martin's Laugh-In," NBC, 1970; "Love,

American Style: Love and the Fur Coat," ABC, 1970; "Match Game '73," CBS, 1973; "What's Happening!: My Three Tons," ABC, 1976; "Cross Wits," SYN, 1977; "What's Happening!: Positive Identification," ABC, 1979.

TV MOVIES AND MINISERIES: "Three's a Crowd," ABC, 1969.

GING, JACK

b. Oklahoma, November 30, 1931. Actor who usually plays tough cops; he was Lt. Ted Quinlan on "Riptide."

AS A REGULAR: "Tales of Wells Fargo," NBC, 1961-62; "The Eleventh Hour," NBC, 1962-64; "Mannix," CBS, 1972; "Dear Detective," CBS, 1979; "Riptide," NBC, 1984-85.

AND: "Wanted Dead or Alive: Bad Gun," CBS, 1959; "The Man and the Challenge: The Visitors," NBC, 1959; "Men Into Space: Sea of Stars," CBS, 1960; "Black Saddle: Means to an End," ABC, 1960; "Wanted Dead or Alive: Jason," CBS, 1960; "Perry Mason: The Case of the Blind Man's Bluff," CBS, 1961; "Shirley Temple's Storybook: The Princess and the Goblins," NBC, 1961; "The Roaring Twenties: Among the Missing," ABC, 1961; "Michael Shayne: It Takes a Heap O' Dyin'," NBC, 1961; "Bob Hope Chrysler Theatre: The War and Eric Kurtz," NBC, 1965; "Perry Mason: The Case of the Lonely Eloper," CBS, 1965; "Trials of O'Brian: A Horse Called Destiny," CBS, 1966; "Judd for the Defense: In a Puff of Smoke," ABC, 1968; "Mannix: End of the Rainbow," CBS, 1968; "The FBI: The Cobra List," ABC, 1969; "Mannix: Medal for a Hero," CBS, 1969; "Hawaii Five-O: Run, Johnny, Run," CBS, 1970; "The Men From Shiloh: The Animal," NBC, 1971; "The Mod Squad: The Poisoned Mind," ABC, 1971; "The Mod Squad: I Am My Brother's Keeper," ABC, 1972; "Medical Center: The Awakening," CBS, 1972; "O'Hara, U.S. Treasury: Operation Smokescreen," CBS, 1972; "My Sister Hank," ABC, 1972; "Ironside: Nightmare Trip," NBC, 1972; "The FBI: Canyon of No Return," ABC, 1972; "Mission: Impossible: Kidnap," CBS, 1972; "Barnaby Jones: Venus as in Fly Trap," CBS, 1974; "Owen Marshall, Counselor at Law: A Killer with a Badge," ABC, 1974; "The FBI: The Two Million Dollar Hit," ABC, 1974; "The Magician: The Illusion of the Deadly Conglomerate," NBC, 1974; "ABC Afternoon Playbreak: Can I Save My Children?," ABC, 1974; "Kojak: The Good Luck Bomber," CBS, 1975; "Little House on the Prairie: Survival," NBC, 1975; "Joe Forrester: Bus Station," NBC, 1975; "Barnaby Jones: The Alpha-Bravo War," CBS, 1975; "The Bionic Woman: Kill Oscar," ABC, 1976; "Kojak: Cry for the Kids," CBS, 1977; "Barnaby Jones: A Desperate Pursuit," CBS, 1979; "Hart to Hart: What Murder?," ABC, 1980; "Quincy: Dead Stop," NBC, 1981; "The A-Team: Bad Time on the Border," NBC, 1983; "Hardcastle and McCormick: Just Another Round of That Old Song," ABC, 1983; "Little House: A New Beginning: May I Have This Dance," NBC, 1983; "Highway to Heaven: Code Name: Freak," NBC, 1985; "Wiseguy: Pilot," CBS, 1987.

TV MOVIES AND MINISERIES: "O'Hara, United States Treasury: Operation Cobra," CBS, 1971; "Terror in the Sky," ABC, 1971; "Murder Impossible," ABC, 1974; "The Imposter," NBC, 1975; "Run, Joe, Run," NBC, 1976; "War and Remembrance," ABC, 1988, 1989.

GINGOLD, HERMIONE
b. London, England, December 9, 1897; d. 1987. Actress and talk show regular with a distinctive, cultured-foghorn voice and witty manner.

AS A REGULAR: "One Minute Please," DUM, 1954-55.

AND: "Elgin TV Hour: A Sting of Death," ABC, 1955; "Ominbus: She Stoops to Conquer," CBS, 1955; "The Last Word," CBS, 1957; "The Tonight Show," NBC, 1957; "The Jack Paar Show," NBC, 1958; "Shower of Stars," CBS, 1958; "The Jack Paar Show," NBC, 1958; "The George Gobel Show," NBC, 1958; "The Ed Sullivan Show," CBS, 1958; "The Garry Moore, CBS, 1958; "The Jack Paar Show," NBC, 1959; "The Perry Como Show," NBC, 1959; "I've Got a Secret," CBS, 1959; "Art Carney Special: Small World, Isn't It?," NBC, 1959; "Arthur Murray Party," NBC, 1959; "Frank Sinatra Timex Show," ABC, 1959; "I've Got a Secret," CBS, 1959; "Frances Langford Special," NBC, 1960; "Startime: Fun Fair," NBC, 1960; "Alfred Hitchcock Presents: The Schartz-Metterklume Method," CBS, 1960; "This Is Your Life," NBC, 1960; "Here's Hollywood," NBC, 1961; "Victor Borge Special," CBS, 1961; "Assassination Plot at Teheran," ABC, 1961; "The Merv Griffin Show," NBC, 1962; "The Merv Griffin Show," NBC, 1963; "Girl Talk," SYN, 1963; "Hallmark Hall of Fame: A Cry of Angels," NBC, 1963; "Get the Message," ABC, 1964; "The Mike Douglas Show," SYN, 1965; "The Merv Griffin Show," SYN, 1967; "The Merv Griffin Show," SYN, 1968; "It Takes a Thief: The Lay of the Land," ABC, 1968; "Love, American Style: Love and the Heist," ABC, 1969; "Ironside: Checkmate and Murder," NBC, 1970; "The Name of the Game: Aquarius Descending," NBC, 1970; "Hotel: Charades," ABC, 1983.

TV MOVIES AND MINISERIES: "Banyon," NBC, 1971.

GINTY, ROBERT
b. Brooklyn, NY, November 14, 1948.

AS A REGULAR: "Baa Baa Black Sheep," NBC, 1976-78; "The Paper Chase," CBS, 1978-79; "Hawaiian Heat," ABC, 1984; "Falcon Crest," CBS, 1989-90.

AND: "The Rockford Files: Caledonia, It's Worth a

Fortune!," NBC, 1974; "Police Woman: Glitter with a Bullet," NBC, 1975; "Jigsaw John: Follow the Yellow Brick Road," NBC, 1976; "The Love Boat: Black Sheep," ABC, 1981; "Quincy: Vigil of Fear," NBC, 1981; "Quincy: Give Me Your Weak," NBC, 1982; "Simon & Simon: The Club Murder Vacation," CBS, 1983;

TV MOVIES AND MINISERIES: "I Want to Live!," ABC, 1983.

GISH, DOROTHY
b. Dorothy de Guiche, Massillon, OH, 1898; d. 1968. Sister of Lillian, and a talented screen comic actress in her own right; her TV appearances were more on the dramatic side.

AS A GUEST: "Ford Theatre: One Day for Keeps," CBS, 1951; "Prudential Family Playhouse: The Bishop Misbehaves," CBS, 1951; "Starlight Theatre: The Magnificent Faker," ABC, 1951; "Robert Montgomery Presents: The Post Road," NBC, 1952; "Goodyear TV Playhouse: The Oil Well," NBC, 1953; "Robert Montgomery Presents: Harvest," NBC, 1953; "U.S. Steel Hour: The Rise and Fall of Silas Lapham," ABC, 1954; "Philco TV Playhouse: The Shadow of Willie Greer," NBC, 1954; "Elgin TV Hour: Flood," ABC, 1954; "Lux Video Theatre: Miss Susie Slagle's," NBC, 1955; "Alcoa Hour: Morning's at Seven," NBC, 1956; "Play of the Week: Morning's at Seven," SYN, 1960.

GISH, LILLIAN
b. Lillian de Guiche, Springfield, OH, October 14, 1896. Incandescent silent-screen actress and beauty whose TV work has ranged from the sublime ("The Defenders," "Morning's at Seven") to the ridiculous ("The Love Boat," "Twin Detectives").

AS A GUEST: "Philco TV Playhouse: The Birth of the Movies," NBC, 1951; "Robert Montgomery Presents: Ladies in Retirement," NBC, 1951; "Pulitzer Prize Playhouse: Detour," ABC, 1951; "Celanese Theatre: The Joyous Season," ABC, 1951; "Schlitz Playhouse of Stars: Grandma Moses," CBS, 1952; "Philco TV Playhouse: The Trip to Bountiful," NBC, 1953; "Robert Montgomery Presents: The Quality of Mercy," NBC, 1954; "Campbell TV Soundstage: The Corner Drugstore," NBC, 1954; "Kraft Television Theatre: I, Mrs. Bibb," NBC, 1955; "Playwrights '56: The Sound and the Fury," NBC, 1955; "Ford Star Jubilee: The Day Lincoln Was Shot," NBC, 1956; "Alcoa Hour: Morning's at Seven," NBC, 1956; "Play of the Week: The Grass Harp," SYN, 1960; "Theatre '62: The Spiral Staircase," NBC, 1961; "The Defenders: Grandma TNT," CBS, 1962; "Mr. Novak: Hello, Miss Phipps," NBC, 1963; "The Alfred Hitchcock Hour: The Body in the Barn," NBC, 1963; "The Breaking Point:

The Gnu, Now Almost Extinct," ABC, 1963; "Arsenic and Old Lace," ABC, 1969; "The Love Boat: Isaac's Teacher," ABC, 1981.
TV MOVIES AND MINISERIES: "Twin Detectives," ABC, 1976; "Thin Ice," CBS, 1981; "Hobson's Choice," CBS, 1983.

GIVENS, ROBIN
b. New York City, NY, November 27, 1964. Attractive actress, and the former Mrs. Mike Tyson.
AS A REGULAR: "Head of the Class," ABC, 1986- .
AND: "The Cosby Show: Theo and the Older Woman," NBC, 1985.
TV MOVIES AND MINISERIES: "Beverly Hills Madam," NBC, 1986; "The Women of Brewster Place," ABC, 1989; "The Penthouse," ABC, 1989.
* The marriage between Givens and heavyweight champion Tyson had already been through several well-publicized battles when Givens told America, via Barbara Walters, that her husband scared her. The on-air marriage therapy didn't work, and they divorced.

GLASER, PAUL MICHAEL
b. Cambridge, MA, March 25, 1943. Dark-featured, curly-headed actor who played Det. Ken Hutchinson on one of the most aggressively mindless cop shows ever.
AS A REGULAR: "Love of Life," CBS, 1971-72; "Starsky and Hutch," ABC, 1975-79.
AND: "The Streets of San Francisco: Bitter Wine," ABC, 1972; "The Waltons: The Air Mail Man," CBS, 1973; "Kojak: Dead on His Feet," CBS, 1974; "Aces High," CBS, 1974; "The Rockford Files: Find Me if You Can," NBC, 1974; "Wide World of Mystery: The Impersonation Murder Case," ABC, 1975; "The Merv Griffin Show," SYN, 1975.
TV MOVIES AND MINISERIES: "Trapped Beneath the Sea," ABC, 1974; "Starsky and Hutch," ABC, 1975; "The Great Houdinis," ABC, 1976; "Wait Til Your Mother Gets Home," NBC, 1983; "Princess Daisy," NBC, 1983; "Attack on Fear," CBS, 1984; "Single Bars, Single Women," ABC, 1984; "Jealousy," ABC, 1984.

GLASS, NED
b. Poland, April 1, 1906; d. 1984. Slight, bald character actor usually in roles that allow him to kvetch; best known as landlord Sol Cooper on "Julia."
AS A REGULAR: "Fair Exchange," CBS, 1962; "Julia," NBC, 1968-71; "Bridget Loves Bernie," CBS, 1972-73.
AND: "Medic: My Very Good Friend Albert," NBC, 1955; "Studio One: Love Me to Pieces," CBS, 1957; "Have Gun, Will Travel: Strange Vendetta," CBS, 1957; "Have Gun, Will Travel:

Show of Force," CBS, 1957; "Court of Last Resort: The Todd-Loomis Case," NBC, 1958; "Gunsmoke: Texas Cowboys," CBS, 1958; "U.S. Marshal: The Champ," SYN, 1958; "Law of the Plainsman: The Comet," NBC, 1960; "Gunsmoke: Crowbait Bob," CBS, 1960; "Peter Gunn: Sentenced," NBC, 1960; "Westinghouse Desilu Playhouse: The Man in the Funny Suit," CBS, 1960; "Peter Gunn: The Heiress," NBC, 1960; "Michael Shayne: Dolls Are Deadly," NBC, 1960; "The Danny Thomas Show: Danny and Durante," CBS, 1961; "Have Gun, Will Travel: The Long Weekend," CBS, 1961; "Slattery's People: Question-What Are You Doing Out There, Waldo?," CBS, 1964; "The Dick Van Dyke Show: I'd Rather Be Bald Than Have No Head at All," CBS, 1964; "Bewitched: Oedipus Hex," ABC, 1966; "The Hero: Curiosity Killed a Key," NBC, 1966; "The Monkees: Monkees in the Ring," NBC, 1967; "Mr. Terrific: Has Mr. Terrific Sold Out?," CBS, 1967; "Love on a Rooftop: The Sellout," ABC, 1967; "The Man From UNCLE: The Hot Number Affair," NBC, 1967; "Hollywood Television Theatre: Enemies," NET, 1971; "The Partridge Family: A Partridge by Any Other Name," ABC, 1971; "Love, American Style: Love and the Black Limousine," ABC, 1972; "Police Woman: Ice," NBC, 1975; "The Mary Tyler Moore Show: My Son, The Genius," CBS, 1976; "Kojak: Justice Deferred," CBS, 1976; "Fish: It Shouldn't Happen to a Dog," ABC, 1978; "Barney Miller: Field Associate," ABC, 1981.
TV MOVIES AND MINISERIES: "The Movie Murderer," NBC, 1970; "Banyon," NBC, 1971; "Mongo's Back in Town," CBS, 1971; "The Adventures of Nick Carter," ABC, 1972; "Crossfire," NBC, 1975.
* Glass played himself in "The Man in the Funny Suit," a retelling of what happened when Ed Wynn was tapped to make his dramatic debut on "Playhouse 90" in "Requiem for a Heavyweight." After disastrous early rehearsals, the nervous producers hired Glass as Wynn's stand-in, but without letting Wynn know about it. Wynn overcame his stage fright and triumphed in the role, and Glass wasn't needed.

GLASS, RON
b. Evansville, IN, July 10, 1945. Actor who played the dapper Det. Harris on "Barney Miller" and Felix in a black version of "The Odd Couple."
AS A REGULAR: "Barney Miller," ABC, 1975-82; "The New Odd Couple," ABC, 1982-83.
AND: "Sanford & Son: The Card Sharps," NBC, 1972; "Maude: Florida's Affair," CBS, 1973; "Hawaii Five-O: Tricks are Not Treats," CBS, 1973; "All in the Family: Everybody Tells the Truth," CBS, 1973; "The Bob Newhart Show: Fit

Fat and Forty-One," CBS, 1973; "Hawaii Five-O: Tricks Are Not Treats," CBS, 1973; "The New Adventures of Perry Mason: The Case of the Tortured Titan," CBS, 1974; "Change at 125th Street," CBS, 1974; "Good Times: Crosstown Busses Run All Day, Doodah, Doodah," CBS, 1974; "Good Times: The Encyclopedia Hustle," CBS, 1974; "Sanford & Son: Once a Thief," NBC, 1974; "Showoffs," ABC, 1975; "When Things Were Rotten: This Lance for Hire," ABC, 1975; "The Streets of San Francisco: The Thrill Killers," ABC, 1976; "Dinah!," SYN, 1978; "Amen: Witness for the Defense," NBC, 1989; "Family Matters: False Arrest," ABC, 1989.

TV MOVIES AND MINISERIES: "Beg, Borrow ... or Steal," CBS, 1973; "Shirts/Skins," ABC, 1973; "Crash," ABC, 1978; "Perry Mason: The Case of the Shooting Star," NBC, 1986.

GLEASON, JACKIE

b. Brooklyn, NY, February 26, 1916; d. 1987. Comic legend with a ferocious appetite for life who gave us Reginald Van Gleason III, the Poor Soul, Joe the Bartender and Ralph Kramden.

AS A REGULAR: "The Life of Riley," NBC, 1949-50; "Cavalcade of Stars," DUM, 1950-52; "The Jackie Gleason Show," CBS, 1952-55; 1956-57; 1958-59; 1961; 1966-70; "The Honeymooners," CBS, 1955-56; 1971; "You're in the Picture," CBS, 1961; "Jackie Gleason and His American Scene Magazine," CBS, 1962-66.

AND: "Studio One: The Laugh Maker," CBS, 1953; "Studio One: Peacock City," CBS, 1954; "Best of Broadway: The Show-Off," CBS, 1955; "Studio One: Uncle Ed and Circumstance," CBS, 1955; "Playhouse 90: The Time of Your Life," CBS, 1958; "This Is Your Life," NBC, 1958; "The Arthur Godfrey Show," CBS, 1958; "All-Star Jazz: The Golden Age of Jazz," CBS, 1959; "The Fabulous Fifties," CBS, 1960; "The Kate Smith Show," CBS, 1960; "Arthur Godfrey Special," CBS, 1960; "The Secret World of Eddie Hodges," CBS, 1960; "Jackie Gleason Special: The Big Sell," CBS, 1960; "The Red Skelton Show," CBS, 1961; "Sunday Sports Spectacular: Jackie Gleason with Putter and Cue," CBS, 1961; "Jackie Gleason Special: The Million Dollar Incident," CBS, 1961; "Here's Lucy: Lucy Visits Jack Benny," CBS, 1968; "Jackie Gleason Special," CBS, 1973; "Two for Three," CBS, 1975; "The Honeymooners-The Second Honeymoon," ABC, 1976.

TV MOVIES AND MINISERIES: "Izzy and Moe," CBS, 1985.

* "You're in the Picture" aired exactly once, on January 20, 1961. The game show—in which celebrities stood behind life-sized pictures, poked their heads through holes and tried to guess what was on the picture surrounding them—was so lousy that the next week, at the appointed time, Gleason emerged on camera and apologized to the audience for insulting their intelligence. He filled the next several weeks with an informal talk show.

* "The Million Dollar Incident" was from a Gleason story idea; the Great One played himself, who'd been kidnapped (by a criminal mastermind played by Everett Sloane) for a million dollar ransom.

TV'S TOP TEN, 1954-55
1. I Love Lucy (CBS)
2. The Jackie Gleason Show (CBS)
3. Dragnet (NBC)
4. You Bet Your Life (NBC)
5. Toast of the Town (CBS)
6. Disneyland (ABC)
7. The Jack Benny Program (CBS)
8. The George Gobel Show (NBC)
9. Ford Theatre (NBC)
10. December Bride (CBS)

GLEASON, JAMES

b. New York City, NY, May 23, 1886; d. 1959. Character actor who played tough-on-the-outside, soft-on-the-inside types in movies and on TV.

AS A GUEST: "Ford Theatre: Sweet Talk Me, Jackson," NBC, 1953; "A Frameup," CBS, 1954; "Shower of Stars: Burlesque," CBS, 1955; "So This Is Hollywood: The Old Timer," NBC, 1955; "Damon Runyon Theatre: The Big Umbrella," CBS, 1955; "Screen Directors Playhouse: Rookie of the Year," NBC, 1955; "Damon Runyon Theatre: Dog About Town," CBS, 1955; "Cheyenne: Decision," ABC, 1956; "Climax!: The Fifth Wheel," CBS, 1956; "The Millionaire: The Story of Charlie Simpson," CBS, 1956; "Ford Theatre: Try Me for Size," NBC, 1956; "Alfred Hitchcock Presents: The End of Indian Summer," CBS, 1957; "Du Pont Theatre: Shark of the Mountain," ABC, 1957; "Leave It to Beaver: The Clubhouse," CBS, 1957; "Restless Gun: The Child," NBC, 1957; "Playhouse 90: The Time of Your Life," CBS, 1958.

GLESS, SHARON

b. Los Angeles, CA, May 31, 1943. Blonde actress who, after a long career playing sidekicks, became a TV favorite as detective Chris Cagney.

AS A REGULAR: "Faraday and Company," NBC, 1973-74; "Marcus Welby, M.D.," ABC, 1974-76; "Switch," CBS, 1975-78; "Turnabout," NBC, 1979; "House Calls," CBS, 1982; "Cagney & Lacey," CBS, 1982-88; "The Trials of Rosie O'Neill," CBS, 1990- .

AND: "McCloud: Encounter with Aries," NBC, 1972; "Cool Million: The Abduction of Bayard

Barnes," NBC, 1972; "Emergency!: Rip-Off," NBC, 1973; "Ironside: House of Terror," NBC, 1973; "Adam 12: Clinic on 18th Street," NBC, 1974; "The Bob Newhart Show: The Modernization of Emily," CBS, 1974; "The Rockford Files: This Case Is Closed," NBC, 1974; "Lucas Tanner: Those Who Cannot, Teach," NBC, 1975; "Kojak: Law Dance," CBS, 1976; "The Rockford Files: The Fourth Man," NBC, 1976.

TV MOVIES AND MINISERIES: "All My Darling Daughters," ABC, 1972; "My Darling Daughters' Anniversary," ABC, 1973; "Switch," CBS, 1975; "Richie Brockelman, Private Eye," NBC, 1976; "Crash," ABC, 1978; "The Immigrants," SYN, 1978; "The Islander," CBS, 1978; "Centennial," NBC, 1978-79; "The Last Convertible," NBC, 1979; "Hardhat and Legs," CBS, 1980; "The Revenge of the Stepford Wives," NBC, 1980; "The Miracle of Kathy Miller," CBS, 1981; "Hobson's Choice," CBS, 1983; "The Sky's No Limit," CBS, 1984; "Letting Go," ABC, 1985; "The Outside Woman," CBS, 1989.
* Emmies: 1986, 1987.

GNAGY, JON
b. Varner's Forge, KS, 1907; d. 1981. Goateed artist who hosted a TV drawing program.
AS A REGULAR: "You Are an Artist," NBC, 1946-50.

GOBEL, GEORGE
b. Chicago, IL, May 20, 1920; d. 1991. Flat-topped comic whose low-key style was a marked contrast to the madmen of early fifties' variety shows.
AS A REGULAR: "The George Gobel Show," NBC, 1954-57; CBS, 1959-60; "The George Gobel/Eddie Fisher Show," NBC, 1957-59; "Hollywood Squares," NBC, 1974-81; "Harper Valley PTA," NBC, 1981-82.
AND: "Light's Diamond Jubilee," ABC, CBS, NBC, 1954; "The Jack Benny Program," CBS, 1956; "Dinah Shore Chevy Show," NBC, 1956; "The Perry Como Show," NBC, 1957; "The Garry Moore Show," CBS, 1957; "The Ford Show," NBC, 1957; "The Ray Bolger Show," NBC, 1957; "The Chevy Show," NBC, 1957; "The Steve Allen Show," NBC, 1957; "The Ford Show," NBC, 1958; "The Lux Show with Rosemary Clooney," NBC, 1958; "Dinah Shore Chevy Show," NBC, 1959; "The Chevy Show," NBC, 1959; "The Steve Allen Show," NBC, 1959; "The Garry Moore Show," CBS, 1959; "Startime: Cindy's Fella," NBC, 1959; "G.E. Theatre: They Liked Me Fine," CBS, 1960; "My Three Sons: Lonesome George," ABC, 1960; "The Chevy Show: Four in One," NBC, 1961; "Perry Como's Kraft Music Hall," NBC, 1961; "Candid Camera," CBS, 1961; "The Garry Moore Show," CBS, 1961; "The Ed Sullivan Show," CBS, 1962;

"What's My Line?," CBS, 1962; "The Garry Moore Show," CBS, 1962; "Summer Playhouse: The Apartment House," CBS, 1964; "Dinah Shore Special," ABC, 1964; "Valentine's Day: Hottest Game in Town," ABC, 1964; "The Mike Douglas Show," SYN, 1965; "The Bing Crosby Show: The Image," ABC, 1965; "The Dean Martin Show," NBC, 1965; "Daniel Boone: Four-Leaf Clover," NBC, 1965; "F Troop: Go for Broke," ABC, 1966; "Hollywood Palace," ABC, 1969; "The Saga of Sonora," NBC, 1973; "John Denver Special," ABC, 1974; 'Twas the Night Before Christmas," CBS, 1974; "Joys," NBC, 1976; "Dinah!," SYN, 1976; "Donny and Marie," ABC, 1977; "Chico and the Man: Louie's Can Can," NBC, 1977.
TV MOVIES AND MINISERIES: "Benny and Barney: Las Vegas Undercover," NBC, 1977; "A Guide for the Married Woman," ABC, 1978; "The Invisible Woman," NBC, 1983.
* Emmies: 1955.

GODDARD, MARK
b. Lowell, MA, July 24, 1936. Actor who played the hot-tempered Don West on "Lost in Space" and has migrated to soaps.
AS A REGULAR: "Johnny Ringo," CBS, 1959-60; "The Detectives Starring Robert Taylor," ABC, 1960-61; "Robert Taylor's Detectives," NBC, 1961-62; "Many Happy Returns," CBS, 1964-65; "Lost in Space," CBS, 1965-68; "One Life to Live," ABC, 1981; "The Doctors," NBC, 1982; "General Hospital," ABC, 1984- .
AS A GUEST: "The du Pont Show with June Allyson: Surprise Party," CBS, 1960; "Chevy Mystery Show: Murder Me Nicely," NBC, 1960; "The Rebel: To See the Elephant," ABC, 1960; "Dick Powell's Zane Grey Theatre: The Mormons," CBS, 1960; "Fair Exchange: Lieutenant's Paradise," CBS, 1962; "The Rifleman: Mark's Rifle," ABC, 1962; "Vacation Playhouse: Maggie Brown," CBS, 1963; "Burke's Law: Who Killed April?," ABC, 1964; "The Fugitive: Fun and Games and Party Favors," ABC, 1965; "Barnaby Jones: Dark Legacy," CBS, 1974; "Petrocelli: A Lonely Victim," NBC, 1975; "Switch: Death Squad," CBS, 1976; "Quincy: Sullied Be Thy Name," NBC, 1977; "The Streets of San Francisco: The Cannibals," ABC, 1977; "Benson: War Stories," ABC, 1979; "Barnaby Jones: The Killin' Cousin," CBS, 1980; "The Fall Guy: Devil's Island," ABC, 1983.
TV MOVIES AND MINISERIES: "The Death Squad," ABC, 1973.

GODDARD, PAULETTE
b. Marion Levy, Great Neck, NY, June 3, 1911; d. 1990. Screen actress and former wife of Charles Chaplin who did a little TV.
AS A GUEST: "The Joseph Cotten Show: The

Ghost of Devil's Island," NBC, 1957; "Ford Theatre: Singapore," ABC, 1957; "Errol Flynn Playhouse: Mademoiselle Fifi," SYN, 1957; "Errol Flynn Playhouse: The Doctor's Downfall," SYN, 1957; "Arthur Murray Party," NBC, 1959; "Adventures in Paradise: Lady From South Chicago," ABC, 1959; "Arthur Murray Party," NBC, 1960; "Celebrity Talent Scouts," CBS, 1960.

TV MOVIES AND MINISERIES: "The Snoop Sisters," NBC, 1972.

GODFREY, ARTHUR
b. New York City, NY, August 31, 1903; d. 1983. "The Old Redhead," radio personality who dominated television for the fifties and who was a lot less folksy in his personal dealings than he was on the airwaves.

AS A REGULAR: "Arthur Godfrey's Talent Scouts," CBS, 1948-58; "Arthur Godfrey and His Friends," CBS, 1949-56; "Arthur Godfrey and His Ukelele," CBS, 1950; "Arthur Godfrey Time," CBS, 1952-59; "The Arthur Godfrey Show," CBS, 1958-59; "Candid Camera," CBS, 1960-61; "Your All-American College Show," SYN, 1968.

AND: "Pat Boone Chevy Showroom," ABC, 1959; "The Red Skelton Show: Clem in Miami Beach," CBS, 1959; "A Tribute to Eleanor Roosevelt on Her Diamond Jubilee," NBC, 1959; "The Fabulous Fifties," CBS, 1960; "Arthur Godfrey Special," CBS, 1960; "The Red Skelton Show," CBS, 1961; "Highlights of the 1961 Ringling Bros. Barnum and Bailey Circus," CBS, 1961; "Bulova Watch Time with Arthur Godfrey," CBS, 1961; "Arthur Godfrey in Hollywood," CBS, 1962; "I've Got a Secret," CBS, 1962; "Arthur Godfrey Special: The Sounds of New York," CBS, 1963; "The Jack Paar Program," NBC, 1963; "I've Got a Secret," CBS, 1964; "What's My Line?," CBS, 1964; "The Lucy Show: Lucy and Arthur Godfrey," CBS, 1965; "Ice Capades of 1966," CBS, 1965; "The Dean Martin Show," NBC, 1966; "Bob Hope Chrysler Theatre: The Reason Nobody Hardly Ever Seen a Fat Outlaw in the West Is as Follows," NBC, 1967; "The Smothers Brothers Comedy Hour," CBS, 1968; "The Ed Sullivan Show," CBS, 1970; "Rowan & Martin's Laugh-In," NBC, 1973; "The Love Boat: A Home Is Not a Home," ABC, 1979.

TV MOVIES AND MINISERIES: "Flatbed Annie and Sweetiepie: Lady Truckers," CBS, 1979.

* Godfrey attained nationwide prominence when he tearfully reported on the 1945 funeral of President Franklin D. Roosevelt.
* In 1953 Godfrey fired singer Julius LaRosa on the air, saying he lacked humility; in the next few years he also dumped orchestra leader Archie Bleyer, singers Marion Marlowe and Haleoke and the Chordettes when their popularity threatened to overshadow his.

* Godfrey had a radio show on CBS from 1933-72.

TV'S TOP TEN, 1952-53
1. I Love Lucy (CBS)
2. Arthur Godfrey's Talent Scouts (CBS)
3. Arthur Godfrey and His Friends (CBS)
4. Dragnet (NBC)
5. Texaco Star Theatre (NBC)
6. The Buick Circus Hour (NBC)
7. The Colgate Comedy Hour (NBC)
8. Gangbusters (NBC)
9. You Bet Your Life (NBC)
10. Fireside Theatre (NBC)

GODFREY, KATHY
b. Hasbrouck Heights, NJ, 1910. Younger sister of Arthur Godfrey.

AS A REGULAR: "On Your Way," ABC, 1954.

GOLD, BRANDY
b. Northridge, CA, July 11, 1977. Young actress.

AS A REGULAR: "Baby Makes Five," ABC, 1983; "First Impressions," CBS, 1988.

AND: "St. Elsewhere: Up on the Roof," NBC, 1984; "My Sister Sam: Deep Throat," CBS, 1987.

TV MOVIES AND MINISERIES: "Amityville: The Evil Escapes," NBC, 1989.

GOLD, MISSY
b. Great Falls, MT, July 14, 1970. Actress who played Katie Gatling on "Benson."

AS A REGULAR: "Benson," ABC, 1979-86.

TV MOVIES AND MINISERIES: "Best Sellers: Captains and the Kings," NBC, 1976.

GOLD, TRACEY
b. New York City, NY, May 16, 1969. Young actress who plays Carol Seaver on "Growing Pains."

AS A REGULAR: "Shirley," NBC, 1979-80; "Goodnight Beantown," CBS, 1983-84; "Growing Pains," ABC, 1985- .

AND: "CHiPs: Drive, Lady, Drive," NBC, 1979; "Incredible Sunday," ABC, 1989; "Animal Crack-Ups," ABC, 1989.

TV MOVIES AND MINISERIES: "Best Sellers: Captains and the Kings," NBC, 1976; "The Incredible Journey of Doctor Meg Laurel," CBS, 1979; "Another Woman's Child," CBS, 1983; "Who Will Love My Children?," ABC, 1983; "Thursday's Child," CBS, 1983; "A Reason to Live," NBC, 1985; "Dance 'Til Dawn," NBC, 1988.

GOLDBERG, WHOOPI
b. New York City, NY, 1949. Comic and actress who plays Brenda on "Bagdad Cafe."

AS A REGULAR: "Star Trek: The Next Generation," SYN, 1988- ; "Bagdad Cafe," CBS, 1990- .

AND: "Moonlighting: Camille," ABC, 1986; "Carol, Carl, Whoopi and Robin," ABC, 1986; "Captain EO-Backstage," ABC, 1988; "The Tonight Show Starring Johnny Carson," NBC, 1988; "CBS Schoolbreak Special: My Past Is My Own," CBS, 1989; "The Debbie Allen Special," ABC, 1989; "All Star Tribute to Kareem Abdul-Jabbar," NBC, 1989.

TV MOVIES AND MINISERIES: "Kiss Shot," CBS, 1989.

GOLDBLUM, JEFF

b. Pittsburgh, PA, October 22, 1952. Gangly, dark-featured film actor ("The Big Chill," "The Fly") who played stockbroker Lionel Whitney in the underrated cop show "Tenspeed and Brown Shoe."

AS A REGULAR: "Tenspeed and Brown Shoe," ABC, 1980.

AND: "The Blue Knight: Minnesota," CBS, 1976; "It's Garry Shandling's Show: Go Go Goldblum," FOX, 1988.

GOLDSBORO, BOBBY

b. Marianna, FL, January 18, 1941. Pop singer of the sixties ("Honey").

AS A REGULAR: "The Bobby Goldsboro Show," SYN, 1972-75.

AND: "Where the Action Is," ABC, 1965; "Hollywood Palace," ABC, 1968; "The Merv Griffin Show," SYN, 1968; "The Mike Douglas Show," SYN, 1968; "Jimmy Durante Presents the Lennon Sisters Hour," ABC, 1969; "Bobbie Gentry Special," CBS, 1970; "Stand Up and Cheer," SYN, 1971; "The David Frost Show," SYN, 1971; "The Tonight Show Starring Johnny Carson," NBC, 1972; "Dinah!," SYN, 1976.

GOLONKA, ARLENE

b. Chicago, IL, January 23, 1939. Blonde actress, occasionally in bimbo roles; she played Millie Swanson on "Mayberry RFD."

AS A REGULAR: "Kitty Foyle," NBC, 1958; "Mayberry RFD," CBS, 1968-71; "Joe & Valerie," NBC, 1979.

AND: "U.S. Steel Hour: The Apple of His Eye," CBS, 1959; "Car 54, Where Are You?: The White Elephant," NBC, 1963; "ABC Stage '67: The Love Song of Barney Kempinski," ABC, 1966; "That Girl: Rain, Snow and Rice," ABC, 1967; "The Flying Nun: The Convent," ABC, 1967; "The Andy Griffith Show: Howard and Millie," CBS, 1967; "The Big Valley: Explosion," ABC, 1967; "Get Smart: The Little Black Book," NBC, 1968; "I Spy: Pinwheel," NBC, 1968; "That Girl: The Hijack and the Mighty," ABC, 1968; "It Takes Two," NBC, 1969; "Sarge: A Bad Case of Monogamy," NBC, 1971; "Hollywood Television Theatre: Young Marrieds at Play," NET, 1971; "The Mary Tyler Moore Show: Ted Over Heels,"

CBS, 1971; "Call Holme," NBC, 1972; "Love, American Style: Love and the Ledge," ABC, 1972; "The FBI: The Gopher," ABC, 1972; "Owen Marshall, Counselor at Law: The Trouble with Ralph," ABC, 1972; "M*A*S*H: Edwina," CBS, 1972; "Barnaby Jones: Sing a Song of Murder," CBS, 1973; "All in the Family: Oh Say Can You See," CBS, 1973; "Honeymoon Suite: Two Too Funny People," ABC, 1973; "Maude: The Wallet," CBS, 1974; "Chase: Vacation for a President," NBC, 1974; "The Girl with Something Extra: The Not-So-Good Samaritan," NBC, 1974; "The Mary Tyler Moore Show: I Was a Single for WJM," CBS, 1974; "Police Woman: The Cradle Robbers," NBC, 1974; "Barnaby Jones: Jeopardy for Two," CBS, 1975; "Wide World of Mystery: The Impersonation Murder Case," ABC, 1975; "The Family Holvak: Remembrance of a Guest," NBC, 1975; "The Streets of San Francisco: Dead Air," ABC, 1975; "Maude: Arthur's Medical Convention," CBS, 1975; "The Cop and the Kid: Not with My Teacher," NBC, 1976; "The Streets of San Francisco: Dead or Alive," ABC, 1976; "The Rockford Files: The Gang at Don's Drive-In," NBC, 1977; "Alice: The Pain of No Return," CBS, 1977; "The San Pedro Beach Bums: Sweepstakes Bums," ABC, 1977; "One Day at a Time: Ann's Friends," CBS, 1978; "Taxi: High School Reunion," ABC, 1978; "The Love Boat: Going My Way?," ABC, 1979; "Fantasy Island: Very Strange Affair," ABC, 1982; "The Love Boat: Good Neighbors," ABC, 1982; "Gimme a Break: Eddie Gets Married," NBC, 1983; "Valerie: The Return of Uncle Skip," NBC, 1987; "Growing Pains: The Marrying Kind," ABC, 1988.

TV MOVIES AND MINISERIES: "Nightmare," CBS, 1974; "The Elevator," NBC, 1974; "The Secret Night Caller," NBC, 1975.

GOODEVE, GRANT

b. New Haven, CT, July 6, 1952. Generically handsome actor who played David Bradford on "Eight Is Enough."

AS A REGULAR: "Eight Is Enough," ABC, 1977-81; "Dynasty," ABC, 1983; "One Life to Live," ABC, 1985- .

AND: "Gibbsville: Saturday Night," NBC, 1976; "The Love Boat: A Different Girl," ABC, 1978; "Fantasy Island: Stuntman," ABC, 1979; "The Love Boat: Three in a Bed," ABC, 1982; "The Love Boat: Baby Talk," ABC, 1982; "The Love Boat: Love on Strike," ABC, 1983; "T.J. Hooker: Blue Murder," ABC, 1983; "Murder, She Wrote: Lovers and Other Killers," CBS, 1984.

TV MOVIES AND MINISERIES: "Hot Rod," NBC, 1979; "Eight Is Enough: A Family Reunion," NBC, 1987; "An Eight Is Enough Wedding," NBC, 1989.

GOODMAN, DODY

b. Columbus, OH, October 28, 1929. Comedienne of the isn't-she-daffy variety; she played Martha Shumway, mother of Mary Hartman (Louise Lasser).

AS A REGULAR: "The Jack Paar Show," NBC, 1957-58; "Liar's Club," SYN, 1976-78; "Mary Hartman, Mary Hartman," SYN, 1976-78; "The Mary Tyler Moore Hour," CBS, 1979; "Diff'rent Strokes," NBC, 1981-82; "Texas," NBC, 1982; "One Life to Live," ABC, 1984; "Punky Brewster," NBC, 1984-85.

AND: "The Phil Silvers Show: The Rich Kid," CBS, 1956; "The Eddie Fisher Show," NBC, 1958; "The Steve Allen Show," NBC, 1958; "The Ed Sullivan Show," CBS, 1958; "The Ed Sullivan Show," CBS, 1959; "The Jack Paar Show," NBC, 1961; "The Defenders: The Locked Room," CBS, 1962; "Girl Talk," SYN, 1963; "The Jack Paar Program," NBC, 1964; "The Mike Douglas Show," SYN, 1970; "Cross Wits," SYN, 1976; "The Love Boat: Who's Who," ABC, 1978; "The Merv Griffin Show," SYN, 1979; "Dance Fever," SYN, 1980; "Murder, She Wrote: If It's Thursday, It Must Be Beverly," CBS, 1987; "Duet: Special Delivery," FOX, 1988.

TV MOVIES AND MINISERIES: "I Dream of Jeannie: 15 Years Later," NBC, 1985.

GOODMAN, JOHN

b. St. Louis, MO. Gifted actor who, as Dan Connor, has every bit as much to do with the success of "Roseanne" as its star.

AS A REGULAR: "Roseanne," ABC, 1988-.

AND: "Moonlighting: Come Back, Little Shiksa," ABC, 1987; "The Equalizer: Re-Entry," CBS, 1987; "Saturday Night Live," NBC, 1989; "The Tonight Show Starring Johnny Carson," NBC, 1989.

TV MOVIES AND MINISERIES: "Heart of Steel," ABC, 1983.

GOODSON, MARK & TODMAN, BILL

Producers who've been responsible for just about every daytime game show you've seen.

AS PRODUCERS: "The Web," CBS, 1950-54; "The Name's the Same," ABC, 1951-55; "The Price Is Right," NBC, 1957-63; ABC, 1963-64; CBS, 1972- ; "Split Personality," NBC, 1959-60; "To Tell the Truth," CBS, 1956-67; "The Match Game," NBC, 1962-69; CBS, 1973-79; SYN, 1975-82; ABC, 1990- ; and many, many others.

GOODWIN, BILL

b. San Francisco, CA, July 28, 1910; d. 1958. Announcer who acted on occasion.

AS A REGULAR: "The George Burns and Gracie Allen Show," CBS, 1950-51; "It Pays to Be Married," NBC, 1955; "Penny to a Million," ABC, 1955; "Gerald Mc Boing-Boing," CBS, 1956-58.

AND: "Matinee Theatre: The Serpent's Tooth," NBC, 1957; "The Eve Arden Show: The Rivals," CBS, 1957; "The Red Skelton Show," CBS, 1958.

GORDON, BARRY

b. Brookline, MA, December 21, 1948. Former child actor best remembered from the film "A Thousand Clowns"; he also played Jack Benny as a child on several episodes of his show. Later he played Gary Rabinowitz on "Archie Bunker's Place."

AS A REGULAR: "The Don Rickles Show," CBS, 1972; "The New Dick Van Dyke Show," CBS, 1973-74; "Fish," ABC, 1977-78; "Good Time Harry," NBC, 1980; "Archie Bunker's Place," CBS, 1981-83.

AND: "G.E. Theatre: The Last Lesson," CBS, 1959; "Alfred Hitchcock Presents: The Day of the Bullet," CBS, 1960; "Leave it to Beaver: Beaver's House Guest," ABC, 1960; "Alfred Hitchcock Presents: The Contest for Aaron Gold," NBC, 1960; "The Jack Benny Program: Jack Casting for TV Special," CBS, 1961; "The Jack Benny Program: Musicale," CBS, 1961; "The du Pont Show with June Allyson: Our Man in Rome," CBS, 1961; "Dr. Kildare: Second Chance," NBC, 1961; "Love, American Style: Love and the High School Flop-Out," ABC, 1969; "The Bob Crane Show: An American Fiasco," NBC, 1975; "Good Heavens: I Want Nancy," ABC, 1976; "The Practice: Helen's Beau," NBC, 1976; "Barney Miller: Computer Crime," ABC, 1979; "Three's Company: Secret Admirer," ABC, 1980; "Barney Miller: Inquiry," ABC, 1982; "CBS Summer Playhouse: Dr. Paradise," CBS, 1988.

TV MOVIES AND MINISERIES: "Stark: Mirror Image," CBS, 1986.

GORDON, BRUCE

b. England, June 20, 1919. Heavyset actor usually in threatening roles; he played Frank Nitti on "The Untouchables."

AS A REGULAR: "Behind Closed Doors," NBC, 1958-59; "The Untouchables," ABC, 1959-63; "Peyton Place," ABC, 1965-66; "Run, Buddy, Run," CBS, 1966-67.

AND: "Pond's Theatre: Hang Up My Guns," ABC, 1955; "The Jane Wyman Show: Father Forgets," NBC, 1956; "Kraft Television Theatre: Hang Up My Guns," NBC, 1957; "Hallmark Hall of Fame: The Lark," NBC, 1957; "Westinghouse Desilu Playhouse: Bernadette," CBS, 1958; "Westinghouse Desilu Playhouse: The Untouchables," CBS, 1959; "Playhouse 90: Rank and File," CBS, 1959; "Bat Masterson: Shakedown at St. Joe," NBC, 1959; "Tales of Wells Fargo: Run for the River," NBC, 1960; "The Outlaws: Last Chance," NBC, 1960; "Gunsmoke: Distant Drummer," CBS, 1960; "The Barbara Stanwyck Show: The Secret of Mrs. Randall," NBC, 1960; "Perry Mason: The Case of the Loquacious Liar,"

CBS, 1960; "Stagecoach West: Life Sentence," ABC, 1960; "Maverick: The Ice Man," ABC, 1961; "Peter Gunn: A Kill and a Half," ABC, 1961; "Cheyenne: Angel," ABC, 1961; "The Outlaws: The Cutups," NBC, 1961; "SurfSide 6: Separate Checks," ABC, 1962; "Armstrong Circle Theatre: The Counterfeit League," CBS, 1963; "The Lucy Show: Lucy the Gun Moll," CBS, 1966; "The Man From UNCLE: The Round Table Affair," NBC, 1966; "Get Smart: Don't Look Back," NBC, 1968; "It Takes a Thief: A Sour Note," ABC, 1968; "Here's Lucy: Lucy and the Ex-Con," CBS, 1969; "Here's Lucy: Lucy's Wedding Party," CBS, 1970; "Here's Lucy: Dirtie Gertie," CBS, 1972; "The Doris Day Show: Follow That Dog," CBS, 1973; "Banacek: Now You See Me, Now You Don't," NBC, 1974.

GORDON, GALE
b. Gaylord Aldrich, New York City, NY, February 22, 1906. Longtime comic foil for Eve Arden and then Lucille Ball; former radio actor with a smooth baritone voice and fussy manner.
AS A REGULAR: "Our Miss Brooks," CBS, 1952-56; "The Brothers," CBS, 1956-57; "Sally," NBC, 1958; "Pete and Gladys," CBS, 1960-62; "The Danny Thomas Show," CBS, 1960-61; "Dennis the Menace," CBS, 1962-63; "The Lucy Show," CBS, 1963-68; "Here's Lucy," CBS, 1968-74; "Life with Lucy," ABC, 1986.
AND: "I Love Lucy: Lucy's Schedule," CBS, 1952; "I Love Lucy: Ricky Asks for a Raise," CBS, 1952; "Climax!: A Trophy for Howard Davenport," CBS, 1956; "The Ed Sullivan Show," CBS, 1957; "Playhouse 90: The Jet-Propelled Couch," CBS, 1957; "Studio One: The Award Winner," CBS, 1958; "The Lucille Ball-Desi Arnaz Show: Lucy Makes Room for Danny," CBS, 1958; "The Danny Thomas Show: A Dog's Life," CBS, 1959; "The Real McCoys: The Screen Test," ABC, 1959; "The Danny Thomas Show: Family Portrait," CBS, 1960; "Angel: Unpopular Mechanics," CBS, 1961; "Harrigan and Son: On Broadway," ABC, 1961; "The Donna Reed Show: Dr. Stone and His Horseless Carriage," ABC, 1962; "Here's Hollywood," NBC, 1962; "The Donna Reed Show: Donna Meets Roberta," ABC, 1962; "Lucille Ball Special," CBS, 1964; "Vacation Playhouse: Where There's Smokey," CBS, 1966; "The Dean Martin Show," NBC, 1970; "Lucy Moves to NBC," NBC, 1980.
* Gordon was Lucille Ball's first choice to play Fred Mertz on "I Love Lucy," but he was happy doing "Our Miss Brooks" on the radio.

GORDON, PHIL
b. Meridian, MS, May 5, 1922. Comic actor who played Jasper Depew on "The Beverly Hillbillies."
AS A REGULAR: "Pete Kelly's Blues," NBC, 1959;

"The Beverly Hillbillies," CBS, 1962-63.
AND: "Alfred Hitchcock Presents: Gratitude," NBC, 1961; "The Beverly Hillbillies: The Sheik," CBS, 1965; "Green Acres: My Husband the Rooster Renter," CBS, 1965; "The A-Team: When You Comin' Back, Range Ryder?," NBC, 1983; "Hell Town: Hell Town Goes Bananas," NBC, 1985.

GORDON, RUTH
b. Ruth Jones, Wollaston, MA, October 30, 1896; d. 1985. Oscar winning actress ("Rosemary's Baby") and writer whose TV work consisted mostly of playing free-spirited and/or crazy little old ladies.
AS A GUEST: "Prudential Family Playhouse: Over 21," CBS, 1950; "Hallmark Hall of Fame: Blithe Spirit," NBC, 1966; "The Merv Griffin Show," CBS, 1970; "The Mike Douglas Show," SYN, 1971; "The Flip Wilson Show," NBC, 1971; "The Mike Douglas Show," SYN, 1974; "Kojak: I Want to Report a Dream," CBS, 1975; "Rhoda: Kiss Your Epaulets Goodbye," CBS, 1975; "Medical Story: A Right to Die," NBC, 1975; "Saturday Night Live," NBC, 1976; "The Tonight Show Starring Johnny Carson," NBC, 1976; "Columbo: Try and Catch Me," NBC, 1977; "Taxi: Sugar Mama," ABC, 1979; "Newhart: Grandma, What a Big Mouth You Have," CBS, 1983; "Newhart: Go, Grandma, Go," CBS, 1984.
TV MOVIES AND MINISERIES: "Isn't It Shocking?," ABC, 1973; "The Great Houdinis," ABC, 1976; "Look What's Happened to Rosemary's Baby," ABC, 1976; "Don't Go to Sleep," ABC, 1982.
* Emmies: 1979.

GORE, LESLEY
b. Tenafly, NJ, 1946. Sixties pop vocalist.
AS A GUEST: "The Ed Sullivan Show," CBS, 1965; "Shindig," ABC, 1965; "The Donna Reed Show: By-Line-Jeffrey Stone," ABC, 1966; "Batman: That Darn Catwoman/Scat, Darn Catwoman," ABC, 1967; "American Bandstand," ABC, 1967; "The Match Game," NBC, 1967; "The Mike Douglas Show," SYN, 1969; "The Bobby Vinton Show," SYN, 1977.

GORMAN, CLIFF
b. Jamaica, NY, October 13, 1936. Intense actor who had stage successes with "The Boys in the Band" and as comic Lenny Bruce.
AS A GUEST: "NYPD: Naked in the Streets," ABC, 1968; "NET Playhouse: Paradise Lost," NET, 1971; "Police Story: The Wyatt Earp Syndrome," NBC, 1974; "Hollywood Television Theatre: The Chicago Conspiracy Trial," PBS, 1975; "Police Story: Officer

Needs Help," NBC, 1975; "Medical Story: An Air Full of Death," NBC, 1975; "Hawaii Five-O: Killer Aboard," CBS, 1976; "The Streets of San Francisco: Time Out," ABC, 1977; "Cagney & Lacey: Greed," CBS, 1987; "Murder, She Wrote: If the Frame Fits," CBS, 1986.

TV MOVIES AND MINISERIES: "Class of '63," ABC, 1973; "Strike Force," NBC, 1975; "The Silence," NBC, 1975; "Brinks: The Great Robbery," CBS, 1976; "Having Babies II," ABC, 1977; "The Bunker," CBS, 1981; "Cocaine and Blue Eyes," NBC, 1983; "Doubletake," CBS; 1985.

GORME, EYDIE

b. Bronx, NY, August 16, 1932. Singer, often with husband Steve Lawrence; an Emmy winner for "Steve & Eydie Celebrate Irving Berlin."

AS A REGULAR: "The Tonight Show (Tonight)," NBC, 1954-57; "Steve Allen Presents the Steve Lawrence and Eydie Gorme Show," NBC, 1958.

AND: "Person to Person," CBS, 1956; "The Perry Como Show," NBC, 1957; "The Steve Allen Show," NBC, 1957; "Jerry Lewis Special," NBC, 1957; "The Julius La Rosa Show," NBC, 1957; "The Big Record," CBS, 1957; "The Garry Moore Show," CBS, 1959; "Patti Page Olds Show," ABC, 1959; "The Steve Allen Show," NBC, 1959; "The Perry Como Show," NBC, 1959; "The Andy Williams Show," CBS, 1959; "The Golden Circle," ABC, 1959; "Perry Como's Kraft Music Hall," NBC, 1960; "The Garry Moore Show," CBS, 1960; "The Garry Moore Show," CBS, 1961; "Perry Como's Kraft Music Hall," NBC, 1961; "Queen for a Day," ABC, 1961; "The Garry Moore Show," CBS, 1962; "The Garry Moore Show," CBS, 1963; "The Jimmy Dean Show," ABC, 1964; "Hollywood Palace," ABC, 1964; "The Jack Paar Program," NBC, 1964; "Password," CBS, 1964; "The Tonight Show Starring Johnny Carson," NBC, 1964; "The Jack Paar Program," NBC, 1965; "The Tonight Show Starring Johnny Carson," NBC, 1965; "The Andy Williams Show," NBC, 1967; "This Morning," ABC, 1968; "The Ed Sullivan Show," CBS, 1968; "Hollywood Palace," ABC, 1969; "The Carol Burnett Show," CBS, 1970; "The Carol Burnett Show," CBS, 1973; "The Tonight Show Starring Johnny Carson," NBC, 1973; "Here's Lucy: Lucy the Peacemaker," CBS, 1973; "The Carol Burnett Show," CBS, 1974; "Sanford & Son: Earthquake II," NBC, 1975; "The Carol Burnett Show," CBS, 1977; "Steve & Eydie Celebrate Irving Berlin," NBC, 1978; "The Tonight Show Starring Johnny Carson," NBC, 1988.
* Emmies: 1979.

GORSHIN, FRANK

b. Pittsburgh, PA, April 5, 1934. Comedian and impressionist who had just the right manic touch as the Riddler on "Batman."

AS A REGULAR: "Batman," ABC, 1966-68; "ABC Comedy Hour," ABC, 1972; "The Edge of Night," ABC, 1981-82.

AND: "Navy Log: Amscray," ABC, 1957; "The Steve Allen Show," NBC, 1959; "The Andy Williams Show," CBS, 1959; "Hennesey: Hennesey Meets Honeyboy," CBS, 1959; "Hennesey: Shore Patrol," CBS, 1959; "Steve Allen Plymouth Show," NBC, 1959; "The Detectives Starring Robert Taylor: The Streger Affair," ABC, 1959; "Have Gun, Will Travel: The Sons of Aaron Murdock," CBS, 1959; "Mr. Lucky: The Last Laugh," CBS, 1960; "Perry Como's Kraft Music Hall," NBC, 1960; "The Law and Mr. Jones: One for the Money," ABC, 1961; "The Ed Sullivan Show," CBS, 1961; "The Defenders: The Hundred Lives of Harry Simms," CBS, 1961; "The Ed Sullivan Show," CBS, 1962; "The Lively Ones," NBC, 1962; "The Untouchables: The Pea," ABC, 1962; "Empire: The Fire Dancer," NBC, 1962; "Naked City: Beyond This Place There Be Dragons," ABC, 1963; "Perry Como's Kraft Music Hall," NBC, 1963; "Combat!: The Medal," ABC, 1963; "The Tennessee Ernie Ford Show," ABC, 1964; "The Ed Sullivan Show," CBS, 1964; "Combat!: The Hell Machine," ABC, 1965; "The Munsters: Herman the Tire-Kicker," CBS, 1966; "The Jackie Gleason Show," CBS, 1967; "The Movie Game," SYN, 1969; "Rowan & Martin's Laugh-In," NBC, 1971; "The Flip Wilson Show," NBC, 1972; "The Vin Scully Show," CBS, 1973; "Ironside: What's New with Mark?," NBC, 1974; "Celebrity Sweepstakes," NBC, 1974; "Police Woman: Glitter with a Bullet," NBC, 1975; "SWAT: Ordeal," ABC, 1975; "The Mike Douglas Show," SYN, 1975; "Don Adams Screen Test," SYN, 1976; "Music Hall America," SYN, 1977; "The Mike Douglas Show," SYN, 1977; "Buck Rogers in the 25th Century: Plot to Kill a City," NBC, 1979; "The Fall Guy: Losers, Weepers," ABC, 1984; "Murder, She Wrote: Mourning Among the Wisterias," CBS, 1988.

TV MOVIES AND MINISERIES: "Sky Hei$t," NBC, 1975; "Death Car on the Freeway," CBS, 1979; "A Masterpiece of Murder," NBC, 1986.
* On the night of March 31, 1966, Gorshin was seen on two networks at the same time: On CBS's "The Munsters" he was playing crooked car dealer Fair Deal Dan; on "Batman" he was the Riddler.
* See also "Batman."

GORTNER, MARJOE

b. Long Beach, CA, January 14, 1941. Child evangelist turned actor.

AS A REGULAR: "Speak Up, America," NBC, 1980; "Falcon Crest," CBS, 1986-87.

AND: "Police Story: Requiem for an Informer," NBC, 1973; "Barnaby Jones: Gold Record for Murder," CBS, 1974; "Medical Center: The Demi-God," CBS, 1974; "Archer: The Turkish

Connection," NBC, 1975; "Police Story: War Games," NBC, 1975; "The A-Team: Recipe for Heavy Bread," NBC, 1983.
TV MOVIES AND MINISERIES: "The Marcus-Nelson Murders," CBS, 1973; "Pray for the Wildcats," ABC, 1974; "The Gun and the Pulpit," ABC, 1974; "Mayday at 40,000 Feet," CBS, 1976.

GOSDEN, FREEMAN F.
b. Freeman Fisher Gosden, Richmond, VA, May 5, 1899; d. 1982. Co-creator of "Amos 'n' Andy," which ran on the radio from 1928-60.
AS A REGULAR: "Calvin and the Colonel," ABC, 1961-62.
* See also Charles Correll.

GOSFIELD, MAURICE
b. 1913; d. 1964. Pudgy character actor who played Pvt. Duane Doberman on "The Phil Silvers Show" and the character's cartoon equivalent, Benny the Ball, on "Top Cat."
AS A REGULAR: "The Phil Silvers Show (You'll Never Get Rich)," CBS, 1955-59; "Top Cat," ABC, 1961-62.
AND: "The Perry Como Show," NBC, 1957; "The Steve Allen Show," NBC, 1958; "The Ed Sullivan Show," CBS, 1958; "Perry Como's Kraft Music Hall," NBC, 1959; "The Jack Benny Program," CBS, 1960; "Phil Silvers Special: Summer in New York," CBS, 1960; "One Happy Family: Charlie, Executive at Large," NBC, 1961; "The Jim Backus Show: The Old Army Game," SYN, 1961; "One Happy Family: Big Night Out," NBC, 1961; "The Red Skelton Show: San Fernando and the Kaaka Maami Island," CBS, 1961.

GOSSETT, LOUIS JR.
b. Brooklyn, NY, May 27, 1936. Oscar winning actor ("An Officer and a Gentleman") usually in intense roles.
AS A REGULAR: "The Young Rebels," ABC, 1970-71; "The Lazarus Syndrome," ABC, 1979; "The Powers of Matthew Star," NBC, 1982-83; "Gideon Oliver," ABC, 1988-89.
AND: "The Nurses: The Prisoner," CBS, 1962; "Southern Baptist Hour: Ecclesiastes and the Dying Day," NBC, 1964; "The Mod Squad: When Smitty Comes Marching Home," ABC, 1968; "Daktari: Adam and Jenny," CBS, 1968; "The Bill Cosby Show: The Return of Big, Bad Bubba Bronson," NBC, 1970; "Hollywood Television Theatre: Big Fish, Little Fish," NET, 1971; "The Partridge Family: Soul Club," ABC, 1971; "Bonanza: The Desperado," NBC, 1971; "Longstreet: The Way of the Intercepting Fists," ABC, 1971; "The Bold Ones: One Lonely Step," NBC, 1971; "Alias Smith and Jones: The Bounty Hunter," ABC, 1971; "The Living End," CBS, 1972; "The Rookies: Covenant With Death," ABC, 1972; "The Mod Squad: Good Times Are

Just Memories," ABC, 1972; "Love, American Style: Love and the Mystic," ABC, 1972; "The Fuzz Brothers," ABC, 1973; "Good Times: Thelma's Young Man," CBS, 1974; "McCloud: Shivaree on Delancey Street," NBC, 1974; "Black Bait," CBS, 1975; "Harry O: Shades," ABC, 1975; "Police Story: 50 Cents First Half Hour, $1.75 All Day," NBC, 1976; "Little House on the Prairie: Long Road Home," NBC, 1976; "The Rockford Files: Foul on the First Play," NBC, 1976; "The Rockford Files: Just Another Polish Wedding," NBC, 1977; "Saturday Night Live," NBC, 1982.
TV MOVIES AND MINISERIES: "Companions in Nightmare," NBC, 1968; "It's Good to Be Alive," CBS, 1974; "Sidekicks," CBS, 1974; "Delancey Street," NBC, 1975; "Little Ladies of the Night," ABC, 1977; "Roots," ABC, 1977; "The Critical List," NBC, 1978; "Backstairs at the White House," NBC, 1979; "This Man Stands Alone," NBC, 1979; "A Gathering of Old Men," CBS, 1987; "The Father Clements Story," NBC, 1987; "Roots: The Gift," ABC, 1988.
* Emmies: 1977.

GOULD, ELLIOTT
b. Elliott Goldstein, Brooklyn, NY, August 29, 1938. Hot screen star of the seventies with a slobby everyman quality who's taken a couple of shots at TV acceptance.
AS A REGULAR: "E/R," CBS, 1984-85; "Together We Stand," CBS, 1986-87.
AND: "The Mike Douglas Show," SYN, 1964; "The Steve Allen Show," SYN, 1968; "The David Frost Show," SYN, 1969; "Saturday Night Live," NBC, 1976; "Saturday Night Live," NBC, 1977; "Saturday Night Live," NBC, 1978; "Cher ... and Other Fantasies," NBC, 1979; "Saturday Night Live," NBC, 1980; "The Tonight Show Starring Johnny Carson," NBC, 1981; "Faerie Tale Theatre: Jack and the Beanstalk," SHO, 1983; "Candid Camera on Wheels," CBS, 1989.
TV MOVIES AND MINISERIES: "The Golden Raiders," ABC, 1981; "Vanishing Act," CBS, 1986.

GOULD, HAROLD
b. Schenectady, NY, December 10, 1923. Distinguished actor who worked in TV for over a decade before becoming a familiar face as Rhoda Morgenstern's father, Martin; Gould also does dozens of commercial voice-overs.
AS A REGULAR: "Rhoda," CBS, 1974-76, 1977-78; "The Feather and Father Gang," ABC, 1977; "Park Place," CBS, 1981; "Foot in the Door," CBS, 1983; "Spencer," NBC, 1985; "Dallas," CBS, 1990; "Singer & Sons," NBC, 1990.
AND: "Follow the Sun: Another Part of the Jungle," ABC, 1961; "Dennis the Menace: The Haunted House," CBS, 1961; "Route 66: Go Read the River," CBS, 1962; "The Twilight Zone: Probe

Seven-Over and Out," CBS, 1963; "Mr. Novak: The Private Life of Douglas Morgan, Jr.," NBC, 1964; "The Twilight Zone: The Bewitchin' Pool," CBS, 1964; "The Virginian: Day of the Scorpion," NBC, 1965; "The FBI: The Man Who Went Mad by Mistake," ABC, 1966; "Get Smart: Island of the Darned," NBC, 1966; "The Invaders: The Trial," ABC, 1967; "The Wild Wild West: The Night of the Bubbling Death," CBS, 1967; "He & She: Vote Yes or No," CBS, 1967; "The FBI: The Daughter," ABC, 1968; "He & She: What's in the Kitty?," CBS, 1968; "Lancer: Last Train for Charlie Poe," CBS, 1968; "The Flying Nun: The Rabbi and the Nun," ABC, 1968; "Love, American Style: Love and the Happy Day," ABC, 1972; "The FBI: The Test," ABC, 1972; "Love, American Style: Love and the Newscasters," ABC, 1972; "The Mary Tyler Moore Show: Enter Rhoda's Parents," CBS, 1972; "The Mary Tyler Moore Show: Rhoda's Sister Gets Married," CBS, 1973; "Conflicts: Double Solitaire," PBS, 1974; "Gunsmoke: The Guns of Cibola Blanca," CBS, 1974; "Police Story: Fathers and Sons," NBC, 1974; "Petrocelli: Death in High Places," NBC, 1974; "Hawaii Five-O: The Case Against McGarrett," CBS, 1975; "The Bob Crane Show: An American Fiasco," NBC, 1975; "The Bob Crane Show: The Doctor Sings the Blues," NBC, 1975; "The Rookies: Measure of Mercy," ABC, 1975; "Police Story: Eamon Kinsella Royce," NBC, 1976; "Police Story: The Blue Fog," NBC, 1977; "Family: Acts of Love," ABC, 1977; "The Love Boat: The Caper," ABC, 1978; "Lou Grant: Hype," CBS, 1979; "The Rockford Files: Never Send a Boy King to Do a Man's Job," NBC, 1979; "Webster: The Walnutto," ABC, 1984; "St. Elsewhere: Up on the Roof," NBC, 1984; "Scarecrow and Mrs. King: One Bear Dances, One Bear Doesn't," CBS, 1986; "L.A. Law: Simian Enchanted Evening," NBC, 1986; "CBS Summer Playhouse: Tickets Please," CBS, 1988; "Empty Nest: Man of the Year," NBC, 1989; "Midnight Caller: Blues for Mr. Charlie," NBC, 1989; "Ray Bradbury Theatre: To the Chicago Abyss," USA, 1989.

TV MOVIES AND MINISERIES: "Ransom for a Dead Man," NBC, 1971; "A Death of Innocence," CBS, 1971; "Murdock's Gang," ABC, 1973; "Medical Story," NBC, 1975; "How to Break Up a Happy Divorce," NBC, 1976; "Washington: Behind Closed Doors," ABC, 1977; "Better Late Than Never," NBC, 1979; "The 11th Victim," CBS, 1979; "Hallmark Hall of Fame: Aunt Mary," CBS, 1979; "The Man in the Santa Claus Suit," NBC, 1979; "Born to Be Sold," NBC, 1981; "Help Wanted: Male," CBS, 1982; "The Gambler II: The Adventure Continues," CBS, 1983; "The Red-Light Sting," CBS, 1984; "Mrs. Delafield Wants to Marry," CBS, 1986; "Get Smart, Again!," ABC, 1989.

GOULDING, RAY—See Bob & Ray.

GOULET, ROBERT
b. Lawrence, MA, November 26, 1933. Singer with a smooth baritone and suave manner; also, the guy whose TV appearances drove Elvis Presley to pick up a gun and blow out the tube.

AS A REGULAR: "Blue Light," ABC, 1966.
AND: "The Ed Sullivan Show," CBS, 1961; "Omnibus: An Omnibus of Songs," NBC, 1961; "The Garry Moore Show," CBS, 1961; "Westinghouse Presents: The Enchanted Nutcracker," ABC, 1961; "The Ed Sullivan Show," CBS, 1962; "The Broadway of Lerner and Loewe," NBC, 1962; "The Jack Paar Program," NBC, 1962; "Bell Telephone Hour," NBC, 1962; "The Judy Garland Show," CBS, 1963; "The Joey Bishop Show: Andy Williams Visits Joey," NBC, 1964; "The Ed Sullivan Show," CBS, 1964; "Kraft Suspense Theatre: Operation Grief," NBC, 1964; "I've Got a Secret," CBS, 1964; "The Jack Paar Program," NBC, 1965; "The Red Skelton Hour," CBS, 1965; "The Andy Williams Show," NBC, 1965; "The Mike Douglas Show," SYN, 1965; "The Patty Duke Show: Don't Monkey with Mendel," ABC, 1965; "Brigadoon," ABC, 1966; "The Ed Sullivan Show," CBS, 1966; "The Big Valley: Brother Love," ABC, 1967; "Carousel," ABC, 1967; "The Lucy Show: Lucy and Robert Goulet," CBS, 1967; "The Tonight Show Starring Johnny Carson," NBC, 1968; "The Tonight Show Starring Johnny Carson," NBC, 1968; "Kiss Me, Kate," ABC, 1968; "That's Life: The Honeymoon," ABC, 1968; "The Name of the Game: Keep the Doctor Away," NBC, 1969; "The Glen Campbell Goodtime Hour," CBS, 1969; "Bob Hope Special," NBC, 1971; "Mission: Impossible: Leona," CBS, 1972; "The Julie Andrews Hour," ABC, 1973; "Police Woman: Pawns of Power," NBC, 1975; "The Merv Griffin Show," SYN, 1977; "Police Story: Prime Rib," NBC, 1977; "The Love Boat: The Song Is Ended," ABC, 1978; "Alice: Hello Vegas, Goodbye Diner/Too Many Robert Goulets," CBS, 1980; "The John Davidson Show," SYN, 1981; "Fantasy Island: The Swinger," ABC, 1983; "Murder, She Wrote: Paint Me a Murder," CBS, 1985; "The Tonight Show Starring Johnny Carson," NBC, 1988; "Mr. Belvedere: The Field," ABC, 1989; "Great Performances: An Evening with Alan Jay Lerner," PBS, 1989.

TV MOVIES AND MINISERIES: "The Couple Takes a Wife," ABC, 1972.

GRABLE, BETTY
b. Elizabeth Ruth Grable, St. Louis, MO, December 18, 1916; d. 1973. Star of screen musicals through the forties whose TV appearances were usually on variety shows.
AS A GUEST: "The Jane Wyman Show: Cleopatra

Collins," NBC, 1956; "Ford Star Jubilee: Twentieth Century," NBC, 1956; "Dinah Shore Chevy Show," NBC, 1956; "Do You Trust Your Wife?," CBS, 1957; "The Bob Hope Show," NBC, 1957; "The Ed Sullivan Show," CBS, 1957; "The Eddie Fisher Show," NBC, 1957; "The Lucille Ball-Desi Arnaz Show: Lucy Wins a Racehorse," CBS, 1958; "The Jerry Lewis Show," NBC, 1958; "Shower of Stars," CBS, 1958; "Bob Hope Special," NBC, 1958; "Some of Manie's Friends," NBC, 1959; "Dinah Shore Chevy Show," NBC, 1959; "Dinah Shore Chevy Show," NBC, 1960; "George Burns Special," NBC, 1960; "Perry Como's Kraft Music Hall," NBC, 1960; "The Andy Williams Show," NBC, 1962; "Hollywood Palace," ABC, 1964; "Hollywood Squares," NBC, 1969.

GRADY, DON

b. *Don Agrati, 1944*. Young actor who played Robbie Douglas on "My Three Sons."
AS A REGULAR: "The Mickey Mouse Club," ABC, 1957-59; "My Three Sons," ABC, 1960-65; CBS, 1965-72.
AND: "Restless Gun: Madame Brimstone," NBC, 1959; "Dick Powell's Zane Grey Theatre: Death in a Wood," CBS, 1959; "Wichita Town: Man on a Hill," NBC, 1959; "The Rifleman: The Patsy," ABC, 1960; "Have Gun, Will Travel: The Calf," CBS, 1960; "The Eleventh Hour: Something Crazy's Going on in the Back Room," NBC, 1963; "Mr. Novak: Chin Up, Mr. Novak," NBC, 1964; "Mr. Novak: Once a Clown," NBC, 1965; "The FBI: The Witness," ABC, 1970; "Love, American Style: Love and the Coed Dorm," ABC, 1970; "To Rome with Love: Rome Is Where You Find It," CBS, 1970; "Love, American Style: Love and the Free Weekend," ABC, 1971.
AS CO-WRITER: "My Three Sons: Tramp and the Prince," ABC, 1965.

GRAFF, ILENE

b. *Brooklyn, NY*. Actress who played Marsha Owens on "Mr. Belvedere."
AS A REGULAR: "Supertrain," NBC, 1979; "Lewis & Clark," NBC, 1981-82; "Mr. Belvedere," ABC, 1985-90.
AND: "Barnaby Jones: Child of Love, Child of Vengeance," CBS, 1979; "Remington Steele: Steele Belted," NBC, 1982; "Lottery!: Pilot," ABC, 1983; "St. Elsewhere: Whistle, Wylie Works," NBC, 1985.
TV MOVIES AND MINISERIES: "Beulah Land," NBC, 1980.

GRAHAM, REV. BILLY

b. *William F. Graham, Charlotte, NC, November 7, 1918*. Minister who still preaches on syndicated TV specials.

AS A REGULAR: "Hour of Decision," ABC, 1951-54; "The Billy Graham Crusade," ABC, 1957-59; SYN, 1960- .
AND: "The Jack Paar Show," NBC, 1959; "The Jack Benny Program," CBS, 1963; "Art Linkletter's House Party," CBS, 1963; "Woody Allen Special," CBS, 1969.

GRAHAM, RONNY

b. *Philadelphia, PA, August 26, 1919*. Comedian who played Mr. Dirt in Mobil gasoline commercials of the seventies.
AS A REGULAR: "The New Bill Cosby Show," CBS, 1972-73; "The Hudson Brothers Show," CBS, 1974; "The Bob Crane Show," NBC, 1975; "Chico and the Man," NBC, 1975-76.
AND: "The Phil Silvers Show: Bilko's Bopster," CBS, 1959; "Peter Loves Mary: The Classic Car," NBC, 1960; "The Courtship of Eddie's Father: Two's Company," ABC, 1971; "The Merv Griffin Show," SYN, 1977; "M*A*S*H: Your Hit Parade," CBS, 1978; "Mission: Impossible: The Devils," ABC, 1989.
AS COMPOSER: "Pontiac Star Parade Presents Phil Silvers," CBS, 1959.
AS WRITER: "M*A*S*H," CBS, 1978-79.

GRAHAM, VIRGINIA

b. *Chicago, IL, July 4, 1913*. Talk-show hostess.
AS A REGULAR: "Where Was I?," DUM, 1952; "The Strawhatters," DUM, 1954; "Girl Talk," SYN, 1962-68; "America Alive!," NBC, 1978; "Texas," NBC, 1982.
AND: "The Jack Paar Show," NBC, 1958; "The Jack Paar Show," NBC, 1959; "The Jack Paar Show," NBC, 1960; "To Tell the Truth," CBS, 1961; "The Merv Griffin Show," SYN, 1966; "Snap Judgment," NBC, 1967; "Love, American Style: Love and the Understanding," ABC, 1970; "Virginia Graham: Never a Dull Moment," TNN, 1989.

GRAHAME, GLORIA

b. *Gloria Grahame Hallward, Los Angeles, CA, November 28, 1925; d. 1981*. Oscar-winning fifties "bad girl" who turned to TV when her film career waned.
AS A GUEST: "G.E. Theatre: Don't Let It Throw You," CBS, 1961; "Harrigan and Son: My Fair Lawyer," ABC, 1961; "The New Breed: Blood Money," ABC, 1961; "Sam Benedict: Too Many Strangers," NBC, 1962; "Burke's Law: Who Killed April?," ABC, 1964; "The Outer Limits: The Guests," ABC, 1964; "The Fugitive: The Homecoming," ABC, 1964; "Grindl: Dial G for Grindl," NBC, 1964; "Burke's Law: Who Killed the Rabbit's Husband?," ABC, 1965; "The Iron Horse: Appointment with an Epitaph," ABC, 1967; "Then Came Bronson: The 3:13 Arrives at

Noon," NBC, 1970; "Daniel Boone: Perilous Passage," NBC, 1970; "The Name of the Game: The Takeover," NBC, 1970; "Mannix: Duet for Three," CBS, 1970; "Kojak: Sister Maria," CBS, 1977.
TV MOVIES AND MINISERIES: "Escape," ABC, 1971; "Black Noon," CBS, 1971; "The Girl on the Late, Late Show," NBC, 1974; "Rich Man, Poor Man," ABC, 1976; "Best Sellers: Seventh Avenue," NBC, 1977.
* Grahame's second husband was director Nicholas Ray; her fourth husband was Tony Ray, Nicholas' son from a previous marriage.

GRAMMER, KELSEY
b. *Virgin Islands*. Actor who plays. Dr. Frasier Crane on "Cheers."
AS A REGULAR: "Cheers," NBC, 1984- .
AND: "J.J. Starbuck: Murder in E Minor," NBC, 1987; "227: For Sale," NBC, 1989.
TV MOVIES AND MINISERIES: "Dance 'Til Dawn," NBC, 1988.

GRANDY, FRED
b. *Sioux City, IA, June 29, 1948*. Gopher on "The Love Boat," now U.S. Congressman Gopher from Iowa.
AS A REGULAR: "Maude," CBS, 1973-74; "The Love Boat," ABC, 1977-86.
AND: "Maude: The Double Standard," CBS, 1972; "Love, American Style: Love and the See-Thru Mind," ABC, 1973; "Cross Wits," SYN, 1980; "Cagney & Lacey: Matinee," CBS, 1984.
TV MOVIES AND MINISERIES: "The Girl Most Likely To...," ABC, 1973; "Love Boat II," ABC, 1977; "Blind Ambition," CBS, 1979.

GRANGER, FARLEY
b. *San Jose, CA, July 1, 1925*. Fifties matinee idol who found steady employment on soap operas.
AS A REGULAR: "One Life to Live," ABC, 1976-77; "As the World Turns," CBS, 1986-89.
AND: "Schlitz Playhouse of Stars: Splendid with Swords," CBS, 1955; "U.S. Steel Hour: Incident in an Alley," CBS, 1955; "The Phil Silvers Show: Hollywood," CBS, 1956; "Producers Showcase: Caesar and Cleopatra," NBC, 1956; "Robert Montgomery Presents: Pistolero," NBC, 1956; "Climax!: Fearless Enemy," CBS, 1956; "Playhouse 90: Sizeman and Son," CBS, 1956; "Ford Theatre: Stand by to Dive," ABC, 1956; "The 20th Century-Fox Hour: Men Against Speed," CBS, 1956; "Kraft Theatre: Come to Me," NBC, 1957; "U.S. Steel Hour: Hidden River," CBS, 1958; "U.S. Steel Hour: The Wound Within," CBS, 1958; "Arthur Murray Party," NBC, 1958; "Du Pont Show of the Month: Arrowsmith," CBS, 1960; "Arthur Murray Party," NBC, 1960; "Music for a Summer Night: The

Female of the Species," ABC, 1960; "Dow Hour of Great Mysteries: The Inn of the Flying Dragon," NBC, 1960; "Bell Telephone Hour: The Music of Romance," NBC, 1960; "Our American Heritage: Born a Giant," NBC, 1960; "Du Pont Show of the Month: The Prisoner of Zenda," CBS, 1961; "Family Classics: The Heiress," CBS, 1961; "Bob Hope Chrysler Theatre: Nightmare," NBC, 1966; "Bob Hope Chrysler Theatre: Blind Man's Bluff," NBC, 1967; "Hondo: Hondo and the Apache Kid," ABC, 1967; "Get Smart: Supersonic Boom," NBC, 1967; "Laura," ABC, 1968; "The Outsider: What Flowers Daisies Are," NBC, 1968; "The Name of the Game: The Ordeal," NBC, 1968; "Medical Center: The Loner," CBS, 1969; "Wide World of Mystery: The Haunting of Penthouse D," ABC, 1974; "Medical Story: Million Dollar Baby," NBC, 1975; "Tales From the Darkside: Painkiller," SYN, 1984; "The Love Boat: A Matter of Taste," ABC, 1985.
TV MOVIES AND MINISERIES: "The Challengers," CBS, 1970; "The Lives of Jenny Dolan," NBC, 1975; "Widow," NBC, 1976; "Black Beauty," NBC, 1978.

GRANGER, STEWART
b. *James Stewart, London, England, May 6, 1913*. Actor who appeared in many swashbuckler films of the fifties, and who still pops up on TV.
AS A REGULAR: "The Men From Shiloh," NBC, 1970-71.
AND: "Hotel: Blackout," ABC, 1983; "Murder, She Wrote: Paint Me a Murder," CBS, 1985; "The Love Boat: Call Me Grandma," ABC, 1985.
TV MOVIES AND MINISERIES: "Any Second Now," NBC, 1969; "The Hound of the Baskervilles," ABC, 1972; "The Royal Romance of Charles and Diana," CBS, 1982; "Crossings," ABC, 1986; "Chameleons," NBC, 1989.

GRANT, FAYE
b. *Detroit, MI*. Actress who played Dr. Julie Parrish on "V"; wife of Stephen Collins.
AS A REGULAR: "The Greatest American Hero," ABC, 1981-83; "V," NBC, 1984-85.
AND: "Voyagers!: Pilot," NBC, 1982; "Hardcastle and McCormick: Pilot," ABC, 1983; "Private Eye: Pilot," NBC, 1987; "Tattinger's: Two Men and a Baby," NBC, 1988.
TV MOVIES AND MINISERIES: "Senior Trip!," NBC, 1981; "V," NBC, 1983; "V: The Final Battle," NBC, 1984.

GRANT, KIRBY
b. *Kirby Grant Hoon Jr., Butte, MT, November 24, 1911*. Action hero who played Sky King.
AS A REGULAR: "Sky King," ABC, 1951-54.

GRANT, LEE

b. Lyova Haskell Rosenthal, New York City, NY, October 31, 1930. Stage-trained actress who won an Emmy as Stella Chernak on "Peyton Place" and who now produces and directs films; mother of Dinah Manoff.

AS A REGULAR: "Search for Tomorrow," CBS, 1953-54; "Peyton Place," ABC, 1965-66; "Fay," NBC, 1975-76.

AND: "The Play's the Thing: Screwball," CBS, 1950; "Comedy Theatre: Zone of Quiet," CBS, 1950; "Danger: Dark as Night," CBS, 1952; "Danger: Death to the Lonely," CBS, 1952; "Danger: The Face of Fear," CBS, 1952; "Broadway Television Theatre: The Noose," SYN, 1953; "Playwrights '56: Keyhole," NBC, 1956; "Kraft Television Theatre: Look What's Going On!," NBC, 1958; "The Adventures of Ozzie and Harriet: The Trophy," ABC, 1958; "Kraft Theatre: Three Plays by Tennessee Williams: Moony's Kid Don't Cry," NBC, 1958; "Brenner: Man in the Middle," CBS, 1959; "Play of the Week: The House of Bernard Alba," SYN, 1960; "Great Ghost Tales: Lucy," NBC, 1961; "Breck Golden Showcase: Saturday's Children," CBS, 1962; "The Defenders: The Empty Heart," CBS, 1963; "The Nurses: The Gift," CBS, 1963; "East Side/West Side: Not Bad for Openers," CBS, 1963; "The Nurses: To Spend, to Give, to Want," CBS, 1963; "The Fugitive: Taps for a Dead War," ABC, 1964; "Ben Casey: For a Just Man Falleth Seven Times," ABC, 1964; "Ben Casey: For Jimmy, the Best of Everything," ABC, 1964; "Slattery's People: Question-Where Vanished the Tragic Piper?," CBS, 1964; "The Doctors and the Nurses: A Couple of Dozen Tiny Pills," CBS, 1965; "The Defenders: Nobody Asks What Side You're On," CBS, 1965; "For the People: With Intent to Influence," CBS, 1965; "ABC Stage '67: The Love Song of Barney Kempinski," ABC, 1966; "ABC Stage '67: The People Trap," ABC, 1966; "The Big Valley: The Lady From Mesa," ABC, 1967; "Bob Hope Chrysler Theatre: Deadlock," NBC, 1967; "Judd for the Defense: The Gates of Cerebrus," ABC, 1968; "Mission: Impossible: The Diplomat," CBS, 1968; "Medical Center: The Loner," CBS, 1969; "The Name of the Game: Tarot," NBC, 1970; "The Mod Squad: Mother of Sorrow," ABC, 1970; "The Name of the Game: A Love to Remember," NBC, 1970; "Hollywood Squares," NBC, 1971; "Men at Law: Yesterday Is But a Dream," CBS, 1971; "Robert Young and the Family," CBS, 1973; "The Shape of Things," CBS, 1973; "Three for the Girls: Raincheck," CBS, 1973; "Theatre in America: The Seagull," PBS, 1975; "Why Me?," PBS, 1975; "The Tonight Show Starring Johnny Carson," NBC, 1975; "The Toni Tennille Show," SYN, 1981; "The Pat Sajak Show," CBS, 1989.

TV MOVIES AND MINISERIES: "Night Slaves," ABC, 1970; "The Neon Ceiling," NBC, 1971; "Ransom for a Dead Man," NBC, 1971; "Lieutenant Schuster's Wife," ABC, 1972; "Partners in Crime," NBC, 1973; "What Are Best Friends For?," ABC, 1973; "Perilous Voyage," NBC, 1976; "The Spell," NBC, 1977; "Backstairs at the White House," NBC, 1979; "You Can't Go Home Again," CBS, 1979; "The Million-Dollar Face," NBC, 1981; "Bare Essence," CBS, 1982; "Will There Really Be a Morning?," CBS, 1983; "Mussolini: The Untold Story," NBC, 1985; "The Hijacking of the Achille Lauro," NBC, 1989.

* Grant didn't feel that NBC gave her sitcom "Fay," about a newly divorced woman, a chance. So she went on "The Tonight Show Starring Johnny Carson," and said so, while giving NBC executives the finger.
* Emmies: 1966, 1971.

GRANVILLE, BONITA

b. New York City, NY, February 2, 1923; d. 1988. Actress whose TV appearances were overshadowed by her behind-the-scenes influence as producer of "Lassie" and "The Lone Ranger."

AS A GUEST: "Bigelow Theatre: Make Your Bed," CBS, 1951; "Lux Video Theatre: Not Guilty—of Much," CBS, 1951; "Gruen Guild Theatre: One Strange Day," ABC, 1951; "Schaefer Century Theatre: Annual Honeymoon," NBC, 1952; "Schaefer Century Theatre: Yesterday's World," NBC, 1952; "Campbell TV Soundstage: One Strange Day," NBC, 1952; "Gloria Swanson Theatre: The Antique Shop," SYN, 1955; "Science Fiction Theatre: The Killer Tree," SYN, 1955; "Climax!: The Healer," CBS, 1955; "Climax!: The Fifth Wheel," CBS, 1956; "Ethel Barrymore Theatre: Lady Investigator," SYN, 1956; "Science Fiction Theatre: The Killer Tree," SYN, 1957; "The Bob Cummings Show: Bob Meets Schultzy's Cousin," CBS, 1957; "U.S. Steel Hour: Shadow in the Sky," CBS, 1957; "Studio One: The Fair-Haired Boy," CBS, 1958; "Target: Mercy Killer," SYN, 1958; "This Is the Life: The Burden Made Light," SYN, 1958; "Playhouse 90: The Velvet Alley," CBS, 1959; "Best of the Post: Valley of the Blue Mountain," SYN, 1960.

AS EXECUTIVE-PRODUCER: "The Lone Ranger," ABC, 1949-57; "Lassie," CBS, 1954-71.

GRASSLE, KAREN

b. Berkeley, CA, February 25, 1944. Actress who played Caroline Ingalls on "Little House."

AS A REGULAR: "Little House on the Prairie," NBC, 1974-82.

AND: "Catholic Hour: The Sisters," NBC, 1967;

"The Mike Douglas Show," SYN, 1975; "Dinah!," SYN, 1978; "Hollywood Squares," SYN, 1980; "The Love Boat: Lost and Found," ABC, 1981; "Hotel: Christmas," ABC, 1983; "Murder, She Wrote: Harbinger of Death," CBS, 1988.

TV MOVIES AND MINISERIES: "Battered," NBC, 1978; "Crisis in Mid-Air," CBS, 1979; "Cocaine: One Man's Seduction," NBC, 1983; "Little House: The Last Farewell," NBC, 1984; "Between the Darkness and the Dawn," NBC, 1985.

GRAUER, BEN

b. New York City, NY, June 2, 1908; d. 1977. Announcer best known as the voice who rang in New Year's Eve on TV and the radio.

AS A REGULAR: "Eye Witness," NBC, 1947-48; "Ben Grauer's Americana Quiz," NBC, 1947-49; "Kay Kyser's Kollege of Musical Knowledge," NBC, 1949-50; "What Happened?," NBC, 1952; "The Big Story," NBC, 1955-57; "The March of Medicine," ABC, 1958.

AND: "The Sacco-Vanzetti Story," NBC, 1960.

GRAVES, PETER

b. Peter Aurness, Minneapolis, MN, March 18, 1926. Brother of James Arness who shares his brother's quiet but imposing manner; best known as Jim Phelps, leader of the Impossible Missions Force.

AS A REGULAR: "Fury," NBC, 1955-58; "Whiplash," SYN, 1960-61; "Court-Martial," ABC, 1966; "Mission: Impossible," CBS, 1967-73; ABC, 1988-90.

AND: "Pepsi Cola Playhouse: Melody in Black," ABC, 1953; "Fireside Theatre: The Suitors," NBC, 1953; "Schlitz Playhouse of Stars: Part of the Game," CBS, 1953; "Pepsi Cola Playhouse: Miss Darkness," ABC, 1954; "Fireside Theatre: Beyond the Cross," NBC, 1954; "Fireside Theatre: Bread Upon the Waters," NBC, 1954; "Studio 57: Sauce for the Gander," SYN, 1954; "TV Reader's Digest: Trouble on the Double," ABC, 1955; "Fireside Theatre: Bitter Grapes," NBC, 1955; "Studio One: Circle of Guilt," CBS, 1956; "Cavalcade Theatre: The Major of St. Louis," ABC, 1956; "The Millionaire: The Story of Anna Hartley," CBS, 1956; "Climax!: Carnival at Midnight," CBS, 1957; "Route 66: Hell Is Empty, All the Devils Are Here," CBS, 1962; "The Alfred Hitchcock Hour: You Be Judge, I'll Be Jury," CBS, 1963; "Kraft Suspense Theatre: The Case Against Paul Ryker," NBC, 1963; "The Farmer's Daughter: The Playboy of Capitol Hill," ABC, 1964; "The Virginian: A Matter of Destiny," NBC, 1964; "The Great Adventure: Kentucky's Bloody Ground," CBS, 1964; "Laredo: That's Norway, Thataway," NBC, 1966; "Branded: The Assassins," NBC, 1966; "Run for

Your Life: The Dark Beyond the Door," NBC, 1966; "Walt Disney's Wonderful World of Color: Showdown with the Sundown Kid," NBC, 1966; "The FBI: Rope of Gold," ABC, 1967; "The Invaders: Moonshot," ABC, 1967; "The Mike Douglas Show," SYN, 1968; "The Red Skelton Hour," CBS, 1969; "The Dean Martin Show," NBC, 1970; "The Tim Conway Show," CBS, 1970; "The Sonny and Cher Comedy Hour," CBS, 1977; "The Love Boat: Man of the Cloth," ABC, 1978; "Buck Rogers in the 25th Century: Return of the Fighting 69th," NBC, 1979; "The Love Boat: The Judges," ABC, 1980; "Fantasy Island: The Sailor," ABC, 1982; "Murder, She Wrote: Lovers and Other Killers," CBS, 1984.

TV MOVIES AND MINISERIES: "Valley of Mystery," ABC, 1967; "Call to Danger," CBS, 1973; "The President's Plane Is Missing," ABC, 1973; "Scream of the Wolf," ABC, 1974; "The Underground Man," NBC, 1974; "Where Have All the People Gone?," NBC, 1974; "Dead Man on the Run," ABC, 1975; "SST—Death Flight," ABC, 1977; "The Rebels," SYN, 1979; "Death Car on the Freeway," CBS, 1979; "The Memory of Eva Ryker," CBS, 1980; "300 Miles for Stephanie," NBC, 1981; "The Winds of War," ABC, 1983; "War and Remembrance," ABC, 1988, 1989.

GRAVES, TERESA

b. Houston, TX, January 10, 1949. Actress who danced in bikinis on "Laugh-In" and played spunky cop Christie Love!; a former Doodletown Piper.

AS A REGULAR: "Our Place," CBS, 1967; "Turn-On," ABC, 1969; "Rowan & Martin's Laugh-In," NBC, 1969-70; "The Funny Side," NBC, 1971; "Get Christie Love!," ABC, 1974-75.

AND: "Letters to Laugh-In," NBC, 1969; "Bob Hope Special," NBC, 1970; "Hollywood Squares," NBC, 1971; "The Rookies: Easy Money," ABC, 1973.

TV MOVIES AND MINISERIES: "Get Christie Love!," ABC, 1974.

GRAY, BILLY

b. William Thomas Gray, Los Angeles, CA, January 13, 1938. Clean-cut actor who played clean-cut "Bud" Anderson on "Father Knows Best."

AS A REGULAR: "Father Knows Best," CBS, 1954-55; NBC, 1955-58; CBS, 1958-60.

AND: "Celanese Theatre: On Borrowed Time," ABC, 1952; "Schaefer Century Theatre: Lesson in Hot Lead," NBC, 1952; "Fireside Theatre: The First Prize," NBC, 1954; "Cavalcade of America: Young Andy Jackson," ABC, 1954; "The Steve Allen Show," NBC, 1956; "The Thin Man: Come Back, Darling Asta," NBC, 1957; "Peter Gunn: The Semi-Private Eye," NBC, 1960; "Stagecoach West: Dark Return," ABC, 1960; "Bachelor Father: Ginger's Big Romance," NBC, 1960;

"G.E. Theatre: The Dropout," CBS, 1961; "The Deputy: Two-Way Deal," NBC, 1961; "G.E. Theatre: Sis Bowls 'em Over," CBS, 1961; "Alfred Hitchcock Presents: The Hat Box," NBC, 1961; "The Greatest Show on Earth: Corsicans Don't Cry," ABC, 1964; "Rawhide: Moment in the Sun," CBS, 1965; "I Spy: Lori," NBC, 1966; "Combat!: The Losers," ABC, 1966; "That Girl: Beware of Actors Bearing Gifts," ABC, 1966; "The Bold Ones: Memo From the Class of '76," NBC, 1970.

GRAY, COLEEN

b. Doris Jensen, Staplehurst, NB, October 23, 1922. Attractive actress in film ("Nightmare Alley") and TV; she played Ann Boyd Jones on "Bright Promise."

AS A REGULAR: "Window on Main Street," CBS, 1961-62; "Bright Promise," NBC, 1969-72.

AND: "Matinee Theatre: The Remarkable Mr. Jerome," NBC, 1957; "Playhouse 90: Before I Die," CBS, 1958; "This Is the Life: The Gift," SYN, 1959; "Mother's March," SYN, 1960; "Walt Disney Presents: The Nine Lives of Elfego Baca-Gus Tomlin Is Dead," ABC, 1960; "The Deputy: A Time to Sow," NBC, 1960; "Perry Mason: The Case of the Wandering Widow," CBS, 1960; "Coronado 9: Tramp Steamer," SYN, 1960; "G.E. Theatre: Learn to Say Goodbye," CBS, 1960; "Bus Stop: Jaws of Darkness," ABC, 1961; "Perry Mason: The Case of the Glamorous Ghost," CBS, 1962; "Mr. Ed: Wilbur the Masher," CBS, 1962; "The Wide Country: A Devil in the Chute," NBC, 1962; "77 Sunset Strip: The Floating Man," ABC, 1962; "The Adventures of Ozzie and Harriet: Decorating Dave's Office," ABC, 1963; "Perry Mason: The Case of the Fifty Millionth Frenchman," CBS, 1964; "Branded: Seward's Folly," NBC, 1965; "My Three Sons: Hawaiian Cruise," ABC, 1965; "The Virginian: Men With Guns," NBC, 1966; "The Virginian: Requiem for a Country Doctor," NBC, 1967; "Ironside: The Challenge," NBC, 1968; "The FBI: The Eye of the Needle," ABC, 1971; "Mannix: The Man Outside," CBS, 1971; "Emergency!: The Nuisance," NBC, 1976.

TV MOVIES AND MINISERIES: "Ellery Queen: Don't Look Behind You," NBC, 1971.

GRAY, DOLORES

b. Chicago, IL, June 7, 1930. Musical comedy performer.

AS A REGULAR: "The Buick Circus Hour," NBC, 1952-53.

AND: "Ford Star Jubilee: You're the Top," CBS, 1956; "The Ed Sullivan Show," CBS, 1957; "Person to Person," CBS, 1957; "Pat Boone Chevy Showroom," ABC, 1957; "Texaco Star Theatre: Command Appearance," NBC, 1957; "The Steve Allen Show," NBC, 1958; "The Eddie Fisher Show," NBC, 1958; "The Ed Sullivan Show," CBS, 1958; "The Steve Allen Show," NBC, 1959; "Arthur Murray Party," NBC, 1959; "The Ed Sullivan Show," CBS, 1959; "Bell Telephone Hour: The Golden West," NBC, 1959; "Perry Como's Kraft Music Hall," NBC, 1959; "The Ed Sullivan Show," CBS, 1960; "Bell Telephone Hour: Music Hath Charms," NBC, 1961; "The Ed Sullivan Show," CBS, 1961; "U.S. Steel Hour: Famous," CBS, 1961; "Bell Telephone Hour: The Music of Richard Rodgers," NBC, 1961; "Highways of Melody," NBC, 1961; "The Merv Griffin Show," NBC, 1962; "Stump the Stars," CBS, 1963; "The Ed Sullivan Show," CBS, 1964; "Bell Telephone Hour," NBC, 1965.

GRAY, ERIN

b. Hawaii, January 7, 1952. Attractive brunette actress who's virtually indistinguishable from Connie Selleca, Kristian Alfonso or Emma Samms.

AS A REGULAR: "Buck Rogers in the 25th Century," NBC, 1979-81; "Silver Spoons," NBC, 1982-86; SYN, 1986-87.

AND: "The Rockford Files: With the French Heel Back, Can the Nehru Jacket Be Far Behind?," NBC, 1979; "Hollywood Squares," NBC, 1980; "Vega$: Black Cat Killer," ABC, 1980; "The Fall Guy: License to Kill," ABC, 1981; "Simon & Simon: Matchmaker," CBS, 1981; "Magnum, P.I.: The Black Orchid," CBS, 1981; "Murder, She Wrote: The Wearing of the Green," CBS, 1988; "Hunter: On the Air," NBC, 1989.

TV MOVIES AND MINISERIES: "Evening in Byzantium," SYN, 1978; "The Ultimate Imposter," CBS, 1979; "Coach of the Year," NBC, 1980; "Born Beautiful," NBC, 1982; "Norman Rockwell's Breaking Home Ties," ABC, 1987; "Perry Mason: The Case of the Avenging Ace," NBC, 1988; "Addicted to His Love," ABC, 1988.

GRAY, LINDA

b. Santa Monica, CA, September 12, 1940. Actress who played Sue Ellen on "Dallas."

AS A REGULAR: "Dallas," CBS, 1978-89.

AND: "Marcus Welby, M.D.: The Resident," ABC, 1974; "Women Who Rate a 10," NBC, 1981; "Donahue," SYN, 1981.

TV MOVIES AND MINISERIES: "The Two Worlds of Jennie Logan," CBS, 1979; "Haywire," CBS, 1980; "Not in Front of the Children," CBS, 1982; "The Gambler III: The Legend Continues," CBS, 1987.

GRAYCO, HELEN

b. Tacoma, WA, 1924. Singer and wife of anything-for-a-laugh bandleader Spike "Ah-OOOga" Jones.

AS A REGULAR: "The Spike Jones Show," NBC, 1951; 1954; CBS, 1957; 1960; 1961; "Club

Oasis," NBC, 1958.
AND: "The Frank Sinatra Show," ABC, 1958; "Person to Person," CBS, 1960; "The Dean Martin Show," NBC, 1968.

GRAYSON, KATHRYN
b. Zelma Hednick, Winston-Salem, NC, February 9, 1923. Petite star of MGM musicals with a few TV credits.
AS A GUEST: "G.E. Theatre: Shadow on the Heart," CBS, 1955; "The Perry Como Show," NBC, 1956; "G.E. Theatre: The Invitation," CBS, 1956; "The Jackie Gleason Show: America's Music Makers," CBS, 1957; "Playhouse 90: Lone Woman," CBS, 1957; "The Bob Crosby Show," NBC, 1958; "Pat Boone Chevy Showroom," ABC, 1958; "Lux Playhouse: A Game of Hate," CBS, 1958; "The Ed Sullivan Show," CBS, 1958; "The Perry Como Show," NBC, 1959; "Highways of Melody," NBC, 1961; "The Mike Douglas Show," SYN, 1976; "Murder, She Wrote: If It's Thursday, It Must Be Beverly," CBS, 1987; "Murder, She Wrote: Sins of Castle Cove," CBS, 1989.

GRAZIANO, ROCKY
b. New York City, NY, December 31, 1921; d. 1990. Middleweight champ of the forties, not to be confused with Kathryn Grayson.
AS A REGULAR: "Pantomime Quiz," CBS, 1954; ABC, 1955; CBS, 1955; CBS, 1956; "The Henny and Rocky Show," ABC, 1955; "The Martha Raye Show," NBC, 1955-56; "The Keefe Brasselle Show," CBS, 1963.
AND: "The Steve Allen Show," NBC, 1956; "The Garry Moore Show," CBS, 1958; "The Ed Sullivan Show: Man of the Hour," CBS, 1958; "The Jimmy Dean Show," CBS, 1959; "Naked City: Fallen Star," ABC, 1959; "Naked City: The Canvas Bullet," ABC, 1959; "Be Our Guest," CBS, 1960; "The Arthur Murray Party for Bob Hope," NBC, 1960; "Arthur Murray Party," NBC, 1960; "Car 54, Where Are You?: Puncher and Judy," NBC, 1963; "The Dean Martin Show," NBC, 1970.

GREAZA, WALTER
b. St. Paul, MN, January 1, 1897; d. 1973. Actor who played Winston Grimsley on "The Edge of Night."
AS A REGULAR: "Federal Men (Treasury Men in Action)," ABC, 1950; NBC, 1951-54; ABC, 1954-55; "Martin Kane, Private Eye," NBC, 1951; "The Edge of Night," CBS, 1956-73.
AND: "Hallmark Hall of Fame: Man and Superman," NBC, 1956; "Brenner: Monopoly on Fear," CBS, 1959; "U.S. Steel Hour: A Time to Decide," CBS, 1960; "U.S. Steel Hour: Watching Out for Dulie," CBS, 1961; "U.S. Steel Hour:

Delayed Honeymoon," CBS, 1961; "The Defenders: The Man with the Concrete Thumb," CBS, 1961; "U.S. Steel Hour: Tangle of Truth," CBS, 1961.

GRECO, BUDDY
b. Philadelphia, PA, August 14, 1926. Singer.
AS A REGULAR: "Songs at Twilight," NBC, 1951; "Broadway Open House," NBC, 1951; "Away We Go," CBS, 1967.
AND: "The Rosemary Clooney Show," SYN, 1957; "American Bandstand," ABC, 1958; "The Steve Allen Show," NBC, 1959; "The Ed Sullivan Show," CBS, 1962; "Hollywood Palace," ABC, 1964; "The Pat Boone Show," NBC, 1967; "The Joey Bishop Show," ABC, 1967; "The Joey Bishop Show," ABC, 1969.

GREEN ACRES, CBS, 1965-71.
"Green Acres" was satirical where "The Beverly Hillbillies" was down-home, cynical where "Petticoat Junction" was sentimental. It was in a Twilight Zone all its own—Hooterville, Ill., which might have been an uncharted island somewhere for all its residents knew about modern society. "Petticoat Junction" was also set in Hooterville, but "Green Acres" was clearly on the weird side of town. Whenever characters from "Petticoat" visited "Green Acres," they always looked a little skittish, like they thought toxic waste might be buried in the area.

The main characters in "Green Acres" were Oliver and Lisa Douglas, portrayed by Eddie Albert and Eva Gabor. Oliver had been a successful Manhattan attorney; he and Lisa lived in a penthouse.

The closest Lisa wanted to get to terra firma was buying beauty mud at Bloomingdale's, but Oliver wanted a farm. He wanted to get back to the land, to get his hands dirty, to rekindle the American dream as it had been lived by our forefathers when the country was young and hopes were high. He would talk like that a lot, and every time he did, some patriotic music would start playing and somebody on the show would say, "There goes that patriotic music again."

Anyway, Oliver bought a farm in Hooterville (or "Hootersville," as Lisa called it) that turned out to be a dump. Lisa hated it, but she got along with the residents of Hootersville, most of whom were either selfish, small-minded farmers, genetic misfits or just plain geeks. Like Alf Monroe (Sid Melton) and his sister, Ralph (Mary Grace Canfield). Hank Kimball (Alvy

Moore), the bumbling county agricultural agent. Arnold Ziffel, a pig who went to Harvard, watched "The Dick Van Dyke Show" and who, dear reader, wore hats. And Eb Dawson (Tom Lester), the hired hand who called Oliver and Lisa "mom" and "dad," not necessarily in that order.

The best indication of how good and weird "Green Acres" could be has to be in the episode called "A Square Is Not Round," in which Oliver's chickens keep laying square eggs. Everyone is baffled by this seeming impossibility, especially Hank Kimball, who was always baffled anyway. In one scene, Kimball, watches a square egg clunk down the chute. He picks up, storms into the henhouse and angrily asks, "All right, which one of you mothers laid this?"

GREEN BUSH, LINDSEY & SIDNEY

b. Los Angeles, CA, May 25, 1970. Twin actresses who played Carrie Ingallas on "Little House."
AS A REGULAR: "Little House on the Prairie," NBC, 1974-82.
TV MOVIES AND MINISERIES: "Little House on the Prairie," NBC, 1974.

GREENE, JAMES

Stage actor who plays Davey, the philosophical doorman in Molly Dodd's apartment building.
AS A REGULAR: "The Days and Nights of Molly Dodd," NBC, 1987-88; LIF, 1988- .
AND: "Camera Three: In Tilbury Town," CBS, 1960; "Catholic Hour: The War for Geoffrey Wilson," NBC, 1960; "John Brown's Raid," NBC, 1960; "All in the Family: Mr. Edith Bunker," CBS, 1976; "Perfect Strangers: Tux for Two," ABC, 1987; "Max Headroom: Academy," ABC, 1987; "Columbo: Columbo Goes to the Guillotine," ABC, 1989; "Star Trek: The Next Generation: Who Watches the Watchers?," SYN, 1989; "Alien Nation: Little Lost Lamb," FOX, 1989; "Alien Nation: The First Cigar," FOX, 1989; "Alien Nation: The Night of Screams," FOX, 1989; "Mancuso FBI: Betrayal," NBC, 1989.
TV MOVIES AND MINISERIES: "The Spell," NBC, 1977; "Blind Ambition," CBS, 1979; "Thin Ice," CBS, 1981; "Rage of Angels," NBC, 1983; "Pals," CBS, 1987; "Case Closed," CBS, 1988; "The Hollywood Detective," USA, 1989.

GREENE, LORNE

b. Ottawa, Canada, February 12, 1915; d. 1987. Radio-trained actor with a commanding voice who played pop Ben Cartwright, master of the Ponderosa, on "Bonanza"—and who was about to reprise that role in a TV movie when he died.
AS A REGULAR: "Bonanza, NBC, 1959-73; "Griff,"

ABC, 1973-74; "Lorne Greene's Last of the Wild," SYN, 1974-79; "Battlestar Galactica," ABC, 1978-80; "Code Red," ABC, 1981-82; "Lorne Greene's New Wilderness," SYN, 1982-86.
AND: "Studio One: A Handful of Diamonds," CBS, 1954; "You Are There: The Torment of Beethoven," CBS, 1955; "Studio One: The Cliff," CBS, 1954; "Climax!: Private Worlds," CBS, 1955; "Star Stage: The Toy Lady," NBC, 1955; "Studio 57: Death Dream," SYN, 1955; "Alfred Hitchcock Presents: Help Wanted," CBS, 1956; "Alcoa Hour: Key Largo," NBC, 1956; "Armstrong Circle Theatre: Flareup!," NBC, 1956; "U.S. Steel Hour: Survival," CBS, 1956; "Producers Showcase: Mayerling," NBC, 1957; "Kraft Television Theatre: The Medallion," NBC, 1957; "Playhouse 90: Edge of Innocence," CBS, 1957; "Studio One: 24 Hours to Dawn," CBS, 1957; "Shirley Temple's Storybook: The Little Lame Prince," NBC, 1958; "The Gale Storm Show: Jailmates," CBS, 1959; "Wagon Train: The Vivian Carter Story," NBC, 1959; "Cheyenne: Prairie Skipper," ABC, 1959; "Mickey Spillane's Mike Hammer: A Haze on the Lake," SYN, 1959; "Cheyenne: Gold, Glory and Custer-Requiem," ABC, 1960; "Here's Hollywood," NBC, 1960; "Perry Como's Kraft Music Hall," NBC, 1962; "The Andy Williams Show," NBC, 1963; "The Art Linkletter Show," NBC, 1963; "The Tonight Show Starring Johnny Carson," NBC, 1963; "Missing Links," NBC, 1963; "What's This Song?," NBC, 1964; "Allan Sherman's Funnyland," NBC, 1965; "ABC Nightlife," ABC, 1965; "The Dean Martin Show," NBC, 1968; "The Merv Griffin Show," SYN, 1968; "The Joey Bishop Show," ABC, 1968; "Dinah Shore Special," NBC, 1969; "Jimmy Durante Presents the Lennon Sisters Hour," ABC, 1969; "Movin'," NBC, 1970; "A Salute to Television's 25th Anniversary," ABC, 1972; "The Merv Griffin Show," SYN, 1974; "Sandy in Disneyland," CBS, 1974; "Short Stories of Love: The Fortunate Painter," NBC, 1974; "Tattletales," CBS, 1976; "Happy Days: Hollywood," ABC, 1977; "The Love Boat: The Wedding," ABC, 1979; "Vega$: Aloha, You're Dead," ABC, 1980; "The Love Boat: Love Will Find a Way," ABC, 1982; "The Canadian Conspiracy," MAX, 1986.
TV MOVIES AND MINISERIES: "Destiny of a Spy," NBC, 1969; "The Harness," NBC, 1971; "Nevada Smith," NBC, 1975; "Man on the Outside," ABC, 1975; "The Moneychangers," NBC, 1976; "Roots," ABC, 1977; "SST—Death Flight," ABC, 1977; "The Trial of Lee Harvey Oswald," ABC, 1977; "The Bastard," SYN, 1978; "A Time for Miracles," ABC, 1980; "The Alamo: 13 Days to Glory," NBC, 1987.
* See also "Bonanza."

GREENE, MICHELE

b. Las Vegas, NV. Actress who plays Abby Perkins on "L.A. Law."
AS A REGULAR: "Dorothy," CBS, 1979; "The Bay City Blues," NBC, 1983; "L.A. Law," NBC, 1986- .
AND: "Laverne & Shirley: Bad Girls," ABC, 1979; "The Best Times: Narc," NBC, 1985; "Simon & Simon: Mummy Talks," CBS, 1985; "Matlock: The Billionaire," NBC, 1987.
TV MOVIES AND MINISERIES: "The Miracle of Kathy Miller," CBS, 1981; "Desperate Lives," CBS, 1982; "Perry Mason: The Case of the Notorious Nun," NBC, 1986.

GREENE, RICHARD

b. England, August 25, 1918; d. 1982. Dashing actor in Hollywood films who returned to his homeland for his only TV hit.
AS A REGULAR: "The Adventures of Robin Hood," CBS, 1955-58.
AND: "Prudential Family Playhouse: Berkeley Square," CBS, 1951; "Robert Montgomery Presents: Stairway to Heaven," NBC, 1951; "Lux Video Theatre: Sire de Maletroit's Door," CBS, 1951; "Peter Ibbetson," CBS, 1951; "Studio One: Coriolanus," CBS, 1951; "Somerset Maugham TV Theatre: The Fall of Edward Bernard," NBC, 1951; "Lux Video Theatre: Stolen Years," CBS, 1951; "Robert Montgomery Presents: The Moonstone," NBC, 1952; "A Terribly Strange Bed," CBS, 1953; "G.E. Theatre: The Return of Gentleman Jim," CBS, 1955; "U.S. Steel Hour: The Wayward Widow," CBS, 1959; "G.E. Theatre: Hot Footage," CBS, 1960; "Off to See the Wizard: Island of the Lost," ABC, 1967.

GREENE, SHECKY

b. Chicago, IL, April 8, 1925. Comedian.
AS A REGULAR: "Combat!," ABC, 1962-63.
AND: "The Vic Damone Show," CBS, 1957; "The Tonight Show," NBC, 1957; "The Ed Sullivan Show," CBS, 1958; "The Ed Sullivan Show," CBS, 1959; "Dinah Shore Chevy Show," NBC, 1959; "The Ed Sullivan Show," CBS, 1960; "The Joey Bishop Show: Joey Introduces Shecky Greene," NBC, 1964; "Hollywood Palace," ABC,

1964; "Hollywood Palace," ABC, 1966; "The Merv Griffin Show," SYN, 1968; "This Is Tom Jones," ABC, 1971; "Love, American Style: Love and the Fighting Couple," ABC, 1972; "Love, American Style: Love and the New You," ABC, 1972; "The Tonight Show Starring Johnny Carson," NBC, 1973; "Tattletales," CBS, 1975; "Match Game '75," CBS, 1975; "The Tonight Show Starring Johnny Carson," NBC, 1977; "The Love Boat: Divorce Me, Please!," ABC, 1977; "The Merv Griffin Show," SYN, 1980; "The Fall Guy: T.K.O.," ABC, 1983.
TV MOVIES AND MINISERIES: "Midnight Lace," NBC, 1981.

GREENWOOD, BRUCE

b. Canada. Actor who played Dr. Seth Griffin on "St. Elsewhere."
AS A REGULAR: "Legmen," NBC, 1984; "St. Elsewhere," NBC, 1986-88.
AND: "Matlock: The Billionaire," NBC, 1987; "Jake and the Fatman: Pilot," CBS, 1987.
TV MOVIES AND MINISERIES: "Peyton Place: The Next Generation," NBC, 1985; "Destination: America," ABC, 1987; "Pursuit," NBC, 1988; "Perry Mason: The Case of the All-Star Assassin," NBC, 1989.

GREENWOOD, JOAN

b. London, England, March 4, 1921; d. 1987. Vixenish British actress who practically purred her lines.
AS A GUEST: "Philco TV Playhouse: The King and Mrs. Candle," NBC, 1954; "Hallmark Hall of Fame: Man and Superman," NBC, 1956; "Secret Agent: The Paper Chase," CBS, 1966.
TV MOVIES AND MINISERIES: "The Flame Is Love," NBC, 1979.

GREER, DABBS

b. Fairview, MO, April 2, 1917. Familiar character with a hangdog look; he played Rev. Alden on "Little House."
AS A REGULAR: "Gunsmoke," CBS, 1955-62; "Hank," NBC, 1965-66; "Little House on the Prairie," NBC, 1974-83.
AND: "The Loretta Young Show: Tropical Secretary," NBC, 1955; "Science Fiction Theatre: Strange People of Pecos," SYN, 1955; "Science Fiction Theatre: End of Tomorrow," SYN, 1956; "The Jane Wyman Show: Helpmate," NBC, 1956; "How to Marry a Millionaire: The Penthouse," SYN, 1957; "Perry Mason: The Case of the Fugitive Nurse," CBS, 1958; "Restless Gun: Peligroso," NBC, 1958; "Wanted Dead or Alive: The Martin Poster," CBS, 1958; "The Loretta Young Show: The Accused," NBC, 1959; "Goodyear Theatre: Christabel," NBC, 1959; "The Andy Griffith Show: Sheriff Barney," CBS, 1961; "Have Gun, Will Travel: Lazarus," CBS, 1962; "SurfSide 6: The SurfSide Swindle,"

ABC, 1962; "Robert Taylor's Detectives: The Outsider," NBC, 1962; "The Twilight Zone: Hocus-Pocus and Frisby," CBS, 1962; "The Dick Van Dyke Show: The Attempted Marriage," CBS, 1962; "The Eleventh Hour: Angie, You Made My Heart Stop," NBC, 1962; "The Andy Griffith Show: The Bed Jacket," CBS, 1962; "The Twilight Zone: Valley of the Shadow," CBS, 1963; "Grindl: Grindl, Private Eye," NBC, 1964; "Perry Mason: The Case of the Ice-Cold Hands," CBS, 1964; "The Outer Limits: The Children of Spider County," ABC, 1964; "The Dick Van Dyke Show: 100 Terrible Hours," CBS, 1965; "Gomer Pyle, USMC: Home on the Range," CBS, 1965; "The Dick Van Dyke Show: Fifty-Two Forty-Five or Work," CBS, 1965; "The FBI: By Force and Violence," ABC, 1967; "Gomer Pyle, USMC: The Prize Boat," CBS, 1967; "The Virginian: Bitter Autumn," NBC, 1967; "The Wild Wild West: The Night of the Simian Terror," CBS, 1968; "The Wild Wild West: The Night of the Fire and Brimstone," CBS, 1968; "The FBI: The Ninth Man," ABC, 1968; "Petticoat Junction: Ring-a-Ding-Ding," CBS, 1968; "The FBI: The Runaways," ABC, 1968; "The FBI: Journey Into Night," ABC, 1969; "Mannix: Last Rites for Miss Emma," CBS, 1969; "The FBI: The Architect," ABC, 1970; "The FBI: Dynasty of Hate," ABC, 1971; "James Garner as Nichols: Sleight of Hand," NBC, 1972; "The Rookies: The Commitment," ABC, 1972; "The FBI: Sweet Evil," ABC, 1973; "The Rookies: Down Home Boy," ABC, 1973; "Barnaby Jones: Murder-Go-Round," CBS, 1973; "Ironside: House of Terror," NBC, 1973; "Chopper One: Strain of Innocence," ABC, 1974; "The Streets of San Francisco: Dead or Alive," ABC, 1976; "The Rockford Files: Where's Houston?," NBC, 1976; "Roseanne: Lobocop," ABC, 1989.
TV MOVIES AND MINISERIES: "The Greatest Gift," NBC, 1974.

GREER, JANE
b. Bettejane Greer, Washington, D.C., September 9, 1924. Sultry actress of forties films who's shown a renewed interest in television.
AS A GUEST: "Ford Theatre: Look for Tomorrow," NBC, 1953; "Mirror Theatre: Summer Dance," CBS, 1953; "Ford Theatre: One Man Missing," NBC, 1955; "Ford Theatre: Moment of Decision," ABC, 1957; "Dick Powell's Zane Grey Theatre: A Gun for My Bride," CBS, 1957; "Playhouse 90: No Time at All," CBS, 1958; "Suspicion: Meeting in Paris," NBC, 1958; "Alfred Hitchcock Presents: Going Home," CBS, 1958; "Dick Powell's Zane Grey Theatre: The Vaunted," CBS, 1958; "Bonanza: The Julia Bulette Story," NBC, 1959; "Dick Powell's Zane Grey Theatre: Stagecoach to Yuma," CBS, 1960; "Stagecoach West: High

Lonesome," ABC, 1960; "Thriller: Portrait Without a Face," NBC, 1961; "Burke's Law: Who Killed My Girl?," ABC, 1964; "Columbo: Troubled Waters," NBC, 1975; "Murder, She Wrote: The Last Flight of the Dizzy Damsel," CBS, 1988; "Heartbeat: Stress," ABC, 1989.

GREGORY, BENJI
b. Encino, CA, May 26, 1978. Young actor who played Brian Tanner on "ALF."
AS A REGULAR: "ALF," NBC, 1986-90.
TV MOVIES AND MINISERIES: "Thompson's Last Run," CBS, 1986.

GREGORY, DICK
b. St. Louis, MO, 1932. Black comedian, social crusader and diet-mix salesman.
AS A GUEST: "The Jack Paar Show," NBC, 1961; "The Merv Griffin Show," NBC, 1962; "The Jack Paar Program," NBC, 1963.

GREGORY, JAMES
b. New Rochelle, NY, December 23, 1911. Character actor whose TV fame came late in his career, as Inspector Frank Luger on "Barney Miller."
AS A REGULAR: "The Lawless Years," NBC, 1959-60; 1961; "The Paul Lynde Show," ABC, 1972-73; "Barney Miller," ABC, 1975-82; "Detective School," ABC, 1979.
AND: "Climax!: Island in the City," CBS, 1956; "U.S. Steel Hour: Hidden Fury," CBS, 1957; "Studio One: The Staring Match," CBS, 1957; "Alfred Hitchcock Presents: Cream of the Jest," CBS, 1957; "Kraft Television Theatre: The Long Flight," NBC, 1957; "Kraft Theatre: Polka," NBC, 1957; "Studio One: Presence of the Enemy," CBS, 1958; "The Twilight Zone: Where Is Everybody?," CBS, 1959; "Laramie: Man of God," NBC, 1959; "G.E. Theatre: Sarah's Laughter," CBS, 1960; "Alcoa Theatre: Face to Face," NBC, 1960; "Wagon Train: The Ricky and Laurie Bell Story," NBC, 1960; "Buick Electra Playhouse: The Snows of Kilimanjaro," CBS, 1960; "Moment of Fear: The Third Party," NBC, 1960; "The du Pont Show with June Allyson: I Hit and Ran," CBS, 1960; "Checkmate: Hour of the Execution," CBS, 1961; "Target: The Corrupters: The Malignant Hearts," ABC, 1962; "The Virginian: 50 Days to Moose Jaw," NBC, 1962; "Empire: When the Gods Laugh," NBC, 1962; "Rawhide: Incident at Crooked Hat," CBS, 1963; "Ben Casey: There Was Once a Man in the Land of Uz," ABC, 1964; "F Troop: Too Many Cooks Spoil the Troop," ABC, 1966; "Hogan's Heroes: Hogan Gives a Birthday Party," CBS, 1966; "F Troop: Lieutenant O'Rourke, Front and Center," ABC, 1966; "The Big Valley: The Haunted Gun," ABC, 1966; "Star Trek: Dagger of the Mind," NBC, 1966; "Lancer: The Lawman,"

CBS, 1968; "The Virginian: The Price of Love," NBC, 1969; "All in the Family: Edith Flips Her Wig," CBS, 1972; "The Partridge Family: Danny Drops Out," ABC, 1974; "M*A*S*H: Iron Guts Kelly," CBS, 1974; "The FBI: The Vendetta," ABC, 1974; "Police Story: Fingerprint," NBC, 1974; "Kolchak, the Night Stalker: They Have Been, They Are, They Will Be," ABC, 1974; "Police Story: World Full of Hurt," NBC, 1974; "Emergency!: Prestidigitation," NBC, 1975; "McCoy: Bless the Big Fish," NBC, 1975; "Medical Center: Major Annie, M.D.," CBS, 1976; "Quincy: Death Casts a Vote," NBC, 1977; "The Love Boat: Hey, Jealous Lover," ABC, 1980.

TV MOVIES AND MINISERIES: "Hawaii Five-O," CBS, 1968; "A Very Missing Person," NBC, 1972; "The Weekend Nun," ABC, 1972; "Miracle on 34th Street," CBS, 1973; "The Abduction of Saint Anne," ABC, 1975; "The Bastard," SYN, 1978; "The Great American Traffic Jam," NBC, 1980; "Goldie and the Boxer Go to Holly-wood," NBC, 1981; "Wait Til Your Mother Gets Home," NBC, 1983.

GREY, JOEL
b. Joel Katz, Cleveland, OH, April 11, 1932. Slightly built, award winning musical comedy performer best remembered as the leering, scary emcee in the film and stage versions on "Cabaret"; his TV roles have largely failed to utilize his talent.
AS A GUEST: "Producers Showcase: Jack and the Beanstalk," NBC, 1956; "Telephone Time: The Intruder," CBS, 1957; "December Bride: Crash-ing Hollywood," CBS, 1957; "Pat Boone Chevy Showroom," ABC, 1957; "Court of Last Resort: The Todd-Loomis Case," NBC, 1958; "Little Women," CBS, 1958; "The Chevy Show," NBC, 1959; "Bronco: The Masquerade," ABC, 1960; "Maverick: Full House," ABC, 1960; "Lawman: The Salvation of Owny O'Reilly," ABC, 1960; "Lawman: The Return of Owny O'Reilly," ABC, 1960; "SurfSide 6: The Clown," ABC, 1960; "Yes, Yes Nanette: Nanette's Teenage Suitor," NBC, 1961; "77 Sunset Strip: Open and Close in One," ABC, 1961; "Lawman: Owny O'Reilly, Esquire," ABC, 1961; "The Price Is Right," ABC, 1964; "Missing Links," NBC, 1964; "Missing Links," ABC, 1964; "Get the Message," ABC, 1964; "The Dean Martin Show," NBC, 1966; "Vacation Playhouse: My Lucky Penny," CBS, 1966; "The Mike Douglas Show," SYN, 1969; "George M!," NBC, 1970; "Ironside: A Killing at the Track," NBC, 1971; "Night Gallery: There Aren't Any More MacBanes," NBC, 1972; "The Carol Burnett Show," CBS, 1974; "Twas the Night Before Christmas," CBS, 1974; "The John Davidson Show," SYN, 1981.
TV MOVIES AND MINISERIES: "Man on a String," ABC, 1972; "Queenie," ABC, 1987.

GRIECO, RICHARD
b. 1966, Watertown, NY. Pretty-boy actor who played cop-with-an-attitude Dennis Booker on two cop-shows-with-an-attituide.
AS A REGULAR: "21 Jump Street," FOX, 1988-89; "Booker," FOX, 1989-90.

GRIER, ROOSEVELT
b. Cuthbert, GA, July 14, 1932. Former football player—a member of the L.A. Rams' "Fearsome Foursome" in the sixties—who turned to entertainment.
AS A REGULAR: "Daniel Boone," NBC, 1969-70; "The Rosey Grier Show," SYN, 1970; "Make Room for Granddaddy," ABC, 1970-71; "Movin' On," NBC, 1974-76.
AND: "Truth or Consequences," NBC, 1964; "The Man From UNCLE: The Brain Killer Affair," ABC, 1965; "The Jonathan Winters Show," CBS, 1968; "Bob Hope Christmas Special," NBC, 1969; "Big Daddy," CBS, 1973; "McMillan and Wife: Reunion in Terror," NBC, 1974; "Free to Be You and Me," ABC, 1974; "Cotton Club '75," NBC, 1974; "Kojak: Bad Dude," CBS, 1976; "Kojak: Black Thorn," CBS, 1977; "Chico and the Man: Black Tie Blues," NBC, 1977; "$weepstake$: Cowboy, Linda and Angie, Mark," NBC, 1979; "The Love Boat: The Next Step," ABC, 1979; "The White Shadow: If Your Number's Up...Get It Down," CBS, 1980; "The White Shadow: Georgia on My Mind," CBS, 1980; "Sha Na Na," SYN, 1981; "The White Shadow: Trial and Error," CBS, 1981.
TV MOVIES AND MINISERIES: "Carter's Army," ABC, 1970; "Desperate Mission," NBC, 1971; "Second Chance," ABC, 1972; "Roots: The Next Generations," ABC, 1979; "The Sophisticated Gents," NBC, 1981.

GRIFFIN, MERV
b. San Mateo, CA, July 6, 1925. Former big-band singer, talk-show host, creator of "Jeopardy!" and "Wheel of Fortune."
AS A REGULAR: "The Freddy Martin Show," NBC, 1951; "Summer Holiday," CBS, 1954; "Play Your Hunch," ABC, 1958-59; NBC, 1959-60; 1962-63; "Keep Talking," ABC, 1959-60; "Arthur Murray Party," NBC, 1959-60; "Saturday Prom," NBC, 1960-61; "The Merv Griffin Show," NBC, 1962-63; SYN, 1965-69; 1972-86; CBS, 1969-72; "Talent Scouts," CBS, 1963; "Word for Word," NBC, 1963-64.
AND: "Going Places," ABC, 1956; "The Tonight Show," NBC, 1957; "American Bandstand," ABC, 1958; "Arthur Murray Party," NBC, 1958; "Music for a Summer Night," ABC, 1959; "The Price Is Right," NBC, 1959; "Pantomime Quiz," ABC, 1959; "Music for a Summer Night: Biography of a Boy," ABC, 1960; "To Tell the Truth," CBS, 1961; "The du Pont Show: The

370

Wonderful World of Toys," NBC, 1961; "The Jack Paar Show," NBC, 1962; "To Tell the Truth," CBS, 1962; "The Red Skelton Hour," CBS, 1964; "The Mike Douglas Show," SYN, 1965; "Hippodrome," CBS, 1966; "The Girl with Something Extra: All the Nude That's Fit to Print," NBC, 1973; "Hollywood Squares," NBC, 1975; "Sanford & Son: Earthquake II," NBC, 1975.

GRIFFITH, ANDY

b. Andy Samuel Griffith, Mount Airy, NC, June 1, 1926. Light actor, usually in comedy roles, best known as Sheriff Andy Taylor on a successful sixties sitcom; his relaxed manner betrays a fierce appreciation for good comic writing and performing. Nowadays, he's marking time as criminal lawyer Ben Matlock.

AS A REGULAR: "The Andy Griffith Show," CBS, 1960-68; "The Headmaster," CBS, 1970-71; "The New Andy Griffith Show," CBS, 1971; "Salvage I," ABC, 1979; "Matlock," NBC, 1986- .

AND: "U.S. Steel Hour: No Time for Sergeants," CBS, 1955; "The Steve Allen Show," NBC, 1956; "Strike It Rich," CBS, 1957; "The Steve Allen Show," NBC, 1957; "I've Got a Secret," CBS, 1957; "Person to Person," CBS, 1957; "Dinah Shore Chevy Show," NBC, 1958; "U.S. Steel Hour: Never Know the End," CBS, 1958; "Club Oasis," NBC, 1958; "Playhouse 90: The Male Animal," CBS, 1958; "The Steve Allen Show," NBC, 1958; "Milton Berle Starring in the Kraft Music Hall," NBC, 1958; "The Perry Como Show," NBC, 1958; "The Garry Moore Show," CBS, 1959; "The Steve Allen Show," NBC, 1959; "I've Got a Secret," CBS, 1959; "The Perry Como Show," NBC, 1959; "Arthur Murray Party," NBC, 1959; "The Andy Williams Show," CBS, 1959; "Perry Como's Kraft Music Hall," NBC, 1959; "The Garry Moore Show," CBS, 1960; "The Danny Thomas Show: Danny Meets Andy Griffith," CBS, 1960; "Mike Wallace Interviews," CBS, 1960; "Here's Hollywood," NBC, 1961; "I've Got a Secret," CBS, 1961; "Dean Martin Special," NBC, 1961; "Opening Night," CBS, 1962; "The Andy Williams Show," NBC, 1963; "Opening Night," CBS, 1963; "The Andy Griffith, Don Knotts, Jim Nabors Special," CBS, 1965; "Gomer Pyle, USMC: Opie Joins the Marines," CBS, 1966; "Andy Griffith Special," CBS, 1967; "Mayberry RFD: Andy and Helen Get Married," CBS, 1968; "Mayberry RFD: Help on the Farm," CBS, 1968; "Mayberry RFD: Andy's Baby," CBS, 1969; "The Jim Nabors Hour," CBS, 1969; "The Glen Campbell Goodtime Hour," CBS, 1969; "The Flip Wilson Show," NBC, 1971; "The Carol Burnett Show," CBS, 1971; "The Mod Squad: Big George," ABC, 1972; "Hawaii Five-O: I'm a Family Crook-Don't Shoot," CBS, 1972; "NBC

Follies," NBC, 1973; "The Doris Day Show: The Hoax," CBS, 1973; "The Sonny and Cher Comedy Hour," CBS, 1973; "Here's Lucy: Lucy and Andy Griffith," CBS, 1973; "Mitzi and a Hundred Guys," CBS, 1975; "Adams of Eagle Lake," ABC, 1975; "The Tresaure Chest Murder," ABC, 1975; "The Mike Douglas Show," SYN, 1975; "Tony Orlando and Dawn," CBS, 1976; "Hollywood Television Theatre: Six Characters in Search of an Author," PBS, 1976; "Donny and Marie," ABC, 1976; "Frosty's Wonderland," ABC, 1976; "Captain Kangaroo," CBS, 1978; "Fantasy Island: The Witness," ABC, 1982; "Hotel: Illusions," ABC, 1984; "The Love Boat: Hidden Treasure," ABC, 1985.

TV MOVIES AND MINISERIES: "The Strangers in 7A," CBS, 1972; "Go Ask Alice," ABC, 1973; "Pray for the Wildcats," ABC, 1974; "Winterkill," ABC, 1974; "Savages," ABC, 1974; "Street Killing," ABC, 1976; "The Girl in the Empty Grave," NBC, 1977; "Washington: Behind Closed Doors," ABC, 1977; "Centennial," NBC, 1978-79; "From Here to Eternity," NBC, 1979; "Salvage I," ABC, 1979; "Roots: The Next Generations," ABC, 1979; "Murder in Texas," NBC, 1981; "For Lovers Only," ABC, 1982; "Murder in Coweta County," CBS, 1983; "The Demon Murder Case," NBC, 1983; "Fatal Vision," NBC, 1984; "Crime of Innocence," NBC, 1985; "Diary of a Perfect Murder," NBC, 1986; "Under the Influence," CBS, 1986; "Return to Mayberry," NBC, 1986.

* In case you were wondering, "Salvage I" was about a group of international salvage experts ("Yup, that's junk, all right. Whattya think, Frenchy?" "Oui.").
* Griffith came to TV after making a hugely successful comedy recording called "What It Was, Was Football," a down-home description of a game by someone who'd never seen it played before. Then he went to Broadway as the star of "No Time for Sergeants" and "Destry."
* See also "The Andy Griffith Show."

TV'S TOP TEN, 1967-68

1. The Andy Griffith Show (CBS)
2. The Lucy Show (CBS)
3. Gomer Pyle, USMC (CBS)
4. Gunsmoke (CBS)
4. Family Affair (CBS)
4. Bonanza (NBC)
7. The Red Skelton Hour (CBS)
8. The Dean Martin Show (NBC)
9. The Jackie Gleason Show (CBS)
10. Saturday Night at the Movies (NBC)

GRIFFITH, MELANIE

b. New York City, NY, August 9, 1957. Sexy actress of eighties films ("Working Girl," "Bonfire of the Vanities") who paid her dues in TV.
AS A REGULAR: "Carter Country," ABC, 1978-79.
AND: "Vega$: Redhanded," ABC, 1979; "Alfred Hitchcock Presents: The Man From the South," NBC, 1985; "Miami Vice: By Hooker by Crook," NBC, 1987; "Saturday Night Live," NBC, 1988; "Superstars & Their Moms," TBS, 1989.
TV MOVIES AND MINISERIES: "Steel Cowboy," NBC, 1978; "The Star Maker," NBC, 1981.

GRIMES, TAMMY

b. Lynn, MA, January 30, 1934. Deep-voiced stage actress whose madcap-heiress sitcom was, to that point, one of the quickest-cancelled shows in TV history; now best known for her hundreds of TV commercial voice-overs.
AS A REGULAR: "The Tammy Grimes Show," ABC, 1956.
AND: "U.S. Steel Hour: The Bride Cried," CBS, 1955; "Holiday," NBC, 1956; "Studio One: Babe in the Woods," CBS, 1957; "Omnibus: Forty-Five Minutes From Broadway," NBC, 1959; "Arthur Murray Party," NBC, 1959; "Pontiac Star Parade: Four for Tonight," NBC, 1960; "Sunday Showcase: Hollywood Sings," NBC, 1960; "Dow Hour of Great Mysteries: The Datchet Diamonds," NBC, 1960; "Play of the Week: Archy and Mehitabel," SYN, 1960; "The Ed Sullivan Show," CBS, 1961; "Here's Hollywood," NBC, 1961; "Breck Golden Showcase: The Fourposter," CBS, 1962; "The Andy Williams Show," NBC, 1962; "The Virginian: The Exiles," NBC, 1963; "The Merv Griffin Show," NBC, 1963; "Route 66: Where Are the Sounds of Brahms?," CBS, 1963; "Route 66: Come Home Greta Inger Gruenschaffen," CBS, 1963; "Burke's Law: Who Killed Jason Shaw?," ABC, 1964; "Destry: The Solid Gold Girl," ABC, 1964; "Mr. Broadway: The He-She Chemistry," CBS, 1964; "Trials of O'Brien: A Gaggle of Girls," CBS, 1965; "Tarzan: Mankiller," NBC, 1967; "You're Putting Me On," NBC, 1969; "Love, American Style: Love and the Love Potion," ABC, 1971; "The Snoop Sisters: A Black Day for Bluebeard," NBC, 1974; "'Twas the Night Before Christmas," CBS, 1974; "The Love Boat: Don't Push Me," ABC, 1979; "St. Elsewhere: Playing God," NBC, 1984; "The Equalizer: A Community of Civilized Men," CBS, 1986.
TV MOVIES AND MINISERIES: "The Other Man," NBC, 1970; "Horror at 37,000 Feet," CBS, 1973; "The Borrowers," NBC, 1973; "The Spy Who Returned From the Dead," ABC, 1974; "You Can't Go Home Again," CBS, 1979.

GRIZZARD, GEORGE

b. Roanoke Rapids, NC, April 1, 1928.
Handsome actor with extensive TV guest experience; an Emmy winner for "Attica."
AS A REGULAR: "The Adams Chronicles," PBS, 1976; "Studio 5B," ABC, 1989.
AND: "Justice: The Big Frame," NBC, 1955; "Appointment with Adventure: Escape," CBS, 1955; "U.S. Steel Hour: Bring Me a Dream," CBS, 1956; "Playwrights '56: You and Me ... and the Gatepost!," NBC, 1956; "Goodyear TV Playhouse: The Sentry," NBC, 1956; "Kaiser Aluminum Hour: The Army Game," NBC, 1956; "Alfred Hitchcock Presents: Fog Closing In," CBS, 1956; "Goodyear TV Playhouse: The Gene Austin Story," NBC, 1957; "The Ed Sullivan Show," CBS, 1959; "Alcoa Presents One Step Beyond: Brainwave," ABC, 1959; "Brenner: Good Friend," CBS, 1959; "Lux Playhouse: The Hidden Image," CBS, 1959; "Startime: My Three Angels," NBC, 1959; "U.S. Steel Hour: Act of Terror," CBS, 1959; "The Millionaire: Millionaire Jerry Mitchell," CBS, 1960; "Alfred Hitchcock Presents: Across the Threshhold," CBS, 1960; "The Detectives Starring Robert Taylor: Armed and Dangerous," ABC, 1960; "The Twilight Zone: The Chaser," CBS, 1960; "Thriller: The Twisted Image," NBC, 1960; "U.S. Steel Hour: The Mating Machine," CBS, 1961; "A Story of Love: A String of Beads," NBC, 1961; "Theatre '62: Notorious," NBC, 1961; "Play of the Week: In a Garden," SYN, 1961; "Alfred Hitchcock Presents: Act of Faith," NBC, 1962; "Bus Stop: I Kiss Your Shadow," ABC, 1962; "The Nurses: The Prisoner," CBS, 1962; "The Twilight Zone: In His Image," CBS, 1963; "Vacation Playhouse: Three Wishes," CBS, 1963; "To Tell the Truth," CBS, 1964; "Dr. Kildare: A Hundred Million Tomorrows," NBC, 1964; "Password," CBS, 1965; "Rawhide: A Time for Waiting," CBS, 1965; "Profiles in Courage: Judge Benjamin Barr Lindsey," NBC, 1965; "A Case of Libel," ABC, 1968; "Hallmark Hall of Fame: Teacher, Teacher," NBC, 1969; "On Stage: The Choice," NBC, 1969; "The Front Page," NET, 1970; "Medical Center: Brink of Doom," CBS, 1970; "Ironside: This Could Blow Your Mind," NBC, 1970; "NET Playhouse: A Memory of Two Mondays," NET, 1971; "Marcus Welby, M.D.: A Portrait of Debbie," ABC, 1971; "ABC Theatre: Pueblo," ABC, 1973; "The Country Girl," NBC, 1974; "Wide World of Mystery: The Two Deaths of Sean Doolittle," ABC, 1975; "The Oldest Living Graduate," NBC, 1980; "The Cosby Show: Clair's Toe," NBC, 1985; "Murder, She Wrote: Murder in the Minor Key," CBS, 1987; "Murder, She Wrote: The Body Politic," CBS, 1988; "The Golden Girls: That Old Feeling," NBC, 1989.
TV MOVIES AND MINISERIES: "Travis Logan, D.A.," CBS, 1971; "Indict and Convict," ABC, 1973; "The Stranger Within," ABC, 1974; "Attack on Terror: The FBI Versus the Ku Klux Klan," CBS, 1975; "The Lives of Jenny Dolan," NBC,

1975; "The Night Rider," ABC, 1979; "ABC Theatre: Attica," ABC, 1980; "Not in Front of the Children," CBS, 1982; "Embassy," ABC, 1985; "Under Siege," NBC, 1986; "That Secret Sunday," CBS, 1986; "The Deliberate Stranger," NBC, 1986; "Perry Mason: The Case of the Scandalous Scoundrel," NBC, 1987; "False Witness," NBC, 1989.
* Emmies: 1980.

GRODIN, CHARLES
b. Pittsburgh, PA, April 21, 1935. Comic actor-writer with a dead-on deadpan style who got his start in TV drama; an Emmy winner for co-writing a Paul Simon special.
AS A REGULAR: "The Young Marrieds," ABC, 1964-66.
AND: "The Defenders: The Apostle," CBS, 1962; "My Mother the Car: Burned at the Steak," NBC, 1965; "The FBI: Sky on Fire," ABC, 1967; "NYPD: Money Man," ABC, 1967; "The Guns of Will Sonnett: A Bell for Jeff Sonnett," ABC, 1967; "The Virginian: Reckoning," NBC, 1967; "The Big Valley: The Good Thieves," ABC, 1968; "Saturday Night Live," NBC, 1976; "The Merv Griffin Show," SYN, 1979; "The Tonight Show Starring Johnny Carson," NBC, 1989.
TV MOVIES AND MINISERIES: "The Grass Is Always Greener Over the Septic Tank," CBS, 1978; "Fresno," CBS, 1986.
AS CO-WRITER: "The Paul Simon Special," NBC, 1977.
* Grodin's films include "King Kong," "The Heartbreak Kid," "Heaven Can Wait" and "Taking Care of Business."
* Yikes Dept.: In "A Bell for Jeff Sonnett," Grodin played deadly gunfighter "Bells" Pickering, who pinned bells on his gunbelt to represent his victims.
* Emmies: 1978.

GROH, DAVID
b. Brooklyn, NY, May 21, 1939. Actor who played Joe Gerard, husband of Rhoda Morgenstern (Valerie Harper); when the writers couldn't come up with enough situations for a married Rhoda, she and Joe got a divorce.
AS A REGULAR: "Rhoda," CBS, 1974-77; "Another Day," CBS, 1978; "General Hospital," ABC, 1983-85.
AND: "The Mary Tyler Moore Show: Mary Richards Falls in Love," CBS, 1975; "Police Story: Face for a Shadow," NBC, 1975; "Hollywood Squares," NBC, 1975; "Police Story: The Other Side of the Fence," NBC, 1976; "The Merv Griffin Show," SYN, 1976; "Police Story: Hard Rock Brown," NBC, 1977; "The Love Boat: Help, Murder!," ABC, 1977; "Police Story: Prime Rib," NBC, 1977; "Buck Rogers in the 25th Century: Planet of the Slave Girls," NBC, 1979;

"MacGruder and Loud: The Price of Junk," ABC, 1985; "Murder, She Wrote: Murder Digs Deep," CBS, 1986; "Kate & Allie: The Bully," CBS, 1986; "Hunter: Yesterday's Child," NBC, 1989.
TV MOVIES AND MINISERIES: "Smash-Up on Interstate 5," ABC, 1976; "Victory at Entebbe," ABC, 1976; "The Child-Stealer," ABC, 1979; "Broken Vows," CBS, 1987.

GROSS, MARY
b. Chicago, IL, March 25, 1953. Shrill comic actress; sister of Michael Gross.
AS A REGULAR: "Saturday Night Live," NBC, 1981-85; "The People Next Door," CBS, 1989.
AND: "The Pat Sajak Show," CBS, 1989.

GROSS, MICHAEL
b. Chicago, IL, June 21, 1947. Actor who played good-guy dad Steven Keaton on "Family Ties."
AS A REGULAR: "Family Ties," NBC, 1982-89.
AND: "Love, Sidney: Charlotte's Web," NBC, 1982; "Day by Day: Trading Places," NBC, 1988.
TV MOVIES AND MINISERIES: "A Girl Named Sooner," NBC, 1975; "F.D.R.: The Last Year," NBC, 1980; "Little Gloria ... Happy at Last," NBC, 1982; "Cook & Peary: The Race to the Pole," CBS, 1983; "Family Ties Vacation," NBC, 1985; "A Letter to Three Wives," NBC, 1985; "Right to Die," NBC, 1987; "Quiet Victory: The Charlie Wedemeyer Story," CBS, 1988; "In the Line of Duty: The FBI Murders," NBC, 1988; "A Connecticut Yankee in King Arthur's Court," NBC, 1989.

GRUBBS, GARY
b. Amory, MS, November 14, 1949. Actor who often plays hayseed types, and the occasional bully.
AS A REGULAR: "For Love and Honor," NBC, 1983; "Half Nelson," NBC, 1985.
AND: "Hill Street Blues: Hill Street Station," NBC, 1981; "The Golden Girls: Big Daddy," NBC, 1986; "Married with Children: Poppy's by the Tree," FOX, 1987; "227: Country Cousins," NBC, 1988; "The Magical World of Disney: Davy Crockett-A Natural Man," NBC, 1988; "The Magical World of Disney: Davy Crockett-Guardian Spirit," NBC, 1989.
TV MOVIES AND MINISERIES: "Willa," CBS, 1979; "The Burning Bed," NBC, 1984; "Convicted," NBC, 1986; "Guilty of Innocence: The Lenell Geter Story," CBS, 1987; "Poker Alice," CBS, 1987; "Hallmark Hall of Fame: Foxfire," CBS, 1987.

GUARDINO, HARRY
b. New York City, NY, December 23, 1925. Actor usually in tough-guy roles.
AS A REGULAR: "The Reporter," CBS, 1964; "Monty Nash," SYN, 1971-72; "The New

Adventures of Perry Mason," CBS, 1973-74.
AND: "Kaiser Aluminum Hour: The Deadly
Silence," NBC, 1957; "Studio One: The Mother
Bit," CBS, 1957; "Schlitz Playhouse of Stars: One
Way Out," CBS, 1957; "Suspicion: A Touch of
Evil," NBC, 1958; "Westinghouse Desilu
Playhouse: Chez Rouge," CBS, 1959; "Playhouse
90: Made in Japan," CBS, 1959; "Playhouse 90:
The Killers of Mussolini," CBS, 1959; "Johnny
Staccato: The Wild Reed," NBC, 1959; "The
Untouchables: One-Armed Bandit," ABC, 1960;
"The Overland Trail: Perilous Passage," NBC,
1960; "The Overland Trail: The O'Mara's
Ladies," NBC, 1960; "The Untouchables: The
Nick Moses Story," ABC, 1961; "Checkmate:
Goodbye, Griff," CBS, 1961; "Target: The
Corruptors: Babes in Wall Street," ABC, 1962;
"Cain's Hundred: The Left Side of Canada,"
NBC, 1962; "The Dick Powell Show: The Sea
Witch," NBC, 1962; "Dr. Kildare: Hastings'
Farewell," NBC, 1962; "Alcoa Premiere: The
Masked Marine," ABC, 1962; "The Lloyd
Bridges Show: Wheresoever I Enter," CBS, 1962;
"Route 66: Hey Moth, Come Eat the Flame,"
CBS, 1962; "Bob Hope Chrysler Theatre: It's
Mental Work," NBC, 1963; "Ben Casey: A
Falcon's Eye, a Lion's Heart, a Girl's Hand,"
ABC, 1964; "The Virginian: The Horse Fighter,"
NBC, 1965; "Run for Your Life: Sequenstro,"
NBC, 1966; "The Name of the Game: The
Revolutionary," NBC, 1968; "Hawaii Five-O: A
Thousand Pardons, You're Dead," CBS, 1969;
"Hawaii Five-O: Trouble in Mind," CBS, 1970;
"The FBI: Escape to Terror," ABC, 1970; "Men
at Law: The Dark World of Harry Anders," CBS,
1971; "The Name of the Game: Appointment in
Palermo," NBC, 1971; "Love, American Style:
Love and the Housekeeper," ABC, 1971; "Night
Gallery: The Miracle at Camefeo," NBC, 1972;
"Medical Center: The Torn Man," CBS, 1972;
"McCloud: The Million Dollar Round-Up," NBC,
1973; "Kojak: Dead on His Feet," CBS, 1974;
"Police Story: The Wyatt Earp Syndrome," NBC,
1974; "Police Story: Requiem for C.Z. Smith,"
NBC, 1974; "Hawaii Five-O: McGarret Is
Missing," CBS, 1975; "McCoy: Doubletake,"
NBC, 1975; "Medical Story: Million Dollar
Baby," NBC, 1975; "The Streets of San
Francisco: Till Death Do Us Part," ABC, 1976;
"Kojak: By Silence Betrayed," CBS, 1976;
"Barnaby Jones: The Final Victim," CBS, 1980;
"Murder, She Wrote: Birds of a Feather," CBS,
1984; "Hotel: Resolutions," ABC, 1984; "Murder,
She Wrote: Deadline for Murder," CBS, 1986.
TV MOVIES AND MINISERIES: "Valley of Mystery,"
ABC, 1967; "The Lonely Profession," NBC,
1969; "The Challenge," ABC, 1970; "The Last
Child," ABC, 1971; "The Police Story," NBC,
1973; "Partners in Crime," NBC, 1973;
"Moving Target," ABC, 1973; "Indict and
Convict," ABC, 1973; "Get Christie Love!,"

ABC, 1974; "Street Killing," ABC, 1976;
"Having Babies," ABC, 1976; "Evening in
Byzantium," SYN, 1978; "Pleasure Cove,"
NBC, 1979; "The Neon Empire," SHO, 1989.

GUDAGAST, HANS—See Eric Braeden.

GUEST, CHRISTOPHER
b. New York City, NY, February 5, 1948.
Comic writer and performer; an Emmy winner
for "Lily Tomlin."
AS A REGULAR: "Saturday Night Live," NBC,
1984-85.
AND: "All in the Family: Mike and Gloria Meet,"
CBS, 1977; "St. Elsewhere: Legionnaires," NBC,
1982.
TV MOVIES AND MINISERIES: "Blind Ambition,"
CBS, 1979.
AS CO-WRITER: "Lily Tomlin," ABC, 1976.
AS DIRECTOR: "Trying Times: The Sad Professor,"
PBS, 1989.
* Emmies: 1976.

GUILBERT, ANN MORGAN
b. Minneapolis, MN, 1928. Actress who played
next-door neighbor Millie Helper on "The Dick
Van Dyke Show," and now plays the mother of
the Fanelli boys.
AS A REGULAR: "The Dick Van Dyke Show,"
CBS, 1961-66; "The New Andy Griffith
Show," CBS, 1971; "The Fanelli Boys," NBC,
1990- .
AND: "Hennesey: The Green-Eyed Monster,"
CBS, 1961; "The Bob Newhart Show," NBC,
1961; "Hennesey: Aloha, Dr. Hennesey," CBS,
1961; "Hey, Landlord!: From Out of the Past
Come the Thundering Hoofbeats," NBC, 1966;
"Hey, Landlord!: The Daring Duo vs. the
Incredible Captain Kill," NBC, 1966; "Dick Van
Dyke Special," CBS, 1967; "Dragnet: The Big
Neighbor," NBC, 1967; "Room 222: Fathers and
Sons," ABC, 1969; "Dragnet: Burglary-Helpful
Woman," NBC, 1970; "Emergency!: I'll Fix It,"
NBC, 1974; "Barney Miller: Stress Analyzer,"
ABC, 1981; "Newhart: Aunt Bess," CBS, 1989.
TV MOVIES AND MINISERIES: "The D.A.: Conspiracy
to Kill," NBC, 1971; "Emergency!," NBC,
1972; "Second Chance," ABC, 1972; "Chase,"
NBC, 1973; "The Rangers," NBC, 1974.

GUILLAUME, ROBERT
b. St. Louis, MO, November 30, 1927. Stage-
trained actor-singer who played the wisecracking Benson DuBois for almost ten years as the
character evolved from an "uppity" butler into
a responsible government official.
AS A REGULAR: "Soap," ABC, 1977-79; "Benson,"
ABC, 1979-86; "The Robert Guillaume Show,"
ABC, 1989.
AND: "Julia: The Wheel Deal," NBC, 1969; "All

in the Family: Chain Letter," CBS, 1975; "The Jeffersons: George Won't Talk," CBS, 1975; "Sanford & Son: Steinberg & Son," NBC, 1975; "The Love Boat: The Affair," ABC, 1979; "The Donna Fargo Show," SYN, 1979; "Barbara Mandrell and the Mandrell Sisters," NBC, 1981; "The Toni Tennille Show," SYN, 1981; "Saturday Night Live," NBC, 1983; "The Debbie Allen Special," ABC, 1989; "Sister Kate: Neville's Hired Hand," NBC, 1989.

TV MOVIES AND MINISERIES: "The Kid from Left Field," NBC, 1979; "The Kid with the 200 I.Q.," NBC, 1983; "North and South," ABC, 1985; "Perry Mason: The Case of the Scandalous Scoundrel," NBC, 1987; "The Penthouse," ABC, 1989.

* Bill Cosby wouldn't allow his name to be put in nominations for Emmy Awards after "The Cosby Show" premiered in 1984. So when Robert Guillaume won his Emmy for "Benson" in 1985, he thanked Cosby for not competing.
* Emmies: 1979, 1985.

GULAGER, CLU
b. *Muskogee, OK, November 16, 1928.* Beefy generic leading man who played Emmett Ryker on "The Virginian."

AS A REGULAR: "The Tall Man," NBC, 1960-62; "The Virginian," NBC, 1963-66; 1967-68; "Harold Robbins' The Survivors," ABC, 1969-70; "San Francisco Internationl Airport," NBC, 1970-71; "The MacKenzies of Paradise Cove," ABC, 1979.

AND: "Studio One: A Walk Down the Hill," CBS, 1957; "West Point: The Drowning of the Gun," CBS, 1957; "Goodyear TV Playhouse: Fifteen October 1864," NBC, 1957; "Wanted Dead or Alive: Crossroads," CBS, 1959; "Wagon Train: The Andrew Hale Story," NBC, 1959; "Wagon Train: The Stagecoach Story," NBC, 1959; "The Deputy: Shadow of the Noose," NBC, 1959; "The Untouchables: Vincent 'Mad Dog' Coll," ABC, 1959; "Westinghouse Desilu Playhouse: The Day the Town Stood Up," CBS, 1959; "Laramie: Fugitive Road," NBC, 1959; "Have Gun, Will Travel: The Return of Roy Carter," CBS, 1959; "The Rebel: Paint a House with Scarlet," ABC, 1960; "The Deputy: Trail of Darkness," NBC, 1960; "Alfred Hitchcock Presents: Pen Pal," NBC, 1960; "Here's Hollywood," NBC, 1960; "American Bandstand," ABC, 1961; "Whispering Smith: The Devil's Share," NBC, 1961; "The Defenders: Death Across the Counter," CBS, 1961; "The Alfred Hitchcock Hour: Final Vow," CBS, 1962; "Dr. Kildare: Tyger, Tyger... ," NBC, 1964; "Kraft Suspense Theatre: The Deep End," NBC, 1964; "Journey to the Unknown: The Deep End," ABC, 1968; "The Name of the Game: Swingers Only," NBC, 1969; "Ironside: Price Tag: Death," NBC, 1969; "The Name of the Game: The Perfect Image," NBC, 1969; "The Psychiatrist: A Study of Death," NBC, 1971; "Cannon: County Blues," CBS, 1971; "The FBI: Mastermind," ABC, 1971; "The Bold Ones: A Threatened Species," NBC, 1972; "Medical Center: The Choice," CBS, 1972; "Hawaii Five-O: Fools Die Twice," CBS, 1972; "Bonanza: Stallion," NBC, 1972; "The Mod Squad: Another Final Game," ABC, 1972; "The Bold Ones: Endtheme," NBC, 1972; "Molly and Lawless John," ABC, 1973; "The Wonderful World of Disney: The Mystery in Dracula's Castle," NBC, 1973; "Mannix: The Man Who Wasn't There," CBS, 1973; "Kung Fu: Blood Brothers," ABC, 1973; "Ironside: Murder by One," NBC, 1973; "Barnaby Jones: Trial Run for Death," CBS, 1973; "Owen Marshall, Counselor at Law: The Attacker," ABC, 1974; "Shaft: The Murder Machine," CBS, 1974; "Police Story: Country Boy," NBC, 1974; "Get Christie Love!: Highway to Murder," ABC, 1974; "ABC Afternoon Playbreak: Heart in Hiding," ABC, 1974; "McCloud: Lady on the Run," NBC, 1975; "Khan!: Cloud of Guilt," CBS, 1975; "Cannon: Vengeance," CBS, 1975; "The Streets of San Francisco: Poisoned Snow," ABC, 1975; "Three for the Road: The Cave," CBS, 1975; "Police Story: The Empty Weapon," NBC, 1975; "Barnaby Jones: Eyes of Terror," CBS, 1976; "Hawaii Five-O: Assault on the Palace," CBS, 1976; "Hawaii Five-O: Oldest Profession-Latest Price," CBS, 1976; "The Master: Juggernaut," NBC, 1984; "The Yellow Rose: Villa's Gold," NBC, 1984; "Murder, She Wrote: Funeral at Fifty-Mile," CBS, 1985; "Simon & Simon: The Rookie," CBS, 1986; "Murder, She Wrote: Dead Heat," CBS, 1986; "Murder, She Wrote: Old Habits Die Hard," CBS, 1987.

TV MOVIES AND MINISERIES: "San Francisco International," NBC, 1970; "Truman Capote's The Glass House," CBS, 1972; "Footsteps," CBS, 1972; "Call to Danger," CBS, 1973; "Chant of Silence," ABC, 1973; "Smile Jenny, You're Dead," ABC, 1974; "Houston, We've Got a Problem," ABC, 1974; "Hit Lady," ABC, 1974; "The Killer That Wouldn't Die," ABC, 1976; "Best Sellers: Once an Eagle," NBC, 1976; "Black Beauty," NBC, 1978; "King," NBC, 1978; "A Question of Love," ABC, 1978; "Willa," CBS, 1979; "This Man Stands Alone," NBC, 1979; "Living Proof: The Hank Williams Jr. Story," NBC, 1983; "Bridge Across Time," NBC, 1985.

GUMBEL, BRYANT
b. *Bryant Charles Gumbel, New Orleans, LA, September 29, 1948.* Cool, ultra-competent sportscaster and "Today" show host.

AS A REGULAR: "Games People Play," NBC, 1980-81; "Today," NBC, 1982- .

GUNN, MOSES
b. *St. Louis, MO, October 2, 1929.* Heavyset character actor, usually in intense roles.

AS A REGULAR: "The Cowboys," ABC, 1974;
"Good Times," CBS, 1977; "The Contender,"
CBS, 1980; "Father Murphy," NBC, 1981-84.
AND: "The FBI: Eye of the Storm," ABC, 1969;
"Hawaii Five-O: Nine, Ten, You're Dead," CBS,
1971; "McCloud: A Little Plot at Tranquil
Valley," NBC, 1972; "ABC Theatre: If You Give
a Dance, You Gotta Pay the Band," ABC, 1972;
"Assignment: Vienna: Solider of Fortune," ABC,
1973; "The Jeffersons: George's Skeleton," CBS,
1975; "The Wonderful World of Disney: The
Secret of the Pond," NBC, 1975; "Theatre in
America: The First Breeze of Summer," PBS,
1976; "Quincy: A Blow to the Head, A Blow to
the Heart," NBC, 1977; "Little House on the
Prairie: The Fighter," NBC, 1977; "Little House
on the Prairie: Blind Journey," NBC, 1978; "Little
House on the Prairie: Barn Burner," NBC, 1979;
"The Cosby Show: The Dead End Kids Meet Dr.
Lotus," NBC, 1989; "Amen: Where There's a
Will," NBC, 1989; "The Cosby Show: Grampy
and Nu-Nu Visit the Huxtables," NBC, 1989.
TV MOVIES AND MINISERIES: "Carter's Army,"
ABC, 1970; "The Sheriff," ABC, 1971;
"Haunts of the Very Rich," ABC, 1972;
"Moving Target," ABC, 1973; "Legacy of
Blood," ABC, 1974; "Law of the Land," NBC,
1976; "Roots," ABC, 1977; "The Women of
Brewster Place," ABC, 1989.

GUTTENBERG, STEVE

b. *Brooklyn, NY, August 24, 1958*. Film actor
("Cocoon," "Three Men and a Baby") who
began in TV.
AS A REGULAR: "Billy," CBS, 1979; "No Soap,
Radio," ABC, 1982.
AND: "Saturday Night Live," NBC, 1986.
TV MOVIES AND MINISERIES: "Something for Joey,"
CBS, 1977; "To Race the Wind," CBS, 1980;
"Miracle on Ice," ABC, 1981; "The Day
After," ABC, 1983.

GWENN, EDMUND

b. *London, England, September 26, 1875;
d. 1959*. Character actor fondly remembered as
Kris Kringle in "Miracle on 34th Street" who
did some TV as he entered his late seventies.
AS A GUEST: "Ford Theatre: Heart of Gold," NBC,
1952; "Schlitz Playhouse of Stars: Guardian of
the Clock," CBS, 1953; "Ford Theatre: Come
on, Red," NBC, 1954; "Rheingold Theatre:
The Great Shinin' Saucer of Paddy Faneen,"
NBC, 1955; "Science Fiction Theatre: The

Strange Dr. Lorenz," SYN, 1955; "Eddie
Cantor Theatre: The Man Who Liked Little
People," SYN, 1955; "Science Fiction Theatre:
A Visit From Dr. Pliny," SYN, 1956;
"Playhouse 90: The Greer Case," CBS, 1957;
"Playhouse 90: Winter Dreams," CBS, 1957;
"Alfred Hitchcock Presents: Father and Son,"
CBS, 1957.

GWYNNE, FRED

b. *New York City, NY, July 10, 1926*. Tall, stocky
actor who played patrolman Francis Muldoon
and Herman Munster; now a respected character
actor in films and, less frequently on TV. Also
does commercial voice-overs.
AS A REGULAR: "Car 54, Where Are You?," NBC,
1961-63; "The Munsters," CBS, 1964-66.
AND: "The Phil Silvers Show: Eating Contest,"
CBS, 1955; "The Phil Silvers Show: It's for the
Birds," CBS, 1956; "Studio One: The Landlady's
Daughter," CBS, 1956; "Kaiser Aluminum Hour:
A Man's Game," NBC, 1957; "Kraft Television
Theatre: Sextuplets!," NBC, 1957; "Suspicion:
Hand in Glove," NBC, 1957; "Kraft Television
Theatre: The Big Heist," NBC, 1957; "Du Pont
Show of the Month: Harvey," CBS, 1958; "Du
Pont Show of the Month: The Hasty Heart," CBS,
1958; "Play of the Week: The Old Foolishness,"
SYN, 1961; "Perry Como's Kraft Music Hall,"
NBC, 1962; "U.S. Steel Hour: Don't Shake the
Family Tree," CBS, 1963; "The Danny Kaye
Show," CBS, 1965; "The Danny Kaye Show,"
CBS, 1966; "New York Television Theatre: The
Lesson," NET, 1966; "NET Playhouse: Infancy,"
NET, 1967; "Guess What I Did Today," NBC,
1968; "Arsenic and Old Lace," ABC, 1969;
"Anderson and Company," NBC, 1969;
"Hallmark Hall of Fame: The Littlest Angel,"
NBC, 1969; "The Mike Douglas Show," SYN,
1970; "NET Playhouse: Paradise Lost," NET,
1971; "You Are There: The Siege of the Alamo,"
CBS, 1971; "Hollywood Television Theatre: The
Police," NET, 1971; "Bell System Family
Theatre: Dames at Sea," NBC, 1971; "Hallmark
Hall of Fame: Harvey," NBC, 1971; "Bound for
Freedom," NBC, 1976; "The Dick Cavett Show,"
PBS, 1980; "The Munsters' Revenge," NBC,
1981.
TV MOVIES AND MINISERIES: "Sanctuary of Fear,"
NBC, 1979; "The Mysterious Stranger," PBS,
1982; "Kane & Abel," CBS, 1985; "Vanishing
Act," CBS, 1986; "Murder by the Book," CBS,
1987.

H

HACK, SHELLEY

b. Greenwich, CT. Blonde actress whose last name sums up her acting ability.

AS A REGULAR: "Charlie's Angels," ABC, 1979-80; "Cutter to Houston," CBS, 1983; "Jack and Mike," ABC, 1986-87.

AND: "The Love Boat: Dumb Luck," ABC, 1980.

TV MOVIES AND MINISERIES: "Death Car on the Freeway," CBS, 1979; "Trackdown: Finding the Goodbar Killer," CBS, 1983; "Found Money," NBC, 1983; "Single Bars, Single Women," ABC, 1984; "Kicks," ABC, 1985; "Bridesmaids," CBS, 1989.

* Hack was scheduled to join "Night Court" in 1984 as a public defender, but plans fell through.
* See also "Charlie's Angels."

HACKETT, BUDDY

b. Leonard Hacker, Brooklyn, NY, August 31, 1924. Short, stocky comedian with dozens of TV appearances under his sizable belt.

AS A REGULAR: "School House," DUM, 1949; "Stanley," NBC, 1956-57; "The Jackie Gleason Show," CBS, 1958-59; "The Jack Paar Show," NBC, 1960-62.

AND: "The Perry Como Show," NBC, 1956; "The Steve Allen Show," NBC, 1957; "The Perry Como Show," NBC, 1957; "The Patrice Munsel Show," ABC, 1957; "The Patrice Munsel Show," ABC, 1958; "The Perry Como Show," NBC, 1958; "The Eddie Fisher Show," NBC, 1958; "The Garry Moore Show," CBS, 1959; "The Perry Como Show," NBC, 1959; "Treasure Hunt," NBC, 1959; "The Steve Allen Plymouth Show," NBC, 1960; "The Garry Moore Show," CBS, 1960; "Dan Raven: The Mechanic," NBC, 1960; "Open End," NBC, 1960; "The Danny Thomas Show: Fugitive Father," CBS, 1960; "Perry Como's Kraft Music Hall," NBC, 1961; "The Rifleman: The Clarence Bibs Story," ABC, 1961; "Bulova Watch Time with Arthur Godfrey," CBS, 1961; "Here's Hollywood," NBC, 1961; "What's My Line?," CBS, 1962; "The Jack Paar Program," NBC, 1962; "The Merv Griffin Show," NBC, 1963; "Password," CBS, 1963; "The Joey Bishop Show: My Buddy, My Buddy," NBC, 1963; "Hollywood Palace," ABC, 1964; "What's My Line?," CBS, 1964; "The Joey Bishop Show: Joey and Buddy Hackett Have a Luau," NBC, 1964; "Trials of O'Brien: Notes on a Spanish Prisoner," CBS, 1965; "The Big Valley: The Lost Treasure," ABC, 1966; "The Tonight Show Starring Johnny Carson," NBC, 1967; "Get Smart: Maxwell Smart, Private Eye," NBC, 1967;

"The Lucy Show: Lucy and the Stolen Stole," CBS, 1968; "The Mike Douglas Show," SYN, 1969; "The Tonight Show Starring Johnny Carson," NBC, 1970; "The Glen Campbell Goodtime Hour," CBS, 1972; "Hollywood Squares," NBC, 1973; "McMillan and Wife: Reunion in Terror," NBC, 1974; "Celebrity Sweepstakes," NBC, 1976; "The Love Boat: Going My Way?," ABC, 1979; "The Love Boat: Phantom Bride," ABC, 1981; "The Tonight Show Starring Johnny Carson," NBC, 1981; "The Fall Guy: The Adventures of Ozzie and Harold," ABC, 1982; "Buddy Hackett: Live and Uncensored," HBO, 1984; "Murder, She Wrote: No Laughing Matter," CBS, 1987.

TV MOVIES AND MINISERIES: "Bud and Lou," NBC, 1978.

HACKETT, JOAN

b. New York City, NY, b. 1934, d. 1983. Film and TV actress, often in New York-based dramas.

AS A REGULAR: "Young Dr. Malone," NBC, 1958-63; "The Defenders," CBS, 1961-62; "Another Day," CBS, 1978.

AND: "Ellery Queen: Shadow of the Past," NBC, 1959; "Armstrong Circle Theatre: The Immortal Piano," CBS, 1960; "Alfred Hitchcock Presents: Servant Problem," NBC, 1961; "Westinghouse Presents: Come Again to Carthage," CBS, 1961; "Ben Casey: A Certain Time, a Certain Darkness," ABC, 1961; "The New Breed: Cross the Little Line," ABC, 1962; "The Twilight Zone: A Piano in the House," CBS, 1962; "Combat!: The Chateau," ABC, 1963; "Bob Hope Chrysler Theatre: Echo of Evil," NBC, 1964; "Ben Casey: This Wild, Wild Waltzing World," ABC, 1964; "Bonanza: Woman of Fire," NBC, 1964; "Bob Hope Chrysler Theatre: The Highest Fall of All," NBC, 1965; "Run for Your Life: The Sex Object," NBC, 1966; "The Danny Thomas Hour: It's Greek to Me," NBC, 1967; "The Name of the Game: Witness," NBC, 1968; "Love, American Style: Love and the Proposal," ABC, 1970; "Love, American Style: Love and the Jury," ABC, 1971; "Hollywood Television Theatre: U.S.A.," NET, 1971; "Lights Out: When Widows Weep," SYN, 1971; "Bonanza: Second Sight," NBC, 1972; "Mission: Impossible: Double Dead," CBS, 1972; "Alias Smith and Jones: The Legacy of Charlie O'Rourke," ABC, 1972; "The Love Boat: The Grass Is Always Greener," ABC, 1979.

TV MOVIES AND MINISERIES: "The Young Country," ABC, 1970; "How Awful About Allan," ABC, 1970; "The Other Man," NBC, 1970; "Five Desperate Women," ABC, 1971; "Class of

'63," ABC, 1973; "Reflections on Murder," ABC, 1974; "Stonestreet: Who Killed the Centerfold Model?," NBC, 1977; "Pleasure Cove," NBC, 1979; "The Long Days of Summer," ABC, 1980.

HACKMAN, GENE
b. San Bernadino, CA, January 30, 1931. Fine screen actor who paid his dues in TV until being cast as Buck Barrow in the 1967 film "Bonnie and Clyde."
AS A GUEST: "U.S. Steel Hour: Little Tin God," CBS, 1959; "U.S. Steel Hour: Big Doc's Girl," CBS, 1959; "U.S. Steel Hour: Bride of the Fox," CBS, 1960; "The Defenders: Quality of Mercy," CBS, 1961; "U.S. Steel Hour: Brandenburg Gate," CBS, 1961; "U.S. Steel Hour: Far From the Shade Tree," CBS, 1962; "This Is the Life: Party Line," SYN, 1962; "The Defenders: Judgment Eve," CBS, 1963; "The du Pont Show: Ride with Terror," NBC, 1963; "Trials of O'Brien: The Only Game in Town," CBS, 1966; "Hawk: Do Not Mutilate or Spindle," ABC, 1966; "The FBI: The Courier," ABC, 1967; "The Invaders: The Spores," ABC, 1967; "The Iron Horse: Leopards Try, But Leopards Can't," ABC, 1967; "CBS Playhouse: My Father and My Mother," CBS, 1968; "The Tonight Show Starring Johnny Carson," NBC, 1975.
TV MOVIES AND MINISERIES: "Shadow on the Land," NBC, 1968.

HADLEY, REED
b. Reed Herring, Petrolia, TX, 1911; d. 1974. Handsome TV hero of the early fifties.
AS A REGULAR: "Racket Squad," SYN, 1950; CBS, 1951-53; "Public Defender," CBS, 1954-55.
AND: "Navy Log: One If by Sea," ABC, 1958; "The Red Skelton Show," CBS, 1958; "Restless Gun: The Outlander," NBC, 1958; "Restless Gun: A Very Special Investigator," NBC, 1959; "The Texan: Sheriff of Boothill," CBS, 1959; "Christophers: The Power of the Library," SYN, 1959; "Christophers: The Importance of Being a Teacher," SYN, 1959; "Tightrope!: Borderline," CBS, 1960; "The Deputy: The Shackled Town," NBC, 1961.

HAGEN, JEAN
b. Jean Shirley Verhagen, Chicago, August 3, 1923; d. 1977. Actress who played Margaret, the first wife of Danny Thomas on his TV sitcom; best known as screechy-voiced starlet Lina Lamont in the film "Singin' in the Rain."
AS A REGULAR: "Make Room for Daddy," ABC, 1953-56.
AND: "Climax!: The Lou Gehrig Story," CBS, 1956; "Ford Theatre: The Menace of Hasty

Heights," ABC, 1956; "Alfred Hitchcock Presents: Enough Rope for Two," CBS, 1957; "Westinghouse Desilu Playhouse: Symbol of Authority," CBS, 1959; "Westinghouse Desilu Playhouse: Six Guns for Donegan," CBS, 1959; "Westinghouse Desilu Playhouse: The Hanging Judge," CBS, 1959; "The Detectives Starring Robert Taylor: The Streger Affair," ABC, 1959; "Wagon Train: The Madie Brant Story," NBC, 1960; "Buick Electra Playhouse: The Snows of Kilimanjaro," CBS, 1960; "The du Pont Show with June Allyson: Once Upon a Knight," CBS, 1960; "Stagecoach West: The Brass Lily," ABC, 1961; "Dick Powell's Zane Grey Theatre: The Empty Shell," CBS, 1961; "G.E. Theatre: The Golden Years," CBS, 1961; "The Andy Griffith Show: Andy and the Woman Speeder," CBS, 1961; "Ben Casey: A Story to Be Told Softly," ABC, 1962; "Wagon Train: The Sarah Proctor Story," ABC, 1963; "Dr. Kildare: A Very Infectious Disease," NBC, 1963; "The Streets of San Francisco: Judgment Day," ABC, 1976.

HAGER, JIM & JON
b. Chicago, IL. They're twin country-western singers! They're twin talk-show guests! They're twin Playgirl centerfolds! They're twin detectives!
AS REGULARS: "Hee Haw," CBS, 1969-71; SYN, 1971-86.
AND: "The Merv Griffin Show," SYN, 1974.
TV MOVIES AND MINISERIES: "Twin Detectives," ABC, 1976.

HAGGERTY, DAN
b. Hollywood, CA, November 19, 1941. Beefy, bearded actor who played mountain man Grizzly Adams in the movies and on TV.
AS A REGULAR: "The Life and Times of Grizzly Adams," NBC, 1977-78.
AND: "The Love Boat: The World's Greatest Kisser," ABC, 1983; "Charlie's Angels: Wakiki Angels," ABC, 1981.
TV MOVIES AND MINISERIES: "Desperate Women," NBC, 1978; "Terror Out of the Sky," CBS, 1978; "The Capture of Grizzly Adams," NBC, 1982.

HAGMAN, LARRY
b. Weatherford, TX, September 21, 1931. Actor skilled at light comedy who became a real TV legend as John Ross Ewing, Jr., on "Dallas."
AS A REGULAR: "The Edge of Night," CBS, 1961-63; "I Dream of Jeannie," NBC, 1965-70; "The Good Life," NBC, 1971-72; "Here We Go Again," ABC, 1973; "Dallas," CBS, 1978- .
AND: "Goodyear TV Playhouse: Backwoods Cinderella," NBC, 1957; "Kraft Theatre: The Outcasts of Poker Flat," NBC, 1958; "Du Pont Show of the Month: The Member of the

Wedding," CBS, 1958; "Studio One: Climate of Marriage," CBS, 1958; "Salute to the American Theatre," CBS, 1959; "Diagnosis: Unknown: A Case of Radiant Wine," CBS, 1960; "Play of the Week: Once Around the Block," SYN, 1960; "CBS Television Workshop: How to Shoot Fish in a Barrel," CBS, 1960; "Frontiers of Faith: Count-down - One Man's Decision," NBC, 1961; "The Defenders: The Last Day," CBS, 1964; "Mr. Broadway: Between the Rats and the Finks," CBS, 1964; "The Rogues: Mr. White's Christmas," NBC, 1965; "The Rogues: A Daring Step Backward," NBC, 1965; "The du Pont Show: Ambassador at Large," NBC, 1965; "Love, American Style: Love and the Psychiatrist," ABC, 1970; "Marcus Welby, M.D.: To Get Through the Night," ABC, 1970; "Night Gallery: The Housekeeper," NBC, 1970; "The Name of the Game: A Capitol Affair," NBC, 1971; "Triple Play: The Good Life," NBC, 1971; "Medical Center: Between Two Fires," CBS, 1973; "Applause!," CBS, 1973; "Love Story: The Youngest Lovers," NBC, 1973; "McCloud: The Gang That Stole Manhattan," NBC, 1974; "Police Story: Glamour Boy," NBC, 1974; "Marcus Welby, M.D.: Loser in a Dead Heat," ABC, 1975; "Doctors Hospital: Come at Last to Love," NBC, 1975; "Three for the Road: Ride on a Red Balloon," CBS, 1975; "Detective: Bull in a China Shop," NBC, 1975; "Ellery Queen: The Mad Tea Party," NBC, 1975; "The Streets of San Francisco: Dead Air," ABC, 1975; "Barnaby Jones: Fatal Witness," CBS, 1975; "McMillan: Affair of the Heart," NBC, 1977; "The Rockford Files: Forced Retirement," NBC, 1977; "Donahue," SYN, 1981.

TV MOVIES AND MINISERIES:"Three's a Crowd," ABC, 1969; "Vanished," NBC, 1971; "A Howling in the Woods," NBC, 1971; "Getting Away From It All," ABC, 1972; "No Place to Run," ABC, 1972; "The Alpha Caper," ABC, 1973; "Bloodsport," ABC, 1973; "What Are Best Friends For?," ABC, 1973; "Sidekicks," CBS, 1974; "Hurricane," ABC, 1974; "Sarah T.: Portrait of a Teenage Alcoholic," NBC, 1975; "The Big Ripoff," NBC, 1975; "The Return of the World's Greatest Detective," NBC, 1976; "Best Sellers: The Rhinemann Exchange," NBC, 1977; "Deadly Encounter," CBS, 1982.
* Hagman is the son of Mary Martin.

TV'S TOP TEN, 1980-81
1. Dallas (CBS)
2. The Dukes of Hazzard (CBS)
3. 60 Minutes (CBS)
4. M*A*S*H (CBS)
5. The Love Boat (ABC)
6. The Jeffersons (CBS)
7. Alice (CBS)
8. House Calls (CBS)
8. Three's Company (ABC)
10. Little House on the Prairie (NBC)

HAGUE, ALBERT
b. *Berlin, Germany, October 13, 1920.* Bearded actor-composer who played Benjamin Shorofsky on "Fame."
AS A REGULAR: "Fame," NBC, 1982-83; SYN, 1983-87.
AND: "Amazing Stories: The Doll," NBC, 1986; "ABC Afterschool Specials: The Day My Kid Went Punk," ABC, 1987.
TV MOVIES AND MINISERIES:"Not Just Another Affair," CBS, 1982.

HAID, CHARLES
b. *San Francisco, June 2, 1943.* Husky actor who played Off. Andy Renko on "Hill Street Blues."
AS A REGULAR: "Kate McShane," CBS, 1975; "Delvecchio," CBS, 1976-77; "Hill Street Blues," NBC, 1981-87.
AND: "The Life and Times of Captain Barney Miller," ABC, 1975; "Switch: The Walking Bomb," CBS, 1975; "Police Woman: Task Force: Cop Killer," NBC, 1976; "Jigsaw John: Eclipse," NBC, 1976; "B.J. and the Bear: Eighteen Wheel Ripoff," NBC, 1980; "Murder, She Wrote: Weave a Tangled Web," CBS, 1989.
TV MOVIES AND MINISERIES:"Foster and Laurie," CBS, 1975; "The Bastard," SYN, 1978; "Divorce Wars: A Love Story," ABC, 1982; "Six Against the Rock," NBC, 1987; "Weekend War," ABC, 1988; "The Revenge of Al Capone," NBC, 1989; "A Deadly Silence," ABC, 1989; "Man Against the Mob: The Chinatown Murders," NBC, 1989.
AS A PRODUCER: "Cop Rock," ABC, 1990.
* Haid is Merv Griffin's first cousin.

HAIG, SID
b. *Fresno, CA, July 14, 1939.* Bald actor usually in creepy roles.
AS A REGULAR: "Mary Hartman, Mary Hartman," SYN, 1977-78; "Jason of Star Command," CBS, 1978-80.
AND: "The Lucy Show: Lucy and the Monsters," CBS, 1965; "Batman: The Spell of Tut/The Case Is Shut," ABC, 1966; "Gunsmoke: Stage Stop," CBS, 1966; "The Man From UNCLE: The When in Rome Affair," NBC, 1967; "Get Smart: That Old Gang of Mine," NBC, 1967; "The Flying Nun: The Return of Father Lundigan," ABC, 1968; "Mission: Impossible: Trial by Fury," CBS, 1968; "Here's Lucy: Lucy and the Great Airport Chase," CBS, 1969; "Gunsmoke: Time of the Jackals," CBS, 1969; "Gunsmoke: Jake MacGraw," CBS, 1969; "Mission: Impossible: Commandante," CBS, 1969; "Get Smart: Moonlighting Becomes You," CBS, 1970; "Mannix: Deja Vu," CBS, 1970; "The Rockford Files: Caledonia, It's Worth a Fortune!," NBC, 1974; "Emergency!: The Smoke Eater," NBC,

1975; "Switch: Round Up the Usual Suspects,"
CBS, 1976; "Switch: Photo Finish," CBS, 1978;
"The A-Team: Black Day at Bad Rock," NBC,
1983; "Misfits of Science: Fumble on the One;
Or, How I Recovered the Football and Almost
Saved the Free World," NBC, 1985; "Ohara: Take
the Money and Run," ABC, 1987; "The People
Next Door: Dream Date," CBS, 1989.

TV MOVIES AND MINISERIES:"Alias Smith and
Jones," ABC, 1971; "Who Is the Black
Dahlia?," NBC, 1975; "Kate McShane," CBS,
1975; "The Return of the World's Greatest
Detective," NBC, 1976; "Evening at
Byzantium," SYN, 1978; "Death Car on the
Freeway," CBS, 1979; "The Goddess of Love,"
NBC, 1988.

HAIRSTON, JESTER

b. North Carolina, July 9, 1901. Black actor
whose career dates to playing natives in
"Tarzan" movies; now he plays Rolly Forbes
on "Amen."

AS A REGULAR: "That's My Mama," ABC, 1974-
75; "Amen," NBC, 1986- .

AND: "Gunsmoke: Professor Lute Bone," CBS,
1956; "Studio 57: The Alibi," SYN, 1957; "Court
of Last Resort: The Stephen Elliott Case," NBC,
1958; "The Thin Man: Come Back, Darling
Asta," NBC, 1958; "Pontiac Star Parade: The
Man in the Moon," NBC, 1960; "Thriller: Papa
Benjamin," NBC, 1961; "Have Gun, Will Travel:
The Waiting Room," CBS, 1962.

HAJE, KHRYSTYNE

b. Santa Clara, CA, December 21, 1966.
Attractive redheaded actress who plays Simone
on "Head of the Class."

AS A REGULAR: "Head of the Class," ABC, 1986- .

AND: "CBS SchoolBreak Special: Juvi," CBS,
1987; "The Byron Allen Show," SYN, 1989.

HALE, ALAN JR.

b. Los Angeles, CA, March 8, 1918; d. 1990.
Heavyset actor in gentle giant roles; he played
Skipper Jonas Grumby on "Gilligan's Island."

AS A REGULAR: "Biff Baker, USA," CBS, 1952-
53; "Casey Jones," SYN, 1957-58; "Gilligan's
Island," CBS, 1964-67; "The Good Guys,"
CBS, 1969.

AND: "Stage 7: The Warriors," CBS, 1955; "Stage
7: Three Strikes and Out," CBS, 1955; "Fury:
Pirate Treasure," NBC, 1956; "The 20th Century-
Fox Hour: Young Man From Kentucky," CBS,
1957; "Cheyenne: Hired Gun," ABC, 1957;
"Those Whiting Girls: What Price Publicity?,"
CBS, 1957; "Bonanza: The Saga of Annie
O'Toole," NBC, 1959; "The Untouchables: The
Tri-State Gang," ABC, 1959; "The Texan:
Showdown," CBS, 1960; "The Alaskans:
Partners," ABC, 1960; "Mod Squad: Two Days

for Willy," NBC, 1960; "The Deputy: The
Standoff," NBC, 1960; "Johnny Ringo: Coffin
Sam," CBS, 1960; "Maverick: Arizona Black
Maria," ABC, 1960; "Cheyenne: Road to Three
Graves," ABC, 1960; "Walt Disney Presents:
Moochie of Pop Warner Football," ABC, 1960;
"Hawaiian Eye: Dragon Road," ABC, 1961;
"Gunsmoke: Minnie," CBS, 1961; "Adventures in
Paradise: The Serpent in the Garden," ABC, 1961;
"G.E. Theatre: Louie and the Horseless Buggy,"
CBS, 1961; "Whispering Smith: The Idol," NBC,
1961; "Mr. Ed: Ed the Jumper," CBS, 1961;
"Death Valley Days: Treasure of Elk Creek
Canyon," SYN, 1961; "The Real McCoys: The
Trailer Camp," ABC, 1961; "Perry Mason: The
Case of the Unwelcome Bride," CBS, 1961; "The
Andy Griffith Show: The Farmer Takes a Wife,"
CBS, 1962; "77 Sunset Strip: The Tarnished
Idol," ABC, 1963; "Hazel: Hazel Scores a
Touchdown," NBC, 1963; "The New Phil Silvers
Show: Pay the Two Dollars," CBS, 1964; "My
Favorite Martian: The Disastro-Nauts," CBS,
1964; "Password," CBS, 1965; "Gunsmoke:
Champion of the World," CBS, 1966; "Batman:
The Ogg and I/How to Hatch a Dinosaur," ABC,
1967; "Hondo: Hondo and the Death Drive,"
ABC, 1967; "Daktari: African Showdown," CBS,
1968; "The Virginian: The Bugler," NBC, 1969;
"Green Acres: A Prize in Each and Every
Package," CBS, 1969; "The Flying Nun: The
Great Casino Robbery," ABC, 1969; "The Wild
Wild West: The Night of the Sabatini Death,"
CBS, 1969; "Here's Lucy: Lucy and Wally Cox,"
CBS, 1970; "Ironside: The People Against Judge
McIntire," NBC, 1970; "Alias Smith and Jones:
The Girl in Boxcar Number Three," ABC, 1971;
"Gunsmoke: Jubilee," CBS, 1972; "Marcus
Welby, M.D.: In My Father's House," ABC,
1972; "The Paul Lynde Show: Everything You
Wanted to Know About Your Mother-in-Law But
Were Afraid to Ask," ABC, 1973; "The Love
Boat: The Harder They Fall," ABC, 1979; "Simon
& Simon: The Rough Rider Rides Again," CBS,
1982; "The Love Boat: Meet the Author," ABC,
1982; "Simon & Simon: For Old Crimes's Sake,"
CBS, 1987; "Hollywood Squares," SYN, 1988.

TV MOVIES AND MINISERIES:"Rescue From
Gilligan's Island," NBC, 1978; "The
Castaways on Gilligan's Island," NBC, 1979;
"The Harlem Globetrotters on Gilligan's
Island," NBC, 1981.

HALE, BARBARA

b. DeKalb, IL, April 18, 1921. Brunette actress
who's still Perry Mason's secretary, Della
Street, after all these years.

AS A REGULAR: "Perry Mason," CBS, 1957-66.

AND: "Ford Theatre: The Divided Heart," NBC,
1952; "Schlitz Playhouse of Stars: Vacation for
Ginny," CBS, 1953; "Ford Theatre: Remember to
Live," NBC, 1954; "G.E. Theatre: Meet the

Governor," CBS, 1954; "Schlitz Playhouse of Stars: Tourists Overnight," CBS, 1955; "Science Fiction Theatre: Conversation with an Ape," SYN, 1955; "G.E. Theatre: The Windmill," CBS, 1955; "Science Fiction Theatre: The Hastings Secret," SYN, 1955; "Climax!: The Day They Gave Babies Away," CBS, 1955; "The Loretta Young Show: The Challenge," NBC, 1956; "Damon Runyon Theatre: The Good Luck Kid," CBS, 1956; "Ford Theatre: Behind the Mask," NBC, 1956; "Star Stage: The Guardian," NBC, 1956; "Crossroads: Lifeline," ABC, 1956; "The Millionaire: The Kathy Munson Story," CBS, 1956; "Playhouse 90: The Country Husband," CBS, 1956; "G.E. Theatre: Night Club," CBS, 1959; "Here's Hollywood," NBC, 1960; "Stump the Stars," CBS, 1963; "Custer: Death Hunt," ABC, 1967; "The Most Deadly Game: Model for Murder," ABC, 1970; "Ironside: Murder Impromptu," NBC, 1971; "The Doris Day Show: Doris' House Guest," CBS, 1972; "The Wonderful World of Disney: Chester, Yesterday's Horse," NBC, 1973; "Marcus Welby, M.D.: The Faith of Childish Things," ABC, 1974.

TV MOVIES AND MINISERIES: "Perry Mason: The Case of the Notorious Nun," NBC, 1986; "Perry Mason Returns," NBC, 1985; "Perry Mason: The Case of the Shooting Star," NBC, 1986; "Perry Mason: The Case of the Sinister Spirit," NBC, 1987; "Perry Mason: The Case of the Murdered Madam," NBC, 1987; "Perry Mason: The Case of the Scandalous Scoundrel," NBC, 1987; "Perry Mason: The Case of the Avenging Ace," NBC, 1988; "Perry Mason: The Case of the Lost Love," NBC, 1988; "Perry Mason: The Case of the Lethal Lesson," NBC, 1989; "Perry Mason: The Case of the Musical Murder," NBC, 1989; "Perry Mason: The Case of the All-Star Assassin," NBC, 1989.
* Emmies: 1959.

HALEY, JACK
   b. Boston, MA, August 10, 1899; d. 1979. Pleasant song and dance man of the movies, most notably as the tin man in "The Wizard of Oz," who did a few TV bits.
AS A REGULAR: "Ford Star Revue," NBC, 1950-51.
AND: "Mirror Theatre: Uncle Jack," CBS, 1953; "The Ray Milland Show: Green Thumb," CBS, 1955; "Playhouse 90: No Time at All," CBS, 1958; "Westinghouse Desilu Playhouse: Ballad for a Bad Man," CBS, 1959; "Christophers: Some Facts About Lincoln's Law Practice," SYN, 1959; "The Danny Thomas Show: Battle of the In-Laws," CBS, 1960; "Christophers: Robert E. Lee," SYN, 1960; "The Merv Griffin Show," NBC, 1963; "Burke's Law: Who Killed Beau Sparrow?," ABC, 1963; "Marcus Welby, M.D.: He Could Sell Iceboxes to Eskimos," ABC, 1972.

TV MOVIES AND MINISERIES: "Rolling Man," ABC, 1972.

HALEY, JACKIE EARLE
   b. Northridge, CA, July 14, 1961. Actor who played Moocher in the film and TV versions of "Breaking Away."
AS A REGULAR: "Wait Till Your Father Gets Home," SYN, 1972-74; "Breaking Away," ABC, 1980-81.
AND: "Planet of the Apes: The Legacy," CBS, 1974; "The Love Boat: Rent-a-Family," ABC, 1979.

HALL, ANTHONY MICHAEL
   b. Boston, MA, April 14, 1968.
AS A REGULAR: "Saturday Night Live," NBC, 1985-86.
TV MOVIES AND MINISERIES: "Rascals and Robbers," CBS, 1982; "Running Out," CBS, 1983.

HALL, ARSENIO
   b. Cleveland, OH, February 12, 1960. Comedian with an undisciplined style who's the host of an outrageous late-night talk show.
AS A REGULAR: "The 1/2 Hour Comedy Hour," ABC, 1983; "Thicke of the Night," SYN, 1984; "Solid Gold," SYN, 1985-86; "Motown Revue," NBC, 1985; "The Late Show," FOX, 1987; "The Arsenio Hall Show," SYN, 1989- .
* Hall is the son of a Baptist minister.

HALL, BRAD
   b. Santa Barbara, CA, March 21, 1958.
AS A REGULAR: "Saturday Night Live," NBC, 1982-84.
AND: "CBS Summer Playhouse: Mad Avenue," CBS, 1988; "Empty Nest: Full Nest," NBC, 1989; "Day by Day: Music Man," NBC, 1989.

HALL, CLIFF
   b. Brooklyn, NY, October 4, 1894; d. 1972.
AS A REGULAR: "Crime Photgrapher," CBS, 1951-52.
AND: "Alcoa Presents One Step Beyond: Tidal Wave," ABC, 1960; "The Patty Duke Show: The Wedding Anniversary Caper," ABC, 1964; "Bewitched: A Bum Raps," ABC, 1966.
TV MOVIES AND MINISERIES: "Scalplock," NBC, 1966.

HALL, DEIDRE
   b. Lake Worth, FL, October 31, 1948. Actress who played Dr. Marlena Evans on "Days of Our Lives."
AS A REGULAR: "The Young and the Restless," CBS, 1973-75; "Days of Our Lives," NBC, 1976-88; "Our House," NBC, 1986-88.
AND: "Columbo: Mind Over Mayhem," NBC,

1974; "Wiseguy: The Ripoff Stick," CBS, 1989; "Wiseguy: High Dollar Bop," CBS, 1989; "Wiseguy: Hip Hop on the Gravy Train," CBS, 1989.

TV MOVIES AND MINISERIES: "A Reason to Live," NBC, 1985; "Take My Daughters, Please," NBC, 1988; "Perry Mason: The Case of the All-Star Assassin," NBC, 1989.

HALL, HUNTZ

b. Henry Hall, New York City, NY, 1920. Former Dead End kid who did some TV.

AS A REGULAR: "The Chicago Teddy Bears," CBS, 1971.

AND: "Barefoot in the Park: Disorder in the Court," ABC, 1970; "Diff'rent Strokes: Big Brother," NBC, 1982; "Night Heat: Bless Me Father," CBS, 1988.

TV MOVIES AND MINISERIES: "Escape," ABC, 1971.

HALL, JON

b. Fresno, CA, February 26, 1913; d. 1980. Actor in B-movies, often Arabian Nights-style pictures. He also played Ramar, of the jungle.

AS A REGULAR: "Ramar of the Jungle," SYN, 1952-54.

AND: "The Steve Allen Show," NBC, 1957; "Perry Mason: The Case of the Festive Falcon," CBS, 1963; "Perry Mason: The Case of the Feather Cloak," CBS, 1965.

HALL, JUANITA

b. Keyport, NJ, November 6, 1901; d. 1968. Musical comedy performer; she played Bloody Mary in "South Pacific."

AS A REGULAR: "Captain Billy's Mississippi Music Hall," CBS, 1948.

AND: "Pontiac Star Parade: An Evening with Perry Como," NBC, 1959; "America Pauses for Springtime," CBS, 1959.

HALL, MONTY

b. Winnipeg, Canada, August 25, 1923. Game show emcee.

AS A REGULAR: "The Sky's the Limit," ABC, 1955-56; "Cowboy Theatre," NBC, 1956-57; "Keep Talking," CBS, 1958; "Video Village," CBS, 1961-62; "Video Village Jr.," CBS, 1961-62; "Let's Make a Deal," NBC, 1963-68; ABC, 1968-76; SYN, 1984-86; "NBC Comedy Playhouse," NBC, 1968; "It's Anybody's Guess," NBC, 1977; "Beat the Clock," CBS, 1979-80; "The Joke's on Us," SYN, 1983-84; "Split Second," SYN, 1986-88.

AND: "That Girl: At the Drop of a Bucket," ABC, 1969; "Jimmy Durante Presents the Lennon Sisters Hour," ABC, 1970; "The Odd Couple: Let's Make a Deal," ABC, 1973; "The Flip Wilson Show," NBC, 1973; "Wait Till Your Father Gets Home: Mama Loves Monty," SYN,

1974; "The Odd Couple: A Different Drummer," ABC, 1974; "Love, American Style: Love and the Man of the Year," ABC, 1974; "Mitzi and a Hundred Guys," CBS, 1975; "Tomorrow," NBC, 1977.

HALL, THURSTON

b. Boston, MA, 1882; d. 1958. Character actor often in pompous roles.

AS A REGULAR: "Topper," CBS, 1953-55; "The Adventures of Hiram Holliday," NBC, 1956.

AND: "The Abbott and Costello Show: The Actor's Home," CBS, 1952; "The Abbott and Costello Show: The Tax Return," CBS, 1953; "Circus Boy: Major Buffington," NBC, 1957; "The Adventures of Rin Tin Tin: The Southern Colonel," ABC, 1958.

HALOP, BILLY

b. New York City, NY, February 11, 1920; d. 1976. Former Dead End kid who played rough blue-collar types, including cab company owner Bert Munson on "All in the Family."

AS A REGULAR: "All in the Family," CBS, 1971-76.

AND: "Racket Squad: Accidentally on Purpose," CBS, 1952; "Footlights Theatre: Crossroad," CBS, 1952; "Favorite Story: The World Beyond," SYN, 1953; "Favorite Story: The Lady and the Law," SYN, 1953; "Robert Montgomery Presents: The Pale Blonde of Sand Street," NBC, 1954; "Telephone Time: The Jumping Parson," CBS, 1957; "The Thin Man: The Perfect Servant," NBC, 1959; "I'm Dickens, He's Fenster: Mr. Takeover," ABC, 1963; "The Andy Griffith Show: The Big House," CBS, 1963; "The Adventures of Ozzie and Harriet: The Money Watchers," ABC, 1963; "The Adventures of Ozzie and Harriet: David and the Mermaid," ABC, 1963; "Vacation Playhouse: Papa GI," CBS, 1964; "Perry Mason: The Case of the Antic Angel," CBS, 1964; "The Andy Griffith Show: Opie and the Carnival," CBS, 1965; "Perry Mason: The Case of the Lonely Eloper," CBS, 1965; "The FBI: To Free My Enemy," ABC, 1965; "Gunsmoke: The Returning," CBS, 1967; "Gomer Pyle, USMC: A Dog Is a Dog Is a Dog," CBS, 1968; "The FBI: Escape to Nowhere," ABC, 1972.

HALOP, FLORENCE

b. Queens, NY, January 23, 1923; d. 1986. Short, dumpy actress with a nasal voice; she played Mrs. Hufnagel, who died when a hospital bed folded up with her in it on "St. Elsewhere," and Florence the bailiff on "Night Court."

AS A REGULAR: "Holiday Hotel," ABC, 1951; "Meet Millie," CBS, 1952-56; "St. Elsewhere,"

NBC, 1984-85; "Night Court," NBC, 1985-86.
AND: "I Love Lucy: Redecorating," CBS, 1952;
"Playhouse 90: No Time at All," CBS, 1958;
"Saints and Sinners: A Shame for a Diamond
Wedding," NBC, 1962; "The Danny Thomas
Show: My Fair Uncle," CBS, 1963; "The Alfred
Hitchcock Hour: Starring the Defense," CBS,
1963; "The New Phil Silvers Show: Las Vegas
Was My Mother's Maiden Name," CBS, 1963;
"The Dick Van Dyke Show: The Ugliest Dog In
The World," CBS, 1965; "The Smothers Brothers
Show: How to Succeed in Business and Be Really
Trying," CBS, 1966; "Captain Nice: The Man
with Three Blue Eyes," NBC, 1967; "That Girl: 7
1/4," ABC, 1968; "Allan," NBC, 1971; "Here's
Lucy: Lucy the Sheriff," CBS, 1974; "All in the
Family: Mr. Edith Bunker," CBS, 1976; "Barney
Miller: Massage Parlor," ABC, 1976; "Barney
Miller: Bus Stop," ABC, 1976; "Barney Miller:
Inauguration," ABC, 1978; "Angie: The
Gambler," ABC, 1979; "Angie: Marie Moves
Out," ABC, 1980; "Barney Miller: Field
Associate," ABC, 1981; "Alice: Macho, Macho
Mel," CBS, 1981; "Barney Miller: Stress
Analyzer," ABC, 1981; "Barney Miller:
Landmark," ABC, 1982; "E/R: Son of Sheinfeld,"
CBS, 1984.

HALPIN, LUKE
b. Astoria, NY.
AS A REGULAR: "Flipper," NBC, 1964-68.
AND: "Studio One: A Christmas Surprise," CBS,
1956; "Studio One: A Matter of Guilt," CBS,
1957; "Robert Herridge Theatre: A Trip to
Czardis," SYN, 1960; "Peter Pan," NBC, 1960;
"Robert Herridge Theatre: The Stone Boy," SYN,
1961; "Theatre '62: Intermezzo," NBC, 1961;
"Armstrong Circle Theatre: Battle of Hearts,"
CBS, 1961; "Everglades: Curtains for Kocomo,"
SYN, 1962; "Judd for the Defense: The Worst of
Both Worlds," ABC, 1968.

HALSEY, BRETT
b. Santa Ana, CA, June 20, 1933. Actor who
played John Abbott on "The Young and the
Restless."
AS A REGULAR: "Follow the Sun," ABC, 1961-62;
"Search for Tomorrow," CBS, 1975; "General
Hospital," ABC, 1976-77; "The Young and the
Restless," CBS, 1980-82.
AND: "Gunsmoke: Helping Hand," CBS, 1956;
"Tales of the 77th Bengal Lancers: Hostage,"
NBC, 1956; "West Point: Start Running," CBS,
1957; "West Point: Cold Peril," CBS, 1957;
"Matinee Theatre: The Story of Joseph," NBC,
1957; "Schlitz Playhouse of Stars: Sister Louise
Goes to Town," CBS, 1957; "Perry Mason: The
Case of the Cautious Coquette," CBS, 1958; "The
Millionaire: Millionaire Susan Birchard," CBS,
1958; "Five Fingers: Thin Ice," NBC, 1959;
"Adventures in Paradise: Passage to Tua," ABC,

1960; "Columbo: Death Lends a Hand," NBC,
1971; "Alias Smith and Jones: The Day the
Amnesty Came Through," ABC, 1973; "Toma:
Crime Without Victim," ABC, 1973; "City of
Angels: The Losers," NBC, 1976; "Fantasy Island
A Very Strange Affair," ABC, 1982; "Father
Murphy: Stopover in a One-Horse Town," NBC,
1982; "The New Mike Hammer: Murder in the
Cards," CBS, 1986.
TV MOVIES AND MINISERIES: "Crash," ABC, 1978.

HAMEL, VERONICA
b. Philadelphia, PA, November 20, 1943.
Attractive brunette actress, a former model; she
played Joyce Davenport on "Hill Street Blues."
AS A REGULAR: "Hill Street Blues," NBC, 1981-
87.
AND: "Kojak: How Cruel the Frost, How Bright
the Stars," CBS, 1975; "The Rockford Files: A
Bad Deal in the Valley," NBC, 1976; "The
Rockford Files: Return to the 38th Parallel,"
NBC, 1976; "The Bob Newhart Show: Peeper -
Two," CBS, 1976; "Switch: Round Up the Usual
Suspects," CBS, 1976.
TV MOVIES AND MINISERIES: "Harold Robbins' 79
Park Avenue," NBC, 1977; "The Gathering,
Part II," NBC, 1979; "Sessions," NBC, 1983;
"Kane & Abel," CBS, 1985; "Pursuit," NBC,
1988.

HAMER, RUSTY
b. Tenafly, NJ, February 15, 1947; d. 1990.
Former child actor who played Rusty Williams,
wisecracking TV son of Danny Thomas; he
shot himself.
AS A REGULAR: "The Danny Thomas Show (Make
Room for Daddy)," ABC, 1953-57; CBS,
1957-64; "The Joey Bishop Show," CBS,
1965; "Make Room for Granddaddy," ABC,
1970-71.
AND: "The Perry Como Show," NBC, 1958; "The
Lucille Ball-Desi Arnaz Show: Lucy Makes
Room for Danny," CBS, 1958; "Danny Thomas
Special," NBC, 1965.

HAMILL, MARK
b. Oakland, CA, September 25, 1952. Blonde,
boyish actor who's known worldwide as Luke
Skywalker of "Star Wars" fame, now making
his way back to television.
AS A REGULAR: "General Hospital," ABC, 1972-
73; "The Texas Wheelers," ABC, 1974-75.
AND: "The Bill Cosby Show: The Poet," NBC,
1970; "The Partridge Family: Old Scrapmouth,"
ABC, 1971; "Owen Marshall, Counselor at Law:
Smiles From Yesterday," ABC, 1972; "The FBI:
The Corruptor," ABC, 1972; "Room 222: I've
Got the Hammer, If You've Got the Thumb,"
ABC, 1973; "The Magician: Lightning on a Dry

Day," NBC, 1973; "The Streets of San Francisco: Poisoned Snow," ABC, 1975; "Medical Center: You Can't Annul My Baby," CBS, 1976; "One Day at a Time: Schneider's Pride and Joy," CBS, 1976; "The Streets of San Francisco: Innocent No More," ABC, 1977; "The Muppet Show," SYN, 1980; "Amazing Stories: Gather Ye Acorns," NBC, 1986; "Hooperman: Intolerance," ABC, 1989.

TV MOVIES AND MINISERIES:"Sarah T... Portrait of a Teenage Alcoholic," NBC, 1975; "Delancey Street," NBC, 1975; "Hallmark Hall of Fame: Eric," NBC, 1975; "Mallory: Circumstantial Evidence," NBC, 1976; "The City," NBC, 1977.

HAMILTON, ANTONY
b. England, 1954.
AS A REGULAR: "Cover Up," CBS, 1984-85; "Mission: Immpossible," ABC, 1988-90.
AND: "L.A. Law: The Lung Goodbye," NBC, 1987.
TV MOVIES AND MINISERIES:"Samson and Delilah," ABC, 1984; "Mirrors," NBC, 1985.

HAMILTON, GEORGE
b. Memphis, TN, August 12, 1939. Tanned matinee idol who usually plays smoothies.
AS A REGULAR: "Harold Robbins' The Survivors," ABC, 1969-70; "Paris 7000," ABC, 1970; "Dynasty," ABC, 1985-86; "Spies," CBS, 1987.
AND: "Cimarron City: The Beauty and the Sorrow," NBC, 1959; "The Donna Reed Show: Have Fun," ABC, 1959; "Here's Hollywood," NBC, 1960; "Bob Hope Chrysler Theatre: The Turncoat," NBC, 1964; "The Rogues: Two of a Kind," NBC, 1964; "Burke's Law: Who Killed the Richest Man in the World?," ABC, 1964; "Ben Casey: Where Does the Boomerang Go?," ABC, 1965; "Hullabaloo," NBC, 1965; "Burke's Law: Who Killed Mother Goose?," ABC, 1965; "The Merv Griffin Show," SYN, 1966; "Hullabaloo," NBC, 1966; "Personality," NBC, 1969; "The Ed Sullivan Show," CBS, 1971; "Hollywood Squares," NBC, 1974; "Tattletales," CBS, 1975; "Columbo: A Deadly State of Mind," NBC, 1975; "Tattletales," CBS, 1976; "Police Story: The Other Side of the Fence," NBC, 1976; "The $25,000 Pyramid," SYN, 1976; "McCloud: The Great Taxicab Stampede," NBC, 1977; "Sword of Justice: Blackjack," NBC, 1978; "The Mike Douglas Show," SYN, 1980.
TV MOVIES AND MINISERIES:"The Dead Don't Die," NBC, 1975; "The Strange Possession of Mrs. Oliver," NBC, 1977; "Roots," ABC, 1977; "The Users," ABC, 1978; "Death Car on the Freeway," CBS, 1979; "The Great Cash Giveaway Getaway," NBC, 1980; "Malibu," ABC, 1983; "Two Fathers' Justice," NBC, 1985; "Monte Carlo," CBS, 1986; "Poker Alice," CBS, 1987.

HAMILTON, JOHN
b. 1887; d. 1958. Actor who played editor Perry White on "The Adventures of Superman."
AS A REGULAR: "The Adventures of Superman," SYN, 1951-57.
AND: "Blondie: Howdy, Neighbor," NBC, 1957; "Alfred Hitchcock Presents: Hooked," CBS, 1960.

HAMILTON, LINDA
b. Salisbury, MD. Striking actress who played Catherine Chandler on "Beauty and the Beast."
AS A REGULAR: "Secrets of Midland Heights," CBS, 1980-81; "King's Crossing," ABC, 1982; "Beauty and the Beast," CBS, 1987-89.
AND: "Hill Street Blues: Grace Under Pressure," NBC, 1984; "Hill Street Blues: Fuchs Me? Fuchs You!," NBC, 1984; "Hill Street Blues: Parting Is Such Sweep Sorrow," NBC, 1984; "Murder, She Wrote: Menace, Anyone?," CBS, 1986.
TV MOVIES AND MINISERIES:"Reunion," CBS, 1980; "Country Gold," CBS, 1982; "Secrets of a Mother and Daughter," CBS, 1983; "Secret Weapons," NBC, 1985; "Club Med," ABC, 1986.

HAMILTON, MARGARET
b. Cleveland, OH, December 9, 1902; d. 1985. The wicked witch in "The Wizard of Oz," and tough-as-nails retired editor Thea Taft on a couple of "Lou Grant" episodes.
AS A REGULAR: "The Paul Winchell-Jerry Mahoney Show," NBC, 1953-54; "Valiant Lady," CBS, 1954-57; "As the World Turns," CBS, 1971.
AND: "Silver Theatre: Papa Romani," CBS, 1950; "Gulf Playhouse: The Rose," NBC, 1952; "Studio One: Man of Extinction," CBS, 1954; "Campbell TV Soundstage: An Eye for an Eye," NBC, 1954; "Center Stage: Lucky Louise," ABC, 1954; "U.S. Steel Hour: The Fifth Wheel," ABC, 1954; "Kraft Television Theatre: The Happy Touch," NBC, 1954; "Best of Broadway: The Man Who Came to Dinner," CBS, 1954; "Elgin TV Hour: Warm Clay," ABC, 1954; "Studio One: The Silent Woman," CBS, 1955; "Best of Broadway: The Guardsman," CBS, 1955; "Omnibus: A Different Drummer," CBS, 1955; "Goodyear TV Playhouse: Beloved Stranger," NBC, 1955; "Hallmark Hall of Fame: The Devil's Disciple," NBC, 1955; "Alcoa Hour: Merry Christmas, Mr. Baxter," NBC, 1956; "Omnibus: The Trial of Lizzie Borden," ABC, 1957; "Studio One: My Mother and How She Undid Me," CBS, 1957; "Playhouse 90: The Silver Whistle," CBS, 1959; "Dow Hour of Great Mysteries: The Bat," NBC, 1960; "Startime: Fun Fair," NBC, 1960; "The Secret World of Eddie Hodges," CBS, 1960; "Car 54, Where Are You?: Here Comes Charlie," NBC,

1963; "The Patty Duke Show: Double Date," ABC, 1963; "The Patty Duke Show: Let 'Em Eat Cake," ABC, 1964; "Discovery '64: The Weird World of Witchcraft," ABC, 1964; "The Addams Family: Morticia's Romance," ABC, 1965; "The Addams Family: Happy Birthday, Grandma Frump," ABC, 1966; "Ghostbreaker," ABC, 1967; "Off to See the Wizard: Who's Afraid of Mother Goose?," ABC, 1967; "Triple Play: Is There a Doctor in the House?," NBC, 1971; "Gunsmoke: Quiet Day in Dodge," CBS, 1973; "The Partridge Family: Reuben Kincaid Lives," ABC, 1973; "The Paul Lynde Comedy Hour," ABC, 1976; "Lou Grant: Hollywood," CBS, 1979; "Here's Boomer: Jailbreak," NBC, 1980; "Lou Grant: Review," CBS, 1981; "Nurse: The Gift," CBS, 1981.

TV MOVIES AND MINISERIES:"The Night Strangler," ABC, 1973; "Letters From Frank," CBS, 1979.

HAMILTON, MURRAY

b. Washington, D.C., March 24, 1923; d. 1986.
AS A REGULAR: "Love and Marriage," NBC, 1959-60; "The Man Who Never Was," ABC, 1966-67; "B.J. and the Bear," NBC, 1981; "Hail to the Chief," ABC, 1985.
AND: "Wire Service: Hideout," ABC, 1956; "Wire Service: Confirm or Deny," ABC, 1957; "Warner Bros. Presents Conflict: Girl on a Subway," ABC, 1957; "Have Gun, Will Travel: The Last Laugh," CBS, 1958; "Gunsmoke: Wild West," CBS, 1958; "The Silent Service: The USS Tinosa Story," SYN, 1958; "The Twilight Zone: One for the Angels," CBS, 1959; "Men Into Space: Tankers in Space," CBS, 1960; "Goodyear Theatre: The Ticket," NBC, 1960; "Alfred Hitchcock Presents: Escape to Sonoita," CBS, 1960; "Naked City: The Pedigree Sheet," ABC, 1960; "Route 66: The Swan Bed," CBS, 1960; "The Untouchables: The Tommy Karpeles Story," ABC, 1960; "Way Out: Sideshow," CBS, 1961; "The Untouchables: The Troubleshooter," ABC, 1961; "Naked City: Which Is Joseph Creeley?," ABC, 1961; "The Defenders: The Bedside Murder," CBS, 1962; "Theatre '62: The Farmer's Daughter," NBC, 1962; "U.S. Steel Hour: The Big Laugh," CBS, 1962; "The Untouchables: The Whitey Steele Story," ABC, 1962; "The Defenders: The Hickory Indian," CBS, 1962; "Dr. Kildare: A Time for Every Purpose," NBC, 1962; "The du Pont Show: Windfall," NBC, 1963; "The Defenders: Drink Like a Lady," CBS, 1964; "Trials of O'Brien: Pilot," CBS, 1965; "The FBI: The Camel's Nose," ABC, 1966; "The FBI: The Ninth Man," ABC, 1968; "The FBI: A Life in the Balance," ABC, 1969; "Medical Center: Junkie," CBS, 1970; "The FBI: The Witness," ABC, 1970; "Hollywood Television Theatre: The Police," NET, 1971; "McCloud: Encounter with Aries," NBC, 1972; "Madigan: The Manhattan Beat," NBC, 1972; "Mission: Impossible: Ultimatum," CBS, 1972;

"Love, American Style: Love and the Happy Family," ABC, 1973; "Hawkins: Die, Darling, Die," CBS, 1973; "Police Story: Collision Course," NBC, 1973; "Barnaby Jones: Fatal Flight," CBS, 1973; "Medical Center: Girl From Bedlam," CBS, 1974; "Chase: Eighty-Six Proof TNT," NBC, 1974; "The Streets of San Francisco: License to Kill," ABC, 1974; "Police Story: War Games," NBC, 1975; "Ellery Queen: The Chinese Dog," NBC, 1975; "McMillan and Wife: Secrets for Sale," NBC, 1975; "Alice: Mother-in-Law," CBS, 1976; "Kojak: Sister Maria," CBS, 1977; "Murder, She Wrote: Death Casts a Spell," CBS, 1985; "Blacke's Magic: Ten Tons of Trouble," NBC, 1986; "The Golden Girls: Big Daddy," NBC, 1986.

TV MOVIES AND MINISERIES:"Vanished," NBC, 1971; "Cannon," CBS, 1971; "A Tattered Web," CBS, 1971; "The Harness," NBC, 1971; "The Failing of Raymond," ABC, 1971; "Deadly Harvest," CBS, 1972; "Incident on a Dark Street," CBS, 1973; "Murdock's Gang," ABC, 1973; "Rich Man, Poor Man," ABC, 1976; "Murder at the World Series," ABC, 1977; "Swan Song," ABC, 1980; "Rona Jaffe's Mazes and Monsters," CBS, 1982; "Summer Girl," CBS, 1983; "The Last Days of Patton," CBS, 1986.

HAMILTON, NEIL

b. James Neil Hamilton, Lynn, MA, September 9, 1899. Actor of aristocratic bearing who began in silent films and, on TV, played "That Wonderful Guy" and Commissioner Gordon on "Batman."
AS A REGULAR: "The Hollywood Screen Test," ABC, 1948-53; "That Wonderful Guy," ABC, 1949-50; "Batman," ABC, 1966-68.
AND: "Broadway Television Theatre: The Night of January 16," SYN, 1952; "Best of Broadway: Panama Hattie," CBS, 1954; "U.S. Steel Hour: King's Pawn," ABC, 1954; "Kraft Television Theatre: Five Minutes to Live," NBC, 1956; "Modern Romances: The Tender Age," NBC, 1956; "The Gale Storm Show: Mardi Gras," CBS, 1957; "Telephone Time: Man of Principle," ABC, 1958; "Perry Mason: The Case of the Lazy Lover," CBS, 1958; "Perry Mason: The Case of the Dubious Bridegroom," CBS, 1958; "Maverick: The Rivals," ABC, 1959; "77 Sunset Strip: The Hong Kong Caper," ABC, 1959; "Tightrope!: The Penthouse Story," CBS, 1960; "Bourbon Street Beat: Knock on Any Tombstone," ABC, 1960; "The Man From Blackhawk: The Lady in Yellow," ABC, 1960; "Mr. Garlund: The X-27," CBS, 1960; "Bachelor Father: Bentley and the Big Board," NBC, 1960; "77 Sunset Strip: The Hamlet Caper," ABC, 1961; "The Aquanauts: The Defective Tank Adventure," CBS, 1961; "Perry Mason: The Case of the Difficult Detour," CBS, 1961; "Harrigan and Son: Senior Goes to

Hollywood," ABC, 1961; "The Real McCoys: How to Win Friends," ABC, 1961; "Follow the Sun: Conspiracy of Silence," ABC, 1961; "Bus Stop: Cry to Heaven," ABC, 1962; "Mr. Ed: Horse Sense," CBS, 1962; "Hawaiian Eye: The Meeting on Molokai," ABC, 1962; "Frontier Circus: Naomi Champagne," CBS, 1962; "77 Sunset Strip: Leap, My Lovely," ABC, 1962; "Perry Mason: The Case of Constant Doyle," CBS, 1963; "The Outer Limits: The Invisibles," ABC, 1964; "The Outer Limits: The Bellero Shield," ABC, 1964; "Perry Mason: The Case of the Drifting Dropout," CBS, 1964; "Perry Mason: The Case of the Betrayed Bride," CBS, 1964; "The Munsters: Autumn Croakus," CBS, 1964; "Profiles in Courage: Anne Hutchinson," NBC, 1965; "Kraft Suspense Theatre: In Darkness Waiting," NBC, 1965; "Mr. Ed: Ed's Juice Stand," CBS, 1965; "The Cara Williams Show: The Wig," CBS, 1965; "Art Linkletter's House Party," CBS, 1967.
TV MOVIES AND MINISERIES:"Vanished," NBC, 1971.

HAMLIN, HARRY
b. *Pasadena, CA, October 30, 1951.* Actor who plays Michael Kuzak on "L.A. Law."
AS A REGULAR: "L.A. Law," NBC, 1986- .
TV MOVIES AND MINISERIES: "Studs Lonigan," NBC, 1979; "Master of the Game," CBS, 1984; "Space," CBS, 1985; "Dinner at Eight," TNT, 1989.

HAMNER, EARL JR.
b. *Schuyler, VA, July 10, 1923.* Writer-producer responsible for "The Waltons."
AS WRITER: "The Twilight Zone: The Hunt," CBS, 1962; "The Twilight Zone: A Piano in the House," CBS, 1962.
TV MOVIES AND MINISERIES: "Heidi," NBC, 1968; "The Homecoming," CBS, 1971.
AS WRITER-CREATOR: "The Waltons," CBS, 1972-81; "Falcon Crest," CBS, 1981-90; "Boone," NBC, 1983-84.

HAMPSHIRE, SUSAN
b. *London, England, May 12, 1938.* Attractive British actress who won American TV audiences on some of Public Broadcasting System's first TV hits; she played Fleur on "The Forsyte Saga."
AS A REGULAR: "The Forsyte Saga," NET, 1969-70.
AND: "Adventures in Paradise: Appointment in Tara-Bi," ABC, 1961; "Secret Agent: Are You Going to Be More Permanent?," CBS, 1965; "Secret Agent: You're Not in Any Trouble, Are You?," CBS, 1966; "The Time Tunnel: Rendezvous with Yesterday," ABC, 1966; "NET Playhouse: An Ideal Husband," NET, 1971; "Dr. Jekyll and Mr. Hyde," NBC, 1973; "Wide World

of Mystery: Kill Two Birds," ABC, 1975.
TV MOVIES AND MINISERIES: "David Copperfield," NBC, 1970; "Masterpiece Theatre: The First Churchills," NET, 1971; "Masterpiece Theatre: Vanity Fair," NET, 1972; "Baffled!," NBC, 1973; "The Story of David," ABC, 1976.
* Emmies: 1970, 1971, 1973.

HAMPTON, JAMES
b. *Oklahoma City, OK, July 9, 1939.* Actor usually in good-hearted country-boy roles; he played trooper Dobbs on "F Troop."
AS A REGULAR: "F Troop," ABC, 1965-67; "The Doris Day Show," CBS, 1968-69; "Love, American Style," ABC, 1971-74; "Mary," CBS, 1978; "Maggie," ABC, 1981-82.
AND: "Death Valley Days: The Paper Dynasty," SYN, 1964; "Gomer Pyle, USMC: The Feuding Pyles," CBS, 1965; "The FBI: The Deadly Species," ABC, 1972; "Hawkins: A Life for a Life," CBS, 1973; "The Rockford Files: The Aaron Ironwood School of Success," NBC, 1975; "Goodnight Beantown: Looking Forward to the Past," CBS, 1983; "Matt Houston: Return to 'Nam," ABC, 1984; "Full House: Working Mothers," ABC, 1989; "Full House: El Problema Grande de D.J.," ABC, 1989.
TV MOVIES AND MINISERIES: "Force Five," CBS, 1975; "The Amazing Howard Hughes," CBS, 1977; "Centennial," NBC, 1978-79; "Stand by Your Man," CBS, 1981; "Through the Magic Pyramid," NBC, 1981.

HANDLEMAN, STANLEY MYRON
b. *Brooklyn, NY.* Comedian.
AS A REGULAR: "Dean Martin Presents," NBC, 1968, 1969; "Make Room for Granddaddy," ABC, 1970-71.
AND: "The Merv Griffin Show," SYN, 1968; "The Merv Griffin Show," CBS, 1970; "The Merv Griffin Show," SYN, 1973.

HANKS, TOM
b. *Concord, CA, July 9, 1956.* Light leading man of films ("Big," "Turner and Hooch") and TV.
AS A REGULAR: "Bosom Buddies," ABC, 1980-82.
AND: "The Love Boat: Jealousy," ABC, 1980; "Taxi: The Road Not Taken," ABC, 1982; "Family Ties: The Fugitive," NBC, 1983; "Family Ties: Say Uncle," NBC, 1984; "Saturday Night Live," NBC, 1985; "Saturday Night Live," NBC, 1988; "Saturday Night Live's 15th Anniversary," NBC, 1989; "Late Night with David Letterman," NBC, 1989.
TV MOVIES AND MINISERIES: "Rona Jaffe's Mazes and Monsters," CBS, 1982.

HANLEY, BRIDGET
b. *Minneapolis, MN, February 3, 1941.* Actress

who played Candy, girlfriend of Jeremy Bolt (Bobby Sherman) on "Here Come the Brides." **AS A REGULAR:** "The Second Hundred Years," ABC, 1967-68; "Here Come the Brides," ABC, 1968-70; "Harper Valley PTA," NBC, 1981-82. **AND:** "Gidget: Love and the Single Gidget," ABC, 1966; "The Farmer's Daughter: Is He or Isn't He?," ABC, 1966; "The Pirates of Flounder Bay," ABC, 1966; "Love on a Rooftop: Homecoming," ABC, 1966; "Love on a Rooftop: Who Is Sylvia?," ABC, 1966; "Bewitched: I'd Rather Twitch Than Fight," ABC, 1966; "I Dream of Jeannie: My Master, the Swinging Bachelor," NBC, 1967; "Guess What I Did Today?," ABC, 1968; "The Flying Nun: You Can't Get There From Here," ABC, 1968; "Love, American Style: Love and the Teacher," ABC, 1970; "The Odd Couple: Felix Gets Sick," ABC, 1970; "Nanny and the Professor: The Great Broadcast of 1936," ABC, 1970; "Love, American Style: Love and the Country Girl," ABC, 1971; "Love, American Style: Love and the Singing Suitor," ABC, 1972; "Love, American Style: Love and the Memento," ABC, 1973; "The Rookies: Death Watch," ABC, 1974; "Welcome Back, Kotter: The Reunion," ABC, 1975; "Simon & Simon: The Rough Rider Rides Again," CBS, 1982; "Riptide: Games People Play," NBC, 1985. **TV MOVIES AND MINISERIES:** "Malibu," ABC, 1983.

HANNA, WILLIAM
b. Melrose, NM, July 14, 1910;
& BARBERA, JOSEPH
b. New York City, NY, 1911. Producers who pioneered assembly-line animation for television, filling a vast need and bombarding thirty-five years' worth of kids with cartoons of highly variable quality. **AS PRODUCERS:** "Huckleberry Hound, Quick Draw Mc Graw, Yogi Bear," SYN, 1957-59; "The Flintstones," ABC, 1960-66; "Top Cat," ABC, 1961-62; "The Jetsons," ABC, 1962-63; "Jonny Quest," ABC, 1964-65; and many, many others.

HANSEN, PETER
b. Oakland, CA, December 5, 1921. Actor who plays Lee Baldwin on "General Hospital." **AS A REGULAR:** "Ben Jerrod, Attorney at Law," NBC, 1963; "Mr. Novak," NBC, 1964-65; "General Hospital," ABC, 1965- . **AND:** "Favorite Story: The Robbers," SYN, 1952; "Favorite Story: It Couldn't Happen," SYN, 1952; "Science Fiction Theatre: Beyond Return," SYN, 1955; "Science Fiction Theatre: Signals From the Heart," SYN, 1956; "Science Fiction Theatre: The Strange Lodger," SYN, 1957; "The Adventures of Jim Bowie: Rezin Bowie, Gambler," ABC, 1957; "Panic!: Twenty-Six Hours to Sunrise," NBC, 1957; "Telephone Time: Grandpa Changes the World," ABC, 1957; "Restless Gun: Pressing

Engagement," NBC, 1958; "The Millionaire: The Neal Bowers Story," CBS, 1958; "McKeever and the Colonel: Straight and Narrow," NBC, 1962; "The New Loretta Young Show: Crisis at 8 p.m.," CBS, 1963; "The Lieutenant: Interlude," NBC, 1964; "Dr. Kildare: Why Won't Anyone Listen?," NBC, 1964; "Gomer Pyle, USMC: Gomer Overcomes the Obstacle Course," CBS, 1964; "Gomer Pyle, USMC: Guest in the Barracks," CBS, 1964; "The Outer Limits: The Brain of Colonel Barham," ABC, 1965; "The FBI: The Monster," CBS, 1965; "The Man From UNCLE: The Mad, Mad Tea Party Affair," NBC, 1965; "The FBI: The Predators," ABC, 1968; "Police Woman: Tender Soldier," NBC, 1976; "The Golden Girls: The Triangle," NBC, 1985; "Cagney & Lacey: Exit Stage Center," CBS, 1986; "Simon & Simon: Opposite Attack," CBS, 1987; "Night Court: This Old Man...," NBC, 1989.
* Emmies: 1979.

HARDIN, MELORA
b. Houston, TX, June 29, 1967.
AS A REGULAR: "Secrets of Midland Heights," CBS, 1980-81; "The Family Tree," NBC, 1983; "The Best Times," NBC, 1985; "Dirty Dancing," CBS, 1988. **AND:** "The Love Boat: Julie Falls Hard," ABC, 1978; "Quincy: Never a Child," NBC, 1979; "Quincy: Next Stop Nowhere," NBC, 1982; "Magnum, P.I.: Luther Gillis: File #521," CBS, 1983. **TV MOVIES AND MINISERIES:** "Haywire," CBS, 1980; "Little House: Look Back to Yesterday," NBC, 1983.

HARDIN, TY
b. Orison Whipple Hungerford Jr., New York City, NY, January 1, 1930. Warner Bros. contractee who played Bronco Layne, a replacement for Clint "Cheyenne" Walker when he bolted his series in 1958, and fell into obscurity when "Bronco" left the air. **AS A REGULAR:** "Bronco," ABC, 1958-62. **AND:** "Sugarfoot: The Trial of the Canary Kid," ABC, 1959; "Pat Boone Chevy Showroom," ABC, 1959; "Maverick: Hadley's Hunters," ABC, 1960; "77 Sunset Strip: Strange Bedfellows," ABC, 1961; "The Love Boat: First Voyage, Last Voyage," ABC, 1981. **TV MOVIES AND MINISERIES:** "Red River," CBS, 1988.
* Hardin's films include "I Married a Monster From Outer Space."

HARDWICKE, SIR CEDRIC
b. Stourbridge, England, February 19, 1883; d. 1964. Stage and film actor who did his share of TV. **AS A REGULAR:** "Who Pays?," NBC, 1959; "Mrs. G.

Goes to College (The Gertrude Berg Show),"
CBS, 1961-62.
AND: "Schlitz Playhouse of Stars: Crossroads,"
CBS, 1952; "Lux Video Theatre: The Return of
Ulysses," NBC, 1952; "Omnibus: The Trial of
Mr. Pickwick," CBS, 1952; "G.E. Theatre: Best
Seller," CBS, 1953; "Suspense: Death in the
Passing Lane," CB$, 1953; "Medallion Theatre:
The Big Bow Mystery," CBS, 1953; "Schlitz
Playhouse of Stars: In the Pincers," CBS, 1953;
"Suspense: The Interruption," CBS, 1953;
"Climax!: No Stone Unturned," CBS, 1955; "The
Barretts of Wimpole Street," CBS, 1955; "Cameo
Theatre: The Inca of Jerusalem," NBC, 1955;
"Climax!: Dr. Jekyll and Mr. Hyde," CBS, 1955;
"TV Reader's Digest: The Archer-Shee Case,"
ABC, 1955; "Climax!: The Hanging Judge," CBS,
1956; "Four Star Playhouse: Tunnel of Fear,"
CBS, 1956; "Matinee Theatre: Mr. Krane," NBC,
1957; "Climax!: Strange Deaths at Burnleigh,"
CBS, 1957; "Alfred Hitchcock Presents: A Man
Greatly Beloved," CBS, 1957; "Du Pont Show of
the Month: The Prince and the Pauper," CBS,
1957; "Studio One: The Other Place," CBS, 1958;
"The Last Word," CBS, 1958; "The Red Skelton
Show," CBS, 1958; "The Jack Paar Show," NBC,
1958; "Invisible Fire," CBS, 1958; "Christophers:
Positive Values in Film Making," SYN, 1958;
"Christophers: Advertising the Ten Command-
ments," SYN, 1958; "Eye on New York," CBS,
1959; "Pontiac Star Parade: An Evening with
Perry Como," NBC, 1959; "The Ed Sullivan
Show," CBS, 1959; "The Last Word," CBS, 1959;
"A Tribute to Eleanor Roosevelt on Her Diamond
Jubilee," NBC, 1959; "The Man and the
Challenge: I've Killed Seven Men," NBC, 1959;
"U.S. Steel Hour: The Women of Hadley," CBS,
1960; "U.S. Steel Hour: Revolt in Hadley," CBS,
1960; "Frontiers of Faith: The Grandeur and
Misery of Man," NBC, 1960; "Our American
Heritage: Autocrat and Son," NBC, 1960; "This Is
Your Life," NBC, 1960; "The Red Skelton
Show," CBS, 1960; "Art Linkletter's House
Party," CBS, 1961; "The Breck Golden
Showcase: The Picture of Dorian Gray," CBS,
1961; "Burke's Law: Who Killed Holly
Howard?," ABC, 1963; "The Twilight Zone:
Uncle Simon," CBS, 1963; "The Outer Limits:
The Forms of Things Unknown," ABC, 1964;
"The Nurses: White on White," CBS, 1964.

HAREWOOD, DORIAN
b. *Dayton, OH, 1950.*
AS A REGULAR: "Strike Force," ABC, 1981-82;
"Trauma Center," ABC, 1983; "Glitter," ABC,
1984-85; "The Trial of Rosie O'Neill," CBS,
1990- .
AND: "Swiss Family Robinson: The Slave Ship,"
ABC, 1975; "Kojak: The Condemned," CBS,
1977; "Half 'n' Half," ABC, 1988; "The Magical
World of Disney: Polly," NBC, 1989.

TV MOVIES AND MINISERIES: "Foster and Laurie,"
CBS, 1975; "Roots: The Next Generations,"
ABC, 1979; "Beulah Land," NBC, 1980; "The
Ambush Murders," CBS, 1982; "Guilty of
Innocence: The Lenell Geter Story," CBS,
1987; "ABC Theatre: God Bless the Child,"
ABC, 1988; "Kiss Shot," CBS, 1989.

HARGITAY, MARISKA
b. *Los Angeles, CA, January 23, 1964.* Daughter
of Jayne Mansfield and Mickey Hargitay.
AS A REGULAR: "Downtown," CBS, 1986-87;
"Falcon Crest," CBS, 1988-90.
AND: "In the Heat of the Night: And Then You
Die," NBC, 1988; "Baywatch: Second Wave,"
NBC, 1989; "Wiseguy: The Romp," CBS, 1990.

HARMON, KELLY
b. *Burbank, CA, 1947.* Actress; daughter of
Tom Harmon.
AS A REGULAR: "The Bay City Blues," NBC,
1983.
AND: "The New Loretta Young Show: The
Rivalry," CBS, 1962; "Switch: The Girl on the
Golden Strip," CBS, 1976; "Switch: Death
Squad," CBS, 1976; "CHiPS: Drive, Lady,
Drive," NBC, 1979; "Nero Wolfe: To Catch a
Dead Man," NBC, 1981.

HARMON, KRISTIN
b. *Burbank, CA, 1949.* Actress who was
married to Rick Nelson for a time; sister of
Kelly and Mark Harmon.
AS A REGULAR: "The Adventures of Ozzie and
Harriet," ABC, 1964-66.
AND: "Adam 12: Something Worth Dying For,"
NBC, 1975.
TV MOVIES AND MINISERIES: "The Over-the-Hill
Gang," ABC, 1969.

HARMON, MARK
b. *Burbank, CA, September 2, 1951.* Hunky
actor who played Dr. Bobby Caldwell, who
died of AIDS on "St. Elsewhere"; he also
played Sam, long-lost love of Maddie Hayes
(Cybill Shepherd) on "Moonlighting." Brother
of Kelly and Kristin Harmon.
AS A REGULAR: "Sam," CBS, 1978; "240-Robert,"
ABC, 1979-80; "Flamingo Road," NBC, 1981-
82; "St. Elsewhere," NBC, 1983-86; "Moon-
lighting," ABC, 1987.
AND: "Emergency!: Daisy's Pick," NBC, 1975;
"Police Woman: No Place to Hide," NBC, 1975;
"The Love Boat: The Wedding," ABC, 1979;
"The Love Boat: Set-Up for Romance," ABC,
1983; "The Tonight Show Starring Johnny
Carson," NBC, 1986; "Saturday Night Live,"
NBC, 1987.
TV MOVIES AND MINISERIES: "Little Mo," NBC,
1978; "Centennial," NBC, 1978-79; "Flamingo

Road," NBC, 1980; "Intimate Agony," ABC, 1983; "Prince of Bel Air," ABC, 1986; "The Deliberate Stranger," NBC, 1986; "After the Promise," CBS, 1987; "Tennessee Williams' Sweet Bird of Youth," NBC, 1989.
* Harmon was *People* magazine's "Sexiest Man of 1986."

HARPER, DAVID W.
b. *Abilene, TX, October 4, 1961*. Actor who played Jim-Bob Walton.
AS A REGULAR: "The Waltons," CBS, 1972-81.
TV MOVIES AND MINISERIES: "The Homecoming," CBS, 1971; "A Day for Thanks on Waltons Mountain," NBC, 1982.

HARPER, JESSICA
b. *Chicago, IL, 1949*.
AS A REGULAR: "Little Women," NBC, 1979; "It's Garry Shandling's Show," SHO & FOX, 1989-90.
AND: "Tales From the Darkside: The Tear Collector," SYN, 1985; "The Equalizer: Nocturne," CBS, 1986; "Trying Times: Bedtime Story," PBS, 1988; "Wiseguy: Stairway to Heaven," CBS, 1989.
TV MOVIES AND MINISERIES: "Studs Lonigan," NBC, 1979; "When Dreams Come True," ABC, 1985.

HARPER, RON
b. *Turtle Creek, PA, January 12, 1935*. Generic actor of soaps and sitcoms.
AS A REGULAR: "87th Precinct," NBC, 1961-62; "Wendy & Me," ABC, 1964-65; "The Jean Arthur Show," CBS, 1966; "Garrison's Gorillas," ABC, 1967-68; "Where the Heart Is," CBS, 1969-73; "The Planet of the Apes," CBS, 1974; "Love of Life," CBS, 1977-80; "Another World," NBC, 1980; "Capitol," CBS, 1985-87.
AND: "Tales of Wells Fargo: All That Glitters," NBC, 1960; "Laramie: Duel at Parkison Town," NBC, 1960; "The Deputy: Duty Bound," NBC, 1961; "Love, American Style: Love and the Proposal," ABC, 1970; "Remington Steele: Cast in Steele," NBC, 1984.

HARPER, VALERIE
b. *Suffern, NY, August 22, 1940*. Comic actress with a New York edge whose Emmy-winning role as Rhoda Morgenstern on "The Mary Tyler Moore Show" led to her own show; her series choices since then have been less fortunate.
AS A REGULAR: "The Mary Tyler Moore Show," CBS, 1970-74; "Rhoda," CBS, 1974-78; "Valerie," NBC, 1986-87; "City," CBS, 1990.
AND: "Love, American Style: Love and the Housekeeper," ABC, 1971; "Story Theatre: The

Clever Peasant Lass," SYN, 1972; "Columbo: The Most Crucial Game," NBC, 1972; "The Trouble with People: Double Trouble," NBC, 1972; "The Shape of Things," CBS, 1973; "The Mary Tyler Moore Show: Mary Richards Falls in Love," CBS, 1975; "The Mary Tyler Moore Show: The Last Show," CBS, 1977; "John Denver and the Ladies," ABC, 1979; "The Merv Griffin Show," SYN, 1981; "The Love Boat: Egyptian Cruise," ABC, 1986.
TV MOVIES AND MINISERIES: "Thursday's Game," ABC, 1974; "Fun and Games," ABC, 1980; "The Shadow Box," ABC, 1980; "Don't Go to Sleep," ABC, 1982; "The Execution," NBC, 1985; "Strange Voices," NBC, 1987; "Drop-Out Mother," CBS, 1988; "The People Across the Lake," NBC, 1988.
* Harper walked off "Valerie" in 1987 in a pay dispute; the producers immediately wrote her out of the family sitcom by killing off her character and concentrating on the popular character of her son, played by Jason Bateman. Harper sued the show's producers for violating her contract and bad-mouthing her to the press; the suit was settled out of court.
* Emmies: 1971, 1972, 1973, 1975.

HARRELSON, WOODY
b. *Midland, TX*. Fresh-faced actor who plays Woody Boyd on "Cheers."
AS A REGULAR: "Cheers," NBC, 1985- .
AND: "Dear John: Love and Marriage," NBC, 1989; "Late Night with David Letterman," NBC, 1989; "Saturday Night Live," NBC, 1989.
TV MOVIES AND MINISERIES: "Bay Coven," NBC, 1987; "Killer Instinct," NBC, 1988.

HARRINGTON, AL
b. *Somoa*. Actor who played Det. Ben Kokua on "Hawaii Five-O."
AS A REGULAR: "Hawaii Five-O," CBS, 1972-74.
AND: "Hawaii Five-O: For a Million, Why Not?" CBS, 1971; "Magnum, P.I.: Thank Heaven for Little Girls-and Big Ones, Too," CBS, 1980.

HARRINGTON, PAT
b. *1901; d. 1965*. Vaudeville performer; father of Pat Jr.
AS A REGULAR: "A Couple of Joes," ABC, 1949-50; "The Wonderful John Action," NBC, 1953.
AND: "The Jack Paar Show," NBC, 1959; "The Chevy Show: O'Halloran's Luck," NBC, 1961.

HARRINGTON, PAT JR.
b. *New York City, NY, August 13, 1929*. Comic who began as a master of dialects and played Guido Panzini on "The Steve Allen Show" and "The Jack Paar Show"; he later won an Emmy as handyman Dwayne Schneider on "One Day at a Time."

AS A REGULAR: "The Steve Allen Show," NBC, 1956-59; SYN, 1968; "The Jack Paar Show," NBC, 1958-62; "Laugh Line," NBC, 1959; "The Danny Thomas Show," CBS, 1959-60; "The Steve Allen Plymouth Show," NBC, 1959-60; "The New Steve Allen Show," ABC, 1961; "Stump the Stars (Pantomime Quiz)," CBS, 1962-63; "Mr. Deeds Goes to Town," ABC, 1969-70; "Owen Marshall, Counselor at Law," ABC, 1971-74; "One Day at a Time," CBS, 1975-84; "Steve Allen's Laugh Back," SYN, 1976.

AND: "County Fair," NBC, 1959; "Pantomime Quiz," ABC, 1959; "Alfred Hitchcock Presents: I Can Take Care of Myself," CBS, 1960; "The Chevy Show: Kids Are Funny," NBC, 1961; "Candid Camera," CBS, 1961; "The Spike Jones Show," CBS, 1961; "Westinghouse Presents: The Sound of the Sixties," NBC, 1961; "Password," CBS, 1961; "Grindl: Grindl, Girl Wac," NBC, 1964; "Hootenanny," ABC, 1964; "The Munsters: Pike's Pique," CBS, 1964; "The Tennessee Ernie Ford Show," ABC, 1964; "Mr. Novak: There's a Penguin in My Garden," NBC, 1965; "The Man From UNCLE: The Bow-Wow Affair," NBC, 1965; "The Bing Crosby Show: The Image," ABC, 1965; "The Lucy Show: Lucy the Disc Jockey," CBS, 1965; "The Munsters: Mummy Munster," CBS, 1965; "The Littlest Hobo: Anniversary Guest," SYN, 1965; "The Man From UNCLE: The Hula Doll Affair," NBC, 1967; "Captain Nice: The Week They Stole Payday," NBC, 1967; "It Takes Two," NBC, 1969; "The Flying Nun: The Candid Commercial," ABC, 1970; "The Courtship of Eddie's Father: It's All Write with Me," ABC, 1972; "Love, American Style: Love and Other Mistakes," ABC, 1973; "The Rookies: Cry Wolf," ABC, 1973; "The Partridge Family: The Diplomat," ABC, 1973; "The Girl with Something Extra: John & Sally & Fred & Linda," NBC, 1973; "The New Adventures of Perry Mason: The Case of the Furious Father," CBS, 1973; "Tattletales," CBS, 1974; "Columbo: An Exercise in Fatality," NBC, 1974; "Kolchak, the Night Stalker: Primal Scream," ABC, 1975; "Police Story: To Steal a Million," NBC, 1975; "McMillan and Wife: Greed," NBC, 1975; "The Invisible Man: Go Directly to Jail," NBC, 1975; "Rhyme and Reason," ABC, 1975; "Ellery Queen: The Twelfth Floor Express," NBC, 1975; "Rhyme and Reason," ABC, 1976; "The Love Boat: The Oil Man Cometh," ABC, 1980; "The Love Boat: Dutch Treat," ABC, 1984; "Murder, She Wrote: Footnote to Murder," CBS, 1985; "Duet: Kiss and Break-up," FOX, 1989; "Ray Bradbury Theatre: A Miracle of Rare Device," USA, 1989; "Murder, She Wrote: Jack & Bill," CBS, 1989.

TV MOVIES AND MINISERIES: "Savage," NBC, 1973; "The Affair," ABC, 1973; "The Healers," NBC, 1974; "Let's Switch," ABC, 1975;

"Benny and Barney: Las Vegas Undercover," NBC, 1977; "The Critical List," NBC, 1978; "Between Two Brothers," CBS, 1982.
* Harrington was discovered by Jonathan Winters, who overheard him doing dialect bits.
* Emmies: 1984.

HARRIS, BARBARA
b. Sandra Markowitz, Evanston, IL, 1935. Comic actress of TV and films ("A Thousand Clowns," "Family Plot," "Nashville") who hasn't been well utilized by television.

AS A GUEST: "Alfred Hitchcock Presents: Beta Delta Gamma," NBC, 1961; "Naked City: Daughter, Am I in My Father's House?," ABC, 1962; "As Caesar Sees It," ABC, 1962; "Channing: No Wild Games for Sophie," ABC, 1963; "The Defenders: Claire Cheval Died in Boston," CBS, 1964; "The Jack Paar Program," NBC, 1964; "The Doctors and the Nurses: So Some Girls Play the Cello," CBS, 1964.

TV MOVIES AND MINISERIES: "Ghost of a Chance," CBS, 1987.

HARRIS, JONATHAN
b. New York City, NY, 1914. Actor best known as the cowardly Dr. Zachary Smith on "Lost in Space."

AS A REGULAR: "The Third Man," SYN, 1959-62; "The Bill Dana Show," NBC, 1963-65; "Lost in Space," CBS, 1965-68.

AND: "Shirley Temple's Storybook: Rumpelstiltskin," NBC, 1958; "Telephone Time: Man of Principle," ABC, 1958; "Schlitz Playhouse of Stars: The Kind Mr. Smith," CBS, 1958; "Colgate Theatre: Macreedy's Woman," NBC, 1958; "Climax!: The Big Success," CBS, 1958; "Kraft Mystery Theatre: The Man Who Didn't Fly," NBC, 1958; "G.E. Theatre: Blaze of Glory," CBS, 1958; "G.E. Theatre: The Cold Touch," CBS, 1958; "Shirley Temple's Storybook: The Reluctant Dragon," NBC, 1960; "The Law and Mr. Jones: Exit," ABC, 1961; "The Twilight Zone: Twenty-Two," CBS, 1961; "G.E. Theatre: The Small Elephants," CBS, 1961; "The Twilight Zone: The Silence," CBS, 1961; "The Adventures of Ozzie and Harriet: A Letter of Recommendation," ABC, 1964; "Bewitched: Samantha on the Keyboard," ABC, 1968; "Get Smart: How Green Was My Valet," CBS, 1970; "Bewitched: Paul Revere Rides Again," ABC, 1970; "Love, American Style: Love and the Millionaires," ABC, 1971; "Love, American Style: Love and the Check," ABC, 1972; "Sanford & Son: Pot Luck," NBC, 1973; "Cross Wits," SYN, 1975; "$weepstake$: Billy, Wally and Ludmilla, and Theodore," NBC, 1979; "Fantasy Island: The Winemaker," ABC, 1980.

TV MOVIES AND MINISERIES: "Once Upon a Dead Man," NBC, 1971.

HARRIS, JULIE

b. Julia Ann Harris, Grosse Pointe Park, MI, December 2, 1925. Actress with incandescent TV portrayals to her credit dating to the early fifties; best known to today's audiences for her performance as poet Emily Dickinson in "The Belle of Amherst" and as Lilimae Clements on "Knots Landing."

AS A REGULAR: "Thicker Than Water," ABC, 1973; "Salty," SYN, 1974-75; "The Family Holvak," NBC, 1975; "Knots Landing," CBS, 1981-87.

AND: "Starlight Theatre: Bernice Bobs Her Hair," CBS, 1951; "Goodyear TV Playhouse: October Story," NBC, 1951; "Goodyear TV Playhouse: The Happy Rest," NBC, 1953; "U.S. Steel Hour: A Wind From South," CBS, 1955; "Hallmark Hall of Fame: The Good Fairy," NBC, 1956; "Hallmark Hall of Fame: The Lark," NBC, 1957; "Hallmark Hall of Fame: Little Moon of Alban," NBC, 1958; "Hallmark Hall of Fame: Johnny Belinda," NBC, 1958; "Hallmark Hall of Fame: A Doll's House," NBC, 1959; "Du Pont Show of the Month: Ethan Frome," CBS, 1960; "Sunday Showcase: Turn the Key Deftly," NBC, 1960; "Family Classics: The Heiress," CBS, 1961; "Du Pont Show of the Month: The Night of the Storm," CBS, 1961; "Play of the Week: He Who Gets Slapped," SYN, 1961; "The Power and the Glory," CBS, 1961; "Hallmark Hall of Fame: Victoria Regina," NBC, 1961; "Hallmark Hall of Fame: Pygmalion," NBC, 1963; "Hallmark Hall of Fame: Little Moon of Alban," NBC, 1964; "Kraft Suspense Theatre: The Robrioz Ring," NBC, 1964; "Hamlet," CBS, 1964; "Hallmark Hall of Fame: The Holy Terror," NBC, 1965; "Rawhide: The Calf Woman," CBS, 1965; "Laredo: Rendezvous at Arille," NBC, 1965; "Bob Hope Chrysler: Nightmare," NBC, 1966; "Tarzan: The Perils of Charity Jones," NBC, 1967; "Hallmark Hall of Fame: Anastasia," NBC, 1967; "Garrison's Gorillas: Run From Death," ABC, 1968; "Tarzan: The Four O'Clock Army," NBC, 1968; "Hallmark Hall of Fame: Little Moon of Alban," NBC, 1968; "Bonanza: Dream to Dream," NBC, 1968; "Journey to the Unknown: The Indian Spirit Guide," ABC, 1968; "The Big Valley: A Stranger Everywhere," ABC, 1968; "The Name of the Game: The Bobby Currier Story," NBC, 1969; "The Name of the Game: So Long, Baby and Amen," NBC, 1970; "The Men From Shiloh: Wolf Track," NBC, 1971; "Medical Center: The Guilty," CBS, 1973; "Hawkins: Die, Darling, Die," CBS, 1973; "Columbo: Any Old Port in a Storm," NBC, 1973; "The Bob Newhart Show: Blues for Mr. Borden," CBS, 1973; "Match Game P.M.," SYN, 1975; "The Belle of Amherst," PBS, 1976; "Family Ties: The Freshman and the Senior," NBC, 1986.

TV MOVIES AND MINISERIES: "The House on Greenapple Road," ABC, 1970; "How Awful About Allan," ABC, 1970; "Home for the Holidays," ABC, 1972; "The Greatest Gift," NBC, 1974; "Victory at Entebbe," ABC, 1976; "Backstairs at the White House," NBC, 1979; "The Woman He Loved," CBS, 1988; "Single Women, Married Men," CBS, 1989.

* Emmies: 1959, 1962.

HARRIS, MEL

Attractive brunette actress who plays Hope Steadman on "thirtysomething."

AS A REGULAR: "thirtysomething," ABC, 1987- .

AND: "M*A*S*H: Cementing Relationships," CBS, 1980.

TV MOVIES AND MINISERIES: "Harry's Hong Kong," ABC, 1987; "Cross of Fire," NBC, 1989; "My Brother's Wife," ABC, 1989.

HARRIS, NEIL PATRICK

b. Albuquerque, NM, 1973. Teen heartthrob who plays Doogie Howser, M.D.

AS A REGULAR: "Doogie Howser, M.D.," ABC, 1989- .

TV MOVIES AND MINISERIES: "Hallmark Hall of Fame: Home Fires Burning," CBS, 1989; "Cold Sassy Tree," TNT, 1989.

HARRIS, PHIL

b. Linton, IN, June 24, 1906. Former bandleader whose persona as a lovable, easy-going singer and comic served him well through the heyday of the TV variety show.

AS A GUEST: "The George Gobel Show," NBC, 1956; "Saturday Spectacular: Manhattan Tower," NBC, 1956; "Lux Video Theatre: Movie Songs," NBC, 1956; "The Steve Allen Show," NBC, 1957; "Shower of Stars: Jack Benny's 40th Birthday Celebration," CBS, 1958; "Club Oasis," NBC, 1958; "The Steve Allen Show," NBC, 1958; "The Jack Benny Program," CBS, 1958; "The George Gobel Show," NBC, 1958; "Dean Martin Special," NBC, 1958; "Phil Harris Special," NBC, 1959; "Perry Como's Kraft Music Hall," NBC, 1959; "The Betty Hutton Show: Rock 'n' Roll," CBS, 1960; "Steve Allen Plymouth Show," NBC, 1960; "Jackie Gleason Special: The Big Sell," CBS, 1960; "Bob Hope Buick Show," NBC, 1961; "The Red Skelton Hour," CBS, 1962; "Ben Casey: The Only Place They Know My Name," ABC, 1964; "The Tonight Show Starring Johnny Carson," NBC, 1964; "TheAndy Williams Show," NBC, 1964; "Burke's Law: Who Killed Vaudeville?," ABC, 1964; "Hollywood Palace," ABC, 1964; "Hollywood Palace," ABC, 1965; "The Bing Crosby Show: One for the Birds," ABC, 1965; "The Andy Williams Show," NBC, 1965;

"ABC Stage '67: The People Trap," ABC, 1966; "The Dean Martin Show," NBC, 1967; "Hollywood Palace," ABC, 1967; "F Troop: Where Were You at the Last Massacre?," ABC, 1967; "The Lucy Show: Lucy and Phil Harris," CBS, 1968; "Kraft Music Hall," NBC, 1969; "This Is Tom Jones," ABC, 1970; "Here's Lucy: Lucy and Phil Harris Strike Up the Band," CBS, 1974; "The Love Boat: You Gotta Have Heart," ABC, 1980; "Concrete Cowboys: Pilot," CBS, 1981.

HARRIS, ROSEMARY
b. Ashby, England, September 19, 1930.
AS A REGULAR: "The Chisholms," CBS, 1979-80.
AND: "Studio One: The Great Lady," CBS, 1952; "The Doctor: The World of Nancy Clark," NBC, 1953; "Alfred Hitchcock Presents: I Killed the Count," CBS, 1957; "Alfred Hitchcock Presents: The Glass Eye," CBS, 1957; "Du Pont Show of the Month: The Prince and the Pauper," CBS, 1957; "Hallmark Hall of Fame: Twelfth Night," NBC, 1957; "Suspicion: Lord Arthur Saville's Crime," NBC, 1958; "Omnibus: Moment of Truth," NBC, 1958; "Du Pont Show of the Month: A Tale of Two Cities," CBS, 1958; "Hallmark Hall of Fame: Dial M for Murder," NBC, 1958; "Du Pont Show of the Month: Wuthering Heights," CBS, 1958; "Play of the Week: The Enchanted," SYN, 1961; "A Dickens Chronicle," CBS, 1963; "Profiles in Courage: The Mary S. McDowell Story," NBC, 1964; "New York Television Theatre: Eh, Joe?," NET, 1966; "Hallmark Hall of Fame: Blithe Spirit," NBC, 1966; "NET Playhouse: Uncle Vanya," NET, 1967; "CBS Playhouse: Dear Friends," CBS, 1967.
TV MOVIES AND MINISERIES: "Holocaust," NBC, 1978; "Masterpiece Theatre: Notorious Woman," PBS, 1975-76; "The Chisholms," CBS, 1979.
* Emmies: 1976.

HARRIS, GEORGE
b. Liverpool, England, February 25, 1943.
AS A GUEST:"Saturday Night Live," NBC, 1976.
* See also The Beatles.

HARRISON, GREGORY
b. Catalina Island, CA, May 31, 1950. Hunky TV actor of the seventies and eighties, best known as crazy-but-caring Dr. "Gonzo" Gates on "Trapper John, M.D."
AS A REGULAR: "Logan's Run," CBS, 1977-78; "Trapper John, M.D.," CBS, 1979-86; "Falcon Crest," CBS, 1989-90; "The Family Man," CBS, 1990- .
AND: "M*A*S*H: The Nurses," CBS, 1976; "The Gregory Harrison Show," CBS, 1989; "The Pat Sajak Show," CBS, 1989.

TV MOVIES AND MINISERIES: "Centennial," NBC, 1978-79; "The Fighter," CBS, 1983; "Seduced," CBS, 1985; "Oceans of Fire," CBS, 1986; "Fresno," CBS, 1986; "Hot Paint," CBS, 1988; "Red River," CBS, 1988.

HARRISON, JENILEE
b. Glendale, CA, June 12, 1959. Actress who played Cindy Snow on "Three's Company" and Jamie Ewing on "Dallas."
AS A REGULAR: "Three's Company," ABC, 1980-82; "Dallas," CBS, 1984-86.
AND: "Fantasy Island Natchez Bound," ABC, 1982; "The Love Boat: Here Comes the Bride, Maybe," ABC, 1983; "The Love Boat: Baby Makers," ABC, 1984; "Simon & Simon: Just Because I'm Paranoid," CBS, 1986; "Murder, She Wrote: The Way to Dusty Death," CBS, 1987; "The New Mike Hammer: Lady Killer," CBS, 1987.
TV MOVIES AND MINISERIES: "Malibu," ABC, 1983.

HARRISON, NOEL
b. London, England, January 29, 1936. Son of Rex; he played Mark Slate, sidekick of April Dancer (Stefanie Powers), the girl from UNCLE.
AS A REGULAR: "The Girl From UNCLE," NBC, 1966-67.
AND: "The Ed Sullivan Show," CBS, 1960; "The Man From UNCLE: The Galatea Affair," NBC, 1966; "The Andy Williams Show," NBC, 1967; "Snap Judgment," NBC, 1967; "The Legend of Robin Hood," NBC, 1968; "This Morning," ABC, 1968; "It Takes a Thief: A Case of Red Turnips," ABC, 1968; "The Joey Bishop Show," ABC, 1968; "The Steve Allen Show," SYN, 1968; "The Jerry Lewis Show," NBC, 1968; "Funny You Should Ask," ABC, 1969; "The Spring Thing," NBC, 1969; "Jimmy Durante Presents the Lennon Sisters Hour," ABC, 1969; "Love, American Style: Love and the Burglar," ABC, 1969; "Mission: Impossible: The Falcon," CBS, 1970; "The Mod Squad: A Town Called Sincere," ABC, 1970; "The Name of the Game: The King of Denmark," NBC, 1970; "Call Holme," NBC, 1972; "Ironside: The Deadly Gamesman," NBC, 1972; "The Love Boat: Two Tails of a City," ABC, 1984; "Kate & Allie: Author, Author," CBS, 1985; "Gideon Oliver: Tongs," ABC, 1989.

HARRISON, REX
b. Reginald Carey, Huyton, England, March 5, 1908; d. 1990. Actor and musical comedy performer ("My Fair Lady") usually in charming roles.
AS A GUEST:"Tele-Theatre: The Walking Stick," NBC, 1950; "U.S. Steel Hour: The Man in Possesion," ABC, 1953; "Du Pont Show of the Month: Crescendo," CBS, 1957; "The Fabulous Fifties," CBS, 1960; "Startime: Dear

Arthur," NBC, 1960; "Dow Hour of Great Mysteries: The Datchet Diamonds," NBC, 1960; "Short Stories of Love," NBC, 1974.

TV MOVIES AND MINISERIES: "The Adventures of Don Quixote," CBS, 1973; "Anastasia: The Mystery of Anna," NBC, 1986.

HARROLD, KATHRYN

b. Tazewell, VA, August 2, 1950. Sexy actress who played teacher Sara Newhouse on "The Bronx Zoo"; she also played Lauren Bacall in a TV movie about Humphrey Bogart.

AS A REGULAR: "The Doctors," NBC, 1976-78; "MacGruder and Loud," ABC, 1985; "The Bronx Zoo," NBC, 1987-88.

AND: "The Rockford Files: Black Mirror," NBC, 1978; "The Rockford Files: Love Is the Word," NBC, 1979.

TV MOVIES AND MINISERIES: "Son Rise: A Miracle of Love," NBC, 1979; "Vampire," ABC, 1979; "Bogie," CBS, 1980; "An Uncommon Love," CBS, 1983; "Man Against the Mob," NBC, 1988.

HARRY, JACKEE—See Jackee.

HART, DOLORES

b. Dolores Hicks, Chicago, IL, 1938. Attractive young actress of films ("Where the Boys Are") who left show business in 1963 to become a nun.

AS A GUEST: "Alfred Hitchcock Presents: Silent Witness," CBS, 1957; "The Steve Allen Show," NBC, 1958; "Schlitz Playhouse of Stars: Man on a Rack," CBS, 1958; "Christophers: Some Christopher Ideas," SYN, 1959; "Christophers: The Story Behind the Star-Spangled Banner," SYN, 1959; "The du Pont Show with June Allyson: The Crossing," CBS, 1960; "Playhouse 90: To the Sound of Trumpets," CBS, 1960; "Christophers: The Unique Position of the Teenager," SYN, 1960; "Here's Hollywood," NBC, 1961; "The Virginian: The Mountain of the Sun," NBC, 1963.

HART, DOROTHY

b. Cleveland, Oh, 1923.

AS A REGULAR: "Take a Guess," CBS, 1953; "Pantomime Quiz," CBS, 1953; DUM, 1953-54; CBS, 1954; ABC, 1955; CBS, 1955; CBS, 1956; CBS, 1957; ABC, 1958.

HART, JOHN

b. Los Angeles, CA, 1921.

AS A REGULAR: "The Lone Ranger," SYN, 1952-54; "Hawkeye and the Last of the Mohicans," SYN, 1957.

AND: "I Love Lucy: Lucy Changes Her Mind," CBS, 1953; "I Love Lucy: The Hedda Hopper Story," CBS, 1955; "I Love Lucy: Don Juan Is Shelved," CBS, 1955; "Leave It to Beaver: Lonesome Beaver," ABC, 1958; "Leave It to Beaver: Beaver Plays Hookey," ABC, 1959; "National Velvet: The Fall," NBC, 1961; "Rawhide: Lost Tribe," CBS, 1961; "Father of the Bride: The Boys Go Fishing," CBS, 1961; "Rawhide: The Captain's Wife," CBS, 1962; "Leave It to Beaver: A Night in the Woods," ABC, 1962; "Daktari: The Hostages," CBS, 1966.

HART, MARY

b. Sioux Falls, SD, 1950. TV personality.

AS A REGULAR: "Entertainment Tonight," SYN, 1982- .

AND: "Candid Camera Christmas Special," CBS, 1987.

HART, MOSS

b. New York City, NY, October 24, 1904; d. 1961. Playwright who collaborated with George S. Kaufman on such works as "You Can't Take It with You" and "The Man Who Came to Dinner," and enough of a ham to make a few TV appearances.

AS A REGULAR: "Answer Yes or No," NBC, 1950.

AND: "What's My Line?," CBS, 1959.

HART, RICHARD

b. 1915; d. 1951.

AS A REGULAR: "Ellery Queen," ABC, 1950-51.

AND: "Masterpiece Playhouse: Hedda Gabler," NBC, 1950; "Studio One: The Passionate Pilgrim," CBS, 1950.

HARTFORD, JOHN

b. New York City, NY, December 30, 1937. Singer-songwriter.

AS A REGULAR: "Summer Smothers Brothers Show," CBS, 1968; "The Smothers Brothers Comedy Hour," CBS, 1968-69.

AND: "The Glen Campbell Goodtime Hour," CBS, 1970; "The Glen Campbell Goodtime Hour," CBS, 1971; "The Smothers Brothers Comedy Hour," CBS, 1989.

HARTLEY, MARIETTE

b. New York City, NY, June 21, 1940. Blonde actress who didn't really become a household name until she started doing Polaroid commercials opposite James Garner in the seventies; she won an Emmy as the Incredible Hulk's wife.

AS A REGULAR: "Peyton Place," ABC, 1965; "The Hero," NBC, 1966-67; "Goodnight, Beantown," CBS, 1983-84; "WIOU," CBS, 1990- .

AND: "Stoney Burke: Bandwagon," ABC, 1962; "Gunsmoke: Clarey Cotter," CBS, 1963; "The Twilight Zone: The Long Morrow," CBS, 1964;

"The Breaking Point: No Squares in My Family Circle," ABC, 1964; "The Virginian: The Drifter," NBC, 1964; "The Virginian: Felicity's Spring," NBC, 1964; "My Three Sons: Dublin's Fair City," ABC, 1964; "The FBI: The Impersonator," ABC, 1970; "Gunsmoke: Phoenix," CBS, 1971; "Marcus Welby, M.D.: To Carry the Sun in a Golden Cup," ABC, 1971; "Bonanza: The Iron Butterfly," NBC, 1971; "Mannix: Death Is the Fifth Gear," CBS, 1972; "Love, American Style: Love and the Fighting Couple," ABC, 1972; "The FBI: The Double Play," ABC, 1973; "The Bob Newhart Show: Have You Met Miss Dietz?," CBS, 1973; "Gunsmoke: The Iron Blood of Courage," CBS, 1974; "The Streets of San Francisco: Shield of Honor," ABC, 1974; "The Streets of San Francisco: Cry Help," ABC, 1974; "Barnaby Jones: Image in a Cracked Mirror," CBS, 1974; "Barnaby Jones: Mystery Cycle," CBS, 1974; "Columbo: Publish or Perish," NBC, 1974; "McCloud: Lady on the Run," NBC, 1975; "Little House on the Prairie: The Gift," NBC, 1976; "The Quest: Shanklin," NBC, 1976; "Kingston: Confidential: Shadow Games," NBC, 1977; "Columbo: Try and Catch Me," NBC, 1977; "The Incredible Hulk: Married," CBS, 1978; "M*A*S*H: Inga," CBS, 1979; "The Rockford Files: Trouble in Paradise Cove," NBC, 1979; "The John Davidson Show," SYN, 1980; "The Love Boat: The Captain and the Geisha," ABC, 1983; "Hollywood Squares," SYN, 1988.
TV MOVIES AND MINISERIES: "Earth II," ABC, 1971; "Sandcastles," CBS, 1972; "Genisis II," ABC, 1973; "The Killer Who Wouldn't Die," ABC, 1976; "The Last Hurrah," NBC, 1977; "The Love Tapes," ABC, 1980; "No Place to Hide," CBS, 1981; "Dropout Father," CBS, 1982; "M.A.D.D.: Mothers Against Drunk Driving," NBC, 1983; "Silence of the Heart," CBS, 1984; "My Two Loves," ABC, 1986; "One Terrific Guy," CBS, 1986; "Passion and Paradise," ABC, 1989.
* Emmies: 1979.

HARTMAN, DAVID

b. David Downs Hartman, Pawtucket, RI, May 19, 1935. Nondescript actor who found success as the host of "Good Morning, America," further blurring the line between entertainment and information on television.
AS A REGULAR: "The Virginian," NBC, 1968-69; "The New Doctors," NBC, 1969-73; "Lucas Tanner," NBC, 1974-75; "Good Morning, America," ABC, 1976-85.
AND: "The Virginian: The Masquerade," NBC, 1967; "Marcus Welby, M.D.: Daisy in the Shadow," ABC, 1970; "The Name of the Game: The Men Who Killed a Ghost," NBC, 1971; "Owen Marshall, Counselor at Law: House of Friends," ABC, 1974; "Early Warning," FOX, 1989.

TV MOVIES AND MINISERIES: "San Francisco International," NBC, 1970; "The Feminist and the Fuzz," ABC, 1971; "I Love a Mystery," NBC, 1973; "You'll Never See Me Again," ABC, 1973; "Miracle on 34th Street," CBS, 1973; "Lucas Tanner," NBC, 1974.

HARTMAN, ELIZABETH

b. Youngstown, OH, December 23, 1941; d. 1987. Actress of film ("A Patch of Blue") and some TV.
AS A GUEST: "Night Gallery: The Dark Boy," NBC, 1971; "Wide World of Mystery: A Little Bit Like Murder," ABC, 1975; "Doctors Hospital: Come at Last to Love," NBC, 1975.

HARTMAN, LISA

b. Houston, TX, June 1, 1956. Yet another soap opera goddess; she played Ciji on "Knots Landing" and was so popular that after her character was killed off, she returned to the same soap as Cathy Geary Rush.
AS A REGULAR: "Tabitha," ABC, 1977-78; "Knots Landing," CBS, 1982-83, 1983-86; "High Performance," ABC, 1983.
AND: "Police Woman: Night of the Full Moon," NBC, 1977; "The Love Boat: Reunion Cruise," ABC, 1979; "Fantasy Island Magnolia Blossoms," ABC, 1979; "The Love Boat: The Wedding," ABC, 1979; "Matlock: The Ambassador," NBC, 1988.
TV MOVIES AND MINISERIES: "Where the Ladies Go," ABC, 1980; "The Great American Traffic Jam," NBC, 1980; "Beverly Hills Cowgirl Blues," CBS, 1985; "Roses Are for the Rich," CBS, 1987; "Full Exposure: The Sex Tapes Scandal," NBC, 1989.

HARTMAN, PAUL

b. San Francisco, CA, March 1, 1904; d. 1973. Former vaudeville hoofer with extensive TV credits, best known as fix-it man Emmett Clark on "The Andy Griffith Show" and "Mayberry RFD."
AS A REGULAR: "The Hartmans," NBC, 1949; "The Pride of the Family," ABC, 1953-54; "The Paul Hartman Show," CBS, 1955; "Our Man Higgins," ABC, 1962-63; "The Andy Griffith Show," CBS, 1967-68; "Petticoat Junction," CBS, 1968-69; "Mayberry RFD," CBS, 1968-71.
AND: "Faith Baldwin Playhouse: Henry's Harem," ABC, 1951; "Studio One: The Hero," CBS, 1951; "Gulf Playhouse: The Trial of Charley Christmas," NBC, 1952; "Studio One: Twelve Angry Men," CBS, 1954; "Producers Showcase: Petrified Forest," NBC, 1955; "Producers Showcase: Our Town," NBC, 1955; "Goodyear TV Playhouse: The Expendable House," NBC, 1955; "Playwrights '56: The Heart's a Forgotten

Hotel," NBC, 1955; "Studio One: My Son Johnny," CBS, 1956; "Kraft Television Theatre: Good Old Charlie Fay," NBC, 1956; "Ellery Queen: The Paper Tiger," NBC, 1959; "Alfred Hitchcock Presents: Not the Running Type," CBS, 1960; "Startime: Incident at a Corner," NBC, 1960; "The Outlaws: Ballad for a Badman," NBC, 1960; "Peter Loves Mary: High Society," NBC, 1960; "Thriller: Girl with a Secret," NBC, 1960; "Naked City: Bullets Cost Too Much," ABC, 1961; "The Twilight Zone: Back There," CBS, 1961; "Hallmark Hall of Fame: Time Remembered," NBC, 1961; "Bell Telephone Hour: The Signs of Spring," NBC, 1961; "Alfred Hitchcock Presents: Gratitude," NBC, 1961; "The Shari Lewis Show," NBC, 1961; "Checkmate: The Thrill Seeker," CBS, 1961; "Naked City: The Day the Island Almost Sank," ABC, 1961; "The Defenders: Along Came a Spider," CBS, 1962; "The Lucy Show: Lucy Is a Soda Jerk," CBS, 1963; "The Alfred Hitchcock Hour: Death of a Cop," CBS, 1963; "The Farmer's Daughter: The Speechmaker," ABC, 1963; "The Greatest Show on Earth: Leaves in the Wind," ABC, 1963; "The Alfred Hitchcock Hour: The Magic Shop," CBS, 1964; "Hazel: George's Man Friday," NBC, 1965; "For the People: ... guilt shall not escape nor innocence suffer ...," CBS, 1965; "The Bing Crosby Show: The Test," ABC, 1965; "The Adventures of Ozzie and Harriet: Ghost Town," ABC, 1965; "The Legend of Jesse James: A Real Tough Town," ABC, 1966; "The John Forsythe Show: The Cupid Caper," NBC, 1966; "Family Affair: The Gift Horse," CBS, 1966; "Bob Hope Chrysler Theatre: To Sleep, Perchance to Scream," NBC, 1967; "Petticoat Junction: Girl of Our Dreams," CBS, 1968; "Petticoat Junction: Bad Day at Shady Rest," CBS, 1968; "Love, American Style: Love and the Doorknob," ABC, 1969; "Of Thee I Sing," CBS, 1972.
TV MOVIES AND MINISERIES: "Getting Away From It All," ABC, 1972.

HARTMAN, PHIL
b. Canada. Comic actor and writer.
AS A REGULAR: "Our Time," NBC, 1985; "Saturday Night Live," NBC, 1986- .

HARTY, PATRICIA
b. Washington, D.C., November 5, 1941. Blonde starlet of the sixties; in the seventies she used the name Trisha Hart for a time.
AS A REGULAR: "Search for Tomorrow," CBS, 1964-65; "Occassional Wife," NBC, 1966-67; "Blondie," CBS, 1968-69; "The Bob Crane Show," NBC, 1975; "Herbie, the Love Bug," CBS, 1982.
AND: The FBI: The Messenger," ABC, 1968; "Love, American Style: Love and the Pickup," ABC, 1971; "Alias Smith and Jones: Six Strangers at Apache Springs," ABC, 1972;

"Medical Center: A Game for One Player," CBS, 1972; "The Odd Couple: That Was No Lady," ABC, 1973; "Hardcastle and McCormick: The Day the Music Died," ABC, 1986; "Wiseguy: The Four Letter Word," CBS, 1989.
TV MOVIES AND MINISERIES: "What Are Best Friends For?," ABC, 1973; "The Stranger Who Looks Like Me," ABC, 1974.

HARVEY, LAURENCE
b. Larushka Skikne, Joniskis, Lithuania, 1928; d. 1973. Actor in British and American films ("Room at the Top," "The Manchurian Candidate") and a bit of TV.
AS A GUEST: "Alcoa Hour: The Small Servant," NBC, 1955; "The Jack Paar Show," NBC, 1959; "Alfred Hitchcock Presents: Arthur," CBS, 1959; "I've Got a Secret," CBS, 1960; "Here's Hollywood," NBC, 1960; "The Spirit of the Alamo," ABC, 1960; "The Dinah Shore Chevy Show," NBC, 1961; "The Milton Berle Show," NBC, 1962; "Festival of the Arts: A Month in the Country," NET, 1962; "The Ed Sullivan Show," CBS, 1964; "Dial M for Murder," ABC, 1967; "Night Gallery: The Caterpillar," NBC, 1972; "Columbo: The Most Dangerous Match," NBC, 1973.

HASKELL, PETER
b. Boston, MA, October 15, 1934. Leading man who played Hollis Kirkland on "Ryan's Hope" and Lloyd Kendall on "Search for Tomorrow."
AS A REGULAR: "Bracken's World," NBC, 1969-70; "Rich Man, Poor Man—Book II," ABC, 1976-77; "Ryan's Hope," ABC, 1982-83; "Search for Tomorrow," NBC, 1983-85; "Rituals," SYN, 1985; "The Law and Harry McGraw," CBS, 1987-88.
AND: "The Outer Limits: Wolf 359," ABC, 1964; "Dr. Kildare: Please Let My Baby Live," NBC, 1965; "Ben Casey: A Rambling Discourse on Egyptian Water Clocks," ABC, 1965; "Combat!: Hear No Evil," ABC, 1965; "Rawhide: Incident at Boot Hill," CBS, 1965; "The Man From UNCLE: The Mad, Mad Tea Party Affair," NBC, 1965; "Ben Casey: 26 Ways to Spell Heartbreak: A, B, C, D... ," ABC, 1966; "Ben Casey: Pull the Wool Over Your Eyes, Here Comes the Cold Wind of Truth," ABC, 1966; "Combat!: A Child's Game," ABC, 1966; "Combat!: Jonah," ABC, 1967; "The Green Hornet: Programmed for Death," ABC, 1967; "Mannix: License to Kill," CBS, 1968; "Garrison's Gorillas: Time Bomb," ABC, 1968; "Mannix: To the Swiftest Death," CBS, 1968; "Judd for the Defense: The Sound of the Plastic Axe," ABC, 1968; "The Big Valley: The Prize," ABC, 1968; "The FBI: Three Way Split," ABC, 1971; "McCloud: Encounter with Aries," NBC, 1971; "The Mary Tyler Moore Show: What Is Mary Richards Really Like?," CBS, 1972; "Mission: Impossible: TOD-5," CBS, 1972;

"Medical Center: The Fallen," CBS, 1972; "Hallmark Hall of Fame: The Man Who Came to Dinner," NBC, 1972; "Hawaii Five-O: The Flip Side Is Death," CBS, 1973; "Barnaby Jones: Twenty Million Alibis," CBS, 1973; "The FBI: Selkirk's War," ABC, 1974; "Cannon: Blood Money," CBS, 1974; "Medical Center: Hexed," CBS, 1974; "Amy Prentiss: Baptism of Fire," NBC, 1974; "Medical Center: The Hostile Heart," CBS, 1974; "The Streets of San Francisco: River of Fear," ABC, 1974; "Medical Center: No Hiding Place," CBS, 1975; "Barnaby Jones: The Lonely Victims," CBS, 1976; "Risko," CBS, 1976; "Charlie's Angels: Angel in Love," ABC, 1977; "B.J. and the Bear: Run for the Money," NBC, 1979; "Vega$: Dan Tanna Is Dead," ABC, 1979; "Barnaby Jones: Killer Without a Name," CBS, 1980; "The A-Team: The Heart of Rock and Roll," NBC, 1985; "The Golden Girls: Adult Education," NBC, 1986; "MacGyver: The Human Factor," ABC, 1986; "Murder, She Wrote: Truck Stop," CBS, 1989; "Christine Cromwell: Easy Come, Easy Go," ABC, 1989.
TV MOVIES AND MINISERIES: "Love, Hate, Love," ABC, 1971; "The Eyes of Charles Sand," ABC, 1972; "Suicide Club," ABC, 1973; "The Phantom of Hollywood," CBS, 1974; "The Night They Took Miss Beautiful," NBC, 1977; "The Jordan Chance," CBS, 1978; "Mandrake," NBC, 1979; "The Cracker Factory," ABC, 1979; "Stunt Seven," CBS, 1979.

HASSELHOFF, DAVID

b. Baltimore, MD, July 17, 1952. TV hunk in TV junk; he played Snapper Foster on "The Young and the Restless."
AS A REGULAR: "The Young and the Restless," CBS, 1975-82; "Semi-Tough," ABC, 1980; "Knight Rider," NBC, 1982-86; "Baywatch," NBC, 1989-90.
AND: "The Love Boat: September Song," ABC, 1980; "The Love Boat: Humpty Dumpty," ABC, 1981; "Diff'rent Strokes: Hooray for Hollywood," NBC, 1984; "The Pat Sajak Show," CBS, 1989;
TV MOVIES AND MINISERIES: "Pleasure Cove," NBC, 1979; "The Cartier Affair," NBC, 1984; "Bridge Across Time," NBC, 1985; "Perry Mason: The Case of the Lady in the Lake," NBC, 1988; "Baywatch: Panic at Malibu Pier," NBC, 1989.

HASTINGS, BOB

b. Brooklyn, NY, April 18, 1925. Actor usually in comic roles; best known as apple-polishing Lt. Elroy Carpenter on "McHale's Navy" and as bar owner Tommy Kelsey on "All in the Family"; currently he's Capt. Ramsey on "General Hospital."
AS A REGULAR: "Kitty Foyle," NBC, 1958; "McHale's Navy," ABC, 1962-66; "All in the Family," CBS, 1973-77; "Dealer's Choice,"

SYN, 1973-75; "General Hospital," ABC, 1979- .
AND: "The Phil Silvers Show: The Transfer," CBS, 1956; "The Phil Silvers Show: Bilko's Perfect Day," CBS, 1957; "Hennesey: Space Man," CBS, 1960; "The Donna Reed Show: The First Time We Met," ABC, 1960; "The Real McCoys: How to Paint a House," ABC, 1960; "Hennesey: The Promotion," CBS, 1961; "The Tom Ewell Show: No Fun in the Sun," CBS, 1961; "Peter Loves Mary: The Perfect Father," NBC, 1961; "Pete and Gladys: Lover, Go Away," CBS, 1961; "The Tall Man: Substitute Sheriff," NBC, 1962; "Pete and Gladys: Garden Wedding," CBS, 1962; "The Gertrude Berg Show: High Finance," CBS, 1962; "Room for One More: A New Twist," ABC, 1962; "Dennis the Menace: The Private Eye," CBS, 1962; "Mr. Ed: Ed and the Secret Service," CBS, 1963; "The Twilight Zone: I Dream of Genie," CBS, 1963; "Batman: Penguin Is a Girl's Best Friend/Penguin Sets a Trend/Penguin's Disastrous End," ABC, 1967; "Green Acres: Not Guilty," CBS, 1968; "I Dream of Jeannie: The Used Car Salesman," NBC, 1968; "The Flying Nun: The Boyfriend," ABC, 1969; "Green Acres: Charlie, Homer and Natasha," CBS, 1970; "Love, American Style: Love and the Duel," ABC, 1971; "Ironside: Murder Impromptu," NBC, 1971; "Nanny and the Professor: Aunt Henrietta's Premonition," ABC, 1971; "All in the Family: The Man in the Street," CBS, 1971; "Love, American Style: Love and the Big Surprise," ABC, 1971; "Room 222: Just Call Me Mr. Shigematsu," ABC, 1972; "The Odd Couple: Myrna's Debut," ABC, 1973; "Marcus Welby, M.D.: The Faith of Childish Things," ABC, 1974; "The Manhunter: The Baby Faced Killers," CBS, 1974; "Ironside: Act of Vengeance," NBC, 1974; "The Streets of San Francisco: School of Fear," ABC, 1975; "The Rockford Files: The Great Blue Lake Land and Development Company," NBC, 1975; "The Rockford Files: The Trees, the Bees and T.T. Flowers," NBC, 1977; "The Streets of San Francisco: One Last Trick," ABC, 1977; "Alice: The Last Stow It," CBS, 1979; "Three's Company: The Love Barge," ABC, 1979; "Lou Grant: Guns," CBS, 1980.
TV MOVIES AND MINISERIES: "Any Second Now," NBC, 1969; "Ellery Queen: Don't Look Behind You," NBC, 1971; "A Very Missing Person," NBC, 1972; "Trapped," ABC, 1973; "The Million Dollar Rip-Off," NBC, 1976.

HASTINGS, DON

b. Brooklyn, NY, April 1, 1934. Actor who's played Dr. Bob Hughes on "As the World Turns" for over three decades.
AS A REGULAR: "Captain Video and His Video Rangers," DUM, 1949-55; "The Edge of Night," CBS, 1956-60; "As the World Turns," CBS, 1960- .

HATCH, RICHARD

b. Santa Monica, CA, May 21, 1947.

AS A REGULAR: "All My Children," ABC, 1970-72; "The Streets of San Francisco," ABC, 1976-77; "Mary Hartman, Mary Hartman," SYN, 1977-78; "Battlestar Galactica," ABC, 1978-79; "Santa Barbara," NBC, 1990.

AND: "Room 222: The Quitter," ABC, 1972; "The Rookies: Lots of Trees and a Running Stream," ABC, 1973; "Medical Center: Three on a Tightrope," CBS, 1974; "Hawaii Five-O: Study in Rage," CBS, 1975; "Hawaii Five-O: The Waterfront Stealing," CBS, 1975; "The Rookies: A Deadly Image," ABC, 1975; "The Merv Griffin Show," SYN, 1976; "The Mike Douglas Show," SYN, 1977; "What Really Happened to the Class of '65?: Mr. Potential," NBC, 1978; "The Toni Tennille Show," SYN, 1981; "The Love Boat: Too Many Dads," ABC, 1982; "Hotel: Blackout," ABC, 1983; "Murder, She Wrote: Deadly Lady," CBS, 1984; "MacGruder and Loud: For Better, for Less," ABC, 1985; "Riptide: Wipeout," NBC, 1985; "The Love Boat: The Perfect Arrangement," ABC, 1985; "Blacke's Magic: It's a Jungle Out There," NBC, 1986.

TV MOVIES AND MINISERIES: "Crime Club," CBS, 1973; "F. Scott Fitzgerald and the Last of the Belles," ABC, 1974; "The Hatfields and the McCoys," ABC, 1975; "The Hustler of Muscle Beach," ABC, 1980.

HATFIELD, HURD

b. New York City, NY, 1918. Distinguished-looking stage actor who's done occasional films and lots of TV.

AS A GUEST: "Masterpiece Playhouse: The Rivals," NBC, 1950; "Masterpiece Playhouse: The Importance of Being Ernest," NBC, 1950; "Story Theatre: Mademoiselle Fifi," SYN, 1950; "The Web: Tiger in the Closet," CBS, 1952; "Studio One: The Nativity Play," CBS, 1952; "Summer Studio One: Greed," CBS, 1953; "Broadway Television Theatre: Seventh Heaven," SYN, 1953; "Broadway Television Theatre: The Hasty Heart," SYN, 1953; "Suspense: The Pistol Shot," CBS, 1954; "Robert Montgomery Presents: The Hunchback of Notre Dame," NBC, 1954; "Kraft Television Theatre: The King's Bounty," NBC, 1955; "Armstrong Circle Theatre: I Was Accused," NBC, 1955; "Climax!: The Hanging Judge," CBS, 1956; "Alfred Hitchcock Presents: The Perfect Murder," CBS, 1956; "The Millionaire: The Eric Vincent Story," CBS, 1956; "Hallmark Hall of Fame: Lamp at Midnight," NBC, 1956; "Climax!: The Fog," CBS, 1956; "Alfred Hitchcock Presents: None Are So Blind," CBS, 1956; "Armstrong Circle Theatre: The Trial of Poznan," NBC, 1957; "Du Pont Show of the Month: The Prince and the Pauper," NBC, 1957; "Du Pont Show of the Month: Beyond This Place," CBS, 1957; "Playhouse 90: The Last Man," CBS, 1958; "Climax!: Cabin B-13," CBS, 1958; "Du Pont Show of the Month: The Count of Monte Cristo," CBS, 1958; "Arthur Murray Party," NBC, 1958; "Lux Playhouse: Various Temptations," CBS, 1959; "Ellery Queen: The Curse of Aden," NBC, 1959; "Oldsmobile Music Theatre: Too Bad About Sheila Troy," NBC, 1959; "Du Pont Show of the Month: I, Don Quixote," CBS, 1959; "Play of the Week: Don Juan in Hell," SYN, 1961; "Americans: A Portrait in Verses," CBS, 1962; "Hallmark Hall of Fame: The Invincible Mr. Disraeli," NBC, 1963; "Bob Hope Chrysler Theatre: One Day in the Life of Ivan Denisovich," NBC, 1963; "Hallmark Hall of Fame: A Cry of Angels," NBC, 1963; "Voyage to the Bottom of the Sea: The City Beneath the Sea," ABC, 1964; "NET Playhouse: Ten Blocks on the Camino Real," NET, 1966; "New York Television Theatre: The Movers," NET, 1966; "The Wild Wild West: The Night of the Man-Eating House," CBS, 1966; "The Wild Wild West: Night of the Undead," CBS, 1968; "Hollywood Television Theatre: Monteserrat," NET, 1971; "The FBI: The Hunters," ABC, 1972; "Bonanza: A Place to Hide," NBC, 1972; "Playhouse New York: Between Time and Timbuktu," NET, 1972; "Benjamin Franklin: The Rebel," CBS, 1975; "Kojak: A Hair-Trigger Away," CBS, 1976; "Murder, She Wrote: Death Takes a Curtain Call," CBS, 1985; "Lime Street: Pilot," ABC, 1985; "Blacke's Magic: Knave of Diamonds, Ace of Hearts," NBC, 1986; "Amazing Stories: Gershwin's Trunk," NBC, 1987.

TV MOVIES AND MINISERIES: "Thief," ABC, 1971; "The House and the Brain," ABC, 1973; "The Norliss Tapes," NBC, 1973; "The Word," CBS, 1978; "You Can't Go Home Again," CBS, 1979; "Manions of America," ABC, 1981.

HAVOC, JUNE

b. Ellen Evangeline Hovick, Seattle, November 8, 1916. Actress of films, stage and TV, playwright and a former child star in vaudeville; the sister of Gypsy Rose Lee.

AS A REGULAR: "Willy," CBS, 1954-55; "General Hospital," ABC, 1990.

AND: "Somerset Maugham TV Theatre: Cakes and Ale," NBC, 1951; "Cameo Theatre: Special Delivery," NBC, 1951; "Celanese Theatre: Anna Christie," ABC, 1952; "Pulitzer Prize Playhouse: Daisy Mayme," ABC, 1952; "Robert Montgomery Presents: Fairfield Lady," NBC, 1952; "Omnibus: The Beat," CBS, 1953; "Hollywood Opening Night: The Romantic Type," NBC, 1953; "Omnibus: Aunt Sarah's History," CBS, 1953; "Medallion Theatre: Mrs. Union Station," CBS, 1953; "Fireside Theatre: A Mother's Duty,"

NBC, 1954; "Robert Montgomery Presents: The
Tyrant," NBC, 1956; "Matinee Theatre: Robin
Dow," NBC, 1956; "Arthur Murray Party," NBC,
1957; "Mr. Broadway," NBC, 1957; "Errol Flynn
Theatre: Take the High Road," SYN, 1957;
"Studio One: The Mother Bit," CBS, 1957; "Errol
Flynn Theatre: My Infallible Uncle," SYN, 1957;
"Panic!: The Moth and the Flame," NBC, 1957;
"Masquerade Party," NBC, 1957; "Arthur Murray
Party," NBC, 1959; "The Kraft Music Hall with
Dave King," NBC, 1959; "U.S. Steel Hour: The
Pink Burro," CBS, 1959; "The Last Word," CBS,
1959; "Mike Wallace Interviews," CBS, 1960;
"Arthur Murray Party," NBC, 1960; About Faces,
ABC, 1960; "The Untouchables: The Larry Fay
Story," ABC, 1960; "Password," CBS, 1964;
"Burke's Law: Who Killed Everybody?," ABC,
1964; "The Outer Limits: Cry of Silence," ABC,
1964; "The Wonderful World of Disney: The Boy
Who Stole the Elephants," NBC, 1970;
"McMillan and Wife: The Easy Sunday Murder
Case," NBC, 1971; "Nightside," ABC, 1973;
"Murder, She Wrote: The Days Dwindle Down,"
CBS, 1987.

HAWN, GOLDIE
b. *Washington, D.C., November 21, 1945.*
Former dancer who played a dippy blonde on
"Laugh-In," won an Oscar for "Cactus Flower"
in 1970 and hasn't looked back since.
AS A REGULAR: "Good Morning, World," CBS,
1967-68; "Rowan & Martin's Laugh-In," NBC,
1968-70.
AND: "Andy Griffith Special," CBS, 1967; "The
Spring Thing," NBC, 1969; "I Dream of Jeannie:
The Biggest Star in Hollywood," NBC, 1969.
* Hawn was a dancer in the chorus on the "Andy
Griffith Special" when she was spotted and
cast in "Good Morning, World."

HAYAKAWA, SESSUE
b. *Japan, June 10, 1889; d. 1973.* Actor in
films from 1914 who played evil Orientals and
made a comeback in the fifties as a character
actor, sometimes still playing evil Orientals.
AS A GUEST: "Kraft Theatre: The Sea Is Boiling
Hot," NBC, 1958; "Studio One: Kurishiki
Incident," CBS, 1958; "The Red Skelton
Show," CBS, 1958; "Wagon Train: The Sakae
Ito Story," NBC, 1958; "The Steve Allen
Show," NBC, 1959; "John Gunther's High
Road: Resurgent Japan," ABC, 1960; "Here's
Hollywood," NBC, 1961; "Route 66: Two
Strangers and an Old Enemy," CBS, 1963.

HAYDEN, STERLING
b. *Sterling Relyea Walter, Montclair, NJ, 1916;
d. 1986.* Actor with a bombastic style who kept
busy in movies ("The Killing," "Dr.
Strangelove") and had little time for television.

AS A GUEST: "Schlitz Playhouse of Stars: Some
Delay at Fort Bess," CBS, 1954; "Dick
Powell's Zane Grey Theatre: The Necessary
Breed," CBS, 1957; "Playhouse 90: A Sound
of Different Drummers," CBS, 1957; "Wagon
Train: The Les Rand Story," NBC, 1957; "G.E.
Theatre: The Iron Horse," CBS, 1957;
"Playhouse 90: The Last Man," CBS, 1958;
"Schlitz Playhouse of Stars: East of the Moon,"
CBS, 1958; "Playhouse 90: The Long March,"
CBS, 1958; "Playhouse 90: Old Man," CBS,
1958; "Goodyear Theatre: Points Beyond,"
NBC, 1958; "Du Pont Show of the Month:
Ethan Frome," CBS, 1960; "Carol for Another
Christmas," ABC, 1964; "Banacek: Fly Me-If
You Can Find Me," NBC, 1974.
TV MOVIES AND MINISERIES: "The Blue and the
Gray," CBS, 1982.

HAYDN, RICHARD
b. *England, 1905.* Director and comic actor in
films, radio and on television, usually a
milquetoast type with a nerdy voice.
AS A GUEST: "Schlitz Playhouse of Stars: A
Quarter for Your Trouble," CBS, 1952;
"Disneyland Alice in Wonderland," ABC,
1954; "Producers Showcase: The King and
Mrs. Candle," NBC, 1955; "Playhouse 90:
Charley's Aunt," CBS, 1957; "The Ray Bolger
Show," NBC, 1957; "Playhouse 90: Topaze,"
CBS, 1957; "The Patrice Munsel Show," ABC,
1958; "Shirley Temple's Storybook: The
Emperor's New Clothes," NBC, 1958;
"Playhouse 90: Heart of Darkness," CBS,
1958; "Lux Playhouse: This Will Do Nicely,"
CBS, 1959; "G.E. Theatre: The Ugly
Duckling," CBS, 1960; "The Twilight Zone: A
Thing About Machines," CBS, 1960; "Burke's
Law: Who Killed Jason Shaw?," ABC, 1964;
"The Dick Van Dyke Show: The Return of
Edwin Carp," CBS, 1964; "The Man From
UNCLE: The Mad, Mad Tea Party Affair,"
NBC, 1965; "Bewitched: A Majority of Two,"
ABC, 1968; "It Takes a Thief: The Cold Who
Came in From the Spy," ABC, 1969;
"McCloud: Fifth Man in a String Quartet,"
NBC, 1972; "Love, American Style: Love and
the Impossible Gift," ABC, 1973.

HAYES, BILL
b. *William Foster Hayes, Harvey, IL, Jun. 5,
1925.* Singer of the fifties who had a big hit
with "The Ballad of Davy Crockett"; his career
was revitalized by a character named Doug
Williams on "Days of Our Lives."
AS A REGULAR: "Fireball Fun-for-All," NBC,
1949; "Your Show of Shows," NBC, 1950-53;
"Sid Caesar Presents Comedy Preview," NBC,
1955; "Oldsmobile Music Theatre (Oldsmobile
Presents)," NBC, 1959; "Days of Our Lives,"
NBC, 1970-84, 1985-87.

AND: "Armstrong Circle Theatre: The No-Talent Kid," NBC, 1952; "Hallmark Hall of Fame: The Yeomen of the Guard," NBC, 1957; "Salute to Baseball," NBC, 1957; "The Big Payoff," CBS, 1957; "Club 60," NBC, 1957; "The Big Record," CBS, 1957; "The Big Record," CBS, 1958; "The Jack Paar Show," NBC, 1958; "U.S. Steel Hour: A Family Alliance," CBS, 1958; "Little Women," CBS, 1958; "Hallmark Hall of Fame: Kiss Me, Kate," NBC, 1958; "The Jack Paar Show," NBC, 1959; "Decoy: The Red Clown," SYN, 1959; "Patti Page Olds Show," ABC, 1959; "The Voice of Firestone: The Music of Cole Porter," ABC, 1959; "The Voice of Firestone: Springtime in Paris," ABC, 1959; "Music for a Spring Night: The Holy Days," ABC, 1960; "Bell Telephone Hour: One Nation Indivisible," NBC, 1960; "Music for Christmas Night: The Gift of Song," ABC, 1960; "True Story: Friends Before Freud," NBC, 1961; "The Shari Lewis Show," NBC, 1961; "The du Pont Show: Music of the Thirties," NBC, 1961; "The Tonight Show Starring Johnny Carson," NBC, 1964; "The Mike Douglas Show," SYN, 1964; "Once Upon a Mattress," CBS, 1964; "Cade's County: Jessica," CBS, 1972; "3 for the Money," NBC, 1975; "The Mike Douglas Show," SYN, 1976; "Hollywood Squares," NBC, 1976.
* For a time in 1958 and 1959, Hayes formed a singing team with Florence Henderson.

HAYES, HELEN

b. Helen Hayes Brown, Washington, D.C., October 10, 1900. First lady of the American Stage, as she's known, who's done some live TV drama and other shows on the cultural side—not to mention "Hawaii Five-O" and "The Love Boat."

AS A REGULAR: "The Snoop Sisters," NBC, 1973-74.

AND: "Pulitzer Prize Playhouse: The Late Christopher Bean," ABC, 1950; "Prudential Family Playhouse: The Barretts of Wimpole Street," CBS, 1950; "Robert Montgomery Presents: Victoria Regina," NBC, 1951; "Pulitzer Prize Playhouse: Mary of Scotland," ABC, 1951; "Schlitz Playhouse of Stars: Not a Chance," CBS, 1951; "Schlitz Playhouse of Stars: The Lucky Touch," CBS, 1951; "Schlitz Playhouse of Stars: Dark Fleece," CBS, 1951; "Omnibus: The Twelve Pound Look," CBS, 1952; "Omnibus: The Christmas Tie," CBS, 1952; "Omnibus: The Happy Journey," CBS, 1953; "Omnibus: Irish Linen/Mom and Leo," CBS, 1953; "Motorola TV Hour: Side by Side," ABC, 1954; "U.S. Steel Hour: Welcome Home," ABC, 1954; "Best of Broadway: The Royal Family," CBS, 1954; "Light's Diamond Jubilee: Chance for Adventure," ABC, CBS, NBC, 1954; "Best of Broadway: Arsenic and Old Lace," CBS, 1955; "The Skin of Our Teeth," NBC, 1955; "Omnibus: Dear Brutus," CBS, 1956; "Hallmark Hall of Fame: Cradle Song," NBC, 1956; "President's Birthday Party," CBS, 1956; "Omnibus: The Christmas Tie," ABC, 1956; "Playhouse 90: Four Women in Black," CBS, 1957; "Arthur Murray Party," NBC, 1957; "Alcoa Hour: Mrs. Gilling and the Skyscraper," NBC, 1957; "The General Motors 50th Anniversary Show," NBC, 1957; "Omnibus: Mrs. McThing," NBC, 1958; "Wide, Wide World: American Theatre '58," NBC, 1958; "Arthur Murray Party," NBC, 1958; "U.S. Steel Hour: One Red Rose for Christmas," CBS, 1958; "Hallmark Hall of Fame: Ah, Wilderness!," NBC, 1959; "A Tribute to Eleanor Roosevelt on Her Diamond Jubilee," NBC, 1959; "U.S. Steel Hour: One Red Rose for Christmas," CBS, 1959; "Mother's March," SYN, 1960; "Woman: The Lonely Years," CBS, 1960; "Dow Hour of Great Mysteries: The Bat," NBC, 1960; "Hallmark Hall of Fame: Cradle Song," NBC, 1960; "I've Got a Secret," CBS, 1960; "Play of the Week: The Cherry Orchard," SYN, 1960; "Bell Telephone Hour: The Music of Romance," NBC, 1960; "Michael Shayne: Murder Round My Wrist," NBC, 1961; "Play of the Week: The Velvet Glove," SYN, 1961; "Three Wishes," SYN, 1961; "Tarzan: The Pride of the Lioness," NBC, 1967; "Arsenic and Old Lace," ABC, 1969; "The David Frost Show," SYN, 1969; "Hollywood Television Theatre: The Front Page," NET, 1970; "The Dick Cavett Show," ABC, 1970; "NET Playhouse: Helen Hayes: Portrait of an American Actress," NET, 1970; "Here's Lucy: Lucy and the Little Old Lady," CBS, 1972; "Hallmark Hall of Fame: Harvey," NBC, 1972; "Ghost Story: Alter Ego," NBC, 1972; "Hawaii Five-O: Retire in Sunny Hawaii-Forever," CBS, 1975; "The Love Boat: Marriage of Convenience," ABC, 1980; "Love, Sidney: Pros and Cons," NBC, 1982; "Glitter: The Tribute," ABC, 1984.

TV MOVIES AND MINISERIES: "Do Not Fold, Spindle or Mutilate," ABC, 1971; "The Snoop Sisters," NBC, 1972; "The Moneychangers," NBC, 1976; "Victory at Entebbe," ABC, 1976; "Murder Is Easy," CBS, 1982; "Agatha Christie's Murder with Mirrors," CBS, 1985.
* Emmies: 1953.

HAYES, PETER LIND

b. San Francisco, CA, June 25, 1915. Gifted light comic actor of early TV, often with wife Mary Healy; he had several unsuccesful shows and was a frequent fill-in for Arthur Godfrey.

AS A REGULAR: "Inside USA with Chevrolet," CBS, 1949-50; "The Stork Club," CBS, 1950; "The Peter Lind Hayes Show (The Peter and Mary Show)," NBC, 1950-51; ABC, 1958-59; "Star of the Family," CBS, 1951-52; "Peter Loves Mary," NBC, 1960-61; "Alumni Fun," ABC, 1963; CBS, 1964-66.

AND: "Armstrong Circle Theatre: The Marshal of Misery Gulch," NBC, 1953; "Studio One: Side

Street," CBS, 1954; "Goodyear TV Playhouse: The Way Things Happen," NBC, 1955; "The Arthur Godfrey Show," CBS, 1956; "Ford Star Jubilee: You're the Top," CBS, 1956; "Lux Video Theatre: One Sunday Afternoon," NBC, 1957; "The Jackie Gleason Show," CBS, 1957; "The Arthur Godfrey Show," CBS, 1957; "The Danny Thomas Show: Lose Me in Las Vegas," CBS, 1957; "The Perry Como Show," NBC, 1957; "The Big Party," CBS, 1959; "Alcoa Theatre: The Day the Devil Hid," NBC, 1959; "Miracle on 34th Street," NBC, 1959; "Christophers: How to Write a Good Letter," SYN, 1960; "Play Your Hunch," NBC, 1960; "Password," CBS, 1961; "Password," CBS, 1962; "Dinah Shore Special," NBC, 1962; "The du Pont Show: Regards to George M. Cohan," NBC, 1962; "The Match Game," NBC, 1963; "Perry Como's Kraft Music Hall," NBC, 1963; "Exploring," NBC, 1963; "Password," CBS, 1963; "The Alfred Hitchcock Hour: Body in the Barn," NBC, 1963; "Password," CBS, 1964; "The Outer Limits: Behold, Eck!," ABC, 1964; "Password," CBS, 1965; "Password," CBS, 1966.
AS WRITER: "Kraft Television Theatre: Come to Me," NBC, 1957.

HAYES, SUSAN SEAFORTH—See Susan Seaforth.

HAYMER, JOHNNY
d. 1989. Comedian and actor; he played Sgt. Zale on "M*A*S*H."
AS A REGULAR: "M*A*S*H," CBS, 1974-79; "Madame's Place," SYN, 1982.
AND: "The Jackie Gleason Show," CBS, 1957; "The Garry Moore Show," CBS, 1957; "The Steve Allen Show," NBC, 1958; "The Garry Moore Show," CBS, 1958; "The Ed Sullivan Show," CBS, 1959; "Honey West: Whatever Lola Wants," ABC, 1965; "The Dick Van Dyke Show: Bad Reception in Albany," CBS, 1966; "Captain Nice: That Thing," NBC, 1967; "The Wild Wild West: The Night of the Vipers, 1968; "Gunsmoke: 9:12 to Dodge," CBS, 1968; "My Three Sons: What Did You Do Today, Grandpa?," CBS, 1969; "Get Smart: The Not-So-Great Escape," NBC, 1969; "Switch: Death Squad," CBS, 1976; "Mork & Mindy: Mork in Wonderland," ABC, 1979; "Life Goes On: Paige's Date," ABC, 1989.
TV MOVIES AND MINISERIES: "Mongo's Back in Town," CBS, 1971.

HAYMES, DICK
b. Richard Benjamin Haymes, Argentina, September 13, 1916; d. 1980. Big-band singer with plenty of variety show credits.
AS A GUEST:"Ford Theatre: National Honeymoon," NBC, 1952; "Lux Video Theatre: Song for a Banjo," CBS, 1952; "Suspense: The Deadly Lance," CBS, 1952; "Ford Theatre:

Sweet Talk Me, Jackson," NBC, 1953; "Suspense: Laugh It Off," CBS, 1953; "Screen Directors Playhouse: Cry Justice," NBC, 1956; "Producers Showcase: The Lord Don't Play Favorites," NBC, 1956; "The Jackie Gleason Show: America's Music Makers," CBS, 1957; "The Jackie Gleason Show," CBS, 1957; "The Tonight Show," NBC, 1957; "Music for a Summer Night: Mr. Porter of Indiana," ABC, 1960; "The Jack Paar Show," NBC, 1960; "The Ed Sullivan Show," CBS, 1961; "The Garry Moore Show," CBS, 1961; "Playboy's Penthouse," SYN, 1961; "The Ed Sullivan Show," CBS, 1962; "The Saint: The Contract," NBC, 1965; "McMillan and Wife: Free Fall to Terror," NBC, 1973; "Adam 12: The Clinic on 18th Street," NBC, 1974; "McMillan: All Bets Are Off," NBC, 1976; "The Eddie Capra Mysteries: Murder on the Flip Side," NBC, 1978.
TV MOVIES AND MINISERIES: "Betrayal," ABC, 1974.

HAYNES, LLOYD
b. South Bend, IN, October 19, 1934; d. 1986. Actor who played teacher Pete Dixon on "Room 222."
AS A REGULAR: "Room 222," ABC, 1969-74; "Dynasty," ABC, 1981; "General Hospital," ABC, 1984-86.
AND: "Star Trek: Where No Man Has Gone Before," NBC, 1966; "Batman: King Tut's Coup/ Batman's Waterloo," ABC, 1967; "Tarzan: The Blue Stone of Heaven," NBC, 1967; "Stand Up and Cheer," SYN, 1973; "Emergency!: Equipment," NBC, 1975; "Marcus Welby, M.D.: The Strange Behavior of Paul Kelland," ABC, 1975.
TV MOVIES AND MINISERIES: "Assault on the Wayne," ABC, 1971; "Look What's Happened to Rosemary's Baby," ABC, 1976; "Harold Robbins' 79 Park Avenue," NBC, 1977.

HAYS, ROBERT
b. Bethesda, MD, July 24, 1947. Light leading man.
AS A REGULAR: "Angie," ABC, 1979-80; "Starman," ABC, 1986-87; "FM," NBC, 1989, 1990.
AND: "Marcus Welby, M.D.: The Medea Factor," ABC, 1975; "Laverne & Shirley: Dating Slump," ABC, 1976; "The Blue Knight: Minnesota," CBS, 1976; "Saturday Night Live," NBC, 1981.
TV MOVIES AND MINISERIES: "Young Pioneers," ABC, 1976; "Young Pioneers Christmas," ABC, 1976; "Murder by the Book," CBS, 1987.

HAYWARD, LOUIS
b. Seafield Grant, Johannesburg, South Africa, March 19, 1909; d. 1985. Smooth hero who played the crime solving Lone Wolf.
AS A REGULAR: "The Lone Wolf," SYN, 1954-55;

400

"Harold Robbins' The Survivors," ABC, 1969-70.
AND: "Matinee Theatre: Beginning Now," NBC, 1951; "Ford Theatre: Crossed and Double Crossed," NBC, 1952; "Lux Video Theatre: So Evil, My Love," NBC, 1955; "Climax!: A Promise to Murder," CBS, 1955; "TV Readers Digest: The Voyage of Captain Tom Jones, Pirate," ABC, 1955; "Studio One: Balance of Terror," CBS, 1958; "Schlitz Playhouse of Stars: A Contest of Ladies," CBS, 1958; "Decision: Stand and Deliver," NBC, 1958; "Riverboat: Payment in Full," NBC, 1959; "Breck Golden Showcase: The Picture of Dorian Gray," CBS, 1961; "Kraft Mystery Theatre: Dead on Nine," NBC, 1962; "The Alfred Hitchcock Hour: Day of Reckoning," CBS, 1962; "Rawhide: The Backshooter," CBS, 1964; "Burke's Law: Who Killed the Jackpot?," ABC, 1965; "Night Gallery: Certain Shadows on the Walls," NBC, 1970.

HAYWARD, SUSAN
b. *Edythe Marrener, Brooklyn, NY, 1919; d. 1975.* Oscar-winning film actress who did a couple of TV movies.
TV MOVIES AND MINISERIES: "Heat of Anger," CBS, 1972; "Say Goodbye, Maggie Cole," ABC, 1972.

HAYWORTH, RITA
b. *Margarita Cansino, New York City, NY, October 17, 1918; d. 1987.* Movie sex symbol who did a little TV.
AS A GUEST: "The Ed Sullivan Show," CBS, 1956; "The Poppy Is Also a Flower," ABC, 1966; "Rowan & Martin's Laugh-In," NBC, 1971; "The Carol Burnett Show," CBS, 1972.

HEALY, MARY
b. *New Orleans, LA, April 14, 1918.* Singer-comedienne who often performed with her husband, Peter Lind Hayes.
AS A REGULAR: "Inside USA with Chevrolet," CBS, 1949-50; "The Stork Club," CBS, 1950; "The Peter Lind Hayes Show (The Peter and Mary Show)," NBC, 1950-51; ABC, 1958-59; "Star of the Family," CBS, 1951-52; "Masquerade Party," ABC, 1955-56; "Peter Loves Mary," NBC, 1960-61.
AND: "Armstrong Circle Theatre: The Marshal of Misery Gulch," NBC, 1953; "Studio One: Side Street," CBS, 1954; "Goodyear TV Playhouse: The Way Things Happen," NBC, 1955; "The Arthur Godfrey Show," CBS, 1956; "Ford Star Jubilee: You're the Top," CBS, 1956; "Lux Video Theatre: One Sunday Afternoon," NBC, 1957; "The Jackie Gleason Show," CBS, 1957; "The Arthur Godfrey Show," CBS, 1957; "To Tell the Truth," CBS, 1957; "The Danny Thomas Show: Lose Me in Las Vegas," CBS, 1957; "The Perry Como Show,"

NBC, 1957; "The Big Party," CBS, 1959; "Miracle on 34th Street," NBC, 1959; "Password," CBS, 1962; "Dinah Shore Special," NBC, 1962; "Perry Como's Kraft Music Hall," NBC, 1963.

HEATHERTON, JOEY
b. *Rockville Centre, NY, September 14, 1944.* Sexy, elfin singer-dancer of sixties variety shows who's had her share of legal and career problems since then.
AS A REGULAR: "Perry Como's Kraft Music Hall," NBC, 1961-63; "Dean Martin Presents," NBC, 1968; "Joey & Dad," CBS, 1975.
AND: "The Perry Como Show," NBC, 1956; "Route 66: Three Sides," CBS, 1960; "The Nurses: Night Shift," CBS, 1962; "The Virginian: A Distant Fury," NBC, 1963; "Mr. Novak: To Break a Camel's Back," NBC, 1963; "Arrest and Trial: Some Weeks Are All Mondays," ABC, 1963; "The Nurses: Rally Round My Comrades," CBS, 1963; "Bob Hope Chrysler Theatre: Runaway," NBC, 1964; "Hollywood Palace," ABC, 1964; "Channing: The Trouble with Girls," ABC, 1964; "Hullabaloo," NBC, 1965; "The Dean Martin Show," NBC, 1965; "The Steve Lawrence Show," CBS, 1965; "Of Mice and Men," ABC, 1968; "It Takes a Thief: A Matter of Grey Matter," ABC, 1969; "The Dean Martin Show," NBC, 1969; "The Glen Campbell Goodtime Hour," CBS, 1970; "The Dean Martin Show," NBC, 1970; "The Ed Sullivan Show," CBS, 1970; "Love, American Style: Love and the Hitchhiker," ABC, 1971; "The Militant," NBC, 1971; "Old Faithful," ABC, 1973; "NBC Follies," NBC, 1973; "The Mike Douglas Show," SYN, 1975.
TV MOVIES AND MINISERIES: "The Ballad of Andy Crocker," ABC, 1969.

HEATHERTON, RAY
b. *1910.* Father of Joey.
AS A REGULAR: "Joey & Dad," CBS, 1975.

HECHT, BEN
b. *New York City, NY, February 28, 1893; d. 1964.* Writer ("The Front Page") who did a bit of TV.
AS A REGULAR: "Willys Theatre Presenting Ben Hecht's Tales of the City," CBS, 1953.
AND: "Ellery Queen: This Murder Comes to You Live," NBC, 1959; "Goodyear Theatre: Hello, Charlie," NBC, 1959.
AS WRITER: "Goodyear Theatre: Hello, Charlie," NBC, 1959; "Kaleidoscope: The Third Commandment," NBC, 1959.

HECKART, EILEEN
b. *Columbus, OH, March 29, 1919.* Character actress who played Aunt Flo on "The Mary Tyler Moore Show."
AS A REGULAR: "Out of the Blue," ABC, 1979;

"Trauma Center," ABC, 1983; "Partners in Crime," NBC, 1984; "Annie McGuire," CBS, 1988-89.

AND: "Kraft Television Theatre: Black Sheep," NBC, 1950; "Studio One: Zone Four," CBS, 1950; "Saturday's Children," CBS, 1950; "Danger: The Intruders," CBS, 1952; "Philco TV Playhouse: Segment," NBC, 1952; "Campbell TV Soundstage: A Little Child Shall Lead Them," NBC, 1954; "Goodyear TV Playhouse: My Lost Saints," NBC, 1955; "Philco TV Playhouse: Christmas 'Til Closing," NBC, 1955; "Kraft Television Theatre: Anna Santonello," NBC, 1956; "Hallmark Hall of Fame: The Little Foxes," NBC, 1956; "Alcoa Hour: No License to Kill," NBC, 1957; "Studio One: The Out-of-Towners," CBS, 1957; "Kraft Television Theatre: Success!," NBC, 1957; "Playhouse 90: The Blue Men," CBS, 1959; "Playhouse 90: A Corner of the Garden," CBS, 1959; "Dr. Kildare: The Soul Killer," NBC, 1962; "Naked City: Her Life in Moving Pictures," ABC, 1963; "Ben Casey: Dispel the Black Cyclone That Shakes the Throne," ABC, 1963; "The Eleventh Hour: There Should Be an Outfit Called Families Anonymous," NBC, 1963; "The Defenders: All the Silent Voices," CBS, 1964; "The Fugitive: Angels Travel on Lonely Roads," ABC, 1964; "The Doctors and the Nurses: Night of the Witch," CBS, 1965; "Gunsmoke: Hattie Silks," CBS, 1965; "The FBI: The Insolents," ABC, 1965; "New York Television Theatre: Save Me a Place at Forest Lawn," NET, 1966; "The Felony Squad: The Broken Badge," ABC, 1966; "New York Television Theatre: The Effect of Gamma Rays on Man-in-the-Moon Marigolds," NET, 1966; "The Fugitive: The Breaking of the Habit," ABC, 1967; "CBS Playhouse: Secrets," CBS, 1968; "Gunsmoke: The Innocent," CBS, 1969; "Hallmark Hall of Fame: All the Way Home," NBC, 1971; "The Streets of San Francisco: The 30-Year Pin," ABC, 1972; "Banyon: A Date with Death," NBC, 1972; "Love Story: Love Came Laughing," NBC, 1973; "Barnaby Jones: Dark Legacy," CBS, 1974; "ABC Theatre: Wedding Band," ABC, 1974; "Lily," NBC, 1974; "The Mary Tyler Moore Show: Mary's Aunt," CBS, 1975; "Hawaii Five-O: Honor Is an Unmarked Grave," CBS, 1975; "The Mary Tyler Moore Show: Mary's Aunt Returns," CBS, 1976; "Rhoda: It's Not My Fault-Is It?," CBS, 1976; "The Mary Tyler Moore Show: Lou Proposes," CBS, 1976; "Alice: Mother-in-Law," CBS, 1976; "Flying High: Pilot," CBS, 1978; "Little House on the Prairie: Dance with Me," NBC, 1979; "Lou Grant: Pack," CBS, 1980; "The Cosby Show: Autumn Gifts," NBC, 1987.

TV MOVIES AND MINISERIES: "The Victim," ABC, 1972; "The FBI Story: Alvin Karpis, Public Enemy Number One," CBS, 1974; "Suddenly, Love," NBC, 1978; "Backstairs at the White House," NBC, 1979; "White Mama," CBS, 1980; "F.D.R.: The Last Year," NBC, 1980; "Games Mother Never Taught You," CBS, 1982; "Stuck with Each Other," NBC, 1989.

HEDISON, DAVID

b. Providence, RI, May 20, 1929. Actor who played Captain Lee Crane on "Voyage to the Bottom of the Sea" and Lord Roger Langdon on "The Colbys."

AS A REGULAR: "Five Fingers," NBC, 1959-60; "Voyage to the Bottom of the Sea," ABC, 1964-68; "The Colbys," ABC, 1985-87.

AND: "Hong Kong: Lesson in Fear," ABC, 1961; "Here's Hollywood," NBC, 1961; "Bus Stop: Call Back Yesterday," ABC, 1961; "Perry Mason: The Case of the Dodging Domino," CBS, 1962; "The Farmer's Daughter: The Mink Machine," ABC, 1964; "PDQ," NBC, 1965; "The Saint: Louella," NBC, 1966; "Hollywood Squares," NBC, 1967; "Journey to the Unknown: Somewhere in a Crown," ABC, 1968; "Love, American Style: Love and the Other Love," ABC, 1969; "The FBI: The Buyer," ABC, 1972; "The FBI: The Gathering of Sharks," ABC, 1973; "The New Adventures of Perry Mason: The Case of the Frenzied Feminist," CBS, 1973; "Shaft: The Capricorn Murders," CBS, 1974; "Medical Center: Dark Warning," CBS, 1974; "The Manhunter: The Man Who Thought He Was Dillinger," CBS, 1974; "ABC Afternoon Playbreak: Can I Save My Children?," ABC, 1974; "Family: Coming Apart," ABC, 1976; "Family: Coming of Age," ABC, 1976; "Barnaby Jones: Deadly Charade," CBS, 1977; "The Bob Newhart Show: It Didn't Happen One Night," CBS, 1978; "The Love Boat: Tug of War," ABC, 1979; "Nero Wolfe: Murder by the Book," NBC, 1981; "The Love Boat: April in Boston," ABC, 1982; "The Love Boat: Her Honor the Mayor," ABC, 1985; "Hotel: Distortions," ABC, 1985; "Simon & Simon: Simon Without Simon," CBS, 1985; "Murder, She Wrote: Mirror, Mirror, On the Wall," CBS, 1989.

TV MOVIES AND MINISERIES: "Crime Club," CBS, 1973; "The Cat Creature," ABC, 1973; "Murder Impossible," ABC, 1974; "Adventures of a Queen," CBS, 1975; "The Lives of Jenny Dolan," NBC, 1975; "The Art of Crime," NBC, 1975; "Murder in Peyton Place," NBC, 1977; "The Power Within," ABC, 1979; "The Gambler II: The Adventure Continues," CBS, 1983; "A.D.," NBC, 1985.

HEDREN, TIPPI

b. Nathalie Hedren, Lafayette, MN, 1935. Cool blonde actress in sporadic films and on TV; mother of Melanie Griffith.

AS A REGULAR: "The Bold and the Beautiful," CBS, 1990.

AND: "The Tonight Show Starring Johnny Carson," NBC, 1964; "Run for Your Life: Someone Who Makes Me Feel Beautiful," NBC, 1965; "The Courtship of Eddie's Father: Free Is a Four-Letter Word," ABC, 1970; "Alfred Hitchcock Presents: The Man From the South," NBC, 1985; "Baby Boom: Christmas '88," NBC, 1988; "Superstars & Their Moms," TBS, 1989.

* Alfred Hitchcock spotted Hedren in a commercial for Sego diet drink on the "Today" show in 1961 and signed her to a personal contract. Hedren appeared in Hitchcock's "The Birds" and "Marnie."

HEFLIN, VAN
b. Emmet Evan Heflin, Jr., Walters, OK, December 13, 1910; d. 1971. Film actor in intense roles who did some TV drama.
AS A REGULAR: "The Great Adventure," CBS, 1963-64.
AND: "Nash Airflyte Theatre: A Double-Dyed Deceiver," ABC, 1950; "Robert Montgomery Presents: Arrowsmith," NBC, 1950; "Playhouse 90: The Dark Side of the Earth," CBS, 1957; "Playhouse 90: Rank and File," CBS, 1959; "Playhouse 90: The Cruel Day," CBS, 1960; "The Dick Powell Show: Ricochet," NBC, 1961; "US #1," NBC, 1962; "The Ed Sullivan Show," CBS, 1964; "On Stage: Certain Honorable Men," NBC, 1966; "A Case of Libel," ABC, 1968; "The Danny Thomas Hour: Fear Is the Chain," NBC, 1968; "Hallmark Hall of Fame: Neither Are We Enemies," NBC, 1970.
TV MOVIES AND MINISERIES: "The Last Child," ABC, 1971.

HEGYES, ROBERT
b. New Jersey, May 7, 1951. Actor who played Juan Epstein on "Welcome Back, Kotter."
AS A REGULAR: "Welcome Back, Kotter," ABC, 1975-79; "Cagney & Lacey," CBS, 1986-88.
AND: "The Streets of San Francisco: School of Fear," ABC, 1975; "The Rich Little Show," NBC, 1976; "Break the Bank," SYN, 1977; "Chico and the Man: Raul Runs Away," NBC, 1978; "$weepstake$: Victor, Billy and Bobby, 'Sometimes,'" NBC, 1979.
TV MOVIES AND MINISERIES: "For Lovers Only," ABC, 1982.

HEIDT, HORACE
b. Alameda, CA, May 21, 1901; d. 1986. Bandleader.
AS A REGULAR: "The Horace Heidt Show," CBS, 1950-51; "The Swift Wagon Show," NBC, 1955.

HELMOND, KATHERINE
b. Galveston, TX, July 5, 1934. Actress who played Jessica Tate on "Soap" and plays basically the same role on "Who's the Boss?" as Mona Robinson.
AS A REGULAR: "Soap," ABC, 1977-81; "Who's the Boss?," ABC, 1984- .
AND: "The FBI: The Jug Marker," ABC, 1972; "The Bob Newhart Show: I'm Okay, You're Okay, So What's Wrong?," CBS, 1973; "Adam's Rib: Murder!," ABC, 1973; "Hec Ramsey: Only Birds and Fools," NBC, 1974; "The Snoop Sisters: A Black Day for Bluebeard," NBC, 1974; "Medical Center: Heel of the Tyrant," CBS, 1974; "The Rookies: The Old Neighborhood," ABC, 1975; "Harry O: Portrait of a Murder," ABC, 1975; "The Rookies: Death Lady," ABC, 1975; "Barnaby Jones: The Orchid Killer," CBS, 1975; "Joe Forrester: Pressure Point," NBC, 1976; "Hour Magazine," SYN, 1981; "Benson: God, I Need This Job," ABC, 1983; "The Magical World of Disney: Save the Dog," NBC, 1989.
TV MOVIES AND MINISERIES: "Dr. Max," CBS, 1974; "Locusts," ABC, 1974; "Larry," CBS, 1974; "The Legend of Lizzie Borden," ABC, 1975; "The Family Nobody Wanted," ABC, 1975; "The First 36 Hours of Dr. Durant," ABC, 1975; "James Dean," NBC, 1976; "Wanted: The Sundance Woman," ABC, 1976; "Pearl," ABC, 1978; "Diary of a Teenage Hitchhiker," ABC, 1979; "For Lovers Only," ABC, 1982; "Rosie: The Rosemary Clooney Story," CBS, 1982; "World War III," NBC, 1982.

HELTON, PERCY
b. New York City, NY, 1894; d. 1971. Character actor who played Homer Crachit on the "The Beverly Hillbillies" and usually played mild-mannered elderly types.
AS A REGULAR: "The Beverly Hillbillies," CBS, 1968-71.
AND: "The Abbott and Costello Show: Car Trouble," CBS, 1953; "December Bride: Skid Row," CBS, 1955; "Science Fiction Theatre: Gravity Zero," SYN, 1957; "Alfred Hitchcock Presents: Nightmare in 4-D," CBS, 1957; "Father Knows Best: Trip to Hillsborough," NBC, 1957; "Studio 57: My Friends the Birds," SYN, 1957; "The Thin Man: The Fatal Cliche," NBC, 1957; "Dr. Hudson's Secret Journal: The Foladare Bequest," SYN, 1957; "Alfred Hitchcock Presents: Disappearing Trick," CBS, 1958; "Thriller: Rose's Last Summer," NBC, 1960; "Bringing Up Buddy: Gentleman Callers," ABC, 1960; "Alfred Hitchcock Presents: The Horse-player," NBC, 1961; "Alfred Hitchcock Presents: Services Rendered," NBC, 1961; "The Real McCoys: Double Date," ABC, 1962; "Mr. Ed: Bald Horse," CBS, 1962; "The Real McCoys: Pepino's Inheritance," CBS, 1962; "Mr. Smith Goes to Washington: Miss Ida's Star," ABC, 1963; "The Twilight Zone: Mute," CBS, 1963; "Bonanza: The Hayburner," NBC, 1963; "Hazel:

Hazel's Day Off," NBC, 1963; "The Fugitive: Angels Travel on Lonely Roads," ABC, 1964; "The Twilight Zone: Mr. Garrity and the Graves," CBS, 1964; "Valentine's Day: The Old School Tie," ABC, 1964; "The Baileys of Balboa: My Son, the Dreamer," CBS, 1964; "The Farmer's Daughter: Why Wait Till November?," ABC, 1965; "The FBI: The Sacrifice," ABC, 1966; "Green Acres: Water, Water Everywhere," CBS, 1966; "The Mothers-in-Law: How Do You Moonlight a Meatball?," NBC, 1967; "The Virginian: Execution of Triste," NBC, 1967; "Batman: Louie's Lethal Lilac Time," ABC, 1968; "Get Smart: Spy, Spy, Birdie," NBC, 1968; "Petticoat Junction: Last Train to Pixley," CBS, 1970.

HEMPHILL, SHIRLEY

b. *Asheville, NC*. Pudgy black actress, usually in abrasive comic roles.
AS A REGULAR: "What's Happening!!," ABC, 1976-79, SYN, 1985-88; "One in a Million," ABC, 1980.
AND: "Good Times: Rich Is Better Than Poor...Maybe," CBS, 1976.

HEMSLEY, SHERMAN

b. *Philadelphia, PA, February 1, 1938*. Short black comic actor who's played blustery bumblers on two mediocre sitcoms; he was George Jefferson and Rev. Deacon Frye on "Amen."
AS A REGULAR: "All in the Family," CBS, 1973-75; "The Jeffersons," CBS, 1975-85; "Amen," NBC, 1986- .
AND: "Dean's Place," NBC, 1975; "The Rich Little Show," NBC, 1976; "Donny and Marie," ABC, 1976; "The Love Boat: The Main Event," ABC, 1977; "The John Davidson Show," SYN, 1981; "E/R: Premiere," CBS, 1984; "227: The Big Deal," NBC, 1988; "ALF Takes Over the Network," NBC, 1989.

TV'S TOP TEN, 1981-82
1. Dallas (CBS)
2. 60 Minutes (CBS)
3. The Jeffersons (CBS)
4. Three's Company (ABC)
5. Alice (CBS)
6. The Dukes of Hazzard (CBS)
6. Too Close for Comfort (ABC)
8. ABC Monday Night Movie (ABC)
9. M*A*S*H (CBS)
10. One Day at a Time (CBS)

HENDERSON, FLORENCE

b. *Dale, IN, February 14, 1934*. Actress-singer who'll be known forever as Carol Brady, mother of "The Brady Bunch" in innumerable variations.

AS A REGULAR: "Sing Along," CBS, 1958; "Oldsmobile Music Theatre (Oldsmobile Presents)," NBC, 1959; "The Jack Paar Show," NBC, 1958-62; "Today," NBC, 1959-60; "The Brady Bunch," ABC, 1969-74; "The Brady Bunch Hour," ABC, 1977; "The Brady Brides," NBC, 1981; "The Bradys," CBS, 1990.
AND: "U.S. Steel Hour: Huck Finn," CBS, 1957; "The Big Record," CBS, 1958; "The Big Record," CBS, 1958; "U.S. Steel Hour: A Family Alliance," CBS, 1958; "Little Women," CBS, 1958; "The Voice of Firestone," ABC, 1958; "Patti Page Olds Show," ABC, 1959; "The Voice of Firestone: An Evening with Richard Rodgers," ABC, 1959; "Music for a Winter Night: The Sounds of Christmas," ABC, 1960; "The Gershwin Years," CBS, 1961; "Car 54, Where Are You?: I Love Lucille," NBC, 1962; "The Jack Paar Program," NBC, 1962; "The Voice of Firestone," ABC, 1962; "Bell Telephone Hour: Christmas Program," NBC, 1962; "The Jack Paar Program," NBC, 1963; "Girl Talk," SYN, 1963; "The Garry Moore Show," CBS, 1964; "Password," CBS, 1964; "The Ed Sullivan Show," CBS, 1964; "The Match Game," NBC, 1964; "Get the Message," ABC, 1964; "Bell Telephone Hour: Lyrics by Oscar Hammerstein," NBC, 1964; "The Jack Paar Program," NBC, 1965; "The Match Game," CBS, 1965; "To Tell the Truth," CBS, 1965; "Password," CBS, 1965; "Bell Telephone Hour," NBC, 1965; "Password," CBS, 1966; "I Spy: The Abbe and the Nymph," NBC, 1966; "The Tonight Show Starring Johnny Carson," NBC, 1967; "The Mike Douglas Show," SYN, 1968; "Snap Judgment," NBC, 1968; "Operation: Entertainment," ABC, 1968; "The Tonight Show Starring Johnny Carson," NBC, 1969; "A Salute to Television's 25th Anniversary," ABC, 1972; "Medical Center: Torment," CBS, 1975; "Hollywood Squares," NBC, 1975; "Dinah!," SYN, 1976; "Donny and Marie," ABC, 1976; "The Love Boat: Divorce Me, Please!," ABC, 1977; "The Love Boat: Julie's Aunt," ABC, 1978; "Hollywood Squares," SYN, 1978; "Bonkers!," SYN, 1978; "The Love Boat: The Remake," ABC, 1980; "The Love Boat: Country Cousin Blues," ABC, 1981; "The Love Boat: The Successor," ABC, 1981; "Fantasy Island: The Sailor," ABC, 1982; "Fantasy Island: The Swinger," ABC, 1983; "The Love Boat: Affair on Demand," ABC, 1983; "The Love Boat: The Runaway," ABC, 1985; "ABC Afterschool Special: Just Another Kid: An AIDS Story," ABC, 1987; "Candid Camera Christmas Special," CBS, 1987; "It's Garry Shandling's Show: The Schumakers Go to Hollywood," FOX, 1988; "Day by Day: A Very Brady Episode," NBC, 1989; "The Pat Sajak Show," CBS, 1989; "Free Spirit: The New Secretary," ABC, 1989.
TV MOVIES AND MINISERIES: "The Love Boat,"

ABC, 1976; "The Brady Girls Get Married," NBC, 1981; "A Very Brady Christmas," CBS, 1988.
* "The Brady Bunch" was originally called "The Bradley Bunch."

HENDERSON, SKITCH
b. *Lyle Russell Cedric, Birmingham, England, January 27, 1918.* Bandleader and TV personality.
AS A REGULAR: "Where Was I?," DUM, 1953; "Nothing but the Best," NBC, 1953; "The Dave Garroway Show," NBC, 1953-54; "The Tonight Show," NBC, 1954-57; "The Steve Allen Show," NBC, 1956-59; "The Tonight Show," NBC, 1962; "The Tonight Show Starring Johnny Carson," NBC, 1962-66; "Steve Allen's Laugh Back," SYN, 1976.
AND: "The Kate Smith Show," CBS, 1960; "Captain Kangaroo," CBS, 1961; "To Tell the Truth," CBS, 1962; "Exploring," NBC, 1962; "The Match Game," NBC, 1962; "To Tell the Truth," CBS, 1963; "Exploring," NBC, 1964; "To Tell the Truth," CBS, 1964; "A Wild Winters Night," NBC, 1964; "The Lawrence Welk Show," ABC, 1965; "What's This Song?," NBC, 1965.

HENDLER, LAURI
b. *Ft. Belvoir, VA, April 22, 1965.* Young actress who played Julie Kanisky on "Gimme a Break."
AS A REGULAR: "A New Kind of Family," ABC, 1979-80; "Gimme a Break," NBC, 1981-86.
AND: "Three's Company: The Crush," ABC, 1978; "Magnum, P.I.: Thank Heaven for Little Girls—And Big Ones, Too," CBS, 1980; "Mr. Belevedere: Moonlighting," ABC, 1987.

HENDRIX, WANDA
b. *Dixie Wanda Hendrix, Jacksonville, FL, November 3, 1928; d. 1981.* Forties movie starlet who went to TV in the fifties.
AS A GUEST: "Lux Video Theatre: The Token," CBS, 1950; "Rewrite for Love," SYN, 1951; "Pulitzer Prize Playhouse: The Happy Journey," ABC, 1951; "Bigelow Theatre: A New Year for Margaret," CBS, 1951; "Pulitzer Prize Playhouse: The American Leonardo," ABC, 1952; "Favorite Story: The Fury," SYN, 52; "Robert Montgomery Presents: Keane vs. Keane," NBC, 1952; "Ford Theatre: Something Old, Something New," NBC, 1952; "Plymouth Playhouse: A Tale of Two Cities," ABC, 1953; "Ford Theatre: The Bachelor," NBC, 1953; "Mirror Theatre: The Surprise Party," CBS, 1953; "Schlitz Playhouse of Stars: Fresh Start," CBS, 1953; "Climax!: Avalanche at Devil's Pass," CBS, 1957; "Telephone Time: The Immortal Eye," ABC, 1958; "Wagon Train: The Charles Maury Story," NBC, 1958; "The

Red Skelton Show: San Fernando the Swami," CBS, 1959; "Bat Masterson: The Lady Plays Her Hand," NBC, 1960; "The Deputy: The Lesson," NBC, 1961; "My Three Sons: The Fountain of Youth," CBS, 1968; "Bewitched: TV or Not TV," ABC, 1971.

HENNER, MARILU
b. *Chicago, IL, April 6, 1952.* Sexy redheaded actress who played Elaine Nardo on "Taxi."
AS A REGULAR: "Taxi," ABC, 1978-82; NBC, 1982-83; "Evening Shade," CBS, 1990- .
AND: "Hollywood Squares," NBC, 1978; "Midnight Special," NBC, 1981; "Alfred Hitchcock Presents: The Method Actor," NBC, 1985; "The Tracey Ullman Show: My Baby," FOX, 1989.
TV MOVIES AND MINISERIES: "Stark," CBS, 1985; "Ladykillers," ABC, 1988.

HENNING, LINDA KAYE
b. *Hollywood, CA, 1944.* Pert actress, daughter of producer-writer Paul Henning. She played Betty Jo Bradley on "Petticoat Junction."
AS A REGULAR: "Petticoat Junction," CBS, 1963-70.
AND: "Green Acres: Eb Discovers the Birds and the Bees," CBS, 1966; "Art Linkletter's House Party," CBS, 1967; "The Beverly Hillbillies: The Italian Cook," CBS, 1968; "The Beverly Hillbillies: The Thanksgiving Story," CBS, 1968; "It Takes Two," NBC, 1969; "Family Affair: And Baby Makes Eight," CBS, 1970; "Baffle," NBC, 1973; "Password," ABC, 1974; "Showoffs," ABC, 1975; "Wide World of Mystery: The Nurse Killer," ABC, 1975; "Barnaby Jones: Dangerous Gambit," CBS, 1976; "Happy Days: The Physical," ABC, 1977; "Mork & Mindy: Hold That Mork," ABC, 1979.
TV MOVIES AND MINISERIES: "The Return of the Beverly Hillbillies," CBS, 1981.
* See also "Petticoat Junction."

HENNING, PAUL
Comedy writer who had a hand in some of the most popular rural-oriented sitcoms of the sixties.
AS WRITER: "The George Burns and Gracie Allen Show," CBS, 1950-55; "The Bob Cummings Show," NBC, 1955; CBS, 1955-57; NBC, 1957-59; "The Andy Griffith Show: Crime-Free Mayberry," CBS, 1961.
AS WRITER-PRODUCER: "The Beverly Hillbillies," CBS, 1962-71; "Petticoat Junction," CBS, 1963-70; "Green Acres," CBS, 1965-71.
* See also "The Beverly Hillbillies" and "Green Acres."

HENREID, PAUL
b. *Trieste, Italy, January 10, 1908.* Matinee

idol who often played dour types in the movies ("Casablanca," "Now Voyager"); he's directed as well as appeared on TV shows.

AS A GUEST: "Ford Theatre: The Jewel," NBC, 1953; "Schlitz Playhouse of Stars: The Hoax," CBS, 1954; "Ford Theatre: Mimi," NBC, 1955; "Climax!: Wild Stallion," CBS, 1955; "Ford Theatre: The Connoisseur," ABC, 1957; "Playhouse 90: One Coat of White," CBS, 1957; "Schlitz Playhouse of Stars: Bitter Parting," CBS, 1957; "The Jane Wyman Show: Man of Taste," NBC, 1958; "The Aquanauts: The Atlantis Adventure," CBS, 1960; "Here's Hollywood," NBC, 1961; "It Takes a Thief: The Artist Is for Framing," ABC, 1969; "Judd for the Defense: Elephant in a Cigar Box," ABC, 1969; "Paris 7000: Call Me Ellen," ABC, 1970.

TV MOVIES AND MINISERIES: "The Failing of Raymond," ABC, 1971; "Death Among Friends," NBC, 1975.

AS A DIRECTOR: "Schlitz Playhouse of Stars: Pattern for Death," CBS, 1957; "Alfred Hitchcock Presents: Impromptu Murder," CBS, 1958; "Goodyear Theatre: Author at Work," NBC, 1960.

HENRY, BUCK

b. Buck Henry Zuckerman, New York City, NY, 1930. Comic actor and writer of movies and TV who's been a regular on comedy shows and a frequent guest on "Saturday Night Live."

AS A REGULAR: "The New Steve Allen Show," ABC, 1961; "That Was the Week That Was," NBC, 1964-65; "The New Show," NBC, 1984; "Falcon Crest," CBS, 1987.

AND: "The Dick Cavett Show," ABC, 1969; "Bob Newhart Special: A Last Laugh at the 60's," ABC, 1970; "Saturday Night Live," NBC, 1976; "Saturday Night Live," NBC, 1977; "Saturday Night Live," NBC, 1978; "Saturday Night Live," NBC, 1979; "Saturday Night Live," NBC, 1980; "Alfred Hitchcock Presents: Murder Me Twice," NBC, 1985; "Murphy Brown: My Dinner with Einstein," CBS, 1989; "Late Night with David Letterman," NBC, 1989; "Trying Times: Hunger Chic," PBS, 1989.

AS CO-CREATOR/WRITER: "Get Smart," NBC, 1965-69; CBS, 1969-70.

AS WRITER: "Alfred Hitchcock Presents: Murder Me Twice," NBC, 1985.

AS A DIRECTOR: "Trying Times: Hunger Chic," PBS, 1989.

* Emmies: 1967.

HENRY, EMMALINE

b. Philadelphia, PA, 1930. Blonde actress often in sitcom roles; she played Amanda, wife of Dr. Bellows (Hayden Rorke) on "I Dream of Jeannie."

AS A REGULAR: "I'm Dickens, He's Fenster,"

ABC, 1962-63; "Mickey," ABC, 1964-65; "I Dream of Jeannie," NBC, 1966-70.

AND: "The Red Skelton Show," CBS, 1961; "The Red Skelton Show: Freddie and the Yuletide Doll," CBS, 1961; "The Munsters: Herman, Coach of the Year," CBS, 1965; "The Farmer's Daughter: Simple Joys of Nature," ABC, 1965; "The Farmer's Daughter: Is He or Isn't He?," ABC, 1966; "Petticoat Junction: Second Honeymoon," CBS, 1966; "The Red Skelton Hour," CBS, 1968; "The Don Knotts Show," NBC, 1970; "Love, American Style: Love and the Busy Husband," ABC, 1971; "Green Acres: The Ex-Secretary," CBS, 1971; "The Bob Newhart Show: The Two Loves of Dr. Hartley," CBS, 1973; "The Streets of San Francisco: No Minor Vices," ABC, 1976; "Three's Company: Chrissy's New Boss," ABC, 1978; "Three's Company: The Catered Affair," ABC, 1979; "Eight Is Enough: I Do, I Do, I Do, I Do," ABC, 1979.

TV MOVIES AND MINISERIES: "Backstairs at the White House," NBC, 1979.

* "The Ex-Secretary" was a sitcom pilot in which Henry played—you guessed it—the ex-secretary to Oliver Douglas (Eddie Albert). The plot: Oliver calls his old secretary because she's the only one who knows of a jeweler who can fix his watch. Hard to believe, but that wasn't exciting enough for the folks at CBS, who passed on the series.

HENRY, GLORIA

b. 1923. Actress who played Alice, mother of Dennis "the menace" Mitchell (Jay North).

AS A REGULAR: "The Abbott and Costello Show," CBS, 1952-54; "Dennis the Menace," CBS, 1959-63.

AND: "Navy Log: The Decoy," ABC, 1957; "Perry Mason: The Case of the Careless Redhead," CBS, 1957; "Father Knows Best: Baby in the House," NBC, 1958; "The Farmer's Daughter: The Nesting Instinct," ABC, 1965.

HENSLEY, PAMELA

b. Los Angeles, CA, October 3, 1950. Attractive actress who played C.J. Parsons, sidekick of suave private dick Matt Houston (Lee Horsley).

AS A REGULAR: "Marcus Welby, M.D.," ABC, 1975-76; "Kingston: Confidential," NBC, 1977; "Buck Rogers in the 25th Century," NBC, 1979-80; "240-Robert," ABC, 1981; "Matt Houston," ABC, 1982-85.

AND: "Kojak: Death Is Not a Passing Grade," CBS, 1974; "Ironside: Run Scared," NBC, 1974; "McMillan and Wife: Downshift to Danger," NBC, 1974; "Lucas Tanner: Thirteen Going on Twenty," NBC, 1974; "The Rockford Files: Say Goodbye to Jennifer," NBC, 1975; "Switch: Legends of the Macunas" CBS, 1977;

TV MOVIES AND MINISERIES: "Death Among

Friends," NBC, 1975; "Kingston: The Power Play," NBC, 1976; "The Rebels," SYN, 1979.

HENSON, JIM

b. *Greenville, MS, September 24, 1936; d. 1990.* Puppeteer-performer who created the Muppets; a gentle soul whose humor and creativity have made him as important a cultural figure as Walt Disney.
AS A REGULAR: "Our Place," CBS, 1967; "Sesame Street," PBS, 1969-90; "Saturday Night Live," NBC, 1975-76; "The Muppet Show," SYN, 1976-81; "Jim Henson's The Storyteller," NBC, 1986-87.
AND: "The Steve Allen Show," NBC, 1956; "The Steve Allen Show," NBC, 1957; "The Dick Cavett Show," ABC, 1972; "Sesame Street 20... and Still Counting," NBC, 1989.
* Emmies: 1974, 1976, 1978, 1981, 1987.

HEPBURN, AUDREY

b. *Brussels, Belgium, May 4, 1929.* Screen actress ("Roman Holiday," "My Fair Lady") who's done a little TV.
AS A GUEST: "CBS Television Workshop: Rainy Day in Paradise Junction," CBS, 1952; "Producers Showcase: Mayerling," NBC, 1957.
TV MOVIES AND MINISERIES: "Love Among Thieves," ABC, 1987.

HEPBURN, KATHARINE

b. *Hartford, CT, November 8, 1909.* Legendary movie actress and star who's turned her talent to TV movies, some of which have needed all the help they could get; she won an Emmy for "Love Among the Ruins."
AS A GUEST: "The Dick Cavett Show," ABC, 1973.
TV MOVIES AND MINISERIES: "The Glass Menagerie," ABC, 1973; "Love Among the Ruins," ABC, 1975; "The Corn Is Green," CBS, 1979; "Mrs. Delafield Wants to Marry," CBS, 1986; "Laura Lansing Slept Here," NBC, 1988.
* Emmies: 1975.

HERBERT, DON

b. *Waconia, MN, July 10, 1917.* Gentle TV personality who, as Mr. Wizard, has introduced millions of kids to the wonders of science.
AS A REGULAR: "Watch Mr. Wizard," NBC, 1951-65; NBC, 1971-72; NIK, 1984- .
AND: "Perry Como's Kraft Music Hall," NBC, 1962; "Late Night with David Letterman," NBC, 1982; "The Pat Sajak Show," CBS, 1989.
* Herbert also did commercials for G.E. on "G.E. Theatre" during the fifties.

HERLIHY, ED

b. *Dorchester, MA.* Commercial announcer who hawked Kraft products ("Good food and good food ideas") for years.
AS A REGULAR: "Kraft Television Theatre," NBC, 1947-55; ABC, 1953-55; "The Perry Como Show," NBC, 1959-61; "Perry Como's Kraft Music Hall," NBC, 1961-63; "The Tonight Show," NBC, 1962; "The Kraft Music Hall," NBC, 1967-71.
AND: "Christophers: Everyone Can Be Courteous," SYN, 1962.

HERMAN, PEE-WEE

b. *Paul Reubens.* Comedian with an arrested, childlike style all his own.
AS A REGULAR: "Pee Wee's Playhouse," CBS, 1985- .
AND: "Faerie Tale Theatre: Pinocchio," SHO, 1984; "Saturday Night Live," NBC, 1985.

HERRMANN, EDWARD

b. *Washington, D.C., July 21, 1943.* Actor who played Franklin Roosevelt on two TV dramas and Father McCabe, founder of St. Eligius hospital, on a couple of "St. Elsewhere" episodes.
AS A REGULAR: "Beacon Hill," CBS, 1975.
AND: "M*A*S*H: Heal Thyself," CBS, 1980; "St. Elsewhere: Time Heals," NBC, 1986; "St. Elsewhere: Where There's Hope, There's Crosby," NBC, 1986; "American Playhouse: The Beginning of the Firm," PBS, 1989.
TV MOVIES AND MINISERIES: "Eleanor and Franklin," ABC, 1976; "Eleanor and Franklin: The White House Years," ABC, 1977; "Portrait of a Stripper," CBS, 1979; "Freedom Road," NBC, 1979; "Memorial Day," CBS, 1983; "American Playhouse: Concealed Enemies," PBS, 1984; "Murrow," HBO, 1986.

HERSHEY, BARBARA

b. *Barbara Herzstein, Hollywood, CA, February 5, 1948.* Actress who began in TV, went to movies, became a flower child and came back to TV.
AS A REGULAR: "The Monroes," ABC, 1966-67; "From Here to Eternity," NBC, 1980.
AND: "Gidget: Chivarly Isn't Dead, It's Just Hiding," ABC, 1965; "The Farmer's Daughter: The Fall and Rise of Steven Morley," ABC, 1966; "Gidget: Love and the Single Gidget," ABC, 1966; "Bob Hope Chrysler Theatre: Holloway's Daughters," NBC, 1966; "Daniel Boone: The King Is Smiling," NBC, 1967; "The Invaders: The Miracle," ABC, 1968; "The High Chaparral: The Peace Maker," NBC, 1968; "CBS Playhouse: Secrets," CBS, 1968; "Love Story: The Roller Coaster Stops Here," NBC, 1973; "Kung Fu: Ordeal by Love," ABC, 1974; "The Toni Tennille Show," SYN, 1980; "Faerie Tale Theatre: The Nightingale," SHO, 1984; "Alfred Hitchcock Presents: Murder Me Twice," NBC, 1985.

TV MOVIES AND MINISERIES: "Flood," NBC, 1976; "In the Glitter Palace," NBC, 1977; "Just a Little Inconvenience," NBC, 1977; "A Man Called Intrepid," SYN, 1979; "Angel on My Shoulder," ABC, 1980; "My Wicked, Wicked Ways: The Legend of Errol Flynn," CBS, 1985; "Passion Flower," CBS, 1986.

HERSHOLT, JEAN

b. Copenhagen, Denmark, July 12, 1886; d. 1956. Actor who played the kindly Dr. Christian in movies, on the radio and on TV.
AS A REGULAR: "Doctor Christian," SYN, 1956.
AND: "This Is Your Life," NBC, 1954.

HESLOV, GRANT

b. Los Angeles, CA, May 15, 1963.
AS A REGULAR: "Spencer," NBC, 1984-85.
AND: "Happy Days: The People vs. the Fonz," ABC, 1984; "L.A. Law: The Douglas Fur Ball," NBC, 1987; "Beverly Hills Buntz: Fit to Be Tied," NBC, 1987; "thirtysomething: Tenure," ABC, 1988; "Murder, She Wrote: Jake's Law," CBS, 1989.
TV MOVIES AND MINISERIES: "Gang of Four," ABC, 1989.

HESSEMAN, HOWARD

b. Salem, OR, February 27, 1940. Familiar sitcom presence fondly remembered as Dr. Johnny Fever on "WKRP in Cincinnati," and more recently as teacher Charlie Moore on "Head of the Class"; on "The Bob Newhart Show" he played an occasional member of Bob Hartley's therapy group, a failed writer whose big TV idea was "The Nazi Comedy Hour."
AS A REGULAR: "The Bob Newhart Show," CBS, 1974-76; "WKRP in Cincinnati," CBS, 1978-82; "One Day at a Time," CBS, 1982-84; "Head of the Class," ABC, 1986-90.
AND: "Firehouse: The Hottest Place in Town," ABC, 1974; "Rhoda: I'll Be Loving You, Sometimes," CBS, 1974; "Laverne & Shirley: Christmas Eve at the Booby Hatch," ABC, 1976; "The Bob Newhart Show: Group on a Hot Tin Roof," CBS, 1978; "Saturday Night Live," NBC, 1979; "Women Who Rate a 10," NBC, 1981; "Saturday Night Live," NBC, 1982; "9 to 5: Home Is Where the Hart Is," ABC, 1982; "Saturday Night Live," NBC, 1983; "Murder, She Wrote: Widow, Weep for Me," CBS, 1985; "Woodstock: Return to the Planet of the '60s," CBS, 1989.
TV MOVIES AND MINISERIES: "More Than Friends," ABC, 1978; "Outside Chance," CBS, 1978; "The Great American Traffic Jam," NBC, 1980; "Victims," ABC, 1982; "One Shoe Makes It Murder," CBS, 1982; "Best Kept Secrets," ABC, 1984; "Silence of the Heart," CBS, 1984; "Six Against the Rock," NBC, 1987; "The Diamond Trap," CBS, 1988.

HESTON, CHARLTON

b. Evanston, IL, October 4, 1924. Stiff actor, Moses in "The Ten Commandments," who almost always plays, rather stiffly, heroic figures.
AS A REGULAR: "F.D.R.," ABC, 1965; "The Colbys," ABC, 1985-87.
AND: "Studio One: Smoke," CBS, 1949; "Studio One: Taming of the Shrew," CBS, 1950; "Philco Playhouse: Hear My Heart Speak," NBC, 1950; "Studio One: Letter From Cairo," CBS, 1950; "Suspense: Santa Fe Flight," CBS, 1951; "Curtain Call: The Liar," NBC, 1952; "Robert Montgomery Presents: Dr. Gatskill's Blue Shoes," NBC, 1952; "Philco Playhouse: Elegy," NBC, 1953; "Films of Faith: Three Lives," SYN, 1953; "Climax!: Bailout at 43,000," CBS, 1955; "Playhouse 90: Forbidden Area," CBS, 1956; "The Steve Allen Show," NBC, 1956; "The Jackie Gleason Show," CBS, 1956; "The $64,000 Question," CBS, 1957; "Climax!: The Trial of Captain Wirz," CBS, 1957; "Schlitz Playhouse of Stars: Switch Station," CBS, 1957; "Shirley Temple's Storybook: Beauty and the Beast," NBC, 1958; "Playhouse 90: Point of No Return," CBS, 1958; "The Steve Allen Show," NBC, 1959; The Ed Sullivan Show," CBS, 1959; "The Steve Allen Plymouth Show," NBC, 1960; "The Ed Sullivan Show," CBS, 1960; "Sid Caesar Special: Tiptoe Through TV," CBS, 1960; "The Ed Sullivan Show," CBS, 1961; "Alcoa Premiere: The Fugitive Eye," ABC, 1961; "Westinghouse Presents: An Old-Fashioned Thanksgiving," ABC, 1961; "Perry Como's Kraft Music Hall," NBC, 1963; "Hallmark Hall of Fame: The Patriots," NBC, 1963; "The Mike Douglas Show," SYN, 1964; "The Mike Douglas Show," SYN, 1968; "Hallmark Hall of Fame: Elizabeth the Queen," NBC, 1968; "Don Adams Special: Hooray for Hollywood," CBS, 1970; "The Dick Cavett Show," ABC, 1971; "The Boston Pops in Hollywood," PBS, 1976; "The John Davidson Show," SYN, 1980; "The Mike Douglas Show," SYN, 1980; "Saturday Night Live," NBC, 1987; "Saturday Night Live's 15th Anniversary," NBC, 1989.
TV MOVIES AND MINISERIES: "Chiefs," CBS, 1983; "Nairobi Affair," CBS, 1984; "Proud Men," ABC, 1987; "Original Sin," NBC, 1989.

HEWETT, CHRISTOPHER

b. England. Stage actor who came to TV, mostly in silly roles; best known as Lawrence, assistant to Mr. Rourke (Ricardo Montalban) on "Fantasy Island" after Tattoo (Herve Villechaze) blew the place, and as Mr. Belvedere.
AS A REGULAR: "Ivan the Terrible," CBS, 1976; "Fantasy Island," ABC, 1983-84; "Mr. Belvedere," ABC, 1985-90.
AND: "E/R: Mr. Fix-It," CBS, 1984; "Murder, She

Wrote: It Runs in the Family," CBS, 1987; "The Ice Capades with Jason Bateman and Alyssa Milano," ABC, 1989.

TV MOVIES AND MINISERIES: "ABC Theatre of the Month: The Elephant Man," ABC, 1982.

HEWITT, ALAN
b. New York City, NY, January 21, 1915; d. 1986. Stern-voiced actor who played Det. Bill Brennan on "My Favorite Martian"; often confused with actor James Gregory.
AS A REGULAR: "My Favorite Martian," CBS, 1964-66.
AND: "Matinee Theatre: House of 7 Gables," NBC, 1956; "The Phil Silvers Show: Bilko's Tax Trouble," CBS, 1956; "The Thin Man: Requiem for a Recluse," NBC, 1957; "U.S. Steel Hour: The Change in Chester," CBS, 1957; "Armstrong Circle Theatre: ... and Bring Home a Baby," CBS, 1959; "Peter Loves Mary: Make a Million," NBC, 1960; "Dennis the Menace: Man of the House," CBS, 1960; "National Velvet: Barbecue," NBC, 1960; "The Barbara Stanwyck Show: No One," NBC, 1960; "The Real McCoys: Farmer or Scientist," ABC, 1961; "Perry Mason: The Case of the Wintry Wife," CBS, 1961; "Bachelor Father: Encore in Paris," NBC, 1961; "Maverick: Triple Indemnity," ABC, 1961; "Dennis the Menace: Dennis and the Good Example," CBS, 1961; "McKeever and the Colonel: TV or Not TV," NBC, 1962; "Dennis the Menace: Baby Booties," CBS, 1963; "The Defenders: The Hour Before Doomsday," CBS, 1963; "I'm Dickens, He's Fenster: Table Tennis, Anyone?," ABC, 1963; "Grindl: Grindl, Girl Wac," NBC, 1964; "Hazel: All Mixed Up," NBC, 1964; "The Defenders: The Man Who," CBS, 1964; "No Time for Sergeants: Two Aces in a Hole," ABC, 1964; "No Time for Sergeants: The Day Blue Blew," ABC, 1965; "F Troop: Scourge of the West," ABC, 1965; "Bewitched: Eat at Mario's," ABC, 1965; "Voyage to the Bottom of the Sea: ... And Five of Us Are Left," ABC, 1965; "Dr. Kildare: Fathers and Daughters/A Gift of Love/The Tent-Dwellers/Going Home," NBC, 1965; "Please Don't Eat the Daisies: We're Bigger Than They Are, But...," NBC, 1965; "Gomer Pyle, USMC: Follow That Car," CBS, 1966; "The Wild Wild West: The Night of the Colonel's Ghost," CBS, 1967; "Daktari: Undercover Judy," CBS, 1967; "I Dream of Jeannie: You Can't Arrest Me-I Don't Have a Driver's License," NBC, 1967; "Ironside: The Laying On of Hands," NBC, 1970; "Love, American Style: Love and Accidental Passion," ABC, 1971; "The Bob Newhart Show: I Want to Be Alone," CBS, 1972; "Maude: The Rip-Off," CBS, 1976.
TV MOVIES AND MINISERIES: "Wake Me When the War Is Over," ABC, 1969; "The D.A.: Murder One," NBC, 1969; "The Legend of Lizzie Borden," ABC, 1975; "Best Sellers: Captains and the Kings," NBC, 1976.

HEWITT, MARTIN
b. Claremont, CA, 1960.
AS A REGULAR: "The Family Tree," NBC, 1983.
AND: "Hotel: Christmas," ABC, 1983; "The Love Boat: The Winning Number," ABC, 1986; "Father Dowling Mysteries: Mafia Priest," NBC, 1989.

HEWITT, VIRGINIA
b. Shreveport, LA, 1925; d. 1986. Actress who played Carol on "Space Patrol."
AS A REGULAR: "Space Patrol," ABC, 1951-52.

HEXUM, JON-ERIK
b. Tenafly, NJ, November 5, 1957; d. 1984. Hunky actor who died of a concussion he suffered when he fired a prop pistol at his head.
AS A REGULAR: "Voyagers," NBC, 1982-83; "Cover Up," CBS, 1984.
AND: "Hotel: Cinderella," ABC, 1984.
TV MOVIES AND MINISERIES: "The Making of a Male Model," ABC, 1983.

HEYDT, LOUIS JEAN
b. Montclair, NJ, April 17, 1905; d. 1960. Character actor who usually played heavies.
AS A REGULAR: "Waterfront," SYN, 1954-55; "MacKenzie's Raiders," SYN, 1958-59.
AND: "Science Fiction Theatre: Y.O.R.D.," SYN, 1955; "Kaiser Aluminum Hour: Cracker Money," NBC, 1956; "Wire Service: Violence Preferred," ABC, 1957; "U.S. Steel Hour: A Loud Laugh," CBS, 1957; "My Friend Flicka: The Little Secret," CBS, 1957; "Wagon Train: The Bernal Sierra Story," NBC, 1958; "The Jane Wyman Show: Hide and Seek," NBC, 1958; "Buick Electra Playhouse: The Killers," CBS, 1959; "Tales of Wells Fargo: Cole Younger," NBC, 1960; "Rawhide: Incident of the Devil and His Due," CBS, 1960; "Dick Powell's Zane Grey Theatre: Man in the Middle," CBS, 1960.

HICKMAN, DARRYL
b. Los Angeles, CA, July 28, 1931. Former juvenile actor, brother of Dwayne.
AS A REGULAR: "The Many Loves of Dobie Gillis," CBS, 1959-60; "Walt Disney Presents: Texas John Slaughter," ABC, 1959-60; "The Americans," NBC, 1961.
AND: "Playhouse 90: Winter Dreams," CBS, 1957; "Perry Mason: Case of the Sleepwalker's Niece," CBS, 1957; "Climax!: Tunnel of Fear," CBS, 1957; "Alfred Hitchcock Presents: Heart of Gold," CBS, 1957; "Playhouse 90: The 80 Yard Run," CBS, 1958; "Matinee Theatre: The Odd Ones," NBC, 1958; "G.E. Theatre: Incident," CBS, 1958; "Studio One: The Lonely Stage," CBS, 1958; "The Untouchables: You Can't Pick the Number," ABC, 1959; "Rendezvous: Party for the Kids," SYN, 1960; "The Man and the

Challenge: Man in the Capsule," NBC, 1960; "The Detectives Starring Robert Taylor: Trial by Fire," ABC, 1960; "Here's Hollywood," NBC, 1961; "The Loretta Young Show: The Golden Cord," NBC, 1961; "Rawhide: Incident of the Running Iron," CBS, 1961; "U.S. Steel Hour: Tangle of Truth," CBS, 1961; "87th Precinct: 'Til Death," NBC, 1961; "Walt Disney's Wonderful World of Color: Johnny Shiloh," NBC, 1963; "Missing Links," NBC, 1964; "You Don't Say," NBC, 1964; "The Match Game," NBC, 1965; "Maude: Phillip and Sam," CBS, 1977; "All in the Family: The Commercial," CBS, 1978.

TV MOVIES AND MINISERIES: "High School U.S.A.," NBC, 1983.

AS WRITER: "The Loretta Young Show: The Golden Cord," NBC, 1961.

HICKMAN, DWAYNE

b. Los Angeles, CA, 1934. Former juvenile actor with a gee-whiz quality and a sardonic way with a line that served him well as that philosophical, girl-crazed teen Dobie Gillis.

AS A REGULAR: "The Bob Cummings Show," NBC, 1955; CBS, 1955-57; NBC, 1957-59; "The Many Loves of Dobie Gillis," CBS, 1959-63.

AND: "The Dick Clark Saturday Night Beechnut Show," ABC, 1958; "Dinah Shore Chevy Show," NBC, 1960; "The Ford Show," NBC, 1960; "Here's Hollywood," NBC, 1960; "The Adventures of Ozzie and Harriet: The Kappa Sig Party," ABC, 1961; "Object Is," ABC, 1963; "The Greatest Show on Earth: Rosetta," ABC, 1964; "Wagon Train: The Clay Shelby Story," ABC, 1964; "Combat!: Run, Sheep, Run," ABC, 1966; "We'll Take Manhattan," NBC, 1967; "Ironside: Due Process of Law," NBC, 1968; "The Flying Nun: The Boyfriend," ABC, 1969; "The Wonderful World of Disney: My Dog, the Thief," NBC, 1969; "Love, American Style: Love and the Phone Booth," ABC, 1969; "The Mod Squad: The Healer," ABC, 1969; "Love, American Style: Love and the Topless Policy," ABC, 1972; "Kolchak, the Night Stalker: The Youth Killer," ABC, 1975; "Whatever Happened to Dobie Gillis?," CBS, 1977; "Win, Lose or Draw," SYN, 1988; "Murder, She Wrote: Murder-According to Maggie," CBS, 1990.

TV MOVIES AND MINISERIES: "Bring Me the Head of Dobie Gillis," CBS, 1988.

* "Whatever Happened to Dobie Gillis" was an unsold pilot that looked in on Dobie as an adult. He'd married longtime girlfriend Zelda (Sheila James) and was the owner of the Gillises' grocery store.
* Hickman eventually went to work in TV behind the scenes, as a CBS production executive.

HICKS, CATHERINE

b. Scottsdale, AZ, August 6, 1951.

AS A REGULAR: "Ryan's Hope," ABC, 1976-78; "The Bad News Bears," CBS, 1979-80; "Tucker's Witch," CBS, 1982-83.

AND: "The Tonight Show Starring Johnny Carson," NBC, 1988.

TV MOVIES AND MINISERIES: "Love for Rent," ABC, 1979; "To Race the Wind," CBS, 1980; "Happy Endings," CBS, 1983.

HICKS, HILLY

b. Los Angeles, CA, May 4, 1950. Black actor, often in comic roles.

AS A REGULAR: "Roll Out," CBS, 1973-74.

AND: "The Bill Cosby Show: Let X Equal a Lousy Weekend," NBC, 1969; "Ironside: L'Chayim," NBC, 1969; "Room 222: The Exchange Teacher," ABC, 1970; "Marcus Welby, M.D.: Aura of a New Tomorrow," ABC, 1970; "The Bill Cosby Show: Each According to Appetite," NBC, 1971; "The Mod Squad: Crime Club," ABC, 1972; "The Rookies: Concrete Valley, Neon Sky," ABC, 1972; "The Mod Squad: Crime Club," ABC, 1972; "Adam 12: The Chase," NBC, 1972; "The Rookies: Easy Money," ABC, 1973; "Barnaby Jones: Dangerous Summer," CBS, 1975; "M*A*S*H: White Gold," CBS, 1975; "M*A*S*H: Postop," CBS, 1977; "One Day at a Time: Made for Each Other," CBS, 1979; "Hill Street Blues: Hacked to Pieces," NBC, 1985; "Hill Street Blues: Seoul on Ice," NBC, 1985.

TV MOVIES AND MINISERIES: "Roots," ABC, 1977; "ABC Theatre: Friendly Fire," ABC, 1979; "Turnover Smith," ABC, 1980.

HIGGINS, JOEL

b. Bloomington, IL, September 28, 1943. Light comic actor; he played Edward Stratton III, dad of Ricky (Ricky Schroeder) on "Silver Spoons."

AS A REGULAR: "Search for Tomorrow," CBS, 1975-78; "Salvage I," ABC, 1979; "Best of the West," ABC, 1981-82; "Silver Spoons," NBC, 1982-86; SYN, 1986-87; "Have Faith," ABC, 1989.

TV MOVIES AND MINISERIES: "Salvage I," ABC, 1979; "Killing at Hell's Gate," CBS, 1981; "Bare Essence," CBS, 1982; "Threesome," CBS, 1984; "Laura Lansing Slept Here," NBC, 1988.

HILL, ARTHUR

b. Melfort, Canada, August 1, 1922. Actor who played the uptight Owen Marshall, counselor at law.

AS A REGULAR: "Owen Marshall, Counselor at Law," ABC, 1971-74; "Hagen," CBS, 1980; "Glitter," ABC, 1984-85.

AND: "Hallmark Hall of Fame: Born Yesterday,"

NBC, 1956; "Studio One: The Morning Face," CBS, 1957; "U.S. Steel Hour: The Enemies," CBS, 1958; "Patti Page Olds Show," ABC, 1959; "Alfred Hitchcock Presents: Human Interest Story," CBS, 1959; "Du Pont Show of the Month: Ethan Frome," CBS, 1960; "Play of the Week: The Closing Door," SYN, 1960; "U.S. Steel Hour: The Girl Who Knew Too Much," CBS, 1960; "Lamp Unto My Feet: Best for All Concerned," CBS, 1961; "Ben Casey: The Sweet Kiss of Madness," ABC, 1961; "Westinghouse Presents: Come Again to Carthage," CBS, 1961; "Armstrong Circle Theatre: Battle of Hearts," CBS, 1961; "The Untouchables: Canada Run," ABC, 1962; "U.S. Steel Hour: The Big Laugh," CBS, 1962; "U.S. Steel Hour: Who Is This Woman?," CBS, 1962; "The Defenders: The Last Six Months," CBS, 1962; "Route 66: Kiss the Maiden All Forlorn," CBS, 1962; "Slattery's People: Question: Remember the Dark Sins of Youth?," CBS, 1964; "The Defenders: Go-Between," CBS, 1964; "The Reporter: Vote for Murder," CBS, 1964; "The FBI: Flight to Harbin," ABC, 1966; "Voyage to the Bottom of the Sea: The Monster From the Inferno," ABC, 1966; "The FBI: The Plague Merchant," ABC, 1966; "Mission: Impossible: The Carriers," CBS, 1966; "Bob Hope Chrysler Theatre: The Fatal Mistake," NBC, 1966; "The Invaders: The Leeches," ABC, 1967; "The FBI: By Force and Violence," ABC, 1967; "The Fugitive: Death of a Very Small Killer," ABC, 1967; "CBS Playhouse: Secrets," CBS, 1968; "The FBI: The Attorney," ABC, 1969; "Bracken's World: All the Beautiful Young Girls," NBC, 1969; "The Name of the Game: Echo of a Nightmare," NBC, 1970; "The Bold Ones: Giants Never Kneel," NBC, 1970; "The Name of the Game: Aquarius Descending," NBC, 1970; "Marcus Welby, M.D.: Men Who Care," ABC, 1971; "Hallmark Hall of Fame: The Rivalry," NBC, 1975; "Little House on the Prairie: Journey in the Spring," NBC, 1976; "Murder, She Wrote: The Murder of Sherlock Holmes," CBS, 1984.

TV MOVIES AND MINISERIES: "The Other Man," NBC, 1970; "Vanished," NBC, 1971; "Owen Marshall, Counselor at Law-A Pattern of Morality," ABC, 1971; "Ordeal," ABC, 1973; "Death Be Not Proud," ABC, 1975; "Judge Horton and the Scottsboro Boys," NBC, 1976; "The Ordeal of Dr. Mudd," CBS, 1980; "The Revenge of the Stepford Wives," NBC, 1980; "Angel Dusted," NBC, 1981; "Intimate Agony," ABC, 1983; "Christmas Eve," NBC, 1986; "Perry Mason: The Case of the Notorious Nun," NBC, 1986.

HILL, BENNY

b. England, January 21, 1925. Comedian who believes there's nothing funnier than a man in a dress.

AS A REGULAR: "The Benny Hill Show," SYN, 1979-82.

HILL, DANA

b. Van Nuys, CA, May 6, 1964.

AS A REGULAR: "The Two of Us," CBS, 1981-82; "Sugar and Spice," CBS, 1990.

AND: "The Fall Guy: Child's Play," ABC, 1982; "Faerie Tale Theatre: The Boy Who Left Home to Find Out About the Shivers," SHO, 1984; "Marvin: Baby of the Year," CBS, 1989.

TV MOVIES AND MINISERIES: "The $5.20 an Hour Dream," CBS, 1980; "Silence of the Heart," CBS, 1984; "Combat High," NBC, 1986.

HILL, STEVEN

b. Seattle, WA, February 24, 1922. Actor who played Daniel Briggs, the first leader of the Impossible Missions Force; an Orthodox Jew, he left "Mission: Impossible" when the show's shooting schedule conflicted with his sabbath.

AS A REGULAR: "Mission: Impossible," CBS, 1966-67; "One Life to Live," ABC, 1984-85.

AND: "Suspense: A Pocketful of Murder," ABC, 1950; "Schlitz Playhouse of Stars: The Man I Marry," CBS, 1952; "Lux Video Theatre: Legacy of Love," NBC, 1952; "Goodyear TV Playhouse: The Inward Eye," NBC, 1954; "The Mask: The Young Dancer," ABC, 1954; "The Mask: Marked for Murder," ABC, 1954; "Goodyear TV Playhouse: The Arena," NBC, 1954; "Playhouse 90: For Whom the Bell Tolls," CBS, 1959; "The Lineup: The Strange Return of Army Armitage," CBS, 1959; "The Sacco-Vanzetti Story," NBC, 1960; "The Untouchables: The Jack 'Legs' Diamond Story," ABC, 1960; "Adventures in Paradise: Act of Piracy," ABC, 1961; "Route 66: A City of Wheels," CBS, 1962; "The Untouchables: Downfall," ABC, 1962; "The Eleventh Hour: There Are Dragons in this Forest," NBC, 1962; "Ben Casey: Legacy From a Stranger," ABC, 1962; "Dr. Kildare: Cobweb Chain," NBC, 1962; "Ben Casey: I'll Be All Right in the Morning," ABC, 1963; "Naked City: Barefoot on a Bed of Coals," ABC, 1963; "Bob Hope Chrysler Theatre: Something About Lee Wiley," NBC, 1963; "Espionage: The Incurable One," NBC, 1963; "The Greatest Show on Earth: Corsicans Don't Cry," ABC, 1964; "The Alfred Hitchcock Hour: Who Needs an Enemy?," CBS, 1964; "The Alfred Hitchcock Hour: The Thanatos Palace Hotel," NBC, 1965; "Kraft Suspense Theatre: The Safe House," NBC, 1965; "Rawhide: The Gray Rock Hotel," CBS, 1965; "The Fugitive: The White Knight," ABC, 1966; "Columbo: Murder, Smoke and Shadows," ABC, 1989.

TV MOVIES AND MINISERIES: "King," NBC, 1978; "Between Two Women," ABC, 1986.

HILLAIRE, MARCEL

b. Germany, April 23, 1908. Actor who usually played fussy Europeans.

AS A REGULAR: "Adventures in Paradise," ABC, 1960-62.

AND: "Peter Gunn: A Slight Touch of Homicide," NBC, 1960; "Special Tonight: Ninotchka," ABC, 1960; "The Twilight Zone: A Most Unusual Camera," CBS, 1960; "The Many Loves of Dobie Gillis: Parlez-Vous English," CBS, 1960; "The Dick Powell Show: A Swiss Affair," NBC, 1961; "McHale's Navy: The Big Raffle," ABC, 1963; "The Twilight Zone: The New Exhibit," CBS, 1963; "Combat!: A Rare Vintage," ABC, 1964; "The Man From UNCLE: The Virtue Affair," NBC, 1965; "I Spy: Chrysanthemum," NBC, 1965; "The Man From UNCLE: The See-Paris-and-Die Affair," NBC, 1965; "The Girl From UNCLE: The Dog-Gone Affair," NBC, 1966; "Get Smart: House of Max," CBS, 1970; "Rosetti and Ryan: Ms. Bluebeard," NBC, 1977.

TV MOVIES AND MINISERIES: "Now You See It, Now You Don't," NBC, 1968; "Evening in Byzantium," SYN, 1978; "Amerika," ABC, 1987.

HILLEBRAND, FRED
b. Brooklyn, NY, 1893; d. 1963.
AS A REGULAR: "Martin Kane, Private Eye," NBC, 1949-50.

HILLER, DAME WENDY
b. Bramhall, England, August 15, 1912. British actress, usually playing upper-crust types.
AS A GUEST: "Studio One: The Traveling Lady," CBS, 1957; "Matinee Theatre: Ann Veronica," NBC, 1957; "Matinee Theatre: Eden End," NBC, 1958; "Alfred Hitchcock Presents: Graduating Class," CBS, 1959; "Profiles in Courage: Anne Hutchinson," NBC, 1965.
TV MOVIES AND MINISERIES: "David Copperfield," ABC, 1970; "Hallmark Hall of Fame: Witness for the Prosecution," CBS, 1982; "Masterpiece Theatre: All Passion Spent," PBS, 1989.

HILLERMAN, JOHN
b. Denison, TX, December 20, 1932. Mustachioed, velvet-voiced actor who played Higgins, tsk-tsking sidekick of "Magnum, P.I."
AS A REGULAR: "Ellery Queen," NBC, 1975-76; "The Betty White Show," CBS, 1977-78; "One Day at a Time," CBS, 1977-80; "Magnum P.I.," CBS, 1980-88; "The Hogan Family," CBS, 1990- .
AS A GUEST: "The FBI: The Deadly Species," ABC, 1972; "Mannix: Light and Shadow," CBS, 1973; "Mannix: Silent Target," CBS, 1973; "Kojak: The Only Way Out," CBS, 1974; "The Bob Crane Show: Son of Campus Capers," NBC, 1975; "One Day at a Time: The Maestro," CBS, 1976; "Serpico: Rapid Fire," NBC, 1976; "Flying High: Pilot," CBS, 1978; "Little House on the Prairie: Harriet's Happings," NBC, 1978; "The Love Boat: Rent-a-Family," ABC, 1979; "Lou Grant: Pack," CBS, 1980; "The Love Boat: The

Last Case," ABC, 1983; "Murder, She Wrote: Magnum on Ice," CBS, 1986.

TV MOVIES AND MINISERIES: "Rachel, Sweet Rachel," ABC, 1971; "The Great Man's Whiskers," NBC, 1973; "The Law," NBC, 1974; "Ellery Queen," NBC, 1975; "Kill Me if You Can," NBC, 1977; "Betrayal," NBC, 1978; "A Guide for the Married Woman," ABC, 1978; "The Murder That Wouldn't Die," NBC, 1980; "Marathon," CBS, 1980; "Little Gloria ... Happy at Last," NBC, 1982; "Street of Dreams," CBS, 1988; "Assault and Matrimony," NBC, 1989.

* Emmies: 1987.

HILL STREET BLUES, NBC, 1981-87. This ensemble drama has been as influential in its way as "The Mary Tyler Moore Show" was to sitcoms. Set in a crime-infested neighborhood of a major city, "Hill Street Blues" took an uncompromising look how bad things could get in Ronald Reagan's America and the effect it had on the people we paid to keep the peace. Through it all, like the surgeons surrounded by dying boys on "M*A*S*H," the Hill Street cops fought to keep their sanity through drink, sex, macho bonding and rough talk—the show's producers created a whole new kind of slang for the cops that sounded dirty, but really wasn't. Words like "hairball" and "scumbag" entered the vernacular.

Captain Frank Furillo (Daniel J. Travanti), a recovering alcoholic and uncompromising straight arrow, was saved by his love for public defender Joyce Davenport (Veronica Hamel), and vice versa.

At the calm eye of the storm, Furillo dealt with crooked cops, an endless parade of human misery and the political grandstand-ing of Chief Fletcher Daniels (Jon Cypher). He was forced to negotiate with street gangleaders, flattering them and withstand-ing their verbal abuse to prevent warfare. Still, cops were killed, victims were emotionally scarred, lives were wasted, plate glass was broken—someone always seemed to be flying through a window—and killers were set free on technicalities. In the show's final episode, somebody torched the Hill Street precinct station. The cops would be dispersed, some to neighborhoods even worse. Nothing was resolved, nothing ended. The plate glass would keep breaking somewhere else.

HINDLE, ART
b. Canada, July 21, 1948. Actor who played Jeff Farraday on "Dallas."

AS A REGULAR: "Kingston: Confidential," NBC, 1977; "Dallas," CBS, 1981-82; "Berrenger's," NBC, 1985.

AND: "Scarecrow and Mrs. King: Tale of the Dancing Weasel," CBS, 1985; "Murder, She Wrote: Murder in the Electric Cathedral," CBS, 1986; "Murder, She Wrote: The Days Dwindle Down," CBS, 1987; "Night Heat: Ice," CBS, 1988.

TV MOVIES AND MINISERIES: "Law and Order," NBC, 1976; "The Clone Master," NBC, 1978; "Some Kind of Miracle," CBS, 1979; "The Power Within," ABC, 1979; "Before and After," ABC, 1979; "Fun and Games," ABC, 1980; "Desperate Lives," CBS, 1982; "Mother's Day," FAM, 1989.

HINES, CONNIE
b. Dedham, MA. 1936. Pert actress who played Carol Post, wife of Wilbur (Alan Young), who kept a talking horse in the garage.

AS A REGULAR: "Mr. Ed," SYN, 1961; CBS, 1961-65.

AND: "Bronco: Game at the Beacon Club," ABC, 1959; "The Millionaire: Millionaire Nancy Pearson," CBS, 1959; "The Untouchables: The Doreen Maney Story," ABC, 1960; "Johnny Ringo: The Assassins," CBS, 1960; "Tightrope!: A Matter of Money," CBS, 1960; "Perry Mason: The Case of the Singular Double," CBS, 1960; "Riverboat: Chicota Landing," NBC, 1960; "The Brothers Brannagan: Sunday's Jewels," SYN, 1962; "Stump the Stars," CBS, 1963; "Hollywood Squares," NBC, 1970; "Love, American Style: Love and the Old Boyfriend," ABC, 1971; "The Mod Squad: The Price of Love," ABC, 1971; "Room 222: Here's to the Boy Most Likely," ABC, 1973.

* Hines came to Hollywood on May 24, 1959. That's the kind of thing starlets used to tell interviewers.

HINGLE, PAT
b. Denver, CO, July 19, 1923. Beefy character actor who can play nasty as well as nice.

AS A REGULAR: "Gunsmoke," CBS, 1971; "Stone," ABC, 1980.

AND: "Studio One: An Almanac of Liberty," CBS, 1954; "The Phil Silvers Show: A.W.O.L.," CBS, 1955; "U.S. Steel Hour: A Matter of Pride," CBS, 1957; "Studio One: The Human Barrier," CBS, 1957; "Suspicion: Heartbeat," NBC, 1957; "Alfred Hitchcock Presents: Night of the Execution," CBS, 1957; "Frontiers of Faith: The House of Paper," NBC, 1959; "U.S. Steel Hour: The Last Autumn," CBS, 1959; "Route 66: Burning for Burning," CBS, 1961; "The Twilight Zone: The Incredible World of Horace Ford," CBS, 1963; "Dr. Kildare: The Heart, an Imperfect Machine," NBC, 1963; "Kraft Suspense Theatre: The Name of the Game," NBC, 1963; "The

Fugitive: Search in a Windy City," ABC, 1964; "Carol for Another Christmas," ABC, 1964; "Daniel Boone: The Returning," NBC, 1965; "The Fugitive: Nicest Fella You'd Ever Want to Meet," ABC, 1965; "The Defenders: A Matter of Law and Disorder," CBS, 1965; "The Andy Griffith Show: Wyatt Earp," CBS, 1966; "The Loner: The Mourners for Johnny Sharp," CBS, 1966; "A Man Called Shenandoah: Plunder," ABC, 1966; "The Glass Menagerie," CBS, 1966; "Mission: Impossible: The Confession," CBS, 1967; "Bob Hope Chrysler Theatre: To Sleep, Perchance to Scream," NBC, 1967; "Cimarron Strip: Broken Wing," CBS, 1967; "Run for Your Life: The Company of Scoundrels," NBC, 1967; "The Invaders: The Prophet," ABC, 1967; "The High Chaparral: Threshold of Courage," NBC, 1968; "On Stage: Certain Honorable Men," NBC, 1968; "NET Playhouse: The Trail of Tears," NET, 1970; "Medical Center: Crossroads," CBS, 1971; "Hallmark Hall of Fame: All the Way Home," NBC, 1971; "Owen Marshall, Counselor at Law: A Question of Degree," ABC, 1972; "Kung Fu: The Soul Is the Warrior," ABC, 1973; "The Rookies: Life Robbery," ABC, 1973; "The FBI: Memory of a Legend," ABC, 1973; "The Streets of San Francisco: Web of Lies," ABC, 1975; "Barnaby Jones: Dead Heat," CBS, 1976; "M*A*S*H: April Fools," CBS, 1980; "St. Elsewhere: Brothers," NBC, 1983; "Simon & Simon: Betty Grable Flies Again," CBS, 1983; "Magnum P.I.: Blind Justice," CBS, 1984; "Amazing Stories: Santa '85," NBC, 1985; "Murder, She Wrote: Unfinished Business," CBS, 1986; "Matlock: Santa Claus," NBC, 1986; "Island Son: Everyday People," CBS, 1989.

TV MOVIES AND MINISERIES: "The Ballad of Andy Crocker," ABC, 1969; "A Clear and Present Danger," NBC, 1970; "The City," ABC, 1971; "Rachel, Sweet Rachel," ABC, 1971; "If Tomorrow Comes," ABC, 1971; "Trouble Comes to Town," ABC, 1973; "The Last Angry Man," ABC, 1974; "The Secret Life of John Chapman," ABC, 1976; "Escape From Bogen County," CBS, 1977; "Elvis," ABC, 1979; "Disaster on the Coastliner," ABC, 1979; "Washington Mistress," CBS, 1982; "The Fighter," CBS, 1983; "Lady From Yesterday," CBS, 1985; "ABC Theater: The Rape of Richard Beck," ABC, 1985; "Manhunt for Claude Dallas," CBS, 1986; "LBJ: The Early Years," NBC, 1987; "Kojak: The Price of Justice," CBS, 1987; "Stranger on My Land," ABC, 1988; "The Town Bully," ABC, 1988; "War and Remembrance," ABC, 1988, 1989; "Everybody's Baby: The Rescue of Jessica McClure," ABC, 1989.

HINTON, DARBY
b. Santa Monica, CA, August 19, 1957.

AS A REGULAR: "Daniel Boone," NBC, 1964-70.

AND: "The Adventures of Ozzie and Harriet: An Honor for Oz," ABC, 1966; "Hawaii Five-O: How to Steal a Submarine," CBS, 1975.

HINTON, ED
b. 1928; d. 1958. Father of Darby Hinton.
AS A REGULAR: "I Led Three Lives," SYN, 1953-56.

HIRSCH, JUDD
b. New York City, NY, March 15, 1935. Emmy winning actor who played Alex Rieger on "Taxi" and now plays John Lacey on "Dear John."
AS A REGULAR: "The Law," NBC, 1975; "Delvecchio," CBS, 1976-77; "Taxi," ABC, 1978-82; NBC, 1982-83; "Detective in the House," CBS, 1985; "Dear John," NBC, 1988- .
AND: "Medical Story: Wasteland," NBC, 1975; "Visions: Two Brothers," PBS, 1976; "Rhoda: Rhoda Likes Mike," CBS, 1977; "Rhoda: The Weekend," CBS, 1977.
TV MOVIES AND MINISERIES: "The Law," NBC, 1974; "The Legend of Valentino," ABC, 1975; "The Keegans," CBS, 1976; "Sooner or Later," NBC, 1979; "First Steps," CBS, 1985; "Brotherly Love," CBS, 1985.
* Emmies: 1981, 1983.

HITCHCOCK, ALFRED
b. London, England, August 13, 1899; d. 1980. Much-imitated, much-admired film director who became a universally known face and personality through the anthology shows he hosted.
AS A REGULAR: "Alfred Hitchcock Presents," CBS, 1955-60; NBC, 1960-62; "The Alfred Hitchcock Hour," CBS, 1962-64; NBC, 1964-65.
AS A DIRECTOR: "Alfred Hitchcock Presents: The Perfect Crime," CBS, 1958; "Alfred Hitchcock Presents: Arthur," CBS, 1959; "Startime: Incident at a Corner," NBC, 1960.
AS A PRODUCER: "Suspicion," NBC, 1957-58.
AS A GUEST: "The Perry Como Show," NBC, 1957; "The Mike Douglas Show," SYN, 1970; "The American Film Institute Salute to Alfred Hitchcock," CBS, 1979.

HODGE, AL
b. 1913; d. 1979. Actor who played "Cap-tain VIDEO!," as Ed Norton used to say on "The Honeymooners."
AS A REGULAR: "Captain Video and His Video Rangers," DUM, 1951-55.
AND: "U.S. Steel Hour: Trouble-in-Law," CBS, 1959; "Hawaiian Eye: The Bequest of Arthur Goodwin," CBS, 1960; "Angel: Angel and the Con Men," CBS, 1960; "Michael Shayne: Death Selects the Winner," NBC, 1960.

HODGES, EDDIE
b. Hattiesburg, MS, March 5, 1947. Child actor of the fifties.
AS A GUEST: "The $64,000 Question," CBS, 1957; "The $64,000 Challenge," CBS, 1958; "Omnibus: Mrs. McThing," NBC, 1958; "The Perry Como Show," NBC, 1958; "The Arthur Godfrey Show," CBS, 1958; "Your Hit Parade," CBS, 1958; "The Jimmy Dean Show," CBS, 1958; "The Eddie Fisher Show," NBC, 1959; "Pat Boone Chevy Showroom," ABC, 1959; "Holiday, USA," CBS, 1959; "This Is Your Life (Frank Capra)," NBC, 1959; "The Andy Williams Show," CBS, 1959; "Startime: The Wonderful World of Entertainment," NBC, 1959; "Jimmy Durante Special: Give My Regards to Broadway," NBC, 1959; "Perry Como's Kraft Music Hall," NBC, 1960; "Bell Telephone Hour: Main Street USA," NBC, 1960; "Our American Heritage: Millionaire's Mite," NBC, 1960; "The Secret World of Eddie Hodges," CBS, 1960; "American Bandstand," ABC, 1961; "American Bandstand," ABC, 1962; "Your First Impression," NBC, 1962; "Walt Disney's Wonderful World of Color: Johnny Shiloh," NBC, 1963; "The Dick Van Dyke Show: The Lady and the Babysitter," CBS, 1964; "The John Forsythe Show: Little Miss Egghead," NBC, 1965; "Gunsmoke: Mail Drop," CBS, 1967; "Family Affair: The Flip Side," CBS, 1969.
* Hodges' co-contestant on "The $64,000 Question" was astronaut-to-be John Glenn; his partner on "The $64,000 Challenge" was Patty Duke.
* See also Patty Duke.

HODIAK, JOHN
b. Pittsburgh, PA, April 16, 1914; d. 1955. Actor of forties films, usually in action roles.
AS A GUEST: "Hollywood Playhouse: Task Force Smith," SYN, 1952; "Ford Theatre: They Also Serve," NBC, 1953; "The Loretta Young Show: The Last Spring," NBC, 1955.

HOFFMAN, DUSTIN
b. Los Angeles, CA, August 8, 1937. Screen actor who got his start in TV and who came back to it to perform his award-winning Willy Loman in a stunning production of "Death of a Salesman."
AS A GUEST: "Naked City: Sweet Prince of Delancey Street," ABC, 1961; "The Defenders: A Matter of Law and Disorder," CBS, 1965; "The Doctors and the Nurses: The Heroine," CBS, 1965; "NET Playhouse: The Journey of the Fifth Horse," NET, 1966; "ABC Stage '67: The Trap of Solid Gold," ABC, 1967; "NET Playhouse: The Star Wagon," NET, 1967;

"Higher and Higher, Attorneys at Law," CBS, 1968; "The Merv Griffin Show," SYN, 1969; "The Point," ABC, 1971; "Free to Be You and Me," ABC, 1974; "Camera Three: Circle in the Square's 25th Anniversary," CBS, 1977; "Bette Midler: Old Red Hair Is Back," NBC, 1978.

TV MOVIES AND MINISERIES: "Death of a Salesman," CBS, 1985.

* Emmies: 1986.

HOFFMAN, GERTRUDE
b. 1871; d. 1966. Elderly actress who played Mrs. Odetts on "My Little Margie."
AS A REGULAR: "My Little Margie," CBS, 1952; NBC, 1952; CBS, 1953; NBC, 1953-55.
AND: "Alfred Hitchcock Presents: The Long Shot," CBS, 1955.

HOFMANN, ISABELLA
b. 1957, Chicago, IL. Redheaded beauty who plays Kate on "Dear John."
AS A REGULAR: "Dear John," NBC, 1988- .
AND: "Matlock: The Power Brokers," NBC, 1987.
TV MOVIES AND MINISERIES: "Independence," NBC, 1987; "The Town Bully," ABC, 1988.

HOLBROOK, HAL
b. Harold Rowe Holbrook, Jr., Cleveland, OH, February 17, 1925. Actor who made his mark onstage as Mark Twain; at his best in portrayals of folksy, decent men, including Senator Hays Stowe on "The Bold Ones" and lawyer Reese Watson on "Designing Women."
AS A REGULAR: "The Brighter Day," CBS, 1954-59; "The Bold Ones," NBC, 1970-71; "Sandburg's Lincoln," NBC, 1976; "Designing Women," CBS, 1986-90; "Evening Shade," CBS, 1990- .
AND: "Mr. Citizen: Late for Supper," ABC, 1955; "Wide, Wide World: The Sound of Laughter," NBC, 1958; "The Ed Sullivan Show," CBS, 1963; "The Glass Menagerie," CBS, 1966; "Preview Tonight: The Cliff Dwellers," ABC, 1966; "Mark Twain Tonight!," CBS, 1967; "The Steve Allen Show," SYN, 1968; "The FBI: The Fraud," ABC, 1969; "The Name of the Game: The Perfect Image," NBC, 1969; "The Wonderful World of Disney: The Wacky Zoo of Morgan City," NBC, 1970; "ABC Theatre: Pueblo," ABC, 1973; "The Baboons of Combe," ABC, 1974; "The Grand Ole Opry at 50," ABC, 1975; "The Oath: 33 Hours in the Life of God," ABC, 1976.
TV MOVIES AND MINISERIES: "The Whole World Is Watching," NBC, 1969; "A Clear and Present Danger," NBC, 1970; "Travis Logan, D.A.," CBS, 1971; "Suddenly Single," ABC, 1971; "Goodbye Raggedy Ann," CBS, 1971; "That Certain Summer," ABC, 1972; "The Awakening Land," ABC, 1978; "Murder by Natural

Causes," CBS, 1979; "The Legend of the Golden Gun," NBC, 1979; "Off the Minnesota Strip," ABC, 1980; "The Kidnapping of the President," NBC, 1980; "The Killing of Randy Webster," CBS, 1981; "The Three Wishes of Billy Grier," ABC, 1984; "George Washington," CBS, 1984; "North and South," ABC, 1985; "Behind Enemy Lines," NBC, 1985; "Under Siege," NBC, 1986; "Dress Gray," NBC, 1986; "North and South, Book II," ABC, 1986; "The Fortunate Pilgrim," NBC, 1988; "Emma: Queen of the South Seas," SYN, 1988; "I'll Be Home for Christmas," NBC, 1988; "AT&T Presents: Day One," CBS, 1989; "Sorry, Wrong Number," USA, 1989.

* Emmies: 1971, 1974, 1976.

HOLCOMBE, WENDY
b. Alabaster, AL, 1963.
AS A REGULAR: "Nashville on the Road," SYN, 1975-81; "Lewis & Clark," NBC, 1981-82.

HOLDEN, REBECCA
b. Austin, TX, June 12, 1953. Actress who played April Curtis on "Knight Rider."
AS A REGULAR: "Knight Rider," NBC, 1983-85.
AND: "Three's Company: A Crowded Romance," ABC, 1980; "Barney Miller: Paternity," ABC, 1981; "Magnum, P.I.: All Roads Lead to Floyd," CBS, 1981; "Too Close for Comfort: Seven Month Blues," ABC, 1982; "Taxi: Tony's Lady," ABC, 1982; "Matt Houston: Heritage," ABC, 1983.

HOLDEN, WILLIAM
b. William Franklin Beedle, Jr., O'Fallon, IL, April 17, 1918; d. 1981. Screen idol, usually in anti-hero roles; he played beat cop Bumper Morgan in "The Blue Knight." Also memorable as himself on "I Love Lucy," visiting Lucy Ricardo in Hollywood as she lit her cigarette, setting fire to a putty nose she was wearing because she didn't want Holden to recognize her as the woman who'd just dumped food on him at The Brown Derby. Whew.
AS A GUEST: "I Love Lucy: L.A. at Last!," CBS, 1955; "The Perry Como Show," NBC, 1956; "The Ed Sullivan Show," CBS, 1958; "The Merv Griffin Show," SYN, 1968.
TV MOVIES AND MINISERIES: "The Blue Knight," NBC, 1973; "21 Hours at Munich," ABC, 1976.

* Emmies: 1974.

HOLDRIDGE, CHERYL
b. June 20, 1944. Actress who played the pretty girl-next-door on a number of late fifties sitcoms.
AS A REGULAR: "The Mickey Mouse Club," ABC,

1956-58; "Bachelor Father," NBC, 1958-61.
AND: "Leave It to Beaver: Wally's Pug Nose,"
ABC, 1959; "My Three Sons: Brotherly Love,"
ABC, 1960; "Leave It to Beaver: Teacher's
Daughter," ABC, 1961; "Yes, Yes Nanette: A
Date for Buddy," NBC, 1961; "My Three Sons:
Man in a Trenchcoat," ABC, 1961; "The
Adventures of Ozzie and Harriet: The Pen and
Pencil Set," ABC, 1961; "Bringing Up Buddy:
Buddy and the Teenager," CBS, 1961; "The
Adventures of Ozzie and Harriet: Rick Grades a
Test," ABC, 1961; "Leave It to Beaver: Wally's
Weekend Job," ABC, 1961; "Leave It to Beaver:
Beaver's First Date," ABC, 1961; "The
Adventures of Ozzie and Harriet: The Fraternity
Pin," ABC, 1962; "The Rifleman: A Young
Man's Fancy," ABC, 1962; "Leave It to Beaver:
Wally's Dinner Date," ABC, 1962; "King of
Diamonds: Rain on Wednesday," SYN, 1962;
"The Many Loves of Dobie Gillis: Big Blunder
and Egg Man," CBS, 1962; "The Donna Reed
Show: Mary, Mary, Quite Contrary," ABC, 1962;
"Hawaiian Eye: Go Steady with Danger," ABC,
1963; "Leave It to Beaver: The Moustache,"
ABC, 1963; "Leave It to Beaver: Eddie's
Sweater," ABC, 1963; "The Dick Van Dyke
Show: The Third One From the Left," CBS, 1964;
"Mr. Novak: The Private Life of Douglas Morgan
Jr.," NBC, 1964; "Dr. Kildare: Quid Pro Quo,"
NBC, 1964; "The Eleventh Hour: Does My
Mother Have to Know?", NBC, 1964; "My Three
Sons: The Tree," ABC, 1964; "Wagon Train: The
Story of Annabelle," ABC, 1964; "Bewitched:
The Girl Reporter," ABC, 1964.

TRIVIA QUIZ #11: HOME SWEET SET
Match these TV characters with their places
of residence:

1. Maude Findley	A. Hooterville
2. June Cleaver	B. Honolulu
3. Kenneth Preston	C. Tuckahoe
4. Andy Taylor	D. Boston
5. Socrates Miller	E. Mayberry
6. Spenser	F. Chicago
7. Oliver Douglas	G. New City
8. Michael Kuzak	H. New York City
9. Florida Evans	I. Mayfield
10. Thomas Magnum	J. Los Angeles

(Answers at end of book.)

HOLLAND, KRISTINA
b. *Fayetteville, NC, February 25, 1944.* Actress
who played Tina, secretary to Tom Corbett
(Bill Bixby) on "The Courtship of Eddie's
Father."
AS A REGULAR: "The Courtship of Eddie's
Father," ABC, 1969-72; "Wait Till Your Father
Gets Home," SYN, 1972-74.
AND: "Mr. Deeds Goes to Town: Tricks of the

Trade," ABC, 1970; "Make Room for Grandaddy:
The Arrangement," ABC, 1970; "Love, American
Style: Love and the Old-Fashioned Father," ABC,
1972; "Owen Marshall, Counselor at Law: Words
of Summer," ABC, 1972; "Owen Marshall,
Counselor at Law: The Camerons Are a Special
Clan," ABC, 1973; "The Magician: Lady in a
Trap," NBC, 1973; "Love Story: Joie," NBC,
1973; "Marcus Welby, M.D.: The Working
Heart," ABC, 1973; "Medical Center: Three on a
Tightrope," CBS, 1974; "The Girl with Some-
thing Extra: Irreconcilable Sameness," NBC,
1974; "Barnaby Jones: Murder Once Removed,"
CBS, 1975; "Kolchak, the Night Stalker: Demon
in Lace," ABC, 1975; "The Bob Newhart Show:
A Matter of Vice-Principal," CBS, 1975; "The
Bob Newhart Show: Breaking Up Is Hard to Do,"
CBS, 1976.

HOLLANDER, DAVID
b. *Los Angeles, CA, 1969.*
AS A REGULAR: "The McLean Stevenson Show,"
NBC, 1976-77; "What's Happening!!," ABC,
1978-79; "A New Kind of Family," ABC,
1979-80; "Lewis & Clark," NBC, 1981-82;
"Call to Glory," ABC, 1984-85.
AND: "Switch: Death Squad," CBS, 1976; "House
Calls: A Slight Case of Quartantine," CBS, 1980;
"Lou Grant: Cover-Up," CBS, 1980; "Nero
Wolfe: The Golden Spiders," NBC, 1981; "Nero
Wolfe: Sweet Revenge," NBC, 1981; "Buck
Rogers in the 25th Century: The Golden Man,"
NBC, 1981; "Amazing Stories: Welcome to My
Nightmare," NBC, 1986.
TV MOVIES AND MINISERIES: "The Grass Is Always
Greener Over the Septic Tank," CBS, 1978; "A
Whale for the Killing," ABC, 1981; "Packin' It
In," CBS, 1983.

HOLLIDAY, JUDY
b. *Judith Tuvim, New York City, NY, June 21,
1922; d. 1965.* Stage and screen comedienne,
Billie Dawn in "Born Yesterday," who did a
few variety shows.
AS A GUEST:"The Ed Sullivan Show," CBS, 1957;
"The Perry Como Show," NBC, 1958; "Person
to Person," CBS, 1958; "The Steve Allen
Show," NBC, 1958; "Arthur Murray Party,"
NBC, 1958; "Perry Como's Kraft Music Hall,"
NBC, 1961.

HOLLIDAY, KENE
b. *New York City, NY.* Actor who played Tyler
Hudson on "Matlock."
AS A REGULAR: "Carter Country," ABC, 1977-79;
"Matlock," NBC, 1986-89.
AND: "What's Happening!: Going, Going, Gong,"
ABC, 1978; "Lou Grant: Slammer," CBS, 1979;
"Hill Street Blues: Of Mouse and Man," NBC,
1982; "Hill Street Blues: Zen and the Art of Law

Enforcement," NBC, 1982; "Hill Street Blues: The Young, the Beautiful and the Degraded," NBC, 1982; "Hollywood Beat: Across the Line," ABC, 1985.

TV MOVIES AND MINISERIES: "Roots: The Next Generations," ABC, 1979; "The Chicago Story," NBC, 1981; "Diary of a Perfect Murder," NBC, 1986.

HOLLIDAY, POLLY

b. Jasper, AL, July 2, 1937. Actress who played the outrageous Flo on "Alice"; she got her own sitcom when she started getting more laughs than "Alice" star Linda Lavin.

AS A REGULAR: "Alice," CBS, 1976-80; "Flo," CBS, 1980-81.

AND: "The John Davidson Show," SYN, 1981; "Stir Crazy: Pilot," CBS, 1985; "The Golden Girls: Blind Ambitions," NBC, 1986; "Amazing Stories: The Pumpkin Competition," NBC, 1986; "The Equalizer: Regrets Only," CBS, 1988.

TV MOVIES AND MINISERIES: "Missing Children: A Mother's Story," CBS, 1982; "The Gift of Love: A Christmas Story," CBS, 1983.

HOLLIMAN, EARL

b. Louisiana, September 11, 1928. Macho actor who played Sundance on "Hotel De Paree" and Lt. Bill Crowley, sidekick of Sgt. Pepper Anderson (Angie Dickinson) on "Police Woman."

AS A REGULAR: "Hotel De Paree," CBS, 1959-60; "The Wide Country," NBC, 1962-63; "Police Woman," NBC, 1974-78.

AND: "Playhouse 90: The Dark Side of the Earth," CBS, 1957; "Kraft Television Theatre: The Battle for Wednesday Night," NBC, 1958; "Kraft Television Theatre: The Sea Is Boiling Hot," NBC, 1958; "The Lux Show with Rosemary Clooney," NBC, 1958; "Matinee Theatre: The Man with Pointed Toes," NBC, 1958; "Studio One: The Lady Died at Midnight," CBS, 1958; "Westinghouse Desilu Playhouse: Silent Thunder," CBS, 1958; "You Asked for It," ABC, 1959; "The Twilight Zone: Where Is Everybody?," CBS, 1959; "Here's Hollywood," NBC, 1961; "Our Man Higgins: It's Higgins, Sir," ABC, 1962; "The Great Adventure: Teeth of the Lion," CBS, 1964; "The Virginian: Ring of Silence," NBC, 1965; "Bonanza: The Flannel-Mouth Gun," NBC, 1965; "Twelve O'Clock High: The Ticket," ABC, 1965; "Dr. Kildare: Wings of Hope," NBC, 1965; "Judd for the Defense: No Law Against Murder," ABC, 1968; "Gunsmoke: A Man Called Smith," CBS, 1969; "Marcus Welby, M.D.: Neither Punch Nor Judy," ABC, 1970; "The Wonderful World of Disney: Smoke," NBC, 1970; "It Takes a Thief: Situation Red," ABC, 1970; "Medical Center: The Clash," CBS, 1970; "The FBI: The Quest," ABC, 1970; "Gunsmoke: Hackett," CBS, 1970; "Ironside: The Target,"

NBC, 1971; "The Rookies: A Very Special Piece of Ground," ABC, 1972; "Gunsmoke: Shadler," CBS, 1973; "Medical Center: Impact," CBS, 1973; "The Wonderful World of Disney: The Boy and the Bronc Buster," NBC, 1973; "The FBI: The Pay-Off," ABC, 1973; "The Streets of San Francisco: The Stamp of Death," ABC, 1973; "Police Story: Fingerprint," NBC, 1974; "Celebrity Sweepstakes," NBC, 1974; "Police Story: The Gamble," NBC, 1974; "Hollywood Squares," NBC, 1975; "Hollywood Squares," NBC, 1976.

TV MOVIES AND MINISERIES: "Tribes," ABC, 1970; "Alias Smith and Jones," ABC, 1971; "Cannon," CBS, 1971; "Desperate Mission," NBC, 1971; "Trapped," ABC, 1973; "Cry Panic," ABC, 1974; "I Love You, Goodbye," ABC, 1974; "The Solitary Man," CBS, 1979; "Where the Ladies Go," ABC, 1980; "Country Gold," CBS, 1982; "The Thorn Birds," ABC, 1983; "Gunsmoke: Return to Dodge," CBS, 1987; "American Harvest," CBS, 1987.

HOLLOWAY, STANLEY

b. London, England, October 1, 1890; d. 1982. British musical hall performer who played Alfie Doolittle in "My Fair Lady" and ended up with a TV sitcom as a result.

AS A REGULAR: "Our Man Higgins," ABC, 1962-63.

AND: "The Big Record," CBS, 1957; "Bell Telephone Hour: Groucho Marx in The Mikado," NBC, 1960; "The Jack Paar Show," NBC, 1960; "Bell Telephone Hour: A Galaxy of Music," NBC, 1961; "The Broadway of Lerner and Loewe," NBC, 1962; "Lamp Unto My Feet: The Everlasting Mercy," CBS, 1962; "Hallmark Hall of Fame: The Fantasticks," NBC, 1964; "Perry Como Special," NBC, 1964; "The Dean Martin Show," NBC, 1967.

TV MOVIES AND MINISERIES: "Run a Crooked Mile," NBC, 1969.

HOLLOWAY, STERLING

b. Cedartown, GA, January 4, 1905. Comic actor with unruly hair and a high, raspy voice heard in hundreds of commercials; most recently he narrated the "Moonlighting" version of "Taming of the Shrew."

AS A REGULAR: "The Life of Riley," NBC, 1953-58; "Willy," CBS, 1955; "The Baileys of Balboa," CBS, 1964-65.

AND: "Climax!: Night of a Rebel," CBS, 1957; "The Adventures of Rin Tin Tin: Sorrowful Joe," ABC, 1957; "Circus Boy: Elmer the Aeronaut," NBC, 1957; "Circus Boy: The Magic Lantern," ABC, 1957; "The Adventures of Rin Tin Tin: Sorrowful Joe Returns," ABC, 1957; " Disneyland: Adventures in Fantasy," ABC, 1958; "Circus Boy: Elmer, the Rainmaker," ABC, 1958; "Shirley Temple's Storybook: The Land of

Oz," NBC, 1960; "The Real McCoys: The Jinx," ABC, 1960; "Miami Undercover: The Ghostbreaker," SYN, 1960; "Dick Powell's Zane Grey Theatre: Blood Red," CBS, 1961; "Pete and Gladys: The Projectionist," CBS, 1961; "Margie: False Alarm," ABC, 1962; "Stan Freberg Presents Chinese New Year's Eve," ABC, 1962; "The Andy Griffith Show: The Merchant of Mayberry," CBS, 1962; "Hazel: The Retiring Milkman," NBC, 1963; "The Joey Bishop Show: Joey's Lost Whatchamacallit," NBC, 1963; "The Twilight Zone: What's in the Box?," CBS, 1964; "Burke's Law: Who Killed Annie Foran?," ABC, 1964; "F Troop: Milton the Kid," ABC, 1966; "Please Don't Eat the Daisies: My Son the Genius," NBC, 1966; "That Girl: Phantom of the Horse Opera," ABC, 1966; "Family Affair: Fancy Free," CBS, 1967; "Gilligan's Island: The Pigeon," CBS, 1967; "Love, American Style: Love and the Face Bow," ABC, 1973; "Moonlighting: Atomic Shakespeare," ABC, 1986.

HOLM, CELESTE
b. New York City, NY, April 29, 1919. Screen and TV actress with a warm, pleasant voice, usually playing intelligent, wise women.
AS A REGULAR: "Honestly Celeste," CBS, 1954; "Who Pays?," NBC, 1959; "Nancy," NBC, 1970-71; "Jessie," ABC, 1984; "Falcon Crest," CBS, 1985; "Christine Cromwell," ABC, 1989-90.
AND: "Lux Video Theatre: The Pacing Goose," NBC, 1951; "Lux Video Theatre: The Bargain," NBC, 1952; "Schlitz Playhouse of Stars: Four's a Family," CBS, 1952; "Hollywood Opening Night: Mrs. Genius," NBC, 1953; "Jewelers Showcase: Heart's Desire," CBS, 1953; "U.S. Steel Hour: The Bogey Man," ABC, 1955; "Climax!: The Empty Room Blues," CBS, 1956; "Carolyn," NBC, 1956; "The Vic Damone Show," CBS, 1956; "The Steve Allen Show," NBC, 1956; "Producers Showcase: Jack and the Beanstalk," NBC, 1956; "Schlitz Playhouse of Stars: Wedding Present," CBS, 1957; "Goodyear TV Playhouse: The Princess Back Home," NBC, 1957; "Dick Powell's Zane Grey Theatre: Fugitive," CBS, 1957; "Studio 57: Robin," SYN, 1957; "Hallmark Hall of Fame: The Yeomen of the Guard," NBC, 1957; "The Tonight Show," NBC, 1957; "The $64,000 Question," CBS, 1957; "The Last Word," CBS, 1957; "Pat Boone Chevy Showroom," ABC, 1957; "To Tell the Truth," CBS, 1958; "Christophers: You Need the Law," SYN, 1958; "The Ed Sullivan Show," CBS, 1959; "The Last Word," CBS, 1959; "Perry Como's Kraft Music Hall," NBC, 1959; "Christophers: Famous Women in the Bible," SYN, 1959; "Art Carney Special: The Man in the Dog Suit," NBC, 1960; "Christophers: Abraham Lincoln on Law," SYN, 1960; "Startime: Fun Fair," NBC, 1960; "The Right Man," CBS, 1960; "Follow the Sun: The

Irresistible Miss Bullfinch," ABC, 1962; "Password," CBS, 1962; "Checkmate: So Beats My Plastic Heart," CBS, 1962; "Exploring," NBC, 1962; "Dr. Kildare: The Pack Rat and the Prima Donna," NBC, 1963; "Burke's Law: Who Killed the Kind Doctor?," ABC, 1963; "The Eleventh Hour: How Do I Say 'I Love You'?," NBC, 1964; "Art Linkletter's House Party," CBS, 1964; "Mr. Novak: An Elephant Is Like a Tree," NBC, 1965; "The Mike Douglas Show," SYN, 1965; "Walt Disney's Wonderful World of Color: Kilroy," NBC, 1965; "The Fugitive: The Old Man Picked a Lemon," ABC, 1965; "Run for Your Life: The Cold, Cold War of Paul Bryan," NBC, 1965; "The Long, Hot Summer: Face of Fear," ABC, 1966; "Cinderella," CBS, 1966; "Summer Fun: Meet Me in St. Louis," ABC, 1966; "The Fugitive: Concrete Evidence," ABC, 1967; "The FBI: The Executioners," ABC, 1967; "The Name of the Game: The Brass Ring," NBC, 1970; "Medical Center: No Margin for Error," CBS, 1973; "The Streets of San Francisco: Crossfire," ABC, 1973; "Columbo: Old Fashioned Murder," NBC, 1976; "The Love Boat: A Good and Faithful Servant," ABC, 1979; "Fantasy Island: The Winemaker," ABC, 1980; "The Love Boat: Bet on It," ABC, 1984; "Spenser: For Hire: Haunting," ABC, 1988; "The Magical World of Disney: Polly," NBC, 1989.
TV MOVIES AND MINISERIES: "The Delphi Bureau," ABC, 1972; "The Underground Man," NBC, 1974; "Death Cruise," ABC, 1974; "Best Sellers: The Captains and the Kings," NBC, 1976; "Love Boat II," ABC, 1977; "Backstairs at the White House," NBC, 1979; "Midnight Lace," NBC, 1981; "This Girl for Hire," CBS, 1983.

HOLMES, JENNIFER
b. Fall River, MA. Actress who played Leslie Vanderkellen, short-lived maid at the Stratford Inn on "Newhart" who left and was replaced by her much funnier cousin Stephanie (Julia Duffy).
AS A REGULAR: "Newhart," CBS, 1982-83; "Misfits of Science," NBC, 1985-86.
AND: "Bosom Buddies: Other Than That, She's a Wonderful Person," ABC, 1981; "Lobo: What Are Girls Like You Doing in a Bank Like This?," NBC, 1981; "Simon & Simon: Art for Arthur's Sake," CBS, 1981; "Lou Grant: Friends," CBS, 1981; "Knight Rider: KITT vs. KARR," NBC, 1984; "The Love Boat: Ace Meets the Champ," ABC, 1984; "Webster: Runaway," ABC, 1985; "The Love Boat: Who's the Champ?," ABC, 1986; "Murder, She Wrote: Doom with a View," CBS, 1987; "Who's the Boss?: A Jack Story," ABC, 1988.
TV MOVIES AND MINISERIES: "Hobson's Choice," CBS, 1983.

HOLT, TIM

b. *Charles John Holt, Jr., February 5, 1918; d. 1973*. Actor who played cowboys and who had a couple of other notable screen appearances ("The Magnificent Ambersons," "Treasure of the Sierra Madre"), but with only one TV credit.

AS A GUEST: "The Virginian: A Women of Stone," NBC, 1969.

HOMEIER, SKIP

b. *George Vincent Homeier, Chicago, IL, October 5, 1930*. Former child actor who's worked steadily in television.

AS A REGULAR: "Dan Raven," NBC, 1960-61; "The Interns," CBS, 1970-71.

AND: "Schlitz Playhouse of Stars: Man Out of the Rain," CBS, 1955; "Science Fiction Theatre: Death at 2 a.m.," SYN, 1955; "Science Fiction Theatre: The Other Side of the Moon," SYN, 1956; "Science Fiction Theatre: Living Lights," SYN, 1956; "Climax!: Circle of Destruction," CBS, 1957; "Alcoa Hour: Protege," NBC, 1957; "Studio 57: Palm Springs Incident," SYN, 1957; "Studio One: The Human Barrier," CBS, 1957; "Kraft Television Theatre: Smart Boy," NBC, 1957; "Climax!: Scream in Silence," CBS, 1958; "Walt Disney Presents: The Nine Lives of Elfego Baca-Law and Order, Inc.," ABC, 1958; "Target: Mercy Killer," SYN, 1958; "Playhouse 90: Before I Die," CBS, 1958; "Alfred Hitchcock Presents: The Motive," CBS, 1958; "Kraft Theatre: The Woman at High Hollow," NBC, 1958; "Matinee Theatre: Journey Into Darkness," NBC, 1958; "Dick Powell's Zane Grey Theatre: Black Is for Grief," CBS, 1958; "Studio One: The Shadow of a Genius," CBS, 1958; "Westinghouse Desilu Playhouse: Trial at Devil's Canyon," CBS, 1959; "Alcoa Presents One Step Beyond: The Bride Possessed," ABC, 1959; "Wichita Town: Out of the Past," NBC, 1959; "Rawhide: Incident of the Blue Fire," CBS, 1959; "The Loretta Young Show: Slight Delay," NBC, 1960; "The Rifleman: The Spoiler," ABC, 1960; "The Outlaws: Rape of Red Sky," NBC, 1960; "Walt Disney's Wonderful World of Color: Johnny Shiloh," NBC, 1963; "The Virginian: Strangers at Sundown," NBC, 1963; "The Virginian: A Portrait of Marie Valonne," NBC, 1963; "Combat!: Night Patrol," ABC, 1963; "Combat!: Survival," ABC, 1963; "Combat!: No Hallelujah for Glory," ABC, 1963; "Wagon Train: The Andrew Elliott Story," ABC, 1964; "Combat!: The Imposter," ABC, 1964; "The Addams Family: Halloween with the Addams Family," ABC, 1964; "The Outer Limits: Expanding Human," ABC, 1964; "Rawhide: Brush War at Buford," CBS, 1965; "The Loner: The Mourners for Johnny Sharp," CBS, 1966; "Combat!: Entombed," ABC, 1967; "Garrison's Gorillas: War Games," ABC, 1968; "Mission: Impossible: The Mercenaries," CBS, 1968; "Mannix: A Sleep in the Deep," CBS, 1969; "The Virginian: The Brazos Kid," NBC, 1964; "The Virginian: The Price of Love," NBC, 1969; "Then Came Bronson: A Pickin' an' a Singin'," NBC, 1969; "Quincy: An Ounce of Prevention," NBC, 1979; "Owen Marshall, Counselor at Law: Voice From a Nightmare," ABC, 1971.

TV MOVIES AND MINISERIES: "The Challenge," ABC, 1970; "Two for the Money," ABC, 1972; "The Voyage of the Yes," CBS, 1973; "Washington: Behind Closed Doors," ABC, 1977; "The Wild Wild West Revisited," CBS, 1979.

HOMOLKA, OSCAR

b. *Vienna, Austria, August 12, 1898; d. 1978*. Heavyset actor, often in roles as an evil European.

AS A GUEST: "Robert Montgomery Presents: Pink Hippopotamus," NBC, 1954; "Elgin TV Hour: Love Song," ABC, 1954; "Producers Showcase: Darkness at Noon," NBC, 1955; "Climax!: Carnival at Midnight," CBS, 1957; "Matinee Theatre: The Master Builder," NBC, 1957; "Matinee Theatre: You Touched Me," NBC, 1957; "Kaiser Aluminum Hour: Murder in the House," NBC, 1957; "Du Pont Theatre: Dowry for Ilona," ABC, 1957; "Alfred Hitchcock Presents: Reward to Finder," CBS, 1957; "Playhouse 90: The Plot to Kill Stalin," CBS, 1958; "Playhouse 90: Heart of Darkness," CBS, 1958; "Five Fingers: Operation Ramrod," NBC, 1959; "Alfred Hitchcock Presents: The Ikon of Elijah," CBS, 1960; "Du Pont Show of the Month: Arrowsmith," CBS, 1960; "Art Carney Special: Victory," NBC, 1960; "G.E. Theatre: The Ugly Duckling," CBS, 1960; "Alfred Hitchcock Presents: The Hero," CBS, 1960; "Playhouse 90: In the Presence of Mine Enemies," CBS, 1960; "Play of the Week: A Very Special Baby," SYN, 1960; "Play of the Week: Rashomon," SYN, 1960; "Assassination Plot at Teheran," ABC, 1961; "Thriller: Waxworks," NBC, 1962; "Here's Hollywood," NBC, 1962; "Theatre '62: Spellbound," NBC, 1962; "Walt Disney's Wonderful World of Color: The Mooncussers," NBC, 1962; "The Breaking Point: Solo for B-Flat Clarinet," ABC, 1963; "Burke's Law: Who Killed Jason Shaw?," ABC, 1964; "The du Pont Show: Ambassador at Large," NBC, 1964; "Ben Casey: For This Relief, Many Thanks," ABC, 1964; "Hazel: A Lesson in Diplomacy," NBC, 1964; "The Rogues: Plovonia, Hail and Farewell," NBC, 1964; "Dr. Jekyll and Mr. Hyde," ABC, 1968; "Smithsonian Institution Special: The Legendary Curse of the Hope Diamond," CBS, 1975; "Kojak: The Forgotten Room," CBS, 1975.

HOOD, DARLA

b. *Leedy, OK, November 4, 1931; d. 1979*. Former child actress, a member of Our Gang in movie shorts of the thirties.

AS A REGULAR: "The Ken Murray Show," CBS, 1950-51.
AND: "Tell It to Groucho," CBS, 1962; "The Jack Benny Program," CBS, 1962; "Art Linkletter's House Party," CBS, 1962.

HOOKS, JAN
b. Atlanta, GA, 1957. Gifted comic actress.
AS A REGULAR: "Tush," TBS, 1979-80; "The 1/2 Hour Comedy Hour," ABC, 1983; "Saturday Night Live," NBC, 1986- .

HOOKS, KEVIN
b. Philadelphia, September 19, 1958. Actor who played Morris Thorpe on "The White Shadow."
AS A REGULAR: "The White Shadow," CBS, 1978-81; "He's the Mayor," ABC, 1986.
AND: "The Rookies: Deliver Me from Innocence," ABC, 1976; "Lou Grant: Schools," CBS, 1978.
TV MOVIES AND MINISERIES: "Just an Old Sweet Song," CBS, 1976; "The Greatest Thing That Almost Happened," CBS, 1977; "Backstairs at the White House," NBC, 1979; "Can You Hear the Laughter?: The Story of Freddie Prinze," CBS, 1979.

HOOKS, ROBERT
b. Washington, D.C., April 18, 1937. Actor who played Detective Jeff Ward on "NYPD."
AS A REGULAR: "NYPD," ABC, 1967-69; "Supercarrier," ABC, 1988.
AND: "Profiles in Courage: Frederick Douglass," NBC, 1965; "The Cliff Dwellers," ABC, 1966; "The Mike Douglas Show," SYN, 1968; "Mannix: Last Rites for Miss Emma," CBS, 1969; "The FBI: Silent Partners," ABC, 1969; "Then Came Bronson: A Long Trip to Yesterday," NBC, 1970; "The Bold Ones: Killer on the Loose," NBC, 1970; "The Rookies: The Deadly Cage," ABC, 1973; "McMillan and Wife: The Devil You Say," NBC, 1973; "The Streets of San Francisco: Rampage," ABC, 1973; "Marcus Welby, M.D.: Nguyen," ABC, 1973; "The FBI: Deadly Ambition," ABC, 1974; "ABC Theatre: Ceremonies in Dark Old Men," CBS, 1975; "Petrocelli: Too Many Alibis," NBC, 1975; "Just an Old Sweet Song," CBS, 1976; "The Facts of Life: Overachieving," NBC, 1980; "The White Shadow: Reunion," CBS, 1980; "Quincy: Bitter Pill," NBC, 1982; "The Devlin Connection: Allison," NBC, 1982; "Hardcastle and McCormick: Man in a Glass House," ABC, 1983; "T.J. Hooker: The Trial," ABC, 1983; "J.J. Starbuck: The Six Percent Solution," NBC, 1987; "A Different World: Risky Business," NBC, 1989.
TV MOVIES AND MINISERIES: "Carter's Army," ABC, 1970; "Vanished," NBC, 1971; "The Cable Car Murder," CBS, 1971; "Two for the

Money," ABC, 1972; "Trapped," ABC, 1973; "The Killer Who Wouldn't Die," ABC, 1976; "Just an Old Sweet Song," CBS, 1976; "Backstairs at the White House," NBC, 1979; "The Sophisticated Gents," NBC, 1981.

HOPE, BOB
b. Leslie Townes Hope, Eltham, England, May 29, 1903. Beloved, peripatetic comedian who's been on TV an amazing forty years, and who seems rather stiff on TV these days.
AS A REGULAR: "Bob Hope Special," NBC, 1950- ; "Chesterfield Sound Off Time," NBC, 1951-52; "The Colgate Comedy Hour," NBC, 1952-53; "Bob Hope Presents the Chrysler Theatre," NBC, 1963-67.
AND: "The Charlie Farrell Show: Secrets," CBS, 1956; "I Love Lucy: Lucy Meets Bob Hope," CBS, 1956; "The Perry Como Show," NBC, 1956; "The Jack Benny Program," CBS, 1957; "I've Got a Secret," CBS, 1957; "The Steve Allen Show," NBC, 1957; "The Frank Sinatra Show," ABC, 1957; "The Eddie Fisher Show," NBC, 1957; "The Danny Thomas Show: The Bob Hope Show," CBS, 1958; "The Perry Como Show," NBC, 1958; "The Polly Bergen Show," NBC, 1958; "The Steve Allen Show," NBC, 1958; "The Big Record," CBS, 1958; "Wide, Wide World: The Sound of Laughter," NBC, 1958; "Roberta," NBC, 1958; "Exploring with Hope," NBC, 1958; "The Danny Thomas Show: Danny and Bob Hope Become Directors," CBS, 1959; "Some of Manie's Friends," NBC, 1959; "Frances Langford Special," NBC, 1959; "Jack Benny Special," CBS, 1959; "Dean Martin Special," NBC, 1959; "A Tribute to Eleanor Roosevelt on Her Diamond Jubilee," NBC, 1959; "Hedda Hopper's Hollywood," NBC, 1960; "Project 20: Not So Long Ago," NBC, 1960; "The Arthur Murray Party for Bob Hope," NBC, 1960; "Eleanor Roosevelt's Jubilee," NBC, 1960; "Here's Hollywood," NBC, 1960; "Bob Hope Special: Potomac Madness," NBC, 1960; "Perry Como's Kraft Music Hall," NBC, 1960; "Bobby Darin and Friends," NBC, 1961; "25 Years of Life Magazine," NBC, 1961; "Project 20: The Story of Will Rogers," NBC, 1961; "This Is Your Life (Jayne Mansfield)," NBC, 1961; "The Jimmy Durante Show," NBC, 1961; "The World of Bob Hope," NBC, 1961; "Here's Hollywood," NBC, 1961; "The Danny Thomas Show: Danny and Bob Hope Get Away From It All," CBS, 1962; "The Jack Benny Program," CBS, 1962; "Here's Edie," ABC, 1962; "Lucille Ball Special," CBS, 1964; "The Bing Crosby Show," CBS, 1964; "The Lucy Show: Lucy and the Plumber," CBS, 1964; "The Jack Benny Program," NBC, 1964; "The Tonight Show Starring Johnny Carson," NBC, 1965; "The Andy Williams Show," NBC, 1965; "The Dean Martin Show," NBC, 1966; "Get Smart: 99 Loses

Control," NBC, 1968; "Bing Crosby Special," NBC, 1968; "Roberta," NBC, 1969; "The Many Moods of Perry Como," NBC, 1970; "The Mike Douglas Show," SYN, 1970; "This Is Tom Jones," ABC, 1970; "Festival at Ford's," NBC, 1971; "A Salute to Television's 25th Anniversary," ABC, 1972; "Bing Crosby and His Friends," CBS, 1974; "The Odd Couple: The Hollywood Story," ABC, 1974; "Mitzi and a Hundred Guys," CBS, 1975; "The Flip Wilson Comedy Special," CBS, 1975; "Dinah!," SYN, 1977; "Ann-Margret Special," NBC, 1977; "General Electric's All-Star Anniversary," ABC, 1978; "The John Davidson Show," SYN, 1980; "Highway to Heaven: Heaven Nose, Mr. Smith," NBC, 1988; "The Golden Girls: You Gotta Have Hope," NBC, 1989; "The Jim Henson Hour: Miss Piggy's Hollywood," NBC, 1989; "The Tonight Show Starring Johnny Carson," NBC, 1989; "A Conversation with Dinah," TNN, 1989.

* Hope became an American citizen on December 20, 1920.
* Hope's radio show ran on NBC from 1938-56.
* Hope received an Emmy as executive producer of his 1966 Christmas show, filmed overseas.
* Emmies: 1966.

HOPKINS, ANTHONY
b. *Port Talbot, Wales, December 31, 1937.* Screen actor who's turned to TV movies, in which he's given some of his best performances.
AS A GUEST:"Hollywood Television Theatre: Post Game," NET, 1971; "NET Playhouse: George Jacques Danton," NET, 1971; "Hallmark Hall of Fame: All Creatures Great and Small," NBC, 1975; "Classic Theatre: Three Sisters," PBS, 1975.
TV MOVIES AND MINISERIES: "War and Peace," NET, 1973; "QB VII," ABC, 1974; "Masterpiece Theatre: The Edwardians," NET, 1974; "All Creatures Great and Small," NBC, 1975; "Dark Victory," NBC, 1976; "The Lindbergh Kidnapping Case," NBC, 1976; "Victory at Entebbe," ABC, 1976; "Mayflower: The Pilgrims' Adventure," CBS, 1979; "The Bunker," CBS, 1981; "Peter and Paul," CBS, 1981; "Hollywood Wives," ABC, 1985; "Guilty Conscience," CBS, 1985; "Arch of Triumph," CBS, 1985.
* Hopkins won Emmies for playing accused kidnapped Bruno Hauptmann in "The Lindergh Kidnapping Case" and for playing Adolf Hitler in "The Bunker."
* Emmies: 1976, 1981.

HOPKINS, BO
b. *Greenwood, SC.* Rough-and-tumble leading man who played disbarred lawyer John Cooper on "The Rockford Files."
AS A REGULAR: "Doc Elliot," ABC, 1974; "The

Rockford Files," NBC, 1978-79; "Dynasty," ABC, 1981.
AND: "Gunsmoke: Hard-Luck Henry," CBS, 1967; "The Andy Griffith Show: Emmett's Brother-in-Law," CBS, 1967; "The Virginian: Johnny Moon," NBC, 1967; "The Guns of Will Sonnett: What's in a Name?," ABC, 1968; "The Guns of Will Sonnett: Guilt," ABC, 1968; "The Mod Squad: A Seat by the Window," ABC, 1969; "Ironside: And Then There Was One," NBC, 1972; "James Garner as Nichols: Sleight of Hand," NBC, 1972; "Hawaii Five-O: One Big Happy Family," CBS, 1973; "Conflicts: Gondola," PBS, 1974; "The Rookies: Death at 6 a.m.," ABC, 1974; "ABC Theatre: Judgment: The Court-Martial of Lt. William Calley," ABC, 1975; "Barnaby Jones: Flight to Danger," CBS, 1975; "Charlie's Angels: Love Boat Angels," ABC, 1979; "The A-Team: Pur-Dee Poison," NBC, 1984; "Hotel: Encores," ABC, 1984; "Murder, She Wrote: Armed Response," CBS, 1985; "Scarecrow and Mrs. King: J. Edgar's Ghost," CBS, 1985; "Houston: The Legend of Texas," CBS, 1986; "The New Mike Hammer: Kill John Doe," CBS, 1987.
TV MOVIES AND MINISERIES: "The Runaway Barge," NBC, 1975; "The Kansas City Massacre," ABC, 1975; "Charlie's Angels," ABC, 1976; "Dawn: Portrait of a Teenage Runaway," NBC, 1976; "Casino," ABC, 1980; "The Last Ride of the Dalton Gang," NBC, 1979; "Beggarman, Thief," NBC, 1979; "The Plutonium Incident," CBS, 1980; "A Smokey Mountain Christmas," ABC, 1986.

HOPKINS, MIRIAM
b. *Bainbridge, GA, October 18, 1902; d. 1972.* Screen beauty of screwball comedies and sob stories who turned to live TV in the fifties.
AS A GUEST:"Pulitzer Prize Playhouse: Ned McCobb's Daughter," ABC, 1951; "Betty Crocker Star Matinee: Farewell to Love," ABC, 1951; "Lux Video Theatre: Long Distance," CBS, 1951; "Lux Video Theatre: Julie," CBS, 1952; "Curtain Call: The Party," NBC, 1952; "G.E. Theatre: Desert Crossing," CBS, 1954; "Lux Video Theatre: Sunset Boulevard," NBC, 1955; "The Ray Milland Show: The Molehouse Collection," CBS, 1955; "Studio One: Summer Pavilion," CBS, 1955; "Climax!: Disappearance of Amanda Hale," CBS, 1957; "Matinee Theatre: Woman Alone," NBC, 1957; "The Investigators: Quite a Woman," CBS, 1961; "G.E. Theatre: A Very Special Girl," CBS, 1962; "Route 66: Shadows of an Afternoon," CBS, 1963; "The Outer Limts: Don't Open Till Doomsday," ABC, 1964; "The Flying Nun: Bertrille and the Flicks," ABC, 1969.

HOPKINS, TELMA
b. *Louisville, KY, October 28, 1948.* Wisecracking comedienne and singer best known as one-

third of Tony Orlando and Dawn and as Addy Wilson, sidekick of Nell Harper (Nell Carter) on "Gimme a Break."

AS A REGULAR: "Tony Orlando and Dawn," CBS, 1974-76; "A New Kind of Family," ABC, 1979-80; "Bosom Buddies," ABC, 1980-82; "Gimme a Break," NBC, 1984-87; "Family Matters," ABC, 1989- .

AND: "American Bandstand," ABC, 1972; "The Love Boat: Designated Lover," ABC, 1979; "The Love Boat: A Letter to Babycakes," ABC, 1979; "Battlestars," NBC, 1982; "The Love Boat: Senior Sinners," ABC, 1983; "The Love Boat: Ashes to Ashes," ABC, 1985; "It's Garry Shandling's Show: Save Mr. Peck's," FOX, 1989; "The Pat Sajak Show," CBS, 1989.

TV MOVIES AND MINISERIES: "Roots: The Next Generations," ABC, 1979; "ABC Family Classic: Rock 'n' Roll Mom," ABC, 1989.

HOPPER, DENNIS
b. Dodge City, KS, May 17, 1936. Screen director and actor in intense roles ("Blue Velvet," "Easy Rider") who began his career on television about the same time he appeared in "Rebel Without a Cause" on the big screen.

AS A GUEST: "Medic: Boy in a Storm," NBC, 1955; "Public Defender: Mama's Boy," CBS, 1955; "The Loretta Young Show: Inga," NBC, 1955; "Cheyenne: The Last Train West," ABC, 1956; "Warner Bros. Presents Conflict: Wedding Gift," ABC, 1956; "Warner Bros. Presents Conflict: No Man's Land," ABC, 1956; "Screen Directors Playhouse: High Air," ABC, 1956; "Kaiser Aluminum Hour: Carnival," NBC, 1956; "Cheyenne: The Iron Trail," ABC, 1957; "Warner Bros. Presents Conflict: A Question of Loyalty," ABC, 1957; "Sugarfoot: Brannigan's Boots," ABC, 1957; "Studio One: Trial by Slander," CBS, 1958; "Studio One: The Last Summer," CBS, 1958; "Dick Powell's Zane Grey Theatre: The Sharpshooter," CBS, 1958; "Swiss Family Robinson," NBC, 1958; "Pursuit: Last Night of August," CBS, 1958; "Dick Powell's Zane Grey Theatre: The Sunrise Gun," CBS, 1959; "The Betty Hutton Show: Goldie Meets Mike," CBS, 1960; "The Millionaire: Millionaire Julie Sherman," CBS, 1960; "Naked City: Shoes for Vinnie Winford," ABC, 1961; "Here's Hollywood," NBC, 1961; "87th Precinct: My Friend, My Enemy," NBC, 1961; "The Investigators: The Mind's Own Fire," CBS, 1961; "G.E. Theatre: The Holdout," CBS, 1962; "SurfSide 6: Vendetta Arms," ABC, 1962; "The Defenders: The Indelible Silence," CBS, 1962; "The Twilight Zone: He's Alive," CBS, 1963; "Wagon Train: The Emmett Lawson Story," ABC, 1963; "The Defenders: The Weeping Baboon," CBS, 1963; "Espionage: The Weakling," NBC, 1963; "The

Greatest Show on Earth: The Wrecker," ABC, 1963; "Petticoat Junction: The Beatnik," CBS, 1964; "Arrest and Trial: People in Glass Houses," ABC, 1964; "The Lieutenant: To Set It Right," NBC, 1964; "Bonanza: The Dark Past," NBC, 1964; "Convoy: The Many Colors of Courage," NBC, 1965; "The Legend of Jesse James: South Wind," ABC, 1966; "Court-Martial: Without Spear or Sword," ABC, 1966; "Combat!: A Little Jazz," ABC 1967; "The Big Valley: Night of the Executioner," ABC, 1967; "The Guns of Will Sonnett: Find a Sonnett, Kill a Sonnett," ABC, 1967; "The David Frost Show," SYN, 1971; "Saturday Night Live," NBC, 1987; "Late Night with David Letterman," NBC, 1987.

TV MOVIES AND MINISERIES: "Stark," CBS, 1985; "Stark: Mirror Image," CBS, 1986.

HOPPER, HEDDA
b. Elda Furry, Hollidaysburg, PA, June 2, 1890; d. 1966. Sanctimonious Hollywood gossip columnist who usually played herself on TV.

AS A GUEST: "Goodyear TV Playhouse: Fadeout," NBC, 1953; "I Love Lucy: The Hedda Hopper Story," CBS, 1955; "Bob Hope Show," NBC, 1956; "The Ford Show," NBC, 1957; "Playhouse 90: The Hostess with the Mostess," CBS, 1957; "The Lucille Ball-Desi Arnaz Show: Lucy Takes a Cruise to Havana," CBS, 1957; "Bob Hope Special," NBC, 1958; "The Perry Como Show," NBC, 1958; "The Garry Moore Show," CBS, 1958; "Bob Hope Special," NBC, 1959; "Small World," CBS, 1959; "Hedda Hopper's Hollywood," NBC, 1960; "Person to Person," CBS, 1960; "Here's Hollywood," NBC, 1961; "Art Linkletter's House Party," CBS, 1963; "The Merv Griffin Show," NBC, 1963; "The Beverly Hillbillies: Hedda Hopper's Hollywood," CBS, 1964; "Alice in Wonderland," ABC, 1966.

TV MOVIES AND MINISERIES: "The Lonely Profession," NBC, 1969.

HOPPER, WILLIAM
b. William DeWolf Hopper Jr., New York City, NY, January 26, 1915; d. 1970. Colorless, good-looking actor who played private eye Paul Drake on "Perry Mason"; the son of Hedda Hopper and silent-film star DeWolf Hopper.

AS A REGULAR: "Perry Mason," CBS, 1957-66.

AND: "Warner Bros. Presents Casablanca: The Return," ABC, 1955; "Gunsmoke: Robin Hood," CBS, 1956; "Fury: The Hobo," NBC, 1956; "Studio 57: The Magic Glass," SYN, 1956; "The Millionaire: The Capt. Carroll Story," CBS, 1956; "The Jane Wyman Show: Ten Percent," NBC, 1956; "Lux Video Theatre: Top Rung," NBC, 1956; "Schlitz Playhouse of Stars: The Restless Gun," CBS, 1957; "The Joseph Cotten Show: The

Case of the Jealous Bomber," NBC, 1957; "Command Performance: Mr. November," SYN, 1960.

HORNE, LENA

b. *Brooklyn, NY, June 30, 1917*. Legendary actress and entertainer whose television work has been in a variety vein.

AS A GUEST: "The Ed Sullivan Show," CBS, 1957; "The Steve Allen Show," NBC, 1958; "The Perry Como Show," NBC, 1958; "The Perry Como Show," NBC, 1959; "Perry Como's Kraft Music Hall," NBC, 1960; "The Frank Sinatra Timex Show," ABC, 1960; "Perry Como's Kraft Music Hall," NBC, 1962; "The Milton Berle Show," NBC, 1962; "Password," CBS, 1963; "The Jack Paar Program," NBC, 1963; "Perry Como Special," NBC, 1964; "Bell Telephone Hour," NBC, 1965; "Password," CBS, 1965; "Lena Horne Special," SYN, 1965; "The Tonight Show Starring Johnny Carson," NBC, 1968; "Art Linkletter's House Party," CBS, 1968; "The Dean Martin Show," NBC, 1968; "Kraft Music Hall," NBC, 1970; "The Flip Wilson Show," NBC, 1970; "Sanford & Son: A Visit From Lena Horne," NBC, 1972; "Sanford & Son: The Over-the-Hill Gang," NBC, 1975; "The Cosby Show: Cliff's Birthday," NBC, 1985.

HORSFORD, ANNA MARIA

b. *New York City, NY, March 6, 1945*. Actress who plays Thelma on "Amen."

AS A REGULAR: "Amen," NBC, 1986- .
AND: "Nurse: A Place to Die," CBS, 1982; "Animal Crack-Ups," ABC, 1989.
TV MOVIES AND MINISERIES: "Bill," CBS, 1981; "A Doctor's Story," NBC, 1984; "Stone Pillow," CBS, 1985; "Nobody's Child," CBS, 1986; "Taken Away," CBS, 1989.

HORSLEY, LEE

b. *Muleshoe, TX, May 15, 1955*. TV hunk who played private eye Matt Houston and now plays gunfighter Ethan Cord on "Paradise."

AS A REGULAR: "Nero Wolfe," NBC, 1981; "Matt Houston," ABC, 1982-85; "Paradise," CBS, 1988- .
AND: "The Love Boat: China Cruise," ABC, 1983.
TV MOVIES AND MINISERIES: "The Wild Women of Chastity Gulch," ABC, 1982; "When Dreams Come True," ABC, 1985; "Agatha Christie's Thirteen at Dinner," CBS, 1985; "Crossings," ABC, 1986; "Infidelity," ABC, 1987; "Single Women, Married Men," CBS, 1989.

HORTON, EDWARD EVERETT

b. *Brooklyn, NY, March 18, 1889; d. 1970*. Stage, screen and TV actor who excelled at Milquetoast types; best known to TV audiences as the narrator of "Fractured Fairy Tales" on

"The Bullwinkle Show" and as Hekawi Indian Roaring Chicken on "F Troop."

AS A REGULAR: "Holiday Hotel," ABC, 1950; "The Bullwinkle Show," NBC, 1961-62; "F Troop," ABC, 1965-67.
AND: "Magnavox Theatre: Father, Dear Father," CBS, 1950; "I Love Lucy: Lucy Plays Cupid," CBS, 1952; "Broadway Television Theatre: The Nightcap," SYN, 1952; "Broadway Television Theatre: Whistling in the Dark," SYN, 1953; "Medallion Theatre: The Bartlett Desk," CBS, 1953; "Broadway Television Theatre: The Front Page," SYN, 1953; "Medallion Theatre: The Canterville Ghost," CBS, 1953; "Broadway Television Theatre: Your Uncle Dudley," SYN, 1953; "Best of Broadway: Arsenic and Old Lace," CBS, 1953; "The Merry Widow," NBC, 1955; "Damon Runyon Theatre: A Light in France," CBS, 1955; "Shower of Stars: Time Out for Ginger," CBS, 1955; "G.E. Theatre: The Muse and Mr. Parkinson," CBS, 1956; "Saturday Spectacular: Manhattan Tower," NBC, 1956; "The George Gobel Show," NBC, 1956; "The Red Skelton Show," CBS, 1957; "Playhouse 90: Three Men on a Horse," CBS, 1957; "The Lux Show with Rosemary Clooney," NBC, 1957; "The Steve Allen Show," NBC, 1957; "December Bride: Butler Show," CBS, 1957; "The Ford Show," NBC, 1958; "Art Linkletter's House Party," CBS, 1958; "The Red Skelton Show," CBS, 1959; "The Jack Paar Show," NBC, 1959; "The George Gobel Show," CBS, 1960; "The Red Skelton Show: Freddie in Las Vegas," CBS, 1960; "The Jack Paar Show," NBC, 1960; "The Real McCoys: Teenage Wedding," ABC, 1960; "The Red Skelton Show," CBS, 1962; "Dennis the Menace: Mr. Wilson's Uncle," CBS, 1962; "Dennis the Menace: The Treasure Chest," CBS, 1962; "Dennis the Menace: Dennis's Lovesick Friend," CBS, 1962; "Mr. Smith Goes to Washington: The Senator Baits a Hook," ABC, 1962; "Exploring," NBC, 1962; "Saints and Sinners: A Night of Horns and Bells," NBC, 1962; "Dennis the Menace: My Uncle Ned," CBS, 1963; "Our Man Higgins: Higgins' Understudy," ABC, 1963; "Our Man Higgins: Who's on First?," ABC, 1963; "Burke's Law: Who Killed Eleanora Davis?," ABC, 1963; "The Cara Williams Show: Frank's Old Flame," CBS, 1965; "Valentine's Day: For Me and My Sal," ABC, 1965; "Burke's Law: Who Killed Hamlet?," ABC, 1965; "Camp Runamuck: Spiffy Quits," NBC, 1965; "Batman: An Egg Grows in Gotham/The Yegg Foes in Gotham," ABC, 1966; "The Steve Allen Show," SYN, 1968; "It Takes a Thief: A Matter of Grey Matter," ABC, 1969; "Nanny and the Professor: Strictly for the Birds," ABC, 1970; "Love, American Style: Love and Las Vegas," ABC, 1970; "Johnny Carson Special: The Sun City Scandals," NBC, 1970.

HORTON, PETER

b. *Bellevue, WA*. Blond actor who played Gary

Shepherd on "thirtysomething."
AS A REGULAR: "Seven Brides for Seven Brothers," CBS, 1982-83; "thirtysomething," ABC, 1987- .
AND: "The White Shadow: Just One of the Boys," CBS, 1979; "St. Elsewhere: Lust Et Veritas," NBC, 1983.
TV MOVIES AND MINISERIES: "Miracle on Ice," ABC, 1981.

HORTON, ROBERT

b. Los Angeles, CA, July 29, 1924. Actor who played Flint McCullough on "Wagon Train," announced that he was through with TV westerns, and returned to series TV three years later in another one.
AS A REGULAR: "Warner Bros. Presents Kings Row," ABC, 1955-56; "Wagon Train," NBC, 1957-62; "A Man Called Shenandoah," ABC, 1965-66; "As the World Turns," CBS, 1982-84.
AND: "Ford Theatre: Portrait of Lydia," NBC, 1954; "Studio 57: The Will to Survive," SYN, 1955; "Public Defender: In Memory of Murder," CBS, 1955; "Your Play Time: Call From Robert Jest," NBC, 1955; "The Jane Wyman Show: The Black Road," NBC, 1956; "Cavalcade Theatre: Danger at Clover Ridge," ABC, 1956; "Alfred Hitchcock Presents: The Decoy," CBS, 1956; "Crossroads: False Prophet," ABC, 1956; "Alfred Hitchcock Presents: Crack of Doom," CBS, 1956; "Studio 57: The Road Back," SYN, 1956; "Alfred Hitchcock Presents: Mr. Blanchard's Secret," CBS, 1956; "The Steve Allen Show," NBC, 1957; "The Steve Allen Show," NBC, 1958; "The Ford Show," NBC, 1958; "Alfred Hitchcock Presents: Disappearing Trick," CBS, 1958; "The Lux Show with Rosemary Clooney," NBC, 1958; "Matinee Theatre: Much Ado About Nothing," NBC, 1958; "Studio One: A Delicate Affair," CBS, 1958; "G.E. Theatre: The Last Rodeo," CBS, 1958; "Alfred Hitchcock Presents: The Last Dark Step," CBS, 1959; "The Ford Show," NBC, 1959; "Markham: Deadline Date," CBS, 1959; "The du Pont Show with June Allyson: No Place to Hide," CBS, 1959; "Perry Como's Kraft Music Hall," NBC, 1960; "Alfred Hitchcock Presents: Hooked," CBS, 1960; "Startime: Jeff McLeod: The Last Reb," NBC, 1960; "The Ford Show," NBC, 1960; "About Faces," ABC, 1960; "The Ford Show," NBC, 1961; "The Barbara Stanwyck Show: The Choice," NBC, 1961; "Here's Hollywood," NBC, 1961; "Art Linkletter's House Party," CBS, 1961; "U.S. Steel Hour: The Perfect Accident," CBS, 1962; "Stump the Stars," CBS, 1962; "Your First Impression," NBC, 1962; "Stump the Stars," CBS, 1963; "U.S. Steel Hour: Mission of Fear," CBS, 1963; "Password," CBS, 1964; "To Tell the Truth," CBS, 1964; "What's This Song?," NBC, 1965; "The Man Who Bought Paradise," CBS, 1965; "Art Linkletter's

Hollywood Talent Scouts," CBS, 1966; "Police Woman: The Lifeline Agency," NBC, 1976.
TV MOVIES AND MINISERIES: "The Dangerous Days of Kiowa Jones," ABC, 1966; "The Spy Killer," ABC, 1969; "Foreign Exchange," ABC, 1970; "Red River," CBS, 1988.

HORWICH, FRANCES

Miss Frances to you, pal.
AS A REGULAR: "Ding Dong School," SYN, 1959-60.

HOTCHKIS, JOAN

b. Pasadena, CA.
AS A REGULAR: "The Secret Storm," CBS, 1959; "My World and Welcome to It," NBC, 1969-70; "The Odd Couple," ABC, 1970-72.
AND: "Robert Montgomery Presents: Longing for to Go," NBC, 1957; "Diagnosis: Unknown: The Case of the Elder," CBS, 1960; "Way Out: Soft Focus," CBS, 1961; "Bewitched: The Salem Saga," ABC, 1970; "Bewitched: Samantha's Hot Bedwarmer," ABC, 1970; "The FBI: The Innocents," ABC, 1970; "Mannix: With Intent to Kill," CBS, 1971; "Mannix: To Draw the Lightning," CBS, 1972; "Owen Marshall, Counselor at Law: Sigh No More, Lady," ABC, 1972; "The FBI: A Piece of the Action," ABC, 1974; "Marcus Welby, M.D.: The Time Bomb," ABC, 1975; "Medical Center: If Mine Eye Offends Me," CBS, 1975; "Barnaby Jones: Dangerous Summer," CBS, 1975; "Lou Grant: Dying," CBS, 1978; "Lou Grant: Andrew," CBS, 1979; "St. Elsewhere: All About Eve," NBC, 1983.

HOUGHTON, KATHERINE

b. Hartford, CT, March 10, 1945. Actress who made her film debut in "Guess Who's Coming to Dinner" with her real-life aunt, Katharine Hepburn.
AS A REGULAR: "One Life to Live," ABC, 1990.
AND: "ABC Stage '67: The Confession," ABC, 1966; "Judd for the Defense: In a Puff of Smoke," ABC, 1968; "The Merv Griffin Show," CBS, 1969.

HOULIHAN, KERI

b. Pennsylvania, July 3, 1975.
AS A REGULAR: "Our House," NBC, 1986-88.
AND: "Gimme a Break: Flashback," NBC, 1984; "Webster: Special Friends," ABC, 1984; "ALF: ALF's Special Christmas," NBC, 1987.

HOUSEMAN, JOHN

b. Jacques Haussman, Bucharest, Hungary, 1902; d. 1988. Theatrical producer and director who repeated his film role of Prof. Kingsfield in the TV series version of "The Paper Chase" and did bunches of commercials, making his money the old-fashioned way.
AS A REGULAR: "The Paper Chase," CBS, 1978-79;

SHO, 1984-86; "Silver Spoons," NBC, 1982-86; SYN, 1986-87.

AND: "The Last Word," CBS, 1959; "The Bionic Woman: Kill Oscar," ABC, 1976; "Mork & Mindy: Midas Mork," ABC, 1982.

TV MOVIES AND MINISERIES: "Fear on Trial," CBS, 1975; "Best Sellers: Captains and the Kings," NBC, 1976; "Washington: Behind Closed Doors," ABC, 1977; "Gideon's Trumpet," CBS, 1980; "The Winds of War," ABC, 1983; "A.D.," NBC, 1985; "James Clavell's Noble House," NBC, 1988; "Gore Vidal's Lincoln," NBC, 1988.

AS A PRODUCER: "Playhouse 90," CBS, 1958-59.

AS EXECUTIVE PRODUCER: "The Seven Lively Arts," CBS, 1957-58.

HOUSER, JERRY

b. Los Angeles, CA, July 14, 1952. Actor who played Wally Logan, husband of Marcia Brady (Maureen McCormick).

AS A REGULAR: "We'll Get By," CBS, 1975; "The Brady Brides," NBC, 1981; "The Bradys," CBS, 1990.

AND: "The FBI: The Game of Terror," ABC, 1971; "Room 222: Who Is Benedict Arnold?," ABC, 1971; "The FBI: Ransom," ABC, 1973; "Barnaby Jones: The Murdering Class," CBS, 1973; "The New Temperatures Rising Show: The Mothers," ABC, 1973; "Maude: Maude's Nephew," CBS, 1976; "The McLean Stevenson Show: Pilot," NBC, 1976; "Barnaby Jones: Killer on Campus," CBS, 1977; "One Day at a Time: The Honeymoon Is Over," CBS, 1982; "Duet: No Reservations," FOX, 1988; "The Robert Guillaume Show: Guaranteed Not to Shrink," ABC, 1989; "Trying Times: The Boss," PBS, 1989.

TV MOVIES AND MINISERIES: "S.O.S. Titanic," ABC, 1979; "The Brady Girls Get Married," NBC, 1981; "Miracle on Ice," ABC, 1981; "A Very Brady Christmas," CBS, 1988.

HOVIS, LARRY

b. Wapito, WA, February 20, 1936. Lanky actor who played Carter the chemist on "Hogan's Heroes" and was a regular on "Liar's Club."

AS A REGULAR: "Gomer Pyle, USMC," CBS, 1964-65; "Hogan's Heroes," CBS, 1965-71; "Rowan & Martin's Laugh-In," NBC, 1968, 1971-72; "Liar's Club," SYN, 1976-78.

AND: "American Bandstand," ABC, 1958; "The Andy Griffith Show: Goober Takes a Car Apart," CBS, 1965; "The Andy Griffith Show: The Case of the Punch in the Nose," CBS, 1965; "How's Your Mother-in-Law?," ABC, 1968; "The Ghost and Mrs. Muir: Dog Gone," NBC, 1969; "The Doris Day Show: Peeping Tom," CBS, 1973; "Chico and the Man: Borrowed Trouble," NBC, 1974; "You Don't Say," ABC, 1975; "Alice: The

Indian Taker," CBS, 1977; "Alice: Close Encounters of the Worst Kind," CBS, 1978.

TV MOVIES AND MINISERIES: "The New Daughters of Joshua Cabe," ABC, 1976.

HOWARD, CLINT

b. Burbank, CA, April 20, 1959. Stocky blond child actor; brother of Ron. He played the master of big bear Gentle Ben and sandwich-toting kid Leon on "The Andy Griffith Show."

AS A REGULAR: "The Baileys of Balboa," CBS, 1964-65; "Gentle Ben," CBS, 1967-69; "The Cowboys," ABC, 1974; "Gung Ho," ABC, 1986-87.

AND: "The Andy Griffith Show: One Punch Opie," CBS, 1962; "The Andy Griffith Show: A Black Day for Mayberry," CBS, 1963; "The Fugitive: Home Is the Hunted," ABC, 1964; "The FBI: An Elephant Is Like a Rope," ABC, 1965; "Please Don't Eat the Daisies: Swing That Indian Club," NBC, 1965; "The Patty Duke Show: The Three Little Kittens," ABC, 1966; "Star Trek: The Corbomite Maneuver," NBC, 1966; "Please Don't Eat the Daisies: The Purple Avenger," NBC, 1966; "The Virginian: Ride a Cock-Horse to Laramie Cross," NBC, 1966; "Love, American Style: Love and the Teacher," ABC, 1970; "The FBI: Incident in the Desert," ABC, 1970; "Family Affair: Say Uncle," CBS, 1970; "The Odd Couple: The Big Brothers," ABC, 1970; "Nanny and the Professor: One for the Road," ABC, 1971; "The Mod Squad: The Price of Love," ABC, 1971; "Marcus Welby, M.D.: Tender Comrade," ABC, 1972; "The Rookies: Crossfire," ABC, 1973; "The Streets of San Francisco: The House on Hyde Street," ABC, 1973; "The Streets of San Francisco: Cry Help," ABC, 1974; "Movin' On: Lifeline," NBC, 1974; "Happy Days: Bringing Up Spike," ABC, 1976; "Happy Days: Father and Son," ABC, 1980; "Lou Grant: Recovery," CBS, 1981.

TV MOVIES AND MINISERIES: "The Red Pony," ABC, 1973; "The Death of Richie," NBC, 1977; "Cotton Candy," NBC, 1978.

HOWARD, KEN

b. El Centro, CA, March 28, 1944. Blond actor who played Coach Ken Reeves on "The White Shadow" and Garrett Boydston on two prime-time soaps; also a familiar face in a glossy miniseries or two. An Emmy winner for "The Body Human."

AS A REGULAR: "Adam's Rib," ABC, 1973; "The Manhunter," CBS, 1974-75; "The White Shadow," CBS, 1978-81; "It's Not Easy," ABC, 1983; "The Colbys," ABC, 1985-86; "Dynasty," ABC, 1985-86; "Dream Girl, USA," SYN, 1986.

AND: "Bonanza: The 26th Game," NBC, 1972; "Medical Center: The Outcast," CBS, 1972; "The Mary Tyler Moore Hour," CBS, 1979; "The Body Human: Facts for Boys," CBS, 1980; "Glitter:

Premiere," ABC, 1984; "Murder, She Wrote: Murder at the Oasis," CBS, 1985; "Hotel: Missing Pieces," ABC, 1985; "Murder, She Wrote: Mirror, Mirror, On the Wall," CBS, 1989.

TV MOVIES AND MINISERIES: "The Manhunter," CBS, 1974; "The Critical List," NBC, 1978; "A Real American Hero," CBS, 1978; "Victims," ABC, 1982; "The Thorn Birds," ABC, 1983; "Rage of Angels," NBC, 1983; "He's Not Your Son," CBS, 1984; "Rage of Angels: The Story Continues," NBC, 1986; "The Man in the Brown Suit," CBS, 1989.

* Emmies: 1981.

HOWARD, RON
b. Duncan, OK, March 1, 1954. Former child actor with an unaffected style; he played Opie Taylor on "The Andy Griffith Show" and Richie Cunningham on "Happy Days." Now he's a big-time movie director ("Splash," "Night Shift," "Parenthood") and not a bad one, at that.

AS A REGULAR: "Dennis the Menace," CBS, 1959-60; "The Many Loves of Dobie Gillis," CBS, 1959-60; "The Andy Griffith Show," CBS, 1960-68; "The Smith Family," ABC, 1971-72; "Happy Days," ABC, 1974-80.

AND: "The Twilight Zone: Walking Distance," CBS, 1959; "The du Pont Show with June Allyson: Child Lost," CBS, 1959; "G.E. Theatre: Mr. O'Malley," CBS, 1959; "The Danny Thomas Show: Danny Meets Andy Griffith," CBS, 1960; "Pete and Gladys: The Goat Story," CBS, 1960; "G.E. Theatre: Tippy-Top," CBS, 1961; "The New Breed: So Dark the Night," ABC, 1962; "The Eleventh Hour: Is Mr. Martian Coming Back?," NBC, 1963; "The Great Adventure: Plague," CBS, 1964; "Dr. Kildare: A Candle in the Window," NBC, 1964; "The Fugitive: Cry Uncle," ABC, 1964; "The Big Valley: Night of the Wolf," ABC, 1965; "Gomer Pyle, USMC: Opie Joins the Marines," CBS, 1966; "The Danny Kaye Show," CBS, 1966; "The Monroes: The Race for the Rainbow," ABC, 1967; "Walt Disney's Wonderful World of Color: A Boy Called Nuthin'," NBC, 1967; "Mayberry, RFD: Andy and Helen Get Married," CBS, 1968; "The FBI: The Runaways," ABC, 1968; "Lancer: The Measure of a Man," CBS, 1968; "Judd for the Defense: Between the Dark and the Daylight," ABC, 1969; "Gunsmoke: Charlie Noon," CBS, 1969; "The Wonderful World of Disney: Smoke," NBC, 1970; "Love, American Style: Love and the Happy Day," ABC, 1972; "The Bold Ones: In Sudden Darkness," NBC, 1972; "Bonanza: The Initiation," NBC, 1972; "M*A*S*H: Sometimes You Hear the Bullet," CBS, 1973; "CBS Playhouse 90: The Migrants," CBS, 1973; "Huckleberry Finn," ABC, 1975; "Laverne & Shirley: Excuse Me, May I Cut In?," ABC, 1976; "The Captain & Tennille," ABC, 1976; "Dinah!," SYN, 1978; "Laverne &

Shirley: Shotgun Wedding," ABC, 1979; "Saturday Night Live," NBC, 1982.

TV MOVIES AND MINISERIES: "Locusts," ABC, 1974; "Huckleberry Finn," ABC, 1975; "Return to Mayberry," NBC, 1986.

HOWARD, RONALD
b. England, April 7, 1918. Actor who played Sherlock Holmes on TV; son of Leslie Howard.

AS A REGULAR: "Sherlock Holmes," SYN, 1954; "The Adventures of Robin Hood," CBS, 1956; "Cowboy in Africa," ABC, 1967-68.

AND: "Suspicion: Lord Arthur Saville's Crime," NBC, 1958; "Alfred Hitchcock Presents: An Occurance at Owl Creek Bridge," CBS, 1959; "Alcoa Presents One Step Beyond: The Haunting," ABC, 1960; "Thriller: Well of Doom," NBC, 1961; "Alfred Hitchcock Presents: A Secret Life," NBC, 1961; "Kraft Mystery Theatre: The Hideout," NBC, 1961; "Kraft Mystery Theatre: The Spider's Web," NBC, 1961; "Thriller: God Grante That She Lye Stille," NBC, 1961; "Combat!: What Are the Bugles Blowin' For?," ABC, 1964.

TV MOVIES AND MINISERIES: "Run a Crooked Mile," NBC, 1969.

HOWARD, SUSAN
b. Marshall, TX, January 28, 1946. Actress who played Donna Culver Krebbs on "Dallas."

AS A REGULAR: "Petrocelli," NBC, 1974-76; "Dallas," CBS, 1979-87.

AND: "Love on a Rooftop: Homecoming," ABC, 1966; "Mannix: Who Killed Me?," CBS, 1969; "Mission: Impossible: Committed," CBS, 1971; "Mannix: Round Trip to Nowhere," CBS, 1970; "The FBI: Center of Peril," ABC, 1971; "Love, American Style: Love and the Sweet Sixteen," ABC, 1972; "Columbo: The Most Crucial Game," NBC, 1972; "The Bold Ones: Terminal Career," NBC, 1972; "Marcus Welby, M.D.: A Necessary End," ABC, 1972; "Medical Center: Deadlock," CBS, 1972; "Marcus Welby, M.D.: The Tall Tree," ABC, 1973; "Griff: Premiere," ABC, 1973; "The Virginian: Halfway Back From Hell," NBC, 1969; "Tattletales," CBS, 1976; "City of Angels: The House on Orange Grove Avenue," NBC, 1976; "The Rockford Files: Feeding Frenzy," NBC, 1976; "Barnaby Jones: Yesterday's Terror," CBS, 1977.

TV MOVIES AND MINISERIES: "The Silent Gun," ABC, 1969; "Quarantined," ABC, 1970; "Savage," NBC, 1973; "Indict and Convict," ABC, 1974; "Night Games," NBC, 1974; "The Power Within," ABC, 1979.

HOWARD, TREVOR
b. Kent, England, September 29, 1916; d. 1988. Slight, solid English actor in films and TV.

AS A GUEST: "Producers Showcase: Tonight at 8:30," NBC, 1954; "The 20th Century-Fox Hour: Deception," CBS, 1956; "Studio One: Flower of Pride," CBS, 1956; "Westinghouse Desilu Playhouse: Murder in Gratitude," CBS, 1959; "The Jack Paar Show," NBC, 1960; "Playhouse 90: The Hiding Place," CBS, 1960; "Hallmark Hall of Fame: The Invincible Mr. Disraeli," NBC, 1963; "Hedda Gabler," CBS, 1963; "Hallmark Hall of Fame: Eagle in a Cage," NBC, 1965; "The Poppy Is Also a Flower," ABC, 1966; "The Love Boat: The Death and Life of Sir Albert Demarest," ABC, 1984.

TV MOVIES AND MINISERIES: "Catholics," CBS, 1973; "A Doll's House," ABC, 1973; "The Count of Monte Cristo," NBC, 1975; "George Washington," CBS, 1984; "Peter the Great," NBC, 1986; "Christmas Eve," NBC, 1986.

* Emmies: 1963.

HOWE, QUINCY
b. Boston, MA, 1900; d. 1977. Panelist and commentator.

AS A REGULAR: "U.N. Casebook," CBS, 1948-49; "People's Platform," CBS, 1948-50; "In the First Person," CBS, 1949-50; "It's News to Me," CBS, 1951-52; "Both Sides," ABC, 1953; "Medical Horizons," ABC, 1955; "Outside USA," ABC, 1955-56.

HOWELL, ARLENE
b. Eurlyne Howell, Bossier City, LA, 1940. Fifties starlet; Miss America 1958.

AS A REGULAR: "Bourbon Street Beat," ABC, 1959-60.

AND: "Bob Hope Special," NBC, 1958; "Maverick: Alias Bart Maverick," ABC, 1958; "Maverick: Passage to Fort Doom," ABC, 1959; "Bachelor Father: Ginger's Big Romance," NBC, 1960; "Gomer Pyle, USMC: Sergeant Carter Dates a Pyle," CBS, 1966.

HOWELL, C. THOMAS
b. Los Angeles, CA, December 7, 1966.

AS A REGULAR: "Two Marriages," ABC, 1983-84.

AND: "Nightmare Classics: The Eyes of the Panther," SHO, 1989.

HOWES, SALLY ANN
b. London, England, July 20, 1934. Musical-comedy performer.

AS A GUEST: "The Ed Sullivan Show," CBS, 1958; "The Big Record," CBS, 1958; "The Perry Como Show," NBC, 1958; "The Gift of the Magi," CBS, 1958; "Kraft Music Hall Starring Dave King," NBC, 1959; "Bell Telephone Hour: A Night of Music," NBC, 1959; "The Chevy Show," NBC, 1959; "Buick Electra Playhouse: The Fifth Column," CBS, 1960;

"Sunday Showcase: After Hours," NBC, 1960; "Dinah Shore Chevy Show," NBC, 1960; "Bell Telephone Hour: Holiday in Music," NBC, 1960; "Bell Telephone Hour: Music Hath Charms," NBC, 1961; "The Garry Moore Show," CBS, 1961; "Family Classics: Jane Eyre," CBS, 1961; "U.S. Steel Hour: The Leonardi Code," CBS, 1961; "The Jack Paar Show," NBC, 1961; "Bell Telephone Hour: A Measure of Music," NBC, 1962; "Password," CBS, 1962; "The Voice of Firestone," ABC, 1962; "To Tell the Truth," CBS, 1962; "The Jack Paar Program," NBC, 1962; "The Match Game," NBC, 1963; "To Tell the Truth," CBS, 1963; "The Voice of Firestone," ABC, 1963; "The Jack Paar Program," NBC, 1964; "To Tell the Truth," CBS, 1965; "The Tonight Show Starring Johnny Carson," NBC, 1968; "This Is Tom Jones," ABC, 1969; "Marcus Welby, M.D.: The Day After Forever," ABC, 1973; "Celebrity Sweepstakes," NBC, 1975; "Great Performances: An Evening with Alan Jay Lerner," PBS, 1989.

TV MOVIES AND MINISERIES: "The Hound of the Baskervilles," ABC, 1972; "Female Artillery," ABC, 1973.

HOWLAND, BETH
b. Boston, MA, May 28, 1947. Actress who played the bug-eyed waitress Vera on "Alice."

AS A REGULAR: "Alice," CBS, 1976-85.

AND: "The Mary Tyler Moore Show: Have I Found a Guy For You," CBS, 1972; "Love, American Style: Love and the Cover," ABC, 1974; "The Mary Tyler Moore Show: Mary Richards Falls in Love," CBS, 1975; "The Rookies: Reading, Writing and Angel Dust," ABC, 1975; "Dinah!," SYN, 1980; "The Love Boat: I Remember Helen," ABC, 1982; "The Love Boat: Prisoner of Love," ABC, 1983.

HOYT, JOHN
b. Bronxville, NY, October 5, 1904. Character actor, best known as Grandpa Kaminsky on "Gimme a Break," who specializes in flinty types.

AS A REGULAR: "The Adventures of Rin Tin Tin," ABC, 1954-58; "Tom, Dick and Mary," NBC, 1964-65; "Return to Peyton Place," NBC, 1972-74; "Gimme a Break," NBC, 1982-87;

AND: "The Loretta Young Show: The First Man to Ask Her," NBC, 1956; "G.E. Theatre: The Glorious Gift of Molly Malloy," CBS, 1956; "The George Burns and Gracie Allen Show: The Interview," CBS, 1956; "Matinee Theatre: I Like It Here," NBC, 1956; "The Adventures of Jim Bowie: The Beggar of New Orleans," ABC, 1957; "Studio 57: The Alibi," SYN, 1957; "Alfred Hitchcock Presents: One for the Road," CBS, 1957; "Matinee Theatre: Mr. Krane," NBC, 1957; "Matinee Theatre: Winter in April," NBC, 1957;

"G.E. Theatre: I Will Not Die," CBS, 1957; "O. Henry Playhouse: The Sphinx Apple," SYN, 1957; "Richard Diamond, Private Detective: The Georgie Dale Case," CBS, 1958; "Perry Mason: The Case of the Prodigal Parent," CBS, 1958; "The Thin Man: Housewarming," NBC, 1958; "Playhouse 90: Last Clear Chance," CBS, 1958; "Studio One: The Left-Hand Welcome," CBS, 1958; "Leave It to Beaver: Wally's New Suit," ABC, 1958; "How to Marry a Millionaire: Day in Court," SYN, 1959; "21 Beacon Street: The Trap," NBC, 1959; "Laramie: The General Must Die," NBC, 1959; "Five Fingers: The Final Dream," NBC, 1959; "Johnny Staccato: The Parents," NBC, 1959; "The Alaskans: The Challenge," ABC, 1960; "Lawman: The Judge," ABC, 1960; "The Untouchables: The Big Squeeze," ABC, 1960; "The Deputy: The X Game," NBC, 1960; "Gunslinger: Golden Circle," CBS, 1961; "The Twilight Zone: Will the Real Martian Please Stand Up," CBS, 1961; "Holiday Lodge: Frank the Star," CBS, 1961; "Maverick: The Art Lovers," ABC, 1961; "Have Gun, Will Travel: The Bird of Time," CBS, 1962; "Bonanza: The Decision," NBC, 1962; "Perry Mason: The Case of the Libelous Locket," CBS, 1963; "The Outer Limits: Don't Open Till Doomsday," ABC, 1964; "Destry: Stormy Is a Lady," ABC, 1964; "The Outer Limits: The Bellero Shield," ABC, 1964; "The Munsters: Herman's Happy Valley," CBS, 1965; "The Virginian: Ring of Silence," NBC, 1965; "The Loner: An Echo of Bugles," CBS, 1965; "Amos Burke, Secret Agent: Steam Heat," ABC, 1965; "I Spy: Chrysanthemum," NBC, 1965; "Get Smart: Our Man in Toyland," NBC, 1965; "Petticoat Junction: Temperance, Temperance," CBS, 1967; "The Big Valley: Barbary Red," ABC, 1966; "The Monkees: I Was a Teenage Monkee," NBC, 1967; "T.H.E. Cat: The Blood-Red Night," NBC, 1967; "Mr. Terrific: Stanley Goes to the Dentist," CBS, 1967; "The Virginian: Ah Sing vs. Wyoming," NBC, 1967; "The Wild Wild West: The Night of the Plague," CBS, 1969; "The Virginian: The Shiloh Years," NBC, 1970; "The Flying Nun: Armando and the Pool Table," ABC, 1970; "Planet of the Apes: The Gladiators," CBS, 1974; "Police Woman: Blind Terror," NBC, 1978.

TV MOVIES AND MINISERIES: "Fame Is the Name of the Game," NBC, 1966; "Winchester '73," NBC, 1967; "The Intruders," NBC, 1970; "Welcome Home, Johnny Bristol," CBS, 1972; "The Winds of Kitty Hawk," NBC, 1978.

HUBBARD, JOHN
b. East Chicago, IL, April 14, 1923; d. 1988.
Actor who usually played pompous roles.
AS A REGULAR: "The Mickey Rooney Show," NBC, 1954-55; "Don't Call Me Charlie!," NBC, 1962-63.
AND: "Circus Boy: The Little Fugitive," NBC,

1957; "This Is the Answer: The Six Hour Thief," SYN, 1957; "Maverick: The War of the Silver Kings," ABC, 1957; "The Silent Service: Boomerang," SYN, 1958; "Perry Mason: The Case of the Haunted Husband," CBS, 1958; "The Silent Service: Crevalle's Mine Plant," SYN, 1958; "77 Sunset Strip: Switchburg," ABC, 1959; "The Adventures of Ozzie and Harriet: David the Sleuth," ABC, 1959; "Hawaiian Eye: A Birthday Boy," ABC, 1960; "SurfSide 6: Country Gentleman," ABC, 1960; "Checkmate: Target ... Tycoon," CBS, 1960; "The Adventures of Ozzie and Harriet: David's Almost In-Laws," ABC, 1960; "77 Sunset Strip: Once Upon a Caper," ABC, 1961; "Cheyenne: The Beholden," ABC, 1961; "Hawaiian Eye: The Manchu Formula," ABC, 1961; "Lassie: The Pied Piper," CBS, 1961; "Pete and Gladys: The Three Loves of Gladys," CBS, 1961; "Shannon: The Florentine Prince," SYN, 1962; "Mr. Novak: The Senior Prom," NBC, 1964; "Bonanza: Invention of a Gunfighter," NBC, 1964; "Wendy & Me: Pilot," ABC, 1964; "The Munsters: Herman the Great," CBS, 1964; "Rawhide: A Man Called Mushy," CBS, 1964; "Wendy & Me: Wendy the Waitress," ABC, 1964; "The Virginian: Legend for a Lawman," NBC, 1965; "Bonanza: The Dilemma," NBC, 1965; "Batman: A Riddle a Day Keeps the Riddler Away/When the Rat's Away, the Mice Will Play," ABC, 1966; "Family Affair: The Matter of School," CBS, 1966; "My Three Sons: Good Guys Finish Last," CBS, 1966; "The Wild Wild West: The Night of the Samurai," CBS, 1967.

HUBER, HAROLD
b. New York City, NY, 1910; d. 1959.
AS A REGULAR: "I Cover Times Square," ABC, 1950-51.
AND: "The Web: Trouble at San Rivera," CBS, 1953; "The Jane Wyman Show: Helpmate," NBC, 1956; "The Arlene Francis Show," NBC, 1957; "The Phil Silvers Show: Bilko and the Chaplain," CBS, 1958; "The Phil Silvers Show: Viva Bilko," CBS, 1959.

HUBLEY, SEASON
b. New York City, NY, May 14, 1951.
AS A REGULAR: "Kung Fu," ABC, 1972-75; "Family," ABC, 1976-77.
AND: "The Partridge Family: The Princess and the Partridge," ABC, 1972; "The Rookies: A Time to Mourn," ABC, 1975; "Good Heavens: I Want Nancy," ABC, 1976; "Kojak: Sister Maria," CBS, 1977; "The Twilight Zone: Little Boy Lost," CBS, 1985; "Alfred Hitchcock Presents: Final Escape," NBC, 1985.
TV MOVIES AND MINISERIES: "She Lives," ABC, 1973; "The Healers," NBC, 1974; "SST-Death Flight," ABC, 1977; "Loose Change,"

NBC, 1978; "Elvis," ABC, 1979; "Mrs. R's Daughter," NBC, 1979; "The Three Wishes of Billy Grier," ABC, 1984; "Under the Influence," CBS, 1986; "Christmas Eve," NBC, 1986; "Shakedown on the Sunset Strip," CBS, 1988.

HUCKO, PEANUTS
b. Syracuse, NY, April 7, 1918. Clarinetist.
AS A REGULAR: "The Lawrence Welk Show," ABC, 1970-71; SYN, 1971-72.
AND: "All-Star Jazz: The Golden Age of Jazz," CBS, 1959.

HUDDLESTON, DAVID
b. Vinton, VA, September 17, 1930. Pudgy, heavyset actor usually cast as cops or as threatening rednecks.
AS A REGULAR: "Tenafly," NBC, 1973-74; "Petrocelli," NBC, 1974-76; "The Kallikaks," NBC, 1977; "Hizzonner," NBC, 1979.
AND: "Room 222: Hip Hip Hooray," ABC, 1971; "Bewitched: The Return of Darrin the Bold," ABC, 1971; "Bewitched: Out of the Mouths of Babes," ABC, 1971; "McMillan and Wife: Murder by the Barrel," NBC, 1971; "The Rookies: The Bear That Didn't Get Up," ABC, 1972; "Gunsmoke: The Widowmaker," CBS, 1973; "The New Adventures of Perry Mason: The Case of the Deadly Deeds," CBS, 1973; "Gunsmoke: The Disciple," CBS, 1974; "The Snoop Sisters: A Black Day for Bluebeard," NBC, 1974; "Gunsmoke: In Performance of Duty," CBS, 1974; "Paper Moon: The Imposter," ABC, 1974; "The Mary Tyler Moore Show: What Are Friends For?," CBS, 1974; "The Rookies: A Test of Courage," ABC, 1974; "Emergency!: Daisy's Pick," NBC, 1975; "Police Woman: The Purge," NBC, 1975; "The Rockford Files: The Reincarnation of Angie," NBC, 1975; "Hawaii Five-O: Love Thy Neighbor—Take His Wife," CBS, 1976; "Sanford & Son: The Hawaiian Connection," NBC, 1976; "The Practice: Jules Takes a Partner," NBC, 1976; "Barnaby Jones: Copy-Cat Killing," CBS, 1977; "Supertrain: The Green Girl," NBC, 1979; "Benson: Old Man Gatling," ABC, 1980; "Magnum P.I.: Going Home," CBS, 1985; "J.J. Starbuck: Pilot," NBC, 1987.
TV MOVIES AND MINISERIES: "Sarge: The Badge or the Cross," NBC, 1971; "The Priest Killer," CBS, 1971; "Suddenly Single," ABC, 1971; "Brian's Song," ABC, 1971; "The Homecoming," CBS, 1971; "Tenafly," NBC, 1973; "Brock's Last Case," NBC, 1973; "Hawkins on Murder," CBS, 1973; "Heat Wave," ABC, 1974; "The Gun and the Pulpit," ABC, 1974; "The Oregon Trail," NBC, 1976; "Sherlock Holmes in New York," NBC, 1976; "Best Sellers: Once an Eagle," NBC, 1977; "M.A.D.D.: Mothers Against Drunk Driving,"

NBC, 1983; "When the Bough Breaks," NBC, 1986; "The Tracker," HBO, 1988.

THE HUDSON BROTHERS
b. Portland, OR.—Bill, October 17, 1949; Brett, January 18, 1953; Mark, August 23, 1951.
AS REGULARS: "The Hudson Brothers Show," CBS, 1974; "The Hudson Brothers Razzle-Dazzle Comedy Show," CBS, 1974-75; "Bonkers," SYN, 1978-79.
AND: "The Mike Douglas Show," SYN, 1975; "Hollywood Squares," SYN, 1975; "The Love Boat: Haven't We Met Before?," ABC, 1980.
TV MOVIES AND MINISERIES: "The Millionaire," CBS, 1978.
* See also Mark Hudson.

HUDSON, MARK
AS A REGULAR: "Sara," NBC, 1985; "The Late Show," FOX, 1986-87.
* See also The Hudson Brothers.

HUDSON, ROCHELLE
b. Oklahoma City, OK, March 6, 1914; d. 1972. Character actress.
AS A REGULAR: "That's My Boy," CBS, 1954-55.
AND: "The 20th Century-Fox Hour: That I May Live," CBS, 1955; "77 Sunset Strip: The Legend of Leckonby," ABC, 1961; "Branded: The Mission," NBC, 1965.

HUDSON, ROCK
b. Roy Scherer Jr., Winnetka, IL, November 17, 1925; d. 1985. Screen idol of the fifties at his best in light television fare; he died untimely, due to AIDS.
AS A REGULAR: "McMillan and Wife," NBC, 1971-77; "The Devlin Connection," NBC, 1982; "Dynasty," ABC, 1984-85.
AND: "I Love Lucy: In Palm Springs," CBS, 1955; "The Ed Sullivan Show," CBS, 1956; "Caesar's Hour," NBC, 1957; "The Steve Allen Show," NBC, 1958; "The Big Party," CBS, 1959; "Steve Allen Plymouth Show," CBS, 1959; "The Jack Benny Program: Rock Hudson Visits," CBS, 1962; "Hollywood Squares," NBC, 1974; "The Carol Burnett Show," CBS, 1975.
TV MOVIES AND MINISERIES: "Once Upon a Dead Man," NBC, 1971; "Arthur Hailey's Wheels," NBC, 1978; "The Star Maker," NBC, 1981; "World War III," NBC, 1982.

HUGH-KELLY, DANIEL
b. Hoboken, NJ, 1949. TV hunk who can handle light comedy, best known as Mark McCormick on "Hardcastle and McCormick"; he also played Frank Ryan on "Ryan's Hope."
AS A REGULAR: "Ryan's Hope," ABC, 1977-81; "Chicago Story," NBC, 1982; "Hardcastle and

McCormick," ABC, 1983-86; "I Married Dora," ABC, 1987-88.
TV MOVIES AND MINISERIES: "Thin Ice," CBS, 1981.

HUGHES, BARNARD

b. *Bedford Hills, NY, July 16, 1915.* Stage actor on television as grizzled, sometimes lovable types; best known as "Doc" Joe Bogert, as patriarch Francis Cavanuagh and in an Emmy-winning role as aging judge on "Lou Grant."
AS A REGULAR: "The Guiding Light," CBS, 1961-66; "Doc," CBS, 1975-76; "Mr. Merlin," CBS, 1981-82; "The Cavanaughs," CBS, 1986-88.
AND: "Robert Montgomery Presents: Atomic Quest," NBC, 1957; "The Phil Silvers Show: Bilko's Prize Poodle," CBS, 1958; "Jackie Gleason Special: The Million Dollar Incident," CBS, 1961; "Car 54, Where Are You?: Toody Undercover," NBC, 1962; "Trials of O'Brien: No Justice for the Judge," CBS, 1965; "Trials of O'Brien: A Horse Called Destiny," CBS, 1966; "Catholic Hour: White Man/Black Man," NBC, 1968; "All the Way Home," CBS, 1971; "All in the Family: Edith's Accident," CBS, 1971; "CBS Playhouse 90: Look Homeward, Angel," CBS, 1972; "NET Playhouse: A Memory of Two Mondays," NET, 1972; "All in the Family: Edith Flips Her Wig," CBS, 1972; "You Are There: The Trial of Susan B. Anthony," CBS, 1973; "Much Ado About Nothing," NET, 1973; "All in the Family: Edith's Conversion," CBS, 1973; "Love Story: All My Tomorrows," NBC, 1973; "The Thanksgiving Treasure," CBS, 1973; "Another April," CBS, 1974; "The Bob Newhart Show: An American Family," CBS, 1974; "The Bob Newhart Show: Making Up Is the Thing to Do," CBS, 1976; "Hawaii Five-O: A Capitol Crime," CBS, 1977; "Lou Grant: Judge," CBS, 1977; "The Bob Newhart Show: Grizzly Emily," CBS, 1978; "Captain Kangaroo," CBS, 1979; "The Love Boat: Uncle Joey's Song," ABC, 1984; "The Days and Nights of Molly Dodd: Here's Who Ordered the Pizza," NBC, 1988.
TV MOVIES AND MINISERIES: "The Borgia Stick," NBC, 1967; "Dr. Cook's Garden," ABC, 1971; "The Borrowers," NBC, 1973; "The UFO Incident," ABC, 1975; "Guilty or Innocent: The Sam Sheppard Murder Case," NBC, 1975; "Kill Me if You Can," NBC, 1977; "Sanctuary of Fear," NBC, 1979; "The Sky's No Limit," CBS, 1984; "A Hobo's Christmas," CBS, 1987; "Night of Courage," ABC, 1987; "Hallmark Hall of Fame: Home Fires Burning," CBS, 1989; "AT&T Presents: Day One," CBS, 1989; "The Rise and Fall of Oliver North," CBS, 1989; "AT&T Presents: The Incident," CBS, 1990.
* Emmies: 1978.
* See also Paul Sorvino.

HULL, HENRY

b. *Louisville, KY, October 3, 1890; d. 1977.* Actor, formerly on stage, often in elderly character roles on TV.
AS A GUEST:"Armstrong Circle Theatre: Ghost Town," NBC, 1951; "Lights Out: I, Spy," NBC, 1951; "Lux Video Theatre: Mr. Finchley Versus the Bomb," NBC, 1952; "Favorite Story: The Copper Penny," SYN, 1952; "Suspense: Night of Evil," CBS, 1952; "Lux Video Theatre: Brigadier," CBS, 1952; "Danger: Trial by Jungle," CBS, 1953; "The Web: The Well," CBS, 1954; "Campbell TV Soundstage: Test Case," NBC, 1954; "Campbell TV Soundstage: The Almighty Dollar," NBC, 1954; "Center Stage: Chivarly at Howling Creek," ABC, 1954; "The Ray Milland Show: Battle of the Sexes," CBS, 1954; "U.S. Steel Hour: Freighter," ABC, 1955; "You Are There: The McCoy-Hatfield Feud," CBS, 1955; "Appointment with Adventure: Five in Judgment," CBS, 1955; "Windows: The Calliope Tree," CBS, 1955; "Climax!: Figures in Clay," CBS, 1956; "Kaiser Aluminum Hour: Mr. Finchley Versus the Bomb," NBC, 1956; "Restless Gun: The Last Gray Man," NBC, 1957; "Restless Gun: One on the House," NBC, 1958; "Playhouse 90: Bitter Heritage," CBS, 1958; "Bonanza: The Gunmen," NBC, 1960; "Dick Powell's Zane Grey Theatre: A Small Town That Died," CBS, 1960; "Goodyear Theatre: All in the Family," NBC, 1960; "Wagon Train: Trial for Murder," NBC, 1960; "Bonanza: The Mission," NBC, 1960; "Route 66: The Swan Bed," CBS, 1960; "Laramie: Duel at Parkison Town," NBC, 1960; "Best of the Post: No Enemy," SYN, 1961; "Wagon Train: The Odyssey of Flint McCullough," NBC, 1961; "The Outlaws: Culley," NBC, 1961; "Accent: Ethan Allen and the Green Mountain Boys," CBS, 1962; "Alcoa Premiere: The Man With the Shine on His Shoes," ABC, 1962; "Laramie: The Road to Helena," NBC, 1963.

HULL, JOSEPHINE

b. *Josephine Sherwood, Newton, MA, 1884; d. 1957.* Stage actress ("Arsenic and Old Lace," "Harvey") in dowager roles on TV.
AS A GUEST:"Studio One: Give Us Our Dream," CBS, 1950; "Goodyer TV Playhouse: Dear Ghosts and Guest," NBC, 1950; "Lux Video Theatre: Grandma Was an Acress," CBS, 1951; "Schlitz Playhouse of Stars: Clean Sweep for Lavinia," CBS, 1952; "Lights Out: The Upstairs Floor," NBC, 1952; "Lux Video Theatre: The Wednesday Wish," CBS, 1953; "U.S. Steel Hour: The Meanest Man in the World," CBS, 1955.

HULL, WARREN

b. Gasport, NY, January 17, 1903; d. 1974.
Former actor who turned to TV announcing and game-show hosting, best known as the host of "Strike It Rich."

AS A REGULAR: "A Couple of Joes," ABC, 1949-50; "Cavalcade of Bands," DUM, 1950; "Crawford Mystery Theatre," DUM, 1951; "Strike It Rich," CBS, 1951-58; "Public Prosecutor," SYN, 1951-52; "Who in the World," CBS, 1962.

AND: "Starlight Theatre: With Baited Breath," CBS, 1951; "Armstrong Circle Theatre: The Oldster," NBC, 1951; "Your Hit Parade," CBS, 1959.

* Hull was a guest on the final telecast of "Your Hit Parade" as it ended 24 years on radio and TV.

HUME, BENITA

b. London, England, October 14, 1906; d. 1967. Actress and wife of Ronald Colman.

AS A REGULAR: "The Halls of Ivy," CBS, 1954-55.

HUMPERDINCK, ENGELBERT

b. Arnold George Dorsey, Madras, India, May 2, 1936. Pop singer.

AS A REGULAR: "The Engelbert Humperdinck Show," ABC, 1970.

AND: "The Jerry Lewis Show," NBC, 1968; "This Is Tom Jones," ABC, 1969; "Hollywood Palace," ABC, 1969; "The Ed Sullivan Show," CBS, 1970; "Bob Hope Special," NBC, 1970; "The Mike Douglas Show," SYN, 1980; "The Merv Griffin Show," SYN, 1980; "The Love Boat: Julie and the Bachelor," ABC, 1983; "The Jeffersons: You'll Never Get Rich," CBS, 1983; "The Love Boat: The Crew's Cruise Director," ABC, 1984; "Hotel: Encores," ABC, 1984.

HUNLEY, LEANN

b. Forks, WA. Actress who played Anna on "Days of Our Lives."

AS A REGULAR: "Lobo," NBC, 1979-80; "Days of Our Lives," NBC, 1982-86; "Dynasty," ABC, 1986-88; "Eisenhower and Lutz," CBS, 1988; "FM," NBC, 1989; 1990.

AND: "B.J. and the Bear: Crackers," NBC, 1979; "Highway to Heaven: We Have Forever," NBC, 1987; "Murder, She Wrote: A Little Night Work," CBS, 1988; "Who's the Boss?: Winter Break," ABC, 1989.

TV MOVIES AND MINISERIES: "The Islander," CBS, 1978.

* Emmies: 1986.

HUNNICUT, ARTHUR

b. Gravelly, AR, February 17, 1911; d. 1979. Character actor often in western or hillbilly roles.

AS A REGULAR: "Walt Disney Presents: The Nine Lives of Elfego Baca," ABC, 1959.

AND: "Wire Service: Blood Rock Mine," ABC, 1956; "Cheyenne: Death Deals the Hand," ABC, 1957; "Wanted Dead or Alive: Amos Carter," CBS, 1959; "The Overland Trail: West of Boston," NBC, 1960; "Bonanza: The Hanging Posse," NBC, 1960; "The Andy Griffith Show: A Feud Is a Feud," CBS, 1960; "Laramie: Cactus Lady," NBC, 1961; "My Three Sons: The Horseless Saddle," ABC, 1961; "The Donna Reed Show: One of Those Days," ABC, 1961; "Laramie: Wolf Cub," NBC, 1961; "The Outlaws: The Sisters," NBC, 1962; "The Twilight Zone: The Hunt," CBS, 1962; "Laramie: The Dispossessed," NBC, 1963; "The Virginian: Strangers at Sundown," NBC, 1963; "The Outer Limits: Cry of Silence," ABC, 1964; "Gunsmoke: Cleavus," CBS, 1971.

TV MOVIES AND MINISERIES: "The Trackers," ABC, 1971; "Climb an Angry Mountain," NBC, 1972; "Mrs. Sundance," ABC, 1974.

HUNT, HELEN

b. Los Angeles, CA, June 15, 1963. Blonde actress who played Clancy, girlfriend of Jack Morrison (David Morse) on "St. Elsewhere."

AS A REGULAR: "Amy Prentiss," NBC, 1974-75; "Swiss Family Robinson," ABC, 1975-76; "The Fitzpatricks," CBS, 1977-78; "It Takes Two," ABC, 1982-83.

AND: "Family: Daylight Seranade," ABC, 1980; "The Facts of Life: Dope," NBC, 1980; "St. Elsewhere: Hello and Goodbye," NBC, 1984; "St. Elsewhere: Playing God," NBC, 1984; "St. Elsewhere: Homecoming," NBC, 1984; "St. Elsewhere: Tears of a Clown," NBC, 1985; "St. Elsewhere: Family Ties," NBC, 1986; "St. Elsewhere: Family Feud," NBC, 1986.

TV MOVIES AND MINISERIES: "Pioneer Woman," ABC, 1973; "All Together Now," ABC, 1975; "The Spell," NBC, 1977; "Transplant," CBS, 1979; "Angel Dusted," NBC, 1981; "The Miracle of Kathy Miller," CBS, 1981; "Child Bride of Short Creek," NBC, 1981; "Desperate Lives," CBS, 1982; "Quarterback Princess," CBS, 1983; "Bill: On His Own," CBS, 1983; "Sweet Revenge," CBS, 1984; "Incident at Dark River," TNT, 1989.

HUNT, MARSHA

b. Chicago, IL, October 17, 1917. Former MGM contract player with a string of unexceptional TV credits.

AS A REGULAR: "Peck's Bad Girl," CBS, 1959.

AND: "Studio One: Willow Cabin," CBS, 1950; "Cosmpolitan Theatre: The Secret Front," SYN, 1951; "Ford Theatre: Double Bet," NBC, 1953; "The 20th Century-Fox Hour: Man of the Law," CBS, 1957; "Dick Powell's Zane Grey Theatre: Let the Man Die," CBS, 1958; "Dick Powell's

Zane Grey Theatre: Checkmate," CBS, 1959; "Laramie: Circle of Fire," NBC, 1959; "The Detectives Starring Robert Taylor: The Prowler," ABC, 1960; "The Breaking Point: And James Was a Very Small Snail," ABC, 1963; "Channing: A Rich, Famous, Glamorous Folk Singer Like Me," ABC, 1964; "The Outer Limits: ZZZZZ," ABC, 1964; "The Twilight Zone: Spur of the Moment," CBS, 1964; "The Defenders: Die Laughing," CBS, 1964; "Profiles in Courage: Prof. Richard T. Ely," NBC, 1964; "Ben Casey: A Man, a Maid and a Marionette," ABC, 1965; "Run for Your Life: Hoodlums on Wheels," NBC, 1966; "My Three Sons: The Aunt Who Came to Dinner," CBS, 1967; "The Outsider: Along Came a Spider," NBC, 1968; "The Name of the Game: Goodbye, Harry," NBC, 1969; "Marcus Welby, M.D.: The Daredevil Gesture," ABC, 1970; "Ironside: Little Dog, Gone," NBC, 1970; "The Young Lawyers: We May Be Better Strangers," ABC, 1970; "Ironside: The Riddle in Room Six," NBC, 1971; "Medical Story: A Right to Die," NBC, 1975.
TV MOVIES AND MINISERIES: "Fear No Evil," NBC, 1969; "Jigsaw," ABC, 1972.

HUNTER, JEFFREY

b. Henry H. McKinnies, Jr., New Orleans, LA, November 25, 1925; d. 1969. Handsome fifties actor best known for playing Jesus Christ in "King of Kings."
AS A REGULAR: "Temple Houston," NBC, 1963-64.
AND: "Climax!: South of the Sun," CBS, 1955; "The 20th Century-Fox Hour: The Empty Room," CBS, 1956; "Climax!: Hurricane Dianne," CBS, 1957; "Pursuit: Kiss Me Again, Stranger," CBS, 1958; "Our American Heritage: Destiny West," NBC, 1960; "Checkmate: Waiting for Jocko," CBS, 1961; "Walt Disney Presents: Andrews' Raiders—The Secret Mission," ABC, 1961; "Walt Disney Presents: Andrews' Raiders - Escape to Nowhere," ABC, 1961; "The Alfred Hitchcock Hour: Don't Look Behind You," CBS, 1962; "Combat!: Lost Sheep, Lost Shepard," ABC, 1962; "Bob Hope Chrysler Theatre: Seven Miles of Bad Road," NBC, 1963; "Death Valley Days: Suzie," SYN, 1964; "Bob Hope Chrysler Theatre: Parties to the Crime," NBC, 1964; "Kraft Suspense Theatre: The Trains of Silence," NBC, 1965; "The FBI: The Monster," ABC, 1965; "The Legend of Jesse James: Field of Wild Flowers," ABC, 1966; "Star Trek: The Menagerie," NBC, 1966; "The Green Hornet: Beautiful Dreamer," ABC, 1966; "The Monroes: Mark of Death," ABC, 1967; "The FBI: The Enemies," ABC, 1968.

HUNTER, KIM

b. Janet Cole, Detroit, MI, November 12, 1922. Actress with numerous TV credits whose most famous work has been on stage ("A Streetcar Named Desire") and on film in several "Planet of the Apes" movies.
AS A REGULAR: "The Edge of Night," ABC, 1979-80.
AND: "Robert Montgomery Presents: Rise Up and Walk," NBC, 1952; "Celanese Theatre: The Petrified Forest," ABC, 1952; "Omnibus: The Trial of St. Joan," CBS, 1955; "Appointment with Adventure: Ride the Comet," CBS, 1955; "Screen Directors Playhouse: A Midsummer Daydream," NBC, 1955; "The Joseph Cotten Show: The Person and Property of Margery Hay," NBC, 1956; "Playhouse 90: The Comedian," CBS, 1957; "Person to Person," CBS, 1957; "Kaiser Aluminum Hour: Whereabouts Unknown," NBC, 1957; "Climax!: Cabin B-13," CBS, 1958; "Lamp Unto My Feet: Antigone," CBS, 1958; "Playhouse 90: Free Weekend," CBS, 1958; "Alcoa Theatre: The Dark File," NBC, 1958; "Adventures in Paradise: The Haunted," ABC, 1959; "G.E. Theatre: Early to Die," CBS, 1960; "The Secret of Freedom," NBC, 1960; "Playhouse 90: Alas, Babylon," CBS, 1960; "Rendezvous: In an Early Winter," SYN, 1960; "Special for Women: The Cold Woman," NBC, 1960; "Play of the Week: The Closing Door," SYN, 1960; "Lamp Unto My Feet: The Doorbell," CBS, 1960; "Hallmark Hall of Fame: Give Us Barabbas!," NBC, 1961; "U.S. Steel Hour: Wanted: Someone Innocent," CBS, 1962; "The Eleventh Hour: Of Roses and Nighingales and Other Lovely Things," NBC, 1962; "Russians: Self-Impressions," CBS, 1963; "The Breaking Point: Crack in an Image," ABC, 1963; "Arrest and Trial: Some Weeks Are All Mondays," ABC, 1963; "The Alfred Hitchcock Hour: The Evil of Adelaide Winters," CBS, 1964; "Hawk: Wall of Silence," ABC, 1966; "Mannix: The Name Is Mannix," CBS, 1967; "Bonanza: The Price of Salt," NBC, 1968; "Walt Disney's Wonderful World of Color: The Young Loner," NBC, 1968; "CBS Playhouse: The People Next Door," CBS, 1968; "The Young Lawyers: The Alienation Kick," ABC, 1970; "Bracken's World: A Team of One-Legged Acrobats," NBC, 1970; "Mannix: Deja Vu," CBS, 1970; "Medical Center: The Impostor," CBS, 1971; "Gunsmoke: Ma Colter," CBS, 1971; "Cannon: The Girl in the Electric Chair," CBS, 1971; "Columbo: Suitable for Framing," NBC, 1971; "The Virginia Graham Show," SYN, 1972; "Night Galley: The Late Mr. Peddington," NBC, 1972; "Mission: Impossible: Incarnate," CBS, 1973; "Hec Ramsey: The Detroit Connection," NBC, 1973; "Medical Center: Kiss and Tell," CBS, 1974; "Wide World of Mystery: The Impersonation Murder Case," ABC, 1975; "The Rockford Files: Never Send a Boy King to Do a Man's Job," NBC, 1979.
TV MOVIES AND MINISERIES: "Dial Hot Line," ABC,

1970; "In Search of America," ABC, 1971; "The Magician," NBC, 1973; "Unwed Father," ABC, 1974; "Bad Ronald," ABC, 1974; "Born Innocent," NBC, 1974; "Ellery Queen," NBC, 1975; "The Dark Side of Innocence," NBC, 1976; "Best Sellers: Once an Eagle," NBC, 1976; "Backstairs at the White House," NBC, 1979; "The Golden Gate Murders," CBS, 1979; "F.D.R.: The Last Year," NBC, 1980; "Skokie," CBS, 1981; "Private Sessions," NBC, 1985; "Drop-Out Mother," CBS, 1988; "Cross of Fire," NBC, 1989.

HUNTER, RONALD

b. Boston, MA, June 14, 1943.

AS A REGULAR: "The Lazarus Syndrome," ABC, 1979.

AND: "Kojak: The Pride and the Princess," CBS, 1976; "The Golden Girls: Heart Attack," NBC, 1986; "The Equalizer: Something Green," CBS, 1988.

TV MOVIES AND MINISERIES: "Off the Minnesota Strip," ABC, 1980; "Cagney and Lacey," CBS, 1981; "Rage of Angels," NBC, 1983.

HUNTER, TAB

b. Arthur Andrew Gelien, New York City, NY, July 11, 1931. Fifties hunk who now appears on television from time to time as a curiosity.

AS A REGULAR: "The Tab Hunter Show," NBC, 1960-61; "Mary Hartman, Mary Hartman," SYN, 1977-78.

AND: "Ford Theatre: While We're Young," NBC, 1955; "Lux Video Theatre: Lightning Strikes Twice," NBC, 1955; "Climax!: Fear Strikes Out," CBS, 1955; "The Bob Cummings Show: The Letter," NBC, 1956; "The Perry Como Show," NBC, 1956; "Playhouse 90: Forbidden Area," CBS, 1956; "Warner Bros. Presents Conflict: People Against McQuade," ABC, 1956; "Strike It Rich," CBS, 1957; "I've Got a Secret," CBS, 1957; "Dinah Shore Chevy Show," NBC, 1957; "Pat Boone Chevy Showroom," ABC, 1958; "Hallmark Hall of Fame: Hans Brinker or The Silver Skates," NBC, 1958; "Playhouse 90: Portrait of a Murderer," CBS, 1958; "The Dick Clark Saturday Night Beechnut Show," ABC, 1959; "The Perry Como Show," NBC, 1959; "Pat Boone Chevy Showroom," ABC, 1959; "Arthur Murray Party," NBC, 1959; "Meet Me in St. Louis," CBS, 1959; "American Bandstand," ABC, 1959; "Summer on Ice," NBC, 1959; "I've Got a Secret," CBS, 1959; "Steve Allen Plymouth Show," NBC, 1959; "G.E. Theatre: Disaster," CBS, 1959; "Dick Clark's World of Talent," ABC, 1959; "Startime: Merman on Broadway," NBC, 1959; "Summer on Ice," NBC, 1960; "Play Your Hunch," NBC, 1960; "Celebrity Talent Scouts," CBS, 1960; "Here's Hollywood," NBC, 1960; "The Ford Show," NBC, 1961; "Here's Hollywood," NBC, 1961; "Connie Francis

Special: Kicking Sound Around," ABC, 1961; "Saints and Sinners: Three Columns of Anger," NBC, 1962; "Stump the Stars," CBS, 1962; "Combat!: The Celebrity," ABC, 1962; "Object Is," ABC, 1964; "Stump the Stars," CBS, 1964; "Burke's Law: Who Killed Andy Zygmunt?," ABC, 1964; "The Virginian: The Gift," NBC, 1970; The Wonderful World of Disney: Hacksaw," NBC, 1971; "Cannon: The Treasure of San Iguasio," CBS, 1972; "Owen Marshall, Counselor at Law: Starting Over Again," ABC, 1972; "Circle of Fear: The Ghost of Potter's Field," NBC, 1973; "McMillan and Wife: Deadly Inheritance," NBC, 1976; "Police Woman: Blind Terror," NBC, 1978; "$weepstake$: Victor, Billy and Bobby, 'Sometimes,' " NBC, 1979; "Just Our Luck: Pilot," ABC, 1983.

TV MOVIES AND MINISERIES: "San Francisco International," NBC, 1970; "Katie: Portrait of a Centerfold," NBC, 1978; "The Kid from Left Field," NBC, 1979.

HUNTLEY, CHET

b. Cardwell, MT, December 10, 1911; d. 1974.

AS A REGULAR: "The Huntley-Brinkley Report, NBC, 1956-70; "Chet Huntley Reporting," NBC, 1957-63.

TV MOVIES AND MINISERIES: "Vanished," NBC, 1971.

HURST, RICK

b. Houston, TX. Comic actor usually in gawky roles; he played Deputy Cletus on "The Dukes of Hazzard."

AS A REGULAR: "On the Rocks," ABC, 1975-76; "Amanda's," ABC, 1983; "The Dukes of Hazzard," CBS, 1980-83.

AND: "Sanford & Son: The Piano Movers," NBC, 1972; "The Partridge Family: M Is for the Many Things," ABC, 1972; "Love, American Style: Love and the Family Hour," ABC, 1973; "The Doris Day Show: Anniversary Gift," CBS, 1973; "Kojak: Siege of Terror," CBS, 1973; "Kung Fu: The Chalice," ABC, 1973; "The Girl with Something Extra: It's So Peaceful in the Country," NBC, 1973; "Little House on the Prairie: The 100 Mile Walk," NBC, 1974; "Cross Wits," SYN, 1977; "M*A*S*H: Fade Out, Fade In," CBS, 1977; "CHiPS: Death Watch," NBC, 1979; "The Last Precinct: Gorilla-Gram," NBC, 1986; "Murder, She Wrote: Something Borrowed, Someone Blue," CBS, 1989.

TV MOVIES AND MINISERIES: "The Blue Knight," NBC, 1975; "From Here to Eternity," NBC, 1979; "Mothers, Daughters and Lovers," NBC, 1989.

HUSSEY, RUTH

b. Ruth Carol O'Rourke, Providence, RI, October 30, 1914. Film actress who played

assorted types on TV, from matrons to vixens.
AS A GUEST: "Pulitzer Prize Playhouse: The Magnificent Ambersons," ABC, 1950; "Lux Video Theatre: Gallant Lady," CBS, 1950; "Celanese Theatre: Counselor-at-Law," ABC, 1951; "The Joyful Hour," ABC, 1951; "Ford Theatre: This Is My Heart," NBC, 1953; "G.E. Theatre: Winners Never Lose," CBS, 1953; "Lux Video Theatre: The Moon for Linda," CBS, 1953; "Mirror Theatre: Flight From Home," CBS, 1953; "G.E. Theatre: To Lift a Feather," CBS, 1954; "Studio One: The Boy Who Changed the World," CBS, 1954; "Lux Video Theatre: Craig's Wife," NBC, 1954; "Elgin TV Hour: Warm Clay," ABC, 1954; "Producers Showcase: The Women," NBC, 1955; "Climax!: The Unimportant Man," CBS, 1955; "Science Fiction Theatre: 100 Years Long," SYN, 1955; "Shower of Stars: Time Out for Ginger," CBS, 1955; "Fireside Theatre: Women at Sea," NBC, 1955; "Studio 57: The Magic Glass," SYN, 1956; "Science Fiction Theatre: Unguided Missile," SYN, 1956; "Alfred Hitchcock Presents: Mink," CBS, 1956; "Climax!: A Trophy for Howard Davenport," CBS, 1956; "Lux Video Theatre: Old Acquaintance," NBC, 1956; "The Red Skelton Show," CBS, 1956; "Lux Video Theatre: Payment in Kind," NBC, 1957; "Hill Number One," SYN, 1957; "Climax!: Along Came a Spider," CBS, 1957; "That I May See," SYN, 1957; "Vacation Playhouse: Come A-Runnin'," CBS, 1963; "Marcus Welby, M.D.: The Best Is Yet to Be," ABC, 1972; "The New Adventures of Perry Mason: The Case of the Horoscope Homicide," CBS, 1973.
TV MOVIES AND MINISERIES: "My Darling Daughters' Anniversary," ABC, 1973.

HUSTON, MARTIN
b. 1943.
AS A REGULAR: "My Son Jeep," NBC, 1953; "Jungle Jim," SYN, 1955-56; "Too Young to Go Steady," NBC, 1959; "Diagnosis: Unknown," CBS, 1960; 1961.
AND: "Goodyear TV Playhouse: The Best Wine," NBC, 1957; "Kraft Theatre: Three Plays by Tennessee Williams-This Property Is Condemned," NBC, 1958; "U.S. Steel Hour: The Revolt of Judge Lloyd," CBS, 1960.

HUTCHINS, WILL
b. Marshall Lowell Hutchason, Atwater, CA, May 5, 1932. Likable actor who played reluctant gunfighter Tom "Sugarfoot" Brewster.
AS A REGULAR: "Sugarfoot," ABC, 1957-61; "Hey Landlord," NBC, 1966-67; "Blondie," CBS, 1968-69.
AND: "Warner Bros. Presents Conflict: Magic Brew," ABC, 1956; "Warner Bros. Presents

Conflict: Stranger on the Road," ABC, 1956; "Matinee Theatre: The Wisp End," NBC, 1956; "Warner Bros. Presents Conflict: Capital Punishment," ABC, 1957; "77 Sunset Strip: The Kookie Caper," ABC, 1959; "77 Sunset Strip: Six Superior Skirts," ABC, 1959; "Pat Boone Chevy Showroom," ABC, 1959; "Maverick: Hadley's Hunters," ABC, 1960; "Maverick: Bolt From the Blue," ABC, 1960; "The Roaring Twenties: Pie in the Sky," ABC, 1961; "SurfSide 6: Spring Training," ABC, 1961; "Here's Hollywood," NBC, 1961; "The Alfred Hitchcock Hour: The Star Juror," CBS, 1963; "Perry Mason: The Case of the Scarlet Scandal," CBS, 1966; "The New Adventures of Perry Mason: The Case of the Deadly Deeds," CBS, 1973; "Chase: Hot Beef," NBC, 1974.
TV MOVIES AND MINISERIES: "Horror at 37,000 Feet," CBS, 1973; "The Quest," NBC, 1976.

HUTCHINSON, JOSEPHINE
b. Seattle, WA, October 12, 1904. Actress who played kindly and/or dotty little old ladies.
AS A GUEST: "Pepsi Cola Playhouse: The House Where Time Stopped," ABC, 1955; "Your Play Time: Wait for George," SYN, 1955; "The 20th Century-Fox Hour: Deadline Decision," CBS, 1955; "The 20th Century-Fox Hour: The Man Who Couldn't Wait," CBS, 1957; "Schlitz Playhouse of Stars: Sister Louise Goes to Town," CBS, 1957; "Matinee Theatre: The Ivy Curtain," NBC, 1957; "Perry Mason: The Case of the Screaming Woman," CBS, 1958; "Perry Mason: The Case of the Spanish Cross," CBS, 1959; "The Lineup: Prince of Penmen," CBS, 1959; "Wagon Train: The Tom Tuckett Story," NBC, 1960; "The Rifleman: The Prodigal," ABC, 1960; "The Deputy: Mother and Son," NBC, 1960; "Checkmate: A Matter of Conscience," CBS, 1961; "G.E. Theatre: A Possibility of Oil," CBS, 1961; "Perry Mason: The Case of the Barefaced Witness," CBS, 1961; "Tales of Wells Fargo: Lady Trouble," NBC, 1961; "The Real McCoys: September Song," ABC, 1961; "The Dick Powell Show: Up Jumped the Devil," NBC, 1961; "The New Breed: Mr. Weltschmerz," ABC, 1962; "Rawhide: Grandma's Money," CBS, 1962; "Perry Mason: The Case of the Mystified Miner," CBS, 1962; "The Twilight Zone: I Sing the Body Electric," CBS, 1962; "G.E. True: The Black-Robed Ghost," CBS, 1963; "Kraft Suspense Theatre: The Machine that Played God," NBC, 1963; "Burke's Law: Who Killed the Eleventh Best-Dressed Woman in the World?," ABC, 1964; "Dr. Kildare: The Last Leaves on the Tree," NBC, 1964; "Gunsmoke: The Ladies From St. Louis," CBS, 1967; "The Name of the Game: Nightmare," NBC, 1968; "Then Came Bronson: All the World and God," NBC, 1969;

"The FBI: The Doll Courier," ABC, 1969; "The FBI: Time Bomb," ABC, 1970; "The Bold Ones: If I Can't Sing, I'll Listen," NBC, 1970; "To Rome with Love: The Boy Next Door," CBS, 1970; "The Mod Squad: A Short Course in War," ABC, 1971; "Mannix: Dark So Early, Dark So Long," CBS, 1971; "Longstreet: A World of Perfect Complicity," ABC, 1971; "The Partridge Family: All's War in Love and Fairs," ABC, 1972; "The Sixth Sense: And Scream by the Light of the Moon, the Moon," ABC, 1972; "Little House on the Prairie: If I Should Wake Before I Die," NBC, 1974.

TV MOVIES AND MINISERIES: "Shadow Over Elveron," NBC, 1968; "Travis Logan, D.A.," CBS, 1971; "The Homecoming," CBS, 1971.

HUTTON, BETTY

b. Betty June Thornburg, Battle Creek, MI, February 26, 1921. Exuberant blonde actress of the movies and a bit of TV, including a failed sitcom and a critically panned TV spectacular, "Satins and Spurs."

AS A REGULAR: "The Betty Hutton Show," CBS, 1959-60.

AND: "Satins and Spurs," NBC, 1954; "Dinah Shore Chevy Show," NBC, 1957; "The Nat King Cole Show," NBC, 1957; "The Dinah Shore Chevy Show," NBC, 1958; "The Chevy Show," NBC, 1958; "The Eddie Fisher Show," NBC, 1958; "Phil Harris Special," NBC, 1959; "Dick Clark's World of Talent," ABC, 1959; "The Jack Paar Show," NBC, 1960; "Perry Como's Kraft Music Hall," NBC, 1961; "The Greatest Show on Earth: The Glorious Days of Used to Be," ABC, 1964; "Burke's Law: Who Killed Half of Glory Lee?," ABC, 1964; "Burke's Law: Who Killed the 13th Clown?," ABC, 1965; "Gunsmoke: Bad Lady From Brookline," CBS, 1965; "Donahue," SYN, 1978.
* Hutton's appearance on "Donahue" came after she dropped out of show business, went broke and worked in a Catholic rectory as a cook and housekeeper.

HUTTON, GUNILLA

b. Sweden, May 15, 1944. Blonde sexpot.

AS A REGULAR: "Petticoat Junction," CBS, 1965-66; "Hee Haw," CBS, 1969-71, SYN, 1971- .

AND: "Rhyme and Reason," ABC, 1976; "The Love Boat: The Love Lamp Is Lit," ABC, 1979.

HUTTON, INA RAY

b. Chicago, IL, March 13, 1917; d. 1984. Leader of an all-girl band.

AS A REGULAR: "The Ina Ray Hutton Show," NBC, 1956.

AND: "The Tennesse Ernie Ford Show," NBC, 1956.

HUTTON, JIM

b. Binghamton, NY, 1933; d. 1979. Actor who

played young, earnest types, a pleasant TV presence as the brilliant, distracted detective Ellery Queen.

AS A REGULAR: "Everything's Relative," SYN, 1965; "Ellery Queen," NBC, 1975-76.

AND: "The Twilight Zone: And When the Sky Was Opened," CBS, 1959; "Father Knows Best: Betty's Career Problem," CBS, 1960; "Here's Hollywood," NBC, 1960; "Comedy Spot: You're Only Young Once," CBS, 1962; "The Psychiatrist: The Private World of Martin Dalton," NBC, 1971; "The Name of the Game: The Savage Eye," NBC, 1971; "Love, American Style: Love and Murphy's Bed," ABC, 1972; "Love, American Style: Love and the Small Wedding," ABC, 1972; "Call Holme," NBC, 1972; "Wednesday Night Out," NBC, 1972; "Captain Newman, M.D.," NBC, 1972; "Love, American Style: Love and the Novel Love," ABC, 1973; "Marcus Welby, M.D.: The Mugging," ABC, 1974; "Ironside: A Matter of Life or Death," NBC, 1974; "Joys," NBC, 1976; "One Day at a Time: The Older Man," CBS, 1977; "$weepstake$: Victor, Billy and Bobby, 'Sometimes,' " NBC, 1979.

TV MOVIES AND MINISERIES: "The Deadly Hunt," CBS, 1971; "The Reluctant Heroes," ABC, 1971; "They Call It Murder," NBC, 1971; "Call Her Mom," ABC, 1972; "Don't Be Afraid of the Dark," ABC, 1973; "The Underground Man," NBC, 1974; "Ellery Queen," NBC, 1975; "Flying High," CBS, 1978.

HUTTON, LAUREN

b. Mary Hutton, Charleston, SC, November 17, 1943. Former model and movie actress who's welcomed with open arms by TV soaps and miniseries producers.

AS A REGULAR: "Paper Dolls," ABC, 1984; "Falcon Crest," CBS, 1987.

AND: "The Tonight Show Starring Johnny Carson," NBC, 1975; "Saturday Night Live," NBC, 1981; "Faerie Tale Theatre: The Snow Queen," SHO, 1984.

TV MOVIES AND MINISERIES: "A Time for Love," NBC, 1973; "Best Sellers: The Rhinemann Exchange," NBC, 1977; "Someone Is Watching Me!," NBC, 1978; "Starflight: The Plane That Couldn't Land," ABC, 1983; "The Cradle Will Fall," CBS, 1983; "Scandal Sheet," ABC, 1985; "Sins," CBS, 1986; "The Return of Mickey Spillane's Mike Hammer," CBS, 1986; "Monte Carlo," CBS, 1986; "Perfect People," ABC, 1988.

HUTTON, TIMOTHY

b. Los Angeles, CA, August 16, 1960. Actor who possesses the same youthful intensity of his father, Jim.

TV MOVIES AND MINISERIES: "ABC Theatre: Friendly Fire," ABC, 1979; "Young Love, First

Love," CBS, 1979; "And Baby Makes Six," NBC, 1979; "Father Figure," CBS, 1980; "GE Theatre: A Long Way Home," ABC, 1981.
AS A DIRECTOR: "Amazing Stories: Grandpa's Ghost," NBC, 1986.

HYDE-WHITE, WILFRED
b. *England, May 12, 1903*. Distinguished actor fondly remembered as Emerson Marshall, wily and witty senior partner of a New York law firm in the sitcom "The Associates."
AS A REGULAR: "Peyton Place," ABC, 1967; "The Associates," ABC, 1979-80; "Buck Rogers in the 25th Century," NBC, 1981.
AND: "Douglas Fairbanks Jr. Presents: The Priceless Pocket," SYN, 1953; "Alcoa Hour: Mrs. Gilling and the Skyscraper," NBC, 1957; "Ben Casey: Monument to an Aged Hunter," ABC, 1962; "The Twilight Zone: Passage on the Lady Anne," CBS, 1963; "Ben Casey: Evidence of Things Not Seen," ABC, 1964; "Ben Casey: From Sutter's Crick and Beyond Farewell," ABC, 1965; "Ben Casey: When Givers Prove Unkind/The Man From Quasilia," ABC, 1965; "Ben Casey: Why Did the Day Go Backwards?," ABC, 1965; "Mission: Impossible: Echo of Yesterday," CBS, 1967; "The Donald O'Connor Show," SYN, 1968; "The Name of the Game: The Suntan Mob," NBC, 1969; "It Takes a Thief: To Lure a Man," ABC, 1969; "Paris 7000: Ordeal," ABC, 1970; "The Most Deadly Game: I Said the Sparrow," ABC, 1971; "The Sonny and Cher Comedy Hour," CBS, 1972; "Cool Million: Assault on Gavaloni," NBC, 1972; "Columbo: Dagger of the Mind," NBC, 1972; "Columbo: Last Salute to the Commodore," NBC, 1976; "Vega$: A Way to Live," ABC, 1979; "Laverne & Shirley: Murder on the Moose Jaw Express," ABC, 1980; "Fantasy Island: Wuthering Heights," ABC, 1982.
TV MOVIES AND MINISERIES: "The Sunshine Patriot," NBC, 1968; "Fear No Evil," NBC, 1969; "Run a Crooked Mile," ABC, 1969; "Ritual of Evil," NBC, 1970; "A Brand New Life," ABC, 1973; "The Great Houdinis," ABC, 1976; "The Rebels," SYN, 1979; "The Letter," ABC, 1982.

HYER, MARTHA
b. *Fort Worth, TX, August 10, 1924*. Fifties actress who kept busy in movies and TV.
AS A GUEST: "Jewelers Showcase: Teacher of the Year," CBS, 1952; "The Curtain Rises: Exit—Linda Davis," ABC, 1953; "Four Star Playhouse: Meet a Lonely Man," CBS, 1954; "Best of Broadway: Broadway," CBS, 1955; "Lux Video Theatre: The Lady Gambles," NBC, 1955; "Lux Video Theatre: Jezebel," NBC, 1956; "Playhouse 90: Reunion," CBS, 1958; "Climax!: The Push-Button Giant," CBS, 1958; "Rawhide: Incident West of Lano,"

CBS, 1959; "The Deputy: Hang the Law," NBC, 1960; "Burke's Law: Who Killed Wade Walker?," ABC, 1963; "The Greatest Show on Earth: The Show Must Go On—to Orange City," ABC, 1964; "Burke's Law: Who Killed April?," ABC, 1964; "Bewitched: The Cat's Meow," ABC, 1965; "The Alfred Hitchcock Hour: The Crimson Witness," NBC, 1965; "Burke's Law: Who Killed the Toy Soldier?," ABC, 1965; "Burke's Law: Who Killed the Grand Piano?," ABC, 1965; "The Young Lawyers: The Victims," ABC, 1971; "McCloud: Cowboy in Paradise," NBC, 1974.

HYLAND, DIANA
b. *Cleveland Heights, OH, 1936; d. 1977*. Attractive actress who played mom Joan Bradford on "Eight Is Enough" and, after a long TV career, won an Emmy award for "The Boy in the Plastic Bubble," which was given to her posthumously following her death from cancer.
AS A REGULAR: "Young Doctor Malone," NBC, 1958-63; "Peyton Place," ABC, 1968-69; "Eight Is Enough," ABC, 1977.
AND: "Play of the Week: The Climate of Eden," SYN, 1960; "Armstrong Circle Theatre: Positive Identification," CBS, 1960; "Play of the Week: No Exit," SYN, 1961; "Play of the Week: A Cool Wind Over the Living," SYN, 1961; "The Defenders: The Unwanted," CBS, 1962; "U.S. Steel Hour: Wanted: Someone Innocent," CBS, 1962; "Alcoa Premiere: The Voice of Charlie Pont," ABC, 1962; "Sam Benedict: The Bird of Warning," NBC, 1962; "Dr. Kildare: Love Is a Sad Song," NBC, 1963; "The Alfred Hitchcock Hour: To Catch a Butterfly," CBS, 1963; "Ben Casey: Rigadoon for Three Pianos," ABC, 1963; "Stoney Burke: To Catch the Kaiser," ABC, 1963; "The du Pont Show: The Shark," NBC, 1963; "Wagon Train: The Kitty Pryor Story," ABC, 1963; "The Alfred Hitchcock Hour: Beyond the Sea of Death," CBS, 1964; "The Twilight Zone: Spur of the Moment," CBS, 1964; "The Eleventh Hour: Full Moon Every Night," NBC, 1964; "The Fugitive: When the Bough Breaks," ABC, 1964; "Dr. Kildare: Please Let My Baby Live," NBC, 1965; "Burke's Law: Who Killed the Fat Cat?," ABC, 1965; "The Rogues: Run for the Money," NBC, 1965; "The Doctors and the Nurses: The April Thaw of Dr. Mai," CBS, 1965; "Hercules," ABC, 1965; "Run for Your Life: The Girl Next Door Is a Spy," NBC, 1965; "The Fugitive: Set Fire to a Straw Man," ABC, 1965; "The Wackiest Ship in the Army: I'm Dreaming of a Wide Isthmus," NBC, 1965; "The Man From UNCLE: The Nowhere Affair," NBC, 1966; "Bob Hope Chrysler Theatre: Guilty or Not Guilty," NBC, 1966; "A Man Called Shenandoah: An Unfamiliar Tune," ABC, 1966; "The Iron Horse: Joy Unconfined," ABC, 1966; "The Green Hornet:

Give 'em Enough Rope," ABC, 1966; "Run for Your Life: I Am the Late Diana Hays," NBC, 1966; "Twelve O'Clock High: Practice to Deceive," NBC, 1966; "The Man From UNCLE: The Candidate's Wife Affair," NBC, 1966; "The Fugitive: The Devil's Disciples," ABC, 1966; "The Invaders: Beachhead," ABC, 1967; "The FBI: The Hostage," ABC, 1967; "The Fugitive: Dossier on a Diplomat," ABC, 1967; "Tarzan: The Fanatics," NBC, 1967; "The Invaders: The Summit Meeting," ABC, 1967; "The FBI: Overload," ABC, 1967; "Alias Smith and Jones: Return to Devil's Hole," ABC, 1971; "Dan August: Days of Rage," ABC, 1971; "Medical Center: Suspected," CBS, 1971; "The FBI: Arrangement with Terror," ABC, 1972; "Marcus Welby, M.D.: Dark Fury," ABC, 1974; "Barnaby Jones: Deadly Reunion," CBS, 1976; "Kojak: A Grave Too Soon," CBS, 1976; "Barnaby Jones: Deadly Reunion," CBS, 1976; "Happy Days: Fonzie's Old Lady," ABC, 1977.

TV MOVIES AND MINISERIES: "Scalplock," NBC, 1966; "Ritual of Evil," NBC, 1970; "The Boy in the Plastic Bubble," ABC, 1976.

* Emmies: 1977.

HYLANDS, SCOTT
b. Canada, 1943.

AS A REGULAR: "Night Heat," CBS, 1985-89.
AND: "Ironside: And Then There Was One," NBC, 1972; "Kung Fu: Blood Brothers," ABC, 1973; "The Streets of San Francisco: Shattered Image," ABC, 1973; "Ironside: The Taste of Ashes," NBC, 1974; "Hollywood Television Theatre: The Lady's Not for Burning," NET, 1974; "Police Woman: For the Love of Angela," NBC, 1975; "Medical Center: Major Annie, M.D.," CBS, 1976; "Medical Center: If Wishes Were Horses," CBS, 1976; "Baretta: The Cold Breath of Death," ABC, 1976; "Police Story: Trial Board," NBC, 1977; "Black Sheep Squadron: Divine Wind," NBC, 1977; "The Powers of Matthew Star: Thirty-Six Hours," NBC, 1983.

TV MOVIES AND MINISERIES: "Earth II," ABC, 1971; "Truman Capote's The Glass House," CBS, 1972; "Terror on the Beach," CBS, 1973; "Portrait: A Man Whose Name Was John," ABC, 1973; "The First 36 Hours of Dr. Durant," ABC, 1975; "The Winds of Kitty Hawk," NBC, 1978; "Centennial," NBC, 1978-79; "Jennifer: A Woman's Story," NBC, 1979.

I

I LOVE LUCY, CBS, 1951-57.

CBS wanted Lucille Ball, already a success on the radio with "My Favorite Husband," to come to television in the early 1950s. But they didn't want her husband, Desi Arnaz. Who'd believe that Ball's character would be married to a Cuban bandleader? But Ball wanted Arnaz; he'd been touring with his band and she figured a TV show would keep him at home with steady employment, and they could start a family. So they put together a stage act and shot a pilot with their own money. CBS bought the idea, and Arnaz decided to try something new: A series filmed with three cameras, before a live audience. They did just that, with the help of veteran MGM photographer Karl Freund. That meant the show could be shot in California—unlike most TV at that time. The quality of the image was excellent, and the shows could be rerun forever. Which they have been.

"I Love Lucy" was an instant hit. Ball was a beauty who could take a fall or do a double-take as well as any woman on television; she was ably supported by William Frawley and Vivian Vance as neighbors Fred and Ethel Mertz. When Ball became pregnant in real life in 1952, it was written into the show, though the word "pregnant" couldn't be used. When Lucy Ricardo gave birth to little Ricky in January 1953, more people saw it than saw Dwight Eisenhower inaugurated president.

Ball and Arnaz, who owned the show, parlayed their fortune into TV production, buying the old RKO studios (where Ball had once been under contract) and turning it into Desilu. By the end of the decade, under the leadership of Arnaz, everything from "The Lineup" to "December Bride" to "The Untouchables" was being shot there.

Despite their success, the Ball-Arnaz marriage wasn't any better than it had been when Arnaz was touring, and in 1960 the couple divorced. She would return to television in two years with another long-running sitcom; Arnaz sold his share of Desilu to Ball and dabbled in television through the 1970s.

TRIVIA QUIZ #12: "I LOVE LUCY"

1. What was Lucy Ricardo's maiden name?
2. When the Ricardos and the Mertzes went to Hollywood, Lucy saw two stars in the Brown Derby. Name either one.
3. Why did the Ricardos and the Mertzes go to Hollywood?
4. What song was always requested of Ricky Ricardo?
5. How did Ricky find out Lucy was pregnant?
6. In 1956 the Ricardos and Mertzes moved out of New York City. To which state did they move?
7. Which superhero did Lucy dress as for little Ricky's birthday party?
8. Which cigarette sponsored the show for a time?
9. During their hiatuses from the show, Ball and Arnaz made two movies. Name either one.
10. What was the name of the vaudeville team Fred Mertz had been a part of?

(Answers at end of book.)

INESCOURT, FRIEDA
b. Scotland, 1901; d. 1976.
AS A REGULAR: "Meet Corliss Archer," CBS, 1951.
AND: "Fireside Theatre: Hope Chest," NBC, 1950; "Schaefer Century Theatre: From Such a Seed," NBC, 1952; "Fireside Theatre: The Old Order Changeth," NBC, 1954; "G.E. Theatre: The Crime of Daphne Rutledge," CBS, 1954; "The Ray Milland Show: Stagestruck," CBS, 1954; "Climax!: The Dance," CBS, 1955; "Four Star Playhouse: A Place Full of Strangers," CBS, 1955; "Crossroads: God's Healing," ABC, 1956; "The Millionaire: The Regina Wainwright Story," CBS, 1957; "December Bride: Engagement Show," CBS, 1957; "The Tab Hunter Show: Devil to Pay," NBC, 1960; "The Rebel: Mission—Varina," ABC, 1961.

INGELS, MARTY
b. New York City, NY, March 9, 1936. Raspy-voiced comic actor, often in simpleton roles; now he's an agent who matches up celebrities and TV commercials. Husband of Shirley Jones.
AS A REGULAR: "I'm Dickens, He's Fenster,"

ABC, 1962-63; "The Pruitts of Southhampton," ABC, 1967.

AND: "Hennesey: The Captain's Dilemma," CBS, 1960; "Peter Loves Mary: Peter Joins a Committee," NBC, 1960; "Dan Raven: The Satchel Man," NBC, 1960; "The Ann Sothern Show: Always April," CBS, 1961; "Robert Taylor's Detectives: Tobey's Place," NBC, 1961; "The Dick Van Dyke Show: Oh, How We Met the Night That We Danced," CBS, 1961; "The New Steve Allen Show," ABC, 1961; "The Dick Van Dyke Show: Sol and the Sponsor," CBS, 1962; "The Joey Bishop Show: Once a Bachelor," NBC, 1962; "Hollywood Palace," ABC, 1964; "Burke's Law: Who Killed Madison Cooper?," ABC, 1964; "Get the Message," ABC, 1964; "To Tell the Truth," CBS, 1964; "The Mike Douglas Show," SYN, 1965; "The Addams Family: Cat Addams," ABC, 1966; "Bewitched: Dangerous Diaper Dan," ABC, 1966; "The Mike Douglas Show," SYN, 1967; "Kiss Me, Kate," ABC, 1968; "The Merv Griffin Show," SYN, 1968; "Banacek: Let's Hear It for a Living Legend," NBC, 1972; "The Rookies: Down Home Boy," ABC, 1973; "Police Story: Vice: 24 Hours," NBC, 1975; "The Love Boat: Oh, My Aching Brother," ABC, 1978.

INGRAM, REX

b. Cairo, IL, October 20, 1895; d. 1969. Actor with a powerful voice and manner who played De Lawd in the screen version of "Green Pastures."

AS A GUEST: "Kraft Television Theatre: The Emporer Jones," NBC, 1955; "Your Play Time: The Intolerable Portrait," NBC, 1955; "Crossroads: The Man Who Walked on Water," ABC, 1956; "The Law and Mr. Jones: The Storyville Gang," ABC, 1960; "The Rifleman: Closer Than a Brother," ABC, 1961; "The Dick Powell Show: The Sea Witch," NBC, 1962; "Sam Benedict: A Split Week in San Quentin," NBC, 1962; "The Lloyd Bridges Show: Gentleman in Blue," CBS, 1962; "Mr. Novak: My Name Is Not Legion," NBC, 1963; "Sam Benedict: A Split Week in San Quentin," NBC, 1963; "The Breaking Point: Never Trouble Trouble Until Trouble Troubles You," ABC, 1964; "I Spy: Weight of the World," NBC, 1965; "Daktari: Judy the Poacher," CBS, 1967; "Daktari: The Big Switch," CBS, 1968; "Gunsmoke: The Good Samaritans," CBS, 1969; "The Bill Cosby Show: A Christmas Ballad," NBC, 1969.

IRELAND, JILL

b. London, England, April 24, 1936; d. 1990. Striking actress who matured into character roles; after contracting cancer, she became a powerful and respected spokeswoman for those suffering from the disease.

AS A REGULAR: "Shane," ABC, 1966.

AND: "Kraft Mystery Theatre: The Desperate Man," NBC, 1961; "Ben Casey: The Lonely One," ABC, 1964; "The Man From UNCLE: The Quadripartite Affair," NBC, 1964; "Voyage to the Bottom of the Sea: The Price of Doom," ABC, 1964; "The Man From UNCLE: The Giuoco Piano Affair," NBC, 1964; "Twelve O'Clock High: The Hot Shot," ABC, 1965; "My Favorite Martian: Girl in the Flying Machine," CBS, 1965; "The Man From UNCLE: The Tigers Are Coming Affair," NBC, 1965; "Twelve O'Clock High: The Survivor," ABC, 1966; "Star Trek: This Side of Paradise," NBC, 1967; "The Man From UNCLE: The Five Daughters Affair," NBC, 1967; "Mannix: To the Swiftest Death," CBS, 1968; "Night Gallery: The Ghost of Sorworth Place," NBC, 1972.

IRELAND, JOHN

b. Vancouver, B.C., Canada, January 30, 1914. Handsome actor with rugged good looks; a familiar face on TV westerns from "Zane Grey Theatre" to "Little House on the Prairie."

AS A REGULAR: "The Cheaters," SYN, 1961; "Rawhide," CBS, 1965-66; "Cassie and Company," NBC, 1982.

AND: "Philco TV Playhouse: Confession," NBC, 1951; "Schlitz Playhouse of Stars: The Man I Marry," CBS, 1952; "Schlitz Playhouse of Stars: Prisoner in the Town," CBS, 1954; "Philco TV Playhouse: Time Bomb," NBC, 1954; "Elgin TV Hour: The Bridge," ABC, 1955; "Schlitz Playhouse of Stars: Murder in Paradise," CBS, 1955; "Damon Runyon Theatre: There's No Forever," CBS, 1955; "Studio 57: Lonely Man," SYN, 1955; "Schlitz Playhouse of Stars: Dealer's Choice," CBS, 1956; "G.E. Theatre: Prologue to Glory," CBS, 1956; "Schlitz Playhouse of Stars: Ordeal," CBS, 1956; "Fireside Theatre: This Land Is Mine," NBC, 1956; "Dick Powell's Zane Grey Theatre: Return to Nowhere," CBS, 1956; "Lux Video Theatre: Black Angel," NBC, 1957; "Climax!: Avalanche at Devil's Pass," CBS, 1957; "Playhouse 90: Without Incident," CBS, 1957; "Playhouse 90: A Sound of Different Drummers," CBS, 1957; "Suspicion: End in Violence," NBC, 1958; "Riverboat: The Fight Back," NBC, 1959; "Startime: Closed Set," NBC, 1960; "U.S. Marshal: Rampy's Wife," SYN, 1960; "Rawhide: Incident in the Garden of Eden," CBS, 1960; "Thriller: Papa Benjamin," NBC, 1961; "The Asphalt Jungle: The Last Way Out," ABC, 1961; "Here's Hollywood," NBC, 1962; "The Dick Powell Show: Obituary for Mr. X," NBC, 1962; "The Alfred Hitchcock Hour: The Matched Pearl," NBC, 1962; "Rawhide: Incident of the Portrait," CBS, 1962; "Burke's Law: Who Killed Alex Debbs?," ABC, 1963; "Kraft Suspense Theatre: A Hero for Our Times," NBC, 1963; "Mr. Broadway: Pay Now, Die Later," CBS, 1964; "Branded: Leap Upon Mountains,"

NBC, 1965; "Burke's Law: Who Killed the Rabbit's Husband?," ABC, 1965; "Rawhide: The Spanish Camp," CBS, 1965; "A Man Called Shenandoah: Marlee," ABC, 1966; "Branded: Cowards Die Many Times," NBC, 1966; "The Man Who Never Was: Game of Death," ABC, 1966; "Run for Your Life: The Day Time Stopped," NBC, 1966; "Gunsmoke: Stage Stop," CBS, 1966; "The Iron Horse: Appointment with an Epitaph," ABC, 1967; "Bonanza: Judgement at Red Creek," NBC, 1967; "Gunsmoke: Vengeance," CBS, 1967; "The Name of the Game: The Power," NBC, 1969; "The Men From Shiloh: Jenny," NBC, 1970; "Assignment: Vienna: Hot Potato," ABC, 1972; "Mission: Impossible: Kidnap," CBS, 1972; "Ghost Story: Creatures of the Canyon," NBC, 1972; "Khan!: Cloud of Guilt," CBS, 1975; "Police Story: The Man in the Shadows," NBC, 1975; "Little House on the Prairie: Little Girl Lost," NBC, 1976; "Little House on the Prairie: The Winoka Warriors," NBC, 1978; "$weepstake$: Victor, Billy and Bobby, 'Sometimes,'" NBC, 1979; "Quincy: Murder by S.O.P.," NBC, 1979; "Quincy: Seldom Silent, Never Heard," NBC, 1981; "Hardcastle and McCormick: The Homecoming," ABC, 1984; "Buck James: Quality of Life," ABC, 1988.
TV MOVIES AND MINISERIES: "The Phantom of Hollywood," CBS, 1974; "The Girl on the Late, Late Show," NBC, 1974; "The Millionaire," CBS, 1978; "Bonanza: The Next Generation," SYN, 1988.

IRVING, AMY

b. Palo Alto, CA, September 10, 1953. Actress in film ("Yentl") and TV; ex-wife of Steven Spielberg.
AS A GUEST: "The Rookies: Reading, Writing and Angel Dust," ABC, 1975; "Police Woman: The Hit," NBC, 1975; "Happy Days: Tell It to the Marines," ABC, 1976; "Amazing Stories: Ghost Train," NBC, 1985; "Nightmare Classics: The Turn of the Screw," SHO, 1989.
TV MOVIES AND MINISERIES: "James Dean," NBC, 1976; "James A. Michener's Dynasty," NBC, 1976; "Panache," ABC, 1976; "Best Sellers: Once an Eagle," NBC, 1977; "The Far Pavilions," HBO, 1984; "Anastasia: The Mystery of Anna," NBC, 1986.

IRVING, GEORGE S.

b. Springfield, MA, November 1, 1922.
AS A REGULAR: "The David Frost Revue," SYN, 1971-73; "The Dumplings," NBC, 1976.
AND: "Car 54, Where are You?: Toody and Muldoon Sing Along with Mitch," NBC, 1962; "The Patty Duke Show: Let 'Em Eat Cake," ABC, 1964; "All in the Family: Amelia's Divorce," CBS, 1975.

IRWIN, WYNN

b. New York City, NY, December 11, 1932.
AS A REGULAR: "Lotsa Luck," NBC, 1973-74; "Sugar Time," ABC, 1977-78.
AND: "The Mary Tyler Moore Show: The Happy Homemaker Takes Lou Home," CBS, 1975; "Barney Miller: Ms. Cop," ABC, 1975; "Home Cookin'," ABC, 1975; "Quincy: The Hot Dog Murder," NBC, 1977; "All in the Family: Mike the Pacifist," CBS, 1977; "It's Garry Shandling's Show: Our Town," FOX, 1989.
TV MOVIES AND MINISERIES: "Winner Take All," NBC, 1975; "From Here to Eternity," NBC, 1979; "Hobson's Choice," CBS, 1983.

ISACKSEN, PETER

b. Dover, NH, 1953. Tall, blonde actor often mistaken for Ed Begley Jr.; he played Seaman Pruitt on "CPO Sharkey."
AS A REGULAR: "CPO Sharkey," NBC, 1976-78; "The 1/2 Hour Comedy Hour," ABC, 1983; "Jessie," ABC, 1984.
AND: "Tattletales," CBS, 1977; "Cross Wits," SYN, 1979; "B.J. and the Bear: Wheels of Fortune," NBC, 1979; "Three's Company: Maid to Order," ABC, 1982; "Magnum P.I.: Squeeze Play," CBS, 1983.

ITO, ROBERT

b. Canada, July 2, 1931. Former ballet dancer who played Sam, sidekick of Dr. no-first-name Quincy (Jack Klugman).
AS A REGULAR: "Quincy," NBC, 1976-83.
AND: "Mr. Roberts: Undercover Cook," NBC, 1966; "Nanny and the Professor: Nanny Will Do," ABC, 1970; "Mannix: The Mouse That Died," CBS, 1970; "M*A*S*H: To Market, to Market," CBS, 1972; "Love, American Style: Love and the Fortunate Cookie," ABC, 1973; "Kung Fu: The Assassin," ABC, 1973; "Kojak: The Chinatown Murders," CBS, 1974; "M*A*S*H: The Korean Surgeon," CBS, 1976; "Barnaby Jones: The Fatal Dive," CBS, 1976; "B.J. and the Bear: The Girls of Hollywood High," NBC, 1980; "MacGyver: Children of Light," ABC, 1989.
TV MOVIES AND MINISERIES: "Kung Fu," ABC, 1972; "Men of the Dragon," ABC, 1974; "SST-Death Flight," ABC, 1977.

IVES, BURL

b. Burle Icle Ivanhoe, Hunt, IL, June 14, 1909. Folksinger and character actor best known as millionaire O.K. Crackerby and lawyer Walter Nichols on "The Bold Ones."
AS A REGULAR: "High-Low," NBC, 1957; "O.K. Crackerby," ABC, 1965-66; "The Bold Ones," NBC, 1969-72.
AND: "I've Got a Secret," CBS, 1956; "G.E. Theatre: The Second Stranger," CBS, 1956; "U.S. Steel Hour: To Die Alone," CBS, 1957; "Playhouse

90: The Miracle Worker," CBS, 1957; "The Perry Como Show," NBC, 1958; "Dinah Shore Chevy Show," NBC, 1958; "Holiday USA," CBS, 1959; "Red Skelton Chevy Special," CBS, 1959; "Bell Telephone Hour: The Golden West," NBC, 1959; "G.E. Theatre: Absalom, My Son," CBS, 1959; "Dick Powell's Zane Grey Theatre: The Ox," CBS, 1960; "Bell Telephone Hour: A Galaxy of Music," NBC, 1961; "Accent: Theatre in Dallas," CBS, 1961; "Bell Telephone Hour," NBC, 1964; "The Andy Williams Show," NBC, 1967; "The Name of the Game: The Taker," NBC, 1968; "Hallmark Hall of Fame: Pinocchio," NBC, 1968; "Kraft Music Hall," NBC, 1968; "The Red Skelton Hour," CBS, 1969; "The Glen Campbell Goodtime Hour," CBS, 1971; "Alias Smith and Jones: The McCreedy Bust," ABC, 1971; "Alias Smith and Jones: Going, Going, Gone," ABC, 1972; "Alias Smith and Jones: Which Way to the O.K. Corral?," ABC, 1972; "Alias Smith and Jones: The McCreedy Feud," ABC, 1972; "Night Gallery: The Other Way Out," NBC, 1972; "The First Easter Rabbit," NBC, 1976.

TV MOVIES AND MINISERIES: "The Sound of Anger," NBC, 1968; "The Whole World Is Watching," NBC, 1969; "The Man Who Wanted to Live Forever," ABC, 1970; "Best Sellers: Captains and the Kings," NBC, 1976; "Roots," ABC, 1977; "The Bermuda Depths," ABC, 1978; "The New Adventures of Heidi," NBC, 1978; "Poor Little Rich Girl: The Barbara Hutton Story," NBC, 1987.

IVEY, DANA

b. Atlanta, GA. Actress who played Eleanor Standard, snooty sister-in-law of L.K. McGuire (Loni Anderson) on "Easy Street."

AS A REGULAR: "Easy Street," NBC, 1986-87; "One Life to Live," ABC, 1989-90.

AND: "Death Valley Days: Fort Bowie—Urgent," SYN, 1962; "B.L. Stryker: Die Laughing," ABC, 1989.

IVO, TOMMY

b. Denver, CO, April 18, 1936. Former child actor who became a famous drag racer.

AS A REGULAR: "Margie," ABC, 1961-62.

AND: "The Adventures of Rin Tin Tin: The Gentle Kingdom," ABC, 1957; "Leave It to Beaver: Blind Date Committee," ABC, 1959; "The Many Loves of Dobie Gillis: The Unregistered Nurse," CBS, 1960; "Leave It to Beaver: Wally's Play," ABC, 1960; "The Donna Reed Show: The Mystery Woman," ABC, 1960; "The Donna Reed Show: The Lean and Hungry Look," ABC, 1960; "Lock Up: Breakdown of Trust," SYN, 1960; "The Tall Man: A Kind of Courage," NBC, 1961; "The Donna Reed Show: Military School," ABC, 1961; "Lassie: Lassie's Protege," CBS, 1962; "My Three Sons: The Ballad of Lissa Stratmeyer," ABC, 1964.

* Ivo doubled for Bonnie Bedelia in the film "Heart Like a Wheel," the story of drag racer Shirley Muldowney.

J

JACKEE

b. Winston-Salem, NC. Emmy winning comic actress who played the randy Sandra on "227."
AS A REGULAR: "Another World," NBC, 1983-85; "227," NBC, 1985-90.
AND: "Amen: A Slight Case of Murder," NBC, 1988; "The Arsenio Hall Show," SYN, 1989; "Amen: Don't Rain on My Shower," NBC, 1989.
TV MOVIES AND MINISERIES: "Crash Course," NBC, 1988; "The Women of Brewster Place," ABC, 1989; "Double Your Pleasure," NBC, 1989.
* Emmies: 1987.

JACKSON, ANNE

b. Millvale, PA, September 3, 1926. Stage actress and wife of Eli Wallach; she has extensive TV drama experience.
AS A REGULAR: "Everything's Relative," CBS, 1987.
AND: "Armstrong Circle Theatre: Johnny Pickup," NBC, 1951; "Robert Montgomery Presents: Happy Birthday, George," NBC, 1952; "Lux Video Theatre: Promotion," CBS, 1952; "Kraft Television Theatre: Man on Half-Moon Street," NBC, 1952; "The Vanished Hours," CBS, 1952; "Suspense: Call From a Killer," CBS, 1952; "The Doctor: Marti," NBC, 1952; "The Doctor: Night Riders in Apartment A," NBC, 1952; "The Doctor: The Decision," NBC, 1953; "The Doctor: No Rap Charlie," NBC, 1953; "Philco TV Playhouse: The Big Deal," NBC, 1953; "Philco TV Playhouse: Statute of Limitations," NBC, 1954; "Goodyear TV Playhouse: The Merry-Go-Round," NBC, 1955; "G.E. Theatre: O'Hoolihan and the Leprechaun," CBS, 1955; "Studio One: The Staring Match," CBS, 1957; "Studio One: My Mother and How She Undid Me," CBS, 1957; "Play of the Week: Lullaby," SYN, 1960; "G.E. Theatre: Acres and Pains," CBS, 1962; "The Untouchables: Cooker in the Sky," ABC, 1962; "Girl Talk," SYN, 1963; "ABC Nightlife," ABC, 1964; "The Defenders: Moment of Truth," CBS, 1964; "The Merv Griffin Show," SYN, 1967; "CBS Playhouse: Dear Friends," CBS, 1967; "Hollywood Television Theatre: The Typists," NET, 1971; "Gunsmoke: Blind Man's Bluff," CBS, 1972; "Marcus Welby, M.D.: A Taste of Salt," ABC, 1972; "Sticks and Bones," CBS, 1973; "Orson Welles' Great Mysteries: Come Into My Parlor," SYN, 1973; "G.E. Theatre: Twenty Shades of Pink," CBS, 1976; "84 Charing Cross Road," PBS, 1976; "Maude: Maude's New Friends," CBS, 1976; "Rhoda: One Is a Number," CBS, 1977; "Highway to Heaven: A Father's Faith," NBC, 1986.

TV MOVIES AND MINISERIES: "A Private Battle," CBS, 1980; "Blinded by the Light," CBS, 1980; "Leave 'Em Laughing," CBS, 1981; "A Woman Called Golda," SYN, 1982; "Sam's Son," NBC, 1984; "Out on a Limb," ABC, 1987; "Baby M," ABC, 1988.

JACKSON, EDDIE

b. Brooklyn, NY, 1896; d. 1980. Former vaudeville and nightclub partner of Jimmy Durante.
AS A REGULAR: "Texaco Star Theatre-The Jimmy Durante Show," NBC, 1954-56.
AND: "Club Oasis," NBC, 1957.

JACKSON, GAIL PATRICK

b. Birmingham, AL, June 20, 1911; d. 1980. Hollywood actress who retired from performing in 1947 and then became a producer.
AS PRODUCER: "Perry Mason," CBS, 1957-66.
* Jackson conceived the idea of a "Perry Mason" TV series; her husband, Cornwall Jackson, was the agent of Erle Stanley Gardner, who created Mason.

JACKSON, GLENDA

b. Hoylake, England, May 9, 1936. Much-honored actress of film, stage and TV who won an Emmy for her portrayal of Queen Elizabeth I.
TV MOVIES AND MINISERIES: "Masterpiece Theatre: Elizabeth R," NET, 1972; "The Patricia Neal Story," CBS, 1981.
* Emmies: 1972.

JACKSON, GORDON

b. December 19, 1923; d. 1990. Beloved British actor who had a creative hand in "Upstairs, Downstairs."
AS A REGULAR: "Masterpiece Theatre: Upstairs, Downstairs," PBS, 1973-77.
TV MOVIES AND MINISERIES: "Madame Sin," ABC, 1972; "James Clavell's Noble House," NBC, 1988.
AS CO-CREATOR: "Masterpiece Theatre: Upstairs, Downstairs," PBS, 1973-77.
* Emmies: 1976.

JACKSON, JANET

b. Gary, IN, May 16, 1966. Pop goddess.
AS A REGULAR: "The Jacksons," CBS, 1976-77; "Good Times," CBS, 1977-79; "A New Kind of Family," ABC, 1979-80; "Diff'rent Strokes," NBC, 1980-82; "Fame," SYN, 1984-85.

442

AND: "The Love Boat: Too Many Issacs," ABC, 1985.

JACKSON, KATE

b. *Birmingham, AL, October 29, 1948*. Attractive actress best known as "smart" Charlie's angel Sabrina Duncan and housewife-spy Amanda King.

AS A REGULAR: "Dark Shadows," ABC, 1970-71; "The Rookies," ABC, 1972-76; "Charlie's Angels," ABC, 1976-79; "Scarecrow and Mrs. King," CBS, 1983-87; "Baby Boom," NBC, 1988-89.

AND: "Hollywood Squares," NBC, 1974; "Celebrity Sweepstakes," NBC, 1974; "The $25,000 Pyramid," SYN, 1976; "The San Pedro Beach Bums: The Angels and the Bums," ABC, 1977; "Saturday Night Live," NBC, 1979.

TV MOVIES AND MINISERIES: "Movin' On," NBC, 1972; "The New Healers," ABC, 1972; "Satan's School for Girls," ABC, 1973; "The Killer Bees," ABC, 1974; "Death Cruise," ABC, 1974; "Death Scream," ABC, 1975; "Charlie's Angels," ABC, 1976; "Death at Love House," ABC, 1976; "Topper," ABC, 1979; "Thin Ice," CBS, 1981; "Inmates: A Love Story," ABC, 1981; "Listen to Your Heart," CBS, 1983.

JACKSON, KEITH

b. *Carrolton, GA, October 18, 1926*. Sportscaster.

AS A REGULAR: "Monday Night Football," ABC, 1970; "Monday Night Baseball," ABC, 1978-82; 1986- .

AND: "The Streets of San Francisco: The Hard Breed," ABC, 1973; "Coach: If Keith Jackson Calls, I'll Be at My Therapist's," ABC, 1989.

JACKSON, MARY

b. *Milford, MI*. Actress who played Emily Baldwin on "The Waltons."

AS A REGULAR: "The Waltons," CBS, 1972-81; "Hardcastle and McCormick," ABC, 1983; "Parenthood," NBC, 1990- .

AND: "My Three Sons: Bub Leaves Home," ABC, 1961; "Route 66: Don't Count Stars," CBS, 1961; "The Many Loves of Dobie Gillis: The Truth Session," CBS, 1962; "The Many Loves of Dobie Gillis: I Remember Muu Muu," CBS, 1962; "The Many Loves of Dobie Gillis: When Other Friendships Have Been Forgot," CBS, 1962; "The Many Loves of Dobie Gillis: The Call of the Like Wild," CBS, 1963; "The Andy Griffith Show: Opie's Fortune," CBS, 1964; "The Outer Limits: I, Robot," ABC, 1964; "The FBI: An Elephant Is Like a Rope," ABC, 1965; "The FBI: Vendetta," ABC, 1966; "The FBI: A Sleeper Wakes," ABC, 1967; "The FBI: Conspiracy of Silence," ABC, 1969; "The FBI: Escape to Terror," ABC, 1970;

"The Mary Tyler Moore Show: Howard's Girl," CBS, 1971; "The FBI: Dark Christmas," ABC, 1972; "The Rookies: Death Watch," ABC, 1974; "The Rookies: Walk a Tightrope," ABC, 1974; "The Streets of San Francsisco: One Chance to Live," ABC, 1974; "Columbo: Try and Catch Me," NBC, 1977; "The Runaways: Street of Terror," NBC, 1979; "Open All Night: A Visit From the Folks," ABC, 1982; "Family Ties: Have Gun, Will Unravel," NBC, 1982; "Magnum, P.I.: I Do?," CBS, 1983; "Scarecrow and Mrs. King: The Pharaoh's Engineers," CBS, 1986; "Highway to Heaven: Love and Marriage," NBC, 1986; "Heartbeat: Gestalt and Battery," ABC, 1989.

TV MOVIES AND MINISERIES: "The Failing of Raymond," ABC, 1971; "Letters From Frank," CBS, 1979; "A Small Killing," CBS, 1981; "Between Two Brothers," CBS, 1982; "A Day for Thanks on Walton's Mountain," NBC, 1982.

JACKSON, MICHAEL

b. *Gary, IN, August 29, 1958*. Stunningly successful pop singer and reclusive fellow.

AS A REGULAR: "The Jacksons," CBS, 1976-77.

AND: "The Sonny and Cher Comedy Hour," CBS, 1972; "The Carol Burnett Show," CBS, 1974; "The Tonight Show Starring Johnny Carson," NBC, 1974; "Free to Be You and Me," ABC, 1974; "Sandy in Disneyland," CBS, 1974; "Motown 25th Anniversary Special," NBC, 1983; "Captain EO-Backstage," ABC, 1988.

JACKSON, SAMMY

b. *Henderson, NC, 1937*. Actor who played the Army equivalent of "Gomer Pyle, USMC" over on ABC, without attaining nearly the success of Jim Nabors.

AS A REGULAR: "No Time for Sergeants," ABC, 1964-65.

AND: "Sugarfoot: Short Range," ABC, 1958; "The Adventures of Rin Tin Tin: Apache Stampede," ABC, 1959; "Maverick: Trooper Maverick," ABC, 1959; "Maverick: Greenbacks Unlimited," ABC, 1960; "Maverick: A Bullet for the Teacher," ABC, 1960; "The Virginian: Jed," NBC, 1968; "Police Story: Robbery: 48 Hours," NBC, 1974.

TV MOVIES AND MINISERIES: "Haunts of the Very Rich," ABC, 1972; "The Rebels," SYN, 1979.

JACKSON, SHERRY

b. *Wendell, ID, 1942*. Actress who played Terry Williams, the oldest daughter of Danny Thomas on his sitcom.

AS A REGULAR: "The Danny Thomas Show (Make Room for Daddy)," ABC, 1953-57; CBS, 1957-58; "Make Room for Granddaddy," ABC, 1970-71.

AND: "The Roy Rogers Show: The Unwilling

Outlaw," NBC, 1955; "The Charlie Farrell Show: Secret Love," CBS, 1956; "Maverick: The Naked Gallows," ABC, 1957; "The Perry Como Show," NBC, 1958; "The Lucille Ball-Desi Arnaz Show: Lucy Makes Room for Daddy," CBS, 1958; "77 Sunset Strip: Texas Doll," ABC, 1959; "77 Sunset Strip: The Kookie Caper," ABC, 1959; "Walt Disney Presents: The Swamp Fox-Tory Revenge," ABC, 1960; "The Millionaire: Millionaire Susan Johnson," CBS, 1960; "The Many Loves of Dobie Gillis: The Prettiest Collateral in Town," CBS, 1960; "77 Sunset Strip: The Office Caper," ABC, 1960; "SurfSide 6: High Tide," ABC, 1960; "Riverboat: The Water at Gorgeous Springs," NBC, 1960; "77 Sunset Strip: Trouble in the Middle East," ABC, 1960; "Maverick: Red Dog," ABC, 1961; "Bringing Up Buddy: Buddy and Janie," CBS, 1961; "The Tall Man: Apache Daughter," NBC, 1961; "The New Breed: Care Is No Cure," ABC, 1962; "The Twilight Zone: The Last Rites of Jeff Myrtlebank," CBS, 1962; "Hawaiian Eye: A Scent of Whales," ABC, 1962; "Gunsmoke: Root Down," CBS, 1962; "Vacation Playhouse: Come A-Runnin'," CBS, 1963; "Mr. Novak: The Risk," NBC, 1963; "Perry Mason: The Case of the Festive Falcon," CBS, 1963; "The Lieutenant: Gone the Sun," NBC, 1964; "Wagon Train: The Geneva Balfour Story," ABC, 1964; "Rawhide: Moment in the Sun," CBS, 1965; "Gomer Pyle, USMC: Sergeant Carter Gets a Dear John Letter," CBS, 1965; "The Virginian: Show Me a Hero," NBC, 1965; "My Three Sons: The Wheels," CBS, 1966; "Lost in Space: The Space Croppers," CBS, 1966; "Batman: Death in Slow Motion/The Riddler's False Notion," ABC, 1966; "Death Valley Days: Lady of the Plains," SYN, 1966; "Star Trek: What Are Little Girls Made Of?," NBC, 1966; "The Wild Wild West: The Night of the Vicious Valentine," CBS, 1967; "The Wild Wild West: The Night of the Gruesome Games," CBS, 1968; "The Tonight Show Starring Johnny Carson," NBC, 1968; "The Interns: The Quality of Mercy," CBS, 1970; "Love, American Style: Love and the Waitress," ABC, 1971; "The Rockford Files: The Real Easy Red Dog," NBC, 1975; "The Streets of San Francisco: One Last Trick," ABC, 1977; "Barnaby Jones: Final Judgement," CBS, 1978; "Alice: Good Buddy Flo," CBS, 1980.
TV MOVIES AND MINISERIES: "Wild Women," ABC, 1970; "Cotter," ABC, 1971; "The Girl on the Late, Late Show," NBC, 1974; "Returning Home," ABC, 1975.

JACKSON, STONEY
b. *Richmond, VA, 1960.* Young actor who looks a lot like pop singer Prince—intentionally, apparently.
AS A REGULAR: "The White Shadow," CBS, 1980-81; "The Insiders," ABC, 1985-86; "227," NBC, 1989-90.

AND: "Eight Is Enough: Official Positions," ABC, 1980; "M*A*S*H: Blood and Guts," CBS, 1982; "Hardcastle and McCormick: Prince of Fat City," ABC, 1983; "Highway to Heaven: The Return of the Masked Rider," NBC, 1984.
TV MOVIES AND MINISERIES: "Police Story: Cop Killers," ABC, 1988.

JACKSON, VICTORIA
b. *Miami, FL.* Comic actress.
AS A REGULAR: "The 1/2 Hour Comedy Hour," ABC, 1983; "Half Nelson," NBC, 1985; "Saturday Night Live," NBC, 1986- .
AND: "The Smothers Brothers Comedy Hour: Ghosts, Governments and Other Scary Things," CBS, 1989.

JACOBI, DEREK
b. *London, England, October 22, 1938.*
AS A REGULAR: "The Strauss Family," ABC, 1973.
TV MOVIES AND MINISERIES: "Masterpiece Theatre: I, Claudius," PBS, 1981; "The Hunchback of Notre Dame," CBS, 1982; "Hallmark Hall of Fame: The Secret Garden," CBS, 1987.

JACOBI, LOU
b. *Canada, December 28, 1923.* Rotund, mustachioed comic actor of stage and TV.
AS A REGULAR: "Somerset," NBC, 1970-76; "The Dean Martin Show," NBC, 1971-73; "Ivan the Terrible," CBS, 1976; "Melba," CBS, 1986.
AND: "Douglas Fairbanks Jr. Presents: My Favorite Aunt," SYN, 1953; "Playhouse 90: Child of Our Time," CBS, 1959; "Play of the Week: Volpone," SYN, 1960; "The Defenders: Grandma TNT," CBS, 1962; "Sam Benedict: Season of Vengeance," NBC, 1963; "The Alfred Hitchcock Hour: Ten Minutes From Now," CBS, 1964; "The Dick Van Dyke Show: Young Man with a Shoehorn," CBS, 1965; "Trials of O'Brien: The Trouble with Archie," CBS, 1965; "The Man From UNCLE: The Nowhere Affair," NBC, 1967; "That Girl: Mission: Improbable," ABC, 1969; "Love, American Style: Love and the Unlikely Couple," ABC, 1969; "Allan," NBC, 1971; "Love, American Style: Love and the Boss," ABC, 1971; "The Courtship of Eddie's Father: Tell It Like I'm Telling You It Is," ABC, 1971; "Love, American Style: Love and the Anniversary Crisis," ABC, 1972; "Love, American Style: Love and the Old Swingers," ABC, 1973; "Love, American Style: Love and the Suspicious Husband," ABC, 1974; "Barney Miller: Stakeout," ABC, 1975; "Sanford & Son: Steinberg and Son," NBC, 1975; "Love, Sidney: Sidney's Hero," NBC, 1982; "Tales From the Darkside: Painkiller," SYN, 1984; "Cagney & Lacey: American Dream," CBS, 1985.
TV MOVIES AND MINISERIES: "The Judge and Jake Wyler," NBC, 1972; "Coffee, Tea, or Me?," CBS, 1973; "Better Late Than Never," NBC, 1979.

JACOBS, LAWRENCE-HILTON

b. *New York City, NY, September 4, 1953.*

AS A REGULAR: "Welcome Back, Kotter," ABC, 1975-79; "Rituals," SYN, 1985; "Alien Nation," FOX, 1989-90.

AND: "The Rich Little Show," NBC, 1976; "Paris: Dear John," CBS, 1979; "Barnaby Jones: The Price of Anger," CBS, 1979.

TV MOVIES AND MINISERIES: "Roots," ABC, 1977.

JACOBY, BILLY

b. *Flushing, NY, April 10, 1969.* Brother of Scott Jacoby.

AS A REGULAR: "The Bad News Bears," CBS, 1979-80; "Maggie," ABC, 1981-82; "It's Not Easy," ABC, 1983; "Silver Spoons," NBC, 1985-86.

AND: "Lou Grant: Cover-Up," CBS, 1980; "Hart to Hart: Heart-Shaped Murder," ABC, 1981; "The A-Team: The Out-of-Towners," NBC, 1983; "Highway to Heaven: Dust Child," NBC, 1984; "The Golden Girls: On Golden Girls," NBC, 1985; "21 Jump Street: America, What a Town," FOX, 1987; "The Young Riders: Ten-Cent Hero," ABC, 1989.

TV MOVIES AND MINISERIES: "Angel on my Shoulder," ABC, 1980.

JACOBY, SCOTT

b. *Chicago, IL, November 19, 1956.* Young actor who won an Emmy as the sensitive son of Hal Holbrook in "That Certain Summer," TV's first look at homosexuality.

AS A REGULAR: "One Life to Live," ABC, 1973-74.

AND: "Medical Center: No Way Out," CBS, 1972; "Marcus Welby, M.D.: The Other Martin Loring," ABC, 1972; "A Visiting Angel," CBS, 1973; "Toma: Crime Without Victim," ABC, 1973; "Owen Marshall, Counselor at Law: A Killer with a Badge," ABC, 1974; "Grandpa, Mom, Dad and Richie," NBC, 1974; "Marcus Welby, M.D.: Jake's Okay," ABC, 1975; "The Rookies: Reading, Writing and Angel Dust," ABC, 1975; "Marcus Welby, M.D.: To Live Another Day," ABC, 1975; "Moose," NBC, 1975; "The Golden Girls: Mixed Blessing," NBC, 1988; "The Golden Girls: All That Jazz," NBC, 1989.

TV MOVIES AND MINISERIES: "No Place to Run," ABC, 1972; "That Certain Summer," ABC, 1972; "The Man Who Could Talk to Kids," CBS, 1973; "Bad Ronald," ABC, 1974; "Smash-Up on Interstate 5," ABC, 1976; "Harold Robbins' 79 Park Avenue," NBC, 1977; "No Other Love," CBS, 1979.

* Emmies: 1973.

JACQUET, JEFFREY

b. *Bay City, TX, October 15, 1966.*

AS A REGULAR: "Mork & Mindy," ABC, 1978-79; "Whiz Kids," CBS, 1983-84.

AND: "Sanford: To Keep a Thief," NBC, 1981.

JAECKEL, RICHARD

b. *Long Beach, NY, October 10, 1926.* Actor usually cast as crusty-but-caring bosses and cops.

AS A REGULAR: "Frontier Circus," CBS, 1961-62; "Banyon," NBC, 1972-73; "Firehouse," ABC, 1974; "Salvage I," ABC, 1979; "At Ease," ABC, 1983; "Spenser: For Hire," ABC, 1985-87; "Supercarrier," ABC, 1988.

AND: "Bigelow Theatre: T.K.O.," SYN, 1951; "Four Star Playhouse: The Squeeze," CBS, 1953; "U.S. Steel Hour: The Last Notch," ABC, 1954; "Public Defender: The Prize Fighter Story," CBS, 1954; "Goodyear TV Playhouse: The Big Man," NBC, 1954; "Ford Theatre: Daughter of Mine," NBC, 1954; "Kraft Television Theatre: Papa Was a Sport," NBC, 1954; "Elgin TV Hour: Flood," ABC, 1954; "The Millionaire: The Story of Nancy Marlborough," CBS, 1955; "The Bob Cummings Show: Advice to the Lovelorn," NBC, 1955; "Producers Showcase: The Petrified Forest," NBC, 1955; "Fireside Theatre: Big Joe's Coming Home," NBC, 1955; "Front Row Center: Dinner Date," CBS, 1956; "Matinee Theatre: Night Must Fall," NBC, 1956; "Climax!: To Scream at Midnight," CBS, 1956; "The 20th Century-Fox Hour: Smoke Jumpers," CBS, 1956; "Schlitz Playhouse of Stars: Tower Room 14-A," CBS, 1957; "West Point: One Command," CBS, 1957; "Navy Log: War of the Whaleboats," ABC, 1957; "Crossroads: Paratroop Padre," ABC, 1957; "Crossroads: The Light," ABC, 1957; "Matinee Theatre: Aftermath," NBC, 1957; "Panic: May Day," NBC, 1957; "Playhouse 90: Ain't No Time for Glory," CBS, 1957; "Cimarron City: The Bloodline," NBC, 1959; "The Texan: The Man Behind the Star," CBS, 1959; "Tightrope!: The Cracking Point," CBS, 1960; "Dick Powell's Zane Grey Theatre: Man in the Middle," CBS, 1960; "Tales of Wells Fargo: Kinfolk," NBC, 1960; "77 Sunset Strip: The Office Caper," ABC, 1960; "Alfred Hitchcock Presents: Incident in a Small Jail," NBC, 1961; "Wagon Train: The Chalice," NBC, 1961; "Comedy Spot: The Mighty O," CBS, 1962; "Have Gun, Will Travel: The Predators," CBS, 1962; "The Alfred Hitchcock Hour: Forecast: Low Clouds and Constant Fog," CBS, 1963; "Combat!: Gideon's Army," ABC, 1963; "Temple Houston: The Case for William Gotch," NBC, 1964; "The Virginian: A Matter of Destiny," NBC, 1964; "The Outer Limits: Specimen Unknown," ABC, 1964; "The New Phil Silvers Show: Keep Cool," CBS, 1964; "Bonanza: Between Heaven and Earth," NBC, 1964; "Perry Mason: The Case of the Bogus Buccaneer," CBS, 1966; "The Wild Wild West: The Night of the Grand Emir," CBS, 1966; "The

Wild Wild West: The Night of the Cadre," CBS, 1967; "Bonanza: Night of Reckoning," NBC, 1967; "The Name of the Game: The White Birch," NBC, 1968; "The FBI: Death Watch," ABC, 1971; "Banyon: The Decent Thing to Do," NBC, 1972; "Ironside: The Countdown," NBC, 1972; "Shaft: The Executioners," CBS, 1973; "The FBI: Selkirk's War," ABC, 1974; "Lucas Tanner: Winners and Losers," NBC, 1974; "Police Story: Fathers and Sons," NBC, 1974; "The Wonderful World of Disney: Adventure in Satan's Canyon," NBC, 1974; "Gunsmoke: Larkin," CBS, 1975; "Little House on the Prairie: Long Road Home," NBC, 1976; "Joe Forrester: Pressure Point," NBC, 1976; "Jigsaw John: A Deadly Affair," NBC, 1976; "McCloud: Bonnie and McCloud," NBC, 1976; "Carter Country: Out of the Closet," ABC, 1977; "Lou Grant: Witness," CBS, 1979; "Charlie's Angels: Island Angels," ABC, 1980; "Little House on the Prairie: Sylvia," NBC, 1981; "The Love Boat: Bet on It," ABC, 1984; "Murder, She Wrote: The Way to Dusty Death," CBS, 1987.

TV MOVIES AND MINISERIES: "The Deadly Dream," ABC, 1971; "Firehouse," ABC, 1973; "The Red Pony," ABC, 1973; "Partners in Crime," NBC, 1973; "Born Innocent," NBC, 1974; "The Last Day," NBC, 1975; "Salvage I," ABC, 1979; "The $5.20 an Hour Dream," CBS, 1980; "Reward," ABC, 1980; "The Dirty Dozen: Next Mission," NBC, 1985; "Baywatch: Panic at Malibu Pier," NBC, 1989.

JAFFE, SAM

b. New York City, NY, March 8, 1891; d. 1984.
Slight character actor who radiated a quiet intelligence; after twenty-five years of film work, his greatest popular success came as Dr. David Zorba, mentor to "Ben Casey."
AS A REGULAR: "Ben Casey," ABC, 1961-65.
AND: "Playhouse 90: The Dingaling Girl," CBS, 1959; "Westinghouse Desilu Playhouse: Lepke," CBS, 1959; "Alfred Hitchcock Presents: The Ikon of Elijah," CBS, 1960; "Playhouse 90: To the Sound of Trumpets," CBS, 1960; "Playhouse 90: In the Presence of Mine Enemies," CBS, 1960; "The Eternal Light: The Temptation of Reb Yisroel," NBC, 1960; "Lamp Unto My Feet: No More Songs," CBS, 1960; "Play of the Week: Legend of Lovers," SYN, 1960; "The Law and Mr. Jones: No Sale," ABC, 1960; "Shirley Temple's Storybook: The Terrible Clockman," NBC, 1961; "The Islanders: To Bell a Cat," ABC, 1961; "The Untouchables: Augie 'The Banker' Ciamino," ABC, 1961; "Alfred Hitchcock Presents: The Greatest Monster of Them All," NBC, 1961; "Robert Herridge Theatre: A Cup of Kindness," SYN, 1961; "Naked City: An Economy of Death," ABC, 1961; "The Law and Mr. Jones: The Broken Hand," ABC, 1961; "Cain's Hundred: Final Judgement," NBC, 1961; "The Defenders: The Bedside Murder," CBS, 1962; "The Donna Reed

Show: First Addition," ABC, 1964; "Batman: Shoot a Crooked Arrow/Walk the Straight and Narrow," ABC, 1966; "Tarzan: The Blue Stone of Heaven," NBC, 1967; "Nanny and the Professor: The Astronomers," ABC, 1970; "Alias Smith and Jones: The Great Shell Game," ABC, 1971; "Hollywood Television Theatre: Enemies," NET, 1971; "Alias Smith and Jones: The Day They Hanged Kid Curry," ABC, 1971; "Alias Smith and Jones: A Fistful of Diamonds," ABC, 1971; "Alias Smith and Jones: Bad Night in Big Butte," ABC, 1972; "Ghost Story," NBC, 1972; "Love, American Style: Love and the Wishing Star," ABC, 1972; "Owen Marshall, Counselor at Law: Five Will Get You Six," ABC, 1972; "Ironside: The Countdown," NBC, 1972; "The Saga of Sonora," NBC, 1973; "The Snoop Sisters: Corpse and Robbers," NBC, 1973; "The Streets of San Francisco: Mister Nobody," ABC, 1974; "Columbo: Forgotten Lady," NBC, 1975; "Medical Story: The Moonlight Healer," NBC, 1975; "The Oath: The Sad and Lonely Sundays," ABC, 1976; "The Bionic Woman: Kill Oscar," ABC, 1976; "Kojak: Tears for All Who Loved Her," CBS, 1977; "Flying High: Pilot," CBS, 1978; "Foul Play: Sins of the Fathers," ABC, 1981; "The Love Boat: The Professor Has Class," ABC, 1983.

TV MOVIES AND MINISERIES: "Night Gallery," NBC, 1969; "Quarantined," ABC, 1970; "The Old Man Who Cried Wolf," ABC, 1970; "Sam Hill: Who Killed The Mysterious Mr. Foster?," NBC, 1971; "Gideon's Trumpet," CBS, 1980.

JAFFE, TALIESIN

b. Venice, CA, January 19, 1977.
AS A REGULAR: "Hail to the Chief," ABC, 1985; "She's the Sheriff," SYN, 1987-89.
AND: "Amazing Stories: Magic Saturday," NBC, 1986.
TV MOVIES AND MINISERIES: "Child's Cry," CBS, 1986; "Convicted: A Mother's Story," NBC, 1987.

JAGGER, DEAN

b. Lima, OH, November 7, 1903; d. 1991.
Bespectacled actor who radiated integrity; he played kindly principal Albert Vane on "Mr. Novak." An Emmy winner for "This Is the Life."
AS A REGULAR: "Mr. Novak," NBC, 1963-65.
AND: "Gulf Playhouse: Our 200 Children," NBC, 1952; "Lux Video Theatre: Blind Fury," CBS, 1954; "Cavalcade of America: Night Call," ABC, 1954; "Schlitz Playhouse of Stars: Visibility Zero," CBS, 1955; "Studio 57: My Son Is Gone," SYN, 1955; "The 20th Century-Fox Hour: Smoke Jumpers," CBS, 1956; "Dick Powell's Zane Grey Theatre: There Were Four," CBS, 1957; "Playhouse 90: The Dark Side of the Earth," CBS,

1957; "The Loretta Young Show: Seed From the East," NBC, 1959; "Christophers: Preparing for a Worthwile Life," SYN, 1960; "The Twilight Zone: Static," CBS, 1961; "Our American Heritage: Gentleman's Decision," NBC, 1961; "G.E. Theatre: Mister Doc," CBS, 1962; "The Alfred Hitchcock Hour: The Star Juror," CBS, 1963; "The FBI: The Assassin," ABC, 1966; "The Fugitive: Right in the Middle of the Season," ABC, 1966; "The Storefront Lawyers: A Man's Castle," CBS, 1970; "The Name of the Game: Little Bear Died Running," NBC, 1970; "Bonanza: Shadow of a Hero," NBC, 1971; "The Partridge Family: Don't Bring Your Guns to Town, Santa," ABC, 1971; "Alias Smith and Jones: Only Three to a Bed," ABC, 1972; "Columbo: The Most Crucial Game," NBC, 1972; "Medical Center: End of the Line," CBS, 1973; "CBS Playhouse 90: The Lie," CBS, 1973; "Shaft: The Executioners," CBS, 1973; "Love Story: Time for Love," NBC, 1974; "Harry O: The Mysterious Case of Lester and Dr. Fong," ABC, 1976; "This Is the Life: Independence and 76," SYN, 1980.

TV MOVIES AND MINISERIES: "The Lonely Profession," NBC, 1969; "The Brotherhood of the Bell," CBS, 1970; "Incident in San Francisco," ABC, 1971; "Truman Capote's The Glass House," CBS, 1972; "The Delphi Bureau," ABC, 1972; "The Stranger," NBC, 1973; "I Heard the Owl Call My Name," CBS, 1973; "The Hanged Man," ABC, 1974; "Gideon's Trumpet," CBS, 1980.
* Emmies: 1980.

JAMES, ART

Game-show emcee.
AS A REGULAR: "Concentration, NBC, 1958-73; "Say When!," NBC, 1961-65; "Fractured Phrases," NBC, 1965; "Matches 'n' Mates," ABC, 1967-68; "Temptation," ABC, 1967-68; "Pay Cards!," SYN, 1968-70, 1981-82; "Who, What or Where Game," NBC, 1969-74; "Blank Check," NBC, 1975; "The Magnificent Marble Machine," NBC, 1975-76; "Catch Phrase," SYN, 1985-86.
AND: "The Jack Paar Show," NBC, 1960; "To Tell the Truth," CBS, 1963.

JAMES, CLIFTON

b. New York City, NY, May 29, 1921.
AS A REGULAR: "City of Angels," NBC, 1976; "Lewis & Clark," NBC, 1981-82; "Texas," NBC, 1982.
AND: "Witness: Huey P. Long," CBS, 1960; "Cain's Hundred: Comeback," NBC, 1961; "Slattery's People: Rally Round Your Own Flag, Mister," CBS, 1965; "The Virginian: Linda," NBC, 1966; "Gunsmoke: The Wrong Man," CBS, 1966; "Mannix: A Copy of Murder," CBS, 1968;

"Gunsmoke: Snow Train," CBS, 1970; "Hart to Hart: Pilot," ABC, 1979; "Quincy: Last Rights," NBC, 1980; "The A-Team: Pros and Cons," NBC, 1983; "The A-Team: The White Ballot," NBC, 1983; "Highway to Heaven: Song of the Wild West," NBC, 1984; "Murder, She Wrote: The Last Flight of the Dizzy Damsel," CBS, 1988.

TV MOVIES AND MINISERIES: "The Runaway Barge," NBC, 1975; "Friendly Persuasion," ABC, 1975; "The Deadly Tower," NBC, 1975; "Best Sellers: Captains and the Kings," NBC, 1976; "Undercover with the KKK," NBC, 1979.

JAMES, DENNIS

b. Jersey City, NJ, August 24, 1917. Longtime game-show emcee.
AS A REGULAR: "Cash and Carry," DUM, 1946-47; "The Original Amateur Hour," DUM, 1948-49; NBC, 1949-54; ABC, 1955-57; NBC, 1957-58; CBS, 1959; ABC, 1960; "Chance of a Lifetime," ABC, 1952-53; 1955-56; DUM, 1953-55; "Two for the Money," CBS, 1952-57; "Judge for Yourself," NBC, 1953-54; "The Name's the Same," ABC, 1954-55; "On Your Account," CBS, 1954-56; "High Finance," CBS, 1956; "Haggis Baggis," NBC, 1959; "Your First Impression," NBC, 1962; "People Will Talk," NBC, 1963; "The Price Is Right," ABC, 1963-65; "PDQ," NBC, 1965-69; "Name That Tune," SYN, 1974-81.
AND: "Kraft Television Theatre: Pardon My Prisoner," NBC, 1954; "Club 60," NBC, 1957; "Your First Impression," NBC, 1962; "The Dick Powell Show: The Big Day," NBC, 1962; "The Farmer's Daughter: The Mink Machine," ABC, 1964; "Batman: Hizzoner the Penguin/Dizzoner the Penguin," ABC, 1966; "Tattletales," CBS, 1975.

JAMES, JOHN

b. Minneapolis, MN, April 18, 1956. A regular member of the "Dynasty" crew as Jeff Colby.
AS A REGULAR: "Dynasty," ABC, 1981-85, 1987-89; "The Colbys," ABC, 1985-87.
AND: "The Love Boat: The Arrangement," ABC, 1982.
TV MOVIES AND MINISERIES: "He's Not Your Son," CBS, 1984; "Haunted by Her Past," NBC, 1987.

JAMES, SHEILA

b. Tulsa, OK, 1940. Plain-Jane actress; she played Zelda Gilory, who loved Dobie Gillis (Dwayne Hickman).
AS A REGULAR: "The Stu Erwin Show," ABC, 1950-55; "The Many Loves of Dobie Gillis," CBS, 1959-63; "Broadside," ABC, 1964-65.
AND: "G.E. Theatre: That Other Sunlight," CBS, 1954; "Date with the Angels: Return of the

447

Wheel," ABC, 1957; "The Bob Cummings Show: Bob the Baby Sitter," NBC, 1959; "National Velvet: The Beauty Contest," NBC, 1961; "The New Loretta Young Show: Ponytails and Politics," CBS, 1962; "McHale's Navy: Today I Am a Man!," ABC, 1963; "The Donna Reed Show: A Touch of Glamour," ABC, 1963; "Bob Hope Chrysler Theatre: Wake Up, Darling," NBC, 1964; "Petticoat Junction: The Ladybugs," CBS, 1964; "The Beverly Hillbillies: Cabin in Beverly Hills," CBS, 1964; "The Beverly Hillbillies: Jed Foils a Home Wrecker," CBS, 1964; "The Adventures of Ozzie and Harriet: Rick and the Girl Across the Hall," ABC, 1964; "The Adventures of Ozzie and Harriet: A Message From Kris," ABC, 1965; "The Donna Reed Show: My Son, the Councilman," ABC, 1966; "The John Forsythe Show: On an Island with You and You and You," NBC, 1966; "The Beverly Hillbillies: The Clampett Curse," CBS, 1967; "Marcus Welby, M.D.: The Girl From Rainbow Beach," ABC, 1970; "Whatever Happened to Dobie Gillis?," CBS, 1977.

TV MOVIES AND MINISERIES: "The Feminist and the Fuzz," ABC, 1971; "Bring Me the Head of Dobie Gillis," CBS, 1988.

JAMESON, JOYCE

b. Chicago, IL, September 26, 1932; d. 1987. Squeaky-voiced comic actress with a deep, gasping laugh who was Skippy, one of the "Fun Girls" who plagued Barney Fife and Andy Taylor on "The Andy Griffith Show."

AS A REGULAR: "Club Oasis," NBC, 1958; "The Spike Jones Show," CBS, 1960; "Stump the Stars," CBS, 1964.

AND: "The Abbott and Costello Show: The Birthday Party," CBS, 1952; "Science Fiction Theatre: The Human Circuit," SYN, 1956; "G.E. Theatre: Cab Driver," CBS, 1957; "The Steve Allen Show," NBC, 1958; "Death Valley Days: The Shivaree," SYN, 1958; "The Jack Paar Show," NBC, 1959; "Yancy Derringer: Gone but Not Forgotten," CBS, 1959; "The Chevy Show," NBC, 1959; "The Betty Hutton Show: The Seaton Story," CBS, 1960; "Dante: My Pal, the Bullseye," NBC, 1960; "Checkmate: Murder Game," CBS, 1960; "The Many Loves of Dobie Gillis: Will Success Spoil Dobie's Mother?," CBS, 1961; "Westinghouse Presents: The Sound of the Sixties," NBC, 1961; "Your First Impression," NBC, 1962; "The Many Loves of Dobie Gillis: All Right, Dobie, Drop the Gun," CBS, 1963; "The Many Loves of Dobie Gillis: Requiem for an Underweight Heavyweight," CBS, 1963; "The Twilight Zone: I Dream of Genie," CBS, 1963; "Burke's Law: Who Killed Jason Shaw?," ABC, 1964; "Grindl: The Lucky Piece," NBC, 1964; "Bob Hope Chrysler Theatre: Wake Up, Darling," NBC, 1964; "The Andy Griffith Show: Fun Girls," CBS, 1964; "My

Favorite Martian: The Night Life of Uncle Martin," CBS, 1964; "The Munsters: Dance with Me, Herman," CBS, 1965; "Perry Mason: The Case of the Feather Cloak," CBS, 1965; "The Andy Griffith Show: The Arrest of the Fun Girls," CBS, 1965; "The Man From UNCLE: The Dippy Blonde Affair," NBC, 1966; "The Munsters: Herman Picks a Winner," CBS, 1966; "Gomer Pyle, USMC: Vacation in Las Vegas," CBS, 1966; "The Dick Van Dyke Show: A Day in the Life of Alan Brady," CBS, 1966; "Gomer Pyle, USMC: The Return of Monroe," CBS, 1968; "The Virginian: The Long Ride Home," NBC, 1969; "The Rockford Files: The Dexter Crisis," NBC, 1974; "Police Woman: Bloody Nose," NBC, 1975; "Rhoda: An Elephant Never Forgets," CBS, 1976; "Barney Miller: Rape," ABC, 1978.

TV MOVIES AND MINISERIES: "Run, Simon, Run," ABC, 1970; "The Cable Car Murder," CBS, 1971; "Women in Chains," ABC, 1972; "Crash," ABC, 1978; "The Wild Wild West Revisited," CBS, 1979.

JANIS, CONRAD

b. New York City, NY, February 11, 1928. Actor-musician who played Frederick McConnell, father of Mindy (Pam Dawber) on "Mork & Mindy."

AS A REGULAR: "Bonino," NBC, 1953; "Jimmy Hughes, Rookie Cop," DUM, 1953; "Quark," NBC, 1978; "Mork & Mindy," ABC, 1978-79, 1980-82.

AND: "Actors Studio: Joe McSween's Atomic Machine," CBS, 1950; "Kraft Television Theatre: Spring Green," NBC, 1951; "Suspense: Killers of the City," CBS, 1951; "Suspense: The Deb," CBS, 1952; "The Doctor: Time to Kill," NBC, 1952; "First Person: One Night Stand," NBC, 1953; "Studio One: Cinderella '53," CBS, 1953; "Kraft Television Theatre: The Dashing White Sergeant," ABC, 1954; "Kraft Television Theatre: The Day the Diner Closed," ABC, 1954; "Kraft Television Theatre: One Hill, One River," NBC, 1955; "Danger: Peter River's Blues," CBS, 1955; "Kraft Television Theatre: Gramercy Ghost," NBC, 1955; "Appointment with Adventure: Ride the Comet," CBS, 1955; "U.S. Steel Hour: Ashton Buys a Horse," CBS, 1955; "Armstrong Circle Theatre: The Monkey Ride," CBS, 1959; "Armstrong Circle Theatre: Raid in Beatnik Village," CBS, 1960; "Comedy Spot: Full Speed Anywhere," CBS, 1960; "The Untouchables: The Mark of Cain," ABC, 1960; "U.S. Steel Hour: Shame the Devil," CBS, 1960; "Get Smart: My Nephew the Spy," NBC, 1965; "My Favorite Martian: TV or Not TV," CBS, 1966; "Happy Days: A Place of His Own," ABC, 1976; "The Streets of San Francisco: In Case of Madness," ABC, 1976; "Maude: The Game Show," CBS, 1976; "Police Story: Monster Manor," NBC, 1976; "Barnaby Jones: The Picture Pirates," CBS,

1978; "Kojak: Chains of Custody," CBS, 1978; "The Love Boat: The Vacation," ABC, 1979; "House Calls: Beast of Kensington," CBS, 1980; "Mama's Family: Dear Aunt Fran," NBC, 1984; "St. Elsewhere: Hearing," NBC, 1984; "St. Elsewhere: Cramming," NBC, 1984; "Remington Steele: Stronger Than Steele," NBC, 1985; "Murder, She Wrote: A Little Night Work," CBS, 1988.

TV MOVIES AND MINISERIES: "Miracle on 34th Street," CBS, 1973; "The Red-Light Sting," CBS, 1984.

JANSSEN, DAVID

b. *David Harold Meyer, Naponee, NB, March 27, 1930; d. 1980.* Actor and popular TV presence from the fifties till his death. Best known as Dr. Richard Kimble, "The Fugitive"; and as hard-luck private eye Harry Orwell.

AS A REGULAR: "Richard Diamond, Private Detective," CBS, 1957; 1958; 1959; "The Fugitive," ABC, 1963-67; "O'Hara, U.S. Treasury," CBS, 1971-72; "Harry O," ABC, 1974-76; "Biography," SYN, 1979.

AND: "Lux Video Theatre: It Started with Eve," NBC, 1956; "Warner Bros. Presents Conflict: The Money," ABC, 1957; "Dick Powell's Zane Grey Theatre: There Were Four," CBS, 1957; "Alcoa Theatre: Cupid Wore a Badge," NBC, 1957; "The Millionaire: The Regina Wainwright Story," CBS, 1957; "Dick Powell's Zane Grey Theatre: Trial by Fear," CBS, 1958; "Alcoa Theatre: Decoy Duck," NBC, 1958; "The Millionaire: Millionaire David Barrett," CBS, 1958; "Dick Powell's Zane Grey Theatre: Trail to Nowhere," CBS, 1958; "Dick Powell's Zane Grey Theatre: Hang the Heart High," CBS, 1959; "Arthur Murray Party," NBC, 1959; "Westinghouse Desilu Playhouse: Two Counts of Murder," CBS, 1959; "Death Valley Days: Deadline at Austin," SYN, 1961; "Naked City: A Wednesday Night Story," ABC, 1961; "Adventures in Paradise: Show Me a Hero," ABC, 1961; "Checkmate: Ride a Wild Horse," CBS, 1962; "Target: The Corruptors: The Middleman," ABC, 1962; "G.E. Theatre: Shadow of a Hero," CBS, 1962; "Follow the Sun: A Choice of Weapons," ABC, 1962; "Cain's Hundred: Inside Track," NBC, 1962; "Kraft Mystery Theatre: Two Counts of Murder," NBC, 1962; "Route 66: One Tiger to a Hill," CBS, 1962; "The Eleventh Hour: Make Me a Place," NBC, 1962; "Naked City: On the Battlefront, Every Minute Is Important," ABC, 1963; "The Dick Powell Show: Thunder in a Forgotten Town," NBC, 1963; "Dinah Shore Special," ABC, 1964; "Hollywood Palace," ABC, 1965; "ABC Nightlife," ABC, 1965; "The Dean Martin Show," NBC, 1969; "The Movie Game," SYN, 1969; "Cannon: He Who Digs a Grave," CBS, 1973; "The Tonight Show Starring Johnny Carson," NBC, 1975; "Joys," NBC, 1976; "The

Tonight Show Starring Johnny Carson," NBC, 1976.

TV MOVIES AND MINISERIES: "Night Chase," CBS, 1970; "O'Hara, United States Treasury: Operation Cobra," CBS, 1971; "The Longest Night," ABC, 1972; "Moon of the Wolf," ABC, 1972; "Birds of Prey," CBS, 1973; "Hijack!," ABC, 1973; "Pioneer Woman," ABC, 1973; "Smile, Jenny, You're Dead," ABC, 1974; "Fer-De-Lance," CBS, 1974; "Stalk the Wild Child," NBC, 1976; "Mayday at 40,000 Feet," CBS, 1976; "A Sensitive, Passionate Man," NBC, 1977; "The Word," CBS, 1978; "Centennial," NBC, 1978-79; "S.O.S. Titanic," ABC, 1979; "The Golden Gate Murders," CBS, 1979; "City in Fear," ABC, 1980.

* Janssen made his movie debut at age 15, in the Sonja Henie flick "It's a Pleasure."

* The concluding episode of "The Fugitive" in 1967—in which Janssen, as Dr. Richard Kimble, at last found the one-armed man who had killed his wife—drew an estimated audience of 30 million, or about 45 percent of those watching TV.

JARRETT, RENNE GAIL

b. *Brooklyn, NY, January 28, 1946.* Former child actress who played the President's daughter, Nancy, on a short-lived sitcom.

AS A REGULAR: "Portia Faces Life (The Inner Flame)," CBS, 1954-55; "Nancy," NBC, 1970-71; "Somerset," NBC, 1970-76.

AND: "Startime: The Man," NBC, 1960; "Then Came Bronson: Sybil," NBC, 1970; "Medical Center: The Cambatants," CBS, 1970; "Love, American Style: Love and the Secret Spouse," ABC, 1973; "The Streets of San Francisco: I Ain't Marching Anymore," ABC, 1974; "Barnaby Jones: Death on Deposit," CBS, 1974; "Quincy: Visitors in Paradise," NBC, 1977; "Barnaby Jones: A Simple Case of Terror," CBS, 1977.

TV MOVIES AND MINISERIES: "In Search of America," ABC, 1971; "The Cat Creature," ABC, 1973; "The Family Kovack," CBS, 1974; "The First 36 Hours of Dr. Durant," ABC, 1975; "The New Daughters of Joshua Cabe," ABC, 1976.

JARVIS, GRAHAM

b. *Canada, August 25, 1930.* Actor who played Charlie Haggers on "Mary Hartman, Mary Hartman" and prinicpal Bob Dyrenforth on "Fame."

AS A REGULAR: "The Guiding Light," CBS, 1971-72; "Mary Hartman, Mary Hartman," SYN, 1976-78; "Making the Grade," CBS, 1982; "Fame," SYN, 1985-87.

AND: "The Phil Silvers Show: Bilko the Genius," CBS, 1958; "Naked City: Ooftus Gooftus," ABC,

1961; "The Investigation," NBC, 1967; "NYPD: Walking Target," ABC, 1967; "All in the Family: Archie and the FBI," CBS, 1972; "The Odd Couple: The Big Broadcast," ABC, 1974; "Maude: Walter Gets Religion," CBS, 1975; "M*A*S*H: Big Mac," CBS, 1975; "McMillan and Wife: Secrets for Sale," NBC, 1975; "The Bob Newhart Show: Bob Has to Have His Tonsils Out, So He Spends Christmas Eve in the Hospital," CBS, 1975; "Sanford & Son: Sanford and Rising Son," NBC, 1976; "Alice: Star in the Storeroom," CBS, 1978; "House Calls: Son of Emergency," CBS, 1981; "Father Murphy: False Blessing," NBC, 1981; "Cagney & Lacey: Lost and Found," CBS, 1985; "Rags to Riches: That's Cheating," NBC, 1987; "Murder, She Wrote: Sins of Castle Cove," CBS, 1989.

TV MOVIES AND MINISERIES: "Your Money or Your Wife," CBS, 1972; "The New Maverick," ABC, 1978; "Blind Ambition," CBS, 1979; "Carpool," CBS, 1983; "Vanishing Act," CBS, 1986; "A Cry for Help: The Tracey Thurman Story," NBC, 1989.

JASON, RICK
b. New York City, NY, May 21, 1926. Actor who played Lt. Gil Hanley on "Combat!"
AS A REGULAR: "The Case of the Dangerous Robin," SYN, 1960-61; "Combat!," ABC, 1962-67; "The Young and the Restless," CBS, 1973.
AND: "The Jane Wyman Show: Cleopatra Collins," NBC, 1956; "Damon Runyon Theatre: The Big Umbrella," CBS, 1956; "The 20th Century-Fox Hour: Men Against Speed," CBS, 1956; "Rawhide: Incident of the Coyote Weed," CBS, 1959; "Rawhide: Incident of the Valley in Shadow," CBS, 1959; "The Millionaire: Millionaire Mara Robinson," CBS, 1960; "Police Woman: The Company," NBC, 1975; "Police Woman: The Purge," NBC, 1975; "Police Woman: Tennis Bum," NBC, 1976; "Switch: Who Killed Lila Craig?" CBS, 1977; "Matt Houston: Needle in a Haystack," ABC, 1983; "Murder, She Wrote: A Little Night Work," CBS, 1988.
TV MOVIES AND MINISERIES: "The Monk," ABC, 1969.

JEFFREYS, ANNE
b. Anne Carmichael, Goldsboro, NC, January 26, 1923. Former movie actress best known as the ghostly Marion Kerby on the TV version of "Topper."
AS A REGULAR: "Topper," CBS, 1953-55; "Love That Jill," ABC, 1958; "Bright Promise," NBC, 1970-72; "The Delphi Bureau," ABC, 1972-73; "General Hospital," ABC, 1984-85; "Finder of Lost Loves," ABC, 1984-85.
AND: "Musical Comedy Time: Revenge with

Music," NBC, 1951; "The Merry Widow," NBC, 1955; "Dearest Enemy," NBC, 1955; "The Steve Allen Show," NBC, 1956; "The 20th Century-Fox Hour: City in Flames," CBS, 1957; "Du Pont Theatre: The Widow Was Willing," ABC, 1957; "Telephone Time: Campaign for Marriage," ABC, 1957; "Wagon Train: The Julia Gage Story," NBC, 1957; "The Perry Como Show," NBC, 1958; "Lux Playhouse: Mirror, Mirror," CBS, 1959; "The Bob Cummings Show: Bob and the Pediatrician," NBC, 1959; "The Bob Cummings Show: Bob Gets Hypnotized," NBC, 1959; "Arthur Murray Party," NBC, 1960; "Here's Hollywood," NBC, 1960; "Wagon Train: The Mary Beckett Story," NBC, 1962; "You Don't Say," NBC, 1963; "Dr. Kildare: Believe and Live," NBC, 1965; "Bonanza: The Unwritten Commandment," NBC, 1966; "The Man From UNCLE: The Abominable Snowman Affair," NBC, 1966; "Ghostbreaker," ABC, 1967; "Tarzan: Tiger, Tiger," NBC, 1967; "My Three Sons: What Did You Do Today, Grandpa?," CBS, 1969; "Love, American Style: Love and the President," ABC, 1972; "Police Story: To Steal a Million," NBC, 1975; "Buck Rogers in the 25th Century: Planet of the Amazon Women," NBC, 1979; "Over Easy," PBS, 1981; "Hotel: Cinderella," ABC, 1984.

TRIVIA QUIZ #13: GOOD ANSWER!
Which TV shows gave us these catchphrases?

1. "Goodnight, America, wherever you are."
2. "Man, woman, birth, death, life, infinity."
3. "Let's be careful out there."
4. "Book 'em, Danno."
5. "Right here on our stage ...."
6. "The story you are about to see is true."
7. "Will the real Mr. X please stand up?"
8. "Letters, we get letters ...."
9. "There you go."
10. "Good answer!"

(Answers at end of book.)

JEFFRIES, LANG
b. Canada, June 7, 1931; d. 1987. Actor who played Skip Johnson on "Rescue 8," an action series that was a predecessor to "Emergency!"
AS A REGULAR: "Rescue 8," SYN, 1958-60.
AND: "The Overland Trail: The Most Dangerous Gentleman," NBC, 1960.

JENKINS, ALLEN
b. Al McConegal, New York City, NY, April 9, 1900; d. 1974. Actor who played dim-witted sidekicks and Bronx-accented tough guys in the movies and TV; he provided the voice of

Office Dibble, nemesis of "Top Cat."
AS A REGULAR: "The Duke," NBC, 1954; "Waterfront," SYN, 1954-55; "Damon Runyon Theatre," CBS, 1955-56; "Hey, Jeannie!," CBS, 1956-57; "Top Cat," ABC, 1961-62.
AND: "The Abbott and Costello Show: The Actor's Home," CBS, 1952; "I Love Lucy: New Neighbors," CBS, 1952; "Four Star Playhouse: The Officer and the Lady," CBS, 1952; "I Love Lucy: Ricky and Fred Are TV Fans," CBS, 1953; "I Love Lucy: Too Many Crooks," CBS, 1953; "G.E. Theatre: Here Comes Calvin," CBS, 1954; "Topper: The Blood Brother," CBS, 1955; "It's a Great Life: The Private Line," NBC, 1955; "It's a Great Life: The Palm Springs Story," CBS, 1956; "The Red Skelton Show," CBS, 1956; "Playhouse 90: Three Men on a Horse," CBS, 1957; "The Red Skelton Show," CBS, 1957; "The Red Skelton Show: The Cop and the Anthem," CBS, 1959; "Wagon Train: The Horace Best Story," NBC, 1960; "The Tab Hunter Show: Sultan for a Day," NBC, 1961; "The Red Skelton Show," CBS, 1961; "Valentine's Day: How to Live Without Dying," ABC, 1964; "The Man From UNCLE: The Concrete Overcoat Affair," NBC, 1966; "Batman: That Darn Catwoman/Scat, Darn Catwoman," ABC, 1967; "Bewitched: Darrin Goes Ape," ABC, 1971; "Bewitched: Money Happy Returns," ABC, 1971; "Bewitched: Tabitha's First Day at School," ABC, 1972; "The Paul Lynde Show: No Nudes Is Good Nudes," ABC, 1972.
TV MOVIES AND MINISERIES: "Getting Away From It All," ABC, 1972.

JENNINGS, PETER
b. Canada, July 29, 1938.
AS A REGULAR: "ABC Evening News," 1965-68; "World News Tonight," ABC, 1978- .
AND: "Later with Bob Costas," NBC, 1989.

JENNINGS, WAYLON
b. Littlefield, TX, June 15, 1937. Country-western singer and songwriter who was the narrator on "The Dukes of Hazzard."
AS A REGULAR: "The Dukes of Hazzard," CBS, 1979-85.
AND: "The Glen Campbell Goodtime Hour," CBS, 1969; "Sammy and Company," SYN, 1975.
TV MOVIES AND MINISERIES: "Stagecoach," CBS, 1986.

JENS, SALOME
b. Milwaukee, WI, May 8, 1935.
AS A GUEST: "Play of the Week: The Cherry Orchard," SYN, 1959; "Robert Herridge Theatre: Girl on the Road," SYN, 1960; "Jackie Gleason Special: The Million Dollar Incident," CBS, 1961; "Great Ghost Tales: Who Is the Fairest One of All?," NBC, 1961;

"U.S. Steel Hour: Man on the Mountaintop," CBS, 1961; "Play of the Week: Four by Tennessee Williams," SYN, 1961; "The Defenders: The Naked Heiress," CBS, 1962; "Naked City: Goodbye Mama, Hello Auntie Maud," ABC, 1962; "Stoney Burke: Spin a Golden Web," ABC, 1962; "The Untouchables: The Man in the Cooler," ABC, 1963; "Alcoa Premiere: The Dark Labryinth," ABC, 1963; "U.S. Steel Hour: Mission of Fear," CBS, 1963; "The Outer Limits: Corpus Earthling," ABC, 1963; "Hallmark Hall of Fame: Barefoot in Athens," NBC, 1966; "I Spy: A Room with a Rack," NBC, 1967; "Medical Center: Undercurrent," CBS, 1970; "Bonanza: The Wagon," NBC, 1970; "Gunsmoke: Captain Sligo," CBS, 1971; "Medical Center: Undercurrent," CBS, 1971; "Gunsmoke: Talbot," CBS, 1973; "McMillan and Wife: Reunion in Terror," NBC, 1974; "Wide World of Mystery: The House of Evil," ABC, 1974; "The New Land: The Word Is: Mortal," ABC, 1974; "The Wonderful World of Disney: The Boy Who Talked to Badgers," NBC, 1975; "Medical Center: The Fourth Sex," CBS, 1975; "Kojak: Out of the Shadows," CBS, 1976; "Gibbsville: Saturday Night," NBC, 1976; "Barnaby Jones: Reincarnation," CBS, 1977; "Quincy: Dead Stop," NBC, 1981; "Cagney & Lacey: Exit Stage Center," CBS, 1986; "The Hogan Family: Paris," NBC, 1989.
TV MOVIES AND MINISERIES: "The Satin Murders," ABC, 1974; "In the Glitter Palace," NBC, 1977; "From Here to Eternity," NBC, 1979; "The Golden Moment: An Olympic Love Story," NBC, 1980; "A Matter of Life and Death," CBS, 1981; "Uncommon Valor," CBS, 1983; "Grace Kelly," ABC, 1983; "A Killer in the Family," ABC, 1983; "Playing with Fire," NBC, 1985; "Cast the First Stone," NBC, 1989.

JENSEN, MAREN
b. Arcadia, CA, September 23, 1956.
AS A REGULAR: "Battlestar Galactica," ABC, 1978-79.
AND: "Fantasy Island: Jungle Man," ABC, 1980.

JENSEN, SANFORD
b. South Haven, MI, August 11, 1953.
AS A REGULAR: "Foley Square," CBS, 1985-86; "I Married Dora," ABC, 1987-88.
AND: "Remington Steele: Steele on the Air," NBC, 1986; "Murphy Brown: TV or Not TV," CBS, 1989.

JESSEL, GEORGE
b. New York City, NY, April 3, 1898; d. 1981. Singer-comic of the stage and vaudeville who

was later appointed "Toastmaster General of the United States" by then-President Harry Truman. Having a military title appealed to his right-wing sensibilities; toward the end of his life he took to appearing on talk shows in uniform.

AS A REGULAR: "All Star Revue," NBC, 1952-53; "The Comeback Story," ABC, 1953-54; "The George Jessel Show," ABC, 1953-54; "Jackie Gleason and His American Scene Magazine," CBS, 1965-66.

AND: "Stage Show," CBS, 1956; "The Jackie Gleason Show," CBS, 1957; "The Jack Benny Program," CBS, 1957; "Bob Hope Show," NBC, 1957; "The Ray Bolger Show," NBC, 1957; "The Steve Allen Show," NBC, 1957; "Arthur Murray Party," NBC, 1957; "Mike Wallace Interviews," ABC, 1957; "Tonight," NBC, 1957; "The Jack Paar Show," NBC, 1958; "Pantomime Quiz," ABC, 1958; "Art Linkletter's House Party," CBS, 1958; "Milton Berle Starring in the Kraft Music Hall," NBC, 1958; "Person to Person," CBS, 1959; "The Steve Allen Show," NBC, 1959; "The Sam Levenson Show," CBS, 1959; "Steve Allen Plymouth Show," NBC, 1959; "Startime: George Burns in the Big Time," NBC, 1959; "Be Our Guest," CBS, 1960; "Celebrity Talent Scouts," CBS, 1960; "Play Your Hunch," NBC, 1960; "The Jack Paar Show," NBC, 1960; "The Ed Sullivan Show," CBS, 1961; "The Jack Paar Show," NBC, 1961; "This Is Your Life (Harry Ruby)," NBC, 1961; "Jackie Gleason Special: The Million Dollar Incident," CBS, 1961; "Here's Hollywood," NBC, 1961; "The Ed Sullivan Show," CBS, 1962; "The Tonight Show Starring Johnny Carson," NBC, 1962; "The Merv Griffin Show," NBC, 1962; "Jackie Gleason and His American Scene Magazine," CBS, 1963; "77 Sunset Strip: 5," ABC, 1963; "The Tonight Show Starring Johnny Carson," NBC, 1964; "The Mike Douglas Show," SYN, 1964; "The Tonight Show Starring Johnny Carson," NBC, 1966; "The Tonight Show Starring Johnny Carson," NBC, 1967; "The Dean Martin Show," NBC, 1968; "The Merv Griffin Show," SYN, 1968; "The Mike Douglas Show," SYN, 1969; "The Merv Griffin Show," CBS, 1969; "The Merv Griffin Show," SYN, 1974; "The Merv Griffin Show," SYN, 1977.

* Jessel was set to star in 1927's "The Jazz Singer," the first talking picture, but his salary demands caused Al Jolson to be cast in the role instead.

JILLIAN, ANN

b. Cambridge, MA, January 29, 1951. Blonde singer-dancer-actress who's withstood a double mastectomy to maintain an active TV career; she told her story, playing herself in a TV movie.

AS A REGULAR: "Hazel," CBS, 1965-66; "It's a Living," ABC, 1980-82; SYN, 1985-86; "Jennifer Slept Here," NBC, 1983-84; "Ann Jillian," NBC, 1989-90.

AND: "The Twilight Zone: Mute," CBS, 1963; "My Three Sons: The Ballad of Lissa Stratmeyer," ABC, 1964; "The John Davidson Show," SYN, 1981; "Ooh-La-La—It's Bob Hope's Fun Birthday Spectacular From Paris' Bicentennial," NBC, 1989.

TV MOVIES AND MINISERIES: "Mae West," ABC, 1982; "Malibu," ABC, 1983; "Girls of the White Orchid," NBC, 1983; "This Wife for Hire," CBS, 1985; "Killer in the Mirror," NBC, 1986; "Perry Mason: The Case of the Murdered Madam," NBC, 1987; "Convicted: A Mother's Story," NBC, 1987; "The Ann Jillian Story," NBC, 1988; "Original Sin," NBC, 1989; "Little White Lies," NBC, 1989.

JILLSON, JOYCE

b. Cranston, RI, 1947. Actress who's now an astrologer.

AS A REGULAR: "Peyton Place," ABC, 1968.

AND: "The Man From UNCLE: The My Friend the Gorilla Affair," NBC, 1966; "Columbo: Any Old Port in a Storm," NBC, 1973; "Kolchak, the Night Stalker: The Energy Eater," ABC, 1974; "Police Woman: Blast," NBC, 1975; "Lou Grant: Hostage," CBS, 1977.

TV MOVIES AND MINISERIES: "Murder in Peyton Place," NBC, 1977.

JOHNS, GLYNIS

b. Pretoria, South Africa, October 5, 1923. Blonde actress who played the mother of Diane Chambers on "Cheers"; often in ditsy roles.

AS A REGULAR: "Glynis," CBS, 1963; "Coming of Age," CBS, 1988.

AND: "Studio One: Lily, Queen of the Movies," CBS, 1952; "Lux Video Theatre: Two for Tea," CBS, 1953; "Disneyland: Rob Roy," ABC, 1956; "Errol Flynn Theatre: The Sealed Room," SYN, 1957; "Schlitz Playhouse of Stars: The Dead Are Silent," CBS, 1957; "Errol Flynn Theatre: Girl in Blue Jeans," SYN, 1957; "The Frank Sinatra Show: Face of Fear," ABC, 1958; "The Jack Paar Show," NBC, 1960; "Adventures in Paradise: Beachhead," ABC, 1961; "Kraft Mystery Theatre: The Spider's Web," NBC, 1961; "The Roaring Twenties: Kitty Goes West," ABC, 1961; "G.E. Theatre: The $200 Parlay," CBS, 1961; "Naked City: The Hot Minerva," ABC, 1961; "The Dick Powell Show: Safari," NBC, 1962; "Beachcomber: The Search for Robert Herrick," SYN, 1962; "Dr. Kildare: A Very Present Help," NBC, 1962; "Saints and Sinners: Luscious Lois," NBC, 1962; "The du Pont Show: Windfall," NBC, 1963; "The Lloyd Bridges Show: A Game for Alternate Mondays," CBS, 1963; "Vacation Playhouse: Hide and Seek," CBS, 1963; "Talent Scouts,"

CBS, 1963; "Exploring," NBC, 1963; "Burke's Law: Who Killed Marty Kelso?," ABC, 1964; "The Defenders: The Thief," CBS, 1964; "Twelve O'Clock High: The Hours Before Dawn," ABC, 1964; "Batman: The Londinium Larcenies/The Foggiest Notion/The Bloody Tower," ABC, 1967; "Cheers: Someone Single, Someone Blue," NBC, 1983; "The Love Boat: Side by Side," ABC, 1984; "Murder, She Wrote: Sing a Song of Murder," CBS, 1985.

TV MOVIES AND MINISERIES: "Little Gloria ... Happy at Last," NBC, 1982.

JOHNSON, ARTE

b. Chicago, IL, January 20, 1934. Emmy winning comic who was white-hot in the late sixties, thanks to "Rowan & Martin's Laugh-In," on which he played the "Verrrry interesting" Nazi, dirty old man Tyrone F. Horneye and other assorted characters.

AS A REGULAR: "Sally," NBC, 1958; "Hennesey," CBS, 1959-62; "Don't Call Me Charlie!," NBC, 1962-63; "Rowan & Martin's Laugh-In," NBC, 1968-71; "Ben Vereen ... Comin' at Ya," NBC, 1975; "The Gong Show," SYN, 1976-80; "Knockout," NBC, 1977-78; "Games People Play," NBC, 1980-81; "Glitter," ABC, 1984-85.

AND: "December Bride: Jaywalker," CBS, 1956; "The Twilight Zone: The Whole Truth," CBS, 1961; "Peter Loves Mary: Getting Peter's Putter," NBC, 1961; "Dinah Shore Special: Brief Encounter," NBC, 1961; "Bringing Up Buddy: Auntie's Cake," CBS, 1961; "Alfred Hitchcock Presents: A Secret Life," NBC, 1961; "Yes, Yes Nanette: Nan Suits Dan," NBC, 1961; "Frontier Circus: Journey From Hannibal," CBS, 1961; "The Andy Griffith Show: Andy and Barney in the Big City," CBS, 1962; "G.E. True: The Handmade Private," CBS, 1962; "McHale's Navy: Camera, Action, Panic," ABC, 1963; "No Time for Sergeants: Bloodhounds Are Thicker Than Water," ABC, 1964; "Bob Hope Chrysler Theatre: The Timothy Heist," NBC, 1964; "Many Happy Returns: Krockmeyer on Avon," CBS, 1964; "The Dick Van Dyke Show: I Do Not Choose to Run," CBS, 1966; "The Donna Reed Show: Is There a Small Hotel?," ABC, 1966; "Hollywood Squares," NBC, 1968; "The Beautiful Phyllis Diller Show," NBC, 1968; "I Dream of Jeannie: The Biggest Star in Hollywood," NBC, 1969; "Flip Wilson Special," NBC, 1969; "Kraft Music Hall," NBC, 1970; "Love, American Style: Love and the Living Doll," ABC, 1970; "The Glen Campbell Goodtime Hour," CBS, 1970; "Love, American Style: Love and the Nurse," ABC, 1971; "The Glen Campbell Goodtime Hour," CBS, 1971; "Sesame Street," NET, 1971; "Love, American Style: Love and the Boomerang," ABC, 1972; "The Partridge Family: For Whom the Bell Tolls ... and Tolls ... and Tolls," ABC, 1973; "Hollywood Squares," NBC,

1973; "Baffle," NBC, 1973; "Here's Lucy: Lucy Is a Bird-Sitter," CBS, 1974; "Feeling Good," PBS, 1975; "The Bobby Vinton Show," SYN, 1975; "Hollywood Squares," NBC, 1975; "Jigsaw John: Too Much, Too Soon," NBC, 1976; "Tattletales," CBS, 1976; "The Merv Griffin Show," SYN, 1976; "The Bobby Vinton Show," SYN, 1977; "Kojak: Photo Must Credit Joe Paxton," CBS, 1978; "Captain Kangaroo," CBS, 1978; "The Love Boat: Making the Grade," ABC, 1980; "Dance Fever," SYN, 1980; "The Love Boat: Marrying for Money," ABC, 1982; "The Love Boat: Sly as a Fox," ABC, 1983; "The Love Boat: A Rose Is Not a Rose," ABC, 1984; "The Love Boat: What a Drag," ABC, 1984; "The A-Team: Uncle Buckle-Up," NBC, 1985; "The New Mike Hammer: Murder in the Cards," CBS, 1986; "Murder, She Wrote: No Laughing Matter," CBS, 1987.

TV MOVIES AND MINISERIES: "Twice in a Lifetime," NBC, 1974; "Bud and Lou," NBC, 1978; "The Love Tapes," ABC, 1980; "The Making of a Male Model," ABC, 1983.
* Emmies: 1969.

JOHNSON, BEN

b. Pawhuska, OK, June 13, 1920. Well-known western actor in the films of John Ford ("She Wore a Yellow Ribbon," "Wagonmaster") and an Oscar-winner for "The Last Picture Show"; his TV appearances have also tended to be in oaters.

AS A REGULAR: "The Monroes," ABC, 1966-67.

AND: "The Adventures of Ozzie and Harriet: The Top Gun," ABC, 1958; "Navy Log: Florida Week-End," ABC, 1958; "Alfred Hitchcock Presents: And the Desert Shall Blossom," CBS, 1958; "Laramie: Hour After Dawn," NBC, 1960; "Have Gun, Will Travel: A Head of Hair," CBS, 1960; "Have Gun, Will Travel: The Race," CBS, 1961; "Route 66: A Long Piece of Mischief," CBS, 1962; "Bonanza: The Gamble," NBC, 1962; "Have Gun, Will Travel: The Fifth Bullet," CBS, 1962; "The Virginian: Duel at Shiloh," NBC, 1963; "The Virginian: Dangerous Road," NBC, 1965; "Bob Hope Chrysler Theatre: March From Camp Tyler," NBC, 1965; "Branded: McCord's Way," NBC, 1966; "The Virginian: Johnny Moon," NBC, 1967; "The Virginian: Vision of Blindness," NBC, 1968; "Walt Disney's Wonderful World of Color: Ride a Northbound Horse," NBC, 1969; "Bonanza: The Deserter," NBC, 1969; "Bonanza: Top Hand," NBC, 1971; "Gunsmoke: Drago," CBS, 1971.

TV MOVIES AND MINISERIES: "The Red Pony," ABC, 1973; "Runaway!," ABC, 1973; "Bloodsport," ABC, 1973; "Locusts," ABC, 1974; "The Savage Bees," NBC, 1976; "The Shadow Riders," CBS, 1982; "Wild Horses," CBS, 1985; "Dream West," CBS, 1986; "Stranger on My Land," ABC, 1988.

JOHNSON, BRAD

b. 1924; d. 1981. Actor who played Deputy Lofty Craig on "Annie Oakley."
AS A REGULAR: "Annie Oakley," ABC, 1955-58.
AND: "Death Valley Days: Stagecoach Spy," SYN, 1959; "The Overland Trail: Vigilantes of Montana," NBC, 1960; "Bourbon Street Beat: Wagon Show," ABC, 1960; "Maverick: A Bullet for the Teacher," ABC, 1960; "Wagon Train: The Cathy Eckhardt Story," NBC, 1960; "Gunsmoke: Cattle Barons," CBS, 1967.

JOHNSON, DON

b. Flatt Creek, MO, December 15, 1949. Actor who was rescued from obscurity by "Miami Vice," on which he played pastel-dressed Det. Sonny Crockett.
AS A REGULAR: "From Here to Eternity," NBC, 1980; "Miami Vice," NBC, 1984-89.
AND: "The Bold Ones: Endtheme," NBC, 1972; "Kung Fu: Spirit Helper," ABC, 1973; "The Rookies: The Teacher," ABC, 1974; "The Streets of San Francisco: Hot Dog," ABC, 1976.
TV MOVIES AND MINISERIES: "Law of the Land," NBC, 1976; "The City," NBC, 1977; "Katie: Portrait of a Centerfold," NBC, 1978; "First You Cry," CBS, 1978; "Amateur Night at the Dixie Bar and Grill," NBC, 1979; "The Rebels," SYN, 1979; "Beulah Land," NBC, 1980; "The Revenge of the Stepford Wives," NBC, 1980; "Elvis and the Beauty Queen," NBC, 1981; "The Long Hot Summer," NBC, 1985.

JOHNSON, GEORGANN

b. Decorah, IA, August 15, 1926. Actress who plays the mother of Rosie O'Neill (Sharon Gless).
AS A REGULAR: "Mr. Peepers," NBC, 1952-55; "Somerset," NBC, 1970-76; "As the World Turns," CBS, 1977-79; "Our Family Honor," ABC, 1985-86; "The Colbys," ABC, 1986-87; "The Trials of Rosie O'Neill," CBS, 1990- .
AND: "U.S. Steel Hour: Bang the Drum Slowly," CBS, 1956; "Jonathan," SYN, 1956; "Alfred Hitchcock Presents: One for the Road," CBS, 1957; "Kraft Television Theatre: Men of Prey," NBC, 1957; "Suspicion: The Hollow Man," NBC, 1958; "Phil Silvers on Broadway," CBS, 1958; "Frontiers of Faith: The House of Paper," NBC, 1959; "Ellery Queen: This Murder Comes to You Live," NBC, 1959; "Goodyear Theatre: Christabel," NBC, 1959; "Alcoa Presents One Step Beyond: Rendezvous," ABC, 1960; "Dr. Kildare: Guest Appearance," NBC, 1962; "The Defenders: The Secret," CBS, 1964; "Dr. Kildare: Man Is a Rock," NBC, 1964; "Slattery's People: Question-Is Laura the Name of the Game?," CBS, 1964; "Lou Grant: Hometown," CBS, 1981;

"Quincy: The Flight of the Nightingale," NBC, 1982; "Scarecrow and Mrs. King: Photo Finish," CBS, 1986; "St. Elsewhere: Handoff," NBC, 1987; "thirtysomething: New Parents," ABC, 1989.
TV MOVIES AND MINISERIES: "The Day After," ABC, 1983; "Kate's Secret," NBC, 1986; "Side by Side," CBS, 1988; "Do You Know the Muffin Man?," CBS, 1989.

JOHNSON, JAY

b. Abernathy, TX. Ventriloquist who played Chuck Campbell on "Soap."
AS A REGULAR: "Soap," ABC, 1977-81; "Celebrity Charades," SYN, 1979; "So You Think You've Got Troubles?," SYN, 1982-83.
AND: "Mrs. Columbo: A Game for Puppets," NBC, 1979; "Gimme a Break: Your Prisoner Is Dead," NBC, 1981; "Duet: It's My Party," FOX, 1988; "Something Is Out There: A Message From Mr. Cool," NBC, 1988.

JOHNSON, RUSSELL

b. Ashley, PA, 1924. Actor who played professor Roy Hinkley on "Gilligan's Island."
AS A REGULAR: "Black Saddle," NBC, 1959; ABC, 1959-60; "The Great Adventure," CBS, 1964; "Gilligan's Island," CBS, 1964-67; "Owen Marshall, Counselor at Law," ABC, 1971-74.
AND: "You Are There: Mr. Christian Seizes the Bounty," CBS, 1956; "The Silent Service: The Tirante Plays a Hunch," SYN, 1957; "Wagon Train: The Cliff Grundy Story," NBC, 1957; "Steve Canyon: Operation Heartbeat," ABC, 1959; "Lawman: The Encounter," ABC, 1959; "The Twilight Zone: Execution," CBS, 1960; "The du Pont Show with June Allyson: Intermission," CBS, 1960; "Mr. Garlund: Death of an Enemy," CBS, 1960; "The du Pont Show with June Allyson: The Desperate Challenge," CBS, 1960; "Thriller: The Hungry Glass," NBC, 1961; "The Twilight Zone: Back There," CBS, 1961; "Death Valley Days: Dead Man's Tale," SYN, 1961; "Laramie: Killer Odds," NBC, 1961; "Robert Taylor's Detectives: The Queen of Craven Point," NBC, 1961; "Adventures in Paradise: Survival," ABC, 1961; "Laramie: The Perfect Gift," NBC, 1962; "Laramie: The Dynamiters," NBC, 1962; "The Real McCoys: Allergies Anonymous," ABC, 1962; "The Wide Country: Who Killed Eddie Gannon?," NBC, 1962; "Ben Casey: Go Not Gently Into the Night," ABC, 1962; "Wagon Train: The Shiloh Degnan Story," ABC, 1962; "Laramie: Double Eagles," NBC, 1962; "G.E. True: Mile-Long Shot to Kill," CBS, 1962; "It's a Man's World: Night Beat of the Tom-Tom," NBC, 1962; "Hawaiian Eye: Go for Baroque," ABC, 1963; "The Farmer's Daughter: The Stand-In," ABC, 1963; "The

Greatest Show on Earth: Man in a Hole," ABC, 1964; "The Outer Limits: Specimen Unknown," ABC, 1964; "The Invaders: The Trial," ABC, 1967; "The FBI: The Dynasty," ABC, 1968; "The Big Valley: The Good Thieves," ABC, 1968; "The FBI: Caesar's Wife," ABC, 1969; "Gunsmoke: The Long Night," CBS, 1969; "That Girl: Fly by Night," ABC, 1970; "The FBI: The Quest," ABC, 1970; "Marcus Welby, M.D.: I Can Hardly Tell You Apart," ABC, 1972; "McMillan: Coffee, Tea or Cyanide?," NBC, 1977; "Lou Grant: Babies," CBS, 1978; "Bosom Buddies: Amy's Career," ABC, 1980.

TV MOVIES AND MINISERIES: "The Movie Murderer," NBC, 1970; "Vanished," NBC, 1971; "Beg, Borrow ... or Steal," CBS, 1973; "Aloha Means Goodbye," CBS, 1974; "The Bastard," SYN, 1978; "Rescue From Gilligan's Island," NBC, 1978; "The Castaways on Gilligan's Island," NBC, 1979; "The Harlem Globetrotters on Gilligan's Island," NBC, 1981.

JOHNSON, VAN

b. *Newport, RI, August 20, 1916.* Leading man of forties movies who's done TV variety, drama and comedy.

AS A GUEST: "I Love Lucy: The Dancing Star," CBS, 1955; "The Loretta Young Show: The Last Spring," NBC, 1955; "The Loretta Young Show: Katy," NBC, 1955; "Shower of Stars," CBS, 1957; "The Van Johnson Show," NBC, 1957; "Pied Piper of Hamelin," NBC, 1957; "The Jack Benny Program: Jack's Life Story," CBS, 1957; "Shower of Stars: Jack Benny's 40th Birthday Celebration," CBS, 1958; "The Frank Sinatra Show," ABC, 1958; "Shower of Stars," CBS, 1958; "Dinah Shore Chevy Show," NBC, 1958; "Dinah Shore Chevy Show," NBC, 1959; "Dick Powell's Zane Grey Theatre: Deadfall," CBS, 1959; "G.E. Theatre: At Your Service," CBS, 1960; "I've Got a Secret," CBS, 1960; "The Ann Sothern Show: Loving Arms," CBS, 1960; "Candid Camera," CBS, 1961; "The Ed Sullivan Show," CBS, 1964; "Ben Casey: A Man, a Maid and a Marionette," ABC, 1965; "Batman: The Minstrel's Shakedown/Barbecued Batman," ABC, 1966; "The Danny Thomas Hour: Is Charlie Coming?," NBC, 1967; "The Dean Martin Show," NBC, 1967; "Hollywood Squares," NBC, 1968; "Personality," NBC, 1968; "The Red Skelton Hour," CBS, 1968; "The Dean Martin Show," NBC, 1968; "The Name of the Game: High on a Rainbow," NBC, 1968; "Here's Lucy: Guess Who Owes Lucy $23.50," CBS, 1968; "The Name of the Game: The Brass Ring," NBC, 1970; "The Doris Day Show: Cousin Charlie," CBS, 1970; "The Men From Shiloh: The Angus Killer," NBC, 1971; "The Doris Day Show: The

Albatross," CBS, 1971; "Nanny and the Professor: Seperate Rooms," ABC, 1971; "Love, American Style: Love and the House Bachelor," ABC, 1971; "Wheeler and Murdoch," ABC, 1972; "Man in the Middle," CBS, 1972; "Maude: Flashback," CBS, 1972; "McCloud: This Must Be the Alamo," NBC, 1974; "McMillan and Wife: Downshift to Danger," NBC, 1974; "The Love Boat: Her Own Two Feet," ABC, 1978; "Over Easy," PBS, 1981; "The Love Boat: The Love Boat Musical," ABC, 1982; "Glitter: Premiere," ABC, 1984; "Murder, She Wrote: Hit, Run and Homicide," CBS, 1984; "Murder, She Wrote: Menace, Anyone?," CBS, 1986.

TV MOVIES AND MINISERIES: "San Francisco International," NBC, 1970; "Call Her Mom," ABC, 1972; "The Girl on the Late, Late Show," NBC, 1974; "Rich Man, Poor Man," ABC, 1976; "Black Beauty," NBC, 1978; "The Kidnapping of the President," NBC, 1980.

JONES, ALLAN

b. *Old Forge, PA, October 14, 1908.* Movie singer and father of Jack Jones.

AS A GUEST: "The Spike Jones Show," CBS, 1957; "The Love Boat: That's My Dad," ABC, 1980.

JONES, ANISSA

b. *1958; d. 1976.* Former child actress who played Buffy on "Family Affair"; she died of a drug overdose.

AS A REGULAR: "Family Affair," ABC, 1966-71.

AND: "The Mike Douglas Show," SYN, 1970; "To Rome with Love: Roman Affair," CBS, 1970.

JONES, CAROLYN

b. *Carolyn Sue Jones, Amarillo, TX, April 28, 1929; d. 1983.* Talented actress who appeared extensively on television; best known as Morticia Addams and, later, Myrna Clegg on "Capitol."

AS A REGULAR: "The Addams Family," ABC, 1964-66; "Capitol," CBS, 1982-83.

AND: "City Detective: Best Friend," SYN, 1953; "Pepsi Cola Playhouse: Account Closed," ABC, 1954; "Pepsi Cola Playhouse: The Silence," ABC, 1954; "Dragnet: The Big Frame," NBC, 1954; "Pepsi Cola Playhouse: Double in Danger," ABC, 1954; "Treasury Men in Action: The Case of the Careless Murder," ABC, 1955; "Studio 57: Diagnosis of a Selfish Lady," SYN, 1955; "Fireside Theatre: The Key," NBC, 1955; "Alfred Hitchcock Presents: The Cheney Vase," CBS, 1955; "Four Star Playhouse: The Answer," CBS, 1955; "The 20th Century-Fox Hour: The Heffernan Family," CBS, 1956; "The Jane Wyman Show: Little Black Lie," NBC, 1957; "G.E. Theatre: The Man Who Inherited Everything," CBS, 1957; "Climax!: Disappear-

ance of Amanda Hale," CBS, 1957; "Wagon Train: The John Cameron Story," NBC, 1957; "Schlitz Playhouse of Stars: High Barrier," CBS, 1957; "Playhouse 90: The Last Man," CBS, 1958; "State Trooper: The Paperhanger of Pioche," SYN, 1958; "The David Niven Show: Portrait," NBC, 1959; "This Is Your Life (Frank Capra)," NBC, 1959; "This Is Your Life," NBC, 1959; "Dick Powell's Zane Grey Theatre: Picture of Sal," CBS, 1960; "The Dick Powell Show: Who Killed Julie Greer?," NBC, 1961; "Wagon Train: The Jenna Douglas Story," NBC, 1961; "The Dick Powell Show: Goodbye, Hannah," NBC, 1961; "Art Linkletter's House Party," CBS, 1961; "Frontier Circus: Stopover in Paradise," CBS, 1962; "Burke's Law: Who Killed Sweet Betsy?," ABC, 1963; "Object Is," ABC, 1964; "Password," CBS, 1964; "Burke's Law: Who Killed Madison Cooper?," ABC, 1964; "The du Pont Show: Jeremy Rabbitt, the Secret Avenger," NBC, 1964; "ABC Nightlife," ABC, 1965; "Shindig," ABC, 1965; "Batman: Marsha, Queen of Diamonds/ Marsha's Scheme with Diamonds," ABC, 1966; "Batman: Penguin is a Girl's Best Friend/Penguin Sets a Trend/Penguin's Disastrous End," ABC, 1967; "Rango: What's a Nice Girl Like You Doing Holding Up a Place Like This?," ABC, 1967; "The Danny Thomas Hour: Fame is a Four-Letter Word," NBC, 1967; "You Don't Say," NBC, 1968; "Art Linkletter's House Party," CBS, 1968; "It Takes Two," NBC, 1969; "Bracken's World: King David," NBC, 1969; "The Della Reese Show," SYN, 1969; "Love, American Style: Love and the Geisha," ABC, 1969; "The Name of the Game: Why I Blew Up Dakota," NBC, 1970; "The Movie Game," SYN, 1970; "The Men From Shiloh: The Legacy of Spencer Flats," NBC, 1971; "Ghost Story: The Summer Horse," NBC, 1972; "The New Adventures of Perry Mason: The Case of the Frenzied Feminist," CBS, 1973; "Ironside: Raise the Devil," NBC, 1974; "Ellery Queen: The Hard Headed Huckster," NBC, 1976; "Wonder Woman: The Feminine Mystique," ABC, 1976; "The Love Boat: Cindy," ABC, 1979; "Quincy: Dear Mummy," NBC, 1981.
TV MOVIES AND MINISERIES: "Little Ladies of the Night," ABC, 1977; "Roots," ABC, 1977; "Midnight Lace," NBC, 1981.

JONES, CHARLIE
b. Fort Smith, AR, November 9, 1930.
AS A REGULAR: "Almost Anything Goes," ABC, 1975-76.
AND: "McCloud: Fifth Man in a String Quartet," NBC, 1972.

JONES, CHRISTOPHER
b. Jackson, TN, August 18, 1941. Brooding actor who was pegged to be a big star as Jesse James.
AS A REGULAR: "The Legend of Jesse James," ABC, 1965-66; "Rituals," SYN, 1984-85.
AND: "The Man From UNCLE: The Test Tube Affair," NBC, 1967.

JONES, DAVID
b. England, December 30, 1946. Actor, singer and dancer who was young America's darling as one of "The Monkees."
AS A REGULAR: "The Monkees," NBC, 1966-68.
AND: "The Ed Sullivan Show," CBS, 1964; "The Farmer's Daughter: Moe Hill and the Mountains," ABC, 1966; "Rowan & Martin's Laugh-In," NBC, 1969; "This Is Tom Jones," ABC, 1969; "The Monkees Special," NBC, 1969; "Mannix: Missing: Sun and Sky," CBS, 1969; "Love, American Style: Love and the Elopement," ABC, 1970; "Make Room for Granddaddy: The Teen Idol," ABC, 1970; "The Brady Bunch: Getting Davy Jones," ABC, 1972; "Love, American Style: Love and the Model Apartment," ABC, 1973; "My Two Dads: Fallen Idol," NBC, 1989.
TV MOVIES AND MINISERIES: "Hunter," CBS, 1973.
* Jones appearaned on "The Ed Sullivan Show" February 9, 1964, along with the Beatles. Jones was in the cast of "Oliver!" at the time, doing a number on the show.

JONES, DEAN
b. Morgan County, AL, January 25, 1935. Clean-cut leading man of Walt Disney films and a couple of antiseptic TV shows.
AS A REGULAR: "Ensign O'Toole," NBC, 1962-63; "What's It All About, World?," ABC, 1969; "The Chicago Teddy Bears," CBS, 1971; "Herbie, the Love Bug," CBS, 1982.
AND: "The Steve Allen Show," NBC, 1957; "Dinah Shore Chevy Show," NBC, 1957; "The Chevy Show," NBC, 1958; "Dick Powell's Zane Grey Theatre: The Sunday Man," CBS, 1960; "The Ed Sullivan Show," CBS, 1960; "The Aquanauts: The Frameup Adventure," CBS, 1960; "The Outlaws: Beat the Drum Slowly," NBC, 1960; "Stagecoach West: Red Sand," ABC, 1960; "The Dick Powell Show: Who Killed Julie Greer?," NBC, 1961; "Bonanza: The Friendship," NBC, 1961; "Tales of Wells Fargo: A Killing in Calico," NBC, 1961; "Target: The Corruptors: Play It Blue," ABC, 1962; "Wagon Train: The Lt. Burton Story," NBC, 1962; "Burke's Law: Who Killed Eleanora Davis?," ABC, 1963; "Kraft Suspense Theatre: The Rise and Fall of Eddie Carew," NBC, 1965; "Operation: Entertainment," ABC, 1968; "Art Linkletter's House Party," CBS, 1968; "Medical Center: The Spectre," CBS, 1974; "The Love Boat: Julie and the Producer," ABC, 1984; "Murder, She Wrote: It's a Dogs Life," CBS, 1984; "Murder, She Wrote: Harbinger of Death," CBS, 1988.
TV MOVIES AND MINISERIES: "The Great Man's

Whiskers," NBC, 1973; "Guess Who's Sleeping in My Bed?," ABC, 1973; "The Long Days of Summer," ABC, 1980.

JONES, DICK
b. Snyder, TX, February 25, 1927. Cowboy actor.
AS A REGULAR: "Range Rider," SYN, 1951; "Buffalo Bill Jr.," SYN, 1955.
AND: "Navy Log: The Leave," CBS, 1956; "This Is the Answer: The Tell-Tale Arm," SYN, 1959; "The Blue Angels: Fire Fight," SYN, 1961.

JONES, HENRY
b. Philadelphia, PA, August 1, 1912. TV and film actor who played Judge Jonathan Dexter, father-in-law of "Phyllis" (Cloris Leachman).
AS A REGULAR: "Channing," ABC, 1963-64; "The Girl with Something Extra," NBC, 1973-74; "Phyllis," CBS, 1975-77; "Kate Loves a Mystery," NBC, 1979; "Gun Shy," CBS, 1983; "Code Name: Foxfire," NBC, 1985; "Falcon Crest," CBS, 1985-86; "I Married Dora," ABC, 1987-88.
AND: "Actors Studio: The Timid Guy," CBS, 1950; "Danger: Death Gambles," CBS, 1951; "Schlitz Playhouse of Stars: P.G.," CBS, 1952; "Schlitz Playhouse of Stars: Apple of His Eye," CBS, 1952; "The Web: The Lake," CBS, 1953; "You Are There: The Hanging of Captain Kidd," CBS, 1954; "Center Stage: Lucky Louie," ABC, 1954; "Kraft Television Theatre: The Failure," NBC, 1955; "Studio One: The Genie of Sutton Place," CBS, 1956; "Climax!: Fury at Dawn," CBS, 1956; "Alfred Hitchcock Presents: De Mortuis," CBS, 1956; "The Jane Wyman Show: Where There's Life," NBC, 1956; "Alfred Hitchcock Presents: Nightmare in 4-D," CBS, 1957; "Robert Montgomery Presents: His Name Was Death," NBC, 1957; "Alfred Hitchcock Presents: The West Warlock Time Capsule," CBS, 1957; "Playhouse 90: The Sounds of Eden," CBS, 1959; "Startime: The Wicked Scheme of Jebal Deeks," NBC, 1959; "Alfred Hitchcock Presents: The Blessington Method," CBS, 1959; "Playhouse 90: The Silver Whistle," CBS, 1959; "The Untouchables: Portrait of a Thief," ABC, 1960; "Goodyear Theatre: Author at Work," NBC, 1960; "The Twilight Zone: Mr. Bevis," CBS, 1960; "The Loretta Young Show: The Misfit," NBC, 1960; "Checkmate: The Cyanide Touch," CBS, 1960; "Adventures in Paradise: Away From It All," ABC, 1960; "Best of the Post: The Vision of Henry Whipple," SYN, 1960; "The Real McCoys: Back to West Virginny," CBS, 1961; "The Real McCoys: September Song," ABC, 1961; "The Real McCoys: Fly Away Home," ABC, 1961; "Follow the Sun: The Woman Who Never Was," ABC, 1961; "Thriller: The Weird Taylor," NBC, 1961; "Checkmate:

Juan Moreno's Body," CBS, 1961; "The New Breed: Sweet Bloom of Death," ABC, 1961; "The Investigators: The Dead End Men," CBS, 1961; "Frontier Circus: The Courtship," CBS, 1962; "Wagon Train: The Terry Morrell Story," NBC, 1962; "The du Pont Show: Something to Hide," NBC, 1963; "Kraft Suspense Theatre: The Jack Is High," NBC, 1964; "The Man From UNCLE: The Neptune Affair," NBC, 1964; "Bonanza: A Knight to Remember," NBC, 1964; "Honey West: The Abominable Snowman," ABC, 1965; "Amos Burke, Secret Agent: Peace, It's a Gasser," ABC, 1965; "A Man Called Shenandoah: Town on Fire," ABC, 1965; "Bewitched: The Leprechaun," ABC, 1966; "The Tammy Grimes Show: Pilot," ABC, 1966; "Voyage to the Bottom of the Sea: Night of Terror," ABC, 1966; "Lost in Space: The Curse of Cousin Smith," CBS, 1966; "The Big Valley: Court Martial," ABC, 1967; "The Man From UNCLE: The Caps and Gowns Affair," NBC, 1967; "The Mod Squad: Twinkle, Twinkle Little Starlet," ABC, 1968; "The Mod Squad: My, What a Pretty Bus," ABC, 1968; "The Guns of Will Sonnett: Chapter and Verse," ABC, 1968; "The Name of the Game: Love-In at Ground Zero," NBC, 1969; "Nanny and the Professor: I Think That I Shall Never See a Tree," ABC, 1970; "The Mary Tyler Moore Show: Howard's Girl," CBS, 1971; "Circle of Fear: Doorway to Death," NBC, 1973; "Owen Marshall, Counselor at Law: The Desertion of Keith Ryder," ABC, 1974; "Kolchak, the Night Stalker: The Werewolf," ABC, 1974; "Wide World of Mystery: Please Call It Murder," ABC, 1975; "Barney Miller: The Prisoner," ABC, 1978; "Salvage I: Pilot," ABC, 1979; "Here's Boomer: George and Emma," NBC, 1980; "B.J. and the Bear: For Adults Only," NBC, 1981; "Quincy: The Golden Hour," NBC, 1981; "McClain's Law: Takeover," NBC, 1982; "The Love Boat: Familar Faces," ABC, 1982; "Cagney & Lacey: Entrapment," CBS, 1985; "Scarecrow and Mrs. King: Mission of Gold," CBS, 1987; "Murder, She Wrote: Mr. Penroy's Vacation," CBS, 1988.
TV MOVIES AND MINISERIES: "Something for a Lonely Man," NBC, 1968; "The Movie Murderer," NBC, 1970; "Love, Hate, Love," ABC, 1971; "The Daughters of Joshua Cabe," ABC, 1972; "The Letters," ABC, 1973; "Letters From Three Lovers," ABC, 1973; "Who Is the Black Dahlia?," NBC, 1975; "Code Name: Foxfire," NBC, 1985.

JONES, JACK
b. Los Angeles, CA, January 14, 1938. Singer.
AS A GUEST: "The Big Record," CBS, 1957; "The Steve Allen Show," NBC, 1958; "American Bandstand," ABC, 1958; "Art Linkletter's House Party," CBS, 1958; "The Spike Jones Show," CBS, 1960; "Dinah Shore Chevy Show," NBC, 1961; "The Spike Jones Show,"

CBS, 1961; "The New Steve Allen Show," ABC, 1961; "Highways of Melody," NBC, 1961; "American Bandstand," ABC, 1962; "The Lively Ones," NBC, 1962; "The Jerry Lewis Show," ABC, 1963; "The Judy Garland Show," CBS, 1963; "Bell Telephone Hour," NBC, 1964; "Password," CBS, 1964; "The Judy Garland Show," CBS, 1964; "Object Is," ABC, 1964; "The Joey Bishop Show: Joey, Jack Jones and the Genie," NBC, 1964; "Hollywood Palace," ABC, 1964; "The Ed Sullivan Show," CBS, 1964; "The Jack Benny Program," NBC, 1965; "Hullabaloo," NBC, 1965; "The Jimmy Dean Show," ABC, 1965; "American Bandstand," ABC, 1965; "Bob Hope Special," NBC, 1965; "The Dean Martin Show," NBC, 1965; "Hollywood Palace," ABC, 1965; "What's My Line?," CBS, 1965; "Hollywood Palace," ABC, 1966; "Guys 'n Geishas," NBC, 1967; "Hollywood Palace," ABC, 1968; "The Red Skelton Hour," CBS, 1968; "Kraft Music Hall," NBC, 1969; "The Carol Burnett Show," CBS, 1970; "The Tonight Show Starring Johnny Carson," NBC, 1975; "Dinah!," SYN, 1976; "The Peter Marshall Variety Show," SYN, 1977; "McMillan: Coffee, Tea or Cyanide?," NBC, 1977; "Police Woman: Shark," NBC, 1977; "The Love Boat: That's My Dad," ABC, 1980.

JONES, JAMES EARL
b. Arkabutla, MS, January 17, 1931. Actor with a powerful voice and a presence sometimes too overwhelming for TV.
AS A REGULAR: "As the World Turns," CBS, 1966; "The Guiding Light," CBS, 1967; "Paris," CBS, 1979-80; "Me and Mom," ABC, 1985; "Gabriel's Fire," ABC, 1990- .
AND: "Lamp Unto My Feet: Don't Call Us," CBS, 1962; "Look Up and Live: Room for Death," CBS, 1963; "East Side/West Side: Who Do You Kill?," CBS, 1963; "Channing: Freedom Is a Lovesome Thing, God Wot!" ABC, 1964; "The Defenders: The Non-Violent," CBS, 1965; "Dr. Kildare: A Cry From the States/Adrift in a Sea of Confusion/Gratitude Won't Pay the Bills," NBC, 1966; "Tarzan: To Steal the Rising Sun," NBC, 1967; "Tarzan: The Convert," NBC, 1968; "NET Playhouse: Trumpets of the Lord," NET, 1968; "NYPD: Candy Man," ABC, 1969; "Sesame Street," NET, 1970; "Theatre in America: King Lear," PBS, 1974; "The Cay," NBC, 1974; "Happy Endings: Big Joe and Kansas," ABC, 1975; "Vegetable Soup," NBC, 1975; "Highway to Heaven: A Song of Songs," NBC, 1986; "L.A. Law: Victor Victorious," NBC, 1989; "The Pool Hall," A&E, 1989.
TV MOVIES AND MINISERIES: "The UFO Incident," NBC, 1975; "The Greatest Thing That Almost Happened," CBS, 1977; "Jesus of Nazareth," NBC, 1977; "Roots: The Next Generations,"

ABC, 1979; "The Golden Moment: An Olympic Love Story," NBC, 1980; "The Atlanta Child Murders," CBS, 1985.

JONES, L.Q.
b. Beaumont, TX, 1936. Cowboy actor; he played Belden on "The Virginian."
AS A REGULAR: "Warner Bros. Presents Cheyenne," ABC, 1955-56; "The Virginian," NBC, 1963-67.
AND: "Laramie: Dark Verdict," NBC, 1959; "Buick Electra Playhouse: The Gambler, The Nun and The Radio," CBS, 1960; "The Rebel: The Earl of Durango," ABC, 1960; "Klondike: River of Gold," NBC, 1960; "Klondike: Saints and Stickups," NBC, 1960; "Laramie: The Dark Trail," NBC, 1960; "Klondike: The Unexpected Candidate," NBC, 1960; "The Rebel: Explosion," ABC, 1960; "Laramie: Cactus Lady," NBC, 1961; "The Life and Legend of Wyatt Earp: Casey and the Clowns," ABC, 1961; "Wagon Train: The Christopher Hale Story," NBC, 1961; "Lassie: The Pigeon," CBS, 1961; "The Americans: The Coward," NBC, 1961; "Have Gun, Will Travel: Lazarus," CBS, 1962; "Laramie: The Replacement," NBC, 1962; "Laramie: Shadow of the Past," NBC, 1962; "Have Gun, Will Travel: The Waiting Room," CBS, 1962; "Ben Casey: The Firemen Who Raised Rabbits," ABC, 1962; "Have Gun, Will Travel: The Debutante," CBS, 1963; "Wagon Train: Charlie Wooster, Outlaw," ABC, 1963; "Route 66: ... Shall Forfeit His Dog and Ten Shillings to the King," CBS, 1963; "Rawhide: The Race," CBS, 1964; "My Favorite Martian: That Time Machine Is Waking Up That Old Gang of Mine," CBS, 1965; "Rawhide: Six Weeks to Bent Fork," CBS, 1965; "A Man Called Shenandoah: Rope's End," ABC, 1966; "The Big Valley: Fallen Hawk," ABC, 1966; "The FBI: The Gold Card," ABC, 1967; "The Big Valley: Bounty on a Barkley," ABC, 1968; "Hawaii Five-O: King of the Hill," CBS, 1968; "Gunsmoke: The Good Samaritans," CBS, 1969; "Lancer: Blind Man's Bluff," CBS, 1969; "Gunsmoke: Albert," CBS, 1970; "Gunsmoke: The Gun," CBS, 1970; "The FBI: Dynasty of Hate," ABC, 1971; "Gunsmoke: Tara," CBS, 1972; "Kung Fu: An Eye for an Eye," ABC, 1973; "Kung Fu: The Praying Mantis Kills," ABC, 1973; "Alias Smith and Jones: McGuffin," ABC, 1973; "The Magician: Ripoff," NBC, 1974; "Ironside: Riddle at 24,000," NBC, 1974; "Matt Helm: The Deadly Breed," ABC, 1975; "McCloud: The Moscow Connection," NBC, 1977; "Columbo: The Conspirators," NBC, 1978; "Charlie's Angels: An Angel's Trail," ABC, 1980; "Riker: Pilot," CBS, 1981; "Walking Tall: The Hit Man," NBC, 1981; "The Yellow Rose: A Question of Love," NBC, 1983; "The A-Team: Cowboy George," NBC, 1986.
TV MOVIES AND MINISERIES: "The Bravos," ABC,

1972; "Fireball Forward," ABC, 1972; "Mrs. Sundance," ABC, 1974; "Manhunter," CBS, 1974; "The Strange and Deadly Occurrence," NBC, 1974; "Attack on Terror: The FBI Versus the Ku Klux Klan," CBS, 1975; "Banjo Hackett," NBC, 1976; "Standing Tall," NBC, 1978.

GRANDPA JONES
b. Louis M. Jones, Niagra, KY, October 20, 1913.
AS A REGULAR: "Hee Haw," CBS, 1969-71; SYN, 1971-87.
AND: "Country Music Jubilee," ABC, 1958; "Five Star Jubilee," NBC, 1961; "The Jimmy Dean Show," ABC, 1964; "The Steve Lawrence Show," CBS, 1965; "The Grand Ole Opry at 50," ABC, 1975.

JONES, SHIRLEY
b. Smithtown, PA, March 31, 1934. Oscar-winning actress and musical-comedy star who played Mom Partridge to a pop-singing brood.
AS A REGULAR: "The Partridge Family," ABC, 1970-74; "Shirley," NBC, 1979-80.
AND: "Fireside Theatre: Hired Girl," NBC, 1951; "Gruen Guild Theatre: For Life," SYN, 1952; "Ford Star Jubilee: You're the Top," CBS, 1956; "Playhouse 90: The Big Slide," CBS, 1956; "Lux Video Theatre: Movie Songs," NBC, 1956; "Lux Video Theatre: Dark Victory," NBC, 1957; "U.S. Steel Hour: Shadow of Evil," CBS, 1957; "Pat Boone Chevy Showroom," ABC, 1957; "The Frank Sinatra Show," ABC, 1958; "Pat Boone Chevy Showroom," ABC, 1958; "Du Pont Show of the Month: The Red Mill," CBS, 1958; "The Voice of Firestone: Music From Hollywood," ABC, 1958; "The Eddie Fisher Show," NBC, 1959; "The Danny Thomas Show: Shirley Jones Makes Good," CBS, 1959; "The Garry Moore Show," CBS, 1959; "Bell Telephone Hour: Our Musical Ambassadors," NBC, 1960; "U.S. Steel Hour: Step on the Gas," CBS, 1960; "Bell Telephone Hour: And There Shall Be Music," NBC, 1961; "Dinah Shore Chevy Show," NBC, 1961; "Hollywood Melody," NBC, 1962; "Bell Telephone Hour: Gala Performance," NBC, 1962; "Bell Telephone Hour," NBC, 1964; "Bob Hope Chrysler Theatre: The Shattered Glass," NBC, 1964; "Perry Como Special," NBC, 1965; "The Danny Kaye Show," CBS, 1965; "The Smothers Brothers Comedy Hour," CBS, 1967; "Out of the Blue," CBS, 1968; "The Mike Douglas Show," SYN, 1969; "Alan King Special," NBC, 1969; "This Is Tom Jones," ABC, 1969; "The Name of the Game: The Third Choice," NBC, 1969; "This Is Your Life," SYN, 1971; "Hollywood Squares," NBC, 1974; "Dinah!," SYN, 1975; "McMillan: Philip's Game," NBC, 1977; "The Love Boat: The Dean and the Flunkee," ABC, 1983; "Hotel:

Premiere," ABC, 1983; "Murder, She Wrote: The Body Politic," CBS, 1988.
TV MOVIES AND MINISERIES: "Silent Night, Lonely Night," NBC, 1969; "But I Don't Want to Get Married!," ABC, 1970; "The Girls of Huntington House," ABC, 1973; "The Family Nobody Wanted," ABC, 1975; "Winner Take All," NBC, 1975; "The Lives of Jenny Dolan," NBC, 1975; "Yesterday's Child," NBC, 1977; "Who'll Save Our Children?," CBS, 1978; "Evening in Byzantium," SYN, 1978; "The Children of An Lac," CBS, 1980; "Inmates: A Love Story," ABC, 1981.

JONES, SPIKE
b. Long Beach, CA, December 14, 1911; d. 1965. Bandleader and comedian who performed parody songs and who understood the value of a whoopie-cushion rhythm section.
AS A REGULAR: "The Spike Jones Show," NBC, 1951; 1954; CBS, 1957; 1960; 1961; "Club Oasis," NBC, 1958.
AND: "The Colgate Comedy Hour," NBC, 1951; "The Jack Benny Program," CBS, 1956; "The Ford Show," NBC, 1956; "The Perry Como Show," NBC, 1956; "The Frank Sinatra Show," ABC, 1958; "The Chevy Show," NBC, 1959; "This Is Your Life (Billy Barty)," NBC, 1960; "Person to Person," CBS, 1960; "The Ed Sullivan Show," CBS, 1961; "Person to Person," CBS, 1961; "Burke's Law: Who Killed Victor Barrows?," ABC, 1964.

JONES, STAN
b. Douglas, AZ, June 5, 1914; d. 1963.
AS A REGULAR: "Sheriff of Cochise (U.S. Marshal)," SYN, 1956-58.

JONES, TOM
b. Thomas Jones Woodward, Pontypridd, Wales, June 7, 1940. Singer.
AS A REGULAR: "This Is Tom Jones," ABC, 1969-71.
AND: "The Ed Sullivan Show," CBS, 1965; "The Red Skelton Hour," CBS, 1968; "The Music Scene," ABC, 1969; "Bob Hope Special," NBC, 1969; "Late Night with David Letterman," NBC, 1989.
TV MOVIES AND MINISERIES: "Pleasure Cove," NBC, 1979.

JORDAN, BOBBI
b. Hardinsburg, KY.
AS A REGULAR: "The Rounders," ABC, 1966-67; "Blondie," CBS, 1968-69; "Joe and Sons," CBS, 1975-76; "General Hospital," ABC, 1976-77; "Turnabout," NBC, 1979.
AND: "The Man From UNCLE: The Hula Doll Affair," NBC, 1967; "The FBI: Town of Terror," ABC, 1973; "Quincy: The Eye of the Needle,"

NBC, 1978; "Quincy: Dear Mummy," NBC, 1981; "Highway to Heaven: Man Best Friend," NBC, 1986.

TV MOVIES AND MINISERIES: "The Barbary Coast," ABC, 1975; "Miracle at Beekman's Place," NBC, 1988.

JORDAN, RICHARD

b. New York City, July 19, 1938. Actor who played Kennedy-like patriarch Joseph Armagh in "Captains and the Kings."

AS A REGULAR: "The Equalizer," CBS, 1987-88.
AND: "Naked City: And by the Sweat of Thy Brow," ABC, 1962; "Empire: Long Past, Long Remembered," NBC, 1962; "The Wide Country: Our Ernie Kills People," NBC, 1962; "Ben Casey: Between Summer and Winter, the Glorious Season," ABC, 1962; "Empire: End of an Image," NBC, 1963; "The Bold Ones: Justice Is a Sometime Thing," NBC, 1972; "The FBI: The Detonator," ABC, 1973; "Banacek: If Max Is So Smart, Why Doesn't He Tell Us Where He Is?," NBC, 1973; "Kojak: Dark Sunday," CBS, 1973; "Dinah!," SYN, 1976.

TV MOVIES AND MINISERIES: "Best Sellers: Captains and the Kings," NBC, 1976; "The Defection of Simas Kudirka," CBS, 1978; "Les Miserables," CBS, 1978; "The Bunker," CBS, 1981; "Washington Mistress," CBS, 1982; "The Murder of Mary Phagan," NBC, 1988; "Manhunt: Search for the Night Stalker," NBC, 1989.

JORDAN, WILLIAM

b. Milan, IN.

AS A REGULAR: "Project UFO," NBC, 1978; "Beyond Westworld," CBS, 1980.
AND: "Daktari: The Outsider," CBS, 1968; "Mannix: Lost Sunday," CBS, 1973; "Griff: Premiere," ABC, 1973; "The Magician: Lady in a Trap," NBC, 1973; "The New Adventures of Perry Mason: The Case of the Violent Valley," CBS, 1974; "The Streets of San Francisco: Winterkill," ABC, 1974; "The Rockford Files: Exit Prentiss Carr," NBC, 1974; "Lou Grant: Obituary," CBS, 1981; "Heartbeat: Prison," ABC, 1989; "Paradise: Vengeance," CBS, 1989.

TV MOVIES AND MINISERIES: "The Disappearance of Aimee," NBC, 1976; "The Trial of Lee Harvey Oswald," ABC, 1977; "King," NBC, 1978; "ABC Theatre: Friendly Fire," ABC, 1979.

JORY, VICTOR

b. Dawson City, Yukon Territory, November 28, 1902; d. 1982. Craggy-faced character actor, often in roles as shysters or rugged figures of authority.

AS A REGULAR: "Warner Bros. Presents Kings Row," ABC, 1955-56; "Manhunt," SYN, 1959-61.

AND: "Tele-Theatre: The Wine of Ore Palo," NBC, 1950; "Philco TV Playhouse: The Second Oldest Profession," NBC, 1950; "Sure as Fate: Child's Play," ABC, 1950; "Broadway Television Theatre: Angel Street," SYN, 1952; "Tales of Tomorrow: World of War," ABC, 1952; "Studio One: Captain-General of the Armies," CBS, 1952; "G.E. Theatre: Exit for Margo," CBS, 1954; "Schlitz Playhouse of Stars: Weapon of Courage," CBS, 1954; "Schlitz Playhouse of Stars: The Man Who Escaped From Devil's Island," CBS, 1954; "Kraft Television Theatre: A Connecticut Yankee in King Arthur's Court," ABC, 1954; "Climax!: The Box of Chocolates," CBS, 1955; "Climax!: The Secret of River Lane," CBS, 1956; "Omnibus: One Nation," CBS, 1956; "TV Reader's Digest: The Woman Who Changed Her Mind," ABC, 1956; "Kraft Television Theatre: Profile in Courage," NBC, 1956; "TV Reader's Digest: The Great Banknote Swindle," ABC, 1956; "Kraft Television Theatre: Prairie Night," NBC, 1956; "Science Fiction Theatre: The Flicker," SYN, 1956; "Matinee Theatre: Starmaster," NBC, 1956; "Telephone Time: I Am Not Alone," CBS, 1956; "Alcoa Hour: Key Largo," NBC, 1956; "Matinee Theatre: Savrola," NBC, 1956; "Playhouse 90: Mr. and Mrs. McAdam," CBS, 1957; "Omnibus: The Trial of Captain Kidd," ABC, 1957; "Crossroads: Lone Star Preacher," ABC, 1957; "The 20th Century-Fox Hour: The Still Trumpet," CBS, 1957; "Ford Theatre: Moment of Decision," ABC, 1957; "Kraft Television Theatre: Flesh and Blood," NBC, 1957; "Armstrong Circle Theatre: A Picture of Christmas," CBS, 1958; "U.S. Steel Hour: Night of Betrayal," CBS, 1959; "Wanted Dead or Alive: The Legend," CBS, 1959; "Playhouse 90: Diary of a Nurse," CBS, 1959; "Rawhide: Incident of the Dry Drive," CBS, 1959; "87th Precinct: Dawns an Evil Day," NBC, 1962; "Rawhide: Gold Fever," CBS, 1962; "The Virginian: Dark Challenge," NBC, 1964; "Burke's Law: Who Killed Lenore Wingfield?," ABC, 1964; "Profiles in Courage: The Oscar W. Underwood Story," NBC, 1964; "The Farmer's Daughter: Big Sultan, Little Sultan," ABC, 1964; "Gunsmoke: Chief Joseph," CBS, 1965; "Kraft Suspense Theatre: That Time in Havana," NBC, 1965; "F Troop: Indian Fever," ABC, 1966; "Bonanza: Ride the Wind," NBC, 1966; "Hazel: How to Find Work Without Really Trying," NBC, 1966; "I Spy: Return to Glory," NBC, 1966; "Ironside: The Past Is Prologue," NBC, 1967; "The High Chaparral: The Peace Maker," NBC, 1968; "The Name of the Game: Witness," NBC, 1968; "The Virginian: Fox, Hound and the Widow McCloud," NBC, 1969; "Mannix: Return to Summer Grove," CBS, 1969; "Longstreet: So Who's Fred Hornbeck?," ABC, 1971; "Mannix: Wine From These Grapes," CBS, 1971; "Banacek: No Sign of the Cross," NBC, 1972; "Circle of Fear: The Phantom of Herald Square,"

NBC, 1973; "Kolchak, the Night Stalker: Bad Medicine," ABC, 1974; "The Streets of San Francisco: Cry Help," ABC, 1974; "The Rockford Files: The Italian Bird Fiasco," NBC, 1976; "The Rockford Files: The Becker Connection," NBC, 1976; "Alice: The Indian Taker," CBS, 1977; "The Rockford Files: The Attractive Nuisance," NBC, 1977; "Lou Grant: Cover-Up," CBS, 1980.
TV MOVIES AND MINISERIES: "Call to Danger," CBS, 1973; "Perilous Voyage," NBC, 1976; "Devil Dog: The Hound of Hell," CBS, 1978.

JOSLYN, ALLYN
b. Milford, PA, July 21, 1901; d. 1981. Stage actor best known for his guest shots as Sam Hilliard on "The Addams Family."
AS A REGULAR: "The Ray Bolger Show," ABC, 1953-54; "The Eve Arden Show," CBS, 1957-58; "McKeever and the Colonel," NBC, 1962-63.
AND: "Ford Theatre: Slide, Darling, Slide," NBC, 1954; "Hotel De Paree: Sundance and the Hostiles," CBS, 1959; "Gunsmoke: I Thee Wed," CBS, 1960; "Peter Loves Mary: Make a Million," NBC, 1960; "Michael Shayne: Final Settlement," NBC, 1961; "Have Gun, Will Travel: The Fatal Flaw," CBS, 1961; "The Tom Ewell Show: The Prying Eye," CBS, 1961; "Harrigan and Son: Senior Goes to Hollywood," ABC, 1961; "G.E. Theatre: Go Fight City Hall," CBS, 1962; "The Untouchables: The Silent Partner," ABC, 1962; "Bob Hope Chrysler Theatre: The Square Peg," NBC, 1964; "The Addams Family: The Addams Family Goes to School," ABC, 1964; "The Addams Family: Gomez the Politician," ABC, 1964; "My Three Sons: One of Our Moose Is Missing," ABC, 1964; "F Troop: Iron Horse, Go Home," ABC, 1965; "The Addams Family: Addams Cum Laude," ABC, 1966.

JOURDAN, LOUIS
b. Louis Gendre, Marseilles, France, June 19, 1920. Actor usually in suave, continental roles.
AS A REGULAR: "Paris Precinct," ABC, 1955.
AND: "Robert Montgomery Presents: Wages of Fear," NBC, 1954; "Elgin TV Hour: Warm Clay," ABC, 1954; "Appointment with Adventure: Minus Three Thousand," CBS, 1955; "Studio One: Passage of Arms," CBS, 1955; "Climax!: The Escape of Mendes-France," CBS, 1955; "Ford Theatre: Journey by Moonlight," NBC, 1956; "Playhouse 90: Eloise," CBS, 1956; "Ford Theatre: The Man Who Beat Lupo," ABC, 1957; "G.E. Theatre: The Falling Angel," CBS, 1958; "The Perry Como Show," NBC, 1959; "Shirley MacLaine Special," NBC, 1959; "Pontiac Star Parade: Accent on Love," NBC, 1959; "Louis Jourdan Presents the Timex Show," NBC, 1959; "Bob Hope Chrysler Theatre: War of Nerves," NBC, 1964; "The Judy Garland Show," CBS,

1964; "The Greatest Show on Earth: A Place to Belong," ABC, 1964; "Kraft Suspense Theatre: Graffiti," NBC, 1964; "Bob Hope Chrysler Theatre: A Crash of Cymbals," NBC, 1964; "The FBI: Rope of Gold," ABC, 1967; "The FBI: Wind It Up and It Betrays You," ABC, 1968; "The Name of the Game: Lola in Lipstick," NBC, 1968; "The FBI: The Minerva Tapes," ABC, 1971; "Columbo: Murder Under Glass," NBC, 1978; "Hotel: Prisms," ABC, 1984; "Ooh-La-La-It's Bob Hope's Fun Birthday Spectacular From Paris' Bicentennial," NBC, 1989.
TV MOVIES AND MINISERIES: "Fear No Evil," NBC, 1969; "Run a Crooked Mile," NBC, 1969; "Ritual of Evil," NBC, 1970; "The Great American Beauty Contest," ABC, 1973; "The Count of Monte Cristo," NBC, 1975; "The Man in the Iron Mask," NBC, 1977; "The First Olympics-Athens 1896," NBC, 1984; "Beverly Hills Madam," NBC, 1986.

JOYCE, ELAINE
b. Cleveland, OH, December 19, 1945. Blonde actress whose most recent TV assignment was as the leering hostess on "The Dating Game."
AS A REGULAR: "The Don Knotts Show," NBC, 1970-71; "City of Angels," NBC, 1976; "I've Got a Secret," CBS, 1976; "Mr. Merlin," CBS, 1981-82; "The Dating Game," SYN, 1986-87.
AND: "The Andy Griffith Show: Helen the Authoress," CBS, 1967; "Hawaii Five-O: Just Lucky, I Guess," CBS, 1969; "Hawaii Five-O: Trouble in Mind," CBS, 1970; "Green Acres: The Ex-Secretary," CBS, 1971; "Love, American Style: Love and the Forever Tree," ABC, 1974; "Match Game '74," CBS, 1974; "Police Story: Fathers and Sons," NBC, 1974; "Kojak: Acts of Desperate Men," CBS, 1975; "Hawaii Five-O: Oldest Profession-Latest Price," CBS, 1976; "Cross Wits," SYN, 1977; "The Love Boat: Gopher's Opportunity," ABC, 1978; "The Love Experts," SYN, 1978; "The Love Boat: He's My Brother," ABC, 1981; "The Love Boat: The World's Greatest Kisser," ABC, 1983; "Magnum, P.I.: Legacy From a Friend," CBS, 1983; "Hotel: Faith, Hope and Charity," ABC, 1983; "Simon & Simon: The Disappearance of Harry," CBS, 1984; "Murder, She Wrote: Death Casts a Spell," CBS, 1985.
TV MOVIES AND MINISERIES: "A Guide for the Married Woman," ABC, 1978.

JUMP, GORDON
b. Dayton, OH, April 1, 1932. Pudgy actor who played Mr. Carlson on "WKRP in Cincinnati" and now plays the father of Maggie Seaver (Joanna Kerns) on "Growing Pains." Also the Maytag repairman in TV commercials.
AS A REGULAR: "WKRP in Cincinnati," CBS, 1978-82.

AND: "Get Smart: The Only Way to Die," NBC, 1966; "Get Smart: Casablanca," NBC, 1966; "Mannix: Once Upon a Saturday," CBS, 1969; "The Brady Bunch: The Possible Dream," ABC, 1970; "Love, American Style: Love and the Bowling Ball," ABC, 1970; "Storefront Lawyers: The Emancipation of Bessie Gray," CBS, 1970; "The Mary Tyler Moore Show: The Courtship of Mary's Father's Daughter," CBS, 1972; "The Paul Lynde Show: The Congressman's Son," ABC, 1973; "The Mary Tyler Moore Show: Hi There, Sports Fans," CBS, 1973; "The Partridge Family: The Strikeout King," ABC, 1973; "Love, American Style: Love and the Suspicious Husband," ABC, 1974; "That's My Mama: Cousin Albert," ABC, 1974; "Harry O: Guardian at the Gates," ABC, 1974; "That's My Mama: The Witness," ABC, 1975; "The Streets of San Francisco: Murder by Proxy," ABC, 1975; "Alice: Pay the Fifty Dollars," CBS, 1976; "Good Times: Willona the Fuzz," CBS, 1977; "The Love Boat: The Invisible Maniac," ABC, 1980; "The Love Boat: Putting on the Dog," ABC, 1983; "The Love Boat: Affair on Demand," ABC, 1983; "The Love Boat: The Wager," ABC, 1984; "Amazing Stories: Guilt Trip," NBC, 1985; "Growing Pains: Be a Man," ABC, 1986; "The Golden Girls: Big Daddy," NBC, 1986; "Simon & Simon: Sunrise at Camp Apollo," CBS, 1986; "Murder, She Wrote: If the Frame Fits," CBS, 1986; "Who's the Boss?: A Spirited Christmas," ABC, 1988; "Growing Pains: Anniversary From Hell," ABC, 1989; "Growing Pains: Anger with Love," ABC, 1989; "Growing Pains: Five Grand," ABC, 1989.
TV MOVIES AND MINISERIES: "For Lovers Only," ABC, 1982; "On Fire," ABC, 1987; "Disney Sunday Movie: Justin Case," ABC, 1988; "Perry Mason: The Case of the Lost Love," NBC, 1988.

JURADO, KATY
b. Maria Cristina Jurado Garcia, Mexico, January 16, 1927. Hispanic actress.
AS A REGULAR: "Mr. and Mrs. North," NBC, 1954; "A.K.A. Pablo," ABC, 1984.
AND: "Climax!: Nightmare by Day," CBS, 1956; "Guitar in Guatemala," SYN, 1956; "Playhouse 90: Four Women in Black," CBS, 1957; "The Rifleman: The Boarding House," ABC, 1959; "Here's Hollywood," NBC, 1961; "The Eleventh Hour: The Seventh Day of Creation," NBC, 1962; "The Men From Shiloh: The Best Man," NBC, 1970; "NET Children's Theatre: The Boy and the Turtle," NET, 1971; "Alias Smith and Jones: The McCreedy Feud," ABC, 1972.
TV MOVIES AND MINISERIES: "Any Second Now," NBC, 1969; "A Little Game," ABC, 1971; "Lady Blue," ABC, 1985.

K

KACZMAREK, JANE
> b. Milwaukee, WI.
AS A REGULAR: "The Paper Chase," SHO, 1983-85; "Hill Street Blues," NBC, 1984; "Hometown," CBS, 1985; "Equal Justice," ABC, 1990- .
AND: "Remington Steele: Altered Steele," NBC, 1983; "St. Elsewhere: Release," NBC, 1983; "St. Elsewhere: Graveyard," NBC, 1983; "St. Elsewhere: Family History," NBC, 1983; "Scarecrow and Mrs. King: Always Look a Gift Horse in the Mouth," CBS, 1983.
TV MOVIES AND MINISERIES: "For Lovers Only," ABC, 1982; "Something About Amelia," ABC, 1984; "The Christmas Gift," CBS, 1986; "I'll Take Manhattan," CBS, 1987; "The Three Kings," ABC, 1987.

KAHN, MADELINE
> b. Boston, MA, September 29, 1942. Stage actress with musical-comedy experience who's fared better in movies than on TV, despite a couple of failed sitcom efforts.
AS A REGULAR: "Comedy Tonight," CBS, 1970; "Oh, Madeline," ABC, 1983-84; "Mr. President," FOX, 1987-88.
AND: "The Dick Cavett Show," ABC, 1968; "Hallmark Hall of Fame: Harvey," NBC, 1972; "Adam's Rib: The Unwritten Law," ABC, 1973; "Saturday Night Live," NBC, 1976; "Irving Berlin's 100th Birthday Celebration," CBS, 1988.

KALEMBER, PATRICIA
> b. Schnectady, NY, 1954. Actress who plays Susannah on "thirtysomething."
AS A REGULAR: "Loving," ABC, 1983-84; "Kay O'Brien," CBS, 1986; "Just in Time," ABC, 1988; "thirtysomething," ABC, 1989- .
AND: "The Equalizer: Pilot," CBS, 1985; "The Equalizer: Coal Black Soul," CBS, 1987.
TV MOVIES AND MINISERIES: "Little Girl Lost," ABC, 1988.

KAMEN, MILT
> b. Hurleyville, NY, 1922; d. 1977. Comedian.
AS A REGULAR: "Pantomime Quiz," CBS, 1957; ABC, 1958; ABC, 1959; "The Sid Caesar Show," ABC, 1958; "Perry Como's Kraft Music Hall," NBC, 1961-63; "Love Thy Neighbor," ABC, 1973.
AND: "The Arlene Francis Show," NBC, 1957; "The Garry Moore Show," CBS, 1959; "Play of the Week: Seven Times Monday," SYN, 1961; "Playboy's Penthouse," SYN, 1961; "Route 66: And the Cat Jumped Over the Moon," CBS, 1961; "The Jack Paar Show," NBC, 1962; "The Garry Moore Show," CBS, 1962; "Naked City: Today the Man Who Kills the Ants Is Coming!," ABC, 1962; "The Merv Griffin Show," NBC, 1962; "The Merv Griffin Show," NBC, 1963; "The Match Game," NBC, 1963; "Missing Links," NBC, 1963; "The Nurses: No Score," CBS, 1963; "To Tell the Truth," CBS, 1964; "The Tonight Show Starring Johnny Carson," NBC, 1965; "The Match Game," NBC, 1966; "The Mike Douglas Show," SYN, 1968; "The Della Reese Show," SYN, 1970; "The Dean Martin Show," NBC, 1971; "The Partridge Family: Guess Who's Coming to Drive," ABC, 1971; "The FBI: The Deadly Species," ABC, 1972; "Love, American Style: Love and the Big Mother," ABC, 1972; "The Paul Lynde Show: Howie's Inheritance," ABC, 1973; "Mannix: The Danford File," CBS, 1973; "The FBI: The Rap Taker," ABC, 1973; "The Streets of San Francisco: The Twenty-Four Karat Plague," ABC, 1973; "The Merv Griffin Show," SYN, 1974; "Kolchak, the Night Stalker: They Have Been, They Are, They Will Be," ABC, 1974; "Switch: Case of the Purloined Case," CBS, 1976; "The Merv Griffin Show," SYN, 1977.
TV MOVIES AND MINISERIES: "The Judge and Jake Wyler," NBC, 1972.

KAMPMANN, STEVEN
> b. Philadelphia, PA, May 31, 1940. Writer-actor who played Kirk, original owner of the Yankee Doodle Diner on "Newhart."
AS A REGULAR: "Newhart," CBS, 1982-84.
AS WRITER: "WKRP in Cincinnati," CBS, 1980-81.

KANALY, STEVE
> b. Burbank, CA, March 14, 1946. Actor who plays Ray Krebbs on "Dallas."
AS A REGULAR: "Dallas," CBS, 1978- .
AND: "City of Angels: The November Plan," NBC, 1976; "The Bionic Woman: Assault on the Princess," ABC, 1976; "The Quest: Day of Outrage," NBC, 1976; "Police Story: Trial Board," NBC, 1977; "The Mike Douglas Show," SYN, 1978; "Charlie's Angels: Avenging Angel," ABC, 1979.
TV MOVIES AND MINISERIES: "Melvin Purvis, G-Man," ABC, 1974; "Young Joe, the Forgotten Kennedy," ABC, 1977; "To Find My Son," CBS, 1980.

KANE, CAROL
> b. Cleveland, OH, June 18, 1952. Gifted comic

actress with a waiflike face who's enlivened several sitcoms; best known for her Emmy winning role as Simka, slightly demented wife of Latka Gravas (Andy Kaufman) on "Taxi."

AS A REGULAR: "Taxi," ABC, 1980-82, NBC, 1982-83; "All Is Forgiven," NBC, 1986; "American Dreamer," NBC, 1990- .

AND: "The Virginian: The Return of Golden Tom," NBC, 1966; "The Virginian: Outcast," NBC, 1966; "Cheers: A Ditch in Time," NBC, 1984.

TV MOVIES AND MINISERIES: "Burning Rage," CBS, 1984; "Drop-Out Mother," CBS, 1988.

* Emmies: 1982, 1983.

KANTER, HAL

b. *Savannah, GA, December 18, 1918*. Comedy writer and producer.

AS WRITER/PRODUCER: "The George Gobel Show," NBC, 1954-56; "Milton Berle Starring in the Kraft Music Hall," NBC, 1958-59; "The Danny Kaye Show," CBS, 1961; "All in the Family," CBS, 1975-78.

AS WRITER-CREATOR: "Julia," NBC, 1968-71.

* Emmies: 1955.

KAPLAN, GABE

b. *Brooklyn, NY, March 31, 1945*. Comedian who played teacher Gabe Kotter on a successful seventies sitcom.

AS A REGULAR: "Welcome Back, Kotter," ABC, 1975-79; "Lewis & Clark," NBC, 1981-82.

AND: "The Merv Griffin Show," SYN, 1973; "The Tonight Show Starring Johnny Carson," NBC, 1974; "Wide World in Concert," ABC, 1974; "Celebrity Sweepstakes," NBC, 1975; "The Merv Griffin Show," SYN, 1975; "The Captain & Tennille," ABC, 1976; "Police Story: One of Our Cops Is Crazy," NBC, 1977; "Murder, She Wrote: Birds of a Feather," CBS, 1984.

TV MOVIES AND MINISERIES: "The Love Boat," ABC, 1976.

KAPLAN, MARVIN

b. *New York City, NY, January 24, 1927*. Actor usually in meek roles; he played diner regular Henry on "Alice."

AS A REGULAR: "Meet Millie," CBS, 1952-56; "Top Cat," ABC, 1961-62; "The Chicago Teddy Bears," CBS, 1971; "Alice," CBS, 1977-85.

AND: "Ford Theatre: Double Exposure," NBC, 1953; "G.E. Theatre: The Marriage Fix," CBS, 1953; "The Danny Thomas Show: Evil Eye Schultz," CBS, 1958; "Sally: Look Hans, No Sally," NBC, 1958; "The Red Skelton Show," CBS, 1958; "Comedy Spot: Tom, Dick and Harry," CBS, 1960; "The Many Loves of Dobie Gillis: The Second Childhood of Herbert T. Gillis," CBS, 1961; "Vacation Playhouse: Maggie

Brown," CBS, 1963; "Bob Hope Chrysler Theatre: The Game with Glass Pieces," NBC, 1964; "Allan Sherman's Funnyland," NBC, 1965; "Valentine's Day: The Man Who Shot the World," ABC, 1965; "McHale's Navy: All Ahead Empty," ABC, 1965; "Honey West: The Fun-Fun Killer," ABC, 1966; "Gidget: Don't Defrost the Alligator," ABC, 1966; "Gomer Pyle, USMC: The Carriage Waits," CBS, 1968; "My Three Sons: Gossip, Inc.," CBS, 1968; "Out of the Blue," CBS, 1968; "The Mod Squad: Flight Five Doesn't Answer," ABC, 1969; "The Mod Squad: Lisa," ABC, 1969; "Petticoat Junction: The Other Woman," CBS, 1969; "I Dream of Jeannie: One of Our Hotels Is Growing," NBC, 1970; "Love, American Style: Love and the Latin Lover," ABC, 1972; "Kolchak, the Night Stalker: Bad Medicine," ABC, 1974; "Cagney & Lacey: A Fair Shake," CBS, 1988; "Murphy's Law: When You're Over the Hill, You Pick Up Speed," ABC, 1989; "My Two Dads: Burnin' Vernon," NBC, 1989.

KARLEN, JOHN

b. *Brooklyn, NY*. Actor often in old-shoe roles; he won an Emmy as Harv, loving husband of Mary Beth Lacey (Tyne Daly) on "Cagney & Lacey."

AS A REGULAR: "Dark Shadows," ABC, 1966-71; "Cagney & Lacey," CBS, 1982-88.

AND: "Look Up and Live: The Peddler," CBS, 1961; "The Gallant Men: Signals for an End Run," ABC, 1962; "East Side/West Side: One Drink at a Time," CBS, 1964; "The Magician: The Vanishing Lady," NBC, 1973; "Kojak: Web of Death," CBS, 1973; "Medical Center: No Hiding Place," CBS, 1975; "The Streets of San Francisco: Poisoned Snow," ABC, 1975; "Joe Forrester: The Witness," NBC, 1975; "The Streets of San Francisco: No Minor Vices," ABC, 1976; "Serpico: Rapid Fire," NBC, 1976; "Police Story: Prime Rib," NBC, 1977; "All in the Family: Mike Goes Skiing," CBS, 1977; "The Rockford Files: Rosendahl and Gilda Stern Are Dead," NBC, 1978; "Kojak: Chains of Custody," CBS, 1978; "Lou Grant: Gambling," CBS, 1979; "Quincy: Hot Ice," NBC, 1979; "Quincy: The Final Gift," NBC, 1980; "Strike Force: Sharks," ABC, 1982; "Hill Street Blues: The Spy Who Came From Delgado," NBC, 1982; "The Bay City Blues: Premiere," NBC, 1983; "The Bay City Blues: I Never Swung for My Father," NBC, 1983; "The New Mike Hammer: Green Lipstick," CBS, 1987.

TV MOVIES AND MINISERIES: "Night of Terror," ABC, 1972; "Frankenstein," ABC, 1973; "The Picture of Dorian Gray," ABC, 1973; "Shirts/ Skins," ABC, 1973; "Melvin Purvis, G-Man," ABC, 1974; "Trilogy of Terror," ABC, 1975; "Delancey Street," NBC, 1975; "The Kansas City Massacre," ABC, 1975; "The Return of Mod Squad," ABC, 1979; "Hostage Flight,"

NBC, 1985; "Welcome Home Bobby," CBS, 1986; "The Return of Mickey Spillane's Mike Hammer," CBS, 1986; "Downpayment on Murder," NBC, 1987; "The Cover Girl and the Cop," NBC, 1989; "Babycakes," CBS, 1989.

* Emmies: 1986.

KARLOFF, BORIS

b. *William Henry Pratt, Dulwich, England, November 23, 1887; d. 1969.* Stage actor who was cast as "Frankenstein" in 1931 and associated with horror and suspense projects from then on; in real life he was known as a gentle, caring man and total professional.

AS A REGULAR: "Starring Boris Karloff," ABC, 1949; "Down You Go," DUM, 1954-55; "Col. March of Scotland Yard," SYN, 1957-58; "Thriller," NBC, 1960-62.

AND: "Masterpiece Playhouse: Uncle Vanya," NBC, 1950; "Lights Out: The Leopard Lady," NBC, 1950; "Robert Montgomery Presents: The Kimballs," NBC, 1951; "Studio One: Mutiny on the Nicolette," CBS, 1951; "Suspense: The Lonely Place," CBS, 1951; "Lux Video Theatre: The Jest of Hahalaba," CBS, 1951; "Tales of Tomorrow: Momento," ABC, 1952; "Studio One: A Connecticut Yankee," CBS, 1952; "Curtain Call: The Soul of the Great Bell," NBC, 1952; "Schlitz Playhouse of Stars: Death House," CBS, 1952; "Lux Video Theatre: Fear," NBC, 1952; "Hollywood Opening Night: The Invited Seven," NBC, 1953; "Suspense: The Black Prophet," CBS, 1953; "Robert Montgomery Presents: Burden of Proof," NBC, 1953; "Tales of Tomorrow: Past Tense," ABC, 1953; "Plymouth Playhouse: The Chase," ABC, 1953; "Suspense: The Signal Man," CBS, 1953; "Climax!: White Carnation," CBS, 1954; "Best of Broadway: Arsenic and Old Lace," CBS, 1955; "Elgin TV Hour: A Sting of Death," ABC, 1955; "A Connecticut Yankee," NBC, 1955; "G.E. Theatre: My Blue Ocean," CBS, 1955; "U.S. Steel Hour: Counterfeit," CBS, 1955; "Climax!: Bury Me Later," CBS, 1955; "Alcoa Hour: Even the Weariest River," NBC, 1956; "Playhouse 90: Rendezvous in Black," CBS, 1956; "The Red Skelton Show," CBS, 1956; "Hallmark Hall of Fame: The Lark," NBC, 1957; "Lux Video Theatre: The Man Who Played God," NBC, 1957; "Dinah Shore Chevy Show," NBC, 1957; "The Rosemary Clooney Show," SYN, 1957; "The Lux Show with Rosemary Clooney," NBC, 1957; "The Gisele MacKenzie Show," NBC, 1957; "Suspicion: The Deadly Game," NBC, 1957; "The Betty White Show," ABC, 1958; "Telephone Time: The Vestris," ABC, 1958; "Shirley Temple's Storybook: The Legend of Sleepy Hollow," NBC, 1958; "Studio One: The Shadow of a Genius," CBS, 1958; "Playhouse 90: Heart of Darkness," CBS, 1958; "The Gale Storm Show: It's Murder, My Dear," CBS, 1959; "G.E.

Theatre: The Indian Giver," CBS, 1959; "Playhouse 90: To the Sound of Trumpets," CBS, 1960; "Du Pont Show of the Month: Treasure Island," CBS, 1960; "Sunday Showcase: Hollywood Sings," NBC, 1960; "The Secret World of Eddie Hodges," CBS, 1960; "Here's Hollywood," NBC, 1960; "Hallmark Hall of Fame: Arsenic and Old Lace," NBC, 1962; "Theatre '62: The Paradine Case," NBC, 1962; "Route 66: Lizard's Leg and Owlet's Wing," CBS, 1962; "I've Got a Secret," CBS, 1963; "The Entertainers," CBS, 1965; "The Wild Wild West: The Night of the Golden Cobra," CBS, 1966; "The Man From UNCLE: The Mother Muffin Affair," NBC, 1966; "How the Grinch Stole Christmas," CBS, 1966; "I Spy: Mainly on the Plains," NBC, 1967; "The Name of the Game: The White Birch," NBC, 1968; "The Jonathan Winters Show," CBS, 1968.

KARNS, ROSCOE

b. *San Bernadino, CA, September 7, 1893; d. 1970.* Screen character actor in fast-talking, wisecracking roles; memorable on TV as Rocky King and as Captain Walter Shafer, commanding officer of Chick Hennesey (Jackie Cooper).

AS A REGULAR: "Rocky King, Inside Detective," DUM, 1950-54; "Hennesey," CBS, 1959-62.

AND: "Richard Diamond, Private Detective: The Ed Church Case," CBS, 1958; "December Bride: Bride's Father-in-Law," CBS, 1958; "The Lucy Show: Lucy Becomes a Reporter," CBS, 1963.

KARRAS, ALEX

b. *Gary, IN, July 15, 1935.* Beefy actor, former football star; he played George, foster father of Webster (Emmanuel Lewis). Husband of Susan Clark.

AS A REGULAR: "Webster," ABC, 1983-87, SYN, 1987-88.

AND: "Love, American Style: Love and the Eskimo's Wife," ABC, 1972; "The Odd Couple: That Was No Lady," ABC, 1973; "M*A*S*H: Springtime," CBS, 1974; "McMillan and Wife: Downshift to Danger," NBC, 1974; "Celebrity Sweepstakes," NBC, 1975; "Good Heavens: Jack the Ribber," ABC, 1976; "Faerie Tale Theatre: Goldilocks and the Three Bears," SHO, 1984; "Saturday Night Live," NBC, 1985.

TV MOVIES AND MINISERIES: "Hardcase," ABC, 1972; "The 500-Pound Jerk," CBS, 1973; "Babe," CBS, 1975; "Centennial," NBC, 1978-79; "Jimmy B. and Andre," CBS, 1980; "Maid in America," CBS, 1982.

KASDORF, LENORE

b. *1948.* Actress who played Rita on "The Guiding Light" and now plays Beth, ex-wife of Hayden Fox (Craig T. Nelson) on "Coach."

AS A REGULAR: "The Guiding Light," CBS, 1975-81; "Days of Our Lives," NBC, 1983.

AND: "The FBI: Escape to Nowhere," ABC, 1972; "The Streets of San Francisco: Betrayed," ABC, 1973; "The Magician: The Vanishing Lady," NBC, 1973; "Barnaby Jones: Gold Record for Murder," CBS, 1974; "Barnaby Jones: A Gathering of Thieves," CBS, 1974; "Chase: Hot Beef," NBC, 1974; "The Streets of San Francisco: False Witness," ABC, 1975; "Magnum P.I.: Smaller Than Life," CBS, 1983; "T.J. Hooker: The Trial," ABC, 1983; "Murder, She Wrote: It's a Dog's Life," CBS, 1984; "Knight Rider: Lost Knight," NBC, 1984; "The A-Team: Breakout," NBC, 1984; "Riptide: Girls' Night Out," NBC, 1985; "Matlock: The Quarterback," NBC, 1986; "Murder, She Wrote: Steal Me a Story," CBS, 1987; "Highway to Heaven: Whose Trash Is It Anyway?," NBC, 1988; "Jake and the Fatman: Key Witness," CBS, 1989; "Coach: Parents' Weekend," ABC, 1989; "Coach: If a Coach Falls in the Woods," ABC, 1989.

TV MOVIES AND MINISERIES: "Big Rose," CBS, 1974; "A Different Affair," CBS, 1987; "Dinner at Eight," TNT, 1989.

KASTNER, PETER

b. 1944.

AS A REGULAR: "The Edge of Night," CBS, 1966; "The Ugliest Girl In Town," ABC, 1968-69; "Delta House," ABC, 1979.

AND: "Love, American Style: Love and the Phone Booth," ABC, 1969; "Love, American Style: Love and the Triangle," ABC, 1971; "Love, American Style: Love and the Lovesick Sailor," ABC, 1971; "Love, American Style: Love and the Girlish Groom," ABC, 1973; "Love, American Style: Love and the Mr. and Mrs.," ABC, 1973; "Marcus Welby, M.D.: A Joyful Song," ABC, 1973.

KASZNAR, KURT

b. Kurt Servischer, Vienna, August 13, 1913; d. 1979. Heavyset actor, usually in roles as sweaty villians or offbeat ethnic types.

AS A REGULAR: "Land of the Giants," ABC, 1968-70.

AND: "Philco TV Playhouse: Run Like a Thief," NBC, 1954; "Pond's Theatre: The Forger," ABC, 1955; "Studio One: The Judge and His Hangman," CBS, 1955; "Playwrights '56: Return to Cassino," NBC, 1956; "Lux Video Theatre: A Yankee Cousin," NBC, 1956; "Kraft Television Theatre: One Way West," NBC, 1956; "Climax!: Night of the Heat Wave," CBS, 1956; "The Jane Wyman Show: A Place on the Bay," NBC, 1956; "Schlitz Playhouse of Stars: The Enchanted," CBS, 1957; "Studio 57: The Customs of the Country," SYN, 1957; "Goodyear TV Playhouse: Rumbin Galleries," NBC, 1957; "Climax!: Trail

of Terror," CBS, 1957; "Suspicion: Murder Me Gently," NBC, 1957; "Climax!: The Largest City in Captivity," CBS, 1957; "The Tonight Show," NBC, 1957; "Du Pont Show of the Month: The Bridge of San Luis Rey," CBS, 1958; "Shirley Temple's Storybook: Rumpelstiltskin," NBC, 1958; "Westinghouse Desilu Playhouse: Chez Rouge," CBS, 1959; "Adventures in Paradise: The Black Pearl," ABC, 1959; "Play of the Week: Volpone," SYN, 1960; "Robert Herridge Theatre: The Ballad of Huck Finn," SYN, 1960; "Play of the Week: Thieves' Carnival," SYN, 1960; "Naked City: The Hot Minerva," ABC, 1961; "Play of the Week: Waiting for Godot," SYN, 1961; "Naked City: The Battlefield," ABC, 1963; "The Reporter: Hideout," CBS, 1964; "Trials of O'Brien: How Do You Get to Carnegie Hall?," CBS, 1965; "The Girl From UNCLE: The Dog-Gone Affair," NBC, 1966; "The Hero: The Universal Language," NBC, 1966; "That Girl: Soap Gets in Your Eyes," ABC, 1966; "The Man From UNCLE: The Napoleon's Tomb Affair," NBC, 1967; "My Three Sons: Help, the Gypsies Are Coming," CBS, 1967; "Run for Your Life: The Inhuman Predicament," NBC, 1967; "It Takes a Thief: A Thief Is a Thief Is a Thief," ABC, 1968; "The Men From Shiloh: Crooked Corner," NBC, 1970; "The Name of the Game: A Sister From Napoli," NBC, 1971; "The FBI: The Fatal Showdown," ABC, 1972; "Here's Lucy: Lucy and the Group Encounter," CBS, 1973; "Love, American Style: Love and the Cozy Comrades," ABC, 1973; "Hawkins: Murder on the 13th Floor," CBS, 1974; "ABC Afterschool Special: Cyrano," ABC, 1974.

TV MOVIES AND MINISERIES: "The Smugglers," NBC, 1968; "Once Upon a Dead Man," NBC, 1971; "The Snoop Sisters," NBC, 1972; "Suddenly, Love," NBC, 1978.

KATT, WILLIAM

b. Los Angeles, CA, February 16, 1950. Blonde actor who played "The Greatest American Hero" and Paul Drake Jr. on several "Perry Mason" movies; son of Barbara Hale and Bill Williams.

AS A REGULAR: "The Greatest American Hero," ABC, 1981-83; "Top of the Hill," CBS, 1989-90.

AND: "Kojak: Life, Liberation and the Pursuit of Death," CBS, 1975; "The Rookies: The Old Neighborhood," ABC, 1975.

TV MOVIES AND MINISERIES: "Night Chase," CBS, 1970; "The Daughters of Joshua Cabe," ABC, 1972; "Can Ellen Be Saved?," ABC, 1974; "Perry Mason Returns," NBC, 1985; "Perry Mason: The Case of the Notorious Nun," NBC, 1986; "Perry Mason: The Case of the Shooting Star," NBC, 1986; "Perry Mason: The Case of the Sinister Spirit," NBC, 1987; "Perry Mason: The Case of the Murdered Madam," NBC,

1987; "Perry Mason: The Case of the Scandalous Scoundrel," NBC, 1987; "Perry Mason: The Case of the Avenging Ace," NBC, 1988; "Perry Mason: The Case of the Lady in the Lake," NBC, 1988; "Perry Mason: The Case of the Lost Love," NBC, 1988; "Swimsuit," NBC, 1989.

KAUFMAN, ANDY
b. New York City, NY, January 17, 1949; d. 1984. Comic who experimented with the bizarre; he played Latka Gravas on "Taxi."
AS A REGULAR: "Van Dyke and Company," NBC, 1976; "Taxi," ABC, 1978-82; NBC, 1982-83.
AND: "Saturday Night Live," NBC, 1975; "Dinah!," SYN, 1977; "Cher ... and Other Fantasies," NBC, 1979; "Andy Kaufman Special," ABC, 1980; "Fridays," ABC, 1981.

KAUFMAN, GEORGE S.
b. Pittsburgh, PA, November 14, 1889; d. 1961. Legendary wit and Pulitzer Prize-winning playwright.
AS A REGULAR: "This Is Show Business," CBS, 1949-54; NBC, 1956.
* During the holiday season of 1952, Kaufman spoke on the panel show "This Is Show Business" about the commercialization of Christmas, adding, "Let's make this one program on which no one sings "Silent Night." Viewers, who apparently didn't mind the commercialization, protested; Kaufman was suspended from the show and later reinstated.

KAVNER, JULIE
b. Los Angeles, CA, September 7, 1951. Emmy winning actress who played Brenda Morgenstern on "Rhoda" and was an invaluable second banana to Tracey Ullman; now she provides the voice of Marge Simpson.
AS A REGULAR: "Rhoda," CBS, 1974-78; "The Tracey Ullman Show," FOX, 1987-90; "The Simpsons," FOX, 1990- .
AND: "ABC Afternoon Playbreak: The Girl Who Couldn't Lose," ABC, 1975; "Petrocelli: To See No Evil," NBC, 1975; "Bert D'Angelo/Superstar: The Brown Horse Connection," ABC, 1976; "Lou Grant: House-Warming," CBS, 1977; "Taxi: Tony's Sister and Jim," ABC, 1980.
TV MOVIES AND MINISERIES: "Katherine," ABC, 1975; "No Other Love," CBS, 1979; "The Revenge of the Stepford Wives," NBC, 1980.
* Emmies: 1978.

KAY, BEATRICE
b. New York City, NY, April 21, 1907; d. 1986.
AS A REGULAR: "Calvin and the Colonel," ABC, 1961-62.
AND: "The Rosemary Clooney Show," SYN, 1956; "Art Linkletter's House Party," CBS, 1958;

"M Squad: The Harpies," NBC, 1959; "The Danny Thomas Show: Nightclub Owners," CBS, 1960; "77 Sunset Strip: The Wide-Screen Caper," ABC, 1960; "Bonanza: The Burma Rarity," NBC, 1961; "Hawaiian Eye: The Reluctant Visit," ABC, 1961; "The Real McCoys: Cyrano McCoy," ABC, 1962; "Variety Gardens," CBS, 1962; "Art Linkletter's House Party," CBS, 1963.

KAY, DIANNE
b. Phoenix, AZ, March 29, 1955. Actress who played Nancy Bradford on "Eight Is Enough."
AS A REGULAR: "Eight Is Enough," ABC, 1977-81; "Reggie," ABC, 1983; "Glitter," ABC, 1984-85; "Once a Hero," ABC, 1987.
AND: "The Love Boat: Tugs of the Heart," ABC, 1984; "Simon & Simon: Corpus Delecti," CBS, 1984.
TV MOVIES AND MINISERIES: "Flamingo Road," NBC, 1980; "Portrait of a Showgirl," CBS, 1982; "Eight Is Enough: A Family Reunion," NBC, 1987; "An Eight Is Enough Wedding," NBC, 1989.

KAYE, CAREN
b. 1951, New York City, NY. Attractive actress in sitcom roles.
AS A REGULAR: "Blansky's Beauties," ABC, 1977; "The Betty White Show," CBS, 1977-78; "Who's Watching the Kids?," NBC, 1978; "Empire," CBS, 1984; "It's Your Move," NBC, 1984-85.
AND: "The Mary Tyler Moore Show: What's Wrong with Swimming?," CBS, 1976; "Alice: Pay the Fifty Dollars," CBS, 1976; "Dinah!," SYN, 1978; "The Love Boat: The Wedding," ABC, 1979; "The Misadventures of Sheriff Lobo: Pilot," NBC, 1979; "The Love Boat: Marrying for Money," ABC, 1982; "The Love Boat: The Maid Cleans Up," ABC, 1983; "Taxi: Alex the Gofer," NBC, 1982; "Remington Steele: Hearts of Steele," NBC, 1983; "Hardcastle and McCormick: Goin' Nowhere Fast," ABC, 1983; "Simon & Simon: Reunion at Alcatraz," CBS, 1985; "The Love Boat: Couples," ABC, 1986; "Amazing Stories: Magic Saturday," NBC, 1986.
TV MOVIES AND MINISERIES: "Help Wanted: Male," CBS, 1982.

KAYE, DANNY
b. David Daniel Kaminsky, Brooklyn, NY, 1913; d. 1987. Funnyman of movies and TV; "See It Now," in a well-remembered program, looked at Kaye's activities on behalf of UNICEF.
AS A REGULAR: "The Danny Kaye Show," CBS, 1963-67.
AND: "See It Now: The Secret Life of Danny Kaye," CBS, 1956; "Winter Olympics Opening Ceremonies," CBS, 1960; "An Hour with Danny

Kaye," CBS, 1960; "What's My Line?," CBS, 1961; "The Danny Kaye Show," CBS, 1961; "The Merv Griffin Show," NBC, 1962; "Here's Hollywood," NBC, 1962; "The Danny Kaye Show," NBC, 1962; "The Lucy Show: Lucy Meets Danny Kaye," CBS, 1964; "A Salute to Stan Laurel," CBS, 1965; "Password," CBS, 1966; "The Emporer's New Clothes," ABC, 1972; "Here Comes Peter Cottontail," ABC, 1972; "Pinocchio," CBS, 1976; "Peter Pan," NBC, 1976; "The Muppet Show," SYN, 1979; "The Twilight Zone: Paladin of the Lost Hour," CBS, 1985; "The Cosby Show: A Trip to the Dentist," NBC, 1986.
TV MOVIES AND MINISERIES: "Skokie," CBS, 1981.
* Emmies: 1964.

KAYE, LILA
b. *London, England.* Stage actress who played cooking-show hostess Mama Malone in one of the worst (and shortest-lived) sitcoms ever.
AS A REGULAR: "Mama Malone," CBS, 1984.
AND: "Cheers: The Bartender's Tale," NBC, 1985; "Dear John: The British Are Coming," NBC, 1989.
TV MOVIES AND MINISERIES: "The Return of Sherlock Holmes," CBS, 1987.

KAYE, SAMMY
b. *Cleveland, OH, March 13, 1910; d. 1987.* Bandleader.
AS A REGULAR: "The Sammy Kaye Show," NBC, 1950; CBS, 1951-52; NBC, 1953; ABC, 1954-55; "Sammy Kaye's Music From Manhattan," ABC, 1958-59; "The Keefe Brasselle Show," CBS, 1963.
AND: "The Ed Sullivan Show," CBS, 1957; "The Big Record," CBS, 1957; "Variety Gardens," CBS, 1962.

KAYE, STUBBY
b. *New York City, NY, November 11, 1918.* Pudgy comic actor on TV sitcoms and variety shows; a stage success in "Guys and Dolls" and "L'il Abner."
AS A REGULAR: "Pantomime Quiz," ABC, 1958; ABC, 1959; "Love and Marriage," NBC, 1959-60; "My Sister Eileen," CBS, 1960-61; "Stump the Stars," CBS, 1962-63, 1964; "Shenanigans," ABC, 1964-66.
AND: "The Walter Winchell Show," NBC, 1956; "What's My Line?," CBS, 1956; "Washington Square," NBC, 1956; "Dinah Shore Chevy Show," NBC, 1957; "Washington Square," NBC, 1957; "The Julius La Rosa Show," NBC, 1957; "Du Pont Show of the Month: Crescendo," CBS, 1957; "Pinocchio," NBC, 1957; "Pat Boone Chevy Showroom," ABC, 1957; "The Gisele MacKenzie Show," NBC, 1958; "Hansel and Gretel," ABC, 1958; "The Peter Lind Hayes

Show," ABC, 1959; "Your Hit Parade," CBS, 1959; "The Red Skelton Show: Clem in Dogpatch," CBS, 1960; "The Millionaire: Millionaire Tony Rogers," CBS, 1960; "Music for a Spring Night," ABC, 1960; "Startime: The Nanette Fabray Show—So Help Me, Aphrodite," NBC, 1960; "Comedy Spot: Full Speed Anywhere," CBS, 1960; "Three Wishes," SYN, 1961; "The Red Skelton Hour," CBS, 1962; "The Red Skelton Hour," CBS, 1963; "Ensign O'Toole: Operation: Tubby," NBC, 1963; "The Red Skelton Hour," CBS, 1964; "PDQ," NBC, 1965; "The Monkees: The Monkees Race Again," NBC, 1968; "The Doris Day Show: Dinner for One," CBS, 1970; "Love, American Style: Love and the Dream Burglar," ABC, 1973; "Captain Kangaroo," CBS, 1976; "Harper Valley PTA: Low Noon," NBC, 1981.

KAZAN, LAINIE
b. *New York City, NY, May 15, 1940.* Actress-singer.
AS A REGULAR: "The Dean Martin Summer Show," NBC, 1966; "The Paper Chase," SHO, 1984-86; "Tough Cookies," CBS, 1986; "Karen's Song," FOX, 1987.
AND: "Ben Casey: Why Did the Day Go Backwards?," ABC, 1965; "Hullabaloo," NBC, 1966; "Dream Girl of '67," ABC, 1967; "The Carol Burnett Show," CBS, 1967; "Personality," NBC, 1968; "Operation: Entertainment," ABC, 1968; "When Things Were Rotten: The Spy," ABC, 1975; "Columbo: Make Me a Perfect Murder," NBC, 1978; "Hotel: Premiere," ABC, 1983; "Amazing Stories: Gershwin's Trunk," NBC, 1987; "St. Elsewhere: A Moon for the Misbegotten," NBC, 1987; "St. Elsewhere: The Abby Singer Show," NBC, 1988; "Late Night With David Letterman," NBC, 1989; "Hagar the Horrible," CBS, 1989.
TV MOVIES AND MINISERIES: "Sunset Limousine," CBS, 1983; "Obsessive Love," CBS, 1984.

KAZURINSKY, TIM
b. *Johnstown, PA, March 3, 1950.* Comic actor.
AS A REGULAR: "Saturday Night Live," NBC, 1981-84.
TV MOVIES AND MINISERIES: "Dinner at Eight," TNT, 1989.

KEACH, STACY
b. *William Stacy Keach Jr., June 2, 1941, Savannah, GA.* Stage actor best known on TV as the macho Mike Hammer.
AS A REGULAR: "Caribe," ABC, 1975; "Mickey Spillane's Mike Hammer (The New Mike Hammer)," CBS, 1984-87.
AND: "Hamlet," CBS, 1964; "Actors Company: The Winter's Tale," NET, 1967; "Actors Company: Twelfth Night," NET, 1968; "Actors

Company: Macbeth," NET, 1968; "NET Playhouse: Biograph," NET, 1971; "New York Playhouse: Particular Men," NET, 1972; "New York Playhouse: Antigone," NET, 1972; "Bonanza: The 26th Game," NBC, 1972; "Marcus Welby, M.D.: No Charity for the MacAllisters," ABC, 1974; "Hollywood Television Theatre: The Man of Destiny," PBS, 1975.

TV MOVIES AND MINISERIES: "All the Kind Strangers," ABC, 1974; "James Michener's Dynasty," NBC, 1976; "Jesus of Nazareth," NBC, 1977; "Mickey Spillane's Murder Me, Murder You," CBS, 1983; "Princess Daisy," NBC, 1983; "The Return of Mickey Spillane's Mike Hammer," CBS, 1986; "Intimate Strangers," CBS, 1986; "Hemingway," SYN, 1988; "The Forgotten," USA, 1989.

* See also Rich Little.

KEAN, BETTY

b. *Hartford, CT.* Comic actress; sister of Jane Kean.

AS A REGULAR: "Leave It to Larry," CBS, 1952. **AND:** "The Steve Allen Show," NBC, 1956; "The Jackie Gleason Show," CBS, 1957; "Arthur Murray Party," NBC, 1959; "Pantomime Quiz," ABC, 1959; "Be Our Guest," CBS, 1960; "The Bob Newhart Show: Of Mice and Men," CBS, 1977.

KEAN, JANE

b. *Hartford, CT.* Actress who played Trixie, wife of Ed Norton (Art Carney) on "The Jackie Gleason Show."

AS A REGULAR: "The Jackie Gleason Show," CBS, 1966-71; "Paradise," CBS, 1989- . **AND:** "Club Oasis," NBC, 1958; "The Phil Silvers Show: Doberman, Missing Heir," CBS, 1959; "The Phil Silvers Show: The Bilko Boycott," CBS, 1959; "Be Our Guest," CBS, 1960; "Follow the Sun: Not Aunt Charlotte!," ABC, 1962; "The New Loretta Young Show: Decision at Midnight," CBS, 1962; "Mr. Magoo's Christmas Carol," NBC, 1962; "Love, American Style: Love and the Millionaires," ABC, 1971; "Jackie Gleason Special," CBS, 1973; "Scarecrow and Mrs. King: A Little Sex, a Little Scandal," CBS, 1985.

KEANAN, STACI

b. *Philadelphia, PA, 1975.*

AS A REGULAR: "My Two Dads," NBC, 1987-90; "Going Places," ABC, 1990- . **TV MOVIES AND MINISERIES:** "Many Happy Returns," CBS, 1986; "I'll Take Manhattan," CBS, 1987.

KEARNS, JOSEPH

b. *Salt Lake City, UT, 1907; d. 1962.* Actor who played Mr. Wilson on "Dennis the Menace."

AS A REGULAR: "Our Miss Brooks," CBS, 1953-

55; "Willy," CBS, 1954-55; "How to Marry a Millionaire," SYN, 1957-59; "Dennis the Menace," CBS, 1959-62. **AND:** "I Love Lucy: The Kleptomaniac," CBS, 1952; "December Bride: Sunken Den," CBS, 1956; "Schlitz Playhouse of Stars: Clothes Make the Man," CBS, 1957; "The Real McCoys: You Can't Cheat An Honest Man," ABC, 1957; "The Adventures of Ozzie and Harriet: Tutti Frutti Ice Cream," ABC, 1957; "Studio 57: It's a Small World," SYN, 1957; "I Love Lucy: Lucy's Night in Town," CBS, 1957; "Shower of Stars: Jack Benny's 40th Birthday Celebration," CBS, 1958; "Gunsmoke: The Big Con," CBS, 1958; "The Adventures of Ozzie and Harriet: Ozzie and the Space Age," ABC, 1959; "The Donna Reed Show: Donna Decorates," ABC, 1960; "Angel: Angel the Good Citizen," CBS, 1960; "The Jack Benny Program: Jack Goes to Vault," CBS, 1961.

KEATING, LARRY

b. *St. Paul, MN, 1896; d. 1963.* Actor best known as Harry Morton, exasperated husband of Blanche (Bea Benaderet) and neighbor of George Burns and Gracie Allen.

AS A REGULAR: "The Hank McCune Show," NBC, 1950; "The George Burns and Gracie Allen Show," CBS, 1953-58; "The George Burns Show," NBC, 1958-59; "Mr. Ed," CBS, 1961-63. **AND:** "The Bob Cummings Show: Bob Meets the Mortons," CBS, 1957; "The Lucille Ball-Desi Arnaz Show: Milton Berle Hides Out at the Ricardos," CBS, 1959; "Harrigan and Son: You Can't Fight City Hall," ABC, 1961; "Stump the Stars," CBS, 1963.

KEATON, BUSTER

b. *Joseph Frank Keaton, Piqua, KS, 1896; d. 1966.* Silent-film comic and director whose talent is immortal; TV shows and commercials played a role in rediscovering his talent.

AS A GUEST: "Douglas Fairbanks Jr. Presents: The Awakening," SYN, 1954; "Best of Broadway: The Man Who Came to Dinner," CBS, 1954; "Screen Directors Playhouse: The Silent Partner," NBC, 1956; "Producers Showcase: The Lord Don't Play Favorites," NBC, 1956; "The Rosemary Clooney Show," SYN, 1957; "This Is Your Life," NBC, 1957; "The Ed Sullivan Show," CBS, 1957; "I've Got a Secret," CBS, 1957; "The Betty White Show," ABC, 1958; "Playhouse 90: No Time At All," CBS, 1958; "You Asked For It," ABC, 1958; "Playhouse 90: The Innocent Sleep," CBS, 1958; "The Garry Moore Show," CBS, 1958; "The Donna Reed Show: A Very Merry Christmas," ABC, 1958; "Sunday Showcase: After Hours," NBC, 1960; "Candid Camera," CBS, 1960; "The Jack Paar Show," NBC,

1961; "The Twilight Zone: Once Upon a Time," CBS, 1961; "Scene Stealers," SYN, 1962; "Route 66: Journey to Nineveh," CBS, 1962; "Mr. Smith Goes to Washington: Think Mink," ABC, 1963; "The Greatest Show on Earth: You're All Right, Ivy," ABC, 1964; "Burke's Law: Who Killed Half of Glory Lee?," ABC, 1964; "The Donna Reed Show: Now You See It, Now You Don't," ABC, 1965; "The Man Who Bought Paradise," CBS, 1965; "A Salute to Stan Laurel," CBS, 1965.

KEATON, DIANE

b. *Diane Hall, Los Angeles, CA, January 4, 1946.* Oscar winning actress ("Annie Hall") who did some TV early in her career.

AS A GUEST: "Love, American Style: Love and the Pen Pals," ABC, 1970; "The FBI: Death Watch," ABC, 1971; "Mannix: The Color of Murder," CBS, 1971; "The Tonight Show Starring Johnny Carson," NBC, 1972.

KEATON, MICHAEL

b. *Pittsburgh, PA, September 9, 1951.* Sitcom actor who graduated to films in a big way.

AS A REGULAR: "All's Fair," CBS, 1977; "Mary," CBS, 1978; "The Mary Tyler Moore Hour," CBS, 1979; "Working Stiffs," CBS, 1979; "Report to Murphy," CBS, 1982.

AND: "Saturday Night Live," NBC, 1982.

KEEL, HOWARD

b. *Harold Keel, Gillespie, IL, April 13, 1919.* Baritone star of movie musicals whose TV success has come as Clayton Farlow on "Dallas."

AS A REGULAR: "Dallas," CBS, 1981- .

AND: "Dinah Shore Chevy Show," NBC, 1957; "The General Motors 50th Anniversary Show," NBC, 1957; "The Polly Bergen Show," NBC, 1957; "Dick Powell's Zane Grey Theatre: Gift From a Gunman," CBS, 1957; "The Big Record," CBS, 1958; "Roberta," NBC, 1958; "Bell Telephone Hour," NBC, 1959; "A Toast to Jerome Kern," NBC, 1959; "Bell Telephone Hour: Main Street USA," NBC, 1960; "Bell Telephone Hour: Holiday in Music," NBC, 1960; "Here's Hollywood," NBC, 1961; "Tales of Wells Fargo: Casket 73," NBC, 1961; "Bell Telephone Hour: The Music of Richard Rodgers," NBC, 1961; "Let Freedom Ring," CBS, 1961; "Hollywood Melody," NBC, 1962; "The Voice of Firestone," ABC, 1962; "Death Valley Days: Diamond Jim Brady," SYN, 1963; "The Match Game," NBC, 1964; "Run for Your Life: The Time of the Sharks," NBC, 1965; "Bell Telephone Hour: Salute to Veterans Day," NBC, 1965; "Here's Lucy: Lucy's Safari Man," CBS, 1968; "The Sonny and Cher Comedy Hour," CBS, 1972; "The Quest: Seventy-Two Hours," NBC, 1976;

"The Love Boat: Maid for Each Other," ABC, 1981; "The Love Boat: Kiss and Make-Up," ABC, 1983.

KEESHAN, BOB

b. *1928.* Actor who's entertained and informed millions of children, first as Clarabell the Clown on "Howdy Doody" and then as the gentle "Captain Kangaroo."

AS A REGULAR: "Howdy Doody," NBC, 1948-52; "Captain Kangaroo," CBS, 1955-85; "Mister Mayor," CBS, 1964-65.

AND: "The Jimmy Dean Show," CBS, 1959; "Day by Day: Trading Places," NBC, 1988; "Island Son: Role Models," CBS, 1989.

KEIM, BETTY LOU

b. *Malden, MA, 1938.*

AS A REGULAR: "My Son Jeep," NBC, 1953; "The Deputy," NBC, 1959-60.

AND: "Riverboat: The Wichita Arrows," NBC, 1960.

KEITH, BRIAN

b. *Bayonne, NJ, November 14, 1921.* Reliable TV presence who played Uncle Bill Davis on "Family Affair" and macho judge Milton McCormick.

AS A REGULAR: "Crusader," CBS, 1955-56; "Walt Disney Presents: The Nine Lives of Elfego Baca," ABC, 1959; "The Westerner," NBC, 1960; "Family Affair," CBS, 1966-71; "The Brian Keith Show (The Little People)," NBC, 1972-74; "Archer," NBC, 1975; "Hardcastle & McCormick," ABC, 1983-86; "The Pursuit of Happiness," ABC, 1987-88; "Heartland," CBS, 1989.

AND: "Lux Video Theatre: Inn of Eagles," NBC, 1953; "Motorola TV Hour: Westward the Sun," ABC, 1953; "Campbell TV Soundstage: Journey to Java," NBC, 1954; "Pepsi Cola Playhouse: Pals to the End," ABC, 1955; "Studio 57: The Haven Technique," SYN, 1955; "Pepsi Cola Playhouse: Passage Home," ABC, 1955; "Studio 57: Rescue," SYN, 1955; "Ford Theatre: Sunday Mourn," NBC, 1955; "Elgin TV Hour: Combat Medic," ABC, 1955; "Fireside Theatre: Man on the Window Sill," NBC, 1955; "Lux Video Theatre: Branded," NBC, 1955; "Lux Video Theatre: Possessed," NBC, 1957; "The Brothers: The Runaways," CBS, 1957; "Ford Theatre: Adventure for Hire," ABC, 1957; "Wire Service: Escape to Freedom," ABC, 1957; "Climax!: Hurricane Dianne," CBS, 1957; "Christophers: The Importance of Training Young People," SYN, 1958; "Dick Powell's Zane Grey Theatre: Trouble at Tres Cruces," CBS, 1959; "Alfred Hitchcock Presents: Your Witness," CBS, 1959; "Rawhide: Incident in No Man's Land," CBS, 1959; "Alfred Hitchcock Presents: No Pain,"

CBS, 1959; "Laramie: The General Must Die," NBC, 1959; "Alfred Hitchcock Presents: Cell 227," CBS, 1960; "Here's Hollywood," NBC, 1960; "The Untouchables: Jamaica Ginger," ABC, 1961; "The Americans: The Sentry," NBC, 1961; "Frontier Circus: The Smallest Target," CBS, 1961; "The Outlaws: My Friend, the Horse Thief," NBC, 1961; "Alcoa Premiere: The Breaking Point," ABC, 1961; "The Outlaws: The Bitter Swede," NBC, 1962; "Follow the Sun: The Dumbest Blonde," ABC, 1962; "Alfred Hitchcock Presents: The Test," NBC, 1962; "Target: The Corrupters: The Organizer," ABC, 1962; "The Alfred Hitchcock Hour: Night of the Owl," CBS, 1962; "The Virginian: Duel at Shiloh," NBC, 1963; "Walt Disney's Wonderful World of Color: Johnny Shiloh," NBC, 1963; "Sam Benedict: Run Softly, Oh Softly," NBC, 1963; "Wagon Train: The Tom Tuesday Story," ABC, 1963; "Dr. Kildare: The Gift of the Koodjanuk," NBC, 1963; "The Fugitive: Fear in a Desert City," ABC, 1963; "Wagon Train: The Robert Harrison Clarke Story," ABC, 1963; "77 Sunset Strip: 5," ABC, 1963; "Walt Disney's Wonderful World of Color: Bristle Face," NBC, 1964; "The Great Adventure: The Henry Bergh Story," CBS, 1964; "Walt Disney's Wonderful World of Color: The Tenderfoot," NBC, 1964; "Profiles in Courage: Thomas Hart Benton," NBC, 1964; "You Don't Say," NBC, 1965; "Password," CBS, 1966; "Insight: The Dog That Bit You," SYN, 1967; "The Jonathan Winters Show," CBS, 1969; "Murder, She Wrote: The Murder of Sherlock Holmes," CBS, 1984.

TV MOVIES AND MINISERIES: "Second Chance," ABC, 1972; "The Zoo Gang," NBC, 1975; "The Loneliest Runner," NBC, 1976; "The Quest," NBC, 1976; "Centennial," NBC, 1978-79; "The Chisholms," CBS, 1979; "Cry for the Strangers," CBS, 1982; "World War III," NBC, 1982; "The Alamo: 13 Days to Glory," NBC, 1987; "Perry Mason: The Case of the Lethal Lesson," NBC, 1989; "Lady in a Corner," NBC, 1989.

KEITH, RICHARD
b. *Keith Thibodeaux, Lafayette, LA, December 1, 1950.* Child actor and drummer who played Little Ricky on "I Love Lucy."
AS A REGULAR: "I Love Lucy," CBS, 1956-57; "The Lucille Ball-Desi Arnaz Show," CBS, 1957-59.
AND: "Dick Powell's Zane Grey Theatre: Ride a Lonely Trail," CBS, 1957; "The Phil Silvers Show: Bilko the Potato Sack King," CBS, 1958; "The Andy Griffith Show: One Punch Opie," CBS, 1962; "The Andy Griffith Show: Opie and His Merry Men," CBS, 1963; "The Andy Griffith Show: Andy and Opie's Pal," CBS, 1964; "The Lucy Show: Lucy Is a Process Server," CBS, 1964; "The Joey Bishop Show: Joey the Patient,"

CBS, 1964; "The Andy Griffith Show: Opie and the Carnival," CBS, 1965; "The Andy Griffith Show: Wyatt Earp," CBS, 1966; "The Andy Griffith Show: Look, Paw, I'm Dancing," CBS, 1966; "The Mike Douglas Show," SYN, 1976; "The Pat Sajak Show," CBS, 1989.

KEITH, ROBERT
b. *Fowler, IN, February 10, 1898; d. 1966.* Movie and TV actor; father of Brian Keith.
AS A REGULAR: "The Great Gildersleeve," NBC, 1955-56.
AND: "Pulitzer Prize Playhouse: Robert E. Lee," ABC, 1952; "Philco TV Playhouse: The Basket Weaver," NBC, 1952; "Police Story: The California Case," CBS, 1952; "Armstrong Circle Theatre: Judgment," NBC, 1953; "Studio One: Another Caesar," CBS, 1953; "Motorola TV Hour: Atomic Attack," ABC, 1954; "The Dick Powell Show: The Court-Martial of Captain Wycliff," NBC, 1962; "Alfred Hitchcock Presents: Ten O'Clock Tiger," NBC, 1962; "The Eleventh Hour: Beauty Playing a Mandolin Underneath a Willow Tree," NBC, 1963; "The Fugitive: Home Is the Hunter," ABC, 1964; "The Alfred Hitchcock Hour: Final Escape," NBC, 1964; "The Twilight Zone: The Masks," CBS, 1964.

KELK, JACK
b. *Brooklyn, NY, August 6, 1923.* Actor who played Homer Brown on "The Aldrich Family."
AS A REGULAR: "The Aldrich Family," NBC, 1949-51; "Young Mr. Bobbin," NBC, 1951-52.
AND: "The Donna Reed Show: Donna Plays Cupid," ABC, 1959; "The Donna Reed Show: Jeff vs. Mary," ABC, 1959.

KELLAWAY, CECIL
b. *South Africa, August 22, 1893; d. 1973.* Character actor who often played kindly Irishmen in movies and on TV.
AS A GUEST: "Magnavox Theatre: The Hurricane at Pilgrim Hill," CBS, 1950; "Cavalcade of America: Poor Richard," NBC, 1952; "Cavalcade of America: Sam the Whale," ABC, 1953; "Schlitz Playhouse of Stars: Day of Good News," CBS, 1954; "Ford Theatre: Hanrahan," NBC, 1955; "Schlitz Playhouse of Stars: Visa for X," CBS, 1955; "Studio One: Private History," CBS, 1955; "Ford Theatre: The Fabulous Sycamores," NBC, 1955; "Crossroads: Tenement Saint," ABC, 1956; "Lux Video Theatre: Just Across the Street," NBC, 1957; "Crossroads: Big Sombrero," ABC, 1957; "The Whirlybirds: Buy Me a Miracle," SYN, 1958; "Playhouse 90: Verdict of Three," CBS, 1958; "Studio 57: A Source of Irritation," SYN, 1958; "Studio One: Birthday

Present," CBS, 1958; "The Ann Sothern Show: Hurrah for the Irish," CBS, 1959; "The Ann Sothern Show: The O'Connors Stick Together," CBS, 1959; "The Millioniare: Millionaire Father Gilhooley," CBS, 1959; "The Twilight Zone: Elegy," CBS, 1960; "Adventures in Paradise: The Intruders," ABC, 1960; "Hennesey: Tell It to the Chaplain," CBS, 1960; "Harrigan and Son: You Can't Fight City Hall," ABC, 1961; "Rawhide: Incident in the Middle of Nowhere," CBS, 1961; "Adventures in Paradise: A Touch of Genius," ABC, 1961; "Adventures in Paradise: The Pretender," ABC, 1961; "The Donna Reed Show: The Fabulous O'Hara," ABC, 1961; "The Dick Powell Show: A Swiss Affair," NBC, 1961; "Ben Casey: Imagine a Long, Bright Corridor," ABC, 1962; "The New Breed: Mr. Weltschmerz," ABC, 1962; "Follow the Sun: The Inhuman Equation," ABC, 1962; "Mr. Smith Goes to Washington: For Richer, for Poorer," ABC, 1962; "The Twilight Zone: Passage on the Lady Anne," CBS, 1963; "Ben Casey: If Dreams Were Meant to Sell," ABC, 1963; "My Favorite Martian: Now You See It, Now You Don't," CBS, 1964; "The Greatest Show on Earth: Rosetta," ABC, 1964; "Burke's Law: Who Killed Don Pablo?," ABC, 1964; "Bewitched: A Vision of Sugar Plums," ABC, 1964; "Valentine's Day: Farrow's Last Fling," ABC, 1965; "The FBI: The Hijackers," ABC, 1965; "Kraft Supsense Theatre: Connery's Hands," NBC, 1965; "The FBI: The Hijackers," ABC, 1965; "Kismet," ABC, 1967; "That Girl: Old Man's Darling," ABC, 1968; "The Ghost and Mrs. Muir: Chowderhead," NBC, 1969; "My Friend Tony: Dead Reckoning," NBC, 1969; "Nanny and the Professor: Strictly for the Birds," ABC, 1970; "The Wonderful World of Disney: The Wacky Zoo of Morgan City," NBC, 1970.

KELLERMAN, SALLY

b. Long Beach, CA, June 2, 1938. Blonde actress with a rich, sensuous voice that served her well as "Hot Lips" Houlihan in the movie "M*A*S*H" and for selling, among other things, Hidden Valley salad dressing on TV commercials.

AS A GUEST: "Cheyenne: The Durango Brothers," ABC, 1962; "I'm Dickens, He's Fenster: The Bet," ABC, 1963; "The Adventures of Ozzie and Harriet: Decorating Dave's Office," ABC, 1963; "The Many Loves of Dobie Gillis: The Call of the Like Wild," CBS, 1963; "The Outer Limits: The Human Factor," ABC, 1963; "My Three Sons: Steve and the Viking," ABC, 1963; "The Outer Limits: The Bellero Shield," ABC, 1964; "Ben Casey: The Bark of a Three-Headed Hound," ABC, 1964; "The Greatest

Show on Earth: This Train Don't Stop Until It Gets There," ABC, 1964; "Slattery's People: Question—What Are You Doing Out There, Waldo?," CBS, 1964; "Bob Hope Chrysler Theatre: Parties to the Crime," NBC, 1964; "The Rogues: Bless You, G. Carter Huntington," NBC, 1965; "Twelve O'Clock High: Those Who Are About to Die," ABC, 1965; "The Alfred Hitchcock Hour: Thou Still Unravished Bride," NBC, 1965; "Kraft Suspense Theatre: Connery's Hands," NBC, 1965; "Ben Casey: You Wanna Know What Really Goes on in a Hospital?," ABC, 1965; "A Man Called Shenandoah: Run, Killer, Run," ABC, 1966; "The Legend of Jesse James: The Lonely Place," ABC, 1966; "I Spy: My Mother, the Spy," NBC, 1966; "Bonanza: A Dollar's Worth of Trouble," NBC, 1966; "Star Trek: Where No Man Has Gone Before," NBC, 1966; "That Girl: Break a Leg," ABC, 1966; "T.H.E. Cat: Matter Over Mind," NBC, 1967; "Dundee and the Culhane: The Dead Man's Brief," CBS, 1967; "The Invaders: Labyrinth," ABC, 1967; "Higher and Higher, Attorneys at Law," CBS, 1968; "It Takes a Thief: The Naked Billionaire," ABC, 1969; "Hawaii Five-O: The Big Kahuna," CBS, 1969; "Mannix: The Solid Gold Web," CBS, 1969; "Bonanza: Return Engagement," NBC, 1970; "A Couple of Dons," NBC, 1973; "The Merv Griffin Show," SYN, 1975; "Great Performances: Verna: USO Girl," PBS, 1978; "Saturday Night Live," NBC, 1981; "CBS Summer Playhouse: Dr. Paradise," CBS, 1988.
TV MOVIES AND MINISERIES: "Centennial," NBC, 1978-79; "For Lovers Only," ABC, 1982; "Dempsey," CBS, 1983; "September Gun," CBS, 1983; "Secret Weapons," NBC, 1985.

KELLEY, DEFOREST

b. Atlanta, GA, January 20, 1920. Actor who played Dr. "Bones" McCoy on "Star Trek."
AS A REGULAR: "Star Trek," NBC, 1966-69.
AND: "Favorite Story: Inside Out," SYN, 1952; "Favorite Story: The Man Who Sold His Shadow," SYN, 1952; "Gunsmoke: Indian Scout," CBS, 1956; "Science Fiction Theatre: Survival in Box Canyon," SYN, 1956; "Dick Powell's Zane Grey Theatre: Stage to Tucson," CBS, 1956; "The Lineup: The Ellis Garden Case," CBS, 1957; "You Are There: The Surrender at Corregidor," CBS, 1957; "The Web: Kill and Run," NBC, 1957; "O. Henry Playhouse: Fog in Santone," SYN, 1957; "Trackdown: End of An Outlaw," CBS, 1957; "Playhouse 90: Edge of Innocence," CBS, 1957; "Black Saddle: Apache Trail," ABC, 1959; "Wanted Dead or Alive: Secret Ballot," CBS, 1959; "Alcoa Theatre: 222 Montgomery," NBC, 1959; "Markham: Counterpoint," CBS, 1960; "Two Faces West: Vendetta for January," SYN, 1960; "Riverboat:

472

Listen to the Nightingale," NBC, 1961; "Route 66: The Clover Throne," CBS, 1961; "Lawman: The Squatters," ABC, 1961; "Stagecoach West: Image of a Man," ABC, 1961; "The Deputy: The Means and the End," NBC, 1961; "Bat Masterson: No Amnesty for Death," NBC, 1961; "Stagecoach West: The Big Gun," ABC, 1961; "Bonanza: The Honor of Cochise," NBC, 1961; "Cain's Hundred: The Fixer," NBC, 1961; "Perry Mason: The Case of the Unwelcome Bride," CBS, 1961; "Route 66: 1800 Days to Justice," CBS, 1962; "Have Gun, Will Travel: Protects Ex-Con's Wife," CBS, 1962; "Bonanza: The Decision," NBC, 1962; "The Virginian: Duel at Shiloh," NBC, 1963; "The Virginian: Man of Violence," NBC, 1963; "The Donna Reed Show: Uncle Jeff Needs You," ABC, 1965; "Room 222: The Sins of the Fathers," ABC, 1971; "The Cowboys: David Done It," ABC, 1974.

KELLIN, MIKE
  b. Hartford, CT, April 26, 1922; d. 1983. Character actor with a hangdog face and manner.
  AS A REGULAR: "Bonino," NBC, 1953; "Honestly Celeste," CBS, 1954; "The Wackiest Ship in the Army," NBC, 1965-66; "Fitz and Bones," NBC, 1981.
  AND: "U.S. Steel Hour: Hunted," CBS, 1956; "Kraft Television Theatre: No Warning," NBC, 1957; "Studio One: Dead of Noon," CBS, 1957; "Kraft Television Theatre: Drummer Man," NBC, 1957; "True Story: The Set-Up," NBC, 1957; "Black Saddle: Apache Trial," ABC, 1959; "Have Gun, Will Travel: The Solid Gold Patrol," CBS, 1959; "Tightrope!: Night of the Gun," CBS, 1960; "The Untouchables: The White Slavers," ABC, 1960; "Adventures in Paradise: Once Around the Circuit," ABC, 1960; "Shirley Temple's Storybook: Little Men," NBC, 1960; "Alcoa Presents One Step Beyond: The Trap," ABC, 1960; "Have Gun, Will Travel: Shadow of a Man," CBS, 1961; "Omnibus: Fierce, Funny and Far Out," NBC, 1961; "Naked City: The Deadly Guinea Pig," ABC, 1961; "The Islanders: The World Is Her Oyster," ABC, 1961; "Have Gun, Will Travel: The Siege," CBS, 1961; "Route 66: Birdcage on My Foot," CBS, 1961; "87th Precinct: The Guilt," NBC, 1961; "Have Gun, Will Travel: Drop of Blood," CBS, 1961; "The New Breed: The Valley of the 3 Charlies," ABC, 1961; "The Eternal Light: A Cup of Light," NBC, 1961; "The Untouchables: City Without a Name," ABC, 1961; "The Outlaws: No More Horses," NBC, 1962; "Dr. Kildare: The Mask Makers," NBC, 1962; "Route 66: Hey Moth, Come Eat the Flame," CBS, 1962; "The Twilight Zone: The Thirty-Fathom Grave," CBS, 1963; "Grindl: Some Dogs Have the Biggest Mouths," NBC, 1964; "Mr. Novak: Sparrow on the Wire," NBC, 1964; "The Defenders: Who'll Dig His Grave?,"

CBS, 1964; "Bob Hope Chrysler Theatre: Two Is the Number," NBC, 1964; "Voyage to the Bottom of the Sea: The Mist of Silence," ABC, 1964; "Rawhide: A Man Called Mushy," CBS, 1964; "Mr. Novak: And Then I Wrote," NBC, 1965; "Combat!: Losers Cry Deal," ABC, 1965; "Gunsmoke: The Moonstone," CBS, 1966; "Ironside: A Death in Academe," NBC, 1974; "Kojak: Hush Now or You Die," CBS, 1974; "All in the Family: Archie's Secret Passion," CBS, 1976; "Barney Miller: Noninvolvement," ABC, 1976; "Switch: Blue Crusaders' Reunion," CBS, 1977.
  TV MOVIES AND MINISERIES: "A Clear and Present Danger," NBC, 1970; "Assignment: Munich," ABC, 1972; "The Catcher," NBC, 1972; "Connection," ABC, 1973; "The Art of Crime," NBC, 1975; "Best Sellers: Seventh Avenue," NBC, 1977; "The Murder That Wouldn't Die," NBC, 1980; "F.D.R.: The Last Year," NBC, 1980.

KELLY, AL
  b. 1899; d. 1966. Comedian whose gimmick was double-talk.
  AS A REGULAR: "Back That Fact," ABC, 1953; "The Ernie Kovacs Show," NBC, 1956.
  AND: "The Ed Sullivan Show," CBS, 1957; "The Julius LaRosa Show," NBC, 1957; "The Chevy Show," NBC, 1958; "Make Me Laugh," ABC, 1958; "The Sam Levenson Show," CBS, 1959; "Revlon Revue: Accent on Comedy," CBS, 1960; "Dave's Place," NBC, 1960; "Candid Camera," CBS, 1961; "Play Your Hunch," NBC, 1962; "Trials of O'Brien: Notes on a Spanish Prisoner," CBS, 1965.

KELLY, BRIAN
  b. Detroit, MI. Actor who played Porter Ricks, dad of Sandy (Luke Halpin) and Bud (Tommy Norden) on "Flipper."
  AS A REGULAR: "21 Beacon Street," NBC, 1959; "Straightaway," ABC, 1961-62; "Flipper," NBC, 1964-68.
  AND: "No Warning!: Fingerprints," NBC, 1958; "Here's Hollywood," NBC, 1961; "The Beverly Hillbillies: Elly's Animals," CBS, 1963; "The Beverly Hillbillies: Jed Plays Solomon," CBS, 1963; "You Don't Say," NBC, 1969.
  TV MOVIES AND MINISERIES: "Berlin Affair," ABC, 1970; "Drive Hard, Drive Fast," NBC, 1973.

KELLY, GENE
  b. Pittsburgh, PA, August 23, 1912. Famous dancer on the stage and screen who had little success on two TV series; an Emmy winner for "Jack and the Beanstalk."
  AS A REGULAR: "Going My Way," ABC, 1962-63; "The Funny Side," NBC, 1971.
  AND: "Schlitz Playhouse of Stars: The Life You

Save," CBS, 1957; "Salute to Baseball," NBC, 1957; "The Ed Sullivan Show," CBS, 1957; "The $64,000 Question," CBS, 1957; "Person to Person," CBS, 1958; "Omnibus: Dancing Is a Man's Game," NBC, 1958; "Pontiac Star Parade: The Gene Kelly Show," NBC, 1959; "Here's Hollywood," NBC, 1961; "The Golden Years," NBC, 1961; "Hollywood Palace," ABC, 1964; "Password," CBS, 1965; "October Madness," SYN, 1965; "Jack and the Beanstalk," NBC, 1967; "Peggy Fleming Special," NBC, 1968; "Changing Scene II," ABC, 1970; "The Dean Martin Show," NBC, 1971; "Ol' Blue Eyes Is Back," NBC, 1973; "The Mike Douglas Show," SYN, 1976; "The Mary Tyler Moore Hour," CBS, 1979; "The Love Boat: Two Tails of a City," ABC, 1984.

TV MOVIES AND MINISERIES: "North and South," ABC, 1985; "Sins," CBS, 1986.

* Emmies: 1967.

KELLY, JACK

b. Astoria, NY, September 16, 1927. Handsome actor of fifties TV best known as Bart Maverick, who always suffered a little in comparison to brother Bret (James Garner).

AS A REGULAR: "Warner Bros. Presents Kings Row," ABC, 1955-56; "Dr. Hudson's Secret Journal," SYN, 1955-57; "Maverick," ABC, 1957-62; "Sale of the Century," NBC, 1969-73; "NBC Comedy Playhouse," NBC, 1970; "NBC Comedy Theater," NBC, 1971-72; "Get Christie Love!," ABC, 1975; "The Hardy Boys Mysteries," ABC, 1978-79.

AND: "Pepsi Cola Playhouse: The Sound of Silence," ABC, 1954; "Pepsi Cola Playhouse: The Girl on the Drum," ABC, 1954; "Cavalcade Theatre: Sunrise on a Dirty Face," ABC, 1955; "TV Reader's Digest: My First Bullfight," ABC, 1955; "Fireside Theatre: Kirsti," NBC, 1956; "Fireside Theatre: Scent of Roses," NBC, 1956; "Warner Bros. Presents Conflict: Wedding Gift," ABC, 1956; "The Millionaire: The Story of Fred Graham," CBS, 1956; "Lux Video Theatre: Just Across the Street," NBC, 1957; "Ford Theatre: The Idea Man," ABC, 1957; "State Trooper: Jailbreak at Tonopah," SYN, 1957; "Pantomime Quiz," ABC, 1958; "Pat Boone Chevy Showroom," ABC, 1959; "Here's Hollywood," NBC, 1961; "Wagon Train: The Fenton Canaby Story," ABC, 1963; "Kraft Suspense Theatre: The Name of the Game," NBC, 1963; "Your First Impression," NBC, 1964; "Bob Hope Chrysler Theatre: Red Snow, White Ice," NBC, 1964; "The Lucy Show: Lucy Makes a Pinch," CBS, 1964; "Bob Hope Chrsyler Theatre: Double Jeopardy," NBC, 1965; "Kraft Suspense Theatre: Four Into Zero," NBC, 1965; "Kraft Suspense Theatre: Kill Me on July 20th," NBC, 1965; "Laredo: The Deadliest Kid in the West," NBC, 1966; "Bob Hope Chrsyler Theatre: One Embezzlement and Two Margaritas," NBC, 1966; "Batman: Hot Off the Griddle/The Cat and the

Fiddle," ABC, 1966; "Bob Hope Chrysler Theatre: Time of Flight," NBC, 1966; "Daktari: Daktari's Last Hunt," CBS, 1966; "Run for Your Life: Baby, the World's on Fire," NBC, 1967; "Please Don't Eat the Daisies: Remember Lake Serene," NBC, 1967; "Bob Hope Chrysler Theatre: Deadlock," NBC, 1967; "Ironside: Tagged for Murder," NBC, 1967; "The High Chaparral: Detour From Dodge," NBC, 1967; "The Iron Horse: Dealer's Choice," ABC, 1967; "The Name of the Game: The Inquiry," NBC, 1969; "The Name of the Game: The Civilized Man," NBC, 1969; "Alias Smith and Jones: Night of the Red Dog," ABC, 1972; "Marcus Welby, M.D.: Solomon's Choice," ABC, 1972; "Ghost Story: The Dead We Leave Behind," NBC, 1972; "Ironside: Cold Hard Cash," NBC, 1972; "Banacek: Fly Me-If You Can Find Me," NBC, 1973; "McCloud: This Must Be the Alamo," NBC, 1974; "Hawaii Five-O: Let Death Do Us Part," CBS, 1976; "The Rockford Files: The Becker Connection," NBC, 1976; "Quincy: The Two Sides of Truth," NBC, 1977; "The Rockford Files: Beamer's Last Case," NBC, 1977; "The Hardy Boys Mysteries: Last Kiss of Summer," ABC, 1978; "Bret Maverick: The Hidalgo Thing," NBC, 1982.

TV MOVIES AND MINISERIES: "The New Maverick," ABC, 1978.

KELLY, NANCY

b. Lowell, MA, March 25, 1921. Former child actress; sister of Jack Kelly.

AS A GUEST: "Silver Theatre: Minor Incident," CBS, 1950; "Studio One: The Fathers," CBS, 1953; "Dunninger," SYN, 1953; "Studio One: Conflict," CBS, 1953; "Medallion Theatre: Voyage Back," CBS, 1954; "Kraft Television Theatre: Flowers in a Book," ABC, 1954; "Studio One: The Secret Self," CBS, 1954; "Philco TV Playhouse: Time Bomb," NBC, 1954; "Studio One: The Pilot," CBS, 1956; "Kaiser Aluminum Hour: Roar of the Lion," NBC, 1956; "Playhouse 90: Circle of the Day," CBS, 1957; "The Last Word," CBS, 1957; "Climax!: Murder Is a Witch," CBS, 1957; "Suspicion: Four O'Clock," NBC, 1957; "Alcoa Theatre: Office Party," NBC, 1958; "The Ed Sullivan Show," CBS, 1959; "Thriller: The Storm," NBC, 1962; "Sam Benedict: Nothing Equals Nothing," NBC, 1962; "Girl Talk," SYN, 1963; "The Alfred Hitchcock Hour: The Lonely Hours," CBS, 1963; "Medical Center: Appointment with Danger," CBS, 1974.

TV MOVIES AND MINISERIES: "The Imposter," NBC, 1975; "Murder at the World Series," ABC, 1977.

KELLY, PATSY

b. Sara Veronica Rose Kelly, Brooklyn, NY, January 12, 1910; d. 1981. Movie and stage actress, usually as a wisecracking maid or servant, who turned to television when she "retired."

AS A REGULAR: "The Cop and the Kid," NBC, 1975-76.

AND: "Kraft Television Theatre: The Big Break," NBC, 1957; "The Untouchables: Head of Fire, Feet of Clay," ABC, 1960; "Laramie: Lily," NBC, 1960; "Alfred Hitchcock Presents: Outlaw in Town," NBC, 1960; "The Dick Van Dyke Show: One Angry Man," CBS, 1962; "Burke's Law: Who Killed Mr. Cartwheel?," ABC, 1964; "Valentine's Day: Call Me No Cabs," ABC, 1964; "Vacation Playhouse: My Son, the Doctor," CBS, 1966; "The Wild Wild West: The Night of the Big Blast," CBS, 1966; "Laredo: A Question of Guilt," NBC, 1967; "The Man From UNCLE: The Hula Doll Affair," NBC, 1967; "The Wild Wild West: Night of the Bogus Bandits," CBS, 1967; "Bonanza: A Girl Named George," NBC, 1968; "Love, American Style: Love and the Watchdog," ABC, 1969; "Barefoot in the Park: Pilot," ABC, 1970; "Medical Center: Saturday's Child," CBS, 1974; "The Love Boat: Rent-a-Family," ABC, 1979.

TV MOVIES AND MINISERIES: "The Pigeon," ABC, 1969.

KELLY, PAUL

b. Brooklyn, NY, August 9, 1899; d. 1956. Film actor, often in action roles.

AS A GUEST: "Pulitzer Prize Playhouse: Melville Goodwin, USA," ABC, 1952; "Celanese Theatre: Street Scene," ABC, 1952; "Robert Montgomery Presents: Precinct," NBC, 1952; "Teledrama: Deadline for Murder," CBS, 1953; "Schlitz Playhouse of Stars: The Black Mate," CBS, 1954; "Fireside Theatre: His Brother's Keeper," NBC, 1954; "Schlitz Playhouse of Stars: Underground," CBS, 1955; "Lux Video Theatre: One Foot in Heaven," NBC, 1955; "Fireside Theatre: Marked for Death," NBC, 1955; "Cavalcade Theatre: How to Raise a Boy," ABC, 1955; "Schlitz Playhouse of Stars: Jury of One," CBS, 1955; "Crossroads: Shadow of God," ABC, 1955; "Crossroads: Two-Fisted Saint," ABC, 1956; "Front Row Center: Instant of Truth," CBS, 1956; "Christophers: Atomic Power as a Force for Good," SYN, 1956.

KELLY, PAULA

b. Jacksonville, FL, October 21, 1943. Actress and dancer.

AS A REGULAR: "Night Court," NBC, 1984; "Santa Barbara," NBC, 1984-85.

AND: "This Is Tom Jones," ABC, 1970; "Sanford & Son: Lamont Goes African," NBC, 1972; "The Streets of San Francisco: Men Will Die," ABC, 1975; "Police Woman: The Company," NBC, 1975; "The Streets of San Francisco: The Thrill Killers," ABC, 1976; "Police Woman: Wednesday's Child,"

NBC, 1976; "Police Woman: Once a Snitch," NBC, 1977; "Kojak: The Queen of Hearts is Wild," CBS, 1977; "Good Times: Where Have All the Doctors Gone?," CBS, 1979; "Hot Pursuit: Portrait of a Lady Killer," NBC, 1984; "St. Elsewhere: Cheek to Cheek," NBC, 1986; "Mission: Impossible: Bayou," ABC, 1989.

TV MOVIES AND MINISERIES: "The Women of Brewster Place," ABC, 1989.

KELSEY, LINDA

b. Minneapolis, MN, July 28, 1946. Actress who played Billie Newman on "Lou Grant."

AS A REGULAR: "Lou Grant," CBS, 1977-82; "Day by Day," NBC, 1988-89.

AND: "Emergency!: Frequency," NBC, 1973; "The Rockford Files: The Dexter Crisis," NBC, 1974; "The Mary Tyler Moore Show: A New Sue Ann," CBS, 1974; "Barnaby Jones: Web of Deceit," CBS, 1974; "M*A*S*H: The Nurses," CBS, 1976; "Barnaby Jones: Voice in the Night," CBS, 1976; "The Streets of San Francisco: Let's Pretend We're Strangers," ABC, 1977; "Murder, She Wrote: Capitol Offense," CBS, 1985; "St. Elsewhere: Haunted," NBC, 1985; "Blacke's Magic: Forced Landing," NBC, 1986; "Murder, She Wrote: Jessica Behind Bars," CBS, 1986; "CBS Schoolbreak Special: Home Sweet Homeless," CBS, 1988; "Midnight Caller: End of the Innocence," NBC, 1989.

TV MOVIES AND MINISERIES: "The Picture of Dorian Gray," ABC, 1973; "Eleanor and Franklin," ABC, 1976; "Best Sellers: Captains and the Kings," NBC, 1976; "Something for Joey," CBS, 1977; "A Perfect Match," CBS, 1980; "His Mistress," NBC, 1984; "Attack on Fear," CBS, 1984; "Baby Girl Scott," CBS, 1987.

KELTON, PERT

b. Great Falls, MT, October 14, 1907; d. 1968. Heavyset actress often in roles as domestic or loudmouth, best known as the mother of Marian the Librarian in "The Music Man"; also the first actress to play Alice Kramden opposite Jackie Gleason.

AS A REGULAR: "Calvacade of Stars," DUM, 1950-52; "Henry Morgan's Great Talent Hunt," NBC, 1951.

AND: "The Danny Thomas Show: The Scrubwoman," CBS, 1961; "The Twilight Zone: Miniature," CBS, 1963; "My Three Sons: Back Door Bub," ABC, 1964; "Gomer Pyle, USMC: Show Me the Way to Go Home," CBS, 1966; "T.H.E. Cat: The Canary Who Lost His Voice," NBC, 1966.

KEMP, BRANDIS

b. Palo Alto, CA.

AS A REGULAR: "Fridays," ABC, 1980-82; "AfterMASH," CBS, 1983-84.

AND: "Remington Steele: Steele Trap," NBC, 1982; "Faerie Tale Theatre: Goldilocks and the Three Bears," SHO, 1984; "Perfect Strangers: The Horn Blows at Midnight," ABC, 1987; "227: Country Cousins," NBC, 1988.

KEMP, JEREMY

b. Jeremy Walker, England, February 3, 1935. Actor who usually plays heavies, including Nazis and Soviets.
AS A GUEST: "Murder, She Wrote: From Russia-With Blood," CBS, 1989.
TV MOVIES AND MINISERIES: "Best Sellers: The Rhinemann Exchange," NBC, 1977; "George Washington," CBS, 1984; "Peter the Great," NBC, 1986; "War and Remembrance," ABC, 1988, 1989.

KENDALL, KAY

b. Justine McCarthy, England, 1926; d. 1959. Comic actress of the screen ("Genevieve," "Les Girls") who did a bit of TV.
AS A GUEST: "The Polly Bergen Show," NBC, 1957; "The Phil Silvers Show: Bilko Presents Kay Kendall," CBS, 1958.

KENNEDY, ARTHUR

b. Worcester, MA, February 17, 1914; d. 1990. Rugged actor usually in roles conveying integrity.
AS A REGULAR: "F.D.R.," ABC, 1965; "Nakia," ABC, 1974.
AND: "Ford Theatre: Night Visitor," NBC, 1954; "Ethel Barrymore Theatre: This Is Villa," SYN, 1956; "Dick Powell's Zane Grey Theatre: Make It Look Good," CBS, 1959; "Kaleidoscope: The Third Commandment," NBC, 1959; "Rendezvous: The Sound of Gunfire," CBS, 1959; "Our American Heritage: Divided We Stand," NBC, 1959; "G.E. Theatre: The Web of Guilt," CBS, 1960; "Playhouse 90: In the Presence of Mine Enemies," CBS, 1960; "Our American Heritage: Not Without Honor," NBC, 1960; "Alcoa Premiere: People Need People," ABC, 1961; "The du Pont Show: The Forgery," NBC, 1962; "Espionage: The Whistling Shrimp," NBC, 1963; "Kraft Suspense Theatre: Leviathan Five," NBC, 1964; "Suspense: I, Mike Kenny," CBS, 1964; "The du Pont Show: Ambassador at Large," NBC, 1964; "Kraft Suspense Theatre: Leviathan Five," NBC, 1964; "The Alfred Hitchcock Hour: Change of Address," NBC, 1964; "ABC Stage '67: The Confession," ABC, 1966; "CBS Playhouse: Appalachian Autumn," CBS, 1969.
TV MOVIES AND MINISERIES: "The Movie Murderer," NBC, 1970; "A Death of Innocence," CBS, 1971; "Crawlspace," CBS, 1972; "The President's Plane Is Missing," ABC, 1973; "Nakia," ABC, 1974.

KENNEDY, GEORGE

b. New York City, NY, February 18, 1925. Oscar-winning actor ("Cool Hand Luke") often in take-charge roles.
AS A REGULAR: "Sarge," NBC, 1971-72; "The Blue Knight," CBS, 1976; "Counterattack: Crime in America," ABC, 1982; "Dallas," CBS, 1989- .
AND: "Colt .45: The Rival Gun," ABC, 1959; "Cheyenne: Prisoner of Moon Mesa," ABC, 1959; "The Alaskans: The Golden Fleece," ABC, 1959; "Have Gun, Will Travel: A Head of Hair," CBS, 1960; "Riverboat: River Champion," NBC, 1960; "Peter Gunn: The Crossbow," NBC, 1960; "Have Gun, Will Travel: The Legacy," CBS, 1960; "Gunsmoke: The Blacksmith," CBS, 1960; "My Sister Eileen: Ebenezer Scrooge Appopolous," CBS, 1960; "Klondike: Swing on Your Partner," NBC, 1961; "The Case of the Dangerous Robin: The Missing Manuscript," SYN, 1961; "SurfSide 6: Heels Over Head," ABC, 1961; "Gunsmoke: Kittyshot," CBS, 1961; "Gunsmoke: Big Man," CBS, 1961; "Acapulco: Fisher's Daughter," NBC, 1961; "The Asphalt Jungle: The Friendly Gesture," ABC, 1961; "Bonanza: The Infernal Machine," NBC, 1961; "Bat Masterson: The Fourth Man," NBC, 1961; "The Tall Man: Trial by Hanging," NBC, 1961; "Have Gun, Will Travel: The Road," CBS, 1961; "Have Gun, Will Travel: The Vigil," CBS, 1961; "Have Gun, Will Travel: A Proof of Love," CBS, 1961; "Rawhide: The Peddler," CBS, 1962; "Tales of Wells Fargo: Assignment in Gloribee," NBC, 1962; "The Tall Man: Three for All," NBC, 1962; "Have Gun, Will Travel: Don't Shoot the Piano Player," CBS, 1962; "The Outlaws: Farewell Performance," NBC, 1962; "Thriller: The Innocent Bystanders," NBC, 1962; "The Andy Griffith Show: The Big House," CBS, 1963; "77 Sunset Strip: The Night Was Six Years Long," ABC, 1963; "Bob Hope Chrysler Theatre: One Day in the Life of Ivan Denisovich," NBC, 1963; "The Great Adventure: Rodger Young," CBS, 1964; "McHale's Navy: The Return of Big Frenchy," ABC, 1964; "The Virginian: A Gallows For Sam Horn," NBC, 1964; "Bonanza: The Scapegoat," NBC, 1964; "The Alfred Hitchcock Hour: Misadventure," NBC, 1964; "A Man Called Shenandoah: A Special Talent for Killing," ABC, 1965; "Laredo: Pride of the Rangers," NBC, 1965; "The Outer Limits: The Brain of Colonel Barham," ABC, 1965; "The Virginian: Nobility of Kings," NBC, 1965; "The Virginian: Trail to Ashley Mountain," NBC, 1966; "The Legend of Jesse James: Return to Lawrence," ABC, 1966; "Perry Mason: The Case of the Greek Goddess," CBS, 1966; "The Big Valley: Barbary Red," ABC, 1966; "Dr. Kildare: Mercy or Murder/Strange Sort of Accident," NBC, 1966; "The Jean Arthur Show: Pilot," CBS, 1966; "Tarzan: Thief Catcher," NBC, 1967; "Hawaii Five-O: Draw Me a Killer,"

CBS, 1973; "Hawaii Five-O: Death with Father," CBS, 1974; "Hawaii Five-O: Capsule Kidnapping," CBS, 1976; "Saturday Night Live," NBC, 1981; "Fantasy Island: God Child," ABC, 1983; "The Love Boat: Stolen Years," ABC, 1984; "Half Nelson: Pilot," ABC, 1985.

TV MOVIES AND MINISERIES: "See How They Run," NBC, 1964; "Sarge: The Badge or the Cross," NBC, 1971; "The Priest Killer," CBS, 1971; "A Great American Tragedy," ABC, 1972; "Deliver Us From Evil," ABC, 1973; "A Cry in the Wilderness," ABC, 1974; "The Blue Knight," CBS, 1975; "Backstairs at the White House," NBC, 1979; "On Fire," ABC, 1987; "The Gambler III: The Legend Continues," CBS, 1987; "What Price Victory," ABC, 1988.

* Kennedy served in the Army for 16 years, and was the technical advisor on "The Phil Silvers Show."

KENNEDY, JAYNE

b. *Washington, D.C., October 27, 1951.* TV personality.

AS A REGULAR: "Speak Up, America," NBC, 1980.
AND: "Banacek: Rocket to Oblivion," NBC, 1974; "Sanford & Son: There'll Be Some Changes Made," NBC, 1974; "Police Woman: The Inside Connection," NBC, 1977; "Diff'rent Strokes: The Moonlighter," NBC, 1983; "The Love Boat: Final Score," ABC, 1983.

KENNEDY, MIMI

b. *Rochester, NY, September 25, 1949.* Actress usually in sitcom roles.

AS A REGULAR: "3 Girls 3," NBC, 1977; "Stockard Channing in Just Friends," CBS, 1979; "The Big Show," NBC, 1980; "The Two of Us," CBS, 1981-82; "Spencer," NBC, 1984-85; "Family Man," ABC, 1988.
AND: "St. Elsewhere: Homecoming," NBC, 1984; "St. Elsewhere: The Children's Hour," NBC, 1984; "The Twilight Zone: Aqua Vita," CBS, 1986; "Tales From the Crypt: The Man Who Was Death," HBO, 1989; "Homeroom: Dirty Laundry," ABC, 1989; "Homeroom: It's Not Easy Being Green," ABC, 1989; "Homeroom: Who'll Be My Role Model Now That My Role Model Is Gone?," ABC, 1989.
TV MOVIES AND MINISERIES: "Thin Ice," CBS, 1981; "Baby Girl Scott," CBS, 1987.

KENNEDY, TOM

b. *Jim Narz, Louisville, KY, February 26, 1927.* Game show emcee.

AS A REGULAR: "Dr. I.Q.," ABC, 1953-54, 1958-59; "Break the Bank," NBC, 1956-57; "The Gisele MacKenzie Show," NBC, 1958; "The Big Game," NBC, 1958; "Wingo," CBS, 1958; "The Price Is Right," ABC, 1963-65; "You Don't Say," NBC, 1963-69; ABC, 1975; SYN, 1978-79; "It's Your Bet," SYN, 1969-73; "The Real Tom Kennedy Show," SYN, 1970; "Password," ABC, 1971-75; "Split Second," ABC, 1972-75; "Name That Tune," SYN, 1974-81; "50 Grand Slam," NBC, 1976; "To Say the Least, NBC, 1977-78; "Whew!," CBS, 1979-80; "Body Language," CBS, 1984-86; "Wordplay," NBC, 1986-87.

AND: "My Favorite Martian: Rocket to Mars," CBS, 1963; "I'll Bet," NBC, 1965; "Snap Judgment," NBC, 1968; "Hollywood Squares," NBC, 1970.
TV MOVIES AND MINISERIES: "Having Babies," ABC, 1976.

KERCHEVAL, KEN

b. *Wolcottville, IN, July 15, 1935.* Actor who plays Cliff Barnes on "Dallas."

AS A REGULAR: "Search for Tomorrow," CBS, 1965-67, 1972-73; "The Secret Storm," CBS, 1968; "How to Survive a Marriage," NBC, 1974-75; "Dallas," CBS, 1978- .
AND: "The Defenders: The Tarnished Cross," CBS, 1962; "Kojak: Dark Sunday," CBS, 1975; "The Love Boat: Two for Julie," ABC, 1981; "The Love Boat: Don't Get Mad, Get Even," ABC, 1984; "The New Mike Hammer: A Blinding Fear," CBS, 1987; "Matlock: The Gambler," NBC, 1987; "Highway to Heaven: Whose Trash Is It Anyway?," NBC, 1988; "Super Password," NBC, 1989; "The Pat Sajak Show," CBS, 1989.
TV MOVIES AND MINISERIES: "Judge Horton and the Scottsboro Boys," NBC, 1976; "Devil Dog: The Hound of Hell," CBS, 1978; "Too Far to Go," NBC, 1979; "Walking Through the Fire," CBS, 1979; "The Patricia Neal Story," CBS, 1981; "The Demon Murder Case," NBC, 1983; "Calamity Jane," CBS, 1984.

KERNS, JOANNA

b. *Joanna De Varona, San Francisco, CA, February 12, 1953.* Actress who plays Maggie Seaver on "Growing Pains."

AS A REGULAR: "The Four Seasons," CBS, 1984; "Growing Pains," ABC, 1985- .
AND: "Switch: Play-Off," CBS, 1978; "Three's Company: The Love Lesson," ABC, 1980; "Magnum, P.I.: Wave Goodbye," CBS, 1982; "Magnum, P.I.: Black on White," CBS, 1983; "The A-Team: A Nice Place to Visit," NBC, 1983; "Hill Street Blues: Hair Transplant," NBC, 1984; "Hunter: Pilot," NBC, 1984; "Sea World's Miracle Babies," ABC, 1989; "Animal Crack-Ups," ABC, 1989; "The Pat Sajak Show," CBS, 1989.
TV MOVIES AND MINISERIES: "The Million Dollar Rip-Off," NBC, 1976; "A Bunny's Tale," ABC, 1985; "Stormin' Home," CBS, 1985; "Mistress," CBS, 1987; "Those She Left Behind," NBC, 1989; "The Preppie Murder," ABC, 1989.

KERR, DEBORAH
  b. *Helensburgh, Scotland, September 30, 1921.*
  Film actress who's come lately to TV.
AS A GUEST: "The Steve Allen Show," NBC,
  1958; "Small World," CBS, 1960; "The David
  Frost Show," SYN, 1971; "The Tonight Show
  Starring Johnny Carson," NBC, 1975.
TV MOVIES AND MINISERIES: "Witness for the
  Prosecution," CBS, 1982; "A Woman of
  Substance," SYN, 1984; "Hold the Dream,"
  SYN, 1986.

KERR, JOHN
  b. *New York City, NY, November 15, 1931.*
  Actor who began his career as a young,
  sensitive type.
AS A REGULAR: "Arrest and Trial," ABC, 1963-64;
  "The Long Hot Summer," ABC, 1965; "Peyton
  Place," ABC, 1965-66.
AND: "Summer Studio One: End of the Honey-
  moon," CBS, 1953; "Suspense: The Hunted,"
  CBS, 1954; "Philco TV Playhouse: The Bold and
  the Brave," NBC, 1955; "Elgin TV Hour: Combat
  Medic," ABC, 1955; "Climax!: Man of Taste,"
  CBS, 1955; "Alcoa Hour: Undertow," NBC,
  1955; "Hallmark Hall of Fame: The Corn is
  Green," NBC, 1956; "U.S. Steel Hour: A Fair
  Shake," CBS, 1956; "Climax!: Throw Away the
  Cane," CBS, 1956; "Playhouse 90: Mr. and Mrs.
  McAdam," CBS, 1957; "The Jane Wyman Show:
  Killer's Pride," NBC, 1957; "Climax!: Night of a
  Rebel," CBS, 1957; "Studio One: The Years in
  Between," CBS, 1957; "The Joseph Cotten Show:
  The Case of the Jealous Bomber," NBC, 1957;
  "Playhouse 90: Rumors of Evening," CBS, 1958;
  "Alcoa Theatre: Strange Occurance at Rokesay,"
  NBC, 1958; "G.E. Theatre: A Question of
  Romance," CBS, 1958; "Hallmark Hall of Fame:
  Berkeley Square," NBC, 1959; "Riverboat: The
  Barrier," NBC, 1959; "Walt Disney Presents: The
  Nine Lives of Elfego Baca-Friendly Enemies at
  Law," ABC, 1960; "Rawhide: Incident of the Last
  Chance," CBS, 1960; "Checkmate: The Crimson
  Pool," CBS, 1961; "Bus Stop: Verdict of 12,"
  ABC, 1962; "U.S. Steel Hour: Honor in Love,"
  CBS, 1962; "U.S. Steel Hour: Dry Rain," CBS,
  1962; "The Lloyd Bridges Show: Miracle of Mesa
  Verde," CBS, 1962; "The Defenders: The
  Apostle," CBS, 1962; "The Virginian: The
  Judgment," NBC, 1963; "Wagon Train: The Jim
  Whitlow Story," ABC, 1963; "The Virginian: The
  Judgment," NBC, 1963; "Profiles in Courage:
  John Peter Altgeld," NBC, 1965; "The Alfred
  Hitchcock Hour: An Unlocked Window," NBC,
  1965; "Twelve O'Clock High: Mutiny at 10,000
  Feet," ABC, 1965; "Run for Your Life: The Day
  Time Stopped," NBC, 1966; "The FBI: A Sleeper
  Wakes," ABC, 1967; "The FBI: The Dynasty,"
  ABC, 1968; "The FBI: The Homecoming," ABC,
  1968; "The FBI: The Maze," ABC, 1969; "The

Name of the Game: Wrath of Angels," NBC,
1969; "The Bold Ones: The Verdict," NBC, 1970;
"The FBI: Pressure Point," ABC, 1970; "The FBI:
The Target," ABC, 1970; "The Young Lawyers:
False Witness," ABC, 1971; "Owen Marshall,
Counselor at Law: Men Who Care," ABC, 1971;
"Columbo: Dead Weight," NBC, 1971; "The FBI:
The Watchdog," ABC, 1971; "The Mod Squad:
The Poisoned Mind," ABC, 1971; "The Mod
Squad: I Am My Brother's Keeper," ABC, 1972;
"Alias Smith and Jones: Only Three to a Bed,"
ABC, 1972; The Streets of San Francisco: The
Set-Up," ABC, 1973; "The Mod Squad: Cry
Uncle," ABC, 1973; "The Streets of San
Francisco: The House on Hyde Street," ABC,
1973; "The Streets of San Francisco: The
Albatross," ABC, 1973; "The Streets of San
Francisco: A Wrongful Death," ABC, 1973; "The
Streets of San Francisco: Shield of Honor," ABC,
1974; "Barnaby Jones: Programmed for Killing,"
CBS, 1974; "Police Story: The Gamble," NBC,
1974; "The Streets of San Francisco: False
Witness," ABC, 1975; "The Streets of San
Francisco: Endgame," ABC, 1975; "The Invisible
Man: Eyes Only," NBC, 1975; "McMillan: Affair
of the Heart," NBC, 1977; "The Streets of San
Francisco: Who Killed Helen French?," ABC,
1977.
TV MOVIES AND MINISERIES: "Yuma," ABC, 1971;
  "The Longest Night," ABC, 1972; "Incident on
  a Dark Street," CBS, 1973.

KERRIGAN, J.M.
  b. *Joseph M. Kerrigan, Dublin, Ireland,
  December 16, 1887; d. 1964.* Character actor
  who often played Irishmen.
AS A GUEST: "The Unexpected: Slightly Dead,"
  NBC, 1952; "Easy Chair Theatre: Twilight
  Song," NBC, 1952; "Lux Video Theatre:
  Welcome, Stranger," NBC, 1954; "G.E.
  Theatre: The Martyr," CBS, 1955; "Frontier:
  The Devil and Doctor O'Hara," NBC, 1955;
  "Studio One: Birthday Present," CBS, 1958;
  "Shirley Temple's Storybook: The Magic
  Fishbone," NBC, 1958; "The Loretta Young
  Show: Faith, Hope and Mr. Flaherty," NBC,
  1960.

KERWIN, BRIAN
  b. *Chicago, IL, October 25, 1949.* Actor who
  played Deputy Birdwell Hawkins on "Lobo."
AS A REGULAR: "The Young and the Restless,"
  CBS, 1976-77; "The Chisholms," CBS, 1979;
  "Lobo," NBC, 1979-81.
AND: "The Love Boat: The Family Plan," ABC,
  1980; "St. Elsewhere: Time Heals," NBC, 1986.
TV MOVIES AND MINISERIES: "A Real American
  Hero," CBS, 1978; "The Chisholms," CBS,
  1979; "The Paradise Connection," CBS, 1979;
  "Miss All American Beauty," CBS, 1982;

"Intimate Agony," ABC, 1983; "Wet Gold," ABC, 1984; "Bluegrass," CBS, 1988.

KERWIN, LANCE

b. *Newport Beach, CA, November 6, 1960.* Actor who played James at 15. And 16.

AS A REGULAR: "The Family Holvak," NBC, 1975; "James at 15 (James at 16)," NBC, 1977-78.

AND: "Little House on the Prairie: The 100 Mile Walk," NBC, 1974; "ABC Afterschool Special: The Bridge of Adam Rush," ABC, 1974; "ABC Wide World of Mystery: The Cloning of Clifford Swimmer," ABC, 1974; "Gunsmoke: The Fires of Ignorance," CBS, 1975; "ABC Afterschool Special: The Amazing Cosmic Adventures of Duffy Moon," ABC, 1976; "ABC Afterschool Special: Me and Dad's New Wife," ABC, 1976; "Good Heavens: Jack the Ribber," ABC, 1976; "The Phantom Rebel," NBC, 1976; "ABC Afterschool Special: P.J. and the President's Son," ABC, 1976; "Faerie Tale Theatre: The Snow Queen," SHO, 1984; "Simon & Simon: The Apple Doesn't Fall Far," CBS, 1986.

TV MOVIES AND MINISERIES: "The Greatest Gift," NBC, 1974; "Reflections on Murder," ABC, 1974; "The Loneliest Runner," NBC, 1976; "The Death of Richie," NBC, 1977; "Young Joe, the Forgotten Kennedy," ABC, 1977; "Salem's Lot," CBS, 1979; "The Boy Who Drank Too Much," CBS, 1980; "The Mysterious Stranger," PBS, 1982; "A Killer in the Family," ABC, 1983.

KETCHUM, DAVE

b. *Quincy, IL, 1928.* Comic actor who played Agent 13, the guy who always had to hide in a mailbox or the like, on "Get Smart."

AS A REGULAR: "The New Steve Allen Show," ABC, 1961; "I'm Dickens, He's Fenster," ABC, 1962-63; "Camp Runamuck," NBC, 1965-66; "Get Smart," NBC, 1966-67.

AND: "Angel: The Little Leagues," CBS, 1961; "The Spike Jones Show," CBS, 1961; "The Magic Land of Alakazam," CBS, 1961; "The Real McCoys: The McCoy Sound," CBS, 1963; "The Joey Bishop Show: Joey Insults Jack E. Leonard," NBC, 1964; "The Joey Bishop Show: Joey the Patient," CBS, 1964; "The Munsters: Munster the Magnificent," CBS, 1965; "Hey, Landlord!: The Daring Duo vs. the Incredible Captain Kill," NBC, 1966; "Hey, Landlord!: Divorce, Bachelor Style," NBC, 1966; "Run, Buddy, Run: Dying Is My Life," CBS, 1967; "Hey, Landlord!: Testing, One, Two," NBC, 1967; "Green Acres: Kimball Gets Fired," CBS, 1967; "Petticoat Junction: The Singing Sweethearts," CBS, 1968; "That Girl: Decision Before Dawn," ABC, 1968; "Gomer Pyle, USMC: A Little Chicken Soup Wouldn't Hurt," CBS, 1968; "The Mod Squad: Never Give the Fuzz an Even Break," ABC, 1969; "That Girl: Minnie the Moocher," ABC, 1969; "The Courtship of Eddie's Father: Bully for You," ABC, 1969; "The Courtship of Eddie's Father: A Loaf of Bread, a Bar of Soap and a Jug of Peanut Butter," ABC, 1970; "Love, American Style: Love and the Optimist," ABC, 1970; "The Mary Tyler Moore Show: Divorce Isn't Everything," CBS, 1970; "The Odd Couple: Trapped," ABC, 1971; "The Odd Couple: The Fat Farm," ABC, 1971; "Love, American Style: Love and the Check," ABC, 1972; "The Partridge Family: I'm in Love with a Two-Car Garage," ABC, 1972; "Love, American Style: Love and the Vertical Romance," ABC, 1972; "Happy Days: R.O.T.C.," ABC, 1974; "Alice: Sixty Minutes Man," CBS, 1977; "Happy Days: A Shot in the Head," ABC, 1977; "Mork & Mindy: Christmas Show," ABC, 1978; "Happy Days: Father and Son," ABC, 1980.

TV MOVIES AND MINISERIES: "How to Break Up a Happy Divorce," NBC, 1976; "Get Smart, Again!," ABC, 1989.

AS A WRITER: "M*A*S*H: Tuttle," CBS, 1973.

KEYES, EVELYN

b. *Port Arthur, TX, November 20, 1919.* Actress of thirties and forties films ("Gone with the Wind," "The Jolson Story") who's done a little TV.

AS A GUEST: "Lux Video Theatre: Wild Geese," CBS, 1951; "Climax!: Wild Stallion," CBS, 1955; "The Ugliest Girl in Town: Visitors From a Strange Planet," ABC, 1968; "The Love Boat: Lotions of Love," ABC, 1983; "Amazing Stories: Boo!," NBC, 1986; "Murder, She Wrote: Old Habits Die Hard," CBS, 1987.

KIDDER, MARGOT

b. *Canada, October 17, 1948.* Actress who began in TV, went to movies (Lois Lane in "Superman") and is now back on the tube.

AS A REGULAR: "James Garner as Nichols," NBC, 1971-72; "Shell Game," CBS, 1987.

AND: "The Mod Squad: Call Back Yesterday," ABC, 1970; "Hawaii Five-O: The Diamond That Nobody Stole," CBS, 1973; "Barnaby Jones: Trial Run for Death," CBS, 1973; "Saturday Night Live," NBC, 1979; "The Canadian Conspiracy," MAX, 1986; "Late Night with David Letterman," NBC, 1987.

TV MOVIES AND MINISERIES: "Suddenly Single," ABC, 1971; "The Bounty Man," ABC, 1972; "The Suicide Club," ABC, 1973; "Honky Tonk," NBC, 1974; "Picking Up the Pieces," CBS, 1985; "Vanishing Act," CBS, 1986; "Body of Evidence," CBS, 1988.

KIEL, RICHARD

b. *Redford, MI, September 13, 1939.* Tall,

heavy actor often in freakish roles, including "Jaws" in James Bond movies and as the alien who came to earth with filet of human on his mind in the "To Serve Man" episode of "The Twilight Zone."

AS A REGULAR: "Barbary Coast," ABC, 1975-76; "Van Dyke and Company," NBC, 1976.

AND: "Klondike: Bare Knuckles," NBC, 1960; "Thriller: Well of Doom," NBC, 1961; "The Rifleman: The Decision," ABC, 1961; "The Twilight Zone: To Serve Man," CBS, 1962; "The Man From UNCLE: The Hong Kong Shilling Affair," NBC, 1965; "I Dream of Jeannie: My Hero?," NBC, 1965; "The Wild Wild West: The Night the Wizard Shook the Earth," CBS, 1965; "The Wild Wild West: The Night That Terror Stalked the Town," CBS, 1965; "My Mother the Car: Riddler on the Roof," NBC, 1966; "Honey West: King of the Mountain," ABC, 1966; "Gilligan's Island: Ghost a Go-Go," CBS, 1966; "The Monkees: I Was a Teenage Monkee," NBC, 1967; "Kolchak, the Night Stalker: Bad Medicine," ABC, 1974; "Switch: Death Heist," CBS, 1975; "Simon & Simon: Psyched Out," CBS, 1983.

TV MOVIES AND MINISERIES: "Now You See It, Now You Don't," NBC, 1968.

KIERAN, JOHN

b. New York City, NY, August 2, 1892; d. 1981.

AS A REGULAR: "Kieran's Kaleidoscope," SYN, 1949-52; "Information Please," CBS, 1952.

KIERNAN, WALTER

b. New Haven, CT, January 24, 1902; d. 1978.

AS A REGULAR: "That Reminds Me," ABC, 1948; "Kiernan's Corner," ABC, 1948-49; "Sparring Partners with Walter Kiernan," ABC, 1949; "What's the Story?," DUM, 1951-53; "Who Said That?," NBC, 1951-54; "I've Got a Secret," CBS, 1952; "Who's the Boss?," ABC, 1954; "The Greatest Moments in Sports," NBC, 1954-55.

KIFF, KALEENA

b. Santa Monica, CA, October 23, 1974. Child actress who played Patti on "Love, Sidney" and Kelly, daughter of Wally Cleaver on "The New Leave It to Beaver."

AS A REGULAR: "Love, Sidney," NBC, 1981-83; "The New Leave It to Beaver," DIS, 1985-86; TBS, 1986-89.

AND: "Family Ties: A Keaton Christmas Carol," NBC, 1983.

TV MOVIES AND MINISERIES: "Sidney Shorr," NBC, 1981.

KILEY, RICHARD

b. Chicago, IL, Mar. 31, 1922. Actor whose television career spans from the heyday of live

productions to sprawling miniseries and family dramas; an Emmy winner for "The Thorn Birds" and "A Year in the Life."

AS A REGULAR: "A Year in the Life," NBC, 1987-88.

AND: "Robert Montgomery Presents: The Champion," NBC, 1950; "The Web: Journey by Night," CBS, 1950; "Westinghouse Theatre: The Guinea Pigs," CBS, 1951; "Danger: The Hand of the Enemy," CBS, 1952; "Curtain Call: Azaya," NBC, 1952; "Curtain Call: Season of Divorce," NBC, 1952; "The Web: Kind Stranger," CBS, 1953; "U.S. Steel Hour: P.O.W.," ABC, 1953; "Studio One: A Criminal Design," CBS, 1954; "Studio One: Paul's Apartment," CBS, 1954; "Kraft Television Theatre: Arrowsmith," NBC, 1954; "Justice: Keith's Case," NBC, 1954; "Campbell TV Soundstage: The Corner Drugstore," NBC, 1954; "Philco TV Playhouse: Write Me Out Forever," CBS, 1954; "Studio One: The Small Door," CBS, 1954; "U.S. Steel Hour: The Notebook Warrior," ABC, 1954; "Kraft Television Theatre: Patterns," NBC, 1954; "Omnibus: A Clean Fresh Breeze," CBS, 1954; "Ford Theatre: Summer Memory," NBC, 1954; "Studio One: The Cuckoo in Spring," CBS, 1954; "Kraft Television Theatre: Patterns," NBC, 1955; "You Are There: The Tragedy of John Milton," CBS, 1955; "You Are There: The Death of Socrates," CBS, 1955; "Studio One: Shakedown Cruise," CBS, 1955; "Kraft Television Theatre: The Just and the Unjust," NBC, 1956; "Studio One: The Landlady's Daughter," CBS, 1956; "Kraft Television Theatre: The Discoverers," NBC, 1957; "Kaiser Aluminum Hour: The Story of a Crime," NBC, 1957; "Omnibus: The Trial of Lizzie Borden," ABC, 1957; "Playhouse 90: Homeward Borne," CBS, 1957; "U.S. Steel Hour: Shadow in the Sky," CBS, 1957; "Studio One: Act of Mercy," CBS, 1957; "Kraft Television Theatre: The Other Wise Man," NBC, 1957; "Playhouse 90: Before I Die," CBS, 1958; "Kraft Television Theatre: Material Witness," NBC, 1958; "U.S. Steel Hour: Give Me My Son," CBS, 1958; "Frontiers of Faith: This Prisoner Barabbas," NBC, 1958; "U.S. Steel Hour: Hidden River," CBS, 1958; "Decision: Indemnity," NBC, 1958; "Alfred Hitchcock Presents: The Crooked Road," CBS, 1958; "Goodyear Theatre: The Guy in Ward 4," NBC, 1958; "The Steve Allen Show," NBC, 1959; "U.S. Steel Hour: The Women of Hadley," CBS, 1960; "U.S. Steel Hour: Revolt in Hadley," CBS, 1960; "The Power of the Resurrection," NBC, 1960; "U.S. Steel Hour: Bride of the Fox," CBS, 1960; "U.S. Steel Hour: Trial Without Jury," CBS, 1961; "U.S. Steel Hour: Brandenburg Gate," CBS, 1961; "Alcoa Premiere: The Doctor," ABC, 1962; "The Alfred Hitchcock Hour: Blood Bargain," CBS, 1963; "The Eleventh Hour: This Wonderful Madman Called Me a Beauty," NBC, 1963; "The Great

Adventure: The Colonel From Connecticut," CBS, 1964; "The Defenders: The Last Day," CBS, 1964; "Ben Casey: Keep Out of Reach of Adults," ABC, 1964; "The Nurses: The Forever Child," CBS, 1964; "Kraft Suspense Theatre: Charlie, He Couldn't Kill a Fly," NBC, 1964; "Slattery's People: Question-Whatever Happened to Ezra?," CBS, 1964; "The Long, Hot Summer: The Desperate Innocent," ABC, 1965; "Coronet Blue: The Rebel," CBS, 1967; "The Danny Thomas Hour: Measure of a Man," NBC, 1968; "The FBI: The Homecoming," ABC, 1968; "Garrison's Gorillas: The Plot to Kill," ABC, 1968; "Judd for the Defense: The Holy Ground," ABC, 1969; "The Name of the Game: The Garden," NBC, 1970; "Gunsmoke: Stark," CBS, 1970; "The Mod Squad: Who Are the Keepers, Who Are the Inmates?," ABC, 1970; "Bonanza: Gideon the Good," NBC, 1970; "NET Playhouse: The Ceremony of Innocence," NET, 1970; "The FBI: The Eye of the Needle," ABC, 1971; "Gunsmoke: Bohannon," CBS, 1972; "Gunsmoke: Kitty's Love Affair," CBS, 1973; "The American Parade: The 34th Star," CBS, 1974; "Cannon: The Hit Man," CBS, 1974; "From Sea to Shining Sea," SYN, 1974; "Columbo: A Friend in Deed," NBC, 1974; "Give Me Liberty," SYN, 1975; "Medical Story: Woman in White," NBC, 1975; "Hotel: Promises," ABC, 1985; "The Twilight Zone: The Last Defender of Camelot," CBS, 1986; "Great Performances: An Evening with Alan Jay Lerner," PBS, 1989.

TV MOVIES AND MINISERIES: "Night Gallery," NBC, 1969; "Incident in San Francisco," ABC, 1971; "Murder Once Removed," NBC, 1971; "Jigsaw," ABC, 1972; "Friendly Persuasion," ABC, 1975; "The Macahans," ABC, 1976; "Angel on my Shoulder," ABC, 1980; "Isabel's Choice," CBS, 1981; "The Thorn Birds," ABC, 1983; "George Washington," CBS, 1984; "A.D.," NBC, 1985; "The Bad Seed," ABC, 1985; "Do You Remember Love," CBS, 1985; "If Tomorrow Comes," CBS, 1986; "A Year in the Life," NBC, 1986; "My First Love," ABC, 1988; "AT&T Presents: The Final Days," ABC, 1989.

* Emmies: 1983, 1987.

KILGALLEN, DOROTHY
b. *Chicago, IL, July 3, 1913; d. 1965.* Columnist and regular "What's My Line?" quizzer.
AS A REGULAR: "What's My Line?," CBS, 1950-65.
AND: "The Last Word," CBS, 1957; "The Last Word," CBS, 1958; "Play Your Hunch," NBC, 1960; "I've Got a Secret," CBS, 1961; "Password," CBS, 1961; "Missing Links," NBC, 1964; "The Match Game," NBC, 1964.

KILIAN, VICTOR
b. *Jersey City, NJ, March 6, 1891; d. 1979.* Character who played Grandfather Raymond

Larkin, aka The Fernwood Flasher, on "Mary Hartman, Mary Hartman."
AS A REGULAR: "Mary Hartman, Mary Hartman," SYN, 1976-78.
AND: "Diagnosis: Unknown: The Case of the Elder," CBS, 1960; "Doc Elliot: A Time to Grow," ABC, 1974; "The Jeffersons: Uncle Bertram," CBS, 1975; "The Jeffersons: Jenny's Grandparents," CBS, 1975; "All in the Family: Edith Gets Fired," CBS, 1979; "All in the Family: The Return of Stephanie's Father," CBS, 1979.

KILPATRICK, LINCOLN
b. *St. Louis, MO, February 12, 1932.* Black actor fondly remembered as the right Reverend Deal on "Frank's Place."
AS A REGULAR: "Love of Life," CBS, 1968-70; "The Leslie Uggams Show," CBS, 1969; "Matt Houston," ABC, 1983-85; "Frank's Place," CBS, 1987-88.
AND: "Robert Herridge Theatre: The Ballad of Huck Finn," SYN, 1960; "NYPD: The Golden Fleece," ABC, 1968; "Medical Center: The Last Ten Yards," CBS, 1969; "Then Came Bronson: All the World and God," NBC, 1969; "The Bold Ones: In Dreams They Run," NBC, 1970; "The Bold Ones: A Single Blow of the Sword," NBC, 1971; "Medical Center: Deadlock," CBS, 1972; "McCloud: The Barefoot Stewardess Caper," NBC, 1972; "Police Story: Chief," NBC, 1974; "Harry O: Shades," ABC, 1975; "Good Times: Michael the Warlord," CBS, 1976; "Kojak: Mouse," CBS, 1978; "The White Shadow: Here's Mud in Your Eye," CBS, 1978; "Harris and Company: That's One I Owe You," NBC, 1979; "Lou Grant: Victims," CBS, 1981; "Hill Street Blues: Moon Over Uranus-the Final Legacy," NBC, 1983; "227: The Whiz," NBC, 1988; "Amen: Matchmaker Matchmaker," NBC, 1989.
TV MOVIES AND MINISERIES: "The Mask of Sheba," NBC, 1970; "Just an Old Sweet Song," CBS, 1976; "The Moneychangers," NBC, 1976; "King," NBC, 1978.

KIMBROUGH, CHARLES
Stage-trained actor who plays Jim Dial on "Murphy Brown."
AS A REGULAR: "Murphy Brown," CBS, 1988- .
AND: "Kojak: A Shield for Murder," CBS, 1976; "Nurse: Father," CBS, 1982; "The Pat Sajak Show," CBS, 1989.
TV MOVIES AND MINISERIES: "A Doctor's Story," NBC, 1984; "Cast the First Stone," NBC, 1989.

KIMBROUGH, EMILY
TV personality and author.
AS A REGULAR: "Who's Whose," CBS, 1951.
AND: "U.S. Steel Hour: Wish on the Moon," CBS, 1959; "The Last Word," CBS, 1959.

KING, ALAN

b. Irwin Alan Kniberg, Brooklyn, NY, December 26, 1927. Cigar-smoking comedian whose jokes were fueled by indignation over contemporary life; lately he's been more visible in movies ("Memories of Me," "Enemies-A Love Story").

AND: "The Ed Sullivan Show," CBS, 1957; "Dinah Shore Chevy Show," NBC, 1958; "The Perry Como Show,"NBC, 1958; "The Ed Sullivan Show," CBS, 1958; "The Garry Moore Show," CBS, 1958; "The Ed Sullivan Show," CBS, 1959; "The Garry Moore Show," CBS, 1959; "Arthur Murray Party," NBC, 1959; "Masquerade Party," CBS, 1959; "Dick Clark's World of Talent," ABC, 1959; "The Big Party," CBS, 1959; "The Arthur Murray Party for Bob Hope," NBC, 1960; "The Ed Sullivan Show," CBS, 1960; "What's My Line?," CBS, 1960; "The Garry Moore Show," CBS, 1960; "Perry Como's Kraft Music Hall," NBC, 1960; "Perry Como's Kraft Music Hall," NBC, 1961; "The Garry Moore Show," CBS, 1961; "The Alan King Show," CBS, 1961; "The Jack Benny Program," CBS, 1961; "The Garry Moore Show," CBS, 1962; "What's My Line?," CBS, 1962; "Talent Scouts," CBS, 1963; "The Garry Moore Show," CBS, 1963; "The Garry Moore Show," CBS, 1964; "Password," CBS, 1964; "I've Got a Secret," CBS, 1964; "The Ed Sullivan Show," CBS, 1964; "The Tonight Show Starring Johnny Carson," NBC, 1964; "The Tonight Show Starring Johnny Carson," NBC, 1965; "The Tonight Show Starring Johnny Carson," NBC, 1966; "Personality," NBC, 1967; "The Jackie Gleason Show," CBS, 1967; "Kraft Music Hall: Roast for Johnny Carson," NBC, 1968; "That's Life: The Honeymoon," ABC, 1968; "Alan King Special," NBC, 1968; "Alan King Special," NBC, 1969; "The Ed Sullivan Show," CBS, 1969; "Kraft Music Hall," NBC, 1970; "The Tonight Show Starring Johnny Carson," NBC, 1971; "The Merv Griffin Show," SYN, 1972; "Switch: The Late Show Murders," CBS, 1975; "America's Tribute to Bob Hope," NBC, 1988; "The Tonight Show Starring Johnny Carson," NBC, 1989.

TV MOVIES AND MINISERIES: "Best Sellers: Seventh Avenue," NBC, 1977; "How to Pick Up Girls," ABC, 1978.

AS EXECUTIVE PRODUCER: "The Corner Bar," ABC, 1972-73; "Saturday Night Live with Howard Cosell," ABC, 1975-76.

KING, ALEXANDER

b. 1899; d. 1965. TV personality with a slightly pretentious persona; a big favorite of Jack Paar.

AS A REGULAR: "The Jack Paar Show," NBC, 1958-62; "Alex in Wonderland," SYN, 1959-60.

AND: "Jack Paar Presents," NBC, 1960; "The Jack Paar Program," NBC, 1962; "The Jack Paar Program," NBC, 1963.

KING, B.B.

b. Riley King, Itta Bena, MS, September 19, 1925. Legendary blues guitarist "discovered" by TV in the seventies.

AS A GUEST: "The Barbara McNair Show," SYN, 1970; "The Pearl Bailey Show," ABC, 1971; "The Flip Wilson Show," NBC, 1972; "In Concert," ABC, 1973; "In Session," SYN, 1974; "Sanford & Son: Fred Sings the Blues," NBC, 1977; "The Toni Tennille Show," SYN, 1980; "The Tonight Show Starring Johnny Carson," NBC, 1989; "Booker: Someone Stole Lucille," FOX, 1989.

KING, DAVE

b. England, 1929. Comic brought over to the states and given a summer replacement show in 1959.

AS A REGULAR: "Kraft Music Hall Presents: The Dave King Show," NBC, 1959.

AND: "The Perry Como Show," NBC, 1959; "Perry Como's Kraft Music Hall," NBC, 1959; "Pat Boone Chevy Showroom," ABC, 1960; "Hollywood Palace," ABC, 1964.

KING, JOHN REED

b. Atlantic City, NJ, October 25, 1914; d. 1979. AS A REGULAR: "Missus Goes a-Shopping," CBS, 1944-49; "Chance of a Lifetime," ABC, 1950-51; "Battle of the Ages," DUM, 1952; "Give and Take," CBS, 1952; "Where Was I?," DUM, 1952-53; "Why?," ABC, 1953; "What's Your Bid?," ABC, 1953; "On Your Way," ABC, 1954; "Have a Heart," DUM, 1955.

KING, MABEL

b. Charleston, SC. Heavyset black actress who played Mrs. Thomas on "What's Happening!!"

AS A REGULAR: "What's Happening!!," ABC, 1976-79.

AND: "Barney Miller: Computer Crime," ABC, 1979; "Amazing Stories: The Sitter," NBC, 1986; "Wiseguy: Blood Dance," CBS, 1988.

TV MOVIES AND MINISERIES: "The Jerk, Too," NBC, 1984.

KING, PEE WEE

b. Frank King, Abrams, WI, February 18, 1914. Singer-accordianist.

AS A REGULAR: "Pee Wee King Show," ABC, 1955.

AND: "Country Music Jubilee," ABC, 1958; "Jubilee USA," ABC, 1959; "Jubilee USA," ABC, 1960; "Five Star Jubilee," NBC, 1961.

KING, PEGGY

b. Greensburg, PA, February 16, 1930. Pretty

perky Peggy King, as George Gobel used to call her; pop singer of the fifties.
AS A REGULAR: "The George Gobel Show," NBC, 1954-59.
AND: "The Jonathan Winters Show," NBC, 1956; "The Steve Allen Show," NBC, 1956; "Producers Showcase: Jack and the Beanstalk," NBC, 1956; "The Bob Hope Show," NBC, 1956; "The Ray Anthony Show," ABC, 1957; "Washington Square," NBC, 1957; "The Perry Como Show," NBC, 1957; "The Vic Damone Show," CBS, 1957; "The Julius LaRosa Show," NBC, 1957; "The Guy Mitchell Show," ABC, 1957; "Pat Boone Chevy Showroom," ABC, 1957; "Hallmark Hall of Fame: Hans Brinker or The Silver Skates," NBC, 1958; "The Steve Allen Show," NBC, 1958; "Pantomime Quiz," ABC, 1958; "Matinee Theatre: The Broom and the Groom," NBC, 1958; "The Jimmy Dean Show," CBS, 1958; "The Jack Paar Show," NBC, 1958; "The George Hamilton IV Show," CBS, 1958; "The Arthur Godfrey Show," CBS, 1958; "The Perry Como Show," NBC, 1959; "Maverick: The Strange Journey of Jenny Hill," ABC, 1959; "Your Hit Parade," CBS, 1959; "The Garry Moore Show," CBS, 1959; "Kraft Music Hall Presents: The Dave King Show," NBC, 1959; "Perry Presents," NBC, 1959; "The Andy Williams Show," CBS, 1959; "Perry Como's Kraft Music Hall," NBC, 1959; "Be Our Guest," CBS, 1960.

KING, PERRY
b. Alliance, OH, April 30, 1948. Dashing leading man of eighties television, best known as Cody Allen on "Riptide."
AS A REGULAR: "The Quest," ABC, 1982; "Riptide," NBC, 1984-86.
AND: "Medical Center: Nightmare," CBS, 1973; "Hawaii Five-O: Right Grave, Wrong Body," CBS, 1974; "Hollywood Television Theatre: The Hemingway Play," PBS, 1976; "Half 'n' Half," ABC, 1988.
TV MOVIES AND MINISERIES: "Best Sellers: Captains and the Kings," NBC, 1976; "Foster and Laurie," CBS, 1975; "The Cracker Factory," ABC, 1979; "Love's Savage Fury," ABC, 1979; "City in Fear," ABC, 1980; "The Last Convertible," NBC, 1981; "Inmates: A Love Story," ABC, 1981; "Stranded," NBC, 1986; "I'll Take Manhattan," CBS, 1987; "Perfect People," ABC, 1988; "Shakedown on the Sunset Strip," CBS, 1988; "Disaster at Silo 7," ABC, 1988; "Roxanne: The Prize Pulitzer," NBC, 1989.

KING, REGINA
b. Los Angeles, CA, 1971. Young actress who played Brenda Jenkins on "227."
AS A REGULAR: "227," NBC, 1985-90.

KING, REINA
b. 1976. Young actress who played Carolyn on "What's Happening Now!!"
AS A REGULAR: "What's Happening Now!!," SYN, 1985-86.

KINSELLA, WALTER
b. 1901; d. 1975. Actor who played Happy McMann, owner of the newsstand frequented by Martin Kane, private eye; for a time, Kinsella also did the cigarette commercials on the show.
AS A REGULAR: "Martin Kane, Private Eye," NBC, 1949-54.
AND: "Alfred Hitchcock Presents: You Can't Trust a Man," NBC, 1961; "Perry Mason: The Case of the Duplicate Daughter," CBS, 1961; "The Tall Man: Trial by Hanging," NBC, 1961; "Alfred Hitchcock Presents: The Last Remains," NBC, 1962.

KINSKEY, LEONID
b. Russia, April 18, 1903. Actor who usually plays fussy Europeans.
AS A REGULAR: "The People's Choice," NBC, 1955-56.
AND: "Peter Gunn: The February Girl," NBC, 1959; "Harrigan and Son: There's No Fool Like an Old Fool," ABC, 1960; "The Jack Benny Program: Don's Anniversary," CBS, 1961; "Guestward Ho!: The Hooton Statue," ABC, 1961; "Robert Taylor's Detectives: Tobey's Place," NBC, 1961; "The Joey Bishop Show: A Windfall for Mom," NBC, 1961; "The Joey Bishop Show: A Letter From Stella," NBC, 1962; "Have Gun, Will Travel: The Hunt," CBS, 1962; "Pete and Gladys: Will the Real Michele Tabour Please Stand Up?," CBS, 1962; "Bachelor Father: Will Success Spoil Jasper?," ABC, 1962; "The Real McCoys: The Goodwill Tour," CBS, 1962; "The Joey Bishop Show: Joey's Dramatic Debut," NBC, 1963; "77 Sunset Strip: 5," ABC, 1963; "My Favorite Martian: Extra! Extra! Sensory Perception!," CBS, 1964; "A Salute to Stan Laurel," CBS, 1965; "Honey West: It's Easier Than You Think," ABC, 1966; "The Man From UNCLE: The Jingle Bells Affair," NBC, 1966; "Batman: The Contaminated Cowl/The Mad Hatter Runs a Foul," ABC, 1967; "Daktari: Judy and the Jailbirds," CBS, 1967; "Mayberry RFD: The Harp," CBS, 1970; "Mayberry RFD: Alice and the Professor," CBS, 1971.

KIRBY, BRUNO
b. Bruce Kirby Jr. Actor usually in comic roles, often mistaken for Barry Gordon; best known for his role as the pal of Harry (Billy Crystal) in the film "When Harry Met Sally...".
AS A REGULAR: "The Super," ABC, 1972.
AND: "Room 222: Suitable for Framing," ABC,

1971; "Room 222: Walt Whitman Goes Bananas," ABC, 1972; "Room 222: Twenty-Five Words or Less," ABC, 1973; "Columbo: By Dawn's Early Light," NBC, 1974; "Hill Street Blues: The Russians Are Coming," NBC, 1983; "Late Night With David Letterman," NBC, 1988; "It's Garry Shandling's Show: Save Mr. Peck's," FOX, 1989.
TV MOVIES AND MINISERIES: "All My Darling Daughters," ABC, 1972; "A Summer Without Boys," ABC, 1973; "Some Kind of Miracle," CBS, 1979.

KIRBY, DURWARD
b. Covington, KY. Announcer and straight man to Garry Moore, whom Kirby met in 1939.
AS A REGULAR: "Auction-aire," ABC, 1949-50; "Glamour-Go-Round," CBS, 1950; "The Perry Como Show," CBS, 1950-51; "The Garry Moore Show," CBS, 1950-64; 1966-67; "The Garry Moore Evening Show," CBS, 1951; "G.E. Guest House," CBS, 1951; "Candid Camera," CBS, 1961-66.
AND: "I've Got a Secret," CBS, 1960; "Candid Camera," CBS, 1960; "Password," CBS, 1962; "I've Got a Secret," CBS, 1963; "The Price Is Right," ABC, 1964; "The Carol Burnett Show," CBS, 1968.

KIRBY, GEORGE
b. Chicago, IL, 1923. Comic-impressionist.
AS A REGULAR: "ABC Comedy Hour," ABC, 1972; "Half the George Kirby Comedy Hour," SYN, 1972.
AND: "The Ed Sullivan Show," CBS, 1957; "The Ed Sullivan Show," CBS, 1962; "Perry Como's Kraft Music Hall," NBC, 1963; "The Jimmy Dean Show," ABC, 1964; "The Ed Sullivan Show," CBS, 1964; "The Ed Sullivan Show," CBS, 1965; "The Mike Douglas Show," SYN, 1966; "The Ed Sullivan Show," CBS, 1967; "The Jackie Gleason Show," CBS, 1967; "The Jackie Gleason Show," CBS, 1969; "This Is Tom Jones," ABC, 1970; "Love, American Style: Love and the Mystic," ABC, 1972; "Musical Chairs," CBS, 1975; "Sammy and Company," SYN, 1976; "The Mike Douglas Show," SYN, 1977; "Dinah!," SYN, 1977; "Barney Miller: Eviction," ABC, 1978; "Gimme a Break: The Mayor," NBC, 1983; "Murder, She Wrote: Murder to a Jazz Beat," CBS, 1985; "227: And the Survey Says," NBC, 1988.
TV MOVIES AND MINISERIES: "Sunset Limousine," CBS, 1983.

KIRCHENBAUER, BILL
Portly comedian who played coach Lubbock on "Growing Pains" and "Just the Ten of Us."
AS A REGULAR: "Fernwood 2-Night," SYN, 1977-78; "Growing Pains," ABC, 1987-88; "Just the Ten of Us," ABC, 1988-90; "Totally Hidden Video," FOX, 1990- .

AND: "Mork & Mindy: Mork the Swinging Single," ABC, 1981; "Mork & Mindy: Drive, She Said," ABC, 1982; "Growing Pains: Mike and Julie's Wedding," ABC, 1989; "Animal Crack-Ups," ABC, 1989; "The Byron Allen Show," SYN, 1989.

KIRK, PHYLLIS
b. Phyllis Helene Theodora Kirkegaard, Elizabeth, NJ, September 18, 1930. Sexy actress of fifties television, best known as Nora Charles on "The Thin Man," who eventually moved behind the scenes into TV news.
AS A REGULAR: "The Red Buttons Show," CBS, 1952-53; "The Thin Man," NBC, 1957-59; "The Young Set," ABC, 1965.
AND: "Studio One: Devil in Velvet," CBS, 1952; "Philco TV Playhouse: The Rich Boy," NBC, 1952; "Tales of Tomorrow: Age of Peril," ABC, 1952; "Goodyear TV Playhouse: Wish on the Moon," NBC, 1953; "Lux Video Theatre: Listen, He's Proposing," CBS, 1953; "Armstrong Circle Theatre: Candle in a Bottle," NBC, 1953; "U.S. Steel Hour: P.O.W.," ABC, 1953; "The Web: The Closing Net," CBS, 1953; "Lux Video Theatre: All Dressed in White," NBC, 1954; "Robert Montgomery Presents: Richard Said No," NBC, 1954; "Suspense: The Moonstone," CBS, 1954; "Goodyear TV Playhouse: The Inward Eye," NBC, 1954; "Justice: Keith's Case," NBC, 1954; "Goodyear TV Playhouse: The Power of Suggestion," NBC, 1954; "The Web: Crackpot," CBS, 1954; "Studio One: Prelude to Murder," CBS, 1954; "Robert Montgomery Presents: The Great Gatsby," NBC, 1955; "Appointment with Adventure: Forbidden Holiday," CBS, 1955; "Studio One: Heart Song," CBS, 1955; "Climax!: Edge of Terror," CBS, 1955; "Playwrights '56: The Battler," NBC, 1955; "The Loretta Young Show: Tropical Secretary," NBC, 1955; "Star Stage: The Foreign Wife," NBC, 1955; "Studio One: The Bounty Hunters," CBS, 1956; "Ford Theatre: Tin Can Skipper," NBC, 1956; "Climax!: Gamble on a Thief," CBS, 1956; "Schlitz Playhouse of Stars: The Waiting House," CBS, 1956; "Climax!: Faceless Enemy," CBS, 1956; "Playhouse 90: Made in Heaven," CBS, 1956; "Ford Theatre: Duffy's Man," ABC, 1956; "Robert Montgomery Presents: The Clay Pigeon," NBC, 1957; "Ford Theatre: Mrs. Wane Comes to Call," ABC, 1957; "Celebrity Playhouse: Bachelor Husband," SYN, 1957; "Ford Theatre: Exclusive," ABC, 1957; "The 20th Century-Fox Hour: Men in Her Life," CBS, 1957; "Errol Flynn Theatre: Rustle of Silk," SYN, 1957; "Errol Flynn Theatre: Men in Her Life," ABC, 1957; "Destiny: Foriegn Wife," CBS, 1957; "Errol Flynn Theatre: Declasse," SYN, 1957; "Celebirty Playhouse: Home Is the Soldier," SYN, 1957; "The Steve Allen Show," NBC, 1957; "Suspicion: End in Violence," NBC, 1958; "The Ford Show," NBC,

1958; "Pantomime Quiz," ABC, 1959; "Arthur Murray Party," NBC, 1959; "Dick Clark's World of Talent," ABC, 1959; "Dick Powell's Zane Grey Theatre: Setup," CBS, 1960; "Arthur Murray Party," NBC, 1960; "The Twilight Zone: A World of His Own," CBS, 1960; "Missing Links," NBC, 1964; "To Tell the Truth," CBS, 1964; "Password," CBS, 1964; "Missing Links," ABC, 1964; "Dr. Kildare: A Miracle for Margaret," NBC, 1966; "The Mike Douglas Show," SYN, 1968; "The Donald O'Connor Show," SYN, 1968; "The Name of the Game: Give Till It Hurts," NBC, 1969; "The FBI: The Impersonator," ABC, 1970.

KIRK, TOMMY
b. Louisville, KY, December 10, 1941. Clean-cut actor who began his career with Walt Disney.
AS A REGULAR: "The Mickey Mouse Club," ABC, 1956-59.
AND: "Frontier: The Devil and Doctor O'Hara," NBC, 1955; "Gunsmoke: Ben Pitcher," CBS, 1956; "The Loretta Young Show: Little League," NBC, 1956; "Matinee Theatre: The Outing," NBC, 1956; "Matinee Theatre: The Others," NBC, 1957; "Disneyland: Fourth Anniversary Show," ABC, 1957; "Matinee Theatre: Anxious Night," NBC, 1958; "Matinee Theatre: Look Out for John Tucker," NBC, 1958; "Angel: Goodbye, Young Lovers," CBS, 1961; "Walt Disney's Wonderful World of Color: The Horsemasters," NBC, 1961; "Walt Disney's Wonderful World of Color: Backstage Party," NBC, 1961; "Walt Disney's Wonderful World of Color: Escapade in Florence," NBC, 1962; "Mr. Novak: Love in the Wrong Season," NBC, 1963; "The Streets of San Francisco: Deadline," ABC, 1973.

KIRKWOOD, JAMES JR
Actor-playwright with some TV experience.
AS A REGULAR: "Valiant Lady," CBS, 1953-57.
AND: "Lamp Unto My Feet: Something for Bernice," CBS, 1957.

KIRSHNER, DON
Rock promoter-producer.
AS A REGULAR: "Don Kirshner's Rock Concert," SYN, 1973-81.
AS MUSIC SUPERVISOR: "The Monkees," NBC, 1966 68; "A Year at the Top," CBS, 1977.

KITT, EARTHA
b. North, SC, January 26, 1928. Actress and singer who played Catwoman on "Batman" and whose greatest success has come on the stage.
AS A GUEST: "Omnibus: Salome," CBS, 1955; "The Ed Sullivan Show," CBS, 1956; "Omnibus," ABC, 1956; "Arthur Murray Party," NBC, 1957; "The Big Record," CBS,

1958; "Playhouse 90: Heart of Darkness," CBS, 1958; "Art Linkletter's House Party," CBS, 1958; "The Voice of Firestone: Musical Tour of Manhattan," ABC, 1958; "The Ed Sullivan Show," CBS, 1959; "The Ed Sullivan Show," CBS, 1960; "Stump the Stars," CBS, 1963; "Burke's Law: Who Killed the Rest?," ABC, 1965; "Mission: Impossible: The Traitor," CBS, 1967; "Batman: Catwoman's Dressed to Kill," ABC, 1967; "Batman: The Funny Feline Felonies/The Joke's on Catwoman," ABC, 1967; "The Mike Douglas Show," SYN, 1969; "Police Woman: Tigress," NBC, 1978; "Miami Vice: Whatever Works," NBC, 1986.
TV MOVIES AND MINISERIES: "Lieutenant Schuster's Wife," ABC, 1972.

KJELLIN, ALF
b. Sweden, February 28, 1920.
AS A GUEST: "Fireside Theatre: The Old Talbot," NBC, 1952; "TV Reader's Digest: Comrade Lindemann's Conscience," ABC, 1955; "Pepsi Cola Playhouse: The Nightingale," ABC, 1955; "Crusader: Cross on the Hill," CBS, 1955; "Adventures in Paradise: There Is an Island," ABC, 1960; "Alcoa Presents One Step Beyond: The Peter Hurkos Story," ABC, 1960; "The Loretta Young Show: Emergency in 114," NBC, 1961; "The Alfred Hitchcock Hour: Don't Look Behind You," CBS, 1962; "Combat!: Just for the Record," ABC, 1963; "Combat!: Barrage," ABC, 1963; "Twelve O'Clock High: P.O.W.," ABC, 1965; "Twelve O'Clock High: Back to the Drawing Board," ABC, 1966; "Run for Your Life: The Borders of Barbarism," NBC, 1966; "Tarzan: Last of the Supermen," NBC, 1967; "The FBI: Blueprint for Betrayal," ABC, 1967; "Mission: Impossible: The Phoenix," CBS, 1968; "Mission: Impossible: Doomsday," CBS, 1969; "The FBI: Deadly Reunion," ABC, 1970; "Dan August: Days of Rage," ABC, 1971; "The Sixth Sense: Lady, Lady, Take My Life," ABC, 1972.

KLEIN, ROBERT
b. New York City, NY, February 8, 1942. Comedian.
AS A REGULAR: "Comedy Tonight," CBS, 1970; "TV's Bloopers & Practical Jokes," NBC, 1984-85; "Robert Klein Time," USA, 1986-87.
AND: "The Tonight Show Starring Johnny Carson," NBC, 1969; "Love, American Style: Love and the End of the Line," ABC, 1973; "The Tonight Show Starring Johnny Carson," NBC, 1973; "Saturday Night Live," NBC, 1975; "The Don Ho Show," ABC, 1977; "Saturday Night Live," NBC, 1978; "The Twilight Zone: Wordplay," CBS, 1985; "Family Ties: The Boys

Next Door," NBC, 1987; "The Tonight Show Starring Johnny Carson," NBC, 1989; "Murder, She Wrote: Trevor Hudson's Legacy," CBS, 1989; "Woodstock: Return to the Planet of the '60s," CBS, 1989; "Late Night with David Letterman," NBC, 1989; "Trying Times: A Good Life," PBS, 1989; "Later with Bob Costas," NBC, 1989.
TV MOVIES AND MINISERIES: "Your Place or Mine," CBS, 1983; "This Wife for Hire," CBS, 1985.

KLEMPERER, WERNER
b. Cologne, Germany, Mar. 22, 1920. Character actor who played Nazis in World War II dramas and won two Emmies as Colonel Klink in one of the only sitcoms set in a prison camp, "Hogan's Heroes."
AS A REGULAR: "Hogan's Heroes," CBS, 1965-71.
AND: "Navy Log: After You, Ludwig," ABC, 1957; "Wire Service: The Washington Story," ABC, 1957; "Maverick: Comstock Conspiracy," ABC, 1957; "Studio One: Balance of Terror," CBS, 1958; "The Thin Man: The Pre-Incan Caper," NBC, 1957; "Playhouse 90: The Dungeon," CBS, 1958; "How to Marry a Millionaire: For the Love of Art," SYN, 1958; "Perry Mason: The Case of the Desperate Daughter," CBS, 1958; "Steve Canyon: Iron Curtain," NBC, 1959; "U.S. Border Patrol: Plague Trail," SYN, 1959; "Have Gun, Will Travel: Fragile," CBS, 1959; "How to Marry a Millionaire: Gwen's Secret," SYN, 1959; "The Overland Trail: Vigilantes of Montana," NBC, 1960; "Alcoa Theatre: The Observer," NBC, 1960; "Troubleshooters: Tunnel to Yesterday," NBC, 1960; "Rawhide: Incident of the Music Maker," CBS, 1960; "The Untouchables: The Purple Gang," ABC, 1960; "Peter Loves Mary: Movie Star," NBC, 1961; "Have Gun, Will Travel: The Uneasy Grave," CBS, 1961; "Adventures in Paradise: Survival," ABC, 1961; "The Third Man: The Third Medallion," SYN, 1962; "Checkmate: An Assassin Arrives, Andante," CBS, 1962; "G.E. True: Man with a Suitcase," CBS, 1962; "The Lloyd Bridges Show: The Wonder of Wanda," CBS, 1963; "My Three Sons: The Dream Book," ABC, 1963; "77 Sunset Strip: Escape to Freedom," ABC, 1963; "G.E. True: Heydrich," CBS, 1963; "My Three Sons: Total Recall," ABC, 1963; "The Man From UNCLE: The Project Strigas Affair," NBC, 1964; "Perry Mason: The Case of a Place Called Midnight," CBS, 1964; "Hollywood Squares," NBC, 1968; "The Doris Day Show: Gowns by Louie," CBS, 1972; "Love, American Style: Love and the Unbearable Fiancee," ABC, 1972; "McMillan and Wife: The Devil You Say," NBC, 1973; "Beat the Clock," SYN, 1975; "McMillan: All Bets Are Off," NBC, 1976; "The Love Boat: The Grass Is Always Greener," ABC, 1979; "Mr. Sunshine: The Evaluation," ABC, 1986; "Mr. Sunshine: Great Expectations," ABC, 1986.
TV MOVIES AND MINISERIES: "Wake Me When the

War Is Over," ABC, 1969; "Assignment: Munich," ABC, 1972; "Best Sellers: The Rhinemann Exchange," NBC, 1977; "The Return of the Beverly Hillbillies," CBS, 1981.
* Emmies: 1968, 1969.

KLOUS, PAT
b. Hutchinson, KS, October 19, 1955. Actress who played Judy McCoy, cruise director on "The Love Boat."
AS A REGULAR: "Flying High," CBS, 1978-79; "Aloha, Paradise," ABC, 1981; "The Love Boat," ABC, 1984-86.
AND: "Hotel: Deceptions," ABC, 1983; "Murder, She Wrote: The Bottom Line Is Murder," CBS, 1987.
TV MOVIES AND MINISERIES: "Flying High," CBS, 1978; "Terror Among Us," CBS, 1981.

KLUGMAN, JACK
b. Philadelphia, PA, April 27, 1922. Actor of power and passion whose performances have become less human and more bombastic. Best known as sloppy Oscar Madison of "The Odd Couple" and as self-righteous Dr. No-first-name Quincy, Klugman won his first Emmy as a blacklisted actor on "The Defenders."
AS A REGULAR: "The Greatest Gift," NBC, 1954-55; "Harris Against the World," NBC, 1964-65; "The Odd Couple," ABC, 1970-75; "Quincy," NBC, 1976-83; "You Again?," NBC, 1986-87.
AND: "U.S. Steel Hour: Good for You," ABC, 1954; "U.S. Steel Hour: Two," ABC, 1954; "U.S. Steel Hour: Presento," ABC, 1954; "Studio One: The Missing Men," CBS, 1955; "Producers Showcase: The Petrified Forest," NBC, 1955; "Big Town: Comic Book Murder," NBC, 1955; "Studio One: A Terrible Day," CBS, 1955; "Kraft Television Theatre: Two Times Two," NBC, 1955; "Kraft Television Theatre: The Ninth Hour," NBC, 1956; "Alcoa Hour: Mrs. Gilling and the Skyscraper," NBC, 1957; "Alfred Hitchcock Presents: The Mail Order Prophet," CBS, 1957; "Suspicion: Diary for Death," NBC, 1957; "Gunsmoke: Buffalo Man," CBS, 1958; "Suspicion: Protege," NBC, 1958; "G.E. Theatre: Young and Scared," CBS, 1958; "Studio One: The Man Who Asked for a Funeral," NBC, 1958; "Kraft Mystery Theatre: Night Cry," NBC, 1958; "Playhouse 90: The Time of Your Life," CBS, 1958; "Hallmark Hall of Fame: Kiss Me, Kate," NBC, 1958; "Playhouse 90: The Velvet Alley," CBS, 1959; "Naked City: The Shield," ABC, 1959; "Sunday Showcase: One Loud, Clear Voice," NBC, 1960; "The Twilight Zone: A Passage for Trumpet," CBS, 1960; "Special for Women: The Cold Woman," NBC, 1960; "Naked City: The Well-Dressed Termites," ABC, 1961; "Jackie Gleason Special: The Million Dollar

Incident," CBS, 1961; "Target: The Corruptors: Pier 60," ABC, 1961; "The Twilight Zone: A Game of Pool," CBS, 1961; "Follow the Sun: Busman's Holiday," ABC, 1961; "Straightaway: Die Laughing," ABC, 1961; "Naked City: The Tragic Success of Alfred Tiloff," ABC, 1961; "The Untouchables: The Loophole," ABC, 1961; "The Defenders: The Search," CBS, 1962; "Target: The Corruptors: Chase the Dragon," ABC, 1962; "Ben Casey: Give My Hands an Epitaph," ABC, 1962; "Naked City: Let Me Die Before I Wake," ABC, 1962; "The New Breed: All the Dead Faces," ABC, 1962; "Cain's Hundred: Woman of Silure," NBC, 1962; "Naked City: Stop the Parade! A Baby Is Crying," ABC, 1962; "Naked City: King Stanisulas and the Knights of the Round Stable," ABC, 1962; "The Twilight Zone: Death Ship," CBS, 1963; "The Untouchables: An Eye for an Eye," ABC, 1963; "The Twilight Zone: In Praise of Pip," CBS, 1963; "Arrest and Trial: The Quality of Justice," ABC, 1963; "The Fugitive: Terror at High Point," ABC, 1963; "The Virginian: Roar From the Mountain," NBC, 1964; "The Defenders: Blacklist," CBS, 1964; "The Great Adventure: The Night Raider," CBS, 1964; "Kraft Suspense Theatre: The Threatening Eye," NBC, 1964; "Bob Hope Chrysler Theatre: A Crash of Symbols," NBC, 1964; "The Tonight Show Starring Johnny Carson," NBC, 1964; "Insight: The Prisoner," SYN, 1965; "The Fugitive: Everybody Gets Hit in the Mouth Sometime," ABC, 1965; "Kraft Suspense Theatre: Won't It Ever Be Morning?," NBC, 1965; "Ben Casey: A Slave Is on the Throne," ABC, 1965; "The FBI: Image in a Cracked Mirror," ABC, 1965; "Bob Hope Chrysler Theatre: A Time of Flight," NBC, 1966; "The Name of the Game: For Swingers Only," NBC, 1969; "Then Came Bronson: The Runner," NBC, 1969; "The Name of the Game: Blind Man's Bluff," NBC, 1969; "The FBI: The Diamond Millstone," ABC, 1970; "The Bold Ones: Dark Is the Rainbow, Loud the Silence," NBC, 1971; "The Name of the Game: The Time Is Now," NBC, 1970; "Then Came Bronson: The Runner," NBC, 1970; "Love, American Style: Love and the Big Game," ABC, 1971; "Password," ABC, 1971; "The Carol Burnett Show," CBS, 1972; "Love, American Style: Love and the Cheaters," ABC, 1972; "The Shape of Things," CBS, 1973; "Match Game '73," CBS, 1973; "Willie Mays, All-Star," NBC, 1974; "3 for the Money," NBC, 1975; "The Carol Burnett Show," CBS, 1976; "The Merv Griffin Show," SYN, 1980; "The Merv Griffin Show," SYN, 1981; "The John Davidson Show," SYN, 1981.
TV MOVIES AND MINISERIES: "Fame Is the Name of the Game," NBC, 1966; "Poor Devil," NBC, 1973; "The Underground Man," NBC, 1974; "One of My Wives Is Missing," ABC, 1976.
AS WRITER: "Kraft Television Theatre: The Big Break," NBC, 1957; "Kraft Theatre: Code of the Corner," NBC, 1958.
* Emmies: 1964, 1971, 1973.

KNIGHT, CHRISTOPHER

b. *New York City, NY, 1958.* Actor who plays Peter Brady. A lot.
AS A REGULAR: "The Brady Bunch," ABC, 1969-74; "The Brady Bunch Hour," ABC, 1977; "Joe's World," NBC, 1979-80; "The Bradys," CBS, 1990.
AND: "One Day at a Time: Barbara's Emergence," CBS, 1976; "Happy Days: Be My Valentine," ABC, 1978; "The Love Boat: Baby Sister," ABC, 1985; "Day by Day: A Very Brady Episode," NBC, 1989.
TV MOVIES AND MINISERIES: "Diary of a Teenage Hitchhiker," ABC, 1979; "Valentine Magic on Love Island," NBC, 1980; "The Brady Girls Get Married," NBC, 1981; "A Very Brady Christmas," CBS, 1988.

KNIGHT, FUZZY

b. *John Forrest Knight, Fairmont, WV, May 9, 1901; d. 1976.* Actor usually in woodsy or cowboy roles; longtime sidekick of Tex Ritter.
AS A REGULAR: "Foreign Legionnaire," NBC, 1955-57.
AND: "December Bride: Song Plugging," CBS, 1957; "December Bride: The Texan, Rory Calhoun," CBS, 1959; "Lawman: The Inheritance," ABC, 1961; "The Joey Bishop Show: Very Warm for Christmas," NBC, 1962; "The Joey Bishop Show: Door to Door Salesman," NBC, 1962; "Mr. Smith Goes to Washington: Without a Song," ABC, 1962; "Batman: Hizzoner the Penguin/Dizzoner the Penguin," ABC, 1966.

KNIGHT, GLADYS

b. *Atlanta, GA, May 28, 1944.* Pop singer, fomerly with the Pips.
AS A REGULAR: "The Gladys Knight & the Pips Show," NBC, 1975; "Charlie & Company," CBS, 1985-86.
AND: "Operation: Entertainment," ABC, 1968; "The Mike Douglas Show," SYN, 1968; "The Mike Douglas Show," SYN, 1969; "In Concert," ABC, 1973; "Midnight Special," NBC, 1973; "The Dean Martin Show," NBC, 1974; "The $20,000 Pyramid," ABC, 1976; "The Jeffersons: Who's That Masked Woman?," CBS, 1983; "A Different World: Three Girls Three," NBC, 1988.
TV MOVIES AND MINISERIES: "Desperado," NBC, 1987.

KNIGHT, JACK

b. *Somerville, MA, February 26, 1939.*
AS A REGULAR: "Lotsa Luck," NBC, 1973-74; "James at 15," NBC, 1977-78; "Presenting Susan Anton," NBC, 1979.

AND: "Mannix: A Matter of Principle," CBS, 1973; "CHiPS: Name Your Price," NBC, 1977; "Mrs. Columbo: Caviar with Everything," NBC, 1979; "Diff'rent Strokes: The Athlete," NBC, 1981; "Cheers: Truce or Consequences," NBC, 1982; "Cheers: Let Me Count the Ways," NBC, 1983; "Cheers: Father Knows Last," NBC, 1983; "Cheers: The Boys in the Bar," NBC, 1983; "Annie McGuire: Premiere," CBS, 1988.

TV MOVIES AND MINISERIES: "Dead Man on the Run," ABC, 1975.

KNIGHT, SHIRLEY

b. Goessel, KS, July 4, 1936. Actress of movies, stage and TV; an Emmy winner as the mother of Hope (Mel Harris) on "thirtysomething."

AS A GUEST: "Buckskin: Little Heathen," NBC, 1958; "The Texan: Stampede," CBS, 1959; "Johnny Staccato: The Parents," NBC, 1959; "Hawaiian Eye: A Dime a Dozen," ABC, 1959; "Bourbon Street Beat: Key to the City," ABC, 1960; "Hawaiian Eye: Fatal Cruise," ABC, 1960; "Playhouse 90: The Shape of the River," CBS, 1960; "77 Sunset Strip: Fraternity of Fear," ABC, 1960; "Hawaiian Eye: The Kahuna Curtain," ABC, 1960; "SurfSide 6: Power of Suggestion," ABC, 1960; "SurfSide 6: Little Star Lost," ABC, 1961; "The Roaring Twenties: Big-Town Blues," ABC, 1961; "Cheyenne: The Invaders," ABC, 1961; "Maverick: The Ice Man," ABC, 1961; "Here's Hollywood," NBC, 1961; "Lawman: The Trial," ABC, 1961; "SurfSide 6: Elegy for a Bookeeper," ABC, 1962; "Target: The Corruptors: A Book of Faces," ABC, 1962; "U.S. Steel Hour: You Can't Escape," CBS, 1962; "Naked City: Five Cranks for Winter, Ten Cranks for Spring," ABC, 1962; "The Virginian: Man From the Sea," NBC, 1962; "U.S. Steel Hour: Fair Young Ghost," CBS, 1963; "Girl Talk," SYN, 1963; "Alcoa Premiere: The Broken Year," ABC, 1963; "The du Pont Show: The Takers," NBC, 1963; "The Eleventh Hour: And Man Created Vanity," NBC, 1963; "The Outer Limits: The Man Who Was Never Born," ABC, 1963; "Arrest and Trial: Run Little Man, Run," ABC, 1963; "The Fugitive: The Homecoming," ABC, 1964; "The Defenders: A Voice Loud and Clear," CBS, 1964; "The Virginian: Lost Yesterday," NBC, 1965; "The Fugitive: A.P.B.," ABC, 1965; "The Fugitive: Echo of a Nightmare," ABC, 1966; "Bob Hope Chrysler Theatre: The Faceless Man," NBC, 1966; "The Invaders: The Watchers," ABC, 1967; "The Bold Ones: A Standard for Manhood," CBS, 1972; "Alias Smith and Jones: The Ten Days That Shook Kid Curry," ABC, 1973; "Circle of Fear: Legion of Demons," NBC, 1973; "The Streets of San Francisco: A Room with a View," ABC,

1973; "Jigsaw: Girl on the Run," ABC, 1973; "CBS Playhouse 90: The Lie," CBS, 1973; "Medical Center: Tainted Lady," CBS, 1974; "The Country Girl," NBC, 1974; "Orson Welles' Great Mysteries: Tainted Lady," SYN, 1974; "Barnaby Jones: Fantasy of Fear," CBS, 1975; "Wide World of Mystery: Please Stand by for Murder," ABC, 1975; "Medical Story: Pilot," NBC, 1975; "The Equalizer: Time Present, Time Past," CBS, 1989; "Murder, She Wrote: Smooth Operator," CBS, 1989; "thirtysomething: Arizona," ABC, 1990.

TV MOVIES AND MINISERIES: "The Outsider," NBC, 1967; "Shadow Over Elveron," NBC, 1968; "Friendly Persuasion," ABC, 1975; "Medical Story," NBC, 1975; "21 Hours at Munich," ABC, 1976; "Return to Earth," ABC, 1976; "The Defection of Simas Kudirka," CBS, 1978; "Playing for Time," CBS, 1980; "With Intent to Kill," CBS, 1984.

* Emmies: 1990.

KNIGHT, TED

b. Tadeus Wladslaw Konopka, Terryville, CT, 1923; d. 1986. Deep-voiced actor who played pompous, greedy, selfish, addle-brained anchorman Ted Baxter on "The Mary Tyler Moore Show."

AS A REGULAR: "The Clear Horizon," CBS, 1960-61, 1962; "The Mary Tyler Moore Show," CBS, 1970-77; "The Ted Knight Show," CBS, 1978; "Too Close for Comfort," ABC, 1980-83; SYN, 1984-86.

AND: "How to Marry a Millionaire: A Call to Arms," SYN, 1959; "Gunsmoke: Print Asper," CBS, 1959; "Peter Gunn: Criss Cross," NBC, 1959; "The Twilight Zone: The Lonely," CBS, 1959; "Lawman: The Ugly Man," ABC, 1960; "Pete and Gladys: Crime of Passion," CBS, 1960; "Dr. Kildare: Immunity," NBC, 1961; "G.E. Theatre: Star Witness," CBS, 1961; "The New Loretta Young Show: Pilot," CBS, 1962; "The Virginian: Throw a Long Rope," NBC, 1962; "McHale's Navy: One of Our Engines Is Missing," ABC, 1963; "The Virginian: The Final Hour," NBC, 1963; "Combat!: The Volunteer," ABC, 1963; "Combat!: Weep No More," ABC, 1964; "The Outer Limits: The Invisible Enemy," ABC, 1964; "McHale's Navy: Fountain of Youth," ABC, 1964; "The FBI: An Elephant Is Like a Rope," ABC, 1965; "Gomer Pyle, USMC: Gomer, the Would-Be Hero," CBS, 1966; "The FBI: The Assassin," ABC, 1966; "Combat!: The Brothers," ABC, 1966; "T.H.E. Cat: Brother-hood," NBC, 1967; "Get Smart: Pussycats Galore," NBC, 1967; "The Wild Wild West: The Night of the Kraken," CBS, 1968; "The Dean Martin Show," NBC, 1973; "Music Country USA," NBC, 1974; "Sandy in Disneyland," CBS, 1974; "Hollywood Squares," SYN, 1975; "The Tonight Show Starring Johnny Carson," NBC,

1975; "Saturday Night Live," NBC, 1979; "The Love Boat: Forever Engaged," ABC, 1980; "The Love Boat: Pride of the Pacific," ABC, 1982; "The Love Boat: The Lottery Winners," ABC, 1983.
* Emmies: 1973, 1976.

KNOTTS, DON

b. *Morgantown, WV, July 21, 1924*. Slender comic with bad posture who excelled as high-strung types, especially television's most neurotic lawman, Deputy Barney Fife.

AS A REGULAR: "Search for Tomorrow," CBS, 1953-55; "The Tonight Show," NBC, 1954-57; "The Steve Allen Show," NBC, 1956-59; "Steve Allen Presents the Steve Lawrence and Eydie Gorme Show," NBC, 1958; "Steve Allen Plymouth Show," NBC, 1959-60; "The Andy Griffith Show," CBS, 1960-65; "The Don Knotts Show," NBC, 1970-71; "Steve Allen's Laugh Back," SYN, 1976; "Three's Company," ABC, 1979-84; "What a Country!," SYN, 1987; "Matlock," NBC, 1988- .

AND: "The Lux Show with Rosemary Clooney," NBC, 1958; "The Bob Cummings Show: Bob and Schultzy at Sea," NBC, 1958; "The Many Loves of Dobie Gillis: Almost a Father," CBS, 1960; "Dean Martin Special," NBC, 1960; "The Red Skelton Show: San Fernando and Herbie," CBS, 1961; "Dinah Shore Chevy Show," NBC, 1961; "Hollywood Palace," ABC, 1964; "The Red Skelton Hour," CBS, 1964; "The Red Skelton Hour," CBS, 1965; "The Andy Griffith, Don Knotts, Jim Nabors Special," CBS, 1965; "The Andy Griffith Show: The Return of Barney Fife/The Legend of Barney Fife," CBS, 1966; "McHale's Navy: Little Red Riding Doctor," ABC, 1966; "Andy Griffith Special," CBS, 1967; "The Pat Boone Show," NBC, 1967; "The Andy Griffith Show: A Visit to Barney Fife/Barney Comes to Mayberry," CBS, 1967; "Bob Hope Chrysler Theatre: The Reason Nobody Hardly Ever Seen a Fat Outlaw in the West Is as Follows," NBC, 1967; "The Andy Griffith Show: Barney Hosts a Summit Meeting," CBS, 1968; "Mayberry RFD: Andy and Helen Get Married," CBS, 1968; "The Jim Nabors Hour," CBS, 1969; "The Bill Cosby Show: Swan's Way," NBC, 1970; "Hallmark Hall of Fame: The Man Who Came to Dinner," NBC, 1972; "Here's Lucy: Lucy Goes on Her Last Blind Date," CBS, 1973; "The New Bill Cosby Show," CBS, 1973; "Guess Who's Knott Coming to Dinner," CBS, 1973; "Hollywood Squares," NBC, 1974; "The Spooky Fog," CBS, 1974; "The Girl with Something Extra: The Not-So-Good Samaritan," NBC, 1974; "Wait Till Your Father Gets Home: Don Knotts, the Beekeeper," SYN, 1974; "Hollywood Squares," NBC, 1974; "Harry and Maggie," CBS, 1975; "Hollywood Squares," SYN, 1975; "Tony Orlando and Dawn," CBS, 1975; "Dinah!," SYN,

1976; "Joys," NBC, 1976; "Hollywood Squares," NBC, 1977; "The Captain and Tennille," ABC, 1977; "The Love Boat: Haven't I Seen You ...?," ABC, 1979; "Something Spectacular with Steve Allen," PBS, 1981; "Newhart: Seein' Double," CBS, 1990.

TV MOVIES AND MINISERIES: "Return to Mayberry," NBC, 1986.
* Knotts' Emmies in 1966 and '67 were for guest appearances as Barney on "The Andy Griffith Show."
* Emmies: 1961, 1962, 1963, 1966, 1967.

KNOX, TERENCE

b. *Richland, WA*. Actor who played Dr. Peter White on "St. Elsewhere" and Sgt. Zeke Anderson on "Tour of Duty."

AS A REGULAR: "St. Elsewhere," NBC, 1982-85; "All Is Forgiven," NBC, 1986; "Tour of Duty," CBS, 1987-90.

AND: "Murder, She Wrote: Murder Takes the Bus," CBS, 1985; "Wonderworks: The Mighty Pawns," PBS, 1987.

TV MOVIES AND MINISERIES: "City Killer," NBC, 1984; "Chase," CBS, 1985; "Murder Ordained," CBS, 1987.

KOENIG, WALTER

b. *Chicago, IL*. Actor who played Ensign Chekov on "Star Trek."

AS A REGULAR: "Star Trek," NBC, 1967-69.

AND: "Mr. Novak: The Boy Without a Country," NBC, 1963; "Mr. Novak: With a Hammer in His Hand, Lord, Lord!," NBC, 1964; "Mr. Novak: The Firebrand," NBC, 1965; "Ben Casey: A Rambling Discourse on Egyptian Water Clocks," ABC, 1965; "Gidget: Gidget's Foreign Policy," ABC, 1965; "Columbo: Fade in to Murder," NBC, 1976.

TV MOVIES AND MINISERIES: "Goodbye Raggedy Ann," CBS, 1971.

KOHNER, SUSAN

b. *Los Angeles, CA, November 11, 1936*. Actress of movies ("Imitation of Life") and some fifties and sixties television.

AS A GUEST: "Alcoa Hour: Long After Summer," NBC, 1956; "Matinee Theatre: Letter to a Stranger," NBC, 1956; "Four Star Playhouse: Desert Encounter," CBS, 1956; "Schlitz Playhouse of Stars: Date for Tomorrow," CBS, 1956; "Cavalcade Theatre: Bed of Roses," ABC, 1956; "Climax!: Ten Minutes to Curfew," CBS, 1956; "Schlitz Playhouse of Stars: Dual Control," CBS, 1957; "Wagon Train: The Charles Avery Story," NBC, 1957; "Alfred Hitchcock Presents: Return of the Hero," CBS, 1957; "Suspicion: The Flight," NBC, 1957; "Matinee Theatre: Laugh a Little Tear," NBC, 1958; "Playhouse 90: In the

Presence of Mine Enemies," CBS, 1960; "Route 66: The Quick and the Dead," CBS, 1961; "The du Pont Show with June Allyson: The Guilty Heart," CBS, 1961; "Hong Kong: The Innocent Exile," ABC, 1961; "Here's Hollywood," NBC, 1961; "The Dick Powell Show: Tomorrow, the Man," NBC, 1962; "The Nurses: Root of Violence," CBS, 1963; "Girl Talk," SYN, 1963; "Going My Way: One Small, Unhappy Family," ABC, 1963; "Route 66: But What Do You Do in March?," CBS, 1963; "Temple Houston: Toll the Bell Slowly," NBC, 1963; "Rawhide: Incident at Ten Trees," CBS, 1964; "Channing: A Bang and a Whimper," ABC, 1964.

KOLB, CLARENCE
b. Cleveland, OH, 1875; d. 1964. Tall actor who often played apoplectic bosses in movies and TV.
AS A REGULAR: "My Little Margie," CBS, 1952; NBC, 1952; CBS, 1953; NBC, 1953-55.

KOLB, MINA
Actress who plays the crazy Aunt Mary on "Generations."
AS A REGULAR: "Pete and Gladys," CBS, 1961-62; "Generations," NBC, 1989- .
AND: "Three's Company: Terri Makes Her Move," ABC, 1981; "It's Garry Shandling's Show: Killer Routine," FOX, 1989; "Knots Landing: Grave Misunderstanding," CBS, 1989.

KOMACK, JAMES
b. New York City, NY, August 3, 1930. Comedy writer-producer who began as an actor; he played millionaire dentist Harvey Spencer Blair III on "Hennessey" and freewheeling Norman Tinker on "The Courtship of Eddie's Father."
AS A REGULAR: "Hennesey," CBS, 1959-62; "The Courtship of Eddie's Father," ABC, 1969-72.
AND: "Dick Powell's Zane Grey Theatre: There Were Four," CBS, 1957; "Wagon Train: The Julia Gage Story," NBC, 1957; "This Is Your Life (Carolyn Jones)," NBC, 1959; "The du Pont Show with June Allyson: Emergency," CBS, 1960; "One Happy Family: Sky Diver," NBC, 1961; "Get Smart: The Little Black Book," NBC, 1968; "The Merv Griffin Show," SYN, 1975.
AS WRITER: "Hennesey: Harvey's Doll," CBS, 1961; "The Barbara Stanwyck Show: Size 10," NBC, 1961.
AS DIRECTOR: "The Dick Van Dyke Show: Empress Carlotta's Necklace," CBS, 1961; "The Dick Van Dyke Show: Buddy, Can You Spare a Job?," CBS, 1961; "Get Smart: The Little Black Book," NBC, 1968.
AS PRODUCER-CREATOR-WRITER: "Chico and the Man," NBC, 1974-78; "Welcome Back,

Kotter," ABC, 1975-79; "Mr. T. and Tina," ABC, 1976.

KOOCK, GUICH
b. Austin, TX, July 22, 1944. Actor usually in hayseed roles; he played Deputy Harley Puckett on "Carter Country."
AS A REGULAR: "Carter Country," ABC, 1977-79; "The Chisholms," CBS, 1980; "Lewis & Clark," NBC, 1981-82; "She's the Sheriff," SYN, 1987-89.
AND: "Laverne & Shirley: Dog Day Blind Dates," ABC, 1976; "Alice: Mel's in the Kitchen with Dinah," CBS, 1979; "Match Game '79," CBS, 1979; "The Love Boat: Boomerang," ABC, 1980.
TV MOVIES AND MINISERIES: "The Mysterious Island of Beautiful Women," CBS, 1979.

KOPELL, BERNIE
b. New York City, NY, June 21, 1933. Comic actor best known as Doc on "The Love Boat" and KAOS agent Siegfried on "Get Smart."
AS A REGULAR: "Get Smart," NBC, 1966-69; "That Girl," ABC, 1966-71; "The Doris Day Show," CBS, 1970-71; "Needles and Pins," NBC, 1973; "When Things Were Rotten," ABC, 1975; "The Love Boat," ABC, 1977-86.
AND: "My Favorite Martian: Poor Little Rich Cat," CBS, 1964; "The Lucy Show: Lucy Plays Florence Nightingale," CBS, 1964; "The Beverly Hillbillies: The Movie Starlet," CBS, 1965; "My Favorite Martian: El Senor From Mars," CBS, 1965; "Ben Casey: What to Her Is Plato?," ABC, 1965; "My Favorite Martian: Girl in the Flying Machine," CBS, 1965; "The Farmer's Daughter: High Fashion," ABC, 1965; "The Farmer's Daughter: Anyone for Spindling?," ABC, 1966; "The Dick Van Dyke Show: Remember the Alimony," CBS, 1966; "Death of a Salesman," CBS, 1966; "Green Acres: You Ought to Be in Pictures," CBS, 1966; "Run, Buddy, Run: Did You Ever Have One of Those Days?," CBS, 1966; "The Hero: I Have a Friend," NBC, 1966; "The Flying Nun: The Return of Father Lundigan," ABC, 1968; "Bewitched: Twitching for UNICEF," ABC, 1969; "Bewitched: A Bunny for Tabitha," ABC, 1969; "Bewitched: Samantha's Secret Spell," ABC, 1969; "Bewitched: Samantha's Lost Weekend," ABC, 1970; "Bewitched: Samantha's Secret Is Discovered," ABC, 1970; "Room 222: Goodbye, Mr. Hip," ABC, 1970; "Love, American Style: Love and the Marriage Counselor," ABC, 1970; "Bewitched: Samantha and the Loch Ness Monster," ABC, 1971; "Bewitched: A Plague on Maurice and Samantha," ABC, 1971; "Love, American Style: Love and the Awakening," ABC, 1971; "Love, American Style: Love and the Water Bed," ABC, 1971; "Funny Face: The Repairman Cheateth," CBS, 1971; "Bewitched: The Warlock in the Gray

Flannel Suit," ABC, 1971; "The Odd Couple: Psychic, Shmycic," ABC, 1972; "Room 222: Mr. Wrong," ABC, 1972; "The Bob Newhart Show: I Want to Be Alone," CBS, 1972; "Bewitched: Sam's Witchcraft Blows a Fuse," ABC, 1972; "The Doris Day Show: The Magnificent Fraud," CBS, 1973; "The Paul Lynde Show: Out of Bounds," ABC, 1973; "Diana: Pilot," NBC, 1973; "The Mary Tyler Moore Show: Ted Baxter's Famous Broadcaster's School," CBS, 1975; "Kojak: Money Back Guarantee," CBS, 1975; "Switch: Ain't Nobody Here Named Barney," CBS, 1976; "Chico and the Man: The Face Job," NBC, 1976; "The Merv Griffin Show," SYN, 1976; "Alice: The Failure," CBS, 1977; "The New Mike Hammer: Elegy for a Tramp," CBS, 1987; "ABC Afterschool Specials: The Day My Kid Went Punk," ABC, 1987.

TV MOVIES AND MINISERIES: "Love Boat II," ABC, 1977; "A Guide for the Married Woman," ABC, 1978; "Get Smart, Again!," ABC, 1989.

KOPINS, KAREN
Actress who plays Kay Lloyd on "Dallas."
AS A REGULAR: "Dallas," CBS, 1988- .
AND: "Riptide: Pilot," NBC, 1984; "The Love Boat: Getting Started," ABC, 1985; "Scarecrow and Mrs. King: Stemwinder," CBS, 1986; "The A-Team: The Spy Who Mugged Me," NBC, 1986.
TV MOVIES AND MINISERIES: "The Tracker," HBO, 1988; "Perry Mason: The Case of the Lethal Lesson," NBC, 1989.

KOPPEL, TED
b. England, 1940.
AS A REGULAR: "ABC Weekend News," 1975-77; "Nightline," 1979- .
* Emmies: 1980, 1982, 1985, 1986.

KORMAN, HARVEY
b. Chicago, IL, February 15, 1927. Witty, Emmy-winning second banana to Danny Kaye and Carol Burnett; his solo series attempts have been less successful.
AS A REGULAR: "The Danny Kaye Show," CBS, 1964-67; "The Carol Burnett Show," CBS, 1967-77; "The Tim Conway Show," CBS, 1980-81; "Mama's Family," NBC, 1983-85; "Leo & Liz in Beverly Hills," CBS, 1986; "The Nutt House," NBC, 1989.
AND: "The Donna Reed Show: Decisions, Decisions, Decisions," ABC, 1960; "Hennesey: The Gossip-Go-Round," CBS, 1961; "The Donna Reed Show: Who Needs Glasses?," ABC, 1962; "The Donna Reed Show: Rebel with a Cause," ABC, 1962; "I'm Dickens, He's Fenster: The Acting Game," ABC, 1962; "Empire: Pressure Lock," NBC, 1962; "Dennis the Menace: My Four Boys," CBS, 1963; "Route 66: Suppose I

Said I Was the Queen of Spain," CBS, 1963; "Glynis: Pilot," CBS, 1963; "Hazel: Maid for a Day," NBC, 1964; "The Lucy Show: Lucy the Camp Cook," CBS, 1964; "The Munsters: Family Portrait," CBS, 1964; "Walt Disney's Wonderful World of Color: Gallegher," NBC, 1965; "Walt Disney's Wonderful World of Color: The Further Adventures of Gallegher," NBC, 1965; "Gidget: Daddy Come Home," ABC, 1965; "The Lucy Show: Lucy the Stockholder," CBS, 1965; "The Munsters: Yes Galen, There Is a Herman," CBS, 1965; "The Lucy Show: Lucy at Marineland," CBS, 1965; "A Salute to Stan Laurel," CBS, 1965; "The Munsters: Prehistoric Munster," CBS, 1966; "The Hero: The Big Return of Little Eddie," NBC, 1966; "F Troop: Bye, Bye Balloon," ABC, 1966; "The Wild Wild West: The Night of the Big Blackmail," CBS, 1968; "The Steve Allen Show," SYN, 1968; "Hollywood Squares," NBC, 1974; "Hollywood Squares," NBC, 1975; "Dinah!," SYN, 1976; "Hollywood Squares," SYN, 1979; "Hollywood Squares," SYN, 1980; "The Love Boat: The Emperor's Fortune," ABC, 1983; "The Love Boat: Out of the Blue," ABC, 1985; "Animal Crack-Ups," ABC, 1989.

TV MOVIES AND MINISERIES: "Three's a Crowd," ABC, 1969; "Suddenly Single," ABC, 1971; "The Love Boat," ABC, 1976; "Bud and Lou," NBC, 1978; "The Invisible Woman," NBC, 1983; "Carpool," CBS, 1983; "Crash Course," NBC, 1988.
* Emmies: 1969, 1971, 1972, 1974.

KOTTO, YAPHET
b. New York City, NY, November 15, 1937. Black actor often in action roles.
AS A REGULAR: "For Love and Honor," NBC, 1983.
AND: "Experiment in Terror: Losers Weepers," NBC, 1967; "Death Valley Days: A Man Called Abraham," SYN, 1967; "The Big Valley: The Buffalo Man," ABC, 1967; "The High Chaparral: The Buffalo Soldiers," NBC, 1968; "Hawaii Five-O: King of the Hill," CBS, 1968; "Mannix: Death in a Minor Key," CBS, 1969; "The Name of the Game: The Time Is Now," NBC, 1970; "Gunsmoke: The Scavengers," CBS, 1970; "Night Gallery: The Messiah of Mott Street," NBC, 1971; "Doctors' Hospital: Knives of Chance," NBC, 1975; "The A-Team: The Out-of-Towners," NBC, 1983; "Hill Street Blues: Blues in the Night," NBC, 1985; "Murder, She Wrote: Steal Me a Story," CBS, 1987.
TV MOVIES AND MINISERIES: "Night Chase," CBS, 1970; "Raid on Entebbe," NBC, 1977; "Playing with Fire," NBC, 1985; "Badge of the Assassin," CBS, 1985; "Harem," ABC, 1986; "In Self Defense," ABC, 1987; "Perry Mason: The Case of the Scandalous Scoundrel," NBC, 1987; "Prime Target," NBC, 1989.

KOVACS, ERNIE

b. *Trenton, NJ, 1919; d. 1962.* Driven, pioneering television comic whose camera trickery and wild satire predated TV's penchant for crazy visual blackout comedy in the late 1960s. Endlessly admired today, Kovacs wasn't a huge audience favorite during his lifetime, jumping from show to show and timeslot to timeslot.

AS A REGULAR: "Deadline for Dinner," DUM, 1950; "Kovacs on the Corner," NBC, 1951-52; "It's Time for Ernie," NBC, 1951; "Ernie in Kovacsland," NBC, 1951; "Take a Guess," CBS, 1953; "Time Will Tell," DUM, 1954; "One Minute Please," DUM, 1954-55; "The Ernie Kovacs Show," NBC, 1955-56; "The Tonight Show (Tonight)," NBC, 1956-57; "Take a Good Look," ABC, 1959-61; "Silents Please," ABC, 1961; "The New Ernie Kovacs Show," ABC, 1961-62.

AND: "The Tonight Show," NBC, 1955; "NBC Comedy Hour," NBC, 1956; "The Steve Allen Show," NBC, 1956; "It Could Be You," NBC, 1956; "The Walter Winchell Show," NBC, 1956; "Saturday Spectacular: Sonia Heinie's Holiday on Ice," NBC, 1956; "Ernie Kovacs Special," NBC, 1957; "The Perry Como Show," NBC, 1957; "Producers Showcase: Festival of Magic," NBC, 1957; "The Ed Sullivan Show," CBS, 1957; "What's My Line?," CBS, 1957; "Playhouse 90: Topaze," CBS, 1957; "The Polly Bergen Show," NBC, 1957; "The Perry Como Show," NBC, 1957; "Wide, Wide World: The Fabulous Infant," NBC, 1957; "Dinah Shore Chevy Show," NBC, 1957; "Truth or Consequences," NBC, 1957; "The George Gobel Show," NBC, 1957; "The Big Record," CBS, 1958; "The Ed Sullivan Show," CBS, 1958; "The Eddie Fisher Show," NBC, 1958; "The Ford Show," NBC, 1958; "G.E. Theatre: The World's Greatest Quarterback," CBS, 1958; "Arthur Murray Party," NBC, 1958; "Patti Page Olds Show," ABC, 1958; "The Jack Benny Program," CBS, 1959; "Westinghouse Desilu Playhouse: Symbol of Authority," CBS, 1959; "The Ann Sothern Show: Hurrah for the Irish," CBS, 1959; "The Eddie Fisher Show," NBC, 1959; "The Greatest Show on Earth," ABC, 1959; "You Bet Your Life," NBC, 1959; "G.E. Theatre: I Was a Bloodhound," CBS, 1959; "Schlitz Playhouse of Stars: The Salted Mine," CBS, 1959; "Kovacs on Music," NBC, 1959; "Startime: The Wonderful World of Entertainment," NBC, 1959; "Bob Hope Special," NBC, 1959; "The Westinghouse Lucille Ball-Desi Arnaz Show: Lucy Meets the Moustache," CBS, 1960; "Goodyear Theatre: Author at Work," NBC, 1960; "U.S. Steel Hour: Private Eye, Private Eye," CBS, 1961.

* Kovacs reaped critical and audience acclaim for his half-hour special that aired January 19, 1957 on NBC. The show was thrown together at the last minute when Jerry Lewis announced he'd use only a hour of a 90-minute slot. Kovacs used a set and camera tilted at a 15 degree angle and, without dialogue, played Eugene, a poor soul whose food would keep rolling away from him when he'd place it on a table.

* Kovacs died in an automobile accident on January 13, 1962.

KOVE, MARTIN

b. *Brooklyn, NY.* Hunky actor who played the hunky Det. Victor Isbecki on "Cagney & Lacey."

AS A REGULAR: "Code R," CBS, 1977; "We've Got Each Other," CBS, 1977-78; "Cagney and Lacey," CBS, 1982-88; "Hard Time on Planet Earth," CBS, 1989.

AND: "Rhoda: Anything Wrong?," CBS, 1974; "Switch: The Deadly Missiles Caper," CBS, 1975; "The Rookies: Measure of Mercy," ABC, 1975; "Three for the Road: The Ripoff," CBS, 1975; "Kojak: Law Dance," CBS, 1976; "Petrocelli: Six Strings of Guilt," NBC, 1976; "The Streets of San Francisco: The Drop," ABC, 1976; "Quincy: The Eye of the Needle," NBC, 1978; "Barnaby Jones: Nest of Scorpions," CBS, 1978; "CHiPS: Hot Wheels," NBC, 1979; "Barnaby Jones: Girl on the Road," CBS, 1979; "A Man Called Sloane: Lady Bug," NBC, 1979; "Murder, She Wrote: Armed Response," CBS, 1985; "The Twilight Zone: Opening Day," SYN, 1988.

TV MOVIES AND MINISERIES: "Kingston: The Power Play," NBC, 1976; "Best Sellers: Captains and the Kings," NBC, 1976; "Trouble in High Timber Country," ABC, 1980.

KRAMER, JEFFREY

b. *New York City, NY, 1945.*

AS A REGULAR: "Struck by Lightning," CBS, 1979; "Hard Copy," CBS, 1987.

AND: "Happy Days: Fonzie the Flatfoot," ABC, 1975; "Chico and the Man: In Your Hat," NBC, 1976; "M*A*S*H: Movie Tonight," CBS, 1977; "Laverne & Shirley: Dinner for Four," ABC, 1979; "M*A*S*H: Father's Day," CBS, 1980; "Happy Days: The People vs. the Fonz," ABC, 1984.

KRAMER, STEPFANIE

b. *Los Angeles, CA, August 6, 1956.* Actress who played Det. Sgt. Dee Dee McCall on "Hunter."

AS A REGULAR: "The Secret Empire," NBC, 1979; "Married: The First Year," CBS, 1979; "We Got It Made," NBC, 1983-84; "Hunter," NBC, 1984-90.

AND: "The Runaways: The Breaking Point," NBC, 1979; "Bosom Buddies: All You Need Is Love," ABC, 1982; "The A-Team: Fire!," NBC, 1984.

TV MOVIES AND MINISERIES: "Bridge Across Time," NBC, 1985; "Take My Daughters, Please," NBC, 1988.

KRESKIN

b. Montclair, NJ, January 12, 1935. Mentalist.

AS A REGULAR: "The Amazing World of Kreskin," SYN, 1971-75.

AND: "The Mike Douglas Show," SYN, 1967; "The Mike Douglas Show," SYN, 1968; "The Flip Wilson Show," NBC, 1973; "Sammy and Company," SYN, 1976.

KRISTEN, MARTA

b. Norway, 1945. Blonde actress who played Judy Robinson on "Lost in Space."

AS A REGULAR: "Lost in Space," CBS, 1965-68.

AND: "The Loretta Young Show: The Glass Cage," NBC, 1960; "My Three Sons: Spring Will Be a Little Late This Year," ABC, 1960; "Alfred Hitchcock Presents: The Gloating Place," NBC, 1961; "Alfred Hitchcock Presents: Bang, You're Dead," NBC, 1961; "My Three Sons: Going Steady," ABC, 1962; "Dr. Kildare: Four Feet in the Morning," NBC, 1963; "The Eleventh Hour: Four Feet in the Morning," NBC, 1963; "Mr. Novak: The Senior Prom," NBC, 1964; "The Man From UNCLE: The Neptune Affair," NBC, 1964; "My Three Sons: A Serious Girl," ABC, 1964; "Wagon Train: The Wanda Snow Story," ABC, 1965; "Remington Steele: Sign, Steeled and Delivered," NBC, 1982.

KRISTOFFERSON, KRIS

b. Brownsville, TX, June 22, 1936. Singer-songwriter who was a movie star in the seventies and has turned more to TV films.

AS A GUEST: "Free to Be You and Me," ABC, 1974; "Saturday Night Live," NBC, 1976.

TV MOVIES AND MINISERIES: "Freedom Road," NBC, 1979; "The Lost Honor of Kathryn Beck," CBS, 1984; "The Last Days of Frank and Jesse James," NBC, 1986; "Blood and Orchids," CBS, 1986; "Stagecoach," CBS, 1986; "Amerika," ABC, 1987; "The Tracker," HBO, 1988.

KROEGER, GARY

b. Cedar Falls, IA, April 13, 1957. Comic actor.

AS A REGULAR: "Saturday Night Live," NBC, 1982-85; "Spies," CBS, 1987.

KROFFT, SID

b. Greece, July 30, 1929;

& MARTY

b. Canada. Puppetteers.

AS REGULARS: "Barbara Mandrell and the Mandrell Sisters," NBC, 1980-82; "D.C. Follies," SYN, 1987-89.

AND: "Shower of Stars," CBS, 1957; "The Ed Sullivan Show," CBS, 1959.

KRUGER, OTTO

b. Toledo, OH, Sept 6, 1885; d. 1974. Suave actor who often played evil types.

AS A REGULAR: "Lux Video Theatre," NBC, 1955-56.

AND: "Armstrong Circle Theatre: The Happy Ending," NBC, 1950; "Lights Out: Curtain Call," NBC, 1951; "Somerset Maugham TV Theatre: Outstation," CBS, 1951; "Lux Video Theatre: Something to Live For," CBS, 1953; "G.E. Theatre: Woman's World," CBS, 1953; "Medallion Theatre: Suitable Marriage," CBS, 1954; "Center Stage: Golden Anniversary," ABC, 1954; "Studio One: Prelude to Murder," CBS, 1954; "G.E. Theatre: The Face Is Familiar," CBS, 1954; "Science Fiction Theatre: No Food for Thought," SYN, 1955; "Science Fiction Theatre: Marked Danger," SYN, 1955; "The Desert Song," NBC, 1955; "Climax!: The 78th Floor," CBS, 1956; "Ford Theatre: Miller's Millions," ABC, 1957; "Climax!: Jacob and the Angel," CBS, 1957; "The Rebel: Gun City," ABC, 1959; "The Man and the Challenge: Experiments in Terror," NBC, 1959; "Christophers: Ethics in Journalism," SYN, 1960; "Grand Jury: Final Rest," SYN, 1960; "The Law and Mr. Jones: A Fool for a Client," ABC, 1961; "Perry Mason: The Case of the Grumbling Grandfather," CBS, 1961; "The Investigators: Quite a Woman," CBS, 1961; "The Dick Powell Show: Up Jumped the Devil," NBC, 1961; "Frontier Circus: Lippizan," CBS, 1961; "Thriller: An Attractive Family," NBC, 1962; "Checkmate: A Funny Thing Happened to Me on the Way to the Game," CBS, 1962; "Perry Mason: The Case of the Counterfeit Crank," CBS, 1962; "Dr. Kildare: Gravida One," NBC, 1962; "Sam Benedict: Nothing Equals Nothing," NBC, 1962; "Bonanza: Elegy for a Hangman," NBC, 1963; "The Dick Powell Show: The Judge," NBC, 1963; "Perry Mason: The Case of the Devious Delinquent," CBS, 1963.

KRUSCHEN, JACK

b. Canada, March 20, 1922. Character actor who played Grandpa Papadapolous on "Webster."

AS A REGULAR: "Terry and the Pirates," NBC, 1957; "Hong Kong," ABC, 1960-61; "Busting Loose," CBS, 1977; "Webster," ABC, 1985-87.

AND: "The Jane Wyman Show: Between Jobs," NBC, 1956; "The Jane Wyman Show: The Pendulum," NBC, 1957; "Lux Video Theatre: The Hard Way," NBC, 1957; "Zorro: The Cross of the Andes," ABC, 1958; "Bat Masterson: The Desert Ship," NBC, 1959; "Sugarfoot: The Despera-does," ABC, 1959; "Richard Diamond, Private

Detective: The Lovely Fraud," CBS, 1959; "The Lawless Years: The Big Greeny Story," NBC, 1959; "Tightrope!: Appointment in Jericho," CBS, 1960; "The Rifleman: One Went to Denver," ABC, 1960; "Death Valley Days: Eagle in the Rocks," SYN, 1960; "Harrigan and Son: The Manly Art," ABC, 1961; "The Detectives Starring Robert Taylor: Secret Assignment," ABC, 1961; "Here's Hollywood," NBC, 1961; "Michael Shayne: Date with Death," NBC, 1961; "The Brothers Brannagan: Equinox," SYN, 1961; "Naked City: Which Is Joseph Creeley?," ABC, 1961; "Cain's Hundred: In the Balance," NBC, 1961; "Mr. Ed: Ed's Bed," CBS, 1962; "Route 66: Every Father's Daughter Must Weave Her Own," CBS, 1962; "Batman: Zelda the Great/A Death Worse Than Fate," ABC, 1966; "The Mike Douglas Show," SYN, 1967; "He & She: The Phantom of 84th Street," CBS, 1967; "Ironside: The Macabre Mr. Micawber," NBC, 1968; "Love, American Style: Love and Accidental Passion," ABC, 1971; "Hawaii Five-O: For a Million, Why Not?" CBS, 1971; "Medical Center: Double Jeopardy," CBS, 1971; "Medical Center: No Margin for Error," CBS, 1973; "Columbo: The Most Dangerous Match," NBC, 1973; "Marcus Welby, M.D.: Friends in High Places," ABC, 1973; "McCloud: Shivaree on Delancey Street," NBC, 1974; "Medical Center: Aftershock," CBS, 1975; "City of Angels: The November Plan," NBC, 1976; "Barney Miller: Burial," ABC, 1977; "Switch: Play-Off," CBS, 1978; "Barney Miller: The DNA Story," ABC, 1979; "Alice: Mel, the Magi," CBS, 1979; "Alice: Carrie Chickens Out," CBS, 1981; "Barney Miller: Examination Day," ABC, 1982; "The New Odd Couple: My Strife in Court," ABC, 1983; "Matt Houston: The Crying Clown," ABC, 1983; "E/R: Mr. Fix-It," CBS, 1984; "Remington Steele: Springtime for Steele," NBC, 1985; "Magnum, P.I.: Out of Sync," CBS, 1987.

TV MOVIES AND MINISERIES: "Istanbul Express," NBC, 1968; "Emergency!," NBC, 1972; "Deadly Harvest," CBS, 1972; "The Log of the Black Pearl," NBC, 1975; "The Time Machine," NBC, 1978; "Deadly Intentions," ABC, 1985.

KULKY, HENRY
b. Henry Kulkawich, Hastings-on-the-Hudson, NY, August 11, 1911; d. 1965. Former wrestler; he played Otto Schmidlap on "The Life of Riley" and seaman Max Bronski on "Hennesey."

AS A REGULAR: "The Life of Riley," NBC, 1953-58; "Hennesey," CBS, 1959-62; "Voyage to the Bottom of the Sea," ABC, 1964-65.

AND: "The Abbott and Costello Show: The Paper Hangers," CBS, 1953; "I Love Lucy: Lucy and Bob Hope," CBS, 1956; "The Thin Man: The Pre-Incan Caper," NBC, 1958; "The Red Skelton Show: Cauliflower and the Fight Fix," CBS, 1961;

"Pete and Gladys: Hero in the House," CBS, 1962; "McKeever and the Colonel: The Army Mule," NBC, 1962; "Our Man Higgins: The Manchester Minstrel," ABC, 1963; "The Donna Reed Show: It Grows on Trees," ABC, 1963; "Grindl: The Gruesome Basement," NBC, 1963.

KULP, NANCY
b. Harrisburg, PA, August 28, 1921; d. 1991. Tall, lanky actress who played Jane Hathaway, secretary to banker Milburn Drysdale (Raymond Bailey) on "The Beverly Hillbillies."

AS A REGULAR: "The Bob Cummings Show," NBC, 1955; CBS, 1955-57; NBC, 1957-59; "The Beverly Hillbillies," CBS, 1962-71; "The Brian Keith Show," NBC, 1973-74.

AND: "December Bride: Lily Hires a Maid," CBS, 1954; "I Love Lucy: Lucy Meets the Queen," CBS, 1956; "December Bride: Lily the Matchmaker," CBS, 1956; "The Red Skelton Show: The Magic Shoes," CBS, 1956; "The Adventures of Ozzie and Harriet: The Balloon," ABC, 1956; "Date with the Angels: The Blue Tie," ABC, 1957; "The Frank Sinatra Show," ABC, 1958; "Perry Mason: The Case of the Prodigal Parent," CBS, 1958; "The Gale Storm Show: Captain Courageous," CBS, 1958; "The Real McCoys: The Dancin' Fool," ABC, 1958; "The Gale Storm Show: Passenger Incognito," CBS, 1959; "Milton Berle Special," NBC, 1959; "Comedy Spot: Adventures of a Model," CBS, 1960; "The Jack Benny Program: Don's Anniversary," CBS, 1961; "The Danny Thomas Show: The PTA Bash," CBS, 1962; "My Three Sons: Robbie Valentino," ABC, 1962; "Pete and Gladys: Office Way," CBS, 1962; "The Twilight Zone: The Fugitive," CBS, 1962; "The Jack Benny Program: Alexander Hamilton Story," CBS, 1962; "My Three Sons: The Big Game," ABC, 1962; "The Joey Bishop Show: The Image," NBC, 1962; "The Twilight Zone: The Fugitive," CBS, 1962; "The Lucy Show: Lucy Becomes an Astronaut," CBS, 1962; "Your First Impression," NBC, 1964; "Password," CBS, 1965; "Petticoat Junction: A Cake for Granny," CBS, 1968; "The Mike Douglas Show," SYN, 1971; "Sanford & Son: The Sanford Arms," NBC, 1975; "Sanford & Son: Brother, Can You Spare an Act?," NBC, 1975; "Sanford & Son: Can You Chop This?," NBC, 1976; "Sanford & Son: A Pain in the Neck," NBC, 1976; "The Love Boat: The Kissing Bandit," ABC, 1978; "The Love Boat: The Harder They Fall," ABC, 1979; "Scarecrow and Mrs. King: Billy's Lost Weekend," CBS, 1986; "ABC Afterschool Special: Private Affairs," ABC, 1989.

TV MOVIES AND MINISERIES: "The Return of the Beverly Hillbillies," CBS, 1981.

* In 1984, Kulp was a candidate for a U.S. House seat in Pennsylvania; her Republican opponent got Kulp's old co-star, Buddy Ebsen, to record anti-Kulp campaign ads.

494

KUPCINET, IRV

b. Chicago, IL, July 31, 1912. Newspaper columnist and talk-show host.

AS A REGULAR: "The Tonight Show (Tonight! America After Dark)," NBC, 1957; "Kup's Show," PBS, 1962-86.

KUPCINET, KARYN

b. March 6, 1941; d. 1963. Sixties starlet, daughter of Irv Kupcinet.

AS A REGULAR: "The Gertrude Berg Show (Mrs. G. Goes to College)," CBS, 1961-62.

AND: "Hawaiian Eye: It Ain't Cricket," ABC, 1961; "The Donna Reed Show: Mary's Little Lambs," ABC, 1961; "Hawaiian Eye: The Queen From Kern County," ABC, 1961; "SurfSide 6: Pattern for a Frame," ABC, 1961; "Going My Way: Has Anybody Here Seen Eddie?," ABC, 1963; "Perry Mason: The Case of the Capering Camera," CBS, 1964.

* Kupcinet was found strangled in late 1963; the murder was never solved.

KURALT, CHARLES

b. Wilmington, NC, September 10, 1934. CBS reporter who's been on the road since 1967.

AS A REGULAR: "Eyewitness to History," CBS, 1960-61; "CBS News Adventure," CBS, 1970; "Who's Who," CBS, 1977; "On the Road with Charles Kuralt," CBS, 1983; "The American Parade," CBS, 1984; "Sunday Morning," CBS, 1984- .

* Emmies: 1969, 1978, 1980, 1982, 1985, 1986.

KURTZ, SWOOSIE

b. Omaha, NB, September 6, 1944. Actress who played Laurie Morgan on "Love, Sidney."

AS A REGULAR: "As the World Turns," CBS, 1971; "Mary," CBS, 1978; "Love, Sidney," NBC, 1981-83.

AND: "Kojak: Black Thorn," CBS, 1977.

TV MOVIES AND MINISERIES: "Walking Through the Fire," CBS, 1979; "The Mating Season," CBS, 1980; "Guilty Conscience," CBS, 1985.

KYSER, KAY

b. James Kern Kyser, Rocky Mount, NC, June 18, 1897. Bandleader and personality of radio, TV and movies.

AS A REGULAR: "Kay Kyser's Kollege of Musical Knowledge," NBC, 1949-50, 1954.

L

LABORTEAUX, MATTHEW

b. Los Angeles, CA, December 8, 1966. Actor who played Albert Ingalls on "Little House."
AS A REGULAR: "Little House on the Prairie," NBC, 1978-82; "Whiz Kids," CBS, 1983-84.
AND: "Little House on the Prairie: Journey in the Spring," NBC, 1976; "The Rookies: Lamb to the Slaughter," ABC, 1976; "The Bob Newhart Show: My Boy Guillermo," CBS, 1976; "Mulligan's Stew: Pilot," NBC, 1977; "Lou Grant: Kids," CBS, 1979; "The Love Boat: Winning Isn't Everything," ABC, 1982; "Little House: A New Beginning: Home Again," NBC, 1983; "Amazing Stories: Fine Tuning," NBC, 1985.
TV MOVIES AND MINISERIES: "The Aliens Are Coming," NBC, 1980; "Shattered Spirits," ABC, 1989.

LABORTEAUX, PATRICK

b. Los Angeles, CA, July 22, 1965. Adoptive brother of Matthew, who's also adopted; he played Andy Garvey on "Little House."
AS A REGULAR: "Little House on the Prairie," NBC, 1977-81.
AND: "The Love Boat: Ages of Man," ABC, 1979; "The Love Boat: Vicki Swings," ABC, 1981; "21 Jump Street: A.W.O.L.," FOX, 1989; "Paradise: The Devil's Escort," CBS, 1989.
TV MOVIES AND MINISERIES: "Best Sellers: Captains and the Kings," NBC, 1976; "The Prince of Bel Air," ABC, 1986.

LADD, ALAN

b. Hot Springs, AR, September 3, 1913; d. 1964. Screen star of the forties in occasional TV shows.
AS A GUEST: "G.E. Theatre: Committed," CBS, 1954; "G.E. Theatre: Farewell to Kennedy," CBS, 1955; "The Bob Cummings Show: Bob Gets Schultzy in Pictures," NBC, 1957; "G.E. Theatre: Silent Ambush," CBS, 1958.

LADD, CHERYL

b. Cheryl Stoppelmoor, Huron, SD, July 12, 1951. Blonde sex symbol who played Kris Munroe on "Charlie's Angels."
AS A REGULAR: "Josie and the Pussycats," CBS, 1971-72; "The Ken Berry "WOW" Show," ABC, 1972; "Charlie's Angels," ABC, 1977-81.
AND: "Ironside: A Game of Showdown," NBC, 1973; "The Partridge Family: Double Trouble," ABC, 1973; "Happy Days: Wish Upon a Star,"

ABC, 1974; "Police Woman: Silky Chamberlain," NBC, 1977; "The San Pedro Beach Bums: The Angels and the Bums," ABC, 1977; "The Mike Douglas Show," SYN, 1978; "The Tonight Show Starring Johnny Carson," NBC, 1978; "General Electric's All-Star Anniversary," ABC, 1978; "John Denver and the Ladies," ABC, 1979; "The Presidential Inaugural Gala," CBS, 1989.
TV MOVIES AND MINISERIES: "Satan's School for Girls," ABC, 1973; "When She Was Bad," ABC, 1979; "Grace Kelly," ABC, 1983; "Kentucky Woman," CBS, 1983; "A Death in California," ABC, 1985; "Romance on the Orient Express," NBC, 1985; "Crossings," ABC, 1986; "Deadly Care," CBS, 1987; "Bluegrass," CBS, 1988; "The Fulfillment of Mary Gray," CBS, 1989.
* See also "Charlie's Angels."

LADD, DAVID

b. Los Angeles, CA, February 5, 1947. Actor and son of Alan Ladd; former husband of Cheryl Ladd.
AS A GUEST: "The Steve Allen Show," NBC, 1959; "Bonanza: Feet of Clay," NBC, 1960; "Shirley Temple's Storybook: Tom and Huck," NBC, 1960; "Here's Hollywood," NBC, 1960; "Dick Powell's Zane Grey Theatre: The Broken Wing," CBS, 1961; "Family Affair: Put Your Dreams Away," CBS, 1971; "Kojak: I Could Kill My Wife's Lawyer," CBS, 1977.

LADD, DIANE

b. Rose Diane Ladner, Meridian, MS, November 29, 1932. Actress who played the original Flo in "Alice Doesn't Live Here Anymore," and came to the sitcom version of the movie as waitress Belle Dupree; mother of actress Laura Dern.
AS A REGULAR: "Alice," CBS, 1980-81.
AND: "The Wide Country: Step Over the Sky," NBC, 1963; "Armstrong Circle Theatre: The Counterfeit League," CBS, 1963; "Mr. Novak: I Don't Even Live Here," NBC, 1963; "Hazel: George's 32nd Cousin," NBC, 1963; "Gunsmoke: The Favor," CBS, 1967; "Then Came Bronson: Old Tigers Never Die: They Just Run Away," NBC, 1969; "City of Angels: The November Plan," NBC, 1976; "The Love Boat: The Captain's Ne'er-do-Well Brother," ABC, 1980; "Dinah!," SYN, 1980; "The Love Boat: The Crew's Cruise Director," ABC, 1984.
TV MOVIES AND MINISERIES: "The Devil's Daughter," ABC, 1973; "Black Beauty," NBC,

1978; "Willa," CBS, 1979; "Desperate Lives," CBS, 1982; "Grace Kelly," ABC, 1983; "I Married a Centerfold," NBC, 1984; "Crime of Innocence," NBC, 1985; "Bluegrass," CBS, 1988.

LADD, HANK
b. *Chicago, IL, 1908; d. 1982.*
AS A REGULAR: "The Arrow Show," NBC, 1949: "Waiting for the Break," NBC, 1950.
AND: "I'm Dickens, He's Fenster: The Toupee Story," ABC, 1962.

LAHR, BERT
b. *Irving Lahrheim, New York City, NY, August 13, 1895; d. 1967.* Beloved stage comic who played the cowardly lion in "The Wizard of Oz"; toward the end of his life he charmed a generation of young TV viewers with his commercials for Lay's potato chips.
AS A GUEST: "Prudential Family Playhouse: Burlesque," CBS, 1951; "Omnibus: Vive," CBS, 1953; "Musical Comedy Time: Flying High," NBC, 1951; "The Colgate Comedy Hour: Anything Goes," NBC, 1954; "Best of Broadway: The Man Who Came to Dinner," CBS, 1954; "The Great Waltz," NBC, 1955; "Omnibus: Androcles and the Lion," ABC, 1956; "Washington Square," NBC, 1956; "Omnibus: School for Wives," ABC, 1956; "Omnibus: The Big Wheel," ABC, 1957; "Arthur Murray Party," NBC, 1957; "The Steve Allen Show," NBC, 1957; "Standard Oil 75th Anniversay Show," NBC, 1957; "The Patrice Munsel Show," ABC, 1957; "Kraft Television Theatre: The Big Heist," NBC, 1957; "U.S. Steel Hour: You Can't Win," CBS, 1957; "Omnibus: The Suburban Review," NBC, 1958; "The George Gobel Show," NBC, 1958; "The Ed Sullivan Show," CBS, 1958; "Arthur Murray Party," NBC, 1958; "Arthur Murray Party," NBC, 1959; "G.E. Theatre: Mr. O'Malley," CBS, 1959; "Rendezvous: A Very Fine Deal," SYN, 1960; "Startime: The Greatest Man Alive!," NBC, 1960; "Perry Como's Kraft Music Hall," NBC, 1960; "Arthur Murray Party," NBC, 1960; "The Ed Sullivan Show," CBS, 1960; "The Secret World of Eddie Hodges," CBS, 1960; "The Ed Sullivan Show," CBS, 1961; "The Eleventh Hour: Is Mr. Martian Coming Back?," NBC, 1963; "Hallmark Hall of Fame: The Fantasticks," NBC, 1964; "Bob Hope Chrysler Theatre: Cops and Robbers," NBC, 1965; "Thompson's Ghost," ABC, 1966.

LAINE, FRANKIE
b. *Frank Paul LoVecchio, Chicago, IL, March 30, 1913.* Rip-roaring singer ("Mule Train," "High Noon," "Jezebel") of the fifties.
AS A REGULAR: "Frankie Laine Time," CBS, 1955-56.
AND: "The Perry Como Show," NBC, 1956; "The Perry Como Show," NBC, 1957; "The Nat King Cole Show," NBC, 1957; "The Steve Allen Show," NBC, 1957; "Art Linkletter's House Party," CBS, 1958; "The Big Record," CBS, 1958; "The Perry Como Show," NBC, 1958; "The Ed Sullivan Show," CBS, 1958; "The Garry Moore Show," CBS, 1958; "The Ed Sullivan Show," CBS, 1959; "Perry Mason: The Case of the Jaded Joker," CBS, 1959; "The Garry Moore Show," CBS, 1959; "Art Linkletter's House Party," CBS, 1959; "The Danny Thomas Show: Frankie Laine Sings for Gina," CBS, 1959; "The Perry Como Show," NBC, 1959; "Steve Allen Plymouth Show," NBC, 1959; "The Dick Clark Saturday Night Beechnut Show," ABC, 1959; "Rawhide: Incident on the Road to Yesterday," CBS, 1960; "Bachelor Father: A Party for Peter," ABC, 1961; "The Tennessee Ernie Ford Show," ABC, 1962; "Burke's Law: Who Killed Wade Walker?," ABC, 1963; "Object Is," ABC, 1964; "The Merv Griffin Show," SYN, 1968; "The Della Reese Show," SYN, 1969; "The Mike Douglas Show," SYN, 1980.

LAIRE, JUDSON
b. *New York City, NY, August 3, 1902; d. 1979.* Actor who played Papa Lars Hansen on "Mama."
AS A REGULAR: "The Admiral Broadway Revue," NBC, 1949; "Mama," CBS, 1949-57; "Young Doctor Malone," NBC, 1958-63; "The Nurses," ABC, 1965-67.
AND: "Studio One: The Rockingham Tea Set," CBS, 1950; "Kraft Television Theatre: Valley Forge," NBC, 1950; "Studio One: The Ambassadors," CBS, 1950; "Studio One: Zone Four," CBS, 1950; "Studio One: The Shadow of a Man," CBS, 1950; "Studio One: The Ambassadors," CBS, 1951; "Studio One: Here Is My Life," CBS, 1951; "Studio One: The Other Father," CBS, 1952; "Kraft Television Theatre: Kitty Foyle," NBC, 1954; "Studio One: The Weston Strain," CBS, 1957; "Studio One: Mutiny on the Shark," CBS, 1957; "Our American Heritage: Woodrow Wilson and the Unknown Soldier," NBC, 1961; "The Defenders: The Treadmill," CBS, 1961; "Route 66: To Walk with the Serpent," CBS, 1962; "The Defenders: The Search," CBS, 1962; "The Defenders: The Voices of Death," CBS, 1962; "The Defenders: The Benefactors," CBS, 1962; "Stoney Burke: Child of Luxury," ABC, 1962; "Ben Casey: Legacy From a Stranger," ABC, 1962; "The Defenders: The Weeping Baboon," CBS, 1963; "The Nurses: Show Just Cause Why You Should Weep," CBS, 1963; "Dr. Kildare: The Exploiters," NBC, 1963; "Kraft Suspense Theatre: Leviathan Five," NBC, 1964; "The Nurses: Nurse Is a Feminine Noun," CBS,

1964; "The Defenders: Death on Wheels," CBS, 1965; "The Defenders: Nobody Asks You What Side You're On," CBS, 1965.

LAKE, ARTHUR
b. *Arthur Silverlake, Corbin, KY, April 17, 1905; d. 1987*. Comic actor of the screen who repeated his most famous film and radio role—that of Dagwood Bumstead—on the small screen.
AS A REGULAR: "Blondie," NBC, 1957.

LA LANNE, JACK
Exercise expert who usually played himself.
AS A REGULAR: "The Jack La Lanne Show," SYN, 1962-72; "The Wilton North Report," FOX, 1987-88.
AND: "Peter Gunn: Death Across the Board," ABC, 1960; "The Addams Family: Fester Goes on a Diet," ABC, 1966; "Here's Lucy: Lucy and the Bogie Affair," CBS, 1969.

LAMAS, FERNANDO
b. *Buenos Aires, Argentina, January 9, 1915; d. 1982*. Continental screen star of the forties who turned to TV acting and directing; in the mid-eighties, Billy Crystal lampooned him as the obsequeous talk-show host Fernando on "Saturday Night Live."
AS A GUEST: "The Steve Allen Show," NBC, 1957; "The Big Record," CBS, 1957; "The Patrice Munsel Show," ABC, 1957; "Person to Person," CBS, 1957; "The Lucille Ball-Desi Arnaz Show: Lucy Goes to Sun Valley," CBS, 1958; "The Jane Wyman Show: The Bravado Touch," NBC, 1958; "Climax!: Spider Web," CBS, 1958; "Pursuit: Eagle in the Cage," CBS, 1958; "Art Linkletter's House Party," CBS, 1958; "Dick Powell's Zane Grey Theatre: The Last Raid," CBS, 1959; "Dick Powell's Zane Grey Theatre: Guns for Garibaldi," CBS, 1960; "Esther Williams at Cypress Gardens," NBC, 1960; "Shirley Temple's Storybook: Little Men," NBC, 1960; "Seasons of Youth," ABC, 1961; "Burke's Law: Who Killed Carrie Cornell?," ABC, 1964; "Burke's Law: Who Killed the Man on the White Horse?," ABC, 1965; "The Virginian: We've Lost a Train," NBC, 1965; "Combat!: Breakout," ABC, 1965; "Run for Your Life: Someone Who Makes Me Feel Beautiful," NBC, 1965; "Run for Your Life: The Rediscovery of Charlotte Hyde," NBC, 1966; "The Red Skelton Hour," CBS, 1966; "Laredo: It's the End of the Road, Stanley," NBC, 1966; "Combat!: The Brothers," ABC, 1966; "Run for Your Life: The Sex Object," NBC, 1966; "The Girl From UNCLE: The Horns of the Dilemma Affair," NBC, 1966; "The Girl From UNCLE: The UFO Affair," NBC, 1967; "Run for Your Life:

The Inhuman Predicament," NBC, 1967; "The Red Skelton Hour," CBS, 1967; "Hondo: Hondo and the Commancheros," ABC, 1967; "The High Chaparral: The Firing Wall," NBC, 1967; "Tarzan: Jungle Ransom," NBC, 1968; "He & She: Knock, Knock. Who's There? Fernando. Fernando Who?," CBS, 1968; "Bob Hope Special: For Love or $$$," NBC, 1968; "Mission: Impossible: The Diplomat," CBS, 1968; "It Takes a Thief: One Illegal Angel," ABC, 1969; "Then Came Bronson: Where Will the Trumpets Be?," NBC, 1969; "It Takes a Thief: Cat's Paw," ABC, 1970; "Mission: Impossible: Chico," CBS, 1970; "The Name of the Game: Man of the People," NBC, 1970; "Dan August: The Worst Crime," ABC, 1971; "Alias Smith and Jones: Return to Devil's Hole," ABC, 1971; "The Tonight Show Starring Johnny Carson," NBC, 1971; "The Mod Squad: And Once for My Baby," ABC, 1973; "McCloud: The Gang That Stole Manhattan," NBC, 1974; "Switch: Round Up the Usual Suspects," CBS, 1976; "Police Woman: The Inside Connection," NBC, 1977; "The Love Boat: The Caper," ABC, 1978; "House Calls: Defeat of Clay," CBS, 1980; "Dinah!," SYN, 1980.
TV MOVIES AND MINISERIES: "Valley of Mystery," ABC, 1967; "The Lonely Profession," NBC, 1969; "Powderkeg," CBS, 1971; "Murder on Flight 502," ABC, 1975.
AS DIRECTOR: "Run for Your Life," NBC, 1967-68; "Falcon Crest," CBS, 1981-82.

LAMAS, LORENZO
b. *Los Angeles, CA, January 20, 1956*. Pretty-boy set dressing best known as Lance Cumson of "Falcon Crest"; son of Fernando Lamas.
AS A REGULAR: "California Fever," CBS, 1979; "Secrets of Midland Heights," CBS, 1980-81; "Falcon Crest," CBS, 1981-90; "Dancin' to the Hits," SYN, 1986.
AND: "Switch: 30,000 Witnesses," CBS, 1978.

LAMB, GIL
b. *Minneapolis, MN, June 14, 1904*. Physical comic of films and TV.
AS A GUEST: "Starlight Theatre: Flaxen-Haired Mannequin," CBS, 1951; "Big Town: Shield of a Killer," NBC, 1955; "Shirley Temple's Storybook: The Land of Oz," NBC, 1960; "The Twilight Zone: Once Upon a Time," CBS, 1961; "My Three Sons: What About Harry?," CBS, 1966; "Camp Runamuck: Air Conditioner," NBC, 1966; "The Man From UNCLE: The Apple a Day Affair," NBC, 1967; "Daktari: Judy and the Wizard," CBS, 1967; "My Three Sons: Uncle Charley's Aunt," CBS, 1968; "The Andy Griffith Show: Sam for Town Council," CBS, 1968; "The Wild Wild

West: Night of the Amnesiac," CBS, 1968; "The Ghost and Mrs. Muir: Amateur Night," ABC, 1970; "The Ghost and Mrs. Muir: Curious Cousin, ABC, 1970.

LAMOUR, DOROTHY
b. Dorothy Kaumeyer, New Orleans, LA, October 10, 1914. Movie sex goddess who popularized the sarong in the forties and palled around with Bob Hope and Bing Crosby in their "Road" comedies; in occasional TV guest shots.
AS A GUEST: "Hollywood Opening Night: The Singing Years," NBC, 1952; "This Is Your Life," NBC, 1954; "Damon Runyon Theatre: The Mink Doll," CBS, 1955; "The Herb Shriner Show," ABC, 1956; "Can Do," NBC, 1956; "Circus Time," ABC, 1957; "The Steve Allen Show," NBC, 1957; "The Arthur Murray Party for Bob Hope," NBC, 1960; "Play Your Hunch," NBC, 1960; "The Jack Paar Show," NBC, 1960; "To Tell the Truth," CBS, 1963; "Candid Camera," CBS, 1963; "Burke's Law: Who Killed Madison Cooper?," ABC, 1964; "Burke's Law: Who Killed the Surf Board Broad?," ABC, 1964; "The Name of the Game: Chains of Command," NBC, 1969; "The Tim Conway Show," CBS, 1970; "Bob Hope Special," NBC, 1970; "Marcus Welby, M.D.: Echo From Another World," ABC, 1971; "Love, American Style: Love and the Pickup," ABC, 1971; "Marcus Welby, M.D.: Echo from Another World," ABC, 1972; "The Love Boat: That's My Dad," ABC, 1980; "Hart to Hart: Max's Waltz," ABC, 1984; "Remington Steele: Cast in Steele," NBC, 1984; "Murder, She Wrote: No Accounting for Murder," CBS, 1987.
TV MOVIES AND MINISERIES: "Death at Love House," ABC, 1976.

LAMPERT, ZOHRA
b. New York City, NY, May 13, 1937. Intense leading lady who won an Emmy for her "Kojak" appearance.
AS A REGULAR: "Where the Heart Is," CBS, 1969-73; "The Girl with Something Extra," NBC, 1973-74; "Doctors Hospital," NBC, 1975-76.
AND: "Hallmark Hall of Fame: Cradle Song," NBC, 1956; "Hallmark Hall of Fame: Cradle Song," NBC, 1960; "Route 66: Layout at Glen Canyon," CBS, 1960; "The Defenders: The Prowler," CBS, 1961; "The Defenders: Gideon's Follies," CBS, 1961; "U.S. Steel Hour: Male Call," CBS, 1962; "Sam Benedict: Hear the Mellow Wedding Bells," NBC, 1962; "Dr. Kildare: The Thing Speaks for Itself," NBC, 1963; "The Alfred Hitchcock Hour: A Tangled Web," NBC, 1963; "Dr. Kildare: A Place Among the Monuments," NBC, 1963; "Naked City: Barefoot on a Bed of Coals," ABC, 1963; "The

Reporter: Super Star," CBS, 1964; "The Man From UNCLE: The Mad, Mad Tea Party Affair," NBC, 1965; "Slattery's People: Who You Taking to the Main Event, Eddie?," CBS, 1965; "Trials of O'Brien: How Do You Get to Carnegie Hall?," CBS, 1965; "I Spy: Blackout," NBC, 1965; "Then Came Bronson: Amid Splinters of the Thunderbolt," NBC, 1969;"The FBI: Deadfall," ABC, 1970; "Love, American Style: Love and the Jinx," ABC, 1972; "The Bob Newhart Show: Motel," CBS, 1973; "Kojak: Queen of the Gypsies," CBS, 1975; "Hollywood Television Theatre: The Ladies of the Corridor," PBS, 1975; "Serpico: Trumpet of Time," NBC, 1976; "Hawaii Five-O: Let Death Do Us Part," CBS, 1976; "Switch: Fade Out," CBS, 1977; "Quincy: Ashes to Ashes," NBC, 1978; "Kojak: The Halls of Terror," CBS, 1978.
TV MOVIES AND MINISERIES: "Connection," ABC, 1973; "One of Our Own," NBC, 1975; "Black Beauty," NBC, 1978; "Lady of the House," NBC, 1978; "The Suicide's Wife," CBS, 1979; "Izzy and Moe," CBS, 1985.
* Emmies: 1975.

LAMPKIN, CHARLES
d. 1989. Actor who played Tiger the bartender on "Frank's Place."
AS A REGULAR: "Frank's Place," CBS, 1987-88.
AND: "Straightaway: Full Circle," ABC, 1961; "Mr. Novak: A Single Isolated Incident," NBC, 1963; "Please Don't Eat the Daisies: Who's Kicking That Gong Around?," NBC, 1965; "Daktari: The Killer of Wameru," CBS, 1968; "The FBI: The Sanctuary," ABC, 1969; "Barefoot in the Park: The Bed," ABC, 1970; "Marcus Welby, M.D.: The White Cane," ABC, 1970; "The Interns: The Choice," CBS, 1971; "The Odd Couple: The Odd Monks," ABC, 1972; "The FBI: Fatal Reunion," ABC, 1973; "The Streets of San Francisco: No Badge for Benjy," ABC, 1973; "That's My Mama: Mama Steps Out," ABC, 1974; "Barnaby Jones: Fight to Danger," CBS, 1975; "House Calls: Defeat of Clay," CBS, 1980; "Night Court: Mac and Quon Le-No Reservations," NBC, 1985; "Webster: Seeing It Through," ABC, 1986; "Webster: A Run for the Money," ABC, 1986.
TV MOVIES AND MINISERIES: "Deadlock," NBC, 1969; "Last of the Great Survivors," CBS, 1984.

LANCASTER, BURT
b. New York City, NY, November 2, 1913. Exuberant and talented film actor ("Sweet Smell of Success," "Elmer Gantry," "Local Hero") lately more on TV than in the movies.
AS A GUEST: "The Jackie Gleason Show," CBS, 1957; "The Ed Sullivan Show," CBS, 1957; "Youth Wants to Know," NBC, 1957.
TV MOVIES AND MINISERIES: "Moses, the Law-

giver," CBS, 1975; "Victory at Entebbe," ABC, 1976; "Scandal Sheet," ABC, 1985; "On Wings of Eagles," NBC, 1986; "Barnum," CBS, 1986.

LANCHESTER, ELSA
b. Elsa Sullivan, London, England, October 28, 1902; d. 1986. Actress and wife of actor Charles Laughton, often in scatterbrained roles on TV.
AS A REGULAR: "The John Forsythe Show," NBC, 1965-66; "Nanny and the Professor," ABC, 1971.
AND: "Studio One: Music and Mrs. Pratt," CBS, 1953; "Omnibus: Toine," CBS, 1953; "Schlitz Playhouse of Stars: The Baker of Barbury," CBS, 1953; "Ford Theatre: Hanrahan," NBC, 1955; "Best of Broadway: Stage Door," CBS, 1955; "Heidi," NBC, 1955; "Hallmark Hall of Fame: Alice in Wonderland," NBC, 1955; "Lux Video Theatre: Miss Mabel," NBC, 1956; "The 20th Century-Fox Hour: Stranger in the Night," CBS, 1956; "I Love Lucy: Off to Florida," CBS, 1956; "Robert Montgomery Presents: Miracle at Lensham," NBC, 1956; "Dinah Shore Chevy Show," NBC, 1958; "Art Linkletter's House Party," CBS, 1958; "Shirley Temple's Storybook: Mother Goose," NBC, 1958; "The Ford Show," NBC, 1959; "Wanted Dead or Alive: The Monster," CBS, 1960; "Startime: Academy Award Songs," NBC, 1960; "Adventures in Paradise: The Intruders," ABC, 1960; "The Jack Paar Show," NBC, 1961; "G.E. Theatre: Cat in the Cradle," CBS, 1961; "The Dick Powell Show: The Fifth Caller," NBC, 1961; "Here's Hollywood," NBC, 1962; "Follow the Sun: A Ghost in Her Gazebo," ABC, 1962; "Burke's Law: Who Killed Eleanora Davis?," ABC, 1963; "The Eleventh Hour: A Full Moon Every Night," NBC, 1964; "Burke's Law: Who Killed Cassandra Cass?," ABC, 1964; "The Alfred Hitchcock Hour: The McGregory Affair," NBC, 1964; "Ben Casey: A Boy Is Standing Outside," ABC, 1965; "The Man From UNCLE: The Brain Killer Affair," NBC, 1965; "Slattery's People: What's a Swan Song for a Sparrow?," CBS, 1965; "Walt Disney's Wonderful World of Color: My Dog the Thief," NBC, 1969; "Then Came Bronson: The Circle of Time," NBC, 1969; "It Takes a Thief: The Cold Who Came in From the Spy," ABC, 1969; "The Bill Cosby Show: The Elevator Doesn't Stop Here Anymore," NBC, 1970; "The Bill Cosby Show: Power of the Trees," NBC, 1971; "Night Gallery: Green Finger," NBC, 1972; "Mannix: Death Is the Fifth Gear," CBS, 1972; "Mannix: A Matter of Principle," CBS, 1973; "Here's Lucy: Lucy Goes to Prison," CBS, 1973.
TV MOVIES AND MINISERIES: "In Name Only," ABC, 1969.

LANDAU, MARTIN
b. Brooklyn, NY, June 20, 1931. Striking actor with dark looks who began in TV playing heavies and Indians, best known as smooth master of disguise Rollin Hand on "Mission: Impossible." Lately he's been more visible in movies ("Tucker: The Man and His Dream," "Crimes and Misdemeanors").
AS A REGULAR: "Mission: Impossible," CBS, 1966-69; "Space: 1999," SYN, 1975-77.
AND: "Omnibus: Salome," CBS, 1955; "Harbourmaster: Sanctuary," CBS, 1957; "Tales of Wells Fargo: Doc Holliday," NBC, 1959; "Maverick: High Card Hangs," ABC, 1959; "Playhouse 90: The Sounds of Eden," CBS, 1959; "G.E. Theatre: Survival," CBS, 1959; "The Untouchables: Mexican Standoff," ABC, 1959; "The Twilight Zone: Mr. Denton on Doomsday," CBS, 1960; "Rawhide: Incident Below the Brazos," CBS, 1960; "Adventures in Paradise: Nightmare in Napuka," ABC, 1960; "Wanted Dead or Alive: The Monster," CBS, 1960; "Tate: Tigrero," NBC, 1960; "Wagon Train: The Cathy Eckhardt Story," NBC, 1960; "Checkmate: Moment of Truth," CBS, 1960; "Best of the Post: Frontier Correspondent," SYN, 1960; "The Islanders: Duel of Strangers," ABC, 1960; "Adventures in Paradise: Mr. Flotsam," ABC, 1961; "The Tall Man: Dark Moment," NBC, 1961; "Acapulco: The Gentleman From Brazil," NBC, 1961; "Bonanza: The Gift," NBC, 1961; "The Outlaws: The Avenger," NBC, 1961; "The Rifleman: The Vaqueros," ABC, 1961; "Robert Taylor's Detectives: Shadow of His Brother," NBC, 1961; "The Untouchables: The Loophole," ABC, 1961; "The Outer Limits: Thê Man Who Was Never Born," ABC, 1963; "Mr. Novak: Pay the Two Dollars," NBC, 1963; "The Defenders: The Secret," CBS, 1964; "The Outer Limits: The Bellero Shield," ABC, 1964; "The Greatest Show on Earth: The Night the Monkey Died," ABC, 1964; "The Twilight Zone: The Jeopardy Room," CBS, 1964; "The Alfred Hitchcock Hour: The Second Verdict," NBC, 1964; "Special for Women: Child in Danger," ABC, 1964; "Mr. Novak: Enter a Strange Animal," NBC, 1965; "I Spy: Danny Was a Million Laughs," NBC, 1965; "The Big Valley: The Way to Kill a Killer," ABC, 1965; "The Big Valley: Under a Dark Star," ABC, 1965; "A Man Called Shenandoah: The Locket," ABC, 1965; "The Wild Wild West: The Night of the Red-Eyed Madman," CBS, 1965; "Branded: This Stage of Fools," NBC, 1966; "The Man From UNCLE: The Bat Cave Affair," NBC, 1966; "Gunsmoke: The Goldtakers," CBS, 1966; "Hollywood Squares," NBC, 1968; "The Carol Burnett Show," CBS, 1968; "Columbo: Double Shock," NBC, 1973; "Murder, She Wrote: Birds of a Feather," CBS, 1984; "The Twilight Zone: The Beacon," CBS, 1985; "Blacke's Magic: Last Flight From Moscow," NBC, 1986; "The Pat Sajak Show," CBS, 1989.
TV MOVIES AND MINISERIES: "Welcome Home,

Johnny Bristol," CBS, 1972; "Savage," NBC, 1973; "The Death of Ocean View Park," ABC, 1979; "The Harlem Globetrotters on Gilligan's Island," NBC, 1981; "Kung Fu," CBS, 1986; "The Return of the Six-Million Dollar Man and the Bionic Woman," NBC, 1987; "The Neon Empire," SHO, 1989.

LANDER, DAVID L.

b. Brooklyn, NY, June 22, 1947. Actor who played the buffoonish Andrew "Squiggy" Squiggman on "Laverne & Shirley."
AS A REGULAR: "Laverne & Shirley," ABC, 1976-83.
AND: "The Bob Newhart Show: Ship of Shrinks," CBS, 1974; "Barney Miller: Hot Dogs," ABC, 1975; "Hollywood Squares," SYN, 1980; "The Love Boat: Gopher & Isaac & The Starlet," ABC, 1984; "Matlock: The Convict," NBC, 1987; "Simon & Simon: Bad Betty," CBS, 1988; "Freddy's Nightmares: Lucky Stiff," SYN, 1989.

LANDERS, AUDREY

b. Philadelphia, PA, July 18, 1959. Sexpot actress who reached her peak, success-wise, in the early eighties, thanks to "Dallas," on which she played Afton Cooper.
AS A REGULAR: "Somerset," NBC, 1970-72; "The Secret Storm," CBS, 1972-73; "Highcliffe Manor," NBC, 1979; "Dallas," CBS, 1981-84, 1989-90; "One Life to Live," ABC, 1990- .
AND: "The FBI: The Killing Truth," ABC, 1973; "Marcus Welby, M.D.: The Light at the Threshold," ABC, 1973; "Happy Days: Requiem for a Malph," ABC, 1977; "Police Woman: Screams," NBC, 1977; "B.J. and the Bear: Cain's Son-In-Law," NBC, 1979; "Password Plus," NBC, 1981; "Hee Haw," SYN, 1981; "The Merv Griffin Show," SYN, 1981; "The Love Boat: Substitute Lover," ABC, 1982; "Fantasy Island: Saturday's Child," ABC, 1983; "The Love Boat: Mother Comes First," ABC, 1984; "The Love Boat: All for One," ABC, 1985; "Murder, She Wrote: If a Body Meet a Body," CBS, 1986; "Midnight Caller: The Fall," NBC, 1989; "MacGyver: Two Times Trouble," ABC, 1989.

LANDERS, JUDY

b. Philadelphia, PA, October 7, 1961. Sister of Audrey, another busty blonde who looks about ten years older than she is.
AS A REGULAR: "Vega$," ABC, 1978-79; "B.J. and the Bear," NBC, 1981; "Madame's Place," SYN, 1982.
AND: "Whatever Happened to the Class of '65?: The Bod," NBC, 1977; "The Love Boat: Oh, My Aching Brother," ABC, 1978; "The Jeffersons: The Other Woman," CBS, 1979; "The Love Boat: The Stimulation of Stephanie," ABC, 1979; "The Love Boat: His Girl Friday," ABC, 1982; "The

Love Boat: The Maid Cleans Up," ABC, 1983; "Night Court: The Former Harry Stone," NBC, 1984; "The Love Boat: Love Times Two," ABC, 1985; "The Love Boat: All for One," ABC, 1985; "The A-Team: Where's the Monster When You Need Him?," NBC, 1985; "L.A. Law: The Princess and the Wiener King," NBC, 1986; "Murphy's Law: When You're Over the Hill, You Pick Up Speed," ABC, 1989.

LANDESBERG, STEVE

b. Bronx, NY, November 3, 1945. Dry comedian who played Det. Arthur Dietrich on "Barney Miller."
AS A REGULAR: "Dean Martin Presents," NBC, 1972; "Paul Sand in Friends and Lovers," CBS, 1974-75; "Barney Miller," ABC, 1975-82.
AND: "The Tonight Show Starring Johnny Carson," NBC, 1971; "The Tonight Show Starring Johnny Carson," NBC, 1973; "Black Bart," CBS, 1975; "When Things Were Rotten: Wedding Belle Blue," ABC, 1975; "The Rockford Files: There's One in Every Port," NBC, 1976; "Fish: Fire," ABC, 1977; "The Tonight Show Starring Johnny Carson," NBC, 1978; "The Merv Griffin Show," SYN, 1979; "The Steve Landesberg Television Show," NBC, 1983; "Candid Camera Christmas Special," CBS, 1987; "The Pat Sajak Show," CBS, 1989.

LANDIS, JESSE ROYCE

b. Jessie Royce Medbury, Chicago, IL, November 25, 1904; d. 1972. Actress who often played down-to-earth matrons and mothers.
AS A GUEST: "The Doctor: A Time for Hate," NBC, 1953; "First Person: Comeback," NBC, 1953; "Goodyear TV Playhouse: Fadeout," NBC, 1953; "Armstrong Circle Theatre: Lost Tour," NBC, 1953; "U.S. Steel Hour: Papa Is All," ABC, 1954; "U.S. Steel Hour: Late Date," ABC, 1954; "Kraft Television Theatre: Account Rendered," NBC, 1954; "Climax!: An Episode of Sparrows," CBS, 1955; "Goodyear TV Playhouse: Career Girl," NBC, 1956; "Art Carney Special: The Man in the Dog Suit," NBC, 1960; "Alfred Hitchcock Presents: Mother, May I Go Out to Swim?," CBS, 1960; "U.S. Steel Hour: Girl in the Gold Bathtub," CBS, 1960; "Thriller: The Mark of the Hand," NBC, 1960; "Adventures in Paradise: A Touch of Genuis," ABC, 1961; "The Man From UNCLE: The Adriatic Express Affair," NBC, 1965; "Ironside: Why the Tuesday Afternoon Bridge Club Met on Thursday," NBC, 1969; "NET Playhouse: The Ceremony of Innocence," NET, 1970; "Ironside: Grandmother's House," NBC, 1971; "Columbo: Lady in Waiting," NBC, 1971.
TV MOVIES AND MINISERIES: "Mr. and Mrs. Bo Jo Jones," ABC, 1971.

LANDON, MICHAEL
b. *Eugene Maurice Orowitz, Forest Hills, Queens, NY, October 31, 1936; d. 1991.* Actor-producer given to patronizing preachiness and sentiment; still, a consistent prime-time presence for an amazing thirty years.
AS A REGULAR: "Bonanza," NBC, 1959-73; "Little House on the Prairie," NBC, 1974-82; "Highway to Heaven," NBC, 1984-89.
AND: "Telephone Time: The Mystery of Caspar Hauser," CBS, 1956; "Wire Service: High Adventure," ABC, 1956; "Du Pont Theatre: The Man From St. Paul," ABC, 1957; "Telephone Time: Fight for the Title," ABC, 1957; "G.E. Theatre: Too Good with a Gun," CBS, 1957; "Schlitz Playhouse of Stars: The Restless Gun," CBS, 1957; "Tales of Wells Fargo: Gunshot Messenger," NBC, 1957; "Court of Last Resort: The Forbes-Carroll Case," NBC, 1957; "Tales of Wells Fargo: The Kid," NBC, 1957; "Cheyenne: White Warrior," ABC, 1957; "Schlitz Playhouse of Stars: Hands of the Enemy," CBS, 1957; "The Adventures of Jim Bowie: Deputy Sheriff," ABC, 1958; "Goodyear Theatre: The Giant Step," NBC, 1958; "Schlitz Playhouse of Stars: Way of the West," CBS, 1958; "Tales of Wells Fargo: Sam Bass," NBC, 1958; "Studio One: Man Under Glass," CBS, 1958; "Wanted Dead or Alive: The Martin Poster," CBS, 1958; "The Texan: The Hemp Tree," CBS, 1958; "Dick Powell's Zane Grey Theatre: Living Is a Lonesome Thing," CBS, 1959; "Wanted Dead or Alive: The Legend," CBS, 1959; "Tombstone Territory: The Man From Brewster," ABC, 1959; "Playhouse 90: Project Immortality," CBS, 1959; "Johnny Staccato: The Naked Truth," NBC, 1959; "Here's Hollywood," NBC, 1960; "Your First Impression," NBC, 1962; "Your First Impression," NBC, 1963; "Stump the Stars," CBS, 1963; "Truth or Consequences," NBC, 1964; "You Don't Say," NBC, 1964; "Vacation Playhouse: Luke and the Tenderfoot," CBS, 1965; "Hullabaloo," NBC, 1965; "Red," NBC, 1970; "Mitzi and a Hundred Guys," CBS, 1975; "General Electric's All-Star Anniversary," ABC, 1978; "Little House: A New Beginning: Home Again," NBC, 1983.
TV MOVIES AND MINISERIES: "The Loneliest Runner," NBC, 1976; "Love Is Forever," NBC, 1983; "Little House: Look Back to Yesterday," NBC, 1983; "Little House: The Last Farewell," NBC, 1984; "Sam's Son," NBC, 1984.
AS WRITER-PRODUCER-DIRECTOR: "Love Story: Love Came Laughing," NBC, 1973; "Little House on the Prairie," NBC, 1974-82; "Little House: A New Beginning," NBC, 1982-83; "Highway to Heaven," NBC, 1984-89.

LANE, ABBE
b. *New York City, NY, December 14, 1932.* Statuesque singer-dancer; former wife of Xavier Cugat, who later became the husband of Charo.

AS A REGULAR: "The Xavier Cugat Show," NBC, 1957.
AND: "The Steve Allen Show," NBC, 1957; "The Ed Sullivan Show," CBS, 1957; "Person to Person," CBS, 1957; "The Tonight Show," NBC, 1957; "The Steve Allen Show," NBC, 1958; "The Voice of Firestone," ABC, 1958; "The Ed Sullivan Show," CBS, 1958; "The Ed Sullivan Show: Man of the Hour," CBS, 1958; "Arthur Murray Party," NBC, 1958; "The George Burns Show," NBC, 1959; "The Ed Sullivan Show," CBS, 1959; "The Voice of Firestone," ABC, 1959; "Dick Clark's World of Talent," ABC, 1959; "Louis Jourdan Presents The Timex Show," NBC, 1959; "Arthur Murray Party," NBC, 1960; "The Ed Sullivan Show," CBS, 1960; "Naked City: The Day It Rained Mink," ABC, 1961; "The Ed Sullivan Show," CBS, 1961; "New Year's Eve Party," NBC, 1961; "Password," CBS, 1962; "The Ed Sullivan Show," CBS, 1962; "Missing Links," NBC, 1963; "The Ed Sullivan Show," CBS, 1964; "The Jack Benny Program," NBC, 1964; "Burke's Law: Who Killed the Toy Soldier?," ABC, 1965; "The Dean Martin Show," NBC, 1965; "Amos Burke, Secret Agent: Or No Tomorrow," ABC, 1965; "F Troop: Spy, Counterspy, Counter Counterspy," ABC, 1966; "The Man From UNCLE: The Come With Me to the Casbah Affair," NBC, 1966; "The Mike Douglas Show," SYN, 1967; "Personality," NBC, 1968; "The Flying Nun: The Organ Transplant," ABC, 1968; "Rowan & Martin's Laugh-In," NBC, 1968; "The Brady Bunch: Mike's Horror-Scope," ABC, 1970; "Love, American Style: Love and Other Mistakes," ABC, 1973; "You Don't Say," ABC, 1975; "Cross Wits," SYN, 1978; "Vega$: Best Friends," ABC, 1979; "Amazing Stories: Guilt Trip," NBC, 1985.

LANE, ALLAN "ROCKY"
b. *Harold Albershart, Mishawaka, IN, September 22, 1904; d. 1973.* Longtime cowboy actor who, toward the end of his career, provided the voice of Mr. Ed.
AS A REGULAR: "Mr. Ed," CBS, 1961-65.
AND: "Gunsmoke: Texas Cowboys," CBS, 1958; "Tales of Wells Fargo: The Reward," NBC, 1958; "Gunsmoke: The Badge," CBS, 1960.

LANE, CHARLES
b. *San Francisco, CA, 1899.* Thin, bespectacled character player with a pinched face; he often played sitcom crabs, notably Homer Bedloe on "Petticoat Junction."
AS A REGULAR: "Dear Phoebe," NBC, 1954-55; "The Lucy Show," CBS, 1962-63; "Petticoat Junction," CBS, 1963-68; "The Pruitts of Southhampton," ABC, 1966-67; "The Beverly Hillbillies," CBS, 1971; "Karen," ABC, 1975.
AND: "I Love Lucy: Lucy Goes to the Hospital,"

CBS, 1953; "I Love Lucy: Lucy Tells the Truth," CBS, 1953; "I Love Lucy: The Business Manager," CBS, 1954; "I Love Lucy: Staten Island Ferry," CBS, 1956; "The Gale Storm Show: One Captain Too Many," CBS, 1956; "The Joseph Cotten Show: Alibi for Murder," NBC, 1957; "The People's Choice: Paper Hangers," NBC, 1957; "The Thin Man: The Acrostic Murders," NBC, 1957; "How to Marry a Millionaire: The Truthivac," SYN, 1959; "The Danny Thomas Show: Rusty's Day in Court," CBS, 1959; "Fibber McGee and Molly: The Trailer," NBC, 1959; "Dennis the Menace: Dennis and the Fishing Rod," CBS, 1961; "Guestward Ho!: The Hootons Build a Barbecue," ABC, 1961; "The Many Loves of Dobie Gillis: Move Over, Perry Mason," CBS, 1961; "Dennis the Menace: The 50,000th Customer," CBS, 1961; "Hawaiian Eye: Little Miss Rich Witch," ABC, 1962; "The Many Loves of Dobie Gillis: The Sweet Success of Smell," CBS, 1962; "Dennis the Menace: The New Principal," CBS, 1962; "Mr. Ed: Wilbur in the Lion's Den," CBS, 1962; "McKeever and the Colonel: Blackwell's Stand," NBC, 1962; "The Many Loves of Dobie Gillis: Too Many Kooks Spoil the Broth," CBS, 1963; "The Andy Griffith Show: Aunt Bee the Crusader," CBS, 1964; "Gomer Pyle, USMC: Pay Day," CBS, 1964; "Wendy & Me: Happiness Is a Thing Called Misery," ABC, 1965; "Bewitched: Speak the Truth," ABC, 1965; "The Donna Reed Show: The Big League Shock," ABC, 1965; "The Smothers Brothers Show: A Boarding House Is Not a Home," CBS, 1965; "Get Smart: My Nephew the Spy," NBC, 1965; "Please Don't Eat the Daisies: Say UNCLE," NBC, 1966; "The Man From UNCLE: The Pop Art Affair," NBC, 1966; "Love on a Rooftop: My Husband the Knight," ABC, 1966; "F Troop: Reach for the Sky, Pardner," ABC, 1966; "Gomer Pyle, USMC: The Prize Boat," CBS, 1967; "Love on a Rooftop: Low Calorie Love," ABC, 1967; "He & She: The Old Man and the She," CBS, 1967; "Bewitched: Humbug Not to Be Spoken Here," ABC, 1967; "Green Acres: The Rummage Sale," CBS, 1968; "The Beverly Hillbillies: The Hired Gun," CBS, 1968; "Bewitched: You're So Agreeable," ABC, 1969; "The Flying Nun: The Breakaway Monk," ABC, 1969; "Nanny and the Professor: Nanny on Wheels," ABC, 1970; "Bewitched: Make Love, Not Hate," ABC, 1970; "Bewitched: Samantha's Magic Potion," ABC, 1970; "Bewitched: Laugh, Clown, Laugh," ABC, 1971; "Bewitched: The Warlock in the Gray Flannel Suit," ABC, 1971; "Nanny and the Professor: One for the Road," ABC, 1971; "Bewitched: School Days, School Days," ABC, 1972; "The Odd Couple: Take My Furniture, Please," ABC, 1973; "The Girl with Something Extra: Sally on My Mind," NBC, 1973; "Adam's Rib: Katey at the Bat," ABC, 1973; "The Rookies: Another Beginning for Ben

Fuller," ABC, 1973; "Rhoda: Honeymoon," CBS, 1974; "The Family Holvak: The Long Way Home," NBC, 1975; "One Day at a Time: Julie's Job," CBS, 1976; "Family: Thursday's Child Has Far to Go," ABC, 1976; "Chico and the Man: Old Is Old," NBC, 1976; "Lou Grant: Gambling," CBS, 1979; "Lou Grant: Generations," CBS, 1981; "Little House: A New Beginning: Welcome to Olsenville," NBC, 1982.
TV MOVIES AND MINISERIES: "The Great Man's Whiskers," NBC, 1973.

LANE, SCOTT
b. New York City, NY, January 27, 1951.
AS A REGULAR: "McKeever and the Colonel," NBC, 1962-63.
AND: "Bell Telephone Hour: The Sounds of America," NBC, 1961; "Hazel: Three Little Cubs," NBC, 1962; "Wagon Train: The Grover Allen Story," ABC, 1964; "The Patty Duke Show: Ross Runs Away-But Not Far," ABC, 1966; "The Patty Duke Show: Do a Brother a Favor," ABC, 1966; "Barnaby Jones: Gang War," CBS, 1977.

LANEUVILLE, ERIC
b. New Orleans, LA, July 14, 1952. Actor who played orderly Luther Hawkins on "St. Elsewhere" and also directed episodes of the show.
AS A REGULAR: "Room 222," ABC, 1971-73; "The Cop and the Kid," NBC, 1975-76; "St. Elsewhere," NBC, 1982-88.
AND: "The Bold Ones: Killer on the Loose," NBC, 1970; "Emergency!: Crash," NBC, 1972; "The Rookies: Crossfire," ABC, 1973; "The Rookies: The Saturday Night Special," ABC, 1975; "Sanford & Son: Aunt Esther Meets Her Son," NBC, 1976; "The White Shadow: Needle," CBS, 1979; "The White Shadow: No Blood, No Foul," CBS, 1981; "Hill Street Blues: The Young, the Beautiful and the Degraded," NBC, 1982.
TV MOVIES AND MINISERIES: "Twice in a Lifetime," NBC, 1974; "Foster and Laurie," CBS, 1975.
AS DIRECTOR: "St. Elsewhere," NBC, 1986-88.

LANGDON, SUE ANE
b. Paterson, NJ, March 8, 1936. Blonde actress who played Lillian, wife of Arnie Nuvo (Herschel Bernardi) on "Arnie"; usually in sexy roles in the fifties and sixties.
AS A REGULAR: "Bachelor Father," NBC, 1959-61; "Jackie Gleason and His American Scene Magazine," CBS, 1962-63; "Arnie," CBS, 1970-72; "Grandpa Goes to Washington," NBC, 1978-79; "When the Whistle Blows," ABC, 1980.
AND: "Get Set, Go!," SYN, 1957; "The Steve Allen Show," NBC, 1958; "Lux Playhouse: The Dreamer," CBS, 1959; "Bourbon Street Beat: Light Touch of Terror," ABC, 1959; "Dan Raven:

The High Cost of Fame," NBC, 1960; "SurfSide 6: Local Girl," ABC, 1960; "SurfSide 6: The Bhoyo and the Blonde," ABC, 1961; "77 Sunset Strip: Mr. Goldilocks," ABC, 1961; "Harrigan and Son: On Broadway," ABC, 1961; "The Joey Bishop Show: The Bachelor," NBC, 1961; "Robert Taylor's Detectives: A Barrel Full of Monkeys," NBC, 1961; "Bonanza: The Many Faces of Gideon Flinch," NBC, 1961; "Gunsmoke: Catawomper," CBS, 1962; "Room for One More: Girl From Sweden," ABC, 1962; "Thriller: Cousin Tundifer," NBC, 1962; "Margie: The Dangerous Age," ABC, 1962; "The Dick Van Dyke Show: One Angry Man," CBS, 1962; "Follow the Sun: The Inhuman Equation," ABC, 1962; "The Andy Griffith Show: Three's a Crowd," CBS, 1962; "Bob Hope Chrysler Theatre: The Square Peg," NBC, 1964; "Summer Playhouse: The Apartment House," CBS, 1964; "McHale's Navy: Comrades of PT 73," ABC, 1964; "Perry Mason: The Case of the Scandalous Sculptor," CBS, 1964; "The Man From UNCLE: The Shark Affair," NBC, 1964; "No Time for Sergeants: The Velvet Wiggle," ABC, 1965; "The Wild Wild West: The Night of the Steel Assassin," CBS, 1966; "Ironside: The Challenge," NBC, 1968; "Mannix: Merry-Go-Round for Murder," CBS, 1969; "Hollywood Squares," NBC, 1970; "Love, American Style: Love and the Happy Couple," ABC, 1971; "Love, American Style: Love and the House Bachelor," ABC, 1971; "Police Story: Collision Course," NBC, 1973; "Banacek: The Vanishing Chalice," NBC, 1974; "Celebrity Sweepstakes," NBC, 1974; "Cross Wits," SYN, 1979; "The Love Boat: The Captain's Triangle," ABC, 1980; "Three's Company: Urban Plowboy," ABC, 1982.
TV MOVIES AND MINISERIES: "The Victim," ABC, 1972.

LANGE, HOPE
b. Redding Ridge, CT, November 28, 1933. Movie starlet of the fifties who proved herself a pleasant and able sitcom presence as Mrs. Carolyn Muir and Jenny Preston, Dick Van Dyke's second TV wife.
AS A REGULAR: "Back That Fact," ABC, 1953; "The Ghost and Mrs. Muir," NBC, 1968-69; ABC, 1969-70; "The New Dick Van Dyke Show," CBS, 1971-74.
AND: "Playhouse 90: For I Have Loved Strangers," CBS, 1957; "Playhouse 90: Point of No Return," CBS, 1958; "Playhouse 90: The Innocent Sleep," CBS, 1958; "Art Linkletter's House Party," CBS, 1959; "Hedda Hopper's Hollywood, NBC, 1960; "Hallmark Hall of Fame: Cyrano de Bergerac," NBC, 1962; "The Tonight Show Starring Johnny Carson," NBC, 1963; "Bob Hope Chrysler Theatre: Shipwrecked," NBC, 1966; "The Fugitive: The Last Oasis," ABC, 1966; "CBS Playhouse: Dear Friends," CBS, 1967; "Dinah's Place," NBC, 1971; "Celebrity Sweepstakes," NBC, 1974; "Hollywood

Squares," SYN, 1975; "Medical Story: Woman in White," NBC, 1975; "Hallmark Hall of Fame: The Rivalry," NBC, 1975; "Hazard's People," CBS, 1976; "Police Story: Nightmare on a Sunday Morning," NBC, 1977; "The Love Boat: Going by the Book," ABC, 1978; "Finder of Lost Loves: Premiere," ABC, 1984; "Trying Times: A Family Tree," PBS, 1988.
TV MOVIES AND MINISERIES: "Crowhaven Farm," ABC, 1970; "That Certain Summer," ABC, 1972; "The 500-Pound Jerk," CBS, 1973; "I Love You, Goodbye," ABC, 1974; "Fer-De-Lance," CBS, 1974; "The Secret Night Caller," NBC, 1975; "Love Boat II," ABC, 1977; "Like Normal People," ABC, 1979; "The Day Christ Died," CBS, 1980; "Beulah Land," NBC, 1980; "Private Sessions," NBC, 1985.
* Emmies: 1969, 1970.

LANGE, JIM
b. St. Paul, MN. Announcer and emcee who helmed "The Dating Game" for a dozen years.
AS A REGULAR: "The Tennessee Ernie Ford Show," ABC, 1961-65; "The Dating Game," ABC, 1965-73, 1974-75, 1978-80; "Oh, My Word," SYN, 1966-67; "Spin-off," CBS, 1975; "Give-n-Take," CBS, 1975-76; "Hollywood Connection," SYN, 1977-78; "Bullseye," SYN, 1980-82; "Name That Tune," SYN, 1984-85; "The One Million Dollar Chance of a Lifetime," SYN, 1986-87.
AND: "Bewitched: The Mother-in-Law of the Year," ABC, 1970.

LANGE, TED
b. Oakland, CA, January 5, 1947. Actor who played bartender Isaac on "The Love Boat."
AS A REGULAR: "That's My Mama," ABC, 1974-75; "Mr. T. and Tina," ABC, 1976; "The Love Boat," ABC, 1977-86.
AND: "Rhyme and Reason," ABC, 1975.
TV MOVIES AND MINISERIES: "Love Boat II," ABC, 1977.

LANNING, JERRY
b. Miami, FL, May 17, 1943. Actor-singer who played Justin Marshall on "Texas."
AS A REGULAR: "Search for Tomorrow," CBS, 1978-79; "Texas," NBC, 1980-82.
AND: "The Dick Van Dyke Show: The Twizzle," CBS, 1962; "The Donna Reed Show: Donna Meets Roberta," ABC, 1962; "The Donna Reed Show: Big Star," ABC, 1962; "Damn Yankees," NBC, 1967; "Snap Judgment," NBC, 1968; "The Joey Bishop Show," ABC, 1968; "The Donald O'Connor Show," SYN, 1968.

LANSBURY, ANGELA
b. London, England, October 16, 1925. Honored Broadway and film actress whose fame broadened in the mid-eighties, thanks to a grandmotherly

mystery writer named Jessica B. Fletcher.

AS A REGULAR: "Murder, She Wrote," CBS, 1984- .

AND: "Robert Montgomery Presents: The Citadel," NBC, 1950; "Lux Video Theatre: The Wonderful Night," CBS, 1950; "Lux Video Theatre: Stone's Throw," CBS, 1952; "Robert Montgomery Presents: Cakes and Ale," NBC, 1953; "Mirror Theatre: Dreams Never Lie," CBS, 1953; "Ford Theatre: The Ming Lama," NBC, 1953; "Schlitz Playhouse of Stars: Empty Arms," CBS, 1953; "Four Star Playhouse: A String of Beads," CBS, 1954; "G.E. Theatre: The Crime of Daphne Rutledge," CBS, 1954; "Fireside Theatre: The Indiscreet Mrs. Jarvis," NBC, 1955; "Stage 7: Madeira!, Madeira!," CBS, 1955; "Stage 7: Crisis in Kansas," CBS, 1955; "Stage 7: Billy and the Bride," CBS, 1955; "Rheingold Theatre: The Treasure," NBC, 1955; "Studio 57: The Rarest Stamp," SYN, 1956; "Rheingold Theatre: The Force of Circumstance," NBC, 1956; "Front Row Center: Instant of Truth," CBS, 1956; "Screen Directors Playhouse: Claire," NBC, 1956; "Studio 57: The Brown Leather Case," SYN, 1956; "The George Gobel Show," NBC, 1956; "Strike It Rich," CBS, 1957; "Climax!: The Devil's Brood," CBS, 1957; "Playhouse 90: Verdict of Three," CBS, 1958; "Accused: The Edith Garrison Case," ABC, 1959; "Playhouse 90: The Grey Nurse Said Nothing," CBS, 1959; "The Eleventh Hour: Something Crazy's Going On in the Back Room," NBC, 1963; "The Danny Kaye Show," CBS, 1964; "The Man From UNCLE: The Deadly Toys Affair," NBC, 1965; "Trials of O'Brien: Leave It to Me," CBS, 1965; "The David Frost Show," SYN, 1971; "Story of the First Christmas Snow," NBC, 1975; "Great Performances: Sweeney Todd," PBS, 1984.

TV MOVIES AND MINISERIES: "Little Gloria ... Happy at Last," NBC, 1982; "The Gift of Love: A Christmas Story," CBS, 1983; "Lace," ABC, 1984; "Rage of Angels: The Story Continues," NBC, 1986; "Hallmark Hall of Fame: The Shell Seekers," ABC, 1989.

TV'S TOP TEN, 1986-87

1. The Cosby Show (NBC)
2. Family Ties (NBC)
3. Cheers (NBC)
4. Murder, She Wrote (CBS)
5. The Golden Girls (NBC)
6. 60 Minutes (CBS)
7. Night Court (NBC)
8. Growing Pains (ABC)
9. Moonlighting (ABC)
10. Who's the Boss? (ABC)

LANSING, JOI

b. *Joy Loveland, Salt Lake City, UT, April 6, 1928; d. 1972.* Blonde fifties sexpot.

AS A REGULAR: "The Bob Cummings Show," CBS,

1956-57; NBC, 1957-59; "Klondike," NBC, 1960-61.

AND: "Make Room for Daddy: The Model," ABC, 1956; "Fireside Theatre: Shoot the Moon," NBC, 1956; "I Love Lucy: Desert Island," CBS, 1956; "Warner Bros. Presents Conflict: Magic Brew," ABC, 1956; "The Adventures of Ozzie and Harriet: The Balloon," ABC, 1956; "Noah's Ark: A Girl's Best Friend," NBC, 1956; "The Gale Storm Show: Girls, Girls, Girls," CBS, 1957; "The People's Choice: The Sophisticates," NBC, 1957; "The Adventures of Ozzie and Harriet: Hawaiian Party," ABC, 1957; "Studio 57: Shoot the Moon," SYN, 1957; "Climax!: Mr. Runyon of Broadway," CBS, 1957; "The Adventures of Ozzie and Harriet: The Pony," ABC, 1957; "The Frank Sinatra Show," ABC, 1958; "The Lucille Ball-Desi Arnaz Show: Lucy Wants a Career," CBS, 1959; "The Adventures of Ozzie and Harriet: The Uninvited Guests," ABC, 1960; "Mr. Lucky: Election Bet," CBS, 1960; "Here's Hollywood," NBC, 1960; "The Beverly Hillbillies: Jed Throws a Wingding," CBS, 1963; "The Joey Bishop Show: Joey Leaves Ellie," NBC, 1963; "The Beverly Hillbillies: A Bride for Jed," CBS, 1964; "The Beverly Hillbillies: Flatt and Scruggs Return," CBS, 1966; "The Beverly Hillbillies: Delovely and Scruggs," CBS, 1967; "Petticoat Junction: Steve the Apple Polisher," CBS, 1968; "The Beverly Hillbillies: Bonnie, Flatt and Scruggs," CBS, 1968; "The Mothers-in-Law: Take Hers, He's Mine," NBC, 1969.

LANSING, ROBERT

b. *Robert Howell Brown, San Diego, CA, June 5, 1928.* Actor in thoughtful, quiet roles; best known as Brig. Gen. Frank Savage on "Twelve O'Clock High" and as Control on "The Equalizer."

AS A REGULAR: "Young Doctor Malone," NBC, 1959-61; "87th Precinct," NBC, 1961-62; "Twelve O'Clock High," ABC, 1964-65; "The Man Who Never Was," ABC, 1966-67; "Automan," ABC, 1983-84; "The Equalizer," CBS, 1985-89.

AND: "Kraft Television Theatre: Shadow of Suspicion," NBC, 1956; "U.S. Steel Hour: The Square Egghead," CBS, 1959; "U.S. Steel Hour: Case of Julia Walton," CBS, 1959; "U.S. Steel Hour: Big Doc's Girl," CBS, 1959; "CBS Television Workshop: Friday Dinner on Middle Neck Road," CBS, 1960; "Dow Hour of Great Mysteries: The Burning Court," NBC, 1960; "U.S. Steel Hour: The Great Gold Mountain," CBS, 1960; "Alcoa Presents One Step Beyond: The Voice," ABC, 1960; "Thriller: The Fatal Impulse," NBC, 1960; "The Outlaws: The Daltons Must Die," NBC, 1961; "G.E. Theatre: Image of a Doctor," CBS, 1961; "Checkmate: Phantom Lover," CBS, 1961; "The Tall Man: Rovin' Gambler," NBC, 1961; "Here's Holly-

wood," NBC, 1961; "U.S. Steel Hour: Wanted: Someone Innocent," CBS, 1962; "Sam Benedict: Maddon's Folly," NBC, 1962; "Saints and Sinners: The Year Joan Crawford Won the Oscar," NBC, 1963; "U.S. Steel Hour: Fair Young Ghost," CBS, 1963; "Sam Benedict: Read No Evil," NBC, 1963; "The Eleventh Hour: Fear Begins at Forty," NBC, 1963; "Temple Houston: Gallows in Galilee," NBC, 1963; "The Virginian: Fatal Journey," NBC, 1963; "The Twilight Zone: The Long Morrow," CBS, 1964; "Wagon Train: The Geneva Balfour Story," NBC, 1964; "The Eleventh Hour: Prodigy," NBC, 1964; "The Virginian: The Brothers," NBC, 1965; "Slattery's People: Of Damon, Pythias and Sleeping Dogs," CBS, 1965; "Daniel Boone: The Tamarack Massacre Affair," NBC, 1965; "The Loner: The Trial in Paradise," CBS, 1966; "Branded: Call to Glory," NBC, 1966; "The Monroes: To Break a Colt," ABC, 1967; "Insight: Thunder Over Munich," SYN, 1967; "The High Chaparral: Moon of the Turtle," NBC, 1967; "The Virginian: Execution of Triste," NBC, 1967; "Cimarron Strip: The Assassin," CBS, 1968; "Ironside: The Lonely Hostage," NBC, 1968; "Star Trek: Assignment: Earth," NBC, 1968; "The Mod Squad: A Time to Love, a Time to Cry," ABC, 1968; "Journey to the Unknown: The Beckoning Fair One," ABC, 1968; "The Name of the Game: Swingers Only," NBC, 1969; "Gunsmoke: The Devil's Outpost," CBS, 1969; "Medical Center: Victim," CBS, 1969; "Mannix: Blind Mirror," CBS, 1969; "Mannix: The Judas Touch," CBS, 1970; "Bonanza: Danger Road," NBC, 1970; "The Flying Nun: The Dumbest Kid in School," ABC, 1970; "Marcus Welby, M.D.: False Spring," ABC, 1970; "The Doris Day Show: A Fine Romance," CBS, 1971; "Bonanza: Heritage of Anger," NBC, 1972; "The Rookies: Eye for an Eye," ABC, 1975; "Simon & Simon: The Shadow of Sam Penny," CBS, 1983; "Simon & Simon: Reunion at Alcatraz," CBS, 1985; "Hotel: Recriminations," ABC, 1986.
TV MOVIES AND MINISERIES: "Killer by Night," CBS, 1972; "The Astronaut," NBC, 1972; "The Crime Club," NBC, 1975; "Widow," NBC, 1976; "S*H*E," CBS, 1980; "Bionic Showdown: The Six Million Dollar Man and the Bionic Woman," NBC, 1989.

LANSON, SNOOKY
b. Memphis, TN, March 27, 1914. Singer and "Hit Parade" host.
AS A REGULAR: "Your Hit Parade," NBC, 1950-57; "Chevrolet on Broadway," NBC, 1956; "Five Star Jubilee," NBC, 1961.
AND: "The Tonight Show," NBC, 1957; "The Gisele MacKenzie Show," NBC, 1958; "The George Hamilton IV Show," CBS, 1958; "Your Hit Parade," CBS, 1958; "The Jimmy Dean Show," CBS, 1959; "Jubilee USA," ABC, 1959;

"Jubilee USA," ABC, 1960; "A Salute to Television's 25th Anniversary," ABC, 1972.

LANZA, MARIO
b. Alfred Arnold Cocozza, Philadelphia, PA, January 31, 1925; d. 1959. Ill-fated tenor whose larger-than-life appetites led to his early death.
AS A GUEST: "Shower of Stars: Lend an Ear," CBS, 1954; "The Ed Sullivan Show," CBS, 1958.

LA PLACA, ALISON
b. 1960. Actress who played the selfish Linda Phillips on "Duet" and "Open House."
AS A REGULAR: "Suzanne Pleshette Is Maggie Briggs," CBS, 1984; "Duet," FOX, 1987-89; "Open House," FOX, 1989-90.
AND: "Cheers: Behind Every Great Man," NBC, 1985; "The Pat Sajak Show," CBS, 1989.
TV MOVIES AND MINISERIES: "Murder: By Reason of Insanity," CBS, 1985.

LARKIN, JOHN
b. Oakland, CA, April 11, 1912; d. 1965. Former radio actor who played Mike Karr on "The Edge of Night."
AS A REGULAR: "The Road to Life," CBS, 1954-55; "The Edge of Night," CBS, 1956-62; "Saints and Sinners," NBC, 1962-63; "Twelve O'Clock High," ABC, 1964-65.
AND: "Bonanza: The Colonel," NBC, 1963; "The Dick Powell Show: Tissue of Hate," NBC, 1963; "The Breaking Point: Better Than a Dead Lion," ABC, 1964; "The Alfred Hitchcock Hour: The Evil of Adelaide Winters," CBS, 1964; "Wagon Train: The Duncan McIvor Story," ABC, 1964; "Perry Mason: The Case of the Betrayed Bride," CBS, 1964.

LAROSA, JULIUS
b. Brooklyn, NY, January 2, 1930. Singer who was fired on the air by Arthur Godfrey, who said he lacked humility; in reality, Godfrey was upset because LaRosa was making records without Godfrey's permission.
AS A REGULAR: "Arthur Godfrey and His Friends," CBS, 1952-53; "TV's Top Tunes," CBS, 1955; "The Julius LaRosa Show," CBS, 1955; NBC, 1956-57; "Another World," NBC, 1980.
AND: "The Steve Allen Show," NBC, 1956; "Bandstand," NBC, 1956; "Saturday Spectacular: Sonia Henie's Holiday on Ice," NBC, 1956; "The Steve Allen Show," NBC, 1957; "Matinee Theatre: Three Kids," NBC, 1957; "The Perry Como Show," NBC, 1957; "Galaxy of Stars," NBC, 1957; "The Nat King Cole Show," NBC, 1957; "The Big Record," CBS, 1957; "Kraft Television Theatre: Man in a Trance," NBC, 1957; "The Ed Sullivan Show," CBS, 1957; "The

Patrice Munsel Show," ABC, 1957; "The Polly Bergen Show," NBC, 1958; "The Perry Como Show," NBC, 1958; "The Big Record," CBS, 1958; "The Patrice Munsel Show," ABC, 1958; "Dinah Shore Chevy Show," NBC, 1958; "Steve Allen Presents The Steve Lawrence-Eydie Gorme Show," NBC, 1958; "The Dick Clark Saturday Night Beechnut Show," ABC, 1958; "The Garry Moore Show," CBS, 1958; "Patti Page Olds Show," ABC, 1959; "The Voice of Firestone: The Music of Jerome Kern," ABC, 1959; "The Perry Como Show," NBC, 1959; "The Dick Clark Saturday Night Beechnut Show," ABC, 1959; "The Ed Sullivan Show," CBS, 1959; "Dick Clark's World of Talent," ABC, 1959; "Steve Allen Plymouth Show," NBC, 1960; "Celebrity Talent Scouts," CBS, 1960; "Shirley Temple's Storybook: King Midas," NBC, 1961; "The Jack Paar Show," NBC, 1961; "The Ed Sullivan Show," CBS, 1961; "American Bandstand," ABC, 1962; "U.S. Steel Hour: Marriage Marks the Spot," CBS, 1962; "Candid Camera," CBS, 1962; "Candid Camera," CBS, 1964; "Laverne & Shirley: Separate Tables," ABC, 1980.

LARROQUETTE, JOHN
b. New Orleans, LA, November 25, 1947. Capable comic actor who's won just a few too many Emmy awards as prosecutor Dan Fielding on "Night Court."
AS A REGULAR: "Doctors Hospital," NBC, 1975-76; "Baa Baa Black Sheep," NBC, 1976-78; "Night Court," NBC, 1984- .
AND: "Sanford & Son: Steinberg & Son," NBC, 1975; "Mork & Mindy: Alienation," ABC, 1981; "Remington Steele: Breath of Steele," NBC, 1984; "Saturday Night Live," NBC, 1987; "Saturday Night Live," NBC, 1988; "Late Night with David Letterman," NBC, 1989; "Fifty Years of Television: A Golden Celebration," CBS, 1989.
TV MOVIES AND MINISERIES: "Convicted," NBC, 1986; "Hot Paint," CBS, 1988.
* Emmies: 1985, 1986, 1987.

LARSEN, KEITH
b. Salt Lake City, UT, June 17, 1925.
AS A REGULAR: "The Hunter," NBC, 1954; "Brave Eagle," CBS, 1955-56; "Northwest Passage," NBC, 1958-59; "The Aquanauts (Malibu Run)," CBS, 1960-61.
AND: "Lux Video Theatre: Dark Victory," NBC, 1957; "Playhouse 90: The Blackwell Story," CBS, 1957; "G.E. Theatre: Father and Son Night," CBS, 1958; "The Man and the Challenge: Nightmare Crossing," NBC, 1959; "Wichita Town: Seed of Hate," NBC, 1959; "Men Into Space: Christmas on the Moon," CBS, 1959; "Art Linkletter's House Party," CBS, 1960; "The Roaring Twenties: Blondes Prefer Gentlemen," ABC, 1961; "I'll Bet," NBC, 1965.

LARSON, JACK
b. Los Angeles, CA, February 8, 1933. Actor who played cub reporter Jimmy "Jeepers!" Olson on "The Adventures of Superman."
AS A REGULAR: "The Adventures of Superman," SYN, 1951-57.
AND: "Navy Log: The Big A," ABC, 1956; "Navy Log: Human Bomb," ABC, 1957; "The Dick Van Dyke Show: Big Max Calvada," CBS, 1963; "Gomer Pyle, USMC: PFC Gomer Pyle," CBS, 1965.

LARUE, LASH
b. Al LaRue, Michigan, June 15, 1917. Cowboy actor of films and TV.
AS A REGULAR: "Lash of the West," ABC, 1953; "The Life and Legend of Wyatt Earp," ABC, 1959-60.
TV MOVIES AND MINISERIES: "Stagecoach," CBS, 1986.

LASSER, LOUISE
b. New York City, NY, April 11, 1939. Comic actress and former wife of Woody Allen who played half the title role in "Mary Hartman, Mary Hartman."
AS A REGULAR: "Mary Hartman, Mary Hartman," SYN, 1976-77; "It's a Living," ABC, 1981-82.
AND: "The Tonight Show Starring Johnny Carson," NBC, 1963; "The Bob Newhart Show: Fly the Unfriendly Skies," CBS, 1972; "Love, American Style: Love and the Plumber," ABC, 1972; "The Bob Newhart Show: P-I-L-O-T," CBS, 1972; "The Mary Tyler Moore Show: Mary Richards and the Incredible Plant Lady," CBS, 1973; "CBS Playhouse 90: The Lie," CBS, 1973; "Love Story: The Roller Coaster Stops Here," NBC, 1973; "McCloud: Cowboy in Paradise," NBC, 1974; "Mo and Joe," CBS, 1974; "Medical Center: The Price of a Child," CBS, 1975; "Geraldo Rivera: Good Night America," ABC, 1976; "Saturday Night Live," NBC, 1976; "Taxi: Father of the Bride," ABC, 1980; "Taxi: Take My Ex-Wife, Please," ABC, 1982; "Taxi: Get Me Through the Holidays," NBC, 1982; "St. Elsewhere: In Sickness and in Health," NBC, 1984; "St. Elsewhere: Cramming," NBC, 1984.
TV MOVIES AND MINISERIES: "Coffee, Tea or Me?," CBS, 1973; "Isn't It Shocking?," ABC, 1973.

LAUGHLIN, TOM
b. Minneapolis, MN, 1938. Film actor-director-screenwriter who scored as Billy Jack in several films of the seventies; his career began in TV.
AS A GUEST: "Climax!: Edge of Terror," CBS, 1955; "Navy Log: The Pollywog of Yosu," CBS, 1955; "Navy Log: Bucket of Sand," CBS, 1956; "The Walter Winchell File: The Boy From Mason City," ABC, 1957; "Wagon

Train: The Mary Halstead Story," NBC, 1957; "The Silent Service: Boomerang," SYN, 1958; "Man with a Camera: Second Avenue Assassin," ABC, 1958; "Lux Playhouse: A Game of Hate," CBS, 1958; "M Squad: The Teacher," NBC, 1959; "The Deputy: Like Father," NBC, 1959; "Tales of Wells Fargo: The Quiet Village," NBC, 1960.

LAUGHTON, CHARLES

b. Scarborough, England, July 1, 1899; d. 1962. Corpulent actor often in dignified roles, but handled character parts with equal aplomb; a frequent foil of Tennessee Ernie Ford on his fifties variety show.

AS A REGULAR: "This Is Charles Laughton," SYN, 1953.

AND: "Ford Star Jubilee: The Day Lincoln Was Shot," NBC, 1956; "The Ed Sullivan Show," CBS, 1956; "Washington Square," NBC, 1956; "The Tonight Show," NBC, 1956; "G.E. Theatre: Mr. Kensington's Finest Hour," CBS, 1957; "The George Gobel Show," NBC, 1957; "The Ford Show," NBC, 1957; "Studio 57: Stopover in Bombay," SYN, 1957; "The Lux Show with Rosemary Clooney," NBC, 1957; "The Eddie Fisher Show," NBC, 1957; "The Steve Allen Show," NBC, 1958; "G.E. Theatre: A New York Knight," CBS, 1958; "The George Gobel Show," NBC, 1958; "The Ford Show," NBC, 1958; "The Eddie Fisher Show," NBC, 1958; "G.E. Theatre: The Last Lesson," CBS, 1959; "The Steve Allen Show," NBC, 1959; "Dinah Shore Chevy Show," NBC, 1959; "The Ford Show," NBC, 1959; "The Ed Sullivan Show," CBS, 1960; "Startime: Academy Award Songs," NBC, 1960; "Steve Allen Plymouth Show," NBC, 1960; "Playhouse 90: In the Presence of Mine Enemies," CBS, 1960; "I've Got a Secret," CBS, 1960; "Wagon Train: The Albert Farnsworth Story," NBC, 1960; "Checkmate: Terror From the East," CBS, 1961; "Dinah Shore Chevy Show," NBC, 1961; "The Jack Paar Show," NBC, 1961; "The Ford Show," NBC, 1961.

* When Elvis Presley appeared on "The Ed Sullivan Show" in his famous 1956 appearance from only the waist up, Sullivan didn't introduce him—Laughton did, as guest host that week.
* See also "The Ed Sullivan Show."

LAUREN, TAMMY

b. San Diego, CA, November 16, 1969.

AS A REGULAR: "Who's Watching the Kids?," NBC, 1978; "Out of the Blue," ABC, 1979; "Angie," ABC, 1979-80; "The Best Times," NBC, 1985; "Morningstar/Eveningstar," CBS, 1986.

AND: "The Facts of Life: Runaway," NBC, 1982; "E/R: Premiere," CBS, 1984; "ABC Afterschool

Special: Tattle: When To Tell on a Friend," ABC, 1988.

TV MOVIES AND MINISERIES: "Crime of Innocence," NBC, 1985; "Playing with Fire," NBC, 1985; "The Stepford Children," NBC, 1987; "I Saw What You Did," CBS, 1988; "The People Across the Lake," NBC, 1988; "Desperate for Love," CBS, 1989.

LAURIE, PIPER

b. Rosetta Jacobs, Detroit, MI, January 22, 1932. Actress in fifties films and TV who plays the evil Catherine Martell on "Twin Peaks"; she won an Emmy for the exceptional TV movie "Promise."

AS A REGULAR: "Skag," NBC, 1980; "Twin Peaks," ABC, 1990- .

AND: "Best of Broadway: Broadway," CBS, 1955; "Robert Montgomery Presents: Quality Town," NBC, 1955; "Front Row Center: Winter Dreams," CBS, 1956; "G.E. Theatre: The Road That Led Afar," CBS, 1956; "Playhouse 90: Mr. and Mrs. McAdam," CBS, 1957; "Studio One: The Deaf Heart," CBS, 1957; "The Seven Lively Arts: The Changing Ways of Love," CBS, 1957; "Playhouse 90: The Days of Wine and Roses," CBS, 1958; "Westinghouse Desilu Playhouse: The Innocent Assassin," CBS, 1959; "G.E. Theatre: Caesar and Cleopatra," CBS, 1959; "Hallmark Hall of Fame: Winterset," NBC, 1959; "U.S. Steel Hour: You Can't Have Everything," CBS, 1960; "Play of the Week: Legend of Lovers," SYN, 1961; "G.E. Theatre: A Musket for Jessica," CBS, 1961; "Westinghouse Presents: Come Again to Carthage," CBS, 1961; "The Bob Hope Show," NBC, 1962; "Naked City: Howard Running Bear Is a Turtle," ABC, 1963; "Bob Hope Chrysler Theatre: Something About Lee Wiley," NBC, 1963; "Ben Casey: Light Up the Dark Corners," ABC, 1963; "The Eleventh Hour: My Door Is Locked and Bolted," NBC, 1964; "The Breaking Point: The Summer House," ABC, 1964; "St. Elsewhere: Ties That Bind," NBC, 1983; "St. Elsewhere: Lust Et Veritas," NBC, 1983; "St. Elsewhere: Newheart," NBC, 1983; "Hotel: Illusions," ABC, 1984; "Murder, She Wrote: Murder at the Oasis," CBS, 1985; "The Twilight Zone: The Burning Man," CBS, 1985; "Matlock: The Judge," NBC, 1987.

TV MOVIES AND MINISERIES: "Rainbow," NBC, 1978; "The Bunker," CBS, 1981; "Mae West," ABC, 1982; "The Thorn Birds," ABC, 1983; "Love, Mary," CBS, 1985; "ABC Theatre: Tough Love," ABC, 1985; "Diary of a Perfect Murder," NBC, 1986; "Hallmark Hall of Fame: Promise," CBS, 1986.

* Emmies: 1987.

LAUTER, ED

b. Long Beach, NY, October 30, 1940. Beady-eyed actor usually in sinister roles.

AS A REGULAR: "B.J. and the Bear," NBC, 1979-80.

AND: "The Streets of San Francisco: A Trout in the Milk," ABC, 1972; "Kojak: Mojo," CBS, 1974; "The New Land: The Word Is: Acceptance," ABC, 1974; "Police Story: Odyssey of Death," NBC, 1976; "The Rockford Files: The Dog and Pony Show," NBC, 1977; "Nero Wolfe: Sweet Revenge," NBC, 1981; "The A-Team: Black Day at Bad Rock," NBC, 1983; "St. Elsewhere: Working," NBC, 1983; "Hardcastle and McCormick: Pilot," ABC, 1983; "Simon & Simon: What's in a Gnome?," CBS, 1983; "Magnum, P.I.: Operation: Silent Night," CBS, 1983; "Murder, She Wrote: The Cemetery Vote," CBS, 1987; "The Equalizer: A Place to Stay," CBS, 1987; "The Equalizer: No Place Like Home," CBS, 1988; "Booker: High Rise," FOX, 1989.

TV MOVIES AND MINISERIES: "Class of '63," ABC, 1973; "The Godchild," ABC, 1974; "Satan's Triangle," ABC, 1975; "Shadow in the Street," NBC, 1975; "Last Hours Before Morning," NBC, 1975; "The Clone Master," NBC, 1978; "The Jericho Mile," ABC, 1979; "Love's Savage Fury," ABC, 1979; "Undercover with the KKK," NBC, 1979; "The Cartier Affair," NBC, 1984; "The Defiant Ones," ABC, 1985; "The Boy Who Drank Too Much," CBS, 1980; "The Last Days of Patton," CBS, 1986.

LAVIN, LINDA

b. Portland, ME, October 15, 1937. Actress who played Alice Hyatt in the silly sitcom based on the good movie "Alice Doesn't Live Here Anymore."

AS A REGULAR: "Barney Miller," ABC, 1975-76; "Alice," CBS, 1976-85.

AND: "NET Showcase: The Beggar's Opera," NET, 1967; "Damn Yankees," NBC, 1967; "Alan King Special," NBC, 1969; "CBS Playhouse: Sadbird," CBS, 1969; "Rhoda: The Shower," CBS, 1974; "Dinah!," SYN, 1976; "The Merv Griffin Show," SYN, 1979; "The Mary Tyler Moore Hour," CBS, 1979; "Dinah!," SYN, 1980.

TV MOVIES AND MINISERIES: "Like Mom, Like Me," CBS, 1978; "The $5.20 an Hour Dream," CBS, 1980; "A Matter of Life and Death," CBS, 1981; "Another Woman's Child," CBS, 1983; "A Place to Call Home," CBS, 1987; "Lena: My 100 Children," NBC, 1987.

LAWFORD, PETER

b. London, England, September 7, 1923; d. 1984. Light leading man of forties and fifties movies with varied TV credits.

AS A REGULAR: "Dear Phoebe," NBC, 1954-55; "The Thin Man," NBC, 1957-59; "The Doris Day Show," CBS, 1972-73.

AND: "Ford Theatre: The Son-in-Law," NBC, 1953; "G.E. Theatre: Woman's World," CBS, 1953; "Schlitz Playhouse of Stars: At the Natchez Inn," CBS, 1954; "Ford Theatre: For Value Received," NBC, 1954; "Ford Theatre: Mason-Dixon Line," NBC, 1954; "Texaco Star Theatre," NBC, 1955; "Fireside Theatre: Stephen and Publius Cyrus," NBC, 1955; "Alfred Hitchcock Presents: The Long Shot," CBS, 1955; "Screen Directors Playhouse: Tom and Jerry," NBC, 1955; "The Steve Allen Show," NBC, 1956; "Schlitz Playhouse of Stars: Once Upon a Time," CBS, 1956; "Playhouse 90: Sincerely, Willis Wayde," CBS, 1956; "Ruggles of Red Gap," NBC, 1957; "The Steve Allen Show," NBC, 1957; "Climax!: Bait for the Tiger," CBS, 1957; "The Vic Damone Show," CBS, 1957; "Studio 57: My Friends the Birds," SYN, 1957; "Texaco Star Theatre: Command Appearance," NBC, 1957; "Dinah Shore Chevy Show," NBC, 1958; "Steve Allen Presents the Steve Lawrence-Eydie Gorme Show," NBC, 1958; "The Bob Cummings Show: Bob Judges a Beauty Contest," NBC, 1958; "The Steve Allen Show," NBC, 1959; "Dinah Shore Chevy Show," NBC, 1959; "Milton Berle Special," NBC, 1959; "Goodyear Theatre: Point of Impact," NBC, 1959; "Frank Sinatra Timex Show," ABC, 1959; "Perry Como's Kraft Music Hall," NBC, 1960; "The Garry Moore Show," CBS, 1960; "Frank Sinatra Timex Show," ABC, 1960; "Art Linkletter's House Party," CBS, 1960; "The Garry Moore Show," CBS, 1961; "The Jack Benny Program: English Sketch," CBS, 1961; "Summer on Ice," NBC, 1961; "I've Got a Secret," CBS, 1962; "Theatre '62: The Farmer's Daughter," NBC, 1962; "The Andy Williams Show," NBC, 1963; "The Judy Garland Show," CBS, 1964; "Password," CBS, 1964; "Password," CBS, 1965; "The Alfred Hitchcock Hour: The Crimson Witness," NBC, 1965; "The Entertainers," CBS, 1965; "You Don't Say," NBC, 1965; "Profiles in Courage: General Alexander Doniphan," NBC, 1965; "I've Got a Secret," CBS, 1965; "The Patty Duke Show: Will the Real Sammy Davis Please Hang Up?," ABC, 1965; "Bob Hope Chrysler Theatre: March From Camp Tyler," NBC, 1965; "Run for Your Life: The Carnival Ends at Midnight," NBC, 1966; "The Wild, Wild West: The Night of the Returning Dead," CBS, 1966; "I Spy: Get Thee to a Nunnery," NBC, 1967; "Personality," NBC, 1968; "The Mike Douglas Show," SYN, 1968; "The Tonight Show Starring Johnny Carson," NBC, 1968; "Personality," NBC, 1969; "Rowan & Martin's Laugh-In," NBC, 1969; "Letters to Laugh-In," NBC, 1969; "Dinah's Place," NBC, 1971; "The Men From Shiloh: The Town Killer," NBC, 1971; "The Doris Day Show: Doris and the Doctor," CBS, 1971; "Bewitched: Serena's Richcraft," ABC, 1972; "Password," ABC, 1973; "The $10,000 Pyramid," CBS, 1974; "Born Free: Pilot," NBC, 1974; "The $25,000 Pyramid," SYN, 1976; "Supertrain: A Very Formal Heist," NBC, 1979; "The Love Boat: Murder on the High Seas," ABC, 1979.

TV MOVIES AND MINISERIES: "How I Spent My Summer Vacation," NBC, 1967; "A Step Out of Line," CBS, 1971; "The Deadly Hunt," CBS, 1971; "Ellery Queen: Don't Look Behind You," NBC, 1971; "The Phantom of Hollywood," CBS, 1974; "Fantasy Island," ABC, 1977; "The Mysterious Island of Beautiful Women," CBS, 1979.

LAWRENCE, CAROL
b. Melrose Park, IL, September 5, 1934. Actress and singer who appeared in the Broadway production of "West Side Story"; a familiar face on TV variety shows and as a coffee saleswoman on commercials.
AS A REGULAR: "The Dean Martin Summer Show," NBC, 1967.
AND: "The Ed Sullivan Show," CBS, 1957; "The Ed Sullivan Show," CBS, 1958; "Your Hit Parade," CBS, 1958; "The Ed Sullivan Show," CBS, 1959; "U.S. Steel Hour: Night of Betrayal," CBS, 1959; "Oldsmobile Music Theatre: Too Bad About Sheila Troy," NBC, 1959; "U.S. Steel Hour: The Apple of His Eye," CBS, 1959; "The Kraft Music Hall Starring Dave King," NBC, 1959; "The Andy Williams Show," CBS, 1959; "Pat Boone Chevy Showroom," ABC, 1960; "Phil Silvers Special: Summer in New York," CBS, 1960; "The Bing Crosby Show," ABC, 1960; "Play of the Week: The Dybbuk," SYN, 1960; "Play of the Week: Rashomon," SYN, 1960; "The Garry Moore Show," CBS, 1961; "Bell Telephone Hour: Almanac for February," NBC, 1961; "Bing Crosby Special," ABC, 1961; "G.E. Theatre: The Iron Silence," CBS, 1961; "Westinghouse Presents: The Enchanted Nutcracker," ABC, 1961; "The Garry Moore Show," CBS, 1962; "Bell Telephone Hour: Portraits of Music," NBC, 1962; "Perry Como's Kraft Music Hall," NBC, 1962; "Special for Women: The Indiscriminate Woman," NBC, 1962; "The Ed Sullivan Show," CBS, 1962; "U.S. Steel Hour: Honor in Love," CBS, 1962; "Candid Camera," CBS, 1963; "The Match Game," NBC, 1963; "The Ed Sullivan Show," CBS, 1963; "Wagon Train: The Widow O'Rourke Story," ABC, 1963; "The Breaking Point: There Are the Hip and There Are the Square," ABC, 1963; "Kraft Suspense Theatre: That He Should Weep for Her," NBC, 1964; "Perry Como Special," NBC, 1965; "Bell Telephone Hour," NBC, 1965; "Bob Hope Chrysler Theatre: Terror Island," NBC, 1965; "The Mike Douglas Show," SYN, 1965; "Rawhide: The Vasquez Woman," CBS, 1965; "Bob Hope Chrysler Theatre: Mr. Governess," NBC, 1965; "Run for Your Life: Make the Angels Weep," NBC, 1965; "The Dean Martin Show," NBC, 1965; "Run for Your Life: The Day Time Stopped," NBC, 1966; "The Garry Moore Show: High Button Shoes," CBS, 1966; "Run for Your Life: A Game of Violence," NBC, 1966;

"Combat!: The Furlough," ABC, 1966; "The Fugitive: Death of a Very Small Killer," ABC, 1967; "Kiss Me, Kate!," ABC, 1968; "Bob Hope Special," NBC, 1968; "The Name of the Game: Keep the Doctor Away," NBC, 1969; "What's It All About, World?," ABC, 1969; "The Jackie Gleason Show," CBS, 1969; "Paris 7000: The Shattered Idol," ABC, 1970; "Medical Center: Blood Line," CBS, 1971; "The Courtship of Eddie's Father: A Little Red," ABC, 1971; "The Bold Ones: By Reason of Insanity," NBC, 1972; "Marcus Welby, M.D.: The Light at the Threshold," ABC, 1973; "Hawaii Five-O: Thanks for the Honeymoon," CBS, 1973; "Medical Center: The Enemies," CBS, 1974; "The Six Million Dollar Man: Nuclear Alert," ABC, 1974; "Kung Fu: And Death Will Be Close Behind," ABC, 1974; "Wide World of Mystery: The Centerfold Murders," ABC, 1975; "The $10,000 Pyramid," ABC, 1975; "The Love Boat: Dance with Me," ABC, 1979; "The Love Boat: Country Cousin Blues," ABC, 1981; "Simon & Simon: Break a Leg, Darling," CBS, 1984; "Murder, She Wrote: Birds of a Feather," CBS, 1984; "Hotel: Fallen Idols," ABC, 1985; "Murder, She Wrote: Christopher Bundy-Died on Sunday," CBS, 1986.
TV MOVIES AND MINISERIES: "Stranger in Our House," NBC, 1978.

LAWRENCE, GERTRUDE
b. Gertrud Klasen, London, England, July 4, 1898; d. 1952. Stage actress and comedienne with a few TV credits.
AS A GUEST: "Prudential Family Playhouse: Biography," CBS, 1950; "Prudential Family Playhouse: Skylark," CBS, 1951.

LAWRENCE, JOEY
b. Montgomery, PA, April 20, 1976. Child actor who played Joey Donovan on "Gimme a Break."
AS A REGULAR: "Gimme a Break," NBC, 1983-87.
AND: "Diff'rent Strokes: Big Brother," NBC, 1982; "Silver Spoons: The Best Christmas Ever," NBC, 1982.

LAWRENCE, MARC
b. New York City, NY, February 17, 1910. Actor who often played organized-crime figures and other heavies.
AS A GUEST: "Playhouse 90: Old Man," CBS, 1958; "Playhouse 90: For Whom the Bell Tolls," CBS, 1959; "M Squad: Jeopardy by Fire," NBC, 1959; "Richard Diamond, Private Detective: Running Scared," CBS, 1959; "The Detectives Starring Robert Taylor: Life in the Balance," ABC, 1960; "The Untouchables: Star Witness," ABC, 1960; "Dick Powell's Zane Grey Theatre: Killer Instinct," CBS, 1960; "Bronco: Tangled Trail," ABC, 1960;

"Troubleshooters: High Steel," NBC, 1960; "The Rifleman: Trail of Hate," ABC, 1960; "The Detectives Starring Robert Taylor: The Other Side," ABC, 1960; "The Deputy: The Hard Decision," NBC, 1961; "Lawman: Homecoming," ABC, 1961; "Whispering Smith: Death at Even Money," NBC, 1961; "The Untouchables: The Genna Brothers," ABC, 1961; "Robert Taylor's Detectives: Three Blind Mice," NBC, 1962; "The Untouchables: Blues for a Gone Goose," ABC, 1963; "Bob Hope Chrysler Theatre: The Timothy Heist," NBC, 1964; "Mr. Ed: The Bank Robbery," CBS, 1965; "Mannix: The Nowhere Victim," CBS, 1969; "Here's Lucy: Lucy and Mannix Are Held Hostage," CBS, 1971; "Mannix: Overkill," CBS, 1971; "McCloud: The Gang That Stole Manhattan," NBC, 1974; "Switch: Kiss of Death," CBS, 1975; "The Rookies: Journey to Oblivion," ABC, 1976.

TV MOVIES AND MINISERIES: "Honor Thy Father," CBS, 1973.

LAWRENCE, MATTHEW

b. Montgomery, PA, February 11, 1980. Child actor, brother of Joey Lawrence; he played Matthew Donovan on "Gimme a Break."

AS A REGULAR: "Sara," NBC, 1985; "Gimme a Break," NBC, 1986-87.

LAWRENCE, STEVE

b. Sidney Leibowitz, Brooklyn, NY, July 8, 1935. Smooth-voiced singer of many variety shows, often with wife Eydie Gorme.

AS A REGULAR: "The Tonight Show (Tonight)," NBC, 1954-57; "Steve Allen Presents The Steve Lawrence-Eydie Gorme Show," NBC, 1958; "The Steve Lawrence Show," CBS, 1965; "Foul-Ups, Bleeps & Blunders," ABC, 1984-85.

AND: "Arthur Godfrey's Talent Scouts," CBS, 1951; "The Steve Allen Show," NBC, 1957; "Circus Time," ABC, 1957; "The Julius LaRosa Show," NBC, 1957; "The General Motors 50th Anniversary Show," NBC, 1957; "The Steve Allen Show," NBC, 1958; "Dinah Shore Chevy Show," NBC, 1958; "Pat Boone Chevy Showroom," ABC, 1958; "The Jimmy Dean Show," CBS, 1958; "The Patrice Munsel Show," ABC, 1958; "The Bob Crosby Show," NBC, 1958; "Person to Person," CBS, 1958; "Patti Page Olds Show," ABC, 1958; "The Ed Sullivan Show," CBS, 1959; "The Andy Williams Show," CBS, 1959; "Pat Boone Chevy Showroom," ABC, 1959; "Steve Allen Plymouth Show," NBC, 1960; "Perry Como's Kraft Music Hall," NBC, 1960; "The Garry Moore Show," CBS, 1960; "Perry Como's Kraft Music Hall," NBC, 1960; "Jane Powell Special: Young at Heart," NBC, 1961;

"Queen for a Day," ABC, 1961; "The Garry Moore Show," CBS, 1962; "Bell Telephone Hour: Gala Performance," NBC, 1962; "The Ed Sullivan Show," CBS, 1962; "What's My Line?," CBS, 1962; "What's My Line?," CBS, 1963; "The Garry Moore Show," CBS, 1963; "The Ed Sullivan Show," CBS, 1964; "What's My Line?," CBS, 1964; "Carol for Another Christmas," ABC, 1964; "The Jack Paar Program," NBC, 1965; "The Andy Williams Show," NBC, 1967; "The Ed Sullivan Show," CBS, 1968; "Hollywood Palace," ABC, 1969; "Medical Center: The Corrupted," CBS, 1971; "The Carol Burnett Show," CBS, 1971; "Night Gallery: The Dear Departed," NBC, 1971; "The Carol Burnett Show," CBS, 1972; "Here's Lucy: Lucy the Peacemaker," CBS, 1973; "The Carol Burnett Show," CBS, 1973; "Sanford & Son: Earthquake II," NBC, 1975; "The Carol Burnett Show," CBS, 1975; "Don Adams Screen Test," SYN, 1975; "Police Story: Two Frogs on a Mongoose," NBC, 1976; "Steve & Eydie Celebrate Irving Berlin," NBC, 1978; "The Steve Allen Comedy Hour," NBC, 1980; "Hardcastle and McCormick: Ties My Father Sold Me," ABC, 1984; "Hardcastle and McCormick: McCormick's Bar and Grill," ABC, 1986; "Murder, She Wrote: No Laughing Matter," CBS, 1987; "The Tonight Show Starring Johnny Carson," NBC, 1988.

* Emmies: 1979.
* See also Eydie Gorme.

LAWRENCE, VICKI

b. Inglewood, CA, March 26, 1949. Comedienne who flourished under the wing of Carol Burnett.

AS A REGULAR: "The Carol Burnett Show," CBS, 1967-78; ABC, 1979; "Carol Burnett Presents The Jimmie Rodgers Show," CBS, 1969; "Mama's Family," NBC, 1983-85; SYN, 1986- ; "Win, Lose or Draw," NBC & SYN, 1987-89.

AND: "The Mike Douglas Show," SYN, 1968; "The Donald O'Connor Show," SYN, 1968; "Password," ABC, 1973; "Sammy and Company," SYN, 1975; "The $25,000 Pyramid," SYN, 1976; "The Eddie Capra Mysteries: Murder on the Flip Side," NBC, 1978; "Laverne & Shirley: In the Army," ABC, 1979; "Hollywood Squares," SYN, 1980; "The Love Boat: Rent-a-Romeo," ABC, 1980; "Laverne & Shirley: The Survival Test," ABC, 1980; "Murder, She Wrote: My Johnny Lies Over the Ocean," CBS, 1985; "The Love Boat: Couples," ABC, 1986.

TV MOVIES AND MINISERIES: "Having Babies," ABC, 1976.

* At age 17, Lawrence mailed a letter to Carol Burnett with photos that highlighted the resemblance between the two women. Burnett called Lawrence, and eventually hired her.
* Emmies: 1976.

LAWSON, RICHARD

b. Loma Linda, CA. Actor who plays police detective Nathaniel Hawthorne on "The Days and Nights of Molly Dodd."

AS A REGULAR: "Chicago Story," NBC, 1982; "Dynasty," ABC, 1986-87; "The Days and Nights of Molly Dodd," NBC, 1988; LIF, 1988- .

AND: "Shaft: The Executioners," CBS, 1973; "Medical Center: Survivors," CBS, 1975; "The Streets of San Francisco: Endgame," ABC, 1975; "All in the Family: Mike the Pacifist," CBS, 1977; "The White Shadow: Burnout," CBS, 1981; "Hardcastle and McCormick: The Boxer," ABC, 1983; "227: A Yen for Lester," NBC, 1988.

TV MOVIES AND MINISERIES: "Crossfire," NBC, 1975; "Charleston," NBC, 1979; "The Jericho Mile," ABC, 1979; "The Golden Moment: An Olympic Love Story," NBC, 1980; "V," NBC, 1983; "Johnnie Mae Gibson: FBI," CBS, 1986; "Under the Influence," CBS, 1986; "The Forgotten," USA, 1989; "Double Your Pleasure," NBC, 1989.

LEA, JENIFER

b. Tulsa, OK, 1934. Fifties starlet who was chosen to play Laura Petrie in the pilot for "The Dick Van Dyke Show," but was replaced by Barbara Britton.

AS A GUEST: "Sgt. Preston of the Yukon: Battle at Bradley's," CBS, 1958; "M Squad: The Woman From Paris," NBC, 1958; "The Thin Man: The Fashion Showdown," NBC, 1958; "Wanted Dead or Alive: The Martin Poster," CBS, 1958; "The Rifleman: Smoke Screen," ABC, 1960; "Have Gun, Will Travel: The Twins," CBS, 1960; "The Beverly Hillbillies: Elly Comes Out," CBS, 1967; "Family Affair: The Prize," CBS, 1967.

TV MOVIES AND MINISERIES: "Footsteps," CBS, 1972.

LEACH, ROBIN

b. London, England, 1941. TV "reporter" who pronounces his name Roabin Leiych.

AS A REGULAR: "Entertainment Tonight," SYN, 1983-84; "Lifestyles of the Rich and Famous," SYN, 1984- ; "Fame, Fortune and Romance," ABC, 1986-87; "Runaway with the Rich and Famous," SYN, 1987- .

AND: "thirtysomething: Born to be Mild," ABC, 1988; "Animal Crack-Ups," ABC, 1989; "The People Next Door: Make Room for Abby," CBS, 1989.

LEACHMAN, CLORIS

b. Des Moines, IA, April 30, 1926. Actress with a long history of TV credits; best known as Phyllis Lindstrom on "The Mary Tyler Moore Show" and her own spinoff sitcom.

AS A REGULAR: "Hold It Please," CBS, 1949; "Charlie Wild, Private Detective," CBS, 1950-51; ABC, 1951-52; DUM, 1952; "Bob and Ray," NBC, 1952; "Lassie," CBS, 1957-58; "The Mary Tyler Moore Show," CBS, 1970-75; "Phyllis," CBS, 1975-77; "The Facts of Life," NBC, 1986-88; "The Nutt House," NBC, 1989.

AND: "Philco TV Playhouse: Nocturne," NBC, 1950; "Philco TV Playhouse: Sense and Sensibility," NBC, 1950; "Goodyear TV Playhouse: Matter of Life and Death," NBC, 1951; "Kraft Television Theatre: A Play for Mary," NBC, 1951; "Danger: The Escape Artist," CBS, 1952; "Kraft Television Theatre: Kitty Foyle," ABC, 1954; "Climax!: One Night Stand," CBS, 1955; "Dick Powell's Zane Grey Theatre: The Hanging Tree," CBS, 1957; "Alfred Hitchcock Presents: Don't Interrupt," CBS, 1958; "Alcoa Presents One Step Beyond: The Dark Room," ABC, 1959; "Johnny Staccato: Solomon," NBC, 1960; "Pontiac Star Parade: The Man in the Moon," NBC, 1960; "Rawhide: Arana Sacar," CBS, 1960; "The Twilight Zone: It's a Good Life," CBS, 1961; "The Untouchables: Jigsaw," ABC, 1961; "Cain's Hundred: The Fixer," NBC, 1961; "Alcoa Premiere: The Doctor," ABC, 1962; "Target: The Corruptors: The Wrecker," ABC, 1962; "The Untouchables: Man in the Middle," ABC, 1962; "Route 66: Love Is a Skinny Kid," CBS, 1962; "Laramie: Trial by Fire," NBC, 1962; "G.E. Theatre: The Bar Mitzvah of Major Orlovsky," CBS, 1962; "The New Breed: Judgment at San Belito," ABC, 1962; "The Defenders: Conflict of Interest," CBS, 1964; "Mr. Novak: Faculty Follies," NBC, 1965; "A Man Called Shenandoah: The Caller," ABC, 1965; "Trials of O'Brien: Goodbye and Keep Cool," CBS, 1965; "The Virginian: Requiem for a Country Doctor," NBC, 1967; "The Big Valley: Plunder," ABC, 1967; "The Guns of Will Sonnett: A Killing Rode Into Town," ABC, 1967; "Adam 12: Log #81," NBC, 1968; "The Name of the Game: Nightmare," NBC, 1968; "Mannix: In Need of a Friend," CBS, 1968; "Judd for the Defense: Punishments, Cruel and Unusual," ABC, 1968; "The Virginian: The Land Dreamer," NBC, 1969; "Ironside: Goodbye to Yesterday," CBS, 1969; "Lancer: The Little Darling of the Sierras," CBS, 1969; "That Girl: Don and Sandi and Harry and Snoopy," ABC, 1970; "Marcus Welby, M.D.: A Very Special Sailfish," ABC, 1970; "Men at Law: The Truth, the Whole Truth, and Anything Else That Works," CBS, 1971; "Night Gallery: You Can't Get Help Like That Anymore," NBC, 1972; "Of Thee I Sing," CBS, 1972; "Of Men and Women," ABC, 1972; "America's Romance with the Land," ABC, 1973; "CBS Playhouse 90: The Migrants," CBS, 1974; "Pete 'n' Tillie," CBS, 1974; "Ernie, Madge and Arnie," ABC, 1974; "The Sonny Comedy Revue," ABC, 1974;

"Rhoda: Rhoda's Wedding," CBS, 1974; "The Merv Griffin Show," SYN, 1975; "Cher," CBS, 1975; "Hollywood Television Theatre: The Ladies of the Corridor," PBS, 1975; "The Lorenzo and Henrietta Music Show," SYN, 1976; "The Mary Tyler Moore Show: The Last Show," CBS, 1977; "The Screen Actors Guild 50th Anniversary Celebration," CBS, 1984; "The Love Boat: Stolen Years," ABC, 1984; "The Love Boat: Hidden Treasure," ABC, 1985.

TV MOVIES AND MINISERIES: "Silent Night, Lonely Night," NBC, 1969; "Suddenly Single," ABC, 1971; "Haunts of the Very Rich," ABC, 1972; "A Brand New Life," ABC, 1973; "Crime Club," CBS, 1973; "Dying Room Only," ABC, 1973; "Hitchhike!," ABC, 1974; "Thursday's Game," ABC, 1974; "Death Sentence," ABC, 1974; "Someone I Touched," ABC, 1975; "A Girl Named Sooner," NBC, 1975; "Death Scream," ABC, 1975; "The New, Original Wonder Woman," ABC, 1975; "The Love Boat," ABC, 1976; "Long Journey Back," ABC, 1978; "Backstairs at the White House," NBC, 1979; "Willa," CBS, 1979; "Mrs. R's Daughter," NBC, 1979; "S.O.S. Titanic," ABC, 1979; "The Acorn People," NBC, 1981; "Miss All American Beauty," CBS, 1982; "Dixie: Changing Habits," CBS, 1983; "The Demon Murder Case," NBC, 1983; "Deadly Intentions," ABC, 1985; "The Facts of Life Down Under," NBC, 1987.

* Leachman won two Emmies in 1975; one for her "Cher" appearance, another for "The Mary Tyler Moore Show"; her 1984 Emmy was for "The Screen Actors Guild 50th Anniversary Celebration."
* Emmies: 1973, 1974, 1975, 1984.

LEAHY, FRANK
b. O'Neill, NB, August 27, 1908; d. 1973. Norte Dame football coach who did sports reports and Dodge commercials on "The Ray Anthony Show."

AS A REGULAR: "The Frank Leahy Show," ABC, 1953; "The Ray Anthony Show," ABC, 1956-57.

LEAR, NORMAN
b. New Haven, CT, July 27, 1922. Influential comedy writer and producer whose seventies sitcoms raised issues and provoked discussion; in retrospect, however, they seem shrill and pedantic.

AS CO-WRITER: "Henry Fonda and the Family," CBS, 1962; "All in the Family," CBS, 1971.

AS CREATOR: "All in the Family," CBS, 1971-79; "Fernwood 2-Night," SYN, 1977-78.

AS EXECUTIVE PRODUCER: "All in the Family," CBS, 1971-79; "Maude," CBS, 1972-78; "Good Times," CBS, 1974-79; "The

Jeffersons," CBS, 1975-85; "Mary Hartman, Mary Hartman," SYN, 1975-77; "The Nancy Walker Show," ABC, 1976; "A Year at the Top," CBS, 1977; "Archie Bunker's Place," CBS, 1979-83; "Hanging In," CBS, 1979; "A.K.A. Pablo," ABC, 1984.

AS A GUEST: "Saturday Night Live," NBC, 1976; "All in the Family: The Best of All in the Family," CBS, 1979; "Fifty Years of Television: A Golden Celebration," CBS, 1989.

* Emmies: 1971, 1972, 1973.

LEARNED, MICHAEL
b. Washington, D.C., April 9, 1939. Emmy-winning actress who played Olivia Walton and nurse Mary Benjamin.

AS A REGULAR: "The Waltons," CBS, 1972-80; "Nurse," CBS, 1981-82; "Hothouse," ABC, 1988; "Living Dolls," ABC, 1989.

AND: "NET Playhouse: Glory! Hallelulah!," NET, 1969; "The Doris Day Show: The Chocolate Bar War," CBS, 1969; "Ironside: The Professionals," NBC, 1971; "The Streets of San Francisco: The Takers," ABC, 1972; "The Delphi Bureau: The Top Secret–Secret Project," ABC, 1972; "Gunsmoke: Matt's Love Story," CBS, 1973; "Gunsmoke: A Game of Death ... An Act of Love," CBS, 1973; "Police Story: Love, Mabel," NBC, 1974; "Benjamin Franklin: The Statesman," NBC, 1975; "Dean Martin Special," NBC, 1975; "ABC Theatre: The Missiles of October," ABC, 1976; "St. Elsewhere: Playing God," NBC, 1984; "Murder, She Wrote: Trevor Hudson's Legacy," CBS, 1989; "Who's the Boss?: Life's a Ditch," ABC, 1989.

TV MOVIES AND MINISERIES: "It Couldn't Happen to a Nicer Guy," ABC, 1974; "Hurricane," ABC, 1974; "Widow," NBC, 1976; "Little Mo," NBC, 1978; "Off the Minnesota Strip," ABC, 1980; "The Parade," CBS, 1984; "A Deadly Business," CBS, 1986; "Mercy or Murder?" NBC, 1987; "Roots: The Gift," ABC, 1988.

* Emmies: 1973, 1974, 1976, 1982.

LEBEAUF, SABRINA
b. New Orleans, LA. Actress who plays Sondra Huxtable Thibideaux on "The Cosby Show."

AS A REGULAR: "The Cosby Show," NBC, 1984- .

LEE, ANNA
b. England, January 2, 1913. Character actress of film and TV; best known as Lila Quartermaine on "General Hospital."

AS A REGULAR: "It's News to Me," CBS, 1951-54; "General Hospital," ABC, 1978- .

AND: "Shirley Temple's Storybook: The Little Lame Prince," NBC, 1958; "Alcoa Presents One Step Beyond: Who Are You?," ABC, 1959; "Hawaiian Eye: Beach Boy," ABC, 1959; "Peter

Gunn: Sisters of the Friendless," NBC, 1960; "The Loretta Young Show: The Unwanted, NBC, 1960; "77 Sunset Strip: The Diplomatic Caper," ABC, 1962; "Combat!: The Enemy," ABC, 1965; "Mr. Novak: Faculty Follies," NBC, 1965; "My Three Sons: London Memories," CBS, 1966; "Gunsmoke: Rope Fever," CBS, 1967; "Mannix: Edge of the Knife," CBS, 1968; "The FBI: The Gathering of Sharks," ABC, 1973; "The FBI: The Killing Truth," ABC, 1973; "The Streets of San Francisco: Deadline," ABC, 1973; "B.J. and the Bear: Run for the Money," NBC, 1979; "Glitter: The Tribute," ABC, 1984.

TV MOVIES AND MINISERIES: "Eleanor and Franklin," ABC, 1976; "The Night Rider," ABC, 1979.

LEE, BRENDA

Petite country-western singer with a big voice.
AS A REGULAR: "Ozark Jubilee (Country Music Jubilee, Jubilee USA)," ABC, 1955-61.
AND: "The Perry Como Show," NBC, 1956; "The Perry Como Show," NBC, 1957; "The Steve Allen Show," NBC, 1957; "Navy Log: The Commander and the Kid," ABC, 1957; "The Dick Clark Saturday Night Beechnut Show," ABC, 1960; "Be Our Guest," CBS, 1960; "Perry Como's Kraft Music Hall," NBC, 1960; "The Ford Show," NBC, 1961; "The Danny Thomas Show: Teenage Thrush," CBS, 1961; "Perry Como's Kraft Music Hall," NBC, 1961; "The Ed Sullivan Show," CBS, 1961; "American Bandstand," ABC, 1962; "The Red Skelton Hour," CBS, 1962; "The Ed Sullivan Show," CBS, 1963; "Hullabaloo," NBC, 1965; "Hee Haw," SYN, 1972; "Hee Haw," SYN, 1973; "Hee Haw," SYN, 1977; "Music Hall America," SYN, 1977; "Sha Na Na," SYN, 1978.
* Yipes Dept.: On "Navy Log," Lee played a Korean orphan.

LEE, BRUCE

b. San Francisco, CA, November 27, 1940; d. 1973. Martial artist who did some TV on the way to becoming an international screen star.
AS A REGULAR: "The Green Hornet," ABC, 1966-67.
AND: "Batman: The Spell of Tut/The Case is Shut," ABC, 1966; "Batman: A Piece of the Action/Batman's Satisfaction," ABC, 1967; "Ironside: Tagged for Murder," NBC, 1967; "Longstreet: The Way of the Intercepting Fists," ABC, 1971.

LEE, CHRISTOPHER

b. London, England, May 27, 1922. Lean actor long associated with horror roles.
AS A GUEST: "Douglas Fairbanks Jr. Presents: Destination Milan," SYN, 1953; "The Vise: The Final Column," ABC, 1955; "The Vise:

The Stranglehold," ABC, 1955; "Errol Flynn Theatre: Evil Thought," SYN, 1957; "Errol Flynn Theatre: Love Token," SYN, 1957; "Assignment Foreign Legion: The Anaya," CBS, 1957; "O.S.S.: Operation Firefly," ABC, 1958; "Alcoa Presents One Step Beyond: The Sorceror," ABC, 1961; "The Alfred Hitchcock Hour: The Sign of Satan," CBS, 1964; "The Avengers: Never, Never Say Die," ABC, 1967; "The Avengers: The Interrogators," ABC, 1969; "Saturday Night Live," NBC, 1978; "Charlie's Angels: From Street Models to Hawaiian Angels," ABC, 1980.

TV MOVIES AND MINISERIES: "Poor Devil," NBC, 1973; "The Pirate," CBS, 1978; "Captain America II," CBS, 1979; "Charles & Diana: A Royal Love Story," ABC, 1982.

LEE, GYPSY ROSE

b. Rose Louise Hovick, Seattle, WA, February 9, 1914; d. 1970. Former star of stage, screen and burlesque, with occasional TV credits.
AS A REGULAR: "Think Fast," ABC, 1950; "The Pruitts of Southhampton," ABC, 1966-67.
AND: "U.S. Steel Hour: Sauce for the Goose," CBS, 1956; "The Steve Allen Show," NBC, 1956; "Person to Person," CBS, 1957; "The Last Word," CBS, 1957; "Arthur Murray Party," NBC, 1957; "Pantomime Quiz," CBS, 1957; "The Eddie Fisher Show," NBC, 1957; "U.S. Steel Hour: The Charmer," CBS, 1958; "The Jack Paar Show," NBC, 1958; "Brains and Brawn," NBC, 1958; "Hobby Lobby," ABC, 1959; "The Big Party," CBS, 1959; "Celebrity Talent Scouts," CBS, 1960; "Here's Hollywood," NBC, 1961; "Stump the Stars," CBS, 1962; "Object Is," ABC, 1964; "Burke's Law: Who Killed Vaudeville?," ABC, 1964; "Batman: The Sandman Cometh/The Catwoman Goeth (A Stitch in Time)," ABC, 1966; "The Name of the Game: Shine On, Shine On, Jesse Gill," NBC, 1968; "Hollywood Squares," NBC, 1968; "Hollywood Squares," NBC, 1969; "The Jonathan Winters Show," CBS, 1969; "The Tonight Show Starring Johnny Carson," NBC, 1969.
TV MOVIES AND MINISERIES: "The Over-the-Hill Gang," ABC, 1969.

LEE, MICHELE

b. Michelle Dusiak, Los Angeles, CA, June 24, 1942. Former musical-comedy actress, now soap goddess as Karen Fairgate MacKenzie on "Knots Landing."
AS A REGULAR: "Knots Landing," CBS, 1979- .
AND: "The Many Loves of Dobie Gillis: Crazy Legs Gillis," CBS, 1961; "The Ed Sullivan Show," CBS, 1968; "The Jerry Lewis Show," NBC, 1968; "The Carol Burnett Show," CBS, 1968; "Love, American Style: Love and the Neighbor," ABC, 1969; "Kraft Music Hall,"

NBC, 1970; "Marcus Welby, M.D.: Epidemic,"
ABC, 1970; "Marcus Welby, M.D.: The Basic
Moment," ABC, 1971; "Hollywood Squares,"
NBC, 1971; "Love, American Style: Love and the
Contact Lens," ABC, 1971; "Alias Smith and
Jones: Bad Night in Big Butte," ABC, 1972;
"Love, American Style: Love and the Neglected
Wife," ABC, 1972; "Make Mine Red, White and
Blue," NBC, 1972; "Alias Smith and Jones:
Which Way to the O.K. Corral?," ABC, 1972;
"Alias Smith and Jones: Don't Get Mad, Get
Even," ABC, 1972; "Love, American Style: Love
and the Spaced-Out Chick," ABC, 1973; "Love,
American Style: Love and the Hand Maiden,"
ABC, 1973; "Perry Como's Summer of '74,"
CBS, 1974; "The Carol Burnett Show," CBS,
1974; "The Love Boat: Help, Murder!," ABC,
1977; "The Love Boat: The Caper," ABC, 1978;
"The Love Boat: Musical Cabins," ABC, 1978;
"The Gong Show," SYN, 1978; "Hollywood
Squares," NBC, 1980; "The Love Boat: Pride of
the Pacific," ABC, 1982.

TV MOVIES AND MINISERIES: "Only with Married
Men," ABC, 1974; "Dark Victory," NBC,
1976; "Bud and Lou," NBC, 1978; "A Letter to
Three Wives," NBC, 1985; "Single Women,
Married Men," CBS, 1989.

LEE, PEGGY
*b. Norma Engstrom, Jamestown, ND, May 26,
1920.* Song stylist of the forties and fifties.
AS A REGULAR: "TV's Top Tunes," CBS, 1951;
"Songs for Sale," CBS, 1951-52.
AND: "The Steve Allen Show," NBC, 1957; "The
Jackie Gleason Show," CBS, 1957; "The Nat
King Cole Show," NBC, 1957; "Du Pont Show of
the Month: Crescendo," CBS, 1957; "The Frank
Sinatra Show," ABC, 1957; "The Guy Mitchell
Show," ABC, 1957; "The Perry Como Show,"
NBC, 1958; "Pat Boone Chevy Showroom,"
ABC, 1958; "The Bob Crosby Show," NBC,
1958; "The George Gobel Show," NBC, 1958;
"The Garry Moore Show," CBS, 1959; "Dinah
Shore Chevy Show," NBC, 1959; "Swing Into
Spring," CBS, 1959; "Bing Crosby Special,"
ABC, 1959; "Steve Allen Plymouth Show," NBC,
1959; "The Big Party," CBS, 1959; "Steve Allen
Plymouth Show," NBC, 1960; "Revlon Revue,"
CBS, 1960; "G.E. Theatre: So Deadly, So Evil,"
CBS, 1960; "Night Clubs, New York," CBS,
1960; "Revlon Revue: Seventy-Six Men and
Peggy Lee," CBS, 1960; "The Ed Sullivan
Show," CBS, 1960; "Person to Person," CBS,
1960; "The Chevy Show: Four in One," NBC,
1961; "Perry Como's Kraft Music Hall," NBC,
1961; "The Ed Sullivan Show," CBS, 1961;
"Summer on Ice," NBC, 1961; "The du Pont
Show: Happy with the Blues," NBC, 1961; "The
Lively Ones," NBC, 1962; "The Andy Williams
Show," NBC, 1962; "The Ed Sullivan Show,"
CBS, 1962; "The World of Benny Goodman,"

NBC, 1963; "The Dean Martin Show," NBC,
1965; "The Dean Martin Show," NBC, 1967;
"The Tonight Show Starring Johnny Carson,"
NBC, 1969; "The Andy Williams Show," NBC,
1969; "NET Festival: The World of Peggy Lee,"
NET, 1969; "Petula," ABC, 1970; "Owen
Marshall, Counselor at Law: Smiles From
Yesterday," ABC, 1972; "The Julie Andrews
Hour," ABC, 1973; "The Merv Griffin Show,"
SYN, 1975; "Dinah!," SYN, 1975; "The Music of
Your Life," SYN, 1985.

LEE, PINKY
b. St. Paul, MN, 1916. Child-oriented
performer.
AS A REGULAR: "The Pinky Lee Show," NBC,
1950, 1954-57; "Those Two," NBC, 1951-53;
"Gumby," NBC, 1957.
AND: "The Ed Sullivan Show," CBS, 1960.
* Lee collapsed on camera due to a sinus
  condition in 1955.

LEE, RUTA
b. Montreal, Canada, 1937. Fifties starlet who
found steady employment for a time rolling big
dice and smiling a lot on "High Rollers."
AS A REGULAR: "High Rollers," NBC, 1974-76;
"Coming of Age," CBS, 1988.
AND: "Schlitz Playhouse of Stars: Tower Room
14-A," CBS, 1957; "Bob Hope Show," NBC,
1957; "Suspicion: The Story of Margery
Reardon," NBC, 1957; "Sugarfoot: The Dead
Hills," ABC, 1958; "Perry Mason: The Case of
the Screaming Woman," CBS, 1958; "Maverick:
Plunder of Paradise," ABC, 1958; "Gunsmoke:
Carmen," CBS, 1958; "Mickey Spillane's Mike
Hammer: The Old Folks at Home Blues," SYN,
1958; "Restless Gun: The Painted Beauty," NBC,
1958; "77 Sunset Strip: The Bouncing Chip,"
ABC, 1958; "The Lineup: The Veiled Lady
Case," CBS, 1958; "Tightrope!: Stand on Velvet,"
CBS, 1959; "Maverick: Betrayal," ABC, 1959;
"Peter Gunn: Edie Finds a Corpse," NBC, 1959;
"Hawaiian Eye: With This Ring," ABC, 1960;
"The Tab Hunter Show: Turnabout," NBC, 1961;
"Michael Shayne: Spotlight on a Corpse," NBC,
1961; "Cheyenne: Wanted for the Murder of
Cheyenne Bodie," ABC, 1962; "77 Sunset Strip:
The Snow Job Caper," ABC, 1962; "Perry Mason:
The Case of the Libelous Locket," CBS, 1963;
"Stump the Stars," CBS, 1963; "Arrest and Trial:
Call It a Lifetime," ABC, 1963; "Gomer Pyle,
USMC: Gomer Dates a Movie Star," CBS, 1965;
"The Andy Griffith Show: The Hollywood Party,"
CBS, 1965; "PDQ," NBC, 1965; "The Wild Wild
West: The Night of the Casual Killer," CBS,
1965; "You Don't Say," NBC, 1966; "The Wild
Wild West: The Night of the Gypsy Peril," CBS,
1967; "The Lucy Show: Lucy's Substitute
Secretary," CBS, 1967; "PDQ," NBC, 1967; "The

Lucy Show: Lucy Meets the Berles," CBS, 1967; "Hollywood Squares," NBC, 1968; "The Guns of Will Sonnett: Trail's End," ABC, 1969; "Hogan's Heroes: Who Stole My Copy of Mein Kampf?," CBS, 1969; "Love, American Style: Love and the Comedy Team," ABC, 1969; "The Flying Nun: The Great Casino Robbery," ABC, 1969; "Marcus Welby, M.D.: All Flags Flying," ABC, 1969; "Hogan's Heroes: To Russia with Love," CBS, 1970; "Mayberry RFD: Emmett's Domestic Problem," CBS, 1970; "Mayberry RFD: The City Planner," CBS, 1971; "Love, American Style: Love and the Newscasters," ABC, 1972; "Love, American Style: Love and the Four-Sided Triangle," ABC, 1972; "Password All-Stars," ABC, 1974; "3 for the Money," NBC, 1975; "The Magnificent Marble Machine," NBC, 1976; "Three's Company: An Anniversary Surprise," ABC, 1979; "Mork & Mindy: Mork's Night Out," ABC, 1979; "Simon & Simon: Matchmaker," CBS, 1981; "Three's Company: The Matchbreakers," ABC, 1982; "CHiPS: Journey to a Spacecraft," NBC, 1983; "Fantasy Island: The Butler's Affair," ABC, 1983; "Hotel: Ideals," ABC, 1984; "The Love Boat: Partners to the End," ABC, 1985.
TV MOVIES AND MINISERIES: "A Howling in the Woods," NBC, 1971; "Indict and Convict," ABC, 1973; "Roll, Freddy, Roll," ABC, 1974; "Tennessee Williams' Sweet Bird of Youth," NBC, 1989.

LEE, WILLIAM A.
b. 1908; d. 1982. Character actor who played Mr. Hooper on "Sesame Street."
AS A REGULAR: "Sesame Street," PBS, 1969-82.
AND: "Kraft Television Theatre: The Ninth Hour," NBC, 1956; "Robert Montgomery Presents: Crisis at Sand Cove," NBC, 1957; "Hallmark Hall of Fame: On Borrowed Time," NBC, 1957.

LE GALLIENNE, EVA
b. London, England, January 11, 1899. Stage actress with a few TV credits; an Emmy winner for "The Royal Family."
AS A GUEST: "The Theatre Hour: Uncle Harry," CBS, 1950; "Goodyear TV Playhouse: Roman Fever," NBC, 1952; "Kraft Television Theatre: The Southwest Corner," NBC, 1955; "Hallmark Hall of Fame: Alice in Wonderland," NBC, 1955; "Hallmark Hall of Fame: The Corn Is Green," NBC, 1956; "Du Pont Show of the Month: The Bridge of San Luis Rey," CBS, 1958; "Studio One: The Shadow of a Genius," CBS, 1958; "Playhouse 90: Bitter Heritage," CBS, 1958; "Play of the Week: Mary Stuart," SYN, 1960; "Play of the Week: Therese Raquin," SYN, 1961; "The Royal Family," PBS, 1977; "St. Elsewhere: The Women," NBC, 1984.
* Emmies: 1978.

LEHMAN, TRENT
b. 1961; d. 1982. Child actor who played Butch Everett on "Nanny and the Professor."
AS A REGULAR: "Nanny and the Professor," ABC, 1970-71.
* Lehman hung himself.

LEIBMAN, RON
b. New York City, NY, October 11, 1937. Actor in intense roles, including an Emmy-winning portrayal of attorney Martin "Kaz" Kazinsky.
AS A REGULAR: "Kaz," CBS, 1978-79.
AND: "The du Pont Show: Ride with Terror," NBC, 1963; "The Tonight Show Starring Johnny Carson," NBC, 1973; "Police Story: Vice: 24 Hours," NBC, 1975; "Aaron's Way: The Men Will Cheer, the Boys Will Shout," NBC, 1988.
TV MOVIES AND MINISERIES: "The Art of Crime," NBC, 1975; "Many Happy Returns," CBS, 1986; "Christmas Eve," NBC, 1986.
* Emmies: 1979.

LEIGH, JANET
b. Jeanetta Morrison, Merced, CA, July 6, 1927. Film actress ("Touch of Evil," "Psycho") with varied TV credits; mother of Jamie Lee Curtis.
AS A GUEST: "The Rosemary Clooney Show," SYN, 1956; "Schlitz Playhouse of Stars: Carriage From Britain," CBS, 1957; "The Ed Sullivan Show," CBS, 1957; "Take a Good Look," ABC, 1959; "Mother's March," SYN, 1960; "Here's Hollywood," NBC, 1961; "I've Got a Secret," CBS, 1962; "The Tonight Show Starring Johnny Carson," NBC, 1962; "Art Linkletter's House Party," CBS, 1962; "Andy Williams Special," NBC, 1963; "Bob Hope Special," NBC, 1964; "The Andy Williams Show," NBC, 1964; "Bob Hope Chrysler Theatre: Murder in the First," NBC, 1964; "Bob Hope Chrysler Theatre: Dear Deductible," NBC, 1966; "The Man From UNCLE: The Concrete Overcoat Affair," NBC, 1966; "The Danny Thomas Hour: One for My Baby," NBC, 1968; "Bob Hope Special: For Love or $$$," NBC, 1968; "Bob Hope Special," NBC, 1968; "The Tonight Show Starring Johnny Carson," NBC, 1969; "The Men From Shiloh: Jenny," NBC, 1970; "Comedy Playhouse: My Wives Jane," CBS, 1971; "Hollywood Squares," NBC, 1971; "Circle of Fear: Death's Hand," NBC, 1973; "Love Story: Beginner's Luck," NBC, 1973; "Movin' On: Weddin' Bells," NBC, 1975; "Columbo: Forgotten Lady," NBC, 1975; "Hollywood Squares," SYN, 1975; "Sammy and Company," SYN, 1976; "The Love Boat: Locked Away," ABC, 1978; "The Toni Tennille Show," SYN, 1981; "Matt Houston: Who Would Kill Ramona?," ABC, 1982; "The Love Boat: Unmade for Each

Other," ABC, 1985; "Starman: Society's Pet," ABC, 1986; "Murder, She Wrote: Doom with a View," CBS, 1987.
TV MOVIES AND MINISERIES: "The Monk," ABC, 1969; "Honeymoon with a Stranger," ABC, 1969; "The House on Greenapple Road," ABC, 1970; "The Deadly Dream," ABC, 1971; "Murdock's Gang," ABC, 1973; "Murder at the World Series," ABC, 1977; "Mirror, Mirror," NBC, 1979.
* See also Jamie Lee Curtis.

LEIGH, JENNIFER JASON
b. Los Angeles, CA, 1962.
TV MOVIES AND MINISERIES: "Angel City," CBS, 1980; "The Killing of Randy Webster," CBS, 1981; "The Best Little Girl in the World," ABC, 1981; "Girls of the White Orchid," NBC, 1983.
* Vic Morrow's daughter.

LEIGH, NELSON
b. 1914; d. 1967. Actor who played Pastor Martin on the religious program "This Is the Life," not to be confused with "This Is Your Life."
AS A REGULAR: "This Is the Life," DUM, 1952; ABC, 1952-53; DUM, 1953; ABC, 1953.
AND: "Father Knows Best: Swiss Family Anderson," NBC, 1956; "Navy Log: The Pentagon Story," CBS, 1956; "Lassie: The Hermit," CBS, 1960; "The Ann Sothern Show: The Wedding," CBS, 1961; "The New Breed: Sweet Bloom of Death," ABC, 1961; "The FBI: The Scourge," ABC, 1966.

LEIGHTON, MARGARET
b. Birmingham, England, 1922; d. 1976. British actress specializing in dowager roles.
AS A GUEST: "Suspicion: The Sparkle of Diamonds," NBC, 1957; "Alfred Hitchcock Presents: Tea Time," CBS, 1958; "Playhouse 90: The Second Man," CBS, 1959; "Du Pont Show of the Month: The Browning Version," CBS, 1959; "Westinghouse Presents: The First Day," CBS, 1962; "Festival of the Arts: A Month in the Country," NET, 1962; "The Ed Sullivan Show," CBS, 1962; "Ben Casey: August Is the Month Before Christmas," ABC, 1964; "Burke's Law: Who Killed Everybody?," ABC, 1964; "Dr. Kildare: Lullaby for an Indian Summer," NBC, 1965; "The Alfred Hitchcock Hour: Where the Woodbine Twineth," NBC, 1965; "Dr. Kildare: Behold the Great Man/A Life for a Life/Web of Hate/The Horizontal Hero," NBC, 1965; "The FBI: The Chameleon," ABC, 1966; "Heartbreak House," NET, 1966; "The Autumn Garden," NET, 1966; "Judd for the Defense: The Crystal Maze," ABC, 1969; "The Name of the Game:

The King of Denmark," NBC, 1970; "Hallmark Hall of Fame: Hamlet," NBC, 1970; "NET Playhouse: An Ideal Husband," NET, 1971.
TV MOVIES AND MINISERIES: "Frankenstein: The True Story," NBC, 1973; "Bell System Family Theatre: Great Expectations," NBC, 1974.
* Emmies: 1971.

LEMBECK, MICHAEL
b. Brooklyn, NY, June 25, 1948. Actor who played Max Horvath, husband of Julie (MacKenzie Phillips) on "One Day at a Time."
AS A REGULAR: "The Funny Side," NBC, 1971; "One Day at a Time," CBS, 1979-81; 1981-84; "Foley Square," CBS, 1985-86.
AND: "Room 222: Choose One: And They Lived Happily/Unhappily Ever After," ABC, 1970; "The Partridge Family: To Play or Not to Play," ABC, 1971; "Room 222: You Can't Take a Boy Out of the Country, But ...," ABC, 1971; "Love, American Style: Love and the Mind Reader," ABC, 1973; "Room 222: Cry, Uncle," ABC, 1974; "Happy Days: Cruisin'," ABC, 1975; "Barney Miller: Hair," ABC, 1975; "The Rookies: The Hunting Ground," ABC, 1975; "The Love Boat: Reunion Cruise," ABC, 1979; "The Love Boat: The Lone Ranger," ABC, 1981; "The Love Boat: Too Many Dads," ABC, 1982; "Murder, She Wrote: When Thieves Fall Out," CBS, 1987.
TV MOVIES AND MINISERIES: "Gidget Grows Up," ABC, 1969; "Haunts of the Very Rich," ABC, 1972; "A Summer Without Boys," ABC, 1973; "Bloodsport," ABC, 1973; "Side by Side," CBS, 1988.

LEMMON, CHRIS
b. Los Angeles, January 22, 1954. Actor in light roles; son of Jack. He played Richard, husband of Linda (Alison LaPlaca) of "Duet."
AS A REGULAR: "Brothers & Sisters," NBC, 1979; "Duet," FOX, 1987-89; "Open House," FOX, 1989-90; "Knots Landing," CBS, 1990- .
AND: "CHiPS: Weed Wars," NBC, 1981; "9 to 5: When Violet Gets Blue," ABC, 1983; "Evening at the Improv," A&E, 1989; "The Pat Sajak Show," CBS, 1989.
TV MOVIES AND MINISERIES: "Mirror, Mirror," NBC, 1979; "Uncommon Valor," CBS, 1983.

LEMMON, JACK
b. Boston, MA, February 8, 1925. Actor who began a long movie career in the fifties, stopping for a while in television.
AS A REGULAR: "That Wonderful Guy," ABC, 1949-50; "The Ad-Libbers," ABC, 1949-50, CBS, 1951; "Toni Twin Time," CBS, 1950; "Ad Libbers," CBS, 1951; "Heaven for Betsy," CBS, 1952; "Alcoa-Goodyear Theatre (A Turn of Fate)," NBC, 1957-58.
AND: "Pulitzer Prize Playhouse: The Happy

Journey," ABC, 1951; "Danger: Sparrow Cop," CBS, 1951; "Kraft Television Theatre: The Easy Mark," NBC, 1951; "Newsstand Theatre: Tantrum—Size 12," ABC, 1952; "Kraft Television Theatre: Duet," NBC, 1953; "Kraft Television Theatre: Snooksie," NBC, 1953; "Robert Montgomery Presents: Dinah, Kip and Mr. Barlow," NBC, 1953; "Armstrong Circle Theatre: The Checkerboard Heart," NBC, 1953; "Medallion Theatre: The Grand Cross of the Crescent," CBS, 1953; "Ford Theatre: Marriagable Male," NBC, 1954; "Ford Star Jubilee: The Day Lincoln Was Shot," NBC, 1956; "The Ed Sullivan Show," CBS, 1956; "Dick Powell's Zane Grey Theatre: The Three Graves," CBS, 1957; "Playhouse 90: The Mystery of 13," CBS, 1957; "The Steve Allen Show," NBC, 1958; "What's My Line?," CBS, 1958; "Playhouse 90: Face of a Hero," CBS, 1959; "What's My Line?," CBS, 1959; "What's My Line?," CBS, 1960; "Art Linkletter's House Party," CBS, 1960; "Here's Hollywood," NBC, 1961; "Dinah Shore Special," NBC, 1962; "The Tonight Show Starring Johnny Carson," NBC, 1968; "The Dick Cavett Show," ABC, 1971; "Jack Paar Tonight," ABC, 1973; "Jack Lemmon–Get Happy," NBC, 1973; "Magic of the Stars," HBO, 1981; "The Tonight Show Starring Johnny Carson," NBC, 1988.

TV MOVIES AND MINISERIES: "The Entertainer," NBC, 1976; "The Murder of Mary Phagan," NBC, 1988.

LEMON, MEADOWLARK

b. Lexington County, SC, April 25, 1932. Former Harlem Globetrotter.

AS A REGULAR: "Hello, Larry," NBC, 1979-80.
AND: "Diff'rent Strokes: Feudin' and Fussin'," NBC, 1979.

LENARD, MARK

b. Chicago, IL. Actor often in stern roles; he played Aaron Stempel, rival to Jason Bolt (Robert Brown) on "Here Come the Brides."

AS A REGULAR: "Search for Tomorrow," CBS, 1959-60; "Here Come the Brides," ABC, 1968-70; "The Planet of the Apes," CBS, 1974; "The Secret Empire," NBC, 1979.
AND: "Du Pont Show of the Month: I, Don Quixote," CBS, 1959; "Our American Heritage: Not Without Honor," NBC, 1960; "Family Classics: The Three Musketeers," CBS, 1960; "Robert Herridge Theatre: The Trial and Death of Socrates," SYN, 1961; "The du Pont Show: The Battle of the Paper Bullets," NBC, 1961; "The Power and the Glory," CBS, 1961; "Mission: Impossible: Wheels," CBS, 1966; "Star Trek: Balance of Terror," NBC, 1966; "Mission: Impossible: The Survivors," CBS, 1967; "The Wild Wild West: The Night of the Iron Fist," CBS, 1967; "Run for Your Life: A Dangerous

Proposal," NBC, 1968; "Judd for the Defense: Firebrand," ABC, 1968; "Gunsmoke: Nowhere to Run," CBS, 1968; "Mission: Impossible: The Rebel," CBS, 1970; "The Girl with Something Extra: How Green Was Las Vegas," NBC, 1973; "Hawaii Five-O: Will the Real Mr. Winkler Please Die," CBS, 1973; "The Rookies: Life Robbery," ABC, 1973; "The Bob Newhart Show: Carlin's New Suit," CBS, 1977.

TV MOVIES AND MINISERIES: "Outrage!," ABC, 1973.

LENIHAN, DEIRDRE

b. Atlanta, GA, May 19, 1946. Diminutive actress hailed as another Sandy Duncan until they realized they only needed one.

AS A REGULAR: "Needles and Pins," NBC, 1973.
AND: "The Streets of San Francisco: Men Will Die," ABC, 1975; "Police Woman: Shark," NBC, 1977; "Lou Grant: Guns," CBS, 1980.

THE LENNON SISTERS

b. Los Angeles, CA: Peggy, b. April 8, 1941; Kathy, b. August 22, 1942; Janet, b. November 15, 1946. Singers in close harmony who were pure as driven frozen precipitation.

AS REGULARS: "The Lawrence Welk Show," ABC, 1955-68; "Jimmy Durante Presents the Lennon Sisters Hour," ABC, 1969-70; "The Andy Williams Show," NBC, 1970-71.

AS GUESTS: "Shower of Stars," CBS, 1957; "The Eddie Fisher Show," NBC, 1957; "The Jimmie Rodgers Show," NBC, 1959; "Perry Como's Kraft Music Hall," NBC, 1959; "Bell Telephone Hour: The Gift of Music," NBC, 1959; "Perry Como's Kraft Music Hall," NBC, 1960; "The Garry Moore Show," CBS, 1960; "Here's Hollywood," NBC, 1961; "Perry Como's Kraft Music Hall," NBC, 1961; "Bell Telephone Hour: A Trip to Christmas," NBC, 1961; "The Andy Williams Show," NBC, 1962; "The Roy Rogers and Dale Evans Show," ABC, 1962; "Operation: Entertainment," ABC, 1968; "Love, American Style: Love and the Well-Groomed Bride," ABC, 1972.

LENNON, DIANNE

b. Los Angeles, CA, December 1, 1939. Occasional Lennon sister.

AS A REGULAR: "The Lawrence Welk Show," ABC, 1955-60; 1964-68; "Jimmy Durante Presents: The Lennon Sisters Hour," ABC, 1969-70.
AND: "Shower of Stars," CBS, 1957; "Here's Hollywood," NBC, 1961.

LENNON, JOHN

b. Liverpool, England, 1940; d. 1980.
* See The Beatles.

LENO, JAY
b. *New Rochelle, NY, April 28, 1950*. Popular comedian who specializes in topical humor when he hosts the Johnny Carson show.
AS A REGULAR: "The Marilyn McCoo and Billy Davis Jr. Show," CBS, 1977; "The Tonight Show Starring Johnny Carson," NBC, 1986- .
AND: "One Day at a Time: Going Nowhere," CBS, 1979; "Laverne & Shirley: The Feminine Mistake," ABC, 1979; "Don Kirshner's Rock Concert," SYN, 1980; "Alice: The Wild One," CBS, 1981; "The John Davidson Show," SYN, 1981; "Saturday Night Live," NBC, 1986; "Friday Night Videos," NBC, 1989.

LENYA, LOTTE
b. *Karoline Blamauer, Vienna, Austria, October 18, 1898; d. 1981*. Actress-singer; widow of composer Kurt Weill.
AS A GUEST: "NET Playhouse: Ten Blocks on the Camino Real," NET, 1966; "NET Playhouse: The World of Kurt Weill," NET, 1967.

LENZ, KAY
b. *Los Angeles, CA, March 4, 1953*. Attractive actress who won an Emmy as an AIDS victim on "Midnight Caller."
AS A REGULAR: "Rich Man, Poor Man—Book II," ABC, 1976-77.
AND: "The Streets of San Francisco: Harem," ABC, 1973; "Hill Street Blues: The Other Side of Oneness," NBC, 1984; "Love Story: Time for Love," NBC, 1974; "Gunsmoke: The Foundling," CBS, 1974; "Medical Center: The Conspirators," CBS, 1974; "Kodiak: Death Chase," ABC, 1974; "McCloud: The Barefoot Girls," NBC, 1974; "ABC Afternoon Playbreak: Heart in Hiding," ABC, 1974; "Petrocelli: Face of Evil," NBC, 1975; "Jigsaw John: Eclipse," NBC, 1976; "Magnum P.I.: The Case of the Red-Faced Thespian," CBS, 1984; "The Fall Guy: Losers Weepers," ABC, 1984; "Cagney & Lacey: Victimless Crime," CBS, 1984; "Simon & Simon: Dark Side of the Street," CBS, 1985; "Simon & Simon: Mummy Talks," CBS, 1985; "Riptide: Still Goin' Steady," NBC, 1985; "Murder, She Wrote: Armed Response," CBS, 1985; "Moonlighting: Come Back, Little Shiksa," ABC, 1987; "Midnight Caller: After It Happened," NBC, 1988; "Midnight Caller: Conversations with an Assassin," NBC, 1989; "Hardball: Till Death Do Us Part," NBC, 1989; "ABC Afterschool Special: Private Affairs," ABC, 1989; "Midnight Caller: Someone to Love," NBC, 1989.
TV MOVIES AND MINISERIES: "The Weekend Nun," ABC, 1972; "Lisa, Bright and Dark," NBC, 1973; "A Summer Without Boys," ABC, 1973; "Unwed Father," ABC, 1974; "The Underground Man," NBC, 1974; "The FBI Story: Alvin Karpis, Public Enemy Number One,"

CBS, 1974; "Journey From Darkness," NBC, 1975; "Rich Man, Poor Man," ABC, 1976; "The Seeding of Sarah Burns," CBS, 1979; "Sanctuary of Fear," NBC, 1979; "The Hustler of Muscle Beach," ABC, 1980.
* Emmies: 1989.

LENZ, RICHARD
b. *Springfield, IL, November 21, 1939*.
AS A REGULAR: "Hec Ramsey," NBC, 1972-74.
AND: "Doc," NBC, 1969; "Marcus Welby, M.D.: Don and Denise," ABC, 1972; "Circle of Fear: Spare Parts," NBC, 1973; "Love, American Style: Love and the Growing Romance," ABC, 1973; "Owen Marshall, Counselor at Law: N Is for Nightmare," ABC, 1973; "Wide World of Mystery: Violence in Blue," ABC, 1975; "The Six Million Dollar Man: The Return of the Bionic Woman," ABC, 1975; "Police Woman: Pattern for Evil," NBC, 1975; "Medical Story: A Life in Balance," NBC, 1975; "The Streets of San Francisco: One Last Trick," ABC, 1977; "One Day at a Time: Triple Play," CBS, 1980; "Vega$: Black Cat Killer," ABC, 1980; "Lou Grant: Blacklist," CBS, 1981; "Simon & Simon: Pirate's Key," CBS, 1983; "Magnum P.I.: Tran Quoc Jones," CBS, 1984; "All Is Forgiven: On-Air Committment," NBC, 1986; "Murder, She Wrote: If It's Thursday, It Must Be Beverly," CBS, 1987.
TV MOVIES AND MINISERIES: "Owen Marshall, Counselor at Law," ABC, 1971; "Hec Ramsey," NBC, 1972; "Elvis and the Beauty Queen," NBC, 1981; "In Self Defense," ABC, 1987.

LEONARD, JACK E.
b. *Chicago, IL, April 24, 1911; d. 1973*. Fast-talking insult comic popular in the late fifties and early sixties.
AS A REGULAR: "Jack Leonard," DUM, 1949; "Broadway Open House," NBC, 1951; "Dick Clark's World of Talent," ABC, 1959.
AND: "Best of Broadway: Panama Hattie," CBS, 1954; "Babes in Toyland," NBC, 1954; "Babes in Toyland," NBC, 1955; "Frankie Laine Time," CBS, 1956; "Person to Person," CBS, 1956; "Guy Mitchell Special," CBS, 1957; "Arthur Murray Party," NBC, 1957; "The Jackie Gleason Show," CBS, 1957; "The Steve Allen Show," NBC, 1957; "The Steve Allen Show," NBC, 1958; "The Ed Sullivan Show," CBS, 1958; "The Ed Sullivan Show: Man of the Hour," CBS, 1958; "Arthur Murray Party," NBC, 1959; "The Jimmy Dean Show," CBS, 1959; "I've Got a Secret," CBS, 1959; "The Sam Levenson Show," CBS, 1959; "Pat Boone Chevy Showroom," ABC, 1959; "The Jack Paar Show," NBC, 1961; "Perry Como's Kraft Music Hall," NBC, 1961; "I've Got a Secret," CBS, 1961; "I've Got a Secret," CBS, 1962; "The Jack Paar Program," NBC, 1963;

"The Joey Bishop Show: Joey Insults Jack E. Leonard," NBC, 1964; "The Match Game," NBC, 1964; "I've Got a Secret," CBS, 1965; "Hollywood Palace," ABC, 1965; "The Mike Douglas Show," SYN, 1966; "The Ed Sullivan Show," CBS, 1967; "The Steve Allen Show," SYN, 1968; "The Merv Griffin Show," CBS, 1969; "Rowan & Martin's Laugh-In," NBC, 1969.

LEONARD, SHELDON
b. New York City, NY, February 22, 1907. Tough-guy movie actor whose real talent lay behind the camera; along with producing partner Danny Thomas, Leonard had a hand in some of the best sitcoms of the fifties and sixties.
AS A REGULAR: "The Danny Thomas Show (Make Room for Daddy)," ABC, 1953; CBS, 1959-61; "The Duke," NBC, 1954; "Big Eddie," CBS, 1975.
AND: "I Love Lucy: Sales Resistance," CBS, 1953; "It's a Great Life: I Can Get It for You Whole-sale," NBC, 1954; "Screen Directors Playhouse: It's Always Sunday," ABC, 1956; "Art Linkletter's House Party," CBS, 1959; "The Jack Benny Program," CBS, 1960; "Here's Hollywood," NBC, 1962; "The Joey Bishop Show: Double Time," NBC, 1963; "The Dick Van Dyke Show: Big Max Calvada," CBS, 1963; "Burke's Law: Who Killed His Royal Highness?," ABC, 1964; "Burke's Law: Who Killed Mr. Cartwheel?," ABC, 1964; "The Mike Douglas Show," SYN, 1965; "The Lucy Show: Lucy Meets Sheldon Leonard," CBS, 1967; "Gomer Pyle, USMC: A Star Is Not Born," CBS, 1968; "Rowan & Martin's Laugh-In," NBC, 1970; "3 for the Money," NBC, 1975; "Match Game P.M.," SYN, 1976; "Sanford & Son: The Hawaiian Connection," NBC, 1976; "The Cosby Show: Physician of the Year," NBC, 1985; "The Facts of Life: Rights of Passage," NBC, 1987; "Matlock: The Gambler," NBC, 1987.
TV MOVIES AND MINISERIES: "The Islander," CBS, 1978.
AS PRODUCER-DIRECTOR: "The Danny Thomas Show (Make Room for Daddy)," ABC, 1953-57; CBS, 1957-64; "The Andy Griffith Show," CBS, 1960-68; "The Dick Van Dyke Show," CBS, 1961-66; "I Spy," NBC, 1965-68; "My World and Welcome to It," NBC, 1969-70.
* Emmies: 1957, 1961, 1970.
* See also Bill Cosby.

LEONETTI, TOMMY
b. 1929; d. 1979. Singer and actor.
AS A REGULAR: "Your Hit Parade," NBC, 1957-58; "Gomer Pyle, USMC," CBS, 1964-65.
AND: "The Tonight Show," NBC, 1957; "American Bandstand," ABC, 1957; "The Steve Allen Show," NBC, 1958; "American Bandstand," ABC, 1958; "Arthur Murray Party,"

NBC, 1958; "The Dick Clark Saturday Night Beechnut Show," ABC, 1959; "The Garry Moore Show," CBS, 1959; "Pantomime Quiz," ABC, 1959; "The Garry Moore Show," CBS, 1960; "Art Linkletter's House Party," CBS, 1966; "The Virginia Graham Show," SYN, 1972; "Hawaii Five-O: To Die in Paradise," CBS, 1977.

LESCOULIE, JACK
b. Sacramento, CA, November 17, 1917. Game show emcee and former newsman on the "Today" show.
AS A REGULAR: "Fun and Fortune," ABC, 1949; "The Milton Berle Show," NBC, 1954-55; "The Tonight Show (Tonight! America After Dark)," NBC, 1957; "Today," NBC, 1952-67; "Brains and Brawn," NBC, 1958; "The Jackie Gleason Show," CBS, 1958-59; "1,2,3 Go," NBC, 1961-62.

LESLIE, BETHEL
b. New York City, NY, August 3, 1929.
AS A REGULAR: "The Girls," CBS, 1950; "Love of Life," CBS, 1956; "The Richard Boone Show," NBC, 1963-64; "The Doctors," NBC, 1965-68.
AND: "Goodyear TV Playhouse: The Vine That Grew on 50th Street," NBC, 1950; "Prudential Family Playhouse: The Barretts of Wimpole Street," CBS, 1950; "Cosmopolitan Theatre: The Sighing Sound," SYN, 1951; "Lux Video Theatre: Pick of the Litter," CBS, 1954; "Studio One: The Hero," CBS, 1954; "The Millionaire: The Ruth Ferris Story," CBS, 1957; "Studio 57: The Silent Darkness," SYN, 1957; "M Squad: Blue Indigo," NBC, 1958; "Studio One: Presence of the Enemy," CBS, 1958; "Perry Mason: The Case of the Fugitive Nurse," CBS, 1958; "Dow Hour of Great Mysteries: The Bat," NBC, 1960; "Thriller: Child's Play," NBC, 1960; "Stagecoach West: Unwanted," ABC, 1960; "Riverboat: Trunk Full of Dreams," NBC, 1960; "Route 66: Layout at Glen Canyon," CBS, 1960; "Alfred Hitchcock Presents: The Man with Two Faces," NBC, 1960; "Hong Kong: The Dragon Cup," ABC, 1960; "Adventures in Paradise: Man Eater," ABC, 1961; "Thriller: The Merriweather File," NBC, 1961; "Checkmate: Phantom Lover," CBS, 1961; "The Rifleman: Stopover," ABC, 1961; "Wagon Train: The Janet Hale Story," NBC, 1961; "Adventures in Paradise: Nightmare in the Sun," ABC, 1961; "Follow the Sun: The Woman Who Never Was," ABC, 1961; "The Investigators: Style of Living," CBS, 1961; "Straightaway: The Stranger," ABC, 1961; "Ben Casey: Pavane for a Gentle Lady," ABC, 1961; "Rawhide: The Long Count," CBS, 1962; "Route 66: A City of Wheels," CBS, 1962; "Bonanza: The Jackknife," NBC, 1962; "Cain's Hundred: Inside Track," NBC, 1962; "Checkmate: Referendum on Murder," CBS, 1962; "Alcoa Premiere: The Rules of the Game," ABC,

1962; "The Lloyd Bridges Show: My Child Is Yet a Stranger," CBS, 1962; "Empire: The Tall Shadow," NBC, 1962; "Naked City: Spectre of the Rose Street Gang," ABC, 1962; "Ben Casey: I'll Be All Right in the Morning," ABC, 1963; "The Virginian: The Money Cage," NBC, 1963; "Have Gun, Will Travel: Lady of the Fifth Moon," CBS, 1963; "Bob Hope Chrysler Theatre: A Case of Armed Robbery," NBC, 1964; "The Eleventh Hour: A Pattern of Sunday," NBC, 1964; "The Fugitive: Storm Center," ABC, 1964; "Daniel Boone: The Family Fluellen," NBC, 1964; "Wagon Train: The Mary Lee McIntosh Story," ABC, 1964; "The Defenders: The Merry-Go-Round Murder," CBS, 1965; "Bob Hope Chrysler Theatre: March From Camp Tyler," NBC, 1965; "The Loner: Mantrap," CBS, 1966; "The Name of the Game: The White Birch," NBC, 1968; "The Wild, Wild West: The Night of the Sabatini Death," CBS, 1969; "The Virginian: A Women of Stone," NBC, 1969; "Mannix: Once Upon a Saturday," CBS, 1969; "The Bold Ones: This Day's Child," NBC, 1970; "The Name of the Game: Tarot," NBC, 1970; "The High Chaparral: No Bugles, No Drums," NBC, 1971; "The New Adventures of Perry Mason: The Case of the Tortured Titan," CBS, 1974; "Kung Fu: The Passion of Chen Yi," ABC, 1974; "The White Shadow: Pilot," CBS, 1978.
TV MOVIES AND MINISERIES: "Dr. Cook's Garden," ABC, 1971; "The Last Survivors," NBC, 1975; "The Gift of Love," ABC, 1978.

LESLIE, JOAN

b. Detroit, MI, January 26, 1925. Former Warner Bros. contract actress who's been in a smattering of TV; best known as Mary, wife of George M. Cohan (James Cagney) in "Yankee Doodle Dandy."
AS A GUEST: "Bigelow-Sanford Theatre: Flowers for John," SYN, 1951; "Fireside Theatre: Black Savannah," NBC, 1951; "Fireside Theatre: The Imposter," NBC, 1952; "Schlitz Playhouse of Stars: The Von Linden File," CBS, 1952; "Summer Theatre: Dream Job," ABC, 1953; "Ford Theatre: Old Man's Bride," NBC, 1953; "Lux Video Theatre: Peek of the Letter," NBC, 1954; "Ford Theatre: Wonderful Day for a Wedding," NBC, 1954; "Ford Theatre: Girl in Flight," NBC, 1954; "Stage 7: Conflict," CBS, 1955; "The 20th Century-Fox Hour: Smoke Jumpers," CBS, 1956; "Hill Number One," SYN, 1957; "Christopers: Scientific Power for Good," SYN, 1958; "Christophers: Harness That Power," SYN, 1958; "G.E. Theatre: The Day of the Hanging," CBS, 1959; "Christophers: George Washington and the Making of the Constituiton," SYN, 1960; "Branded: Leap Upon Mountains," NBC, 1965; "Police Story: Headhunter," NBC, 1975; "Simon & Simon: The Shadow of Sam Penny,"
CBS, 1983; "Murder, She Wrote: Mr. Penroy's Vacation," CBS, 1988.
TV MOVIES AND MINISERIES: "The Keegans," CBS, 1976; "Charley Hannah," ABC, 1986; "Turn Back the Clock," NBC, 1989.

LESTER, BUDDY

b. Chicago, IL, January 16, 1917. Comedian.
AS A REGULAR: "The New Phil Silvers Show," CBS, 1963-64.
AND: "Make Me Laugh," ABC, 1958; "Schlitz Playhouse of Stars: Portrait of a Legend," CBS, 1958; "Truth or Consequences," NBC, 1958; "The Danny Thomas Show: Danny and the Hoodlums," CBS, 1961; "I'm Dickens, He's Fenster: How Not to Succeed in Business," ABC, 1963; "Gomer Pyle, USMC: Gomer and the Card Shark," CBS, 1967; "That Girl: 7 1/4," ABC, 1968; "Dragnet: Bunco-$9000," NBC, 1969; "It Takes a Thief: Sing a Song of Murder," ABC, 1970; "The Doris Day Show: The Prizefighter and the Lady," CBS, 1970; "Petticoat Junction: Whiplash, Whiplash," CBS, 1970; "The Odd Couple: And Leave the Greyhound to Us," ABC, 1971; "The Mod Squad: Home Is the Street," ABC, 1971; "Emergency!: Crash," NBC, 1972; "Barney Miller: Ramon," ABC, 1975; "Barney Miller: Graft," ABC, 1975; "Barney Miller: Abduction," ABC, 1977.
TV MOVIES AND MINISERIES: "Ellery Queen: Don't Look Behind You," NBC, 1971.

LESTER, JERRY

b. Chicago, IL, 1911. Comedian.
AS A REGULAR: "Broadway Open House," NBC, 1950-51; "Cavalcade of Stars," DUM, 1950; "Chesterfield Sound-Off Time," NBC, 1951-52; "Saturday Night Dance Party," NBC, 1952; "Pantomime Quiz," CBS, 1953; DUM, 1953-54; ABC, 1955; CBS, 1955; "Weekend," SYN, 1963.
AND: "Robert Montgomery Presents: Plainfield Teachers College," NBC, 1956; "The Steve Allen Show," NBC, 1957; "Miami Undercover: No Laughing Matter," SYN, 1960; "The du Pont Show: The Battle of the Paper Bullets," NBC, 1961; "The Mike Douglas Show," SYN, 1964; "The Monkees: Monkees in the Movies," NBC, 1967; "Li'l Abner," NBC, 1967; "Barnaby Jones: The Black Art of Dying," CBS, 1973.

LESTER, KETTY

b. August 16, 1938. Black actress-singer who played Hester Sue Terhune on "Little House."
AS A REGULAR: "Days of Our Lives," NBC, 1975; "Little House on the Prairie," NBC, 1978-83; "Morningstar/Eveningstar," CBS, 1986.
AND: "The Vic Damone Show," CBS, 1957; "Art Linkletter's House Party," CBS, 1958; "Shindig," ABC, 1964; "American Bandstand,"

ABC, 1965; "Where the Action Is," ABC, 1965; "The Donald O'Connor Show," SYN, 1968; "The FBI: Eye of the Storm," ABC, 1969; "Sanford & Son: The Infernal Triangle," NBC, 1973; "Marcus Welby, M.D.: The Fatal Challenge," ABC, 1974; "Marcus Welby, M.D.: Public Secrets," ABC, 1974; "Lou Grant: Murder," CBS, 1978; "The White Shadow: Mainstream," CBS, 1979; "Hill Street Blues: Life in the Minors," NBC, 1983; "Hill Street Blues: Eugene's Comedy Empire Strikes Back," NBC, 1983; "Webster: San Francisco," SYN, 1987; "St. Elsewhere: Curtains," NBC, 1988; "In the Heat of the Night: Gunshot," NBC, 1989; "Quantum Leap: So Help Me God: July 29, 1957," NBC, 1989.
TV MOVIES AND MINISERIES: "Louis Armstrong–Chicago Style," ABC, 1976; "Battered," NBC, 1978.

LESTER, MARK

b. Richmond, England, July 11, 1958. Young actor in films ("Oliver!") and on TV.
AS A REGULAR: "H.R. Pufnstuf," NBC, 1969-71.
AND: "The Dating Game," ABC, 1969; "The Ghost and Mrs. Muir: Spirit of the Law," ABC, 1969; "The Wonderful World of Disney: The Boy Who Stole the Elephants," NBC, 1970; "Then Came Bronson: The Runner," NBC, 1970.

LESTER, TOM

b. Jackson, MS, 1938. Lanky actor who played Eb on "Green Acres."
AS A REGULAR: "Green Acres," CBS, 1965-71; "Petticoat Junction," CBS, 1966-70.
AND: "The Beverly Hillbillies: The Thanksgiving Story," CBS, 1968; "The Beverly Hillbillies: The Courtship of Homer Noodleman," CBS, 1968; "The Beverly Hillbillies: Christmas in Hooterville," CBS, 1968; "Love, American Style: Love and the Competitors," ABC, 1973; "Marcus Welby, M.D.: No Charity for the MacAllisters," ABC, 1974.
* See also "Green Acres."

LETTERMAN, DAVID

b. Indianapolis, IN, April 12, 1947. Former bagboy who became a big-time comedian.
AS A REGULAR: "The Starland Vocal Band Show," CBS, 1977; "Mary," CBS, 1978; "The David Letterman Show," NBC, 1980; "Late Night with David Letterman," NBC, 1982- .
AND: "The Tonight Show Starring Johnny Carson," NBC, 1978; "The Love Experts," SYN, 1978; "The Merv Griffin Show," SYN, 1979; "The Tonight Show Starring Johnny Carson," NBC, 1980; "Later with Bob Costas," NBC, 1989; "The Tonight Show Starring Johnny Carson," NBC, 1989.
TV MOVIES AND MINISERIES: "Fast Friends," NBC, 1979.

* Strictly in the interest of posterity, here were Letterman's fellow celebrity judges the week he appeared on "The Love Experts": Jo Anne Worley, Jo Ann Pflug and the man himself, Soupy Sales.
* Letterman was the warm-up comedian before tapings of "Barney Miller."
* Emmies: 1984, 1985, 1986, 1987.
* See also Teri Garr.

LEVANT, OSCAR

b. Pittsburgh, PA, December 27, 1906; d. 1972. Pianist and comic performer.
AS A REGULAR: "G.E. Guest House," CBS, 1951.
AND: "The Eddie Fisher Show," NBC, 1958; "The Steve Allen Show," NBC, 1958; "The Jack Benny Program," CBS, 1958; "The Jack Paar Program," NBC, 1963; "The Joey Bishop Show: Joey vs. Oscar Levant," CBS, 1964.
* Someone once asked Levant if he ever watched Dinah Shore's TV show. "I can't," he replied, "I'm a diabetic."

LEVENE, SAM

b. Russia, August 28, 1905; d. 1980. Actor in hard-boiled, soft-hearted roles in film and TV.
AS A GUEST: "Medallion Theatre: The Alibi Kid," CBS, 1954; "Douglas Fairbanks Jr. Presents: Johnny Blue," SYN, 1954; "Studio One: The Playwright and the Star," CBS, 1957; "Studio One: The Mother Bit," CBS, 1957; "Kraft Television Theatre: The Old Ticker," NBC, 1957; "Omnibus: Mrs. McThing," NBC, 1958; "Play of the Week: The World of Sholom Alechiem," SYN, 1960; "The Ed Sullivan Show," CBS, 1960; "The Aquanauts: The Frameup Adventure," CBS, 1960; "The Untouchables: The Larry Fay Story," ABC, 1960; "The Ed Sullivan Show," CBS, 1961; "The Tonight Show Starring Johnny Carson," NBC, 1963; "Bob Hope Chrysler Theatre: A Small Rebellion," NBC, 1966.
* On stage, Levene originated the role of Nathan Detroit in "Guys and Dolls" and Al Lewis in "The Sunshine Boys."

LEVENSON, SAM

b. New York City, NY, December 28, 1911; d. 1980. Former high-school teacher who turned his experiences into comedic paydirt.
AS A REGULAR: "This Is Show Business," CBS, 1949-54; "The Sam Levenson Show," CBS, 1951-52; "Two for the Money," CBS, 1955-57; "Masquerade Party," CBS, 1958; NBC, 1958-59; CBS, 1959-60; NBC, 1960; "The Sam Levenson Show," CBS, 1959; "Celebrity Talent Scouts," CBS, 1960.
AND: "Toast of the Town," CBS, 1949; "The Jack Benny Program," CBS, 1949; "The Jack Benny Program," CBS, 1950; "The Ed Sullivan Show,"

CBS, 1956; "Arthur Murray Party," NBC, 1957; "The Steve Allen Show," NBC, 1957; "Person to Person," CBS, 1958; "The Ed Sullivan Show," CBS, 1958; "The Arthur Godfrey Show," CBS, 1959; "Dick Clark's World of Talent," ABC, 1959; "The Ed Sullivan Show," CBS, 1959; "The Ed Sullivan Show," CBS, 1960; "Something Special," NBC, 1960; "The Jack Paar Show," NBC, 1961; "The Ed Sullivan Show," CBS, 1961; "The Ed Sullivan Show," CBS, 1962; "To Tell the Truth," CBS, 1962; "To Tell the Truth," CBS, 1963; "Password," CBS, 1963; "The Match Game," NBC, 1963; "The Jack Paar Program," NBC, 1963; "Missing Links," NBC, 1963; "The Tonight Show Starring Johnny Carson," NBC, 1964; "To Tell the Truth," CBS, 1964; "The Jack Paar Program," NBC, 1964; "The Price Is Right," ABC, 1964; "Missing Links," NBC, 1964; "On Broadway Tonight," CBS, 1965; "To Tell the Truth," CBS, 1965; "The Match Game," NBC, 1965; "The Tonight Show Starring Johnny Carson," NBC, 1967; "The Merv Griffin Show," SYN, 1968; "The Mike Douglas Show," SYN, 1973.
* Levenson entertained at bar mitzvahs and nightclubs when he was spotted by one of Ed Sullivan's producers in 1949. He dropped out of television by the mid-sixties, feeling his gently humorous stories weren't right for the increasingly fast-paced medium.

LEVINSON, RICHARD
b. 1934, d. 1987;
& LINK, WILLIAM
Talented writing team who created "Columbo" and wrote several memorable TV movies.
AS WRITERS: "Chevy Mystery Show: Enough Rope," NBC, 1960; "Alfred Hitchcock Presents: Profit-Sharing Plan," NBC, 1962; "Columbo: Death Lends a Hand," NBC, 1971.
AS CREATORS: "Columbo," NBC, 1971-78; ABC, 1989-90.
TV MOVIES AND MINISERIES: "Prescription: Murder," NBC, 1968; "Istanbul Express," NBC, 1968; "The Whole World Is Watching," NBC, 1969; "My Sweet Charlie," NBC, 1970; "McCloud: Who Killed Miss U.S.A.?," NBC, 1970; "Sam Hill: Who Killed the Mysterious Mr. Foster?," NBC, 1971; "Two on a Bench," ABC, 1971; "That Certain Summer," ABC, 1972; "The Judge and Jake Wyler," NBC, 1972; "Tenafly," NBC, 1973; "Savage," NBC, 1973.
* Emmies: 1970, 1972.

LEVY, EUGENE
b. Canada, December 17, 1946. Gifted comic performer who played such characters on "SCTV" as old guy Sid Dithers, newsman Earl Camembert and no-talent comic Bobby Bittman.
AS A REGULAR: "Second City TV," SYN, 1977-81;

"SCTV Network 90," NBC, 1981-83.
AND: "The Enigma of Bobby Bittman," MAX, 1988.
* Emmies: 1983.

LEWIS, AL
Comic actor who played Off. Leo Schnauzer on "Car 54, Where Are You?" and Grandpa on "The Munsters."
AS A REGULAR: "Car 54, Where Are You?," NBC, 1961-63; "The Munsters," CBS, 1964-66.
AND: "U.S. Steel Hour: Trouble-in-Law," CBS, 1959; "Naked City: The Pedigree Sheet," ABC, 1960; "Gomer Pyle, USMC: Hit and Write," CBS, 1969; "Green Acres: Star Witness," CBS, 1971; "Here's Lucy: Lucy Plays Cops and Robbers," CBS, 1973; "Love, American Style: Love and the Love Nest," ABC, 1973; "Taxi: On the Job," ABC, 1981; "Best of the West: They're Hanging Parker Tillman," ABC, 1981.
* Lewis now runs a restaurant in New York City called "Grandpa's"; he's also been a high school basketball scout and he holds a Ph.D in child psychology from Columbia University.

LEWIS, EMMANUEL
b. Brooklyn, NY, March 9, 1971. Tiny black comic actor who played elementary schooler Webster Papadopalous until he was—that's right—17 years old.
AS A REGULAR: "Webster," ABC, 1983-87; SYN, 1987-88.
AND: "The Love Boat: Only the Good Die Young," ABC, 1984.

LEWIS, GEOFFREY
b. Plainfield, NJ, July 31, 1935. Weatherbeaten actor usually in low-key good-guy roles.
AS A REGULAR: "Flo," CBS, 1980-81; "Gun Shy," CBS, 1983.
AND: "Mannix: Days Beyond Recall," CBS, 1971; "Alias Smith and Jones: The Bounty Hunter," ABC, 1971; "Alias Smith and Jones: What Happened at the XST?," ABC, 1972; "Gunsmoke: Hostage," CBS, 1972; "Barnaby Jones: Murder-Go-Round," CBS, 1973; "Police Woman: Sidewinder," NBC, 1975; "SWAT: The Killing Ground," ABC, 1975; "Starsky and Hutch: The Fix," ABC, 1975; "Police Woman: Farewell, Mary Jane," NBC, 1975; "The Streets of San Francisco: School of Fear," ABC, 1975; "Police Woman: The Death of a Dream," NBC, 1976; "Little House on the Prairie: The Bully Boys," NBC, 1976; "Bert D'Angelo/Superstar: Cops Who Sleep Together," ABC, 1976; "City of Angels: The Bloodshot Eye," NBC, 1976; "The Rookies: Journey to Oblivion," ABC, 1976; "McCloud: Bonnie and McCloud," NBC, 1976; "Alice: A Call to Arms," CBS, 1976; "Laverne & Shirley: Honeymoon Hotel," ABC, 1977; "Lou

Grant: Hen-House," CBS, 1977; "Quark: The Good, the Bad and the Ficus," NBC, 1978; "A Man Called Sloane: Tuned for Destruction," NBC, 1979; "B.J. and the Bear: B.J.'s Sweethearts," NBC, 1979; "Lou Grant: Dogs," CBS, 1980; "Little House: A New Beginning: Older Brothers," NBC, 1983; "The Yellow Rose: Villa's Gold," NBC, 1984; "Magnum P.I.: The Return of Luther Gillis," CBS, 1984; "Scarecrow and Mrs. King: Utopia Now," CBS, 1985; "Amazing Stories: One for the Road," NBC, 1986; "Easy Street: The Check Is in the Mail," NBC, 1987; "Murder, She Wrote: No Accounting for Murder," CBS, 1987; "Murder, She Wrote: Who Threw the Barbitals in Mrs. Fletcher's Chowder?," CBS, 1987; "Webster: The Wild, Wild Webst," SYN, 1988; "Paradise: The Burial Ground," CBS, 1989.

TV MOVIES AND MINISERIES: "Moon of the Wolf," ABC, 1972; "Honky Tonk," NBC, 1974; "The Great Ice Rip-Off," ABC, 1974; "Attack on Terror: The FBI Versus the Ku Klux Klan," CBS, 1975; "The New Daughters of Joshua Cabe," ABC, 1976; "Centennial," NBC, 1978-79; "The Jericho Mile," ABC, 1979; "Samurai," ABC, 1979; "Salem's Lot," CBS, 1979; "Belle Starr," CBS, 1980; "The Shadow Riders," CBS, 1982; "Life of the Party: The Story of Beatrice," CBS, 1982; "Return of the Man From UNCLE," CBS, 1983; "Travis McGee," ABC, 1983; "September Gun," CBS, 1983; "Stormin' Home," CBS, 1985; "Dallas: The Early Years," CBS, 1986; "The Annihilator," NBC, 1986.

LEWIS, GEORGE J.

b. Mexico, December 10, 1903. Actor who played Don Alejandro on "Zorro."

AS A REGULAR: "Zorro," ABC, 1957-59.

AND: "The Life and Legend of Wyatt Earp: Bat Masterson Wins His Star," ABC, 1957; "Broken Arrow: The Broken Wire," ABC, 1957; "77 Sunset Strip: Return to San Dede—Capital City," ABC, 1960; "Walt Disney Presents: El Bandido," ABC, 1960; "77 Sunset Strip: Trouble in the Middle East," ABC, 1960; "Daniel Boone: Tekawitha McLeod," NBC, 1964.

LEWIS, JERRY

b. Joseph Levitch, Newark, NJ, March 16, 1926. Frantic comic whose style is a matter of personal taste; he left a partnership with Dean Martin in 1956, had a succesful solo movie career, one flop TV variety show and one moderately successful one, and now channels almost all his energies toward his annual telethon.

AS A REGULAR: "The Colgate Comedy Hour," NBC, 1950-55; "The Jerry Lewis Show," ABC, 1963; NBC, 1967-69; "Jerry Lewis Telethon for Muscular Dystrophy," SYN, 1963- ; "Will the Real Jerry Lewis Please Sit Down?," ABC, 1970-72.

AND: "Toast of the Town," CBS, 1948; "Jerry Lewis Special," NBC, 1957; "The Steve Allen Show," NBC, 1957; "Youth Wants to Know," NBC, 1957; "Arthur Murray Party," NBC, 1957; "Jerry Lewis Show," NBC, 1958; "Person to Person," CBS, 1958; "The Eddie Fisher Show," NBC, 1958; "The Jack Paar Show," NBC, 1958; "Startime: The Jazz Singer," NBC, 1959; "Louis Jourdan Presents The Timex Show," NBC, 1959; "Jerry Lewis Special," NBC, 1960; "The Jack Paar Show," NBC, 1960; "Here's Hollywood," NBC, 1960; "The Ed Sullivan Show," CBS, 1960; "The Ed Sullivan Show," CBS, 1961; "The Garry Moore Show," CBS, 1961; "I've Got a Secret," CBS, 1961; "High Hopes," SYN, 1961; "Stump the Stars," CBS, 1962; "The Joey Bishop Show: Joey Goes to CBS," CBS, 1964; "Ben Casey: A Little Fun to Match the Sorrow," ABC, 1965; "Hullabaloo," NBC, 1965; "The Tonight Show Starring Johnny Carson," NBC, 1965; "Batman: The Bookworm Turns/While Gotham City Burns," ABC, 1966; "The Tonight Show Starring Johnny Carson," NBC, 1968; "The David Frost Show," SYN, 1970; "Red," NBC, 1970; "The Tonight Show Starring Johnny Carson," NBC, 1973; "The Dick Cavett Show," ABC, 1973; "NBC Follies," NBC, 1973; "Dinah!," SYN, 1975; "Oral Roberts' Christmas Is Love," SYN, 1975; "The Mike Douglas Show," SYN, 1977; "Saturday Night Live," NBC, 1983; "HBO Comedy Hour: An Evening with Sammy Davis Jr. and Jerry Lewis," HBO, 1989.

TV MOVIES AND MINISERIES: "Fight for Life," ABC, 1987.

* Lewis and Dean Martin were a comedy team from 1946-56. They've reunited twice—once in 1976, when Martin made a surprise appearance on Lewis' telethon and again in 1989, when Martin was doing a Las Vegas show on his 72nd birthday and Lewis wheeled in a big cake. "Why we broke up, I'll never know," Lewis said. "I love you, and I mean it," Martin said.
* See also Ernie Kovacs.

LEWIS, JERRY LEE

b. Ferriday, LA, September 29, 1935. Outrageous rock 'n' roller of the fifties and beyond.

AS A GUEST: "The Steve Allen Show," NBC, 1957; "The Big Beat," ABC, 1957; "American Bandstand," ABC, 1957; "The Big Record," CBS, 1958; "American Bandstand," ABC, 1958; "The Dick Clark Saturday Night Beechnut Show," ABC, 1958; "American Bandstand," ABC, 1964; "Shindig," ABC, 1965; "The Monkees Special," NBC, 1969; "The David Frost Show," SYN, 1970; "Police Story: Collision Course," NBC, 1973; "In Concert," ABC, 1974.

* The film "Great Balls of Fire" was about

Lewis' early career; in the film, Steve Allen played himself.

LEWIS, ROBERT Q.

b. New York City, NY, April 5, 1921. Bespectacled emcee and game-show contestant; former radio announcer.

AS A REGULAR: "The Show Goes On," CBS, 1950-52; "The Robert Q. Lewis Show," CBS, 1950-51; "The Name's the Same," ABC, 1951-54; "Masquerade Party," CBS, 1958; "Make Me Laugh," ABC, 1958; "Play Your Hunch," CBS, 1958-59; "Get the Message," ABC, 1964.
AND: "Studio One: A Christmas Surprise," CBS, 1956; "Hidden Treasure," SYN, 1957; "What's My Line?," CBS, 1957; Christophers: Education and American Heritage," SYN, 1959; "The Gale Storm Show: Susannah's True Confession," CBS, 1958; "The Price Is Right," NBC, 1960; "Arthur Murray Party," NBC, 1960; "Number Please," ABC, 1961; "The Hathaways: TV or Not TV," ABC, 1961; "Room for One More: The Right Wrong Number," ABC, 1962; "Play Your Hunch," NBC, 1962; "To Tell the Truth," CBS, 1962; "What's My Line?," CBS, 1963; "Missing Links," NBC, 1964; "Password," CBS, 1964; "The Patty Duke Show: The Tycoons," ABC, 1964; "The Match Game," NBC, 1964; "To Tell the Truth," CBS, 1964; "Grindl: It's in the Bag," NBC, 1964; "To Tell the Truth," CBS, 1965; "Camp Runamuck: Turtle???," NBC, 1965; "Bob Hope Chrysler Theatre: The Highest Fall of All," NBC, 1965; "Bewitched: Nobody's Perfect," ABC, 1966; "To Tell the Truth," CBS, 1967; "Bewitched: The Mother-in-Law of the Year," ABC, 1970; "Love, American Style: Love and the Unhappy Couple," ABC, 1971; "Cross Wits," SYN, 1976.

LEWIS, SHARI

b. Shari Hurwitz, New York City, NY, January 17, 1934. Petite, talented ventriloquist who had a Saturday morning network show for a time.
AS A REGULAR: "The Shari Lewis Show," NBC, 1960-63.
AND: "The Steve Allen Show," NBC, 1958; "Steve Allen Presents: The Steve Lawrence-Eydie Gorme Show," NBC, 1958; "Patti Page Olds Show," ABC, 1958; "Arthur Murray Party," NBC, 1958; "Patti Page Olds Show," ABC, 1959; "Arthur Murray Party," NBC, 1959; "Your Hit Parade," CBS, 1959; "Pat Boone Chevy Showroom," ABC, 1959; "The Garry Moore Show," CBS, 1959; "The Chevy Show," NBC, 1959; "The Andy Williams Show," CBS, 1959; "Person to Person," CBS, 1959; "Perry Como's Kraft Music Hall," NBC, 1959; "Arthur Murray Party," NBC, 1960; "The Chevy Show," NBC, 1960; "The Ford Show," NBC, 1960; "Keep Talking," ABC, 1960; "The Ed Sullivan Show," CBS, 1960; "The Jack

Paar Show," NBC, 1960; "Christmas in September," SYN, 1960; "U.S. Steel Hour: Step on the Gas," CBS, 1960; "The Ford Show," NBC, 1961; "The Ed Sullivan Show," CBS, 1961; "U.S. Steel Hour: Watching Out for Dulie," CBS, 1961; "Car 54, Where Are You?: How High Is Up?," NBC, 1962; "The Jack Benny Program: Shari Lewis Show," CBS, 1962; "Play Your Hunch," NBC, 1962; "Car 54, Where Are You?: Puncher and Judy," NBC, 1963; "Missing Links," NBC, 1963; "The Match Game," NBC, 1963; "Missing Links," NBC, 1964; "The Danny Kaye Show," CBS, 1964; "The Ed Sullivan Show," CBS, 1965; "To Tell the Truth," CBS, 1965; "The Dean Martin Show," NBC, 1965; "You Don't Say," NBC, 1965; "The Man From UNCLE: The Off-Broadway Affair," NBC, 1966; "Hollywood Palace," ABC, 1968; "The Tonight Show Starring Johnny Carson," NBC, 1968; "Snap Judgment," NBC, 1969; "Love, American Style: Love and the Dummies," ABC, 1971; "Love, American Style: Love and the Alibi," ABC, 1972; "Baffle," NBC, 1973; "Rhyme and Reason," ABC, 1975; "Dummies," HBO, 1981.

LEYDEN, BILL

b. Chicago, IL. Emcee.
AS A REGULAR: "Musical Chairs," NBC, 1955; "It Could Be You," NBC, 1956-61; "Your First Impression," NBC, 1962-64; "Call My Bluff," NBC, 1965; "You're Putting Me On," NBC, 1969.
AND: "Arthur Murray Party," NBC, 1959; "Here's Hollywood," NBC, 1960.

LIBERACE

b. Wladziu Valentino Liberace, West Allis, WI, 1919; d. 1987. Pianist and entertainer with a glitzy, flamboyant style—and wardrobe to match—that made for entertaining television.
AS A REGULAR: "The Liberace Show," NBC, 1952; SYN, 1953-55; ABC, 1958-59; CBS, 1969; "Liberace," SYN, 1960.
AND: "Shower of Stars," CBS, 1957; "The Perry Como Show," NBC, 1957; "The Steve Allen Show," NBC, 1957; "The Big Record," CBS, 1957; "Art Linkletter's House Party,"CBS, 1958; "The Big Record," CBS, 1958; "The Red Skelton Show," CBS, 1958; "The Steve Allen Show," NBC, 1959; "The Ford Show," NBC, 1959; "Celebrity Talent Scouts," CBS, 1960; "I've Got a Secret," CBS, 1961; "Variety Gardens," CBS, 1962; "The Ed Sullivan Show," CBS, 1962; "Dinah Shore Special," NBC, 1963; "Art Linkletter's House Party," CBS, 1963; "The Red Skelton Hour," CBS, 1964; "Hollywood Palace," ABC, 1964; "The Andy Williams Show," NBC, 1964; "Hollywood Palace," ABC, 1965; "Batman: The Devil's Fingers/The Dead Ringers," ABC, 1966; "Hollywood Palace," ABC, 1967; "The

Jackie Gleason Show," CBS, 1967; "Kraft Music Hall," NBC, 1967; "The Dean Martin Show," NBC, 1968; "Here's Lucy: Lucy and Liberace," CBS, 1970; "The Tonight Show Starring Johnny Carson," NBC, 1975; "Kojak: Sixty Miles to Hell," CBS, 1978; "The Mike Douglas Show," SYN, 1980; "Liberace in Las Vegas," PBS, 1986; "Leo & Liz in Beverly Hills: Premiere," CBS, 1986.

LIBERTINI, RICHARD
b. Cambridge, MA. Tall, bearded actor usually in comic roles.
AS A REGULAR: "Story Theatre," SYN, 1971-72; "The Melba Moore-Clifton Davis Show," CBS, 1972; "Soap," ABC, 1977-78; "Family Man," ABC, 1988; "The Fanelli Boys," NBC, 1990- .
AND: "The Mary Tyler Moore Show: The Forty-Five-Year Old Man," CBS, 1971; "The Bob Newhart Show: Halls of Hartley," CBS, 1977; "Good Times: Love Has a Spot on Its Lung," CBS, 1977; "The Bob Newhart Show: Shallow Throat," CBS, 1977; "CPO Sharkey: Fear of Flying," NBC, 1978; "Alice: Florence of Arabia," CBS, 1978; "Barney Miller: Evaluation," ABC, 1978; "Barney Miller: Middle Age," ABC, 1979; "Barney Miller: The Child Stealers," ABC, 1980; "Captain Kangaroo," CBS, 1981; "Mork & Mindy: Twelve Angry Appliances," ABC, 1981; "The Twilight Zone: Saucer of Loneliness," CBS, 1986; "Moonlighting: It's a Wonderful Job," ABC, 1986.
TV MOVIES AND MINISERIES: "American Playhouse: The Trial of Bernhard Goetz," PBS, 1988; "Fair Game," NBC, 1989.

LICHT, JEREMY
b. Los Angeles, CA, January 4, 1971. Young actor who plays Mark on "The Hogan Family."
AS A REGULAR: "Valerie," NBC, 1986-87; "Valerie's Family," NBC, 1987-88; "The Hogan Family," NBC, 1988-90; CBS, 1990- .
AND: "St. Elsewhere: Samuels and the Kid," NBC, 1982; "Hotel: Deceptions," ABC, 1983; "Jessie: Pilot," NBC, 1984; "Totally Hidden Video," FOX, 1989.
TV MOVIES AND MINISERIES: "And Your Name Is Jonah," CBS, 1979; "Father Figure," CBS, 1980; "Lois Gibbs and the Love Canal," CBS, 1982.

LIGHT, JUDITH
b. Trenton, NJ, February 9, 1949. Emmy-winning actress who played Karen Wolek on "One Life to Live" and then made the jump to prime-time as Angela Bower on "Who's the Boss?"
AS A REGULAR: "One Live to Live," ABC, 1977-83; "Who's the Boss?," ABC, 1984- .
AND: "Kojak: Monkey on a Sting," CBS, 1977;

"St. Elsewhere: Dog Day Hospital," NBC, 1983; "Family Ties: Not an Affair to Remember," NBC, 1983; "Remington Steele: Dreams of Steele," NBC, 1984; "The Tonight Show Starring Johnny Carson," NBC, 1989.
TV MOVIES AND MINISERIES: "Intimate Agony," ABC, 1983; "Dangerous Affection," NBC, 1987; "The Ryan White Story," ABC, 1989; "My Boyfriend's Back," NBC, 1989.
* Emmies: 1980, 1981.

LIME, YVONNE
b. Glendale, CA, April 7, 1938. Young actress who played Dotty Snow, pal of Betty Anderson (Elinor Donahue) on "Father Knows Best."
AS A REGULAR: "Father Knows Best," CBS, 1954-55; NBC, 1955-57; "The Many Loves of Dobie Gillis," CBS, 1959-60; "Happy," NBC, 1960; 1961; "Bringing Up Buddy," CBS, 1960-61.
AND: "The Adventures of Ozzie and Harriet: Gentleman Dave," ABC, 1958; "West Point: Blind Date," ABC, 1958; "The George Burns and Gracie Allen Show: Grammar School Dance," CBS, 1958; "This Is the Life: Rebellion," SYN, 1959; "Wichita Town: Biggest Man in Town," NBC, 1959; "Father Knows Best: Betty Makes a Choice," CBS, 1960; "Bat Masterson: The Snare," NBC, 1960; "The Adventures of Ozzie and Harriet: The Uninvited Guests," ABC, 1960; "The Adventures of Ozzie and Harriet: The Professor's Experiment," ABC, 1960; "Here's Hollywood," NBC, 1961; "The Joey Bishop Show: The Baby Nurse," NBC, 1963; "Gomer Pyle, USMC: Captain Ironpants " CBS, 1964; "Gomer Pyle, USMC: Sergeant Carter's Farewell to His Troops," CBS, 1965; "The Andy Griffith Show: The Taylors in Hollywood," CBS, 1965; "Gomer Pyle, USMC: And Baby Makes Three," CBS, 1968; "My Three Sons: The Grandfathers," CBS, 1968; "Dragnet: Management Services," NBC, 1968.

LINDEN, HAL
b. Harold Lipschitz, New York City, NY, March 20, 1931. Former singer with the Sammy Kaye band who played police Capt. Barney Miller; he won Emmies for the informational "FYI" series.
AS A REGULAR: "Search for Tomorrow," CBS, 1969; "Barney Miller," ABC, 1975-82; "FYI," ABC, 1982-84; "Blacke's Magic," NBC, 1986.
AND: "Ruggles of Red Gap," NBC, 1956; "Car 54, Where Are You?: Benny the Bookie's Last Chance," NBC, 1963; "Saga of the Western World," ABC, 1963; "The Shameful Secrets of Hastings Corners," NBC, 1970; "Ghost Story: Elegy for a Vampire," NBC, 1972; "The FBI: The Confession," ABC, 1973; "Password All-Stars," ABC, 1975; "Cher," CBS, 1975; "Lola Falana Special," ABC, 1975; "Tattletales," CBS, 1976;

"Hollywood Squares," SYN, 1980; "Hal Linden's Big Apple," ABC, 1980; "The John Davidson Show," SYN, 1981; "Something Spectacular with Steve Allen," PBS, 1981; "Bob Hope Lampoons Television 1985," NBC, 1985; "Great Performances: An Evening with Alan Jay Lerner," PBS, 1989.

TV MOVIES AND MINISERIES: "Mr. Inside/Mr. Outside," NBC, 1973; "The Love Boat," ABC, 1976; "How to Break Up a Happy Divorce," NBC, 1976; "Father Figure," CBS, 1980; "Starflight: The Plane That Couldn't Land," ABC, 1983; "The Other Woman," CBS, 1983; "My Wicked, Wicked Ways: The Legend of Errol Flynn," CBS, 1985; "Dream Breakers," CBS, 1989.

AS A DIRECTOR: "Barney Miller: Corporation," ABC, 1977; "Barney Miller: Hostage," ABC, 1978.

* Emmies: 1983, 1984.

LINDFORS, VIVECA

b. Elsa Viveca Torstensdotter Lindfors, Sweden, December 29, 1920. Actress of stage, screen and TV; an Emmy winner for her role as a dancing teacher on "Life Goes On."

AS A REGULAR: "All My Children," ABC, 1983.

AND: "Ford Theatre: The Bet," NBC, 1953; "Lux Video Theatre: Autumn Nocturne," CBS, 1953; "Suspense: The Riddle of Mayerling," CBS, 1953; "Playhouse 90: Rendezvous in Black," CBS, 1956; "Alcoa Hour: Adventure in Diamonds," NBC, 1956; "U.S. Steel Hour: They Never Forget," CBS, 1957; "Climax!: The Long Count," CBS, 1957; "The Loretta Young Show: Louise," NBC, 1957; "Playhouse 90: The Last Tycoon," CBS, 1957; "Climax!: The Largest City in Captivity," CBS, 1957; "Five Fingers: Temple of the Swinging Doll," NBC, 1959; "Rawhide: Incident of the Day of the Dead," CBS, 1959; "Adventures in Paradise: Castaways," ABC, 1960; "Naked City: The Deadly Guinea Pig," ABC, 1961; "The Untouchables: Ring of Terror," ABC, 1961; "Play of the Week: The Emporer's Clothes," SYN, 1961; "The Defenders: The Locked Room," CBS, 1962; "Theatre '62: The Paradine Case," NBC, 1962; "The Nurses: Night Shift," CBS, 1962; "Twelve O'Clock High: The Climate of Doubt," ABC, 1964; "The Defenders: Comeback," CBS, 1964; "Voyage to the Bottom of the Sea: Hail to the Chief," ABC, 1964; "Ben Casey: A Dipperful of Water From a Poisoned Well," ABC, 1965; "Bonanza: Angela," NBC, 1965; "Ben Casey: Where Did All the Roses Go?," ABC, 1966; "Coronet Blue: The Presence of Evil," CBS, 1967; "The FBI: A Sleeper Wakes," ABC, 1967; "The Diary of Anne Frank," ABC, 1967; "Medical Center: The Fallen Image," CBS, 1969; "The FBI: The Doll Courier," ABC, 1969; "The Interns: The Fever," CBS, 1970; "Glitter: On Your Toes," ABC, 1984; "Hotel:

Missing Pieces," ABC, 1985; "CBS Schoolbreak Special: A Matter of Conscience," CBS, 1989; "Life Goes On: Save the Last Dance for Me," ABC, 1990.

TV MOVIES AND MINISERIES: "The Best Little Girl in the World," ABC, 1981; "Divorce Wars: A Love Story," ABC, 1982; "Playing for Time," CBS, 1980; "Passions," CBS, 1984; "A Doctor's Story," NBC, 1984; "Secret Weapons," NBC, 1985; "The Ann Jillian Story," NBC, 1988.

* Emmies: 1990.

LINDLEY, AUDRA

b. Los Angeles, CA. Stage-trained actress who played Helen Roper, wisecracking sex-starved wife of Stanley (Norman Fell) on "Three's Company" and a spinoff sitcom.

AS A REGULAR: "Search for Tomorrow," CBS, 1962; "Another World," NBC, 1964-69; "Bridget Loves Bernie," CBS, 1972-73; "Fay," NBC, 1975-76; "Doc," CBS, 1976; "Three's Company," ABC, 1977-79; "The Ropers," ABC, 1979-80.

AND: "Kraft Television Theatre: Shadow of Suspicion," NBC, 1956; "U.S. Steel Hour: Victim," CBS, 1957; "Modern Romances: The Accursed," NBC, 1957; "Kraft Theatre: Angry Angel," NBC, 1958; "An American Girl," NBC, 1958; "Armstrong Circle Theatre: Legend of Murder: The Untold Story of Lizzie Borden," CBS, 1961; "Maude: Then There Were None," CBS, 1975; "Chico and the Man: The Beard," NBC, 1975; "Barnaby Jones: Image of Evil," CBS, 1975; "The Love Boat: Gotcha!," ABC, 1977; "The Love Boat: Marooned," ABC, 1978; "The Love Boat: The Wedding," ABC, 1979.

TV MOVIES AND MINISERIES: "Pearl," ABC, 1978; "The Revenge of the Stepford Wives," NBC, 1980; "Dangerous Affection," NBC, 1987; "Perry Mason: The Case of the Lady in the Lake," NBC, 1988; "Take My Daughters, Please," NBC, 1988; "Bridesmaids," CBS, 1989.

LINDSAY, MARK

b. Eugene, OR, March 9, 1944. Pop singer who was leader of Paul Revere and the Raiders.

AS A REGULAR: "Where the Action Is," ABC, 1965-66; "Make Your Own Kind of Music," NBC, 1971; "Rock 'n' Roll Summer Action," ABC, 1985.

AND: "Hullabaloo," NBC, 1965; "Batman: Hizzoner the Penguin/Dizzoner the Penguin," ABC, 1966.

LINDSEY, GEORGE

b. Jasper, AL. Actor who played Goober Pyle on "The Andy Griffith Show" and "Mayberry RFD," now a regular on "Hee Haw."

AS A REGULAR: "The Andy Griffith Show," CBS, 1963-68; "Mayberry RFD," CBS, 1968-71; "Hee Haw," SYN, 1972- .
AND: "The Real McCoys: The McCoy Sound," CBS, 1963; "The Twilight Zone: I Am the Night-Color Me Black," CBS, 1964; "Daniel Boone: Pilot," NBC, 1964; "The Alfred Hitchcock Hour: The Return of Verge Likens," NBC, 1964; "The Joey Bishop Show: Joey and Larry Split," CBS, 1964; "Gomer Pyle, USMC: A Visit From Cousin Goober," CBS, 1965; "Gunsmoke: Mad Dog," CBS, 1967; "The Jonathan Winters Show," CBS, 1969; "The Steve Allen Show," SYN, 1969; "Love, American Style: Love and the Modern Wife," ABC, 1969; "The Johnny Cash Show," ABC, 1970; "Love, American Style: Love and the Duel," ABC, 1971; "Gunsmoke: Blindman's Buff," CBS, 1972; "M*A*S*H: Temporary Duty," CBS, 1978.
TV MOVIES AND MINISERIES: "Return to Mayberry," NBC, 1986.

LINK, MICHAEL
b. Provo, UT, June 12, 1962. Child actor who played Earl J. Waggedorn on "Julia."
AS A REGULAR: "Julia," NBC, 1968-71.
AND: "Hollywood Palace," ABC, 1968; "The Courtship of Eddie's Father: Time for a Change," ABC, 1972; "Three for the Road: The Albatross," CBS, 1975.
TV MOVIES AND MINISERIES: "Stowaway to the Moon," CBS, 1975.

LINKER, AMY
b. Brooklyn, NY, October 19, 1966. Actress who played teenager Lauren Hutchinson, best friend of Patty Greene (Sarah Jessica Parker) on "Square Pegs."
AS A REGULAR: "Square Pegs," CBS, 1982-83.
AND: "Fantasy Island: Saturday's Child," ABC, 1983; "E/R: All's Well That Ends," CBS, 1984.

LINKLETTER, ART
b. Moose Jaw, Sasketchewan, Canada, July 17, 1912. Jolly TV personality who was a staple on the tube for almost twenty years.
AS A REGULAR: "Art Linkletter's House Party," CBS, 1952-69; "People Are Funny," NBC, 1954-61; "Haggis Baggis," NBC, 1958-59; "The Art Linkletter Show," NBC, 1963; "Art Linkletter's Hollywood Talent Scouts," CBS, 1965-66.
AND: "Saturday Spectacular: Sonia Henie's Holiday on Ice," NBC, 1956; "G.E. Theatre: The Big Shooter," CBS, 1957; "Person to Person," CBS, 1957; "G.E. Theatre: Kid at the Stick," CBS, 1958; "I've Got a Secret," CBS, 1958; "The Perry Como Show," NBC, 1958; "G.E. Theatre: The Odd Ball," CBS, 1958; "The Bob Cummings Show: Bob vs. Linkletter," NBC, 1959;

"Disneyland '59," ABC, 1959; "America Pauses in September," NBC, 1959; "Startime: Art Linkletter's Secret World of Kids," NBC, 1959; "The Jack Paar Show," NBC, 1960; "On the Go," CBS, 1960; "The Chevy Show: Love Is Funny," NBC, 1960; "Something Special," NBC, 1960; "Here's Hollywood," NBC, 1961; "Dick Powell's Zane Grey Theatre: The Bible Man," CBS, 1961; "What's My Line?," CBS, 1961; "The Chevy Show: Kids Are Funny," NBC, 1961; "I've Got a Secret," CBS, 1961; "High Hopes," SYN, 1961; "Here's Hollywood," NBC, 1961; "Perry Como's Kraft Music Hall," NBC, 1962; "G.E. Theatre: Badge of Honor," CBS, 1962; "The Danny Thomas Show: A Promise Is a Promise," CBS, 1962; "Wagon Train: The Sam Darland Story," ABC, 1962; "The Tonight Show," NBC, 1962; "Stump the Stars," CBS, 1962; "What's My Line?," CBS, 1962; "The Lucy Show: Lucy and Art Linkletter," CBS, 1966; "Batman: Catwoman Goes to College/Batman Displays His Knowledge," ABC, 1967; "The Tonight Show Starring Johnny Carson," NBC, 1968; "Hollywood Squares," NBC, 1968; "It Takes Two," NBC, 1970; "Here's Lucy: Lucy and Art Linkletter," CBS, 1970; "The Virginia Graham Show," SYN, 1972.
* See also John Frankenheimer.

LINKLETTER, JACK
b. San Francisco, CA, November 20, 1937. Son of Art.
AS A REGULAR: "Art Linkletter's House Party," CBS, 1957-63; "Haggis Baggis," NBC, 1958-59; "On the Go," CBS, 1959-60; "Here's Hollywood," NBC, 1960-62; "Hootenanny," ABC, 1963-64; "The Rebus Game, ABC, 1965.
AND: "Dick Powell's Zane Grey Theatre: The Bible Man," CBS, 1961; "Art Linkletter's House Party," CBS, 1964.

LINN-BAKER, MARK
b. St. Louis, MO, June 17, 1953. Comic actor who plays Larry on "Perfect Strangers."
AS A REGULAR: "Comedy Zone," CBS, 1984; "Perfect Strangers," ABC, 1986- .
AND: "American Playhouse: The Ghost Writer," PBS, 1985; "The Equalizer: Bump and Run," CBS, 1986; "The Hogan Family: Stan and Deliver," NBC, 1989; "The Arsenio Hall Show," SYN, 1989.

LINVILLE, LARRY
b. Ojai, CA, September 29, 1939. Actor who played Maj. Frank Burns on "M*A*S*H"; he left the show early to avoid typecasting as weasels, but it was too late.
AS A REGULAR: "Mannix," CBS, 1968-69; "M*A*S*H," CBS, 1972-77; "Grandpa Goes to Washington," NBC, 1978-79; "Checking

In," CBS, 1981; "Herbie, The Love Bug," CBS, 1982; "Paper Dolls," ABC, 1984.
AND: "The Outsider: The Secret of Mareno Bay," NBC, 1969; "Mission: Impossible: The Glass Cage," CBS, 1969; "Room 222: Arizona State Loves You," ABC, 1969; "The FBI: Flight," ABC, 1969; "Mission: Impossible: Submarine," CBS, 1969; "Gunsmoke: The Cage," CBS, 1969; "Mannix: Who Is Sylvia?," CBS, 1970; "Mission: Impossible: The Innocent," CBS, 1970; "The Young Rebels: Ring of Freedom," ABC, 1970; "The Young Lawyers: Remember Chris Gately," ABC, 1970; "The FBI: The Inheritors," ABC, 1970; "Marcus Welby, M.D.: The White Cane," ABC, 1970; "Mission: Impossible: Robot," CBS, 1970; "Mannix: Bang, Bang, You're Dead," CBS, 1971; "Marcus Welby, M.D.: Once There Was a Bantu Prince," ABC, 1972; "Kolchak, the Night Stalker: Chopper," ABC, 1975; "The Rockford Files: The Deadly Maze," NBC, 1977; "Hollywood Squares," NBC, 1978; "CHiPS: Roller Disco," NBC, 1979; "Barnaby Jones: Deadly Sanctuary," CBS, 1979; "The Love Boat: The Love Lamp Is Lit," ABC, 1979; "Lou Grant: Sting," CBS, 1980; "The Love Boat: First Voyage, Last Voyage," ABC, 1981; "Murder, She Wrote: Murder Takes the Bus," CBS, 1985; "Misfits of Science: Pilot," NBC, 1985; "Murder, She Wrote: Curse of the Daanav," CBS, 1987.
TV MOVIES AND MINISERIES: "Marcus Welby, M.D.," ABC, 1969; "Vanished," NBC, 1971; "The Night Stalker," ABC, 1972; "Night Partners," CBS, 1983.

LIPTON, PEGGY
b. Lawrence, NY, 1948. Actress who played Julie Barnes on "The Mod Squad"; almost twenty years later, looking much the same, she plays Norma Jennings on "Twin Peaks."
AS A REGULAR: "The John Forsythe Show," NBC, 1965-66; "The Mod Squad," ABC, 1968-73; "Twin Peaks," ABC, 1990- .
AND: "Mr. Novak: And Then I Wrote," NBC, 1965; "The Virginian: The Wolves Up Front, the Jackals Behind," NBC, 1966; "Walt Disney's Wonderful World of Color: Willie and the Yank," NBC, 1967; "The Invaders: Condition: Red," ABC, 1967; "Hollywood Squares," NBC, 1969; "This Is Tom Jones," ABC, 1969.
TV MOVIES AND MINISERIES: "The Return of Mod Squad," ABC, 1979; "Addicted to His Love," ABC, 1988.

LITEL, JOHN
b. Albany, WI, December 30, 1894; d. 1972. Longtime character actor, often in westerns.
AS A REGULAR: "My Hero," NBC, 1952-53; "Stagecoach West," ABC, 1960-61.
AND: "I Love Lucy: Mr. and Mrs. TV Show,"

CBS, 1954; "Kaiser Aluminum Hour: So Short a Season," NBC, 1957; "Du Pont Theatre: One Day at a Time," ABC, 1957; "Maverick: The War of the Silver Kings," ABC, 1957; "Tales of Wells Fargo: Apache Gold," NBC, 1957; "Sugarfoot: Quicksilver," ABC, 1957; "Climax!: Time of the Hanging," CBS, 1958; "Restless Gun: Gratitude," NBC, 1958; "77 Sunset Strip: The Court-Martial of Johnny Murdo," ABC, 1958; "Restless Gun: A Bell for Santo Domingo," NBC, 1958; "Cimarron City: Kid on a Calico Horse," NBC, 1958; "Maverick: The People's Friend," ABC, 1960; "Hawaiian Eye: Stamped for Danger," ABC, 1960; "Wanted Dead or Alive: The Inheritance," CBS, 1960; "Bronco: Winter Kill," ABC, 1960; "G.E. Theatre: The Money Driver," CBS, 1960; "Have Gun, Will Travel: Ben Jalisco," CBS, 1961; "Bonanza: The Tin Badge," NBC, 1961; "Hazel: Hazel Quits," NBC, 1962; "The Virginian: The Judgment," NBC, 1963; "The Virginian: Legend for a Lawman," NBC, 1965; "Branded: The Vindicator," NBC, 1965.

LITTLE, CLEAVON
b. Chickasaw, OK, June 1, 1939. Talented actor with stage training, at home in comedy or drama.
AS A REGULAR: "The David Frost Revue," SYN, 1971-73; "Temperatures Rising," ABC, 1972-74; "Bagdad Cafe," CBS, 1990- .
AND: "All in the Family: Edith Writes a Song," CBS, 1971; "The Mod Squad: The Connection," ABC, 1972; "Police Story: A Community of Victims," NBC, 1975; "The Rookies: Measure of Mercy," ABC, 1975; "The Rockford Files: Sticks and Stones May Break Your Bones, But Waterbury Will Bury You," NBC, 1977; "Supertrain: The Green Girl," NBC, 1979; "The Love Boat: The Matchmaker," ABC, 1980; "American Short Story: The Sky Is Gray," PBS, 1980; "ALF: ALF's Special Christmas," NBC, 1987; "CBS Summer Playhouse: Tickets Please," CBS, 1988; "Dear John: Stand by Your Man," NBC, 1989; "227: For Richer, for Poorer," NBC, 1989.
TV MOVIES AND MINISERIES: "The Homecoming," CBS, 1971; "Money to Burn," ABC, 1973; "The Day the Earth Moved," ABC, 1974.

LITTLE, RICH
b. Ottawa, Canada, November 26, 1938. Impressionist at the peak of his popularity during the seventies.
AS A REGULAR: "Love on a Rooftop," ABC, 1966-67; "The John Davidson Show," ABC, 1969; "ABC Comedy Hour," ABC, 1972; "The Julie Andrews Hour," ABC, 1972-73; "The Rich Little Show," NBC, 1976; "The New You Asked for It," SYN, 1981-82.
AND: "The Judy Garland Show," CBS, 1964; "On

Broadway Tonight," CBS, 1964; "On Broadway Tonight," CBS, 1965; "Hollywood Palace," ABC, 1965; "The Dean Martin Show," NBC, 1965; "The Flying Nun: With a Friend Like Him," ABC, 1967; "Operation: Entertainment," ABC, 1968; "The Tonight Show Starring Johnny Carson," NBC, 1968; "The Joey Bishop Show," ABC, 1968; "This Is Tom Jones," ABC, 1969; "Petticoat Junction: Billie Jo and the Big, Big Star," CBS, 1969; "The Flying Nun: The Breakaway Monk," ABC, 1969; "Love, American Style: Love and the Big Leap," ABC, 1969; "The Beverly Hillbillies: The Pollution Solution," CBS, 1970; "Love, American Style: Love and the Hypnotist," ABC, 1970; "Here's Lucy: Lucy and the Celebrities," CBS, 1971; "Mannix: The Other Game in Town," CBS, 1971; "Love, American Style: Love and the Plane Truth," ABC, 1972; "Hollywood Squares," NBC, 1973; "Love, American Style: Love and the Impressionist," ABC, 1973; "Love, American Style: Love and the Last Joke," ABC, 1974; "Wait Till Your Father Gets Home: Rich Little, Supersleuth," SYN, 1974; "The Perry Como Christmas Show," CBS, 1974; "The Merv Griffin Show," SYN, 1975; "The Mac Davis Show," NBC, 1975; "Doris Day Today," CBS, 1975; "Chico and the Man: The Hallowed Garage," NBC, 1975; "Police Woman: Screams," NBC, 1977; "Hollywood Squares," NBC, 1978; "The Love Boat: Kin Folk," ABC, 1979; "Something Spectacular with Steve Allen," PBS, 1981; "The Love Boat: A Rose Is Not a Rose," ABC, 1984; "ALF: Tonight, Tonight," NBC, 1988; "Murder, She Wrote: Deadpan," CBS, 1988.
* The producers of "Mickey Spillane's Mike Hammer" hired Little to impersonate the show's star, Stacy Keach, while Keach served a jail sentence in England for possessing cocaine. Little did the voice-over narration for several episodes in 1985.

LITTLEFIELD, LUCIEN
b. San Antonio, TX, August 16, 1895; d. 1960. Character actor, usually in comic roles.
AS A REGULAR: "The Abbott and Costello Show," CBS, 1952-54; "Blondie," NBC, 1957.
AND: "Favorite Story: A Tale of Negative Gravity," SYN, 1952; "Ford Theatre: On the Beach," ABC, 1956; "The Life of Riley: Foriegn Intrigue," NBC, 1957; "Ford Theatre: The Gentle Deceiver," ABC, 1957; "Circus Boy: Uncle Cyrus," ABC, 1958.

LIVINGSTON, BARRY
b. Los Angeles, CA, December 17, 1953. Bespectacled child actor who played Ernie Douglas on "My Three Sons"; brother of Stanley Livingston.
AS A REGULAR: "The Adventures of Ozzie and

Harriet," ABC, 1961-62; "My Three Sons," ABC, 1963-65; CBS, 1965-72; "Sons and Daughters," CBS, 1974.
AND: "The Dick Van Dyke Show: The Talented Neighborhood," CBS, 1962; "The Lucy Show: Lucy Gets Locked in the Vault," CBS, 1963; "The Breaking Point: A Land More Cruel," ABC, 1964; "Room 222: Pardon Me, Your Apathy Is Showing," ABC, 1972; "Ironside: The Caller," NBC, 1973; "The Streets of San Francisco: The Runaways," ABC, 1974; "Police Woman: Smack," NBC, 1974; "Simon & Simon: Double Play," CBS, 1984.
TV MOVIES AND MINISERIES: "The Elevator," CBS, 1974; "Senior Year," CBS, 1974.

LIVINGSTON, STANLEY
b. Los Angeles, CA, 1950. Child actor who played Chip Douglas on "My Three Sons."
AS A REGULAR: "The Adventures of Ozzie and Harriet," ABC, 1958-59; "My Three Sons," ABC, 1960-65; CBS, 1965-72.
AND: "Room 222: A Hairy Escape," ABC, 1973.
TV MOVIES AND MINISERIES: "Sarge: The Badge or the Cross," NBC, 1971.

LIVINGSTONE, MARY
b. Sadye Marks, Seattle, WA, 1909; d. 1983. Wife of Jack Benny, who appeared extensively with him on radio and occasionally on TV.
AS A REGULAR: "The Jack Benny Program," CBS, 1950-64.
AND: "The George Burns and Gracie Allen Show: The Plumber's Friend," CBS, 1957; "Shower of Stars: Jack Benny's 40th Birthday Party Celebration," CBS, 1958; "Jack Benny's 20th Anniversary Special," NBC, 1970.

LLOYD, CHRISTOPHER
b. Stamford, CT, October 22, 1938. Lanky comic actor who won two Emmies as the Reverend Jim on "Taxi."
AS A REGULAR: "Taxi," ABC, 1979-82; NBC, 1982-83.
AND: "Barney Miller: The Vandal," ABC, 1978; "Barney Miller: Open House," ABC, 1979; "Freebie and the Bean: Bolo's Lady," CBS, 1980; "Best of the West: The Calico Kid Goes to School," ABC, 1982; "Cheers: I'll Be Seeing You," NBC, 1984; "Street Hawk: Pilot," ABC, 1985; "Amazing Stories: Go to the Head of the Class," NBC, 1986.
TV MOVIES AND MINISERIES: "Stunt Seven," CBS, 1979; "Money on the Side," ABC, 1982; "September Gun," CBS, 1983; "The Cowboy and the Ballerina," CBS, 1984.
* Emmies: 1982, 1983.

LLOYD, NORMAN
b. Jersey City, NJ, November 8, 1914. Actor-

producer who worked behind the scenes with Alfred Hitchcock on his television shows; in front of the camera, he was memorable as the dying Dr. Daniel Auschlander on "St. Elsewhere."

AS A REGULAR: "St. Elsewhere," NBC, 1982-88; "Wiseguy," CBS, 1989-90.

AND: "The 20th Century-Fox Hour: We Must Kill Toni," CBS, 1956; "G.E. Theatre: The Earring," CBS, 1957; "Alfred Hitchcock Presents: Nightmare in 4-D," CBS, 1957; "Alfred Hitchcock Presents: Design for Loving," CBS, 1958; "Alfred Hitchcock Presents: The Little Man Who Was There," CBS, 1960; "Alfred Hitchcock Presents: Maria," NBC, 1961; "Kojak: Night of the Piraeus," CBS, 1975; "The Twilight Zone: The Last Defender of Camelot," CBS, 1986; "Murder, She Wrote: If the Frame Fits," CBS, 1986.

TV MOVIES AND MINISERIES: "The Dark Secret of Harvest Home," NBC, 1978; "Amityville: The Evil Escapes," NBC, 1989.

AS A DIRECTOR: "Companions in Nightmare," NBC, 1968; "The Smugglers," NBC, 1968, "Columbo: Lady in Waiting," NBC, 1971.

AS CO-PRODUCER: "Alfred Hitchcock Presents," CBS, 1955-60; NBC, 1960-62.

* Lloyd played the title role in Alfred Hitchcock's 1942 film "Saboteur."

LO BIANCO, TONY
b. Brooklyn, NY.

AS A REGULAR: "Hidden Faces," NBC, 1968-69; "Love of Life," CBS, 1972-73; "Jessie," ABC, 1984.

AND: "Get Smart: Smart, the Assassin," NBC, 1966; "Hawk: H Is a Dirty Letter," ABC, 1966; "NYPD: Cry Brute," ABC, 1968; "NYPD: Stones," ABC, 1968; "NET Playhouse: A Memory of Two Mondays," NET, 1971; "Madigan: The Manhattan Beat," NBC, 1972; "Police Story: Requiem for an Informer," NBC, 1973; "Police Story: The Hunters," NBC, 1974; "Police Story: Glamour Boy," NBC, 1974; "The Streets of San Francisco: Solitaire," ABC, 1974; "Police Story: Explosion!," NBC, 1974; "Police Story: Sniper," NBC, 1975; "Police Story: Firebird," NBC, 1976; "The Twilight Zone: If She Dies," CBS, 1985; "CBS Summer Playhouse: Off Duty," CBS, 1988.

TV MOVIES AND MINISERIES: "Mr. Inside/Mr. Outside," NBC, 1973; "The Story of Jacob and Joseph," NBC, 1974; "Shadow in the Street," NBC, 1975; "Jesus of Nazareth," NBC, 1977; "Marciano," ABC, 1979; "Another Woman's Child," CBS, 1983; "Lady Blue," ABC, 1985; "Welcome Home Bobby," CBS, 1986; "Police Story: The Freeway Killings," NBC, 1987; "The Ann Jillian Story," NBC, 1988; "Body of Evidence," CBS, 1988; "True Blue," NBC, 1989.

LOCANE, AMY
b. Trenton, NJ, December 19, 1971.

AS A REGULAR: "Spencer," NBC, 1984-85.

AND: "Hothouse: Nancy," ABC, 1988.

LOCKHART, GENE
b. London, Ontario, Canada, July 18, 1891; d. 1957. Roly-poly character actor with a long career in films and TV; father of June Lockhart.

AS A REGULAR: "His Honor, Homer Bell," SYN, 1955.

AND: "Lights Out: Dr. Heidegger's Experiment," NBC, 1950; "Prudential Family Playhouse: The Barretts of Wimpole Street," CBS, 1950; "Nash Airfylte Theatre: The Windfall," CBS, 1950; "Lux Video Theatre: A Child Is Born," CBS, 1950; "Robert Montgomery Presents: The House of Seven Gables," NBC, 1951; "Tales of Tomorrow: The Golden Ingot," ABC, 1952; "Lux Video Theatre: Ile," CBS, 1952; "Broadway Television Theatre: The Bishop Misbehaves," SYN, 1952; "Gulf Playhouse: The Rose," NBC, 1952; "Robert Montgomery Presents: The Biarritz Scandal," NBC, 1952; "Gulf Playhouse: An Afternoon in Caribou," NBC, 1952; "Lux Video Theatre: Fear," NBC, 1952; "Robert Montgomery Presents: The Burtons," NBC, 1953; "Ford Theatre: My Daughter's Husband," NBC, 1953; "Danger: But the Patient Died," CBS, 1953; "Armstrong Circle Theatre: The Bells of Cockaigne," NBC, 1953; "Schlitz Playhouse of Stars: The Closed Door," CBS, 1953; "Campbell TV Soundstage: The Test Case," NBC, 1954; "Motorola TV Hour: The Sins of the Fathers," ABC, 1954; "Armstrong Circle Theatre: Treasure Trove," NBC, 1954; "Lux Video Theatre: The Queen's English," CBS, 1954; "The 20th Century-Fox Hour: The Late Christopher Bean," CBS, 1955; "Science Fiction Theatre: When a Camera Fails," SYN, 1956; "Science Fiction Theatre: The Miracle of Dr. Dove," SYN, 1956; "Lux Video Theatre: Has Anybody Seen My Gal?," NBC, 1956; "The Jane Wyman Show: This Way to Heaven," NBC, 1956; "Telephone Time: Vicksburg, 5:35 p.m.," CBS, 1956; "The Joseph Cotten Show: Law Is for Lovers," NBC, 1956; "Lux Video Theatre: It Happened on Fifth Avenue," NBC, 1957; "Hill Number One," SYN, 1957; "Climax!: Don't Ever Come Back," CBS, 1957; "World's Greatest Mother," SYN, 1958.

LOCKHART, JUNE
b. New York City, NY, June 25, 1925. Actress with extensive TV experience, best known as understanding mom Ruth Martin on "Lassie" and Maureen Robinson on "Lost in Space."

AS A REGULAR: "Who Said That?," NBC, 1952-54; ABC, 1955; "Lassie," CBS, 1958-64; "Lost in Space," CBS, 1965-68; "Petticoat Junction,"

CBS, 1968-70; "General Hospital," ABC, 1984-85.

AND: "Pulitzer Prize Playhouse: The Just and the Unjust," ABC, 1951; "Prudential Family Playhouse: One Sunday Afternoon," CBS, 1951; "Lux Video Theatre: Happily, But Not Forever," CBS, 1952; "Studio One: The Doctor's Wife," CBS, 1952; "U.S. Steel Hour: Goodbye ... But It Doesn't Go Away," ABC, 1954; "Studio One: The Deserter," CBS, 1954; "Elgin TV Hour: Midsummer Melody," ABC, 1955; "Kraft Television Theatre: My Aunt Daisy," NBC, 1955; "Science Fiction Theatre: Brain Unlimited," SYN, 1956; "Telephone Time: Vicksburg, 5:35 p.m.," CBS, 1956; "Alcoa Hour: Morning's at Seven," NBC, 1956; "Studio 57: Teacher," SYN, 1956; "Schlitz Playhouse of Stars: The Night They Won the Oscar," CBS, 1956; "Studio One: A Matter of Guilt," CBS, 1957; "Arthur Murray Party," NBC, 1957; "U.S. Steel Hour: A Loud Laugh," CBS, 1957; "Pantomime Quiz," CBS, 1957; "Climax!: Jacob and the Angel," CBS, 1957; "U.S. Steel Hour: The Locked Door," CBS, 1957; "Have Gun, Will Travel: No Visitors," CBS, 1957; "U.S. Steel Hour: Little Charlie Don't Want a Saddle," CBS, 1957; "Shirley Temple's Storybook: Beauty and the Beast," NBC, 1958; "Cimarron City: Medicine Man," NBC, 1958; "Playhouse 90: The Nutcracker," CBS, 1958; "Rawhide: Incident at Barker Springs," CBS, 1959; "U.S. Steel Hour: The Square Egghead," CBS, 1959; "G.E. Theatre: Night Club," CBS, 1959; "Mother's March," SYN, 1960; "Arthur Murray Party," NBC, 1960; "Wagon Train: The Ricky and Laurie Bell Story," NBC, 1960; "Best of the Post: The Marriage That Couldn't Succeed," SYN, 1960; "Art Linkletter's House Party," CBS, 1964; "Perry Mason: The Case of the Scandalous Sculptor," CBS, 1964; "The Alfred Hitchcock Hour: The Second Wife," NBC, 1965; "Mr. Novak: Once a Clown," NBC, 1965; "Death Valley Days: The Magic Locket," SYN, 1965; "Password," CBS, 1966; "You Don't Say," NBC, 1966; "Family Affair: The Substitute Teacher," CBS, 1968; "The Steve Allen Show," SYN, 1968; "The Beverly Hillbillies: The Thanksgiving Story," CBS, 1968; "The Man and the City: Hands of Love," ABC, 1971; "Honeymoon Suite," ABC, 1972; "Love, American Style: Love and the Favorite Family," ABC, 1973; "ABC's Matinee Today: I Never Said Goodbye," ABC, 1973; "Adam 12: Camp," NBC, 1974; "Marcus Welby, M.D.: Last Flight to Babylon," ABC, 1974; "The $10,000 Pyramid," ABC, 1975; "You Don't Say," ABC, 1975; "Happy Days: Two Angry Men," ABC, 1976; "Quincy: A Star Is Dead," NBC, 1976; "The Hardy Boys Mysteries: Search for Atlantis," ABC, 1978; "The Love Experts," SYN, 1978; "Quincy: Physician, Heal Thyself," NBC, 1979; "Magnum, P.I.: Thicker Than Blood," CBS, 1981; "Quincy: Quincy's

Wedding," NBC, 1983; "Murder, She Wrote: School for Scandal," CBS, 1985; "Amazing Stories: The Pumpkin Competition," NBC, 1986; "CBS Schoolbreak Special: Never Say Goodbye," CBS, 1989.

TV MOVIES AND MINISERIES: "But I Don't Want to Get Married!," ABC, 1970; "The Bait," ABC, 1973; "Loose Change," NBC, 1978; "The Gift of Love," ABC, 1978; "Walking Through the Fire," CBS, 1979; "Perfect People," ABC, 1988; "A Whisper Kills," ABC, 1988.

LOCKLEAR, HEATHER

b. Los Angeles, CA, September 25, 1961. Blonde actress who played Sammy Jo on "Dynasty" and officer Stacy Sheridan on "T.J. Hooker"; not to be confused with Heather Thomas. Then again, go ahead.

AS A REGULAR: "Dynasty," ABC, 1981-89; "T.J. Hooker," ABC, 1982-85; CBS, 1985-87; "Going Places," ABC, 1990- .

AND: "The Love Boat: Youth Takes a Holiday," ABC, 1983.

TV MOVIES AND MINISERIES: "City Killer," NBC, 1984; "ABC Family Classic: Rock 'n' Roll Mom," ABC, 1989.

LOCKWOOD, GARY

b. John Gary Yusolfksy, Van Nuys, CA, February 21, 1937. Generically handsome TV actor.

AS A REGULAR: "Follow the Sun," ABC, 1961-62; "The Lieutenant," NBC, 1963-64.

AND: "Bus Stop: Cherie," ABC, 1961; "Saints and Sinners: Dear George, the Siamese Cat Is Missing," NBC, 1962; "Perry Mason: The Case of the Playboy Pugilist," CBS, 1962; "The Lloyd Bridges Show: My Daddy Can Lick Your Daddy," CBS, 1963; "Missing Links," NBC, 1964; "Twelve O'Clock High: The Idolater," ABC, 1965; "The Long Hot Summer: A Day of Trouble," ABC, 1966; "Gunsmoke: The Raid," CBS, 1966; "Star Trek: Where No Man Has Gone Before," NBC, 1966; "Love, American Style: Love and the Doorknob," ABC, 1969; "Medical Center: The Assailant," CBS, 1970; "Medical Center: Man at Bay," CBS, 1970; "The Young Rebels: To Kill a Traitor," ABC, 1971; "Love, American Style: Love and the Phone Book," ABC, 1971; "The Young Lawyers: I've Got a Problem," ABC, 1971; "Night Gallery: The Ring with the Red Velvet Ropes," NBC, 1972; "Mission: Impossible: The Question," CBS, 1973; "Barnaby Jones: Sunday: Doomsday," CBS, 1973; "Banacek: No Stone Unturned," NBC, 1973; "Medical Center: Stranger in Two Worlds," CBS, 1973; "Barnaby Jones: The Platinum Connection," CBS, 1974; "The FBI: The Animal," ABC, 1974; "The Six Million Dollar Man: Eyewitness to Murder," ABC, 1974;

"Ironside: The Faded Image," NBC, 1974; "Barnaby Jones: Blueprint for a Caper," CBS, 1974; "The Six Million Dollar Man: Steve Austin, Fugitive," ABC, 1975; "Three for the Road: Match Point," CBS, 1975; "Cannon: Coffin Corner," CBS, 1976; "Police Story: End of the Line," NBC, 1977; "Barnaby Jones: Man on Fire," CBS, 1979; "The Fall Guy: King of the Cowboys," ABC, 1984; "Simon & Simon: Corpus Delecti," CBS, 1984; "Simon & Simon: Tonsillitis," CBS, 1986; "Simon & Simon: Family Forecast," CBS, 1986; "Scarecrow and Mrs. King: The Eyes Have It," CBS, 1986; "Murder, She Wrote: Indian Giver," CBS, 1987.
TV MOVIES AND MINISERIES: "Earth II," ABC, 1971; "The Manhunter," CBS, 1974; "The FBI Story: Alvin Karpis, Public Enemy Number One," CBS, 1974; "The Incredible Journey of Doctor Meg Laurel," CBS, 1979; "The Return of the Six Million Dollar Man and the Bionic Woman," NBC, 1987.

LOEB, PHILIP
b. *Philadelphia, PA, 1894; d. 1955.* Actor who played Jake on "The Goldbergs"; he committed suicide after being blacklisted in the early fifties.
AS A REGULAR: "The Goldbergs," CBS, 1949-51.

LOGAN, ROBERT
b. *May 29, 1941, Brooklyn, NY.* Actor who played J.R. Hale on "77 Sunset Strip."
AS A REGULAR: "77 Sunset Strip," ABC, 1961-63; "Daniel Boone," NBC, 1965-66.
AND: "Maverick: The Cactus Switch," ABC, 1961; "Dr. Kildare: Tyger, Tyger ...," NBC, 1964; "Mr. Novak: Johnny Ride the Pony," NBC, 1964; "The Merv Griffin Show," SYN, 1979; "Riptide: Father's Day," NBC, 1984.
TV MOVIES AND MINISERIES: "Snowbeast," NBC, 1977; "Death Ray 2000," NBC, 1981.

LOGGIA, ROBERT
b. *Staten Island, NY, January 3, 1930.* Actor in films ("Prizzi's Honor") and TV; he played jewel thief gone straight "T.H.E. Cat" and FBI agent Nick Mancuso in the miniseries "Favorite Son" and a subesquent series.
AS A REGULAR: "Walt Disney Presents: The Nine Lives of Elfego Baca," ABC, 1958-60; "T.H.E. Cat," NBC, 1966-67; "The Secret Storm," CBS, 1972; "Search for Tomorrow," CBS, 1973; "Emerald Point NAS," CBS, 1983-84; "Mancuso, FBI," NBC, 1989-90.
AND: "Studio One: The Traveling Lady," CBS, 1957; "Studio One: Mutiny on the Shark," CBS, 1957; "Playhouse 90: Rumors of Evening," CBS, 1958; "Wagon Train: The Jose Maria Moran Story," NBC, 1959; "G.E. Theatre: Hitler's Secret," CBS, 1959; "Westinghouse Desilu

Playhouse: Come Back to Sorrento," CBS, 1959; "Alcoa Presents One Step Beyond: The Hand," ABC, 1959; "U.S. Steel Hour: How to Make a Killing," CBS, 1960; "Frontiers of Faith: From the Dark Source," NBC, 1960; "The Overland Trail: Mission to Mexico," NBC, 1960; "Play of the Week: Strindberg on Love," SYN, 1960; "Alfred Hitchcock Presents: The Money," NBC, 1960; "Play of the Week: Legend of Lovers," SYN, 1961; "Naked City: The Fingers of Henri Tourelle," ABC, 1961; "Target: The Corruptors: The Poppy Vendor," ABC, 1961; "The Defenders: Perjury," CBS, 1961; "Alcoa Premiere: The End of a World," ABC, 1961; "Alfred Hitchcock Presents: The Case of M.J.H.," NBC, 1962; "The Untouchables: Takeover," ABC, 1962; "The Dick Powell Show: The Hook," NBC, 1962; "The du Pont Show: The Interrogator," NBC, 1962; "Kraft Suspense Theatre: The Robrioz Ring," NBC, 1964; "Gunsmoke: Chief Joseph," CBS, 1965; "Combat!: The Tree of Moray," ABC, 1965; "Run for Your Life: The Cold, Cold War of Paul Bryan," NBC, 1965; "The Wild Wild West: The Night of the Sudden Death," CBS, 1965; "Voyage to the Bottom of the Sea: Graveyard of Fear," ABC, 1966; "The Wild Wild West: The Night of the Assassin," CBS, 1967; "Then Came Bronson: Against a Blank, Cold Wall," NBC, 1969; "The FBI: The Deadly Pact," ABC, 1970; "The FBI: Arrangement with Terror," ABC, 1972; "McMillan and Wife: Aftershock," NBC, 1975; "Starsky and Hutch: The Fix," ABC, 1975; "Columbo: Now You See Him," NBC, 1976; "Police Woman: Wednesday's Child," NBC, 1976; "The Rockford Files: Drought at Indianhead River," NBC, 1976; "The Rockford Files: Beamer's Last Case," NBC, 1977; "Police Woman: Shadow of Doubt," NBC, 1977; "The Rockford Files: Rosendahl and Gilda Stern Are Dead," NBC, 1978; "The Hardy Boys Mysteries: Search for Atlantis," ABC, 1978; "Sword of Justice: Deadly Fashion," NBC, 1978; "Charlie's Angels: Toni's Boys," ABC, 1980; "Nero Wolfe: In the Best Families," NBC, 1981; "Matt Houston: Return to 'Nam," ABC, 1984; "The Tonight Show Starring Johnny Carson," NBC, 1989.
TV MOVIES AND MINISERIES: "Mallory: Circumstantial Evidence," NBC, 1976; "Street Killing," ABC, 1976; "Scott Free," NBC, 1976; "The Moneychangers," NBC, 1976; "No Other Love," CBS, 1979; "Casino," ABC, 1980; "A Woman Called Golda," SYN, 1982; "A Touch of Scandal," CBS, 1984; "Streets of Justice," NBC, 1985; "Echoes in the Darkness," CBS, 1987; "Favorite Son," NBC, 1988; "Dream Breakers," CBS, 1989.

LOLLOBRIGIDA, GINA
b. *Subiaco, Italy, July 4, 1928.* Fifties movie sexpot who's been on a TV soap or two.

AS A REGULAR: "Falcon Crest," CBS, 1984.
AND: "Person to Person," CBS, 1958; "The Ed
Sullivan Show," CBS, 1958; "I've Got a Secret,"
CBS, 1958; "Bob Hope Special," NBC, 1959;
"The Ed Sullivan Show," CBS, 1959.
TV MOVIES AND MINISERIES: "Deceptions," NBC,
1985.

LOMBARDO, GUY

b. London, Ontario, Canada, 1902; d. 1977.
Bandleader who ushered in the New Year on
TV and radio from 1929 until the mid
seventies.
AS A REGULAR: "Guy Lombardo's Diamond
Jubilee," CBS, 1956; "The Guy Lombardo
Show," SYN, 1957.
AND: "The Perry Como Show," NBC, 1956; "The
Ed Sullivan Show," CBS, 1957; "The Steve Allen
Show," NBC, 1957; "The Ed Sullivan Show,"
CBS, 1958; "Startime: The Swingin' Years,"
NBC, 1960; "Celebrity Talent Scouts," CBS,
1960; "I've Got a Secret," CBS, 1962; "Missing
Links," NBC, 1964; "Bell Telephone Hour,"
NBC, 1965.

LON, ALICE

b. Kilgore, TX, 1926; d. 1981. "Champagne
Lady" on the Lawrence Welk show, a vocalist
who was dumped by Welk when she showed
too much knee on camera. Really.
AS A REGULAR: "The Lawrence Welk Show,"
ABC, 1955-59.
AND: "Art Linkletter's House Party," CBS, 1957.

LONDON, JULIE

*b. Julie Peck, Santa Rosa, CA, September 26,
1916.* Smoky-voiced fifties songstress who
played nurse Dixie McCall on "Emergency!"
AS A REGULAR: "Emergency!," NBC, 1972-77.
AND: "Bob Hope Show," NBC, 1956; "The
Rosemary Clooney Show," SYN, 1957; "The Ed
Sullivan Show," CBS, 1957; "Dick Powell's Zane
Grey Theatre: A Time to Live," CBS, 1957;
"Shower of Stars," CBS, 1957; "Playhouse 90:
Without Incident," CBS, 1957; "The Big Record,"
CBS, 1957; "The Steve Allen Show," NBC, 1958;
"Stars of Jazz," ABC, 1958; "The Bob Crosby
Show," NBC, 1958; "The Garry Moore Show,"
CBS, 1959; "Bob Hope Special," NBC, 1959;
"Frances Langford Special," NBC, 1959; "The
Perry Como Show," NBC, 1959; "The David
Niven Show: Maggie Malone," NBC, 1959; "The
Andy Williams Show," CBS, 1959; "America
Pauses in September," NBC, 1959; "Dinah Shore
Chevy Show," NBC, 1959; "Adventures in
Paradise: Mission to Manila," ABC, 1959; "Pat
Boone Chevy Show," ABC, 1959; "The Red
Skelton Show: Clem the Disk Jockey," CBS,
1960; "Steve Allen Plymouth Show," NBC, 1960;
"The Chevy Show: Pleasant Dreams," NBC,

1960; "Laramie: Queen of Diamonds," NBC,
1960; "Rawhide: Incident at Rojo Canyon,"
CBS, 1960; "Here's Hollywood," NBC, 1960;
"Michael Shayne: Die Like a Dog," NBC, 1960;
"Dave's Place," NBC, 1960; "Dan Raven: Tinge
of Red," NBC, 1960; "Hong Kong: Suitable for
Framing," ABC, 1961; "The Barbara Stanwyck
Show: Night Visitors," NBC, 1961; "The
Gershwin Years," CBS, 1961; "Bob Hope Buick
Show," NBC, 1961; "Checkmate: Goodbye,
Griff," CBS, 1961; "The Garry Moore Show,"
CBS, 1961; "Bob Hope Buick Show," NBC,
1961; "Follow the Sun: Night Song," ABC,
1961; "The Jack Benny Program: Julie London
Show," CBS, 1962; "The Voice of Firestone,"
ABC, 1962; "The Dick Powell Show: Charlie's
Duet," NBC, 1963; "The Eleventh Hour: Like a
Diamond in the Sky," NBC, 1963; "Bob Hope
Special," NBC, 1964; "The Alfred Hitchcock
Hour: The Crimson Witness," NBC, 1965; "I'll
Bet," NBC, 1965; "I Spy: Three Hours on a
Sunday Night," NBC, 1965; "The Man From
UNCLE: The Prince of Darkness Affair," NBC,
1967; "The Big Valley: Alias Nellie Handley,"
ABC, 1968; "The Big Valley: They Called Her
Death," ABC, 1968; "Adam 12: Emergency!,"
NBC, 1972; "Celebrity Sweepstakes," NBC,
1974; "Tattletales," CBS, 1975; "Match Game
'75," CBS, 1975; "Celebrity Sweepstakes,"
NBC, 1976.
TV MOVIES AND MINISERIES: "Emergency!," NBC,
1972.

LONG, RICHARD

b. Chicago, IL, December 17, 1927; d. 1974.
Popular TV leading man who played private
dick Rex Randolph on "Bourbon Street Beat"
and "77 Sunset Strip," Jarrod Barkley on "The
Big Valley" and professor Harold Everett on
"Nanny and the Professor."
AS A REGULAR: "Bourbon Street Beat," ABC,
1959-60; "77 Sunset Strip," ABC, 1960-61;
"Stump the Stars," CBS, 1962-63, 1964; "The
Big Valley," ABC, 1965-69; "Nanny and the
Professor," ABC, 1970-71; "Thicker Than
Water," ABC, 1973.
AND: "TV Reader's Digest: Holiday in Mexico,"
ABC, 1955; "Climax!: Wild Stallion," CBS, 1955;
"Matinee Theatre: The Gate," NBC, 1956; "U.S.
Steel Hour: The Great Adventure," CBS,
1956; "TV Reader's Digest: Down on the
Tennessee," ABC, 1956; "Hey, Jeannie!: Lost
Jacket," CBS, 1956; "Schlitz Playhouse of Stars:
Terror in the Streets," CBS, 1957; "Suspicion: Four
O'Clock," NBC, 1957; "Alcoa Theatre: In the
Dark," NBC, 1958; "Wagon Train: The Annie
MacGregor Story," NBC, 1958; "The Millionaire:
The Johanna Judson Story," CBS, 1958;
"Maverick: Alias Bart Maverick," ABC, 1958;
"77 Sunset Strip: One False Step," ABC,
1958; "Have Gun, Will Travel: The Singer,"

CBS, 1958; "Sugarfoot: The Vultures," ABC, 1959; "Lawman: The Ring," ABC, 1959; "Maverick: The Spanish Dancer," ABC, 1959; "Maverick: The Goose-Drownder," ABC, 1959; "77 Sunset Strip: The President's Daughter," ABC, 1960; "Target: The Corruptors: Quicksand," ABC, 1961; "Thriller: An Attractive Family," NBC, 1962; "Tales of Wells Fargo: Hometown Doctor," NBC, 1962; "The Outlaws: No More Horses," NBC, 1962; "The Twilight Zone: Person or Persons Unknown," CBS, 1962; "77 Sunset Strip: Nine to Five," ABC, 1963; "Going My Way: Hear No Evil," ABC, 1963; "The Alfred Hitchcock Hour: Blonde Bargain," NBC, 1963; "77 Sunset Strip: The Fumble," ABC, 1963; "The Twilight Zone: Number Twelve Looks Just Like You," CBS, 1964; "Walt Disney's Wonderful World of Color: Tenderfoot," NBC, 1964; "Kraft Suspense Theatre: Streetcar, Do You Read Me?," NBC, 1965; "I'll Bet," NBC, 1965; "You Don't Say," NBC, 1965; "Hollywood Squares," NBC, 1967; "Love, American Style: Love and the Minister," ABC, 1970; "The ABC Saturday Superstar Movie: Mini-Munsters," ABC, 1973; "Nanny and the Professor and the Phantom of the Circus," ABC, 1974.
TV MOVIES AND MINISERIES: "The Girl Who Came Gift-Wrapped," ABC, 1974; "Death Cruise," ABC, 1974.

LONG, SHELLEY
b. Fort Wayne, IN, August 23, 1949. Emmy winning actress who played Diane Chambers on "Cheers"—and frankly, really isn't missed all that much since she left the show.
AS A REGULAR: "Cheers," NBC, 1982-87.
AND: "M*A*S*H: Bottle Fatigue," CBS, 1980; "Bob Hope's Super Bowl Party," NBC, 1989.
TV MOVIES AND MINISERIES: "The Cracker Factory," ABC, 1979; "The Princess and the Cabbie," CBS, 1981.
* Emmies: 1983.

LONTOC, LEON
b. 1909; d. 1974. Asian actor who played Henry, chauffeur of playboy detective Amos Burke (Gene Barry) on "Burke's Law."
AS A REGULAR: "Burke's Law," ABC, 1963-65.
AND: "Hawaiian Eye: Assignment: Manila," ABC, 1960; "Hong Kong: Murder by Proxy," ABC, 1960; "Alfred Hitchcock Presents: A Woman's Help," NBC, 1960; "Hong Kong: The Runaway," ABC, 1961; "Adventures in Paradise: Hurricane Audrey," ABC, 1962; "McHale's Navy: Movies Are Your Best Diversion," ABC, 1962; "McHale's Navy: The Natives Get Restless," ABC, 1963; "The Man From UNCLE: The Abominable Snowman Affair," NBC, 1966.
TV MOVIES AND MINISERIES: "The Brotherhood of the Bell," CBS, 1970.

LOOKINLAND, MIKE
b. Mount Pleasant, UT, 1960. Actor who played Bobby Brady.
AS A REGULAR: "The Brady Bunch," ABC, 1969-74; "The Brady Bunch Hour," ABC, 1977; "The Bradys," CBS, 1990.
AND: "Day by Day: A Very Brady Episode," NBC, 1989.
TV MOVIES AND MINISERIES: "Dead Men Tell No Tales," CBS, 1971; "The Brady Girls Get Married," NBC, 1981; "A Very Brady Christmas," CBS, 1988.

LOPEZ, PRISCILLA
b. Bronx, NY, February 26, 1948.
AS A REGULAR: "In the Beginning," CBS, 1978; "Kay O'Brien," CBS, 1986.
AND: "All in the Family: Mike and Gloria Meet," CBS, 1977; "Family: Disco Queen," ABC, 1979.
TV MOVIES AND MINISERIES: "Intimate Strangers," CBS, 1986.

LOPEZ, VINCENT
b. Brooklyn, NY, 1898; d. 1975. Pianist.
AS A REGULAR: "Welcome Aboard," NBC, 1948-49; "Vincent Lopez," DUM, 1949-50; "The Vincent Lopez Show," CBS, 1957.
AND: "The Ed Sullivan Show," CBS, 1960.

LOR, DENISE
b. California. Singer long associated with Garry Moore.
AS A REGULAR: "The Garry Moore Show," CBS, 1950-58; "The Garry Moore Evening Show," CBS, 1951; "Seven at Eleven," NBC, 1951; "Droodles," NBC, 1954; "The Arthur Murray Show," CBS, 1956.
AND: "The Jonathan Winters Show," NBC, 1957; "Get Set, Go!," SYN, 1957; "The Jimmy Dean Show," CBS, 1957; "The Jack Paar Show," NBC, 1958; "The Bob Crosby Show," NBC, 1958; "The George Hamilton IV Show," CBS, 1958; "The Jimmy Dean Show," CBS, 1958; "Arthur Murray Party," NBC, 1958; "The Jack Paar Show," NBC, 1959; "The Garry Moore Show," CBS, 1961; "The Alan King Show," CBS, 1961; "The Garry Moore Show," CBS, 1962.

LORD, JACK
b. John Joseph Patrick Ryan, Brooklyn, NY, December 30, 1930. Macho, humorless TV leading man who had a long, comfortable run as Steve "Book 'em, Danno" McGarrett on "Hawaii Five-O."
AS A REGULAR: "Stoney Burke," ABC, 1962-63; "Hawaii Five-O," CBS, 1968-80.
AND: "Omnibus: One Nation," CBS, 1956; "Studio One: An Incident of Love," CBS, 1956; "Philco TV Playhouse: This Land Is Mine," NBC, 1956; "Warner Bros. Presents Conflict: Pattern for

535

Violence," ABC, 1957; "Climax!: Mr. Runyon of Broadway," CBS, 1957; "Playhouse 90: Lone Woman," CBS, 1957; "Have Gun, Will Travel: Three Bells to Perdido," CBS, 1957; "Playhouse 90: Reunion," CBS, 1958; "The Millionaire: The Lee Randolph Story," CBS, 1958; "The Loretta Young Show: Marriage Crisis," NBC, 1959; "Alcoa Presents One Step Beyond: Father Image," ABC, 1959; "The Lineup: The Strange Return of Army Armitage," CBS, 1959; "The Untouchables: The Jake Lingle Killing," ABC, 1959; "Bonanza: The Outcast," NBC, 1960; "Naked City: The Human Trap," ABC, 1960; "Route 66: Play it Glissando," CBS, 1961; "The Americans: Half Moon Road," NBC, 1961; "The Outlaws: The Bell," NBC, 1961; "Stagecoach West: House of Violence," ABC, 1961; "Stagecoach West: El Carnicero," ABC, 1961; "Rawhide: Incident of His Brother's Keeper," CBS, 1961; "Checkmate: The Star System," CBS, 1962; "The Greatest Show on Earth: Man in a Hole," ABC, 1964; "The Reporter: How Much for a Prince?," CBS, 1964; "Wagon Train: The Lee Barton Story," ABC, 1965; "Kraft Suspense Theatre: The Long Ravine," NBC, 1965; "Bob Hope Chrysler Theatre: The Crime," NBC, 1965; "The Loner: The Vespers," CBS, 1965; "Twelve O'Clock High: Big Brother," ABC, 1965; "Combat!: The Linesman," ABC, 1965; "Laredo: Above the Law," NBC, 1966; "Bob Hope Chrysler Theatre: The Faceless Man," NBC, 1966; "Twelve O'Clock High: Face of a Shadow," ABC, 1966; "The FBI: Collision Course," ABC, 1966; "The Virginian: High Stakes," NBC, 1966; "Bob Hope Chrysler Theatre: Storm Crossing," NBC, 1966; "The Invaders: Vikor," ABC, 1967; "The Fugitive: Goodbye, My Love," ABC, 1967; "Ironside: Dead Man's Tale," NBC, 1967; "The Man From UNCLE: The His Master's Touch Affair," NBC, 1967; "The High Chaparral: The Kinsman," NBC, 1968.

TV MOVIES AND MINISERIES: "The Doomsday Flight," NBC, 1966; "Hawaii Five-O," CBS, 1968.

* In 1962, Lord told a *TV Guide* interviewer that he turned down the leading roles on "Wagon Train" ("westerns were getting tired") and "Ben Casey" ("I can't stand an atmosphere of human misery").

LORD, MARJORIE

b. *Marjorie Wollenberg, San Fransisco, CA, July 26, 1918.* Attractive actress in unmemorable TV roles until Danny Thomas came along, looking for a second TV wife.

AS A REGULAR: "The Danny Thomas Show (Make Room for Daddy)," ABC, 1957; CBS, 1957-64; "Make Room for Granddaddy," ABC, 1970-71; "Sweet Surrender," NBC, 1987.
AND: "Magnavox Theatre: The Three Muske-teers," CBS, 1950; "Story Theatre: The Real

Thing," SYN, 1951; "Fireside Theatre: Mirage," NBC, 1952; "Fireside Theatre: Visit From a Stranger," NBC, 1952; "Fireside Theatre: The Visitor," NBC, 1953; "Ford Theatre: Shadow of Truth," NBC, 1954; "Ramar of the Jungle: Call to Danger," SYN, 1955; "Cavalcade of America: Take Off Zero," ABC, 1955; "Cavalcade of America: Decision for Justice," ABC, 1955; "The Loretta Young Show: A Shadow Between," NBC, 1955; "Omnibus: The Billy Mitchell Court-Martial," CBS, 1956; "Wire Service: Hideout," ABC, 1956; "The Return," SYN, 1956; "The Life of Riley: Summer Job for Junior," NBC, 1957; "Dick Powell's Zane Grey Theatre: Decision at Wilson's Creek," CBS, 1957; "Wagon Train: The Willy Moran Story," NBC, 1957; "The Lucille Ball-Desi Arnaz Show: Lucy Makes Room for Danny," CBS, 1958; "The Joey Bishop Show: This Is Your Life," NBC, 1961; "Your First Impression," NBC, 1962; "Special for Women: The Menace of Age," ABC, 1964; "Password," CBS, 1965; "Danny Thomas Special," NBC, 1965; "The Danny Thomas Hour: Make More Room for Daddy," NBC, 1967; "Make Room for Granddaddy," CBS, 1969; "Love, American Style: Love and the Single Couple," ABC, 1969; "ABC Afternoon Playbreak: This Child Is Mine," ABC, 1972.
TV MOVIES AND MINISERIES: "The Missing Are Deadly," ABC, 1975; "Side by Side," CBS, 1988.

LOREN, DONNA

b. *Boston, MA, March 7, 1947.* Sixties starlet who was the Dr. Pepper girl on TV commercials.
AS A REGULAR: "Shindig," ABC, 1964-66.
AND: "American Bandstand," ABC, 1965; "Dr. Kildare: The Life Machine/Toast the Golden Couple/Wives and Losers/Welcome Home, Dear Anna/Hour of Decision/Aftermath," NBC, 1965; "Where the Action Is," ABC, 1966; "Batman: The Joker Goes to School/He Meets His Match, the Grisly Ghoul," ABC, 1966; "The Danny Thomas Hour: Two for Penny," NBC, 1968.

LOREN, SOPHIA

b. *Sofia Scicolone, Rome, Italy, September 20, 1934.* Italian actress and sex symbol.
AS A GUEST: "Person to Person," CBS, 1957; "Person to Person," CBS, 1958; "The Ed Sullivan Show," CBS, 1958; "The New Steve Allen Show," ABC, 1961; "The World of Sophia Loren," NBC, 1962; "Sophia Loren in Rome," ABC, 1964; "Sophia," ABC, 1968.
TV MOVIES AND MINISERIES: "Brief Encounter," NBC, 1974; "Aurora," NBC, 1984; "The Fortunate Pilgrim," NBC, 1988.

LORING, LISA

b. *February 16, 1958.* Former child actress

who played Wednesday on "The Addams Family" and Cricket Montgomery on "As the World Turns."
AS A REGULAR: "The Addams Family," ABC, 1964-66; "As the World Turns," CBS, 1981-83.
AND: "Dr. Kildare: Maybe Love Will Save My Apartment House," NBC, 1964; "Bonanza: Something Hurt, Something Wild," NBC, 1966.

LORNE, MARION
b. Wilkes Barre, PA, 1886; d. 1968. Actress who gained attention as a dotty regular on Garry Moore's show; then she played the equally dotty Aunt Clara on "Bewitched."
AS A REGULAR: "Mr. Peepers," NBC, 1952-55; "The Steve Allen Show," NBC, 1957; "Sally," NBC, 1957-58; "The Garry Moore Show," CBS, 1958-62; "Bewitched," ABC, 1964-68.
AND: "Suspicion: The Way Up to Heaven," NBC, 1958; "Du Pont Show of the Month: Harvey," CBS, 1958.
* Emmies: 1968.

LORRE, PETER
b. Laszlo Loewenstein, Rosenberg, Czechoslovakia, 1904; d. 1964. Actor who played many sinister roles in forties movies ("The Maltese Falcon," "Casablanca") and on TV.
AS A GUEST: "Lux Video Theatre: Taste," CBS, 1952; "Suspense: The Tortured Hand," CBS, 1952; "U.S. Steel Hour: The Vanishing Point," ABC, 1953; "Schlitz Playhouse of Stars: The Pipe," CBS, 1954; "Climax!: Casino Royale," CBS, 1954; "Best of Broadway: Arsenic and Old Lace," CBS, 1955; "Producers Showcase: Reunion in Vienna," NBC, 1955; "Climax!: The Fifth Wheel," CBS, 1956; "Climax!: The Man Who Lost His Head," CBS, 1956; "Encore Theatre: Queen's Bracelet," NBC, 1956; "Playhouse 90: Sizeman and Son," CBS, 1956; "The 20th Century-Fox Hour: Operation Cicero," CBS, 1956; "Playhouse 90: The Last Tycoon," CBS, 1957; "Climax!: A Taste for Crime," CBS, 1957; "The Red Skelton Show," CBS, 1957; "The Red Skelton Show: Appleby the Weatherman," CBS, 1959; "Five Fingers: Thin Ice," NBC, 1959; "Alfred Hitchcock Presents: The Man From the South," CBS, 1960; "Playhouse 90: The Cruel Day," CBS, 1960; "Wagon Train: The Alexander Portlass Story," NBC, 1960; "The Red Skelton Show," CBS, 1960; "Rawhide: Incident of the Slavemaster," CBS, 1960; "Best of the Post: The Baron Loved His Wife," SYN, 1960; "Checkmate: The Human Touch," CBS, 1961; "Mrs. G. Goes to College: First Test," CBS, 1961; "Mrs. G. Goes to College: The Trouble with Crayton," CBS, 1961; "Route 66: Lizard's Leg and Owlet's Wing," CBS, 1962; "The Jack Benny Program," CBS, 1963; "The Tonight Show Starring Johnny Carson," NBC, 1963; "The Tennessee Ernie Ford Show," ABC, 1963; "The du Pont Show: Diamond Fever," NBC, 1963; "77 Sunset Strip: 5," ABC, 1963; "Kraft Suspense Theatre: The End of the World, Baby," NBC, 1963.

LOUDON, DOROTHY
b. Boston, MA, September 17, 1933. Singer-actress on TV and the stage ("Annie").
AS A REGULAR: "It's a Business?," DUM, 1952; "Laugh Line," NBC, 1959; "The Garry Moore Show," CBS, 1962-64; "Dorothy," CBS, 1979.
AND: "The Peter Lind Hayes Show," ABC, 1958; "The Jack Paar Show," NBC, 1959; "Revlon Revue: Accent on Comedy," CBS, 1960; "Project 20: Those Ragtime Years," NBC, 1960; "The Dinah Shore Chevy Show," NBC, 1961; "The Dinah Shore Chevy Show: Like Young," NBC, 1961; "The Ed Sullivan Show," CBS, 1961; "The du Pont Show: Music of the Thirties," NBC, 1961; "The du Pont Show: Regards to George M. Cohan," NBC, 1962; "Password," CBS, 1962; "The Lively Ones," NBC, 1962; "The Mike Douglas Show," SYN, 1964; "The Jonathan Winters Show," CBS, 1968; "The Merv Griffin Show," CBS, 1969; "Murder, She Wrote: Magnum on Ice," CBS, 1986.

LOUISE, ANITA
b. New York City, NY, January 9, 1915; d. 1970.
AS A REGULAR: "My Friend Flicka," CBS, 1956-57; "Theater Time," ABC, 1957; "Spotlight Playhouse," CBS, 1958.
AND: "Stars Over Hollywood: Landing at Daybreak," NBC, 1950; "Favorite Story: The Magician," SYN, 1952; "Ford Theatre: Heart of Gold," NBC, 1952; "Fireside Theatre: The Juror," NBC, 1953; "Ford Theatre: The Fugitives," NBC, 1954; "Ford Theatre: Favorite Son," NBC, 1955; "Ethel Barrymore Theatre: Dear Miss Lovelace," SYN, 1956; "The Loretta Young Show: Power Play," NBC, 1956; "The Millionaire: Story of Nancy Wellington," CBS, 1957; "Playhouse 90: The Greer Case," CBS, 1957; "U.S. Steel Hour: Far From the Shade Tree," CBS, 1962; "Mannix: Missing: Sun and Sky," CBS, 1969.

LOUISE, TINA
b. New York City, NY, February 11, 1937. Lip-quivering actress who played Ginger Grant, the movie star on "Gilligan's Island"; reportedly she didn't get along with the other castaways, so she wasn't invited to appear in the "Gilligan's Island" TV movies.
AS A REGULAR: "Jan Murray Time," NBC, 1955; "Gilligan's Island," CBS, 1964-67; "Dallas," CBS, 1978; "Rituals," SYN, 1984-85.
AND: "Studio One: The Bounty Hunters," CBS,

1956; "Appointment with Adventure: All Through the Night," CBS, 1956; "Producers Showcase: Happy Birthday," NBC, 1956; "The Phil Silvers Show: Bilko Goes South," CBS, 1957; "Climax!: A Matter of Life and Death," CBS, 1957; "Dean Martin Special," NBC, 1961; "Tales of Wells Fargo: New Orleans Trackdown," NBC, 1961; "The New Breed: I Remember Murder," ABC, 1961; "Checkmate: A Funny Thing Happened to Me on the Way to the Game," CBS, 1962; "The Real McCoys: Grandpa Pygmalion," CBS, 1962; "Route 66: Tex, I'm Here to Kill a King," CBS, 1963; "Burke's Law: Who Killed Billy Jo?," ABC, 1963; "Kraft Suspense Theatre: The Deep End," NBC, 1964; "Mr. Broadway: Smelling Like a Rose," CBS, 1964; "A Salute to Stan Laurel," CBS, 1965; "Bonanza: Desperate Passage," NBC, 1967; "Suspense Theatre: The Deep End," ABC, 1968; "Bob Hope Special," NBC, 1969; "Love, American Style: Love and the Advice Givers," ABC, 1969; "Mannix: Missing: Sun and Sky," CBS, 1969; "Ironside: Beware the Wiles of the Stranger," NBC, 1970; "The Mod Squad: Call Back Yesterday," ABC, 1970; "Love, American Style: Love and the Duel," ABC, 1971; "Love, American Style: Love and the Lady Athlete," ABC, 1972; "Mannix: The Faces of Murder," CBS, 1973; "Love, American Style: Love and the See-Thru Mind," ABC, 1973; "Police Story: Death on Credit," NBC, 1973; "Kojak: Die Before They Wake," CBS, 1974; "Police Story: Requiem for C.Z. Smith," NBC, 1974; "Marcus Welby, M.D.: All Passions Spent," ABC, 1976; "The Love Boat: My Sister, Irene," ABC, 1979; "Simon & Simon: Full Moon Blues," CBS, 1986; "Blacke's Magic: Death Goes to the Movies," NBC, 1986.

TV MOVIES AND MINISERIES: "But I Don't Want To Get Married!," ABC, 1970; "Call to Danger," CBS, 1973; "Death Scream," ABC, 1975; "Nightmare in Badham County," ABC, 1976; "Look What's Happened to Rosemary's Baby," ABC, 1976; "SST-Death Flight," ABC, 1977; "Friendships, Secrets and Lies," NBC, 1979.

LOVEJOY, FRANK
b. Bronx, NY, March 28, 1914; d. 1962. Rough-and-tumble leading man, best known as private eye McGraw.
AS A REGULAR: "Man Against Crime," NBC, 1956; "Meet McGraw (The Adventures of McGraw)," NBC, 1957-58.
AND: "Lux Video Theatre: Second Meeting," CBS, 1953; "Four Star Playhouse: Out of the Night," CBS, 1953; "Four Star Playhouse: Meet McGraw," CBS, 1954; "Four Star Playhouse: Search in the Night," CBS, 1954; "Ford Star Jubilee: The Caine Mutiny Court Martial," CBS, 1955; "Climax!: The Passport," CBS, 1955; "Rheingold Theatre: Act of Decision," NBC, 1956; "Rheingold Theatre: The Whizzer," NBC,

1956; "The Loretta Young Show: Case 258," NBC, 1956; "Four Star Playhouse: Yellowbelly," CBS, 1956; "Playhouse 90: The Country Husband," CBS, 1956; "Dick Powell's Zane Grey Theatre: No Man Living," CBS, 1957; "Du Pont Theatre: Chicago 2-1-2," ABC, 1957; "The Loretta Young Show: Out of Control," NBC, 1958; "Christophers: Good Reading Will Help You," SYN, 1959; "Playhouse 90: The Raider," CBS, 1959; "Dick Powell's Zane Grey Theatre: Hanging Fever," CBS, 1959; "The Red Skelton Show," CBS, 1959; "The David Niven Show: Backtrack," NBC, 1959; "The Loretta Young Show: Circles of Panic," NBC, 1959; "Dick Powell's Zane Grey Theatre: Shadows," CBS, 1959; "The du Pont Show with June Allyson: Escape," CBS, 1960; "Wichita Town: The Hanging Judge," NBC, 1960; "Arthur Murray Party," NBC, 1960; "U.S. Steel Hour: Shadow of a Pale Horse," CBS, 1960; "The du Pont Show: The Battle of the Paper Bullets," NBC, 1961; "Target: The Corruptors: The Fix," ABC, 1961; "Bus Stop: County General," ABC, 1962.

LOVITZ, JON
b. Tarzana, CA, July 21, 1957. Comic actor.
AS A REGULAR: "Foley Square," CBS, 1985-86; "Saturday Night Live," NBC, 1985-90.

LOWE, CHAD
b. Dayton, OH, January 15, 1968. Young actor; brother of Rob.
AS A REGULAR: "Spencer," NBC, 1984-85.
TV MOVIES AND MINISERIES: "Silence of the Heart," CBS, 1984; "There Must Be a Pony," ABC, 1986; "Hallmark Hall of Fame: April Morning," CBS, 1988.

LOWE, EDMUND
b. San Jose, CA, 1890; d. 1971.
AS A REGULAR: "Your Witness," ABC, 1949-50; "Front Page Detective," DUM, SYN, 1951-53.
AND: "Warner Bros. Presents Conflict: Thunder in the Night," ABC, 1956; "Conflict: Execution Night," ABC, 1957; "Maverick: The War of the Silver Kings," ABC, 1957.

LOWE, ROB
b. Charlottesville, VA, March 17, 1964. Actor-moviemaker.
AS A REGULAR: "A New Kind of Family," ABC, 1979-80.
TV MOVIES AND MINISERIES: "Thursday's Child," CBS, 1983.
* Lowe made worldwide headlines when a pornographic videotape surfaced that he shot (and participated in). The incident was widely predicted to either help or harm its career; it hasn't really done much of either.

LOWERY, ROBERT

b. Robert Lowery Hanke, Kansas City, MO, 1914; d. 1971. Colorless B-movie actor who played circus owner Big Tim Champion, guardian of Corky (Mickey Dolenz) on "Circus Boy."

AS A REGULAR: "Circus Boy," NBC, 1956-57; ABC, 1957-58; "Pistols 'n' Petticoats," CBS, 1966-67.

AND: "A Far, Far Better Thing," SYN, 1956; "Playhouse 90: Helen Morgan," CBS, 1957; "The Life and Legend of Wyatt Earp: Mr. Buntline's Vacation," ABC, 1957; "The Adventures of Rin Tin Tin: Fort Adventure," ABC, 1959; "Rawhide: Incident of the Shambling Man," CBS, 1959; "Death Valley Days: Whirlwind Courtship," SYN, 1959; "Riverboat: Race to Cincinnati," NBC, 1959; "Cheyenne: Riding Solo," ABC, 1959; "Hawaiian Eye: Beach Boy," ABC, 1959; "The Man From Blackhawk: Portrait of Cynthia," ABC, 1960; "77 Sunset Strip: Condor's Lair," ABC, 1960; "Maverick: Full House," ABC, 1960; "Tales of Wells Fargo: Dealer's Choice," NBC, 1960; "Tightrope!: The Horse Runs High," CBS, 1960; "The Alaskans: Kangaroo Court," ABC, 1960; "Cheyenne: Counterfeit Gun," ABC, 1960; "The Roaring Twenties: Champagne Lady?," ABC, 1960; "Perry Mason: The Case of the Provocative Protege," CBS, 1960; "Hawaiian Eye: Swan Song for a Hero," ABC, 1960; "77 Sunset Strip: Old Cardsharps Never Die," ABC, 1961; "Whispering Smith: Death at Even Money," NBC, 1961; "Perry Mason: The Case of the Roving River," CBS, 1961; "Rawhide: The Captain's Wife," CBS, 1962; "Hawaiian Eye: Total Eclipse," ABC, 1962; "Hazel: New Man in Town," NBC, 1962; "The Farmer's Daughter: Bless Our Happy Home," ABC, 1964.

LOWRY, JUDITH

b. Ft. Sill, OK, July 27, 1890; d. 1977. Elderly actress who played smart-mouthed Mother Dexter on "Phyllis"; also appeared in dozens of TV commercials.

AS A REGULAR: "Phyllis," CBS, 1975-77.

AND: "The Phil Silvers Show: Miss America," CBS, 1956; "Diagnosis: Unknown: The Case of the Elder," CBS, 1960; "The Patty Duke Show: It Takes a Heap of Livin'," ABC, 1965; "Maude: The Election," CBS, 1975; "Kojak: A Long Way From Times Square," CBS, 1975.

* See also Burt Mustin.

LOY, MYRNA

b. Myrna Williams, Helena, MT, August 2, 1905. Warmly sexy, skilled film actress ("The Thin Man," "The Best Years of Our Lives," "Mr. Blandings Builds His Dream House") with occasional TV credits.

AS A GUEST: "G.E. Theatre: It Gives Me Great Pleasure," CBS, 1955; "G.E. Theatre: Lady of the House," CBS, 1957; "The Perry Como Show," NBC, 1957; "G.E. Theatre: Love Came Late," CBS, 1957; "Schlitz Playhouse of Stars: No Second Helping," CBS, 1957; "The George Gobel Show," NBC, 1959; "Meet Me in St. Louis," CBS, 1959; "The du Pont Show with June Allyson: Surprise Party," CBS, 1960; "Celebrity Talent Scouts," CBS, 1960; "I've Got a Secret," CBS, 1960; "Family Affair: A Helping Hand," CBS, 1967; "The Virginian: Lady of the House," NBC, 1967; "Columbo: Etude in Black," NBC, 1972; "Ironside: All About Andrea," NBC, 1973.

TV MOVIES AND MINISERIES: "Death Takes a Holiday," ABC, 1971; "Do Not Fold, Spindle or Mutilate," ABC, 1971; "The Couple Takes a Wife," ABC, 1972; "Indict and Convict," ABC, 1973; "The Elevator," ABC, 1974.

LU, LISA

b. Peking, China, 1932. Actress who played Hey Girl on "Have Gun, Will Travel."

AS A REGULAR: "Yancy Derringer," CBS, 1958-59; "Have Gun, Will Travel," CBS, 1960-61; "Anna and the King," CBS, 1972.

AND: "Shirley Temple's Storybook: The Nightingale," NBC, 1958; "Have Gun, Will Travel: Hey Boy's Revenge," CBS, 1958; "The Gale Storm Show: The Case of the Chinese Puzzle," CBS, 1959; "Bachelor Father: Peter Meets His Match," NBC, 1959; "The Rebel: Blind Marriage," ABC, 1960; "Hawaiian Eye: Shadow of the Blade," ABC, 1960; "Hawaiian Eye: Jade Song," ABC, 1960; "Bachelor Father: Peter Gets Jury Duty," NBC, 1960; "Dante: The Misfortune Cookie," NBC, 1960; "Hong Kong: The Turncoat," ABC, 1960; "Checkmate: Terror From the East," CBS, 1961; "Hawaiian Eye: The Manchu Formula," ABC, 1961; "Bonanza: Day of the Dragon," NBC, 1961; "The Dick Powell Show: Three Soldiers," NBC, 1961; "The Brothers Brannagan: Key of Jade," SYN, 1962; "Cheyenne: Pocketful of Stars," ABC, 1962; "Hawaiian Eye: Two Too Many," ABC, 1963; "My Three Sons: Cherry Blossoms in Bryant Park," ABC, 1964; "My Three Sons: The Lotus Blossom," ABC, 1964; "The Big Valley: Hunter's Moon," ABC, 1968; "Family Affair: The Great Kow-Tow," CBS, 1968.

TV MOVIES AND MINISERIES: "James Clavell's Noble House," NBC, 1988.

LUCCI, SUSAN

b. Westchester, NY, December 23, 1948. Actress who built a career as the scheming Erica Kane on "All My Children."

AS A REGULAR: "All My Children," ABC, 1970-90; "Dallas," CBS, 1990- .

TV MOVIES AND MINISERIES: "Invitation to Hell,"

ABC, 1984; "Anastasia: The Mystery of Anna," NBC, 1986; "Haunted by Her Past," NBC, 1987; "Lady Mobster," ABC, 1988.

LUCKINBILL, LAURENCE
b. Fort Smith, AR, November 21, 1934.
AS A REGULAR: "The Secret Storm," CBS, 1967-68; "Where the Heart Is," CBS, 1970-71; "The Delphi Bureau," ABC, 1972-73.
AND: "NYPD: Naked in the Streets," ABC, 1968; "The Bold Ones: The Continual Roar of Musketry," NBC, 1970; "Bonanza: Shadow of a Hero," NBC, 1971; "NET Playhouse: Biography," NET, 1971; "Mission: Impossible: Double Dead," CBS, 1972; "And the Bones Came Together," ABC, 1973; "ABC Afternoon Playbreak: A Special Act of Love," ABC, 1973; "The FBI: Diamond Run," ABC, 1974; "Barnaby Jones: Time to Kill," CBS, 1974; "The Mary Tyler Moore Show: Anyone Who Hates Kids and Dogs," CBS, 1975; "Someone to Watch Over Me," NBC, 1975; "The Rookies: Vendetta," ABC, 1975; "City of Angels: The November Plan," NBC, 1976; "Columbo: Make Me a Perfect Murder," NBC, 1978; "Barnaby Jones: Echo of a Distant Battle," CBS, 1979; "Murder, She Wrote: A Lady in the Lake," CBS, 1986; "Murder, She Wrote: Murder Through the Looking Glass," CBS, 1988.
TV MOVIES AND MINISERIES: "Murder Impossible," ABC, 1974; "Panic on the 5:22," ABC, 1974; "Death Sentence," ABC, 1974; "Winner Take All," NBC, 1975; "The Lindbergh Kidnapping Case," NBC, 1976; "Ike," ABC, 1979; "The Mating Season," CBS, 1980; "One Terrific Guy," CBS, 1986.

LUDDEN, ALLEN
b. Mineral Point, WI, October 5, 1919; d. 1981. Game show emcee most associated with "Password" and "G.E. College Bowl."
AS A REGULAR: "G.E. College Bowl," CBS, 1959-63; "Password," CBS, 1961-68; ABC, 1969-76; "Win with the Stars," SYN, 1968-69; "Liar's Club," SYN, 1970, 1974-80; "Stumpers!," NBC, 1976.
AND: "To Tell the Truth," CBS, 1962; "ABC Nightlife," ABC, 1965; "Batman: Hizzoner the Penguin/Dizzoner the Penguin," ABC, 1966; "The Mike Douglas Show," SYN, 1967; "You Don't Say," NBC, 1967; "The Mike Douglas Show," SYN, 1968; "The Odd Couple: Password," ABC, 1972; "Match Game '74," CBS, 1974; "Tattletales," CBS, 1974; "Tattletales," CBS, 1976; "The Love Boat: Taking Sides," ABC, 1978.
* Emmies: 1976.

LUFT, LORNA
b. Los Angeles, CA, November 21, 1952. Daughter of Judy Garland; she played nurse Libby Kegler on "Trapper John, M.D."
AS A REGULAR: "Trapper John, M.D.," CBS, 1985-86.
AND: "The Judy Garland Show," CBS, 1963; "Love, American Style: Love and the Blue Plate Special," ABC, 1973; "McCloud: The Park Avenue Pirates," NBC, 1975; "Murder, She Wrote: Broadway Malady," CBS, 1985.

LUKAS, PAUL
b. Budapest, Hungary, May 26, 1894; d. 1971. Stage and TV actor and Oscar winner for the 1943 film "Watch on the Rhine."
AS A GUEST: "Sure as Fate: Tremolo," CBS, 1950; "Robert Montgomery Presents: The Ringmaster," NBC, 1952; "Armstrong Circle Theatre: Caprice," NBC, 1952; "Lux Video Theatre: Something to Celebrate," CBS, 1952; "Orient Express: Red Sash," CBS, 1953; "U.S. Steel Hour: The Thief," ABC, 1955; "Mr. Citizen: The Friendly Stranger," ABC, 1955; "Playhouse 90: Judgment at Nuremberg," CBS, 1959; "Sam Benedict: Season of Vengeance," NBC, 1963; "Bob Hope Chrysler Theatre: Four Kings," NBC, 1963; "The Man Who Bought Paradise," CBS, 1965; "The FBI: The Defector," ABC, 1966; "Run for Your Life: The Day Time Stopped," NBC, 1966; "The FBI: The Defector," ABC, 1966; "The FBI: The Hostage," ABC, 1967; "The Man From UNCLE: The Test Tube Affair," NBC, 1967; "The Name of the Game: Collector's Edition," NBC, 1968.
TV MOVIES AND MINISERIES: "The Challenge," ABC, 1970.

LUKE, KEYE
b. China, June 18, 1904; d. 1991. Actor who began as Charlie Chan's number one son in the movies. Best known as Master Po on "Kung Fu" and as the voice of Charlie Chan in a cartoon series; Luke remained active in movies ("Gremlins") and on TV.
AS A REGULAR: "Kentucky Jones," NBC, 1964-65; "Anna and the King," CBS, 1972; "The Amazing Chan and the Chan Clan," CBS, 1972-74; "Kung Fu," ABC, 1972-75; "Harry O," ABC, 1976; "Sidekicks," ABC, 1986-87.
AND: "Hollywood Playhouse: Task Force Smith," SYN, 1952; "Fireside Theatre: The Traitor," NBC, 1953; "Fireside Theatre: The Reign of Amelia Jo," NBC, 1954; "Studio 57: Ring Once for Death," SYN, 1955; "The Ray Milland Show: Chinese Luck," CBS, 1955; "My Little Margie: The San Francisco Story," NBC, 1955; "Gunsmoke: The Queue," CBS, 1955; "Crusader: Christmas in Burma," CBS, 1955; "Crossroads: Calvary in China," ABC, 1956; "Telephone Time: Time Bomb," CBS, 1956; "TV Reader's Digest: The Smuggler," ABC, 1956; "Wire Service: No

Peace at Lo Dao," ABC, 1957; "Climax!: Jacob and the Angel," CBS, 1957; "Panic: May Day," NBC, 1957; "Alcoa Theatre: In the Dark," NBC, 1958; "The Gale Storm Show: The Case of the Chinese Puzzle," CBS, 1959; "America Pauses for Springtime," CBS, 1959; "Richard Diamond, Private Detective: Chinese Honeymoon," CBS, 1958; "Follow the Sun: Little Girl Lost," ABC, 1961; "Target: The Corruptors: Chase the Dragon," ABC, 1962; "Fair Exchange: Pilot," CBS, 1962; "The Mickey Rooney Show: That's the Way the Fortune Cookie Crumbles," ABC, 1964; "Perry Mason: The Case of the Feather Cloak," CBS, 1965; "Jonny Quest: The Sea Haunt," ABC, 1965; "I Spy: Danny Was a Million Laughs," NBC, 1965; "The Wackiest Ship in the Army: Last Path to Garcia," NBC, 1965; "The Smothers Brothers Show: The Hawaiian Caper," CBS, 1966; "The FBI: Spy Master," ABC, 1966; "The FBI: The Courier," ABC, 1967; "The Andy Griffith Show: Aunt Bee's Restaurant," CBS, 1967; "Family Affair: The Great Kow-Tow," CBS, 1968; "The Big Valley: Emperor of Rice," ABC, 1968; "The Outsider: As Cold as Ashes," NBC, 1968; "Star Trek: Whom Gods Destroy," NBC, 1968; "Hawaii Five-O: All the King's Horses," CBS, 1969; "It Takes a Thief: Project X," ABC, 1970; "Marcus Welby, M.D.: A Portrait of Debbie," ABC, 1971; "Here's Lucy: Lucy and the Chinese Curse," CBS, 1972; "The FBI: Memory of a Legend," ABC, 1973; "Love, American Style: Love and the Golden Worm," ABC, 1974; "ABC Theatre: Judgment: The Court Martial of the Tiger of Malaya—General Yamashita," ABC, 1974; "M*A*S*H: Patent 4077," CBS, 1978; "M*A*S*H: A Night at Rosie's," CBS, 1979; "M*A*S*H: Death Takes a Holiday," CBS, 1980; "Charlie's Angels: Island Angels," ABC, 1980; "Bret Maverick: The Yellow Rose," NBC, 1981; "Remington Steele: You're Steele the One for Me," NBC, 1982; "Magnum, P.I.: Forty Years From Sand Island," CBS, 1983; "The A-Team: The Maltese Cow," NBC, 1983; "Miami Vice: Golden Triangle," NBC, 1985.
TV MOVIES AND MINISERIES: "Kung Fu," ABC, 1972; "The Cat Creature," ABC, 1973; "Judge Dee in the Monastery Murders," ABC, 1974; "Blade in Hong Kong," CBS, 1985; "Kung Fu," CBS, 1986.

LULU
b. Scotland, November 3, 1948. Singer.
AS A REGULAR: "Andy Williams Presents Ray Stevens," NBC, 1970.
AND: "Operation: Entertainment," ABC, 1968; "The Ugliest Girl in Town: Popped Star," ABC, 1968.

LUND, ART
b. Salt Lake City, UT, April 1, 1915; d. 1990. Singer-actor.
AS A REGULAR: "The Ken Murray Show," CBS, 1951-52.
AND: "The Ed Sullivan Show," CBS, 1956; "The

Tonight Show," NBC, 1957; "Bell Telephone Hour: The Golden West," NBC, 1959; "Salute to the American Theatre," CBS, 1959; "Gunsmoke: False Front," CBS, 1962; "Gunsmoke: Susan Was Evil," CBS, 1974; "Kojak: A Very Deadly Game," CBS, 1974; "The Rockford Files: The Countess," NBC, 1974; "Little House on the Prairie: Money Crop," NBC, 1975; "City of Angels: The Parting Shot," NBC, 1976.
TV MOVIES AND MINISERIES: "The Quest," NBC, 1976; "Man From Atlantis," NBC, 1977.

LUNDIGAN, WILLIAM
b. Syracuse, NY, June 12, 1914; d. 1975. Actor and commercial spokesman who sold Chryslers during each episode of "Climax!"
AS A REGULAR: "Climax," CBS, 1954-58; "Shower of Stars," CBS, 1956-57; "Men Into Space," CBS, 1959-60.
AND: "Lux Video Theatre: A Man in the Kitchen," CBS, 1953; "Ford Theatre: The Bachelor," NBC, 1953; "Schlitz Playhouse of Stars: Give the Guy a Break," CBS, 1954; "G.E. Theatre: To Lift a Feather," CBS, 1954; "Ford Theatre: The Tryst," NBC, 1954; "Fireside Theatre: The Indiscreet Mrs. Jarvis," NBC, 1955; "Rheingold Theatre: Total Recall," NBC, 1955; "Science Fiction Theatre: Beyond," SYN, 1955; "Playhouse 90: No Time at All," CBS, 1958; "Christophers: Preparing for the Future," SYN, 1958; "Christophers: Positive Values in Film Making," SYN, 1958; "Westinghouse Desilu Playhouse: K.O. Kitty," CBS, 1958; "Christophers: Some Facts on Robert E. Lee," SYN, 1959; "Mrs. America Pageant," SYN, 1959; "Christophers: George Washington and the Making of the Constitution," SYN, 1960; "Death Valley Days: Dangerous Crossing," SYN, 1961; "Here's Hollywood," NBC, 1962; "The Dick Powell Show: Last of the Private Eyes," NBC, 1963; "Run for Your Life: In Search of April," NBC, 1966; "Marcus Welby, M.D.: Cynthia," ABC, 1970.

LUNT, ALFRED
b. Milwaukee, WI, August 19, 1892; d. 1977. Stage legend with a few TV credits; an Emmy winner for "The Magnificent Yankee."
AS A GUEST: "Producers Showcase: The Great Sebastians," NBC, 1957; "The Last Word," CBS, 1958; "U.S. Steel Hour: The Old Lady Shows Her Medals," CBS, 1963; "Hallmark Hall of Fame: The Magnificent Yankee," NBC, 1965.
* Emmies: 1965.

LUPINO, IDA
b. London, England, February 4, 1918. Actress and director with extensive TV experience.
AS A REGULAR: "Four Star Playhouse," CBS,

1952-56; "Mr. Adams and Eve," CBS, 1957-58.

AND: "Ford Theatre: Marriageable Male," NBC, 1954; "Ford Theatre: A Season to Love," NBC, 1954; "Dick Powell's Zane Grey Theatre: The Fearful Courage," CBS, 1956; "I've Got a Secret," CBS, 1957; "The Ed Sullivan Show," CBS, 1957; "Art Linkletter's House Party," CBS, 1958; "Dinah Shore Chevy Show," NBC, 1958; "Lux Playhouse: Various Temptations," CBS, 1959; "The Perry Como Show," NBC, 1959; "The Lucille Ball-Desi Arnaz Show: Lucy's Summer Vacation," CBS, 1959; "The Twilight Zone: The 16-Millimeter Shrine," CBS, 1959; "Bonanza: The Saga of Annie O'Toole," NBC, 1959; "Dinah Shore Chevy Show," NBC, 1960; "Here's Hollywood," NBC, 1960; "G.E. Theatre: Image of a Doctor," CBS, 1961; "The Investigators: Something for Charity," CBS, 1961; "Sam Benedict: Not Even the Gulls Shall Weep," NBC, 1962; "The Virginian: A Distant Fury," NBC, 1963; "Kraft Suspense Theatre: One Step Down," NBC, 1963; "Burke's Law: Who Killed Billy Jo?," ABC, 1963; "You Don't Say," NBC, 1964; "Burke's Law: Who Killed Lenore Wingfield?," ABC, 1964; "The Rogues: Two of a Kind," NBC, 1965; "The Virginian: We've Lost a Train," NBC, 1965; "The Wild Wild West: The Night of the Big Blast," CBS, 1966; "Judd for the Defense: Kingdom of the Blind," ABC, 1968; "Batman: The Entrancing Dr. Cassandra," ABC, 1968; "It Takes a Thief: Turnabout," ABC, 1969; "The Outcasts: The Thin Edge," ABC, 1969; "The Mod Squad: Peace Now-Arly Blau!," ABC, 1969; "The Name of the Game: The Perfect Image," NBC, 1969; "Family Affair: Maudie," CBS, 1969; "Bracken's World: The Anonymous Star," NBC, 1970; "Family Affair: The Return of Maudie," CBS, 1970; "Nanny and the Professor: The Balloon Ladies," ABC, 1971; "Columbo: Short Fuse," NBC, 1972; "Alias Smith and Jones: What's in It for Mia?," ABC, 1972; "Medical Center: Conflict," CBS, 1972; "The Bold Ones: A Terminal Career," NBC, 1972; "Barnaby Jones: The Deadly Jinx," CBS, 1974; "The Streets of San Francisco: Blockade," ABC, 1974; "The Manhunter: The Ma Gentry Gang," CBS, 1974; "Columbo: Swan Song," NBC, 1974; "Switch: Stung From Beyond," CBS, 1975; "Police Woman: The Chasers," NBC, 1975.

TV MOVIES AND MINISERIES: "Women in Chains," ABC, 1972; "The Strangers in 7A," CBS, 1972; "Female Artillery," ABC, 1973; "I Love a Mystery," NBC, 1973; "The Letters," ABC, 1973.

AS DIRECTOR: "Have Gun, Will Travel," CBS, 1958-59; "The Donna Reed Show: A Difference of Opinion," ABC, 1959; "Hong Kong: Clear for Action," ABC, 1960; "Thriller: The Last of the Sommervilles," NBC, 1961; "G.E. Theatre: A Very Special Girl," CBS,

1962; "Mr. Novak: Love in the Wrong Season," NBC, 1963; "Mr. Novak: Day in the Year," NBC, 1964; "Dr. Kildare: To Walk in Grace," NBC, 1964.

LUPONE, PATTI

b. Northport, NJ, April 21, 1949. Musical-comedy actress who plays Libby on "Life Goes On."

AS A REGULAR: "Life Goes On," ABC, 1989- .

AND: "Cowboy Joe," ABC, 1988.

TV MOVIES AND MINISERIES: "LBJ: The Early Years," NBC, 1987.

LUPTON, JOHN

b. Highland Park, IL, August 22, 1926. Actor who played Tom Jeffords on "Broken Arrow" and Tom Horton on "Days of Our Lives."

AS A REGULAR: "The Halls of Ivy," CBS, 1954-55; "Broken Arrow," ABC, 1956-58; "Never Too Young," ABC, 1965; "Days of Our Lives," NBC, 1965-72, 1975-79.

AND: "Fireside Theatre: The Relentless Weavers," NBC, 1954; "My Little Margie: The Shipboard Story," NBC, 1954; "Studio 57: Step Lightly, Please," SYN, 1954; "Studio One: Always Welcome," CBS, 1956; "Matinee Theatre: A Cowboy for Chris," NBC, 1956; "The 20th Century-Fox Hour: Broken Arrow," CBS, 1956; "Schlitz Playhouse of Stars: The Press Agent," CBS, 1956; "The Millionaire: Story of Jimmy Reilly," CBS, 1957; "Restless Gun: Ricochet," NBC, 1959; "Playhouse 90: The Second Happiest Day," CBS, 1959; "Behind Closed Doors: The Antidote," NBC, 1959; "Yancy Derringer: A State of Crisis," CBS, 1959; "Black Saddle: Client: Peter Warren," ABC, 1959; "Goodyear Theatre: Wait Till Spring," NBC, 1959; "Death Valley Days: The Grand Duke," SYN, 1959; "Richard Diamond, Private Detective: Fallen Star," CBS, 1959; "G.E. Theatre: The Tallest Marine," CBS, 1959; "Perry Mason: The Case of the Bartered Bikini," CBS, 1959; "Men Into Space: Rocket to Venus, CBS, 1960; "Tales of Wells Fargo: Day of Judgment," NBC, 1960; "Checkmate: Target ... Tycoon," CBS, 1960; "Gunsmoke: Ben Tolliver's Stud," CBS, 1960; "SurfSide 6: Circumstantial Evidence," ABC, 1961; "Laramie: Killer Odds," NBC, 1961; "Walt Disney Presents: Andrews' Raiders—Escape to Nowhere," ABC, 1961; "Malibu Run: Kidnap Adventure," CBS, 1961; "Target: The Corruptors: The Platinum Highway," ABC, 1961; "Window on Main Street: The Return of Buzz Neldrum," CBS, 1961; "Wagon Train: The Jenna Douglas Story," NBC, 1961; "Laramie: The Day of the Savage," NBC, 1962; "Alfred Hitchcock Presents: Victim Found," NBC, 1962; "Death Valley Days: The Private Mint of Clark, Gruber & Co.," SYN, 1963; "Alcoa Premiere: Five, Six, Pick Up Sticks,"

ABC, 1963; "Wagon Train: The Trace McCloud Story," ABC, 1964; "Rawhide: Incident at Zebulon," CBS, 1964; "The Littlest Hobo: Dark Encounter," SYN, 1964; "The Virginian: A Gallows for Sam Horn," NBC, 1964; "Gomer Pyle, USMC: Pay Day," CBS, 1964; "Gunsmoke: Chicken," CBS, 1964; "Gomer Pyle, USMC: Sergeant of the Week," CBS, 1964; "Flipper: The Lifeguard," NBC, 1965; "Slattery's People: Does Nero Still at Ringside Sit?," CBS, 1965; "Gomer Pyle, USMC: My Buddy-War Hero," CBS, 1965; "The Cara Williams Show: The Dog Sitter," CBS, 1965; "Gomer Pyle, USMC: Gomer the M.P.," CBS, 1965; "Wagon Train: The Chief Crazy Bear Story," ABC, 1965; "T.H.E. Cat: A Slight Family Trait," NBC, 1967; "The FBI: The Conspirators," ABC, 1967; "Ironside: The Gambling Game," NBC, 1971; "Owen Marshall, Counselor at Law: Eulogy for a Wide Receiver," ABC, 1971; "Marcus Welby, M.D.: Solomon's Choice," ABC, 1972; "The FBI: The Deadly Species," ABC, 1972; "The FBI: Dark Christmas," ABC, 1972; "ABC Afterschool Special: Alexander," ABC, 1973; "Medical Center: The Guilty," CBS, 1973; "ABC's Matinee Today: I Never Said Goodbye," ABC, 1973; "Marcus Welby, M.D.: The Mugging," ABC, 1974; "Doc Elliot: The Carrier," ABC, 1974; "The FBI: Survival," ABC, 1974; "Apple's Way: The Pen Pal," CBS, 1974; "Ironside: Setup: Danger," NBC, 1974; "Police Story: Explosion!," NBC, 1974; "Kung Fu: Barbary House," ABC, 1975; "The Rockford Files: A Bad Deal in the Valley," NBC, 1976; "The Rockford Files: So Help Me God," NBC, 1976; "The Rockford Files: The Competitive Edge," NBC, 1977; "Charlie's Angels: An Angel's Trail," ABC, 1980.
TV MOVIES AND MINISERIES: "The Astronaut," NBC, 1972; "All My Darling Daughters," ABC, 1972; "The Judge and Jake Wyler," NBC, 1972; "Anna Karenina," CBS, 1985; "Red River," CBS, 1988.

LUPUS, PETER
b. 1937. Muscular actor who played strongman Willie Armitage on "Mission: Impossible."
AS A REGULAR: "Mission: Impossible," CBS, 1966-73.
AND: "I'm Dickens, He's Fenster: Nurse Dickens," ABC, 1962; "The Joey Bishop Show: Chance of a Lifetime," NBC, 1962; "The Many Loves of Dobie Gillis: Beauty Is Only Kin Deep," CBS, 1963; "Police Squad!: Terror in the Neighborhood," ABC, 1982.

LUZ, FRANC
b. Cambridge, MA. Actor usually in sensitive-hunk roles.
AS A REGULAR: "The Doctors," NBC, 1979-81; "Ryan's Hope," ABC, 1984; "Hometown,"

CBS, 1985; "Kay O'Brien," CBS, 1986; "Free Spirit," ABC, 1989-90.
AND: "Remington Steele: Steele Eligible," NBC, 1984; "Kate & Allie: Allie's Affair," CBS, 1985; "My Sister Sam: Fog Bound," CBS, 1987; "The Facts of Life: Peeksill Law," NBC, 1988; "Cheers: Norm, Is That You?," NBC, 1988; "Empty Nest: Strange Bedfellows," NBC, 1989.
TV MOVIES AND MINISERIES: "Classified Love," CBS, 1986.

LYDON, JAMES
b. Harrington Park, NJ, May 30, 1923. Former child actor in comic and dramatic roles; now he works behind the camera as a producer.
AS A REGULAR: "The First Hundred Years," CBS, 1950-52; "So This Is Hollywood," NBC, 1955; "The Gale Storm Show," CBS, 1956; "Love That Jill," ABC, 1958.
AND: "Navy Log: Incident at Formosa," ABC, 1956; "Navy Log: Human Bomb," ABC, 1957; "Trackdown: Law in Lampasas," CBS, 1957; "Wanted Dead or Alive: Twelve Hours to Crazy Horse," CBS, 1959; "77 Sunset Strip: Secret Island," ABC, 1959; "Wagon Train: The Vittorio Bottecelli Story," NBC, 1959; "Hotel De Paree: Sundance and the Barren Soil," CBS, 1960; "Bronco: End of a Rope," ABC, 1960; "Wagon Train: The Jeremy Dow Story," NBC, 1960; "The Twilight Zone: Back There," CBS, 1961; "Wanted Dead or Alive: Dead Reckoning," CBS, 1961; "The Life and Legend of Wyatt Earp: Until Proven Guilty," ABC, 1961; "The Barbara Stanwyck Show: The Choice," NBC, 1961; "Stagecoach West: The Raider," ABC, 1961; "The Real McCoys: Baseball vs. Love," ABC, 1961; "Whispering Smith: The Devil's Share," NBC, 1961; "Checkmate: Kill the Sound," CBS, 1961; "Hennesey: Hystersis Synchronous Can Be Fun," CBS, 1962; "Wagon Train: The Dr. Denker Story," NBC, 1962; "Many Happy Returns: The Woodsman," CBS, 1965; "Gunsmoke: First People," CBS, 1968; "The FBI: Act of Violence," ABC, 1968; "The FBI: The Traitor," ABC, 1970; "Adam 12: Suspect #1," NBC, 1974; "The Rockford Files: Joey Blue Eyes," NBC, 1976; "Simon & Simon: Facets," CBS, 1985.
TV MOVIES AND MINISERIES: "The New Daughters of Joshua Cabe," ABC, 1976.

LYMAN, DOROTHY
b. Minneapolis, MN, April 18, 1947. Emmy winning soap actress who now plays Naomi on "Mama's Family"; she was Opal Gardner on "All My Children."
AS A REGULAR: "A World Apart," ABC, 1970-71; "The Edge of Night," CBS, 1972-73; "One Life to Live," ABC, 1975; "Another World," NBC, 1976-80; "All My Children," ABC, 1981-83; "Mama's Family," NBC, 1983-85; SYN, 1986- .

AND: "Hunter: The Pit," NBC, 1989; "American Playhouse: Ollie Hopnoodle's Haven of Bliss," PBS, 1989.

TV MOVIES AND MINISERIES: "The People Across the Lake," NBC, 1988.

* Emmies: 1982, 1983.

LYN, DAWN

b. 1963. Child actress who played Dodie on "My Three Sons."

AS A REGULAR: "My Three Sons," CBS, 1969-72.
AND: "Marcus Welby, M.D.: Tender Comrade," ABC, 1972; "Gunsmoke: The Sodbusters," CBS, 1972; "Gunsmoke: Women for Sale," CBS, 1973; "Mannix: Little Girl Lost," CBS, 1973; "Marcus Welby, M.D.: Child of Silence," ABC, 1974; "Born Free: Africa's Child," NBC, 1974; "Barnaby Jones: Theatre of Fear," CBS, 1975; "Emergency!: Involvement," NBC, 1976; "The Streets of San Francisco: Castle of Fear," ABC, 1976.

LYNCH, KEN

b. 1910; d. 1990. Veteran character actor who spent virtually all of his career playing cops.

AS A REGULAR: "The Plainclothesman," DUM, 1949-54; "Checkmate," CBS, 1960-61; "McCloud," NBC, 1970-77; "The Doris Day Show," CBS, 1972-73.
AND: "Gunsmoke: Born to Hang," CBS, 1957; "Dick Powell's Zane Grey Theatre: A Time to Live," CBS, 1957; "Playhouse 90: The Dungeon," CBS, 1958; "Steve Canyon: Big Thunder," NBC, 1958; "Maverick: The Brasada Spur," ABC, 1959; "Bat Masterson: Deadline," NBC, 1959; "The Twilight Zone: Mr. Denton on Doomsday," CBS, 1959; "The Untouchables: Mexican Standoff," ABC, 1959; "Playhouse 90: The Tunnel," CBS, 1959; "Hotel De Paree: Sundance and the Bare-Knuckled Fighters," CBS, 1959; "Have Gun, Will Travel: The Wager," CBS, 1959; "Peter Gunn: Hot Money," NBC, 1960; "Hennesey: Hennesey Joins the Marines," CBS, 1960; "Have Gun, Will Travel: Fight at Adobe Wells," CBS, 1960; "77 Sunset Strip: Publicity Brat," ABC, 1960; "The Overland Trail, The Baron Comes Back," NBC, 1960; "Perry Mason: The Case of the Irate Inventor," CBS, 1960; "Have Gun, Will Travel: The Marshal's Boy," CBS, 1960; "Lawman: The Escape of Joe Killmer," ABC, 1960; "Angel: The Pool Shark," CBS, 1960; "Angel: The Bank Account," CBS, 1960; "The Tall Man: First Blood," NBC, 1961; "Gunsmoke: Bad Sheriff," CBS, 1961; "Malibu Run: The Radioactive-Object Adventure," CBS, 1961; "Thriller: A Good Imagination," NBC, 1961; "Lawman: The Promise," ABC, 1961; "Follow the Sun: Journey Into Darkness," ABC, 1961; "The Dick Van Dyke Show: The Talented Neighborhood," CBS, 1961; "The Andy Griffith Show: Jailbreak," CBS, 1962; "The Donna Reed Show: Winner Take All," ABC, 1962; "Rawhide: Abiline," CBS, 1962; "The Eleventh Hour: My Name Is Judith, I'm Lost, You See," NBC, 1963; "The Andy Griffith Show: A Black Day for Mayberry," CBS, 1963; "The Great Adventure: The Treasure Train of Jefferson Davis," CBS, 1963; "The Dick Van Dyke Show: The Sound of the Trumpets of Conscience Falls Deafly on a Brain That Holds Its Ears," CBS, 1963; "Wagon Train: The Alice Whitetree Story," ABC, 1964; "The Dick Van Dyke Show: The Alan Brady Show Goes to Jail," CBS, 1964; "The Baileys of Balboa: The Hot Turkey," CBS, 1964; "Mr. Novak: An Elephant Is Like a Tree," NBC, 1965; "The Big Valley: The Young Marauders," ABC, 1965; "Bonanza: The Lonely Runner," NBC, 1965; "The Munsters: Follow That Munster," CBS, 1965; "Gomer Pyle, USMC: Sergeant of the Guard," CBS, 1965; "The FBI: The Exiles," ABC, 1965; "Honey West: The Flame and the Pussycat," ABC, 1965; "Gomer Pyle, USMC: Gomer Minds His Sergeant's Car," CBS, 1965; "Run, Buddy, Run: Buddy Overstreet, Forgive Me," CBS, 1966; "The FBI: Blood Verdict," ABC, 1967; "The FBI: The Predators," ABC, 1968; "The FBI: Conspiracy of Silence," ABC, 1969; "The FBI: Flight," ABC, 1969; "The Virginian: The Substitute," NBC, 1969; "Gunsmoke: Snow Train," CBS, 1970; "The FBI: Escape to Terror," ABC, 1970; "Gunsmoke: Lynott," CBS, 1971; "All in the Family: Archie and the Lock-Up," CBS, 1971; "The Doris Day Show: Whodunnit, Doris?," CBS, 1971; "The Streets of San Francisco: The First Day of Forever," ABC, 1972; "All in the Family: Everybody Tells the Truth," CBS, 1973; "Mannix: The Man Who Wasn't There," CBS, 1973; "The Rookies: The Wheel of Death," ABC, 1973; "The FBI: The Animal," ABC, 1974; "Marcus Welby, M.D.: Last Flight to Babylon," ABC, 1974; "Police Story: The Empty Weapon," NBC, 1975; "Barnaby Jones: Price of Terror," CBS, 1975; "The Rockford Files: The Attractive Nuisance," NBC, 1977; "Barnaby Jones: The Deadly Valentine," CBS, 1977; "Switch: Photo Finish," CBS, 1978.

TV MOVIES AND MINISERIES: "Run, Simon, Run," ABC, 1970; "Incident in San Francisco," ABC, 1971; "Jigsaw," ABC, 1972.

* "The Plainclothesman" was told entirely from the point of view of the title character, played by Lynch. Only his voice was heard.

LYNCH, PEG

b. Lincoln, NB. Actress who played Ethel to Alan Bunce's Albert.

AS A REGULAR: "Ethel and Albert," NBC, 1953-54; CBS, 1955; ABC, 1955-56.
AND: "The General Motors 50th Anniversary Show," NBC, 1957.

544

LYNCH, RICHARD

b. April 26, 1936.

AS A REGULAR: "Battlestar Galactica," ABC, 1980; "The Phoenix," ABC, 1982.

AND: "Serpico: Prime Evil," NBC, 1976; "The Streets of San Francisco: Time Out," ABC, 1977; "Police Woman: Solitaire," NBC, 1977; "Charlie's Angels: Angels on the Street," ABC, 1979; "Buck Rogers in the 25th Century: Vegas in Space," NBC, 1979; "The A-Team: Hot Styles," NBC, 1984; "MacGruder and Loud: The Inside Man," ABC, 1985; "Scarecrow and Mrs. King: You Only Die Twice," CBS, 1985; "The Last Precinct: Never Cross a Vampire," NBC, 1986; "Werewolf: Nightmares at the Braine Hotel," FOX, 1987; "Hunter: The Legion of Hate," NBC, 1989.

TV MOVIES AND MINISERIES: "Starsky and Hutch," ABC, 1975; "Sizzle," ABC, 1981.

LYNDE, PAUL

b. Mt. Vernon, OH, June 13, 1926; d. 1982. Comic actor who usually played smug, fussy types; he was the longtime center square on "Hollywood Squares," mouthing scripted jokes as if they were spontaneous witticisms.

AS A REGULAR: "The Red Buttons Show," CBS, 1952-53; "Stanley," NBC, 1956-57; "Perry Como's Kraft Music Hall," NBC, 1961-62; "Bewitched," ABC, 1965-72; "The Pruitts of Southhampton," ABC, 1967; "The Jonathan Winters Show," CBS, 1968-69; "Hollywood Squares," NBC, 1968-81; "Dean Martin Presents," NBC, 1968-69; "That's Life," ABC, 1968-69; "Where's Huddles?," CBS, 1970; "The Paul Lynde Show," ABC, 1972-73; "Temperatures Rising," ABC, 1973-74.

AND: "The Ed Sullivan Show," CBS, 1952; "Ruggles of Red Gap," NBC, 1957; "The Tonight Show," NBC, 1957; "The Phil Silvers Show: Bilko's Big Woman Hunt," CBS, 1958; "The Lux Show with Rosemary Clooney," NBC, 1958; "Steve Allen Presents The Steve Lawrence-Eydie Gorme Show," NBC, 1958; "The Jack Paar Show," NBC, 1959; "The George Gobel Show," NBC, 1959; "The Phil Silvers Show: Bilko in Outer Space," CBS, 1959; "The Jack Paar Show," NBC, 1960; "The Andy Williams Show," NBC, 1962; "The Jackie Gleason Show," CBS, 1962; "Henry Fonda and the Family," CBS, 1962; "The Patty Duke Show: The Genius," ABC, 1963; "Burke's Law: Who Killed Cable Roberts?," ABC, 1963; "Grindl: Twas the Week Before Christmas," NBC, 1963; "The Jack Paar Program," NBC, 1964; "Burke's Law: Who Killed Merlin the Great?," ABC, 1964; "The Mike Douglas Show," SYN, 1964; "The Munsters: Rock-a-Bye Munster," CBS, 1964; "The Munsters: Low-Cal Munster," CBS, 1964; "The Munsters: Eddie's Nickname," CBS, 1965;

"Bewitched: Driving Is the Only Way to Fly," ABC, 1965; "The Farmer's Daughter: Rich Man, Poor Man," ABC, 1965; "Burke's Law: Who Killed Mr. Colby in Ladies' Lingerie?," ABC, 1965; "The Farmer's Daughter: Stag at Bay," ABC, 1965; "Hollywood Palace," ABC, 1965; "Gidget: Take a Lesson," ABC, 1966; "F Troop: The Singing Mountie," ABC, 1966; "I Dream of Jeannie: My Master the Rich Tycoon," NBC, 1966; "Bob Hope Chrysler Theatre: The Blue-Eyed Horse," NBC, 1966; "That Girl: These Boots Weren't Made for Walking," ABC, 1967; "Hey, Landlord!: A Little Off the Top," NBC, 1967; "The Beverly Hillbillies: Jed Inherits a Castle," CBS, 1967; "Everybody's Talking," ABC, 1967; "I Dream of Jeannie: Everybody's a Movie Star," NBC, 1967; "Hollywood Palace," ABC, 1967; "I Dream of Jeannie: Please Don't Feed the Astronauts," NBC, 1968; "The Mothers-in-Law: The Match Game," NBC, 1968; "The Jonathan Winters Show," CBS, 1968; "The Flying Nun: The Return of Father Lundigan," ABC, 1968; "Kraft Music Hall," NBC, 1969; "Kraft Music Hall," NBC, 1970; "Love, American Style: Love and the Nervous Executive," ABC, 1970; "The Glen Campbell Goodtime Hour," CBS, 1970; "Love, American Style: Love and the Pregnancy," ABC, 1971; "Love, American Style: Love and the House Bachelor," ABC, 1971; "Rowan & Martin's Laugh-In," NBC, 1972; "Password," ABC, 1972; "The Dating Game," ABC, 1972; "Perry Como's Summer of '74," CBS, 1974; "The Mac Davis Show," NBC, 1974; "The $10,000 Pyramid," ABC, 1975; "Paul Lynde Special," ABC, 1975.

TV MOVIES AND MINISERIES: "Gidget Grows Up," ABC, 1969; "Gidget Gets Married," ABC, 1972.

* On "The Ed Sullivan Show," Lynde reprised his routine from the Broadway show "New Faces of 1952" as a battered tourist in Africa.

LYNLEY, CAROL

b. Carolyn Lee, New York City, NY, February 13, 1942. Former child actress.

AS A REGULAR: "The Immortal," ABC, 1970-71.

AND: "Goodyear TV Playhouse: Grow Up," NBC, 1956; "Alfred Hitchcock Presents: The Young One," CBS, 1957; "Art Linkletter's House Party," CBS, 1957; "Du Pont Show of the Month: Junior Miss," CBS, 1957; "G.E. Theatre: Young and Scared," CBS, 1958; "Pursuit: The Vengeance," CBS, 1958; "Shirley Temple's Storybook: Rapunzel," NBC, 1958; "G.E. Theatre: Deed of Mercy," CBS, 1959; "G.E. Theatre: The Last Dance," CBS, 1959; "Walt Disney's Wonderful World of Color: The Light in the Forest," NBC, 1961; "Henry Fonda and the Family," CBS, 1962; "The Alfred Hitchcock Hour: Final Vow," CBS, 1962; "Alcoa Premiere: Whatever Happened to Miss Illinois?," ABC, 1962; "The Virginian: Man

From the Sea," NBC, 1962; "Stump the Stars," CBS, 1963; "The Dick Powell Show: The Rage of Silence," NBC, 1963; "The Young Set," ABC, 1965; "Bob Hope Chrysler Theatre: The Fliers," NBC, 1965; "Run for Your Life: In Search of April," NBC, 1966; "Bob Hope Chrysler Theatre: Runaway Boy," NBC, 1966; "The FBI: False Witness," ABC, 1967; "The Man From UNCLE: The Prince of Darkness Affair," NBC, 1967; "The Invaders: The Believers," ABC, 1967; "Journey to the Unknown: Eve," ABC, 1968; "It Takes a Thief: Boom at the Top," ABC, 1969; "The Bold Ones: Giants Never Kneel," NBC, 1970; "The Most Deadly Game: Who Killed Kindness?," ABC, 1970; "Mannix: Voice in the Dark," CBS, 1971; "Night Gallery: Last Rites for a Dead Druid," NBC, 1972; "The Sixth Sense: The House that Cried Murder," ABC, 1972; "Orson Welles' Great Mysteries: Death of an Old-Fashioned Girl," SYN, 1973; "The Magician: Ripoff," NBC, 1974; "Wide World of Mystery: If It's a Man, Hang Up," ABC, 1975; "Quincy: Who's Who in Neverland," NBC, 1976; "Police Woman: Trial by Prejudice," NBC, 1976; "Kojak: Kiss It All Goodbye," CBS, 1977; "The Love Boat: Best of Friends," ABC, 1979; "All Star Secrets," NBC, 1979; "Charlie's Angels: Island Angels," ABC, 1980; "Fantasy Island: Shadow Games," ABC, 1982; "Hotel: Faith, Hope and Charity," ABC, 1983.

TV MOVIES AND MINISERIES: "Shadow on the Land," NBC, 1968; "The Smugglers," NBC, 1968; "The Immortal," ABC, 1969; "Weekend of Terror," ABC, 1970; "The Cable Car Murder," CBS, 1971; "The Night Stalker," ABC, 1972; "The Elevator," ABC, 1974; "Death Stalk," NBC, 1974; "Flood," NBC, 1976; "Fantasy Island," ABC, 1977; "Having Babies II," ABC, 1977.

LYNN, DIANA

b. Dolores Loehr, Los Angeles, CA, October 7, 1926; d. 1971. Former Paramount contract actress who matured from a precocious ingenue into an attractive, talented performer.

AS A GUEST: "Silver Theatre: Double Feature," CBS, 1950; "Silver Theatre: Walt and Lavinia," CBS, 1950; "Lux Video Theatre: Down Bayou DuBac," CBS, 1950; "Lux Video Theatre: The Twinkle in Her Eye," CBS, 1951; "Hollywood Opening Night: The Shepard Touch," SYN, 1953; "Robert Montgomery Presents: Dinah, Kip and Mr. Barlow," NBC, 1953; "G.E. Theatre: Best Seller," CBS, 1953; "You Are There: The Last Hours of Joan of Arc," CBS, 1953; "Robert Montgomery Presents: World by the Tail," NBC, 1953; "Medallion Theatre: The Blue Serge Suit," CBS, 1954; "Climax!: A Leaf Out of the Book," CBS, 1955; "Stage 7: Down From the Stars," CBS, 1955; "Best of Broadway: Stage Door," CBS, 1955; "Climax!: A Farewell to Arms," CBS, 1955; "Schlitz Playhouse: O'Connor and the Blue-Eyed Felon," CBS, 1955; "U.S. Steel Hour: The Seventh Veil," CBS, 1955; "The Loretta Young Show: Moment of Decision," NBC, 1955; "Alcoa Hour: A Girl Can Tell," NBC, 1955; "Matinee Theatre: Anything But Love," NBC, 1956; "Lux Video Theatre: Princess O'Rourke," NBC, 1956; "Climax!: To Scream at Midnight," CBS, 1956; "Matinee Theatre: The Hollow Woman," NBC, 1956; "The Joseph Cotten Show: Nevada Nightengale," NBC, 1956; "Playhouse 90: Forbidden Area," CBS, 1956; "Schlitz Playhouse of Stars: The House That Jackson Built," CBS, 1956; "Playhouse 90: The Star Wagon," CBS, 1957; "Climax!: Trail of Terror," CBS, 1957; "Climax!: Jacob and the Angel," CBS, 1957; "Playhouse 90: A Sound of Different Drummers," CBS, 1957; "Du Pont Show of the Month: Junior Miss," CBS, 1957; "Playhouse 90: The Return of Ansel Gibbs," CBS, 1958; "Playhouse 90: A Marriage of Strangers," CBS, 1959; "Lux Playhouse: Boy on a Fence," CBS, 1959; "Arthur Murray Party," NBC, 1959; "Adventures in Paradise: Safari at Sea," ABC, 1959; "The Phildelphia Story," NBC, 1959; "Chevy Mystery Show: Dark Possession," NBC, 1960; "Here's Hollywood," NBC, 1960; "U.S. Steel Hour: The Mating Machine," CBS, 1961; "Checkmate: The Deadly Silence," CBS, 1961; "Checkmate: Juan Moreno's Body," CBS, 1961; "The Investigators: In a Mirror, Darkly," CBS, 1961; "Bus Stop: How Does Charlie Feel?," ABC, 1962; "Burke's Law: Who Killed Carrie Cornell?," ABC, 1964; "The Nurses: A Kind of Loving," CBS, 1964; "The Virginian: You Take the High Road," NBC, 1965.

LYNN, JEFFREY

b. Ragner Godfrey Lind, Auburn, MA, February 16, 1909. Rather bland leading man of movies and TV; he played Charles Clemens on "The Secret Storm."

AS A REGULAR: "My Son Jeep," NBC, 1953; "Star Stage," NBC, 1955-56; "The Secret Storm," CBS, 1968-74.

AND: "Studio One: Miracle in the Rain," CBS, 1950; "Lights Out: The Dispossessed," NBC, 1951; "Lux Video Theatre: Sweet Sorrow," CBS, 1951; "The Clock: Affliction," NBC, 1951; "Schlitz Playhouse of Stars: The Man I Marry," CBS, 1952; "Robert Montgomery Presents: Happy Birthday, George," NBC, 1952; "Tales of Tomorrow: Sleep No More," ABC, 1952; "Lux Video Theatre: Stone's Throw," CBS, 1952; "Philco TV Playhouse: The Black Sheep," NBC, 1952; "Lux Video Theatre: Thanks for a Lovely Evening," CBS, 1953; "Suspense: The Quarry," CBS, 1953; "Goodyear TV Playhouse: The

546

Accident," NBC, 1953; "Robert Montgomery Presents: The Woman Who Hated Children," NBC, 1953; "Medallion Theatre: The Trouble Train," CBS, 1953; "Suspense: Before the Fact," CBS, 1954; "Elgin TV Hour: High Man," ABC, 1954; "Kraft Television Theatre: The Independent," NBC, 1954; "Danger: A Taste for Murder," CBS, 1954; "Robert Montgomery Presents: Death and the Sky Above," NBC, 1955; "True Story: Dream No More," NBC, 1957; "That I May See," SYN, 1957; "U.S. Steel Hour: The Case of Julia Walton," CBS, 1959; "Theatre '62: The Spiral Staircase," NBC, 1961; "Play of the Week: The Magic and the Loss," SYN, 1961; "Ironside: Love My Enemy," NBC, 1969; "The Bold Ones: Crisis," NBC, 1969; "Murder, She Wrote: The Days Dwindle Down," CBS, 1987.

LYON, SUE

b. Davenport, IA, July 10, 1946. Former film ingenue ("Lolita") who worked in TV during the mid-seventies.

AS A GUEST: "Arsenic and Old Lace," ABC, 1969; "Funny You Should Ask," ABC, 1969; "The Bold Ones: Crisis," NBC, 1969; "Love, American Style: Love and the Bed," ABC, 1969; "The Men From Shiloh: Nightmare at New Life," NBC, 1970; "Men at Law: Marathon," CBS, 1971; "Night Gallery: Miss Lovecraft Sent Me," NBC, 1971; "Love, American Style: Love and the Extra Job," ABC, 1974.

TV MOVIES AND MINISERIES: "But I Don't Want to Get Married!," ABC, 1970; "Smash-Up on Interstate 5," ABC, 1976.

LYONS, GENE

b. Pittsburgh, PA, 1923; d. 1974. Actor often in stern roles; he played police commissioner Dennis Randall on "Ironside."

AS A REGULAR: "Woman with a Past," CBS, 1954; "Ironside," NBC, 1967-75.

AND: "Kraft Television Theatre: Give Me the Courage," NBC, 1957; "Rendezvous: The White Circle," CBS, 1959; "Have Gun, Will Travel: Episode in Laredo," CBS, 1959; "The Twilight Zone: King Nine Will Not Return," CBS, 1960; "The du Pont Show with June Allyson: The Visitor," CBS, 1960; "Naked City: The Human Trap," ABC, 1960; "Hong Kong: Murder by Proxy," ABC, 1961; "The Americans: The Bounty Jumpers," NBC, 1961; "Have Gun, Will Travel: The Road," CBS, 1961; "Stoney Burke: The Mob Riders," ABC, 1962; "The Alfred Hitchcock Hour: What Really Happened?," CBS, 1963; "The Dick Van Dyke Show: Ray Murdock's X Ray," CBS, 1963; "The Virginian: If You Have Tears," NBC, 1963; "The Great Adventure: Six Wagons to the Sea," CBS, 1964; "The Alfred Hitchcock Hour: The Evil of Adelaide Winters," CBS, 1964; "Perry Mason: The Case of the Wrathful Wraith," CBS, 1965; "The FBI: The Courier," ABC, 1967; "The FBI: Pressure Point," ABC, 1970; "The FBI: Escape to Nowhere," ABC, 1972.

TV MOVIES AND MINISERIES: "Ironside," NBC, 1967.

LYTELL, BERT

b. New York City, NY, February 24, 1885; zd. 1954. Actor whose career dated to silent films; usually in dignified roles.

AS A REGULAR: "The Hollywood Screen Test," ABC, 1948; "Philco TV Playhouse," NBC, 1948-49; "One Man's Family," NBC, 1949-52; "The Orchid Award," ABC, 1953.

AND: "Tales of Tomorrow: A Child Is Crying," ABC, 1952; "Broadway Television Theatre: I Like It Here," SYN, 1952; "Broadway Television Theatre: Janie," SYN, 1953.

M

MACARTHUR, JAMES
b. *Los Angeles, CA, December 8, 1937.* Actor who played Danny Williams, sidekick to Steve McGarrett (Jack Lord) on "Hawaii Five-O."
AS A REGULAR: "Hawaii Five-O," CBS, 1968-79.
AND: "Climax!: Deal a Blow," CBS, 1955; "Arthur Murray Party," NBC, 1957; "Studio One: Tongues of Angels," CBS, 1958; "G.E. Theatre: Young and Scared," CBS, 1958; "Studio One: Ticket to Tahiti," CBS, 1958; "Westinghouse Desilu Playhouse: The Innocent Assassin," CBS, 1959; "The Dick Powell Show: The Court-Martial of Captain Wycliff," NBC, 1962; "Sam Benedict: Some Fires Die Slowly," NBC, 1963; "Twelve O'Clock High: The Outsider," ABC, 1966; "Walt Disney's Wonderful World of Color: Willie and the Yank," NBC, 1967; "Hondo: Hondo and the Mad Dog," ABC, 1967; "Tarzan: Pride of the Lioness," NBC, 1967; "Combat!: Encounter," ABC, 1967; "Death Valley Days: Kit Carson," SYN, 1968; "Lassiter," CBS, 1968; "Hollywood Squares," NBC, 1972; "The Love Boat: Next-Door Wife," ABC, 1979; "The Love Boat: Marriage of Convenience," ABC, 1980; "The Love Boat: Vicki's Gentlemen Caller," ABC, 1985.
TV MOVIES AND MINISERIES: "The Night The Bridge Fell Down," NBC, 1983.

MCBRIDE, MARY MARGARET
b. *Paris, MO, November 16, 1899; d. 1976.* Personality of radio and early TV; Bob and Ray parodied her with their character Mary Margaret McGoon.
AS A REGULAR: "Mary Margaret McBride," NBC, 1948.
AND: "Mike Wallace Interviews," ABC, 1957; "The Tonight Show," NBC, 1957; "Modern Romances," NBC, 1958.

MCCALLA, IRISH
b. *Pawnee City, NB, December 25, 1929.* Sexy starlet of the fifties.
AS A REGULAR: "Sheena, Queen of the Jungle," SYN, 1955-56.
AND: "You Bet Your Life," NBC, 1961; "Have Gun, Will Travel: Bob Wire," CBS, 1963.

MCCALLUM, DAVID
b. *Glasgow, Scotland, September 19, 1933.* Blonde actor and sixties teen heartthrob who played Illya Kuryakin on "The Man From UNCLE."
AS A REGULAR: "The Man From UNCLE," NBC,

1964-68; "The Invisible Man," NBC, 1975-76.
AND: "The Outer Limits: The Sixth Finger," ABC, 1963; "The Travels of Jaimie McPheeters: The Day of the Search," ABC, 1964; "Perry Mason: The Case of the Fifty Millionth Frenchman," CBS, 1964; "The Andy Williams Show," NBC, 1965; "Hullabaloo," NBC, 1965; "Festival of the Arts: Wuthering Heights," NET, 1965; "Please Don't Eat the Daisies: Say UNCLE," NBC, 1966; "This Morning," ABC, 1968; "Hallmark Hall of Fame: Teacher, Teacher," NBC, 1969; "Hallmark Hall of Fame: The File on Devlin," NBC, 1969; "Night Gallery: The Phantom Farmhouse," NBC, 1971; "The Man and the City: Pipe Me a Loving Tune," ABC, 1971; "Marcus Welby, M.D.: Just a Little Courage," ABC, 1972; "The Screaming Skull," ABC, 1973; "The Six Million Dollar Man: Doomsday, and Counting," ABC, 1973; "The Six Million Dollar Man: The Last of the Fourth of Julys," ABC, 1974; "Bert D'Angelo/Superstar: A Noise in the Street," ABC, 1976; "Strike Force: Ice," ABC, 1982; "The A-Team: The Say Uncle Affair," NBC, 1986; "Matlock: The Billionaire," NBC, 1987; "Murder, She Wrote: From Russia— with Blood," CBS, 1989.
TV MOVIES AND MINISERIES: "Hauser's Memory," NBC, 1974; "She Waits," CBS, 1972; "Frankenstein: The True Story," NBC, 1973; "The Invisible Man," NBC, 1975; "Return of the Man From UNCLE," CBS, 1983; "Behind Enemy Lines," NBC, 1985; "Freedom Fighter," NBC, 1988.

MCCARTNEY, PAUL
b. *Liverpool, England, June 18, 1942.*
AS A GUEST: "Saturday Night Live," NBC, 1980.
* See also The Beatles.

MACCHIO, RALPH
b. *Huntington, NY, November 4, 1962.* Teen hunk of TV and the "Karate Kid" movies.
AS A REGULAR: "Eight Is Enough," ABC, 1980-81.
TV MOVIES AND MINISERIES: "The Three Wishes of Billy Grier," ABC, 1984.

MCCLANAHAN, RUE
b. *Healdton, OK, February 2, 1934.* Emmy winning actress who plays Blanche Devereaux on "The Golden Girls"; she also played Vivian, friend of "Maude" (Beatrice Arthur).
AS A REGULAR: "Where the Heart Is," CBS, 1969-70; "Another World," NBC, 1970-71; "Maude," CBS, 1972-78; "Apple Pie," ABC, 1978; "Mama's Family," NBC, 1983-85; "The

Golden Girls," NBC, 1985- .

AND: "Hogan's Goat," NET, 1971; "All in the Family: The Bunkers and the Swingers," CBS, 1972; "ABC's Matinee Today: My Secret Mother," ABC, 1973; "Mannix: A Daughter's Life at Stake," CBS, 1974; "Theatre in America: Who's Happy Now?," PBS, 1975; "Theatre in America: The Rimers of Eldritch," PBS, 1975; "Hollywood Squares," NBC, 1977; "Gimme a Break: The Second Time Around," NBC, 1981; "The Love Boat: His Girl Friday," ABC, 1982; "The Love Boat: How Do I Love Thee?," ABC, 1984; "Gimme a Break: Grandpa's Secret Life," NBC, 1984; "Murder, She Wrote: Murder Takes the Bus," CBS, 1985; "Empty Nest: Fatal Attraction," NBC, 1988; "Animal Crack-Ups," ABC, 1989; "Let Me Hear You Whisper," A&E, 1989; "The Wickedest Witch," NBC, 1989; "Nightmare Classics: The Strange Case of Dr. Jekyll and Mr. Hyde," SHO, 1989.

TV MOVIES AND MINISERIES: "Sergeant Matlovich vs. the U.S. Air Force," NBC, 1978; "Rainbow," NBC, 1978; "Topper," ABC, 1979; "The Great American Traffic Jam," NBC, 1980; "Word of Honor," CBS, 1981; "The Little Match Girl," NBC, 1987; "Liberace," ABC, 1988; "Take My Daughters, Please," NBC, 1988; "The Man in the Brown Suit," CBS, 1989.

* Emmies: 1987.

MCCLURE, DOUG

b. Pacific Palisades, CA, May 11, 1938. Hunky blond leading man of the sixties who played Trampas on "The Virginian."

AS A REGULAR: "The Overland Trail," NBC, 1960; "Checkmate," CBS, 1960-62; "The Virginian," NBC, 1962-71; "Search," NBC, 1972-73; "Barbary Coast," ABC, 1975-76; "Out of This World," SYN, 1987- .

AND: "The Adventures of Jim Bowie: Bad Medicine," ABC, 1958; "Court of Last Resort: The Todd-Loomis Case," NBC, 1958; "Death Valley Days: Gold Rush in Reverse," SYN, 1958; "The Gale Storm Show: The Honeymoon Suite," CBS, 1959; "U.S. Steel Hour: Street of Love," CBS, 1961; "Dream Girl of '67," ABC, 1967; "It Takes a Thief: A Thief Is a Thief Is a Thief," ABC, 1968; "The Mike Douglas Show," SYN, 1969; "Name Droppers," NBC, 1969; "Ghost Story: Cry of the Cat," NBC, 1972; "Hardcastle and McCormick: School for Scandal," ABC, 1984; "Scarecrow and Mrs. King: Remembrance of Things Past," CBS, 1984; "Magnum P.I.: Way of the Stalking Horse," CBS, 1985; "Murder, She Wrote: Night of the Headless Horseman," CBS, 1986; "Murder, She Wrote: Steal Me a Story," CBS, 1987; "B.L. Stryker: The King of Jazz," ABC, 1989.

TV MOVIES AND MINISERIES: "The Longest Hundred Miles," NBC, 1967; "Terror in the Sky," ABC,

1971; "The Birdmen," CBS, 1971; "The Death of Me Yet," ABC, 1971; "Playmates," ABC, 1972; "The Judge and Jake Wyler," NBC, 1972; "Shirts/Skins," ABC, 1973; "Death Race," ABC, 1973; "Satan's Triangle," ABC, 1975; "SST-Death Flight," ABC, 1977; "Roots," ABC, 1977; "The Rebels," SYN, 1979; "Nightside," ABC, 1980.

MCCONNELL, ED

b. 1892; d. 1955. "Smilin' Ed," host of a long-running kiddie show.

AS A REGULAR: "The Buster Brown TV Show with Smilin' Ed McConnell and the Buster Brown Gang," NBC, 1950-51; "Smilin' Ed McConnell and His Gang," NBC, 1951-54.

* McConnell also provided the voice of one of the show's characters, Froggie the Gremlin.

MCCORD, KENT

b. Los Angeles, CA, September 26, 1942. Actor usually in straight-arrow roles; he played Off. Jim Reed on "Adam 12."

AS A REGULAR: "Adam 12," NBC, 1968-75; "Battlestar Galactica," ABC, 1980.

AND: "The Virginian: A Bald-Faced Boy," NBC, 1966; "The Virginian: A Welcoming Town," NBC, 1967; "Dragnet: The Big Interrogation," NBC, 1967; "Dragnet: The Big Magazine," NBC, 1967; "Dragnet: The Big Bank," NBC, 1967; "Dragnet: The Big Search," NBC, 1968; "The Outsider: The Land of the Fox," NBC, 1968; "Hollywood Squares," NBC, 1971; "Marcus Welby, M.D.: Strike II," ABC, 1975; "Baa Baa Black Sheep: Presumed Dead," NBC, 1976; "The Love Boat: The Perfect Match," ABC, 1980; "Private Eye: Star," NBC, 1988; "21 Jump Street: Chapel of Love," FOX, 1988.

TV MOVIES AND MINISERIES: "The Outsider," NBC, 1967; "Shadow Over Elveron," NBC, 1968; "Dragnet," NBC, 1969; "Emergency!," NBC, 1972; "Beg, Borrow ... or Steal," CBS, 1973; "Nashville Beat," TNN, 1989.

MCCORMACK, PATTY

b. New York City, NY, August 21, 1945. Child actress ("The Bad Seed") who still does a fair amount of TV; she played Ingeborg on "Mama."

AS A REGULAR: "Mama," CBS, 1953-56; "Peck's Bad Girl," CBS, 1959; "Young Doctor Malone," NBC, 1962-63; "The Best of Everything," ABC, 1970; "As the World Turns," CBS, 1975-76; "The Ropers," ABC, 1979-80.

AND: "Mirror Theatre: The Party," NBC, 1953; "Campbell TV Soundstage: I Remember, I Remember," NBC, 1954; "The Web: Handful of Stars," CBS, 1954; "Playhouse 90: The Miracle Worker," CBS, 1957; "Du Pont Theatre: Dan

Marshall's Brat," ABC, 1957; "Matinee Theatre: There Won't Be Any Trouble," NBC, 1957; "Studio 57: Robin," SYN, 1957; "U.S. Steel Hour: Rachel's Summer," CBS, 1959; "Alcoa Presents One Step Beyond: Make Me Not a Witch," ABC, 1959; "Chevy Mystery Show: Summer Hero," NBC, 1960; "Route 66: Black November," CBS, 1960; "Route 66: Sleep on Four Pillows," CBS, 1961; "Death Valley Days: A Girl Named Virginia," SYN, 1962; "The New Breed: Thousands and Thousand of Miles," ABC, 62; "Rawhide: Incident of the Wolvers," CBS, 1962; "Rawhide: Incident at Paradise," CBS, 1963; "The Doctors: Pride and Mrs. Cobb," NBC, 1963; "The Farmer's Daughter: Cousin Helga Came to Dinner," ABC, 1964; "The Wild Wild West: Night of the Death Masks," CBS, 1968; "Police Story: Chain of Command," NBC, 1974; "The Streets of San Francisco: Blockade," ABC, 1974; "Barnaby Jones: Image in a Cracked Mirror," CBS, 1974; "Emergency!: The Convention," NBC, 1978; "Friends: Going Out," ABC, 1979; "Three's Company: Moving On," ABC, 1979; "Three's Company: Stanley the Ladies' Man," ABC, 1979; "Hotel: The Wedding," ABC, 1984; "Partners in Crime: Fashioned for Murder," NBC, 1984; "Murder, She Wrote: The Wearing of the Green," CBS, 1988; "Freddy's Nightmares: Photo Finish," SYN, 1989. TV MOVIES AND MINISERIES: "Night Partners," CBS, 1983.

MCCORMICK, MAUREEN
b. *California, 1956*. Marcia Brady.
AS A REGULAR: "The Brady Bunch," ABC, 1969-74; "The Brady Bunch Hour," ABC, 1977; "The Brady Brides," NBC, 1981; "The Bradys," CBS, 1990.
AND: "The Farmer's Daughter: Why Don't They Ever Pick Me?," ABC, 1965; "Honey West: In the Bag," ABC, 1965; "Camp Runamuck: Tomboy," NBC, 1966; "I Dream of Jeannie: My Master, the Doctor," NBC, 1966; "Marcus Welby, M.D.: The Day After Forever," ABC, 1973; "Happy Days: Cruisin'," ABC, 1975; "Joe Forrester: Bus Station," NBC, 1975; "The Streets of San Francisco: No Minor Vices," ABC, 1976; "Gibbsville: All the Young Girls," NBC, 1976; "Lou Grant: Sweep," CBS, 1979; "The Love Boat: Doc's Exchange," ABC, 1980; "The Love Boat: The Christmas Presence," ABC, 1982; "Day by Day: A Very Brady Episode," NBC, 1989.
TV MOVIES AND MINISERIES: "A Vacation in Hell," ABC, 1979; "A Very Brady Christmas," CBS, 1988.

MCCREA, JOEL
b. *Los Angeles, CA, November 5, 1905*. Screen actor who jumped on the TV western bandwagon of the fifties.
AS A REGULAR: "Four Star Playhouse," CBS,

1952-53; "Wichita Town," NBC, 1959-60.
AND: "Art Linkletter's House Party," CBS, 1957; "I've Got a Secret," CBS, 1959; "The Merv Griffin Show," CBS, 1970; "This Is Your Life," SYN, 1972.

MCDEVITT, RUTH
b. *Coldwater, MI, September 13, 1895; d. 1976*. Actress who often played spunky old ladies; she played columnist Emily Cowles on "Kolchak, the Night Stalker."
AS A REGULAR: "A Woman to Remember," DUM, 1947; "Mr. Peepers," NBC, 1953-55; "Young Doctor Malone," NBC, 1958-63; "Pistols 'n' Petticoats," CBS, 1966-67; "Johnny Cash Presents The Everly Brothers Show," ABC, 1970; "Bright Promise," NBC, 1969-72; "All in the Family," CBS, 1973-75; "Kolchak, the Night Stalker," ABC, 1974-75.
AND: "Kraft Television Theatre: The Wonderful Gift," NBC, 1956; "Robert Montgomery Presents: Slice of Life," NBC, 1957; "True Story: Mother's Day," NBC, 1957; "Naked City: Bridge Party," ABC, 1961; "Dr. Kildare: Gravida One," NBC, 1962; "The Nurses: Night Shift," CBS, 1962; "The Doctors: Call Me Charity," NBC, 1963; "The Alfred Hitchcock Hour: The Cadaver," CBS, 1964; "Bewitched: Long Live the Queen," ABC, 1967; "Bewitched: Mrs. Stephens, Where Are You?," ABC, 1969; "Marcus Welby, M.D.: Child of Silence," ABC, 1974; "The Rookies: Blue Christmas," ABC, 1974; "Little House on the Prairie: If I Should Wake Before I Die," NBC, 1974; "The Streets of San Francisco: School of Fear," ABC, 1975; "The Bob Newhart Show: Seemed Like a Good Idea at the Time," CBS, 1975; "Ellery Queen: The Twelfth Floor Express," NBC, 1975; "Medical Center: Two Against Death," CBS, 1975.
TV MOVIES AND MINISERIES: "In Search of America," ABC, 1971; "The Girl Most Likely to...," ABC, 1973; "Skyway to Death," ABC, 1974; "My Father's House," NBC, 1975; "One of My Wives Is Missing," ABC, 1976.

MCDOWALL, RODDY
b. *London, England, September 17, 1928*. Former child actor with extensive TV experience; memorable as the Bookworm on "Batman" and in an Emmy-award winning role as Alexander Hamilton's brother, Philip, in "Not Without Honor."
AS A REGULAR: "The Planet of the Apes," CBS, 1974; "Fantastic Journey," NBC, 1977; "Tales of the Gold Monkey," ABC, 1982-83; "Bridges to Cross," CBS, 1986.
AND: "Robert Montgomery Presents: When We Are Married," NBC, 1951; "Kraft Television Theatre: Philip Goes Forth," NBC, 1952; "Lux Video Theatre: Salad Days," CBS, 1952; "Broadway Television Theatre: It Pays to

Advertise," SYN, 1952; "Medallion Theatre: A Suitable Marriage," CBS, 1954; "Goodyear TV Playhouse: Buy Me Blue Ribbons," NBC, 1954; "Armstrong Circle Theatre: My Client, McDuff," NBC, 1954; "Robert Montgomery Presents: The Reality," NBC, 1954; "Matinee Theatre: White Headed Boy," NBC, 1957; "Alcoa Hour: He's for Me," NBC, 1957; "The Arlene Francis Show," NBC, 1957; "Suspicion: The Woman with Red Hair," NBC, 1958; "Playhouse 90: Heart of Darkness," CBS, 1958; "Arthur Murray Party," NBC, 1958; "U.S. Steel Hour: Night of Betrayal," CBS, 1959; "Oldsmobile Music Theatre: Too Bad About Sheila Troy," NBC, 1959; "Art Carney Special: The Best of Anything," NBC, 1960; "The Twilight Zone: People Are Alike All Over," CBS, 1960; "Person to Person," CBS, 1960; "Our American Heritage: Not Without Honor," NBC, 1960; "Naked City: The Fault in Our Stars," ABC, 1961; "Person to Person," CBS, 1961; "The Power and the Glory," CBS, 1961; "Hallmark Hall of Fame: The Tempest," NBC, 1963; "Password," CBS, 1964; "The Eleventh Hour: The Only Remaining Copy Is in the British Museum," NBC, 1964; "Bob Hope Chrysler Theatre: Mr. Biddle's Crime Wave," NBC, 1964; "Batman: The Bookworm Turns/While Gotham City Burns," ABC, 1966; "Bob Hope Chrysler Theatre: The Fatal Mistake," NBC, 1966; "The Invaders: The Organization," ABC, 1967; "Hallmark Hall of Fame: Saint Joan," NBC, 1967; "Journey to the Unknown: The Killing Bottle," ABC, 1969; "It Takes a Thief: Boom at the Top," ABC, 1969; "Love, American Style: Love and the Sensuous Twin," ABC, 1972; "The Carol Burnett Show," CBS, 1974; "Hollywood Squares," NBC, 1974; "The Snoop Sisters: A Black Day for Bluebeard," NBC, 1974; "Hollywood Squares," SYN, 1975; "The White Seal," CBS, 1975; "The Magnificent Marble Machine," NBC, 1975; "Police Woman: Pawns of Power," NBC, 1975; "Hollywood Squares," NBC, 1976; "Mowgli's Brothers," CBS, 1976; "Harry O: The Mysterious Case of Lester and Dr. Fong," ABC, 1976; "Hollywood Squares," NBC, 1977; "The Love Boat: Don't Push Me," ABC, 1979; "$weepstake$: Billy, Wally and Ludmilla, and Theodore," NBC, 1979; "Mork & Mindy: Dr. Morkenstein," ABC, 1979; "Hotel: Intimate Stranger," ABC, 1984; "Murder, She Wrote: School for Scandal," CBS, 1985; "Matlock: The Chef," NBC, 1987; "Murder, She Wrote: Fire Burn, Cauldron Bubble," CBS, 1989; "Matlock: The Starlet," NBC, 1989; "Nightmare Classics: Carmilla," SHO, 1989.

TV MOVIES AND MINISERIES: "Night Gallery," NBC, 1969; "Terror in the Sky," ABC, 1971; "A Taste of Evil," ABC, 1971; "What's a Nice Girl Like You...?," ABC, 1971; "Miracle on 34th Street," CBS, 1973; "The Elevator," ABC, 1974; "Flood," NBC, 1976; "Best Sellers: The

Rhinemann Exchange," NBC, 1977; "The Thief of Baghdad," NBC, 1978; "The Immigrants," SYN, 1978; "The Memory of Eva Ryker," CBS, 1980; "The Million-Dollar Face," NBC, 1981; "Mae West," ABC, 1982; "This Girl for Hire," CBS, 1983.
* Emmies: 1961.

MCGAVIN, DARREN
b. San Joaquin, CA, May 7, 1922. Dependable actor who played Carl Kolchak, reporter and reluctant investigator into the occult, in two highly-rated TV movies and a series; also, an Emmy winner as the dad of Murphy Brown (Candice Bergen).

AS A REGULAR: "Crime Photgrapher," CBS, 1951-52; "Mickey Spillane's Mike Hammer," SYN, 1957-58; "Riverboat," NBC, 1959-61; "The Outsider," NBC, 1968-69; "Kolchak, the Night Stalker," ABC, 1974-75; "Small & Frye," CBS, 1983.

AND: "Tales of Tomorrow: The Duplicates," ABC, 1952; "Goodyear TV Playhouse: The Witness," NBC, 1952; "Armstrong Circle Theatre: Recapture," NBC, 1952; "Armstrong Circle Theatre: The Town That Refused to Die," NBC, 1955; "Alfred Hitchcock Presents: The Cheney Vase," CBS, 1955; "Studio One: First Prize for Murder," CBS, 1957; "Studio One: The Fair-Haired Boy," CBS, 1958; "Decision: Man Against Crime," NBC, 1958; "The Ford Show," NBC, 1959; "Arthur Murray Party," NBC, 1960; "Here's Hollywood," NBC, 1960; "The Islanders: Island Witness," ABC, 1961; "Stagecoach West: A Place of Still Waters," ABC, 1961; "Death Valley Days: The Stolen City," SYN, 1961; "Route 66: The Opponent," CBS, 1961; "Rawhide: The Sendoff," CBS, 1961; "Pass-word," CBS, 1961; "To Tell the Truth," CBS, 1961; "Password," CBS, 1962; "To Tell the Truth," CBS, 1962; "U.S. Steel Hour: Marriage Marks the Spot," CBS, 1962; "The Match Game," NBC, 1963; "The Defenders: Everybody Else Is Dead," CBS, 1963; "Object Is," ABC, 1964; "To Tell the Truth," CBS, 1964; "The Virginian: The Intruders," NBC, 1964; "The Alfred Hitchcock Hour: A Matter of Murder," CBS, 1964; "The Doctors and the Nurses: Hildie," CBS, 1964; "Ben Casey: Kill the Dream but Spare the Dreamer," ABC, 1964; "The Defenders: A Taste of Ashes," CBS, 1964; "Bob Hope Chrysler Theatre: Parties to the Crime," NBC, 1964; "The Rogues: The Diamond-Studded Pie," NBC, 1965; "The Name of the Game: Goodbye, Harry," NBC, 1969; "Love, American Style: Love and the Fly," ABC, 1970; "Mannix: A Ticket to the Eclipse," CBS, 1970; "The Name of the Game: The Battle of Gannon's Bridge," NBC, 1970; "Bracken's World: Infinity," NBC, 1970; "Matt Lincoln: Billy," ABC, 1970; "The Bold Ones: The

Invasion of Kevin Ireland," NBC, 1971; "Father on Trial," NBC, 1972; "The Wonderful World of Disney: High-Flying Spy," NBC, 1972; "Shaft: The Meat-Eaters," CBS, 1974; "Owen Marshall, Counselor at Law: A Foreigner Among Us," ABC, 1974; "Police Story: The Ripper," NBC, 1974; "Don Adams Screen Test," SYN, 1975; "Anyone for Tennyson?," PBS, 1977; "The Love Boat: The Promoter," ABC, 1980; "Nero Wolfe: Gambit," NBC, 1981; "Highway to Heaven: The Correspondent," NBC, 1987; "Murphy Brown: Brown Like Me," CBS, 1989.

TV MOVIES AND MINISERIES: "The Outsider," NBC, 1967; "The Challenge," ABC, 1970; "The Challengers," CBS, 1970; "Berlin Affair," ABC, 1970; "Tribes," ABC, 1970; "Banyon," NBC, 1971; "The Death of Me Yet," ABC, 1971; "The Night Stalker," ABC, 1972; "Something Evil," CBS, 1972; "The Rookies," ABC, 1972; "Say Goodbye, Maggie Cole," ABC, 1972; "The Night Strangler," ABC, 1973; "The Six-Million Dollar Man," ABC, 1973; "Brinks: The Great Robbery," CBS, 1976; "Law and Order," NBC, 1976; "The Users," ABC, 1978; "Ike," ABC, 1979; "Battle of the Generations," NBC, 1979; "Love for Rent," ABC, 1979; "Waikiki," ABC, 1980; "My Wicked, Wicked Ways: The Legend of Errol Flynn," CBS, 1985; "AT&T Presents: Inherit the Wind," NBC, 1988; "The Diamond Trap," CBS, 1988.
* Emmies: 1990.

MCGEE, FRANK
b. Monroe, LA, September 12, 1921; d. 1974.
AS A REGULAR: "World Wide '60," NBC, 1960; "Here and Now," NBC, 1961; "NBC Weekend News," NBC, 1965-71; "NBC Evening News," NBC, 1970-71; "Today," NBC, 1971-74.

MACGIBBON, HARRIET
b. Chicago, IL, 1905; d. 1987. Actress who usually played snooty matrons; she was Mrs. Drysdale on "The Beverly Hillbillies."
AS A REGULAR: "Three Steps to Heaven," NBC, 1953-54; "Golden Windows," NBC, 1954-55; "Peter Loves Mary," NBC, 1960-61; "The Beverly Hillbillies," CBS, 1962-69; "The Smothers Brothers Show," CBS, 1965-66.
AND: "Hennesey: Hennesey Meets Mrs. Horatio Grief," CBS, 1959; "Hennesey: Senior Nurse," CBS, 1960; "The Donna Reed Show: The Wedding Present," ABC, 1960; "Margie: Riches to Rags," ABC, 1961; "Dr. Kildare: The Bed I've Made," NBC, 1962; "Our Man Higgins: Mr. Gilbert and Mr. Sullivan," ABC, 1962; "Grindl: It's in the Bag," NBC, 1964; "The Eleventh Hour: The Secret in the Stone," NBC, 1964; "Ben Casey: A Thousand Words Are Mute," ABC, 1964; "Many Happy Returns: The Shoplifter," CBS, 1964; "Dragnet: The Big Bank Examiners,"

NBC, 1967; "Bewitched: The Battle of Burning Creek," ABC, 1969; "The Mod Squad: Never Give the Fuzz an Even Break," ABC, 1969; "The Doris Day Show: Happiness Is Not Being Fired," CBS, 1972.

MCGIVER, JOHN
b. New York City, NY, November 5, 1913; d. 1975. Rotund actor with a stuffy voice and formal manner who usually played floorwalkers or authority figures; best known as Dr. Luther Quince on "The Jimmy Stewart Show" and as the salesman at Tiffany's in the film "Breakfast at Tiffany's."
AS A REGULAR: "The Patty Duke Show," ABC, 1963-64; "Many Happy Returns," CBS, 1964-65; "Mr. Terrific," CBS, 1967; "The Jimmy Stewart Show," NBC, 1971-72.
AND: "Kraft Television Theatre: Most Blessed Woman," NBC, 1957; "U.S. Steel Hour: The Change in Chester," CBS, 1957; "Schlitz Playhouse of Stars: The Kind Mr. Smith," CBS, 1958; "U.S. Steel Hour: Trouble-in-Law," CBS, 1959; "Du Pont Show of the Month: Oliver Twist," CBS, 1959; "Five Fingers: The Assassin," NBC, 1959; "The Secret of Freedom," NBC, 1960; "The Tab Hunter Show: My Brother, the Hero," NBC, 1960; "Peter Loves Mary: The Last Train From Oakdell," NBC, 1961; "Malibu Run: The Tidal Wave Adventure," CBS, 1961; "U.S. Steel Hour: Marriage Marks the Spot," CBS, 1962; "The Lucy Show: Lucy Is a Kangaroo for a Day," CBS, 1962; "Ensign O'Toole: Operation: Psychology," NBC, 1963; "Mr. Novak: A Feeling for Friday," NBC, 1963; "The Twilight Zone: The Bard," CBS, 1963; "The Twilight Zone: Sounds and Silences," CBS, 1964; "The Lucy Show: Lucy Is Her Own Lawyer," CBS, 1964; "The du Pont Show: The Missing Bank of Rupert X. Humperdink," NBC, 1964; "The Beverly Hillbillies: Granny vs. the Weather Bureau," CBS, 1964; "Candid Camera," CBS, 1965; "The Dick Van Dyke Show: See Rob Write, Write Rob, Write," CBS, 1965; "Honey West: How Brillig, O Beamish Boy?," ABC, 1966; "The Wild Wild West: The Night of the Turncoat," CBS, 1967; "The Doris Day Show: Doris the Spy," CBS, 1970; "Bewitched: The Mother-in-Law of the Year," ABC, 1970; "Love, American Style: Love and the Trip," ABC, 1971; "Hollywood Television Theatre: The Police," NET, 1971; "Alias Smith and Jones: A Fistful of Diamonds," ABC, 1971; "Alias Smith and Jones: Witness to a Lynching," ABC, 1972; "Love, American Style: Love and the Christmas Punch," ABC, 1972; "McCoy: Bless the Big Fish," NBC, 1975.
TV MOVIES AND MINISERIES: "The Feminist and the Fuzz," ABC, 1971; "Sam Hill: Who Killed the Mysterious Mr. Foster?," NBC, 1971; "The Great Man's Whiskers," NBC, 1973; "Tom Sawyer," CBS, 1973.

MCGOOHAN, PATRICK

b. *Astoria, Queens, NY, 1928.* Actor associated
with British television, especially as "Secret
Agent" John Drake and as "The Prisoner," both
exceptional shows that have become cult
classics; an Emmy winner as a crazed military
school commander on "Columbo."
AS A REGULAR: "Danger Man," CBS, 1961;
"Secret Agent," CBS, 1965-66; "The Prisoner,"
CBS, 1968-69; "Rafferty," CBS, 1977.
AND: "The Vise: Gift From Heaven," ABC, 1955;
"Walt Disney's Wonderful World of Color: The
Scarecrow of Romney Marsh," NBC, 1964;
"Columbo: By Dawn's Early Light," NBC, 1974;
"Columbo: Identity Crisis," NBC, 1975.
TV MOVIES AND MINISERIES: "Koroshi," NET, 1968;
"The Man in the Iron Mask," NBC, 1977; "Of
Pure Blood," CBS, 1986.
AS DIRECTOR: "Columbo: Identity Crisis," NBC,
1975; "Columbo: Last Salute to the Commo-
dore," NBC, 1976.
AS CREATOR-PRODUCER: "The Prisoner," CBS,
1968-69.
* Emmies: 1975.

MCGRATH, FRANK

b. *Mound City, MO, February 2, 1903; d.
1967.* Grizzled actor who played cook Charlie
Wooster on "Wagon Train."
AS A REGULAR: "Wagon Train," NBC, 1957-62;
ABC, 1962-65; "Tammy," ABC, 1965-66.
AND: "Art Linkletter's House Party," CBS, 1962;
"The Virginian: Linda," NBC, 1966.

MCINTIRE, JOHN

b. *Spokane, WA, June 27, 1907; d. 1991.*
Character actor often in western roles; he
played wagonmaster Christopher Hale on
"Wagon Train" and Clay Grainger on "The
Virginian."
AS A REGULAR: "Naked City," ABC, 1958-59;
"Wagon Train," NBC, 1961-62; ABC, 1962-
65; "The Virginian," NBC, 1967-68; "Shirley,"
NBC, 1979-80; "American Dream," ABC,
1981.
AND: "G.E. Theatre: The Windmill," CBS, 1955;
"Cavalcade of America: Six Hours to Deadline,"
ABC, 1955; "Front Row Center: Expert Witness,"
CBS, 1956; "Cavalcade Theatre: Wild April,"
ABC, 1956; "Lux Video Theatre: The Taggart
Light," NBC, 1957; "Father Knows Best: Bud, the
Caretaker," CBS, 1957; "G.E. Theatre: The Trail
to Christmas," CBS, 1957; "Alfred Hitchcock
Presents: Sylvia," CBS, 1958; "Goodyear Theatre:
Decision by Terror," NBC, 1958; "Wichita Town:
Drifting," NBC, 1959; "Westinghouse Desilu
Playhouse: The Hanging Judge," CBS, 1959;
"Laramie: The Passing of Kuba Smith," NBC,
1960; "Arrest and Trial: Run Little Man, Run,"
ABC, 1963; "Daniel Boone: The Reunion," NBC,

1965; "The FBI: The Hijackers," ABC, 1965; "Walt
Disney's Wonderful World of Color: The Mystery
of Edward Sims," NBC, 1968; "The Wonderful
World of Disney: Snow Bear," NBC, 1970;
"Homewood: The Plot to Overthrow Christmas,"
NET, 1970; "The Wonderful World of Disney:
Bayou Boy," NBC, 1971; "The FBI: The Last Job,"
ABC, 1971; "Love, American Style: Love and the
Old Cowboy," ABC, 1971; "Longstreet: Please
Leave the Wreck for Others to Enjoy," ABC, 1972;
"Dirty Sally: Right of Way," CBS, 1974; "Quincy:
Quincy's Wedding," NBC, 1983; "The Love Boat:
The Problem with Poppa," ABC, 1985.
TV MOVIES AND MINISERIES: "Longstreet," ABC,
1971; "Powderkeg," CBS, 1971; "Linda," ABC,
1973; "The Healers," NBC, 1974; "The New
Daughters of Joshua Cabe," ABC, 1976; "The
Jordan Chance," CBS, 1978; "Mrs. R's
Daughter," NBC, 1979; "The Cowboy and the
Ballerina," CBS, 1984; "Dream Breakers," CBS,
1989.

MACK, TED

b. *Greeley, CO, February 12, 1904; d. 1976.*
Emcee of a long-running amateur talent
program.
AS A REGULAR: "The Original Amateur Hour,"
DUM, 1948-49; NBC, 1949-54; ABC, 1955-57;
NBC, 1957-58; CBS, 1959; ABC, 1960; CBS,
1960-70; "The Ted Mack Family Hour," ABC,
1951.
AND: "Christophers: Set Big Goals," SYN, 1962;
"Christophers: Reach Out to the World," SYN,
1963; "The Red Skelton Hour," CBS, 1969.

MCKAY, GARDNER

b. *George Cadogan Gardner McKay, New York
City, June 10, 1932.* Good-looking actor who
played adventurer Adam Troy, captain of the
good ship Tiki, on "Adventures in Paradise."
After the show folded, he got out of the acting
business.
AS A REGULAR: "Adventures in Paradise," ABC,
1959-62.
AND: "Death Valley Days: The Big Rendezvous,"
SYN, 1956; "The Thin Man: The Angel Biz," NBC,
1957; "Boots and Saddles: The Politician," SYN,
1957; "Boots and Saddles: The Decision," SYN, 1957;
"Vacation Playhouse: A Love Affair Just for Three,"
CBS, 1963.

MCKAY, JIM

b. *Philadelphia, PA.* Sportscaster who's been
covering the Olympics since 1960.
AS A REGULAR: "Make the Connection," NBC,
1955; "The Verdict Is Yours," CBS, 1957-62;
"Sports Spot," CBS, 1951; "Make the Connection," NBC, 1955; "Eye on New York," CBS,
1958; "ABC Wide World of Sports," ABC,
1961- .

MCKEAN, MICHAEL

b. New York City, NY, October 17, 1947. Actor who played Lenny Kosnowski on "Laverne & Shirley."

AS A REGULAR: "Laverne & Shirley," ABC, 1976-83; "Grand," NBC, 1990.

AND: "Hollywood Squares," SYN, 1980; "Saturday Night Live," NBC, 1984.

TV MOVIES AND MINISERIES: "More Than Friends," ABC, 1978; "Classified Love," CBS, 1986.

MACKENZIE, GISELE

b. Gisele Marie Louise Marguerite la Fleche, Winnipeg, Manitoba, Canada, January 10, 1927. Popular singer of the fifties.

AS A REGULAR: "Your Hit Parade," NBC, 1953-57; "The Gisele MacKenzie Show," NBC, 1957-58; "The Sid Caesar Show," ABC, 1963-64.

AND: "Kraft Television Theatre: Now, Where Was I?," NBC, 1955; "Justice: Hard to Get," NBC, 1955; "Studio One: The Man Who Caught the Ball at Coogan's Bluff," CBS, 1955; "G.E. Theatre: The Hat with the Roses," CBS, 1956; "The Jack Benny Program," CBS, 1958; "Dinah Shore Chevy Show," NBC, 1958; "Arthur Murray Party," NBC, 1959; "U.S. Steel Hour: Holiday on Wheels," CBS, 1959; "The Ford Show," NBC, 1959; "The Chevy Show," NBC, 1959; "Perry Como's Kraft Music Hall," NBC, 1960; "Summer on Ice," NBC, 1960; "I've Got a Secret," CBS, 1960; "The Jack Benny Program," CBS, 1960; "Bell Telephone Hour: And Freedom Sings," NBC, 1960; "The Garry Moore Show," CBS, 1960; "The Garry Moore Show," CBS, 1962; "The Jack Benny Program: Ghost Town Western Sketch," CBS, 1962; "Here's Hollywood," NBC, 1962; "Stump the Stars," CBS, 1962; "The Jack Paar Program," NBC, 1962; "The Merv Griffin Show," NBC, 1963; "The Match Game," NBC, 1963; "Sid Caesar and Edie Adams Together," ABC, 1963; "You Don't Say," NBC, 1964; "To Tell the Truth," CBS, 1964; "Burke's Law: Who Killed Half of Glory Lee?," ABC, 1964; "The Price Is Right," ABC, 1965; "PDQ," NBC, 1965; "PDQ," NBC, 1966; "The Match Game," NBC, 1966; "The Mike Douglas Show," SYN, 1972; "A Salute to Television's 25th Anniversary," ABC, 1972; "MacGyver: The Secret of Parker House," ABC, 1988.

MCKEON, NANCY

b. Westbury, NY, April 5, 1966.

AS A REGULAR: "The Facts of Life," NBC, 1980-88.

AND: "Alice: Who Ordered the Hot Turkey?," CBS, 1978; "The Love Boat: Daddy's Pride," ABC, 1979; "Alice: Alice's Halloween Surprise," CBS, 1981.

TV MOVIES AND MINISERIES: "A Question of Love," ABC, 1978; "The Facts of Life Goes to Paris," NBC, 1982; "High School USA," NBC, 1983; "This Child Is Mine," 1985, NBC; "Strange Voices," NBC, 1987; "The Facts of Life Down

Under," NBC, 1987; "A Cry for Help: The Tracey Thurman Story," NBC, 1989.

MCKEON, PHILLIP

b. Westbury, NY, November 11, 1964. Young actor who played Tommy Hyatt, son of Alice (Linda Lavin). Brother of Nancy.

AS A REGULAR: "Alice," CBS, 1976-85.

AND: "Dinah!," SYN, 1980.

MACLAINE, SHIRLEY

b. Shirley MacLean Beaty, Richmond, VA, April 24, 1934. Oscar and Emmy-winning dancer-actress who played herself in a 1987 miniseries about her introduction to the spiritual world.

AS A REGULAR: "Shirley's World," ABC, 1971-72.

AND: "Shower of Stars," CBS, 1956; "The Bob Hope Show," NBC, 1956; "Dinah Shore Chevy Show," NBC, 1957; "The Chevy Show," NBC, 1957; "The Chevy Show," NBC, 1958; "Dinah Shore Chevy Show," NBC, 1958; "The Sid Caesar Show," NBC, 1958; "Shirley MacLaine Special," NBC, 1959; "Person to Person," CBS, 1959; "Here's Hollywood," NBC, 1961; "Shirley MacLaine Special," CBS, 1974; "The Carol Burnett Show," CBS, 1975; "Shirley MacLaine Special: Gypsy in My Soul," CBS, 1975; "Inaugural Eve Special," CBS, 1977; "Shirley MacLaine Special: Every Little Movement," CBS, 1980; "Shirley MacLaine," SHO, 1985; "Irving Berlin's 100th Birthday Celebration," CBS, 1988; "Late Night with David Letterman," NBC, 1988.

TV MOVIES AND MINISERIES: "Out on a Limb," ABC, 1987.

* Emmies: 1980.

MACLEOD, GAVIN

b. Mt. Kisco, NY, February 28, 1931. Bald actor lucky enough to be in three successful series: He was Happy Haines on "McHale's Navy," Murray Slaughter on "The Mary Tyler Moore Show" and "Love Boat" Capt. Merrill Stubing.

AS A REGULAR: "McHale's Navy," ABC, 1962-64; "The Mary Tyler Moore Show," CBS, 1970-77; "The Love Boat," ABC, 1977-86.

AND: "U.S. Marshal: Undercover," SYN, 1958; "The Untouchables: The Tri-State Gang," ABC, 1959; "Mr. Lucky: Hair of the Dog," CBS, 1960; "Straightaway: The Heist," ABC, 1961; "The Untouchables: The Loophole," ABC, 1961; "The Dick Van Dyke Show: Empress Carlotta's Necklace," CBS, 1961; "My Favorite Martian: The Man From Uncle Martin," CBS, 1966; "Combat!: The Masquers," ABC, 1967; "Hogan's Heroes: The Collector General," CBS, 1968; "Hogan's Heroes: Clearance Sale at the Black Market," CBS, 1968; "The Flying Nun: A Star Is Reborn," ABC, 1969; "Love, American Style:

Love and the Image Makers," ABC, 1974; "Dinah!," SYN, 1974; "The Merv Griffin Show," SYN, 1974; "Rhoda: Rhoda's Wedding," CBS, 1974; "Charlie's Angels: Love Boat Angels," ABC, 1979; "Hotel: Fallen Idols," ABC, 1985.

TV MOVIES AND MINISERIES: "The Intruders," NBC, 1970; "Only with Married Men," ABC, 1974; "Scruples," CBS, 1980; "Murder Can Hurt You!," ABC, 1980.

MCLERIE, ALLYN ANN

b. Canada, December 1, 1926. Musical comedy actress who plays Florence, worried mother of Molly Dodd (Blair Brown).

AS A REGULAR: "The Tony Randall Show," ABC, 1976-77; CBS, 1977-78; "The Days and Nights of Molly Dodd," NBC, 1987-88; LIF, 1988- .

AND: "The Jimmy Dean Show," CBS, 1959; "Music for a Summer Night: Mr. Porter of Indiana," ABC, 1960; "Westinghouse Presents: An Old-Fashioned Thanksgiving," ABC, 1961; "The FBI: The Minerva Tapes," ABC, 1971; "The FBI: The Jug Marker," ABC, 1972; "Love Story: Time for Love," NBC, 1974; "The FBI: The Lost Man," ABC, 1974; "Medical Center: Three on a Tightrope," CBS, 1974; "Medical Center: Too Late for Tomorrow," CBS, 1975; "Lou Grant: Hit," CBS, 1979; "WKRP in Cincinnati: The Patter of Little Feet," CBS, 1979; "Lou Grant: Inheritance," CBS, 1980; "Barney Miller: Homicide," ABC, 1980; "WKRP in Cincinnati: The Baby," CBS, 1980; "Hart to Hart: Ex-Wives Can Be Murder," ABC, 1981; "WKRP in Cincinnati: A Simple Little Wedding," CBS, 1981; "The Love Boat: The Last Case," ABC, 1983; "St. Elsewhere: Drama Center," NBC, 1984; "Punky Brewster: Henry Falls in Love," NBC, 1985; "Webster: Almost Home," ABC, 1985; "Simon & Simon: Love and/or Marriage," CBS, 1986.

TV MOVIES AND MINISERIES: "A Tree Grows in Brooklyn," NBC, 1974; "Born Innocent," NBC, 1974; "Someone I Touched," ABC, 1975; "Death Scream," ABC, 1975; "The Entertainer," NBC, 1976; "And Baby Makes Six," NBC, 1979; "To Find My Son," CBS, 1980; "Rascals and Robbers," CBS, 1982; "Living Proof: The Hank Williams Jr. Story," NBC, 1983; "Two Kinds of Love," CBS, 1983; "Fantasies," ABC, 1982; "Stranger in My Bed," NBC, 1987.

MCMAHON, ED

b. Detroit, MI, March 6, 1923. Longtime sidekick of Johnny Carson, "Star Search" host and pitchman in thousands of commercials; he also toadies to the great God Jerry Lewis each Labor Day weekend.

AS A REGULAR: "Big Top," CBS, 1950-51; "Who Do You Trust?," ABC, 1958-62; "The Tonight Show Starring Johnny Carson," NBC, 1962- ; "Missing Links," NBC, 1963-64; "Snap Judgment," NBC, 1967-68; "Concentration," NBC, 1969; "NBC Adventure Theatre," NBC,

1972; "Whodunnit?," NBC, 1979; "Star Search," SYN, 1983- ; "Jerry Lewis Labor Day Telethon," SYN, 1983- ; "TV's Bloopers & Practical Jokes," NBC, 1984-88.

AND: "The Joey Bishop Show: Joey, Jack Jones and the Genie," NBC, 1964; "Kraft Music Hall," NBC, 1968; "Kraft Music Hall: Roast for Johnny Carson," NBC, 1968; "Here's Lucy: Lucy and Johnny Carson," CBS, 1969; "Here's Lucy: Lucy the Wealthy Widow," CBS, 1973; "The Sonny and Cher Comedy Hour," CBS, 1973; "The Mike Douglas Show," SYN, 1974; "Dinah!," SYN, 1975; "Sanford & Son: The Hawaiian Connection," NBC, 1976; "The Sonny and Cher Comedy Hour," CBS, 1976; "The Peter Marshall Variety Show," SYN, 1977; "Hollywood Squares," SYN, 1980; "ALF: Tonight, Tonight," NBC, 1988; "Newhart: The Nice Man Cometh," CBS, 1989.

TV MOVIES AND MINISERIES: "The Kid From Left Field," NBC, 1979; "The Golden Moment: An Olympic Love Story," NBC, 1980; "The Great American Traffic Jam," NBC, 1980; "The Star Maker," NBC, 1981.

MCMAHON, HORACE

b. South Norwalk, CT, 1906; d. 1971. Tough-guy actor best known as Lt. Mike Parker on "Naked City."

AS A REGULAR: "Martin Kane, Private Eye," NBC, 1950-51; "Make Room for Daddy," ABC, 1953-54; "Naked City," ABC, 1959; 1960-63; "Jackie Gleason and His American Scene Magazine," CBS, 1963-64; "Mr. Broadway," CBS, 1964.

AND: "Ford Theatre: To Any Soldier," NBC, 1953; "Schlitz Playhouse of Stars: The Pearl Street Incident," CBS, 1954; "Climax!: The Long Goodbye," CBS, 1954; "Ford Theatre: Stars Don't Shine," NBC, 1955; "Pond's Theatre: The Cornered Man," ABC, 1955; "Damon Runyon Theatre: Situation Wanted," CBS, 1955; "Studio One: The Man Who Caught the Ball at Coogan's Bluff," CBS, 1955; "Star Tonight: Faith and Patience," ABC, 1956; "Robert Montgomery Presents: The Misfortunes of Mr. Minihan," NBC, 1956; "Ford Theatre: Front Page Father," ABC, 1956; "Father Knows Best: Trip to Hillsborough," NBC, 1957; "The 20th Century-Fox Hour: Threat to a Happy Ending," CBS, 1957; "Suspicion: Death Watch," NBC, 1958; "The Phil Silvers Show: Bilko's Big Woman Hunt," CBS, 1958; "Sunday Showcase: What Makes Sammy Run?," NBC, 1959; "The Alaskans: Counterblow," ABC, 1960; "Sugarfoot: The Captive Locomotives," ABC, 1960; "Bourbon Street Beat: Wagon Show," ABC, 1960; "Bronco: End of a Rope," ABC, 1960; "77 Sunset Strip: Sierra," ABC, 1960; "The Twilight Zone: Mr. Bevis," CBS, 1960; "Route 66: Where Are the Sounds of Celi Brahms?," CBS, 1963; "The Tonight Show Starring Johnny Carson," NBC, 1963; "For the

People: The Right to Kill," CBS, 1965; "Batman: The Sport of Penguins/A Horse of Another Color," ABC, 1967; "My Three Sons: Casanova O'Casey," CBS, 1968; "Family Affair: A Lesson for Grownups," CBS, 1969.

MACMURRAY, FRED
b. Kankakee, IL, August 30, 1908. Actor who had a solid movie career behind him when he came to TV as dad Steve Douglas on "My Three Sons"; reportedly one of Hollywood's wealthiest men.

AS A REGULAR: "My Three Sons," ABC, 1960-65; CBS, 1965-72.

AND: "The George Gobel Show," NBC, 1954; "G.E. Theatre: Bachelor's Bride," CBS, 1955; "The George Gobel Show," NBC, 1955; "The George Gobel Show," NBC, 1956; "Screen Directors Playhouse: It's a Most Unusual Day," NBC, 1956; "The George Gobel Show," NBC, 1956; "The 20th Century-Fox Hour: False Witness," CBS, 1957; "Dinah Shore Chevy Show," NBC, 1957; "The George Gobel Show," NBC, 1957; "The $64,000 Question," CBS, 1957; "Shower of Stars," CBS, 1957; "The Lucille Ball-Desi Arnaz Show: Lucy Hunts Uranium," CBS, 1958; "December Bride: Fred MacMurray Show," CBS, 1958; "The George Gobel Show," NBC, 1958; "G.E. Theatre: One Is a Wanderer," CBS, 1958; "Cimarron City: I, the People," NBC, 1958; "The Ed Sullivan Show," CBS, 1959; "Hobby Lobby," ABC, 1959; "U.S. Steel Hour: The American Cowboy," CBS, 1960; "The Andy Williams Show," NBC, 1963; "Andy Williams Special," NBC, 1963; "Summer Playhouse: The Apartment House," CBS, 1964; "Joys," NBC, 1976.

TV MOVIES AND MINISERIES: "The Chadwick Family," ABC, 1974; "Beyond the Bermuda Triangle," NBC, 1975.

MCNEAR, HOWARD
b. Los Angeles, CA, 1905; d. 1969. Comic actor fondly remembered as Mayberry barber Floyd Lawson on "The Andy Griffith Show."

AS A REGULAR: "The Brothers," CBS, 1956-57; "The Andy Griffith Show," CBS, 1960-67; "The Jetsons," ABC, 1962-63.

AND: "December Bride: Texas Show," CBS, 1956; "I Love Lucy: Little Ricky Gets Stage Fright," CBS, 1956; "December Bride: Jaywalker," CBS, 1956; "The George Burns and Gracie Allen Show: September and May," CBS, 1957; "George Sanders Mystery Theatre: The Night I Died," NBC, 1957; "Schlitz Playhouse of Stars: The Hole Card," CBS, 1957; "Bachelor Father: Bentley Leads a Dog's Life," CBS, 1958; "Peter Gunn: The Missing Night Watchman," NBC, 1959; "Maverick: Dodge City or Bust," ABC, 1960; "Have Gun, Will Travel: The Prisoner," CBS, 1960; "The Many Loves of Dobie Gillis:

Dr. Jekyll and Mr. Gillis," CBS, 1962; "The Twilight Zone: Hocus-Pocus and Frisby," CBS, 1962; "The Wide Country: Straitjacket for an Indian," NBC, 1962; "The Twilight Zone: The Bard," CBS, 1963; "Please Don't Eat the Daisies: The Leaning Tower of Ridgemont," NBC, 1966.
* McNear left "The Andy Griffith Show" in 1966, suffering from a debilitating muscle disease. He returned to the show shortly thereafer, but he stayed seated during his scenes or stood behind the barber chair with the aid of an unseen prop.

MACNEE, PATRICK
b. England, February 6, 1922. Actor who played debonair secret agent John Steed on two TV versions of "The Avengers."

AS A REGULAR: "The Avengers," ABC, 1966-69; "The New Avengers," CBS, 1976; "Gavilan," NBC, 1982-83; "Empire," CBS, 1984.

AND: "Matinee Theatre: Jane Eyre," NBC, 1956; "Suspicion: The Voice in the Night," NBC, 1958; "Schlitz Playhouse of Stars: No Boat for Four Months," CBS, 1958; "Studio One: Man Under Glass," CBS, 1958; "Alcoa Theatre: Strange Occurance at Rokesay," NBC, 1958; "Playhouse 90: Misalliance," CBS, 1959; "U.S. Steel Hour: Dangerous Interlude," CBS, 1959; "Alcoa Presents One Step Beyond: Night of April 14," ABC, 1959; "Alfred Hitchcock Presents: Arthur," CBS, 1959; "The Virginian: A King's Ransom," NBC, 1970; "Alias Smith and Jones: The Man Who Murdered Himself," ABC, 1972; "Columbo: Troubled Waters," NBC, 1975; "House Calls: Uncle Digby," CBS, 1981; "The Love Boat: The Last Heist," ABC, 1984; "Magnum P.I.: Holmes Is Where the Heart Is," CBS, 1984; "Murder, She Wrote: Sing a Song of Murder," CBS, 1985; "Blacke's Magic: It's a Jungle Out There," NBC, 1986; "Murphy's Law: Do Someone a Favor and It Becomes Your Job," ABC, 1988.

TV MOVIES AND MINISERIES: "Mister Jerico," ABC, 1970; "Portrait: The Woman I Love," ABC, 1974; "Matt Helm," ABC, 1975; "Sherlock Holmes in New York," NBC, 1976; "Evening in Byzantium," SYN, 1978; "The Billion Dollar Threat," ABC, 1979; "Stunt Seven," CBS, 1979; "Return of the Man From UNCLE," CBS, 1983; "Club Med," ABC, 1986; "Sorry, Wrong Number," USA, 1989.

MCNEILL, DON
b. Galena, IL, December 23, 1907. Longtime morning-show host on TV and radio.

AS A REGULAR: "Don McNeill TV Club," ABC, 1950-51, 1954; "Take Two," ABC, 1963.

AND: "Person to Person," CBS, 1958; "The Jack Benny Program," CBS, 1960.

MCNICHOL, KRISTY
b. Los Angeles, CA, September 11, 1962. Former

child actress who won two Emmies as Buddy on "Family"; she plays Barbara on "Empty Nest."
AS A REGULAR: "Apple's Way," CBS, 1974-75; "Family," ABC, 1976-80; "Empty Nest," NBC, 1988- .
AND: "Love, American Style: Love and the Unsteady Steady," ABC, 1973; "Summer of My German Soldier," NBC, 1978; "Murder, She Wrote: Showdown in Saskatchewan," CBS, 1989.
TV MOVIES AND MINISERIES: "Like Mom, Like Me," CBS, 1978; "My Old Man," CBS, 1979; "Blinded by the Light," CBS, 1980; "Love Mary," CBS, 1985; "Women of Valor," CBS, 1986.
* Emmies: 1977, 1979.

MCQUEEN, BUTTERFLY
b. Thelma McQueen, Tampa, FL, January 8, 1911. Actress best known as Prissy in "Gone with the Wind," with sporadic TV credits; she played Oriole, sidekick of Beulah, on that sitcom about a black maid.
AS A REGULAR: "Beulah," ABC, 1950-53.
AND: "Studio One: Give Us Our Dream," CBS, 1950; "Hallmark Hall of Fame: The Green Pastures," NBC, 1959; "The Dating Game," ABC, 1969; "ABC Afterschool Special: The Seven Wishes of a Rich Kid," ABC, 1980; "The Magical World of Disney: Polly," NBC, 1989.
* Emmies: 1980.

MCQUEEN, STEVE
b. Terence Stephen McQueen, Indianapolis, IN, March 24, 1930; d. 1980. Handsome blond actor who moved into movie stardom after scoring as bounty hunter Josh Randall on "Wanted Dead or Alive."
AS A REGULAR: "Wanted Dead or Alive," CBS, 1958-61.
AND: "Goodyear TV Playhouse: The Chivington Raid," NBC, 1955; "U.S. Steel Hour: Bring Me a Dream," CBS, 1956; "Studio One: The Defender," CBS, 1957; "Tales of Wells Fargo: Bill Longley," NBC, 1958; "West Point: Ambush," CBS, 1957; "Climax!: Four Hours in White," CBS, 1958; "Trackdown: The Bounty Hunter," CBS, 1958; "Alfred Hitchcock Presents: Human Interest Story," CBS, 1959; "Alfred Hitchcock Presents: The Man From the South," CBS, 1960; "Perry Como's Kraft Music Hall," NBC, 1960; "The Bob Hope Buick Show," NBC, 1960; "The Dick Powell Show: Thunder in a Forgotten Town," NBC, 1963.

MACRAE, ELIZABETH
b. Elizabeth Herndon MacRae, Fayetteville, NC. Actress who played Lou Ann Poovie, girlfriend of Gomer Pyle, USMC.
AS A REGULAR: "Gomer Pyle, USMC," CBS, 1966-69; "General Hospital," ABC, 1969-70, 1972-73.
AND: "Harrigan and Son: Junior Goes Society,"

ABC, 1961; "Maverick: Benefit of Doubt," ABC, 1961; "SurfSide 6: One for the Road," ABC, 1961; "Surfside 6: The Roust," ABC, 1962; "77 Sunset Strip: Mr. Bailey's Honeymoon," ABC, 1962; "Route 66: Go Read the River," CBS, 1962; "Gunsmoke: Us Haggens," CBS, 1962; "Sam Benedict: The Boiling Point," NBC, 1963; "Stoney Burke: A Matter of Percentage," ABC, 1963; "The Fugitive: Dark Corner," ABC, 1964; "The Virginian: Two Men Named Laredo," NBC, 1965; "The Andy Griffith Show: Big Brothers," CBS, 1967; "Kojak: Night of the Piraeus," CBS, 1975; "Kojak: Secret Snow-Deadly Snow," CBS, 1975; "Barnaby Jones: Eyes of Terror," CBS, 1976; "Rhoda: Nose Job," CBS, 1977.

MACRAE, GORDON
b. East Orange, NJ, 1921; d. 1986. Musical comedy star and singer with plenty of variety-show credits.
AS A REGULAR: "The Colgate Comedy Hour," NBC, 1954-55; "The Gordon MacRae Show," NBC, 1956; "Lux Video Theatre," NBC, 1956-57.
AND: "Ford Star Jubilee: You're the Top," CBS, 1956; "President's Birthday Party," CBS, 1956; "The Jackie Gleason Show," CBS, 1957; "The Spike Jones Show," CBS, 1957; "Five Stars in Springtime," NBC, 1957; "The Polly Bergen Show," NBC, 1958; "The Eddie Fisher Show," NBC, 1958; "Pat Boone Chevy Showroom," ABC, 1959; "The Ed Sullivan Show," CBS, 1959; "The Bell Telephone Hour: We Two," NBC, 1960; "Revlon Revue," CBS, 1960; "Dinah Shore Chevy Show," NBC, 1960; "Person to Person," CBS, 1960; "Highways of Melody," NBC, 1961; "Westinghouse Presents: Carnival at Sun Valley," ABC, 1962; "The Jack Paar Program," NBC, 1962; "The Ed Sullivan Show," CBS, 1964; "On Broadway Tonight," CBS, 1965; "Aqua Varieties," ABC, 1965; "The Dean Martin Show," NBC, 1965; "Bell Telephone Hour," NBC, 1965; "The Mike Douglas Show," SYN, 1966; "The Merv Griffin Show," SYN, 1974; "McCloud: The Barefoot Girls," NBC, 1974; "Dinah!," SYN, 1975.

MACRAE, MEREDITH
b. Houston, TX, 1945. Actress who played Sally, girlfriend and later wife of Mike Douglas (Tim Matheson) on "My Three Sons"; then she jumped over to "Petticoat Junction" as Billie Jo Bradley.
AS A REGULAR: "My Three Sons," ABC, 1963-65; "Petticoat Junction," CBS, 1966-70; "ValueTelevision," SYN, 1987.
AND: "Person to Person," CBS, 1960; "Art Linkletter's House Party," CBS, 1967; "Personality," NBC, 1968; "The Match Game," NBC, 1968; "The Beverly Hillbillies: The Thanksgiving Story," CBS, 1968; "The Beverly Hillbillies: The Week Before Christmas," CBS, 1968; "The Spring Thing," NBC, 1969; "Love, American Style: Love

and Grandma," ABC, 1970; "Alias Smith and Jones: Something to Get Hung About," ABC, 1972; "Love, American Style: Love and the Bashful Groom," ABC, 1972; "The FBI: The Detonator," ABC, 1973; "The $10,000 Pyramid," CBS, 1974; "Tattletales," CBS, 1974; "The Merv Griffin Show," SYN, 1974; "3 for the Money," NBC, 1975; "Dinah!," SYN, 1976; "The Rockford Files: Requiem for a Funny Box," NBC, 1977; "CHiPS: Off-Road," NBC, 1980; "Webster: The Uh-Oh Feeling," ABC, 1984; "Magnum P.I.: This Island Isn't Big Enough," CBS, 1986.
* See also James Brown.

MACRAE, SHEILA
b. London, England, September 24, 1924. Comedienne and singer who performed frequently with ex-husband Gordon; the last actress to date to play Alice Kramden.
AS A REGULAR: "The Jackie Gleason Show," CBS, 1966-70; "The Honeymooners," CBS, 1971; "Parenthood," NBC, 1990- .
AND: "I Love Lucy: The Fashion Show," CBS, 1955; "Lux Video Theatre: One Sunday Afternoon," NBC, 1957; "The Dinah Shore Chevy Show," NBC, 1958; "The Garry Moore Show," CBS, 1959; "The Ed Sullivan Show," CBS, 1959; "The Bell Telephone Hour: We Two," NBC, 1960; "Revlon Revue," CBS, 1960; "The Dinah Shore Chevy Show," NBC, 1960; "Person to Person," CBS, 1960; "Highways of Melody," NBC, 1961; "Westinghouse Presents: Carnival at Sun Valley," ABC, 1962; "The Jack Paar Program," NBC, 1962; "The Red Skelton Hour," CBS, 1962; "Stump the Stars," CBS, 1963; "The Jack Paar Program," NBC, 1963; "The Ed Sullivan Show," CBS, 1964; "Missing Links," ABC, 1964; "On Broadway Tonight," CBS, 1965; "Aqua Varieties," ABC, 1965; "The Dean Martin Show," NBC, 1965; "The Young Set," ABC, 1965; "Personality," NBC, 1968; "Jackie Gleason Special," CBS, 1973; "Musical Chairs," CBS, 1975; "The Love Boat: The Harder They Fall," ABC, 1979.
TV MOVIES AND MINISERIES: "Goldie and the Boxer Go to Hollywood," NBC, 1981.

MCRANEY, GERALD
b. Collins, MS, August 19, 1947. Popular TV performer with an old-shoe charm who played private detective Rick Simon and now plays Major "Mack" MacGillis on "Major Dad."
AS A REGULAR: "The Law," NBC, 1975; "Simon & Simon," CBS, 1981-88; "Major Dad," CBS, 1989- .
AND: "Gunsmoke: Whelan's Men," CBS, 1973; "Alias Smith and Jones: The Day the Amnesty Came Through," ABC, 1973; "The FBI: Deadly Ambition," ABC, 1974; "Barnaby Jones: Mystery Cycle," CBS, 1974; "Gunsmoke: Hard Labor," CBS, 1975; "The Streets of San Francisco:

Deadly Silence," ABC, 1975; "Petrocelli: Death Ride," NBC, 1975; "Petrocelli: Terror on Wheels," NBC, 1975; "The Streets of San Francisco: Hot Dog," ABC, 1976; "Barnaby Jones: Dangerous Gambit," CBS, 1976; "Police Woman: Task Force: Cop Killer," NBC, 1976; "Lobo: Keep on Buckin'," NBC, 1981; "Designing Women: Dash Goff, the Writer," CBS, 1987.
TV MOVIES AND MINISERIES: "The Jordan Chance," CBS, 1978; "Where the Ladies Go," ABC, 1980; "Memories Never Die," CBS, 1982; "City Killer," NBC, 1984; "Easy Prey," ABC, 1986; "A Hobo's Christmas," CBS, 1987; "Where the Hell's That Gold?," CBS, 1988; "The People Across the Lake," NBC, 1988.
* McRaney was the last guest star to draw against Matt Dillon (James Arness) on "Gunsmoke."

MCVEY, PATRICK
b. 1910; d. 1973. Actor who played crusading newspaper editor Steve Wilson, of Big Town.
AS A REGULAR: "Big Town," CBS, 1950-54; "Boots and Saddles," SYN, 1957-59; "Manhunt," SYN, 1959-61.
AND: "Kraft Television Theatre: Wish Tonight," NBC, 1954; "Studio One: The Laughter of Giants," CBS, 1956; "Armstrong Circle Theatre: Seventy-Three Seconds Into Space," NBC, 1956; "Kaiser Aluminum Hour: The Old Army Game," NBC, 1956; "Tombstone Territory: Pick Up the Gun," ABC, 1958; "Maverick: The Jail at Junction Flats," ABC, 1958; "Restless Gun: Strange Family in Town," NBC, 1958; "Perry Mason: The Case of the Dubious Bridegroom," CBS, 1958; "Dick Powell's Zane Grey Theatre: Hanging Fever," CBS, 1959; "Maverick: The Brasada Spur," ABC, 1959; "Tombstone Territory: Day of the Amnesty," ABC, 1959; "G.E. Theatre: My Dark Days," CBS, 1962; "Have Gun, Will Travel: Shootout at Hogtooth," CBS, 1962; "The Lucy Show: Lucy and Viv Are Volunteer Firemen," CBS, 1963; "The Virginian: The Judgment," NBC, 1963; "Hazel: So Long, Brown Eyes," NBC, 1963; "Perry Mason: The Case of the Bigamous Spouse," CBS, 1963; "The Great Adventure: Rodger Young," CBS, 1964; "Perry Mason: The Case of the Paper Bullets," CBS, 1964; "For the People: ... to prosecute all crimes ...," CBS, 1965; "Hawk: The Man Who Owned Everyone," ABC, 1966; "Hogan's Goat," NET, 1971.

MACY, BILL
b. Revere, MA, May 18, 1922. Actor who played Walter, husband of Maude Findlay (Beatrice Arthur) now he usually plays aging crabs.
AS A REGULAR: "Maude," CBS, 1972-78; "Hanging In," CBS, 1979; "Nothing in Common," NBC, 1987.

AND: "All in the Family: Archie Sees a Mugging," CBS, 1972; "All in the Family: Maude," CBS, 1972; "Celebrity Sweepstakes," NBC, 1974; "Tony Orlando and Dawn," CBS, 1975; "The Lorenzo and Henrietta Music Show," SYN, 1976; "Hotel: Premiere," ABC, 1983; "The Love Boat: A Match Made in Heaven," ABC, 1984; "St. Elsewhere: Up on the Roof," NBC, 1984; "Riptide: Games People Play," NBC, 1985; "Murder, She Wrote: Corned Beef and Carnage," CBS, 1986; "L.A. Law: The Princess and the Wiener King," NBC, 1986; "The Love Boat: We'll Meet Again," ABC, 1986; "The New Mike Hammer: Requiem for Billy," CBS, 1986; "Starman: The Grifters," ABC, 1987; "Highway to Heaven: Heaven Nose, Mr. Smith," NBC, 1988; "The Facts of Life: Golden Oldies," NBC, 1988; "CBS Summer Playhouse: Tickets Please," CBS, 1988; "Murder, She Wrote: Something Borrowed, Someone Blue," CBS, 1989.
TV MOVIES AND MINISERIES: "All Together Now," ABC, 1975; "Death at Love House," ABC, 1976; "Stunt Seven," CBS, 1979; "Perry Mason: The Case of the Murdered Madam," NBC, 1987.

MADDEN, DAVE

b. Canada, 1933. Long-faced comic actor who played diner regular Earl Hicks on "Alice" and manager Reuben Kincaid on "The Partridge Family."
AS A REGULAR: "Camp Runamuck," NBC, 1965-66; "Rowan & Martin's Laugh-In," NBC, 1968-69; "The Partridge Family," ABC, 1970-74; "Alice," CBS, 1978-85.
AND: "The Ed Sullivan Show," CBS, 1963; "Bewitched: Super Car," ABC, 1967; "Bewitched: Samantha's Shopping Spree," ABC, 1969; "Love, American Style: Love and the Topless Policy," ABC, 1972; "Love, American Style: Love and the Singing Suitor," ABC, 1972; "Happy Days: Big Money," ABC, 1974; "Starsky and Hutch: Starsky and Hutch on Playboy Island," ABC, 1977; "Barney Miller: Eviction," ABC, 1978.
TV MOVIES AND MINISERIES: "The Girl Who Came Gift-Wrapped," ABC, 1974; "More Wild Wild West," CBS, 1980.

MADISON, GUY

b. Robert Moseley, Bakersfield, CA, January 19, 1922. Yee-hah! It's Wild Bill Hickok!
AS A REGULAR: "The Adventures of Wild Bill Hickok," SYN, 1951-54.
AND: "Light's Diamond Jubilee: A Kiss for the Lieutenant," ABC, CBS, NBC, 1954; "Climax!: A Farewell to Arms," CBS, 1955; "Ford Theatre: Passage to Yesterday," NBC, 1955; "The Perry Como Show," NBC, 1956; "The Steve Allen Show," NBC, 1956; "Ford Theatre: Sometimes It Happens," ABC, 1956; "Climax!: The Man Who Stole the Bible," CBS, 1957; "Not One Shall Die," SYN, 1957; "Wagon Train: The Riley Gratton Story," NBC, 1957; "G.E. Theatre: Bold Loser," CBS, 1958; "Schlitz Playhouse of Stars: You Can't Win 'Em All," CBS, 1959; "The Ann Sothern Show: Katy and the Cowboy," CBS, 1959; "Arthur Murray Party," NBC, 1959; "The Red Skelton Show: San Fernando's Treasure Hunt," CBS, 1959; "Hobby Lobby," ABC, 1959; "Death Valley Days: Extra Guns," SYN, 1961; "Dick Powell's Zane Grey Theatre: Jericho," CBS, 1961; "The Love Boat: Yesterday's Love," ABC, 1979.
TV MOVIES AND MINISERIES: "Red River," CBS, 1988.

MAHARIS, GEORGE

b. Astoria, NY, September 1, 1928. Actor with a brooding quality; he played Buz Murdock, who went looking for America with Tod Stiles (Martin Milner) in a Corvette on "Route 66." He left TV for the movies, but by the seventies he was back making the game-show rounds.
AS A REGULAR: "Search for Tomorrow," CBS, 1959-60; "Route 66," CBS, 1960-63; "The Most Deadly Game," ABC, 1970-71.
AND: "Naked City: Manhole," ABC, 1959; "Naked City: Four Sweet Corners," ABC, 1959; "Naked City: Fire Island," ABC, 1959; "Alcoa Theatre: Action Off Screen," NBC, 1960; "Naked City: A Death of Princes," ABC, 1960; "Here's Hollywood," NBC, 1961; "The Chevy Show," NBC, 1961; "The Merv Griffin Show," NBC, 1962; "Password," CBS, 1962; "The Tennessee Ernie Ford Show," ABC, 1963; "To Tell the Truth," CBS, 1965; "The Mike Douglas Show," SYN, 1965; "Hullabaloo," NBC, 1965; "Bob Hope Chrysler Theatre: A Small Rebellion," NBC, 1966; "The Danny Thomas Hour: The Demon Under the Bed," NBC, 1967; "Journey to the Unknown: Miss Belle," ABC, 1968; "The Steve Allen Show," SYN, 1970; "Night Gallery: The Hand of Borgus Weems," NBC, 1971; "Medical Center: The Pawn," CBS, 1971; "The FBI: The Rip-Off," ABC, 1972; "Of Men and Women: The Brave and the Free," ABC, 1972; "Barnaby Jones: Deadly Prize," CBS, 1973; "Mission: Impossible: The Fountain," CBS, 1973; "Barnaby Jones: Deadly Prize," CBS, 1973; "Shaft: The Meat-Eaters," CBS, 1974; "The Snoop Sisters: The Devil Made Me Do It," NBC, 1974; "Cross Wits," SYN, 1976; "The $20,000 Pyramid," ABC, 1977; "Police Story: Six Foot Stretch," NBC, 1977; "Kojak: Lady in the Squad Room," CBS, 1977; "Switch: Legends of the Macunas," CBS, 1977; "Matt Houston: The Bikini Murders," ABC, 1984.
TV MOVIES AND MINISERIES: "Escape to Mindanao," NBC, 1968; "The Monk," ABC, 1969; "The Victim," ABC, 1972; "Come Die with Me," ABC, 1974; "Death to Sister Mary," ABC,

559

1974; "Death in Space," ABC, 1974; "Murder on Flight 502," ABC, 1975; "Look What's Happened to Rosemary's Baby," ABC, 1976; "Rich Man, Poor Man," ABC, 1976; "SST-Death Flight," ABC, 1977; "Crash," ABC, 1978.

* Maharis left "Route 66" on bad terms. He missed several episodes after contracting hepatitis in 1962, and he claimed the producers rushed him back into production without giving him enough time to recover. He was replaced by Glenn Corbett.

MAHONEY, JOCK

b. *Jacques Joseph O'Mahoney, Chicago, IL, February 7, 1919.* Rugged actor who played super-cool western lawman Yancy Derringer; also, Sally Field's stepfather.

AS A REGULAR: "Range Rider," SYN, 1951; "Yancy Derringer," CBS, 1958-59.

AND: "The Loretta Young Show: The First Man to Ask Her," NBC, 1954; "The Loretta Young Show: No Help Wanted," NBC, 1954; "The Loretta Young Show: Decision," NBC, 1955; "The Loretta Young Show: Option on a Wife," NBC, 1955; "The Loretta Young Show: Tale of a Cayuse," NBC, 1955; "Christophers: Some Facts About Valley Forge," SYN, 1959; "Rawhide: Incident of the Sharpshooter," CBS, 1960; "The Millionaire: Millionaire Vance Ludlow," CBS, 1960; "Laramie: Ladies' Day," NBC, 1961; "Batman: The Purr-fect Crime/Better Luck Next Time," ABC, 1966; "Tarzan: The Ultimate Weapon," NBC, 1966; "Tarzan: Deadly Silence," NBC, 1966; "Tarzan: Mask of Roma," NBC, 1967; "Batman: I'll Be a Mummy's Uncle," ABC, 1968; "Kung Fu: The Hoots," ABC, 1973; "The Streets of San Francisco: Blockade," ABC, 1974; "The Streets of San Francisco: One Last Shot," ABC, 1974; "B.J. and the Bear: Fly a Wild Horse," NBC, 1979; "Simon & Simon: The Rough Rider Rides Again," CBS, 1982; "The Fall Guy: King of the Cowboys," ABC, 1984.

MAJORS, LEE

b. *Lee Yeary, Wyandotte, MI, April 23, 1940.* Beefy leading man in action roles; best known as bionic man Steve Austin and stuntman-bounty hunter Colt Seavers, "The Fall Guy."

AS A REGULAR: "The Big Valley," ABC, 1965-69; "The Virginian," NBC, 1970-71; "Owen Marshall, Counselor at Law," ABC, 1971-74; "The Six Million Dollar Man," ABC, 1974-78; "The Fall Guy," ABC, 1981-86; "Tour of Duty," CBS, 1990.

AND: "Gunsmoke: A Song for Dying," CBS, 1965; "The Alfred Hitchcock Hour: The Monkey's Paw," NBC, 1965; "Marcus Welby, M.D.: Men Who Care," ABC, 1971; "Alias Smith and Jones: The McCreedy Bust: Going, Going, Gone," ABC, 1972; "Funshine Saturday Sneakpeek," ABC,

1974; "The Bionic Woman: Welcome Home, Jaime," ABC, 1976; "Dinah!," SYN, 1976; "The Bionic Woman: Return of Bigfoot," ABC, 1976; "The Bionic Woman: Kill Oscar," ABC, 1976; "The Love Boat: China Cruise," ABC, 1983.

TV MOVIES AND MINISERIES: "The Ballad of Andy Crocker," ABC, 1969; "Weekend of Terror," ABC, 1970; "The Six Million Dollar Man," ABC, 1973; "Francis Gary Powers: The True Story of the U-2 Spy Incident," NBC, 1976; "Just a Little Inconvenience," NBC, 1977; "Starflight: The Plane That Couldn't Land," ABC, 1983; "The Cowboy and the Ballerina," CBS, 1984; "A Smokey Mountain Christmas," ABC, 1986; "The Return of the Six Million Dollar Man and the Bionic Woman," NBC, 1987; "Danger Down Under," NBC, 1988; "Bionic Showdown: The Six Million Dollar Man and the Bionic Woman," NBC, 1989.

MALDEN, KARL

b. *Mladen Sulkilovich, Gary, IN, March 23, 1914.* Stage and film actor who came to TV for a long stay as detective Lt. Mike Stone in "The Streets of San Francisco," and now he sells credit cards; an Emmy winner for "Fatal Vision."

AS A REGULAR: "The Streets of San Francisco," ABC, 1972-77; "Skag," NBC, 1980.

AND: "Wide, Wide World: The Western," NBC, 1958; "Here's Hollywood," NBC, 1960.

TV MOVIES AND MINISERIES: "The Streets of San Francisco," ABC, 1972; "Word of Honor," CBS, 1981; "Miracle on Ice," ABC, 1981; "Fatal Vision," NBC, 1984; "With Intent to Kill," CBS, 1984; "My Father, My Son," CBS, 1988; "The Hijacking of the Achille Lauro," NBC, 1989.

* Emmies: 1985.

MALONE, DOROTHY

b. *Chicago, IL, January 30, 1925.* Oscar-winning actress who was busy as heck in TV and movies ("Written on the Wind," "Too Much Too Soon") during the fifties, and who played Constance MacKenzie Carson, a leading citizen, more or less, of "Peyton Place."

AS A REGULAR: "Peyton Place," ABC, 1964-68; "High Hopes," SYN, 1978.

AND: "The Doctor: The Runaways," NBC, 1953; "Four Star Playhouse: Moorings," CBS, 1953; "Campbell TV Soundstage: Surprise Party," NBC, 1954; "Fireside Theatre: Afraid to Live," NBC, 1954; "Fireside Theatre: Our Son," NBC, 1954; "Fireside Theatre: Mr. Onion," NBC, 1955; "G.E. Theatre: Clown," CBS, 1955; "Four Star Playhouse: A Study in Panic," CBS, 1955; "The Loretta Young Show: A Ticket for May," NBC, 1956; "The Rosemary Clooney Show," SYN, 1957; "Bob Hope Special," NBC, 1958; "Cimarron City: A Respectable Girl," NBC, 1958;

"Alcoa Theatre: The Last Flight Out," NBC, 1960; "G.E. Theatre: A Little White Lye," CBS, 1961; "Route 66: Fly Away Home," CBS, 1961; "Checkmate: The Heat of Passion," CBS, 1961; "The Dick Powell Show: Open Season," NBC, 1961; "Dr. Kildare: The Administrator," NBC, 1962; "Death Valley Days: The Watch," SYN, 1962; "The Untouchables: The Floyd Gibbons Story," ABC, 1962; "The Greatest Show on Earth: Where the Wire Ends," ABC, 1964; "Insight: The Edith Stein Story," SYN, 1967; "The Beautiful Phyllis Diller Show," NBC, 1968; "The Bold Ones: Is This Operation Necessary?," NBC, 1972; "Ironside: Confessions: From a Lady of the Evening," NBC, 1973; "City of Angels: The November Plan," NBC, 1976; "Police Woman: The Trick Book," NBC, 1976; "The Streets of San Francisco: Child of Anger," ABC, 1976.

TV MOVIES AND MINISERIES: "The Pigeon," ABC, 1969; "Rich Man, Poor Man," ABC, 1976; "Little Ladies of the Night," ABC, 1977; "Murder in Peyton Place," NBC, 1977; "Katie: Portrait of a Centerfold," NBC, 1978; "He's Not Your Son," CBS, 1984; "Peyton Place: The Next Generation," NBC, 1985.

MANDAN, ROBERT

b. Clever, MO, February 2, 1932. Actor who played Chester Tate on "Soap" and Col. Fielding on "Private Benjamin."

AS A REGULAR: "From These Roots," NBC, 1958-61; "The Edge of Night," CBS, 1963; "Search for Tomorrow," CBS, 1965-70; "Caribe," ABC, 1975; "Soap," ABC, 1977-81; "Private Benjamin," CBS, 1982-83; "Three's a Crowd," ABC, 1984-85.

AND: "Mission: Impossible: Shape-Up," CBS, 1971; "Mannix: To Save a Dead Man," CBS, 1971; "Cannon: To Kill a Guinea Pig," CBS, 1972; "Mannix: The Inside Man," CBS, 1972; "Barney Miller: Hotel," ABC, 1975; "Barnaby Jones: Counterfall," CBS, 1975; "Maude: Walter's Ethics," CBS, 1975; "Police Story: The Jar," NBC, 1976; "The Rockford Files: Where's Houston?," NBC, 1976; "Barnaby Jones: Killer on Campus," CBS, 1977; "The Love Boat: Like Father, Like Son," ABC, 1979; "$weepstake$: Cowboy, Linda and Angie, Mark," NBC, 1979; "Fantasy Island: An Audience with the King," ABC, 1982; "Highway to Heaven: Love and Marriage," NBC, 1986; "The Facts of Life: Out of Peekskill," NBC, 1986.

TV MOVIES AND MINISERIES: "A Great American Tragedy," ABC, 1972; "The Heist," ABC, 1972; "Panic on the 5:22," ABC, 1974; "Goldie and the Boxer Go to Hollywood," NBC, 1981; "In Love with an Older Woman," CBS, 1982.

MANDEL, HOWIE

b. Canada. Actor best known as Dr. Wayne Fiscus on "St. Elsewhere"; as a stand-up comic, he's more frantic than funny.

AS A REGULAR: "St. Elsewhere," NBC, 1982-88; "Good Grief," FOX, 1990- ; "Bobby's World," FOX, 1990- .

AND: "The Byron Allen Show," SYN, 1989.

MANDRELL, BARBARA

b. Houston, TX, December 25, 1948. Country-pop performer.

AS A REGULAR: "Barbara Mandrell and the Mandrell Sisters," NBC, 1980-82.

AND: "Five Star Jubilee," NBC, 1961; "The Wilburn Brothers Show," SYN, 1974; "The Grand Ole Opry at 50," ABC, 1975; "Tattletales," CBS, 1977; "The Rockford Files: Love Is the Word," NBC, 1979; "Marty Robbins' Spotlight," SYN, 1979; "Dolly," ABC, 1988; "America's Tribute to Bob Hope," NBC, 1988; "The Pat Sajak Show," CBS, 1989; "Bob Hope's Easter Vacation in the Bahamas," NBC, 1989.

TV MOVIES AND MINISERIES: "Murder in Music City," NBC, 1979; "The Concrete Cowboys," CBS, 1979; "Burning Rage," CBS, 1984.

MANETTI, LARRY

b. Pendleton, OR. Actor who played Rick on "Magnum, P.I."

AS A REGULAR: "Baa Baa Black Sheep," NBC, 1976-78; "The Duke," NBC, 1979; "Magnum P.I.," CBS, 1980-88.

AND: "Switch: The Walking Bomb," CBS, 1975; "The Streets of San Francisco: The Honorable Profession," ABC, 1976; "Emergency!: Rules of Order," NBC, 1976; "Tenspeed and Brown Shoe: Pilot," ABC, 1980; "The Rockford Files: Nice Guys Finish Dead," NBC, 1980.

MANN, JOHNNY

b. Baltimore, August 30, 1928. Choral director and performer.

AS A REGULAR: "The George Gobel/Eddie Fisher Show," NBC, 1957-59; "The Danny Kaye Show," CBS, 1963-64; "The Joey Bishop Show," ABC, 1967-69; "Johnny Mann's Stand Up and Cheer," SYN, 1971-73.

MANOFF, DINAH

b. New York City, NY, January 25, 1958. Actress who plays Carol, neurotic daughter of Dr. Harry Weston (Richard Mulligan) on "Empty Nest"; daughter of Lee Grant.

AS A REGULAR: "Soap," ABC, 1978-79; "Empty Nest," NBC, 1988- .

AND: "Family: Sleeping Gypsy," ABC, 1978; "$weepstake$: Dewey and Harold and Sarah and Maggie," NBC, 1979; "Lou Grant: Bomb," CBS, 1979; "Mork & Mindy: Mork's Baby Blues," ABC, 1979; "Cagney & Lacey: Fathers & Daughters," CBS, 1984; "Night Court: The Nun," NBC, 1984; "Murder, She Wrote: Murder in the Minor Key," CBS, 1987.

TV MOVIES AND MINISERIES: "A Matter of Sex," NBC, 1984; "Flight #90: Disaster on the Potomac," NBC, 1984; "Classified Love," CBS, 1986; "The Cover Girl and the Cop," NBC, 1989.

MANTOOTH, RANDOLPH

b. Sacramento, CA, September 19, 1945. Actor who played John Gage on "Emergency!" and Alex Masters on "Loving."

AS A REGULAR: "Emergency!," NBC, 1972-77; "Operation Petticoat," ABC, 1978-79; "Loving," ABC, 1987-90.

AND: "Owen Marshall, Counselor at Law: Until Proven Innocent," ABC, 1971; "Marcus Welby, M.D.: Solomon's Choice," ABC, 1972; "Owen Marshall, Counselor at Law: The Desertion of Keith Ryder," ABC, 1974; "Project UFO: The Pipeline Incident," NBC, 1978; "The Love Boat: Like Father, Like Son," ABC, 1979; "The Fall Guy: The Winner," ABC, 1984.

TV MOVIES AND MINISERIES: "Vanished," NBC, 1971; "Marriage: Year One," NBC, 1971; "The Bravos," ABC, 1972; "Emergency!," NBC, 1972; "Testimony of Two Men," SYN, 1977; "Bridge Across Time," NBC, 1985.

MARCH, FREDRIC

b. Ernest Frederick McIntyre Bickel, Racine, WI, August 31, 1897; d. 1975. Gifted film actor ("A Star Is Born," "The Best Years of Our Lives," "Death of a Salesman") who did some TV drama.

AS A GUEST: "Nash Airflyte Theatre: The Boor," CBS, 1950; "Lux Video Theatre: The Speech," CBS, 1951; "Lux Video Theatre: Ferry Crisis at Friday Point," CBS, 1952; "Omnibus: The Last Night of Don Juan," CBS, 1953; "The Best of Broadway: The Royal Family," CBS, 1954; "Shower of Stars: A Christmas Carol," CBS, 1956; "The Ed Sullivan Show," CBS, 1957; "The Ed Sullivan Show," CBS, 1958; "Du Pont Show of the Month: The Winslow Boy," CBS, 1958; "Du Pont Show of the Month: Hamlet," CBS, 1959; "25 Years of Life Magazine," NBC, 1961; "Hallmark Hall of Fame: Inherit the Wind," NBC, 1965.

MARCH, HAL

b. San Francisco, CA, April 22, 1920; d. 1970. Light actor and TV personality, best known as the host of "The $64,000 Question."

AS A REGULAR: "The George Burns and Gracie Allen Show," CBS, 1950-51; "The RCA Victor Show," NBC, 1952-53; "My Friend Irma," CBS, 1953-54; "The Soldiers," NBC, 1955; "The Imogene Coca Show," NBC, 1955; "The $64,000 Question," CBS, 1955-58; "What's It For?," NBC, 1957-58; "Laughs

for Sale," ABC, 1963; "It's Your Bet," SYN, 1969-73.

AND: "I Love Lucy: Lucy Fakes Illness," CBS, 1952; "I Love Lucy: Lucy Is Matchmaker," CBS, 1953; "Four Star Playhouse: Marked Down," CBS, 1954; "Hallmark Hall of Fame: Dream Girl," NBC, 1955; "Omnibus: The Great Forgery," CBS, 1956; "The Bachelor," NBC, 1956; "The Most Beautiful Girl in the World," NBC, 1956; "Dinah Shore Chevy Show," NBC, 1956; "Saturday Spectacular: High Button Shoes," NBC, 1956; "The Jack Paar Show," NBC, 1959; "Arthur Murray Party," NBC, 1960; "The Jack Paar Show," NBC, 1960; "The Merv Griffin Show," NBC, 1963; "The du Pont Show: Holdup!," NBC, 1963; "I've Got a Secret," CBS, 1963; "You Don't Say," NBC, 1964; "Burke's Law: Who Killed the Tall One in the Middle?," ABC, 1964; "Mr. Broadway: Smelling Like a Rose," CBS, 1964; "You Don't Say," NBC, 1965; "Burke's Law: Who Killed Cop Robin?," ABC, 1965; "Trials of O'Brien: Dead End on Flugel Street," CBS, 1965; "Gidget: In and Out with the In-Laws," ABC, 1966; "Hey, Landlord!: Sizzling Sidney," NBC, 1966; "The Lucy Show: Mooney the Monkey," CBS, 1966; "The Monkees: Dance, Monkee, Dance," NBC, 1966; "The Danny Thomas Hour: My Pal Tony," NBC, 1968; "It Takes Two," NBC, 1969.

MARCHAND, NANCY

b. Buffalo, NY, June 19, 1928. Emmy-winning actress who worked in TV for 25 years before becoming a star as Margaret Pynchon, owner-publisher of the Los Angeles Tribune on "Lou Grant."

AS A REGULAR: "Love of Life," CBS, 1970-74; "Beacon Hill," CBS, 1975; "Another World," NBC, 1976; "Lovers and Friends (For Richer, for Poorer)," NBC, 1977; "Lou Grant," CBS, 1977-82.

AND: "Studio One: Little Women," CBS, 1950; "Kraft Television Theatre: Of Famous Memory," NBC, 1951; "Kraft Television Theatre: The Peaceful Warrior," NBC, 1952; "Studio One: The Hospital," CBS, 1952; "Kraft Television Theatre: Marty," NBC, 1953; "Kraft Television Theatre: The Old Maid," ABC, 1954; "Kraft Television Theatre: The Office Dance," NBC, 1954; "Kraft Television Theatre: Career," NBC, 1954; "Kraft Television Theatre: A Child Is Born," ABC, 1954; "Omnibus: The Renaissance," CBS, 1955; "Producers Showcase: Mayerling," NBC, 1957; "Playhouse 90: The Hidden Image," CBS, 1959; "Sunday Showcase: The Indestructable Mr. Gore," NBC, 1959; "Play of the Week: A Piece of Blue Sky," SYN, 1960; "Play of the Week: The House of Bernarda Alba," SYN, 1960; "The Law and Mr. Jones: The Long Echo," ABC, 1960; "The Defenders: The Attack," CBS, 1961; "Repertory Theatre: Don Juan in Hell," NET,

1965; "Southern Baptist Hour: The Statesman," NBC, 1966; "The Lower Depths," NET, 1966; "New York Television Theatre: Dark Lady of the Sonnets," NET, 1966; "NYPD: What's a Nice Girl Like You," ABC, 1968; "Cheers: Diane Meets Mom," NBC, 1984.

TV MOVIES AND MINISERIES: "Some Kind of Miracle," CBS, 1979; "Willa," CBS, 1979; "The Golden Moment: An Olympic Love Story," NBC, 1980; "Killjoy," CBS, 1981; "Agatha Christie's Sparkling Cyanide," CBS, 1983.

* Emmies: 1978, 1980, 1981, 1982.

MARGO

b. Marie Marguerita Guadalupe Teresa Estela Bolado Castilla y O'Donnell, Mexico City, Mexico, May 10, 1917. Actress and wife of Eddie Albert.

AS A GUEST: "The Unexpected: Eclipse," SYN, 1952; "Schlitz Playhouse of Stars: Enchanted Evening," CBS, 1952; "Wagon Train: The John Darro Story," NBC, 1957; "Westinghouse Desilu Playhouse: The Night the Phone Rang," CBS, 1958; "Arthur Murray Party," NBC, 1959; "The Jack Paar Show," NBC, 1959; "Westinghouse Desilu Playhouse: So Tender, So Profane," CBS, 1959; "Person to Person," CBS, 1960; "Here's Hollywood," NBC, 1961; "Rawhide: A Man Called Mushy," CBS, 1964.

MARGOLIN, STUART

b. Davenport, IA, January 31, 1940. Familiar TV face who was a regular in "Love, American Style" blackouts and who played Angel Martin on "The Rockford Files."

AS A REGULAR: "Occassional Wife," NBC, 1966-67; "Love American Style," ABC, 1969-73; "James Garner as Nichols," NBC, 1971-72; "The Rockford Files," NBC, 1974-80; "Bret Maverick," NBC, 1981-82; "Mr. Smith," NBC, 1983.

AND: "Mrs. G. Goes to College: Lonely Sunday," CBS, 1961; "The Gertrude Berg Show: High Finance," CBS, 1962; "Blue Light: The Deserters," ABC, 1966; "Hey, Landlord!: The Long, Hot Bus," NBC, 1966; "He & She: The Midgets From Broadway," CBS, 1968; "The FBI: The Homecoming," ABC, 1968; "The Monkees: Monkees Watch Their Feet," NBC, 1968; "M*A*S*H: Bananas, Crackers and Nuts," CBS, 1972; "Gunsmoke: Homecoming," CBS, 1973; "The Mary Tyler Moore Show: Romeo and Mary," CBS, 1973; "Cops," CBS, 1973; "M*A*S*H: Operation Noselift," CBS, 1974; "Rhoda: The Party," CBS, 1975; "Rhoda: If You Want to Shoot the Rapids You Have to Get Wet," CBS, 1976; "Magnum, P.I.: Basket Case," CBS, 1983; "Hill Street Blues: Hacked to Pieces," NBC, 1985; "Hill Street Blues: Seoul on Ice," NBC, 1985.

TV MOVIES AND MINISERIES: "The Ballad of Andy Crocker," ABC, 1969; "The Intruders," NBC, 1970; "The California Kid," ABC, 1974; "This Is the West That Was," NBC, 1974; "Perilous Voyage," NBC, 1976; "Lanigan's Rabbi," NBC, 1976; "A Killer in the Family," ABC, 1983; "Three of a Kind," ABC, 1989.

AS DIRECTOR: "The Mary Tyler Moore Show: The Seminar," CBS, 1976.

* Emmies: 1979, 1980.

MARIE, ROSE

b. Rose Marie Mazetta, New York City, NY, August 15, 1923. Blonde actress-comedian who was on the radio as a tot; best known as a Hollywood Square and as man-hungry comedy writer Sally Rogers on "The Dick Van Dyke Show."

AS A REGULAR: "My Sister Eileen," CBS, 1960-61; "The Dick Van Dyke Show," CBS, 1961-66; "Hollywood Squares," NBC, 1966-82; "The Doris Day Show," CBS, 1969-71.

AND: "The Jackie Gleason Show," CBS, 1957; "The Julius LaRosa Show," NBC, 1957; "The Bob Cummings Show: Collins the Crooner," NBC, 1958; "M Squad: The System," NBC, 1958; "The Chevy Show," NBC, 1959; "The Many Loves of Dobie Gillis: The Prettiest Collateral in Town," CBS, 1960; "Art Linkletter's House Party," CBS, 1961; "Stump the Stars," CBS, 1962; "Your First Impression," NBC, 1963; "Dinah Shore Special," ABC, 1964; "Password," CBS, 1964; "You Don't Say," NBC, 1964; "The Monkees: Monkees in a Ghost Town," NBC, 1966; "The Monkees: Monkee Mother," NBC, 1967; "Hey, Landlord!: Aunt Harriet Wants You," NBC, 1967; "The Virginian: The Lady from Wichita," NBC, 1967; "You Don't Say," NBC, 1968; "My Three Sons: First Night Out," CBS, 1968; "Funny You Should Ask," ABC, 1969; "The Tonight Show Starring Johnny Carson," NBC, 1970; "Can You Top This?," SYN, 1970; "Baffle," NBC, 1973; "Petrocelli: Pilot," NBC, 1974; "The Merv Griffin Show," SYN, 1975; "Kojak: Twenty-Four Six for Two-Hundred," CBS, 1975; "Get Christie Love!: Uncle Harry," ABC, 1975; "The Magnificent Marble Machine," NBC, 1976; "Something Spectacular with Steve Allen," PBS, 1981; "The Love Boat: Teach Me Tonight," ABC, 1981; "Cagney & Lacey: Stress," CBS, 1985.

* See also Selma Diamond.

MARINARO, ED

b. New York City, NY, March 31, 1951. Beefy actor and former football player who played Off. Joe Coffey on "Hill Street Blues."

AS A REGULAR: "Laverne & Shirley," ABC, 1980-81; "Hill Street Blues," NBC, 1981-86.

AND: "The Gong Show," SYN, 1978; "Hill Street Blues: Jungle Madness," NBC, 1981; "Private Eye: Nicky the Rose," NBC, 1987; "Dynasty:

House of the Falling Son," ABC, 1989.

TV MOVIES AND MINISERIES: "Born Beautiful,"
NBC, 1982; "Tonight's the Night," ABC,
1987; "Sharing Richard," CBS, 1988; "The
Diamond Trap," CBS, 1988.

* Marinaro was a running back with the
Minnesota Vikings and New York Jets.

MARKEY, ENID

b. Dillon, CO, February 22, 1896; d. 1981.
Slight, elderly actress best known for comic
roles; she played Mrs. Mendlebright, landlady
of Barney Fife (Don Knotts) on "The Andy
Griffith Show."

AS A REGULAR: "Bringing Up Buddy," CBS, 1960-
61.

AND: "Kraft Television Theatre: The 19th Hole,"
NBC, 1950; "Armstrong Circle Theatre: Enter
Rosalind," NBC, 1951; "Philco TV Playhouse:
Up Above the World So High," NBC, 1953;
"Kraft Television Theatre: The Rose Garden,"
NBC, 1953; "Goodyear TV Playhouse: Buy Me
Blue Ribbons," NBC, 1954; "Motorola TV Hour:
Love Song," ABC, 1954; "Armstrong Circle
Theatre: Man Talk," NBC, 1954; "Kraft
Television Theatre: Citizen Miller," NBC, 1954;
"U.S. Steel Hour: Flint and Fire," CBS, 1958;
"Playhouse 90: The Silver Whistle," CBS, 1959;
"The Defenders: Grandma TNT," CBS, 1962;
"The Andy Griffith Show: Up in Barney's
Room," CBS, 1963; "Repertory Theatre: The
Wedding," NET, 1965; "Gomer Pyle, USMC:
Grandma Pyle, Fortune Teller," CBS, 1966; "The
Adventures of Ozzie and Harriet: Wally's Traffic
Ticket," ABC, 1966; "Please Don't Eat the
Daisies: Who's Walking Under the Bed?," NBC,
1966.

MARKHAM, DEWEY "PIGMEAT"

b. Durham, NC, April 18, 1904; d. 1981. Black
nightclub comic whose "Here Come the Judge"
routine was appropriated by Sammy Davis Jr.
on a "Rowan & Martin's Laugh-In" guest shot;
after they heard it, the producers decided to
hire the originator of the phrase.

AS A REGULAR: "Rowan & Martin's Laugh-In,"
NBC, 1968-69.

AND: "The Ed Sullivan Show," CBS, 1957; "The
Ed Sullivan Show," CBS, 1958; "The Ed Sullivan
Show," CBS, 1959; "The Ed Sullivan Show,"
CBS, 1960; "The Ed Sullivan Show," CBS, 1961;
"The Tonight Show Starring Johnny Carson,"
NBC, 1968; "The Merv Griffin Show," SYN,
1969; "The Tonight Show Starring Johnny
Carson," NBC, 1969.

* Markham toured with James Brown in 1961,
and later with Jackie Wilson and Chuck Berry.

MARKHAM, MONTE

b. Manatee, FL, June 21, 1935. Handsome

actor who played simple-living millionaire
Longfellow Deeds and Perry Mason on
unsuccessful shows.

AS A REGULAR: "The Second Hundred Years,"
ABC, 1967-68; "Mr. Deeds Goes to Town,"
ABC, 1969-70; "The New Adventures of Perry
Mason," CBS, 1973-74; "Dallas," CBS, 1981;
"Rituals," SYN, 1984-85; "Baywatch," NBC,
1989-90.

AND: "Mission: Impossible: Odd Man Out," CBS,
1966; "The Iron Horse: Death by Triangulation,"
ABC, 1967; "The FBI: The Intermediary," ABC,
1968; "Here Come the Brides: The Firemaker,"
ABC, 1968; "The Mod Squad: Fear Is a Bucking
Horse," ABC, 1969; "The Mike Douglas Show,"
SYN, 1969; "The Young Rebels: Valley of
Guns," ABC, 1970; "Hawaii Five-O: The Payoff,"
CBS, 1970; "Hawaii Five-O: To Kill or Be
Killed," CBS, 1971; "The Mary Tyler Moore
Show: Just a Lunch," CBS, 1971; "Dan August:
Witness to a Killing," ABC, 1971; "The Name of
the Game: A Capitol Affair," NBC, 1971; "Love,
American Style: Love and the Married Bachelor,"
ABC, 1971; "Sarge: A Bad Case of Monogamy,"
NBC, 1971; "McNaughton's Daughter: Love Is a
Four-Letter Word," NBC, 1976; "Quincy: Who's
Who in Neverland," NBC, 1976; "Police Woman:
Guns," NBC, 1977; "What Really Happened to
the Class of '65?: The Class Renegade," NBC,
1978; "Lucan: How Do You Run Forever?,"
ABC, 1978; "The Love Boat: The Captain's
Triangle," ABC, 1980; "The Fall Guy: License to
Kill," ABC, 1981; "The Love Boat: Off Course
Romance," ABC, 1983; "The A-Team: There's
Always a Catch," NBC, 1984; "Blacke's Magic:
Death Goes to the Movies," NBC, 1986; "Murder,
She Wrote: Doom with a View," CBS, 1987;
"The Golden Girls: Scared Straight," NBC, 1988.

TV MOVIES AND MINISERIES: "Death Takes a
Holiday," ABC, 1971; "The Astronaut," NBC,
1972; "Visions...," CBS, 1972; "Visions of
Death," CBS, 1973; "Hustling," ABC, 1975;
"Ellery Queen," NBC, 1975; "Dropout Father,"
CBS, 1982; "Baywatch: Panic at Malibu Pier,"
NBC, 1989.

MARLOWE, HUGH

*b. Hugh Herbert Hipple, Philadelphia, PA,
January 30, 1911; d. 1982.* Good-guy actor of
films and TV; best known as Jim Matthews on
"Another World."

AS A REGULAR: "Ellery Queen," SYN, 1954-56;
"Another World," NBC, 1969-82.

AND: "Schlitz Playhouse of Stars: Her Kind of
Honor," CBS, 1954; "Studio One: Cross My
Heart," CBS, 1955; "U.S. Steel Hour: Hung for a
Sheep," ABC, 1955; "G.E. Theatre: The Crime of
Daphne Rutledge," CBS, 1954; "Crossroads: Dig
or Die, Brother Hyde," ABC, 1956; "Alfred
Hitchcock Presents: John Brown's Body," CBS,
1956; "On Trial: The Case of the Abandoned

Horse," NBC, 1957; "Alfred Hitchcock Presents: A Man Greatly Beloved," CBS, 1957; "Crossroads: Jhonakehunkga—Called John," ABC, 1957; "Alfred Hitchcock Presents: Touche," CBS, 1959; "Rawhide: Incident of the Champagne Bottles," CBS, 1960; "Perry Mason: The Case of the Slandered Submarine," CBS, 1960; "Michael Shayne: The Poison Pen Club," NBC, 1960; "The Andy Griffith Show: Mayberry on Record," CBS, 1961; "Alfred Hitchcock Presents: Services Rendered," NBC, 1961; "Rawhide: The Pitchwagon," CBS, 1962; "Perry Mason: The Case of the Borrowed Baby," CBS, 1962; "The Law and Mr. Jones: Poor Eddie's Dead," ABC, 1962; "The Dick Powell Show: The Third Side of the Coin," NBC, 1963; "Perry Mason: The Case of the Nebulous Nephew," CBS, 1963; "The Alfred Hitchcock Hour: Day of Reckoning," NBC, 1963; "Arrest and Trial: An Echo of Conscience," ABC, 1964; "The Virginian: The Intruders," NBC, 1965; "Perry Mason: The Case of the Sleepy Slayer," CBS, 1964; "Hazel: Hazel's Day in Court," NBC, 1965; "Perry Mason: The Case of the Hasty Honeymooner," CBS, 1965; "The Virginian: Trail to Ashley Mountain," NBC, 1966; "The Man From UNCLE: The Seven Wonders of the World Affair," NBC, 1968; "Judd for the Defense: Murder on a Square Hole," ABC, 1968.

MARS, KENNETH

b. *Chicago, IL, 1936.* Beefy comic actor who played sensitive fireman Harry Zarakardos on "He & She" and has lent support to various variety shows.

AS A REGULAR: "He & She," CBS, 1967-68; "The Don Knotts Show," NBC, 1970-71; "Sha Na Na," SYN, 1977-78; "The Carol Burnett Show," ABC, 1979.

AND: "Trials of O'Brien: Never Bet on Anything That Talks," CBS, 1966; "Gunsmoke: The Returning," CBS, 1967; "Get Smart: A Man Called Smart," NBC, 1967; "The Debbie Reynolds Show: The Paper Butterfly," NBC, 1968; "The Ghost and Mrs. Muir: Captain Gregg's Whiz-Bang," NBC, 1968; "Room 222: Clothes Make the Boy," ABC, 1969; "Love, American Style: Love and the Good Samaritan," ABC, 1969; "Mannix: Merry-Go-Round for Murder," CBS, 1969; "The Ghost and Mrs. Muir: Tourist Go Home," ABC, 1970; "That Girl: I Ain't Got Nobody," ABC, 1970; "Sheperd's Flock," CBS, 1971; "McMillan and Wife: Murder by the Barrel," NBC, 1971; "Love, American Style: Love and the Mistress," ABC, 1971; "Love, American Style: Love and the Newscasters," ABC, 1972; "McMillan and Wife: Cop of the Year," NBC, 1972; "Ironside: Ollinger's Last Case," NBC, 1973; "Love, American Style: Love and the Missing Mister," ABC, 1973; "Hollywood Television Theatre: Steambath," NET, 1974;

"Hello Mother, Goodbye," NBC, 1974; "Alice: The Odd Couple," CBS, 1977; "Columbo: The Bye-Bye Sky High I.Q. Murder Case," NBC, 1977; "Barnaby Jones: The Killin' Cousin," CBS, 1980; "Simon & Simon: The Dead Letter File," CBS, 1981; "Alice: Mel Wins by a Nose," CBS, 1982; "Hardcastle and McCormick: Too Rich and Too Thin," ABC, 1985; "Murder, She Wrote: Footnote to Murder," CBS, 1985; "The Twilight Zone: Tooth or Consequences," CBS, 1986; "Hardcastle and McCormick: Brother, Can You Spare a Crime?," ABC, 1986; "Simon & Simon: Family Forecast," CBS, 1986; "The Last Precinct: I Want My Mummy," NBC, 1986; "Simon & Simon: The Case of Don Diablo," CBS, 1986.

TV MOVIES AND MINISERIES: "Second Chance," ABC, 1972; "Guess Who's Sleeping in My Bed?," ABC, 1973; "Someone I Touched," ABC, 1975; "The New, Original Wonder Woman," ABC, 1975; "Before and After," ABC, 1979; "Get Smart, Again!," ABC, 1989.

MARSH, JEAN

b. *July 1, 1934.* Emmy-winning actress who played Rose the maid on "Upstairs, Downstairs" and had a hand in creating the series.

AS A REGULAR: "Masterpiece Theatre: Upstairs, Downstairs," PBS, 1974-77; "9 to 5," ABC, 1982-83.

AND: "The Moon and Sixpence," NBC, 1959; "The Twilight Zone: The Lonely," CBS, 1959; "Walt Disney's Wonderful World of Color: The Horsemasters," NBC, 1961; "The Love Boat: The Emperor's Fortune," ABC, 1983.

TV MOVIES AND MINISERIES: "Jane Eyre," NBC, 1971; "Master of the Game," CBS, 1984; "The Corsican Brothers," CBS, 1985; "A Connecticut Yankee in King Arthur's Court," NBC, 1989.

AS CO-CREATOR: "Masterpiece Theatre: Upstairs, Downstairs," PBS, 1974-77.

* Emmies: 1975, 1976, 1977.

MARSHALL, E.G.

b. *Everett G. Marshall, Owatonna, MN, June 18, 1910.* Actor with extensive experience in live TV drama; he played attorney Lawrence Preston on "The Defenders" and Dr. David Craig on "The Bold Ones."

AS A REGULAR: "The Defenders," CBS, 1961-65; "The Bold Ones," NBC, 1969-73; "The Gangster Chronicles," NBC, 1981.

AND: "Kraft Television Theatre: On Stage," NBC, 1947; "Kraft Television Theatre: The Dark Tower," NBC, 1950; "Kraft Television Theatre: Kelly," NBC, 1950; "Philco TV Playhouse: By-Line for Murder," NBC, 1951; "Kraft Television Theatre: New Gossoon," NBC, 1952; "You Are There: The Triumph of Alexander the Great," CBS, 1955; "Hallmark Hall of Fame: The Little Foxes," NBC, 1956; "Kraft Television Theatre:

The Duel," NBC, 1957; "Alcoa Hour: The Big Build-Up," NBC, 1957; "Studio One: The Out-of-Towners," CBS, 1957; "Playhouse 90: Clash by Night," CBS, 1957; "Alcoa Hour: Night," NBC, 1957; "Suspicion: Four O'Clock," NBC, 1957; "Alfred Hitchcock Presents: The Mail-Order Prophet," CBS, 1957; "Shirley Temple's Storybook: Beauty and the Beast," NBC, 1958; "Studio One: Presence of the Enemy," CBS, 1958; "Shirley Temple's Storybook: Rip Van Winkle," NBC, 1958; "Playhouse 90: The Plot to Kill Stalin," CBS, 1958; "The Eternal Light: The Gift," NBC, 1958; "Pursuit: Calculated Risk," CBS, 1958; "Playhouse 90: A Quiet Game of Cards," CBS, 1959; "Du Pont Show of the Month: The Night of the Storm," CBS, 1961; "Exploring," NBC, 1963; "The Presidency: A Splendid Misery," CBS, 1964; "ABC Nightlife," ABC, 1965; "The Poppy Is Also a Flower," ABC, 1966; "A Case of Libel," ABC, 1968; "On Stage: This Town Will Never Be the Same," NBC, 1969; "Hallmark Hall of Fame: The Littlest Angel," NBC, 1969; "The Brady Bunch: The Slumber Caper," ABC, 1970; "The Men From Shiloh: Lady at the Bar," NBC, 1970; "You Are There: Paul Revere's Ride," CBS, 1972; "CBS Playhouse 90: Look Homeward, Angel," CBS, 1972; "Ironside: Five Days in the Death of Sergeant Brown," NBC, 1972; "Drink, Drank, Drunk," PBS, 1974; "ABC Theatre: Collision Course," ABC, 1976; "Nurse: Father," CBS, 1982; "The Equalizer: The Last Campaign," CBS, 1988.

TV MOVIES AND MINISERIES: "A Clear and Present Danger," NBC, 1970; "Vanished," NBC, 1971; "The City," ABC, 1971; "Ellery Queen: Don't Look Behind You," NBC, 1971; "Pursuit," ABC, 1972; "Money to Burn," ABC, 1973; "The Abduction of Saint Anne," ABC, 1975; "Vampire," ABC, 1979; "Disaster on the Coastliner," ABC, 1979; "The Phoenix," ABC, 1981; "Kennedy," NBC, 1983; "Hallmark Hall of Fame: The Winter of Our Discontent," CBS, 1983; "Under Siege," NBC, 1986; "At Mother's Request," CBS, 1987; "The Hijacking of the Achille Lauro," NBC, 1989.
* Emmies: 1962, 1963.

MARSHALL, HERBERT
b. London, England, May 23, 1890; d. 1968. Film and TV actor with a smooth manner and cultured voice.
AS A REGULAR: "The Unexpected," SYN, 1952; "Times Square Playhouse," SYN, 1957.
AND: "Nash Airflyte Theatre: Municipal Report," CBS, 1950; "Robert Montgomery Presents: An Inspector Calls," NBC, 1951; "Ford Theatre: The Girl in the Park," NBC, 1952; "Best of Broadway: The Philadelphia Story," CBS, 1954; "Elgin TV Hour: Yesterday's Magic," ABC, 1954; "Lux Video Theatre: The Browning Version," NBC, 1955; "December Bride: The Laundromat Show,"

CBS, 1955; "The George Gobel Show," NBC, 1956; "Lux Video Theatre: Now Voyager," NBC, 1956; "Alfred Hitchcock Presents: A Bottle of Wine," CBS, 1957; "I've Got a Secret," CBS, 1957; "The Loretta Young Show: Louise," NBC, 1957; "Playhouse 90: The Mystery of 13," CBS, 1957; "Studio One: Balance of Terror," CBS, 1958; "Alfred Hitchcock Presents: Little White Frock," CBS, 1958; "Adventures in Paradise: Nightmare on Napuka," ABC, 1960; "Adventures in Paradise: There Is an Island," ABC, 1960; "Hong Kong: Colonel Cat," ABC, 1960; "Michael Shayne: Spotlight on a Corpse," NBC, 1961; "Dick Powell's Zane Grey Theatre: The Atoner," CBS, 1961; "77 Sunset Strip: 5," ABC, 1963.

MARSHALL, PENNY
b. New York City, NY, October 15, 1942. Comic actress who left her mark on sitcom history as Laverne De Fazio in "Laverne & Shirley"; now a film director ("Big").
AS A REGULAR: "The Odd Couple," ABC, 1971-75; "The Bob Newhart Show," CBS, 1972-73; "Paul Sand in Friends and Lovers," CBS, 1974-75; "Laverne & Shirley," ABC, 1976-83.
AND: "Then Came Bronson: The Runner," NBC, 1970; "Barefoot in the Park: In Sickness and in Health," ABC, 1970; "Love, American Style: Love and the Pickup," ABC, 1971; "The Mary Tyler Moore Show: I Was A Single For WJM," CBS, 1974; "Wives," CBS, 1975; "The Mary Tyler Moore Show: Murray in Love," CBS, 1975; "Chico and the Man: Chico and the Van," NBC, 1975; "Happy Days: A Date with the Fonz," ABC, 1975; "Happy Days: Football Frolic," ABC, 1976; "The Merv Griffin Show," SYN, 1976; "The Mary Tyler Moore Show: Menage a Lou," CBS, 1976; "Happy Days: Beauty Contest," ABC, 1976; "Happy Days: Fonzie the Superstar," ABC, 1976; "General Electric's All-Star Anniversary," ABC, 1978; "Mork & Mindy: Mork Moves In," ABC, 1978; "Happy Days: Shotgun Wedding," ABC, 1979; "Taxi: Louie Moves Uptown," NBC, 1982.
TV MOVIES AND MINISERIES: "The Feminist and the Fuzz," ABC, 1971; "The Crooked Hearts," ABC, 1972; "The Couple Takes a Wife," ABC, 1972; "Let's Switch," ABC, 1975; "More Than Friends," ABC, 1978; "Love Thy Neighbor," ABC, 1984; "Challenge of a Lifetime," ABC, 1985.

MARSHALL, PETER
b. Huntington, WV, March 30, 1927. Game-show host, occasional singer and former comic, teamed with Tommy Noonan.
AS A REGULAR: "Hollywood Squares," NBC, 1966-82; "Storybook Squares," NBC, 1968; "NBC Action Playhouse," NBC, 1971-72; "The Peter Marshall Variety Show," SYN, 1976-77; "Fantasy," NBC, 1982-83; "All-Star Blitz," ABC, 1985.

AND: "Saturday Spectacular: Manhattan Tower," NBC, 1956; "The Millionaire: Millioniare Jeff Mercer," CBS, 1959; "The Lucy Show: Lucy's Sister Pays a Visit," CBS, 1963; "The Merv Griffin Show," SYN, 1968; "Love, American Style: Love and the Mountain Cabin," ABC, 1969; "Love, American Style: Love and the Amateur Night," ABC, 1973; "Love, American Style: Love and the Weirdo," ABC, 1973; "Banacek: Now You See Me, Now You Don't," NBC, 1974; "The Magnificent Marble Machine," NBC, 1976; "The Love Boat: The Now Marriage," ABC, 1979; "Lou Grant: Witness," CBS, 1979; "WKRP in Cincinnati: Real Families," CBS, 1980; "The Love Boat: Programmed for Love," ABC, 1982; "CHiPS: Rock, Devil, Rock," NBC, 1982; "Jessie: The Long Fuse," ABC, 1984; "Sledge Hammer!: To Live and Die on TV," ABC, 1986; "Married with Children: Married with Queen," FOX, 1989.

TV MOVIES AND MINISERIES: "Harold Robbins' 79 Park Avenue," NBC, 1977; "A Guide for the Married Woman," ABC, 1978.

WITH TOMMY NOONAN: "The George Gobel Show," NBC, 1958; "The Ed Sullivan Show," CBS, 1960; "The Ed Sullivan Show," CBS, 1961.

MARTIN, ANDREA

b. *Portland, ME.* Emmy-winning comic actress.

AS A REGULAR: "Second City TV," SYN, 1977-81; "SCTV Network 90," NBC, 1981-83; "Roxie," CBS, 1987.

AND: "Kate & Allie: Stage Mother," CBS, 1986; "Kate & Allie: The Goodbye Girl," CBS, 1986.

TV MOVIES AND MINISERIES: "Torn Between Two Lovers," CBS, 1979.

* Emmies: 1982, 1983.

MARTIN, DEAN

b. *Dino Crocetti, Steubenville, OH, June 7, 1917.* Smooth singer and laid-back personality who's been on everyone's variety shows, and vice versa.

AS A REGULAR: "The Colgate Comedy Hour," NBC, 1950-55; "Dean Martin Special," NBC, 1957-61; "The Dean Martin Show," NBC, 1965-74; "Half Nelson," NBC, 1985.

AND: "Dinah Shore Chevy Show," NBC, 1957; "The Steve Allen Show," NBC, 1957; "Club Oasis," NBC, 1957; "Club Oasis," NBC, 1958; "Person to Person," CBS, 1958; "The Danny Thomas Show: Terry's Crush," CBS, 1958; "The Bing Crosby Show," ABC, 1958; "Phil Harris Special," NBC, 1959; "Frank Sinatra Timex Show," ABC, 1959; "Startime: The Dean Martin Show," NBC, 1959; "Startime: The Dean Martin Show," NBC, 1960; "Bob Hope Buick Show," NBC, 1961; "Dinah Shore Special," NBC, 1961; "Judy Garland Special," CBS, 1962; "Dinah Shore Special," NBC, 1962; "Bob Hope Special," NBC, 1963; "Perry Como Special," NBC, 1964;

"The Bing Crosby Show," CBS, 1964; "Hollywood Palace," ABC, 1964; "Bob Hope Special," NBC, 1964; "Rawhide: Canliss," CBS, 1964; "Perry Como Special," NBC, 1965; "The Tonight Show Starring Johnny Carson," NBC, 1965; "The Lucy Show: Lucy Dates Dean Martin," CBS, 1966; "The Merv Griffin Show," CBS, 1970; "The Carol Burnett Show," CBS, 1970; "Changing Scene II," ABC, 1970; "Music Country USA," NBC, 1974; "Lucille Ball," CBS, 1975; "Dean's Place," NBC, 1975; "Dean Martin Special," NBC, 1975; "Dean's Place," NBC, 1976; "Joys," NBC, 1976; "Charlie's Angels: Angels in Vegas," ABC, 1978; "The Misadventures of Sheriff Lobo: Dean Martin and the Moonshiners," NBC, 1979; "Dean Martin in London," SHO, 1984.

* See also Jerry Lewis.

MARTIN, DEAN PAUL

b. *Santa Monica, CA, November 17, 1951; d. 1987.* Son of Dean; he played Dr. Billy Hayes on "Misfits of Science" and died when the National Guard jet he was piloting crashed.

AS A REGULAR: "Misfits of Science," NBC, 1985-86.

AND: "The Love Boat: Father in the Cradle," ABC, 1984.

MARTIN, DICK

b. *Detroit, MI, January 30, 1922.* Comedian long teamed with Dan Rowan.

AS A REGULAR: "The Chevy Show," NBC, 1958; "The Lucy Show," CBS, 1962-64; "The Dean Martin Summer Show," NBC, 1966; "Rowan & Martin's Laugh-In," NBC, 1968-73; "Match Game P.M.," SYN, 1975-82; "The Cheap Show," SYN, 1978-79; "Mindreaders," NBC, 1979-80.

AND: "Off to See the Wizard: Who's Afraid of Mother Goose?," ABC, 1967; "The Tim Conway Show," CBS, 1970; "The Carol Burnett Show," CBS, 1970; "The Dean Martin Show," NBC, 1971; "Celebrity Sweepstakes," NBC, 1974; "Password All-Stars," ABC, 1975; "Celebrity Sweepstakes," NBC, 1976; "Tattletales," CBS, 1976; "The Love Boat: Marooned," ABC, 1978; "The Love Boat: Life Begins at 40," ABC, 1979; "The Mike Douglas Show," SYN, 1981; "Here's Boomer: Make 'Em Laugh," NBC, 1981.

AS DIRECTOR: "The Bob Newhart Show," CBS, 1977-78.

* Emmies: 1969.
* See also Dan Rowan.

MARTIN, JARED

b. *New York City, NY, December 21, 1944.* Actor who played Dusty Farlow on "Dallas."

AS A REGULAR: "Fantastic Journey," NBC, 1977; "Dallas," CBS, 1979-82, 1985; "War of the

Worlds," SYN, 1988-89.
AND: "The Partridge Family: See Here, Private Partridge," ABC, 1970; "The Bold Ones: Trial of a PFC," NBC, 1970; "The Rookies: A Bloody Shade of Blue," ABC, 1972; "The Rookies: Sound of Silence," ABC, 1973; "Columbo: A Stitch in Crime," NBC, 1973; "Shaft: The Killing," CBS, 1973; "Switch: The Cruise Ship Murders," CBS, 1975; "CHiPS: Hot Wheels," NBC, 1979; "Big Shamus, Little Shamus: Pilot," CBS, 1979; "The Love Boat: Meet the Author," ABC, 1982; "Knight Rider: Knight of the Drones," NBC, 1984; "Murder, She Wrote: It's a Dog's Life," CBS, 1984; "Scarecrow and Mrs. King: The Artful Dodger," CBS, 1984; "Finder of Lost Loves: Tricks," ABC, 1985; "Hotel: Fallen Idols," ABC, 1985; "Murder, She Wrote: Magnum on Ice," CBS, 1986; "The Love Boat: The Perfect Divorce," ABC, 1985; "Hunter: Shades," NBC, 1987; "The New Mike Hammer: Who Killed Sister Lorna?," CBS, 1987.
TV MOVIES AND MINISERIES: "Men of the Dragon," ABC, 1974; "M Station: Hawaii," CBS, 1980.

MARTIN, KIEL
b. Pittsburgh, PA, 1944; d. 1990. Actor who played Det. John LaRue on "Hill Street Blues."
AS A REGULAR: "Hill Street Blues," NBC, 1981-87; "Second Chance," FOX, 1987.
AND: "The Virginian: Star Crossed," NBC, 1967; "The Virginian: The Hell Wind," NBC, 1968; "Dragnet: The Big Little Victim," NBC, 1968; "The Virginian: Incident at Diablo Crossing," NBC, 1969; "Paris: Pilot," CBS, 1979; "Matt Houston: Who Would Kill Ramona?," ABC, 1982; "Father Dowling Mysteries: Missing Body Mystery," NBC, 1989; "Miami Vice: Leap of Faith," NBC, 1989; "Ray Bradbury Theatre: A Sound of Thunder," USA, 1989.
TV MOVIES AND MINISERIES: "The Catcher," NBC, 1972; "The Log of the Black Pearl," NBC, 1975; "Child Bride of Short Creek," NBC, 1981; "Convicted: A Mother's Story," NBC, 1987; "If It's Tuesday, It Still Must Be Belgium," NBC, 1987.

MARTIN, LORI
b. Dawn Catherine Menzer, Glendale, CA, April 18, 1947. Teen actress who played Velvet Brown, mistress of King the horse on "National Velvet."
AS A REGULAR: "National Velvet," NBC, 1960-62.
AND: "Here's Hollywood," NBC, 1960; "Here's Hollywood," NBC, 1961; "Sam Benedict: Run Softly, Oh Softly," NBC, 1963; "The Donna Reed Show: All Women Are Dangerous," ABC, 1963; "Leave It to Beaver: Beaver Sees America," ABC, 1963; "The Breaking Point: The Tides of Darkness," ABC, 1964; "Slattery's People: Question-Do the Ignorant Sleep in Pure White Beds?," CBS, 1964; "My Three Sons: Robbie's Double Life," CBS, 1966.

MARTIN, MARY
b. Weatherford, TX, December 1, 1913; d. 1990. Musical-comedy legend who recreated her stage role as Peter Pan on TV; thanks to video, today's audiences continue to enjoy it.
AS A REGULAR: "Over Easy," PBS, 1981-82.
AND: "Producers Showcase: Peter Pan," NBC, 1955; "The Skin of Our Teeth," NBC, 1955; "Producers Showcase: Peter Pan," NBC, 1956; "Hallmark Hall of Fame: Born Yesterday," NBC, 1956; "Annie Get Your Gun," NBC, 1957; "Magic with Mary Martin," NBC, 1959; "Music with Mary Martin," NBC, 1959; "Eleanor Roosevelt's Jubilee," NBC, 1960; "Peter Pan," NBC, 1960; "25 Years of Life Magazine," NBC, 1961; "Bing Crosby Special," ABC, 1962; "The Jack Paar Program," NBC, 1964; "Dinah!," SYN, 1976; "The Love Boat: So Help Me Hanna," ABC, 1983; "Hardcastle and McCormick: Hardcastle, Hardcastle, Hardcastle and McCormick," ABC, 1985.
TV MOVIES AND MINISERIES: "Valentine," ABC, 1979.
* Mother of Larry Hagman.
* Emmies: 1956.

MARTIN, PAMELA SUE
b. Westport, CT, January 5, 1953. Actress who played Fallon Carrington Colby on "Dynasty."
AS A REGULAR: "The Nancy Drew Mysteries," ABC, 1977-78; "The Hardy Boys Mysteries," ABC, 1977-78; "Dynasty," ABC, 1981-84; "Star Games," SYN, 1985-86.
AND: "Hollywood Television Theatre: The Hemingway Play," PBS, 1976; "The Quest: Day of Outrage," NBC, 1976; "The Love Boat: Boomerang," ABC, 1980; "The John Davidson Show," SYN, 1981; "Saturday Night Live," NBC, 1985.
TV MOVIES AND MINISERIES: "The Girls of Huntington House," ABC, 1973; "The Gun and the Pulpit," ABC, 1974; "Human Feelings," NBC, 1978; "Bay Coven," NBC, 1987.

MARTIN, QUINN
b. 1922; d. 1987. Producer of crime shows that seemed fresh at first and quickly degenerated into run-of-the-mill prime-time fodder.
AS PRODUCER-CREATOR: "Westinghouse Desilu Playhouse: The Untouchables," CBS, 1959; "The Untouchables," ABC, 1959-63; "The Fugitive," ABC, 1963-67; "Twelve O'Clock High," ABC, 1964-67; "The FBI," ABC, 1965-74; "The Invaders," ABC, 1967-68; "Cannon," CBS, 1971-76; "The Streets of San Francisco," ABC, 1972-77; "Barnaby Jones," CBS, 1973-80; "The Manhunter," CBS, 1974-75; "Most Wanted," ABC, 1976-77; "Tales of the Unexpected," NBC, 1977.

MARTIN, ROSS

b. *Martin Rosenblatt, Grodek, Poland, March 22, 1920; d. 1981.* Character actor who brought a touch of humor to his roles, a commodity especially needed to counterbalance the dour Robert Conrad on "The Wild Wild West," on which Martin played Artemus Gordon.

AS A REGULAR: "Mr. Lucky," CBS, 1959-60; "Stump the Stars," CBS, 1962-63, 1964; "The Wild Wild West," CBS, 1965-69.

AND: "U.S. Steel Hour: Wetback Run," CBS, 1956; "Modern Romances: Unwanted Diamonds," NBC, 1957; "Studio One: The Human Barrier," CBS, 1957; "Gunsmoke: Bottleman," CBS, 1958; "Bat Masterson: The Treasure of Worry Hill," NBC, 1958; "U.S. Marshal: The Check Artist," SYN, 1959; "Peter Gunn: The Fuse," NBC, 1959; "The Twilight Zone: The Four of Us Are Dying," CBS, 1960; "Comedy Spot: The Sky's the Limit," CBS, 1960; "Dr. Kildare: Second Chance," NBC, 1961; "The Whirlybirds: The Midnight Show," SYN, 1962; "The Dick Powell Show: Everybody Loves Sweeney," NBC, 1963; "Your First Impression," NBC, 1963; "Object Is," ABC, 1964; "Password," CBS, 1966; "Mitzi's Second Special," NBC, 1969; "Love, American Style: Love and the Nutsy Girl," ABC, 1969; "Columbo: Suitable for Framing," NBC, 1971; "Night Gallery: Camera Obscura," NBC, 1971; "Ironside: Mind for Murder," NBC, 1973; "Tenafly: The Cash and Carry Caper," NBC, 1973; "McCloud: The Solid Gold Swingers," NBC, 1973; "Barnaby Jones: Friends Till Death," CBS, 1974; "The Invisible Man: The Fine Art of Diplomacy," NBC, 1975; "Don Adams Screen Test," SYN, 1976; "Sanford & Son: California Crude," NBC, 1976; "Gemini Man: Minotaur," NBC, 1976; "Quark: All the Emporer's Quasi-Norms," NBC, 1978; "The American Girls: Pilot," CBS, 1978; "Whew!," CBS, 1980; "Fantasy Island: The Winemaker," ABC, 1980; "Card Sharks," NBC, 1980; "Mork & Mindy: Mork and the Bum Rap," ABC, 1981.

TV MOVIES AND MINISERIES: "The Sheriff," ABC, 1971; "The Crooked Hearts," ABC, 1972; "Dying Room Only," ABC, 1973; "Skyway to Death," ABC, 1974; "Yesterday's Child," NBC, 1977; "The Wild Wild West Revisited," CBS, 1979; "The Return of Mod Squad," ABC, 1979; "More Wild Wild West," CBS, 1980.

MARTIN, STEVE

b. *Waco, TX, 1945.* Silver-haired, original, influential comic of the seventies and eighties who's turned almost totally toward feature films.

AS A REGULAR: "Andy Williams Presents Ray Stevens," NBC, 1970; "The Ken Berry "WOW" Show," ABC, 1972; "Half the George Kirby Comedy Hour," SYN, 1972; "The Sonny and Cher Comedy Hour," CBS, 1972-73; "The Smothers Brothers Comedy Hour," NBC, 1975;

"The Johnny Cash Show," CBS, 1976.

AND: "The Smothers Brothers Comedy Hour," CBS, 1969; "Cher," CBS, 1975; "Saturday Night Live," NBC, 1976; "The Merv Griffin Show," SYN, 1977; "The Tonight Show Starring Johnny Carson," NBC, 1977; "Saturday Night Live," NBC, 1977; "The Tonight Show Starring Johnny Carson," NBC, 1978; "The Carol Burnett Show," CBS, 1978; "Saturday Night Live," NBC, 1978; "Saturday Night Live," NBC, 1979; "Saturday Night Live," NBC, 1980; "The Steve Allen Comedy Hour," NBC, 1980; "Saturday Night Live," NBC, 1986; "Saturday Night Live," NBC, 1987; "Saturday Night Live," NBC, 1989; "The Tonight Show Starring Johnny Carson," NBC, 1989; "Saturday Night Live's 15th Anniversary," NBC, 1989.

AS WRITER: "The Smothers Brothers Comedy Hour," CBS, 1967-69.

AS PRODUCER: "Domestic Life," CBS, 1984.

* Emmies: 1969.

MARTIN, STROTHER

b. *Kokomo, IN, March 26, 1919; d. 1980.* Reliable character actor at his best in downhome roles or as backwoods heavies.

AS A REGULAR: "Hotel De Paree," CBS, 1959-60; "Hawkins," CBS, 1973-74.

AND: "Gunsmoke: Professor Lute Bone," CBS, 1956; "I Love Lucy: Off to Florida," CBS, 1956; "Matinee Theatre: Eugenie Grandet," NBC, 1956; "Broken Arrow: Apache Dowry," ABC, 1957; "The Millionaire: Story of Jerry Patterson," CBS, 1957; "Have Gun, Will Travel: High Wire," CBS, 1957; "The Dick Van Dyke Show: Baby Fat," CBS, 1965; "The Virginian: The Claim," NBC, 1965; "The Big Valley: Brother Love," ABC, 1967; "Gilligan's Island: Take a Dare," CBS, 1967; "The Virginian: You Can Lead a Horse to Water," NBC, 1970; "Marcus Welby, M.D.: Nobody Wants a Fat Jockey," ABC, 1970; "Love, American Style: Love and the Old Boyfriend," ABC, 1971; "Gunsmoke: Island in the Desert," CBS, 1974; "The Rookies: The Teacher," ABC, 1974; "The Rockford Files: The Trees, the Bees and T.T. Flowers," NBC, 1977; "Saturday Night Live," NBC, 1980.

TV MOVIES AND MINISERIES: "One of Our Own," NBC, 1975; "Steel Cowboy," NBC, 1978; "Better Late Than Never," NBC, 1979.

MARTIN, TONY

b. *Alvin Morris, San Francisco, CA, December 25, 1912.* Former big-band singer who oozed passion and romance; husband of Cyd Charisse.

AS A REGULAR: "The Tony Martin Show," NBC, 1954-56.

AND: "Shower of Stars: High Pitch," CBS, 1955; "The Ed Sullivan Show," CBS, 1957; "Galaxy of Stars," NBC, 1957; "Tony Martin Special," NBC,

1957; "Startime: Meet Cyd Charisse," NBC, 1959; "Steve Allen Plymouth Show," NBC, 1960; "The Ed Sullivan Show," CBS, 1960; "The Donna Reed Show: Tony Martin Visits," ABC, 1961; "Dean Martin Special," NBC, 1961; "The Garry Moore Show," CBS, 1961; "Perry Como's Kraft Music Hall," NBC, 1961; "Death Valley Days: The Unshakable Man," SYN, 1962; "The Tonight Show Starring Johnny Carson," NBC, 1963; "Hollywood Palace," ABC, 1965; "Hollywood Squares," NBC, 1967; "The Mike Douglas Show," SYN, 1967; "The Name of the Game: I Love You, Billy Baker," NBC, 1970; "Donny and Marie," ABC, 1977.

MARTINDALE, WINK

b. *Winston Conrad, Jackson, TN, December 4, 1934.* Game-show host with a perpetual smile; he had a pop hit, "Deck of Cards," in the late fifties.

AS A REGULAR: "What's This Song?," NBC, 1964-65; "Dream Girl of '67," ABC, 1966-67; "How's Your Mother-in-Law?," ABC, 1967-68; "Can You Top This?, SYN, 1970-72; "Words and Music," NBC, 1970-71; "Gambit," CBS, 1972-76; NBC, 1980-81; "High Rollers," NBC, 1974-76, 1980; SYN, 1976-77; 1987-88; "Tic Tac Dough," SYN, 1978-86; "Las Vegas Gambit," NBC, 1980-81; "Headline Chasers," SYN, 1985-86.

AND: "Jubilee USA," ABC, 1959.

MARTINEZ, A

b. *Adolf Martinez III, Glendale, CA.* Actor who plays Cruz Castillo on "Santa Barbara."

AS A REGULAR: "Storefront Lawyers," CBS, 1970-71; "The Cowboys," ABC, 1974; "Born to the Wind," NBC, 1982; "Cassie and Company," NBC, 1982; "Whiz Kids," CBS, 1983-84; "Santa Barbara," NBC, 1984- .

AND: "Mannix: Time Out of Mind," CBS, 1970; "The Man and the City: Reprisal," ABC, 1971; "The Bold Ones: Justice Is a Sometime Thing," NBC, 1972; "The Streets of San Francisco: Hall of Mirrors," ABC, 1972; "Police Story: Man on a Rack," NBC, 1973; "Hawaii Five-O: A Bullet for El Diablo," CBS, 1973; "Kung Fu: And Death Will Be Close Behind," ABC, 1974; "McCloud: Sharks!," NBC, 1975; "The Streets of San Francisco: False Witness," ABC, 1975; "Police Woman: The Buttercup Killer," NBC, 1977; "Quincy: Walk Softly Through the Night," NBC, 1979; "Barney Miller: The DNA Story," ABC, 1979; "B.J. and the Bear: The Murphy Contingent," NBC, 1979; "Barney Miller: The Doll," ABC, 1981; "CHiPS: A Simple Operation," NBC, 1981; "The White Shadow: Cops," CBS, 1981; "Remington Steele: High Flying Steele," NBC, 1984.

TV MOVIES AND MINISERIES: "Hunters Are for Killing," CBS, 1970; "Probe," NBC, 1972;

"The Abduction of Saint Anne," ABC, 1975; "Death Among Friends," NBC, 1975; "Mallory: Circumstantial Evidence," NBC, 1976; "Centennial," NBC, 1978-79; "Manhunt: Search for the Night Stalker," NBC, 1989.

MARVIN, LEE

b. *New York City, NY, February 19, 1924; d. 1987.* Rugged actor who played Chicago cop Frank Ballinger on "M Squad." He also played heavies, and virtually dropped TV acting after winning an Oscar for "Cat Ballou" in 1966.

AS A REGULAR: "M Squad," NBC, 1957-60.

AND: "Dragnet: The Big Cast," NBC, 1952; "Rebound: The Mine," ABC, 1952; "Easy Chair Theatre: Sound in the Night," SYN, 1953; "The Doctors: The Runaways," NBC, 1953; "The American Hour: Outlaw's Reckoning," ABC, 1953; "Pepsi Cola Playhouse: Open Season," ABC, 1954; "Campbell TV Soundstage: The Psychopathic Nurse," NBC, 1954; "Center Stage: The Day Before Atlanta," ABC, 1954; "The Ford Show," NBC, 1957; "G.E. Theatre: All I Survey," CBS, 1958; "Climax!: Time of the Hanging," CBS, 1958; "Schlitz Playhouse of Stars: A Fistful of Love," CBS, 1959; "The Steve Allen Show," NBC, 1959; "Westinghouse Desilu Playhouse: Man in Orbit," CBS, 1959; "The Twilight Zone: The Mighty Casey," CBS, 1959; "Steve Allen Plymouth Show," NBC, 1959; "Sunday Showcase: The American," NBC, 1960; "G.E. Theatre: Don't You Remember?," CBS, 1960; "Wagon Train: The Jose Morales Story," NBC, 1960; "G.E. Theatre: The Joke's on Me," CBS, 1961; "The Untouchables: The Nick Acropolis Story," ABC, 1961; "Alcoa Premiere: People Need People," ABC, 1961; "The Investigators: The Oracle," CBS, 1961; "The Twilight Zone: The Grave," CBS, 1961; "Route 66: Mon Petit Chou," CBS, 1961; "Ben Casey: A Story to Be Told Softly," ABC, 1962; "The Twilight Zone: Steel," CBS, 1963; "Kraft Suspense Theatre: The Case Against Paul Ryker," NBC, 1963; "You Don't Say," NBC, 1963; "Bob Hope Chrysler Theatre: The Loving Cup," NBC, 1965; "Bob Hope Special," NBC, 1966; "The Joey Bishop Show," ABC, 1968; "The Ed Sullivan Show," CBS, 1969; "The Merv Griffin Show," CBS, 1970; "Changing Scene II," ABC, 1970; "Bob Hope Special," NBC, 1971; "The Tonight Show Starring Johnny Carson," NBC, 1972; "The Flip Wilson Show," NBC, 1972.

TV MOVIES AND MINISERIES: "The Dirty Dozen: Next Mission," NBC, 1985.

MARX, CHICO

b. *Leonard Marx, New York City, NY, March 26, 1886; d. 1961.* Piano-playing Marx brother.

AS A REGULAR: "The College Bowl," ABC, 1950-51.

AND: "Silver Theatre: Papa Romani," CBS, 1950;

"Art Linkletter's House Party," CBS, 1957; "Playhouse 90: No Time at All," CBS, 1958; "G.E. Theatre: The Great Jewel Robbery," CBS, 1959.

MARX, GROUCHO

b. *Julius Marx, New York City, NY, October 2, 1890; d. 1977.* Noted wit, film comic and wisecracking game-show host, only with him around the game didn't matter all that much.
AS A REGULAR: "You Bet Your Life," NBC, 1950-61; "Tell It to Groucho," NBC, 1962.
AND: "The Perry Como Show," NBC, 1956; "G.E. Theatre: The Great Jewel Robbery," CBS, 1959; "The Last Word," CBS, 1959; "I've Got a Secret," CBS, 1959; "What's My Line?," CBS, 1959; "Dinah Shore Chevy Show," NBC, 1959; "Bell Telephone Hour: Groucho Marx in the Mikado, NBC, 1960; "Open End," NBC, 1960; "G.E. Theatre: The Holdout," CBS, 1962; "Bob Hope Chrysler Theatre: Time for Elizabeth," NBC, 1964; "Hollywood Palace," ABC, 1964; "Hollywood Palace," ABC, 1965; "I Dream of Jeannie: The Greatest Invention in the World," NBC, 1967; "Kraft Music Hall: Roast for Johnny Carson," NBC, 1968; "The Jackie Gleason Show," CBS, 1969; "The Music Scene," ABC, 1969; "Joys," NBC, 1976.
* Emmies: 1951.

MARX, HARPO

b. *Adolph Marx, New York City, NY, November 21, 1888; d. 1964.* Screen comic and mime who did an amazing "mirror" bit opposite Lucille Ball that's even more amazing when you consider he was in his late sixties at the time.
AS A GUEST: "I Love Lucy: Harpo Marx," CBS, 1955; "Art Linkletter's House Party," CBS, 1957; "Person to Person," CBS, 1958; "Du Pont Show of the Month: The Red Mill," CBS, 1958; "G.E. Theatre: The Great Jewel Robbery," CBS, 1959; "The du Pont Show with June Allyson: Silent Panic," CBS, 1960; "The Chevy Show: Swinging at the Summit," NBC, 1961; "The Ed Sullivan Show," CBS, 1961; "Play Your Hunch," NBC, 1961; "I've Got a Secret," CBS, 1961; "Here's Hollywood," NBC, 1961; "You Bet Your Life," NBC, 1961; "Art Linkletter's House Party," CBS, 1961; "The du Pont Show: The Wonderful World of Toys," NBC, 1961; "The Red Skelton Hour," CBS, 1962; "Mr. Smith Goes to Washington: The Musicale," ABC, 1962.

MASON, JAMES

b. *Huddersfield, England, May 15, 1909; d. 1984.* Debonair actor with a cultured voice equally adept at playing troubled men with deep flaws.

AS A REGULAR: "Lux Video Theatre," NBC, 1954-55.
AND: "Panic!: Marooned," NBC, 1957; "Dean Martin Special," NBC, 1957; "G.E. Theatre: The Questioning Note," CBS, 1957; "Playhouse 90: The Thundering Wave," CBS, 1957; "Schlitz Playhouse of Stars: No Boat for Four Months," CBS, 1958; "Playhouse 90: Not the Glory," CBS, 1958; "The Jack Paar Show," NBC, 1958; "Playhouse 90: The Second Man," CBS, 1959; "Alcoa Theatre: A Sword for Marius," NBC, 1959; "Person to Person," NBC, 1959; "About Faces," ABC, 1960; "Stoney Burke: The Scavenger," ABC, 1962; "Dr. Kildare: Behold the Great Man/A Life for a Life/Web of Hate/The Horizontal Hero," NBC, 1965; "Lena Horne Special," SYN, 1965; "ABC Stage '67: Dare I Weep, Dare I Mourn," ABC, 1966; "Password," CBS, 1967; "The Mike Douglas Show," SYN, 1967; "Personality," NBC, 1968; "The Tonight Show Starring Johnny Carson," NBC, 1968; "The Legend of Silent Night," ABC, 1968; "The Movie Game," SYN, 1970.
TV MOVIES AND MINISERIES: "Frankenstein: The True Story," NBC, 1973; "Bell System Family Theatre: Great Expectations," NBC, 1974; "Jesus of Nazareth," NBC, 1977; "Salem's Lot," CBS, 1979; "George Washington," CBS, 1984; "A.D.," NBC, 1985.
AS DIRECTOR: "Telephone Time: Death of a Nobody," ABC, 1957.

MASON, JACKIE

b. *New York City, NY.* Comedian.
AS A REGULAR: "Chicken Soup," ABC, 1989.
AND: "The Garry Moore Show," CBS, 1960; "The Garry Moore Show," CBS, 1961; "Perry Como's Kraft Music Hall," NBC, 1961; "The Ed Sullivan Show," CBS, 1961; "The Jack Paar Show," NBC, 1961; "The Jack Paar Show," NBC, 1962; "The Jack Paar Program," NBC, 1962; "The Ed Sullivan Show," CBS, 1962; "To Tell the Truth," CBS, 1962; "The Ed Sullivan Show," CBS, 1963; "The Merv Griffin Show," NBC, 1963; "The Jack Paar Program," NBC, 1963; "Talent Scouts," CBS, 1963; "The Garry Moore Show," CBS, 1964; "The Tennessee Ernie Ford Show," ABC, 1964; "Hollywood Palace," ABC, 1964; "The Ed Sullivan Show," CBS, 1964; "Candid Camera," CBS, 1965; "Hollywood Palace," ABC, 1965; "ABC Nightlife," ABC, 1965; "The Ed Sullivan Show," CBS, 1967; "The Smothers Brothers Comedy Hour," CBS, 1967; "The Merv Griffin Show," SYN, 1968; "The Dean Martin Show," NBC, 1968; "The Merv Griffin Show," CBS, 1969; "Dolly," ABC, 1988; "Later with Bob Costas," NBC, 1989.
* On October 18, 1964, Mason appeared on "The Ed Sullivan Show." The program was running late, and behind the camera Sullivan raised two fingers in an effort to speed up Mason's act.

Mason made it part of his act and held up a finger. Sullivan thought it was THE finger; Mason denied it. Sullivan cancelled Mason's $45,000, six-show contract and the comedian claims to have been blackballed by the entertainment industry for the next twenty-odd years.

MASSEY, RAYMOND

b. Toronto, August 30, 1896; d. 1983. Actor who was "Abe Lincoln in Illinois" to one generation and Dr. Kildare's mentor, Dr. Gillespie, to another.

AS A REGULAR: "I Spy," SYN, 1956-57; "Dr. Kildare," NBC, 1961-66.

AND: "Laburnum Grove," CBS, 1950; "The Clock: The Morning After," NBC, 1950; "Lux Video Theatre: Abe Lincoln in Illinois," CBS, 1951; "Betty Crocker Star Matinee: The Linden Tree," ABC, 1951; "Robert Montgomery Presents: For These Services," NBC, 1954; "Producers Showcase: Yellow Jack," NBC, 1955; "Goodyear TV Playhouse: All Summer Long," NBC, 1956; "Climax!: Strange Hostage," CBS, 1956; "Producers Showcase: Mayerling," NBC, 1957; "Kraft Television Theatre: A Matter of Life," NBC, 1957; "G.E. Theatre: Hitler's Secret," CBS, 1959; "Alfred Hitchcock Presents: Road Hog," CBS, 1959; "Perry Como's Kraft Music Hall," NBC, 1960; "Playhouse 90: The Cruel Day," CBS, 1960; "Dick Powell's Zane Grey Theatre: Seed of Evil," CBS, 1960; "Riverboat: Trunk Full of Dreams," NBC, 1960; "Wagon Train: Princess of a Lost Tribe," NBC, 1960; "Here's Hollywood," NBC, 1961; "Our American Heritage: Not in Vain," NBC, 1961; "Adventures in Paradise: Command at Sea," ABC, 1961; "Kraft Mystery Theatre: Two Counts of Murder," NBC, 1962; "Play Your Hunch," NBC, 1962; "The Merv Griffin Show," NBC, 1962; "Insight: The Cross in Crisis," SYN, 1962; "The Eleventh Hour: Four Feet in the Morning," NBC, 1963; "Missing Links," NBC, 1964; "The Match Game," NBC, 1964; "Hallmark Hall of Fame: Saint Joan," NBC, 1967; "Night Gallery: Clean Kills and Other Trophies," NBC, 1971; "Night Gallery: Rare Objects," NBC, 1972.

TV MOVIES AND MINISERIES: "All My Darling Daughters," ABC, 1972; "The President's Plane Is Missing," ABC, 1973; "My Darling Daughters' Anniversary," ABC, 1973.

MASUR, RICHARD

b. New York City. Actor who played David Kane, suitor of Ann Romano (Bonnie Franklin) on "One Day at a Time."

AS A REGULAR: "Hot L Baltimore," ABC, 1975; "One Day at a Time," CBS, 1975-76; "Empire," CBS, 1984.

AND: "All in the Family: Gloria's Boyfriend," CBS, 1974; "The Mary Tyler Moore Show: The Outsider," CBS, 1974; "Switch: The Man Who

Couldn't Lose," CBS, 1975; "Rhoda: A Night in the Emergency Room," CBS, 1976; "Happy Days: Allison," ABC, 1980; "One Day at a Time: The Indianapolis Story," CBS, 1981; "Cagney & Lacey: I'll Be Home for Christmas," CBS, 1982; "Amazing Stories: The Amazing Falsworth," NBC, 1985; "Wonderworks: Hiroshima Maiden," PBS, 1988; "L.A. Law: Open Heart Perjury," NBC, 1988; "Wonderworks: Two Daddies?," PBS, 1989; "Island Son: Life Sentence," CBS, 1989.

TV MOVIES AND MINISERIES: "Having Babies," ABC, 1976; "Betrayal," NBC, 1978; "Walking Through the Fire," CBS, 1979; "East of Eden," ABC, 1981; "Money on the Side," ABC, 1982; "The Demon Murder Case," NBC, 1983; "Adam," NBC, 1983; "Hallmark Hall of Fame: The Winter of Our Discontent," CBS, 1983; "The Burning Bed," NBC, 1984; "Flight #90: Disaster on the Potomac," NBC, 1984; "Obsessed with a Married Woman," ABC, 1985; "Embassy," ABC, 1985; "Wild Horses," CBS, 1985; "When the Bough Breaks," NBC, 1986; "The George McKenna Story," CBS, 1986; "Roses Are for the Rich," CBS, 1987; "Settle the Score," NBC, 1989; "Cast the First Stone," NBC, 1989.

AS DIRECTOR: "ABC Afterschool Special: Torn Between Two Fathers," ABC, 1989.

MATHERS, JERRY

b. Sioux City, IA, June 2, 1948. Former child actor who played Theodore "Beaver" Cleaver in a well-written fifties sitcom.

AS A REGULAR: "Disneyland: The Adventures of Davy Crockett," ABC, 1954-55; "Leave It to Beaver," CBS, 1957-58; ABC, 1958-63; "The New Leave It to Beaver," DIS, 1985-86; TBS, 1986-89.

AND: "All Star Revue" (as Baby New Year 1951), NBC, 1950; "The Bing Crosby Show," ABC, 1951; "Lux Video Theatre: The Great McGinty," NBC, 1954; "The Colgate Comedy Hour," NBC, 1955; "Mickey Mouse Club: Adventure Time," ABC, 1955; "The Adventures of Ozzie and Harriet: Halloween Show," ABC, 1955; "December Bride: Trailer Show," CBS, 1956; "Studio 57: It's a Small World," SYN, 1957; "The George Gobel Show," NBC, 1958; "The Chevy Show: Children Are People?," NBC, 1960; "Batman: The Great Escape/The Great Train Robbery," ABC, 1968; "Lassie: Area," CBS, 1970; "My Three Sons: Love Thy Neighbor," CBS, 1970; "Flying High: Pilot," CBS, 1978; "The Match Game-Hollywood Squares Hour," NBC, 1983; "The Love Boat: The Final Cruise," ABC, 1988.

TV MOVIES AND MINISERIES: "The Girl, the Gold Watch and the Dynamite," SYN, 1981; "Still the Beaver," CBS, 1983.

* Mathers didn't actually appear in "Davy Crockett," but he dubbed the voices for Crockett's children.

* In high school Mathers played in a band called Beaver and the Trappers.

MATHESON, TIM

b. *Glendale, CA, December 31, 1947.* Former child actor; he supplied the voice for cartoon hero Jonny Quest.

AS A REGULAR: "Window on Main Street," CBS, 1961-62; "Jonny Quest," ABC, 1964-65; "The Virginian," NBC, 1969-70; "Bonanza," NBC, 1972-73; "The Quest," NBC, 1976; "Tucker's Witch," CBS, 1982-83; "Just in Time," ABC, 1988.

AND: "Leave It to Beaver: Tell It to Ella," ABC, 1962; "Leave It to Beaver: The Clothing Drive," ABC, 1963; "Bracken's World: The Country Boy," NBC, 1970; "Room 222: The Long Honeymoon," ABC, 1971; "Ironside: His Fiddlers Three," NBC, 1972; "Here's Lucy: Kim Moves Out," CBS, 1972; "Medical Center: Impasse," CBS, 1973; "Kung Fu: The Soldier," ABC, 1973; "Police Story: Fingerprint," NBC, 1974; "Owen Marshall, Counselor at Law: A Killer with a Badge," ABC, 1974; "Three for the Road: Match Point," CBS, 1975; "Jigsaw John: Thicker Than Blood," NBC, 1976; "Hollywood Television Theatre: The Hemingway Play," PBS, 1976; "Hawaii Five-O: East Wind, Ill Wind," CBS, 1977; "Trying Times: Get a Job," PBS, 1988.

TV MOVIES AND MINISERIES: "Owen Marshall, Counselor at Law," ABC, 1971; "Lock, Stock and Barrel," NBC, 1971; "Hitched," NBC, 1973; "Remember When," NBC, 1974; "The Last Day," NBC, 1975; "The Runaway Barge," NBC, 1975; "Best Sellers: Captains and the Kings," NBC, 1976; "The Quest," NBC, 1976; "Listen to Your Heart," CBS, 1983; "Obsessed with a Married Woman," ABC, 1985; "Blind Justice," CBS, 1986; "Bay Coven," NBC, 1987; "Warm Hearts, Cold Feet," CBS, 1987; "The Littlest Vicims," CBS, 1989; "Little White Lies," NBC, 1989; "Buried Alive," USA, 1990.

MATHEWS, LARRY

b. *Larry Mazzeo, Burbank, CA, August 15, 1955.* Former child actor who played Richie Petrie on "The Dick Van Dyke Show."

AS A REGULAR: "The Dick Van Dyke Show," CBS, 1961-66.

MATTHAU, WALTER

b. *Walter Matuschanskayasky, New York City, NY, October 1, 1920.* Rumpled actor who began in television and shows signs of returning to it after a successful movie career.

AS A REGULAR: "Talahassee 7000," SYN, 1961.

AND: "Philco TV Playhouse: Tour of Duty," NBC, 1952; "Armstrong Circle Theatre: The Straight Forward Narrow," NBC, 1952; "Philco TV Playhouse: The Basket Weaver," NBC, 1952; "Schlitz Playhouse of Stars: Should Doctors Ever Marry?," CBS, 1952; "Suspense: F.O.B. Vienna,"

CBS, 1953; "Plymouth Playhouse: Nightmare Number Three," ABC, 1953; "Goodyear TV Playhouse: Nothing to Sneeze At," NBC, 1953; "U.S. Steel Hour: Late Date," ABC, 1954; "Robert Montgomery Presents: The Lost Weekend," NBC, 1955; "Alcoa Hour: The Big Vote," NBC, 1956; "Goodyear TV Playhouse: A Will to Live," NBC, 1957; "Goodyear TV Playhouse: The Legacy," NBC, 1957; "U.S. Steel Hour: Victim," CBS, 1957; "Alcoa Hour: The Trouble with Women," NBC, 1957; "Climax!: To Walk the Night," CBS, 1957; "Kraft Theatre: Code of the Corner," NBC, 1958; "Alfred Hitchcock Presents: The Crooked Road," CBS, 1958; "Alfred Hitchcock Presents: Dry Run," CBS, 1959; "Alfred Hitchcock Presents: Very Moral Theft," NBC, 1960; "Play of the Week: The Rope Dancers," SYN, 1960; "Play of the Week: Juno and the Paycock," SYN, 1960; "Play of the Week: My Heart's in the Highlands," SYN, 1960; "Our American Heritage: Born a Giant," NBC, 1960; "Naked City: The Man Who Bit the Diamond in Half," ABC, 1960; "Route 66: Eleven, the Hard Way," CBS, 1961; "Target: The Corrupters: The Million-Dollar Dump," ABC, 1961; "Alfred Hitchcock Presents: Cop for a Day," NBC, 1961; "Target: The Corruptors: One for the Road," ABC, 1962; "Westinghouse Presents: Footnote to Fame," CBS, 1962; "The du Pont Show: Police Emergency," NBC, 1962; "G.E. Theatre: Acres and Pains," CBS, 1962; "The du Pont Show: Big Deal in Laredo," NBC, 1962; "Naked City: Don't Knock It Till You've Tried It," ABC, 1962; "The Eleventh Hour: A Tumble From a High White Horse," NBC, 1963; "The du Pont Show: The Takers," NBC, 1963; "Bob Hope Chrysler Theatre: White Snow, Red Ice," NBC, 1964; "The du Pont Show: Jeremy Rabbitt, the Secret Avenger," NBC, 1964; "The Rogues: The Personal Touch," NBC, 1964; "Dr. Kildare: Man Is a Rock," NBC, 1964; "Profiles in Courage: John M. Slaton," NBC, 1964; "Profiles in Courage: Andrew Johnson," NBC, 1965; "Carol Channing Special," CBS, 1968; "Hollywood Television Theatre: Awake and Sing," NET, 1972; "The Tonight Show Starring Johnny Carson," NBC, 1974; "The Mike Douglas Show," SYN, 1975; "Saturday Night Live," NBC, 1978; "Magic of the Stars," HBO, 1981.

TV MOVIES AND MINISERIES: "AT&T Presents: The Incident," CBS, 1990.

MAY, ELAINE

b. *Elaine Berlin, Philadelphia, PA, April 21, 1932.* Comedienne who teamed with Mike Nichols; now a film director ("The Heartbreak Kid," "Ishtar").

AS A REGULAR: "Keep Talking," CBS, 1958-59; "The Jack Paar Program," NBC, 1964.

* See also Mike Nichols.

MAYEHOFF, EDDIE

b. Baltimore, MD, July 7, 1911. Comic actor usually in blustery roles.

AS A REGULAR: "Hour Glass," NBC, 1946-47; "Doc Corkle," NBC, 1952; "That's My Boy," CBS, 1954-55.

AND: "Studio One: The Star Spangled Soldier," CBS, 1956; "Playhouse 90: Made in Heaven," CBS, 1956; "The Ed Sullivan Show," CBS, 1957; "Strike It Rich," CBS, 1957; "The Standard Oil 75th Anniversary Show," NBC, 1957; "Arthur Murray Party," NBC, 1958; "Bob Hope Chrysler Theatre: Brilliant Benjamin Boggs," NBC, 1966; "Love, American Style: Love and the Athlete," ABC, 1969; "Nanny and the Professor: From Butch with Love," ABC, 1970.

MAYO, WHITMAN

b. New York, November 15, 1930. Actor who played Grady Wilson, pal of Fred Sanford (Redd Foxx).

AS A REGULAR: "Sanford & Son," NBC, 1973-77; "Grady," NBC, 1975-76; "The Sanford Arms," NBC, 1977; "Hell Town," NBC, 1985; "The Van Dyke Show," CBS, 1988.

AND: "Hollywood Squares," NBC, 1975; "Diff'rent Strokes: The Adoption," NBC, 1979; "Sanford: The Freeway," NBC, 1981; "Lou Grant: Generations," CBS, 1981; "Hill Street Blues: The Belles of St. Mary's," NBC, 1983.

TV MOVIES AND MINISERIES: "Hell Town," NBC, 1985.

MAYRON, MELANIE

Actress who plays Melissa Steadman on "thirtysomething."

AS A REGULAR: "thirtysomething," ABC, 1987- .

AND: "Rhoda: With Friends Like These," CBS, 1975; "Medical Center: Two Against Death," CBS, 1975; "Cagney & Lacey: Con Games," CBS, 1985.

TV MOVIES AND MINISERIES: "Hustling," ABC, 1975; "Katie: Portrait of a Centerfold," NBC, 1978; "The Best Little Girl in the World," ABC, 1981; "Will There Really Be a Morning?," CBS, 1983; "Playing for Time," CBS, 1980; "Wallenberg: A Hero's Story," NBC, 1985.

MAZURKI, MIKE

b. Mikhail Mazurwski, Austria, Dec. 25, 1909. Hulking actor usually in hulking roles; he played caveman Clon in "It's About Time."

AS A REGULAR: "It's About Time," CBS, 1966-67; "The Chicago Teddy Bears," CBS, 1971.

AND: "Disneyland: The Adventures of Davy Crockett-Davy Crockett Goes to Congress," NBC, 1955; "Have Gun, Will Travel: Ella West," CBS, 1958; "Tightrope!: The Long Odds," CBS, 1960; "Have Gun, Will Travel: Love's Young Dream,"

CBS, 1960; "Bachelor Father: Kelly the Match-maker," NBC, 1960; "The Roaring Twenties: Duke on the Bum," ABC, 1961; "Stan Freberg Presents Chinese New Year's Eve," ABC, 1962; "The Munsters: Knock Wood, Here Comes Charlie," CBS, 1964; "The John Forsythe Show: School for Spies," NBC, 1966; "Gilligan's Island: The Friendly Physician," CBS, 1966; "Rango: Diamonds Look Better Around Your Neck Than a Rope," ABC, 1967; "Batman: The Wail of the Siren," ABC, 1967; "The Jerry Lewis Show," NBC, 1967; "I Dream of Jeannie: Jeannie and the Great Bank Robbery," NBC, 1967; "The Beverly Hillbillies: The Great Tag-Team Match," CBS, 1968; "My Three Sons: What Did You Do Today, Grandpa?," CBS, 1969; "Love, American Style: Love and the Gangster," ABC, 1971; "Mannix: Days Beyond Recall," CBS, 1971; "Gunsmoke: Trafton," CBS, 1971.

MAZURSKY, PAUL

b. Brooklyn, NY, April 25, 1930. Noted movie director ("Down and Out in Beverly Hills") who began as a film and TV actor.

AS A GUEST: "The Lineup: My Son Is a Stranger," CBS, 1959; "The Rifleman: Shotgun Man," ABC, 1960; "Chevy Mystery Show: Dead Man's Walk," NBC, 1960; "Michael Shayne: The Trouble with Ernie," NBC, 1961; "Adventures in Paradise: The Closing Circle," ABC, 1961; "The Dick Powell Show: Somebody's Waiting," NBC, 1961; "G.E. Theatre: Call to Danger," CBS, 1961; "Hennesey: Tight Quarters," CBS, 1962; "Robert Taylor's Detectives: The Jagged Edge," NBC, 1962; "The Twilight Zone: He's Alive," CBS, 1963; "Alcoa Premiere: George Gobel Presents," ABC, 1963; "The Real McCoys: The Auction," CBS, 1963; "Channing: The Face in the Sun," ABC, 1964; "Love on a Rooftop: The Fifty Dollar Misunderstanding," ABC, 1966.

AS CO-WRITER: "The Danny Kaye Show," CBS, 1965-67.

* "George Gobel Presents" was the pilot for a variety show; Mazursky's appearance was as a comedy team with Joyce Van Patten.

MEADE, JULIA

b. Ridgewood, NJ, 1928. Actress who was also a commercial spokeswoman on "The Ed Sullivan Show," and "Playhouse 90."

AS A REGULAR: "Club Embassy," NBC, 1952-53; "Spotlight Playhouse," CBS, 1959; "Gas Company Playhouse," NBC, 1960.

AND: "The Tonight Show," NBC, 1956; "Armstrong Circle Theatre: The Complex Mummy Complex," CBS, 1958; "The Ed Sullivan Show: Man of the Hour," CBS, 1958; "Christophers: Making Government Your Business," SYN, 1960; "Here's Hollywood," NBC, 1961; "Get the Message," ABC, 1964.

TV MOVIES AND MINISERIES: "My First Love," ABC, 1988.

MEADER, VAUGHN

Impressionist whose hit comedy album satirizing the Kennedys, "The First Family," made him a household name in the early sixties; his guest shots dried up following the events of November 22, 1963.

AS A GUEST: "Talent Scouts," CBS, 1962; "The Ed Sullivan Show," CBS, 1962; "The Jack Paar Program," NBC, 1962; "The Jack Paar Program," NBC, 1963; "The Ed Sullivan Show," CBS, 1963; "Hootenanny," ABC, 1963; "The Match Game," NBC, 1963; "To Tell the Truth," CBS, 1964; "Hootenanny," ABC, 1964.

MEADOWS, AUDREY

b. Wu Chang, China, February 8, 1924. Comic actress who had a way with a tart comeback; she played Alice Kramden, of course.

AS A REGULAR: "Cavalcade of Stars," DUM, 1950-52; "Bob and Ray," NBC, 1951-53; "Club Embassy," NBC, 1952-53; "The Jackie Gleason Show, CBS, 1952-55; 1956-57; "What's Going On?," ABC, 1954; "What's in a Word?," CBS, 1954; "The Name's the Same," ABC, 1955; "The Honeymooners," CBS, 1955-56; "Masquerade Party," CBS, 1958; NBC, 1958-59; CBS, 1959-60; NBC, 1960; "Keep Talking," CBS, 1958-59; "Too Close for Comfort," ABC, 1982-83; "Uncle Buck," CBS, 1990- .

AND: "The Steve Allen Show," NBC, 1957; "I've Got a Secret," CBS, 1957; "The Jack Benny Program," CBS, 1958; "The Steve Allen Show," NBC, 1958; "The Garry Moore Show," CBS, 1958; "Dinah Shore Chevy Show," NBC, 1959; "Person to Person" (as substitute host), CBS, 1959; "Alfred Hitchcock Presents: Mrs. Bixby and the Colonel's Coat," NBC, 1960; "Candid Camera," CBS, 1960; "Play of the Week: The Grand Tour," SYN, 1961; "Wagon Train: The Nancy Palmer Story," NBC, 1961; "Dinah Shore Special," NBC, 1962; "The du Pont Show: The Action in New Orleans," NBC, 1962; "Sam Benedict: Life Is a Lie, Love a Cheat," NBC, 1962; "The Red Skelton Hour," CBS, 1962; "The Match Game," NBC, 1963; "Password," CBS, 1964; "Please Don't Eat the Daisies: Big Brass Blonde," NBC, 1965; "A Salute to Stan Laurel," CBS, 1965; "The Red Skelton Hour," CBS, 1969; "The Carol Burnett Show," CBS, 1970; "The Red Skelton Hour," CBS, 1970; "The Tim Conway Show," CBS, 1970; "Love, American Style: Love and Dear Old Mom and Dad," ABC, 1972; "Honeymooners-The Second Honeymoon," ABC, 1976; "The Love Boat: Doc's Exchange," ABC, 1980; "Diff'rent Strokes: The Squatter," NBC, 1982; "The Love Boat: Novelties," ABC, 1984;

"Murder, She Wrote: If the Frame Fits," CBS, 1986.
* Emmies: 1955.

MEADOWS, JAYNE

b. Wu Chang, China, September 27, 1926. Sister of Audrey and wife of Steve Allen; comic actress and a quiz show staple.

AS A REGULAR: "I've Got a Secret," CBS, 1952-59; "The Art Linkletter Show," NBC, 1963; "The Steve Allen Comedy Hour," CBS, 1967; "Medical Center," CBS, 1969-72; "Steve Allen's Laugh Back," SYN, 1976; "Meeting of Minds," PBS, 1977-78; "It's Not Easy," ABC, 1983.

AND: "Danger: Love Trap," CBS, 1952; "Robert Montgomery Presents: Eva? Caroline?," NBC, 1952; "Chesterfield Playhouse: C.O.D.," SYN, 1952; "The Web: End of the Line," CBS, 1953; "Kraft Television Theatre: The Old Maid," ABC, 1954; "U.S. Steel Hour: Red Gulch," ABC, 1955; "Fireside Theatre: The Sport," NBC, 1955; "Studio One: The Drop of a Hat," CBS, 1956; "The Red Skelton Show," CBS, 1957; "The Steve Allen Show," NBC, 1958; "The Red Skelton Show," CBS, 1958; "Arthur Murray Party," NBC, 1959; "The Steve Allen Show," NBC, 1959; "The Jimmy Dean Show," CBS, 1959; "What's My Line?," CBS, 1959; "Steve Allen Plymouth Show," NBC, 1959; "The Red Skelton Show: San Fernando's Thanksgiving," CBS, 1959; "The Ann Sothern Show: Top Executive," CBS, 1959; "Steve Allen Plymouth Show," NBC, 1960; "Masquerade Party," NBC, 1960; "G.E. Theatre: The Man Who Thought for Himself," CBS, 1960; "Play Your Hunch," NBC, 1962; "Your First Impression," NBC, 1963; "The Judy Garland Show," CBS, 1964; "Object Is," ABC, 1964; "The Eleventh Hour: Does My Mother Have to Know?," NBC, 1964; "The Match Game," NBC, 1965; "The Match Game," NBC, 1967; "You Don't Say," NBC, 1968; "Hollywood Squares," NBC, 1968; "The Steve Allen Show," SYN, 1968; "The Outsider: Through a Stained-Glass Window," NBC, 1969; "Love, American Style: Love and the Many-Married Couple," ABC, 1970; "Here's Lucy: Lucy Stops a Marriage," CBS, 1970; "Adam 12: Hollywood Division," NBC, 1973; "Hi-Ho, Steverino: A 25th Anniversary Salute to Steve Allen," ABC, 1974; "The Tonight Show Starring Johnny Carson," NBC, 1974; "Tattletales," CBS, 1974; "The Girl with Something Extra: The Cost of Giving," NBC, 1974; "Tenspeed and Brown Shoe: Pilot," ABC, 1980; "The Love Boat: Hey, Jealous Lover," ABC, 1980; "The Love Boat: Meet the Author," ABC, 1982; "The Love Boat: Breaks of Life," ABC, 1982; "The Love Boat: Soap Gets in Your Eyes," ABC, 1984; "St. Elsewhere: Russian Roulette," NBC, 1987; "St. Elsewhere: Visiting Daze," NBC, 1987; "St. Elsewhere: The Abby

Singer Show," NBC, 1988; "The Magical World of Disney: Parent Trap Hawaiian Honeymoon," NBC, 1989.

TV MOVIES AND MINISERIES: "Now You See It, Now You Don't," NBC, 1968; "James Dean," NBC, 1976; "Miss All American Beauty," CBS, 1982; "A Masterpiece of Murder," NBC, 1986.

MEARA, ANNE

b. New York City, NY, September 20, 1929. Comedienne who played Veronica Rooney on "Archie Bunker's Place" and Dorothy Halligan on "ALF"; frequently teamed with husband Jerry Stiller.

AS A REGULAR: "The Greatest Gift," NBC, 1954-55; "The Paul Lynde Show" ABC, 1972-73; "The Corner Bar," ABC, 1973; "Kate McShane," CBS, 1975; "Rhoda," CBS, 1976-77; "Archie Bunker's Place," CBS, 1979-82; "ALF," NBC, 1987-90.

AND: "Special Tonight: Ninotchka," ABC, 1960; "Bell System Family Theatre: Dames at Sea," NBC, 1971; "Medical Center: Trial by Knife," CBS, 1974; "The $25,000 Pyramid," SYN, 1975; "Captain Kangaroo," CBS, 1977; "The $20,000 Pyramid," ABC, 1977; "The Sonny and Cher Comedy Hour," CBS, 1977; "The $20,000 Pyramid," ABC, 1979; "Captain Kangaroo," CBS, 1980; "Murder, She Wrote: Who Threw the Barbitals in Mrs. Fletcher's Chowder?," CBS, 1987.

TV MOVIES AND MINISERIES: "Kate McShane," CBS, 1975; "The Other Woman," CBS, 1983.

* See also Jerry Stiller.

MEKKA, EDDIE

b. Worcester, MA, June 14, 1952. Actor who played Carmine Ragusa on "Laverne & Shirley."

AS A REGULAR: "Laverne & Shirley," ABC, 1976-83; "Blansky's Beauties," ABC, 1977.

AND: "The Mike Douglas Show," SYN, 1977; "Happy Days: Joanie's Weird Boyfriend," ABC, 1977; "The Love Boat: The Three Stages of Love," ABC, 1979; "Dance Fever," SYN, 1981; "The Love Boat: Momma and Me," ABC, 1981; "The Love Boat: Substitute Lover," ABC, 1982; "Moonlighting: In 'n' Outlaws," ABC, 1989.

MELTON, SID

b. Brooklyn, NY, May 23, 1920. Worried-looking comic actor who played club owner Charley Halper on "The Danny Thomas Show," un-handyman Alf Monroe on "Green Acres" and con man Friendly Freddy on "Gomer Pyle, USMC."

AS A REGULAR: "Captain Midnight," CBS, 1954-55; "It's Always Jan," CBS, 1955-56; "The Danny Thomas Show," CBS, 1959-64; "Green Acres," CBS, 1966-69; "Make Room for Granddaddy," ABC, 1970-71.

AND: "December Bride: Song Plugging," CBS, 1957; "Schlitz Playhouse of Stars: The Hole Card," CBS, 1957; "The Lucille Ball-Desi Arnaz Show: Milton Berle Hides Out at the Ricardos," CBS, 1959; "The Ann Sothern Show: Johnny Moves Up," CBS, 1959; "December Bride: The Texan, Rory Calhoun," CBS, 1959; "The Gale Storm Show: It's Magic," ABC, 1960; "The Tab Hunter Show: For Money or Love," NBC, 1960; "The Joey Bishop Show: This Is Your Life," NBC, 1961; "The Bob Hope Show," NBC, 1962; "The Munsters: Rock-a-Bye Munster," CBS, 1964; "The Dick Van Dyke Show: Romance, Roses and Rye Bread," CBS, 1964; "The Andy Griffith Show: The Hollywood Party," CBS, 1965; "Gomer Pyle, USMC: Caution: Low Overhead," CBS, 1966; "Run, Buddy, Run: The Bank Holdup," CBS, 1966; "Hey, Landlord!: The Shapes of Wrath," NBC, 1966; "Gomer Pyle, USMC: Friendly Freddy Strikes Again," CBS, 1967; "Gomer Pyle, USMC: Friendly Freddy, the Gentleman's Tailor," CBS, 1968; "Petticoat Junction: The Singing Sweethearts," CBS, 1968; "Gomer Pyle, USMC: Freddy's Friendly Computer," CBS, 1969; "Love, American Style: Love and the Newscasters," ABC, 1972; "The Doris Day Show: Welcome to Big Sur," CBS, 1973; "Tenafly: The Cash and Carry Caper," NBC, 1973; "Rhoda: Brenda's Unemployment," CBS, 1975; "The Golden Girls: Mother's Day," NBC, 1988; "The Golden Girls: Sophia's Wedding," NBC, 1988.

MELVILLE, SAM

b. Utah, August 20, 1940. Lantern-jawed actor who played Off. Mike Danko on "The Rookies."

AS A REGULAR: "The Rookies," ABC, 1972-76.

AND: "That Girl: Rich Little Rich Girl," ABC, 1966; "T.H.E. Cat: Curtains for Miss Winslow," NBC, 1966; "Hogan's Heroes: Information Please," CBS, 1966; "Gunsmoke: Death Train," CBS, 1967; "The Guns of Will Sonnett: Message at Noon," ABC, 1967; "The Iron Horse: Leopards Try, But Leopards Can't," ABC, 1967; "Gunsmoke: Mistaken Identity," CBS, 1967; "Here Come the Brides: Logjam," ABC, 1969; "Gunsmoke: The Good Samaritans," CBS, 1969; "Gunsmoke: The War Priest," CBS, 1970; "Gunsmoke: The Gun," CBS, 1970; "Mannix: Dark So Early, Dark So Long," CBS, 1971; "Gunsmoke: The Bullet," CBS, 1971; "Hawaii Five-O: For a Million, Why Not?" CBS, 1971; "The A-Team: There's Always a Catch," NBC, 1984; "Scarecrow and Mrs. King: The Wrong Way Home," CBS, 1985; "The A-Team: Body Slam," NBC, 1985; "Scarecrow and Mrs. King: Stemwinder," CBS, 1986; "Starman: Fatal Flaw," ABC, 1986; "Scarecrow and Mrs. King: Santa's

Got a Brand New Bag," CBS, 1986; "Scarecrow and Mrs. King: Rumors of My Death," CBS, 1987. **TV MOVIES AND MINISERIES:** "Terror in the Sky," ABC, 1971; "The Rookies," ABC, 1972.

MELVIN, ALLAN

b. *Kansas City, MO*. Character actor long in comic roles; he played Sgt. Hacker on "Gomer Pyle, USMC," Sam the butcher on "The Brady Bunch," Barney Hefner on "All in the Family" and "Archie Bunker's Place" and the guy in the Liquid Plumr commercials.
AS A REGULAR: "You'll Never Get Rich (The Phil Silvers Show)," CBS, 1955-59; "The Joey Bishop Show," CBS, 1964-65; "Gomer Pyle, USMC," CBS, 1965-69; "The Brady Bunch," ABC, 1969-73; "All in the Family," CBS, 1973-79; "Archie Bunker's Place," CBS, 1979-83.
AND: "The Dick Van Dyke Show: Harrison B. Harding of Camp Crowder, Mo.," CBS, 1961; "The Andy Griffith Show: Jailbreak," CBS, 1962; "The Andy Griffith Show: Andy and Barney in the Big City," CBS, 1962; "The Andy Griffith Show: Lawman Barney," CBS, 1962; "The Dick Van Dyke Show: Will You Two Be My Wife?," CBS, 1963; "Empire: The Loner," NBC, 1963; "McHale's Navy: A Wreath for McHale," ABC, 1963; "The Andy Griffith Show: Barney's First Car," CBS, 1963; "The Andy Griffith Show: Ernest T. Bass Joins the Army," CBS, 1963; "Grindl: Grindl, The Impractical Nurse," NBC, 1963; "The Danny Thomas Show: The Leprechaun," CBS, 1964; "The Dick Van Dyke Show: Honeymoons Are for the Lucky," CBS, 1964; "My Favorite Martian: The Sinkable Mrs. Brown," CBS, 1964; "The Andy Griffith Show: Andy's Vacation," CBS, 1964; "The Flintstones: Monster Fred," ABC, 1964; "The Andy Griffith Show: Barney's Uniform," CBS, 1964; "Ben Casey: Kill the Dream But Spare the Dreamer," ABC, 1964; "The Dick Van Dyke Show: The Alan Brady Show Goes to Jail," CBS, 1964; "Slattery's People: He Who Has Ears, Let Him Bug Somebody Else," CBS, 1965; "The Dick Van Dyke Show: No Rice at My Wedding," CBS, 1965; "The Dick Van Dyke Show: Body and Sol," CBS, 1965; "My Favorite Martian: Heir Today, Gone Tomorrow," CBS, 1966; "The Dick Van Dyke Show: Remember the Alimony," CBS, 1966; "The Dick Van Dyke Show: The Gunslinger," CBS, 1966; "Run, Buddy, Run: I Want a Piece of That Boy," CBS, 1966; "Love, American Style: Love and the Modern Wife," ABC, 1969; "Love, American Style: Love and the Bowling Ball," ABC, 1970; "Love, American Style: Love and the Happy Couple," ABC, 1971.

MENJOU, ADOLPHE

b. *Pittsburgh, PA, February 18, 1890; d. 1963*. Suave actor and fancy dresser.
AS A REGULAR: "Favorite Story," SYN, 1952; "Target," SYN, 1958-59.

AND: "Science Fiction Theatre: Barrier of Silence," SYN, 1955; "The Ford Show," NBC, 1956; "Art Linkletter's House Party," CBS, 1957; "I've Got a Secret," CBS, 1957; "Art Linkletter's House Party," CBS, 1958; "The Ford Show," NBC, 1959; "On the Go," CBS, 1960; "Here's Hollywood," NBC, 1961; "The du Pont Show with June Allyson: The Secret Life of James Thurber," CBS, 1961; "The Merv Griffin Show," NBC, 1962.

MERCER, MARIAN

b. *Akron, OH, November 26, 1935*. Blonde stage actress often in comic roles; memorable as heart-transplant patient Eve Leighton on "St. Elsewhere."
AS A REGULAR: "The Andy Williams Show," NBC, 1962-63; "The Dom DeLuise Show," CBS, 1968; "The Dean Martin Show," NBC, 1971-72; "The Sandy Duncan Show," CBS, 1972; "The Wacky World of Jonathan Winters," SYN, 1972-74; "A Touch of Grace," ABC, 1973; "Mary Hartman, Mary Hartman," SYN, 1976-78; "It's a Living," ABC, 1980-82; SYN, 1985-88; "Foot in the Door," CBS, 1983; "St. Elsewhere," NBC, 1983.
AND: "The Golddiggers," SYN, 1971; "Police Woman: Fish," NBC, 1974; "The Bob Crane Show: The Lyle Principle," NBC, 1975; "9 to 5: Loverwear," ABC, 1982; "The Love Boat: Mother Comes First," ABC, 1984; "St. Elsewhere: Afterlife," NBC, 1986; "Open House: Married Without Children," FOX, 1989.
TV MOVIES AND MINISERIES: "The Cracker Factory," ABC, 1979; "Life of the Party: The Story of Beatrice," CBS, 1982; "Agatha Christie's Murder in Three Acts," CBS, 1986.

MEREDITH, BURGESS

b. *Cleveland, OH, November 16, 1908*. Versatile movie, stage and TV actor best known as Batman's nemesis, The Penguin, for his appearances on "The Twilight Zone" and for his Emmy-winning role as Joseph Welch, the lawyer who shot down Sen. Joe McCarthy (Peter Boyle) in "Tailgunner Joe."
AS A REGULAR: "Mr. Novak," NBC, 1964-65; "Batman," ABC, 1966-68; "Search," NBC, 1972-73; "Those Amazing Animals," ABC, 1980-81; "Gloria," CBS, 1982-83.
AND: "Robert Montgomery Presents: Our Town," NBC, 1950; "Studio One: The Horse's Mouth," CBS, 1950; "Omnibus: The Christmas Tie," CBS, 1952; "Tales of Tomorrow: The Great Silence," ABC, 1953; "Omnibus: Everyman," CBS, 1953; "G.E. Theatre: Edison the Man," CBS, 1954; "What's My Line?," CBS, 1956; "U.S. Steel Hour: Haunted Harbor," CBS, 1957; "Suspicion: Hand in Glove," NBC, 1957; "G.E. Theatre: The Unfamiliar," CBS, 1958; "Du Pont Show of the Month: The Human Comedy," CBS, 1959;

"America Pauses for Springtime," CBS, 1959; "Hallmark Hall of Fame: Ah, Wilderness!," NBC, 1959; "The Twilight Zone: Time Enough at Last," CBS, 1959; "The Twilight Zone: Mr. Dingle, the Strong," CBS, 1961; "The Twilight Zone: The Obsolete Man," CBS, 1961; "Play of the Week: Waiting for Godot," SYN, 1961; "Doctor B.," NBC, 1961; "Ben Casey: Pack Up All My Care and Woe," ABC, 1962; "The Twilight Zone: Printer's Devil," CBS, 1963; "77 Sunset Strip: 5," ABC, 1963; "Trials of O'Brien: No Justice for the Judge," CBS, 1965; "The Wild Wild West: The Night of the Human Trigger," CBS, 1965; "Twelve O'Clock High: Back to the Drawing Board," ABC, 1966; "Please Don't Eat the Daisies: The Magnificent Muldoon," NBC, 1966; "Ironside: The Macabre Mr. Micawber," NBC, 1968; "Love, American Style: Love and the Hypnotist," ABC, 1970; "The Bold Ones: Power Play," NBC, 1970; "The Name of the Game: All the Old Familiar Faces," NBC, 1970; "Night Gallery: The Little Black Bag," NBC, 1970; "The Man and the City: Pipe Me a Loving Tune," ABC, 1971; "The FBI: Dynasty of Hate," ABC, 1971; "Ironside: Unreasonable Facsimile," NBC, 1972; "McCloud: A Little Plot at Tranquil Valley," NBC, 1972; "From Sea to Shining Sea," SYN, 1974; "Over Easy," PBS, 1981; "CHiPs: In the Best of Families," NBC, 1982; "Faerie Tale Theatre: Thumbelina," SHO, 1984; "The Wickedest Witch," NBC, 1989.

TV MOVIES AND MINISERIES: "Lock, Stock and Barrel," NBC, 1971; "Getting Away From It All," ABC, 1972; "Probe," NBC, 1972; "Tailgunner Joe," NBC, 1977; "Johnny, We Hardly Knew Ye," NBC, 1977; "SST-Death Flight," ABC, 1977; "The Last Hurrah," NBC, 1977; "Wet Gold," ABC, 1984; "Outrage!," CBS, 1986.

AS CO-DIRECTOR: "Playhouse 90: The Jet-Propelled Couch," CBS, 1957.
* Emmies: 1977.

MEREDITH, DON
b. Mount Vernon, TX. Ex-gridiron star turned sportscaster-actor—and Lipton tea lover on commercials.
AS A REGULAR: "Monday Night Football," ABC, 1970-73; 1977-84.
AND: "Police Story: Requiem for an Informer," NBC, 1973; "Police Story: The Hunted," NBC, 1974; "Police Story: Glamour Boy," NBC, 1974; "Police Story: Explosion!," NBC, 1974; "Police Story: The Witness," NBC, 1975; "Police Story: Face for a Shadow," NBC, 1975; "Police Woman: The Loner," NBC, 1975; "McCloud: The Man From Taos," NBC, 1975; "The Quest: Shanklin," NBC, 1976; "Police Story: The Jar," NBC, 1976.
TV MOVIES AND MINISERIES: "Terror on the 40th Floor," NBC, 1974; "Sky Hei$t," NBC, 1975; "Banjo Hackett," NBC, 1976; "Mayday at

40,000 Feet," CBS, 1976; "Undercover with the KKK," NBC, 1979; "The Night the City Screamed," ABC, 1980; "Terror Among Us," CBS, 1981; "Police Story: The Freeway Killings," NBC, 1987.
* Emmies: 1971.

MERIWETHER, LEE
b. Los Angeles, CA, May 27, 1935. Actress who played Betty, daughter-in-law of Barnaby Jones (Buddy Ebsen); now she plays Lily Munster.
AS A REGULAR: "The Clear Horizon," CBS, 1960-61; 1962; "The Time Tunnel," ABC, 1966-67; "The New Andy Griffith Show," CBS, 1971; "Barnaby Jones," CBS, 1973-80; "The New Masquerade Party," SYN, 1974-75; "The New Munsters," SYN, 1988- .
AND: "Alcoa Hour: Protege," NBC, 1957; "The Phil Silvers Show: Cyrano De Bilko," CBS, 1957; "Modern Romances: Honeymoon," NBC, 1957; "Omnibus: Mrs. McThing," NBC, 1958; "Bringing Up Buddy: Buddy and the Amazon," CBS, 1961; "Perry Mason: The Case of the Frustrated Folk Singer," CBS, 1965; "Dr. Kildare: My Name Is Lisa, and I Am Lost," NBC, 1965; "The Man From UNCLE: The Mad, Mad Tea Party Affair," NBC, 1965; "The FBI: Slow March Up a Steep Hill," ABC, 1965; "F Troop: O'Rourke vs. O'Reilly," ABC, 1965; "My Three Sons: What About Harry?," CBS, 1966; "Family Affair: First Love," CBS, 1967; "Mission: Impossible: Doomsday," CBS, 1969; "The Doris Day Show: Hospital Benefit," CBS, 1973; "Hollywood Squares," NBC, 1974; "The $10,000 Pyramid," CBS, 1974; "Password All-Stars," ABC, 1975; "Break the Bank," SYN, 1976; "Cross Wits," SYN, 1977; "The Love Boat: Clothes Make the Girl," ABC, 1981; "The Love Boat: The Captain's Portrait," ABC, 1982; "Fantasy Island: The Butler's Affair," ABC, 1983; "The Love Boat: Father in the Cradle," ABC, 1984; "Murder, She Wrote: A Lady in the Lake," CBS, 1986.
TV MOVIES AND MINISERIES: "Mirror, Mirror," NBC, 1979.

MERMAN, ETHEL
b. Ethel Zimmerman, Astoria, Queens, NY, January 16, 1909; d. 1984. Leather-lunged musical-comedy star who belted out a song or two on TV variety shows; she later played the mother of Gopher (Fred Grandy) on "The Love Boat."
AS A GUEST: "The Colgate Comedy Hour: Anything Goes," NBC, 1954; "Best of Broadway: Panama Hattie," CBS, 1954; "G.E. Theatre: Reflected Glory," CBS, 1956; "U.S. Steel Hour: Honest in the Rain," CBS, 1956; "The Perry Como Show," NBC, 1957; "Dinah Shore Chevy Show," NBC, 1958; "The Arthur

Murray Party for Bob Hope," NBC, 1960; "The Judy Garland Show," CBS, 1964; "The Lucy Show: Lucy Teaches Ethel Merman to Sing/Ethel Merman and the Boy Scout Show," CBS, 1964; "Annie Get Your Gun," NBC, 1967; "That Girl: Pass the Potatoes, Ethel Merman," ABC, 1967; "Batman: The Sport of Penguins/A Horse of Another Color," ABC, 1967; "The Mike Douglas Show," SYN, 1967; "Tarzan: Mountains of the Moon," NBC, 1967; "That Girl: The Other Woman," ABC, 1968; "Hollywood Palace," ABC, 1968; "The Merv Griffin Show," SYN, 1968; "The Tonight Show Starring Johnny Carson," NBC, 1969; "The Tonight Show Starring Johnny Carson," NBC, 1974; "Dinah!," SYN, 1975; "Hollywood Squares," SYN, 1975; "Evening at Pops," PBS, 1976; "The Love Boat: Not-so-Fast Gopher," ABC, 1980; "The Love Boat: The Love Boat Musical," ABC, 1982; "The Love Boat: Gopher Farnsworth Smith," ABC, 1982.

MERRILL, GARY
b. *Hartford, CT, August 2, 1914; d. 1990.* Screen and TV actor who played Dr. Gillespie to young Dr. Kildare (Mark Jenkins); former husband of Bette Davis.
AS A REGULAR: "The Mask," ABC, 1954; "Justice," NBC, 1954-55; "Winston Churchill," ABC, 1960-61; "The Reporter," CBS, 1964; "Young Dr. Kildare," SYN, 1972-73.
AND: "Danger: Family Jewels," CBS, 1953; "U.S. Steel Hour: The Man with the Gun," ABC, 1954; "Warner Bros. Presents Conflict: Yacht on the High Seas," ABC, 1956; "Playhouse 90: If You Knew Elizabeth," CBS, 1957; "Schlitz Playhouse of Stars: Hey, Mac," CBS, 1957; "Dick Powell's Zane Grey Theatre: The Promise," CBS, 1957; "The Loretta Young Show: The Understanding Heart," NBC, 1957; "Laramie: The Lonesome Gun," NBC, 1959; "Alfred Hitchcock Presents: Oh, Youth and Beauty," NBC, 1960; "Here's Hollywood," NBC, 1960; "The Twilight Zone: Still Valley," CBS, 1961; "G.E. Theatre: Money and the Minister," CBS, 1961; "The Dick Powell Show: Obituary for Mr. X," NBC, 1962; "Bus Stop: Put Your Dreams Away," ABC, 1962; "Alcoa Premiere: Tiger," ABC, 1962; "Sam Benedict: The Boiling Point," NBC, 1963; "Ben Casey: Use Neon for My Epitaph," ABC, 1963; "The Alfred Hitchcock Hour: The Paragon," CBS, 1963; "Combat!: The Walking Wounded," ABC, 1963; "The Alfred Hitchcock Hour: Nothing Ever Happens in Linvale," CBS, 1963; "The Outer Limits: The Human Factor," ABC, 1963; "Kraft Suspense Theatre: The Machine That Played God," NBC, 1963; "Suspense: The Hunter," CBS, 1964; "The Doctors and the Nurses: A Dangerous Silence," CBS, 1965; "For the People: The Right to Kill," CBS, 1965; "Bob Hope Chrysler Theatre:

The Highest Fall of All," NBC, 1965; "Branded: Romany Roundup," NBC, 1965; "Voyage to the Bottom of the Sea: The Menfish," ABC, 1966; "The Time Tunnel: Rendezvous with Yesterday," ABC, 1966; "Hondo: Hondo and the Eagle Claw," ABC, 1967; "NET Playhouse: They," NET, 1970; "Marcus Welby, M.D.: The Worth of a Man," ABC, 1970; "CBS Children's Hour: Summer's Forever," CBS, 1972; "Medical Center: Fatal Memory," CBS, 1973; "Jackie Gleason Special," CBS, 1973; "ABC Theatre: Pueblo," ABC, 1973; "Movin' On: Prosperity #1," NBC, 1975.
TV MOVIES AND MINISERIES: "The Dangerous Days of Kiowa Jones," ABC, 1966; "Then Came Bronson," NBC, 1969; "Earth II," ABC, 1971; "The Murderers," ABC, 1973; "Murder in the Computer," ABC, 1973.

MERRITT, THERESA
b. *Newport News, VA, September 24, 1922.* Heavy black actress who played Mama.
AS A REGULAR: "That's My Mama," ABC, 1974-75.
AND: "Password All-Stars," ABC, 1975; "Police Story: Face for a Shadow," NBC, 1975; "NBC Special Treat: Sunshine's on the Way," NBC, 1980; "The Love Boat: Senior Sinners," ABC, 1981.
TV MOVIES AND MINISERIES: "Miracle at Beekman's Place," NBC, 1988.

MICHELL, KEITH
b. *Australia, December 1, 1926.* Actor who won an Emmy as King Henry VIII.
AS A REGULAR: "The Six Wives of Henry VIII," CBS, 1971.
AND: "Dow Hour of Great Mysteries: The Great Impersonation," NBC, 1960; "Leonard Bernstein Special: Oedipus Rex," CBS, 1961; "Murder, She Wrote: A Little Night Work," CBS, 1988.
TV MOVIES AND MINISERIES: "The Story of Jacob and Joseph," ABC, 1974; "The Tenth Month," CBS, 1979; "The Day Christ Died," CBS, 1980.
* Emmies: 1972.

MILANO, ALYSSA
b. *Brooklyn, NY, December 19, 1972.* Actress who plays Sam Micelli on "Who's the Boss?"
AS A REGULAR: "Who's the Boss?," ABC, 1984- .
AND: "Living Dolls: It's All Done with Mirrors," ABC, 1989; "Living Dolls: It's My Party," ABC, 1989; "The Ice Capades with Jason Bateman and Alyssa Milano," ABC, 1989.
TV MOVIES AND MINISERIES: "Crash Course," NBC, 1988; "Dance 'Til Dawn," NBC, 1988.

MILLAND, RAY
b. *Reginald Truscott-Jones, Neath, Wales, 1907; d. 1986.* Leading man of films ("The Lost Weekend") and TV.

AS A REGULAR: "The Ray Milland Show (Meet Mr. McNutley)," CBS, 1953-55; "Markham," CBS, 1959-60.
AND: "Screen Directors Playhouse: Markheim," NBC, 1956; "G.E. Theatre: That's the Man," CBS, 1956; "Ford Theatre: Catch at Straws," ABC, 1956; "G.E. Theatre: Never Turn Back," CBS, 1957; "Schlitz Playhouse of Stars: The Girl in the Grass," CBS, 1957; "G.E. Theatre: Angel of Wrath," CBS, 1957; "Suspicion: Eye for an Eye," NBC, 1958; "G.E. Theatre: A Battle for a Soul," CBS, 1958; "Goodyear Theatre: A London Affair," NBC, 1959; "I've Got a Secret," CBS, 1959; "Alcoa Premiere: Pattern of Guilt," ABC, 1962; "Here's Hollywood," NBC, 1962; "The Alfred Hitchcock Hour: Home Away From Home," CBS, 1963; "The du Pont Show: The Silver Burro," NBC, 1963; "The Name of the Game: A Love to Remember," NBC, 1970; "Night Gallery: The Hand of Borgus Weems," NBC, 1971; "The Movie Game," SYN, 1971; "Columbo: Death Lends a Hand," NBC, 1971; "Columbo: The Greenhouse Jungle," NBC, 1972; "Hollywood Squares," NBC, 1972; "Cool Million: Hunt for a Lonely Girl," NBC, 1972; "The Merv Griffin Show," SYN, 1974; "From Sea to Shining Sea: The Unwanted," SYN, 1975; "The Love Boat: The Wedding," ABC, 1979; "Charlie's Angels: Angel in Love," ABC, 1980; "Hart to Hart: Long Lost Love," ABC, 1983.
TV MOVIES AND MINISERIES: "Daughter of the Mind," ABC, 1969; "River of Gold," ABC, 1971; "Black Noon," CBS, 1971; "The Screaming Lady," ABC, 1972; "The Dead Don't Die," NBC, 1975; "Ellery Queen," NBC, 1975; "Rich Man, Poor Man," ABC, 1976; "Look What's Happened to Rosemary's Baby," ABC, 1976; "Mayday at 40,000 Feet," CBS, 1976; "Best Sellers: Seventh Avenue," NBC, 1977; "Testimony of Two Men," SYN, 1977; "The Darker Side of Terror," CBS, 1979; "The Royal Romance of Charles and Diana," CBS, 1982; "Starflight: The Plane That Couldn't Land," ABC, 1983.
* On "Markham," Milland played crime-solving adventurer Roy Markham. Why that name? So Milland could wear his own monogrammed shirts on the show.

MILLER, ANN
b. *Lucille Ann Collier, Cherino, TX, April 12, 1923.* Dancer and actress who made a comeback of sorts tapping atop a giant can of Great American Soup on a seventies TV commercial.
AS A GUEST: "Bob Hope Special," NBC, 1957; "Dinah Shore Chevy Show," NBC, 1957; "The Perry Como Show," NBC, 1958; "Arthur Murray Party," NBC, 1958; "The Ed Sullivan Show," CBS, 1960; "Dream Girl of '67," ABC, 1967; "The Mike Douglas Show," SYN, 1968;

"The Jonathan Winters Show," CBS, 1968; "Bell System Family Theatre: Dames at Sea," NBC, 1971; "The Virginia Graham Show," SYN, 1972; "Love, American Style: Love and the Christmas Punch," ABC, 1972; "The Love Boat: The Love Boat Musical," ABC, 1982.

MILLER, CHERYL
b. *Sherman Oaks, CA, February 4, 1943.* Young actress who played Paula, daughter of Dr. Marsh Tracy (Marshall Thompson) on "Daktari."
AS A REGULAR: "Daktari," CBS, 1966-69.
AND: "Leave It to Beaver: The Party Spoiler," ABC, 1962; "Our Man Higgins: The Royal and Ancient Game," ABC, 1963; "The Donna Reed Show: Boys and Girls," ABC, 1963; "The Farmer's Daughter: Turkish Delight," ABC, 1964; "Flipper: Love and Sandy," NBC, 1965; "The Donna Reed Show: That Mysterious Smile," ABC, 1965; "Love, American Style: Love and the Oldy Weds," ABC, 1971; "The Streets of San Francisco: Target: Red," ABC, 1974; "Barnaby Jones: The Challenge," CBS, 1974.
TV MOVIES AND MINISERIES: "Gemini Man," NBC, 1976.

MILLER, DENISE
b. *Brooklyn, NY, July 17, 1963.* Actress who played Billie Bunker on "Archie Bunker's Place."
AS A REGULAR: "Fish," ABC, 1977-78; "Makin' It," ABC, 1979; "Archie Bunker's Place," CBS, 1981-83.
AND: "Barney Miller: Evacuation," ABC, 1976; "Barney Miller: The Recluse," ABC, 1976; "The Love Boat: The Girl Who Stood Still," ABC, 1982; "The Love Boat: The Victims," ABC, 1982; "Knight Rider: Custom KITT," NBC, 1983.
TV MOVIES AND MINISERIES: "Sooner or Later," NBC, 1979.

MILLER, DENNY SCOTT
b. *Bloomington, IN, April 25, 1934.* Beefy blond actor who played Duke Shannon on "Wagon Train."
AS A REGULAR: "The Life of Riley," NBC, 1953-58; "Wagon Train," NBC, 1961-62; ABC, 1962-64; "Mona McCluskey," NBC, 1965-66.
AND: "The Overland Trail: The Reckoning," NBC, 1960; "G.E. Theatre: The Playoff," CBS, 1960; "Laramie: License to Kill," NBC, 1960; "The Rifleman: The Promoter," ABC, 1960; "Have Gun, Will Travel: Saturday Night," CBS, 1960; "Michael Shayne: The Body Beautiful," NBC, 1961; "The Deputy: Brother in Arms," NBC, 1961; "Gilligan's Island: Big Man on a Little Stick," CBS, 1965; "Gilligan's Island: Our Vines Have Tender Apes," CBS, 1967; "Love, American Style: Love and the Legal Agreement,"

ABC, 1969; "I Dream of Jeannie: Eternally Yours, Jeannie," NBC, 1970; "Gunsmoke: Lijah," CBS, 1971; "The Brady Bunch: Quarterback Sneak," ABC, 1973; "Quincy: Go Fight City Hall-To the Death," NBC, 1976; "The Streets of San Francisco: Commitment," ABC, 1974; "Emergency!: Nagging Suspicion," NBC, 1974; "Alice: Alice Gets a Pass," CBS, 1976; "The Rockford Files: Forced Retirement," NBC, 1977; "The Rockford Files: Black Mirror," NBC, 1978; "Quark: Goodbye Polumbus," NBC, 1978; "Vega$: Redhanded," ABC, 1979; "M*A*S*H: Tell It to the Marines," CBS, 1981; "House Calls: Dr. Solomon, Mr. Hide," CBS, 1981; "Voyagers!: An Arrow Pointing East," NBC, 1982; "Simon & Simon: Design for Murder," CBS, 1983; "Magnum P.I.: A Sense of Doubt," CBS, 1983; "Knight Rider: The Rotten Appels," NBC, 1984; "Hardcastle and McCormick: McCormick's Bar and Grill," ABC, 1986; "Magnum, P.I.: Photo Play," CBS, 1986.
TV MOVIES AND MINISERIES: "Vanished," NBC, 1971; "V," NBC, 1983.

MILLER, JEREMY

b. *West Covina, CA, October 21, 1976.* Young actor who plays Ben Seaver on "Growing Pains."
AS A REGULAR: "Growing Pains," ABC, 1985- .
AND: "Animal Crack-Ups," ABC, 1989.

MILLER, LARA JILL

b. *Allentown, PA, April 20, 1967.* Actress who played Samantha Kanisky on "Gimme a Break."
AS A REGULAR: "Gimme a Break," NBC, 1981-87.

MILLER, MARK

b. *Houston, TX.* Actor best known as Jim Nash, husband of Joan (Patricia Crowley) on "Please Don't Eat the Daisies."
AS A REGULAR: "Portia Faces Life (The Inner Flame)," CBS, 1954-55; "Guestward Ho!," ABC, 1960-61; "General Hospital," ABC, 1964; "Please Don't Eat the Daisies," NBC, 1965-67; "The Name of the Game," NBC, 1968-71; "Bright Promise," NBC, 1969-72.
AND: "Robert Montgomery Presents: Sturdevant's Daughter," NBC, 1957; "The Millionaire: Millionaire Patricia Collins," CBS, 1960; "The Andy Griffith Show: Barney's Replacement," CBS, 1961; "Follow the Sun: The Hunters," ABC, 1961; "The Tall Man: Property of the Crown," NBC, 1962; "Alfred Hitchcock Presents: Apex," NBC, 1962; "Stoney Burke: Sidewinder," ABC, 1962; "Hawaiian Eye: The After Hours Heart," ABC, 1962; "The Twilight Zone: I Dream of Genie," CBS, 1963; "I Dream of Jeannie: Ride 'Em Astronaut," NBC, 1969; "The FBI: Holiday with Terror," ABC, 1972; "Marcus Welby, M.D.: The Other Martin Loring," ABC, 1972; "Griff:

Death by Prescription," ABC, 1973; "The Streets of San Francisco: No Badge for Benjy," ABC, 1973; "Marcus Welby, M.D.: Public Secrets," ABC, 1974; "Barnaby Jones: The Deadly Jinx," CBS, 1974; "The Streets of San Francisco: The Cat's Paw," ABC, 1975; "Matt Helm: The Deadly Breed," ABC, 1975.
TV MOVIES AND MINISERIES: "Harpy," CBS, 1971; "Terror on Highway 91," CBS, 1989.
AS WRITER: "Please Don't Eat the Daisies: The Magnificent Muldoon," NBC, 1966.

MILLER, MARVIN

b. *St. Louis, MO, July 18, 1913; d. 1985.* Heavyset character actor with a smooth, deep voice best known as Michael Anthony, the guy who gave someone a million dollars each week on "The Millionaire."
AS A REGULAR: "Mysteries of Chinatown," ABC, 1949-50; "Space Patrol," ABC, 1951-52; "The Millionaire," CBS, 1955-60; "Gerald McBoing-Boing," CBS, 1956-58; "The Chevy Show," NBC, 1958-61; "The Famous Adventures of Mr. Magoo," NBC, 1964-65.
AND: "The Jack Benny Program," CBS, 1958; "State Trooper: The Case of the Happy Dragon," SYN, 1959; "The Danny Thomas Show: The Chinese Doll," CBS, 1959; "The Adventures of Ozzie and Harriet: Rick's Twenty-First Birthday" (as Michael Anthony), ABC, 1961; "Bat Masterson: The Marble Slab," NBC, 1961; "Here's Hollywood," NBC, 1961; "Insight: The Cross in Crisis," SYN, 1962; "Batman: A Riddle a Day Keeps the Riddler Away/When the Rat's Away, the Mice Will Play," ABC, 1966; "Love, American Style: Love and the Wee He," ABC, 1972; "Kolchak, the Night Stalker: The Trevi Collection," ABC, 1975.
TV MOVIES AND MINISERIES: "Eva Peron," NBC, 1981.

MILLER, MITCH

b. *Rochester, NY, July 4, 1911.* Goateed former recording executive who hit paydirt in the early sixties with a sing-along show.
AS A REGULAR: "Songs for Sale," CBS, 1951; "Sing Along with Mitch," NBC, 1961-64.
AND: "The Last Word," CBS, 1957; "The Big Record," CBS, 1957; "Your Hit Parade," CBS, 1958; "The Arthur Godfrey Show," CBS, 1958; "The Dick Clark Saturday Night Beechnut Show," ABC, 1959; "Startime: Sing Along with Mitch," NBC, 1960; "The du Pont Show: The Wonderful World of Toys," NBC, 1961; "Here's Hollywood," NBC, 1961; "Car 54, Where Are You?: Toody and Muldoon Sing Along with Mitch," NBC, 1962; "The Tonight Show Starring Johnny Carson," NBC, 1962; "The Merv Griffin Show," NBC, 1962; "The Merv Griffin Show," NBC, 1963; "Password," CBS, 1963; "Get the Message," ABC, 1964.

MILLER, ROGER

b. Fort Worth, TX, January 2, 1936. Pop singer-songwriter of the sixties; now he's a Broadway composer ("Big River").

AS A REGULAR: "The Roger Miller Show," NBC, 1966.

AND: "The Jimmy Dean Show," ABC, 1964; "The Jimmy Dean Show," ABC, 1965; "The Andy Williams Show," NBC, 1965; "Ice Capades of 1966," CBS, 1965; "Hollywood Palace," ABC, 1967; "Operation: Entertainment," ABC, 1968; "The Mike Douglas Show," SYN, 1969; "The Mike Douglas Show," SYN, 1970; "Love, American Style: Love and the Longest Night," ABC, 1971; "Rollin' on the River," SYN, 1971; "Dinah's Place," NBC, 1973; "Sammy and Company," SYN, 1975.

MILLS, ALLEY

b. Chicago, IL. Actress who plays mom Norma Arnold on "The Wonder Years."

AS A REGULAR: "The Associates," ABC, 1979-80; "Making the Grade," CBS, 1982; "The Wonder Years," ABC, 1988- .

AND: "Lou Grant: Search," CBS, 1981; "Hill Street Blues: Zen and the Art of Law Enforcement," NBC, 1982; "Hill Street Blues: Personal Foul," NBC, 1982; "Hill Street Blues: Invasion of the Third World Mutant Body Snatchers," NBC, 1982; "Mr. President: Pilot," FOX, 1987.

TV MOVIES AND MINISERIES: "The Other Woman," CBS, 1983; "I Love You Perfect," ABC, 1989.

MILLS, DONNA

b. Chicago, December 11, 1943. Actress who was the evil Abby Cunningham Ewing on "Knots Landing."

AS A REGULAR: "Love Is a Many Splendored Thing," CBS, 1967-70; "The Good Life," NBC, 1971-72; "Knots Landing," CBS, 1980-89.

AND: "The FBI: The Hitchhiker," ABC, 1971; "Owen Marshall, Counselor at Law: The Triangle," ABC, 1972; "Someone at the Top of the Stairs," ABC, 1973; "Gunsmoke: A Game of Death ... An Act of Love," CBS, 1973; "Marcus Welby, M.D.: A Fevered Angel," ABC, 1974; "McMillan and Wife: Buried Alive," NBC, 1974; "Wide World of Mystery: Killer with Two Faces," ABC, 1974; "Police Story: Explosion!," NBC, 1974; "Police Story: Officer Needs Help," NBC, 1975; "The Six Million Dollar Man: The Cross-Country Kidnap," ABC, 1975; "Hawaii Five-O: McGarrett Is Missing," CBS, 1975; "Medical Center: If Mine Eye Offends Me," CBS, 1975; "City of Angels: The Parting Shot," NBC, 1976; "Police Woman: Mother Love," NBC, 1976; "Quincy: A Star Is Dead," NBC, 1976; "Quincy: A Star Is Dead," NBC, 1976; "The Love Boat: Lonely at the Top," ABC, 1977; "The Love Boat: Marooned," ABC, 1978; "Bob

Hope Lampoons Television 1985," NBC, 1985.

TV MOVIES AND MINISERIES: "Haunts of the Very Rich," ABC, 1972; "Rolling Man," ABC, 1972; "Night of Terror," ABC, 1972; "The Bait," ABC, 1973; "One Deadly Owner," ABC, 1973; "Live Again, Die Again," ABC, 1974; "Who Is the Black Dahlia?," NBC, 1975; "Beyond the Bermuda Triangle," NBC, 1975; "Look What's Happened to Rosemary's Baby," ABC, 1976; "Smash-Up on Interstate 5," ABC, 1976; "Hanging by a Thread," NBC, 1979; "Waikiki," ABC, 1980; "Bare Essence," CBS, 1982; "He's Not Your Son," CBS, 1984; "Outback Bound," CBS, 1988; "The Lady Forgets," CBS, 1989.

MILLS, HAYLEY

b. London, England, April 18, 1946. Former ingenue more visible on TV as of late.

AS A GUEST: "Here's Hollywood," NBC, 1960; "The Danny Kaye Show," CBS, 1964; "Walt Disney's Wonderful World of Color: Disneyland's 10th Anniversary," NBC, 1965; "The Love Boat: The Secret Life of Burl Smith," ABC, 1979; "The Love Boat: Haven't We Met Before?," ABC, 1980; "The Love Boat: The Perfect Divorce," ABC, 1985; "Amazing Stories: The Greibble," NBC, 1986; "Murder, She Wrote: Unfinished Business," CBS, 1986; "The Magical World of Disney: Parent Trap III," NBC, 1989; "The Magical World of Disney: Parent Trap Hawaiian Honeymoon," NBC, 1989.

TV MOVIES AND MINISERIES: "Disney Sunday Movie: Parent Trap II," ABC, 1987.

MILLS, JOHN

b. Felixstowe, England, February 22, 1908. Actor and father of Hayley and Juliet.

AS A REGULAR: "Dundee and the Culhane," CBS, 1967.

AND: "Producers Showcase: The Letter," NBC, 1956; "Here's Hollywood," NBC, 1960; "The du Pont Show: The Interrogator," NBC, 1962; "The Danny Kaye Show," CBS, 1964; "The du Pont Show: The Hell Walkers," NBC, 1964; "Walt Disney's Wonderful World of Color: Disneyland's 10th Anniversary," NBC, 1965; "Nanny and the Professor: The Human Fly," ABC, 1971; "The Love Boat: A Good and Faithful Servant," ABC, 1979.

TV MOVIES AND MINISERIES: "The Zoo Gang," NBC, 1975; "Agatha Christie's Murder with Mirrors," CBS, 1985.

MILLS, JULIET

b. London, England, November 21, 1941. Actress who played Phoebe Figalilly, better known as Nanny; an Emmy winner for "QB VII."

AS A REGULAR: "Nanny and the Professor," ABC,

1970-71.

AND: "Special Tonight: Mrs. Miniver," CBS, 1960; "The Man From UNCLE: The Vienna-Venice Affair," NBC, 1965; "The Man From UNCLE: The Adriatic Express Affair," NBC, 1965; "Twelve O'Clock High: The Slaughter Pen," ABC, 1966; "Ben Casey: Pull the Wool Over Your Eyes; Here Comes the Cold Wind of Truth," ABC, 1966; "Bob Hope Chrysler Theatre: Time of Flight," NBC, 1966; "Mr. Dickens of London," ABC, 1967; "Alias Smith and Jones: The Man Who Murdered Himself," ABC, 1972; "ABC's Matinee Today: Alone with Terror," ABC, 1973; "Match Game '74," CBS, 1974; "Nanny and the Professor and the Phantom of the Circus," ABC, 1974; "Wide World of Mystery: Demon, Demon," ABC, 1975; "Ellery Queen: The Hard Headed Huckster," NBC, 1976; "Switch: Coronado Circle," CBS, 1977; "The Love Boat: Masquerade," ABC, 1978; "Police Woman: Sixth Sense," NBC, 1978; "The Love Boat: The Song Is Ended," ABC, 1978; "The Love Boat: Tug of War," ABC, 1979; "The Love Boat: Phantom Bride," ABC, 1981; "The Love Boat: Sally's Paradise," ABC, 1981; "The Love Boat: A Match Made in Heaven," ABC, 1984; "Hotel: Fallen Idols," ABC, 1985.

TV MOVIES AND MINISERIES: "Wings of Fire," NBC, 1967; "The Challengers," CBS, 1970; "Letters From Three Lovers," ABC, 1973; "QB VII," ABC, 1974; "Best Sellers: Once an Eagle," NBC, 1977; "The Cracker Factory," ABC, 1979.

* On the night of February 17, 1979, Hayley, John and Juliet Mills all appeared on the same episode—in different segments—of "The Love Boat." Awwww.

* Emmies: 1975.

MILNER, MARTIN

b. Detroit, MI, December 26, 1927. Clean-cut, freckled leading man who played adventurer Tod Stiles on "Route 66" and L.A. cop Pete Malloy on "Adam 12."

AS A REGULAR: "The Stu Erwin Show," ABC, 1954-55; "The Life of Riley," NBC, 1957-58; "Route 66," CBS, 1960-64; "Adam 12," NBC, 1968-75; "Swiss Family Robinson," ABC, 1975-76.

AND: "Schlitz Playhouse of Stars: Rim of Violence," CBS, 1954; "Schlitz Playhouse of Stars: Mr. Schoolmarm," CBS, 1955; "TV Reader's Digest: The Old, Old Story," ABC, 1956; "Science Fiction Theatre: Three Minute Mile," SYN, 1956; "Telephone Time: The Churchill Club," ABC, 1956; "Crossroads: Timberland Preacher," ABC, 1956; "Navy Log: Incident at Formosa," ABC, 1956; "West Point: No Reason," ABC, 1957; "Wagon Train: The Sally Potter Story," NBC, 1958; "The Millionaire: The Neal Bowers Story," CBS, 1958;

"Westinghouse Desilu Playhouse: Debut," CBS, 1958; "Westinghouse Desilu Playhouse: Chain of Command," CBS, 1959; "Hotel De Paree: Vein of Ore," CBS, 1959; "The Twilight Zone: Mirror Image," CBS, 1960; "The Chevy Show," NBC, 1961; "Slattery's People: What's a Requiem for a Loser?," CBS, 1964; "Kraft Suspense Theatre: Streetcar, Do You Read Me?," NBC, 1965; "Bob Hope Chrysler Theatre: The War and Eric Kurtz," NBC, 1965; "The Virginian: Timberland," NBC, 1965; "Bob Hope Chrysler Theatre: Memorandum for a Spy," NBC, 1965; "Vacation Playhouse: Joe Starr," CBS, 1965; "Gidget: The Great Kahuna," ABC, 1965; "Laredo: Yahoo," NBC, 1965; "Bob Hope Chrysler Theatre: When Hell Froze," NBC, 1966; "A Man Called Shenandoah: Requiem for the Second," ABC, 1966; "The Virginian: Trail to Ashley Mountain," NBC, 1966; "Run for Your Life: Rendezvous in Tokyo," NBC, 1967; "The Rat Patrol: The Wild Goose Raid," ABC, 1967; "Twelve O'Clock High: Six Feet Under," ABC, 1967; "Insight: Fat Hands and a Diamond Ring," SYN, 1967; "Land's End," ABC, 1968; "Dragnet: Internal Affairs," NBC, 1968; "The Mike Douglas Show," SYN, 1968; "NBC Comedy Playhouse: Simon Says Get Married," NBC, 1970; "Columbo: Murder by the Book," NBC, 1971; "Hollywood Squares," NBC, 1971; "Password," ABC, 1974; "Tattletales," CBS, 1977; "Charlie's Angels: Island Angels," ABC, 1980; "Murder, She Wrote: Reflections of the Mind," CBS, 1985; "Murder, She Wrote: The Last Flight of the Dizzy Damsel," CBS, 1988.

TV MOVIES AND MINISERIES: "Emergency!," NBC, 1972; "Runaway!," ABC, 1973; "Hurricane," NBC, 1974; "The Swiss Family Robinson," ABC, 1975; "Flood," NBC, 1976; "SST-Death Flight," ABC, 1977; "Black Beauty," NBC, 1978; "Little Mo," NBC, 1978; "Crisis in Mid-Air," CBS, 1979; "Nashville Beat," TNN, 1989.

MINEO, SAL

b. New York City, NY, January 10, 1939; d. 1976. Actor who broke into TV and movies ("Rebel Without a Cause") while in his teens; he found work a little harder to come by as he grew older.

AS A GUEST: "Big Town: Juvenile Gangs," NBC, 1955; "Philco TV Playhouse: The Trees," NBC, 1955; "Frontiers of Faith: The Man on the 6:02," NBC, 1955; "Studio One: Dino," CBS, 1956; "Kraft Television Theatre: Drummer Man," NBC, 1957; "Rock 'n' Roll," ABC, 1957; "Arthur Murray Party," NBC, 1957; "The Ed Sullivan Show," CBS, 1957; "American Bandstand," ABC, 1957; "American Bandstand," ABC, 1958; "The Big Record," CBS, 1958; "Du Pont Show of the Month: Aladdin," CBS, 1958; "The Ed Sullivan Show," CBS, 1958; "Pursuit: The

Vengeance," CBS, 1958; "An Evening with Durante," NBC, 1959; "The Big Party," CBS, 1959; "The Greatest Show on Earth: The Loser," ABC, 1963; "Combat!: The Hard Road Back," ABC, 1964; "What's This Song?," NBC, 1964; "Dr. Kildare: Tomorrow Is a Fickle Girl," NBC, 1964; "Shindig," ABC, 1965; "The Patty Duke Show: Patty Meets a Celebrity," ABC, 1965; "Burke's Law: Who Killed the Rabbit's Husband?," ABC, 1965; "Mona McCluskey: The Beatnik," NBC, 1966; "Combat!: Nothing to Lose," ABC, 1966; "Run for Your Life: Sequenstro," NBC, 1966; "Court-Martial: The House Where He Lived," ABC, 1966; "Combat!: Nothing to Lose," ABC, 1966; "Combat!: The Brothers," ABC, 1966; "Bob Hope Chrysler Theatre: A Song Called Revenge," NBC, 1967; "Hawaii Five-O: Tiger by the Tail," CBS, 1968; "The Name of the Game: A Hard Case of the Blues," NBC, 1969; "The Name of the Game: So Long, Baby, and Amen," NBC, 1970; "Mission: Impossible: Flip Side," CBS, 1970; "My Three Sons: Proxy Parents," CBS, 1971; "Harry O: Pilot," ABC, 1973; "Griff: Prey," ABC, 1973; "Tenafly: Man Running," NBC, 1974; "Police Story: The Hunters," NBC, 1974; "Hawaii Five-O: Hit Gun for Sale," CBS, 1975; "SWAT: Coven of Killers," ABC, 1975; "SWAT: Deadly Tide," ABC, 1975; "Columbo: A Case of Immunity," NBC, 1975; "Police Story: Jurisdiction," NBC, 1975.
TV MOVIES AND MINISERIES: "The Dangerous Days of Kiowa Jones," ABC, 1966; "Stranger on the Run," NBC, 1967; "The Challengers," CBS, 1970; "In Search of America," ABC, 1971; "How to Steal an Airplane," NBC, 1971; "The Family Rico," CBS, 1972.
* Mineo was stabbed to death in a Hollywood alley.

MINER, JAN
b. *Boston, MA, October 15, 1917.* Actress best known as Madge the manicurist on TV commercials.
AS A REGULAR: "Crime Photgrapher," CBS, 1951-52; "Robert Montgomery Presents," NBC, 1954-56; "Paul Sand in Friends and Lovers," CBS, 1974-75.
AND: "Robert Montgomery Presents: The Weather Lover," NBC, 1957; "True Story: Mother's Day," NBC, 1957; "Alcoa Presents: The Inheritance," ABC, 1959; "Naked City: A Death of Princes," ABC, 1960; "The Doctors and the Nurses: The Patient Nurse," CBS, 1965.
TV MOVIES AND MINISERIES: "F.D.R.: The Last Year," NBC, 1980.

MINNELLI, LIZA
b. *Hollywood, CA, March 12, 1946.* Actress and singer with a few TV credits, including an

Emmy-winning 1972 special.
AS A GUEST: "Pontiac Star Parade Presents the Gene Kelly Show," CBS, 1959; "Hedda Hopper's Hollywood," NBC, 1960; "The Jack Paar Show," NBC, 1961; "The Judy Garland Show," CBS, 1963; "Bell Telephone Hour," NBC, 1964; "Mr. Broadway: Nightingale for Sale," NBC, 1964; "The Ed Sullivan Show," CBS, 1965; "Ice Capades of 1966," CBS, 1965; "The Dangerous Christmas of Red Riding Hood," ABC, 1965; "The Carol Burnett Show," CBS, 1968; "The Ed Sullivan Show," CBS, 1968; "The Merv Griffin Show," SYN, 1968; "The Dick Cavett Show," ABC, 1969; "The Glen Campbell Goodtime Hour," CBS, 1969; "The Red Skelton Hour," CBS, 1969; "Movin'," NBC, 1970; "Liza with a Z," NBC, 1972; "The Merv Griffin Show," SYN, 1973; "Sammy and Company," SYN, 1975; "Mac Davis Special," NBC, 1975; "The Tonight Show Starring Johnny Carson," NBC, 1975; "Baryshnikov on Broadway," ABC, 1980; "Faerie Tale Theatre: The Princess and the Pea," SHO, 1984; "Frank, Liza & Sammy: The Ultimate Event," SHO, 1989.
TV MOVIES AND MINISERIES: "A Time to Live," NBC, 1985.
* Paar introduced Minnelli on his show as "Dujy Landgar," an anagram of her mother's name. He didn't tell the audience who she really was until after she belted out "They Can't Take That Away From Me"—from a wheelchair, because she'd broken her leg a few days before.

MINOR, MICHAEL
b. *San Francisco, CA.* Actor who played Steve Elliott, husband of Betty Jo (Linda Kaye Henning) on "Petticoat Junction"; he then moved to soaps, playing, among other characters, Dr. Royal Dunning on "Another World."
AS A REGULAR: "Petticoat Junction," CBS, 1966-70; "The Beverly Hillbillies," CBS, 1971; "As the World Turns," CBS, 1975; "All My Children," ABC, 1980-82; "Another World," NBC, 1983-84.
AND: "My Three Sons: First Things First," ABC, 1963; "My Three Sons: The Guys and the Dolls," ABC, 1964; "My Three Sons: First You're a Tadpole," ABC, 1964; "The Beverly Hillbillies: The Italian Cook," CBS, 1968; "The Beverly Hillbillies: The Thanksgiving Story," CBS, 1968; "The Beverly Hillbillies: Buss Bodine, Boy General," CBS, 1970; "My Three Sons: After the Honeymoon," CBS, 1971.

MINTZ, ELI
b. *Austria, 1904.* Actor who played Uncle David on "The Goldbergs."
AS A REGULAR: "The Goldbergs," CBS, 1949-51;

NBC, 1952-53; DUM, 1954.
AND: "Studio One: The Little Black Bag," CBS, 1951; "The Doctor: Jules," NBC, 1953; "Kraft Television Theatre: The Man Most Likely," NBC, 1954; "Studio One: An Almanac of Liberty," CBS, 1954; "Studio One: Three Empty Rooms," CBS, 1955; "The Garry Moore Show," CBS, 1956; "The Garry Moore Show," CBS, 1957; "Playhouse 90: The Fabulous Irishman," CBS, 1957; "Lamp Unto My Feet: Nachshon's Leap," CBS, 1958; "Play of the Week: The Dybbuk," SYN, 1960; "U.S. Steel Hour: Honor in Love," CBS, 1962; "Ben Casey: Saturday, Surgery and Stanley Schultz," ABC, 1962; "New York Television Theatre: Whisper in My Good Ear," NET, 1965.

MITCHELL, CAMERON
b. Dallastown, PA, April 11, 1918. Heavyset actor who played Buck Cannon on "The High Chaparral."
AS A REGULAR: "Beachcomber," SYN, 1961-62; "The High Chaparral," NBC, 1967-71; "Swiss Family Robinson," ABC, 1975-76.
AND: "Hollywood Opening Night: The Kirbys," CBS, 1952; "Hollywood Opening Night: Prison Doctor," CBS, 1952; "Campbell Playhouse: Return to Vienna," NBC, 1952; "Lux Video Theatre: Kill That Story!," CBS, 1953; "The 20th Century-Fox Hour: The Ox-Bow Incident," CBS, 1955; "The 20th Century-Fox Hour: Man on the Ledge," CBS, 1955; "Climax!: The Prowler," CBS, 1955; "Studio One: The Bounty Hunter," CBS, 1956; "Studio One: The Brotherhood of the Bell," CBS, 1958; "U.S. Steel Hour: The Bromley Touch," CBS, 1958; "Kraft Theatre: Dog in a Bush Tunnel," NBC, 1958; "The Untouchables: Ain't We Got Fun?," ABC, 1959; "Death Valley Days: Pete Kitchen's Wedding Night," SYN, 1959; "Dick Powell's Zane Grey Theatre: The Grubstake," CBS, 1959; "Goodyear Theatre: Omaha Beach—Plus 15," NBC, 1960; "Bonanza: House Divided," NBC, 1960; "Westinghouse Desilu Playhouse: Meeting at Apalachin," CBS, 1960; "Court-Martial: Where There's No Echo," ABC, 1966; "The Joey Bishop Show," ABC, 1968; "Lassiter," CBS, 1968; "Hollywood Television Theatre: The Andersonville Trial," NET, 1970; "The Mod Squad: Home Is the Street," ABC, 1971; "This Is Your Life" (Shirley Jones), SYN, 1971; "McCloud: Someone's Out to Get Jenny," NBC, 1971; "The FBI: Bitter Harbor," ABC, 1971; "Night Gallery: Green Fingers," NBC, 1972; "The Bold Ones: Short Flight to a Distant Star," NBC, 1972; "Alias Smith and Jones: Which Way to the O.K. Corral?," ABC, 1972; "Hawkins: Murder in Hollywood," CBS, 1973; "The Magician: Illusion in Terror," NBC, 1973; "Police Story: Line of Fire," NBC, 1973; "Medical Center: The Shattered Mask," CBS, 1974; "Ironside: What's

New with Mark?," NBC, 1974; "Medical Center: Trial by Knife," CBS, 1974; "Gunsmoke: The Iron Men," CBS, 1974; "Petrocelli: Death in High Places," NBC, 1974; "Bronk: The Vigilante," CBS, 1976; "The Quest: Seventy-Two Hours," NBC, 1976; "Project UFO: The Pipeline Incident," NBC, 1978; "Charlie's Angels: Avenging Angel," ABC, 1979; "Magnum, P.I.: Adelaide," CBS, 1981; "Hardcastle and McCormick: The Homecoming," ABC, 1984; "Murder, She Wrote: Murder to a Jazz Beat," CBS, 1985; "Simon & Simon: Something for Sarah," CBS, 1986; "Matlock: The Producer," NBC, 1987; "Mama's Boy: Hamlet," NBC, 1988.
TV MOVIES AND MINISERIES: "Thief," ABC, 1971; "The Reluctant Heroes," ABC, 1971; "The Delphi Bureau," ABC, 1972; "The Rookies," ABC, 1972; "The Stranger," NBC, 1973; "Hitchhike!," ABC, 1974; "The Hanged Man," ABC, 1974; "The Girl on the Late, Late Show," NBC, 1974; "Death in Space," ABC, 1974; "The Swiss Family Robinson," ABC, 1975; "Flood," NBC, 1976; "The Quest," NBC, 1976; "Testimony of Two Men," SYN, 1977; "Black Beauty," NBC, 1978; "The Bastard," SYN, 1978; "Hanging by a Thread," NBC, 1979; "Turnover Smith," ABC, 1980; "The Gambler II: The Adventure Continues," CBS, 1983.

MITCHELL, THOMAS
b. Elizabeth, NJ, July 11, 1892; d. 1962. Beloved movie character actor ("Gone with the Wind," "It's a Wonderful Life") who turned to TV in the fifties. He won an Emmy Award as simply "Best Actor" in 1953.
AS A REGULAR: "Mayor of the Town," SYN, 1954; "O. Henry Playhouse," SYN, 1957; "Glencannon," SYN, 1959.
AND: "Celanese Theatre: Ah, Wilderness," ABC, 1951; "Tales of Tomorrow: The Crystal Egg," ABC, 1951; "Armstrong Circle Theatre: The Long View," NBC, 1951; "Tales of Tomorrow: 20,000 Leagues Under the Sea," ABC, 1952; "Lights Out: The Eyes From San Francisco," NBC, 1952; "Lux Video Theatre: Promotion," CBS, 1952; "Hallmark Hall of Fame: Of Time and the River," NBC, 1953; "Backbone of America: They Flee by Night," NBC, 1953; "Medallion Theatre: The Gentle Deception," CBS, 1954; "Ford Theatre: The Good of His Soul," NBC, 1954; "Light's Diamond Jubilee: Chance for Adventure," ABC, CBS, NBC, 1954; "Ford Theatre: Shadow of Truth," NBC, 1954; "U.S. Steel Hour: Freight," ABC, 1955; "Rheingold Theatre: The Unforgivable," NBC, 1955; "Ford Theatre: P.J. and the Lady," NBC, 1955; "Screen Directors Playhouse: Final Tribute," NBC, 1955; "Ford Theatre: Remembrance Day," NBC, 1955; "Alcoa Hour: Undertow," NBC, 1955; "The 20th Century-Fox

Hour: Miracle on 34th Street," CBS, 1955; "Telephone Time: The Gadfly," ABC, 1957; "Kraft Theatre: The Velvet Trap," NBC, 1958; "Shirley Temple's Storybook: The Nightingale," NBC, 1958; "Dick Powell's Zane Grey Theatre: A Handful of Ashes," CBS, 1958; "Playhouse 90: Natchez," CBS, 1958; "Quest for Adventure: The White-Tail Buck," SYN, 1958; "Dick Powell's Zane Grey Theatre: Man Alone," CBS, 1959; "Laramie: Dark Verdict," NBC, 1959; "Bell Telephone Hour: The Gift of Music," NBC, 1959; "Alcoa Theatre: Lady Bug," NBC, 1959; "The Secret of Freedom," NBC, 1960; "The Untouchables: Underworld Bank," ABC, 1960; "The Right Man," CBS, 1960; "The Islanders: Deadly Tomorrow," ABC, 1960; "Our American Heritage: The Invincible Teddy," NBC, 1961; "Stagecoach West: Image of a Man," ABC, 1961; "Dick Powell's Zane Grey Theatre: A Warm Day in Heaven," CBS, 1961; "Adventures in Paradise: A Penny a Day," ABC, 1961; "Hallmark Hall of Fame: The Joke and the Valley," NBC, 1961; "Here's Hollywood," NBC, 1961; "Lee, the Virginian," NBC, 1962; "Perry Como's Kraft Music Hall," NBC, 1962.
* Emmies: 1953.

MITCHLLL, SCOEY

b. Newburgh, NY, March 12, 1930. Actor in comic roles who's turned to producing some pretty awful sitcoms and TV movies.
AS A REGULAR: "What's It All About, World?," ABC, 1969; "Barefoot in the Park," ABC, 1970-71; "Rhoda," CBS, 1975-76.
AND: "The Mike Douglas Show," SYN, 1968; "The Mothers-in-Law: Guess Who's Coming Forever?," NBC, 1969; "Here Come the Brides: A Far Cry From Yesterday," ABC, 1969; "That Girl: Shake Hands and Come Out Acting," ABC, 1969; "The Ed Sullivan Show," CBS, 1970; "Cops," CBS, 1973; "The Six Million Dollar Man: Little Orphan Airplane," ABC, 1974; "Match Game '74," CBS, 1974; "Password," ABC, 1974; "Police Story: The Execution," NBC, 1975; "Joe Forrester: Pilot," NBC, 1975; "Joe Forrester: Fashion Mart," NBC, 1975; "Tattletales," CBS, 1976; "Taxi: Cab 804," ABC, 1978; "Lou Grant: Skids," CBS, 1979; "Me & Mrs. C.: Ladies' Choice," NBC, 1986.
TV MOVIES AND MINISERIES: "The Voyage of the Yes," CBS, 1973; "Miracle at Beekman's Place," NBC, 1988.
AS PRODUCER-CREATOR: "Me & Mrs. C.," NBC, 1986-87; "13 East," NBC, 1989-90.
TV MOVIES AND MINISERIES: "Miracle at Beekman's Place," NBC, 1988.

MITCHUM, ROBERT

b. Bridgeport, CT, August 6, 1917. Movie icon ("Thunder Road," "Night of the Hunter") who's warmed to television recently; he

sleepwalked his way through the role of "Pug" Henry in "War and Remembrance."
AS A REGULAR: "A Family for Joe," NBC, 1990.
AND: "The Ed Sullivan Show," CBS, 1957; "The Nat King Cole Show," NBC, 1957; "The Frank Sinatra Show," ABC, 1958; "Here's Hollywood," NBC, 1961; "The Equalizer: Mission: McCall," CBS, 1987; "Saturday Night Live," NBC, 1987.
TV MOVIES AND MINISERIES: "Nightkill," NBC, 1980; "One Shoe Makes It Murder," CBS, 1982; "The Winds of War," ABC, 1983; "A Killer in the Family," ABC, 1983; "North and South," ABC, 1985; "The Hearst and Davies Affair," ABC, 1985; "Promises to Keep," CBS, 1985; "Thompson's Last Run," CBS, 1986; "War and Remembrance," ABC, 1988, 1989; "Brotherhood of the Rose," NBC, 1989.
* Mitchum sang and danced on "The Ed Sullivan Show" to promote the Calypso album he'd just made.

MOBLEY, MARY ANN

b. Biloxi, MS, February 17, 1939. Miss America 1959; perky TV personality.
AS A REGULAR: "Be Our Guest," CBS, 1960; "General Hospital," ABC, 1979; "Diff'rent Strokes," ABC, 1985-86.
AND: "Burke's Law: Who Killed Lenore Wingfield?," ABC, 1964; "Burke's Law: Who Killed the Tall One in the Middle?," ABC, 1964; "You Don't Say," NBC, 1965; "The Man From UNCLE: The Moonglow Affair," NBC, 1966; "The Virginian: Vengeance Trail," NBC, 1967; "Love, American Style: Love and the Other Love," ABC, 1969; "Love, American Style: Love and the Young Unmarrieds," ABC, 1969; "To Rome with Love: Baby of the Family," CBS, 1970; "Love, American Style: Love and the Sex Survey," ABC, 1972; "The New Adventures of Perry Mason: The Case of the Telltale Trunk," CBS, 1973; "Tattletales," CBS, 1974; "Love, American Style: Love and the Seven-Year Wait," ABC, 1974; "Police Story: Fingerprint," NBC, 1974; "Match Game '75," CBS, 1975; "The Love Boat: Ship of Ghouls," ABC, 1978; "Diff'rent Strokes: Teacher's Pet," NBC, 1980; "Card Sharks," NBC, 1980; "Hotel: Ideals," ABC, 1984; "The Love Boat: The Odd Triple," ABC, 1985.
TV MOVIES AND MINISERIES: "Istanbul Express," NBC, 1968.

MOLINARO, AL

b. Kenosha, WI, June 24, 1919. Roly-poly actor often cast as a bumbler; best known as restaurant owner Al Delvecchio on "Happy Days."
AS A REGULAR: "The Odd Couple," ABC, 1970-75; "Happy Days," ABC, 1976-82; "Joanie Loves Chachi," ABC, 1982-83; "The Family Man," CBS, 1990- .

AND: "Get Smart: Ironhand," CBS, 1969; "Get Smart: Ice Station Siegfried," CBS, 1970; "Bewitched: Bewitched, Bothered and Baldoni," ABC, 1971; "Love, American Style: Love and the Advice Column," ABC, 1972; "Love, American Style: Love and the Secret Life," ABC, 1973; "Love, American Style: Love and the Patrol Person," ABC, 1973; "Laverne & Shirley: Falter at the Altar," ABC, 1976.

MOLL, RICHARD
b. Pasadena, CA. Tall, beefy actor who plays bailiff Bull Shannon on "Night Court."
AS A REGULAR: "Night Court," NBC, 1984- .
AND: "Best of the West: The Prisoner," ABC, 1981; "Remington Steele: Steele in the News," NBC, 1983; "The Facts of Life: Down and Out in Malibu," NBC, 1987; "Sledge Hammer!: Hammeroid!," ABC, 1987; "My Two Dads: A Judge Dies in Soho, All the Neighbors Burn and Other Stories," NBC, 1989; "Totally Hidden Video," FOX, 1989.
TV MOVIES AND MINISERIES: "The Jericho Mile," ABC, 1979; "Combat High," NBC, 1986; "Dream Date," NBC, 1989; "Class Cruise," NBC, 1989.
* Moll stands six feet eight inches tall.

MONICA, CORBETT
b. St. Louis, MO. Comedian who played Larry Corbett, Joey Bishop's TV manager.
AS A REGULAR: "The Joey Bishop Show," NBC, 1963-64; CBS, 1964-65.
AND: "The Julius LaRosa Show," NBC, 1957; "The Bob Crosby Show," NBC, 1958; "The Ed Sullivan Show," CBS, 1959; "Perry Como's Kraft Music Hall," NBC, 1960; "The Ed Sullivan Show," CBS, 1960; "The Ed Sullivan Show," CBS, 1961; "The Joey Bishop Show: Joey's Replacement," NBC, 1962; "The Tonight Show Starring Johnny Carson," NBC, 1964; "The Jimmy Dean Show," ABC, 1964; "Hollywood Palace," ABC, 1964; "Hollywood Palace," ABC, 1965; "The Jimmy Dean Show," ABC, 1965; "The Sammy Davis Jr. Show," NBC, 1966; "Get Smart: The Little Black Book," NBC, 1968; "Personality," NBC, 1969; "Love, American Style: Love and the Instant Father," ABC, 1972; "Chicken Soup: The Reservation," ABC, 1989.
TV MOVIES AND MINISERIES: "Call Her Mom," ABC, 1972.

MONROE, MARILYN
b. Norma Jean Mortenson, Los Angeles, CA, June 1, 1926; d. 1962. Troubled movie actress and sex symbol.
AS A GUEST: "Person to Person," CBS, 1955; "The Ed Sullivan Show," CBS, 1957.
* Monroe was scheduled to play Sadie Thompson in a full-color production of "Rain"

for NBC in the late fifties, but it never came to pass.

MONROE, VAUGHN
b. Wilton Monroe, Akron, OH, 1912; d. 1973. Pop singer ("Ghost Riders in the Sky," "Dance, Ballerina, Dance") and TV personality of the fifties.
AS A REGULAR: "The Vaughn Monroe Show," CBS, 1950-51; NBC, 1954-55; "Your Show of Shows," NBC, 1950-54; "Caesar's Hour," NBC, 1954-57; "Air Time '57," ABC, 1957.
AND: "The Perry Como Show," NBC, 1957; "Arthur Murray Party," NBC, 1957; "Galaxy of Stars," NBC, 1957; "The George Gobel Show," NBC, 1957; "The Jimmy Dean Show," CBS, 1957; "The Jack Paar Show," NBC, 1958; "American Bandstand," ABC, 1958; "The Big Record," CBS, 1958; "The Bob Crosby Show," NBC, 1958; "The George Gobel Show," NBC, 1958; "The Steve Allen Show," NBC, 1959; "Startime: The Swingin' Singin' Years," NBC, 1960; "Bonanza: The Wooing of Abigail Jones," NBC, 1962; "Missing Links," ABC, 1964; "The Ed Sullivan Show," CBS, 1965.

MONTALBAN, RICARDO
b. Mexico City, Mexico, November 25, 1920. Dashing actor in films and TV best known as Mr. Roarke on "Fantasy Island" and as a TV pitchman for those Chrysler Cordobas with their rich Corinthian leather; an Emmy winner for "How the West Was Won."
AS A REGULAR: "McNaughton's Daughter," NBC, 1976; "Fantasy Island," ABC, 1978-84; "The Colbys," ABC, 1985-87.
AND: "Climax!: The Mojave Kid," CBS, 1955; "Ford Theatre: Cardboard Casanova," NBC, 1955; "The Loretta Young Show: Gina," NBC, 1955; "Climax!: Island in the City," CBS, 1956; "The Loretta Young Show: Rhubarb in Apartment 7-B," NBC, 1956; "The 20th Century-Fox Hour: Operation Cicero," CBS, 1956; "The Loretta Young Show: The Man on Top," NBC, 1957; "Arthur Murray Party," NBC, 1959; "The Loretta Young Show: Each Man's Island," NBC, 1959; "Playhouse 90: Target for Three," CBS, 1959; "Riverboat: A Night at Trapper's Landing," NBC, 1959; "Adventures in Paradise: The Derelict," ABC, 1959; "Bonanza: Day of Reckoning," NBC, 1960; "The Loretta Young Show: No Margin for Error," NBC, 1960; "Alfred Hitchcock Presents: Outlaw in Town," NBC, 1960; "The Chevy Show: Autumn Crocus," NBC, 1961; "Walt Disney Presents: Zorro—Auld Acquaintance," ABC, 1961; "The Loretta Young Show: The Man Who Couldn't Smile," NBC, 1961; "The Lloyd Bridges Show: War Song," CBS, 1962; "The Tennessee Ernie Ford Show," ABC, 1963; "Alcoa Premiere: The Glass Palace," ABC, 1963; "The Dick Powell Show: Epilogue," NBC, 1963; "The Great

Adventure: The Death of Sitting Bull," CBS, 1963; "Ben Casey: Six Impossible Things Before Breakfast," ABC, 1963; "Hallmark Hall of Fame: The Fantasticks," NBC, 1964; "Bob Hope Chrysler Theate: In Any Language," NBC, 1965; "The Long Hot Summer: Man with Two Faces," ABC, 1966; "Alice Through the Looking Glass," ABC, 1966; "The Wild Wild West: The Night of the Lord of Limbo," CBS, 1966; "Bob Hope Chrysler Theatre: Code Name: Heraclitus," NBC, 1967; "Star Trek: Space Seed," NBC, 1967; "Danny Thomas Special," NBC, 1967; "Mission: Impossible: Snowball in Hell," CBS, 1967; "I Spy: Magic Mirror," NBC, 1967; "Ironside: The Sacrifice," NBC, 1968; "The Virginian: Wind of Outrage," NBC, 1968; "It Takes a Thief: The Thingamabob Heist," ABC, 1968; "Bracken's World: Hey Gringo-Hey Cholo," NBC, 1970; "Marcus Welby, M.D.: The Labyrinth," ABC, 1970; "The Men From Shiloh: Last of the Comancheros," NBC, 1970; "The Carol Burnett Show," CBS, 1970; "The Doris Day Show: Billy's First Date," CBS, 1971; "James Garner as Nichols: The Siege," NBC, 1971; "The Wonderful World of Disney: Mustang War," NBC, 1973; "Griff: Countdown to Terror," ABC, 1973; "The Sonny and Cher Comedy Hour," CBS, 1974; "Switch: Kiss of Death," CBS, 1975; "Columbo: A Matter of Honor," NBC, 1976; "The Mike Douglas Show," SYN, 1976; "Police Story: Hard Rock Brown," NBC, 1977.

TV MOVIES AND MINISERIES: "The Longest Hundred Miles," NBC, 1967; "The Pigeon," ABC, 1969; "Black Water Gold," ABC, 1970; "The Aquarians," NBC, 1970; "Sarge: The Badge or the Cross," NBC, 1971; "The Face of Fear," CBS, 1971; "Desperate Mission," NBC, 1971; "Fireball Forward," ABC, 1972; "Wonder Woman," ABC, 1974; "The Mark of Zorro," ABC, 1974; "McNaughton's Daughter," NBC, 1976; "Fantasy Island," ABC, 1977; "How the West Was Won," ABC, 1978.

* Emmies: 1978.

MONTGOMERY, ELIZABETH

b. *Los Angeles, CA, April 15, 1933.* Attractive actress who played the nose-twitching Samantha Stevens on "Bewitched"; daughter of Robert.

AS A REGULAR: "Robert Montgomery Presents," NBC, 1953-54; 1956; "Bewitched," ABC, 1964-72.

AND: "Robert Montgomery Presents: Top Secret," NBC, 1951; "Armstrong Circle Theatre: The Right Approach," NBC, 1953; "Armstrong Circle Theatre: Millstone," NBC, 1954; "Kraft Television Theatre: The Lift Is Cold," NBC, 1954; "Studio One: Summer Pavilion," CBS, 1955; "Kraft Television Theatre: Patterns," NBC, 1955; "Kraft Television Theatre: The Diamond as Big as the Ritz," NBC, 1955; "Appointment with

Adventure: Relative Stranger," CBS, 1955; "Warner Bros. Presents Conflict: Siege," ABC, 1956; "Climax!: The Shadow of Evil," CBS, 1956; "Studio One: The Drop of a Hat," CBS, 1956; "Kraft Television Theatre: The Duel," NBC, 1957; "Studio One: A Dead Ringer," CBS, 1958; "Suspicion: The Velvet Vault," NBC, 1958; "Playhouse 90: Bitter Heritage," CBS, 1958; "Cimarron City: Hired Hand," NBC, 1958; "Du Pont Show of the Month: Harvey," CBS, 1958; "Alfred Hitchcock Presents: Man with a Problem," CBS, 1958; "The Loretta Young Show: Marriage Crisis," NBC, 1959; "Riverboat: The Barrier," NBC, 1959; "Wagon Train: The Vittorio Bottecelli Story," NBC, 1959; "Johnny Staccato: Tempted," NBC, 1960; "The Tab Hunter Show: For Money or Love," NBC, 1960; "Alcoa Presents One Step Beyond: The Death Waltz," ABC, 1960; "The Untouchables: The Rusty Heller Story," ABC, 1960; "The Twilight Zone: Two," CBS, 1961; "Theatre '62: The Spiral Staircase," NBC, 1961; "Thriller: Masquerade," NBC, 1961; "Frontier Circus: Karina," CBS, 1961; "Checkmate: The Star System," CBS, 1962; "Alcoa Premiere: Mr. Lucifer," ABC, 1962; "Saints and Sinners: The Homecoming Bit," NBC, 1963; "Boston Terrier," ABC, 1963; "Rawhide: Incident at El Crucero," CBS, 1963; "The Eleventh Hour: The Bronze Locust," NBC, 1963; "77 Sunset Strip: White Lie," ABC, 1963; "Burke's Law: Who Killed Mr. X?," ABC, 1964; "Burke's Law: Who Killed His Royal Highness?," ABC, 1964; "The Flintstones: Samantha," ABC, 1965; "Hollywood Squares," SYN, 1978.

TV MOVIES AND MINISERIES: "The Victim," ABC, 1972; "Mrs. Sundance," ABC, 1974; "A Case of Rape," NBC, 1974; "The Legend of Lizzie Borden," ABC, 1975; "Dark Victory," NBC, 1976; "A Killing Affair," CBS, 1977; "The Awakening Land," ABC, 1978; "Jennifer: A Woman's Story," NBC, 1979; "An Act of Violence," CBS, 1979; "Belle Starr," 1980; "Missing Pieces," CBS, 1983; "Second Sight: A Love Story," CBS, 1984; "Amos," CBS, 1985; "Between the Darkness and the Dawn," NBC, 1985; "Stone Fox," NBC, 1987.

MONTGOMERY, GEORGE

b. *George Montgomery Letz, Brady, MT, August 29, 1916.* Burly actor in cowboy roles and former husband of Dinah Shore; in the seventies he hawked furniture polish on TV commercials.

AS A REGULAR: "Cimarron City," NBC, 1958-59.

AND: "Stage 7: The Traveling Salesman," CBS, 1955; "Screen Directors Playhouse: Claire," NBC, 1956; "The Jane Wyman Show: Ten Percent," NBC, 1956; "Ford Theatre: The Quiet Stranger," ABC, 1957; "Arthur Murray Party," NBC, 1957; "G.E. Theatre: Thousand Dollar Gun," CBS, 1957; "Dinah Shore Chevy Show," NBC, 1957;

"The Gisele MacKenzie Show," NBC, 1958; "Wagon Train: The Jessie Cowan Story," NBC, 1958; "The Life of Riley: Movie Struck," NBC, 1958; "Dinah Shore Chevy Show," NBC, 1958; "The Bob Cummings Show: Bob Goes Western," NBC, 1959; "About Faces," ABC, 1960; "Dinah Shore Special," NBC, 1961; "Here's Hollywood," NBC, 1961; "Hawaiian Eye: Boar Hunt," ABC, 1963; "Talent Scouts," CBS, 1963; "Exploring," NBC, 1964; "Bonanza: The Code," NBC, 1966; "I Spy: A Day Called Four Jaguar," NBC, 1966; "Alias Smith and Jones: Jailbreak at Junction City," ABC, 1972; "NET Playhouse: Portait of a Hero As a Young Man," NET, 1972; "The Six Million Dollar Man: The Coward," ABC, 1974; "The Odd Couple: The Hollywood Story," ABC, 1974; "Over Easy," PBS, 1978.

MONTGOMERY, ROBERT

b. Henry Montgomery Jr., Beacon, NY, May 21, 1904; d. 1981. Screen star of the thirties and forties who hosted a well-done anthology series and became the first media consultant to a president.
AS A REGULAR: "Robert Montgomery Presents," NBC, 1950-57; "Eye Witness," NBC, 1953.
AND: "The Jack Paar Show," NBC, 1960; "The Ed Sullivan Show," CBS, 1960; "The Jack Paar Show," NBC, 1961; "The Merv Griffin Show," NBC, 1963.
* Montgomery campaigned actively for Dwight Eisenhower, and after Eisenhower was elected, Montgomery was Ike's media consultant, overseeing his television appearances.

MOORE, CLAYTON

b. Chicago, IL, September 14, 1914. Action hero of the movies, and the Lone Ranger, aka John Reid, to a generation of TV viewers.
AS A REGULAR: "The Lone Ranger," ABC, 1949-56.
AND: "Lassie: Peace Patrol," CBS, 1959.
* Moore was caught in the center of controversy in the early eighties. He'd been making personal appearances as the Lone Ranger for years, but when a new Lone Ranger movie was planned, the producers told Moore to stop passing himself off as the masked man. Moore appealed to public sentiment and made worldwide headlines; he also started making personal appearances wearing a pair of wrap-around sunglasses. The movie, by the way, starring Klinton Spilsbury as the Lone Ranger, was a huge flop.

MOORE, DUDLEY

b. Dagenham, Essex, April 19, 1935. Comic actor in films ("10," "Arthur") and occasionally on the tube; he was teamed for a time with Peter Cook.

AS A GUEST: "The Jack Paar Program," NBC, 1962; "Chronicle: A Trip to the Moon," CBS, 1964; "The Mike Douglas Show," SYN, 1968; "Kraft Music Hall," NBC, 1969; "When Things Were Rotten: Wedding Belle Blue," ABC, 1975; "Saturday Night Live," NBC, 1976; "The Muppet Show," SYN, 1980; "Saturday Night Live," NBC, 1986; "The Tonight Show Starring Johnny Carson," NBC, 1989; "The Jim Henson Hour: Miss Piggy's Hollywood," NBC, 1989.

MOORE, GARRY

b. Thomas Garrison Morfit, Baltimore, January 31, 1915. Comic and TV personality who relied on a warm charm rather than socko jokes to win popularity.
AS A REGULAR: "The Garry Moore Show," CBS, 1950-58; 1958-64; 1966-67; "The Garry Moore Evening Show," CBS, 1951; "I've Got a Secret," CBS, 1952-66; "To Tell the Truth," SYN, 1969-76.
AND: "The Ed Sullivan Show," CBS, 1956; "The George Gobel Show," NBC, 1957; "Mr. Broadway," NBC, 1957; "The Perry Como Show," NBC, 1957; "Mike Todd Party," CBS, 1957; "The Last Word," CBS, 1958; "Person to Person," CBS, 1958; "All-Star Jazz," CBS, 1958; "The Red Skelton Show," CBS, 1959; "The Year Gone By," CBS, 1959; "Steve Allen Plymouth Show," NBC, 1959; "The Right Man," CBS, 1960; "Candid Camera," CBS, 1960; "Tomorrow: Big City—1980," CBS, 1960; "Something Special," NBC, 1960; "The Jimmy Durante Show," NBC, 1961; "What's My Line?," CBS, 1961; "The Jack Benny Program," CBS, 1961; "Password," CBS, 1961; "The du Pont Show: Chicago and All That Jazz," NBC, 1961; "Password," CBS, 1962; "Opening Night," CBS, 1962; "To Tell the Truth," CBS, 1962; "Opening Night," CBS, 1963; "Hollywood Squares," NBC, 1968; "The Mike Douglas Show," SYN, 1968; "The Carol Burnett Show," CBS, 1968; "The Mike Douglas Show," SYN, 1975.

MOORE, JOANNA

b. Americus, GA, 1935. Sultry actress of fifties and sixties TV; memorable as Peggy, the country nurse and girlfriend of Andy Taylor on "The Andy Griffith Show." She's the former wife of Ryan O'Neal and mother of Tatum.
AS A REGULAR: "The Andy Griffith Show," CBS, 1962.
AS A GUEST: "Wagon Train: The Jean LeBec Story," NBC, 1957; "Alfred Hitchcock Presents: Post Mortem," CBS, 1958; "The Millionaire: The Doris Winslow Story," CBS, 1958; "Perry Mason: The Case of the Terrified Typist," CBS, 1958; "Kraft Mystery Theatre: Death for Sale," NBC, 1958; "The Millionaire: Millionaire Jackson Greene," CBS, 1959; "Adventures in Paradise:

The Siege of Troy," ABC, 1960; "Gunsmoke: Colleen So Green," CBS, 1960; "The Rebel: Lady of Quality," ABC, 1960; "Gunsmoke: Cherry Red," CBS, 1960; "Hong Kong: Blind Bargain," ABC, 1960; "The Untouchables: The Nero Rankin Story," ABC, 1961; "Route 66: A Skill for Hunting," CBS, 1961; "U.S. Steel Hour: My Wife's Best Friend," CBS, 1961; "Follow the Sun: The Far Edge of Nowhere," ABC, 1961; "Alcoa Premiere: Pattern of Guilt," ABC, 1962; "Hawaiian Eye: Go for Baroque," ABC, 1963; "The Virginian: The Money Cage," NBC, 1963; "The Lieutenant: Interlude," NBC, 1964; "The Fugitive: Crack in a Crystal Ball," ABC, 1965; "The Wild Wild West: The Night of the Fatal Trap," CBS, 1965; "The Man From UNCLE: The Deadly Decoy Affair," NBC, 1965; "My Three Sons: Charley and the Dancing Lesson," CBS, 1965; "Bewitched: Charlie Harper, Winner," ABC, 1967; "The FBI: The Gold Card," ABC, 1967; "T.H.E. Cat: Design for Death," NBC, 1967; "The Virginian: To Bear Witness," NBC, 1967; "The FBI: The Tunnel," ABC, 1968; "The FBI: The Prey," ABC, 1969; "Nanny and the Professor: The Wiblet Will Get You If You Don't Watch Out," ABC, 1970; "Police Story: Explosion!," NBC, 1974; "Kung Fu: Barbary House," ABC, 1975.

MOORE, MARY TYLER

b. Brooklyn, NY, December 29, 1937. Gifted comic actress who learned her stuff as Laura Petrie on "The Dick Van Dyke Show"; her brilliant seventies sitcom continues to influence contemporary TV fare.
AS A REGULAR: "Richard Diamond, Private Detective," CBS, 1959; "The Dick Van Dyke Show," CBS, 1961-66; "The Mary Tyler Moore Show," CBS, 1970-77; "Mary," CBS, 1978; 1985-86; "The Mary Tyler Moore Hour," CBS, 1979; "Annie McGuire," CBS, 1988-89.
AND: "77 Sunset Strip: The Kookie Caper," ABC, 1959; "77 Sunset Strip: Thanks for Tomorrow," ABC, 1959; "Bourbon Street Beat: The Black Magnolia," ABC, 1959; "Johnny Staccato: The Mask of Jason," NBC, 1960; "77 Sunset Strip: The Fix," ABC, 1960; "Hawaiian Eye: Typhoon," ABC, 1960; "The Millionaire: Millionaire Vance Ludlow," CBS, 1960; "The Tab Hunter Show: One Blonde Too Many," NBC, 1960; "Wanted Dead or Alive: The Twain Shall Meet," CBS, 1960; "Hawaiian Eye: Vanessa Vanishes," ABC, 1960; "Bachelor Father: Bentley and the Big Board," NBC, 1960; "Thriller: The Fatal Impulse," NBC, 1960; "The Deputy: Day of Fear," NBC, 1960; "The Aquanauts: The Trophy Adventure," CBS, 1961; "SurfSide 6: Inside Job," ABC, 1961; "Hawaiian Eye: The Comics," ABC, 1961; "The Jack Paar Show," NBC, 1961; "Hawaiian Eye: Two for the Money," ABC, 1961;

"Straightaway: Sounds of Fury," ABC, 1962; "Thriller: Men of Mystery," NBC, 1962; "Stump the Stars," CBS, 1962; "The Danny Kaye Show," CBS, 1963; "The Danny Kaye Show," CBS, 1964; "The Andy Williams Show," NBC, 1965; "Dick Van Dyke and the Other Woman," CBS, 1969; "The Movie Game," SYN, 1970; "The American Parade: We the Women," CBS, 1974; "Rhoda: Joe," CBS, 1974; "Rhoda: Pop Goes the Question," CBS, 1974; "Rhoda: Rhoda's Wedding," CBS, 1974; "Rhoda: Along Comes Mary," CBS, 1975; "Late Night with David Letterman," NBC, 1986; "Saturday Night Live," NBC, 1989; "Saturday Night Live's 15th Anniversary," NBC, 1989.
TV MOVIES AND MINISERIES: "Run a Crooked Mile," NBC, 1969; "First You Cry," CBS, 1978; "ABC Theatre: Heartsounds," ABC, 1984; "Finnegan Begin Again," HBO, 1985; "Gore Vidal's Lincoln," NBC, 1988.
AS DIRECTOR: "The Mary Tyler Moore Show: A Boy's Best Friend," CBS, 1974.
* Moore actually made her TV debut in 1955, as "Happy Hotpoint" on appliance commercials during "The Adventures of Ozzie and Harriet"; then she played Sam, secreatry to TV flatfoot Richard Diamond (David Janssen): only her legs were shown.
* Emmies: 1964, 1966, 1973, 1974, 1976.
* See also Dick Van Dyke.

MOORE, MELBA

b. Beatrice Moore, New York City, NY, October 27, 1945. Actress most often on comedy or musical shows; her sitcom "Melba" was pulled after just one episode; a few more were run in the summer-rerun graveyard.
AS A REGULAR: "The Melba Moore-Clifton Davis Show," CBS, 1972; "Melba," CBS, 1986.
AND: "Festival at Ford's," NBC, 1971; "The Love Boat: The Next Step," ABC, 1979; "Dance Fever," SYN, 1980; "The Love Boat: Gopher & Isaac & the Starlet," ABC, 1984; "The Cosby Show: Twinkle, Twinkle Little Star," NBC, 1988.
TV MOVIES AND MINISERIES: "Mother's Day," FAM, 1989.

MOORE, ROGER

b. London, England, October 14, 1927. Dashing actor tabbed to replace Sean Connery as James Bond in the seventies and eighties; he played the Saint, Simon Templar, on TV.
AS A REGULAR: "Ivanhoe," SYN, 1958; "The Alaskans," ABC, 1959-60; "Maverick," ABC, 1960-61; "The Saint," NBC, 1967-69; "The Persuaders," ABC, 1971-72.
AND: "Goodyear TV Playhouse: A Murder Is Announced," NBC, 1956; "Lux Video Theatre: The Taggart Light," NBC, 1957; "Matinee Theatre: The Remarkable Mr. Jerome," NBC, 1957; "Maverick: The Rivals," ABC, 1959;

"Alfred Hitchcock Presents: The Avon Emeralds," CBS, 1959; "77 Sunset Strip: Tiger by the Tail," ABC, 1961; "The Roaring Twenties: Right Off the Boat," ABC, 1961; "The Third Man: Angry Young Man," SYN, 1961; "Trials of O'Brien: What Can Go Wrong?," CBS, 1965; "The Tonight Show Starring Johnny Carson," NBC, 1966.
TV MOVIES AND MINISERIES: "Sherlock Holmes in New York," NBC, 1976; "The Golden Raiders," ABC, 1981.

MOORE, TIM

b. *Rock Island, IL, 1888; d. 1958.* Actor who played George "Kingfish" Stevens on "Amos 'n Andy."
AS A REGULAR: "Amos 'n Andy," CBS, 1951-53.
AND: "The Jack Paar Show," NBC, 1958.

MOOREHEAD, AGNES

b. *Clinton, MA, December 6, 1906; d. 1974.* Stage and screen actress with many notable credits, including "Citizen Kane," but best remembered as the evil Endora, mother-in-law of Darrin Stephens (Dick York, later Dick Sargent) on "Bewitched."
AS A REGULAR: "Bewitched," ABC, 1964-72.
AND: "Mirror Theatre: Lullaby," CBS, 1953; "The Colgate Comedy Hour: Roberta," NBC, 1955; "Matinee Theatre: Graybeards and Witches," NBC, 1956; "Studio 57: Teacher," SYN, 1956; "Schlitz Playhouse of Stars: The Life You Save," CBS, 1957; "Climax!: False Witness," CBS, 1957; "Not One Shall Die," SYN, 1957; "Wagon Train: The Mary Halstead Story," NBC, 1957; "Du Pont Show of the Month: A Tale of Two Cities," CBS, 1958; "Playhouse 90: The Dungeon," CBS, 1958; "Suspicion: Protege," NBC, 1958; "Shirley Temple's Storybook: Rapunzel," NBC, 1958; "The Twilight Zone: The Invaders," CBS, 1961; "My Sister Eileen: Aunt Harriet's Way," CBS, 1961; "My Sister Eileen: The Protectors," CBS, 1961; "The Greatest Show on Earth: This Train Doesn't Stop Till It Gets There," ABC, 1964; "Burke's Law: Who Killed Don Pablo?," ABC, 1964; "Burke's Law: Who Killed Hamlet?," ABC, 1965; "Alice Through the Looking Glass," NBC, 1966; "The Wild Wild West: The Night of the Vicious Valentine," CBS, 1967; "Custer: Spirit Woman," ABC, 1967; "Password," CBS, 1967; "Hollywood Squares," NBC, 1968; "The Dick Cavett Show," ABC, 1969; "Barefoot in the Park: Pilot," ABC, 1970; "The Men From Shiloh: Gun Quest," NBC, 1970; "Night Gallery: Certain Shadows on the Walls," NBC, 1970; "The Wonderful World of Disney: The Strange Monster of Strawberry Cove," NBC, 1971; "Love, American Style: Love and the Particular Girl," ABC, 1971; "Marcus Welby, M.D.: He Could Sell Iceboxes to Eskimos," ABC, 1972; "Short Stories of Love: The Fortunate

Painters," NBC, 1974.
TV MOVIES AND MINISERIES: "The Ballad of Andy Crocker," ABC, 1969; "Marriage: Year One," NBC, 1971; "Suddenly Single," ABC, 1971; "Rolling Man," ABC, 1972; "Night of Terror," ABC, 1972; "Frankenstein: The True Story," NBC, 1973.
* Moorehead's Emmy came not for "Bewitched," but for her "Wild Wild West" guest role.
* Emmies: 1967.

MORAN, ERIN

b. *Burbank, CA, October 18, 1961.* Young actress with deep-dish dimples; she played Joanie Cunningham on "Happy Days" and in a short-lived spinoff with TV boyfriend Scott Baio.
AS A REGULAR: "Daktari," CBS, 1968-69; "The Don Rickles Show," CBS, 1972; "Happy Days," ABC, 1974-84; "Joanie Loves Chachi," ABC, 1982-83.
AND: "Family Affair: There Goes New York," CBS, 1970; "The FBI: Deadfall," ABC, 1970; "My Three Sons: Dodie's Dilemma," CBS, 1970; "Bearcats!: Hostages," CBS, 1971; "Gunsmoke: Lijah," CBS, 1971; "The FBI: The Wedding Gift," ABC, 1973; "The FBI: Town of Terror," ABC, 1973; "The Captain & Tennille," ABC, 1976; "The Love Boat: The Family Plan," ABC, 1980; "The Love Boat: China Cruise," ABC, 1983; "Hotel: Premiere," ABC, 1983; "Glitter: In Tennis Love Means Nothing," ABC, 1984; "The Love Boat: The Counterfeit Couple," ABC, 1985; "The Love Boat: Forties Fantasy," ABC, 1985; "Murder, She Wrote: Unfinished Business," CBS, 1986.

MORANIS, RICK

b. *Canada.* Emmy-winning comic performer and writer; on "SCTV" he played comic Skip Bittman and did deadly impersonations of Dick Cavett, Woody Allen and David Brinkley, among others; now he's in the movies ("Honey, I Shrunk the Kids," "Parenthood").
AS A REGULAR: "Second City TV," SYN, 1980-81; "SCTV Network 90," NBC, 1981-82.
AND: "Saturday Night Live," NBC, 1983; "Saturday Night Live," NBC, 1989.
* Emmies: 1982.

MORENO, RITA

b. *Rosita Dolores Alverio, Humacao, Puerto Rico, December 11, 1931.* Actress and singer in many a dramatic role and on many a variety show; she won Emmies for her appearance on "The Muppet Show" and for an appearance as prostitute Rita Capovick on "The Rockford Files."
AS A REGULAR: "9 to 5," ABC, 1982-83; "B.L.

Stryker," ABC, 1989-90.

AND: "Fireside Theatre: Saint and Senorita," NBC, 1952; "Fireside Theatre: M'Liss," NBC, 1952; "G.E. Theatre: The Cat with the Crimson Eyes," CBS, 1953; "Ford Theatre: Wonderful Day for a Wedding," NBC, 1954; "The 20th Century-Fox Hour: Broken Arrow," CBS, 1956; "Climax!: The Chinese Game," CBS, 1956; "Climax!: Strange Sanctuary," CBS, 1957; "Father Knows Best: Fair Exchange," CBS, 1958; "Tales of Wells Fargo: Lola Montez," NBC, 1959; "Cimarron City: The Town Is a Prisoner," NBC, 1959; "The Millionaire: Millionaire Alicia Osante," CBS, 1959; "Playhouse 90: Alas, Babylon," CBS, 1960; "Bourbon Street Beat: Suitable for Framing," ABC, 1960; "Perry Como's Kraft Music Hall," NBC, 1961; "Highways of Melody," NBC, 1961; "The Andy Williams Show," NBC, 1962; "To Tell the Truth," CBS, 1962; "The Jack Benny Program," CBS, 1963; "Password," CBS, 1963; "Burke's Law: Who Killed Julian Buck?," ABC, 1963; "Trials of O'Brien: Dead End on Flugel Street," CBS, 1965; "The Match Game," NBC, 1966; "Run for Your Life: Who's Che Guevara?," NBC, 1967; "Sesame Street," NET, 1971; "Hec Ramsey: The Hard Road to Vengeance," NBC, 1973; "Dominic's Dream," CBS, 1974; "Medical Center: May God Have Mercy," CBS, 1974; "The $10,000 Pyramid," ABC, 1975; "Shoot for the Stars," NBC, 1977; "The Rockford Files: The Paper Palace," NBC, 1977; "The Muppet Show," SYN, 1977; "The Rockford Files: Rosendahl and Gilda Stern Are Dead," NBC, 1978; "Hollywood Squares," SYN, 1978; "The Rockford Files: The No Fault Affair," NBC, 1979; "Whew!," CBS, 1980; "The Toni Tennille Show," SYN, 1980; "The Love Boat: The Lottery Winners," ABC, 1983; "The Cosby Show: You Only Hurt the One You Love," NBC, 1987; "Miami Vice: Miami Squeeze," NBC, 1989.

TV MOVIES AND MINISERIES: "Anatomy of a Seduction," CBS, 1979; "Portrait of a Showgirl," CBS, 1982.

* Emmies: 1977, 1978.

MORGAN, DENNIS
b. Stanley Morner, Prentice, WI, December 30, 1910. Leading man of the movies with a smattering of TV experience.

AS A REGULAR: "21 Beacon Street," NBC, 1959.

AND: "G.E. Theatre: Atomic Love," CBS, 1953; "Pepsi Cola Playhouse: Open Season," ABC, 1954; "Fireside Theatre: Not Captain Material," NBC, 1955; "Ford Theatre: Celebrity," NBC, 1955; "Stage 7: Press Conference," CBS, 1955; "Best of Broadway: Stage Door," CBS, 1955; "Stage 7: The Fox Hunt," CBS, 1955; "Star Stage: Dr. Jordan," NBC, 1956; "Telephone Time: Line Chief," ABC, 1957; "Alfred Hitchcock Presents: Bull in a China Shop," CBS, 1958; "Here's Hollywood," NBC, 1961; "Saints and Sinners:

Source of Information," NBC, 1962; "The Dick Powell Show: The Old Man and the City," NBC, 1963; "Petticoat Junction: Bye, Bye, Doctor," CBS, 1968; "The Love Boat: The Gift," ABC, 1980.

MORGAN, HARRY
b. Harry Bratsburg, Detroit, MI, April 10, 1915. Bald, slight actor who played henpecked Pete Porter on "December Bride" and "Pete and Gladys," cop Bill Gannon on "Dragnet" and Colonel Sherman Potter on "M*A*S*H" and its spinoff.

AS A REGULAR: "December Bride," CBS, 1954-59; "Pete and Gladys," CBS, 1960-62; "The Richard Boone Show," NBC, 1963-64; "Kentucky Jones," NBC, 1964-65; "Dragnet," NBC, 1967-70; "The D.A.," NBC, 1971-72; "Hec Ramsey," NBC, 1972-74; "M*A*S*H," CBS, 1975-83; "AfterMASH," CBS, 1983-84; "Blacke's Magic," NBC, 1986; "You Can't Take It with You," SYN, 1987-88.

AND: "Cavalcade Theatre: Who Is Byington?," ABC, 1956; "The 20th Century-Fox Hour: The Marriage Broker," CBS, 1957; "Have Gun, Will Travel: A Snare for Murder," CBS, 1959; "Alfred Hitchcock Presents: Anniversary Gift," CBS, 1959; "Going My Way: Like My Own Brother," ABC, 1962; "Ensign O'Toole: Operation: Mess," NBC, 1962; "The Untouchables: Double Cross," ABC, 1962; "Have Gun, Will Travel: American Primitive," CBS, 1963; "The Virginian: Strangers at Sundown," NBC, 1963; "The Virginian: Strangers at Sundown," NBC, 1963; "The Wackiest Ship in the Army: The Lady and the Luluai," NBC, 1965; "Dr. Kildare: A Gift of Love/The Tent Dwellers/Going Home," NBC, 1965; "The Jerry Lewis Show," NBC, 1968; "Love, American Style: Love and the Motel," ABC, 1970; "The Partridge Family: The Sound of Money," ABC, 1970; "Gunsmoke: The Witness," CBS, 1970; "Night Gallery: The Last Mr. Peddington," NBC, 1972; "The Partridge Family: All's War in Love and Fairs," ABC, 1972; "Gunsmoke: Milligan," CBS, 1972; "M*A*S*H: The General Flipped at Dawn," CBS, 1974; "Gunsmoke: The Wiving," CBS, 1974; "Gunsmoke: Brides and Grooms," CBS, 1975; "The Love Boat: The Racer's Edge," ABC, 1985; "Murder, She Wrote: The Days Dwindle Down," CBS, 1987.

TV MOVIES AND MINISERIES: "Dragnet," NBC, 1969; "But I Don't Want to Get Married!," ABC, 1970; "The Feminist and the Fuzz," ABC, 1971; "Ellery Queen: Don't Look Behind You," NBC, 1971; "Sidekicks," CBS, 1974; "The Bastard," SYN, 1978; "Backstairs at the White House," NBC, 1979; "Roots: The Next Generations," ABC, 1979; "The Wild Wild West Revisited," CBS, 1979; "Better Late Than Never," NBC, 1979; "More Wild Wild

West," CBS, 1980; "Agatha Christie's Sparkling Cyanide," CBS, 1983; "AT&T Presents: The Incident," CBS, 1990.
* Emmies: 1980.

MORGAN, HENRY
b. New York City, NY, March 31, 1915. Radio and TV personality who specialized in sardonic humor.
AS A REGULAR: "On the Corner," ABC, 1948; "Henry Morgan's Great Talent Hunt," NBC, 1951; "Draw to Win," CBS, 1952; "I've Got a Secret," CBS, 1952-67; 1976; "That Was the Week That Was," NBC, 1964; "My World and Welcome to It," NBC, 1969-70.
AND: "A Tribute to Eleanor Roosevelt On Her Diamond Jubilee," NBC, 1959; "The Garry Moore Show," CBS, 1959; "Here's Hollywood," NBC, 1961; "The Merv Griffin Show," NBC, 1962; "The Match Game," NBC, 1964; "Get the Message," ABC, 1964; "The Price Is Right," ABC, 1965; "The Mike Douglas Show," SYN, 1966; "Snap Judgment," NBC, 1968; "The Match Game," NBC, 1968; "The Match Game," NBC, 1969.
AS WRITER: "Victor Borge Special," CBS, 1958.

MORGAN, ROBIN
b. Lake Worth, FL, January 29, 1942. Child actress who played Dagmar on "Mama."
AS A REGULAR: "Mama," CBS, 1949-56.
AND: "Suspense: The Lonely Place," CBS, 1951; "Kraft Television Theatre: 40 Weeks of Uncle Tom," NBC, 1954; "Robert Montgomery Presents: Halfway House," NBC, 1955; "Robert Montgomery Presents: The Tall Dark Man," NBC, 1955; "Alcoa Hour: Kiss and Tell," NBC, 1956.

MORIARTY, MICHAEL
b. Detroit, MI, April 5, 1941. Intense actor whose TV appearances have been sporadic and impressive; an Emmy winner for "The Glass Menagerie" and "Holocaust."
AS A REGULAR: "Law & Order," NBC, 1990- .
AND: "The Equalizer: Encounter in a Closed Room," CBS, 1987; "The Equalizer: Starfire," CBS, 1989.
TV MOVIES AND MINISERIES: "A Summer Without Boys," ABC, 1973; "The Glass Menagerie," ABC, 1973; "The Deadliest Season," CBS, 1977; "The Winds of Kitty Hawk," NBC, 1978; "Holocaust," NBC, 1978; "Too Far to Go," NBC, 1979; "Windmills of the Gods," CBS, 1988; "Frank Nitti: The Enforcer," ABC, 1988.
* Emmies: 1974, 1978.

MORITA, PAT
b. California, 1930. Actor who began as a comedian; best known as Arnold on "Happy Days" and as the co-star of the "Karate Kid" movies.

AS A REGULAR: "The Queen and I," CBS, 1969; "Sanford & Son," NBC, 1974-75; "Happy Days," ABC, 1975-76; 1982-83; "Mr. T. and Tina," ABC, 1976; "Blansky's Beauties," ABC, 1977; "Ohara," ABC, 1987-88.
AND: "Hollywood Palace," ABC, 1964; "Hollywood Palace," ABC, 1966; "Gomer Pyle, USMC: The Recruiting Poster," CBS, 1967; "Rowan & Martin's Laugh-In," NBC, 1968; "The Outsider: Love Is Under L," NBC, 1968; "The Courtship of Eddie's Father: Gentleman Friend," ABC, 1969; "The Courtship of Eddie's Father: The Littlest Kidnapper," ABC, 1970; "Nanny and the Professor: My Son the Sitter," ABC, 1970; "The Bill Cosby Show: Power of the Trees," NBC, 1971; "Love, American Style: Love and the Love Potion," ABC, 1971; "The Odd Couple: Partner's Investment," ABC, 1972; "Columbo: Etude in Black," NBC, 1972; "Love, American Style: Love and Lady Luck," ABC, 1972; "Hawaii Five-O: Tricks Are Not Treats," CBS, 1973; "Love, American Style: Love and the Woman in White," ABC, 1973; "M*A*S*H: Deal Me Out," CBS, 1973; "M*A*S*H: The Chosan People," CBS, 1974; "Wives," CBS, 1975; "Grady: Be It Ever So Humble," NBC, 1975; "Lola Falana Special," ABC, 1975; "Welcome Back, Kotter: Career Day," ABC, 1976; "The Merv Griffin Show," SYN, 1976; "Laverne & Shirley: Separate Tables," ABC, 1980; "Lou Grant: Recovery," CBS, 1981; "Lobo: The Roller Disco Karate Kaper," NBC, 1981.
TV MOVIES AND MINISERIES: "Evil Roy Slade," NBC, 1972; "A Very Missing Person," NBC, 1972; "Brock's Last Case," NBC, 1973; "Human Feelings," NBC, 1978; "Amos," CBS, 1985.

MORLEY, ROBERT
b. Semley, England, May 26, 1908. Actor and raconteur.
AS A GUEST: "U.S. Steel Hour: Edward, My Son," CBS, 1955; "Playhouse 90: Misalliance," CBS, 1959; "du Pont Show of the Month: Oliver Twist," CBS, 1959; "Alfred Hitchcock Presents: Speciality of the House," CBS, 1959; "du Pont Show of the Month: Heaven Can Wait," CBS, 1960; "The Dick Powell Show: The Big Day," NBC, 1962; "Espionage: The Life of a Friendly Star," NBC, 1963; "The Jack Paar Program," NBC, 1965; "The Danny Kaye Show," CBS, 1967.
TV MOVIES AND MINISERIES: "Bell System Family Theatre: Great Expectations," NBC, 1974; "The Winds of War," ABC, 1983; "War and Remembrance," ABC, 1988, 1989.

MORRIS, CHESTER
b. John Chester Brooks Morris, New York City, NY, February 16, 1901; d. 1970. Actor in action roles, and a frequent guest on talk and game shows.
AS A REGULAR: "Gangbusters," SYN, 1951;

"Diagnosis: Unknown," CBS, 1960.
AND: "NBC Showcase: The Great Merlini," NBC, 1950; "Starlight Theatre: Act of God Notwithstanding," CBS, 1951; "Schlitz Playhouse of Stars: Billy Budd," CBS, 1952; "Suspense: Point Blank," CBS, 1953; "Danger: Towerman," CBS, 1953; "Robert Montgomery Presents: The Greatest Man in the World," NBC, 1953; "The Web: Rock-Bound," CBS, 1954; "Studio One: Jack Sparling, 46," CBS, 1954; "Studio One: Blow-Up at Cortland," CBS, 1955; "Studio One: The Arena," CBS, 1956; "The Tonight Show," NBC, 1956; "Kraft Television Theatre: Time Lock," NBC, 1956; "The Red Skelton Show," CBS, 1957; "Dick Powell's Zane Grey Theatre: Black Is for Grief," CBS, 1957; "Playhouse 90: Child of Trouble," CBS, 1957; "Kraft Television Theatre: Men of Prey," NBC, 1957; "Pursuit: Tiger on a Bicycle," CBS, 1958; "Oldsmobile Music Theatre: Too Bad About Sheila Troy," NBC, 1959; "U.S. Steel Hour: Whisper of Evil," CBS, 1959; "To Tell the Truth," CBS, 1959; "Rawhide: Incident on the Road to Yesterday," CBS, 1960; "The Jack Paar Show," NBC, 1961; "Play of the Week: Morning's at Seven," SYN, 1961; "A Story of Love: A String of Beads," NBC, 1961; "Naked City: Make-Believe Man," ABC, 1961; "Checkmate: Portrait of a Man Running," CBS, 1961; "Ben Casey: An Expensive Glass of Water," ABC, 1961; "The Defenders: The Empty Chute," CBS, 1962; "Candid Camera," CBS, 1962; "Alcoa Premiere: The Contenders," ABC, 1962; "The Eleventh Hour: Along About Late in the Afternoon," NBC, 1962; "Alcoa Premiere: The Glass Palace," ABC, 1963; "To Tell the Truth," CBS, 1963; "Route 66: Soda Pop and Paper Flags," CBS, 1963; "The Defenders: The Bagman," CBS, 1963; "Route 66: Child of a Night," CBS, 1964; "Espionage: Castles in Spain," NBC, 1964; "East Side/West Side: The Name of the Game," CBS, 1964; "Kraft Suspense Theatre: The Gambit," NBC, 1964; "Dr. Kildare: Dolly's Dilemma," NBC, 1964; "Suspense: The Hunger," CBS, 1964; "The Price Is Right," ABC, 1964; "Mr. Broadway: Don't Mention My Name in Sheboygan," CBS, 1964; "Bob Hope Chrysler Theatre: The Fliers," NBC, 1965; "The Defenders: A Matter of Law and Disorder," CBS, 1965; "Gentle Ben: Busman's Holiday," CBS, 1969; "Personality," NBC, 1969.

MORRIS, GARRETT

b. New Orleans, LA, February 1, 1937. Comic actor best-known as baseball player Chico Esquela on "Saturday Night Live."
AS A REGULAR: "Roll Out," CBS, 1973-74; "Saturday Night Live," NBC, 1975-80; "It's Your Move," NBC, 1984-85; "Hunter," NBC, 1986- .
AND: "CBS Television Workshop: The Bible Salesman," CBS, 1960; "Diff'rent Strokes:

Santa's Helper," NBC, 1982; "Hill Street Blues: Passage to Libya," NBC, 1985; "Murder, She Wrote: Murder to a Jazz Beat," CBS, 1985; "Scarecrow and Mrs. King: The Wrong Way Home," CBS, 1985; "The Love Boat: The Will," ABC, 1986; "Who's the Boss?: SAMSCAR," ABC, 1988; "Saturday Night Live's 15th Anniversary," NBC, 1989.
TV MOVIES AND MINISERIES: "The Invisible Woman," NBC, 1983.

MORRIS, GREG

b. Cleveland, OH, September 27, 1934. Actor who played Barney Collier on "Mission: Impossible."
AS A REGULAR: "Mission: Impossible," CBS, 1966-73; "Vega$," ABC, 1979-81.
AND: "Dr. Kildare: The Gift of the Koodjanuk," NBC, 1963; "The Dick Van Dyke Show: That's My Boy??," CBS, 1963; "Ben Casey: Allie," ABC, 1963; "The Twilight Zone: The Seventh Is Made Up of Phantoms," CBS, 1963; "The Dick Van Dyke Show: Bupkiss," CBS, 1965; "The Fugitive: Wings of an Angel," ABC, 1965; "Branded: Fill No Glass for Me," NBC, 1965; "I Spy: Lori," NBC, 1966; "Dream Girl of '67," ABC, 1967; "Hollywood Squares," NBC, 1969; "Dinah Shore Special," NBC, 1969; "Love, American Style: Love and the Unloved Couple," ABC, 1970; "Mannix: Climb a Deadly Mountain," CBS, 1973; "Love Story: A Glow of Dying Embers," NBC, 1973; "Password," ABC, 1974; "Match Game '74," CBS, 1974; "The Snoop Sisters: The Devil Made Me Do It," NBC, 1974; "You Don't Say," ABC, 1975; "The Streets of San Francisco: Merchants of Death," ABC, 1975; "Captain Kangaroo," CBS, 1976; "Sanford & Son: The Hawaiian Connection," NBC, 1976; "Tattletales," CBS, 1977; "Break the Bank," SYN, 1977; "What's Happening!: If I'm Elected," ABC, 1977; "The Love Boat: Till Death Do Us Part," ABC, 1978; "What's Happening!: Dwayne's Debate," ABC, 1979; "Murder, She Wrote: Lovers and Other Killers," CBS, 1984; "Mission: Immpossible: The Condemned," ABC, 1988; "Mission: Impossible: The Golden Serpent," ABC, 1989.
TV MOVIES AND MINISERIES: "The Doomsday Flight," NBC, 1966; "Killer by Night," CBS, 1972; "Flight to Holocaust," NBC, 1977; "Crisis in Mid-Air," CBS, 1979; "Roots: The Next Generations," ABC, 1979.

MORRIS, HOWARD

b. September 4, 1919. Gifted physical comic and clown, first as a sidekick to Sid Caesar and later as rock-throwing Ernest T. Bass on "The Andy Griffith Show."
AS A REGULAR: "Your Show of Shows," NBC, 1950-54; "Caesar's Hour," NBC, 1954-57; "The Jetsons," ABC, 1962-63; "The

Flintstones," ABC, 1962-63; "The Famous Adventures of Mr. Magoo," NBC, 1964-65.
AND: "Two for the Money," CBS, 1957; "The Polly Bergen Show," NBC, 1957; "Hallmark Hall of Fame: Twelfth Night," NBC, 1957; "Kraft Theatre: Code of the Corner," NBC, 1958; "The Sid Caesar Show," ABC, 1958; "The Patrice Munsel Show," ABC, 1958; "Du Pont Show of the Month: Aladdin," CBS, 1958; "The Chevy Show," NBC, 1959; "Pantomime Quiz," ABC, 1959; "Sid Caesar Special: Tiptoe Through TV," CBS, 1960; "Sid Caesar Special: Variety—World of Show Biz," CBS, 1960; "U.S. Steel Hour: When in Rome," CBS, 1960; "Wanted Dead or Alive: Detour," CBS, 1961; "Here's Hollywood," NBC, 1962; "Ensign O'Toole: Operation: Intrigue," NBC, 1963; "The Andy Griffith Show: Mountain Wedding," CBS, 1963; "The Dick Van Dyke Show: The Masterpiece," CBS, 1963; "The Andy Griffith Show: Ernest T. Bass Joins the Army," CBS, 1963; "The Twilight Zone: I Dream of Genie," CBS, 1963; "The Danny Kaye Show," CBS, 1964; "The Danny Thomas Show: The Leprechaun," CBS, 1964; "The Andy Griffith Show: My Fair Ernest T. Bass," CBS, 1964; "The Flintstones: The Gruesomes," ABC, 1964; "The Andy Griffith Show: The Education of Ernest T. Bass," CBS, 1964; "The Andy Griffith Show: Andy and Helen Have Their Day," CBS, 1964: "The Flintstones: The Hatrocks and the Gruesomes," ABC, 1965; "The Andy Griffith Show: Malcolm at the Crossroads," CBS, 1965; "The Lucy Show: Lucy Dates a Lifeguard," CBS, 1965; "The Sid Caesar, Imogene Coca, Carl Reiner, Howard Morris Special," CBS, 1967; "PDQ," NBC, 1967; "Love, American Style: Love and the Plumber," ABC, 1972; "The Bob Newhart Show: Jerry's Retirement," CBS, 1976; "Fantasy Island: Curtain Call," ABC, 1983; "The Yellow Rose: Sport of Kings," NBC, 1984; "The Love Boat: Another Dog Gone Christmas," ABC, 1985; "Murder, She Wrote: Something Borrowed, Someone Blue," CBS, 1989.
TV MOVIES AND MINISERIES: "The Munsters' Revenge," NBC, 1981; "Portrait of a Showgirl," CBS, 1982; "Return to Mayberry," NBC, 1986.
AS DIRECTOR: "The Dick Van Dyke Show," CBS, 1963-65; "The Andy Griffith Show," CBS, 1964-65.
AS PRODUCER: "The Corner Bar," ABC, 1972-73.

MORROW, VIC
b. *Bronx, NY, February 14, 1932; d. 1982.* Actor best known as Sgt. Chip Saunders on "Combat!"
AS A REGULAR: "Combat!," ABC, 1962-67; "B.A.D. Cats," ABC, 1980.
AND: "The Millionaire: The Story of Joey Diamond," CBS, 1956; "Climax!: Strange Hostage," CBS, 1956; "Restless Gun: Duel at

Lockwood," NBC, 1957; "The Lineup: My Son Is a Stranger," CBS, 1959; "Wichita Town: They Won't Hang Jimmy Relson," NBC, 1959; "Bonanza: The Avenger," NBC, 1960; "The Outlaws: Beat the Drum Slowly," NBC, 1960; "The Barbara Stanwyck Show: The Key to a Killer," NBC, 1960; "The Untouchables: The Tommy Karpeles Story," ABC, 1960; "The Law and Mr. Jones: A Very Special Citizen," ABC, 1961; "The Outlaws: The Avenger," NBC, 1961; "The Lawless Years: Little Augie," NBC, 1961; "G.E. Theatre: The Iron Silence," CBS, 1961; "The Tall Man: Time of Foreshadowing," NBC, 1961; "The Outlaws: No Luck on Friday," NBC, 1961; "Bonanza: The Tin Badge," NBC, 1961; "The New Breed: To Sell a Human Being," ABC, 1962; "The Untouchables: The Maggie Storm Story," ABC, 1962; "Death Valley Days: A Matter of Honor," SYN, 1963; "Mannix: Days Beyond Recall," CBS, 1971; "Hawaii Five-O: Two Doves and Mr. Heron," CBS, 1971; "The FBI: Center of Peril," ABC, 1971; "Mission: Impossible: Two Thousand," CBS, 1972; "McCloud: A Little Plot at Tranquil Valley," NBC, 1972; "The FBI: Desperate Journey," ABC, 1973; "The Streets of San Francisco: The Twenty-Four Karat Plague," ABC, 1973; "Love Story: The Cardboard House," NBC, 1973; "Police Story: Countdown," NBC, 1974; "Paris: Pilot," CBS, 1979; "Charlie's Angels: From Street Models to Hawaiian Angels," ABC, 1980.
TV MOVIES AND MINISERIES: "A Step Out of Line," CBS, 1971; "Travis Logan, D.A.," CBS, 1971; "River of Mystery," NBC, 1971; "Truman Capote's The Glass House," CBS, 1972; "The Weekend Nun," ABC, 1972; "The Police Story," NBC, 1973; "Tom Sawyer," CBS, 1973; "Nightmare," CBS, 1973; "The California Kid," ABC, 1974; "Death Stalk," NBC, 1974; "The Night That Panicked America," ABC, 1975; "Best Sellers: Captains and the Kings," NBC, 1976; "Roots," ABC, 1977.
* Morrow died July 23, 1982 while shooting a sequence for the film version of "The Twilight Zone." A helicopter was hit by debris from an explosion and the rotor blade struck and killed Morrow and two children.

MORSE, BARRY
b. *London, England, 1919.* Actor who played Lt. Philip Gerard, pursuer of "The Fugitive" (David Janssen).
AS A REGULAR: "The Fugitive," ABC, 1963-67; "Space: 1999," SYN, 1975-76.
AND: "U.S. Steel Hour: This Day in Fear," CBS, 1958; "Du Pont Show of the Month: Treasure Island," CBS, 1960; "Dow Hour of Great Mysteries: The Inn of the Flying Dragon," NBC, 1960; "Family Classics: The Three Musketeers," CBS, 1960; "Family Classics: The Heiress," CBS,

1961; "Naked City: The Deadly Guinea Pig," ABC, 1961; "U.S. Steel Hour: The Leonardi Code," CBS, 1961; "The Untouchables: The King of Champagne," ABC, 1961; "Way Out: Soft Focus," CBS, 1961; "Adventures in Paradise: The Fires of Kanua," ABC, 1961; "U.S. Steel Hour: The Bitter Sex," CBS, 1961; "The Defenders: The Bedside Murder," CBS, 1962; "Naked City: Portrait of a Painter," ABC, 1962; "The Twilight Zone: A Piano in the House," CBS, 1962; "The New Breed: Wings for a Plush Horse," ABC, 1962; "Wagon Train: The Shiloh Degnan Story," ABC, 1962; "The Alfred Hitchcock Hour: A Tangled Web, CBS, 1963; "The Untouchables: Kiss of Death," ABC, 1963; "The Defenders: Who'll Dig His Grave?," CBS, 1964; "The Outer Limits: Controlled Experiment," ABC, 1964; "The FBI: The Flaw," ABC, 1968.
TV MOVIES AND MINISERIES: "Master of the Game," CBS, 1984; "Fight for Life," ABC, 1987; "War and Remembrance," ABC, 1988, 1989.

MORSE, DAVID
b. *Beverly, MA, October 11, 1953.* Actor who played disaster-prone Dr. Jack Morrison on "St. Elsewhere."
AS A REGULAR: "St. Elsewhere," NBC, 1982-88.
AND: "Nurse: Equal Opportunity," CBS, 1981; "A Place at the Table," NBC, 1988.
TV MOVIES AND MINISERIES: "Shattered Vows," NBC, 1984; "When Dreams Come True," ABC, 1985; "Downpayment on Murder," NBC, 1987; "Six Against the Rock," NBC, 1987; "Brotherhood of the Rose," NBC, 1989; "Cross of Fire," NBC, 1989.

MORSE, ROBERT
b. *Newton, MA, May 18, 1931.* Stage actor with some TV experience who made a comeback in the late eighties as Truman Capote in a one-man Broadway show.
AS A REGULAR: "The Secret Storm," CBS, 1954; "That's Life," ABC, 1968-69.
AND: "Goodyear TV Playhouse: Man on Spikes," NBC, 1955; "The Phil Silvers Show: Bilko Goes to College," CBS, 1956; "Matinee Theatre: Rain in the Morning," NBC, 1957; "The Jack Paar Show," NBC, 1958; "Pantomime Quiz," ABC, 1959; "Omnibus: Forty-Five Minutes From Broadway," NBC, 1959; "Alfred Hitchcock Presents: Touche," CBS, 1959; "Perry Como's Kraft Music Hall," NBC, 1960; "Alfred Hitchcock Presents: Hitchhike," CBS, 1960; "Shirley Temple's Storybook: Rebel Gun," NBC, 1961; "Play of the Week: The Velvet Glove," SYN, 1961; "Naked City: Sweet Prince of Delancey Street," ABC, 1961; "The Jack Paar Show," NBC, 1961; "Password," CBS, 1962; "The Smothers Brothers Comedy Hour," CBS, 1967; "Hollywood Squares," NBC, 1968; "The Jonathan Winters Show," CBS, 1968; "The Don

Knotts Show," NBC, 1970; "Alias Smith and Jones: The Day They Hanged Kid Curry," ABC, 1970; "Night Gallery: Marmalade Wine," NBC, 1971; "Love, American Style: Love and the Ledge," ABC, 1972; "Free to Be You and Me," ABC, 1974; "Love, American Style: Love and the Forever Tree," ABC, 1974; "The Merv Griffin Show," SYN, 1974; "Showoffs," ABC, 1975; "The First Easter Rabbit," NBC, 1976; "Murder, She Wrote: Broadway Malady," CBS, 1985; "The Twilight Zone: Ye Gods," CBS, 1985.
TV MOVIES AND MINISERIES: "Calender Girl Murders," ABC, 1984.

MOSES, WILLIAM R.
b. *Los Angeles, CA, November 17, 1959.* Actor who played Cole Gioberti on "Falcon Crest."
AS A REGULAR: "Falcon Crest," CBS, 1981-86.
AND: "The Love Boat: The Dean and the Flunkee," ABC, 1983; "The Love Boat: Revenge With the Proper Stranger," ABC, 1984; "Finder of Lost Loves: Premiere," ABC, 1984; "Murder, She Wrote: Coal Miner's Slaughter," CBS, 1988; "Father Dowling Mysteries: The Man Who Came to Dinner Mystery," NBC, 1989.
TV MOVIES AND MINISERIES: "War and Remembrance," ABC, 1988, 1989; "Perry Mason: The Case of the Lethal Lesson," NBC, 1989; "Perry Mason: The Case of the Musical Murder," NBC, 1989; "Perry Mason: The Case of the All-Star Assassin," NBC, 1989; "Rock Hudson," ABC, 1990.

MOST, DONNY
b. *Brooklyn, NY, August 8, 1953.* Actor who played Ralph Malph on "Happy Days."
AS A REGULAR: "Happy Days," ABC, 1974-80.
AND: "Police Story: Explosion!," NBC, 1974; "The Captain & Tennille," ABC, 1976; "The Peter Marshall Variety Show," SYN, 1977; "The Love Boat: The Wedding," ABC, 1979; "The Love Boat: May the Best Man Win," ABC, 1980; "Fantasy Island: Shadow Games," ABC, 1982; "CHiPS: Rock, Devil, Rock," NBC, 1982; "The Love Boat: Zinging Valentine," ABC, 1983; "Murder, She Wrote: Stage Struck," CBS, 1986; "Hagar the Horrible," CBS, 1989.
TV MOVIES AND MINISERIES: "Huckleberry Finn," ABC, 1975.

MOSTEL, JOSHUA
b. *New York City, NY, December 21, 1957.* Roly-poly actor, son of Zero.
AS A REGULAR: "Delta House," ABC, 1979; "At Ease," ABC, 1983; "Murphy's Law," ABC, 1988-89.
AND: "The Equalizer: Beyond Control," CBS, 1987.
TV MOVIES AND MINISERIES: "Best Sellers: Seventh Avenue," NBC, 1977.

MOSTEL, ZERO

b. Samuel Joel Mostel, Brooklyn, NY, 1915; d.
1977. Actor and comic who had his biggest
successes on film ("The Producers") and on
stage ("A Funny Thing Happened on the Way
to the Forum," "Fiddler on the Roof").

AS A GUEST: "Play of the Week: The World of
Sholom Aleichem," SYN, 1960; "Play of the
Week: Waiting for Godot," SYN, 1961; "The
Tonight Show Starring Johnny Carson," NBC,
1968; "Old Faithful," ABC, 1973; "Saga of
Sonora," NBC, 1973; "Festival of Lively Arts
for Young People: Gianni Schicchi," CBS,
1975; "The Mike Douglas Show," SYN, 1976;
"Love, Life, Liberty and Lunch," ABC, 1976;
"The Little Drummer Boy, Book II," NBC,
1976.

MOWBRAY, ALAN

b. London, England, August 18, 1896; d. 1969.
Comic character actor who played the blustery
but quick-witted conman Colonel Flack.

AS A REGULAR: "The Mickey Rooney Show,"
NBC, 1954-55; "Colonel Flack," SYN, 1957-
58; "Dante," NBC, 1960-61.

AND: "Stars Over Hollywood: Small Town Story,"
NBC, 1950; "Bigelow Theatre: Agent From
Scotland Yard," CBS, 1951; "Robert Montgomery
Presents: The Young in Heart," NBC, 1951;
"Gruen Guild Theatre: Unfinished Business,"
ABC, 1951; "Schaefer Century Theatre: Annual
Honeymoon," NBC, 1952; "The Unexpected:
Confidentially Yours," NBC, 1952; "Mr. Lucky at
Seven: It Happened in Heaven," ABC, 1952;
"Plymouth Playhouse: Col. Humphrey J. Flack,"
ABC, 1953; "Four Star Playhouse: The House
Always Wins," CBS, 1955; "Four Star Playhouse:
Alias Mr. Hepp," CBS, 1955; "The Red Skelton
Show," CBS, 1957; "The Adventures of McGraw:
Escape," NBC, 1958; "Schlitz Playhouse of Stars:
A Contest of Ladies," CBS, 1958; "Maverick: The
Misfortune Tellers," ABC, 1960; "The Gale
Storm Show: It's Magic," ABC, 1960; "Startime:
Tennesse Ernie Meets King Arthur," NBC, 1960;
"Whispering Smith: The Poet and Peasant Case,"
NBC, 1961; "The Patty Duke Show: The
Actress," ABC, 1963; "Burke's Law: Who Killed
Everybody?," ABC, 1964; "Profiles in Courage:
Anne Hutchinson," NBC, 1965; "Mr. Roberts:
Eight in Every Port," NBC, 1966; "Mr. Roberts:
Son of Eight in Every Port," NBC, 1966; "The
Man From UNCLE: The My Friend the Gorilla
Affair," NBC, 1966; "The Beverly Hillbillies: A
Bundle for Britain," CBS, 1968; "The Flying
Nun: The Great Casino Robbery," ABC, 1969.

MOYERS, BILL

b. Billy Don Moyers, Hugo, OK, June 5, 1934.
TV journalist and commentator; former press
secretary to Lyndon Johnson.

AS A REGULAR: "Bill Moyers' Journal," PBS,
1979-81; "Creativity with Bill Moyers," PBS,
1981-82; "Our Times with Bill Moyers," CBS,
1983; "A Walk Through the 20th Century,"
PBS, 1984.
* Emmies: 1974, 1978, 1979, 1980, 1981, 1984,
1985, 1986.

MUDD, ROGER

b. Washington, D.C., February 9, 1928.
AS A REGULAR: "CBS Weekend News," 1966-73;
"NBC Evening News," NBC, 1982-83; "1986,"
NBC, 1986; "The MacNeil-Lehrer News
Hour," PBS, 1986- .
* Emmies: 1973, 1974, 1980.

MUIR, JEAN

b. Jean Muir Fullarton, New York City, NY,
February 13, 1911. Film and TV actress whose
name appeared in an pamphlet that accused her
of being a Communist. She claimed she was
blacklisted.

AS A GUEST: "Philco TV Playhouse: The Sudden
Guest," NBC, 1950; "Naked City: Hey
Teach!," ABC, 1959; "Route 66: Bridge
Across Five Days," CBS, 1961.

MULDAUR, DIANA

b. New York City, NY, August 19, 1943. Coolly
attractive actress who played mean attorney
Rosalind Shays on "L.A. Law."

AS A REGULAR: "The Secret Storm," CBS, 1965;
"Harold Robbins' The Survivors," ABC, 1969-
70; "McCloud," NBC, 1970-77; "Born Free,"
NBC, 1974; "The Tony Randall Show," ABC,
1976-77; CBS, 1977-78; "Hizzonner," NBC,
1979; "Fitz and Bones," NBC, 1981; "A Year
in the Life," NBC, 1987-88; "L.A. Law," NBC,
1989-91 .

AND: "The Americans: On to Richmond," NBC,
1961; "The Doctors and the Nurses: A Couple of
Dozen Tiny Pills," CBS, 1965; "Dr. Kildare: The
Encroachment/A Patient Lost/What Happened to
All the Sunshine and Roses?/The Taste of Crow/
Out of a Concrete Tower," NBC, 1966;
"Gunsmoke: Fandango," CBS, 1967; "The FBI:
Act of Violence," ABC, 1968; "I Spy: This Guy
Smith," NBC, 1968; "Star Trek: Return to
Tomorrow," NBC, 1968; "The Invaders: The Life
Seekers," ABC, 1968; "Star Trek: Is There in
Truth No Beauty?," NBC, 1968; "The Felony
Squad: The Distant Shore," ABC, 1968; "The
Courtship of Eddie's Father: And Eddie Makes
Three," ABC, 1969; "The Mod Squad: The
Loser," ABC, 1970; "Dan August: Murder by
Proxy," ABC, 1970; "Ironside: Good Samaritan,"
NBC, 1971; "Marcus Welby, M.D.: Tender
Comrade," ABC, 1972; "The FBI: Escape to
Nowhere," ABC, 1972; "Hawaii Five-O: Death

Wish on Tantalus Mountain," CBS, 1972; "Medical Center: Doctor and Mr. Harper," CBS, 1972; "Banyon: Dead Run," NBC, 1972; "Owen Marshall, Counselor at Law: Charlie Gave Me Your Number," ABC, 1972; "The Bold Ones: The Velvet Prison," NBC, 1972; "Alias Smith and Jones: The Great Shell Game," ABC, 1972; "Hec Ramsey: The Mystery of the Yellow Rose," NBC, 1973; "Owen Marshall, Counselor at Law: A Lesson in Loving," ABC, 1973; "ABC Afternoon Playbreak: A Special Act of Love," ABC, 1973; "Kung Fu: Theodora," ABC, 1973; "The Wonderful World of Disney: Hog Wild," NBC, 1974; "Cannon: Blood Money," CBS, 1974; "The Rockford Files: Charlie Harris at Large," NBC, 1974; "The Streets of San Francisco: Dead Lift," ABC, 1976; "Police Woman: Solitaire," NBC, 1977; "Lucan: How Do You Run Forever?," ABC, 1978; "$weepstake$: Dewey and Harold and Sarah and Maggie," NBC, 1979; "The Love Boat: Aftermath," ABC, 1979; "B.J. and the Bear: Bear Bondage," NBC, 1980; "Quincy: Slow Boat to Madness," NBC, 1981; "Murder, She Wrote: Footnote to Murder," CBS, 1985.

TV MOVIES AND MINISERIES: "McCloud: Who Killed Miss USA?," NBC, 1970; "Call to Danger," CBS, 1973; "Ordeal," ABC, 1973; "Planet Earth," ABC, 1974; "Charlie's Angels," ABC, 1976; "Black Beauty," NBC, 1978; "The Word," CBS, 1978; "Agatha Christie's Murder in Three Acts," CBS, 1986.

MULGREW, KATE

b. Dubuque, IA, April 29, 1955. Actress who played Mrs. Columbo in a misbegotten series; most recently she played Dr. Joanne Springsteen on "Heartbeat."

AS A REGULAR: "Ryan's Hope," ABC, 1975-77, 1983; "Kate Loves a Mystery (Kate Columbo, Mrs. Columbo)," NBC, 1979; "Heartbeat," ABC, 1988.

AND: "St. Elsewhere: Time Heals," NBC, 1986; "Cheers: Strange Bedfellows," NBC, 1986; "Murder, She Wrote: The Corpse Flew First Class," CBS, 1987.

TV MOVIES AND MINISERIES: "The Word," CBS, 1978; "Jennifer: A Woman's Story," NBC, 1979; "A Time for Miracles," ABC, 1980; "Manions of America," ABC, 1981; "Roses Are for the Rich," CBS, 1987; "Roots: The Gift," ABC, 1988.

MULHARE, EDWARD

b. Ireland, 1923. Dashing leading man who played the ghost of Capt. Daniel Gregg opposite Hope Lange as Carolyn Muir.

AS A REGULAR: "The Ghost and Mrs. Muir," NBC, 1968-69; ABC, 1969-70; "Knight Rider," NBC, 1982-86.

AND: "The Adventures of Robin Hood: The Imposters," CBS, 1956; "The Ed Sullivan Show,"

CBS, 1957; "Kraft Television Theatre: Night of the Plague," NBC, 1957; "Lamp Unto My Feet: The Hand of God," CBS, 1957; "Kraft Television Theatre: The First and the Last," NBC, 1957; "U.S. Steel Hour: Who's Earnest?," CBS, 1957; "Look Up and Live: Priest and Poet—Gerard Manley Hopkins," CBS, 1959; "Look Up and Live: The Glory of the Heart," CBS, 1960; "Catholic Hour: The Theatre and Love," NBC, 1961; "The Outer Limits: The Sixth Finger," ABC, 1963; "The Farmer's Daughter: Katy and the Prince," ABC, 1964; "Mr. Novak: He Who Can, Does So," NBC, 1964; "Convoy: The Duel," NBC, 1965; "Twelve O'Clock High: Siren Voices," ABC, 1966; "Run for Your Life: The Savage Machines," NBC, 1966; "The Girl From UNCLE: The Mata Hari Affair," NBC, 1966; "The FBI: The Hostage," ABC, 1967; "The Streets of San Francisco: Tower Beyond Tragedy," ABC, 1972; "The FBI: The Fatal Showdown," ABC, 1972; "Cannon: Death of a Hunter," CBS, 1974; "The Streets of San Francisco: One Chance to Live," ABC, 1974; "Benjamin Franklin: The Ambassador," CBS, 1974; "Ellery Queen: Two-Faced Woman," NBC, 1976; "Murder, She Wrote: One Good Bid Deserves a Murder," CBS, 1986; "Murder, She Wrote: Stage Struck," CBS, 1986.

TV MOVIES AND MINISERIES: "Gidget Grows Up," ABC, 1969.

MULL, MARTIN

b. Chicago, IL, August 18, 1943. Comedian who played Garth Gimble on "Mary Hartman, Mary Hartman" and twin brother Barth on "Fernwood 2-Night."

AS A REGULAR: "Mary Hartman, Mary Hartman," SYN, 1976-77; "Fernwood 2-Night," SYN, 1977-78; "Domestic Life," CBS, 1984; "His & Hers," CBS, 1990.

AND: "Cher," CBS, 1975; "Music Hall America," SYN, 1977; "Taxi: Hollywood Calling," ABC, 1979; "The Tom and Dick Smothers Brothers Special," NBC, 1980; "The Mike Douglas Show," SYN, 1981; "Candid Camera Christmas Special," CBS, 1987; "It's Garry Shandling's Show: Save Mr. Peck's," FOX, 1989; "Woodstock: Return to the Planet of the '60s," CBS, 1989; "It's Garry Shandling's Show: Garry Goes Golfing," FOX, 1989.

TV MOVIES AND MINISERIES: "Lots of Luck," DIS, 1985; "California Girls," ABC, 1985.

MULLANEY, JACK

b. Pittsburgh, PA, September 18, 1932; d. 1982. Comic actor on several short-lived sitcoms.

AS A REGULAR: "The Ann Sothern Show," CBS, 1958-60; "Ensign O'Toole," NBC, 1962-63; "My Living Doll," CBS, 1964-65; "It's About Time," CBS, 1966-67.

AND: "Alfred Hitchcock Presents: Never Again,"

CBS, 1956; "Playhouse 90: Eloise," CBS, 1956; "Studio One: A Walk in the Forest," CBS, 1957; "Studio One: Kurishiki Incident," CBS, 1958; "The Thin Man: The Kappa Kappa Kappa Caper," NBC, 1958; "Thriller: Child's Play," NBC, 1960; "Alcoa Presents One Step Beyond: The Return," ABC, 1960; "The Barbara Stanwyck Show: House in Order," NBC, 1960; "The Outlaws: Last Chance," NBC, 1960; "The du Pont Show with June Allyson: Love on Credit," CBS, 1960; "The Law and Mr. Jones: The Concert," ABC, 1961; "The du Pont Show with June Allyson: Our Man in Rome," CBS, 1961; "Thriller: The Prisoner in the Mirror," NBC, 1961; "G.E. Theatre: Star Witness," CBS, 1961; "The Joey Bishop Show: Barney the Bloodhound," NBC, 1961; "The Joey Bishop Show: The Income Tax Caper," NBC, 1962; "Grindl: Grindl, She-Wolf of Wall Street," NBC, 1963; "That Girl: Many Happy Returns," ABC, 1969; "Love, American Style: Love and the Monsters," ABC, 1971; "Love, American Style: Love and the Lovely Evening," ABC, 1972.
TV MOVIES AND MINISERIES: "Love, Hate, Love," ABC, 1971.

MULLAVEY, GREG

b. Buffalo, NY, September 10, 1939. Actor who played Tom, husband of Mary Hartman (Louise Lasser).
AS A REGULAR: "Mary Hartman, Mary Hartman," SYN, 1976-78; "Number 96," NBC, 1980-81; "Rituals," SYN, 1984-85.
AND: "Gomer Pyle, USMC: Sergeant Carter, Marine Baby Sitter," CBS, 1964; "The Fugitive: When the Wind Blows," ABC, 1965; "Combat!: Beneath the Ashes," ABC, 1965; "Gidget: Ring-a-Ding Dingbat," ABC, 1966; "Blue Light: How to Kill a Soldier," ABC, 1966; "Mission: Impossible: The Heir Apparent," CBS, 1968; "The Virginian: The Girl in the Shadows," NBC, 1969; "The Outside: A Lot of Muscle," NBC, 1969; "It Takes a Thief: The Great Chess Gambit," ABC, 1969; "Ironside: L'Chayim," NBC, 1969; "Petticoat Junction: How to Arrange a Marriage," CBS, 1970; "Medical Center: The Deceived," CBS, 1970; "Paris 7000: Ordeal," ABC, 1970; "The Most Deadly Game: Break-down," ABC, 1970; "The Mary Tyler Moore Show: Bob and Rhoda and Teddy and Mary," CBS, 1970; "The Mod Squad: The Hot, Hot Car," ABC, 1971; "Men at Law: Marathon," CBS, 1971; "Alias Smith and Jones: How to Rob a Bank in One Hard Lesson," ABC, 1971; "Gunsmoke: Ma Colter," CBS, 1971; "Medical Center: The Loser," CBS, 1971; "Wednesday Night Out," NBC, 1972; "Hawaii Five-O: Thanks for the Honeymoon," CBS, 1973; "Marcus Welby, M.D.: The Problem with Charlie," ABC, 1973; "The Streets of San Francisco: Deadline," ABC, 1973; "The Streets of San Francisco: Trail of Terror," ABC, 1975; "McCloud: Three Guns for New York," NBC, 1975; "Cross Wits," SYN, 1976; "Dinah!," SYN, 1976; "M*A*S*H: Major Ego," CBS, 1978; "Diff'rent Strokes: Football Father," NBC, 1980; "House Calls: Jailhouse Doc," CBS, 1980; "Card Sharks," NBC, 1980; "Magnum P.I.: A Sense of Doubt," CBS, 1983; "Cagney & Lacey: A Cry for Help," CBS, 1983; "Hardcastle and McCormick: D-Day," ABC, 1984; "The Fall Guy: Dead Ringer," ABC, 1985; "The Twilight Zone: A Little Peace and Quiet," CBS, 1985; "Hill Street Blues: Seoul on Ice," NBC, 1985; "Life with Lucy: Lucy Makes a Hit with John Ritter," ABC, 1986; "Matlock: Blind Justice," NBC, 1987.
TV MOVIES AND MINISERIES: "Companions in Nightmare," NBC, 1968; "Quarantined," ABC, 1970; "The Birdmen," CBS, 1971; "Cry Rape!," CBS, 1973; "The Disappearance of Flight 412," NBC, 1974; "Switch," CBS, 1975; "Having Babies," ABC, 1976; "Centennial," NBC, 1978-79; "Who Gets the Friends?," CBS, 1988; "Not Quite Human II," DIS, 1989; "The Hollywood Detective," USA, 1989.

MULLIGAN, RICHARD

b. Bronx, NY, November 13, 1932. Emmy-winning actor who played Bert Campbell on "Soap" and now seems settled in for a comfortable run as Dr. Harry Weston on "Empty Nest."
AS A REGULAR: "The Hero," NBC, 1966-67; "Diana," NBC, 1973-74; "Soap," ABC, 1977-81; "Reggie," ABC, 1983; "Empty Nest," NBC, 1988- .
AND: "Gunsmoke: Wonder," CBS, 1967; "I Dream of Jeannie: Around the World in 80 Blinks," NBC, 1969; "The Partridge Family: Why Did the Music Stop?," ABC, 1971; "Love, American Style: Love and the Jury," ABC, 1971; "The Partridge Family: The Diplomat," ABC, 1973; "Matt Helm: Pilot," ABC, 1975; "Medical Story: The Right to Die," NBC, 1975; "Doctors' Hospital: But Who Will Bless Thy Daughter Norah?," NBC, 1975; "Gibbsville: Saturday Night," NBC, 1976; "Little House on the Prairie: Soldier's Return," NBC, 1976; "The Love Boat: Going by the Book," ABC, 1978; "$weepstake$: Dewey and Harold and Sarah and Maggie," NBC, 1979; "Highway to Heaven: Basinger's New York," NBC, 1985; "The Twilight Zone: Night of the Meek," CBS, 1985; "The Twilight Zone: The Toys of Caliban," CBS, 1986; "J.J. Starbuck: The Blimpy That Yelled Blue," NBC, 1987; "The Golden Girls: Yokel Hero," NBC, 1988; "The Golden Girls: Sick and Tired," NBC, 1989; "The Golden Girls: Not Another Monday," NBC, 1989.
TV MOVIES AND MINISERIES: "Malibu," ABC, 1983; "Jealousy," ABC, 1984; "Poker Alice," CBS, 1987; "Gore Vidal's Lincoln," NBC, 1988.
* Emmies: 1980, 1989.

MUMY, BILLY

b. 1954. Freckled child actor who played Will Robinson on "Lost in Space."

AS A REGULAR: "Lost in Space," CBS, 1965-68; "Sunshine," NBC, 1975.

AND: "The Loretta Young Show: My Own Master," NBC, 1960; "The Loretta Young Show: The Lie," NBC, 1961; "The Twilight Zone: Long-Distance Call," CBS, 1961; "Alfred Hitchcock Presents: Bang, You're Dead," NBC, 1961; "The Twilight Zone: It's a Good Life," CBS, 1961; "G.E. Theatre: A Friendly Tribe," CBS, 1961; "Alfred Hitchcock Presents: The Door Without a Key," NBC, 1962; "Father of the Bride: Furnishing the Apartment," CBS, 1962; "Dr. Kildare: The Bronc Buster," NBC, 1962; "Walt Disney's Wonderful World of Color: Sammy the Way-Out Seal," NBC, 1962; "The Alfred Hitchcock Hour: House Guest," CBS, 1962; "The Twilight Zone: In Praise of Pip," CBS, 1963; "The Fugitive: Home Is the Hunted," ABC, 1964; "The Eleventh Hour: Sunday Father," NBC, 1964; "Walt Disney's Wonderful World of Color: A Taste of Melon," NBC, 1964; "The Adventures of Ozzie and Harriet: Rick's Old Printing Press," ABC, 1964; "Bewitched: A Vision of Sugar Plums," ABC, 1964; "The Munsters: Come Back Little Googie," CBS, 1965; "Bewitched: Junior Executive," ABC, 1965; "The Virginian: The Old Cowboy," NBC, 1965; "I Dream of Jeannie: Whatever Happened to Baby Custer?," NBC, 1965; "Lancer: The Kid," CBS, 1969; "The Rockford Files: Backlash of the Hunter," NBC, 1978; "Alfred Hitchcock Presents: Bang! You're Dead," NBC, 1985.

TV MOVIES AND MINISERIES: "Sunshine," NBC, 1973; "The Rockford Files," NBC, 1974.

* In "Bang! You're Dead," Mumy played a little boy who was toting around a loaded pistol; in the 1985 remake, he played a bit role.

MUNI, PAUL

b. Muni Weisenfreund, Lemburg, Ukraine, September 22, 1895; d. 1967. Celebrated film ("I Was a Fugitive From a Chain Gang") and stage actor, occasionally on TV.

AS A GUEST: "Ford Theatre: The People vs. Johnson," NBC, 1953; "G.E. Theatre: Letter From the Queen," CBS, 1956; "Playhouse 90: Last Clear Chance," CBS, 1958; "Saints and Sinners: A Shame for a Diamond Wedding," NBC, 1962.

MUNSEL, PATRICE

b. Spokane, WA, May 14, 1925. Operatic singer who did many TV guest shots and had her own show in the late fifties.

AS A REGULAR: "The Patrice Munsel Show," ABC, 1957-58.

AND: "The Buick Berle Show," NBC, 1952;

"Omnibus: The Merry Widow," CBS, 1954; "Naughty Marietta," NBC, 1955; "The Great Waltz," NBC, 1955; "The Walter Winchell Show," NBC, 1956; "Alcoa Hour: The Stingiest Man in Town," NBC, 1956; "Checkmate: The Gift," CBS, 1961; "Bell Telephone Hour: Much Ado About Music," NBC, 1961; "Home for the Holidays," NBC, 1961; "Play Your Hunch," NBC, 1962; "The Merv Griffin Show," NBC, 1962; "Perry Como's Kraft Music Hall," NBC, 1963; "The Red Skelton Hour," CBS, 1965; "The Mike Douglas Show," SYN, 1966; "The Wild Wild West: The Night of the Diva," CBS, 1969; "The Red Skelton Hour," CBS, 1969.

MURPHY, AUDIE

b. Kingston, TX, June 20, 1924; d. 1971. Heavily-decorated World War II veteran whose heroics led to a mildly successful screen and TV career.

AS A REGULAR: "Whispering Smith," NBC, 1961.

AND: "Suspicion: The Flight," NBC, 1957; "G.E. Theatre: Incident, CBS, 1958; "The Chevy Show," NBC, 1959; "Startime: The Man," NBC, 1960; "Here's Hollywood," NBC, 1961.

MURPHY, BEN

b. Jonesboro, AR, March 6, 1941. Generic TV hunk in standard-issue TV, except his role as Jed "Kid" Curry on "Alias Smith and Jones."

AS A REGULAR: "The Name of the Game," NBC, 1968-71; "Alias Smith and Jones," ABC, 1971-73; "Griff," ABC, 1973-74; "Gemini Man," NBC, 1976; "The Chisholms," CBS, 1979-80; "Lottery!," ABC, 1983-84; "Berrenger's," NBC, 1985.

AND: "It Takes a Thief: A Matter of Loyal Larceny," ABC, 1968; "The Virginian: The Orchard," NBC, 1968; "The Virginian: The Decision," NBC, 1968; "The Outsider: Tell It Like It Was ... and You're Dead," NBC, 1969; "Medical Center: His Brother's Keeper," CBS, 1970; "The Mod Squad: A Far Away Place So Near," ABC, 1970; "Kojak: A Summer Madness," CBS, 1976; "The Love Boat: Best of Friends," ABC, 1979; "$weepstake$: Cowboy, Linda and Angie, Mark," NBC, 1979; "The Love Boat: The Maid Cleans Up," ABC, 1983; "The Love Boat: Two Tails of a City," ABC, 1984; "Hotel: Fantasies," ABC, 1984; "Finder of Lost Loves: Losing Touch," ABC, 1984; "The Love Boat: The Wager," ABC, 1984; "MacGruder and Loud: The Odds Favor Death," ABC, 1985; "Scarecrow and Mrs. King: A Lovely Little Affair," CBS, 1985; "Murder, She Wrote: Reflections of the Mind," CBS, 1985; "The Love Boat: Miss Mom," ABC, 1986.

TV MOVIES AND MINISERIES: "Alias Smith and Jones," ABC, 1971; "The Letters," ABC, 1973; "Runaway!," ABC, 1973; "Heat Wave," ABC,

1974; "This Is the West That Was," NBC, 1974; "Gemini Man," NBC, 1976; "Bridger," ABC, 1976; "The Chisholms," CBS, 1979; "Uncommon Valor," CBS, 1983; "The Cradle Will Fall," CBS, 1983; "Stark: Mirror Image," CBS, 1986.

MURPHY, EDDIE
b. *Brooklyn NY, April 3, 1961.* Comedian.
AS A REGULAR: "Saturday Night Live," NBC, 1981-84.
AND: "Late Night with David Letterman," NBC, 1988; "The Arsenio Hall Show," SYN, 1988; "What's Alan Watching?," CBS, 1989; "Saturday Night Live's 15th Anniversary," NBC, 1989.
AS PRODUCER: "What's Alan Watching?," CBS, 1989.

MURPHY, ERIN & DIANE
b. *1964.* Twins who played Tabitha on "Bewitched."
AS REGULARS: "Bewitched," ABC, 1966-72.

MURPHY, GEORGE
b. *New Haven, CT, July 4, 1902.* Dancer and actor who went into politics, becoming a one-term U.S. Senator from California.
AS A REGULAR: "MGM Parade," ABC, 1955-56.
AND: "The Thin Man: The Scene Stealer," NBC, 1958; "Westinghouse Desilu Playhouse: So Tender, So Profane," CBS, 1959; "The Jack Paar Show," NBC, 1960; "New Comedy Showcase: You're Only Young Twice," CBS, 1960; "Here's Hollywood," NBC, 1960.

MURPHY, MICHAEL
b. *Los Angeles, CA, May 5, 1949.* Actor in movies ("An Unmarried Woman") and TV; he played presidential candidate Tanner on a satirical HBO miniseries.
AS A REGULAR: "Two Marriages," ABC, 1983-84; "Hard Copy," CBS, 1987.
AND: "The Man From UNCLE: The Love Affair," NBC, 1965.
TV MOVIES AND MINISERIES: "The Crooked Hearts," ABC, 1972; "The Autobiography of Miss Jane Pittman," CBS, 1974; "I Love You, Goodbye," ABC, 1974; "Tanner '88," HBO, 1988; "The Caine Mutiny Court-Martial," CBS, 1988.

MURRAY, ARTHUR
b. *New York City, NY, April 4, 1895, d. 1991;*
& KATHRYN
b. *Jersey City, NJ, 1906.* Dancing instructors and TV variety show hosts.
AS REGULARS: "Arthur Murray Party," ABC, 1950; DUM, 1950-51; ABC, 1951-52; CBS, 1952; DUM, 1952-53; CBS, 1953; NBC, 1953-55; CBS, 1956; NBC, 1957; 1958-60.
AND: "The Steve Allen Show," NBC, 1956;

"Arthur Murray Special," NBC, 1957; "American Bandstand," ABC, 1961; "The Merv Griffin Show," SYN, 1976; "The Merv Griffin Show," SYN, 1980.

MURRAY, BILL
b. *Evanston, IL, September 21, 1950.* A nut, a knucklehead, a zany lame-brained comic.
AS A REGULAR AND WRITER: "Saturday Night Live," NBC, 1977-80.
AND: "Saturday Night Live," NBC, 1981; "Late Night with David Letterman," NBC, 1982; "Saturday Night Live," NBC, 1987.
* Murray was a guest on the first "Late Night with David Letterman."
* Emmies: 1977.

MURRAY, DON
b. *Hollywood, CA, July 31, 1929.* Fifties screen star who played Sid Fairgate on "Knots Landing."
AS A REGULAR: "Made in America," CBS, 1964; "The Outcasts," ABC, 1968-69; "Knots Landing," CBS, 1979-81; "The Magical World of Disney: Brand New Life," NBC, 1989-90; "Sons and Daughters," CBS, 1990- .
AND: "Kraft Television Theatre: The Music Master," NBC, 1952; "Kraft Television Theatre: Mr. Lazarus," NBC, 1952; "The Skin of Our Teeth," NBC, 1955; "Philco TV Playhouse: A Man Is Ten Feet Tall," NBC, 1955; "U.S. Steel Hour: Moment of Courage," CBS, 1956; "The Ed Sullivan Show," CBS, 1957; "Playhouse 90: For I Have Loved Strangers," CBS, 1957; "Du Pont Show of the Month: The Hasty Heart," CBS, 1958; "Art Linkletter's House Party," CBS, 1959; "Du Pont Show of the Month: Billy Budd," CBS, 1959; "Hallmark Hall of Fame: Winterset," NBC, 1959; "Hedda Hopper's Hollywood," NBC, 1960; "Playhouse 90: Alas, Babylon," CBS, 1960; "Here's Hollywood," NBC, 1960; "The Match Game," NBC, 1964; "The Mike Douglas Show," SYN, 1967; "The Steve Allen Show," SYN, 1970; "The Wonderful World of Disney: Justin Morgan Had a Horse," NBC, 1972; "Love Story: The Roller Coaster Stops Here," NBC, 1973; "Police Story: The Big Walk," NBC, 1973; "Orson Welles' Great Mysteries: The Power of Lea," SYN, 1974; "Amy Prentiss: The Desperate World of Jane Doe," NBC, 1974; "Police Story: Headhunter," NBC, 1975.
TV MOVIES AND MINISERIES: "The Borgia Stick," NBC, 1967; "Daughter of the Mind," ABC, 1969; "The Intruders," NBC, 1970; "Cotter," ABC, 1972; "The Girl on the Late, Late Show," NBC, 1974; "The Sex Symbol," ABC, 1974; "A Girl Named Sooner," NBC, 1975; "Rainbow," NBC, 1978; "Crisis in Mid-Air," CBS, 1979; "The Boy Who Drank Too Much," CBS, 1980; "Quarterback Princess," CBS, 1983; "A Touch of Scandal," CBS, 1984;

"Thursday's Child," CBS, 1983; "Something in Common," CBS, 1986; "Stillwatch," CBS, 1987; "The Stepford Children," NBC, 1987; "Mistress," CBS, 1987.

MURRAY, JAN

b. October 4, 1917. Borscht-belt comic who was a busy fellow in the fifties and sixties.

AS A REGULAR: "Songs for Sale," CBS, 1950-51; "Sing It Again," CBS, 1951; "Go Lucky," CBS, 1951; "Blind Date," DUM, 1953; "Dollar a Second," DUM, 1953-54; NBC, 1954; ABC, 1954-55; NBC, 1955; ABC, 1955-56; NBC, 1957; "Jan Murray Time," NBC, 1955; "Treasure Hunt," ABC, 1956-57, NBC, 1957-60; "The Jan Murray Show (Charge Account)," NBC, 1960-62; "Chain Letter," NBC, 1966.

AND: "Jerry Lewis Special," NBC, 1957; "The Ed Sullivan Show," CBS, 1959; "The Ed Sullivan Show," CBS, 1960; "The Steve Allen Plymouth Show," NBC, 1960; "Celebrity Talent Scouts," CBS, 1960; "The Jack Paar Show," NBC, 1960; "The Garry Moore Show," CBS, 1960; "Dick Powell's Zane Grey Theatre: The Empty Shell," CBS, 1961; "Here's Hollywood," NBC, 1961; "Dr. Kildare: A Million-Dollar Property," NBC, 1961; "Car 54, Where Are You?: Boom, Boom, Boom," NBC, 1962; "The Ed Sullivan Show," CBS, 1962; "To Tell the Truth," CBS, 1963; "The Tonight Show Starring Johnny Carson," NBC, 1963; "To Tell the Truth," CBS, 1964; "The Joey Bishop Show: In This Corner, Jan Murray," CBS, 1964; "Burke's Law: Who Killed Mother Goose?," ABC, 1964; "PDQ," NBC, 1965; "ABC Nightlife," ABC, 1965; "PDQ," NBC, 1966; "The Lucy Show: Lucy and the Soap Opera," CBS, 1966; "The Man From UNCLE: The Hula Doll Affair," NBC, 1967; "The Pat Boone Show," NBC, 1967; "Hollywood Squares," NBC, 1968; "The Joey Bishop Show," ABC, 1968; "Hollywood Squares," NBC, 1969; "Funny You Should Ask," ABC, 1969; "It Takes Two," NBC, 1970; "The Name of the Game: The Battle of Gannon's Bridge," NBC, 1970; "Love, American Style: Love and the Happy Couple," ABC, 1971; "Hollywood Squares," NBC, 1972; "Mannix: Shadow Play," CBS, 1973; "Kolchak, the Night Stalker: The Vampire," ABC, 1974; "Joys," NBC, 1976; "Ellery Queen: Caesar's Last Siege," NBC, 1976; "The Practice: Oh Brother," NBC, 1977; "Hardcastle and McCormick: What's So Funny?," ABC, 1985.

TV MOVIES AND MINISERIES: "Roll, Freddy, Roll," ABC, 1974.

MURRAY, KEN

b. Don Court, Nyack, NY, July 14, 1903; d. 1988. Comic whose home movies of Hollywood stars made him a popular guest on TV shows.

AS A REGULAR: "The Ken Murray Show," CBS,

1950-53; "The Judy Garland Show," CBS, 1964.

AND: "The Ford Show," NBC, 1956; "Do You Trust Your Wife?," CBS, 1957; "The Ed Sullivan Show," CBS, 1960; "Frances Langford Special," NBC, 1960; "Art Linkletter's House Party," CBS, 1960; "Here's Hollywood," NBC, 1961; "Death Valley Days: Gamble with Death," SYN, 1961; "Here's Hollywood," NBC, 1962; "The du Pont Show: Hollywood—My Home Town," NBC, 1962; "The Ed Sullivan Show," CBS, 1962; "Burke's Law: Who Killed Beau Sparrow?," ABC, 1963; "The Greatest Show on Earth: The Show Must Go On—to Orange City," ABC, 1964; "Art Linkletter's House Party," CBS, 1965; "The Bing Crosby Show: Are Parents People?," ABC, 1965; "The Man From UNCLE: The Fiddlesticks Affair," NBC, 1965.

MURROW, EDWARD R.

b. Greensboro, NC, April 25, 1908; d. 1965. Legendary TV journalist who began in radio; after various quarrels with CBS brass, he left to work for the Kennedy administration. A lifetime smoker who often had cigarette in hand when he visited notables on "Person to Person," he died of cancer.

AS A REGULAR: "See It Now," CBS, 1951-58; "Person to Person," CBS, 1953-59; "Small World," CBS, 1958-60; "CBS Reports," CBS, 1959-61.

AND: "Years of Crisis," CBS, 1956; "The Ed Sullivan Show," CBS, 1956; "The Jackie Gleason Show," CBS, 1957; "Studio One: The Night America Trembled," CBS, 1957; "Years of Crisis, 1949-1959," CBS, 1958; "Lost Class of '59," CBS, 1959; "The Press and the People: The Responsibility of TV," CBS, 1959.

* Emmies: 1954, 1956, 1957, 1958.

MUSANTE, TONY

b. Bridgeport, CT, June 30, 1936. Intense actor who played undercover cop Dave Toma and My Lai officer Lt. William Calley on a special.

AS A REGULAR: "Toma," ABC, 1973-74.

AND: "The du Pont Show: Ride with Terror," NBC, 1963; "Bob Hope Chrysler Theatre: A Wind of Hurricane Force," NBC, 1964; "The Alfred Hitchcock Hour: Memo From Purgatory," NBC, 1964; "Trials of O'Brien: Bargain Day on the Street of Regret," CBS, 1965; "The Fugitive: The One That Got Away," ABC, 1966; "Marcus Welby, M.D.: The Tall Tree," ABC, 1973; "ABC Theatre: Judgment: The Court-Martial of Lt. William Calley," ABC, 1974; "Police Story: Fathers and Sons," NBC, 1974; "The Rockford Files: Charlie Harris at Large," NBC, 1975; "Medical Story: The God Syndrome," NBC, 1975; "Police Story: The Other Side of the Badge," NBC, 1976; "MacGruder and Loud: Pilot," ABC, 1985; "The Equalizer: Pretenders,"

CBS, 1986; "Jesse Hawkes: Pilot," CBS, 1989.
TV MOVIES AND MINISERIES: "Toma," ABC, 1973; "The Desperate Miles," ABC, 1975; "My Husband Is Missing," NBC, 1978.

MUSE, CLARENCE
b. Baltimore, MD, October 7, 1889; d. 1979. Actor who played Sam the piano player in a series version of "Casablanca."
AS A REGULAR: "Warner Bros. Presents Casablanca," ABC, 1955-56.
AND: "Four Star Playhouse: Bourbon Street," CBS, 1954; "Daktari: Toto the Great," CBS, 1968.
TV MOVIES AND MINISERIES: "A Dream for Christmas," CBS, 1973.

MUSIC, LORENZO
b. Brooklyn, NY, May 2, 1937. Comic writer and actor; he played Carlton the doorman on "Rhoda."
AS A REGULAR: "Rhoda," CBS, 1974-78; "The Lorenzo and Henrietta Music Show," SYN, 1978-79.
AND: "Carlton, Your Doorman," CBS, 1979.
AS WRITER: "The Mary Tyler Moore Show," CBS, 1970-71; "The Bob Newhart Show," CBS, 1972-73.
* Emmies: 1980.

MUSTIN, BURT
b. Pittsburgh, PA, February 8, 1884; d. 1977. Retired car salesman who took to acting in 1950; best known as Gus the kindly fireman on "Leave It to Beaver" and Arthur Lanson on "Phyllis."
AS A REGULAR: "Date with the Angels," ABC, 1957-58; "Leave It to Beaver," CBS, 1957-58; ABC, 1958-63; "The Andy Griffith Show," CBS, 1960-67; "Ichabod and Me," CBS, 1961-62; "The Funny Side," NBC, 1971; "Phyllis," CBS, 1976-77.
AND: "Abbott and Costello Show: Little Old Lady," CBS, 1952; "Father Knows Best: Grandpa Jim's Rejuvenation," CBS, 1954; "Our Miss Brooks: Safari O'Toole," CBS, 1954; "The Jane Wyman Show: Married to a Stranger," NBC, 1957; "Restless Gun: Pressing Engagement," NBC, 1958; "The Gale Storm Show: Happily Unmarried," CBS, 1959; "Mr. Lucky: The Leadville Kid Gang," CBS, 1960; "The Many Loves of Dobie Gillis: Here Comes the Groom,"

CBS, 1960; "G.E. Theatre: Adams' Apples," CBS, 1960; "Harrigan and Son: Pipes are Pipes," ABC, 1960; "The Twilight Zone: Night of the Meek," CBS, 1960; "77 Sunset Strip: Mr. Bailey's Honeymoon," ABC, 1962; "My Three Sons: Kibitzers," ABC, 1962; "The Twilight Zone: Kick the Can," CBS, 1962; "The Beverly Hillbillies: Another Neighbor," CBS, 1963; "The Many Loves of Dobie Gillis: Where Is Thy Sting?" CBS, 1963; "The Dick Van Dyke Show: Very Old Shoes, Very Old Rice," CBS, 1964; "The Fugitive: Nicest Fella You'd Ever Want to Meet," ABC, 1965; "The Virginian: Farewell to Honesty," NBC, 1965; "Get Smart: Dear Diary," NBC, 1966; "Batman: An Egg Grows in Gotham/The Yegg Foes in Gotham," ABC, 1966; "Camp Runamuck: Senior Citizens," NBC, 1966; "Gomer Pyle, USMC: Gomer Goes Home," CBS, 1968; "Nanny and the Professor: The Great Broadcast of 1936," ABC, 1970; "Mayberry RFD: Goober the Hero," CBS, 1971; "The Mary Tyler Moore Show: The Second-Story Story," CBS, 1971; "All in the Family: Archie is Worried About His Job," CBS, 1971; "Rowan & Martin's Laugh-In," NBC, 1972; "Love, American Style: Love and the Return of Raymond," ABC, 1973; "Sanford & Son: Home Sweet Home for the Aged," NBC, 1973; "The Brady Bunch: Bobby's Hero," ABC, 1973; "All in the Family: Edith Finds an Old Man," CBS, 1973; "Here's Lucy: Lucy and Joan Rivers Do Jury Duty," CBS, 1973; "All in the Family: Archie Feels Left Out," CBS, 1974; "Love, American Style: Love and the Parent's Sake," ABC, 1974; "The Streets of San Francisco: Winterkill," ABC, 1974; "Rhoda: Honeymoon," CBS, 1974; "All in the Family: Mike Makes His Move," CBS, 1975; "All in the Family: Archie's Weighty Problem," CBS, 1976.
TV MOVIES AND MINISERIES: "The Over-the-Hill Gang Rides Again," ABC, 1970. "The Moneychangers," NBC, 1976.

MYERSON, BESS
b. Bronx, NY, July 16, 1924. Miss America 1945, game-show regular; in 1988 she was acquitted of bribery charges.
AS A REGULAR: "The Big Payoff," NBC, 1952-53; CBS, 1953-59; "The Name's the Same," ABC, 1954-55; "I've Got a Secret," CBS, 1958-67; "Candid Camera," CBS, 1966-67.
AND: "The Ed Sullivan Show," CBS, 1960; "Here's Hollywood," NBC, 1962; "To Tell the Truth," CBS, 1964.

N

NABORS, JIM

b. Sylacauga, AL, June 12, 1932. Comic actor and singer who was Gomer Pyle, USMC and an immensely popular TV presence during the sixties.

AS A REGULAR: "The Andy Griffith Show," CBS, 1963-64; "Gomer Pyle, USMC," CBS, 1964-69; "The Jim Nabors Hour," CBS, 1969-71; "The Lost Saucer," ABC, 1975-76; "The Jim Nabors Show," SYN, 1978-79.

AND: "The New Steve Allen Show," ABC, 1961; "Mr. Smith Goes to Washington: Grand Ol' Opry," ABC, 1963; "Mr. Smith Goes to Washington: To Be or Not to Be," ABC, 1963; "Art Linkletter's House Party," CBS, 1964; "ABC Nightlife," ABC, 1965; "The Andy Griffith, Don Knotts, Jim Nabors Special," CBS, 1965; "Art Linkletter's Hollywood Talent Scouts," CBS, 1966; "The Lucy Show: Lucy Gets Caught in the Draft," CBS, 1966; "The Carol Burnett Show," CBS, 1967; "Girlfriends and Nabors," CBS, 1968; "The Steve Allen Show," SYN, 1968; "The Carol Burnett Show," CBS, 1968; "The Don Rickles Show," ABC, 1969; "The Carol Burnett Show," CBS, 1969; "The Carol Burnett Show," CBS, 1970; "The Carol Burnett Show," CBS, 1971; "The Carol Burnett Show," CBS, 1972; "The Sonny and Cher Comedy Hour," CBS, 1973; "The Mike Douglas Show," SYN, 1973; "The Rookies: Down Home Boy," ABC, 1973; "Funshine Saturday Sneak Peek," ABC, 1975; "The Merv Griffin Show," SYN, 1975; "The Love Boat: Mr. Popularity," ABC, 1977; "Hollywood Squares," SYN, 1980; "The Love Boat: I Remember Helen," ABC, 1982.

* See also Jack Benny.

NADER, GEORGE

b. Los Angeles, CA, October 19, 1921. Actor in action roles, busiest in the fifties.

AS A REGULAR: "Ellery Queen," NBC, 1958-59; "The Man and the Challenge," NBC, 1959-60; "Shannon," SYN, 1961-62.

AND: "Fireside Theatre: The Lady Wears a Star," NBC, 1953; "Jewelers Showcase: Heart's Desire," CBS, 1953; "Your Play Time: The Tin Bridge," CBS, 1953; "The Loretta Young Show: Oh, My Aching Heart," NBC, 1954; "Stage 7: The Legacy," CBS, 1955; "Lux Video Theatre: The Glass Web," NBC, 1956; "Lux Video Theatre: One Way Street," NBC, 1957; "The Steve Allen Show," NBC, 1957; "Climax!: The Stranger Within," CBS, 1957; "Laramie: .45 Calibre," NBC, 1960; "The Loretta Young Show: The Choice," NBC, 1961; "The Andy Griffith Show: The New Doctor," CBS, 1961; "Here's Hollywood," NBC, 1961; "Alfred Hitchcock Presents: Self-Defense," NBC, 1961; "Alfred Hitchcock Presents: Where Beauty Lies," NBC, 1962; "Burke's Law: Who Killed the Jackpot?," ABC, 1965; "Owen Marshall, Counselor at Law: Warlock at Mach 3," ABC, 1972; "The FBI: The Game of Chess," ABC, 1972.

NAISH, J. CARROL

b. New York City, NY, January 21, 1900; d. 1973. Actor who specialized in dialects, playing an Italian in "Life with Luigi," Charlie Chan and an Indian in "Guestward Ho!"

AS A REGULAR: "Life with Luigi," CBS, 1952; "The Adventures of Charlie Chan," SYN, 1957-58; "Guestward Ho!," ABC, 1960-61.

AND: "Westinghouse Desilu Playhouse: My Father, the Fool," CBS, 1958; "Restless Gun: Red Blood of Courage," NBC, 1958; "Cimarron City: The Bloodline, NBC, 1959; "Wagon Train: The Old Man Charvanaugh Story," NBC, 1959; "Christophers: Some Facts on John Witherspoon," SYN, 1959; "The Untouchables: The Joe Bucco Story," ABC, 1959; "The Untouchables: The Noise of Death," ABC, 1960; "Wagon Train: The Benjamin Burns Story," NBC, 1960; "Route 66: And Make Thunder His Tribute," CBS, 1963; "Burke's Law: Who Killed Super Sleuth?," ABC, 1964; "I Dream of Jeannie: Djinn and Water," NBC, 1965; "The Man From UNCLE: The Super-Colossal Affair," NBC, 1966; "Green Acres: His Honor," CBS, 1967; "Bob Hope Special: For Love or $$$," NBC, 1968; "Get Smart: The Secret of Sam Vittorio," NBC, 1968.

TV MOVIES AND MINISERIES: "The Hanged Man," NBC, 1964; "Cutter's Trail," CBS, 1970.

NAMATH, JOE

b. Beaver Falls, PA, May 31, 1943. Football quarterback who turned to acting.

AS A REGULAR: "The Waverly Wonders," NBC, 1978.

AND: "Here's Lucy: Lucy and Joe Namath," CBS, 1972; "The Flip Wilson Show," NBC, 1973; "The Brady Bunch: Mail Order Hero," ABC, 1973; "The Love Boat: Rent-a-Romeo," ABC, 1980; "The Toni Tennille Show," SYN, 1980; "The Love Boat: Then There Were Two," ABC, 1981; "The A-Team: Quarterback Sneak," NBC, 1986; "Kate & Allie: The Namath of the Game," CBS, 1988; "Later with Bob Costas," NBC, 1989; "The Pat Sajak Show," CBS, 1989.

NAPIER, ALAN

b. *Alan Napier-Clavering, England, January 7, 1903; d. 1988.* Tall, slender actor who played Alfred, butler to Batman.

AS A REGULAR:"Don't Call Me Charlie!," NBC, 1962-63; "Batman," ABC, 1966-68.

AND: "The 20th Century-Fox Hour: Operation Cicero," CBS, 1956; "The Loretta Young Show: The Bronte Story," NBC, 1956; "Alfred Hitchcock Presents: I Killed the Count," CBS, 1957; "Matinee Theatre: The Little Minister," NBC, 1957; "G.E. Theatre: Mischief at Bandy Leg," CBS, 1957; "The Detectives Starring Robert Taylor: The Bait," ABC, 1959; "Shirley Temple's Storybook: Kim," NBC, 1960; "Thriller: The Purple Room," NBC, 1960; "Adventures in Paradise: Daughter of Illusion," ABC, 1960; "Thriller: Hay-Fork and Bill-Hook," NBC, 1961; "Thriller: Dark Legacy," NBC, 1961; "Assassination Plot at Teheran," ABC, 1961; "The Bob Cummings Show: North by Southeast," CBS, 1962; "The Third Man: Dark Island," SYN, 1962; "Checkmate: A Chant of Silence," CBS, 1962; "Alcoa Premiere: Impact of an Execution," ABC, 1963; "The Twilight Zone: Passage on the Lady Anne," CBS, 1963; "The Breaking Point: So Many Pretty Girls, So Little Time," ABC, 1964; "The Rogues: Money Is for Burning," NBC, 1965; "Laredo: The Land Grabbers," NBC, 1965; "Daktari: The Killer Lion," CBS, 1966; "The Beverly Hillbillies: The Clampetts in London," CBS, 1967; "Family Affair: Oh, to Be in England," CBS, 1969; "Ironside: The Last Cotillion," NBC, 1974.

TV MOVIES AND MINISERIES: "Crime Club," CBS, 1973; "The Bastard," SYN, 1978.

NARZ, JACK

b. *Louisville, KY, November 13, 1922.* Emcee.

AS A REGULAR:"Life with Elizabeth," SYN, 1953-55; "Kollege of Musical Knowledge," NBC, 1954; "The Bob Crosby Show," CBS, 1957; "The Gisele MacKenzie Show," NBC, 1957-58; "The Ford Show," NBC, 1958-60; "Dotto," CBS, 1958; NBC, 1958; "Top Dollar," CBS, 1959; "Video Village," CBS, 1960-61; "Seven Keys," ABC, 1961-64; "I'll Bet," NBC, 1965; "Beat the Clock," SYN, 1969; "Concentration," SYN, 1973-79; "Now You See It," CBS, 1974-75.

AND: "The Price Is Right," NBC, 1960; "The Farmer's Daughter: My Papa the Politician," ABC, 1966.

NASH, BRIAN

b. *Glendale, CA, 1956.* Child actor who played Joel Nash on "Please Don't Eat the Daisies."

AS A REGULAR:"Mickey," ABC, 1964-65; "Please Don't Eat the Daisies," NBC, 1965-67.

AND: "My Three Sons: High on the Hog," ABC,

1963; "Grindl: Active Retirement," NBC, 1964; "The Dick Van Dyke Show: Brother, Can You Spare $2,500?," CBS, 1965; "Bewitched: There's No Witch Like an Old Witch," ABC, 1965; "Many Happy Returns: The Woodsman," CBS, 1965; "The Munsters: Yes Galen, There Is a Herman," CBS, 1965; "The Flying Nun: A Young Man with a Coronet," ABC, 1967; "The Virginian: Star Crossed," NBC, 1967; "The Brady Bunch: Brace Yourself," ABC, 1970.

NATWICK, MILDRED

b. *Baltimore, MD, June 19, 1908.* Actress of film, stage and TV; she won an Emmy as crime-solving Gwendolyn Snoop.

AS A REGULAR:"The Snoop Sisters," NBC, 1973-74; "Little Women," NBC, 1979.

AND: "Suspense: The Horizontal Man," CBS, 1950; "Lights Out: The Queen Is Dead," NBC, 1950; "Philco TV Playhouse: The Tempest of Tick Creek," NBC, 1952; "Armstrong Circle Theatre: The Marmalade Scandal," NBC, 1953; "Suspense: The Suitor," CBS, 1953; "Tales of Tomorrow: Ink," ABC, 1953; "Campbell TV Soundstage: The Almighty Dollar," NBC, 1954; "Kraft Television Theatre: Mr. Simmons," ABC, 1954; "U.S. Steel Hour: A Garden in the Sea," ABC, 1954; "Studio One: Uncle Ed and Circumstances," CBS, 1955; "Ford Star Jubilee: Blithe Spirit," CBS, 1956; "Studio One: Always Welcome," CBS, 1956; "Alfred Hitchcock Presents: The Perfect Murder," CBS, 1956; "The Loretta Young Show: Hapless Holiday," NBC, 1956; "Kaiser Aluminum Hour: Antigone," NBC, 1956; "Playhouse 90: Eloise," CBS, 1956; "Kraft Television Theatre: The Big Heist," NBC, 1957; "Alfred Hitchcock Presents: Miss Bracegirdle Does Her Duty," CBS, 1958; "Play of the Week: Waltz of the Toreadors," SYN, 1960; "Naked City: Take and Put," ABC, 1961; "Hallmark Hall of Fame: Arsenic and Old Lace," NBC, 1962; "The Most Deadly Game: I Said the Sparrow," ABC, 1971; "The House Without a Christmas Tree," CBS, 1972; "The Thanksgiving Treasure," CBS, 1973; "McMillan and Wife: Love, Honor and Swindle," NBC, 1975; "The Easter Promise," CBS, 1975; "McMillan and Wife: Greed," NBC, 1975; "Addie and the King of Hearts," CBS, 1976; "Family: A Right and Proper Good Life," ABC, 1976; "The Bob Newhart Show: A Girl in Her Twenties," CBS, 1977; "Alice: Vera's Aunt Agatha," CBS, 1980; "The Love Boat: Marriage of Convenience," ABC, 1980; "Hardcastle and McCormick: Hardcastle, Hardcastle, Hardcastle and McCormick," ABC, 1985; "Murder, She Wrote: Murder in the Electric Cathedral," CBS, 1986.

TV MOVIES AND MINISERIES: "Do Not Fold, Spindle or Mutilate," ABC, 1971; "The Snoop Sisters," NBC, 1972; "Money to Burn," ABC, 1973; "Maid in America," CBS, 1982; "Deadly Deception," CBS, 1987.

* Emmies: 1974.

NAUGHTON, DAVID

b. Hartford, CT, February 13, 1951. Fresh-faced actor who sang and danced in Dr. Pepper "I'm a Pepper" commercials.

AS A REGULAR: "Makin' It," ABC, 1979; "At Ease," ABC, 1983; "My Sister Sam," CBS, 1986-88.

AND: "Murder, She Wrote: The Wearing of the Green," CBS, 1988.

TV MOVIES AND MINISERIES: "Getting Physical," CBS, 1984; "The Goddess of Love," NBC, 1988.

NAUGHTON, JAMES

b. Middletown, CT, December 6, 1945.

AS A REGULAR: "Faraday and Company," NBC, 1973-74; "The Planet of the Apes," CBS, 1974; "Making the Grade," CBS, 1982; "Trauma Center," ABC, 1983; "Raising Miranda," CBS, 1988.

AND: "Barnaby Jones: Voice in the Night," CBS, 1976; "Who's the Boss?: Custody," ABC, 1985.

TV MOVIES AND MINISERIES: "F. Scott Fitzgerald and The Last of the Belles," ABC, 1973; "The First 36 Hours of Dr. Durant," ABC, 1975; "The Bunker," CBS, 1981; "Parole," CBS, 1982; "Last of the Great Survivors," CBS, 1984; "Between the Darkness and the Dawn," NBC, 1985; "Sins of Innocence," CBS, 1986; "Necessity," CBS, 1988.

NEAL, PATRICIA

b. Packard, KY, January 20, 1926. Talented, Oscar-winning actress ("Hud") who worked her way back from a 1965 stroke that could have devastated her career.

AS A GUEST: "Goodyear TV Playhouse: Spring Reunion," NBC, 1954; "Studio One: A Handful of Diamonds," CBS, 1954; "Omnibus: Salome," CBS, 1955; "Playhouse 90: The Playroom," CBS, 1957; "Suspicion: Someone Is After Me," NBC, 1958; "Playhouse 90: The Gentleman from Seventh Avenue," CBS, 1958; "Studio One: Tide of Corruption," CBS, 1958; "Pursuit: The Silent Night," CBS, 1958; "Play of the Week: Strindberg on Love," SYN, 1960; "Play of the Week: The Magic and the Loss," SYN, 1961; "Special for Women: Mother and Daughter," NBC, 1961; "Checkmate: The Yacht Club Gang," CBS, 1962; "The Untouchables: The Maggie Storm Story," ABC, 1962; "Westinghouse Presents: That's Where the Town's Going," CBS, 1962; "Ben Casey: My Enemy Is a Bright Green Sparrow," ABC, 1963; "Espionage: The Weakling," NBC, 1963; "Ghost Story: Time of Terror," NBC, 1972; "Kung Fu: Blood of the Dragon," ABC, 1974; "G.E. Theatre: Things in Their Season," CBS, 1974; "Little House on the Prairie: Remember Me," NBC, 1975; "Movin'

On: Prosperity #1," NBC, 1975; "Glitter: Premiere," ABC, 1984.

TV MOVIES AND MINISERIES: "The Homecoming," CBS, 1971; "Things in Their Season," CBS, 1974; "Hallmark Hall of Fame: Eric," NBC, 1975; "The Bastard," SYN, 1978; "Shattered Vows," NBC, 1984.

* Neal's story was dramatized in a 1981 TV movie with Glenda Jackson.

NEILL, NOEL

b. Minneapolis, MN. Actress who played Lois Lane on "The Adventures of Superman."

AS A REGULAR: "The Adventures of Superman," SYN, 1951-57.

NELSON, BARRY

b. Barry Neilsen, San Francisco, CA, April 16, 1920. Leading man of stage and TV; he played James Bond in "Casino Royale" on "Climax!"

AS A REGULAR: "The Hunter," CBS, 1952; "My Favorite Husband," CBS, 1953-55.

AND: "Suspense: My Old Man's Badge," CBS, 1950; "Suspense: The Gentleman From America," CBS, 1950; "Starlight Theatre: The Roman Kid," CBS, 1950; "Climax!: Casino Royale," CBS, 1954; "Schlitz Playhouse of Stars: The Uninhibited Female," CBS, 1955; "Screen Directors Playhouse: Every Man Has Two Wives," NBC, 1955; "Producers Showcase: Happy Birthday," NBC, 1956; "Climax!: The Push-Button Giant," CBS, 1958; "Lux Playhouse: Drive a Desert Road," CBS, 1958; "Alfred Hitchcock Presents: The Waxwork," CBS, 1959; "To Tell the Truth," CBS, 1962; "To Tell the Truth," CBS, 1963; "The Match Game," NBC, 1963; "The du Pont Show: The Bachelor Game," NBC, 1963; "Ben Casey: My Love, My Love," ABC, 1963; "To Tell the Truth," CBS, 1964; "Bob Hope Chrysler Theatre: Wake Up, Darling," NBC, 1964; "The Alfred Hitchcock Hour: Anyone for Murder?," CBS, 1964; "Special for Women: Just a Housewife," ABC, 1965; "Password," CBS, 1965; "Password," CBS, 1966; "To Tell the Truth," CBS, 1967; "Heaven Help Us," CBS, 1967; "Password," CBS, 1967; "Personality," NBC, 1968; "CBS Playhouse: Secrets," CBS, 1968; "The Name of the Game: Break Out to a Fast Buck," NBC, 1969; "The FBI: Tug-of-War," ABC, 1969; "My Wives Jane," CBS, 1971; "Longstreet: Spell Legacy Like Death," ABC, 1972; "Owen Marshall, Counselor at Law: A Piece of God," ABC, 1972; "Circle of Fear: Doorway to Death," NBC, 1973; "Is There a Doctor in the House?," NBC, 1974; "Salvage I: Golden Orbit," ABC, 1979; "Taxi: Mr. Personalities," ABC, 1981; "Here's Boomer: The Prince and the Boomer," NBC, 1981; "Magnum, P.I.: Tropical Madness," CBS, 1982; "Murder, She Wrote: Mourning Among the Wisterias," CBS, 1988.

TV MOVIES AND MINISERIES: "The Borgia Stick," NBC, 1967; "Seven in Darkness," ABC, 1969; "Climb an Angry Mountain," NBC, 1972; "Washington: Behind Closed Doors," ABC, 1977.

NELSON, CRAIG T.

b. Spokane, WA, April 4, 1946. Former comedy writer who's also an exceptional dramatic actor; he plays Hayden Fox on "Coach."

AS A REGULAR:"Chicago Story," NBC, 1982; "Call to Glory," ABC, 1984-85; "Coach," ABC, 1989- .

AND: "Taxi: The Great Race," ABC, 1979; "The White Shadow: Christmas Story," CBS, 1980; "WKRP in Cincinnati: Out to Lunch," CBS, 1981.

TV MOVIES AND MINISERIES: "The Chicago Story," NBC, 1981; "Murder in Texas," NBC, 1981; "The Ted Kennedy Jr. Story," NBC, 1986.

AS WRITER: "The Tim Conway Comedy Hour," CBS, 1970.

NELSON, DAVID

b. New York City, NY, October 24, 1936. The Nelson brother who wasn't Ricky on "The Adventures of Ozzie and Harriet."

AS A REGULAR:"The Adventures of Ozzie and Harriet," ABC, 1952-66.

AND: "The Steve Allen Show," NBC, 1959; "Here's Hollywood," NBC, 1961; "Hollywood Palace," ABC, 1966; "Hondo: Hondo and the Apache Trail," ABC, 1967; "The Love Boat: Julie Falls Hard," ABC, 1978.

TV MOVIES AND MINISERIES: "Smash-Up on Interstate 5," ABC, 1976.

AS DIRECTOR: "The Adventures of Ozzie and Harriet," ABC, 1963-66.

* See also "The Adventures of Ozzie and Harriet."

NELSON, FRANK

b. 1911; d. 1986. Comic actor who was the store clerk who'd always show up in the stores Jack Benny would visit and greet him by saying, "Yeuuuueees?"

AS A REGULAR:"The Hank McCune Show," NBC, 1950; "The Jack Benny Program," CBS, 1950-64; NBC, 1964-65; "I Love Lucy," CBS, 1951-56; "The Jetsons," ABC, 1962-63.

AND: "Our Miss Brooks: Safari O'Toole," CBS, 1954; "The Lucille Ball-Desi Arnaz Show: Lucy Takes a Cruise to Havana," CBS, 1957; "The Betty White Show," ABC, 1958; "Shower of Stars: Jack Benny's 40th Birthday Celebration," CBS, 1958; "The Real McCoys: Weekend in Los Angeles," ABC, 1960; "The Tom Ewell Show: Tom Takes Over," CBS, 1960; "Angel: The Honest Man," CBS, 1961; "Pete and Gladys: The Live-In Couple," CBS, 1961; "Pete and Gladys: Office Way," CBS, 1962; "The Danny Thomas

Show: Rusty's Birthday," CBS, 1963; "The Lucy Show: Lucy Visits the White House," CBS, 1963; "The Addams Family: The Addams Family Tree," ABC, 1964; "Petticoat Junction: Don't Call Us," CBS, 1967; "Sanford & Son: Lamont in Love," NBC, 1976; "Sanford & Son: Sergeant Gork," NBC, 1976.

NELSON, HARRIET

b. Peggy Lou Snyder, Des Moines, IA, 1914. Thirties movie starlet who was on- and off-screen wife to Ozzie Nelson.

AS A REGULAR:"The Adventures of Ozzie and Harriet," ABC, 1952-66; "Ozzie's Girls," SYN, 1973.

AND: "The Tonight Show Starring Johnny Carson," NBC, 1969; "Love, American Style: Love and Take Me Along," ABC, 1969; "The Tonight Show Starring Johnny Carson," NBC, 1970; "Love, American Style: Love and the Only Child," ABC, 1971; "Night Gallery: You Can Come Up Now, Mrs. Millikan," NBC, 1972; "Love, American Style: Love and the Unmarriage," ABC, 1973; "Father Dowling Mystries: The Man Who Came to Dinner Mystery," NBC, 1989.

TV MOVIES AND MINISERIES: "Smash-Up on Interstate 5," ABC, 1976; "Best Sellers: Once an Eagle," NBC, 1977; "Death Car on the Freeway," CBS, 1979; "The Kid with the 200 I.Q.," NBC, 1983.

* See also "The Adventures of Ozzie and Harriet."

NELSON, JIMMY

b. Chicago, IL, December 15, 1928. Ventriloquist who had a dummy named Velvel; during the fifties and sixties they did commercials for Nestle's ("N-E-S-T-L-E-S, Nestle's makes the very best—chocolate").

AS A REGULAR:"Texaco Star Theatre," NBC, 1952-53; "Quick as a Flash," ABC, 1953-54; "Bank on the Stars," NBC, 1954; "Come Closer," ABC, 1954; "Down You Go," NBC, 1956.

AND: "The Jackie Gleason Show," CBS, 1957; "The Jimmy Dean Show," CBS, 1957; "Pat Boone Chevy Showroom," ABC, 1957; "The Jimmy Dean Show," CBS, 1958.

NELSON, KRIS—See Kris Harmon.

NELSON, OZZIE

b. Oswald Nelson, Jersey City, NJ, 1907; d. 1975. Former bandleder who was well-meaning dad Ozzie Nelson on TV, and behind the scenes was the brains behind "The Adventures of Ozzie and Harriet."

AS A REGULAR:"The Adventures of Ozzie and Harriet," ABC, 1952-66; "Ozzie's Girls," SYN, 1973.

AND: "Fireside Theatre: Shoot the Moon," NBC, 1956; "The Bob Cummings Show: Bob Becomes a Stage Uncle," NBC, 1958; "The Mothers-in-Law:

Didn't You Used to Be Ossie Snick?," NBC, 1968; "The Tonight Show Starring Johnny Carson," NBC, 1969; "Love, American Style: Love and Take Me Along," ABC, 1969; "The Tonight Show Starring Johnny Carson," NBC, 1970; "Love, American Style: Love and the Only Child," ABC, 1971; "Adam 12: The Grandmothers," NBC, 1971; "Ozzie's Girls: Pilot," NBC, 1972; "Night Gallery: You Can Come Up Now, Mrs. Millikan," NBC, 1972; "Love, American Style: Love and the Unmarriage," ABC, 1973.
AS DIRECTOR: "Adam 12: The Grandmothers," NBC, 1971.
AS PRODUCER: "Ozzie's Girls," SYN, 1973.
AS PRODUCER-DIRECTOR-WRITER: "The Adventures of Ozzie and Harriet," ABC, 1952-66.
* See also "The Adventures of Ozzie and Harriet."

NELSON, RICK
b. Eric Hilliard Nelson, Teaneck, NJ, 1940; d. 1985. Sitcom star and rock 'n' roll idol of the fifties.
AS A REGULAR: "The Adventures of Ozzie and Harriet," ABC, 1952-66; "Malibu U," ABC, 1967.
AND: "Five Stars in Springtime," NBC, 1957; "Wide, Wide World: The Western," NBC, 1958; "G.E. Theatre: The Wish Book," CBS, 1961; "ABC Stage '67: On the Flip Side," ABC, 1966; "Hondo: Hondo and the Judas," ABC, 1967; "Bobbie Gentry Special," CBS, 1970; "The Jim Nabors Hour," CBS, 1970; "Owen Marshall, Counselor at Law: Victim in Shadow," ABC, 1972; "McCloud: Encounter with Aries," NBC, 1972; "The Streets of San Francisco: Harem," ABC, 1973; "Don Kirshner's Rock Concert," SYN, 1974; "Owen Marshall, Counselor at Law: A Foreigner Among Us," ABC, 1974; "Saturday Night Live," NBC, 1979; "The Mike Douglas Show," SYN, 1981.
TV MOVIES AND MINISERIES: "The Over-the-Hill Gang," ABC, 1969.
* See also "The Adventures of Ozzie and Harriet."

NELSON, TRACY
b. Santa Monica, CA, October 25, 1963. Daughter of Rick; she plays Sister Steve on "The Father Dowling Mysteries."
AS A REGULAR: "Square Pegs," CBS, 1982-83; "Glitter," ABC, 1984-85; "The Father Dowling Mysteries," NBC, 1988; ABC, 1989- .
AND: "Hotel: Blackout," ABC, 1983; "The Love Boat: The Runaway," ABC, 1985; "St. Elsewhere: The Women," NBC, 1984; "Family Ties: Ladies Man," NBC, 1984.
TV MOVIES AND MINISERIES: "Pleasures," ABC, 1986; "Kate's Secret," NBC, 1986; "Tonight's the Night," ABC, 1987; "If It's Tuesday, It

Still Must Be Belgium," NBC, 1987; "Fatal Confession: A Father Dowling Mystery," NBC, 1988.

NESBITT, CATHLEEN
b. Cheshire, England, November 24, 1888; d. 1982. Actress in refined roles; she played Agatha Morley, mother of Glen Morley (William Windom) on "The Farmer's Daughter."
AS A REGULAR: "The Farmer's Daughter," ABC, 1963-66; "Masterpiece Theatre: Upstairs, Downstairs," PBS. 1975-77.
AND: "Robert Montgomery Presents: Candles for Theresa," NBC, 1952; "Philco TV Playhouse: The Mother," NBC, 1954; "Studio One: You're Only Young Twice," CBS, 1955; "Producers Showcase: Reunion in Vienna," NBC, 1955; "Alcoa Hour: Sister," NBC, 1956; "Studio One: The Playwright and the Star," CBS, 1957; "Goodyear TV Playhouse: A Will to Live," NBC, 1957; "Alcoa Hour: No License to Kill," NBC, 1957; "Suspicion: Hand in Glove," NBC, 1957; "Studio One: Bend in the Road," CBS, 1957; "Kraft Theatre: Eddie," NBC, 1958; "U.S. Steel Hour: The Reward," CBS, 1958; "Wagon Train: The Matthew Lowry Story," NBC, 1959; "Special Tonight: Mrs. Miniver," CBS, 1960; "U.S. Steel Hour: A Time to Decide," CBS, 1960; "Play of the Week: Thieves' Carnival," SYN, 1960; "Shirley Temple's Storybook: The Little Mermaid," NBC, 1961; "Adventures in Paradise: Flamin' Lady," ABC, 1961; "Play of the Week: The House of Bernarda Alba," SYN, 1961; "Empire: Pressure Lock," NBC, 1962; "Camera Three: The Love Affair of the Golden Top and Other Tales," CBS, 1962; "U.S. Steel Hour: Fair Young Ghost," CBS, 1963; "The Nurses: The Third Generation," CBS, 1963; "U.S. Steel Hour: The Many Ways of Heaven," CBS, 1963; "U.S. Steel Hour: The Old Lady Shows Her Medals," CBS, 1963; "Kraft Mystery Theatre: Go Look at Roses," NBC, 1963; "The Autumn Garden," NET, 1966; "T.H.E. Cat: The Blood-Red Night," NBC, 1967; "The Crucible," CBS, 1967.

NESMITH, MICHAEL
b. Houston, TX, December 30, 1942. Member of the Monkees who's gone into video production.
AS A REGULAR: "The Monkees," NBC, 1966-68; "Michael Nesmith in Televison Parts," NBC, 1985.
AND: "The Monkees Special," NBC, 1969.

NEWHART, BOB
b. Chicago, IL, September 5, 1929. Witty comedian with a low-key style; his sitcoms of the seventies and eighties have been consistent bright spots.

AS A REGULAR: "The Bob Newhart Show," NBC, 1961-62; CBS, 1972-78; "The Entertainers," CBS, 1964; "Newhart," CBS, 1982-90.
AND: "The Jack Paar Show, " NBC, 1960; "The Garry Moore Show," CBS, 1960; "The Ed Sullivan Show," CBS, 1960; "The Ed Sullivan Show," CBS, 1961; "Dinah Shore Chevy Show," NBC, 1961; "The Garry Moore Show," CBS, 1961; "Here's Hollywood," NBC, 1961; "The Ed Sullivan Show," CBS, 1962; "Playboy's Penthouse," SYN, 1962; "The Jack Paar Show," NBC, 1962; "The Judy Garland Show," CBS, 1963; "Hollywood Palace," ABC, 1964; "The Jack Paar Program," NBC, 1964; "The Dean Martin Show," NBC, 1965; "The Tonight Show Starring Johnny Carson," NBC, 1965; "A Salute to Stan Laurel," CBS, 1965; "Hollywood Palace," ABC, 1966; "Captain Nice: One Rotten Apple," NBC, 1967; "Jack Paar Special," NBC, 1967; "The Jackie Gleason Show," CBS, 1968; "The Dean Martin Show," NBC, 1968; "The Glen Campbell Goodtime Hour," CBS, 1969; "Bob Newhart Special: A Last Laugh at the 60's," ABC, 1970; "The Dean Martin Show," NBC, 1970; "The Merv Griffin Show," SYN, 1974; "Tattletales," CBS, 1976; "The Tonight Show Starring Johnny Carson," NBC, 1979; "Saturday Night Live," NBC, 1980; "The Tonight Show Starring Johnny Carson," NBC, 1989; "The Tonight Show Starring Johnny Carson: 27th Anniversary," NBC, 1989.
TV MOVIES AND MINISERIES: "Thursday's Game," ABC, 1974; "Marathon," CBS, 1980.

NEWLAND, JOHN
b. Cincinnati, OH, November 23, 1917. Handsome actor with extensive live TV experience; he hosted "One Step Beyond."
AS A REGULAR: "One Man's Family," NBC, 1950; "Robert Montgomery Presents," NBC, 1952-54; "The Loretta Young Show," NBC, 1955-58; "Alcoa Presents One Step Beyond," ABC, 1959-61; "The Next Step Beyond," SYN, 1978.
AND: "Philco TV Playhouse: Little Boy Lost," NBC, 1950; "Philco TV Playhouse: The American," NBC, 1950; "Philco TV Playhouse: Birth of the Movies," NBC, 1951; "Tales of Tomorrow: The Picture of Dorian Gray," ABC, 1953; "Schlitz Playhouse of Stars: Allen of Harper," CBS, 1953; "Eye Witness: Youth from Vienna," NBC, 1953; "Schlitz Playhouse of Stars: The Perfect Secretary," CBS, 1953; "Schlitz Playhouse of Stars: Square Shootin'," CBS, 1954; "Robert Montgomery Presents: The Great Gatsby," NBC, 1955; "Robert Montgomery Presents: Lucifer," NBC, 1955; "Schlitz Playhouse of Stars: The Bitter Land," CBS, 1956; "Robert Montgomety Presents: September Affair," NBC, 1956; "Robert Montgomery Presents: The Grand Prize," NBC, 1957; "G.E.

Theatre: At Miss Minner's," CBS, 1958; "The Loretta Young Show: The Seducer," NBC, 1960; "The Loretta Young Show: Unconditional Surrender," NBC, 1960; "Here's Hollywood," NBC, 1961; "Thriller: The Return of Andrew Bentley," NBC, 1961; "Thriller: Portrait Without a Face," NBC, 1961; "Dr. Kildare: Tyger, Tyger," NBC, 1964.
AS DIRECTOR: "Alcoa Presents One Step Beyond: Anniversary of a Murder," ABC, 1960.
TV MOVIES AND MINISERIES: "The Deadly Hunt," CBS, 1971; "Crawlspace," CBS, 1972; "Don't Be Afraid of the Dark," ABC, 1973.

NEWMAN, BARRY
b. Boston, MA, November 7, 1938. Ruggedly handsome actor who played attorney Tony Petrocelli.
AS A REGULAR: "The Edge of Night," CBS, 1964-65; "Petrocelli," NBC, 1974-76; "Nightingales," NBC, 1989.
AND: "U.S. Steel Hour: Two Black Kings," CBS, 1962; "Get Smart: The Groovy Guru," NBC, 1968; "The Mike Douglas Show," SYN, 1975; "Don Adams Screen Test," SYN, 1975; "The Peter Marshall Variety Show," SYN, 1977; "Quincy: The Cutting Edge," NBC, 1983; "Murder, She Wrote: Snow White, Blood Red," CBS, 1988; "Murder, She Wrote: Jake's Law," CBS, 1989.
TV MOVIES AND MINISERIES: "Night Games," NBC, 1974; "Having It All," ABC, 1982; "Fantasies," ABC, 1982; "Second Sight: A Love Story," CBS, 1984; "My Two Loves," ABC, 1986.

NEWMAN, EDWIN
b. New York City, NY, January 25, 1919. NBC newsman from 1949-84.
AS A REGULAR: "Edwin Newman Reporting," NBC, 1960; "The Nation's Future," NBC, 1961; "What's Happening to America," NBC, 1968; "Comment," NBC, 1971-72.
AND: "Saturday Night Live," NBC, 1984; "Newhart: Dr. Jekyll & Mr. Loudon," CBS, 1987.
* Emmies: 1983.

NEWMAN, LARAINE
b. Los Angeles, CA, March 2, 1952.
AS A REGULAR: "Manhattan Transfer," CBS, 1975; "Saturday Night Live," NBC, 1975-80.
AND: "St. Elsewhere: Legionnaires," NBC, 1982; "St. Elsewhere: Tweety and Ralph," NBC, 1982; "Alfred Hitchcock Presents: The Jar," NBC, 1986; "Amazing Stories: Miss Stardust," NBC, 1987; "Duet: The New and Improved Linda," FOX, 1989; "Saturday Night Live's 15th Anniversary," NBC, 1989.
TV MOVIES AND MINISERIES: "Her Life as a Man," NBC, 1984.

NEWMAN, PAUL

b. *Cleveland, OH, January 26, 1925*. Blue-eyed screen idol of the fifties, sixties, seventies, eighties and probably the nineties; he got his start in live TV drama.

AS A GUEST: "The Web: The Bells of Damon," CBS, 1953; "The Web: One for the Road," CBS, 1953; "The Mask: Party Night," ABC, 1954; "Goodyear TV Playhouse: Guilty Is the Stranger," NBC, 1954; "Danger: Knife in the Dark," CBS, 1954; "Appointment with Adventure: Five in Judgment," CBS, 1955; "Appointment with Adventure: Bridge of the Devil," CBS, 1955; "Philco TV Playhouse: The Death of Billy the Kid," NBC, 1955; "Producers Showcase: Our Town," NBC, 1955; "Playwrights '56: The Battler," NBC, 1955; "Kaiser Aluminum Hour: The Army Game," NBC, 1956; "U.S. Steel Hour: The Five Fathers of Pepi," CBS, 1956; "U.S. Steel Hour: Bang the Drum Slowly," CBS, 1956; "Kaiser Aluminum Hour: The Rag Jungle," NBC, 1956; "I've Got a Secret," CBS, 1957; "Playhouse 90: The 80-Yard Run," CBS, 1958; "Person to Person," CBS, 1958; "The Glass Wall," SYN, 1959; "Mike Wallace Interviews," CBS, 1960; "Eleanor Roosevelt's Jubilee," NBC, 1960; "Here's Hollywood," NBC, 1961; "The Tonight Show Starring Johnny Carson," NBC, 1968; "Once Upon a Wheel," NBC, 1974; "The Wild Places," NBC, 1974; "Inaugural Eve Special," CBS, 1977.
* Newman wasn't a talk-show regular, but he may have appeared on the "Tonight" show on February 8, 1968 because of another guest: The Rev. Martin Luther King Jr.

NEWMAR, JULIE

b. *Julie Newmeyer, Los Angeles, CA, August 16, 1935*. Statuesque actress in bombshell roles; on her only sitcom she played a robot in the shape of a woman.

AS A REGULAR: "My Living Doll," CBS, 1964-65.
AND: "The Phil Silvers Show: The Big Scandal," CBS, 1957; "Adventures in Paradise: Open for Diving," ABC, 1960; "Perry Como's Kraft Music Hall," NBC, 1961; "Person to Person," CBS, 1961; "The Defenders: Gideon's Follies," CBS, 1961; "Route 66: How Much a Pound Is Albatross?," CBS, 1962; "Route 66: Give the Old Cat a Tender Mouse," CBS, 1962; "Girl Talk," SYN, 1963; "The Twilight Zone: Of Late I Think of Cliffordville," CBS, 1963; "The Beverly Hillbillies: The Beautiful Maid," CBS, 1966; "F Troop: Yellow Bird," ABC, 1966; "The Monkees: Monkees Get Out More Dirt," NBC, 1967; "Get Smart: The Laser Blazer," NBC, 1968; "The Mike Douglas Show," SYN, 1968; "Personality," NBC, 1969; "Love, American Style: Love and the Big Night," ABC, 1970; "Love, American Style: Love

and the Cake," ABC, 1970; "Bewitched: The Eight-Year Witch," ABC, 1971; "Love, American Style: Love and the Bathtub," ABC, 1972; "Columbo: Double Shock," NBC, 1973; "McMillan and Wife: Aftershock," NBC, 1975; "The Love Boat: Haven't I Seen You ...?," ABC, 1979; "CHiPs: This Year's Riot," NBC, 1982; "Half-Nelson: The Deadly Vase," NBC, 1985.

TV MOVIES AND MINISERIES: "McCloud: Who Killed Miss USA?," NBC, 1970; "The Feminist and the Fuzz," ABC, 1971; "A Very Missing Person," NBC, 1972.
* See also Bob Cummings.

NEWSOM, TOMMY

b. *Portsmouth, VA, February 25, 1929*. Musician-bandleader.

AS A REGULAR: "The Tonight Show Starring Johnny Carson," NBC, 1968- .
AND: "Newhart: A Midseason's Night Dream," CBS, 1988; "ALF: Tonight, Tonight," NBC, 1988.

NEWTON, WAYNE

b. *Norfolk, VA, April 3, 1942*. Singer-performer.

AS A GUEST: "Jackie Gleason and His American Scene Magazine," CBS, 1962; "Truth or Consequences," NBC, 1964; "American Bandstand," ABC, 1964; "The Ed Sullivan Show," CBS, 1965; "Hollywood Palace," ABC, 1965; "The Lucy Show: Lucy Discovers Wayne Newton," CBS, 1965; "Here's Lucy: Lucy Sells Craig to Wayne Newton," CBS, 1968; "The Jim Nabors Hour," CBS, 1969; "Here's Lucy: Lucy and Wayne Newton," CBS, 1969; "The Merv Griffin Show," SYN, 1973; "NBC Follies," NBC, 1973; "Music Country USA," NBC, 1974; "The Tonight Show Starring Johnny Carson," NBC, 1974; "Cher," CBS, 1975; "Switch: The Girl on the Golden Strip," CBS, 1976; "Switch: Legends of the Macunas," CBS, 1977; "The Pat Sajak Show," CBS, 1989; "Late Night with David Letterman," NBC, 1989.

NICHOLAS, DENISE

b. *Detroit, MI, 1944*. Actress who played counselor Liz McIntyre on "Room 222."

AS A REGULAR: "Room 222," ABC, 1969-74; "Baby I'm Back," CBS, 1978.
AND: "NYPD: The Witness," ABC, 1967; "NYPD: Bomber," ABC, 1967; "NYPD: Encounter on a Rooftop," ABC, 1968; "The FBI: Eye of the Storm," ABC, 1969; "NYPD: The Night Watch," ABC, 1969; "The Flip Wilson Show," NBC, 1970; "Love, American Style: Love and the Split-Up," ABC, 1971; "Police Story: A Community of Victims," NBC, 1975; "Marcus Welby, M.D.: The Strange Behavior of Paul

Kelland," ABC, 1975; "Rhoda: The Party," CBS, 1975; "The Love Boat: The Affair," ABC, 1979; "Diff'rent Strokes: Substitute Mother," NBC, 1980; "Supercarrier: Give Me Liberty," ABC, 1988; "The Cosby Show: Birthday Blues," NBC, 1989.

TV MOVIES AND MINISERIES: "Five Desperate Women," ABC, 1971; "The Sophisticated Gents," NBC, 1981; "Mother's Day," FAM, 1989.

NICHOLS, BARBARA
b. Barbara Nickerauer, Queens, NY, December 30, 1929; d. 1976. Comic actress, sometimes in dumb blonde roles.
AS A REGULAR: "Broadway Open House," NBC, 1951; "Sid Caesar Presents Comedy Preview," NBC, 1955; "Love That Jill," ABC, 1958.
AND: "Studio One: Confessions of a Nervous Man," CBS, 1953; "U.S. Steel Hour: Good for You," ABC, 1954; "Center Stage: The Heart of a Clown," ABC, 1954; "Armstrong Circle Theatre: Fred Allen's Sketchbook," NBC, 1954; "Danger: Peter River Blues," CBS, 1955; "The Thin Man: The Case of the Baggy Pants," NBC, 1958; "The Bob Cummings Show: Bob and the Dumb Blonde," NBC, 1958; "The Bob Cummings Show: Bob and Schultzy Reunite," NBC, 1958; "The Jack Benny Program," CBS, 1958; "Westinghouse Desilu Playhouse: The Untouchables," CBS, 1959; "The Jack Benny Program: Jimmy Stewart Show," CBS, 1959; "The Dick Powell Show: No Strings Attached," NBC, 1962; "Alcoa Premiere: Five, Six, Pick Up Sticks," ABC, 1963; "Going My Way: Has Anybody Here Seen Eddie?," ABC, 1963; "The Tonight Show Starring Johnny Carson," NBC, 1963; "Arrest and Trial: Isn't It a Lovely View?," ABC, 1963; "The Beverly Hillbillies: Jethro's First Love," CBS, 1963; "The Beverly Hillbillies: Chickadee Returns," CBS, 1963; "Laredo: A Question of Discipline," NBC, 1965; "The Wild Wild West: The Night of the Whirring Death," CBS, 1966; "Batman: Shoot a Crooked Arrow/Walk the Straight and Narrow," ABC, 1966; "Green Acres: Never Take Your Wife to a Convention," CBS, 1967; "The Man from UNCLE: The Summit Five Affair," NBC, 1967; "Hawaii Five-O: A Thousand Pardons, You're Dead," CBS, 1969; "The Doris Day Show: A Weighty Problem," CBS, 1971; "Adam 12: Vendetta," NBC, 1972; "The Rookies: Blue Christmas," ABC, 1974.

NICHOLS, MIKE
b. Michael Peschkowsky, Berlin, Germany, November 6, 1931. Comedian, writer and film director ("The Graduate," "Postcards From the Edge") who was a familiar face on fifties TV, often with partner Elaine May.
AS A REGULAR: "Laugh Line," NBC, 1959; "The

Jack Paar Program," NBC, 1964.
AND: "Playhouse 90: Journey to the Day," CBS, 1960; "Password," CBS, 1961.
WITH ELAINE MAY: "The Jack Paar Show," NBC, 1957; "The Steve Allen Show," NBC, 1957; "Omnibus: The Suburban Review," NBC, 1958; "The Perry Como Show," NBC, 1958; "Du Pont Show of the Month: The Red Mill," CBS, 1958; "Dinah Shore Chevy Show," NBC, 1958; "Keep Talking," CBS, 1958; "Pontiac Star Parade: Accent on Love," NBC, 1959; "Dinah Shore Chevy Show," NBC, 1959; "The Jack Paar Show," NBC, 1959; "The Big Party," CBS, 1959; "The Fabulous Fifties," CBS, 1960; "Jack Paar Presents," NBC, 1960; "Person to Person," CBS, 1960; "Perry Como's Kraft Music Hall," NBC, 1961; "The Smothers Brothers Comedy Hour," CBS, 1967; "The Great American Dream Machine," NET, 1971.
* Nichols and May were scheduled to appear on the Emmy Awards in 1960, but they dropped out when one of the sponsors objected to a sketch they were planning that would have made fun of home permanents.
* See also Elaine May.

NICHOLS, NICHELLE
b. Chicago, IL, 1936. Actress who played Lt. Uhura on "Star Trek."
AS A REGULAR: "Star Trek," NBC, 1966-69; 1973-75.
AND: "The Lieutenant: To Set It Right," NBC, 1964; "Tarzan: Deadly Silence," NBC, 1966.

NICHOLSON, JACK
b. Neptune, NJ, April 22, 1937. Screen icon of the last twenty-odd years who began his career in TV roles and grade-B drive-in quickies.
AS A GUEST: "Tales of Wells Fargo: The Washburn Girl," NBC, 1961; "Cheyenne: The Equalizer," ABC, 1961; "Hawaiian Eye: Total Eclipse," ABC, 1962; "Dr. Kildare: The Encroachment/A Patient Lost/What Happened to All the Sunshine and Roses?/The Taste of Crow/Out of a Concrete Tower," NBC, 1966; "The Andy Griffith Show: Opie Finds a Baby," CBS, 1966; "The Andy Griffith Show: Aunt Bee the Juror," CBS, 1967; "The Guns of Will Sonnett: A Son for a Son," ABC, 1967.

NIELSEN, LESLIE
b. Canada, February 11, 1926. All-purpose leading man of fifties and sixties television, usually in stern roles; in the late seventies he got a new lease on life as a deadpan comic actor, thanks to the movie "Airplane!"
AS A REGULAR: "Walt Disney Presents: The Swamp Fox," ABC, 1959-61; "The New Breed," ABC, 1961-62; "Peyton Place," ABC, 1965; "The Bold Ones," NBC, 1969-70;

"Bracken's World," NBC, 1970; "The Explorers," SYN, 1972-73; "Police Squad!," ABC, 1982; "Shaping Up," ABC, 1984.

AND: "Actor's Studio: Hannah," CBS, 1950; "Studio One: The Survivors," CBS, 1950; "The Trap: Sentence of Death," CBS, 1950; "Tales of Tomorrow: Black Planet," ABC, 1952; "Tales of Tomorrow: Appointment to Mars," ABC, 1952; "Man Behind the Badge: The Case of the Yankee II," SYN, 1954; "Studio One: A Guest at the Embassy," CBS, 1954; "Alfred Hitchcock Presents: The Two-Million Dollar Defense," CBS, 1958; "Playhouse 90: The Velvet Alley," CBS, 1959; "G.E. Theatre: Nora," CBS, 1959; "Goodyear Theatre: Any Friend of Julie's," NBC, 1959; "Rawhide: Incident Below the Brazos," CBS, 1960; "The Untouchables: Three Thousand Suspects," ABC, 1960; "Moment of Fear: Total Recall," NBC, 1960; "Thriller: The Twisted Image," NBC, 1960; "G.E. Theatre: Journal of Hope," CBS, 1960; "Route 66: Poor Little Kangaroo Rat," CBS, 1962; "Ben Casey: He Thought He Saw an Albatross," ABC, 1963; "Channing: Exercise in a Shark Tank," ABC, 1963; "Kraft Suspense Theatre: One Step Down," NBC, 1963; "The Fugitive: The Glass Tightrope," ABC, 1963; "The Alfred Hitchcock Hour: The Magic Shop," CBS, 1964; "Object Is," ABC, 1964; "The Defenders: Survival," CBS, 1964; "The Virginian: Ryker," NBC, 1964; "The Fugitive: Tiger Left, Tiger Right," ABC, 1964; "Wagon Train: The Brian Conlin Story," ABC, 1964; "The Defenders: Death on Wheels," CBS, 1965; "Dr. Kildare: Do You Trust Your Doctor?," NBC, 1965; "Voyage to the Bottom of the Sea: The Creature," ABC, 1965; "Dr. Kildare: She Loves Me, She Loves Me Not," NBC, 1965; "Bob Hope Chrysler Theatre: Guilty or Not Guilty," NBC, 1966; "The Virginian: No Drums, No Trumpets," NBC, 1966; "The Virginian: The Fortress," NBC, 1967; "Bob Hope Chrysler Theatre: Code Name: Heraclitus," NBC, 1967; "Judd for the Defense: A Civil Case of Murder," ABC, 1967; "The Man from UNCLE: The Seven Wonders of the World Affair," NBC, 1968; "It Takes a Thief: A Thief Is a Thief Is a Thief," ABC, 1968; "Gunsmoke: Time of the Jackals," CBS, 1969; "The Big Valley: Town of No Exit," ABC, 1969; "The Virginian: The Long Ride Home," NBC, 1969; "Night Gallery: The Phantom of What Opera?," NBC, 1971; "Medical Center: Conspiracy," CBS, 1971; "The FBI: Fool's Gold," ABC, 1973; "Barnaby Jones: Killing Defense," CBS, 1973; "The Streets of San Francisco: One Last Shot," ABC, 1974; "Hawaii Five-O: Right Grave, Wrong Body," CBS, 1974; "Ironside: The Over-the-Hill Blues," NBC, 1974; "Celebrity Sweepstakes," NBC, 1974; "Kojak: Loser Takes All," CBS, 1974; "Kung Fu: Barbary House," ABC, 1975; "Columbo: Identity Crisis," NBC, 1975; "Don Adams Screen Test," SYN, 1976; "The Love Boat: Bo 'n' Sam," ABC, 1979; "Murder, She Wrote: Dead Men's Gold," CBS, 1986; "Highway to Heaven: Gift of Life," NBC, 1986; "Day by Day: Harper and Son," NBC, 1988; "Saturday Night Live," NBC, 1989; "Later with Bob Costas," NBC, 1989.

TV MOVIES AND MINISERIES: "See How They Run," NBC, 1964; "Shadow Over Elveron," NBC, 1968; "Hawaii Five-O," CBS, 1968; "Companions in Nightmare," NBC, 1968; "Trial Run," NBC, 1969; "Deadlock," NBC, 1969; "Night Slaves," ABC, 1970; "The Aquarians," NBC, 1970; "Hauser's Memory," NBC, 1970; "Incident in San Francisco," ABC, 1971; "They Call It Murder," NBC, 1971; "Snatched," ABC, 1973; "The Letters," ABC, 1973; "Can Ellen Be Saved?," ABC, 1974; "Brinks: The Great Robbery," CBS, 1976; "Little Mo," NBC, 1978; "Backstairs at the White House," NBC, 1979; "The Night the Bridge Fell Down," NBC, 1983; "Blade in Hong Kong," CBS, 1985; "Fatal Confession: A Father Dowling Mystery," NBC, 1988.

NIMOY, LEONARD

b. Boston, MA, March 26, 1931. Mr. Spock.

AS A REGULAR: "Star Trek," NBC, 1966-69; 1973-75; "Mission: Impossible," CBS, 1969-71; "In Search of...," SYN, 1976-82.

AND: "Favorite Story: The Adoption," SYN, 1952; "Dragnet: The Big Boys," NBC, 1954; "West Point: His Brother's Fist," CBS, 1956; "West Point: Cold Peril," CBS, 1957; "M Squad: The Firemakers," NBC, 1959; "Rough Riders: Gunpoint Persuasion," ABC, 1959; "Wagon Train: The Estaban Zamora Story," NBC, 1959; "M Squad: Badge for a Coward," NBC, 1960; "Tate: Comanche Scalps," NBC, 1960; "The Tall Man: A Bounty for Billy," NBC, 1960; "The Rebel: The Hunted," ABC, 1960; "Bonanza: The Ape," NBC, 1960; "The Tall Man: A Gun Is for Killing," NBC, 1961; "Wagon Train: The Tiburcio Mendez Story," NBC, 1961; "87th Precinct: The Very Hard Sell," NBC, 1961; "The Twilight Zone: A Quality of Mercy," CBS, 1961; "Cain's Hundred: Murder by Proxy," NBC, 1962; "Laramie: The Runt," NBC, 1962; "Wagon Train: The Baylor Crofoot Story," NBC, 1962; "Perry Mason: The Case of the Shoplifter's Shoe," CBS, 1963; "The Man From UNCLE: The Project Strigas Affair," NBC, 1964; "Kraft Suspense Theatre: Kill No More," NBC, 1965; "Death Valley Days: The Journey," SYN, 1965; "The Virginian: Show Me a Hero," NBC, 1965; "The Virginian: The Showdown," NBC, 1965; "Combat!: The Raider," ABC, 1965; "A Man Called Shenandoah: Run, Killer, Run," ABC, 1966; "Get Smart: The Dead Spy Scrawls," NBC, 1966; "The Beautiful Phyllis Diller Show," NBC, 1968; "Night Gallery: She'll Be Company for

You," NBC, 1972; "Columbo: A Stitch in Crime," NBC, 1973; "Short Stories of Love: Kiss Me Again, Stranger," NBC, 1974; "The $10,000 Pyramid," ABC, 1975; "T.J. Hooker: Vengeance Is Mine," ABC, 1983.

TV MOVIES AND MINISERIES: "Assault on the Wayne," ABC, 1971; "Baffled!," NBC, 1973; "The Alpha Caper," ABC, 1973; "The Missing Are Deadly," ABC, 1975; "Seizure: The Story of Kathy Morris," CBS, 1980; "The Sun Also Rises," NBC, 1984.

NIVEN, DAVID

b. *James David Graham Niven, Kirriemuir, Scotland, March 1, 1910; d. 1983.* Suave actor of films and TV, in dramatic and comedy roles; later a best-selling author.

AS A REGULAR:"Four Star Playhouse," CBS, 1952-56; "Alcoa-Goodyear Theatre (A Turn of Fate)," NBC, 1957-58; "The David Niven Show," NBC, 1959; "The Rogues," NBC, 1964-65.

AND: "Schlitz Playhouse of Stars: Not a Chance," CBS, 1951; "Celanese Theatre: The Petrified Forest," ABC, 1952; "Robert Montgomery Presents: The Sheffield Story," NBC, 1952; "Hollywood Opening Night: Sword Play," NBC, 1952; "Light's Diamond Jubilee: The Girls in Their Summer Dresses," ABC, CBS, NBC, 1954; "The 20th Century-Fox Hour: Thank You, Jeeves," CBS, 1956; "Dick Powell's Zane Grey Theatre: Village of Fear," CBS, 1957; "Mr. Adams and Eve: Taming of the Shrew," CBS, 1957; "What's My Line?," CBS, 1958; "Dick Powell's Zane Grey Theatre: The Accuser," CBS, 1958; "What's My Line?," CBS, 1960; "The du Pont Show with June Allyson: The Trench Coat," CBS, 1960; "Here's Hollywood," NBC, 1961; "The Bluffers," NBC, 1974; "Dinah!," SYN, 1975; "The Merv Griffin Show," SYN, 1975; "Bell System Family Theatre: The Canterville Ghost," NBC, 1975; "The Mike Douglas Show," SYN, 1977.

TV MOVIES AND MINISERIES: "A Man Called Intrepid," SYN, 1979; "The Golden Raiders," ABC, 1981.

NOBLE, JAMES

b. *Dallas, TX, March 5, 1922.* Lanky actor who played Gov. James Gatling on "Benson."

AS A REGULAR:"The Brighter Day," CBS, 1959-60; "As the World Turns," CBS, 1962; "A World Apart," ABC, 1970-71; "Benson," ABC, 1979-86; "First Impressions," CBS, 1988.

AND: "Hart to Hart: Pilot," ABC, 1979; "The Love Boat: Country Cousin Blues," ABC, 1981; "The Love Boat: Why Johnny Can't Read," ABC, 1984; "The Love Boat: Doc's Big Case," ABC, 1983; "Scarecrow and Mrs. King: Any Number

Can Play," CBS, 1987; "Murder, She Wrote: No Accounting for Murder," CBS, 1987; "ABC Afterschool Specials: The Day My Kid Went Punk," ABC, 1987; "The Magical World of Disney: The Absent-Minded Professor," NBC, 1988; "Father Dowling Mysteries: What Do You Call a Call Girl Mystery?," NBC, 1989; "Perfect Strangers: Father Knows Best," ABC, 1989.

TV MOVIES AND MINISERIES: "Lovey: A Circle of Children, Part II," CBS, 1978; "When the Bough Breaks," NBC, 1986; "Perry Mason: The Case of the Murdered Madam," NBC, 1987; "Deadly Deception," CBS, 1987.

NOLAN, JEANETTE

b. *Los Angeles, CA, December 30, 1911.* Longtime character actress, often in western roles; wife of John McIntire.

AS A REGULAR:"Hotel De Paree," CBS, 1959-60; "The Richard Boone Show," NBC, 1963-64; "The Virginian," NBC, 1967-68; "Dirty Sally," CBS, 1974.

AND: "The Jane Wyman Show: Between Jobs," NBC, 1956; "The Jane Wyman Show: Birthright," NBC, 1957; "Richard Diamond, Private Detective: Escape From Oak Lane," CBS, 1957; "G.E. Theatre: Stopover," CBS, 1958; "Alfred Hitchcock Presents: The Right Kind of House," CBS, 1958; "Have Gun, Will Travel: Gun Shy," CBS, 1958; "Have Gun, Will Travel: The Tender Gun," CBS, 1960; "Klondike: Swoger's Mules," NBC, 1960; "Wanted Dead or Alive: Witch Woman," CBS, 1960; "Gunsmoke: Love Thy Neighbor," CBS, 1961; "Guestward Ho!: Hawkeye's First Love," ABC, 1961; "Adventures in Paradise: Who Is Sylvia?," ABC, 1961; "Bat Masterson: The Good and the Bad," NBC, 1961; "The Outlaws: The Avenger," NBC, 1961; "Thriller: Parasite Mansion," NBC, 1961; "Wagon Train: The Janet Hale Story," NBC, 1961; "Yes, Yes Nanette: Behind Every Great Man," NBC, 1961; "Alfred Hitchcock Presents: Coming Home," NBC, 1961; "Adventures in Paradise: The Closing Circle," ABC, 1961; "Thriller: La Strega," NBC, 1962; "The Twilight Zone: The Hunt," CBS, 1962; "Frontier Circus: The Courtship," CBS, 1962; "Bus Stop: The Opposite Virtues," ABC, 1962; "The Twilight Zone: Jess-Belle," CBS, 1963; "Wagon Train: Charlie Wooster, Outlaw," ABC, 1963; "Laramie: The Renegade Brand," NBC, 1963; "Combat!: Infant of Prague," ABC, 1964; "The Fugitive: Ill Wind," ABC, 1966; "My Three Sons: Grandma's Girl," CBS, 1966; "The Invaders: Nightmare," ABC, 1967; "The Mothers-in-Law: Nanny, Go Home," NBC, 1969; "The FBI: The Last Job," ABC, 1971; "Love, American Style: Love and the Old Cowboy," ABC, 1971; "Gunsmoke: Pike," CBS, 1971; "Gunsmoke: P.S. Murry Christmas," CBS, 1971; "The Sonny and Cher Comedy Hour," CBS, 1974; "The Streets of San Francisco: The

Runaways," ABC, 1974; "Police Woman: Don't Feed the Pigeons," NBC, 1975; "Columbo: The Conspirators," NBC, 1978; "The Misadventures of Sheriff Lobo: The Boom Boom Lady," NBC, 1979; "Here's Boomer: George and Emma," NBC, 1980; "Strike Force: Sharks," ABC, 1982; "Quincy: Quincy's Wedding," NBC, 1983; "Hell Town: Hell Town Goes Bananas," NBC, 1985; "St. Elsewhere: To Tell the Truth," NBC, 1986; "Cagney & Lacey: A Different Drummer," CBS, 1987; "MacGyver: The Madonna," ABC, 1989.

TV MOVIES AND MINISERIES: "Longstreet," ABC, 1971; "Say Goodbye, Maggie Cole," ABC, 1972; "Hijack!," ABC, 1973; "The Desperate Miles," ABC, 1975; "Babe," CBS, 1975; "Law and Order," NBC, 1976; "The New Daughters of Joshua Cabe," ABC, 1976; "The Awakening Land," ABC, 1978; "Better Late Than Never," NBC, 1979; "The Hustler of Muscle Beach," ABC, 1980; "The Wild Women of Chastity Gulch," ABC, 1982.

NOLAN, KATHLEEN

b. Joycelyn Schrum, St. Louis, MO, September 27, 1933. Actress who played Kate, wife of Luke (Richard Crenna) on "The Real McCoys."

AS A REGULAR: "Jamie," ABC, 1953-54; "The Real McCoys," ABC, 1957-62; "Broadside," ABC, 1964-65.

AND: "Producers Showcase: Peter Pan," NBC, 1955; "Elgin TV Hour: Midsummer Melody," ABC, 1955; "Producers Showcase: Peter Pan," NBC, 1956; "The Millionaire: The Story of Waldo Francis Turner," CBS, 1956; "Warner Bros. Presents Conflict: Stranger on the Road," ABC, 1956; "Broken Arrow: The Rescue," ABC, 1957; "Make Room for Daddy: Girl From Iowa," ABC, 1957; "Warner Bros. Presents Conflict: The Money," ABC, 1957; "Meet McGraw: The Girl from Molina," NBC, 1957; "Bob Hope Special," NBC, 1958; "Here's Hollywood," NBC, 1961; "Saints and Sinners: The Man on the Rim," NBC, 1962; "The Alfred Hitchcock Hour: Annabel," CBS, 1962; "The Untouchables: Blues for a Gone Goose," ABC, 1963; "Ben Casey: Hang No Hats on Dreams," ABC, 1963; "Burke's Law: Who Killed Cynthia Royal?," ABC, 1963; "The Lloyd Bridges Show: The Rising of the Moon," CBS, 1963; "The Alfred Hitchcock Hour: Beast in View," CBS, 1964; "The Breaking Point: Confounding Her Astronomers," ABC, 1964; "The Big Valley: Into the Widow's Web," ABC, 1966; "Bewitched: A Most Unusual Wood Nymph," ABC, 1966; "Love, American Style: Love and the Bowling Ball," ABC, 1970; "The Name of the Game: Seek and Destroy," NBC, 1971; "Wednesday Night Out," NBC, 1972; "The Bold Ones: A Substitute Womb," NBC, 1973; "Gunsmoke: Susan Was Evil," CBS, 1973; "Kolchak, the Night Stalker: The Vampire," ABC, 1974; "The Rockford Files: New Life, Old

Dragons," NBC, 1977; "Quincy: Sugar and Spice," NBC, 1981; "Magnum, P.I.: Tropical Madness," CBS, 1982.

TV MOVIES AND MINISERIES: "Alias Smith and Jones," ABC, 1971; "Testimony of Two Men," SYN, 1977; "The Immigrants," SYN, 1978.

NOLAN, LLOYD

b. San Francisco, CA, August 11, 1902; d. 1985. Movie and TV leading man who played Dr. Morton Chegley, boss of "Julia" (Diahann Carroll) and who won an Emmy as Captain Quegg in a production of "The Caine Mutiny Court Martial."

AS A REGULAR: "Martin Kane, Private Eye," NBC, 1951-52; "Special Agent 7," SYN, 1959; "Julia," NBC, 1968-71.

AND: "Theatre Hour: The Barker," CBS, 1950; "Ford Theatre: Protect Her Honor," NBC, 1952; "Climax!: Sailor on Horseback," CBS, 1955; "Ford Star Jubilee: The Caine Mutiny Court Martial," CBS, 1955; "Playhouse 90: Galvanized Yankee," CBS, 1957; "The Big Record," CBS, 1957; "Dick Powell's Zane Grey Theatre: Homecoming," CBS, 1958; "The Ford Show," NBC, 1959; "Wagon Train: The Hunter Malloy Story," NBC, 1959; "Hallmark Hall of Fame: Ah, Wilderness!," NBC, 1959; "The Untouchables: The George "Bugs" Moran Story," ABC, 1960; "Startime: Crime, Inc.," NBC, 1960; "Christophers: The Adamses," SYN, 1960; "Bonanza: The Stranger," NBC, 1960; "This Is Your Life," NBC, 1960; "The Barbara Stanwyck Show: The Seventh Miracle," NBC, 1960; "Dick Powell's Zane Grey Theatre: Knife of Hate," CBS, 1960; "Here's Hollywood," NBC, 1961; "Bus Stop: The Glass Jungle," ABC, 1961; "Laramie: Deadly Is the Night," NBC, 1961; "G.E. Theatre: Call to Danger," CBS, 1961; "The Outlaws: The Old Man," NBC, 1962; "The Dick Powell Show: Special Assignment," NBC, 1962; "The du Pont Show: Two Faces of Treason," NBC, 1963; "The Great Adventure: The Death of Sitting Bull," CBS, 1963; "Kraft Suspense Theatre: The Case Against Paul Ryker," NBC, 1963; "77 Sunset Strip: 5," ABC, 1963; "The Virginian: It Takes a Big Man," NBC, 1963; "The Outer Limits: Soldier," ABC, 1964; "Slattery's People: Rally Round Your Own Flag, Mister," CBS, 1965; "Mannix: The Name Is Mannix," CBS, 1967; "The Virginian: The Masquerade," NBC, 1967; "Custer: Breakout," ABC, 1967; "The Danny Thomas Hour: The Cage," NBC, 1968; "I Spy: The Name of the Game," NBC, 1968; "Owen Marshall, Counselor at Law: A Question of Degree," ABC, 1972; "The Bold Ones: A Nation of Human Pincushions," NBC, 1972; "McCloud: Butch Cassidy Rides Again," NBC, 1973; "The FBI: The Killing Truth," ABC, 1973; "The Magician: Ripoff," NBC, 1974; "The Wonderful World of Disney: The Sky's the

Limit," NBC, 1975; "Sandburg's Lincoln: The Unwilling Warrior," NBC, 1975; "City of Angels: The November Plan," NBC, 1976; "McMillan: Affair of the Heart," NBC, 1977; "Police Woman: Merry Christmas, Waldo," NBC, 1977; "$weepstake$: Dewey and Harold and Sarah and Maggie," NBC, 1979; "Remington Steele: Cast in Steele," NBC, 1984; "Murder, She Wrote: Death in the Afternoon," CBS, 1985.

TV MOVIES AND MINISERIES: "Wings of Fire," NBC, 1967; "Isn't It Shocking?," ABC, 1973; "The Abduction of Saint Anne," ABC, 1975; "Flight to Holocaust," NBC, 1977; "Valentine," ABC, 1979.

* Emmies: 1956.

NOLAN, TOMMY
> *b. Bernard Maurice Joseph Girouard Jr., Montreal, Canada, January 15, 1948.* Child actor of the late fifties, also known as Butch Bernard.

AS A REGULAR: "Buckskin," NBC, 1958-59; "The Dennis O'Keefe Show," CBS, 1959-60.

AND: "Studio 57: The Face of a Killer," SYN, 1957; "G.E. Theatre: Stopover," CBS, 1958; "G.E. Theatre: Angel in the Air," CBS, 1958; "G.E. Theatre: A Turkey for the President," CBS, 1958; "The Ford Show," NBC, 1959; "Wagon Train: The Cappy Darrin Story," NBC, 1959; "Markham: The Young Conspirator," CBS, 1959; "Wagon Train: The Dick Jarvis Story," NBC, 1960; "Thriller: Child's Play," NBC, 1960; "Lassie: Blind Dog," CBS, 1960; "G.E. Theatre: Graduation Dress," CBS, 1960; "Rawhide: Incident of the Night Visitor," CBS, 1960; "Lassie: The Lynx," CBS, 1960; "Thriller: Parasite Mansion," NBC, 1961.

NOLTE, NICK
> *b. Omaha, NB, February 8, 1941.* Bearish actor of TV and, later of movies, thanks to his role in "Rich Man, Poor Man."

AS A GUEST: "Walt Disney's Wonderful World of Color: The Feather Farm," NBC, 1969; "Medical Center: Impasse," CBS, 1973; "Griff: Premiere," ABC, 1973; "The Streets of San Francisco: Crossfire," ABC, 1973; "Emergency!: Body Language," NBC, 1974; "Medical Center: The Conspirators," CBS, 1974; "The Rookies: The Teacher," ABC, 1974; "Barnaby Jones: Dark Legacy," CBS, 1974; "Barnaby Jones: Trap Play," CBS, 1975.

TV MOVIES AND MINISERIES: "The California Kid," ABC, 1974; "Death Sentence," ABC, 1974; "The Runaway Barge," NBC, 1975; "Rich Man, Poor Man," ABC, 1976.

NOONAN, TOMMY
> *b. Bellingham, WA, April 29, 1922; d. 1968.* Comic who teamed for a time with Peter Marshall; later a writer and director of nudie movies.

AS A REGULAR: "Stump the Stars," CBS, 1962-63.

AND: "The Millionaire: Millionaire Jim Hayes," CBS, 1959; "Here's Hollywood," NBC, 1960; "The Rebel: Shriek of Silence," ABC, 1961; "Perry Mason: The Case of the Crying Comedian," CBS, 1961; "G.E. Theatre: The Free Wheelers," CBS, 1962; "The Red Skelton Hour," CBS, 1963; "The Real McCoys: How You Gonna Keep 'Em Down on the Farm After They've Seen San Quentin?," CBS, 1963; "My Three Sons: A Real Nice Time," CBS, 1966; "Batman: King Tut's Coup/Batman's Waterloo," ABC, 1967; "Gomer Pyle, USMC: A Visit from Aunt Bee," CBS, 1967.

* See also Peter Marshall.

NORRIS, CHRISTOPHER
> *b. New York City, NY, October 7, 1953.* Blonde actress who played Nurse Brancusi on "Trapper John, M.D." and Laura on "Santa Barbara."

AS A REGULAR: "The Doctors," NBC, 1967; "The Edge of Night," CBS, 1968-70; "Trapper John, M.D.," CBS, 1979-85; "Santa Barbara," NBC, 1988-90.

AND: "The Paul Lynde Show: Springtime for Paul," ABC, 1973; "Police Story: Open City," NBC, 1976; "The Love Boat: The Caller," ABC, 1980; "The Love Boat: Arrivederci, Gopher," ABC, 1982; "Hotel: Charades," ABC, 1983; "Finder of Lost Loves: Losing Touch," ABC, 1984; "The Love Boat: Girl of the Midnight Sun," ABC, 1985; "Murder, She Wrote: Stage Struck," CBS, 1986; "The New Mike Hammer: The Last Laugh," CBS, 1987; "Matlock: The Husband," NBC, 1987; "Murder, She Wrote: Deadpan," CBS, 1988; "The Pat Sajak Show," CBS, 1989.

TV MOVIES AND MINISERIES: "Mr. and Mrs. Bo Jo Jones," ABC, 1971; "The Great American Beauty Contest," ABC, 1973; "Mayday at 40,000 Feet!," CBS, 1976; "Suddenly, Love," NBC, 1978; "The Great American Traffic Jam," NBC, 1980.

NORTH, JAY
> *b. August 3, 1952.* Blond actor who played Dennis "the Menace" Mitchell, the Bart Simpson of his day, and later supplied cartoon voices.

AS A REGULAR: "Dennis the Menace," CBS, 1959-63; "Maya," NBC, 1967-68; "Pebbles and Bamm-Bamm," CBS, 1971-72; "The Flintstones Comedy Hour," CBS, 1972-73; "The Flintstones Show," CBS, 1973-74.

AND: "Wanted Dead or Alive: Eight-Cent Reward," CBS, 1958; "Westinghouse Desilu Playhouse: Martin's Folly," CBS, 1959; "Sugarfoot: The Giant Killer," ABC, 1959; "77 Sunset Strip: Eyewitness," ABC, 1959; "Art Linkletter's House Party," CBS, 1959; "The

Detectives Starring Robert Taylor: The Hiding Place," ABC, 1959; "The Ford Show," NBC, 1959; "The Red Skelton Show," CBS, 1960; "The Chevy Show: Children Are People?," NBC, 1960; "The Ed Sullivan Show," CBS, 1960; "The Donna Reed Show: Donna Decorates," ABC, 1960; "The Chevy Show: Ghosts, Goblins and Kids," NBC, 1960; "Here's Hollywood," NBC, 1960; "The Red Skelton Show," CBS, 1961; "Art Linkletter's House Party," CBS, 1961; "This Is the Answer: Valley of Shadows," SYN, 1964; "Wagon Train: Those Who Stay Behind," ABC, 1964; "The Man from UNCLE: The Deadly Toys Affair," NBC, 1965; "My Three Sons: Whatever Happened to Baby Chip?," CBS, 1966; "The Lucy Show: Lucy and the Robot," CBS, 1966; "My Three Sons: Good Guys Finish Last," CBS, 1966; "Jericho: Eric the Redhead," CBS, 1966.

TV MOVIES AND MINISERIES: "Scout's Honor," NBC, 1980.

NORTH, SHEREE
b. Los Angeles, CA, January 17, 1933. Fifties starlet who moved to regular TV roles in the sixties.

AS A REGULAR: "Big Eddie," CBS, 1975; "I'm a Big Girl Now," ABC, 1980-81; "The Bay City Blues, NBC, 1983.

AND: "Shower of Stars: Lend an Ear," CBS, 1954; "The Ed Sullivan Show," CBS, 1956; "The Perry Como Show," NBC, 1956; "Playhouse 90: Topaz," CBS, 1957; "Bob Hope Special," NBC, 1957; "Steve Allen Plymouth Show," NBC, 1960; "The Untouchables: Search for a Dead Man," ABC, 1963; "The Breaking Point: Solo for B-Flat Clarinet," ABC, 1963; "Burke's Law: Who Killed the Kind Doctor?," ABC, 1963; "The Eleventh Hour: There Should Be an Outfit Called Families Anonymous," NBC, 1963; "The Greatest Show on Earth: This Train Doesn't Stop Until It Gets There," ABC, 1964; "Burke's Law: Who Killed Davidian Jones?," ABC, 1964; "Burke's Law: Who Killed Rosie Sunset?," ABC, 1965; "The Virginian: That Saunders Woman," NBC, 1966; "Confidential for Women: The Story of Susan Durrell," ABC, 1966; "The Big Valley: The Man from Nowhere," ABC, 1966; "Bob Hope Chrysler Theatre: Code Name: Heraclitus," NBC, 1967; "The Fugitive: Walls of Night," ABC, 1967; "Mannix: Comes Up Rose," CBS, 1968; "The Name of the Game: One of the Girls in Research," NBC, 1970; "The Most Deadly Game: Who Killed Kindness?," ABC, 1970; "The Interns: The Challengers," CBS, 1971; "Medical Center: Shock," CBS, 1971; "Alias Smith and Jones: The Men That Corrupted Hadleyburg," ABC, 1972; "Cannon: Stakeout," CBS, 1972; "Kojak: The Chinatown Murders," CBS, 1974; "Hawaii Five-O: Hawaiian Nightmare," CBS, 1974; "The Mary Tyler Moore Show: Lou and That Woman," CBS, 1974; "Barnaby Jones: Forfeit by Death," CBS,

1974; "Wide World of Mystery: The Cloning of Clifford Swimmer," ABC, 1974; "Benjamin Franklin: The Whirlwind," CBS, 1974; "The Mary Tyler Moore Show: The Shame of the Cities," CBS, 1975; "Medical Center: Half a Life," CBS, 1975; "Marcus Welby, M.D.: How Do You Know What Hurts Me?," ABC, 1976; "Magnum P.I.: The Return of Luther Gillis," CBS, 1984; "The Golden Girls: Transplant," NBC, 1985; "Matlock: The Don," NBC, 1986; "The Golden Girls: Ebb Tide," NBC, 1989.

TV MOVIES AND MINISERIES: "Then Came Bronson," NBC, 1969; "Vanished," NBC, 1971; "Rolling Man," ABC, 1972; "Trouble Comes to Town," ABC, 1973; "Snatched," ABC, 1973; "Maneater," CBS, 1973; "Key West," NBC, 1973; "Winter Kill," ABC, 1974; "Shadow in the Street," NBC, 1975; "Most Wanted," ABC, 1976; "The Night They Took Miss Beautiful," NBC, 1977; "A Real American Hero," CBS, 1978; "Amateur Night at the Dixie Bar and Grill," NBC, 1979; "Portrait of a Stripper," CBS, 1979; "Legs," ABC, 1983; "Scorned and Swindled," CBS, 1984.

NORTON, CLIFF
b. Scarsdale, NY. Comedian.

AS A REGULAR: "Garroway at Large," NBC, 1949-51; "Your Show of Shows," NBC, 1950-54; "The Public Life of Cliff Norton," NBC, 1952; "The Dave Garroway Show," 1953-54; "What's Going On?," ABC, 1954; "Caesar's Hour," NBC, 1954-57; "Sid Caesar Presents Comedy Preview," NBC, 1955; "It's About Time," CBS, 1966-67; "Where's Huddles?," CBS, 1970.

AND: "The Jonathan Winters Show," NBC, 1956; "The George Gobel Show," NBC, 1957; "The Garry Moore Show," CBS, 1957; "U.S. Steel Hour: Sideshow," CBS, 1957; "Studio One: Love Me to Pieces," CBS, 1957; "Pantomime Quiz," CBS, 1957; "The Garry Moore Show," CBS, 1958; "Dave's Place," NBC, 1960; "Play of the Week: The Grand Tour," SYN, 1961; "The du Pont Show: The Battle of the Paper Bullets," NBC, 1961; "Pete and Gladys: Never Forget a Friend," CBS, 1962; "The Gertrude Berg Show: Dad's Day," CBS, 1962; "The Dick Van Dyke Show: A Bird in the Head Hurts," CBS, 1962; "Alcoa Premiere: George Gobel Presents," ABC, 1963; "My Favorite Martian: Rocket to Mars," CBS, 1963; "Grindl: One Angry Grindl," NBC, 1963; "The Edie Adams Show," ABC, 1964; "Bewitched: It's Magic," ABC, 1965; "The Andy Griffith Show: Goober's Replacement," CBS, 1966; "The Lucy Show: Lucy the Fight Manager," CBS, 1967; "The Monkees: The Picture Frame," NBC, 1967; "Bewitched: Cousin Serena Strikes Again," ABC, 1969; "Bewitched: One Touch of Midas," ABC, 1969; "Bewitched:

Samantha the Sculptress," ABC, 1969; "I Dream of Jeannie: The Wedding," NBC, 1969; "The Wild Wild West: The Night of the Plague," CBS, 1969; "Get Smart: Ice Station Siegfried," CBS, 1970; "Bewitched: The Phrase Is Familiar," ABC, 1970; "The Paul Lynde Show: How to Be Unhappy, Though Poor," ABC, 1972; "The Doris Day Show: It's a Dog's Life," CBS, 1973; "The Odd Couple: The Odd Decathalon," ABC, 1973; "Here's Lucy: Mary Jane's Boyfriend," CBS, 1974; "The Odd Couple: The Dog Story," ABC, 1974; "The Bob Newhart Show: The New Look," CBS, 1975; "Alice: Pay the Fifty Dollars," CBS, 1976; "One Day at a Time: Peabody's War," CBS, 1978; "Lou Grant: Sting," CBS, 1980; "Gimme a Break: Do or Diet," NBC, 1981; "Remington Steele: To Stop a Steele," NBC, 1983; "Love, Sidney: Sidney's Bar Mitzvah," NBC, 1983; "Gimme a Break: Ship of Fools," NBC, 1985; "Highway to Heaven: With Love, the Claus," NBC, 1986.

NORTON-TAYLOR, JUDY

b. Santa Monica, CA, January 29, 1958. Actress who played Mary Ellen on "The Waltons."

AS A REGULAR:"The Waltons," CBS, 1972-81. AND: "The Felony Squad: The Distant Shore," ABC, 1968; "Cross Wits," SYN, 1980; "The Love Boat: A Business Affair," ABC, 1982. TV MOVIES AND MINISERIES: "The Homecoming," CBS, 1971; "Valentine," ABC, 1979; "A Wedding on Walton's Mountain," NBC, 1982; "A Day for Thanks on Walton's Mountain," NBC, 1982.

NOURI, MICHAEL

b. Washington, D.C., December 9, 1945. Hunky dark-featured actor in movies ("Flashdance") and TV.

AS A REGULAR:"Beacon Hill," CBS, 1975; "Search for Tomorrow," CBS, 1975-78; "The Curse of Dracula," NBC, 1979; "The Last Convertible," NBC, 1981; "The Gangster Chronicles," NBC, 1981; "The Bay City Blues," NBC, 1983; "Downtown," CBS, 1986-87. TV MOVIES AND MINISERIES: "Fun and Games," ABC, 1980; "Secrets of a Mother and Daughter," CBS, 1983; "Between Two Women," ABC, 1986; "Rage of Angels: The Story Continues," NBC, 1986; "Quiet Victory: the Charlie Wedemeyer Story," CBS, 1988.

NOVAK, KIM

b. Marilyn Novak, Chicago, IL, February 13, 1933. Sexy actress in films of the fifties who left the business and returned briefly in the eighties.

AS A REGULAR:"Falcon Crest," CBS, 1986-87. AND: "Light's Diamond Jubilee: A Kiss for the Lieutenant," ABC, CBS, NBC, 1954; "The Frank Sinatra Show," ABC, 1957; "Alfred Hitchcock Presents: The Man From the South," NBC, 1985. TV MOVIES AND MINISERIES: "The Third Girl from the Left," ABC, 1973; "Satan's Triangle," ABC, 1975; "Malibu," ABC, 1983.

NOVELLO, DON

b. Ashtabula, OH, January 1, 1943. Comic who created Father Guido Sarducci.

AS A REGULAR:"The Smothers Brothers Comedy Hour," NBC, 1975; "Saturday Night Live," NBC, 1978-80; 1985-86. AND: "Late Night with David Letterman," NBC, 1989.

NOVELLO, JAY

b. 1904; d. 1982. Slight, bald character actor who usually played charlatans, shysters or the occasional kindly ethnic.

AS A REGULAR:"McHale's Navy," ABC, 1965-66. AND: "I Love Lucy: The Seance," CBS, 1951; "Gangbusters: The Willie Sutton Story," SYN, 1954; "I Love Lucy: The Sublease," CBS, 1954; "I Love Lucy: Visitor from Italy," CBS, 1956; "Schlitz Playhouse of Stars: Markheim," CBS, 1956; "Maverick: Plunder of Paradise," ABC, 1958; "Richard Diamond, Private Detective: Arson," CBS, 1958; "The Millionaire: Millionaire Martha Crockett," CBS, 1958; "The Unchained Goddess," NBC, 1958; "Bat Masterson: Barbary Castle," NBC, 1959; "Maverick: The Marquesa," ABC, 1960; "Wagon Train: The Lita Foldaire Story," NBC, 1960; "Adventures in Paradise: One Little Pearl," ABC, 1960; "Alcoa Presents One Step Beyond: Persons Unknown," ABC, 1961; "The Islanders: A Rope for Charlie Munday," ABC, 1961; "Hong Kong: The Innocent Exile," ABC, 1961; "77 Sunset Strip: The Six Out of Eight Caper," ABC, 1961; "Naked City: Make-Believe Man," ABC, 1961; "Hawaiian Eye: My Love, but Lightly," ABC, 1962; "The Andy Griffith Show: Guest of Honor," CBS, 1962; "The Lucy Show: Lucy Meets a Millionaire," CBS, 1964; "Combat!: The Town That Went Away," ABC, 1964; "The Andy Griffith Show: Otis Sues the County," CBS, 1964; "Bonanza: Woman of Fire," NBC, 1965; "F Troop: La Dolce Courage," ABC, 1966; "The Smothers Brothers Show: The Girl From RALPH," CBS, 1966; "My Three Sons: Arrivederci, Robbie," CBS, 1966; "Gomer Pyle, USMC: Sue the Pants Off 'Em," CBS, 1967; "The Mothers-in-Law: Through the Lurking Glass," NBC, 1967; "The Flying Nun: The Landlord Cometh," ABC, 1969; "Family Affair: Lost in Spain," CBS, 1969; "Gomer Pyle, USMC: The Short Voyage Home," CBS, 1969; "The Mod Squad: The Debt," ABC, 1969; "Then Came Bronson: The Gleam of the Eagle Mind," NBC, 1970; "Love, American Style: Love and the

Duel," ABC, 1971; "The FBI: The Test," ABC, 1972; "McCloud: The Million Dollar Round Up," NBC, 1973; "The Streets of San Francisco: For the Love of God," ABC, 1973; "Chico and the Man: Old Is Old," NBC, 1976; "Kojak: A Grave Too Soon," CBS, 1976.

TV MOVIES AND MINISERIES: "Powderkeg," CBS, 1971.

NUYEN, FRANCE
b. *Marseilles, France, July 31, 1939.* Actress first noticed in "The World of Suzie Wong"; she played Dr. Paulette Kiem on "St. Elsewhere."

AS A REGULAR: "St. Elsewhere," NBC, 1986-88; "Knots Landing," CBS, 1989.

AND: "The Ed Sullivan Show," CBS, 1958; "Pontiac Star Parade: An Evening with Perry Como," NBC, 1959; "Hong Kong: Clear for Action," ABC, 1960; "Adventures in Paradise: One Little Pearl," ABC, 1960; "Play Your Hunch," NBC, 1963; "Girl Talk," SYN, 1963; "Amos Burke, Secret Agent: The Prisoners of Mr. Sin," ABC, 1965; "The Man from UNCLE: The Cherry Blossom Affair," NBC, 1965; "I Spy: Tiger," NBC, 1966; "I Spy: Always Say Goodbye," NBC, 1966; "Gunsmoke: Gunfighter, R.I.P.," CBS, 1966; "I Spy: An American Empress," NBC, 1967; "Star Trek: Elaan of Troyius," NBC, 1968; "Medical Center: The Battle of Lily Wu," CBS, 1969; "Hawaii Five-O: Highest Castle, Deepest Grave," CBS, 1971; "The Magician: The Illusion of the Lost Dragon," NBC, 1974; "The Six Million Dollar Man: The Coward," ABC, 1974; "Kung Fu: A Small Beheading," ABC, 1974; "Hawaii Five-O: Small Witness, Large Crime," CBS, 1975; "Medical Center: Child of Conflict," CBS, 1976; "Police Story: Thanksgiving," NBC, 1976; "Police Woman: Death of a Dream," NBC, 1976; "Hawaii Five-O: Ready, Aim," CBS, 1977; "Columbo: Murder Under Glass," NBC, 1978; "Fantasy Island: Jungle Man," ABC, 1980; "Magnum P.I.: Torah, Torah, Torah," CBS, 1985.

TV MOVIES AND MINISERIES: "Black Water Gold," ABC, 1970; "Horror at 37,000 Feet," CBS, 1973; "Chopper One," ABC, 1974.

NYE, LOUIS
b. *Hartford, CT.* Funnyman who played the smug Gordon Hathaway on "The Steve Allen Show" and Sonny Drysdale on "The Beverly Hillbillies."

AS A REGULAR: "The Tonight Show," NBC, 1954-57; "The Steve Allen Show," NBC, 1956-59; "Steve Allen Plymouth Show," NBC, 1959-60; "The Ann Sothern Show," CBS, 1960-61; "The New Steve Allen Show," ABC, 1961; "The Beverly Hillbillies," CBS, 1962; "The Steve Allen Comedy Hour," CBS, 1967; "Happy Days," CBS, 1970; "Needles and Pins," NBC, 1973; "Steve Allen's Laugh Back," SYN, 1976.

AND: "The Arlene Francis Show," NBC, 1957; "The Tonight Show," NBC, 1958; "The Arlene Francis Show," NBC, 1958; "The Jack Paar Show," NBC, 1958; "Make Me Laugh," ABC, 1958; "Naked City: The Bloodhounds," ABC, 1959; "The Chevy Show: Arabian Nights," NBC, 1960; "Here's Hollywood," NBC, 1960; "Dinah Shore Chevy Show," NBC, 1961; "Guestward Ho!: The Beatniks," ABC, 1961; "The Spike Jones Show," CBS, 1961; "The Danny Thomas Show: Bunny Cooks a Meal," CBS, 1962; "The Jack Benny Program: Jack and the Cab Driver," CBS, 1962; "You Don't Say," NBC, 1963; "The Judy Garland Show," CBS, 1964; "The Edie Adams Show," ABC, 1964; "The Beverly Hillbillies: Sonny Drysdale Returns," CBS, 1966; "The Munsters: Zombo," CBS, 1966; "Hollywood Squares," NBC, 1967; "Dream Girl of '67," ABC, 1967; "Operation: Entertainment," ABC, 1968; "The Jackie Gleason Show," CBS, 1969; "The Jonathan Winters Show," CBS, 1969; "The Della Reese Show," SYN, 1969; "The Della Reese Show," SYN, 1970; "Love, American Style: Love and the Unhappy Couple," ABC, 1971; "The Don Knotts Show," NBC, 1971; "Evening at Pops," NET, 1972; "Hi-Ho, Steverino: A 25th Anniversary Salute to Steve Allen," ABC, 1974; "Mitzi and a Hundred Guys," CBS, 1975; "The Merv Griffin Show," SYN, 1976; "Laverne & Shirley: Guilty Until Proven Not," ABC, 1977; "Police Woman: Ambition," NBC, 1977; "Starsky and Hutch: Starsky and Hutch on Playboy Island," ABC, 1977; "The Love Boat: A New Woman," ABC, 1979; "The Love Boat: Aquaphobiac," ABC, 1981; "The Love Boat: Youth Takes a Holiday," ABC, 1983; "St. Elsewhere: Schwartzwald," NBC, 1987; "St. Elsewhere: The Abby Singer Show," NBC, 1988.

O

OAKLAND, SIMON
b. New York City, NY, 1922; d. 1983. Heavyset character actor who often played heavies and/or stern bosses.

AS A REGULAR: "House on High Street," NBC, 1960; "Toma," ABC, 1973-74; "Kolchak, the Night Stalker," ABC, 1974-75; "Baa Baa Black Sheep," NBC, 1976-78; "David Cassidy, Man Undercover," NBC, 1978-79.

AND: "Gunsmoke: How to Cure a Friend," CBS, 1956; "Producers Showcase: The Great Sebastians," NBC, 1957; "O. Henry Playhouse: The Atavism of John Tom Little Bear," SYN, 1957; "Armstrong Circle Theatre: The Dead Sea Scrolls," CBS, 1957; "Kraft Mystery Theatre: Web of Guilt," CBS, 1958; "Have Gun, Will Travel: The Statue of San Sebastian," CBS, 1958; "Armstrong Circle Theatre: House of Cards," CBS, 1959; "Car 54, Where Are You?: Hail to the Chief," NBC, 1962; "The Twilight Zone: The Thirty-Fathom Grave," CBS, 1963; "Stoney Burke: Image of Glory," ABC, 1963; "My Favorite Martian: Pilot," CBS, 1963; "Combat!: The Long Way Home," ABC, 1963; "Mr. Novak: With a Hammer in His Hand, Lord, Lord!," NBC, 1964; "The Outer Limits: Second Chance," ABC, 1964; "Mr. Broadway: Try to Find a Spy," CBS, 1964; "Mission: Impossible: The Frame," CBS, 1967; "The Mike Douglas Show," SYN, 1968; "Hawaii Five-O: One Day We Shall Be Strangers in Our Own Land," CBS, 1968; "The Wild Wild West: The Night of the Fugitives," CBS, 1968; "Judd for the Defense: A Swim with Sharks," ABC, 1968; "The FBI: The Maze," ABC, 1969; "Medical Center: The Runaway," CBS, 1970; "Hawaii Five-O: Didn't We Meet at a Murder?" CBS, 1972; "Medical Center: No Sanctuary," CBS, 1972; "Hawaii Five-O: Engaged to Be Buried," CBS, 1973; "Hawaii Five-O: The Waterfront Stealing," CBS, 1975; "Marcus Welby, M.D.: How Do You Know What Hurts Me?," ABC, 1976; "Police Story: The Jar," NBC, 1976; "Gibbsville: All the Young Girls," NBC, 1976; "The Rockford Files: Sticks and Stones May Break Your Bones, But Waterbury Will Bury You," NBC, 1977; "Switch: Blue Crusaders' Reunion," CBS, 1977; "The Rockford Files: The House on Willis Avenue," NBC, 1978; "The Rockford Files: Just a Coupla Guys," NBC, 1979; "CHiPS: Drive, Lady, Drive," NBC, 1979; "The Rockford Files: Nice Guys Finish Dead," NBC, 1980; "Lou Grant: Obituary," CBS, 1981; "Quincy: Bitter Pill," NBC, 1982; "Quincy: Give Me Your Weak," NBC, 1982; "CHiPS: Alarmed," NBC, 1982.

TV MOVIES AND MINISERIES: "The Cable Car Murder," CBS, 1971; "The Night Stalker," ABC, 1972; "The Night Strangler," ABC, 1973; "Toma," ABC, 1973; "Key West," NBC, 1973; "Young Joe, the Forgotten Kennedy," ABC, 1977; "Evening in Byzantium," SYN, 1978.

OATES, WARREN
b. Depoy, KY, July 5, 1930; d. 1982. Gifted actor in films and TV who was almost always better than his material; he specialized in grizzled characters who could be funny or frightening.

AS A REGULAR: "Stoney Burke," ABC, 1962-63.

AND: "Studio One: The Night America Trembled," CBS, 1957; "Wanted Dead or Alive: Die by the Gun," CBS, 1958; "Have Gun, Will Travel: Three Sons," CBS, 1958; "The Adventures of Rin Tin Tin: The Epidemic," ABC, 1959; "Wanted Dead or Alive: The Legend," CBS, 1959; "Buckskin: Charlie, My Boy," NBC, 1959; "Wanted Dead or Alive: Amos Carter," CBS, 1959; "77 Sunset Strip: Blackout," ABC, 1960; "Tate: Before Sunup," NBC, 1960; "Wrangler: Affair at the Trading Post," NBC, 1960; "Gunsmoke: Small Water," CBS, 1960; "The Outlaws: Thirty a Month," NBC, 1960; "Stagecoach West: The Renegades," ABC, 1961; "The Dick Powell Show: Somebody's Waiting," NBC, 1961; "Thriller: The Hollow Watcher," NBC, 1962; "The Rifleman: Day of Reckoning," ABC, 1962; "Bonanza: The Mountain Girl," NBC, 1962; "77 Sunset Strip: Terror in a Small Town," ABC, 1962; "The Travels of Jaimie McPheeters: The Day of the First Sailor," ABC, 1963; "The Twilight Zone: The Seventh Is Made Up of Phantoms," CBS, 1963; "Bob Hope Chrysler Theatre: The War and Eric Kurtz," NBC, 1965; "Branded: Judge Not," NBC, 1965; "A Man Called Shenandoah: The Fort," ABC, 1965; "Slattery's People: Rally Round Your Own Flag, Mister," CBS, 1965; "The Virginian: One Spring Like Long Ago," NBC, 1966; "The Monroes: The Forest Devil," ABC, 1966; "Shane: An Echo of Anger," ABC, 1966; "Gunsmoke: The Mission," CBS, 1966; "The Big Valley: The Murdered Party," ABC, 1966; "Dundee and the Culhane: The Turn the Other Cheek Brief," CBS, 1967; "Gunsmoke: The Wreckers," CBS, 1967; "Cimarron Strip: The Battle Ground," CBS, 1967; "The Iron Horse: The Return of Hode Avery," ABC, 1967; "Walt Disney's Wonderful World of Color: The Mystery of Edward Sims," NBC, 1968; "The FBI: Turnabout," ABC, 1971; "The

Name of the Game: The Showdown," NBC, 1971.
TV MOVIES AND MINISERIES: "Something for a Lonely Man," NBC, 1968; "The Movie Murderer," NBC, 1970; "The Reluctant Heroes," ABC, 1971; "Black Beauty," NBC, 1978; "My Old Man," CBS, 1979; "And Baby Makes Six," NBC, 1979; "Baby Comes Home," CBS, 1980; "East of Eden," ABC, 1981.

O'BRIAN, HUGH

b. *Hugh J. Krampe, Rochester, NY, April 19, 1925.* One of the biggest stars of fifties TV as Wyatt Earp; off camera he's involved in several charitable organizations. In 1989 he played Wyatt Earp again on an episode of "Paradise."

AS A REGULAR: "The Life and Legend of Wyatt Earp," ABC, 1955-61; "Search," NBC, 1972-73.
AND: "Fireside Theatre: Going Home," NBC, 1951; "Royal Playhouse: Shifting Sands," SYN, 1952; "The Loretta Young Show: Guest in the House," NBC, 1954; "The Loretta Young Show: Double Trouble," NBC, 1954; "The Loretta Young Show: Three Minutes Too Late," NBC, 1954; "Studio 57: The Engagement Ring," SYN, 1955; "The Millionaire: Millionaire Luke Foreman," CBS, 1955; "The Loretta Young Show: Feeling No Pain," NBC, 1955; "Stage 7: Billy and the Bride," CBS, 1955; "Damon Runyon Theatre: A Light in France," CBS, 1955; "Make Room for Daddy: A Visit From Wyatt Earp," ABC, 1955; "Matinee Theatre: Tall Dark Stranger," NBC, 1956; "Ford Theatre: Ringside Seat," ABC, 1957; "The Ed Sullivan Show," CBS, 1957; "Playhouse 90: Invitation to a Gunfighter," CBS, 1957; "The Jackie Gleason Show," CBS, 1957; "Dinah Shore Chevy Show," NBC, 1957; "Queen for a Day," NBC, 1957; "Date with the Angels: Star Struck," ABC, 1957; "Playhouse 90: Reunion," CBS, 1958; "The Big Record," CBS, 1958; "The Ed Sullivan Show," CBS, 1958; "Frances Langford Special," NBC, 1959; "Westinghouse Desilu Playhouse: Chain of Command," CBS, 1959; "Westinghouse Desilu Playhouse: Circle of Evil," CBS, 1960; "About Faces," ABC, 1960; "Christophers: The Importance of Attending Labor Meetings," SYN, 1960; "Person to Person," CBS, 1960; "The Secret World of Eddie Hodges," CBS, 1960; "G.E. Theatre: Graduation Dress," CBS, 1960; "The Dick Powell Show: Up Jumped the Devil," NBC, 1961; "I've Got a Secret," CBS, 1962; "Here's Hollywood," NBC, 1962; "Theatre '62: Spellbound," NBC, 1962; "Alcoa Premiere: The Rules of the Game," ABC, 1962; "Dr. Kildare: The Administrator," NBC, 1962; "The Alfred Hitchcock Hour: Ride the Nightmare," CBS, 1962; "The Virginian: The Executioners," NBC, 1962; "Stump the Stars," CBS, 1963; "Perry

Mason: The Case of the Two-Faced Turnabout," CBS, 1963; "Password," CBS, 1965; "Bob Hope Chrysler Theatre: Exit From a Plane in Flight," NBC, 1965; "What's This Song?," NBC, 1965; "Shindig," ABC, 1965; "The Virginian: The Executioners," NBC, 1965; "The Merv Griffin Show," SYN, 1966; "Great Bible Adventures: Seven Rich Years ... and Seven Lean," ABC, 1966; "Dial M for Murder," ABC, 1967; "The Merv Griffin Show," SYN, 1967; "The Movie Game," SYN, 1969; "Police Story: Collision Course," NBC, 1973; "Police Story: Open City," NBC, 1976; "Police Story: Spitfire," NBC, 1977; "Fantasy Island: Wuthering Heights," ABC, 1982; "The Love Boat: Saving Grace," ABC, 1982; "The Pat Sajak Show," CBS, 1989; "Paradise: A Gathering of Guns," CBS, 1989.
TV MOVIES AND MINISERIES: "Wild Women," ABC, 1970; "Harpy," CBS, 1971; "Probe," NBC, 1972; "Murder on Flight 502," ABC, 1975; "Benny and Barney: Las Vegas Undercover," NBC, 1977; "Fantasy Island," ABC, 1977; "Murder at the World Series," ABC, 1977.

O'BRIEN, EDMOND

b. *New York City, NY, September 10, 1915; d. 1985.* Bombastic film actor ("The Killers," "White Heat") who played attorney Sam Benedict and mean old Will Varner on "The Long Hot Summer."

AS A REGULAR: "Johnny Midnight," SYN, 1960; "Sam Benedict," NBC, 1962-63; "The Long Hot Summer," ABC, 1965.
AND: "Stars Over Hollywood: Not a Bad Guy," NBC, 1950; "Pulitzer Prize Playhouse: Ice Bound," ABC, 1951; "Lux Video Theatre: Hit and Run," CBS, 1951; "Schlitz Playhouse of Stars: The Net Draws Tight," CBS, 1954; "Rheingold Theatre: Dark Stranger," NBC, 1955; "Schlitz Playhouse of Stars: Tower Room 14-A," CBS, 1957; "The George Gobel Show," NBC, 1957; "Lux Video Theatre: To Have and Have Not," NBC, 1957; "Playhouse 90: The Comedian," CBS, 1957; "Dick Powell's Zane Grey Theatre: A Gun Is for Killing," CBS, 1957; "Playhouse 90: The Male Animal," CBS, 1958; "Schlitz Playhouse of Stars: The Town That Slept with the Lights On," CBS, 1958; "Suspicion: Death Watch," NBC, 1958; "Lux Playhouse: Coney Island Winter," CBS, 1958; "Playhouse 90: The Blue Men," CBS, 1959; "Laramie: The Iron Captain," NBC, 1959; "Dick Powell's Zane Grey Theatre: Lonesome Road," CBS, 1959; "The Dick Powell Show: Killer in the House," NBC, 1961; "Target: The Corruptors: The Visible Govern-ment," ABC, 1961; "The Breaking Point: Tides of Darkness," ABC, 1964; "Walt Disney's Wonderful World of Color: Gallegher," NBC, 1965; "Walt Disney's Wonderful World of Color: The Further Adventures of Gallegher," NBC, 1965; "The Virginian: Ah Sing vs. Wyoming,"

NBC, 1967; "Flesh and Blood," NBC, 1968; "Mission: Impossible: The Counterfeiter," CBS, 1968; "It Takes a Thief: Roar-a-Bye, Baby," ABC, 1969; "The Young Lawyers: MacGillicuddy Always Was a Pain in the Neck," ABC, 1970; "The Name of the Game: L.A. 2017," NBC, 1971; "The High Chaparral: The Hostage," NBC, 1971; "The Streets of San Francisco: The Thirty Year Pin," ABC, 1972; "McMillan and Wife: Cop of the Year," NBC, 1972; "Police Story: Chain of Command," NBC, 1974.

TV MOVIES AND MINISERIES: "The Hanged Man," NBC, 1964; "The Doomsday Flight," NBC, 1966; "The Outsider," NBC, 1967; "The Intruders," NBC, 1970; "River of Mystery," NBC, 1971; "What's a Nice Girl Like You...?," ABC, 1971; "Jigsaw," ABC, 1972; "Isn't It Shocking?," ABC, 1973.

O'BRIEN, MARGARET

b. Angela Maxine O'Brien, San Diego, CA, January 15, 1937. Former MGM child star ("Journey for Margaret," "Meet Me in St. Louis") who spent her teens and early twenties in television.

AS A GUEST: "Robert Montgomery Presents: The Canterville Ghost," NBC, 1950; "Lux Video Theatre: To Lovely Margaret," CBS, 1951; "Lux Video Theatre: The White Gown," CBS, 1953; "Studio One: A Breath of Air," CBS, 1953; "Ford Theatre: Daughter of Mine," NBC, 1954; "Climax!: South of the Sun," CBS, 1955; "Matinee Theatre: Midsummer," NBC, 1955; "Front Row Center: Innocent Witness," CBS, 1956; "Climax!: Night of a Rebel," CBS, 1957; "Matinee Theatre: Winter in April," NBC, 1957; "Climax!: The Necessary Evil," CBS, 1957; "Plahyouse 90: The Mystery of 13," CBS, 1957; "Suspicion: The Story of Margery Reardon," NBC, 1957; "The Jane Wyman Show: Roadblock No. 7," NBC, 1957; "Kraft Television Theatre: Come to Me," NBC, 1957; "G.E. Theatre: The Young Years," CBS, 1957; "Matinee Theatre: The Little Minister," NBC, 1957; "The Steve Allen Show," NBC, 1957; "Studio One: Trial by Slander," CBS, 1958; "Studio One: Tongues of Angels," CBS, 1958; "Person to Person," CBS, 1958; "Wagon Train: The Sacramento Story," NBC, 1958; "Steve Allen Presents The Steve Lawrence-Eydie Gorme Show," NBC, 1958; "I've Got a Secret," CBS, 1958; "Little Women," CBS, 1958; "Pursuit: Kiss Me Again, Stranger," CBS, 1958; "Rawhide: Incident of the Town in Terror," CBS, 1959; "Playhouse 90: The Second Happiest Day," CBS, 1959; "Arthur Murray Party," NBC, 1959; "U.S. Steel Hour: Big Doc's Girl," CBS, 1959; "The du Pont Show with June Allyson: Escape," CBS, 1960; "New Comedy Showcase: Maggie," CBS, 1960; "Checkmate: Deadly Shadow," CBS,

1960; "The Aquanauts: River Gold," CBS, 1961; "Here's Hollywood," NBC, 1961; "Adventures in Paradise: The Trial of Adam Troy," ABC, 1961; "Dr. Kildare: The Dragon," NBC, 1962; "The du Pont Show: The Betrayal," NBC, 1962; "Perry Mason: The Case of the Shoplifter's Shoe," CBS, 1963; "Bob Hope Chrysler Theatre: The Turncoat," NBC, 1964; "The Mike Douglas Show," SYN, 1964; "Combat!: Entombed," ABC, 1967; "Love, American Style: Love and the Letter," ABC, 1969; "The Movie Game," SYN, 1970; "Marcus Welby, M.D.: Dinner of Herbs," ABC, 1972; "Quincy: Across the Line," NBC, 1982.

TV MOVIES AND MINISERIES: "Split Second to an Epitaph," NBC, 1968; "Death in Space," ABC, 1974; "Testimony of Two Men," SYN, 1977.

O'BRIEN, PAT

b. William Joseph Patrick O'Brien, Milwaukee, WI, 1899; d. 1983. Actor who excelled at playing tough, sentimental Irishmen; he appeared in dozens of Warner Bros. movies of the thirties and forties and a wide variety of television, including his own short-lived sitcom.

AS A REGULAR: "Harrigan and Son," ABC, 1960-61.

AND: "The Ed Sullivan Show," CBS, 1950; "Lux Video Theatre: The Irish Drifter," CBS, 1951; "Lux Video Theatre: Tin Badge," CBS, 1951; "The Joyful Hour," ABC, 1951; "Schlitz Playhouse of Stars: It's a Man's World," CBS, 1952; "Lux Video Theatre: The Face of Autumn, CBS, 1952; "G.E. Theatre: Winners Never Lose," CBS, 1953; "Lux Video Theatre: One for the Road," CBS, 1953; "Lux Video Theatre: The Chase," NBC, 1954; "Climax!: The Box of Chocolates," CBS, 1955; "Climax: The Prowler," CBS, 1955; "Science Fiction Theatre: Are We Invaded?," SYN, 1956; "Studio 57: Who's Calling?," SYN, 1956; "Kraft Theatre: Eddie," NBC, 1958; "Christophers: Our National Heritage," SYN, 1958; "Art Linkletter's House Party," CBS, 1959; "Walt Disney Presents: I Captured the King of the Leprechauns," ABC, 1959; "You Asked For It," ABC, 1959; "Christophers: About Daniel Webster," SYN, 1959; "Christophers: The Life of John Hart," SYN, 1960; "Person to Person," CBS, 1960; "What's My Line?," CBS, 1960; "Best of the Post: Cop Without a Badge," SYN, 1960; "The Ed Sullivan Show," CBS, 1961; "The Merv Griffin Show," NBC, 1962; "The Dick Powell Show: Thunder in a Forgotten Town," NBC, 1963; "Going My Way: Boss of the Ward," ABC, 1963; "The Virginian: The Fortunes of Jimerson Jones," NBC, 1964; "Kraft Suspense Theatre: Threatening Eye," NBC, 1964; "Bob Hope Chrysler Theatre: A Case of Armed Robbery," NBC, 1964; "Kraft Suspense Theatre: The Jack Is

High," NBC, 1964; "Bob Hope Chrysler Theatre: The Crime," NBC, 1965; "The David Frost Show," SYN, 1970; "Alias Smith and Jones: Shootout at Diablo Station," ABC, 1971; "Owen Marshall, Counselor at Law: Words of Summer," ABC, 1972; "Banyon: The Graveyard Vote," NBC, 1972; "McCloud: Butch Cassidy Rides Again," NBC, 1973; "ABC's Matinee Today: The Other Woman," ABC, 1973; "Tenafly: Joyride to Nowhere," NBC, 1973; "The Wonderful World of Disney: The Sky's the Limit," NBC, 1975; "Happy Days: The Roaring Twenties," ABC, 1980.

TV MOVIES AND MINISERIES: "The Over-the-Hill Gang," ABC, 1969; "Welcome Home, Johnny Bristol," CBS, 1972; "The Adventures of Nick Carter," ABC, 1972; "Kiss Me, Kill Me," ABC, 1976.

O'CONNELL, ARTHUR
b. New York City, NY, March 29, 1908; d. 1981. White haired, mustachioed actor good at comedy and light drama; on TV he often played kindly elders.
AS A REGULAR: "Mr. Peepers," NBC, 1953-54; "The Second Hundred Years," ABC, 1967-68.
AND: "Comedy Theatre: Summer Had Better Be Good," ABC, 1950; "Philco TV Playhouse: 0 for 37," NBC, 1953; "Kraft Television Theatre: All Our Yesterdays," ABC, 1954; "Kraft Television Theatre: Mr. Simmons," ABC, 1954; "Philco TV Playhouse: The Outsiders," NBC, 1955; "Omnibus: The Blue Hotel," ABC, 1956; "Father Knows Best: Hard Luck Leo," NBC, 1956; "Goodyear Theatre: Christabel," NBC, 1959; "Startime: The Wonderful World of Entertainment," NBC, 1959; "Dick Powell's Zane Grey Theatre: The Broken Wing," CBS, 1961; "Stagecoach West: Songs My Mother Told Me," ABC, 1961; "Window on Main Street: The Old West Show," CBS, 1962; "The New Breed: Judgment at San Belito," ABC, 1962; "Route 66: From an Enchantress Fleeing," CBS, 1962; "The Dick Powell Show: Pericles on 31st Street," NBC, 1962; "Empire: Green, Green Hills," NBC, 1962; "Sam Benedict: Sugar and Spice and Everything," NBC, 1963; "The Breaking Point: A Little Anger Is a Good Thing," ABC, 1964; "Summer Playhouse: The Human Comedy," CBS, 1964; "The Fugitive: Tug of War," ABC, 1964; "Special for Women: The Menace of Age," ABC, 1964; "The FBI: The Hijackers," ABC, 1965; "Wagon Train: The Wanda Snow Story," ABC, 1965; "Wagon Train: The Silver Lady," ABC, 1965; "Ironside: Why the Tuesday Afternoon Club Met on Thursday," NBC, 1969; "The Name of the Game: Breakout to a Fast Buck," NBC, 1969; "Nanny and the Professor: Star Bright," ABC, 1970; "Bonanza: Fallen Woman," NBC, 1971; "Cannon: No Pockets in a Shroud," CBS, 1971; "McCloud: The Disposal Man," NBC, 1971;

"Room 222: The Fading of the Elegant Beast," ABC, 1971; "Alias Smith and Jones: Bad Night in Big Butte," ABC, 1972; "The Jimmy Stewart Show: Old School Ties," NBC, 1972; "Honeymoon Suite," ABC, 1972; "The Paul Lynde Show: No Nudes Is Good Nudes," ABC, 1972; "Ghost Story: Elegy for a Vampire," NBC, 1972; "Adam's Rib: The Unwritten Law," ABC, 1973; "The New Adventures of Perry Mason: The Case of the Tortured Titan," CBS, 1974; "Shaft: The Capricorn Murders," CBS, 1974; "Medical Story: A Right to Die," NBC, 1975.

TV MOVIES AND MINISERIES: "Seven in Darkness," ABC, 1969; "A Taste of Evil," ABC, 1971; "Shootout in a One-Dog Town," ABC, 1974.

O'CONNOR, CARROLL
b. New York City, NY, August 2, 1924. Actor who made Archie Bunker a television icon; now he plays Chief Bill Gillespie on "In the Heat of the Night," and has won Emmies for both roles.
AS A REGULAR: "All in the Family," CBS, 1971-79; "Archie Bunker's Place," CBS, 1979-83; "In the Heat of the Night," NBC, 1988- .
AND: "Armstrong Circle Theatre: Full Disclosure," CBS, 1960; "Armstrong Circle Theatre: Positive Identification," CBS, 1960; "The Sacco-Vanzetti Story," NBC, 1960; "The Untouchables: Power Play," ABC, 1961; "Dr. Kildare: The Burning Sky," NBC, 1962; "The Untouchables: Bird in the Hand," ABC, 1962; "The Dick Powell Show: Luxury Liner," NBC, 1963; "Stoney Burke: Web of Fear," ABC, 1963; "Alcoa Premiere: The Dark Labyrinth," ABC, 1963; "The Eleventh Hour: Pressure Breakdown," NBC, 1963; "Bonanza: The Boss," NBC, 1963; "East Side/West Side: Age of Consent," CBS, 1963; "Slattery's People: Question-What Did You Do All Day, Mr. Slattery?," CBS, 1965; "Ben Casey: Three Li'l Lambs," ABC, 1965; "Profiles in Courage: Grover Cleveland," NBC, 1965; "Dr. Kildare: The Time Buyer," NBC, 1965; "Slattery's People: A Sitting Duck Named Slattery," CBS, 1965; "I Spy: It's All Done with Mirrors," NBC, 1966; "Bob Hope Chrysler Theatre: Massacre at Ft. Phil Kearney," NBC, 1966; "Gunsmoke: The Wrong Man," CBS, 1966; "The Wild Wild West: The Night of the Ready-Made Corpse," CBS, 1966; "That Girl: A Tenor's Loving Care," ABC, 1967; "Gunsmoke: Major Glory," CBS, 1967; "A Walk in the Night," NBC, 1968; "Walt Disney's Wonderful World of Color: Ride a Northbound Horse," NBC, 1969; "The Governor and J.J.: Pilot," CBS, 1969; "The Virginia Graham Show," SYN, 1971; "The Funny Papers," CBS, 1972; "Of Thee I Sing," CBS, 1972; "The Vin Scully Show," CBS, 1973; "Three for the Girls," CBS, 1973; "The Tonight Show Starring Johnny Carson," NBC, 1974; "Tony Orlando and Dawn," CBS, 1974; "Sammy and Company," SYN, 1975; "The Merv Griffin Show," SYN, 1976.

TV MOVIES AND MINISERIES: "Fear No Evil," NBC, 1969; "The Last Hurrah," NBC, 1977; "Convicted," NBC, 1986; "Hallmark Hall of Fame: Foxfire," CBS, 1987.

* Emmies: 1972, 1977, 1978, 1979, 1989.
* See also "All in the Family," Jean Stapleton.

O'CONNOR, DONALD

b. *Chicago, IL, August 28, 1925.* Gifted song-and-dance man ("Singin' in the Rain") who did lots of TV variety shows, including a couple of his own.

AS A REGULAR: "The Colgate Comedy Hour," NBC, 1951-54; "The Donald O'Connor Texaco Show," NBC, 1954-55; "The Donald O'Connor Show," SYN, 1968.

AND: "Dinah Shore Chevy Show," NBC, 1956; "The Ed Sullivan Show," CBS, 1957; "Standard Oil 75th Anniversary Show," NBC, 1957; "Playhouse 90: The Jet-Propelled Couch," CBS, 1957; "Du Pont Show of the Month: The Red Mill," CBS, 1958; "Dean Martin Special," NBC, 1959; "Pontiac Star Parade: The Gene Kelly Show," NBC, 1959; "The Donald O'Connor Show," NBC, 1960; "Here's Hollywood," NBC, 1961; "Dinah Shore Special," NBC, 1961; "High Hopes," SYN, 1961; "Hollywood Melody," NBC, 1962; "The Tonight Show," NBC, 1962; "Hollywood Palace," ABC, 1964; "Hollywood Palace," ABC, 1966; "Bob Hope Chrysler Theatre: Brilliant Benjamin Boggs," NBC, 1966; "Vacation Playhouse: The Hoofer," CBS, 1966; "ABC Stage '67: Olympus 7-0000," ABC, 1966; "Bob Hope Special," NBC, 1969; "The Carol Burnett Show," CBS, 1969; "The Andy Williams Show," NBC, 1970; "The Julie Andrews Hour," ABC, 1972; "The Bobby Darin Show," NBC, 1973; "The Girl with Something Extra: Irreconcilable Sameness," NBC, 1974; "Ellery Queen: The 12th Floor Express," NBC, 1975; "Police Story: Payment Deferred," NBC, 1976; "Dinah!," SYN, 1976; "Tony Orlando and Dawn," CBS, 1976; "Dinah!," SYN, 1977; "The Love Boat: Seal of Approval," ABC, 1981; "Alice: Guinness on Tap," CBS, 1981; "Simon & Simon: Grand Illusion," CBS, 1983; "The Love Boat: Paying the Piper," ABC, 1985; "The Love Boat: Second Banana," ABC, 1986; "Highway to Heaven: Playing for Keeps," NBC, 1986; "America's Tribute to Bob Hope," NBC, 1988.

* Emmies: 1954.

O'HANLON, GEORGE

b. *Brooklyn, NY, November 23, 1917.* Actor who provided the voice of George Jetson.

AS A REGULAR: "The Life of Riley," NBC, 1955-56; "Pantomime Quiz," ABC, 1958; "The Jetsons," ABC, 1962-63; "The Reporter," CBS, 1964.

AND: "I Love Lucy: Lucy and Superman," CBS, 1957; "Sugarfoot: Bunch Quitter," ABC, 1957;

"Schlitz Playhouse of Stars: The Hole Card," CBS, 1957; "Maverick: Black Fire," ABC, 1958; "How to Marry a Millionaire: Loco and the Cowboy," SYN, 1959; "The Red Skelton Show," CBS, 1960; "The Ann Sothern Show: Secret Admirer," CBS, 1960; "Checkmate: Melody for Murder," CBS, 1961; "The Ann Sothern Show: Invitation," CBS, 1961; "The Roaring Twenties: Footlights," ABC, 1962; "Love, American Style: Love and the Dummies," ABC, 1971; "The Odd Couple: My Strife in Court," ABC, 1973.

TV MOVIES AND MINISERIES: "Where Have All the People Gone?," NBC, 1974; "The Missing Are Deadly," ABC, 1975.

O'HARA, CATHERINE

b. *Canada, March 4, 1954.* Blonde comic actress of film ("Home Alone") and TV.

AS A REGULAR: "Second City TV," SYN, 1977-80; "The Steve Allen Comedy Hour," NBC, 1980-81; "SCTV Network 90," NBC, 1981-82.

AND: "Trying Times: Get a Job," PBS, 1988; "Late Night with David Letterman," NBC, 1989.

O'HARA, MAUREEN

b. *Maureen FitzSimons, Dublin, Ireland, August 17, 1921.* Attractive redheaded film actress ("Miracle on 34th Street," "The Quiet Man," "McLintock!") who sang and danced a fair amount in TV.

AS A GUEST: "This Is Your Life," NBC, 1957; "Dinah Shore Chevy Show," NBC, 1957; "The Perry Como Show," NBC, 1958; "The George Gobel Show," NBC, 1958; "Bob Hope Special," NBC, 1959; "Pat Boone Chevy Showroom," ABC, 1959; "The Perry Como Show," NBC, 1959; "Dick Clark's World of Talent," ABC, 1959; "Hobby Lobby," ABC, 1959; "The Ford Show," NBC, 1959; "Perry Como's Kraft Music Hall," NBC, 1959; "Special Tonight: Mrs. Miniver," CBS, 1960; "The Jack Paar Show," NBC, 1960; "Family Classics: The Scarlet Pimpernel," CBS, 1960; "Bell Telephone Hour: 'Twas the Night Before ...," NBC, 1960; "The Chevy Show," NBC, 1961; "The Ed Sullivan Show," CBS, 1961; "Theatre '62: Spellbound," NBC, 1962; "The Ed Sullivan Show," CBS, 1962; "Bell Telephone Hour: Gala Performance," NBC, 1962; "Hallmark Hall of Fame: A Cry of Angels," NBC, 1963; "The Garry Moore Show: High Button Shoes," CBS, 1966; "Off to See the Wizard: Who's Afraid of Mother Goose?," ABC, 1967.

TV MOVIES AND MINISERIES: "The Red Pony," NBC, 1973.

O'HEANEY, CAITLIN

b. *Whitefish Bay, WI, August 16, 1953.*
AS A REGULAR: "Apple Pie," ABC, 1978; "Tales

of the Gold Monkey," ABC, 1982-83; "The Charmings," ABC, 1987.
AND: "St. Elsewhere: Getting Ahead," NBC, 1987; "Murder, She Wrote: When Thieves Fall Out," CBS, 1987; "Badlands 2005," ABC, 1988; "Alien Nation: Chains of Love," FOX, 1989.
TV MOVIES AND MINISERIES: "The Seeding of Sarah Burns," CBS, 1979.

O'KEEFE, DENNIS

b. Edward Vance Flanagan, Fort Madison, IA, March 29, 1908; d. 1968. Light leading man of the movies who tried the widowed-father sitcom route in the late fifties.
AS A REGULAR: "Suspicion," NBC, 1957; "The Dennis O'Keefe Show," CBS, 1959-60.
AND: "Nash Airflyte Theatre: Scandalous Conduct," CBS, 1951; "Lux Video Theatre: Route Nineteen," CBS, 1951; "Gulf Playhouse: Double Byline," NBC, 1952; "Lux Video Theatre: A Time for Heroes," CBS, 1953; "Robert Montgomery Presents: Head for Moonlight," NBC, 1953; "Climax!: The Thirteenth Chair," CBS, 1954; "Producers Showcase: Yellow Jack," NBC, 1955; "Climax!: Edge of Terror," CBS, 1955; "Lux Video Theatre: The Human Jungle," NBC, 1955; "Climax!: Scheme to Defraud," CBS, 1955; "Screen Directors Playhouse: It's Always Sunday," CBS, 1956; "Kraft Television Theatre: Five Minutes to Live," NBC, 1956; "Studio One: Manhattan Duet," CBS, 1956; "Climax!: A Trophy for Howard Davenport," CBS, 1956; "Playhouse 90: Confession," CBS, 1956; "Schlitz Playhouse of Stars: The Traveling Corpse," CBS, 1957; "The Ford Show," NBC, 1957; "Suspicion: The Woman With Red Hair," NBC, 1958; "Suspicion: The Devil Makes Three," NBC, 1958; "Studio 57: Take Five," SYN, 1958; "Riverboat: River Champion," NBC, 1960; "Riverboat: Return of River Champion," NBC, 1961; "The Joey Bishop Show: The Bachelor," NBC, 1961; "Follow the Sun: The Longest Crap Game in History," ABC, 1961; "The Dick Powell Show: Open Season," NBC, 1961; "Follow the Sun: Annie Beeler's Place," ABC, 1962; "The Price Is Right," ABC, 1965; "Petticoat Junction: Twenty-Five Years Too Late," CBS, 1966.

OLIN, KEN

b. Chicago, IL, July 30, 1954. Actor who plays Michael Steadman on "thirtysomething."
AS A REGULAR: "The Bay City Blues," NBC, 1983; "Hill Street Blues," NBC, 1984-85; "Falcon Crest," CBS, 1985-86; "thirtysomething," ABC, 1987- .
AND: "Murder, She Wrote: Deadline for Murder," CBS, 1986; "The Tonight Show Starring Johnny Carson," NBC, 1989.
TV MOVIES AND MINISERIES: "Tonight's the Night,"

ABC, 1987; "I'll Take Manhattan," CBS, 1987; "Police Story: Cop Killers," ABC, 1988.

OLIVIER, LORD LAURENCE

b. Dorking, England, May 22, 1907; d. 1989. Legendary actor and former director of England's National Theatre Company whose TV work was limited to pretigious, Emmy-winning productions, an occasional visit with Dick Cavett and a few commercials for Polaroid in the seventies.
AS A GUEST: "The Moon and Sixpence," NBC, 1959; "The Power and the Glory," CBS, 1961; "NET Playhouse: Uncle Vanya," NET, 1967; "On Stage: Male of the Species," NBC, 1969; "Long Day's Journey Into Night," ABC, 1973; "The Dick Cavett Show," ABC, 1973; "ABC Theatre: The Merchant of Venice," ABC, 1974; "The Dick Cavett Show," PBS, 1980.
TV MOVIES AND MINISERIES: "David Copperfield," ABC, 1970; "Love Among the Ruins," ABC, 1976; "Cat on a Hot Tin Roof," NBC, 1976; "Jesus of Nazareth," NBC, 1977; "Great Performances: Brideshead Revisited," PBS, 1981-82; "King Lear," SYN, 1984; "Peter the Great," NBC, 1986.
* Emmies: 1960, 1973, 1975, 1982, 1984.

OLMOS, EDWARD JAMES

b. East Los Angeles, CA, February 24, 1947. Gaunt, dark-featured actor who won an Emmy as the glowering Lt. Martin Castillo on "Miami Vice."
AS A REGULAR: "Miami Vice," NBC, 1984-89.
AND: "Police Woman: Sara Who?," NBC, 1976; "Hawaii Five-O: Ready, Aim," CBS, 1977; "Hill Street Blues: Of Mouse and Man," NBC, 1982; "Hill Street Blues: Zen and the Art of Law Enforcement," NBC, 1982; "Hill Street Blues: Parting Is Such Sweep Sorrow," NBC, 1984; "Later with Bob Costas," NBC, 1989.
TV MOVIES AND MINISERIES: "Evening in Byzantium," SYN, 1978; "300 Miles for Stephanie," NBC, 1981; "The Fortunate Pilgrim," NBC, 1988.
* Emmies: 1985.

O'LOUGHLIN, GERALD S.

b. New York City, NY, December 23, 1921. Actor who played Lt. Eddie Ryker on "The Rookies" and Joe Kaplan on "Our House."
AS A REGULAR: "Storefront Lawyers," CBS, 1970-71; "The Rookies," ABC, 1972-76; "Automan," ABC, 1983-84; "Our House," NBC, 1986-88.
AND: "Our American Heritage: The Secret Rebel," NBC, 1961; "The Asphalt Jungle: The Fighter," ABC, 1961; "Lamp Unto My Feet: The Gift," CBS, 1961; "Going My Way: A Man for Mary," ABC, 1962; "Ben Casey: Of All Save Pain

Bereft," ABC, 1962; "The Defenders: Kill or Be Killed," CBS, 1963; "For the People: ... to prosecute all crimes ...," CBS, 1965; "The FBI: Ordeal," ABC, 1966; "Mission: Impossible: The Killing," CBS, 1968; "Mannix: Comes Up Rose," CBS, 1968; "Judd for the Defense: A Swim with Sharks," ABC, 1968; "Medical Center: Emergency in Ward E," CBS, 1969; "The FBI: Fatal Impostor," ABC, 1970; "The Virginian: Train of Darkness," NBC, 1970; "Then Came Bronson: The Mary R," NBC, 1970; "Mission: Impossible: Shape-Up," CBS, 1971; "Room 222: The Quitter," ABC, 1972; "Mission: Impossible: The Killing," CBS, 1968; "McClain's Law: Pilot," NBC, 1981; "M*A*S*H: Bombshells," CBS, 1982; "Simon & Simon: Room 3502," CBS, 1983; "Quincy: A Loss for Words," NBC, 1983; "Riptide: The Orange Grove," NBC, 1984; "Murder, She Wrote: Jake's Law," CBS, 1989.
TV MOVIES AND MINISERIES: "The D.A.: Murder One," NBC, 1969; "Murder at the World Series," ABC, 1977; "Something for Joey," CBS, 1977; "Crash," ABC, 1978; "Arthur Hailey's Wheels," NBC, 1978; "Roots: The Next Generations," ABC, 1979; "Blind Ambition," CBS, 1979; "A Matter of Life and Death," CBS, 1981; "The Blue and the Gray," CBS, 1982; "Brothers-in-Law," ABC, 1985; "Under Siege," NBC, 1986; "Child's Cry," CBS, 1986.

OLSEN, JOHNNY
b. Windon, MN, 1910; d. 1985. Jovial announcer who did hundreds of game shows; best known for his work for Jackie Gleason ("From Miami Beach—The Sun and Fun Capital of the World") and "The Price Is Right" ("Come on down!").
AS A REGULAR: "Doorway to Fame," DUM, 1947-49; "Fun for the Money," ABC, 1949; "The Strawhatters," DUM, 1953; "Hold That Note," NBC, 1957; "Keep It in the Family," ABC, 1957-58; "Play Your Hunch," NBC, 1960; 1962; "Jackie Gleason and His American Scene Magazine," CBS, 1962-66; "The Jackie Gleason Show," CBS, 1966-70; "The Price Is Right," CBS, 1972-85.

OLSEN, MERLIN
b. Logan, UT, September 15, 1940. Former football star who seems to be repenting for it by appearing in as many gentle roles as possible; he played Jonathan Garvey on "Little House" and Father Murphy.
AS A REGULAR: "Little House on the Prairie," NBC, 1977-81; "Father Murphy," NBC, 1981-84; "Fathers and Sons," NBC, 1986; "Aaron's Way," NBC, 1988.
AND: "Shindig," ABC, 1965; "Petticoat Junction: With This Ring," CBS, 1970; "Walking Tall: The

Hit Man," NBC, 1981.
TV MOVIES AND MINISERIES: "A Fire in the Sky," NBC, 1978; "Time Bomb," NBC, 1984.

OLSEN, SUSAN
b. Santa Monica, CA, 1961. Blonde moppet who played Cindy Brady; she was on her honeymoon when "A Very Brady Christmas" was shot, given rise to rumors that she'd been killed or sold into bondage.
AS A REGULAR: "The Brady Bunch," ABC, 1969-74; "The Brady Bunch Hour," ABC, 1977; "The Bradys," CBS, 1990.
AND: "Julia: The Grass Is Sometimes Greener," NBC, 1968; "Gunsmoke: A Man Called Smith," CBS, 1969.
TV MOVIES AND MINISERIES: "The Brady Girls Get Married," NBC, 1981.

O'MALLEY, J. PAT
b. England, 1901; d. 1985. Bald character actor often cast as a rascal; he played Bert Beasley, fiance of the randy Mrs. Naugatuck (Hermione Baddeley) on "Maude" and was the father of Rob Petrie on "The Dick Van Dyke Show."
AS A REGULAR: "My Favorite Martian," CBS, 1963-64; "Wendy & Me," ABC, 1964-65; "The Rounders," ABC, 1966-67; "A Touch of Grace," ABC, 1973; "Maude," CBS, 1975-77.
AND: "The Adventures of Hiram Holliday: Wrong Rembrandt," NBC, 1956; "Kraft Television Theatre: The Just and the Unjust," NBC, 1956; "Schlitz Playhouse of Stars: The Lady Was a Flop," CBS, 1957; "Robert Montgomery Presents: Slice of Life," NBC, 1957; "Gunsmoke: Monopoly," CBS, 1958; "Peter Gunn: The Vicious Dog," NBC, 1958; "Rawhide: Incident at the Buffalo Smoke House," CBS, 1959; "Walt Disney Presents: The Swamp Fox-A Case of Treason," ABC, 1960; "Have Gun, Will Travel: Out at the Old Ballpark," CBS, 1960; "The Law and Mr. Jones: What's in a Name?," ABC, 1960; "National Velvet: The Drought," NBC, 1960; "Wanted Dead or Alive: The Medicine Man," CBS, 1960; "Adventures in Paradise: The Jonah Stone," ABC, 1961; "Thriller: Yours Truly, Jack the Ripper," NBC, 1961; "The Dick Van Dyke Show: What's in a Middle Name?," CBS, 1962; "Frontier Circus: The Inheritance," CBS, 1962; "Sam Benedict: Not Even the Gulls Shall Weep," NBC, 1963; "The Real McCoys: Sir Fergus McCoy," CBS, 1963; "The Andy Griffith Show: Up in Barney's Room," CBS, 1963; "The Lloyd Bridges Show: The Rising of the Moon," CBS, 1963; "The Twilight Zone: The Self-Improvement of Salvadore Ross," CBS, 1964; "The Lucy Show: Lucy Goes Into Politics," CBS, 1964; "The Twilight Zone: Mr. Garrity and the Graves," CBS, 1964; "The Dick Van Dyke Show: The Plot

Thickens," CBS, 1964; "The Man From UNCLE: The Nowhere Affair," NBC, 1966; "Run, Buddy, Run: Win, Place, Die," CBS, 1966; "Bewitched: Sam's Spooky Chair," ABC, 1966; "The Man From UNCLE: The Jingle Bells Affair," NBC, 1966; "Batman: That Darn Catwoman/Scat, Darn Catwoman," ABC, 1967; "The Mod Squad: Bad Man on Campus," ABC, 1968; "The Ghost and Mrs. Muir: It's a Gift," NBC, 1969; "I Dream of Jeannie: Jeannie for the Defense," NBC, 1969; "The Beverly Hillbillies: Drysdale and Friend," CBS, 1969; "The Brady Bunch: The Honey-moon," ABC, 1969; "Nanny and the Professor: Strictly for the Birds," ABC, 1970; "Storefront Lawyers: The Electric Kid," CBS, 1970; "Love, American Style: Love and the Golden Memory," ABC, 1973; "Barney Miller: You Dirty Rat," ABC, 1975; "Harry O: Mr. Five and Dime," ABC, 1976; "Switch: Dancer," CBS, 1977; "The Rockford Files: The Deadly Maze," NBC, 1977; "One Day at a Time: Peabody's War," CBS, 1978; "Lou Grant: Scam," CBS, 1979; "Hizzonner: Mr. Perfect," NBC, 1979; "Barney Miller: The Counterfeiter," ABC, 1979; "Three's Company: Old Folks at Home," ABC, 1979; "Family: 'Tis the Season," ABC, 1979; "Barney Miller: The Rainmaker," ABC, 1981; "Taxi: The Road Not Taken," ABC, 1982.

TV MOVIES AND MINISERIES: "Getting Away From It All," ABC, 1972; "A Matter of Life and Death," CBS, 1981; "A Small Killing," CBS, 1981.

O'NEAL, PATRICK

b. *Ocala, FL, September 26, 1927.* Graying actor in bossy roles, sometimes as a bad guy.

AS A REGULAR: "Dick and the Duchess," CBS, 1957-58; "Diagnosis: Unknown," CBS, 1960; "Kaz," CBS, 1978-79; "Emerald Point NAS," CBS, 1983.

AND: "Hallmark Hall of Fame: The Road to Tara," NBC, 1954; "Cavalcade of America: The Paper Sword," ABC, 1954; "Treasury Men in Action: Case of the Still Waters," ABC, 1955; "Appoint-ment with Adventure: Design for Trouble," CBS, 1955; "Matinee Theatre: The Catamaran," NBC, 1956; "The Joseph Cotten Show: The Deadly Chain," NBC, 1957; "Wagon Train: The Beauty Jamison Story," NBC, 1958; "The Millionaire: Millionaire Elizabeth Tander," CBS, 1960; "Special for Women: The Single Woman," NBC, 1961; "Play of the Week: The Magic of the Loss," SYN, 1961; "Look Up and Live: The Interior Life," CBS, 1961; "Look Up and Live: The Moment," CBS, 1961; "Naked City: The Sweetly Smiling Face of Truth," ABC, 1962; "The Defenders: Poltergeist," CBS, 1963; "The Nurses: The Perfect Nurse," CBS, 1963; "The Twilight Zone: A Short Drink From a Certain Fountain," CBS, 1963; "The Defenders: Fugue for Trumpet and Small Boy," CBS, 1963; "Route 66: Where

There's a Will There's a Way," CBS, 1964; "The Alfred Hitchcock Hour: Bed of Roses," CBS, 1964; "The Outer Limits: Wolf 359," ABC, 1964; "The Defenders: The Man Who," CBS, 1964; "Coronet Blue: Six Months to Mars," CBS, 1967; "Snap Judgment," NBC, 1969; "Night Gallery: A Fear of Spiders," NBC, 1971; "Alias Smith and Jones: Everything Else You Can Steal," ABC, 1971; "McCloud: The Disposal Man," NBC, 1971; "Columbo: Blueprint for Murder," NBC, 1972; "Marcus Welby, M.D.: House of Mirrors," ABC, 1972; "Cannon: Stakeout," CBS, 1972; "The FBI: The Game of Chess," ABC, 1972; "The Doris Day Show: The Press Secretary," CBS, 1972; "McCloud: The Barefoot Stewardess Caper," NBC, 1972; "The Doris Day Show: Welcome to Big Sur," CBS, 1973; "The Doris Day Show: Meant for Each Other," CBS, 1973; "Search: Moment of Madness," NBC, 1973; "Barnaby Jones: Secret of the Dunes," CBS, 1973; "Barnaby Jones: The Challenge," CBS, 1974; "The Streets of San Francisco: The Glass Dart Board," ABC, 1975; "Medical Center: Too Late for Tomorrow," CBS, 1975; "Barnaby Jones: Sins of the Father," CBS, 1976; "Columbo: Make Me a Perfect Murder," NBC, 1978; "Nurse: To Life," CBS, 1982; "Murder, She Wrote: Broadway Malady," CBS, 1985; "Blacke's Magic: Knave of Diamonds, Ace of Hearts," NBC, 1986; "J.J. Starbuck: The Six Percent Solution," NBC, 1987; "A Man Called Hawk: Choice of Chance," ABC, 1989.

TV MOVIES AND MINISERIES: "Companions in Nightmare," NBC, 1968; "Cool Million," NBC, 1972; "Once the Killing Starts," ABC, 1974; "Crossfire," NBC, 1975; "The Killer Who Wouldn't Die," ABC, 1976; "Twin Detectives," ABC, 1976; "The Moneychangers," NBC, 1976; "The Deadliest Season," CBS, 1977; "The Last Hurrah," NBC, 1977; "Like Mom, Like Me," CBS, 1978; "Make Me an Offer," ABC, 1980; "Fantasies," ABC, 1982.

O'NEAL, RYAN

b. *Ryan Patrick O'Neal, Los Angeles, CA, April 20, 1941.* Handsome leading man of movies ("Love Story," "Paper Moon") and TV, though he hasn't been very successful in either medium as of late; companion of Farrah Fawcett.

AS A REGULAR: "The Vikings," SYN, 1960; "Empire," NBC, 1962-63; "Peyton Place," ABC, 1964-69.

AND: "The Many Loves of Dobie Gillis: The Hunger Strike," CBS, 1960; "G.E. Theatre: The Playoff," CBS, 1960; "Yes, Yes Nanette: Nanette's Teenage Suitor," NBC, 1961; "Bachelor Father: Bentley and the Great Debate," NBC, 1961; "Yes, Yes Nanette: Nancy Comes Home," NBC, 1961; "Leave It to Beaver: Wally Goes

Steady," ABC, 1961; "My Three Sons: Chug and Robbie," ABC, 1962; "Our Man Higgins: It's Higgins, Sir," ABC, 1962; "Play Your Hunch," NBC, 1963; "The Virginian: It Takes a Big Man," NBC, 1963; "Perry Mason: The Case of the Bountiful Beauty," CBS, 1964; "Wagon Train: The Nancy Styles Story," ABC, 1964; "Everybody's Talking," ABC, 1967; "The Search," CBS, 1968; "Under the Yum Yum Tree," ABC, 1969; "The Mike Douglas Show," SYN, 1975.
TV MOVIES AND MINISERIES: "Love, Hate, Love," ABC, 1971; "Small Sacrifices," ABC, 1989.

O'NEAL, TATUM

b. Los Angeles, CA, November 5, 1963. Oscar-winning former child actress; daughter of Ryan O'Neal and actress Joanna Moore.
AS A GUEST: "Cher," CBS, 1975; "Faerie Tale Theatre: Goldilocks and the Three Bears," SHO, 1984; "CBS Schoolbreak Special: 15 and Getting Straight," CBS, 1989.

O'NEILL, DICK

b. Bronx, NY. Heavyset character actor who usually plays East-coast types; he was Charlie, father of Chris Cagney on "Cagney & Lacey."
AS A REGULAR: "Rosetti and Ryan," NBC, 1977; "Kaz," CBS, 1978-79; "Cagney & Lacey," CBS, 1983-87; "Empire," CBS, 1984; "Better Days," CBS, 1986; "Falcon Crest," CBS, 1987.
AND: "The Chevy Show: O'Halloran's Luck," NBC, 1961; "Look Up and Live: Comedies of Terror—A Likely Story," CBS, 1961; "Good Times: Florida's Big Gig," CBS, 1974; "Barney Miller: Graft," ABC, 1975; "The Law: Prior Consent," NBC, 1975; "Barney Miller: Ambush," ABC, 1975; "Rhoda: Rhoda's Sellout," CBS, 1976; "M*A*S*H: Thirty-Eight Across," CBS, 1977; "M*A*S*H: B.J. Papa San," CBS, 1979; "Three's Company: Jack on the Lam," ABC, 1979; "One Day at a Time: Happy New Year II," CBS, 1979; "Diff'rent Strokes: Bank Job," NBC, 1980; "The Facts of Life: Shoplifting," NBC, 1980; "One Day at a Time: Orville and Emily Strike Back," CBS, 1982; "M*A*S*H: Sons and Bowlers," CBS, 1982; "St. Elsewhere: Monday, Tuesday, Sven's Day," NBC, 1983; "St. Elsewhere: Remission," NBC, 1983; "Magnum, P.I.: I Do?," CBS, 1983; "Cheers: The Barstoolie," NBC, 1985; "Simon & Simon: New Cop in Town," CBS, 1987; "Murder, She Wrote: Benedict Arnold Slipped Here," CBS, 1988; "Growing Pains: Birth of a Seaver," ABC, 1988.
TV MOVIES AND MINISERIES: "The UFO Incident," NBC, 1975; "The Entertainer," NBC, 1976; "Woman of the Year," CBS, 1976; "A Man Called Intrepid," SYN, 1979; "Chiller," CBS, 1985; "Passion Flower," CBS, 1986; "The Diamond Trap," CBS, 1988.

O'NEILL, ED

Actor who plays Al Bundy on "Married with Children."
AS A REGULAR: "Married with Children," FOX, 1987- .
AND: "Miami Vice: Heart of Darkness," NBC, 1984; "Hunter: The Garbage Man," NBC, 1985; "Midnight Caller: .12 Gauge," NBC, 1988; "Late Night with David Letterman," NBC, 1989.
TV MOVIES AND MINISERIES: "When Your Lover Leaves," NBC, 1983; "Police Story: Gladiator School," ABC, 1988.

O'NEILL, JENNIFER

b. Rio de Janeiro, Brazil, February 20, 1949. Former model and rather stiff film ("Summer of '42") and TV actress.
AS A REGULAR: "Bare Essence," NBC, 1983; "Cover Up," CBS, 1984-85.
AND: "The Tonight Show Starring Johnny Carson," NBC, 1972.
TV MOVIES AND MINISERIES: "Love's Savage Fury," ABC, 1979; "The Other Victim," CBS, 1981; "A.D.," NBC, 1985; "Chase," CBS, 1985; "Perry Mason: The Case of the Shooting Star," NBC, 1986; "The Red Spider," CBS, 1988; "Glory Days," CBS, 1988; "Full Exposure: The Sex Tapes Scandal," NBC, 1989.

ONTKEAN, MICHAEL

b. Canada, January 24, 1946. Actor who plays Sheriff Harry Truman on "Twin Peaks."
AS A REGULAR: "The Rookies," ABC, 1972-74; "Twin Peaks," ABC, 1990- .
AND: "The Partridge Family: Not with My Sister, You Don't," ABC, 1971.
TV MOVIES AND MINISERIES: "The Rookies," ABC, 1972; "The Blood of Others," HBO, 1984; "Kids Don't Tell," CBS, 1985.

ORBACH, JERRY

b. Bronx, NY, October 20, 1935. Stage actor and singer ("The Fantasticks") best known as seedy private dick Harry McGraw on "Murder, She Wrote" and on his own short-lived series.
AS A REGULAR: "The Law and Harry McGraw," CBS, 1987-88.
AND: "The Jack Paar Show," NBC, 1960; "Twenty-Four Hours in a Woman's Life," CBS, 1961; "The Ed Sullivan Show," CBS, 1961; "The Shari Lewis Show," NBC, 1962; "The Defenders: The Chosen Twelve," CBS, 1965; "Annie Get Your Gun," NBC, 1967; "The Mike Douglas Show," SYN, 1968; "The David Frost Show," SYN, 1969; "The Tonight Show Starring Johnny Carson," NBC, 1969; "The Tonight Show Starring Johnny Carson," NBC, 1970; "Love, American Style: Love and the Hoodwinked Honey," ABC, 1973; "Kojak: A Question of Answers," CBS, 1975; "Medical Center: The

Captives," CBS, 1975; "Murder, She Wrote: One Good Bid Deserves a Murder," CBS, 1986; "Irving Berlin's 100th Birthday Celebration," CBS, 1988; "Murder, She Wrote: Double Exposure," CBS, 1989.
TV MOVIES AND MINISERIES: "Out on a Limb," ABC, 1987; "Love Among Thieves," ABC, 1987; "Perry Mason: The Case of the Musical Murder," NBC, 1989.

ORLANDO, TONY
b. Michael Anthony Orlando Cassavitis, New York City, NY, April 3, 1944. Pop music performer who sang annoying songs with his group, Dawn; he was just as annoying as a variety-show host for a time.
AS A REGULAR: "Tony Orlando and Dawn," CBS, 1974-76.
AND: "American Bandstand," ABC, 1961; "American Bandstand," ABC, 1972; "Chico and the Man: The Big Brush-Off," NBC, 1975; "The Mike Douglas Show," SYN, 1975; "The Mike Douglas Show," SYN, 1980; "The Cosby Show: Mr. Quiet," NBC, 1985; "It's Garry Shandling's Show: Save Mr. Peck's," FOX, 1989; "The Pat Sajak Show," CBS, 1989.
TV MOVIES AND MINISERIES: "300 Miles for Stephanie," NBC, 1981; "Rosie: The Rosemary Clooney Story," CBS, 1982.

O'ROURKE, HEATHER
b. San Diego, CA, December 27, 1975; d. 1987. Child actress best known as the girl who said "They're heee-ere" in the "Poltergeist" movies.
AS A REGULAR: "Happy Days," ABC, 1982-83.
AND: "Webster: Travis," ABC, 1983; "Webster: Katherine's Swan Song," ABC, 1983; "Webster: Second Time Around," ABC, 1983.
TV MOVIES AND MINISERIES: "Surviving," ABC, 1985.

OSBORN, LYN
b. Detroit, MI, 1922; d. 1958. Actress who played Cadet Happy on "Space Patrol."
AS A REGULAR: "Space Patrol," ABC, 1951-52.

OSBORNE, MADOLYN SMITH—See
Madolyn Smith.

OSMOND BROTHERS
b. Ogden, UT—Wayne, August 28, 1951; Merrill, b. April 30, 1953; Jay, b. Ogden, UT, March 2, 1955; Alan, b. Ogden, UT, December 9, 1957.
AS REGULARS: "The Andy Williams Show," NBC, 1962-63; 1964-67; "The Travels of Jaimie McPheeters," ABC, 1963-64; "Donny and Marie," ABC, 1976-79.

AND: "Andy Williams Special," NBC, 1963; "Andy Williams Special," NBC, 1964; "Bob Hope Chrysler Theatre: The Seven Little Foys," NBC, 1964; "The Jerry Lewis Show," NBC, 1968; "The Jerry Lewis Show," NBC, 1969; "The Glen Campbell Goodtime Hour," CBS, 1970; "Paul Lynde Special," ABC, 1975.

OSMOND, DONNY
b. Ogden, UT, December 9, 1957.
AS A REGULAR: "Donny and Marie," ABC, 1976-79.
AND: "The Jerry Lewis Show," NBC, 1968; "Here's Lucy: Lucy and Donny Osmond," CBS, 1972; "The Perry Como Sunshine Show," CBS, 1974; "Andy Williams Special," NBC, 1974; "Hollywood Squares," NBC, 1975; "Bob Hope's Christmas Party," NBC, 1975; "General Electric's All-Star Anniversary," ABC, 1978; "The Love Boat: Kin Folk," ABC, 1979; "The Love Boat: The Christmas Presence," ABC, 1982.
TV MOVIES AND MINISERIES: "The Wild Women of Chastity Gulch," ABC, 1982.

OSMOND, JIMMY
b. Canoga Park, CA, April 16, 1963.
AS A REGULAR: "Donny and Marie," ABC, 1976-79.
AND: "Fame: Your Own Song," NBC, 1982; "The Love Boat: The Girl Who Stood Still," ABC, 1982; "The Love Boat: The Importance of Being Johnny," ABC, 1984; "The Love Boat: Getting Started," ABC, 1985.

OSMOND, KEN
b. Los Angeles, June 7, 1943. Former child actor who played Eddie "My, what a pretty dress you're wearing, Mrs. Cleaver" Haskell on "Leave It to Beaver."
AS A REGULAR: "Leave It to Beaver," CBS, 1957-58; ABC, 1958-63; "The New Leave It to Beaver," DIS, 1985-86; TBS, 1986-89.
AND: "Circus Boy: Corky's Big Parade," NBC, 1957; "Lassie: Fire Watchers," CBS, 1958; "The Munsters: Herman's Sorority Caper," CBS, 1966; "Happy Days: Vocational Education," ABC, 1983.
TV MOVIES AND MINISERIES: "Still the Beaver," CBS, 1983.

OSMOND, MARIE
b. Ogden, UT, October 13, 1959.
AS A REGULAR: "Donny and Marie," ABC, 1976-79; "Marie," NBC, 1980-81; "Ripley's Believe It or Not," ABC, 1985-86.
AND: "The Perry Como Sunshine Show," CBS, 1974; "Andy Williams Special," NBC, 1974; "Hollywood Squares," NBC, 1975; "Bob Hope's Christmas Party," NBC, 1975; "General Electric's All-Star Anniversary," ABC, 1978; "Doug

Henning Special," NBC, 1981; "The Love Boat: The Arrangement," ABC, 1982; "Marie Osmond at Church Street Station," TNN, 1989.
TV MOVIES AND MINISERIES: "The Gift of Love," ABC, 1978.

O'SULLIVAN, MAUREEN
b. *County Roscommon, Ireland, May 17, 1911.* Screen actress who was Tarzan's Jane, with occasional TV credits; mother of Mia and Tisa Farrow.
AS A REGULAR: "The Guiding Light," CBS, 1984.
AND: "Hollywood Opening Night: The Lucky Cloth," NBC, 1952; "Ford Theatre: They Also Serve," NBC, 1953; "Schlitz Playhouse of Stars: Parents' Weekend," CBS, 1953; "Ford Theatre: The Trestle," NBC, 1953; "Lux Video Theatre: Message in a Bottle," CBS, 1953; "Four Star Playhouse: The Gift," CBS, 1953; "Ford Theatre: Daughter of Mine," NBC, 1954; "Fireside Theatre: Brian," NBC, 1955; "Stage 7: Roommates," CBS, 1955; "Climax!: The Great Impersonation," CBS, 1955; "Warner Bros. Presents Casablanca: The Return," ABC, 1955; "The Whistler: Trademark," SYN, 1956; "Du Pont Theatre: The Blessed Midnight," ABC, 1956; "Lux Video Theatre: Michael and Mary," NBC, 1956; "Crossroads: The Man Who Walked on Water," ABC, 1957; "Climax!: Let It Be Me," CBS, 1957; "Playhouse 90: Edge of Innocence," CBS, 1957; "Alcoa Premiere: Moment of Decision," ABC, 1961; "Ben Casey: A Boy Is Standing Outside the Door," ABC, 1965.
TV MOVIES AND MINISERIES: "The Crooked Hearts," ABC, 1972; "The Great Houdinis," ABC, 1976.

OWEN, REGINALD
b. *England, August 5, 1887; d. 1972.* Film and stage actor who played lots of elderly gentlemen on TV, mainly because that's what he was by then.
AS A GUEST: "Climax!: The Trouble at Number 5," CBS, 1957; "Alcoa Presents One Step Beyond: The Dream," ABC, 1959; "Walt Disney Presents: Moochie of Pop Warner Football," ABC, 1960; "Walt Disney Presents: From Ticonderoga to Disneyland," ABC, 1960; "Thriller: Trio for Terror," NBC, 1961; "Peter Loves Mary: The Bridey Lindsey Story," NBC, 1961; "Maverick: A Technical Error," ABC, 1961; "Adventures in Paradise: The Quest of Ambrose Feather," ABC, 1962; "Camp Runamuck: Spiffy Quits," NBC, 1965; "Run for Your Life: The Borders of Barbarism," NBC, 1966; "Bewitched: The Short Happy

Circuit of Aunt Clara," ABC, 1966; "Bewitched: McTavish," ABC, 1968; "McCloud: Give My Regards to Broadway," CBS, 1972; "Topper Returns," NBC, 1973.

OWENS, BUCK
b. *Alvis Edgar Owens, Sherman, TX, August 12, 1929.*
AS A REGULAR: "Hee Haw," CBS, 1969-71; SYN, 1971-86.
AND: "Jubilee USA," ABC, 1960; "The Jimmy Dean Show," ABC, 1964; "The Jimmy Dean Show," ABC, 1965; "Operation: Entertainment," ABC, 1968; "The Jonathan Winters Show," CBS, 1969; "The Music Scene," ABC, 1969; "The Merv Griffin Show," CBS, 1970.
TV MOVIES AND MINISERIES: "Murder Can Hurt You!," ABC, 1980.

OWENS, GARY
b. *Mitchell, SD, May 10, 1936.* Comic actor and announcer who was one of the few regulars to stay with "Rowan & Martin's Laugh-In" from beginning to end.
AS A REGULAR: "Rowan & Martin's Laugh-In," NBC, 1968-73; "Letters to Laugh-In," NBC, 1969; "The Hudson Brothers Show," CBS, 1974; "The Gong Show," SYN, 1976-77; "Games People Play," NBC, 1980-81.
AND: "McHale's Navy: The Seven Faces of Ensign Parker," ABC, 1965; "McHale's Navy: A Star Falls on Taratupa," ABC, 1965; "The Munsters: Will Success Spoil Herman Munster?," CBS, 1965; "Batman: True or False-Face/Holy Rat Race," ABC, 1966; "Batman: The Sport of Penguins/A Horse of Another Color," ABC, 1967; "I Dream of Jeannie: The Biggest Star in Hollywood," NBC, 1969; "Barnaby Jones: Twenty Million Alibis," CBS, 1973.

OXENBERG, CATHERINE
b. *New York City, September 22, 1961.* Actress who played Amanda Carrington on "Dynasty."
AS A REGULAR: "Dynasty," ABC, 1984-86.
AND: "The Love Boat: The Present," ABC, 1984; "Saturday Night Live," NBC, 1986.
TV MOVIES AND MINISERIES: "The Royal Romance of Charles and Diana," CBS, 1982; "Still Crazy Like a Fox," CBS, 1987; "Swimsuit," NBC, 1989; "Trenchcoat in Paradise," CBS, 1989.

OZ, FRANK
b. *England, May 25, 1944.* Puppeteer.
AS A REGULAR: "Sesame Street," PBS, 1969- ; "The Muppet Show," SYN, 1976-81.
* Emmies: 1974, 1976, 1978.

P

PAAR, JACK

b. Canton, OH, May 1, 1918. Comedian and talk-show host prone to pretense and emotionalism, and a television legend because of it.

AS A REGULAR: "Up to Paar," NBC, 1952; "I've Got News for You," NBC, 1952; "Bank on the Stars," CBS, 1953; "The Jack Paar Show," CBS, 1953-56; "The Morning Show," CBS, 1954; "The Tonight Show (The Jack Paar Show)," NBC, 1957-62; "The Jack Paar Program," NBC, 1962-65; "Jack Paar Tonight," ABC, 1973.

AND: "The Ed Sullivan Show," CBS, 1956; "The Ed Sullivan Show," CBS, 1957; "Person to Person," CBS, 1957; "To Tell the Truth," CBS, 1957; "Startime: Jack Paar's World," NBC, 1960; "Jack Paar Presents," NBC, 1960; "Perry Como's Kraft Music Hall," NBC, 1960; "The Joey Bishop Show: Joey Meets Jack Paar," NBC, 1961; "The Jack Benny Program," CBS, 1961; "The Bob Newhart Show," NBC, 1962; "The Bob Hope Show," NBC, 1962; "Password," CBS, 1962; "Candid Camera," CBS, 1963; "Jack Paar Special," NBC, 1969; "The Jack Paar Diary," NBC, 1970; "Jack Paar Comes Home," NBC, 1986; "Jack Paar Remembers," NBC, 1987; "Late Night with David Letterman," NBC, 1988; "The Pat Sajak Show," CBS, 1989.

* Paar walked off his show February 1960 when network censors wouldn't let him tell a joke that included the phrase "W.C.," as in "water closet," as in "bathroom." The incident made nationwide headlines, with the joke being printed in newspapers and being read and heard by millions more people than would have heard it if Paar had told it on TV without incident.

* See also Liza Minnelli.

PAGE, GERALDINE

b. Kirksville, MO, November 22, 1924; d. 1987. Sensitive Oscar-winning actress ("A Trip to Bountiful") who won Emmy awards as the eccentric cousin Sookie in two Truman Capote stories, "A Christmas Memory" and "The Thanksgiving Visitor."

AS A GUEST: "Lux Video Theatre: The Lesson," NBC, 1952; "Summer Theatre: The Shadowy Third," CBS, 1952; "Robert Montgomery Presents: The Fall Guy," NBC, 1952; "Philco TV Playhouse: Miss Look-Alike," NBC, 1954; "Omnibus: The Turn of the Screw," CBS, 1955; "Windows: A Domestic Dilemma," CBS, 1955; "U.S. Steel Hour: Shoot It Again,"

CBS, 1955; "U.S. Steel Hour: The Hill Wife," CBS, 1957; "Kraft Television Theatre: Fire and Ice," NBC, 1957; "Playhouse 90: Portrait of a Murder," CBS, 1958; "G.E. Theatre: No Hiding Place," CBS, 1958; "Playhouse 90: Old Man," CBS, 1958; "Sunday Showcase: People Kill People Sometimes," NBC, 1959; "The Long Hot Summer: Evil Angel," ABC, 1966; "Hallmark Hall of Fame: Barefoot in Athens," NBC, 1966; "ABC Stage '67: A Christmas Memory," ABC, 1966; "The Thanksgiving Visitor," ABC, 1968; "Night Gallery: The Sins of the Fathers," NBC, 1972; "CBS Playhouse: Look Homeward, Angel," CBS, 1972; "Medical Center: The Betrayed," CBS, 1972; "Night Gallery: Something in the Woodwork," NBC, 1973; "The Snoop Sisters: Corpse and Robbers," NBC, 1973; "Kojak: A Shield for Murder," CBS, 1976.

TV MOVIES AND MINISERIES: "Live Again, Die Again," ABC, 1974; "Something for Joey," CBS, 1977; "The Parade," CBS, 1984; "Nazi Hunter: The Beate Klarsfeld Story," ABC, 1986.

* Emmies: 1967, 1969.

PAGE, LAWANDA

b. Cleveland, OH, October 19, 1920. Comic actress who played Aunt Esther on "Sanford & Son" and a spinoff series.

AS A REGULAR: "Sanford & Son," NBC, 1973-77; "The Sanford Arms," NBC, 1977; "Detective School," ABC, 1979; "B.A.D. Cats," ABC, 1980.

AND: "The Love Boat: The Main Event," ABC, 1977; "Diff'rent Strokes: The Relative," NBC, 1979; "The Mike Douglas Show," SYN, 1981.

PAGE, PATTI

b. Clara Ann Fowler, Claremore, OK, November 8, 1927. Singer of the fifties.

AS A REGULAR: "Music Hall," CBS, 1952; "Scott Music Hall," NBC, 1952-53; "The Patti Page Show," NBC, 1956; "The Big Record," CBS, 1957-58; "Patti Page Olds Show," ABC, 1958-59.

AND: "Appointment with Adventure: Paris Venture," CBS, 1956; "The Ed Sullivan Show," CBS, 1956; "The Perry Como Show," NBC, 1957; "Washington Square," NBC, 1957; "Five Stars in Springtime," NBC, 1957; "U.S. Steel Hour: Upbeat," CBS, 1957; "The Vic Damone Show," CBS, 1957; "The Perry Como Show," NBC, 1958; "The Bing Crosby Show," ABC,

1958; "Dinah Shore Chevy Show," NBC, 1960; "Bob Hope Buick Show," NBC, 1961; "Perry Como's Kraft Music Hall," NBC, 1961; "Bachelor Father: A Song Is Born," ABC, 1961; "Bell Telephone Hour: The Music of Love," NBC, 1962; "The Pat Boone Show," NBC, 1962; "Bell Telephone Hour," NBC, 1963; "The Ed Sullivan Show," CBS, 1963; "The Jimmy Dean Show," ABC, 1964; "The Tonight Show Starring Johnny Carson," NBC, 1964; "The Jonathan Winters Show," CBS, 1968; "Operation: Entertainment," ABC, 1968; "Bob Hope Special," NBC, 1969; "The David Frost Show," SYN, 1970; "The Mike Douglas Show," SYN, 1977; "The Music of Your Life," SYN, 1985.

PAIGE, JANIS

b. *Tacoma, WA, September 16, 1922.* Earthy actress-dancer in dramatic and variety shows; she played hospital administrator Catherine Hackett on "Trapper John, M.D."

AS A REGULAR: "It's Always Jan," CBS, 1955-56; "Lanigan's Rabbi," NBC, 1977; "Baby Makes Five," ABC, 1983; "Gun Shy," CBS, 1983; "Trapper John, M.D.," CBS, 1985-86.

AND: "Bob Hope Show," NBC, 1957; "Salute to Baseball," NBC, 1957; "The Perry Como Show," NBC, 1957; "Lux Video Theatre: The Latch Key," NBC, 1957; "The Big Record," CBS, 1957; "Pat Boone Chevy Showroom," ABC, 1957; "The Garry Moore Show," CBS, 1958; "The George Gobel Show," NBC, 1958; "Milton Berle Starring in the Kraft Music Hall," NBC, 1958; "The Red Skelton Show," CBS, 1959; "Westinghouse Desilu Playhouse: Chez Rouge," CBS, 1959; "The Secret World of Eddie Hodges," CBS, 1960; "The Milton Berle Show," NBC, 1962; "87th Precinct: The Lover," NBC, 1962; "The Red Skelton Hour," CBS, 1962; "Alcoa Premiere: Blues for a Hanging," ABC, 1962; "The Bob Hope Christmas Show," NBC, 1963; "The Dick Powell Show: The Last of the Private Eyes," NBC, 1963; "Burke's Law: Who Killed the Swinger on a Hook?," ABC, 1964; "You Don't Say," NBC, 1964; "The Fugitive: Ballad for a Ghost," ABC, 1964; "Bob Hope Christmas Special," NBC, 1965; "Roberta," NBC, 1969; "Sarge: Psst! Wanna Buy a Dirty Picture?," NBC, 1971; "Columbo: Blueprint for Murder," NBC, 1972; "Mannix: A Way to Dusty Death," CBS, 1973; "Police Story: A Dangerous Age," NBC, 1974; "The Mary Tyler Moore Show: Menage a Lou," CBS, 1976; "All in the Family: Archie's Brief Encounter," CBS, 1976; "The Rockford Files: A Three Day Affair with a Thirty Day Escrow," NBC, 1978; "Alice: The Cuban Connection," CBS, 1978; "All in the Family: The Return of the Waitress," CBS, 1978; "Eight Is Enough: Fathers and Other Strangers," ABC, 1979; "St. Elsewhere: Remission," NBC, 1983; "Mission: Impossible: The Haunting," ABC, 1989.

TV MOVIES AND MINISERIES: "The Turning Point of Jim Malloy," NBC, 1975; "Lanigan's Rabbi," NBC, 1976; "Angel on my Shoulder," ABC, 1980; "Valentine Magic on Love Island," NBC, 1980; "The Other Woman," CBS, 1983.

PALANCE, JACK

b. *Walter Palanuik, Lattimer, PA, February 18, 1920.* Burly actor who won an Emmy as punchdrunk prizefighter Mountain McClintock in "Requiem for a Heavyweight" and used his soft, threatening voice to good effect as the host of "Ripley's Believe It or Not."

AS A REGULAR: "The Greatest Show on Earth," ABC, 1963-64; "Bronk," CBS, 1975-76; "Ripley's Believe It or Not," ABC, 1982-86.

AND: "Lights Out: The Man Who Couldn't Remember," NBC, 1950; "Studio One: Little Man, Big World," CBS, 1952; "Gulf Playhouse: Necktie Party," NBC, 1952; "The Web: The Last Chance," CBS, 1953; "Suspense: The Kiss-Off," CBS, 1953; "Suspense: Cagliostro and the Chess Player," CBS, 1953; "Playhouse 90: Requiem for a Heavyweight," CBS, 1956; "Dick Powell's Zane Grey Theatre: The Lariat," CBS, 1956; "Playhouse 90: The Last Tycoon," CBS, 1957; "The Perry Como Show," NBC, 1957; "Playhouse 90: The Death of Manolete," CBS, 1957; "Texaco Star Theatre: Command Appearance," NBC, 1957; "Rivak the Barbarian," NBC, 1960; "Password," CBS, 1965; "Convoy: The Many Colors of Courage," NBC, 1965; "Run for Your Life: I Am the Late Diana Hays," NBC, 1966; "Alice Through the Looking Glass," NBC, 1966; "The Man From UNCLE: The Concrete Overcoat Affair," NBC, 1966; "The Mike Douglas Show," SYN, 1967; "The Carol Burnett Show," CBS, 1968; "The Strange Case of Dr. Jekyll and Mr. Hyde," NBC, 1968; "NET Playhouse: The Trail of Tears," NET, 1970; "The Mike Douglas Show," SYN, 1970; "NET Playhouse: Biography," NET, 1971; "The Sonny and Cher Comedy Hour," CBS, 1973; "The Tonight Show Starring Johnny Carson," NBC, 1974; "Buck Rogers in the 25th Century: Planet of the Slave Girls," NBC, 1979.

TV MOVIES AND MINISERIES: "Dracula," CBS, 1974; "The Godchild," ABC, 1974; "The Hatfields and McCoys," ABC, 1975; "Bronk," CBS, 1975; "The Last Ride of the Dalton Gang," NBC, 1979; "The Golden Moment: An Olympic Love Story," NBC, 1980; "The Ivory Ape," ABC, 1980.

* Emmies: 1957.

PALILLO, RON

b. *Connecticut, April 2, 1954.* Actor who played Arnold Horshack on "Welcome Back, Kotter"; his comic trademark was a wheezing laugh.

AS A REGULAR: "Welcome Back, Kotter," ABC, 1975-79.

AND: "The Rich Little Show," NBC, 1976; "Match Game '77," CBS, 1977; "The Love Boat: The Switch," ABC, 1978; "$weepstake$: Dewey and Harold and Sarah and Maggie," NBC, 1979; "The Love Boat: For the Record," ABC, 1981; "Alice: The Wild One," CBS, 1981.

TV MOVIES AND MINISERIES: "The Invisible Woman," NBC, 1983.

PALLANTE, ALADDIN—See Aladdin.

PALMER, BETSY

b. Betsy Hrunek, East Chicago, IN, November 1, 1926. Blonde actress who was the dumb one, usually, on "I've Got a Secret"; more recently she played Aunt Ginny on "Knots Landing."

AS A REGULAR: "Masquerade Party," ABC, 1956; NBC, 1957; "What's It For," NBC, 1957-58; "I've Got a Secret," CBS, 1957-67; "Number 96," NBC, 1980-81; "Knots Landing," CBS, 1989-90.

AND: "Summer Studio One: Sentence of Death," CBS, 1953; "Summer Studio One: Look Homeward, Hayseed," CBS, 1953; "Armstrong Circle Theatre: A Story to Whisper," NBC, 1953; "The Web: The Bait," CBS, 1954; "Philco TV Playhouse: The Ghost Writer," NBC, 1955; "Appointment with Adventure: The Secret of Juan Valdez," CBS, 1955; "Kraft Television Theatre: The Girl Who Saw Too Much," NBC, 1956; "Climax!: Burst of Violence," CBS, 1956; "Studio One: Goodbye, Picadilly," CBS, 1956; "Climax!: Stain of Honor," CBS, 1957; "Alcoa Hour: Protege," NBC, 1957; "U.S. Steel Hour: The Wayward Widow," CBS, 1959; "Phil Silvers Special: The Ballad of Louie the Louse," CBS, 1959; "Our American Heritage: The Pratical Dreamer," NBC, 1959; "Oscar Night in Hollywood," NBC, 1960; "U.S. Steel Hour: Game of Hearts," CBS, 1960; "The Garry Moore Show," CBS, 1960; "U.S. Steel Hour: Shame the Devil," CBS, 1960; "Password," CBS, 1961; "Password," CBS, 1962; "The Tonight Show Starring Johnny Carson," NBC, 1962; "Password," CBS, 1963; "The Price Is Right," ABC, 1963; "Password," CBS, 1964; "To Tell the Truth," CBS, 1964; "Candid Camera," CBS, 1964; "The Ed Sullivan Show," CBS, 1965; "Password," CBS, 1965; "The Mike Douglas Show," SYN, 1967; "Personality," NBC, 1967; "Personality," NBC, 1968; "Hallmark Hall of Fame: A Punt, a Pass and a Prayer," NBC, 1968; "Love, American Style: Love and the Ghost," ABC, 1972; "Captain Kangaroo," CBS, 1976; "Newhart: Me and My Gayle," CBS, 1987; "Murder, She Wrote: Something Borrowed, Someone Blue," CBS, 1989.

TV MOVIES AND MINISERIES: "The Zoo Gang," NBC, 1975; "Isabel's Choice," CBS, 1981; "The Goddess of Love," NBC, 1988.

PARDO, DON

b. Westfield, MA. Announcer extraordinaire.

AS A REGULAR: "Jeopardy!," NBC, 1964-75; "Saturday Night Live," NBC, 1975-81; 1982- .

AND: "ALF Takes Over the Network," NBC, 1989.

PARIS, JERRY

b. San Francisco, CA, July 25, 1925; d. 1986. Reliable supporting actor of fifties TV; in the sixties he played neighbor Jerry Helper on "The Dick Van Dyke Show" and got into sitcom directing.

AS A REGULAR: "Those Whiting Girls," CBS, 1957; "Steve Canyon," NBC, 1959; "The Untouchables," ABC, 1959-60; "Michael Shayne," NBC, 1960-61; "The Dick Van Dyke Show," CBS, 1961-66.

AND: "Matinee Theatre: Sound of Fear," NBC, 1956; "Navy Log: The Big A," ABC, 1956; "Schlitz Playhouse of Stars: Tower Room 14-A," CBS, 1957; "The 20th Century-Fox Hour: The Great American Hoax," CBS, 1957; "The Millionaire: The Bob Fielding Story," CBS, 1957; "The Bob Cummings Show: Scramble for Grandpa," CBS, 1957; "Startime: Incident at a Corner," NBC, 1960; "77 Sunset Strip: Big Boy Blue," ABC, 1961; "Robert Taylor's Detectives: Point of No Return," NBC, 1962; "G.E. Theatre: Ten Days in the Sun," CBS, 1962; "The Lloyd Bridges Show: Little Man, Big Bridge," CBS, 1962; "77 Sunset Strip: Falling Stars," ABC, 1963; "Death Valley Days: The Private Mint of Clark, Gruber & Co.," SYN, 1963; "Love, American Style: Love and the Psychiatrist," ABC, 1970.

TV MOVIES AND MINISERIES: "But I Don't Want To Get Married!," ABC, 1970; "Every Man Needs One," ABC, 1972;

AS DIRECTOR: "The Dick Van Dyke Show," CBS, 1963-66; "The Mary Tyler Moore Show," CBS, 1971; "Happy Days," ABC, 1974-84.

TV MOVIES AND MINISERIES: "But I Don't Want to Get Married!," ABC, 1970; "What's a Nice Girl Like You...?," ABC, 1971; "The Feminist and the Fuzz," ABC, 1971; "Two on a Bench," ABC, 1971; "Call Her Mom," ABC, 1972; "Evil Roy Slade," NBC, 1972; "The Couple Takes a Wife," ABC, 1972; "Every Man Needs One," ABC, 1972.

* Emmies: 1964.

PARKER, FESS

b. Fort Worth, TX, August 16, 1926. Actor who was a pop-culture phenomenon of the mid-fifties as coonskin-cap wearing Davy, Davy Crockett, King of the Wild Frontier, on "Disneyland"; in the sixties he played another coonskin-cap wearing fellow, Daniel Boone.

AS A REGULAR: "Disneyland: The Adventures of

Davy Crockett," ABC, 1954-55; "Disneyland: Doc Grayson," ABC, 1956-57; "Mr. Smith Goes to Washington," ABC, 1962-63; "Daniel Boone," NBC, 1964-70.

AND: "My Little Margie: The All-American," NBC, 1955; "Death Valley Days: Kickapoo Run," SYN, 1956; "The George Gobel Show," NBC, 1956; "The Ed Sullivan Show," CBS, 1957; "Disneyland: Fourth Anniversary Show," ABC, 1957; "The Mickey Mouse Club," ABC, 1958; "Playhouse 90: Turn Left at Mt. Everest," CBS, 1958; "Schlitz Playhouse of Stars: The Hasty Hanging," CBS, 1958; "Bob Hope Special," NBC, 1959; "Startime: Merman on Broadway," NBC, 1959; "G.E. Theatre: Aftermath," CBS, 1960; "Walt Disney Presents: Andrews' Raiders," ABC, 1961; "Here's Hollywood," NBC, 1961; "Walt Disney's Wonderful World of Color: The Light in the Forest," NBC, 1961; "Death Valley Days: Miracle at Whiskey Gulch," SYN, 1963; "The Alfred Hitchcock Hour: Nothing Ever Happens in Linvale," CBS, 1963; "Destry: Destry Had a Little Lamb," ABC, 1964; "The Danny Kaye Show," CBS, 1965; "The Fess Parker Show," CBS, 1974.

TV MOVIES AND MINISERIES: "Climb an Angry Mountain," NBC, 1972.

PARKER, JAMESON
b. Baltimore, November 18, 1947. Actor who played A.J. Simon on "Simon & Simon."

AS A REGULAR: "Somerset," NBC, 1970-76; "One Life to Live," ABC, 1976-78; "Simon & Simon," CBS, 1981-89.

TV MOVIES AND MINISERIES: "Women at West Point," CBS, 1979; "Anatomy of a Seduction," CBS, 1979; "The Gathering, Part II," NBC, 1979; "The Promise of Love," CBS, 1980; "Callie & Son," CBS, 1981; "Who Is Julia?" CBS, 1986.

PARKER, LEW
b. October 28, 1907; d. 1972. Comedian who played Lew Marie, father of Marlo Thomas on "That Girl."

AS A REGULAR: "Star Time," DUM, 1950-51; "Your Surprise Store," CBS, 1952; "That Girl," ABC, 1966-71.

AND: "The Steve Allen Show," NBC, 1956; "Kaiser Aluminum Hour: A Man's Game," NBC, 1957; "The Jackie Gleason Show," CBS, 1957; "Arthur Murray Party," NBC, 1959; "Pantomime Quiz," ABC, 1959; "Be Our Guest," CBS, 1960; "Gidget: Operation Shaggy Dog," ABC, 1966; "F Troop: The Ballot of Corporal Agarn," ABC, 1966; "The Lucy Show: Mooney the Monkey," CBS, 1966; "The Lucy Show: Lucy the Star Maker," CBS, 1967; "The Lucy Show: Lucy and Phil Harris," CBS, 1968; "The Lucy Show: Lucy and the Lost Star," CBS, 1968.

PARKER, SARAH JESSICA
b. Nelsonville, OH, March 25, 1965.

AS A REGULAR: "Square Pegs," CBS, 1982-83; "A Year in the Life," NBC, 1987-88; "Equal Justice," ABC, 1990- .

TV MOVIES AND MINISERIES: "Going for the Gold: The Bill Johnson Story," CBS, 1985; "A Year in the Life," NBC, 1986; "The Room Upstairs," CBS, 1987; "Pursuit," NBC, 1988; "The Ryan White Story," ABC, 1989.

PARKINS, BARBARA
b. Canada, May 22, 1942. Sexy sixties actress who played Betty Anderson Harrington Cord Harrington, one of the busier young women in "Peyton Place".

AS A REGULAR: "Peyton Place," ABC, 1964-69.

AND: "Leave It to Beaver: No Time for Babysitters," ABC, 1961; "Wagon Train: The Mark Minor Story," NBC, 1961; "The Tall Man: Shadow of the Past," NBC, 1961; "G.E. Theatre: We're Holding Your Son," CBS, 1961; "G.E. Theatre: A Friendly Tribe," CBS, 1961; "My Three Sons: Coincidence," ABC, 1962; "Perry Mason: The Case of the Unsuitable Uncle," CBS, 1962; "Dr. Kildare: The Soul Killer," NBC, 1962; "Laramie: The Wedding Party," NBC, 1963; "The Wide Country: The Lucky Punch," NBC, 1963; "The Merv Griffin Show," CBS, 1970; "Double Play: Ghost Story," NBC, 1972; "Great Performances: Jennie," PBS, 1975; "Gibbsville: All the Young Girls," NBC, 1976; "Hotel: Faith, Hope and Charity," ABC, 1983; "The Love Boat: The Light of Another Day," ABC, 1984.

TV MOVIES AND MINISERIES: "A Taste of Evil," ABC, 1971; "Snatched," ABC, 1973; "Law of the Land," NBC, 1976; "Best Sellers: Captains and the Kings," NBC, 1976; "Young Joe, the Forgotten Kennedy," ABC, 1977; "Testimony of Two Men," SYN, 1977; "The Critical List," NBC, 1978; "Manions of America," ABC, 1981; "Uncommon Valor," CBS, 1983; "Calender Girl Murders," ABC, 1984; "Peyton Place: The Next Generation," NBC, 1985.

PARKS, BERT
b. Bert Jacobson, Atlanta, GA, December 30, 1914. Host of the Miss America pageant from 1955-80, appearing again in 1990.

AS A REGULAR: "Party Line," NBC, 1947; "Break the Bank," ABC, 1948-49; NBC, 1949-52; CBS, 1952-53; NBC, 1953; ABC, 1954-56; "Stop the Music," ABC, 1949-52; 1954-56; "Balance Your Budget," CBS, 1952-53; "Double or Nothing," CBS, 1952-54; NBC, 1953; "Two in Love," CBS, 1954; "Break the $250,000 Bank," NBC, 1956-57; "Giant Step," CBS, 1956-57; "Hold That Note," NBC, 1957; "Masquerade Party," NBC, 1958-59; CBS,

1959-60; NBC, 1960; "Bid 'n' Buy," CBS, 1958; "County Fair," NBC, 1958-59; "Haggis Baggis," NBC, 1958-59; "The Big Payoff," CBS, 1959-60; "Yours for a Song," ABC, 1961-63; "Circus," SYN, 1971-73.
AND: "Bandstand," NBC, 1956; "Arthur Murray Party," NBC, 1959; "The Jack Paar Show," NBC, 1960; "The Tonight Show Starring Johnny Carson," NBC, 1963; "Burke's Law: Who Killed Mr. X?," ABC, 1963; "Burke's Law: Who Killed His Royal Highness?," ABC, 1964; "Burke's Law: Who Killed Mr. Colby in Ladies' Lingerie?," ABC, 1965; "Ellery Queen: Miss Aggie's Farewell Performance," NBC, 1975; "The Bionic Woman: Bionic Beauty," ABC, 1976; "The Love Boat: Making the Grade," ABC, 1980; "WKRP in Cincinnati: Herb's Dad," CBS, 1980; "227: A Funny Thing Happened on the Way to the Pageant," NBC, 1988; "Roseanne: Sweet Dreams," ABC, 1989.
* Bert Parks sang this song at the 1969 Miss America Pageant: "You Can't Be Caught Nappin' with Your Generation Gappin'."
* Parks was a regular host of the Miss America Pageant until 1980, at which time he was dumped for being too old and reaped reams of publicity because of it.

PARKS, LARRY
b. Samuel Lawrence Klausman Parks, Olathe, KS, December 13, 1914; d. 1975. Screen actor ("The Jolson Story") who was suddenly unemployable in the early fifties because of past Communist ties; TV roles helped a little. Husband of actress Betty Garrett.
AS A GUEST: "Ford Theatre: The Happiest Day," NBC, 1954; "Ford Theatre: Wedding March," NBC, 1954; "Ford Theatre: Tomorrow We'll Love," NBC, 1955; "Ford Theatre: A Smattering of Bliss," NBC, 1955; "Ford Theatre: The Penlands and the Poodle," ABC, 1957; "Arthur Murray Party," NBC, 1957; "Suspicion: Diagnosis: Death," NBC, 1958; "The Untouchables: The Lily Dallas Story," ABC, 1961; "Dr. Kildare: Breakdown," NBC, 1962.

PARKS, MICHAEL
b. Corona, CA, 1938. Actor who often plays loners or surly types; he was the motorcycle-riding Jim Bronson and more recently he played Jean Reneau on "Twin Peaks."
AS A REGULAR: "Then Came Bronson," NBC, 1969-70; "The Colbys," ABC, 1987; "Twin Peaks," ABC, 1990.
AND: "The Detectives Starring Robert Taylor: The Frightened Ones," ABC, 1961; "The Detectives Starring Robert Taylor: Personal Enemy," ABC, 1961; "Bus Stop: The Opposite Virtues," ABC, 1962; "The Real McCoys: George's Nephew," ABC, 1962; "Target: The Corruptors: Nobody

Gets Hurt," ABC, 1962; "Stoney Burke: The Riders," ABC, 1962; "Sam Benedict: Too Many Strangers," NBC, 1962; "Perry Mason: The Case of Constant Doyle," CBS, 1963; "77 Sunset Strip: Crashout," ABC, 1963; "The Alfred Hitchcock Hour: Diagnosis: Danger," CBS, 1963; "Bob Hope Chrysler Theatre: A Time for Killing," NBC, 1965; "A Hatful of Rain," ABC, 1968; "Owen Marshall, Counselor at Law: Sometimes Tough Is Good," ABC, 1973; "Medical Center: Fatal Memory," CBS, 1973; "Ironside: A Death in Academe," NBC, 1974; "McCloud: The 42nd Street Cavalry," NBC, 1974; "Wide World of Mystery: The Werewolf of Woodstock," ABC, 1975; "Police Woman: Ice," NBC, 1975; "Police Story: War Games," NBC, 1975; "Baretta: Half-Million Dollar Baby," ABC, 1975; "Wide World of Mystery: Murder at Malibu," ABC, 1975; "The Rookies: One-Way Street to Nowhere," ABC, 1975; "The Streets of San Francisco: Men Will Die," ABC, 1975; "Wide World of Mystery: Distant Early Warning," ABC, 1975; "Police Woman: A Shadow on the Sea," NBC, 1978; "Fantasy Island: The Golden Hour," ABC, 1978; "Shirley: Play on Words," NBC, 1979; "The Equalizer: Nocturne," CBS, 1986; "The Equalizer: Target of Choice," CBS, 1988; "Murder, She Wrote: Prediction: Murder," CBS, 1988.
TV MOVIES AND MINISERIES: "Stranger on the Run," NBC, 1967; "Then Came Bronson," NBC, 1969; "The Young Lawyers," CBS, 1969; "Can Ellen Be Saved?," ABC, 1974; "The Story of Pretty Boy Floyd," ABC, 1974; "Royce," CBS, 1976; "Perilous Voyage," NBC, 1976; "The Savage Bees," NBC, 1976; "Escape From Bogen County," CBS, 1977; "Rainbow," NBC, 1978; "Fast Friends," NBC, 1979; "Reward," ABC, 1980; "Turnover Smith," ABC, 1980; "Dial M for Murder," NBC, 1981; "Chase," CBS, 1985; "Dangerous Affection," NBC, 1987; "Spiker," CBS, 1988.

PARKYAKARKUS—See Harry Einstein.

PARRISH, HELEN
b. Columbus, GA, March 12, 1922; d. 1959. Former child actress who was a regular on one of television's first variety shows, "Hour Glass"; on "Leave It to Beaver" she played the mother of Lumpy Rutherford (Frank Bank).
AS A REGULAR: "Hour Glass," NBC, 1946; "Show Business Inc.," NBC, 1947.
AND: "Racket Squad: Bill of Sale," CBS, 1951; "Fireside Theatre: The Critic," NBC, 1953; "Twentieth Century Tales: Stepdaughter," ABC, 1953; "The Curtain Rises: Yang, Yin and Mrs. Wiswell," ABC, 1953; "Cavalcade of America: John Yankee," NBC, 1953; "TV Reader's Digest: If I Were Rich," ABC, 1955; "Crossroads: God in the Street," ABC, 1956; "Leave It to Beaver: Lumpy Rutherford," CBS, 1958.

PARTON, DOLLY

b. *Locust Ridge, TN, January 19, 1946.*
Pneumatic country-pop singer.

AS A REGULAR: "The Porter Wagoner Show," SYN, 1965-70; "Dolly," SYN, 1976-77; ABC, 1987-88.

AND: "The Wilburn Brothers Show," SYN, 1974; "The New Candid Camera," SYN, 1975; "The Grand Ole Opry at 50," ABC, 1975; "The Tonight Show Starring Johnny Carson," NBC, 1981; "The Mike Douglas Show," SYN, 1981; "Saturday Night Live," NBC, 1989; "Designing Women: The First Day of the Last Decade of the Entire Twentieth Century," CBS, 1990.

TV MOVIES AND MINISERIES: "A Smokey Mountain Christmas," ABC, 1986.

PATRICK, BUTCH

b. *Inglewood, CA, 1957.* Young actor who played Eddie Munster, vampire kid with the sharpest widow's peak in the third grade.

AS A REGULAR: "The Real McCoys," CBS, 1963; "The Munsters," CBS, 1964-66.

AND: "Robert Taylor's Detectives: The Legend of Jim Riva," NBC, 1961; "Don't Call Me Charlie!: The Dog Show," NBC, 1962; "My Favorite Martian: How to Be a Hero Without Really Trying," CBS, 1963; "I Dream of Jeannie: My Master the Author," NBC, 1966; "Gunsmoke: Mad Dog," CBS, 1967; "The Monkees: Christmas Show," NBC, 1967; "Family Affair: By a Whisker," CBS, 1968; "My Three Sons: Life Begins in Katie," CBS, 1968; "My Three Sons: Tea for Three," CBS, 1968; "My Three Sons: Three's a Crowd," CBS, 1969; "My Three Sons: Goodbye Forever," CBS, 1969; "Ironside: Act of Vengeance," NBC, 1974.

PATRICK, GAIL—See Gail Patrick Jackson.

PATRICK, LEE

b. *November 22, 1911.* Actress who played tough blondes in the movies, and dotty older women on TV.

AS A REGULAR: "Boss Lady," NBC, 1952; "Topper," CBS, 1953-55.

AND: "The Abbott and Costello Show: Hillary's Birthday," CBS, 1952; "Those Whiting Girls: What Price Publicity?," CBS, 1955; "The 20th Century-Fox Hour: The Marriage Broker," CBS, 1957; "The Dennis O'Keefe Show: Aunt Millie," CBS, 1960; "Lawman: The Old War Horse," ABC, 1960; "Harrigan and Son: Shall We Dance?," ABC, 1961; "The Real McCoys: George's Housekeeper," ABC, 1961; "Pete and Gladys: Lover, Go Away," CBS, 1961; "Follow the Sun: Chicago Style," ABC, 1962; "Adventures in Paradise: The Baby Sitters," ABC, 1962; "The Real McCoys: The Skeleton in the Closet," CBS, 1963; "The Farmer's Daughter: Scandal in Washington," ABC, 1964; "Hazel: It's a Dog's World," NBC, 1965; "The Donna Reed Show: The Gladiators," ABC, 1965; "Hazel: Noblesse Oblige," CBS, 1965.

PATTERSON, HANK

b. *Alabama, October 9, 1888; d. 1975.* Fred Ziffel. Enough said.

AS A REGULAR: "Gunsmoke," CBS, 1957-75; "Green Acres," CBS, 1965-71.

AND: "The Abbott and Costello Show: The Pigeon," CBS, 1953; "Ford Theatre: Fear Has Many Faces," ABC, 1957; "Ford Theatre: Desperation," ABC, 1957; "Death Valley Days: Halfway Girl," SYN, 1957; "Broken Arrow: The Teacher," ABC, 1957; "Restless Gun: Pressing Engagement," NBC, 1958; "Restless Gun: Sheriff Billy," NBC, 1958; "Dick Powell's Zane Grey Theatre: A Warm Day in Heaven," CBS, 1961; "Straightaway: The Tin Caesar," ABC, 1961; "Tales of Wells Fargo: Kelly's Clover Girls," NBC, 1961; "Have Gun, Will Travel: El Paso Stage," CBS, 1961; "The Twilight Zone: Kick the Can," CBS, 1962; "The Rifleman: The Debit," ABC, 1962; "Ripcord: Last Chance," SYN, 1962; "The Twilight Zone: Ring-a-Ding Girl," CBS, 1963; "Death Valley Days: Three Minutes to Eternity," SYN, 1964; "The Twilight Zone: Come Wander with Me," CBS, 1964; "The Andy Griffith Show: If I Had a Quarter Million," CBS, 1965; "Petticoat Junction: The Windfall," CBS, 1966; "Petticoat Junction: Kate Sells the Hotel," CBS, 1966; "The Beverly Hillbillies: Drysdale and Friend," CBS, 1969; "Love, American Style: Love and the Return of Raymond," ABC, 1973.

PATTERSON, LEE

b. *Canada, March 31, 1929.* Actor who played private eye Ken Madison on "SurfSide Six" and Joe Riley on "One Life to Live."

AS A REGULAR: "SurfSide Six," ABC, 1960-62; "The Nurses," ABC, 1965-67; "One Life to Live," ABC, 1968-70, 1972-79; "Texas," NBC, 1980-81.

AND: "The Alaskans: Behind the Moon," ABC, 1960; "The Deputy: The Chain of Action," NBC, 1960; "The Alaskans: Sign of the Kodiak," ABC, 1960; "The Virginian: Show Me a Hero," NBC, 1965; "Combat!: Nine Place Vendee," ABC, 1965; "Twelve O'Clock High: Angel Babe," ABC, 1966; "The Mike Douglas Show," SYN, 1981; "Magnum, P.I.: Flashback," CBS, 1982; "Riptide: Pilot," NBC, 1984; "The A-Team: Chopping Spree," NBC, 1984.

TV MOVIES AND MINISERIES: "The Last Days of Patton," CBS, 1986.

PATTERSON, LORNA

b. *Whittier, CA, July 1, 1956.* Actress who played Pvt. Judy Benjamin.

AS A REGULAR: "Working Stiffs," CBS, 1979; "Goodtime Girls," ABC, 1980; "Private

Benjamin," CBS, 1981-83.
AND: "Murder, She Wrote: The Search for Peter Kerry," CBS, 1989.
TV MOVIES AND MINISERIES: "Sidney Shorr," NBC, 1981; "The Imposter," ABC, 1984.

PATTERSON, MELODY
b. Los Angeles, CA, 1947. Shapely blonde starlet who played Wrangler Jane on "F Troop."
AS A REGULAR: "F Troop," ABC, 1965-67.
AND: "Wendy & Me: You Can't Fight City Hall," ABC, 1965; "The Monkees: Hillbilly Honeymoon," NBC, 1967; "Green Acres: Eb's Romance," CBS, 1968; "Hawaii Five-O: Bomb, Bomb, Who's Got the Bomb?" CBS, 1974.

PAULEY, JANE
b. Indianapolis, IN, October 31, 1950.
AS A REGULAR: "Today," NBC, 1976-90; "NBC Weekend News," NBC, 1980-83; "Real Life with Jane Pauley," NBC, 1990- .

PAULSEN, PAT
b. South Bend, IN. Deadpan comic and presidential candidate.
AS A REGULAR: "The Smothers Brothers Comedy Hour," CBS, 1967-69; ABC, 1970; NBC, 1975; CBS, 1988-89; "Summer Smothers Brothers Show," CBS, 1968; "Pat Paulsen's Half a Comedy Hour," ABC, 1970; "Joey & Dad," CBS, 1975.
AND: "The Wild Wild West: The Night of the Camera," CBS, 1968; "The Monkees: Monkees Watch Their Feet," NBC, 1968; "The Mike Douglas Show," SYN, 1969; "This Is Tom Jones," ABC, 1969; "Sesame Street," NET, 1970; "Get Smart: The Mess of Adrian Listenger," CBS, 1970; "Love, American Style: Love and the Decision," ABC, 1971; "Love, American Style: Love and the Security Building," ABC, 1971; "The Mike Douglas Show," SYN, 1973; "Dinah!," SYN, 1974; "The Misadventures of Sheriff Lobo: Perkins Bombs Out," NBC, 1980; "The Tom and Dick Smothers Brothers Special," NBC, 1980.
* Emmies: 1968.

PAYNE, JOHN
b. Roanoke, VA, May 23, 1912; d. 1989. Matinee idol who played gunfighter Vint Bonner on "Restless Gun."
AS A REGULAR: "Restless Gun," NBC, 1957-59.
AND: "Schlitz Playhouse of Stars: The Name Is Bellingham," CBS, 1951; "Schlitz Playhouse of Stars: Exit," CBS, 1951; "Robert Montgomery Presents: The Deep Six," NBC, 1953; "Best of Broadway: The Philadelphia Story," CBS, 1954; "G.E. Theatre: Lash of Fear," CBS, 1955; "Hallmark Hall of Fame: Alice in Wonderland," NBC, 1955; "Studio 57: Deadline," SYN, 1956;

"G.E. Theatre: Fastest Gun in the West," CBS, 1957; "Dick Powell's Zane Grey Theatre: Until the Man Dies," CBS, 1957; "Schlitz Playhouse of Stars: The Restless Gun," CBS, 1957; "The Steve Allen Show," NBC, 1957; "The Ford Show," NBC, 1957; "Perry Como's Kraft Music Hall," NBC, 1959; "What's My Line?," CBS, 1959; "The Garry Moore Show," CBS, 1960; "O'Conner's Ocean," NBC, 1960; "G.E. Theatre: The Little Hours," CBS, 1962; "The Dick Powell Show: Borderline," NBC, 1962; "The Name of the Game: Fear of High Places," NBC, 1968; "Gunsmoke: Gentry's Law," CBS, 1970; "Columbo: Forgotten Lady," NBC, 1975.
AS EXECUTIVE PRODUCER: "Restless Gun," NBC, 1957-59.

PAYTON-FRANCE, JO MARIE
Actress who plays Hariette Winslow on "Family Matters"; she originated the role on "Perfect Strangers."
AS A REGULAR: "The New Odd Couple," ABC, 1982-83; "Perfect Strangers," ABC, 1987-89; "Family Matters," ABC, 1989- .
AND: "Frank's Place: The Recruiting Game," CBS, 1988.

PEARCE, ALICE
b. New York City, NY, October 16, 1913; d. 1966. Comic actress who often played homely, loud types; she was an Emmy winner as nosy neighbor Gladys Kravitz on "Bewitched."
AS A REGULAR: "Alice Pearce," ABC, 1949; "Jamie," ABC, 1953-54; "One Minute Please," DUM, 1954-55; "Bewitched," ABC, 1964-66.
AND: "The Tonight Show," NBC, 1956; "The Patrice Munsel Show," ABC, 1958; "The Paul Winchell Show," ABC, 1959; "The Jack Paar Show," NBC, 1960; "Startime: Jack Paar's World," NBC, 1960; "The Ann Sothern Show: Operation Pudney," CBS, 1961; "The Twilight Zone: Static," CBS, 1961; "Shirley Temple's Storybook: The Princess and the Goblins," NBC, 1961; "The Ann Sothern Show: The Beginning," CBS, 1961; "Angel: Angel of Mercy," CBS, 1961; "Look Up and Live: Comedies of Terror—A Likely Story," CBS, 1961; "Dennis the Menace: You Go Your Way," CBS, 1962; "The Many Loves of Dobie Gillis: And Now a Word From Our Sponsor," CBS, 1963; "The Donna Reed Show: A Touch of Glamour," ABC, 1963; "Hazel: Hot Potato a la Hazel," NBC, 1964; "Many Happy Returns: A Date for Walter," CBS, 1965.
* Emmies: 1966.

PEARL, MINNIE
b. Sarah Ophelia Colley Cannon, Centerville, TN, October 25, 1912. Country-flavored comedienne.
AS A REGULAR: "Grand Ole Opry," ABC, 1955-56;

"Hee Haw," CBS, 1970-71; SYN, 1971- ; "On Stage America," SYN, 1984.

AND: "Dinah Shore Chevy Show," NBC, 1957; "This Is Your Life," NBC, 1957; "Country Music Jubilee," ABC, 1957; "The Ford Show," NBC, 1957; "The Jack Paar Show," NBC, 1958; "Jubilee USA," ABC, 1959; "The Chevy Show," NBC, 1959; "The Tennessee Ernie Ford Show," ABC, 1964; "The Jimmy Dean Show," ABC, 1965; "The Tennessee Ernie Ford Show," ABC, 1965; "The Steve Lawrence Show," CBS, 1965; "The Mike Douglas Show," SYN, 1966; "Swingin' Country," NBC, 1966; "The Joey Bishop Show," ABC, 1968; "Operation: Entertainment," ABC, 1968; "The Mike Douglas Show," SYN, 1968; "The Jonathan Winters Show," CBS, 1968; "The Grand Ole Opry at 50," ABC, 1975; "The Merv Griffin Show," SYN, 1975; "The Porter Wagoner Show," SYN, 1976; "Ann-Margret Special," NBC, 1977; "The Love Boat: A Home Is Not a Home," ABC, 1979; "George Burns in Nashville?," NBC, 1980; "Backstage at the Grand Ole Opry," SYN, 1981.

PEARY, HAROLD

b. 1908; d. 1985. Pudgy comic actor who played "The Great Gildersleeve" on the radio, while Willard Waterman, a virtual lookalike, played the role on TV.

AS A REGULAR: "Willy," CBS, 1955; "Blondie," NBC, 1957; "Fibber McGee and Molly," NBC, 1959-60.

AND: "The Bob Cummings Show: Miss Coffee Break," CBS, 1956; "The Bob Cummings Show: Bob Plays Cupid," CBS, 1956; "Mr. Smith Goes to Washington: The Senator and the Page Boy," ABC, 1962; "The Dick Van Dyke Show: Who and Where Was Antonio Stradivarius?," CBS, 1963; "The Patty Duke Show: Partying Is Such Sweet Sorrow," ABC, 1965; "My Mother the Car: TV or Not TV," NBC, 1965; "My Mother the Car: My Son the Ventriloquist," NBC, 1965; "My Three Sons: Whatever Happened to Baby Chip?," CBS, 1966; "Petticoat Junction: The Three Queens," CBS, 1969; "That Girl: I Ain't Got Nobody," ABC, 1970; "The Doris Day Show: The People's Choice," CBS, 1971.

PEEPLES, NIA

b. December 10, 1961. Actress-dancer who played Nicole on "Fame."

AS A REGULAR: "Fame," SYN, 1984-87; "Top of the Pops," CBS, 1987-88; "Nia Peeples Party Machine," SYN, 1990- .

AND: "Matlock: The Starlet," NBC, 1989.

TV MOVIES AND MINISERIES: "Swimsuit," NBC, 1989; "Nasty Boys," NBC, 1989.

PELUCE, MEENO

b. Amsterdam, Holland, February 26, 1970. Child actor; brother of Soleil Moon Frye.

AS A REGULAR: "The Bad News Bears," CBS, 1979-80; "Best of the West," ABC, 1981-82; "Voyagers!," NBC, 1982-83; "Detective in the House," CBS, 1985.

AND: "Lou Grant: Denial," CBS, 1979; "The Love Boat: Captive Audience," ABC, 1980; "The A-Team: Pros and Cons," NBC, 1983; "Scarecrow and Mrs. King: The ACM Kid," CBS, 1983; "Silver Spoons: Spare the Rod," NBC, 1984; "Punky Brewster: George Falls in Love," NBC, 1985.

TV MOVIES AND MINISERIES: "Fast Friends," NBC, 1979.

PENNY, JOE

b. London, England, September 14, 1956. Dark-featured TV hunk who plays Jake Styles to William Conrad's Fatman.

AS A REGULAR: "The Gangster Chronicles," NBC, 1981; "Riptide," NBC, 1984-86; "Jake and the Fatman," CBS, 1987- .

AND: "Lou Grant: Cop," CBS, 1979; "Paris: Fitz's Boys," CBS, 1979; "T.J. Hooker: Cheerleader Murder," ABC, 1983; "Matlock: The Don," NBC, 1986; "The Twilight Zone: The Convict's Piano," CBS, 1986.

TV MOVIES AND MINISERIES: "Samurai," ABC, 1979; "Perry Mason: The Case of the Shooting Star," NBC, 1986; "Blood Vows: The Story of a Mafia Wife," NBC, 1987; "Roses Are for the Rich," CBS, 1987; "A Whisper Kills," ABC, 1988.

PEPPARD, GEORGE

b. Detroit, MI, October 1, 1928. Handsome actor who played cool insurance investigator Banacek and A-Team commander Hannibal Smith.

AS A REGULAR: "Banacek," NBC, 1972-74; "Doctors Hospital," NBC, 1975-76; "The A-Team," NBC, 1983-87.

AND: "Kraft Television Theatre: Flying Object at Three O'Clock High," NBC, 1956; "Matinee Theatre: End of the Rope," NBC, 1956; "Kraft Television Theatre: Out to Kill," NBC, 1956; "U.S. Steel Hour: Bang the Drum Slowly," CBS, 1956; "Studio One: A Walk in the Forest," CBS, 1957; "Alcoa Hour: The Big Build-Up," NBC, 1957; "Matinee Theatre: Aftermath," NBC, 1957; "Kraft Television Theatre: The Long Flight," NBC, 1957; "Alfred Hitchcock Presents: The Diplomatic Corpse," CBS, 1957; "Suspicion: The Eye of Truth," NBC, 1958; "Hallmark Hall of Fame: Little Moon of Alban," NBC, 1958; "Startime: Incident at a Corner," NBC, 1960; "Our American Heritage: The Invincible Teddy," NBC, 1961; "Password," CBS, 1964; "Bob Hope Chrysler Theatre: The Game with Glass Pieces," NBC, 1964; "The Mike Douglas Show," SYN, 1976.

TV MOVIES AND MINISERIES: "The Bravos," ABC, 1972; "Banacek: Detour to Nowhere," NBC,

1972; "One of Our Own," NBC, 1975; "Guilty or Innocent: The Sam Sheppard Murder Case," NBC, 1975; "Torn Between Two Lovers," CBS, 1979; "Crisis in Mid-Air," CBS, 1979; "Man Against the Mob," NBC, 1988; "Man Against the Mob: The Chinatown Murders," NBC, 1989.

PEREZ, JOSE
b. New York City, NY, 1940.
AS A REGULAR: "Calucci's Department," CBS, 1973; "On the Rocks," ABC, 1975-76.
AND: "Kraft Television Theatre: Welcome to a Stranger," NBC, 1957; "Studio One: Guitar," CBS, 1957; "The Nurses: Root of Violence," CBS, 1963; "East Side/West Side: The Street," CBS, 1964; "NYPD: Macho," ABC, 1968; "Hollywood Television Theatre: Steambath," NET, 1973; "Aces Up," CBS, 1974; "Murder, She Wrote: Hooray for Homicide," CBS, 1984; "Miami Vice: Junk Love," NBC, 1986; "Tattinger's: Two Men and a Baby," NBC, 1988; "Miami Vice: Miracle Man," NBC, 1989.
TV MOVIES AND MINISERIES: "The Godchild," ABC, 1974; "One Shoe Makes It Murder," CBS, 1982.

PERKINS, ANTHONY
b. New York City, NY, April 14, 1932. Actor who began on films ("Fear Strikes Out") and TV in sensitive roles; nowadays he virtually makes his living as Norman Bates, the character he played in Alfred Hitchcock's 1960 film, "Psycho."
AS A GUEST: "Kraft Television Theatre: The Missing Year," NBC, 1954; "Armstrong Circle Theatre: The Fugitive," NBC, 1954; "Man Behind the Badge: The Case of the Narcotics Rackets," CBS, 1954; "G.E. Theatre: Mr. Blue Ocean," CBS, 1955; "Windows: The World Out There," CBS, 1955; "The Ed Sullivan Show," CBS, 1956; "The Ed Sullivan Show," CBS, 1957; "The Steve Allen Show," NBC, 1957; "Person to Person," CBS, 1957; "Look Here," NBC, 1958; "The Jack Paar Show," NBC, 1958; "American Bandstand," ABC, 1958; "Hedda Hopper's Hollywood," NBC, 1960; "What's My Line?," CBS, 1960; "I've Got a Secret," CBS, 1960; "The World of Sophia Loren," NBC, 1962; "Password," CBS, 1962; "Password," CBS, 1963; "I've Got a Secret," CBS, 1963; "ABC Stage '67: Evening Primrose," ABC, 1966; "Saturday Night Live," NBC, 1976.
TV MOVIES AND MINISERIES: "How Awful About Allan," ABC, 1970; "Les Miserables," CBS, 1978; "First You Cry," CBS, 1978; "The Sins of Dorian Gray," ABC, 1983.

PERKINS, MARLIN
b. Carthage, MO, March 28, 1905; d. 1986. Zoo director turned animal-show host.
AS A REGULAR: "Zoo Parade," NBC, 1950-57; " Wild Kingdom," NBC, 1968-71; SYN, 1971-85.

PERKINS, MILLIE
b. Passaic, NJ, May 12, 1938. Former ingenue who played Anne Frank in the honored 1959 film; more recently she played Gladys Presley, mother of Elvis.
AS A REGULAR: "Knots Landing," CBS, 1983-84; "Elvis," ABC, 1990.
AND: "Bob Hope Special," NBC, 1960; "Wagon Train: The Will Santee Story," NBC, 1961; "U.S. Steel Hour: Street of Love," CBS, 1961; "The Breaking Point: Solo for B-Flat Clarinet," ABC, 1963; "The Reporter: Rope's End," CBS, 1964; "thirtysomething: In Re the Marriage of Weston," ABC, 1988.
TV MOVIES AND MINISERIES: "Shattered Vows," NBC, 1984; "The Other Lover," CBS, 1985; "Penalty Phase," CBS, 1986; "Strange Voices," NBC, 1987; "Broken Angel," ABC, 1988.

PERLMAN, RHEA
b. Brooklyn, NY, March 31, 1948. Comic actress who's been honored three times for her one-note role as mean waitress Carla on "Cheers."
AS A REGULAR: "Cheers," NBC, 1982- .
AND: "Taxi: Louie and the Nice Girl," ABC, 1979; "Taxi: Louie Meets the Folks," ABC, 1979; "Taxi: Louie's Rival," ABC, 1980; "Taxi: Louie's Fling," ABC, 1981; "Taxi: Zena's Honeymoon," NBC, 1982; "Saturday Night Live," NBC, 1983; "St. Elsewhere: Cheers," NBC, 1985; "Amazing Stories: The Wedding Ring," NBC, 1986; "Matlock: The Producer," NBC, 1987; "ABC Family Theater: Together Again," ABC, 1988; "Wonderworks: Two Daddies?," PBS, 1989.
TV MOVIES AND MINISERIES: "I Want to Keep My Baby," CBS, 1976; "Dangerous Affection," NBC, 1987.
* Emmies: 1984, 1985, 1986.

PERREAU, GIGI
b. Ghislaine Elizabeth Marie Therese Perreau-Saussine, Los Angeles, CA, February 6, 1941. Former child actress in some television; her real-life brother, Richard Miles, played her brother on "The Betty Hutton Show."
AS A REGULAR: "The Betty Hutton Show," CBS, 1959-60; "Follow the Sun," ABC, 1961-62.
AND: "Lux Video Theatre: The Girl Who Couldn't Cry," CBS, 1954; "Ford Theatre: Unbroken Promise," NBC, 1954; "Gloria Swanson Theatre: Was It Red?," SYN, 1955; "Alfred Hitchcock Presents: Graduating Class," CBS, 1959; "The Rifleman: Heller," ABC, 1960; "The Islanders: Flight From Terror," ABC, 1960; "Stagecoach West: The Land Beyond," ABC, 1960; "The Rifleman: Death Trap," ABC, 1961; "Lassie: Avalanche," CBS, 1964; "Perry Mason: The Case of the Sleepy Slayer," CBS, 1964; "Gunsmoke: Chicken," CBS, 1964; "Many Happy Returns:

The Diamond," CBS, 1965; "My Three Sons: Be My Guest," ABC, 1965; "Gomer Pyle, USMC: Arrivederci, Gomer," CBS, 1966; "Tarzan: The Prodigal Puma," NBC, 1966; "The Iron Horse: Death by Triangulation," ABC, 1967; "The Brady Bunch: Vote for Brady," ABC, 1970.

PERRINE, VALERIE

b. Galveston, TX, September 3, 1944. Screen sex symbol of the seventies ("Slaughterhouse Five," "Lenny") who appeared nude on the television production of "Steambath."
AS A REGULAR: "Leo & Liz in Beverly Hills," CBS, 1986.
AND: "Lady Luck," NBC, 1973; "Hollywood Television Theatre: Steambath," NET, 1973; "Love Story: When the Girls Came Out to Play," NBC, 1973; "Dinah!," SYN, 1975; "The Mike Douglas Show," SYN, 1976.
TV MOVIES AND MINISERIES: "The Couple Takes a Wife," ABC, 1972; "Malibu," ABC, 1983; "When Your Lover Leaves," NBC, 1983; "Tennessee Williams' Sweet Bird of Youth," NBC, 1989.

PERRY, JOHN BENNETT

b. Williamstown, MA, January 4, 1941. Conventionally handsome actor who played Sheriff Gilmore on "Falcon Crest."
AS A REGULAR: "240-Robert," ABC, 1979-81; "Paper Dolls," ABC, 1984; "Falcon Crest," CBS, 1985-86.
AND: "Police Story: Death on Credit," NBC, 1973; "SWAT: Vendetta," ABC, 1975; "Little House: A New Beginning: Once Upon a Time," NBC, 1983; "The Love Boat: The Light of Another Day," ABC, 1984; "Murder, She Wrote: When Thieves Fall Out," CBS, 1987; "Rags to Riches: Wilderness Blues," NBC, 1987.
TV MOVIES AND MINISERIES: "The Police Story," NBC, 1973; "A Matter of Life and Death," CBS, 1981; "The Other Lover," CBS, 1985; "The Last Fling," ABC, 1987; "She Knows Too Much," NBC, 1989; "False Witness," NBC, 1989.

PESCOW, DONNA

b. Brooklyn, NY, March 24, 1954. Actress who plays Donna Garland on "Out of This World."
AS A REGULAR: "Angie," ABC, 1979-80; "All My Children," ABC, 1983; "Out of This World," SYN, 1987- .
AND: "Match Game '79," CBS, 1979; "The Love Boat: Best of Friends," ABC, 1979; "The Love Boat: Baby Talk," ABC, 1982; "The Love Boat: For Love of Money," ABC, 1983.
TV MOVIES AND MINISERIES: "Human Feelings," NBC, 1978; "Rainbow," NBC, 1978; "Police-woman Centerfold," NBC, 1983; "Obsessed with a Married Woman," ABC, 1985.

PETERS, BERNADETTE

b. Bernadette Lazzara, New York City, NY, February 28, 1944. Singer-actress.
AS A REGULAR: "All's Fair," CBS, 1976-77.
AND: "Hallmark Hall of Fame: Hallmark Christmas Tree-The Miracle of the Orphanage," NBC, 1958; "NBC Experiment in Television: We Interrupt This Season," NBC, 1967; "The Mike Douglas Show," SYN, 1969; "Kraft Music Hall," NBC, 1969; "The Dick Cavett Show," ABC, 1970; "George M!," NBC, 1970; "The Ed Sullivan Show," CBS, 1971; "NET Playhouse: Clifford Odets' Paradise Lost," NET, 1971; "Once Upon a Mattress," CBS, 1972; "Love, American Style: Love and the Hoodwinked Honey," ABC, 1973; "The Carol Burnett Show," CBS, 1974; "All in the Family: Gloria Suspects Mike," CBS, 1975; "The Owl and the Pussycat," NBC, 1975; "Maude: Rumpus in the Rumpus Room," CBS, 1975; "The $25,000 Pyramid," SYN, 1975; "Showoffs," ABC, 1975; "McCoy: In Again, Out Again," NBC, 1976; "McCloud: The Night New York Turned Blue," NBC, 1976; "The Mike Douglas Show," SYN, 1977; "Saturday Night Live," NBC, 1981; "The Merv Griffin Show," SYN, 1981.
TV MOVIES AND MINISERIES: "The Islander," CBS, 1978.

PETERSEN, PATTY

b. 1955. Young actress, sister of Paul Petersen; she played Trisha, adopted daughter of the Stones on "The Donna Reed Show."
AS A REGULAR: "The Donna Reed Show," ABC, 1963-66.

PETERSEN, PAUL

b. Glendale, CA, September 23, 1945. Child actor who played Jeff Stone on "The Donna Reed Show."
AS A REGULAR: "The Donna Reed Show," ABC, 1958-66; "Dream Girl of '67," ABC, 1966-67.
AND: "Ford Theatre: Black Jim Hawk," ABC, 1956; "American Bandstand," ABC, 1962; "Shindig," ABC, 1965; "Where the Action Is," ABC, 1965; "F Troop: Johnny Eagle Eye," ABC, 1966; "The Flying Nun: Song of Bertrille," ABC, 1968; "The Big Valley: The Long Ride," ABC, 1968; "Lassie: Track of the Jaguar," CBS, 1968; "My Three Sons: Mexican Honeymoon," CBS, 1969; "Love, American Style: Love and the Bashful Groom," ABC, 1972.
TV MOVIES AND MINISERIES: "Something for a Lonely Man," NBC, 1968; "Gidget Grows Up," ABC, 1969.
AS CO-WRITER: "The Donna Reed Show: Never Look a Gift Horse in the Mouth," ABC, 1965.
* Petersen sang two songs on "The Donna Reed Show" that made the pop charts—"She Can't Find Her Keys" peaked at number 19 in March

1962, and "My Dad" hit number six in November 1962.
* See also Brenda Benet.

PETRIE, GEORGE O.
Actor with extensive TV experience; he was a stock company player with Jackie Gleason, in various roles on "The Honeymooners," and now plays Harve Smithfield on "Dallas" and Don Auippo on "Wiseguy."
AS A REGULAR: "Search for Tomorrow," CBS, 1954-58; "The Honeymooners," CBS, 1955-56; "The Jackie Gleason Show," CBS, 1956-57; 1958-61; "Dallas," CBS, 1978- ; "Hard Copy," CBS, 1987.
AND: "The Tom Ewell Show: Passenger Pending," CBS, 1961; "Mrs. G. Goes to College: Sam's Car," CBS, 1961; "SurfSide 6: A Slight Case of Chivalry," ABC, 1961; "Leave It to Beaver: Summer in Alaska," ABC, 1963; "The Twilight Zone: In His Image," CBS, 1963; "The Farmer's Daughter: The Gypsy Love Song," ABC, 1963; "Dr. Kildare: Tyger, Tyger ...," NBC, 1964; "Ben Casey: A Falcon's Eye, a Lion's Heart, a Girl's Hand," ABC, 1964; "The Andy Griffith Show: A Deal Is a Deal," CBS, 1964; "Gomer Pyle, USMC: A Star Is Born," CBS, 1966; "The Munsters: Prehistoric Munster," CBS, 1966; "Gunsmoke: Celia," CBS, 1970; "The Streets of San Francisco: Spooks for Sale," ABC, 1975; "Medical Center: The Last Performance," CBS, 1975; "Maude: Walter's Crisis," CBS, 1976; "Switch: Play-Off," CBS, 1978; "House Calls: Officer Needs Assistance," CBS, 1980; "House Calls: A Man for All Surgeons," CBS, 1982; "Hill Street Blues: Eugene's Comedy Empire Strikes Back," NBC, 1983; "St. Elsewhere: Brand New Bag," NBC, 1986; "Wiseguy: The Squeeze," CBS, 1988; "Wiseguy: Aria for Don Auippo," CBS, 1988; "Heartbeat: Gestalt and Battery," ABC, 1989.
TV MOVIES AND MINISERIES: "The Deadliest Season," CBS, 1977; "Silent Victory: The Kitty O'Neil Story," CBS, 1979.

PEYSER, PENNY
b. Irvington, NY, February 9, 1951. Actress who played Cindy, wife of Harrison Fox (John Rubinstein) on "Crazy Like a Fox."
AS A REGULAR: "Rich Man, Poor Man—Book II," ABC, 1976-77; "The Tony Randall Show," CBS, 1977-78; "Crazy Like a Fox," CBS, 1984-86; "Knots Landing," CBS, 1989.
AND: "Barnaby Jones: Stages of Fear," CBS, 1978; "$weepstake$: Billy, Wally and Ludmilla, and Theodore," NBC, 1979; "The White Shadow: Christmas Story," CBS, 1980; "The Powers of Matthew Star: Thirty-Six Hours," NBC, 1983; "The Fall Guy: Dirty Laundry," ABC, 1983; "The A-Team: Labor Pains," NBC, 1983; "Amazing Stories: Secret Cinema," NBC, 1986; "MacGyver:

The Battle of Jimmy Giordano," ABC, 1989.
TV MOVIES AND MINISERIES: "B.J. and the Bear," NBC, 1978; "The Girls in the Office," ABC, 1979; "Still Crazy Like a Fox," CBS, 1987.

PFEIFFER, MICHELLE
b. Orange County, CA, April 29, 1962. Movie sex goddess ("The Fabulous Baker Boys") who went from being a supermarket cashier to TV actress.
AS A REGULAR: "Delta House," ABC, 1979; "B.A.D. Cats," ABC, 1980.
AND: "ABC Afterschool Special: One Too Many," ABC, 1985.
TV MOVIES AND MINISERIES: "The Children Nobody Wanted," CBS, 1981; "Callie & Son," CBS, 1981.

PFLUG, JO ANN
b. Atlanta, GA. Sexy actress of the seventies; she played Lt. Dish in the movie "M*A*S*H."
AS A REGULAR: "Operation Petticoat," ABC, 1978-79; "The Fall Guy," ABC, 1981-82; "Rituals," SYN, 1984.
AND: "The Beverly Hillbillies: Granny Lives It Up," CBS, 1966; "Marcus Welby, M.D.: To Carry the Sun in a Golden Cup," ABC, 1971; "Love, American Style: Love and the Doctor's Honeymoon," ABC, 1971; "The Dean Martin Show," NBC, 1971; "Wide World of Mystery: Nick and Nora," ABC, 1975; "Adam 12: Dana Hall," NBC, 1975; "The Bob Crane Show: Campus Capers," NBC, 1975; "The $25,000 Pyramid," SYN, 1975; "Match Game '76," CBS, 1976; "Cross Wits," SYN, 1976; "Dinah!," SYN, 1976; "The Love Experts," SYN, 1978; "Quincy: The Eye of the Needle," NBC, 1978; "The Love Boat: The Man Who Loved Women," ABC, 1978; "The Love Boat: Trial Romance," ABC, 1979; "Vega$: Redhanded," ABC, 1979; "The Love Boat: The Major's Wife," ABC, 1980; "One Day at a Time: Social Security," CBS, 1983; "The Love Boat: The Buck Stops Here," ABC, 1984; "B.L. Stryker: The King of Jazz," ABC, 1989.
TV MOVIES AND MINISERIES: "A Step Out of Line," CBS, 1971; "They Call it Murder," NBC, 1971; "The Night Strangler," ABC, 1973; "Scream of the Wolf," ABC, 1974; "The Underground Man," NBC, 1974.

PHILBIN, REGIS
Talk-show host.
AS A REGULAR: "The Joey Bishop Show," ABC, 1967-69; "Neighbors," ABC, 1975-76; "Almost Anything Goes," ABC, 1976; "The Regis Philbin Show," NBC, 1982; "Regis Philbin's Health Styles," LIF, 1983-86; "Live with Regis & Kathie Lee," SYN, 1988- .
AND: "Get Smart: The Hot Line," NBC, 1968; "That Girl: That Cake," ABC, 1970; "Love, American

Style: Love and the Old Cowboy," ABC, 1971;
"The San Pedro Beach Bums: Sweepstakes Bums,"
ABC, 1977; "Super Dave," SHO, 1989.
TV MOVIES AND MINISERIES: "SST-Death Flight,"
ABC, 1977.

PHILLIPS, BARNEY
b. *St. Louis, MO, October 20, 1913; d. 1982.*
Deadpan actor who played Sgt. Ed Jacobs on
"Dragnet" and Capt. Franks on "The Felony
Squad"; he kidded his image as actor-playing-a-
cop Fletcher Huff on "The Betty White Show."
AS A REGULAR: "Dragnet," NBC, 1952; "The
Brothers Brannagan," SYN, 1961-62; "Twelve
O'Clock High," ABC, 1964-67; "The Felony
Squad," ABC, 1967-68; "The Betty White
Show," CBS, 1977-78.
AND: "I Love Lucy: Ricky's European Booking,"
CBS, 1955; "G.E. Theatre: The Earring," CBS,
1957; "The Adventures of Ozzie and Harriet: The
Duenna," ABC, 1957; "Peter Gunn: The Blind
Pianist," NBC, 1958; "Black Saddle: Four From
Stillwater," NBC, 1958; "The Loretta Young Show:
The Accused," NBC, 1959; "Have Gun, Will
Travel: The Shooting of Jessie May," CBS, 1960;
"Tales of Wells Fargo: Dead Man's Street," NBC,
1960; "The Andy Griffith Show: Barney Gets His
Man," CBS, 1961; "Malibu Run: The Landslide
Adventure," CBS, 1961; "The Twilight Zone: Will
the Real Martian Please Stand Up," CBS, 1961;
"Death Valley Days: The Truth Teller," SYN,
1962; "The Dick Van Dyke Show: The Cat
Burglar," CBS, 1963; "The Twilight Zone:
Miniature," CBS, 1963; "Kraft Suspense Theatre:
Doesn't Anyone Know Who I Am?," NBC, 1964;
"Get Smart: Greer Window," NBC, 1969; "The
Doris Day Show: The Tiger," CBS, 1969; "Mannix:
Tooth of the Serpent," CBS, 1969; "Columbo:
Suitable for Framing," NBC, 1971; "Hawaii Five-
O: AOR Cargo-Dial for Murder," CBS, 1971;
"Owen Marshall, Counselor at Law: Smiles From
Yesterday," ABC, 1972; "The Paul Lynde Show:
Out of Bounds," ABC, 1973; "The Streets of San
Francisco: The Bullet," ABC, 1973; "Medical
Center: Three-Cornered Cage," CBS, 1974;
"Petrocelli: Death in High Places," NBC, 1974;
"Medical Center: No Escape," CBS, 1974; "Archer:
The Turkish Connection," NBC, 1975; "Lou Grant:
Scam," CBS, 1979; "One Day at a Time: Old
Horizons," CBS, 1980; "Lou Grant: Obituary,"
CBS, 1981.
TV MOVIES AND MINISERIES: "Run, Simon, Run,"
ABC, 1970; "Longstreet," ABC, 1971; "A Death
of Innocence," CBS, 1971; "Beg, Borrow ... or
Steal," CBS, 1973; "Shirts/Skins," ABC, 1973;
"Law of the Land," NBC, 1976.

PHILLIPS, MACKENZIE
b. *Alexandria, VA, November 10, 1959.* Actress
who played Julie Cooper Horvath on "One Day
at a Time."
AS A REGULAR: "One Day at a Time," CBS, 1975-
80; 1981-83.
AND: "Baretta: On the Road," ABC, 1975; "The
Mary Tyler Moore Show: Mary's Delinquent,"
CBS, 1975; "The Love Boat: Going by the Book,"
ABC, 1978; "Murder, She Wrote: Death in the
Afternoon," CBS, 1985.
TV MOVIES AND MINISERIES: "G.E. Theatre: Miles to
Go Before I Sleep," CBS, 1975; "Eleanor and
Franklin," ABC, 1976; "Fast Friends," NBC,
1979.

PHILLIPS, MICHELLE
b. *Long Beach, CA, April 6, 1944.* Former
member of The Mamas and the Papas, now an
actress on prime-time soaps.
AS A REGULAR: "Hotel," ABC, 1986; "Knots
Landing," CBS, 1987; 1989- .
AND: "The Tonight Show Starring Johnny Carson,"
NBC, 1968; "Dinah!," SYN, 1978; "Fantasy Island:
The Mermaid," ABC, 1979; "Fantasy Island:
Mermaid Returns," ABC, 1980; "Fantasy Island:
Three's a Crowd," ABC, 1983; "Hotel: Secrets,"
ABC, 1983; "The Love Boat: No More Alimony,"
ABC, 1984; "The Love Boat: Doc's Slump," ABC,
1984.
TV MOVIES AND MINISERIES: "The Death Squad,"
ABC, 1973; "Aspen," NBC, 1977; "The Users,"
ABC, 1978; "Moonlight," CBS, 1982; "Mickey
Spillane's Murder Me, Murder You," CBS,
1983; "Secrets of a Married Man," NBC, 1984;
"Stark: Mirror Image," CBS, 1986; "Assault and
Matrimony," NBC, 1989; "Trenchcoat in
Paradise," CBS, 1989.
* Phillips and Dennis Hopper were married for
eight days.

PHILLIPS, WENDY
b. *Brooklyn, NY, January 2, 1952.* Blonde actress
who played Anne Gardner Maxwell on "A Year
in the Life" and the white romantic interest of
Robert Guillaume on a short-lived sitcom.
AS A REGULAR: "Executive Suite," CBS, 1976-77;
"The Eddie Capra Mysteries," NBC, 1978-79;
"A Year in the Life," NBC, 1987-88; "The
Robert Guillaume Show," ABC, 1989; "Falcon
Crest," CBS, 1989-90.
AND: "B.J. and the Bear: Eighteen Wheel Ripoff,"
NBC, 1980; "Jigsaw John: A Deadly Affair," NBC,
1976; "Lou Grant: Frame-Up," CBS, 1979; "Paris:
Pawn," CBS, 1979; "Taxi: The Road Not Taken,"
ABC, 1982; "Matlock: The Court-Martial," NBC,
1987; "Murder, She Wrote: Murder, She Spoke,"
CBS, 1987.
TV MOVIES AND MINISERIES: "The Love Tapes,"
ABC, 1980; "A Year in the Life," NBC, 1986.

PICKENS, SLIM
b. *Louis Bert Lindley Jr., Kingsberg, CA, June
29, 1919.* Former rodeo rider who got into

movies and TV, almost always in cowboy roles.

AS A REGULAR: "The Outlaws," NBC, 1961-62; "The Wide Country," NBC, 1962-63; "Custer," ABC, 1967; "B.J. and the Bear," NBC, 1979; "Hee Haw," SYN, 1981-83; "The Nashville Palace," NBC, 1981-82; "Filthy Rich," CBS, 1982.

AND: "Death Valley Days: The Telescope Eye," SYN, 1956; "Disneyland: The Saga of Andy Burnett," ABC, 1957; "Circus Boy: The Proud Pagliacci," ABC, 1957; "Wagon Train: The Tent City Story," NBC, 1958; "Alfred Hitchcock Presents: Final Arrangements," NBC, 1961; "Route 66: A Long Piece of Mischief," CBS, 1962; "Wagon Train: The Eve Newhope Story," NBC, 1962; "The Virginian: Run Quiet," NBC, 1963; "The Alfred Hitchcock Hour: The Jar," NBC, 1964; "The Man From UNCLE: The Iowa Scuba Affair," NBC, 1964; "The Virginian: Big Image...Little Man," NBC, 1964; "Rawhide: The Backshooter," CBS, 1964; "Mannix: Only Giants Can Play," CBS, 1969; "Ironside: Goodbye to Yesterday," NBC, 1969; "That Girl: Nobody Here Knows Chickens," ABC, 1969; "Medical Center: The Professional," CBS, 1970; "Bonanza: What Are Pardners For?," NBC, 1970; "The Name of the Game: Little Bear Died Running," NBC, 1970; "The Mary Tyler Moore Show: The Forty-Five-Year-Old Man," CBS, 1971; "Kung Fu: The Lawman," ABC, 1974; "Baretta: Sharper Than a Serpent's Tooth," ABC, 1975; "McMillan and Wife: Deadly Inheritance," NBC, 1976; "The Life and Times of Grizzly Adams: The Unholy Beast," NBC, 1977; "The Love Boat: Kin Folk," ABC, 1979; "Best of the West: The Prisoner," ABC, 1981.

TV MOVIES AND MINISERIES: "Sam Hill: Who Killed The Mysterious Mr. Foster?," NBC, 1971; "Desperate Mission," NBC, 1971; "The Devil and Miss Sarah," ABC, 1971; "Rolling Man," ABC, 1972; "Hitched," NBC, 1973; "Twice in a Lifetime," NBC, 1974; "The Gun and the Pulpit," ABC, 1974; "Babe," CBS, 1975; "Banjo Hackett," NBC, 1976; "Undercover with the KKK," NBC, 1979; "Swan Song," ABC, 1980; "This House Possessed," ABC, 1981.

PICKETT, CINDY

b. *Norman, OK, April 18, 1947.* Actress who played Jackie Marler on "The Guiding Light" and Dr. Carol Novino on "St. Elsewhere."

AS A REGULAR: "The Guiding Light," CBS, 1976-80; "Call to Glory," ABC, 1984-85; "St. Elsewhere," NBC, 1986-88.

AND: "Simon & Simon: The Dillinger Print," CBS, 1984; "Magnum P.I.: The Look," CBS, 1984.

TV MOVIES AND MINISERIES: "The Ivory Ape," ABC, 1980; "Cry for the Strangers," CBS, 1982; "Cocaine and Blue Eyes," NBC, 1983;

"Amerika," ABC, 1987; "Echoes in the Darkness," CBS, 1987; "I Know My First Name Is Steven," NBC, 1989.

PICKLES, CHRISTINA

b. *England.* Actress who played Nurse Helen Rosenthal on "St. Elsewhere."

AS A REGULAR: "The Guiding Light," CBS, 1970-71; "Another World," NBC, 1977-79; "St. Elsewhere," NBC, 1982-88; "The People Next Door," CBS, 1989.

AND: "Family Classics: Vanity Fair," CBS, 1961; "Du Pont Show of the Month: The Lincoln Murder Case," CBS, 1961; "Lou Grant: Suspect," CBS, 1981; "The White Shadow: Psyched-Out," CBS, 1981; "Who's the Boss?: A Spirited Christmas," ABC, 1988; "Family Ties: Heartstrings," NBC, 1988.

TV MOVIES AND MINISERIES: "The Hijacking of the Achille Lauro," NBC, 1989.

PICON, MOLLY

b. *New York City, NY, June 1, 1898.* Diminutive comic actress, usually in Jewish roles.

AS A REGULAR: "Somerset," NBC, 1971-76.

AND: "Startime: The Jazz Singer," NBC, 1959; "Car 54, Where Are You?: I Won't Go," NBC, 1961; "The Jack Paar Show," NBC, 1961; "Car 54, Where Are You?: Occupancy, August First," NBC, 1962; "Car 54, Where Are You?: Joan Crawford Didn't Say No," NBC, 1963; "Dr. Kildare: The Eleventh Commandment," NBC, 1963; "The Merv Griffin Show," SYN, 1966; "The Joey Bishop Show," ABC, 1968; "Gomer Pyle, USMC: A Little Chicken Soup Wouldn't Hurt," CBS, 1968; "The David Frost Show," SYN, 1971; "The Mike Douglas Show," SYN, 1977; "Vega$: Mother Mishkin," ABC, 1979; "The Facts of Life: From Russia with Love," NBC, 1981.

TV MOVIES AND MINISERIES: "Murder on Flight 502," ABC, 1975.

PIDGEON, WALTER

b. *East St. John, New Brunswick, Canada, 1898; d. 1984.* Distinguished actor, long with MGM, often in character roles on TV, including the King in the 1966 CBS version of "Cinderella."

AS A REGULAR: "MGM Parade," ABC, 1956.

AND: "The Perry Como Show," NBC, 1957; "What's My Line?," CBS, 1957; "The Ed Sullivan Show," CBS, 1957; "The Chevy Show," NBC, 1958; "Patti Page Olds Show," ABC, 1958; "Swiss Family Robinson," NBC, 1958; "Dick Powell's Zane Grey Theatre: Pressure Point," CBS, 1958; "Meet Me in St. Louis," CBS, 1959; "Dick Powell's Zane Grey Theatre: King of the Valley," CBS, 1959; "The Ed Sullivan Show," CBS, 1960; "Checkmate: Death Beyond Recall,"

CBS, 1962; "Rawhide: The Reunion," CBS, 1962; "Perry Mason: The Case of the Surplus Suitor," CBS, 1963; "The Breaking Point: The Gnu, Now Almost Extinct," ABC, 1963; "Daniel Boone: Not in Our Stars," NBC, 1964; "Dr. Kildare: Never Too Old for the Circus," NBC, 1964; "Burke's Law: Who Killed Mother Goose?," ABC, 1965; "Cinderella," CBS, 1965; "The FBI: The Executioners," ABC, 1967; "The Danny Thomas Hour: My Pal Tony," NBC, 1968; "Marcus Welby, M.D.: A Passing of Torches," ABC, 1970; "Dan August: The Law," ABC, 1971; "The Snoop Sisters: Fear Is a Free Throw," NBC, 1974; "Gibbsville: Premiere," NBC, 1976.

TV MOVIES AND MINISERIES: "How I Spent My Summer Vacation," NBC, 1967; "The House on Greenapple Road," ABC, 1970; "The Mask of Sheba," NBC, 1970; "The Screaming Woman," ABC, 1972; "Live Again, Die Again," ABC, 1974; "The Girl on the Late, Late Show," NBC, 1974; "You Lie So Deep, My Love," ABC, 1975; "Murder on Flight 502," ABC, 1975; "The Lindbergh Kidnapping Case," NBC, 1976.

PINCHOT, BRONSON
b. *New York City, NY, May 20, 1959.* Comic actor who plays Balki on "Perfect Strangers."
AS A REGULAR: "Sara," NBC, 1985; "Perfect Strangers," ABC, 1986- .
AND: "Amazing Stories: Mummy, Daddy," NBC, 1985; "Saturday Night Live," NBC, 1987.

PINK LADY
Japanese singing duo composed of Mie Nemoto & Kei Masuda. They were hired to host an NBC variety show, but there was just one problem—they didn't speak English.
AS REGULARS: "Pink Lady," NBC, 1980.

PINTAURO, DANNY
b. *Milltown, NJ, January 6, 1976.* Young actor who plays Jonathan on "Who's the Boss?"
AS A REGULAR: "As the World Turns," CBS, 1983-84; "Who's the Boss?," ABC, 1984- .
AND: "Highway to Heaven: Man's Best Friend," NBC, 1986; "Sea World's Miracle Babies," ABC, 1989; "Animal Crack-Ups," ABC, 1989; "Totally Hidden Video," FOX, 1989.

PINZA, EZIO
b. *Rome, Italy, May 8, 1892; d. 1957.* Basso popular in early TV.
AS A REGULAR: "The RCA Victor Show," NBC, 1951-52; "Bonino," NBC, 1953.
AND: "Robert Montgomery Presents: The Valari Special," NBC, 1952; "Hollywood Opening Night: Interlude," NBC, 1953; "G.E. Theatre: The Half-Promised Land," CBS, 1955.

PISCOPO, JOE
b. *Passaic, NJ, June 17, 1951.* Comic actor as famous for beer commercials as for imaginative bits.
AS A REGULAR: "Saturday Night Live," NBC, 1980-84.
AND: "The Joe Piscopo Special," HBO, 1984.

PITTS, ZASU
b. *Parsons, KS, January 3, 1898; d. 1963.* Slender, gawky actress in comic spinster roles in films and TV; best known as Esmerelda "Nugey" Nugent, the nutty sidekick of Gale Storm on her sitcom.
AS A REGULAR: "The Gale Storm Show," CBS, 1956-59; ABC, 1959-60.
AND: "G.E. Theatre: Pardon My Aunt," CBS, 1954; "Kraft Television Theatre: The Happy Touch," NBC, 1954; "Best of Broadway: The Man Who Came to Dinner," CBS, 1954; "Screen Directors Playhouse: The Silent Partner," NBC, 1955; "The 20th Century-Fox Hour: Mr. Belvedere," CBS, 1956; "Private Secretary: Not Quite Paradise," CBS, 1957; "The Dennis O'Keefe Show: The Crush," CBS, 1960; "Guestward Ho!: Lonesome's Gal," ABC, 1961; "The Jim Backus Show: Advice Column," SYN, 1961; "Here's Hollywood," NBC, 1962; "Art Linkletter's House Party," CBS, 1962; "Perry Mason: The Case of the Absent Artist," CBS, 1962; "Burke's Law: Who Killed Holly Howard?," ABC, 1963.

PLACE, MARY KAY
b. *Tulsa, OK, September 23, 1947.* Blonde actress of film ("The Big Chill") and TV; she played Loretta Haggers on "Mary Hartman, Mary Hartman."
AS A REGULAR: "Mary Hartman, Mary Hartman," SYN, 1976-78.
AND: "All in the Family: Archie Goes Too Far," CBS, 1973; "M*A*S*H: Springtime," CBS, 1974; "M*A*S*H: Mad Dogs and Servicemen," CBS, 1974; "The Mary Tyler Moore Show: Murray in Love," CBS, 1975; "Saturday Night Live," NBC, 1976; "Traitor in my House," PBS, 1988.
TV MOVIES AND MINISERIES: "Out on the Edge," CBS, 1989.
AS WRITER: "M*A*S*H: Hot Lips and Empty Arms," CBS, 1973; "M*A*S*H: Springtime," CBS, 1974; "The Mary Tyler Moore Show: Mary's Delinquent," CBS, 1975.
* Emmies: 1977.

PLATO, DANA
b. *Maywood, CA, November 7, 1964.* Actress who played Kimberly Drummond on "Diff'rent Strokes."
AS A REGULAR: "Diff'rent Strokes," NBC, 1978-84.
AND: "CHiPS: Nightingale," NBC, 1980; "Growing Pains: Mike's Madonna Story," ABC, 1985; "The

Love Boat: Baby Sister," ABC, 1985.
TV MOVIES AND MINISERIES: "Beyond the Bermuda Triangle," NBC, 1975.

PLATT, EDWARD C.
b. Staten Island, NY, February 4, 1916; d. 1974. Bald character actor best known as the Chief on "Get Smart."
AS A REGULAR: "Get Smart," NBC, 1965-69; CBS, 1969-70.
AND: "Wire Service: Until I Die," ABC, 1956; "Telephone Time: The Man the Navy Couldn't Sink," ABC, 1957; "The Jane Wyman Show: Death Rides the 12:15," NBC, 1957; "Tales of Wells Fargo: Doc Bell," NBC, 1958; "Dick Powell's Zane Grey Theatre: Trial by Fear," CBS, 1958; "Westinghouse Desilu Playhouse: Trial at Devil's Canyon," CBS, 1959; "Whispering Smith: The Hemp Reeger Case," NBC, 1961; "The Dick Powell Show: Who Killed Julie Greer?," NBC, 1961; "Cheyenne: Ride the Whirlwind," ABC, 1962; "Death Valley Days: A Girl Named Virginia," SYN, 1962; "Bonanza: The Guilty," NBC, 1962; "The Dick Van Dyke Show: A Nice Friendly Game of Cards," CBS, 1964; "The Breaking Point: The Tides of Darkness," ABC, 1964; "The Outer Limits: The Special One," ABC, 1964; "Grindl: Grindl, Private Eye," NBC, 1964; "Burke's Law: Who Killed the Horne of Plenty?," ABC, 1964; "The Outer Limits: Keeper of the Purple Twilight," ABC, 1964; "The Virginian: The Secret of Brymar Hall," NBC, 1964; "The Mike Douglas Show," SYN, 1967; "The Jerry Lewis Show," NBC, 1968; "The Governor and J.J.: A Day in the Life...," CBS, 1970; "Love, American Style: Love and the Man Next Door," ABC, 1970; "The Odd Couple: Oscar's New Life," ABC, 1971; "Owen Marshall, Counselor at Law: A Foreigner Among Us," ABC, 1974.
TV MOVIES AND MINISERIES: "The Snoop Sisters," NBC, 1972.

PLEASANCE, DONALD
b. Worksop, England, October 5, 1919. Actor often in evil roles, including Robin Hood's nemesis Prince John.
AS A REGULAR: "The Adventures of Robin Hood," CBS, 1955-58.
AND: "Alcoa Presents One Step Beyond: The Confession," ABC, 1961; "Danger Man: Find and Return," CBS, 1961; "Walt Disney's Wonderful World of Color: The Horsemasters," NBC, 1961; "The Twilight Zone: The Changing of the Guard," CBS, 1962; "The Outer Limits: The Man with the Power," ABC, 1963; "Espionage: The Liberators," NBC, 1964; "The Defenders: Fires of the Mind," CBS, 1965; "The Fugitive: With Strings Attached," ABC, 1966; "The Diary of Anne Frank," ABC, 1967; "Hawaii Five-O: The Ninety Second War," CBS, 1972; "Dr. Jekyll and Mr.

Hyde," NBC, 1973; "Orson Welles' Great Mysteries: Captain Rogers," SYN, 1973; "Columbo: Any Old Port in a Storm," NBC, 1973; "Saturday Night Live," NBC, 1981.
TV MOVIES AND MINISERIES: "The Count of Monte Cristo," NBC, 1975; "Jesus of Nazareth," NBC, 1977; "The Defection of Simas Kudirka," CBS, 1978; "The Bastard," SYN, 1978; "Centennial," NBC, 1978-79; "Gold of the Amazon Women," NBC, 1979; "Better Late Than Never," NBC, 1979; "Witness for the Prosecution," CBS, 1982; "Master of the Game," CBS, 1984; "The Corsican Brothers," CBS, 1985; "Arch of Triumph," CBS, 1985.

PLESHETTE, JOHN
b. New York City, NY, July 27, 1942. Actor who played Richard Avery on "Knots Landing" and Lee Harvey Oswald in a TV movie.
AS A REGULAR: "Doctors Hospital," NBC, 1975-76; "Knots Landing," CBS, 1979-83.
AND: "The Patty Duke Show: Simon Says," ABC, 1964; "The Rockford Files: Dwarf in a Helium Hat," NBC, 1978; "The Rockford Files: Black Mirror," ABC, 1978; "Simon & Simon: Under the Knife," CBS, 1984; "MacGruder and Loud: Pilot," ABC, 1985; "Highway to Heaven: All That Glitters," NBC, 1985; "Simon & Simon: Love and/or Marriage," CBS, 1986; "Highway to Heaven: Heaven Nose, Mr. Smith," NBC, 1988.
TV MOVIES AND MINISERIES: "The Trial of Lee Harvey Oswald," ABC, 1977; "Best Sellers: Seventh Avenue," NBC, 1977; "Burning Rage," CBS, 1984; "Stormin' Home," CBS, 1985; "Welcome Home Bobby," CBS, 1986; "Mrs. Delafield Wants to Marry," CBS, 1986; "Windmills of the Gods," CBS, 1988; "Shattered Innocence," CBS, 1988.

PLESHETTE, SUZANNE
b. New York City, NY, January 31, 1937. Attractive actress who played Emily Hartley, patient wife of Bob Newhart on his seventies sitcom.
AS A REGULAR: "The Bob Newhart Show," CBS, 1972-78; "Suzanne Pleshette Is Maggie Briggs," CBS, 1984; "Bridges to Cross," CBS, 1986; "Nightingales," NBC, 1989.
AND: "Harbourmaster: Night Rescue," CBS, 1957; "G.E. Theatre: The World's Greatest Quarterback," CBS, 1958; "Have Gun, Will Travel: Death of a Gunfighter," CBS, 1958; "Playhouse 90: Diary of a Nurse," CBS, 1959; "The Ed Sullivan Show," CBS, 1959; "Adventures in Paradise: Lady From South Chicago," ABC, 1959; "Naked City: The Pedigree Sheet," ABC, 1960; "Route 66: The Strengthening Angels," CBS, 1960; "The Islanders: Forbidden Cargo," ABC, 1960; "Alcoa Presents One Step Beyond: Delusion," ABC, 1960; "Dr. Kildare: Shining Image," NBC, 1961; "Target: The Corruptors: Viva Vegas," ABC, 1962; "Ben Casey: Behold a

Pale Horse," ABC, 1962; "The Dick Powell Show: Days of Glory," NBC, 1962; "Dr. Kildare: The Soul Killer," NBC, 1962; "Channing: The Potato Bash World," ABC, 1963; "Bob Hope Chrysler Theatre: Corridor 400," NBC, 1963; "Dr. Kildare: Goodbye, Mr. Jersey," NBC, 1964; "The Fugitive: World's End," ABC, 1964; "The Wild Wild West: The Night of the Inferno," CBS, 1965; "The Fugitive: All the Scared Rabbits," ABC, 1965; "Bob Hope Chrysler Theatre: After the Lion, Jackals," NBC, 1966; "The Invaders: The Pursued," ABC, 1968; "The FBI: The Mercenary," ABC, 1968; "It Takes a Thief: A Sour Note," ABC, 1968; "The Name of the Game: The Suntan Mob," NBC, 1969; "Name Droppers," NBC, 1970; "The Name of the Game: The Skin Game," NBC, 1970; "Love, American Style: Love and the Fly," ABC, 1970; "Gunsmoke: Stark," CBS, 1970; "Marcus Welby, M.D.: Daisy in the Shadow," ABC, 1970; "The Courtship of Eddie's Father: Hello, Miss Bessinger," ABC, 1970; "The FBI: The Inheritors," ABC, 1970; "Hollywood Squares," NBC, 1970; "The Name of the Game: A Capitol Affair," NBC, 1971; "Medical Center: Conspiracy," CBS, 1971; "Columbo: Dead Weight," NBC, 1971; "Ironside: When She Was Bad," NBC, 1971; "Hollywood Squares," NBC, 1972; "Bonanza: A Place to Hide," NBC, 1972; "The Tonight Show Starring Johnny Carson," NBC, 1976; "The Tonight Show Starring Johnny Carson," NBC, 1989; "Newhart: The Last Newhart," CBS, 1990.

TV MOVIES AND MINISERIES: "Wings of Fire," NBC, 1967; "Along Came a Spider," ABC, 1970; "Hunters Are for Killing," CBS, 1970; "River of Gold," ABC, 1971; "In Broad Daylight," ABC, 1971; "The Legend of Valentino," ABC, 1975; "Law and Order," NBC, 1976; "Richie Brockelman, Private Eye," NBC, 1976; "Flesh and Blood," CBS, 1979; "The Star Maker," NBC, 1981; "Help Wanted: Male," CBS, 1982; "Fantasies," ABC, 1982; "One Cooks, the Other Doesn't," CBS, 1983; "Dixie: Changing Habits," CBS, 1983; "Kojak: The Belarus File," CBS, 1985; "A Stranger Waits," CBS, 1987.

* Pleshette guest-starred on the final episode of "Newhart" as Emily Hartley, lying in bed next to TV husband Bob Newhart as he awakened from a dream that had been the eighties sitcom.

PLUMB, EVE

b. Burbank, CA, 1957. Blonde actress who played Jan Brady, of the bunch.

AS A REGULAR: "The Brady Bunch," ABC, 1969-74; "Little Women," NBC, 1979; "The Brady Brides," NBC, 1981; "The Bradys," CBS, 1990.

AND: "The Virginian: A Small Taste of Justice," NBC, 1967; "Family Affair: Christmas Came a Little Early," CBS, 1968; "Lancer: The Heart of Pony Alice," CBS, 1968; "Mannix: Edge of the Knife," CBS, 1968; "Here's Lucy: Lucy and Donny Osmond," CBS, 1972; "Fantasy Island: The Swimmer," ABC, 1980; "The Love Boat: Honeymoon Pressure," ABC, 1980.

TV MOVIES AND MINISERIES: "The House on Greenapple Road," ABC, 1970; "Dawn: Portrait of a Teenage Runaway," NBC, 1976; "Little Women," NBC, 1978; "Secrets of Three Hungry Wives," NBC, 1978; "The Night The Bridge Fell Down," NBC, 1983; "A Very Brady Christmas," CBS, 1988.

PLUMMER, CHRISTOPHER

b. Toronto, Canada, December 13, 1929. Dashing leading man often in prestigious TV projects; he won an Emmy for "The Moneychangers."

AS A GUEST: "Summer Studio One: The Gathering Night," CBS, 1953; "Broadway Television Theatre: Dark Victory," SYN, 1953; "The Web: Sheep's Clothing," CBS, 1954; "Kraft Television Theatre: The Dashing White Sergeant," ABC, 1954; "Kraft Television Theatre: The King's Bounty," NBC, 1955; "Producers Showcase: Cyrano de Bergerac," NBC, 1955; "Appointment with Adventure: A Thief There Was," CBS, 1956; "Alcoa Hour: Even the Weariest River," NBC, 1956; "Omnibus: Oedipus Rex," ABC, 1957; "Du Pont Show of the Month: The Prince and the Pauper," CBS, 1957; "Hallmark Hall of Fame: Little Moon of Alban," NBC, 1958; "Hallmark Hall of Fame: Johnny Belinda," NBC, 1958; "Omnibus: The Lady's Not for Burning," NBC, 1958; "Omnibus: Prince Orestes," NBC, 1959; "Hallmark Hall of Fame: A Doll's House," NBC, 1959; "The Phildelphia Story," NBC, 1959; "Sunday Showcase: After Hours," NBC, 1960; "Our American Heritage: Autocrat and Son," NBC, 1960; "Hallmark Hall of Fame: Captain Brassbound's Conversion," NBC, 1960; "Du Pont Show of the Month: The Prisoner of Zenda," CBS, 1961; "Hallmark Hall of Fame: Time Remembered," NBC, 1961; "Hallmark Hall of Fame: Cyrano de Bergerac," NBC, 1962; "Hamlet," NET, 1964; "Hallmark Hall of Fame: After the Fall," NBC, 1974; "The Cosby Show: Shakespeare," NBC, 1987.

TV MOVIES AND MINISERIES: "The Moneychangers," NBC, 1976; "Jesus of Nazareth," NBC, 1977; "The Shadow Box," ABC, 1980; "Dial M for Murder," NBC, 1981; "Little Gloria ... Happy at Last," NBC, 1982; "The Thorn Birds," ABC, 1983; "Crossings," ABC, 1986; "A Hazard of Hearts," CBS, 1987.

* Emmies: 1977.

POITIER, SIDNEY

b. Miami, FL, February 20, 1927. Oscar-winning actor ("Lilies of the Field") who began on TV.

AS A GUEST: "Philco TV Playhouse: Parole Chief," NBC, 1952; "Pond's Theatre: Fascinating Stranger," ABC, 1955; "Philco TV Playhouse: A Man Is Ten Feet Tall," NBC, 1955; "A Tribute to Eleanor Roosevelt on Her Diamond Jubilee," NBC, 1959; "The Strollin' 20s," CBS, 1966; "ABC Stage '67: A Time for Laughter," ABC, 1967; "The Tonight Show Starring Johnny Carson," NBC, 1968; "The Great American Dream Machine," NET, 1970; "The New Bill Cosby Show," CBS, 1972; "The Merv Griffin Show," SYN, 1975; "Inaugural Eve Special," CBS, 1977.

POLLACK, SYDNEY
b. *South Bend, IN, July 1, 1934.* Actor and film director ("Tootsie," "Out of Africa"); an Emmy-winner for "Bob Hope Chrysler Theatre."
AS A GUEST: "Kraft Television Theatre: Time Lock," NBC, 1956; "Playhouse 90: For Whom the Bell Tolls," CBS, 1959; "U.S. Steel Hour: The Case of Julia Walton," CBS, 1959; "Armstrong Circle Theatre: 35 Rue du Marche," CBS, 1959; "Alfred Hitchcock Presents: The Contest for Aaron Gold," NBC, 1960; "The Twilight Zone: The Trouble with Templeton," CBS, 1960; "Have Gun, Will Travel: A Quiet Night in Town," CBS, 1961; "Robert Herridge Theatre: The Chrysanthemums," SYN, 1961; "The Deputy: Spoken in Silence," NBC, 1961; "The New Breed: Compulsion to Confess," ABC, 1961.
AS DIRECTOR: "Bob Hope Chrysler Theatre: The Game," NBC, 1965.
* Emmies: 1966.

POLLARD, MICHAEL J.
b. *Michael J. Pollack, Passaic, NJ, May 30, 1939.* Actor often in offbeat, dimwitted roles; memorable as C.W. Moss in "Bonnie and Clyde" and as the bumbling cousin of Barney Fife (Don Knotts) on an episode of "The Andy Griffith Show."
AS A REGULAR: "Leo & Liz in Beverly Hills," CBS, 1986.
AND: "Alfred Hitchcock Presents: Appointment at Eleven," CBS, 1959; "Alfred Hitchcock Presents: Anniversary Gift," CBS, 1959; "Startime: The Man," NBC, 1960; "The Secret of Freedom," NBC, 1960; "Look Up and Live: Two Alone-The Stranger," CBS, 1960; "Henry Fonda and the Family," CBS, 1962; "The Andy Griffith Show: Cousin Virgil," CBS, 1962; "Going My Way: Tell Me When You Get to Heaven," ABC, 1963; "Route 66: And Make Thunder His Tribute," CBS, 1963; "The Lucy Show: Chris Goes Steady," CBS, 1964; "Mr. Novak: Honor and All That," NBC, 1965; "Honey West: The Princess and the Paupers," ABC, 1965; "The Virginian: The Wolves Up Front, the Jackals Behind," NBC,

1966; "I Spy: Trial by Treehouse," NBC, 1966; "Star Trek: Miri," NBC, 1966; "The Danny Thomas Hour: The Scene," NBC, 1967; "This Morning," ABC, 1968; "Movin' On: Pilot," NBC, 1974; "Crime Story: Desert Justice," NBC, 1988.
TV MOVIES AND MINISERIES: "The Smugglers," NBC, 1968; "Stuck with Each Other," NBC, 1989.

PONCE, DANNY
b. *Waltham, MA, September 4, 1972.* Actor who plays Willie Hogan on "The Hogan Family."
AS A REGULAR: "Knots Landing," CBS, 1983-85; "Valerie," NBC, 1986-87; "Valerie's Family," NBC, 1987; "The Hogan Family," NBC, 1987- .
AND: "Hell Town: Father Love," NBC, 1985; "Hunter: Rape and Revenge," NBC, 1985.

PONCE, PONCIE
b. *Hawaii, April 10, 1933.* Actor who played Kim, sidekick to the private dicks on "Hawaiian Eye."
AS A REGULAR: "Hawaiian Eye," ABC, 1959-63.
AND: "77 Sunset Strip: Only Zeroes Count," ABC, 1959; "77 Sunset Strip: Perfect Setup," ABC, 1960.

PORTER, DON
b. *Miami, OK, September 24, 1912.* Actor who played Ann Sothern's boss/romantic interest in two sitcoms, and Sally Field's father in the third; often cast as stern types on drama series.
AS A REGULAR: "Private Secretary," CBS, 1953-57; "The Ann Sothern Show," CBS, 1959-61; "Gidget," ABC, 1965-66.
AND: "Here's Hollywood," NBC, 1961; "Comedy Spot: I Love My Doctor," CBS, 1962; "Vacation Playhouse: Tallie," CBS, 1965; "Judd for the Defense: Epitaph on a Computer Card," ABC, 1969; "Love, American Style: Love and the Single Couple," ABC, 1969; "The Mod Squad: The Judas Trap," ABC, 1970; "Love, American Style: Love and the Teddy Bear," ABC, 1971; "Green Acres: Hawaiian Honeymoon," CBS, 1971; "The Rookies: A Deadly Velocity," ABC, 1972; "The Fuzz Brothers," ABC, 1973; "The New Adventures of Perry Mason: The Case of the Deadly Deeds," CBS, 1973; "Barnaby Jones: Secret of the Dunes," CBS, 1973; "Hawaii Five-O: Murder is a Taxing Affair," CBS, 1973; "Tenafly: The Cash and Carry Caper," NBC, 1973; "Barnaby Jones: Secret of the Dunes," CBS, 1973; "The Mod Squad: Scion of Death," ABC, 1973; "Here's Lucy: Meanwhile, Back at the Office," CBS, 1974; "Happy Anniversary and Goodbye," CBS, 1974; "The FBI: The Lost Man," ABC, 1974; "Switch: Death by Resurrection," CBS, 1975; "McMillan and Wife: Secrets for

Sale," NBC, 1975; "Ellery Queen: Veronica's Veils," NBC, 1975; "Hawaii Five-O: Anatomy of a Bribe," CBS, 1976; "Three's Company: Jack's Uncle," ABC, 1977; "Switch: Lady of the Deep," CBS, 1978; "Sword of Justice: Judgement Day," NBC, 1978; "Turnabout: Till Dad Do Us Part," NBC, 1979; "Hotel: Faith, Hope and Charity," ABC, 1983; "The Love Boat: He Ain't Heavy," ABC, 1983; "CBS Summer Playhouse: Old Money," CBS, 1988.

TV MOVIES AND MINISERIES: "The Norliss Tapes," NBC, 1973; "The Morning After," ABC, 1974; "Murder or Mercy," ABC, 1974; "The Legend of Lizzie Borden," ABC, 1975; "The Murder That Wouldn't Die," NBC, 1980.

POST, MARKIE
b. Palo Alto, CA, November 4, 1950. Pert blonde actress who plays Christine Sullivan on "Night Court."

AS A REGULAR: "Semi-Tough," ABC, 1980; "The Gangster Chronicles," NBC, 1981; "The Fall Guy," ABC, 1982-85; "Night Court," NBC, 1985- .

AND: "B.J. and the Bear: B.J.'s Sweethearts," NBC, 1979; "Barnaby Jones: Master of Deception," CBS, 1979; "Buck Rogers in the 25th Century: Plot to Kill a City," NBC, 1979; "Lou Grant: Censored," CBS, 1980; "House Calls: A Slight Case of Quarantine," CBS, 1980; "The Love Boat: A Dress to Remember," ABC, 1981; "Cheers: Just Three Friends," NBC, 1983; "The A-Team: The Only Church in Town," NBC, 1983; "The Love Boat: Dee Dee's Dilemma," ABC, 1983; "Hotel: Prisms," ABC, 1984; "Glitter: Premiere," ABC, 1984; "The A-Team: Hot Styles," NBC, 1984; "The Pat Sajak Show," CBS, 1989;

TV MOVIES AND MINISERIES: "Not Just Another Affair," CBS, 1982; "Triplecross," ABC, 1986.

POSTON, TOM
b. Columbus, OH, October 17, 1927. Talented, dependable comic actor and game-show regular who was a longtime foil for Steve Allen; more recently he played easygoing handyman George Utley on "Newhart."

AS A REGULAR: "The Tonight Show," NBC, 1954-57; "The Steve Allen Show," NBC, 1956-59; "To Tell the Truth," CBS, 1958-67; "Pantomime Quiz," ABC, 1958; "Split Personality," NBC, 1959-60; "On the Rocks," ABC, 1975-76; "We've Got Each Other," CBS, 1977-78; "Mork & Mindy," ABC, 1978-82; "Newhart," CBS, 1982-90.

AND: "Goodyear TV Playhouse: Tangled Web," NBC, 1955; "Playwrights '56: You Sometimes Get Rich," NBC, 1956; "Robert Montgomery Presents: Who?," NBC, 1956; "The Phil Silvers Show: The Face on the Recruiting Poster," CBS, 1956; "The Phil Silvers Show: Love That

Guardhouse," CBS, 1956; "U.S. Steel Hour: The Change in Chester," CBS, 1957; "Look Up and Live: Humor and Faith," CBS, 1957; "What's My Line?," CBS, 1958; "Hallmark Hall of Fame: Hallmark Christmas Tree-Before the Stores Close," NBC, 1958; "Arthur Murray Party," NBC, 1958; "Person to Person," CBS, 1959; "Arthur Murray Party," NBC, 1959; "The Ed Sullivan Show," CBS, 1959; "Startime: Merman on Broadway," NBC, 1959; "Salute to the American Theatre," CBS, 1959; "Hallmark Hall of Fame: The Tempest," NBC, 1960; "Steve Allen Plymouth Show," NBC, 1960; "Way Back in 1960," ABC, 1960; "Celebrity Talent Scouts," CBS, 1960; "Play of the Week: The Enchanted," SYN, 1961; "I've Got a Secret," CBS, 1961; "Password" (first guest), CBS, 1961; "Lamp Unto My Feet: The Journal of Clarence Candide," CBS, 1961; "Thriller: Masquerade," NBC, 1961; "Password," CBS, 1962; "Hallmark Hall of Fame: The Tempest," NBC, 1963; "Missing Links," NBC, 1963; "The Defenders: The Seven-Hundred-Year-Old Gang," CBS, 1964; "Get the Message," ABC, 1964; "Bob Hope Chrysler Theatre: Double Jeopardy," NBC, 1965; "Get Smart: Shock It to Me," NBC, 1969; "Harry and Maggie," CBS, 1975; "The Bob Newhart Show: The Longest Good-Bye," CBS, 1975; "The Bob Newhart Show: Peeper—Two," CBS, 1976; "Alice: Vera's Mortician," CBS, 1976; "The Bob Newhart Show: Enter Mrs. Peeper," CBS, 1976; "The Bob Newhart Show: The Slammer," CBS, 1976; "The Bob Newhart Show: You're Having My Hartley," CBS, 1977; "$weepstake$: Dewey and Harold and Sarah and Maggie," NBC, 1979; "The Steve Allen Comedy Hour," NBC, 1980; "Hollywood Squares," NBC, 1980; "The Love Boat: The Prize Winner," ABC, 1983; "Late Night with David Letterman," NBC, 1986; "St. Elsewhere: The Abby Singer Show," NBC, 1988; "The Magical World of Disney: Save the Dog," NBC, 1989; "The Pat Sajak Show," CBS, 1989; "Super Password," NBC, 1989; "Animal Crack-Ups," ABC, 1989.

TV MOVIES AND MINISERIES: "A Guide for the Married Woman," ABC, 1978.

* Emmies: 1959.

POTTS, ANNIE
b. Nashville, TN, 1949. Actress who plays Mary Jo Shively on "Designing Women."

AS A REGULAR: "Goodtime Girls," ABC, 1980; "Designing Women," CBS, 1986- .

AND: "Sirota's Court: Court Fear," NBC, 1976; "Remington Steele: Steele Crazy After All These Years," NBC, 1983; "Magnum, P.I.: Two Birds of a Feather," CBS, 1983; "The Twilight Zone: Wordplay," CBS, 1985; "Lime Street: Swiss Watch and Wait," ABC, 1985; "Amazing Stories: Family Dog," NBC, 1987.

TV MOVIES AND MINISERIES: "Black Market Baby,"

ABC, 1977; "Flatbed Annie and Sweetiepie: Lady Truckers," CBS, 1979; "Something So Right," CBS, 1982; "Cowboy," CBS, 1983; "Why Me?," ABC, 1984.

* See also Jean Smart.

POWELL, DICK

b. Mountain View, AR, November 14, 1904; d. 1963. Thirties leading man in hokey musicals who made the jump to serious actor; then he became a popular TV star and co-producer of several successful TV shows of the fifties.

AS A REGULAR: "Four Star Playhouse," CBS, 1952-56; "Dick Powell's Zane Grey Theatre," CBS, 1956-62; "The Dick Powell Show," NBC, 1961-63.

AND: "Climax!: The Long Goodbye," CBS, 1954; "Mr. Adams and Eve: Backwash," CBS, 1958; "The Ed Sullivan Show," CBS, 1958; "What's My Line?," CBS, 1959; "I've Got a Secret," CBS, 1959; "The du Pont Show with June Allyson: A Summer's Ending," CBS, 1959; "The du Pont Show with June Allyson: The Doctor and the Redhead," CBS, 1960; "Art Linkletter's House Party," CBS, 1960; "The Tom Ewell Show: Site Unseen," CBS, 1960; "The Law and Mr. Jones: Everybody vs. Timmy Drayton," ABC, 1961; "This Is Your Life" (Debbie Reynolds), NBC, 1961; "Ensign O'Toole: Operation: Benefit," NBC, 1962.

AS PRODUCER-DIRECTOR: "Four Star Playhouse," CBS, 1952-56; "Dick Powell's Zane Grey Theatre," CBS, 1956-62; "The Dick Powell Show," NBC, 1961-63.

* Powell played Raymond Chandler's private eye Philip Marlowe in the 1944 film "Murder, My Sweet" and on TV on "Climax!"

POWELL, JANE

b. Suzanne Burce, Portland, OR, April 1, 1929. Oh-so-wholesome leading lady of fifties musicals who plays the mother of Jason Seaver (Alan Thicke) on "Growing Pains."

AS A REGULAR: "Alcoa-Goodyear Theatre (A Turn of Fate)," NBC, 1957-58; "Growing Pains," ABC, 1988- .

AND: "Ruggles of Red Gap," NBC, 1957; "The Standard Oil 75th Anniversary Show," NBC, 1957; "Tex and Jinx," NBC, 1957; "The Steve Allen Show," NBC, 1958; "The Eddie Fisher Show," NBC, 1958; "The George Gobel Show," NBC, 1958; "Dinah Shore Chevy Show," NBC, 1959; "The Garry Moore Show," CBS, 1959; "I've Got a Secret," CBS, 1959; "Meet Me in St. Louis," CBS, 1959; "The du Pont Show with June Allyson: The Girl," CBS, 1959; "Hooray for Love," CBS, 1960; "Bell Telephone Hour: The Music of Romance," NBC, 1960; "Jane Powell Special: Young at Heart," NBC, 1961; "Feathertop," ABC, 1961; "I've Got a Secret," CBS, 1962; "Bell Telephone Hour: A Measure of

Music," NBC, 1962; "The Dick Powell Show: View From the Eiffel Tower," NBC, 1962; "Password," CBS, 1962; "The Red Skelton Hour," CBS, 1962; "Perry Como's Kraft Music Hall," NBC, 1963; "The Garry Moore Show," CBS, 1963; "The Ed Sullivan Show," CBS, 1964; "Andy Williams Special," NBC, 1964; "The Judy Garland Show," CBS, 1964; "Hollywood Palace," ABC, 1964; "Bell Telephone Hour," NBC, 1965; "Danny Thomas Special," NBC, 1967; "Snap Judgment," NBC, 1968; "The Love Boat: Maid for Each Other," ABC, 1981; "The Love Boat: Saving Grace," ABC, 1982; "Murder, She Wrote: Old Habits Die Hard," CBS, 1987; "Great Performances: An Evening with Alan Jay Lerner," PBS, 1989.

TV MOVIES AND MINISERIES: "The Letters," ABC, 1973; "Mayday at 40,000 Feet," CBS, 1976.

POWERS, STEFANIE

b. Stefania Federkiewicz, Hollywood, CA, November 12, 1942. Sixties starlet who left a so-so movie career to become a big TV star; most recently she was crime-solving Jennifer Hart, wife of Jonathan (Robert Wagner) on the silly "Hart to Hart" and a heroine in some impressive miniseries.

AS A REGULAR: "The Girl From UNCLE," NBC, 1966-67; "The Feather and Father Gang," ABC, 1977; "Hart to Hart," ABC, 1979-84.

AND: "Vacation Playhouse: Swingin' Together," CBS, 1963; "Bonanza: Calamity Over the Comstock," NBC, 1963; "The Steve Allen Show," SYN, 1968; "Operation: Entertainment," ABC, 1968; "Love, American Style: Love and the Tattoo," ABC, 1969; "Love, American Style: Love and the Doorknob," ABC, 1969; "It Takes a Thief: Fortune City," ABC, 1970; "Medical Center: Man at Bay," CBS, 1970; "The Movie Game," SYN, 1970; "Love, American Style: Love and the Big Surprise," ABC, 1971; "The Mod Squad: The Connection," ABC, 1972; "Barnaby Jones: Echoes of a Murder," CBS, 1973; "McCloud: Butch Cassidy Rides Again," NBC, 1973; "Marcus Welby, M.D.: The Endless Moment," ABC, 1973; "Medical Center: Fatal Memory," CBS, 1973; "Kodiak: Pilot," ABC, 1974; "McMillan and Wife: The Game of Survival," NBC, 1974; "The Rookies: Judgement," ABC, 1974; "The Streets of San Francisco: No Place to Hide," ABC, 1975; "Three for the Road: The Ghost Story," CBS, 1975; "The Rockford Files: The Real Easy Red Dog," NBC, 1975; "McMillan: Affair of the Heart," NBC, 1977.

TV MOVIES AND MINISERIES: "Five Desperate Women," ABC, 1971; "Rachel, Sweet Rachel," ABC, 1971; "Paper Man," CBS, 1971; "Ellery Queen: Don't Look Behind You," NBC, 1971; "Hardcase," ABC, 1972; "No Place to Run," ABC, 1972; "Shootout in a One-Dog Town,"

ABC, 1974; "Skyway to Death," ABC, 1974; "The Manhunter," CBS, 1974; "Night Games," NBC, 1974; "Sky Hei$t," NBC, 1975; "Return to Earth," ABC, 1976; "Feather and Father," ABC, 1976; "Washington: Behind Closed Doors," ABC, 1977; "The Golden Raiders," ABC, 1981; "Hollywood Wives," ABC, 1985; "Deceptions," NBC, 1985; "At Mother's Request," CBS, 1987; "Beryl Markham: A Shadow on the Sun," CBS, 1988; "Marked for Murder," NBC, 1988; "Love and Betrayal," CBS, 1989.

PREMINGER, OTTO
b. Vienna, Austria, December 5, 1906; d. 1986. Autocratic movie director ("Laura," "The Moon Is Blue," "Advise and Consent") who played occasional bad guy roles on TV, including a go-round as Mr. Freeze on "Batman." (Eli Wallach and George Sanders also played the role.)
AS A GUEST: "Suspense: Operation Barracuda," CBS, 1954; "Small World," CBS, 1960; "Here's Hollywood," NBC, 1962; "Password," CBS, 1964; "ABC Nightlife," ABC, 1965; "Batman: Green Ice/Deep Freeze," ABC, 1966; "The Merv Griffin Show," SYN, 1967.

PRENTISS, ANN
b. Ann Ragusa, San Antonio, TX, 1941. Comic actress, sister of Paula; she played police-woman Candy Kane on the superhero spoof "Captain Nice."
AS A REGULAR: "Captain Nice," NBC, 1967.
AND: "Get Smart: The Little Black Book," NBC, 1968; "The Courtship of Eddie's Father: The Road to You Know Where Is Paved with You Know What," ABC, 1969; "The Virginian: Crime Wave in Buffalo Springs," NBC, 1969; "McCloud: Walk in the Dark," NBC, 1970; "Love, American Style: Love and the Lady Barber," ABC, 1972; "Love, American Style: Love and the Hairy Excuse," ABC, 1972; "Baretta: This Ain't My Bag," ABC, 1975; "Switch: Through the Past Deadly," CBS, 1975; "Switch: Through the Past Deadly," CBS, 1975; "Switch: Ain't Nobody Here Named Barney," CBS, 1976.
TV MOVIES AND MINISERIES: "In Name Only," ABC, 1969.

PRENTISS, PAULA
b. Paula Ragusa, San Antonio, TX, March 4, 1939. Tall, dark leading lady of some TV, notably the witty sitcom "He & She," in which she starred opposite real-life husband Richard Benjamin.
AS A REGULAR: "He & She," CBS, 1967-68.
AND: "Here's Hollywood," NBC, 1960; "The Ed Sullivan Show," CBS, 1962; "Password," CBS,

1964; "The Merv Griffin Show," SYN, 1969; "Saturday Night Live," NBC, 1980.
TV MOVIES AND MINISERIES: "The Couple Takes a Wife," ABC, 1972; "Having Babies II," ABC, 1977; "Friendships, Secrets and Lies," NBC, 1979; "Packin' It In," CBS, 1983; "M.A.D.D.: Mothers Against Drunk Driving," NBC, 1983.

PRESLEY, ELVIS
b. Tupelo, MS, January 8, 1935; d. 1977. Entertainment legend whose influence is still everywhere.
AS A GUEST: "Stage Show," CBS, 1956; "The Milton Berle Show," NBC, 1956; "The Steve Allen Show," NBC, 1956; "The Ed Sullivan Show," CBS, 1956; "The Ed Sullivan Show," CBS, 1957; "Frank Sinatra Timex Show," ABC, 1960; "Elvis Presley Special," NBC, 1968; "Aloha From Hawaii," NBC, 1972.
* When he appeared with Steve Allen, Presley was forced to wear a tuxedo as he sang "Hound Dog" to a real live hound dog.
* Presley tried—and failed—to appear on "Arthur Godfrey's Talent Scouts" in 1955.
* On TV, Presley has been portrayed by Kurt Russell ("Elvis" the TV movie), Don Johnson ("Elvis and the Beauty Queen"), Dale Midkiff ("Elvis and Me") and Michael St. Gerard ("Elvis" the TV series).
* See also "The Ed Sullivan Show," Robert Goulet, Charles Laughton, Kurt Russell.

PRESLEY, PRISCILLA
b. Brooklyn, NY, May 24, 1945. Striking actress with more beauty than talent. Former wife of Elvis Presley; best known as Jenna Wade on "Dallas."
AS A REGULAR: "Those Amazing Animals," ABC, 1980-81; "Dallas," CBS, 1983-88.
TV MOVIES AND MINISERIES: "Love Is Forever," NBC, 1983.
AS CO-EXECUTIVE PRODUCER: "Elvis," ABC, 1990.

PRESSMAN, LAWRENCE
b. Cynthiana, KY, July 10, 1939. Actor who plays Dr. Canfield on "Doogie Howser, M.D."
AS A REGULAR: "Mulligan's Stew," NBC, 1977; "Ladies' Man," CBS, 1980-81; "Doogie Howser, M.D.," ABC, 1989- .
AND: "The FBI: The Stalking Horse," ABC, 1971; "The Mary Tyler Moore Show: The Six-and-a-Half-Year Itch," CBS, 1971; "Hollywood Television Theatre: Young Marrieds at Play," NET, 1971; "Marcus Welby, M.D.: Please Don't Send Flowers," ABC, 1972; "Owen Marshall, Counselor at Law: Who Saw Him Die?," ABC, 1972; "Marcus Welby, M.D.: Blood Kin," ABC, 1973; "Griff: All the Lonely People," ABC, 1973; "Hawaii Five-O: Why Wait Until Uncle Kevin Dies?," CBS, 1973; "Barnaby Jones: Dead Man's

Run," CBS, 1974; "6 Rms Riv Vu," CBS, 1974; "The Bob Newhart Show: Brutally Yours, Bob Hartley," CBS, 1974; "Paper Moon: Long Division," ABC, 1974; "The Bob Newhart Show: A Matter of Vice-Principal," CBS, 1975; "McMillan and Wife: Requiem for a Bride," NBC, 1975; "The Streets of San Francisco: Breakup," ABC, 1976; "Police Woman: Father to the Man," NBC, 1976; "Barnaby Jones: Final Ransom," CBS, 1976; "M*A*S*H: Are You Now, Margaret?," CBS, 1979; "One Day at a Time: Teacher's Pet," CBS, 1980; "United States: Broccoli," NBC, 1980; "The Love Boat: Father, Dear Father," ABC, 1982; "Hill Street Blues: Here's Adventure, Here's Romance," NBC, 1983; "Street Hawk: Pilot," ABC, 1985; "Murder, She Wrote: My Johnny Lies Over the Ocean," CBS, 1985; "Matlock: Diary of a Perfect Murder," NBC, 1986; "Murder, She Wrote: The Way to Dusty Death," CBS, 1987; "St. Elsewhere: The Naked Civil Surgeon," NBC, 1988; "CBS Summer Playhouse: Baby on Board," CBS, 1988; "Moonlighting: Take My Wife, for Example," ABC, 1989.

TV MOVIES AND MINISERIES: "Cannon," CBS, 1971; "The Snoop Sisters," NBC, 1972; "The First 36 Hours of Dr. Durant," ABC, 1975; "Rich Man, Poor Man," ABC, 1976; "Man From Atlantis," NBC, 1977; "The Trial of Lee Harvey Oswald," ABC, 1977; "Like Mom, Like Me," CBS, 1978; "Blind Ambition," CBS, 1979; "The Gathering, Part II," NBC, 1979; "Cry for the Strangers," CBS, 1982; "The Three Wishes of Billy Grier," ABC, 1984; "The Red-Light Sting," CBS, 1984; "Victims for Victims: The Theresa Saldana Story," NBC, 1984; "The Deliberate Stranger," NBC, 1986; "On Wings of Eagles," NBC, 1986; "Little Girl Lost," ABC, 1988; "She Knows Too Much," NBC, 1989.

PRESTON, J.A.

b. *Washington, D.C.* Black actor often in distinguished roles; he played Mayor Ozzie Cleveland on "Hill Street Blues."

AS A REGULAR: "All's Fair," CBS, 1976-77; "Hill Street Blues," NBC, 1982-85.

AND: "New York Television Theatre: Hard Travelin'," NET, 1969; "All in the Family: Archie the Donor," CBS, 1975; "Good Times: Willona's Dilemma," CBS, 1975; "James at 15: Friends," NBC, 1977; "Freebie and the Bean: Bolo's Lady," CBS, 1980; "The New Odd Couple: Bachelor of the Year," ABC, 1983; "Gimme a Break: Daddy's Little Girl," NBC, 1984; "The Yellow Rose: Sport of Kings," NBC, 1984; "Punky Brewster: Punky Finds a Home," NBC, 1984; "The A-Team: Dishpan Man," NBC, 1986; "Amazing Stories: The Pumpkin Competition," NBC, 1986; "Simon & Simon: Little Boy Dead," CBS, 1988; "Hunter: No Good Deed Ever Goes Unpunished," NBC,

1988; "In the Heat of the Night: Intruders," NBC, 1989; "It's Garry Shandling's Show: Kramer vs. Grant," FOX, 1989.

TV MOVIES AND MINISERIES: "The Plutonium Incident," CBS, 1980; "The George McKenna Story," CBS, 1986.

PRESTON, ROBERT

b. *Robert Preston Meservey, Newton Highlands, MA, June 8, 1918; d. 1987.* Dynamic, likable actor of stage, TV and films, best known as Professor Harold Hill, "The Music Man."

AS A REGULAR: "Man Against Crime," CBS, 1951; "Anywhere, USA," ABC, 1952; "The Chisholms," CBS, 1979-80.

AND: "Pulitzer Prize Playhouse: Blockade," ABC, 1951; "Lux Video Theatre: Cafe Ami," CBS, 1951; "Schlitz Playhouse of Stars: The Nymph and the Lamp," CBS, 1951; "Lux Video Theatre: Kelly," CBS, 1952; "U.S. Steel Hour: Hope for a Harvest," ABC, 1953; "Campbell TV Soundstage: Al Toolum and His Buddy Leo," NBC, 1954; "U.S. Steel Hour: The End of Paul Dane," ABC, CBS, 1954; "U.S. Steel Hour: The Bogey Man," ABC, 1955; "The 20th Century-Fox Hour: Child of the Regiment," CBS, 1956; "Goodyear TV Playhouse: Missouri Legend," NBC, 1956; "Climax!: The Midas Touch," CBS, 1956; "Playhouse 90: Made in Heaven," CBS, 1956; "Alcoa Hour: The Animal Kingdom," NBC, 1957; "Omnibus: The Trial of Lizzie Borden," ABC, 1957; "Kraft Television Theatre: Nothing Personal," NBC, 1957; "Climax!: Trail of Terror," CBS, 1957; "Wide, Wide World: American Theatre '58," NBC, 1958; "The Perry Como Show," NBC, 1958; "The Bells of St. Mary's," CBS, 1959; "Du Pont Show of the Month: Years Ago," CBS, 1960; "Bell Telephone Hour: One Nation Indivisible," NBC, 1960; "Dinner with the President," CBS, 1963; "Carol & Company," CBS, 1963; "What's My Line?," CBS, 1964; "Happy Endings: A Commercial Break," ABC, 1975.

TV MOVIES AND MINISERIES: "My Father's House," ABC, 1975; "The Chisholms," CBS, 1979; "September Gun," CBS, 1983; "Finnegan Begin Again," HBO, 1985; "Outrage!," CBS, 1986.

PRESTON, WAYDE

b. *Steamboat Springs, CO, September 10, 1930.* Fifties western hero who played government agent Christopher Colt on "Colt .45."

AS A REGULAR: "Colt .45," ABC, 1957-60.

AND: "Sugarfoot: The Trial of the Canary Kid," ABC, 1959; "Sugarfoot: The Return of the Canary Kid," ABC, 1959; "Maverick: The Saga of Waco Williams," ABC, 1959; "Pat Boone Chevy Showroom," ABC, 1959; "Sugarfoot: The Canary

Kid, Inc.," ABC, 1959; "Maverick: The Witch of Hound Dog," ABC, 1960.

PRICE, KENNY
b. *Florence, KY, May 27, 1931.* Country-western singer and comic.
AS A REGULAR: "Midwestern Hayride," NBC, 1959; "Hee Haw," SYN, 1974- ; "Hee Haw Honeys," SYN, 1978-79.
AND: "Hee Haw," CBS, 1970.

PRICE, MARC
b: *February 23, 1968.* Actor who played Skippy on "Family Ties."
AS A REGULAR: "Family Ties," NBC, 1982-89; "Condo," ABC, 1983; "Teen Win, Lose or Draw," DIS, 1989- .
AND: "One Day at a Time: Mrs. O'Leary's Kid," CBS, 1982.
TV MOVIES AND MINISERIES: "Class Cruise," NBC, 1989.

PRICE, ROGER
b. *Charleston, WV, March 6, 1920.* Comedian.
AS A REGULAR: "School House," DUM, 1949; "How To," CBS, 1951; "What Happened?," NBC, 1952; "Who's There?," CBS, 1952; "Droodles," NBC, 1954; "The Name's the Same," ABC, 1954-55; "You Can't Do That on Television," NIK, 1986- .
AND: "Circus Time," ABC, 1957; "The Steve Allen Show," NBC, 1957; "Two for the Money," CBS, 1957; "Sunday Showcase: After Hours," NBC, 1960; "The Many Loves of Dobie Gillis: Almost a Father," CBS, 1960; "Get Smart: Weekend Vampire," NBC, 1965; "Faraday and Company: A Wheelbarrow Full of Trouble," NBC, 1973.
TV MOVIES AND MINISERIES: "Get Smart, Again!," ABC, 1989.

PRICE, VINCENT
b. *St. Louis, May 27, 1911.* Lean, dignified actor who began his career playing cads, moved into horror and remained versatile enough to perform in horror parodies as well. His TV credits—commercials as well as guest apearances—are extensive.
AS A REGULAR: "Pantomime Quiz," CBS, 1950; CBS, 1951; NBC, 1952; "ESP," ABC, 1958; "The Hilarious House of Frightenstein," SYN, 1975; "Time Express," CBS, 1979; "Mystery," PBS, 1982-89.
AND: "Lux Video Theatre: The Promise," CBS, 1951; "Lights Out: The Third Door," NBC, 1952; "Lux Video Theatre: The Game of Chess," CBS, 1952; "Summer Theatre: Dream Job," ABC, 1953; "Schlitz Playhouse of Stars: Sheila," CBS, 1953; "Philip Morris Playhouse: Bullet for a Stranger," CBS, 1953; "Climax!: Night of Execution," CBS, 1955; "Alcoa Hour: Sister," NBC, 1956; "Science

Fiction Theatre: One Thousand Eyes," NBC, 1956; "The $64,000 Question," CBS, 1956; "Playhouse 90: Forbidden Area," CBS, 1956; "Crossroads: God's Healing," ABC, 1956; "Washington Square," NBC, 1956; "Shower of Stars," CBS, 1957; "The Red Skelton Show," CBS, 1957; "The $64,000 Challenge," CBS, 1957; "Schlitz Playhouse of Stars: The Blue Hotel," CBS, 1957; "Odyssey: Revolution of the Eye," CBS, 1957; "Playhouse 90: Lone Woman," CBS, 1957; "G.E. Theatre: Angel in the Air," CBS, 1958; "Schlitz Playhouse of Stars: The Kind Mr. Smith," CBS, 1958; "The Jack Benny Program," CBS, 1958; "Matinee Theatre: Angel Street," NBC, 1958; "The Jack Paar Show," NBC, 1958; "Person to Person," CBS, 1958; "Have Gun, Will Travel: The Moor's Revenge," CBS, 1959; "The Jack Benny Program," CBS, 1959; "The Red Skelton Show," CBS, 1959; "The Red Skelton Show," CBS, 1960; "Startime: Tennesse Ernie Meets King Arthur," NBC, 1960; "Chevy Mystery Show: Run-Around," NBC, 1960; "Here's Hollywood," NBC, 1960; "Family Classics: The Three Musketeers," CBS, 1960; "U.S. Steel Hour: Shame the Devil," CBS, 1960; "Tell It to Groucho," CBS, 1962; "Stump the Stars," CBS, 1963; "The Red Skelton Hour," CBS, 1964; "The Danny Kaye Show," CBS, 1965; "The Red Skelton Hour," CBS, 1965; "The Man From UNCLE: The Foxes and the Hounds Affair," NBC, 1965; "Batman: An Egg Grows in Gotham/The Yegg Foes in Gotham," ABC, 1966; "F Troop: V Is for Vampire," ABC, 1967; "Voyage to the Bottom of the Sea: The Deadly Dolls," ABC, 1967; "Batman: The Ogg and I/ How to Hatch a Dinosaur," ABC, 1967; "Batman: The Ogg Couple," ABC, 1967; "The Mike Douglas Show," SYN, 1968; "Get Smart: Is This Trip Necessary?," CBS, 1969; "The Red Skelton Hour," CBS, 1970; "Love, American Style: Love and the Haunted House," ABC, 1970; "Here's Lucy: Lucy Cuts Vincent's Price," CBS, 1970; "The Mod Squad: A Time for Hyacinths," ABC, 1970; "Night Gallery: The Class of '99," NBC, 1971; "Here Comes Peter Cottontail," ABC, 1972; "Night Gallery: The Return of the Sorcerer," NBC, 1972; "The Carol Burnett Show," CBS, 1972; "The Brady Bunch: The Tiki Caves," ABC, 1972; "Columbo: Lovely But Lethal," NBC, 1973; "The Carol Burnett Show," CBS, 1974; "The Snoop Sisters: A Black Day for Bluebeard," NBC, 1974; "Hollywood Squares," SYN, 1975; "The Merv Griffin Show," SYN, 1975; "Joys," NBC, 1976; "Hollywood Squares," NBC, 1977; "The Captain and Tennille," ABC, 1977; "The Love Boat: Ship of Ghouls," ABC, 1978; "Freddy the Freeloader's Christmas Dinner," HBO, 1981; "Blacke's Magic: Wax Poetic," NBC, 1986.
TV MOVIES AND MINISERIES: "What's a Nice Girl Like You...?," ABC, 1971.

PRIEST, PAT

b. *Bountiful, UT, 1936*. Actress who played Marilyn on "The Munsters."

AS A REGULAR: "The Munsters," CBS, 1964-66.
AND: "The Many Loves of Dobie Gillis: The Gigolo," CBS, 1961; "Valentine's Day: The Life You Save Is Yours," ABC, 1964; "My Favorite Martian: My Uncle the Folk Singer," CBS, 1964; "The Lucy Show: Lucy Flies to London," CBS, 1966; "Bewitched: And Something Makes Four," ABC, 1969; "Bewitched: Samantha's Lost Weekend," ABC, 1970; "The Mary Tyler Moore Show: Sue Ann's Sister," CBS, 1976.
* Priest is the daughter of former U.S. Treasurer Ivy Baker Priest.

PRIMUS, BARRY

b. *New York City, NY, February 16, 1938*. Actor who played Sgt. Dory McKenna on "Cagney & Lacey."

AS A REGULAR: "Cagney & Lacey," CBS, 1984-85.
AND: "The Defenders: The Tarnished Cross," CBS, 1962; "The Virginian: The Mark of a Man," NBC, 1966; "Medical Center: Woman for Hire," CBS, 1973; "The Streets of San Francisco: A Good Cop...But," ABC, 1977; "Lou Grant: Victims," CBS, 1981; "Cagney & Lacey: Recreational Use," CBS, 1982; "T.J. Hooker: Undercover Affair," ABC, 1983; "MacGruder and Loud: A Very Scary Man," ABC, 1985; "The Equalizer: Out of the Past," CBS, 1986; "Miami Vice: Line of Fire," NBC, 1988.
TV MOVIES AND MINISERIES: "Big Rose," CBS, 1974; "Washington: Behind Closed Doors," ABC, 1977; "Portrait of a Showgirl," CBS, 1982; "I Want to Live!," ABC, 1983; "Heart of Steel," ABC, 1983; "Brotherly Love," CBS, 1985.

PRINCIPAL, VICTORIA

b. *Japan, January 3, 1945*. Actress who began in sexpot roles; then she played Pamela Barnes Ewing on "Dallas."

AS A REGULAR: "Dallas," CBS, 1978-87.
AND: "Love, American Style: Love and the Perfect Setup," ABC, 1973; "Love, American Style: Love and the Mr. and Mrs.," ABC, 1973; "Love Story: When the Girls Came Out to Play," NBC, 1973; "Banacek: Fly Me-If You Can Find Me," NBC, 1974; "The John Davidson Show," SYN, 1981; "The Merv Griffin Show," SYN, 1981.
TV MOVIES AND MINISERIES: "Last Hours Before Morning," NBC, 1975; "Fantasy Island," ABC, 1977; "The Night They Took Miss Beautiful," NBC, 1977; "Not Just Another Affair," CBS, 1982; "Mistress," CBS, 1987; "Naked Lie," CBS, 1989; "Blind Witness," ABC, 1989.

PRINZE, FREDDIE

b. *New York City, NY, June 22, 1954; d. 1977*. Ill-fated comedian whose success was instantaneous and, apparently, terrifying; he committed suicide.

AS A REGULAR: "Chico and the Man," NBC, 1974-77.
AND: "The Tonight Show Starring Johnny Carson," NBC, 1974; "The Merv Griffin Show," SYN, 1974; "Celebrity Sweepstakes," NBC, 1974; "The Mike Douglas Show," SYN, 1974; "Midnight Special," NBC, 1975; "The Merv Griffin Show," SYN, 1975; "Joys," NBC, 1976; "Celebrity Sweepstakes," SYN, 1976; "Tony Orlando and Dawn," CBS, 1976; "Inaugural Eve Special," CBS, 1977.
TV MOVIES AND MINISERIES: "The Million Dollar Ripoff," NBC, 1976.

PROSKY, ROBERT

b. *Philadelphia, PA, December 13, 1920*. Heavyset stage-trained actor who played Sgt. Stan Jablonski on "Hill Street Blues."

AS A REGULAR: "Hill Street Blues," NBC, 1984-87.
AND: "Lou Grant: Hometown," CBS, 1981; "Murder, She Wrote: Old Habits Die Hard," CBS, 1987; "American Playhouse: A Walk in the Woods," PBS, 1989.
TV MOVIES AND MINISERIES: "World War III," NBC, 1982; "Into Thin Air," CBS, 1985; "The Murder of Mary Phagan," NBC, 1988; "Home Fires Burning," CBS, 1989; "From the Dead of the Night," NBC, 1989; "The Heist," SHO, 1989.

PROVINE, DOROTHY

b. *Dorothy Michele Provine, Deadwood, SD, January 20, 1937*. Fifties starlet who played flapper Pinky Pinkham in "The Roaring Twenties."

AS A REGULAR: "The Alaskans," ABC, 1959-60; "The Roaring Twenties," ABC, 1960-62.
AND: "The Bob Cummings Show: Bob in Surgery," NBC, 1958; "The Millionaire: The David Barrett Story," CBS, 1958; "Lawman: Lady in Question," ABC, 1958; "The Real McCoys: The McCoys Visit Hollywood," ABC, 1959; "Alfred Hitchcock Presents: The Morning After," CBS, 1959; "Cimarron City: The Bitter Lesson," NBC, 1959; "Sugarfoot: The Giant Killer," ABC, 1959; "77 Sunset Strip: Downbeat," ABC, 1959; "Cheyenne: Red Water North," ABC, 1959; "Dean Martin Special," NBC, 1960; "American Bandstand," ABC, 1960; "Bulova Watch Time with Pat Boone," ABC, 1961; "The Bob Hope Christmas Show," NBC, 1962; "Hawaiian Eye: A Likely Story," ABC, 1962; "The Red Skelton Show: Bride of Bolivar," CBS, 1962; "Comedy Spot: You're Only Young Once," CBS, 1962; "Perry Como's Kraft Music Hall," NBC, 1962; "Hawaiian Eye: A Night with Nora Stewart," ABC, 1962; "The Gallant Men: Tommy," ABC, 1963; "Perry Como Special,"

NBC, 1964; "The Garry Moore Show," CBS, 1964; "Hollywood Palace," ABC, 1964; "Dr. Kildare: Music Hath Charms," NBC, 1965; "The Man From UNCLE: The Alexander the Greater Affair," NBC, 1965; "The Jerry Lewis Show," NBC, 1967; "The Danny Thomas Hour: My Pal Tony," NBC, 1968; "The FBI: Breakthrough," ABC, 1968; "Love, American Style: Love and Those Poor Crusaders' Wives," ABC, 1970; "NBC Comedy Playhouse: Simon Says Get Married," NBC, 1970; "Police Story: The Big Walk," NBC, 1973.
TV MOVIES AND MINISERIES: "The Sound of Anger," NBC, 1968.

PROVOST, JON

b. Los Angeles, CA, March 12, 1950. Former child actor who began his career on "Lassie" and now is back on a revived version of the show.
AS A REGULAR: "Lassie," CBS, 1957-64; SYN, 1989- .
AND: "The Ford Show," NBC, 1958; "Startime: Art Linkletter's Secret World of Kids," NBC, 1959; "Mr. Ed: Jon Provost Meets Mr. Ed," CBS, 1965.

PROWSE, JULIET

b. Bombay, India, September 25, 1936. Dancer-actress who was most popular in the sixties.
AS A REGULAR: "Mona McCluskey," NBC, 1965-66.
AND: "Frank Sinatra Timex Show," ABC, 1959; "Frank Sinatra Timex Show," ABC, 1960; "Steve Allen Plymouth Show," NBC, 1960; "Here's Hollywood," NBC, 1960; "Adventures in Paradise: A Whale of a Tale," ABC, 1960; "Perry Como's Kraft Music Hall," NBC, 1960; "Remember How Great," NBC, 1961; "Bob Hope Buick Show," NBC, 1961; "Perry Como's Kraft Music Hall," NBC, 1962; "Hollywood Melody," NBC, 1962; "The Red Skelton Hour," CBS, 1962; "The Bob Hope Show," NBC, 1962; "Burke's Law: Who Killed Harris Crown?," ABC, 1963; "Password," CBS, 1964; "The Ed Sullivan Show," CBS, 1964; "Danny Thomas Special," NBC, 1964; "Burke's Law: Who Killed the Tall One in the Middle?," ABC, 1964; "Password," CBS, 1965; "The Tonight Show Starring Johnny Carson," NBC, 1965; "The Dean Martin Show," NBC, 1966; "The Danny Thomas Hour: It's Greek to Me," NBC, 1967; "The Dean Martin Show," NBC, 1968; "Bob Hope Special," NBC, 1968; "The Name of the Game: Shine On, Shine On Jessie Gill," NBC, 1968; "The Dean Martin Show," NBC, 1971; "Dinah!," SYN, 1976; "The Devlin Connection: Claudine," NBC, 1982; "Fantasy Island: Forbidden Love," ABC, 1983; "Glitter: Premiere," ABC, 1984; "The Love Boat: The Dream Boat," ABC, 1984; "Murder, She Wrote: No Fashionable Way to Die," CBS, 1987.
TV MOVIES AND MINISERIES: "Second Chance," ABC, 1972.

PRYOR, RICHARD

b. Peoria, IL, December 1, 1940. Hard-edged black comic whose NBC variety show was too spicy for the censors; an Emmy winner for "Lily."
AS A REGULAR: "The Richard Pryor Show," NBC, 1977; "Pryor's Place," CBS, 1984-85.
AND: "On Broadway Tonight," CBS, 1965; "The Wild Wild West: The Night of the Eccentrics," CBS, 1966; "The Ed Sullivan Show," CBS, 1967; "Operation: Entertainment," ABC, 1968; "The Tonight Show Starring Johnny Carson," NBC, 1968; "Bob Newhart Special: A Last Laugh at the 60's," ABC, 1970; "The Ed Sullivan Show," CBS, 1970; "The Partridge Family: Soul Club," ABC, 1971; "The Mod Squad: The Connection," ABC, 1972; "The New Bill Cosby Show," CBS, 1973; "Lily," CBS, 1973; "Saturday Night Live," NBC, 1975; "Dinah!," SYN, 1976; "Sammy and Company," SYN, 1977.
TV MOVIES AND MINISERIES: "The Young Lawyers," CBS, 1969; "Carter's Army," ABC, 1970.
AS CO-WRITER: "Lily," CBS, 1973.
* Yipes Dept.: "Soul Club" was about what happened when the Partridge Family was mistakenly booked into a Detroit nightclub.
* Emmies: 1974.

PULLIAM, KESHIA KNIGHT

b. Newark, NJ, April 9, 1979. Young actress who plays Rudy on "The Cosby Show."
AS A REGULAR: "The Cosby Show," NBC, 1984- .
AND: "A Different World: Rudy and the Snow Queen," NBC, 1988; "A Different World: Clair's Last Stand," NBC, 1988; "The Magical World of Disney: Polly," NBC, 1989.
TV MOVIES AND MINISERIES: "The Little Match Girl," NBC, 1987; "A Connecticut Yankee in King Arthur's Court," NBC, 1989.

PURCELL, SARAH

b. Richmond, IN, October 8, 1948.
AS A REGULAR: "The Better Sex," ABC, 1977-78; "Real People," NBC, 1979-84.
AND: "Charlie's Angels: Marathon Angels," ABC, 1979; "Candid Camera Christmas Special," CBS, 1987.
TV MOVIES AND MINISERIES: "A Guide for the Married Woman," ABC, 1978; "Terror Among Us," CBS, 1981.

PURL, LINDA

b. Greenwich, CT, September 2, 1955. Actress who most recently played Charlene, daughter of Ben Matlock (Andy Griffith); she played Ashley, girlfriend of Fonzie (Henry Winkler) on "Happy Days."
AS A REGULAR: "The Secret Storm," CBS, 1973-74; "Happy Days," ABC, 1974-75; 1982-83;

"Beacon Hill," CBS, 1975; "Matlock," NBC, 1986-87.

AND: "Lucas Tanner: Thirteen Going on Twenty," NBC, 1974; "Medical Center: Street Girl," CBS, 1975; "Hawaii Five-O: The Hostage," CBS, 1975; "Murder, She Wrote: Murder at the Oasis," CBS, 1985; "Alfred Hitchcock Presents: Revenge," NBC, 1985; "Murder, She Wrote: Mourning Among the Wisterias," CBS, 1988; "Trying Times: The Sad Professor," PBS, 1989.

TV MOVIES AND MINISERIES: "The Oregon Trail," NBC, 1976; "Eleanor and Franklin," ABC, 1976; "Young Pioneers," ABC, 1976; "Young Pioneers Christmas," ABC, 1976; "Having Babies," ABC, 1976; "Little Ladies of the Night," ABC, 1977; "Black Market Baby," ABC, 1977; "Testimony of Two Men," SYN, 1977; "Women at West Point," CBS, 1979; "Like Normal People," ABC, 1979; "The Flame Is Love," NBC, 1979; "The Night the City Screamed," ABC, 1980; "Manions of America," ABC, 1981; "Money on the Side," ABC, 1982; "The Love Boat: A Gentleman of Discrimination," ABC, 1985; "Pleasures," ABC, 1986; "Diary of a Perfect Murder," NBC, 1986; "Outrage!," CBS, 1986; "In Self Defense," ABC, 1987; "Addicted to His Love," ABC, 1988.

PYLE, DENVER

b. Bethune, CO, May 11, 1920. Craggy character actor fondly remembered as mountaineer Briscoe Darling on "The Andy Griffith Show," and not-so-fondly remembered as Uncle Jesse on "The Dukes of Hazzard."

AS A REGULAR: "The Life and Legend of Wyatt Earp," ABC, 1955-56; "Code Three," SYN, 1956-57; "Tammy," ABC, 1965-66; "The Doris Day Show," CBS, 1968-70; "The Life and Times of Grizzly Adams," NBC, 1977-78; "The Dukes of Hazzard," CBS, 1979-85; "Dallas," CBS, 1990.

AND: "Medic: Death Rides a Wagon," NBC, 1955; "The Millionaire: Millionaire Arthur Darner," CBS, 1955; "Crossroads: Sky Pilot of the Cumberlands," ABC, 1956; "My Friend Flicka: Big Red," CBS, 1957; "The Adventures of Jim Bowie: Master at Arms," ABC, 1957; "Gunsmoke: Liar From Blackhawk," CBS, 1957; "O. Henry Playhouse: The Sphinx Apple," SYN, 1957; "Have Gun, Will Travel: The Colonel and the Lady," CBS, 1957; "The Overland Trail: Lawyer in Petticoats," NBC, 1960; "Hotel De Paree: Sundance and the Long Trek," CBS, 1960; "Laramie: Vengeance," NBC, 1963; "Ripcord: Where Do the Elephants Go to Die?," SYN, 1963; "The Virginian: Vengeance Is the Spur," NBC, 1963; "The Andy Griffith Show: The Darlings Are Coming," CBS, 1963; "The Andy Griffith Show: Mountain Wedding," CBS, 1963; "The Dick Van Dyke Show: Uncle George," CBS, 1963; "The Andy Griffith Show: Briscoe Declares for Aunt Bee," CBS, 1963; "Dr. Kildare: A Willing Suspension of Disbelief," NBC, 1964; "The Twilight Zone: Black Leather Jackets," CBS, 1964; "The Great Adventure: The Special Courage of Captain Pratt," CBS, 1964; "Bonanza: Bullet for a Bride," NBC, 1964; "The Andy Griffith Show: Divorce, Mountain Style," CBS, 1964; "Death Valley Days: Greydon's Charge," SYN, 1964; "The Andy Griffith Show: The Darling Baby," CBS, 1964; "Mr. Novak: Johnny Ride the Pony," NBC, 1964; "Slattery's People: Question-What Did You Do All Day, Mr. Slattery?," CBS, 1965; "The Andy Griffith Show: The Darling Fortune," CBS, 1966; "Gunsmoke: The Goldtakers," CBS, 1966; "Gunsmoke: Mad Dog," CBS, 1967; "The Guns of Will Sonnett: The Warriors," ABC, 1968; "Gomer Pyle, USMC: The Price of Tomatoes," CBS, 1968; "Gunsmoke: Shadler," CBS, 1973; "Kung Fu: The Ancient Warrior," ABC, 1973; "The New Adventures of Perry Mason: The Case of the Violent Valley," CBS, 1974; "The Streets of San Francisco: Winterkill," ABC, 1974; "The Manhunter: The Baby Faced Killers," CBS, 1974; "Karen: Premiere," ABC, 1975; "Petrocelli: Blood Money," NBC, 1976; "Barnaby Jones: Stalking Horse," CBS, 1976; "Password Plus," NBC, 1981; "Murder, She Wrote: Coal Miner's Slaughter," CBS, 1988.

TV MOVIES AND MINISERIES: "Hitched," NBC, 1973; "Sidekicks," CBS, 1974; "Murder or Mercy," ABC, 1974.

Q

QUAYLE, ANTHONY

b. Ainsdale, England, September 7, 1913; d. 1989. Film and TV actor in distinguished roles; he won an Emmy for "QB VII."

AS A REGULAR: "Strange Report," NBC, 1971; "The Six Wives of Henry VIII," CBS, 1971.

AND: "Suspicion: The Man with the Gun," NBC, 1958.

TV MOVIES AND MINISERIES: "Destiny of a Spy," NBC, 1969; "Jarrett," ABC, 1973; "QB VII," ABC, 1974; "Bell System Family Theatre: Great Expectations," NBC, 1974; "Moses, the Lawgiver," CBS, 1975; "21 Hours at Munich," ABC, 1976; "Dial M for Murder," NBC, 1981; "Manions of America," ABC, 1981.

* Emmies: 1975.

QUINN, ANTHONY

b. Chihuahua, Mexico, April 21, 1916. Macho, Oscar-winning actor in larger-than-life roles; he played the mayor of a southwestern city in his only TV series to date.

AS A REGULAR: "The Man and the City," ABC, 1971-72.

AND: "Lights Out: The House of Dust," NBC, 1951; "Ford Theatre: Ticket to Oblivion," CBS, 1951; "Danger: Blue Murder," CBS, 1951; "Schlitz Playhouse of Stars: Dark Fleece," CBS, 1951; "Schlitz Playhouse of Stars: The Long Trail," CBS, 1954; "Schlitz Playhouse of Stars: Bandit's Hideout," CBS, 1955; "Person to Person," CBS, 1958; "Here's Hollywood," NBC, 1961; "The Ed Sullivan Show," CBS, 1962; "The Dick Cavett Show," ABC, 1971; "The Cosby Show: Surf's Up," NBC, 1989.

TV MOVIES AND MINISERIES: "The City," ABC, 1971; "Jesus of Nazareth," NBC, 1977; "Onassis: The Richest Man in the World," ABC, 1988.

QUINN, BILL

b. New York City, May 6, 1912. Reliable character actor; he played Mr. Van Ranseleer on "Archie Bunker's Place" and Mary Tyler Moore's TV father.

AS A REGULAR: "The Rifleman," ABC, 1958-63; "McHale's Navy," ABC, 1964-66; "Please Don't Eat the Daisies," NBC, 1966-67; "The Mary Tyler Moore Show," CBS, 1972; "All in the Family," 1978-79; "Archie Bunker's Place," CBS, 1979-83.

AND: "Bonanza: Vendetta," NBC, 1959; "The Detectives Starring Robert Taylor: Back-Seat Driver," ABC, 1959; "The Twilight Zone: Nightmare as a Child," CBS, 1960; "The Westerner: School Days," NBC, 1960; "Wanted Dead or Alive: Surprise

Witness," CBS, 1960; "Hawaiian Eye: The Money Blossom," ABC, 1960; "Wanted Dead or Alive: Monday Morning," CBS, 1961; "Wanted Dead or Alive: Barney's Bounty," CBS, 1961; "The Brothers Brannagan: Equinox," SYN, 1961; "The Jack Benny Program: The Income Tax Show," NBC, 1964; "The Beverly Hillbillies: Elly in the Movies," CBS, 1965; "The Munsters: Herman's Child Psychology," CBS, 1965; "Mr. Roberts: Getting There Is Half the Fun," NBC, 1965; "The FBI: Southwind," ABC, 1968; "The FBI: The Swindler," ABC, 1969; "Ironside: L'Chayim," NBC, 1969; "That Girl: The Night They Raided Daddy's," ABC, 1970; "Mannix: War of Nerves," CBS, 1970; "Alias Smith and Jones: The Ten Days That Shook Kid Curry," ABC, 1973; "The Bob Newhart Show: Mister Emily Hartley," CBS, 1973; "The Bob Newhart Show: The Ceiling Hits Bob," CBS, 1975; "The Rockford Files: Pastoria Prime Pick," NBC, 1975; "Barnaby Jones: Murder Once Removed," CBS, 1975; "Little House on the Prairie: The Long Road Home," NBC, 1976; "The Rockford Files: Backlash of the Hunter," NBC, 1978; "The Bob Newhart Show: Happy Trails to You," CBS, 1978; "Stone: Homicide," ABC, 1980; "Newhart: Mrs. Newton's Body Lies a Mould'rin in the Grave," CBS, 1982; "The Golden Girls: The Operation," NBC, 1986.

TV MOVIES AND MINISERIES: "The Pigeon," ABC, 1969; "The Challenge," ABC, 1970; "Incident in San Francisco," ABC, 1971; "Dead Men Tell No Tales," CBS, 1971; "Set This Town on Fire," NBC, 1973; "Satan's School for Girls," ABC, 1973; "Best Sellers: Captains and the Kings," NBC, 1976; "Backstairs at the White House," NBC, 1979.

QUINN, LOUIS

b. Louis Quinn Frackt, Chicago, IL, 1915. Comedian and gag writer who played Roscoe on "77 Sunset Strip."

AS A REGULAR: "77 Sunset Strip," ABC, 1958-63.

AND: "The Donna Reed Show: The Daughter Complex," ABC, 1964; "Hollywood Palace," ABC, 1964; "Gilligan's Island: Little Island, Big Gun," CBS, 1965; "Hazel: Hazel Needs a Car," CBS, 1965; "Honey West: Pandora's Box," ABC, 1966; "The Farmer's Daughter: Alias Katy Morley," ABC, 1966; "Batman: The Impractical Joker/The Joker's Provokers," ABC, 1966; "Please Don't Eat the Daisies: My Mother's Name Is Fred," NBC, 1966; "The Monkees: Your Friendly Neighborhood Kidnappers," NBC, 1966; "The Hero: I Have a Friend," NBC, 1966; "Batman: The Funny Feline Felonies/The Joke's on Catwoman," ABC, 1967; "Chico and the Man: Garage Sale," NBC, 1975.

R

RACHINS, ALAN

b. Cambridge, MA. Actor who plays Douglas Brackman on "L.A. Law."
AS A REGULAR: "L.A. Law," NBC, 1986- .
AND: "Hollywood Squares," SYN, 1988; "The Pat Sajak Show," CBS, 1989.
TV MOVIES AND MINISERIES: "Mistress," CBS, 1987; "Single Women, Married Men," CBS, 1989.

RADNER, GILDA

b. Detroit, June 28, 1946; d. 1989. Gifted comic actress who died of cancer.
AS A REGULAR: "Saturday Night Live," NBC, 1975-80.
AND: "The Muppet Show," SYN, 1981; "It's Garry Shandling's Show: Mr. Smith Goes to Nam," FOX, 1988.
* Emmies: 1978.

RAE, CHARLOTTE

b. Milwaukee, WI, April 22, 1926. Heavyset actress who played Edna Garrett on "Diff'rent Strokes" and "The Facts of Life."
AS A REGULAR: "Car 54, Where Are You?," NBC, 1961-63; "Hot L Baltimore," ABC, 1975; "The Rich Little Show," NBC, 1976; "Diff'rent Strokes," NBC, 1978-79; "The Facts of Life," NBC, 1979-86.
AND: "U.S. Steel Hour: Two," ABC, 1954; "Armstrong Circle Theatre: Fred Allen's Sketchbook," NBC, 1954; "Pond's Theatre: 30, Honey, 30," ABC, 1955; "Opera Theatre: The Would-Be Gentleman," NBC, 1955; "Appointment with Adventure: Stranger on a Plane," CBS, 1955; "Philco TV Playhouse: The Miss America Story," NBC, 1955; "The Phil Silvers Show: The Twitch," CBS, 1955; "The Ed Sullivan Show," CBS, 1957; "The Garry Moore Show," CBS, 1958; "Du Pont Show of the Month: Harvey," CBS, 1958; "The Eternal Light: The Broken Sabbath of Rabbi Asher," NBC, 1958; "The Phil Silvers Show: Bilko and the Medium," CBS, 1958; "Play of the Week: The World of Sholom Aleichem," SYN, 1959; "Camera Three: The Best and the Worst," CBS, 1960; "The Sid Caesar Show," ABC, 1963; "The Defenders: Comeback," CBS, 1964; "The Garry Moore Show," CBS, 1964; "New York Television Theatre: The Immovable Gordons," NET, 1966; "The Paul Lynde Show: Martha's Last Hurrah," ABC, 1972; "Love, American Style: Love and the Clinic," ABC, 1973; "All in the Family: Where's Archie?," CBS, 1974; "Good Times: Florida's

Big Gig," CBS, 1974; "Barney Miller: Sniper," ABC, 1976; "The Eddie Capra Mysteries: Dirge for a Dead Dachshund," NBC, 1978; "The Love Boat: Pride of the Pacific," ABC, 1982; "The Love Boat: Youth Takes a Holiday," ABC, 1983; "The Love Boat: Your Money or Your Wife," ABC, 1985; "Murder, She Wrote: Doom with a View," CBS, 1987; "St. Elsewhere: Rites of Passage," NBC, 1987; "The Magical World of Disney: Save the Dog," NBC, 1989; "227: Reunion Blues," NBC, 1989.
TV MOVIES AND MINISERIES: "Queen of the Stardust Ballroom," CBS, 1975; "The Triangle Factory Fire Scandal," NBC, 1979; "The Facts of Life Goes to Paris," NBC, 1982.

RAFFIN, DEBORAH

b. Los Angeles, CA, March 13, 1953. Actress who went from minor movies to slick miniseries.
AS A REGULAR: "Foul Play," ABC, 1981.
AND: "Dinah!," SYN, 1975; "B.L. Stryker: Royal Gambit," ABC, 1989.
TV MOVIES AND MINISERIES: "Nightmare in Badham County," ABC, 1976; "How to Pick Up Girls," ABC, 1978; "Willa," CBS, 1979; "Mind Over Murder," CBS, 1979; "The Last Convertible," NBC, 1979; "Haywire," CBS, 1980; "The Last Convertible," NBC, 1979; "Killing at Hell's Gate," CBS, 1981; "For Lovers Only," ABC, 1982; "Running Out," CBS, 1983; "Agatha Christie's Sparkling Cyanide," CBS, 1983; "Threesome," CBS, 1984; "Lace II," ABC, 1985; "James Clavell's Noble House," NBC, 1988.

RAFT, GEORGE

b. George Ranft, New York City, NY, September 26, 1895; d. 1980. Movie tough-guy ("Scarface," "They Drive by Night," "Some Like It Hot") who did a bit of television.
AS A REGULAR: "I'm the Law," SYN, 1952-53.
AND: "The Red Skelton Show," CBS, 1957; "The Ed Sullivan Show," CBS, 1957; "The Gisele MacKenzie Show," NBC, 1957; "Arthur Murray Party," NBC, 1959; "Red Skelton Special," CBS, 1960; "Here's Hollywood," NBC, 1961; "Batman: Black Widow Strikes Again/Caught in the Spider's Den," ABC, 1967; "The Tonight Show Starring Johnny Carson," NBC, 1969; "The Tonight Show Starring Johnny Carson," NBC, 1970.
* Raft did a commercial for Alka-Seltzer in the late 1960s in which he led a group of convicts in a mess hall rebellion.

RAINER, LUISE

b. Vienna, Austria, 1912. Actress who won back-to-back Oscars in 1936 and 1937 and then virtually retired from acting; her TV appearances have been sporadic.

AS A GUEST: "Rosalind," CBS, 1950; "Schlitz Playhouse of Stars: Love Came Late," CBS, 1952; "Lux Video Theatre: Bouquet for Caroline," CBS, 1953; "Suspense: Torment," CBS, 1954; "The Ed Sullivan Show," CBS, 1959; "Arthur Murray Party," NBC, 1959; "Combat!: Their Finest Hour," ABC, 1965; "The Merv Griffin Show," SYN, 1974; "The Love Boat: The Lady and the Maid," ABC, 1984.

RAINS, CLAUDE

b. London, England, November 10, 1889; d. 1967. Gifted actor in films ("Casablanca," "Notorious") and TV.

AS A GUEST: "Medallion Theatre: The Man Who Liked Dickens," CBS, 1953; "Medallion Theatre: The Archer Case," CBS, 1953; "Alfred Hitchcock Presents: And So Died Riabouchinska," CBS, 1956; "Kraft Television Theatre: A Night to Remember," NBC, 1956; "Alcoa Hour: President," NBC, 1956; "Kaiser Aluminum Hour: Antigone," NBC, 1956; "Alfred Hitchcock Presents: The Cream of the Jest," CBS, 1957; "Hallmark Hall of Fame: On Borrowed Time," NBC, 1957; "The Pied Piper of Hamelin," NBC, 1957; "Alfred Hitchcock Presents: The Diamond Necklace," CBS, 1959; "Playhouse 90: Judgement at Nuremberg," CBS, 1959; "Once Upon a Christmas Time," NBC, 1959; "Hallmark Hall of Fame: Shangri-La," NBC, 1960; "Naked City: To Walk in Silence," ABC, 1960; "Alfred Hitchcock Presents: The Horseplayer," NBC, 1961; "Alfred Hitchcock Presents: The Door Without a Key," NBC, 1962; "Rawhide: Incident of Judgment Day," CBS, 1962; "Wagon Train: The Daniel Clay Story," NBC, 1962; "The du Pont Show: The Outpost," NBC, 1962; "Sam Benedict: Nor Practice Makes Perfect," NBC, 1962; "Rawhide: Incident of Judgment Day," CBS, 1963; "Bob Hope Chrysler Theatre: Something About Lee Wiley," NBC, 1963; "The du Pont Show: The Takers," NBC, 1963; "Dr. Kildare: Why Won't Anybody Listen?," NBC, 1964; "The Reporter: A Time to Be Silent," CBS, 1964; "Bob Hope Chrysler Theatre: Cops and Robbers," NBC, 1965.

RAITT, JOHN

b. Santa Ana, CA, January 29, 1917.

AS A REGULAR: "The Buick Circus Hour," NBC, 1952-53; "The Chevy Show," NBC, 1958, 1959.

AND: "Pulitzer Prize Playhouse: Knickerbocker

Holiday," ABC, 1950; "Musical Comedy Time: Revenge with Music," NBC, 1951; "The Web: The Dark Shore," CBS, 1952; "Motorola TV Hour: The Thirteen Clocks," ABC, 1953; "The Ed Sullivan Show," CBS, 1957; "Annie Get Your Gun," NBC, 1957; "Dinah Shore Chevy Show," NBC, 1957; "Shirley Temple's Storybook: Rumpelstiltskin," NBC, 1958; "The Patrice Munsel Show," ABC, 1958; "The Lux Show with Rosemary Clooney," NBC, 1958; "Art Linkletter's House Party," CBS, 1958; "Shower of Stars," CBS, 1958; "Dinah Shore Chevy Show," NBC, 1958; "Pat Boone Chevy Showroom," ABC, 1958; "The Voice of Firestone," ABC, 1958; "G.E. Theatre: No Man Can Tame Me," CBS, 1959; "Bell Telephone Hour: Twas the Night Before ... ," NBC, 1960; "The Ford Show," NBC, 1961; "Bell Telephone Hour: The Signs of Spring," NBC, 1961; "Yves Montand Special," ABC, 1961; "Bell Telephone Hour: A Trip to Christmas," NBC, 1961; "Bell Telephone Hour: The Songs of Irving Berlin," NBC, 1962; "Bell Telephone Hour: Thanksgiving Show," NBC, 1962; "Bell Telephone Hour: The Music of Cole Porter," NBC, 1964; "The Edie Adams Show," ABC, 1964; "Bell Telephone Hour: Lyrics by Oscar Hammerstein," NBC, 1964; "The Mike Douglas Show," SYN, 1966.

RAMBO, DACK

b. Delano, CA, November 13, 1941. Hunky actor who played Jack Ewing on "Dallas."

AS A REGULAR: "The New Loretta Young Show," CBS, 1962-63; "Never Too Young," ABC, 1965-66; "The Guns of Will Sonnett," ABC, 1967-69; "Dirty Sally," CBS, 1974; "Sword of Justice," NBC, 1978-79; "All My Children," ABC, 1982-83; "Paper Dolls," ABC, 1984; "Dallas," CBS, 1985-87; "Another World," NBC, 1990.

AND: "Gunsmoke: The Witness," CBS, 1970; "Gunsmoke: Pike," CBS, 1971; "The Man and the City: Disaster on Turner Street," ABC, 1971; "Gunsmoke: Dirty Sally," CBS, 1973; "Marcus Welby, M.D.: Dark Fury," ABC, 1975; "The Rookies: Angel," ABC, 1975; "Fantasy Island: Magnolia Blossoms," ABC, 1979; "The Love Boat: Not Now, I'm Dying," ABC, 1979; "House Calls: All About Adam," CBS, 1980; "The Love Boat: Two for Julie," ABC, 1981; "Hotel: Secrets," ABC, 1983; "Hotel: Distortions," ABC, 1985; "Murder, She Wrote: When Thieves Fall Out," CBS, 1987; "Hunter: Presumed Guilty," NBC, 1988; "Highway to Heaven: The Source," NBC, 1989.

TV MOVIES AND MINISERIES: "River of Gold," ABC, 1971; "Hit Lady," ABC, 1974; "Waikiki," ABC, 1980.

RAMBO, DIRK

b. Delano, CA, November 13, 1941; d. 1967. Actor and twin brother of Dack who died in a motorcycle accident.

AS A REGULAR: "The New Loretta Young Show," CBS, 1962-63.
AND: "The Virginian: High Stakes," NBC, 1966.

RANDALL, SUE

b. *Philadelphia, PA, 1935; d. 1984.* Actress who played Beaver Cleaver's teacher, Miss Landers; her career came to an end in the mid-sixties after she was seriously injured in an automobile accident.

AS A REGULAR: "Leave It to Beaver," ABC, 1958-62.

AND: "77 Sunset Strip: Hit and Run," ABC, 1958; "Cheyenne: The Besieged," ABC, 1959; "77 Sunset Strip: Strange Girl in Town," ABC, 1959; "Hennesey: The Matchmaker," CBS, 1959; "The Real McCoys: The Girls at Mom's Place," ABC, 1959; "The Twilight Zone: And When the Sky was Opened," CBS, 1959; "Have Gun, Will Travel: Shot by Request," CBS, 1959; "Have Gun, Will Travel: Day of the Badman," CBS, 1960; "The Man and the Challenge: The Windowless Room," NBC, 1960; "New Comedy Showcase: You're Only Young Twice," CBS, 1960; "Perry Mason: The Case of the Ill-Fated Faker," CBS, 1960; "Bat Masterson: The Hunter," NBC, 1960; "The Life and Legend of Wyatt Earp: Big Brother," ABC, 1960; "The Aquanauts: The Frameup Adventure," CBS, 1960; "The Roaring Twenties: Judge Seward's Secret," ABC, 1960; "77 Sunset Strip: The Affairs of Adam Gallante," ABC, 1960; "Thriller: Man in the Middle," NBC, 1960; "The Tom Ewell Show: Storm Over Shangri-La," CBS, 1961; "The du Pont Show with June Allyson: The Secret Life of James Thurber," CBS, 1961; "The Detectives Starring Robert Taylor: Time for Decision," ABC, 1961; "Hennesey: The Green-eyed Monster," CBS, 1961; "Michael Shayne: The Trouble with Ernie," NBC, 1961; "SurfSide 6: Spinout at Sebring," ABC, 1961; "Bonanza: The Horse Breaker," NBC, 1961; "Ichabod and Me: The Love Letter," CBS, 1962; "Margie: A Lesson in Teaching," ABC, 1962; "I'm Dickens, He's Fenster: The Acting Game," ABC, 1962; "The Twilight Zone: From Agnes-With Love," CBS, 1964; "The Fugitive: When the Bough Breaks," ABC, 1964; "Wendy & Me: It Takes Two to Tangle," ABC, 1964; "Profiles in Courage: The Robert Taft Story," NBC, 1965; "My Favorite Martian: Crash Diet," CBS, 1965; "The Fugitive: Wings of an Angel," ABC, 1965; "The Virginian: Show Me a Hero," NBC, 1965; "Bonanza: Mighty Is the Word," NBC, 1965.

RANDALL, TONY

b. *Leonard Rosenberg, Tulsa, OK, February 26, 1920.* Slight comic leading man of film ("Will Success Spoil Rock Hunter?", "Lover Come Back") and TV, often in neurotic roles; best known as Felix Unger of "The Odd Couple" and the star of his own sitcom.

AS A REGULAR: "One Man's Family," NBC, 1950-52; "Mr. Peepers," NBC, 1952-55; "The Odd Couple," ABC, 1970-75; "The Tony Randall Show," ABC, 1976-77; CBS, 1977-78; "Love, Sidney," NBC, 1981-83.

AND: "Studio One: Mrs. Hargraves," CBS, 1952; "Philco TV Playhouse: A Little Something in Reserve," NBC, 1953; "The Web: The Badger Game," CBS, 1953; "Kraft Television Theatre: In Albert's Room," NBC, 1953; "Pepsi Cola Playhouse: When, Lovely Woman," ABC, 1953; "Kraft Television Theatre: The Antique Touch," NBC, 1954; "Goodyear TV Playhouse: The Huntress," NBC, 1954; "Motorola TV Hour: Nightmare in Algiers," ABC, 1954; "Armstrong Circle Theatre: The Beautiful Wife," NBC, 1954; "Philco TV Playhouse: One Mummy Too Many," NBC, 1955; "Alcoa Hour: Man on a Tiger," NBC, 1956; "The Tonight Show," NBC, 1956; "Studio One: The Hollywood Complex," CBS, 1957; "Goodyear TV Playhouse: Weekend in Vermont," NBC, 1957; "Playhouse 90: The Playroom," CBS, 1957; "Holiday in Las Vegas," NBC, 1957; "The Dick Clark Saturday Night Beechnut Show," NBC, 1958; "The Arthur Godfrey Show," CBS, 1958; "Steve Allen Presents The Steve Lawrence-Eydie Gorme Show," NBC, 1958; "Dinah Shore Chevy Show," NBC, 1958; "Goodyear Theatre: Coogan's Reward," NBC, 1959; "Person to Person," CBS, 1959; "The George Gobel Show," NBC, 1959; "Westinghouse Desilu Playhouse: Martin's Folly," CBS, 1959; "Pontiac Star Parade: The Man in the Moon," NBC, 1960; "Take a Good Look," ABC, 1960; "Startime: The Nanette Fabray Show-So Help Me, Aphrodite," NBC, 1960; "What's My Line?," CBS, 1960; "The Jack Paar Show," NBC, 1960; "I've Got a Secret," CBS, 1960; "Hooray for Love," CBS, 1960; "The Garry Moore Show," CBS, 1960; "G.E. Theatre: Strictly Solo," CBS, 1960; "Hallmark Hall of Fame: Arsenic and Old Lace," NBC, 1962; "That's Life: Pilot," ABC, 1968; "The Smothers Brothers Comedy Hour," CBS, 1968; "The Merv Griffin Show," SYN, 1969; "Alan King Special," NBC, 1969; "Love, American Style: Love and the Big Night," ABC, 1970; "The Flip Wilson Show," NBC, 1970; "Here's Lucy: Lucy the Mountain Climber," CBS, 1971; "The David Frost Revue," SYN, 1971; "The Comedians," SYN, 1971; "Hallmark Hall of Fame: The Littlest Angel," NBC, 1971; "The Sonny and Cher Comedy Hour," CBS, 1972; "The Carol Burnett Show," CBS, 1972; "Hollywood Squares," SYN, 1978; "The Tonight Show Starring Johnny Carson," NBC, 1981; "Gimme a Break: Big Apple," NBC, 1984; "The Magical World of Disney: Save the Dog," NBC, 1989; "Bob Hope's Easter Vacation in the Bahamas," NBC, 1989.

TV MOVIES AND MINISERIES: "Sidney Shorr," NBC, 1981; "Hitler's SS: Portrait in Evil," NBC, 1985; "The Man in the Brown Suit," CBS, 1989.
* Emmies: 1975.

RANDOLPH, AMANDA
b. Louisville, KY, 1902; d. 1967. Actress who played Louise the maid on "The Danny Thomas Show."
AS A REGULAR: "The Laytons," DUM, 1948; "Amos 'n Andy," CBS, 1951-53; "The Danny Thomas Show (Make Room for Daddy)," ABC, 1953-57; CBS, 1957-64.
AND: "Matinee Theatre: The Serpent's Tooth," NBC, 1957; "The Man From Blackhawk: The Ghost of Lafitte," ABC, 1959; "The New Breed: Sweet Bloom of Death," ABC, 1961; "Danny Thomas Special," NBC, 1965.

RANDOLPH, JOHN
b. 1917. Older actor who usually plays rascally types; he currently plays Harris Crown on "Grand."
AS A REGULAR: "Lucas Tanner," NBC, 1975; "Lucan," ABC, 1977-78; "Angie," ABC, 1979-80; "Annie McGuire," CBS, 1988-89; "Grand," NBC, 1990- .
AND: "The Defenders: Go-Between," CBS, 1964; "Slattery's People: The Unborn," CBS, 1965; "The Patty Duke Show: Take Me Out to the Ball Game," ABC, 1965; "Judd for the Defense: The Worst of Both Worlds," ABC, 1968; "Mannix: A Problem of Innocence," CBS, 1973; "The Bob Newhart Show: My Wife Belongs to Daddy," CBS, 1973; "Columbo: Swan Song," NBC, 1974; "The Bob Newhart Show: An American Family," CBS, 1974; "Medical Center: Faces of Peril," CBS, 1974; "Kojak: The Best Judge Money Can Buy," CBS, 1974; "Police Story: Countdown," NBC, 1974; "The Bob Newhart Show: Jerry's Retirement," CBS, 1976; "Medical Center: Major Annie, M.D.," CBS, 1976; "Sirota's Court: The Judge," NBC, 1977; "Lou Grant: Sports," CBS, 1978; "M*A*S*H: Too Many Cooks," CBS, 1979; "Nero Wolfe: Murder by the Book," NBC, 1981; "Best of the West: The Railroad," ABC, 1982; "Family Ties: I Never Killed for My Father," NBC, 1982; "Quincy: Baby Rattlesnakes," NBC, 1982; "The Equalizer: Suspicion of Innocence," CBS, 1987; "Matlock: The Investigation," NBC, 1988; "Roseanne: Dear Mom and Dad," ABC, 1989; "Roseanne: We Gather Together," ABC, 1989.
TV MOVIES AND MINISERIES: "The Borgia Stick," NBC, 1967; "A Step Out of Line," CBS, 1971; "The Cable Car Murder," CBS, 1971; "A Death of Innocence," CBS, 1971; "The Family Rico," CBS, 1972; "The Judge and Jake Wyler," NBC, 1972; "Partners in Crime," NBC, 1973; "Tell Me Where It Hurts," CBS, 1974; "Adventures of the Queen," CBS, 1975; "The Runaways," CBS, 1975; "The New, Original Wonder Woman,"

ABC, 1975; "F. Scott Fitzgerald in Hollywood," ABC, 1976; "Secrets," ABC, 1977; "Kill Me if You Can," NBC, 1977; Washington: Behind Closed Doors," ABC, 1977; "The Winds of Kitty Hawk," NBC, 1978; "Backstairs at the White House," NBC, 1979; "Blind Ambition," CBS, 1979; "Vital Signs," CBS, 1986.

RANDOLPH, JOYCE
b. Detroit, MI, October 21, 1925. Blonde actress who played Trixie Norton, loving wife of Ed (Art Carney) on "The Honeymooners."
AS A REGULAR: "Cavalcade of Stars," DUM, 1950-52; "The Jackie Gleason Show," CBS, 1952-55; 1956-57; "The Honeymooners," CBS, 1955-56.

RANDOLPH, LILLIAN
b. 1915; d. 1980. Sister of Amanda; she played Bill Cosby's TV mom and Madame Queen on "Amos 'n Andy."
AS A REGULAR: "Amos 'n Andy," CBS, 1951-53; "The Great Gildersleeve," NBC, 1955-56; "The Bill Cosby Show," NBC, 1969-70.
AND: "Room 222: Only a Rose," ABC, 1970; "Mannix: The World Between," CBS, 1970.
TV MOVIES AND MINISERIES: "Tenafly," NBC, 1973; "Roots," ABC, 1977.

RAPHAEL, SALLY JESSE
Talk-show hostess.
AS A REGULAR: "Sally Jesse Raphael," SYN, 1986- .
AND: "The Virginia Graham Show," SYN, 1967; "The Equalizer: Making of a Martyr," CBS, 1989; "Later with Bob Costas," NBC, 1989; "Kojak: Fatal Flaw," ABC, 1989.

RAPPAPORT, DAVID
b. England, November 23, 1952; d. 1990. Dwarf actor who played toymaker-crimefighter Simon McKay on "The Wizard" and manipulative attorney Hamilton Schuyler on "L.A. Law." He committed suicide.
AS A REGULAR: "The Wizard," CBS, 1986-87.
AND: "Hardcastle and McCormick: In the Eye of the Beholder," ABC, 1986; "Amazing Stories: Gather Ye Acorns," NBC, 1986; "L.A. Law: The Wizard of Odds," NBC, 1987; "Hooperman: Nick Derringer, P.I.," ABC, 1988; "Mr. Belvedere: Duel," ABC, 1988; "L.A. Law: The Mouse That Soared," NBC, 1989.
TV MOVIES AND MINISERIES: "Peter Gunn," ABC, 1989.

RASCHE, DAVID
b. Illinois. Comic actor who played macho cop Sledge Hammer!
AS A REGULAR: "Ryan's Hope," ABC, 1975;

"Sledge Hammer!," ABC, 1986-88.
AND: "Love, Sidney: Welcome Home," NBC, 1981; "Miami Vice: Bushido," NBC, 1986; "Kate & Allie: Winning," CBS, 1986.
TV MOVIES AND MINISERIES: "Sanctuary of Fear," NBC, 1979; "Special Bulletin," NBC, 1983; "The Lost Honor of Kathryn Beck," CBS, 1984; "Secret Witness," CBS, 1988.

RASHAD, PHYLICIA

b. Houston, TX, June 19, 1948. Attractive actress who more than holds her own as Bill Cosby's TV wife, Clair Huxtable.
AS A REGULAR: "One Life to Live," ABC, 1983-84; "The Cosby Show," NBC, 1984- .
AND: "A Different World: Clair's Last Stand," NBC, 1988; "Later with Bob Costas," NBC, 1989; "The Magical World of Disney: Polly," NBC, 1989.
TV MOVIES AND MINISERIES: "False Witness," NBC, 1989.

RATHBONE, BASIL

b. Johannesburg, South Africa, June 13, 1892; d. 1967. Slim, intense actor who played Sherlock Holmes in the movies, and at least once on TV.
AS A REGULAR: "Your Lucky Clue," CBS, 1952; "Dunninger," SYN, 1953.
AND: "Tele-Theatre: Queen of Spades," NBC, 1950; "NBC Showcase: Sherlock Holmes," NBC, 1950; "Nash Airfylte Theatre: The Kind Mr. Smith," CBS, 1950; "Lux Video Theatre: The General's Boots," CBS, 1951; "Shower of Stars: A Christmas Carol," CBS, 1954; "Svengali and the Blonde," NBC, 1955; "Science Fiction Theatre: The Stones Began to Move," SYN, 1955; "Star Tonight: The Selfish Giant," ABC, 1955; "Kraft Television Theatre: Five Minutes to Live," NBC, 1956; "Alcoa Hour: The Stingiest Man in Town," NBC, 1956; "Hallmark Hall of Fame: The Lark," NBC, 1957; "U.S. Steel Hour: Huck Finn," CBS, 1957; "Kraft Theatre: Heroes Walk on Sand," NBC, 1957; "The Arlene Francis Show," NBC, 1958; "Hallmark Hall of Fame: Hans Brinker or The Silver Skates," NBC, 1958; "Du Pont Show of the Month: Aladdin," CBS, 1958; "The Betty White Show," ABC, 1958; "Pantomime Quiz," ABC, 1958; "Frigidaire Summer Theatre: Affair in Sumatra," ABC, 1958; "The Jack Paar Show," NBC, 1959; "The Red Skelton Show: Super Cauliflower," CBS, 1960; "Arthur Murray Party," NBC, 1960; "Here's Hollywood," NBC, 1961; "1,2,3, Go!," NBC, 1961; "Hallmark Hall of Fame: Victoria Regina," NBC, 1961; "Burke's Law: Who Killed Hamlet?," ABC, 1965; "Dr. Kildare: Perfect Is Too Hard to Be/ Duet for One Hand," NBC, 1965; "Summer Fun: The Pirates of Flounder Bay," ABC, 1966; "Hallmark Hall of Fame: Soldier in Love," NBC, 1967.

RATHER, DAN

b. Wharton, TX, October 31, 1931.
AS A REGULAR: "60 Minutes," CBS, 1975-81; "Who's Who," CBS, 1977; "The CBS Evening News with Dan Rather," CBS, 1981- ; "48 Hours," CBS, 1987- .
* Emmies: 1973, 1974, 1980, 1985, 1986.

RATZENBERGER, JOHN

b. Bridgeport, CT, April 6, 1947. Comic actor who plays mail carrier Cliff Claven on "Cheers."
AS A REGULAR: "Cheers," NBC, 1982- ; "Captain Planet and the Planeteers," TBS, 1990- .
AND: "St. Elsewhere: Cheers," NBC, 1985.

RAYBURN, GENE

b. Christopher, IL, December 22, 1917. Emcee best known for his tenure on "The Match Game."
AS A REGULAR: "The Name's the Same," ABC, 1953-55; "The Tonight Show (Tonight)," NBC, 1954-57; "Make the Connection," NBC, 1955; "Choose Up Sides," NBC, 1956; "The Steve Allen Show," NBC, 1956-59; "Dough Re Mi," NBC, 1958-60; "Steve Allen Presents The Steve Lawrence-Eydie Gorme Show," NBC, 1958; "Play Your Hunch," NBC, 1959-62; "Head of the Class," NBC, 1960; "Match Game," NBC, 1962-69; CBS, 1973-79; SYN, 1976-81; "Snap Judgment," NBC, 1969; "Match Game P.M.," SYN, 1975-82; "Break the Bank," SYN, 1976-77; "Tic Tac Dough," CBS, 1978; "The Match Game/Hollywood Squares Hour," NBC, 1983-84.
AND: "Kraft Theatre: Heroes Walk on Sand," NBC, 1957; "To Tell the Truth," CBS, 1964; "The Mike Douglas Show," SYN, 1974; "Dinah!," SYN, 1975; "Tattletales," CBS, 1975.

RAYE, MARTHA

b. Margie Yvonne Reed, Butte, MT, August 27, 1916. "The Big Mouth" of TV denture-cleaner commercials, longtime comedienne with a brash, anything-goes style; she played the mother of diner owner Mel (Vic Tayback) on "Alice."
AS A REGULAR: "All Star Revue," NBC, 1951-53; "The Martha Raye Show," NBC, 1955-56; "The Bugaloos," NBC, 1970-71; "Amateur's Guide to Love," CBS, 1972; "Steve Allen's Laugh Back," SYN, 1976; "McMillan," NBC, 1976-77; "Alice," CBS, 1982-84.
AND: "Musical Comedy Time: Anything Goes," NBC, 1950; "The Walter Winchell Show," NBC, 1956; "Washington Square," NBC, 1956; "The Steve Allen Show," NBC, 1956; "Washington Square," NBC, 1957; "The Steve Allen Show," NBC, 1957; "The Steve Allen Show," NBC, 1958; "The Patrice Munsel Show," ABC, 1958;

"Club Oasis," NBC, 1958; "Steve Allen Plymouth Show," NBC, 1960; "Candid Camera," CBS, 1960; "Perry Como's Kraft Music Hall," NBC, 1961; "I've Got a Secret," CBS, 1961; "The Red Skelton Hour," CBS, 1964; "Burke's Law: Who Killed the Fat Cat?," ABC, 1965; "The Mike Douglas Show," SYN, 1968; "The Jackie Gleason Show," CBS, 1969; "The Red Skelton Hour," CBS, 1969; "Jimmy Durante Presents the Lennon Sisters Hour," ABC, 1969; "Bob Hope Special," NBC, 1970; "Love, American Style: Love and the Hidden Meaning," ABC, 1973; "The New Candid Camera," SYN, 1975; "McMillan and Wife: Deadly Inheritance," NBC, 1976.

RAYMOND, GENE

b. *Raymond Guion, New York City, NY, August 13, 1908.* Film and TV actor who was busy during the heyday of live TV drama; he also starred in the first made-for-TV movie.

AS A REGULAR: "Fireside Theatre," NBC, 1953-55; "What's Going On?," ABC, 1954; "TV Reader's Digest," ABC, 1956; "Hollywood Summer Theatre," CBS, 1956; "Paris 7000," ABC, 1970.

AND: "Pulitzer Prize Playhouse: The Pharmacist's Mate," ABC, 1950; "Tales of Tomorrow: Plague From Space," ABC, 1952; "Pulitzer Prize Playhouse: The American Leonardo," ABC, 1952; "Lux Video Theatre: The Lesson," NBC, 1952; "Footlights Theatre: Mechanic on Duty," CBS, 1952; "Lux Video Theatre: Some Call It Love," CBS, 1953; "Schlitz Playhouse of Stars: Dawn at Damascus," CBS, 1954; "Kraft Television Theatre: The Hickory Limb," ABC, 1955; "The Loretta Young Show: Weekend in Winnetka," NBC, 1955; "Ford Theatre: Dear Diane," NBC, 1956; "Playhouse 90: Charley's Aunt," CBS, 1957; "Matinee Theatre: The Ivy Curtain," NBC, 1957; "Climax!: The Secret Love of Johnny Spain," CBS, 1958; "Climax!: House of Doubt," CBS, 1958; "The Red Skelton Show," CBS, 1958; "Person to Person," CBS, 1958; "U.S. Steel Hour: Big Doc's Girl," CBS, 1959; "The Barbara Stanwyck Show: Big Career," NBC, 1961; "U.S. Steel Hour: The Shame of Paula Marsten," CBS, 1961; "U.S. Steel Hour: The Haven," CBS, 1961; "Sam Benedict: Hannigan," NBC, 1962; "Route 66: Journey to Nineveh," CBS, 1962; "The Dick Powell Show: The Old Man and the City," NBC, 1963; "The Defenders: The Brother Killers," CBS, 1963; "Channing: Dragon in the Den," ABC, 1963; "The Outer Limits: The Borderland," ABC, 1963; "Burke's Law: Who Killed My Girl?," ABC, 1964; "The Man From UNCLE: The Secret Sceptre Affair," NBC, 1965; "The Defenders: The Non-Violent," CBS, 1965; "Laredo: The Land Slickers," NBC, 1966; "The Girl From UNCLE: The Fountain of Youth Affair," NBC, 1967; "Judd for the Defense: Death From a Flower Girl," ABC, 1967; "Hondo: Hondo

and the Sudden Town," ABC, 1967; "Ironside: Desperate Encounter," NBC, 1968; "The Bold Ones: To Save a Life," NBC, 1969; "The Name of the Game: High Card," NBC, 1969; "The Name of the Game: The Power," NBC, 1969; "Mannix: Missing: Sun and Sky," CBS, 1969; "The Interns: The Price of Love," CBS, 1970; "The FBI: The Inheritors," ABC, 1970.

TV MOVIES AND MINISERIES: "The Hanged Man," NBC, 1964.

REAGAN, NANCY DAVIS

Actress and former U.S. First Lady.

AS A GUEST: "Ford Theatre: First Born," NBC, 1953; "G.E. Theatre: That's the Man," CBS, 1956; "G.E. Theatre: A Turkey for the President," CBS, 1958; "G.E. Theatre: The Playoff," CBS, 1960; "Dick Powell's Zane Grey Theatre: The Long Shadow," CBS, 1961; "The Tall Man: Shadow of the Past," NBC, 1961; "G.E. Theatre: Money and the Minister," CBS, 1961; "87th Precinct: King's Ransom," NBC, 1962; "Diff'rent Strokes: The Reporter," NBC, 1983.

* Ms. Davis' co-star in "A Turkey for the President" was—well, guess.

REAGAN, RONALD

b. *Tampico, IL, February 6, 1911.* Film and TV actor who had his own successful sitcom, "Mr. President," which ran on all networks from 1980-89.

AS A REGULAR: "The Orchid Award," ABC, 1953-54; "G.E. Theatre," CBS, 1954-61; "Death Valley Days," SYN, 1965-66.

AND: "Nash Airflyte Theatre: Disappearance of Mrs. Gordon," CBS, 1950; "Hollywood Opening Night: The Priceless Gift," NBC, 1952; "Ford Theatre: First Born," NBC, 1953; "Medallion Theatre: A Job for Jimmy Valentine," CBS, 1953; "Schlitz Playhouse of Stars: The Doctor Goes Home," CBS, 1953; "Lux Video Theatre: Message in a Bottle," CBS, 1953; "Mirror Theatre: Next Stop Bethlehem," CBS, 1953; "Ford Theatre: And Suddenly You Knew," NBC, 1953; "Lux Video Theatre: A Place in the Sun," CBS, 1954; "Schlitz Playhouse of Stars: The Jungle Trap," CBS, 1954; "Schlitz Playhouse of Stars: The Edge of Battle," CBS, 1954; "Ford Theatre: Beneath These Waters," NBC, 1954; "The Gisele MacKenzie Show," NBC, 1957; "The Ford Show," NBC, 1957; "The Ford Show," NBC, 1959; "The du Pont Show with June Allyson: The Way Home," CBS, 1960; "Startime: The Swingin' Years," NBC, 1960; "Startime: The Swingin' Singin' Years," NBC, 1960; "Here's Hollywood," NBC, 1960; "Art Linkletter's House Party," CBS, 1960; "Dick Powell's Zane Grey Theatre: The Long Shadow," CBS, 1961; "I've Got a Secret," CBS, 1961; "Bob Hope Buick

Show," NBC, 1961; "The Dick Powell Show: Who Killed Julie Greer?," NBC, 1961; "Wagon Train: The Fort Pierce Story," ABC, 1963; "Kraft Suspense Theatre: Cruel and Unusual Night," NBC, 1964; "The Sonny and Cher Comedy Hour," CBS, 1972; "The Dean Martin Show," NBC, 1973; "The Mike Douglas Show," SYN, 1973; "Dean's Place," NBC, 1975.

* Reagan also made a TV movie, 1964's "The Killers," in which he slaps around his girlfriend, Angie Dickinson. The film was deemed too violent for TV, however, and released to theatres instead.

REASON, REX
b. Berlin, Germany, November 20, 1928.
Action hero of the late fifties.
AS A REGULAR: "Man Without a Gun," SYN, 1958-59; "The Roaring Twenties," ABC, 1960-62.
AND: "Warner Bros. Presents Conflict: Passage to Maranga," ABC, 1957; "Ford Theatre: Singapore," ABC, 1957; "Undercurrent: Fatal Alibi," CBS, 1958; "77 Sunset Strip: Blackout," ABC, 1960; "The Alaskans: Disaster at Gold Hill," ABC, 1960; "Bourbon Street Beat: Swamp Fire," ABC, 1960; "The Alaskans: Calico," ABC, 1960; "Sugarfoot: The Captive Locomotives," ABC, 1960; "The Alaskans: The Ballad of Whitehorse," ABC, 1960.

REASON, RHODES
b. Berlin, Germany, November 20, 1928.
Cowboy actor; twin of Rex.
AS A REGULAR: "White Hunter," SYN, 1958; "Bus Stop," ABC, 1961-62.
AND: "Cheyenne: The Trap," ABC, 1956; "Ford Theatre: The Man Who Beat Lupo," ABC, 1957; "Du Pont Theatre: The Man Who Asked No Favors," ABC, 1957; "Wire Service: The Indictment," ABC, 1957; "Maverick: Ghost Rider," ABC, 1957; "Sugarfoot: Strange Land," ABC, 1957; "Bronco: The Burning Springs," ABC, 1959; "Death Valley Days: California's First Ice Man," SYN, 1959; "Bourbon Street Beat: Key to the City," ABC, 1960; "The Rifleman: Conflict," ABC, 1962; "77 Sunset Strip: Scream Softly, Dear," ABC, 1963; "Daniel Boone: The Hostages," NBC, 1965; "Perry Mason: The Case of the Bogus Buccaneer," CBS, 1966; "The Lucy Show: Lucy and Carol Burnett," CBS, 1967; "Star Trek: Bread and Circuses," NBC, 1968; "Here's Lucy: Lucy the Matchmaker," CBS, 1968; "Here's Lucy: Lucy the Sky Diver," CBS, 1970; "Here's Lucy: Lucy's Tenant," CBS, 1973.

REASONER, HARRY
b. Dakota City, IA., April 17, 1923; d. 1991.
AS A REGULAR: "CBS Weekend News," CBS, 1963-70; "60 Minutes," CBS, 1968-70;

1978-91; "ABC Evening News," ABC, 1970-78; "The Reasoner Report," ABC, 1973-75.
* Emmies: 1968, 1974, 1981, 1982.

REDDY, HELEN
b. Melbourne, Australia, October 25, 1941.
Pop singer most popular in the seventies.
AS A REGULAR: "The Helen Reddy Show," NBC, 1973; "Midnight Special," NBC, 1975-76.
AND: "The Virginia Graham Show," SYN, 1972; "The Flip Wilson Show," NBC, 1973; "The New Bill Cosby Show," CBS, 1973; "Midnight Special," NBC, 1973; "The Carol Burnett Show," CBS, 1973; "The Carol Burnett Show," CBS, 1975; "Dinah!," SYN, 1976; "The Love Boat: Out of This World," ABC, 1980.

REDFORD, ROBERT
b. Charles Robert Redford Jr. Santa Monica, CA, August 18, 1937. Screen idol who got his feet wet on the tube.
AS A GUEST: "Maverick: Iron Hand," ABC, 1960; "The Deputy: Last Gunfight, NBC, 1960; "Hallmark Hall of Fame: Captain Brassbound's Conversion," NBC, 1960; "Playhouse 90: In the Presence of Mine Enemies," CBS, 1960; "Tate: The Bounty Hunter," NBC, 1960; "Tate: Comanche Scalps," NBC, 1960; "Perry Mason: The Case of the Treacherous Toupee," CBS, 1960; "Play of the Week: The Iceman Cometh," SYN, 1960; "Our American Heritage: Born a Giant," NBC, 1960; "Play of the Week: Black Monday," SYN, 1960; "Alfred Hitchcock Presents: The Greatest Monster of Them All," NBC, 1961; "Naked City: Tombstone for a Derelict," ABC, 1961; "Jackie Gleason Special: The Million Dollar Incident," CBS, 1961; "The Americans: The Coward," NBC, 1961; "Whispering Smith: The Grudge," NBC, 1961; "Route 66: First Class Mouliak," CBS, 1961; "Bus Stop: The Covering Darkness," ABC, 1961; "Alfred Hitchcock Presents: The Right Kind of Medicine," NBC, 1961; "The Twilight Zone: Nothing in the Dark," CBS, 1962; "The Alfred Hitchcock Hour: A Piece of the Action," CBS, 1962; "Dr. Kildare: The Burning Sky," NBC, 1962; "Alcoa Premiere: The Voice of Charlie Post," ABC, 1962; "The Untouchables: Snowball," ABC, 1963; "The Alfred Hitchcock Hour: A Tangled Web," NBC, 1963; "The Dick Powell Show: The Last of the Big Spenders," NBC, 1963; "The Breaking Point: Bird and Snake," ABC, 1963; "The Virginian: The Evil That Men Do," NBC, 1963; "The Defenders: The Siege," CBS, 1964.

REDGRAVE, LYNN
b. London, England, March 8, 1943. Red-headed actress in films ("Georgy Girl"); she

now hawks Weight Watcher foods on TV and has been a regular on a couple of sitcoms, including "Chicken Soup," where the romantic chemistry between her and Jackie Mason was as potent as ice water.

AS A REGULAR: "House Calls," CBS, 1979-81; "Teachers Only," NBC, 1982-83; "Chicken Soup," ABC, 1989.

AND: "The Carol Burnett Show," CBS, 1968; "Personality," NBC, 1968; "Dinah!," SYN, 1975; "Kojak: A Hair-Trigger Away," CBS, 1976; "Hollywood Squares," SYN, 1976; "The $20,000 Pyramid," ABC, 1977; "The John Davidson Show," SYN, 1980; "The John Davidson Show," SYN, 1981; "Murder, She Wrote: It's a Dog's Life," CBS, 1984; "Candid Camera Christmas Special," CBS, 1987; "The Pat Sajak Show," CBS, 1989.

TV MOVIES AND MINISERIES: "Turn of the Screw," ABC, 1974; "Centennial," NBC, 1978-79; "Sooner or Later," NBC, 1979; "Beggarman, Thief," NBC, 1979; "Gauguin the Savage," CBS, 1980; "The Seduction of Miss Leona," CBS, 1980; "The Bad Seed," ABC, 1985; "My Two Loves," ABC, 1986.

REDGRAVE, VANESSA

b. London, England, January 30, 1937. Gifted actress who's contributed memorable portrayals to TV, particularly as a concentration-camp inmate in "Playing for Time" and as transsexual tennis played Renee Richards in "Second Serve."

AS A GUEST: "Camera Three: Circle in the Square's 25th Anniversary," CBS, 1977; "Faerie Tale Theatre: Snow White and the Seven Dwarfs," SHO, 1984.

TV MOVIES AND MINISERIES: "Playing for Time," CBS, 1980; "Peter the Great," NBC, 1986; "Second Serve," CBS, 1986.

* Emmies: 1981.

REED, ALAINA

b. Springfield, OH, November 10, 1946. Actress who played Olivia on "Sesame Street" and Rose on "227."

AS A REGULAR: "Sesame Street," PBS, 1978-85; "227," NBC, 1985-90.

AND: "Animal Crack-Ups," ABC, 1989.

REED, ALAN

b. Teddy Bergman, New York City, NY, August 20, 1907; d. 1977. Heavyset character actor who was the voice of Fred Flintstone.

AS A REGULAR: "Smilin' Ed McConnell and His Gang," NBC, 1951-55; "Life with Luigi," CBS, 1952; "Andy's Gang," NBC, 1955-60; "Mr. Adams and Eve," CBS, 1957-58; "The Flintstones," ABC, 1960-66; "Peter Loves Mary," NBC, 1960-61; "Mickey," ABC, 1964-65; "Where's Huddles?," CBS, 1970.

AND: "Make Room for Daddy: Hollywood Story,"

ABC, 1955; "Action Tonight: Crackdown," NBC, 1957; "The People's Choice: The Practical Joker," NBC, 1958; "The Bob Cummings Show: Bob Helps Anna Maria," NBC, 1958; "The Donna Reed Show: Operation Deadbeat," ABC, 1959; "Startime: The Jazz Singer," NBC, 1959; "Tightrope!, The Casino," CBS, 1959; "Michael Shayne: The Poison Pen Club," NBC, 1960; "Angel: The Wedding Gift," CBS, 1961; "Hennesey: The Wedding," CBS, 1961; "The Gertrude Berg Show: Dad's Day," CBS, 1962; "The Lucy Show: Lucy Visits the White House," CBS, 1963; "The Dick Van Dyke Show: The Masterpiece," CBS, 1963; "The Andy Griffith Show: Gomer Pyle, USMC," CBS, 1964; "The Beverly Hillbillies: Teenage Idol," CBS, 1964; "The Beverly Hillbillies: The Widow Poke Arrives," CBS, 1964; "Harris Against the World: Pilot," NBC, 1964; "The Addams Family: Cousin Itt Visits the Addams Family," ABC, 1965; "The Smothers Brothers Show: Outside Inside Hollywood," CBS, 1966; "Honey West: Pandora's Box," ABC, 1966; "Batman: Penguin is a Girl's Best Friend/Penguin Sets a Trend/Penguin's Disastrous End," ABC, 1967; "The Beverly Hillbillies: Robin Hood of Griffith Park," CBS, 1967; "The Beverly Hillbillies: Robin Hood and the Sheriff," CBS, 1967; "The Mothers-in-Law: Through the Lurking Glass," NBC, 1967; "The Beverly Hillbillies: The Great Tag-Team Match," CBS, 1968.

TV MOVIES AND MINISERIES: "In Name Only," ABC, 1969.

REED, DONNA

b. Donna Belle Mullenger, Denison, IA, January 27, 1921; d. 1986. Oscar-winning screen actress who, when good roles dried up, moved to television and her own sitcom, as perfect mom Donna Stone.

AS A REGULAR: "The Donna Reed Show," ABC, 1958-66; "Dallas," CBS, 1984-85.

AND: "Ford Theatre: Portrait of Lydia," NBC, 1954; "G.E. Theatre: Flight From Tormendero," CBS, 1957; "Suspicion: The Other Side of the Curtain," NBC, 1957; "Art Linkletter's House Party," CBS, 1958; "Arthur Murray Party," NBC, 1958; "This Is Your Life," NBC, 1958; "The Love Boat: Polly's Poker Palace," ABC, 1984.

TV MOVIES AND MINISERIES: "The Best Place to Be," NBC, 1979; "Deadly Lessons," ABC, 1983.

* Reed signed a long-term contract to replace Barbara Bel Geddes as Miss Ellie on "Dallas," but when Bel Geddes wanted to return to the series in 1985, Reed was dumped. She sued the show's producers and received a reported $1 million contract settlement.

REED, JERRY

b. Atlanta, GA, March 20, 1937. Singer-comedian.

AS A REGULAR: "The Glen Campbell Goodtime Hour," CBS, 1970-72; "The Jerry Reed When

You're Hot, You're Hot Hour," CBS, 1972; "Dean Martin Presents," NBC, 1973; "Nashville 99," CBS, 1977; "Concrete Cowboys," CBS, 1981.
AND: "Music Country USA," NBC, 1974; "Nashville on the Road," SYN, 1975; "The Tonight Show Starring Johnny Carson," NBC, 1975; "Alice: Star in the Storeroom," CBS, 1978; "Alice: The Jerry Reed Fish Story," CBS, 1981.
TV MOVIES AND MINISERIES: "The Concrete Cowboys," CBS, 1979.

REED, PAMELA
b. Tacoma, WA, 1953. Attractive actress who plays Janice Pasetti on "Grand."
AS A REGULAR: "The Andros Targets," CBS, 1977; "Grand," NBC, 1990- .
AND: "L.A. Law: Romancing the Drone," NBC, 1988.
TV MOVIES AND MINISERIES: "I Want to Live!," ABC, 1983; "Heart of Steel," ABC, 1983; "Scandal Sheet," ABC, 1985; "Tanner '88," HBO, 1988.

REED, PAUL
Heavyset character actor who played Capt. Block on "Car 54, Where Are You?"
AS A REGULAR: "Caesar's Hour," NBC, 1956; "The Sid Caesar Show," ABC, 1958; "Car 54, Where Are You?," NBC, 1961-63; "The Cara Williams Show," CBS, 1964-65.
AND: "Sid Caesar Special: Variety —World of Show Biz," CBS, 1960; "Du Pont Show of the Month: Heaven Can Wait," CBS, 1960; "The Patty Duke Show: The Con Artists," ABC, 1964; "The Donna Reed Show: Trees," ABC, 1965; "I Dream of Jeannie: Russian Roulette," NBC, 1965; "The Munsters: The Fregosi Emerald," CBS, 1966; "The Donna Reed Show: My Son, the Councilman," ABC, 1966; "The Beverly Hillbillies: Jed in Politics," CBS, 1966; "Hey, Landlord!: The Daring Duo vs. the Incredible Captain Kill," NBC, 1966; "Bewitched: A Gazebo Never Forgets," ABC, 1966; "The Beverly Hillbillies: The Army Game," CBS, 1967.

REED, ROBERT
b. Highland Park, IL, October 19, 1932. Actor who played Kenneth Preston on "The Defenders" and Mike Brady, dad to the bunch.
AS A REGULAR: "The Defenders," CBS, 1961-65; "Mannix," CBS, 1969-75; "The Brady Bunch," ABC, 1969-74; "The Brady Bunch Hour," ABC, 1977; "The Runaways," NBC, 1978; "Nurse," CBS, 1981-82; "The Bradys," CBS, 1990.
AND: "Father Knows Best: The Impostor," CBS, 1959; "Men Into Space: Earthbound," CBS, 1960; "Bronco: Volunteers from Aberdeen,"

ABC, 1960; "Password," CBS, 1963; "Dr. Kildare: The Life Machine/Toast the Golden Couple/Wives and Losers/Welcome Home, Dear Anna/Hour of Decision/Aftermath," NBC, 1965; "Love, American Style: Love and the Wild Party," ABC, 1969; "Love, American Style: Love and the Vampire," ABC, 1971; "Love, American Style: Love and the Reincarnation," ABC, 1971; "The Mod Squad: The Connection," ABC, 1972; "Jigsaw John: Promise to Kill," NBC, 1976; "Stumpers," NBC, 1976; "Barnaby Jones: Death Beat," CBS, 1977; "The Love Boat: The Witness," ABC, 1978; "Charlie's Angels: Angel in Love," ABC, 1980; "The Love Boat: Friend of the Family," ABC, 1983; "The Love Boat: Seems Like Old Time," ABC, 1984; "The Love Boat: Joint Custody," ABC, 1985; "Half-Nelson: The Deadly Vase," NBC, 1985; "Murder, She Wrote: Footnote to Murder," CBS, 1985; "Murder, She Wrote: Murder Through the Looking Glass," CBS, 1988; "Day by Day: A Very Brady Episode," NBC, 1989; "Free Spirit: The New Secretary," ABC, 1989.
TV MOVIES AND MINISERIES: "The City," ABC, 1971; "Assignment: Munich," ABC, 1972; "Haunts of the Very Rich," ABC, 1972; "Snatched," ABC, 1973; "The Man Who Could Talk to Kids," CBS, 1973; "Pray for the Wildcats," ABC, 1974; "The Secret Night Caller," NBC, 1975; "Rich Man, Poor Man," ABC, 1976; "Law and Order," NBC, 1976; "Nightmare in Badham County," ABC, 1976; "The Boy in the Plastic Bubble," ABC, 1976; "Revenge for a Rape," ABC, 1976; "The New, Original Wonder Woman," ABC, 1976; "Lanigan's Rabbi," NBC, 1976; "Roots," ABC, 1977; "Love Boat II," ABC, 1977; "SST-Death Flight," ABC, 1977; "Bud and Lou," NBC, 1978; "Thou Shalt Not Commit Adultery," NBC, 1978; "Mandrake," NBC, 1979; "Love's Savage Fury," ABC, 1979; "Scruples," CBS, 1980; "Casino," ABC, 1980; "The Brady Girls Get Married," NBC, 1981; "Death of a Centerfold: The Dorothy Stratton Story," NBC, 1981; "A Very Brady Christmas," CBS, 1988.

REESE, DELLA
b. Deloreese Patricia Early, Detroit, MI, July 6, 1932. Singer-actress, more of the latter these days.
AS A REGULAR: "The Della Reese Show," SYN, 1969-70; "Chico and the Man," NBC, 1976-78; "It Takes Two," ABC, 1982-83; "Charlie & Company," CBS, 1986.
AND: "The Ed Sullivan Show," CBS, 1957; "The Ed Sullivan Show," CBS, 1958; "The Ed Sullivan Show," CBS, 1959; "Dick Clark's World of Talent," ABC, 1959; "The Ed Sullivan Show," CBS, 1960; "Perry Como's Kraft Music Hall," NBC, 1960; "American Bandstand," ABC, 1960; "The Ed Sullivan Show," CBS, 1961; "Play Your

Hunch," NBC, 1962; "Hollywood Palace," ABC, 1964; "To Tell the Truth," CBS, 1964; "ABC Nightlife," ABC, 1965; "The Mike Douglas Show," SYN, 1967; "Funny You Should Ask," ABC, 1969; "The David Frost Show," SYN, 1969; "The Tonight Show Starring Johnny Carson," NBC, 1970; "The Bold Ones: Killer on the Loose," NBC, 1970; "Rowan & Martin's Laugh-In," NBC, 1972; "Hollywood Squares," NBC, 1973; "McCloud: This Must Be the Alamo," NBC, 1974; "The Tonight Show Starring Johnny Carson," NBC, 1974; "Police Woman: Requiem for Bored Wives," NBC, 1974; "Sanford & Son: Della, Della, Della," NBC, 1975; "Chico and the Man: The Juror," NBC, 1975; "The Rookies: Ladies' Day," ABC, 1975; "The Magnificent Marble Machine," NBC, 1976; "McCloud: The Night New York Turned Blue," NBC, 1976; "Medical Center: Major Annie, M.D.," CBS, 1976; "Welcome Back, Kotter: The Gong Show," ABC, 1979; "With Ossie & Ruby," PBS, 1981; "Sha Na Na," SYN, 1981; "The Love Boat: The Love Boat Musical," ABC, 1982; "The A-Team: Lease with an Option," NBC, 1985; "Night Court: Auntie Maim," NBC, 1989.

TV MOVIES AND MINISERIES: "The Voyage of the Yes," CBS, 1973; "Twice in a Lifetime," NBC, 1974; "Nightmare in Badham County," ABC, 1976; "Roots: The Next Generations," ABC, 1979.

* On "The A-Team," Reese had the honor of playing the mother of B.A. Baracus (Mr. T).

REEVES, GEORGE

b. George Besselo, Woodstock, IA, April 6, 1914; d. 1959. Film and TV actor best known as Superman.

AS A REGULAR: "The Adventures of Superman," SYN, 1950-57.

AND: "Silver Theatre: The First Show of 1950," CBS, 1950; "Kraft Television Theatre: Kelly," NBC, 1950; "Kraft Television Theatre: Storm in a Teacup," NBC, 1950; "The Trap: Sentence of Death," CBS, 1950; "Kraft Television Theatre: The Wind Is 90," NBC, 1950; "Kraft Television Theatre: Feathers in a Gale," NBC, 1950; "Fireside Theatre: Hurry, Hurry," NBC, 1952; "Kraft Television Theatre: Six by Six," NBC, 1952; "Footlights Theatre: Heart of Gold," CBS, 1953; "Walt Disney Presents: Doc Grayson-White Man's Medicine," ABC, 1956; "I Love Lucy: Lucy and Superman," CBS, 1957.

* Reeves died of a gunshot wound; reportedly he was upset over not being able to find any work after "Superman" ended its run, but friends say that wasn't the case.

REGALBUTO, JOE

b. Brooklyn, NY. Slight, balding actor often in nerdy roles; he plays Frank Fontana on "Murphy Brown."

AS A REGULAR: "The Associates," ABC, 1979-80; "Ace Crawford, Private Eye," CBS, 1983; "Street Hawk," ABC, 1985; "Knots Landing," CBS, 1985; "Murphy Brown," CBS, 1988- .

AND: "Lou Grant: Pack," CBS, 1980; "Barney Miller: Agent Orange," ABC, 1980; "Bosom Buddies: There's No Business," ABC, 1981; "Barney Miller: The Car," ABC, 1981; "Best of the West: Sam's Life Is Threatened," ABC, 1982; "Mork & Mindy: Gotta Run," ABC, 1982; "St. Elsewhere: Hearing," NBC, 1984; "Magnum P.I.: Going Home," CBS, 1985; "Hardcastle and McCormick: The Yankee Clipper," ABC, 1985; "Amazing Stories: Dorothy and Ben," NBC, 1986; "The Love Boat: What Ever Happened to Jumpin' Jack Flash?," ABC, 1986; "Cagney & Lacey: No Vacancy," CBS, 1987; "The Pat Sajak Show," CBS, 1989.

TV MOVIES AND MINISERIES: "Divorce Wars: A Love Story," ABC, 1982; "The Other Woman," CBS, 1983; "Love Lives On," ABC, 1985; "Police Story: Cop Killers," ABC, 1988; "Prime Target," NBC, 1989.

REID, DAPHNE MAXWELL

Attractive actress fondly remembered as mortician Hannah Griffin on "Frank's Place"; wife of Tim Reid.

AS A REGULAR: "Simon & Simon," CBS, 1985-87; "CBS Summer Playhouse," CBS, 1987; "Frank's Place," CBS, 1987-88; "Snoops," CBS, 1989-90.

AND: "WKRP in Cincinnati: Real Families," CBS, 1980; "Hill Street Blues: Chipped Beef," NBC, 1981; "The A-Team: Skins," NBC, 1985; "Murder, She Wrote: The Body Politic," CBS, 1988.

TV MOVIES AND MINISERIES: "The Long Journey Home," NBC, 1987.

REID, TIM

b. Norfolk, VA, December 19, 1944. Gifted light comic performer; memorable as Venus Flytrap on "WKRP in Cincinnati" and as Frank Parrish on the underrated comedy-drama "Frank's Place."

AS A REGULAR: "Easy Does It ... Starring Frankie Avalon," CBS, 1976; "The Richard Pryor Show," NBC, 1977; "The Marilyn McCoo and Billy Davis, Jr. Show," CBS, 1977; "WKRP in Cincinnati," CBS, 1978-82; "Teachers Only," NBC, 1983; "Simon & Simon," CBS, 1983-87; "CBS Summer Playhouse," CBS, 1987; "Frank's Place," CBS, 1987-88; "Snoops," CBS, 1989-90.

AND: "That's My Mama: Clifton's Persuasion," ABC, 1974; "Rhoda: Guess Who I Saw Today?," CBS, 1976; "What's Happening!: It's All in Your Head," ABC, 1977; "Matlock: The Court-Martial," NBC, 1987.

665

AS CO-EXECUTIVE PRODUCER: "Frank's Place," CBS, 1987-88; "Snoops," CBS, 1989-90.

REILLY, CHARLES NELSON

b. New York City, NY, January 13, 1931. Manic comic actor, a game show regular.

AS A REGULAR: "The Steve Lawrence Show," CBS, 1965; "The Ghost and Mrs. Muir," NBC, 1968-69; ABC, 1969-70; "Dean Martin Presents," NBC, 1970; "Arnie," CBS, 1971-72; "It Pays to Be Ignorant," SYN, 1972-73; "Match Game," CBS, 1973-79; ABC, 1990- ; "Match Game P.M.," SYN, 1975-82.

AND: "Car 54, Where Are You?: Occupancy August First," NBC, 1962; "Car 54, Where Are You?: The Loves of Sylvia Schnauser," NBC, 1963; "The Farmer's Daughter: An Affair of State," ABC, 1963; "The Dean Martin Show," NBC, 1969; "Love, American Style: Love and the Neighbor," ABC, 1969; "The Steve Allen Show," SYN, 1970; "Here's Lucy: Lucy's Vacuum," CBS, 1970; "Kraft Music Hall," NBC, 1970; "The Doris Day Show: Whodunnit, Doris?," CBS, 1971; "Love, American Style: Love and the Detective," ABC, 1972; "Love, American Style: Love and the Laughing Lover," ABC, 1973; "Love, American Style: Love and the Return of Raymond," ABC, 1973; "Password," ABC, 1974; "The Peter Marshall Variety Show," SYN, 1976; "Dinah!," SYN, 1980; "Sha Na Na," SYN, 1981; "The Love Boat: Pride of the Pacific," ABC, 1982; "Amazing Stories: Guilt Trip," NBC, 1985; "Animal Crack-Ups," ABC, 1989.

TV MOVIES AND MINISERIES: "Call Her Mom," ABC, 1972.

REILLY, HUGH

b. Newark, NJ, 1920. Actor who played Paul Martin, father of Timmy (Jon Provost) on "Lassie."

AS A REGULAR: "Claudia, the Story of a Marriage," NBC, 1952; CBS, 1952; "TV Reader's Digest," ABC, 1955; "Lassie," CBS, 1958-64.

AND: "Armstrong Circle Theatre: Three Cents Worth of Fear," NBC, 1957; "Alcoa Hour: No License to Kill," NBC, 1957; "Harbourmaster: Dangerous Channel," CBS, 1957; "U.S. Steel Hour: The Reward," CBS, 1958; "Frontiers of Faith: The Hair Shirt," NBC, 1959; "True Story: The Accident," NBC, 1960.

REINER, CARL

b. New York City, NY, March 20, 1922. Gifted comic writer, entertainer and director.

AS A REGULAR: "The Fashion Story," ABC, 1948-49; "The Fifty-Fourth Street Revue," CBS, 1949; "Eddie Condon's Floor Show," CBS, 1950; "Your Show of Shows," NBC, 1950-54; "Droodles," NBC, 1954; "Caesar's Hour," NBC, 1954-57; "Keep Talking," CBS, 1958-59; "The Sid Caesar Show," ABC, 1958; "Dinah Shore Chevy Show," NBC, 1959-60; "Take a Good Look," ABC, 1960-61; "The Dick Van Dyke Show," CBS, 1963-66; "The Art Linkletter Show," NBC, 1963; "The Celebrity Game," CBS, 1964-65, 1967-68; "Good Heavens," ABC, 1976.

AND: "I've Got a Secret," CBS, 1957; "Masquerade Party," NBC, 1957; "Playhouse 90: Topaze," CBS, 1957; "The Patrice Munsel Show," ABC, 1957; "Comedy Spot: Head of the Family," CBS, 1960; "A Date with Debbie," ABC, 1960; "Art Linkletter's House Party," CBS, 1960; "Here's Hollywood," NBC, 1960; "The Ed Sullivan Show," CBS, 1961; "The New Steve Allen Show," ABC, 1961; "The Bob Newhart Show," NBC, 1962; "The Tonight Show Starring Johnny Carson," NBC, 1963; "Burke's Law: Who Killed Snooky Martinelli?," ABC, 1964; "Hollywood Palace," ABC, 1964; "The Jack Paar Program," NBC, 1964; "Burke's Law: Who Killed Supersleuth?," ABC, 1964; "Hollywood Palace," ABC, 1965; "The Sid Caesar, Imogene Coca, Carl Reiner, Howard Morris Special," CBS, 1967; "Hollywood Squares," NBC, 1967; "Paulsen for President," CBS, 1968; "That Girl: I Don't Have the Vegas Notion," ABC, 1969; "The Movie Game," SYN, 1970; "The Comedians," SYN, 1971; "Night Gallery: Professor Peabody's Last Lecture," NBC, 1972; "Hollywood Squares," NBC, 1973; "The Tonight Show Starring Johnny Carson," NBC, 1974; "Annie and the Hoods," ABC, 1974; "The 2000 Year Old Man," CBS, 1975; "The Merv Griffin Show," SYN, 1976; "Mary," CBS, 1978; "Dinah!," SYN, 1980; "Something Spectacular with Steve Allen," PBS, 1981; "Faerie Tale Theatre: Pinocchio," SHO, 1984; "Carol, Carl, Whoopi and Robin," ABC, 1986; "It's Garry Shandling's Show: Killer Routine," FOX, 1989; "It's Garry Shandling's Show: Save Mr. Peck's," FOX, 1989; "Fifty Years of Television: A Golden Celebration," CBS, 1989.

TV MOVIES AND MINISERIES: "Medical Story," NBC, 1975; "Skokie," CBS, 1981.

AS WRITER: "Your Show of Shows," NBC, 1950-54; "Caesar's Hour," NBC, 1954-57; "Dinah Shore Chevy Show," NBC, 1959-60; "Comedy Spot: Head of the Family," CBS, 1960; "The Sid Caesar, Imogene Coca, Carl Reiner, Howard Morris Special," CBS, 1967.

AS PRODUCER-CREATOR-WRITER: "The Dick Van Dyke Show," CBS, 1961-66; "The New Dick Van Dyke Show," CBS, 1971-74.

* "The Dick Van Dyke Show" was born when Reiner decided to write about what he knew—a TV comedy writer's home and work life. Before the idea was even bought by a network, Reiner had written a season's worth of scripts. He appeared in the show's pilot, called "Head of the Family" (and produced it with money

raised from John F. Kennedy's father, Joe), but the network didn't like him in the lead.
* Emmies: 1957, 1958, 1962, 1963, 1964, 1965, 1966, 1967.

REINER, ROB

b. Bronx, NY, March 6, 1945. Comic actor who played Mike Stivic on "All in the Family," and now he's a movie director ("When Harry Met Sally..."); son of Carl.
AS A REGULAR: "All in the Family," CBS, 1971-78; "Free Country," ABC, 1978.
AND: "Hey, Landlord!: From Out of the Past Come the Thundering Hoofbeats," NBC, 1966; "Gomer Pyle, USMC: Gomer the Recruiter," CBS, 1967; "Hey, Landlord!: Testing, One, Two," NBC, 1967; "Batman: The Zodiac Crimes/The Joker's Hard Times/The Penguin Declines," ABC, 1967; "The Mothers-in-Law: The Career Girls," NBC, 1967; "Gomer Pyle, USMC: Lost-the Colonel's Daughter," CBS, 1967; "Gomer Pyle, USMC: Flower Power," CBS, 1969; "The Beverly Hillbillies: Back to the Hills," CBS, 1969; "The Beverly Hillbillies: The Hills of Home," CBS, 1969; "Room 222: Funny Money," ABC, 1970; "The Partridge Family: A Man Called Snake," ABC, 1971; "Hollywood Squares," NBC, 1971; "The Odd Couple: The Rain in Spain," ABC, 1974; "The $25,000 Pyramid," SYN, 1975; "Saturday Night Live," NBC, 1975; "The Rockford Files: The No-Cut Contract," NBC, 1976; "Good Heavens: Take Me Out to the Ball Game," ABC, 1976; "It's Garry Shandling's Show: Dial L for Laundry," FOX, 1988; "It's Garry Shandling's Show: Home Sweet Home," FOX, 1989; "It's Garry Shandling's Show: Save Mr. Peck's," FOX, 1989.
TV MOVIES AND MINISERIES: "Thursday's Game," ABC, 1974; "More Than Friends," ABC, 1978.
AS CO-WRITER: "All in the Family: Now That You Know the Way, Let's Be Strangers," CBS, 1971; "All in the Family: Flashback: Mike Meets Archie," CBS, 1971; "All in the Family: Flashback: Mike and Gloria's Wedding," CBS, 1972; "Free Country," ABC, 1978.
* Emmies: 1974, 1978.

REMICK, LEE

b. Boston, MA, December 14, 1935; d. 1991. Talented movie actress ("Anatomy of a Murder") who began in live TV.
AS A GUEST: "Armstrong Circle Theatre: Judy and the Brain," NBC, 1953; "Kraft Television Theatre: Double in Ivory," NBC, 1953; "Robert Montgomery Presents: My Little Girl," NBC, 1954; "Studio One: Death and Life of Larry Benson," CBS, 1954; "Robert Montgomery Presents: It Depends on You," NBC, 1955; "Kraft Television Theatre: The Diamond as Big as the Ritz," NBC, 1955; "Robert Montgomery Presents: Man Lost," NBC, 1955; "Robert Montgomery Presents: Three Men From

Tomorrow," NBC, 1956; "Robert Montgomery Presents: All Expenses Paid," NBC, 1956; "Studio One: The Landlady's Daughter," CBS, 1956; "Robert Montgomery Presents: The Young and Beautiful," NBC, 1956; "Playhouse 90: The Last Tycoon," CBS, 1957; "Kraft Television Theatre: Circle of Fear," NBC, 1957; "Playhouse 90: Last Clear Chance," CBS, 1958; "Hallmark Hall of Fame: The Tempest," NBC, 1960; "Art Carney Special: Everybody's Doin' It," NBC, 1961; "Theatre '62: The Farmer's Daughter," NBC, 1962; "Damn Yankees," NBC, 1967; "Hallmark Hall of Fame: The Man Who Came to Dinner," NBC, 1972; "Of Men and Women," ABC, 1972; "Great Performances: Jennie," PBS, 1975; "Faerie Tale Theatre: The Snow Queen," SHO, 1984.
TV MOVIES AND MINISERIES: "And No One Could Save Her," ABC, 1973; "The Blue Knight," NBC, 1973; "QB VII," ABC, 1974; "Hustling," ABC, 1975; "A Girl Named Sooner," NBC, 1975; "Arthur Hailey's Wheels," NBC, 1978; "Ike," ABC, 1979; "Torn Between Two Lovers," CBS, 1979; "Haywire," CBS, 1980; "The Letter," ABC, 1982; "The Gift of Love: A Christmas Story," CBS, 1983; "A Good Sport," CBS, 1984; "ABC Theatre: Tough Love," ABC, 1985; "Of Pure Blood," CBS, 1986; "Bridge to Silence," CBS, 1989; "Dark Holiday," NBC, 1989.

RENALDO, DUNCAN

b. Spain, April 23, 1904; d. 1981. The Cisco Kid.
AS A REGULAR: "The Cisco Kid," SYN, 1950-56.
AND: "Art Linkletter's House Party," CBS, 1958.

REPP, STAFFORD

b. California, April 26, 1918; d. 1974. Heavyset actor best known as Chief O'Hara on "Batman."
AS A REGULAR: "The Thin Man," NBC, 1957-58; "The New Phil Silvers Show," CBS, 1963-64; "Batman," ABC, 1966-68.
AND: "Science Fiction Theatre: The Missing Waveband," SYN, 1956; "Big Town: Waterfront," NBC, 1956; "Cheyenne: The Law Man," ABC, 1956; "Noah's Ark: Kangaroo's Tale," NBC, 1957; "The Jane Wyman Show: A Dangerous Thing," NBC, 1957; "The Millionaire: The Bob Fielding Story," CBS, 1957; "Hennesey: Shore Patrol," CBS, 1959; "Richard Diamond, Private Detective: Popskull," CBS, 1960; "Mr. Lucky: Vote the Bullet," CBS, 1960; "Comedy Spot: McGarry and Me," CBS, 1960; "Guestward Ho!: Babs' Mother," ABC, 1960; "The Twilight Zone: Nick of Time," CBS, 1960; "Tales of Wells Fargo: Assignment in Gloribee," NBC, 1962; "The Virginian: The Exiles," NBC, 1963; "Grindl: The Mad Bomber," NBC, 1964; "The

Twilight Zone: Caesar and Me," CBS, 1964; "My Favorite Martian: That Time Machine Is Waking Up That Old Gang of Mine," CBS, 1965; "The Mothers-in-Law: Through the Lurking Glass," NBC, 1967; "The Ghost and Mrs. Muir: The Real James Gatley," NBC, 1968; "The Mothers-in-Law: The First Anniversary Is the Hardest," NBC, 1968; "I Dream of Jeannie: Never Put a Genie on a Budget," NBC, 1969; "Love, American Style: Love and the Doorknob," ABC, 1969; "Gunsmoke: Hostage," CBS, 1972; "Kung Fu: The Chalice," ABC, 1973; "M*A*S*H: White Gold," CBS, 1975.

RETTIG, TOMMY
b. Jackson Heights, NY, December 10, 1941. Child actor who played Jeff, Lassie's master B.T. (Before Timmy).
AS A REGULAR: "Lassie," CBS, 1954-57; "Never Too Young," ABC, 1965-66.
AND: "Your Play Time: The Tin Bridge," CBS, 1953; "Footlights Theatre: Heart of Gold," CBS, 1953; "You Play Time: Long, Long Ago," CBS, 1953; "Four Star Playhouse: No Identity," CBS, 1953; "Ford Theatre: First Born," NBC, 1953; "Omnibus: Nothing So Monstrous," CBS, 1954; "Ford Theatre: Good of His Soul," NBC, 1954; "Schlitz Playhouse of Stars: Mr. Ears," CBS, 1955; "Studio One: Presence of the Enemy," CBS, 1958; "Studio One: No Place to Run," CBS, 1958; "Sugarfoot: The Ghost," ABC, 1958; "The Man From Blackhawk: The Ghost of Lafitte," ABC, 1959; "Lawman: The Town Boys," ABC, 1960; "Wagon Train: Weight of Command," NBC, 1961; "Peter Gunn: I Know It's Murder," ABC, 1961; "Cheyenne: Trouble at Sand Springs," ABC, 1961; "Death Valley Days: Davy's Friend," SYN, 1962; "Many Happy Returns: The Diamond," CBS, 1965; "Mr. Novak: The Firebrand," NBC, 1965; "The Fugitive: Trial by Fire," ABC, 1965; "The Littlest Hobo: Curse of Smoky Ridge," SYN, 1965.

REY, ALEJANDRO
b. Argentina, February 8, 1930; d. 1987. Actor best known as casino owner Carlos Ramirez on "The Flying Nun."
AS A REGULAR: "Slattery's People," CBS, 1965; "The Flying Nun," ABC, 1967-70; "Days of Our Lives," NBC, 1976; "Santa Barbara," NBC, 1984; "Dallas," CBS, 1986.
AND: "SurfSide 6: Spinout at Sebring," ABC, 1961; "Thriller: Guillotine," NBC, 1961; "Perry Mason: The Case of the Injured Innocent," CBS, 1961; "Thriller: La Strega," NBC, 1962; "The Dick Powell Show: The Price of Tomatoes," NBC, 1962; "Route 66: Peace, Pity, Pardon," CBS, 1963; "The Fugitive: Smoke Screen," ABC, 1963; "The Greatest Show on Earth: Where the Wire Ends," ABC, 1964; "Arrest and Trial: The Best There Is," ABC, 1964; "I Spy: My Mother, the Spy," NBC, 1966; "The Girl From UNCLE: The Horns of the Dilemma Affair," NBC, 1966; "Run for Your Life: Edge of the Volcano," NBC, 1966; "The FBI: The Grey Passenger," ABC, 1967; "My Three Sons: My Son, the Bullfighter," CBS, 1967; "The Iron Horse: The Passenger," ABC, 1967; "That Girl: The Mating Game," ABC, 1967; "Three for Danger," NBC, 1967; "It Takes a Thief: Guess Who's Coming to Rio," ABC, 1969; "The FBI: The Catalyst," ABC, 1969; "The Outcasts: And Then There Was One," ABC, 1969; "The Merv Griffin Show," CBS, 1969; "The Game Game," SYN, 1969; "The David Frost Show," SYN, 1969; "The Dick Cavett Show," ABC, 1970; "Night Gallery: The Doll of Death," NBC, 1971; "Owen Marshall, Counselor at Law: Eighteen Years Next April," ABC, 1971; "Gunsmoke: The Bullet," CBS, 1971; "Cannon: Treasure of Saulguasion," CBS, 1972; "Alias Smith and Jones: The Clementine Ingredient," ABC, 1972; "Night Gallery: The Doccal Death," NBC, 1973; "Police Story: Across the Line," NBC, 1974; "Kung Fu: A Lamb to the Slaughter," ABC, 1975; "McMillan and Wife: Deadly Inheritance," NBC, 1976; "The Love Boat: The Duel," ABC, 1981; "The Love Boat: The Christmas Presence," ABC, 1982; "Hotel: Premiere," ABC, 1983; "E/R: Sentimental Journey," CBS, 1984; "The A-Team: The Theory of Revolution," NBC, 1986.
TV MOVIES AND MINISERIES: "Seven in Darkness," ABC, 1969; "Money to Burn," ABC, 1973; "Satan's Triangle," ABC, 1975; "Grace Kelly," ABC, 1983; "Rita Hayworth: The Love Goddess," CBS, 1983.

REYNOLDS, BURT
b. Waycross, GA, February 11, 1936. Likably macho leading man of silly, successful seventies movies; he began his career in TV and has come back to it.
AS A REGULAR: "Riverboat," NBC, 1959-60; "Gunsmoke," CBS, 1962-65; "Hawk," ABC, 1966; "Dan August," ABC, 1970-71; "Out of This World," SYN, 1987-89; "B.L. Stryker," ABC, 1988-90; "Evening Shade," CBS, 1990- .
AND: "M Squad: The Teacher," NBC, 1959; "Schlitz Playhouse of Stars: You Can't Win 'Em All," CBS, 1959; "The Lawless Years: The Payoff," NBC, 1959; "Playhouse 90: Alas, Babylon," CBS, 1960; "Johnny Ringo: The Stranger," CBS, 1960; "Alfred Hitchcock Presents: Escape to Sonoita," CBS, 1960; "Pony Express: The Kidnapping," SYN, 1960; "The Aquanauts: The Big Swim," CBS, 1960; "Michael Shayne: The Boat Caper," NBC, 1961; "Dick Powell's Zane Grey Theatre: The Man From Everywhere," CBS, 1961; "The Blue Angels: Fire Fight," SYN, 1961; "Malibu Run: Kidnap Adventure," CBS, 1961; "Route 66: Love Is a Skinny Kid," CBS, 1962; "The Twilight Zone:

The Bard," CBS, 1963; "Branded: Now Join the Human Race," NBC, 1965; "The FBI: All the Streets Are Silent," ABC, 1965; "Twelve O'Clock High: The Jones Boy," ABC, 1965; "Gentle Ben: Hurricane Coming," CBS, 1967; "The FBI: Act of Violence," ABC, 1968; "Lassiter," CBS, 1968; "The Mike Douglas Show," SYN, 1969; "You're Putting Me On," NBC, 1969; "Love, American Style: Love and the Banned Book," ABC, 1970; "Hollywood Squares," NBC, 1971; "Hollywood Squares," NBC, 1972; "The Tonight Show Starring Johnny Carson," NBC, 1972; "The Wacky World of Jonathan Winters," SYN, 1974; "The Tonight Show Starring Johnny Carson," NBC, 1974; "The Tonight Show Starring Johnny Carson," NBC, 1975; "David Steinberg's Noonday," NBC, 1975; "Saturday Night Live," NBC, 1980; "The Golden Girls: Ladies of the Evening," NBC, 1987.

TV MOVIES AND MINISERIES: "Hunters Are for Killing," CBS, 1970; "Run, Simon, Run," ABC, 1970.

AS DIRECTOR: "Alfred Hitchcock Presents: The Method Actor," NBC, 1985; "Amazing Stories: Guilt Trip," NBC, 1985.

REYNOLDS, DEBBIE

b. Marie Frances Reynolds, El Paso, TX, April 1, 1932. Musical-comedy star of films and TV; mother of Carrie Fisher.

AS A REGULAR: "The Debbie Reynolds Show," NBC, 1969-70; "Aloha Paradise," ABC, 1981. AND: "The Ed Sullivan Show," CBS, 1956; "Can Do," NBC, 1956; "The Eddie Fisher Show," NBC, 1957; "The Eddie Fisher Show," NBC, 1958; "The Steve Allen Show," NBC, 1959; "Hedda Hopper's Hollywood," NBC, 1960; "A Date with Debbie," ABC, 1960; "Here's Hollywood," NBC, 1960; "Three Wishes," SYN, 1961; "This Is Your Life," NBC, 1961; "Jackpot Bowling Starring Milton Berle," NBC, 1961; "The Art Linkletter Show," NBC, 1963; "Hollywood Palace," ABC, 1964; "Hollywood Palace," ABC, 1965; "Girlfriends and Nabors," CBS, 1968; "Kraft Music Hall," NBC, 1969; "Bracken's World: It's the Power Structure, Baby," NBC, 1969; "Pat Paulsen's Half a Comedy Hour," ABC, 1970; "This Is Tom Jones," ABC, 1970; "Rowan & Martin's Laugh-In," NBC, 1970; "The Pearl Bailey Show," ABC, 1971; "Rowan & Martin's Laugh-In," NBC, 1972; "The Merv Griffin Show," SYN, 1974; "The Perry Como Sunshine Show," CBS, 1974; "Hollywood Squares," SYN, 1975; "The Love Boat: The Promoter," ABC, 1980; "Barbara Mandrell and the Mandrell Sisters," NBC, 1981; "Jennifer Slept Here: Boo!," NBC, 1983; "Hollywood Squares," SYN, 1988.

TV MOVIES AND MINISERIES: "Sadie and Son," CBS, 1987; "Perry Mason: The Case of the Musical Murder," NBC, 1989.

REYNOLDS, FRANK

b. East Chicago, IN, November 29, 1923; d. 1983.

AS A REGULAR: "ABC Evening News," ABC, 1968-70, 1978-83.

RHOADES, BARBARA

b. Poughkeepsie, NY, March 23, 1947. Attractive actress usually in light comic roles.

AS A REGULAR: "Busting Loose," CBS, 1977; "Celebrity Challenge of the Sexes," CBS, 1978; "Hanging In," CBS, 1979; "Soap," ABC, 1980-81; "You Again?," NBC, 1986-87.

AND: "The Virginian: With Help From Ulysses," NBC, 1968; "Mannix: Comes Up Rose," CBS, 1968; "Love, American Style: Love and the Unlikely Couple," ABC, 1969; "Mannix: Once Upon a Saturday," CBS, 1969; "Ironside: Dora," NBC, 1970; "The Partridge Family: Danny and the Mob," ABC, 1970; "Bewitched: The House That Uncle Arthur Built," ABC, 1971; "Columbo: Lady in Waiting," NBC, 1971; "The Paul Lynde Show: Whose Lib?," ABC, 1972; "McMillan and Wife: Two Dollars' Trouble," NBC, 1973; "Love, American Style: Love and the Amateur Night," ABC, 1973; "Griff: All the Lonely People," ABC, 1973; "Kojak: Web of Death," CBS, 1973; "McMillan and Wife: Free Fall to Terror," NBC, 1973; "Kojak: Web of Death," CBS, 1973; "Happy Days: The Skin Game," ABC, 1974; "The Odd Couple: Our Fathers," ABC, 1974; "Kolchak, the Night Stalker: Primal Scream," ABC, 1975; "The Six Million Dollar Man: The White Lightning War," ABC, 1975; "Columbo: Identity Crisis," NBC, 1975; "Joe Forrester: Weekend," NBC, 1975; "Ellery Queen: Veronica's Veils," NBC, 1975; "Sanford & Son: The Hawaiian Connection," NBC, 1976; "Police Story: Monster Manor," NBC, 1976; "What's Happening!: Going, Going, Gong," ABC, 1978; "The Love Boat: Musical Cabins," ABC, 1978; "Quark: The Old and the Beautiful," NBC, 1978; "The Eddie Capra Mysteries: Murder, Murder," NBC, 1978; "Rhoda: Jack's New Image," CBS, 1978; "Cross Wits," SYN, 1979; "Password Plus," NBC, 1980; "Murder, She Wrote: Birds of a Feather," CBS, 1984; "Cagney & Lacey: Happily Ever After," CBS, 1985; "Murder, She Wrote: Who Threw the Barbitals in Mrs. Fletcher's Chowder?," CBS, 1987.

TV MOVIES AND MINISERIES: "The Judge and Jake Wyler," NBC, 1972; "Hunter," CBS, 1973; "The Police Story," NBC, 1973; "What Are Best Friends For?," ABC, 1973; "Crime Club," NBC, 1975; "Conspiracy of Terror," NBC, 1975; "Twin Detectives," ABC, 1976; "Sex and the Single Parent," CBS, 1979.

RHODES, HARI

b. Cincinnati, OH, April 10, 1932. Actor who played Mike on "Daktari."

AS A REGULAR: "Daktari," CBS, 1966-69; "The Bold Ones," NBC, 1969-70; "Most Wanted," ABC, 1976-77.

AND: "G.E. Theatre: The Patsy," CBS, 1960; "Adventures in Paradise: The Death-Divers," ABC, 1960; "Adventures in Paradise: Open for Diving," ABC, 1960; "Have Gun, Will Travel: The Shooting of Jessie May," CBS, 1960; "Follow the Sun: The Hunters," ABC, 1961; "Ben Casey: To a Grand and Natural Finale," ABC, 1962; "King of Diamonds: Alias Willie Hogan," SYN, 1962; "Channing: Another Kind of Music," ABC, 1964; "The Outer Limits: Moonstone," ABC, 1964; "Profiles in Courage: Frederick Douglass," NBC, 1965; "The FBI: The Deadly Pact," ABC, 1970; "Medical Center: The World Between," CBS, 1970; "The Steve Allen Show," SYN, 1970; "Mission: Impossible: Cat's Paw," CBS, 1971; "The FBI: Fatal Reunion," ABC, 1973; "The Streets of San Francisco: A Collection of Eagles," ABC, 1973; "The Streets of San Francisco: The Bullet," ABC, 1973; "The Streets of San Francisco: Deathwatch," ABC, 1973; "The Streets of San Francisco: A String of Puppets," ABC, 1973; "The Streets of San Francisco: For Good or Evil," ABC, 1974; "Police Story: Requiem for C.Z. Smith," NBC, 1974; "Police Story: Vice: 24 Hours," NBC, 1975; "Police Story: Oxford Gray," NBC, 1976; "The Streets of San Francisco: Breakup," ABC, 1976; "Quincy: Go Fight City Hall-To the Death," NBC, 1976; "Quincy: Death by Good Intentions," NBC, 1978; "The White Shadow: The Cross Town Hustle," CBS, 1979.

TV MOVIES AND MINISERIES: "Deadlock," NBC, 1969; "Earth II," ABC, 1971; "Trouble Comes to Town," ABC, 1973; "A Dream for Christmas," CBS, 1973; "Mayday at 40,000 Feet!," CBS, 1976; "Roots," ABC, 1977; "Backstairs at the White House," NBC, 1979.

RICH, ADAM

b. New York City, NY, October 12, 1968. Actor who played Nicholas Bradford on "Eight Is Enough."

AS A REGULAR: "Eight Is Enough," ABC, 1977-81; "Code Red," ABC, 1981-82; "Gun Shy," CBS, 1983.

AND: "The Love Boat: The Grass Is Always Greener," ABC, 1979; "The John Davidson Show," SYN, 1981; "St. Elsewhere: Family Affair," NBC, 1986.

TV MOVIES AND MINISERIES: "Eight Is Enough: A Family Reunion," NBC, 1987; "An Eight Is Enough Wedding," NBC, 1989.

RICH, BUDDY

b. Bernard Rich, Brooklyn, NY, June 30, 1917; d. 1987. Drummer.

AS A REGULAR: "The Marge and Gower Champion Show," CBS, 1957; "Away We Go," CBS, 1967.

AND: "The Steve Allen Show," NBC, 1957; "The Big Record," CBS, 1958; "Stars of Jazz," ABC, 1958; "The Ed Sullivan Show," CBS, 1967; "Here's Lucy: Lucy and the Drum Contest," CBS, 1970; "The David Frost Show," SYN, 1971; "The Tonight Show Starring Johnny Carson," NBC, 1974; "Cotton Club '75," NBC, 1974.

RICHARDS, KIM

b. Long Island, NY, September 19, 1964. Child actress who played Prudence on "Nanny and the Professor" and Ruthie Adler on "Hello, Larry."

AS A REGULAR: "Nanny and the Professor," ABC, 1970-71; "Here We Go Again," ABC, 1973; "James at 15," NBC, 1977-78; "Hello, Larry," NBC, 1979-80.

AND: "The FBI: Dark Christmas," ABC, 1972; "The Streets of San Francisco: River of Fear," ABC, 1974; "Little House on the Prairie: Town Party-Country Pary," NBC, 1974; "Medical Story: Million Dollar Baby," NBC, 1975; "Medical Center: If Wishes Were Horses," CBS, 1976; "Family: Monday Is Forever," ABC, 1976; "Police Woman: Father to the Man," NBC, 1976; "The Rockford Files: The Family Hour," NBC, 1976; "Hizzonner: Mizzonner," NBC, 1979; "Diff'rent Strokes: The Trip," NBC, 1979; "Diff'rent Strokes: Feudin' and Fussin'," NBC, 1979; "Diff'rent Strokes: Thanksgiving Crossover," NBC, 1979; "Alice: Not with My Niece, You Don't," CBS, 1982; "Magnum, P.I.: Mixed Doubles," CBS, 1982; "Lottery!: Boston: False Illusion," ABC, 1983.

TV MOVIES AND MINISERIES: "Devil Dog: The Hound of Hell," CBS, 1978.

RICHARDSON, SUSAN

b. Coatesville, PA, March 11, 1952. Actress who played Susan Bradford Stockwell on "Eight Is Enough."

AS A REGULAR: "Eight Is Enough," ABC, 1977-81.

AND: "Happy Days: Fonzie Joins the Band," ABC, 1975; "The Mike Douglas Show," SYN, 1981; "One Day at a Time: The Honeymoon Is Over," CBS, 1982; "One Day at a Time: First Things First," CBS, 1982.

TV MOVIES AND MINISERIES: "Eight Is Enough: A Family Reunion," NBC, 1987; "An Eight Is Enough Wedding," NBC, 1989.

RICHMAN, PETER MARK

b. Philadelphia, PA, April 16, 1927. Actor who played Andrew Laird on "Dynasty" and the minister father of Suzanne Somers on "Three's Company."

AS A REGULAR: "Cain's Hundred," NBC, 1961-62; "Longstreet," ABC, 1971-72; "Dynasty," ABC, 1981-84; "Santa Barbara," NBC, 1984.

AND: "Goodyear TV Playhouse: Star in the Night," NBC, 1954; "Philco TV Playhouse: Middle of the

Night," NBC, 1954; "Goodyear TV Playhouse: Backfire," NBC, 1955; "Kraft Television Theatre: Sheriff's Man," NBC, 1957; "Studio 57: Typhoon," SYN, 1957; "Alfred Hitchcock Presents: The Cure," CBS, 1960; "Moment of Fear: Fire by Night," NBC, 1960; "Play of the Week: Emmanuel," SYN, 1960; "U.S. Steel Hour: You Can't Escape," CBS, 1962; "The Virginian: A Portrait of Marie Valonne," NBC, 1963; "Ben Casey: From Too Much Love of Living," ABC, 1963; "The Outer Limits: The Borderland," ABC, 1963; "Combat!: The Hostages," ABC, 1964; "The Virginian: The Girl From Yesterday," NBC, 1964; "The Fugitive: Ballad for a Ghost," ABC, 1964; "The Twilight Zone: The Fear," CBS, 1964; "The Outer Limits: The Probe," ABC, 1965; "Profiles in Courage: Ulysses S. Grant," NBC, 1965; "The FBI: The Problem of the Honorable Wife," ABC, 1965; "The Wild Wild West: The Night of the Dancing Death," CBS, 1965; "Twelve O'Clock High: The Jones Boy," ABC, 1965; "Combat!: Counterplay," ABC, 1966; "The Loner: Incident in the Middle of Nowhere," CBS, 1966; "The FBI: Breakthrough," ABC, 1968; "The Name of the Game: Pineapple Rose," NBC, 1968; "Bonanza: A World Full of Cannibals," NBC, 1968; "Mission: Impossible: My Friend, My Enemy," CBS, 1970; "The New Adventures of Perry Mason: The Case of the Horoscope Homicide," CBS, 1973; "The Streets of San Francisco: Shield of Honor," ABC, 1974; "Barnaby Jones: Silent Vendetta," CBS, 1976; "Quincy: A Dead Man's Truth," NBC, 1977; "Three's Company: Chrissy Come Home," ABC, 1978; "Three's Company: Triangle Troubles," ABC, 1979; "Three's Company: The Reverend Steps Out," ABC, 1979; "B.J. and the Bear: B.J. and the Witch," NBC, 1980; "Fantasy Island: Shadow Games," ABC, 1982; "The Love Boat: The Runaway," ABC, 1985; "Hardcastle and McCormick: Round Up the Old Gang," ABC, 1986; "Murder, She Wrote: Deadline for Murder," CBS, 1986.

TV MOVIES AND MINISERIES: "The House on Greenapple Road," ABC, 1970; "McCloud: Who Killed Miss U.S.A.?," NBC, 1970; "Yuma," ABC, 1971; "The Islander," CBS, 1978; "Blind Ambition," CBS, 1979; "Dempsey," CBS, 1983; "City Killer," NBC, 1984.

RICKLES, DON

b. New York City, NY, May 8, 1926. Insult comic.
AS A REGULAR: "The Don Rickles Show," ABC, 1968-69; CBS, 1972; "CPO Sharkey," NBC, 1976-78; "Foul-Ups, Bleeps & Blunders," ABC, 1984-85.
AND: "Stage 7: A Note of Fear," CBS, 1955; "Four Star Playhouse: The Listener," CBS, 1956; "The Eddie Fisher Show," NBC, 1957; "The Thin Man: The Cat Kicker," NBC, 1959; "Christophers:

Ways to Help the Handicapped," SYN, 1960; "Here's Hollywood," NBC, 1961; "The Twilight Zone: Mr. Dingle, the Strong," CBS, 1961; "Hennesey: Professional Sailor," CBS, 1961; "Cain's Hundred: Blood Money," NBC, 1962; "Burke's Law: Who Killed Harris Crown?," ABC, 1963; "The Addams Family: Halloween with the Addams Family," ABC, 1964; "The Dick Van Dyke Show: 4 1/2/The Alan Brady Show Goes to Jail," CBS, 1964; "Burke's Law: Who Killed the Swinger on a Hook?," ABC, 1964; "Burke's Law: Who Killed the Fat Cat?," ABC, 1965; "The Beverly Hillbillies: Jed's Temptation," CBS, 1965; "The Munsters: Dance with Me, Herman," CBS, 1965; "Gomer Pyle, USMC: My Buddy-War Hero," CBS, 1965; "The Andy Griffith Show: The Luck of Newton Monroe," CBS, 1965; "Summer Playhouse: Kibbee Hates Fitch," CBS, 1965; "F Troop: The Return of Bald Eagle," ABC, 1965; "Run for Your Life: In Search of April," NBC, 1966; "The Wild Wild West: The Night of the Druid's Blood," CBS, 1966; "Gilligan's Island: The Kidnapper," CBS, 1966; "The Lucy Show: Lucy the Fight Manager," CBS, 1967; "Bob Hope Chrysler Theatre: Murder at NBC," NBC, 1967; "I Spy: Night Train to Madrid," NBC, 1967; "I Dream of Jeannie: My Master the Weakling," NBC, 1967; "The Jerry Lewis Show," NBC, 1968; "Kraft Music Hall: Roast for Johnny Carson," NBC, 1968; "The Ed Sullivan Show," CBS, 1969; "The Carol Burnett Show," CBS, 1969; "Get Smart: To Sire, with Love," NBC, 1969; "The Mothers-in-Law: Show Business Is No Business," NBC, 1969; "Bob Newhart Special: A Last Laugh at the 60's," ABC, 1970; "A Couple of Dons," NBC, 1973; "The Tonight Show Starring Johnny Carson," NBC, 1974; "Sanford & Son: Once a Thief," NBC, 1974; "The Merv Griffin Show," SYN, 1974; "Don Adams Screen Test," SYN, 1975; "The Mike Douglas Show," SYN, 1975; "Joys," NBC, 1976; "Medical Center: The Happy State of Depression," CBS, 1976; "The Tonight Show Starring Johnny Carson," NBC, 1978; "The Mike Douglas Show," SYN, 1980; "Saturday Night Live," NBC, 1983; "Gimme a Break: Nell and the Kid," NBC, 1984; "The Tonight Show Starring Johnny Carson," NBC, 1989; "Newhart: The Nice Man Cometh," CBS, 1989.

RIGG, DIANA

b. Doncaster, England, July 20, 1938. Striking actress of film, stage and TV who played Emma Peel on "The Avengers" and tried her own mid-seventies sitcom in the mold of "The Mary Tyler Moore Show."
AS A REGULAR: "The Avengers," ABC, 1966-68; "Diana," NBC, 1973-74; "Mystery," PBS, 1989- .
AND: "NET Playhouse: Women Beware Women," NET, 1968; "On Stage: Married Alive," NBC,

1970; "Hollywood Squares," NBC, 1974.

TV MOVIES AND MINISERIES: "G.E. Theatre: In This House of Brede," CBS, 1975; "Hallmark Hall of Fame: Witness for the Prosecution," CBS, 1982; "A Hazard of Hearts," CBS, 1987.

RILEY, JACK

b. Cleveland, OH. Deadpan comic actor who played the world's biggest neurotic, Elliot Carlin, on "The Bob Newhart Show."

AS A REGULAR: "Occassional Wife," NBC, 1966-67; "The Bob Newhart Show," CBS, 1972-78; "The Tim Conway Show," CBS, 1980; "Roxie," CBS, 1987.

AND: "Gomer Pyle, USMC: The Great Talent Hunt," CBS, 1967; "Rowan & Martin's Laugh-In," NBC, 1968; "Hogan's Heroes: At Last-Schultz Knows Something," CBS, 1969; "The Mary Tyler Moore Show: Didn't You Used to Be ... Wait ... Don't Tell Me!," CBS, 1971; "The Mary Tyler Moore Show: Rhoda Morgenstern: Minneapolis to New York," CBS, 1972; "M*A*S*H: Chief Surgeon Who?," CBS, 1972; "Cannon: Catch Me If You Can," CBS, 1973; "Columbo: Candidate for Crime," NBC, 1973; "Kung Fu: The Gunman," ABC, 1974; "The Snoop Sisters: Fear Is a Free Throw," NBC, 1974; "Happy Days: The Deadly Dares," ABC, 1974; "Barnaby Jones: Poisoned Pigeon," CBS, 1975; "Barney Miller: Fear of Flying," ABC, 1976; "Alice: A Call to Arms," CBS, 1976; "The Rockford Files: There's One in Every Port," NBC, 1976; "Diff'rent Strokes: Goodbye, Dolly," NBC, 1978; "Diff'rent Strokes: The New Landlord," NBC, 1979; "Barney Miller: The Counterfeiter," ABC, 1979; "Family Ties: Have Gun, Will Unravel," NBC, 1982; "One Day at a Time: The Travel Agent," CBS, 1983; "Night Court: Wonder Drug," NBC, 1984; "The Love Boat: Honey Beats the Odds," ABC, 1984; "Mama's Boy: Hamlet," NBC, 1988; "Night Court: The Clip Show," NBC, 1989; "Duet: Role Call," FOX, 1989.

RILEY, JEANNINE

b. Madera, CA, 1939. Starlet who played Billie Jo Bradley on "Petticoat Junction."

AS A REGULAR: "Petticoat Junction," CBS, 1963-65; "Hee Haw," CBS, 1969-71; "Dusty's Trail," SYN, 1973.

AND: "Route 66: Lizard's Leg and Owlet's Wing," CBS, 1962; "Wagon Train: The Davey Baxter Story," ABC, 1963; "The Adventures of Ozzie and Harriet: Ozzie & Joe and the Fashion Models," ABC, 1963; "The Virginian: Run Away Home," NBC, 1963; "The Adventures of Ozzie and Harriet: A Message From Kris," ABC, 1965; "Convoy: The Many Colors of Courage," NBC, 1965; "The Smothers Brothers Show: The Girl From R.A.L.P.H.," CBS, 1966; "The Man From UNCLE: The Sort of Do-It-Yourself Dreadful

Affair," NBC, 1966; "The Smothers Brothers Show: I'm in Love with a Mortal," CBS, 1966; "The Wild Wild West: The Night of the Arrow," CBS, 1967; "The Man From UNCLE: The Apple a Day Affair," NBC, 1967; "The Wild Wild West: The Night of the Arrow," CBS, 1967; "Gomer Pyle, USMC: Win-a-Date," CBS, 1969; "Love, American Style: Love and the Big Date," ABC, 1970; "Love, American Style: Love and the Traveling Salesman," ABC, 1971; "James at 16: Queen of the Silver Dollar," NBC, 1978.

RINGWALD, MOLLY

b. Sacramento, CA, February 16, 1968. Film actress ("The Breakfast Club") in some TV; the way her movies are doing at the box office, she should be heading back to the tube any second now.

AS A REGULAR: "The Facts of Life," NBC, 1979-80.

AND: "Diff'rent Strokes: Slumber Party," NBC, 1979; "Tall Tales & Legends: Johnny Appleseed," SHO, 1986; "Late Night with David Letterman," NBC, 1987.

TV MOVIES AND MINISERIES: "Packin' It In," CBS, 1983; "Surviving," ABC, 1985.

RITCHARD, CYRIL

b. 1898, Sydney, Australia; d. 1977. Actor skilled in comic and dramatic roles, best known as Captian Hook opposite Mary Martin's Peter Pan.

AS A GUEST: "Prudential Family Playhouse: Ruggles of Red Gap," CBS, 1951; "Kraft Television Theatre: Mrs. Dane's Defense," NBC, 1951; "Goodyear TV Playhouse: Tresaure Chest," NBC, 1952; "Studio One: Pontius Pilate," CBS, 1952; "Producers Showcase: Peter Pan," NBC, 1955; "Goodyear TV Playhouse: Visit to a Small Planet," NBC, 1955; "Studio One: The Spongers," CBS, 1955; "Producers Showcase: The King and Mrs. Candle," NBC, 1955; "Dearest Enemy," NBC, 1955; "Producers Showcase: Peter Pan," NBC, 1956; "Hallmark Hall of Fame: The Good Fairy," NBC, 1956; "The Steve Allen Show," NBC, 1956; "Producers Showcase: Jack and the Beanstalk," NBC, 1956; "The Last Word," CBS, 1957; "The Patrice Munsel Show," ABC, 1957; "The General Motors 50th Anniversary Show," NBC, 1957; "Dinah Shore Chevy Show," NBC, 1958; "Omnibus: La Perichole," NBC, 1958; "Person to Person," CBS, 1958; "Du Pont Show of the Month: Aladdin," CBS, 1958; "Hallmark Hall of Fame: Hallmark Christmas Tree-Promenade on Christmas Day," NBC, 1958; "Pontiac Star Parade: An Evening with Perry Como," NBC, 1959; "Omnibus: H.M.S. Pinafore," NBC, 1959; "The Steve Allen Show," NBC, 1959; "Pontiac Star Parade: Four for Tonight," NBC, 1960; "Steve Allen

Plymouth Show," NBC, 1960; "Peter Pan," NBC, 1960; "What's My Line?," CBS, 1961; "Bell Telephone Hour," NBC, 1962; "Exploring: The Owl and the Pussycat," NBC, 1962; "The Red Skelton Hour," CBS, 1962; "Stump the Stars," CBS, 1963; "Dr. Kildare: A Sense of Tempo," NBC, 1964; "The Man Who Bought Paradise," CBS, 1965; "The Irregular Verb to Love," NET, 1965; "The Dangerous Christmas of Red Riding Hood," ABC, 1965; "Hans Brinker," NBC, 1969; "NET Playhouse: Foul," NET, 1970; "The Emporer's New Clothes," ABC, 1972; "The Snoop Sisters: The Devil Made Me Do It," NBC, 1974; "Story of the First Christmas Snow," NBC, 1975; "Love, Life, Liberty and Lunch," ABC, 1976.

RITTER, JOHN

b. *Jonathan Ritter, Burbank, CA, September 17, 1948.* Capable light leading man of TV who won an Emmy as Jack Tripper on "Three's Company"; then he took on the semi-dramatic role of San Francisco cop Harry Hooperman.

AS A REGULAR: "The Waltons," CBS, 1972-77; "Three's Company," ABC, 1977-84; "Three's a Crowd," ABC, 1984-85; "Hooperman," ABC, 1987-89.

AND: "Hawaii Five-O: Two Doves and Mr. Hernon," CBS, 1971; "Medical Center: End of the Line," CBS, 1973; "M*A*S*H: Deal Me Out," CBS, 1973; "The Bob Newhart Show: Sorry, Wrong Mother," CBS, 1974; "Kojak: Deliver Us Some Evil," CBS, 1974; "Owen Marshall, Counselor at Law: To Keep and Bear Arms," ABC, 1974; "Barnaby Jones: Price of Terror," CBS, 1975; "The Bob Crane Show: Son of Campus Capers," NBC, 1975; "The Rookies: Reluctant Hero," ABC, 1975; "The Mary Tyler Moore Show: Ted's Wedding," CBS, 1975; "The Streets of San Francisco: Murder by Proxy," ABC, 1975; "Rhoda: Attack on Mr. Right," CBS, 1976; "Hawaii Five-O: Dealer's Choice-Blackmail," CBS, 1977; "The Love Boat: Oh, Dale!," ABC, 1977; "The Tonight Show Starring Johnny Carson," NBC, 1980; "The Love Boat: The Emperor's Fortune," ABC, 1983; "Life with Lucy: Lucy Makes a Hit with John Ritter," ABC, 1986; "Have Faith: The Window," ABC, 1989.

TV MOVIES AND MINISERIES: "The Night That Panicked America," ABC, 1975; "In Love with an Older Woman," CBS, 1982; "Pray TV," ABC, 1982; "Sunset Limousine," CBS, 1983; "Love Thy Neighbor," ABC, 1984; "Letting Go," ABC, 1985; "Unnatural Causes," NBC, 1986; "The Last Fling," ABC, 1987; "Prison for Children," CBS, 1987; "My Brother's Wife," ABC, 1989.

AS EXECUTIVE PRODUCER: "Have Faith," ABC, 1989; "Anything But Love," ABC, 1989- .
* Emmies: 1984.

RITTER, THELMA

b. *Brooklyn, NY, February 14, 1905; d. 1969.* Wisecracking character actress who was always a welcome sight in films ("All About Eve," "Rear Window") and on TV.

AS A GUEST: "Best of Broadway: The Show-Off," CBS, 1955; "Goodyear TV Playhouse: The Catered Affair," NBC, 1955; "The 20th Century-Fox Hour: The Late Christoper Bean," CBS, 1955; "Alfred Hitchcock Presents: The Baby Sitter," CBS, 1956; "U.S. Steel Hour: The Human Pattern," CBS, 1957; "Telephone Time: Plot to Save a Boy," ABC, 1957; "The Jack Paar Show," NBC, 1958; "The Perry Como Show," NBC, 1958; "Arthur Murray Party," NBC, 1959; "G.E. Theatre: Sarah's Laughter," CBS, 1960; "Startime: The Man," NBC, 1960; "Frontier Circus: Journey from Hannibal," CBS, 1961; "Wagon Train: The Madame Sagittarius Story," ABC, 1963; "The Jack Paar Program," NBC, 1964.

RIVERA, CHITA

b. *Dolores Conchita Figuero del Rivero, Washington, D.C., January 23, 1933.* Dancer-actress.

AS A REGULAR: "The New Dick Van Dyke Show," CBS, 1973-74.

AND: "The General Motors 50th Anniversary Show," NBC, 1957; "Dinah Shore Chevy Show," NBC, 1958; "Sid Caesar Special: Tiptoe Through TV," CBS, 1960; "The Ed Sullivan Show," CBS, 1960; "Sid Caesar Special: Variety—World of Show Biz," CBS, 1960; "The Garry Moore Show," CBS, 1960; "The Ed Sullivan Show," CBS, 1960; "Arthur Godfrey Special: The Sounds of New York," CBS, 1963; "The Judy Garland Show," CBS, 1964; "The Outer Limits: The Bellero Shield," ABC, 1964; "The Entertainers," CBS, 1965; "The Jonathan Winters Show," CBS, 1968; "Hollywood Palace," ABC, 1968; "Saturday Night Live with Howard Cosell," ABC, 1975; "Sammy and Company," SYN, 1975.

TV MOVIES AND MINISERIES: "Mayflower Madam," CBS, 1987.

RIVERA, GERALDO

b. *New York City, NY, July 3, 1943.* Grandstanding, self-important reporter-talk show host who never hesitates to make himself more important than whatever story he's covering.

AS A REGULAR: "20/20," ABC, 1978-85; "Geraldo," SYN, 1987- .

AND: "Candid Camera on Wheels," CBS, 1989.
* Emmies: 1980, 1981.

RIVERS, JOAN

b. *Brooklyn, NY, June 8, 1933.* Comedienne.

AS A REGULAR: "The Tonight Show Starring Johnny Carson," NBC, 1983-86; "The Late Show,"

FOX, 1986-87; "The Joan Rivers Show," SYN, 1989- .
AND: "The Tonight Show Starring Johnny Carson," NBC, 1966; "The Ed Sullivan Show," CBS, 1966; "The Ed Sullivan Show," CBS, 1967; "Kraft Music Hall," NBC, 1968; "Personality," NBC, 1969; "Hollywood Squares," NBC, 1970; "The Carol Burnett Show," CBS, 1970; "The Merv Griffin Show," SYN, 1972; "The Flip Wilson Show," NBC, 1972; "Here's Lucy: Lucy and Joan Rivers Do Jury Duty," CBS, 1973; "The Flip Wilson Show," NBC, 1973; "The Mac Davis Show," NBC, 1975; "Hollywood Squares," SYN, 1975; "The Tonight Show Starring Johnny Carson," NBC, 1976; "The Tonight Show Starring Johnny Carson," NBC, 1977; "The Mike Douglas Show," SYN, 1978; "Hollywood Squares," SYN, 1979; "Hollywood Squares," SYN, 1980; "The Mike Douglas Show," SYN, 1980; "Saturday Night Live," NBC, 1983; "The Pat Sajak Show," CBS, 1989; "Later with Bob Costas," NBC, 1989.
AS WRITER-TV MOVIES AND MINISERIES: "The Girl Most Likely to...," ABC, 1973.

RIZZUTO, PHIL
b. New York City, NY, September 25, 1918.
AS A REGULAR: "Down You Go," DUM, 1954-55.

ROBARDS, JASON JR.
b. Chicago, IL, July 26, 1922. Gifted actor who specializes in hard-bitten, principaled types.
AS A GUEST: "Studio One: A Picture in the Paper," CBS, 1955; "Studio One: The Incredible World of Horace Ford," CBS, 1955; "Studio One: 24 Hours to Dawn," CBS, 1957; "Omnibus: Moment of Truth," NBC, 1958; "The Ed Sullivan Show," CBS, 1959; "Playhouse 90: For Whom the Bell Tolls," CBS, 1959; "Du Pont Show of the Month: Billy Budd," CBS, 1959; "Sunday Showcase: People Kill People Sometimes," NBC, 1959; "Westinghouse Presents: That's Where the Town's Going," CBS, 1962; "Bob Hope Chrysler Theatre: One Day in the Life of Ivan Denisovich," NBC, 1963; "Hallmark Hall of Fame: Abe Lincoln in Illinois," NBC, 1964; "The Presidency: A Splendid Misery," CBS, 1964; "Bob Hope Chrysler Theatre: Shipwrecked," NBC, 1966; "ABC Stage '67: Noon Wine," ABC, 1966; "Barbra Streisand Special: Belle of 14th Street," CBS, 1967; "Ghost Story: The Dead We Leave Behind," NBC, 1972; "The House Without a Christmas Tree," CBS, 1972; "Old Faithful," ABC, 1973; "The Thanksgiving Treasure," CBS, 1973; "The Country Girl," NBC, 1974; "The Easter Promise," CBS, 1975; "ABC Theatre: A Moon for the Misbegotten," ABC, 1975; "Addie and the King of Hearts," CBS, 1976; "Thomas Hart Benton," PBS, 1989.

TV MOVIES AND MINISERIES: "Washington: Behind Closed Doors," ABC, 1977; "A Christmas to Remember," CBS, 1978; "Haywire," CBS, 1980; "F.D.R.: The Last Year," NBC, 1980; "The Day After," ABC, 1983; "The Atlanta Child Murders," CBS, 1985; "The Long Hot Summer," NBC, 1985; "Johnny Bull," ABC, 1986; "The Last Frontier," CBS, 1986; "Norman Rockwell's Breaking Home Ties," ABC, 1987; "AT&T Presents: Inherit the Wind," NBC, 1988.

ROBARDS, JASON SR.
b. Hillsdale, MI, December 31, 1892; d. 1963. Character actor and father of Jason Robards.
AS A REGULAR: "Acapulco," NBC, 1961.
AND: "G.E. Theatre: The Coward of Fort Bennett," CBS, 1958; "Studio One: Man Under Glass," CBS, 1958; "Cimarron City: I, the Jury," NBC, 1958; "Cimarron City: To Become a Man," NBC, 1958; "Laramie: Ride Into Darkness," NBC, 1960; "G.E. Theatre: Journey to a Wedding," CBS, 1960; "G.E. Theatre: The Wish Book," CBS, 1961; "The Adventures of Ozzie and Harriet: The Secret Agent," ABC, 1963.

ROBBINS, A
Comic also known as the Banana Man.
AS A GUEST: "The Garry Moore Show," CBS, 1957; "Captain Kangaroo," CBS, 1957; "Captain Kangaroo," CBS, 1958; "The Paul Winchell Show," ABC, 1959; "Music on Ice," NBC, 1960.

ROBERTS, DORIS
b. St. Louis, November 4, 1930. Actress who played Mildred Krebs on "Remington Steele"; also an Emmy winner as a homeless woman on an episode of "St. Elsewhere."
AS A REGULAR: "Angie," ABC, 1979-80; "Maggie," ABC, 1981-82; "Remington Steele," NBC, 1983-87.
AND: "The Defenders: Claire Cheval Died in Boston," CBS, 1964; "The Doctors and the Nurses: The Patient Nurse," CBS, 1965; "The Mary Tyler Moore Show: Phyllis Whips Inflation," CBS, 1975; "Medical Center: Two Against Death," CBS, 1975; "All in the Family: Edith's Night Out," CBS, 1976; "Rhoda: Meet the Levys," CBS, 1976; "The Streets of San Francisco: The Thrill Killers," ABC, 1976; "Barney Miller: Sex Surrogate," ABC, 1977; "Barney Miller: The Sighting," ABC, 1978; "Barney Miller: Wojo's Girl," ABC, 1979; "Barney Miller: Agent Orange," ABC, 1980; "The Love Boat: Trigamist," ABC, 1980; "Alice: Alice's Big Four-Oh!," CBS, 1981; "St. Elsewhere: Cora and Arnie," NBC, 1982; "Cagney & Lacey: Jane Doe #37," CBS, 1983; "The Love Boat: Call Me a Doctor," ABC, 1984; "Cagney & Lacey:

School Daze," CBS, 1988; "Perfect Strangers: Maid to Order," ABC, 1989; "Full House: Granny Tanny," ABC, 1989.

TV MOVIES AND MINISERIES: "Jennifer: A Woman's Story," NBC, 1979; "Another Woman's Child," CBS, 1983; "Ordinary Heroes," ABC, 1986; "Remington Steele: The Steele That Wouldn't Die," NBC, 1987.

* Emmies: 1983.

ROBERTS, PERNELL

b. Waycross, GA, May 18, 1928. Actor who played Adam Cartwright on "Bonanza" and Dr. Trapper John McIntyre.

AS A REGULAR: "Bonanza," NBC, 1959-65; "Trapper John, M.D.," CBS, 1979-86.

AND: "Kraft Television Theatre: Shadow of Suspicion," NBC, 1956; "Gunsmoke: How to Kill a Woman," CBS, 1957; "Sugarfoot: Misfire," ABC, 1957; "Trackdown: The Reward," CBS, 1958; "Have Gun, Will Travel: Hey Boy's Revenge," CBS, 1958; "Shirley Temple's Storybook: Rumpelstiltskin," NBC, 1958; "Dick Powell's Zane Grey Theatre: Utopia, Wyo.," CBS, 1958; "Shirley Temple's Storybook: The Sleeping Beauty," NBC, 1958; "You Don't Say," NBC, 1964; "You Don't Say," NBC, 1965; "The Virginian: The Long Way Home," NBC, 1966; "Gunsmoke: Stranger in Town," CBS, 1967; "The Wild Wild West: The Night of the Firebird," CBS, 1967; "Mission: Impossible: Operation-Heart," CBS, 1967; "The Big Valley: Hunter's Moon," ABC, 1968; "Alias Smith and Jones: Twenty-One Days to Tenstrike," ABC, 1972; "Marcus Welby, M.D.: Tender Comrade," ABC, 1972; "Mission: Impossible: Imitation," CBS, 1973; "Marcus Welby, M.D.: The Day After Forever," ABC, 1973; "Mannix: Little Girl Lost," CBS, 1973; "Hawkins: Candidate for Murder," CBS, 1974; "Police Story: Chief," NBC, 1974; "The Odd Couple: Strike Up the Band-or Else," ABC, 1974; "Police Story: To Steal a Million," NBC, 1975; "Jigsaw John: The Death of the Party," NBC, 1976; "The Streets of San Francisco: Breakup," ABC, 1976; "Quincy: The Two Sides of Truth," NBC, 1977; "Police Woman: Deadline: Death," NBC, 1977; "Barnaby Jones: Testament of Power," CBS, 1977; "Quincy: Death By Good Intentions," NBC, 1978; "The Rockford Files: The House on Willis Avenue," NBC, 1978; "Hotel: Premiere," ABC, 1983.

TV MOVIES AND MINISERIES: "The Silent Gun," ABC, 1969; "San Francisco International," NBC, 1970; "The Bravos," ABC, 1972; "The Adventures of Nick Carter," ABC, 1972; "Dead Man on the Run," ABC, 1975; "The Deadly Tower," NBC, 1975; "The Lives of Jenny Dolan," NBC, 1975; "Best Sellers: Captains and the Kings," NBC, 1976; "The Immigrants," SYN, 1978; "Centennial," NBC,

1978-79; "The Night Rider," ABC, 1979; "Hot Rod," NBC, 1979; "Desperado," NBC, 1987; "Perry Mason: The Case of the All-Star Assassin," NBC, 1989.

ROBERTS, ROY

b. Tampa, FL, March 19, 1900; d. 1975. Character actor who played blustery Captain Huxley on "The Gale Storm Show," blustery banker John Cushing on "The Beverly Hillbillies" and blustery bank president Harrison Cheever on "The Lucy Show."

AS A REGULAR: "The Gale Storm Show," CBS, 1956-59; ABC, 1959-60; "Petticoat Junction," CBS, 1963-64; "The Beverly Hillbillies," CBS, 1964-67; "The Lucy Show," CBS, 1965-68; "Gunsmoke," CBS, 1965-75.

AND: "Ford Theatre: Dr. Jordan," NBC, 1955; "Playhouse 90: Massacre at Sand Creek," CBS, 1956; "The 20th Century-Fox Hour: The Marriage Broker," CBS, 1957; "The Dick Van Dyke Show: Sol and the Sponsor," CBS, 1962; "The Dick Van Dyke Show: My Husband Is Not a Drunk," CBS, 1962; "Lawman: Heritage of Hate," ABC, 1962; "The Andy Griffith Show: Andy on Trial," CBS, 1962; "Bonanza: A Hot Day for a Hanging," NBC, 1962; "The Beverly Hillbillies: The Clampetts in Court," CBS, 1963; "The Twilight Zone: A Kind of a Stopwatch," CBS, 1963; "McHale's Navy: The Day the War Stood Still," ABC, 1963; "The Adventures of Ozzie and Harriet: Dave Takes a Client to Dinner," ABC, 1963; "The Munsters: A Walk on the Mild Side," CBS, 1964; "The Munsters: Family Portrait," CBS, 1964; "My Three Sons: Be My Guest," ABC, 1965; "Green Acres: One of Our Assembly-men Is Missing," CBS, 1966; "The Road West: This Savage Land," NBC, 1966; "Petticoat Junction: The Santa Claus Special," CBS, 1966; "Family Affair: Fancy Free," CBS, 1967; "The Outsider: The Land of the Fox," NBC, 1968; "Petticoat Junction: Love Rears Its Ugly Head," CBS, 1970; "Here's Lucy: Lucy and the Astronauts," CBS, 1971; "Here's Lucy: Lucy Is N.G. as R.N.," CBS, 1974.

TV MOVIES AND MINISERIES: "Now You See It, Now You Don't," NBC, 1968.

ROBERTS, TANYA

b. Bronx, NY, October 15, 1955. Actress who played Charlie's angel Julie Rogers.

AS A REGULAR: "Charlie's Angels," ABC, 1980-81.

TV MOVIES AND MINISERIES: "Pleasure Cove," NBC, 1979; "Mickey Spillane's Murder Me, Murder You," CBS, 1983.

* See also "Charlie's Angels."

ROBERTSON, CLIFF

b. La Jolla, CA, September 9, 1925. Handsome

Oscar-winning actor ("Charly") who won an Emmy for his appearance on a "Bob Hope Chrysler Theatre" episode; now he sells phones and phone service on commercials for AT&T.

AS A REGULAR: "Rod Brown of the Rocket Rangers," CBS, 1953-54; "Robert Montgomery Presents," NBC, 1954; "Falcon Crest," CBS, 1983-84.

AND: "Short Story Drama: A Portrait of General Garrity," NBC, 1952; "Hallmark Hall of Fame: 10,000 Words," NBC, 1952; "Armstrong Circle Theatre: The Use of Dignity," NBC, 1954; "U.S. Steel Hour: A Fair Shake," CBS, 1956; "Kraft Television Theatre: The Big Break," NBC, 1957; "Kraft Television Theatre: Vengeance," NBC, 1957; "Playhouse 90: Natchez," CBS, 1958; "The Untouchables: Underground Railway," ABC, 1959; "Riverboat: End of a Dream," NBC, 1960; "U.S. Steel Hour: The Man Who Knew Tomorrow," CBS, 1960; "The Outlaws: Ballad for a Badman," NBC, 1960; "Here's Hollywood," NBC, 1961; "U.S. Steel Hour: The Two Worlds of Charlie Gordon," CBS, 1961; "G.E. Theatre: The Small Elephants," CBS, 1961; "The Twilight Zone: A Hundred Yards Over the Rim," CBS, 1961; "The Outlaws: The Connie Masters Story," NBC, 1961; "The Dick Powell Show: The Geetas Box," NBC, 1961; "U.S. Steel Hour: Man on the Mountaintop," CBS, 1961; "The Outlaws: The Dark Sunrise of Griff Kincaid," NBC, 1962; "Bus Stop: How Does Charlie Feel?," ABC, 1962; "The Breck Golden Showcase: Saturday's Children," CBS, 1962; "Ben Casey: For the Ladybug, One Dozen Roses," ABC, 1962; "Alcoa Premiere: Second Chance," ABC, 1962; "The Twilight Zone: The Dummy," CBS, 1962; "The Eleventh Hour: The Man Who Came Home Late," NBC, 1963; "The Outer Limits: The Galaxy Being," ABC, 1963; "The Greatest Show on Earth: The Circus Came to Town," ABC, 1963; "Object Is," ABC, 1964; "The Breaking Point: So Many Pretty Girls, So Little Time," ABC, 1964; "Bob Hope Chrysler Theatre: The Meal Ticket," NBC, 1964; "To Tell the Truth," CBS, 1965; "Bob Hope Chrysler Theatre: The Game," NBC, 1965; "Bob Hope Chrysler Theatre: And Baby Makes Five," NBC, 1966; "The Match Game," NBC, 1966; "Batman: Come Back, Shame/It's the Way You Play the Game," ABC, 1966; "ABC Stage '67: The People Trap," ABC, 1967; "Bob Hope Chrysler Theatre: Verdict for Terror," NBC, 1967; "The Match Game," NBC, 1968; "Batman: The Great Escape/The Great Train Robbery," ABC, 1968; "Personality," NBC, 1968; "Bracken's World: Stop Date," NBC, 1969; "American Heritage: Lincoln: Trial by Fire," ABC, 1974; "American Heritage: The Yanks Are Coming," ABC, 1974.

TV MOVIES AND MINISERIES: "The Sunshine Patriot," NBC, 1968; "The Man Without a Country," ABC, 1973; "A Tree Grows in Brooklyn," NBC, 1974; "My Father's House," ABC, 1975; "Return to Earth," ABC, 1976; "Washington: Behind Closed Doors," ABC, 1977; "Overboard," NBC, 1978; "G.E. Theater: Two of a Kind," CBS, 1982; "Dreams of Gold: The Mel Fisher Story," CBS, 1986.

* **Emmies:** 1966.

ROBERTSON, DALE

b. Dayle Robertson, Oklahoma City, OK, July 14, 1923. Rugged leading man who played Wells Fargo troubleshooter Jim Hardie and, more recently, the crime-solving J.J. Starbuck.

AS A REGULAR: "Tales of Wells Fargo," NBC, 1957-62; "The Iron Horse," ABC, 1966-68; "Death Valley Days," SYN, 1968-72; "Dynasty," ABC, 1981; "J.J. Starbuck," NBC, 1987-88.

AND: "Ford Theatre: The Face," NBC, 1956; "Schlitz Playhouse of Stars: Flowers for Jenny," CBS, 1956; "Schlitz Playhouse of Stars: A Tale of Wells Fargo," CBS, 1956; "Climax!: Circle of Destruction," CBS, 1957; "The 20th Century-Fox Hour: The Still Trumpet," CBS, 1957; "The Steve Allen Show," NBC, 1958; "The Perry Como Show," NBC, 1958; "The George Burns Show," NBC, 1958; "The Chevy Show," NBC, 1960; "The Ford Show," NBC, 1960; "The Roy Rogers and Dale Evans Show," ABC, 1962; "Hollywood Palace," ABC, 1964; "The Red Skelton Hour," CBS, 1968; "The Merv Griffin Show," SYN, 1974; "Fantasy Island: Stuntman," ABC, 1979; "The Love Boat: The Oil Man Cometh," ABC, 1980; "Matt Houston: Pilot," ABC, 1982; "Murder, She Wrote: Prediction: Murder," CBS, 1988; "Murder, She Wrote: The Last Flight of the Dizzy Damsel," CBS, 1988.

TV MOVIES AND MINISERIES: "Scalplock," NBC, 1966; "Melvin Purvis, G-Man," ABC, 1974; "The Kansas City Massacre," ABC, 1975; "Return to Earth," CBS, 1976; "The Last Ride of the Dalton Gang," NBC, 1979.

ROBINSON, CHARLES

b. Houston, TX. Actor who played Newdell on "Buffalo Bill" and Mac Robinson on "Night Court."

AS A REGULAR: "Buffalo Bill," NBC, 1983-84; "Night Court," NBC, 1985-86.

AND: "Switch: Go for Broke," CBS, 1977; "The White Shadow: Bonus Baby," CBS, 1978; "Lou Grant: Vet," CBS, 1979; "Hill Street Blues: Pestolozzi's Revenge," NBC, 1982; "St. Elsewhere: Tweety and Ralph," NBC, 1982.

TV MOVIES AND MINISERIES: "Crash Course," NBC, 1988.

ROBINSON, EDWARD G.

b. Emanuel Goldenberg, Bucharest, Hungary, 1893; d. 1973. Screen actor ("Little Caesar,"

"Double Indemnity," "The Cincinnati Kid") who turned to stage and TV work in the fifties.

AS A GUEST: "Lux Video Theatre: Witness for the Prosecution," CBS, 1953; "Climax!: Epitaph for a Spy," CBS, 1954; "For the Defense: The Case of Kenny Jason," SYN, 1954; "Ford Theatre: ... And Son," NBC, 1955; "Ford Theatre: A Set of Values," NBC, 1955; "The Ed Sullivan Show," CBS, 1956; "The $64,000 Question," CBS, 1956; "The Steve Allen Show," NBC, 1957; "Playhouse 90: Shadows Tremble," CBS, 1958; "Goodyear Theatre: A Good Name," NBC, 1959; "This Is Your Life" (Frank Capra), NBC, 1959; "This Is Your Life" (Mervyn LeRoy), NBC, 1959; "Dick Powell's Zane Grey Theatre: Heritage," CBS, 1959; "The Devil and Daniel Webster," NBC, 1960; "The Right Man," CBS, 1960; "G.E. Theatre: The Dropout," CBS, 1961; "Here's Hollywood," NBC, 1961; "Robert Taylor's Detectives: The Legend of Jim Riva," NBC, 1961; "The du Pont Show: Cops and Robbers," NBC, 1962; "Hollywood Palace," ABC, 1965; "Who Has Seen the Wind?," ABC, 1965; "Hollywood Palace," ABC, 1966; "The Lucy Show: Lucy Goes to a Hollywood Premiere," CBS, 1966; "Batman: A Piece of the Action/ Batman's Satisfaction," ABC, 1967; "Bracken's World: The Mary Tree," NBC, 1970; "Night Gallery: The Messiah on Mott Street," NBC, 1971; "Rowan & Martin's Laugh-In," NBC, 1971; "America's Romance with the Land," ABC, 1973.

TV MOVIES AND MINISERIES: "U.M.C.," CBS, 1969; "The Old Man Who Cried Wolf," ABC, 1970.

ROCCO, ALEX

b. Boston, MA, February 29, 1936. Character actor who won an Emmy as craven show-biz agent Al Floss on "The Famous Teddy Z"; he also played the blue-collar father of Jo (Nancy McKeon) on "The Facts of Life."

AS A REGULAR: "Three for the Road," CBS, 1975; "The Facts of Life," NBC, 1981-88; "The Famous Teddy Z," CBS, 1989-90.

AND: "Get Smart: How to Succeed in the Spy Business Without Really Trying," NBC, 1967; "Batman: A Piece of the Action/Batman's Satisfaction," ABC, 1967; "That Girl: Chef's Night Out," ABC, 1970; "The FBI: The Outcast," ABC, 1972; "Portrait: Legend in Granite," ABC, 1973; "Get Christie Love!: Death on Delivery," ABC, 1974; "The Rookies: A Legacy of Death," ABC, 1974; "Kojak: Close Cover Before Killing," CBS, 1975; "Twigs," CBS, 1975; "Police Story: Bought and Paid For," NBC, 1976; "The Mary Tyler Moore Show: Lou's Army Reunion," CBS, 1977; "Police Story: Nightmare on a Sunday Morning," NBC, 1977; "The Rockford Files: The Trees, the Bees and T.T. Flowers," NBC, 1977; "Barnaby Jones: Circle of Treachery," CBS,

1977; "Simon & Simon: Almost Completely Out to Sea," CBS, 1984; "Hardcastle and McCormick: Ties My Father Sold Me," ABC, 1984; "The Love Boat: Seems Like Old Times," ABC, 1984; "The A-Team: The Champ," NBC, 1985; "The Golden Girls: That Was No Lady," NBC, 1985; "Rags to Riches: Vegas Rock," NBC, 1987; "The Pat Sajak Show," CBS, 1989; "Murphy Brown: And the Whiner Is ... ," CBS, 1989.

TV MOVIES AND MINISERIES: "Hustling," ABC, 1975; "Three for the Road," CBS, 1975; "The Blue Knight," CBS, 1975; "Harold Robbins' 79 Park Avenue," NBC, 1977; "The Grass Is Always Greener Over the Septic Tank," CBS, 1978; "Badge of the Assassin," CBS, 1985; "ABC Family Classic: Rock 'n' Roll Mom," ABC, 1989.

ROCHE, EUGENE

b. Boston, MA, September 22, 1928. Heavyset actor who played private eye Luther Gillis on "Magnum, P.I."

AS A REGULAR: "The Corner Bar," ABC, 1973; "Soap," ABC, 1978-81; "Good Time Harry," NBC, 1980; "Webster," ABC, 1984-86; "Take Five," CBS, 1987; "Perfect Strangers," ABC, 1987-88.

AND: "Catholic Hour: In Word and in Song," NBC, 1963; "Profiles in Courage: The Robert Taft Story," NBC, 1965; "Ironside: Down Two Roads," NBC, 1972; "McCloud: This Must Be the Alamo," NBC, 1974; "The Magician: The Illusion of the Deadly Conglomerate," NBC, 1974; "Hawaii Five-O: A Woman's Work Is With a Gun," CBS, 1975; "Kojak: Out of the Frying Pan," CBS, 1975; "Sunshine: Why Sam's Paid," NBC, 1975; "Ellery Queen: The Chinese Dog," NBC, 1975; "Kojak: Acts of Desperate Men," CBS, 1975; "The Streets of San Francisco: The Drop," ABC, 1976; "All in the Family: Beverly Rides Again," CBS, 1976; "All in the Family: The Draft Dodger," CBS, 1976; "Barnaby Jones: The Bounty Hunter," CBS, 1976; "Lou Grant: Hoax," CBS, 1977; "Police Woman: Solitaire," NBC, 1977; "All in the Family: Archie's Other Wife," CBS, 1978; "Hart to Hart: Pilot," ABC, 1979; "Taxi: The Road Not Taken," ABC, 1982; "Magnum, P.I.: Luther Gillis: File #521," CBS, 1983; "Magnum P.I.: The Return of Luther Gillis," CBS, 1984; "Magnum P.I.: Luther Gillis: File #001," CBS, 1984; "Highway to Heaven: Another Kind of War, Another Kind of Peace," NBC, 1985; "Hardcastle and McCormick: Something's Going On On This Train," ABC, 1985; "Murder, She Wrote: Deadline for Murder," CBS, 1986; "Murder, She Wrote: Deadpan," CBS, 1988; "Murder, She Wrote: Something Borrowed, Someone Blue," CBS, 1989.

TV MOVIES AND MINISERIES: "Crawlspace," CBS, 1972; "Crime Club," NBC, 1975; "The Art of Crime," NBC, 1975; "The Winds of Kitty

Hawk," NBC, 1978; "The New Maverick," ABC, 1978; "The Child-Stealer," ABC, 1979; "Love for Rent," ABC, 1979; "Miracle on Ice," ABC, 1981; "Cocaine and Blue Eyes," NBC, 1983.

ROCK, BLOSSOM
b. Blossom MacDonald, Philadelphia, PA, August 21, 1896; d. 1978. Older sister of Jeanette MacDonald; she played Grandmama on "The Addams Family."
AS A REGULAR: "The Addams Family," ABC, 1964-66.
AND: "It's About Time: Mark Your Ballots," CBS, 1966.

ROCKWELL, ROBERT
b. Lake Bluff, IL, October 5, 1921. Actor who played Philip Boynton, the object of Eve Arden's affection on "Our Miss Brooks"; nowadays he plays Wally, husband of Jane Powell on "Growing Pains."
AS A REGULAR: "Our Miss Brooks," CBS, 1952-55; "The Man From Blackhawk," ABC, 1959-60; "Search for Tomorrow," CBS, 1977-78; "Growing Pains," ABC, 1988- .
AND: "The Adventures of Superman: Superman on Earth," SYN, 1951; "Schaefer Century Theatre: Yesterday's World," NBC, 1952; "Campbell TV Soundstage: The Little Pig Cried," NBC, 1952; "Telephone Time: She Sette Her Little Foote," CBS, 1956; "The Millionaire: The Story of Professor Amberson Adams," CBS, 1957; "Private Secretary: The Reunion," CBS, 1957; "Tales of Wells Fargo: The Time to Kill," NBC, 1957; "Meet McGraw: The Texas Story," NBC, 1957; "The Gale Storm Show: The Phantom Valise," CBS, 1957; "The Loretta Young Show: Dear Milkman," NBC, 1958; "SurfSide 6: Odd Job," ABC, 1960; "Death Valley Days: Death Ride," SYN, 1961; "Maverick: Substitute Gun," ABC, 1961; "Perry Mason: The Case of the Misguided Missle," CBS, 1961; "Perry Mason: The Case of the Shapely Shadow," CBS, 1962; "Cheyenne: A Town That Lived and Died," ABC, 1962; "Room for One More: Happiness Is Just a State of Mind," ABC, 1962; "The Lucy Show: Lucy Digs Up a Date," CBS, 1962; "Perry Mason: The Case of the Lurid Letter," CBS, 1962; "Perry Mason: The Case of the Candy Queen," CBS, 1965; "Thompson's Ghost," ABC, 1966; "Petticoat Junction: Spare That Cottage," CBS, 1970; "Lassie: Lassie's Saga," CBS, 1970; "Here's Lucy: The Not-So-Popular Mechanics," CBS, 1973; "Diff'rent Strokes: The Adoption," NBC, 1979; "Eight Is Enough: I Do, I Do, I Do, I Do," ABC, 1979; "Lou Grant: Nightside," CBS, 1980; "Diff'rent Strokes: The Wedding," NBC, 1984; "E/R: Premiere," CBS, 1984; "E/R: Son of Sheinfeld," CBS, 1984; "E/R: Only a Nurse," CBS, 1984; "The Equalizer: The Child Broker,"

CBS, 1988; "Newhart: The Nice Man Cometh," CBS, 1989.

RODD, MARCIA
b. Lyons, KS, July 8, 1940. Actress usually in light roles; she played E.J. Riverside, wife of Stanley (Charles Siebert) on "Trapper John, M.D."
AS A REGULAR: "The David Frost Revue," SYN, 1971-73; "The Dumplings," NBC, 1976; "13 Queens Boulevard," ABC, 1979; "Flamingo Road," NBC, 1981-82; "Trapper John, M.D.," CBS, 1983-86; "The Four Seasons," CBS, 1984.
AND: "All in the Family: Mike's Mysterious Son," CBS, 1972; "All in the Family: Maude," CBS, 1972; "Medical Center: The Torn Man," CBS, 1972; "Barnaby Jones: Fatal Witness," CBS, 1975; "Medical Center: The Captives," CBS, 1975; "Match Game '76," CBS, 1976; "Maude: Walter's Temptation," CBS, 1977; "M*A*S*H: Temporary Duty," CBS, 1978; "Lou Grant: The Samaritan," CBS, 1979; "Lou Grant: Cameras," CBS, 1981; "Bret Maverick: The Yellow Rose," NBC, 1981; "Night Court: Hi Honey, I'm Home," NBC, 1984; "Gimme a Break: Carl's Delicate Moment," NBC, 1984; "Murder, She Wrote: Keep the Home Fries Burning," CBS, 1986; "21 Jump Street: After School Special," FOX, 1987; "Murder, She Wrote: Harbinger of Death," CBS, 1988; "Empty Nest: Harry's Vacation," NBC, 1988.
TV MOVIES AND MINISERIES: "How to Break Up a Happy Divorce," NBC, 1976.

RODGERS, JIMMIE
b. Camas, WA, September 18, 1933. Folksinger ("Kisses Sweeter Than Wine") most popular in the late fifties.
AS A REGULAR: "The Jimmie Rodgers Show," NBC, 1959; "Carol Burnett Presents The Jimmie Rodgers Show," CBS, 1969.
AND: "The Ed Sullivan Show," CBS, 1957; "American Bandstand," ABC, 1957; "Shower of Stars," CBS, 1957; "The Big Record," CBS, 1957; "The Ed Sullivan Show," CBS, 1958; "The Gisele MacKenzie Show," NBC, 1958; "Dinah Shore Chevy Show," NBC, 1958; "The Big Record," CBS, 1958; "Club Oasis," NBC, 1958; "The Dick Clark Saturday Night Beechnut Show," ABC, 1958; "Jimmy Durante Special: Give My Regards to Broadway," NBC, 1959; "The Ford Show," NBC, 1960; "Pat Boone Chevy Showroom," ABC, 1960; "The Dick Clark Saturday Night Beechnut Show," ABC, 1960; "The Chevy Show: Love Is Funny," NBC, 1960; "Here's Hollywood," NBC, 1960; "Art Linkletter's House Party," CBS, 1961; "Checkmate: Melody for Murder," CBS, 1961; "Art Linkletter's House Party," CBS, 1962; "Art Linkletter's House Party," CBS, 1963; "Hootenanny," ABC, 1964; "Shindig," ABC, 1965; "Jimmy Durante Presents The Lennon Sisters

Hour," ABC, 1969; "Barnaby Jones: Murder in the Key of C," CBS, 1980.

RODRIGUEZ, PAUL
b. Mexico. Comedian.
AS A REGULAR: "A.K.A. Pablo," ABC, 1984; "Trial and Error," CBS, 1988; "The Newlywed Game," SYN, 1989- ; "Grand Slam," CBS, 1990.
AND: "The Smothers Brothers Comedy Hour: Ghosts, Governments and Other Scary Things," CBS, 1989; "The Pat Sajak Show," CBS, 1989.

ROGERS, BUDDY
b. Charles Rogers, Olathe, KS, August 13, 1904. Silent-screen star and husband of the late Mary Pickford, occasionally on TV.
AS A REGULAR: "Calvacade of Bands," DUM, 1951.
AND: "This Is Your Life" (Richard Arlen), NBC, 1961; "The Lucy Show: Lucy and Carol Burnett," CBS, 1967; "Petticoat Junction: Wings," CBS, 1968.
* See also Richard Arlen.

ROGERS, GINGER
b. Virginia Katherine McMath, Independence, MO, July 16, 1911. Oscar-winning screen actress and frequent dancing partner of Fred Astaire; she made the TV variety show rounds in the fifties and sixties.
AS A GUEST: "Producers Showcase: Tonight at 8:30-Three by Coward," NBC, 1954; "The Bob Hope Show," NBC, 1956; "The Perry Como Show," NBC, 1957; "The Steve Allen Show," NBC, 1957; "The $64,000 Question," CBS, 1957; "The Jack Benny Program: Ginger Rogers Show," CBS, 1957; "The Perry Como Show," NBC, 1958; "Person to Person," CBS, 1958; "Dinah Shore Chevy Show," NBC, 1958; "Pontiac Star Parade: The Ginger Rogers Show," CBS, 1958; "Pat Boone Chevy Showroom," ABC, 1959; "Pontiac Star Parade: Accent on Love," NBC, 1959; "Dinah Shore Chevy Show," NBC, 1959; "Steve Allen Plymouth Show," NBC, 1960; "Bob Hope Special: Potomac Madness," NBC, 1960; "Bob Hope Buick Show," NBC, 1961; "Dinah Shore Special," NBC, 1961; "I've Got a Secret," CBS, 1962; "Bell Telephone Hour: The Songs of Irving Berlin," NBC, 1962; "Password," CBS, 1962; "Vacation Playhouse: A Love Affair Just for Three," CBS, 1963; "Hollywood Palace," ABC, 1964; "Cinderella," CBS, 1965; "Bob Hope Chrysler Theatre: Terror Island," NBC, 1965; "Bell Telephone Hour: The Music of Jerome Kern," NBC, 1965; "Here's Lucy: Ginger Rogers Comes to Tea," CBS, 1971; "Hollywood Squares," NBC, 1972; "The Dean Martin Show," NBC, 1973; "The Love Boat: Critical Success," ABC, 1979; "Glitter: In Tennis Love Means Nothing," ABC, 1984.

ROGERS, KENNY
b. Houston, TX, August 21, 1937. Country-pop vocalist whose TV work—especially his "Gambler" westerns—has been the visual equivalent of his slick, cliched music.
AS A REGULAR: "Rollin' on the River," SYN, 1971-73.
AND: "The Glen Campbell Goodtime Hour," CBS, 1970; "The Mike Douglas Show," SYN, 1973; "Hee Haw," SYN, 1976; "Christmas in America: A Love Story," NBC, 1989.
TV MOVIES AND MINISERIES: "The Dream Makers," NBC, 1975; "The Gambler," CBS, 1980; "Coward of the County," CBS, 1981; "The Gambler II: The Adventure Continues," CBS, 1983; "Wild Horses," CBS, 1985; "The Gambler III: The Legend Continues," CBS, 1987.

ROGERS, ROY
b. Leonard Slye, Cincinnati, OH, November 5, 1912. Cowboy star who usually appeared with his wife, Dale Evans.
AS A REGULAR: "The Roy Rogers Show," NBC, 1951-57; "The Chevy Show," NBC, 1958-62; "The Roy Rogers and Dale Evans Show," ABC, 1962.
AND: "Cavalcade of America: A Medal for Miss Walker," ABC, 1954; "Bold Journey: I Follow the Western Star," ABC, 1958; "I've Got a Secret," CBS, 1958; "I've Got a Secret," CBS, 1961; "The Beverly Hillbillies: Doctor Jed Clampett," CBS, 1964; "The Fall Guy: King of the Cowboys," ABC, 1984.
WITH DALE EVANS: "This Is Your Life" (Roy Rogers), NBC, 1953; "The Perry Como Show," NBC, 1956; "Dinah Shore Chevy Show," NBC, 1956; "The Perry Como Show," NBC, 1957; "Hollywood Palace," ABC, 1964; "The Andy Williams Show," NBC, 1964; "Bell Telephone Hour," NBC, 1965; "The Tonight Show Starring Johnny Carson," NBC, 1965; "The Andy Williams Show," NBC, 1965; "The Andy Williams Show," NBC, 1966; "Kraft Music Hall," NBC, 1968; "Hollywood Palace," ABC, 1969; "The Ed Sullivan Show," CBS, 1970; "The Jim Nabors Hour," CBS, 1970; "Hee Haw," SYN, 1972; "Music Hall America," SYN, 1977; "Barbara Mandrell and the Mandrell Sisters," NBC, 1981.
* See also Dale Evans.

ROGERS, WAYNE
b. Birmingham, AL, April 7, 1933. Actor who played Trapper John on "M*A*S*H" and Dr. Charley Michaels on "House Calls."
AS A REGULAR: "Search for Tomorrow," CBS, 1959; "Stagecoach West," ABC, 1960-61; "M*A*S*H," CBS, 1972-75; "City of Angels," NBC, 1976; "House Calls," CBS, 1979-82.

AND: "Dick Powell's Zane Grey Theatre: The Lonely Gun," CBS, 1959; "The Millionaire: Millionaire Sylvia Merrick," CBS, 1960; "Law of the Plainsman: Dangeorus Barriers," NBC, 1960; "The Dick Powell Show: The Clocks," NBC, 1962; "Have Gun, Will Travel: The Debutante," CBS, 1963; "Honey West: Invitation to Limbo," ABC, 1965; "Combat!: The Gun," ABC, 1966; "The FBI: The Tormentors," ABC, 1966; "The FBI: The Extortionist," ABC, 1967; "Celebrity Sweepstakes," NBC, 1974; "The Mike Douglas Show," SYN, 1974; "Cher," CBS, 1975; "Dinah!," SYN, 1975; "The Merv Griffin Show," SYN, 1977; "The John Davidson Show," SYN, 1980.

TV MOVIES AND MINISERIES: "Attack on Terror: The FBI Versus the Ku Klux Klan," CBS, 1975; "Having Babies II," ABC, 1977; "Thou Shalt Not Commit Adultery," NBC, 1978; "He's Fired, She's Hired," CBS, 1984; "Lady From Yesterday," CBS, 1985; "I Dream of Jeannie: 15 Years Later," NBC, 1985; "One Terrific Guy," CBS, 1986; "American Harvest," CBS, 1987; "Drop-Out Mother," CBS, 1988; "Bluegrass," CBS, 1988; "Passion and Paradise," ABC, 1989.

ROGERS, WILL JR.

b. New York City, NY, October 20, 1911. Son of humorist Will Rogers and occasional TV actor; also one in a long line of morning-show hosts who tried to unseat NBC's "Today" show.

AS A REGULAR: "Good Morning!," CBS, 1957.

AND: "Ford Theatre: Life, Liberty and Orrin Dooley," NBC, 1952; "Ford Theatre: Lucky Tommy Jordan," NBC, 1954; "Schlitz Playhouse of Stars: Gift of the Devil," CBS, 1954; "Schlitz Playhouse of Stars: Mr. Schoolmarm," CBS, 1955; "Schlitz Playhouse of Stars: A Mule for Santa Fe," CBS, 1955; "Schlitz Playhouse of Stars: On a Dark Night," CBS, 1956; "Bandwagon '56," CBS, 1956; "Thanksgiving Festival of Music," CBS, 1956; "Burke's Law: Who Killed Holly Howard?," ABC, 1963; "The Merv Griffin Show," SYN, 1974.

ROKER, ROXIE

b. Miami, FL, August 28, 1929. Actress who played Helen Willis on "The Jeffersons."

AS A REGULAR: "The Jeffersons," CBS, 1975-85.

AND: "Kojak: Law Dance," CBS, 1976; "$weepstake$: Roscoe, Elizabeth and the MC," NBC, 1979; "Cross Wits," SYN, 1980; "Dance Fever," SYN, 1981; "The John Davidson Show," SYN, 1981; "The Love Boat: The Will," ABC, 1986; "ABC Afterschool Special: The Day My Kid Went Punk," ABC, 1987; "The New Mike Hammer: Mike Gets Married," CBS, 1987.

TV MOVIES AND MINISERIES: "Roots," ABC, 1977; "The Making of a Male Model," ABC, 1983.

ROLLE, ESTHER

b. Pompano, FL; November 8, 1922. Black actress who played Florida Evans on "Maude" and "Good Times"; she left the latter show for a time when Jimmie Walker's buffonish antics began to dominate. An Emmy winner for "Summer of My German Soldier."

AS A REGULAR: "One Life to Live," ABC, 1971; "Maude," CBS, 1972-74; "Good Times," CBS, 1974-77, 1978-79; "Singer & Sons," NBC, 1990.

AND: "Hollywood Squares," SYN, 1975; "The New Odd Couple: Pilot," ABC, 1982; "The Love Boat: I Like to Be in America," ABC, 1983; "Murder, She Wrote: Reflections of the Mind," CBS, 1985; "The Love Boat: Daughter's Dilemma," ABC, 1985.

TV MOVIES AND MINISERIES: "Summer of My German Soldier," NBC, 1978; "I Know Why the Caged Bird Sings," CBS, 1979.

* Emmies: 1979.

ROLLINS, HOWARD E. JR.

b. Baltimore, MD, October 17, 1952. Actor who plays Virgil Tibbs on "In the Heat of the Night."

AS A REGULAR: "Another World," NBC, 1982; "Wildside," ABC, 1985; "In the Heat of the Night," NBC, 1988- .

TV MOVIES AND MINISERIES: "King," NBC, 1978; "Roots: The Next Generations," ABC, 1979; "Johnnie Mae Gibson: FBI," CBS, 1986; "A Doctor's Story," NBC, 1984; "He's Fired, She's Hired," CBS, 1984; "The Children of Times Square," ABC, 1986.

ROMAN, LULU

b. Dallas, TX, 1947. Heavyset comic actress.

AS A REGULAR: "Hee Haw," CBS, 1969-71; SYN, 1971- ; "Hee Haw Honeys," SYN, 1978-79.

ROMAN, RUTH

b. Boston, MA, December 22, 1924. Fifties film actress who's done some TV, including two prime-time soaps; she played Sylvia Lean on "Knots Landing."

AS A REGULAR: "The Long Hot Summer," ABC, 1965-66; "Knots Landing," CBS, 1986.

AND: "Story Theatre: Mme. Fifi," NBC, 1951; "Lux Video Theatre: The Chase," NBC, 1954; "Ford Theatre: The Lilac Bush," NBC, 1955; "Producers Showcase: Darkness at Noon," NBC, 1955; "G.E. Theatre: Into the Night," CBS, 1955; "Climax!: Spin Into Darkness," CBS, 1956; "Ford Theatre: Panic," NBC, 1956; "The Jane Wyman Show: He Came for the Money," NBC, 1958; "Bonanza: Magnificent Adah," NBC, 1959; "Arthur Murray Party," NBC, 1959; "The Phildelphia Story," NBC, 1959; "G.E. Theatre: The Book of Silence," CBS, 1960; "Naked City: The Human Trap," ABC, 1960; "The Untouchables: Man Killer," ABC, 1961; "Bus Stop: Turn

Again Home," ABC, 1962; "The Defenders: The Voices of Death," CBS, 1962; "The Alfred Hitchcock Hour: What Really Happened?," CBS, 1963; "Sam Benedict: Green Room, Gray Morning," NBC, 1963; "The Eleventh Hour: Advice to the Lovelorn and Shopworn," NBC, 1963; "Route 66: In the Closing of a Trunk," CBS, 1963; "The Greatest Show on Earth: Silent Love, Secret Love," ABC, 1963; "Burke's Law: Who Killed Harris Crown?," ABC, 1963; "Dr. Kildare: Four Feet in the Morning," NBC, 1963; "The Eleventh Hour: Four Feet in the Morning," NBC, 1963; "The Breaking Point: Who Is Mimi—What Is She?," ABC, 1963; "Bob Hope Chrysler Theatre: The Candidate," NBC, 1963; "The Outer Limits: Moonstone," ABC, 1964; "Dr. Kildare: A Candle in the Window," NBC, 1964; "The Bing Crosby Show: Real Estate Venture," ABC, 1965; "The FBI: The Courier," ABC, 1967; "I Spy: Let's Kill Karlovassi," NBC, 1967; "Gunsmoke: Coreyville," CBS, 1969; "The Name of the Game: Witness," NBC, 1968; "Mission: Impossible: The Elixer," CBS, 1968; "The Outsider: The Town That Wouldn't," NBC, 1969; "Gunsmoke: Coreyville," CBS, 1969; "Marcus Welby, M.D.: Diagnosis: Fear," ABC, 1969; "Crisis," CBS, 1970; "Mannix: The Judas Touch," CBS, 1971; "The Men From Shiloh: The Angus Killer," NBC, 1971; "Gunsmoke: Waste," CBS, 1971; "Ironside: Gentle Oaks," NBC, 1971; "The Mod Squad: Belinda-End of Little Miss Bubble Gum," ABC, 1972; "Cops," CBS, 1973; "Faraday and Company: Premiere," NBC, 1973; "Hec Ramsey: The Hard Road to Vengeance," NBC, 1973; "Police Woman: Disco Killer," NBC, 1977; "Murder, She Wrote: If It's Thursday, It Must Be Beverly," CBS, 1987; "Murder, She Wrote: Sins of Castle Cove," CBS, 1989.

TV MOVIES AND MINISERIES: "The Old Man Who Cried Wolf," ABC, 1970; "Incident in San Francisco," ABC, 1971; "Go Ask Alice," ABC, 1973; "Punch and Jody," NBC, 1974.

ROMERO, CESAR

b. *New York City, NY, February 15, 1907.*
Suave screen actor to one generation of Americans; the Joker to another.

AS A REGULAR: "Your Chevrolet Showroom," ABC, 1953-54; "Passport to Danger," SYN, 1954-56; "Take a Good Look," ABC, 1959-60; "Batman," ABC, 1966-68; "Falcon Crest," CBS, 1985-87.

AND: "Bigelow Theatre: The Big Hello," CBS, 1951; "Campbell TV Soundstage: The Cavorting Statue," NBC, 1952; "Schlitz Playhouse of Stars: Tango," CBS, 1952; "Mr. Lucky at Seven: A Letter From Home," ABC, 1952; "Ford Theatre: All's Fair in Love," NBC, 1953; "Pepsi Cola Playhouse: The Police Arrive," ABC, 1954; "Climax!: The Long Goodbye," CBS, 1954; "The Lucille Ball-Desi Arnaz Show: Lucy Takes a

Cruise to Havana," CBS, 1957; "The Gisele MacKenzie Show," NBC, 1957; "The Ford Show," NBC, 1958; "Wagon Train: The Honorable Don Charlie Story," NBC, 1958; "The Patrice Munsel Show," ABC, 1958; "What's My Line?," CBS, 1958; "Zorro: The Gay Caballero," ABC, 1959; "Keep Talking," CBS, 1959; "Zorro: The Legend of Zorro," ABC, 1959; "The Ford Show," NBC, 1959; "The Red Skelton Show," CBS, 1959; "Dinah Shore Chevy Show," NBC, 1959; "The Texan: South of the Border," CBS, 1959; "Arthur Murray Party," NBC, 1959; "John Gunther's High Road: Cuba," ABC, 1959; "Death Valley Days: Olvera," SYN, 1959; "Rawhide: Incident of the Stalking Death," CBS, 1959; "Love and Marriage: Jealousy," NBC, 1960; "Dick Powell's Zane Grey Theatre: The Reckoning," CBS, 1960; "The Betty Hutton Show: Goldie Falls in Love," CBS, 1960; "The Red Skelton Show: San Fernando's Marriage Mill," CBS, 1960; "The Red Skelton Show: Deadeye and the Alamo," CBS, 1961; "Dick Powell's Zane Grey Theatre: The Man From Everywhere," CBS, 1961; "Stagecoach West: The Big Gun," ABC, 1961; "The du Pont Show: The Battle of the Paper Bullets," NBC, 1961; "Beachcomber: The Spaniard," SYN, 1962; "Target: The Corruptors: My Native Land," ABC, 1962; "Follow the Sun: A Ghost in Her Gazebo," ABC, 1962; "Burke's Law: Who Killed Snooky Martinelli?," ABC, 1964; "Object Is," ABC, 1964; "Dr. Kildare: Onions, Garlic and Flowers That Bloom in the Spring," NBC, 1964; "Burke's Law: Who Killed Don Pablo?," ABC, 1964; "Burke's Law: Who Killed Davidian Jones?," ABC, 1964; "Bonanza: The Deadliest Game," NBC, 1965; "Burke's Law: Who Killed the Rest?," ABC, 1965; "T.H.E. Cat: Queen of Diamonds, Knave of Hearts," NBC, 1967; "Art Linkletter's House Party," CBS, 1967; "Get Smart: The Reluctant Redhead," NBC, 1968; "Here's Lucy: A Date for Lucy," CBS, 1969; "The Merv Griffin Show," CBS, 1970; "It Takes a Thief: Beyond a Treasonable Doubt," ABC, 1970; "Julia: Half Past Sick," NBC, 1970; "Bewitched: Salem, Here We Come," ABC, 1970; "Alias Smith and Jones: The McCreedy Bust," ABC, 1971; "Nanny and the Professor: The Man Who Came to Pasta," ABC, 1971; "Love, American Style: Love and the Duel," ABC, 1971; "Night Gallery: A Matter of Semantics," NBC, 1971; "O'Hara, U.S. Treasury: Operation: Mr. Felix," CBS, 1972; "Alias Smith and Jones: The McCreedy Bust: Going, Going, Gone," ABC, 1972; "The Mod Squad: The Connection," ABC, 1972; "Alias Smith and Jones: The McCreedy Feud," ABC, 1972; "Chase: A Bit of Class," NBC, 1973; "Banacek: The Vanishing Chalice," NBC, 1974; "Ironside: The Last Cotillion," NBC, 1974; "Medical Center: The High Cost of Winning," CBS, 1975; "Chico and the Man:

Chico's Padre," NBC, 1977; "Buck Rogers in the 25th Century: Vegas in Space," NBC, 1979; "Matt Houston: Who Would Kill Ramona?," ABC, 1982; "Fantasy Island: The Butler's Affair," ABC, 1983; "The Love Boat: Authoress, Authoress," ABC, 1984; "The Love Boat: Love in a Vacuum," ABC, 1985; "Magnum P.I.: Little Games," CBS, 1985; "Riptide: Arrivederci, Baby," NBC, 1985; "Half-Nelson: The Deadly Vase," NBC, 1985; "Murder, She Wrote: Paint Me a Murder," CBS, 1985; "Blacke's Magic: Ten Tons of Trouble," NBC, 1986; "The Tracey Ullman Show: Tell and Kiss," FOX, 1988.

ROONEY, ANDREW

b. Albany, NY, January 14, 1919.
AS A REGULAR: "60 Minutes," CBS, 1978- .
* Rooney wrote material for Arthur Godfrey and Garry Moore in the fifties and sixties and began writing for CBS news in the sixties.
* Emmies: 1969, 1979, 1981, 1982.

ROONEY, MICKEY

b. Joe Yule Jr., Brooklyn, NY, September 23, 1920. Pint-sized actor in comic and serious roles, not to mention knocking himself out on variety shows; he won an Emmy for his touching, unhammy performance as the mildly retarded "Bill."
AS A REGULAR: "The Mickey Rooney Show," NBC, 1954-55; "Mickey," ABC, 1964-65; "NBC Follies," NBC, 1973; "One of the Boys," NBC, 1982; "The Adventures of the Black Stallion," FAM, 1990- .
AND: "Celanese Theatre: Saturday's Children," ABC, 1952; "The Steve Allen Show," NBC, 1956; "The George Gobel Show," NBC, 1956; "Schlitz Playhouse of Stars: The Lady Was a Flop," CBS, 1957; "The Red Skelton Show," CBS, 1957; "Playhouse 90: The Comedian," CBS, 1957; "The Perry Como Show," NBC, 1957; "The Steve Allen Show," NBC, 1957; "I've Got a Secret," CBS, 1957; "Arthur Murray Party," NBC, 1957; "Mr. Broadway," CBS, 1957; "Pinocchio," NBC, 1957; "The Ed Sullivan Show," CBS, 1957; "Person to Person," CBS, 1958; "December Bride: Mickey Rooney Show," CBS, 1958; "The Ed Sullivan Show," CBS, 1958; "Alcoa Theatre: Eddie," NBC, 1958; "The Red Skelton Show: George's Band," CBS, 1959; "Wagon Train: The Greenhorn Story," NBC, 1959; "Startime: The Dean Martin Show," NBC, 1959; "Steve Allen Plymouth Show," NBC, 1959; "The Jack Paar Show," NBC, 1959; "Mickey Rooney Special," CBS, 1960; "This Is Your Life" (Billy Barty), NBC, 1960; "Revlon Revue: The Many Sides of Mickey Rooney," CBS, 1960; "Wagon Train: Wagons Ho!," NBC, 1960; "The Ed Sullivan Show," CBS, 1960; "Here's Hollywood," NBC, 1960; "G.E. Theatre: The Money Driver," CBS, 1960; "The Jackie Gleason Show," CBS, 1961; "Checkmate: The Paper Killer," CBS, 1961; "Hennesey: Shore Patrol Revisited," CBS, 1961; "The Ed Sullivan Show," CBS, 1961; "The Dick Powell Show: Who Killed Julie Greer?," NBC, 1961; "The Investigators: I Thee Kill," CBS, 1961; "The Dick Powell Show: Somebody's Waiting," NBC, 1961; "Naked City: Ooftus Gooftus," ABC, 1961; "Candid Camera," CBS, 1961; "The Ed Sullivan Show," CBS, 1962; "Frontier Circus: Calamity Circus," CBS, 1962; "The Dick Powell Show: Special Assignment," NBC, 1962; "Stump the Stars," CBS, 1962; "The Andy Williams Show," NBC, 1962; "The Dick Powell Show: Everybody Loves Sweeney," NBC, 1963; "Alcoa Premiere: Five, Six, Pick Up Sticks," ABC, 1963; "The Red Skelton Hour," CBS, 1963; "The Twilight Zone: The Last Night of a Jockey," CBS, 1963; "The Judy Garland Show," CBS, 1963; "Kraft Suspense Theatre: The Hunt," NBC, 1963; "Hollywood Palace," ABC, 1964; "Bob Hope Chrysler Theatre: Kicks," NBC, 1965; "The Fugitive: This'll Kill You," ABC, 1966; "The Lucy Show: Lucy Meets Mickey Rooney," CBS, 1966; "The Jean Arthur Show: Pilot," CBS, 1966; "Hollywood Palace," ABC, 1967; "The Jackie Gleason Show," CBS, 1969; "Hollywood Squares," NBC, 1970; "The Red Skelton Hour," CBS, 1970; "The Name of the Game: Cynthia Is Alive and Living in Avalon," NBC, 1970; "The Tonight Show Starring Johnny Carson," NBC, 1970; "The Tim Conway Show," CBS, 1970; "Santa Claus Is Coming to Town," ABC, 1970; "Hollywood Squares," NBC, 1970; "Dan August: The Manufactured Man," ABC, 1971; "Night Gallery: Rare Objects," NBC, 1972; "The Love Boat: The Christmas Presence," ABC, 1982; "The Golden Girls: Larceny and Old Lace," NBC, 1987.
TV MOVIES AND MINISERIES: "Evil Roy Slade," NBC, 1972; "Leave 'Em Laughing," CBS, 1981; "Bill," CBS, 1981; "Senior Trip!," NBC, 1981; "Bill: On His Own," CBS, 1983; "Disney Sunday Movie: The Little Spies," ABC, 1986; "The Return of Mickey Spillane's Mike Hammer," CBS, 1986; "Bluegrass," CBS, 1988.
* Rooney probably wasn't the first celebrity to turn up drunk on a talk show, but his 1959 encounter with Jack Paar made nationwide headlines. TV Guide reported that Rooney and Paar traded insults as the audience gasped, and later Paar got his last licks in: "It's a shame—he used to be such a great talent."
* Emmies: 1982.

RORKE, HAYDEN

b. Brooklyn, NY, October 23, 1910; d. 1987. Character actor who played Dr. Bellows on "I Dream of Jeannie."
AS A REGULAR: "Mr. Adams and Eve," CBS, 1957-58; "No Time for Sergeants," ABC,

1964-65; "I Dream of Jeannie," NBC, 1965-70.
AND: "I Love Lucy: New Neighbors," CBS, 1952;
"West Point: The Right to Choose," CBS, 1956;
"Schlitz Playhouse of Stars: The Night They Won
the Oscar," CBS, 1956; "Schlitz Playhouse of
Stars: The Lady Was a Flop," CBS, 1957; "The
George Burns and Gracie Allen Show: The
Aptitude Test," CBS, 1957; "The Thin Man:
Scene of the Crime," NBC, 1958; "Perry Mason:
The Case of the Flighty Father," CBS, 1960;
"Riverboat: No Bridge on the River," NBC, 1960;
"Dante: Don't Come On a My House," NBC,
1961; "The Jack Benny Program: Jack Goes to
Vault," CBS, 1961; "My Sister Eileen: The
Perfect Secretary," CBS, 1961; "The Twilight
Zone: A Penny for Your Thoughts," CBS, 1961;
"Harrigan and Son: The Magnificent Borough,"
ABC, 1961; "The Brothers Brannagan: She's
Leaving," SYN, 1961; "Perry Mason: The Case of
the Violent Vest," CBS, 1961; "Dr. Kildare:
Winter Harvest," NBC, 1961; "Dr. Kildare:
Season to Be Jolly," NBC, 1961; "Cheyenne:
Beginner's Luck," ABC, 1962; "Bonanza: The
Lady From Baltimore," NBC, 1962; "The Donna
Reed Show: The Baby Buggy," ABC, 1962;
"Walt Disney's Wonderful World of Color:
Johnny Shiloh," NBC, 1963; "The Beverly
Hillbillies: Jethro's Friend," CBS, 1963; "The
Adventures of Ozzie and Harriet: Publicity for the
Fraternity," ABC, 1963; "The Andy Griffith
Show: The Taylors in Hollywood," CBS, 1965;
"Here's Lucy: Lucy and the Raffle," CBS, 1971;
"Hizzonner: Mr. Perfect," NBC, 1979.
TV MOVIES AND MINISERIES: "The Moneychangers,"
NBC, 1976; "Best Sellers: Once an Eagle,"
NBC, 1977; "Suddenly, Love," NBC, 1978; "I
Dream of Jeannie: 15 Years Later," NBC,
1985.

ROSATO, TONY
b. Italy, December 26, 1954. Comic actor.
AS A REGULAR: "Second City TV," SYN, 1980-81;
"Saturday Night Live," NBC, 1981-82;
"Amanda's," ABC, 1983; "Night Heat," CBS,
1985- ; "Diamonds," CBS, SYN, 1987- .
TV MOVIES AND MINISERIES: "Hands of a Stranger,"
NBC, 1987.

ROSE, JAMIE
b. New York City, NY, November 26, 1959.
Actress who played tough cop Katy Mahoney,
who would run out of a beauty parlor to gun down
bad guys on "Lady Blue," one of the dumbest
shows ever on ABC—and that's saying a lot.
AS A REGULAR: "Falcon Crest," CBS, 1981-83;
"Lady Blue," ABC, 1985-86; "St. Elsewhere,"
NBC, 1987.
AND: "Jessie: Flesh Wounds," ABC, 1984; "Duet:
Fugue," FOX, 1987; "The Hogan Family: Dad's
First Date," NBC, 1988; "Murder, She Wrote:
Snow White, Blood Red," CBS, 1988; "My Two

Dads: Say Goodnight, Gracie," NBC, 1989.
TV MOVIES AND MINISERIES: "In Love with an Older
Woman," CBS, 1982; "Flight #90: Disaster on
the Potomac," NBC, 1984; "Lady Blue," ABC,
1985.

ROSE, JANE
b. Spokane, WA, February 7, 1912; d. 1979.
Actress who played Audrey Dexter, Cloris
Leachman's TV mother-in-law on "Phyllis."
AS A REGULAR: "Love of Life," CBS, 1951-56;
"The Wonderful John Action," NBC, 1953;
"Phyllis," CBS, 1975-77; "Co-ed Fever," CBS,
1979.
AND: "Kraft Television Theatre: Most Blessed
Woman," NBC, 1957; "Suspicion: The Woman
Turned to Salt," NBC, 1958; "True Story: The
Diamond M," NBC, 1958; "U.S. Steel Hour: Flint
and Fire," CBS, 1958; "Dillinger: A Year to Kill,"
CBS, 1960; "Shirley Temple's Storybook:
Madeline," NBC, 1960; "The Defenders: The
Seven-Hundred-Year-Old Gang," CBS, 1964;
"The Doctors and the Nurses: Night of the
Witch," CBS, 1965; "All in the Family: Edith's
Friend," CBS, 1975; "Lou Grant: Murder," CBS,
1978; "Rhoda: In Search of Martin," CBS, 1978.
TV MOVIES AND MINISERIES: "Roots: The Next
Generations," ABC, 1979.

ROSS, DIANA
b. Detroit, MI, March 26, 1944. Singer-actress,
formerly leader of The Supremes.
AS A GUEST: "The Ed Sullivan Show," CBS, 1968;
"Tarzan: The Convert," NBC, 1968; "Bing
Crosby Special," NBC, 1968; "Dinah Shore
Special," NBC, 1969; "Rowan & Martin's
Laugh-In," NBC, 1969.

ROSS, JOE E.
b. New York City, NY, March 15, 1905; d.
1982. Round-faced, stocky character actor
usually in comic roles in which he could say,
"Ooo! Ooo!"; he played Sgt. Rupert Ritzik on
"The Phil Silvers Show" and Off. Gunther
Toody on "Car 54, Where Are You?"
AS A REGULAR: "The Phil Silvers Show (You'll
Never Get Rich)," CBS, 1955-59; "Car 54,
Where Are You?," NBC, 1961-63; "It's About
Time," CBS, 1966-67; "Hong Kong Phooey,"
ABC, 1974-76.
AND: "The Ed Sullivan Show," CBS, 1958; "Perry
Como's Kraft Music Hall," NBC, 1959;
"Goodyear Theatre: Hello Charlie," NBC, 1959;
"Phil Silvers Special: Summer in New York,"
CBS, 1960; "Perry Como's Kraft Music Hall,"
NBC, 1962; "Art Linkletter's House Party," CBS,
1962; "Batman: The Funny Feline Felonies/The
Joke's on Catwoman," ABC, 1967; "The Ed
Sullivan Show," CBS, 1968; "Love, American
Style: Love and the Sexpert," ABC, 1973; "When

Things Were Rotten: Quarantine," ABC, 1975.
TV MOVIES AND MINISERIES: "Getting Away From It
All," ABC, 1972.
* See also Steve Rossi.

ROSS, KATHARINE
b. *Hollywood, CA, January 29, 1943.* Attractive
actress who did some sixties television before
moving on to films ("The Graduate," "Butch
Cassidy and the Sundance Kid") toward the end
of the decade; she played Francesca Scott Colby
Hamilton Langdon.
AS A REGULAR: "The Colbys," ABC, 1985-87.
AND: "Sam Benedict: A Split Week in San
Quentin," NBC, 1962; "Kraft Suspense Theatre:
Are There Any More Out There Like You?," NBC,
1963; "The Lieutenant: Fall From a White Horse,"
NBC, 1963; "The Alfred Hitchcock Hour: The
Dividing Wall," CBS, 1963; "The Virginian: Dark
Challenge," NBC, 1964; "The Big Valley: Winner
Loses All," ABC, 1965; "The Loner: Widow on
the Evening Stage," CBS, 1965; "Mr. Novak:
Faculty Follies," NBC, 1965; "Great Bible
Adventures: Seven Rich Years ... and Seven Lean,"
ABC, 1966; "ABC Afterschool Special: Tattle:
When to Tell on a Friend," ABC, 1988.
TV MOVIES AND MINISERIES: "The Longest Hundred
Miles," NBC, 1967; "Wanted: The Sundance
Woman," ABC, 1976; "Murder by Natural
Causes," CBS, 1979; "Murder in Texas," NBC,
1981; "The Shadow Riders," CBS, 1982;
"Travis McGee," ABC, 1983; "Secrets of a
Mother and Daughter," CBS, 1983.

ROSS, MARION
b. *Albert Lea, MN, October 25, 1928.* Motherly
actress who played mom Marion Cunningham
on "Happy Days."
AS A REGULAR: "Life with Father," CBS, 1953-55;
"The Gertrude Berg Show (Mrs. G. Goes to
College)," CBS, 1961; "Mr. Novak," NBC,
1963-64; "Paradise Bay," NBC, 1965-66;
"Happy Days," ABC, 1974-84;
AND: "Buckskin: Hunter's Moon," NBC, 1958;
"Steve Canyon: Operation Zero Launch," NBC,
1958; "M Squad: High School Bride," NBC,
1959; "The Donna Reed Show: Flowers for the
Teacher," ABC, 1960; "G.E. Theatre: Sarah's
Laughter," CBS, 1960; "Thriller: The Prisoner in
the Mirror," NBC, 1961; "Route 66: 1800 Days to
Justice," CBS, 1962; "The Brothers Brannagan:
Duet," SYN, 1962; "Channing: Exercise in a Shark
Tank," ABC, 1963; "The Outer Limits: The
Special One," ABC, 1964; "Mr. Novak: An
Elephant Is Like a Tree," NBC, 1965; "The
Fugitive: Trial by Fire," ABC, 1965; "The Brady
Bunch: Is There a Doctor in the House?," ABC,
1969; "Mannix: Return to Summer Grove," CBS,
1969; "Hawaii Five-O: Blind Tiger," CBS, 1969;
"Hawaii Five-O: AOR Cargo-Dial for Murder,"
CBS, 1971; "Love, American Style: Love and

the Happy Day," ABC, 1972; "Marcus Welby,
M.D.: He Could Sell Iceboxes to Eskimos," ABC,
1972; "Mannix: A Problem of Innocence," CBS,
1973; "Emergency!: Inheritance Tax," NBC,
1973; "Break the Bank," SYN, 1977; "The Love
Boat: Kin Folk," ABC, 1979; "Joanie Loves
Chachi: Who Gives a Hootenanny?," ABC,
1982; "The Love Boat: Picture From the Past,"
ABC, 1985; "The Love Boat: The Second Time
Around," ABC, 1986; "The Love Boat: Hello,
Emily," ABC, 1986; "Night Court: The Trouble
Is Not in Your Set," NBC, 1989; "Sister Kate:
The Nun," NBC, 1989; "Living Dolls: And
I Thought Modeling Was Hard," ABC,
1989.
TV MOVIES AND MINISERIES: "Any Second Now,"
NBC, 1969; "The Psychiatrist: God Bless the
Children," NBC, 1970; "Pearl," ABC, 1978;
"Survival of Dana," CBS, 1979; "Sins of the
Father," NBC, 1985.

ROSSI, STEVE
Singer who was teamed for a time with Marty
Allen; for their joint credits, see Allen.
AS A GUEST: "Lawrence Welk's Top Tunes and
New Talent," ABC, 1957; "Art Linkletter's
House Party," CBS, 1958; "The Mike Douglas
Show," SYN, 1968; "The Ed Sullivan Show,"
CBS, 1968; "The Merv Griffin Show," SYN,
1969.
* Rossi and Marty "Hello Dere!" Allen broke up
in 1968, and Rossi formed a comedy team for a
time with Joe E. "Ooo! Ooo!" Ross. Then in
1969, he formed a team with Slappy White.

ROTH, LILLIAN
b. *Lillian Rutstein, Boston, MA, December 13,
1910; d. 1980.* Singer of the thirties whose
career crashed due to personal problems; her
career revived slightly in the fifties after she
appeared on "This Is Your Life," wrote her
autobiography, "I'll Cry Tomorrow," and it was
made into a movie with Susan Hayward.
AS A GUEST: "This Is Your Life," NBC, 1953; "U.S.
Steel Hour: Outcast," CBS, 1955; "Playhouse
90: Child of Trouble," CBS, 1957; "Mike
Wallace Interviews," ABC, 1958; "The Ed
Sullivan Show," CBS, 1958; "Witness: Dutch
Schultz," CBS, 1960.

ROUNDTREE, RICHARD
b. *New Rochelle, NY, September 7, 1942.* Actor
who was a smash as "Shaft" in the movies, less
so on TV; still, he keeps busy.
AS A REGULAR: "Shaft," CBS, 1973-74; "Outlaws,"
CBS, 1986-87; "Generations," NBC, 1990- .
AND: "Hollywood Squares," SYN, 1975; "Freedom
Is," SYN, 1976; "The Love Boat: The Affair,"
ABC, 1979; "Magnum, P.I.: Black on White,"
CBS, 1983; "Murder, She Wrote: The Last Flight

of the Dizzy Damsel," CBS, 1988; "Cadets," ABC, 1988; "ABC Afterschool Special: Daddy Can't Read," ABC, 1989; "Amen: Thelma and the D.I.," NBC, 1989; "A Different World: Great Expectations," NBC, 1989; "Amen: Sergeant in Arms," NBC, 1989.
TV MOVIES AND MINISERIES: "Firehouse," ABC, 1973; "Roots," ABC, 1977; "A.D.," NBC, 1985; "The Fifth Missile," NBC, 1986.

ROUNTREE, MARTHA
b. Gainesville, FL, 1916.
AS A REGULAR: "Leave It to the Girls," NBC, 1949-51; ABC, 1953-54; "Keep Posted," DUM, 1951-53; "The Big Issue," DUM, 1953.
AS PRODUCER-CREATOR: "Leave It to the Girls," NBC, 1949-51; ABC, 1953-54.

ROWAN, DAN
b. Beggs, OK, July 2, 1922; d. 1987. Comedian who was co-host of one of the sixties' most popular shows.
AS A REGULAR: "The Chevy Show," NBC, 1958; "The Dean Martin Summer Show," NBC, 1966; "Rowan & Martin's Laugh-In," NBC, 1968-73.
AND: "The Lucy Show: Lucy and Carol in Palm Springs," CBS, 1966; "The Lucy Show: Mainstreet USA/Lucy Puts Main Street on the Map," CBS, 1967; "It Takes Two," NBC, 1969; "Celebrity Sweepstakes," NBC, 1974; "Celebrity Sweepstakes," NBC, 1975; "The Love Boat: Masquerade," ABC, 1978.
WITH DICK MARTIN: "The Walter Winchell Show," NBC, 1956; "The Bob Hope Show," NBC, 1957; "The Perry Como Show," NBC, 1957; "Jerry Lewis Special," NBC, 1957; "The Perry Como Show," NBC, 1958; "The Perry Como Show," NBC, 1959; "Chevy Show Special," NBC, 1959; "The Chevy Show," NBC, 1959; "The Ed Sullivan Show," CBS, 1960; "Art Linkletter's House Party," CBS, 1960; "Here's Hollywood," NBC, 1961; "The Ed Sullivan Show," CBS, 1961; "Art Linkletter's House Party," CBS, 1961; "The Ed Sullivan Show," CBS, 1962; "The Mike Douglas Show," SYN, 1964; "Hollywood Palace," ABC, 1964; "Hollywood Palace," ABC, 1965; "The Ed Sullivan Show," CBS, 1965; "PDQ," NBC, 1966; "The Andy Williams Show," NBC, 1967; "Bob Hope Chrysler Theatre: Murder at NBC," NBC, 1967; "The Dean Martin Show," NBC, 1967; "Rowan & Martin's Laugh-In Special," NBC, 1967; "Off to See the Wizard: Who's Afraid of Mother Goose?," ABC, 1967; "The Smothers Brothers Comedy Hour," CBS, 1968; "The Dean Martin Show," NBC, 1974.

ROWE, MISTY
Blonde starlet, usually in bimbo roles, who'll have a job as long as there's a "Hee Haw."

AS A REGULAR: "Hee Haw," SYN, 1972- ; "Happy Days," ABC, 1974-75; "When Things Were Rotten," ABC, 1975; "Hee Haw Honeys," SYN, 1978-79; "Joe's World," NBC, 1979-80.
AND: "Love, American Style: Love and the Sexpert," ABC, 1973; "The Love Boat: Rent-a-Romeo," ABC, 1980; "Silver Spoons: Trouble with Grandfather," NBC, 1984.
TV MOVIES AND MINISERIES: "Bloodsport," ABC, 1973; "SST-Death Flight," ABC, 1977.

ROWLAND, JADA
b. New York City, NY, February 23, 1943. Actress who grew up on the soaps; she was Amy Ames on "The Secret Storm" and later Caroline Aldrich on "The Doctors."
AS A REGULAR: "The Secret Storm," CBS, 1954-64; "As the World Turns," CBS, 1967-68; "The Doctors," NBC, 1976-82; "The Hamptons," ABC, 1983.
AND: "U.S. Steel Hour: Whisper of Evil," CBS, 1959.

ROWLANDS, GENA
b. Cambria, WI, June 19, 1936. Striking actress of films and some TV; she played Teddy Carella, deaf-mute wife of Det. Steve Carella (Robert Lansing) on "87th Precinct" and won an Emmy as former First Lady Betty Ford.
AS A REGULAR: "87th Precinct," NBC, 1961-62; "Peyton Place," ABC, 1967.
AND: "Goodyear TV Playhouse: Do It Yourself," NBC, 1955; "Robert Montgomery Presents: The Great Gatsby," NBC, 1955; "G.E. Theatre: The Girl with Flaxen Hair," CBS, 1958; "Laramie: The Run to Tumavaca," NBC, 1959; "Riverboat: Guns for Empire," NBC, 1959; "Johnny Staccato: Fly, Baby, Fly," NBC, 1960; "Adventures in Paradise: The Death-Divers," ABC, 1960; "Alfred Hitchcock Presents: The Doubtful Doctor," NBC, 1960; "The Tab Hunter Show: Double Trouble," NBC, 1960; "The Islanders: Island Witness," ABC, 1961; "Target: The Corruptors: The Poppy Vendor," ABC, 1961; "The Alfred Hitchcock Hour: Ride the Nightmare," CBS, 1962; "The Dick Powell Show: Project X," NBC, 1963; "The Lloyd Bridges Show: A Personal Matter," CBS, 1963; "The Alfred Hitchcock Hour: The Lonely Hours," CBS, 1963; "77 Sunset Strip: Flight 307," ABC, 1963; "The Virginian: No Tears for Savannah," NBC, 1963; "Bonanza: She Walks in Beauty," NBC, 1963; "Kraft Suspense Theatre: One Step Down," NBC, 1963; "Bob Hope Chrysler Theatre: It's Mental Work," NBC, 1963; "The Breaking Point: Heart of Marble, Body of Stone," ABC, 1963; "Burke's Law: Who Killed Victor Barrows?," ABC, 1964; "Dr. Kildare: To Walk in Grace," NBC, 1964; "The Alfred Hitchcock Hour: Murder Case," CBS, 1964; "Burke's Law: Who Killed Annie Foran?," ABC, 1964; "Kraft Suspense Theatre: Won't It Ever Be Morning?," NBC, 1965; "Run for Your Life: The

Rediscovery of Charlotte Hyde," NBC, 1966; "The Long Hot Summer: From This Day Forward," ABC, 1966; "The Road West: Beyond the Hill," NBC, 1967; "Garrison's Gorillas: The Frame-Up," ABC, 1968; "Medical Center: Man in Hiding," CBS, 1971; "Ghost Story: The Concrete Captain," NBC, 1972; "Medical Center: Child of Violence," CBS, 1973; "Marcus Welby, M.D.: The 266 Days," ABC, 1974; "Columbo: Playback," NBC, 1975.

TV MOVIES AND MINISERIES: "A Question of Love," ABC, 1978; "Strangers: The Story of a Mother and Daughter," CBS, 1979; "Thursday's Child," CBS, 1983; "An Early Frost," NBC, 1985; "The Betty Ford Story," ABC, 1986.
* Emmies: 1987.

RUBINSTEIN, JOHN
b. Los Angeles, CA, December 8, 1946. Actor who played Jeff Maitland on "Family" and Harrison K. Fox on "Crazy Like a Fox."
AS A REGULAR: "Family," ABC, 1976-80; "Crazy Like a Fox," CBS, 1984-86.
AND: "Dragnet: The Big Bang," NBC, 1967; "Room 222: Flu," ABC, 1969; "The Bold Ones: A Thing Not of God," NBC, 1970; "The Young Lawyers: We May Be Better Strangers," ABC, 1970; "Men at Law: Hostage," CBS, 1971; "The Psychiatrist: Ex-Sgt. Randall," NBC, 1971; "The Mod Squad: Survival," ABC, 1971; "The Mary Tyler Moore Show: You Certainly Are a Big Boy," CBS, 1972; "Hawaii Five-O: Chain of Events," CBS, 1972; "Barnaby Jones: Dangerous Summer," CBS, 1975; "Police Woman: Glitter with a Bullet," NBC, 1975; "Wide World of Mystery: Mr. and Ms. and the Bandstand Mystery," ABC, 1975; "Barnaby Jones: Dangerous Summer," CBS, 1975; "The Rookies: The Mugging," ABC, 1976; "Barnaby Jones: Deadline for Dying," CBS, 1976; "The Streets of San Francisco: Once a Con," ABC, 1977; "Lou Grant: Hostage," CBS, 1977; "Vega$: Best Friends," ABC, 1979; "The Love Boat: Reunion Cruise," ABC, 1979; "Matlock: The Investigation," NBC, 1988.
TV MOVIES AND MINISERIES: "The Psychiatrist: God Bless The Children," NBC, 1970; "A Howling in the Woods," NBC, 1971; "Something Evil," CBS, 1972; "The Streets of San Francisco," ABC, 1972; "All Together Now," ABC, 1975; "Happily Ever After," CBS, 1978; "Roots: The Next Generations," ABC, 1979; "She's Dressed to Kill," NBC, 1979; "Make Me an Offer," ABC, 1980; "In Search of Historic Jesus," NBC, 1981; "Skokie," CBS, 1981; "Killjoy," CBS, 1981; "I Take These Men," CBS, 1983; "M.A.D.D.: Mothers Against Drunk Driving," NBC, 1983; "Still Crazy Like a Fox," CBS, 1987; "The Two Mrs. Grenvilles," NBC, 1987; "Beryl Markham: A Shadow on the Sun," CBS, 1988; "Liberace," ABC, 1988.

RUDIE, EVELYN
b. 1950. Child actress best known as Eloise, the little girl who terrorized the Plaza Hotel, in a "Playhouse 90" production.
AS A GUEST: "Ford Theatre: The Woman at Fog Point," NBC, 1955; "Playhouse 90: Eloise," CBS, 1956; "Omnibus: Madeline and the Bat Hat," ABC, 1956; "The George Gobel Show," NBC, 1957; "Playhouse 90: The Hostess with the Mostess," CBS, 1957; "The Red Skelton Show," CBS, 1957; "Alfred Hitchcock Presents: A Man Greatly Beloved," CBS, 1957; "The Patrice Munsel Show," ABC, 1957; "The Gale Storm Show: Angela the Angel," CBS, 1958; "Du Pont Show of the Month: The Red Mill," CBS, 1958; "Wagon Train: The Millie Davis Story," NBC, 1958; "Lux Playhouse: Small Wonder," CBS, 1958; "G.E. Theatre: Nobody's Child," CBS, 1959; "You Bet Your Life," NBC, 1959; "Lawman: The Kids," ABC, 1960; "77 Sunset Strip: Publicity Brat," ABC, 1960; "Here's Hollywood," NBC, 1960; "Holiday Lodge: The Kid," CBS, 1961.

RUGGLES, CHARLIE
b. Los Angeles, CA, February 8, 1886; d. 1970. Actor of films and TV, usually in mild-mannered or henpecked roles; he had his own family sitcom for a time and played Mr. Farquhar, fortune-hunting beau of Granny Clampett (Irene Ryan) on "The Beverly Hillbillies."
AS A REGULAR: "The Ruggles," ABC, 1949-52; "The World of Mr. Sweeney," NBC, 1953-55; "The Bullwinkle Show," NBC, 1961-62.
AND: "Medallion Theatre: The Consul," CBS, 1953; "Studio One: Runaway," CBS, 1954; "Motorola TV Hour: The Muldoon Matter," ABC, 1954; "U.S. Steel Hour: Welcome Home," CBS, 1954; "Matinee Theatre: The Luck of Amos Currie," NBC, 1956; "Playhouse 90: Eloise," CBS, 1956; "Warner Bros. Presents Conflict: The Man From 1997," ABC, 1956; "Warner Bros. Presents Conflict: Girl on a Subway," ABC, 1957; "The Red Skelton Show," CBS, 1957; "Climax!: Let It Be Me," CBS, 1957; "The Life of Riley: Riley's Ups and Downs," NBC, 1957; "U.S. Steel Hour: Crisis in Coroma," CBS, 1957; "The Steve Allen Show," NBC, 1957; "The Life of Riley: The Letter," NBC, 1958; "Playhouse 90: The Male Animal," CBS, 1958; "The Red Skelton Show," CBS, 1958; "Studio One: A Delicate Affair," CBS, 1958; "The Bells of St. Mary's," CBS, 1959; "Once Upon a Christmas Time," NBC, 1959; "The Red Skelton Show: Deadeye Turns in His Badge," CBS, 1959; "Goodyear Theatre: The Sitter's Baby," NBC, 1960; "A Date with Debbie," ABC, 1960; "Best of the Post: The Little Terror," SYN, 1960; "Here's Hollywood," NBC, 1961; "The Chevy Show: The Happiest Day," NBC, 1961; "The Jim Backus Show:

Marriage-Go-Round," SYN, 1961; "Follow the Sun: The Highest Wall," ABC, 1961; "The Real McCoys: Hassie's European Trip," ABC, 1961; "Frontier Circus: Mr. Brady Regrets," CBS, 1962; "The Red Skelton Show: Calling Dr. Kadiddlehopper," CBS, 1962; "The Red Skelton Hour," CBS, 1962; "Saints and Sinners: A Servant in the House of My Party," NBC, 1962; "The Dick Powell Show: The Court-Martial of Captain Wycliff," NBC, 1962; "McKeever and the Colonel: The Big Charade," NBC, 1963; "The Dick Powell Show: The Old Man and the City," NBC, 1963; "Burke's Law: Who Killed Mr. X?," ABC, 1963; "Burke's Law: Who Killed Purity Mather?," ABC, 1963; "Ben Casey: I'll Get on My Icefloe and Wave Goodbye," ABC, 1964; "Destry: Deputy for a Day," ABC, 1964; "Bewitched: Help, Help, Don't Save Me," ABC, 1964; "Burke's Law: Who Killed Lenore Wingfield?," ABC, 1964; "Burke's Law: Who Killed Merlin the Great?," ABC, 1964; "My Living Doll: Rhoda's Legacy," CBS, 1964; "Wagon Train: The Jamison Hershey Story," ABC, 1965; "The Man From UNCLE: The Ultimate Computer Affair," NBC, 1965; "The Andy Griffith Show: Aunt Bee the Swinger," CBS, 1965; "The Munsters: Herman's Driving Test," CBS, 1965; "The Beverly Hillbillies: Mrs. Drysdale's Father," CBS, 1965; "The Beverly Hillbillies: Mr. Farquhar Stays On," CBS, 1965; "Bewitched: Aunt Clara's Old Flame," ABC, 1965; "Laredo: A Taste of Money," NBC, 1966; "Bonanza: Horse of a Different Hue," NBC, 1966; "Pistols 'n' Petticoats: The Triangle," CBS, 1966; "The Beverly Hillbillies: Granny Lives It Up," CBS, 1966; "Please Don't Eat the Daisies: Just for Laughs," NBC, 1966; "Carousel," ABC, 1967; "The Danny Thomas Hour: One for My Baby," NBC, 1968.

RUSH, BARBARA

b. *Santa Barbara, CA, 1927.* Film and TV actress, usually in dramatic roles; she played Eudora Weldon on "Flamingo Road."
AS A REGULAR: "Saints and Sinners," NBC, 1962-63; "Peyton Place," ABC, 1968-69; "The New Dick Van Dyke Show," CBS, 1973-74; "Flamingo Road," NBC, 1981-82.
AND: "Lux Video Theatre: Gavin's Darling," CBS, 1954; "Lux Video Theatre: Shadow of a Doubt," NBC, 1955; "Playhouse 90: The Troublemakers," CBS, 1957; "Suspicion: The Voice in the Night," NBC, 1958; "Lux Playhouse: The Connoisseur," CBS, 1958; "Sunday Showcase: What Makes Sammy Run?," NBC, 1959; "Theatre '62: Notorious," NBC, 1961; "G.E. Theatre: A Very Special Girl," CBS, 1962; "The Eleventh Hour: Make Me a Place," NBC, 1962; "The Dick Powell Show: The Honorable Albert Higgins," NBC, 1963; "Ben Casey: From Too Much Love of Living," ABC, 1963; "The Outer Limits: The

Forms of Things Unknown," ABC, 1964; "The Fugitive: Landscape with Running Figures," ABC, 1965; "Laredo: Miracle at Massacre Mansion," NBC, 1966; "Bob Hope Chrysler Theatre: Storm Crossing," NBC, 1966; "Batman: Nora Clavicle and the Ladies' Crime Club," ABC, 1968; "Mannix: A Copy of Murder," CBS, 1968; "Marcus Welby, M.D.: Silken Threads and Silver Hooks," ABC, 1969; "Medical Center: A Life Is Waiting," CBS, 1969; "Love, American Style: Love and the Motel," ABC, 1970; "The Mod Squad: Kicks, Incorporated," ABC, 1971; "Ironside: Ring of Prayer," NBC, 1971; "Night Gallery: Cool Air," NBC, 1971; "Marcus Welby, M.D.: Don't Talk About Darkness," ABC, 1972; "Medical Center: The Awakening," CBS, 1972; "The Streets of San Francisco: Shattered Image," ABC, 1973; "Medical Center: A Choice of Evils," CBS, 1974; "Police Story: The Chief," NBC, 1974; "Is There a Doctor in the House?," NBC, 1974; "The Love Boat: The Now Marriage," ABC, 1979; "The Love Boat: Eleanor's Return," ABC, 1979; "Knight Rider: Goliath," NBC, 1983; "Finder of Lost Loves: A Gift," ABC, 1984; "Murder, She Wrote: No Fashionable Way to Die," CBS, 1987; "Magnum, P.I.: The Aunt Who Came to Dinner," CBS, 1987; "Hooperman: Nick Derringer, P.I.," ABC, 1988.
TV MOVIES AND MINISERIES: "Suddenly Single," ABC, 1971; "The Eyes of Charles Sand," ABC, 1972; "Moon of the Wolf," ABC, 1972; "Crime Club," CBS, 1973; "The Last Day," NBC, 1975; "Death Car on the Freeway," CBS, 1979; "Flamingo Road," NBC, 1980; "The Night The Bridge Fell Down," NBC, 1983.

RUSSELL, JANE

b. *Ernestine Jane Geraldine Russell, Bemidji, MI, June 21, 1921.* Forties sex symbol and "full-figured gal" of the eighties who's best-known for her bra commercials.
AS A GUEST: "The Steve Allen Show," NBC, 1957; "Colgate Theatre: Macreedy's Woman," NBC, 1958; "The Steve Allen Show," NBC, 1958; "Westinghouse Desilu Playhouse: Ballad for a Bad Man," CBS, 1959; "The Ed Sullivan Show," CBS, 1959; "The Red Skelton Show," CBS, 1959; "The Arthur Murray Party for Bob Hope," NBC, 1960; "Celebrity Talent Scouts," CBS, 1960; "Bob Hope Buick Show," NBC, 1961; "I've Got a Secret," CBS, 1961; "Death Valley Days: Splinter Station," SYN, 1962; "Stump the Stars," CBS, 1962; "Don Adams Screen Test," SYN, 1975.

RUSSELL, JOHN

b. *Los Angeles, CA, January 8, 1921; d. 1991.* Lantern-jawed leading man of the fifties, most notably as Marshal Dan Troop, "Lawman."
AS A REGULAR: "Soldiers of Fortune," SYN, 1955-56; "Lawman," ABC, 1958-62.

AND: "The Gale Storm Show: It's Only Money," CBS, 1957; "Maverick: A Rage for Vengeance," ABC, 1958; "Cheyenne: The Empty Gun," ABC, 1958; "Cheyenne: Dead to Rights," ABC, 1958; "Sugarfoot: Ring of Sand," ABC, 1958; "Pat Boone Chevy Showroom," ABC, 1959; "Northwest Passage: The Killers," NBC, 1959; "Maverick: Hadley's Hunters," ABC, 1960; "Daniel Boone: The Prophet," NBC, 1965; "It Takes a Thief: Guess Who's Coming to Rio?," ABC, 1969; "It Takes a Thief: The Blue Blue Danube," ABC, 1969; "Alias Smith and Jones: Witness to a Lynching," ABC, 1972; "Alias Smith and Jones: The Day the Amnesty Came Through," ABC, 1973; "Emergency!: Inferno," NBC, 1973; "Gunsmoke: The Iron Men," CBS, 1974; "McCloud: The Concrete Jungle Caper," NBC, 1974; "Police Story: Love, Mabel," NBC, 1974; "Simon & Simon: The Rough Rider Rides Again," CBS, 1982; "The Fall Guy: King of the Cowboys," ABC, 1984.

TV MOVIES AND MINISERIES: "Alias Smith and Jones," ABC, 1971.

RUSSELL, KURT

b. *Springfield, MA, March 17, 1951.* Former child actor who became a familiar TV face and is now a big-screen star ("Tequila Sunrise," "Tango and Cash").

AS A REGULAR: "The Travels of Jaimie McPheeters," ABC, 1963-64; "The New Land," ABC, 1974; "The Quest," NBC, 1976.

AND: "The Fugitive: Nemesis," ABC, 1964; "The Man From UNCLE: The Finny Foot Affair," NBC, 1964; "The Virginian: A Father for Toby," NBC, 1964; "Daniel Boone: The First Stone," NBC, 1965; "The Virginian: The Brothers," NBC, 1965; "Gilligan's Island: Gilligan Meets Jungle Boy," CBS, 1965; "The Legend of Jesse James: The Colt," ABC, 1966; "The FBI: The Tormentors," ABC, 1966; "Then Came Bronson: The Spitball Kid," NBC, 1969; "Love, American Style: Love and the First-Nighters," ABC, 1970; "Room 222: Paul Revere Rides Again," ABC, 1971; "Love Story: Beginner's Luck," NBC, 1973; "Gunsmoke: A Trail of Bloodshed," CBS, 1974; "Police Story: Country Boy," NBC, 1974; "Harry O: Double Jeopardy," ABC, 1975; "Police Story: The Empty Weapon," NBC, 1975; "Hawaii Five-O: East Wind, Ill Wind," CBS, 1977.

TV MOVIES AND MINISERIES: "Search for the Gods," ABC, 1975; "The Deadly Tower," NBC, 1975; "The Quest," NBC, 1976; "Elvis," ABC, 1979; "Amber Waves," ABC, 1980.

* "Elvis" aired on Sunday, February 11, 1979, opposite "Gone with the Wind" on CBS and "One Flew Over the Cuckoo's Nest" on NBC— and beat both of them in the ratings.

RUSSELL, MARK

b. *Buffalo, NY, August 23, 1932.* Political satirist.

AS A REGULAR: "Mark Russell Special," PBS,

1976- ; "The Starland Vocal Band Show," CBS, 1977; "Real People," NBC, 1979-84.

RUSSELL, NIPSEY

b. *Atlanta, GA, October 13, 1924.*

AS A REGULAR: "Car 54, Where Are You?," NBC, 1961-62; "ABC Nightlife," ABC, 1965; "Barefoot in the Park," ABC, 1970-71; "The Dean Martin Show," NBC, 1972-73; "The Dean Martin Comedy World," NBC, 1974; "The New Masquerade Party," SYN, 1974-75; "Your Number's Up," NBC, 1985.

AND: "The Jack Paar Show," NBC, 1961; "Missing Links," NBC, 1963; "Missing Links," NBC, 1964; "The Ed Sullivan Show," CBS, 1964; "To Tell the Truth," CBS, 1965; "Dream Girl of '67," ABC, 1967; "Personality," NBC, 1968; "The Tonight Show Starring Johnny Carson," NBC, 1968; "The Joey Bishop Show," ABC, 1968; "Alan King Special," NBC, 1969; "Rhyme and Reason," ABC, 1975; "Rhyme and Reason," ABC, 1976; "Police Woman: Guns," NBC, 1977; "$weepstake$: Roscoe, Elizabeth and the MC," NBC, 1979; "The Love Boat: Trigamist," ABC, 1980; "Password Plus," NBC, 1981.

RUTTAN, SUSAN

Actress who plays Roxanne Melman on "L.A. Law."

AS A REGULAR: "L.A. Law," NBC, 1986- .

AND: "Bosom Buddies: What Price Glory?," ABC, 1980; "Best of the West: The New Jail," ABC, 1981; "Buffalo Bill: A Hero," NBC, 1984; "Newhart: Georgie's Girl," CBS, 1984; "Night Court: Wheels of Justice," NBC, 1985.

TV MOVIES AND MINISERIES: "Packin' It In," CBS, 1983; "Scorned and Swindled," CBS, 1984; "Second Sight: A Love Story," CBS, 1984; "Kicks," ABC, 1985; "Bay Coven," NBC, 1987; "Take My Daughters, Please," NBC, 1988.

RYAN, FRAN

b. *Los Angeles, CA.* Actress often in gruff-but-kindly roles; she played Miss Hannah, who took over the Long Branch Saloon when Miss Kitty (Amanda Blake) vamoosed from "Gunsmoke" and also played the mother of Hungry Jack on TV commercials.

AS A REGULAR: "The Doris Day Show," CBS, 1968; "Green Acres," CBS, 1969-70; "Gunsmoke," CBS, 1974-75; "No Soap, Radio," ABC, 1982; "The Wizard," CBS, 1986-87; "The Dave Thomas Comedy Show," CBS, 1990.

AND: "Batman: The Greatest Mother of Them All/ Ma Parker," ABC, 1966; "The Beverly Hillbillies: The Housekeeper," CBS, 1968; "I Dream of Jeannie: One of Our Hotels Is Growing," NBC, 1970; "The Bill Cosby Show: Rules Is Rules,"

NBC, 1970; "The Brady Bunch: To Move or Not to Move," ABC, 1970; "The Odd Couple: The Odd Couples," ABC, 1972; "The Rookies: Ladies' Day," ABC, 1975; "The Family Holvak: The Long Way Home," NBC, 1975; "The Quest: Seventy-Two Hours," NBC, 1976; "Barney Miller: Corporation," ABC, 1977; "Foul Play: Postage Due," ABC, 1981; "Taxi: Elegant Iggy," ABC, 1982; "Hill Street Blues: The Rise and Fall of Paul the Wall," NBC, 1984; "Highway to Heaven: Man Best Friend," NBC, 1986; "Webster: Grab Bag," SYN, 1987; "Murphy Brown: Nowhere to Run," CBS, 1988; "Murder, She Wrote: Sins of Castle Cove," CBS, 1989.

TV MOVIES AND MINISERIES: "Marcus Welby, M.D.," ABC, 1969; "Stalk the Wild Child," NBC, 1976; "Life of the Party: The Story of Beatrice," CBS, 1982; "Gunsmoke: Return to Dodge," CBS, 1987.

RYAN, IRENE

b. Irene Noblette, El Paso, TX, October 17, 1903; d. 1973. Vaudeville comedienne, teamed with husband Tim; she later became a household face as Granny Clampett on "The Beverly Hillbillies."

AS A REGULAR: "Bringing Up Buddy," CBS, 1960-61; "The Beverly Hillbillies," CBS, 1962-71.

AND: "The Whistler: Lucky Night," SYN, 1955; "The Ray Bolger Show," ABC, 1955; "Front Row Center: Uncle Barney," CBS, 1956; "Matinee Theatre: One of the Family," NBC, 1956; "The Betty White Show," ABC, 1958; "Restless Gun: The Battle of Tower Rock," NBC, 1958; "My Three Sons: Romance of the Silver Pines," ABC, 1962; "Wagon Train: The Malachi Hobart Story," NBC, 1962; "Andy Williams Special," NBC, 1964; "The Danny Kaye Show," CBS, 1965; "Mr. Ed: Love and the Single Horse," CBS, 1965; "Petticoat Junction: Granny, the Baby Expert," CBS, 1968; "Petticoat Junction: A Cake for Granny," CBS, 1968; "The Don Knotts Show," NBC, 1970; "Love, American Style: Love and the Lost Dog," ABC, 1972; "Love, American Style: Love and the Old Swingers," ABC, 1973.
* See also "The Beverly Hillbillies."

RYAN, ROBERT

b. Chicago, IL, November 11, 1909; d. 1973. Rugged, talented leading man of films ("Crossfire," "Bad Day at Black Rock," "The Wild Bunch") who did a bit of above-average TV and worked behind the scenes for peace-related causes.

AS A REGULAR: "Alcoa-Goodyear Theatre (A Turn of Fate)," NBC, 1957-58; "World War I," CBS, 1964-65.

AND: "Screen Directors Playhouse: Lincoln's

Doctor's Bag," NBC, 1955; "Dick Powell's Zane Grey Theatre: You Only Run Once," CBS, 1956; "Dick Powell's Zane Grey Theatre: The Hanging Tree," CBS, 1957; "The Steve Allen Show," NBC, 1957; "Dick Powell's Zane Grey Theatre: Trial by Fear," CBS, 1958; "What's My Line?," CBS, 1958; "Playhouse 90: The Great Gatsby," CBS, 1958; "Dick Powell's Zane Grey Theatre: To Sit in Judgment," CBS, 1958; "Dick Powell's Zane Grey Theatre: Interrogation," CBS, 1959; "Buick Electra Playhouse: The Snows of Kilimanjaro," CBS, 1960; "Person to Person," CBS, 1960; "Here's Hollywood," NBC, 1961; "The New Steve Allen Show," ABC, 1961; "Wagon Train: The John Bernard Story," ABC, 1962; "Kraft Suspense Theatre: Are There Any More Out There Like You?," NBC, 1963; "The Breaking Point: Better Than a Dead Lion," ABC, 1964; "The Eleventh Hour: Who Chopped Down the Cherry Tree?," NBC, 1964; "Bell Telephone Hour," NBC, 1964; "Wagon Train: The Bob Stuart Story," ABC, 1964; "Bob Hope Chrysler Theatre: Guilty or Not Guilty," NBC, 1966; "This Morning," ABC, 1968; "The Front Page," NET, 1970.

TV MOVIES AND MINISERIES: "The Man Without a Country," ABC, 1973.

RYDELL, BOBBY

b. Philadelphia, PA, April 26, 1942. Pop singer of the fifties and sixties.

AS A REGULAR: "Paul Whiteman's TV Teen Club," ABC, 1951-53.

AND: "American Bandstand," ABC, 1959; "The Dick Clark Saturday Night Beechnut Show," ABC, 1959; "The Red Skelton Show: Bolivar, the Songwriter," CBS, 1959; "The Dick Clark Saturday Night Beechnut Show," ABC, 1960; "The Danny Thomas Show: The Singing Delinquent," CBS, 1960; "Perry Como's Kraft Music Hall," NBC, 1960; "The Ed Sullivan Show," CBS, 1962; "The Red Skelton Hour," CBS, 1962; "American Bandstand," ABC, 1963; "The Joey Bishop Show: Bobby Rydell Plugs Ellie's Song," NBC, 1963; "Combat!: The Duel," ABC, 1964; "The Red Skelton Hour," CBS, 1964; "The Jimmy Dean Show," ABC, 1965; "The Mike Douglas Show," SYN, 1965; "Where the Action Is," ABC, 1965; "PDQ," NBC, 1965; "The Red Skelton Hour," CBS, 1965; "The Merv Griffin Show," SYN, 1966; "The Red Skelton Hour," CBS, 1969; "Beat the Clock," SYN, 1970; "Cagney & Lacey: Child Witness," CBS, 1984; "American Bandstand's 33 1/3 Anniversary," ABC, 1985; "On Stage at Wolf Trap: The Golden Boys of Bandstand," PBS, 1986; "The Facts of Life: '62 Pick-Up," NBC, 1986; "Hollywood Squares," SYN, 1988.

S

SAGAL, KATEY

b. Los Angeles, CA, 1956. Actress who plays Peg Bundy on "Married with Children."
AS A REGULAR: "Mary," CBS, 1985-86; "Married with Children," FOX, 1987- .
AND: "Columbo: Candidate for Crime," NBC, 1973.
TV MOVIES AND MINISERIES: "The Failing of Raymond," ABC, 1971.

SAGET, BOB

Comedian; he plays Danny Tanner on "Full House."
AS A REGULAR: "Full House," ABC, 1987- ; "America's Funniest Home Videos," ABC, 1990- .
AND: "The Tonight Show Starring Johnny Carson," NBC, 1989; "America's Funniest Home Videos," ABC, 1989.

SAINT, EVA MARIE

b. Newark, NJ, July 4, 1924. Blonde actress of films ("On the Waterfront," "North by Northwest") and early TV; she later played the mother of Maddie Hayes (Cybill Shepherd) on "Moonlighting."
AS A REGULAR: "Campus Hoopla," NBC, 1946-47; "One Man's Family," NBC, 1950-52; "Moonlighting," ABC, 1987-89.
AND: "City Hospital: In His Image," ABC, 1953; "The Web: Last Chance," CBS, 1953; "Goodyear TV Playhouse: A Trip to Bountiful," NBC, 1953; "Philco TV Playhouse: Middle of the Night," NBC, 1954; "Omnibus: A Clean, Fresh Breeze," CBS, 1954; "G.E. Theatre: Mr. Death and the Red-Headed Woman," CBS, 1954; "Producers Showcase: Yellow Jack," NBC, 1955; "Producers Showcase: Our Town," NBC, 1955; "The Ed Sullivan Show," CBS, 1957; "Bob Hope Chrysler Theatre: Her School for Bachelors," NBC, 1964; "Carol for Another Christmas," ABC, 1964; "The First Woman President," CBS, 1974; "Hollywood Television Theatre: The Fatal Weakness," PBS, 1976; "The Love Boat: Poor Rich Man," ABC, 1983.
TV MOVIES AND MINISERIES: "The Macahans," ABC, 1976; "A Christmas to Remember," CBS, 1978; "The Curse of King Tut's Tomb," NBC, 1980; "The Best Little Girl in the World," ABC, 1981; "Malibu," ABC, 1983; "Jane Doe," CBS, 1983; "Fatal Vision," NBC, 1984; "The Last Days of Patton," CBS, 1986; "A Year in the Life," NBC, 1986; "Norman Rockwell's Breaking Home Ties," ABC, 1987; "I'll Be Home for Christmas," NBC, 1988.

SAINT JAMES, SUSAN

b. Susan Miller, Los Angeles, CA, August 14, 1946. Sexpot actress of the sixties who began her career at the Universal TV factory; she played Sally McMillan, wife of Stewart (Rock Hudson) and then she spent five years as independent divorcee Kate McArdle, pal of Allie Lowell (Jane Curtin).
AS A REGULAR: "The Name of the Game," NBC, 1968-71; "McMillan and Wife," NBC, 1971-76; "Kate & Allie," CBS, 1984-89.
AND: "Ironside: Girl in the Night," NBC, 1967; "It Takes a Thief: A Thief Is a Thief Is a Thief/It Takes One to Know One," ABC, 1968; "Ironside: Something for Nothing," NBC, 1968; "It Takes a Thief: When Theives Fall In," ABC, 1968; "It Takes a Thief: Payoff at the Piazza," ABC, 1969; "It Takes a Thief: The Suzie Simone Caper," ABC, 1970; "McCloud: Walk in the Dark," NBC, 1970; "M*A*S*H: War Co-Respondent," CBS, 1980; "Saturday Night Live," NBC, 1981; "Saturday Night Live," NBC, 1983; "Late Night with David Letterman," NBC, 1987; "Tattinger's: Broken Windows," NBC, 1988; "Woodstock: Return to the Planet of the '60s," CBS, 1989.
TV MOVIES AND MINISERIES: "Fame Is the Name of the Game," NBC, 1966; "Alias Smith and Jones," ABC, 1971; "Once Upon a Dead Man," NBC, 1971; "Magic Carpet," NBC, 1972; "Scott Free," NBC, 1976; "Desperate Women," NBC, 1978; "The Girls in the Office," ABC, 1979; "Sex and the Single Parent," CBS, 1979; "S.O.S. Titanic," ABC, 1979; "The Kid From Nowhere," NBC, 1982; "I Take These Men," CBS, 1983.
* Emmies: 1969.

ST. JOHN, JILL

b. Los Angeles, CA, August 19, 1940. Redheaded starlet of the sixties.
AS A REGULAR: "Emerald Point NAS," CBS, 1983-84.
AND: "Schlitz Playhouse: No Second Helping," CBS, 1957; "Du Pont Show of the Month: Junior Miss," CBS, 1957; "Bob Hope Special," NBC, 1958; "Here's Hollywood," NBC, 1961; "Bob Hope Chrysler Theatre: Have Girls, Will Travel," NBC, 1964; "Burke's Law: Who Killed Merlin the Great?," ABC, 1964; "The Andy Williams Show," NBC, 1965; "The Name of the Game: The Civilized Man," NBC, 1969; "The Tonight Show Starring Johnny Carson," NBC, 1969; "The Don Knotts Show," NBC, 1970; "Decisions, Decisions," NBC, 1971; "Rowan & Martin's

Laugh-In," NBC, 1972; "Old Faithful," ABC, 1973; "Saga of Sonora," NBC, 1973; "The Love Boat: Cyrano De Bricker," ABC, 1979; "Hart to Hart: Pilot," ABC, 1979; "The Love Boat: Spider Seranade," ABC, 1979; "Vega$: Sudden Death," ABC, 1980; "The Love Boat: Mind My Wife," ABC, 1981; "The Love Boat: Does Father Know Best?," ABC, 1982; "Matt Houston: Pilot," ABC, 1982; "Magnum, P.I.: Italian Ice," CBS, 1982; "J.J. Starbuck: Song From the Sequel," NBC, 1987.

TV MOVIES AND MINISERIES: "Fame Is the Name of the Game," NBC, 1966; "How I Spent My Summer Vacation," NBC, 1967; "The Spy Killer," ABC, 1969; "Foreign Exchange," ABC, 1970; "Brenda Starr," ABC, 1976.

SAJAK, PAT
b. Chicago, IL, 1947. Former deejay and weatherman who's just a shade less inane and a shade wittier than most game show hosts, so it was decided he'd make a great talk show host. He didn't.

AS A REGULAR: "Wheel of Fortune," NBC, 1981-89; SYN, 1983- ; "The Pat Sajak Show," CBS, 1989-90.

AND: "Gimme a Break: Big Apple," NBC, 1984; "The A-Team: Wheel of Fortune," NBC, 1985; "Santa Barbara," NBC, 1988.

SALES, SOUPY
b. Milton Hines, Franklinton, NC, January 8, 1926. Wacky comic who began on New York TV; his big gimmick was getting hit in the face with a pie. He was also the funniest member of the "What's My Line?" panel, which wasn't saying much.

AS A REGULAR: "The Soupy Sales Show," ABC, 1955, 1959-60, 1962; SYN, 1966-68; "What's My Line?," SYN, 1968-75; "Junior Almost Anything Goes," ABC, 1976-77; "Sha Na Na," SYN, 1978-81.

AND: "The Rebel: A Wife for Johnny Yuma," ABC, 1960; "Hennesey: Hennesey Meets Soupy Sales," CBS, 1962; "The Jack Paar Show," NBC, 1962; "Ensign O'Toole: Operation: Jinx," NBC, 1962; "McKeever and the Colonel: The Old Grad," NBC, 1963; "The Real McCoys: The McCoy Sound," CBS, 1963; "Burke's Law: Who Killed Mr. X?," ABC, 1963; "Your First Impression," NBC, 1963; "Route 66: This Is Going to Hurt Me More Than It Hurts You," CBS, 1964; "The Ed Sullivan Show," CBS, 1965; "The Match Game," NBC, 1969; "The Merv Griffin Show," SYN, 1969; "The Beverly Hillbillies: The Hero," CBS, 1969; "The Beverly Hillbillies: Our Hero the Banker," CBS, 1970; "Hollywood Squares," NBC, 1971; "Love, American Style: Love and the Big Surprise," ABC, 1971; "Love, American Style: Love and the Wishing Star," ABC, 1972; "The $10,000

Pyramid," CBS, 1974; "Tony Orlando and Dawn," CBS, 1976; "The Love Experts," SYN, 1978; "The Love Boat: Accidental Cruise," ABC, 1978.

SAMMS, EMMA
b. England, August 28, 1961. Soap vixen who was Holly on "General Hospital" and Fallon Carrington Colby on "Dynasty" and "The Colbys."

AS A REGULAR: "General Hospital," ABC, 1982-85; "Dynasty," ABC, 1985; 1987-89; "The Colbys," ABC, 1985-87.

AND: "Hotel: Cinderella," ABC, 1984; "The New Mike Hammer: Green Lipstick," CBS, 1987; "Murder, She Wrote: Snow White, Blood Red," CBS, 1988; "Newhart: A Midseason's Night Dream," CBS, 1988; "Super Password," NBC, 1989; "My Two Dads: In Her Dreams," NBC, 1989; "Animal Crack-Ups," ABC, 1989.

TV MOVIES AND MINISERIES: "Agatha Christie's Murder in Three Acts," CBS, 1986; "A Connecticut Yankee in King Arthur's Court," NBC, 1989.

SAMPLES, JUNIOR
b. Alvin Samples, Cumming, GA, April 10, 1926; d. 1983. Fat, slow-talking comic on "Hee Haw."

AS A REGULAR: "Hee Haw," CBS, 1969-71; SYN, 1971-83.

SAND, PAUL
b. Paul Sanchez, Los Angeles, CA, March 4, 1944. Thin, dark-featured actor often in sensitive or comic roles.

AS A REGULAR: "Story Theatre," SYN, 1971-72; "Paul Sand in Friends and Lovers," CBS, 1974-75; "St. Elsewhere," NBC, 1983-84; "Gimme a Break," NBC, 1986-87.

AND: "As Caesar Sees It," ABC, 1962; "The Governor and J.J.: A Day in the Life...," CBS, 1970; "The Mary Tyler Moore Show: 1040 or Fight," CBS, 1970; "The Carol Burnett Show," CBS, 1973; "The Carol Burnett Show," CBS, 1974; "Dinah!," SYN, 1975; "Taxi: Fledgling," ABC, 1981; "The Love Boat: For Love of Money," ABC, 1983; "Cagney & Lacey: Happily Ever After," CBS, 1985; "Murder, She Wrote: Footnote to Murder," CBS, 1985; "Magnum P.I.: All Thieves on Deck," CBS, 1986; "Empty Nest: Tears of a Clown," NBC, 1989.

TV MOVIES AND MINISERIES: "The Last Fling," ABC, 1987; "Disney Sunday Movie: Justin Case," ABC, 1988.

SANDERS, RICHARD
b. Harrisburg, PA, August 23, 1940. Les Nessman, WKRP News, winner of the coveted Silver Sow Award.

AS A REGULAR: "WKRP in Cincinnati," CBS, 1978-82; "Spencer," NBC, 1984-85; "Berrenger's,"

NBC, 1985; "You Can't Take It with You,"
SYN, 1987-88.

AND: "McCloud: London Bridges," NBC, 1977;
"Goodnight Beantown: Peace on Earth," CBS,
1983; "Murder, She Wrote: We're Off to Kill the
Wizard," CBS, 1984; "Simon & Simon: Corpus
Delecti," CBS, 1984; "Newhart: Leave It to the
Beavers," CBS, 1984; "Who's the Boss?: It
Happened One Summer," ABC, 1985; "ALF:
Pennsylvania 6-5000," NBC, 1986; "Easy Street:
The Mad Gardener," NBC, 1987; "Night Court:
The Clip Show," NBC, 1989.

TV MOVIES AND MINISERIES: "Diary of a Teenage
Hitchhiker," ABC, 1979.

SANDRICH, JAY

b. Los Angeles, CA. Emmy-winning director; the
son of film director Mark Sandrich.

AS DIRECTOR: "The Ghost and Mrs. Muir: The
Great Power Failure," ABC, 1969; "Nanny and
the Professor: I Think I Shall Never See a Tree,"
ABC, 1970; "The Ghost and Mrs. Muir:
Amateur Night," ABC, 1970; "Nanny and the
Professor: A Letter for Nanny," ABC, 1970;
"The Mary Tyler Moore Show," CBS, 1970-77;
"The Odd Couple," ABC, 1970-75; "The Bob
Newhart Show," CBS, 1972-75; "WKRP in
Cincinnati: Pilot-Part 1," CBS, 1978; "The
Cosby Show," NBC, 1984-89.

TV MOVIES AND MINISERIES: "The Crooked Hearts,"
ABC, 1972; "What Are Best Friends For?,"
ABC, 1973.

* Emmies: 1970, 1973, 1985, 1986.

SANDS, TOMMY

b. Chicago, IL, August 27, 1937. Teen idol of the
fifties whose career took off when he played an
Elvis-like singer on "Kraft Television Theatre";
married for a time to Nancy Sinatra.

AS A GUEST: "Kraft Television Theatre: The Singin'
Idol," NBC, 1957; "The Ford Show," NBC,
1957; "The Steve Allen Show," NBC, 1957;
"Shower of Stars," CBS, 1957; "This Is Your
Life," NBC, 1957; "Kraft Television Theatre:
Flesh and Blood," NBC, 1957; "The Ed Sullivan
Show," CBS, 1957; "The Ford Show," NBC,
1958; "The Big Record," CBS, 1958; "The
Garry Moore Show," CBS, 1959; "The Ford
Show," NBC, 1959; "The Dick Clark Saturday
Night Beechnut Show," ABC, 1959; "Red
Skelton Chevy Special," CBS, 1959; "Perry
Como's Kraft Music Hall," NBC, 1959; "Wagon
Train: The Larry Hanify Story," NBC, 1960;
"The Ed Sullivan Show," CBS, 1962; "U.S.
Steel Hour: The Inner Panic," CBS, 1962;
"Stump the Stars," CBS, 1962; "Wagon Train:
The Davey Baxter Story," ABC, 1963; "Alcoa
Premiere: Blow High, Blow Clear," ABC, 1963;
"Wagon Train: The Gus Morgan Story," ABC,
1963; "Laramie: Trapped," NBC, 1963; "Wagon
Train: The Bob Stuart Story," ABC, 1964;

"Slattery's People: Question—Why the Lonely?
Why the Misbegotten?," CBS, 1964; "Kraft
Suspense Theatre: Rumble on the Docks," NBC,
1964; "Mr. Novak: Let's Dig a Little Grammar,"
NBC, 1964; "What's This Song?," NBC, 1965;
"Combat!: More Than a Soldier," ABC, 1965;
"Mr. Novak: And Then I Wrote," NBC, 1965;
"Branded: That the Brave Endure," NBC, 1965;
"Bonanza: The Debt," NBC, 1965; "Hawaii
Five-O: By the Numbers," CBS, 1968; "Hawaii
Five-O: Hit Gun for Sale," CBS, 1975.

* On "The Singin' Idol," Sands introduced a song,
"Teenage Crush," that reached number three on
the pop charts in 1957.

SANDY, GARY

b. Dayton, OH, December 25, 1943. Actor who
played station manager Andy Travis on "WKRP
in Cincinnati."

AS A REGULAR: "As the World Turns," CBS, 1970;
"The Secret Storm," CBS, 1973-74; "Somerset,"
NBC, 1974-76; "WKRP in Cincinnati," CBS,
1978-82.

AND: "Medical Center: The Happy State of
Depression," CBS, 1976; "Murder, She Wrote:
Capitol Offense," CBS, 1985; "Blacke's Magic: A
Friendly Game of Showdown," NBC, 1986.

TV MOVIES AND MINISERIES: "For Lovers Only,"
ABC, 1982.

SANFORD, ISABEL

b. New York City, NY, August 29, 1917. Emmy
winning actress who played Louise Jefferson.

AS A REGULAR: "All in the Family," CBS, 1971-75;
"The Jeffersons," CBS, 1975-85.

AND: "Bewitched: Samantha Goes South for a
Spell," ABC, 1968; "The Mod Squad: Hello
Mother, My Name Is Julie," ABC, 1968; "On
Being Black: Fare Thee Well, Reverend Taylor,"
NET, 1969; "The Interns: The Choice," CBS,
1970; "The Mary Tyler Moore Show: His Two
Right Arms," CBS, 1972; "Love, American Style:
Love and the Perfect Wedding," ABC, 1972;
"The New Temperatures Rising Show: The
Mothers," ABC, 1973; "Kojak: Die Before They
Wake," CBS, 1974; "Dean's Place," NBC, 1976;
"All in the Family: The Family Next Door,"
CBS, 1979; "Hollywood Squares," NBC, 1980;
"The John Davidson Show," SYN, 1981; "The
Love Boat: Going to the Dogs," ABC, 1983;
"The New Mike Hammer: Harlem Nocturne,"
CBS, 1986.

TV MOVIES AND MINISERIES: "The Great Man's
Whiskers," NBC, 1973.

* Emmies: 1981.

SANTOS, JOE

b. Brooklyn, NY, June 9, 1934. Dark-featured
character actor best known as Det. Dennis
Becker on "The Rockford Files."

692

AS A REGULAR: "The Rockford Files," NBC, 1974-80; "Me and Maxx," NBC, 1980; "A.K.A. Pablo," ABC, 1984; "Hardcastle and McCormick," ABC, 1985-86; "Santa Barbara," NBC, 1990- .

AND: "Room 222: The Impostor," ABC, 1972; "The Streets of San Francisco: Rampage," ABC, 1973; "Barnaby Jones: Rendezvous with Terror," CBS, 1974; "Police Story: Countdown," NBC, 1974; "Police Story: Robbery: 48 Hours," NBC, 1974; "Kung Fu: A Lamb to the Slaughter," ABC, 1975; "Police Story: Spanish Class," NBC, 1976; "Police Story: Two Frogs on a Mongoose," NBC, 1976; "Police Story: Monster Manor," NBC, 1976; "Police Story: Trial Board," NBC, 1977; "Joe Forrester: A Game of Lose," NBC, 1976; "Lou Grant: Barrio," CBS, 1977; "Eischied: Spanish Eight," NBC, 1979; "Paris: Pay The Two Bucks," CBS, 1980; "Hill Street Blues: Hair Transplant," NBC, 1984; "Hill Street Blues: Lucky Ducks," NBC, 1984; "Hill Street Blues: Eva's Brawn," NBC, 1984; "The A-Team: Trouble on Wheels," NBC, 1984; "Magnum, P.I.: Murder by Night," CBS, 1986; "Magnum, P.I.: Out of Sync," CBS, 1987; "Murder, She Wrote: A Little Night Work," CBS, 1988; "Miami Vice: Hostile Takeover," NBC, 1988.

TV MOVIES AND MINISERIES: "The Blue Knight," NBC, 1973; "The Rockford Files," NBC, 1974; "The Girl on the Late-Late Show," NBC, 1974; "A Matter of Wife and Death," NBC, 1975; "The Hustler of Muscle Beach," ABC, 1980; "Deadline," ABC, 1988.

SARGENT, DICK

b. Richard Cox, Carmel, CA, April 19, 1933. Actor who replaced Dick York as Darrin Stephens on "Bewitched."

AS A REGULAR: "One Happy Family," NBC, 1961; "Broadside," ABC, 1964-65; "The Tammy Grimes Show," ABC, 1966; "Bewitched," ABC, 1969-72; "Down to Earth," TBS, 1985-87.

AND: "West Point: Wrong Fight," CBS, 1957; "The Loretta Young Show: Ten Men and a Girl," NBC, 1959; "Wichita Town: Afternoon in Town," NBC, 1960; "Black Saddle: The Freebooters," ABC, 1960; "Gunsmoke: Catawomper," CBS, 1962; "The Alfred Hitchcock Hour: Don't Look Behind You," CBS, 1962; "The Adventures of Ozzie and Harriet: An Old Friend of June's," ABC, 1962; "Hazel: Mr. Griffin Throws a Wedding," NBC, 1963; "Wagon Train: The Naomi Kaylor Story," ABC, 1963; "Wagon Train: The Andrew Elliott Story," ABC, 1964; "I Dream of Jeannie: Jeannie for the Defense," NBC, 1969; "Love, American Style: Love and the Love Potion," ABC, 1971; "Love, American Style: Love and the Fighting Couple," ABC, 1972; "Love, American Style: Love and Lover's Lane," ABC, 1972; "Here's Lucy: Lucy Plays Cops and Robbers," CBS, 1973; "Love, American Style: Love and the Playwright," ABC, 1973; "The Streets of San Francisco: Shattered Image," ABC, 1973; "Pass-word," ABC, 1974; "McMillan and Wife: The Deadly Cure," NBC, 1976; "Marcus Welby, M.D.: Prisoner of the Island Cell," ABC, 1976; "Switch: Formula for Murder," CBS, 1977; "Three's Company: Chrissy's Date," ABC, 1977; "The Love Boat: Silent Night," ABC, 1977; "Charlie's Angels: Love Boat Angels," ABC, 1979; "Taxi: Jim's Inheritance," NBC, 1982; "Family Ties: No Nukes Is Good Nukes," NBC, 1982; "Diff'rent Strokes: Arnold's Strike," NBC, 1984; "Murder, She Wrote: Simon Says, Color Me Dead," CBS, 1987.

TV MOVIES AND MINISERIES: "Melvin Purvis, G-Man," ABC, 1974; "Fantasy Island," ABC, 1977; "The Power Within," ABC, 1979; "Battle of the Generations," NBC, 1979.

SAUNDERS, LORI

b. 1941. Attractive actress who played Bobbie Jo Bradley on "Petticoat Junction."

AS A REGULAR: "Petticoat Junction," CBS, 1965-70; "Dusty's Trail," SYN, 1973.

AND: "Art Linkletter's House Party," CBS, 1967; "The Beverly Hillbillies: The Thanksgiving Story," CBS, 1968; "The Beverly Hillbillies: The Week Before Christmas," CBS, 1968; "The Beverly Hillbillies: Sam Drucker's Visit," CBS, 1969; "The Courtship of Eddie's Father: When the Shoe Is on the Other Foot, It Doesn't Fit," ABC, 1970; "The Beverly Hillbillies: Welcome to the Family," CBS, 1971; "The Beverly Hillbillies: The Teahouse of Jed Clampett," CBS, 1971; "Love, American Style: Love and the Love Kit," ABC, 1973.

SAVAGE, FRED A.

Young actor who plays Kevin Arnold on "The Wonder Years."

AS A REGULAR: "Morningstar/ Eveningstar," CBS, 1986; "The Wonder Years," ABC, 1988- .

AND: "The Twilight Zone: What Are Friends For?," CBS, 1986; "ABC Afterschool Special: Runaway Ralph," ABC, 1988; "The Tonight Show Starring Johnny Carson," NBC, 1989.

TV MOVIES AND MINISERIES: "Convicted: A Mother's Story," NBC, 1987.

SAVALAS, TELLY

b. Aristoteles Savalas, Garden City, NY, January 21, 1924. Chrome-domed actor who began his career in menacing character roles and then found fame—and even a brief tenure as a minor-league sex symbol—as detective Theo Kojak.

AS A REGULAR: "Acapulco," NBC, 1961; "Kojak," CBS, 1973-78; ABC, 1989-90.

AND: "Armstrong Circle Theatre: House of Cards," CBS, 1959; "Brenner: Man in the Middle," CBS, 1959; "Armstrong Circle Theatre: 35 Rue du Marche," CBS, 1959; "Diagnosis: Unknown: Gina, Gina," CBS, 1960; "Armstrong Circle Theatre: Engineer of Death: The Eichmann Story," CBS, 1960; "Naked City: To Walk in Silence," ABC,

1960; "U.S. Steel Hour: Operation North Star," CBS, 1960; "The Aquanauts: The Storm Adventure," CBS, 1961; ABC, 1963; "77 Sunset Strip: 5," ABC, 1963; "The Twilight Zone: The Living Doll," CBS, 1963; "Burke's Law: Who Killed Purity Mather?," ABC, 1963; "Grindl: The Gruesome Basement," NBC, 1963; "The Rogues: Viva Diaz!," NBC, 1964; "Burke's Law: Who Killed the Man on the White Horse?," ABC, 1965; "The Fugitive: May God Have Mercy," ABC, 1965; "The FBI: The Executioners," ABC, 1967; "The Man From UNCLE: The Five Daughters Affair," NBC, 1967; "Cimarron Strip: The Battleground," CBS, 1967; "Nobody's Perfect," CBS, 1974; "The Merv Griffin Show," SYN, 1974; "Joys," NBC, 1976; "Celebrity Sweepstakes," SYN, 1976; "Alice: Has Anyone Here Seen Telly?," CBS, 1979; "The Love Boat: Too Many Issacs," ABC, 1985; "The Equalizer: Blood and Wine," CBS, 1987; "J.J. Starbuck: Gold From the Rainbow," NBC, 1987.

TV MOVIES AND MINISERIES: "Mongo's Back in Town," CBS, 1971; "Visions...," CBS, 1972; "The Marcus-Nelson Murders," CBS, 1973; "She Cried Murder!," CBS, 1973; "Hellinger's Law," CBS, 1981; "The Golden Raiders," ABC, 1981; "The Cartier Affair," NBC, 1984; "Kojak: The Belarus File," CBS, 1985; "The Dirty Dozen: The Deadly Mission," NBC, 1987; "Kojak: The Price of Justice," CBS, 1987; "The Dirty Dozen: The Fatal Mission," NBC, 1988; "The Hollywood Detective," USA, 1989.
* Emmies: 1974.

SAVITCH, JESSICA
b. Margate, NJ, 1947; d. 1983. Blonde news anchorwoman with little experience who died in a car accident; in the late eighties two tell-all biographies told of Savitch's tragic insecurities and ambition and of a TV news industry where looks matter more than ability.
AS A REGULAR: "NBC Weekend News," NBC, 1977-83; "Prime Time Sunday," NBC, 1979-80; "Frontline," PBS, 1983.

SAWYER, DIANE
b. Glasgow, KY, December 22, 1945. Anchorwoman-reporter.
AS A REGULAR: "CBS Morning News," CBS, 1981-84; "The American Parade," CBS, 1984; "60 Minutes," CBS, 1984-89; "PrimeTime Live," ABC, 1989- .

SAXON, JOHN
b. Brooklyn, NY, August 5, 1935. Actor who played Dr. Ted Stuart on "The Bold Ones" and Tony Cumson on "Falcon Crest."
AS A REGULAR: "The Bold Ones," NBC, 1969-72; "Falcon Crest," CBS, 1981-82; 1986-90 .

AND: "Medic: Walk with Lions," NBC, 1955; "G.E. Theatre: Cat in the Cradle," CBS, 1961; "Here's Hollywood," NBC, 1961; "The Dick Powell Show: A Time to Die," NBC, 1962; "Burke's Law: Who Killed Cable Roberts?," ABC, 1963; "Bob Hope Chrysler Theatre: Echo of Evil," NBC, 1964; "Burke's Law: Who Killed the Horne of Plenty?," ABC, 1964; "Gunsmoke: Dry Road to Nowhere," CBS, 1965; "Bob Hope Chrysler Theatre: After the Lion, Jackals," NBC, 1966; "The Virginian: Vision of Blindness," NBC, 1968; "The Name of the Game: Collector's Edition," NBC, 1968; "The Men From Shiloh: The Regimental Line," NBC, 1971; "The Sixth Sense: Lady, Lady, Take My Life," ABC, 1972; "Night Gallery: I'll Never Leave You—Ever," NBC, 1972; "Kung Fu: King of the Mountain," ABC, 1972; "Banyon: The Clay Clarinet," NBC, 1972; "The Streets of San Francisco: A Collection of Eagles," ABC, 1973; "The Mary Tyler Moore Show: Menage a Phyllis," CBS, 1974; "Gunsmoke: The Squaw," CBS, 1975; "Petrocelli: The Mark of Cain," NBC, 1975; "The Rockford Files: A Portrait of Elizabeth," NBC, 1976; "The Six Million Dollar Man: The Return of Bigfoot," ABC, 1976; "Scarecrow and Mrs. King: The First Time," CBS, 1983; "Hardcastle and McCormick: Pilot," ABC, 1983; "Scarecrow and Mrs. King: Saved by the Bells," CBS, 1983; "Murder, She Wrote: Hooray for Homicide," CBS, 1984; "Half-Nelson: Diplomatic Immunity," NBC, 1985; "Murder, She Wrote: A Very Good Year for Murder," CBS, 1988.

TV MOVIES AND MINISERIES: "The Doomsday Flight," NBC, 1966; "Winchester '73," NBC, 1967; "Istanbul Express," NBC, 1968; "The Intruders," NBC, 1970; "Snatched," ABC, 1973; "Linda," ABC, 1973; "Can Ellen Be Saved?," ABC, 1974; "Planet Earth," ABC, 1974; "Crossfire," NBC, 1975; "Strange New World," ABC, 1975; "Best Sellers: Once an Eagle," NBC, 1976; "Raid on Entebbe," NBC, 1977; "Harold Robbins' 79 Park Avenue," NBC, 1977; "The Immigrants," SYN, 1978; "Brothers-in-Law," ABC, 1985.

SCALIA, JACK
b. Brooklyn, NY, November 10, 1951. Hunky actor; he played Nicholas Pearce, who had an affair with Sue Ellen (Linda Gray) on "Dallas."
AS A REGULAR: "The Devlin Connection," NBC, 1982; "High Performance," ABC, 1983; "Berrenger's," NBC, 1985; "Hollywood Beat," ABC, 1985; "Dallas," CBS, 1987-89; "Wolf," CBS, 1989-90.
TV MOVIES AND MINISERIES: "The Star Maker," NBC, 1981; "Amazon," ABC, 1984; "The Other Lover," CBS, 1985; "Club Med," ABC, 1986; "Remington Steele: The Steele That Wouldn't Die," NBC, 1987.

SCHAAL, RICHARD

b. *Chicago, IL.* Father of Wendy Schaal. Comic actor who played photographer Leo Heatherton on "Phyllis," Dr. Sandler on "Trapper John, M.D." and the dense date of Mary Tyler Moore on a couple of episodes of her sitcom; former husband of Valerie Harper.

AS A REGULAR: "Phyllis," CBS, 1975-76; "Please Stand By," SYN, 1978-79; "Trapper John, M.D.," CBS, 1980-84; "Just Our Luck," ABC, 1983.

AND: "The Dick Van Dyke Show: Dear Sally Rogers," CBS, 1966; "I Dream of Jeannie: Jeannie and the Secret Weapon," NBC, 1969; "The FBI: Antennae of Death," ABC, 1970; "The Mary Tyler Moore Show: Today I Am a Ma'am," CBS, 1970; "Love, American Style: Love and the Out-of-Town Client," ABC, 1970; "The Mary Tyler Moore Show: The Snow Must Go On," CBS, 1970; "The Mary Tyler Moore Show: Howard's Girl," CBS, 1971; "The Mary Tyler Moore Show: Didn't You Used To Be ... Wait ... Don't Tell Me!," CBS, 1971; "Love, American Style: Love and the Black Limousine," ABC, 1972; "The Bob Newhart Show: Goodnight, Nancy," CBS, 1972; "Shaft: The Meat-Eaters," CBS, 1974; "The Mary Tyler Moore Show: I Was a Single for WJM," CBS, 1974; "The Bob Newhart Show: By the Way ... You're Fired," CBS, 1974; "The Bob Newhart Show: Life Is a Hamburger," CBS, 1974; "The Rockford Files: Caledonia, It's Worth a Fortune!," NBC, 1974; "Rhoda: Not Made for Each Other," CBS, 1975; "Celebrity Sweepstakes," NBC, 1975; "Rhoda: Man of the Year," CBS, 1976; "Police Woman: Death Game," NBC, 1977; "Nero Wolfe: Wolfe at the Door," NBC, 1981; "Hardcastle and McCormick: Something's Going On On This Train," ABC, 1985.

TV MOVIES AND MINISERIES: "Nightmare," CBS, 1973; "Let's Switch," ABC, 1975; "Almost Grown," CBS, 1988.

SCHAEFFER, REBECCA

b. *Eugene, OR, 1964; d. 1989.* Pert actress who played Patti, sister of Samantha Russell (Pam Dawber) on "My Sister Sam"; she was shot by an obsessed fan.

AS A REGULAR: "My Sister Sam," CBS, 1986-88.

SCHAFER, NATALIE

b. *New York City, NY, November 5, 1912.* Actress who played Mrs. Thurston Howell III (Lovey to her friends) on "Gilligan's Island."

AS A REGULAR: "Gilligan's Island," CBS, 1964-67; "Harold Robbins' The Survivors," ABC, 1969-70; "Search for Tomorrow," CBS, 1971-72.

AND: "I Love Lucy: The Charm School," CBS, 1954; "Producers Showcase: The Petrified Forest," NBC, 1955; "The Loretta Young Show: The Bronte Story," NBC, 1956; "Ford Theatre: Footnote on a Doll," ABC, 1957; "The Phil Silvers Show: Bilko's Formula 7," CBS, 1959; "Sunday Showcase: After Hours," NBC, 1960; "Guestward Ho!: Babs' Mother," ABC, 1960; "Thriller: The Grim Reaper," NBC, 1961; "Route 66: Give the Old Cat a Tender Mouse," CBS, 1962; "Girl Talk," SYN, 1963; "The Beverly Hillbillies: The Dress Shop," CBS, 1964; "Mannix: A Game of Shadows," CBS, 1972; "Diana: New Marshall in Town," NBC, 1973; "Love, American Style: Love and the Man of the Year," ABC, 1974; "Marcus Welby, M.D.: An End and a Beginning," ABC, 1975; "McCoy: In Again, Out Again," NBC, 1976; "Three's Company: Jack in the Flower Shop," ABC, 1978; "CHiPS: Journey to a Spacecraft," NBC, 1983; "Simon & Simon: The Secret of Chrome Eagle," CBS, 1983.

TV MOVIES AND MINISERIES: "Rescue From Gilligan's Island," NBC, 1978; "The Castaways on Gilligan's Island," NBC, 1979; "The Harlem Globetrotters on Gilligan's Island," NBC, 1981.

SCHALLERT, WILLIAM

b. *Los Angeles, CA, July 6, 1922.* Reliable character actor in dozens of shows; he played Martin Lane, Patty Duke's TV father and father of the Hardy boys.

AS A REGULAR: "Commando Cody," NBC, 1955; "The Many Loves of Dobie Gillis," CBS, 1959-63; "Philip Marlowe," ABC, 1959-60; "The Patty Duke Show," ABC, 1963-66; "The Nancy Walker Show," ABC, 1976; "The Nancy Drew Mysteries," ABC, 1977-78; "The Hardy Boys Mysteries," ABC, 1977-78; "Little Women," NBC, 1979; "The New Gidget," SYN, 1986-88.

AND: "Playhouse 90: Massacre at Sand Creek," CBS, 1956; "The Adventures of Jim Bowie: The Pearl and Crown," ABC, 1957; "Telephone Time: The Koshetz Story," ABC, 1957; "Perry Mason: The Case of the Lonely Heiress," CBS, 1957; "Leave It to Beaver: Beaver's Short Pants," CBS, 1957; "Have Gun, Will Travel: The Long Night," CBS, 1957; "The Texan: Troubled Town," CBS, 1958; "Steve Canyon: Crash Landing," NBC, 1958; "Wanted Dead or Alive: The Littlest Client," CBS, 1959; "Maverick: The Strange Journey of Jenny Hill," ABC, 1959; "Buick Electra Playhouse: The Gambler, the Nun and the Radio," CBS, 1960; "My Sister Eileen: Ruth the Starmaker," CBS, 1961; "Checkmate: The Paper Killer," CBS, 1961; "The Rifleman: Short Rope for a Tall Man," ABC, 1961; "Hennesey: Admiral and Son," CBS, 1961; "The Andy Griffith Show: Quiet Sam," CBS, 1961; "The Lucy Show: Lucy and Viv Play Softball," CBS, 1963; "Combat!: Head Count," ABC, 1966; "The Virginian: Dead-Eye Dick," NBC, 1966; "Mission: Impossible: The Train," CBS, 1967; "Get Smart: A Man Called Smart," NBC, 1967; "Ironside: The Taker," NBC, 1967; "The Wild Wild West: The Night of the Bubbling Death," CBS, 1967; "Hawaii Five-O: To Kill or Be Killed," CBS, 1971; "Love Story: Beginner's Luck," NBC, 1973; "Little House on the Prairie: Centennial," NBC, 1976; "Lou Grant: Expose," CBS, 1979; "Little House on the Prairie: Annabelle," NBC, 1979; "Lou Grant: Blacklist," CBS, 1981; "St. Elsewhere: Family Ties," NBC, 1986; "Scarecrow and Mrs. King: The Boy Who Could Be King," CBS, 1986; "Highway to Heaven: Man's Best Friend," NBC, 1986; "Simon & Simon: Competition-Who Needs It?," CBS, 1987; "Matlock: The Gift," NBC, 1987; "St. Elsewhere: Handoff," NBC, 1987.

TV MOVIES AND MINISERIES: "Escape," ABC, 1971; "Man on a String," ABC, 1972; "Partners in Crime," NBC, 1973; "Hijack!," ABC, 1973; "Remember When," NBC, 1974; "Death Sentence," ABC, 1974; "Promise Him Anything," ABC, 1975; "Dawn: Portrait of a Teenage Runaway," NBC, 1976; "Ike," ABC, 1979; "Blind Ambition," CBS, 1979; "The Winds of War," ABC, 1983; "Grace Kelly," ABC, 1983; "Through Naked Eyes," ABC, 1983; "Under the Influence," CBS, 1986; "War and Remembrance," ABC, 1988; "Bring Me the Head of Dobie Gillis," CBS, 1988; "Cross of Fire," NBC, 1989.

SCHEDEEN, ANNE
b. *Portland, OR*. Actress who played Kate Tanner on "ALF."

AS A REGULAR: "Marcus Welby, M.D.," ABC, 1975-76; "Paper Dolls," ABC, 1984; "ALF," NBC, 1986-90.

AND: "Emergency!: The Bash," NBC, 1974; "Lucas Tanner: Merry Gentlemen," NBC, 1974; "McCloud: The Park Avenue Pirates," NBC, 1975; "Three for the Road: Trail of Bigfoot," CBS, 1975; "Emergency!: Fair Fight," NBC, 1976; "Switch: Dangerous Curves," CBS, 1977; "Kingston: Confidential: Seed of Corruption," NBC, 1977; "Three's Company: Will the Real Jack Tripper," ABC, 1978; "Three's Company: Double Date," ABC, 1978; "Three's Company: Stanley's Hotline," ABC, 1978; "Three's Company: Honest Jack Tripper," ABC, 1981; "Simon & Simon: Thin Air," CBS, 1982; "Cheers: Norm's Conquest," NBC, 1984; "E/R: The Sister," CBS, 1984; "Murder, She Wrote: If the Frame Fits," CBS, 1986.

TV MOVIES AND MINISERIES: "You Lie So Deep, My Love," ABC, 1975; "Flight to Holocaust," NBC, 1977; "Cast the First Stone," NBC, 1989.

SCHELL, RONNIE
b. *Richmond, CA, December 23, 1931*. Comic actor and performer in hundreds of TV commercials; he played Duke Slater on "Gomer Pyle, USMC."

AS A REGULAR: "Gomer Pyle, USMC," CBS, 1964-67, 1968-69; "That Girl," ABC, 1966-67; "Good Morning, World," CBS, 1967-68; "The Jim Nabors Hour," CBS, 1969-71.

AND: "The Bob Newhart Show," NBC, 1962; "The Merv Griffin Show," NBC, 1962; "The Merv Griffin Show," NBC, 1963; "The Patty Duke Show: Our Daughter the Artist," ABC, 1965; "The Patty Duke Show: Patty the Candy Striper," ABC, 1965; "The Patty Duke Show: Fiance for a Day," ABC, 1966; "The Andy Griffith Show: The Foster Lady," CBS, 1966; "Love, American Style: Love and the Safely Married Man," ABC, 1970; "That Girl: Counter Proposal," ABC, 1970; "The Mike Douglas Show," SYN, 1971; "Love, American Style: Love and the Naked Stranger," ABC, 1972; "Happy Days: Be the First on Your Block," ABC, 1974; "Adam 12: Camp," NBC, 1974; "Happy Days: A Star Is Bored," ABC, 1974; "Dinah!," SYN, 1975; "Alice: Mel's Happy Burger," CBS, 1976; "One Day at a Time: Schneider Gets Fired," CBS, 1979; "Charlie's Angels: Marathon Angels," ABC, 1979; "Mork & Mindy: Mork in Wonderland," ABC, 1979; "Alice: Mel's in the Kitchen with Dinah," CBS, 1979; "Dance Fever," SYN, 1980; "Sledge Hammer!: Pilot," ABC, 1986; "Mr. Belvedere: Marsha's Secret," ABC, 1988; "Hard Time on Planet Earth: Wrestlemania," CBS, 1989; "227: There Go the Clowns," NBC, 1989.

SCHNEIDER, JOHN
b. *Mt. Kisco, NY, April 8, 1954*. Blond actor who played Bo Duke.

AS A REGULAR: "The Dukes of Hazzard," CBS, 1979-85; "Grand Slam," CBS, 1990.

AND: "The Mike Douglas Show," SYN, 1980; "The Magical World of Disney: Wild Jack," NBC, 1989.

TV MOVIES AND MINISERIES: "Happy Endings," CBS, 1983; "Stagecoach," CBS, 1986; "Christmas Comes to Willow Creek," CBS, 1987; "Outback Bound," CBS, 1988.

SCHREIBER, AVERY
b. *Chicago, IL, April 9, 1935*. Roly-poly, mustachioed comic actor, often with Jack Burns; best known for his Doritos commericals.

AS A REGULAR: "My Mother the Car," NBC, 1965-66; "Our Place," CBS, 1967; "The Burns and Schreiber Comedy Hour," ABC, 1973; "Ben Vereen... Comin' at Ya," NBC, 1975; "Sammy and Company," SYN, 1975-77; "Sha Na Na," SYN, 1977-78.

AND: "The Jack Paar Program," NBC, 1965; "Hollywood Palace," ABC, 1965; "Perry Como Special," NBC, 1967; "Get Smart: The Worst Best Man," NBC, 1968; "The Mothers-in-Law: And Baby Makes Four," NBC, 1969; "The Glen Campbell Goodtime Hour," CBS, 1969; "Love, American Style: Love and the Advice Givers," ABC, 1969; "That Girl: Mission: Improbable," ABC, 1969; "The Ghost and Mrs. Muir: The Firehouse Five Plus Ghost," ABC, 1969; "That

Girl: Counter Proposal," ABC, 1970; "Barefoot in the Park: Corie's Rear Window," ABC, 1970; "McCloud: Fifth Man in a String Quartet," NBC, 1972; "Love, American Style: Love and the Perfect Wife," ABC, 1972; "The Dean Martin Show," NBC, 1973; "The Mike Douglas Show," SYN, 1974; "Love, American Style: Love and the Opera Singer," ABC, 1974; "Chico and the Man: Play Gypsy," NBC, 1975; "Chico and the Man: The Misfortune Teller," NBC, 1975; "Match Game '76," CBS, 1976; "The Rockford Files: Rattlers' Class of '63," NBC, 1977; "The Love Boat: Marooned," ABC, 1978; "Shadow Chasers: Pilot," ABC, 1985; "The Love Boat: Santa, Santa, Santa," ABC, 1985.

TV MOVIES AND MINISERIES: "Escape," ABC, 1971; "Second Chance," ABC, 1972; "Flatbed Annie and Sweetiepie: Lady Truckers," CBS, 1979.

SCHRODER, RICKY

b. Staten Island, NY, April 13, 1970. Former child actor who's turned to TV movies.
AS A REGULAR: "Silver Spoons," NBC, 1982-86; SYN, 1986-87.
AND: "Doug Henning Special," NBC, 1981.
TV MOVIES AND MINISERIES: "Something So Right," CBS, 1982; "Two Kinds of Love," CBS, 1983; "A Reason to Live," NBC, 1985; "Too Young the Hero," CBS, 1988; "Terror on Highway 91," CBS, 1989; "Lonesome Dove," CBS, 1989; "Out on the Edge," CBS, 1989.

SCHUCK, JOHN

b. Boston, MA, February 4, 1940. Husky actor who played Sgt. Enright on "Mc Millan and Wife"; he now plays Herman Munster.
AS A REGULAR: "McMillan and Wife," NBC, 1971-76; "Holmes and Yoyo," ABC, 1976; "Turnabout," NBC, 1979; "The New Odd Couple," ABC, 1982-83; "The Munsters Today," SYN, 1988- .
AND: "Gunsmoke: Coreyville," CBS, 1969; "Mission: Impossible: Death Squad," CBS, 1970; "The Mary Tyler Moore Show: Keep Your Guard Up," CBS, 1970; "Room 222: The Fuzz That Grooved," ABC, 1970; "Gunsmoke: The Thieves," CBS, 1970; "Bonanza: A Single Pilgrim," NBC, 1971; "Cade's County: Slay Ride," CBS, 1972; "Ironside: Bubble, Bubble, Toil and Murder," NBC, 1972; "Love, American Style: Love and the President," ABC, 1972; "If I Had a Million," NBC, 1973; "Movin' On: The Price of Loving," NBC, 1975; "The $25,000 Pyramid," SYN, 1975; "The Love Boat: The Caper," ABC, 1978; "St. Elsewhere: Up on the Roof," NBC, 1984; "St. Elsewhere: Homecoming," NBC, 1984; "St. Elsewhere: The Children's Hour," NBC, 1984; "E/R: Both Sides Now," CBS, 1985; "Blacke's Magic: Forced Landing," NBC, 1986; "Murder, She Wrote: Stage Struck," CBS, 1986; "Simon & Simon: Love and/or Marriage,"

CBS, 1986; "The Golden Girls: Strange Bedfellows," NBC, 1987; "Simon & Simon: Second Swell," CBS, 1988.
TV MOVIES AND MINISERIES: "Once Upon a Dead Man," NBC, 1971; "Hunter," CBS, 1973; "Roots," ABC, 1977.

SCHULTZ, DWIGHT

b. Baltimore, MD, November 24, 1947. Actor who played Murdock on "The A-Team."
AS A REGULAR: "The A-Team," NBC, 1983-87.
AND: "Hill Street Blues: Life, Death, Eternity, Etcetera," NBC, 1981; "Nurse: Going Home," CBS, 1981.
TV MOVIES AND MINISERIES: "When Your Lover Leaves," NBC, 1983; "Perry Mason: The Case of the Sinister Spirit," NBC, 1987; "Perry Mason: The Case of the Musical Murder," NBC, 1989.

SCOLARI, PETER

b. New Rochelle, NY, September 12, 1954. Light comic actor who played, memorably, the self-absorbed Michael Harris on "Newhart."
AS A REGULAR: "Goodtime Girls," ABC, 1980; "Bosom Buddies," ABC, 1980-82; "Baby Makes Five," ABC, 1983; "Newhart," CBS, 1984-90.
AND: "Remington Steele: Steele Waters Run Deep," NBC, 1982; "The Love Boat: Daredevil," ABC, 1986; "Family Ties: Once in Love with Elyse," NBC, 1986; "The New Mike Hammer: Green Blizzard," CBS, 1987; "Trying Times: Death and Taxes," PBS, 1989; "The Arsenio Hall Show," SYN, 1989; "Later with Bob Costas," NBC, 1989.
TV MOVIES AND MINISERIES: "Carpool," CBS, 1983; "Amazon," ABC, 1984; "Fatal Confession: A Father Dowling Mystery," NBC, 1988; "The Ryan White Story," ABC, 1989.

SCOTT, GEORGE C.

b. Wise, VA, October 18, 1927. Intense film actor ("Dr. Strangelove," "Patton") who's come to TV to star in a socially-conscious drama series and a mediocre sitcom; he won an Emmy (which he refused) for "The Price."
AS A REGULAR: "East Side/West Side," CBS, 1963-64; "Mr. President," FOX, 1987-88.
AND: "Du Pont Show of the Month: A Tale of Two Cities," CBS, 1958; "Kraft Theatre: The Outcasts of Poker Flat," NBC, 1958; "Sunday Showcase: People Kill People Sometimes," NBC, 1959; "Ben Casey: I Remember a Lemon Tree," ABC, 1961; "The Power and the Glory," CBS, 1961; "Breck Golden Showcase: The Picture of Dorian Gray," CBS, 1961; "Naked City: Strike a Statue," ABC, 1962; "The Virginian: The Brazen Bell," NBC, 1962; "The Eleventh Hour: I Don't Belong in a White Painted House," NBC, 1962;

"The Virginian: The Brazen Bell," NBC, 1962; "Bob Hope Chrysler Theatre: A Time for Killing," NBC, 1965; "The Road West: This Savage Land," NBC, 1966; "The Crucible," CBS, 1967; "Personality," NBC, 1968; "On Stage: Mirror, Mirror on the Wall," NBC, 1969; "Hallmark Hall of Fame: The Price," NBC, 1971; "The Trouble with People," NBC, 1972; "A Salute to Television's 25th Anniversary," ABC, 1972; "Hollywood Squares," SYN, 1975; "The American Parade: Power and the Presidency," CBS, 1976; "Camera Three: Circle in the Square's 25th Anniversary," CBS, 1977.

TV MOVIES AND MINISERIES: "Jane Eyre," NBC, 1971; "Fear on Trial," CBS, 1975; "Hallmark Hall of Fame: Beauty and the Beast," NBC, 1976; "Oliver Twist," CBS, 1982; "China Rose," CBS, 1983; "A Christmas Carol," CBS, 1984; "Mussolini: The Untold Story," NBC, 1985; "Choices," ABC, 1986; "The Last Days of Patton," CBS, 1986; "The Murders in the Rue Morgue," CBS, 1986; "Pals," CBS, 1987; "The Ryan White Story," ABC, 1989.

AS A DIRECTOR: "Hollywood Television Theatre: The Andersonville Trial," NET, 1970.

* Emmies: 1971.

SCOTT, WILLARD

Rotund weatherman-clown on the "Today" show; he occasionally plays Mr. Poole on "The Hogan Family."

AS A REGULAR: "Today," NBC, 1984- ; "Valerie," NBC, 1987-88; "Valerie's Family," NBC, 1988; "The Hogan Family," NBC, 1988-90; CBS, 1990- .

SCOTTI, VITO

b. San Francisco, CA, January 26, 1918. Character actor usually called upon for dialect roles, mostly Italian and Japanese; on "Gilligan's Island" he played a grossly stereotyped Japanese soldier unaware that World War II was over, and in another episode he was a mad scientist.

AS A REGULAR: "Mama Rosa," ABC, 1950; "Andy's Gang," NBC, 1955-60; "The Flying Nun," ABC, 1968-69; "To Rome with Love," CBS, 1969-71; "Barefoot in the Park," ABC, 1970-71.

AND: "Schlitz Playhouse of Stars: Clothes Make the Man," CBS, 1957; "The Californians: Deadly Tintype," NBC, 1958; "How to Marry a Millionaire: Loco and the Gambler," SYN, 1959; "Johnny Staccato: The Mask of Jason," NBC, 1960; "The Deputy: Trail of Darkness," NBC, 1960; "Mr. Lucky: Election Bet," CBS, 1960; "Cheyenne: Counterfeit Gun," ABC, 1960; "SurfSide 6: The Clown," ABC, 1960; "Tales of Wells Fargo: The Hand That Shook the Hand," NBC, 1961; "Bachelor Father: Star Light, Star Not So Bright," ABC, 1961; "Surfside 6: The

Roust," ABC, 1962; "The Addams Family: Art and the Addams Family," ABC, 1964; "Gilligan's Island: So Sorry, My Island Now," CBS, 1965; "The Jack Benny Program," NBC, 1965; "The Addams Family: The Addams Family and the Spacemen," ABC, 1965; "Wendy & Me: Tacos, Enchiladas and Wendy," ABC, 1965; "Get Smart: Mr. Big," NBC, 1965; "Laredo: I See by Your Outfit," NBC, 1965; "Gilligan's Island: The Friendly Physician," CBS, 1966; "Batman: The Penguin's Nest/The Bird's Last Jest," ABC, 1966; "McMillan and Wife: Murder by the Barrel," NBC, 1971; "Columbo: Any Old Port in a Storm," NBC, 1973; "Shaft: The Killing," CBS, 1973; "Columbo: Candidate for Crime," NBC, 1973; "McMillan and Wife: Man Without a Face," NBC, 1974; "Columbo: Swan Song," NBC, 1974; "Columbo: Negative Reaction," NBC, 1974; "Columbo: Identity Crisis," NBC, 1975; "McCoy: Bless the Big Fish," NBC, 1975; "The Bionic Woman: Assault on the Princess," ABC, 1976; "Police Woman: Silky Chamberlain," NBC, 1977; "Happy Days: Married Strangers," ABC, 1979; "CHiPS: Journey to a Spacecraft," NBC, 1983; "Columbo: Murder-A Self Portrait," ABC, 1989.

TV MOVIES AND MINISERIES: "Twice in a Lifetime," NBC, 1974.

SEAFORTH, SUSAN

b. San Francisco, CA, July 11, 1943. Actress in fifties TV as a starlet and later in soaps; she plays Julie Williams on "Days of Our Lives" and was JoAnna Manning on "The Young and the Restless."

AS A REGULAR: "General Hospital," ABC, 1963; "The Young Marrieds," ABC, 1964-66; "Days of Our Lives," NBC, 1968-84; 1990- ; "The Young and the Restless," CBS, 1984-89.

AND: "The Life and Legend of Wyatt Earp: The Sharpshooter," ABC, 1957; "The 20th Century-Fox Hour: Threat to a Happy Ending," CBS, 1957; "Leave It to Beaver: Wally's Girl Trouble," CBS, 1957; "The Loretta Young Show: My Two Hands," NBC, 1958; "SurfSide 6: The Empty House," ABC, 1961; "National Velvet: The Scandal," NBC, 1962; "SurfSide 6: Find Leroy Burdette," ABC, 1962; "Hawaiian Eye: Blackmail in Satin," ABC, 1962; "Cheyenne: The Bad Penny," ABC, 1962; "77 Sunset Strip: Flight From Escondido," ABC, 1962; "Hawaiian Eye: The Long Way Home," ABC, 1963; "The Travels of Jaimie McPheeters: The Day of the Search," ABC, 1964; "My Three Sons: The Leopard's Spots," ABC, 1965; "The FBI: The Insolents," ABC, 1965; "My Three Sons: Weekend in Paradise," CBS, 1967; "The FBI: The Traitor," ABC, 1967; "Dragnet: The Big Starlet," NBC, 1968; "Dragnet: The Big Investigation," NBC, 1968; "The Wild Wild West: The Night of the Miguelito's Revenge," CBS, 1968; "The Felony

Squad: The Fatal Hours," ABC, 1968; "Emergency!: Botulism," NBC, 1972; "The Mike Douglas Show," SYN, 1976; "Hollywood Squares," NBC, 1976; "Heartbeat: Stress," ABC, 1989.

SEGAL, GEORGE
b. *New York City, NY, February 13, 1936*. Leading man of films in two short-lived TV series.
AS A REGULAR: "Take Five," CBS, 1987; "Murphy's Law," ABC, 1988-89.
AND: "Armstrong Circle Theatre: Ghost Bomber: The Lady Be Good," CBS, 1960; "Play of the Week: The Closing Door," SYN, 1960; "Look Up and Live: The Tender Falcon," CBS, 1960; "Accent: Ethan Allen and the Green Mountain Boys," CBS, 1962; "Armstrong Circle Theatre: The Friendly Thieves," CBS, 1962; "U.S. Steel Hour: The Inner Panic," CBS, 1962; "The Nurses: Root of Violence," CBS, 1963; "Naked City: Man Without a Skin," ABC, 1963; "The Alfred Hitchcock Hour: A Nice Touch," CBS, 1963; "Channing: A Patron Saint for the Cargo Cult," ABC, 1963; "The Nurses: Climb a Broken Ladder," CBS, 1964; "Death of a Salesman," CBS, 1966; "The Desperate Hours," ABC, 1967; "The Mike Douglas Show," SYN, 1967; "Of Mice and Men," ABC, 1968; "CBS Playhouse 90: The Lie," CBS, 1973; "The Merv Griffin Show," SYN, 1974; "Dinah!," SYN, 1975; "Later with Bob Costas," NBC, 1989.
TV MOVIES AND MINISERIES: "Trackdown: Finding the Goodbar Killer," CBS, 1983; "Not My Kid," CBS, 1985; "Many Happy Returns," CBS, 1986.

SELBY, DAVID
b. *Morgantown, WV, February 5, 1941*. Actor who played Quentin Collins on "Dark Shadows" and Richard Channing on "Falcon Crest."
AS A REGULAR: "Dark Shadows," ABC, 1966-71; "Flamingo Road," NBC, 1981-82; "Falcon Crest," CBS, 1982-90.
AND: "Kojak: An Unfair Trade," CBS, 1976; "The Pat Sajak Show," CBS, 1989; "Doogie Howser, M.D.: She Ain't Heavy, She's My Cousin," ABC, 1989.
TV MOVIES AND MINISERIES: "Washington: Behind Closed Doors," ABC, 1977; "The Night Rider," ABC, 1979; "Love for Rent," ABC, 1979.

SELLECCA, CONNIE
b. *Bronx, NY, May 25, 1955*. Attractive actress who may yet be in something worth watching; she played Christine Francis on "Hotel."
AS A REGULAR: "Flying High," CBS, 1978-79; "Beyond Westworld," CBS, 1980; "The Greatest American Hero," ABC, 1981-83;

"Hotel," ABC, 1983-88.
AND: "The John Davidson Show," SYN, 1981.
TV MOVIES AND MINISERIES: "The Bermuda Depths," ABC, 1978; "Flying High," CBS, 1978; "Captain America II," CBS, 1979; "She's Dressed to Kill," NBC, 1979; "Downpayment on Murder," NBC, 1987; "The Last Fling," ABC, 1987; "Brotherhood of the Rose," NBC, 1989; "Turn Back the Clock," NBC, 1989.

SELLECK, TOM
b. *Detroit, MI, January 29, 1945*. Handsome, likable leading man who made his mark as Thomas Magnum, P.I.
AS A REGULAR: "The Young and the Restless," CBS, 1974-75; "Magnum P.I.," CBS, 1980-88.
AND: "Lancer: Yesterday's Vengeance," CBS, 1969; "The FBI: The Confession," ABC, 1973; "Marcus Welby, M.D.: Dark Fury," ABC, 1974; "The Streets of San Francisco: Spooks for Sale," ABC, 1975; "Taxi: Cab 804," ABC, 1978; "The Rockford Files: White on White and Nearly Perfect," NBC, 1978; "The Rockford Files: Nice Guys Finish Dead," NBC, 1980; "The John Davidson Show," SYN, 1982; "Murder, She Wrote: Magnum on Ice," CBS, 1986; "Dolly," ABC, 1988; "The Tonight Show Starring Johnny Carson," NBC, 1989.
TV MOVIES AND MINISERIES: "The Movie Murderer," NBC, 1970; "Returning Home," ABC, 1975; "Most Wanted," ABC, 1976; "The Concrete Cowboys," CBS, 1979; "Divorce Wars: A Love Story," ABC, 1982; "The Shadow Riders," CBS, 1982.
* Emmies: 1984.

SERLING, ROD
b. *Syracuse, NY, December 25, 1924; d. 1975*. Writer-producer given at times to preaching; still, his "Twilight Zone" stands as the model of a classic anthology series.
AS A REGULAR: "The Twilight Zone," CBS, 1959-64; "Liar's Club," SYN, 1969; "Night Gallery," NBC, 1970-73.
AND: "The Last Word, CBS, 1957; "Look Here," NBC, 1958; "On the Go," CBS, 1959; "Art Linkletter's House Party," CBS, 1960; "Westinghouse Desilu Playhouse: The Man in the Funny Suit," CBS, 1960; "Here's Hollywood," NBC, 1961; "Ichabod and Me: The Author," CBS, 1962; "The Jack Benny Program," CBS, 1963; "The Art Linkletter Show," NBC, 1963; "The Match Game," NBC, 1964; "The Danny Kaye Show," CBS, 1964; "You Don't Say," NBC, 1964; "The Tonight Show Starring Johnny Carson," NBC, 1964; "To Tell the Truth," CBS, 1964; "The Mike Douglas Show," SYN, 1965; "The Match Game," NBC, 1966; "You Don't Say," NBC, 1968; "You Don't Say," NBC, 1969; "Appointment with Adventure," CBS, 1971;

"Password," ABC, 1972; "A Salute to Television's 25th Anniversary," ABC, 1972; "Ironside: Bubble, Bubble, Toil and Murder," NBC, 1972; "Smithsonian Institution Special: Monsters! Mysteries or Myths?," CBS, 1974.

AS A WRITER: "Kraft Television Theatre: The Blues for Joey Menotti," NBC, 1953; "Kraft Television Theatre: Patterns," NBC, 1956; "Kaiser Aluminum Hour: Mr. Finchley Versus the Bomb," NBC, 1956; "Playhouse 90: Requiem for a Heavyweight," CBS, 1956; "Playhouse 90: The Comedian," CBS, 1957; "Playhouse 90: The Dark Side of the Earth," CBS, 1957; "Playhouse 90: Panic Button," CBS, 1957; "Matinee Theatre: The Cause," NBC, 1958; "Playhouse 90: Bomber's Moon," CBS, 1958; "Playhouse 90: A Town Has Turned to Dust," CBS, 1958; "Pursuit: Last Night of August," CBS, 1958; "Westinghouse Desilu Playhouse: Time Element," CBS, 1958; "Playhouse 90: The Velvet Alley," CBS, 1959; "Playhouse 90: Rank and File," CBS, 1959; "Playhouse 90: In the Presence of Mine Enemies," CBS, 1960; "Bob Hope Chrysler Theatre: It's Mental Work," NBC, 1964; "Carol for Another Christmas," ABC, 1964.

TV MOVIES AND MINISERIES: "The Doomsday Flight," NBC, 1966; "Night Gallery," NBC, 1969.

AS WRITER-PRODUCER-CREATOR: "The Twilight Zone," CBS, 1959-64; "The Loner," CBS, 1965-66; "Night Gallery," NBC, 1970-73.

AS CREATOR: "The New People," ABC, 1969-70.

* Emmies: 1956, 1957, 1958, 1960, 1961, 1964.

SEVAREID, ERIC
b. Velva, ND, November 26, 1912. CBS news reporter-commentator from 1940-77.

AS A REGULAR: "Capitol Cloak Room," CBS, 1949-50; "The American Week," CBS, 1954; "Conquest," CBS, 1957-58; "The March of Medicine," ABC, 1958; "CBS Weekend News," CBS, 1962-63; "Conversations with Eric Sevareid," CBS, 1975; "Eric Sevareid's Chronicle," SYN, 1982.

AND: "Taxi: Fantasy Borough," ABC, 1980.

* Emmies: 1973, 1974, 1977.

SEVERINSON, DOC
b. Carl Severinson, Arlington, OR, July 7, 1927. Trumpeter-bandleader.

AS A REGULAR: "The Tonight Show Starring Johnny Carson," NBC, 1967- .

AND: "Jack Lemmon-Get Happy," NBC, 1973; "The Merv Griffin Show," SYN, 1973; "Love, American Style: Love and the Cover," ABC, 1974; "Sandy in Disneyland," CBS, 1974; "Hollywood Squares," SYN, 1975; "Dinah!," SYN, 1977; "The Merv Griffin Show," SYN, 1977; "Midnight Special," NBC, 1977; "The Peter Marshall Variety Show," SYN, 1977; "Hollywood Squares," NBC,

1978; "NBC Special Treat: Sunshine's on the Way," NBC, 1980; "It's Garry Shandling's Show: No Baby, No Show," FOX, 1988; "The Ice Capades with Jason Bateman and Alyssa Milano," ABC, 1989.

SEYMOUR, JANE
b. England, February 15, 1951. Goddess of the TV movie.

AS A GUEST: "McCloud: The Great Taxicab Stampede," NBC, 1977; "Dinah!," SYN, 1978; "Dance Fever," SYN, 1981; "The John Davidson Show," SYN, 1981; "Late Night with David Letterman," NBC, 1987; "Fifty Years of Television: A Golden Celebration," CBS, 1989.

TV MOVIES AND MINISERIES: "Frankenstein: The True Story," NBC, 1973; "Best Sellers: Captains and the Kings," NBC, 1976; "Benny and Barney: Las Vegas Undercover," NBC, 1977; "Best Sellers: Seventh Avenue," NBC, 1977; "The Awakening Land," ABC, 1978; "Dallas Cowboy Cheerleaders," ABC, 1979; "East of Eden," ABC, 1981; "Dark Mirror," ABC, 1984; "The Sun Also Rises," NBC, 1984; "Obsessed with a Married Woman," ABC, 1985; "Crossings," ABC, 1986; "The Woman He Loved," CBS, 1988; "Onassis: The Richest Man in the World," ABC, 1988; "War and Remembrance," ABC, 1988, 1989.

SHACKELFORD, TED
b. Oklahoma City, OK, June 23, 1946. Actor who's played Gary Ewing on "Dallas" and "Knots Landing."

AS A REGULAR: "Another World," NBC, 1975-77; "Dallas," CBS, 1979-81; "Knots Landing," CBS, 1979- .

AND: "Paradise: Home Again," CBS, 1989; "The Young Riders: The Keepsake," ABC, 1989.

TV MOVIES AND MINISERIES: "The Jordan Chance," CBS, 1978; "Terror Among Us," CBS, 1981.

SHANDLING, GARRY
b. Chicago, IL, 1950. Comedian.

AS A REGULAR: "It's Garry Shandling's Show," FOX & SHO, 1988-90.

AND: "Saturday Night Live," NBC, 1987; "The Tonight Show Starring Johnny Carson," NBC, 1989.

SHATNER, WILLIAM
b. Montreal, Canada, March 22, 1931. Captain Kirk and T.J. Hooker, rolled into one.

AS A REGULAR: "For the People," CBS, 1965; "Star Trek," NBC, 1966-69; 1973-75; "The Barbary Coast," ABC, 1975-76; "T.J. Hooker," ABC, 1982-85; CBS, 1985-87.

AND: "Goodyear TV Playhouse: All Summer Long," NBC, 1956; "Omnibus: School for Wives," ABC, 1956; "Kaiser Aluminum Hour:

Gwyneth," NBC, 1956; "Omnibus: Oedipus Rex," ABC, 1957; "Kraft Television Theatre: The Discoverers, NBC, 1957; "Studio One: The Defender," CBS, 1957; "Kaiser Aluminum Hour: The Deadly Silence," NBC, 1957; "Alfred Hitchcock Presents: The Glass Eye," CBS, 1957; "Studio One: The Deaf Heart," CBS, 1957; "Studio One: No Deadly Medicine," CBS, 1957; "Kraft Theatre: The Velvet Trap," NBC, 1958; "U.S. Steel Hour: Walk with a Stranger," CBS, 1958; "U.S. Steel Hour: A Man in Hiding," CBS, 1958; "Suspicion: Protege," NBC, 1958; "Climax!: Time of the Hanging," CBS, 1958; "Playhouse 90: A Town Has Turned to Dust," CBS, 1958; "Kraft Mystery Theatre: The Man Who Didn't Fly," NBC, 1958; "U.S. Steel Hour: Old Marshals Never Die," CBS, 1958; "The Ed Sullivan Show," CBS, 1958; "Hallmark Hall of Fame: Hallmark Christmas Tree-Light One Candle," NBC, 1958; "Sunday Showcase: The Indestructable Mr. Gore," NBC, 1959; "Salute to the American Theatre," CBS, 1959; "Alfred Hitchcock Presents: Mother, May I Go Out to Swim?," CBS, 1960; "Family Classics: The Scarlet Pimpernel," CBS, 1960; "Play of the Week: The Night of the Auk," SYN, 1960; "The Twilight Zone: Nick of Time," CBS, 1960; "The Outlaws: Starfall," NBC, 1960; "Alcoa Presents One Step Beyond: The Promise," ABC, 1960; "Thriller: The Hungry Glass," NBC, 1961; "Robert Herridge Theatre: A Story of a Gunfighter," SYN, 1961; "Thriller: The Grim Reaper," NBC, 1961; "The Defenders: Killer Instinct," CBS, 1961; "Dr. Kildare: Admitting Service," NBC, 1961; "Naked City: Portrait of a Painter," ABC, 1962; "Naked City: Without Stick or Sword," ABC, 1962; "The Defenders: The Invisible Badge," CBS, 1962; "The Nurses: A Difference of Years," CBS, 1963; "The Dick Powell Show: Colossus," NBC, 1963; "The Nurses: A Question of Mercy," CBS, 1963; "Alcoa Premiere: Million Dollar Hospital," ABC, 1963; "77 Sunset Strip: 5," ABC, 1963; "The Twilight Zone: Nightmare at 20,000 Feet," CBS, 1963; "Twelve O'Clock High: I Am the Enemy," ABC, 1965; "The Fugitive: Stranger in the Mirror," ABC, 1965; "The Virginian: The Claim," NBC, 1965; "The Big Valley: A Time to Kill," ABC, 1966; "Dr. Kildare: The Encroachment/A Patient Lost/What Happened to All the Sunshine and Roses?/The Taste of Crow/Out of a Concrete Tower," NBC, 1966; "Bob Hope Chrysler Theatre: Wind Fever," NBC, 1966; "Gunsmoke: Quaker Girl," CBS, 1966; "Everybody's Talking," ABC, 1967; "Hollywood Squares," NBC, 1968; "Alexander the Great," ABC, 1968; "The Skirts of Happy Chance," NET, 1969; "The Virginian: Black Jade," NBC, 1969; "CBS Playhouse: Shadow Game," CBS, 1969; "Hollywood Squares," NBC, 1970; "The Name of the Game: Tarot," NBC, 1970; "Paris 7000: Shattered Idol," ABC, 1970; "Ironside: Little Jerry Jessup," NBC, 1970; "Medical Center: The Combatants," CBS, 1970; "Hollywood Television

Theatre: The Andersonville Trial," NET, 1970; "Mission: Impossible: Encore," CBS, 1971; "Cade's County: The Armageddon Contract," CBS, 1971; "The Sixth Sense: Can a Dead Man Strike From the Grave?," ABC, 1972; "Hawaii Five-O: You Don't Have to Kill to Get Rich—But It Helps," CBS, 1972; "Mission: Impossible: Cocaine," CBS, 1972; "Owen Marshall, Counselor at Law: Five Will Get You Six," ABC, 1972; "Marcus Welby, M.D.: Heartbeat for Yesterday," ABC, 1972; "The Bold Ones: A Tightrope to Tomorrow," NBC, 1973; "Kung Fu; A Small Beheading," ABC, 1974; "Police Story: Love, Mabel," NBC, 1974; "Amy Prentiss: Baptism of Fire," NBC, 1974; "Police Woman: Smack," NBC, 1974; "The Rookies: The Hunting Ground," ABC, 1975; "Benjamin Franklin: The Statesman," CBS, 1975; "Don Adams Screen Test," SYN, 1975; "The 10th Level," CBS, 1976; "Columbo: Fade in to Murder," NBC, 1976; "The John Davidson Show," SYN, 1981; "Mork & Mindy: Midas Mork," ABC, 1982; "Saturday Night Live," NBC, 1986.

TV MOVIES AND MINISERIES: "Sole Survivor," CBS, 1970; "Vanished," NBC, 1971; "Owen Marshall, Counselor at Law," ABC, 1971; "The People," ABC, 1972; "The Hound of the Baskervilles," ABC, 1972; "Incident on a Dark Street," CBS, 1973; "Go Ask Alice," ABC, 1973; "Horror at 37,000 Feet," CBS, 1973; "Pioneer Woman," ABC, 1973; "Indict and Convict," ABC, 1974; "Pray for the Wildcats," ABC, 1974; "The Barbary Coast," ABC, 1975; "Perilous Voyage," NBC, 1976; "Testimony of Two Men," SYN, 1977; "Crash," ABC, 1978; "The Bastard," SYN, 1978; "Disaster on the Coastliner," ABC, 1979; "The Kidnapping of the President," NBC, 1980; "Secrets of a Married Man," NBC, 1984; "North Beach and Rawhide," CBS, 1985; "Broken Angel," ABC, 1988.

SHAW, RETA

b. South Paris, ME, September 13, 1912; d. 1982. Actress who usually played stern housekeepers or domineering mothers; she played housekeeper Martha Grant on "The Ghost and Mrs. Muir."

AS A REGULAR: "Mr. Peepers," NBC, 1954; "The Ann Sothern Show," CBS, 1958-59; "The Tab Hunter Show," NBC, 1960-61; "Ichabod and Me," CBS, 1961-62; "Oh, Those Bells," CBS, 1962; "The Cara Williams Show," CBS, 1964-65; "The Ghost and Mrs. Muir," NBC, 1968-69; ABC, 1969-70.

AND: "The Millionaire: Story of Anna Hartley," CBS, 1956; "The Life of Riley: World's Greatest Grandson," NBC, 1956; "Annie Get Your Gun," NBC, 1957; "The Betty White Show," ABC, 1958; "The Millionaire: The Johanna Judson

Story," CBS, 1958; "Meet Me in St. Louis," CBS, 1959; "Pete and Gladys: Uncle Paul's New Wife," CBS, 1961; "The Real McCoys: The New Piano," ABC, 1962; "Thriller: Til Death Do Us Part," NBC, 1962; "The Many Loves of Dobie Gillis: Bachelor Father ... and Son," CBS, 1962; "The Lucy Show: Lucy Misplaces Two Thousand Dollars," CBS, 1962; "The Andy Griffith Show: Convicts at Large," CBS, 1962; "The Farmer's Daughter: Cousin Helga Came to Dinner," ABC, 1964; "The Andy Griffith Show: The Song Festers," CBS, 1964; "Bob Hope Chrysler Theatre: Think Pretty," NBC, 1964; "Bewitched: The Witches Are Out," ABC, 1964; "My Three Sons: Here Comes Charley," ABC, 1965; "The Lucy Show: My Fair Lucy," CBS, 1965; "The Dick Van Dyke Show: Fifty-Two Forty-Five or Work," CBS, 1965; "The Man From UNCLE: The Suburbia Affair," NBC, 1967; "Here's Lucy: Lucy the Process Server," CBS, 1968; "I Dream of Jeannie: Jeannie and the Wild Pipchicks," NBC, 1968; "The FBI: The Hero," ABC, 1968; "Bewitched: Sam's Witchcraft Blows a Fuse," ABC, 1972; "Here's Lucy: Lucy and the Group Encounter," CBS, 1972; "The Odd Couple: Maid for Each Other," ABC, 1973; "Emergency!: Snake Bite," NBC, 1973; "Happy Days: Breaking Up Is Hard to Do," ABC, 1974.

TV MOVIES AND MINISERIES: "Murder Once Removed," NBC, 1971; "Guess Who's Sleeping in My Bed?," ABC, 1973; "The Girl Who Came Gift-Wrapped," ABC, 1974.

SHAWLEE, JOAN
b. Queens, NY, March 5, 1925; d. 1987. Comic actress, often in shrill showgirl roles; she played Pickles, wife of Buddy Sorrell (Morey Amsterdam) on "The Dick Van Dyke Show."
AS A REGULAR: "The Abbott and Costello Show," CBS, 1952-54; "Aggie," SYN, 1957; "The Betty Hutton Show," CBS, 1959-60; "The Dick Van Dyke Show," CBS, 1963-66; "The Feather and Father Gang," ABC, 1977.
AND: "Maverick: Stampede," ABC, 1958; "The Rifleman: The Lonesome Bride," ABC, 1961; "Columbo: Suitable for Framing," NBC, 1971; "The Rookies: Covenant with Death," ABC, 1972.
TV MOVIES AND MINISERIES: "Something for a Lonely Man," NBC, 1968; "Dead Men Tell No Tales," CBS, 1971; "Child Bride of Short Creek," NBC, 1981.

SHAWN, DICK
b. Richard Schulefand, Buffalo, NY, December 1, 1929; d. 1987. Underrated comedian at his best on variety shows; he also played Marshal Bing Bell in the well-remembered TV movie "Evil Roy Slade."
AS A REGULAR: "Mary," CBS, 1978; "Hail to the Chief," ABC, 1985.

AND: "The Ed Sullivan Show," CBS, 1956; "The Ed Sullivan Show," CBS, 1958; "The Eddie Fisher Show," NBC, 1958; "Dinah Shore Chevy Show," NBC, 1959; "Mickey Rooney Special," CBS, 1960; "Here's Hollywood," NBC, 1960; "G.E. Theatre: Don't Let It Throw You," CBS, 1961; "Checkmate: Laugh Till I Die," CBS, 1961; "The du Pont Show with June Allyson: The Old-Fashioned Way," CBS, 1961; "Michael Shayne: The Trouble with Ernie," NBC, 1961; "Here's Edie," ABC, 1962; "The Jimmy Dean Show," ABC, 1963; "To Tell the Truth," CBS, 1963; "That Girl: The Mailman Cometh Out," ABC, 1967; "Off to See the Wizard: Who's Afraid of Mother Goose?," ABC, 1967; "Personality," NBC, 1968; "Operation: Entertainment," ABC, 1968; "The Lucy Show: Lucy and the Pool Hustler," CBS, 1968; "Hollywood Palace," ABC, 1969; "This Is Tom Jones," ABC, 1970; "The Bold Ones: The Glass Cage," NBC, 1971; "Bell System Family Theatre: Dames at Sea," NBC, 1971; "Love, American Style: Love and the Hairy Excuse," ABC, 1972; "Love, American Style: Love and the Memento," ABC, 1973; "Medical Center: The Price of a Child," CBS, 1975; "Beat the Clock," SYN, 1975; "Dinah!," SYN, 1976; "The Gong Show," SYN, 1978; "The Merv Griffin Show," SYN, 1978; "Laverne & Shirley: Upstairs, Downstairs," ABC, 1979; "Magnum P.I.: Squeeze Play," CBS, 1983; "The Fall Guy: Losers Weepers," ABC, 1984; "The Twilight Zone: Cold Reading," CBS, 1986; "Amazing Stories: Miss Stardust," NBC, 1987.
TV MOVIES AND MINISERIES: "Evil Roy Slade," NBC, 1972; "Fast Friends," NBC, 1979.
* Shawn had a heart attack while performing onstage; the audience thought it part of the show, laughing until they realized something was seriously wrong. By then, he was dead.

SHAYNE, ROBERT
b. Robert Shaen Dawe, Yonkers, NY, 1910. Actor who played Inspector Henderson, who couldn't quite figure out why Clark Kent and Superman were never around at the same time.
AS A REGULAR: "The Adventures of Superman," SYN, 1951-57.
AND: "Navy Log: Peril on the Sea," ABC, 1956; "The Donna Reed Show: Donna's Helping Hand," ABC, 1961; "The Hathaways: Elinor's Best Friend," ABC, 1962; "Hazel: Never Trouble Trouble," NBC, 1964.
TV MOVIES AND MINISERIES: "The Priest Killer," CBS, 1971.

SHEARER, HARRY
Witty comic and writer who provides various voices on "The Simpsons"; he began his career as a child actor, and appeared in "It's a Small World," the pilot for "Leave It to Beaver."
AS A REGULAR: "Saturday Night Live," NBC,

1984-85; "The Simpsons," FOX, 1990- .
AND: "G.E. Theatre: Cab Driver," CBS, 1957;
"Studio 57: It's a Small World," SYN, 1957;
"Laverne & Shirley: Guinea Pig," ABC, 1977;
"Harry Shearer Special: The Magic of Live," HBO,
1988; "ALF Takes Over the Network," NBC,
1989.
* Shearer made his film debut in "Abbott and
Costello Go to Mars."

SHEEHAN, DOUGLAS
b. Santa Monica, CA, April 27, 1949. Actor who
played Ben Gibson on "Knots Landing" and
Brian Harper on "Day by Day."
AS A REGULAR: "General Hospital," ABC, 1979-82;
"Knots Landing," CBS, 1983-87; "Day by
Day," NBC, 1988-89.
AND: "Cheers: Diane's Perfect Date," NBC, 1983.
TV MOVIES AND MINISERIES: "Stranger in My Bed,"
NBC, 1987; "In the Line of Duty: The FBI
Murders," NBC, 1988.

SHEEN, BISHOP FULTON J.
b. El Paso, IL, May 8, 1895; d. 1979.
AS A REGULAR: "Life Is Worth Living," DUM,
1952-55; ABC, 1955-57.
AND: "The Steve Allen Show," NBC, 1956; "The
Ed Sullivan Show," CBS, 1956.
* Emmies: 1953.

SHEEN, MARTIN
b. Ramon Estevez, Dayton, OH, August 3, 1940.
Actor who divides his time between films
("Apocalypse Now," "Wall Street") and the
tube, where he's appeared in several superior
TV movies and does Toyota and Pepsi
commercials.
AS A GUEST: "The Defenders: The Attack," CBS,
1961; "Route 66: And the Cat Jumped Over the
Moon," CBS, 1961; "Naked City: The Night the
Saints Lost Their Halos," ABC, 1962; "The
Defenders: The Tarnished Cross," CBS, 1962;
"East Side/West Side: You Can't Beat the
System," CBS, 1964; "Trials of O'Brien:
Charlie Has All the Luck," CBS, 1965;
"Mission: Impossible: Live Bait," CBS, 1968;
"Hawaii Five-O: Cry Lie!," CBS, 1970;
"Medical Center: A Duel with Doom," CBS,
1970; "Hollywood Television Theatre: The
Andersonville Trial," NET, 1970; "The FBI:
The Condemned," ABC, 1970; "Ironside: No
Game for Amateurs," ABC, 1970; "Hawaii
Five-O: Time and Memories," CBS, 1970; "The
Young Lawyers: Are You Running with One,
Denny?," ABC, 1970; "The Interns: The
Secret," CBS, 1971; "Dan August: Dead
Witness to a Killing," ABC, 1971; "Hollywood
Television Theatre: Monserrat," NET, 1971;
"Love, American Style: Love and the Swinging
Surgeon," ABC, 1973; "Cannon: Memo From a

Dead Man," CBS, 1973; "The Streets of San
Francisco: Betrayed," ABC, 1973; "Columbo:
Lovely But Lethal," NBC, 1973; "Toma: The
Oberon Contract," ABC, 1973; "Medical
Center: Clash of Shadows," CBS, 1973; "Love
Story: Mirabelle's Summer," NBC, 1973;
"Saturday Night Live," NBC, 1979; "The
Fourth Wise Man," ABC, 1985; "Alfred
Hitchcock Presents: The Method Actor," NBC,
1985; "The Pat Sajak Show," CBS, 1989.
TV MOVIES AND MINISERIES: "Then Came Bronson,"
NBC, 1969; "Goodbye Raggedy Ann," CBS,
1971; "Mongo's Back in Town," CBS, 1971;
"Welcome Home, Johnny Bristol," CBS, 1972;
"That Certain Summer," ABC, 1972; "Pursuit,"
ABC, 1972; "Crime Club," CBS, 1973; "A
Prowler in the Heart," ABC, 1973; "Letters
From Three Lovers," ABC, 1973; "Catholics,"
CBS, 1973; "Message to My Daughter," ABC,
1973; "The Execution of Private Slovik," NBC,
1974; "The Story of Pretty Boy Floyd," ABC,
1974; "The California Kid," ABC, 1974; "The
Last Survivors," NBC, 1975; "Sweet Hostage,"
ABC, 1975; "Blind Ambition," CBS, 1979;
"Kennedy," NBC, 1983; "The Atlanta Child
Murders," CBS, 1985; "Out of the Darkness,"
CBS, 1985; "Consenting Adult," ABC, 1985;
"News at Eleven," CBS, 1986; "Samaritan: The
Mitch Snyder Story," CBS, 1986; "Shattered
Spirits," ABC, 1989; "Nightbreaker," TNT,
1989.

SHELDON, JACK
b. Jacksonville, FL, November 30, 1931.
Trumpeter-comedian.
AS A REGULAR: "The Cara Williams Show,"
CBS, 1964-65; "Run, Buddy, Run," CBS, 1966-
67; "The Merv Griffin Show," SYN, 1972-79;
"The Girl with Something Extra," NBC, 1973-
74.
AND: "The Edie Adams Show," ABC, 1964;
"Gilligan's Island: Little Island, Big Gun," CBS,
1965; "Dragnet: Narcotics-DR-21," NBC, 1969;
"Petticoat Junction: Selma Plout's Plot," CBS,
1970; "Dragnet: A.I.D.-The Weekend," NBC,
1970; "Dragnet: Burglary-Baseball," NBC, 1970;
"Marcus Welby, M.D.: Go Get 'Em, Tiger," ABC,
1970.

SHEPHERD, CYBILL
b. Memphis, TN, February 18, 1950. Actress
and former model whose comatose career got
a shot in the arm when she played former
model-turned-detective Maddie Hayes on
"Moonlighting."
AS A REGULAR: "The Yellow Rose," NBC, 1983-
84; "Moonlighting," ABC, 1985-89.
TV MOVIES AND MINISERIES: "A Guide for the
Married Woman," ABC, 1978; "Secrets of a
Married Man," NBC, 1984; "Seduced," CBS,
1985; "The Long Hot Summer," NBC, 1985.

SHEPODD, JON

b. 1927. Actor who played Paul Martin on "Lassie," being quickly succeeded in the role by Hugh Reilly.

AS A REGULAR: "Lassie," CBS, 1957-58.

AND: "Schlitz Playhouse of Stars: The Bankmouse," CBS, 1956; "Navy Log: Captain's Choice," ABC, 1956; "Wire Service: Blood Rock Mine," ABC, 1956; "Matinee Theatre: Daughter of the Seventh," NBC, 1957; "Alcoa Theatre: Circumstantial," NBC, 1957; "Men Into Space: Water Tank Rescue," CBS, 1959; "Power of the Resurrection," NBC, 1960; "The Brothers Brannagan: Damaged Dolls," SYN, 1961.

SHERIDAN, ANN

b. Clara Lou Sheridan, Denton, TX, February 21, 1915; d. 1967. Thirties sex symbol, known as the "Oomph" girl, who was also a capable dramatic and comic actress; she played crack shot Henrietta Hanks in a short-lived western sitcom.

AS A REGULAR: "Another World," NBC, 1965-66; "Pistols 'n' Petticoats," CBS, 1966-67.

AND: "Ford Theatre: Malaya Incident," NBC, 1953; "Dunninger," SYN, 1953; "Lux Video Theatre: The Lovely Day," CBS, 1953; "Schlitz Playhouse of Stars: The Prize," CBS, 1953; "Calling Terry Conway," NBC, 1956; "U.S. Steel Hour: Hunted," CBS, 1956; "Lux Video Theatre: The Hard Way," NBC, 1957; "Playhouse 90: Without Incident," CBS, 1957; "Ford Theatre: Cross Hairs," ABC, 1957; "The Perry Como Show," NBC, 1958; "Pursuit: The Dark Cloud," CBS, 1958; "Arthur Murray Party," NBC, 1959; "Arthur Murray Party," NBC, 1960; "U.S. Steel Hour: The Impostor," CBS, 1960; "Celebrity Talent Scouts," CBS, 1960; "Wagon Train: The Mavis Grant Story," ABC, 1962; "To Tell the Truth," CBS, 1964; "To Tell the Truth," CBS, 1965; "The Tonight Show Starring Johnny Carson," NBC, 1966.

SHERIDAN, NICOLLETTE

b. England, November 21, 1963. Actress who plays Paige Matheson on "Knots Landing."

AS A REGULAR: "Paper Dolls," ABC, 1984; "Knots Landing," CBS, 1986- .

TV MOVIES AND MINISERIES: "Agatha Christie's Dead Man's Folly," CBS, 1986.

SHERMAN, ALLAN

Comedian-songwriter of the sixties; he also created "I've Got a Secret."

AS A GUEST: "The Garry Moore Show," CBS, 1963; "The Tonight Show Starring Johnny Carson," NBC, 1964; "The Tennessee Ernie Ford Show," ABC, 1964; "Get the Message," ABC, 1964; "Mr. Novak: Let's Dig a Little Grammar," NBC, 1964; "Allan Sherman's Funnyland," NBC, 1965; "The Tonight Show Starring Johnny Carson," NBC, 1965; "The Dean Martin Show," NBC, 1965; "The Ed Sullivan Show," CBS, 1966; "You Don't Say," NBC, 1966; "Hippodrome," CBS, 1966; "The Mike Douglas Show," SYN, 1969; "Hollywood Squares," NBC, 1969.

AS CREATOR: "I've Got a Secret," CBS, 1952-67, 1976.

SHERMAN, BOBBY

b. Santa Monica, CA, July 18, 1943. Pop singer-actor of the late sixties; he played Jeremy Bolt on "Here Come the Brides."

AS A REGULAR: "Shindig," ABC, 1964-66; "Here Come the Brides," ABC, 1968-70; "Getting Together," ABC, 1971-72.

AND: "Honey West: The Princess and the Paupers," ABC, 1965; "The Monkees: Monkees in the Movies," NBC, 1967; "The FBI: The Mechanized Accomplice," ABC, 1968; "The Many Moods of Perry Como," NBC, 1970; "The Don Knotts Show," NBC, 1970; "The Partridge Family: A Knight in Shining Armor," ABC, 1971; "The Mod Squad: The Connection," ABC, 1972; "Old Faithful," ABC, 1973; "Emergency!: Messin' Around," NBC, 1974; "Jigsaw John: Too Much, Too Soon," NBC, 1976; "Three's Company: Jack's Other Mother," ABC, 1981; "The Love Boat: Palimony O' Mine," ABC, 1982; "Murder, She Wrote: Murder to a Jazz Beat," CBS, 1985; "Blacke's Magic: Forced Landing," NBC, 1986.

TV MOVIES AND MINISERIES: "Skyway to Death," ABC, 1974.

SHORE, DINAH

b. Fanny Rose Shore, Winchester, TN, March 1, 1917. Popular variety-show songstress of the fifties and sixties, later moving into the talk-show business.

AS A REGULAR: "The Dinah Shore Show," NBC, 1951-57; "Dinah Shore Chevy Show," NBC, 1956-57; 1957-62; "Dinah Shore Special," NBC, 1961-63; ABC, 1964-65; "Dinah's Place," NBC, 1970-74; "Dinah!," SYN, 1974-80; "Dinah and Her New Best Friends," CBS, 1976; "A Conversation with Dinah," TNN, 1989- .

AND: "The Bob Hope Show," NBC, 1950; "The Perry Como Show," NBC, 1956; "Wide, Wide World," NBC, 1957; "The Steve Allen Show," NBC, 1957; "The Danny Thomas Show: The Dinah Shore Show," CBS, 1957; "The General Motors 50th Anniversary Show," NBC, 1957; "The Frank Sinatra Show," ABC, 1958; "The Steve Allen Show," NBC, 1958; "The Danny Thomas Show: Dinah Shore and Danny Are Rivals," CBS, 1958; "Cimarron City: Cimarron Holiday," NBC, 1958; "Pat Boone Chevy Showroom," ABC, 1959; "Some of Manie's Friends," NBC, 1959; "Red Skelton Special,"

CBS, 1960; "Dinah Shore Special: Brief Encounter," NBC, 1961; "Here's Hollywood," NBC, 1961; "Special for Women: Child in Danger," ABC, 1964; "The Ed Sullivan Show," CBS, 1965; "Bob Hope Special," NBC, 1965; "Dinah Shore Special," NBC, 1969; "The Movie Game," SYN, 1969; "Jimmy Durante Presents the Lennon Sisters Hour," ABC, 1970; "Here's Lucy: Someone's On the Ski Lift with Dinah," CBS, 1971; "The Mike Douglas Show," SYN, 1971; "A Salute to Television's 25th Anniversary," ABC, 1972; "Jack Lemmon-Get Happy," NBC, 1973; "Tony Orlando and Dawn," CBS, 1975; "Alice: Mel's in the Kitchen with Dinah," CBS, 1979; "240-Robert: Applicant," ABC, 1979; "America's Tribute to Bob Hope," NBC, 1988; "CBS News Special: Lucy," CBS, 1989.
TV MOVIES AND MINISERIES: "Death Car on the Freeway," CBS, 1979.
* Emmies: 1955, 1956, 1957, 1958, 1959.

SHORT, MARTIN
b. Canada. Gifted comic actor who played Ed Grimley on "SCTV" and "Saturday Night Live."
AS A REGULAR: "The Associates," ABC, 1979-80; "I'm a Big Girl Now," ABC, 1980-81; "SCTV Network 90," NBC, 1982-83; "Saturday Night Live," NBC, 1984-85.
AND: "Taxi: Jim Joins the Network," ABC, 1981; "Tall Tales & Legends: Johnny Appleseed," SHO, 1986; "The Canadian Conspiracy," MAX, 1986; "Saturday Night Live," NBC, 1986; "Really Weird Tales," HBO, 1986; "The Tonight Show Starring Johnny Carson," NBC, 1988; "The Tonight Show Starring Johnny Carson," NBC, 1989; "Late Night with David Letterman," NBC, 1989; "The Tracey Ullman Show: Needle in a Haystack," FOX, 1989.
TV MOVIES AND MINISERIES: "Sunset Limousine," CBS, 1983.
* Emmies: 1983.

SHOWALTER, MAX
b. Caldwell, KS, June 2, 1917. Actor with a brash, intense manner, also known as Casey Adams; he was the first Ward Cleaver (wearing a silk robe and smoking cigarettes) in the "Leave It to Beaver" pilot, "It's a Small World."
AS A REGULAR: "The Swift Show," NBC, 1949; "The Stockard Channing Show," CBS, 1980.
AND: "The Jane Wyman Show: Cleopatra Collins," NBC, 1956; "Schlitz Playhouse of Stars: Carriage From Britian," CBS, 1957; "Studio 57: It's a Small World," SYN, 1957; "Navy Log: The Web Feet," ABC, 1958; "The Real McCoys: Foreman of the Jury," ABC, 1960; "Perry Mason: The Case of the Wandering Widow," CBS, 1960; "The Andy Griffith Show: The Horse Trader," CBS, 1961; "Stagecoach West: The Guardian

Angels," ABC, 1961; "Perry Mason: The Case of the Malicious Mariner," CBS, 1961; "The Many Loves of Dobie Gillis: Names My Mother Called Me," CBS, 1962; "Empire: The Earth Mover," NBC, 1962; "Hazel: Hazel and the Stockholders Meeting," NBC, 1963; "Hazel: I Been Singin' All My Life," NBC, 1963; "Dr. Kildare: Goodbye, Mr. Jersey," NBC, 1964; "Hazel: Hazel's Midas Touch," NBC, 1964; "The Lucy Show: Lucy Gets the Bird," CBS, 1964; "The Lucy Show: Lucy and Arthur Godfrey," CBS, 1965; "Bewitched: The Very Informal Dress," ABC, 1965; "Jimmy Durante Meets the Lively Arts," ABC, 1965; "The Doris Day Show: The Chocolate Bar War," CBS, 1969; "Kojak: A Long Way From Times Square," CBS, 1975; "The Bob Newhart Show: The Ironwood Experience," CBS, 1977; "Foul Play: Sins of the Fathers," ABC, 1981; "The Love Boat: Meet the Author," ABC, 1982; "The Love Boat: So Help Me Hanna," ABC, 1983.

SHRINER, HERB
b. Toledo, OH, May 29, 1918; d. 1970. Humorist of early TV.
AS A REGULAR: "The Herb Shriner Show," CBS, 1949-50; 1956; ABC, 1951-52; "Two for the Money," NBC, 1952-53; CBS, 1953-57.
AND: "Screen Directors Playhouse: Meet the Governor," NBC, 1955; "Pat Boone Chevy Showroom," ABC, 1958; "The Ed Sullivan Show," CBS, 1958; "America Pauses for Springtime," CBS, 1959; "Revlon Revue," CBS, 1960; "Way Back in 1960," ABC, 1960; "Revlon Revue: Accent on Comedy," CBS, 1960; "High Road: A Trip to Jamaica," ABC, 1960; "World Wide 60: Jamboree," NBC, 1960.

SHRINER, KIN
b. New York City, NY, December 6, 1953. Son of humorist Herb Shriner, a soap hunk as Scott Baldwin on "General Hospital."
AS A REGULAR: "General Hospital," ABC, 1977-83, 1985, 1987- ; "Texas," NBC, 1984; "Rituals," SYN, 1984-85.
AND: "The Love Boat: Baby Makers," ABC, 1984.
TV MOVIES AND MINISERIES: "Obsessive Love," CBS, 1984; "War and Remembrance," ABC, 1988, 1989.

SHRINER, WIL
b. New York City, NY, December 6, 1953. Comic and twin of Kin.
AS A REGULAR: "Television: Inside and Out," NBC, 1981-82; "TV's Bloopers & Practical Jokes," NBC, 1985-86; "The Wil Shriner Show," SYN, 1987-88; "Prime Time Pets," CBS, 1990.
AND: "Candid Camera: Eat! Eat! Eat!," CBS, 1989.

SHROYER, SONNY

b. Valdosta, GA. Lanky comic actor who played Deputy Enos on "The Dukes of Hazzard" and a spinoff series.

AS A REGULAR: "The Dukes of Hazzard," CBS, 1979-80; 1982-85; "Enos," CBS, 1980-81.

AND: "Today's FBI: El Paso Murder," ABC, 1981; "The Love Boat: Good Neighbors," ABC, 1982.

TV MOVIES AND MINISERIES: "Freedom Road," NBC, 1979.

SHUSTER, FRANK—See Wayne and Shuster.

SIEBERT, CHARLES

b. Kenosha, WI, March 9, 1938. Actor who played the priggish Dr. Stanley Riverside on "Trapper John, M.D."

AS A REGULAR: "Search for Tomorrow," CBS, 1969-71; "The Blue Knight," CBS, 1976; "One Day at a Time," CBS, 1976-79; "Husbands, Wives & Lovers," CBS, 1978; "Trapper John, M.D.," CBS, 1979-86; "Mancuso, FBI," NBC, 1989-90.

AND: "You Are There: The Fall of Troy," CBS, 1971; "All in the Family: Archie's Civil Rights," CBS, 1975; "The Rockford Files: The Reincarnation of Angie," NBC, 1975; "Kojak: By Silence Betrayed," CBS, 1976; "Barnaby Jones: The Fatal Dive," CBS, 1976; "Police Woman: Shark," NBC, 1977; "The Rockford Files: New Life, Old Dragons," NBC, 1977; "What's Happening!: Nothing Personal," ABC, 1977; "All in the Family: Stretch Cunningham, Goodbye," CBS, 1977; "Rhoda: Rhoda vs. Ida," CBS, 1978; "All in the Family: Edith's Final Respects," CBS, 1978; "Barnaby Jones: Stages of Fear," CBS, 1978; "Good Times: Househunting," CBS, 1979; "The Love Boat: Same Wave Length," ABC, 1982; "The Love Boat: The Wager," ABC, 1984; "Murder, She Wrote: Night of the Headless Horseman," CBS, 1986; "The New Mike Hammer: Lady Killer," CBS, 1987; "Murder, She Wrote: Indian Giver," CBS, 1987; "ABC Afterschool Special: Tattle: When to Tell on a Friend," ABC, 1988.

TV MOVIES AND MINISERIES: "Panache," ABC, 1976; "The Seeding of Sarah Burns," CBS, 1979; "Topper," ABC, 1979; "F.D.R.: The Last Year," NBC, 1980; "Perry Mason: The Case of the Avenging Ace," NBC, 1988; "Shakedown on the Sunset Strip," CBS, 1988.

SIKES, CYNTHIA

b. Coffeyville, KS. Miss Kansas 1972; she played Dr. Annie Cavanero on "St. Elsewhere."

AS A REGULAR: "Big Shamus, Little Shamus," CBS, 1979; "Flamingo Road," NBC, 1981-82; "St. Elsewhere," NBC, 1982-85.

AND: "Joe Forrester: Fashion Mart," NBC, 1975; "Columbo: Now You See Him," NBC, 1976; "Police Woman: Task Force: Cop Killer," NBC,

1976; "The Rockford Files: A Portrait of Elizabeth," NBC, 1976; "Hart to Hart: 'Tis the Season to Be Murdered," ABC, 1980; "The Fall Guy: Soldiers of Misfortune," ABC, 1982; "Magnum P.I.: A Little Bit of Luck, a Little Bit of Grief," CBS, 1985; "Hotel: Imperfect Union," ABC, 1985; "L.A. Law: Open Heart Perjury," NBC, 1988.

TV MOVIES AND MINISERIES: "Best Sellers: Captains and the Kings," NBC, 1976; "His Mistress," NBC, 1984; "Oceans of Fire," CBS, 1986.

SIKKING, JAMES B.

b. Los Angeles, CA, March 5, 1934. Actor who played Lt. Howard Hunter, commander of the Emergency Action Team (EAT) on "Hill Street Blues"; now he's the dad of Doogie Howser, M.D.

AS A REGULAR: "General Hospital," ABC, 1973-76; "Turnabout," NBC, 1979; "Hill Street Blues," NBC, 1981-87; "Doogie Howser, M.D.," ABC, 1989- .

AND: "Assignment: Underwater: The Trap," SYN, 1961; "Combat!: The Long Way Home," ABC, 1963; "The Outer Limits: The Human Factor," ABC, 1963; "The Outer Limits: Cold Hands, Warm Heart," ABC, 1964; "The Virginian: Nobility of Kings," NBC, 1965; "Honey West: A Stitch in Crime," ABC, 1965; "The FBI: Wind It Up and It Betrays You," ABC, 1968; "The FBI: The Condemned," ABC, 1970; "The Doris Day Show: Doris vs. Pollution," CBS, 1970; "Mannix: One for the Lady," CBS, 1970; "Mission: Impossible: Decoy," CBS, 1970; "The FBI: Three Way Split," ABC, 1971; "The FBI: The Game of Terror," ABC, 1971; "The Bob Newhart Show: Goodnight, Nancy," CBS, 1972; "Room 222: Lift, Thrust and Drag," ABC, 1972; "M*A*S*H: Tuttle," CBS, 1973; "The Rookies: Cauldron," ABC, 1973; "Room 222: Pi in the Sky," ABC, 1973; "The FBI: Deadly Ambition," ABC, 1974; "Little House on the Prairie: To Live with Fear," NBC, 1977; "The Rockford Files: A Good Clean Bust with Sequel Rights," NBC, 1978; "Paris: Burnout," CBS, 1979; "The Misadventures of Sheriff Lobo: The Senator Votes Absentee," NBC, 1979; "CBS Summer Playhouse: Mad Avenue," CBS, 1988; "American Playhouse: Ollie Hopnoodle's Haven of Bliss," PBS, 1989.

TV MOVIES AND MINISERIES: "The Astronaut," NBC, 1972; "Man on a String," ABC, 1972; "Family Flight," ABC, 1972; "Coffee, Tea or Me?," CBS, 1973; "The Alpha Caper," ABC, 1973; "First Steps," CBS, 1985; "Dress Gray," NBC, 1986; "Bay Coven," NBC, 1987; "Police Story: The Freeway Killings," NBC, 1987; "Brotherhood of the Rose," NBC, 1989; " AT&T Presents: The Final Days," ABC, 1989; "Desperado: Badlands Justice," NBC, 1989.

SILVER, RON

b. New York City, NY, July 2, 1946. Gifted film actor ("Enemies, a Love Story," "Reversal of Fortune") who played Gary Levy, friend of Brenda Morgenstern (Julie Kavner) on "Rhoda."

AS A REGULAR: "The Mac Davis Show," NBC, 1976; "Rhoda," CBS, 1975-78; "Dear Detective," CBS, 1979; "The Stockard Channing Show," CBS, 1980; "Baker's Dozen," CBS, 1982.

AND: "McMillan and Wife: Secrets for Sale," NBC, 1975; "The Rockford Files: The Italian Bird Fiasco," NBC, 1976; "Here's Boomer: The Private Eye," NBC, 1980; "Hill Street Blues: Life in the Minors," NBC, 1983; "Hill Street Blues: Eugene's Comedy Empire Strikes Back," NBC, 1983; "Trying Times: Drive, She Said," PBS, 1988.

TV MOVIES AND MINISERIES: "Betrayal," NBC, 1978; "Word of Honor," CBS, 1981; "Kane & Abel," CBS, 1985; "Trapped in Silence," CBS, 1986; "Billionaire Boys Club," NBC, 1987; "A Father's Revenge," ABC, 1988.

SILVERHEELS, JAY

b. Harold J. Smith, Six Nations Indian Reservation, Ontario, Canada, May 26, 1919; d. 1980. Hmmm. Tonto, kemosabe.

AS A REGULAR: "The Lone Ranger," ABC, 1949-60.

AND: "Wide Wide World: The Western," NBC, 1958; "Walt Disney Presents: Texas John Slaughter-Geronimo's Revenge," ABC, 1959; "Wanted Dead or Alive: Man on Horseback," CBS, 1959; "Walt Disney Presents: Texas John Slaughter-Apache Friendship," CBS, 1960; "Wagon Train: Path of the Serpent," NBC, 1961; "Laramie: The Day of the Savage," NBC, 1962; "Your First Impression," NBC, 1964; "The Virginian: The Heritage," NBC, 1968; "The Brady Bunch: The Brady Braves," ABC, 1971; "Love, American Style: Love and the Test of Manhood," ABC, 1972.

* In 1974 Silverheels obtained a harness racing license and spent the rest of his life as a jockey.

SILVERMAN, JONATHAN

b. Los Angeles, CA, August 5, 1966. Actor who played Jonathan Maxwell on "Gimme a Break."

AS A REGULAR: "Gimme a Break," NBC, 1984-86.

TV MOVIES AND MINISERIES: "Challenge of a Lifetime," ABC, 1985.

SILVERS, CATHY

b. New York City, NY, May 27, 1961. Daughter of Phil; she played Jenny Piccalo on "Happy Days."

AS A REGULAR: "Happy Days," ABC, 1980-83;

"Foley Square," CBS, 1985-86.

AND: "Person to Person," CBS, 1960; "The Love Boat: No Dad of Mine," ABC, 1985.

SILVERS, PHIL

b. Philip Silversmith, Brooklyn, NY, 1912; d. 1985. Bespectacled, fast-talking comic actor whose sitcom was a highlight of fifties TV; he played conniving Sgt. Ernie Bilko.

AS A REGULAR: "The Arrow Show," NBC, 1948-49; "You'll Never Get Rich (The Phil Silvers Show)," CBS, 1955-59; "The New Phil Silvers Show," CBS, 1963-64; "The Beverly Hillbillies," CBS, 1969-70.

AND: "The Ed Sullivan Show," CBS, 1956; "I've Got a Secret," CBS, 1958; "Phil Silvers on Broadway," CBS, 1958; "The Ed Sullivan Show: Man of the Hour," CBS, 1958; "Pontiac Star Parade Presents Phil Silvers," CBS, 1959; "Jack Benny Special," CBS, 1959; "Phil Silvers Special: The Ballad of Louie the Louse," CBS, 1959; "Jack Benny Special," CBS, 1960; "Phil Silvers Special: The Slowest Gun in the West," CBS, 1960; "Phil Silvers Special: Summer in New York," CBS, 1960; "Celebrity Talent Scouts," CBS, 1960; "Candid Camera," CBS, 1960; "Person to Person," CBS, 1960; "The Ed Sullivan Show," CBS, 1961; "The Jack Benny Program," CBS, 1961; "The Jack Benny Program," CBS, 1962; "Talent Scouts," CBS, 1963; "Opening Night," CBS, 1963; "Art Linkletter's House Party," CBS, 1964; "The Danny Kaye Show," CBS, 1964; "A Salute to Stan Laurel," CBS, 1965; "Gilligan's Island: The Producer," CBS, 1966; "The Lucy Show: Lucy and the Efficiency Expert," CBS, 1966; "Damn Yankees," NBC, 1967; "The Dean Martin Show," NBC, 1968; "Hollywood Palace," ABC, 1968; "The Jackie Gleason Show," CBS, 1968; "The Movie Game," SYN, 1969; "Name Droppers," NBC, 1970; "Rowan & Martin's Laugh-In," NBC, 1970; "Eddie Skinner," CBS, 1971; "The Flip Wilson Show," NBC, 1972; "Kolchak, the Night Stalker: Horror of the Heights," ABC, 1974; "Get Christie Love!: Uncle Harry," ABC, 1975; "SWAT: Deadly Tide," ABC, 1975; "Joys," NBC, 1976; "Charlie's Angels: Angels on Ice," ABC, 1977.

TV MOVIES AND MINISERIES: "The Night They Took Miss Beautiful," NBC, 1977.

* Emmies: 1956.

SIMMONS, JEAN

b. Crouch Hill, London, January 31, 1929. Gifted and beautiful film actress ("Hamlet," "Guys and Dolls," "Elmer Gantry") who's now a familiar face on glossy miniseries; an Emmy winner for "The Thorn Birds."

AS A GUEST: "Here's Hollywood," NBC, 1960; "Bob Hope Chrysler Theatre: Crazier Than Cotton," NBC, 1966; "Bob Hope Chrysler Theatre: The Lady Is My Wife," NBC, 1967;

"Hallmark Hall of Fame: Soldier in Love," NBC, 1967; "Decisions! Decisions!," NBC, 1971; "The Odd Couple: The Princess," ABC, 1972; "The Easter Promise," CBS, 1975; "Hawaii Five-O: The Cop on the Cover," CBS, 1977; "Hotel: Deceptions," ABC, 1983; "Murder, She Wrote: Mirror, Mirror, On the Wall," CBS, 1989.

TV MOVIES AND MINISERIES: "Heidi," NBC, 1968; "The Dain Curse," CBS, 1978; "Beggarman, Thief," NBC, 1979; "A Small Killing," CBS, 1981; "The Thorn Birds," ABC, 1983; "North and South," ABC, 1985; "North and South, Book II," ABC, 1986; "AT&T Presents: Inherit the Wind," NBC, 1988; "Perry Mason: The Case of the Lost Love," NBC, 1988.

* Emmies: 1983.

SIMMONS, RICHARD
b. *St. Paul, MN, 1918.* Heavy-set actor of the heroic type.
AS A REGULAR: "Sgt. Preston of the Yukon," CBS, 1955-58.
AND: "Favorite Story: The Diamond Lens," SYN, 1952; "Captain Kangaroo," CBS, 1958; "Leave It to Beaver: The Parking Attendants," ABC, 1963; "Leave It to Beaver: Beaver the Caddy," ABC, 1963; "The Munsters: Tin Can Man," CBS, 1964; "The Brady Bunch: Tell It Like It Is," ABC, 1970.

SIMMONS, RICHARD
The other one.
AS A REGULAR: "General Hospital," ABC, 1979-81; "The Richard Simmons Show," SYN, 1982-85.
AND: "Fame: Teachers," NBC, 1982; "CHiPS: Meet the New Guy," NBC, 1982.

SIMPSON, O.J.
b. *Orenthal Jones Simpson, San Francisco, CA, July 9, 1947.* Sportscaster-actor.
AS A REGULAR: "Monday Night Football," ABC, 1983-85.
AND: "Medical Center: The Last Ten Yards," CBS, 1969; "Here's Lucy: The Big Game," CBS, 1973; "Saturday Night Live," NBC, 1978; "In the Heat of the Night: Walkout," NBC, 1989.
TV MOVIES AND MINISERIES: "A Killing Affair," CBS, 1977; "Goldie and the Boxer Go to Hollywood," NBC, 1981; "Cocaine and Blue Eyes," NBC, 1983.

SINATRA, FRANK
b. *Francis Albert Sinatra, Hoboken, NJ, December 12, 1915.* Chairman of the board, Francis Albert, Rat Packer, a man who did it his way, now in the December of his years. Myyyyy, my.
AS A REGULAR: "The Frank Sinatra Show," CBS, 1950-52; ABC, 1957-58; "Frank Sinatra Timex Show," ABC, 1959-60.
AND: "Colgate Comedy Hour: Anything Goes," NBC, 1954; "Producers Showcase: Our Town," NBC, 1955; "The Dinah Shore Show," NBC, 1956; "The Ed Sullivan Show," CBS, 1956; "The Walter Winchell Show," NBC, 1956; "The Bob Hope Show," NBC, 1957; "The Edsel Show," CBS, 1957; "Club Oasis," NBC, 1958; "Dinah Shore Chevy Show," NBC, 1958; "Dean Martin Special," NBC, 1958; "The Ed Sullivan Show," CBS, 1958; "Some of Manie's Friends," NBC, 1959; "Bing Crosby Special," ABC, 1959; "Startime: The Dean Martin Show," NBC, 1959; "Dean Martin Special," NBC, 1960; "Red Skelton Special," CBS, 1960; "The Gershwin Years," CBS, 1961; "Judy Garland Special," CBS, 1962; "Dinah Shore Special," NBC, 1962; "Burke's Law: Who Killed Wade Walker?," ABC, 1963; "The Bing Crosby Show," CBS, 1964; "The Dean Martin Show," NBC, 1965; "Hollywood Palace," ABC, 1965; "Frank Sinatra: A Man and His Music," NBC, 1965; "Francis Albert Sinatra Does His Thing," CBS, 1968; "Ol' Blue Eyes Is Back," NBC, 1973; "Magnum, P.I.: Out of Sync," CBS, 1987; "Irving Berlin's 100th Birthday Celebration," CBS, 1988; "The Presidential Inaugural Gala," CBS, 1989; "Who's the Boss?: Party Double," ABC, 1989; "Frank, Liza & Sammy: The Ultimate Event," SHO, 1989.

SINATRA, FRANK JR.
b. *Jersey City, NJ, January 10, 1944.*
AS A REGULAR: "Dean Martin Presents," NBC, 1968.
AND: "The Jack Benny Program," CBS, 1962; "Sam Benedict: Read No Evil," NBC, 1963; "The Ed Sullivan Show," CBS, 1964; "Hullabaloo," NBC, 1965; "The Patty Duke Show: Every Girl Should Be Married," ABC, 1965; "Everybody's Talking," ABC, 1967; "The Red Skelton Hour," CBS, 1970; "Dinah's Place," NBC, 1970; "Alias Smith and Jones: The Long Chase," ABC, 1972; "Marcus Welby, M.D.: The Working Heart," ABC, 1973; "Adam 12: Clinic on 18th Street," NBC, 1974; "The Love Boat: Play by Play," ABC, 1979.

SINATRA, NANCY
b. *1940.* Singer of the sixties and daughter of Frank; she played herself on "China Beach."
AS A GUEST: "The Frank Sinatra Show," ABC, 1957; "Frank Sinatra Timex Show," ABC, 1960; "Here's Hollywood," NBC, 1961; "Perry Como's Kraft Music Hall," NBC, 1961; "Stump the Stars," CBS, 1962; "The Virginian: If You Have Tears," NBC, 1963; "What's This Song?," NBC, 1965; "The Man From UNCLE: The Take Me To Your Leader Affair," NBC, 1966; "Off to See the Wizard: Who's Afraid of Mother Goose?," ABC, 1967; "The Ed Sullivan Show," CBS, 1968; "The Glen

Campbell Goodtime Hour," CBS, 1969; "Rowan & Martin's Laugh-In," NBC, 1969; "The Many Moods of Perry Como," NBC, 1970; "The Bobby Darin Show," NBC, 1973; "Dinah!," SYN, 1974; "Hollywood Squares," NBC, 1974; "China Beach: Chao Ong," ABC, 1988.

SINCLAIR, MADGE
b. *Jamaica, April 28, 1938*. Actress who played Nurse Ernstine Shoop on "Trapper John, M.D."
AS A REGULAR: "Grandpa Goes to Washington," NBC, 1978-79; "Trapper John, M.D.," CBS, 1980-86; "Ohara," ABC, 1987; "Gabriel's Fire," ABC, 1990- .
AND: "Joe Forrester: Pilot," NBC, 1975; "Doctors Hospital: Come at Last to Love," NBC, 1975; "Serpico: One Long Tomorrow," NBC, 1977; "The White Shadow: Sudden Death," CBS, 1979; "Gideon Oliver: By the Rivers of Babylon," ABC, 1989; "Homeroom: Dinner at Fiveish," ABC, 1989; "Homeroom: Who'll Be My Role Model Now That My Role Model Is Gone?," ABC, 1989; "Midnight Caller: Take Back the Streets," NBC, 1989.
TV MOVIES AND MINISERIES: "Roots," ABC, 1977; "One in a Million: The Ron LeFlore Story," CBS, 1978; "I Know Why the Caged Bird Sings," CBS, 1979; "Jimmy B. and Andre," CBS, 1980; "Victims," ABC, 1982.

SINGER, LORI
b. *Corpus Christi, TX, November 6, 1962*. Actress who repeated her film role of Julie Miller on the TV version of "Fame."
AS A REGULAR: "Fame," NBC, 1982-83.
TV MOVIES AND MINISERIES: "Born Beautiful," NBC, 1982.

SKELTON, RED
b. *Richard Skelton, Vincennes, IN, July 18, 1913*. Legendary TV comic and mime who was a Tuesday night TV tradition for almost twenty years. Dumped by CBS because his show didn't draw enough younger viewers, he jumped to NBC for a season and then, bitter, virtually left the TV business.
AS A REGULAR: "The Red Skelton Show," NBC, 1951-53; CBS, 1953-62; "The Red Skelton Hour," CBS, 1962-70; "Red," NBC, 1970-71.
AND: "Climax!: Public Pigeon Number One," CBS, 1955; "Playhouse 90: The Big Slide," CBS, 1956; "The Garry Moore Show," CBS, 1958; "Milton Berle Starring in The Kraft Music Hall," NBC, 1958; "The Arthur Godfrey Show," CBS, 1959; "The Westinghouse Lucille Ball-Desi Arnaz Show: Lucy Goes to Alaska, CBS, 1959; "The Jack Paar Show," NBC, 1959; "The Wizard of Oz" (host), CBS, 1959; "Steve Allen Plymouth Show," NBC, 1959; "On the Go," CBS, 1960; "Westinghouse Desilu Playhouse: The Man in the Funny Suit" (as himself), CBS, 1960; "Dinah Shore Chevy Show,"

NBC, 1960; "The Jack Paar Show," NBC, 1960; "Red Skelton Special," CBS, 1960; "The Jack Paar Show," NBC, 1961; "The Garry Moore Show," CBS, 1962; "Talent Scouts," CBS, 1963; "The Ed Sullivan Show," CBS, 1966; "Art Linkletter's House Party," CBS, 1968; "The Ed Sullivan Show," CBS, 1968; "Rudolph's Shiny New Year," ABC, 1976; "General Electric's All-Star Anniversary," ABC, 1978; "Freddy the Freeloader's Christmas Dinner," HBO, 1981.
* Emmies: 1952.

SKULNIK, MENASHA
b. *Russia, 1892; d. 1970*. Yiddish comic.
AS A REGULAR: "Menasha the Magnificent," NBC, 1950; "The Goldbergs," NBC, 1953-54.
AND: "U.S. Steel Hour: Ashton Buys a Horse," CBS, 1955; "Kraft Television Theatre: The Plunge," NBC, 1956; "Omnibus: The So-Called Human Race," NBC, 1958; "The Ed Sullivan Show," CBS, 1966.

SLATTERY, RICHARD X.
b. *Bronx, NY*. Burly actor and former New York City policeman who usually played gruff characters.
AS A REGULAR: "The Gallant Men," ABC, 1962-63; "Mr. Roberts," NBC, 1965-66; "Switch," CBS, 1976-77; "CPO Sharkey," NBC, 1977-78.
AND: "Naked City: A Hole in the City," ABC, 1961; "Bus Stop: Door Without a Key," ABC, 1962; "The Eleventh Hour: A Full Moon Every Night," NBC, 1964; "No Time for Sergeants: The Spirit of Seventy-Five," ABC, 1964; "Mr. Terrific: My Partner the Jailbreaker," CBS, 1967; "The Virginian: Bitter Autumn," NBC, 1967; "Bewitched: How Green Was My Grass," ABC, 1968; "The FBI: The Predators," ABC, 1968; "I Dream of Jeannie: Strongest Man in the World," NBC, 1968; "Bewitched: Cousin Serena Strikes Again," ABC, 1969; "Room 222: Fathers and Sons," ABC, 1969; "The Courtship of Eddie's Father: Getting Back on the Horse," ABC, 1971; "My Three Sons: After the Honeymoon," CBS, 1971; "Bewitched: The Return of Darrin the Bold," ABC, 1971; "Room 222: Suing Means Saying You're Sorry," ABC, 1972; "The Paul Lynde Show: The Bare Facts," ABC, 1973; "The Paul Lynde Show: Everything You Wanted to Know About Your Mother-in-Law But Were Afraid to Ask," ABC, 1973; "Emergency!: Snake Bite," NBC, 1973; "Chico and the Man: Garage Sale," NBC, 1975; "Paris: Fitz's Boys," CBS, 1979.
TV MOVIES AND MINISERIES: "Now You See It, Now You Don't," NBC, 1968.

SLEZAK, ERIKA
b. *Los Angeles, CA, 1945*. Actress and daughter

of Walter; she plays Victoria Lord Buchanan on "One Life to Live."
AS A REGULAR: "One Live to Live," ABC, 1971- .

SLEZAK, WALTER

b. *Vienna, Austria, May 3, 1902; d. 1983.*
Pudgy character actor.
AS A REGULAR: "This Is Show Business," NBC, 1956; "High-Low," NBC, 1957; "Chevy Mystery Show," NBC, 1960; "Made in America," CBS, 1964; "One Life to Live," 1974.
AND: "Studio One: Collector's Item," CBS, 1951; "Danger: The Knave of Diamonds," CBS, 1951; "Suspense: Dr. Anonymous," CBS, 1951; "Studio One: The Innocence of Pastor Muller," CBS, 1951; "Danger: Footfalls," CBS, 1952; "Schlitz Playhouse of Stars: The White Cream Pitcher," CBS, 1952; "Omnibus: Arms and the Man," CBS, 1953; "U.S. Steel Hour: Papa Is All," ABC, 1954; "Hallmark Hall of Fame: The Good Fairy," NBC, 1956; "Person to Person," CBS, 1957; "The Big Record," CBS, 1957; "The Patrice Munsel Show," ABC, 1957; "Art Linkletter's House Party," CBS, 1958; "Playhouse 90: The Gentleman From Seventh Avenue," CBS, 1958; "Telephone Time: Recipe for Success," ABC, 1958; "U.S. Steel Hour: Beaver Patrol," CBS, 1958; "U.S. Steel Hour: The Public Prosecutor," CBS, 1958; "Alcoa Theatre: The Slightly Fallen Angel," NBC, 1959; "The Big Party," CBS, 1959; "Here's Hollywood," NBC, 1961; "The Outlaws: Masterpiece," NBC, 1961; "Cain's Hundred: The Cost of Living," NBC, 1962; "Here's Hollywood," NBC, 1962; "The Jack Paar Program," NBC, 1962; "Play Your Hunch," NBC, 1962; "The Merv Griffin Show," NBC, 1963; "Stump the Stars," CBS, 1963; "Rawhide: Incident of the Black Ace," CBS, 1963; "77 Sunset Strip: 5," ABC, 1963; "Hallmark Hall of Fame: A Cry of Angels," NBC, 1963; "Dr. Kildare: Never Is a Long Day," NBC, 1964; "The Man Who Bought Paradise," CBS, 1965; "Batman: The Clock King's Crazy Crimes/The King Gets Crowned," ABC, 1966; "The Legend of Robin Hood," NBC, 1968; "Assignment: Vienna: A Deadly Shade of Green," ABC, 1973.
TV MOVIES AND MINISERIES: "Heidi," NBC, 1968.

SLOANE, EVERETT

b. *New York City, NY, October 1, 1909; d. 1965.* Character actor in film ("Citizen Kane," "The Lady From Shanghai") and extensive TV; memorable as a ruthless, hard-driving executive in "Patterns."
AS A REGULAR: "Official Detective," SYN, 1957-58; "The Famous Adventures of Mr. Magoo," NBC, 1964-65.
AND: "Philco TV Playhouse: Vincent Van Gogh," NBC, 1950; "Philco TV Playhouse:

Semmelweis," NBC, 1950; "Philco TV Playhouse: The Great Escape," NBC, 1951; "Danger: Mad Man of Middletown," CBS, 1951; "Studio One: Mark of Cain," CBS, 1953; "Studio One: A Breath of Air," CBS, 1953; "Tales of Tomorrow: Read to Me, Herr Doktor," ABC, 1953; "Omnibus: The Trial of St. Joan," CBS, 1955; "Kraft Television Theatre: Patterns," NBC, 1955; "Studio One: The Silent Woman," CBS, 1955; "Kraft Television Theatre: The Emperor Jones," NBC, 1955; "Front Row Center: Dinner at Eight," CBS, 1955; "Studio One: Heart Song," CBS, 1955; "Kraft Television Theatre: The King's Bounty," NBC, 1955; "Omnibus: The Renaissance," CBS, 1955; "Alfred Hitchcock Presents: Our Cook's a Treasure," CBS, 1955; "Alfred Hitchcock Presents: Place of Shadows," CBS, 1956; "Ford Star Jubilee: High Tor," CBS, 1956; "Studio One: Rachel," CBS, 1956; "The Joseph Cotten Show: The Jameson Case," NBC, 1956; "Playhouse 90: Massacre at Sand Creek," CBS, 1956; "Schlitz Playhouse of Stars: Night Drive," CBS, 1957; "Climax!: Don't Ever Come Back," CBS, 1957; "Ford Theatre: Exclusive," ABC, 1957; "Studio 57: The Customs of the Country," SYN, 1957; "Climax!: Trial of Captain Wirz," CBS, 1957; "Kraft Television Theatre: Success!," NBC, 1957; "Suspicion: Diary for Death," NBC, 1957; "Suspicion: The Flight," NBC, 1957; "Climax!: Thieves of Tokyo," CBS, 1958; "Schlitz Playhouse of Stars: Man on a Rack," CBS, 1958; "Jerry Lewis Special," NBC, 1958; "No Warning!: Ashley and Son," NBC, 1958; "The Jane Wyman Show: Hide and Seek," NBC, 1958; "Climax!: The Push-Button Giant," CBS, 1958; "Studio One: The Strong Man," CBS, 1958; "Wanted Dead or Alive: Shawnee Bill," CBS, 1958; "Goodyear Theatre: The Spy," NBC, 1958; "Wagon Train: The Flint McCullough Story," NBC, 1959; "Cimarron City: The Ratman," NBC, 1959; "Zorro: The Man From Spain," ABC, 1959; "Alfred Hitchcock Presents: The Waxwork," CBS, 1959; "Zorro: Treasure for the King," ABC, 1959; "Zorro: Exposing the Tyrant," ABC, 1959; "Wanted Dead or Alive: Reckless," CBS, 1959; "The Loretta Young Show: Shower of Ashes," NBC, 1959; "The Twilight Zone: The Fever," CBS, 1959; "Best of the Post: Command," SYN, 1960; "The Aquanauts: The Floating Mine Adventure," CBS, 1960; "A Question of Chairs: The Challenge of American Education," CBS, 1961; "Jackie Gleason Special: The Million Dollar Incident," CBS, 1961; "The Asphalt Jungle: The Gomez Affair," ABC, 1961; "Follow the Sun: Cry Fraud," ABC, 1961; "Rawhide: Incident at Sugar Creek," CBS, 1962; "Sam Benedict: The Target Over the Hill," NBC, 1962; "Saints and Sinners: The Homecoming Bit," NBC, 1963; "Rawhide: Incident of the Pied Piper," CBS, 1964; "Wagon Train: The Andrew Elliott Story," ABC, 1964; "Jonny Quest:

Tresaure of the Temple," ABC, 1964; "Voyage to the Bottom of the Sea: Hotline," ABC, 1964; "The Rogues: The Laughing Lady of Luxor," NBC, 1965; "Bonanza: Right Is the Fourth R," NBC, 1965; "Rawhide: The Empty Sleeve," CBS, 1965; "Ben Casey: A Horse Named Stravinsky," ABC, 1965; "Hercules," ABC, 1965; "Honey West: In the Bag," ABC, 1965.

AS DIRECTOR: "The Loretta Young Show: The Misfit," NBC, 1960; "The Loretta Young Show: Switchblade," NBC, 1960.

AS WRITER: "77 Sunset Strip: The Hamlet Caper," ABC, 1960.

SMART, JEAN
b. *Seattle.* Attractive blonde actress who plays Charlene Stillfield on "Designing Women."

AS A REGULAR: "Teachers Only," NBC, 1983; "Reggie," ABC, 1983; "Designing Women," CBS, 1986- .

AND: "Goodnight Beantown: The Source," CBS, 1983; "Remington Steele: Steele in the Chips," NBC, 1984; "Lime Street: Swiss Watch and Wait," ABC, 1985; "A Place at the Table," NBC, 1988.

* Smart's appearance on "Lime Street"—with Annie Potts as her sister—led to the two women being cast as regulars on "Designing Women." Both shows were created by Linda Bloodworth-Thomason.

SMIRNOFF, YAKOV
b. *Russia.* Soviet comedian whose anti-Communism routine has aged like bad cheese.

AS A REGULAR: "What a Country!," SYN, 1986-87.

AND: "Scarecrow and Mrs. King: Sudden Death," CBS, 1983; "Night Court: Some Like It Hot," NBC, 1984; "Night Court: World War III," NBC, 1985; "The Love Boat: Picture Me a Spy," ABC, 1986; "The Tonight Show Starring Johnny Carson," NBC, 1987; "Night Court: Russkie Business," NBC, 1988.

SMITH, ALEXIS
b. *Penticon, Canada, June 8, 1921.* Forties film actress with an active career on the stage and TV; she plays Jessica Montford on "Dallas."

AS A REGULAR: "Dallas," CBS, 1984; 1990; "Hothouse," ABC, 1988.

AND: "Rheingold Theatre: The Back of Beyond," NBC, 1955; "Stage 7: To Kill a Man," CBS, 1955; "The 20th Century-Fox Hour: The Heffernan Family," CBS, 1956; "On Trial: We Who Love Her," NBC, 1956; "Robert Montgomery Presents: September Affair," NBC, 1956; "Lux Video Theatre: The Gay Sisters," NBC, 1956; "The Steve Allen Show," NBC, 1957; "Schlitz Playhouse of Stars: I Shot a Prowler," CBS, 1958; "U.S. Steel Hour: The Last Autumn," CBS, 1959; "Adventures in Paradise: Somewhere South of Suva," ABC, 1959; "Person to Person," CBS, 1960;

"Michael Shayne: A Night with Nora," NBC, 1960; "Route 66: Incident on a Bridge," CBS, 1961; "Password," CBS, 1964; "The Price Is Right," ABC, 1964; "Marcus Welby, M.D.: The Windfall," ABC, 1971; "Nightside," ABC, 1973; "The Merv Griffin Show," SYN, 1974; "The Love Boat: The Importance of Being Johnny," ABC, 1984; "The Love Boat: The Villa," ABC, 1985.

TV MOVIES AND MINISERIES: "A Death in California," ABC, 1985; "Dress Gray," NBC, 1986; "Marcus Welby, M. D.: A Family Affair," NBC, 1988.

SMITH, ALLISON
b. *Bronx, NY, December 9, 1969.* Blonde actress who played Jennie, daughter of Jane Curtin on "Kate & Allie."

AS A REGULAR: "Kate & Allie," CBS, 1984-89.

AND: "ABC Afterschool Special: Tattle: When to Tell on a Friend," ABC, 1988; "Animal Crack-ups," ABC, 1989.

SMITH, "BUFFALO" BOB
b. *Buffalo, NY, November 27, 1917.* TV personality who played opposite a puppet.

AS A REGULAR: "The Gulf Road Show Starring Bob Smith," NBC, 1948-49; "Howdy Doody," NBC, 1947-60.

AND: "Gumby," NBC, 1957; "Treasure Hunt," NBC, 1958; "Happy Days: The Howdy Doody Show," ABC, 1975; "The Pat Sajak Show," CBS, 1989.

SMITH, BUBBA
b. *Beaumont, TX, February 28, 1945.* Beefy ex-football player.

AS A REGULAR: "Semi-Tough," ABC, 1980; "Open All Night," ABC, 1981-82; "Blue Thunder," ABC, 1984; "Half-Nelson," NBC, 1985.

AND: "The Odd Couple: Take My Furniture, Please," ABC, 1973; "The White Shadow: The Hitter," CBS, 1980; "Taxi: Tony's Comeback," ABC, 1982; "Hart to Hart: Bahama-Bound Harts," ABC, 1983.

TV MOVIES AND MINISERIES: "Stuck with Each Other," NBC, 1989.

SMITH, HAL
b. *Petosky, MI, 1917.* Comic character actor who played Otis Campbell, town drunk of Mayberry, on "The Andy Griffith Show."

AS A REGULAR: "I Married Joan," NBC, 1952-55; "The Adventures of Ozzie and Harriet," ABC, 1959-60; "The Andy Griffith Show," CBS, 1961-66; "Pat Paulsen's Half a Comedy Hour," ABC, 1970.

AND: "Have Gun, Will Travel: The Great Mojave Chase," CBS, 1957; "The Loretta Young Show: The Prettiest Girl in Town," NBC, 1958; "Broken Arrow: The Outlaw," ABC, 1958; "Jefferson

Drum: Arrival," NBC, 1958; "Jefferson Drum: The Hanging of Joe Lavetti," NBC, 1958; "Tombstone Territory: The Tin Gunman," ABC, 1959; "Bonanza: Magnificent Adah," NBC, 1959; "Have Gun, Will Travel: The Marshal's Boy," CBS, 1960; "Gunsmoke: Old Flame," CBS, 1960; "Lassie: The Chase," CBS, 1960; "Leave It to Beaver: Beaver Won't Eat," ABC, 1960; "Dennis the Menace: Dennis and the Radio Set," CBS, 1960; "The Flintstones: Baby Barney," ABC, 1962; "Fair Exchange: Nothing Ventured," CBS, 1962; "My Favorite Martian: If You Can't Lick 'Em," CBS, 1964; "The Lucy Show: Lucy Becomes a Father," CBS, 1964; "The Flintstones: Deep in the Heart of Texarock," ABC, 1965; "The Addams Family: The Addams Family Goes to Court," ABC, 1965; "The Man From UNCLE: The Matterhorn Affair," NBC, 1967; "The Virginian: The Hell Wind," NBC, 1968; "Gomer Pyle, USMC: Here Today, Gone Tomorrow," CBS, 1969; "Petticoat Junction: The Great Race," CBS, 1969; "The Brady Bunch: The Voice of Christmas," ABC, 1969; "The Doris Day Show: You're As Old As You Feel," CBS, 1969; "The Odd Couple: Surprise! Surprise!," ABC, 1971; "Here's Lucy: Dirtie Gertie," CBS, 1972; "The Odd Couple: Oscar's Birthday," ABC, 1972; "The Streets of San Francisco: Trail of the Serpent," ABC, 1973; "Ellery Queen: The Chinese Dog," NBC, 1975.
TV MOVIES AND MINISERIES: "Getting Away From It All," ABC, 1972.

SMITH, HOWARD K.
b. Ferriday, LA, May 12, 1914. A CBS reporter from 1941-61, and an ABC reporter from 1961-79.
AS A REGULAR: "Behind the News," CBS, 1959; "Eyewitness to History," CBS, 1960; "Howard K. Smith-News and Comment," ABC, 1962-63; "ABC Evening News," 1969-75; "V," NBC, 1984-85.

SMITH, JACK
b. 1919.
AS A REGULAR: "Place the Face," NBC, 1953; "You Asked for It," ABC, 1958-60.
AND: "I Dream of Jeannie: Jeannie the Governor's Wife," NBC, 1969; "Happy Days: Fearless Fonzie/The Other Richie Cunningham," ABC, 1975;
* Smith played himself as the host of "You Asked for It" in "Fearless Fonzie," in which the Fonz (Henry Winkler) tried a motorcycle leap over 14 garbage cans.

SMITH, JACLYN
b. Houston, TX, October 26, 1947. Actress who played Kelly Garrett, the one Charlie's Angel to remain for the entire run of that fine, fine series.
AS A REGULAR: "Charlie's Angels," ABC, 1976-81; "Christine Cromwell," ABC, 1989-90.

AND: "McCloud: The Park Avenue Rustlers," NBC, 1973; "McCloud: The Man with the Golden Hat," NBC, 1975; "The Rookies: The Code Five Affair," ABC, 1975; "Switch: The Late Show Murders," CBS, 1975; "Switch: Death Heist," CBS, 1975; "The Love Boat: A Tasteful Affair," ABC, 1977; "The San Pedro Beach Bums: The Angels and the Bums," ABC, 1977; "Dinah!," SYN, 1978; "Donny and Marie," ABC, 1978; "The Toni Tennille Show," SYN, 1981; "The Pat Sajak Show," CBS, 1989.
TV MOVIES AND MINISERIES: "Probe," NBC, 1972; "Switch," CBS, 1975; "Charlie's Angels," ABC, 1976; "Escape From Bogen County," CBS, 1977; "The Users," ABC, 1978; "Nightkill," NBC, 1980; "Jacqueline Bouvier Kennedy," ABC, 1981; "Rage of Angels," NBC, 1983; "The Night They Saved Christmas," ABC, 1984; "George Washington," CBS, 1984; "Florence Nightingale," NBC, 1985; "Rage of Angels: The Story Continues," NBC, 1986; "Windmills of the Gods," CBS, 1988; "The Bourne Identity," ABC, 1988; "Settle the Score," NBC, 1989.

SMITH, KATE
b. Greenville, VA, May 1, 1907; d. 1986. Beloved singer of radio and TV.
AS A REGULAR: "The Kate Smith Evening Hour," NBC, 1951-52; "The Kate Smith Show," CBS, 1960.
AND: "Hallmark Hall of Fame: The Small One," NBC, 1952; "The Ed Sullivan Show," CBS, 1956; "The Ed Sullivan Show," CBS, 1957; "The Jackie Gleason Show," CBS, 1957; "The Big Record," CBS, 1957; "The Perry Como Show," NBC, 1958; "The Eddie Fisher Show," NBC, 1959; "The Ford Show," NBC, 1959; "The Garry Moore Show," CBS, 1959; "Startime: The Wonderful World of Entertainment," NBC, 1959; "Once Upon a Christmas Time," NBC, 1959; "The Ford Show," NBC, 1960; "The Ed Sullivan Show," CBS, 1962; "The Andy Williams Show," NBC, 1963; "The Ed Sullivan Show," CBS, 1964; "Hollywood Palace," ABC, 1964; "Hollywood Palace," ABC, 1965; "The Ed Sullivan Show," CBS, 1965; "Kraft Music Hall," NBC, 1968; "The Beautiful Phyllis Diller Show," NBC, 1968; "The Jonathan Winters Show," CBS, 1969; "Kraft Music Hall," NBC, 1969; "The Jim Nabors Hour," CBS, 1969.

SMITH, REX
b. Jacksonville, FL, September 19, 1956.
AS A REGULAR: "Solid Gold," SYN, 1982-83; "Street Hawk," ABC, 1985.
AND: "Cagney & Lacey: Old Flames," CBS, 1988.
TV MOVIES AND MINISERIES: "Sooner or Later," NBC, 1979; "The Trial of the Incredible Hulk," NBC, 1989.

SMITH, ROGER

b. Southgate, CA, December 18, 1932. Actor who played gumshoe Jeff Spencer on "77 Sunset Strip"; husband of Ann-Margret.

AS A REGULAR: "Father Knows Best," NBC, 1957-58; "77 Sunset Strip," ABC, 1958-63; "Mr. Roberts," NBC, 1965-66.

AND: "Ford Theatre: Never Lend Money to a Woman," NBC, 1956; "Ford Theatre: Stand by to Dive," ABC, 1956; "Hawaiian Eye: I Wed Three Wives," ABC, 1960; "The Ford Show," NBC, 1960; "SurfSide 6: Love Song for a Deadly Redhead," ABC, 1962; "Truth or Consequences," NBC, 1964; "Kraft Suspense Theatre: Knight's Gambit," NBC, 1964; "The Farmer's Daughter: The One-Eyed Sloth," ABC, 1964; "The Mike Douglas Show," SYN, 1964; "The Mike Douglas Show," SYN, 1965; "Call My Bluff," NBC, 1965; "The Merv Griffin Show," SYN, 1967; "The Tonight Show Starring Johnny Carson," NBC, 1968; "The Joey Bishop Show," ABC, 1968.

AS WRITER: "77 Sunset Strip: The Man in the Crowd," ABC, 1961; "77 Sunset Strip: The Down Under Caper," ABC, 1962.

SMITHERS, JAN

b. North Hollywood, CA, July 3, 1949. Attractive actress who played Bailey Quarters on "WKRP"; wife of James Brolin.

AS A REGULAR: "WKRP in Cincinnati," CBS, 1978-82.

AND: "Love Story: Beginner's Luck," NBC, 1973; "The Love Boat: Kiss and Make-Up," ABC, 1983; "The Love Boat: Don't Get Mad, Get Even," ABC, 1984; "Legmen: Pilot," NBC, 1984; "Hotel: Encores," ABC, 1984.

TV MOVIES AND MINISERIES: "The Love Tapes," ABC, 1980.

SMITS, JIMMY

b. New York City, NY, July 9, 1958. Handsome dark-featured actor who plays Victor Sifuentes on "L.A. Law."

AS A REGULAR: "L.A. Law," NBC, 1986- .

TV MOVIES AND MINISERIES: "Rockabye," CBS, 1986; "The Highwayman," NBC, 1987; "Dangerous Affection," NBC, 1987.

SMOTHERS, TOM

b. Governors Island, NY, February 2, 1937;

& DICK

b. Governors Island, NY, November 20, 1939. Brothers whose CBS variety show was too satirical for the network to handle; but twenty years later they were welcomed back by CBS for a reunion special that became a regular series.

AS REGULARS: "The New Steve Allen Show," ABC, 1961; "The Smothers Brothers Show," CBS, 1965-66; "The Smothers Brothers Comedy Hour," CBS, 1967-69; ABC, 1970; NBC, 1975; CBS, 1988-89; "Fitz and Bones," NBC, 1981.

AND: "The Jack Paar Show," NBC, 1961; "The Jack Paar Show," NBC, 1962; "The Roy Rogers and Dale Evans Show," ABC, 1962; "The Merv Griffin Show," NBC, 1962; "The Danny Thomas Show: Rusty's Campaign," CBS, 1962; "The Jack Paar Program," NBC, 1963; "The Garry Moore Show," CBS, 1964; "Burke's Law: Who Killed the Richest Man in the World?," ABC, 1964; "Hollywood Palace," ABC, 1964; "Alice Through the Looking Glass," NBC, 1966; "The Andy Williams Show," NBC, 1966; "The Jonathan Winters Show," CBS, 1968; "Paulsen for President," CBS, 1968; "What's It All About, World?," ABC, 1969; "Dinah Shore Special," NBC, 1969; "The Glen Campbell Goodtime Hour," CBS, 1969; "Smothers Brothers Special," ABC, 1970; "A Salute to Television's 25th Anniversary," ABC, 1972; "NBC Follies," NBC, 1973; "Dinah!," SYN, 1974; "The Sonny and Cher Comedy Hour," CBS, 1976; "The Tom and Dick Smothers Brothers Special," NBC, 1980; "Saturday Night Live," NBC, 1982; "Saturday Night Live," NBC, 1983; "The Tonight Show Starring Johnny Carson," NBC, 1985; "What's Alan Watching?," CBS, 1989; "Fifty Years of Television: A Golden Celebration," CBS, 1989.

DICK SOLO: "Fantasy Island: A Very Strange Affair," ABC, 1982.

TOM SOLO: "Love, American Style: Love and the Kidnapper," ABC, 1969; "Rollin' on the River," SYN, 1971; "The Bear Who Slept Through Christmas," NBC, 1973; "Free to Be You and Me," ABC, 1974; "Captain Kangaroo," CBS, 1978; "The Love Boat: Out of This World," ABC, 1980; "The Love Boat: A Wife for Wilfred," ABC, 1982; "Fantasy Island: An Audience with the King," ABC, 1982.

SNYDER, TOM

b. Milwaukee, May 12, 1936. Pompous interviewer.

AS A REGULAR: "Tomorrow," NBC, 1973-82; "Prime Time Sunday," NBC, 1979-80.

* Emmies: 1974.

SOLOMON, BRUCE

b. New York City, NY, 1944.

AS A REGULAR: "Mary Hartman, Mary Hartman," SYN, 1976-77; "Lanigan's Rabbi," NBC, 1977; "E/R," CBS, 1984-85.

AND: "Barney Miller: Horse Thief," ABC, 1975; "One Day at a Time: Between Mother and Daughter," CBS, 1979; "The Facts of Life: Summer of '84," NBC, 1984; "St. Elsewhere: Where There's Hope, There's Crosby," NBC, 1986.

SOMERS, BRETT

b. Canada. Comic actress who played Blanche,

ex-wife of Oscar Madison (Jack Klugman) on "The Odd Couple"; at the time, Somers was married to Klugman.

AS A REGULAR: "The Odd Couple," ABC, 1971-75; "The New Adventures of Perry Mason," CBS, 1973-74; "Match Game," CBS, 1973-79; "Match Game P.M.," SYN, 1975-82.

AND: "Kraft Television Theatre: Teddy Bear," NBC, 1956; "Kraft Television Theatre: Give Me the Courage," NBC, 1957; "Have Gun, Will Travel: The Poker Addict," CBS, 1960; "The New Breed: Wave Goodbye to Grandpa," ABC, 1961; "Ben Casey: And If I Die," ABC, 1962; "The New Breed: All the Dead Faces," ABC, 1962; "Have Gun, Will Travel: The Eve of St. Elmo," CBS, 1963; "The FBI: Image in a Cracked Mirror," ABC, 1965; "Password," ABC, 1971; "Love, American Style: Love and the Cheaters," ABC, 1972; "The FBI: Memory of a Legend," ABC, 1973; "The Bob Crane Show: The Doctor Sings the Blues," NBC, 1975; "Barney Miller: Stakeout," ABC, 1975; "Barney Miller: The Election," ABC, 1976; "The Love Boat: The Man Who Loved Women," ABC, 1978; "The Love Boat: You Gotta Have Heart," ABC, 1980.

TV MOVIES AND MINISERIES: "The Great American Beauty Contest," ABC, 1973.

SOMERS, SUZANNE
b. Suzanne Mahoney, San Bruno, CA, October 16, 1946. Blonde sexpot who rocketed to stardom as Chrissy in "Three's Company," left the show in a well-publicized dispute and quickly fell into obscurity; the strange part is how surprised she seemed by that.

AS A REGULAR: "The Anniversary Game," SYN, 1969; "Three's Company," ABC, 1977-81; "She's the Sheriff," SYN, 1987-89.

AND: "The Rockford Files: The Big Ripoff," NBC, 1974; "The Peter Marshall Variety Show," SYN, 1977; "The Love Boat: Centerfold," ABC, 1977; "Dick Clark's Live Wednesday," NBC, 1978; "General Electric's All-Star Anniversary," ABC, 1978; "The Tonight Show Starring Johnny Carson," NBC, 1978; "Hollywood Squares," SYN, 1980; "Donahue," SYN, 1981.

TV MOVIES AND MINISERIES: "Zuma Beach," NBC, 1978; "Happily Ever After," CBS, 1978; "Hollywood Wives," ABC, 1985.

SOMMARS, JULIE
b. Fremont, NB. Attractive actress who plays prosecutor Julie March on "Matlock."

AS A REGULAR: "The Governor & J.J.," CBS, 1969-72; "Matlock," NBC, 1987- .

AND: "The Loretta Young Show: The Trouble with Laury's Men," NBC, 1960; "Shirley Temple's Storybook: The Prince and the Pauper," NBC, 1960; "Holiday Lodge: The Boss," CBS, 1961; "The Great Adventure: Teeth of the Lion," CBS, 1964; "Slattery's People: Question-How Do You

Fall in Love with a Town?," CBS, 1965; "Mr. Novak: The Firebrand," NBC, 1965; "Ben Casey: What to Her Is Plato?," ABC, 1965; "The Man From UNCLE: The Foxes and Hounds Affair," NBC, 1965; "Gunsmoke: The Jailer," CBS, 1966; "Run, Buddy, Run: Down on the Farm," CBS, 1966; "The FBI: The Conspirators," ABC, 1967; "The Man From UNCLE: The When in Rome Affair," NBC, 1967; "The Virginian: Big Tiny," NBC, 1968; "The FBI: The Daughter," ABC, 1968; "Get Smart: The Reluctant Redhead," NBC, 1968; "Judd for the Defense: Transplant," ABC, 1968; "The FBI: A Life in the Balance," ABC, 1969; "Love, American Style: Love and the Nurse," ABC, 1971; "Harry O: The Admiral's Lady," ABC, 1974; "Barnaby Jones: Web of Deceit," CBS, 1974; "The Rockford Files: The Kirkoff Case," NBC, 1974; "McCloud: The 42nd Street Cavalry," NBC, 1974; "Switch: James Caan Con," CBS, 1975; "Ellery Queen: The Mad Tea Party," NBC, 1975; "Jigsaw John: The Executioner," NBC, 1976; "McMillan: Coffee, Tea or Cyanide?," NBC, 1977; "Barnaby Jones: Design for Madness," CBS, 1979; "Magnum, P.I.: From Moscow to Maui," CBS, 1982.

TV MOVIES AND MINISERIES: "Five Desperate Women," ABC, 1971; "The Harness," NBC, 1971; "How to Steal an Airplane," NBC, 1971; "Centennial," NBC, 1978-79; "Sex and the Single Parent," CBS, 1979.

SONDERGAARD, GALE
b. Edith Holm Sondergaard, Lichtfield, MI, February 15, 1899. Film ("Rebecca") and TV actress often in sinister roles; she played Marguerite Beaulac on "Ryan's Hope."

AS A REGULAR: "The Best of Everything," ABC, 1970; "Ryan's Hope," ABC, 1976-77.

AND: "It Takes a Thief: The Scorpio Drop," ABC, 1969; "Get Smart: Rebecca of Funny-Folk Farm," CBS, 1970; "Tango," NET, 1970; "Night Gallery: The Dark Boy," NBC, 1971; "The Bold Ones: The Letter of the Law," NBC, 1971; "Medical Center: Adults Only," CBS, 1974; "Nakia: Walking in Another Man's Skin," ABC, 1974; "Police Story: World Full of Hurt," NBC, 1974.

TV MOVIES AND MINISERIES: "The Cat Creature," ABC, 1973; "Centennial," NBC, 1978-79.

SOO, JACK
b. Oakland, CA, 1915; d. 1979. Deadpan comic actor who played Det. Nick Yemana on "Barney Miller."

AS A REGULAR: "Valentine's Day," ABC, 1964-65; "Barney Miller," ABC, 1975-78.

AND: "The Jack Benny Program," CBS, 1962; "The Red Skelton Hour," CBS, 1964; "Wackiest Ship in the Army: Pilot," NBC, 1965; "The Odd Couple: Oscar's Promotion," ABC, 1972; "M*A*S*H: To Market, to Market," CBS, 1972; "Amy Prentiss: Profile in Evil," NBC, 1975; "M*A*S*H: Payday,"

CBS, 1975; "Police Woman: Bloody Nose," NBC, 1975.

TV MOVIES AND MINISERIES: "The Monk," ABC, 1969; "She Lives," ABC, 1973.

SORVINO, PAUL

b. *New York City, NY, 1939*. Character actor often in comic roles on TV and active in films ("GoodFellas").

AS A REGULAR: "We'll Get By," CBS, 1975; "Bert D'Angelo/Superstar," ABC, 1976; "The Oldest Rookie," CBS, 1987-88.

AND: "The Streets of San Francisco: Superstar," ABC, 1976; "Captain Kangaroo," CBS, 1977; "Moonlighting: The Son Also Rises," ABC, 1986.

TV MOVIES AND MINISERIES: "Tell Me Where It Hurts," CBS, 1974; "It Couldn't Happen to a Nicer Guy," ABC, 1974; "Best Sellers: Seventh Avenue," NBC, 1977; "Dummy," CBS, 1979; "My Mother's Secret Life," ABC, 1984; "With Intent to Kill," CBS, 1984; "Surviving," ABC, 1985; "Chiller," CBS, 1985; "Betrayed by Innocence," CBS, 1986; "Almost Partners," PBS, 1989.

* In the early 1970s, Sorvino made a pilot that didn't sell. Barnard Hughes played his junkman father. Recast, the show was a hit for most of the 1970s: "Sanford & Son."

SOTHERN, ANN

b. *Harriette Lake, Valley City, ND., January 22, 1909*. Wisecracking film and TV actress who played quick-witted big-city "career gals" in two fifties sitcoms.

AS A REGULAR: "Private Secretary," CBS, 1953-57; "The Ann Sothern Show," CBS, 1958-61; "My Mother the Car," NBC, 1965-66.

AND: "Schlitz Playhouse of Stars: Lady with a Will," CBS, 1952; "Hollywood Opening Night: Let George Do It," NBC, 1952; "Ford Theatre: With No Regrets," ABC, 1957; "Washington Square," NBC, 1957; "The Steve Allen Show," NBC, 1957; "The Perry Como Show," NBC, 1957; "The Lucille Ball-Desi Arnaz Show: Lucy Takes a Cruise to Havana," CBS, 1957; "I've Got a Secret," CBS, 1962; "The Merv Griffin Show," NBC, 1962; "To Tell the Truth," CBS, 1962; "Password," CBS, 1963; "The Andy Williams Show," NBC, 1963; "The Match Game," NBC, 1963; "I've Got a Secret," CBS, 1963; "The Alfred Hitchcock Hour: Water's Edge," NBC, 1964; "The Lucy Show: My Fair Lucy," CBS, 1965; "The Lucy Show: Lucy and the Countess Lose Weight," CBS, 1965; "The Lucy Show: Lucy and the Old Mansion," CBS, 1965; "The Lucy Show: Lucy and the Countess," CBS, 1965; "The Lucy Show: Lucy and the Countess Have a Horse Guest," CBS, 1965; "The Lucy Show: Lucy Helps the Countess," CBS, 1965; "The Lucy Show: Lucy the Undercover Agent," CBS, 1965; "The Legend of Jesse James: The Widow Fay," ABC, 1965; "Family Affair: A Man's

Place," CBS, 1968; "Love, American Style: Love and the Bachelor," ABC, 1969; "Love, American Style: Love and the Positive Man," ABC, 1969; "The Movie Game," SYN, 1970; "The Man From Shiloh: The Legacy of Spencer Flats," NBC, 1971; "Alias Smith and Jones: Everything Else You Can Steal," ABC, 1971; "Medical Story: The Moonlight Healer," NBC, 1975.

TV MOVIES AND MINISERIES: "The Outsider," NBC, 1967; "Congratulations, It's a Boy!," ABC, 1971; "The Death of Me Yet," ABC, 1971; "A Death of Innocence," CBS, 1971; "The Weekend Nun," ABC, 1972; "The Great Man's Whiskers," NBC, 1973; "Best Sellers: Captains and the Kings," NBC, 1976; "A Letter to Three Wives," NBC, 1985.

SOUL, DAVID

b. *Chicago, IL, August 28, 1943*. Blond actor who played detective Dave Starsky and mysterious saloon owner Rick Blaine in a silly TV revival of "Casablanca."

AS A REGULAR: "Here Come the Brides," ABC, 1968-70; "Owen Marshall, Counselor at Law," ABC, 1974; "Starsky and Hutch," ABC, 1975-79; "Casablanca," NBC, 1983; "The Yellow Rose," NBC, 1983-84.

AND: "The Merv Griffin Show," SYN, 1966; "Star Trek: The Apple," NBC, 1967; "The Merv Griffin Show," SYN, 1968; "The Young Rebels: The Age of Independence," ABC, 1970; "Dan August: The Manufactured Man," ABC, 1971; "Ironside: Lesson in Terror," NBC, 1971; "All in the Family: Gloria Poses in the Nude," CBS, 1971; "Movin' On," NBC, 1972; "The FBI: The Runner," ABC, 1972; "The Streets of San Francisco: Hall of Mirrors," ABC, 1972; "Owen Marshall, Counselor at Law: Love Child," ABC, 1972; "Intersect," ABC, 1973; "Circle of Fear: The Phantom of Herald Square," NBC, 1973; "The Rookies: A Test of Courage," ABC, 1974; "McMillan and Wife: Guilt by Association," NBC, 1974; "Medical Center: Kiss and Tell," CBS, 1974; "Gunsmoke: Brides and Grooms," CBS, 1975; "The Merv Griffin Show," SYN, 1975; "Crime Story: Blast From the Past," NBC, 1987.

TV MOVIES AND MINISERIES: "The Disappearance of Flight 412," NBC, 1974; "Starsky and Hutch," ABC, 1975; "Little Ladies of the Night," ABC, 1977; "Salem's Lot," CBS, 1979; "Swan Song," ABC, 1980; "Manions of America," ABC, 1981; "World War III," NBC, 1982; "Through Naked Eyes," ABC, 1983; "The Fifth Missile," NBC, 1986; "Harry's Hong Kong," ABC, 1987; "In the Line of Duty: The FBI Murders," NBC, 1988; "Prime Target," NBC, 1989.

SOULE, OLAN

b. *La Harpe, IL, February 28, 1909*. Slight, bespectacled actor who often played fussy or officious types.

AS A REGULAR: "Captain Midnight," CBS, 1954-55; "Dragnet," NBC, 1955-58; "Arnie," CBS, 1970-72.

AND: "I Love Lucy: Nursery School," CBS, 1955; "Schlitz Playhouse of Stars: Clothes Make the Man," CBS, 1957; "Tales of Wells Fargo: Bounty," NBC, 1957; "Studio One: Tongues of Angels," CBS, 1958; "Bachelor Father: Bentley Leads a Dog's Life," CBS, 1958; "Hennesey: Harvey and His Electric Money Machine," CBS, 1961; "Pete and Gladys: Pop's Girlfriend," CBS, 1961; "Have Gun, Will Travel: The Taxgatherer," CBS, 1961; "The Real McCoys: George Retires," ABC, 1961; "Stagecoach West: The Marker," ABC, 1961; "Alfred Hitchcock Presents: Bang, You're Dead," NBC, 1961; "The Andy Griffith Show: Barney and the Choir," CBS, 1962; "Room for One More: A Trip to the Beach," ABC, 1962; "The Andy Griffith Show: Rafe Hollister Sings," CBS, 1963; "McHale's Navy: Instant Democracy," ABC, 1963; "My Three Sons: An Evening with a Star," ABC, 1963; "The Andy Griffith Show: The Darlings Are Coming," CBS, 1963; "The Twilight Zone: Caesar and Me," CBS, 1964; "The Andy Griffith Show: The Song Festers," CBS, 1964; "Mr. Ed: Ed the Pool Player," CBS, 1964; "The Andy Griffith Show: The Pageant," CBS, 1964; "My Favorite Martian: Martian Report #1," CBS, 1965; "My Favorite Martian: Martin's Favorite Martian," CBS, 1965; "Gomer Pyle, USMC: Gomer and the Phone Company," CBS, 1966; "Batman: The Curse of Tut/The Pharoah's in a Rut," ABC, 1966; "The FBI: Ordeal," ABC, 1966; "Family Affair: The Prize," CBS, 1967; "My Three Sons: Heartbeat," CBS, 1967; "Petticoat Junction: The Christening," CBS, 1969; "Dragnet: D.H.Q.-Medical," NBC, 1969; "Dragnet: Burglary-Courtroom," NBC, 1969; "The FBI: Eye of the Storm," ABC, 1969; "That Girl: 10% of Nothing Is Nothing," ABC, 1970.

TV MOVIES AND MINISERIES: "The D.A.: Conspiracy to Kill," NBC, 1971; "The Six Million Dollar Man," ABC, 1973.

SPANO, JOE

b. San Francisco, CA, July 7, 1946. Actor who played Lt. Henry Goldblume on "Hill Street Blues."

AS A REGULAR: "Hill Street Blues," NBC, 1981-87.

AND: "Lou Grant: Bomb," CBS, 1979; "L.A. Law: Hey, Lick Me Over," NBC, 1988; "Midnight Caller: The Execution of John Saringo," NBC, 1989; "Mission: Impossible: The Greek," ABC, 1989.

TV MOVIES AND MINISERIES: "Northern Lights," PBS, 1979; "Brotherhood of Justice," ABC, 1986; "Deep Dark Secrets," NBC, 1987; "Disaster at Silo 7," ABC, 1988; "Cast the First Stone," NBC, 1989.

SPELLING, AARON

A great American TV schlockmeister; producer whose shows are more successful financially than artistically.

AS A GUEST: "I Love Lucy: Tennessee Bound," CBS, 1955; "The Millionaire: The Story of Joey Diamond," CBS, 1956; "This is Your Life (Carolyn Jones)," NBC, 1959; "Here's Hollywood," NBC, 1960; "Here's Hollywood," NBC, 1961.

AS WRITER: "Playhouse 90: The Last Man," CBS, 1958; "Westinghouse Desilu Playhouse: The Night the Phone Rang," CBS, 1958; "The David Niven Show: Portrait," NBC, 1959; "Dick Powell's Zane Grey Theatre: Mission," CBS, 1959; "The Dick Powell Show: A Time to Die," NBC, 1962;

TV MOVIES AND MINISERIES: "Carter's Army," ABC, 1970.

AS WRITER-PRODUCER: "Johnny Ringo," CBS, 1959-60; "The du Pont Show with June Allyson," CBS, 1959-61; "Burke's Law," ABC, 1963-65; "Amos Burke, Secret Agent," ABC, 1965-66; "Family," ABC, 1976-80; "Charlie's Angels," ABC, 1976-81; "The Love Boat," ABC, 1977-86; "Fantasy Island," ABC, 1978-84, many others.

SPIELBERG, DAVID

b. Weslaco, TX, March 6, 1939. Familiar actor often in authoritative roles.

AS A REGULAR: "Where the Heart Is," CBS, 1969-73; "Bob & Carol & Ted & Alice," ABC, 1973; "The Practice," NBC, 1976-77; "The American Girls," CBS, 1978; "From Here to Eternity," NBC, 1980; "Jessica Novak," CBS, 1981; "Wiseguy," CBS, 1988.

AND: "The Bold Ones: In the Defense of Ellen McKay," NBC, 1971; "The Bold Ones: By Reason of Insanity," NBC, 1972; "Ironside: Down Two Roads," NBC, 1972; "Owen Marshall, Counselor at Law: A Piece of God," ABC, 1972; "Love, American Style: Love and the Flying Finletters," ABC, 1974; "The Rockford Files: Charlie Harris at Large," NBC, 1975; "McMillan and Wife: Love, Honor and Swindle," NBC, 1975; "The Rockford Files: Just by Accident," NBC, 1975; "Police Story: Ice Time," NBC, 1977; "CPO Sharkey: Sharkey the Actor," NBC, 1977; "One Day at a Time: The Married Man," CBS, 1978; "Lou Grant: Harassment," CBS, 1980; "Mork & Mindy: Mork in Never-Never Land," ABC, 1980; "CHiPs: Wheels of Justice," NBC, 1980; "Foul Play: Hit and Run," ABC, 1981; "Here's Boomer: Boomer and the Muskrat Cove Treasure," NBC, 1981; "Lou Grant: Business," CBS, 1981; "Quincy: Dying for a Drink," NBC, 1982; "Family Ties: Give Uncle Arthur a Kiss," NBC, 1983; "Hardcastle and McCormick: Too Rich and Too Thin," ABC, 1985; "Highway to Heaven: The People Next Door," NBC, 1986; "Highway to Heaven: Whose Trash Is

It Anyway?," NBC, 1988; "Wiseguy: Phantom Pain," CBS, 1988; "Wiseguy: Dirty Little Wars," CBS, 1988; "Wiseguy: Date with an Angel," CBS, 1988; "Hunter: Heir of Neglect," NBC, 1988; "Murphy's Law: Do Someone a Favor and It Becomes Your Job," ABC, 1988.

TV MOVIES AND MINISERIES: "Night of Terror," ABC, 1972; "Toma," ABC, 1973; "Force Five," CBS, 1975; "The Lindbergh Kidnapping Case," NBC, 1976; "King," NBC, 1978; "Arthur Hailey's Wheels," NBC, 1978; "Sergeant Matlovich vs. the U.S. Air Force," NBC, 1978; "From Here to Eternity," NBC, 1979; "The Henderson Monster," CBS, 1980; "Maid in America," CBS, 1982; "Games Mother Never Taught You," CBS, 1982; "Space," CBS, 1985; "Sworn to Silence," ABC; 1987; "The Rise and Fall of Oliver North," CBS, 1989; "The Preppie Murder," ABC, 1989.

SPIELBERG, STEVEN

b. Cincinnati, OH, December 18, 1947. Immensely successful director ("Jaws," "E.T.") and producer who began directing TV shows after bluffing his way onto the Universal lot, finding an empty office and then acting as if he belonged there.

AS DIRECTOR: "Columbo: Murder by the Book," NBC, 1971; "Amazing Stories: Ghost Train," NBC, 1985; "Amazing Stories: The Mission," NBC, 1985.

TV MOVIES AND MINISERIES: "Night Gallery," NBC, 1969; "Duel," ABC, 1971; "Something Evil," CBS, 1972; "Savage," NBC, 1973.

AS PRODUCER: "Amazing Stories," NBC, 1985-87.

AS A GUEST: "The Tracey Ullman Show: The Gate," FOX, 1989.

TV MOVIES AND MINISERIES: "Something Evil," CBS, 1972.

SPIVAK, LAWRENCE E.

b. Brooklyn, NY, 1900.

AS A REGULAR: "Meet the Press," NBC, 1947-75; "Keep Posted," DUM, 1951-53; "The Big Issue," DUM, 1953.

STACK, ROBERT

b. Los Angeles, CA, January 13, 1919. Familiar TV face, first as the unsmiling Eliot Ness, leader of "The Untouchables," then as the unsmiling Dan Farrell of "The Name of the Game," and now as the unsmiling host of "Unsolved Mysteries."

AS A REGULAR: "The Untouchables," ABC, 1959-63; "The Name of the Game," NBC, 1968-71; "Most Wanted," ABC, 1976-77; "Strike Force," ABC, 1981-82; "Falcon Crest," CBS, 1987; "Unsolved Mysteries," NBC, 1988- .

AND: "Lux Video Theatre: Inside Story," CBS, 1951; "Lights Out: Will-o'-the-Wisp," NBC, 1951; "Lux Video Theatre: Route 19," CBS, 1951; "Celanese Theatre: They Knew What They Wanted," ABC, 1952; "Hollywood Opening Night: Thirty Days," NBC, 1952; "Schlitz Playhouse of Stars: Storm Warnings," CBS, 1953; "Ford Theatre: Ever Since the Day," NBC, 1953; "Ford Theatre: Indirect Approach," NBC, 1954; "The 20th Century-Fox Hour: Laura," CBS, 1955; "Producers Showcase: The Lord Don't Play Favorites," NBC, 1956; "Playhouse 90: Panic Button," CBS, 1957; "Westinghouse Desilu Playhouse: The Untouchables," CBS, 1959; "The Lawless Years: The Billy Boy Rockabye Creel Story," NBC, 1959; "Person to Person," CBS, 1960; "Here's Hollywood," NBC, 1961; "Bob Hope Chrysler Theatre: The Command," NBC, 1964; "Bob Hope Chrysler Theatre: Memorandum for a Spy," NBC, 1965; "The Lucy Show: Lucy the Gun Moll," CBS, 1966; "The Danny Thomas Hour: The Scene," NBC, 1967; "Laura," ABC, 1968; "Police Story: Odyssey of Death," NBC, 1976; "The John Davidson Show," SYN, 1981; "Hotel: The Wedding," ABC, 1984; "Murder, She Wrote: Christopher Bundy-Died on Sunday," CBS, 1986.

TV MOVIES AND MINISERIES: "The Strange and Deadly Occurrence," NBC, 1974; "Houston, We've Got a Problem," ABC, 1975; "Adventures of the Queen," CBS, 1975; "Murder on Flight 502," ABC, 1975; "Most Wanted," ABC, 1976; "George Washington," CBS, 1984; "Hollywood Wives," ABC, 1985; "Perry Mason: The Case of the Sinister Spirit," NBC, 1987.

* Emmies: 1960.

STALLONE, SYLVESTER

b. New York City, NY, July 6, 1946. Burly actor who now plays cartoon figures on the big screen.

AS A GUEST: "Kojak: My Brother, My Enemy," CBS, 1975; "Police Story: The Cutting Edge," NBC, 1975; "The Merv Griffin Show," SYN, 1977.

STAMOS, JOHN

Hunky young TV actor who plays the super-cool Jesse on "Full House"; he earlier played Blackie Parrish on "General Hospital."

AS A REGULAR: "General Hospital," ABC, 1982-84; "Dreams," CBS, 1984; "You Again?," NBC, 1986-87; "Full House," ABC, 1987- .

STANDER, LIONEL

b. New York City, NY, January 11, 1908. Gravel-voiced character player of films ("A Star Is Born") and occasional TV; best known as the lovable Max on "Hart to Hart," a role he

reprised on a fantasy episode of "Moonlighting."
AS A REGULAR: "Hart to Hart," ABC, 1979-84.
AND: "Moonlighting: It's a Wonderful Job," ABC,
1986; "It's Garry Shandling's Show: Save Mr.
Peck's," FOX, 1989.

STANG, ARNOLD
b. Chelsea, MA, September 28, 1925. Comic
actor with a nerdy, high-pitched voice; he was a
comic foil to Milton Berle and the voice of the
wily Top Cat.
AS A REGULAR: "School House," DUM, 1949;
"Henry Morgan's Great Talent Hunt," NBC,
1951; "Doc Corkle," NBC, 1952; "The Buick-
Berle Show," NBC, 1953-54; "The Milton Berle
Show," NBC, 1954-55; "Washington Square,"
NBC, 1956-57; "Top Cat," ABC, 1961-62;
"Broadside," ABC, 1965.
AND: "Ford Theatre: Lady in His Life," NBC, 1954;
"December Bride: Pete's Brother-in-Law," CBS,
1956; "Bulletin From Bertie," CBS, 1956;
"Producers Showcase: Jack and the Beanstalk,"
NBC, 1956; "December Bride: The Prize Fighter,"
CBS, 1956; "The Red Skelton Show," CBS, 1957;
"Playhouse 90: Three Men on a Horse," CBS,
1957; "The Jane Wyman Show: The Man in the
Car," NBC, 1957; "The Vic Damone Show," CBS,
1957; "Arthur Murray Party," NBC, 1957; "The
Patrice Munsel Show," ABC, 1958; "Playhouse 90:
Turn Left at Mt. Everest," CBS, 1958; "Art
Linkletter's House Party," CBS, 1958; "The Ed
Sullivan Show," CBS, 1958; "The Ed Sullivan
Show," CBS, 1959; "Arthur Murray Party," NBC,
1960; "Wagon Train: The Ah Chong Story," NBC,
1961; "Bonanza: The Many Faces of Gideon
Flinch," NBC, 1961; "Batman: The Great Escape/
The Great Train Robbery," ABC, 1968; "The
Donald O'Connor Show," SYN, 1968; "The Cosby
Show: No Way, Baby," NBC, 1989.

STANLEY, FLORENCE
Gravel-voiced character actress in the Selma
Diamond mode; she played Bernice, wife of
Det. Fish (Abe Vigoda) on "Barney Miller" and
a spinoff; more recently she played Judge
Wilbur on "My Two Dads."
AS A REGULAR: "Barney Miller," ABC, 1975-77;
"Joe and Sons," CBS, 1975-76; "Fish," ABC,
1977-78; "My Two Dads," NBC, 1987-90.
AND: "Du Pont Show of the Month: Men in White,"
CBS, 1960; "Cry Vengeance!," NBC, 1961; "The
Power and the Glory," CBS, 1961; "Night Court:
The Game Show," NBC, 1989.
TV MOVIES AND MINISERIES: "Maybe Baby," NBC,
1988.

STANLEY, KIM
*b. Patricia Reid, Tularosa, NM, February 11,
1925.* Stage actress with extensive experience in
live TV; she won an Emmy for a guest role on

"Ben Casey" and for her performance as Big
Mama in "Cat on a Hot Tin Roof."
AS A GUEST: "The Trap: Sentence of Death," CBS,
1950; "Danger: The Anniversary," CBS, 1951;
"Danger: The System," CBS, 1952; "Goodyear
TV Playhouse: The Witness," NBC, 1952;
"Goodyear TV Playhouse: The Darkness
Below," NBC, 1952; "Philco TV Playhouse: A
Young Lady of Property," NBC, 1953;
"Goodyear TV Playhouse: The Brownstone,"
NBC, 1954; "Kraft Television Theatre: The
Scarlet Letter," NBC, 1954; "Philco TV
Playhouse: Somebody Special," NBC, 1954;
"Elgin TV Hour: The Bridge," ABC, 1955;
"Playwrights '56: The Writing Place," NBC,
1955; "Playwrights '56: Flight," NBC, 1956;
"Goodyear TV Playhouse: Conspiracy of
Hearts," NBC, 1956; "Goodyear TV Play-
house: Joey," NBC, 1956; "Kraft Television
Theatre: Death Is a Spanish Dancer," NBC,
1956; "Goodyear TV Playhouse: In the Days of
Our Youth," NBC, 1956; "Studio One: The
Traveling Lady," CBS, 1957; "Kraft Television
Theatre: The Glass Wall," NBC, 1957;
"Playhouse 90: Clash by Night," CBS, 1957;
"Playhouse 90: Tomorrow," CBS, 1960;
"Westinghouse Presents: That's Where the
Town's Going," CBS, 1962; "Ben Casey: A
Cardinal Act of Mercy," ABC, 1963; "The
Eleventh Hour: Does My Mother Have to
Know?," NBC, 1964; "Flesh and Blood,"
NBC, 1968; "NET Playhouse: I Can't Imagine
Tomorrow," NET, 1971; "The Name of the
Game: The Man Who Killed a Ghost," NBC,
1971; "Medical Center: Secret Heritage," CBS,
1971; "Night Gallery: A Fear of Spiders,"
NBC, 1971; "Cat on a Hot Tin Roof," SHO,
1984.
TV MOVIES AND MINISERIES: "U.M.C.," CBS, 1969.
* Emmies: 1963, 1985.

STANWYCK, BARBARA
*b. Ruby Stevens, Brooklyn, NY, July 16, 1907;
d. 1990.* Screen star and skilled actress ("The
Lady Eve," "Double Indemnity") who won
Emmies for her role as Victoria Barkley in
"The Big Valley," for "The Thorn Birds" and
for her own anthology series.
AS A REGULAR: "The Barbara Stanwyck Show,"
NBC, 1960-61; "The Big Valley," ABC, 1965-
69; "The Colbys," ABC, 1985-86.
AND: "Ford Theatre: Sudden Silence," ABC, 1956;
"Dick Powell's Zane Grey Theatre: The
Freighter," CBS, 1958; "Goodyear Theatre: Three
Dark Years," NBC, 1958; "Dick Powell's Zane
Grey Theatre: Trail to Nowhere," CBS, 1958;
"The Real McCoys: The McCoys Visit Holly-
wood," ABC, 1958; "The Jack Benny Program:
Autolight," CBS, 1959; "Dick Powell's Zane
Grey Theatre: Hang the Heart High," CBS, 1959;
"Christophers: The Price of Happiness," SYN,

1959; "Dick Powell's Zane Grey Theatre: Lone Woman," CBS, 1959; "The Joey Bishop Show: A Windfall for Mom," NBC, 1961; "Wagon Train: The Maud Frazer Story," NBC, 1961; "G.E. Theatre: Star Witness," CBS, 1961; "Rawhide: The Captain's Wife," CBS, 1962; "The Dick Powell Show: Special Assignment," NBC, 1962; "Wagon Train: The Caroline Casteel Story," ABC, 1962; "The Untouchables: Elegy," ABC, 1962; "The Untouchables: Search for a Dead Man," ABC, 1963; "Wagon Train: The Molly Kincaid Story," ABC, 1963; "Wagon Train: The Kate Crawley Story," ABC, 1964; "Charlie's Angels: Toni's Boys," ABC, 1980; "The American Film Institute Salute to Barbara Stanwyck," CBS, 1989.

TV MOVIES AND MINISERIES: "The House That Would Not Die," ABC, 1970; "A Taste of Evil," ABC, 1971; "The Letters," ABC, 1973; "The Thorn Birds," ABC, 1983.

* Emmies: 1961, 1966, 1983.
* See also Ann-Margret.

STAPLETON, JEAN
b. Jeanne Murray, New York City, NY, January 19, 1923. Gifted comic actress who made Edith Bunker a television legend.
AS A REGULAR: "Woman with a Past," CBS, 1954; "Today Is Ours," NBC, 1958; "All in the Family," CBS, 1971-79; "Archie Bunker's Place," CBS, 1979-80; "Bagdad Cafe," CBS, 1990- .
AND: "Philco TV Playhouse: A Business Proposition," NBC, 1955; "Dr. Kildare: The Patient," NBC, 1961; "Follow the Sun: The Inhuman Equation," ABC, 1962; "Dennis the Menace: Mr. Wilson's Housekeeper," CBS, 1962; "The Nurses: The Barbara Bowers Story," CBS, 1962; "The Defenders: The Hidden Jungle," CBS, 1962; "Car 54, Where Are You?: J'Adore Muldoon," NBC, 1962; "The Eleventh Hour: The Bride Wore Pink," NBC, 1963; "My Three Sons: The People's House," ABC, 1964; "The Patty Duke Show: The Raffle," ABC, 1965; "Acts of Love-and Other Comedies," ABC, 1973; "Inaugural Eve Special," CBS, 1977; "The Mike Douglas Show," SYN, 1979; "Faerie Tale Theatre: Jack and the Beanstalk," SHO, 1983; "Scarecrow and Mrs. King: The Legend of Das Geisterschloss," CBS, 1984; "Scarecrow and Mrs. King: The Three Faces of Emily," CBS, 1984; "Faerie Tale Theatre: Cinderella," SHO, 1986; "The Love Boat: Egyptian Cruise," ABC, 1986; "Let Me Hear You Whisper," A&E, 1989; "Trying Times: The Boss," PBS, 1989.

TV MOVIES AND MINISERIES: "Hallmark Hall of Fame: Aunt Mary," CBS, 1979; "Angel Dusted," NBC, 1981; "Isabel's Choice," CBS, 1981; "A Matter of Sex," NBC, 1984; "Agatha Christie's Dead Man's Folly," CBS, 1986.

* One of Stapleton's co-stars on "The Hidden Jungle" episode of "The Defenders" was an actor she'd work with later—Carroll O'Connor.
* Emmies: 1971, 1972, 1978.

STAPLETON, MAUREEN
b. Troy, NY, June 21, 1925. Versatile actress in early television; best remembered as "Queen of the Stardust Ballroom"; an Emmy winner for "Among the Paths to Eden."
AS A REGULAR: "What Happened?," NBC, 1952; "The Thorns," ABC, 1988.
AND: "Curtain Call: Carrie Marr," NBC, 1952; "Goodyear TV Playhouse: The Accident," NBC, 1953; "Philco TV Playhouse: The Mother," NBC, 1954; "Philco TV Playhouse: Incident in July," NBC, 1955; "Armstrong Circle Theatre: Actual," NBC, 1955; "Justice: Track of Fear," NBC, 1955; "Studio One: Rachel," CBS, 1956; "Alcoa Hour: No License to Kill," NBC, 1957; "Kraft Theatre: All the King's Men," NBC, 1958; "Arthur Murray Party," NBC, 1958; "Playhouse 90: For Whom the Bell Tolls," CBS, 1959; "CBS Television Workshop: Tessie Malfitan," CBS, 1960; "Robert Herridge Theatre: Riders to the Sea," SYN, 1960; "A Question of Chairs: The Challenge of American Education," CBS, 1961; "Car 54, Where Are You?: The Gypsy Curse," NBC, 1961; "Naked City: Ooftus Gooftus," ABC, 1961; "Naked City: Kill Me When I'm Young So I Can Die Happy," ABC, 1962; "The du Pont Show: The Betrayal," NBC, 1962; "East Side/West Side: One Drink at a Time," CBS, 1964; "New York Television Theatre: Save Me a Piece of Forest Lawn," NET, 1966; "Among the Paths to Eden," ABC, 1967; "On Stage: Mirror, Mirror Off the Wall," NBC, 1969; "Dig," CBS, 1973; "The Mike Douglas Show," SYN, 1977; "Saturday Night Live," NBC, 1979; "B.L. Stryker: Auntie Sue," NBC, 1989.

TV MOVIES AND MINISERIES: "Tell Me Where It Hurts," CBS, 1974; "Queen of the Stardust Ballroom," CBS, 1975; "Cat on a Hot Tin Roof," NBC, 1976; "Letters From Frank," CBS, 1979; "The Gathering," NBC, 1979; "Little Gloria ... Happy at Last," NBC, 1982; "Private Sessions," NBC, 1985.

* Emmies: 1968.

STARR, RINGO
b. Richard Starkey, Liverpool, England, July 7, 1940.
AS A GUEST: "Rowan & Martin's Laugh-In," NBC, 1970; "Saturday Night Live," NBC, 1984.
TV MOVIES AND MINISERIES: "Princess Daisy," NBC, 1983.

* See also The Beatles.

STEELE, BOB
b. Robert North Bradbury Jr., Pendelton, OR, Jan, 23, 1906. Cowboy actor who played Duffy on "F Troop."

AS A REGULAR: "F Troop," ABC, 1965-67.
AND: "Cheyenne: Lone Gun," ABC, 1956; "The
Californians: The Marshal," NBC, 1957; "Have
Gun, Will Travel: The High-Graders," CBS,
1958; "Hotel De Paree: Sundance and the Bare-
Knuckled Fighters," CBS, 1959; "Rawhide:
Incident of the Deserter," CBS, 1960; "National
Velvet: A Matter of Pride," NBC, 1960; "Family
Affair: The Old Cowhand," CBS, 1969; "Then
Came Bronson: The 3:13 Arrives at Noon," NBC,
1970.

STEINBERG, DAVID
*b. Winnipeg, Manitoba, Canada, August 19,
1942.* Actor-comedian.
AS A REGULAR: "The Music Scene," ABC, 1969-
70; "The David Steinberg Show," CBS, 1972;
"David Steinberg's Noonday," NBC, 1975-76.
AND: "The Merv Griffin Show," SYN, 1966; "The
Smothers Brothers Comedy Hour," CBS, 1969;
"The Ed Sullivan Show," CBS, 1970; "The Odd
Couple: The Odd Couple Meet Their Host," ABC,
1971; "Movies, Movies, Movies," ABC, 1974;
"Dinah!," SYN, 1974; "The Mike Douglas
Show," SYN, 1975; "Late Night with David
Letterman," NBC, 1989.

STEPHENS, JAMES
b. Mt. Kisco, NY, May 18, 1951. Actor who
played Hart on "The Paper Chase."
AS A REGULAR: "The Paper Chase," CBS, 1978-
79; SHO, 1984-86.
AND: "M*A*S*H: Morale Victory," CBS, 1980;
"Murder, She Wrote: We're Off to Kill the
Wizard," CBS, 1984; "St. Elsewhere: Time
Heals," NBC, 1986; "Cagney & Lacey: Shadow
of Doubt," CBS, 1987; "Cagney & Lacey:
Trading Places," CBS, 1988; "Cagney & Lacey:
Amends," CBS, 1988; "21 Jump Street: I'm
Okay, You Need Work," FOX, 1988; "Father
Dowling Mysteries: The Pretty Baby Mystery,"
NBC, 1989.
TV MOVIES AND MINISERIES: "The Death of Ocean
View Park," ABC, 1979; "Houston: The
Legend of Texas," CBS, 1986.

STERLING, ROBERT
*b. William Hart, New Castle, PA, November
13, 1917.* Popular light actor of fifties TV; he
played the ghostly George Kerby on "Topper."
AS A REGULAR: "Topper," CBS, 1953-55; "The
20th Century-Fox Hour," CBS, 1956-57;
"Love That Jill," ABC, 1958; "Ichabod and
Me," CBS, 1961-62.
AND: "Studio One: The Ambassadors," CBS,
1950; "Studio One: The Man Who Had
Influence," CBS, 1950; "Celanese Theatre: Brief
Moment," ABC, 1952; "Lights Out: The Borgia
Lamp," NBC, 1952; "Robert Montgomery
Presents: The Lonely," NBC, 1952; "Robert

Montgomery Presents: Candles for Therese,"
NBC, 1952; "The Web: Homecoming," CBS,
1952; "Climax!: Thin Air," CBS, 1955; "Dearest
Enemy," NBC, 1955; "The Loretta Young Show:
Tightwad Millioniare," NBC, 1956; "Lux Video
Theatre: Here Comes the Groom," NBC, 1956;
"Ford Theatre: Clay Pigeon," NBC, 1956;
"Warner Bros. Presents Conflict: Yesterday's
Hero," ABC, 1956; "The Steve Allen Show,"
NBC, 1956; "Ford Theatre: The Man Across the
Hall," ABC, 1957; "Du Pont Theatre: The Widow
Was Willing," ABC, 1957; "Telephone Time:
Campaign for Marriage," ABC, 1957; "Wagon
Train: The Julia Gage Story," NBC, 1957; "The
Perry Como Show," NBC, 1958; "Arthur Murray
Party," NBC, 1960; "U.S. Steel Hour: The Yum-
Yum Girl," CBS, 1960; "Here's Hollywood,"
NBC, 1960; "Art Linkletter's House Party," CBS,
1961; "The Alfred Hitchcock Hour: House
Guest," CBS, 1962; "The Twilight Zone: Printer's
Devil," CBS, 1963; "Naked City: Alive and Still a
Second Lieutenant," ABC, 1963; "Nanny and the
Professor: The Conversion of Brother Ben," ABC,
1971; "The Bold Ones: Dagger in the Mind,"
NBC, 1971; "Love, American Style: Love and the
President," ABC, 1972; "Over Easy," PBS, 1981;
"Simon & Simon: The Last Time I Saw Michael,"
CBS, 1982; "Hotel: Cinderella," ABC, 1984.
TV MOVIES AND MINISERIES: "Letters From Three
Lovers," ABC, 1973; "Beggarman, Thief,"
NBC, 1979.

STERN, BILL
b. Rochester, NY, July 1, 1907; d. 1971.
Sportscaster whose melodramatic, anecdote-
filled style was parodied by Woody Allen in
his film "Radio Days."
AS A REGULAR: "Spotlight on Sports," NBC, 1950;
"Are You Positive?," NBC, 1952; "The
Name's the Same," ABC, 1953-54.

STERN, DANIEL
b. Stamford, CT, August 28, 1957. Light comic
actor who provides the voice-overs on "The
Wonder Years."
AS A REGULAR: "Hometown," CBS, 1985; "The
Wonder Years," ABC, 1988- .
AND: "Later with Bob Costas," NBC, 1989.
TV MOVIES AND MINISERIES: "Samson and Delilah,"
ABC, 1984; "Weekend War," ABC, 1988.

STEVENS, ANDREW
b. Memphis, TN, June 10, 1955. Hunky actor
who plays Casey Denault on "Dallas"; son of
Stella Stevens.
AS A REGULAR: "The Oregon Trail," NBC, 1977;
"Code Red," ABC, 1981-82; "Emerald Point
NAS," CBS, 1983-84; "Dallas," CBS, 1987- .
AND: "Police Story: The Empty Weapon," NBC,
1975; "The John Davidson Show," SYN, 1981;

"Murder, She Wrote: Lovers and Other Killers," CBS, 1984; "The Love Boat: A Gentleman of Discrimination," ABC, 1985; "Murder, She Wrote: Double Exposure," CBS, 1989.

TV MOVIES AND MINISERIES: "The Oregon Trail," NBC, 1976; "Secrets," ABC, 1977; "The Bastard," SYN, 1978; "The Rebels," SYN, 1979; "Women at West Point," CBS, 1979; "Topper," ABC, 1979; "Beggarman, Thief," NBC, 1979; "Miracle on Ice," ABC, 1981; "Hollywood Wives," ABC, 1985.

STEVENS, CONNIE

b. Concetta Ann Ingolia, Brooklyn, NY, August 8, 1938. Petite blonde actress who scored a hit as Cricket Blake on "Hawaiian Eye"; in 1974 she played "The Sex Symbol" in a controversial TV movie that was released with nude scenes overseas.

AS A REGULAR: "Hawaiian Eye," ABC, 1959-63; "Stump the Stars," CBS, 1964; "Wendy & Me," ABC, 1964-65; "Kraft Music Hall Presents The Des O'Connor Show," NBC, 1971; "Starting From Scratch," SYN, 1988-89.

AND: "Sugarfoot: Misfire," ABC, 1957; "The Bob Cummings Show: Bob Goes Hillbilly," NBC, 1958; "Art Linkletter's House Party," CBS, 1958; "Maverick: Two Tickets to Ten Strike," ABC, 1959; "77 Sunset Strip: Honey From the Bee," ABC, 1959; "Pat Boone Chevy Showroom," ABC, 1959; "The Dick Clark Beechnut Show," ABC, 1959; "77 Sunset Strip: Perfect Setup," ABC, 1960; "Cheyenne: Reprieve," ABC, 1963; "The Tonight Show Starring Johnny Carson," NBC, 1964; "Temple Houston: The Town That Trespassed," NBC, 1964; "Hollywood Palace," ABC, 1965; "The Steve Lawrence Show," CBS, 1965; "ABC Stage '67: The People Trap," ABC, 1966; "The Mike Douglas Show," SYN, 1967; "The Tonight Show Starring Johnny Carson," NBC, 1967; "Hollywood Palace," ABC, 1968; "Funny You Should Ask," ABC, 1968; "Love, American Style: Love and the Legal Agreement," ABC, 1969; "Hallmark Hall of Fame: The Littlest Angel," NBC, 1969; "This Is Tom Jones," ABC, 1971; "NBC Follies," NBC, 1973; "The Mac Davis Show," NBC, 1974; "Hollywood Squares," NBC, 1976; "Dinah!," SYN, 1979; "The Love Boat: The Decision," ABC, 1979; "The Love Boat: The Perfect Match," ABC, 1980; "Dance Fever," SYN, 1980; "Dance Fever," SYN, 1982; "The Love Boat: Same Wave Length," ABC, 1982; "The Love Boat: A Wife for Wilfred," ABC, 1982; "The Love Boat: Your Money or Your Wife," ABC, 1985; "Murder, She Wrote: Murder Digs Deep," CBS, 1986; "Win, Lose or Draw," SYN, 1988; "Animal Crack-Ups," ABC, 1989.

TV MOVIES AND MINISERIES: "Call Her Mom," ABC, 1972; "Playmates," ABC, 1972; "Every Man Needs One," ABC, 1972; "The Sex Symbol," ABC, 1974; "Love's Savage Fury," ABC, 1979; "Scruples," CBS, 1980; "Murder Can Hurt You!," ABC, 1980; "Bring Me the Head of Dobie Gillis," CBS, 1988.

STEVENS, CRAIG

b. Gail Shikles Jr., Liberty, MO, July 8, 1918. Handsome actor whose facial and vocal resemblance to Cary Grant was used to good effect when he played super-cool, jazz-loving gumshoe Peter Gunn.

AS A REGULAR: "Peter Gunn," NBC, 1958-60; ABC, 1960-61; "Mr. Broadway," CBS, 1964; "The Invisible Man," NBC, 1975-76; "Dallas," CBS, 1981.

AND: "Fireside Theatre: The Imposter," NBC, 1952; "Gruen Guild Theatre: The Corner Shop," SYN, 1952; "Fireside Theatre: Let the Cards Decide," NBC, 1953; "Pepsi Cola Playhouse: The Night Light at Vorden's," ABC, 1953; "Four Star Playhouse: Beneath the Surface," CBS, 1956; "Matinee Theatre: From the Desk of Margaret Tydings," NBC, 1957; "Ford Theatre: Fate Travels East," ABC, 1957; "The Jane Wyman Show: The Man in the Car," NBC, 1957; "The Eve Arden Show: The Reunion," CBS, 1957; "Lux Video Theatre: Diagnosis: Homicide," NBC, 1957; "State Trooper: The Wennemucca Weskit," SYN, 1958; "Schlitz Playhouse of Stars: I Shot a Prowler," CBS, 1958; "The Music Shop," NBC, 1959; "The Gale Storm Show: Sing, Susannah, Sing," CBS, 1959; "Dinah Shore Chevy Show," NBC, 1959; "The Ford Show," NBC, 1959; "The Chevy Show," NBC, 1959; "The Chevy Show," NBC, 1960; "Person to Person," CBS, 1960; "Summer on Ice," NBC, 1960; "The Chevy Show: The Happiest Day," NBC, 1961; "Dinah Shore Chevy Show," NBC, 1961; "Comedy Spot: The Mighty O," CBS, 1962; "The Entertainers," CBS, 1965; "The Best Years," NBC, 1969; "The Name of the Game: The Emissary," NBC, 1969; "The Bold Ones: Shriek of Silence," NBC, 1969; "My Three Sons: The Return of Albert," CBS, 1970; "To Rome with Love: The Catnip Club," CBS, 1970; "Marcus Welby, M.D.: The Windfall," ABC, 1971; "Love, American Style: Love and the Swinging Philosophy," ABC, 1972; "Ghost Story: Time of Terror," NBC, 1972; "Search: The Clayton Lewis Document," NBC, 1973; "Faraday and Company: Premiere," NBC, 1973; "Chase: The Dice Rolled Dead," NBC, 1973; "Gunsmoke: A Trail of Bloodshed," CBS, 1974; "Wide World of Mystery: Nick and Nora," ABC, 1975; "Ellery Queen: Premiere," NBC, 1975; "Starsky and Hutch: Starsky and Hutch on Playboy Island," ABC, 1977; "Quincy: Holding Pattern," NBC, 1977; "Police Woman: Sweet Kathleen," NBC, 1978; "The Love Boat: I'll See You Again," ABC, 1979; "B.J. and the Bear: The Girls of Hollywood High," NBC, 1980; "The Love Boat:

All for One," ABC, 1985; "Murder, She Wrote: Power Keg," CBS, 1986.

TV MOVIES AND MINISERIES: "McCloud: Who Killed Miss USA?," NBC, 1970; "Mister Jerico," ABC, 1970; "The Snoop Sisters," NBC, 1972; "The Elevator," ABC, 1974; "Killer Bees," ABC, 1974; "Rich Man, Poor Man," ABC, 1976; "Love Boat II," ABC, 1977; "Secrets of Three Hungry Wives," NBC, 1978; "Marcus Welby, M.D.: A Family Affair," NBC, 1988.

STEVENS, INGER

b. Inger Stensland, Stockholm, Sweden, October 18, 1934; d. 1970. Sexy blonde actress who played Katy Holstrum on "The Farmer's Daughter"; personal problems led to her suicide in 1970.

AS A REGULAR: "The Farmer's Daughter," ABC, 1963-66.

AND: "Studio One: Sue Ellen," CBS, 1954; "Kraft Television Theatre: Strangers in Hiding," NBC, 1954; "Playhouse 90: Eloise," CBS, 1956; "The Millionaire: Story of Betty Perkins," CBS, 1956; "Alfred Hitchcock Presents: My Brother Richard," CBS, 1957; "Climax!: The Giant Killer," CBS, 1957; "Pantomime Quiz," ABC, 1958; "Playhouse 90: Diary of a Nurse," CBS, 1959; "Bonanza: The Newcomers," NBC, 1959; "Sunday Showcase: The Indestructable Mr. Gore," NBC, 1959; "The Twilight Zone: The Hitchhiker," CBS, 1960; "Dick Powell's Zane Grey Theatre: Calico Bait," CBS, 1960; "Moment of Fear: Total Recall," NBC, 1960; "Malibu Run: The Margot Run," CBS, 1961; "Follow the Sun: Cry Fraud," ABC, 1961; "Robert Taylor's Detectives: Song of the Guilty Heart," NBC, 1961; "Route 66: Burning for Burning," CBS, 1961; "Follow the Sun: The Girl From the Brandenburg Gate," ABC, 1961; "The Dick Powell Show: The Price of Tomatoes," NBC, 1962; "Breck Golden Showcase: Saturday's Children," CBS, 1962; "Your First Impression," NBC, 1962; "The Eleventh Hour: The Blues My Baby Gave to Me," NBC, 1962; "Sam Benedict: The Target Over the Hill," NBC, 1962; "What's My Line?," CBS, 1963; "The Alfred Hitchcock Hour: Forecast: Low Clouds and Coastal Fog," CBS, 1963; "Girl Talk," SYN, 1963; "Your First Impression," NBC, 1963; "The Nurses: Party Girl," CBS, 1963; "The Dick Powell Show: The Last of the Big Spenders," NBC, 1963; "Empire: Duet for Eight Wheels," NBC, 1963.

TV MOVIES AND MINISERIES: "The Borgia Stick," NBC, 1967; "The Mask of Sheba," NBC, 1970; "Run, Simon, Run," ABC, 1970.

STEVENS, MARK

b. Richard Stevens, Cleveland, OH, December 13, 1915. Action hero of fifties TV who played crusading newspaper editor Steve Wilson on "Big Town"; he was also the show's producer-director, but his career faded quickly after it went off the air.

AS A REGULAR: "Martin Kane, Private Eye," NBC, 1953-54; "Big Town," NBC, 1954-56.

AND: "Story Theatre: Mysterious Picture," SYN, 1951; "Schlitz Playhouse of Stars: Silver Saddle," CBS, 1952; "Ford Theatre: Birth of a Hero," NBC, 1952; "Schlitz Playhouse of Stars: Knave of Hearts," CBS, 1953; "G.E. Theatre: Confession," CBS, 1953; "Ford Theatre: Kiss and Forget," NBC, 1953; "Schlitz Playhouse of Stars: Washington Incident," CBS, 1956; "Wagon Train: The Nels Stack Story," NBC, 1957; "Dick Powell's Zane Grey Theatre: Dangerous Orders," CBS, 1957; "Schlitz Playhouse of Stars: Sporting Chance," CBS, 1957; "The Loretta Young Show: The Defense," NBC, 1957; "Studio 57: The Face of a Killer," SYN, 1957; "The Jane Wyman Show: A Reasonable Doubt," NBC, 1957; "The Gisele MacKenzie Show," NBC, 1958; "Dick Powell's Zane Grey Theatre: The Stranger," CBS, 1958; "Schlitz Playhouse of Stars: Man on a Raft, CBS, 1958; "The Loretta Young Show: For Better or for Worse," NBC, 1958; "Our American Heritage: The Practical Dreamer," NBC, 1959; "Stagecoach West: The Saga of Jeremy Boone," ABC, 1960; "Bus Stop: The Ordeal of Kevin Brooke," ABC, 1962; "Rawhide: Incident of the Hunter," CBS, 1962; "Kojak: The Trade-Off," CBS, 1975; "Simon & Simon: For Old Crimes's Sake," CBS, 1987; "Murder, She Wrote: Obituary for a Dead Anchor," CBS, 1986; "Magnum, P.I.: The Aunt Who Came to Dinner," CBS, 1987; "Scarecrow and Mrs. King: One Flew East," CBS, 1987.

AS PRODUCER-DIRECTOR: "Big Town," NBC, 1955-56.

STEVENS, RAY

b. Clarksdale, GA, January 24, 1939. Comic-singer ("Everything Is Beautiful") of the seventies.

AS A REGULAR: "The Andy Williams Show," NBC, 1969-71; "Andy Williams Presents Ray Stevens," NBC, 1970; "Dean Martin Presents," NBC, 1973.

AND: "American Bandstand," ABC, 1961.

TV MOVIES AND MINISERIES: "Murder in Music City," NBC, 1979; "The Concrete Cowboys," CBS, 1979.

STEVENS, STELLA

b. Estelle Eggleston, Yazoo City, MS, October 1, 1936. Blonde actress who now plays Phyllis Blake on "Santa Barbara" and was Lute-Mae on "Flamingo Road."

AS A REGULAR: "Ben Casey," ABC, 1964-65; "Flamingo Road," NBC, 1981-82; "Santa Barbara," NBC, 1989- .

AND: "Alfred Hitchcock Presents: Craig's Will," CBS, 1960; "Johnny Ringo: Uncertain Vengeance," CBS, 1960; "Here's Hollywood," NBC,

1960; "G.E. Theatre: Graduation Dress," CBS, 1960; "Hawaiian Eye: Kakua Woman," ABC, 1960; "Bonanza: Silent Thunder," NBC, 1960; "Riverboat: Zigzag," NBC, 1960; "G.E. Theatre: The Great Alberti," CBS, 1961; "Follow the Sun: Conspiracy of Silence," ABC, 1961; "Frontier Circus: The Balloon Girl," CBS, 1962; "Hawaiian Eye: Hatau Woman," ABC, 1963; "The Steve Allen Show," SYN, 1968; "Bob Hope Special," NBC, 1968; "Ghost Story: The Dead We Leave Behind," NBC, 1972; "Hec Ramsey: Hangman's Wages," NBC, 1972; "Police Story: The Losing Game," NBC, 1975; "Hart to Hart: Pilot," ABC, 1979; "The John Davidson Show," SYN, 1981; "Fantasy Island: Saturday's Child," ABC, 1983; "The Love Boat: Off Course Romance," ABC, 1983; "The Love Boat: One Last Time," ABC, 1983; "Highway to Heaven: Help Wanted: Angel," NBC, 1984; "Night Court: Harry and the Madam," NBC, 1984; "Murder, She Wrote: Funeral at Fifty-Mile," CBS, 1985; "Magnum P.I.: Find Me a Rainbow," CBS, 1986; "Newhart: It Happened One Afternoon," CBS, 1983.

TV MOVIES AND MINISERIES: "In Broad Daylight," ABC, 1971; "Climb an Angry Mountain," NBC, 1972; "Linda," ABC, 1973; "Honky Tonk," NBC, 1974; "The Day the Earth Moved," ABC, 1974; "The New, Original Wonder Woman," ABC, 1975; "Kiss Me, Kill Me," ABC, 1976; "Wanted: The Sundance Woman," ABC, 1976; "Murder in Peyton Place," NBC, 1977; "The Night They Took Miss Beautiful," NBC, 1977; "The Jordan Chance," CBS, 1978; "Friendships, Secrets and Lies," NBC, 1979; "Make Me an Offer," ABC, 1980; "Flamingo Road," NBC, 1980; "Amazon," ABC, 1984; "A Masterpiece of Murder," NBC, 1986; "Man Against the Mob," NBC, 1988.

STEVENSON, MCLEAN
b. Bloomington, IL, November 14, 1929. Comic actor who left "M*A*S*H," on which he played Col. Henry Blake, for his own sitcom. And then another, and another, and another ....

AS A REGULAR: "The Doris Day Show," CBS, 1969-71; "The Tim Conway Comedy Hour," CBS, 1970; "M*A*S*H," CBS, 1972-75; "The McLean Stevenson Show," NBC, 1976-77; "Celebrity Challenge of the Sexes," CBS, 1978; "In the Beginning," CBS, 1978; "Hello, Larry," NBC, 1979-80; "Condo," ABC, 1983; "Dirty Dancing," CBS, 1988.

AND: "That Girl: My Sister's Keeper," ABC, 1969; "The Wacky World of Jonathan Winters," SYN, 1973; "Baffle," NBC, 1973; "Hollywood Squares," NBC, 1974; "The Tonight Show Starring Johnny Carson," NBC, 1974; "Dinah!," SYN, 1975; "The Rich Little Show," NBC, 1976; "Hollywood Squares," NBC, 1976; "Hollywood Squares," NBC, 1977; "Diff'rent Strokes: The

Trip," NBC, 1979; "Diff'rent Strokes: Feudin' and Fussin'," NBC, 1979; "Diff'rent Strokes: Thanksgiving Crossover," NBC, 1979; "The Love Boat: The Captain's Replacement," ABC, 1983; "The Love Boat: The Buck Stops Here," ABC, 1984.

TV MOVIES AND MINISERIES: "Shirts/Skins," ABC, 1973; "Class Cruise," NBC, 1989.

AS WRITER: "M*A*S*H: The Trial of Henry Blake," CBS, 1973.

STEVENSON, PARKER
b. Philadelphia, PA, June 4, 1952. Generic TV hunk.

AS A REGULAR: "The Hardy Boys Mysteries," ABC, 1977-79; "Falcon Crest," CBS, 1984-85; "Probe," ABC, 1988; "Baywatch," NBC, 1989-90.

AND: "Gunsmoke: To Ride a Yellow Horse," CBS, 1974; "The Streets of San Francisco: The Drop," ABC, 1976; "The Love Boat: Poor Rich Man," ABC, 1983; "The Love Boat: Don't Take My Wife, Please," ABC, 1983; "Alfred Hitchcock Presents: The Method Actor," NBC, 1985; "Murder, She Wrote: Sticks and Stones," CBS, 1986; "Mission: Impossible: The Haunting," ABC, 1989.

TV MOVIES AND MINISERIES: "This House Possessed," ABC, 1981; "North and South, Book II," ABC, 1986; "That Secret Sunday," CBS, 1986; "Baywatch: Panic at Malibu Pier," NBC, 1989; "The Cover Girl and the Cop," NBC, 1989.

STEWART, BYRON
b. Baxter Springs, KS, May 1, 1956. Beefy actor who played Warren Coolidge on "The White Shadow" and then on "St. Elsewhere."

AS A REGULAR: "The White Shadow," CBS, 1978-81; "St. Elsewhere," NBC, 1984-88.

TV MOVIES AND MINISERIES: "The Return of Mod Squad," ABC, 1979; "Grambling's White Tiger," NBC, 1981.

STEWART, ELAINE
b. Elsa Steinberg, Montclair, NJ, May 31, 1929. Fifties starlet who became seventies game show ornamentation, flipping over large playing cards and doing less work—if that's possible—than even Vanna White.

AS A REGULAR: "Gambit," CBS, 1972-76; NBC, 1980-81.

AND: "Pantomime Quiz," ABC, 1958; "Bat Masterson: The Rage of Princess Ann," NBC, 1960; "The Tab Hunter Show: The Doll in the Bathing Suit," NBC, 1960; "Girl Talk," SYN, 1963; "Burke's Law: Who Killed Billy Jo?," ABC, 1963; "Perry Mason: The Case of the Capering Camera," CBS, 1964.

STEWART, JAMES
b. Indiana, PA, May 20, 1908. Legendary screen leading man whose characters exemplify

simplicity and decency; he tried his hand at a family sitcom and a lawyer show in the seventies.

AS A REGULAR: "The Jimmy Stewart Show," NBC, 1971-72; "Hawkins," CBS, 1973-74.

AND: "G.E. Theatre: The Windmill," CBS, 1955; "Cowboy Five-Seven," NBC, 1956; "President's Birthday Party," CBS, 1956; "G.E. Theatre: The Town with a Past," CBS, 1957; "G.E. Theatre: The Trail to Christmas," CBS, 1957; "Let's Take a Trip," CBS, 1958; "The Jack Benny Program," CBS, 1958; "Then There Were Four," SYN, 1958; "The Jack Benny Program: Jimmy Stewart Show," CBS, 1959; "Startime: Cindy's Fella," NBC, 1959; "Hedda Hopper's Hollywood," NBC, 1960; "The George Gobel Show," CBS, 1960; "The Jack Benny Program: Jack Goes to a Concert," CBS, 1960; "A Tribute to President Eisenhower," NBC, 1961; "The Jack Benny Program: Auction Show," CBS, 1961; "Alcoa Premiere: Flashing Spikes," ABC, 1962; "The Jack Benny Program," CBS, 1962; "My Three Sons: Robbie Wins His Letter," ABC, 1963; "Password," CBS, 1964; "The Jack Benny Program: The Income Tax Show," NBC, 1964; "Julia: A Little Chicken Soup Never Hurt Anyone," NBC, 1969; "The American West of John Ford," CBS, 1971; "Hallmark Hall of Fame: Harvey," NBC, 1972; "Music Country USA," NBC, 1974; "The Tonight Show Starring Johnny Carson," NBC, 1977; "General Electric's All-Star Anniversary," ABC, 1978; "Hour Magazine," SYN, 1982; "The Tonight Show Starring Johnny Carson," NBC, 1989.

TV MOVIES AND MINISERIES: "Hawkins on Murder," CBS, 1973.

STEWART, PAUL

b. New York City, NY, March 13, 1908. Dour-faced character actor often in threatening roles.

AS A REGULAR: "Deadline," SYN, 1959-60; "The Man Who Never Was," ABC, 1966-67; "The New Adventures of Huckleberry Finn," NBC, 1968-69; "Harold Robbins' The Survivors," ABC, 1969-70.

AND: "Prudential Family Playhouse: Over 21," CBS, 1950; "Lights Out: The Man with the Astrakan Hat," NBC, 1951; "TV Reader's Digest: The Only Way Out," ABC, 1956; "Playhouse 90: Confession," CBS, 1956; "Panic!: Fingerprints," NBC, 1957; "Climax!: The Long Count," CBS, 1957; "Climax!: Mask for the Devil," CBS, 1957; "Alcoa Theatre: The First Star," NBC, 1958; "Johnny Staccato: The List of Death," NBC, 1959; "Alfred Hitchcock Presents: Craig's Will," CBS, 1960; "The Asphalt Jungle: The Kidnapping," ABC, 1961; "Cain's Hundred: Final Judgement," NBC, 1961; "The Breaking Point: Crack in an Image," ABC, 1963; "Bob Hope Chrysler Theatre: A Case of Armed Robbery," NBC, 1964; "Mannix: Pressure Point," CBS, 1968; "My Friend Tony: Death Comes in Small Packages," NBC, 1969;

"The Name of the Game: Swingers Only," NBC, 1969; "Ironside: The Prophecy," NBC, 1969; "The Outsider: Handle with Care," NBC, 1969; "Mannix: A Sleep in the Deep," CBS, 1969; "Mission: Impossible: Robot," CBS, 1969; "The Name of the Game: High Card," NBC, 1969; "Storefront Lawyers: The Emancipation of Bessie Gray," CBS, 1970; "The Bold Ones: The Continual Roar of Musketry," NBC, 1970; "The Name of the Game: Why I Blew Up Dakota," NBC, 1970; "Mannix: Deja Vu," CBS, 1970; "Ironside: Ring of Prayer," NBC, 1971; "The Name of the Game: Los Angeles 2017," NBC, 1971; "Medical Center: The Martyr," CBS, 1971; "The Doris Day Show: Follow That Dog," CBS, 1973; "Columbo: Double Shock," NBC, 1973; "The FBI: Rules of the Game," ABC, 1973; "Cannon: The Hit Man," CBS, 1974; "The Streets of San Francisco: Letters From the Grave," ABC, 1975; "Ellery Queen: The Twelfth Floor Express," NBC, 1975; "The Rockford Files: Irving the Explainer," NBC, 1977; "Lou Grant: Hollywood," CBS, 1979; "Remington Steele: Steele Knuckles and Glass Jaws," NBC, 1983; "Riptide: Catch a Fallen Star," NBC, 1984.

TV MOVIES AND MINISERIES: "Carter's Army," ABC, 1970; "City Beneath the Sea," NBC, 1971; "The Nativity," ABC, 1978; "The Dain Curse," CBS, 1978; "Seduced," CBS, 1985.

STICKNEY, DOROTHY

b. Dickinson, ND, June 21, 1903. Actress usually in spinsterish roles.

AS A GUEST: "Lights Out: I Spy," NBC, 1951; "Robert Montgomery Presents: The Cypress Tree," NBC, 1955; "Studio One: A Special Announcement," CBS, 1956; "Alcoa Hour: Morning's at Seven," NBC, 1956; "Alfred Hitchcock Presents: Conversation with a Corpse," CBS, 1956; "Cinderella," CBS, 1957; "Studio 57: My Friends the Birds," SYN, 1957; "Goodyear TV Playhouse: Weekend in Vermont," NBC, 1957; "Alfred Hitchcock Presents: Miss Paisley's Cat," CBS, 1957; "G.E. Theatre: The Young Years," CBS, 1957; "Telephone Time: Abby, Julia and the Seven Pet Cows," ABC, 1958; "Camera Three: Actor's Choice," CBS, 1959; "Hallmark Hall of Fame: Arsenic and Old Lace," NBC, 1962; "ABC Stage '67: Evening Primrose," ABC, 1966; "On Stage: Certain Honorable Men," NBC, 1968.

TV MOVIES AND MINISERIES: "The Homecoming," CBS, 1971.

STIERS, DAVID OGDEN

b. Peoria, IL, October 31, 1942. Actor who played Dr. Charles Emerson Winchester on "M*A*S*H" and now plays the courtroom opponent of Perry Mason (Raymond Burr).

AS A REGULAR: "Doc," CBS, 1976; "M*A*S*H,"

CBS, 1977-83.
AND: "Kojak: Money Back Guarantee," CBS, 1975; "Rhoda: If You Want to Shoot the Rapids, You Have to Get Wet," CBS, 1976; "The Mary Tyler Moore Show: Look at Us, We're Walking," CBS, 1976; "The Mary Tyler Moore Show: The Critic," CBS, 1977; "The Mary Tyler Moore Show: The Ted and Georgette Show," CBS, 1977; "Rhoda: Nose Job," CBS, 1977; "$weepstake$: Billy, Wally and Ludmilla, and Theodore," NBC, 1979; "Matlock: Blind Justice," NBC, 1987; "ALF: Turkey in the Straw," NBC, 1988; "Matlock: The Ambassador," NBC, 1988; "Ray Bradbury Theatre: The Pedestrian," USA, 1989.
TV MOVIES AND MINISERIES: "Charlie's Angels," ABC, 1976; "A Circle of Children," CBS, 1977; "Sergeant Matlovich vs. the U.S. Air Force," NBC, 1978; "The First Olympics-Athens 1896," NBC, 1984; "The Bad Seed," ABC, 1985; "North and South," ABC, 1985; "North and South, Book II," ABC, 1986; "Mrs. Delafield Wants to Marry," CBS, 1986; "Perry Mason: The Case of the Notorious Nun," NBC, 1986; "The Alamo: 13 Days to Glory," NBC, 1987; "Perry Mason: The Case of the Sinister Spirit," NBC, 1987; "Perry Mason: The Case of the Murdered Madam," NBC, 1987; "Perry Mason: The Case of the Scandalous Scoundrel," NBC, 1987; "Perry Mason: The Case of the Avenging Ace," NBC, 1988; "Perry Mason: The Case of the Lady in the Lake," NBC, 1988; "Perry Mason: The Case of the Lost Love," NBC, 1988; "AT&T Presents: Day One," CBS, 1989; "AT&T Presents: The Final Days," ABC, 1989.
AS DIRECTOR: "M*A*S*H: Identity Crisis," CBS, 1981; "M*A*S*H: That Darn Kid," CBS, 1982.

STILLER, JERRY

b. Brooklyn, NY, June 8, 1929. Stocky actor usually in comic roles, often with wife Anne Meara.
AS A REGULAR: "The Paul Lynde Show," ABC, 1972-73; "Joe and Sons," CBS, 1975-76; "Tattinger's," NBC, 1988; "Nick and Hillary," NBC, 1989.
AND: "Studio One: The Furlough," CBS, 1957; "Camera Three," CBS, 1959; "Lamp Unto My Feet: The Journal of Clarence Candide," CBS, 1961; "Rhoda: Touch of Classy," CBS, 1976; "Captain Kangaroo," CBS, 1977.
TV MOVIES AND MINISERIES: "Madame X," NBC, 1981; "The Other Woman," CBS, 1983.
WITH ANNE MEARA: "The Merv Griffin Show," NBC, 1963; "The Ed Sullivan Show," CBS, 1964; "Hootenanny," ABC, 1964; "The Ed Sullivan Show," CBS, 1965; "The Ed Sullivan Show," CBS, 1966; "The Mike Douglas Show," SYN, 1967; "The Ed Sullivan Show," CBS, 1968; "The Mike Douglas Show," SYN, 1968; "The Merv

Griffin Show," SYN, 1968; "Kraft Music Hall," NBC, 1968; "Kraft Music Hall," NBC, 1970; "Love, American Style: Love and the Conjugal Visit," ABC, 1971; "The Courtship of Eddie's Father: Thy Neighbor Loves Thee," ABC, 1971; "ABC Comedy Hour," ABC, 1972; "The Courtship of Eddie's Father: We Love Annie," ABC, 1972; "Love, American Style: Love and the Clinical Problem," ABC, 1973; "The Love Boat: Super Mom," ABC, 1979; "The Love Boat: We the Jury," ABC, 1983.

STOCKWELL, DEAN

Actor who's contributed memorable recent movie cameos ("Blue Velvet," "Tucker: The Man and His Dream"); now he plays Al on "Quantum Leap."
AS A REGULAR: "Quantum Leap," NBC, 1989-
AND: "Front Row Center: Innocent Witness," CBS, 1956; "Matinee Theatre: Class of '58," NBC, 1956; "Matinee Theatre: Horsepower," NBC, 1956; "Matinee Theatre: Julie," NBC, 1956; "Schlitz Playhouse of Stars: Washington Incident," CBS, 1956; "U.S. Steel Hour: Victim," CBS, 1957; "Playhouse 90: Made in Japan," CBS, 1959; "Wagon Train: The Rodney Lawrence Story," NBC, 1959; "Johnny Staccato: The Nature of the Night," NBC, 1959; "Buick Electra Playhouse: The Killers," CBS, 1959; "Checkmate: The Cyanide Touch," CBS, 1960; "The du Pont Show with June Allyson: The Dance Man," CBS, 1960; "Alfred Hitchcock Presents: The Landlady," NBC, 1961; "The Outlaws: Assassin," NBC, 1961; "Wagon Train: The Will Santee Story," NBC, 1961; "Hallmark Hall of Fame: The Joke and the Valley," NBC, 1961; "Here's Hollywood," NBC, 1961; "Bus Stop: Afternoon of a Cowboy," ABC, 1961; "The Dick Powell Show: The Geetas Box," NBC, 1961; "The Twilight Zone: A Quality of Mercy," CBS, 1961; "The Alfred Hitchcock Hour: Annabel," CBS, 1962; "The Dick Powell Show: In Search of a Son," NBC, 1962; "The Greatest Show on Earth: The Wrecker," ABC, 1963; "The Danny Thomas Hour: The Cage," NBC, 1968; "The FBI: The Quarry," ABC, 1968; "Bonanza: The Medal," NBC, 1969; "Mannix: A Step in Time," CBS, 1971; "The FBI: End of a Nightmare," ABC, 1972; "Columbo: The Most Crucial Game," NBC, 1972; "Mission: Impossible: The Pendulum," CBS, 1973; "The Streets of San Francisco: Legion of the Lost," ABC, 1973; "Orson Welles' Great Mysteries: Unseen Alibi," SYN, 1973; "Police Story: Collision Course," NBC, 1973; "Police Story: Love, Mabel," NBC, 1974; "The Streets of San Francisco: The Programming of Charlie Blake," ABC, 1975; "Columbo: Troubled Waters," NBC, 1975; "Police Story: The Return of Joe Forrester," NBC, 1975; "Three for the Road: Trail of Bigfoot," CBS, 1975; "McCloud: 'Twas the Fight Before Christmas," NBC, 1976;

"Miami Vice: Bushido," NBC, 1986; "Murder, She Wrote: Deadpan," CBS, 1988.

TV MOVIES AND MINISERIES: "Paper Man," CBS, 1971; "The Failing of Raymond," ABC, 1971; "The Adventures of Nick Carter," ABC, 1972; "The Return of Joe Forrester," NBC, 1975; "A Killing Affair," CBS, 1977; "Born to Be Sold," NBC, 1981; "The Gambler III: The Legend Continues," CBS, 1987.

STOKEY, MIKE

Emcee.

AS A REGULAR: "Armchair Detective," CBS, 1949; "Pantomime Quiz," CBS, 1949-51; NBC, 1952; CBS, 1952-53; DUM, 1953-54; CBS, 1954; ABC, 1955; CBS, 1955-57; ABC, 1958-59; "Stump the Stars," CBS, 1962-63.

AND: "The FBI: The Recruiter," ABC, 1971.

STONE, CYNTHIA

b. Peoria, IL, February 26, 1926. Actress and one-time wife of Jack Lemmon; she starred opposite him on "That Wonderful Guy" and "Heaven for Betsy."

AS A REGULAR: "That Wonderful Guy," ABC, 1949-50; "Ad Libbers," CBS, 1951; "Heaven for Betsy," CBS, 1952.

AND: "Dr. Kildare: Why Won't Anyone Listen?," NBC, 1964.

STONE, HAROLD J.

b. New York City, NY, 1911. Beefy actor often in threatening roles; he played Sam, father of Bernie Steinberg (David Birney) on "Bridget Loves Bernie."

AS A REGULAR: "The Hartmans," NBC, 1949; "The Goldbergs," NBC, 1952; "Grand Jury," SYN, 1959-60; "My World and Welcome to It," NBC, 1969-70; "Bridget Loves Bernie," CBS, 1972-73.

AND: "Du Pont Theatre: Frightened Witness," ABC, 1957; "Wire Service: The Indictment," ABC, 1957; "Alfred Hitchcock Presents: The Night the World Ended," CBS, 1957; "Robert Taylor's Detectives: Three Blind Mice," NBC, 1962; "Rawhide: Incident of the Trail's End," CBS, 1963; "Empire: The Tiger Inside," NBC, 1963; "Ben Casey: A Hundred More Pipers," ABC, 1963; "The Rifleman: The Bullet," ABC, 1963; "Dr. Kildare: A Place Among the Monuments," NBC, 1963; "Voyage to the Bottom of the Sea: Mutiny," ABC, 1965; "Mr. Novak: Beat the Plowshare, Edge the Sword," NBC, 1965; "Gilligan's Island: Goodbye, Old Paint," CBS, 1965; "Bob Hope Chrysler Theatre: Kicks," NBC, 1965; "The Big Valley: Teacher of Outlaws," ABC, 1966; "The Virginian: The Laramie Road," NBC, 1965; "The Virginian: The Mark of a Man," NBC, 1966; "The Virginian: Ride to Delphi," NBC, 1966; "Get Smart: Ship of Spies," NBC, 1966; "Mr. Terrific: Matchless," CBS, 1967; "The Man From UNCLE: The It's All Greek to Me Affair," NBC, 1967; "Ironside: Force of Arms," NBC, 1968; "The Virginian: The Shiloh Years," NBC, 1970; "Hogan's Heroes: Look at the Pretty Snowflakes," CBS, 1971; "Longstreet: Anatomy of a Mayday," ABC, 1972; "Medical Center: Woman for Hire," CBS, 1973; "Ironside: The Hidden Man," NBC, 1973; "Ironside: Run Scared," NBC, 1974; "The Rockford Files: The Countess," NBC, 1974; "The Rookies: Take Over," ABC, 1974; "Police Woman: Pattern for Evil," NBC, 1975; "Kojak: A Grave Too Soon," CBS, 1976; "Welcome Back, Kotter: Kotter & Son," ABC, 1977; "Three's Company: The Loan Shark," ABC, 1979; "Paris: Dear John," CBS, 1979; "Barney Miller: Homicide," ABC, 1980; "Lou Grant: Law," CBS, 1981; "Simon & Simon: The Dillinger Print," CBS, 1984.

TV MOVIES AND MINISERIES: "Breakout," NBC, 1970; "The Legend of Valentino," ABC, 1975.

STONE, MILBURN

b. Burrton, KS, July 5, 1940; d. 1980. Doctor Galen Adams.

AS A REGULAR: "Gunsmoke," CBS, 1955-75.

AND: "Dragnet: The Big Jump," NBC, 1952; "Front Row Center: The Morals Squad," CBS, 1956; "Climax!: The Great World and Timothy Colt," CBS, 1958; "Art Linkletter's House Party," CBS, 1958; "Perry Como's Kraft Music Hall," NBC, 1961.

* Stone to *TV Guide*: "I never had an identity until Doc, so there was no problem losing my own."
* Stone criticized "Gunsmoke" co-star Dennis Weaver for his tardiness to the set and his "high spirits" during work hours.
* Emmies: 1968.

STONE, ROB

b. Chicago, IL, September 22, 1962. Actor who played Kevin on "Mr. Belvedere."

AS A REGULAR: "Mr. Belvedere," ABC, 1985-90.

AND: "21 Jump Street: Two for the Road," FOX, 1987; "Rags to Riches: That's Cheating," NBC, 1987; "ABC Family Theater: A Family Again," ABC, 1988.

TV MOVIES AND MINISERIES: "Crash Course," NBC, 1988.

STORCH, LARRY

b. New York City, NY, January 8, 1923. Comedian with a frantic style who played Cpl. Randolph Agarn on "F Troop."

AS A REGULAR: "Cavalcade of Stars," DUM, 1951-52; "The Larry Storch Show," CBS, 1953; "F Troop," ABC, 1965-67; "The Queen and I," CBS, 1969.

AND: "Arthur Murray Party," NBC, 1957; "The Steve Allen Show," NBC, 1957; "The Big Record,"

CBS, 1957; "The Phil Silvers Show: Bilko's Bopster," CBS, 1959; "The Chevy Show," NBC, 1959; "Hennesey: Shore Patrol," CBS, 1959; "Playboy's Penthouse," SYN, 1962; "Car 54, Where Are You?: Remember St. Petersburg," NBC, 1962; "Car 54, Where Are You?: That's Show Business," NBC, 1962; "Your First Impression," NBC, 1962; "Car 54, Where Are You?: Pretzel Mary," NBC, 1962; "Jackie Gleason and His American Scene Magazine," CBS, 1963; "Car 54, Where Are You?: Here Comes Charlie," NBC, 1963; "The Tonight Show Starring Johnny Carson," NBC, 1963; "Gilligan's Island: Little Island, Big Gun," CBS, 1965; "I Dream of Jeannie: Fly Me to the Moon," NBC, 1967; "Gomer Pyle, USMC: Wild Bull of the Pampas," CBS, 1967; "The Mothers-in-Law: I Thought He'd Never Leave," NBC, 1967; "Get Smart: The Groovy Guru," NBC, 1968; "He & She: Dog's Best Friend," CBS, 1968; "The Doris Day Show: The Prizefighter and the Lady," CBS, 1970; "The Doris Day Show: The Duke Returns," CBS, 1970; "The Glen Campbell Goodtime Hour," CBS, 1970; "The Doris Day Show: Duke the Performer," CBS, 1970; "Love, American Style: Love and the Arctic Station," ABC, 1971; "The Doris Day Show: Duke's Girlfriend," CBS, 1971; "Love, American Style: Love and the Joker," ABC, 1971; "Alias Smith and Jones: The Long Chase," ABC, 1972; "The Sonny and Cher Comedy Hour," CBS, 1972; "Emergency!: School Days," NBC, 1972; "Love, American Style: Love and the Dream Burglar," ABC, 1973; "All in the Family: Oh Say Can You See," CBS, 1973; "Tenafly: Joy Ride to Nowhere," NBC, 1973; "Love, American Style: Love and the Woman in White," ABC, 1973; "Love, American Style: Love and Mr. Bunny," ABC, 1974; "Columbo: Negative Reaction," NBC, 1974; "Kolchak, the Night Stalker: The Vampire," ABC, 1974; "Police Story: Love, Mabel," NBC, 1974; "The Merv Griffin Show," SYN, 1975; "Switch: Case of the Purloined Case," CBS, 1976; "The Life and Times of Grizzly Adams: Gold Is Where You Find It," NBC, 1977; "The Love Boat: The Caper," ABC, 1978; "The Love Boat: Tony's Family," ABC, 1978; "Fantasy Island: Eagleman," ABC, 1980; "Fantasy Island: House of Dolls," ABC, 1982; "The Fall Guy: Losers Weepers," ABC, 1984.
TV MOVIES AND MINISERIES: "Hunters Are for Killing," CBS, 1970; "The Woman Hunter," CBS, 1972; "The Couple Takes a Wife," ABC, 1972.

STORM, GALE
b. Bloomington, TX, April 5, 1922. Brunette actress who went from forgettable films to silly sitcoms.
AS A REGULAR: "My Little Margie," CBS, 1952; NBC, 1952; CBS, 1953; NBC, 1953-55; "NBC Comedy Hour," NBC, 1956; "The Gale Storm Show," CBS, 1956-59; ABC, 1959-60.
AND: "Hollywood Premiere: Mr. and Mrs.

Detective," ABC, 1950; "Bigelow Theatre: Mechanic on Duty," SYN, 1951; "The Unexpected: The Puppeteers," NBC, 1952; "Pitfall: The Hot Welcome," SYN, 1954; "Robert Montgomery Presents: Tomorrow Is Forever," NBC, 1955; "This Is Your Life," NBC, 1955; "Ford Theatre: Johnny, Where Are You?," NBC, 1955; "Stage Show," CBS, 1956; "Shower of Stars," CBS, 1957; "The Perry Como Show," NBC, 1957; "Dinah Shore Chevy Show," NBC, 1957; "The Big Record," CBS, 1957; "Pat Boone Chevy Showroom," ABC, 1958; "Dinah Shore Chevy Show," NBC, 1958; "Person to Person," CBS, 1959; "The Chevy Show: Home for Christmas," NBC, 1960; "The Garry Moore Show," CBS, 1961; "The Mike Douglas Show," SYN, 1964; "Burke's Law: Who Killed His Royal Highness?," ABC, 1964; "Burke's Law: Who Killed Wimbledon Hastings?," ABC, 1965; "Tomorrow," NBC, 1976; "The Love Boat: A New Woman," ABC, 1979; "Murder, She Wrote: Something Borrowed, Someone Blue," CBS, 1989.

STORY, RALPH
Emcee-personality.
AS A REGULAR: "What Do You Have in Common?," CBS, 1954; "The $64,000 Challenege," CBS, 1956-58; NBC, 1958.
AND: "The Jimmy Dean Show," CBS, 1957; "The Red Skelton Show," CBS, 1958; "Art Linkletter's House Party," CBS, 1959; "My Three Sons: Soap-Box Derby," ABC, 1961; "The Lucy Show: Lucy and Ken Berry," CBS, 1968; "Bewitched: Hippie, Hippie, Hippie," ABC, 1968; "The Smothers Brothers Comedy Hour," CBS, 1969; "The Name of the Game: Aquarius Descending," NBC, 1970.

STOSSEL, LUDWIG
b. Austria, February 12, 1883; d. 1973. Actor often in ethnic roles, perhaps best known as "The little old winemaker, me," in TV commercials of the sixties.
AS A REGULAR: "Warner Bros. Presents Casablanca," ABC, 1955-56; "Man with a Camera," ABC, 1958-60; "Alias Smith and Jones," ABC, 1972-73.
AND: "Public Defender: Destiny," CBS, 1954; "December Bride: The Sentimentalist," CBS, 1955; "Science Fiction Theatre: Spider, Incorporated," SYN, 1955; "TV Reader's Digest: A Bell for Okinawa," ABC, 1956; "Crusader: Man of Medicine," CBS, 1956; "Science Fiction Theatre: The Sound That Kills," SYN, 1956; "Father Knows Best: The Angel's Sweater," NBC, 1956; "Window on Main Street: Christmas Memory," CBS, 1961; "Window on Main Street: The Women," CBS, 1962.

STRANGE, GLENN
b. Weed. NM, August 16, 1899; d. 1973. Heavyset actor who played Frankenstein in the

movies and Long Branch Saloon bartender Sam on "Gunsmoke."

AS A REGULAR: "Gunsmoke," CBS, 1961-73.
AND: "The Abbott and Costello Show: The Birthday Party," CBS, 1952; "Cheyenne: Welcome Enemy," ABC, 1960; "The Rifleman: Miss Bertie," ABC, 1960; "Thriller: A Good Imagination," NBC, 1961.

STRASBERG, SUSAN

b. New York City, NY, May 22, 1938. Daughter of Lee, a fresh-faced actress in film ("Picnic") and TV who played the wife of cop David Toma (Tony Musante).

AS A REGULAR: "The Marriage," NBC, 1954; "Toma," ABC, 1973-74.
AND: "Goodyear TV Playhouse: Catch a Falling Star," NBC, 1953; "Kraft Television Theatre: Romeo and Juliet," NBC, 1954; "G.E. Theatre: Mr. Blue Ocean," CBS, 1955; "Omnibus: Dear Brutus," CBS, 1956; "Hallmark Hall of Fame: Cradle Song," NBC, 1956; "Person to Person," CBS, 1956; "Westinghouse Desilu Playhouse: Debut," CBS, 1958; "Our American Heritage: Destiny West," NBC, 1960; "Play of the Week: The Cherry Orchard," SYN, 1960; "Here's Hollywood," NBC, 1961; "Dr. Kildare: A Game for Three," NBC, 1963; "Bob Hope Chrysler Theatre: Four Kings," NBC, 1963; "The Breaking Point: A Child of the Center Ring," ABC, 1964; "Burke's Law: Who Killed the Eleventh Best-Dressed Woman in the World?," ABC, 1964; "The Rogues: The Stefanini Dowry," NBC, 1964; "Burke's Law: Who Killed Cop Robin?," ABC, 1965; "Run for Your Life: The Voice of Gina Milan," NBC, 1965; "The Virginian: The Captive," NBC, 1966; "The Invaders: Quantity Unknown," ABC, 1967; "The FBI: The Executioners," ABC, 1967; "The Big Valley: Night in a Small Town," ABC, 1967; "The FBI: The Quarry," ABC, 1968; "The Name of the Game: Pineapple Rose," NBC, 1968; "The Steve Allen Show," SYN, 1968; "CBS Playhouse: The Experiment," CBS, 1969; "Crisis," CBS, 1970; "McCloud: Our Man in Paris," NBC, 1970; "The Men From Shiloh: Crooked Corner," NBC, 1970; "The Movie Game," SYN, 1970; "Alias Smith and Jones: Exit From Wickenburg," ABC, 1971; "The Sixth Sense: Through a Flame Darkly," ABC, 1972; "Mannix: The Faces of Murder," CBS, 1973; "Night Gallery: The Doll of Death," NBC, 1973; "The Streets of San Francisco: One Last Shot," ABC, 1974; "The Rockford Files: The Countess," NBC, 1974; "McMillan and Wife: Guilt by Association," NBC, 1974; "Wide World of Mystery: Murder at Malibu," ABC, 1975; "Medical Story: Wasteland," ABC, 1975; "Harry O: Past Imperfect," ABC, 1976; "Medical Center: The Touch of Sight," CBS, 1976; "The Rockford Files: A Bad Deal in the Valley," NBC, 1976; "Cagney & Lacey: A Different Drummer," CBS, 1987.
TV MOVIES AND MINISERIES: "Marcus Welby, M.D.," ABC, 1969; "Hauser's Memory," NBC, 1970;

"Mr. and Mrs. Bo Jo Jones," ABC, 1971; "Frankenstein," ABC, 1973; "Toma," ABC, 1973; "SST-Death Flight," ABC, 1977; "The Immigrants," SYN, 1978; "Beggarman, Thief," NBC, 1979; "Rona Jaffe's Mazes and Monsters," CBS, 1982.

STRASSER, ROBIN

b. New York City, NY, May 7, 1945. Actress who played Rachel on "Another World," Dr. Christina Karras on "All My Children" and Dorian on "One Life to Live."

AS A REGULAR: "Another World," NBC, 1967-71, 1972; "All My Children," ABC, 1976-79; "One Life to Live," ABC, 1979-89; "Knots Landing," CBS, 1990- .
AND: "The Irregular Verb to Love," NET, 1965; "The Rookies: A Legacy of Death," ABC, 1974; "The John Davidson Show," SYN, 1981; "Murder, She Wrote: The Last Flight of the Dizzy Damsel," CBS, 1988; "China Beach: Women in White," ABC, 1989.
TV MOVIES AND MINISERIES: "Baby M," ABC, 1988.

STRASSMAN, MARCIA

b. New York City, NY, April 28, 1948. Actress who played the wife of Gabe Kaplan on "Welcome Back, Kotter."

AS A REGULAR: "M*A*S*H," CBS, 1972-73; "Welcome Back, Kotter," ABC, 1975-79; "Good Time Harry," NBC, 1980; "Booker," FOX, 1989-90.
AND: "The Patty Duke Show: How to Succeed in Romance," ABC, 1964; "The Patty Duke Show: The Raffle," ABC, 1965; "The Paul Lynde Show: No More Mr. Nice Guy," ABC, 1973; "Love Story: Mirabelle's Summer," NBC, 1973; "Marcus Welby, M.D.: The Latch-Key Child," ABC, 1974; "Police Story: The Ripper," NBC, 1974; "City of Angels: The Losers," NBC, 1976; "The Rockford Files: Only Rock 'n' Roll Will Never Die," NBC, 1979; "Magnum, P.I.: Heal Thyself," CBS, 1982; "E/R: Premiere," CBS, 1984; "Shadow Chasers: Pilot," ABC, 1985; "Amazing Stories: Such Interesting Neighbors," NBC, 1987; "CBS Summer Playhouse: Tickets Please," CBS, 1988; "TV 101: First Love," CBS, 1989; "ABC Afterschool Special: Daddy Can't Read," ABC, 1989.
TV MOVIES AND MINISERIES: "Brenda Starr," ABC, 1976; "Brave New World," NBC, 1980; "Haunted by Her Past," NBC, 1987.

STRAUSS, PETER

b. Croton-on-Hudson, NY, February 20, 1942. Hunky, dashing actor who played Rudy Jorache on "Rich Man, Poor Man" and most recently played gumshoe Peter Gunn; an Emmy winner for "The Jericho Mile."

AS A REGULAR: "Rich Man, Poor Man-Book II," ABC, 1976-77.
AND: "Medical Center: Countdown," CBS, 1971; "The Mary Tyler Moore Show: Angels in the Snow," CBS, 1973; "The Streets of San Francisco: Timelock," ABC, 1973; "The Streets of San Francisco: For the Love of God," ABC, 1973; "Hawaii Five-O: Death With Father," CBS, 1974; "Barnaby Jones: The Last Contract," CBS, 1974; "The Streets of San Francisco: Letters from the Grave," ABC, 1975; "Medical Center: Survivors," CBS, 1975.
TV MOVIES AND MINISERIES: "The Man Without a Country," ABC, 1973; "Attack on Terror: The FBI Versus the Ku Klux Klan," CBS, 1975; "Rich Man, Poor Man," ABC, 1976; "Young Joe, the Forgotten Kennedy," ABC, 1977; "The Jericho Mile," ABC, 1979; "Angel on my Shoulder," ABC, 1980; "A Whale for the Killing," ABC, 1981; "Masada," ABC, 1981; "Heart of Steel," ABC, 1983; "Tender Is the Night," SHO, 1985; "Kane & Abel," CBS, 1985; "Under Siege," NBC, 1986; "Penalty Phase," CBS, 1986; "Proud Men," ABC, 1987; "Brotherhood of the Rose," NBC, 1989; "Peter Gunn," ABC, 1989.
* Emmies: 1979.

STREEP, MERYL
b. Mary Louise Streep, Summit, NJ, June 22, 1949. Chameleon-like actress of movies ("Sophie's Choice," "Out of Africa," "Postcards From the Edge"); she won an Emmy for her work in "Holocaust."
TV MOVIES AND MINISERIES: "The Deadliest Season," CBS, 1977; "Holocaust," NBC, 1978.
* Emmies: 1978.

STREISAND, BARBRA
b. Brooklyn, NY, April 24, 1942. Talented, driven singer-actress who turned to TV specials to solidify her star status in the mid-sixties.
AS A GUEST: "The Tonight Show Starring Johnny Carson," NBC, 1962; "The Merv Griffin Show," NBC, 1962; "The Ed Sullivan Show," CBS, 1962; "Bob Hope Special," NBC, 1963; "The Judy Garland Show," CBS, 1963; "My Name Is Barbra," CBS, 1965; "Color Me Barbra," CBS, 1966; "Barbra Streisand Special: Belle of 14th Street," CBS, 1967; "A Happening in Central Park," CBS, 1968; "Barbra Streisand—And Other Musical Instruments," CBS, 1973; "Putting It Together—The Making of The Broadway Album," HBO, 1986; "One Voice," HBO, 1986.
* Emmies: 1965.

STRICKLAND, GAIL
b. Birmingham, AL. Actress who played Dr.

Marilyn McGrath on "Heartbeat."
AS A REGULAR: "The Insiders," ABC, 1985-86; "What a Country!," SYN, 1986-87; "Heartbeat," ABC, 1988-89.
AND: "The Mary Tyler Moore Show: Almost a Nun's Story," CBS, 1973; "Barnaby Jones: Friends Till Death," CBS, 1974; "Hawaii Five-0: Killer at Sea," CBS, 1974; "Hawaii Five-0: How to Steal a Masterpiece," CBS, 1974; "The Bob Newhart Show: My Boy Guillermo," CBS, 1976; "Lou Grant: Scandal," CBS, 1978; "M*A*S*H: Bottoms Up," CBS, 1981; "Alice: Give My Regards to Broadway," CBS, 1982; "Hill Street Blues: Invasion of the Third World Mutant Body Snatchers," NBC, 1982; "Hardcastle and McCormick: Flying Down to Rio," ABC, 1983; "Night Court: Pilot," NBC, 1984; "Hill Street Blues: The Other Side of Oneness," NBC, 1984; "Cagney & Lacey: Fathers & Daughters," CBS, 1984; "Family Ties: Ladies Man," NBC, 1984; "Highway to Heaven: A Dream of Wild Horses," NBC, 1987; "Murder, She Wrote: Steal Me a Story," CBS, 1987.
TV MOVIES AND MINISERIES: "Ellery Queen," NBC, 1975; "The Dark Side of Innocence," NBC, 1976; "The Gathering, Part II," NBC, 1979; "Letters From Frank," CBS, 1979; "A Matter of Life and Death," CBS, 1981; "Life of the Party: The Story of Beatrice," CBS, 1982.

STRIMPELL, STEPHEN
b. New York City, NY, 1939. Actor who played Stanley Beamish, aka Mr. Terrific, on a sixties superhero spoof.
AS A REGULAR: "Mr. Terrific," CBS, 1967.
AND: "Westinghouse Presents: The Dispossessed," CBS, 1961; "Run, Buddy, Run: Wild Wild Wake," CBS, 1966.

STRITCH, ELAINE
b. Detroit, MI, February 2, 1925. Character actress at her best playing warmly cynical survivors.
AS A REGULAR: "The Growing Paynes," DUM, 1949; "Pantomime Quiz," CBS, 1953; DUM, 1953-54; ABC, 1955; CBS, 1955; ABC, 1958; "My Sister Eileen," CBS, 1960-61; "Trials of O'Brien," CBS, 1965-66; "The Ellen Burstyn Show," ABC, 1986-87.
AND: "Goodyear TV Playhouse: Nothing to Sneeze At," NBC, 1953; "Goodyear TV Playhouse: Here's Father," NBC, 1954; "Motorola TV Hour: The Family Man," ABC, 1954; "Appointment with Adventure: The House on Gellen Street," CBS, 1955; "Washington Square," NBC, 1956; "Alcoa Hour: He's for Me," NBC, 1957; "Du Pont Show of the Month: The Red Mill," CBS, 1958; "Climax!: The Disappearance of Daphne," CBS, 1958; "Studio One: The Left-Handed Welcome," CBS, 1958; "Your Hit Parade," CBS, 1959; "Adventures in Paradise: The Haunted," ABC, 1959; "Art Carney Special:

3-in-1," NBC, 1960; "Wagon Train: The Tracy Sadler Story," NBC, 1960; "Arthur Murray Party," NBC, 1960; "Art Carney Special: Full Moon Over Brooklyn," NBC, 1960; "Alcoa Theatre: You Should Meet My Sister," NBC, 1960; "Password," CBS, 1962; "The Nurses: The Witch of the West Wing," CBS, 1963; "Repertory Theatre: The Wedding," NET, 1965; "New York Television Theatre: Pins and Needles," NET, 1966; "The Mike Douglas Show," SYN, 1969; "The Mourner," NBC, 1971; "Shades of Greene: Two Gentle People," PBS, 1976; "Tattinger's: Rest in Peas," NBC, 1988.

TV MOVIES AND MINISERIES: "Stranded," NBC, 1986.

STRINGBEAN

b. David Akeman, Annville, KY, June 17, 1915; d. 1973. Banjoist and comic who was murdered.

AS A REGULAR: "Hee Haw," CBS, 1969-71; SYN, 1971-73.

AND: "Country Music Jubilee," ABC, 1958.

STRUNK, JUD

b. Jamestown, NY, June 11, 1933.

AS A REGULAR: "Rowan & Martin's Laugh-In," NBC, 1972-73.

AND: "The Merv Griffin Show," SYN, 1968.

STRUTHERS, SALLY

b. Portland, OR, July 28, 1948. Blonde actress who played Gloria, daughter of Archie Bunker (Carroll O'Connor) on "All in the Family" and her own short-lived sitcom.

AS A REGULAR: "The Smothers Brothers Comedy Hour," ABC, 1970; "The Tim Conway Comedy Hour," CBS, 1970; "All in the Family," CBS, 1971-78; "Pebbles and Bamm-Bamm," CBS, 1971-72; "The Flintstones Comedy Hour," CBS, 1972-73; "The Flintstone Show," CBS, 1973-74; "Gloria," CBS, 1982-83; "9 to 5," SYN, 1986-88.

AND: "Ironside: Love, Peace, Brotherhood," NBC, 1970; "Love, American Style: Love and the Triangle," ABC, 1971; "The Courtship of Eddie's Father: The Blarney Stone Girl," ABC, 1971; "The David Frost Show," SYN, 1971; "Hollywood Squares," NBC, 1972; "Hotel Nincty," CBS, 1973; "Password All-Stars," ABC, 1975; "The Carol Burnett Show," CBS, 1975; "Rhyme and Reason," ABC, 1975; "Hollywood Squares," NBC, 1975; "Dinah!," SYN, 1976; "The John Davidson Show," SYN, 1981; "Archie Bunker's Place: Gloria Comes Home," CBS, 1982; "Super Password," NBC, 1989; "Animal Crack-Ups," ABC, 1989.

TV MOVIES AND MINISERIES: "Aloha Means Goodbye," CBS, 1974; "Hey, I'm Alive!," ABC, 1975; "The Great Houdinis," ABC,

1976; "My Husband Is Missing," NBC, 1978; "And Your Name Is Jonah," CBS, 1979; "A Gun in the House," CBS, 1981; "A Deadly Silence," ABC, 1989.

* Emmies: 1972, 1979.

STUART, BARBARA

b. Paris, IL. Actress who played Bunny, girlfriend of Sgt. Carter (Frank Sutton) on "Gomer Pyle, USMC."

AS A REGULAR: "The George Burns Show," NBC, 1958-59; "Pete and Gladys," CBS, 1960-61; "Gomer Pyle, USMC," CBS, 1964-70; "The Queen and I," CBS, 1969; "The McLean Stevenson Show," NBC, 1976-77; "Our Family Honor," ABC, 1985-86.

AND: "Jefferson Drum: The Outlaw," NBC, 1958; "The Lawless Years: The Maxey Gordon Story," NBC, 1959; "Markham: The Man From Salzburg," CBS, 1960; "Chevy Mystery Show: Dead Man's Walk," NBC, 1960; "Tales of Wells Fargo: All That Glitters," NBC, 1960; "Coronado 9: Smugglers of Death," SYN, 1960; "The Twilight Zone: A Thing About Machines," CBS, 1960; "Sam Benedict: Run Softly, Oh Softly," NBC, 1963; "Destry: Destry Had a Little Lamb," ABC, 1964; "The Dick Van Dyke Show: Dear Mrs. Petrie, Your Husband Is in Jail," CBS, 1964; "The Joey Bishop Show: In This Corner, Jan Murray," CBS, 1964; "The Andy Griffith Show: TV or Not TV," CBS, 1965; "The Adventures of Ozzie and Harriet: Helpful June," ABC, 1965; "The Joey Bishop Show: Joey the Star Maker," CBS, 1965; "The Joey Bishop Show: What'll You Have?," CBS, 1965; "The Farmer's Daughter: Glen a Gogh-Gogh," ABC, 1965; "Mr. Roberts: A Turn for the Nurse," NBC, 1966; "Batman: The Puzzles Are Coming/The Duo Is Slumming," ABC, 1966; "Mr. Terrific: Stanley the Safecracker," CBS, 1967; "T.H.E. Cat: Queen of Diamonds, Knave of Hearts," NBC, 1967; "Captain Nice: Whatever Lola Wants," NBC, 1967; "Kung Fu: The Third Man," ABC, 1973; "Three's Company: Chrissy's Cousin," ABC, 1980; "Hotel: Outsiders," ABC, 1984; "Highway to Heaven: Love and Marriage," NBC, 1986; "Simon & Simon: Second Swell," CBS, 1988.

STUART, MARY

b. Mary Houchins, Miami, FL, July 4, 1926. Actress who played Joanne Tourneur for the entire run of "Search for Tomorrow."

AS A REGULAR: "Search for Tomorrow," CBS, 1951-82; NBC, 1982-86.

SUES, ALAN

b. Ross, CA. Comedian.

AS A REGULAR: "Rowan & Martin's Laugh-In," NBC, 1968-72.

AND: "The Twilight Zone: The Masks," CBS,

1964; "Shindig," ABC, 1964; "Art Linkletter's Hollywood Talent Scouts," CBS, 1966; "Letters to Laugh-In," NBC, 1969; "Hollywood Squares," NBC, 1970; "Love, American Style: Love and the Baker's Half Dozen," ABC, 1971; "The David Frost Show," SYN, 1971; "Love, American Style: Love and the Intruder," ABC, 1972; "$weepstake$: Victor, Billy and Bobby, 'Sometimes,' " NBC, 1979.

SULLAVAN, MARGARET

b. Margaret Brooke, Norfolk, VA, May 16, 1911; d. 1960. Film actress of the thirties and forties ("The Good Fairy," "The Shop Around the Corner"); her story was chronicled by her daughter, actress Brooke Hayward, in "Haywire." The book was made into a TV movie with Lee Remick as Sullavan.

AS A GUEST: "Ford Theatre: Touchstone," ABC, 1951; "Schlitz Playhouse of Stars: Still Life," CBS, 1951; "Schlitz Playhouse of Stars: The Nymph and the Lamp," CBS, 1951; "Producers Showcase: State of the Union," NBC, 1954.

SULLIVAN, BARRY

b. Patrick Francis Barry Sullivan, Boston, MA, August 29, 1912. All-purpose leading man who played Pat Garrett in the western series "The Tall Man."

AS A REGULAR: "The Man Called X," SYN, 1956; "Harbourmaster (Adventures at Scott Island)," CBS, 1957; ABC, 1958; "The Tall Man," NBC, 1960-62; "The Road West," NBC, 1966-67; "Rich Man, Poor Man-Book II," ABC, 1976-77.

AND: "Ford Theatre: As the Flame Dies," NBC, 1953; "Ford Theatre: The Fugitives," NBC, 1954; "Medallion Theatre: Book Overdue," CBS, 1954; "Ford Star Jubilee: The Caine Mutiny Court Martial," CBS, 1955; "Ford Star Jubilee: A Bell for Adano," CBS, 1956; "Studio One: Career," CBS, 1956; "The Ford Show," NBC, 1958; "Playhouse 90: Nightmare at Ground Zero," CBS, 1958; "Climax!: Cabin B-13," CBS, 1958; "Alfred Hitchcock Presents: The Two-Million Dollar Defense," CBS, 1958; "Playhouse 90: Dark December," CBS, 1959; "Bonanza: The Sun Mountain Herd," NBC, 1959; "Dick Powell's Zane Grey Theatre: The Lonely Gun," CBS, 1959; "Startime: My Three Angels," NBC, 1959; "The du Pont Show with June Allyson: The Crossing," CBS, 1959; "Westinghouse Desilu Playhouse: City in Bondage," CBS, 1960; "Sam Benedict: Some Fires Die Slowly," NBC, 1963; "The Virginian: Woman From White Wing," NBC, 1963; "Ben Casey: The Echo of a Silent Cheer," ABC, 1963; "The Great Adventure: The Great Diamond Mountain," CBS, 1963; "You Don't Say," NBC, 1964; "Object Is," ABC, 1964; "The Great Adventure: The President Vanishes,"

CBS, 1964; "The Reporter: The Lost Lady Blues," CBS, 1964; "Kraft Suspense Theatre: The Last Clear Chance," NBC, 1965; "Run for Your Life: Never Pick Up a Stranger," NBC, 1965; "Twelve O'Clock High: Grant Me No Favor," ABC, 1965; "The Loner: The Oath," CBS, 1965; "The Poppy Is Also a Flower," ABC, 1966; "Mission: Impossible: The Psychic," CBS, 1967; "Insight: Fat Hands and a Diamond Ring," SYN, 1967; "The Man From UNCLE: The Seven Wonders of the World Affair," NBC, 1968; "That Girl: Sock It to Me," ABC, 1968; "The Name of the Game: The Inquiry," NBC, 1969; "It Takes a Thief: Boom at the Top," ABC, 1969; "CBS Playhouse: The Experiment," CBS, 1969; "On Stage: This Town Will Never Be the Same," NBC, 1969; "The Virginian: The Power Seekers," NBC, 1969; "The Name of the Game: High Card," NBC, 1969; "The Dating Game," ABC, 1970; "It Takes a Thief: Situation Red," ABC, 1970; "The High Chaparral: A Matter of Survival," NBC, 1970; "Medical Center: Deadly Encounter," CBS, 1970; "The High Chaparral: A Matter of Vengeance," NBC, 1970; "Dan August: The Titan," ABC, 1971; "The Name of the Game: Los Angeles 2017," NBC, 1971; "Hallmark Hall of Fame: The Price," NBC, 1971; "Medical Center: Circle of Power," CBS, 1971; "McCloud: Somebody's Out to Get Jennie," NBC, 1971; "Longstreet: This Little Piggy Went to Market," ABC, 1971; "Marcus Welby, M.D.: Of Magic Shadow Shapes," ABC, 1972; "Mannix: Cry Pigeon," CBS, 1972; "Hawaii Five-O: While You're at It, Bring in the Moon," CBS, 1972; "Hollywood Television Theatre: Another Part of the Forest," NET, 1972; "Cool Million: The Abduction of Bayard Barnes," NBC, 1972; "The Sixth Sense: Five Widows Weeping," ABC, 1972; "Night Gallery: Finnegan's Flight," NBC, 1972; "Ironside: The Countdown," NBC, 1973; "The Streets of San Francisco: Deadline," ABC, 1973; "The Magician," NBC, 1973; "Barnaby Jones: A Little Glory, A Little Death," CBS, 1973; "Cannon: He Who Digs a Grave," CBS, 1973; "The Streets of San Francisco: Inferno," ABC, 1973; "The Streets of San Francisco: The Most Deadly Species," ABC, 1974; "Harry O: Guardian at the Gates," ABC, 1974; "Ironside: Trial of Terror," NBC, 1974; "The Streets of San Francisco: The Thrill Killers," ABC, 1976; "Quincy: Sullied Be Thy Name," NBC, 1977; "The Runaways: Street of Terror," NBC, 1979; "Charlie's Angels: Love Boat Angels," ABC, 1979; "Little House on the Prairie: Author, Author," NBC, 1979; "The Love Boat: The Grass Is Always Greener," ABC, 1979; "Vega$: The Day the Gambling Stopped," ABC, 1980.

TV MOVIES AND MINISERIES: "The Immortal," ABC, 1969; "Night Gallery," NBC, 1969; "The House on Greenapple Road," ABC, 1970; "Yuma," ABC, 1971; "Cannon," CBS, 1971;

"Kung Fu," ABC, 1972; "The Magician," NBC, 1973; "Savage," NBC, 1973; "Letters From Three Lovers," ABC, 1973; "Hurricane," ABC, 1974; "Best Sellers: Once an Eagle," NBC, 1977; "The Bastard," SYN, 1978; "The Immigrants," SYN, 1978; "Backstairs at the White House," NBC, 1979; "Casino," ABC, 1980.

SULLIVAN, ED
b. New York City, NY, 1901; d. 1974. Newspaper columnist and TV impressario whose variety show was an American institution for almost 25 years.
AS A REGULAR: "Toast of the Town," CBS, 1948-1955; "The Ed Sullivan Show," CBS, 1955-71.
AND: "The Phil Silvers Show: Sgt. Bilko Presents Ed Sullivan," CBS, 1956; "The Phil Silvers Show: Show Segments," CBS, 1957; "The $64,000 Question," CBS, 1957; "Mr. Adams and Eve: Back Page," CBS, 1958; "Eye On New York," CBS, 1958; "G.E. Theatre: Bill Bailey Won't You Please Come Home?," CBS, 1959; "The Jack Benny Program," CBS, 1959; "The Red Skelton Show," CBS, 1961; "Jackie Gleason Special: The Million Dollar Incident," CBS, 1961; "Kraft Music Hall: Roast for Johnny Carson," NBC, 1968; "The Red Skelton Hour," CBS, 1969; "A Salute to Television's 25th Anniversary," ABC, 1972; "Clownaround," CBS, 1973.
* See also "The Ed Sullivan Show."

SULLIVAN, KATHLEEN
b. Pasadena, CA, 1953.
AS A REGULAR: "ABC Weekend News," ABC, 1985-87; "CBS This Morning," CBS, 1987-90.

SULLIVAN, SUSAN
b. New York City, NY, November 18, 1944. Actress who played Maggie Gioberti on "Falcon Crest" and the nice lady who knows everything on Tylenol commercials.
AS A REGULAR: "A World Apart," ABC, 1970-71; "Another World," NBC, 1971-76; "Rich Man, Poor Man-Book II," ABC, 1976-77; "Having Babies," ABC, 1978-79; "It's a Living," ABC, 1980-81; "Falcon Crest," CBS, 1981-89.
AND: "Medical Center: No Hiding Place," CBS, 1975; "Kojak: Both Sides of the Law," CBS, 1975; "McMillan and Wife: Requiem for a Bride," NBC, 1975; "City of Angels: The House on Orange Grove Avenue," NBC, 1976; "Barnaby Jones: Deadline for Dying," CBS, 1976; "Kojak: When You Hear the Beep, Drop Dead," CBS, 1977; "Barnaby Jones: Final Judgment," CBS, 1978; "The Love Boat: Doc Be Patient," ABC, 1979; "Taxi: What Price Bobby?," ABC, 1980.
TV MOVIES AND MINISERIES: "No Place to Run," ABC, 1972; "The City," NBC, 1977; "Having Babies II," ABC, 1977; "The New Maverick," ABC, 1978; "The Ordeal of Dr. Mudd," CBS,

1980; "City in Fear," ABC, 1980; "Rage of Angels: The Story Continues," NBC, 1986.

SUMMERS, HOPE
b. Mattoon, IL, 1901; d. 1979. Actress who played Clara Edwards, friend-rival of Aunt Bee (Frances Bavier) on "The Andy Griffith Show."
AS A REGULAR: "Hawkins Falls, Population 6,200," NBC, 1951-55; "The Rifleman," ABC, 1958-63; "The Andy Griffith Show," CBS, 1961-68; "Another Day," CBS, 1978.
AND: "The Loretta Young Show: Three and Two, Please," NBC, 1957; "The Gale Storm Show: Family Reunion," CBS, 1958; "The Thin Man: The Pre-Incan Caper," NBC, 1958; "The Danny Thomas Show: The Big Fight," CBS, 1962; "Dr. Kildare: The Bronc Buster," NBC, 1962; "Divorce Court: Talbot vs. Talbot," SYN, 1962; "The Danny Thomas Show: Howdy Neighbor," CBS, 1964; "Hazel: Hot Potato a la Hazel," NBC, 1964; "No Time for Sergeants: Will's Misfortune Cookie," ABC, 1965; "The Dick Van Dyke Show: Odd But True," CBS, 1965; "Petticoat Junction: The Crowded Wedding Ring," CBS, 1965; "The Beverly Hillbillies: Jethro Goes to College," CBS, 1966; "Love on a Rooftop: My Husband the Knight," ABC, 1966; "Gomer Pyle, USMC: The Secret Life of Gomer Pyle," CBS, 1967; "That Girl: Decision Before Dawn," ABC, 1968; "Mayberry RFD: The Mayberry Float," CBS, 1970; "Mayberry RFD: The New Housekeeper," CBS, 1970; "Marcus Welby, M.D.: Epidemic," ABC, 1970; "M*A*S*H: The Trial of Henry Blake," CBS, 1973; "The Girl with Something Extra: All the Nude That's Fit to Print," NBC, 1973; "Chico and the Man: Garage Sale," NBC, 1975; "Welcome Back, Kotter: Mr. Kotter, Teacher," ABC, 1975; "Little House on the Prairie: The Collection," NBC, 1976; "Starsky and Hutch: Savage Sunday," ABC, 1975.
TV MOVIES AND MINISERIES: "Death Sentence," ABC, 1974.

SUSANN, JACQUELINE
b. Philadelphia, PA, August 20, 1921; d. 1974. Trash novelist ("Valley of the Dolls") who began in early TV.
AS A REGULAR: "The Morey Amsterdam Show," CBS, 1948-49; DUM, 1949-50; "Your Surprise Store," CBS, 1952.
AND: "Suspense: Pigeons in the Cave," CBS, 1953; "Danger: A Day's Pay," CBS, 1954; "Mannix: The Crime That Wasn't," CBS, 1971; "Love, American Style: Love and the Hidden Meaning," ABC, 1973; "Celebrity Sweepstakes," NBC, 1974.

SUSMAN, TODD
b. St. Louis, MO, January 17, 1947. Actor who most recently played Constable Shiftlet on "Newhart."

AS A REGULAR: "The Bob Crane Show," NBC, 1975; "Spencer's Pilots," CBS, 1976; "Number 96," NBC, 1980-81; "Star of the Family," ABC, 1982; "Goodnight Beantown," CBS, 1983-84; "Newhart," CBS, 1985-90; "Laugh!s," SHO, 1990- .

AND: "The Young Rebels: The Infiltrator," ABC, 1970; "Room 222: You Can't Take a Boy Out of the Country, But ...," ABC, 1971; "Room 222: I Hate You, Silas Marner," ABC, 1971; "Love, American Style: Love and Lady Luck," ABC, 1972; "Room 222: Pete's Protege," ABC, 1973; "M*A*S*H: Operation Noselift," CBS, 1974; "Kojak: Hush Now, or You Die!," CBS, 1974; "Barney Miller: Kidnapping," ABC, 1978; "Barney Miller: Strip Joint," ABC, 1979; "The White Shadow: Feeling No Pain," CBS, 1979; "Lou Grant: Jazz," CBS, 1981; "Barney Miller: Altercation," ABC, 1982; "Remington Steele: Steele Crazy After All These Years," NBC, 1983; "Webster: Burn-Out," ABC, 1984; "Webster: TV or Not TV," ABC, 1985; "St. Elsewhere: Slice o'Life," NBC, 1985; "St. Elsewhere: Once Upon a Mattress," NBC, 1986; "Webster: The Strike," SYN, 1987; "St. Elsewhere: Final Cut," NBC, 1988; "ALF: Hide Away," NBC, 1989; "Highway to Heaven: Goodbye, Mr. Zelinka," NBC, 1989; "Have Faith: Holy Smoke," ABC, 1989; "Have Faith: The Window," ABC, 1989.

TV MOVIES AND MINISERIES: "Death Scream," ABC, 1975; "Spencer's Pilots," CBS, 1976; "The Other Victim," CBS, 1981; "City Killer," NBC, 1984.

SUSSKIND, DAVID

b. *New York City, NY, December 19, 1920; d. 1987.* Television producer and talk-show host famed for his offbeat, controversial guests.

AS PRODUCER: "Kraft Television Theatre," NBC, 1947-58; ABC, 1953-55; "Justice," NBC, 1954-56; "Du Pont Show of the Month," CBS, 1957-61; "Swiss Family Robinson," NBC, 1958; "Oldsmobile Music Theatre," NBC, 1959; "Too Young to Go Steady," NBC, 1959; "Hooray for Love," CBS, 1960; "The Power and the Glory," CBS, 1961; "East Side/West Side," CBS, 1963-64.

TV MOVIES AND MINISERIES: "Eleanor and Franklin," ABC, 1976; "Eleanor and Franklin: The White House Years," ABC, 1977.

AS HOST: "The David Susskind Show," SYN, 1958-87; "Good Company," ABC, 1967.

AND: "East Side/West Side: Nothing But the Half-Truth," CBS, 1964.

TV MOVIES AND MINISERIES: "Fear on Trial," CBS, 1975.

* Emmies: 1966, 1967, 1976, 1977.

SUTTON, FRANK

b. *Clarksville, TN, October 23, 1923; d. 1974.* Character actor who hit TV paydirt as Sgt.

Vince Carter, continually exasperated by Gomer Pyle (Jim Nabors).

AS A REGULAR: "The Secret Storm," CBS, 1960-61; "Gomer Pyle, USMC," CBS, 1964-69; "The Jim Nabors Hour," CBS, 1969-71.

AND: "Studio One: Walk Down the Hill," CBS, 1957; "Kaiser Aluminum Hour: Passion for Revenge," NBC, 1957; "True Story: A Matter of Suspicion," NBC, 1957; "Brenner: Word of Honor," CBS, 1959; "Armstrong Circle Theatre: Sound of Violence," CBS, 1959; "Witness: 'Shoeless Joe' Jackson," CBS, 1960; "Deadline: The New Nurses," SYN, 1960; "Naked City: New York to L.A.," ABC, 1961; "The Defenders: The Riot," CBS, 1961; "Combat!: The Chateau," ABC, 1963; "Empire: Seven Days on Rough Street," NBC, 1963; "The Andy Griffith Show: Gomer Pyle, USMC," CBS, 1964; "Password," CBS, 1965; "Love, American Style: Love and the Haunted House," ABC, 1970; "Love, American Style: Love and the Guru," ABC, 1972; "Love, American Style: Love and the Lady Barber," ABC, 1972; "Love, American Style: Love and the Secret Life," ABC, 1973.

TV MOVIES AND MINISERIES: "Hurricane," ABC, 1974.

SWANSON, GLORIA

b. *Gloria May Josephine Svensson, Chicago, IL, March 27, 1899; d. 1983.* Legendary actress and sex symbol of the twenties; she appeared often on TV in the sixties.

AS A REGULAR: "Gloria Swanson Presents," SYN, 1954-55.

AND: "Hollywood Opening Night: The Pattern," NBC, 1953; "Mike Wallace Interviews," ABC, 1957; "The Steve Allen Show," NBC, 1957; "Bob Hope Special," NBC, 1958; "Hedda Hopper's Hollywood," NBC, 1960; "Straightaway: A Toast to Yesterday," ABC, 1961; "Dr. Kildare: The Good Luck Charm," 1963; "Burke's Law: Who Killed Purity Mather?," ABC, 1963; "The Alfred Hitchcock Hour: Behind the Locked Door," CBS, 1964; "Kraft Suspense Theatre: Who Is Jennifer?," NBC, 1964; "Burke's Law: Who Killed Vaudeville?," ABC, 1964; "My Three Sons: Fountain of Youth," ABC, 1965; "Ben Casey: Minus That Rusty Old Hacksaw," ABC, 1965; "The Beverly Hillbillies: The Gloria Swanson Story," CBS, 1966; "Johnny Carson Special: The Sun City Scandals," NBC, 1970; "The Carol Burnett Show," CBS, 1975.

TV MOVIES AND MINISERIES: "The Killer Bees," ABC, 1974.

SWAYZE, JOHN CAMERON

b. *Wichita, KS, April 4, 1906.*

AS A REGULAR: "Who Said That?," NBC, 1948-51; "Guess What Happened?," NBC, 1952; "Armstrong Circle Theatre," NBC, 1955-57; "Chance for Romance," ABC, 1958.

733

AND: "To Tell the Truth," CBS, 1956; "Studio One: The Human Barrier," CBS, 1957; "To Tell the Truth," CBS, 1958.

SWAYZE, PATRICK

b. *Houston, TX, August 18, 1954.* Film hunk ("Dirty Dancing," "Ghost") who began in TV.
AS A REGULAR: "Renegades," ABC, 1983.
AND: "M*A*S*H: Blood Brothers," CBS, 1981; "Amazing Stories: Life on Death Row," NBC, 1986; "The Pat Sajak Show," CBS, 1989.
TV MOVIES AND MINISERIES: "North and South," ABC, 1985; "North and South, Book II," ABC, 1986.

SWEENEY, TERRY

b. *St. Albans, NY, March 23, 1960.* Comic actor who did a good Nancy Reagan on "Saturday Night Live."
AS A REGULAR: "Saturday Night Live," NBC, 1985-86.

SWEET, DOLPH

b. *New York City, NY, July 18, 1920; d. 1985.* Heavyset actor who played Chief Carl Kanisky on "Gimme a Break"; he also played Gil McGowan on "Another World."
AS A REGULAR: "Trials of O'Brien," CBS, 1965-66; "The Edge of Night," CBS, 1967-68; "Another World," NBC, 1972-77; "When the Whistle Blows," ABC, 1980; "Gimme a Break," NBC, 1981-85.
AND: "The Defenders: The Eye of Fear," CBS, 1963; "For the People: ... to prosecute all crimes ...," CBS, 1965; "Little House on the Prairie: The Godsister," NBC, 1978; "Taxi: The Great Line, ABC, 1978; "Paris: America the Beautiful," CBS, 1980; "Hagen: Pilot," CBS, 1980; "Hill Street Blues: Life, Death, Eternity, Etcetera," NBC, 1981; "Hill Street Blues: Gatorbait," NBC, 1981.
TV MOVIES AND MINISERIES: "A Killing Affair," CBS, 1977; "King," NBC, 1978; "Studs Lonigan," NBC, 1979; "Flesh and Blood," CBS, 1979; "Marciano," ABC, 1979; "Hallmark Hall of Fame: Aunt Mary," CBS, 1979; "Gideon's Trumpet," CBS, 1980; "The Acorn People," NBC, 1981.

SWENSON, INGA

b. *Omaha, NB, December 29, 1932.* Actress who played Gretchen Kraus on "Benson."
AS A REGULAR: "Benson," ABC, 1979-86.
AND: "Goodyear TV Playhouse: The Best Wine," NBC, 1957; "Playhouse 90: Heart of Darkness," CBS, 1958; "U.S. Steel Hour: Goodbye ... But It Doesn't Go Away," CBS, 1958; "Playhouse 90: The Wings of the Dove," CBS, 1959; "Du Pont Show of the Month: Oliver Twist," CBS, 1959; "Hallmark Hall of Fame: Victoria Regina," NBC,

1961; "The Defenders: The Locked Room," CBS, 1962; "Bonanza: Inger, My Love," NBC, 1962; "Dr. Kildare: Breakdown," NBC, 1962; "The Nurses: Party Girl," CBS, 1963; "Bonanza: Journey Remembered," NBC, 1963; "CBS Playhouse: My Father and My Mother," CBS, 1968; "Medical Center: The Deceived," CBS, 1970; "NET Playhouse: The Tape Recorder," NET, 1970; "Medical Center: Secret Heritage," CBS, 1971; "The Rookies: Eye for an Eye," ABC, 1975; "Barnaby Jones: The Lonely Victims," CBS, 1976; "The Golden Girls: Little Sister," NBC, 1989.
TV MOVIES AND MINISERIES: "Earth II," ABC, 1971; "Testimony of Two Men," SYN, 1977; "North and South," ABC, 1985; "Bay Coven," NBC, 1987.

SWENSON, KARL

b. *Brooklyn, NY, July 23, 1908; d. 1978.* Actor who played Lars Hanson on "Little House."
AS A REGULAR: "Portia Faces Life (The Inner Flame)," CBS, 1954-55; "Little House on the Prairie," NBC, 1974-78.
AND: "U.S. Steel Hour: To Die Alone," CBS, 1957; "Circus Boy: The Magic Lantern," ABC, 1957; "Gunsmoke: Fingered," CBS, 1957; "Sugarfoot: Small War at Custer Junction," ABC, 1958; "Jefferson Drum: The Lawless," NBC, 1958; "Black Saddle: Four From Stillwater," NBC, 1958; "Bat Masterson: Cheyenne Club," NBC, 1958; "Rawhide: Incident at the Buffalo Smoke House," CBS, 1959; "Dick Powell's Zane Grey Theatre: King of the Valley," CBS, 1959; "Bonanza: The Sun Mountain Herd," NBC, 1959; "Hotel De Paree: Sundance and the Marshal of Water's End," CBS, 1960; "The Rifleman: The Jailbird," ABC, 1960; "Death Valley Days: Eagle in the Rocks," SYN, 1960; "The Rifleman: The Vision," ABC, 1960; "The Man and the Challenge: Breakoff," NBC, 1960; "Mr. Lucky: Odyssey of Hate," CBS, 1960; "Klondike: Klondike Fever," NBC, 1960; "Alfred Hitchcock Presents: Very Moral Theft," NBC, 1960; "Hawaiian Eye: The Blue Goddess," ABC, 1960; "The Andy Griffith Show: Mr. McBeevee," CBS, 1962; "The Virginian: Riff-Raff," NBC, 1962; "Ripcord: Day of the Hunter," SYN, 1962; "It's a Man's World: Chicago Gains a Number," NBC, 1962; "Gomer Pyle, USMC: A Date for the Colonel's Daughter," CBS, 1964; "The Virginian: The Heritage," NBC, 1968; "The Virginian: The Substitute," NBC, 1969; "Gunsmoke: The Devil's Outpost," CBS, 1969; "The Mod Squad: The Sands of Anger," ABC, 1971; "The Odd Couple: Sometimes a Great Ocean," ABC, 1972; "Barnaby Jones: Trial Run for Death," CBS, 1973; "Happy Days: Richie's Car," ABC, 1974; "The Streets of San Francisco: Blockade," ABC, 1974.
TV MOVIES AND MINISERIES: "The Birdmen," CBS, 1971; "A Howling in the Woods," NBC, 1971; "The Gun and the Pulpit," ABC, 1974.

SWIT, LORETTA

b. Passaic, NJ, November 4, 1937. Actress who played Maj. Margaret Houlihan on "M*A*S*H" as the character "evolved" from a sex-crazed harpy to a responsible, competent, reliable (yawn) professional admired by all. And the longer the Korean War raged, the more makeup she wore and the blonder her hair got.

AS A REGULAR: "M*A*S*H," CBS, 1972-83.
AND: "Hawaii Five-O: A Thousand Pardons, You're Dead," CBS, 1969; "Gunsmoke: The Pack Rat," CBS, 1970; "Mannix: Only One Death to a Customer," CBS, 1970; "Ironside: Ollinger's Last Case," NBC, 1973; "Love, American Style: Love and the Pick-Up Fantasy," ABC, 1973; "Love, American Style: Love and the Locksmith," ABC, 1974; "Password," ABC, 1974; "Tony Orlando and Dawn," CBS, 1975; "It's a Bird, It's a Plane, It's Superman," ABC, 1975; "The $25,000 Pyramid," SYN, 1975; "The Bobby Vinton Show," SYN, 1975; "The $25,000 Pyramid," SYN, 1976; "The Love Boat: Anoushka," ABC, 1978; "The Best Christmas Pageant Ever," ABC, 1983; "The Love Boat: The Present," ABC, 1984.
TV MOVIES AND MINISERIES: "Shirts/Skins," ABC, 1973; "The Last Day," NBC, 1975; "Mirror, Mirror," NBC, 1979; "Friendships, Secrets and Lies," NBC, 1979; "Valentine," ABC, 1979; "The Love Tapes," ABC, 1980; "Cagney & Lacey," CBS, 1981; "The Kid From Nowhere," NBC, 1982; "Games Mother Never Taught You," CBS, 1982; "The Execution," NBC, 1985; "Dreams of Gold: The Mel Fisher Story," CBS, 1986.
* Emmies: 1980, 1982.

T

MR. T
b. Lawrence Tero, Chicago, IL, May 21, 1952.
Hulking, macho black actor who was hot in the
early eighties, especially as B.A. Baracus on
"The A-Team."
AS A REGULAR: "The A-Team," NBC, 1983-87;
"T. and T.," SYN, 1987-89.
AND: "Silver Spoons: Me and Mr. T," NBC, 1982;
"Saturday Night Live," NBC, 1985; "Bob Hope
Lampoons Television 1985," NBC, 1985.
TV MOVIES AND MINISERIES: "The Toughest Man in
the World," CBS, 1984.

TAKEI, GEORGE
b. Los Angeles, CA, April 20, 1940. Actor who
played Sulu on "Star Trek."
AS A REGULAR: "Star Trek," NBC, 1966-69.
AND: "Hawaiian Eye: Sword of the Samurai,"
ABC, 1960; "Hawaiian Eye: Jade Song," ABC,
1960; "The Islanders: Our Girl in Saigon," ABC,
1960; "Hawaiian Eye: The Manchu Formula,"
ABC, 1961; "Hawaiian Eye: Thomas Jefferson
Chu," ABC, 1961; "The Twilight Zone: The
Encounter," CBS, 1964; "My Three Sons: The
Hong Kong Story," CBS, 1965; "Mr. Roberts:
Which Way Did the War Go?," NBC, 1965; "Mr.
Roberts: Getting There Is Half the Fun," NBC,
1965; "Mission: Impossible: The Carriers," CBS,
1966; "Ironside: No Motive for Murder," NBC,
1971; "Chico and the Man: Ms. Liz," NBC, 1975;
"Hawaii Five-O: Death's Name Is Sam," CBS,
1975; "Baa Baa Black Sheep: Up for Grabs,"
NBC, 1976; "Blacke's Magic: A Friendly Game
of Showdown," NBC, 1986; "Miami Vice: By
Hooker by Crook," NBC, 1987.

TALMAN, WILLIAM
b. Detroit, MI, February 4, 1915; d. 1968. B-
movie actor who played always-losing district
attorney Hamilton Berger on "Perry Mason."
AS A REGULAR: "Perry Mason," CBS, 1957-66.
AND: "Lux Video Theatre: Pick of the Litter,"
CBS, 1954; "Cavalcade Theatre: Texas Rangers,"
ABC, 1955; "TV Reader's Digest: Old Master
Detective," ABC, 1955; "Science Fiction Theatre:
Water Maker," SYN, 1955; "Ford Theatre: South
of Selanger," NBC, 1955; "Screen Directors
Playhouse: Number Five Checked Out," NBC,
1956; "Climax!: Sit Down with Death," CBS,
1956; "Cimarron City: To Become a Man," NBC,
1958; "Goodyear Theatre: Disappearance," NBC,
1958; "Have Gun, Will Travel: The Shooting of
Jessie May," CBS, 1960; "Have Gun, Will Travel:
Long Way Home," CBS, 1961; "The Wild Wild
West: Night of the Ready-Made Corpse," CBS,
1966; "The Wild Wild West: The Night of the
Man-Eating House," CBS, 1966; "The Invaders:
Quantity Unknown," ABC, 1967.
* Talman was fired from "Perry Mason" in 1960
  when he was one of several folks found nude at
  a wild Hollywood party raided by police, who
  said they found marijuana and narcotics at the
  scene. Talman denied any wrongdoing, and he
  was eventually cleared of narcotics and morals
  charges. "Perry Mason" star Raymond Burr
  and other cast members lobbied for Talman's
  return, and he was rehired that December.
  Richard Boone helped tide Talman over during
  his unemployment by hiring him for some
  guest shots on "Have Gun, Will Travel."

TAMBOR, JEFFREY
b. San Francisco, CA. Actor who played the
cross-dressing attorney-judge Alan Wachtel on
"Hill Street Blues."
AS A REGULAR: "The Ropers," ABC, 1979-80;
"Hill Street Blues," NBC, 1981-87; "9 to 5,"
ABC, 1982; "Mr. Sunshine," ABC, 1986;
"Max Headroom," ABC, 1987; "Studio 5B,"
ABC, 1989; "American Dreamer," NBC,
1990- .
AND: "Three's Company: Moving On," ABC,
1979; "Three's Company: Stanley the Ladies'
Man," ABC, 1979; "Taxi: Elaine and the Lame
Duck," ABC, 1979; "The Love Boat: The
Successor," ABC, 1981; "Three's Company:
Father of the Bride," ABC, 1981; "Barney Miller:
Field Associate," ABC, 1981; "Three's Company:
Two Flew Over the Cuckoo's Nest," ABC, 1981;
"M*A*S*H: Foreign Affairs," CBS, 1982; "The
Love Boat: Out of My Hair," ABC, 1983; "The
Twilight Zone: Dead Woman's Shoes," CBS,
1985; "The Twilight Zone: The World Next
Door," CBS, 1986; "Murder, She Wrote:
Harbinger of Death," CBS, 1988; "Doogie
Howser, M.D.: Every Dog Has His Doogie,"
ABC, 1989.
TV MOVIES AND MINISERIES: "A Gun in the House,"
CBS, 1981; "The Star Maker," NBC, 1981;
"Take Your Best Shot," CBS, 1982; "Cocaine:
One Man's Seduction," NBC, 1983; "The
Three Wishes of Billy Grier," ABC, 1984.

TANDY, JESSICA
b. London, England, June 7, 1909. Award-
winning actress who's arguably in the period of
her greatest fame, thanks to the films "Cocoon"
and "Driving Miss Daisy."
AS A REGULAR: "The Marriage," NBC, 1954.

AND: "Masterpiece Playhouse: Hedda Gabler," NBC, 1950; "Prudential Family Playhouse: Icebound," CBS, 1951; "Studio One: Hangman's House," CBS, 1951; "Omnibus: Glory in the Flower," CBS, 1953; "Omnibus: John Quincy Adams," CBS, 1955; "Alcoa Hour: The Confidence Man," NBC, 1956; "G.E. Theatre: Pot of Gold," CBS, 1956; "Alfred Hitchcock Presents: Toby," CBS, 1956; "Goodyear TV Playhouse: A Murder Is Announced," NBC, 1956; "Studio One: The Five Dollar Bill," CBS, 1957; "Schlitz Playhouse of Stars: Clothes Make the Man," CBS, 1957; "Studio 57: Little Miss Bedford," SYN, 1957; "Alfred Hitchcock Presents: The Glass Eye," CBS, 1957; "Suspicion: Murder Me Gently," NBC, 1957; "Telephone Time: War Against War," ABC, 1958; "Person to Person," CBS, 1958; "Telephone Time: War Against War," ABC, 1958; "Hallmark Hall of Fame: Hallmark Christmas Tree-The Miracle of the Orphanage," NBC, 1958; "The Ed Sullivan Show," CBS, 1959; "Du Pont Show of the Month: The Fallen Idol," CBS, 1959; "The Moon and Sixpence," NBC, 1959; "The Breaking Point: Glass Flowers Never Drop Petals," ABC, 1964; "Password," CBS, 1964; "Judd for the Defense: Punishments, Cruel and Unusual," ABC, 1968; "The FBI: The Set-Up," ABC, 1972.

TV MOVIES AND MINISERIES: "Hallmark Hall of Fame: Foxfire," CBS, 1987.

TARKENTON, FRAN

b. Richmond, VA, February 3, 1940. Sports-caster formerly with the Minnesota Vikings and New York Giants.

AS A REGULAR: "Monday Night Football," ABC, 1979-82; "That's Incredible," ABC, 1980-84.

AND: "Saturday Night Live," NBC, 1976.

TARSES, JAY

b. Baltimore, MD, July 3, 1939. Comedy writer-producer, formerly a stand-up team with Tom Patchett; he plays garbageman Nick Donatello on one of his creations, "The Days and Nights of Molly Dodd."

AS A REGULAR: "Make Your Own Kind of Music," NBC, 1971; "Open All Night," ABC, 1981-82; "The Duck Factory," NBC, 1984; "The Days and Nights of Molly Dodd," NBC, 1987-88; LIF, 1988- .

AND: "The Bob Newhart Show: Mister Emily Hartley," CBS, 1973; "The Bob Newhart Show: Enter Mrs. Peeper," CBS, 1976; "Lou Grant: Pack," CBS, 1980; "Family Ties: Not with My Sister You Don't," NBC, 1982; "Family Ties: Suzanne Takes You Down," NBC, 1982; "St. Elsewhere: Whistle, Wylie Works," NBC, 1985.

AS CO-WRITER: "The Bob Newhart Show," CBS, 1972-76; "The Carol Burnett Show," CBS, 1972-73.

AS CREATOR-WRITER: "The Days and Night of Molly Dodd," NBC, 1987-88; LIF, 1988- ; "The Slap Maxwell Story," ABC, 1988-89.

* Emmies: 1973.
* See also Tom Patchett.

TATE, SHARON

b. Dallas, TX, 1943; d. 1969. Sixties starlet who played a bank secretary on "The Beverly Hillbillies"; she married director Roman Polanski and was brutally murdered in 1969 by members of Charles Manson's "family."

AS A REGULAR: "The Beverly Hillbillies," CBS, 1963-65.

AND: "The Man From UNCLE: The Girls of Nazarone," NBC, 1965.

TAYBACK, VIC

b. Brooklyn, NY, January 6, 1930; d. 1990. Beefy actor who parlayed a film role as diner owner Mel into a cushy job on a successful, below-average sitcom.

AS A REGULAR: "Morning Star," NBC, 1965-66; "Griff," ABC, 1973-74; "Khan," CBS, 1975; "Alice," CBS, 1976-85.

AND: "Hotel De Paree: Sundance and the Blood Money," CBS, 1960; "Bewitched: Red Light, Green Light," ABC, 1965; "The Man From UNCLE: The Recollectors Affair," NBC, 1965; "F Troop: Corporal Agarn's Farewell to the Troops," ABC, 1965; "Family Affair: Who's Afraid of Nural Shipeni?," CBS, 1966; "I Dream of Jeannie: This Is Murder," NBC, 1966; "Get Smart: Maxwell Smart, Alias Jimmy Ballantine," NBC, 1966; "The Monkees: Your Friendly Neighborhood Kidnappers," NBC, 1966; "Love on a Rooftop: The Big Brass Bed," ABC, 1966; "The Monkees: Son of a Gypsy," NBC, 1966; "Family Affair: All Around the Town," CBS, 1967; "Captain Nice: Is Big Town Burning?," NBC, 1967; "Bewitched: Samantha Fights City Hall," ABC, 1968; "Mission: Impossible: The Mercenaries," CBS, 1968; "The Bill Cosby Show: The Fatal Phone Call," NBC, 1969; "The Mary Tyler Moore Show: Second-Story Story," CBS, 1971; "Columbo: Suitable for Framing," NBC, 1971; "Medical Center: May God Have Mercy," CBS, 1974; "The Rookies: Take Over," ABC, 1974; "Hawaii Five-O: Bone of Contention," CBS, 1975; "Barney Miller: Stakeout," ABC, 1975; "Switch: The Body at the Bottom," CBS, 1975; "The Practice: The Choice," NBC, 1976; "Medical Center: The Touch of Sight," CBS, 1976; "Family: A Point of Departure," ABC, 1976; "Tattletales," CBS, 1976; "McCloud: Bonnie and McCloud," NBC, 1976; "The Love Boat: Trial Romance," ABC, 1979; "$weepstake$: Billy, Wally and Ludmilla, and Theodore," NBC, 1979; "The Love Boat: Trigamist," ABC, 1980; "Dinah!," SYN, 1980; "The Love Boat: Love Below Decks," ABC,

1983; "The Love Boat: Unmade for Each Other," ABC, 1985; "The Love Boat: Your Money or Your Wife," ABC, 1985.

TV MOVIES AND MINISERIES: "The Alpha Caper," ABC, 1973; "The Blue Knight," CBS, 1973; "Dark Victory," NBC, 1976; "Portrait of a Stripper," CBS, 1979; "The Night the City Screamed," ABC, 1980; "The Great American Traffic Jam," NBC, 1980; "Through the Magic Pyramid," NBC, 1981.

TAYLOR, ELIZABETH

b. London, England, February 27, 1932. Oscar-winning actress, sex symbol to a generation, wife of a U.S. Senator and tempestuous mate of Richard Burton. And she's done a bit of TV, too.

AS A GUEST: "Person to Person," CBS, 1957; "Mike Todd Party," CBS, 1957; "A Tribute to Eleanor Roosevelt on Her Diamond Jubilee," NBC, 1959; "The Sammy Davis Jr. Show," NBC, 1966; "Here's Lucy: Lucy Meets the Burtons," CBS, 1970; "General Electric's All-Star Anniversary," ABC, 1978; "General Hospital: The Wedding of Luke and Laura," ABC, 1981; "All My Children," ABC, 1983; "Hotel: Intimate Stranger," ABC, 1984.

TV MOVIES AND MINISERIES: "Divorce His/Divorce Hers," ABC, 1973; "Victory at Entebbe," ABC, 1976; "Between Friends," HBO, 1983; "North and South," ABC, 1985; "Malice in Wonderland," CBS, 1985; "There Must Be a Pony," ABC, 1986; "Poker Alice," CBS, 1987; "Tennessee Williams' Sweet Bird of Youth," NBC, 1989.

* In "Lucy Meets the Burtons," Lucille Ball tries on Elizabeth Taylor's 69-carat diamond ring and can't get it off. The episode gave Ball her second-highest rating ever, a whopping 34 percent of the TV audience. (Ball's highest rating came when she gave birth to Little Ricky on "I Love Lucy" in 1953.)
* See also Richard Burton.

TAYLOR, KENT

b. Louis Weiss, Nashua, IA, May 11, 1907; d. 1987. Actor best remembered as the suave, mustachioed Boston Blackie, a private eye with a really neat streamlined car.

AS A REGULAR: "Boston Blackie," SYN, 1951-53; "Rough Riders," ABC, 1958-59.

AND: "Bigelow Theatre: A Case of Marriage," CBS, 1951; "Teledrama: Deadline for Murder," CBS, 1953; "Damon Runyon Theatre: Judy the Jinx," CBS, 1956; "Crossroads: Lifeline," ABC, 1956; "Ford Theatre: The Menace of Hasty Heights," ABC, 1956; "The Joseph Cotten Show: The Case of the Absent Man," NBC, 1957; "Tales of Wells Fargo: Alias Jim Hardie," NBC, 1958; "Zorro: The Man with the Whip," ABC, 1958; "Sugarfoot: Funeral at Forty Mile," ABC, 1960; "Peter Gunn: Sepi," ABC, 1960; "The Rifleman:

The Wyoming Story," ABC, 1961; "Hawaiian Eye: Man From Manila," ABC, 1961; "Cheyenne: Stage to the Sky," ABC, 1961; "77 Sunset Strip: The Celluloid Cowboy," ABC, 1961; "Hawaiian Eye: Tusitala," ABC, 1961; "Voyage to the Bottom of the Sea: ... And Five of Us Are Left," ABC, 1965; "Rango: The Daring Holdup of the Deadwood Stage," ABC, 1967; "Land of the Giants: The Deadly Dart," ABC, 1970.

TV MOVIES AND MINISERIES: "The Phantom of Hollywood," CBS, 1974.

TAYLOR, RENEE

b. New York City, NY, March 19, 1935. Comedienne and comic writer, often with Joe Bologna.

AS A REGULAR: "Perry Como's Kraft Music Hall," NBC, 1960; "Mary Hartman, Mary Hartman," SYN, 1977-78.

AND: "The Jack Paar Show," NBC, 1960; "Girl Talk," SYN, 1963; "The Reporter: Rope's End," CBS, 1964; "On Broadway Tonight," CBS, 1965; "The Mike Douglas Show," SYN, 1967; "The Dick Cavett Show," ABC, 1968; "The Merv Griffin Show," SYN, 1968; "The Merv Griffin Show," SYN, 1975; "Lottery!: Pilot," ABC, 1983; "St. Elsewhere: Strike Out," NBC, 1984; "St. Elsewhere: Breathless," NBC, 1984.

TV MOVIES AND MINISERIES: "Woman of the Year," CBS, 1976.

AS CO-WRITER: "Acts of Love-And Other Comedies," ABC, 1973.

* Emmies: 1973.

TAYLOR, RIP

b. January 13, 1934. Confetti-throwing comedian.

AS A REGULAR: "The Beautiful Phyllis Diller Show," NBC, 1968; "Dean Martin Presents," NBC, 1972; "The Gong Show," SYN, 1976-80; "The $1.98 Beauty Show," SYN, 1978-80.

AND: "The Ed Sullivan Show," CBS, 1961; "The Ed Sullivan Show," CBS, 1962; "The Ed Sullivan Show," CBS, 1963; "Jackie Gleason and His American Scene Magazine," CBS, 1963; "The Mike Douglas Show," SYN, 1965; "The Monkees: Monkees on the Wheel," NBC, 1967; "It's Happening," ABC, 1968; "The Monkees: Mijacged," NBC, 1968; "The Tonight Show Starring Johnny Carson," NBC, 1968; "The Mike Douglas Show," SYN, 1969; "The Merv Griffin Show," CBS, 1969; "The Della Reese Show," SYN, 1969; "The David Frost Show," SYN, 1969; "Animal Crack-Ups," ABC, 1989; "Santa Barbara," NBC, 1989.

TAYLOR, ROBERT

b. Spangler Arlington Brugh, Filley, NB, August 5, 1911; d. 1969. Screen hunk of the thirties, usually at MGM, who came to TV in the late fifties as macho detective Capt. Matt Holbrook.

AS A REGULAR: "The Detectives Starring Robert Taylor," ABC, 1959-61; "Robert Taylor's Detectives," NBC, 1961-62; "Death Valley Days," SYN, 1966-68.

AND: "The Thin Man: The Scene Stealer," NBC, 1958; "The du Pont Show with June Allyson: So Dim the Light," CBS, 1960; "Art Linkletter's House Party," CBS, 1960; "The Tonight Show Starring Johnny Carson," NBC, 1963; "Play Your Hunch," NBC, 1963; "The Merv Griffin Show," NBC, 1963; "Hondo: Hondo and the Eagle Claw," ABC, 1967.

TV MOVIES AND MINISERIES: "The Return of the Gunfighter," ABC, 1967.

TAYLOR, ROD

b. Sydney, Australia, January 11, 1930. Action hero who recently played Frank Agretti on "Falcon Crest."

AS A REGULAR: "Hong Kong," ABC, 1960-61; "Bearcats!," CBS, 1971; "The Oregan Trail," NBC, 1977; "Masquerade," ABC, 1983-84; "Outlaws," CBS, 1986-87; "Falcon Crest," CBS, 1988-90.

AND: "Lux Video Theatre: The Browning Version," NBC, 1955; "Studio 57: Killer Whale," SYN, 1955; "Studio 57: The Last Day on Earth," SYN, 1955; "Schlitz Playhouse of Stars: A Thing to Fight For," CBS, 1955; "Suspicion: The Story of Margery Reardon," NBC, 1957; "G.E. Theatre: The Young Years," CBS, 1957; "Playhouse 90: Verdict of Three," CBS, 1958; "Playhouse 90: The Great Gatsby," CBS, 1958; "Lux Playhouse: The Best House in the Valley," CBS, 1958; "Playhouse 90: The Long March," CBS, 1958; "Playhouse 90: The Raider," CBS, 1959; "Playhouse 90: Misalliance," CBS, 1959; "The Twilight Zone: And When the Sky Was Opened," CBS, 1959; "Dick Powell's Zane Grey Theatre: Picture of Sal," CBS, 1960; "Goodyear Theatre: Capital Gain," NBC, 1960; "G.E. Theatre: Early to Die," CBS, 1960; "Westinghouse Desilu Playhouse: Thunder in the Night," CBS, 1960; "Bus Stop: Portrait of a Hero," ABC, 1961; "The du Pont Show: The Ordeal of Dr. Shannon," NBC, 1962.

TV MOVIES AND MINISERIES: "Powderkeg," CBS, 1971; "Family Flight," ABC, 1972; "A Matter of Wife and Death," NBC, 1975; "The Oregon Trail," NBC, 1976; "Hellinger's Law," CBS, 1981; "Jacqueline Bouvier Kennedy," ABC, 1981; "Charles & Diana: A Royal Love Story," ABC, 1982.

TEMPLE, SHIRLEY

b. Santa Monica, CA, April 23, 1928. Screen moppet of the thirties who returned to show biz as a mother to host a TV anthology series.

AS A REGULAR: "Shirley Temple's Storybook," ABC, 1959; NBC, 1960-61.

AND: "Dinah Shore Chevy Show," NBC, 1958;

"Chevy Show Special," NBC, 1959; "The Red Skelton Hour," CBS, 1963.

TENNANT, VICTORIA

b. London, September 30, 1950. Blonde actress in film ("All of Me") and TV; she played Pamela Tudsbury in "The Winds of War" and "War and Remembrance." Wife of Steve Martin.

AS A GUEST: "The Twilight Zone: Red Snow," CBS, 1986.

TV MOVIES AND MINISERIES: "The Winds of War," ABC, 1983; "Dempsey," CBS, 1983; "Under Siege," NBC, 1986; "War and Remembrance," ABC, 1988, 1989.

TENNILLE, TONI

b. Montgomery, AL, May 8, 1943. Pop singer of the seventies.

AS A REGULAR: "The Captain and Tennille," ABC, 1976-77; "The Toni Tennille Show," SYN, 1980-81.

AND: "Perry Como's Christmas in Mexico," CBS, 1975; "Fantasy Island: The Golden Hour," ABC, 1978; "The Love Boat: The Witness," ABC, 1978; "The Music of Your Life," SYN, 1985.

TEWES, LAUREN

b. Trafford, PA, October 28, 1953. Actress who played Julie McCoy on "The Love Boat."

AS A REGULAR: "The Love Boat," ABC, 1977-84.

AND: "Fantasy Island: Mrs. Brandell's Favorites," ABC, 1984; "Murder, She Wrote: A Lady in the Lake," CBS, 1986.

TV MOVIES AND MINISERIES: "Dallas Cowboy Cheerleaders," ABC, 1979.

* In 1985, Tewes talked about her cocaine addiction to the Hollywood equivalent of a father confessor—a *TV Guide* reporter. In the ensuing article, designed to make Tewes employable again after being dropped from "The Love Boat," she said she was saved from death by a broadcast of "Mister Rogers' Neighborhood": "He said 'I'll be your friend, will you be mine?' And I burst into tears, and I said, 'Yes.'"

THIBODEAUX, KEITH—See Richard Keith.

THICKE, ALAN

b. Canada, March 1, 1947. Light comic actor whose highly touted talk show flopped; he bounced back to star as dad Jason Seaver on "Growing Pains."

AS A REGULAR: "Thicke of the Night," SYN, 1983-84; "Growing Pains," ABC, 1985- ; "Animal Crack-Ups," ABC, 1987- .

AND: "The Love Boat: No More Alimony," ABC, 1984; "The Love Boat: Sleeper," ABC, 1986.

TV MOVIES AND MINISERIES: "Calendar Girl
Murders," ABC, 1984; "Perry Mason: The
Case of the Shooting Star," NBC, 1986;
"Dance 'Til Dawn," NBC, 1988; "Not Quite
Human II," DIS, 1989.
AS PRODUCER: "Fernwood 2-Night," SYN, 1977-
78.

THINNES, ROY

b. Chicago, IL, April 6, 1938. Actor who
played David Vincent on "The Invaders" and
Nick Hogan on "Falcon Crest."
AS A REGULAR: "General Hospital," ABC, 1963-
66; "The Long Hot Summer," ABC, 1965-66;
"The Invaders," ABC, 1967-68; "The
Psychiatrist," NBC, 1971; "From Here to
Eternity," NBC, 1980; "Falcon Crest," CBS,
1982-83.
AND: "Du Pont Theatre: Chicago 2-1-2," ABC,
1957; "Meet McGraw: McGraw Meets
McGinley," NBC, 1958; "Peter Gunn: The Man
with the Scar," NBC, 1960; "The Untouchables:
Fist of Five," ABC, 1962; "The Eleventh Hour:
Something Crazy's Going on in the Back Room,"
NBC, 1963; "Twelve O'Clock High: In Search of
My Enemy," ABC, 1965; "The FBI: The
Escape," ABC, 1966; "Twelve O'Clock High: A
Distant Cry," ABC, 1966; "The Fugitive: Wine Is
a Traitor," ABC, 1966; "Highway to Heaven: Oh
Lucky Man," NBC, 1985; "The Love Boat: Frat
Brothers Forever," ABC, 1985; "Murder, She
Wrote: Dead Heat," CBS, 1986; "Murder, She
Wrote: Trouble in Eden," CBS, 1987.
TV MOVIES AND MINISERIES: "The Other Man,"
NBC, 1970; "The Psychiatrist: God Bless the
Children," NBC, 1970; "Black Noon," CBS,
1971; "Horror at 37,000 Feet," CBS, 1973;
"The Norliss Tapes," NBC, 1973; "Satan's
School for Girls," ABC, 1973; "Death Race,"
ABC, 1973; "The Manhunter," NBC, 1976;
"Secrets," ABC, 1977; "From Here to
Eternity," NBC, 1979; "The Return of Mod
Squad," ABC, 1979; "Sizzle," ABC, 1981;
"Dark Holiday," NBC, 1989.

THOMAS, BETTY

b. St. Louis, MO, July 27, 1948. Actress who
played Sgt. Lucy Bates on "Hill Street Blues."
AS A REGULAR: "Hill Street Blues," NBC, 1981-
87.
AND: "Password Plus," NBC, 1981; "Saturday
Night Live," NBC, 1983; "Saturday Night Live,"
NBC, 1984.
TV MOVIES AND MINISERIES: "Outside Chance,"
CBS, 1978; "When Your Lover Leaves,"
NBC, 1983; "Prison for Children," CBS, 1987.
AS DIRECTOR: "Doogie Howser, M.D.," ABC,
1989- .
* Emmies: 1985.

THOMAS, DANNY

b. Muzyad Yaghoob, Deerfield, MI, January 6,
1912; d. 1991. Comedian and storyteller who
found TV fame as big-mouthed, soft-hearted
night club comic Danny Williams; his visibility
slipped quickly in the sixties, but by then he
was into TV production and had probably
already made a zillion dollars.
AS A REGULAR: "All Star Revue," NBC, 1950-52;
"The Danny Thomas Show (Make Room for
Daddy)," ABC, 1953-57; CBS, 1957-64;
"Danny Thomas Special," NBC, 1964-65; "
The Danny Thomas Hour," NBC, 1967-68;
"Make Room for Granddaddy," ABC, 1970-
71; "The Practice," NBC, 1976-77; "I'm a Big
Girl Now," ABC, 1980-81; "One Big Family,"
SYN, 1986-87.
AND: "The Ed Sullivan Show," CBS, 1957;
"Dinah Shore Chevy Show," NBC, 1957; "Bob
Hope Special," NBC, 1957; "Dean Martin
Special," NBC, 1958; "Christophers: Lincoln
Speaks for Himself," SYN, 1958; "Christophers:
A Visit with Danny Thomas," SYN, 1958; "The
Ed Sullivan Show," CBS, 1958; "Dinah Shore
Chevy Show," NBC, 1958; "The Lucille Ball-
Desi Arnaz Show: Lucy Makes Room for
Danny," CBS, 1958; "The Ford Show," NBC,
1958; "The Jack Benny Program: Jack Goes to a
Nightclub," CBS, 1959; "Bob Hope Special,"
NBC, 1959; "Dick Powell's Zane Grey Theatre:
A Thread of Respect," CBS, 1959; "Opening
Night," CBS, 1962; "The Dick Van Dyke Show:
It May Look Like a Walnut!," CBS, 1963;
"Opening Night," CBS, 1963; "The Joey Bishop
Show: Danny Gives Joey Advice," NBC, 1963;
"The Tonight Show Starring Johnny Carson,"
NBC, 1964; "The Joey Bishop Show: Andy
Williams Visits Joey," NBC, 1964; "The Mike
Douglas Show," SYN, 1964; "The Lucy Show:
Lucy Helps Danny Thomas," CBS, 1965; "Perry
Como Special," NBC, 1965; "The Dean Martin
Show," NBC, 1965; "Hollywood Palace," ABC,
1966; "Guys 'n' Geishas," NBC, 1967; "The
Generation Gap," CBS, 1968; "Carol Channing
Special," ABC, 1969; "That Girl: My Sister's
Keeper," ABC, 1969; "The Andy Williams
Show," NBC, 1969; "Jimmy Durante Presents the
Lennon Sisters Hour," ABC, 1969; "The Movie
Game," SYN, 1970; "Can You Top This?," SYN,
1970; "That Girl: Those Friars," ABC, 1971; "The
Pearl Bailey Show," ABC, 1971; "The Mod
Squad: Kicks, Incorporated," ABC, 1972; "Here's
Lucy: Lucy and Danny Thomas," CBS, 1973;
"The Sonny and Cher Comedy Hour," CBS, 1974;
"McCloud: Shivaree on Delancey Street," NBC,
1974; "Happy Days: Grandpa's Visit," ABC,
1977; "Kojak: In Full Command," CBS, 1978;
"America's Tribute to Bob Hope," NBC, 1988;
"A Conversation with Dinah," TNN, 1989; "Fifty
Years of Television: A Golden Celebration,"
CBS, 1989.

TV MOVIES AND MINISERIES: "Side by Side," CBS, 1988.
AS DIRECTOR: "The Danny Thomas Show: The Leprechaun," CBS, 1964.
* Aside from his own shows, Thomas also owned a piece of "The Andy Griffith Show," "The Joey Bishop Show," "The Dick Van Dyke Show" and "The Mod Squad."
* Emmies: 1955.

THOMAS, DAVE
b. *Canada*. Gifted comic actor who played Bill Needle on "SCTV"; he also does a great Bob Hope.
AS A REGULAR: "Second City TV," SYN, 1977-81; "SCTV Network 90," NBC, 1981-82; "The New Show," NBC, 1984; "The Dave Thomas Comedy Show," CBS, 1990.
AND: "Saturday Night Live," NBC, 1983; "The Pat Sajak Show," CBS, 1989.

THOMAS, FRANKIE
b. *New York City, NY, April 9, 1921*. Tom Corbett, space cadet.
AS A REGULAR: "A Woman to Remember," DUM, 1947; "One Man's Family," NBC, 1949; "Tom Corbett, Space Cadet," CBS, 1950; ABC, 1951-52; NBC, 1951; "First Love," NBC, 1954-55.

THOMAS, HEATHER
b. *Greenwich, CT, September 8, 1957*. Blonde actress who played Jody Banks on "The Fall Guy."
AS A REGULAR: "Co-ed Fever," CBS, 1979; "The Fall Guy," ABC, 1981-86.
AND: "David Cassidy, Man Undercover: Flashpoint," NBC, 1978; "B.J. and the Bear: The Girls of Hollywood High," NBC, 1980; "Battle of the Network Stars," ABC, 1982; "The Love Boat: When Worlds Collide," ABC, 1983; "The Love Boat: Putting on the Dog," ABC, 1983; "The New Mike Hammer: A Blinding Fear," CBS, 1987.
TV MOVIES AND MINISERIES: "The Dirty Dozen: The Fatal Mission," NBC, 1988.

THOMAS, LOWELL
b. *Woodington, OH, April 6, 1892; d. 1981*.
AS A REGULAR: "High Adventure with Lowell Thomas," CBS, 1957-60; "Our American Heritage," NBC, 1960.
AND: "This Is Your Life," NBC, 1959; "The Jack Paar Program," NBC, 1964.
TV MOVIES AND MINISERIES: "Ike," ABC, 1979.

THOMAS, MARLO
b. *Detroit, MI, November 21, 1943*. Actress and daughter of Danny Thomas; she was a fresh sitcom presence as Ann Marie on "That Girl."
AS A REGULAR: "The Joey Bishop Show," NBC, 1961-62; "That Girl," ABC, 1966-71.

AND: "Dick Powell's Zane Grey Theatre: A Thread of Respect," CBS, 1959; "The Many Loves of Dobie Gillis: The Hunger Strike," CBS, 1960; "77 Sunset Strip: The Fanatics," ABC, 1960; "Dick Powell's Zane Grey Theatre: Honor Bright," CBS, 1961; "Thriller: The Ordeal of Dr. Cordell," NBC, 1961; "The Danny Thomas Show: Everything Happens to Me," CBS, 1961; "Insight: The Sophomore," SYN, 1963; "Arrest and Trial: Tigers Are for Jungles," ABC, 1964; "Bonanza: A Pink Cloud Comes From Old Cathay," NBC, 1964; "McHale's Navy: The Missing Link," ABC, 1964; "My Favorite Martian: Miss Jekyll and Hyde," CBS, 1964; "Wendy & Me: Wendy's Anniversary Fun?," ABC, 1964; "The Young Set," ABC, 1965; "Valentine's Day: Follow the Broken Pretzel," ABC, 1965; "The Donna Reed Show: Guests, Guests, Who Wants Them?," ABC, 1965; "Ben Casey: Three Li'l Lambs," ABC, 1965; "Saturday Superstar Movie: That Girl in Wonderland," ABC, 1973; "Acts of Love—And Other Comedies," ABC, 1973; "Free to Be You and Me," ABC, 1974; "The Practice: Judy Sinclair," NBC, 1976; "The Body Human: Facts for Girls," CBS, 1981.
TV MOVIES AND MINISERIES: "The Lost Honor of Kathryn Beck," CBS, 1984; "Consenting Adult," ABC, 1985; "Nobody's Child," CBS, 1986.
AS CO-PRODUCER: "Taken Away," CBS, 1989.
* Yikes Dept.: In her "Bonanza" guest shot, Thomas played a Chinese mail-order bride destined for—gulp—Hoss Cartwright.
* "That Girl" was originally titled "Miss Independence."
* Emmies: 1974, 1981, 1986, 1989.

THOMAS, PHILIP MICHAEL
b. *Columbus, OH, May 26, 1949*. Handsome actor who played Det. Ricardo Tubbs on "Miami Vice"; while the show was hot he gave interviews that seemed to indicate massive confidence in his talent; he hasn't been heard from since.
AS A REGULAR: "Miami Vice," NBC, 1984-89.
AND: "Griff: Premiere," ABC, 1973; "Police Woman: It's Only a Game," NBC, 1974; "Medical Center: If Wishes Were Horses," CBS, 1976; "Sirota's Court: Pilot," NBC, 1976; "The Debbie Allen Special," ABC, 1989.
TV MOVIES AND MINISERIES: "Toma," ABC, 1973; "This Man Stands Alone," NBC, 1979; "Valentine," ABC, 1979; "False Witness," NBC, 1989.

THOMAS, RICHARD
b. *New York City, NY, June 13, 1951*. Emmy-winning actor who shone as the sensitive John-Boy Walton.
AS A REGULAR: "1-2-3, Go!," NBC, 1961-62; "Flame in the Wind (A Time for Us)," ABC,

1964-66; "As the World Turns," CBS, 1966-67; "The Waltons," CBS, 1972-77.
AND: "The Seven Lively Arts: The Nutcracker," CBS, 1957; "Hallmark Hall of Fame: A Doll's House," NBC, 1959; "Hallmark Hall of Fame: Give Us Barabbas!," NBC, 1961; "Great Ghost Tales: Sredni Vashtar," NBC, 1961; "The Defenders: The Boy Between," CBS, 1961; "Marcus Welby, M.D.: Echo of a Baby's Laugh," ABC, 1969; "Marcus Welby, M.D.: All the Golden Dandelions Are Gone," ABC, 1970; "Medical Center: Runaway," CBS, 1970; "Bonanza: The Weary Willies," NBC, 1970; "Bracken's World: Fallen, Fallen in Babylon," NBC, 1971; "The FBI: The Game of Terror," ABC, 1971; "Night Gallery: The Sins of the Fathers," NBC, 1972; "H.M.S. Pinafore," CBS, 1973; "Barefoot in the Park," SHO, 1982.
TV MOVIES AND MINISERIES: "The Homecoming," CBS, 1971; "The Red Badge of Courage," NBC, 1974; "The Silence," NBC, 1975; "Roots: The Next Generations," ABC, 1979; "No Other Love," CBS, 1979; "To Find My Son," CBS, 1980; "Berlin Tunnel 21," CBS, 1981; "Living Proof: The Hank Williams Jr. Story," NBC, 1983; "Hobson's Choice," CBS, 1983; "The Master of Ballantrae," CBS, 1984; "Final Jeopardy," NBC, 1985.
* Emmies: 1973.

THOMPSON, MARSHALL
b. James Marshall Thompson, Peoria, IL, November 27, 1925. B-movie actor who played Dr. Marsh Tracy on "Daktari," a veterinarian who was always getting upstaged by Clarence the cross-eyed lion and Judy the chimp.
AS A REGULAR: "Angel," CBS, 1960-61; "Daktari," CBS, 1966-69.
AND: "Fireside Theatre: Visit From a Stranger," NBC, 1952; "Favorite Story: Sudden Impulse," SYN, 1952; "Science Fiction Theatre: Stranger in the Desert," SYN, 1955; "Private Secretary: The Root of All Evil," CBS, 1955; "Science Fiction Theatre: The Frozen Sound," SYN, 1955; "Matinee Theatre: Bread Upon the Waters," NBC, 1957; "Ford Theatre: Moment of Decision," ABC, 1957; "Panic: Botulish," NBC, 1957; "Those Whiting Girls: The Feminine Touch," CBS, 1957; "Matinee Theatre: Fall of the House of Usher," NBC, 1957; "Dick Powell's Zane Grey Theatre: The Open Cell," CBS, 1957; "The Loretta Young Show: Vengeance Is Thine," NBC, 1959; "Perry Mason: The Case of the Wayward Wife," CBS, 1960; "Startime: Jeff McLeod, the Last Rebel," NBC, 1960; "Wagon Train: Trial for Murder," NBC, 1960; "Art Linkletter's House Party," CBS, 1960; "Here's Hollywood," NBC, 1960; "Wagon Train: The Grover Allen Story," ABC, 1964; "The Partridge Family: Anatomy of a Tonsil," ABC, 1971; "Owen Marshall, Counselor at Law: A Matter of Degree," ABC, 1972; "Hec Ramsey:

The Detroit Connection," NBC, 1973; "The Streets of San Francisco: For the Love of God," ABC, 1973; "Ironside: Friend or Foe," NBC, 1974; "Planet of the Apes: Premiere," CBS, 1974; "Quincy: Sweet Land of Liberty," NBC, 1979; "Lou Grant: Brushfire," CBS, 1980; "Lou Grant: Inheritance," CBS, 1980.
TV MOVIES AND MINISERIES: "Centennial," NBC, 1978-79.

THOMPSON, SADA
b. Des Moines, IA, September 27, 1929. Actress who played Kate Lawrence on "Family."
AS A REGULAR: "Family," ABC, 1976-80.
AND: "Camera Three: The Cracked Looking Glass," CBS, 1961; "Love Story: Joie," NBC, 1973.
TV MOVIES AND MINISERIES: "The Entertainer," NBC, 1976; "Princess Daisy," NBC, 1983; "My Two Loves," ABC, 1986; "Fatal Confession: A Father Dowling Mystery," NBC, 1988; "Hallmark Hall of Fame: Home Fires Burning," CBS, 1989.
* Emmies: 1978.

THORSON, LINDA
b. Canada, 1947. Actress who played Tara King on "The Avengers," and now plays Julia Medina on "One Life to Live."
AS A REGULAR: "The Avengers," ABC, 1968-69; "Marblehead Manor," SYN, 1987-88; "One Life to Live," ABC, 1989- .
AND: "McClain's Law: Portrait of a Playmate," NBC, 1981; "Lime Street: Swiss Watch and Wait," ABC, 1985; "St. Elsewhere: Lost and Found in Space," NBC, 1985; "St. Elsewhere: Close Encounter," NBC, 1985; "St. Elsewhere: Watch the Skies," NBC, 1985; "The Bronx Zoo: Signs of Life," NBC, 1987.
TV MOVIES AND MINISERIES: "Blind Justice," CBS, 1986.

TIGHE, KEVIN
b. Los Angeles, CA, August 13, 1944. Actor who played paramedic Roy DeSoto on "Emergency!"
AS A REGULAR: "Emergency!," NBC, 1972-77.
AND: "Hollywood Squares," NBC, 1975; "Ellery Queen: Caesar's Last Siege," NBC, 1976; "The Love Boat: Dumb Luck," ABC, 1980.
TV MOVIES AND MINISERIES: "Emergency!," NBC, 1972; "The Rebels," SYN, 1979.

TILLSTROM, BURR
b. Chicago, IL, October 13, 1917; d. 1985. Puppeteer.
AS A REGULAR: "Kukla, Fran & Ollie," NBC, 1948-54; ABC, 1954-57; NBC, 1961-62; PBS, 1969-71; SYN, 1975-76; "That Was the Week That Was," NBC, 1964-65.

742

AND: "The Polly Bergen Show," NBC, 1958; "The Perry Como Show," NBC, 1958; "The Chevy Show," NBC, 1959.
* Emmies: 1966.

TILTON, CHARLENE

b. San Diego, CA, December 1, 1958. Blonde actress who plays Lucy Ewing on "Dallas."
AS A REGULAR: "Dallas," CBS, 1978-85; 1989- .
AND: "Happy Days: They Shoot Fonzies, Don't They?," ABC, 1976; "Fernwood 2-Night," SYN, 1977; "The Mike Douglas Show," SYN, 1978; "Laverne & Shirley: Murder on the Moose Jaw Express," ABC, 1980; "The Love Boat: May the Best Man Win," ABC, 1980; "Hollywood Squares," SYN, 1980; "Saturday Night Live," NBC, 1981; "The Love Boat: The Courier," ABC, 1985; "Murder, She Wrote: The Cemetery Vote," CBS, 1987.
TV MOVIES AND MINISERIES: "Diary of a Teenage Hitchhiker," ABC, 1979.

TINY TIM

b. Herbert Khaury, New York City, NY, 1923. Sixties curiosity, an ugly troubador who sang in a shaky soprano voice and plinked a ukelele.
AS A GUEST: "Rowan & Martin's Laugh-In," NBC, 1968; "The Tonight Show Starring Johnny Carson," NBC, 1968; "You Don't Say," NBC, 1969; "The Tonight Show Starring Johnny Carson," NBC, 1969; "Bob Newhart Special: A Last Laugh at the 60's," ABC, 1970; "The Red Skelton Hour," CBS, 1970; "The Ed Sullivan Show," CBS, 1970; "Love, American Style: Love and the Vampire," ABC, 1971.
TV MOVIES AND MINISERIES: "Ironside," NBC, 1967.
* Tiny Tim married Miss Vicki on "The Tonight Show" December 17, 1969.

TOBIAS, GEORGE

b. New York City, NY, 1901; d. 1980. Dependable character actor in dozens of films ("The Strawberry Blonde," "The Glenn Miller Story") and as next-door neighbor Abner Kravitz on "Bewitched."
AS A REGULAR: "Adventures in Paradise," ABC, 1960-61; "Bewitched," ABC, 1964-72.
AND: "Make Room for Daddy: Christmas and Clowns," ABC, 1956; "Telephone Time: Here Lies Francois Gold," ABC, 1957; "Climax!: To Walk the Night," CBS, 1957; "The Loretta Young Show: The Last Witness," NBC, 1958; "77 Sunset Strip: Vicious Circle," ABC, 1958; "Laramie: Lily," NBC, 1960; "Tightrope!: Big Business," CBS, 1960; "The Overland Trail: Lawyer in Petticoats," NBC, 1960; "The Deputy: Lucifer Urge," NBC, 1960; "The Rebel: The Earl of Durango," ABC, 1960; "77 Sunset Strip: The President's Daughter," ABC, 1960; "Angel: The Valedictorian," CBS, 1960; "The Untouchables: The Loophole," ABC,

1961; "Sam Benedict: The Bird of Warning," NBC, 1962; "The Real McCoys: How You Gonna Keep 'Em Down on the Farm After They've Seen San Quentin?," CBS, 1963; "Bob Hope Chrysler Theatre: The Seven Little Foys," NBC, 1964; "The Joey Bishop Show: Joey Goes to CBS," CBS, 1964; "The Man From UNCLE: The Hot Number Affair," NBC, 1967; "Love, American Style: Love and the Bed," ABC, 1969; "Mannix: Time Out of Mind," CBS, 1970; "Medical Center: The Fallen," CBS, 1972; "Medical Center: Survivors," CBS, 1975.

TOLSKY, SUSAN

b. Houston, TX, April 6, 1943. Comic actress.
AS A REGULAR: "Here Come the Brides," ABC, 1968-70; "The New Bill Cosby Show," CBS, 1972-73; "Madame's Place," SYN, 1982.
AND: "Here's Lucy: Kim Finally Cuts You-Know-Who's Apron Strings," CBS, 1972; "Here's Lucy: A Home Is Not an Office," CBS, 1972; "Love, American Style: Love and the Trampled Passion," ABC, 1973; "Love, American Style: Love and the Tycoon," ABC, 1973; "Alice: Tommy's T.K.O.," CBS, 1980; "Barney Miller: Riot," ABC, 1981; "Barney Miller: Landmark," ABC, 1982; "Alice: Vera, Queen of the Soaps," CBS, 1982; "Alice: Mel Wins by a Nose," CBS, 1982.

TOMLIN, LILY

b. Detroit, MI, September 1, 1939. Gifted comedienne.
AS A REGULAR: "The Music Scene," ABC, 1969-70; "Rowan & Martin's Laugh-In," NBC, 1970-73.
AND: "Hollywood Squares," NBC, 1970; "The Tonight Show Starring Johnny Carson," NBC, 1971; "Hollywood Squares," NBC, 1972; "The Carol Burnett Show," CBS, 1972; "The Mike Douglas Show," SYN, 1973; "Lily," CBS, 1973; "John Denver Special," ABC, 1974; "Hollywood Squares," NBC, 1975; "The Merv Griffin Show," SYN, 1975; "Saturday Night Live," NBC, 1975; "Lily Tomlin," ABC, 1976; "Saturday Night Live," NBC, 1976; "Inaugural Eve Special," CBS, 1977; "The Paul Simon Special," NBC, 1977; "The Mike Douglas Show," SYN, 1981; "Lily: Sold Out," CBS, 1981; "Saturday Night Live," NBC, 1983; "Fifty Years of Television: A Golden Celebration," CBS, 1989.
AS CO-WRITER: "Lily," CBS, 1973; "Lily Tomlin," ABC, 1976; "The Paul Simon Special," NBC, 1977; "Lily: Sold Out," CBS, 1981.
* Emmies: 1974, 1976, 1977, 1981.

TONG, SAMMEE

b. San Francisco, CA, 1901; d. 1964. Actor who played Peter Tong, wisecracking houseboy of Bentley Gregg (John Forsythe) on "Bachelor Father."

AS A REGULAR: "Bachelor Father," CBS, 1957-59; NBC, 1959-61; ABC, 1961-62; "Mickey," ABC, 1964-65.

AND: "Hey, Jeannie!: Jeannie the Proprietor," CBS, 1956; "G.E. Theatre: A New Girl in His Life," CBS, 1957; "You Are There: The Surrender of Corregidor," CBS, 1957; "Hawaiian Eye: Dead Ringer," ABC, 1960.

TOOMEY, REGIS

b. Pittsburgh, PA, August 13, 1902. Seasoned character actor in dozens of movies who usually played easygoing cops or detectives; he played Doc Stuart on "Petticoat Junction."

AS A REGULAR: "The Mickey Rooney Show," NBC, 1954-55; "Richard Diamond, Private Detective," CBS, 1957; 1958; "Shannon," SYN, 1961-62; "Burke's Law," ABC, 1963-65; "Petticoat Junction," CBS, 1968-69.

AND: "Bigelow-Sanford Theatre: T.K.O.," SYN, 1950; "Four Star Playhouse: Dante's Inferno," CBS, 1953; "Schlitz Playhouse of Stars: The Ledge," CBS, 1953; "Four Star Playhouse: The Hard Way," CBS, 1953; "Stage 7: Young Girl in an Apple Tree," CBS, 1955; "Four Star Playhouse: The House Always Wins," CBS, 1955; "The Loretta Young Show: The Bad Apple," NBC, 1957; "The Adventures of Ozzie and Harriet: The Reading Room," ABC, 1957; "The 20th Century-Fox Hour: The Still Trumpet," CBS, 1957; "Cheyenne: Hard Bargain," ABC, 1957; "Restless Gun: Hill of Death," NBC, 1957; "The Danny Thomas Show: Man's Best Friend," CBS, 1957; "The Millionaire: The Pete Marlow Story," CBS, 1957; "Navy Log: One Grand Marine," ABC, 1958; "The Loretta Young Show: South American Uncle," NBC, 1958; "Broken Arrow: Transfer," ABC, 1958; "Playhouse 90: No Time At All," CBS, 1958; "Maverick: Shady Deal at Sunny Acres," ABC, 1959; "The David Niven Show: Maggie Malone," NBC, 1959; "Markham: The Long Haul," CBS, 1959; "Rawhide: Incident of the Stalking Death," CBS, 1959; "The Tall Man: And the Beast," NBC, 1960; "Perry Mason: The Case of the Loquacious Liar," CBS, 1960; "Peter Gunn: Dream Big, Dream Deadly," ABC, 1960; "Route 66: The Quick and the Dead," CBS, 1961; "Cheyenne: Shepherd with a Gun," ABC, 1961; "Death Valley Days: The Hold-Up Proof Safe," SYN, 1961; "Cain's Hundred: Murder by Proxy," NBC, 1962; "Perry Mason: The Case of the Twelfth Wildcat," CBS, 1965; "The Farmer's Daughter: To Have and to Hold," ABC, 1965; "Green Acres: Sprained Ankle, Country Style," CBS, 1966; "The Legend of Jesse James: Things Don't Just Happen," ABC, 1966; "Insight: A Reason to Live, A Reason to Die," SYN, 1966; "The Doris Day Show: Who's Got the Trenchcoat?," CBS, 1972; "Ghost Story: The Summer House," NBC, 1972; "The FBI: Till Death Do Us Part," ABC, 1972; "The FBI: End of a Nightmare," ABC, 1972; "Adam 12: A Fool and His Money," NBC,

1973; "Owen Marshall, Counselor at Law: The Desertion of Keith Ryder," ABC, 1974.

TV MOVIES AND MINISERIES: "The Phantom of Hollywood," CBS, 1974.

TORK, PETER

b. Washington, D.C., February 13, 1944.

AS A REGULAR: "The Monkees," NBC, 1966-68.

AND: "The Monkees Special," NBC, 1969.

TORME, MEL

b. Chicago, IL, September 13, 1925. Smooth vocalist.

AS A REGULAR: "TV's Top Tunes," CBS, 1951; "Summertime USA," CBS, 1953; "The Judy Garland Show," CBS, 1963-64; "It Was a Very Good Year," ABC, 1971.

AND: "The Steve Allen Show," NBC, 1956; "Playhouse 90: The Comedian," CBS, 1957; "Art Linkletter's House Party," CBS, 1957; "The Rosemary Clooney Show," SYN, 1957; "The Nat King Cole Show," NBC, 1957; "The Jimmy Dean Show," CBS, 1957; "The Big Record," CBS, 1957; "The Jimmy Dean Show," CBS, 1958; "The Lux Show with Rosemary Clooney," NBC, 1958; "Art Linkletter's House Party," CBS, 1958; "Stars of Jazz," ABC, 1958; "Your Hit Parade," CBS, 1959; "The Garry Moore Show," CBS, 1959; "The Andy Williams Show," CBS, 1959; "Steve Allen Plymouth Show," NBC, 1959; "Revlon Revue: Seventy-Six Men and Peggy Lee," CBS, 1960; "Pat Boone Chevy Showroom," ABC, 1960; "Play Your Hunch," NBC, 1960; "What's My Line?," CBS, 1960; "The Garry Moore Show," CBS, 1960; "Dan Raven: The Junket," NBC, 1960; "Art Carney Special: Everybody's Doin' It," NBC, 1961; "The Garry Moore Show," CBS, 1961; "The Spike Jones Show," CBS, 1961; "The Garry Moore Show," CBS, 1962; "Password," CBS, 1962; "American Bandstand," ABC, 1962; "Password," CBS, 1964; "The Tennessee Ernie Ford Show," ABC, 1965; "Jackie Gleason and His American Scene Magazine," CBS, 1965; "The Bing Crosby Show: Moonlighting Becomes You," ABC, 1965; "The Lucy Show: Lucy and the Music World," CBS, 1965; "You Don't Say," NBC, 1966; "The Lucy Show: Mainstreet USA," CBS, 1967; "The Virginian: The Handy Man," NBC, 1968; "The Carol Burnett Show," CBS, 1969; "The Jackie Gleason Show," CBS, 1969; "Kraft Music Hall," NBC, 1969; "Jimmy Durante Presents the Lennon Sisters Hour," ABC, 1970; "Love, American Style: Love and the Singles Apartment," ABC, 1970; "The Carol Burnett Show," CBS, 1970; "The Carol Burnett Show," CBS, 1971; "Mel Torme and Woody Herman," PBS, 1976; "Something Spectacular with Steve Allen," PBS, 1981; "Hotel: Premiere," ABC, 1983; "Webster: Burn-Out," ABC, 1984; "Night Court: Strange Bedfellows," NBC, 1989.

TRACY, LEE

b. William Lee Tracy, Atlanta, GA, April 14, 1898; d. 1968. Actor at his best in wisecracking roles; he was Martin Kane, private eye.

AS A REGULAR: "The Amazing Mr. Malone," ABC, 1951-52; "Martin Kane, Private Eye," NBC, 1952-53; "New York Confidential," SYN, 1958-59.

AND: "Theatre Hour: The Traitor," ABC, 1950; "Danger: Green and Gold String," CBS, 1950; "Billy Rose's Playbill: If You Can Act, Act," SYN, 1950; "Lights Out: Men on the Mountain," NBC, 1950; "Pulitzer Prize Playhouse: Light Up the Sky," ABC, 1951; "Billy Rose's Playbill: Sugar O'Hara," SYN, 1951; "Cosmopolitan Theatre: The Secret Front," SYN, 1951; "Kraft Television Theatre: Good Old Charlie Fay," NBC, 1956; "Follow the Sun: The Last of the Big Spenders," ABC, 1962; "87th Precinct: Square Cop," NBC, 1962; "Wagon Train: The George B. Hanrahan Story," NBC, 1962; "Going My Way: Cornelius Come Home," ABC, 1963; "Profiles in Courage: The Robert Taft Story," NBC, 1965; "Slattery's People: Question-How Do You Fall in Love with a Town?," CBS, 1965; "Ben Casey: Eulogy in Four Flats," ABC, 1965.

TRAVALENA, FRED

b. New York City, NY, October 6, 1942. Comedian.

AS A REGULAR: "ABC Comedy Hour," ABC, 1972; "Keep on Truckin'," ABC, 1975; "Anything for Money," SYN, 1984-85.

AND: "The Mike Douglas Show," SYN, 1977; "Hollywood Squares," NBC, 1977; "The Love Boat: Double Wedding," ABC, 1978; "The John Davidson Show," SYN, 1981; "Newhart: A Midseason's Night Dream," CBS, 1988; "Murphy Brown: Buddies Schmuddies," CBS, 1989.

TRAVANTI, DANIEL J.

b. Kenosha, WI, March 7, 1940. Emmy winning actor who played Capt. Frank Furillo, who kept his head while everyone about him was losing theirs, on "Hill Street Blues."

AS A REGULAR: "General Hospital," ABC, 1979; "Hill Street Blues," NBC, 1981-87.

AND: "Route 66: Child of a Night," CBS, 1964; "East Side/West Side: The Name of the Game," CBS, 1964; "The Patty Duke Show: Block That Statue," ABC, 1964; "Gidget: Now There's a Face," ABC, 1965; "The Man From UNCLE: The Deadly Goddess Affair," NBC, 1966; "Love on a Rooftop: One Picture Is Worth ...," ABC, 1966; "The FBI: Death of a Fixer," ABC, 1968; "Medical Center: The Savage Image," CBS, 1970; "The FBI: The Diamond Millstone," ABC, 1970; "The Interns: The Choice," CBS, 1971; "Mannix: Murder Times Three," CBS, 1971; "Mission: Impossible: Image," CBS, 1971; "The FBI: The Franklin Papers," ABC, 1972; "Barnaby Jones: Echoes of a Murder," CBS, 1973; "Love Story: Joie," NBC, 1973; "The Bob Newhart Show: The Battle of the Groups," CBS, 1974; "The FBI: Confessions of a Madman," ABC, 1974; "Kojak: A Souvenir From Atlantic City," CBS, 1974; "Barnaby Jones: Theatre of Fear," CBS, 1975; "Kojak: A Grave Too Soon," CBS, 1976; "Saturday Night Live," NBC, 1982; "Later with Bob Costas," NBC, 1989.

TV MOVIES AND MINISERIES: "The Love War," ABC, 1970; "Adam," NBC, 1983; "Aurora," NBC, 1984; "Murrow," HBO, 1986; "Howard Beach: Making the Case for Murder," NBC, 1989.

* Emmies: 1981, 1982.
* See also "Hill Street Blues."

TRAVOLTA, ELLEN

b. Englewood, NJ. Sister of John, which is pretty much the only reason she's in show business.

AS A REGULAR: "Makin' It," ABC, 1979; "Number 96," NBC, 1980-81; "Joanie Loves Chachi," ABC, 1982-83; "Charles in Charge," SYN, 1987- .

AND: "All in the Family: The Unemployment Story," CBS, 1976; "What's Happening!: Nothing Personal," ABC, 1977; "Welcome Back, Kotter: Whatever Happened to Arnold?," ABC, 1977; "The Love Boat: Rocky," ABC, 1978; "Lou Grant: Charlatan," CBS, 1979; "Angie: The Gambler," ABC, 1979; "Three's Company: ... And Justice for Jack," ABC, 1980.

TV MOVIES AND MINISERIES: "Are You in the House Alone?," CBS, 1978.

TRAVOLTA, JOHN

b. Englewood, NJ, February 18, 1954. Movie actor ("Saturday Night Fever," "Look Who's Talking") who began his career in TV commercials and as Vinnie Horshack on "Welcome Back, Kotter."

AS A REGULAR: "Welcome Back, Kotter," ABC, 1975-79.

AND: "Owen Marshall, Counselor at Law: A Piece of God," ABC, 1972; "Medical Center: Saturday's Child," CBS, 1974; "Late Night with David Letterman," NBC, 1989.

TV MOVIES AND MINISERIES: "The Boy in the Plastic Bubble," ABC, 1976.

TREACHER, ARTHUR

b. Arthur Veary, Brighton, England, July 23, 1894; d. 1975. Movie actor who almost always played butlers; in the sixties he became a British version of Ed McMahon to Merv Griffin on his talk show.

AS A REGULAR: "Down You Go," NBC, 1956; "You're in the Picture," CBS, 1961; "The Merv Griffin Show," SYN, 1964-74; CBS, 1969-72.

AND: "Philco TV Playhouse: Uncle Dynamite,"

NBC, 1950; "Philco TV Playhouse: The Room Next Door," NBC, 1952; "Goodyear TV Playhouse: It's a Small World," NBC, 1952; "Philco TV Playhouse: Mr. Pettengill Here," NBC, 1953; "Armstrong Circle Theatre: Tom O'Shanter," NBC, 1954; "Armstrong Circle Theatre: The Three Tasks," NBC, 1954; "Kraft Television Theatre: Alice in Wonderland," NBC, 1954; "Climax!: The Fifth Wheel," CBS, 1956; "The 20th Century-Fox Hour: Thank You, Jeeves," CBS, 1956; "Bulletin From Bertie," CBS, 1956; "The Jack Paar Show," NBC, 1958; "The Garry Moore Show," CBS, 1958; "Arthur Murray Party," NBC, 1960; "Play Your Hunch," NBC, 1960; "Shirley Temple's Storybook: The Land of Oz," NBC, 1960; "The Jack Paar Show," NBC, 1960; "Play of the Week: The Enchanted," SYN, 1960; "Shirley Temple's Storybook: King Midas," NBC, 1961; "The Merv Griffin Show," NBC, 1962; "The Beverly Hillbillies: The Boarder," CBS, 1964; "The Beverly Hillbillies: The Boarder Stays," CBS, 1964; "The Price Is Right," ABC, 1965.

TREBEK, ALEX

b. Canada, July 22, 1940. Game show emcee.
AS A REGULAR: "The Wizard of Odds," NBC, 1973-74; "High Rollers," NBC, 1974-76, 1980; SYN, 1976-77, 1987; "Double Dare," CBS, 1976-77; "The $128,000 Question," SYN, 1977-78; "Battlestars," NBC, 1981-83; "Pitfall," SYN, 1981-82; "Jeopardy!," SYN, 1984- ; "ValueTelevision," SYN, 1987; "Classic Concentration," NBC, 1987- ; "Super Jeopardy!," ABC, 1990.
AND: "The Magnificent Marble Machine," NBC, 1976; "Dinah!," SYN, 1977; "What's Alan Watching?," CBS, 1989; "Later with Bob Costas," NBC, 1989.

TREVOR, CLAIRE

b. Claire Wemlinger, New York City, NY, March 8, 1909. Actress often in tough roles; she won an Emmy for "Dodsworth."
AS A GUEST: "Ford Theatre: Alias Nora Hale," NBC, 1953; "G.E. Theatre: Foggy Night," CBS, 1954; "Ford Theatre: Summer Memory," NBC, 1954; "Lux Video Theatre: No Sad Songs for Me," NBC, 1955; "Stage 7: Billy and the Bride," CBS, 1955; "The 20th Century-Fox Hour: Walking Down Broadway," CBS, 1955; "Climax!: The Prowler," CBS, 1956; "Schlitz Playhouse of Stars: Foolproof," CBS, 1956; "Alfred Hitchcock Presents: Safe Conduct," CBS, 1956; "Producers Showcase: Dodsworth," NBC, 1956; "G.E. Theatre: Emergency Call," CBS, 1956; "Masquerade Party," ABC, 1956; "Playhouse 90: If You Knew Elizabeth," CBS, 1957; "Westinghouse Desilu Playhouse: Happy Hill," CBS, 1959; "Wagon Train: The C.L. Harding Story," NBC,

1959; "The Untouchables: The Ma Barker Story," ABC, 1959; "U.S. Steel Hour: The Revolt of Judge Lloyd," CBS, 1960; "Alfred Hitchcock Presents: A Crime for Mothers," NBC, 1961; "Person to Person," CBS, 1961; "The Investigators: New Sound for the Blues," CBS, 1961; "Dr. Kildare: The Bed I've Made," NBC, 1962; "The Love Boat: Misunderstanding," ABC, 1983; "Murder, She Wrote: Witness for the Defense," CBS, 1987.
TV MOVIES AND MINISERIES: "Norman Rockwell's Breaking Home Ties," ABC, 1987.
* Emmies: 1957.

TROUP, BOBBY

b. Harrisburg, PA, October 18, 1918. Songwriter and singer turned actor; he played Dr. Joe Early on "Emergency!"
AS A REGULAR: "Acapulco," NBC, 1961; "Emergency!," NBC, 1972-77.
AND: "Stars of Jazz," ABC, 1958; "The Rosemary Clooney Show," SYN, 1957; "The Bob Cummings Show: Bob Slows Down," NBC, 1957; "American Bandstand," ABC, 1958; "Perry Mason: The Case of the Jaded Joker," CBS, 1959; "Frances Langford Special," NBC, 1959; "Markham: The Bad Spell," CBS, 1959; "Rawhide: Incident at Rojo Canyon," CBS, 1960; "Here's Hollywood," NBC, 1960; "Perry Mason: The Case of the Missing Melody," CBS, 1961; "King of Diamonds: A Diamond for Mr. Smith," SYN, 1962; "I'll Bet," NBC, 1965; "Dragnet: The Big Explosion," NBC, 1967; "Dragnet: The Big Bookie," NBC, 1967; "Dragnet: The Christmas Story," NBC, 1967; "Dragnet: Vice-DR-30," NBC, 1969; "Mannix: A Pittance of Faith," CBS, 1969; "Mannix: Medal for a Hero," CBS, 1969; "Tattletales," CBS, 1975; "Simon & Simon: Marlowe, Come Home," CBS, 1985; "Highway to Heaven: The Inner Limits," NBC, 1989; "Highway to Heaven: Goodbye, Mr. Zelinka," NBC, 1989.
TV MOVIES AND MINISERIES: "Dragnet," NBC, 1969; "Emergency!," NBC, 1972; "The Rebels," SYN, 1979.

TRUEX, ERNEST

b. Kansas City, MO, September 19, 1890; d. 1973. Comic actor in milquetoast roles; he was hotel manager Jason Macauley during the first season of "The Ann Sothern Show."
AS A REGULAR: "The Truex Family," SYN, 1950; "Jamie," ABC, 1953-54; "Mr. Peepers," NBC, 1954-55; "The Ann Sothern Show," CBS, 1958-59; "Pete and Gladys," CBS, 1961.
AND: "Starlight Theatre: Much Ado About Spring," CBS, 1950; "Ford Theatre: The Ghost Patrol," CBS, 1951; "Danger: Final Rejection," CBS, 1951; "Kraft Television Theatre: The Mollusk," NBC, 1952; "Cameo Theatre: The Canon's Curtains," NBC, 1952; "Goodyear TV Playhouse: The New Process," NBC, 1953; "Inner Sanctum: The Yellow

Parakeet," SYN, 1954; "Kraft Television Theatre: Alice in Wonderland," NBC, 1954; "Armstrong Circle Theatre: Fred Allen's Sketchbook," NBC, 1954; "Pond's Theatre: 30, Honey, 30," ABC, 1955; "Elgin TV Hour: Midsummer Melody," ABC, 1955; "Lux Video Theatre: Make Way for Tomorrow," NBC, 1955; "Studio One: The Spongers," CBS, 1955; "Producers Showcase: Our Town," NBC, 1955; "Climax!: House of Shadows," CBS, 1955; "Star Tonight: Have Faith in Your Agent," ABC, 1955; "Justice: Eyewitness," NBC, 1956; "Matinee Theatre: The Middle Son," NBC, 1956; "Alfred Hitchcock Presents: A Pearl Necklace," NBC, 1961; "The Red Skelton Show: Mr. K. Goes to College," CBS, 1961; "The Dick Powell Show: A Time to Die," NBC, 1962; "The Twilight Zone: Kick the Can," CBS, 1962; "Alfred Hitchcock Presents: The Matched Pearl," NBC, 1962; "The Farmer's Daughter: One Rainy Night," ABC, 1963; "Bonanza: Square Deal Sam," NBC, 1964; "Grindl: Everyone's Coming Up Roses," NBC, 1964; "Petticoat Junction: Billie Jo's Job," CBS, 1965; "Hazel: Who's in Charge Here?," CBS, 1965; "Summer Fun: The Kwimpers of New Jersey," ABC, 1966; "Petticoat Junction: Young Love," CBS, 1966.

TUCKER, FORREST

b. *Plainfield, IN, February 12, 1919; d. 1986.* Burly actor often in action roles; he played con artist Sgt. Morgan O'Rourke on "F Troop."
AS A REGULAR: "Crunch and Des," SYN, 1955; "Pantomime Quiz," ABC, 1958; "F Troop," ABC, 1965-67; "Dusty's Trail," SYN, 1973; "Filthy Rich," CBS, 1982-83.
AND: "Tele-Theatre: The Hoosier Schoolmaster," NBC, 1950; "Schlitz Playhouse of Stars: Blizzard-Bound," CBS, 1954; "Appointment with Adventure: Two Falls for Satan," CBS, 1956; "Robert Montgomery Presents: The Right Thing," NBC, 1956; "Lux Video Theatre: Rebuke Me Not," NBC, 1956; "Kaiser Aluminum Hour: Member in Good Standing," NBC, 1957; "Ford Theatre: The Quiet Stranger," ABC, 1957; "Secret Agent 7: Rags to Riches," SYN, 1959; "Whispering Smith: The Trademark," NBC, 1961; "The Wide Country: Speckle Bird," NBC, 1963; "Dr. Kildare: Island Like a Peacock," NBC, 1963; "Channing: Collision Course," ABC, 1963; "Death Valley Days: Three Minutes to Eternity," SYN, 1964; "Burke's Law: Who Killed Don Pablo?," ABC, 1964; "The Virginian: Hideout," NBC, 1965; "Slattery's People: Bill Bailey, Why Did You Come Home?," CBS, 1965; "Gunsmoke: The Storm," CBS, 1965; "Gunsmoke: Cattle Barons," CBS, 1967; "Hondo: Hondo and the Judas," ABC, 1967; "Walt Disney's Wonderful World of Color: A Boy Called Nuthin'," NBC, 1967; "Doc," NBC, 1969; "Gunsmoke: The War Priest," CBS, 1970; "Medical Center: The Professional," CBS, 1970; "Love, American

Style: Love and the Double Bed," ABC, 1970; "Bracken's World: Love It or Leave It, Change It or Lose It," NBC, 1970; "Gunsmoke: Yankton," CBS, 1972; "Columbo: Blueprint for Murder," NBC, 1972; "Bobbie Joe and the Big Apple Good Time Band," CBS, 1972; "Marcus Welby, M.D.: The Brittle Warrior," ABC, 1974; "Little House on the Prairie: Founder's Day," NBC, 1975; "Kojak: On the Edge," CBS, 1976; "Ellery Queen: Two-Faced Woman," NBC, 1976; "The Life and Times of Grizzly Adams: Gold Is Where You Find It," NBC, 1977; "Police Woman: A Shadow on the Sea," NBC, 1978; "Alice: Flo Finds Her Father," CBS, 1979; "The Love Boat: A Dress to Remember," ABC, 1981; "Matt Houston: Killing Isn't Everything," ABC, 1982; "Murder, She Wrote: It's a Dog's Life," CBS, 1984.
TV MOVIES AND MINISERIES: "Alias Smith and Jones," ABC, 1971; "Lock, Stock and Barrel," NBC, 1971; "Welcome Home, Johnny Bristol," CBS, 1972; "Footsteps," CBS, 1972; "Jarrett," ABC, 1973; "Best Sellers: Once an Eagle," NBC, 1976; "Black Beauty," NBC, 1978; "A Real American Hero," CBS, 1978; "The Rebels," SYN, 1979.

TUCKER, MICHAEL

b. *Baltimore, MD, February 6, 1944.* Pudgy actor who plays Stuart Markowitz on "L.A. Law."
AS A REGULAR: "L.A. Law," NBC, 1986- .
AND: "Hill Street Blues: Fecund Hand Rose," NBC, 1981; "ABC Family Theater: A Family Again," ABC, 1988; "The Tracey Ullman Show: The Baltimore Stoops," FOX, 1989.
TV MOVIES AND MINISERIES: "Vampire," ABC, 1979; "AT&T Presents: Day One," CBS, 1989; "Assault and Matrimony," NBC, 1989.

TUCKER, SOPHIE

b. *Sophie Abuza, Europe, 1884; d. 1966.* Vaudeville singer and storyteller who was singing off-key and telling unfunny stories by the time she was appearing on fifties variety shows.
AS A GUEST: "The Ed Sullivan Show," CBS, 1956; "The Jerry Lewis Show," NBC, 1958; "The Ed Sullivan Show," CBS, 1958; "The Ed Sullivan Show," CBS, 1959; "The Ed Sullivan Show," CBS, 1960; "The Ed Sullivan Show," CBS, 1961; "The Ed Sullivan Show," CBS, 1963; "The Ed Sullivan Show," CBS, 1965.

TULLY, TOM

b. *Durango, CO, 1908; d. 1982.* Bald, average-guy character actor who played Inspector Matt Grebb on "The Lineup" and Sam Petrie, father of Rob on "The Dick Van Dyke Show."
AS A REGULAR: "The Lineup," CBS, 1954-59; "Shane," ABC, 1966.
AND: "Personal Appearance Theatre: The Death

Chase," ABC, 1952; "Cavalcade of America: In This Crisis," NBC, 1952; "Ford Theatre: The Lady and the Champ," NBC, 1953; "Schlitz Playhouse of Stars: Showdown at Sunset," CBS, 1954; "Make Room for Daddy: Rusty's Pal," ABC, 1954; "Dick Powell's Zane Grey Theatre: Badge of Honor," CBS, 1957; "The Danny Thomas Show: The Chess Game," CBS, 1957; "Dick Powell's Zane Grey Theatre: Black Is for Grief," CBS, 1958; "Alfred Hitchcock Presents: Backward, Turn Backward," CBS, 1960; "U.S. Steel Hour: Summer Rhapsody," CBS, 1961; "Rawhide: Incident in Rio Salado," CBS, 1961; "Tales of Wells Fargo: Defiant at the Gate," NBC, 1961; "Empire: Long Past, Long Remembered," NBC, 1962; "The Untouchables: A Taste for Pineapple," ABC, 1963; "Perry Mason: The Case of the Arrogant Astronaut," CBS, 1964; "Perry Mason: The Case of the Nautical Knot," CBS, 1964; "The Dick Van Dyke Show: Pink Pills and Purple Parents," CBS, 1964; "The Virginian: The Hour of the Tiger," NBC, 1964; "My Living Doll: Rhoda the Shoplifter," CBS, 1965; "Rawhide: Blood Harvest," CBS, 1965; "The Farmer's Daughter: The Woman Behind the Man," ABC, 1965; "Bonanza: The Dilemma," NBC, 1965; "The Loner: Hunt the Man Down," CBS, 1965; "The Dick Van Dyke Show: The Curse of the Petrie People," CBS, 1966; "Hey, Landlord!: Woody, Can You Spare a Sister?," NBC, 1967; "The Andy Griffith Show: Goodbye, Dolly," CBS, 1967; "The Guns of Will Sonnett: The Favor," ABC, 1967; "Bonanza: The Sure Thing," NBC, 1967; "The Guns of Will Sonnett: Meeting in a Small Town," ABC, 1969; "The High Chaparral: The Last Hundred Miles," NBC, 1969; "The Mod Squad: A Place to Run, a Place to Hide," ABC, 1969; "Mission: Impossible: Trapped," CBS, 1972; "The Rookies: Dead, Like a Lost Dream," ABC, 1972; "The Rookies: Down Home Boy," ABC, 1973; "St. Elsewhere: Craig in Love," NBC, 1983.
TV MOVIES AND MINISERIES: "Any Second Now," NBC, 1969; "Hijack!," ABC, 1973.

TURNER, KATHLEEN
b. Springfield, MO, 1956. Film actress ("War of the Roses") who began as Nola Aldrich on "The Doctors."
AS A REGULAR: "The Doctors," NBC, 1978-79.
AND: "Saturday Night Live," NBC, 1985; "Saturday Night Live," NBC, 1989.

TURNER, LANA
b. Julia Jean Mildred Frances Turner, Wallace, ID, February 8, 1920. Movie sex symbol who showed up as—gasp—a grandma on "The Love Boat."
AS A REGULAR: "Harold Robbins' The Survivors," ABC, 1969-70; "Falcon Crest," CBS, 1982-83.
AND: "The Bob Hope Show," NBC, 1957; "Dinah

Shore Chevy Show," NBC, 1959; "Milton Berle Special," NBC, 1959; "The Bob Hope Christmas Show," NBC, 1963; "The Smothers Brothers Comedy Hour," CBS, 1967; "The Love Boat: Call Me Grandma," ABC, 1985.

TUTTLE, LURENE
b. Pleasant Lake, IN, August 29, 1906; d. 1986. Character actress; she played Nurse Hannah Yarby on "Julia."
AS A REGULAR: "Life with Father," CBS, 1953-55; "Father of the Bride," CBS, 1961-62; "Julia," NBC, 1968-70.
AND: "I Love Lucy: The Club Election," CBS, 1953; "The Bob Cummings Show: Bob Buys a Plane," CBS, 1956; "Du Pont Theatre: Decision for a Hero," ABC, 1957; "Leave It to Beaver: Beaver Gets Adopted," ABC, 1959; "The Californians: Skeletons in the Closet," NBC, 1959; "Playhouse 90: The Wings of the Dove," CBS, 1959; "Bourbon Street Beat: The Missing Queen," ABC, 1960; "Goodyear Theatre: All in the Family," NBC, 1960; "Johnny Ringo: Killer, Choose a Card," CBS, 1960; "Michael Shayne: Die Like a Dog," NBC, 1960; "Harrigan and Son: Young Man's World," ABC, 1960; "The Andy Griffith Show: Opie's Charity," CBS, 1960; "Hazel: The Fire's Never Dead While the Ashes Are Red," NBC, 1963; "Mr. Novak: The Risk," NBC, 1963; "The Andy Griffith Show: The Shoplifters," CBS, 1964; "The Munsters: Munster Masquerade," CBS, 1964; "I Dream of Jeannie: What House Across the Street?," NBC, 1965; "My Favorite Martian: The Avenue C Mob," CBS, 1965; "The Beverly Hillbillies: The Marriage Machine," CBS, 1967; "Petticoat Junction: Cannonball for Sale," CBS, 1968; "The Mary Tyler Moore Show: Farmer Ted and the News," CBS, 1972; "Gunsmoke: Homecoming," CBS, 1972; "The Partridge Family: For Sale by Owner," ABC, 1972; "The Rookies: Eyewitness," ABC, 1974; "Little House on the Prairie: A Matter of Faith," NBC, 1975; "Little House on the Prairie: Going Home," NBC, 1976; "Switch: Ain't Nobody Here Named Barney," CBS, 1976; "Alice: A Piece of the Rock," CBS, 1977; "Police Woman: Merry Christmas, Waldo," NBC, 1977; "Barnaby Jones: The Killin' Cousin," CBS, 1980; "St. Elsewhere: In Sickness and in Health," NBC, 1984; "Murder, She Wrote: Death in the Afternoon," CBS, 1985.
TV MOVIES AND MINISERIES: "Mrs. Sundance," ABC, 1974; "Live Again, Die Again," ABC, 1974; "White Mama," CBS, 1980.

TYLER, JUDY
b. Milwaukee, WI, 1932; d. 1957. Attractive actress who played Princess Summerfallwinterspring on "Howdy Doody" and had just finished filming "Jailhouse Rock" with Elvis Presley when she was killed in a car accident.

AS A REGULAR: "Howdy Doody," NBC, 1952-57; "Sid Caesar Presents Comedy Preview," NBC, 1955.
AND: "Pantomime Quiz," CBS, 1957; "Perry Mason: Case of the Fan Dancer's Horse," CBS, 1957.

TYLER, KIM

b. Hollywood, CA, April 17, 1954. Child actor who played Kyle Nash on "Please Don't Eat the Daisies."
AS A REGULAR: "Please Don't Eat the Daisies," NBC, 1965-67.
AND: "The Adventures of Ozzie and Harriet: Ten for the Tigers," ABC, 1961; "The Adventures of Ozzie and Harriet: Backyard Pet Show," ABC, 1962; "The Andy Griffith Show: One Punch Opie," CBS, 1962; "The Addams Family: The Addams Family Tree," ABC, 1964; "My Favorite Martian: Martin's Favorite Martian," CBS, 1965.

TYLER, WILLIE

b. Red Level, AL, September 8, 1940. Black ventriloquist; his dummy is Lester.
AS A REGULAR: "Rowan & Martin's Laugh-In," NBC, 1972-73.
AND: "Sammy and Company," SYN, 1975; "Lola Falana Special," ABC, 1975; "The Jeffersons: George's New Stockbroker," CBS, 1978; "The White Shadow: If Your Number's Up...Get It Down," CBS, 1980; "Comic Strip Live," FOX, 1989; "Super Dave," SHO, 1989.

TYSON, CICELY

b. New York City, NY, December 19, 1939. Actress who won an Emmy for her incandescant performamce in "The Autobiography of Miss Jane Pittman."
AS A REGULAR: "East Side/West Side," CBS, 1963-64; "The Guiding Light," CBS, 1966.
AND: "Slattery's People: Who You Taking to the Main Event, Eddie?," CBS, 1965; "I Spy: So Long," NBC, 1965; "I Spy: Trial by Treehouse," NBC, 1966; "The FBI: The Enemies," ABC, 1968; "Medical Center: The Last Ten Yards," CBS, 1969; "The FBI: Silent Partners," ABC, 1969; "On Being Black: Johnny Ghost," NET, 1969; "The Courtship of Eddie's Father: Guess Who's Coming for Lunch," ABC, 1969; "The Bill Cosby Show: The Blind Date," NBC, 1970; "Mission: Impossible: Death Squad," CBS, 1970; "Gunsmoke: The Scavengers," CBS, 1970; "Hollywood Television Theatre: Neighbors," NET, 1971; "Emergency!: Crash," NBC, 1972; "Wednesday Night Out," NBC, 1972; "Free to Be You and Me," ABC, 1974; "G.E. Theatre: Just an Old Sweet Song," CBS, 1976; "Saturday Night Live," NBC, 1979.
TV MOVIES AND MINISERIES: "Marriage: Year One," NBC, 1971; "The Autobiography of Miss Jane Pittman," CBS, 1974; "Just an Old Sweet Song," CBS, 1976; "Roots," ABC, 1977; "King," NBC, 1978; "Playing with Fire," NBC, 1985; "Samaritan: The Mitch Snyder Story," CBS, 1986; "Acceptable Risks," ABC, 1986; "The Women of Brewster Place," ABC, 1989.
* Emmies: 1974.

U

UECKER, BOB

b. *Milwaukee, WI, January 26, 1935.* Baseball player with the Braves, Cardinals and Phillies; he played George Owens on "Mr. Belvedere."
AS A REGULAR: "Monday Night Baseball," ABC, 1976-82; "Mr. Belvedere," ABC, 1985-90.
AND: "The Peter Marshall Variety Show," SYN, 1977; "Saturday Night Live," NBC, 1984; "Later with Bob Costas," NBC, 1989; "The Tonight Show Starring Johnny Carson," NBC, 1989.

UGGAMS, LESLIE

b. *New York City, NY, May 25, 1943.* Singer-actress; an Emmy winner for "Fantasy."
AS A REGULAR: "Beulah," ABC, 1950; "Paul Whiteman's TV Teen Club," ABC, 1952; "Sing Along with Mitch," NBC, 1961-64; "The Leslie Uggams Show," CBS, 1969; "Fantasy," NBC, 1982-83.
AND: "Arthur Godfrey's Talent Scouts," CBS, 1952; "Name That Tune," CBS, 1958; "American Bandstand," ABC, 1958; "The Bob Crosby Show," NBC, 1958; "The Jimmy Dean Show," CBS, 1958; "Patti Page Olds Show," ABC, 1958; "Music for a Summer Night," ABC, 1959; "The Jack Paar Show," NBC, 1959; "The Andy Williams Show," CBS, 1959; "Startime: Sing Along with Mitch," NBC, 1960; "The Ed Sullivan Show," CBS, 1964; "The Price Is Right," ABC, 1964; "The Ed Sullivan Show," CBS, 1965; "Hullabaloo," NBC, 1965; "Alan King Special," NBC, 1969; "The Tonight Show Starring Johnny Carson," NBC, 1969; "The Andy Williams Show," NBC, 1970; "The Dean Martin Show," NBC, 1971; "The Mod Squad: Deal with the Devil," ABC, 1972; "The Merv Griffin Show," SYN, 1972; "Marcus Welby, M.D.: Feedback," ABC, 1974; "Dinah!," SYN, 1976; "The Peter Marshall Variety Show," SYN, 1977; "The Muppet Show," SYN, 1980; "Magnum P.I.: Dream a Little Dream," CBS, 1984; "The Ice Capades with Jason Bateman and Alyssa Milano," ABC, 1989.
TV MOVIES AND MINISERIES: "Roots," ABC, 1977; "Backstairs at the White House," NBC, 1979; "Sizzle," ABC, 1981.
* Emmies: 1983.

ULLMAN, TRACEY

b. *England, 1961.* Chameleon-like comic actress whose sketch-oriented show was critically acclaimed and virtually abandoned by the viewing public.
AS A REGULAR: "The Tracey Ullman Show," FOX, 1987-90.
AND: "Late Night with David Letterman," NBC, 1988; "Late Night with David Letterman," NBC, 1989.
* Emmies: 1989, 1990.

URICH, ROBERT

b. *Toronto, OH, December 19, 1946.* Hunky actor who played TV dicks Dan Tanna on "Vegas" and No-first-name Spenser.
AS A REGULAR: "Bob & Carol & Ted & Alice," ABC, 1973; "SWAT," ABC, 1975-76; "Soap," ABC, 1977; "Tabitha," ABC, 1977-78; "Vega$," ABC, 1978-81; "Gavilan," NBC, 1982-83; "Spenser: For Hire," ABC, 1985-88; "American Dreamer," NBC, 1990- .
AND: "The FBI: The Runner," ABC, 1972; "Kung Fu: Blood Brothers," ABC, 1973; "Marcus Welby, M.D.: Death Is Only a Side Effect," ABC, 1973; "Gunsmoke: Manolo," CBS, 1975; "Cross Wits," SYN, 1976; "Charlie's Angels: Angels in Vegas," ABC, 1978; "The Love Boat: Love Me, Love My Dog," ABC, 1979; "Saturday Night Live," NBC, 1982.
TV MOVIES AND MINISERIES: "When She Was Bad," ABC, 1979; "Killing at Hell's Gate," CBS, 1981; "Take Your Best Shot," CBS, 1982; "Princess Daisy," NBC, 1983; "Invitation to Hell," ABC, 1984; "His Mistress," NBC, 1984; "Scandal Sheet," ABC, 1985; "The Defiant Ones," ABC, 1985; "Amerika," ABC, 1987; "Hallmark Hall of Fame: April Morning," CBS, 1988; "She Knows Too Much," NBC, 1989; "The Comeback," CBS, 1989; "The Defiant Ones," ABC, 1989; "Lonesome Dove," CBS, 1989; "Night Walk," CBS, 1989.

V

VACCARO, BRENDA
b. Brooklyn, NY, November 18, 1939. Deep-voiced, dark-featured actress in intense roles; an Emmy winner for the comedy special "The Shape of Things."
AS A REGULAR: "Sara," CBS, 1976; "Dear Detective," CBS, 1979; "Paper Dolls," ABC, 1984.
AND: "True Story: Revenge," NBC, 1960; "The Greatest Show on Earth: Don't Look Down, Don't Look Back," ABC, 1963; "The Fugitive: See Hollywood and Die," ABC, 1963; "The Defenders: The Sworn Twelve," CBS, 1965; "The Doctors and Nurses: The Heroine," CBS, 1965; "Vacation Playhouse: My Lucky Penny," CBS, 1966; "Coronet Blue: A Charade for Murder," CBS, 1967; "You're Putting Me On," NBC, 1969; "The FBI: Scapegoat," ABC, 1969; "The Name of the Game: One of the Girls in Research," NBC, 1970; "The Name of the Game: Appointment in Palermo," NBC, 1971; "The Name of the Game: Jenny," NBC, 1971; "Marcus Welby, M.D.: House of Mirrors," ABC, 1972; "Banacek: To Steal a King," NBC, 1972; "McCloud: The Park Avenue Rustlers," NBC, 1972; "The Streets of San Francisco: Act of Duty," ABC, 1973; "The Shape of Things," CBS, 1973; "ABC Theatre: Judgment: The Trial of Julius and Ethel Rosenberg," ABC, 1974; "Lily," NBC, 1974; "The Streets of San Francisco: The Most Deadly Species," ABC, 1974; "Good Heavens: Take Me Out to the Ball Game," ABC, 1976; "The Love Boat: Shop Ahoy," ABC, 1984; "St. Elsewhere: The Women," NBC, 1984; "Murder, She Wrote: Just Another Fish Story," CBS, 1988; "The Pat Sajak Show," CBS, 1989.
TV MOVIES AND MINISERIES: "Travis Logan, D.A.," CBS, 1971; "What's a Nice Girl Like You...?," ABC, 1971; "Honor Thy Father," CBS, 1973; "Sunshine," NBC, 1973; "The Big Ripoff," NBC, 1975; "The Pride of Jesse Hallam," CBS, 1981; "The Star Maker," NBC, 1981; "GE Theatre: A Long Way Home," ABC, 1981; "Deceptions," NBC, 1985.
* Emmies: 1974.

VALENTINE, KAREN
b. Santa Rosa, CA, May 25, 1947. Actress who won an Emmy as idealistic teacher Alice Johnson on "Room 222."
AS A REGULAR: "Room 222," ABC, 1969-74; "Karen," ABC, 1975; "Our Time," NBC, 1985.
AND: "It's About Time: The Cave Family Singers," CBS, 1967; "Hollywood Squares," NBC, 1970; "Love, American Style: Love and the Elopement," ABC, 1970; "Love, American Style: Love and the

Coed Dorm," ABC, 1970; "The Bold Ones: Tender Predator," NBC, 1971; "Hollywood Squares," NBC, 1971; "The Tonight Show Starring Johnny Carson," NBC, 1971; "The Tonight Show Starring Johnny Carson," NBC, 1972; "Love, American Style: Love and the Scroungers," ABC, 1972; "Owen Marshall, Counselor at Law: Murder in the Abstract," ABC, 1972; "Love, American Style: Love and the Four-Sided Triangle," ABC, 1972; "Hollywood Squares," NBC, 1973; "The Karen Valentine Show," ABC, 1973; "Hollywood Squares," NBC, 1974; "Bell System Family Theatre: Christmas with the Bing Crosbys," NBC, 1974; "Baretta: A Bite of the Apple," ABC, 1975; "The Magnificent Marble Machine," NBC, 1975; "The Bobby Vinton Show," SYN, 1975; "Bill Cosby Special," ABC, 1975; "Sammy and Company," SYN, 1975; "The Magnificent Marble Machine," NBC, 1976; "The Rich Little Show," NBC, 1976; "McMillan: Dark Sunrise," NBC, 1977; "The Love Boat: The Caper," ABC, 1978; "Hollywood Squares," SYN, 1980; "The New Mike Hammer: Who Killed Sister Lorna?," CBS, 1987; "Murder, She Wrote: Murder Through the Looking Glass," CBS, 1988.
TV MOVIES AND MINISERIES: "Gidget Grows Up," ABC, 1969; "The Daughters of Joshua Cabe," ABC, 1972; "Coffee, Tea or Me?," CBS, 1973; "The Girl Who Came Gift-Wrapped," ABC, 1974; "The Love Boat," ABC, 1976; "Having Babies," ABC, 1976; "Murder at the World Series," ABC, 1977; "Muggable Mary: Street Cop," CBS, 1982; "Money on the Side," ABC, 1982; "Skeezer," NBC, 1982; "Illusions," CBS, 1983; "Jane Doe," CBS, 1983; "He's Fired, She's Hired," CBS, 1984; "Perfect People," ABC, 1988.
* Emmies: 1970.

VALENTINE, SCOTT
b. June 3, 1958. Actor who played Nick, boyfriend of Mallory Keaton (Justine Bateman) on "Family Ties."
AS A REGULAR: "Family Ties," NBC, 1985-89.
AND: "Knight Rider: The Wrong Crowd," NBC, 1985; "Matlock: The Angel," NBC, 1986.

VALLEE, RUDY
b. Hubert Prior Rudy Vallee, Island Pond, VT, July 28, 1901; d. 1986. Popular singer of the twenties who turned to acting.
AS A REGULAR: "On Broadway Tonight," CBS, 1964-65.
AND: "Eddie Cantor Theatre: The Playboy," SYN, 1955; "December Bride: Rudy Vallee Show," CBS,

1956; "The Vic Damone Show," CBS, 1956; "Matinee Theatre: Jenny Kissed Me," NBC, 1956; "Texaco Star Theatre: Command Appearance," NBC, 1957; "December Bride: Crashing Hollywood," CBS, 1957; "The Lucille Ball-Desi Arnaz Show: Lucy Takes a Cruise to Havana," CBS, 1957; "Kraft Theatre: The Battle for Wednesday Night," NBC, 1958; "Mike Wallace Interviews," ABC, 1958; "Hansel and Gretel," NBC, 1958; "The Jack Paar Show," NBC, 1958; "The Jimmy Dean Show," CBS, 1958; "The Red Skelton Show: Clem Sings," CBS, 1958; "The Garry Moore Show," CBS, 1959; "The George Gobel Show," CBS, 1959; "The Golden Circle," ABC, 1959; "Perry Como's Kraft Music Hall," NBC, 1961; "The Tonight Show Starring Johnny Carson," NBC, 1962; "Batman: The Londinium Larcenies/The Foggiest Notion/The Bloody Tower," ABC, 1967; "Death Valley Days: The Friend," SYN, 1968; "The Mike Douglas Show," SYN, 1969; "Petticoat Junction: But I've Never Been in Erie, PA," CBS, 1969; "Here's Lucy: Lucy and Rudy Vallee," CBS, 1970; "Night Gallery: Dandelion Wine," NBC, 1971; "Alias Smith and Jones: Dreadful Sorry, Clementine," ABC, 1971; "Alias Smith and Jones: The Man Who Broke the Bank at Red Gap," ABC, 1972.

VAN ARK, JOAN

b. New York City, NY, June 16, 1943. Blonde actress who plays Valene Ewing on "Knots Landing."
AS A REGULAR: "Temperatures Rising," ABC, 1972-73; "We've Got Each Other," CBS, 1977-78; "Dallas," CBS, 1978-81; "Knots Landing," CBS, 1979- .
AND: "The Guns of Will Sonnett: The Man Who Killed James Sonnett," ABC, 1968; "The Mod Squad: Twinkle, Twinkle Little Starlet," ABC, 1968; "Gunsmoke: Stryker," CBS, 1969; "The FBI: The Maze," ABC, 1969; "Love, American Style: Love and the Proposal," ABC, 1970; "The FBI: The Condemned," ABC, 1970; "Hawaii Five-O: To Kill or Be Killed," CBS, 1971; "Medical Center: Edge of Violence," CBS, 1971; "Love, American Style: Love and the Triple Threat," ABC, 1971; "The FBI: The Deadly Gift," ABC, 1971; "The Odd Couple: A Night to Dismember," ABC, 1972; "M*A*S*H: Radar's Report," CBS, 1973; "Mannix: The Girl in the Polka Dot Dress," CBS, 1973; "Ironside: Run Scared," NBC, 1974; "Barnaby Jones: The Challenge," CBS, 1974; "The Rockford Files: Find Me if You Can," NBC, 1974; "The Girl with Something Extra: A Zircon in the Rough," NBC, 1974; "The FBI: The Vendetta," ABC, 1974; "Medical Center: Adults Only," CBS, 1974; "Medical Center: Too Late for Tomorrow," CBS, 1975; "Rhoda: Rhoda Meets the Ex-Wife," CBS, 1975; "The Rockford Files: Resurrection in Black and White," NBC, 1975; "Medical Story: Woman in White," NBC, 1975; "The Rockford Files: There's One in Every Port," NBC, 1976; "Kojak: Lady in the Squad Room," CBS, 1977; "McMillan: Have

You Heard the One About ...," NBC, 1977; "Quark: All the Emporer's Quasi-Norms," NBC, 1978; "The Love Boat: What's a Brother For?," ABC, 1979; "Glitter: Premiere," ABC, 1984; "The Love Boat: Seems Like Old Times," ABC, 1984.
TV MOVIES AND MINISERIES: "The Judge and Jake Wyler," NBC, 1972; "Big Rose," CBS, 1974; "Shell Game," CBS, 1975; "Testimony of Two Men," SYN, 1977; "Red Flag: The Ultimate Game," CBS, 1981; "Shakedown on the Sunset Strip," CBS, 1988; "My First Love," ABC, 1988.

VANCE, VIVIAN

b. Vivian Roberta Jones, Cherryville, KS, July 26, 1912; d. 1979. Comic actress who was a longtime foil and friend of Lucille Ball.
AS A REGULAR: "I Love Lucy," CBS, 1951-57; "The Lucille Ball-Desi Arnaz Show," CBS, 1957-59; "The Lucy Show," CBS, 1962-65.
AND: "Shower of Stars: High Pitch," CBS, 1955; "The Ed Sullivan Show," CBS, 1956; "I've Got A Secret," CBS, 1959; "Arthur Murray Party," NBC, 1959; "The Deputy: Land Greed," NBC, 1959; "The Jack Paar Show," NBC, 1960; "The Red Skelton Show: Appleby's Fallout Shelter," CBS, 1960; "The Red Skelton Show: Appleby's Predictions," CBS, 1960; "Candid Camera," CBS, 1961; "The Red Skelton Show: Appleby's Sleepwalk," CBS, 1961; "Password," CBS, 1961; "Candid Camera," CBS, 1962; "The Jack Paar Show," NBC, 1962; "The Red Skelton Show: The Iceman Cometh," CBS, 1962; "ABC Nightlife," ABC, 1965; "The Mike Douglas Show," SYN, 1965; "I've Got a Secret," CBS, 1966; "The Lucy Show: Viv Visits Lucy," CBS, 1967; "Here's Lucy: Lucy the Matchmaker," CBS, 1968; "The Dick Cavett Show," ABC, 1968; "Love, American Style: Love and the Medium," ABC, 1969; "Here's Lucy: Lucy and Lawrence Welk," CBS, 1970; "Here's Lucy: Lucy and Viv Visit Tijuana," CBS, 1970; "The Front Page," NET, 1970; "Here's Lucy: Lucy Goes Hawaiian," CBS, 1971; "Here's Lucy: With Viv as a Friend, Who Needs an Enemy?," CBS, 1972; "Rhoda: Friends and Mothers," CBS, 1975; "Dinah!," SYN, 1975.
TV MOVIES AND MINISERIES: "Getting Away From It All," ABC, 1972; "The Great Houdinis," ABC, 1976.
* Emmies: 1954.

VANDER PYL, JEAN

Actress who was the voice of Wilma Flintstone and Rosey the Robot on "The Jetsons."
AS A REGULAR: "The Flinstones," ABC, 1960-66; "The Jetsons," ABC, 1962-63; "Please Don't Eat the Daisies," NBC, 1966-67; "Where's Huddles?," CBS, 1970.
AND: "Leave It to Beaver: Beaver and Alma," ABC, 1960; "Top Cat: Choo Choo's Romance," ABC, 1961; "Top Cat: Choo Choo Goes Ga Ga," ABC, 1962; "The Donna Reed Show: With This Ring," ABC, 1965.

VAN DYKE, BARRY

b. Atlanta, GA, July 31, 1951. Son of Dick Van Dyke; he played St. John Hawke on "Airwolf" and opposite his gifted father on a short-lived sitcom.

AS A REGULAR: "Battlestar Galactica," ABC, 1980; "Gun Shy," CBS, 1983; "The Redd Foxx Show," ABC, 1986; "Airwolf," USA, 1987; "The Van Dyke Show," CBS, 1988.

AND: "The Wizard of Oz," CBS, 1961; "The Dick Van Dyke Show: The Talented Neighborhood," CBS, 1962; "Mork & Mindy: A Mommy for Mork," ABC, 1978; "Mork & Mindy: Young Love," ABC, 1978; "The Love Boat: Boomerang," ABC, 1980; "Remington Steele: Steele Belted," NBC, 1982; "The Love Boat: When the Magic Disappears," ABC, 1983; "The A-Team: Bend in the River," NBC, 1984; "The Love Boat: Love Times Two," ABC, 1985; "The Love Boat: The Tour Guide," ABC, 1986.

TV MOVIES AND MINISERIES: "Casino," ABC, 1980.

VAN DYKE, DICK

b. West Plains, MO, December 13, 1925. Limber Emmy- and Tony-award winning leading man of movies, the tube and Broadway; his recent TV work hasn't been up to his talent.

AS A REGULAR: "The Morning Show," CBS, 1955; "CBS Cartoon Theatre," CBS, 1956; "The Garry Moore Show," CBS, 1957-58; "The Chevy Showroom," ABC, 1958; "Mother's Day," ABC, 1958-59; "Pantomime Quiz," ABC, 1958, 1959; "Laugh Line," NBC, 1959; "The Dick Van Dyke Show," CBS, 1961-66; "The New Dick Van Dyke Show," CBS, 1971-74; "Van Dyke and Company," NBC, 1976; "The Carol Burnett Show," CBS, 1978; "The Van Dyke Show," CBS, 1988.

AND: "Nothing But the Truth," CBS, 1956; "The Phil Silvers Show: Hillbilly Whiz," CBS, 1957; "The Phil Silvers Show: Bilko's Cousin," CBS, 1958; "Pat Boone Chevy Showroom," ABC, 1958; "The Polly Bergen Show," NBC, 1958; "True Story: The Imperfect Secretary," NBC, 1958; "Armstrong Circle Theatre: A Picture of Christmas," CBS, 1958; "The Jack Paar Show," NBC, 1959; "The Perry Como Show," NBC, 1959; "U.S. Steel Hour: Trap for a Stranger," CBS, 1959; "The Andy Williams Show," CBS, 1959; "The Ed Sullivan Show," CBS, 1959; "Art Carney Special: Very Important People," NBC, 1959; "The Fabulous Fifties," CBS, 1960; "Arthur Murray Party," NBC, 1960; "Alfred Hitchcock Presents: Craig's Will," CBS, 1960; "The Garry Moore Show," CBS, 1960; "Play Your Hunch," NBC, 1960; "The Jack Paar Show," NBC, 1960; "The Ed Sullivan Show," CBS, 1960; "Look Up and Live: Two Alone," CBS, 1960; "New Comedy Showcase: The Trouble with Richard," CBS, 1960; "No Place Like Home," NBC, 1960; "The Garry Moore Show," CBS, 1961; "Dinah Shore Chevy Show," NBC, 1961; "The Jack Paar Show," NBC, 1961; "I've Got a Secret," CBS, 1962; "Password," CBS, 1962; "Play Your Hunch," NBC,

1962; "Stump the Stars," CBS, 1962; "The Wizard of Oz," CBS, 1962; "Henry Fonda and the Family," CBS, 1962; "The Jack Benny Program," CBS, 1963; "The Garry Moore Show," CBS, 1963; "I've Got a Secret," CBS, 1963; "A Salute to Stan Laurel," CBS, 1965; "Walt Disney's Wonderful World of Color: A Tribute to Walt Disney," NBC, 1966; "The Dick Van Dyke Special," CBS, 1967; "The Dick Van Dyke Special," CBS, 1968; "Dick Van Dyke and the Other Woman," CBS, 1969; "The Bill Cosby Show: Miraculous Marvin," NBC, 1971; "The First Nine Months Are the Hardest," NBC, 1971; "I'm a Fan," CBS, 1972; "Dick Van Dyke Meets Bill Cosby," CBS, 1972; "America's Romance with the Land," ABC, 1973; "Columbo: Negative Reaction," NBC, 1974; "Julie and Dick in Covent Garden," ABC, 1974; "The Confessions of Dick Van Dyke," ABC, 1975; "Lola!," ABC, 1976; "CBS: On the Air," CBS, 1978; "How to Survive the 70s and Maybe Even Bump Into Happiness," CBS, 1978; "The Mary Tyler Moore Hour," CBS, 1979; "The Merv Griffin Show," SYN, 1980; "Harry's Battles," ABC, 1981; "True Life Stories," ABC, 1981; "CBS Library: The Wrong Way Kid," CBS, 1984; "Highway to Heaven: Wally," NBC, 1986; "Disney's Golden Anniversary of 'Snow White and the Seven Dwarfs,'" ABC, 1987; "Airwolf: Malduke," USA, 1987; "Sylvia Fine Kaye's Musical Comedy Tonight III," PBS, 1988; "Ringling Bros. and Barnum & Bailey Clown College: 20th Anniversary," CBS, 1988; "Roger Rabbit and the Secrets of Toon Town," CBS, 1988; "Super Bloopers and New Practical Jokes," NBC, 1988; "CBS News Special: Lucy," CBS, 1989; "The Magical World of Disney: Disney-MGM Studios Theme Park Grand Opening," NBC, 1989; "The Golden Girls: Under the Big Top," NBC, 1989.

TV MOVIES AND MINISERIES: "The Morning After," ABC, 1974; "Dropout Father," CBS, 1982; "Found Money," NBC, 1983; "The Country Girl," SHO, 1985; "Diary of a Perfect Murder," NBC, 1986; "Two of a Kind," CBS, 1987; "Ghost of a Chance," CBS, 1987.

AS DIRECTOR: "The Nancy Dussault Show," CBS, 1973.

* Van Dyke and his wife, Marjorie Willets, were married February 12, 1948 on the ABC radio program "Bride and Groom."
* Van Dyke's 1969 special with Mary Tyler Moore, "Dick Van Dyke and the Other Woman," convinced CBS executives that Moore could carry her own series; "The Mary Tyler Moore Show" premiered the next fall.
* Van Dyke and Moore reprised their roles as Rob and Laura Petrie on Moore's short-lived variety show in 1979; in the sketch, Alan Brady passes away and Rob has to write his eulogy.
* Emmies: 1964, 1965, 1966, 1984.

VAN DYKE, JERRY

b. *Danville, IL, July 27, 1931.* Brother of Dick, an underrated comedian who's never quite found his ideal TV vehicle; best known as Luther Van Dam on "Coach."

AS A REGULAR: "Picture This," CBS, 1963; "The Judy Garland Show," CBS, 1963; "My Mother the Car," NBC, 1965-66; "Accidental Family," NBC, 1967-68; "The Headmaster," CBS, 1970-71; "13 Queens Boulevard," ABC, 1979; "Coach," ABC, 1989- .

AND: "The Dick Van Dyke Show: I Am My Brother's Keeper/The Sleeping Brother," CBS, 1962; "The Ed Sullivan Show," CBS, 1962; "G.E. True: The Handmade Private," CBS, 1962; "The Andy Williams Show," NBC, 1962; "You Don't Say," NBC, 1964; "Art Linkletter's House Party," CBS, 1964; "The Dick Van Dyke Show: Stacey Petrie," CBS, 1965; "The Andy Griffith Show: Banjo-Playing Deputy," CBS, 1965; "The Young Set," ABC, 1965; "Gomer Pyle, USMC: Gomer and the Nightclub Comic," CBS, 1968; "Funny You Should Ask," ABC, 1969; "Love, American Style: Love and the Nutsy Girl," ABC, 1969; "The Jim Nabors Hour," CBS, 1970; "The Merv Griffin Show," CBS, 1970; "Love, American Style: Love and the Gangster," ABC, 1971; "Love, American Style: Love and the Jealous Husband," ABC, 1971; "The Mary Tyler Moore Show: But Seriously, Folks," CBS, 1972; "The Mary Tyler Moore Show: Son of But Seriously, Folks," CBS, 1973; "House Calls: The Dead Beat," CBS, 1980; "The Merv Griffin Show," SYN, 1980; "Newhart: You're Homebody 'Til Somebody Loves You," CBS, 1983.

TV MOVIES AND MINISERIES: "Fresno," CBS, 1986.

VAN FLEET, JO

b. *Oakland, CA, December 30, 1919.* Stage and TV actress often in threatening or intense roles; she played Lesley Ann Warren's wicked stepmother in "Cinderella."

AS A GUEST: "Philco TV Playhouse: The Thin Air," NBC, 1952; "Armstrong Circle Theatre: Last Tour," NBC, 1953; "U.S. Steel Hour: Morning Star," ABC, 1954; "Philco TV Playhouse: Assassin," NBC, 1955; "Alfred Hitchcock Presents: Reward to Finder," CBS, 1957; "Westinghouse Desilu Playhouse: The Crazy Hunter," CBS, 1958; "Alcoa Theatre: 30 Pieces of Silver," NBC, 1959; "Du Pont Show of the Month: The Night of the Storm," CBS, 1961; "Alfred Hitchcock Presents: Servant Problem," NBC, 1961; "Thriller: The Remarkable Mrs. Hawk," NBC, 1961; "Naked City: The Night the Saints Lost Their Halos," ABC, 1962; "Frontier Circus: The Courtship," CBS, 1962; "Russians: Self-Impressions," CBS, 1963; "77 Sunset Strip: Don't Wait for Me," ABC, 1963; "Route 66: The Stone Guest," CBS, 1963; "Summer Playhouse: Satan's Waitin'," CBS, 1964; "Kraft

Suspense Theatre: The World I Want to Know," NBC, 1964; "Cinderella," CBS, 1965; "The Virginian: Legacy of Hate," NBC, 1966; "Experiment in Television: Good Day," NBC, 1967; "The Mod Squad: A Is for Annie," ABC, 1970; "NET Playhouse: Paradise Lost," NET, 1971; "Bonanza: The Stillness Within," NBC, 1971; "Medical Center: The Martyr," CBS, 1971; "Medical Center: Time of Darkness," CBS, 1973; "Police Woman: The Buttercup Killer," NBC, 1977.

TV MOVIES AND MINISERIES: "The Family Rico," CBS, 1972; "Satan's School for Girls," ABC, 1973.

VANOCUR, SANDER

b. *Cleveland, OH.* NBC reporter from 1957-71, NET reporter from 1971-73, ABC reporter from 1977.

AS A REGULAR: "NBC Weekend News," NBC, 1961-65; "First Tuesday," NBC, 1969-70.

VAN PATTEN, DICK

b. *Kew Gardens, NY, December 9, 1928.* Actor who began his career as the wavy-haired Nels Hansen on "Mama" and was that epitome of white squareness, bald-headed pop Tom Bradford on "Eight Is Enough."

AS A REGULAR: "Mama," CBS, 1949-57; "Young Doctor Malone," NBC, 1958-63; "The Partners," NBC, 1971-72; "The New Dick Van Dyke Show," CBS, 1973-74; "When Things Were Rotten," ABC, 1975; "Eight Is Enough," ABC, 1977-81; "WIOU," CBS, 1990- .

AND: "Rawhide: Incident of the Power and the Plow," CBS, 1959; "Du Pont Show of the Month: Men in White," CBS, 1960; "Hawaii Five-O: The Payoff," CBS, 1970; "Medical Center: The Awakening," CBS, 1972; "Sanford & Son: The Great Sanford Siege," NBC, 1972; "The Paul Lynde Show: Howie Comes Home to Roost," ABC, 1972; "The Streets of San Francsisco: 45 Minutes from Home," ABC, 1972; "McMillan and Wife: No Hearts, No Flowers," NBC, 1973; "The Doris Day Show: Anniversary Gift," CBS, 1973; "The Paul Lynde Show: Back Talk," ABC, 1973; "Banacek: Rocket to Oblivion," NBC, 1974; "The Girl with Something Extra: The New Broom," NBC, 1974; "Sierra: Cruncher," NBC, 1974; "Kolchak the Night Stalker: They Have Been, They Are, They Will Be," ABC, 1974; "Barnaby Jones: Dark Homecoming," CBS, 1974; "Medical Center: Street Girl," CBS, 1975; "Barnaby Jones: Deadly Reunion," CBS, 1976; "What's Happening!: The Burger Queen," ABC, 1976; "CPO Sharkey: Kowalksi the Somnambulist," NBC, 1977; "One Day at a Time: Ginny's Child," CBS, 1977; "Happy Days: Graduation," ABC, 1977; "Hollywood Squares," SYN, 1978; "Dance Fever," SYN, 1979; "The Mike Douglas Show," SYN, 1980; "The Love Boat: His Girl Friday," ABC, 1982; "The Love Boat: When the Magic Disappears," ABC, 1983; "Hotel: Charades," ABC, 1983; "The Love Boat: How Do I

Love Thee?," ABC, 1984; "Hotel: Missing Pieces," ABC, 1985; "Growing Pains: Fortunate Son," ABC, 1989.
TV MOVIES AND MINISERIES: "Hec Ramsey," NBC, 1972; "The Crooked Hearts," ABC, 1972; "The Love Boat," ABC, 1976; "Diary of a Teenage Hitchhiker," ABC, 1979; "Picking Up the Pieces," CBS, 1985; "The Midnight Hour," ABC, 1985; "Eight Is Enough: A Family Reunion," NBC, 1987; "An Eight Is Enough Wedding," NBC, 1989.

VAN PATTEN, JOYCE
b. New York City, NY, March 9, 1934. Former child actress, usually in comic roles. Sister of Dick Van Patten.
AS A REGULAR: "As the World Turns," CBS, 1956-57; "Young Doctor Malone," NBC, 1958-63; "The Danny Kaye Show," CBS, 1964-67; "The Good Guys," CBS, 1968-70; "The Don Rickles Show," CBS, 1972; "The Mary Tyler Moore Hour," CBS, 1979.
AND: "The Law and Mr. Jones: Cold Turkey," ABC, 1961; "The Many Loves of Dobie Gillis: Crazy Legs Gillis," CBS, 1961; "Bus Stop: Turn Again Home," ABC, 1962; "Target: The Corruptors: Fortress of Despair," ABC, 1962; "Checkmate: Remembrance of Crimes Past," CBS, 1962; "Robert Taylor's Detectives: Night Boat," NBC, 1962; "The Many Loves of Dobie Gillis: Wanted Dead or Alive," CBS, 1962; "The New Loretta Young Show: First Assignment," CBS, 1962; "Alcoa Premiere: George Gobel Presents," ABC, 1963; "The Many Loves of Dobie Gillis: Lassie, Get Lost," CBS, 1963; "The Twilight Zone: Passage on the Lady Anne," CBS, 1963; "The Outer Limits: A Feasibility Study," ABC, 1964; "Mr. Novak: From the Brow of Zeus," NBC, 1965; "Perry Mason: The Case of the Thermal Thief," CBS, 1965; "The Virginian: Ring of Silence," NBC, 1965; "Slattery's People: The Unborn," CBS, 1965; "The Loner: The Mourners for Johnny Sharp," CBS, 1966; "The Andy Griffith Show: Opie Steps Up in Class," CBS, 1967; "Family Affair: Class Clown," CBS, 1970; "The FBI: Turnabout," ABC, 1971; "McCloud: A Little Plot at Tranquil Valley," NBC, 1972; "Love, American Style: Love and the Naked Stranger," ABC, 1972; "The Bob Newhart Show: Let's Get Away From It Almost," CBS, 1973; "Love, American Style: Love and the Playwright," ABC, 1973; "The Streets of San Francisco: The House on Hyde Street," ABC, 1973; "Owen Marshall, Counselor at Law: House of Friends," ABC, 1974; "The Rockford Files: To Protect and Serve," NBC, 1977; "Lou Grant: After-Shock," CBS, 1977; "Amazing Stories: One for the Books," NBC, 1986.
TV MOVIES AND MINISERIES: "But I Don't Want to Get Married!," ABC, 1970; "The Stranger Within," ABC, 1974; "Let's Switch," ABC, 1975; "Winner Take All," NBC, 1975; "Another Woman's Child," CBS, 1983; "The Demon

Murder Case," NBC, 1983; "In Defense of Kids," CBS, 1983; "Malice in Wonderland," CBS, 1985; "Under the Influence," CBS, 1986.
* See also Paul Mazursky.

VAN PATTEN, TIMOTHY
b. Brooklyn, NY, June 10, 1959. Half-brother of Dick Van Patten; he played Mario "Salami" Pettrino on "The White Shadow."
AS A REGULAR: "The White Shadow," CBS, 1978-81; "The Master," NBC, 1984; "True Blue," NBC, 1989-90.
AND: "St. Elsewhere: Give the Boy a Hand," NBC, 1985; "Night Heat: Fighting Back," CBS, 1986.
TV MOVIES AND MINISERIES: "Dress Gray," NBC, 1986.

VAN PATTEN, VINCENT
b. Bellrose, NY, October 17, 1957. Son of Dick Van Patten.
AS A REGULAR: "Apple's Way," CBS, 1974-75; "Three for the Road," CBS, 1975.
AND: "Nanny and the Professor: The Humanization of Herbert T. Peabody," ABC, 1970; "Marcus Welby, M.D.: This Is Max!," ABC, 1972; "Medical Center: Impact," CBS, 1973; "What Really Happened to the Class of '65?: The Most Likely to Succeed," NBC, 1978; "$weepstake$: Cowboy, Linda and Angie, Mark," NBC, 1979; "The Love Boat: First Voyage, Last Voyage," ABC, 1981.
TV MOVIES AND MINISERIES: "Dial Hot Line," ABC, 1970; "The Bravos," ABC, 1972.

VAN VALKENBURGH, DEBORAH
b. Schenectady, NY, August 29, 1952. Actress who played Jackie Rush on "Too Close for Comfort."
AS A REGULAR: "Too Close for Comfort," ABC, 1980-83; SYN, 1984-85.
AND: "Hotel: Resolutions," ABC, 1984; "Crime Story: Shockwaves," NBC, 1987; "Cagney & Lacey: Button, Button," CBS, 1988; "Heartbeat: Prison," ABC, 1989.
TV MOVIES AND MINISERIES: "A Bunny's Tale," ABC, 1985; "Going for the Gold: The Bill Johnson Story," CBS, 1985; "CAT Squad: Python Wolf," NBC, 1988.

VARNEY, JIM
b. Lexington, KY, 1946. Comic actor who's a legend in the annals of lowbrow TV humor thanks to his "Hey, Vern" commercials.
AS A REGULAR: "The Johnny Cash Show," CBS, 1976; "Fernwood 2-Night," SYN, 1977-78; "Operation Petticoat," ABC, 1977-79; "Pink Lady," NBC, 1980; "Pop! Goes the Country," SYN, 1982; "The Rousters," NBC, 1983-84.
AND: "Alice: Better Late Than Never," CBS, 1978.

VAUGHN, ROBERT
b. New York City, NY, November 22, 1932. Dark-

haired, chin-dimpled actor who played Napoleon Solo, the man from UNCLE and now sells hairpieces on late-night TV; he won an Emmy for "Washington: Behind Closed Doors."

AS A REGULAR: "The Lieutenant," NBC, 1963-64; "The Man From UNCLE," NBC, 1964-68; "The Protectors," SYN, 1972-73; "Emerald Point NAS," CBS, 1983-84; "The A-Team," NBC, 1986-87.

AND: "Medic: Black Friday," NBC, 1955; "Big Town: Marine Story," NBC, 1956; "West Point: The Operator," CBS, 1956; "The Millionaire: The Story of Jay Powers," CBS, 1956; "Father Knows Best: Betty Goes Steady," NBC, 1956; "Dick Powell's Zane Grey Theatre: Courage Is a Gun," CBS, 1956; "Wichita Town: Passage to the Enemy," NBC, 1959; "The Rebel: Noblesse Oblige," ABC, 1960; "The Man From Blackhawk: Remember Me Not," ABC, 1960; "Men Into Space: Moon Cloud," CBS, 1960; "Law of the Plainsman: The Dude," NBC, 1960; "Checkmate: Interrupted Honeymoon," CBS, 1960; "Laramie: The Dark Trail," NBC, 1960; "The Garlund Touch: The Awakening," CBS, 1960; "The du Pont Show with June Allyson: Emergency," CBS, 1960; "Wagon Train: The Roger Bigelow Story," NBC, 1960; "Stagecoach West: Object: Patrimony," ABC, 1961; "Bonanza: The Way Station," NBC, 1962; "The Eleventh Hour: The Blues My Baby Gave to Me," NBC, 1962; "The Dick Van Dyke Show: It's a Shame She Married Me," CBS, 1963; "The Eleventh Hour: The Silence of Good Men," NBC, 1963; "You Don't Say," NBC, 1964; "Jimmy Durante Meets the Lively Arts," ABC, 1965; "The Danny Kaye Show," CBS, 1966; "Please Don't Eat the Daisies: Say UNCLE," NBC, 1966; "The Girl From UNCLE: The Mother Muffin Affair," NBC, 1966; "Hollywood Palace," ABC, 1968; "Snap Judgment," NBC, 1968; "Portrait: The Man From Independence," ABC, 1974; "Police Woman: Blast," NBC, 1975; "Columbo: Troubled Waters," NBC, 1975; "The $25,000 Pyramid," SYN, 1975; "Police Woman: Generation of Evil," NBC, 1976; "Columbo: Last Salute to the Commodore," NBC, 1976; "Hotel: Charades," ABC, 1983; "Murder, She Wrote: Murder Digs Deep," CBS, 1986.

TV MOVIES AND MINISERIES: "The Woman Hunter," CBS, 1972; "Kiss Me, Kill Me," ABC, 1976; "Best Sellers: Captains and the Kings," NBC, 1976; "Washington: Behind Closed Doors," ABC, 1977; "The Islander," CBS, 1978; "Backstairs at the White House," NBC, 1979; "Centennial," NBC, 1978-79; "The Rebels," SYN, 1979; "Mirror, Mirror," NBC, 1979; "City in Fear," ABC, 1980; "Fantasies," ABC, 1982; "Intimate Agony," ABC, 1983; "Return of the Man From UNCLE," CBS, 1983; "Private Sessions," NBC, 1985; "The Prince of Bel Air," ABC, 1986; "Murrow," HBO, 1986;

"Desperado," NBC, 1987.

AS DIRECTOR: "Police Woman: The Melting Point of Ice," NBC, 1976.

* Emmies: 1978.

VERDUGO, ELENA

b. Hollywood, CA, 1926. Film and TV actress who played Millie Bronson in "Meet Millie" and faithful nurse Consuelo Lopez to Marcus Welby, M.D.

AS A REGULAR: "Meet Millie," CBS, 1952-56; "Redigo," NBC, 1963; "The New Phil Silvers Show," CBS, 1964; "Many Happy Returns," CBS., 1964-65; "Mona McCluskey," NBC, 1965-66; "Marcus Welby, M.D.," ABC, 1969-76.

AND: "Cavalcade of America: Arrow and the Bow," NBC, 1953; "The Red Skelton Show," CBS, 1957; "The Rosemary Clooney Show," SYN, 1957; "Pantomime Quiz," CBS, 1957; "The Bob Cummings Show: Bob and the Ravishing Realtor," NBC, 1958; "The Red Skelton Show," CBS, 1958; "Wanted Dead or Alive: Call Your Shot," CBS, 1959; "The Bob Cummings Show: Bob Helps Von Zell," NBC, 1959; "The Red Skelton Show," CBS, 1959; "Rawhide: Incident at Spanish Rock," CBS, 1959; "The Red Skelton Show: Super Cauliflower," CBS, 1960; "Here's Hollywood," NBC, 1960; "Preview Theatre: Harry's Business," NBC, 1961; "Holiday Lodge: The Target," CBS, 1961; "Route 66: Kiss the Maiden All Forlorn," CBS, 1962; "77 Sunset Strip: Paper Chase," ABC, 1963; "Your First Impression," NBC, 1963; "Mona McCluskey: My Fair Sergeant," NBC, 1965; "Mona McCluskey: The Present," NBC, 1966; "Ironside: The Sacrifice," NBC, 1968; "Love, American Style: Love and the Modern Wife," ABC, 1969; "The Steve Allen Show," SYN, 1970.

TV MOVIES AND MINISERIES: "Marcus Welby, M.D.," ABC, 1969; "The Alpha Caper," ABC, 1973.

VEREEN, BEN

b. Miami, FL, October 10, 1946. Musical-comedy performer in TV variety and light drama; he played Uncle Philip on "Webster" and con artist E.L. "Tenspeed" Turner on the underrated "Tenspeed and Brown Shoe" and "J.J. Starbuck."

AS A REGULAR: "Ben Vereen... Comin' at Ya," NBC, 1975; "Tenspeed and Brown Shoe," ABC, 1980; "Webster," ABC, 1984-85; "You Write the Songs," SYN, 1986-87; "J.J. Starbuck," NBC, 1988-89.

AND: "The Mike Douglas Show," SYN, 1975; "Sammy and Company," SYN, 1977; "The Tonight Show Starring Johnny Carson," NBC, 1978; "Ben Vereen-His Roots," ABC, 1978; "The Love Boat: The Dream Boat," ABC, 1984.

TV MOVIES AND MINISERIES: "Louis Armstrong-Chicago Style," ABC, 1976; "Roots," ABC, 1977; "A.D.," NBC, 1985; "Lost in London," CBS, 1985.

VERNON, JACKIE
b. *New York City, NY, 1929; d. 1987.* Deadpan comedian who also played off-key trumpet.
AS A REGULAR: "The Garry Moore Show," CBS, 1966-67.
AND: "The Jack Paar Program," NBC, 1964; "Hootenanny," ABC, 1964; "The Ed Sullivan Show," CBS, 1964; "The Jack Paar Program," NBC, 1965; "The Ed Sullivan Show," CBS, 1965; "The Ed Sullivan Show," CBS, 1967; "Hollywood Squares," NBC, 1968; "The Ed Sullivan Show," CBS, 1968; "That's Life: Bachelor Days," ABC, 1968; "The Merv Griffin Show," SYN, 1969; "The Merv Griffin Show," CBS, 1970; "The Flip Wilson Show," NBC, 1972; "The Merv Griffin Show," SYN, 1973; "The Merv Griffin Show," SYN, 1977.

VIGODA, ABE
b. *New York City, NY, February 24, 1921.* Long-faced actor who played Det. Phil Fish on "Barney Miller."
AS A REGULAR: "Barney Miller," ABC, 1975-77; "Fish," ABC, 1977-78; "One Life to Live," ABC, 1984.
AND: "Mannix: A Matter of Principle," CBS, 1973; "Kojak: 18 Hours of Fear," CBS, 1974; "Kojak: The Best Judge Money Can Buy," CBS, 1974; "Hawaii Five-O: The Two-Faced Corpse," CBS, 1974; "The Rockford Files: The Kirkoff Case," NBC, 1974; "The Rookies: Something Less Than a Man," ABC, 1974; "Cos," ABC, 1976; "Break the Bank," SYN, 1976; "Dean Martin's Red Hot Scandals of 1926," NBC, 1976; "Break the Bank," SYN, 1977; "Barney Miller: Burial," ABC, 1977; "The Mike Douglas Show," SYN, 1978; "The Rockford Files: Rosendahl and Gilda Stern Are Dead," NBC, 1978; "The Love Boat: Home Sweet Home," ABC, 1978; "Supertrain: A Very Formal Heist," NBC, 1979; "B.J. and the Bear: Mary Ellen," NBC, 1979; "Barney Miller: Lady and the Bomb," ABC, 1981; "Late Night with David Letterman," NBC, 1989; "B.L. Stryker: The Dancer's Touch," ABC, 1989; "Santa Barbara," NBC, 1989.
TV MOVIES AND MINISERIES: "The Devil's Daughter," ABC, 1973; "Toma," ABC, 1973; "Having Babies," ABC, 1976; "How to Pick Up Girls," ABC, 1978; "Death Car on the Freeway," CBS, 1979.
* When a tabloid newspaper incorrectly reported that Vigoda was dead in 1989, David Letterman allowed him on his show for about two minutes to prove otherwise. And just to make sure the report wasn't true, Dave had Vigoda breathe on a mirror.

VILLECHAIZE, HERVE
b. *France, April 23, 1943.* Dwarf actor who hit it big, no pun intended, as Tattoo on "Fantasy Island" and left the show for greener pastures. He's still waiting.
AS A REGULAR: "Fantasy Island," ABC, 1978-83.
AND: "Taxi: Fantasy Borough," ABC, 1980.
* Villechaize stands three feet ten inches tall.

VINCENT, JAN-MICHAEL
b. *Denver, CO, July 15, 1944.* Actor usually in macho roles; he played the helicopter pilot Stringfellow Hawke on "Airwolf" and was a marine recruit in the good TV movie "Tribes."
AS A REGULAR: "Banana Splits Adventure Hour: Danger Island," NBC, 1968-69; "Harold Robbins' The Survivors," ABC, 1969-70; "Airwolf," CBS, 1984-86.
AND: "Dragnet: The Big Bang," NBC, 1967; "Dan August: Death Chain," ABC, 1971; "Men at Law: One American," CBS, 1971; "Gunsmoke: Ma Colter," CBS, 1971; "Marcus Welby, M.D.: Catch a Ring That Isn't There," ABC, 1973; "Police Story: Line of Fire," NBC, 1973; "Police Story: Incident in the Kill Zone," NBC, 1975.
TV MOVIES AND MINISERIES: "Tribes," ABC, 1970; "The Catcher," NBC, 1972; "Sandcastles," CBS, 1972; "Deliver Us From Evil," ABC, 1973; "The Winds of War," ABC, 1983; "Six Against the Rock," NBC, 1987; "Tarzan in Manhattan," CBS, 1989.

VINTON, BOBBY
b. *Canonsburg, PA, April 16, 1935.* Whiny-voiced pop singer.
AS A REGULAR: "The Bobby Vinton Show," SYN, 1975-78.
AND: "Saturday Prom," NBC, 1960; "The Lawrence Welk Show," ABC, 1963; "The Ed Sullivan Show," CBS, 1964; "The Jimmy Dean Show," ABC, 1964; "The Patty Duke Show: Patty and the Newspaper Game," ABC, 1965; "American Bandstand," ABC, 1965; "The Jimmy Dean Show," ABC, 1965; "The Sonny and Cher Comedy Hour," CBS, 1972; "Wide World in Concert," ABC, 1975; "Boone: Chance of a Lifetime," NBC, 1983; "Hee Haw," SYN, 1985.

VIVYAN, JOHN
b. *Chicago, IL, May 31, 1916; d. 1983.* Handsome actor who played "Mr. Lucky."
AS A REGULAR: "Mr. Lucky," CBS, 1959-60.
AND: "The Joseph Cotten Show: Alibi for Murder," NBC, 1957; "The Loretta Young Show: The Little Witness," NBC, 1957; "Maverick: Black Fire," ABC, 1958; "Colt .45: The Mirage," ABC, 1958; "The Millionaire: The Laura Hunter Story," CBS, 1958; "Rough Riders: The Counterfeiters," ABC, 1958; "Maverick: The Judas Mask," ABC, 1958; "Bat Masterson: A Matter of Honor," NBC, 1959;

"77 Sunset Strip: The Girl Who Couldn't Remember," ABC, 1959; "The Lawless Years: The Big Greeny Story," NBC, 1959; "The Lawless Years: The Big Man," NBC, 1959; "Walt Disney Presents: Texas John Slaughter-Wild Horse Revenge," ABC, 1959; "Maverick: A Cure for Johnny Rain," ABC, 1959; "Bat Masterson: The Hunter," NBC, 1960; "The Chevy Show: Arabian Nights," NBC, 1960; "Death Valley Days: The Lady Was an M.D.," SYN, 1961; "Beachcomber: The Con Man," SYN, 1961; "King of Diamonds: The Magic Act," SYN, 1962; "Comedy Spot: His Model Wife," CBS, 1962; "The Lucy Show: Lucy Becomes a Reporter," CBS, 1963; "Mr. Terrific: The Sultan Has Five Wives," CBS, 1967; "Batman: Penguin's Clean Sweep," ABC, 1968; "The FBI: The Witness," ABC, 1970; "Simon & Simon: Betty Grable Flies Again," CBS, 1983.

VOGEL, MITCH

b. *Alhambra, CA, January 17, 1956*. Actor who played Jamie Hunter on "Bonanza."
AS A REGULAR: "Bonanza," NBC, 1970-73.
AND: "The Virginian: The Storm Gate," NBC, 1968; "Gunsmoke: McCabe," CBS, 1970; "Gunsmoke: Lynch Town," CBS, 1973; "The Streets of San Francisco: Jacob's Boy," ABC, 1974; "Little House on the Prairie: The Love of Johnny Johnson," NBC, 1974; "Little House on the Prairie: To See the World," NBC, 1975; "Gunsmoke: The Hiders," CBS, 1975; "The Quest: Seventy-Two Hours," NBC, 1976.

VOIGHT, JON

b. *Yonkers, NY, December 29, 1938*. Blond screen actor ("Midnight Cowboy," "Coming Home," "Runaway Train"), usually in intense roles.
AS A GUEST: "Naked City: Alive and Still a Second Lieutenant," ABC, 1963; "The Defenders: The Brother Killers," CBS, 1963; "Gunsmoke: The Newcomers," CBS, 1966; "NET Playhouse: A Sleep of Prisoners," NET, 1966; "Coronet Blue: The Rebel," CBS, 1967; "Gunsmoke: Prairie Wolfer," CBS, 1967; "NYPD: Bomber," ABC, 1967; "Gunsmoke: The Prisoner," CBS, 1969.

VOLAND, HERBERT

Actor usually in stern, authoritative roles on sitcoms; he played Gen. Clayton on "M*A*S*H."
AS A REGULAR: "Love on a Rooftop," ABC, 1966-67, 1971; "Mr. Deeds Goes to Town," ABC,

1969-70; "Arnie," CBS, 1970-72; "M*A*S*H," CBS, 1972-73; "The Paul Lynde Show," ABC, 1972-73.
AND: "Kraft Television Theatre: No Warning," NBC, 1957; "Studio One: A Matter of Guilt," CBS, 1957; "Frontiers of Faith: The Rainy Season," NBC, 1958; "Look Up and Live: Two Alone—The Stranger," CBS, 1960; "Du Pont Show of the Month: The Lincoln Murder Case," CBS, 1961; "The Virginian: Farewell to Honesty," NBC, 1965; "I Dream of Jeannie: Whatever Happened to Baby Custer?," NBC, 1965; "Gidget: I Have This Friend Who ...," ABC, 1966; "The Iron Horse: Joy Unconfined," ABC, 1966; "Bewitched: That Was No Chick, That Was My Wife," ABC, 1967; "Bewitched: Mirror, Mirror on the Wall," ABC, 1968; "The Mothers-in-Law: The Birth of Everything But the Blues," NBC, 1968; "The Mothers-in-Law: Haven't You Had That Baby Yet?," NBC, 1969; "Love, American Style: Love and the Nervous Executive," ABC, 1970; "Get Smart: Do I Hear a Vaults?," CBS, 1970; "Sanford & Son: Pot Luck," NBC, 1973; "All in the Family: Birth of the Baby," CBS, 1975; "Harry O: Forbidden City," ABC, 1976.
TV MOVIES AND MINISERIES: "Scalplock," NBC, 1966; "In Name Only," ABC, 1969.

VON ZELL, HARRY

b. *Indianapolis, IN, July 11, 1906; d. 1981*. Longtime announcer-straight man to George Burns and Gracie Allen.
AS A REGULAR: "The George Burns and Gracie Allen Show," CBS, 1951-58; "The George Burns Show," NBC, 1958-59; "The George Gobel Show," CBS, 1959-60; "Celebrity Golf," NBC, 1960-61.
AND: "Wagon Train: The Tobias Jones Story," NBC, 1958; "The Bob Cummings Show: Bob Helps Martha," NBC, 1959; "The Bob Cummings Show: Bob Helps Von Zell," NBC, 1959; "Christophers: Participating in School Affairs," SYN, 1959; "The Many Loves of Dobie Gillis: Dobie's Navy Blues," CBS, 1960; "Bachelor Father: Bentley and the Blood Bank," NBC, 1960; "Bachelor Father: There's No Place Like Home," NBC, 1961; "The Tall Man: Petticoat Crusade," NBC, 1961; "Wagon Train: Clyde," NBC, 1961; "McHale's Navy: Uncle Admiral," ABC, 1963.
AS WRITER: "Wagon Train: The Tobias Jones Story," NBC, 1958; "Wagon Train: The Dr. Willoughby Story," NBC, 1958; "Wagon Train: The Flint McCullough Story," NBC, 1959.

W

WAGGONER, LYLE

b. Kansas City, KS, April 13, 1935. Beefy actor who was a second banana to Carol Burnett; he played Steve Trevor on "Wonder Woman."

AS A REGULAR: "The Carol Burnett Show," CBS, 1967-74; ABC, 1979; "Carol Burnett Presents the Jimmie Rodgers Show," CBS, 1969; "It's Your Bet," SYN, 1969-73; "Wonder Woman," ABC, 1976-77; CBS, 1977-79.

AND: "It Takes Two," NBC, 1969; "Marcus Welby, M.D.: The Day After Forever," ABC, 1973; "Don Adams Screen Test," SYN, 1975; "Maude: The Case of the Broken Bowl," CBS, 1976; "The Merv Griffin Show," SYN, 1976; "The Love Boat: My Boyfriend's Back," ABC, 1979; "Supertrain: A Very Formal Heist," NBC, 1979; "Charlie's Angels: Island Angels," ABC, 1980; "Mork & Mindy: Mork and the Family Reunion," ABC, 1981; "The Love Boat: A Dress to Remember," ABC, 1981; "Happy Days: Good News, Bad News," ABC, 1984; "Hardcastle and McCormick: If You Could See What I See," ABC, 1986; "The New Mike Hammer: Requiem for Billy," CBS, 1986.

TV MOVIES AND MINISERIES: "Letters From Three Lovers," ABC, 1973."The New, Original Wonder Woman," ABC, 1975; "Love Boat II," ABC, 1977; "The Great American Traffic Jam," NBC, 1980.

WAGNER, LINDSAY

b. Los Angeles, CA, June 22, 1949. Attractive actress who hasn't much TV series success since she played Jaime Sommers, the bionic woman.

AS A REGULAR: "The Bionic Woman," ABC, 1976-77; NBC, 1977-78; "Jessie," ABC, 1984; "A Peaceable Kingdom," CBS, 1989.

AND: "The Bold Ones; In the Defense of Ellen McKay," NBC, 1971; "Man and the City: Disaster on Turner Street," ABC, 1971; "Sarge: The Combatants," NBC, 1971; "Owen Marshall, Counselor at Law: Until Proven Innocent," ABC, 1971; "Marcus Welby, M.D.: All the Pretty People," ABC, 1972; "The FBI: Dark Journey," ABC, 1972; "Marcus Welby, M.D.: Don and Denise," ABC, 1972; "Marcus Welby, M.D.: The Best Is Yet to Be," ABC, 1972; "Marcus Welby, M.D.: Dark Fury," ABC, 1974; "The Rockford Files: Aura Lee, Farewell," NBC, 1975; "The Six Million Dollar Man: The Bionic Woman," ABC, 1975; "The Six Million Dollar Man: The Return of the Bionic Woman," ABC, 1975; "The Six Million Dollar Man: The Secret of Bigfoot," ABC, 1976; "The Six Million Dollar Man: The Return of

Bigfoot," ABC, 1976; "The Rockford Files: Backlash of the Hunter," NBC, 1978; "The Fall Guy: Devil's Island," ABC, 1983; "Kate & Allie: Late Bloomer," CBS, 1986; "The Pat Sajak Show," CBS, 1989.

TV MOVIES AND MINISERIES: "The Rockford Files," NBC, 1974; "The Incredible Journey of Doctor Meg Laurel," CBS, 1979; "The Two Worlds of Jennie Logan," CBS, 1979; "Scruples," CBS, 1980; "Callie & Son," CBS, 1981; "Memories Never Die," CBS, 1982; "I Want to Live!," ABC, 1983; "Princess Daisy," NBC, 1983; "Two Kinds of Love," CBS, 1983; "Passions," CBS, 1984; "The Other Lover," CBS, 1985; "This Child Is Mine," NBC, 1985; "Child's Cry," CBS, 1986; "Convicted," NBC, 1986; "Stranger in my Bed," NBC, 1987; "The Return of the Six Million Dollar Man and the Bionic Woman," NBC, 1987; "The Taking of Flight 847: The Uli Derickson Story," NBC, 1988; "Nightmare at Bitter Creek," CBS, 1988; "From the Dead of the Night," NBC, 1989; "The Bionic Showdown: The Six Million Dollar Man and the Bionic Woman," NBC, 1989.

* Emmies: 1977.

WAGNER, ROBERT

b. Detroit, MI, February 10, 1930. Smooth, handsome actor of fifties movies and throughly routine TV; he played professional thief Alexander Mundy and crime-solving Jonathan Hart.

AS A REGULAR: "It Takes a Thief," ABC, 1968-70; "Switch," CBS, 1975-78; "Hart to Hart," ABC, 1979-84; "Lime Street," ABC, 1985.

AND: "The 20th Century-Fox Hour: The Ox-Bow Incident," CBS, 1955; "The 20th Century-Fox Hour: Gun in His Hand," CBS, 1956; "The Ed Sullivan Show," CBS, 1957; "Dinah Shore Chevy Show," NBC, 1957; "Bob Hope Special," NBC, 1958; "The Jack Benny Program," CBS, 1960; "The Eleventh Hour: And Man Created Vanity," NBC, 1963; "Bob Hope Chrysler Theatre: The Enemy on the Beach," NBC, 1966; "Bob Hope Chrysler Theatre: Runaway Bay," NBC, 1966; "The Name of the Game: The War Merchants," NBC, 1970; "The Name of the Game: The Man Who Killed a Ghost," NBC, 1971; "Don Adams Screen Test," SYN, 1975.

TV MOVIES AND MINISERIES: "How I Spent My Summer Vacation," NBC, 1967; "City Beneath the Sea," NBC, 1971; "The Cable Car Murder," CBS, 1971; "Killer by Night," CBS, 1972; "Madame Sin," ABC, 1972; "The Streets of San Francisco," ABC, 1972; "The Affair," ABC, 1973; "The Abduction of Saint Anne," ABC, 1975; "Switch," CBS, 1975; "Cat on a Hot Tin Roof," NBC, 1976; "Death at Love House," ABC, 1976; "Pearl," ABC, 1978; "The Critical List," NBC, 1978; "There Must Be a Pony," ABC, 1986; "Love Among Thieves," ABC, 1987; "Indiscreet," CBS, 1988; "Windmills of the Gods," CBS, 1988.

WAHL, KEN
b. Chicago, IL, 1953. Hunky actor who played Vinnie Terranova on "Wiseguy."
AS A REGULAR: "Double Dare," CBS, 1985; "Wiseguy," CBS, 1987-90.
TV MOVIES AND MINISERIES: "The Dirty Dozen: Next Mission," NBC, 1985; "The Gladiator," ABC, 1986.

WAITE, RALPH
b. White Plains, NY, June 22, 1928. Graying actor who played father John Walton and attorney Ben Walker on "The Mississippi."
AS A REGULAR: "The Waltons," CBS, 1972-81; "The Mississippi," CBS, 1983-84.
TV MOVIES AND MINISERIES: "The Borgia Stick," NBC, 1967; "Roots," ABC, 1977; "Angel City," CBS, 1980; "A Wedding on Walton's Mountain," NBC, 1982; "A Day for Thanks on Walton's Mountain," NBC, 1982; "A Good Sport," CBS, 1984; "Crime of Innocence," NBC, 1985; "Red Earth, White Earth," CBS, 1989.

WALDEN, ROBERT
b. New York City, NY, September 25, 1943. Actor who played reporter Joe Rossi on "Lou Grant."
AS A REGULAR: "The Bold Ones," NBC, 1972-73; "Lou Grant," CBS, 1977-82; "Brothers," SHO, 1984-89.
AND: "The Rookies: Margin for Error," ABC, 1973; "Columbo: Any Old Port in a Storm," NBC, 1973; "Adam's Rib: Murder!," ABC, 1973; "Medical Center: Faces of Peril," CBS, 1974; "The Streets of San Francisco: Jacob's Boy," ABC, 1974; "The Rookies: Time Lock," ABC, 1974; "The Streets of San Francisco: Web of Lies," ABC, 1975; "Medical Center: Torment," CBS, 1975; "Police Woman: Broken Angels," NBC, 1976; "The Rockford Files: The Oracle Wore a Cashmere Suit," NBC, 1976; "Starsky and Hutch: Murder at Sea," ABC, 1976; "Rhoda: Somebody Has to Say They're Sorry," CBS, 1977; "The Streets of San Francisco: A Good Cop...But," ABC, 1977; "Police Story: Spitfire," NBC, 1977; "Murder, She Wrote: Death in the Afternoon," CBS, 1985; "The New Mike Hammer: The Last Laugh," CBS, 1987; "Matlock: The Convict," NBC, 1987; "Father Dowling Mysteries: Missing Body Mystery," NBC, 1989.
TV MOVIES AND MINISERIES: "Shirts/Skins," ABC,

1973; "The Great Ice Rip-Off," ABC, 1974; "Panic on the 5:22," ABC, 1974; "Larry," CBS, 1974; "The Kansas City Massacre," ABC, 1975; "Centennial," NBC, 1978-79; "Memorial Day," CBS, 1983; "Perry Mason: The Case of the Lost Love," NBC, 1988.

WALKER, CLINT
b. Hartford, IL, May 30, 1927. Beefy actor who stands over six feet tall; he played wandering crimefighter Cheyenne Bodie in one of the most popular westerns of the fifties.
AS A REGULAR: "Cheyenne (Warner Bros. Presents Cheyenne)," ABC, 1955-58, 1959-63; "Kodiak," ABC, 1974.
AND: "Maverick: Hadley's Hunters," ABC, 1960; "77 Sunset Strip: 5," ABC, 1963; "Kraft Suspense Theatre: Portrait of an Unknown Man," NBC, 1964; "The Lucy Show: Lucy and Clint Walker," CBS, 1965; "The Lucy Show: Lucy and the Sleeping Beauty," CBS, 1966; "The Love Boat: Friend of the Family," ABC, 1983.
TV MOVIES AND MINISERIES: "Yuma," ABC, 1971; "Hardcase," ABC, 1972; "The Bounty Man," ABC, 1972; "Scream of the Wolf," ABC, 1974; "Killdozer," ABC, 1974; "Snowbeast," NBC, 1977; "Centennial," NBC, 1978-79; "The Mysterious Island of Beautiful Women," CBS, 1979.
* Walker walked off the "Cheyenne" set in 1958 in a contract dispute with Warner Bros. The studio began another western series under the "Cheyenne" title, with Ty Hardin as "Bronco" Layne. Walker returned to the show in 1959.

WALKER, JIMMIE
b. Bronx, NY, June 25, 1949. Lanky black comic who was hot in the mid-seventies; he played J.J. Walker on "Good Times" and his trademark was the phrase "Dy-no-MITE!" Well, it seemed funny at the time.
AS A REGULAR: "Good Times," CBS, 1974-79; "B.A.D. Cats," ABC, 1980; "At Ease," ABC, 1983; "Bustin' Loose," SYN, 1987-88.
AND: "The Merv Griffin Show," SYN, 1974; "Perry Como's Summer of '74," CBS, 1974; "Cotton Club '75," NBC, 1974; "Dyn-O-Mite Saturday," CBS, 1975; "Cher," CBS, 1975; "Hollywood Squares," NBC, 1975; "The Merv Griffin Show," SYN, 1975; "Rhyme and Reason," ABC, 1975; "Joys," NBC, 1976; "Match Game '76," CBS, 1976; "The Love Boat: One If by Land," ABC, 1977; "The Love Boat: Till Death Do Us Part," ABC, 1978; "Hollywood Squares," SYN, 1979; "The Love Boat: A Letter to Babycakes," ABC, 1979; "The White Shadow: If Your Number's Up...Get It Down," CBS, 1980; "The John Davidson Show," SYN, 1981; "Cagney & Lacey: Chop Shop," CBS, 1983; "The Fall Guy: Losers Weepers," ABC, 1984; "The Love Boat: Ashes to Ashes," ABC, 1985; "Late Night with David Letterman," NBC, 1987; "Jimmie

Walker and Friends," SHO, 1989.

TV MOVIES AND MINISERIES: "The Greatest Thing
That Almost Happened," CBS, 1977; "Murder
Can Hurt You!," ABC, 1980.

WALKER, NANCY

*b. Anna Myrtle Swoyer, Philadelphia, PA, May
10, 1922.* Diminutive character actress, usually
in comic roles. After a long stage career and some
TV, she hit paydirt as Ida Morgenstern, mother
of Rhoda (Valerie Harper) on "The Mary Tyler
Moore Show" and "Rhoda." She also played
wiseacre maid Mildred on "McMillan and Wife"
and Rosie of paper-towel commercial fame.

AS A REGULAR: "Family Affair," CBS, 1970-71;
"McMillan and Wife," NBC, 1971-76; "Rhoda,"
CBS, 1974-76, 1977-78; "The Nancy Walker
Show," ABC, 1976; "Blansky's Beauties," ABC,
1977; "Mama's Boy," NBC, 1988-89; "True
Colors," FOX, 1990- .

AND: "Medallion Theatre: Voyage Back," CBS,
1954; "Playwrights '56: Nick and Letty," NBC,
1956; "Kraft Theatre: Code of the Corner," NBC,
1958; "The Red Skelton Show," CBS, 1958; "The
Patrice Munsel Show," ABC, 1958; "Arthur Murray
Party," NBC, 1959; "The Big Party," CBS, 1959;
"Perry Como's Kraft Music Hall," NBC, 1960;
"Music for a Spring Night: The Sounds of a City,"
ABC, 1960; "The Tab Hunter Show: I Love a
Marine," NBC, 1960; "Play of the Week: The Girls
in 509," SYN, 1961; "Perry Como's Kraft Music
Hall," NBC, 1961; "The Jack Paar Show," NBC,
1961; "The Ed Sullivan Show," CBS, 1961; "The
Garry Moore Show," CBS, 1962; "The Andy
Williams Show," NBC, 1962; "The Garry Moore
Show," CBS, 1963; "The Garry Moore Show,"
CBS, 1964; "The Mary Tyler Moore Show: Support
Your Local Mother," CBS, 1970; "Kraft Music
Hall," NBC, 1970; "Love, American Style: Love
and the See-Through Man," ABC, 1971; "The Mary
Tyler Moore Show: A Girl's Best Mother Is Not
Her Friend," CBS, 1971; "Love, American Style:
Love and the Oldy-Weds," ABC, 1971; "Keep the
Faith," CBS, 1972; "Medical Center: Cycle of
Peril," CBS, 1972; "The Mary Tyler Moore Show:
Enter Rhoda's Parents," CBS, 1972; "The Partridge
Family: Aspirin at 7, Dinner at 8," ABC, 1972;
"The Mary Tyler Moore Show: Rhoda's Sister Gets
Married," CBS, 1973; "Police Story: Fingerprint,"
NBC, 1974; "Hollywood Squares," NBC, 1974;
"Dinah!," SYN, 1974; "The Carol Burnett Show,"
CBS, 1975; "Tony Orlando and Dawn," CBS, 1975;
"Paul Lynde Special," ABC, 1975; "Happy Days:
Second Anniversary Special," ABC, 1976; "The
Love Boat: Home Sweet Home," ABC, 1978; "The
Mary Tyler Moore Hour," CBS, 1979; "The Love
Boat: A Honeymoon for Horace," ABC, 1982.

TV MOVIES AND MINISERIES: "Every Man Needs
One," ABC, 1972; "Thursday's Game," ABC,
1974; "Death Scream," ABC, 1975; "Human
Feelings," NBC, 1978.

AS DIRECTOR: "The Mary Tyler Moore Show: Just
Friends," CBS, 1973; "The Mary Tyler Moore
Show: Two Wrongs Don't Make a Writer,"
CBS, 1974.

WALLACE, MARCIA

b. Creston, IA, November 1, 1942. Lanky actress
who played dry-witted receptionist Carol Kester
on "The Bob Newhart Show."

AS A REGULAR: "The Bob Newhart Show," CBS,
1972-78.

AND: "The Merv Griffin Show," SYN, 1968; "The
Brady Bunch: Will the Real Jan Brady," ABC,
1970; "The Merv Griffin Show," CBS, 1970;
"Columbo: Murder by the Book," NBC, 1971;
"The $10,000 Pyramid," ABC, 1975; "Hollywood
Squares," SYN, 1975; "The Love Boat: Musical
Cabins," ABC, 1978; "Cross Wits," SYN, 1979;
"Hollywood Squares," SYN, 1980; "Card Sharks,"
NBC, 1980; "Taxi: The Shloogel Show," NBC,
1982.

TV MOVIES AND MINISERIES: "Flying High," CBS,
1978.

WALLACE, MIKE

b. Myron Wallace, Brookline, MA, May 9, 1918.
Legendary TV reporter who began as a game
show emcee and announcer; he didn't get a
reputation as a hard-nosed interviewer until the
late fifties.

AS A REGULAR: "Stand by for Crime," ABC, 1949;
"Majority Rules," ABC, 1949-50; "Guess
Again," CBS, 1951; "All Around the Town,"
CBS, 1951-52; "I'll Buy That," CBS, 1953-54;
"Who's the Boss?," ABC, 1954; "What's in a
Word?," CBS, 1954; "The Big Surprise," NBC,
1956-57; "Mike Wallace Interviews," ABC,
1957-58; CBS, 1959-60; "Who Pays?," NBC,
1959; "Race for Space," SYN, 1960; "Biography," SYN, 1961-64; "60 Minutes," CBS,
1968- .

AND: "The Colgate Comedy Hour," NBC, 1951;
"Summer Studio One: The Roman Kid," CBS,
1953; "Studio One: For the Defense," CBS, 1955;
"To Tell the Truth," CBS, 1956; "The Seven Lively
Arts: The Changing Ways of Love," CBS, 1957;
"Night Clubs, New York," CBS, 1960; "Startime:
Well, What About You?," NBC, 1960; "Revlon
Revue: Accent on Comedy," CBS, 1960; "The Jack
Benny Program," CBS, 1960.

* Emmies: 1971, 1972, 1973.

WALLACH, ELI

b. Brooklyn, NY, December 7, 1915. Stage and
film actor ("Baby Doll," "The Magnificent
Seven") who used live TV drama as his training
ground.

AS A REGULAR: "Our Family Honor," ABC, 1985-
86.

AND: "Lights Out: Rappaccini's Daughter," NBC,

1951; "Danger: The System," CBS, 1952; "Summer Theatre: Stan, the Killer," CBS, 1952; "The Web: Deadlock," CBS, 1952; "Philco TV Playhouse: The Baby," NBC, 1953; "Goodyear TV Playhouse: The Brownstone," NBC, 1954; "Philco TV Playhouse: Shadow of the Champ," NBC, 1955; "G.E. Theatre: Mr. Blue Ocean," CBS, 1955; "Philco TV Playhouse: The Outsiders," NBC, 1955; "Kaiser Aluminum Hour: A Fragile Affair," NBC, 1956; "Hallmark Hall of Fame: The Lark," NBC, 1957; "Studio One: The Man Who Wasn't Himself," CBS, 1957; "Arthur Murray Party," NBC, 1958; "Playhouse 90: For Whom the Bell Tolls," CBS, 1959; "Du Pont Show of the Month: I, Don Quixote," CBS, 1959; "Salute to the American Theatre," CBS, 1959; "Sunday Showcase: The Margaret Bourke-White Story," NBC, 1960; "Goodyear Theatre: Birthright," NBC, 1960; "Naked City: A Death of Princes," ABC, 1960; "Robert Herridge Theatre: Hope is the Thing with Feathers," SYN, 1960; "Play of the Week: Lullaby," SYN, 1960; "Camera Three: The Synagogue and the Sacred," CBS, 1961; "The Outlaws: A Bit of Glory," NBC, 1962; "Naked City: A Run for the Money," ABC, 1962; "The Dick Powell Show: Tomorrow the Man," NBC, 1962; "The Merv Griffin Show," NBC, 1963; "ABC Nightlife," ABC, 1964; "The Poppy Is Also a Flower," ABC, 1966; "Batman: Ice Spy/The Duo Defy," ABC, 1967; "The Merv Griffin Show," SYN, 1967; "CBS Playhouse: Dear Friends," CBS, 1967; "NET Playhouse: Paradise Lost," NET, 1971; "Hollywood Television Theatre: The Typists," NET, 1971; "The Great American Dream Machine," NET, 1971; "Orson Welles' Great Mysteries: Compliments of the Season," SYN, 1973; "Kojak: A Question of Answers," CBS, 1975; CBS, 1975; "G.E. Theatre: Twenty Shades of Pink," CBS, 1976; "Highway to Heaven: A Father's Faith," NBC, 1986; "Murder, She Wrote: A Very Good Year for Murder," CBS, 1988; "CBS Schoolbreak Special: A Matter of Conscience," CBS, 1989.

TV MOVIES AND MINISERIES: "A Cold Night's Death," ABC, 1973; "Indict and Convict," ABC, 1973; "Best Sellers: Seventh Avenue," NBC, 1977; "The Pirate," CBS, 1978; "The Pride of Jesse Hallam," CBS, 1981; "Skokie," CBS, 1981; "The Wall," CBS, 1982; "The Executioner's Song," NBC, 1982; "Embassy," ABC, 1985; "Christopher Columbus," CBS, 1985; "Murder: By Reason of Insanity," CBS, 1985; "Sam's Son," NBC, 1984; "Something in Common," CBS, 1986.
* Emmies: 1967.

WALLEY, DEBORAH
b. Bridgeport, CT, August 12, 1943. Actress who played Susie Hubbard Buell on "The Mothers-in-Law."

AS A REGULAR: "The Mothers-in-Law," NBC, 1967-69.
AND: "Route 66: Ten Drops of Water," CBS, 1960; "The Ed Sullivan Show," CBS, 1962; "Gomer Pyle, USMC: Lies, Lies, Lies," CBS, 1966; "Love, American Style: Love and the Anxious Mama," ABC, 1972; "Simon & Simon: The Last Big Break," CBS, 1986.

WALMSLEY, JON
b. England, February 6, 1956. Actor who played Jason Walton.
AS A REGULAR: "The Waltons," CBS, 1972-81.
AND: "The Bill Cosby Show: A Word From Our Sponsor," NBC, 1969; "Combat!: The Furlough," ABC, 1966; "$weepstake$: Billy, Wally and Ludmilla, and Theodore," NBC, 1979.
TV MOVIES AND MINISERIES: "The Homecoming," CBS, 1971; "A Wedding on Walton's Mountain," NBC, 1982; "A Day for Thanks on Waltons Mountain," NBC, 1982.

WALSTON, RAY
b. New Orleans, LA, November 22, 1918. Stage actor best known as Uncle Martin on "My Favorite Martian" and as nerdy high school Mr. Hand in the film "Fast Times at Ridgemont High" and its TV spinoff.
AS A REGULAR: "My Favorite Martian," CBS, 1963-66; "Stop Susan Williams," NBC, 1979; "Silver Spoons," NBC, 1985; "Fast Times," CBS, 1986.
AND: "Studio One: The Hero," CBS, 1954; "Producers Showcase: State of the Union," NBC, 1954; "Hallmark Hall of Fame: There Shall Be No Night," NBC, 1957; "The Perry Como Show," NBC, 1958; "The Arthur Godfrey Show," CBS, 1958; "Playhouse 90: Shadows Tremble," CBS, 1958; "Ellery Queen: This Murder Comes to You Live," NBC, 1959; "Music From Shubert Alley," NBC, 1959; "Buick Electra Playhouse: The Killers," CBS, 1959; "Perry Como's Kraft Music Hall," NBC, 1960; "Saints and Sinners: Judgment in Jazz Alley," NBC, 1962; "The Wide Country: The Girl in the Sunshine Smile," NBC, 1962; "Ben Casey: The White Ones Are Dolphins," ABC, 1963; "Going My Way: The Reformation of Willie," ABC, 1963; "Talent Scouts," CBS, 1963; "Summer Playhouse: Satan's Waitin'," CBS, 1964; "The Man Who Bought Paradise," CBS, 1965; "Art Linkletter's Hollywood Talent Scouts," CBS, 1966; "The Wild Wild West: The Night of Montezuma's Hordes," CBS, 1967; "Garrison's Gorillas: The Crime Wave," ABC, 1967; "Custer: Breakout," ABC, 1967; "The Donald O'Connor Show," SYN, 1968; "Love, American Style: Love and the Boss's Ex," ABC, 1970; "The Mod Squad: A Double for Danger," ABC, 1971; "Ironside: Ring of Prayer," NBC, 1971; "Love, American Style: Love and the Fullback," ABC, 1972; "Mission: Impossible: TOD-5," CBS, 1972; "The Paul Lynde Show: Meet Aunt Charlotte," ABC, 1972; "Buck Rogers in the

25th Century: Cosmic Whiz Kid," NBC, 1979; "Little House on the Prairie: The King Is Dead," NBC, 1979; "Simon & Simon: Murder Between the Lines," CBS, 1983; "Gimme a Break: The Center," NBC, 1984; "Newhart: Tell a Lie, Get a Check," CBS, 1984; "The Love Boat: Santa, Santa, Santa," ABC, 1985; "St. Elsewhere: Getting Ahead," NBC, 1987; "Simon & Simon: For Old Crimes's Sake," CBS, 1987; "Murder, She Wrote: The Way to Dusty Death," CBS, 1987; "ABC Afterschool Special: Runaway Ralph," ABC, 1988.

TV MOVIES AND MINISERIES: "This Girl for Hire," CBS, 1983; "The Jerk, Too," NBC, 1984; "Amos," CBS, 1985; "Red River," CBS, 1988; "I Know My First Name Is Steven," NBC, 1989; "Class Cruise," NBC, 1989.

WALTER, JESSICA

b. Brooklyn, NY, January 31, 1940. Attractive brunette actress who won an Emmy as police chief Amy Prentiss.

AS A REGULAR: "Love of Life," CBS, 1962-65; "For the People," CBS, 1965; "Amy Prentiss," NBC, 1974-75; "Bare Essence," NBC, 1983; "Aaron's Way," NBC, 1988.

AND: "Route 66: A Long Way From St. Louis," CBS, 1963; "East Side/West Side: Take Sides with the Sun," CBS, 1964; "The Alfred Hitchcock Hour: The Ordeal of Mrs. Snow," CBS, 1964; "Ben Casey: August Is the Month Before Christmas," ABC, 1964; "Flipper: 300 Feet Below," NBC, 1964; "The Doctors and the Nurses: The Suspect," CBS, 1964; "The Reporter: How Much for a Prince?," CBS, 1964; "The Fugitive: The White Knight," ABC, 1966; "Pursue and Destroy," ABC, 1966; "The FBI: Rope of Gold," ABC, 1967; "The FBI: Counter-Stroke," ABC, 1967; "Kiss Me, Kate," ABC, 1968; "The FBI: Death of a Fixer," ABC, 1968; "The Name of the Game: The Ordeal," NBC, 1968; "Then Came Bronson: Where Will the Trumpets Be?," NBC, 1969; "Love, American Style: Love and the Big Leap," ABC, 1969; "Mannix: Who Is Sylvia?," CBS, 1970; "Mission: Impossible: Orpheus," CBS, 1970; "The Most Deadly Game: Breakdown," ABC, 1970; "Love, American Style: Love and the Kidnapper," ABC, 1971; "Marcus Welby, M.D.: A More Exciting Case," ABC, 1972; "The FBI: The Gathering of Sharks," ABC, 1973; "Love, American Style: Love and the Twanger Tutor," ABC, 1973; "Banacek: The Two Million Clams of Cap'n Jack," NBC, 1973; "Mannix: The Danford File," CBS, 1973; "The Streets of San Francisco: The Stamp of Death," ABC, 1973; "Tenafly: The Cash and Carry Caper," NBC, 1973; "Medical Center: Woman for Hire," CBS, 1973; "Love, American Style: Love and the Weirdo," ABC, 1973; "Barnaby Jones: Venus as in Fly Trap," CBS, 1974; "Columbo: Mind Over Mayhem," NBC, 1974; "The Magician: The Illusion of the Evil Spikes," NBC, 1974; "Ironside: Amy Prentiss, A.K.A. The Chief," NBC,

1974; "The Rookies: Take Over," ABC, 1974; "Barnaby Jones: Dead Man's Run," CBS, 1974; "Hawaii Five-O: The Two-Faced Corpse," CBS, 1974; "McCloud: The Park Avenue Pirates," NBC, 1975; "The Carol Burnett Show," CBS, 1975; "The Streets of San Francisco: Till Death Do Us Part," ABC, 1976; "McMillan: All Bets Are Off," NBC, 1976; "Quincy: Images," NBC, 1978; "The Love Boat: We Three," ABC, 1979; "The Love Boat: Doc's Dismissal," ABC, 1981; "The Love Boat: Three in a Bed," ABC, 1982; "Three's a Crowd: The Maternal Triangle," ABC, 1984; "The Love Boat: The Problem with Poppa," ABC, 1985; "Murder, She Wrote: Magnum on Ice," CBS, 1986; "ABC Afterschool Specials: Just Another Kid: An AIDS Story," ABC, 1987; "J.J. Starbuck: Murder by Design," NBC, 1988.

TV MOVIES AND MINISERIES: "The Immortal," ABC, 1969; "Three's a Crowd," ABC, 1969; "They Call It Murder," NBC, 1971; "Women in Chains," ABC, 1972; "Hurricane," ABC, 1974; "Having Babies," ABC, 1976; "Black Market Baby," ABC, 1977; "Arthur Hailey's Wheels," NBC, 1978; "Secrets of Three Hungry Wives," NBC, 1978; "Vampire," ABC, 1979; "She's Dressed to Kill," NBC, 1979; "Miracle on Ice," ABC, 1981; "Thursday's Child," CBS, 1983; "The Execution," NBC, 1985; "Killer in the Mirror," NBC, 1986.

* Emmies: 1975.

WALTERS, BARBARA

b. Boston, MA, September 25, 1931. Interviewer who's as much, if not more, of a celebrity than the people she grills; ABC lured her from NBC in 1976 with a million dollar-a-year contract.

AS A REGULAR: "Today," NBC, 1963-76; "Not for Women Only," SYN, 1972-76; "ABC Evening News," ABC, 1976-78; "Barbara Walters Special," ABC, 1976- ; "20/20," ABC, 1981- .

AND: "The Mike Douglas Show," SYN, 1965; "The Mike Douglas Show," SYN, 1967; "ABC Comedy Hour," ABC, 1972; "Fifty Years of Television: A Golden Celebration," CBS, 1989.

WARD, BURT

b. Los Angeles, CA, July 6, 1945. Holy leotards, Batman! It's Robin, the boy wonder!

AS A REGULAR: "Batman," ABC, 1966-68; "The New Adventures of Batman," CBS, 1977-78.

WARD, JAY

b. 1920; d. 1989. Brilliant animation producer-writer reponsible for Bullwinkle J. Moose, Super Chicken, Tom Slick, time-traveling Mr. Peabody and his boy, Sherman, and many others.

AS PRODUCER-CREATOR-WRITER: "Rocky and His Friends," ABC, 1959-61; "The Bullwinkle Show," NBC, 1961-73; "George of the Jungle," ABC, 1967-70.

WARDEN, JACK

b. Newark, NJ, September 18, 1930. Former prizefighter who specializes in playing lovable lugs; he was "Jigsaw John" and detective Harry Fox on "Crazy Like a Fox," and he won an Emmy for "Brian's Song."

AS A REGULAR: "Mr. Peepers," NBC, 1953-55; "Norby," NBC, 1955; "The Asphalt Jungle," ABC, 1961; "The Wackiest Ship in the Army," NBC, 1965-66; "NYPD," ABC, 1967-69; "Jigsaw John," NBC, 1976; "The Bad News Bears," CBS, 1979-80; "Crazy Like a Fox," CBS, 1984-86; "Knight and Daye," NBC, 1989.

AND: "Kaiser Aluminum Hour: A Real Fine Cutting Edge," NBC, 1957; "Hallmark Hall of Fame: The Lark," NBC, 1957; "U.S. Steel Hour: Up Above the World So High," CBS, 1957; "Suspicion: The Flight," NBC, 1957; "The Ed Sullivan Show," CBS, 1958; "Playhouse 90: Nightmare at Ground Zero," CBS, 1958; "Playhouse 90: The Blue Men," CBS, 1959; "Playhouse 90: The Day Before Atlanta," CBS, 1959; "The Twilight Zone: The Lonely," CBS, 1959; "The Untouchables: The George 'Bugs' Moran Story," ABC, 1960; "Ben Casey: The Trouble with Charlie," ABC, 1962; "Tales of Wells Fargo: The Traveler," NBC, 1962; "The Virginian: Throw a Long Rope," NBC, 1962; "Going My Way: Not Good Enough for My Sister," ABC, 1962; "Ben Casey: I Hear America Singing," ABC, 1962; "Naked City: Spectre of the Rose Street Gang," ABC, 1962; "Route 66: Two Strangers and an Old Enemy," CBS, 1963; "The Breaking Point: No Squares in My Family Circle," ABC, 1964; "Bob Hope Chrysler Theatre: Out on the Outskirts of Town," NBC, 1964; "Slattery's People: Question-Is Laura the Name of the Game?," CBS, 1964; "Bewitched: It Shouldn't Happen to a Dog," ABC, 1964; "Wagon Train: The Mary Lee McIntosh Story," ABC, 1965; "Walt Disney's Wonderful World of Color: Gallegher," NBC, 1965; "Dr. Kildare: No Mother to Guide Them," NBC, 1965; "The Virginian: Shadows of the Past," NBC, 1965.

TV MOVIES AND MINISERIES: "The Face of Fear," CBS, 1971; "Brian's Song," ABC, 1971; "What's a Nice Girl Like You...?," ABC, 1971; "Man on a String," ABC, 1972; "Lieutenant Schuster's Wife," ABC, 1972; "Remember When," NBC, 1974; "The Godchild," ABC, 1974; "Journey from Darkness," NBC, 1975; "They Only Come Out at Night," NBC, 1975; "Raid on Entebbe," NBC, 1977; "Topper," ABC, 1979; "A Private Battle," CBS, 1980; "Hobson's Choice," CBS, 1983; "A.D.," NBC, 1985; "Still Crazy Like a Fox," CBS, 1987; "The Three Kings," ABC, 1987; "Police Story: The Watch Commander," ABC, 1988.

* **Emmies:** 1972.

WARING, FRED

b. Tyrone, PA, June 9, 1900; d. 1984. Bandleader and blender inventor.

AS A REGULAR: "The Fred Waring Show," CBS, 1949-54.

AND: "President's Birthday Party," CBS, 1956; "The Perry Como Show," NBC, 1956; "Club Oasis," NBC, 1957; "The Voice of Firestone," ABC, 1958; "The Voice of Firestone: Easter Program," ABC, 1959; "The du Pont Show: Fred Waring's Unforgettables," NBC, 1961; "Bell Telephone Hour," NBC, 1963.

WARNER, MALCOLM-JAMAL

b. Jersey City, NJ, August 18, 1970. Actor who plays Theo Huxtable on "The Cosby Show."

AS A REGULAR: "The Cosby Show," NBC, 1984- .

AND: "Call to Glory: A Nation Divided," ABC, 1984; "Saturday Night Live," NBC, 1986; "Matlock: The Producer," NBC, 1987; "A Different World: Risky Business," NBC, 1989.

TV MOVIES AND MINISERIES: "Hallmark Hall of Fame: Foxfire," CBS, 1987; "Mother's Day," FAM, 1989.

WARREN, LESLEY ANN

b. New York City, NY, August 16, 1946. Actress-singer who was cast as Cinderella just out of her teens; now she often plays women of easy virtue in TV movies.

AS A REGULAR: "Mission: Impossible," CBS, 1970-71.

AND: "Cinderella," CBS, 1966; "Love, American Style: Love and the Divorce Sale," ABC, 1969; "The Don Knotts Show," NBC, 1970; "Columbo: A Deadly State of Mind," NBC, 1975; "SWAT: Deadly Tide," ABC, 1975; "Jigsaw John: Too Much, Too Soon," NBC, 1976; "The Andy Williams Show," SYN, 1977.

TV MOVIES AND MINISERIES: "Seven in Darkness," ABC, 1969; "Love, Hate, Love," ABC, 1971; "Assignment: Munich," ABC, 1972; "The Daughters of Joshua Cabe," ABC, 1972; "The Letters," ABC, 1973; "The Legend of Valentino," ABC, 1975; "Harold Robbins' 79 Park Avenue," NBC, 1977; "Betrayal," NBC, 1978; "Pearl," ABC, 1978; "Portrait of a Stripper," CBS, 1979; "Beulah Land," NBC, 1980; "Portrait of a Showgirl," CBS, 1982; "Evergreen," NBC, 1985.

WARREN, MICHAEL

b. South Bend, IN, March 5, 1946. Actor who played Off. Bobby Hill on "Hill Street Blues."

AS A REGULAR: "Sierra," NBC, 1974; "Paris," CBS, 1979-80; "Hill Street Blues," NBC, 1981-87.

AND: "Marcus Welby, M.D.: Cross-Match," ABC, 1972; "The White Shadow: Wanna Bet," CBS, 1979; "Lou Grant: Marathon," CBS, 1979; "In the

Heat of the Night: The Hammer and the Glove,"
NBC, 1988; "L.A. Law: Izzy Ackerman, Or Is He
Not?," NBC, 1989; "A Little Bit Strange," NBC,
1989; "ABC Afterschool Special: Private
Affairs," ABC, 1989.
TV MOVIES AND MINISERIES: "The Child Saver,"
NBC, 1988.

WARRICK, RUTH
b. St. Joseph, MO, June 29, 1916. Film actress
who plays soap-villianess-for-all-seasons
Phoebe Tyler on "All My Children."
AS A REGULAR: "The Guiding Light," CBS, 1955-
56; "As the World Turns," CBS, 1956-60;
"Father of the Bride," CBS, 1961-62; "Peyton
Place," ABC, 1965-67; "All My Children,"
ABC, 1970- .
AND: "Ellery Queen: Body of the Crime," NBC,
1959; "Ellery Queen: The Chemistry Set," NBC,
1959; "Here's Hollywood," NBC, 1962; "Art
Linkletter's House Party," CBS, 1962;
"Gunsmoke: The Storm," CBS, 1965; "The Man
From UNCLE: The Seven Wonders of the World
Affair," NBC, 1968; "The Mike Douglas Show,"
SYN, 1977; "The Love Boat: The Victims," ABC,
1982.

WASHINGTON, DENZEL
b. Mount Vernon, NY, December 28, 1954.
Actor who played Dr. Phil Chandler on "St.
Elsewhere"; now he's in the movies ("Cry
Freedom," "Mo' Better Blues").
AS A REGULAR: "St. Elsewhere," NBC, 1982-88.
TV MOVIES AND MINISERIES: "Flesh and Blood,"
CBS, 1979; "The George McKenna Story,"
CBS, 1986.

WATERS, ETHEL
b. Chester, PA, October 31, 1900; d. 1977.
Legendary actress and singer of the twenties
and thirties; she played Beulah, the level-
headed maid who always had to rescue her
bumbling white employers and toward the end
of her life she did many religious broadcasts.
AS A REGULAR: "Beulah," ABC, 1950-52.
AND: "Favorite Playhouse: Speaking of Hannah,"
CBS, 1955; "Climax!: The Dance," CBS, 1955;
"G.E. Theatre: Winner by Decision," CBS, 1955;
"Playwrights '56: The Sound and the Fury," NBC,
1955; "Break the $250,000 Bank," NBC, 1956;
"Saturday Spectacular: Manhattan Tower," NBC,
1956; "The Steve Allen Show," NBC, 1956;
"Matinee Theatre: Sing for Me," NBC, 1957;
"Whirlybirds: The Big Lie," SYN, 1959; "Route
66: Good Night, Sweet Blues," CBS, 1961; "The
Great Adventure: Go Down, Moses," CBS, 1963;
"Professor Hubert Abernathy," CBS, 1967;
"Owen Marshall, Counselor at Law: Run, Carol,
Run," ABC, 1972; "The Mike Douglas Show,"
SYN, 1976.

* Waters went on "Break the $250,000 Bank" to
win money to pay back taxes; she won
$10,000.

WATERSTON, SAM
b. Cambridge, MA, November 15, 1940. Film
("Interiors," "Crimes and Misdemeanors") and
TV actor, usually in cerebral roles.
AS A REGULAR: "QED," CBS, 1982.
AND: "Much Ado About Nothing," NET, 1973;
"Amazing Stories: Mirror, Mirror," NBC, 1986;
"American Playhouse: A Walk in the Woods,"
PBS, 1989.
TV MOVIES AND MINISERIES: "The Glass Menag-
erie," ABC, 1973; "Reflections on Murder,"
ABC, 1974; "ABC Theatre: Friendly Fire,"
ABC, 1979; "Games Mother Never Taught
You," CBS, 1982; "In Defense of Kids," CBS,
1983; "Dempsey," CBS, 1983; "American
Playhouse: Oppenheimer," PBS, 1983-84;
"Finnegan Begin Again," HBO, 1985; "Love
Lives On," ABC, 1985; "The Fifth Missile,"
NBC, 1986; "The Room Upstairs," CBS, 1987;
"Gore Vidal's Lincoln," NBC, 1988; "Terrorist
on Trial: The United States vs. Salim Ajami,"
CBS, 1988.

WATKINS, CARLENE
b. Hartford, CT, June 4, 1952. Attractive,
talented actress usually in comic roles; she
plays the ex-wife of "Dear John" (Judd
Hirsch).
AS A REGULAR: "The Secret Empire," NBC, 1979;
"Best of the West," ABC, 1981-82; "It's Not
Easy," ABC, 1983; "Mary," CBS, 1985-86;
"The Tortellis," NBC, 1987; "Dear John,"
NBC, 1988- .
AND: "Columbo: The Bye-Bye Sky High I.Q.
Murder Case," NBC, 1977; "B.J. and the Bear:
Snow White and the Seven Truckers," NBC,
1979; "The Love Boat: The Joy of Celebacy,"
ABC, 1981; "Nero Wolfe: The Golden Spiders,"
NBC, 1981; "Taxi: The Shloogel Show," NBC,
1982; "Remington Steele: In the Steele of the
Night," NBC, 1982; "Magnum, P.I.: Basket
Case," CBS, 1983; "The Love Boat: Ace in the
Hole," ABC, 1984; "The Love Boat: Hippies and
Yuppies," ABC, 1986.

WATSON, DEBBIE
b. Los Angeles, CA, January 17, 1949. Perky
actress of sixties TV who played cute-as-a-bug
teenagers in two sitcoms.
AS A REGULAR: "Karen," NBC, 1964-65;
"Tammy," ABC, 1965-66.
AND: "The Virginian: Requiem for a Country
Doctor," NBC, 1967; "The Virginian: Eileen,"
NBC, 1969; "Love, American Style: Love and the
First-Nighters," ABC, 1970.

WATSON, DOUGLASS

b. Larkin Douglass Watson III, Jackson, GA, February 24, 1921; d. 1989. Actor who played the beloved Mackenzie Cory on "Another World."

AS A REGULAR: "Moment of Truth," NBC, 1965; "Search for Tomorrow," CBS, 1967-68; "Love of Life," CBS, 1972-73; "Another World," NBC, 1974-89.

AND: "Starlight Theatre: The Sire de Maletroit's Door," CBS, 1950; "Masterpiece Playhouse: Richard III," NBC, 1950; "Kraft Television Theatre: Brief Candle," NBC, 1951; "Robert Montgomery Presents: The Young and Beautiful," NBC, 1956; "Hallmark Hall of Fame: Man and Superman," NBC, 1956; "Goodyear TV Playhouse: The Dark Side of the Moon," NBC, 1957; "CBS Television Workshop: The Conversion of Buster Drumwright," CBS, 1960; "Look Up and Live: Belief, Work and Charity - Job," CBS, 1962; "Hallmark Hall of Fame: Abe Lincoln in Illinois," NBC, 1964; "The Eternal Light: Inscription for a Blank Page," NBC, 1964; "The Doctors and the Nurses: A Couple of Dozen Tiny Pills," CBS, 1965; "Liquid Fire," NET, 1968; "The Bold Ones: Lisa, I Hardly Knew You," NBC, 1972; "Much Ado About Nothing," NET, 1973.

WAXMAN, AL

b. Canada, March 2, 1935. Heavyset actor who played Lt. Bert Samuels on "Cagney & Lacey."
AS A REGULAR: "Cagney & Lacey," CBS, 1982-88.
TV MOVIES AND MINISERIES: "When Michael Calls," ABC, 1972; "Cagney & Lacey," CBS, 1981.

WAYNE, DAVID

b. David McMeekan, Traverse City, MI, January 30, 1914. Slight, engaging actor often in comic roles in film ("Adam's Rib," "How to Marry a Millionaire") and TV; he played Willard "Digger" Barnes on "Dallas" and Dr. Amos Weatherby on "House Calls."

AS A REGULAR: "Norby," NBC, 1955; "The Good Life," NBC, 1971-72; "Ellery Queen," NBC, 1975-76; "Dallas," CBS, 1978; "House Calls," CBS, 1979-82.

AND: "Studio One: The Dreams of Jasper Hornby," CBS, 1950; "Omnibus: The Sojourner," CBS, 1953; "Producers Showcase: Darkness at Noon," NBC, 1955; "Alcoa Hour: Morning's at Seven," NBC, 1956; "Ruggles of Red Gap," NBC, 1957; "Alfred Hitchcock Presents: One More Mile to Go," CBS, 1957; "The Big Record," CBS, 1957; "Suspicion: Heartbeat," NBC, 1957; "Playhouse 90: The Jet-Propelled Couch," CBS, 1957; "Du Pont Show of the Month: Junior Miss," CBS, 1957; "The Frank Sinatra Show: The Feeling Is Mutual," ABC, 1957; "The Ed Sullivan Show," CBS, 1958; "The Perry Como Show," NBC, 1958; "Rendez-vous: The Incurable Wound," CBS, 1959; "Alcoa

Theatre: Operation Spark," NBC, 1959; "The Jack Paar Show," NBC, 1959; "The Strawberry Blonde," NBC, 1959; "The Twilight Zone: Escape Clause," CBS, 1959; "The Devil and Daniel Webster," NBC, 1960; "Arthur Murray Party," NBC, 1960; "G.E. Theatre: Do Not Disturb," CBS, 1960; "Our American Heritage: Millionaire's Mite," NBC, 1960; "Arthur Murray Party," NBC, 1960; "The Overland Trail: Escort Detail," NBC, 1960; "Wagon Train: The Shad Bennington Story," NBC, 1960; "The Outlaws: No More Pencils - No More Books," NBC, 1961; "Here's Hollywood," NBC, 1961; "The Outlaws: Roly," NBC, 1961; "Alcoa Premiere: Delbert, Texas," ABC, 1961; "Password," CBS, 1961; "Route 66: Aren't You Surprised to See Me?," CBS, 1962; "U.S. Steel Hour: The White Lie," CBS, 1962; "Hallmark Hall of Fame: Teahouse of the August Moon," NBC, 1962; "The Alfred Hitchcock Hour: The Thirty-First of February," CBS, 1963; "Sam Benedict: The Boiling Point," NBC, 1963; "The Dick Powell Show: Apples Don't Fall Far," NBC, 1963; "The Virginian: The Small Parade," NBC, 1963; "The Cowboy and the Tiger," NBC, 1963; "Channing: The Last Testament of Buddy Crown," ABC, 1963; "Burke's Law: Who Killed the Horne of Plenty?," ABC, 1964; "Mr. Broadway: Pay Now, Die Later," CBS, 1964; "The Bing Crosby Show: Music Hath Charms," ABC, 1964; "Hallmark Hall of Fame: Lamp at Midnight," NBC, 1966; "Batman: The Thirteenth Hat/Batman Stands Pat," ABC, 1966; "Bob Hope Chrysler Theatre: Holloway's Daughter," NBC, 1966; "Batman: The Contaminated Cowl/The Mad Hatter Runs a Foul," ABC, 1967; "CBS Playhouse: Dear Friends," CBS, 1967; "The Merv Griffin Show," SYN, 1968; "Arsenic and Old Lace," ABC, 1969; "Walt Disney's Wonderful World of Color: The Boy Who Stole the Elephants," NBC, 1970; "The Name of the Game: A Sister From Napoli," NBC, 1971; "The Good Life," NBC, 1971; "Men at Law: The Truth, the Whole Truth and Anything Else That Works," CBS, 1971; "Medical Center: The Shattered Man," CBS, 1971; "Night Gallery: The Diary," NBC, 1971; "Cade's County: One Small, Acceptable Death," CBS, 1972; "The Streets of San Francisco: In the Midst of Strangers," ABC, 1972; "Mannix: To Quote a Dead Man," CBS, 1973; "Faraday and Company: Premiere," NBC, 1973; "Ironside: Downhill All the Way," NBC, 1973; "Gunsmoke: Lynch Town," CBS, 1973; "Hawaii Five-O: 30,000 Rooms, and I Have the Key," CBS, 1974; "Barnaby Jones: Dark Legacy," CBS, 1974; "Gunsmoke: I Have Promises to Keep," CBS, 1975; "Benjamin Franklin: The Statesman," CBS, 1975; "It's a Bird, It's a Plane, It's Superman," ABC, 1975; "The Treasure Chest Murder," ABC, 1975; "Barney Miller: Bureaucrat," ABC, 1975; "Switch: Dancer," CBS, 1977; "Family: The

Covenant," ABC, 1978; "Eight Is Enough: Fathers and Other Strangers," ABC, 1979; "Matt Houston: Heritage," ABC, 1983; "St. Elsewhere: Dr. Wylie, I Presume?," NBC, 1984; "St. Elsewhere: Whistle, Wylie Works," NBC, 1985; "St. Elsewhere: Bye George," NBC, 1985; "Murder, She Wrote: Murder Takes the Bus," CBS, 1985; "Newhart: Pirate Pete," CBS, 1985.

TV MOVIES AND MINISERIES: "The Catcher," NBC, 1972; "The FBI Story: Alvin Karpis, Public Enemy Number One," CBS, 1974; "Ellery Queen," NBC, 1975; "Best Sellers: Once an Eagle," NBC, 1976; "In the Glitter Palace," NBC, 1977; "Black Beauty," NBC, 1978; "Loose Change," NBC, 1978; "The Gift of Love," ABC, 1978; "The Girls in the Office," ABC, 1979; "Poker Alice," CBS, 1987.

WAYNE, JOHN
b. Marion Michael Morrison, Winterset, IA, May 26, 1907; d. 1979. Movie legend who warmed to TV toward the end of his career.

AS A GUEST: "I Love Lucy: Lucy and John Wayne," CBS, 1955; "Screen Directors Playhouse: Rookie of the Year," NBC, 1955; "Wide, Wide World: The Western," NBC, 1958; "The Spirit of the Alamo," ABC, 1960; "The Jack Benny Program," CBS, 1960; "Wagon Train: The Colter Craven Story," NBC, 1960; "Alcoa Premiere: Flashing Spikes," ABC, 1962; "The Dean Martin Show," NBC, 1965; "The Lucy Show: Lucy and John Wayne," CBS, 1966; "The Dean Martin Show," NBC, 1966; "The Beverly Hillbillies: The Indians Are Coming," CBS, 1967; "The Red Skelton Hour," CBS, 1969; "The Movie Game," SYN, 1970; "Plimpton! Shootout at Rio Lobo," ABC, 1970; "The American West of John Ford," CBS, 1971; "Rowan & Martin's Laugh-In," NBC, 1972; "A Salute to Television's 25th Anniversary," ABC, 1972; "Maude: Maude Meets the Duke," CBS, 1974; "Inaugural Eve Special," CBS, 1977; "General Electric's All-Star Anniversary," ABC, 1978.

WAYNE, JOHNNY
b. Canada;
& SHUSTER, FRANK
b. Canada. Canadian comedy team who apparently were big favorites of Ed Sullivan.

AS REGULARS: "Holiday Lodge," CBS, 1961; "Wayne and Shuster Take an Affectionate Look at ...," CBS, 1966.

AND: "The Lux Show with Rosemary Clooney," NBC, 1958; "The Ed Sullivan Show," CBS, 1958; "The Ed Sullivan Show: Man of the Hour," CBS, 1958; "The Ed Sullivan Show," CBS, 1959; "The Ed Sullivan Show," CBS, 1960; "The Dinah Shore Chevy Show," NBC, 1961; "The Red Skelton Show," CBS, 1961; "The Ed Sullivan Show," CBS, 1961; "The Ed Sullivan Show," CBS, 1962; "The Ed Sullivan Show," CBS, 1963; "The Ed Sullivan Show," CBS, 1967.

WEATHERLY, SHAWN
b. Sumter, SC, 1960. Attractive actress who's functioned as window dressing on a couple of routine shows; when Weatherly wanted out of "Baywatch," the producers obliged by having her lifeguard character eaten by a shark.

AS A REGULAR: "Shaping Up," ABC, 1984; "Oceanquest," NBC, 1985; "J.J. Starbuck," NBC, 1987-88; "Baywatch," NBC, 1989-90.

AND: "Hunter: The Shooter," CBS, 1985; "Private Eye: Star," NBC, 1988.

TV MOVIES AND MINISERIES: "Baywatch: Panic at Malibu Pier," NBC, 1989.

WEAVER, DENNIS
b. Joplin, MO, June 4, 1925. Lanky actor usually in easy-going roles; he won an Emmy as limping deputy Chester Goode on "Gunsmoke," played lawman Sam McCloud and then Buck Jones, a Texas surgeon who was a little too intense for his own good.

AS A REGULAR: "Gunsmoke," CBS, 1955-64; "Kentucky Jones," NBC, 1964-65; "Gentle Ben," CBS, 1967-69; "McCloud," NBC, 1970-77; "Stone," ABC, 1980; "Emerald Point NAS," CBS, 1983-84; "Buck James," ABC, 1987-88.

AND: "Schlitz Playhouse of Stars: Underground," CBS, 1955; "Big Town: Crime in the City Room," NBC, 1956; "The Silent Service: Two Davids and a Goliath," SYN, 1957; "Climax!: Burst of Fire," CBS, 1958; "Playhouse 90: The Dungeon," CBS, 1958; "The Ed Sullivan Show," CBS, 1959; "Christmas at the Circus," CBS, 1959; "On the Go," CBS, 1960; "Alfred Hitchcock Presents: Insomnia," CBS, 1960; "The Twilight Zone: Shadow Play," CBS, 1961; "The Garry Moore Show," CBS, 1962; "You Don't Say," NBC, 1964; "Combat!: The Farmer," ABC, 1965; "Walt Disney's Wonderful World of Color: Showdown with the Sundown Kid," NBC, 1966; "The Dean Martin Show," NBC, 1968; "Judd for the Defense: The View From the Ivy Tower," ABC, 1969; "The Name of the Game: Give Till It Hurts," NBC, 1969; "That Girl: That Metermaid," ABC, 1970; "The Virginian: Train of Darkness," NBC, 1970; "The Dean Martin Show," NBC, 1971; "Hollywood Squares," SYN, 1976; "Hollywood Squares," SYN, 1980; "Magnum P.I.: Let Me Hear the Music," CBS, 1985; "The Pat Sajak Show," CBS, 1989.

TV MOVIES AND MINISERIES: "McCloud: Who Killed Miss U.S.A.?," NBC, 1970; "The Forgotten Man," ABC, 1971; "Duel," ABC, 1971; "Rolling Man," ABC, 1972; "Female Artillery," ABC, 1973; "The Great Man's

Whiskers," NBC, 1973; "Terror on the Beach," CBS, 1973; "Ishi: The Last of His Tribe," NBC, 1978; "Pearl," ABC, 1978; "The Islander," CBS, 1978; "Centennial," NBC, 1978-79; "The Ordeal of Patty Hearst," ABC, 1979; "Amber Waves," ABC, 1980; "The Ordeal of Dr. Mudd," CBS, 1980; "Don't Go to Sleep," ABC, 1982; "Cocaine: One Man's Seduction," NBC, 1983; "Going for the Gold: The Bill Johnson Story," CBS, 1985; "A Winner Never Quits," ABC, 1986; "Bluffing It," ABC, 1987; "Disaster at Silo 7," ABC, 1988.
* Emmies: 1959.
* See also Milburn Stone.

WEAVER, DOODLES

b. Los Angeles, CA, May 11, 1911; d. 1983. Lowbrow comedian with Spike Jones's band; uncle of Sigourney.
AS A REGULAR: "Doodles Weaver," NBC, 1951; "A Day with Doodles," SYN, 1965-66.
AND: "The Colgate Comedy Hour," NBC, 1951; "Pied Piper of Hamelin," NBC, 1957; "Art Linkletter's House Party," CBS, 1957; "Lawman: The Lady Belle," ABC, 1960; "You Bet Your Life," NBC, 1960; "Lawman: The Parting," ABC, 1960; "The Tab Hunter Show: I Love a Marine," NBC, 1960; "Wagon Train: The Joe Muharich Story," NBC, 1961; "The Donna Reed Show: Jeff, the Treasurer," ABC, 1961; "The Donna Reed Show: The Mustache," ABC, 1961; "The Andy Griffith Show: Aunt Bee's Brief Encounter," CBS, 1961; "The Hathaways: A Man for Amanda," ABC, 1962; "The Dick Van Dyke Show: One Angry Man," CBS, 1962; "Mr. Smith Goes to Washington: The Country Sculptor," ABC, 1962; "Dennis the Menace: Poor Mr. Wilson," CBS, 1962; "Have Gun, Will Travel: Shootout at Hogtooth," CBS, 1962; "The Donna Reed Show: The Handy Man," ABC, 1963; "Please Don't Eat the Daisies: Knight of Knights," NBC, 1966; "Batman: Shoot a Crooked Arrow/Walk the Straight and Narrow," ABC, 1966; "My Three Sons: The Good Earth," CBS, 1967; "The Monkees: Monkees in Manhattan," NBC, 1967; "Dragnet: The Big Solicitor," NBC, 1967; "Dragnet: The Big Dog," NBC, 1967; "Little House on the Prairie: The Lord Is My Sheperd," NBC, 1974.
* Weaver shot himself.

WEBB, JACK

b. John Randolph Webb, Santa Monica, CA, April 2, 1902; d. 1982. Movie character actor ("Sunset Boulevard") who turned to radio and then TV as no-nonsense cop Sgt. Joe Friday on "Dragnet"; he made a fortune producing deadpan action shows.
AS A REGULAR: "Dragnet," NBC, 1952-59, 1967-70; "G.E. True," CBS, 1962-63; "Escape," NBC, 1973.
AND: "The Ed Sullivan Show," CBS, 1957; "Club

60," NBC, 1957; "Wide, Wide World: The Fabulous Infant," NBC, 1957; "Look Here," NBC, 1958; "Art Linkletter's House Party," CBS, 1958; "Some of Manie's Friends," NBC, 1959; "Person to Person," CBS, 1959; "The Jack Benny Program," CBS, 1959; "Play Your Hunch," NBC, 1961; "Here's Hollywood," NBC, 1961; "Art Linkletter's House Party," CBS, 1962; "The Jerry Lewis Show," NBC, 1968.
TV MOVIES AND MINISERIES: "Dragnet," NBC, 1969; "O'Hara, United States Treasury: Operation Cobra," CBS, 1971.
AS PRODUCER: "Dragnet," NBC, 1952-59, 1967-70; "Noah's Ark," NBC, 1956-57; "The D.A.'s Man," NBC, 1959; "Pete Kelly's Blues," NBC, 1959; "77 Sunset Strip," ABC, 1963-64; "Adam 12," NBC, 1968-75; "Emergency," NBC, 1972-77; "Escape," NBC, 1973; "Mobile One," ABC, 1975; "Project UFO," NBC, 1978-79.
AS DIRECTOR: "Adam 12: Pilot," NBC, 1968; "Dragnet," NBC, 1969; "O'Hara, United States Treasury: Operation Cobra," CBS, 1971.

WEBBER, ROBERT

b. Santa Ana, CA, October 14, 1924; d. 1989. Beefy actor who was a memorable villian of a couple of episodes of "The Rockford Files" and played Alexander Hayes, father of Maddie (Cybill Shepherd) on "Moonlighting."
AS A REGULAR: "Three Steps to Heaven," NBC, 1953-54; "The Brighter Day," CBS, 1958; "The Edge of Night," CBS, 1959; "Moonlighting," ABC, 1987-89.
AND: "The Phil Silvers Show: Bilko Gets Some Sleep," CBS, 1956; "New York Confidential: Come Home to Death," SYN, 1958; "Art Carney Special: Full Moon Over Brooklyn," NBC, 1960; "U.S. Steel Hour: Game of Hearts," CBS, 1960; "Play of the Week: A Palm Tree in a Rose Garden," SYN, 1960; "The Dick Powell Show: Three Soldiers," NBC, 1961; "The Investigators: Panic Wagon," CBS, 1961; "Thriller: Portrait Without a Face," NBC, 1961; "Westinghouse Presents: Footnote to Fame," CBS, 1962; "Alfred Hitchcock Presents: Burglar Proof," NBC, 1962; "Theatre '62: The Paradine Case," NBC, 1962; "Stoney Burke: Spin a Golden Web," ABC, 1962; "The Dick Powell Show: The Court-Martial of Captain Wycliff," NBC, 1962; "Route 66: Give the Old Cat a Tender Mouse," CBS, 1962; "The Defenders: Ordeal," CBS, 1963; "The Greatest Show on Earth: Silent Love, Secret Love," ABC, 1963; "The Fugitive: Garden House," ABC, 1964; "Kraft Suspense Theatre: Leviathan Five," NBC, 1964; "The Outer Limits: Keeper of the Purple Twilight," ABC, 1964; "Mr. Broadway: Don't Mention My Name in Sheboygan," CBS, 1964; "Kraft Suspense Theatre: Kill No More," NBC, 1965; "The Bold Ones: The People Against Ortega," NBC, 1969; "Mannix: A Gathering of Ghosts," CBS, 1971; "McCloud: The New Mexican Connection," NBC, 1971; "Banacek:

Let's Hear It for a Living Legend," NBC, 1972; "Love, American Style: Love and the Confession," ABC, 1972; "Mission: Impossible: The Deal," CBS, 1972; "Griff: Premiere," ABC, 1973; "Kojak: The Corrupter," CBS, 1973; "Ironside: A Game of Showdown," NBC, 1973; "The Magician: Lady in a Trap," NBC, 1973; "Ironside: Amy Prentiss, A.K.A. The Chief," NBC, 1974; "The Streets of San Francisco: The Twenty-Five Caliber Plague," ABC, 1974; "McCloud: The Man with the Golden Hat," NBC, 1975; "The Rockford Files: The Deep Blue Sleep," NBC, 1975; "Switch: The Old Diamond Game," CBS, 1975; "The Rockford Files: Aura Lee, Farewell," NBC, 1975; "Barnaby Jones: Price of Terror," CBS, 1975; "The Rockford Files: The Oracle Wore a Cashmere Suit," NBC, 1976; "McMillan: Coffee, Tea or Cyanide?," NBC, 1977; "Barnaby Jones: Final Judgment," CBS, 1978; "The Rockford Files: Never Send a Boy King to Do a Man's Job," NBC, 1979; "Tenspeed and Brown Shoe: Pilot," ABC, 1980; "Darkroom: Closed Circuit," ABC, 1981.

TV MOVIES AND MINISERIES: "The Movie Murderer," NBC, 1970; "Hauser's Memory," NBC, 1970; "Thief," ABC, 1971; "Hawkins on Murder," CBS, 1973; "Double Indemnity," ABC, 1973; "Death Stalk," NBC, 1974; "Murder or Mercy," ABC, 1974; "Harold Robbins' 79 Park Avenue," NBC, 1977; "Not Just Another Affair," CBS, 1982; "Don't Go to Sleep," ABC, 1982; "Starflight: The Plane That Couldn't Land," ABC, 1983; "Getting Physical," CBS, 1984; "In Like Flynn," ABC, 1985; "Assassin," CBS, 1986; "Something Is Out There," NBC, 1988.

WEDGEWORTH, ANN

b. Abilene, TX, January 21, 1935. Actress usually in breathy Southern-lady roles, often in comedies.
AS A REGULAR: "The Edge of Night," CBS, 1966; "Another World," NBC, 1967-70; "Somerset," NBC, 1970-76; "Three's Company," ABC, 1979-80; "Filthy Rich," CBS, 1982-83; "Evening Shade," CBS, 1990- .
AND: "Kraft Television Theatre: Vengeance," NBC, 1957; "Kraft Suspense Theatre: Operation Grief," NBC, 1964; "The Equalizer: Suspicion of Innocence," CBS, 1987; "Doodle's," ABC, 1988; "Roseanne: We Gather Together," ABC, 1989.
TV MOVIES AND MINISERIES: "Bogie," CBS, 1980; "Elvis and the Beauty Queen," NBC, 1981; "Killjoy," CBS, 1981; "Right to Kill?," ABC, 1985; "A Stranger Waits," CBS, 1987.

WEINBERGER, ED

Writer-producer; he provided the voice for talking orangutan Mr. Smith.
AS A REGULAR: "Mr. Smith," NBC, 1983.
AND: "Taxi: The Ten Percent Solution," ABC, 1981.
AS WRITER: "The Mary Tyler Moore Show," CBS, 1972-75; "The Mary Tyler Moore Show: The

Last Show," CBS, 1977; "Taxi," ABC, 1978-79; "Mr. Smith," NBC, 1983; "The Cosby Show," NBC, 1984-87; "Family Man," ABC, 1988; "Major Dad," CBS, 1989- .
AS DIRECTOR: "Taxi: Alex's Romance," ABC, 1979.
* Emmies: 1975, 1976, 1977, 1979, 1980, 1981, 1985.

WEISSMULLER, JOHNNY

b. Peter John Weissmuller, Windber, PA, June 2, 1904; d. 1984. Him Tarzan.
AS A REGULAR: "Jungle Jim," SYN, 1955.
AND: "Here's Hollywood," NBC, 1961.

WEITZ, BRUCE

b. Norwalk, CT, May 27, 1943. Short, wiry, dark-featured actor who played Det. Mick Belker on "Hill Street Blues."
AS A REGULAR: "Hill Street Blues," NBC, 1981-87; "Mama's Boy," NBC, 1988-89.
AND: "Happy Days: Kid Stuff," ABC, 1978; "The White Shadow: Just One of the Boys," CBS, 1979; "Paris: Burnout," CBS, 1979; "Matlock: The Gambler," NBC, 1987; "Midnight Caller: Mercy Me," NBC, 1989.
TV MOVIES AND MINISERIES: "Death of a Centerfold: The Dorothy Stratten Story," NBC, 1981; "A Reason to Live," NBC, 1985; "If It's Tuesday, It Still Must Be Belgium," NBC, 1987; "Baby M," ABC, 1988; "A Deadly Silence," ABC, 1989; "Fair Game," NBC, 1989; "A Cry for Help: The Tracey Thurman Story," NBC, 1989.
* Emmies: 1984.

WELCH, RAQUEL

b. Raquel Tejada, Chicago, IL, September 5, 1942. Movie sex symbol who's lately turned to TV movies.
AS A GUEST: "The Virginian: Ryker," NBC, 1964; "McHale's Navy: McHale the Desk Commander," ABC, 1964; "Bewitched: Witch or Wife?," ABC, 1964; "The Rogues: Hugger-Mugger by the Sea," NBC, 1964; "Wendy & Me: Wendy Sails in the Sunset," ABC, 1965; "The Baileys of Balboa: Sam's Nephew," CBS, 1965; "Bracken's World: Fade-In," NBC, 1969; "This Is Tom Jones," ABC, 1970; "The Funny Papers," CBS, 1972; "The Mike Douglas Show," SYN, 1975; "Cher," CBS, 1975; "Saturday Night Live," NBC, 1976; "Mork & Mindy: Mork vs. the Necrotrons," ABC, 1979; "The Muppet Show," SYN, 1980; "The Dick Cavett Show," PBS, 1980.
TV MOVIES AND MINISERIES: "Right to Die," NBC, 1987; "Scandal in a Small Town," NBC, 1988; "Trouble in Paradise," CBS, 1989.

WELD, TUESDAY

b. Susan Weld, New York City, NY, August 27, 1943. Blonde actress of fifties and sixties movies and TV; she played Dobie Gillis' unattainable romantic goal, the predatory Thalia Menninger, and now keeps busy in TV movies.

AS A REGULAR: "The Many Loves of Dobie Gillis," CBS, 1959-60, 1962.

AND: "Goodyear TV Playhouse: Backwoods Cinderella," NBC, 1957; "Bob Hope Special," NBC, 1958; "The Adventures of Ozzie and Harriet: The Other Guy's Girl," ABC, 1959; "77 Sunset Strip: Secret Island," ABC, 1959; "The Red Skelton Show: Appleby the Big Producer," CBS, 1959; "The Adventures of Ozzie and Harriet: Rick Gets Even," ABC, 1959; "77 Sunset Strip: Condor's Lair," ABC, 1960; "About Faces," ABC, 1960; "The Millionaire: Millionare Katherine Boland," CBS, 1960; "Dinah Shore Chevy Show," NBC, 1960; "The Tab Hunter Show: The Doll in the Bathing Suit," NBC, 1960; "Dick Powell's Zane Grey Theatre: The Mormons," CBS, 1960; "Bob Hope Buick Show," NBC, 1961; "Follow the Sun: The Highest Wall," ABC, 1961; "Bus Stop: Cherie," ABC, 1961; "The Dick Powell Show: A Time to Die," NBC, 1962; "Adventures in Paradise: The Velvet Trap," ABC, 1962; "Naked City: A Case Study of Two Savages," ABC, 1962; "The Dick Powell Show: Run Till It's Dark," NBC, 1962; "The Eleventh Hour: Something Crazy's Going on in the Back Room," NBC, 1963; "The du Pont Show: The Legend of Lylah Clare," NBC, 1963; "The Greatest Show on Earth: Silent Love, Secret Love," ABC, 1963; "Bob Hope Special," NBC, 1963; "Bob Hope Christmas Special," NBC, 1964; "Mr. Broadway: Keep an Eye on Emily," CBS, 1964; "The Fugitive: Dark Corner," ABC, 1964; "The Crucible," CBS, 1967.

TV MOVIES AND MINISERIES: "Reflections on Murder," ABC, 1974; "F. Scott Fitzgerald in Hollywood," ABC, 1976; "Madame X," NBC, 1981; "The Winter of Our Discontent," CBS, 1983; "Scorned and Swindled," CBS, 1984; "Circle of Violence: A Family Drama," CBS, 1986; "Something in Common," CBS, 1986.

WELK, LAWRENCE

b. Strasburg, ND, March 11, 1903. Bandleader whose conglomeration had a decidedly ricky-tick style; still, he was an audience favorite for 27 years—and still is, in reruns.

AS A REGULAR: "The Lawrence Welk Show," ABC, 1955-71; SYN, 1971-82; "Lawrence Welk's Top Tunes and New Talent," ABC, 1956-59.

AND: "Person to Person," CBS, 1956; "Shower of Stars," CBS, 1957; "This Is Your Life," NBC, 1957; "I've Got a Secret," CBS, 1957; "An Evening with Durante," NBC, 1959; "The Jack Benny Program," CBS, 1962; "The Andy Williams Show," NBC, 1962; "Danny Thomas Special," NBC, 1967; "Here's Lucy: Lucy and Lawrence Welk," CBS, 1970; "The Tonight Show Starring Johnny Carson," NBC, 1974.

WELLES, ORSON

b. Kenosha, WI, May 6, 1915; d. 1985. Film legend whose best-known TV role might be that as the unseen voice of Robin Masters on "Magnum, P.I."

AS A REGULAR: "The Marty Feldman Comedy Machine," ABC, 1972; "Orson Welles' Great Mysteries," SYN, 1973-74; "Magnum P.I.," CBS, 1981-85; "Scene of the Crime," NBC, 1985.

AND: "Omnibus: King Lear," CBS, 1953; "Ford Star Jubilee: Twentieth Century," CBS, 1956; "The Herb Shriner Show," CBS, 1956; "I Love Lucy: Lucy Meets Orson Welles," CBS, 1956; "The Steve Allen Show," NBC, 1957; "The Steve Allen Show," NBC, 1958; "Colgate Theatre: Fountain of Youth," NBC, 1958; "Shindig," ABC, 1965; "The Dean Martin Show," NBC, 1969; "The Name of the Game: The Enemy Before Us," NBC, 1970; "Night Gallery: Silent Snow, Secret Snow," NBC, 1971; "Rikki-Tikki-Tavi," CBS, 1975; "Moonlighting: The Dream Sequence Always Rings Twice," ABC, 1985.

AS WRITER-DIRECTOR: "Colgate Theatre: Fountain of Youth," NBC, 1958.

* Welles won a Peabody Award for "Fountain of Youth."

* What did Welles do on "Shindig"? He sang a song—"So Many Things to Remember."

WELLS, DAWN

b. Reno, NV. Pert actress who played Mary Ann Summers, the farm girl on "Gilligan's Island."

AS A REGULAR: "Gilligan's Island," CBS, 1964-67.

AND: "The Roaring Twenties: War with the Night Hawkers," ABC, 1961; "Maverick: Deadly Image," ABC, 1961; "77 Sunset Strip: The Rival Eye Caper," ABC, 1961; "Wagon Train: The Captain Dan Brady Story," NBC, 1961; "77 Sunset Strip: The Inverness Cape Caper," ABC, 1961; "Tales of Wells Fargo: Kelly's Clover Girls," NBC, 1961; "87th Precinct: Out of Order," NBC, 1962; "Everglades: Fight at Boca Chico," SYN, 1962; "Lawman: No Contest," ABC, 1962; "The Joey Bishop Show: A Young Man's Fancy," NBC, 1962; "Bonanza: The Way Station," NBC, 1962; "It's a Man's World: The Bravest Man in Cordella," NBC, 1962; "Hawaiian Eye: The Sign-Off," ABC, 1962; "It's a Man's World: Chicago Gains a Number," NBC, 1962; "Channing: Swing for the Moon," ABC, 1964; "The Joey Bishop Show: Joey and Roberta Sherwood Play a Benefit," NBC, 1964; "Password," CBS, 1965; "The Wild Wild West: The Night of the Headless Woman," CBS, 1968; "The FBI: The Attorney," ABC, 1969; "High Rollers," NBC, 1976; "Growing Pains: Broadway Bound," ABC, 1987.

TV MOVIES AND MINISERIES: "Rescue From Gilligan's Island," NBC, 1978; "The Castaways on Gilligan's Island," NBC, 1979;

"The Harlem Globetrotters on Gilligan's Island," NBC, 1981.
* Wells showed up on "High Rollers" as a substitute dice roller for Ruta Lee, who was having a severe dimple attack.

WENDT, GEORGE

b. *Chicago, IL, October 17, 1948*. Rotund actor who plays Norm Peterson on "Cheers."
AS A REGULAR: "Making the Grade," CBS, 1982; "Cheers," NBC, 1982- .
AND: "Taxi: Latka the Playboy," ABC, 1981; "Alice: Monty Falls for Alice," CBS, 1981; "M*A*S*H: Trick or Treatment," CBS, 1982; "St. Elsewhere: Cheers," NBC, 1985; "Saturday Night Live," NBC, 1986; "The Twilight Zone: The World Next Door," CBS, 1986; "The Jim Henson Hour: Miss Piggy's Hollywood," NBC, 1989; "Day by Day: Fraternity," NBC, 1989.
* Coach: "What's shakin', Normie?" Norm: "All four cheeks and a couple of chins, Coach."

WEST, ADAM

b. *William Anderson, Walla Walla, WA, September 19, 1928*. Handsome actor who'll be forever known as millionaire Bruce Wayne, aka "Batman."
AS A REGULAR: "Robert Taylor's Detectives," NBC, 1961-62; "Batman," ABC, 1966-68; "The New Adventures of Batman," CBS, 1977-78; "The Last Precinct," NBC, 1986.
AND: "Sugarfoot: The Mysterious Stranger," ABC, 1959; "Maverick: Two Tickets to Ten Strike," ABC, 1959; "Colt .45: The Escape," ABC, 1959; "Cheyenne: Blind Spot," ABC, 1959; "Lawman: The Wayfarer," ABC, 1959; "Maverick: Pappy," ABC, 1959; "77 Sunset Strip: Thanks for Tomorrow," ABC, 1959; "Bronco: The Burning Springs," ABC, 1959; "Maverick: A Fellow's Brother," ABC, 1959; "Hawaiian Eye: Quick Return," ABC, 1959; "Goodyear Theatre: All in the Family," NBC, 1960; "Colt .45: The Devil's Godson," ABC, 1960; "Westinghouse Desilu Playhouse: Murder Is a Private Affair," CBS, 1960; "Laramie: Man From Kansas," NBC, 1961; "Tales of Wells Fargo: The Has-Been," NBC, 1961; "Bonanza: The Bride," NBC, 1961; "Perry Mason: The Case of the Barefaced Witness," CBS, 1961; "Michael Shayne: Date with Death," NBC, 1961; "The Rifleman: Stopover," ABC, 1961; "Guestward Ho!: Bill the Fireman," ABC, 1961; "Here's Hollywood," NBC, 1961; "Beachcomber: Captain Huckabee's Beard," SYN, 1962; "Perry Mason: The Case of the Bogus Books," CBS, 1962; "The Real McCoys: The Crop Dusters," CBS, 1963; "Laramie: The Betrayers," NBC, 1963; "Petticoat Junction: The Talent Scout," CBS, 1964; "The Outer Limits: The Invisible Enemy," ABC, 1964; "Bewitched: Love Is Blind," ABC, 1964; "The Virginian: Legend for a Lawman," NBC, 1965; "Alexander the Great," ABC, 1968; "Hollywood Squares," NBC, 1968; "The Big Valley: In Silent Battle," ABC, 1968; "Love, American Style: Love and the Great Catch," ABC, 1970; "Night Gallery: With Apologies to Mr. Hyde," NBC, 1971; "Alias Smith and Jones: The Men That Corrupted Hadleyburg," ABC, 1972; "This Is the Life: The Revenge of Cho Lin," SYN, 1972; "Mannix: A Puzzle for One," CBS, 1972; "Emergency!: The Parade," NBC, 1974; "Alice: Sex Education," CBS, 1976; "The Love Boat: Booming Romance," ABC, 1983.
TV MOVIES AND MINISERIES: "The Eyes of Charles Sand," ABC, 1972; "Poor Devil," NBC, 1973; "Nevada Smith," NBC, 1975; "I Take These Men," CBS, 1983; "The Last Precinct," NBC, 1986.

WESTHEIMER, DR. RUTH

b. *Karola Ruth Siegel, Frankfurt, Germany, 1928*. Impish sex therapist who craves, yearns for, desires, must have, media attention.
AS A REGULAR: "Ask Dr. Ruth," SYN, 1987-88.
AND: "Late Night with David Letterman," NBC, 1983; "The Arsenio Hall Show," SYN, 1989; "Dr. Ruth's House," ABC, 1990.

WESTON, JACK

b. *Jack Weinstein, Cleveland, OH, 1925*. Pudgy actor best known in films ("The Incredible Mr. Limpet," "The Four Seasons"); he played Walter Hathaway, father to a brood of chimpanzees, on "The Hathaways."
AS A REGULAR: "Rod Brown of the Rocket Rangers," CBS, 1953-54; "My Sister Eileen," CBS, 1960-61; "The Hathaways," ABC, 1961-62; "The Four Seasons," CBS, 1984.
AND: "Big Town: Waterfront," NBC, 1956; "The George Burns and Gracie Allen Show: Locked Out," CBS, 1958; "Du Pont Show of the Month: Harvey," CBS, 1958; "Playhouse 90: The Tunnel," CBS, 1959; "The Untouchables: Ain't We Got Fun?," ABC, 1959; "Rawhide: Incident at the Buffalo Smoke House," CBS, 1959; "Markham: A Cry From the Penthouse," CBS, 1960; "The Twilight Zone: The Monsters Are Due on Maple Street," CBS, 1960; "Have Gun, Will Travel: Lady with a Gun," CBS, 1960; "Alfred Hitchcock Presents: Forty Detectives Later," CBS, 1960; "Have Gun, Will Travel: The Poker Fiend," CBS, 1960; "Thriller: The Cheaters," NBC, 1960; "Harrigan and Son: Shall We Dance?," ABC, 1961; "Peter Loves Mary: Peter Writes a Book," NBC, 1961; "G.E. Theatre: Love Is a Lion's Roar," CBS, 1961; "The Lawless Years: The Kid Dropper Story," NBC, 1961; "Dr. Kildare: Twenty-Four Hours," NBC, 1961; "Thriller: Flowers of Evil," NBC, 1962; "Sam Benedict: A Split Week in San Quentin," NBC, 1962; "Stoney Burke: A Matter of Percentage,"

ABC, 1963; "The Twilight Zone: The Bard," CBS, 1963; "The Danny Kaye Show," CBS, 1964; "Grindl: Grindl Goes West," NBC, 1964; "Burke's Law: Who Killed Andy Zygmunt?," ABC, 1964; "Bob Hope Chrysler Theatre: The Turncoat," NBC, 1964; "Burke's Law: Who Killed the 13th Clown?," ABC, 1965; "Bob Hope Chrysler Theatre: Kicks," NBC, 1965; "Bewitched: Prodigy," ABC, 1966; "Ben Casey: 26 Ways to Spell Heartbreak: A, B, C, D... ," ABC, 1966; "The Man From U.N.C.L.E: The Project Deephole Affair," NBC, 1966; "The Don Knotts Show," NBC, 1970; "All in the Family: Edith the Judge," CBS, 1972; "The Carol Burnett Show," CBS, 1974.

TV MOVIES AND MINISERIES: "Fame Is the Name of the Game," NBC, 1966; "Now You See It, Now You Don't," NBC, 1968; "I Love a Mystery," NBC, 1973; "Deliver Us From Evil," ABC, 1973; "Harold Robbins' 79 Park Avenue," NBC, 1977; "If Tomorrow Comes," CBS, 1986.

WETTIG, PATRICIA

Emmy winning actress who plays Nancy Weston on "thirtysomething"; she was formerly the wife of Dr. Jack Morrison (David Morse) on "St. Elsewhere" and she's the real-life wife of Ken Olin, who plays Michael on "thirtysomething."

AS A REGULAR: "St. Elsewhere," NBC, 1986-87; "thirtysomething," ABC, 1987- .

AND: "Remington Steele: Blood Is Thicker Than Steele," NBC, 1984; "Hill Street Blues: The Life and Time of Dominic Florio Jr.," NBC, 1985.

TV MOVIES AND MINISERIES: "Police Story: Cop Killers," ABC, 1988.

* Emmies: 1989, 1990.

WHEELER, BERT

b. Albert Jerome Wheeler, Paterson, NJ, April 7, 1895; d. 1968. Vaudeville comic who turned to character acting on TV; he played Smokey Joe on "Brave Eagle."

AS A REGULAR: "Brave Eagle," CBS, 1955-56.

AND: "Robert Montgomery Presents: Rio Rita," NBC, 1950; "Pat Boone Chevy Showroom," ABC, 1958; "The Jimmy Dean Show," CBS, 1958; "Brains and Brawn," NBC, 1958; "The Sam Levenson Show," CBS, 1959; "Robert Herridge Theatre: Hope is the Thing with Feathers," SYN, 1960; "The Defenders: The Invisible Badge," CBS, 1962.

WHELAN, JILL

b. Oakland, CA, September 29, 1966. Actress who played Vicki Stubing on "The Love Boat."

AS A REGULAR: "The Love Boat," ABC, 1979-86.

AND: "Matt Houston: Who Would Kill Ramona?," ABC, 1982.

WHELCHEL, LISA

b. Fort Worth, TX, May 29, 1963. Blonde actress who played Blair on "The Facts of Life."

AS A REGULAR: "The New Mickey Mouse Club," SYN, 1977-78; "The Facts of Life," NBC, 1979-88.

AND: "Family: All for Love," ABC, 1978; "The Love Boat: Poor Rich Man," ABC, 1983; "The Love Boat: The Racer's Edge," ABC, 1985.

TV MOVIES AND MINISERIES: "The Facts of Life Goes to Paris," NBC, 1982; "The Wild Women of Chastity Gulch," ABC, 1982; "The Facts of Life Down Under," NBC, 1987.

WHITE, BETTY

b. January 17, 1924. Durable actress who began as a game-show and talk-show fixture, won several Emmies as Sue Ann Nivens on "The Mary Tyler Moore Show" and now plays the dotty Rose Nylund on "The Golden Girls."

AS A REGULAR: "Life with Elizabeth," SYN, 1953-55; "Make the Connection," NBC, 1955; "Date with the Angels," ABC, 1957-58; "The Betty White Show," ABC, 1958; CBS, 1977-78; "The Jack Paar Show," NBC, 1958-62; "The Pet Set," SYN, 1971-72; "Match Game," CBS, 1973-79; "The Mary Tyler Moore Show," CBS, 1973-77; "Match Game P.M.," SYN, 1975-82; "Liar's Club," SYN, 1976-78; "Just Men," NBC, 1983; "Mama's Family," NBC, 1983-85; "The Golden Girls," NBC, 1985- .

AND: "The Millionaire: The Story of Virginia Lennart," CBS, 1956; "To Tell the Truth," CBS, 1958; "I've Got a Secret," CBS, 1958; "To Tell the Truth," CBS, 1959; "Masquerade Party," NBC, 1959; "To Tell the Truth," CBS, 1961; "Candid Camera," CBS, 1961; "Password," CBS, 1961; "Password," CBS, 1962; "U.S. Steel Hour: Scene of the Crime," CBS, 1962; "To Tell the Truth," CBS, 1962; "Your First Impression," NBC, 1962; "Your First Impression," NBC, 1963; "The Match Game," NBC, 1963; "Password," CBS, 1963; "Password," CBS, 1964; "The Match Game," NBC, 1964; "The Price Is Right," ABC, 1964; "The Tennessee Ernie Ford Show," ABC, 1964; "What's This Song?," NBC, 1965; "The Match Game," NBC, 1965; "Call My Bluff," NBC, 1965; "The Mike Douglas Show," SYN, 1966; "You Don't Say," NBC, 1967; "That's Life: Buying a House," ABC, 1968; "Petticoat Junction: The Cannonball Bookmobile," CBS, 1969; "The Odd Couple: Password," ABC, 1972; "Password," ABC, 1974; "Tattletales," CBS, 1974; "You Don't Say," ABC, 1975; "Ellery Queen: Miss Aggie's Farewell Performance," NBC, 1975; "The Merv Griffin Show," SYN, 1975; "Tattletales," CBS, 1976; "The Sonny and Cher Comedy Hour," CBS, 1976; "The Sonny and Cher Comedy Hour," CBS, 1977; "The Carol Burnett Show," CBS, 1978; "Best of the West: Mail Order Bride," ABC, 1981; "The Love Boat: My Friend, The Executrix," ABC, 1982; "Love, Sidney: Charlotte's

Web," NBC, 1982; "The Love Boat: Authoress, Authoress," ABC, 1984; "Hotel: Outsiders," ABC, 1984; "St. Elsewhere: Red, White, Black and Blue," NBC, 1984; "St. Elsewhere: Close Encounter," NBC, 1985; "Matlock: The Producer," NBC, 1987; "The Tonight Show Starring Johnny Carson," NBC, 1988; "Empty Nest: Strange Bedfellows," NBC, 1989; "The Pat Sajak Show," CBS, 1989; "A Conversation with Betty White," DIS, 1989; "Later with Bob Costas," NBC, 1989; "Empty Nest: Rambo of Neiman Marcus," NBC, 1989.
TV MOVIES AND MINISERIES: "Vanished," NBC, 1971; "Before and After," ABC, 1979.
* Emmies: 1975, 1976, 1986.
* See also Oliver Clark.

WHITE, DAVID
b. 1916; d. 1990. Actor who played Larry Tate on "Bewitched."
AS A REGULAR: "Bewitched," ABC, 1964-72.
AND: "The Phil Silvers Show: The Rest Cure," CBS, 1956; "The Phil Silvers Show: The Song of the Motor Pool," CBS, 1956; "Alcoa Hour: Protege," NBC, 1957; "True Story: The Dinner Party," NBC, 1958; "Armstrong Circle Theatre: House of Cards," CBS, 1959; "Alfred Hitchcock Presents: Dry Run," CBS, 1959; "Have Gun, Will Travel: The Unforgiven," CBS, 1959; "The Untouchables: The Rusty Heller Story," ABC, 1960; "The Outlaws: Starfall," NBC, 1960; "The du Pont Show with June Allyson: A Thief or Two," CBS, 1960; "SurfSide 6: Little Star Lost," ABC, 1961; "The Outlaws: Chalk's Lot," NBC, 1961; "Target: The Corruptors: The Poppy Vendor," ABC, 1961; "Hawaiian Eye: Kill a Grey Fox," ABC, 1961; "SurfSide 6: The Roust," ABC, 1962; "Alcoa Premiere: Mr. Easy," ABC, 1962; "Cain's Hundred: The Cost of Living," NBC, 1962; "The Twilight Zone: I Sing the Body Electric," CBS, 1962; "The Lloyd Bridges Show: Yankee Stay Here," CBS, 1962; "77 Sunset Strip: The Catspaw Caper," ABC, 1962; "Have Gun, Will Travel: The Marshal of Sweetwater," CBS, 1962; "Saints and Sinners: Judith Was a Lady," NBC, 1962; "Our Man Higgins: Golf Partner," ABC, 1962; "My Favorite Martian: A Nose for News," CBS, 1963; "McKeever and the Colonel: Project: Walkie-Talkie," NBC, 1963; "The Virginian: The Man Who Couldn't Die," NBC, 1963; "Mr. Novak: Hello, Miss Phipps," NBC, 1963; "The Alfred Hitchcock Hour: Night Caller," CBS, 1964; "My Favorite Martian: The Memory Pill," CBS, 1964; "Destry: Destry Had a Little Lamb," ABC, 1964; "Slattery's People: Question-Whatever Happened to Ezra?," CBS, 1964; "The Farmer's Daughter: A Locket for Agatha," ABC, 1964; "Mission: Impossible: Two Thousand," CBS, 1972; "Banacek: The Two Million Clams of Cap'n Jack," NBC, 1973; "Love, American Style: Love and the Legend," ABC, 1973; "Room 222: Of Smoke-Filled Rooms," ABC, 1973; "The Odd Couple: Felix Directs," ABC, 1973; "Kojak: Before the Devil

Knows," CBS, 1974; "Police Woman: The Shoefly Days," NBC, 1974; "The Rookies: Johnny Lost His Gun," ABC, 1974; "Columbo: Identity Crisis," NBC, 1975; "The Streets of San Francisco: Underground," ABC, 1976; "What's Happening!: The Burger Queen," ABC, 1976; "Police Woman: The Trick Book," NBC, 1976; "The Rockford Files: Foul on the First Play," NBC, 1976; "Quincy: Sugar and Spice," NBC, 1981; "Cagney & Lacey: Two Grand," CBS, 1985; "Remington Steele: Steele of Approval," NBC, 1985; "The A-Team: Duke of Whispering Pines," NBC, 1986.
TV MOVIES AND MINISERIES: "Twin Detectives," ABC, 1976.

WHITE, JALEEL
b. Los Angeles, CA, November 27, 1976. Young actor who plays the nerdy Steve Urkel on "Family Matters."
AS A REGULAR: "Charlie & Company," CBS, 1985-86; "Family Matters," ABC, 1989- .
AND: "Cadets," ABC, 1988.

WHITE, JESSE
b. Buffalo, NY, January 3, 1919. Heavyset actor, usually puffing on a stogie, who played con artists Shifty Shafer and Oscar Pudney on Ann Sothern's two sitcoms; best known as the lonely Maytag repairman on TV commercials of the sixties, seventies and eighties.
AS A REGULAR: "Private Secretary," CBS, 1953-57; "Make Room for Daddy," ABC, 1955-57; "The Ann Sothern Show," CBS, 1960-61.
AND: "TV Reader's Digest: Old Master Detective," ABC, 1955; "Cavalcade Theatre: Wild April," ABC, 1956; "Schlitz Playhouse of Stars: Carriage From Britain," CBS, 1957; "The 20th Century-Fox Hour: The Great American Hoax," CBS, 1957; "Climax!: Mr. Runyon of Broadway," CBS, 1957; "The 20th Century-Fox Hour: The Marriage Broker," CBS, 1957; "The Frank Sinatra Show," ABC, 1958; "The Thin Man: The Perfect Servant," NBC, 1959; "The Texan: Private Account," CBS, 1959; "Lux Playhouse: Boy on a Fence," CBS, 1959; "Tightrope!: The Money Fight," CBS, 1959; "Man with a Camera: Fragment of a Murder," ABC, 1960; "Tightrope!: The Shark," CBS, 1960; "The Andy Griffith Show: Andy, the Marriage Counselor," CBS, 1961; "The Law and Mr. Jones: One for the Money," ABC, 1961; "Yes, Yes Nanette: A Special Special," NBC, 1961; "Yes, Yes Nanette: The Show Must Not Go On," NBC, 1961; "Angel: Promise to a Friend," CBS, 1961; "The Dick Van Dyke Show: Washington Versus the Bunny," CBS, 1961; "The Jack Benny Program: Auction Show," CBS, 1961; "G.E. Theatre: A Voice on the Phone," CBS, 1961; "The Roaring Twenties: Pinky Goes to College," ABC, 1961; "The Twilight Zone: Once Upon a Time," CBS, 1961; "Hawaiian Eye: The Missile Rogues," ABC, 1962; "Pete and Gladys: Pete's Hobby," CBS, 1962; "Ichabod and Me: A

Visit From Lippy," CBS, 1962; "The Roaring Twenties: The People People Marry," ABC, 1962; "Adventures in Paradise: The Quest of Ambrose Feather," ABC, 1962; "The Addams Family: Wednesday Leaves Home," ABC, 1964; "The Munsters: Movie Star Munster," CBS, 1965; "Perry Mason: The Case of the Fatal Fortune," CBS, 1965; "Green Acres: Parity Begins at Home," CBS, 1965; "Petticoat Junction: Hooterville, You're All Heart," CBS, 1966; "Please Don't Eat the Daisies: How Now, Hausfrau?," NBC, 1966; "The Wild Wild West: The Night of the Whirring Death," CBS, 1966; "Rango: My Teepee Runneth Over," ABC, 1967; "That Girl: There Is Time for Ann the Pieman," ABC, 1969; "Hawaii Five-O: Golden Boy in Black Trunks," CBS, 1969; "Make Room for Granddaddy: This Granddaddy Rated X," ABC, 1970; "Mannix: Nightshade," CBS, 1972; "Here's Lucy: The Case of the Reckless Wheelchair," CBS, 1972; "Kolchak, the Night Stalker: Chopper," ABC, 1975; "Happy Days: Richie's Flip Side," ABC, 1975.

WHITE, VANNA

b. Conway, SC, February 18, 1957. Human hula-hoop who inexplicably became a fad in the mid-1980s.

AS A REGULAR: "Wheel of Fortune," NBC, 1983-89; CBS, 1989-90; SYN, 1983- .

AND: "The A-Team: Wheel of Fortune," NBC, 1985; "Simon & Simon: Walking Point," CBS, 1987; "Santa Barbara," NBC, 1988; "The Pat Sajak Show," CBS, 1989.

TV MOVIES AND MINISERIES: "The Goddess of Love," NBC, 1988.

WHITEMAN, PAUL

b. Denver, CO, March 28, 1890; d. 1967. Bandleader of the twenties and thirties.

AS A REGULAR: "Paul Whiteman's TV Teen Club," ABC, 1949-54; "Paul Whiteman's Goodyear Revue," ABC, 1949-52; "On Stage with Paul Whiteman," ABC, 1954; "America's Greatest Bands," CBS, 1955.

AND: "The Big Payoff," CBS, 1957; "The Big Record," CBS, 1957; "The Voice of Firestone: An Evening with Paul Whiteman," ABC, 1959; "Revlon Revue: Salute to Paul Whiteman," CBS, 1960; "Bell Telephone Hour: Almanac for February," NBC, 1961; "The du Pont Show: Music of the Thirties," NBC, 1961.

WHITMAN, STUART

b. San Francisco, CA, February 1, 1926. Actor often in solid cowboy roles; he played marshal Jim Crown on "Cimarron Strip."

AS A REGULAR: "Cimarron Strip," CBS, 1967-68.

AND: "Four Star Playhouse: Desert Encounter," CBS, 1956; "Gunsmoke: Cholera," CBS, 1956;

"Dick Powell's Zane Grey Theatre: Until the Man Dies," CBS, 1957; "Mr. Adams and Eve: Teenage Daughter," CBS, 1957; "Alcoa Theatre: Encounter on a Second Class Coach," NBC, 1957; "Court of Last Resort: The Westover Case," NBC, 1958; "Have Gun, Will Travel: The Last Laugh," CBS, 1958; "Trackdown: The Town," CBS, 1958; "Bob Hope Chrysler Theatre: A Killing Sundial," NBC, 1963; "ABC Stage '67: The People Trap," ABC, 1966; "Bracken's World: Murder-Off Camera," NBC, 1970; "The FBI: The Impersonator," ABC, 1970; "The FBI: The Watchdog," ABC, 1971; "Night Gallery: Lindemann's Catch," NBC, 1972; "Ghost Story: The Concrete Captain," NBC, 1972; "Night Gallery: Fright Night," NBC, 1972; "Walt Disney's Wonderful World of Color: High Flying," NBC, 1972; "The Streets of San Francisco: The Set-Up," ABC, 1973; "The FBI: The Double Play," ABC, 1973; "Intersect," ABC, 1973; "Love, American Style: Love and the Lie," ABC, 1973; "Hec Ramsey: A Hard Road to Vengeance," NBC, 1973; "Police Story: Chain of Command," NBC, 1974; "Ellery Queen: Caesar's Last Stand," NBC, 1976; "Harry O: The Mysterious Case of Lester and Dr. Fong," ABC, 1976; "Simon & Simon: The Rough Rider Rides Again," CBS, 1982; "The A-Team: West Coast Turnaround," NBC, 1983; "The A-Team: Blood, Sweat and Cheers," NBC, 1985; "Blacke's Magic: Revenge of the Esperanza," NBC, 1986; "Hardcastle and McCormick: Round Up the Old Gang," ABC, 1986; "Simon & Simon: Still Phil After All These Years," CBS, 1986; "Murder, She Wrote: Trouble in Eden," CBS, 1987; "J.J. Starbuck: Cactus Jack's Last Call," NBC, 1988.

TV MOVIES AND MINISERIES: "The Man Who Wanted to Live Forever," ABC, 1970; "City Beneath the Sea," NBC, 1971; "Revenge," ABC, 1971; "The Woman Hunter," CBS, 1972; "The Man Who Died Twice," CBS, 1973; "The Cat Creature," ABC, 1973; "Beverly Hills Cowgirl Blues," CBS, 1985; "Stillwatch," CBS, 1987.

WHITMORE, JAMES

b. White Plains, NY, October 1, 1921. Actor who specializes in roles that radiate honor and honesty; he played President Harry S Truman in the stage and film versions of "Give 'Em Hell, Harry!" and was lawyer Abraham Lincoln Jones in "The Law and Mr. Jones."

AS A REGULAR: "The Law and Mr. Jones," ABC, 1960-62; "My Friend Tony," NBC, 1969; "Temperatures Rising," ABC, 1972-73.

AND: "Ford Theatre: For Value Received," NBC, 1954; "Crossroads: The Good Thief," ABC, 1955; "Stage 7: The Bequest," CBS, 1955; "Schlitz Playhouse of Stars: Midnight Kill," CBS, 1955; "Damon Runyon Theatre: The Blonde Mink," CBS, 1956; "Schlitz Playhouse of Stars: The Big Payday," CBS, 1956; "Playwrights '56: This

Business of Murder," NBC, 1956; "Fireside Theatre: The Velvet Trap," NBC, 1956; "Studio One: A Favor for Sam," CBS, 1956; "Kraft Television Theatre: Profile in Courage," NBC, 1956; "Dick Powell's Zane Grey Theatre: Debt of Gratitude," CBS, 1956; "Kraft Television Theatre: Out to Kill," NBC, 1956; "Dick Powell's Zane Grey Theatre: The Fearful Courage," CBS, 1956; Climax!: The Fog," CBS, 1956; "Ford Theatre: Fear Has Many Faces," ABC, 1957; "Playhouse 90: Dark December," CBS, 1959; "Playhouse 90: The Sounds of Eden," CBS, 1959; "Westinghouse Desilu Playhouse: The Hanging Judge," CBS, 1959; "Dick Powell's Zane Grey Theatre: Wayfarers," CBS, 1960; "Our American Heritage: Shadow of a Soldier," NBC, 1960; "Chevy Mystery Show: Thunder of Silence," NBC, 1960; "Alcoa Premiere: The Witch Next Door," ABC, 1961; "Checkmate: Nice Guys Finish Last," CBS, 1961; "Robert Taylor's Detectives: Act of God," NBC, 1961; "Focus," NBC, 1962; "Rawhide: The Incident of the Dogfaces," CBS, 1962; "Americans: A Portrait in Verses," CBS, 1962; "U.S. Steel Hour: Big Day for a Scrambler," CBS, 1962; "Going My Way: Tell Me When You Get to Heaven," ABC, 1963; "Route 66: A Gift From a Warrior," CBS, 1963; "Ben Casey: Father Was an Intern," ABC, 1963; "The Twilight Zone: On Thursday We Leave for Home," CBS, 1963; "Rawhide: Incident of the Iron Bull," CBS, 1963; "The Travels of Jaimie McPheeters: The Day of the Golden Fleece," ABC, 1963; "Dr. Kildare: If You Can't Believe the Truth," NBC, 1963; "Arrest and Trial: My Name Is Martin Burnham," ABC, 1963; "Kraft Suspense Theatre: The Long, Lost Life of Edward Smalley," NBC, 1963; "The Greatest Show on Earth: Love the Giver," ABC, 1964; "Slattery's People: Question-What Is Truth?," CBS, 1964; "Kraft Suspense Theatre: Rumble on the Docks," NBC, 1964; "Walt Disney's Wonderful World of Color: The Tenderfoot," NBC, 1964; "Combat!: The Cossack," ABC, 1965; "Burke's Law: Who Killed Cop Robin?," ABC, 1965; "Gunsmoke: Dry Road to Nowhere," CBS, 1965; "For the People: Any Benevolent Purpose," CBS, 1965; "Run for Your Life: This Town for Sale," NBC, 1965; "The Virginian: Nobody Said Hello," NBC, 1966; "The Loner: The Mourners for Johnny Sharp," CBS, 1966; "The Big Valley: The Death Merchant," ABC, 1966; "The Big Valley: Forty Rifles," ABC, 1966; "The Big Valley: Target," ABC, 1966; "Assault: The Legend," ABC, 1966; "T.H.E. Cat: Little Arnie From Long Ago," NBC, 1966; "Shane: Day of the Hawk," ABC, 1966; "The Monroes: The Hunter," ABC, 1966; "The Big Valley: Target," ABC, 1966; "The Big Valley: Night in a Small Town," ABC, 1967; "The Invaders: Quantity Unknown," ABC, 1967; "Tarzan: Tiger, Tiger," NBC, 1967; "The Big Valley: Night in a Small Town," ABC, 1967;

"The Virginian: Paid in Full," NBC, 1967; "Custer: Spirit Woman," ABC, 1967; "The Big Valley: Shadow of a Giant," ABC, 1968; "The Danny Thomas Hour: My Pal Tony," NBC, 1968; "Bonanza: To Die in Darkness," NBC, 1968; "The Virginian: A Flash of Darkness," NBC, 1969; "The Name of the Game: Goodbye, Harry," NBC, 1969; "Then Came Bronson: The Mountain," NBC, 1970; "The Men From Shiloh: Lady at the Bar," NBC, 1970; "Gunsmoke: Women for Sale," CBS, 1973; "The Merv Griffin Show," SYN, 1974; "John Denver Special," ABC, 1974; "Dinah!," SYN, 1975; "Bell System Family Theatre: The Canterville Ghost," NBC, 1975.
TV MOVIES AND MINISERIES: "The Challenge," ABC, 1970; "If Tomorrow Comes," ABC, 1971; "I Will Fight No More Forever," ABC, 1975; "The Word," CBS, 1978.

WHITTAKER, JOHNNIE
Child actor who played Jody Davis on "Family Affair"; he was the first actor to play Scotty Baldwin on "General Hospital."
AS A REGULAR: "General Hospital," ABC, 1963; "Family Affair," ABC, 1966-71; "Sigmund and the Sea Monsters," NBC, 1974-76.
AND: "Gunsmoke: The Returning," CBS, 1967; "Bewitched: Sam and the Beanstalk," ABC, 1969; "The Virginian: The Runaway Boy," NBC, 1969; "To Rome with Love: Roman Affair," CBS, 1970; "Gunsmoke: Waste," CBS, 1971; "Marcus Welby, M.D.: Cross-Match," ABC, 1972.
TV MOVIES AND MINISERIES: "Something Evil," CBS, 1972.

WICKER, IREENE
b. Quincy, IL. Singer whose career was tarnished when she was wrongly accused of supporting leftists causes in the early fifties.
AS A REGULAR: "The Singing Lady," ABC, 1948-50, 1953-54.

WICKES, MARY
b. Mary Isabelle Wickenhauser, St. Louis, MO, June 13, 1912. Slender actress who almost always plays good-hearted but tart-tongued housekeepers or nurses; she's still going strong on "The Father Dowling Mysteries."
AS A REGULAR: "Inside USA with Chevrolet," CBS, 1949-50; "The Peter Lind Hayes Show (The Peter and Mary Show)," NBC, 1950; "Bonino," NBC, 1953; "The Halls of Ivy," CBS, 1954-55; "Make Room for Daddy (The Danny Thomas Show)," ABC, 1956-57; CBS, 1957-58; "Mrs. G. Goes to College (The Gertrude Berg Show)," CBS, 1961-62; "Temple Houston," NBC, 1963-64; "Julia," NBC, 1968-71; "Doc," CBS, 1975-76; "The Father Dowling Mysteries," NBC, 1989; ABC, 1990- .

AND: "Studio One: Mary Poppins," CBS, 1949; "I Love Lucy: The Ballet," CBS, 1952; "Playhouse 90: Circle of the Day," CBS, 1957; "Startime: Cindy's Fella," NBC, 1959; "Dennis the Menace: Dennis and the Starlings," CBS, 1960; "Buick Electra Playhouse: The Gambler, The Nun and The Radio," CBS, 1960; "Shirley Temple's Storybook: The Princess and the Goblins," NBC, 1961; "Bonanza: The Colonel," NBC, 1963; "The Donna Reed Show: First Addition," ABC, 1964; "My Three Sons: Carribean Cruise," ABC, 1964; "The Lucy Show: Lucy and Clint Walker," CBS, 1965; "The Lucy Show: Lucy the Baby Sitter," CBS, 1967; "F Troop: Marriage, Fort Courage Style," ABC, 1967; "The Beverly Hillbillies: The Social Climbers," CBS, 1967; "The Lucy Show: Lucy and Robert Goulet," CBS, 1967; "The Lucy Show: Lucy's Mystery Guest," CBS, 1967; "Here's Lucy: Lucy Goes on Strike," CBS, 1969; "Here's Lucy: Lucy and Harry's Tonsils," CBS, 1969; "Columbo: Suitable for Framing," NBC, 1971; "Here's Lucy: Lucy and Her All-Nun Band," CBS, 1971; "The Jimmy Stewart Show: Period of Readjustment," NBC, 1971; "Sanford & Son: The Light House-keeper," NBC, 1972; "Here's Lucy: Lucy's Big Break," CBS, 1972; "Here's Lucy: Lucy and Eva Gabor Are Hospital Roommates," CBS, 1972; "Here's Lucy: Lucy Plays Cops and Robbers," CBS, 1973; "Here's Lucy: Lucy the Sheriff," CBS, 1974; "Kolchak, the Night Stalker: They Have Been, They Are, They Will Be," ABC, 1974; "M*A*S*H: House Arrest," CBS, 1975; "Match Game '76," CBS, 1976; "Highway to Heaven: Country Doctor," NBC, 1986.
TV MOVIES AND MINISERIES: "The Monk," ABC, 1969; "Willa," CBS, 1979; "The Christmas Gift," CBS, 1986; "Fatal Confession: A Father Dowling Mystery," NBC, 1988; "Almost Partners," PBS, 1989.

WIDMARK, RICHARD
b. Sunrise, MN, December 26, 1914. Screen actor at his best in tough roles ("Kiss of Death," "Murder on the Orient Express"); he played New York detective Sgt. Dan Madigan in a 1968 film and on TV.
AS A REGULAR: "Madigan," NBC, 1972-73.
AND: "I Love Lucy: The Tour," CBS, 1955; "The Spirit of the Alamo," ABC, 1960; "Here's Hollywood," NBC, 1962; "Benjamin Franklin: The Rebel," CBS, 1975.
TV MOVIES AND MINISERIES: "Vanished," NBC, 1971; "Brock's Last Case," NBC, 1973; "The Last Day," NBC, 1975; "All God's Children," ABC, 1980; "A Whale for the Killing," ABC, 1981; "Blackout," HBO, 1985; "A Gathering of Old Men," CBS, 1987; "Cold Sassy Tree," TNT, 1989.

THE WIERE BROTHERS
Harry, b. Berlin, Germany, 1908; Herbert, b.

Vienna, Austria, 1909; Sylvester, b. Prague, Czechoslovakia, 1910; d. 1970. Vaudeville comedy team without much TV success.
AS REGULARS: "Ford Festival," NBC, 1951-52; "Oh, Those Bells," CBS, 1962.
AND: "The Ed Sullivan Show," CBS, 1957; "The Perry Como Show," NBC, 1957; "Jerry Lewis Special," NBC, 1958; "The Garry Moore Show," CBS, 1959; "Perry Como's Kraft Music Hall," NBC, 1959; "Perry Como's Kraft Music Hall," NBC, 1960; "The Chevy Show," NBC, 1961; "High Hopes," SYN, 1961; "Art Linkletter's House Party," CBS, 1962; "Hollywood Palace," ABC, 1964.

WILCOX, LARRY
b. San Diego, CA, August 8, 1947. Blond actor who played Off. Jon Baker on "CHiPS."
AS A REGULAR: "Lassie," SYN, 1972-74; "CHiPS," NBC, 1977-82.
AND: "Room 222: Stay Awhile, Mr. Dreamchaser," ABC, 1971; "The Partridge Family: Heartbreak Keith," ABC, 1973; "Hawaii Five-O: The Young Assassins," CBS, 1974; "The Streets of San Francisco: The Runaways," ABC, 1974; "The Love Boat: Witness for the Prosecution," ABC, 1980; "Hardcastle and McCormick: Outlaw Champion," ABC, 1984; "Hotel: Ideals," ABC, 1984; "The Love Boat: Hippies and Yuppies," ABC, 1986; "Matlock: The Convict," NBC, 1987; "The New Mike Hammer: Body Shot," CBS, 1987; "Murder, She Wrote: Showdown in Saskatchewan," CBS, 1989.
TV MOVIES AND MINISERIES: "Mr. and Mrs. Bo Jo Jones," ABC, 1971; "The Great American Beauty Contest," ABC, 1973; "Death Stalk," NBC, 1974; "Sky Hei$t," NBC, 1975; "The Last Ride of the Dalton Gang," NBC, 1979; "The Love Tapes," ABC, 1980; "Deadly Lessons," ABC, 1983; "The Dirty Dozen: Next Mission," NBC, 1985; "Perry Mason: The Case of the Avenging Ace," NBC, 1988.

WILDER, GENE
b. Jerome Silberman, Milwaukee, WI, June 11, 1935. Frizzy-haired comic actor at his best in seventies films ("Blazing Saddles," "Young Frankenstein") and TV.
AS A GUEST: "Armstrong Circle Theatre: The Man Who Refused to Die," CBS, 1962; "Death of a Salesman," CBS, 1966; "Hollywood Television Theatre: The Scarecrow," NET, 1972; "The Trouble with People," NBC, 1972; "Acts of Love-And Other Comedies," ABC, 1973; "Home for Passover," NBC, 1973; "Annie and the Hoods," ABC, 1974.
TV MOVIES AND MINISERIES: "Thursday's Game," ABC, 1974.

WILLARD, FRED
b. Shaker Heights, OH, September 18, 1939.

Comedian who played dim co-host Jerry Hubbard on "Fernwood 2-Night."
AS A REGULAR: "The Burns and Schreiber Comedy Hour," ABC, 1973; "Sirota's Court," NBC, 1976-77; "Fernwood 2-Night," SYN, 1977-78; "Real People," NBC, 1979, 1981-83; "Thicke of the Night," SYN, 1983-84; "D.C. Follies," SYN, 1987-89.
AND: "The Ed Sullivan Show," CBS, 1964; "The Garry Moore Show," CBS, 1964; "Hey, Landlord!: The Big Fumble," NBC, 1966; "Get Smart: A Tale of Two Tails," NBC, 1968; "Love, American Style: Love and the Nuisance," ABC, 1970; "The Bob Newhart Show: Tobin's Back in Town," CBS, 1975; "Laverne & Shirley: Dog Day Blind Dates," ABC, 1976; "Saturday Night Live," NBC, 1978; "The Love Boat: Then There Were Two," ABC, 1981; "The Love Boat: Couples," ABC, 1986; "Late Night with David Letterman," NBC, 1987; "Animal Crack-Ups," ABC, 1989.
TV MOVIES AND MINISERIES: "How to Break Up a Happy Divorce," NBC, 1976; "Escape From Bogen County," CBS, 1977; "Flatbed Annie and Sweetiepie: Lady Truckers," CBS, 1979; "Salem's Lot," CBS, 1979.
* Willard made his TV debut with Ed Sullivan as part of a comedy team with Vic Grecco.

WILLIAMS, ANDY
b. Wall Lake, IA, December 3, 1930. Smooth-voiced, cardigan-wearing sixties singer; he began as part of a brother group.
AS A REGULAR: "The College Bowl," ABC, 1950-51; "The Tonight Show (Tonight)," NBC, 1954-57; "The Andy Williams and June Valli Show," NBC, 1957; "The Chevy Showroom," ABC, 1958; "The Andy Williams Show," ABC, 1958; CBS, 1959; NBC, 1962-67, 1969-71; SYN, 1976-77.
AND: "The Jonathan Winters Show," NBC, 1957; "Club 60," NBC, 1957; "Rock 'n' Roll," ABC, 1957; "Five Stars in Springtime," NBC, 1957; "The Big Beat," ABC, 1957; "The Steve Allen Show," NBC, 1957; "American Bandstand," ABC, 1957; "The Big Record," CBS, 1957; "The Patrice Munsel Show," ABC, 1957; "Pat Boone Chevy Showroom," ABC, 1958; "American Bandstand," ABC, 1958; "The Dick Clark Saturday Night Beechnut Show," ABC, 1958; "The Chevy Show," NBC, 1958; "The Perry Como Show," NBC, 1958; "Pat Boone Chevy Showroom," ABC, 1959; "The Garry Moore Show," CBS, 1959; "Music From Shubert Alley," NBC, 1959; "Pontiac Star Parade: The Man in the Moon," NBC, 1960; "The Dick Powell Show: A Time to Die," NBC, 1962; "The Joey Bishop Show: Andy Williams Visits Joey," NBC, 1964; "The Jack Benny Program," NBC, 1964; "Feliciano-Very Special," NBC, 1969; "Flip Wilson Special," NBC, 1969; "Movin'," NBC, 1970; "Andy Williams Special," NBC, 1974;

"Paul Lynde Special," ABC, 1975; "Barbara Mandrell and the Mandrell Sisters," NBC, 1981; "Bob Hope's Easter Vacation in the Bahamas," NBC, 1989.

WILLIAMS, ANSON
b. Los Angeles, CA, September 25, 1949. Actor who played Warren "Potsie" Weber on "Happy Days."
AS A REGULAR: "Happy Days," ABC, 1974-83.
AND: "The Paul Lynde Show: Whiz Kid Sizzles as Quiz Fizzles," ABC, 1972; "Love, American Style: Love and the Happy Day," ABC, 1972; "Marcus Welby, M.D.: The Panic Path," ABC, 1973; "The $10,000 Pyramid," CBS, 1974; "Laverne & Shirley: Excuse Me, May I Cut In?," ABC, 1976; "Break the Bank," SYN, 1976; "Tattletales," CBS, 1977; "Dolly," SYN, 1979; "Dance Fever," SYN, 1981; "The John Davidson Show," SYN, 1981.
TV MOVIES AND MINISERIES: "Lisa, Bright and Dark," CBS, 1973; "I Married a Centerfold," NBC, 1984.
AS DIRECTOR: "Little White Lies," NBC, 1989.

WILLIAMS, BARRY
b. Santa Monica, CA, September 30, 1954. Actor who played Greg, the oldest Brady child in the bunch.
AS A REGULAR: "The Brady Bunch," ABC, 1969-74; "The Brady Bunch Hour," ABC, 1977; "The Bradys," CBS, 1990.
AND: "The FBI: The Messenger," ABC, 1968; "Lancer: Blood Rock," CBS, 1968; "Marcus Welby, M.D.: The Chemistry of Hope," ABC, 1969; "Mission: Impossible: Gitano," CBS, 1970; "Police Woman: Generation of Evil," NBC, 1976; "Three's Company: Up in the Air," ABC, 1982; "Murder, She Wrote: Night of the Headless Horseman," CBS, 1986.
TV MOVIES AND MINISERIES: "The Brady Girls Get Married," NBC, 1981; "A Very Brady Christmas," CBS, 1988.

WILLIAMS, BILL
b. Brooklyn, NY, May 15, 1916. Actor who'll probably always be known, to his chagrin, as Kit Carson.
AS A REGULAR: "Adventures in Jazz," CBS, 1949; "Starlit Time," DUM, 1950; "The Adventures of Kit Carson," SYN, 1951-55; "Music at the Meadowbrook," ABC, 1953, 1956; "Date with the Angels," ABC, 1957-58; "Walt Disney Presents: Texas John Slaughter," ABC, 1958-59; "Assignment: Underwater," SYN, 1960-61.
AND: "Bigelow Theatre: Make Your Bed," CBS, 1951; "Twilight Theatre: Crew Cut," ABC, 1953; "Science Fiction Theatre: The Hastings Secret," SYN, 1955; "Schlitz Playhouse of Stars: Well of Anger," CBS, 1955; "Science Fiction Theatre:

Project 44," SYN, 1956; "Schlitz Playhouse of
Stars: Angels in the Sky," CBS, 1956; "Damon
Runyon Theatre: Miracle Jones," CBS, 1956;
"Science Fiction Theatre: The Mind Machine,"
SYN, 1956; "The Millionaire: Millionaire Martha
Halloran," CBS, 1959; "G.E. Theatre: The Flying
Wife," CBS, 1959; "Westinghouse Desilu
Playhouse: The Untouchables," CBS, 1959;
"Bachelor Father: East Meets West," CBS, 1959;
"Men Into Space: Asteroid," CBS, 1959;
"Laramie: Man of God," NBC, 1959; "Here's
Hollywood," NBC, 1960; "My Sister Eileen:
Marty's Best Friend," CBS, 1961; "Perry Mason:
The Case of the Crippled Cougar," CBS, 1962;
"Lawman: Get Out of Town," ABC, 1962; "77
Sunset Strip: The Snow Job Caper," ABC, 1962;
"Perry Mason: The Case of the Bluffing Blast,"
CBS, 1963; "Rawhide: The Last Herd," CBS,
1964; "The Littlest Hobo: Ninety Dollars for
Mary," SYN, 1964; "Perry Mason: The Case of
the Murderous Mermaid," CBS, 1965; "The Wild
Wild West: The Night of the Casual Killer," CBS,
1965; "Perry Mason: The Case of the Twelfth
Wildcat," CBS, 1965; "Batman: Fine Finny
Fiends/Batman Makes the Scenes," ABC, 1966;
"Walt Disney's Wonderful World of Color: Trial
by Error," NBC, 1967; "Dragnet: The Big Blank,"
NBC, 1967; "Lassie: A Chance to Live," CBS,
1968; "The FBI: The Runaways," ABC, 1968;
"Marcus Welby, M.D.: To Carry the Sun in a
Golden Cup," ABC, 1970; "Ironside: Nightmare
Trip," NBC, 1972; "O'Hara, U.S. Treasury:
Operation Smokescreen," CBS, 1972;
"Gunsmoke: Talbot," CBS, 1973; "Walt Disney's
Wonderful World of Color: Chester, Yesterday's
Horse," NBC, 1973; "The Streets of San
Francisco: The Unicorn," ABC, 1973; "The
Rookies: Three Hours to Kill," ABC, 1973; "The
Rookies: Get Ryker," ABC, 1973; "Adam 12:
West Valley Division," NBC, 1974; "The
Rookies: Something Less Than a Man," ABC,
1974; "The FBI: The Lost Man," ABC, 1974;
"The Wonderful World of Disney: The Flight of
the Grey Wolf," NBC, 1976; "Police Woman:
Sara Who?," NBC, 1976.
TV MOVIES AND MINISERIES: "Carter's Army,"
ABC, 1970; "The Phantom of Hollywood,"
CBS, 1974; "Goldie and the Boxer Go to
Hollywood," NBC, 1981.

WILLIAMS, BILLY DEE
b. *New York City, NY, April 6, 1937*. Black
actor in debonair roles; also a spokesman for
Colt 45 malt liquor ("It works every time") in
some controversial TV spots.
AS A REGULAR: "The Guiding Light," CBS, 1966;
"Double Dare," CBS, 1985.
AND: "The FBI: Eye of the Storm," ABC, 1969;
"The FBI: The Sanctuary," ABC, 1969; "The
New People: The Prisoner of Bomano," ABC,
1969; "The FBI: The Architect," ABC, 1970;

"The Jeffersons: Me and Billy Dee," CBS, 1978;
"227: Play It Again, Stan," NBC, 1989.
TV MOVIES AND MINISERIES: "Brian's Song," ABC,
1971; "Truman Capote's The Glass House,"
CBS, 1972; "The Hostage Tower," CBS, 1980;
"Time Bomb," NBC, 1984; "The Imposter,"
ABC, 1984; "Oceans of Fire," CBS, 1986;
"The Return of Desperado," NBC, 1988.

WILLIAMS, CARA
b. *Bernice Kamiat, Brooklyn, NY, June 29,
1925*. Redheaded actress who played a
scatterbrain on two sixties sitcoms; her
reputation for temperament and a stormy
marriage to John Barrymore Jr. hampered her
employment.
AS A REGULAR: "Pete and Gladys," CBS, 1960-62;
"The Cara Williams Show," CBS, 1964-65;
"Rhoda," CBS, 1974-75.
AND: "The Trap: Lonely Boy," CBS, 1950;
"Armstrong Circle Theatre: Man and Wife,"
NBC, 1950; "Broadway TV Theatre: Within the
Law," SYN, 1950; "Matinee Theatre: Beyond a
Reasonable Doubt," NBC, 1955; "Alfred
Hitchcock Presents: The Decoy," CBS, 1956;
"Alfred Hitchcock Presents: De Mortius," CBS,
1956; "The Jane Wyman Show: Harbor Patrol,"
NBC, 1957; "Alfred Hitchcock Presents: Last
Request," CBS, 1957; "Westinghouse Desilu
Playhouse: Meeting at Apalachin," CBS, 1960;
"Alfred Hitchcock Presents: The Cure," CBS,
1960; "Dick Powell's Zane Grey Theatre: Seed of
Evil," CBS, 1960; "The Red Skelton Show:
Appleby's Remote Control," CBS, 1961; "The
Red Skelton Show: Freddie and the Yuletide
Doll," CBS, 1961; "Jackie Gleason and His
American Scene Magazine," CBS, 1962; "Henry
Fonda and the Family," CBS, 1962; "Art
Linkletter's House Party," CBS, 1964; "Medical
Center: The Happy State of Depression," CBS,
1976.

WILLIAMS, CINDY
b. *Van Nuys, CA, August 22, 1947*. Petite
comic actress who played Shirley Feeney to
Penny Marshall's Laverne De Fazio.
AS A REGULAR: "The Funny Side," NBC, 1971;
"Laverne & Shirley," ABC, 1976-82; "Normal
Life," CBS, 1990.
AND: "Room 222: The Exchange Teacher," ABC,
1970; "Room 222: I Love You, Charlie-I Love
You, Abbie," ABC, 1970; "Room 222: Laura Fay,
You're Okay!," ABC, 1971; "Nanny and the
Professor: The Art of Relationships," ABC, 1971;
"Love, American Style: Love and the Face Bow,"
ABC, 1973; "Love, American Style: Love and the
Time Machine," ABC, 1973; "CBS Playhouse 90:
The Migrants," CBS, 1974; "Happy Days: A Date
with the Fonz," ABC, 1975; "Happy Days: Fonzie
the Superstar," ABC, 1976; "Petrocelli: Survival,"
NBC, 1976; "Dinah!," SYN, 1976; "General

Electric's All-Star Anniversary," ABC, 1978; "Mork & Mindy: Mork Moves In," ABC, 1978; "Happy Days: Shotgun Wedding," ABC, 1979; "Andy Kaufman Special," ABC, 1980; "The Magical World of Disney: Save the Dog," NBC, 1989.

TV MOVIES AND MINISERIES: "Suddenly, Love," NBC, 1978; "When Dreams Come True," ABC, 1985.

* Williams left "Laverne & Shirley" when she claimed the show's producers wouldn't make her work load easier to accomodate her pregnancy. Then she claimed she was treated unfairly by the show's producer-creator, Garry Marshall, the brother of Williams' co-star, Penny Marshall. The Marshalls claimed that Williams was paranoid and difficult to work with.

WILLIAMS, CLARENCE III
b. *New York City, NY, August 21, 1939.* Actor who played Lincoln Hayes on "The Mod Squad."
AS A REGULAR: "The Mod Squad," ABC, 1968-73.
AND: "Directions '66: J.F. Power: The Darkness and the Grace," ABC, 1966; "Daktari: Goodbye, Wameru," CBS, 1967; "Tarzan: The Professional," NBC, 1968; "The Danny Thomas Hour: Measure of a Man," NBC, 1968; "Orson Welles' Great Mysteries: The Furnished Room," SYN, 1974; "Hill Street Blues: Parting Is Such Sweep Sorrow," NBC, 1984; "The Cosby Show: Cliff's Birthday," NBC, 1985; "Miami Vice: Tale of the Goat," NBC, 1986.
TV MOVIES AND MINISERIES: "The Return of Mod Squad," ABC, 1979.

WILLIAMS, GRANT
b. *New York City, NY, August 18, 1930; d. 1985.* Generic TV hunk who played gumshoe Greg MacKenzie on "Hawaiian Eye" and "The Incredible Shrinking Man" on the big screen.
AS A REGULAR: "Hawaiian Eye," ABC, 1960-63.
AND: "Lux Video Theatre: Paris Calling," NBC, 1957; "Matinee Theatre: The Little Minister," NBC, 1957; "Shirley Temple's Storybook: The Wild Swans," NBC, 1958; "Yancy Derringer: Longhair," CBS, 1959; "Walt Disney Presents: The Peter Tchaikovsky Story," ABC, 1959; "Gunsmoke: The Bear," CBS, 1959; "The Millionaire: Millionaire Grant Burton," CBS, 1959; "Alcoa Presents One Step Beyond: Dead Ringer," ABC, 1959; "Bonanza: Escape to the Ponderosa," NBC, 1960; "Mr. Lucky: Stacked Deck," CBS, 1960; "SurfSide 6: Par-a-kee," ABC, 1960; "The Roaring Twenties: Brother's Keeper," ABC, 1960; "SurfSide 6: Bride and Seek," ABC, 1960; "The Munsters: Sleeping Cutie," CBS, 1964; "The Outer Limits: The Brain of Colonel Barham," ABC, 1965; "The FBI: Breakthrough," ABC, 1968; "Dragnet: B.O.D.-Dr-27," NBC, 1969.

WILLIAMS, GUY
b. *Armando Catalano, New York City, NY, January 14, 1924; d. 1989.* Actor who played Zorro and stern-but-understanding dad John Robinson on "Lost in Space."
AS A REGULAR: "Zorro," ABC, 1957-59; "Walt Disney Presents: Zorro," ABC, 1960-61; "Lost in Space," CBS, 1965-68.
AND: "Disneyland: Fourth Anniversary Show," ABC, 1957; "Maverick: Dade City Dodge," ABC, 1961; "Here's Hollywood," NBC, 1961; "Walt Disney's Wonderful World of Color: The Prince and the Pauper," NBC, 1962; "You Don't Say," NBC, 1966.

WILLIAMS, HAL
b. *Columbus, OH, December 14, 1938.* Burly black actor who played Sgt. Major Ross on "Private Benjamin" and Lester Jenkins on "227."
AS A REGULAR: "Sanford & Son," NBC, 1972-76; "On the Rocks," ABC, 1975-76; "Private Benjamin," CBS, 1981-83; "227," NBC, 1985-90.
AND: "Kung Fu: The Well," ABC, 1973; "The Magician: The Man Who Lost Himself," NBC, 1973; "Good Times: Getting Up the Rent," CBS, 1974; "Police Woman: Anatomy of Two Rapes," NBC, 1974; "Harry O: Shadows at Noon," ABC, 1974; "Harry O: Double Jeopardy," ABC, 1975; "Quincy: The Hot Dog Murder," NBC, 1977; "The Jeffersons: Louise's Friend," CBS, 1977; "Good Times: The Teacher," CBS, 1978; "What's Happening!: The Eviction," ABC, 1979; "The White Shadow: Sudden Death," CBS, 1979; "American Short Story: The Sky Is Gray," PBS, 1980; "Sanford: Cal the Coward," NBC, 1981; "Gimme a Break: TV or Not TV," NBC, 1984; "Webster: Webster Long," ABC, 1984.
TV MOVIES AND MINISERIES: "Sidekicks," CBS, 1974; "Thou Shalt Not Commit Adultery," NBC, 1978; "Roots: The Next Generations," ABC, 1979.

WILLIAMS, JOHN
b. *England, April 15, 1903.* Solid, mustachioed British actor who played Giles French on "Family Affair" and appeared in several memorable episodes of "Alfred Hitchcock Presents"; he appeared as the canny inspector in the stage, screen and TV versions of "Dial M for Murder."
AS A REGULAR: "The Rogues," NBC, 1964-65; "Family Affair," CBS, 1967.
AND: "Alfred Hitchcock Presents: Back for Christmas," CBS, 1956; "Alfred Hitchcock Presents: Wet Saturday," CBS, 1956; "Alfred Hitchcock Presents: The Rose Garden," CBS, 1956; "Alfred Hitchcock Presents: One for the Road," CBS, 1957; "Alcoa Hour: The Original

Miss Chase," NBC, 1957; "Alfred Hitchcock Presents: I Killed the Count," CBS, 1957; "Playhouse 90: The Clouded Image," CBS, 1957; "Suspicion: Rainy Day," NBC, 1957; "Father Knows Best: Mr. Beal Meets His Match," NBC, 1957; "Playhouse 90: Point of No Return," CBS, 1958; "Hallmark Hall of Fame: Dial M for Murder," NBC, 1958; "Du Pont Show of the Month: What Every Woman Knows," CBS, 1959; "Alfred Hitchcock Presents: Banquo's Chair," CBS, 1959; "Westinghouse Desilu Playhouse: Perilous," CBS, 1959; "Playhouse 90: Misalliance," CBS, 1959; "Checkmate: Murder Game," CBS, 1960; "Twenty-Four Hours in a Woman's Life," CBS, 1961; "Malibu Run: The Radioactive-Object Adventure," CBS, 1961; "Thriller: Yours Truly, Jack the Ripper," NBC, 1961; "Bus Stop: Accessory by Consent," ABC, 1961; "Alcoa Premiere: The Hands of Danofrio," ABC, 1962; "Dr. Kildare: The Thing Speaks for Itself," NBC, 1963; "Hallmark Hall of Fame: Pygmalion," NBC, 1963; "My Three Sons: Bub's Butler," ABC, 1963; "The Twilight Zone: The Bard," CBS, 1963; "The Lucy Show: Lucy and the Great Bank Robbery," CBS, 1964; "Valentine's Day: If Africa Speaks, Don't Answer," ABC, 1964; "The Wild Wild West: The Night of the Bleak Island," CBS, 1966; "Combat!: The Furlough," ABC, 1966; "Mission: Impossible: Lover's Knot," CBS, 1970; "Columbo: Dagger of the Mind," NBC, 1972; "Love, American Style: Love and the Generation Gap," ABC, 1973.

TV MOVIES AND MINISERIES: "The Hound of the Baskervilles," ABC, 1972.

WILLIAMS, PAUL

b. Omaha, NB, September 19, 1940. Tiny composer who's played his own sardonic self on TV variety shows and done a bit of dramatic TV as well.

AS A GUEST: "Midnight Special," NBC, 1973; "The Merv Griffin Show," SYN, 1974; "The Odd Couple: The Paul Williams Show," ABC, 1974; "Password," ABC, 1974; "The Mac Davis Show," NBC, 1974; "Password All-Stars," ABC, 1975; "When Things Were Rotten: The House Band," ABC, 1975; "Sammy and Company," SYN, 1977; "Donny and Marie," ABC, 1977; "Police Woman: Ambition," NBC, 1977; "The Love Boat: Musical Cabins," ABC, 1978; "Bonkers!," SYN, 1978; "B.J. and the Bear: Blonde in a Gilded Cell," NBC, 1981; "The Love Boat: Rhymes, Riddles and Romance," ABC, 1982; "Fantasy Island: The Witness," ABC, 1982; "Wonderworks: Frog," PBS, 1988; "227: Play It Again, Stan," NBC, 1989.

TV MOVIES AND MINISERIES: "Flight to Holocaust," NBC, 1977; "The Wild Wild West Revisited," CBS, 1979; "Battle of the Generations," NBC,

WILLIAMS, ROBIN

b. Chicago, IL, July 21, 1952. Manic comedian

who played Mork the martian on a hugely successful sitcom.

AS A REGULAR: "The Richard Pryor Show," NBC, 1977; "Laugh-In," NBC, 1977-78; "Mork & Mindy," ABC, 1978-82.

AND: "Happy Days: My Favorite Orkan," ABC, 1978; "Happy Days: Mork Returns," ABC, 1979; "Out of the Blue: Random's Arrival," ABC, 1979; "Faerie Tale Theatre: Tale of the Frog Prince," SHO, 1982; "An Evening with Robin Williams," HBO, 1983; "Saturday Night Live," NBC, 1984; "Saturday Night Live," NBC, 1986; "Carol, Carl, Whoopi and Robin," ABC, 1986; "Saturday Night Live," NBC, 1988; "Late Night with David Letterman," NBC, 1988.

* Emmies: 1987.

WILLIAMS, SPENCER

b. Vidalia, LA, July 14, 1893; d. 1969. Actor who played Andy Brown on "Amos 'n Andy."

AS A REGULAR: "Amos 'n Andy," CBS, 1951-53.

WILLIAMS, VAN

b. Fort Worth, TX, February 27, 1934. Actor who played private eye Ken Madison on "Bourbon Street Beat" and "SurfSide 6" and who also played Britt Reid, aka the Green Hornet.

AS A REGULAR: "Bourbon Street Beat," ABC, 1959-60; "SurfSide 6," ABC, 1960-62; "The Tycoon," ABC, 1964-65; "The Green Hornet," ABC, 1966-67.

AND: "Cheyenne: Vengeance Is Mine," ABC, 1962; "77 Sunset Strip: The Tarnished Idol," ABC, 1963; "The Gallant Men: The Leathernecks," ABC, 1963; "Hawaiian Eye: Two Million Too Much," ABC, 1963; "Temple Houston: Ten Rounds for Baby," NBC, 1964; "The Dick Van Dyke Show: No Rice at My Wedding," CBS, 1965; "The Beverly Hillbillies: The Courtship of Elly," CBS, 1965; "Batman: The Spell of Tut/The Case is Shut," ABC, 1966; "Batman: A Piece of the Action/Batman's Satisfaction," ABC, 1967; "Love, American Style: Love and the Minister," ABC, 1970; "Mannix: The Search for Darrell Andrews," CBS, 1970; "Nanny and the Professor: The Visitor," ABC, 1970; "Mission: Impossible: The Deal," CBS, 1972; "Gunsmoke: Thirty a Month and Found," CBS, 1974; "Barnaby Jones: Circle of Treachery," CBS, 1977.

TV MOVIES AND MINISERIES: "The Runaways," CBS, 1975; "The Night Rider," ABC, 1979.

WILLIAMSON, FRED

b. Gary, IN, March 5, 1938. Former football player, now an actor in macho roles; he played Steve Bruce, gentleman friend of Julia Baker (Diahann Carroll) on "Julia."

AS A REGULAR: "Julia," NBC, 1970-71; "Half Nelson," NBC, 1985.

AND: "Police Story: Dangerous Games," NBC,

1973; "The Rookies: Johnny Lost His Gun," ABC, 1974; "Police Story: Thanksgiving," NBC, 1976; "CHiPS: Roller Disco," NBC, 1979; "Lou Grant: Violence," CBS, 1981.
TV MOVIES AND MINISERIES: "Deadlock," NBC, 1969; "Arthur Hailey's Wheels," NBC, 1978.

WILLIS, BRUCE
b. March 19, 1955, Germany. Emmy winning actor who played gumshoe David Addison on "Moonlighting."
AS A REGULAR: "Moonlighting," ABC, 1985-89.
AND: "Miami Vice: No Exit," NBC, 1984; "The Twilight Zone: Shatterday," CBS, 1985; "All Star Tribute to Kareem Abdul-Jabbar," NBC, 1989; "Saturday Night Live," NBC, 1989.
* Emmies: 1987.

WILLS, BEVERLY
b. Los Angeles, 1934; d. 1963. Daughter of comic Joan Davis, who played her sister on TV.
AS A REGULAR: "I Married Joan," NBC, 1952-55.
AND: "Tales of Wells Fargo: Man in the Box," NBC, 1957; "Matinee Theatre: Out of the Frying Pan," NBC, 1958; "The Tall Man: The Impatient Brides," NBC, 1962; "Mr. Ed: Ed the Shiskabob," CBS, 1964.
* Wills died in a house fire.
* See also Joan Davis.

WILLSON, MEREDITH
b. Mason City, IA, May 18, 1902; d. 1984. Orchestra leader and composer; he wrote "The Music Man."
AS A REGULAR: "The Meredith Willson Show," NBC, 1949; "The Name's the Same," ABC, 1951-53.
AND: "The Garry Moore Show," CBS, 1959; "Art Linkletter's House Party," CBS, 1959; "Dinah Shore Chevy Show," NBC, 1961; "Here's Hollywood," NBC, 1961.

WILSON, DEMOND
b. Valdosta, GA, October 13, 1946. Actor who played Lamont, son of Fred Sanford (Redd Foxx).
AS A REGULAR: "Sanford & Son," NBC, 1972-77; "Baby I'm Back," CBS, 1978; "The New Odd Couple," ABC, 1982-83.
AND: "All in the Family: Edith Writes a Song," CBS, 1971; "Hollywood Squares," NBC, 1973; "Hollywood Squares," NBC, 1974; "Hollywood Squares," SYN, 1975; "The Love Boat: A Letter to Babycakes," ABC, 1979; "The Love Boat: Black Sheep," ABC, 1981; "Today's FBI: Terror," ABC, 1981.

WILSON, DON
b. Lincoln, NB, 1900; d. 1982. Jolly, jowly announcer and sidekick to Jack Benny.

AS A REGULAR: "The Jack Benny Program," CBS, 1950-64; NBC, 1964-65.
AND: "Shower of Stars: Jack Benny's 40th Birthday Celebration," CBS, 1958; "The Red Skelton Show," CBS, 1958; "The Perry Como Show," NBC, 1958; "Christophers: The Life of Robert E. Lee," SYN, 1958; "The Red Skelton Show," CBS, 1959; "Christophers: Some Facts on Nathaniel Greene," SYN, 1959; "Death Valley Days: Gates Ajar Morgan, SYN, 1959; "Harrigan and Son: Junior's Other Job," ABC, 1961; "Batman: Hizzoner the Penguin/Dizzoner the Penguin," ABC, 1966.

WILSON, DOOLEY
b. Arthur Wilson, Tyler, TX, April 3, 1894; d. 1953. Character actor best known as the piano-playing Sam in the film "Casablanca."
AS A REGULAR: "Beulah," ABC, 1951-52.

WILSON, EARL
b. Rockford, OH, May 3, 1907; d. 1987. Newspaper columnist.
AS A REGULAR: "Stage Entrance," DUM, 1951-52; "The Tonight Show (Tonight! America After Dark)," NBC, 1957.
AND: "The Garry Moore Show," CBS, 1957; "Play Your Hunch," NBC, 1962.

WILSON, ELIZABETH
b. Grand Rapids, MI, April 4, 1925.
AS A REGULAR: "East Side/West Side," CBS, 1963-64; "Doc," CBS, 1975-76; "Morningstar/Eveningstar," CBS, 1986.
AND: "Omnibus: School for Wives," ABC, 1956; "U.S. Steel Hour: The Pink Burro," CBS, 1959; "U.S. Steel Hour: Rachel's Summer," CBS, 1959; "U.S. Steel Hour: Queen of the Orange Bowl," CBS, 1960; "Armstrong Circle Theatre: Black-Market Babies," CBS, 1961; "U.S. Steel Hour: Welcome Home," CBS, 1961; "The Doctors and the Nurses: Sixteen Hours to Chicago," CBS, 1965; "Maude: The Wife Swappers," CBS, 1975; "All in the Family: Amelia's Divorce," CBS, 1975; "Love, Sidney: A Piece of the Rock," NBC, 1981.
TV MOVIES AND MINISERIES: "G.E. Theatre: Miles to Go Before I Sleep," CBS, 1975; "Sanctuary of Fear," NBC, 1979; "Conspiracy of Love," CBS, 1987.

WILSON, FLIP
b. Clerow Wilson, Jersey City, NJ, December 8, 1933. Comedian whose career peaked in the seventies.
AS A REGULAR: "The Flip Wilson Show," NBC, 1970-74; "People Are Funny," NBC, 1984; "Charlie & Company," CBS, 1985-86.
AND: "The Mike Douglas Show," SYN, 1967; "Hollywood Squares," NBC, 1968; "Rowan &

Martin's Laugh-In," NBC, 1968; "Kraft Music Hall: Roast for Johnny Carson," NBC, 1968; "The Carol Burnett Show," CBS, 1968; "Flip Wilson Special," NBC, 1969; "Hollywood Palace," ABC, 1969; "Love, American Style: Love and the Hustler," ABC, 1969; "The Many Moods of Perry Como," NBC, 1970; "Here's Lucy: Lucy and Flip Go Legit," CBS, 1971; "The David Frost Revue," SYN, 1971; "Clerow Wilson and the Miracle of P.S. 114," NBC, 1973; "Clerow Wilson's Great Escape," NBC, 1974; "Joys," NBC, 1976; "Pinocchio," CBS, 1976; "The Six Million Dollar Man: Privacy of the Mind," ABC, 1976; "The Sonny and Cher Comedy Hour," CBS, 1977; "Saturday Night Live," NBC, 1983; "227: Mary's Cookies," NBC, 1989.

WILSON, JOYCE VINCENT
b. Detroit, MI, December 14, 1946. One-third of the seventies singing group Dawn.
AS A REGULAR: "Tony Orlando and Dawn," CBS, 1974-76.
AND: "American Bandstand," ABC, 1972; "It's Garry Shandling's Show: Save Mr. Peck's," FOX, 1989; "The Pat Sajak Show," CBS, 1989.

WILSON, MARIE
b. Katherine Elizabeth Wilson, Anaheim, CA, December 30, 1916; d. 1972. Attractive blonde actress who played the scatterbrained Irma Peterson in a popular radio and TV sitcom.
AS A REGULAR: "My Friend Irma," CBS, 1952-54; "Where's Huddles?," CBS, 1970.
AND: "The Ed Sullivan Show," CBS, 1957; "The Red Skelton Show," CBS, 1957; "The Ford Show," NBC, 1957; "The Eddie Fisher Show," NBC, 1957; "The Lux Show with Rosemary Clooney," NBC, 1957; "The Red Skelton Show," CBS, 1958; "The Garry Moore Show," CBS, 1959; "The Ed Sullivan Show," CBS, 1960; "Arthur Murray Party," NBC, 1960; "Here's Hollywood," NBC, 1961; "Empire: Hidden Asset," NBC, 1963; "Burke's Law: Who Killed Marty Kelso?," ABC, 1964; "Burke's Law: Who Killed Wimbeldon Hastings?," ABC, 1965.

WILSON, TERRY
b. Huntington Park, CA, September 3, 1923. Actor who played Bill Hawks on "Wagon Train."
AS A REGULAR: "Wagon Train," NBC, 1957-62; ABC, 1962-65.
AND: "The Road West: This Savage Land," NBC, 1966; "The Virginian: The Sins of the Fathers," NBC, 1970.
TV MOVIES AND MINISERIES: "The Daughters of Joshua Cabe Return," ABC, 1975.
AS WRITER: "Wagon Train: The Ah Chong Story," NBC, 1961.

WILSON, THEODORE
b. New York City, NY, December 10, 1943. Black actor usually in sitcom roles.
AS A REGULAR: "Roll Out," CBS, 1973-74; "That's My Mama," ABC, 1974-75; "The Sanford Arms," NBC, 1977; "Good Times," CBS, 1978-79; "Crazy Like a Fox," CBS, 1985-86; "The Redd Foxx Show," ABC, 1986; "You Can't Take It with You," SYN, 1987-88.
AND: "First Family of Washington," ABC, 1973; "The Partridge Family: Hate Thy Neighbor," ABC, 1973; "Police Story: Requiem for Bored Wives," NBC, 1974; "M*A*S*H: The General Flipped at Dawn," CBS, 1974; "Good Times: Sweet Daddy Williams," CBS, 1976; "Good Heavens: Jack the Ribber," ABC, 1976; "What's Happening!: The Runaway," ABC, 1976; "All in the Family: Archie's Brief Encounter," CBS, 1976; "Police Woman: Shadow of Doubt," NBC, 1977; "Kojak: Once More From Birdland," CBS, 1977; "What's Happening!: Doobie or Doobie Not," ABC, 1978; "The White Shadow: A Christmas Present," CBS, 1979; "The White Shadow: Salami's Affair," CBS, 1980; "Gimme a Break: Flashback," NBC, 1984; "Cagney & Lacey: Play It Again, Santa," CBS, 1985; "The Twilight Zone: Night of the Meek," CBS, 1985; "Hardcastle and McCormick: McCormick's Bar and Grill," ABC, 1986; "Easy Street: Be-Bop Man," NBC, 1986; "Cagney & Lacey: Easy Does It," CBS, 1987; "The New Mike Hammer: Body Shot," CBS, 1987; "L.A. Law: Victor Victorious," NBC, 1989; "Alien Nation: Chains of Love," FOX, 1989; "Alien Nation: The Game," FOX, 1989; "Midnight Caller: Take Back the Streets," NBC, 1989.
TV MOVIES AND MINISERIES: "The Love Boat," ABC, 1976; "Malice in Wonderland," CBS, 1985; "Kiss Shot," CBS, 1989.

WINCHELL, PAUL
b. New York City, NY, December 21, 1922. Ventriloquist, with dummies Jerry Mahoney and Knucklehead Smith.
AS A REGULAR: "The Bigelow Show," NBC, 1948-49; CBS, 1949; "The Paul Winchell-Jerry Mahoney Show," NBC, 1950-54; "What's My Name?," NBC, 1952-54; "Circus Time," ABC, 1956-57; "The Paul Winchell Show," ABC, 1957-60; "Keep Talking," CBS, 1958-59; ABC, 1959-60; "Runaround, NBC, 1972-73.
AND: "Five Star Comedy Party," ABC, 1957; "Arthur Murray Party," NBC, 1957; "The Vic Damone Show," CBS, 1957; "Pat Boone Chevy Showroom," ABC, 1957; "The Polly Bergen Show," NBC, 1957; "Ted Mack's Amateur Hour," NBC, 1958; "Arthur Murray Party," NBC, 1959; "The Lineup: Death of a Puppet," CBS, 1959; "Arthur Murray Party," NBC, 1960; "All-Star Circus," NBC, 1960; "Dan Raven: Man on the Ledge," NBC, 1960; "American Bandstand,"

ABC, 1960; "Candid Camera," CBS, 1961; "Your First Impression," NBC, 1962; "The Beverly Hillbillies: Home for Christmas," CBS, 1962; "The Beverly Hillbillies: No Place Like Home," CBS, 1962; "77 Sunset Strip: Falling Stars," ABC, 1963; "Your First Impression," NBC, 1963; "The Donna Reed Show: The Chinese Horse," ABC, 1963; "The Donna Reed Show: All Those Dreams," ABC, 1963; "Object Is," ABC, 1964; "Perry Mason: The Case of the Nervous Neighbor," CBS, 1964; "The Dick Van Dyke Show: Talk to the Snail," CBS, 1966; "The Lucy Show: Lucy and Paul Winchell," CBS, 1966; "The Lucy Show: Mainstreet USA," CBS, 1967; "Rowan & Martin's Laugh-In," NBC, 1968; "The Virginian: Dark Corridor," NBC, 1968; "The Steve Allen Show," SYN, 1968; "Rowan & Martin's Laugh-In," NBC, 1969; "Here's Lucy: Lucy the Cement Worker," CBS, 1969; "Love, American Style: Love and the Serious Wedding," ABC, 1969; "Hollywood Squares," NBC, 1970; "Nanny and the Professor: The Humanization of Herbert T. Peabody," ABC, 1970; "Love, American Style: Love and the Dummies," ABC, 1971; "The Brady Bunch: And Now a Word From Our Sponsor," ABC, 1971; "Love, American Style: Love and Lover's Lane," ABC, 1972; "Love, American Style: Love and the New Act," ABC, 1972.

* Winchell was as interested in medical research as he was in show business—in 1965 he patented a prototype of an artificial heart and he's patented at least 10 other medical inventions.

WINCHELL, WALTER
b. New York City, NY, April 7, 1897; d. 1972.
Columnist-personality who wanted to become as big a TV name as fellow columnist and competitor Ed Sullivan; he didn't.
AS A REGULAR: "The Walter Winchell Show," ABC, 1952-55; NBC, 1956; ABC, 1960; "The Walter Winchell File," ABC, 1957-58; "The Untouchables," ABC, 1959-63.
AND: "The Perry Como Show," NBC, 1956; "Westinghouse Desilu Playhouse: The Untouchables," CBS, 1959; "Westinghouse Desilu Playhouse: Lepke," CBS, 1959; "John Gunther's High Road: New York—The Day People, The Night People," ABC, 1959.

WINDOM, WILLIAM
b. New York City, NY, September 28, 1923.
Actor with tons of TV credits; he played Congressman Glen Morley on "The Farmer's Daughter," curmudgeonly cartoonist John Monroe on "My World and Welcome to It" and Dr. Seth Hazlitt on "Murder, She Wrote"; and Frank, family patriarch on "Parenthood."
AS A REGULAR: "The Farmer's Daughter," ABC,

1963-66; "My World and Welcome to It," NBC, 1969-70; "The Girl with Something Extra," NBC, 1973-74; "Brothers and Sisters," NBC, 1979; "Murder, She Wrote," CBS, 1985-90; "Parenthood," NBC, 1990.
AND: "Masterpiece Playhouse: Richard III," NBC, 1950; "Omnibus: The Education of Henry Adams," CBS, 1955; "Robert Montgomery Presents: The Drifter," NBC, 1955; "Robert Montgomery Presents: Tomorrow Is Forever," NBC, 1955; "Robert Montgomery Presents: The Grand Prize," NBC, 1957; "Hallmark Hall of Fame: Dial M for Murder," NBC, 1958; "Armstrong Circle Theatre: Black-Market Babies," CBS, 1961; "Checkmate: Through a Dark Glass," CBS, 1961; "The Donna Reed Show: All is Forgiven," ABC, 1961; "SurfSide 6: Affairs at Hotel Delight," ABC, 1961; "Ben Casey: The Sweet Kiss of Madness," ABC, 1961; "The Twilight Zone: Five Characters in Search of an Exit," CBS, 1961; "77 Sunset Strip: Mr. Bailey's Honeymoon," ABC, 1962; "SurfSide 6: Anniversary Special," ABC, 1962; "The Gertrude Berg Show: Goodbye, Mr. Howell," CBS, 1962; "Bus Stop: The Ordeal of Kevin Brooke," ABC, 1962; "The Donna Reed Show: The Wide Open Spaces," ABC, 1962; "Follow the Sun: A Ghost in Her Gazebo," ABC, 1962; "Kraft Mystery Theatre: In Close Pursuit," NBC, 1962; "The Gallant Men: The Gallant Men," ABC, 1962; "The Lucy Show: Lucy Digs Up a Date," CBS, 1962; "Stoney Burke: A Matter of Pride," ABC, 1962; "Gunsmoke: False Front," CBS, 1962; "Combat!: Off Limits," ABC, 1963; "The Twilight Zone: Miniature," CBS, 1963; "Twelve O'Clock High: Gauntlet of Fire," ABC, 1966; "The FBI: The Assassin," ABC, 1966; "The Wild Wild West: The Night of the Flying Pie Plate," CBS, 1966; "Run for Your Life: The List of Alice McKenna," NBC, 1967; "The Virginian: To Bear Witness," NBC, 1967; "The Fugitive: The Ivy Maze," ABC, 1967; "The Invaders: Doomsday Minus One," ABC, 1967; "Mission: Impossible: The Train," CBS, 1967; "Bob Hope Chrysler Theatre: Wipeout," NBC, 1967; "Mission: Impossible: The Widow," CBS, 1967; "Star Trek: The Doomsday Machine," NBC, 1967; "The FBI: By Force and Violence," ABC, 1967; "The Invaders: The Summit Meeting," ABC, 1967; "Custer: Under Fire," ABC, 1967; "Bonanza: Star Crossed," NBC, 1968; "Mannix: The Girl in the Frame," CBS, 1968; "Ironside: Trip to Hashbury," NBC, 1968; "The Virginian: The Orchard," NBC, 1968; "The Name of the Game: Lola in Lipstick," NBC, 1968; "The Virginian: Halfway Back From Hell," NBC, 1969; "Hawaii Five-O: Which Way Did They Go?," CBS, 1969; "The Name of the Game: The Time Is Now," NBC, 1970; "Love, American Style: Love and the Visitor," ABC, 1970; "That Girl: That Script," ABC, 1971; "Hollywood Television Theatre: Big Fish, Little

Fish," NET, 1971; "The Men From Shiloh: The Politician," NBC, 1971; "Night Gallery: They're Tearing Down Tim Riley's Bar," NBC, 1971; "Gunsmoke: The Judgement," CBS, 1972; "Ghost Story: The Summer House," NBC, 1972; "The Rookies: Time is the Fire," ABC, 1972; "The Streets of San Francisco: 45 Minutes From Home," ABC, 1972; "The FBI: The Jug Marker," ABC, 1972; "Marcus Welby, M.D.: Ask Me Again Tomorrow," ABC, 1972; "Robert Young and the Family," CBS, 1973; "The Flip Wilson Show," NBC, 1973; "Mission: Impossible: The Fighter," CBS, 1973; "The Partridge Family: Bedknobs and Drumsticks," ABC, 1973; "Hollywood Television Theatre: Winesburg, Ohio," NET, 1973; "McMillan and Wife: Game of Survival," NBC, 1974; "The Streets of San Francisco: Requiem for Murder," ABC, 1975; "The Streets of San Francisco: Letters from the Grave," ABC, 1975; "Lucas Tanner: Shattered," NBC, 1975; "SWAT: Coven of Killers," ABC, 1975; "Barney Miller: Doomsday," ABC, 1975; "Petrocelli: Shadow of Fear," NBC, 1975; "Medical Center: If Wishes Were Horses," CBS, 1976; "Heck's Angels," CBS, 1976; "Gibbsville: Saturday Night," NBC, 1976; "McMillan: Philip's Game," NBC, 1977; "Kojak: Once More From Birdland," CBS, 1977; "Police Woman: Silky Chamberlain," NBC, 1977; "Quincy: The Hot Dog Murder," NBC, 1977; "The Love Boat: Man in Her Life," ABC, 1979; "Barney Miller: Contempt," ABC, 1981; "Foul Play: Play It Again, Tuck," ABC, 1981; "Hart to Hart: With This Hart I Thee Wed," ABC, 1982; "The Love Boat: Here Comes the Bride, Maybe," ABC, 1981; "The A-Team: Pilot," NBC, 1983; "Lottery!: Boston: False Illusion," ABC, 1983; "Matt Houston: Heritage," ABC, 1983; "St. Elsewhere: In Sickness and in Health," NBC, 1984; "Simon & Simon: Under the Knife," CBS, 1984; "Hunter: The Hot Grounder," NBC, 1984; "Hardcastle and McCormick: Surprise on Seagull Beach," ABC, 1985; "Newhart: Goodbye and Good Riddance, Mr. Chips," CBS, 1987; "Have Faith: Letters From Home," ABC, 1989.

TV MOVIES AND MINISERIES: "Prescription: Murder," NBC, 1968; "U.M.C.," CBS, 1969; "The House on Greenapple Road," ABC, 1970; "Assault on the Wayne," ABC, 1971; "Escape," ABC, 1971; "A Taste of Evil," ABC, 1971; "Marriage: Year One," NBC, 1971; "The Homecoming," CBS, 1971; "Second Chance," ABC, 1972; "A Great American Tragedy," ABC, 1972; "Pursuit," ABC, 1972; "The Girls of Huntington House," ABC, 1973; "Murder in the First Person Singular," ABC, 1974; "The Day the Earth Moved," ABC, 1974; "The Abduction of Saint Anne," ABC, 1975; "Journey From Darkness," NBC, 1975; "Guilty or Innocent: The Sam Sheppard Murder Case," NBC, 1975;

"Bridger," ABC, 1976; "Richie Brockelman, Private Eye," NBC, 1976; "Best Sellers: Once an Eagle," NBC, 1977; "Best Sellers: Seventh Avenue," NBC, 1977; "Blind Ambition," CBS, 1979; "Portrait of a Rebel: Margaret Sanger," CBS, 1980; "Leave 'Em Laughing," CBS, 1981; "Desperate Lives," CBS, 1982; "Why Me?," ABC, 1984; "Surviving," ABC, 1985.
* Emmies: 1970.

WINFIELD, PAUL
b. Los Angeles, CA, May 22, 1941. Heavyset actor who played the mean landlord on "227."
AS A REGULAR: "Julia," NBC, 1968-70; "The Charmings," ABC, 1987-88; "Wiseguy," CBS, 1989; "227," NBC, 1989-90.
AND: "Daktari: The Diamond Smugglers," CBS, 1966; "Mission: Impossible: Trial by Fury," CBS, 1968; "Ironside: Robert Phillips vs. the Man," NBC, 1968; "The Name of the Game: The Suntan Mob," NBC, 1969; "Mannix: The Odds Against Donald Jordan," CBS, 1969; "Julia: It Takes Two to Tangle," NBC, 1969; "Room 222: Arizona State Loves You," ABC, 1969; "The Young Lawyers: A Simple Thing Called Justice," ABC, 1970; "The Young Rebels: Unbroken Chains," ABC, 1970; "James Garner as Nichols: Eddie Joe," NBC, 1972; "Ironside: Find a Victim," NBC, 1972; "G.E. Theatre: It's Good to Be Alive," CBS, 1974; "Blacke's Magic: Knave of Diamonds, Ace of Hearts," NBC, 1986; "Wonderworks: The Mighty Pawns," PBS, 1987.
TV MOVIES AND MINISERIES: "Horror at 37,000 Feet," CBS, 1973; "It's Good to Be Alive," CBS, 1974; "King," NBC, 1978; "Backstairs at the White House," NBC, 1979; "Roots: The Next Generation," ABC, 1979; "Angel City," CBS, 1980; "The Sophisticated Gents," NBC, 1981; "Under Siege," NBC, 1986; "Guilty of Innocence: The Lenell Geter Story," CBS, 1987.

WINFREY, OPRAH
b. Kosciuska, MS, January 29, 1954. Popular TV interviewer and mother confessor to oddballs on her daily show.
AS A REGULAR: "The Oprah Winfrey Show," SYN, 1986- ; "Brewster Place," ABC, 1990.
AND: "Saturday Night Live," NBC, 1986.
TV MOVIES AND MINISERIES: "The Women of Brewster Place," ABC, 1989.

WINGREEN, JASON
b. Brooklyn, NY. Heavyset actor who played Harry Snowden on "All in the Family" and "Archie Bunker's Place."
AS A REGULAR: "The Rounders," ABC, 1966-67; "All in the Family," CBS, 1976-79; "Archie Bunker's Place," CBS, 1979-83.
AND: "Rough Riders: The Duelists," ABC, 1958;

"Steve Canyon: Operation Heartbeat," ABC, 1959; "Goodyear Theatre: Coogan's Reward," NBC, 1959; "Bourbon Street Beat: Swamp Fire," ABC, 1960; "The Twilight Zone: A Stop at Willoughby," CBS, 1960; "Wanted Dead or Alive: Journey for Josh," CBS, 1960; "The Twilight Zone: The Midnight Sun," CBS, 1961; "The New Breed: All the Dead Faces," ABC, 1962; "The Outer Limits: O.B.I.T.," ABC, 1963; "The Fugitive: Angels Travel on Lonely Roads," ABC, 1964; "The Outer Limits: The Special One," ABC, 1964; "The Outer Limits: Expanding Human," ABC, 1964; "Slattery's People: Question-Where Vanished the Tragic Piper?," CBS, 1964; "Profiles in Courage: The Robert Taft Story," NBC, 1965; "The Long Hot Summer: A Stranger to the House," ABC, 1965; "The Big Valley: A Time to Kill," ABC, 1966; "The Man From UNCLE: The Five Daughters Affair," NBC, 1967; "The FBI: Counter-stroke," ABC, 1967; "The FBI: The Mechanized Accomplice," ABC, 1968; "The FBI: Conspiracy of Silence," ABC, 1969; "The FBI: The Challenge," ABC, 1969; "Mannix: The Solid Gold Web," CBS, 1969; "Mannix: Figures in a Landscape," CBS, 1970; "Mannix: A Puzzle for One," CBS, 1972; "The FBI: The Corruptor," ABC, 1972; "Columbo: Short Fuse," NBC, 1972; "Kung Fu: The Praying Mantis Kills," ABC, 1973; "Marcus Welby, M.D.: The Fatal Challenge," ABC, 1974; "Ironside: What's New with Mark?," NBC, 1974; "Medical Center: The Captives," CBS, 1975; "Barnaby Jones: Fatal Witness," CBS, 1975; "The Rockford Files: So Help Me God," NBC, 1976; "Scarecrow and Mrs. King: Weekend," CBS, 1984; "Highway to Heaven: Playing for Keeps," NBC, 1986; "Matlock: The Gigolo," NBC, 1988; "Freddy's Nightmares: Photo Finish," SYN, 1989.
TV MOVIES AND MINISERIES: "U.M.C.," CBS, 1969; "San Francisco International," NBC, 1970; "Banyon," NBC, 1971; "Paper Man," CBS, 1971; "Killer by Night," CBS, 1972; "Getting Away From It All," ABC, 1972; "Cry Panic!," ABC, 1974; "Roots: The Next Generations," ABC, 1979.

WINKELMAN, MICHAEL
b. 1946. Young actor who played Little Luke McCoy, brother of Big Luke (Richard Crenna); long before the Darryls on "Newhart," they were the first two TV brothers to have the same first name.
AS A REGULAR: "The Real McCoys," ABC, 1957-62; CBS, 1962-63.
AND: "The Loretta Young Show: The Last Spring," NBC, 1956; "Studio 57: Teacher," SYN, 1956; "The Joseph Cotten Show: The Fourth Witness," NBC, 1956; "The Loretta Young Show: Imperfect Balance," NBC, 1956; "Lassie: The Vigil," CBS, 1956; "Wire Service: The Johnny Rath Story," ABC, 1957; "The Millionaire: Story

of Judge William Westholme," CBS, 1957; "Panic!: Twenty-Six Hours to Sunrise," NBC, 1957; "Mr. Novak: To Lodge and Dislodge," NBC, 1963; "Mr. Novak: Love in the Wrong Season," NBC, 1963; "Mr. Novak: He Who Can Does," NBC, 1963.

WINKLER, HENRY
b. New York City, NY, October 30, 1945. Actor who scored as Arthur "Fonzie" Fonzarelli on "Happy Days" and now is more active behind the scenes.
AS A REGULAR: "Happy Days," ABC, 1974-84.
AND: "The Mary Tyler Moore Show: The Dinner Party," CBS, 1973; "The Bob Newhart Show: Clink Shrink," CBS, 1974; "Rhoda: You Can Go Home Again," CBS, 1974; "Laverne & Shirley: The Society Party," ABC, 1976; "Friends," NBC, 1976; "Laverne & Shirley: The Bachelor Party," ABC, 1976; "Laverne & Shirley: Goodtime Girls," ABC, 1976; "General Electric's All-Star Anniversary," ABC, 1978; "Mork & Mindy: Mork Moves In," ABC, 1978; "Laverne & Shirley: Shotgun Wedding," ABC, 1979; "Joanie Loves Chachi: Fonzie's Visit," ABC, 1982; "Wonderworks: Two Daddies?," PBS, 1989; "It's Garry Shandling's Show: First Show of the Fourth Season," FOX, 1989.
TV MOVIES AND MINISERIES: "Katherine," ABC, 1975.
AS CO-EXECUTIVE PRODUCER: "MacGyver," ABC, 1985- ; "Mr. Sunshine," ABC, 1986.

WINNINGER, CHARLES
b. Athens, WI, May 26, 1884; d. 1969. Comic character actor in many movies; he played the old vaudeville partner of Fred Mertz (William Frawley) on "I Love Lucy."
AS A REGULAR: "The Charlie Farrell Show," CBS, 1956.
AND: "Schlitz Playhouse of Stars: The Whale on the Beach," CBS, 1954; "I Love Lucy: Mertz and Kurtz," CBS, 1954; "Best of Broadway: The Philadelphia Story," CBS, 1954; "Fireside Theatre: His Maiden Voyage," NBC, 1955; "Science Fiction Theatre: The Magic Suitcase," SYN, 1957; "Art Linkletter's House Party," CBS, 1959; "The Millionaire: Millionaire Terrence Costigan," CBS, 1959.

WINNINGHAM, MARE
b. 1959. Actress who's become the Meryl Streep of television, immersing herself in her roles totally and often producing memorable performances. She won an Emmy for "Amber Waves."
AS A GUEST: "Police Woman: Battered Teachers," NBC, 1978; "ABC Afterschool Special: One Too Many," ABC, 1985; "The Twilight Zone: Button, Button," CBS, 1986.

TV MOVIES AND MINISERIES: "The Death of Ocean View Park," ABC, 1979; "Amber Waves," ABC, 1980; "Off the Minnesota Strip," ABC, 1980; "Missing Children: A Mother's Story," CBS, 1982; "The Thorn Birds," ABC, 1983; "Single Bars, Single Women," ABC, 1984; "Helen Keller: The Miracle Continues," SYN, 1985; "Hallmark Hall of Fame: Love Is Never Silent," NBC, 1985; "A Winner Never Quits," ABC, 1986; "Who Is Julia?" CBS, 1986; "Eye on the Sparrow," NBC, 1987; "ABC Theatre: God Bless the Child," ABC, 1988.
* Emmies: 1980.

WINTER, EDWARD
b. Ventura, CA. Actor best known as the crazy CIA agent Col. Flagg on "M*A*S*H."
AS A REGULAR: "The Secret Storm," CBS, 1969; "Adam's Rib," ABC, 1973; "M*A*S*H," CBS, 1973-79; "Project UFO," NBC, 1978-79; "Empire," CBS, 1984; "Hollywood Beat," ABC, 1985; "9 to 5," SYN, 1986-88.
AND: "Mannix: Climb a Deadly Mountain," CBS, 1973; "The New Adventures of Perry Mason: The Case of the Furious Father," CBS, 1973; "The Bob Newhart Show: The Gray Flannel Shrink," CBS, 1974; "Marcus Welby, M.D.: The Outrage," ABC, 1974; "Karen: Premiere," ABC, 1975; "The Bob Crane Show: A Case of Misdiagnosis," NBC, 1975; "The Mary Tyler Moore Show: A Reliable Source," CBS, 1976; "Jigsaw John: A Deadly Affair," NBC, 1976; "Barnaby Jones: Shadow of Fear," CBS, 1977; "Maude: The Ecologist," CBS, 1977; "Alice: That Old Back Magic," CBS, 1977; "Lou Grant: House-Warming," CBS, 1977; "Police Woman: Sixth Sense," NBC, 1978; "The Love Boat: Julie's Dilemma," ABC, 1978; "Lou Grant: Cop," CBS, 1979; "Salvage I: Golden Orbit," ABC, 1979; "Shirley: Separate Agendas," NBC, 1979; "Lou Grant: Business," CBS, 1981; "Magnum, P.I.: Heal Thyself," CBS, 1982; "The A-Team: Holiday in the Hills," NBC, 1983; "Simon & Simon: Psyched Out," CBS, 1983; "Hardcastle and McCormick: Killer B's," ABC, 1983; "The A-Team: Road Games," NBC, 1985; "Misfits of Science: Pilot," NBC, 1985; "Cagney & Lacey: Con Games," CBS, 1985; "The Golden Girls: Blind Date," NBC, 1989; "Father Dowling Mysteries: What Do You Call a Call Girl Mystery?," NBC, 1989; "Murder, She Wrote: Smooth Operator," CBS, 1989.
TV MOVIES AND MINISERIES: "Eleanor and Franklin," ABC, 1976; "The Girl in the Empty Grave," NBC, 1977; "The Lost Honor of Kathryn Beck," CBS, 1984; "Perry Mason: The Case of the Notorious Nun," NBC, 1986; "Stranded," NBC, 1986; "The Christmas Gift," CBS, 1986.

WINTERS, GLORIA
b. Los Angeles, CA. Actress who played Penny, niece of Sky King.
AS A REGULAR: "The Life of Riley," NBC, 1949-50; "Sky King," NBC, 1951-52; ABC, 1952-54.
AND: "Richard Diamond, Private Detective: The Merry-Go-Round Case," CBS, 1957; "Death Valley Days: Solomon in All His Glory," SYN, 1959.

WINTERS, JONATHAN
b. Dayton, OH, November 11, 1925. Pudgy, introverted comic genius at his best improvising. He was a talk-show staple in the fifties; later Robin Williams, a longtime admirer, had Winters join "Mork & Mindy" as his son, Mearth.
AS A REGULAR: "And Here's the Show," NBC, 1955; "The Jonathan Winters Show," NBC, 1956-57; "NBC Comedy Hour," NBC, 1956; "The Jack Paar Show," NBC, 1958-62; "Masquerade Party," CBS, 1958; "Jonathan Winters Special," NBC, 1964-65; "The Jonathan Winters Show," CBS, 1967-69; "Hot Dog," NBC, 1970-71; "The Wacky World of Jonathan Winters," SYN, 1972-74; "Mork & Mindy," ABC, 1981-82; "Hee Haw," SYN, 1983-84.
AND: "The Jackie Gleason Show," CBS, 1957; "The Steve Allen Show," NBC, 1957; "The Arlene Francis Show," NBC, 1957; "The Tonight Show," NBC, 1957; "The Arlene Francis Show," NBC, 1958; "The George Gobel Show," NBC, 1958; "The Steve Allen Show," NBC, 1958; "The Arthur Godfrey Show," CBS, 1959; "The Steve Allen Show," NBC, 1959; "Startime: Jack Paar's World," NBC, 1960; "Be Our Guest," CBS, 1960; "Steve Allen Plymouth Show," NBC, 1960; "Shirley Temple's Storybook: The Land of Oz," NBC, 1960; "Candid Camera," CBS, 1960; "Dinah Shore Chevy Show: South Pacific Holiday," NBC, 1960; "The Garry Moore Show," CBS, 1960; "Shirley Temple's Storybook: Babes in Toyland," NBC, 1960; "Art Carney Special: Everybody's Doin' It," NBC, 1961; "The Garry Moore Show," CBS, 1961; "I've Got a Secret," CBS, 1961; "The Chevy Show," NBC, 1961; "The Twilight Zone: A Game of Pool," CBS, 1961; "The Jack Paar Program," NBC, 1962; "The Andy Williams Show," NBC, 1963; "The Garry Moore Show," CBS, 1963; "The Jack Paar Program," NBC, 1964; "I've Got a Secret," CBS, 1964; "A Wild Winters Night," NBC, 1964; "The Andy Williams Show," NBC, 1964; "The Andy Williams Show," NBC, 1965; "Bob Hope Special," NBC, 1966; "The Andy Williams Show," NBC, 1966; "Guys 'n Geishas," NBC, 1967; "Flip Wilson Special," NBC, 1969; "The Andy Williams Show," NBC, 1969; "The Rosey Grier Show," SYN, 1970; "Movin'," NBC, 1970; "The Andy Williams Show," NBC, 1970; "The Andy Williams Show," NBC, 1971; "Festival at Ford's," NBC, 1971; "Jack Paar Tonight," ABC, 1973; "The Fricker Fracus," CBS, 1973; "Wait Till Your Father Gets Home: Maude Loves Papa,"

SYN, 1974; "Hollywood Squares," SYN, 1975; "Freedom Is," SYN, 1976; "Dean Martin's Red Hot Scandals of 1926," NBC, 1976; "Hollywood Squares," NBC, 1980; "The Muppet Show," SYN, 1980; "Jonathan Winters and Friends," SHO, 1989.

TV MOVIES AND MINISERIES: "Now You See It, Now You Don't," NBC, 1968; "More Wild Wild West," CBS, 1980.

WINTERS, ROLAND

b. Boston, MA, November 22, 1904. Heavyset character who often played stern bosses.

AS A REGULAR: "Mama," CBS, 1951-52; "Doorway to Danger," NBC, 1952; "Meet Millie," CBS, 1953-55; "The Peter Lind Hayes Show," ABC, 1959; "The Smothers Brothers Show," CBS, 1965-66.

AND: "Kraft Television Theatre: The Man on Half-Moon Street," NBC, 1952; "Lux Video Theatre: Ferry Crisis," NBC, 1952; "Kraft Television Theatre: The Music Master," NBC, 1952; "Star Playhouse: Mr. Greentree and Friend," SYN, 1955; "Lux Video Theatre: The Wayward Saint," CBS, 1956; "Kaiser Aluminum Hour: Mr. Finchley Versus the Bomb," NBC, 1956; "The Red Skelton Show: The Magic Shoes," CBS, 1956; "Kaiser Aluminium Hour: Throw Me a Rope," NBC, 1957; "Broken Arrow: Powder Keg," ABC, 1957; "Kraft Television Theatre: The Duel," NBC, 1957; "The 20th Century-Fox Hour: City in Flames," CBS, 1957; "You Are There: The Attempt to Assassinate Theodore Roosevelt," CBS, 1957; "Kraft Television Theatre: The Roaring 20th," NBC, 1957; "Goodyear TV Playhouse: The Legacy," NBC, 1957; "Matinee Theatre: The Remarkable Mr. Jerome," NBC, 1957; "Studio One: The Unmentionable Blues," CBS, 1957; "Studio One: The Dark Intruder," CBS, 1957; "Kraft Television Theatre: A Cook for Mr. General," NBC, 1957; "Schlitz Playhouse of Stars: Outlaw's Boots," CBS, 1957; "Date with the Angels: Double Trouble," ABC, 1958; "The Millionaire: The Doris Winslow Story," CBS, 1958; "Little Women," CBS, 1958; "Startime: The Wicked Scheme of Jebal Deeks," NBC, 1959; "Comedy Spot: Adventures of a Model," CBS, 1960; "Omnibus: He Shall Have Power," NBC, 1960; "Play of the Week: The Iceman Cometh," SYN, 1960; "A Story of Love: A String of Beads," NBC, 1961; "The Red Skelton Show: Clem the Genius," CBS, 1961; "Naked City: Take and Put," ABC, 1961; "Holiday Lodge: Love Visits," CBS, 1961; "The Defenders: The Crusaders," CBS, 1962; "Alcoa Premiere: The Rules of the Game," ABC, 1962; "The Alfred Hitchcock Hour: Captive Audience," CBS, 1962; "Dennis the Menace: Henry's New Job," CBS, 1962; "The Defenders: Climate of Evil," CBS, 1963; "The Lucy Show: Lucy's College Reunion," CBS, 1963; "Hazel: Scheherazade and

Her Frying Pan," NBC, 1964; "Burke's Law: Who Killed Carrie Cornell?," ABC, 1964; "Route 66: This Is Going to Hurt Me More Than It Hurts You," CBS, 1964; "The Farmer's Daughter: Turkish Delight," ABC, 1964; "Bob Hope Chrysler Theatre: Time for Elizabeth," NBC, 1964; "The Addams Family: The Addams Family Splurges," ABC, 1965; "The Farmer's Daughter: Katy's Castle," ABC, 1965; "The Cara Williams Show: The Offer," CBS, 1965; "Perry Mason: The Case of the Telltale Tap," CBS, 1965; "Profiles in Courage: John Quincy Adams," NBC, 1965; "Summer Playhouse: Hello Dere!," CBS, 1965; "Mr. Roberts: Bookser's Honeymoon," NBC, 1965; "Green Acres: Don't Call Us, We'll Call You," CBS, 1965; "Gomer Pyle, USMC: The Show Must Go On," CBS, 1967; "Bewitched: Man of the Year," ABC, 1968; "Doc," NBC, 1969.

TV MOVIES AND MINISERIES: "Miracle on 34th Street," CBS, 1973; "The Dain Curse," CBS, 1978; "You Can't Go Home Again," CBS, 1979.

WINTERS, SHELLEY

b. Shirley Schrift, St. Louis, MO, August 18, 1922. Fifties bombshell who matured into character roles; still, she's best known for her tell-all autobiography and as a loud-mouthed guest on talk shows. An Emmy winner for "Two Is the Number."

AS A GUEST: "Ford Theatre: Mantrap," NBC, 1954; "Climax!: Sorry, Wrong Number," CBS, 1954; "Producers Showcase: The Women," NBC, 1955; "Climax!: Dark Wall," CBS, 1956; "Alcoa Hour: A Double Life," NBC, 1957; "U.S. Steel Hour: Inspired Alibi," CBS, 1957; "Climax!: Don't Touch Me," CBS, 1957; "The Bob Hope Show," NBC, 1957; "The Steve Allen Show," NBC, 1957; "Arthur Murray Party," NBC, 1957; "Wagon Train: The Ruth Owens Story," NBC, 1957; "Schlitz Playhouse of Stars: Smarty," CBS, 1957; "Du Pont Show of the Month: Beyond This Place," CBS, 1957; "Kraft Theatre: Polka," NBC, 1957; "The Ed Sullivan Show," CBS, 1959; "The Jack Paar Show," NBC, 1960; "Play of the Week: A Piece of Blue Sky," SYN, 1961; "Alcoa Premiere: The Cake Baker," ABC, 1962; "Alcoa Premiere: The Way From Darkness," ABC, 1962; "To Tell the Truth," CBS, 1963; "Bob Hope Chrysler Theatre: Two Is the Number," NBC, 1964; "To Tell the Truth," CBS, 1964; "Ben Casey: A Disease of the Heart Called Love," ABC, 1964; "Bob Hope Chrysler Theatre: Back to Back," NBC, 1965; "Batman: The Greatest Mother of Them All/Ma Parker," ABC, 1966; "Hollywood Squares," NBC, 1967; "Bob Hope Chrysler Theatre: Wipeout," NBC, 1967; "Here's Lucy: Lucy and Miss Shelley Winters," CBS, 1968;

"That's Life: The Ninth Month," ABC, 1968; "Funny You Should Ask," ABC, 1968; "The Dick Cavett Show," ABC, 1970; "McCloud: The Barefoot Girls," NBC, 1974; "Password All-Stars," ABC, 1974; "Chico and the Man: Ed Steps Out," NBC, 1975; "Frosty's Winter Wonderland," ABC, 1976; "Kojak: Chains of Custody," CBS, 1978; "Cher ... and Other Fantasies," NBC, 1979; "Hollywood Squares," SYN, 1980; "Vega$: Macho Murders," ABC, 1980; "The Love Boat: Venetian Love Song," ABC, 1982; "The Tonight Show Starring Johnny Carson," NBC, 1985.

TV MOVIES AND MINISERIES: "Revenge," ABC, 1971; "A Death of Innocence," CBS, 1971; "The Adventures of Nick Carter," ABC, 1972; "The Devil's Daughter," ABC, 1973; "Double Indemnity," CBS, 1973; "The Sex Symbol," ABC, 1974; "Big Rose," CBS, 1974; "Elvis," ABC, 1979.

* Emmies: 1964.

WINWOOD, ESTELLE

b. Estelle Goodwin, England, January 24, 1883; d. 1984. Character actress in extensive TV, often as crazed spinsters; when she died she was the oldest member of the Screen Actors Guild.

AS A GUEST: "Lights Out: Masque," NBC, 1950; "Suspense: The Rose Garden," CBS, 1951; "Broadway Television Theatre: Outward Bound," SYN, 1952; "Broadway Television Theatre: Criminal at Large," SYN, 1953; "Kraft Television Theatre: Miss Mabel," NBC, 1953; "Studio One: Birthright," CBS, 1953; "Studio One: A Bargain with God," CBS, 1953; "Broadway Television Theatre: The Bat," SYN, 1953; "Motorola TV Hour: A Dash of Bitter," ABC, 1954; "Robert Montgomery Presents: The Promise/The Reality," NBC, 1954; "Producers Showcase: Tonight at 8:30," NBC, 1954; "Playwrights '56: Adam and Evening," NBC, 1956; "Alfred Hitchcock Presents: There Was an Old Woman," CBS, 1956; "Climax!: The Mad Bomber," CBS, 1957; "Climax!: Deadly Climate," CBS, 1957; "Matinee Theatre: The Conversation Table," NBC, 1957; "Kraft Theatre: The Woman at High Hollow," NBC, 1958; "Alfred Hitchcock Presents: Bull in a China Shop," CBS, 1958; "Shirley Temple's Storybook: The Magic Fishbone," NBC, 1958; "The Donna Reed Show: Miss Lovelace Comes to Tea," ABC, 1959; "The Twilight Zone: Long Live Walter Jameson," CBS, 1960; "The Ann Sothern Show: One for the Books," CBS, 1960; "Bourbon Street Beat: Ferry to Algiers," ABC, 1960; "The Real McCoys: Where There's a Will," ABC, 1960; "Adventures in Paradise: A Penny a Day," ABC, 1961; "Thriller: Dialogues with Death," NBC, 1961; "Dennis the Menace: Calling All Bird Lovers," CBS, 1962; "Dr. Kildare: The Last Leaves on the Tree," NBC,

1964; "The Rogues: Wherefore Are Thou, Harold?," NBC, 1965; "The FBI: The Monster," ABC, 1965; "Perry Mason: The Case of the Final Fadeout," CBS, 1966; "Bewitched: Witches and Warlocks Are My Favorite Things," ABC, 1966; "The Man From UNCLE: The Her Master's Voice Affair," NBC, 1966; "ABC Stage '67: The People Trap," ABC, 1966; "Batman: Marsha, Queen of Diamonds/Marsha's Scheme with Diamonds," ABC, 1966; "Batman: Penguin is a Girl's Best Friend/Penguin Sets a Trend/Penguin's Disastrous End," ABC, 1967; "The Name of the Game: The Taker," NBC, 1968; "The Doris Day Show: The Antique," CBS, 1968; "The Doris Day Show: The Still," CBS, 1968; "The Outsider: The Secret of Mareno Bay," NBC, 1969; "Love, American Style: Love and the Living Doll," ABC, 1969; "CBS Playhouse: Appalachian Autumn," CBS, 1969; "Love, American Style: Love and the Old Flames," ABC, 1972; "Banyon: Time Lapse," NBC, 1973; "Barnaby Jones: Murder in the Doll's House," CBS, 1973; "Switch: One of Our Zeppelins Is Missing," CBS, 1976; "Police Story: Monster Manor," NBC, 1976; "Quincy: Honor Thy Elders," NBC, 1979.

WITHERS, JANE

b. Atlanta, GA, April 12, 1927. Former child actress who plays goofy roles on TV; she was also Josephine the plumber, saleswoman for Comet cleanser in sixties TV commercials.

AS A GUEST: "U.S. Steel Hour: The Pink Burro," CBS, 1959; "Peck's Bad Girl: The Breadwinner," CBS, 1959; "Here's Hollywood," NBC, 1961; "G.E. Theatre: A Very Special Girl," CBS, 1962; "Pete and Gladys: Step on Me," CBS, 1962; "Girl Talk," SYN, 1963; "The Alfred Hitchcock Hour: How to Get Rid of Your Wife," CBS, 1963; "The Match Game," NBC, 1964; "Your First Impression," NBC, 1964; "Summer Playhouse: The Apartment House," CBS, 1964; "The Munsters: Pike's Pique," CBS, 1964; "The Price Is Right," ABC, 1965; "The Match Game," NBC, 1965; "The Munsters: Grandpa's Lost Wife," CBS, 1966; "The Mike Douglas Show," SYN, 1970; "The Love Boat: The Invisible Maniac," ABC, 1980.

TV MOVIES AND MINISERIES: "All Together Now," ABC, 1975.

WOLFMAN JACK

b. Bob Smith, Brooklyn, NY, January 21, 1939. Deejay who became a celebrity when his voice was heard throughout the film "American Graffiti."

AS A REGULAR: "Midnight Special," NBC, 1973-81.
AND: "The Odd Couple: The Songwriter," ABC, 1973; "Sanford & Son: Sergeant Gork," NBC, 1976; "What's Happening!: My Three Tons," ABC, 1976; "What's Happening!: Going, Going,

Gong," ABC, 1978; "All Star Secrets," NBC, 1979; "Vega$: The Man Who Was Twice," ABC, 1980.

WONDER, STEVIE

b. Steveland Judkins, Saginaw, MI, May 13, 1950. Pop legend, usually on variety shows.

AS A GUEST: "The Ed Sullivan Show," CBS, 1964; "The Ed Sullivan Show," CBS, 1968; "The Flip Wilson Show," NBC, 1971; "Burt Bacharach: Opus No. III," ABC, 1973; "Dinah!," SYN, 1976; "Inaugural Eve Special," CBS, 1977; "Saturday Night Live," NBC, 1983.

* See also "The Ed Sullivan Show."

WONG, ANNA MAY

b. Wong Lui-Tsong, Los Angeles, CA, January 3, 1907; d. 1961. Actress often cast as (of course) inscrutable types.

AS A REGULAR: "The Gallery of Mme. Lui-Tsong," DUM, 1951.

AND: "Producers Showcase: The Letter," NBC, 1956; "Climax!: The Chinese Game," CBS, 1956; "Climax!: Deadly Tattoo," CBS, 1958; "The Life and Legend of Wyatt Earp: China Mary," ABC, 1960; "The Barbara Stanwyck Show: Dragon by the Tail," NBC, 1961; "Danger Man: The Journey Ends Halfway," CBS, 1961.

WOOD, NATALIE

b. Natasha Gurdin, San Francisco, CA, July 20, 1938; d. 1981. Former child actress turned sexy movie star ("Rebel Without a Cause," "Splendor in the Grass," "Love with the Proper Stranger"); between her child star and sexpot days, she spent some time in TV.

AS A REGULAR: "The Pride of the Family," ABC, 1953-54.

AND: "Schaefer Century Theatre: Playmaters," NBC, 1952; "Hollywood Playhouse: Quite a Viking," SYN, 1952; "G.E. Theatre: I'm a Fool," CBS, 1954; "Studio 57: The Plot Against Miss Pomeroy," SYN, 1954; "Four Star Playhouse: The Wild Bunch," CBS, 1955; "Ford Theatre: Too Old for Dolls," NBC, 1955; "Heidi," NBC, 1955; "Mayor of the Town: The Old Triangle," SYN, 1955; "Studio One: Miracle at Potter's Farm," CBS, 1955; "G.E. Theatre: Feathertop," CBS, 1955; "Warner Bros. Presents Conflict: The Deadly Riddle," ABC, 1955; "Warner Bros. Presents Conflict: Wedding Gift," ABC, 1956; "The Perry Como Show," NBC, 1956; "Kaiser Aluminium Hour: Carnival," NBC, 1956; "The Ed Sullivan Show," CBS, 1956; "Warner Bros. Presents Conflict: Girl on a Subway," ABC, 1957; "The Bob Hope Show," NBC, 1957; "Bob Hope Special," NBC, 1958; "The Frank Sinatra Show," ABC, 1958; "The Jack Benny Program," CBS, 1960; "Eleanor Roosevelt's Jubilee," NBC, 1960;

"A Tribute to American Theatre: Cat on a Hot Tin Roof," NBC, 1976; "The Mike Douglas Show," SYN, 1979; "Hart to Hart: Pilot," ABC, 1979; "The Mike Douglas Show," SYN, 1980.

TV MOVIES AND MINISERIES: "The Affair," ABC, 1973; "Cat on a Hot Tin Roof," NBC, 1976; "From Here to Eternity," NBC, 1979; "The Cracker Factory," ABC, 1979; "The Memory of Eva Ryker," CBS, 1980.

* Wood was married to Robert Wagner from 1957 to 1962, and remarried him in 1972.

WOOD, PEGGY

b. Margaret Wood, Brooklyn, NY, February 9, 1892; d. 1978. Actress who was memorable as Marta Hansen, better known as Mama.

AS A REGULAR: "Mama," CBS, 1949-57; "One Life to Live," ABC, 1969-70.

AND: "Pulitzer Prize Playhouse: The Skin of Our Teeth," ABC, 1951; "The Ed Sullivan Show," CBS, 1957; "Strike It Rich," CBS, 1957; "Dick Powell's Zane Grey Theatre: The Bitter Land," CBS, 1957; "The Last Word," CBS, 1958; "U.S. Steel Hour: Seed of Guilt," CBS, 1959; "Dr. Kildare: An Ancient Office," NBC, 1962; "Americans: A Portrait in Verses," CBS, 1962; "The Nurses: The Saturday Evening of Time," CBS, 1963; "For the People: ... the killing of one human being ...," CBS, 1965; "New York Television Theatre: Opening Night," NET, 1966.

WOODARD, ALFRE

b. Tulsa, OK, November 2, 1953. Talented actress who played Dr. Roxanne Turner on "St. Elsewhere"; she won Emmies for guest roles on "Hill Street Blues" and "L.A. Law."

AS A REGULAR: "Tucker's Witch," CBS, 1982-83; "Sara," NBC, 1985; "St. Elsewhere," NBC, 1985-87.

AND: "Hill Street Blues: Praise Dilaudid," NBC, 1983; "Hill Street Blues: Doris in Wonderland," NBC, 1983; "Hill Street Blues: Goodbye, Mr. Scripps," NBC, 1983; "L.A. Law: Pilot," NBC, 1986; "The Magical World of Disney: A Mother's Courage-The Mary Thomas Story," NBC, 1989.

TV MOVIES AND MINISERIES: "The Ambush Murders," CBS, 1982; "Sweet Revenge," CBS, 1984; "Unnatural Causes," NBC, 1986; "The Child Saver," NBC, 1988.

* Emmies: 1984, 1987.

WOODELL, PAT

b. Winthrop, MA, 1944. Actress who was the original Bobbie Jo Bradley on "Petticoat Junction."

AS A REGULAR: "Petticoat Junction," CBS, 1963-65.

AND: "Hawaiian Eye: Go Steady with Danger," ABC, 1963; "The Gallant Men: To Hold Up a Mirror," ABC, 1963; "Hollywood Palace," ABC,

1965; "The Mike Douglas Show," SYN, 1965; "The Munsters: A Visit From the Teacher," CBS, 1966; "The New Adventures of Perry Mason: The Case of the Murdered Murderer," CBS, 1973.

WOODS, JAMES
b. Warwick, RI, April 18, 1947. Gaunt actor usually in intense roles; he won Emmies for the superlative "Promise" and "My Name Is Bill W."
AS A GUEST: "Kojak: Death Is Not a Passing Grade," CBS, 1974; "The Rockford Files: The Kirkoff Case," NBC, 1974; "The Streets of San Francisco: Trail of Terror," ABC, 1975; "The Rookies: A Time to Mourn," ABC, 1975; "Bert D'Angelo/Superstar: Cops Who Sleep Together," ABC, 1976; "Police Story: Thanksgiving," NBC, 1976; "Saturday Night Live," NBC, 1989.
TV MOVIES AND MINISERIES: "Footsteps," CBS, 1972; "A Great American Tragedy," ABC, 1972; "Foster and Laurie," CBS, 1975; "The Disappearance of Aimee," NBC, 1976; "F. Scott Fitzgerald in Hollywood," ABC, 1976; "Holocaust," NBC, 1978; "The Gift of Love," ABC, 1978; "The Incredible Journey of Doctor Meg Laurel," CBS, 1979; "And Your Name Is Jonah," CBS, 1979; "Badge of the Assassin," CBS, 1985; "Hallmark Hall of Fame: Promise," CBS, 1986; "In Love and War," NBC, 1987; "Hallmark Hall of Fame: My Name Is Bill W.," ABC, 1989.
* Emmies: 1986, 1989.

WOODWARD, EDWARD
b. June 1, 1930, Surrey, England. Dashing actor who played former spy Robert McCall, "The Equalizer."
AS A REGULAR: "The Equalizer," CBS, 1985-89; "Over My Dead Body," CBS, 1990.
AND: "The Defenders: Conflict of Interests," CBS, 1964; "The Tonight Show Starring Johnny Carson," NBC, 1989.
TV MOVIES AND MINISERIES: "Love Is Forever," NBC, 1983; "A Christmas Carol," CBS, 1984; "Arthur the King," CBS, 1985; "Codename: Kyril," SHO, 1988; "The Man in the Brown Suit," CBS, 1989.

WOODWARD, JOANNE
b. Thomasville, GA, February 27, 1930. Oscar-winning actress ("The Three Faces of Eve") and wife of Paul Newman, usually in above-average TV fare; she won Emmies for "See How She Runs" and "Do You Remember Love."
AS A GUEST: "Omnibus: Abraham Lincoln: The Early Years," CBS, 1952; "Robert Montgomery Presents: Penny," NBC, 1952; "Omnibus: New Salem," CBS, 1953; "The Web: Welcome

Home," CBS, 1954; "Elgin TV Hour: High Man," ABC, 1954; "Robert Montgomery Presents: Homecoming," NBC, 1954; "Rheingold Theatre: Dark Stranger," NBC, 1955; "Pond's Theatre: Cynara," ABC, 1955; "Four Star Playhouse: Full Circle," CBS, 1955; "The 20th Century-Fox Hour: "The Late George Apley," CBS, 1955; "Four Star Playhouse: Watch the Sunset," CBS, 1956; "Person to Person," CBS, 1957; "Playhouse 90: The 80-Yard Run," CBS, 1958; "Wide, Wide World: A Star's Story," NBC, 1958; "Person to Person," CBS, 1958; "Here's Hollywood," NBC, 1961; "Hallmark Hall of Fame: All the Way Home," NBC, 1971; "The Mike Douglas Show," SYN, 1973; "The Wild Places," NBC, 1974; "Dinah's Place," NBC, 1974; "The Carol Burnett Show," CBS, 1976; "Inaugural Eve Special," CBS, 1977.
TV MOVIES AND MINISERIES: "Sybil," NBC, 1976; "Little Women," NBC, 1976; "See How She Runs," CBS, 1977; "A Christmas to Remember," CBS, 1978; "The Shadow Box," ABC, 1980; "Crisis at Central High," CBS, 1981; "Passions," CBS, 1984; "Do You Remember Love," CBS, 1985.
* Emmies: 1978, 1985.

WOOLERY, CHUCK
b. Ashland, KY.
AS A REGULAR: "Your Hit Parade," CBS, 1974; "Wheel of Fortune," NBC & SYN, 1975-83; "Love Connection," SYN, 1983- ; "Scrabble," NBC, 1984- .
AND: "Love, American Style: Love and the Cozy Comrades," ABC, 1973; "Celebrity Sweepstakes," NBC, 1975; "Dinah!," SYN, 1976; "Dinah!," SYN, 1977; "$weepstake$: Billy, Wally and Ludmilla, and Theodore," NBC, 1979; "The John Davidson Show," SYN, 1981; "It's Garry Shandling's Show: Anjelica," FOX, 1988; "227: A Date to Remember," NBC, 1989.
TV MOVIES AND MINISERIES: "A Guide for the Married Woman," ABC, 1978.

WOOLEY, SHEB
b. Erick, OK. Actor who played Pete Nolan on "Rawhide," had a hit song with "Purple People Eater" and wrote the theme song for "Hee Haw."
AS A REGULAR: "Rawhide," CBS, 1959-65; "Hee Haw," CBS, 1969.
AND: "My Friend Flicka: The Unmasking," CBS, 1956; "Dick Powell's Zane Grey Theatre: Vengeance Canyon," CBS, 1956; "Cheyenne: The Iron Trail," ABC, 1957; "Ford Theatre: Fate Travels East," ABC, 1957; "Tales of Wells Fargo: Man in the Box," NBC, 1957; "The Life and Legend of Wyatt Earp: Indian Wife," ABC, 1957; "The Bob Crosby Show," NBC, 1958; "The Ed Sullivan Show," CBS, 1958; "Music USA," CBS,

1958; "Truth or Consequences," NBC, 1964;
"Hootenanny," ABC, 1964; "The Jimmy Dean
Show," ABC, 1964; "Death Valley Days: Paid in
Full," SYN, 1965.

WOOLLEY, MONTY
b. *Edgar Montillion Woolley, New York City,
August 17, 1888; d. 1963*. Bearded actor and
former drama coach who repeated his stage and
film role as "The Man Who Came to Dinner"
on TV.
AS A GUEST: "Best of Broadway: The Man Who
Came to Dinner," CBS, 1954; "Christmas
Story Hour," CBS, 1954; "Playhouse 90:
Eloise," CBS, 1956; "Five Fingers: The Man
with the Triangle Heads," NBC, 1959.

WOPAT, TOM
b. *Lodi, WI, September 9, 1950*. Generic TV
hunk who played Luke Duke.
AS A REGULAR: "The Dukes of Hazzard," CBS,
1979-85; "Blue Skies," CBS, 1988; "A
Peaceable Kingdom," CBS, 1989-90.
AND: "The Merv Griffin Show," SYN, 1980; "The
Pat Sajak Show," CBS, 1989.
TV MOVIES AND MINISERIES: "Burning Rage," CBS,
1984; "Christmas Comes to Willow Creek,"
CBS, 1987.

WORLEY, JO ANNE
b. *Lowell, IN, 1942*. Big-mouthed comedienne
who was hot in the late sixties.
AS A REGULAR: "Rowan & Martin's Laugh-In,"
NBC, 1968-70; "Hot Dog," NBC, 1970-71; "It
Pays to Be Ignorant," SYN, 1972-73.
AND: "The Many Loves of Dobie Gillis: Goodbye
Mr. Pomfritt, Hello Mr. Chips," CBS, 1961; "On
Broadway Tonight," CBS, 1965; "The Merv
Griffin Show," SYN, 1966; "Captain Nice: One
Rotten Apple," NBC, 1967; "The Merv Griffin
Show," SYN, 1967; "The Merv Griffin Show,"
SYN, 1968; "Funny You Should Ask," ABC,
1968; "Hollywood Palace," ABC, 1969; "This Is
Tom Jones," ABC, 1969; "The Andy Williams
Show," NBC, 1969; "Love, American Style: Love
and the Optimist," ABC, 1970; "Hollywood
Squares," NBC, 1970; "Love, American Style:
Love and the Pregnancy," ABC, 1971; "Love,
American Style: Love and the Unhappy Couple,"
ABC, 1971; "The Mouse Factory," SYN, 1972;
"Love, American Style: Love and the Big
Mother," ABC, 1972; "Love, American Style:
Love and the Guilty Conscience," ABC, 1972;
"The Paul Lynde Show: An Affair to Forget,"
ABC, 1972; "Honeymoon Suite," ABC, 1973;
"Emergency!: Women," NBC, 1973; "Love,
American Style: Love and the Games People
Play," ABC, 1974; "Match Game '74," CBS,
1974; "Tattletales," CBS, 1974; "The Six Million
Dollar Man: Survival of the Fittest," ABC, 1974;

"Rhyme and Reason," ABC, 1975; "Rhyme and
Reason," ABC, 1976; "Hawaii Five-O: Blood
Money Is Hard to Wash," CBS, 1977; "Junior
Almost Anything Goes," ABC, 1977; "The Love
Boat: Accidental Cruise," ABC, 1978; "The Love
Experts," SYN, 1978; "The Love Boat: The
Stimulation of Stephanie," ABC, 1979; "The
Love Boat: Putting on the Dog," ABC, 1983;
"Murder, She Wrote: My Johnny Lies Over the
Ocean," CBS, 1985.
TV MOVIES AND MINISERIES: "The Feminist and the
Fuzz," ABC, 1971; "What's a Nice Girl Like
You...?," ABC, 1971.

WRIGHT, MAX
b. *Detroit, MI*. Lean, bespectacled comic actor
who played station manager Karl Shub on
"Buffalo Bill" and Willie Tanner on "ALF."
AS A REGULAR: "Buffalo Bill," NBC, 1983-84;
"Misfits of Science," NBC, 1985-86; "ALF,"
NBC, 1986-90.
AND: "Taxi: The Road Not Taken," ABC, 1982;
"E/R: Mr. Fix-It," CBS, 1984; "Cheers: Strange
Bedfellows," NBC, 1986.
TV MOVIES AND MINISERIES: "Playing for Time,"
CBS, 1980.

WRIGHT, TERESA
b. *Muriel Teresa Wright, New York City, NY,
October 27, 1918*. Gifted film ("The Little
Foxes," "Shadow of a Doubt") and TV actress.
AS A GUEST: "Lux Video Theatre: The Sound of
Waves Breaking," CBS, 1952; "Robert
Montgomery Presents: And Never Come
Back," NBC, 1952; "Schlitz Playhouse of
Stars: Dress in the Window," CBS, 1952;
"Hollywood Opening Night: Alicia," NBC,
1952; "Ford Theatre: And Suddenly You
Knew," NBC, 1953; "Ford Theatre: The
Happiest Day," NBC, 1954; "U.S. Steel Hour:
The End of Paul Dane," ABC, 1954; "Climax!:
The Long Goodbye," CBS, 1954; "Ford
Theatre: Stars Don't Shine," NBC, 1955; "Four
Star Playhouse: The Good Sisters," CBS, 1955;
"G.E. Theatre: Love Is Eternal," CBS, 1955;
"Climax!: The Gay Illiterate," CBS, 1956;
"Star Stage: The Secret Place," NBC, 1956;
"Rheingold Theatre: The Lonely Ones," NBC,
1956; "Studio 57: The Faithful Heart," SYN,
1956; "Schlitz Playhouse of Stars: Witness to
Condemn," CBS, 1956; "The 20th Century-
Fox Hour: Child of the Regiment," CBS, 1956;
"Playhouse 90: The Miracle Worker," CBS,
1957; "Schlitz Playhouse of Stars: Sister
Louise Goes to Town," CBS, 1957; "Ford
Theatre: Desperation, ABC, 1957; "Undercur-
rent: No Escape," CBS, 1957; "Playhouse 90:
Edge of Innocence," CBS, 1957; "U.S. Steel
Hour: Trap for a Stranger," CBS, 1959; "U.S.
Steel Hour: The Hours Before Dawn," CBS,
1959; "Adventures in Paradise: Pit of Silence,"

ABC, 1959; "Sunday Showcase: The Margaret Bourke-White Story," NBC, 1960; "Our American Heritage: Shadow of a Soldier," NBC, 1960; "The Alfred Hitchcock Hour: Three Wives Too Many," CBS, 1964; "Bonanza: My Son, My Son," NBC, 1964; "The Defenders: The Pill Man," CBS, 1964; "The Alfred Hitchcock Hour: Lonely Place," NBC, 1964; "The Defenders: The Prosecutor," CBS, 1965; "The Desperate Hours," ABC, 1967; "CBS Playhouse: Appalachian Autumn," ABC, 1969; "Owen Marshall, Counselor at Law: The Camerons Are a Special Clan," ABC, 1973; "Hawkins: Murder on the 13th Floor," CBS, 1974; "Mystery of the Week: Terror in the Night," ABC, 1976; "The Love Boat: The Christmas Presence," ABC, 1982; "Murder, She Wrote: Mr. Penroy's Vacation," CBS, 1988.

TV MOVIES AND MINISERIES: "Crawlspace," CBS, 1972; "The Elevator," ABC, 1974; "Flood," NBC, 1976; "Bill: On His Own," CBS, 1983.

WYATT, JANE

b. Campgaw, NJ, August 12, 1912. Emmy-winning actress who played the mother of Betty, Bud, Kitten and Mr. Spock.

AS A REGULAR: "Father Knows Best," CBS, 1954-55; NBC, 1955-58; CBS, 1958-60.

AND: "Robert Montgomery Presents: Kitty Foyle," NBC, 1950; "Robert Montgomery Presents: The Awful Truth," NBC, 1950; "Nash Airflyte Theatre: The Lipstick," CBS, 1951; "Lights Out: The Intruder," CBS, 1952; "Robert Montgomery Presents: The Wall," NBC, 1952; "Studio One: Lovers and Friends," CBS, 1952; "Schlitz Playhouse of Stars: A Southern Lady," CBS, 1952; "Ford Theatre: Protect Her Honor," NBC, 1952; "Fireside Theatre: Love Without Wings," NBC, 1952; "Robert Montgomery Presents: The Inward Eye," NBC, 1952; "Studio One: The Walsh Girls," CBS, 1953; "The American Hour: Outlaw's Reckoning," ABC, 1953; "P.M. Playhouse: To Love and to Cherish," CBS, 1953; "Motorola TV Hour: The Family Man," ABC, 1954; "Playwrights '56: Daisy, Daisy," NBC, 1955; "The Steve Allen Show," NBC, 1956; "Studio One: The Laughing Willow," CBS, 1958; "Christophers: The Importance of Rehabilitation Work," SYN, 1959; "Steve Allen Plymouth Show," NBC, 1959; "Take a Good Look," ABC, 1960; "Story of a Family," NBC, 1960; "Something Special," NBC, 1960; "Going My Way: Don't Forget to Say Goodbye," ABC, 1963; "Alcoa Premire: Blow High, Blow Clear," ABC, 1963; "The Virginian: The Secret of Brynmar Hall," NBC, 1964; "Bob Hope Chrysler Theatre: Echo of Evil," NBC, 1964; "The Alfred Hitchcock Hour: The Monkey's Paw," NBC, 1965; "Password," CBS, 1965; "Insight: The Edith Stein Story," SYN, 1967; "Star Trek:

Journey to Bavel," NBC, 1967; "CBS Playhouse: My Father and My Mother," CBS, 1968; "Love, American Style: Love and the Pill," ABC, 1969; "Love, American Style: Love and the Good Deal," ABC, 1969; "The Ghost and Mrs. Muir: Wedding Day????," ABC, 1970; "The Men From Shiloh: The Price of the Hanging," NBC, 1970; "Hollywood Television Theatre: Neighbors," NET, 1971; "Alias Smith and Jones: The Reformation of Harry Briscoe," ABC, 1972; "Owen Marshall, Counselor at Law: The Break-in," ABC, 1974; "Marcus Welby, M.D.: Designs," ABC, 1974; "Hollywood Television Theatre: The Ladies of the Corridor," PBS, 1975; "Gibbsville: Premiere," NBC, 1976; "The Love Boat: The Reunion," ABC, 1979; "Quincy: A Woman's Place," NBC, 1980; "The Love Boat: Here Comes the Bride, Maybe," ABC, 1981; "St. Elsewhere: A Wing and a Prayer," NBC, 1983; "Hotel: Christmas," ABC, 1983; "The Love Boat: Love in a Vacuum," ABC, 1985; "St. Elsewhere: E/R," NBC, 1986; "St. Elsewhere: Once Upon a Mattress," NBC, 1986; "St. Elsewhere: Jose, Can You See?," NBC, 1987; "St. Elsewhere: Split Decision," NBC, 1988; "Baby Boom: Guilt," NBC, 1988; "The Pat Sajak Show," CBS, 1989.

TV MOVIES AND MINISERIES: "See How They Run," NBC, 1964; "Weekend Of Terror," ABC, 1970; "You'll Never See Me Again," ABC, 1973; "Tom Sawyer," CBS, 1973; "Katherine," ABC, 1975; "Amelia Earhart," NBC, 1976; "The Nativity," ABC, 1978; "Missing Children: A Mother's Story," CBS, 1982; "Amityville: The Evil Escapes," NBC, 1989.

* Emmies: 1958, 1959, 1960.

WYMAN, JANE

b. Sarah Jane Fulks, St. Joseph, MO, January 4, 1914. Oscar-winning actress ("Johnny Belinda") who most recently played that mean Angela Channing on "Falcon Crest"; ex-wife of Ronald Reagan, whom she left because she was tired of listening to him talk about politics.

AS A REGULAR: "The Jane Wyman Show (Fireside Theatre)," NBC, 1955-58; "Summer Playhouse," NBC, 1957; "Falcon Crest," CBS, 1981-90.

AND: "G.E. Theatre: Amelia," CBS, 1955; "The Steve Allen Show," NBC, 1957; "The Ford Show," NBC, 1957; "The Perry Como Show," NBC, 1958; "Wagon Train: The Dr. Willoughby Story," NBC, 1958; "The Ford Show," NBC, 1958; "Lux Playhouse: A Deadly Guest," CBS, 1959; "The Perry Como Show," NBC, 1959; "Some of Manie's Friends," NBC, 1959; "America Pauses for Springtime," CBS, 1959; "Startime: Academy Award Songs," NBC, 1960; "I've Got a Secret," CBS, 1960; "Checkmate: Lady on the Brink," CBS, 1960; "Bob Hope Buick Show," NBC, 1961; "The Investigators: Death Leaves a Tip," CBS, 1961; "Wagon Train:

The Wagon Train Mutiny," ABC, 1962; "Insight: The Cross in Crisis," SYN, 1962; "The Andy Williams Show," NBC, 1963; "Naked City: The South American Dream," ABC, 1963; "Bell Telephone Hour," NBC, 1964; "The Match Game," NBC, 1964; "Password," CBS, 1964; "Password," CBS, 1965; "The FBI: The Cave-in," ABC, 1966; "Bob Hope Chrysler Theatre: When Hell Froze," NBC, 1966; "The Red Skelton Hour," CBS, 1968; "Bob Hope Special," NBC, 1969; "My Three Sons: Who Is Sylvia?," CBS, 1970; "The Mike Douglas Show," SYN, 1970; "The Bold Ones: In Sudden Darkness," NBC, 1972; "The Sixth Sense: If I Should Die Before I Wake," ABC, 1972; "Hollywood Squares," NBC, 1972; "Owen Marshall, Counselor at Law: The Desertion of Keith Ryder," ABC, 1974; "The Love Boat: The Gift," ABC, 1980.

TV MOVIES AND MINISERIES: "The Failing of Raymond," ABC, 1971; "The Incredible Journey of Doctor Meg Laurel," CBS, 1979.

WYNN, ED

b. Isaiah Edwin Leopold, Philadelphia, November 6, 1886; d. 1966. Vaudeville clown and radio star who made a comeback as a dramatic actor and viable TV property with "Requiem for a Heavyweight."

AS A REGULAR: "The Ed Wynn Show," CBS, 1949-50; NBC, 1958-59; "All Star Revue," NBC, 1950-52.

AND: "Playhouse 90: Requiem for a Heavy-weight," CBS, 1956; "The Perry Como Show," NBC, 1957; "Shower of Stars," CBS, 1957; "The Kate Smith Hour," ABC, 1957; "I've Got a Secret," CBS, 1957; "The 20th Century-Fox Hour: The Great American Hoax," CBS, 1957; "Alcoa Hour: Protege," NBC, 1957; "Texaco Star Theatre: Command Appearance," NBC, 1957; "The Perry Como Show," NBC, 1957; "Hallmark Hall of Fame: On Borrowed Time," NBC, 1957; "Shower of Stars," CBS, 1958; "Dinah Shore Chevy Show," NBC, 1958; "December Bride: Ed Wynn Show," CBS, 1958; "Milton Berle Starring in the Kraft Music Hall," NBC, 1959; "The Garry Moore Show," CBS, 1959; "Meet Me in St. Louis," CBS, 1959; "The Ed Sullivan Show," CBS, 1959; "G.E. Theatre: Miracle at the Opera," CBS, 1959; "The Twilight Zone: One for the Angels," CBS, 1959; "Startime: Art Linkletter's Secret World of Kids," NBC, 1959; "Wagon Train: The Cappy Darrin Story," NBC, 1959; "Miracle on 34th Street," NBC, 1959; "Startime: The Greatest Man Alive!," NBC, 1960; "Westinghouse Desilu Playhouse: The Man in the Funny Suit," CBS, 1960; "The Garry Moore Show," CBS, 1960; "The Garry Moore Show," CBS, 1961; "The Red Skelton Show," CBS, 1961; "Walt Disney's Wonderful World of Color: Backstage Party," NBC, 1961; "Rawhide: Twenty-Five Santa Clauses," CBS, 1961; "Scene

Stealers," SYN, 1962; "The Garry Moore Show," CBS, 1962; "G.E. Theatre: Ten Days in the Sun," CBS, 1962; "Walt Disney's Wonderful World of Color: Golden Horseshoe Revue," NBC, 1962; "77 Sunset Strip: 5," ABC, 1963; "The Twilight Zone: Ninety Years Without Slumbering," CBS, 1963; "Burke's Law: Who Killed Avery Lord?," ABC, 1964; "Hollywood Palace," ABC, 1964; "Slattery's People: Question-Whatever Happened to Ezra?," CBS, 1964; "The Red Skelton Hour," CBS, 1964; "Walt Disney's Wonderful World of Color: Treasure in the Haunted House," NBC, 1964; "Hollywood Palace," ABC, 1965; "The Entertainers," CBS, 1965; "Bonanza: The Ponderosa Birdman," NBC, 1965; "Professor Hubert Abernathy," CBS, 1967.

* Wynn's "Requiem for a Heavyweight" comeback was far from a sure thing. After disastrous early rehearsals, the producers secretly hired actor Ned Glass to understudy Wynn in case he couldn't perform in the live broadcast. In 1960, the whole story was told, with Wynn and virtually everyone else playing themselves, on an episode of "Westinghouse Desilu Playhouse" called "The Man in the Funny Suit."

* Emmies: 1950.

WYNN, KEENAN

b. Francis Xavier Aloysius Wynn, New York City, NY, July 27, 1916; d. 1986. Gifted actor and son of Ed, often in blustery roles; he played Willard "Digger" Barnes on "Dallas" after David Wayne left the show.

AS A REGULAR: "Troubleshooters," NBC, 1959-60; "You're in the Picture," CBS, 1961; "Dallas," CBS, 1979-80; "Call to Glory," ABC, 1984-85; "The Last Precinct," NBC, 1986.

AND: "U.S. Steel Hour: The Rack," ABC, 1955; "Best of Broadway: Broadway," CBS, 1955; "Studio One: Like Father, Like Son," CBS, 1955; "Fireside Theatre: The Sport," NBC, 1955; "Schlitz Playhouse of Stars: Two-Bit Gangster," CBS, 1955; "G.E. Theatre: Lash of Fear," CBS, 1955; "Screen Directors Playhouse: A Midsummer Daydream," NBC, 1955; "Damon Runyon Theatre: Cleo," CBS, 1956; "Studio One: Circle of Guilt," CBS, 1956; "Ford Star Jubilee: Twentieth Century," CBS, 1956; "Wagon Train: The Luke O'Malley Story," NBC, 1958; "Art Linkletter's House Party," CBS, 1958; "Steve Allen Plymouth Show," NBC, 1960; "The du Pont Show with June Allyson: Piano Man," CBS, 1960; "Westinghouse Desilu Playhouse: The Man in the Funny Suit," CBS, 1960; "The Twilight Zone: A World of His Own," CBS, 1960; "The Aquanauts: The Scotland Yard Adventure," CBS, 1960; "The Islanders: The Cold War of Adam Smith," ABC, 1960; "Alfred Hitchcock Presents: The Last Escape," NBC, 1961; "The Untouchables: Augie 'The Banker' Ciamino," ABC, 1961;

"Candid Camera," CBS, 1961; "Naked City: The Day It Rained Mink," ABC, 1961; "Hallmark Hall of Fame: The Joke and the Valley," NBC, 1961; "Checkmate: A Slight Touch of Venom," CBS, 1961; "The Roaring Twenties: Standing Room Only," ABC, 1961; "The Power and the Glory," CBS, 1961; "Route 66: Some of the People, Some of the Time," CBS, 1961; "The New Breed: The Valley of the 3 Charlies," ABC, 1961; "The Dick Powell Show: The Last of the Private Eyes," NBC, 1963; "77 Sunset Strip: 5," ABC, 1963; "Burke's Law: Who Killed Cable Roberts?," ABC, 1963; "The Littlest Hobo: Die Hard," SYN, 1965; "Vacation Playhouse: Patrick Stone," CBS, 1965; "Combat!: The Flying Machine," ABC, 1966; "The Wild Wild West: The Night of the Freebooters," CBS, 1966; "Summer Fun: The Pirates of Flounder Bay," ABC, 1966; "The Road West: No Sanctuary," NBC, 1967; "The Name of the Game: Love-In at Ground Zero," NBC, 1969; "Then Came Bronson: The Old Motorcycle Fiasco," NBC, 1969; "The Name of the Game: A Hard Case of the Blues," NBC, 1969; "Lancer: Blue Skies for Willie Sharp," CBS, 1970; "The Name of the Game: Battle at Gannon's Bridge," NBC, 1970; "Love, American Style: Love and the Father," ABC, 1970; "Medical Center: Crisis," CBS, 1970; "Santa Claus Is Coming to Town," ABC, 1970; "Alias Smith and Jones: Stagecoach Seven," ABC, 1971; "Alias Smith and Jones: Dreadful Sorry, Clementine," ABC, 1971; "Bearcats!: Bitter Flats," CBS, 1971; "The Mod Squad: Exit the Closer," ABC, 1971; "Owen Marshall, Counselor at Law: Run, Carol, Run," ABC, 1972; "Alias Smith and Jones: What Happened at the XST?," ABC, 1972; "Hawaii Five-O: Journey Out of Limbo," CBS, 1972; "The New Adventures of Perry Mason: The Case of the Telltale Trunk," CBS, 1973; "McMillan and Wife: The Devil You Say," NBC, 1973; "Honeymoon Suite," ABC, 1973; "Hec Ramsey: Hard Road to Vengeance," NBC, 1973; "The Girl with Something Extra: Guess Who's Feeding the Pigeons," NBC, 1974; "Kolchak, the Night Stalker: The Spanish Moss Murders," ABC, 1974; "Kolchak, the Night Stalker: Demon in Lace," ABC, 1975; "Emergency!: 905-Wild," NBC, 1975; "The Bob Newhart Show: What's It All About, Albert?," CBS, 1975; "Medical Center: Too Late for Tomorrow," CBS, 1975; "The Rookies: From Out of Darkness," ABC, 1976; "G.E. Theatre: Twenty Shades of Pink," CBS, 1976; "The Life and Times of Grizzly Adams: The Seekers," NBC, 1978; "Police Woman: Good Old Uncle Ben," NBC, 1978; "One Day at a Time: Small Wonder Returns," CBS, 1981; "The Love Boat: The Christmas Presence," ABC, 1982; "Taxi: Tony's Baby," NBC, 1983; "St. Elsewhere: Family History," NBC, 1983; "Hardcastle and McCormick: Just Another Round of That Old Song," ABC, 1983; "Quincy: Whatever Happened to Morris Perlmutter?" NBC, 1983.

TV MOVIES AND MINISERIES: "The Young Lawyers," CBS, 1969; "The House On Greenapple Road," ABC, 1970; "Assault on the Wayne," ABC, 1971; "Cannon," CBS, 1971; "Terror in the Sky," ABC, 1971; "Assignment: Munich," ABC, 1972; "Night Train to Terror," ABC, 1973; "Hijack!," ABC, 1973; "Message to My Daughter," ABC, 1973; "Hit Lady," ABC, 1974; "Target Risk," NBC, 1975; "The Lindbergh Kidnapping Case," NBC, 1976; "The Quest," NBC, 1976; "The Bastard," SYN, 1978; "The Billion Dollar Threat," ABC, 1979; "The Monkey Mission," NBC, 1981; "The Capture of Grizzly Adams," NBC, 1982; "Return of the Man From UNCLE," CBS, 1983; "Mirrors," NBC, 1985.

* Wynn encouraged his father to turn to dramatic acting in the mid-fifties and appeared with him in "Requiem for a Heavyweight."
* See also Ed Wynn.

YZ

YORK, DICK
b. Fort Wayne, IN, September 4, 1928. Actor skilled at light comedy, best known as Darrin Stephens on "Bewitched."

AS A REGULAR: "Going My Way," ABC, 1962-63; "Bewitched," ABC, 1964-69.

AND: "Goodyear TV Playhouse: Visit to a Small Planet," NBC, 1955; "Kraft Television Theatre: Million Dollar Rookie," NBC, 1955; "Kaiser Aluminium Hour: A Real Fine Cutting Edge," NBC, 1957; "Alfred Hitchcock Presents: Vicious Circle," CBS, 1957; "Studio One: The Weston Strain," CBS, 1957; "Kraft Television Theatre: Ride Into Danger," NBC, 1957; "The Seven Lively Arts: The Changing Ways of Love," CBS, 1957; "Playhouse 90: The Time of Your Life," CBS, 1958; "Father Knows Best: Betty, Pioneer Woman," CBS, 1958; "Playhouse 90: Made in Japan," CBS, 1959; "Alcoa Theatre: The Glorious Fourth," NBC, 1960; "The Americans: The War Between the States," NBC, 1961; "Frontier Circus: The Shaggy Kings," CBS, 1961; "G.E. Theatre: A Musket for Jessica," CBS, 1961; "Adventures in Paradise: The Reluctant Hero," ABC, 1961; "Rawhide: Incident at Confidence Creek," CBS, 1963; "Wagon Train: The Michael Malone Story," ABC, 1964; "The Flintstones: Samantha," ABC, 1965; "Simon & Simon: The Wrong Stuff," CBS, 1983.

TV MOVIES AND MINISERIES: "High School, USA," NBC, 1983.

* York left "Bewitched" after long enduring pain as the result of a 1959 back injury. Today, suffering from emphysema, York lives in Michigan and spends most of his time on the phone, putting different relief agencies for the homeless in touch with the people who need them.

YORKIN, BUD
b. Alan David Yorkin, Washington, PA, February 22, 1926. Writer-director-producer, long in collaboration with Norman Lear.

AS PRODUCER-DIRECTOR: "The George Gobel Show," NBC, 1954-56; "The Ford Show," NBC, 1956-61; "An Evening with Fred Astaire," NBC, 1958; "Jack Benny Special," CBS, 1959; "Another Evening with Fred Astaire," NBC, 1959; "Henry Fonda and the Family," CBS, 1962; "Carter Country," ABC, 1977-79.

WITH NORMAN LEAR: "TV Guide Awards," NBC, 1960; "Bobby Darin and Friends," NBC, 1961; "The Danny Kaye Show," CBS, 1961; "All in the Family," CBS, 1971-79.

* Yorkin began at NBC in 1948 as a cameraman.
* Emmies: 1959, 1960.

YOTHERS, TINA
b. Whittier, CA, May 5, 1973. Actress who played Jennifer Keaton on "Family Ties."

AS A REGULAR: "Family Ties," NBC, 1982-89.

AND: "Father Murphy: The Dream Day," NBC, 1982; "Domestic Life: Pilot," CBS, 1984; "The Jim Henson Hour: Miss Piggy's Hollywood," NBC, 1989; "Animal Crack-Ups," ABC, 1989; "Totally Hidden Video," FOX, 1989.

TV MOVIES AND MINISERIES: "Family Ties Vacation," NBC, 1985; "Crash Course," NBC, 1988.

YOUNG, ALAN
b. Angus Young, North Shields, Northumberland, England, November 19, 1919. Comic actor who played Wilbur Post, master of Mr. Ed.

AS A REGULAR: "The Alan Young Show," CBS, 1950-53; "Saturday Night Revue," NBC, 1954; "Mr. Ed," CBS, 1961-65; "Coming of Age," CBS, 1988.

AND: "G.E. Theatre: Wild Luke's Boy," CBS, 1954; "Stage 7: I Killed John Harrington," CBS, 1955; "Studio One: The Man Who Caught the Ball at Coogan's Bluff," CBS, 1955; "Studio One: This Will Do Nicely," CBS, 1956; "Matinee Theatre: Ask Me No Questions," NBC, 1956; "Studio 57: Swing Your Partner, Hector," SYN, 1956; "The Steve Allen Show," NBC, 1956; "Startime: Tennesse Ernie Meets King Arthur," NBC, 1960; "Arthur Murray Party," NBC, 1960; "The Chevy Show: Love is Funny," NBC, 1960; "Art Linkletter's House Party," CBS, 1961; "Art Linkletter's House Party," CBS, 1962; "The Andy Williams Show," NBC, 1962; "Death Valley Days: The Hat That Won the West," SYN, 1962; "Stump the Stars," CBS, 1963; "You Don't Say," NBC, 1964; "Gibbsville: Saturday Night," NBC, 1976; "The Love Boat: Booming Romance," ABC, 1983; "Murder, She Wrote: Keep the Home Fries Burning," CBS, 1986; "The Pat Sajak Show," CBS, 1989.

* "Mr. Ed" was originally called "The Wonderful World of Wilbur Pope," and Scott McKay played Pope in the pilot.
* Emmies: 1951.

YOUNG, GIG
b. Byron Barr, St. Cloud, MN, November 4, 1913; d. 1978. Actor usually in light comic or

795

dramatic roles; he won an Oscar for "They Shoot Horses, Don't They?"

AS A REGULAR: "Warner Bros. Presents," ABC, 1955-56; "The Rogues," NBC, 1964-65; "Gibbsville," NBC, 1976.

AND: "Silver Theatre: Lady with Ideas," CBS, 1950; "Rewrite for Love," SYN, 1951; "Robert Montgomery Presents: The Sunday Punch," NBC, 1953; "Schlitz Playhouse of Stars: Part of the Game," CBS, 1953; "Producers Showcase: Tonight at 8:30," NBC, 1954; "U.S. Steel Hour: Sauce for the Goose," NBC, 1956; "Climax!: Jacob and the Angel," CBS, 1957; "Studio One: A Dead Ringer," CBS, 1958; "Goodyear Theatre: The Spy," NBC, 1958; "The Twilight Zone: Walking Distance," CBS, 1959; "The Phildelphia Story," NBC, 1959; "Special Tonight: Ninotchka," ABC, 1960; "Shirley Temple's Storybook: The Prince and the Pauper," NBC, 1960; "Here's Hollywood," NBC, 1961; "Theatre '62: The Spiral Staircase," NBC, 1961; "The Alfred Hitchcock Hour: A Piece of the Action," CBS, 1962; "Kraft Suspense Theatre: The End of the World," NBC, 1963; "Hollywood Palace," ABC, 1964; "The Mike Douglas Show," SYN, 1964; "The Andy Williams Show," NBC, 1965; "The Red Skelton Hour," CBS, 1966; "The Merv Griffin Show," CBS, 1970; "Benjamin Franklin: The Ambassador," CBS, 1974; "The Merv Griffin Show," SYN, 1975; "McCloud: The Night New York Turned Blue," NBC, 1976.

TV MOVIES AND MINISERIES: "Companions in Nightmare," NBC, 1968; "The Neon Ceiling," NBC, 1971; "The Great Ice Rip-Off," ABC, 1974; "The Turning Point of Jim Malloy," NBC, 1975; "Sherlock Holmes in New York," NBC, 1976.

* In 1978, Young shot his newlywed wife and then killed himself.

YOUNG, LORETTA

b. Gretchen Young, Salt Lake City, UT, January 6, 1913. Grande dame of the fifties anthology series, and an Oscar-winning film actress ("The Farmer's Daughter").

AS A REGULAR: "A Letter to Loretta," NBC, 1953-54; "The Loretta Young Show," NBC, 1954-61; "The New Loretta Young Show," CBS, 1962-63.

AND: "World's Greatest Mother," SYN, 1958.

TV MOVIES AND MINISERIES: "Christmas Eve," NBC, 1986; "Lady in a Corner," NBC, 1989.

* In 1972, Young sued NBC because they were showing her television shows abroad. That was bad enough, Young said, but the old shows included her familiar opening, emerging through a door in the best gowns fifties high fashion had to offer. And those outfits were very much out of style, Miss Young huffed. She won $600,000.

* Emmies: 1955, 1957, 1959.

YOUNG, ROBERT

b. Chicago, IL, February 22, 1907. Actor who played dad-who-knew-best Jim Anderson and doctor-who-knew-best Marcus Welby.

AS A REGULAR: "Father Knows Best," CBS, 1954-55; NBC, 1955-58; CBS, 1958-60; "Window on Main Street," CBS, 1961-62; "Marcus Welby, M.D.," ABC, 1969-76; "Little Women," NBC, 1979.

AND: "Ford Theatre: Keep It in the Family," NBC, 1954; "Climax!: The Valiant Men," CBS, 1955; "I've Got a Secret," CBS, 1956; "The Steve Allen Show," NBC, 1956; "Art Linkletter's House Party," CBS, 1957; "Moment of Decision: Stage to Yuma," ABC, 1957; "The Steve Allen Show," NBC, 1957; "Art Linkletter's House Party," CBS, 1959; "Christophers: The Story Behind the Star-Spangled Banner," SYN, 1959; "Steve Allen Plymouth Show," NBC, 1959; "This Is Your Life," NBC, 1960; "Something Special," NBC, 1960; "Dr. Kildare: Lullaby for an Indian Summer," NBC, 1965; "Bob Hope Chrysler Theatre: The Admiral," NBC, 1965; "Bob Hope Chrysler Theatre: Holloway's Daughters," NBC, 1966; "ABC Stage '67: KO's," ABC, 1967; "The Name of the Game: The Protector," NBC, 1968; "Owen Marshall, Counselor at Law: Men Who Care," ABC, 1971; "ABC Comedy Hour," ABC, 1972; "A Salute to Television's 25th Anniversary," ABC, 1972; "Robert Young and the Family," CBS, 1973; "Owen Marshall, Counselor at Law: I've Promised You a Father," ABC, 1974.

TV MOVIES AND MINISERIES: "Marcus Welby, M.D.," ABC, 1969; "Vanished," NBC, 1971; "All My Darling Daughters," ABC, 1972; "My Darling Daughters' Anniversary," ABC, 1973; "Little Women," NBC, 1978; "Mercy or Murder?" NBC, 1987; "Conspiracy of Love," CBS, 1987; "Marcus Welby, M.D.: A Family Affair," NBC, 1988.

* Emmies: 1957, 1958, 1970.

YOUNGMAN, HENNY

b. Liverpool, England, January 12, 1906. Comedian. Please.

AS A REGULAR: "Texaco Star Theatre," NBC, 1948; "The Henny and Rocky Show," ABC, 1955; "Joey & Dad," CBS, 1975.

AND: "The Julius LaRosa Show," NBC, 1957; "The Steve Allen Show," NBC, 1958; "The Jack Paar Show," NBC, 1958; "Make Me Laugh," ABC, 1958; "The Ed Sullivan Show," CBS, 1959; "Steve Allen Plymouth Show," NBC, 1960; "The Ed Sullivan Show," CBS, 1961; "U.S. Steel Hour: The Golden Thirty," CBS, 1961; "The Ed Sullivan Show," CBS, 1962; "Jackie Gleason and His American Scene Magazine," CBS, 1963; "The Tonight Show Starring Johnny Carson," NBC, 1963; "The Tonight Show Starring Johnny Carson," NBC, 1964; "Hollywood Palace," ABC, 1964; "Jackie Gleason and His American Scene

Magazine," CBS, 1965; "The Jimmy Dean Show," ABC, 1965; "The Merv Griffin Show," SYN, 1966; "Kraft Music Hall," NBC, 1967; "The Dean Martin Show," NBC, 1968; "Hollywood Palace," ABC, 1968; "Batman: I'll Be a Mummy's Uncle," ABC, 1968; "The Tonight Show Starring Johnny Carson," NBC, 1973; "The Merv Griffin Show," SYN, 1974; "Dinah!," SYN, 1975; "The Mike Douglas Show," SYN, 1977; "Hollywood Squares," SYN, 1980; "Woodstock: Return to the Planet of the '60s," CBS, 1989; "The People Next Door: Town Without Pity," CBS, 1989; "The Pat Sajak Show," CBS, 1989.

ZERBE, ANTHONY
b. California, 1936. Actor who plays Teaspoon on "The Young Riders."
AS A REGULAR: "Harry O," ABC, 1975-76; "The Young Riders," ABC, 1989- .
AND: "The Big Valley: The Guilt of Matt Bentell," ABC, 1965; "Mission: Impossible: The Astrologer," CBS, 1967; "Gunsmoke: Blood Money," CBS, 1968; "The Virginian: The Good-Hearted Badman," NBC, 1968; "Mission: Impossible: The Amateur," CBS, 1970; "Gunsmoke: Noon Day Devil," CBS, 1970; "Storefront Lawyers: Where Were We, Waldo?," CBS, 1970; "Mission: Impossible: The Connection," CBS, 1971; "Cannon: The Torch," CBS, 1972; "Ironside: The Savage Sentry," NBC, 1972; "Mannix: Cry Silence," CBS, 1972; "Hollywood Television Theatre: Carola," NET, 1973; "Gunsmoke: Talbot," CBS, 1973; "Cannon: Catch Me If You Can," CBS, 1973; "The Streets of San Francisco: The Twenty-Four Karat Plague," ABC, 1973; "The FBI: Rules of the Game," ABC, 1973; "Kung Fu: The Hoots," CBS, 1973; "Hawaii Five-O: Mother's Deadly Helper," CBS, 1974; "The Rookies: Death Watch," ABC, 1974; "Benjamin Franklin: The Statesman," CBS, 1975; "The Wonderful World of Disney: The Secret of the Pond," NBC, 1975; "The Rockford Files: The Gang at Don's Drive-in," NBC, 1977; "Little House: A New Beginning: The Wild Boy," NBC, 1982; "Nurse: On the Line," CBS, 1982; "Nurse: Impressions," CBS, 1982; "The Equalizer: Memories of Manon," CBS, 1987; "The Equalizer: The Mystery of Manon," CBS, 1988; "Columbo: Columbo Goes to the Guillotine," ABC, 1989.
TV MOVIES AND MINISERIES: "The Priest Killer," CBS, 1971; "The Hound of the Baskervilles," ABC, 1972; "Snatched," ABC, 1973; "She Lives," ABC, 1973; "The Healers," ABC, 1974; "In the Glitter Palace," NBC, 1977; "Best Sellers: Once an Eagle," NBC, 1977; "Kiss Meets the Phantom of the Park," NBC, 1978; "Centennial," NBC, 1978-79; "The Chisholms," CBS, 1979; "ABC Theatre: Attica," ABC, 1980; "The Seduction of Miss Leona," CBS, 1980; "Rascals and Robbers,"

CBS, 1982; "Return of the Man From UNCLE," CBS, 1983; "A.D.," NBC, 1985; "One Police Plaza," CBS, 1986; "Independence," NBC; 1987.
* Emmies: 1976.

ZIMBALIST, EFREM JR.
b. New York City, NY, November 30, 1923. Actor who played private eye Stu Bailey on "77 Sunset Strip" and agent Lew Erskine on "The FBI."
AS A REGULAR: "Concerning Miss Marlowe," NBC, 1954-55; "77 Sunset Strip," ABC, 1958-64; "The FBI," ABC, 1965-74; "Hotel," ABC, 1986.
AND: "Goodyear TV Playhouse: The Film Maker," NBC, 1956; "U.S. Steel Hour: Stopover at Sublimity," CBS, 1956; "The Phil Silvers Show: The Blue Blood of Bilko," CBS, 1957; "Warner Bros. Presents Conflict: Execution Night," ABC, 1957; "Maverick: Shady Deal at Sunny Acres," ABC, 1959; "Hawaiian Eye: Three Tickets to Lani," ABC, 1959; "The Alaskans: The Trial of Reno McKee," ABC, 1960; "Hawaiian Eye: I Wed Three Wives," ABC, 1960; "Wonderland on Ice," NBC, 1960; "Person to Person," CBS, 1961; "Cheyenne: The Prince of Darkness," ABC, 1961; "Object Is," ABC, 1964; "Hollywood Palace," ABC, 1964; "The Mike Douglas Show," SYN, 1964; "What's This Song?," NBC, 1964; "Bob Hope Chrysler Theatre: The Sojourner," NBC, 1964; "The Alfred Hitchcock Hour: See the Monkey Dance," NBC, 1964; "The Reporter: Super Star," CBS, 1964; "Password," CBS, 1965; "Rawhide: The Last Order," CBS, 1965; "Insight: Stranger in My Shoes," SYN, 1967; "A Salute to Television's 25th Anniversary," ABC, 1972; "Remington Steele: Sting of Steele," NBC, 1983; "Fantasy Island: The Butler's Affair," ABC, 1983; "Hardcastle and McCormick: The Georgia Street Motors," ABC, 1984; "Remington Steele: Blue-Blooded Steele," NBC, 1984; "The Love Boat: Polly's Poker Palace," ABC, 1984; "Murder, She Wrote: The Last Flight of the Dizzy Damsel," CBS, 1988.
TV MOVIES AND MINISERIES: "Who Is the Black Dahlia?," NBC, 1975; "Terror Out of the Sky," CBS, 1978; "The Gathering, Part II," NBC, 1979; "Scruples," CBS, 1980; "Baby Sister," ABC, 1983.

ZIMBALIST, STEPHANIE
b. New York City, October 8, 1956.
AS A REGULAR: "Remington Steele," NBC, 1982-87.
AND: "Person to Person," CBS, 1961; "The Love Boat: Eyes of Love," ABC, 1978; "Family: Ballerina," ABC, 1979.
TV MOVIES AND MINISERIES: "Yesterday's Child," NBC, 1977; "Long Journey Back," ABC, 1978; "Forever," NBC, 1978; "Centennial,"

NBC, 1978-79; "The Triangle Factory Fire Scandal," NBC, 1979; "The Golden Moment: An Olympic Love Story," NBC, 1980; "Elvis and the Beauty Queen," NBC, 1981; "Love on the Run," NBC, 1985; "A Letter to Three Wives," NBC, 1985; "Remington Steele: The Steele That Wouldn't Die," NBC, 1987; "Celebration Family," ABC, 1987; "The Man in the Brown Suit," CBS, 1989.

ZIMMER, KIM

b. Grand Rapids, MI, February 2, 1955. Actress who played Nola Aldrich on "The Doctors" and Reva Shayne on "The Guiding Light."
AS A REGULAR: "One Life to Live," ABC, 1978; "The Doctors," NBC, 1979-82; "One Life to Live," ABC, 1983; "The Guiding Light," CBS, 1983-90.
AND: "MacGyver: Deadly Dreams," ABC, 1989.
TV Movies and Miniseries: "Trenchcoat in Paradise," CBS, 1989.

ZIMMER, NORMA

b. Larsen, ID. Lawrence Welk's "Champagne Lady."
AS A REGULAR: "The Meredith Willson Show," NBC, 1949; "The Lawrence Welk Show," ABC, 1960-71; SYN, 1971-82 .
AND: "I Love Lucy: Lucy Goes to Scotland," CBS, 1956.

ZMED, ADRIAN

b. Chicago, IL, March 14, 1954. Actor who played Off. Vince Romano on "T.J. Hooker."
AS A REGULAR: Flatbush," CBS, 1979; "Goodtime Girls," ABC, 1980; "T.J. Hooker," ABC, 1982-85; "Dance Fever," SYN, 1985-87;
AND: "Angie: Marie Moves Out," ABC, 1980; "Bosom Buddies: Best Friends," ABC, 1981; "Empty Nest: The Check Isn't in the Mail," NBC, 1988; "Murder, She Wrote: From Russia—With Blood," CBS, 1989.
TV MOVIES AND MINISERIES: "Victims for Victims: The Theresa Saldana Story," NBC, 1984.

ZULU

b. Gilbert Kauhi, Hawaii. Actor who played Kono on "Hawaii Five-O."
AS A REGULAR: "Hawaii Five-O," CBS, 1968-72.
TV M OVIES AND MINISERIES: "Hawaii Five-O," CBS, 1968.

ZUNIGA, DAPHNE

Actress in film ("The Sure Thing") and TV.
AS A GUEST: "Family Ties: Double Date," NBC, 1984; "Family Ties: The Graduate," NBC, 1984; "Nightmare Classics: The Eyes of the Panther," SHO, 1989.
TV MOVIES AND MINISERIES: "Stone Pillow," CBS, 1985.

TRIVIA QUIZ ANSWERS

QUIZ #1
1. "Maude."
2. "Harry."
3. "Hazel."
4. "Sam."
5. "Fay."
6. "Angie."
7. "Julia."
8. "Billy."
9. "Willy."
10. "Mickey."

QUIZ #2
1. Barney Fife. Who else?
2. Barney's landlady, Mrs. Mendlebright.
3. Andy Taylor. Usually said to Barney.
4. Ernest T. Bass, from the "My Fair Ernest T. Bass" episode. In an effort to clean up Ernest T. so he can be presented to polite society, Barney and Andy teach him one line of unaccented English, aimed at party hostess Mrs. Wiley.
5. Opie Taylor, looking on the bright side when his father burns breakfast.
6. Goober Pyle. His impersonations, respectively, of Cary Grant and Edward G. Robinson.
7. Gomer Pyle. A standard response.
8. Barney Fife. Ditto.
9. Gomer, from the "Barney's First Car" episode. He's carsick, but enjoying the ride.
10. Barney, from the "Barney and the Choir" episode.

QUIZ #3
1. Question marks.
2. Harriet (played by Madge Blake).
3. Barbara Gordon, the commissioner's daughter.
4. True.
5. Bob Kane.
6. Gordon.
7. O'Hara.
8. Batman. What else?
9. Bat-time, Bat-channel.
10. False.

QUIZ #4
1. Jethrine, also played by Max Baer, Jr.
2. The Commerce Bank of Beverly Hills.
3. Sonny.
4. Louis Nye.
5. Homer Noodleman.
6. The cement pond.
7. Mammoth Pictures.
8. Kellogg's.
9. Winston.
10. Hathaway.

QUIZ #5
1. McMann and Tate.
2. Chevrolet.
3. Abner.
4. Gladys.
5. Serena.
6. Elizabeth Montgomery, using the joke name Pandora Spocks. (Say it fast.)
7. Dr. Bombay, played by Bernard Fox.
8. Adam.
9. Lisa Hartman.
10. Her nose.

QUIZ #6
1. E. ("Cannon.")
2. H. ("Hill Street Blues.")
3. A. ("The Rockford Files.")
4. D. ("Mannix.")
5. J. ("Remington Steele.")
6. G. ("Hawaii Five-O.")
7. B. ("Magnum P.I.")
8. F. ("Starsky and Hutch.")
9. C. ("Hart to Hart.")
10. I. ("Charlie's Angels.")

QUIZ #7
1. John.
2. "Somebody Killed Her Husband."
3. Lee Majors.
4. False.
5. Barbara Stanwyck.
6. "The Rookies."
7. "Christine Cromwell."
8. "The Burning Bed."
9. "Once upon a time ...."
10. Charlie.

QUIZ #8
1. "Mayday."
2. William Devane.
3. An accountant.
4. A bottle cap.
5. Indiana.
6. Hanover.
7. Florida.
8. Evan Drake, played by Tom Skerritt.
9. He was a hockey player.
10. He was run over by a Zamboni machine.

QUIZ #9
1. Camp Crowder, Missouri.
2. New Rochelle, New York. (Bonus: Bonnie Meadow Road.)
3. He was a dentist.
4. A Tarantula.
5. He was in the Army; she was a dancer with the USO.
6. Cooley.

d—an acronym for the names
, Oscar, Sam, Edward, Benjamin,
es and David.
...es.
...iny Thomas, who played the alien
...lak from the planet Twylo.
...leehan.

...IZ #10
1. The drive-in.
2. Winston.
3. The Great Gazoo, voiced by Harvey Korman.
4. The Water Buffalos.
5. Dino.
6. A small elephant.
7. Mr. Slate.
8. She played a Bedrock version of herself: Ann-Margrock.
9. Flaghoople.
10. Hoppy the hopperoo.

QUIZ #11
1. C.
2. I.
3. H.
4. E.
5. G.
6. D.
7. A.
8. J.

9. F.
10. B.

QUIZ #12
1. McGillicuddy.
2. Eve Arden and William Holden.
3. MGM wanted Ricky to do a screen test for a possible movie role.
4. "Babaloo."
5. She told him while he was doing his nightclub act.
6. Connecticut.
7. Superman.
8. Philip Morris.
9. "The Long, Long Trailer" and "Forever Darling."
10. Mertz and Kurtz (played in one episode by Charles Winninger).

QUIZ #13
1. "Midnight Caller."
2. "Ben Casey."
3. "Hill Street Blues."
4. "Hawaii Five-O."
5. "The Ed Sullivan Show."
6. "Dragnet."
7. "To Tell the Truth."
8. "The Perry Como Show" (or "Perry Como's Kraft Music Hall").
9. "McCloud."
10. "Family Feud."

ABOUT THE AUTHOR

David Inman grew up watching too much TV. As a child his mother would punish him by sending him outside to play. When he did go out, it was to play "Gilligan's Island" (he usually was the professor) or "Hogan's Heroes" (he'd usually play LeBeau) with the neighborhood kids. In 1981 he began writing a TV question-and-answer column, "The Incredible Inman," for *The Louisville* (Kentucky) *Times*; the column now appears in *The* (Louisville) *Courier-Journal* and is syndicated nationwide by Gannett News Service. Inman was born in Louisville and grew up across the Ohio River in Jeffersonville, Indiana. He and his wife, Rebecca Terry, have a son, Sam.